WEST'S LAW SCHOOL ADVISORY BOARD

THE LAW OF TORTS

By

Dan B. Dobbs
Professor of Law
The University of Arizona
James E. Rogers College of Law

HORNBOOK SERIES®

WEST GROUP
A THOMSON COMPANY

ST. PAUL, MINN., 2000

610 Opperman Drive
P.O. Box 64526
St. Paul, MN 55164–0526
1–800–328–9352

Printed in the United States of America

ISBN 0–314–21187–X

TEXT IS PRINTED ON 10% POST CONSUMER RECYCLED PAPER

1st Reprint–2001

In Memory of W. Page Keeton

*

Preface

This book is intended to provide a single-volume summary of contemporary tort law, somewhat along the lines provided by the five editions of Prosser and Prosser & Keeton on Torts. In fact, I originally intended to write a new edition of those works. But the law has changed a good deal and so have ideas about it, and ultimately it seemed better to write an entirely new book built from the ground up. This is that book. Except for a quotation or two, it contains not a word of Prosser or Prosser and Keeton text. On the other hand, it covers all of the same ground and a good deal of wholly new legal issues as well. It attempts to cover not merely favorite or best-known subject matter, but the whole range of topics, including the fast-growing economic torts.

Changes in tort law since the last edition of Prosser & Keeton in 1984 are enormous. The changes certainly include changes in attitudes of judges and legislators. When Prosser last wrote, immunities were on the wane and grounds for liability increasing. In more recent years, immunities have been increasingly invoked by courts and erected by legislatures, sometimes expanding older immunities, sometimes creating new ones. Federal preemption of state law often effectively immunizes defendants and displaces traditional tort law altogether. Tort reform statutes have had similar effects, capping damages, abolishing joint and several liability, and otherwise posing barriers to full compensation. The sweeping march of strict liability in products liability law, largely a result of Prosser's Restatement draft, is now in retreat with a wholly new Restatement of Products Liability. The ultimate effect of some changes is yet uncertain. The development of managed care or HMO-medicine is changing medical issues, probably forever, and there are some new kinds of liabilities not contemplated before, but also new kinds of harms that may go unredressed.

Another change that has become apparent is that statistical thinking is more common and more commonly accepted by judges. This is important in proof and trials on many common issues such as calculation of future losses expected to occur after a trial is over. But it has also affected the way many courts deal with the standard issue of causation in negligence cases, so that if a doctor deprives the plaintiff of a chance at health, he might be liable for the value of the lost chance, even if he would not be liable under traditional causal rules.

Changes have also occurred incrementally in obscure corners of the law that may turn out to be more important than their obscurity indicates. The tiny tort law of trespass to chattels has been invoked to protect commercial abuse of email and computer hacking. The tort of battery may now be a weapon in the fight against second-hand smoke. The

list of changes is very long and inappropriate to a preface, but the reader of this book will find them aplenty.

The organization of this book is similar enough to be roughly familiar, but it is not identical to Prosser. One difference that will be obvious to those who love the Prosser editions is that this book contains no separate chapter on the contract-tort connection; those materials have been distributed where they seemed most relevant and the contemporary conflict between contract and tort approaches is heightened in the materials on interference with contract and interference with business opportunity. Another difference is that it attempts to separate purely economic torts and economic/dignitary torts that involve no physical harm, from the more familiar personal injury/property damage torts.

Other differences between this and the Prosser editions lie in the case citations. For the most part, the cases cited here are very recent ones. I have tried to resist including long lists of case citations except where unfamiliar subject matter or holdings make such lists especially helpful. It is usually sufficient to cite one or two cases for any given point. The cases are important, however, and the aim is to cite enough in each section to permit the reader to begin more detailed research.

On the other hand, it is increasingly important to recognize statutes and their impact on tort law. If ten states have *Tarasoff* statutes but the words of each are different, only a more specialized treatise could hope to parse the statutes separately. Even so, if you are trying to understand the general law of torts, it is useful to know that such statutes exist and that they impose a duty upon therapists, even if the duty differs slightly from state to state. Some statutes have developed a large jurisprudence of their own. That is so with the Federal Employers Liability Act (FELA) and with civil rights statutes as well as a number of others. The details must be left to specialized works, but it is important to recognize that statutory torts do exist, that, like other torts, they have elements the plaintiff must prove, and defenses that can rescue the defendant.

This book's approach to statutes is illustrated by the two statutory areas named. Some civil rights materials are not so well known, so several sections are devoted to them. On the other hand, the FELA materials, however specialized, are variations on the ordinary negligence rules, so that no separate section is devoted to them. In particular cases lawyers and students will no doubt wish for a different emphasis, but I hope that overall this approach commends itself as a sensible and useful one.

This book attempts to give formal statements of many rules, but perhaps just as often it attempts to state the gist or aim of the rule and to spell out examples of its application. Examples are particularly useful with materials that are often difficult for students. One or two good examples will often work like pictures; they can explain more than a thousand words. Although spelled out examples or hypotheticals take up valuable space, I hope readers will find them useful.

I have tried hard to make material accessible, both in the sense that they can be readily found and in the sense that material secondary or extraneous to the user's immediate need can be avoided until the reader is ready for it. With this in mind, the sections are shorter than many of Prosser's sections. While Prosser and Keeton contained less than 140 sections, this book, not many pages longer, contains 492. The idea is that if readers can locate an appropriate section, they can quickly access what is most important to them. In many instances, readers will want additional material to be found in other sections, but I hope no one will be required to read 50 pages to find the two sentences in point. A good index is also required to make material quickly accessible. I have rejected computer or concordance type indexing. I hope and believe that the index will take the user of this book to appropriate materials with ease.

This book does not consciously attempt to advance any particular approach to, or theory of torts. It attempts instead to acknowledge and point to overriding policy goals, to economic analysis, and to concerns of corrective justice or accountability as well as to practical problems in administering tort law. But it is not *about* any of those things. It is *about* today's tort law. If I have a view about economic analysis vs. corrective justice or utilitarianism vs. some "moral" approach, it is probably that all these approaches and their variations have a good deal to offer.

On the other hand, this book does occasionally offer comments or assessments of particular cases or legal rules, in the belief that any position taken offers students and lawyers a beginning point for their own analysis.

Conventions

"Defendant" and "actor." This book uses several conventions. Like the Restatement, it sometimes uses the term "actor" to refer to the person whose acts are in issue. But more often it uses the term defendant. "Actor" is admittedly more accurate because "actor" covers the case in which the plaintiff's acts are in issue as well as the case in which we are concerned with the defendant's act. Nevertheless, "actor" is often confusing to first-year students and professional usage makes it easy to understand that "defendant" can include other actors if the context demands.

"He" and "she." The pronouns he and she can be distributed more or less equally by using "she" for all plaintiffs and "he" for all defendants and that is what I have done here. One person objected to this idea on the ground that women were no more greedy or dishonest than men and should not be put in the position of always appearing as plaintiffs. That criticism assumes that plaintiffs are greedier or more dishonest than others. I do not believe that to be the case. A neutral judicial system should not in any event assume any such thing. So, intending no implications about anyone's character, I use she in referring to plaintiffs and he (or "it" with corporations) in referring to defendants. It turns out that this system sometimes yields greater clarity.

Citations and quotations. Interior quotation marks are almost always omitted as are case citations appearing without a quotation. The denial of certiorari by the United States Supreme Court does not connote approval of the decision and denial is not noted. Short forms of repeated citations are used as follows:

Restatement Second of Torts (1965–1977): Restatement.

W. Page Keeton, Dan B. Dobbs, Robert E. Keeton, & David G. Owens, Prosser & Keeton on Torts (5th ed. 1984): Prosser and Keeton.

Fowler V. Harper, Fleming James, Jr. & Oscar S. Gray, The Law of Torts (2d ed. 1986): Harper, James & Gray.

Restatement Third, Torts: Products Liability (1997): Restatement of Products Liability.

Restatement Third, Torts: Unfair Competition (1995): Restatement of Unfair Competition.

J. Thomas McCarthy, Trademarks and Unfair Competition (4th ed. 1998): McCarthy Trademarks.

Acknowledgments

I am grateful for the efforts of Paul Hayden for his kind reading of and important suggestions about Chapter 36. Many persons helped with this book while they were law students at the James E. Rogers College of Law at the University of Arizona. They found cases, checked citations, and proofed manuscript. I am grateful to David Benton, Julia Corty, Lindsay Franke, Patrick J. Dooley, Robyn Kool, Kevin Harper, Jennifer Lehman, Pat Lewis, Kathryn Maxwell, Kelley Myers, Anoma Phanthourath Nolan, Wyatt Pickett, Chris Simpson, Dawn Throne, and Barbara Vidal all of whom gave me fine research and much other help for very substantial periods. I am likewise grateful to Melissa Berren, Adrien Edelman, Virginia Escobar, Elisa Gill Donnadieu, Chris Jenks, Jennifer Johnson, Ruth Mendus, Josh Moya, Taylor Nguyen, Carrie Rednour, Roger Reiersen, Amy Ruskin, Erin Simpson, Ken Spafford, and Jess Walsh, all of whom generously read and cite-checked many pages of final manuscript, often making helpful suggestions about revision.

The law library at the James E. Rogers College of Law, under the Directorship of Ron Cherry and later Mike Chirorazzi gave me generous support. Reference librarians Carol Elliott, Maureen Garmon, Jacquelyn Kaspar, and Foreign Law Librarian Francisco Avalos were always cheerfully helpful. Under the wonderful supervision of Carolyn Scott, Heather Brossard made painstaking corrections in the manuscript. I am always grateful for the moral and personal support provided by Associate Dean Kathleen Kavanagh and by my friend Loretta Taylor.

DAN B. DOBBS

Tucson, Arizona

*

WESTLAW® Overview

The Law of Torts, by Dan B. Dobbs, offers a detailed and comprehensive treatment of basic rules, principles and issues relating to tort law. To supplement the information contained in this book, you can access Westlaw, a computer-assisted legal research service of West Group. Westlaw contains a broad array of legal resources, including case law, statutes, expert commentary, current developments and various other types of information.

Learning how to use these materials effectively will enhance your legal research abilities. To help you coordinate the information in the book with your Westlaw research, this volume contains an appendix listing Westlaw databases, search techniques and sample problems.

THE PUBLISHER

*

Summary of Contents

Page

PART III. OPERATING AND ALTERING THE TORT SYSTEM IN PERSONAL INJURY CASES

PART IV. ECONOMIC AND DIGNITARY INJURY

Table of Contents

Page

PART III. OPERATING AND ALTERING THE TORT SYSTEM IN PERSONAL INJURY CASES

PART IV. ECONOMIC AND DIGNITARY INJURY

*

THE LAW OF TORTS

*

PART I. INTRODUCING TORT LAW
CHAPTER 1

INTRODUCING AND SURVEYING TORT AND INJURY LAW

TOPIC A. TORTS AND THE SCOPE OF TORT AND INJURY LAW

§ 1. Defining Torts

Tort and Compensation

Defining torts. Much of formal tort law is an attempt to define what counts as a legal wrong in particular settings. For instance, the rules of assault define what counts as the tort that goes by that name. This section, in contrast, speaks more generally to some of the important defining characteristics of torts in general. A tort is conduct that amounts to a legal wrong and that causes harm for which courts will impose civil liability. Conduct that counts only as breach of contract will lead to legal liability but breach of contract is not considered to be a tortious wrong. Some torts are also crimes; but tort law is not concerned with the separate issue of criminal responsibility. The essence of tort is the defendant's potential for civil liability to the victim for harmful wrongdoing and correspondingly the victim's potential for compensation or other relief.

Sources: common law and statute. Tort law is predominantly common law. That is, judges rather than legislatures usually define what counts as a tort and how compensation is to be measured. Nevertheless, a statute or even the Constitution itself may make certain conduct legally wrongful and may permit recovery of damages for such conduct. So violation of statute or constitution is sometimes a tort for which the violator is subject to liability.

Examples of torts. Examples of torts can be found everywhere. In the absence of some defense or special facts, it is a tort to punch another in the nose, to negligently run an automobile into another, or to negligently perform a medical operation. It may be a tort to sell a defective product that causes harm. Some torts cause no physical harms at all but are nonetheless actionable. For example, it is tortious to maliciously prosecute a person without probable cause, to damage reputation by libel, to interfere intentionally with a contract, or to mislead a person by misrepresenting material facts in connection with a sale. Many other torts can

be described or named, and in fact courts are free to recognize variations and even to recognize "new torts" at any time.

Damages and other remedies. Tort law is primarily intended to redress legally recognized harms by rendering a judgment against the wrongdoer.[1] This award is usually a money award called "damages," and it is usually intended as a kind of compensation for the harm suffered. In some cases, a punitive damages award may be added to compensatory damages to deter further misconduct. Other remedies that are infrequently available include restitution, which forces the tortfeasor to disgorge gains he wrongfully obtained by tort, and injunction, which compels him to cease his tortious conduct. In the great majority of tort cases, however, a favorable judgment for the victim means an award of money as compensation for harm caused.

Bases of Tort Liability

The fault basis. Tort liability can be defined in part by the grounds on which it is invoked. The term "tort" is derived from Latin roots meaning "twisted," as if to say tortious conduct is twisted conduct, conduct that departs from the existing norm. As the word itself suggests, torts are traditionally associated with wrongdoing in some moral sense. In the great majority of cases today, tort liability is grounded in the conclusion that the wrongdoer was at fault in a legally recognizable way. It is not ordinarily enough to impose liability that the defendant has merely caused harm by accident or happenstance; he must also be at fault. This fault approach is often associated with ideals of freedom; you will be free to act without liability, so long as you are not at fault in your actions.

Kinds of fault. There are many kinds of fault that have no legal significance at all. It is a fault to be lazy or to use the salad fork for a meat dish, but neither fault is a tort. Faulty conduct that is legally important can be described in many ways. For present purposes, it is enough to recognize that legal fault in the law of torts is usually sorted in two categories: (1) intentional wrongs or (2) negligent wrongs.[2]

Intentional torts. Intentional wrongs entail at least an intent on the part of the defendant to engage in conduct that the law regards as wrongful. Most commonly, the intentional tort defendant is consciously aware of his wrongdoing; he is always aware of his act.

Negligence. Negligent wrongs entail unreasonably risky behavior that actually results in harm. The defendant in the negligence case is sometimes aware that he is taking unreasonable risks; he is always in

§ 1

1. See Chapter 26.

2. Sometimes courts recognize a third category, placed between the first two. A willful or wanton wrong is a species of negligence because the wanton defendant does not intend an invasion of the plaintiff's rights. At the same time, it has some resemblance to an intentional wrong because the the defendant has an anti-social state of mind; he is conscious of creating a high risk of harm.

violation of reasonableness standards whether he is consciously aware of that fact or not.

Expanding and limiting liability for fault. Although fault of some kind is commonly found in tort cases, courts may at times seem to expand liability beyond the limits of fault. Sometimes this occurs when courts seem to define fault to include rather ordinary conduct. At other times, even faulty behavior does not result in liability. Several reasons explain these apparent departures from the fault principle. For instance, courts do not ordinarily impose tort liability for negligence unless the negligence causes harm. Beyond this, courts may refuse to impose liability for wrongful conduct that in fact causes harm when the harm it causes is remote or fortuitous. These and some other instances may qualify or limit the fault principle. Nevertheless, fault remains the basis of tort liability in the overwhelming number of cases.

Strict liability. In a few instances tort law imposes strict liability. Strict liability is liability without proof of fault. Apart from these few instances, an accidentally caused harm is ordinarily not a tort at all; there is no general strict liability. In contrast, intentional or negligent infliction of physical harm is almost always tortious, even if it is subject to defenses in a particular case. The two best-known instances of common law strict liability are cases in which the defendant engages in some abnormally dangerous activity and those in which the defendant manufactures a defective product. In both of those cases liability may be imposed as a matter of legal policy, irrespective of the defendant's fault. In many instances of strict liability, however, the defendant may be at fault in fact, even if the plaintiff has not proved it.

Types of Harm—The Interests Protected

Types of interests protected. Tort liability can also be defined in part by the types of interests or values it protects. Tort law recognizes three distinct legal interests that deserve protection against wrongdoing. These interests are a person's interest in (1) physical security and autonomy; (2) emotional security and other intangible interests such as privacy and reputation; and (3) economic security and opportunity.

Legal rules give the greatest protection to physical security of persons and property. Intentional and negligent physical interference with persons are both ordinarily tortious in the absence of a good justification. The negligent driver who strikes a pedestrian unintentionally is liable in tort just as the intentional bully who sexually harasses his victim. When the defendant physically interferes with the plaintiff's person or the plaintiff's property in a way that counts as a tort, the plaintiff can recover for all her reasonably connected damages, including reasonable damages for emotional harm and damages for economic losses.

When it comes to intangible harm without physical interference or physical harm, courts are much more reluctant to impose tort liability. One form of intangible harm is pure emotional harm. For example, one

might intentionally or negligently cause distress to the plaintiff by the use of unpleasant words. In such cases the plaintiff may suffer emotional injury but no physical interference with her person. Some conduct that causes only intangible harm is tortious and some is not, but courts often demonstrate great caution about imposing liability for intangible harm unless the defendant has physically interfered with the plaintiff's person or property.

Economic harms. Very similar statements can be made about pure economic harm, that is, pocketbook harms that do not result from physical interference with person or property. The sign-carrying protester or religious speaker who posts himself outside the plaintiff's shop may drive the plaintiff's customers away. This is economic harm, but unless the protestor or speaker is guilty of physical interference with the plaintiff or her property, the chances are very good that the economic harm to the plaintiff will not be redressed at all. In this particular example, the right we all have to comment honestly and truthfully would be most significant. In other economic harm cases, cases that do not necessarily involve free speech issues, different reasons may lead to the same result. There are assuredly many economic torts that will result in liability. The point is that courts are more cautious in protecting the economic interest, as distinct from the physical security interest.

§ 2. Tort and Crime

Purposes of criminal and tort law. The relationship between tort law and criminal law is largely explained by their respective purposes. The purpose of criminal punishment is primarily to vindicate the state's interests in deterring crime and imposing justice. The purpose of tort liability is in no way inconsistent, but its emphasis is different. It is primarily to vindicate the individual victim and the victim's rights and secondarily to confirm and reinforce public standards of behavior.

Tort law growing out of criminal law. In the development of English law, tort law arose out of criminal law. Judges who imposed punishment upon lawbreakers at one time also occasionally imposed civil liability. Judges and lawyers gradually perceived that criminal punishment and civil liability had related but distinct purposes. Tort law developed into a separate field in itself, aimed at providing distinctly civil remedies.

Conduct as both criminal and tortious. Today, a single act might constitute both a crime and a tort. For example, if a defendant beats a person, he is almost certainly committing a crime for which the state can prosecute and punish. He is also committing a tort, for which the injured individual may sue and recover compensation. The individual's tort suit may proceed whether or not the crime is prosecuted.

Interaction of criminal and tort law. In tort cases, courts will often take notice of the fact that the defendant's conduct amounted to a crime and will give weight to this fact in determining whether the conduct also amounted to a tort. But this does not work the other way around. Crime

is usually defined by statute; whether the defendant's conduct is a tort is not important in determining whether conduct violates criminal law.

Substantive comparisons: intent and harm. Substantively speaking, there is no necessary correlation between tort and crime. The most fundamental basis for criminal liability is intent, often very specific intent. Some kind of intent is also required for some torts, but more commonly mere negligence coupled with actual harm will suffice for liability. A second important difference in the two fields can be seen in the different ways in which actual harm is treated. Criminal law redresses the state's interests in the security of society. It may punish conduct that threatens those interests even when no harm has been done. Speeding increases risks to others and so may be punished criminally. Tort law, aimed at protection of individuals, would never impose liability for speeding alone; tort law would impose liability only if harm results.

Procedural comparisons. On the procedural side, tort and crime differ enormously. Criminal prosecutions ordinarily must be initiated by the government; tort suits may be brought by an aggrieved individual. Criminal prosecutions can succeed only if the proof shows guilt beyond a reasonable doubt; tort suits can succeed if the proof shows an actionable tort by a more-likely-than-not standard.

§ 3. Tort and Contract

Breach of contract is not in itself a tort. The conventional view goes further. It holds that the fields of tort and contract are entirely distinct because contract duties are created by the promises of the parties, while tort duties are created by the courts and imposed as rules of law. On this view, the province of torts is wrongs and the province of contract is agreements or promises. This perception is that the fields of tort and contract hardly touch each other, much less overlap. Another conventional view supports the same conclusion. It asserts that contracts are largely about economic matters such as buying and selling; many torts typically involve physical harms.

A third point is not so often mentioned, but it is important. Contract law is at least formally strict liability law. Most of tort law, on the other hand, is at least formally fault-based. Specifically, a person is often liable for a contract breach even if he is not at fault and made every effort to perform the contract as promised. But one is not ordinarily liable under tort law even for conduct that causes horrible injuries unless he is at fault in some way. The reasoning and the formal themes of tort law thus differ enormously from those of contract law.

Finally, in the actual practice of law, lawyers who negotiate and draft contracts are seldom focused on litigation. Tort law, with its emphasis on compensation after the fact rather than on planning, is preeminently a law of litigation and litigators. Most cases are settled, but they are settled on the basis of expected litigation outcomes.

Some of the conventional views stated above are partly correct but they are not wholly so. The fields of tort and contract do in fact overlap and share many of the same premises.

First, it is usually true that rules of law govern tort cases, while the parties' agreement determines contract liabilities; but the parties' agreement controls their rights only because courts accept a rule of law that says so. For this reason, a rule of law ultimately lies behind both tort and contract. Second, contractual promises sometimes create or at least underlie tort duties, so that what begins as contract ends as tort if one of the parties is injured. For example, if I promise to provide you a safety net for your work as a roofer, but the net I provide will not hold when you fall into it with the result that you are injured, courts may hold me liable in tort even though I would not be responsible to provide a net unless I had contracted to do so. A third area of overlap occurs when tort law is invoked to protect contract rights. If I interfere with your contract with another person so you cannot reap its benefits, I may be liable to you in tort.

Perhaps most importantly, much of tort law is shaped by the expectations of the parties, even when those expectations are not explicitly made part of any contract. Expectations in a relationship have some consensual qualities, in that respect resembling contract. As the New Jersey Court said, when a person is in a consensual relationship, courts judge the reasonableness of his conduct by reference to his "consent and mutual understanding" and by the "common expectations that serve to identify what conduct is acceptable" among people in the relationship.[1] When the parties stand in some particular relationship, like that of lawyer and client or bailor and bailee, or seller and buyer, courts historically constructed the tort duties out of the parties' expectations. Finally, tort duties may at times be limited by the parties' expectations, undertakings, or tacit agreements. So the contract cousins, consent and expectation, play a very large role indeed in shaping tort duties.

A more radical view is that the distinction between tort and contract is entirely manipulative; courts might characterize a case as a contract case when they wish to focus exclusively on the promises of the parties and their enforceability but characterize a case as a tort case when they wish to focus on or emphasize public policy or rules imposed by courts that do not necessarily vindicate the parties' promises. In this view, the distinction between tort and contract does not represent any underlying legal reality; it is merely instead a distinction invoked to facilitate the court's analysis and conclusions.

A more moderate view is that in some cases, the distinctions between tort and contract may be distinctions of degree rather than kind, or they may reflect only factual setting or professional habit. Further than that, contract cases always involve promises. Tort cases

§ 3

1. Crawn v. Campo, 136 N.J. 494, 507, 643 A.2d 600, 606 (1994).

often involve expectations of the parties, but only occasionally do they involve explicit promises. Numerous tort cases are characteristically disputes between strangers, that is, people who have no special relationship marked by contract. Such cases cannot be thought of as involving any contract law or any overlap with the field of contracts.

But if the basic division between tort and contract continues to dominate legal thinking and research, that fact should not obscure the importance of contract, informal understandings, and even relationships between the parties in determining duties under the rules of tort law. When a contract is in the picture, tort law almost always treats the contract as important and worth examining.

§ 4. Tort and Property

Crime, Tort, Contract and Property designate the traditional great fields of the common law. The preceding sections have indicated that tort law has affinities with both the law of crimes and the law of contracts. Tort law also has affinities with the law of property.

Property law aims at defining rights of people with respect to things rather than with respect to other people. The things at issue in property law can be intangible as well as tangible; one can own a patent or copyright as well as a farm called Blackacre. Property law is fundamentally concerned with establishing ownership of property, with the incidents of ownership, and with the means by which ownership can be changed. The incidents of ownership may include the right to physical integrity of property, the right to exclusive possession of property, and the right to reasonable enjoyment of property.

Because tort law is necessarily centered on conduct of persons, or at least on results of that conduct, it does not seem at first glance to be concerned at all with static ownership. On this ground it is clearly distinguishable from property law. In addition, property law resembles contract law in that it is largely a matter of consensual agreements and in that lawyers engaged in property practice are likely to be drafters, negotiators, planners, and facilitators rather than litigators.

Yet ownership of property underlies many torts, and some tort actions are expressly brought for the purpose of establishing or confirming rights in property, while others are brought to vindicate or protect those rights. The ancient action of trespass was a tort action brought to assess damages for invasion of the plaintiff's real property (and later for trespass to chattels as well). In this kind of case, tort law can be viewed as a kind of helper or action arm for property law.

In defining the tort of trespass the courts necessarily define something of the incidents of ownership of real property. If I enter your land in good faith and in the reasonable belief that it is my own, courts may nevertheless declare that I am a trespasser and liable to you for damages. In so saying, courts in the tort suit determine important incidents of your ownership. By this tort law rule, courts are saying that you have rights to exclusive possession even against a person who enters in good

faith, not merely against those who know the land is yours. In the same way, if courts hold that my factory smoke is a nuisance that prevents your reasonable use and enjoyment of land, they have not only defined the legal limits of my conduct; they have also defined the incidents of your land ownership.

So tort law blends with property law just as it does with contract law. Sometimes the only viable issue in a tort case is truly an issue of property rights. At other times the issue will emphasize the defendant's conduct and its possible wrongful character. Differences must often be described in terms of emphasis or focus rather than in terms of essentialities. As a practical matter, however, when the issue is mainly about underlying property rights rather than about the wrongfulness of the defendant's conduct, the case must be left to the law of property rather than the law of tort.

§ 5. Torts and Regulatory Control

The immediately preceding sections have compared tort law with other fields of law. A different way to help define the scope of tort law is to contrast it with governmental regulation, which is not a field of law but a different mechanism for enforcing rules. The reason for making the contrast is that both institutions—tort law and regulation—can be seen as means of imposing a degree of social control by preventing injury or compensating it. There are endless debates about whether tort law is effective in its aims, but that is another question.

Government regulation (of dangerous activities, for example) is always derived ultimately from legislation. A statute passed by the Congress or a state or commonwealth legislature might specifically forbid some dangerous activities. Or, it might set standards for safety and create an administrative agency to enforce those standards. The Occupational Safety and Health Acts passed by the Congress and by many state legislatures are examples. The statutes require employers to observe certain levels of safety and empower an agency (a) to make concrete standards by promulgating regulations, (b) to inspect, and (c) to enforce the standards. The administrative agency might, for example, prescribe the amount and design of bracing required to protect workers in trenches from cave-ins.[1]

Regulatory systems govern many important activities in society. They are not limited to health and safety risks. Extensive statutes and regulations govern the way in which securities like stocks and bonds are sold and the kind of information that must be provided to prospective buyers. This is economic, not safety regulation. But like safety regulation, it differs enormously from tort law, yet has its tort law counterparts.

§ 5

1. 29 C.F.R. § 1926.652 prescribes details about slopes, soil types, shoring systems, and shield systems. An appendix gives details on shoring construction.

What are the important differences between a tort law way and the regulatory way of trying to control conduct and make compensation? First, regulators look forward: regulation is always formulated in advance. If four-by-four timbers must be used to shore up a trench, the regulation will say so in advance. Tort cases look backward: they decide that conduct that has already taken place was wrongful.

In part this difference derives from another. Regulation is often quite specific and detailed (about the size of the timbers, for example). Tort law standards are usually broad and general until a specific case is decided. Tort law standards are never likely to provide for the use of four-by-four timbers. Instead, tort law standards are likely to provide that the contractor constructing a trench should exercise reasonable care. After an injury has occurred, the court in a tort case will decide whether the contractor's shoring-up methods were reasonable or not. Once the tort case is decided, however, it has effect as precedent, and as precedent it looks forward in time just as regulation does. Some jurists once thought that as precedents accumulated they would eventually provide a kind of catalog or code of all possible answers, but precedents in torts do not work this way, partly because each case is likely to be a little different.

A signal difference between regulation and tort law is that regulation does not ordinarily aim at compensation. The OSHA regulation on trenches, for example, aims at preventing injury, not at compensating injury that actually occurs. If an OSHA regulation is violated, the OSHA regulators might ultimately enforce a civil penalty, but that penalty will not go to an injured person. This point shows that regulatory control is closely analogous to criminal law. Tort law, in contrast, aims specifically at compensating the victim of a wrong by awarding damages. Only occasionally does it attempt to prevent injury in advance by issuing an injunction.

Many lawyers distinguishing regulation from tort law would perhaps think first of the procedural incidents of the two systems. Tort law is court law. The victim of a wrong sues. The victim does not rely on others to enforce rights. Suit is in a court (usually nearby) and one that is open to all individuals. Most notably, the facts in the suit are decided by a jury if either party requests it, not by a judge or an administrator.

Probably no practicing lawyers would think that tort law and regulatory law systems are alike. Yet for all their differences, they are not located in impenetrable compartments. Courts in tort cases may adopt administrative regulations as guidelines for tort law. And courts as well as administrative agencies sometimes provide rules in advance by issuing injunctions. Sometimes the injunction will be just as specific and detailed as an administrative regulation.

§ 6. Torts and Personal Injury Law

Many people think of personal injury cases when they think of tort law. But tort law is more than injury law because it includes rules for

wrongs that cause economic and emotional injury even when no physical harm of any kind has been done. Tort law is also less than personal injury law. Other social institutions in addition to tort law attempt to control and compensate personal injury. Tort law is, in fact, only one of a number of ways in contemporary American society aimed at creating incentives for safety or at providing compensation for loss or both.

The alternative institutions are not even the institutions of the common law, much less of tort law. Yet they account for most of the compensation paid for injury. Tort law cannot be meaningfully understood without understanding that such alternative systems exist. Alternative non-tort systems include social security support for totally disabled persons, medical benefits derived from social security or otherwise, workers' compensation benefits for those injured on the job, no-fault automobile injury systems operating under insurance plans, and others. In some cases dangerous products are subjected to special taxes, which are then used as a fund to pay for injuries those products cause. Mass torts claims, in which hundreds of thousands of people are injured by a product such as asbestos, begin with tort law but are so large and complex that they have generated unique adaptive behaviors within the law. Global settlements of these claims may prescribe more definitions and rules than an administrative agency administering, say, workers' compensation.[1]

Alternative, non-tort systems seek to compensate for injury even when injury is not caused by wrongdoing. In that sense they are strict liability systems. So the element of fault so prominent in most of tort law is almost wholly missing in the alternative systems. Non-tort systems usually attempt to resolve the injury-compensation question outside of court; although the administrators may hold some court-like hearings, there will be no jury. They also almost always reject or limit recovery for the victim's pain and suffering. For lawyers dealing with personal injury cases, torts does not cover all of their work; they must also work with alternative systems. Some of these alternative, non-tort systems are discussed later in this book.[2]

§ 7. Is Tort Law A Coherent Field?

The boundaries of torts and tort law staked loosely in the preceding sections may suggest that torts cannot be a coherent field. It is not only large in itself, including all kinds of wrongs of which there are many if not infinite varieties; it also has family ties to criminal, contract, property, and regulatory law, not to mention alternative compensation schemes. The size and diversity of tort law is emphasized by the fact that lawyers do not specialize in tort law but only in some patch of it. Probably no lawyer could be said to "specialize" in a field so diverse that

§ 6

1. See Peter H. Schuck, Mass Torts: an Institutional Evolutionist Perspective, 80 Cornell L. Rev. 941 (1995).

2. See Chapter 27.

it includes medical malpractice, products liability, interference with contract, libel, privacy, sexual harassment, civil rights, malicious prosecution, and other torts. If size and diversity of tort law threatens to render it incoherent, so does the fact that tort law is always changing.

The unity in tort law, if there is any, does not lie in factual similarities among the different torts. The common threads in tort law may not be satisfying, especially to a beginning student of the field, but they are real even if they sometimes break. First, the issue of fault dominates most of tort law. Although fault may be defined quite differently according to the factual setting and relationships of the parties, courts are deeply involved with defining fault in a large proportion of all tort cases. The fact that fault is not always properly defined, or is defined with policy problems as well as with justice in mind, does not reflect a rejection of the fault standard, only a difference of opinion about how it should be applied. Where courts have deviated from the fault principle, either in their formal rules or in their unconscious applications of it, they have nevertheless struggled hard to articulate a meaningful basis for legal responsibility that matches in at least some degree the community's sense of justice. Fault, or some aspect of fault, often finds its way into the case by the back door when it is denied entry at the front.

Second, tort cases have developed and continue to develop a cluster of analytical tools or ways of thinking that are special to tort cases. They say that the defendant's conduct must have in fact caused the plaintiff's harm, and more than that, the defendant's conduct must be a significant or proximate cause of the harm. Those concepts are not unique to tort law, but they are uniquely important in tort law.

Third, the process of lawyering tort claims is, overall, enormously different from the process of, say, contract drafting or estate planning. Part of that difference lies in the fact that tort law is litigation law. Tort litigation usually entails a jury, so the members of the public are present to participate and view the professional judges and lawyers at work. The public presence transforms the private world of legal professionals and affects the way they think of themselves and the proceedings, so that the culture of decision-making in American tort law is indeed quite special. The jury's role has made judges and lawyers especially sensitive in tort cases not only to procedures and remedies, but also to the problems of proof and evidence. One of the enduring concerns of the tort law process in the United States is the role of the jury in relation to the role of the judge. Other process differences are generated through a cluster of tort law institutions, including the contingent percentage fee and the prevalence of liability insurance as well as the special role of the jury.

If tort law is a coherent field, its coherence is thus not derived from the factual unity of the cases it determines, but from its focus on wrongdoing, its increased emphasis on certain analytical tools, and its virtually unique process of lawyering and deciding cases.

TOPIC B. AIMS, POLICIES AND METHODS OF TORT LAW

§ 8. Justice, Policy, and Process Aims of Tort Law

What are the conscious and articulated aims and policies of judges when they choose or apply tort rules? Because judges are humans and can fall prey to bias and cultural assumptions, their decisions will no doubt reflect social or personal attitudes from time to time, attitudes that may hold rational persuasion at bay. The question here, though, is not what judges do as fate-or culture-determined creatures, but what judges do when they are at their best, acting consciously and explaining rationally their decisions. Put differently, what kinds of arguments of justice or policy, as distinct from arguments of self-interest or bias, can lawyers make to judges who are faced with a choice of different tort rules?

In medieval England, the law of torts, like the law of crimes, had modest aims, principally to discourage violence and revenge. Today's tort law has much grander aims. All of the aims are laudable, but sometimes one of them will conflict with another. The most commonly mentioned aims of tort law are (1) compensation of injured persons and (2) deterrence of undesirable behavior. Both of these aims, however, are subsumed in whole or part under broader goals.

Morality or corrective justice. Particular aims of tort law are usually erected under one of two large systems of thought. The first bases tort law on moral responsibility or corrective justice. It attempts to hold defendants liable for harms they wrongfully caused and no others. Good social effects may result when courts act to right the wrongs done by defendants, but in this system of thought that is not the point of imposing liability. Liability is imposed instead when and only when it is "right" to do so.

Social utility or policy. The second large system of thought reverses the emphasis; it bases tort law on social policy or a good-for-all-of-us view. Social policy may coincide with justice in particular cases, but the dominant concern is not justice to the individual; it is to provide a system of rules that, overall, works toward the good of society.

Process. One kind of utility or social policy is inward looking. Rules must be made with the legal process itself in mind. They must be the kind of rules judges and juries can understand and apply in a practical way, and they must not leave too much to the judge's or the jury's discretion. These and a host of similar considerations focus on the litigation process itself as a good to be preserved rather than on the abstract ideal of justice or social utility.

Potential conflicts. The first two ways of looking at tort law are usually regarded as antithetical to each other.[1] Although justice and

§ 8

1. George P. Fletcher, Corrective Justice for Moderns, 106 HARV. L. REV. 1658 (1993) (Reviewing Jules Coleman, Risks and Wrongs) ("The passion to do justice

policy often point to the same result, they do not always do so, and when they do not, one of these views must prevail or both must be compromised. The legal process view might also conflict with the aims of justice or those of policy.

Suppose a city, facing a raging and spreading fire, attempts to create a firebreak by blowing up a row of houses. Because time is critical, the city insists upon doing so before the plaintiff, who owns one of the houses, can remove his furniture. When the whole thing is over, the plaintiff claims damages from the city for the value of the furniture he could have saved. The city has acted for the good of its residents generally, but the plaintiff is the one who pays the costs. If the city's action is to be judged by a standard of social policy, some jurists might say the city should not be liable. On the other hand, if it is judged by corrective justice standards, the city should pay for the damage it did. Otherwise, the city would get the advantage of its action (whatever that advantage might be) but would pay none of the costs. There are more subtle examples, but this one is enough to suggest the potential conflict between a decision based upon (supposed) social policy and one based upon justice to the individual.

The goals summarized in this section are discussed in many, many tort cases. These goals influence results and they also stand as measures for evaluating cases and making arguments. They are central in the practice as well as the theory of tort law. They also play a large part in evaluating subsidiary aims such as compensation and deterrence discussed in the sections that follow.

§ 9. Ideas of Corrective Justice[1]

Tort law is at least partly rights-based. That is, it is at least partly based on ideals of corrective justice, ideals of righting wrongs, or (somewhat relatedly) ideals about accountability or personal responsibility for harm-causing conduct.[2] Every claim is unique because it is about individual human beings, or at least individual corporations acting in particular circumstances.[3]

Distributive justice distinguished. One part of the corrective justice ideal disclaims any intent to effect *distributive* justice.[4] Distributive

does not admit of trade offs against utilitarian criteria"). Some writers have tried to find some middle ground in which both morality and social utility are given appropriate room for operation. See IZHAK ENGLARD, THE PHILOSOPHY OF TORT LAW (1993).

§ 9

1. Many books and articles are devoted to ideas about corrective justice. Symposia are reflected in 37 ARIZ. L. REV. 3 (1995) and 77 IOWA L. REV. 1 (1992).

2. Kenneth W. Simons, Negligence, 16 SOCIAL PHILOSOPHY & POLICY 2 52, 91 (1999) argues that fault is a more basic conception in tort law than corrective justice and explains the legal rules better.

3. See Kenneth S. Abraham, What Is a Tort Claim? An Interpretation of Contemporary Tort Reform, 51 MD. L. REV. 172 (1992).

4. See Weinrib, Corrective Justice, 77 IOWA L. REV. 403 (1992).

justice ideals deal with the question, "How should goods in society be distributed among people?" If you worry that some people do not have enough to eat and think that children should not starve even if their parents do not work, then you might think the basic goods of life are not justly distributed. The most traditional elements of tort law do not in fact aim at a redistribution of goods but are concerned with corrective justice instead.

Policy and utility distinguished. As already indicated, corrective justice ideals or standards are also distinguished from ideals or standards based on policy or utility. Tort law often takes policy and utility into account as well as rights or corrective justice.[5] Policy and utility questions ask what is good for society as a whole. Those questions definitely do not address issues of right and wrong in individual cases. For instance, defendants sometimes argue that they should not be required to pay full damages for harms they cause because tort liability for full damages will drive up the costs of insurance and might even cause some defendants to go out of business. The public in general, they say, would be the loser. This kind of argument is an argument based on policy or utility. Regardless whether the argument is factually sound and logically valid, it is an argument that attempts to establish ideals of public good, not ideals of justice between two individuals. A corrective justice approach in contrast asks whether the defendant wronged the plaintiff and how to right that wrong, even if righting the wrong turns out to cost more than the plaintiff lost.

Plaintiffs also present arguments of policy. They often argue that the defendant as a business enterprise can better "distribute the risk" or "distribute the loss" that results from accidental injury. Even if the defendant is not at fault, they argue, the defendant can better absorb the costs of injuries associated with its enterprise, or even pass those losses on to others, by raising its prices. In certain areas this kind of argument, associated with the phrase "enterprise liability" or "collective liability,"[6] has sometimes but not always been effective. Arguments for liabilities divorced from rights might also have a special place in mass tort litigation where hundreds of thousands of people have been injured by products like asbestos or the Dalkon Shield.[7] Such arguments, however, are not about corrective justice—righting wrongs—but about finding effective ways of dealing with injury.

Fault and corrective justice. Tort law imposes liability upon defendants for conduct the law treats as wrong. In most instances, the conduct adjudged as wrong can be viewed as morally faulty conduct: it is intentional misconduct or at least unreasonably risky conduct likely to cause harm to others. In these cases, tort law seems to be commensurate

5. See IZHAK ENGLARD, THE PHILOSOPHY OF TORT LAW 227–229 (1992). You could also say that our understanding of corrective justice might be modified according to context, perhaps in a way to take policy and process needs into account.

6. See Robert L. Rabin, Some Thoughts on the Ideology of Enterprise Liability, 55 MD. L. REV. 1190 (1996).

7. See Francis E. McGovern, Resolving Mature Mass Tort Litigation, 69 B. U. L. REV. 659 (1989).

with corrective justice ideals. The defendant's fault is a wrong that has harmed the plaintiff in some recognizable way; tort liability, by requiring the wrongdoer to compensate the plaintiff,[8] can put the accounts right between the parties.

Conversely, it can be argued that in a corrective justice scheme, it would be wrong to impose liability upon a defendant who is not at fault in causing the plaintiff's harm. Society may wish to compensate injured people by the use of public funds, but it cannot justly force one innocent individual to compensate another.

These views emphasize individual accountability for fault, accompanied by individual freedom to act without fault. They are consistent with an ideal of social responsibility for victims, however; they do not speak against government compensation for victims when the defendant is not at fault, only against compensation by the faultless defendant.

Strict liability and corrective justice. When tort law imposes liability without fault, does it go beyond the principle of corrective justice? At least *some* strict liability seems commensurate with corrective justice. For example, suppose a long-standing custom in our neighborhood permits any neighbor to borrow garden equipment from any other neighbor, but the custom is equally strong that if the equipment is damaged or lost while in the borrower's possession, the borrower must make the loss good. Suppose I borrow your lawnmower and without my fault it is damaged when a truck backs over it in my driveway. A rule that imposes liability upon me would be a strict liability rule because I was not at fault. Even so, liability seems to accord with corrective justice so long as you and I both know of the custom.

Uniting the potential for gains and losses. Some thinkers have advocated a general regime of strict liability on the ground that strict liability is a morally based system and therefore within the principle of corrective justice. One idea behind this view is that when I make choices about my conduct, I am entitled to the gains that may result from that conduct (including my personal pleasure), so I should also take responsibility for the losses.[9] If I choose to hang-glide off the mountainside, either for personal pleasure or as part of a demonstration that brings me profit, then I should pay any damages I do when I cannot control the glider and land on your vegetable garden or your cat.[10] This line of

8. It may be argued that if anyone, wrongdoer or not, compensates the plaintiff, corrective justice has been done. In this view, the state or an insurance company could compensate victims in the interests of corrective justice. Others have emphasized that corrective justice is not merely compensation, but compensation *from* the wrongdoer; that is, it requires a demonstration of "public respect for rights and public recognition of the transgressor's fault by requiring something important to be given up on one side and received on the other, even if there is no equivalence of value possible." Margaret Jane Radin, Compensation and Commensurability, 43 Duke L. J. 56 (1993).

9. A most elaborate theory of strict liability based on corrective justice was presented many years ago by Richard Epstein in A Theory of Strict Liability (1980). His theory is much too complex to permit adequate summary.

10. This idea can be viewed as a moral idea and hence an appropriate part of corrective justice reasoning, but it is also an economic idea which says that an enterprise

thought works best when an active person causes harm to a person or thing at rest. When two hang-gliders (or car drivers) crash into each other without fault, it is much harder to work out a system of strict liability that is also based on corrective justice.

Nonreciprocal risks. A different view about the corrective justice basis of strict liability is that strict liability can justly be imposed when the defendant imposes nonreciprocal risks on the plaintiff. For example, an airplane pilot imposes only small and quite reasonable risks to people on the ground, since crashes are extremely rare. Nevertheless, the pilot imposes some risks to people below while they impose none upon him. If reciprocity is a moral test of liability, then strict liability should be imposed upon the pilot, and such liability would be commensurate with corrective justice reasoning.[11]

Community standards. A third view might emphasize community standards as the basis for corrective justice liability. Community standards might be embodied in an explicit custom, like the neighborhood custom in the lawnmower example above. Or they might be embodied only in the views of the jury that decides the case. If the jury is representative of the community as a whole, its verdict is likely to reflect the implicit standards of fault and liability that already exist at that time and that place. This, too, is a view of corrective justice.[12] Presumably it would permit strict liability where the community standard called for it, perhaps in cases like that of the borrowed lawnmower.

Fault again. Although innovative thinkers have sought to justify strict liability within a corrective justice framework, many of the cases put seem to be cases of special kinds of fault, for example, fault as judged by the fairness of imposing non-reciprocal risks or as judged by deviations from community-accepted norms. Whatever is to be said of strict liability theories of corrective justice, the great majority of tort cases turn on some kind of perception that the defendant is at fault in a significant way. At least for those cases, tort law begins with corrective justice ideals, even if those ideals may be modified by pragmatic, process, or policy considerations in particular cases.

should not be permitted to externalize its costs. See § 11. Both forms of the idea are attractive but both raise additional questions. What costs should be regarded as part of the potential costs or losses that go with hang-gliding? If the answer is "foreseeable harms to others," then the argument sounds like an argument for negligence liability, not strict liability, because the judgment that a defendant has taken unreasonable or negligent risks is based on the conclusion that the risks were foreseeable.

11. George Fletcher, Fairness and Utility in Tort Theory, 85 Harv. L. Rev. 537 (1972), developed the reciprocity idea. Later, Fletcher modified his views a little to speak of "dominance" as ground for liability in contrast to "failed cooperation" which calls for dividing liability between the parties. Fletcher, Corrective Justice for Moderns, 106 Harv. L. Rev. 1658 (1993) (Reviewing Jules Coleman, Risks and Wrongs).

12. Catherine Wells, Tort Law as Corrective Justice: A Pragmatic Justification for Jury Adjudication, 88 Mich. L. Rev. 2348 (1990). Other writers emphasizing community standards as a basis for liability include Michael Wells, Scientific Policymaking and the Torts Revolution: The Revenge of the Ordinary Observer, 26 Ga. L. Rev. 725 (1992); Patrick Kelley, Who Decides? Community Safety Conventions at the Heart of Tort Liability, 38 Clev. State. L. Rev. 315 (1990).

§ 10. Compensation, Risk Distribution, Fault

Compensation. Compensation of injured persons is one of the generally accepted aims of tort law. Payment of compensation to injured persons is desirable. If a person has been wronged by a defendant, it is just that the defendant make compensation.[1] Compensation is also socially desirable, for otherwise the uncompensated injured persons will represent further costs and problems for society. However, a corrective justice system of tort law will compensate only those who are injured by some conduct that can be called a wrong. A tort system based solely on social policy might conceivably seek to exact compensation from defendants who have caused harms by accident but not by wrongdoing or, alternatively, might provide a social system of insurance for everyone.

Magnitude of injury problem. Injury costs are socially as well as individually significant. A study published in 1991 estimated that at that time non-fatal personal injuries resulted in $98 billion in annual direct costs with an additional $175 billion in annual economic costs.[2] Compensation for injury may actually help reduce personal injury costs. Appropriate medical attention, for example, may allow an injured person to return to work sooner. Injury also has ripple effects especially when it promotes economic hardship. Children and others within a family stressed by serious injury and consequent economic difficulty may reflect that stress by inflicting still further economic costs upon society, for example, by abusing alcohol or drugs.

Social costs of injury as grounds for strict liability. The social costs of injury suggest that compensation for injury might be desirable for policy or social reasons. It is true that compensation is usually stated to be one of the goals of tort law. In that bald form, the statement suggests that compensation should be recoverable in all cases, not merely when corrective justice demands it. In other words, if compensation is an unqualified goal in itself, defendants would be liable whenever they caused harm, even if they were not at fault.

Risk distribution or loss spreading. With this in mind, some commentators have argued that tort liability should be strict or expansive in order to secure compensation for more injured persons. Some defendants if not all were seen as good "risk distributors" who should be liable for any harms they cause regardless of fault because they can "distribute" the costs of paying compensation. This means that some defendants, such as products manufacturers, could pay compensation for injuries they cause and then recoup some or all of those costs by raising the price of products. In this view, each individual purchaser of the products will pay a tiny fraction of the costs of injuries inflicted, by those products and

§ 10

1. What counts as "compensation" is in part the subject matter of remedies. Conceivably corrective justice might accept some response from the wrongdoer-defendant that is not measured by money losses. See Margaret Jane Radin, Compensation and Commensurability, 43 Duke L. J. 56 (1993).

2. Deborah R. Hensler, et al., Compensation for Accidental Injuries in the United States (RAND 1991).

the injured person will not be compelled to bear the entire cost alone.[3] Loss would thus cause less social dislocation. At the same time, an enterprise would be forced to internalize losses typically generated by the business itself.

Limited acceptance of risk distribution arguments. The common law of tort has not in fact generally adopted views that compensation is more important than corrective justice or that liability should be strict. Distribution arguments and strict liability have gone hand in hand, but only in a few kinds of cases.[4] They have not supplanted fault as the most common basis for tort liability.

Moral and policy reasons for limiting compensation to cases of fault. Since compensation *is* indeed important and one of the goals of tort law, why is it that courts do not adopt strict liability across the board and order compensation in every case in which the defendant causes harm? The most obvious possibility is that judges feel heavily committed to a system of corrective justice and turn to social policy only when they feel social policy and corrective justice coincide at least in part. It is also possible, however, that in spite of social policy favoring compensation, other social policies counsel only limited compensation through the tort system.

First, the role of judges in framing schemes of distribution is doubtful. The risk distribution arguments may be sound, but sometimes may better be addressed to legislation. In fact, some legislation in effect adopts such arguments. Workers' compensation statutes, for example, impose strict liability upon employers when workers are injured on the job. The cost or loss is distributed in part to workers themselves, whose wages might be higher but for the employer's cost of insuring against their injury. Part of it is distributed to customers who buy the employer's products or services. Second, an invariable award of compensation that must be paid by a defendant may eliminate any deterrent effect that the award would have if it were confined to cases of fault. Third, the tort system is an extremely expensive system to operate. If compensation is the most important goal, the tort system is a poor way to accomplish it because other means are cheaper. For instance, workers' compensation insurance is usually more efficient than liability insurance used to pay tort judgments. Relatedly, the tort system is not in *fact* the source of most compensation for injury. Private insurance, such as the injured person's medical insurance, and public assistance programs provide most of the compensation that goes for injury.[5] Finally, the injured person

3. See Escola v. Coca Cola Bottling Co. of Fresno, 24 Cal.2d 453, 462, 150 P.2d 436, 441 (1944) (Traynor, J., concurring); George L. Priest, The Invention of Enterprise Liability: A Critical History of the Intellectual Foundations of Modern Tort Law, 14 J. LEG. STUD. 461 (1985); VIRGINIA E. NOLAN AND EDMUND URSIN, UNDERSTANDING ENTERPRISE LIABILITY 168 (1995).

4. See Gary T. Schwartz, The Beginning and the Possible End of the Rise of Modern American Tort Law, 26 GA. L. REV. 601(1992).

5. DEBORAH R. HENSLER, ET AL., COMPENSATION FOR ACCIDENTAL INJURIES IN THE UNITED STATES (Rand 1991). This study concludes that only 10% of all persons who get some kind of compensation for injuries receive

often bears some of the responsibility for her own injury, and in addition the parties may be equally good at "distributing" the risk by purchasing their own insurance.

§ 11. Fostering Freedom, Deterring Unsafe Conduct; Economic Analysis

Deterrence. Courts and writers almost always recognize that another aim of tort law is to deter certain kinds of conduct by imposing liability when that conduct causes harm. The idea of deterrence is not so much that an individual, having been held liable for a tort, would thereafter conduct himself better. It is rather the idea that all persons, recognizing potential tort liability, would tend to avoid conduct that could lead to tort liability. They might sometimes engage in the conduct in question, but only if they would get more out of it than the tort liability would cost. Some critics believe that tort law fails to provide systematic deterrence.[1]

Deterrence in corrective justice and social policy systems. Both corrective justice and social policy goals can agree that deterrence is acceptable, but the two approaches might call for deterring quite different conduct. If you focus on conduct that is wrongful in the sense of being unjust to an individual, you might regard any given act as wrongful even though it is economically useful in society. If you focus on social policy, you might want to forgive defendants who cause harms by their socially useful activities.

Suppose for example that there are two methods of constructing a building the defendant intends to build. One is quick, easy, and cheap. The other is slow and expensive. The trouble is that the quick, easy, cheap building is also a little more dangerous to build, so that, overall, more injuries occur in construction of the cheaper buildings than in construction of the more expensive ones that are slower to build. Not surprisingly, the defendant chooses to build the cheaper, quicker version. Suppose he builds it with care, but, as will inevitably happen sooner or later, someone is injured in a construction accident. Should the injured person have a claim against the builder-defendant?

A corrective justice approach to the builder. A corrective justice approach would not necessarily say that the builder had committed a wrong. However, in deciding whether a wrong was done, a hard-line corrective justice approach might give no weight to the fact that the defendant was doing something economically sound or socially useful. So it is quite possible that from a corrective justice standpoint, a jurist might say that the defendant was a wrongdoer in choosing to build the

payments under the tort system, that is, from the tortfeasor or his insurer. These payments amount to even less: 7% of the compensation dollar. The tort system plays a greater role, however, when it comes to auto cases.

§ 1

1. See, with different arguments, STEPHEN D. SUGARMAN, DOING AWAY WITH PERSONAL INJURY LAW 7–9 (1989); Daniel Shuman, The Psychology of Deterrence in Tort Law, 42 KAN. L. REV. 115 (1993).

riskier building, even though he built it with great care. That conclusion would lead to liability.

A social policy approach to the builder. A social policy approach would not necessarily approve the builder's choice any more than a corrective justice approach would necessarily disapprove it. However, in deciding whether the builder committed a legal wrong, a social policy approach would ask whether it would be good for society as a whole either to deter the builder's conduct or force him to pay for the harms done. So a social policy approach might well decide that it is socially desirable to foster economically sound decisions, such as the decision to build a cheaper building, at least if the money saved was more than the cost of injuries.

Economic analysis. As the example suggests, one particular kind of social policy consideration is the economic one. If economics is defined broadly enough to include a consideration of all human wants and desires, then perhaps all social policies are in a sense economic policies.

For instance, economic analysis of the personal injury part of tort law might attempt to suggest rules for finding the right balance between the number of injuries and the freedom of defendants to act. People in general ought to be free to build buildings, including cheaper ones, if they do so carefully; the law wants to protect their freedom and indeed encourage the enterprise because economically sound decisions are indeed good for the community as a whole. So one line of economic thought suggests that in deciding the builder's tort liability, the costs of injury should be weighed, but so should the social (economic) utility of the cheaper building.[2] This line of thought in fact accords with a great many decisions in the courts that do not mention economics at all. Depending on how much the builder saved and how high the injury costs were, this line of thought might lead a court to deny any recovery against the builder.

A different line of economic/public policy thinking might assert that if it is statistically likely that more injuries occur when the cheaper building is constructed, then the costs of those injuries should be regarded as a part of the builder's costs of doing business. Even if he is not regarded as being at fault, nevertheless, he chose the riskier method and got its benefits (less investment in the building); so he should take the disadvantages.[3] In economic terms, he should not be permitted to externalize his costs. This line of reasoning leads to the conclusion that the builder should be held liable for the injuries caused.[4]

Tort law has tended, although not universally, to resolve many disputes in a way consistent with the first line of economic analysis,

2. See §§ 144–146.

3. In § 9 this line of thought was presented as a moral rather than an economic principle.

4. Cf. Guido Calabresi, The Costs of Accidents (1970) (suggesting that if the activity (building, in this case) bears the costs of accidents associated with that activity, the costs of the activity will rise and accidents will be reduced either because people will seek alternate ways of avoiding the higher costs or ways of making the activity safer).

taking into account the benefits and costs of a particular activity in judging fault. On the other hand, workers' compensation and some other alternatives to tort law have resolved certain disputes in a way consistent with the second kind of analysis, holding the defendant liable even if he was not at fault.

§ 12. Individual Accountability and Social Responsibility: Alternative Compensation Schemes

Some of the large differences in approach sketched in the preceding sections can be understood in terms of the constant tension in our society between individual accountability and a measure of social responsibility. We are all individuals and we are all members of society. That duality shapes our dilemma with many issues in life, not merely tort issues.

Part of the tensions between personal accountability and social responsibility are minimized or resolved when an individual injured by an innocent defendant can seek compensation from public sources rather than from the defendant. Such an approach treats innocently caused injury as a social responsibility rather than a matter of the defendant's personal accountability. The argument is that when both the plaintiff and defendant are innocent, there is no justice in shifting the plaintiff's suffering to the equally innocent defendant, but there might be a point in alleviating the plaintiff's suffering through some kind of insurance or public benefit system.

Plans like workers' compensation, which requires employers to pay compensation for workers' injuries even when employers are not at fault, may be rationalized on the ground that injury is a regular cost of business to be borne by the business itself. If injury is seen to be as much a part of the worker's life as a part of the business, however, that explanation becomes less convincing. A different explanation for workers' compensation plans is that the employer is held liable without fault because he can pass on the costs of employee injury to the public who buys his product or services. In this view, the employer is not himself ultimately responsible for worker injuries; rather he is a conduit for public liability.

Although alternative compensation plans help fulfil a sense of social responsibility or at least help solve a social problem, they may raise doubts about whether they give enough scope for either corrective justice or deterrence in the form of individual accountability for wrongs. The workers' compensation system, for example, substitutes limited compensation obligations for tort liability, so that the negligent employer escapes any obligation to make full tort payment to a wronged individual. From the employer's point of view, this reduction in tort liability may be balanced by the employer's obligation to pay other workers even when the employer is not at fault, but even so, the employer's incentive for safety is reduced.

Justice and accountability go hand in hand with the individualization that has been characteristic of the traditional legal system. The plaintiff in a tort case tells her own story, the individual facts of injury and grievance. The plaintiff speaks for herself, not as a representative of asbestos victims, or workers, or some other class. The defendant's story is also his own. Traditional tort law is not about workers against employers or about claimants who demand a supportive share of a state's treasury but about Mary Smith's particular grievance against John Jones.[1] The advent of mass tort litigation, and bureaucratic systems of compensation such as those found in social security disability cases, however, has put the individual claimant far from the center of the torts universe.

Many forms of social response to injury are now in place. The next generation of tort lawyers and policy thinkers must tackle the job of getting a good mixture of personal accountability and social responsibility.

§ 13. Process Values in Tort Law

Judges of course wish to formulate and apply rules to obtain both justice and public policy goals. They also wish to promote and protect process values. Process values are values we attach to the legal process itself, in particular, the process of deciding disputes.[1] Jury trial rights, discussed later, are one part of the dispute resolution process, but there are others. Many process values are represented in procedural codes and in constitutional prescriptions. Due process is a prized right even if it is not precisely formulated: we should hold the trial before the verdict; each party should be entitled to know what the other claims; disputing parties must be able to present their side of the dispute.

Adopting, formulating, and applying tort rules. Procedural specifications do not cover all considerations of process. Judges consider process values in choosing, formulating, and applying rules of tort law. A judge might justly award damages to an injured plaintiff even if there were no rules at all, but the process of adjudication would then itself be suspect and in a sense unjust. So rules adopted must be rules that can be seen, understood, and applied, at least by the professionals involved in litigation. Judges striving to formulate or apply tort rules attempt to meet this modest concern for the litigation process itself.

Process goals. No authoritative list of process values guides judges, so lawyers can argue that any given rule is undesirable because it does not appropriately respect process concerns. Broadly phrased, the legal process should be designed not only to get good results in accord with justice and policy, but also to leave participants with a sense of humane

§ 12

1. See Abraham, What Is A Tort Claim? An Interpretation of Contemporary Tort Reform, 51 MD. L. REV. 172 (1992); Robinson and Abraham, Collective Justice in Tort Law, 78 VA. L. REV. 1481 (1992).

§ 13

1. Distinguish the process *theory,* proposed in Jay Tidmarsh, A Process Theory of Torts, WASH. & LEE L. REV. 1313 (1994).

participation in the process.[2] That might include the felt need to tell one's side of the story and relate a sense of injustice. It might also include a sense that justice is not only done but seen to be done. There is also a practical side to process. Rules should be structured to permit efficient decision making—no litigant should be compelled to spend weeks getting a decision that can be made as well in a day.

Loose rule formulation that diminishes judicial accountability. These broadly phrased ideas suggest many more specific concerns. If rules are too abstract, they may fail to constrain the judge or the jury. They may instead effectively permit the decision makers to do as they like. Rules like this can undermine the process of justice because professional lawyers and other observers cannot confidently say whether the judge or jury applied the law or not. A rule that merely told people "be good" has at least two process defects. First, it fails to point to evidence a lawyer could adduce or arguments she could make. Second, the rule is so undefined that it fails to constrain the judge in appropriate ways. If too many rules were like this, the judge's decision would be a ukase of a judicial czar, not an adjudication of facts and law. The judges' rational explanations of what they do is usually the only effective check on them. If their decisions are not subject to professional scrutiny because the rules are so uncertain that anything goes, judges are likely to become in time more arbitrary and ultimately less just.[3]

Tight rule formulation that eliminates needed flexibility. Conversely, however, precise rules may constrain the decision makers too much, leaving no room for justly deciding the individual's case which is at the heart of our concept of justice. A rule that says "be good" violates the process interest in understandable, reasonably precise rules. At the other extreme, a rule that says "never, ever, drive more than 40 miles per hour in this zone" may leave too little flexibility for the case of the driver rushing his child to the emergency room.

Rules guiding lawyers' investigation and arguments. Although some rules are actually read and understood by the people whose conduct they regulate, many tort rules are not. Rules often attempt to reflect the way people should behave even if they have not read the statutes and the cases. Thus, many tort rules are mainly read and understood by lawyers. Judges formulating tort rules must have in mind that lawyers use rules in very practical ways, to know what arguments and what facts are relevant so that investigation can proceed accordingly. Rules devalue the process when they fail to point to arguments and facts that are relevant

2. See Robert S. Summers, Evaluating and Improving Legal Processes—A Plea for "Process Values", 60 Cornell L. Rev. 1 (1974).

3. James Henderson, Process Constraints in Tort, 67 Cornell L. Rev. 901 (1982), contains an excellent and well-known discussion of similar ideas. Professor Henderson, however, argues a step further: rules requiring a balance and evaluation of a number of factors detract from legal process partly because they turn judges into intuitive decision-makers, or managers, or planners, (or, one might fear, autocrats). If, however, balancing several factors is a matter of degree, one might think that the process value asserted here is itself merely one factor among many and as intuitive as some of the rules it condemns.

to the litigation. That was one of the objections to a rule that simply commanded people to be good. The rule gives no hint what facts might impress the judge on the goodness scale or what arguments might be structured in favor of one side or the other.

Rules failing to specify provable facts. Rules also detract from good process when they call for facts that cannot be proved with reasonable confidence or proved within a reasonable length of time. Suppose that it is normally a tort to touch someone who has not consented to a touching, but that it is not a tort to touch someone who has consented to it. If the plaintiff plays in a game of tag or football, consent seems apparent even if it is not expressed. If judges were to say that anyone touching the plaintiff is liable unless the plaintiff actually, subjectively consents to the touching, the rule would not point to evidence that can be reached by the defendant's lawyer, since no one can produce evidence about the plaintiff's state of mind except so far as it is outwardly or objectively expressed. That might or might not lead to unjust results, but it leads to process concerns because we would not be very sure of our basis for judging the question of subjective consent if we are not permitted to consider the outward signs.

Deciding by avoiding decision. In some situations, judges believe that their basis for judging is too limited to permit them to act at all. Sometimes this feeling leads to rules that reject tort law solutions altogether. For example, no judge wishes to condone parental abuse of children, but few judges want to tell parents that they cannot punish their children in ways accepted in the community. So if a child were to sue her parent, claiming that punishment was unjust or harmful, some judges might fear their ability to discriminate between abuse and punishment. They might refuse to entertain the case altogether, or if they entertained it, they might demand especially clear proof from the child. Judges might have other reasons besides those related to the legal process for reaching such a decision. Official interference with family life is a troubling and dangerous matter. Nevertheless, inability to decide in a way that can be rationally understood by citizens and lawyers is one of the reasons why judges may refuse to recognize a tort or, if they recognize it, to apply the rules with great caution.

On the other hand, resolution of human disputes cannot await the certainty of a long-term scientific study. Judges must be (and are) prepared to tolerate a degree of uncertainty in many claims. The amount of acceptable uncertainty in proof depends a lot on the judge's assessment of the net cost of error.

Process value arguments as judgment, not logic. Process value arguments probably should be taken as important factors in deciding what rules to formulate and how to apply them, but they probably should not be taken as sovereign commands. They appeal to judgment, not to a sense of inexorable logic. They should be evaluated, too, with the possibility in mind that they tend to favor defendants, for example, by

demanding clarity in rules that cannot always be supplied or by insisting upon certainty of evidence or logic that is seldom available.

Topic C. History and Methods of Tort Law

§ 14. Historical Development of Tort Law

Tort law's traits can often be understood through its history. This section reflects only a small part of that history that bears on some specific tools of thought that sometimes still affect our resolution of cases.

Common Law Writs of Trespass and Case

Common law writs. The early common law was based upon decisions by judges developed gradually in England after the Norman Conquest. Local lords or the courts they controlled decided some cases, but the medieval English King as the chief feudal lord claimed the right to decide cases involving property rights and the "King's peace." Gradually a procedure developed under which the King, through his Chancellor, would issue a "writ" which had the effect of conferring jurisdiction on the King's courts to hear the case.

The writ of trespass. The writs were stylized documents or forms containing certain words that remained more or less the same from case to case. Lawyers and judges naturally called these writs by a short name based on that commonly used language. Certain early writs, all in Latin, asserted a claim that the defendant had transgressed by force and violence. An English word for "transgress" was trespass, so these writs were called writs of trespass. The trespass writ developed several sub-forms. For instance, one version asserted that the defendant acted "vi et armis," that is, by use of force. Another asserted that the defendant "broke the close," that is, invaded land and disrupted the plaintiff's rightful possession of it.

The characteristic instance for which an aggrieved person might obtain the writ of *trespass* was one in which the defendant applied direct force to the plaintiff's interests: he rode onto the plaintiff's land or he struck the plaintiff with a stick. The *trespass* action was not so much about land as about direct physical force. You could have trespass to persons, chattels, or land.[1]

The writ of trespass on the case. Over time, the king's agents began to issue some new writs, covering instances in which the force applied by the defendant was not direct. The defendant throws a log which strikes the plaintiff. A claim on those facts calls for the writ of *trespass*. The defendant throws a log in the plaintiff's path and he trips over it after it has come to rest. A claim on those facts does not justify the use of the

§ 14

1. Judge Arnold collected many early cases of trespass, only a few of which involved trespass to land alone in Morris Arnold, Select Cases of Trespass from the King's Courts—1307–1399 (1985).

writ of *trespass*.[2] Nevertheless, the claim might appeal to one's sense of justice and in the late 14th century the Chancellor began to issue writs to cover such indirect injuries.[3] The new kind of writ was called *trespass on the case.* As this writ became common, legal professionals began to refer to the new writ simply as *case* and the plaintiff was said to bring an action *on the case.*

Strict liability under the writ of trespass. The writ of *trespass* was based on direct force, which sounds like intentional wrongdoing. However, if we understand the obscure history of this action, intentional wrongdoing was not a required part of the trespass claim. If the defendant threw a log that hit the plaintiff, the defendant was liable even if he had never intended to strike the plaintiff. So, at least according to the dominant view, *trespass* was initially a kind of strict liability tort.[4] Perhaps this was so because trespassory torts were likely in earlier culture to promote revenge and blood feuds, and because, from very early times, the law sought to substitute payment for the continuing violence that would erupt without it.[5]

Recovery without harm under the writ of trespass. In addition, if *trespass* were the appropriate writ, the plaintiff could recover without proving any actual pecuniary loss. For example, if the defendant directly entered upon the plaintiff's land without a justification, he would be liable for at least nominal damages, even if no harm was done. In the case of more violent torts this rule may also demonstrate the connection between trespass as a tort and trespass as a criminal or quasi-criminal action. As a kind of deterrent, the action inflicted a cost upon the defendant even if the plaintiff suffered no loss.

Fault under the writ of case. The writ of *case*, on the other hand, was associated with fault such as intent or negligence on the part of the defendant. If the plaintiff tripped over the log the defendant had left on the path, the defendant would not be liable unless he was guilty of wrongful intent or negligence.

Damages under the writ of case. Furthermore, where *case* was the appropriate writ, the plaintiff could not recover unless he proved, in addition to fault, some legally recognizable harm such as physical injury or pecuniary loss. If the defendant negligently cut a tree so that it would

2. "[I]f a man throws a log into the highway, and in that act it hits me, I may maintain trespass, because it is an immediate wrong; but if as it lies there I tumble over it and receive an injury, I must bring an action upon the case, because it is only prejudicial in consequence.... " Reynolds v. Clarke, 1 Str. 634, 93 Eng.Rep. 747, 748 (K.B. 1726) (Forescue, J.).

3. Before that time, the royal courts did entertain some indirect injury suits under the Trespass writ. See M.J. PRICHARD, *Scott v. Shepherd* (1773) AND THE EMERGENCE OF THE TORT OF NEGLIGENCE 5, 13 ff. (1976).

4. Some scholars are skeptical. See Gary Schwartz, Tort Law and the Economy in Nineteenth–Century America: A Reinterpretation, 90 YALE L. J. 1717 (1981); cf. Stephen Young, Reconceptualizing Accountability in the Early Nineteenth Century: How the Tort of Negligence Appeared, 21 CONN. L. REV. 197 (1989).

5. On the bót or fixed payment that could be demanded for each kind of affront and the blood-feud basis for this procedure, see 2 SIR FREDERICK POLLOCK AND FREDERIC WILLIAM MAITLAND, HISTORY OF ENGLISH LAW 451, 525 (1952).

narrowly miss striking the plaintiff as it fell, the plaintiff would have no claim for this fault unless he could show harm to himself. This rule is still the ordinary rule today: a negligence action lies only if the plaintiff has suffered in a way the courts will recognize as legal harm.

Coming to America

The Spanish conquerors of Mexico and settlers in what is now the American West left a legacy of the civil or code-oriented law. The French version of civil law likewise came to those areas settled by the French. The English colonists in the East brought with them common law assumptions. But colonial institutions did not quite match those of England. No chancellor was there to issue writs even if Americans assumed that the writs matched some more or less immutable form of thinking about law.

The strict liability elements of the *trespass* writ were eroded in the 19th century. In the United States, the year 1850 brought a leading decision of the Massachusetts Court in *Brown v. Kendall*.[6] A man striking at fighting dogs with a stick unintentionally struck the plaintiff when he raised the stick over his shoulder. The case fit the model of the *trespass* writ because the injury was both direct and forcible, so strict liability might have been imposed under the older rules. But the court rejected that approach and substituted a fault standard instead.

From that time on, courts tended to assume that some kind of fault—negligence or intentional wrong—was required to establish tort liability in most cases. Yet the appeal of strict liability for special cases remained, and courts began to find new occasions to impose liability without fault. *Brown v. Kendall* made fault the dominant approach to resolution of tort disputes, but it also opened up the courts to new kinds of strict liability, not based on the writs or forms of action at all, but on some sense of justice or policy. *Brown v. Kendall* signaled the acceptance of new kinds of reasoning in tort cases, a reasoning that left the formal writs behind.

§ 15. Common Law Methods of Analysis and the Doctrine of Precedent

Civil law codes, common law decisions. Roman legal principles were stated in the form of a Code. Many countries today initially state tort law as general principles arranged in a code of laws. These are the civil law countries, including Mexico and the countries of continental Europe and many others. Common law countries—those which, like Canada and the United States, took their early legal thought from England—did not begin with a set of principles but began by deciding cases. Gradually, decisions in individual cases came to be seen as operating on certain principles or rules, which were then taken as the basis for future decisions on similar facts. American tort law, though now often supplemented by statutory law, initially developed from common law decisions

6. Brown v. Kendall, 60 Mass. (6 Cush.) 292 (1850).

and those decisions still constitute the main source to which judges turn for guidance in deciding new cases.

Statutes in common law countries. In spite of the preeminent importance of case decision in the common law of torts, many statutes affect tort law today. Statutes may indirectly affect tort law by setting some standard that courts adopt. Statutes may directly affect tort law by creating some claim or defense that would not otherwise be recognized or enforced by the judges. Even ordinances or administrative rules may have some effect in the tort process. Since about 1960, the United States Constitution, too, has been instrumental in creating tort rights by way of a federal statute recognizing civil rights torts. So statutory instruments today are part of tort law. Statutes in the United States, however, often differ from codes in that they do not attempt to provide a coherent set of rules or principles. Instead, they prescribe very particular rules for a particular situation. When statutes do not wholly govern a tort claim, how do appellate judges go about deciding a case?

Precedent and other sources. Besides considering the particular facts of the case, judges today are likely to consider logic, public policy, and justice. Most of these considerations will be expressed in terms of rules, principles or policies derived from earlier case decisions. Under the doctrine of precedent, judges are "bound" to follow the rules previously adopted by the same court or a higher court in the same judicial system.

In the United States, the court of one state is not ordinarily required to consider the precedents of another state court. Indeed, precedents of federal courts can be ignored by state courts unless the issue before the state court is an issue of federal law. However, courts in the United States are staffed with judges who received similar legal training and who know the common law background of the cases they decide. So quite frequently the courts of one state will consider decisions of another state persuasive. By the same token, if the state has no precedent on point, its courts will frequently look to general principles of common law or to the opinions of commentators or respected professional groups like the American Law Institute.

Deviating from precedent. But in the United States today precedents are usually regarded as important guides, to be taken seriously but not necessarily slavishly followed. If the precedent was decided in a feudal society it may not be apt to govern disputes in a highly mechanized society. Perhaps just as important, social values change over time. A precedent that is now perceived as unfairly discriminatory is likely to be overruled. Precedents may also be modified because with time and experience judges come to perceive that the precedent was stated too broadly or too narrowly, or that when the precedent case was decided, its logical or social implications were not fully grasped.

Application to new cases. Application of precedent to new cases is sometimes rather mechanical but mostly it is not. Lawyers do not litigate clear cases. Unless the lawyers are very bad or the parties very angry, clear cases are settled because lawyers can determine from

precedent what the result will be. Sometimes the law is the clearest thing in the case; it is the facts or the inferences to be drawn from the facts that are disputed. Facts are usually resolved by the time the case reaches an appellate court. If a case is on appeal, there is usually a dispute about legal rules. Does a certain rule exist at all, and if so, should it be overruled? If it does exist, should it be applied to the facts of the particular case? How, exactly, should the rule be worded?

Uncertainty. Many beginning students are surprised to learn that after hundreds of years of common law development, so much remains that can be disputed. Part of that surprise is due to some distortion in the picture. Cases reaching the appellate courts are not necessarily representative of the many thousands of other cases that are readily resolved by settlement because the law is clear. But part of the surprise is accurately grounded. Tort law is very much litigation law; it is often somewhat indeterminate or uncertain until the particular case is actually decided. In one way that is unfortunate. In another it is not. A society with a precise rule for every possible human act and every configuration of circumstances would probably be a society with a great deal of injustice and very little freedom. Change is part of the nature of tort law.

§ 16. Tort Rules and What They Do

Tort law is better understood when its limits are appreciated. Law cannot effectively solve all problems. Even issues capable of legal resolution are sometimes resolved outside the law by community standards and practices that do not depend heavily upon formal tort law.[1] In many other instances, however, tort law tends to articulate and reinforce community standards and to provide a framework for discussion and argument about their application. If it does a great deal more than that, it is very successful indeed.

Some tort rules or principles may be precise enough and well-known enough to guide conduct, at least in a general way. This may be especially so in the case of defendants who act repeatedly and plan their conduct to avoid legal liability. Manufacturers know that dangerous products can lead to tort liability, even if they do not know detailed rules.

Many of the technical or professional rules of tort law, the rules that affect litigation outcomes, however, are not known or understood by people in general. Even if they were known, the tort rules seldom determine outcomes of litigation by themselves. That is, the technical tort rules are almost never detailed enough to lead inexorably to a given conclusion except in extreme cases. The law directs people to use reasonable care under the circumstances, but it does not attempt in advance to define fully what counts as reasonable care in all possible circumstances.

§ 16

1. See ROBERT C. ELLICKSON, ORDER WITHOUT LAW (1991).

Some tort rules are not even about conduct at all, but about how to interpret its effects. Rules about how to judge whether the defendant's conduct caused harm would almost never guide anyone's actual conduct even if the rules were precise and well-understood.

Why have tort rules if people do not know them and cannot use them to guide their conduct?

First, the traditional tort rules governing conduct to a large extent reflect social values and norms already in existence in the culture. They do not create new standards imposed by authoritarian judges; they merely enforce what society already believes. This view also explains why tort rules can be announced after the dispute arises; they do not invent a new standard and impose it on past conduct but instead resolve disputes about events in the past in the light of standards we generally share but perhaps have not fully articulated. So in a sense it is not tort rules that we expect to shape conduct. The tort rule confirms or articulates social ideals and perhaps reinforces them by imposing liability.

Second, even if tort rules had no effect whatever on actual conduct, they are professional tools. They alert lawyers to issues in a dispute that judges and others can recognize as legitimate issues. They tell lawyers what kind of evidence to look for and introduce in court. They help lawyers formulate the terms and structure of their arguments. For example, if a rule says that people must use reasonable care in the circumstances, and that custom of the relevant community is to be considered in judging reasonable care, you would not know from the rule alone what conduct is or is not acceptable. You would know, however, that you could look for evidence of community custom, introduce it in evidence, and construct your argument on the basis of that custom. Rules are thus tools for practical and moral discourse and for legal argumentation. As tools, they work in a setting that not only includes the facts of particular cases but social facts and institutional environment as well.

This book attempts to present a full statement of tort doctrine. At the same time, it attempts to preserve some awareness of major conditions that affect it. For example, tort law cannot be understood apart from institutions like the jury or the liability insurance system. Particular practices, as well as grand institutions like the jury, also affect the operation and ultimate effective meaning of tort rules. How a rule works is the best test of what a rule really is. It will be hard to understand tort law unless you understand some of the methods for allocating the costs among several defendants, methods that are often critical if a settlement is to be achieved. Yet, a full description of tort law's operation in practice or its social effects is not possible for a single volume.

Chapter 2

Operating Conditions of Tort Law

§ 17. Trials and Appeals

Tort law as practiced by professionals operates in settings and under conditions that determine much about the impact the formal rules will have on the parties. The characteristics of trials and appeals are among those conditions. Although the details of trial must be left to treatises on procedure, several traits of the trial and appeal system directly affect the way tort law works.

Determining facts. Disputes in litigation are usually about the facts or about the law. Factual disputes arise when the parties or witnesses contradict one another and when there are gaps in the evidence that might be filled by different inferences of fact. There is, of course, no guarantee that any witnesses will be found, or that they will have good memories, or that they will be reputable and convincing. Factual disputes are decided by the jury if there is one.

Determining law. Disputes about law commonly include issues of interpretation and application. The parties may interpret earlier decisions of the court in a different way; or one of them may argue that precedent does not apply because the particular facts of the case differ from those in earlier decisions. Disputes about law are decided by the judge.

Evaluating facts in the light of the law. A third kind of dispute is about how conduct is evaluated. If the trier of fact determines that the defendant drove his car at a speed of 60 mph, and the judge determines that the law required the defendant to exercise reasonable care under the circumstances, someone must still evaluate the defendant's conduct by applying the legal rule of reasonable care to the facts. Sometimes 60 mph is unreasonable (around children playing, for example) and sometimes not (on an interstate highway, for example). This third or evaluative kind of dispute is frequently decided by the jury, but sometimes judges make a rule of law to cover the particular evaluation.

Adversary presentation. The adversary system of the common law permits and requires the parties to present their respective cases. The plaintiff must initiate a case by filing a complaint summarizing the main facts on which her claim is based and by serving the defendant with a copy. The defendant must ordinarily file an answer summarizing defenses. At trial, the plaintiff must present her evidence, subject to the defendant's cross examination. In turn, the defendant must present his evidence, subject to the plaintiff's cross examination. The judge may ask

questions of a witness but seldom does so. Almost never does the judge direct any investigation of facts.

Trials and appeals. All three kinds of disputes are initially decided in the trial court, where the parties present their evidence, usually in the form of witnesses' testimony. The trial judge must decide all issues of law that arise and instruct the jury about the law it is to apply in evaluating the parties' conduct. Appeals are quite different. Judges in the appeals court only determine issues or rules of law; they do not weigh evidence or substitute their own evaluations for those of the jury.[1]

Expense. Trial of a substantial tort claim is expensive. Preparation for trial consumes large amounts of lawyer time. It may entail many expenses, too, such as expenses of finding experts, learning from them, and planning their testimony. If the parties do not settle the case and trial actually takes place, additional costs will be incurred. The parties may dispute both the facts and the application of law to the case. If the amounts in issue are large, both parties will have some incentive to settle to avoid a total loss. Most cases are in fact settled.

Credible threats. The strategy of both parties in tort litigation is to create a credible threat to the other party. The plaintiff makes a credible threat by asserting a claim for damages that the law recognizes as a valid claim and by asserting facts that support the claim. The defendant makes a credible threat by asserting a defense the law recognizes, along with supporting facts. If the law supports the plaintiff's claim only uncertainly, the plaintiff's claim is less threatening than if the law clearly favored the plaintiff. In that case, the defendant would either refuse to settle or pay the plaintiff less in settlement than otherwise. And vice versa. The weaker the defendant's facts and arguments for the defense, the more the defendant would tend to pay in settlement. However, even a weak claim with only a 10% chance of success may become threatening if the plaintiff can plausibly assert that her injuries are very great and her damages are very high.

Non-objective claims. Claims for pain, suffering, and emotional distress as well as claims for punitive damages are more threatening in many cases than claims for wage loss or medical expenses. The claim for damages for pain or the like is an open-ended, non-objective claim, without any measurement. So it is a potential threat for large sums of money. Such a claim adds magnitude to the threat and tends to encourage the defendant to think of settlement.

Motion to dismiss. Two important procedural devices can be used before trial to exclude claims that are not legally justified. The first is a motion to dismiss (called a general demurrer under earlier common law procedure). The motion to dismiss asserts that the adversary's claim or defense is not legally valid even if all the facts are exactly as claimed by the adversary. This motion is not about facts at all, but about the legal

§ 17

1. Judges do review for sufficiency of evidence, but not its weight. See § 18.

validity of the claim or defense. The judge considers the written complaint of the plaintiff or answer of the defendant to decide this motion.

Summary judgment. The other major device used to exclude claims or defenses is the motion for summary judgment. This motion also attempts to interdict a claim or defense before trial, but it is made after the parties have completed discovery. The process of discovery permits the parties to question witnesses under oath to discover what their testimony will be, or to obtain their testimony in written form. Written records of discovered material can be filed with the court. The motion for summary judgment asks the court to consider the *undisputed* testimony as shown in discovery documents and to dismiss a claim or defense as legally invalid or inadequate on that basis. Unlike the motion to dismiss, the summary judgment permits the judge to consider facts (as shown in the discovery documents). But the summary judgment motion does not permit the judge to decide any disputed fact; that is an issue to be resolved at trial after the live witnesses are heard.

Other procedures to establish or eliminate threats. Even if the parties are unable to settle and thus forced to try the case, they will continue to attempt to interdict threatening claims. Partly this is to reduce the danger that the jury will make an unfavorable award and partly it is to continue to create a climate for favorable settlement. In the trial itself parties argue legal rules (1) to exclude or admit evidence and (2) to support or avoid instructions to the jury according to whether the evidence or instruction is favorable.

Even a very superficial discussion of trial strategies affecting legal rules shows how difficult it is to translate abstract ideals of tort law into practice. Whatever the aims of tort law—justice, compensation, deterrence—they are not likely to be fully realized in all cases. A good claim may founder on an unimpressive or confused witness. Or a doubtful claim combined with expenses of trial and risks of loss may induce a settlement justified only by the expense, not by the merits of the claim. This may be an unavoidable part of human limitations. If so, it is also true that tort goals will be realized only in some cases, not all.

§ 18. Judge, Jury, and Community Values

Judge and Jury

The role of the jury is central in tort litigation in the United States. In most cases, a jury trial is available as a matter of right. Jury trial is traditionally almost invariable in substantial tort cases.

Jury functions. The jury's function is to determine the facts. In part, this means that the jury will decide whether a witness is speaking truthfully and without mistake. It also means that the jury will decide what factual inferences are to be drawn from the evidence. In many instances juries also evaluate conduct at issue, for instance by determining that the defendant's conduct was unreasonably risky and amounted to negligence. In so doing, they bring their own knowledge of "social

facts" to bear on the case. Finally, the jury will determine the amount of damages, subject to the judge's instructions about the legal measures to be used.

Judge control by reviewing sufficiency of evidence. The trial judge has considerable power to affect the jury's determinations. The trial judge in the first instance will submit to the jury only those claims for which there is sufficient evidence adduced at the trial. If the plaintiff says she was injured when struck by the defendant's car but presents no other facts showing how the injury occurred, the trial judge may not submit the claim to the jury at all. The claim is consistent with the idea that the defendant is at fault but also consistent with the idea that the plaintiff is at fault. So the judge might direct a verdict, telling the jury it must find for the defendant. In this extreme kind of case, the judge is not weighing testimony or evidence but is considering its logical or rational sufficiency to establish the plaintiff's claim. Evaluative decisions by the jury are treated similarly. If reasonable people could differ, the claim will be decided by the jury; if not, the judge will direct a verdict for the defendant. Appellate judges may address the same issue on the basis of written transcripts of the testimony. Judges can also control jury determinations to some extent by excluding testimony that is irrelevant and prejudicial.

Judge control by rules of law. Judges may minimize or eliminate the jury's role in a different way by making a rule of law that demands a precise result or that casts the judge in the role of decision maker. For example, the traditional rule of law was that trespassers could not recover damages for injuries suffered by conditions negligently created by the landowner on his own land. If the trespasser were a neighboring Girl Scout taking a short cut across the defendant's land, the jury might think the defendant negligent in creating a dangerous, life-threatening condition. But under this rule, if a trespasser asserted a claim against the landowner, there was literally nothing for the jury to decide and the judge would direct a verdict. The effect is to eliminate any role for the jury in evaluating the driver's conduct.

Jury performance. For some, civil juries embody democratic values and represent the community's ability to resist harsh rules handed down from above.[1] For others, juries are perceived as an almost lawless threat, bent on exercising their prejudices and inflicting undeserved losses upon unpopular defendants. Juries in individual cases can no doubt fit either view, but actual studies, as distinct from anecdotes about particular cases, seem to suggest that juries often get the same result judges would get in the same case and that in some important kinds of tort cases juries actually favor the defendant more than the plaintiff.[2]

§ 18

1. Stephan Landsman, The Civil Jury in America: Scenes from an Unappreciated History, 44 Hastings L. J. 579 (1993) and others see political values in the jury as well as "equity."

2. Juries are by no means always better for plaintiffs than judges. See Kevin Clermont and Theodore Eisenberg, Trial by Jury or Judge: Transcending Empiricism, 77 Cornell L. Rev. 1124 (1992); Michael J. Sakes, Public Opinion about the Civil Jury:

Strategic effects. If the defendant is no more at risk when a jury decides the case than when the judge does so, the judge's decision to permit the jury to be the decision maker in a given case still has strategic impact. A judge's decision to reject a defendant's motion for summary judgment, for example, helps to make the plaintiff's claim a more credible threat and hence may increase pressure upon the defendant to settle in a way favorable to the plaintiff.[3] This effect may occur even before the judge makes an actual decision. Because litigators are like chess players, thinking at least several moves in advance, the defendants' lawyers will also be inclined to settle when they believe that the judge will leave the case to the jury's decision at the end of any trial.

The Jury as Meliorator and Repository of Community Values

One view of juries sees them as an institution for meliorating the rigors of the law when it applies too harshly in particular cases. In this respect juries could be compared to the chancellor sitting in the old separate equity courts and using discretion rather than law to obtain equitable or fair results.[4] Like the chancellor, the jury decides a particular case; it does not make law.[5] Perhaps this gives juries the freedom to act in accord with the community conscience when a judge who is bound to make a record of the legal rulings and who acts in the sight of lawyers and appellate judges may feel more constrained.

At any rate, the view of the jury as meliorator of harshness or dispenser of equity is related to the idea that the jury represents the community and its values. And if the jury is drawn from all members of society at random, it will in some sense represent the community. In many tort cases, community values form the basis for moral judgment about the parties' fault and justifications. In those cases, a significant role for the jury may be especially desirable.[6]

On the other hand, one might believe that one's *rights* should not be subject to a judge's or jury's discretionary veto. If the plaintiff has a right not to be discriminated against on the job or subjected to sexual

Can Realty Be Found in the Illusions?, 48 DePaul L. Rev. 221 (1998); Leon Green, Judge and Jury 406 (1930). Nor do jurors generally disfavor corporate defendants. See Valerie P. Hans, The Illusions and Realities of Jurors' Treatment of Corporate Defendants, 48 DePaul L. Rev. 327 (1998).

3. This effect does not depend upon whether juries favor plaintiffs more than judges would. First, the effect will be the same if juries in fact get the same results as judges but lawyers wrongly believe that juries favor plaintiffs. Second, the effect will be similar if there are no juries at all, only judges, and the judge announces that the case calls for judgment rather than a rule of law. (That would be analogous to letting the case go to the jury.) Once the defense lawyer forecasts that the judge will treat the case as a judgment call, he will be willing to recommend a higher settlement than if he forecast that the judge would rule for the defendant as a matter of law.

4. 1 Dan B. Dobbs, Law of Remedies § 2.4 (7) (1993).

5. The chancellor's theory was that he only acted to compel the particular defendant to act in accordance with conscience; he did not make law.

6. Michael Wells, Scientific Policymaking and the Torts Revolution: The Revenge of the Ordinary Observer, 26 Ga. L. Rev. 725 (1992); Patrick Kelley, Who Decides? Community Safety Conventions at the Heart of Tort Liability, 38 Clev. St. L. Rev. 315 (1990); Catharine Wells, Tort Law as Corrective Justice: A Pragmatic Justification for Jury Adjudication, 88 Mich. L. Rev. 2348 (1990).

harassment, a judge should not undermine that right by a discretionary refusal to enforce it. Nor should a jury. When the law seeks to uphold a right that does not fully conform to community feelings, courts are likely to reduce the jury's role for the very reason that it *does* represent working values in the community. In libel cases, for example, the fear is that the jury may lose sight of the value of free speech when faced with derogatory statements about the plaintiff. Accordingly, legal rules constrain liability and give the judges more power in these cases.

Because juries (like judges) both protect community values and undermine them, judges in tort cases play out a considerable ambivalence, sometimes relying heavily on the jury, sometimes manipulating rules and judgments to sideline it. Many of the tort rules and practices seen in this book can be understood as taking one side or another about the jury's appropriate role.

§ 19. The Prima Facie Case, the Burden of Proof, and Affirmative Defenses

"The prima facie case" is a standard term for lawyers but a bemusing one for students. The term represents two important features of litigation law in general and tort law in particular.

"Elements" of the case. The plaintiff in a tort case cannot prevail in her claim without providing evidence of facts that show certain specific elements or features of the claim. The elements differ according to the tort claimed. For instance, the plaintiff who sues for false imprisonment must prove that the defendant confined her; that is one of the elements of that particular kind of claim. The plaintiff who sues for battery need not prove confinement at all, but must prove that the defendant wrongfully touched her. Sometimes the elements to be proved are generalized very broadly or even vaguely. Nevertheless, when the plaintiff knows all the elements she must prove to avoid losing, she has at least a general idea, maybe a specific one, about the kind of evidence she needs.

The prima facie case. When the plaintiff provides testimony about facts that show all the elements necessary for the tort she claims, she has made a prima facie case. What this means is best understood by noticing that we cannot say the plaintiff *wins* when she offers testimony on all the elements of the claim. First, the jury might disbelieve her evidence on some essential element. Second, the defendant may have a valid defense. When the plaintiff has made out a prima facie case she qualifies as a starter in the race. Her case goes to the jury. The procedural form of the same idea is that if the plaintiff proves the elements of her case, the judge will not direct a verdict against her.

The burden of proof. "Prima facie case" implies a second important rule. It implies that the plaintiff has the burden of proof on each of the elements of her case. The term "burden of proof" is itself a troublesome one. Agonizing details can be left for treatment elsewhere,[1] but the

§ 19

1. See §§ 150–152.

burden of proof rules are too important in tort litigation to ignore altogether. The term means at least two things. First, if nothing is proven on a point, the point must be decided against the party with the burden of proof. If the plaintiff must prove confinement to prove a false imprisonment, but fails to do so, the plaintiff has not met her burden of proving the elements of the claim and she will lose. Second, if the plaintiff has presented testimony, but the jury is not sure it is convinced by the testimony, the burden of proof rules tell the jury what to do. A juror whose mind is evenly balanced on the issue, not sure that the testimony is true or untrue, must vote against the plaintiff because she has the burden of convincing jurors by the weight of the evidence.

Preponderance of the evidence or probability. The doubtful jury problem is related to the idea that the plaintiff's burden is not merely to offer testimony, but to persuade the jury by a preponderance of the evidence.[2] Preponderance means only "greater weight" of the evidence. Contemporary thinking usually translates this to probabilities. The plaintiff need not prove that each fact necessary for her prima facie case is certainly true or true beyond a doubt. Instead, she must prove that each fact is more probable than not. Expressed statistically, she must persuade the jury or other trier of fact that the likelihood of each fact in her case exceeds 50%.[3]

Affirmative defenses. The plaintiff has the burden of proving the elements of her prima facie case (like confinement in the false imprisonment claim). The defendant has the burden of proving affirmative defenses. Facts showing affirmative defenses, if believed by the trier of fact, will exculpate the defendant or at least reduce the damages he must pay. Self-defense is a familiar affirmative defense. The important point is that the burden is on the defendant when it comes to affirmative defenses. If the defendant asserts self-defense but proves nothing about it, the jury cannot properly relieve the defendant of liability. Likewise, if the defendant offers testimony to show self-defense but the juror's mind is evenly balanced whether the testimony is true or not, the juror must reject the defense.

Affirmative defenses are relevant only if the plaintiff has made a prima facie case by providing testimony to show all the required elements and if the jury believes that testimony. If the plaintiff has not offered evidence of some element in her case, the trial judge will direct a verdict against her. If she offered evidence but the jury does not believe it, the jury will find against her for failing to sustain her burden. Only if the jury believes the plaintiff's evidence does the question of a defense enter into the picture. So rejection of the defendant's defense does not

2. There are some very limited exceptions on matters of causation. See §§ 176–179.

3. Everyday language sometimes uses the term "probable" standing alone to mean "more probable than not," and that is also often the usage of judges and lawyers. See, e.g., Stinson v. England, 69 Ohio St.3d 451, 633 N.E.2d 532 (1994). Statisticians and other experts may use probability to refer to any degree of probability, so it is possible to speak of a probability at the 40% level.

necessarily mean the plaintiff will prevail; the jury might also reject the plaintiff's testimony.

Why are these rules important in tort law? Rules establishing elements of the plaintiff's case (and elements of the affirmative defenses) operate to tell lawyers and judges what kind of evidence will be important and what kind of arguments will be relevant. They permit the lawyers to evaluate their cases. Rules allocating the burden of proof and persuasion provide practical means for resolving cases when proof is not forthcoming and when it is doubtful. Perhaps more importantly, they establish one further means by which judges can limit the role of the jury.

§ 20. Remedies and Attorney Fees

The proof and measures of tort damages and other remedies can be discussed later, but one facet of tort remedies is so much a part of the operating system of tort law that it must be mentioned here. That facet is described by three interrelated rules and practices.

The American rule on attorney fees. First, the "American rule" about attorney fees is that the losing party is not required to pay the winning party's fees. Regardless who wins the case, the plaintiff pays her own attorney and the defendant pays his. There are exceptions,[1] but in the overwhelming number of common law tort cases, this is the rule. One result of this rule is that the plaintiff who prevails in the litigation may not be fully compensated after she deducts the costs of attorney fees and other litigation expense.

Contingent percentage fees. Second, plaintiffs' attorneys accept most tort cases on a contingent, percentage fee. If the plaintiff does not recover, the attorney is not paid at all. If the plaintiff does recover, the attorney's fee is a percentage of the recovery. The percentage is fixed or limited in some states, but not in others. It may vary from a low of around 25% to a high of about 50%; most are probably between these figures. This practice, combined with the American rule, means that a plaintiff who fully recovers from the defendant may still be uncompensated for anywhere from one-fourth to one-half of her loss. It should not be assumed that a high percentage fee overcompensates lawyers. Since they are not paid at all when a client does not recover, the percentage fee must pay for the time spent in losing cases as well as in winning them.[2]

§ 20

1. The largest number of cases in which a losing party must pay a prevailing party's reasonable attorney fees are based on a specific statute authorizing a fee recovery. Federal civil rights cases are a major example. See 1 DAN B. DOBBS, LAW OF REMEDIES § 3.10 (2d ed. 1993).

2. This is a complex subject. Lawyers whose reputation and skill allow them to pick only cases that will be won and will produce large damages may be skimming the cream, and if they charge the same percentage on the cream that other lawyers charge on the milk, these lawyers will have proportionately higher incomes. Lawyers who accept some cases that are not likely to win or to recover large damages verdicts should not be regarded in a negative light. On the contrary, plaintiffs are entitled to their day in court even if their cases are not certain.

Defendants' lawyers usually charge an hourly rate. They usually represent liability insurers or large corporations that are self-insured.

Non-objective awards. Third, in personal injury tort cases, pain and suffering damage awards are often quite substantial. Punitive damages awards, when they are made at all, can also be very large. These two kinds of damages have it in common that they cannot be measured by any objective criterion. Consequently, the jury's award may be quite difficult to challenge on appeal. In the case of some intangible harms, such as reputation harm in libel cases, juries are allowed to make a similar award, that is, one that is not limited by pecuniary loss or measurable in any objective way.

Non-objective awards and the attorney fee. One characteristic of non-objective awards has already been noticed.[3] Non-objective awards create substantial threats to defendants. After all, if the plaintiff has pain and suffering, a jury might award $1 million just as well as $500,000 or $100,000. These threats in turn create incentives to pay larger sums in settlement. A different characteristic is equally important. Non-objective awards such as damages for pain provide a fund from which the prevailing plaintiff can pay her attorney fees.

In the light of these rules and practices it is easy to understand why plaintiffs' lawyers find it important to assert non-objective damages claims. Besides whatever pressure such claims exert upon defendants and their lawyers, they also increase the chance that the plaintiff will receive full compensation for her actual economic losses. There may be other justifications and needs for such non-objective claims, but these reasons show why they are almost imperative. If the "American rule" on attorney fees is eventually displaced by a loser-pay rule, non-objective damages will find much less obvious justification.

§ 21. State and Federal Laws

Older treatises on torts have had little occasion to notice that the legal system of the United States is a federal system with tort law emanating not only from local jurisdictions like states but also from the national government itself. The omission of federal law has become a luxury that is no longer affordable. Federal tort law will appear in a number of places throughout this book. This section does not address the substance of that law but its place in the structure of tort law generally.

Common law as state law. The common law of torts is almost exclusively state law. The federal government is circumscribed, having only those powers specifically provided for by the federal Constitution. States, on the other hand, enjoy plenary power except as limited by the Constitution. These understandings leave the federal courts with almost no admitted common law work to do. Instead, they interpret and enforce federal statutes and the federal constitution.

3. § 17.

Admiralty law and maritime torts. One body of federal tort law is, however, analogous to the common law in that it is a body of law developed by judicial decisions. This body of law is known as general maritime law. "Drawn from state and federal sources, the general maritime law is an amalgam of traditional common-law rules, modifications of those rules, and newly created rules."[1] This body of law is created by federal courts to deal with torts on or associated with navigable waters. The unusual power to create this general maritime law is derived from the federal constitutional grant of "Admiralty" power to the federal courts.

Federal statutes protecting constitutional rights. Federal statutes have not adopted any general tort law, and if they attempted to do so they would be constitutionally questioned. Federal statutes create or deeply affect tort law only when they are related to some field constitutionally placed in the hands of the federal rather than the state governments. For example, the Congress has created statutory tort law for the protection of constitutional and other federal rights.[2]

Federal statutes granting claims against the federal government. Federal statutes also grant—and limit—tort claims against the federal government itself.[3] These statutes are peculiar because they contain federally imposed limits on the tort liability of the federal government, yet otherwise rely upon state law to prescribe the tort rules.

Federal statutes under commerce and other powers. Another field for Congressional action is interstate commerce. Congress can regulate matters affecting commerce and on this ground has enacted tort statutes creating claims for interstate railroad and maritime workers.[4] These statutes are favorable to the workers's claims, providing more expansive rights than would be granted under state law, which of course is displaced by the federal statutes.

Federal environmental statutes supplement the common law tort of nuisance and the common law of strict liability for abnormal danger, sometimes creating surprising liabilities in connection with the release of hazardous substances.[5]

§ 21

1. East River Steamship Corp. v. Transamerica Delaval, Inc., 476 U.S. 858, 864, 106 S.Ct. 2295, 2298, 90 L.Ed.2d 865 (1986).

2. One statute of very general application is 42 U.S.C.A. § 1983, creating a tort claim for violation of federal rights. Other statutes go further, adding new rules or procedures to implement federal constitutional rights. For example, various federal statutes prohibit discrimination in employment, including sexual harassment. Some of these are enforced by both regulatory systems and by tort claims. See, e.g., 42 U.S.C.A. § 2000e ("Title VII"); Franklin v. Gwinnett County Public Schools, 503 U.S. 60, 112 S.Ct. 1028, 117 L.Ed.2d 208 (1992) (teacher's sexual harassment of student actionable in tort under Title IX, 20 U.S.C.A. § 1681).

3. The Federal Tort Claims Act (FTCA), principally found in 28 U.S.C.A. §§ 2671–2680.

4. The Federal Employers Liability Act (FELA), 45 U.S.C.A. § 51 creates a tort claim for interstate railroad workers and, for that claim, abolishes certain common law defenses. The Jones Act does the same for maritime workers. 46 App. U.S.C.A. § 688.

5. 42 U.S.C.A. § 9607 et seq. represents one of several important environmental statutes. This one, known as the Superfund

The federal trademark statute creates rights in trademarks and in practice it has largely displaced the common law of trademark.[6] Under other constitutional provisions, Congress has enacted patent[7] and copyright[8] statutes. These in effect define certain intellectual property interests and set up tort claims for their infringement. A number of federal statutes create claims in particular settings, for example, claims for misrepresentation in the sale of securities[9] and claims for certain kinds of acts that state tort law would classify as privacy invasions.[10]

Preemption. Sometimes Congress does not actually create a claim in tort but does set a standard of some kind. Congress and its regulatory agencies set safety standards for automobile manufacturers, for example, by requiring seat-belts or airbags. If a manufacturer complies with federal standards, but the product is nevertheless unsafe and causes harm, can state tort law hold the manufacturer liable? The question peels open a new layer of tort issues that in turn opens into the federal system itself.

Since the federal system is supreme (within its constitutional powers), Congress could provide for preemption or displacement of state tort law as it has done with the copyright statute. Even if it does not do so explicitly, its legislation might still imply such a preemption. Or preemption might be thought necessary to carry out the federal scheme of things. On one or more such grounds, courts have found that various federal statutes displaced or preempted state tort law.[11] For instance, a tobacco manufacturer who complies with the warning prescribed by federal statute cannot be held liable under state tort law for failure to give a better warning.[12] The effect is to make the federal standard the only standard and to relieve the defendant who has complied with that standard, even if, by state law, that defendant was guilty of negligence or other tortious conduct. This is the opposite effect of federal legislation creating a claim for railroad workers.

Act or CERCLA, creates liabilities for contamination of lands, including one's own land where release of hazardous materials into the environment is a danger. See, e.g., Bedford Affiliates v. Sills, 156 F.3d 416 (2d Cir. 1998) (discussing strict liability under CERCLA and the affirmative defenses available). Basic CERCLA liability is described briefly in Tom Kuhnle, Note, The Rebirth of Common Law Actions for Addressing Hazardous Waste Contamination, 15 Stan. Envtl. L. J. 187 (1996).

6. 15 U.S.C.A. § 1051 et seq. See § 457 below.

7. 35 U.S.C.A. § 101 et seq.

8. 17 U.S.C.A. § 101; see § 461 below.

9. E.g., 15 U.S.C. §§ 77k & 77l; 15 U. S. C. § 78j (securities); 15 U.S.C. § 1701 et seq. (interstate land sales); 15 U.S.C. § 1601 et seq. (certain disclosures to consumers).

10. 29 U. S. C. § 2001 et seq. (lie detector tests by employers forbidden, tort claim created); 18 U.S.C. §§ 2510–2520 (wiretapping, claim created).

11. CSX Transportation, Inc. v. Easterwood, 507 U.S. 658, 113 S.Ct. 1732, 123 L.Ed.2d 387 (1993) (federal speed limits for trains, preemption); Wood v. General Motors Corp., 865 F.2d 395 (1st Cir.1988) (federal airbag regulations for motor preemption); King v. Collagen Corporation, 983 F.2d 1130 (1st Cir.1993) (federal regulation of medical "devices," preemption); Papas v. Upjohn Co., 985 F.2d 516 (11th Cir.1993) (federal statute on pesticides; preemption). See §§ 224, 256, 274, & 373.

12. Cipollone v. Liggett Group, Inc., 505 U.S. 504, 112 S.Ct. 2608, 120 L.Ed.2d 407 (1992) (but leaving certain other claims available); see § 373.

Constitutional defenses or limits on state tort law. Because federal law, within its sphere, is supreme, states may not impose tort liability in a way that violates the United States Constitution. The Supreme Court seldom strikes down an ordinary state-law tort claim on constitutional grounds, but it is possible. Suits for libel, quintessentially state-law tort claims, are now limited in several ways by the Constitution's free speech provisions, so that, for example, those discussing issues of public concern may not be held strictly liable.[13]

Federal claims in state courts. In some instances, federal legislation not only preempts state-law claims but also gives federal courts exclusive jurisdiction to hear the claims. For example, patent and copyright claims must be tried in federal courts, not state courts. In other instances, however, federal claims can be tried in either state or federal courts, as the plaintiff wishes. One example is the general federal civil rights claim.[14] When federal claims are enforced in state courts, the states are of course compelled to follow the federal law for those claims, although they may follow their own trial procedures.

State claims in federal court. In a few cases state-law tort claims may be tried in federal courts. Sometimes this is because the state-law claim is so closely related to a purely federal claim that the two should be tried together. At other times this is because Congress has permitted federal jurisdiction over certain claims when the parties are of diverse citizenship, the plaintiff a citizen of one state and the defendant a citizen of another.[15] When state-law tort claims are tried in federal courts, they are still state-law claims and federal courts must apply the state law rules for those claims, even though they follow their own federal procedural rules.[16]

Scope of federal supremacy. Federal law is supreme and must prevail when it conflicts with state law. However, in many instances a federal rule applies only to a federal claim or a federal statute; it has no application at all to a state-law claim. In such cases, even if the federal and state rules are different, they are not in conflict because they do not deal with the same thing. For instance, federal decisions determine the incidents of a tort claim under a federal tort statute like the Federal Employers Liability Act, and state courts trying such cases must follow federal decisions as well as the federal statute. But the federal rules apply only to the tort claims created under that statute, not to similar tort claims brought under state law.

Similarly, a federal rule may set a minimum standard but may at the same time permit states to set a higher one. The Supreme Court, to protect free speech rights, requires that in most libel actions, the

13. Critics of public officials and public figures can be held liable only for knowing or reckless falsehoods, while critics of private persons on matters of public concern can be held liable for any fault. See § 417.

14. 42 U.S.C.A. § 1983.

15. 28 U.S.C.A. § 1332.

16. The point was established in Erie Railroad v. Tompkins, 304 U.S. 64, 58 S.Ct. 817, 82 L.Ed. 1188 (1938). A long line of federal decisions has explained the details and applied the rule.

plaintiff must prove at least some degree of fault on the defendant's part to justify a recovery.[17] But states may provide even more protection for free speech by requiring a high degree of fault as a prerequisite to liability.[18]

In the same way, the fact that a state law does not violate the federal constitution does not mean that it meets the demands of the state's own constitution, and the state courts are of course free to strike down their own rules on state law grounds, even if those rules have been upheld as valid under the United States Constitution.[19]

The relationship of state law to federal law and to the law of other states is the topic of treatises in federal jurisdiction[20] and conflicts of law.[21] The points sketched in this section suffice to show that tort law today operates in a complex environment. Lawyers are required not only to take into account the interaction of statutes and common law decisions, but the interaction of state and federal law as well.

§ 22. Liability Insurance

No one will understand tort law in the United States without understanding that liability insurance fuels the system, limits its capacity for compensation and deterrence, shapes the litigation, and affects the costs and choices in the system as a whole.

Insurer's obligations. Liability insurance protects the insured against tort liability by paying the insured's tort victims. Liability insurance is not health or accident insurance; it pays only when the insured is legally liable to pay because of his tort. Once a claim covered by the policy is asserted against the insured, the liability insurer is obliged to defend the claim and to pay any judgment rendered against the insured, subject to the limits of the policy.

The insurer's/insured's attorney. The insurer has the right and sometimes the duty to settle with the claimant as a way of protecting the insured. As part of the insurer's obligation to defend the insured, it provides an attorney who must, at least in some major degree, represent the individual insured. At the same time, the attorney is usually one who represents the insurer (and others like it) in other cases as well. Although in most states the insurer is not a party to the law suit, it

17. Gertz v. Robert Welch, Inc., 418 U.S. 323, 94 S.Ct. 2997, 41 L.Ed.2d 789 (1974). See § 417.

18. E.g., Chang v. Michiana Telecasting Corp., 900 F.2d 1085 (7th Cir.1990).

19. For instance, guest statutes limiting the tort claims that could be brought by automobile passengers have sometimes been stricken as unconstitutional under state law, as in Brown v. Merlo, 8 Cal.3d 855, 106 Cal.Rptr. 388, 506 P.2d 212 (1973), even though guest statutes had been held valid under the federal constitution. Silver v. Silver, 280 U.S. 117, 50 S.Ct. 57, 74 L.Ed. 221 (1929).

20. Charles Alan Wright, The Law of Federal Courts (4th ed. 1983 & Supps.).

21. Eugene Scoles & Peter Hay, Conflict of Laws (2d ed. 1992); Robert Leflar, Luther McDougal & Robert Felix, American Conflicts Law (4th ed. 1986); Russell Weintraub, Commentary on the Conflict of Laws (3d ed. 1986).

stands responsible for almost everything that happens on the defense side of the case.

Social function of insurance and individual veto. Liability insurance fuels a large number of tort cases, especially automobile cases. It does so because many individuals who cause harm do not have sufficient assets to pay for the harm they do and because the chief assets, such as one's home, may be protected by law. The existence of insurance and its amount become central practical issues for the tort lawyers on both sides. If the insured defendant does not have a sufficient amount of insurance, the plaintiff can be only partly compensated. A few states require liability insurance to cover automobile drivers. Otherwise, the decision to purchase insurance and the decision about its limits is up to the individual policyholder.

The compensation goal. Whether the tort system's goal of compensation for victims of wrongdoing can be fulfilled depends on whether the tortfeasor has assets or insurance. Insurance contributes to the compensation goal by providing a means of payment in many cases that would otherwise go uncompensated. On the other hand, the compensation goal can readily be frustrated because many individuals purchase no liability insurance or if they purchase it, they procure only the most limited amounts.

The deterrence goal. Is the tort system's goal of deterring wrongdoing undermined by insurance? The defendant who fully insures himself in advance helps serve the compensation goals of tort law. But by the same token, he is fully protected against the immediate economic consequences of tort liability, so arguably the deterrence function of tort law is lost when full liability insurance enters the picture.

The presence of insurance is not likely to *wholly* dispel any deterrent effect tort law has. An insured's fear of increased premiums may work as well in some cases, although premium adjustments do not often correlate fully to the insured's risk-taking conduct.[1] And if tort law is less a matter of deterrence and more a matter of reinforcing values the community and the defendant already accept, insurance probably does not undermine the effects of tort law. These and other reasons suggest that tort law may retain a residual effect on conduct even in a system dominated by liability insurance.[2] But whether this in fact is so and whether the residuum is big enough to count is a specific empirical question that cannot be solved by reasoning about human behavior in general. So anyone can justifiably entertain the suspicion that the more insurance serves the compensation goal, the less it will serve the deterrence goal.

§ 22

1. See STEPHEN D. SUGARMAN, DOING AWAY WITH PERSONAL INJURY LAW 13–14 (1989).

2. One commentator suggests that uninsurable costs, reputational loss in the case of professional persons who are sued, and the time losses entailed in defending a suit even when fully insured might affect deterrence. At the same time he argues that people are not necessarily rational wealth-maximizers and hence do not change their behavior because of insurance. Daniel Shuman, The Psychology of Deterrence in Tort Law, 42 U. KAN. L. REV. 115, 130 (1993).

Insurance affecting decisions on liability? It is probably fair to say that tort law expanded the rights of injured persons during much of the 20th century[3] and that the expansion was probably due in part to the perception of courts and juries that an insurer, not the individual defendant, would pay the judgment and that no other way of assuring some aid for the injured effectively existed. Many tort doctrines have changed in the 20th century, usually to expand liability.[4] Practices in the field may have done the same.

Ironically, expanded liability tends to drive up insurance costs,[5] which in turn may lead some people to reduce or eliminate their insurance, with concomitant reduction in funds available to make compensation. Alternatively, increased costs of insurance has led some groups to seek exemption from tort liability or at least a limitation on the amount of damages they must pay. As this pressure increases, some courts seem inclined, not to expand liability in order to utilize insurance funds, but to restrict liability in order to protect those funds from excessive demands.

Insurance affects more aspects of tort law than can be readily summarized and a great deal on this subject must be left for discussions elsewhere. What has been said should be enough to indicate that tort law does not operate in a sterile laboratory. Its hope for compensation and its hopes for deterrence, for corrective justice and for social utility are all among the aspects of tort law affected by the presence of liability insurance.

3. Distinguish expanded rules of tort liability from the claim that (a) litigation has increased and the claim that (b) awards have risen dramatically. The latter two points are heavily debated, but the incomplete figures suggest that the increased litigation is modest. See, e.g., Michael Saks, Do We Really Know Anything About the Behavior of the Tort Litigation System—And Why Not?, 140 U. Pa. L. Rev. 1147 (1992); Joseph Sanders and Craig Joyce, "Off to the Races:" The 1980s Tort Crisis and the Law Reform Process, 27 Hous. L. Rev. 207 (1990). Most of the heavy debate is centered on personal injury tort law, although much of the recent expansion of liability has appeared in the economic tort area.

4. In terms of doctrine, which is readily identifiable if not fully reliable, consider these examples: (1) Specific protections for landowners have been restricted in a number of states; (2) immunities of the federal government, state government, and local governments have been substantially reduced, mostly in the second half of the 20th century; (3) family immunities have been substantially reduced or abolished; (4) civil rights torts, which hardly existed before about 1960, have become a major field; (5) environmental torts, in the modern sense largely statutory, are even more recent; (6) contributory negligence and assumed risk defenses, which once barred negligence claims, are now considered only in determining the plaintiff's damages, again a liberalization that has occurred almost entirely after 1960. The list is much longer.

5. Insurance premium costs are complicated and tort liability is by no means the only factor. Downward fluctuation in the insurer's investment income in a sluggish economy will necessarily affect the insurer's need for premium income.

*

Part II. Physical Interference with Person or Property

Subpart A. Intended Interference

Chapter 3

Direct and Intentional Interference with the Person

Topic A. Scope

§ 23. Scope of the Chapter

This chapter addresses the elements of one group of intentional torts to individual persons, part of a group anciently called "trespassory" torts. Similar torts to property are covered in the next chapter and defenses to these torts in the chapter after that. Trespassory torts are accomplished through the use of physical force, rather than, say, the use of words. Torts like libel and misrepresentation are not trespassory torts, for they are not accomplished by force, and they are accordingly covered much later. Liability for trespassory torts to the person is based upon the defendant's intent to commit some particular act, not upon some generalized assessment of the defendant's behavior. The acts that count as torts in this chapter impact the plaintiff's need for physical security. They also impair the plaintiff's freedom rights, that is, the plaintiff's rights of autonomy and self-determination.

All of these torts are actionable even if the plaintiff has no proven physical harm. Perhaps courts assume that the plaintiff suing for a trespassory tort has some kind of emotional harm, but if so, the plaintiff is not required to prove it. Put differently, these trespassory torts are regarded as harmful in themselves, and in this respect they differ fundamentally from claims for negligence, which always require proof of actual harm.

Topic B. Intent and Related Concepts

§ 24. The Meaning of Intent

Non-tortious intent. Intent itself is a neutral word that does not imply wrong. This is so first because intent by itself is never a tort and second because many intents are perfectly honorable. Your intent to pet your dog or paint your house is not a tortious intent; if carried out, no tort is committed. Which intents are tortious are determined by the rules

of particular torts such as battery. (In the case of battery, intent to touch another person in a way not consented to is the relevant intent.)

State of mind showing intent. What is the state of mind required for an intent? The defendant has an intent to achieve a specified result when the defendant either (1) has a purpose to accomplish that result or (2) lacks such a purpose but knows to a substantial certainty that the defendant's actions will bring about the result.[1]

The purpose test. To illustrate the purpose clause, suppose the defendant attempts to hit a target by firing a rifle from a great distance. It may be unlikely that he can do so, but it is his purpose to do so if he can. Under the first clause, he has intent to hit the target because he has a purpose to do so. The intent is not necessarily tortious or wrong; to see whether the defendant has committed a tort will require other steps in proof and reasoning. The illustration given merely shows the intent element in what may or may not turn out to be a tort.

The certainty test. To see the certainty clause in operation, suppose that the defendant puts sleeping powders in the food served by the cafeteria at a summer camp. His purpose is limited: he knows X will eat the food and wishes to put X to sleep. By the purpose clause, the defendant does not intend to put others to sleep at all. However, if he knows that others will also be eating the cafeteria food at the same time, he must know to a substantial or virtual certainty that they, too, will be affected. Under the certainty clause of the intent definition, the defendant intends to affect others who eat the same cafeteria food at the same time. Mere risk, however, even a very high risk, is not enough to show substantial certainty.[2]

The focused viewpoint of substantial certainty. The substantial certainty test is focused on the plaintiff (or a particular group of plaintiffs) and on the source of the harm and a particular time and place. It will not suffice to say that the defendant maintains a dangerous condition on his land that, over a period of years, is almost certain to cause injury to someone. That might be negligence, but it is not an intent to harm or to commit any trespassory tort.[3]

Deviations. Courts occasionally ignore one or the other of the tests or definitions of intent, seemingly to obtain results that could better be

§ 24

1. Frey v. Kouf, 484 N.W.2d 864 (S.D. 1992); Garratt v. Dailey, 46 Wash. 2d 197, 279 P.2d 1091 (1955); Restatement § 8A.

2. See State Farm Fire & Casualty Co. v. S.S. & G.W., 858 S.W.2d 374 (Tex.1993) (if defendant mistakenly believed he could not communicate disease to consenting sexual partner, he lacked the substantial certainty intent).

3. Cf. Brown v. Diversified Hospitality Group, Inc., 600 So.2d 902 (La.App.1992) (deliberate decision to use inadequate staff increased the risk of robbery and thus of injury to the plaintiff-employee but this is not substantial certainty); but cf. Bradley v. American Smelting & Refining Co., 104 Wash.2d 677, 683, 709 P.2d 782, 786 (1985) (operator of copper smelter had substantial certainty intent that the law of gravity would visit known microscopic particles in its gases "upon someone, somewhere"). A few cases appear to distort the rules of intent in order to avoid the exclusive remedy provisions of workers' compensation statutes and to permit recovery for "intentional" torts. See § 395.

explained on other grounds. One case, for example, insisted that smokers did not intend to touch the plaintiff with their second-hand smoke, even though they allegedly knew their smoke was not only touching the plaintiff but also causing her harm.[4] Such a case implicitly rejects the substantial certainty test, but it might better be understood as establishing a privilege or insisting that a more material touching is required to establish a battery.

Intent is specific. Intent is not a general state of mind. One has a purpose to, or a substantial certainty of accomplishing one or more specific objectives. The defendant might intend to touch and also intend his touching to have harmful effects. These are two different intents. Quite possibly one is tortious and the other is not. Consequently, analysis of intent must be quite specific.

Intent is subjective. Since intent is a state of mind, it is necessarily subjective. That is, the relevant state of mind is that of the person whose intent is in question. This differs from negligence, which is judged by an objective standard. Thus a defendant is negligent if he departs from the standard of care expected of people generally, but he is not necessarily acting intentionally merely because other people acting in like circumstances would harbor an intent.

Evidence of intent is objective. Although the relevant intent is subjective, the trier of fact has no mind reading machine to determine that subjective intent. One's subjective intent is necessarily determined from external or objective evidence. If the defendant pushes the plaintiff into a room, locks the door and throws away the key, the trier of fact is entitled to infer that the defendant intends to confine the plaintiff, at least for a time. So evidence that the defendant intended any given act may be good evidence that he also intended results that tend to follow such an act.

§ 25. Intent and Motive

Motive. A bad motive is occasionally important in determining tort liability, especially in cases involving certain economic torts[1] and claims for punitive damages.[2] But the concept of intent is not the same as the concept of motive. A defendant whose conduct is intentional is not necessarily a defendant who has a bad motive or who is conscious that he is committing a legal wrong.

The difference between intent and motive is illustrated by the case of the physician who forces treatment on an unwilling patient. He may act from the motives of good will and in the belief that his treatment will

4. Pechan v. DynaPro, Inc., 251 Ill. App.3d 1072, 190 Ill.Dec. 698, 622 N.E.2d 108 (1993).

§ 25

1. As in the case of interference with business opportunity without physical threat or harm. See Chapter 32.

2. See § 381.

be best for the patient; he might even believe that he has the legal right to force the treatment upon the patient. But neither his good motives nor his erroneous belief that he is acting rightfully will excuse his intended touching of the patient against the patient's will.[3] Intent, not motive, is the basis of liability for the torts discussed in this chapter.

Capacity: children and mentally disabled persons. In most jurisdictions,[4] neither infancy nor mental disability provides any general immunity from tort liability.[5] Both children[6] and mentally disabled persons[7] may be held responsible for intentional torts. The real question in intentional tort claims against them is the same as in other suits, that is, whether they in fact entertained the intent required to establish a particular tort. Very small children or babies may lack the capacity to entertain an intent, and perhaps some mentally disabled persons lack capacity as well. If they have the requisite intent, however, they do not escape liability because of their age or disability.

§ 26. Intent and Negligence

Intent and negligence distinguished. Intent and negligence are entirely different concepts. Negligence entails unreasonably risky conduct; the emphasis is on risk as it would be perceived by a reasonable person, not on the defendant's purpose or on the certainty required to show intent. The defendant may create *risks* of harm without having either a purpose or a certainty that harm will result.[1] Indeed, negligence does not require a state of mind at all but focuses instead on outward conduct. Even if the defendant recognizes the risk and deliberately decides to chance it without having purpose or certainty required for intent, he is not liable for an intentional tort, only for negligence.[2]

3. Rodriguez v. Pino, 634 So.2d 681 (Fla.App.1994) (thus physician not liable for respecting the patient's expressed wish not to have certain treatment); Fox v. Smith, 594 So.2d 596 (Miss.1992) ("no matter how slight or well intentioned without that patient's informed consent, and violation of this rule constitutes a battery").

4. A few jurisdictions protect certain minors. See Horton v. Hinely, 261 Ga. 863, 413 S.E.2d 199 (1992) (nine-year-old boys allegedly set fire to a seven-year-old; minors under 13 were immune).

5. Restatement, § 895I (infants) & § 895J (mentally disabled persons).

6. Cleveland Park Club v. Perry, 165 A.2d 485, 487 (D.C.Mun.App.1960); Farm Bureau Mut. Ins. Co. of Arkansas v. Henley, 275 Ark. 122, 628 S.W.2d 301 (1982); Gymnastics USA v. McDougal, 92 Or.App. 453, 758 P.2d 881 (1988); cf. Ellis v. D'Angelo, 116 Cal.App.2d 310, 253 P.2d 675 (1953) (4-year-old boy could have the intent required to commit a battery, but might lack capacity to be negligent).

7. Polmatier v. Russ, 206 Conn. 229, 537 A.2d 468 (1988); Williams v. Kearbey, 13 Kan.App.2d 564, 775 P.2d 670 (1989). See W v. Meah, [1986] 1 All E.R. 935 (defendant had suffered a blow to his head that caused a personality change and had recovered from the person who caused the blow, but he was nonetheless held responsible for the rape he perpetrated as a result of his new personality).

§ 26

1. E.g., Spivey v. Battaglia, 258 So.2d 815 (Fla.1972); Frey v. Kouf, 484 N.W.2d 864 (S.D.1992); Funeral Services by Gregory, Inc. v. Bluefield Community Hospital, 186 W.Va. 424, 413 S.E.2d 79 (1991), overruled on other grounds by Courtney v. Courtney, 190 W.Va. 126, 437 S.E.2d 436 (1993).

2. Some decisions may misstate this rule but may be justified on other grounds. See Doe v. Johnson, 817 F.Supp. 1382 (W.D.Mich.1993) (perhaps confusing risk with certainty but also perhaps justified because the plaintiff's consent to inter-

Intent and negligence as mutually exclusive. Any given act may be intentional or it may be negligent, but it cannot be both. Intent and negligence are regarded as mutually exclusive grounds for liability. As the saying goes, there is no such thing as a negligent battery, since battery is defined as an intentional touching, not as a negligent one. So under traditional conceptions, there was no overlap between intentional and negligent torts.[3]

Categorizing conduct. Although there is no overlap between intent and negligence, it is sometimes difficult to discern whether a given set of conduct falls in one category or another. The evidence offered in a case may permit the trier to draw different inferences, so that some jurors would conclude that a defendant acted intentionally while others would conclude that he acted only negligently. If the evidence warrants either a finding that the defendant acted with substantial certainty or that he took an unreasonable risk, the jury might be permitted to find either negligence or intent.[4]

§ 27. Intent and Reckless or Wanton Misconduct

Courts often recognize a kind of third category of fault that is distinguishable both from intent and from negligence. This category is called recklessness or willful or wanton misconduct. Not surprisingly, reckless conduct resembles both intentional conduct and negligence, so this category adds a degree of confusion or uncertainty.

Elements. In civil cases, courts find conduct to be reckless, willful or wanton when two elements concur. First, the conduct must not only create an unreasonable risk of harm to others, it must create a high degree of risk or a risk of very serious harm. Second, the defendant must be conscious of the risk and proceed without concern for the safety of others.[1] Driving while voluntarily intoxicated or drag racing on the public highway are examples.[2] Sometimes authorities say that the defendant need not actually be aware of the risk if it is obvious. However, obviousness of the risk is probably not the test of recklessness. Instead, obviousness is only evidence about the defendant's probable state of mind. If the risk is obvious enough, the trier can infer that the defendant was in fact conscious of it,[3] and if it is also a serious risk of substantial

course may not have included intercourse with a person who knew himself to be infected).

3. American National Fire Ins. Co. v. Schuss, 221 Conn. 768, 607 A.2d 418 (1992). Statutes on particular topics may blur negligence and intent. See Central Pathology Service Medical Clinic, Inc. v. Superior Court, 3 Cal.4th 181, 10 Cal.Rptr.2d 208, 832 P.2d 924 (1992).

4. In spite of what may be broader language, this may be the idea behind Ghassemieh v. Schafer, 52 Md.App. 31, 447 A.2d 84 (Md.Ct.Sp.App. 1982).

§ 27

1. Restatement § 500. Some courts may de-emphasize the state of mind in "wanton" as distinct from "willful" torts. E.g., Seeholzer v. Kellstone, Inc., 80 Ohio App.3d 726, 610 N.E.2d 594 (1992) (defining willful to require a state of mind but wanton to require only a high probability of harm).

2. Booker, Inc. v. Morrill, 639 N.E.2d 358 (Ind.App.1994) (intoxicated driving is wanton misconduct); Lewis v. Miller, 374 Pa.Super. 515, 543 A.2d 590 (1988) (drinking and drag racing).

3. See Farmer v. Brennan, 511 U.S. 825, 114 S.Ct. 1970, 128 L.Ed.2d 811 (1994).

harm, the trier can find recklessness, willful or wanton misconduct, or "deliberate indifference."[4]

Relation to intent and to negligence. Both elements of recklessness—high risk and consciousness of the risk—bear some relationship to intent, but both fall somewhat short of intent. Conduct that imposes only a moderate risk of harm to others is clearly at most only negligent conduct. As the risk becomes greater it may tend to approach virtual certainty and thus become a species of intent. In the case of recklessness, the risk is very high (or very grave), but it is somewhat short of the certainty required to justify a finding that the defendant was acting with intent to cause harm.

Consciousness of risk or indifference to it also bears some resemblance to intent. In fact, the defendant harbors one kind of intent, namely, an intent to take a risk. An intent to take a risk, however, is far short of an intent to inflict an actual harm or an invasion of the plaintiff's rights, so intentional risk-taking is not itself the basis for finding an intentional tort. Nevertheless, it is a cousin to the intentional tort even while it is at home in the negligence family.

Relevance of recklessness in determining liability. In the overwhelming number of tort cases, the defendant's liability turns on intent or negligence, so that recklessness is irrelevant except perhaps to show grounds for punitive damages. In a few instances, however, recklessness is important when mere negligence is not a sufficient ground for liability.[5] In those cases, the plaintiff may be permitted to recover upon a showing of either intent or recklessness. The plaintiff may be able to show reckless misconduct even if she cannot show intentional misconduct, so the category of recklessness in such cases becomes significant.

Topic C. Battery

§ 28. Simple Battery

Intent. The defendant is subject to liability for a simple battery when he intentionally causes bodily contact[1] to the plaintiff in a way not

4. The deliberate indifference standard used in certain civil rights cases is congruent with the definition of recklessness given in this book. See Farmer v. Brennen, supra, n.3.

5. *Examples:* (1) Some statutes make parents liable (usually in limited amounts) for certain reckless or malicious acts of their children, but in the absence of an agency relationship, not for merely negligent acts. E.g., Conn. Gen. Stat. § 52–572. See Walker v. Kelly, 8 Conn.Cir. 715, 314 A.2d 785 (1973). (2) Guest statutes, now almost entirely obsolete in American law, protected automobile drivers from liability to their passengers for ordinary negligence but held them liable for some higher degree of fault such as wanton or reckless misconduct. E.g., Ala. Code § 32–1–2. (3) The common law tort of intentional infliction of emotional distress requires either intent or recklessness on the defendant's part. See Chapter 20. (4) Some common law rules for the liability of landowners to visitors on the land impose liability under standards similar to a recklessness standard. See Chapter 13. (5) Some civil rights liabilities are imposed only in cases of deliberate indifference, which appears to be a species of recklessness or wanton misconduct. See § 45 below. (6) Contributory negligence of a plaintiff was no defense if the defendant was guilty of wanton misconduct. See § 200 below.

§ 28

1. Occasionally courts speak of bodily harm, not merely bodily contact, as in Van-

justified by the plaintiff's apparent wishes or by a privilege,[2] and the contact is in fact harmful or against the plaintiff's will.[3] An accidental touching may count as negligence, but it is not a battery.[4] The defendant may also be subject to liability for a secondary or extended battery. In that case, the defendant unintentionally touches the plaintiff in the course of tortious activity that goes awry.[5]

Harm or offense. Many batteries represent intentional harm, as where one spouse beats or shoots another.[6] An intent to cause actual harm is a sufficient intent but not a necessary one.[7] It is enough that the defendant intends bodily contact that is "offensive,"[8] which is to say a bodily contact that does not appear acceptable to the plaintiff and that is not permitted by a rule of law. Any touching that violates ordinary social usages may thus be a battery unless the plaintiff has given signs that it is acceptable. So an aggressive shove that causes no physical harm is a battery.[9] Violence or ill will is not required. A caress, for example, is a battery unless circumstances indicate that it is acceptable.[10] Even medical treatment that involves a touching is a battery if the health care provider has no reason to believe it is consented to.[11]

Direct vs. indirect harm. In early common law, battery claims were pursued by an action for trespass to the person and thus fell under the rule that trespass actions would lie only if the harm was done directly.[12] If the defendant dug a hole intending the plaintiff to fall into it in the dark, that would not have been a direct harm and hence the trespass claim would not lie. With the abolition of the forms of action, the

dervelden v. Victoria, 177 Wis.2d 243, 502 N.W.2d 276 (Ct.App.1993). This implies a rejection of the offensive battery, but sometimes "bodily harm" is merely loose language and not intended to be such a rejection.

2. As to privileges, see Chapter 5. Even when the defendant is privileged to touch the plaintiff, as where the defendant is privileged to make a lawful arrest, the touching may exceed the privilege because it is excessively forceful or unnecessary. Jackson v. District of Columbia, 412 A.2d 948 (D.C.App.1980).

3. Restatement § 13.

4. Janelsins v. Button, 102 Md.App. 30, 648 A.2d 1039 (1994). By definition, there is no such thing as a negligent battery.

5. § 40 below.

6. Cain v. McKinnon, 552 So.2d 91(Miss.1989); Noble v. Noble, 761 P.2d 1369 (Utah 1988).

7. Frey v. Kouf, 484 N.W.2d 864 (S.D. 1992).

8. § 29 below.

9. Whitley v. Andersen, 37 Colo.App. 486, 551 P.2d 1083 (1976), aff'd, 194 Colo. 87, 570 P.2d 525 (1977).

10. Cf. Kerans v. Porter Paint Co., 61 Ohio St.3d 486, 575 N.E.2d 428 (1991) (intimate touchings as well as other sexual misconduct by plaintiff's superior at work, employer liability for failure to prevent the misconduct); Johnson v. Ramsey County, 424 N.W.2d 800 (Minn.App.1988) (kiss implanted by employer); Rogers v. Loews L'Enfant Plaza Hotel, 526 F.Supp. 523, (D.D.C.1981) (male superior on the job, unwanted touching of the plaintiff's hair). Some sexual harassment does not involve a touching and hence is not a battery but may constitute some other tort. E.g., International Union, United Automobile, Aerospace And Agricultural Implement Workers of America, UAW v. Johnson Controls, Inc., 499 U.S. 187, 111 S.Ct. 1196, 113 L.Ed.2d 158 (1991).

11. E.g., Mims v. Boland, 110 Ga.App. 477, 138 S.E.2d 902 (1964).

12. See § 14, supra and §§ 50, 111 below.

distinction is meaningless or confusing. In any event, it has been subsumed by the intent rules: if the defendant acts on an intention to inflict a harmful or offensive bodily contact, and he succeeds, he is liable for the battery whether the harm is direct or not.

Damages. Once a battery is established, the defendant becomes liable for the harms resulting, including unintended ones. He may intend only an offensive touching, but he is liable for any actual harm that results. Recovery is permitted for trespassory torts without proof of pecuniary loss or actual physical harm.[13] The defendant is of course liable for physical harms resulting from the battery, but he is also liable for impermissible touchings that are not physically harmful.

Policy. The law of battery, an outgrowth of the old trespass writ, was originally conceived solely in terms of force and violence.[14] Like much other early law, it served to substitute a legal recovery for revenge and to discourage actual violence. Tort law today of course shares those goals; but as the rules show, it adopts more subtle ones as well. Battery today vindicates the plaintiff's rights of autonomy and self-determination, her right to decide for herself how her body will be treated by others, and to exclude their invasions as a matter of personal preference, whether physical harm is done or not.[15]

§ 29. Harm or Offense Required to Establish Simple Battery

The central core. The central core of the battery rules is simple. Subject only to the most limited exception,[1] the defendant must respect the plaintiff's apparent wishes to avoid intentional bodily contact. Hostile, aggressive, or harmful touchings are batteries because the plaintiff wishes to avoid them. But the plaintiff's right to avoid unwanted intentional contact does not depend upon the defendant's hostile intent or even upon the reasonableness of the plaintiff's wishes. A person is entitled to refuse well-intentioned medical treatment[2] as well as the bumptious grapplings of an unwelcome swain.[3] In a world full of uncon-

13. § 42 below.

14. Cole v. Turner, 6 Mod.Rep. 149, 90 Eng.Rep. 958 (Nisi Prius 1704) ("the least touching of another in anger is a battery.... If any of them use violence against the other ... it is a battery").

15. In the Interest of Baby Boy Doe, 260 Ill.App.3d 392, 198 Ill.Dec. 267, 632 N.E.2d 326 (Ill.App. 1994) (right to refuse medical treatment includes right to refuse cesarian operation that might improve chances of fetus or child); James Henderson, Why Vosburg Comes First, 1992 Wis. L. Rev. 853, 859.

§ 29

1. See the paragraph below, *The case of social usage or conflicting rights.* In addition, there are of course affirmative defenses or privileges, such as self-defense.

2. Rodriguez v. Pino, 634 So.2d 681 (Fla.App.1994); Gragg v. Calandra, 297 Ill. App.3d 639, 231 Ill.Dec. 711, 696 N.E.2d 1282 (1998); cf. Anderson v. St. Francis–St. George Hospital, 83 Ohio App.3d 221, 614 N.E.2d 841 (1992) (if life-saving treatment was given against the plaintiff's will, the plaintiff had a battery claim), rev'd on other grounds, 77 Ohio St.3d 82, 671 N.E.2d 225 (1996).

3. Stockett v. Tolin, 791 F.Supp. 1536 (S.D.Fla.1992) (employer touched employee's breasts, licked her); Johnson v. Ramsey County, 424 N.W.2d 800 (Minn.Ct.App. 1988) (kissing battery); cf. R. v. Burden, 1 W.W.R. 193 (B.C. C.A.) [1982] (defendant

trollable events, all persons are at least entitled to prohibit unwanted intentional touchings of any kind.

Formulating a rule: the Restatement's "harmful or offensive" test. How is this central policy to be formulated in a rule? The Restatement attempts to convey the policy by saying that the defendant is subject to liability for causing bodily contact that is either (a) harmful or (b) "offensive." The Restatement does not use "offense" in the sense that a person might be huffy or irritable. Rather, an offensive touching is one that infringes a reasonable sense of personal dignity.[4] More broadly put, a touching is "offensive" if it infringes upon the plaintiff's actual and apparent wishes to avoid it. Although liability may be imposed for harmful attacks, liability does not depend upon harm[5] or even upon emotional distress[6] to the plaintiff; it depends upon violating the plaintiff's right to herself.

"Offense": plaintiff's apparent consent as the central issue. The Restatement formula has the advantage of singling out some specific forms of battery—those that are "harmful" and those that are "offensive." But the terms may be distracting. The gist of the battery is that the plaintiff has been touched, intentionally, in a way that she has not even apparently consented to and that is not justified by some generally recognized privilege.[7] The defendant's intent to touch in a way the plaintiff has not apparently permitted is what counts; it is what makes the touching "offensive."[8] At least this is true when the plaintiff is competent to give or withhold consent.

The same idea may apply when the defendant has consent to touch but goes beyond the consent in some particular way. For instance, the surgeon who has consent to remove one organ does not necessarily have consent, even implicit consent, to remove another.[9]

sat next to plaintiff on virtually empty bus and put his hand on her thigh; this is a criminal battery).

4. The Restatement uses the term "personal dignity," which is again accurate but must not be understood to mean reserved bearing or social distance. It means only the right of every person to determine how her or his body is to be touched, subject perhaps to some social conventions that permit the more or less unavoidable touchings in a crowd or the like.

5. E.g., Whitley v. Andersen, 37 Colo. App. 486, 551 P.2d 1083 (1976), aff'd, 194 Colo. 87, 570 P.2d 525 (1977).

6. This is congruent with the rule for certain kinds of sexual harassment claims under some federal statutes: an abusive or hostile environment is required, but not emotional distress. See Harris v. Forklift Systems, Inc., 510 U.S. 17, 114 S.Ct. 367, 126 L.Ed.2d 295 (1993).

7. Privileges, as affirmative defenses, are discussed in Chapter 5.

8. The whole course of decisions bears this out. Courts sometimes expressly recognize the point as well. See Cohen v. Smith, 269 Ill.App.3d 1087, 207 Ill.Dec. 873, 648 N.E.2d 329 (1995) ("Liability for battery emphasizes the plaintiff's lack of consent to the touching").

9. Mohr v. Williams, 95 Minn. 261, 104 N.W. 12 (1905) (consent to operate on right ear, actual operation on left ear, held a battery, but benefits of the operation are to be considered in fixing damages); Bommareddy v. Superior Court (Williams), 222 Cal. App.3d 1017, 272 Cal.Rptr. 246 (1990), overruled on other grounds, Central Pathology Service Med. Clinic, Inc. v. Superior Court (Hull), 3 Cal.4th 181, 832 P.2d 924, 10 Cal.Rptr.2d 208 (1992) (statute limiting punitive damages claims in medical negligence cases applied to intentional torts); see Cobbs v. Grant, 8 Cal.3d 229, 239, 502 P.2d 1, 7, 104 Cal.Rptr. 505, 511 (1972) ("Where a doctor obtains consent of the patient to perform one type of treatment and subse-

What counts as an apparent consent is an important topic considered later. The central point to note here is that the plaintiff's apparent consent shows that the defendant is not intending to touch in an offensive way and that no right of the plaintiff has been invaded by permitted touchings, even if it turns out to be unintentionally harmful.[10] In such a case the defendant may be responsible for negligence if he has unreasonably risked harm, but he is not liable for the intended touching to which the plaintiff apparently consented. Conversely, if it is apparent that the plaintiff is not consenting to the defendant's touching, it becomes clear that the touching is intended to be offensive at least under the substantial certainty definition of intent.

The case of social usage and conflicting rights. In one narrow kind of case a defendant may escape liability for an intentional touching even when he knows that the plaintiff wishes to avoid it. A plaintiff who rides the subway may implicitly consent to a certain amount of intentional jostling as other riders leave the car, and if so, the touching would not transgress the plaintiff's rights; in the Restatement's words, it would not be offensive. Suppose, however, the subway rider makes it plain to all passengers that she must not be touched by others as they attempt to exit the crowded car. Would other riders be liable for a battery if they must push through the throng to reach the exit? Presumably not. Not only are such jostlings socially accepted, they are necessary to protect the rights of others who must also live in an unpleasantly crowded world. The plaintiff's right to avoid bodily contact is important, but so is the defendant's right to take the subway and get to work. The plaintiff cannot preempt the subway space for herself alone.[11]

The Restatement's "reasonable sense of personal dignity." The problem of conflicting rights is a small one in the actual cases, but the Restatement gives an answer to it that may be too large. It formulates the solution by saying that the touching must be one that would offend a reasonable sense of personal dignity.[12] This formulation uses an objective standard, what people in general regard as an acceptable touching.[13] In doing so, it disregards the plaintiff's own wishes. Yet if adequately expressed, the plaintiff's wishes usually count for everything; she has a right to reject unprivileged touchings that others would find reasonable.

quently performs a substantially different treatment for which consent was not obtained, there is a clear case of battery"). In some circumstances, including genuine emergencies, an implied consent may be found. Cf. Kennedy v. Parrott, 243 N.C. 355, 90 S.E.2d 754 (1956). Distinguishable problems arise in the case of mistaken consent, uninformed consent, and conditioned consent.

10. Hellriegel v. Tholl, 69 Wash.2d 97, 417 P.2d 362 (1966).

11. Cf. McCracken v. O.B. Sloan, 40 N.C.App. 214, 252 S.E.2d 250 (1979) (plaintiff touched by smoke).

12. Restatement § 19 (1965). "Dignity," like "offense," may mislead inexperienced readers in the law. Dignity here has nothing to do with gravity, formality, or reserve. It is instead a reflection of self-respect or a sense of one's self.

13. Other objective formulations are sometimes used. See Zgraggen v. Wilsey, 200 A.D.2d 818, 606 N.Y.S.2d 444 (App.Div. 1994) (touching is offensive if it is "wrongful under all the circumstances").

The real point seems to be, not that the plaintiff's wishes are to be evaluated by others, but that others are as entitled as she to ride subways. When the entitlement of others disappears, as where the subway car is not crowded, the plaintiff is free to insist that she not be touched even if many others would not object to an unnecessary jostle.

Reasonable sense of dignity when the plaintiff lacks capacity to consent. What is the relevance, if any, of the "reasonable sense of personal dignity"? First, when the plaintiff lacks capacity to consent or to withhold consent, an objective standard based on the objective reasonable sense of personal dignity may be desirable. For example, sexual touchings of a very small child who understands nothing of what is happening might be regarded as batteries even if they caused no identifiable harm, either because the touchings are unlawful in themselves or because they would offend an objective idea of a reasonable sense of personal dignity.

Reasonable sense of dignity as evidence of what the plaintiff in fact permitted or prohibited. In a second kind of case, the plaintiff has full capacity to consent or withhold consent and has not expressly prohibited the touching. The ultimate questions will be whether the touching was *in fact* against the plaintiff's apparent wishes as reasonably understood by the defendant. A touching that would not ordinarily offend a reasonable sense of personal dignity would presumably not be against the plaintiff's wishes, in the absence of some expression to the contrary. So a reasonable sense of personal dignity is also indirectly relevant in trying to decide whether the defendant had any notice that his touching would be unacceptable. It is a matter of evidence, not a rule of law. By the same token, the objective reasonable sense of dignity is irrelevant when the plaintiff has manifested a desire to avoid the contact and the defendant has no privilege (like the subway rider) that justifies the touching.

This analysis suggests that the uses of the "reasonable sense of personal dignity" test should have a quite narrow impact. The Restatement may have gone too far in suggesting that offensiveness or a reasonable sense of dignity are of general importance in determining battery liability.[14]

Burden of proof. In some instances, the plaintiff's consent or apparent consent is analyzed as an affirmative defense, to be proved by the defendant. However, in the case of battery, the plaintiff's burden is to show that the defendant intended to and did cause either harm or "offense," a burden that ordinarily requires the plaintiff to show that the defendant's touching was not apparently consented to. Consent or

14. The Restatement's illustrations are all in line with these comments. Illustrations 1 and 3 actually use the test affirmatively, as a basis for liability, not as a defense against it. In another illustration the defendant is not liable because he has held a child who is being sick in his cab. This illustration is in accord with the idea that the touching, being generally acceptable in society, would inferentially be acceptable to the particular plaintiff as well, in the absence of an expression to the contrary. Illustration 2 approximates the subway example; the defendant "deliberately but not discourteously pushes" the plaintiff to pass him in a "densely crowded street." This accords with a privilege analysis.

apparent consent is certainly relevant, but not because it is an affirmative defense. Rather it is relevant on two issues that are a part of the plaintiff's case: (1) did the defendant intend an offensive touching? or (2) was there in fact an offensive touching?

§ 30. Nature of Intent Required to Establish Simple Battery

Intent to ... Intent has been defined to include either a purpose to effect some result or a substantial certainty that the result will follow from the defendant's actions.[1] What *results* must the defendant intend to establish a simple battery?

The Restatement formula. The Restatement's formula is that the defendant must intend a "harmful or offensive contact." As already explained, an intent to touch in a way the defendant understands is not consented to is sufficient. So is an actual intent to harm. The question is whether the plaintiff shows intent by showing merely an intent to touch that turned out to be offensive or harmful, or whether she must show that the harm or offense was also intended. On this point the Restatement and some of the cases are ambiguous.[2]

Ambiguity illustrated. Suppose the defendant intends to touch the plaintiff but he intends the touching to be friendly and comforting, not either harmful or offensive. That is, he believes the touching is consented to. In this state of mind, he hugs the plaintiff, but the plaintiff is unexpectedly harmed by the hug or revolted by it. A little authority phrases the rule in a way that suggests the defendant will be liable.[3] Other courts seems to think that the defendant must intend not only a touching but also must intended it to be harmful or offensive.[4]

§ 30

1. § 24.

2. One court, for example, says that the plaintiff "must prove that there was bodily contact, that the contact was offensive, and that the defendant intended to make the contact." But of course the statement itself is ambiguous. It says that the plaintiff "must prove" the stated elements but it does not say that the plaintiff need prove *only* those elements. Laurie Marie M. v. Jeffrey T. M., 159 A.D.2d 52, 559 N.Y.S.2d 336 (1990) aff'd, 77 N.Y.2d 981, 575 N.E.2d 393, 571 N.Y.S.2d 907 (1991). In Masters v. Becker, 22 A.D.2d 118, 254 N.Y.S.2d 633 (1964), the court said that the plaintiff needed "only" to prove bodily contact, that the contact was offensive, and that the defendant intended to make the contact.

3. Cf. White v. University of Idaho, 118 Idaho 400, 797 P.2d 108 (1990) (intent to "act" required but not either intent to harm or to offend). In *White*, a professor and piano enthusiast touched the plaintiff's back with his hands as if playing a piano. The plaintiff was a social acquaintance and fellow enthusiast; neither harm nor offense was intended. An unexpected injury occurred. The victim sued the professor's employer, a state university, which might be held liable for an employee's negligence but not the employee's battery. The court held that the professor's act was a battery so that the university was not liable. In other words, the result of the court's expansive conception of battery in this particular case is not liability but non-liability.

4. "A harmful or offensive contact with a person, resulting from an act intended to cause the plaintiff to suffer such a contact, is a battery." Caudle v. Betts, 512 So.2d 389, 390 (La.1987). Many cases, some of them prosecutions for criminal battery, have emphasized the need for wrongful intent, sometimes overstating the intent required by saying that it must be an intent to harm. Other cases support the intent requirement by analyzing unintended harm as negligence, not battery. Cf. Spivey v. Battaglia, 258 So.2d 815 (Fla.1972) (friend-

The fault principle argument. The Restatement's formula is perhaps ambiguous, but it probably means intent to harm or offend as well as an intent to touch is required. This is in line with the fault principle and also with the freedom to act encouraged by that principle. To see this, suppose that in the illustrative example, the defendant is a wife who hugs her husband, but the hug unexpectedly causes a bone spur to break off and impinge upon a nerve in her husband's spine. If the wife intended neither harm nor any violation of the husband's implicit consent to friendly physical contact, the intent is not tortious or faulty. Except under a general regime of strict liability that is inconsistent with the fault principle, the physical contact alone seems to furnish no ground for liability.

That is not the whole story, because the wife might be at fault in some other way. Specifically, she might be negligent in creating an unreasonable risk to the husband. But liability for negligence rests on entirely different grounds and such a liability is imposed only in cases of actual harm, not cases of touchings that are merely offensive.[5] If the only claim is liability for battery, the fault principle seems to require that the defendant (a) intend to touch the plaintiff, and (b) intend to harm the plaintiff by the touching or to touch in a way that is not consented to.

The strict liability argument. One argument for strict liability based on intent to touch without an intent to harm or offend is rooted in some particular circumstances. Some insensitive defendants may honestly believe that the plaintiff will welcome their sexual touchings and some abusive defendants will certainly claim so. Should a defendant who fondles strangers be permitted to escape liability if the jury believes that he really thought his attentions were welcome?

One answer is that the jury is free to and presumably would reject such a preposterous claim. A second solution is more subtle. Even if the jury believes that the defendant had no intent to offend, it might find him to be negligent and liable on that ground if he causes actual harm. However, that solution would leave the victim with no redress for merely offensive touchings if the jury believed the defendant had no intent to offend. A third solution is to impose strict liability, holding all defendants liable for the offenses or harms resulting from an intended touching, even if it was apparently consented to. The best solution, however, may be to recognize that the plaintiff's apparent lack of consent must be judged objectively. If the plaintiff says, in words or deeds, "Don't touch me," and the defendant intentionally touches the plaintiff anyway, the defendant, not the plaintiff, must bear the cost of the defendant's foolish belief that no means yes. These solutions do not, however, suggest that the wife who hugs her husband is liable for an unexpected harm.

ly, unsolicited hug caused unintended and unexpected paralysis, no liability for battery, but potential liability for negligence).

5. §§ 110 & 114.

Substituting unlawfulness for intent. Historically, battery was a tort brought by use of the trespass writ. It was thus originally a strict liability tort in which the only requirement was a direct application of force to the person without regard to fault or even any specific intent. For a time, illegality of the defendant's act was sufficient.[6] With the general adoption of the fault principle beginning around 1850,[7] courts began to insist on intent that was in some way wrongful, or on proof of negligence.

The roots of the battery tort in a regime of strict liability still occasionally produce its tart fruits in the form of liability of defendants who acted without intent to transgress the plaintiff's wishes at all. A famous case is *Vosburg v. Putney*,[8] where a 12–year old school boy kicked the 14–year-old plaintiff during a class period. The 12–year old was held liable for battery, although he intended no harm. Because the kick was in the school room, not on the playground, the court thought it was "unlawful" and that unlawfulness was enough to justify liability. The facts given by the court are consistent with liability based on intent to inflict an offensive touching, and if the defendant intended an offensive touching, standard rules would make him liable for the unintended harm.[9] So *Vosburg* may not stand for any form of liability without intent, much less liability without fault.

Vosburg does suggest, however, that sometimes courts may substitute unlawfulness of the defendant's conduct for a wrongful intent, although *Vosburg* does not seem to be a very convincing exemplar of that viewpoint and may in fact have been compromised as an authority by the very court that decided it.[10] If defendants are to be held liable for battery on the ground that the touching was "unlawful," the logic of liability will deprive the plaintiff of the legal power to consent to such a touching, a result that is wholly at odds with the autonomy battery law seeks to

6. E.G. Roberts, Negligence: Blackstone to Shaw to ?, 50 Cornell L. Q. 191 (1965).

7. §§ 112, 342.

8. 80 Wis. 523, 50 N.W. 403 (1891). *Vosburg v. Putney* has produced literally reams of material from scholars. For its centennial, the Wisconsin Law Review published some 150 pages of scholarly material. See Zigurds Zile, Vosburg v. Putney: A Centennial Story, 1992 Wis. L. Rev. 877; James Henderson, Why Vosburg Comes First, 1992 Wis. L. Rev. 854; Robert Rabin, Vosburg v. Putney in Three–Part Disharmony, 1992 Wis. L. Rev. 863; James Willard Hurst, The Use of Case Histories, 1992 Wis. L. Rev. 875. The authors are not concerned with the fact that something like "unlawfulness" became a kind of substitute for intent in *Vosburg*, but with other issues such as the extensive costs of litigation as compared with the non-existent benefit.

9. § 28.

10. Gouger v. Hardtke, 167 Wis.2d 504, 482 N.W.2d 84 (1992), used several peculiar standards in holding that a school boy had not committed a battery when he threw a soapstone at another boy in shop class. First, the court focused on intent to *injure* (not on intent to inflict an unwanted touching). Second, the court ignored the defendant's admitted purpose to strike the plaintiff; instead it treated substantial certainty as the sole test of intent. Third, the apparent consent of the plaintiff was ignored. The court may have been striving to find a negligent tort rather than an intentional one to preserve insurance coverage. Whatever the reasons, the decision seems formally at odds with *Vosburg*. In Vandervelden v. Victoria, 177 Wis.2d 243, 502 N.W.2d 276 (Ct.App.1993) the Wisconsin court also departed from the offensive branch of battery, saying that bodily harm was required.

protect.[11] Nevertheless, unlawfulness or some other objective standard of liability would sometimes fulfill important policies without imposing strict liability.[12]

§ 31. The Bodily Contact Required to Establish Simple Battery

Material touching. The size of the object that touches the plaintiff does not matter. The plaintiff is of course touched if she is struck by a bullet, but she is also touched if she drinks poison put in her cup by the defendant.[1] On the other hand, odors, smokes, or gases have been traditionally treated as intangibles, even though they do have a physical presence.[2] Whether a touching by second-hand tobacco smoke would count as a battery under some circumstances is perhaps uncertain.[3] However, several decisions have found a battery resulting from smoke, with the qualification that the defendant must have a purpose to harm or offend and is not liable merely for substantial certainty touchings.[4]

Extended personality. The plaintiff is also touched if the defendant touches some intimate extension of the plaintiff's person,[5] as when the

11. In *Vosburg* the parties were minors, and possibly the plaintiff-victim was in no position to give either an understanding consent or a legally binding one. In such a case, imposition of liability upon the defendant does not imply any loss of the plaintiff's power to decide for himself, since the plaintiff lacks that power anyway.

12. Sexual touchings of a small child who lacks capacity to consent and power to prohibit might be an example of an unlawful touching for which liability should be imposed even if the child was also too young to experience a sense of offense and is not harmed, and even if neither harm nor offense were intended. Given the character of such an act as one always considered wrongful, liability would not be "strict" even though the defendant lacked intent to harm or offend.

§ 31

1. Snouffer v. Snouffer, 87 Ohio App.3d 89, 621 N.E.2d 879 (1993) (administering poison is a battery).

2. This distinction is one of the factual bases for the traditional legal difference between trespass to land (physical, tangible entry) and nuisance (intangible invasions affecting enjoyment but not possession).

3. See McCracken v. O.B. Sloan, 40 N.C.App. 214, 252 S.E.2d 250 (1979) (upholding smokers' rights and refusing to find battery); see Renee Vintzel Loridas, Annotation, Secondary Smoke as Battery, 46 A.L.R.5th 813 (1997).

4. Richardson v. Hennly, 209 Ga.App. 868, 434 S.E.2d 772 (1993) (claim that defendant deliberately directed pipe smoke at plaintiff knowing it would cause her actual harm; pipe smoke is visible and capable of "touching" the plaintiff), rev'd on other grounds, 264 Ga. 355, 444 S.E.2d 317 (1994); Leichtman v. WLW Jacor Communications, Inc., 92 Ohio App.3d 232, 634 N.E.2d 697 (1994) (allegations that defendant repeatedly blew cigar smoke in the plaintiff's face for the very purpose of causing physical discomfort and distress). Cf. Pechan v. DynaPro, Inc., 251 Ill.App.3d 1072, 190 Ill.Dec. 698, 622 N.E.2d 108 (1993) (employer not liable for battery merely because it authorized employees to smoke in plaintiff's presence; it would be liable only if smokers themselves had a purpose to touch; substantial certainty of a touching would not suffice, semble). See, David Ezra, Smoker Battery: An Antidote to Second-Hand Smoke, 63 So.Cal.L.Rev. 1061 (1990) (canvassing theories for claims against smokers). Exposure to second-hand smoke on the job might conceivably be covered by workers' compensation if harm is caused or possibly even by anti-discrimination statutes. See Hinman v. Yakima Sch. Dist. No. 7, 69 Wash.App. 445, 850 P.2d 536 (1993) (state job-discrimination statute).

5. Espinoza v. Thomas, 189 Mich.App. 110, 472 N.W.2d 16 (1991) (group of strikers blocking, rocking, and beating on the car plaintiff was driving is a battery); Picard v. Barry Pontiac-Buick, Inc., 654 A.2d 690 (R.I.1995).

defendant jerks a plate from the plaintiff's hand, even if the hand itself is not touched.[6]

Causing a touching by other objects or by other persons. Touching is not limited to physical contact between the defendant's body and the plaintiff's. The defendant who wears gloves to slap the plaintiff is no less guilty of a battery than one who strikes the plaintiff bare-handed. More than that, the plaintiff is touched and a battery committed if the defendant intentionally pulls the chair from under the plaintiff as she sits, with the result that she falls to the ground.[7] Finally, the defendant may be responsible for a battery if he directly causes other persons to effectuate or complete the harmful or offensive bodily contact with the plaintiff.[8]

§ 32. Battery and Other Torts: Acts and Omissions

Acts distinguished from intent and from involuntary motion. The Restatement structures analysis of battery and other trespassory torts by requiring an "act" of the defendant.[1] An act in the Restatement's terminology is an external manifestation of will, a voluntary contraction of muscles, nothing more.[2] Involuntary muscle spasms, convulsions, bodily movements during sleep are thus not acts. On the other hand, an instantaneous response to emergency, as where the defendant grabs the plaintiff to avoid falling, constitutes an act.[3] The term "act" has no moral content. The defendant "acts" when he strikes another even if he is prompted by insane impulses.[4]

Act distinguished from inaction. The term "act" is also used to emphasize a distinction between affirmative deeds on the one hand and omissions or passive behavior on the other. Battery normally results from the defendant's affirmative acts or deeds: the defendant strikes the plaintiff or spits on him or poisons his drink. Can a defendant be liable for a battery when the defendant does nothing to stop another's bodily contact with the plaintiff? Analogies from negligence law suggest that the defendant who has no special relationship with the plaintiff or her

6. Fisher v. Carrousel Motor Hotel, Inc., 424 S.W.2d 627 (Tex.1967) (plate jerked from the plaintiff's hand is a battery).

7. Garratt v. Dailey, 46 Wash.2d 197, 279 P.2d 1091 (1955).

8. Richardson v. Hennly, 209 Ga.App. 868, 434 S.E.2d 772 (1993) (it is enough that defendant sets a force in motion that touches the plaintiff, quoting PROSSER & KEETON ON TORTS § 9), rev'd on other grounds, 264 Ga. 355, 444 S.E.2d 317 (1994); Wilder v. Gardner, 39 Ga.App. 608, 147 S.E. 911 (Ga.App.1929) ("One who by advice, counsel, or command procures another to commit a wrong" is equally liable); Mock v. Polley, 116 Ind.App. 580, 66 N.E.2d 78 (1946) (one aiding and abetting or encouraging battery is "equally guilty" and liable in tort); Leichtman v. WLW Jacor Communications, Inc., 92 Ohio App.3d 232, 236, 634 N.E.2d 697, 699 (1994) ("one who is present and encourages or incites commission of a battery ... can be equally liable as a principal").

§ 32

1. E.g., Restatement § 13 (liability for harmful battery requires act, intention, and harmful contact).

2. Restatement § 2.

3. Restatement § 2, Cmt. b.

4. Polmatier v. Russ, 206 Conn. 229, 537 A.2d 468 (1988).

attacker would not be liable for a battery if he merely failed to prevent the attacker from hitting the plaintiff.

Duty to protect the plaintiff from others' batteries? On the other hand, the defendant might be under a duty to protect the plaintiff. Employers, for example, are under a duty to protect employees from sexual batteries (and other forms of sexual harassment). If an employer knows that an employee is being sexually battered by another employee, it is not implausible to say that the employer is also guilty of a battery, though he has not committed any "act" and in some instances the battery claim might be advantageous.[5] Similarly, a hospital is under a duty to protect patients from attack, and a knowing failure to do so might be thought of as a battery by inaction. In practice, however, courts are likely to think of both kinds of claims as negligence claims turning on reasonableness rather than battery claims turning upon intent.[6] That is not necessarily the plaintiff's loss, since the defendant's liability insurance may cover negligence but not battery. The upshot is that an affirmative act is at least ordinarily if not invariably required to establish a battery.

Vicarious liability for battery. Liability may, of course, be imposed upon one who instigates a battery or other trespassory tort by another. That is not a case of inaction[7] but a case of liability of one person for the actions of another.[8] It may also be imposed upon employers and persons in analogous roles for the actions of their employees committed within the scope of employment.

Topic D. Assault

§ 33. Simple Assault

Nature of the tort. Newspapers and even judges and lawyers sometimes use the term assault to mean a battery. More technically, assault is a quite different tort, although it often precedes a battery. An assault is an act that is intended to and does place the plaintiff in apprehension of an immediate unconsented-to touching that would amount to a battery.[1] The plaintiff's subjective recognition or apprehension that she is about to be touched in an impermissible way is at the core of the assault claim.

Intent and transferred intent. As in other cases, intent may be based either on the defendant's purpose or on his substantial certainty that a

5. Because employers are generally protected from negligence claims under workers' compensation laws, but sometimes not for intentional tort claims. See generally, Jean Love, Actions for Nonphysical Harm: The Relationship Between the Tort System and No-Fault Compensation (With an Emphasis on Workers' Compensation), 73 Cal. L. Rev. 857 (1985).

6. *Employers liable for negligence:* E.g., Ford v. Revlon, Inc., 153 Ariz. 38, 734 P.2d 580 (1987). *Hospital liable for negligence:* Sumblin v. Craven County Hospital Corp., 86 N.C.App. 358, 357 S.E.2d 376 (1987) (viewing claim against hospital for failure to protect psychiatric patient from molestation as a negligence case).

7. E.g., West v. LTV Steel Co., 839 F.Supp. 559 (N.D.Ind.1993).

8. See Chapter 22 on vicarious liability generally.

§ 33

1. Restatement §§ 21 & 32.

trespassory tort will occur. A risk that the plaintiff will be touched or put in apprehension does not qualify as substantial certainty and it forms no basis for liability based on intent. In the case of a secondary or extended assault, the defendant may be held liable if his misconduct is directed at a third person but miscarries so that it is the plaintiff who apprehends the immediate or "imminent" touching.[2]

Examples of simple assault. An example of an intended battery that actually culminates only in an assault is the case of the defendant who attempts to strike the plaintiff from behind. If the plaintiff turns in time to see the blow about to be delivered and escapes it, there is no battery since there is no touching. But if the plaintiff apprehended an imminent touching from the blow, the defendant is liable for an assault. If the plaintiff is not aware of the impending blow, there is no assault at all, although if the blow is actually delivered there will be a battery.[3]

In some instances, the defendant's whole purpose is to convince the plaintiff that a battery is imminent even though the defendant never intends to deliver the threatened blow. In the absence of a privilege, the defendant is liable for assault in such cases as well, so long as he intends to put the plaintiff in apprehension of a battery. For example, the defendant may shoot a pistol at the plaintiff with the intent to frighten but not to touch. Again, if the plaintiff apprehends an imminent battery, the defendant is liable for the assault.

Damages. Since assault is a tort that is historically derived from the writ of trespass, the tort carries with it a right to a damages award even when no physical harm is done.[4]

§ 34. Apprehension of Imminent Touching

Apprehension vs. fear. Courts often define assault in terms of the plaintiff's fear of an imminent touching, but they probably do not literally mean fear, as much as a recognition that a touching is threatened.[1] The courageous plaintiff who fears nothing or is sure he can avoid the threatened touch is entitled to recover for assault if he is aware that the defendant is attempting to land a blow or to shoot him.[2]

Apprehension: reasonableness, words alone. Many opinions have asserted that the plaintiff's apprehension must be reasonable or well-

2. § 40.

3. This results from the rule that the plaintiff must apprehend an imminent touching. See McCraney v. Flanagan, 47 N.C.App. 498, 267 S.E.2d 404 (1980) (when plaintiff awoke, she found that defendant had had sexual intercourse with her, but as she had not been aware of an imminent sexual touching, she had no assault claim).

4. See § 42.

§ 34

1. Lamb v. State, 93 Md.App. 422, 613 A.2d 402 (Ct. Spec. App. 1993) (words like fear sometimes used loosely as shorthand for apprehension, but fear is not literally required, citing PROSSER & KEETON ON TORTS § 10).

2. Brady v. Schatzel, Q.St.R. 206 (1911) (pointing a rifle at victim, criminal responsibility should turn on the assailant's intent, not on the timidity or courage of the victim); R. v. Gardner, 69 N.B.R.2d 135 (N.B. Q.B. 1986) ("degree of alarm felt" is irrelevant, criminal case); Restatement § 24, cmt. b and ilus. 1 & 2.

founded,[3] that the defendant must have the apparent present ability to complete the battery,[4] and that words alone, without accompanying action, cannot count as an assault.[5] These rules are sometimes criticized as too restrictive for extreme cases.[6] For example, in one sense there is no such thing as a "words alone" case; all words occur in a social context and that context may reinforce and add substance to the verbal threat.[7] The apparent reality of the threat, not its form, is what counts.

Imminence. Although the plaintiff need not suffer fear, she must in fact conclude that the threatened battery is imminent, meaning that it will occur without delay unless an intervening force prevents it or the plaintiff is able to flee. Future danger,[8] or a threatening atmosphere without reason to expect some immediate touching,[9] in other words, is not enough. On the other hand, the threat of imminent touching need not be explicit or verbal. If an angry crowd of men block, rock, and beat on the plaintiff's car, the plaintiff may justly feel apprehension of a battery even if none is expressly threatened.[10]

Conditional threats. The defendant cannot defeat the plaintiff's assault claim on the ground that he gave the plaintiff an unprivileged alternative to the threatened battery. The robber who points a gun and says "your money or your life" is guilty of an assault because he has no right to take either.[11] The rule is different, however, if the defendant has a privilege to insist upon the alternative. "Leave my property or I'll

3. Allen v. Walker, 569 So.2d 350, 351 (Ala.1990) ("well-founded fear of an imminent battery, coupled with the apparent present ability to effectuate the attempt, if not prevented"); Espinoza v. Thomas, 189 Mich.App. 110, 472 N.W.2d 16 (1991).

4. Muslow v. A.G. Edwards & Sons, Inc., 509 So.2d 1012 (La.App.1987) ("reasonable apprehension" based on "present ability"); Hawkins v. Hawkins, 101 N.C.App. 529, 400 S.E.2d 472 (1991) ("reasonable apprehension, apparent ability"), aff'd, 331 N.C. 743, 417 S.E.2d 447 (1992).

5. Webbier v. Thoroughbred Racing Protective Bureau, Inc., 105 R.I. 605, 614, 254 A.2d 285, 290 (1969) ("Words alone are never a sufficient basis for a finding for assault"). However, words-alone cases now tend to recognize that words must be interpreted in light of circumstances and may, in that light, count as an assault. See Muslow v. A.G. Edwards & Sons, Inc., 509 So.2d 1012, 1020 (La.App.1987); Johnson v. Bollinger, 86 N.C.App. 1, 356 S.E.2d 378 (1987); Restatement § 31.

6. Restatement § 27 (apprehension need not be well-founded).

7. Words that do not threaten a battery in one setting may do so in another. In Cullison v. Medley, 570 N.E.2d 27 (Ind. 1991), the defendants entered the plaintiff's home at night after he had gone to bed. They accused him of bothering a young woman in their family and berated him extensively. One of them kept slapping at a gun he wore on his thigh, but did not draw it. The court held that these facts would support a claim for assault. Similarly, "I'll get you," spoken by a defendant who wears a pistol in violation of law may be an assault even though he does not draw the pistol. Johnson v. Bollinger, 86 N.C.App. 1, 356 S.E.2d 378 (1987). The Restatement modifies the traditional statement by adding that threatening words may suffice if accompanied by action or circumstances that put the plaintiff in reasonable apprehension of imminent battery. Restatement § 31.

8. Dickens v. Puryear, 302 N.C. 437, 276 S.E.2d 325 (1981); cf. Johnson v. Brooks, 567 So.2d 34 (Fla.App.1990) (numerous threatening telephone calls not "acts," at most they are statements of intention to act).

9. Vietnamese Fishermen's Ass'n v. Knights of the Ku Klux Klan, 518 F.Supp. 993 (S.D.Tex.1981); State Rubbish Collectors Assn. v. Siliznoff, 38 Cal.2d 330, 240 P.2d 282 (1952).

10. Espinoza v. Thomas, 189 Mich.App. 110, 472 N.W.2d 16 (1991).

11. Holcombe v. Whitaker, 294 Ala. 430, 318 So.2d 289 (1975); Restatement § 30.

carry you off myself'' may be a threat of battery that the defendant is entitled to make in the protection of his property.[12]

§ 35. Assault, Crime, and Other Torts

Tort and crime. Assault may be a crime as well as a tort, but criminal law definitions of assault sometimes emphasize the intent to injure and the risk of escalating violence rather than the victim's apprehension of a battery,[1] so criminal assault cases are not necessarily sound authority in the tort setting. For example, under some criminal statutes, the defendant may be criminally responsible for an attempt to batter the victim.[2] The logic of this kind of provision is that the victim's awareness or lack of awareness is unimportant, since one may attempt to commit a battery the victim does not see or anticipate, as where the victim is hit from behind. Tort law, on the other hand, emphasizes and demands the plaintiff's awareness of the threat.

Assault and emotional distress. The law of assault represents a narrow segment in the spectrum of emotional harms. Because of its narrow definition, it is not a very important segment in itself. Lawyers may thus find it more relevant to consider the broader topic of emotional distress in Chapter 20. As that chapter shows, claims that may fail as assault claims may succeed under the rubric of some other tort that also protects interests in emotional security. For instance, some forms of sexual harassment may fall short of a battery or an assault but may be actionable as an intentional infliction of emotional distress,[3] or an invasion of privacy,[4] or as a violation of constitutional[5] or statutory rights.[6] Similarly, stalking, the harassment of victims by following, calling, and otherwise pursuing them,[7] may be addressed in criminal[8] or civil statutes.[9]

12. Restatement § 30, illus. 1.

§ 35

1. See Wayne LaFave and Austin Scott, Jr., Criminal Law 7.16 (1986) (discussing two types of assault statutes, those that make attempted battery an assault and those that make intentional scaring of the victim an assault).

2. E.g., Cal. Penal Code § 240 ("An assault is an unlawful attempt, coupled with a present ability, to commit a violent injury on the person of another").

3. E.g., Ford v. Revlon, Inc., 153 Ariz. 38, 734 P.2d 580 (1987). See § 305.

4. Phillips v. Smalley Maintenance Services, Inc., 435 So.2d 705 (Ala.1983) (sexual demands in employment treated as privacy suit). See § 426.

5. Assault-like behavior might sometimes count as excessive force prohibited by the Fourth or Eighth Amendments and made actionable by civil rights statutes. See Northington v. Jackson, 973 F.2d 1518 (10th Cir.1992). See §§ 45 & 48 below.

6. 42 U.S.C.A. § 2000e.

7. See Silvija Strikis, Stopping Stalking, 81 Geo. L. J. 2771 (1993). Stalkers may begin by seeking attention and end by repeated threats and ultimately by killing their victims. As many as 200,000 roam the streets. Stalkers make their victims' lives miserable and fearful. Probably no legal remedy, civil or criminal, will protect the victims without incarcerating the stalkers on a long-term or permanent basis. Since that is improbable, self-help may represent the victim's only hope of survival and a life without constant fear.

8. E.g., Ariz. Rev. Stat. § 13–2921 ("harassment").

9. E.g., Cal. Civ. Code § 1708.7. The California statute creates a statutory tort called stalking based on a pattern of conduct the "intent of which was to follow, alarm, or harass the plaintiff," with result-

Topic E. False Imprisonment

§ 36. Simple False Imprisonment

Elements of the tort. Courts protect personal freedom of movement by imposing liability for false imprisonment. False imprisonment in its simple form[1] is established by proof that the defendant intentionally confined[2] or instigated[3] the confinement of the plaintiff. Confinement implies that the plaintiff is constrained against her will.[4] A third element, according to the Restatement and some authority, is that the plaintiff must have been aware of the confinement at the time.[5]

"False arrest." False arrest is a term that describes the setting for false imprisonment when it is committed by an officer or by one who claims the power to make an arrest. Although false arrest is not essentially different from false imprisonment,[6] detention by an officer or one acting under color of law may also amount to a civil rights violation.[7]

Burden of proof. When intent, confinement, and awareness are established, the plaintiff is entitled to recover unless the defendant can establish an affirmative defense. Many false imprisonment cases actually

ing reasonable fear by the plaintiff for herself or an immediate family member. In addition, the defendant must either make a credible threat or violate a restraining order.

§ 36

1. As to false imprisonment secondary to some other tort, see § 40.

2. Restatement § 35. Confinement, detention, restraint are all terms used; they appear to refer to the same underlying idea.

3. Deadman v. Valley Nat. Bank of Arizona, 154 Ariz. 452, 743 P.2d 961 (Ct. App. 1987); Desai v. SSM Health Care, 865 S.W.2d 833 (Mo.App.1993); Restatement § 45A. This rule explains why a physician who testifies that he examined the plaintiff and found her mentally ill when in fact he never examined her at all may be held for the plaintiff's false imprisonment when she is later confined as a mentally ill person. See Crouch v. Cameron, 414 S.W.2d 408, 30 A.L.R.3d 520 (Ky. 1967). The rule is presumably the basis for imposing liability upon one who makes a false report of crime to police in the expectation that police will arrest the plaintiff. Washington v. Farlice, 1 Cal.App.4th 766, 2 Cal.Rptr.2d 607 (1991) (defendant reported her car stolen, knowing it was rightfully in possession of plaintiff's family; plaintiff was subjected to a humiliating arrest for which defendant was liable). When the defendant instigates an inappropriate *warrant* for prosecution, however, the action must be for malicious prosecution. See Montgomery Ward v. Wilson, 339 Md. 701, 664 A.2d 916 (1995) . Nor does a mere report of facts to the police qualify as instigation of the arrest. See Lusk v. Ira Watson Company, 185 W.Va. 680, 408 S.E.2d 630 (1991).

4. A plaintiff who voluntarily accepts apparent confinement is not confined if she can leave at any time. See Pounders v. Trinity Court Nursing Home, 265 Ark. 1, 576 S.W.2d 934, 4 A.L.R.4th 442 (1979). In other cases the plaintiff consents in advance to a confinement from which she cannot escape, in which case the confinement is real but the consent is a defense until it is properly revoked. See Day v. Providence Hospital, 622 So.2d 1273 (Ala.1993) (consent to stay overnight in locked psychiatric ward).

5. Douthit v. Jones, 619 F.2d 527 (5th Cir.1980); Parvi v. City of Kingston, 41 N.Y.2d 553, 362 N.E.2d 960, 394 N.Y.S.2d 161 (1977); Restatement §§ 35, 42; but cf. Scofield v. Critical Air Medicine, Inc., 45 Cal.App.4th 990, 52 Cal.Rptr.2d 915 (1996) (seemingly, liability without actual knowledge or actual harm). Consciousness of confinement is required only for the purely dignitary tort; the plaintiff can recover for actual harm without consciousness of confinement.

6. See, e.g., Asgari v. City of Los Angeles, 15 Cal.4th 744, 937 P.2d 273, 63 Cal. Rptr.2d 842 (1997).

7. §§ 44–48.

turn on affirmative defenses such as the privilege to detain a person legally committed to a mental institution or the privilege to detain a person for investigation, but the burden is on the defendant to prove these defenses and they are considered in a separate chapter.[8]

Motive and duration. Bad motive or hostility to the plaintiff is not required to establish false imprisonment; an intent to confine plus actual confinement is sufficient.[9] Nor need the plaintiff show confinement for a substantial length of time. Unless the defendant is privileged, a confinement for "any appreciable time, however short" is actionable.[10] However, the role of privilege is quite significant in false imprisonment cases, and where the defendant claims a privilege to detain the plaintiff, both his motive in detaining and the duration of the detention may become important in determining whether the defendant exceeded his privilege.[11]

Confinement. Confinement means that the plaintiff is not permitted to go beyond boundaries fixed by the defendant. The plaintiff whose road is obstructed is not confined and neither is the plaintiff who is excluded from a place of public accommodation, although in both instances the plaintiff may have some other kind of tort claim.[12] On the other hand, the boundaries of the plaintiff's confinement may be much less precise than four walls. The plaintiff who is detained on the street by a gang may be confined even if the gang does not specify the exact limits of her free movement. One is not confined at all if there is a reasonable means of egress.[13]

Examples of false imprisonment. False imprisonment is effected in many ways and in diverse social settings, but not surprisingly it most frequently involves a relatively powerful defendant. A storekeeper detains a customer or employee suspected of theft, sometimes by physical restraint and sometimes by threat;[14] a hospital, nursing home, or substance abuse center holds a patient against her will;[15] a driver refuses to

8. §§ 82–87.

9. Fair Oaks Hospital v. Pocrass, 266 N.J.Super. 140, 628 A.2d 829 (1993); cf. Smith v. Holeman, 212 Ga.App. 158, 441 S.E.2d 487 (1994) (malice is not required).

10. West v. King's Dept. Store, Inc., 321 N.C. 698, 365 S.E.2d 621 (1988); Bennett v. Ohio Dept. of Rehab. and Correction, 60 Ohio St.3d 107, 573 N.E.2d 633 (1991); Moody v. McElroy, 513 A.2d 5 (R.I.1986).

11. Cf. Taylor v. Super Discount Market, Inc., 212 Ga.App. 155, 441 S.E.2d 433 (1994) (implicitly a privilege case; store clerk briefly retained the plaintiff's $20 bill to investigate whether it was counterfeit, no false imprisonment).

12. Obstruction of a public road may be a public nuisance for which a seriously affected individual may have a private right of action. See § 467. Refusal to admit the plaintiff to a place of public accommodation may violate civil rights laws and at least permit an injunction. See 42 U.S.C.A. § 2000a–5(a).

13. Restatement Torts § 36, cmt. a; Krochalis v. Insurance Company of North America, 629 F.Supp. 1360 (E.D.Pa.1985). To be reasonable, the means of egress must be (a) readily knowable and (b) reasonably safe and appropriate. See Noguchi v. Nakamura, 2 Haw.App. 655, 638 P.2d 1383 (1982) (egress from moving car not reasonable).

14. See § 84.

15. Collins v. Straight, Inc., 748 F.2d 916 (4th Cir.1984) (drug treatment center, intimidation in what reads like the brainwashing pattern); Geddes v. Daughters of Charity of St. Vincent De Paul, Inc., 348 F.2d 144 (5th Cir.1965) (private mental hospital without commitment); Stowers v. Ardmore Acres Hospital, 19 Mich.App. 115, 172 N.W.2d 497 (1969) (mental health examination under court order, but if re-

stop his car so a passenger can get out;[16] a police officer lacking a warrant and lacking probable cause nevertheless detains or jails an individual.[17] In all these cases the main question in the first place is whether the plaintiff was in fact confined against her will and in the second whether the defendant was privileged to detain her.

§ 37. Methods of Confinement

Methods of confinement—physical restraint of person or property. The most obvious kind of confinement is that imposed by a physical barrier or physical force. For example, the defendant may lock the plaintiff in a room,[1] or physically restrain the plaintiff from moving.[2] Similarly, the plaintiff might be confined by blocking her automobile[3] or taking its keys when use of the vehicle furnished the only reasonable means of egress[4] or by detaining her property so that she herself is effectively confined if she is to protect or retrieve it.[5]

Submission to legal authority. Short of such physical restraints, an officer may effectuate a confinement merely by asserting authority to do so. If the plaintiff submits to a law enforcement officer's assertion of authority to detain her, she has been confined, and unless the officer enjoys a privilege or an immunity, he is liable for false arrest.[6] But there

straint was greater than authorized by court it was unlawful; verdict for plaintiff reinstated and affirmed); Big Town Nursing Home, Inc. v. Newman, 461 S.W.2d 195 (Tex.Civ.App.1970) (mentally healthy plaintiff forcibly brought back when he walked out of nursing home, locked in ward with mentally disabled patients, strapped to chair, all without justification in fact or any legal proceedings whatever); see generally Annotation, False Imprisonment in Connection with Confinement in Nursing Home or Hospital, 4 A.L.R.4th 449 (1981); see also, Annotation, Liability for False Imprisonment Predicated upon Institution of, or Conduct in Connection with, Insanity Proceedings, 30 A.L.R.3d 523 (1970); cf. Candy H. v. Redemption Ranch, Inc., 563 F.Supp. 505 (M.D.Ala.1983) (unwed, pregnant young woman detained under severe rules of home to which she was admitted, facts claimed would show false imprisonment and violation of a civil rights statute, 42 U.S.C.A. § 1985(3)). See also § 37, below.

16. Noguchi v. Nakamura, 2 Haw.App. 655, 638 P.2d 1383 (1982) (injury trying to escape, potential liability); Sindle v. New York City Transit Authority, 33 N.Y.2d 293, 352 N.Y.S.2d 183, 307 N.E.2d 245 (1973) (similar); cf. Drabek v. Sabley, 31 Wis.2d 184, 142 N.W.2d 798, 20 A.L.R.3d 1435 (1966) (defendant told boy to get in car, then drove him to police station to complain about boy's conduct).

17. E.g., Gordon v. Villegas, 1994 WL 86373 (Conn.Super.1994).

§ 37

1. Geddes v. Daughters of Charity of St. Vincent De Paul, Inc., 348 F.2d 144 (5th Cir.1965) (plaintiff locked in private mental hospital without commitment, two locked doors and an implicit threat that plaintiff would be stopped if she tried to leave).

2. E.g., Stockett v. Tolin, 791 F.Supp. 1536 (S.D.Fla.1992) (among many misdeeds, employer pinned employee to chair for a few moments; false imprisonment and other torts were established); Big Town Nursing Home, Inc. v. Newman, 461 S.W.2d 195 (Tex.Civ.App.1970) (plaintiff forcibly brought back to nursing home, then locked up); Verstraelen v. Kellog, 60 Wash. 2d 115, 372 P.2d 543 (1962) (dragging plaintiff down the road and announcing, "you are not going anywhere").

3. Schanafelt v. Seaboard Finance Co., 108 Cal.App.2d 420, 239 P.2d 42 (1951).

4. Verstraelen v. Kellog, 60 Wash.2d 115, 372 P.2d 543 (1962) (holding keys to plaintiff's car, false imprisonment).

5. Burrow v. K–Mart Corp., 166 Ga.App. 284, 304 S.E.2d 460 (1983); Ashland Dry Goods Co. v. Wages, 302 Ky. 577, 195 S.W.2d 312 (1946); Clarke v. K Mart Corp., 197 Mich.App. 541, 495 N.W.2d 820 (1992).

6. Martin v. Houck, 141 N.C. 317, 54 S.E. 291 (1906); Restatement § 41 (if plaintiff believes authority is valid or is in doubt about its validity and submits to it); cf.

may be a factual question for the jury about whether the plaintiff submitted to authority or merely acquiesced in the detention to clear her name or to provide assistance.[7]

Threats and duress. A number of cases involve confinement effectuated by conduct that expresses or implies a threat that the plaintiff will be restrained or subjected to an offensive touching if she attempts to leave.[8] Intimidation in an isolated or coercive environment may effect a confinement in some instances.[9] Threats of actual bodily harm are not required but they are of course sufficient.[10] Threats of harm to the plaintiff's property or to another person may have the effect of restraining the plaintiff.[11] When a threat, express or implied, is the basis for claiming confinement, the plaintiff must show, as in assault cases, that there is a reason to believe the threat can be carried out.[12] And of course the harm threatened must be immediate, not some time in the future.[13]

Implicit threats effecting a confinement. Sometimes plaintiffs feel implicitly threatened when the defendant has made no overt threat at all. One such case occurs when a retailer's manager or security guards invite a customer or employee to a back room for a discussion of suspected theft. If the customer or employee goes along to clear matters up and not as the result of any express or implied threat, there has been no confinement against the customer's will and no false imprisonment.[14]

Campbell v. S.S. Kresge Co., 21 N.S.R. 2d 236, 74 D.L.R. 3d 717 (Nova Scotia 1976) (store security guard showed his police badge to shopper-suspect, shopper was not consenting but acceding to his requests out of fear). See also Rollin Perkins, The Law of Arrest, 25 Iowa L. Rev. 201, 203 (1940).

7. Covell v. McCarthy, 123 Vt. 472, 194 A.2d 394 (1963) (after using a siren and flashing lights to pull driver over, officer asked, "will you come with me to the station?"; the driver accompanied the officer; held, a factual question whether this was submission to authority and therefore a false arrest).

8. Schanafelt v. Seaboard Finance Co., 108 Cal.App.2d 420, 239 P.2d 42, 43 (1951) ("Words or conduct furnishing a reasonable apprehension on the part of the one restrained that he will not be allowed to depart is sufficient"); Burrow v. K-Mart Corp., 166 Ga.App. 284, 287 304 S.E.2d 460, 463 (1983) ("reasonable apprehension that force will be used if the plaintiff does not submit"); Jacques v. Childs Dining Hall Co., 244 Mass. 438, 138 N.E. 843, 26 A.L.R. 1329 (1923) ("any demonstration of physical power which to all appearances can be avoided only by submission operates as effectually to constitute an imprisonment if submitted to as if any amount of force had been exercised"); Dendekker v. F.W. Woolworth Co. Limited, [1975] 3 W.W.R. 429 (Alberta).

9. See Collins v. Straight, Inc., 748 F.2d 916 (4th Cir.1984) (drug treatment center, six and one-half hours of intimidation with door blocked, false imprisonment verdict upheld). See also the paragraph *Implicit threats effecting a confinement*, below.

10. Cassady v. Tackett, 938 F.2d 693 (6th Cir.1991) (civil rights claim against jailer whose threats allegedly forced the plaintiff to barricade herself in her office).

11. Restatement § 40A (threats to member of plaintiff's immediate family). The Restatement's "immediate family" rule seems unduly restrictive. If the plaintiff would be privileged to defend a third person against the action threatened, it seems logical to say that she could attempt to avoid the threatened action by sacrificing her own freedom of movement.

12. Herbst v. Wuennenberg, 83 Wis.2d 768, 266 N.W.2d 391 (1978).

13. Restatement § 40, cmt. b (1965); The Limited Stores, Inc. v. Wilson-Robinson, 317 Ark. 80, 876 S.W.2d 248 (1994).

14. E.g., Hardy v. LaBelle's Distributing Co., 203 Mont. 263, 661 P.2d 35 (1983); cf. Pounders v. Trinity Court Nursing Home, 265 Ark. 1, 576 S.W.2d 934, 4 A.L.R.4th 442 (1979) (although nursing home told resident that she could not leave and even had her shoes, she was not confined because she had consented to being there initially and could walk out [barefooted?] at any time).

If the customer wishes to leave but does not attempt to do so for fear that she will be restrained or otherwise harmed if she does, she must demonstrate at least an implicit threat to prevent her exit.

Evidentiary detail matters greatly in presenting this kind of claim. In one case[15] the plaintiff, an 18–year-old employee, was taken to an "office" that consisted of a windowless room with bare light bulbs. It had one door only and any exit required passage through two other rooms. The employee was confronted with several persons who insisted that she admit to a kind of theft and make immediate restitution in cash. Their voices, she said, were not soft. She made no effort to leave and testified that she believed she would not be permitted to do so. In this and similar cases[16] courts have held that the evidence sufficed to permit the jury to infer that the plaintiff was confined by implicit threats found in the circumstances.

A threat may be implied in the fact that the plaintiff is isolated and outnumbered,[17] confronted by figures of authority or power, or subjected to hostility and verbal abuse. Other evidence of a threat might include the relative ages, independence, education, and power of the parties. A ten-year-old might feel intimidated when a 28–year-old lawyer would not.[18] When such factors do not weigh in favor of the plaintiff, however, there is no confinement merely because the defendant asserts that the plaintiff must stay,[19] much less because the defendant requests the plaintiff's assistance.[20]

Undue influence: affecting the plaintiff's will. Conceivably, the concept of confinement could be expanded to permit liability not only when

15. Black v. Kroger Co., 527 S.W.2d 794 (Tex.Civ.App.1975).

16. DeAngelis v. Jamesway Dept. Store, 205 N.J.Super. 519, 501 A.2d 561 (1985) (17–year-old employee, shouting, verbal refusal to permit her to leave or talk to parents); Dupler v. Seubert, 69 Wis.2d 373, 230 N.W.2d 626 (1975) (one man stood at the door and another demanded the plaintiff sit down when she attempted to leave). In Johnson v. Randall's Food Markets, Inc., 869 S.W.2d 390 (Tex.App.1993), rev'd on other grounds, 891 S.W.2d 640 (1995), the court went so far as to say that "An unlawful detention may be accomplished by words alone if their effect is to restrain the plaintiff," but seemed to have in mind a verbal threat that "was such as would inspire in the threatened person a just fear of injury to his person, reputation, or property."

17. Compare Dupler v. Seubert, 69 Wis.2d 373, 230 N.W.2d 626 (1975) (plaintiff outnumbered, evidence of threats sufficient) with Herbst v. Wuennenberg, 83 Wis.2d 768, 266 N.W.2d 391 (1978) (three male plaintiffs claimed to have been confined by woman who stood in the doorway, evidence insufficient). See also Collins v. Straight, Inc., 748 F.2d 916 (4th Cir.1984) (drug treatment center, to induce the plaintiff to accept treatment/confinement used more than one staff member to intimidate the plaintiff for hours in an isolated, windowless room).

18. Drabek v. Sabley, 31 Wis.2d 184, 142 N.W.2d 798, 20 A.L.R.3d 1435 (1966).

19. E.g., Pounders v. Trinity Court Nursing Home, 265 Ark. 1, 576 S.W.2d 934, 4 A.L.R.4th 442 (1979); Covell v. McCarthy, 123 Vt. 472, 194 A.2d 394 (1963) (jury question whether the plaintiff had submitted to legal authority or had waited in the police station voluntarily while facts were checked); Herbst v. Wuennenberg, 83 Wis.2d 768, 266 N.W.2d 391 (1978).

20. The Limited Stores, Inc. v. Wilson–Robinson, 317 Ark. 80, 876 S.W.2d 248 (1994) (when the store's alarm went off as plaintiff left the store, employees asked the plaintiff if she would return to the store, and when she did, then established that she carried a calculator that might have set off the alarm; no false imprisonment).

the plaintiff is physically restrained or threatened but also when the defendant's conduct destroys the capacity of the plaintiff to exert her own will. For instance, a nursing home patient may lose her ability for independent action when she is removed from friends and social support and made dependent on the staff, so that she submits to their assertion of authority to confine her. It has been argued in such cases that the assertion of authority against the vulnerable patient should itself count as false imprisonment or at least that little more should be required.[21] When the defendant systematically uses techniques calculated to destroy the plaintiff's ability to act as an independent human being and then asserts that the plaintiff may not leave, the claim for false imprisonment becomes almost compelling.[22]

This kind of issue has arisen when a religious group isolates the plaintiff and subjects her to sleep deprivation and other techniques that critics call brainwashing.[23] Although it is plausible to argue that a false imprisonment claim lies when the defendant effectively confines a person by systematically destroying the plaintiff's individuality and personhood, religious groups cannot be held liable merely because their assertion of religious doctrine has led the plaintiff to accept confinement. In *Molko v. Holy Spirit Ass'n for the Unification of World Christianity*,[24] the plaintiff claimed to have been confined by the defendant's teaching that, if the plaintiff left the religious community, her family "would be damned in Hell forever." The Court refused to permit the claim of false imprisonment to go forward on this ground, since to do so would impose a penalty upon the religious group for asserting its religious belief. The court did not appear to pass on the validity of a false imprisonment claim based on manipulative techniques that are independent of the doctrine asserted by the defendant.[25]

21. Cathrael Kazin, "Nowhere to Go and Chose to Stay": Using the Tort of False Imprisonment to Redress Involuntary Confinement of the Elderly in Nursing Homes and Hospitals, 137 U. Pa. L. Rev. 903, 904 (1989), criticizing Pounders v. Trinity Court Nursing Home, 265 Ark. 1, 576 S.W.2d 934, 4 A.L.R.4th 442 (1979) (concluding, over dissents, that plaintiff "voluntarily" remained in nursing home).

22. Cf. Collins v. Straight, Inc., 748 F.2d 916 (4th Cir.1984) (drug treatment center, intimidation in what reads like the brainwashing pattern); Candy H. v. Redemption Ranch, Inc., 563 F.Supp. 505 (M.D.Ala. 1983) (unwed, pregnant young woman allegedly held incommunicado at "redemption" home, facts alleged would establish common law false imprisonment or civil rights tort).

23. Laura Brown, He Who Controls the Mind Controls the Body: False Imprisonment, Religious Cults, and the Destruction of Volitional Capacity, 25 Val. U. L. Rev. 407 (1991). As to the sometimes similar techniques in "deprogramming" alleged cult victims, see Taylor v. Gilmartin, 686 F.2d 1346 (10th Cir.1982). As to the possible privilege to de-program an alleged victim of mind-control, see § 104.

24. 46 Cal.3d 1092, 762 P.2d 46, 252 Cal.Rptr. 122 (1988).

25. *Molko* appears to imply that a physical restraint or threat would *suffice*, but it does not appear to say that such a restraint or threat is *required*. However, it has been read otherwise, to require physical force or threat. George v. ISKCON of California, 4 Cal.Rptr.2d 473, 494 (1992) (ordered not published); see Brown, supra n. 23. In *George*, supra, the court expanded protections for religious groups by saying that "Tort liability based on dietary restrictions, methods of worship, and communal living arrangements and schedules is just as surely inimical to the free exercise of religious liberty as that based on threats of divine retribution."

§ 38. Duty to Release from Confinement

The ordinary false imprisonment case is one in which the defendant has acted in some affirmative way to effect the plaintiff's confinement, directly or indirectly. If the plaintiff is confined, but not as a result of the defendant's act, does the defendant ever owe a duty to assist in the plaintiff's release?

Custodians. Jailers, at least, owe a duty to release a prisoner when her sentence is up,[1] and no doubt analogous rules apply to other custodians such as psychiatric hospitals to which a person may be committed for a limited period only.

Failure to provide opportunity for bond or hearing. Even if the plaintiff is properly arrested, officers may owe him the opportunity to make bond or to be taken before a magistrate without delay, either of which could lead to immediate release. In such a case, if the officer refuses to give the arrested person an opportunity to make bond or to take him before a magistrate without delay, the officer will be liable for a false imprisonment.[2] The liability in such a case is not based on the legal arrest but on the failure to present the plaintiff with legal opportunities for release.

Promise to release. A defendant who induces a person to accept confinement in reliance on a promise or implicit promise to end the confinement on demand may be obliged to take affirmative action to effect the release when it is demanded. In one well-known case[3] the defendant induced the plaintiff to board his yacht on the promise that he would release her at any time she desired. But while the yacht was anchored offshore, the defendant refused to provide a boat to shore demanded by the plaintiff. The court found a false imprisonment on the basis of the promise or implicit promise that a boat would be made available. In a similar vein, automobile drivers might be expected to make reasonable stops to permit passengers to alight.[4]

Defendant innocently causing imprisonment. Limited authority suggests that the defendant who innocently or under a privilege causes a confinement of the plaintiff has a duty to release the plaintiff or to inform him of an exit he could not otherwise locate once the privilege

§ 38

1. Douthit v. Jones, 619 F.2d 527 (5th Cir.1980); Bennett v. Ohio Dept. of Rehab. and Correction, 60 Ohio St.3d 107, 573 N.E.2d 633 (1991).

2. Valadez v. City of Des Moines, 324 N.W.2d 475 (Iowa 1982) (holding, however, that where magistrate was not available until morning the delay was not unreasonable; reviewing authorities on that issue pro and con); Jackson v. Thompson, 188 S.W.2d 853 (Mo.App.1945) (bond opportunity Denied); Annotation, Delay in Taking Before Magistrate or Denial of Opportunity to Give Bail as Supporting Action for False Imprisonment, 98 A.L.R.2d 966 (1964).

3. Whittaker v. Sandford, 110 Me. 77, 85 A. 399 (1912).

4. Cf. Drabek v. Sabley, 31 Wis.2d 184, 142 N.W.2d 798, 20 A.L.R.3d 1435 (1966) (10–year old child in car being driven to police station); Sindle v. New York City Transit Authority, 33 N.Y.2d 293, 352 N.Y.S.2d 183, 307 N.E.2d 245 (1973) (school bus driver driving boisterous passengers to police station, refusing to stop).

terminates and release becomes feasible.[5] The rule is congruent with the rule in negligence cases, where it is said that one who innocently causes harm must take reasonable steps to minimize that harm.[6] Under these conditions, if the defendant is aware of the plaintiff's confinement and intentionally refuses to aid the plaintiff's escape, then the false imprisonment tort seems established. On the other hand, if the defendant does not refuse aid for the purpose of imprisoning the plaintiff or in substantial certainty that such imprisonment will result, then the tort, if any, seems to be one of negligence.[7]

Relationship between parties. Perhaps some special relationships between plaintiff and defendant would warrant an extension of the affirmative duty to others,[8] but there seem to be few cases. In *Andrews v. Piedmont Air Lines*,[9] the plaintiff was a stroke victim using a wheelchair and evidently unable to move himself or the chair without assistance. An airline refused to honor his ticket because he could not reach the restroom unassisted but then left him alone at some distance from the immediate departure area. The court found no false imprisonment, but did not expressly address the question whether the airline owed an affirmative duty to provide assistance.

§ 39. False Imprisonment and Other Torts

Civil rights. The common law action for false imprisonment does not stand alone. Confinement imposed by state officials is often privileged, but when it is not, an improperly confined person may also have a federal civil rights claim.[1]

Malicious prosecution. When the confinement takes place as a result of legal process such as a warrant for arrest, the plaintiff will seldom have an actionable claim for false imprisonment, since the legal process ordinarily furnishes a privilege or defense. If the legal proceeding against the plaintiff was itself brought without probable cause and for bad motives, the plaintiff may have a claim for malicious prosecution rather than false imprisonment. The difference, aside from damages measures and potential immunities,[2] is that the malicious prosecution plaintiff must affirmatively prove that the defendant prosecuted without probable cause to do so and prosecuted in bad faith.[3] This is a heavy burden that is not ordinarily imposed upon the plaintiff who can assert a false imprisonment claim, since the plaintiff makes her case for false impris-

5. Talcott v. National Exhibition Co., 144 App.Div. 337, 128 N.Y.S. 1059 (1911).

6. § 316.

7. Cf. Restatement § 45 (refusal with intent required).

8. Restatement § 45, cmt. a (store's duty to customer who accidently locks himself in the washroom).

9. Andrews v. Piedmont Airlines, 297 S.C. 367, 377 S.E.2d 127 (App. 1989).

§ 39

1. See § 46 below.

2. Once a formal charge has been made and the plaintiff is confined by judicial order after arraignment, the false imprisonment is terminated and the claim for any remaining damages must ordinarily be one for malicious prosecution. See Asgari v. City of Los Angeles, 15 Cal.4th 744, 937 P.2d 273, 63 Cal.Rptr.2d 842 (1997).

3. See Chapter 30.

onment by showing only an intentional confinement, with justifications coming in only by way of affirmative defenses.

Emotional harm claims. False imprisonment is a direct interference with the person and thus a trespassory tort like the others in this chapter. But its effect is not merely to redress physical or pecuniary harms. In most instances, recovery for false imprisonment redresses a dignitary or intangible interest, a species of emotional distress or insult that one feels at the loss of freedom and the subjugation to the will of another. False imprisonment is thus as much part of the universe of emotional harm as it is part of the universe of potential violence associated with trespassory torts. As a practical matter, lawyers considering a false imprisonment suit may also consider asserting not only claims for malicious prosecution, civil rights, and invasion of privacy, but also claims for emotional harm, which are discussed in Chapter 20.

Topic F. Extended Liability and Damages

§ 40. Extended Liability or Transferred Intent

Extending liability beyond simple trespassory torts. Courts tend to hold an intentional wrongdoer responsible for an extensive range of consequences, including consequences he never intended, at least in the case of trespassory torts to the person. At least three levels of this extended liability can be demonstrated by examples:

(1) Offense intended with harm resulting or vice-versa. Defendant intends to touch the plaintiff in an offensive way, but he intends no harm. The touching actually causes harm to the plaintiff. The defendant is liable for the unintended harm as well as any intended offense.[1] For example, the defendant kisses the plaintiff against her will, but intending no physical harm. In fact, however, the plaintiff suffers an immediate allergic reaction to the defendant's touch. The defendant is liable for the harm as well as for the intended offense. The same principle works to impose liability if the defendant intends a harmful touching but succeeds only in imposing an offensive one.[2]

(2) Tortious conduct directed at A with resulting invasion of B's rights. Defendant hurls a stone, intending a harmful battery to A; the stone misses A but strikes B. Defendant is liable for the harm to B although he never intended to touch B at all.[3] The idea might also be applied if the defendant attempts to put A in apprehension of a battery but puts B in apprehension instead,[4] or if defendant intends to imprison

§ 40

1. Bettel v. Yim, 20 O.R.2d 617, 88 D.L.R.3d 543 (Ont.Co.Ct. 1978); Restatement § 16 (1965).

2. Restatement §§ 18 & 20.

3. Davis v. White, 18 B.R. 246 (Bkrtcy. Va.1982); Singer v. Marx, 144 Cal.App.2d 637, 301 P.2d 440 (1956); Talmage v. Smith, 101 Mich. 370, 59 N.W. 656 (1894); Carnes v. Thompson, 48 S.W.2d 903 (Mo. 1932).

4. Holloway v. Wachovia Bank & Trust Co., 109 N.C.App. 403, 428 S.E.2d 453 (1993), rev'd on other grounds, 339 N.C. 338, 452 S.E.2d 233 (1994).

A but by mistake or misadventure imprisons B instead.[5]

The rule of liability may not extend to indirect harms. Suppose the defendant fires a pistol at A, intending harm to A but none to B. No harm comes to B from the defendant's fire, but A responds in self-defense, firing at the defendant. A's fire, not the defendant's, causes harm to B. It is not clear that the defendant would be liable for battery by way of transferred intent, although he might be liable for negligence if foreseeable actual harm comes to B.[6]

(3) One tort intended with another tort resulting. Defendant fires a pistol intending to put A in apprehension of an immediate and unconsented-to bodily touching but intending no actual touching. Without defendant's fault, the bullet actually strikes A. Defendant is liable to A for battery although he never intended a battery at all.[7]

Combining the rules. The rules may be combined. For example, if defendant intends to commit a mere assault on A, but actual touching results to B, the defendant is liable to B for the battery.[8] It has thus been suggested that the doctrine could apply as between any two trespassory torts, including, perhaps, property torts as well as personal torts.[9] For example, acts intended to imprison the plaintiff might result in a battery or an assault. If the extended liability rule applied, the defendant would be liable for the battery or assault even though he only intended a false imprisonment.[10]

Expressing the principle. The Restatement recognizes these rules but fragments the principle of extended liability by building extended liability into the definition of each separate tort.[11] Traditional discussion, on the other hand, expresses the extended liability doctrine as a result of "transferred intent:" the defendant's intent to harm A is "transferred" to B, for example. Although often called a fiction, the transferred intent expression is merely a metaphor. If taken literally, it can lead to mechanical analysis and unjustified imposition of liability upon defendants who have been guilty of no wrong at all. It may be more accurate to state the rule as an extended liability rule by saying that the defendant, who acts in such a way that the intended injury would be

5. Du Lac v. Perma Trans Products, Inc., 103 Cal.App.3d 937, 163 Cal.Rptr. 335 (1980); Restatement § 43.

6. See, As to the Analogous Case of Felony Murder, Annotation, 56 A.L.R.3d 239 (1974).

7. Manning v. Grimsley, 643 F.2d 20 (1st Cir.1981) (heckled baseball pitcher may have thrown at hecklers protected behind the screen, intending to put them in apprehension of imminent bodily touching; the screen broke and the plaintiff was actually injured); Brown v. Martinez, 68 N.M. 271, 361 P.2d 152 (1961); Restatement § 20.

8. Alteiri v. Colasso, 168 Conn. 329, 362 A.2d 798 (1975) (boy threw a stone intended to scare but not hit A; the stone actually hit B, who was injured; liability).

9. William Prosser, Transferred Intent, 45 Tex. L. Rev. 650 (1967).

10. Cf. Sindle v. New York City Transit Authority, 33 N.Y.2d 293, 352 N.Y.S.2d 183, 307 N.E.2d 245 (1973) (bus driver refused to stop to permit rowdy passengers to depart; plaintiff was injured in trying to escape).

11. The Restatement defines each tort to include cases in which some other tort or harm was intended, and to include as well cases in which the tort was intended to another person. See §§ 13, 16, 18, 20 & 21.

actionable, is liable for all direct consequences even though they are not intended.

Non-tortious or privileged intent. The formulation just suggested makes it clear that the extended liability doctrine properly applies only when the defendant's act would have been a tort if carried out as intended. The defendant who fires a pistol in target practice, intending to hit his own target, has no tortious intent at all. If the bullet strikes the plaintiff instead of the target, then quite possibly the evidence will show that the defendant was negligent, but he has not committed a battery. In the same way, the defendant must not be held liable if his conduct was protected by a privilege and the plaintiff is injured without fault. For example, the defendant may act intentionally in justified self-defense; if his act of self-defense causes injury to a bystander, there is no reason to impose liability unless the defendant was negligent.[12]

Scope of the doctrine. Should the defendant be responsible for any unexpected harm resulting from any trespassory tort? Although it is appropriate to impose responsibility for intentional wrongs that go awry, the same grounds cannot make it appropriate to impose responsibility for purely technical wrongs. The defendant's entry upon another's land by mistake is potentially a tort even if the defendant has no intent to invade another's interests or to cause harm, but a general extension of liability for unintended harm does not seem justified. So the doctrine may well be limited to cases of conscious wrongdoing and to those in which harm that results directly from an intended intervention. Such a limitation would not exclude liability of a technical tortfeasor for negligence.

§ 41. Extended Liability: The Pros and Cons

The rules of extended liability may reflect criminal law doctrine carried over into tort law. Criminal liability for miscarried criminal activity may seem entirely appropriate, since from the state's point of view the defendant's act justifies punishment whether the harm is done

12. Morris v. Platt, 32 Conn. 75 (1864); Moore v. City of Detroit, 128 Mich.App. 491, 340 N.W.2d 640 (1983); William Prosser, Transferred Intent, 45 Tex. L. Rev. 650 (1967); Restatement § 75.

Prosser saw the privilege rule as a "limitation" on the transferred intent doctrine. See William Prosser, Torts 112 (4th ed. 1971). A fuller statement might be that the privilege rule reflects the inherent scope of the transferred intent doctrine; it is a rule of extended liability that applies when the defendant's acts are intentionally tortious and not otherwise.

In Brown v. Martinez, 68 N.M. 271, 361 P.2d 152 (1961), a farmer, hearing noises of boys stealing watermelons in one direction, fired a gun in the opposite direction to frighten the thieves. The shot actually hit the plaintiff. Applying transferred intent rules, the court imposed liability without considering whether the farmer might have been privileged to create an apprehension of a touching in defense of his property. In Talmage v. Smith, 101 Mich. 370, 59 N.W. 656 (1894), the facts were similar except that the defendant threw a stick at one boy he could see and injured another whom he could not. The court there approved an instruction that applied transferred intent rules to establish liability only if the defendant intended to hit one boy; if he intended to frighten only, he would not be liable. Presumably this reflects the court's idea that he would have been privileged to frighten, although not to hit.

to A or to B. Skeptics might argue, however, that the same justification does not apply when it comes to tort liability.

Consider the case in which the defendant intends a battery to A but causes a battery to B instead. Given that the defendant intended no touching of B, one possibility is that the defendant was nonetheless negligent toward B. If that is the case, the argument against extended liability says that the defendant should be liable to B under the rules for negligence, but not under the rules for battery, since he never intended to batter B. The difference between the two forms of tort liability can be enormous, so the argument is not merely a formal distinction. For example, the defendant might take bankruptcy to escape ultimate responsibility for his negligent torts, but may not be permitted to do so in the case of certain intentional torts.[1]

A second possibility in this situation is that the defendant was *not* negligent towards B; that is, B's presence was unknown and not foreseeable, so a stone hurled at A did not create any recognizable risk to B. In that case, the injury to B is pure accident, and one opposed to the extended liability principle would be compelled to say that B could not recover at all, since, as to him, the defendant intended no tort of any kind and was not negligent.

If these positions against extended liability are plausible, it is because of the broader idea that if tort liability is justly based on intent rather than on strict responsibility, then that liability should not be more extensive than the wrongful intent or the moral fault of the defendant.[2] It is not so clear, however, that the defendant who is held liable for harm to B when he intended only harm to A is being held liable for harms beyond the range of his fault. If his fault lies in his intent and his act rather than in identification of a particular victim, then liability for the intent and the act seems perfectly appropriate even if the particular victim was not the intended one.

Extended liability may be harder to justify in some other kinds of cases. One might think there really is a signal moral difference between a defendant's intention to put the plaintiff in apprehension of a battery and the defendant's intention to accomplish the battery itself. But even here, the argument against extended liability turns on how you conceive the basis for liability in the first place. If the real basis is intended interference with the plaintiff's autonomy with respect to her own body, then the defendant who batters when he means to assault is properly held liable because the core wrong is the same in either case, namely an infringement of the plaintiff's autonomy. The same can be said with respect to the harm-offense dichotomy.

§ 41

1. See Davis v. White, 18 B.R. 246 (Bkrtcy.Va.1982).

2. It is possible to think of liability in excess of moral fault as a species of strict or absolute liability. In Manning v. Grimsley, 643 F.2d 20 (1st Cir.1981), the court regarded the transferred intent rules as imposing absolute liability, although the court also thought that to be justified.

In addition, it can be said that an intentional aggressor should bear the risk that his aggression will lead to unintended injury or that the aggressor should be subjected to appropriate incentives to deter the aggression.[3]

§ 42. Damages for Trespassory Torts to the Person

Physical harm: pecuniary losses. Damages awards usually aim to compensate the plaintiff for the losses resulting from the tort. Rules for compensation of physical harms are the same whether the harm results from a trespassory tort or from ordinary negligence. The plaintiff is entitled, for example, to recover for wage loss and reasonable medical expenses, if any, resulting from a battery, assault, or false imprisonment.[1]

Physical harm: pain, distress, emotional harm. Victims who sustain physical harm are always entitled to recover not only for the consequent pecuniary losses but also for any pain and suffering resulting from that physical harm. In this context, pain and suffering includes mental or emotional suffering, so the plaintiff can also recover for any proven mental distress or emotional harm.[2] Victims are not limited to a recovery for some standard amount of suffering. If they suffer more than most people, they are nevertheless entitled to recover for the suffering they actually undergo; the defendant, it is said, takes his victims as he finds them, with any special vulnerability they may have.[3]

Dignitary harm without physical harm. When the trespassory tort causes no physical harm, the traditional tort rule is that the plaintiff can nevertheless recover substantial as distinct from nominal damages. The idea is loosely linked to the idea of mental distress, but no actual proof of mental distress is required. The invasion of the plaintiff's rights is regarded as a harm in itself and subject to an award of damages. If the plaintiff suffers emotional distress as a result of any of these torts, even without physical harm, she is entitled to recover for that emotional distress as a separate element of damages.

3. See Manning v. Grimsley, 643 F.2d 20 (1st Cir.1981) (strong social policy to induce obedience to criminal law by imposing liability); John Fleming, The Law of Torts 25 (8th ed. 1992). Cf. William Prosser, Transferred Intent, 45 Tex. L. Rev. 650 (1967) (as between innocent plaintiff and defendant guilty of moral wrong towards someone, it is better that defendant bear the loss).

§ 42

1. E.g., Caudle v. Betts, 512 So.2d 389 (La.1987) (nerve damage); Garratt v. Dailey, 46 Wash. 2d 197, 279 P.2d 1091 (1955) (broken bone). Chapter 25 covers damages generally.

2. Kennan v. Checker Taxi Co., Inc., 250 Ill.App.3d 155, 189 Ill.Dec. 891, 620 N.E.2d 1208 (1993) ("pain and suffering incurred by the plaintiff as a result of the blows inflicted, and for the humiliation, indignity, and vexation suffered by the plaintiff as a result of his assailant's conduct"); Rosenbloom v. Flygare, 501 N.W.2d 597 (Minn.1993); Laurie Marie M. v. Jeffrey T. M., 159 A.D.2d 52, 559 N.Y.S.2d 336 (1990) (sexual abuse of child by stepparent, plaintiff's emotional reactions resulting in "lessened capacity to participate fully as wife, mother, lover, or friend" to be considered in awarding damages), aff'd, 77 N.Y.2d 981, 575 N.E.2d 393, 571 N.Y.S.2d 907 (1991).

3. Stockett v. Tolin, 791 F.Supp. 1536 (S.D.Fla.1992).

Under these rules, the plaintiff who is falsely imprisoned may recover substantial damages even if she suffers neither physical harm nor loss of wages and even if she does not testify to any kind of distress.[4] The circumstances of the imprisonment and its duration will of course affect the amount of damages the trier will be willing to award.[5]

An offensive battery gets similar treatment, so that damages may be awarded without any separate proof of mental distress aside from a preference not to be touched by the defendant.[6] Even beneficial touchings such as medical procedures may warrant damages if they are batteries, although the benefit is no doubt to be considered in determining the appropriate amount of the award.[7] The case of assault is treated in the same way.[8]

Punitive damages. In addition to compensatory damages, most states permit the plaintiff to recover an additional sum as punitive damages when the defendant's conduct and state of mind are especially odious, usually where he acts with malice or oppression, or at least with recklessness. Intentional torts are often candidates for punitive damages where the defendant intends actual harm or serious offense.[9] Punitive damages may be awarded in quite substantial sums, but there are constitutional standards to be met and some states now impose limitations on the amount of punitive damages.[10]

§ 43. Infliction of Mental Distress[1]

Intentional infliction of emotional distress describes a separate but nontrespassory tort dealt with in Chapter 20. It also describes a possible

4. E.g., Phillips v. District of Columbia, 458 A.2d 722, 725 (D.C.App.1983).

5. West v. King's Dept. Store, Inc., 321 N.C. 698, 365 S.E.2d 621, 624 (1988) (duration of restraint).

6. Johnson v. Ramsey County, 424 N.W.2d 800 (Minn.App.1988) (unwanted kiss is actionable).

7. Mohr v. Williams, 95 Minn. 261, 104 N.W. 12 (1905), overruled on other grounds by Genzel v. Halvorson, 248 Minn. 527, 80 N.W.2d 854 (1957); McCandless v. State, 3 A.D.2d 600, 162 N.Y.S.2d 570 (1957), aff'd mem., 4 N.Y.2d 797, 173 N.Y.S.2d 30, 149 N.E.2d 530 (1958) (abortion that was less painful than labor and delivery would have been and that improved the plaintiff's mental health, nevertheless warranted $2,000 in compensatory damages).

8. The traditional case on the whole topic of such damages was an assault case, I de S et ux. v. W de S., Y.B. Lib. Ass. f 99, pl. 60 (1348).

9. E.g., Stockett v. Tolin, 791 F.Supp. 1536 (S.D.Fla.1992) (persistent sexual harassment including battery and other torts, $1 million against individual defendant for punitive damages); Kennan v. Checker Taxi Co., Inc., 250 Ill.App.3d 155, 189 Ill.Dec. 891, 620 N.E.2d 1208 (1993) (taxi driver battered unsighted passenger; $193,000 punitive award); Deborah S. v. Diorio, 153 Misc.2d 708, 583 N.Y.S.2d 872 (1992) (acquaintance rape); Rosenbloom v. Flygare, 501 N.W.2d 597 (Minn.1993) (officer defendant coupled battery with racial animus).

10. See § 383.

§ 43

1. See Calvert Magruder, Mental and Emotional Disturbance in the Law of Torts, 49 HARV. L. REV. 1033 (1936); Daniel Givelber, The Right to Minimum Social Decency and the Limits of Evenhandedness: Intentional Infliction of Emotional Distress by Outrageous Conduct, 82 COLUM. L. REV. 42 (1982); Paul Hayden, Religiously Motivated "Outrageous" Conduct: Intentional Infliction of Emotional Distress as a Weapon against "Other People's Faiths," 34 WM. & MARY L. REV. 579 (1993).

motive for some intentional trespassory torts. It is worth mention here mainly because certain comparisons and contrasts are useful.

The tort was recognized by the Restatement around the middle of the 20th century[2] and courts have widely accepted the Restatement's formulation of the tort. Under this formulation, the defendant's conduct must be (1) extreme and outrageous, (2) based on an intent to cause severe emotional harm or at least on a reckless disregard of such harm, and (3) in fact a cause of severe emotional harm. Special rules add a recovery for interference with dead bodies[3] and for gross insults by common carriers and utilities.[4]

To the three elements in the Restatement formulation, some courts are beginning to add a requirement that (4) the distress suffered must be of the kind people in general would suffer and not merely an idiosyncratic reaction.[5] On the other hand, there is no requirement of physical injury resulting from the distress, since the outrageousness of the defendant's conduct is a good guarantee that the emotional harm is real.[6]

Sexual harassment may count as intentional infliction of emotional distress although it involves no touching that would qualify as a battery.[7] Threats of future harm, if they are serious enough, may count as intentional infliction of emotional distress for which the plaintiff can recover, even though they would not threaten the immediate touching required to show an assault.[8] On the other hand, doctrines peculiar to trespassory torts have no application. The defendant is not liable under the extended liability or transferred intent rule for emotional distress,[9] nor is he subject to liability for damages without proof of harm.

Topic G. Civil Rights Torts

§ 44. Civil Rights Torts Based on Intentional Invasion of the Person

Scope. Civil rights violations are torts.[1] They have generated an important specialty,[2] in which the courts look to common law tort rules

2. Restatement § 46.

3. See Cates v. Taylor, 428 So.2d 637 (Ala.1983).

4. Restatement § 48 recognizes the traditional "special liability" of common carriers and public utilities for gross insults to patrons or intending patrons.

5. 49 Prospect Street Tenants Ass'n v. Sheva Gardens, Inc., 227 N.J.Super. 449, 547 A.2d 1134 (1988).

6. State Rubbish Collectors Ass'n v. Siliznoff, 38 Cal.2d 330, 240 P.2d 282 (1952).

7. Ford v. Revlon, Inc., 153 Ariz. 38, 734 P.2d 580 (1987).

8. State Rubbish Collectors Ass'n v. Siliznoff, 38 Cal.2d 330, 240 P.2d 282 (1952); Dickens v. Puryear, 302 N.C. 437, 276 S.E.2d 325 (1981).

9. If defendant beats or threatens A's mother, A may recover if she is present (at least if his presence is known to the defendant) because that fits the substantial certainty test of intent. But A cannot recover if she learns about the beating later. This is in effect a rejection of transferred intent, which historically applied only to trespassory torts. Restatement § 46 (2) & cmt. l.

§ 44

1. Imbler v. Pachtman, 424 U.S. 409, 417, 96 S.Ct. 984, 988, 47 L.Ed.2d 128 (1976).

2. Among the books see Chester Antieau, Federal Civil Rights Acts (2d ed. 1980, 2 vols. & Supp.); Chester Antieau & Milo Mecham, Tort Liability of Government Officers and Employees (1990); Martin

as models without necessarily accepting their limitations.[3] Some civil rights claims are quite similar to claims for common law trespassory torts to the person. This chapter focuses only on those.

Statutes generally. A number of federal statutes, as well as some state statutes, address various forms of discrimination[4] and other civil rights issues.[5] Statutes prohibit discrimination against persons with disability,[6] as well as discrimination in employment,[7] education,[8] and housing.[9] Perhaps the most important single federal statute is 42 U.S.C.A. § 1983.

Section 1983. Section 1983 authorizes tort claims for deprivation of federal rights[10] under color of state law.[11] The defendants are usually state or local officials or local governments, although the victim may also assert a claim against a private individual who uses state law to violate federal rights. (Against *federal* officials, the victim can claim directly under the constitution for violation of constitutional rights.)[12]

SCHWARTZ & JOHN KIRKLIN, SECTION 1983 LITIGATION: CLAIMS, DEFENSES, AND FEES (2d ed. 1991, 2 vols. & Supp.).

3. Common law torts provide a starting place for analysis and suggest appropriate substantive rules in some cases. See Heck v. Humphrey, 512 U.S. 477, 114 S.Ct. 2364, 129 L.Ed.2d 383 (1994).

4. Violation of anti-discrimination statutes does not ordinarily wreak a trespassory tort but causes economic, emotional, or dignitary harm instead. However, 42 U.S.C.A. 1985 addresses a number of instances of intimidation and hence can cover physical force cases if the requisite discrimination is found. The statute covers acts of private individuals even when they are not acting under color of state law. So a conspiracy to block the highway to African–American civil rights workers, followed by assault and battery, may state a claim under § 1985 against private conspirators. Griffin v. Breckenridge, 403 U.S. 88, 91 S.Ct. 1790, 29 L.Ed.2d 338 (1971). Not all violence or intimidation, however, is discrimination within the purview of the statute. See Bray v. Alexandria Women's Health Clinic, 506 U.S. 263, 113 S.Ct. 753, 122 L.Ed.2d 34 (1993) (anti-abortion intimidation construed not to be directed at women as a group).

5. Some civil rights claims are so denominated because they involve governmental wrongs against individuals, or at least abuse of governmental power under color of law. Other civil rights claims are so denominated because they involve impermissible discrimination against a person or group. Most direct physical harm cases (trespassory tort cases) involve abuse of governmental power. The Violence Against Women Act, 42 U.S.C.A. § 13981, created a claim for "a crime of violence committed because of gender or on the basis of gender, and due, at least in part, to an animus based on the victim's gender" even when there was no abuse of governmental power. At this writing, the Fourth Circuit has held the statute unconstitutional as exceeding the powers of Congress. Brzonkala v. Virginia Polytechnic Institute and State University, 169 F.3d 820 (4th Cir.1999).

6. See 42 U.S.C.A. § 12112.

7. Title VII claims, 42 U.S.C.A. § 2000e. See Meritor Savings Bank, FSB v. Vinson, 477 U.S. 57, 106 S.Ct. 2399, 91 L.Ed.2d 49 (1986).

8. 20 U. S. C. A. § 1681(a). See Gebser v. Lago Vista Independent School Dist., 524 U.S. 274, 118 S.Ct. 1989, 141 L.Ed.2d 277 (1998).

9. See 42 U.S.C.A. §§ 3601 & 42 U.S.C.A. § 1982.

10. Including some but not all federal statutory rights. See § 275.

11. A person acts under the color of state law when he exercises power "possessed by virtue of state law and made possible only because [of] the authority of state law.... " See West v. Atkins, 487 U.S. 42, 108 S.Ct. 2250, 101 L.Ed.2d 40 (1988). Private individuals ordinarily do not act under color of state law, but sometimes they do. See Adickes v. S. H. Kress & Co., 398 U.S. 144, 90 S.Ct. 1598, 26 L.Ed.2d 142 (1970).

12. Bivens v. Six Unknown Named Agents of Federal Bureau of Narcotics, 403 U.S. 388, 91 S.Ct. 1999, 29 L.Ed.2d 619 (1971).

Advantages for the plaintiff. For the plaintiff, the § 1983 suit has several potential advantages over common law theories like battery or false imprisonment. Although officers can sometimes claim the benefits of a federal immunity from suit in a § 1983 action,[13] the state-law immunities will not protect him as they might in a state-law tort claim.[14] In addition, civil rights suits almost always permit the prevailing plaintiff or her attorney to recover a reasonable attorney fee, which is definitely not available in the common law action.[15] The plaintiff also has a choice of forum; she may sue in either federal or state court, whichever she believes is strategically more advantageous.[16]

Trespassory torts compared. Many constitutional torts redressed under § 1983 would also qualify as a prima facie common law tort. Trespassory torts such as battery,[17] false imprisonment,[18] or assault[19] are examples. Possibly even an intentional infliction of severe distress under color of law will entail liability under § 1983.[20] Certainly some of the misconduct condemned as a civil rights violation is conduct that would constitute a property tort such as conversion[21] or trespass.[22] And of course some constitutional torts may be recognized even though they are not analogues to trespassory common law torts.[23] In all cases, however, the substantive basis for the claim must be found in the words of the federal law.

Major Constitutional bases. Section 1983 claims may arise out of statutory rights or any provision of the Constitution designed to protect

13. § 273 below.

14. E.g., Anderson v. Village of Forest Park, 238 Ill.App.3d 83, 179 Ill.Dec. 373, 606 N.E.2d 205 (1992) (state tort immunities cannot bar the § 1983 claim).

15. See 1 Dan B. Dobbs, Law of Remedies § 3.10 (2d ed. 1993).

16. See Howlett v. Rose, 496 U.S. 356, 110 S.Ct. 2430, 110 L.Ed.2d 332 (1990) (state court must entertain plaintiff's § 1983 action).

17. Webster v. City of Houston, 689 F.2d 1220 (5th Cir.1982), on hearing en banc, 739 F.2d 993 (1984) (police shot decedent as he came out of his van with his hands up, then planted a gun on him to justify their actions); Cottrell v. Kaysville City, Utah, 994 F.2d 730 (10th Cir.1993) (strip search, trial court erred in holding it reasonable as a matter of law under the facts of the case).

18. Harper v. McDonald, 679 F.2d 955 (D.C.Cir.1982) (detention without warrant or probable cause).

19. McDonald v. Haskins, 966 F.2d 292 (7th Cir.1992) (pointing gun at head of 9–year-old-child and threatening to pull the trigger where child presented no threat of any kind was excessive force and officer was not immune); cf. Herrera v. Valentine, 653 F.2d 1220 (8th Cir.1981) (deputy, taking pregnant plaintiff to jail, stopped the car and told her "I don't know whether to take you people out in the country and shoot you or take you to jail;" there was other misconduct as well).

20. See Smith v. Aldingers, 999 F.2d 109 (5th Cir.1993) (remanding for consideration of that issue).

21. Cf. United States v. Eight Thousand Eight Hundred and Fifty Dollars, 461 U.S. 555, 103 S.Ct. 2005, 76 L.Ed.2d 143 (1983) (customs officers may seize property without a prior hearing but under some circumstances must institute forfeiture proceedings thereafter).

22. See Monroe v. Pape, 365 U.S. 167, 81 S.Ct. 473, 5 L.Ed.2d 492 (1961) (police invaded plaintiffs' home without a warrant and committed other violations as well), overruled on other grounds by Monell v. Department of Social Svs. of the City of N.Y., 436 U.S. 658, 98 S.Ct. 2018, 56 L.Ed.2d 611 (1978).

23. The common law tort of malicious prosecution, which is not a trespassory tort, might have a civil rights counterpart. See Malley v. Briggs, 475 U.S. 335, 106 S.Ct. 1092, 89 L.Ed.2d 271 (1986).

the plaintiff against the harm inflicted. Most § 1983 suits, however, are generated from one of three constitutional provisions. These are (1) the 14th Amendment's guarantees of substantive and procedural due process of law and equal protection of the laws; (2) the Fourth Amendment's provision against unreasonable searches and seizures, and (3) the Eighth Amendment's provisions against cruel and unusual punishments.

§ 45. Fourteenth Amendment Claims

Provisions; substantive and procedural rights. The 14th Amendment provides that states may not deny "equal protection of the laws" to any person. It also provides that states must not "deprive any person of life, liberty, or property, without due process of law." Similar clauses in the 5th Amendment apply to the federal government.

The most obvious meaning of due process is related to fair procedure; a state must not have the sentence first and the trial afterward. The procedural rights do not involve direct physical harm cases and hence are not considered in this section. However, the due process clause may also create substantive rights, that is, it may protect against "serious, shocking, deprivation of life, liberty, or property" that is in some sense "wrong" regardless of legal procedures.[1]

Fourteenth Amendment applying Bill of Rights to the States. The first ten amendments (the Bill of Rights) constrain the power of the federal government, not the power of the states.[2] However, at least some of the provisions of the first ten amendments also limit state powers because they represent specific instances of the due process guaranteed by the Fourteenth Amendment, which definitely does apply to the states.[3] A claim against a state official for violating the Fourth Amendment's unreasonable search and seizure rules is therefore technically a claim that he violated the 14th Amendment, which in turn applies the Fourth Amendment rules to the states.

Preference for specific provisions. The test of substantive due process is whether the official conduct shocks the conscience of the court.[4] The Court has been reluctant to expand the idea of substantive due process because that idea provides few guides to decision.[5] Consequently, the Court has given clear indication that if the case is one that fits Fourth Amendment patterns, the Fourteenth Amendment rule would look to the

§ 45

1. See Planned Parenthood of Southeastern Pennsylvania v. Casey, 505 U.S. 833, 112 S.Ct. 2791, 120 L.Ed.2d 674 (1992) (reviewing some of the substantive due process history).

2. See RONALD ROTUNDA, JOHN NOVAK & NELSON YOUNG, TREATISE ON CONSTITUTIONAL LAW: SUBSTANCE AND PROCEDURE § 14.2(1986).

3. See, e.g., Duncan v. Louisiana, 391 U.S. 145, 147–148 88 S.Ct. 1444, 1446–1447, 20 L.Ed.2d 491 (1968) (reviewing instances of selective incorporation of the Bill of Rights provisions in the Fourteenth Amendment's due process clause).

4. Collins v. City of Harker Heights, Texas, 503 U.S. 115, 112 S.Ct. 1061, 117 L.Ed.2d 261 (1992); Williams v. Denver, 99 F.3d 1009 (10th Cir.1996). In some cases, as where the victim is in custody, willful indifference may count as shocking the conscience. See County of Sacramento v. Lewis, 523 U.S. 833, 118 S.Ct. 1708, 140 L.Ed.2d 1043 (1998).

5. See Collins v. City of Harker Heights, Texas, supra n.4.

more specific rule under the Fourth Amendment, which would therefore govern most excessive force claims.[6] The result is that the substantive due process claim seems to be displaced when the defendant has directly and intentionally applied excessive force because the Fourth Amendment's test of unreasonable force is used instead.

Fourteenth Amendment cases NOT based on specific provisions of the Bill of Rights. Does the 14th Amendment create any protections against direct physical harm not already furnished by a specific provision of the Bill of Rights? The answer seems to be a qualified yes, but the content of those substantive due process rights, apart from the rights imported from the Bill of Rights,[7] is uncertain. Some of the cases involve non-action rather than direct action against an individual. Others turn on questions of discrimination under the equal protection clause. Still others protect against such intangible interests as privacy rights rather than interests in physical security or liberty. The plaintiff might, for example, be able to show deliberate official indifference to the victim's equal protection when a city[8] fails to protect domestic violence victims,[9] or a denial of substantive due process rights when a city fails to give its officers proper training to prevent unnecessarily dangerous or violent activities.[10]

Roots in specific constitutional provisions. Even in some of these non-action cases some more specific constitutional provision is the root of the claim. Suppose a superior officer fails to take action to investigate, discipline, or control a subordinate against whom complaints of brutality

6. Graham v. Connor, 490 U.S. 386, 109 S.Ct. 1865, 104 L.Ed.2d 443 (1989); Albright v. Oliver, 510 U.S. 266, 114 S.Ct. 807, 127 L.Ed.2d 114 (1994). If the particular amendment does not "cover" the conduct, the case can still proceed for adjudication as a substantive due process claim. The difference between not covering the conduct and not proscribing it may be hard to discern in some cases, however. If the case proceeds under the substantive due process claim, the claim may fail under the "shock the conscience" test. See County of Sacramento v. Lewis, 523 U.S. 833, 118 S.Ct. 1708, 140 L.Ed.2d 1043 (1998).

7. The Bill of Rights provisions may furnish guides even if the Court concludes that they do not literally apply. In Ingraham v. Wright, 430 U.S. 651, 97 S.Ct. 1401, 51 L.Ed.2d 711 (1977) a child sued for what he claimed was excessive physical punishment at school. The Court viewed the case as a pure due process case rather than as a Fourth Amendment case because it thought the Fourth Amendment was directed at criminal investigations. Nevertheless, as the Court recognized, the ideas of freedom from restraint and bodily seizure, central in the Fourth Amendment, were part of the Fourteenth Amendment as well.

8. A city's liability for § 1983 violations must be based on a "policy" pursued by the city, not on random violence of the officer. See § 277.

9. Balistreri v. Pacifica Police Department, 901 F.2d 696 (9th Cir.1988) (although police owed no due process duty to protect battered wife, the plaintiff should have been permitted to amend her complaint to state, if she could; an equal protection claim based on an allegation that police refusal was based on gender and marital status).

10. Fagan v. City of Vineland, 22 F.3d 1283 (3d Cir.1994) (high speed chases); Bordanaro v. McLeod, 871 F.2d 1151 (1st Cir. 1989) (massive police rampage through a motel with clubs, bat, tire-irons, an axe, and revolvers, followed by a savage beating, policy of inadequate recruitment, training, and discipline by city as one ground of city's liability). See City of Canton, Ohio v. Harris, 489 U.S. 378, 109 S.Ct. 1197, 103 L.Ed.2d 412 (1989); but cf. Board of County Comn'rs of Bryan County v. Brown, 520 U.S. 397, 117 S.Ct. 1382, 137 L.Ed.2d 626 (1997) (sheriff's failure to read background check before hiring deputy did not reflect deliberate indifference).

have been lodged in the past and who in turn continues to use excessive force against individuals. The superior officer may be found liable for his non-action.[11] Or a city may be found liable for its failure to train officers to avoid excessive force or to discipline those who inflict it.[12] In such cases the substance of the victim's claim seems to be the Fourth Amendment's prohibition against unreasonable searches and seizures even if the vehicle for that claim is sometimes the more general due process clause.

Trespassory torts contrasted. Fourteenth Amendment cases based on non-action differ from traditional trespassory torts. Although the Court has said that an officer does not violate the 14th Amendment merely by being negligent,[13] non-action cases do share some characteristics of negligence cases. First, official failure to act usually creates only risks, not certainties of injury. For example, the city that fails to train officers may create a statistical likelihood that sooner or later officers will use excessive force or make unjustified seizures of individuals.[14] Or the prison which refuses to protect the plaintiff from unhealthy exposures may create a risk that eventuates in harm.[15] These are cases of risk, not intent, and even high risk does not meet the substantial certainty test of intent.[16] Nor does the city ordinarily have a purpose or desire to cause harm through its inadequate training or failure to discipline. Courts have not always permitted a finding of deliberate indifference in such cases,[17] but when they do, liability seems to be based upon a kind of recklessness, not upon the intent required in common law analogues.[18]

§ 46. Fourth Amendment Claims

The Fourth Amendment claim. The Fourth Amendment, which limits the powers of the states by way of the Fourteenth Amendment, provides that

11. E.g., Shaw v. Stroud, 13 F.3d 791 (4th Cir.1994).

12. E.g., Cox v. District of Columbia, 821 F.Supp. 1 (D.D.C. 1993).

13. Daniels v. Williams, 474 U.S. 327, 106 S.Ct. 662, 88 L.Ed.2d 662 (1986) (due process); Washington v. Davis, 426 U.S. 229, 96 S.Ct. 2040, 48 L.Ed.2d 597 (1976) (equal protection).

14. See Board of County Comn'rs of Bryan County v. Brown, 520 U.S. 397, 117 S.Ct. 1382, 137 L.Ed.2d 626 (1997).

15. Helling v. McKinney, 509 U.S. 25, 113 S.Ct. 2475, 125 L.Ed.2d 22 (1993) (Eighth Amendment claim could be based on potential future harm to health as well as on present harm).

16. However, if the defendant is actually present when another officer uses excessive force and the defendant does nothing about it, intent to harm in the substantial certainty sense could be found. See Czajkowski v. City of Chicago, Illinois, 810 F.Supp. 1428 (N.D.Ill.1992) (one officer allegedly stood by while his partner attacked the partner's divorcing wife; summary judgment denied to the nonacting officer).

17. See Board of County Comn'rs of Bryan County v. Brown, 520 U.S. 397, 117 S.Ct. 1382, 137 L.Ed.2d 626 (1997).

18. Some courts have said specifically that recklessness is enough. See Wood v. Ostrander, 879 F.2d 583, 587–88 (9th Cir. 1989) (reviewing cases and deliberate indifference formula). It might be better to recognize that some deliberate risk-taking, which is only "negligence" in common law terms, could nevertheless violate some constitutional rights. Although deliberate risk-taking is often only negligence, it is quite different from thoughtlessness or bad judgment.

> The right of the people to be secure in their persons, houses, papers, and effects, against unreasonable searches and seizures, shall not be violated, and no Warrants shall issue, but upon probable cause, supported by Oath or affirmation, and particularly describing the place to be searched, and the persons or things to be seized.

The Fourth Amendment's objective reasonableness standard. The Fourth Amendment limits the powers of officers in their treatment of free individuals.[1] The violation is objectively judged by a reasonableness standard. Neither the officer's malice nor his good faith is important if his objective conduct was reasonable, and neither is important if he lacks probable cause for the arrest or justification for an investigatory stop.[2] As this objective standard implies, specific intent to violate the plaintiff's constitutional rights is not required.[3] However, the § 1983 defendant must intend to take physical control of a person or thing.[4] The word "seizure" implies as much. And the defendant may still assert affirmative defenses or an "immunity" as to which the defendant must carry the burden of proof.[5]

Seizure (1): unjustified arrest or search. Seizure can take many forms. It includes, for example, an unjustified entry into[6] or physical seizure of[7] a home analogous to trespass, as well as at least two distinct classes of interference with the person. First, an officer seizes a person in violation of the Fourth Amendment when the officer restricts a person's liberty.[8] The unconstitutionality of this kind of seizure does not depend upon excessive force or intent to harm, only an intent to detain in a way that is not objectively justified.

Short of a full scale arrest, officers may constitutionally stop a person for questions, so long as the person knows she is free to leave.[9] In other words, the officer may talk to the plaintiff as long as she consents. In addition, the officer may make a limited investigatory stop, even

§ 46

1. As to rights of prisoners, see § 48. Some Fourth Amendment rights may carry over to protect those in custody. Needless strip searches, for example, might be forbidden by the Fourth Amendment.

2. Graham v. Connor, 490 U.S. 386, 109 S.Ct. 1865, 104 L.Ed.2d 443 (1989).

3. Caballero v. City of Concord, 956 F.2d 204 (9th Cir.1992).

4. Brower v. County of Inyo, 489 U.S. 593, 596, 109 S.Ct. 1378, 1381, 103 L.Ed.2d 628 (1989).

5. See § 276. In practice, the *prima facie* case for Fourth Amendment violation and the immunity are closely related and must be considered together.

6. E.g., Monroe v. Pape, 365 U.S. 167, 81 S.Ct. 473, 5 L.Ed.2d 492 (1961), overruled on other grounds by Monell v. Dept. of Social Svcs. of the City of N.Y., 436 U.S. 658, 98 S.Ct. 2018, 56 L.Ed.2d 611 (1978). A warrant is normally required to justify a search and even when the officer has probable cause, there must be a special excuse to justify proceeding without one.

7. Soldal v. Cook County, Illinois, 506 U.S. 56, 113 S.Ct. 538, 121 L.Ed.2d 450 (1992) (illegal eviction accomplished by disconnection and hauling of the plaintiff's house gave new meaning to the term mobile home and counted as a seizure, actionable under the Fourth Amendment's standards if unreasonable).

8. "It must be recognized that whenever a police officer accosts an individual and restrains his freedom to walk away, he has 'seized' that person." Terry v. Ohio, 392 U.S. 1, 16, 88 S.Ct. 1868, 1877, 20 L.Ed.2d 889, 903 (1968).

9. E.g., Florida v. Bostick, 501 U.S. 429, 111 S.Ct. 2382, 115 L.Ed.2d 389 (1991).

without the consent of the person, but in that case the officer must entertain a reasonable suspicion.[10] He is subject to liability for an unconstitutional seizure if the suspicion is not reasonable or if his conduct exceeds that suspicion.[11] Even reasonable suspicion is not enough to justify a full arrest, as distinct from an investigatory stop. For an arrest, the officer must either have a warrant[12] or probable cause to believe that the person being arrested committed a crime.[13]

Seizure (2): excessive force or unjustified search. A second class of unconstitutional "seizure" occurs when an officer, intending to take control of a person applies excessive or "unreasonable" force in doing so. An officer commits an unconstitutional seizure actionable under § 1983 if he shoots down an unarmed and non-violent suspect,[14] sets up a road block calculated to cause death,[15] or beats a non-threatening citizen with a riot baton.[16] Under the objective reasonableness test, the amount of force that is permissible will depend heavily upon the circumstances, including, for example, the threat posed by the suspect and the seriousness of her supposed crimes.[17] Analogously, excessive force by a public school teacher in punishing a child will be actionable, although perhaps on slightly different theories.[18] It is thus often impossible to determine as a matter of legal rules whether the force used was unconstitutionally excessive. Instead, the question will be one for the jury.[19]

§ 47. The Fourth Amendment and Common Law Torts

Comparing false imprisonment. The first class of unconstitutional seizure—based on detention unjustified by warrant or probable cause—closely resembles the common law false arrest or false imprisonment. The intent to seize is comparable to the purposeful intent to detain at

10. Terry v. Ohio, 392 U.S. 1, 88 S.Ct. 1868, 20 L.Ed.2d 889 (1968).

11. Morgan v. Woessner, 997 F.2d 1244 (9th Cir.1993).

12. See § 83.

13. Ripson v. Alles, 21 F.3d 805 (8th Cir.1994) (probable cause required); Oliveira v. Mayer, 23 F.3d 642 (2d Cir.1994) (distinguishing "stop" cases which can be justified on reasonable suspicion from "arrest" cases that require probable cause); Leydens v. City of Des Moines, 484 N.W.2d 594 (Iowa 1992) (probable cause plus exigent circumstances required).

14. Tennessee v. Garner, 471 U.S. 1, 105 S.Ct. 1694, 85 L.Ed.2d 1 (1985); cf. Chew v. Gates, 27 F.3d 1432 (9th Cir.1994) (policy to release police dog trained to bite against all concealed suspects regardless of their danger).

15. Brower v. County of Inyo, 489 U.S. 593, 109 S.Ct. 1378, 103 L.Ed.2d 628 (1989).

16. Cf. Baker v. Chaplin, 497 N.W.2d 314 (Minn.App.1993) (demonstrator who was offering no threat allegedly struck with deadly force, although it did not in fact cause death, a clear violation of the Fourth Amendment).

17. Graham v. Connor, 490 U.S. 386, 109 S.Ct. 1865, 104 L.Ed.2d 443 (1989); Dixon v. Richer, 922 F.2d 1456 (10th Cir. 1991).

18. See Ingraham v. Wright, 430 U.S. 651, 97 S.Ct. 1401, 51 L.Ed.2d 711 (1977) (viewing the claim as one under the Fourteenth Amendment, not even indirectly under the Fourth Amendment, and applying the common law privilege to discipline children but recognizing potential liability for excessive force).

19. See Chew v. Gates, 27 F.3d 1432 (9th Cir.1994) (police dog released to find hiding suspect was trained to bite repeatedly until he got a grip, then to hold on; policy to release such dogs against all suspects whether they were resistant or not, whether they were armed or violent or not; excessive force was a jury question).

common law. The wrongful detention itself, without other harm, seems to suffice to make the plaintiff's case, barring a privilege to detain. The issue of probable cause is also an issue that arises in the common law false imprisonment case. In the case of a common law warrantless arrest, however, the officer's probable cause is an affirmative defense,[1] while in the Fourth Amendment claim it looks as if the plaintiff has the burden to show an absence of probable cause in the first place.[2]

Comparing battery and assault. This second class of unconstitutional search or seizure—based on excessive force in making a seizure otherwise justified—resembles the common law battery or occasionally the common law assault. The intent to seize is quite comparable to the intent to touch in a battery case, although it may be that seizure implies more than a fleeting touch. If the force is excessive or unreasonable under the circumstances, there is no reason to think that physical harm is required, although of course such harm is commonly the result. For instance, a strip search that is not justified as reasonable under the circumstances[3] is a violation of the Fourth Amendment.[4]

The requirement of excessive or unreasonable force is not matched by any element of the common law battery but is precisely matched by the affirmative defense that can be asserted by an arresting officer at common law: he is privileged to make an otherwise justified arrest by the use of reasonable force. The difference, if there is any, lies in the fact that the reasonableness of the force is usually considered in determining the prima facie case for violation of the Fourth Amendment, but is considered as an affirmative defense in the common law battery case.[5]

Transferred intent or extended liability. It also seems that the extended liability or transferred intent rules applied in common law trespassory torts has at least some scope in the Fourth Amendment

§ 47

1. E.g., Miller v. City of Jacksonville, 603 So.2d 1310 (Fla.App.1992); Budgar v. State, 98 Misc.2d 588, 414 N.Y.S.2d 463 (Ct.Cl. 1979). But in malicious prosecution, the burden is upon the plaintiff to show want of probable cause. See Rotte v. City of Jacksonville, 509 So.2d 1252 (1987).

2. See § 87.

3. Reasonableness depends both upon the grounds for the search and its extent. Strip searches of traffic offenders or those who failed to register their dogs but who pose no threat of any kind seem obviously unreasonable, and courts have been ready to protect against such searches. E.g., Watt v. City of Richardson, 849 F.2d 195 (5th Cir.1988). In contrast, strip searches of prisoners who have been in contact with outsiders and who may thus present security problems are readily permissible, at least where the search is conducted visually but not by body probes. Bell v. Wolfish, 441 U.S. 520, 99 S.Ct. 1861, 60 L.Ed.2d 447 (1979). In between, strip searches with manipulation of body parts may not be called for in the case of prison visitors upon whom no particular suspicion has fallen. Blackburn v. Snow, 771 F.2d 556 (1st Cir.1985) (blanket rule for searching all visitors in this way violated Fourth Amendment, $177,000 in damages plus almost as much more in prejudgment interest approved).

4. Bilbrey v. Brown, 738 F.2d 1462 (9th Cir.1984); Hill v. Bogans, 735 F.2d 391 (10th Cir.1984); Franz v. Lytle, 997 F.2d 784 (10th Cir.1993).

5. In federal civil rights cases, the officer may assert "immunity" to suit, apparently with the burden of establishing the facts that show immunity. See § 87. Unfortunately for clarity of analysis and jury instructions, the immunity claim may raise issues similar to those in the prima facie case. Cf. Wyatt v. Cole, 504 U.S. 158, 112 S.Ct. 1827, 118 L.Ed.2d 504 (1992) (Rehnquist, C.J. dissenting).

§ 1983 tort. Thus the Court has said that even if the officer detains a person who is not the intended one, a seizure occurs.[6] Similarly, an intended seizure includes unintended consequences. If the officer intends to shoot the plaintiff in the leg but misses and shoots in the heart instead, there is still a seizure. "[I]t is enough for a seizure that a person be stopped by the very instrumentality set in motion or put in place in order to achieve that result."[7]

Acts and omissions; duty to protect or release. In the absence of special relationships between the parties or some specific provision of law, the common law rules usually impose no duty to protect another from attack[8] or to release another from detention.[9] The Fourth Amendment seems to be generally in accord. It does not seem to suggest that officers owe any general affirmative duties to assist those under attack or to release persons imprisoned by others. Other provisions of the Constitution may demand affirmative action for protection of individuals in special circumstances,[10] but such cases are usually easier to think of as negligence cases.[11]

§ 48. Eighth Amendment Claims

Cruel and unusual punishment. The Eighth Amendment to the United States Constitution prohibits "cruel and unusual punishments."[1] It applies to treatment of a person who has actually been convicted of crime[2] and at least indirectly to pretrial detainees.[3] The Eighth Amend-

6. "A seizure occurs even when an unintended person or thing is the object of the detention or taking" provided "the detention or taking itself [is] willful." Brower v. County of Inyo, 489 U.S. 593, 596, 109 S.Ct. 1378, 1381, 103 L.Ed.2d 628 (1989).

7. Brower v. County of Inyo, 489 U.S. 593, 599, 109 S.Ct. 1378, 1382, 103 L.Ed.2d 628, 637 (1989).

8. See Chapter 21.

9. See § 38.

10. For example: (a) The due process clause in particular may require affirmative action for the protection of individuals held in custody. E.g., the jailer must use care to prevent an inmate's suicide. (b) The equal protection clause may require municipalities who protect some citizens by enforcing laws against violence to enforce those same laws for the protection of all citizens, such as victims of domestic violence; (c) Municipalities may be liable for failure to train officers sufficiently if, because of inadequate training, officers inflict constitutionally proscribed invasions; (d) The Eighth Amendment may require affirmative action to protect prisoners.

11. Courts are reluctant to find constitutional violations based on "mere negligence," but in common law terms many of the cases of liability would be described as negligence cases and certainly not as intentional trespassory harms. For example: a prison assigns a violent male sex offender to work in proximity to a female nurse although he was considered likely to commit a violent crime if alone with her. The prison neither provided protection nor warned the nurse. The prison officials were held subject to § 1983 liability. L.W. v. Grubbs, 974 F.2d 119 (9th Cir.1992). But in common law terms, unless an attack on the plaintiff was certain to occur, the prison was guilty of negligence or unreasonable risk-taking, not intended harm.

§ 48

1. "Excessive bail shall not be required, nor excessive fines imposed, nor cruel and unusual punishments inflicted."

2. Ingraham v. Wright, 430 U.S. 651, 97 S.Ct. 1401, 51 L.Ed.2d 711 (1977) (The Eighth Amendment does not apply to punishments inflicted in a public school; "it was designed to protect those convicted of crimes").

3. Johnson v. Summers, 411 Mass. 82, 86, 577 N.E.2d 301, 304 (1991) (pretrial detainee's 14th Amendment right to medical attention is "at least as great as the

ment is not limited to protections against formal judicial sentences;[4] it applies to any conduct of officers that in effect imposes "punishment."[5]

Types of cases. Examples of cruel and unusual punishment that count as constitutional torts include (1) cases of excessive force inflicted upon prisoners by prison guards, (2) cases of excessively harsh conditions of confinement, and (3) cases in which necessary medical attention is denied. In some instances prisoners or detainees may enjoy protections of the Fourth and 14th Amendment as well.[6]

Excessive force cases: the subjective component. The Eighth Amendment is implicated when an officer wantonly inflicts unnecessary pain upon a prisoner.[7] A guard who beats a prisoner who poses no threat may thus be liable to the prisoner under § 1983.[8] On the other hand, it is no violation of the Eighth Amendment at all if the guard uses force in good faith in the exercise of appropriate discipline or to control a prison disturbance. The prison officials' subjective state of mind is thus in issue.[9] The burden appears to be upon the plaintiff to prove in the first instance that the force was excessive and administered wantonly, in bad faith, sadistically, or maliciously.

The objective component. The officer's malicious or culpable state of mind may be enough by itself to show that the force used is excessive and violates the cruel and unusual punishment clause. Yet the Court has also said that not "every malevolent touch by a prison guard gives rise to

corresponding Eighth Amendment right of a prisoner").

4. Justice Thomas has argued that only judges and juries impose punishments and that acts of jailers do not come within the Eighth Amendment. E.g., Farmer v. Brennan, 511 U.S. 825, 114 S.Ct. 1970, 128 L.Ed.2d 811 (1994) (Thomas, J. concurring in the judgment).

5. Pelfrey v. Chambers, 43 F.3d 1034 (6th Cir.1995) holds that an unwarranted attack by a prison guard can be cruel and unusual punishment even though the attack is not a response to any act of the prisoner but is instead wholly unprovoked. There was a dissent, based on earlier decisions rendered under the Due Process clause.

6. Strip searches of prisoners are often analyzed under the Fourth Amendment. See Annotation, Fourth Amendment as Prohibiting Strip Searches of Arrestees or Pretrial Detainees, 78 A.L.R. Fed. 201 (1986). Sometimes treatment of prisoners is condemned on 14th Amendment substantive due process grounds. E.g., Rushing v. Wayne County, 436 Mich. 247, 462 N.W.2d 23 (1990) (prisoner stripped, held in public view). In Jordan v. Gardner, 986 F.2d 1521 (9th Cir.1993), the court held that "cross gender," clothed body searches, with grabbing, rubbing, and upward thrust motions violated the Eighth Amendment where there was no emergency or suspicion.

7. See Whitley v. Albers, 475 U.S. 312, 106 S.Ct. 1078, 89 L.Ed.2d 251 (1986); cf. White v. Napoleon, 897 F.2d 103 (3d Cir. 1990) (allegations that doctor deliberately inflicted pain by continuing treatments known to be ineffective were sufficient).

8. Hickey v. Reeder, 12 F.3d 754 (8th Cir.1993) (prisoner refused to clean his cell, stun gun applied); Burgin v. Iowa Dept. of Corrections, 923 F.2d 637 (8th Cir.1991) (excessive force in removing inmate's coat); Felix v. McCarthy, 939 F.2d 699 (9th Cir. 1991) (prison officer spat at prisoner's feet and ordered a cleanup, then handcuffed and threw him against a wall); Davis v. Locke, 936 F.2d 1208 (11th Cir.1991) (pulling shackled prisoner from dog cage on a truck and dropping him on his head). Cf. McRorie v. Shimoda, 795 F.2d 780 (9th Cir.1986) (allegation that guard attempted to "plunge the riot stick into McRorie's anus," states Eighth Amendment claim). Strip searches of prisoners, generally permissible, may violate the 14th Amendment's due process clause when unnecessarily carried out by guards of opposite sex. Canedy v. Boardman, 16 F.3d 183 (7th Cir.1994).

9. Wilson v. Seiter, 501 U.S. 294, 299, 111 S.Ct. 2321, 2324, 115 L.Ed.2d 271 (1991).

a federal cause of action." Instead, the physical force used must be objectively as well as subjectively wrong.[10] That is, it must be a violation of contemporary standards of decency.[11] This does not mean, however, that the plaintiff must show any particular amount of physical harm, much less a significant injury.[12]

Conditions of confinement and medical attention. The excessive force cases resemble common law battery cases.[13] Two other claims of cruel or unusual punishment are not so direct and forcible. First, prisoners may claim that some conditions of confinement are so harsh or dangerous that they count as punishment separate from the punishment authorized by a judge's sentence. For example, the prison might house a prisoner where she is in serious danger of substantial injury from attacks by others.[14] It might also fail to deal with a subordinate who demonstrates violent proclivities,[15] or to intervene in a reasonable way when an attack occurs.[16]

Second, prisoners may claim that they were injured or ill and that the prison officials failed to provide appropriate medical attention.[17]

10. In Wilson v. Seiter, 501 U.S. 294, 111 S.Ct. 2321, 115 L.Ed.2d 271 (1991), a conditions-of-confinement case, the Court said the objective component of the test was whether "the deprivation [was] sufficiently serious," while the subjective component was whether the officer acted "with a sufficiently culpable state of mind."

11. Hudson v. McMillian, 503 U.S. 1, 112 S.Ct. 995, 117 L.Ed.2d 156 (1992).

12. Hudson v. McMillian, supra. n.11. In Northington v. Jackson, 973 F.2d 1518 (10th Cir.1992), the allegation was that the defendant put a gun to the prisoner's head and threatened to kill him. This resembles a common law assault. The court thought that the complaint stated a claim under the Eighth Amendment even if no physical harm at all resulted. Although prisoners have no claim for verbal abuse, they have a right to be free from the terror of instant death.

13. Resemblance to false imprisonment cases is more subtle, since to begin with the defendants have the legal authority to impose imprisonment in Eighth Amendment cases. On analogy to common law cases in which the defendant exceeds his privilege to detain the plaintiff, however, it is possible to view the Eighth Amendment excessive force cases as a species of false imprisonment. The battery comparison seems more direct and to the point.

14. E.g., Farmer v. Brennan, 511 U.S. 825, 114 S.Ct. 1970, 128 L.Ed.2d 811 (1994) (rape); Butler v. Dowd, 979 F.2d 661 (8th Cir.1992) (rape, but nominal damage award was not unjust because some of the rapes might have occurred even if defendants had not violated constitution by deliberate indifference).

15. Supervising officers who know or have notice of a pattern of unconstitutional conduct by subordinates may be held liable for failing to respond to that pattern if the facts warrant an inference that the supervisor was willfully indifferent to the violations and if his failure to act can be considered a cause of the injury later inflicted. Slakan v. Porter, 737 F.2d 368 (4th Cir. 1984).

16. Buckner v. Hollins, 983 F.2d 119 (8th Cir.1993).

17. Estelle v. Gamble, 429 U.S. 97, 104–105, 97 S.Ct. 285, 291, 50 L.Ed.2d 251 (1976) ("[D]eliberate indifference to serious medical needs of prisoners constitutes the 'unnecessary and wanton infliction of pain' ... proscribed by the Eighth Amendment. This is true whether the indifference is manifested by prison doctors in their response to the prisoner's needs or by prison guards in intentionally denying or delaying access to medical care or intentionally interfering with the treatment once prescribed"); Patterson v. Pearson, 19 F.3d 439 (8th Cir.1994) (delay in treating known infection); Weeks v. Chaboudy, 984 F.2d 185 (6th Cir.1993) (paraplegic prisoner not admitted to area where he could use his wheelchair, left for some days where he was unable to clean himself; this involved a "medical need" even if his paraplegia was the result of a "conversion reaction" or mental condition); cf. City of Canton, Ohio v. Harris, 489 U.S. 378, 109 S.Ct. 1197, 103 L.Ed.2d 412 (1989) (city's liability for policy

Prisoners might even obtain relief (perhaps by injunction) from conditions that put them at risk for serious health injuries in the future.[18]

The subjective component in conditions and medical deprivation cases. In the conditions/medical attention cases, the Court has developed a special set of fault rules. One rule is subjective, based on the official's state of mind: the official is liable only if he is guilty of deliberate indifference[19] to the prisoner's danger or medical needs. In this context,[20] deliberate indifference is an explicitly subjective standard. The official is not guilty of deliberate indifference if he does not in fact know of the risk, nor if he makes reasonable provisions against a known risk, even if those provisions prove to be ineffective to prevent harm.[21] Although this deliberate indifference standard verbally differs from the "wanton infliction of pain" standard used in excessive force cases, it may represent merely an adaptation of that standard to situations in which the official or the governmental wrong lies in failing to act rather than in action—here, in failing to provide better conditions or protections against others rather than in active misconduct.

The objective components in conditions and medical deprivation cases. Two elements required for liability under the Eighth Amendment appear to be objective. First, in the danger/conditions of confinement cases, the risk must be substantial and the threatened injury serious. Essentially the same idea is re-worded for the deprivation cases: the deprivation must be serious and it must be a denial of "the minimal civilized measures of life's necessities." The Court appears to regard these formulations as addressing an objectively judged risk.[22] If this is correct, then the plaintiff apparently would be required to show both an objectively serious risk and a subjective indifference by the defendants.

The other objective component in the conditions cases is that once the substantial and serious risk is known by officials, their response to it is judged by a reasonableness standard. The official is not liable if he

of deliberate indifference to need for training officers to provide appropriate medical attention to prisoners).

18. Helling v. McKinney, 509 U.S. 25, 113 S.Ct. 2475, 125 L.Ed.2d 22 (1993) (prisoner's exposure to second hand tobacco smoke; Eighth Amendment claim can be based on willful indifference to possible future harm).

19. Wilson v. Seiter, 501 U.S. 294, 111 S.Ct. 2321, 115 L.Ed.2d 271 (1991) (prison conditions); Estelle v. Gamble, 429 U.S. 97, 97 S.Ct. 285, 50 L.Ed.2d 251 (1976) (medical attention in prison); Johnson v. Summers, 411 Mass. 82, 577 N.E.2d 301 (1991) (officers saw arrestee's fall down stairs but ignored repeated complaints of pain and requests for medical attention).

20. Deliberate indifference may be an objective standard in some situations. See City of Canton v. Harris, 489 U.S. 378, 109 S.Ct. 1197, 103 L.Ed.2d 412 (1989) (municipal liability for failure to train employees).

21. Farmer v. Brennan, 511 U.S. 825, 114 S.Ct. 1970, 128 L.Ed.2d 811 (1994); see also Wilson v. Seiter, 501 U.S. 294, 111 S.Ct. 2321, 115 L.Ed.2d 271 (1991).

22. See Wilson v. Seiter, 501 U.S. 294, 298, 111 S.Ct. 2321, 2324, 115 L.Ed.2d 271 (1991) ("Our holding in Rhodes turned on the objective component of an Eighth Amendment prison claim (was the deprivation sufficiently serious?).... "); Farmer v. Brennan, 511 U.S. 825, 834, 114 S.Ct. 1970, 1977, 128 L.Ed.2d 811 (1994) ("the inmate must show that he is incarcerated under conditions posing a substantial risk of serious harm"). If the seriousness element were subjective, the *Farmer* Court would presumably have said that the inmate was required to show the official *knew* of a substantial risk.

provides reasonable protection for a known substantial risk, even if it turns out that the protection provided was insufficient and the plaintiff was harmed.[23] At least in its verbal formulation, this is essentially like the rule used in ordinary common law negligence cases and it turns, not on good faith or subjective qualities of the actor, but on an objective reasonableness standard, taking all the circumstances into account.

Acts and omissions. When a public entity holds a person in custody, the entity and its officers owe such a person affirmative duties as described above. These are duties that are not owed to people in general. The principle that puts a custodian under a duty to take reasonable affirmative action is broader than the Eighth Amendment but is reflected in its condition-of-confinement and medical deprivation jurisprudence. In this respect, the Eighth Amendment offers certain benefits to persons convicted of crime that are not afforded to persons who must rely upon the Fourth Amendment or other bases for a claim. Only to a limited degree does a governmental entity owe affirmative acts of protection to persons who have not been convicted.[24]

23. Farmer v. Brennan, supra, n.21.

24. Thus, in Hilliard v. City and County of Denver, 930 F.2d 1516 (10th Cir.1991), an officer arrested the driver of a car for suspected intoxication, impounded the car, and left the plaintiff passenger stranded in a high crime area, where she was robbed, sexually assaulted, stripped naked and left bleeding. The court thought it not clearly established that the officer owed any duty to provide for the helpless passenger, since she had not been taken into custody. A number of cases are similar to *Hilliard.* Unless the plaintiff is in custody, only a little authority has ventured to require more from the officer. See Wood v. Ostrander, 879 F.2d 583 (9th Cir.1989).

CHAPTER 4

DIRECT AND INTENTIONAL INTERFERENCE WITH PROPERTY

TOPIC A. SCOPE

§ 49. Scope of the Chapter

This chapter covers intentional torts to tangible property interests resulting from the direct application of physical force. It thus continues the discussion of "trespassory" torts initiated in Chapter 3. Defenses are covered in the next chapter.

An actor can interfere with property interests in ways not covered in this chapter. The most common example is private nuisance, an interference with one's use and enjoyment of land by such means as pollution. Such forms of interference are discussed in the chapter on nuisance.

Property itself may be intangible and thus not covered in this chapter. Trademarks, copyrights, patents, trade secrets, bank accounts, even the expectation of obtaining the benefits of a contract might be considered as property in some sense or treated like property in some ways. The law protects interests in such property by recognizing a number of torts, but they are not the trespassory torts covered in this chapter. So if I convince someone to breach his contract to sell his basketball tickets to you and to sell them to me instead, I may have committed a tort such as interference with contract, but it is not a tort covered in this chapter, which focuses on intentional physical interferences, not on economic or purely emotional harm.

TOPIC B. TRESPASS TO LAND

§ 50. Trespass to Land—Elements and Terms

Elements. One who intentionally[1] enters or causes[2] direct and tangible[3] entry upon the land in possession[4] of another is a trespasser and liable for the tort of trespass, unless the entry is privileged or consented to. Physical harm to the land is not required.[5] The gist of the tort is

§ 50

1. Intent: see § 51.

2. E.g., Brown Jug, Inc. v. International Brotherhood of Teamsters, Chauffeurs, Warehousemen & Helpers of America, Local 959, 688 p.2d 932 (Alaska 1984) (union liable for causing individuals to trespass while picketing the plaintiff).

3. Direct and tangible: see § 53.

4. Possession: § 52.

5. See nn. 12 & 13 below; § 56.

intentional interference with rights of exclusive possession; no other harm is required. In modern law, the defendant is a trespasser not only if he intentionally enters or causes entry but also if he refuses to leave or remove his goods from the land when he is under an obligation to do so; hence a refusal to leave is equivalent to entry for this purpose.[6] One who has consent to be on the land may become a trespasser by exceeding the consent.[7] One who enters above[8] or below[9] the surface may also be a trespasser.

Regimes of rights and regimes of accommodation. Trespass is one of two major tort regimes for protecting an occupant's interest in property. The other regime is the law of nuisance. The law of nuisance deals with indirect or intangible interference with an owner's use and enjoyment of land, while trespass deals with direct and tangible interferences with the right to exclusive possession of land. To invoke the law of nuisance is to invoke a regime of accommodation between conflicting land uses. The noise from your radio bothers me, but it is not a trespass because it does not interfere with my possession and does not intrude in a tangible way. Courts seek accommodation in such cases by considering the reasonableness and amount. If the noise is too loud or too long it may be a nuisance, otherwise not. On the other hand, the law of trespass is a law of rights that does not depend upon reasonableness except with certain defenses. Trespass is not traditionally a matter of a lot or a little; it is a yes-or-no kind of tort. If the defendant has committed an act equivalent to an intentional entry and the plaintiff is a possessor, then, prima facie, a trespass has occurred. The line between nuisance and trespass has never been precisely marked, and some modern cases have blurred it further by calling the intrusion of harmful microscopic particles as trespasses rather than as nuisances and then by using some of the techniques of nuisance law to weigh the amount and reasonableness of the intrusion.[10]

Trespass terminology. The term trespass is confusing because legal professionals use it in at least three quite different ways. *First*, the term refers to the tort, made up of facts and a set of rules. One commits the tort of trespass only when in addition to an entry or its equivalent, one has an intent to enter. To use the term trespass in this sense is to say

6. Crawford v. French, 633 P.2d 524 (Colo.App.1981) (refusal to remove materials after permission had been revoked); Busada v. Ransom Motors, Inc., 31 Md.App. 704, 358 A.2d 258 (1976) (automobile bodies and parts left after notice to remove; the fact that the defendant deposited nothing after the notice is of no significance); Suggs v. Carroll, 76 N.C.App. 420, 333 S.E.2d 510 (1985) (defendants became trespassers when they refused to leave on request); Restatement § 158. In earlier common law, a forcible entry was required to establish an action under the writ of *Trespass* and remaining on the land was actionable only in *Case*R with its requirement of actual damages. The writ system was abolished in the American states beginning around 1850, so the distinction does not seem viable today.

7. Brown v. Dellinger, 355 S.W.2d 742 (Tex.Civ.App.1962); Restatement § 168. Consent might be restricted or conditional as to the area or as to activities on the land.

8. § 54.

9. § 55.

10. See § 463.

that the trespass set of rules applies to determine the case and not, say, the set of rules invoked if the claim is for negligence or nuisance.

Second, the term sometimes refers only to the *fact* of entry on or harm to land rather than to the legal effect of an entry or the set of rules that attends the trespass theory. One can enter land without committing the tort of trespass, but it is possible, using the term in this second and more limited sense, to say the defendant trespassed on the plaintiff's land even when the tort of trespass was not committed. This explains why, confusing and unfortunate as it is, courts occasionally refer to a negligent trespass, meaning only a negligent entry.[11] This treatise attempts to avoid this kind of usage.

Third, the term trespass can refer to the form of action by the same name, the old writ of *Trespass* used in the earlier common law. The modern tort claim for trespass originated in that writ. Under its rules the plaintiff is not required to prove actual harm to the land or to persons or things on it;[12] interference with possession is itself an injury for which the plaintiff can recover at least nominal damages.[13] These rules still hold.

Trespass: the writ or form of action. Forms of the writ of *Trespass* were used for all claims resulting from direct use of force.[14] The form of the *Trespass* writ or the declaration used for trespass to land was known as *Trespass Quare Clausem Fregit,*[15] because it demanded that the defendant answer to the court wherefore he broke the close, that is, whether or why he entered the plaintiff's land, which was fictionally treated as if it were enclosed.

Ejectment. An offshoot of the *Trespass* form of action was and is ejectment. Ejectment became a kind of trespass suit available to the owner of land who was out of possession. Ejectment today lies against a

11. For example, in this sentence the term trespass does not mean the tort of trespass to land but merely entry that is legally actionable on *any* ground: "A trespass may arise from an intrusion upon plaintiffs' land which is either intentional, negligent or the result of ultrahazardous conduct." Lunda v. Matthews, 46 Or.App. 701, 613 P.2d 63, 66 (1980). Although one may be liable for negligent harm to land, the set of rules that determine liability are quite different from those that determine trespass liability.

12. Restatement § 163.

13. Gross v. Capital Electric Line Builders, 253 Kan. 798, 861 P.2d 1326 (1993); Snow v. City of Columbia, 305 S.C. 544, 409 S.E.2d 797, 802 (Ct.App.1991) ("Thus, for example if one . . . walks upon it, or casts a twig upon it, or pours a bucket of water upon it, he commits a trespass by the very act of breaking the enclosure. . . . The mere entry entitles the party in possession at least to nominal damages").

14. The old common law writ called *Trespass* directly or indirectly generated six torts—battery, assault, and false imprisonment on the personal side, trespass to land, conversion, and trespass to chattels on the property side. All of those torts entailed a direct application of force; that is, they invaded or threatened to invade the plaintiff's physical security of person or property. See § 14.

15. Joseph Koffler & Alison Reppy, Common Law Pleading 155 (1969) (defendant "with force and arms broke and entered the close of the said [plaintiff] . . . and with his feet, in walking, trod down, trampled upon, consumed, and spoiled the grass and herbage . . . there growing, and being of great value, and other wrongs to the said [plaintiff] there did, to the damages of said [plaintiff] and against the peace of our lord the now king").

trespasser who was not merely a transient intruder but who had actually himself gone into possession of the land. Ejectment today gives the owner-plaintiff damages traditionally called *mesne profits*.[16] It goes beyond trespass mainly in that its end result is to put the plaintiff-owner in possession of the land.[17]

Trouble with trespass. The trespass to land rules are clear and work well in the simple paradigm on which they were built: defendant walks or rides onto the plaintiff's land. The trespass to land rules are also clear when the variations on that paradigm are insubstantial: the defendant drives his cattle onto the land. But trespass rules become too inflexible or difficult to apply when the entry is by smoke or pollution,[18] the migration of underground liquids, the growth of tree roots, or high overflights by aircraft.[19] In all those cases courts have often put aside the trespass theory and analyzed the case on different terms, usually as a potential nuisance.

Alternatives. Trespass to land is not the only set of tort rules affecting rights in land. For example, one might sue for negligent invasion of land if intent cannot be shown. Or the plaintiff might assert federal civil rights laws as a basis for a claim if the trespass is committed under color of state law.[20] When the facts fall far outside the simple trespass paradigm, the plaintiff might assert a claim based on nuisance theory instead. [21]

§ 51. Intent Required to Show Trespass

Intent required. The intent required to show a trespass to land is the intent[1] to enter[2] or to commit the equivalent of an entry. To cause an

16. The plaintiff was once required to sue separately in *Trespass* for the mesne profits. *Mesne profits* is a term, not a description; the plaintiff recovers damages for lost possession, which might, for example, include rental value.

17. See 1 Dan B. Dobbs, Law of Remedies §§ 4.2 (2), 5.8 (2), 5.10 (1) (2d ed. 1993).

18. § 53.

19. § 54.

20. See Monroe v. Pape, 365 U.S. 167, 81 S.Ct. 473, 5 L.Ed.2d 492 (1961) overruled on other grounds, Monell v. Dep't of Soc. Svcs. of City of N.Y., 436 U.S. 658, 98 S.Ct. 2018, 56 L.Ed.2d 611 (1978); cf. Soldal v. Cook County, Illinois, 506 U.S. 56, 113 S.Ct. 538, 121 L.Ed.2d 450 (1992) (plaintiff's mobile home disconnected in improper eviction). The Fourth Amendment's prohibition against unreasonable searches and seizures is one basis for this kind of claim. The Fourth Amendment is discussed in connection with a civil rights claim for personal torts in §§ 46 & 47. The prohibitions of the Fourteenth and Fifth Amendments against governmental takings of property without just compensation is another possible basis if the governmental entity uses the land. For cases involving attachments of land or chattels without a prior hearing and hence potentially involving a denial of due process, see § 67.

21. See Chapter 34.

§ 51

1. "Although neither deliberation, purpose, motive, nor malice are necessary elements of intent, the defendant must intend the act which in law constitutes the invasion of the plaintiff's right. Trespass is an intentional tort; and while the trespasser, to be liable, need not intend or expect the damaging consequence of his entry, he must intent the act which constitutes the unwarranted entry on another's land." Snow v. City of Columbia, 305 S.C. 544, 409 S.E.2d 797, 802 (S.C.App.1991). Occasionally a case appears to say that an entry is a trespass without specifying that intent is required. See Gliptis v. Fifteen Oil Co., 204 La. 896, 16 So.2d 471 (1943) (unintended slant of oil well that bottoms on the plaintiff's property beneath the surface is a sub-

entry upon the land by another[3] or by an object,[4] to remain upon the land after a privilege to be there has terminated,[5] to exceed the permitted use of the land,[6] and to refuse to remove goods or materials left there[7] are all equivalent to entry under modern law.

Intent to harm not required. Since intent to enter is sufficient, the plaintiff need not show an intent to cause harm or even to invade the plaintiff's possessory rights.[8] Thus one who intends to and does enter a parcel of land in the mistaken belief that it is his own land or that he has a right to be there is nonetheless a technical trespasser and liable for nominal damages and any actual harm done.[9] Even a child can be a

surface trespass whether the deviation is intended or not).

2. Taft v. Ball, Ball & Brosamer, Inc., 169 Ariz. 173, 818 P.2d 158 (Ariz.App. 1991); Restatement § 158. Early common law envisioned the plaintiff's land as an enclosed parcel and required an entry that "broke the close."

3. E.g., Greyhound Lines, Inc. v. Peter Pan Bus Lines, Inc., 845 F.Supp. 295 (E.D.Pa.1994) (intentional entry or causing a third person to enter is trespass); Houston Lighting and Power Co. v. Sue, 644 S.W.2d 835 (Tex.App.1982) (same); Prahl v. Brosamle, 98 Wis.2d 130, 295 N.W.2d 768 (1980) (officer's permission for another to enter private property was a trespass by the officer).

4. Armitage v. Decker, 218 Cal.App.3d 887, 267 Cal.Rptr. 399 (1990).

5. Metromedia Co. v. WCBM Maryland, Inc., 327 Md. 514, 610 A.2d 791 (1992) ("An occupancy rightful because permissive becomes tortious when a proper demand to vacate is ignored and it is then the occupants become trespassers and damages for their wrongful occupancy begin to accrue"); Suggs v. Carroll, 76 N.C.App. 420, 333 S.E.2d 510 (1985) (defendants refused to leave when told); Shlim v. CML, Inc., 112 Or.App. 597, 829 P.2d 1012 (1992).

If the privilege to be on the land was created by law rather than by consent of the owner, the defendant who abused or exceeded the privilege was at one time said to be a trespasser from the beginning, *ab initio*, with damages figured accordingly. See § 90.

6. For example, grazing cattle on public lands in excess of the permitted use is viewed as a "trespass." See John S. Harbison, Hohfeld and Herefords: the Concept of Property and the Law of the Range, 22 N.M. L. Rev. 459 (1992).

7. Crawford v. French, 633 P.2d 524 (Colo.App.1981) (refusal to remove materials after permission had been revoked); Hector v. Metro Centers, Inc., 498 N.W.2d 113 (N.D.1993) (plaintiff permitted defendant to pile dirt on the plaintiff's land, but later revoked the consent; defendant was a trespasser in failing to remove the dirt after consent was revoked). *Prior owners*: When pollution or chemical contamination is left behind by a prior owner, however, the new owner may be denied recovery on the ground that since she had contractual relations with the seller, she should protect herself by contract provisions. See Rosenblatt v. Exxon Company, 335 Md. 58, 642 A.2d 180 (1994). Newhall Land and Farming Co. v. Superior Court (Mobil Oil Corp.), 19 Cal.App.4th 334, 23 Cal.Rptr.2d 377 (1993) upheld a complaint against former owners of the land who had allegedly contaminated it, but the reasoning rested ultimately on the defendants' creation of a nuisance and on their intent to contaminate at the time of their occupancy, not on mere refusal to remove.

8. Baugh v. CBS, Inc., 828 F.Supp. 745, 756 (N.D.Cal.1993) (if there is intentional entry, good faith and mistaken belief are irrelevant); Kibbe v. Rohde, 285 Pa.Super. 379, 427 A.2d 1163 (1981) (trespasser's good faith belief that he had the right to repossess goods from the landowner does not "excuse" the trespass nor prevent punitive damages).

9. Miller v. National Broadcasting Co., 187 Cal.App.3d 1463, 232 Cal.Rptr. 668, 69 A.L.R.4th 1027 (1986) (trial court was in error in exonerating intrusive NBC camera crew because it had no malice; intent to enter is enough); Kopka v. Bell Telephone Co. of Pa., 371 Pa. 444, 91 A.2d 232 (1952); Restatement § 164. The Restatement recognizes other mistakes as well and takes the position that none of them affect the defendant's liability if he entered the land intentionally. Good faith of the trespasser usually operates (a) to exclude punitive damages, see § 56, and (b) in the mining context to prevent use of harsh measures of damages.

trespasser if he has the intent to enter another's land, or a part of the land not permitted to him.[10]

Harm without intent. The intent rule, however, does not subject the plaintiff to liability for unintended harm when he is rightfully on the land. The negative import of the intent rule is that the defendant is not liable for trespass when he enters by negligence, by accident, or without an act of his own.[11] For example, if he is carried onto the land against his will,[12] if his car goes out of control and runs onto the land,[13] or if his golf game is bad and he slices a ball into the plaintiff's house,[14] the defendant is no trespasser.[15] In such cases, the defendant will be liable only if he is shown to have been negligent in causing the harm. A contractor properly on the owner's land is not a trespasser on the land and his liability to the telephone company when he cuts its buried cable depends upon proof that he either did so intentionally or negligently.[16]

Scope of the intent requirement. The requirement of intent applies only to the trespass claim; the plaintiff is still free to prove, if she can, that the defendant who lacked intent to enter was nevertheless negligent in causing a harmful entry,[17] or else that he is subject to strict liability for abnormally dangerous activities.[18] However, if the plaintiff must rely upon a negligence or abnormal danger theory rather than upon a trespass theory, she must prove not only that the defendant was in fact negligent, but also that the plaintiff suffered actual damages, not merely an interference with technical possession.

Intent as purpose or certainty. The term intent in trespass to land cases means what it means in other torts.[19] The defendant intends an entry if it is his purpose to enter. He also intends an entry if he knows

See Reynolds v. Pardee & Curtin Lumber Co., 172 W.Va. 804, 310 S.E.2d 870 (1983).

10. Cleveland Park Club v. Perry, 165 A.2d 485 (D.C.Mun.Ct.App.1960); Farm Bureau Mutual Ins. Co. of Arkansas, Inc. v. Henley, 275 Ark. 122, 628 S.W.2d 301 (1982); Brown v. Dellinger, 355 S.W.2d 742 (Tex.Civ.App.1962) (7–8 year old boys liable for trespass which unintentionally caused $28,000 in harm to house and contents).

11. Phillips v. Sun Oil Co., 307 N.Y. 328, 121 N.E.2d 249 (1954).

12. Smith v. Stone, Style 65, 82 Eng. Rep. 533 (K.B. 1647).

13. Hawke v. Maus, 141 Ind.App. 126, 226 N.E.2d 713 (1967); Smith v. Pate, 246 N.C. 63, 97 S.E.2d 457 (1957); cf. Cereghino v. Boeing Company, 826 F.Supp. 1243 (D.Or.1993) (defendants who disposed of contaminants on their own land were not trespassers to nearby landowner when the contaminants migrated to the plaintiff's land, since they did not intend to cause entry upon that land).

14. Malouf v. Dallas Athletic Country Club, 837 S.W.2d 674 (Tex.App.1992).

15. He may intrude upon the land and since "trespass" can be used nontechnically to mean intrusion as a matter of fact, it is possible to say that one negligently trespasses. But such a one is not a trespasser in the legal sense that the trespass rules apply. The negligent intruder, for example, is liable only if he causes harm, while the trespasser is liable whether harm results or not. See Restatement § 165.

16. Two older decisions that may be to the contrary are extant in Massachusetts and Texas. See § 55.

17. E.g, Pennsylvania R. Co. v. City of Pittsburgh, 335 Pa. 449, 6 A.2d 907 (1939). Since the term trespass is sometimes used loosely to mean an entry upon land or a harm to it, courts occasionally speak of a negligent trespass, meaning only a negligent entry upon land that causes harm. The phrase is nonsensical when the term trespass is defined to require intent.

18. See the paragraph, "Strict Liability for trespass" below.

19. §§ 24–27.

that his actions make entry substantially or virtually certain to follow.[20] The defendant who releases his hounds for the fox hunt adjacent to the plaintiff's croplands may know to a virtual certainty that they will run on the plaintiff's land; if so, the defendant has the requisite intent and is liable as a trespasser.[21]

Strict liability for trespass. Since the intent required to show a trespass is only an intent to enter land, and since that intent might be wholly innocent, the rules may sometimes impose a limited kind of strict liability. But this appearance may be somewhat misleading.

One possible case of theoretical strict liability is that of the innocent trespasser who enters the land in the reasonable belief that he has a right to be there. But in today's world, suit is unlikely to be brought at all if the defendant is a casual trespasser rather than one who claims a right to be on the land. On the other hand, if the trespasser claims the land as his own, his liability may still be nominal and it may serve to establish the plaintiff's title or right to possession at a cost to the defendant essentially no different from the cost he would incur if a declaratory judgment or some other suit were brought to obtain a judicial determination of the parties' rights. If this is strict liability, not much is to be made of it.

A second possible case of theoretical strict liability occurs if the trespasser exploits the land or its resources in the innocent and reasonable belief that he is entitled to do so. But in that case the trespasser himself has made a gain from the trespass and liability for that enrichment derived from another's property is appropriate quite apart from tort law and regardless of his innocence.[22]

A third kind of case that might impose strict liability for trespass to land involves harms to land caused by the defendant's use of explosives or other high energy sources, as where the defendant's blasting with dynamite throws stones or debris onto the plaintiff's land. Strict liability

20. See Malouf v. Dallas Athletic Country Club, 837 S.W.2d 674, 676 (Tex.App. 1992) (trespass requires "an intent to commit an act which violates a property right, or would be practically certain to have that effect, although the actor may not know that the act he intends to commit is such a violation"); Cover v. Phillips Pipe Line Co., 454 S.W.2d 507 (Mo.1970).

21. Pegg v. Gray, 240 N.C. 548, 82 S.E.2d 757 (1954). Note that the defendant might be liable for negligence if he merely took a risk that the hounds would enter the plaintiff's lands and if actual harm were inflicted. Cf. Ream v. Keen, 314 Or. 370, 838 P.2d 1073 (1992) (defendant would be liable for trespass where he knew smoke from burning field would drift onto the plaintiff's property).

22. The unjust enrichment justification may be present even though the court itself uses a trespass analysis. In Maye v. Yappen, 23 Cal. 306 (1863), for example, the defendant was liable for unintentionally mining gold that was part of the plaintiff's claim; the reasoning was the reasoning of trespass, but the facts were the facts of unjust enrichment. Liability to make restitution for unjust enrichment is independent of liability in tort for wrongdoing. So long as the defendant's liability is limited to his enrichment resulting from the trespass, it cannot be said that liability is "strict." See generally 1 Dan B. Dobbs, Law of Remedies §§ 4.1 (1) & 5.4 (2d ed. 1993). Liability for the gains is no less justified if the trespasser is in fact at fault. Cf. Santa Clarita Water Co. v. Lyons, 161 Cal.App.3d 450, 207 Cal.Rptr. 698 (1984).

was imposed in such cases, sometimes on a trespass theory.[23] Strict liability is still imposed on the same facts, but the cases are no longer perceived as trespass to land cases. Instead, trespass is seen as an accidental or unimportant feature in the cases, which are viewed as turning on the defendant's abnormally dangerous activity.[24] Liability is strict whether the resulting harm is a trespass to land or an injury to the person.[25] The result is that trespass itself generates little or no strict liability.[26]

§ 52. Protected Interests: Possession and Physical Integrity

Interests protected. The common law recognized and protected major kinds of rights or interests in land from direct invasion by physical forces: (1) The right to exclusive possession of land; that is, the right to exclude others from the land,[1] somewhat analogous to the right of a person to prohibit touchings by others. (2) The right of physical integrity of the land itself; that is, the right to prevent others from doing physical harm to or taking any part of the land such as trees or minerals.[2]

A third major interest of land owners and occupiers did not entail either direct or tangible force. This was (3) The right to the use and enjoyment of the land; that is, the right to prevent those outside of the land from unreasonably interfering with its enjoyment, for example, by activities that made the land too smelly or uncomfortable for occupation.

Protecting possession. The right to sue for the tort of trespass was originally conceived as a means of protecting the exclusive possession of one on the land. For this reason, the owner of an easement, who has no possessory interest in the land but only a right to its use, has no claim for trespass interfering with possession.[3] On the other hand, anyone who had possession or the right to possession of land could sue whether that

23. E.g., Green v. General Petroleum Corp., 205 Cal. 328, 270 P. 952, 60 A.L.R. 475 (1928) (oil well blow-out depositing 4–7 inches of oil and debris on the plaintiff's house. Judgment was based on trespass theory affirmed with some language suggesting nuisance-type thinking); Mulchanock v. Whitehall Cement Mfg. Co., 253 Pa. 262, 98 A. 554 (1916) (blasting at a stone quarry a "direct trespass" by casting stones on the plaintiff's property). Similarly, according to the Restatement, operators of aircraft are strictly liable for ground damage from airplane crashes and the like. Restatement § 520A. This was rejected in recent years. See Crosby v. Cox Aircraft Co. of Washington, 109 Wash.2d 581, 746 P.2d 1198 (1987).

24. See § 348.

25. Even the older cases extend strict liability to personal injuries on a public highway when they resulted from blasting. Sullivan v. Dunham, 161 N.Y. 290, 55 N.E. 923 (1900).

26. The most significant possibility for strict liability based on trespass (as distinct from that based on grounds of abnormally dangerous activity) arises under the extended liability rule discussed in § 58.

§ 52

1. E.g., Allred v. Harris, 14 Cal.App.4th 1386, 1390, 18 Cal.Rptr.2d 530, 533 (1993) (abortion protest case; "right to exclude persons is a fundamental aspect of private property").

2. The main issue in many cases, including trespass cases, is the measure of damages for physical harm to land or severance of minerals or timber. E.g., Dethloff v. Zeigler Coal Co., 82 Ill.2d 393, 45 Ill.Dec. 175, 412 N.E.2d 526 (1980) (coal).

3. See P & A Construction, Inc. v. Hackensack Water Co., 115 N.J.Super. 550, 280 A.2d 497 (1971); Socony–Vacuum Oil Co. v. Bailey, 202 Misc. 364, 109 N.Y.S.2d 799 (Sup.Ct. 1952). The easement holder might

person was the owner in fee or not. For instance, a tenant in possession had a claim for a trespassory entry.[4] Even an adverse possessor of the land might have a claim against a mere trespasser.[5] The owner of vacant land is accounted the possessor and hence has standing to sue the trespasser.[6]

Protecting physical integrity of the land; the owner's reversionary interests. If the entry also causes harm to the land's physical integrity that reduces the value of the owner's interests as well as the possessor's, today's law will also allow the owner to recover for any actual damages he will ultimately suffer. For instance, if the trespasser enters a tenant's apartment, the tenant has an action for trespass; if the trespasser rips the door off, the landlord who must repair it has an action for the damages resulting whether the theory is one of trespass or of case.[7]

To say that the owner's claim is in case rather than trespass implies three things: (1) The owner, as distinct from the possessor, will have an action only if the trespass causes actual harm to the owner's interest. Mere interference with possession is not itself enough. (2) The owner would be required to prove fault with respect to the damages he claims. That might mean that the trespasser's intent to enter, if innocent, would not support the owner's claim for actual damages. That result is consistent with the argument that "transferred intent" should not apply in the absence of fault.[8] (3) The trespass statute of limitations is inappropriate so that some other, possibly shorter statute would apply.[9]

Wrongful possessor's suit against the owner. As will appear,[10] a landowner who is in possession of the land is privileged to use reasonable

have a claim for actual damages if the defendant is negligent and he might obtain injunctive relief if the defendant continues to interfere with the easement's use.

4. Indian Bayou Hunting Club, Inc. v. Taylor, 261 So.2d 669 (La.App.1972) (injunction in favor of tenant against trespasser); Neilan v. Braun, 354 N.W.2d 856 (Minn.App.1984) (tenant in possession could recover from landlord-owner for landlord's cattle trespass).

5. Spring Valley Estates, Inc. v. Cunningham, 181 Colo. 435, 438, 510 P.2d 336, 338 (1973) ("from the beginning of his possession period, an adverse possessor has an interest in a given piece of property enforceable against everyone *except* the owner or one claiming through the owner.... Once the 18–year period has passed, all remedies, including those for quiet title, ejectment and trespass may be utilized even against the record title holder"); Myrick v. Bishop, 8 N.C. 485, 486 (1821). Not every person on the land is a possessor; one who is there sporadically and without title is not, for example.

6. E.g., Waters v. Dennis Simmons Lumber Co., 154 N.C. 232, 70 S.E. 284 (1911).

7. AmSouth Bank, N.A. v. City of Mobile, 500 So.2d 1072 (Ala.1986) ("the landlord may sue for an injury to the reversion interest, even while a tenant is in possession"); Smith v. Cap Concrete, 133 Cal. App.3d 769, 184 Cal.Rptr. 308 (1982); Motchan v. STL Cablevision, Inc., 796 S.W.2d 896 (Mo.App.1990). If the tenant himself does damage to the landlord's reversion, the landlord's claim may be technically for *Waste*.

8. § 58.

9. In AmSouth Bank, N.A. v. City of Mobile, 500 So.2d 1072 (Ala.1986) the owner had leased the premises. The defendant's operations caused physical damage to the premises, and the landlord sued more than one year later. The trespass statute of limitations was six years, but the statute of limitations applicable to the action on the case was only one year. The landlord's claim was barred since it was not for injury to possession (it had none), only injury to its reversionary or ownership interest.

10. § 76.

force to defend the land against trespass by others. When another person has gone into possession of the land, however, the landowner's use of force to gain possession has long been proscribed by statute[11] in the belief that even reasonable force asserted by the owner will begat violence. It is thus theoretically possible for a wrongful possessor to recover from the true owner who attempts to recover the property by force. The scope of this rule depends primarily upon the owner's privilege, or lack of privilege to retake the property. That privilege is discussed along with other defenses in Chapter 5.

§ 53. Direct and Tangible Entry

Intrusion. Entry upon the land or the equivalent to entry upon land, is definitionally essential to the tort of trespass. Actions outside the land that do not cause intrusions upon it may sometimes warrant liability, as where the adjoining landowner's excavation of his own soil allows the plaintiff's soil to subside.[1] But they are not trespasses because no intrusion has taken place. Courts sometimes speak loosely in such cases, using the term trespass to refer to any case of harms to land rather than to cases that would be actionable only because intent and entry are shown.[2]

Tangible intrusion. Because the action for trespass was conceived as a means of protecting possession, a tangible entry upon the land was traditionally required. Anything less than a tangible entry, such as penetration of the land by smoke, noise, or light, might affect enjoyment, but it would not affect possession. If the defendant who caused air pollution was guilty of any tort at all, it was not the tort of trespass.[3]

Direct vs. indirect intrusion. Because the old common law writ of *Trespass* was used in trespass to land cases, the entry upon land originally had to be "direct."[4] The directness requirement, intended to mark the boundaries appropriate for the old writ of trespass that has long since been abolished, seems irrelevant today. The intent requirement in trespass cases is now well defined enough to exclude inappropriate liabilities without the addition of a directness test.[5] Indirect interfer-

11. Since 1381, with the state of 5 Richard II, c. 7.

§ 53

1. Removal of lateral or subjacent support subjects the defendant to strict liability as well as to liability for negligence. See Restatement §§ 817–821.

2. Nida v. American Rock Crusher Co., 253 Kan. 230, 855 P.2d 81 (1993). A similar problem arises when one pumps water from wells upon his own land, but in doing so draws off water for miles around, lowering the water table and depriving others of access to water that was previously under and part of their own land. Courts have also called this a trespass. Forbell v. City of New York, 164 N.Y. 522, 58 N.E. 644 (1900).

3. E.g., Williams v. Monsanto Co., 856 S.W.2d 338 (Mo.App.1993) ("For trespass to lie the pollution must be at a level so as to constitute an actual interference with the possession of the land, not merely interference with its use and enjoyment").

4. §§ 14, 111 & 112.

5. Older expressions of the intent requirement in trespass cases sometimes defined intent so broadly that an indirectness test was needed to narrow it. Thus the trespass "must intend the act which amounts to or produces the unlawful invasion, and the intrusion must at least be the immediate or inevitable consequence of what he willfully does.... " Phillips v. Sun Oil Co., 307 N.Y. 328, 121 N.E.2d 249

ence with possession today, at least if it causes actual harm, is assuredly actionable whether it is called trespass or not.[6]

In any event the direct-indirect dichotomy is too vague to work well with some forces. For instance, if the defendant's conduct on his own land causes diffuse surface waters to drain upon the plaintiff's land, or the defendant's obstruction causes unwanted matter to back up on to the plaintiff's land, the intrusion can plausibly be regarded either as direct[7] or indirect[8] and liability in trespass can be accepted or rejected accordingly.

Policy in requiring tangible entry. The rule requiring tangible entry reflects ancient history reinforced by contemporary policy. Pollution, noise, gases, unpleasant sights, and dangerous conditions such as stored explosives can all reduce one's enjoyment of land, but courts were unwilling to say that a landowner would have a claim for damages any time she heard a noise or smelled burning leaves. The policy view was that the law of trespass with its automatic responsibility for any purposeful or certain entry would produce too much liability. It provided no mechanism for limiting liability to serious or substantial invasions. If smoke drifting onto the plaintiff's land were held to be a trespass, even a little smoke would count.

The traditional nuisance alternative. With this in mind, courts traditionally considered "intangible" invasions as potential interference with a landowner's right of use and enjoyment rather than her right to possession. That is to say, courts traditionally invoked the law of nuisance rather than the law of trespass.[9] Under the law of nuisance, courts could reject liability for, say, smoke that blows across the plaintiff's land, if the smoke did not much interfere with the plaintiff's enjoyment and if it would be costly or difficult for the defendant to avoid it. Nuisance law aims more at reasonable accommodation of conflicting

(1954). The first clause (the intent clause) standing alone would impose liability for "intended acts" that cause a trespass, which could include, say, driving a car without intent to enter the land. The second or directness clause operates to narrow the definition so that it operates like the current definition of intent: the trespasser must intend to enter or affect the land.

6. E.g., a creditor levied on a debtor's property stored on the plaintiff's premises. Notice of the levy interfered with the plaintiff's ability to rent the premises. This was actionable. Shopfner v. Clark, 246 Ark. 70, 436 S.W.2d 475 (1969).

7. Dial v. City of O'Fallon, 81 Ill.2d 548, 44 Ill.Dec. 248, 411 N.E.2d 217 (1980) (defendant closed its sewer system because it was overloaded, with the predictable result that raw sewage backed up into Mrs. Dial's house; held trespass).

8. Looney v. Hindman, 649 S.W.2d 207 (Mo.1983) (surface waters "collected" and discharged into plaintiff's property; although trespass would be a suitable theory if the defendant had discharged sewage or silt, trespass theory could not be used here to impose liability if defendant's act were reasonable). Some indirect injuries might not be actionable on any theory. Cf. Letterman v. English Mica Co., 249 N.C. 769, 107 S.E.2d 753 (1959) (defendant's downstream dam backed waters up to flood plaintiff's upstream property, but only after T had dumped so much dirt into the river that the bed was raised in the dam's still water area; the dam was not a "direct" cause of waters entering the plaintiff's property).

9. Chapter 34.

uses rather than at protection of absolute rights under trespass doctrines.

Waters and liquids. Cases involving waters have also often been removed from the domain of trespass law. States differ in their formal rules about liability for surface waters cast upon the plaintiff's land, but, whether on a nuisance theory or not, the courts' tendency is to permit both parties maximum reasonable use so that an intrusion of waters is actionable when it is unreasonable or when independent grounds for strict liability exist, otherwise not.[10] If the defendant's dam breaks, causing downstream flooding, the defendant may be liable for trespass if he intentionally caused the waters to enter the plaintiff's property. Otherwise, his liability is for negligence or nuisance.[11]

Similarly, courts are likely to hold that the trespass theory invokes the wrong set of rules for riparian flooding. They instead incline toward nuisance or negligence theories to invoke rules requiring proof of unreasonable actions by the defendant or separate grounds for strict liability.[12]

Underground liquids that seep into the plaintiff's soil and cause harm represent still another category. Although courts sometimes speak of "trespass" in the underground pollution cases,[13] their actual approach

10. Pendergrast v. Aiken, 293 N.C. 201, 236 S.E.2d 787 (1977) ("Each possessor is legally privileged to make a reasonable use of his land, even though the flow of surface water is altered thereby and causes some harm to others, but liability is incurred when his harmful interference with the flow of surface waters is unreasonable and causes substantial damages;" nuisance rules are the appropriate set of rule for analysis). States use three different formal doctrines. (1) The common enemy rule treats unwanted surface waters as a common enemy, so that each landowner is free to dispose of them as best he can. (2) The civil law rule is largely the reverse; no landowner is free to alter natural drainage. These two rules are often modified in practice and at times tend to resemble (3) the reasonable use rule under which landowners are free to alter their own natural drainage to the plaintiff's detriment until that alteration causes unreasonable interference. See Roger Cunningham, William Stoebuck & Dale Whitman, The Law of Property § 7.6 (2d ed. 1993).

11. See Cooper v. Horn, 248 Va. 417, 448 S.E.2d 403 (1994) (upholding a trespass instruction where the defendant did not argue that intent was required, but mainly discussing negligence).

12. Ellis v. Alabama Power Co., 431 So.2d 1242 (Ala.1983) (dam operator discharging waters in accord with Corps of Engineers flood control plan; liability for release of water must be predicated upon negligence, not trespass); Kunz v. Utah Power & Light Co., 117 Idaho 901, 792 P.2d 926 (1990). In Saden v. Kirby, 635 So.2d 277 (La.App.1994), the court rejected a trespass approach to liability for flooding caused by a governmental entity. The entity in effect raised a levee to protect certain areas from flooding, but that act caused greater flooding of the plaintiffs' properties. The court invoked a provision of the Louisiana Code that has some affinities with common law nuisance theories and on the basis of the code provision, imposed strict liability.

13. E.g., Cassinos v. Union Oil Co. of California, 14 Cal.App.4th 1770, 18 Cal. Rptr.2d 574 (1993). Sometimes it does not matter whether the case is thought of as one of nuisance or trespass because the rules are the same for the issue before the court. See Wilson v. McLeod Oil Co., Inc., 327 N.C. 491, 398 S.E.2d 586, 11 A.L.R.5th 1019 (1990) (statute of limitations). Sometimes courts use the term trespass to refer, not to the set of rules that attend the trespass theory but to the mere fact of entry. In this sense, courts can speak of a negligent trespass, as in Fortier v. Flambeau Plastics Co., 164 Wis.2d 639, 476 N.W.2d 593 (Wis.App.1991); but as the Restatement points out, when negligence or strict liability is the basis for the liability, the intrusion alone is not enough and actual damages must be shown. See Restatement § 165, Cmt. b.

often more closely resembles the reasonableness approach of nuisance law in which the courts see maximum freedom for the legitimate interests of both landowners.[14] Nuisance or negligence rather than trespass is definitely the approach courts take when liquids percolate underground to enter the plaintiff's land beneath the surface.[15]

Changing views. What counts as an "intangible" entry or one that falls short of affecting possession is obviously a matter of degree. Even smoke or gases might carry microscopic particles to the plaintiff's land, and some such particles can do great harm. With this in mind, some contemporary cases reject the traditional view and treat any discernible entry of particles as a trespass, at least if it causes actual harm.[16] The main effect of this may be that the defendant cannot take advantage of the traditional nuisance-law rules that limit liability to cases of "unreasonable" intrusions and those that actually interfere with use and enjoyment of the land. A secondary effect may be that in some cases that these courts now call trespass cases, the plaintiff will be denied recovery for utterly trifling intrusions upon the land. Most cases continue to use a nuisance, not a trespass analysis for intangible or small-particle intrusions, and for convenience, this book considers all such claims together in connection with nuisance.

§ 54. Entries Above the Surface[1]

General rule. Possessory interests are not limited to the surface of the land. Possessory interests may include chattels, structures, and growth on the land. They also include the right to exclusive possession of reasonably usable airspace above the ground as well as space below the

14. The Restatement treats interference with the flow of surface waters as a nuisance issue, not a trespass issue. Restatement § 833. Interference with one's rights to *use* water of course raises an entirely different issue. See Restatement §§ 850–864. Water rights are now an important form of property law and subject to considerable regulation.

15. Pan American Petroleum Co. v. Byars, 228 Ala. 372, 153 So. 616 (1934) (underground leak of gasoline, trespass claim is inappropriate because the intrusion is indirect, not direct); United Fuel Gas Co. v. Sawyers, 259 S.W.2d 466, 38 A.L.R.2d 1261 (Ky. 1953) (pollution by subterraneous waters by oil, salt water or the like is actionable only upon showing of either nuisance or negligence); Phillips v. Sun Oil Co., 307 N.Y. 328, 121 N.E.2d 249 (1954) (gasoline storage tank leaks, but since there was no intended entry, trespass would not lie); Kulpa v. Stewart's Ice Cream, 144 A.D.2d 205, 534 N.Y.S.2d 518 (1988) (gasoline storage tank leaked into the plaintiff's water well; no trespass action because there was no intent, but triable issues were raised as to nuisance); Norman v. Greenland Drilling Co., 403 P.2d 507 (Okla.1965) (plaintiff must either show nuisance or negligence for pollution by way of underground sources); cf. Williams v. Amoco Production Co., 241 Kan. 102, 734 P.2d 1113 (1987) (rejecting strict liability, finding no nuisance, holding that negligence could be a basis for liability); Fortier v. Flambeau Plastics Co., 164 Wis.2d 639, 476 N.W.2d 593 (Wis.App.1991) (rejecting strict liability for disposal of hazardous wastes in landfill, requiring proof of negligence).

16. Ream v. Keen, 314 Or. 370, 838 P.2d 1073 (1992) (smoke from burning field); Bradley v. American Smelting & Ref. Co., 104 Wash.2d 677, 709 P.2d 782 (1985).

§ 54

1. See generally ROBERT R. WRIGHT, THE LAW OF AIRSPACE (1968) (covering ownership of airspace, aircraft and other aerial intrusions, theories of relief, and valuation, among other issues).

surface.[2] It is a trespass to intrude upon non-navigable waters upon the land,[3] to fire a bullet across it,[4] to maintain a utility line above it,[5] or even to extend an arm into the airspace.[6] Put the other way around, the owner has the right to the exclusive use of the airspace.[7] She may simply enjoy possession of the space, or, unless zoning rules or covenants prohibit it, she may erect tall buildings or sell the airspace to others.[8]

Qualifications and doubts. Ownership of airspace is qualified by the traditional rule that intangible intrusions like smoke are not trespassory.[9] It is also qualified somewhat by the practice of courts to treat natural intrusions of tree limbs or roots under rules like those for nuisance rather than under the rules of trespass. The victim of a leafy intrusion may usually lop the leaf and branch at the property line, but she has no action for damages based on the intrusion alone.[10] A New Jersey case goes further and holds that an intentional use of a scaffold in the airspace above the plaintiff's three story building was not actionable.[11] The scaffold was used in the renovation of the defendant's nine-story structure, which adjoined the plaintiff's building. The intrusion was temporary and although it was directly over the plaintiff's roof, it did not interfere with any current use.

The problem of aircraft overflights. The development of aircraft, especially powered aircraft, has raised substantial questions about airspace rights. The traditional view of land ownership was expressed as a maxim, *cujus est solum ejus est utque ad coelum*, one who owns the

2. Restatement § 159.

3. Steel Creek Development Corp. v. James, 58 N.C.App. 506, 294 S.E.2d 23 (1982).

4. Whittaker v. Stangvick, 100 Minn. 386, 111 N.W. 295 (1907); see Racine v. Glendale Shooting Club, Inc., 755 S.W.2d 369 (Mo.App.1988).

5. United States v. Gates of the Mountains Lakeshore Homes, Inc., 732 F.2d 1411 (9th Cir.1984); Butler v. Frontier Telephone Co., 186 N.Y. 486, 79 N.E. 716 (1906) (wires 30 feet above the soil, suspended from supports entirely outside the land; ejectment lay). In Ward v. McGlory, 358 Mass. 322, 265 N.E.2d 78 (1970) one defendant transmitted electricity through wires constructed by another defendant above the plaintiff's land. The wires were trespassing objects and the court held that the transmission of electricity was also a trespass.

6. Kenney v. Barna, 215 Neb. 863, 341 N.W.2d 901 (1983) (seven year-old girl stuck her arm through a wire fence to pet the dog, she was a trespasser so that the owner could defend against dog-bite liability).

7. See Atlantic Aviation Ltd. v. N.S. Light & Power Co. Ltd., 55 D.L.R. 2d 554 (N.S.S.C. 1965) (flier claimed defendant's electricity transmission towers interfered with an air "highway;" held, no such highway exists apart from statute or zoning rule).

8. The fee in land may be divided by the owner, who can sell airspace above it or interests in minerals below the surface. See Cheape v. Town of Chapel Hill, 320 N.C. 549, 359 S.E.2d 792 (1987) (air rights can be sold).

9. § 53.

10. The plaintiff can sometimes recover actual damages, at least if there is a "sensible injury," but otherwise the remedy is limited to self-help of the limb-lopping variety. The requirement of actual damages and "sensible injury" treats the case as closer to nuisance than to trespass. Jones v. Wagner, 425 Pa.Super. 102, 624 A.2d 166 (1993) called the claim one for trespass but seemed to have in mind only a recovery of actual expenses which of course is not the usual rule in trespass. In other tree-limb and tree-root cases, courts treat the claim as one for nuisance, or require a showing of some substantial harm. See, e.g., Cannon v. Dunn, 145 Ariz. 115, 700 P.2d 502 (Ct.App. 1985) (nuisance requiring "sensible injury" to permit suit).

11. Slotoroff v. Nassau Associates, 178 N.J.Super. 292, 428 A.2d 956 (1980).

surface owns "up to the heavens." The statement is a literary, not technical view of the law and the cosmos. No one possesses the upper reaches of airspace, but the maxim clouded all analysis of the problem. The expansive terms of the maxim herded thought into two channels. First, the rights of the owner extended infinitely upward. Second, the problem was one of ownership and trespass law.

Neither proposition seems sound. Very low overflights can interfere with possession; some of them may be close to the simple trespass paradigm. Sometimes trespass liability is imposed or recognized in such cases,[12] at least where they actually interfere with existing possession.[13] But most of the problems lie with higher flights, with the special problems of airport takeoffs and landings, or with low flights over unoccupied land that interferes with nothing. For these problem cases, many different versions of a trespass rule have been taken, a summary of which can be relegated to a note.[14] No firm rule has emerged, perhaps because trespass rules furnish poor tools for analysis.

For most problem flights, the known or foreseeable harm done to the plaintiff is a better index to the justice of the case than the mere entry into a column of air. Thus nuisance law, which explicitly limits the landowner's rights to reasonable use and enjoyment,[15] is likely to provide better access to appropriate considerations of justice and policy. A pure trespass analysis would merely ask whether the plane intruded in the airspace, while nuisance law is concerned with a reasonable accommodation of the conflicting interests. Under nuisance rules, some noisy flights

12. Smith v. New England Aircraft Co., 270 Mass. 511, 170 N.E. 385, 69 A.L.R. 300 (1930) (no liability for overflights in navigable airspace, that above 500 feet, but it is a trespass to fly over the wooded part of rural estate at altitudes of 100 feet on takeoff or landing).

13. Hinman v. Pacific Air Lines Transport, 84 F.2d 755 (9th Cir.1936) ("We own so much of the space above the ground as we can occupy or make use of, in connection with the enjoyment of our land. This right is not fixed. It varies with our varying needs and is coextensive with them. The owner of land owns as much of the space above him as he uses, but only so long as he uses it. All that lies beyond belongs to the world.... traversing the airspace above appellants' land is not, of itself, a trespass at all, but it is a lawful act unless it is done under circumstances which will cause injury to appellants' possession"); United States v. Gaidys, 194 F.2d 762 (10th Cir. 1952).

14. No one actually advocates an unregenerate *ad coelum* theory, which would treat all overflights at any altitude as trespasses. Among the theories someone has supported, are these: (1) The landowner does indeed own to the sky or at least to some very high altitude, but the public has an easement for flight. Only if the flight exceeds the (implied) terms of the easement would there be liability. This works much like a nuisance theory. (2) The landowner owns the column of airspace of the land, but the defendant enjoys a privilege of reasonable flight across the column. This, too, has or could have at least some resemblance to reasonableness judgments invoked in nuisance cases. (3) The plaintiff does not own to the heavens but only to the limits of his potential effective possession; (4) The plaintiff does not own to the heavens but to the limits of his actual possession or use; (5) The plaintiff owns to a fixed height prescribed by positive law; in the stratum of ownership, any entry is a trespass; above that stratum, no entry is a trespass. This theory is usually geared to certain core federal definitions of navigable airspace which begins, except for takeoff and landing, at 500 feet. See, summarizing all these theories, Cahoon, Comment, Low Altitude Airspace: A Property Rights No-Man's Land, 56 J. Air L. & Com. 157 (1990). A sixth solution leaves trespass law and resorts to nuisance analysis.

15. See Chapter 34.

might be actionable even if they don't actually overfly the plaintiff's land, while some less troublesome flights might be permissible even if they do. Nuisance rules likewise permit degrees of accommodation, for example, by limiting the number of flights over the plaintiff's land rather than barring all of them.[16]

The Restatement purports to address the problem as one of trespass, but in fact invokes some ideas of nuisance law. It provides that overflights are trespasses if (a) they are in the "immediate reaches" of the land *and* (b) they interfere with use and enjoyment.[17] By substituting use and enjoyment for possession, the Restatement in effect tacitly supports at least a partial nuisance analysis.[18] Nuisance analysis may also conform better to federal regulations, which define navigable airspace for aviation purposes and which may be inconsistent with liability for a mere technical trespass but consistent with liability for actual interference with use and enjoyment.

§ 55. Entries Below the Surface

Subsurface trespass. According to the traditional maxim, the landowner owns to the depths as well as to the heavens. Just as intrusions in the immediate airspace above land are trespasses, so are intrusions immediately below its surface so long as they are intended and without permission. If the defendant mines beneath the plaintiff's land, he is clearly a trespasser.[1] He is also a trespasser if the foundation of his house projects into the plaintiff's land below the surface,[2] or his televi-

16. See Atkinson v. Bernard, Inc., 223 Or. 624, 355 P.2d 229 (1960).

17. Restatement § 159.

18. Courts in fact often seem to confuse the concepts and the rules attached to each. See Robert R. Wright, The Law of Airspace 164 (1967).

§ 55

1. National Lead Co. v. Magnet Cove Barium Corp., 231 F.Supp. 208 (W.D.Ark. 1964); Maye v. Yappen, 23 Cal. 306 (1863) (gold mine); cf. Gliptis v. Fifteen Oil Co., 204 La. 896, 16 So.2d 471 (1943) (oil well slanted so that it crosses the property line beneath the surface; "subsurface trespass"). Differing forms of trespass and the remedies therefor are discussed in W.L. Summers, Oil and Gas §§ 22 et seq. (1954 & Supp.) Rights in underground waters, petroleum, and gas are now frequently regulated by statute in ways that change the traditional rights, often in favor of conservation for mutual advantage. Thus where an oil field is regulated and unitized so that all owners in the area share in the oil produced, subsurface entries on one owner's land may no longer be actionable, or if actionable may yield a limited damages measure. See Nunez v. Wainoco Oil & Gas Co., 488 So.2d 955 (La.1986).

2. 509 Sixth Avenue Corp. v. New York City Transit Authority, 15 N.Y.2d 48, 203 N.E.2d 486, 255 N.Y.S.2d 89, 12 A.L.R.3d 1258 (1964) (encroachment 30 feet underground is a continuing trespass); Epstein v. Cressey Development Corp., 89 D.L.R.4th 32 (B.C.Ct.App. 1992) (anchor rods and concrete angled under the plaintiff's property to support the defendant's building without surface disruption of the plaintiff's property, but with probable economic effect if the plaintiff chose to build); cf. L'Enfant Plaza East, Inc. v. John McShain, Inc., 359 A.2d 5 (D.C.App.1976) (contractor installed support for building that projected into plaintiff's property 23 feet below the surface, action not barred by the statute of limitations); Pennsylvania once affirmed a decree ordering a defendant to remove the entire wall of a four-story building because the footing beneath the surface projected 1 1/2 inches onto the plaintiff's land and the offending projection could be removed otherwise only by entry upon the plaintiff's land to chip off the stones. Pile v. Pedrick, 167 Pa. 296, 31 A. 646 (1895).

sion cable or his sewer lies beneath the plaintiff's land.[3] In one well-known case, a natural cave lay beneath the land of both the plaintiff and the defendant. The only entrance, however, was on the defendant's land, so that the plaintiff could not have used the cave at all. Nevertheless, the defendant was held liable when he used that part of the cave below the plaintiff's land.[4]

Underground cable or conduit cases. Underground cable cases once generated some confusion about liability for trespass. If a telephone company has a non-exclusive easement for an underground cable, it has no right to exclude contractors from digging in the easement area. Its right is only to prevent an intended trespass to the cable itself. So the contractor who is rightfully upon the owner's land is not a trespasser merely because he digs in the area. Under the logic of the intent rule, he is not liable for an unintended harm to the cable.[5] It would of course be otherwise if the contractor were trespassing upon the telephone company's own land. Older cases sometimes imposed strict liability for unintended and non-negligent entry upon land, but these now appear to be largely overruled or obsolete.[6]

3. Neely v. Coffey, 81 Ill.2d 439, 43 Ill. Dec. 706, 410 N.E.2d 839 (1980).

4. Edwards v. Lee's Adm'r, 265 Ky. 418, 96 S.W.2d 1028 (1936) (defendant made commercial use of the cave; the plaintiff was permitted to recover the profits resulting from the underground trespass). As to profits award, the case was overruled or limited in Triple Elkhorn Min. Co., Inc. v. Anderson, 646 S.W.2d 725 (Ky.1983). Cf. Barnett v. St. Anthony Falls Water–Power Co., 33 Minn. 265, 22 N.W. 535 (1885) (defendant's tunnel, not on the plaintiff's land, caused Mississippi River waters to carve out a cavern under the plaintiff's land, making the land unsuitable for erecting large buildings; plaintiff could recover for depreciated value).

5. General Telephone Co. of the Southwest v. Bi–Co Pavers, Inc., 514 S.W.2d 168, 73 A.L.R.3d 978 (Tex.Civ.App. 1974); Socony–Vacuum Oil Co. v. Bailey, 202 Misc. 364, 109 N.Y.S.2d 799 (1952) (pipe line). Most of the cases proceed on a negligence theory. See Annotation, Liability of one excavating in highway for injury to public utility cables, conduits, or the like, 73 A.L.R.3d 987 (1977).

One Texas Supreme Court decision, difficult to interpret, seems to the contrary. Mountain States Tel. and Tel. Co. v. Vowell Construction Co., 161 Tex. 432, 341 S.W.2d 148 (1960), defined trespass to personalty broadly to include injury or interference, with or without physical force and with or without an intent to affect the property. This departs widely from contemporary understanding, and the case might be limited to conduits on public property. Some Texas courts have sidestepped the case, as in General Telephone Co. of the Southwest v. Bi–Co Pavers, Inc., supra. But the case has also been accepted at face value. General Telephone Company of the Southwest v. Blacksher, 742 S.W.2d 465 (Tex.App.1987) (liability imposed for damage to buried telephone cable).

Massachusetts imposed liability for harm to an underground conduct in United Electric Light Co. v. Deliso Constr. Co., 315 Mass. 313, 52 N.E.2d 553 (1943) but that decision was at least in part made in reliance on blasting cases, which are now treated as abnormal danger strict liability cases rather than as trespass cases.

6. For instance, Kentucky once held that if the goods hauled by the defendant accidently rolled onto the plaintiff's property, the defendant was liable for a trespass even if he did not intend to invade the plaintiff's land and even if he was not negligent. Happy Coal Co. v. Smith, 229 Ky. 716, 17 S.W.2d 1008 (1929). That view was overruled in Randall v. Shelton, 293 S.W.2d 559 (Ky.1956) (rock thrown onto the plaintiff's land by truck's wheels, injuring the plaintiff who was on her own land, no liability without fault). Cf. Wood v. United Air Lines, Inc., 32 Misc.2d 955, 223 N.Y.S.2d 692 (Sup.Ct. 1961) (airplane crash with ground damage, no intent and no trespass); Smith v. VonCannon, 283 N.C. 656, 197 S.E.2d 524 (1973) (right of owner to recovery for entrance upon land "must rest on proof of some wrongful act or neglect of the defen-

Percolation of liquids underground. Subsurface pollution of water or oil reserves may be regarded as a trespass in some cases. In a California case,[7] the defendant disposed of waste water in a way that contaminated the plaintiff's underground oil. This was regarded as a trespass and actionable on that ground. But migration or percolation of wastes beneath the surface is often considered to be in the domain of nuisance law rather than the domain of trespass.[8] Tree roots that penetrate a neighbor's soil have also been accorded treatment more in line with the milder demands of nuisance law.[9]

Remote intrusions. Remote entries, far underground or far above it, have become technologically feasible. That feasibility challenges the traditional rule which suggests infinite extension of possessory rights above and below the ground just as the airplane challenged the corresponding rule above ground. It seems likely that courts will respond pragmatically. A tunnel hundreds of feet below the surface that does not affect the value of the land or remove minerals probably should not be regarded as a trespass.[10] When the defendant injected industrial wastes far below the surface of its land and they migrated to a position below the surface of the plaintiff's land, the Ohio Court denied the plaintiff's trespass claim, saying that "ownership rights in today's world are not so clear-cut as they were before the advent of airplanes and injection wells."[11]

§ 56. Remedies for Trespass to Land

Harm to rights of exclusive possession. Courts will issue injunctions to prevent trespasses that threaten to continue or to be repeated.[1] More

dant"). The Supreme Court insisted upon a negligence analysis in Parrot v. Wells, Fargo & Co. (The Nitro-glycerine Case), 82 U.S. (15 Wall.) 524, 21 L.Ed. 206 (1872) (a carrier opened a leaking case that had been deposited with it; it contained nitroglycerine, but the defendant had no reason to know it; an explosion occurred causing damage to the plaintiff's property nearby; defendant was not liable without negligence). But see United Electric Light Co. v. Deliso Constr. Co., 315 Mass. 313, 52 N.E.2d 553 (1943) and Mountain States Tel. and Tel. Co. v. Vowell Construction Co., 161 Tex. 432, 341 S.W.2d 148 (1960), both discussed supra n. 5.

7. Cassinos v. Union Oil Co. of California, 14 Cal.App.4th 1770, 18 Cal.Rptr.2d 574 (1993).

8. Cambridge Water Co. Ltd. v. Eastern Counties Leather, [1994] 2 W.L.R. 53, [1994] 1 All ER 53 (H.L.) (migration of chemical wastes from a tannery polluted the plaintiff's water wells many miles away; this was regarded as a potential nuisance, although no liability was imposed).

9. Cannon v. Dunn, 145 Ariz. 115, 700 P.2d 502 (Ct.App.1985).

10. Cf. Application of Gillespie, 173 Misc. 591, 17 N.Y.S.2d 560 (Sup. Ct. 1940) (tunnel 500 feet below ground, nominal damages only); Boehringer v. Montalto, 142 Misc.Rep. 560, 254 N.Y.S. 276 (Sup.Ct. 1931) (easement for sewer construction 150 feet below the surface could not affect any conceivable use by buyer of land, so the grantor was not in breach of a covenant against encumbrances).

11. Chance v. BP Chemicals, 77 Ohio St.3d 17, 670 N.E.2d 985 (1996). The court used the language of trespass but it required the kind of substantial injury usually associated with nuisance claims.

§ 56

1. E.g., Allred v. Harris, 18 Cal.Rptr.2d 530, 14 Cal.App.4th 1386 (1993); Charleston Joint Venture v. McPherson, 308 S.C. 145, 417 S.E.2d 544 (1992) (mall protestor enjoined); Planned Parenthood of Mid–Iowa v. Maki, 478 N.W.2d 637 (Iowa 1991) (abortion clinic protestor enjoined); Walsh v. Johnston, 608 A.2d 776 (Me.1992) (injunc-

commonly, the trespasser is liable for damages. He is always liable to the possessor for at least nominal damages for the intrusion upon possession.[2] So far as he occupies the land, he is liable for the rental value of its use;[3] somewhat similarly, he may be held for gains he makes directly from use of the land or its resources.[4] He is, of course, liable for other torts he commits in the course of a trespass.

Harm to rights of physical integrity. For any actual harm done to the land, or to things or people upon the land, he is also liable to the possessor or the owner as their interests appear. In the usual case his liability is measured by the diminution in value of the land resulting from the trespass, or, in some cases, by the reasonable costs of making repairs or restoring the land.[5]

Courts are generally reluctant to approve recovery for repairs or restoration when costs exceed the amount by which the land's value has been diminished. But sometimes the excess repair cost recovery is justified, as it usually is in cases of environmental damage,[6] since in those cases the defendant's tort has caused harm to others besides the plaintiff and is likely to continue in the future unless abated.[7]

Emotional distress. Damages for trespass can always include damages for loss of use and for discomfort and annoyance resulting from the trespass.[8] In some cases, the plaintiff will be entitled to have more general forms of emotional distress considered in fixing his damages.[9] Courts sometimes begin analysis by stating a "general rule" against recovery for distress in the absence of physical impact or harm to the plaintiff's person,[10] but then quickly turn to "exceptions" broad enough

tion requiring removing of structure encroaching on the owner's land); see generally, 1 Dan B. Dobbs, Law of Remedies §§ 5.5, 5.10 (2d ed. 1993) (injunction protecting physical integrity, injunctions protecting possession, injunction requiring removal of encroachments).

2. Neely v. Coffey, 81 Ill.2d 439, 43 Ill. Dec. 706, 410 N.E.2d 839 (1980); Gross v. Capital Electric Line Builders, Inc., 253 Kan. 798, 861 P.2d 1326 (1993); Marvin E. Nieberg Real Estate Co., v. Taylor–Morley–Simon, Inc., 867 S.W.2d 618 (Mo.App.1993). Nominal damages are damages in name only, usually $1 or six cents. By recovery of nominal damages, the plaintiff becomes the prevailing party and thus usually entitled to recovery statutory costs.

3. Salesian Society, Inc. v. Village of Ellenville, 121 A.D.2d 823, 505 N.Y.S.2d 197 (1986); Uhlhorn v. Keltner, 723 S.W.2d 131 (Tenn.App.1986). When a trespasser occupies the plaintiff's land at the time of suit, the plaintiff's claim was traditionally called one for ejectment. The ejectment suit would give the prevailing plaintiff possession of the land and damages called "mesne profits" equal to rental value.

4. 1 Dan B. Dobbs, Law of Remedies § 5.9 (2d ed. 1993). Cf. Austin v. Rescon Construction, Ltd., 57 D.L.R.4th 591 (B.C.Ct. App. 1989) (savings accrued to defendant from using plaintiff's land to be awarded as punitive damages).

5. See 1 Dan B. Dobbs, Law of Remedies §

6. E.g., Davey Compressor Co. v. City of Delray Beach, 639 So.2nd 595 (Fla.1994); cf Mailman's Steam Carpet Cleaning Corp. v. Lizotte, 415 Mass. 865, 616 N.E.2d 85 (1993).

7. See Dan B. Dobbs, Law of Remedies § 5.2 (5) (2d ed. 1993).

8. Restatement § 929 (1) (c).

9. Britt Builders, Inc. v. Brister, 618 So.2d 899 (1993) ("Anguish, humiliation, and embarrassment are appropriate considerations"). See generally Comment Note, Recovery for mental shock or distress in connection with injury to or interference with tangible property, 28 A.L.R.2d 1070 (1953).

10. E.g., Valley Development Co. v. Weeks, 147 Colo. 591, 364 P.2d 730 (1961).

to permit awards in any cases in which emotional distress is reasonably foreseeable.[11] At the other end of the spectrum, some courts have declared without qualification that emotional distress damages may be recovered for the trespass.[12]

The actual results in the cases suggest, however, that courts neither routinely grant nor routinely deny emotional harm damages in trespass cases. Emotional harm damages are awarded generally only when the trespass is more than a transient passage.[13] Courts approve such damages when the trespass is repeated or continuing,[14] when it threatens physical harm or is a deliberate or hostile infringement of the plaintiff's rights,[15] when it physically alters or destroys property of aesthetic value,[16] or afflicts some personal sensibility[17] or when it is accompanied by some other tort.[18]

Punitive damages.[19] Punitive damages may generally be awarded by the trier of fact only when the defendant has been guilty of some very serious wrongdoing, often described as malice, oppression, or wanton misconduct. Casual, transient trespass cases without other wrongdoing would seldom meet standards for punitive awards. But deliberate and

11. Indeed, the "exception" stated is often only the requirement that the harms claimed be the natural or foreseeable result of the trespass. E.g., Douglas v. Humble Oil & Refining Co., 251 Or. 310, 445 P.2d 590 (1968) (if a direct and natural result of trespass or some other tort).

12. Armitage v. Decker, 218 Cal.App.3d 887, 267 Cal.Rptr. 399 (1990) ("The general rule is simply that damages may be recovered for annoyance and distress, including mental anguish, proximately caused by a trespass"); Cullison v. Medley, 570 N.E.2d 27 (Ind.1991) (reasonably foreseeable emotional injury may be recovered regardless of the traditional rule requiring impact or physical injury to the person).

13. In fact, lawyers usually attempt to claim emotional distress damages in trespass to land cases by attempting to allege an independent tort, such as intentional or negligent infliction of mental distress.

14. E.g., McGregor v. Barton Sand & Gravel, Inc., 62 Or.App. 24, 660 P.2d 175 (1983) (spillage of pond water onto plaintiff's lower land and threat of landslides over a long period of time).

15. E.g., Tran v. General Motors Acceptance Corp., 1989 WL 64564 (E.D.Pa.1989) (aggression effort to repossess a car); Valley Development Co. v. Weeks, 147 Colo. 591, 364 P.2d 730 (1961) (dictum).

16. Pearce v. L.J. Earnest, Inc., 411 So.2d 1276 (La.App.1982) (ornamental trees); Phillips v. Town of Many, 538 So.2d 745 (La.App.1989) (road crew altered plaintiff's property over her repeated protests).

17. Jefferies v. Bush, 608 So.2d 361 (Ala.1992) ("Unless the trespass is attended with words or acts of insult or contumely, damages for mental anguish are not recoverable"). For examples: In Douglas v. Humble Oil & Refining Co., 251 Or. 310, 445 P.2d 590 (1968), a repossession case, the defendant entered the plaintiff's home while plaintiff was away, ransacked it and took papers and equipment. "An invasion of a home by strangers is not so impersonal in its effect upon the householders that we can say as a matter of law that mental distress is never compensable." An old fashioned example is May v. Western Union Tel. Co., 157 N.C. 416, 72 S.E. 1059 (1911) where the trespasser sang bawdy songs to members of the household.

18. For example, the trespass in Cullison v. Medley, 570 N.E.2d 27 (Ind.1991) (was in fact accompanied by intimidating conduct and an assault). Since nuisance always involves invasion of use and enjoyment interests for which some kind of distress damages are appropriate, those trespasses that are accompanied by a nuisance or that resemble nuisance cases are good candidates for distress claims. E.g., Lunda v. Matthews, 46 Or.App. 701, 613 P.2d 63 (1980) (clouds of cement dust and fumes from plant prevented plaintiffs from going outdoors, nuisance and trespass claim combined and mental distress recovery justified).

19. Punitive damages generally, § 381; 1 Dan B. Dobbs, Law of Remedies § 3.11 (2d ed. 1993).

known trespass, coupled with factors such as repetition, destruction or taking of property, or other aggravating elements, warrant substantial punitive awards.[20] Statutes sometimes prescribe double or treble damages where timber or minerals are taken.[21]

§ 57. Damages for Temporary and Continuing Trespass vs. Damages for Permanent Single Trespass

Persisting invasions of land, whether by way of trespass or by way of nuisance, create varied and difficult problems in determining damages and a number of other issues.[1] For instance, if an embankment on the defendant's land periodically causes floods on the plaintiff's land, one question will be whether to permit or require the plaintiff to sue for each flooding, or whether to say the plaintiff can or must sue for all future damages at once. Conflicting decisions and factual variety make statement of a general rule perilous. This section attempts to state the general tendencies.

Temporary vs. permanent. If the defendant's nuisance or trespass continues to cause harm to the plaintiff's interests in land, courts usually begin by classifying the invasion as either permanent (completed) or temporary and continuing.[2]

Damages-rules effects of permanent (or completed) classification. If the invasion is permanent, courts award damages only once and assess all future damages in the one law suit. The permanent or future damages measure is usually the diminished value of the land resulting from the invasion.[3] Once the defendant has paid permanent damages, he will not be liable again for the continuance of the same invasion.

If the *defendant* is the party successfully demanding that damages be measured by the permanent measure, he is in effect forcing the plaintiff to make a sale of an interest in the land.[4] If the *plaintiff* is the

20. E.g., Holliday v. Campbell, 873 S.W.2d 839 (Ky.App.1994) (timber taken); Hamilton Development Co. v. Broad Rock Club, Inc., 248 Va. 40, 445 S.E.2d 140 (Va. 1994) ("blatant recklessness in seizing a neighbor's land, clearing it, grading it, and appropriating it for its own use, resulting in compensatory damages of $20,000"); Epstein v. Cressey Development Corp., 89 D.L.R.4th 32 (B.C.Ct.App. 1992) (deliberate underground trespass after plaintiff had refused permission was arrogant and high handed and warranted $45,000 in exemplary damages).

21. See 1 Dan B. Dobbs, Law of Remedies § 5.3 (3) (2d ed. 1993).

§ 57

1. Other matters that may be determined by the classification but that are not directly covered in this section include: (1) whether the statute of limitations has run on the entire claim or only on the claims for harms done outside the statutory period; (2) whether more than one suit can be brought (res judicata issues); (3) whether the plaintiff as a purchaser of the land has standing to sue for the invasion or whether the owner at the time of the invasion has standing instead. See, e.g., Vaughn v. Missouri Public Service Co., 616 S.W.2d 540 (Mo.App.1981).

2. See Restatement § 930.

3. Mel Foster Co. Properties, Inc. v. American Oil Co., 427 N.W.2d 171 (Iowa 1988); Scantlin v. City of Pevely, Mo., 741 S.W.2d 48 (Mo.App.1987).

4. This is analogous to the power of eminent domain. Private eminent domain, the power of one individual intentionally to take another's rights in land by paying market value of those rights, is generally unacceptable.

party successfully demanding damages measured by the permanent measure, she is in effect forcing the defendant to make a purchase of an interest in the plaintiff's land.[5]

Damages rules effects of temporary (or continuing) classification. If the invasion is temporary or continuing, it is treated as if it were renewed daily, with a new trespass or nuisance each day. The plaintiff may sue for all harms that have occurred to the time of suit or trial, but may not sue for future harms that would be incurred only if the trespass continues; that is so because harm linked directly to continued trespass may terminate at any time and may never be incurred at all.[6] This measure of damages contemplates the possibility of successive suits. After the plaintiff recovers once, she may sue again for damages that have occurred since the first suit.[7]

Classification of an invasion as temporary or continuing does not give the defendant any permanent rights to continue the invasion. For that reason, a decision to classify the invasion as temporary can provide the defendant an incentive to eliminate the invasion, since if he does so, he will not be liable for damages in the future.[8]

Example of a permanent invasion. It is not easy to find harmony in the case results. However, some courts would classify the invasion as permanent with a single one-time recovery on facts similar to the illustration that follows.

A city with the power of eminent domain erects a dam, one effect of which is that water periodically floods parts of the plaintiff's land and will continue to do so indefinitely into the future. The dam is durable. Its physical or factual permanence, together with the city's power to condemn a flooding easement in the plaintiff's land, suggests that the case should be treated as a kind of taking of property. The city should be liable to pay all the damages the plaintiff will ever suffer in one suit. If the value of the land is worth $10,000 less because of the prospects of flooding, the city will be liable for that, but not ever liable again for the same kind of invasion flooding resulting from the dam.[9]

Example of a temporary or continuing invasion. A temporary or continuing invasion might take several forms. One might look like this: defendant parks his truck on the plaintiff's land and never takes it off. The plaintiff can sue at any time and, having recovered, can sue again for further damages accruing later. The damages for temporary or

5. The effect is to force a sale of a limited interest in the land, the right to pollute or continue a trespass. Subject to this limit, it is analogous to the remedy in conversion. See § 67.

6. E.g., Baker v. Burbank–Glendale–Pasadena Airport Authority, 39 Cal.3d 862, 705 P.2d 866, 218 Cal.Rptr. 293 (1985); Webb v. Virginia-Carolina Chemical Co., 170 N.C. 662, 87 S.E. 633 (1916).

7. E.g., City of Holdenville v. Kiser, 195 Okla. 189, 156 P.2d 363 (1945).

8. See note 19 below.

9. Town of Troy v. Cheshire R.R., 23 N.H. 83 (1851). But, to repeat, cases are not consistent; some courts have refused to consider the structure or harm as permanent. See Uline v. New York Cent. & H. R.R., 101 N.Y. 98, 4 N.E. 536 (1886). A number of cases are analogous on the facts, for example, where a city's street embankment causes flooding. City of Sioux Falls v. Miller, 492 N.W.2d 116 (S.D.1992).

continuing nuisance will not give the plaintiff the diminished value of the land. That measure assumes that the land could never recover from the parked truck, but that is absurd. Instead, the plaintiff could recover damages measured by the harm suffered up to suit or trial. In this illustration, that is probably the rental value of the land for truck-parking purposes. When the invasion is caused, not by a structure, but by the defendant's method of operation, courts usually treat the invasion as temporary.[10] The fact that the invasion can be abated is central but not exclusive in making that determination.[11]

Many cases are less clear than these models. The neighbor who builds a part of his house on your property may be compelled to remove it, in which case the trespass is clearly temporary. But equally, the court might decide that removal is too costly or wasteful and allow him to keep the house there, paying permanent damages.[12] Courts may likewise consider hazardous wastes that percolate into the plaintiff's lands or waters temporary in some instances[13] but permanent in others.[14]

Basis for classification. Classification as permanent or temporary is partly a matter of fact and partly a matter of policy seemingly governed by a number of factors. The most significant factors favoring a classification as temporary seem to be:

(1) the invasion can in fact be terminated or abated;[15]

(2) the cost of termination is not wasteful or oppressive;[16]

(3) no privilege or public policy favors a continuation of the inva-

10. E.g., Ryan v. City of Emmetsburg, 232 Iowa 600, 4 N.W.2d 435 (1942); Webb v. Virginia–Carolina Chemical Co., 170 N.C. 662, 87 S.E. 633 (1916).

11. See Spar v. Pacific Bell, 235 Cal. App.3d 1480, 1 Cal.Rptr.2d 480 (1991); Mel Foster Co. Properties, Inc. v. American Oil Co., 427 N.W.2d 171 (Iowa 1988), both discussed below in note 19.

12. Kratze v. Independent Order of Oddfellows, Garden City Lodge #11, 442 Mich. 136, 500 N.W.2d 115 (1993). See 1 DAN B. DOBBS, LAW OF REMEDIES § 5.10 (4) (2d ed. 1993). Similarly, the trespasser may build entirely on the plaintiff's land, as where he mistakes the lot number. See id., § 5.8 (3).

13. Wilson v. McLeod Oil Co., Inc., 327 N.C. 491, 398 S.E.2d 586, 11 A.L.R.5th 1019 (1990) (temporary, statute of limitations did not bar).

14. If the harm to the land continues even though the structure that caused the invasion no longer exists, or the acts that caused it are no longer being carried out, there is some tendency to regard the invasion as permanent. Cf. Mel Foster Co. Properties, Inc. v. American Oil Co., 427 N.W.2d 171 (Iowa 1988); Sustrik v. Jones & Laughlin Steel Corp., 413 Pa. 324, 197 A.2d 44 (1964). Mangini v. Aerojet–General Corp., 12 Cal.4th 1087, 1103, 912 P.2d 1220, 1229, 51 Cal.Rptr.2d 272, 281 (1996) treats the invasion as permanent unless it can be "remedied at a reasonable cost by reasonable means."

15. E.g., Mangini v. Aerojet–General Corp., 12 Cal.4th 1087, 1103, 912 P.2d 1220, 1229, 51 Cal.Rptr.2d 272, 281 (1996); Knight v. City of Missoula, 252 Mont. 232, 827 P.2d 1270 (1992).

16. If the defendant can efficiently terminate the invasion it is not unfair to expect him to do so or to be liable in successive actions as long as he permits the invasion to continue. Where the converse is true, and abatement of the invasion and the harm is extremely costly compared to alternatives, the defendant may in effect be permitted to purchase the right to continue the invasion by paying permanent damages. See Kratze v. Independent Order of Oddfellows, Garden City Lodge #11, 442 Mich. 136, 500 N.W.2d 115 (1993).

sion;[17]

(4) incentive to abate the invasion can be provided by permitting repeated suits for damages as they accrue;[18] and

(5) the plaintiff prefers temporary damages;[19]

(6) overall, it is not just to permit the defendant to acquire the permanent right to invade the plaintiff's interests in land by paying market price for that right against the plaintiff's wishes.[20]

Plaintiff's election. Writers[21] and courts[22] have sometimes suggested that the plaintiff should simply have an election to treat the invasion as either temporary or permanent. A plaintiff's election to recover tempo-

17. When the invasion could be considered the exercise of eminent domain power, the invasion can be considered to be an informal taking by the defendant, who is entitled by statute to acquire the right by paying its value. See Spaulding v. Cameron, 38 Cal.2d 265, 239 P.2d 625 (1952). Less obviously, the court might simply hold that the defendant's invasive conduct or structure would not be enjoined and hence would permit the defendant to acquire a permanent right to invade the plaintiff's land apart from any eminent domain power. See Restatement § 930. The text states that when these conditions are *not* present, their absence favors the plaintiff's use of temporary measures. If a defendant who lacks the power of eminent domain purposefully tries to acquire rights in the plaintiff's land by the invasion (rather than by bargaining), courts are more likely to issue an injunction to require termination of the invasion and hence more likely to treat the invasion as temporary.

18. See Mangini v. Aerojet–General Corp., 12 Cal.4th 1087, 1103, 912 P.2d 1220, 1229, 51 Cal.Rptr.2d 272, 281 (1996). Temporary damages do not invariably furnish incentives for avoiding further harm. Where they are not, this factor does not counsel classification as a temporary nuisance. In Spar v. Pacific Bell, 235 Cal. App.3d 1480, 1 Cal.Rptr.2d 480 (1991) the defendant had buried a substantial telephone conduit under the plaintiff's land. When it was discovered, the plaintiff demanded removal and the defendant in fact removed it. The plaintiff then sued, but the court held that the invasion was permanent even though it was removable and in fact removed. Note that the use of temporary damages measures here would not impose incentives upon the defendant to cleanup; the invasion has already been removed. The result is consistent with the view that incentives are an important factor. The same is only partly true with Mel Foster Co. Properties, Inc. v. American Oil Co., 427 N.W.2d 171 (Iowa 1988), where the defendant caused pollution of the plaintiff's land by chemicals. The defendant had ceased to pollute, so in that respect incentives were not required. On the other hand, the pollution remained on the land. Even so, a permanent measure of damages should ordinarily suffice to permit the plaintiff to clean up the land herself.

19. When it is the defendant's preference for temporary damages, other factors may counsel holding for the defendant, but not the defendant's preference alone. When it is the *plaintiff's* preference for temporary damages, that is a strong factor in favor of the temporary measure simply because the plaintiff is the victim, not the perpetrator of the tort. This is equivalent to saying that the plaintiff should usually have the power to elect a temporary damages measure. If the defendant has a power of eminent domain with respect to the interest involved, or wasteful costs would be imposed by temporary damages, the plaintiff's preference might be disregarded.

20. This factor in effect imports the factors used in conversion cases, where the issue is quite similar. In those cases, the defendant who interferes with possession of the plaintiff's chattel is or is not required to "buy" the chattel, depending ultimately upon the justice of forcing him to do so under the circumstances. This is turn is analyzed by considering a number of factors, such as the extent of interference and the defendant's consciousness of wrongdoing. See § 64.

21. McCormick, Damages for Anticipated Injury to Land, 37 Harv. L. Rev. 574 (1924).

22. Baker v. Burbank–Glendale–Pasadena Airport Authority, 39 Cal.3d 862, 705 P.2d 866, 218 Cal.Rptr. 293 (1985).

rary damages, however, would be inconsistent with the defendant's power of eminent domain, which implies that the defendant can take the right to invade the land by paying market value of that right. Similarly, the plaintiff's right of election would be inconsistent with justice or judicial policy where the court has concluded that the defendant should be allowed to continue the invasion as if he had eminent domain power. A contrary election, to take permanent damages, might simply be unjustified where the defendant can terminate the harm and is likely to do so. Nevertheless, the plaintiff is by definition a victim whose rights have been invaded, and whatever may be said where the statute of limitations is in issue, the plaintiff's choice of temporary damages should be respected where the other factors do not clearly weigh against it.

§ 58. Extended Liability for Unintended and Non-Negligent Harms

Extended liability for unintended and non-negligent harms. Doctrine has it that the trespasser is liable for all harms directly caused by his trespass, not merely those he caused intentionally or negligently. The Restatement puts the point by saying that the trespasser is subject to liability for harms caused by acts done and conditions he created on the land, even if he would not have been liable for such harms had he not been a trespasser.[1] And the trespasser's liability extends not only to the possessor of land but also to members of her household. The rule of extended liability for trespass appears to be the general form of the rule from which the "transferred intent" rule is logically derived.

Examples. Under the extended liability rule, the trespasser may be held liable for a personal injury innocently caused in the course of a trespass, as where a trespasser's truck runs over a child,[2] or where his trespass opens a door which allows a mentally disabled but apparently normal person to leave and suffer injury,[3] or where his chemicals cause an allergic reaction.[4] Or he may be held responsible for a fire innocently caused in the course of a trespass.[5] Other cases impose a similar liability.[6]

§ 58

1. Restatement § 162.

2. St. Petersburg Coca-Cola Bottling Co. v. Cuccinello, 44 So.2d 670 (Fla.1950) (child struck by trespasser's truck; lack of fault no defense since he was a trespasser).

3. Keesecker v. G.M. McKelvey Co., 141 Ohio St. 162, 47 N.E.2d 211 (1943) (defendant's agent delivered a package at the wrong house; his entry allowed a mentally disabled but apparently normal child to get out and be injured).

4. Cf. Brabazon v. Joannes Bros., 231 Wis. 426, 286 N.W. 21 (1939) (demonstrating fly spray over the plaintiff's objection, plaintiff became ill from it).

5. Wyant v. Crouse, 127 Mich. 158, 86 N.W. 527 (1901); Lee v. Stewart, 218 N.C. 287, 10 S.E.2d 804 (1940); cf. Brown v. Dellinger, 355 S.W.2d 742 (Tex.Civ.App. 1962) (7–8 year-old boys intentionally started fire in charcoal grill; the fire got out of hand and burned the garage and house; since the boys were trespassers, they were liable for $28,000 in damages resulting from the unintended spread of the fire).

6. See Williams v. River Lakes Ranch Development Corporation, 41 Cal.App.3d 496, 116 Cal.Rptr. 200 (1974) (strict liability for cattle trespass and also liability for cattle's "foreseeable" injury to owner); Beavers v. West Penn Power Co., 436 F.2d 869 (3d Cir.1971) (poles carrying high tension wires tilted over the years and may have

Extended liability for indirect injuries or not. In line with the common law rules for trespassory torts generally, courts may distinguish direct from indirect injuries, allocating the latter to an action on the case. In this view, liability for trespass would not extend to indirect injuries that were also unintended and unforeseeable.[7] However, some courts have held the trespasser responsible even for unintended injuries that are also indirect.[8]

As between a conscious wrongdoer on the one hand and an innocent possessor or her family on the other, courts are fully justified in imposing the unexpected loss upon the wrongdoer. The same is not so obviously so in the case of the trespasser who is innocently mistaken in believing the land is his or that he has permission to enter it.

TOPIC C. INTERFERENCE WITH CHATTELS

§ 59. Development of Liability for Interference with Chattels

Interference with chattels, which can come about in many different ways and in many different degrees, has not been treated quite like interference with land. Two sets of distinctions bedeviled the development of liability for interference with chattels and to some extent continue to produce litigation or confusion.

First, the defendant could interfere with your goods in two radically different ways or in two radically different settings. In one scenario, the defendant physically takes your chattel, say a horse. In the other, he is rightfully in possession of your chattel to begin with, say as the stable owner who is paid to feed your horse, but he refuses to give it up when you demand it.

Second, the defendant's interference might be transitory and inconsequential or it might be substantial. He might pet your horse although you have told him not to do so. Or he might steal your horse and ride him to exhaustion.

The Trespass writ. These variables in chattel interference—taking vs. keeping on the one hand and minor vs. substantial interference on

hung over the land of another; if the defendant's wires were trespassing objects, the defendant would be liable for death of a child who came in contract with the wires).

7. Connolley v. Omaha Pub. Power District, 185 Neb. 501, 177 N.W.2d 492 (1970); cf. Wawanesa Mutual Insurance Co. v. Matlock, 60 Cal.App.4th 583, 70 Cal.Rptr.2d 512 (1997) (one smoking and trespassing teenager accidentally set a fire; his fellow trespasser, who had furnished the cigarette, was not liable).

8. Kopka v. Bell Telephone Co. of Pa., 371 Pa. 444, 91 A.2d 232 (1952) (telephone company was responsible for a hole dug on the plaintiff's land; the plaintiff, hearing of the hole, went looking for it and fell in; the defendant was held liable); Turner v. Thorne and Thorne, O.W.N. 20, 21 D.L.R.2d 29 (Ontario H.C. 1959) (defendant mistakenly delivered packages intended for another to plaintiff's home; upon returning home, the plaintiff fell over them in the dark; defendant was held liable). The *Kopka* court recognized a limitation, however: "[I]f the owner or possessor of the land, wilfully, voluntarily, or by negligence, himself brings about the injury to his person, such an injury cannot be said to be consequent upon the trespass to the land, and in that event the trespasser would not be liable therefor."

the other—led to the use of different common law writs depending on the facts of the case. The simplest case was an intentional taking or damage to a chattel. Because the taking was physical ("forcible") and direct, the writ of *Trespass* could be used to recover damages.[1] This form of trespass was called *Trespass de bonis asportatis*, that is, for the taking of goods. So far, so good.

The Detinue background. But the defendant might not *take* the chattel at all. He might be a bailee, that is, a person who rightfully possessed the chattel but was not its owner. A borrower is a bailee; so is someone who is paid to care for the chattel. If the bailee refused to return the chattel upon demand, he was not guilty of a trespass because he had not wrongfully taken it. In this situation the plaintiff could use *Detinue*.

In *Detinue* the defendant had the option of paying for the chattel or returning it.[2] So if he had damaged the chattel he could return it and thus escape liability. The plaintiff could not recover the damages by then invoking Trespass, so *Detinue* might prove to be quite inadequate for the plaintiff. A second disadvantage in *Detinue* was that the defendant could also opt to have the case tried by wager of law. This meant that the defendant could defeat the claim altogether if he could produce a specific number of oath-helpers, that is persons who would swear that the defendant was generally a truthful person.[3]

Action on the Case for Trover develops. Since neither *Trespass* nor *Detinue* was a wholly satisfactory solution for the plaintiff, and since they left gaps in which no remedy at all was found, plaintiffs' lawyers eventually succeeded in developing an action of *Trespass on the Case for Trover*. *Trover* was a word that had been earlier used in certain *Detinue* cases. As the word suggests, the allegation in the new *Trover* action was that the defendant had found the goods belonging to the plaintiff. The allegation of a finding was a happy fiction. It negated both trespass and bailment and hence left the way open for an action on the case,[4] because

§ 59

1. Originally, a complete dispossession was required, and even that did not suffice if the chattel was taken by way of Distress, that is, by a lord who has (wrongfully) seized the chattel as security for rent. In that case the plaintiff had to proceed by an action called Replevin. See Ames, The History of Trover, 11 Harv. L. Rev. 277, 286 (1897).

2. The writ of Replevin allowed specific recovery of the chattels, but it originally lay only for chattels wrongfully distrained by the lord as security for the tenant's rent due. See Ames, The History of Trover, 11 Harv. L. Rev. 277, 287 (1897).

3. "... with a dozen or half-a-dozen ruffians he might swear an honest man out of his goods." Bereford, C.J., in a Yearbook case quoted in C.H.S. Fifoot, History and Sources of the Common Law 29 (1949). Milsom thinks that in the local courts the procedure might not have been so bad, although when the trial was in the central courts and the defendant used hired compurgators it was obviously undesirable to say the least. See S.F.C. Milsom, Historical Foundations of the Common Law 67 (2d ed. 1981).

4. To use *Case* the plaintiff had to show that no other writ was appropriate to the facts. That meant that the plaintiff had to claim that neither *Trespass* nor *Detinue* fit the facts alleged. The allegation of a finding and the allegation that the goods were converted to the defendant's own use both played a significant part in showing that *Trespass* and *Detinue* could not apply. The rule that the allegation of finding could not be denied then left the plaintiff almost com-

the bare allegation of finding was enough and the plaintiff was never required to prove it.[5] The allegation went on to say that the defendant, having found the goods, "converted them to his own use," that is, kept them or altered them or sold them and retained the money.

Trespassory and non-trespassory claims combined in one action. With the advent of the action on the case for trover, both settings were reflected in a single tort we today call conversion. The old allegations explain why the tort is so called and also why if you research the topic you must look in the Digest for the topic *Trover* rather than the topic Conversion.[6] Conversion's parentage—part *Trespass*, part *Case*—helps explain the fact that it sometimes seems trespassory and sometimes does not. Although there is now one tort of conversion rather than several writs, the two major settings for that tort remain important. Failure to return cases—the second setting—raise problems that are not much like the problems raised in the taking cases. The writs are gone but the factual skeleton on which they hung remains.

Substantial vs. insubstantial interference. What of the distinction between substantial and insubstantial interferences? On this point, the development of *Trover* also had its effects. *Trespass* had originally been dedicated to the physical taking cases, but at least by the 1840s, *Trespass* had become the repository for claims of less substantial interference or damage.[7] Substantial interference cases were redressed in *Trover*. The difference was that *Trespass* permitted the plaintiff to recover actual damages, but *Trover* allowed the plaintiff to recover the full value of the chattel. It was in effect a forced sale. That remains the law today.

§ 60. Trespass to Chattels

General rule. The tort of trespass to chattels, known in old law as *trespass de bonis asportatis*, is committed by intentionally interfering with the plaintiff's possession in a way that causes recognizable harm. The defendant may interfere with the chattel by interfering with the plaintiff's access or use[1] or by causing actual harm to the chattel.[2] As the

pletely free to use *Case* for *Trover* in lieu of the earlier actions. See, recounting the details and the gaps, Simpson, The Introduction of the Action on the Case for Conversion, 75 L. Q. Rev. 364 (1959).

5. Ames, The History of Trover, 11 Harv. L. Rev. 277 (1897).

6. There is a topic "Conversion," but it refers to equitable conversion, which has no relationship to trover. Conversion cases may of course be digested under more specific topics rather than under Trover. These include Automobiles, Bailments, Carriers, Sales, and Secured Transactions.

7. See Fouldes v. Willoughby, 8 M. & W. 540, 151 Eng.Rep. 1153 (1841)

§ 60

1. See Zaslow v. Kroenert, 29 Cal.2d 541, 176 P.2d 1 (1946) (removing cotenant's goods and putting them in storage, not enough to be a conversion, trespass to chattels only warranting damages based on impairment of the goods or their loss of use); Huffman and Wright Logging Co. v. Wade, 317 Or. 445, 857 P.2d 101 (1993) (demonstrators chained themselves to logging equipment; on appeal they conceded that this was a trespass to chattels, arguing only that the punitive damages award was impermissible; but the judgment for both compensatory and punitive damages was upheld).

term chattel implies, the tort aims to protect interests in tangible property. Recent cases, however, have extended it to protect computer systems from electronic invasions by way of unsolicited email or the like.[3]

Intent. The intent required is familiar from the trespass to land and conversion cases. It is enough if the defendant had an intent to act upon the property; if his interference is substantial enough, he is liable even though he had no intent to harm or even to invade another's interests.[4] On the other hand, he is not liable for trespass to a chattel if he never intended to touch it at all and does so only accidently, as where a contractor excavating land strikes a buried telephone cable.[5]

Direct vs. indirect interference. Trespass was the proper form of action under earlier common law only when the interference with land, chattel, or person was direct and physical. Under this rule, the defendant who locked the door to a room where the plaintiff's goods were located might not be guilty of a trespass,[6] although he might be liable in an action on the case for the intentional interference.[7] The forms of action have long since been abolished, so the distinction between trespass and case (as forms of action) are no longer important. The defendant who places poisoned meat before the plaintiff's dog, intending that the dog will eat it, is no doubt liable if the dog does eat, even though he does not put the meat in the dog's mouth or otherwise touch the dog. With the

2. See Restatement § 218. The Restatement's structure may be confusing. It begins in § 217 by saying that any intermeddling with a chattel is a trespass. On this basis, the court in Hernandez v. United States, 353 F.2d 624 (9th Cir.1965) said that an officer's manual compression of baggage and his smelling the escaping air, for marihuana was a trespass to chattels. However, such a trespass would not be actionable under Restatement § 218, which, provides that no intermeddling is *actionable* unless it causes dispossession, loss of use or other harm.

3. CompuServe Inc. v. Cyber Promotions, Inc., 962 F.Supp. 1015 (S.D.Oh. 1997) (spam email on plaintiff's system to thousands of plaintiff's subscribers); Thrifty–Tel, Inc. v. Myron Bezenek, 46 Cal. App.4th 1559, 54 Cal.Rptr.2d 468 (1996) (computer hackers breaking into telephone company's long-distance system, using confidential access code, and making calls was trespass to chattels); Intel Corp. v. Hamidi, 1999 WL 450944 (App.Dept.Superior Ct. 1999)(not published) (email on plaintiff's computer system to all plaintiff's employees).

4. Restatement § 217, Cmt. c.

5. Mountain States Tel. & Tel. Co. v. Horn Tower Const. Co., 147 Colo. 166, 363 P.2d 175 (1961); Cover v. Phillips Pipe Line Co., 454 S.W.2d 507 (Mo.1970); Southwestern Bell Tel. Co. v. M.H. Burton Construction Co., 549 P.2d 1214 (Okla.1976). Cf. National Coal Board v. J.E. Evans & Co., (Cardiff), Ltd., [1951] 2 KB 861, [1962] 2 Alkl. E.R. 310 (Ct. of Appeal) (similar, plaintiff itself was faulty). United Electric Light Co. v. Deliso Constr. Co., 315 Mass. 313, 52 N.E.2d 553 (1943) reached a contrary result where a contractor injected cement beneath the earth under high pressure and the cement damaged a nearby cable of which the contractor knew. The court invoked the blasting cases, which are now treated as strict liability cases under the abnormal danger rule. It also approved a nuisance theory.

When the owner of the cable is also owner of the land, the contractor may be a trespasser to the land if he is intentionally upon the land, but in the common case the cable or pipeline owner merely has an easement, a non-possessory interest. The focus, in such cases should be on the contractor's intent to act on the cable or pipeline, not merely his intent to be on the land. The contractor may, of course, be liable for negligence.

6. See Clerk & Lindsell on Torts 1295 (16th ed. 1989).

7. Restatement § 217, cmt. d.

abolition of the forms of action, it is not confusing to call the defendant's tort a trespass.

Possession. Trespass to chattels parallels trespass to land on some issues and not on others. Although physical interference is required, direct harm has become less important and so has possession. So if the defendant intentionally harms a chattel that the owner has loaned or leased to someone else, the owner is not in possession, but he has an action if his interests in the chattel are adversely affected.[8] In this respect the trespass to chattel rules resemble those for trespass to land.

Harm or dispossession required. Trespass to chattels differs from trespass to land in one important respect. An intended entry upon land is a trespass whether it is harmful or not. An intended touching of a chattel is not. To establish liability for trespass to chattels, the possessor must show legally recognizable harm.[9] Harm can be any one of four kinds: (1) actual dispossession or, short of that, (2) loss of use for an appreciable period;[10] (3) damage to the chattel; or (4) personal harm to the plaintiff or to someone or something in which the plaintiff had a legal interest.[11]

Trivial interference and measurable harm. One way to measure the harm caused by dispossession is to estimate the rental value of the chattel during the period in which the plaintiff was deprived of possession. Conceivably, the cost of renting a substitute chattel would be an acceptable measure under some circumstances.[12] When an object has no rental value, other means for estimating value of lost possession may be available. For example, it may be possible to estimate the price people might pay for an option to purchase for the period of dispossession.[13] As these comments suggest, trivial interference should never count as dispossession. For instance, suppose that for my own convenience in parking, I release the brake on your car and push it four feet forward. This should not count as a dispossession and if no other harm is done, I am not liable for a trespass to your car.[14]

But the reverse is also true; whenever the intentional intermeddling causes objectively harm measurable by rental value or otherwise, the intermeddler should be liable for that harm.

Extended liability. The harm necessary to trigger liability for trespass to chattels can be, according to the Restatement, harm to something

8. Restatement § 220.

9. Glidden v. Szybiak, 95 N.H. 318, 63 A.2d 233 (1949) (not a trespass to pull dog's ears since dog was not hurt); see Johnson v. Weedman, 5 Ill. 495 (1843); cf. Zaslow v. Kroenert, 29 Cal.2d 541, 176 P.2d 1 (1946) (liability is for actual dispossession or harm).

10. See Koepnick v. Sears Roebuck & Co., 158 Ariz. 322, 762 P.2d 609 (Ct.App. 1988) (two-minute search of plaintiff's truck not a trespass to the truck). Distinguish Hernandez v. United States, 353 F.2d 624 (9th Cir.1965). The court there held that an officer's momentary handling of luggage was a trespass, but the court did not say it was an *actionable* trespass.

11. Restatement § 218.

12. See 1 Dan B. Dobbs, Law of Remedies § 5.15 (2) (2d ed. 1993) (loss of use).

13. 2 Dan B. Dobbs, Law of Remedies § 6.9 (2) (2d ed 1993).

14. Restatement § 218, Illustration 3.

other than the chattel itself.[15] Suppose, as in the example above, I push your car to make more room for me to park. The car rolls out of control and knocks you down without damaging the car at all. Although you have not been dispossessed or deprived of the car's use, and although no harm has been done to the car, the rule seems to say that I would be liable for your injuries.[16] This rule is inspired by the familiar rule of extended liability or transferred intent.[17] Mere emotional distress is not bodily harm under this rule. When no other harm is done by a trivial interference, the plaintiff's emotional distress does not activate the extended liability rule and does not permit the claim.[18]

Substantial interference. If the defendant's interference with the chattel is substantial, amounting to an exercise of ownership rights or "dominion" over the chattel, the plaintiff may have an option to claim either trespass to chattels or conversion.[19] As the following sections indicate, however, the interference must be quite substantial to justify the conversion claim, which in effect forces the defendant to buy the chattel.

§ 61. Conversion of Chattels—Elements and Issues

The Basic Case for Conversion

This section summarizes the main rules and issues in conversion cases. The rules are treated in more detail in the sections that follow.

The core case. The essential point of the tort now called conversion[1] is simple: if I intentionally exercise dominion or control over your chattel in a way that is inconsistent with your rights and deprives you of the chattel, then I must pay you for it unless you decide to and actually do

15. Restatement § 218 (d), and cmt. j.

16. Cf. Buchanan Marine, Inc. v. McCormack Sand Co., Inc., 743 F.Supp. 139 (E.D.N.Y.1990) (defendant moored at a mooring buoy owned by the plaintiff; as a result of the defendant's unauthorized acts, some barges broke away and the plaintiff's barge was damaged and it also incurred costs of cleaning up a beach where the barges drifted; held, all proximately caused damages are recoverable).

17. See §§ 40 & 58. The rule seems to differ from ordinary transferred intent in that the defendant in the trespass to chattels case may have no actionable intent at all. The Restatement seems to attempt a fudge on this by implying in § 217 that it is tortious to intermeddle at all, and then to provide in § 218 that while it is tortious, it is nevertheless not actionable unless harm is done. The effect would then be to make the defendant liable for unexpected harm to something other than the chattel under the extended liability rules. The implication of § 217 seems doubtful. The justification for extending liability to harms that were neither intended nor reasonably foreseeable does not seem to apply to many cases of chattel touchings. I intentionally lean on the fender of a stranger's car while chatting in the parking lot. It turns out to be an eggshell fender and collapses under the slight pressure. Harm is done, but it is not far from clear that I should be regarded as morally at fault.

18. Morrow v. First Interstate Bank of Oregon, 118 Or.App. 164, 847 P.2d 411 (1993).

19. Vines v. Branch, 244 Va. 185, 418 S.E.2d 890, 893–894 (1992) ("Where a person has illegally seized the personal property of another and converted it to his own use, the owner may bring an action in trespass, trover, detinue, or assumpsit").

§ 61

1. The tort was once referred to by the name of a writ used, *Trover*. See § 59.

get it back.[2] I take your watch and sell it. I have converted it and I am liable to you for conversion. The price I must pay as a converter is the value of the watch, usually figured by its value at the time and place of conversion.

Glimpsing beyond the core. Beyond the core case, any form of interference with another's chattel can count as a conversion, provided the interference is substantial enough to warrant a forced sale to the defendant. If the interference with your possession is enough and I enjoy no privilege, I am a converter if I dispossess you, if I transfer title or possession, if I fail to return your chattel on demand,[3] and even if I acquire title to your chattel in good faith from a thief who stole it from you.[4]

Possession. The conversion rules, like those of trespass to land, traditionally protected possessory rights.[5] So a bailee who had no title to the chattel could sue if the defendant seized the chattel.[6] Even a finder could sue for conversion and the fact that the title and right to possession are in the owner was no defense.[7] Today the owner who is not in possession can also sue to the extent her interests are adversely affected by the conversion.[8]

Substantial interference by control. Everyone agrees that conversion requires more than intermeddling or interference; it requires very substantial exercise of control or dominion inconsistent with the plaintiff's rights. Jurists have found it impossible to define with precision the amount of control that will count as a conversion. Perhaps the best approach is to ask, with the Restatement, whether the defendant exercised so much control over the chattel that courts can justly require him to pay its full value.[9]

Insubstantial interference. If the defendant's dominion over the chattel was limited, as where he takes the plaintiff's car for a one-block joy ride, the court is unlikely to find a conversion. In that case, the defendant may be liable for the tort of trespass to chattels.[10] But in that

2. Collin v. American Empire Ins. Co., 21 Cal.App.4th 787, 26 Cal.Rptr.2d 391 (1994) ("act of dominion wrongfully exerted over another's personal property in denial of or inconsistent with his rights therein);" P.F. Jurgs & Co. v. O'Brien, 160 Vt. 294, 629 A.2d 325 (1993) (conversion occurs when defendant "has exercised dominion over [property] in exclusion and defiance of the owner's right, or has withheld possession from the owner under a claim of title inconsistent with the owner's title"). As to getting the property back, see § 67.

3. § 65.

4. § 66.

5. E.g., Car Transportation v. Garden Spot Distributors, 305 Ark. 82, 805 S.W.2d 632 (1991).

6. See Lawrence v. State, 231 Ga.App. 739, 501 S.E.2d 254 (1998)

7. Restatement § 895. This is the *jus tertii* rule, that is, the rule that rights of third persons constitute no defense to the converter.

8. Restatement § 243. The right to recover is not in doubt. The only possible question is whether the action by the owner out of possession should be called one for conversion. If the possessor has already recovered full value of the chattel in a conversion suit, the owner's right may be limited to a claim against the possessor. See Restatement § 895, Illustration 7.

9. Restatement § 222 A. See § 64.

10. § 60.

case the defendant will not be liable for the entire value of the car, only for actual damages caused.

Alternatives to conversion. The plaintiff who cannot prevail on a conversion claim may have a number of alternatives. The defendant who has committed no conversion may still be liable for a trespass to chattels or for negligent harm to the chattel.[11] If interference occurs through use of the judicial process, the plaintiff's claim may be for malicious prosecution or the like,[12] or even for infringement of civil rights in certain cases.[13] Statutes may create claims that redress interference with chattels under a set of rules different from those used in conversion cases. For example, Florida's civil theft statute permits recovery of treble damages, but only when criminal intent is shown.[14] When the property in question is intangible, conversion may or may not be the appropriate theory, but a congregation of economic tort claims stands ready for such cases.[15]

Issues in Conversion Cases

Property and tort issues. Two radically different kinds of problems arise in conversion cases. In many cases, the broad issue is whether or not the plaintiff's property interest prevails over the defendant's. In such cases, the focus of inquiry is not on the defendant's conduct but on the plaintiff's property rights. For example, a creditor who loans money to a farmer to buy cows, may take a mortgage or other security interest in the cows, even though the farmer keeps them on the farm. If the farmer sells the cows to defendant, contrary to a provision of the mortgage, the defendant will be a converter if the plaintiff's mortgage is a property interest superior to the defendant's. That issue is resolved by rules about the rights or property interests of creditors; tort law is merely the vehicle for enforcing those underlying property rights.[16] So many conversion cases turn primarily on the law of personal property ownership, or on the law of secured transactions, warehouse receipts, or other rules under the Uniform Commercial Code,[17] where the rules attempt to

11. The most common tort case of all is such a case—negligent damage to an automobile. The ordinary rules of negligence law apply in such cases. See Chapters 6–11.

12. See Chapter 30.

13. See § 65 on unconstitutional creditor uses of the judicial process.

14. Fla. Stat. Ann. § 812.35 (6) permits a civil action for injunctive relief by private persons; subsec. (7) appears to permit the treble damage remedy only in favor of governmental entities.

15. See § 63.

16. In Production Credit Assn. of Madison v. Nowatzski, 90 Wis.2d 344, 280 N.W.2d 118 (1979) the court considered the UCC rules dealing with the rights of secured creditors and concluded the creditor who had filed its papers in the proper office had a conversion action against the buyer of the goods under certain circumstances.

17. The Uniform Commercial Code and the decisions that emanate from it resolve many issues about conflicting rights in personal property. As one example of many, the UCC provides for resolution of conflicting claims to goods bailed to a warehouse in § 7–403 (1). See 2 James White & Robert Summers, Uniform Commercial Code § 21–3 (3d ed. 1988). The UCC also occasionally speaks to some issues about conduct as well as about conflicting rights, for instance in its provision that a creditor may repossess goods only without causing a breach of the peace. UCC § 9–503.

delineate the interests held by adverse parties rather than to prescribe conduct.

In other cases the plaintiff's property interest is clear and the question is whether the defendant's conduct should count as a substantial interference with that interest. If I drive your car without your permission, but only take it across the street, the question whether I am a converter focuses heavily on my conduct, not on your property interest.

It is true that a court indirectly determines something about your property rights when it decides that my conduct did or did not violate those rights, conduct is the central focus of the inquiry. So in a sense, the two kinds of cases cannot be wholly separated. Yet the first kind of case, with its concern for determining conflicting interests in property, must be mainly understood through the law of personal property and the Uniform Commercial Code, not through the law of torts.

The tort issues in conversion cases. The main tort issues to be considered in conversion cases fall into three groups.

(1) Did the defendant have the requisite intent? Put the other way around, can the defendant escape liability if he acted in good faith?[18]

(2) Did the defendant exercise sufficient control to be counted as a converter?[19] Or is he, perhaps, guilty only of a trespass to chattels?

(3) What kind of property is subject to conversion? Does it include intangible property such as stocks or bonds? Does it include real property?[20]

§ 62. Conversion: Intent Required

Intent required. Conversion is an intentional tort. There is no such thing as a conversion by accident. The defendant may accidently damage property and may be liable for doing so if he is negligent or if the facts warrant imposition of strict liability; but negligent damage, destruction, or taking without an intent to affect the chattel at all is not a conversion.[1]

The intent required is the defendant's intent to exercise control of or dominion over the goods, no more.[2] As in other cases, intent is shown either by the defendant's purpose to affect the goods in question or by his substantial certainty that they will be affected.[3] For example, the

18. § 62.

19. § 64.

20. § 63.

§ 62

1. Collin v. American Empire Ins. Co., 21 Cal.App.4th 787, 26 Cal.Rptr.2d 391 (1994)

2. Restatement § 217, cmt. c; Northeast Bank of Lewiston and Auburn v. Murphy, 512 A.2d 344 (Me.1986).

3. Restatement § 217, cmt. c.

defendant who intentionally seizes the plaintiff's automobile intends to seize its contents, even if his only purpose is to repossess the car.[4]

Bad or good faith irrelevant. The intent required to show conversion is exactly analogous to the intent required to prove a trespass to land. In neither case is the defendant's bad motive or good faith ordinarily[5] relevant except on the question of punitive damages. The defendant might believe the goods are his and that he has every right to deal with them, but, even so, he harbors the requisite intent if he intends to act upon the goods.[6] For example, if I mistakenly pick up your book from a library table, intending to take my own, and then sell it, I am a converter. In the same way, an innocent agent, who negotiates a sale of goods on behalf of his principal is liable for conversion when it turns out that the principal had no right to the goods and that they belong to the plaintiff instead.[7]

Where the defendant does not benefit from the conversion. The intent rule would be easy to understand if the defendant intending to treat goods as his own always retained the benefit of those goods. If I take your book by mistake, it is not harsh to require me to pay for it if I am then allowed to have title to the book. Conversion law is a kind of informal forced sale, and I do indeed have a right to the book once I have paid you for it.[8] The rule in conversion, however, does not limit liability to cases in which the defendant has himself received or retained a benefit.[9] As applied to the book example, this rule means that I would

4. See Jones v. Petty, 577 So.2d 821 (La.App.1991)

5. Good faith of a stakeholder who refuses to deliver a chattel until he can determine which of two claimants is the rightful owner is one exception. See Paris American Corp. v. McCausland, 52 Wash.App. 434, 759 P.2d 1210 (1988). Good faith of a purchaser is relevant to defeat a conversion claim only in very limited circumstances discussed below. As to carrier's limited liability, see § 65.

6. Car Transportation v. Garden Spot Distributors, 305 Ark. 82, 805 S.W.2d 632 (1991) ("Conscious wrongdoing is not the requisite intent for conversion"); P.F. Jurgs & Co. v. O'Brien, 160 Vt. 294, 629 A.2d 325 (1993) ("Specific intent to convert, that is, knowledge that the property is owned by another, is not required for liability in tort. It follows that the converter's good faith belief in ownership of the property, or lack of knowledge as to its true ownership, is irrelevant"); Paris American Corp. v. McCausland, 52 Wash.App. 434, 759 P.2d 1210 (Wash.App. 1988) ("good faith cannot be shown as a defense to conversion"); Restatement § 244. See Martel Enterprises v. City of Chicago, 223 Ill.App.3d 1028, 164 Ill.Dec. 945, 584 N.E.2d 157 (Ill.App. 1991); Rensch v. Riddle's Diamonds of Rapid City, Inc., 393 N.W.2d 269 (S.D.1986) (inadvertent misdelivery, conversion). In Wiseman v. Schaffer, 115 Idaho 537, 768 P.2d 800 (Idaho App.1989) an imposter paid a tow truck driver to tow a car he claimed to own but that in fact belonged to the plaintiff. The truck driver towed the car to the designated place, from which it was stolen. The court reversed a jury verdict for the defendant, observing that the driver indisputably exercised dominion over the car without a right to do so and that his mistaken belief that he had been empowered to tow the car was not defense.

7. Ensminger v. Burton, 805 S.W.2d 207 (Mo.App.1991) (auctioneer selling goods he did not know were subject to the plaintiff's mortgage is liable to the plaintiff for conversion); Restatement § 233.

8. See O'Keeffe v. Snyder, 83 N.J. 478, 416 A.2d 862, 873–74 (1980).

9. Reed v. Hamilton, 315 Ark. 56, 864 S.W.2d 845 (1993) (defendant who misdelivered the item never obtained any benefit from it but he is liable); Rodgers v. Rodgers, 184 W.Va. 82, 95, 399 S.E.2d 664, 677 (1990).

remain liable for conversion of your book even if I had later lost the book or it had been destroyed in a fire without my fault.

One stringent example of the intent rule occurs when a thief converts your watch, then sells it to an innocent purchaser who reasonably believed that the thief was the owner. Although some innocent purchasers are protected from liability by special rules, the innocent purchaser in the case just described is not.[10] His intent to deal with the goods as owner is a sufficient basis for liability. The effect is that the good faith buyer pays twice, once when he paid the thief and once when he pays the conversion judgment. Economically, then, he is a no-benefit defendant, financially in the same position as the defendant who is held for conversion even though he no longer has the converted goods.

When the intent rule is not determinative. The intent rule does not necessarily mean that I am liable for any touching of your book, because the interference must be substantial and it must deprive you of control or dominion. Nor does the intent rule mean that am never liable for harm to a chattel without intent. One of the most common torts of all is the negligent automobile accident. If I damage or destroy your car by my negligent driving, I am liable for the harm done, but not because I am a converter.

§ 63. Property Subject to Conversion

Traditional Rules

Tangible personal property. Under the traditional common law rule, only tangible personal property could be converted. This meant three things.

First, no action for conversion would lie for dispossession of an interest in real property or damage to it.[1] If timber, minerals, or soil were severed from the land, they became personal property and subject to conversion,[2] but if I occupied your land, you could not effect a forced sale by claiming a conversion.[3]

Second, no action for conversion would lie for interference with intangible rights such as choses in action.[4] Although some courts adopt

10. See § 66.

§ 63

1. Emerick v. Mutual Benefit Life Ins. Co., 756 S.W.2d 513 (Mo.1988) (no conversion of leasehold interests).

2. Pan American Petroleum Corporation v. Long, 340 F.2d 211 (5th Cir.1964) (oil taken from beneath plaintiff's land by slant drilling was subject to conversion); Lubecki v. Omega Logging, Inc., 674 F.Supp. 501, 508 (W.D.Pa.1987) (severance of timber from the land converts it to personal property); Embrey v. Weissman, 74 Mich.App. 138, 253 N.W.2d 687 (1977) (soil, timber); Smith v. Shiflett, 66 Wash.2d 462, 403 P.2d 364 (1965) (timber cutting treated as trespass followed by conversion).

3. Rowe v. Burrup, 95 Idaho 747, 518 P.2d 1386 (1974). The landowner could sue in ejectment to recover possession and damages for loss of use. If the interloper obtained legal title, the court might impose a constructive trust in favor of the victim. So relief is available, but does not take the form of a forced sale.

4. Southern Cellular Telecom v. Banks, 208 Ga.App. 286, 431 S.E.2d 115 (1993) (plaintiff's contract right to become a 49% owner of a corporation divested by fraud; fraud claim would lie but not one for con-

the terminology of conversion in intellectual property and unfair competition cases,[5] the import of the general rule is that such torts as infringement of a copyright[6] or trademark, interference with business opportunities,[7] the "taking" one's personality or performance for commercial purposes,[8] and the misappropriation of ideas[9] must be governed by their own particular rules and not by the rules of conversion.

Third, no action for conversion would lie for interference with rights that do not count as property rights.[10] In each case, other actions might conceivably lie, but if so they would not have the characteristics of conversion, such as a forced sale or liability for intended but good faith interference.

Historical bases. The general rule against the use of the conversion action for interference with intangibles or real property is often traced to the ancient writ of trover, which alleged the property had been lost by

version of an intangible property interest); Shebester v. Triple Crown Insurers, 826 P.2d 603 (1992) ("chose in action" not subject to conversion). In *Shebester* the buyer of a horse on an installment contract was contractually obliged to procure insurance payable to the seller. The buyer procured insurance payment to himself instead. When the horse died, the seller informed the insurer of the contract, but the insurer paid the proceeds to the buyer in accord with the policy, not to the seller. This was not a conversion, the court said, since the seller's claim was a chose in action, an intangible right to recover money.

5. National Surety Corporation v. Applied Systems, Inc., 418 So.2d 847 (Ala. 1982) held that computer software was subject to conversion. But the "conversion" was a use by a new competitor who had gained the information while employed by the plaintiff. This looks much more like a trade secrets case or a violation of fiduciary duty. Similarly, In Blue Cross & Blue Shield of Connecticut, Inc. v. DiMartino, 1991 WL 127094 (Conn.Super.1991) the court found that an employee's use of confidential data from a computer was a misappropriation of trade secrets; then it added that it was also a conversion, but it did not explain how use that does not affect the owner's possession could count as conversion. Nor did it apply the conversion measure of damages (the value of the thing converted), saying that the plaintiff could recover "actual damages" and restitution for unjust enrichment. In Veeco Instruments, Inc. v. Candido, 70 Misc.2d 333, 334 N.Y.S.2d 321, 324 (Sup. Ct. 1972) a discharged employee was held liable for intentionally converting computer program materials, but since he had a definite intent to take the physical materials and would have been aware of the interference this caused in the plaintiff's business, the conversion rule that permits liability for innocent but intended dominion was not really involved. For further discussion of intellectual property and unfair competition cases see Chapter 33.

6. Federal copyright law preempts state law on the general topic, so that if the complaint is that the defendant "converted" the plaintiff's property by publishing material regulated by copyright law, no state claim is permitted. See Maheu v. CBS, Inc., 201 Cal.App.3d 662, 247 Cal.Rptr. 304 (1988). This seems to have been overlooked in Charter Hospital of Mobile, Inc. v. Weinberg, 558 So.2d 909 (Ala.1990) where a copyrighted treatment program was said to have been converted.

7. H.J., Inc. v. International Telephone & Telegraph Corp., 867 F.2d 1531 (8th Cir. 1989) (manufacturer who terminated distributor and sold directly to dealers was not liable for "conversion" of the dealer network; the claim was properly one for interference with business relations).

8. Ippolito v. Lennon, 150 A.D.2d 300, 542 N.Y.S.2d 3 (1989) (rights in a performance, no conversion action unless right is merged in and identified with a document). "Taking" a performance or a personality characteristic may be actionable on other grounds.

9. Bloom v. Hennepin County, 783 F.Supp. 418, 440 (D.Minn.1992) (medical procedure or "protocol" allegedly misappropriated by defendants, intellectual property law, not conversion law should govern).

10. See the paragraph "Non-property rights" below.

the plaintiff and found by the defendant.[11] Since an intangible right could not be lost or found, conversion would not lie for interference with such a right. Conversion also had roots in *Trespass* and consequently emphasized the direct and the physical aspects of the tort. An intangible right cannot be directly and physically taken, so the use of conversion to protect such rights is historically inappropriate on this ground as well.

The history of pernicious and ancient writs in a primitive legal system seems to furnish little basis for contemporary legal decisions. The real question is whether a conversion action for intangibles would serve justice and public policy, so it is not surprising that courts have not always adhered to the traditional rule.

Modern Expansion of Conversion

Contemporary tort decisions often adhere to the traditional rules, but sometimes go beyond them by imposing liability on a conversion theory for the taking of intangibles. Some of the decisions seem formally but not substantively different from the traditional ones. If the defendant obtains the electrical company's electricity by circumventing its meter, it is sure that the defendant should be liable for what he got and conversion is as good an explanation as any.[12]

Other decisions are more troubling, because the claim would be more fairly assessed under the rules and policies of some other tort or because the conversion rules seem too harsh for the circumstances. Most of the cases fall in one of the categories discussed below.

Money and money credits. Identifiable, specific coins or bills are subject to conversion if they are identifiable as the particular coins or bills taken from the plaintiff.[13] The old idea that money could be converted only if it was in a "bag" now seems obsolete.[14] Today, it might be plausible to say that when the defendant commits an affirmative act and physically takes control of particular paper monies he is guilty of conversion, even if the particular bills or coins cannot be identified.[15]

11. § 59.

12. DeLong v. Osage Valley Elec. Cooperative Ass'n, 716 S.W.2d 320 (Mo.App. 1986) (recognizing liability for conversion).

13. In In re Moody, 899 F.2d 383 (5th Cir.1990) the defendant was held guilty of converting a pedigreed 1879 gold four-dollar coin worth between $75,000 and $88,000. In Little v. Gibbs, 4 N.J.L. 211 (1818) the court thought identification by numbers on bills would suffice: "If money or cash be lost or stolen the loser cannot maintain trover to recover it, because it cannot be distinguished. But notes and bank bills may be recovered in such an action, because the interest of the owner in them is sufficient, and they may be distinguished by names, marks and numbers on them."

14. See Kinaston v. Moor, Cro. Car. 89, 79 Eng.Rep. 678 (1627) (perhaps suggesting that the bag was only important as one piece of evidence showing that it was the plaintiff's money held by the defendant, but an unnecessary piece of evidence if the evidence showed that the defendant took the money directly from the plaintiff).

15. Cf. Lappe and Associates, Inc. v. Palmen, 811 S.W.2d 468 (Mo.App.1991) (check payable to defendant for one purpose, fund diverted to another purpose, held, conversion). Replevin, a forced return of converted goods, of course requires identification of the goods. See § 65.

Certainly the plaintiff is entitled to recover on some theory, even if not on the basis of conversion.[16]

Courts have actually gone beyond the case of physical taking of bills; they have sometimes said that if a bank improperly transfers funds from the plaintiff's account that is also a conversion, even though the "transfer" is purely a bookkeeping entry.[17]

Some courts have gone even further, losing sight of the difference between contract obligations and conversion. If your life insurer fails to credit your premium payment, it does not sound so reasonable to say it has converted the whole policy and must pay you its face value or its accumulated sums. What you should get is the proper credit and the resulting increase in policy value, not a forced sale of the policy. This is borne out in the commonly accepted rule that conversion does not lie for failure to pay a debt.[18] Yet some courts have purported to find a conversion in cases that do not involve a physical seizure of a document, but merely turn on the defendant's failure to enter bookkeeping credits[19] or to pay money owed.[20]

Documents embodying rights; negotiable instruments. One of the more clearly justified departures from the traditional rules comes when the defendant takes or wrongly retains a negotiable instrument that is not merely evidence of a right but that embodies it and can itself be bought and sold as an embodiment of the right to collect. A promissory note payable to the plaintiff, for example, represents the plaintiff's rights to recover money from the maker of the note and courts have generally recognized that such a note can be converted.[21] A deed to land, once

16. Assumpsit, to use the name of an old form of action, would lie for money received by the defendant that belongs to the plaintiff. See 1 DAN B. DOBBS, LAW OF REMEDIES § 6.1 (1) (2d ed. 1993).

17. Brown v. Oklahoma State Bank & Trust Co. of Vinita, 860 P.2d 230 (1993). Many cases use the term conversion when nothing seems to hinge on the label. If the bank was wrongful in its transfer, the plaintiff is entitled to recover the money. Nothing seems to have been added in *Brown* by the conversion label.

18. Morris v. National Western Life Ins. Co., 208 Ga.App. 443, 430 S.E.2d 813, 815 (1993); Faircloth v. A.L. Williams & Associates, Inc., 206 Ga.App. 764, 426 S.E.2d 601 (1992); Lappe and Associates, Inc. v. Palmen, 811 S.W.2d 468 (Mo.App.1991). Cf. Shebester v. Triple Crown Insurers, 826 P.2d 603 (Okl.1992) (insurer allegedly paid wrong person, held not a conversion).

19. Federal Deposit Insurance Corporation v. S. Prawer & Co., 829 F.Supp. 439 (D.Me.1993) (holder of note converted "credits" when it failed to credit payments, then transferred the note).

20. Omar v. Mezvinsky, 13 Conn.App. 533, 537 A.2d 1039 (1988). Contra: Covington v. Exxon Company, U.S.A., 551 So.2d 935 (Ala.1989) (suspension of royalty payments due was not a conversion since no specific monies were identified or segregated as the plaintiff's). No reason is apparent why an ordinary claim for debt or for money had and received would not have been appropriate in *Omar*. Nor does the conversion theory utilized appear to add to or subtract from anyone's rights. In other words, using the conversion theory here simply adds something else to discuss in briefs and books without adding any protection to the underlying right. In some cases, however, the plaintiff pursues a conversion theory instead of a more appropriate one in the hope of applying a more favorable statute of limitations.

21. Teper v. Weiss, 115 Ga.App. 621, 155 S.E.2d 730 (1967); Lappe and Associates, Inc. v. Palmen, 811 S.W.2d 468 (Mo. App.1991); Save Charleston Foundation v. Murray, 286 S.C. 170, 333 S.E.2d 60 (S.C.App.1985); United Leasing Corp. v. Thrift Ins. Corp., 247 Va. 299, 440 S.E.2d 902 (1994); cf. Federal Deposit Insurance

recorded, has a similar quality and its recording may count as a conversion.[22] Checks, bonds, stock certificates and other similar instruments have been treated the same way,[23] and the plaintiff can recover for their conversion, provided she was entitled to possession of the instrument.[24] The measurement of damages in such cases, however, frequently presents a problem; a promissory note for $100 is not necessarily worth that sum, and certainly is not if the maker is insolvent or has a good defense.[25]

Documents that merely evidence rights. Many documents are important only because they furnish some evidence of a right or a convenient means of enforcing it, but do not in any sense embody that right. If the defendant takes your insurance policy or your ATM card, but does not collect the insurance or draw on your bank account, it seems plausible to say that he is guilty of a trespass to chattels and should be liable for the costs and inconvenience caused, but not so plausible to say that he has converted your life insurance policy or your bank account and must pay the full value. Similarly, a card specifying your entitlement to medical services may facilitate medical attention without controlling your right to that attention. In such a case, the taking of your card is not a conversion of your right to medical care.[26]

Nevertheless, in a number of factually varied cases, courts have permitted a recovery for conversion of assets reflected in such documents as accounts showing amounts owed,[27] savings account pass books,[28] life insurance policies,[29] and other evidentiary documents.[30] These cases are

Corporation v. S. Prawer & Co., 829 F.Supp. 439 (D.Me.1993) (failure to credit promissory note, conversion).

22. Montano v. Land Title Guarantee Co. 778 P.2d 328 (Colo.App.1989) (deed from A to C held by bailee in three-party transaction; bailee recorded it without authority, whereupon C borrowed money on it; B, who was to pay A left for parts unknown; held, the bailee is a converter).

23. Carmichael v. Halstead Nursing Center, Ltd., 237 Kan. 495, 701 P.2d 934 (1985) (corporate defendant, with name similar to payee's, deposited check in its own bank account; this was a conversion); Dayton Construction, Inc. v. Meinhardt, 882 S.W.2d 206 (Mo.App.1994) (specific checks). In addition, payment of a negotiable instrument on a forged endorsement is a conversion. Restatement § 241A.

24. Great Lakes Higher Education Corp. v. Austin Bank of Chicago, 837 F.Supp. 892 (N.D.Ill.1993).

25. See Annotation, Measure of damages for conversion or loss of commercial paper, 85 A.L.R.2d 1349 (1962).

26. Robinson v. St. Clair County, 144 Ill.App.3d 118, 98 Ill.Dec. 133, 493 N.E.2d 1154 (1986) (card could not be bought, sold, or transferred and care could be obtained without it; hence defendant was not liable for death of child allegedly resulting because card was not available).

27. *Plunkett-Jarrell Grocery Co. v. Terry*, 222 Ark. 784, 263 S.W.2d 229, 44 A.L.R.2d 917 (1953).

28. Stebbins v. North Adams Trust Co., 243 Mass. 69, 136 N.E. 880 (1922) (under a system in which the passbook was required to make a withdrawal and in which its assignment operated to assign the account and not merely the book itself; defendant liable for the amount in the account).

29. Gauntt v. United Ins. Co. of America, 853 F.Supp. 1382 (M.D.Ala.1994) (life insurance policy; because it is the sole evidence of the terms, the defendant's retention of the policy denied the plaintiff the ability to know her rights; but query whether the court has in mind damages based on the value of that knowledge or the value of the policy itself).

30. See Annotation, Nature of property or rights other than tangible chattels which may be subject to conversion, 44 A.L.R.2d 927 (1955).

far removed from the paradigm case of physical conversion; they are essentially financial or economic tort cases, not physical interference cases and it might be better to so view them.[31]

Intellectual property, unfair competition, economic opportunities. Many important intangible rights are covered by the terms intellectual property and unfair competition and interference with contract. Use of a conversion analysis for these cases runs risks that important issues will be overlooked or that inappropriate liabilities will be imposed.[32] For instance, the rule that ideas cannot be protected by copyright may be subverted if a court allows a claim for their conversion.[33] These rights, like rights in other intangibles, are best considered elsewhere, along with other economic torts.[34]

Limiting Conversion to Property Rights

Non-property rights; body tissue. One traditional limitation continues to be applied without exception. Courts recognize a conversion only when the right interfered with can be considered to be a property right.[35] Even if conversion is exported from its foundation in physical tort law to cover some economic tort cases, it is not likely to cover purely personal rights. One might not have a property interest in one's own body, for example; taking control of a person's body might be a battery or a false imprisonment but not a conversion. The California Supreme Court has held that taking unique body cells of a patient for use in developing a commercially valuable product is not a conversion.[36] A California federal district court on the same kind of facts has taken the position that although body cells could not be converted, the abstract right to commercialize those cells was property, even if cells themselves were not. At the same time, that court refused to permit an action for conversion, leaving the plaintiff to rights under contract or patent law.[37]

Similarly, intentional interference with dead bodies may constitute a tort to living relatives, but it seems less than helpful to say that the claim arises because relatives have a property interest in the body. It is not preposterous to say that someone might own a dead body or that someone might own his own body cells, since both are in fact bought and sold. But the claim of relatives that a body was mishandled is not a claim for the market value of the body but rather for the relative's emotional distress, so such a claim is not about the body as property but the body as the physical remains of a loved one. Conversion is thus the wrong theory for such a case.[38]

31. See Chapters 32 and 33.

32. Cf. Val D. Ricks, The Conversion of Intangible Property: Bursting the Ancient Trover Bottle with New Wine, 1991 B. Y. U. L. Rev. 1681 (1991).

33. Cf. Charter Hospital of Mobile, Inc. v. Weinberg, 558 So.2d 909 (Ala.1990).

34. Chapters 32 & 33.

35. H.J., Inc. v. International Telephone & Telegraph Corp., 867 F.2d 1531, 1547 (8th Cir.1989).

36. Moore v. Regents of the University of California, 51 Cal.3d 120, 271 Cal.Rptr. 146, 793 P.2d 479 (1990).

37. Miles, Inc. v. Scripps Clinic and Research Foundation, 810 F.Supp. 1091 (S.D.Cal.1993).

38. Culpepper v. Pearl Street Building, Inc., 877 P.2d 877 (Colo.1994) rejected the

In the same way it can be said that although one might interfere with another's contracts or business opportunities, one person cannot "convert" another's employees, since they are not property.[39]

§ 64. Dominion or Control Required

Tests and Factors

The Cooley general definition. Cooley defined conversion[1] as "Any distinct act of dominion, wrongfully exerted over one's property in denial of his right or inconsistent with it." Many courts have stated this formula or some variation on it.[2] The plaintiff's consent to the defendant's conduct of course negates a conversion, since if the defendant is acting with the plaintiff's consent, he cannot be acting inconsistently with the plaintiff's rights, much less can he be doing so in a way that counts as "dominion."[3]

Everyone gets the general idea in the Cooley definition: if the defendant behaves toward the chattel in a way that would suggest to an objective viewer that the defendant was the owner, he is a converter. If his behavior falls short of that, he may be no more than a mere trespasser to the chattel. But the definition is too abstract to furnish a strong guide to attorneys who must seek useful evidence and formulate arguments.

The Restatement's test: justice of a forced sale. The Restatement drafters, well aware of the difficulty, offered a rule that requires dominion over the plaintiff's chattel that is so extensive that it will be just to force the defendant to pay full value of the chattel.[4] The conversion

conversion theory, saying the claim was really one for infliction of emotional distress and could not proceed unless the requirement for emotional distress claims were met.

39. Equity Group Ltd. v. Painewebber Incorporated, 839 F.Supp. 930, 933 (D.D.C. 1993).

§ 64

1. Thomas M. Cooley, Law of Torts 448 (1878). Courts picked up Cooley's definition from various editions.

2. E.g., Plunkett–Jarrell Grocery Co. v. Terry, 222 Ark. 784, 263 S.W.2d 229, 44 A.L.R.2d 917 (1953); Roebuck Auto Sales, Inc. v. Wallace, 293 Ala. 231, 301 So.2d 546 (1974); Collin v. American Empire Ins. Co., 21 Cal.App.4th 787, 26 Cal.Rptr.2d 391 (1994); Kummer v. City of Fargo, 516 N.W.2d 294 (N.D.1994); Rodgers Rodgers, 184 W.Va. 82, 399 S.E.2d 664 (1990). Some courts list demand for the goods and a refusal to yield them by the defendant as an element. E.g., Stathis v. Geldermann, Inc., 258 Ill.App.3d 690, 196 Ill.Dec. 761, 630 N.E.2d 926 (1994) ("(1) an unauthorized and wrongful assumption of control, domination, or ownership by a person over the personalty of another; (2) a right in the property; (3) a right to the immediate possession of the property, absolute and unconditional; and (4) a demand for possession thereof"). But the demand-and-refusal element is required only when the defendant has come into possession of the goods rightfully and has not otherwise exercised dominion over them.

3. See Jones v. DCH Health Care Authority, 621 So.2d 1322, 1324 (Ala.1993).

4. Restatement § 222A (1). The Restatement's formula does not make reasonableness the test of conversion; intent to exercise dominion over the chattel is still required. However, the Restatement's formula may have the effect of making some case outcomes turn in part on the reasonableness of the defendant's intentional interference. In Mustola v. Toddy, 253 Or. 658, 456 P.2d 1004 (1969) a police officer stopped a car because the driver appeared to be under the influence of intoxicants. After some roadside discussion, the officer decided that a passenger named Joe was the

action in effect results in a judicially forced sale of the goods to the defendant; this forced sale is the action's most significant feature.[5] The Restatement's principle is to declare a conversion when, but only when, the facts justify such an extreme remedy—when the defendant exercised quite extensive dominion over the chattel. The Restatement's rule does not eliminate judgment calls, but it does tell lawyers and judges what kind of judgment must be made.

The Restatement's factors. The Restatement attempts to provide more specific bases for developing evidence, formulating arguments, and making decisions. It lists six factors that courts should consider in determining whether the defendant's interference with the chattel is serious enough to justify a finding of conversion. The list provides a convenient evidentiary template, suggesting that evidence on the following points will be helpful to a decision:

(1) the extent and duration of the defendant's dominion or control;

(2) the defendant's intent to assert a right in the goods that is inconsistent with the plaintiff's ownership;

(3) the defendant's good faith;

(4) the amount of actual interference with the plaintiff's right to use the chattel;

(5) any harm done; and

(6) the inconvenience or expense caused.[6]

Applying the factors to an example. For example, suppose that by happenstance the defendant's car key fits the plaintiff's identical car and the defendant mistakenly takes the wrong car from a parking lot but discovers his mistake and returns the car two hours later with apologies. He has not harmed the car. The first factor tells the lawyer to inquire about the length of time the defendant had the car; it was not long, so that factor perhaps favors the defendant. The second and third factors tell lawyers to consider the defendant's state of mind; and since he did not intend to assert ownership and acted in good faith, those factors also favor the defendant.

The fourth factor suggests that lawyers should find out whether the plaintiff was actually inconvenienced by loss of the car's use. For example, if the plaintiff did not actually attempt to use the car and did not even know of its absence, her abstract right to possession has been invaded but she has suffered no actual interference at all. The fifth

"soberest of the bunch" and told him to take off. Joe did, in the plaintiff's car. Joe was not known to the plaintiff except as a person he had given a ride to on an interstate trip. The court concluded that the officer's direction to Joe to "take off" was not a conversion in light of the Restatement's factors, because it was reasonable for him to assume that passengers were not unfriendly to the owner's interests. The court added a factor of its own: "the desirability of permitting police officers acting in emergency situations to have sufficient leeway in dealing with property ... that they are not unduly inhibited.... "

5. Pearson v. Dodd, 410 F.2d 701, 706 (D.C.Cir.1969); Louisiana State Bar Association v. Hinrichs, 486 So.2d 116 (La.1986).

6. Restatement § 222A (2).

factor, harm done, and the sixth, actual expense caused, both seem to work for the defendant in this example. The conclusion almost certainly is that the defendant should be liable for trespass to chattels for any harm actually done but should not be compelled to purchase the car by way of a conversion action.[7]

§ 65. Methods of Committing Conversion

(1) Dispossession

General rule. As the Restatement recognizes, conversion can be committed in many different ways.[1] A taking of the chattel by a thief is a simple and core example. But the defendant can commit conversion by any act that counts as dominion over the chattel and that is not privileged[2] or protected by law.[3] Dispossessing the plaintiff,[4] or preventing the plaintiff's possession when she is entitled to it,[5] is a common form of conversion, so long as the interference with the plaintiff's interests is substantial. For example, even the sheriff who tows away the plaintiff's tractor in the good faith belief that it is stolen property may be liable for conversion.[6]

Seriousness of dispossession. Whether the dispossession is serious enough to count as a conversion is largely a matter of degree, but the defendant's intent or lack of intent to assert a right in the property is also significant. Returning a rental car hours after it is due is not necessarily a conversion, even if it is a trespass or breach of contract.[7] Driving the plaintiff's car across the street without permission is conceivably a dispossession, but if the plaintiff can recover the car by crossing the street, it is not a conversion, only a trespass.[8] Taking the car

7. Cf. Johnson v. Weedman, 5 Ill. 495 (1843) (holding in accord with the argument by A. Lincoln for the defendant that a bailee's wrongful riding of the bailed horse was not a conversion).

§ 65

1. Restatement § 223 lists seven ways in which conversion can be committed. These include (1) dispossession, (2) destruction or alteration, (3) using a chattel, (4) receiving it, (5) disposing of it, (6) delivering it to the wrong person, or (7) refusing to surrender it to the owner. All of course require intent to deal with the chattel and a substantial interference.

2. See § 81 (repossession of chattels wrongfully taken) and Chapter 5 generally.

3. When the conversion takes place by use of judicial processes, conversion rules may be too stringent and courts may invoke the rules of malicious prosecution or similar torts instead in order to provide appropriate protection for resort to courts. See n. 12 below.

4. Restatement § 223.

5. Hartford Financial Corp. v. Burns, 96 Cal.App.3d 591, 158 Cal.Rptr. 169 (1979) (after tenant's departure, landlord locked premises and prevented secured creditor from reaching tenant's personal property).

6. E.J. Strickland Construction, Inc. v. Department of Agriculture and Consumer Services of Florida, 515 So.2d 1331 (Fla. App.1987) (in the absence of probable cause, the sheriff's interference with property is analogous to false arrest).

7. See Stupak v. Winter Park Leasing, Inc., 585 So.2d 283 (Fla.1991) (a question of insurance coverage, lessee was 13 hours overdue when accident occurred, whether this was a conversion was a jury question).

8. Zaslow v. Kroenert, 29 Cal.2d 541, 176 P.2d 1 (1946); cf. Western States Mutual Ins. Co. v. Verucchi, 66 Ill.2d 527, 6 Ill.Dec. 879, 363 N.E.2d 826 (1977) (not a conversion to drive car across the street, or, because of traffic conditions, to drive it several blocks to get there; insurance coverage issue).

from Mississippi to Kansas, on the other hand, is easily a conversion.[9].

Creditor cases. A number of dispossession cases arise in the context of creditors' efforts to recover the debt owed or the property allocated to secure that debt. The defendant's mere assertion of a lien or security interest against the plaintiff's property is not necessarily a conversion of the property even though the defendant has no right to a lien on it.[10] But a creditor-lienor who sells property not subject to its lien is guilty of conversion[11] and so is a sheriff who enforces a judgment by seizing property of the wrong person.[12] So is a creditor who wrongfully repossesses the debtor's car,[13] and one who conducts a sale of it that is not commercially reasonable.[14]

A creditor who can rightfully take possession of mortgaged chattels cannot rightfully seize unmortgaged chattels as well, or if he does, he must make prompt and reasonable efforts to identify and return those not mortgaged.[15] Even if a creditor is entitled to repossess the chattel in an honest and peaceable way, he may be a converter if he repossesses by a breach of the peace,[16] or in some states if he does so by fraud or

9. Cf. PACCAR Financial Corp. v. Howard, 615 So.2d 583 (Miss.1993) (defendant repossessed the plaintiff's 18–wheeler; the plaintiff intentionally left goods in the truck intending to get them later, but the defendant moved the truck from Mississippi to Kansas and did not help get the goods back to the plaintiff; held, conversion of the plaintiff's personal items).

10. Prewitt v. Branham, 643 S.W.2d 122 (Tex.1982).

11. Central GMC, Inc. v. Helms, 303 Md. 266, 492 A.2d 1313 (1985) (garageman's lien discharged as against innocent purchaser when repairer relinquished vehicle, so that garagemen's subsequent sale of vehicle was a conversion).

12. See Lake Philgas Service v. Valley Bank & Trust Co., 845 P.2d 951 (Utah App.1993); Curtis v. Carey, 393 S.W.2d 185 (Tex.Civ.App.1965) (affirming judgment for wrongful levy and conversion); cf. Tunnell v. Hicks, 574 So.2d 264 (Fla.App.1991) (sheriff's unjustified seizure was a conversion). Not every seizure is actionable. Seizure under legal process may be privileged in some instances. When the sheriff executes upon property of the plaintiff rather than property of the judgment debtor, a statute may provide the exclusive remedy. See the remarkable tribulations of almost everyone in Elliott v. Denton & Denton, 109 Nev. 979, 860 P.2d 725 (1993). Where the sheriff seizes property of the debtor but the process is defective or invalid, conversion rules might defeat the policy of encouraging resort to courts. Some courts therefore hold that in such cases the plaintiff will be obliged to prove one of the malicious prosecution family of torts. See Crouter v. United Adjusters, 259 Or. 348, 485 P.2d 1208 (1971). Malicious prosecution and related torts, see § Chapter 30.

13. E.g., Wiley v. General Motors Acceptance Corp., 624 So.2d 518 (Ala.1993) (creditor who provided disability insurance to pay debt in case of debtor's disability and was thus fully protected by insurance it arranged was liable for conversion for repossession when debtor suffered disability and fell behind in payments); Security Pacific Housing Services, Inc. v. Friddle, 315 Ark. 178, 866 S.W.2d 375 (1993) (mobile home owner not shown to be in default); Jones v. Petty, 577 So.2d 821 (La.App. 1991); Entriken v. Motor Coach Federal Credit Union, 256 Mont. 85, 845 P.2d 93 (1992) (repossession when debt was covered in part by disability insurance payments was a conversion).

14. E.g., Klooster v. North Iowa State Bank, 404 N.W.2d 564 (Iowa 1987) (creditor's sale); Kearns v. McNeill Brothers Moving and Storage Company, 509 A.2d 1132 (D.C.App.1986) (warehouse's sale of bailed goods to pay storage costs).

15. See Boisdore v. International City Bank & Trust Co., 361 So.2d 925 (La.App. 1978) ("That it was difficult to distinguish those items under the chattel mortgage from those belonging to the plaintiff is no excuse for delay of an entire year in allowing plaintiff access to his property").

16. Ivy v. General Motors Acceptance Corp., 612 So.2d 1108 (Miss.1992); McCall v. Owens, 820 S.W.2d 748 (Tenn.App.1991).

trickery.[17]

So far as the creditor's interference results from a judicial proceeding, the plaintiff's grievance may not rest on conversion but on malicious prosecution or even on a civil rights tort instead.[18]

(2) Destruction, alteration, or damage

Intentional destruction, major alteration, or serious damage is often an extreme case of dispossession and it counts as a conversion.[19] For example, the defendant who throws away the plaintiff's possessions is exercising complete dominion over them and is liable for conversion.[20]

Destruction or serious damage may also amount to a conversion in a rather different way. If the defendant intermeddles with a chattel, without intent to cause harm to it but substantial harm or destruction nevertheless occurs, the defendant becomes a converter liable for the destruction.[21]

(3) Sale, disposal, transfer of possession

One step beyond this, the defendant's unauthorized transfer of an interest in the plaintiff's property is ordinarily a substantial exercise of dominion over that property and if so is a conversion.[22] For example, a jeweler who holds the plaintiff's rubies for appraisal is not a converter so long as he holds them, but he becomes one when he sells them. Even the jeweler's innocent employee, who believes the jewels to be part of the stock in trade, may be a converter if he negotiates a sale of the rubies and delivers possession of them.[23] Similarly, one who holds property pledged to secure payment of a debt is a converter of the pledge if he

UCC § 9–503 provides for repossession of collateral security if it "can be done without breach of the peace."

17. See Ford Motor Credit Co. v. Byrd, 351 So.2d 557 (Ala.1977) (possession by trickery, held conversion).

18. As to creditors' unconstitutional use of legal process see § 67 below; 1 Dan B. Dobbs, Law of Remedies § 5.17 (2) (2d ed. 1993); as to malicious prosecution see note 12 and Chapter 30.

19. Iemma v. Adventure RV Rentals, Inc., 632 N.E.2d 1178 (Ind.App.1994); Restatement § 226.

20. Bowler v. Joyner, 562 A.2d 1210 (D.C.1989).

21. Restatement § 228. In Gelder v. Puritan Ins. Co., 100 N.M. 240, 668 P.2d 1117 (Ct.App.1983) Kirchner leased an airplane from Gelder, promising that it would not be used in transporting controlled substances. The plane carried marijuana. After unloading over 300 pounds, the plane took off, was unable to remain airborne, and crashed. Since the use was unauthorized and resulted in serious damage, this was a conversion. In consequence, the insurer had no responsibility under its policy.

22. Northeast Bank of Lewiston and Auburn v. Murphy, 512 A.2d 344 (Me.1986) (insurer's release of check to attorney without protecting lien of a bank was exercise of dominion over it and a conversion); Rudnitski v. Seely, 452 N.W.2d 664 (Minn.1990); Hofland v. Elgin–Butler Brick Co., 834 S.W.2d 409 (Tex.App.1992) (defendant selling business sold the plaintiff's brick which was stored on the premises, seemingly without intent; held a conversion). But cf. Installment Finance Corp. v. Hudiburg Chevrolet, Inc., 794 P.2d 751 (Okla.1990) (official's innocent discharge of lien on automobile in reliance on forged release of lien was not a conversion of the lienor's interest, because this was not dominion; perhaps explicable on other grounds).

23. Restatement § 233 (1).

sells it in violation of any of the terms of the pledge or after the underlying debt has been paid.[24]

A transfer of possession without an actual sale and without gain to the defendant may still operate as a conversion. For example, a bailee of goods who rebails them to another warehouse in violation of his contract to hold them himself may be a converter, at least if the transfer leads to the loss of the goods.[25]

(4) Misdelivery

A warehouse or other bailee who holds the plaintiff's goods must deliver them only to the plaintiff or to persons the plaintiff designates. If the bailee misdelivers the goods to the wrong person, even by honest mistake, he is a converter and liable for the value of the goods.[26] For instance, the jeweler who does not sell the plaintiff's rubies but mistakenly delivers them to another customer is a converter.[27]

In a classic case,[28] the bailor instructed the bailee to return bailed goods by shipping them Railway Express. The bailee packed the goods and addressed them to the plaintiff, then gave them to a person dressed in an appropriate uniform and who represented that he was from the express agency. But the person was an imposter and the plaintiff never

24. "A pledge is a bailment for security. It is effected by delivery of possession of the pledged property, although title remains in the pledgor.... A pledgee owes a fiduciary duty of care to preserve and protect the pledged property, and may be liable for conversion if the pledge is wrongfully sold or transferred without authority." Hartford v. State Bar of California, 50 Cal.3d 1139, 791 P.2d 598, 270 Cal.Rptr. 12 (1990).

25. Fotos v. Firemen's Ins. Co. of Washington, D.C., 533 A.2d 1264, 76 A.L.R.4th 875 (D.C. 1987) (fur coat stored with the defendant was then stored by the defendant with a third person where it was stolen, seemingly without the defendant's fault; liability for conversion could be predicated upon a breach of the bailment contract if it provided for storage only by the defendant); Johnson v. Johnson, 849 P.2d 1361 (Alaska 1993) (city police seized funds in search under a warrant, then turned them over to federal authorities in violation of state laws on handling seized currency; held, city was subject to conversion claim); cf. MacGuire v. Elometa Corp., 189 A.D.2d 708, 592 N.Y.S.2d 730 (1993) (release of pledge to pledgor before underlying debt had been paid to the plaintiff).

26. S/M Industries, Inc. v. Hapag–Lloyd A.G., 586 So.2d 876 (Ala.1991) (cartons of furniture stored in a warehouse); Montano v. Land Title Guarantee Co., 778 P.2d 328 (Colo.App.1989) (deed prematurely turned over by title company); B & Y Heavy Movers, Inc. v. Fluor Constructors, Inc., 211 Ill.App.3d 975, 156 Ill.Dec. 301, 570 N.E.2d 777 (1991) (heavy equipment); cf. Shepherd Fleets, Inc. v. Opryland USA, Inc., 759 S.W.2d 914 (Tenn.App.1988) (damage to guest's car in hotel valet parking lot, implicit analogy to misdelivery cases).

In Johnson v. Johnson, 849 P.2d 1361 (Alaska 1993), city police officers seized drugs and cash in a search of plaintiff's home, then turned the cash over to federal Drug Enforcement Administration. This handling of the money violated state laws. The DEA retained the cash as forfeited funds. Thereafter, in the plaintiff's criminal case, the evidence was suppressed and the court ordered its return. The police officers, no longer holding the cash they had turned over to the DEA, were held subject to liability for conversion. In Turner v. Scobey Moving and Storage Co., 515 S.W.2d 253 (Tex.1974) someone forged an "authorization" from the plaintiff to receive her goods. The warehouse responded to the authorization in good faith and delivered the goods to the person presenting the forgery. It failed to require the non-negotiable warehouse receipt and was held liable to the plaintiff for a conversion.

27. Rensch v. Riddle's Diamonds of Rapid City, Inc., 393 N.W.2d 269 (S.D. 1986).

28. Baer v. Slater, 261 Mass. 153, 158 N.E. 328, 54 A.L.R. 1328 (1927).

got the goods. Although the bailee was both innocent and reasonable in delivering the goods to the apparent employee of the express company, he was held for conversion even though he was a gratuitous bailee and not one for hire.

(5) Nondelivery

When demand and refusal is required. Somewhat strangely, a bailee's non-delivery may be treated more leniently than misdelivery. A bailee who is under an obligation to return goods when a specific event occurs may be liable as a converter when the event occurs and he fails to return the goods, whether or not the plaintiff demands them.[29] But when the plaintiff bails goods for an indefinite time, the bailee is not a converter until the plaintiff has made a demand for their return, unless the bailee commits some affirmative act of dominion by asserting ownership, disposing of or damaging the goods. The rule requiring a demand has even been applied when the defendant is a third person who acquired the goods in good faith from the bailee and who asserts title to them.[30] The date of the demand or refusal may be significant in starting the statute of limitations clock running or in assessing damages.[31]

What counts as refusal. When a demand is required, the defendant becomes a converter only if he refuses to return the property after the demand is made or if he engages in conduct equivalent to a refusal.[32]

29. Albrecht v. Zwaanshoek Holding En Financiering, B.V., 816 P.2d 808 (Wyo. 1991) (pledgee of share certificates had duty to return them when debt secured by the pledge was satisfied, no demand necessary).

30. Lawrence v. Meloni, 163 A.D.2d 827, 558 N.Y.S.2d 360 (1990); Lowney v. Knott, 84 R.I. 425, 125 A.2d 98, 57 A.L.R.2d 1042 (1956) (the bailee borrowed a ring, then gave it to his fiance, the defendant; "Unless defendant also performed some distinct and positive act amounting to the exercise of dominion over the ring in a way that was necessarily in exclusion or defiance of plaintiff's right of ownership, there would be no conversion on her part until demand and refusal").

31. E.g., Kornegay v. Thompson, 157 Ga.App. 558, 278 S.E.2d 140 (1981) (plaintiff allegedly loaned a ring to defendant many years before suit, but demand was made within the statute of limitations period). Sometimes courts worry that the plaintiff could manipulate the statute of limitations or possibly pursue false claims by delaying a demand in the case of a gratuitous bailment for an indefinite time. This is not a problem if the bailee has converted by some affirmative act such as sale of the goods, since it is then the sale, not the withholding of possession that is the conversion, and no demand is necessary to trigger the plaintiff's claim. See, e.g., Elghanayan v. Victory, 192 A.D.2d 355, 596 N.Y.S.2d 35 (1993) (statute starts at conversion of time when it should have been or was discovered). In the absence of affirmative acts of conversion by the bailee, some courts have said that the plaintiff must make a demand within a reasonable time, else the plaintiff might sue for their return fifty years later. See Annotation, When statute of limitations starts to run against bailor's action for recovery, or for damages for conversion or detention, of property deposited for an indefinite time, 57 A.L.R.2d 1044 (1958). The rule that bases damages on the value of the goods at the time and place of conversion must also be accommodated when conversion is triggered by a demand and refusal. See § 65.

32. Put the other way around, "Where, however, there is no wrongful taking and the defendant rightfully comes into possession of the chattels, a demand by the rightful owner and a refusal by the alleged tortfeasor are necessary elements of the tort." Production Credit Assn. of Madison v. Nowatzski,90 Wis.2d 344, 280 N.W.2d 118 (1979) (closely paraphrasing Prosser, 4th ed. p. 89; Emerick v. Mutual Benefit Life Ins. Co.), 756 S.W.2d 513 (Mo.1988) (similar; defendant who came rightfully into possession of leasehold was not a converter of furniture on the premises in the absence of a demand).

"Refusal" is a shorthand expression in this context. Once the demand has been made, any conduct of the defendant that is inconsistent with the plaintiff's rights in the property counts as a refusal or its legal equivalent. Explicit verbal refusal is not required.

The defendant's unreasonable and serious delay in returning the property[33] or giving access[34] to it after a demand might be enough to make a jury question on this point. The defendant who continues to withhold the plaintiff's goods is a converter if he denies that goods belong to the plaintiff or that he himself holds them,[35] or refuses to respond to the plaintiff's repeated letters and telephone demands,[36] or if he demands payment of charges he has no legal right to.[37]

Qualified or limited refusal. On the other hand, a bailee may have a number of legitimate reasons for refusing to make an immediate return of the goods. Where the goods are not represented by a negotiable instrument, the defendant may refuse immediate delivery of the goods so that he can make reasonable efforts to ascertain the plaintiff's identity as the bailor[38] and where he is a stakeholder, he may refuse delivery until he can reasonably ascertain ownership or take other appropriate steps,[39] so long as the refusal is made in good faith and properly communicated to the plaintiff.[40] Although the bailee may not subject the return of the goods to conditions he has no right to impose,[41] he may assuredly condition their return upon presentation of appropriate receipts or payment of storage charges that are in fact due.[42]

Bailee's burden of proving his innocence. Once the plaintiff has made a demand upon the bailee and the bailee has refused to deliver up the goods, the picture becomes a little more complicated. Suitors who claim that a bailee has failed to return the bailed goods often assert both

33. Willis v. Midland Finance Co., 97 Ga.App. 443, 103 S.E.2d 185 (1958) (delay of "days"); see Schroeder v. Auto Driveaway Company, 11 Cal.3d 908, 523 P.2d 662, 114 Cal.Rptr. 622 (1974). Delay in delivery, if coupled with other circumstances, might conceivably count as some other tort, or as breach of a contract. See Hanke v. Global Van Lines, Inc., 533 F.2d 396 (8th Cir.1976) (repeated and outrageous delay by movers of household goods coupled with repeated assurance that delivery would be made soon might support emotional distress claim).

34. Russell–Vaughn Ford, Inc. v. Rouse, 281 Ala. 567, 206 So.2d 371 (1968) (plaintiff, looking at new cars at a dealer's, gave up keys to his car on a salesman's request; when he did not trade, the dealer's employees "couldn't find the keys" until the police were called; held a conversion of the car); cf. Clayton X–Ray Co. v. Professional Systems Corp., 812 S.W.2d 565 (Mo.App.1991) (seller of computer system, not fully paid, installed a program that would lock up the computer at a certain time; after the computer locked up the buyer sued for "conversion" and recovered punitive damages, but damages seem not to have been computed by the conversion rule).

35. Driver v. Hice, 618 So.2d 129 (Ala. Civ.App.1993).

36. McKinley v. Flaherty, 390 N.W.2d 30 (Minn.App.1986).

37. Car Transportation v. Garden Spot Distributors, 305 Ark. 82, 805 S.W.2d 632 (1991); Phillips v. Catania, 155 A.D.2d 866, 547 N.Y.S.2d 476 (1989).

38. Restatement § 239.

39. Paris American Corp. v. McCausland, 52 Wash.App. 434, 759 P.2d 1210 (1988).

40. Restatement § 241.

41. He cannot, for example, withhold the goods until the plaintiff pays charges someone owes. See note 37, supra.

42. Hofland v. Elgin–Butler Brick Co., 834 S.W.2d 409 (Tex.App.1992).

a breach of the bailment contract and a conversion.[43] The bailee's liability for failure to return the plaintiff's goods arises only if he is negligent. However, in most states[44] the bailee must prove that he is not negligent in failing to deliver the goods.[45] If he fails to prove his innocence, he is either presumptively negligent or has presumptively misdelivered the property and thus has either breached the bailment contract or is guilty of a conversion.

If the bailee is deemed guilty of a conversion, he loses the benefit of his contractual limitation on liability.[46] Some courts hold that he loses the limitation and becomes fully liable if he fails to sustain his burden of proving that he did not convert the goods,[47] although this stringent rule has been rejected in the case of common carriers regulated by statute.[48] The burden of proving your innocence when no one knows what happened is understandably a difficult one.[49]

(6) Use or interference short of dispossession

When the defendant uses the plaintiff's chattel or interferes with it but does not damage it or dispossess the plaintiff for any significant time, rules provide little assistance. If the use or interference is substantial enough, the court may find a conversion. If it is not, the court will reject a conversion approach[50] and the defendant will be liable at most for a trespass to chattels. In this setting the defendant's intent or bad

43. Contract, negligence, and conversion and theoretically separable bases of liability. Thus "a warehouse which fails to redeliver goods to the person entitled to their return upon a proper demand, may be liable for either negligence *or* conversion, depending upon the circumstances". I.C.C. Metals v. Municipal Warehouse Co., 50 N.Y.2d 657, 662, 409 N.E.2d 849, 852, 431 N.Y.S.2d 372, 376 (1980) (emphasis added). But these theories are often rolled up together. For example, in Fotos v. Firemen's Ins. Co. of Washington, D.C., 533 A.2d 1264, 1267, 76 A.L.R.4th 875 (D.C.App. 1987) the court said that breach of the bailment contract *is* a conversion.

44. The Uniform Commercial Code section covering the warehouseman's liability for nondelivery permits states to adopt an alternative which puts the burden on the plaintiff to show the negligence. More than a quarter of the states have adopted this alternative, of which some leading commentators express hearty disapproval. 2 James White & Robert Summers, Uniform Commercial Code § 31–3 (3d ed. 1988).

45. E.g., Kearns v. McNeill Brothers Moving and Storage Company, 509 A.2d 1132 (D.C.1986); D'Aloisio v. Morton's, Inc., 342 Mass. 231, 172 N.E.2d 819 (1961); Procter & Gamble Distributing Co. v. Lawrence American Field Warehousing Corp., 16 N.Y.2d 344, 213 N.E.2d 873, 266 N.Y.S.2d 785, 21 A.L.R.3d 1320 (1965).

46. Lipman v. Petersen, 223 Kan. 483, 575 P.2d 19 (1978) (holding that under UCC § 7–204 (2), which strikes the limited liability provision of a contract when the bailee converts goods to his own use, a technical conversion is a conversion to the bailee's own use so as to allow a full recovery).

47. I.C.C. Metals v. Municipal Warehouse Co., 50 N.Y.2d 657, 409 N.E.2d 849, 431 N.Y.S.2d 372 (1980). For cases going both ways on this, see 2 James White & Robert Summers, Uniform Commercial Code § 21–3, pp. 145–146 (3d ed. 1988).

48. Art Masters Associates, Ltd. v. United Parcel Service, 77 N.Y.2d 200, 567 N.E.2d 226, 566 N.Y.S.2d 184 (1990).

49. See, e.g., I.C.C. Metals v. Municipal Warehouse Co., 50 N.Y.2d 657, 665, 409 N.E.2d 849, 854, 431 N.Y.S.2d 372, 377 (note 3) (1980) (detailing unsuccessful efforts of the warehouse to prove that goods were stolen without its fault).

50. Johnson v. Weedman, 5 Ill. 495 (1843); Fouldes v. Willoughby, 8 M. & W. 540, 151 Eng. Rep. 1143 (1841).

faith becomes important,[51] along with the duration of the interference. The defendant who uses your desk to write a letter is probably not a converter even if you have told him not to do so; if he uses it for months and claims ownership, he probably is.[52]

As already indicated, even a minor trespass may warrant liability for conversion if, in the course of the trespass, substantial though unintended harm results to the chattel.[53] This rule is a manifestation of the extended liability rule seen in other intentional torts such as trespass to land and battery.[54]

(7) Acquiring possession, ownership, or security interests

General rule. Subject to the special rule for agents stated below, one who acquires possession of a chattel often exercises substantial dominion over the chattel merely by acquiring possession, title or a claim to title, or a security interest in it.[55]

All acquisitions are not conversions, of course; one who acquires possession with appropriate consent of the owner is not a converter, nor is one who acquires transient possession that does not interfere substantially with the plaintiff's rights in the chattel.

On the other hand, the plaintiff who purchases a chattel is surely asserting ownership and the right of dominion, and if this is inconsistent with the rights of the plaintiff, then it is a conversion. In particular, the good faith purchaser from a thief is a converter even though he purchases in utter good faith.[56]

Agent receiving goods innocently. A thief steals your computer, then has it stored in the ABCo. Warehouse, which knew nothing of the theft. The thief has converted your computer and is liable to you. If recovery against the thief is not possible, can you recover for conversion against the ABCo. Warehouse? The answer is no. The warehouse can be viewed as an agent or bailee of the thief. An agent or bailee who receives goods for storage, safekeeping, or transport is not a converter merely because he acquires possession.[57] The rule is supported by policy; it is commercially convenient to permit storage and transport. It is also supported by

51. See Veeco Instruments, Inc. v. Candido, 70 Misc.2d 333, 334 N.Y.S.2d 321, 324 (Sup.Ct. 1972) ("a conscious and determined act"); Restatement § 222A (2) (b) & (c).

52. Restatement § 227, Ills. 1–4. Illustration 2 indicates that use of the desk daily for six months would be a conversion even without harm or a claim of ownership. That seems extreme. The illustration was based on Miller v. Uhl, 37 Ohio App. 276, 174 N.E. 591 (1929), where the defendant was a bailee of a bus for storage. Instead of storing it, he used it to carry passengers for a period of five weeks and put 2,000 miles on it. This was a conversion but it is not much like writing letters at a desk.

53. See note 21, supra.

54. See §§ 40 & 58.

55. For example, if a bank knowingly accepts the pledge of a trust's securities to secure the individual obligation of a trustee. Maloney v. Stone, 195 A.D.2d 1065, 601 N.Y.S.2d 731 (1993). Or accepts stock as collateral for a loan to T that was pledged by the plaintiff solely to secure a different loan to T. Ocean National Bank of Kennebunk v. Diment, 462 A.2d 35 (Me.1983).

56. See § 66.

57. Restatement § 230.

the fact that a bailment by itself seldom puts the goods beyond the owner's reach, so that there is relatively little to be gained by imposing liability upon the innocent bailee.

The protective rule for agents and bailees does not extend to those who accept the goods when they knew or had reason to know of the plaintiff's rights. Nor to those who take an active role in negotiating for their principals a transfer or sale[58] on the one hand or a purchase or receipt of the goods on the other.[59]

§ 66. The Bona Fide Purchaser of Converted Goods

Tangible Goods

Three rules. Innocent purchasers of tangible converted goods—bona fide purchasers as they are usually called—are sometimes themselves treated as converters in spite of their innocence. At other times they are protected from liability. Depending upon the setting, one of three different rules is invoked to determine whether a bona fide purchaser is liable for conversion.

(1) The first rule applies when an innocent purchaser buys from a thief-converter; the purchaser is fully liable for conversion.

(2) The second rule applies when the innocent purchaser buys from someone who obtained voidable title to the goods by fraud or other misdoings; the innocent purchaser is not liable for conversion under this rule; his title is good and he retains the chattel without liability.

(3) The third rule is a statutory provision of the Uniform Commercial code that protects innocent purchasers who buy goods from merchants who deal in such goods, even though the merchant has wrongfully sold goods entrusted to him by another customer.

(1) Traditional rule of liability. Under the traditional common law rule, one who purchases converted goods is himself a converter by the very act of purchase. The purchaser may be wholly innocent, he may pay value for the goods, he may act in good faith. He is nevertheless a converter.[1] If he is held liable to the owner, the innocent purchaser has a

58. Ensminger v. Burton, 805 S.W.2d 207 (Mo.App.1991); Restatement § 233.

59. Restatement § 231.

§ 66

1. Kahn v. Quintana, 811 P.2d 458 (Colo.App.1991) (good faith buyer of silverware from thief who stole it from the plaintiffs is liable for common law conversion); Inmi–Etti v. Aluisi, 63 Md.App. 293, 492 A.2d 917 (1985) (Butler obtained certificate of title to the plaintiff's car by submitting a false affidavit to the motor vehicle administration, then sold the car to defendant; held, the defendant is liable for conversion since the title was void); O'Keeffe v. Snyder, 83 N.J. 478, 416 A.2d 862 (1980) (three Georgia O'Keeffe paintings, owned by her, allegedly stolen in 1946; defendant bought them in good faith in 1975 for $35,000, and would be liable for conversion unless the statute of limitations had run; new purchases such as defendant's do not start the statute of limitations running anew); Nat Koslow, Inc. v. Bletterman, 23 Misc.2d 340, 197 N.Y.S.2d 583 (Sup.Ct. 1960). In England there is an exception for goods purchased in the market overt, which is at a location specified in various town charters or by ancient custom, or in London any public sales by dealers in goods of the particular kinds. See Ray Brown, Law of Personal Property § 9.4 (3d ed. Walter Rauschenbush 1975).

claim against the person who sold him the goods, but this claim is seldom of any value to the innocent purchaser, who is usually sued only because the converter cannot be found or has no funds.

Rationale. The innocent purchaser rule is usually derived by reasoning in this way: a thief who converts goods does not get title to the goods by converting them. Title to the goods thus remains in the original owner even after the conversion. Since the thief-converter has no title, he cannot pass title to a purchaser, and this is true whether the purchaser is innocent or not. The rationale stands on two well-accepted rules about conversion: first, intent to deal with the goods is enough and bad faith is not required; and second, a purchase of goods is sufficient exercise of dominion or control to count as a conversion.

The rationale is formalistic in the sense that it does not turn on either an assessment of policy or justice. On the policy scale one might consider the value of commercial certainty and whether the innocent victim or the innocent buyer can most efficiently protect against the thief's machinations. Although the common law rule is not built upon a rationale of policy, it might conceivably help minimize certain kinds of systematic theft. Some important civil law countries protect the bona fide purchaser rather than the original owner.[2] In the case of art theft, the civil law rule might conceivably abet art laundering operations. The thief can sell to a bona fide purchaser in, say, Italy, then directly or indirectly repurchase it himself, acquiring good title in that country that he can then pass on to a buyer in any other country.[3] In any event, the purchaser in Italy need not be hesitant about making the purchase.

(2) Traditional rule of non-liability: the bona fide purchaser from one who has voidable title. Conversion is only one of the methods by which a wrongdoer can separate victims from their property. Some others include fraud and duress. If the wrongdoer does not steal the plaintiff's property but instead uses fraudulent representations to induce the plaintiff to give it to him, the wrongdoer acquires a voidable title. When the plaintiff discovers the fraud, she might decide to leave the property with the defendant and to recover damages. Or she might decide to avoid the transfer because it was tainted with fraud. This right to avoid the fraudulent deal and get the property back is usually thought of as an equitable right or an "equity."

2. See Winkworth v. Christie, Manson & Wood, Ltd., [1980] 1 Ch. 496, [1980] 1 All E.R. 1121 (1979). In *Winkworth*, Japanese works of art were stolen from the plaintiff in England. They were taken to Italy where they eventually passed to D'Annone, who bought them as a bona fide purchaser and who, under Italian law, would have good title so long as he was not aware of the theft and there was no irregularity in the sale. D'Annone at some later time delivered the goods to Christies for sale by auction in England. The English Court held that Italian law applied and that, barring development of different facts, D'Annone would not be liable.

3. See Grover, Note, The Need for Civil–Law Nations to Adopt Discovery Rules in Art Replevin Actions: A Comparative Study, 70 TEX. L. REV. 1431 (1992) (detailing the process of laundering and suggesting that the original owner should be given a limited time for full recovery from the bona fide purchaser).

The victim who loses her property because of a wrongdoer's fraud may pursue either the damages remedy or the avoidance remedy, but unless and until she avoids the transaction, the wrongdoer still has title. He is therefore not in the same position as the ordinary converter. Since he has title, he can pass that title to a bona fide purchaser who pays value for the goods and who has no notice of the wrongdoing.[4] The bona fide purchaser who takes title from the wrongdoer is thus not a converter and not liable to the victim. In the traditional view, a bona fide purchase "cuts off equities" like the owner's right to avoid the fraudulent deal,[5] even though it does not cut off rights based on legal title.

Some difficulties with innocent purchaser liability. The two rules operate together to impose liability upon some innocent purchasers and not upon others. The difference between those who are liable and those who are not does not lie in their own merit or in their claim to fairness, but in the logic of title. The rationale for the liability of innocent purchasers also ignores commercial needs. In many instances, it may be desirable to encourage the movement of goods in commerce. People who buy a watch at the mall should not be at risk for liability if it turns out that the jewelry store had purchased a stolen item. Nor would it be desirable for people to expend time and money checking on the store's title. Either result would slow economic activity and add to the costs of getting goods.

(3) The Uniform Commercial Code rule. The Uniform Commercial Code, adopted in almost all states, adds a third rule about innocent purchasers that partly addresses the criticisms above. It provides that if I entrust my goods to a "merchant who deals in goods of that kind," then the merchant has a "power" to transfer all the title I had.[6]

For example, I leave my bicycle at a shop that sells bikes, solely for the purpose of repair. The owner repairs my bike, then sells it to you. You do not know that the bike is mine, so you are a bona fide purchaser. Under the traditional rule you would still be liable as a converter because the shop owner did not have any title to pass to you. Under the UCC provision, however, the owner had power to pass you all the title I had in the bike.[7] So you own the bike and you are therefore not a converter. The shop owner definitely is a converter, however; he had a *power* to pass title in a way that protects you as the purchaser; but he had no title himself and no *right* to pass title. The Code provision

4. This common law rule is now included in the Uniform Commercial Code, § 2–403 (1). See Jernigan v. Ham, 691 S.W.2d 553 (Tenn.App.1984). If title is obtained other than by the owner's voluntary transfer, however, the title is void, not merely voidable. See Inmi–Etti v. Aluisi, 63 Md. App. 293, 492 A.2d 917 (1985).

5. Western Idaho Production Credit Ass'n v. Simplot Feed Lots, Inc., 106 Idaho 260, 678 P.2d 52 (1984).

6. UCC § 2–403 (2).

7. See, e.g., Perez–Medina v. First Team Auction, Inc., 206 Ga.App. 719, 426 S.E.2d 397 (1992) (the entrusting provision does not apply unless the owner should objectively recognize that the person with whom goods are left is a merchant dealing in goods of that kind; but he should have so recognized here and the merchant's buyer took good title).

protects the bona fide purchaser from the merchant, not the thieving merchant himself.

Money and Intangibles

Rule for money. Money and negotiable instruments such as checks are treated differently from tangible chattels. Although conversion did not traditionally lie for taking paper money, the plaintiff had an action of some kind[8] and today the action may well be called one for conversion. Whatever the action is called, special rules apply to protect innocent persons to whom the stolen money is paid. The rule is that the person who innocently accepts money from a thief or embezzler is not a converter at all and not liable to the original owner.[9]

Example and rationale. An example makes it clear why the rule is all but inevitable. Suppose a thief steals the plaintiff's money, then buys a loaf of bread from the baker. The baker has no knowledge of the money's provenance. If money were treated like a tangible chattel, the baker would be liable to the plaintiff who could make appropriate proof of the facts. But if the baker were liable, he would want to make inquiries about the source of monies offered him by customers, or perhaps he would only sell to customers known to him, or to those who could put up collateral security. Perhaps instead he would raise all prices to cover the costs of potential liability. In any event, trade would be slower or goods would be more costly; some customers might find it difficult to buy goods at all. The legal policy is to avoid the unimaginable inconvenience, commercial lethargy, higher costs, and perhaps discrimination that would result if the baker could not accept currency without inquiry into their source. Hence the rule protects those who receive money innocently, even if the money was in fact stolen from the plaintiff.

Negotiable instruments. The policy to permit free passage of money in trade applies as well to negotiable instruments like checks and negotiable promissory notes.[10] In *Hinkle v. Cornwell Quality Tool Co.*[11] Zelnar embezzled $57,000 from Hinkle. When discovered, she agreed repay Hinkle. She embezzled sufficient sums from Cornwell, deposited them in her bank account, and then wrote checks to Hinkle for $57,000. Hinkle cashed the checks and was thus fully repaid. At that point

8. Assumpsit or a debt claim would suffice. Constructive trusts could be applied when the owner could trace the actual funds. See 1 Dan B. Dobbs, Law of Remedies §§ 4.3 (2), 6.1 (2d ed. 1993).

9. Kelley Kar Company v. Maryland Casualty Co., 142 Cal.App.2d 263, 298 P.2d 590, 62 A.L.R.2d 533 (1956); Hinkle v. Cornwell Quality Tool Co., 40 Ohio App.3d 162, 532 N.E.2d 772 (1987); City of Portland v. Berry, 86 Or.App. 376, 739 P.2d 1041 (1987). If the plaintiff attempts to proceed on a constructive trust theory instead, she must trace the funds precisely, and if if she can do so, she will be defeated by the rule that a constructive trust claim is an "equity" that is always cut off by a bona fide purchase for value or its equivalent.

10. See Federal Ins. Co. I.C. v. Banco de Ponce, 751 F.2d 38 (1st Cir.1984); Hinkle v. Cornwell Quality Tool Co., 40 Ohio App.3d 162, 532 N.E.2d 772 (1987); City of Portland v. Berry, 86 Or.App. 376, 739 P.2d 1041 (1987).

11. Hinkle v. Cornwell Quality Tool Co., 40 Ohio App.3d 162, 532 N.E.2d 772 (1987).

Cornwell discovered that Hinkle had been paid with funds embezzled from Cornwell. Cornwell sued Hinkle. The court refused to permit Cornwell to recover.

Other and more complex doctrines may explain cases like *Hinkle*[12] and in any event special rules and terminology of negotiable instrument law are codified in the Uniform Commercial Code.[13] However, the underlying policy is essentially the same as the policy towards money with the result that those who are holders in due course of negotiable instruments are protected in much the same way as those who innocently accept money from a thief.

§ 67. Remedies for Conversion

Damages

*General rule.*The normal remedy for conversion is an award of damages. The traditional measure of damages is the value of the chattel at the time and place of conversion, subject to limitations on liability the parties have validly contracted for,[1] plus interest from the time of conversion.[2] In three different settings the recovery may be measured differently.

(1) Recovery of trespass damages instead. The plaintiff may treat the conversion as a trespass to chattels and sue for her actual damages rather than for the value of the chattel.[3]

(2) Recovery of defendant's gain. The plaintiff may "waive the tort and sue in assumpsit," meaning that the plaintiff can have a restitutionary recovery for the gains the defendant made by converting the chattel. For example, if the chattel was worth $10 when it was converted by the defendant, and he later sells it for $20, the plaintiff would choose this option.[4]

12. See 1 DAN B. DOBBS, LAW OF REMEDIES §§ 4.7 (1) & 4.7 (2) (2d ed. 1993) (bona fide purchases and discharge for value rules).

13. See 1 JAMES WHITE & ROBERT SUMMERS, UNIFORM COMMERCIAL CODE 621 ff (3d ed. 1988).

§ 67

1. A bailee may validly contract to limit liability for damage or nondelivery of the goods, at least if the bailee provides an opportunity to the bailor to contract for increased liability at an increased storage charge.UCC § 7–204. However, some courts hold that this rule cannot be invoked to limit the bailee's liability in the case of an actual conversion, as distinct from a loss, or in a case in which the bailee cannot prove what happened to the nondelivered goods. I.C.C. Metals v. Municipal Warehouse Co., 50 N.Y.2d 657, 409 N.E.2d 849, 431 N.Y.S.2d 372 (1980).

2. E.g., Florida Farm Bureau Casualty Ins. Co. v. Patterson, 611 So.2d 558 (Fla. App.1992). The traditional rule held that in cases of conversion or destruction of a chattel, the plaintiff could recover interest on its value but not rental value for loss of its use. Rental value recoveries are, however, sometimes appropriate, especially if the plaintiff is reasonable in not immediately replacing the converted chattel and does in fact rent a reasonable substitute. When rental value is awarded, no interest should be awarded for the same time period. See 1 DAN B. DOBBS, LAW OF REMEDIES § 5.15 (2) (2d ed. 1993).

3. Vines v. Branch, 244 Va. 185, 418 S.E.2d 890 (1992).

4. The rule, its peculiar terminology, and its practical effects are explained in 1 DAN B. DOBBS, LAW OF REMEDIES § 5.18 (2d ed. 1993).

(3) Recovery of a later price increase. When the value of the converted goods tends to fluctuate, as with commodities and with shares of corporate stock, some states permit the plaintiff to recover the value of the chattel at some time after conversion. For instance, if the plaintiff's wheat is worth $1 per bushel in November when it is converted, but the plaintiff only discovers the conversion the following May when wheat is selling for $2 a bushel, it seems obviously wrong to limit the plaintiff to the $1; had the wheat not been converted the plaintiff could have sold it at the $2 price. Even if the plaintiff discovers the conversion immediately, the price may rise before she can effectuate a replacement, so a recovery of the value of the wheat at the time of conversion would not fully compensate.

Some states cope with this problem by allowing the plaintiff the highest price or market value of the goods between conversion and the time of trial,[5] but this may permit the plaintiff to speculate at the defendant's expense by delaying trial. New York uses a slightly different rule: the highest value of the goods between the time of conversion and a reasonable time for replacing them.[6] This rule seems to offer the better chance for compensation without speculation.[7]

When the goods are bailed and lost, it may be that neither the bailor nor the bailee knows the date of conversion. Courts can use the demand and refusal rules to fix the date of conversion and hence the date for calculating damages, but this technique is artificial and misses both the policy and the justice concerns. Suppose you bail goods worth $100 at the time of bailment and you demand their return one year later when their market price has dropped to $50. At that time the bailee discovers their loss and hence refuses a return. If the date of the demand and refusal is the date of the conversion you would recover only $50. This may in fact account for your loss because you can apparently replace the goods at that price at the time you want them. However, it may fail to account for the bailee's possible gain. We cannot be sure that the bailee is innocent (that is one of the reasons why we impose liability). If the bailee took the goods early in the bailment period, he may have received the full $100 value. In this situation, the New York Court has said that the measurement rule must give the plaintiff the highest value from the time of

5. E.g., Brown v. Campbell, 536 So.2d 920 (Ala.1988). Variations include "time of time," "time of verdict," and "time of filing suit."

6. E.g., Newburger Cotton Co. v. Stevens, 167 Ark. 257, 267 S.W. 777, 40 A.L.R. 1279 (1925); Mayer v. Monzo, 221 N.Y. 442, 117 N.E. 948 (1917); Ahles v. Aztec Enterprises, Inc., 120 A.D.2d 903, 502 N.Y.S.2d 821 (1986).

7. See 1 Dan B. Dobbs, Law of Remedies § 5.13 (2). This rule may not be satisfactory when the property is not replaceable. When prices are extremely volatile, a further refinement might be thought desirable. Suppose the date of conversion is November 1, and the market price at that time is $1, but that the price in December rises to $3. The following May the plaintiff discovers the conversion, at which time the price is $2. The plaintiff can reasonably be expected to sue within one week. During that week, the price rises to $2.25. A literal reading of the rule stated in the text would give the plaintiff $3, even though the $3 price was never known to the plaintiff and he did not lose that price. So some thinkers might prefer the highest price from the date of *discovery* to a reasonable time thereafter.

bailment, not merely the highest value from time of conversion or its discovery.[8]

Consequential damages. Under the traditional rule and also under the rule for fluctuating markets, the plaintiff recovers the market value of the chattel at some relevant date. Such a recovery measures loss to the plaintiff by the capital value of the chattel as an asset. But it is also possible that the plaintiff has additional losses often called special or consequential damages. For example, the plaintiff may be required to expend monies in trying to find the chattel or in providing a substitute.[9] In general, the plaintiff may recover reasonably proven consequential damages that could not have been reasonably avoided. However, courts usually do not permit a recovery for emotional distress resulting solely from the conversion of a chattel.[10] When the chattel is not an item of value in the market place courts offer a wooley rule that gives the jury a little leeway but not too much: the plaintiff can recover the value to the owner herself but not anything for sentimental attachment.[11]

Punitive damages. Although the rules for allowing punitive damages may be expressed in many ways, the general principle is that punitive damages are permissible only when the defendant has engaged in serious misconduct coupled with a reckless or malicious state of mind.[12] Some conversion cases fall into this category and permit the award of punitive damages.[13]

Nominal damages. Courts have said that nominal damages, such as $1 or six cents, may be recovered in conversion actions where there are no provable actual damages.[14]

Return of the chattel. Suppose the defendant converts the plaintiff's chattels so that an action lies, but that the defendant has returned the chattels before the plaintiff brought suit. The rational thing to say is that if the plaintiff has accepted the return of the chattels he has no action for conversion, only an action for trespass. That would yield the plaintiff's actual damages. But it has long been said that the plaintiff can

8. Procter & Gamble Distributing Co. v. Lawrence American Field Warehousing Corp., 16 N.Y.2d 344, 213 N.E.2d 873, 266 N.Y.S.2d 785 (1965).

9. E.g., Veeco Instruments, Inc. v. Candido, 70 Misc.2d 333, 334 N.Y.S.2d 321, 324 (Sup. Ct. 1972) (computer program materials converted, plaintiff recovered costs of reprogramming). The cost of renting a substitute is often not compensable. See n. 2, supra.

10. Lance Productions, Inc. v. Commerce Union Bank, 764 S.W.2d 207 (Tenn. App.1988) (in the absence of malicious acts by the defendant, no emotional distress damages in conversion).

11. 1 Dan B. Dobbs, Law of Remedies § 5.15 (3), 5.16 (3) (2d ed. 1993).

12. 1 Dan B. Dobbs, Law of Remedies § 3.11 (2) (2d ed. 1993).

13. See, e.g., Schroeder v. Auto Driveaway Company, 11 Cal.3d 908, 523 P.2d 662, 114 Cal.Rptr. 622 (1974) (conversion coupled with fraud, jury "could reasonably infer that defendants acted in callous disregard of plaintiffs' rights, knowing that their conduct was substantially certain to vex, annoy, and injure plaintiffs", punitive damages affirmed); Veeco Instruments, Inc. v. Candido, 70 Misc.2d 333, 334 N.Y.S.2d 321 (Sup.Ct. 1972) (conscious, deliberate conversion); Zimprich v. North Dakota Harvestore Systems, Inc. 461 N.W.2d 425 (N.D. 1990) (creditor repossessing after agreement to postpone repossession).

14. MacGuire v. Elometa Corp., 189 A.D.2d 708, 592 N.Y.S.2d 730 (1993).

recover full value of the goods, subject to a credit to the defendant for their return.[15] This way of looking at the damages leads courts to call the claim one of conversion. But since the damages are not like conversion damages, it might be better to say that the claim is one for trespass to chattels if a credit is given for return of the goods. The suggestion that the plaintiff might be *required* to take the chattel back to minimize her damages seems to be totally inconsistent with the whole point of the conversion claim,[16] that the plaintiff has a right to force the defendant to pay for what he took, that is, to regard the tort as a sale rather than as a merely trespass.

Recovery of the Chattel: Replevin

If the plaintiff can identify the specific chattel converted by the defendant, the plaintiff usually has the option to recover the chattel itself, together with any harms or losses resulting from its taking. Common law actions to recover the chattel[17] gave way in the United States to statutory actions often called replevin actions after one of their common law predecessors. Particular jurisdictions sometimes use other terminology.

In the traditional statutory replevin action, the sheriff seized the disputed property. If the plaintiff had posted a bond or other security, the sheriff could turn the property over to the plaintiff before trial. The plaintiff's bond guaranteed a return of the property or payment for it if it turned out on trial that the plaintiff was not entitled to it after all.

Pre-trial seizure of the property is known as a provisional remedy. It obviously runs serious risks of error and abuse. In a series of cases, the Supreme Court of the United States has held that some kind of hearing ordinarily[18] must be held before a pre-trial seizure will be constitutional.[19] In response to these decisions, some jurisdictions have modified their statutes to require a brief adversary hearing before the property is seized. In some instances, the statute now authorizes a more straightforward procedure under which the judge, like the old equity judge, orders

15. See Ames, The History of Trover, 11 Harv. L. Rev. 277, 185 (1897)

16. Lance Productions, Inc. v. Commerce Union Bank, 764 S.W.2d 207 (Tenn. App.1988)

17. The common law rights to recover the chattel grew out of the writs of *Detinue* and *Replevin* each circumscribed in particular ways. See 1 Dan B. Dobbs, Law of Remedies § 4.2 (2) (2d ed. 1993).

18. Mitchell v. W. T. Grant Co., 416 U.S. 600, 94 S.Ct. 1895, 40 L.Ed.2d 406 (1974) took a more lenient view where a lienholder sequestered property without notice, but where there was judicial supervision and a factual rather than a conclusory affidavit.

19. Sniadach v. Family Finance Corp. of Bay View, 395 U.S. 337, 89 S.Ct. 1820, 23 L.Ed.2d 349 (1969) (garnishment of wages without notice or hearing violates due process); Fuentes v. Shevin, 407 U.S. 67, 92 S.Ct. 1983, 32 L.Ed.2d 556 (1972) (provisional relief under replevin statutes without a hearing before seizure violates due process); North Georgia Finishing, Inc. v. Di–Chem, Inc., 419 U.S. 601, 95 S.Ct. 719, 42 L.Ed.2d 751 (1975) (garnishment of corporate bank account without hearing, with no provision for early hearing after garnishment violates due process). See also Connecticut v. Doehr, 501 U.S. 1, 111 S.Ct. 2105, 115 L.Ed.2d 1 (1991) (pre-trial, ex parte attachment statute unconstitutional for want of notice and opportunity to be heard before the attachment, where the plaintiff could attach property in which it had no pre-existing interest).

the defendant to deliver the property to the plaintiff or to deposit it in court.

CHAPTER 5

DEFENSES TO DIRECT AND INTENTIONAL INTERFERENCE WITH PERSON OR PROPERTY

TOPIC A. GENERAL PRINCIPLES

§ 68. Privileges and Defenses Defeating a Claim

Privileges defeat claims. Courts recognize many privileges or justifications that can be invoked by a defendant to defeat a claim that would otherwise be actionable. Many privileges are well-established; many are called by commonly used names. But there is no closed master list of privileges any more than there is a closed list of claims. Courts can and do recognize new privileges or modify old ones as required by the changes in social conditions or by the facts of individual cases and they do not necessarily append a name to the privilege in the process.[1]

Scope. Defenses, privileges, and immunities permeate tort law; they are not limited to trespassory torts. This chapter considers justifications that furnish the defendant a legal privilege to commit acts that would, except for the justification, count as a trespassory tort such as battery or trespass to land. It deals with justifications for the defendant's conduct, not with defenses like the statute of limitations that are based on policy, defenses like contributory negligence that are based on the plaintiff's own misconduct, or defenses like governmental immunity based on the defendant's status.

Examples of privileges covered. Common examples include the defendant's privilege of self-defense and defense of property. The plaintiff's consent to the defendant's conduct may count as a justification or else may show that the conduct is not tortious at all. Other justifications include the privilege of some non-judicial authorities to impose discipline by acts that would be tortious among strangers, and the limited justification to cause harm to save life or property in cases of overwhelming necessity.

The significance of affirmative defenses. The term "defenses" usually refers to affirmative defenses, meaning those on which the defendant has the burden of proof and the burden of persuasion. This burden means that the defendant must produce appropriate evidence on his

§ 68

1. See, e.g., Peterson v. Sorlien, 299 N.W.2d 123, 11 A.L.R.4th 208 (1980) (recognizing an unique privilege on the part of parents to detain an adult child under certain circumstances).

defense and must also persuade the jury to believe it. The jury's doubts about facts necessary to show the plaintiff's prima facie case work against the plaintiff; the jury's doubts about the facts necessary to the defendant's defense work against the defendant.

Liability for exceeding the privilege. The issue of privilege as an affirmative defense arises only when the plaintiff has made a prima facie case showing that the defendant committed a tort. The privilege, if proven, then defeats the plaintiff's claim. But if the privilege does not apply, the defendant is liable for the tort. Similarly, if the defendant exceeds the privilege he is liable for harms caused by his unprivileged acts. The defendant would be liable, for instance, for harms caused by using more force than reasonably necessary to defend himself or his property.

Liability limits that are not privileges. Sometimes the word privilege is used loosely and may refer to liability-defeating rules that are not *affirmative* defenses at all. To show a battery the plaintiff must show that the defendant touched her in a way that was harmful or offensive; and, ordinarily at least, such a showing entails an implicit claim that she did not consent to the touching. So the burden in such a case is on the plaintiff to show non-consent rather than upon the defendant to show that consent was affirmatively given. Although consent is not an affirmative defense in such a case, it is routinely called a privilege.[2] In spite of this anomaly, consent is considered in this chapter.

How rights differ from privileges. Finally, privileges differ from rights. A privilege exempts a potential defendant from liability to another. A right gives a potential plaintiff a claim enforceable against another. It is incorrect to say that you have a right of self-defense because you cannot go to court to enforce such a right. But it is correct to say that you have a privilege of self-defense under appropriate conditions. To say you have a privilege of self-defense is only to say you will not be held liable for defending yourself.

But while privilege and right are different, they often go hand in hand. If you have a privilege to enter my land to recover your boat washed up on my beach, you probably can sue if I do not permit your entry. If so, you have a right as well as a privilege.

§ 69. Justification and Excuse: Mistake and Disability

In most instances, tort law recognizes justifications for conduct that otherwise would be tortious, but recognizes only limited excuses.

Justification. When a judge believes the defendant's harmful act was justified, the judge believes that people in general can rightly act as the defendant did. For instance, reasonable acts in self-defense may cause harm, but the judge who sanctions self-defense as a justification believes that, even so, people in general can rightly act as the defendant did under the circumstances that confronted him. Justifications tend to

2. See 1 Harper, James & Gray, Law of Torts § 3.10 (1986 & Supps.).

invoke objective standards of reasonableness to modify the flat rules of trespassory torts.

Excuse. Excuses differ from justifications. They do not assert that the defendant's act was rightful and that others should act in the same way. They rather assert that the defendant's conduct was understandable given his personal condition and that he is not personally blameworthy for matters not within his control. Excuses focus on subjective mental or psychological characteristics of the actor; they include mental disability, infancy, and mistake. In general, excuses do not furnish defenses to intentional tort claims,[1] but justifications do. This reinforces the idea that the tort systems tends to work with objective, not subjective standards of liability.

Mistake

Although other privileges may provide a defense to the defendant, mistake, infancy, and mental disability are not themselves separate defenses. In many cases torts are committed by one who acts under a mistake of fact or mistake of law or legal rights. For example, the defendant who mistakenly believes that he is entering his own land when in fact he is entering land that belongs to the plaintiff is a trespasser.[2] That is to say, mistake is no defense to the trespass claim. The same rule applies with conversion of chattels.[3] Similarly, the defendant's mistaken belief that the plaintiff is a criminal does not give the defendant a privilege to effect an arrest[4] or commit a battery.

Several specific privileges protect the defendant who acts as a reasonable person under the circumstances. If one of these privileges applies, and if the defendant acts under a mistake that a reasonable person would make, then mistake is at least relevant in determining whether the defendant acted as a reasonable person.[5] Self defense is an example of a privilege to act as a reasonable person under the circumstances. If the plaintiff appears to menace the defendant with guns and knives, the defendant is privileged to respond with a reasonable amount of force in self defense. In a sense the defendant may be mistaken, but it is not his subjective mistake that relieves him of liability; it is the objective reasonableness of his conduct.

§ 69

1. Personal disabilities are important in tort law, but not always because they are defenses. For instance, the plaintiff's infancy or mental disability or ignorance-mistake is very likely to "excuse" delay in bringing suit. In addition, if the defendant knows of the plaintiff's disability, the defendant will be expected to adjust his conduct accordingly. For example, the defendant could not take advantage of the professed consent of a mentally disabled person or a small child. See § 98.

2. Restatement § 164; See § 51, supra.

3. P.F. Jurgs & Co. v. O'Brien, 160 Vt. 294, 629 A.2d 325 (Vt. 1993); see § 62, supra.

4. See National Food Stores, Inc. v. Utley, 303 F.2d 284 (8th Cir.1962) (honest mistaken identity, liability for arrest of wrong person although arrest of right person would have been justified).

5. See W.V.H. Rogers, Winfield & Jolowicz on Tort 745 (14th ed. 1994). Examples include mistakes in self-defense § 72, and defense of property, § 76 below. The rule that protects a defendant who acts upon reasonable appearances necessarily means that a reasonable mistake about the underlying reality is tolerated. See § 96.

Mistake as negating required intent. The defendant's mistake may also be relevant in determining whether the defendant had the intent required to show a tort. For instance, the defendant who honestly but mistakenly identifies the plaintiff as the person who committed a crime is not guilty of an intentional infliction of mental distress. To say that the defendant was honestly mistaken in such a case is to say that the defendant lacked intent to inflict distress.[6] The point applies to defenses as well. If consent is given under a substantial mistake as to the nature of the transaction, and the mistake is known to the other party, the consent may be ineffective.[7]

To a very large extent, liability of a mistaken defendant turns on the nature of the tort asserted against him and on the particular privilege invoked. It can be said that mistake as such is not a recognized defense, but that said, lawyers must turn to the elements of and privileges for the particular tort to determine whether a mistake could negate the intent required or whether the privilege invokes the reasonable person standard and thus takes at least reasonable mistakes into account.

Infancy

What has been said about mistake is largely true with infancy and mental disability as well. The general rule is that children—infants as they are often called in the old language of the law—are liable for their intentional torts.[8] Very small children and those who are infants in the popular sense, however, are usually thought incapable of committing intentional torts. But from around the age of four or so, children can clearly form tortious intent[9] and the only question is whether they formed and acted upon such intent in fact.

Although infancy is not a defense in itself, infancy is a fact that is more or less probative of intent or lack of intent in a particular case. So in some instances a child may escape liability for harm he has done simply because he had formed none of the intent required to establish an intentional tort.[10] This is a fact-specific result, not a rule that childhood furnishes a defense. It is at least in form an application of the same rules that apply to adults, namely rules requiring a subjective intent to act in a way that the law declares to be tortious.

Mental Disability

The same essential rules apply to mental disability, not to mention

6. See Adams v. National Bank of Detroit, 444 Mich. 329, 508 N.W.2d 464 (1993).

7. See § 100.

8. Brown v. Dellinger, 355 S.W.2d 742 (Tex.Civ.App.1962) (trespass); Restatement, § 895I (infants) & § 895J (mentally disabled persons). As to negligence of children, see §§ 124–127 below.

9. Ellis v. D'Angelo, 116 Cal.App.2d 310, 253 P.2d 675 (1953) (battery, four-year-old boy)

10. Shiflet v. Segovia, 40 Ohio App.2d 244, 318 N.E.2d 876 (1974) (minor can show absence of intent as basis to negative liability). Colorado modified the intent required of infants in battery cases, requiring an intent to effect a harmful, not merely offensive result. But no infancy defense is created by this rule. Horton v. Reaves, 186 Colo. 149, 526 P.2d 304 (1974).

voluntary intoxication.[11] The mentally disabled are subject to liability for their intentional torts under the same rules applicable to other persons.[12] The mentally disabled defendant, however, like the infant or the victim of mistake, may escape ultimate liability for reasons only tangentially related to his disability.[13] Perhaps more importantly, there is no liability unless intent is in fact formed and acted upon. If the mentally disabled person has no capacity for or does not in fact entertain an intent to touch, he cannot be guilty of a battery.

Topic B. Defense of Self and Others

§ 70. Self Defense and Defense of Others Generally

Rule summary. The defendant is privileged to use reasonable force to defend himself against unprivileged acts[1] that he reasonably believes will cause him bodily harm or offensive bodily contact. The privilege exists even though the defendant's use of reasonable force would otherwise amount to a tort such as a battery or assault, but limits are imposed upon the use of deadly force or force likely to cause grave bodily injury. Similar rules afford the defendant a privilege to protect other persons from harm.[2] These privileges to defend self or others are affirmative defenses, on which the defendant ordinarily has the burden of proof.[3]

Relation to criminal law self-defense. The common law self-defense rules are often elaborated from the rules used in criminal prosecutions. Criminal law precedents on self-defense are therefore often good guides to the tort law rule. However, the rules applied in criminal prosecutions are usually derived from statutes, which may specifically enact provisions at odds with the common law tort rules and the concerns of both policy and justice in criminal cases may be sufficiently different to call for different results in particular instances. For instance, self-defense is

11. E.g., Janelsins v. Button, 102 Md. App. 30, 648 A.2d 1039 (1994).

12. Polmatier v. Russ, 206 Conn. 229, 537 A.2d 468 (1988); Williams v. Kearbey, 13 Kan.App.2d 564, 775 P.2d 670 (1989); Goff v. Taylor, 708 S.W.2d 113 (Ky.App. 1986).

13. See Anicet v. Gant, 580 So.2d 273 (Fla.App.1991) (one whose job it is to attend a violently insane person cannot recover for injuries that person intentionally inflicts because the attendant has been paid to face these harms).

§ 70

1. The privilege of another to make an arrest may trump the defendant's privilege of self defense as indicated in § 73 below.

2. § 73 below.

3. E.g., Boyer v. Waples, 206 Cal.App.2d 725, 24 Cal.Rptr. 192 (1962); Winn v. Inman, 119 Ill.App.3d 836, 75 Ill.Dec. 351, 457 N.E.2d 141 (1983); Hartley v. Oidtman, 410 S.W.2d 537 (Mo.App.1966). When the plaintiff claims excessive force by an arresting officer, however, the plaintiff may be required to prove excessive force as part of his prima facie case. Some states have choreographed a trial in which the burden dances from defendant to plaintiff under some circumstances. See Liveoak v. Ingham, 644 S.W.2d 566 (1982); Grieger v. Vega, 153 Tex. 498, 506, 271 S.W.2d 85, 90 (1954) (wrongful death claim; "When defendant's evidence raises an issue of justification, the presumption that the killing was wrongful is balanced, and the matter is set at large. The plaintiff can then no longer rely alone upon the presumption, but must prove the wrong by a preponderance of the evidence").

an affirmative defense in tort law, but courts and statutes often require the prosecution to prove the absence of self-defense in a criminal case.[4]

Timing; threat of harm requiring immediate action. The privilege of self-defense is a privilege to avoid or minimize harm to oneself. It is not a privilege to retaliate or avenge harm already inflicted.[5] Likewise, it is a privilege based on immediate need to prevent an imminent invasion of one's person,[6] or at least on an immediate necessity to prevent a future harm.[7] If the danger reasonably appears to be imminent, the defendant need not await the first blow before asserting himself. On the other hand, the privilege of self-defense cannot be invoked to justify a preemptive strike against someone who threatens no immediate harm merely on the ground that he might attack in the future.[8]

Reasonable force. The force used by the defendant in the exercise of his privilege must be reasonable under the circumstances as they reasonably appeared to the defendant. If the circumstances warrant, the defendant may commit acts that would otherwise constitute a battery, an assault, or a false imprisonment.[9] A technical assault, being a mere threat of battery, may be privileged even when a battery itself would constitute excessive force.[10]

The force that is reasonable depends in large measure upon the harm threatened and in some measure on the whole circumstances of the case, including the alternatives available. In judging reasonableness of the force, courts do not expect the defendant to make a "microscopic analysis" of the situation, only to act reasonably considering the emergency.[11] But deadly force, or force threatening grave bodily harm, is

4. State v. Mitchell, 639 So.2d 391, 393 (La.App.1994) ("the burden is on the state to prove that the defendant did not act in self-defense"); Commonwealth v. Curtis, 417 Mass. 619, 631, 632 N.E.2d 821, 829 (1994) ("where the issue of self-defense has been sufficiently raised by the evidence, the defendant is entitled to an instruction which places on the Commonwealth the burden of disproving the factor of self-defense beyond a reasonable doubt").

5. Restatement § 63, cmt. g.

6. E.g., Martin v. Estrella, 107 R.I. 247, 266 A.2d 41 (1970). Imminent, impending, "then and there" are phrases used in most of the definitions. Courts sometimes emphasize that the privilege depends upon the fact that resort to courts is impractical.

7. See Robert Schopp, Bargara Sturgis, and Megan Sullivan, Battered Woman Syndrome, Expert Testimony, and the Distinction between Justification and Excuse, 1994 U. Ill. L. Rev. 45, 66 ff. (1994).

8. Restatement § 63, cmt. k; but see § 72. As to the threat of future harm that can only be prevented by present actions, however, see supra n. 7.

9. Restatement § 70.

10. Restatement § 70 (2). Cf. Jackson v. District of Columbia, 412 A.2d 948, 956 (D.C.App.1980) ("In making an arrest, however, a police officer is privileged even to use force unless the 'means employed are in excess of those which the actor reasonably believes to be necessary.'... a police officer is protected to an even greater degree against assault claims arising from arrests: unless the threatened use of force is clearly excessive, an officer is protected against liability for assault").

11. In re Paul F., 543 A.2d 255, 257 (R.I.1988) ("Rather we should view the disruptive and emotional furor that was created by Addison as the events must have appeared to Paul at the time"); Wackett v. Calder, 51 D.L.R.2d 598 (B.C.C.A. 1965) (defendant being attacked "is not held down to measure with exactitude or nicety the weight or power of his blows"). When the defendant uses excessive or unreasonable force, he may intend to do out of retaliation or vengeance; but he may also merely have gauged the amount of necessary force wrongly, in which case his actions closely resemble negligence. Cf.

excessive except as a last resort, when the defendant reasonably believes himself to be attacked by such force.[12]

Liability for excess force. If he uses excessive force, the defendant himself becomes, to that extent, a tortfeasor and he will himself be liable for harms caused by the excess.[13] In that case, the original attacker is privileged to defend against the excess force,[14] once the original attacker has attempted to withdraw from his aggressive posture and no longer poses a threat.[15] The defendant is only liable for the excess, not for the privileged force, but if he has caused an indivisible harm, one that cannot practically be separated, he is liable for the entire harm.[16]

§ 71. When Retreat Is Required in Lieu of Force in Self Defense

Avoidance or retreat generally. In the usual case, the defendant may defend himself from harm by using non-deadly force, even if he could avoid injury by retreating or by complying with some improper demand asserted by the plaintiff and even if his self-defense will inflict harm on the plaintiff.[1] This is also the rule in criminal law.[2]

Negligently threatened harm. But if the harm threatened is unintentional, merely the result of the plaintiff's negligence, the defendant should reasonably avoid the harm if possible, rather than inflict harm upon the negligent plaintiff.[3] In many imaginable cases, this rule may represent only a specific instance of the more general rule that only reasonable force should be used. The plaintiff should not avoid harm to himself by derailing the negligently driven trolley if he can avoid harm by stepping off the track.

Evasion or retreat to avoid the use of deadly force. If the attacker is threatening immediate use of force that reasonably appears likely to cause death or serious bodily harm, the defendant may respond with deadly force if that is the only safe alternative.[4] But if the defendant can avoid the use of deadly force and harm to himself by a retreat, authorities are divided.

The Restatement, speaking only to tort claims and not to criminal prosecutions, has it that an invalorous retreat is required to avoid deadly

Transamerica Ins. Group v. Meere, 143 Ariz. 351, 694 P.2d 181 (1984).

12. Martin v. Yeoham, 419 S.W.2d 937, 950 (Mo.App.1967) (to justify deadly force "[t]here must be reasonable cause of apprehension of imminent danger of death or great bodily harm").

13. E.g., Jahner v. Jacob, 233 N.W.2d 791 (N.D.1975). One who inflicts bodily harm or offense by using more force than permitted by the privilege is liable for a battery, whether the force is used in self-defense or in the exercise of some other privilege, such as the privilege to make an arrest. Schumann v. McGinn, 307 Minn. 446, 240 N.W.2d 525 (1976).

14. Fraguglia v. Sala, 17 Cal.App.2d 738, 62 P.2d 783 (1936); Restatement § 71.

15. Gortarez v. Smitty's Super Valu, Inc., 140 Ariz. 97, 680 P.2d 807 (1984); Jelly v. Dabney, 581 P.2d 622 (Wyo.1978).

16. Restatement § 71, cmt. b.

§ 71

1. Restatement § 63.

2. Wayne LaFave and Austin Scott, Jr. Criminal Law § 5.7 (f) (2d ed. 1986).

3. Restatement § 64.

4. Restatement § 65 (1).

force, provided the retreat can be effected in complete safety.[5] Likewise, if the defendant can avoid the use of deadly force and protect himself adequately by relinquishing some privilege, he must do that.[6]

Many courts, usually said to be a majority, traditionally permit the use of deadly force to counter deadly force without any general requirement of retreat. Such courts might require some kind of retreat to show withdrawal by one who was initially the aggressor, but otherwise allowed the defendant to defend himself with deadly force so long as such force was otherwise a reasonable response to an apparent threat.[7]

Most of the cases involve criminal prosecutions, not tort claims, so the legal ideas on this subject are principally generated in the criminal process, which in turn may be largely based on criminal statutes. As criminal statutes are amended or recodified, they may require a retreat when it can be made in complete safety.[8] This process of change in criminal statutes is likely to encourage courts to adopt a corresponding rule for self-defense in tort cases. Consequently the tort rule in a given jurisdiction may be discovered lurking in the implications of criminal statutes.

Reasons for a retreat requirement. Reasons given for a retreat requirement usually emphasize the value of human life, as well as the danger of an escalating affray. However, it is quite possible that courts also have in mind a number of practical dangers. History is written by the winners and lethal self-defense may leave few or no independent witnesses to contradict the easy claim of self-defense. In many cases the risk of error on the whole question of self-defense is quite high because the sudden unfolding of events and the shifting behaviors of the antagonists baffle attempts to determine who, at any given moment, is actually the aggressor. Because the risk of error in determining whether the defendant is standing his ground or acting on a license to kill is potentially so high, a requirement of retreat might seem better protection than some alteration of the proof burdens.

Exceptions to the retreat requirement. Even under the rule that a safe retreat is preferable to use of deadly force, the defendant is not required to retreat when he is already in his own home or dwelling place.[9] Nor need the defendant abandon an attempt at a lawful arrest to

5. Restatement § 65.

6. Restatement § 65 (3). But he need not relinquish his dwelling place or the privilege of making a lawful arrest. Nor of course need he sacrifice his own body to a rape or sodomy. Restatement § 65 (1) (b).

7. E.g., People v. Willner, 879 P.2d 19 (Colo.1994).

8. E.g., CONN. GEN. STATS. ANN. § 53a–19 (b) ("a person is not justified in using deadly physical force upon another person if he knows that he can avoid the necessity of using such force with complete safety (1) by retreating, except that the actor shall not be required to retreat if he is in his dwelling... or place of work and was not the initial aggressor, or if he is a peace officer ... or (2) by surrendering possession of property to a person asserting a claim of right thereto, or (3) by complying with a demand that he abstain from performing an act which he is not obliged to perform").

9. E.g., State v. Johnson, 261 N.C. 727, 136 S.E.2d 84 (1964). Even in one's own home, retreat may be required if the deadly attack comes from a cohabitant; Restatement § 65 (2) (a). Compare Hanauer v. Coscia, 157 Conn. 49, 54, 244 A.2d 611, 614

avoid using deadly force in self-defense.[10] That is not to say, of course, that deadly force can always be used to effect an arrest, only that it can be used in self-defense against deadly force.[11]

§ 72. Appearance and Reality: Objective vs. Subjective Perceptions of Threat

Objectively Judged Appearances

Appearance of attack; objective standards. The defendant can claim the privilege of self defense only if he in fact or subjectively believes that the defense was needed because of harm about to occur.[1] But, with only a little authority to the contrary,[2] a mere subjective belief is not sufficient to invoke the privilege. The defendant must also entertain an objectively warranted basis for belief that defense is required. That is, he may use force only if reasonable people in the same situation would perceive the need for force.[3] The amount of force used as well as the need for it comes under the same objective standard: it is justified only to the extent that it is reasonable in light of the apparent need.[4]

(1968) ("Where a person, without fault, is assaulted in his home, he is not required to retreat from his assailant but may resist even to the extent of seriously injuring his adversary when it becomes necessary").

10. Fields v. Dailey, 68 Ohio App.3d 33, 587 N.E.2d 400 (1990); Restatement § 65 (2) (c).

11. See Tennessee v. Garner, 471 U.S. 1, 105 S.Ct. 1694, 85 L.Ed.2d 1 (1985).

§ 72

1. E.g., McCoy v. Taylor Tire Co., 254 S.W.2d 923, 924 (Ky.1953) (defense applies when defendant "had reasonable grounds to believe, and in good faith did believe, that the plaintiff was then and there about to inflict upon him bodily harm"); Hartley v. Oidtman, 410 S.W.2d 537 (Mo.App.1966) (reasonable ground to believe and does believe attack is imminent); Tatman v. Cordingly, 672 P.2d 1286 (Wyo.1983).

Some writers have tried to draw a distinction among the the various verbal formulations, but imminent, immediate, impending and other words used by the courts and in the statutes are probably not intended to mean different things, nor can any of these terms be reduced to more precise conceptions. See Robert Schopp, Barbara Sturgis, and Megan Sullivan, Battered Woman Syndrome, Expert Testimony, and the Distinction between Justification and Excuse, 1994 U. Ill. L. Rev. 45.

2. Delaware, by statute, imposed a subjective standard in criminal cases and the Delaware Court carried this over to civil cases. Moor v. Licciardello, 463 A.2d 268 (Del.1983). See Annotation, John Wagner, Jr., Standard for Determination of Reasonableness of Criminal Defendant's Belief, for Purposes of Self-defense Claim, That Physical Force Is Necessary–Modern Cases, 73 A.L.R.4th 993 (1989). See also the segment *The "Battered Woman" Cases* below.

3. Crabtree v. Dawson, 119 Ky. 148, 83 S.W. 557 (1904) (defendant, believing that one Noble was about to attack him with bricks, and that the plaintiff was Noble, struck the plaintiff and knocked him down a flight of stairs; the defendant could rely on reasonable appearances even though he struck the wrong person); Jahner v. Jacob, 233 N.W.2d 791 (N.D.1975); Glover v. Berger, 72 Wyo. 221, 263 P.2d 498 (1953); Restatement § 63, cmt. i. In Maichle v. Jonovic, 69 Wis.2d 622, 230 N.W.2d 789 (1975) where the defendant was a boy eight years of age, the court implied that appearance of an attack would be judged by the "beliefs, instincts and impulses" of reasonable children "of like age, intelligence and experiences."

4. "The degree of force which may be used by a person in defense of himself, his family or his property must be limited to such force as would have appeared to be necessary to a reasonable man in all of the circumstances, knowing what the defendant knew, and facing the facts which presented themselves at the time to the defendant." Boyer v. Waples, 206 Cal.App.2d 725, 727, 24 Cal.Rptr. 192 (1962); Winn v. Inman,

Objective judgment about subjectively known facts. The tort law standard is objective in the sense that it refuses to justify the use of force on the basis of bizarre perceptions. "Good morning" cannot ordinarily be construed as an attack. However, the tort-law objective standard is not an abstract standard. It requires objective reasonableness, but it does so on the basis of facts known to the defendant.

For example, if the defendant knows that his attacker has violent propensities,[5] or if he has been hostile to the defendant in the past,[6] he may reasonably perceive an attack, even though bystanders who have no such information would not recognize the need for defense. Thus in judging whether the defense was reasonable, tort law accepts the facts known to the defendant and all the perceptions of events that reasonably grow out of those facts.

Unjustified use of force. The objective standard means that the defendant's unusual or irrational fears, or a belief that attack is imminent when there is no evidence of it, do not justify an attack on another, much less an attack with deadly force.[7] Although the facts subjectively known to the defendant are accepted as a basis for action, the action itself must reasonably grow out of those facts, or out of appearances that would be shared by reasonable others, not out of idiosyncratic fears or biases.[8]

This application of the objective standard is sometime meliorated in practice, however, by the recognition that even the hypothetical reasonable person cannot make a perfectly cool judgment about the force needed in an emergency such as a burglary or a robbery.[9]

Justified use of force. The objective standard leaves the honest but irrational defendant subject to tort liability. But it also excuses the

119 Ill.App.3d 836, 75 Ill.Dec. 351, 457 N.E.2d 141 (1983).

5. If the defendant knows the plaintiff's reputation for violence, for example, that reputation may be admissible to show the apparent need for self-defense, Martin v. Estrella, 107 R.I. 247, 266 A.2d 41 (1970). Or the court may permit him to "offer evidence of prior specific acts of violence or prior threats of violence to show that plaintiff is a turbulent and dangerous man and the defendant's knowledge thereof." Villines v. Tomerlin, 206 Cal.App.2d 448, 452, 23 Cal.Rptr. 617 (1962).

6. Bradley v. Hunter, 413 So.2d 674 (La. App.1982) (woman's past trouble with man who came toward her cursing and threatening; a shot in the head was self-defense, though the man appeared to have no weapon); Maichle v. Jonovic, 69 Wis.2d 622, 230 N.W.2d 789 (1975) (course of attacks by two boys upon another).

7. Tatman v. Cordingly, 672 P.2d 1286, 1290 (Wyo.1983) ("A subjective fear does not by itself entitle the defendant to use self-defense").

8. One group of commentators gives the example of a defendant who sees a man approaching with a baseball bat. Because the man approaching with the bat is of a different race, the defendant interprets the approach as an attack and responds with a gunshot. But all the objective facts indicate that no attack is threatened; many people are leaving a nearby baseball field, all carrying bats and gloves. The objective rule would not permit the defense. Robert Schopp, Barbara Sturgis, and Megan Sullivan, supra n. 1 at 98–99 (1994).

9. In Bennett v. Dunn, 507 So.2d 451 (Ala.1987) the "attacker" seemed to have been stealing a truck and driving away when the homeowner shot him, but the court thought that "Given ... the late hour, with Dunn being aroused from his sleep" fear of attack and response to it were reasonable. In O'Neal v. Church's Fried Chicken, Inc., 580 So.2d 706 (La.App.1991) a would-be robber was leaving the premises; he "turned slightly," whereupon the defendant shot and killed him. This was self-defense.

honest and rational response even if that response is mistaken. The defendant is privileged to respond to an apparent threat of attack by the plaintiff, even if it turns out later that the plaintiff never intended to attack at all. So, although mistake itself is not a defense, the defendant's mistaken perception of an attack will warrant reasonable use of force in response, so long as reasonable people in possession of the facts known to the defendant would have perceived the plaintiff's conduct as a threat warranting the response.[10]

The "Battered Woman"[11] Cases

In recent years a number of women who have killed or injured their intimate companions, usually a spouse, have claimed to be battered women entitled to some kind of defense arising from their long-term mistreatment. The cases so far are criminal prosecutions, not tort cases.[12] In some, the ordinary self-defense rules might apply, but in others the defendant kills a sleeping spouse who is not engaged in any threat of imminent or immediate harm to anyone.

Some judicial decisions, following an early hypothesis by a clinician, have painted a picture of battered women as those subjected to repeated physical and psychological attacks by husbands or others in an intimate relationship. They are seen to have undergone such degrading and demoralizing brutality that they are often unable to escape the demeaning relationship because of "learned helplessness."[13]

One argument based on the claim that the defendant is a battered woman is that experts should be permitted to testify about the putative battered woman syndrome in order to establish that the defendant's testimony is credible and not a fantasy. This would be significant in some ordinary self-defense cases because it might bear on the reasonableness of a woman's perception that she is being attacked.

A second argument is that because of the defendant's history as a battered woman, she can somehow claim self-defense when she kills her sleeping husband even though to a bystander no attack would appear to be in progress and no harm would appear to be imminent.

10. Boyer v. Waples, 206 Cal.App.2d 725, 24 Cal.Rptr. 192 (1962); Hanauer v. Coscia, 157 Conn. 49, 54, 244 A.2d 611, 614 (1968) (it is enough if the defendant entertained "the reasonable belief that the plaintiff intended to do him bodily harm whether or not the danger which gave rise to the belief actually existed if, in resorting to self-defense, he reasonably believed in the existence of such a danger"); Keep v. Quallman, 68 Wis. 451, 32 N.W. 233 (1887) (when accused of slander, the plaintiff reached for his pocket, whereupon the defendant hit him with a cane in the belief that the plaintiff was reaching for a gun); Restatement § 63, cmts. h & i.

11. Although women are not the only victims, the familiar case of the woman battered by spouse or cohabitant will be used here as the exemplar of the problem.

12. In Cusseaux v. Pickett, 279 N.J.Super. 335, 652 A.2d 789 (1994), the court said it recognized a new, battered woman tort, but this was seemingly for the purpose of extending a statute of limitations to permit the woman to sue.

13. See the description in State v. Kelly, 97 N.J. 178, 478 A.2d 364 (1984).

These criminal cases have generated a whirlwind of argument and commentary that is quite beyond this work,[14] but it can be said that some jurisdictions have adopted a supposed subjective standard for criminal cases. In *State v. Leidholm*[15] the North Dakota Court said that the jury is to consider the "physical and psychological properties peculiar to the accused," and then to judge whether she had a "sincere and reasonable belief that the use of force was necessary".[16] A few other courts have supported similar approaches in the battered woman case or under the specific wording of a criminal statute. Whether these results will carry over to civil tort liability is most uncertain. Most courts appear to have stood firmly on the objective standard, in effect insisting that the defense is based on moral justification rather than forgiveness or understanding.[17]

The claim of self-defense may seem preposterous by objective standards if, for example, a woman kills her husband while he is soundly sleeping and presenting no present evidence of attack. Such a case appears on the surface to be either retaliation and revenge or a preemptive strike against prospective future harm. Perhaps, however, no one should reject the subjective standard without examining the evidence of seemingly subhuman cruelty to which some women are subjected.

One matter distinguishes the typical battered woman case from many other cases in which a subjective standard might be claimed. The battered woman is in fact responding, however inappropriately, to her tormentor. The adult who beats children because he was himself a victim of child abuse is not responding to a tormentor, even if the child is the source of his immediate irritation. But if such distinctions might explain why a subjective rule for battered women differs from a subjective rule for many others, it may look uncomfortably like a rule that permits effective revenge on a subjective basis.

§ 73. Types of Harm Appropriate for Self Defenses; Defending against Arrest

Self-help. In some instances the law permits a person to remedy past wrongs by self-help and in so doing, to protect himself against future

14. One careful analysis is Robert Schopp, Barbara Sturgis, and Megan Sullivan, Battered Woman Syndrome, Expert Testimony, and the Distinction between Justification and Excuse, 1994 U. Ill. L. Rev. 45 (1994).

15. State v. Leidholm, 334 N.W.2d 811, 818 (N.D.1983).

16. Some of the court's language sounds objective. The same physical properties of the accused is an objective fact and would often be relevant under a completely objective test. The court's "sincere and reasonable" test seems to demand both subjective sincerity and objective reasonableness, but perhaps the court meant reasonable only in the light of the accused's subjective condition.

17. E.g., State v. Norman, 324 N.C. 253, 378 S.E.2d 8 (1989); see Annotation, John Wagner, Jr., Standard for Determination of Reasonableness of Criminal Defendant's Belief, for Purposes of Self-defense Claim, That Physical Force Is Necessary—Modern Cases, 73 A.L.R.4th 993 (1989). In criminal prosecutions, a separate defense based on some form of mental disability may be acceptable but that defense would operate quite differently from self-defense. See Robert Schopp, Barbara Sturgis, and Megan Sullivan, supra n. 1.

wrongs. Within limits, for example, a person harmed by a nuisance might be privileged to abate it, just as a landowner might be privileged to remove a trespassing object. Self-help is closely analogous to self-defense but may be broader.

Self-defense against physical harms. The self defense privilege as such is usually raised when the defendant is subjected to physical threat—assault, battery, false imprisonment. The usual case is a threatened harmful battery. The plaintiff advances upon the defendant with a pitchfork; the defendant responds with a whip. But self-defense is equally warranted against the elevator cowboy's furtive gropings that threaten only offensive, not harmful batteries.[1] The privilege of self-defense can also be invoked to protect against unintended physical harm[2] and against false imprisonment. The defendant is also privileged to defend himself against negligently caused harm by committing acts that would otherwise amount to a trespassory tort such as battery.[3]

Self defense against words. But the hurtful or provocative words of an antagonist do not justify a battery to silence the antagonist's utterances.[4] As this perhaps implies, verbal provocation is no defense, although it does bear on the propriety of punitive damages.[5]

Self-defense against false imprisonment. The defendant who is about to be subjected to confinement, or reasonably appears to be, is ordinarily entitled to use reasonable force to protect himself against such confinement.[6] When the confinement is threatened by an officer, however, special rules may apply.

Self-defense against an officer's unlawful arrest. Courts do not agree about whether the privilege to resist confinement extends to the case of an unlawful arrest by an officer. A number of courts hold that even

§ 73

1. Restatement § 63 (1) (privilege extends to offensive as well as harmful contact).

2. Restatement § 64 (privilege to protect against negligent conduct).

3. Restatement § 64. Sterling v. City of Albany, 276 Or. 403, 408, 555 P.2d 23, 27 (1976) seems to have recognized some kind of privilege but rejected the term self defense as to negligence. "The defense of self-defense is properly confined to cases where the action is for an assault. In an action for negligence, the fact that the defendant acted in the belief that it was necessary for his own protection to injure the plaintiff may be germane to the question of the reasonableness of his conduct, but it does not constitute a separate defense in the sense that it does where the tort is intentional."

4. Crotteau v. Karlgaard, 48 Wis.2d 245, 179 N.W.2d 797 (1970).

5. Manning v. Michael, 188 Conn. 607, 616, 452 A.2d 1157, 1162 (1982) ("A finding of provocation does not justify an assault, but merely limits liability to actual damages sustained"). Louisiana, however, traditionally considered provocation on the issue of compensatory damages as well. E.g., Eddy v. A.L. Litton, 586 So.2d 670 (La.App.1991); Cappo v. Vinson Guard Service, Inc., 400 So.2d 1148 (La.App.1981) ("old bastard" sufficiently provocative to bear on damages). A line of cases that permitted verbal provocation to bar the claim altogether was rejected in the Louisiana Supreme Court in Morneau v. American Oil Co., 272 So.2d 313 (1973). In 1996 the Louisiana Civil Code was amended to eliminate comparative negligence defenses against intentional torts, La. Stat. Ann. Civ. Code Art. 2323 (C). Whether that implies an end to the partial defense of provocation in Louisiana has not been determined at this writing. In Wijngaarde v. Parents of Guy, 720 So.2d 6 (1998) the court thought that the statute required "the intentional tortfeasor to absorb the negligent plaintiff's fault."

6. Restatement § 68.

though an officer's arrest is unlawful, the victim of that arrest has no privilege to resist.[7] For this view it is said that resistance to an officer's arrest encourages expanding violence and that the victim of such an arrest today enjoys a good probability that bail will be available so that he can promptly be released, that illegally obtained evidence will be excluded from any trial, and that he will have a damages action to redress the wrong.[8]

The contrary view, however, is still maintained in some courts.[9] That view has a degree of appeal in tort suits. The officer who has attempted an unlawful arrest meets resistance that causes him harm, then sues the citizen he wrongfully attacked, so that the citizen might understandably perceive himself to be twice victimized by the officer. In such cases the policy of minimizing the risk of expanding violence conflicts directly with the demands of justice. Although the choice is no easy matter, the victim's opportunity for redress in the courts at a later date suggests that a rule against a right to resist might substantially satisfy both the desire for peace and the desire for justice.

§ 74. Protecting Third Persons from Apparent Attack

Privilege to Protect a Third Person

A person is privileged not only to defend himself but also others from an attack that appears to threaten imminent harm. Defense of others follows the same analysis as defense of one's own person. The defendant who intervenes to defend another must believe that the victim would have the privilege of self-defense, that is that the attack makes defense necessary to avoid imminent harm. Reasonable appearances must also justify that belief, and the force used by the defendant must be reasonable in light of the threat. Under such conditions, one is privileged to defend another as well as himself.[1]

Two views once restricted the intervener's privilege. The first was that only family members or those with a special duty of protection enjoyed the privilege. This now seems to be obsolete.[2]

A second restriction was that the intervener stood in the shoes of the apparent victim of the attack and had no more privilege than the "victim" had. So if the intervener came to the defense of a "victim" who in fact was an aggressor or who was being lawfully arrested by an officer, he would be liable civilly or to criminal prosecution. Put differently, the

7. Evans v. City of Bakersfield, 22 Cal. App.4th 321, 27 Cal.Rptr.2d 406 (1994); Rhiner v. City of Clive, 373 N.W.2d 466 (Iowa 1985); State v. Haas, 134 N.H. 480, 596 A.2d 127 (1991).

8. See State v. Hatton, 116 Ariz. 142, 568 P.2d 1040 (1977).

9. White v. Morris, 345 So.2d 461, 466 (La.1977) ("we cannot abrogate our citizens' time honored right to resist an unlawful arrest"); State v. Wiegmann, 350 Md. 585, 714 A.2d 841 (1998).

§ 74

1. Restatement § 76.

2. See Gortarez v. Smitty's Super Valu, Inc., 140 Ariz. 97, 680 P.2d 807 (1984); Hartley v. Oidtman, 410 S.W.2d 537 (Mo. App.1966).

good samaritan who intervened to assist the victim of an attack took the risk that appearances might be deceiving.[3]

At the middle of the twentieth century, the view just stated may have been the common one, so that the privilege for protection of third persons was limited to interveners who correctly perceived the need for protection. However, many states have now enacted statutes as part of the criminal codes that specifically permit the defense of third persons based on apparent need for such a defense.[4] Accordingly, in criminal prosecutions, the reasonably mistaken intervener may be fully protected.[5] The criminal statutes do not by their terms prescribe a tort-law rule, but they reflect an attitude and a policy that will presumably carry over easily to protect the reasonably mistaken intervener in tort cases.

§ 75. Harms to Third Persons in the Course of Defending Self

When the defendant's self-defensive conduct causes harm to a third person who is not his attacker, has the privilege any role to play? The brief answer is no.

If the defendant intentionally injures the plaintiff as a means of protecting himself from attack by others, he is liable under the ordinary rules of law. For example, if an attacker says to the defendant, "you must shoot P or I will shoot you," we may understand the defendant who shoots P to save himself, but the law does not exempt him from liability for the battery.[1] This is a version of the necessity defense, under which defendants acting for their own good must pay for what they take or damage.[2]

The answer is reversed if the defendant injures a bystander in self-defense, but without any of the intents that would be required to show a tort. Suppose that, in justified self-defense, the defendant fires a pistol at an attacker but that the bullet strikes a bystander instead and that the bystander is neither attacking the defendant nor giving any appearance of doing so. If the defendant's conduct were not privileged under the

3. People v. Young, 11 N.Y.2d 274, 183 N.E.2d 319, 229 N.Y.S.2d 1 (1962). It may be that the arrest setting colored this ruling. The issue could arise just as well when the intervening defendant mistakenly came to the aid of the aggressor.

4. E.g., N.Y. Penal Law § 35.15 (subject to qualifications, "A person may ... use physical force upon another person when and to the extent he reasonably believes such to be necessary to defend himself or a third person from what he reasonably believes to be the use or imminent use of unlawful physical force by such other person... ."). See also Danny Veilleux, Annotation, Construction and Application of Statutes Justifying the Use of Force to Prevent the Use of Force Against Another, 71 A.L.R.4th 940 (1989).

5. See People v. Smith, 19 Ill.App.3d 704, 312 N.E.2d 355 (1974); People v. Melendez, 155 Misc.2d 196, 588 N.Y.S.2d 718 (1992) (doubting that People v. Young, supra n. 3 is still a majority and holding that in any event a New York statute overruled that case). The Model Penal Code § 3.05 provides for full protection of the mistaken intervener if "under the circumstances as the actor believes them to be, the person whom he seeks to protect would be justified in using such protective force."

§ 75

1. Restatement § 73 and Ill. 1.

2. § 107 below.

rules of self-defense, he would be liable to the bystander-plaintiff for battery, under the extended liability or transferred intent rules.[3] But the defendant's conduct is not tortious; it is justified by the self-defense privilege, so there is no occasion to apply the transferred intent or extended liability doctrine.

The Restatement and other authority hold that the defendant is liable in such a case only if he is negligent in causing harm to the bystander.[4] Negligent he may or may not be, depending upon the facts, but the focus of the negligence issue will be on the question whether his behavior was unreasonably risky, not merely on the fact of injury.

Topic C. Defense and Recovery of Property

§ 76. Defense of Possession: Land and Chattels

General Rule

The possessor of land or chattels is privileged to use reasonable force when necessary to defend possession of land or chattels against intrusion, taking, harm, or continuing trespass.

A place of business, for example, may remove an unruly customer if the customer will not leave voluntarily, even though the act of touching the customer would otherwise amount to a battery.[1] Or the possessor of land may remove a trespassing chattel left on his land, even though the act of doing so would otherwise amount to a conversion or a trespass to chattels.[2]

Similar rules give a privilege of one in possession of a chattel to use reasonable force to prevent a person from harming or carrying it away,[3] and even deadly force against an animal to prevent its destruction of the defendant's property, at least where the defendant's property is more valuable.[4]

Courts usually distinguish between defense of property and its recovery. Once an owner completely loses possession of the land or the chattel the privilege of defense is exhausted; to recover the property he must resort to the courts.[5]

This section summarizes the rules for defense of property, as distinct from its recovery. The defense of property rules closely track those applied in self-defense cases, with the obvious difference that less force

3. See § 40, supra.

4. Morris v. Platt, 32 Conn. 75 (1864); Restatement § 75.

§ 76

1. Griego v. Wilson, 91 N.M. 74, 570 P.2d 612 (Ct.App.1977).

2. Restatement § 260.

3. Vacanti v. Master Electronics Corp., 245 Neb. 586, 514 N.W.2d 319 (1994); Restatement §§ 77 & 260.

4. Grabenstein v. Sunsted, 237 Mont. 254, 772 P.2d 865 (1989) (defendant, finding most of his chickens dead and the plaintiff's dog about to pounce on the last one, shot the dog and killed it instantly; finding that the defendant was preventing imminent harm upheld; the defendant was privileged).

5. §§ 80 & 81 below.

may be justified in defense of property than in defense of person. Because of this similarity, this section states the rules as briefly as possible. The main qualifications or limitations on the privilege to defend property follow.

Qualifying and Explaining the General Rule

Reasonable force. It must reasonably appear that such force is needed, adapted, and proportioned to the protection of the possessor's interest in preventing the intrusion or ousting the intruder.[6] The defendant is not ordinarily expected to resort to the courts in the face of an attempted intrusion or dispossession, but he might be required to do so if the only alternative is to use force that is clearly disproportionate to the interests he seeks to protect. For example, if the plaintiff's underground telephone cable trespasses on the defendant's land without interfering with the land's use, a destruction of the cable might be disproportionate to the harm suffered by the defendant. In such a case, the defendant might be well advised to seek the aid of the courts rather than to destroy the cable.[7]

The defendant must limit the force applied to meet the apparent need for it. If the defendant uses excess force, he has exceeded his privilege and will be liable for harms caused by the excess force.[8] As long as there is room for reasonable people to differ in applying the standards, the question of excessive force is one for the jury.[9]

The force justified for the defense of property interests alone is relatively limited, but if the conflict escalates, self-defense or other privileges may be invoked and greater force may become appropriate.[10] Most commonly, the defendant's force will be the kind that counts as a battery, but in appropriate circumstances, a mere threat of a battery (an assault) or a confinement of the intruder may also be appropriate.[11]

6. Person v. Children's Hospital National Medical Center, 562 A.2d 648 (D.C.1989); Restatement § 77.

7. State v. Patch, 145 Vt. 344, 488 A.2d 755 (1985).

8. E.g., Terrell v. Hester, 182 Ga.App. 160, 355 S.E.2d 97 (1987). The intruder remains liable for her trespass, however.

9. See Vancherie v. Siperly, 243 Md. 366, 221 A.2d 356 (1966); Fields v. State, 21 So.2d 412 (Miss.1945).

10. See Restatement § 79 (deadly force if intruder appears to threaten serious bodily harm). In Bennett v. Dunn, 507 So.2d 451 (Ala.1987) the court thought a landowner justified in firing a .22 rifle repeatedly at a man who was apparently attempting to steal a truck because there might have been some basis, although seemingly not much, (for thinking the man might attack the defendant or his family). The court In re Paul F., 543 A.2d 255 (R.I.1988) justified a pursuit of an intruder in the home on the ground that the intruder was a felon and that a 17-year-old young man was privileged not only to defend the home but to use force to restrain the felon.

11. Restatement § 80. The Restatement expressly recognizes that an assault may may be privileged even if it threatens harm that would, if actually inflicted, be excessive. Restatement § 81 (2). State v. Lord, 617 A.2d 536 (Me.1992) (defendant who threatened to use deadly force to keep children off his property, claiming he had read the law and had a right to do so, was prosecuted for terrorizing; held, the trial court should have instructed on the use of threats to defend one's property; "A threat to use deadly force is the equivalent of nondeadly force").

In Brown v. Martinez, 68 N.M. 271, 361 P.2d 152 (1961), a farmer shot in the opposite direction from watermelon thieves, intending only to frighten them. That would count as an assault. The shot actually hit

Deadly force. Deadly force, including force likely to cause grave bodily harm, may not be used against an apparently peaceable intruder.[12] Even a demonstration of deadly force as a threat might be excessive.[13] But under many criminal-law statutes, such force may be used, if otherwise reasonable, to defend possession of a home[14] and in all likelihood this rule would be applied as well in tort cases. Deadly force may also be used, under the rules for self-defense and defense of third persons, if the intruder's attack itself appears to threaten a person with deadly force.[15]

Least force that will be effective. Reasonable force is ordinarily the least force that is reasonably likely to be effective in defense of the property interests. If the intruder is peaceable, the defendant must first request the intruder to depart[16] or must otherwise give him a chance to leave peaceably,[17] unless it is apparent that such a request is futile or dangerous. If the intruder enters forcibly, immediate resistance, without

one of the would-be intruders who was fleeing the patch. The court did not consider the possibility that, although deadly force would not be justified in defense of watermelons, a threat of such force might be a permissible way of defending property. But perhaps the court assumed that a demonstration of deadly force, with all the chances that it might go awry, was excessive even though the landowner never intended to do more than frighten. In Appelgren v. Walsh, 136 Ill.App.3d 700, 91 Ill.Dec. 340, 483 N.E.2d 686 (1985) the owner of a farm found his tenant cutting some dead trees. The owner allegedly held a shotgun to the tenant's head, then kept it pointed at him and his friends until the sheriff arrived. The court held that the jury could find an assault because even the threat of such force was excessive under the circumstances. In Scheufele v. Newman, 187 Or. 263, 210 P.2d 573 (1949) the court thought that firing a rifle away from the plaintiff but a spot ten feet away from him was excessive force for ejecting a peaceable trespasser who was fishing.

12. Restatement § 79.

13. See n. 11, supra.

14. E.g., FLA. STAT. ANN. § 782.02 ("The use of deadly force is justifiable when a person is resisting any attempt to murder such person or to commit any felony upon him or upon or in any dwelling house in which such person shall be"). See State v. White, 642 So.2d 842 (Fla.App.1994).

Statutes sometimes provide protection indirectly by calling for a presumption that force used inside a dwelling is used for self-defense, thus invoking whatever privilege exists to use deadly force in self-defense. E.g., CAL.PENAL CODE § 198.5 ("Any person using force intended or likely to cause death or great bodily injury within his or her residence shall be presumed to have held a reasonable fear of imminent peril of death or great bodily injury to self, family, or a member of the household when that force is used against another person, not a member of the family or household, who unlawfully and forcibly enters....")

In State v. Clothier, 243 Kan. 81, 753 P.2d 1267 (1988) a statute permitted use of deadly force in defense of a dwelling where the defendant "reasonably believes that such conduct is necessary to prevent or terminate such other's unlawful entry into or attack upon his dwelling." The state argued that the statute was unconstitutional under Tennessee v. Garner, 471 U.S. 1, 105 S.Ct. 1694, 85 L.Ed.2d 1 (1985) where the Court allowed a civil rights claim for the shooting of a runaway but unarmed suspect. The Court refused to hold that the privilege conferred by the statute to defend a dwelling was unconstitutional. Cf. Cavillo–Silva v. Home Grocery, 19 Cal.4th 714, 968 P.2d 65, 80 Cal.Rptr.2d 506 (1998) (statutory immunity of all landowners, including businesses, protects use of deadly force used in self-defense).

15. Restatement § 79.

16. MacDonald v. Hees, 46 D.L.R. 3d 720 (N.S. 1974); Restatement § 77 (c) & cmt. j.

17. In Ramirez v. Chavez, 71 Ariz. 239, 242, 226 P.2d 143, 145 (1951) the court concluded that "when Chavez informed Ramirez he was going to put him out, this was sufficient to convey to Ramirez the information that it was desirable that he leave the

a polite request, may be reasonable, but if deadly force is contemplated, a warning would be necessary if it is safe to give one.

Intruder's superior privilege. The intruder's privilege to enter or remain in cases of necessity to save herself from death or grave bodily harm will be superior to the possessor's privilege, at least for a reasonable period of time.[18] Put otherwise, the possessor may not eject the intruder from a fast-moving train.[19] Other privileges of an intruder, such as the privilege to arrest under a warrant or legal authority, will likewise supersede or override the possessor's privilege.[20]

Mistake; appearances. The rule governing mistakes in the exercise of a privilege against an apparent attacker must be stated in a series of switchbacks, as follows:

(A) Reasonable appearances, not hidden actualities, determine the existence and scope of the privilege. If it reasonably appears to the possessor that an intruder is breaking into the house, the possessor may be justified in using force even if the intruder turns out to be a paper boy.[21]

(B) The rule in paragraph (A) is qualified by the rule that if the intruder is acting in the exercise of his superior privilege, the defendant's mistake as to the extent or nature of the intruder's privilege is no defense.[22] For instance, the possessor presumably has no privilege to use force to defend his property against a lawful search or seizure.[23]

(C) The rule in paragraph (B) is also qualified. If the intruder misleads the defendant or causes the defendant's mistake of facts, the defendant is entitled to act on the reasonable appearances induced by the intruder. For example, in a Florida case, testimony was that a number of police officers in possession of a warrant did not knock or announce their warrant, but instead cut the power lines, broke open the door with a sledge hammer, and appeared in plain clothes with ski masks to raid a poker game. In such circumstances, the defendant might reasonably mistake his masked visitors for violent attackers, not guardians of order. Their superior privilege based on the warrant was nullified because they actively created a misimpression.[24]

premises and amounted to a request to leave." There are no doubt many permutations that would suffice.

18. E.g., Depue v. Flateau, 100 Minn. 299, 111 N.W. 1 (1907); see § 107.

19. See Restatement § 77, cmt. i and Ill. 10.

20. State v. Haas, 134 N.H. 480, 596 A.2d 127 (1991); cf. Commonwealth v. Kuyamjian, 18 Mass.App.Ct. 680, 469 N.E.2d 1291 (1984).

21. Smith v. Delery, 238 La. 180, 114 So.2d 857 (1959).

22. Magnuson v. Billmayer, 189 Mont. 458, 616 P.2d 368 (1980) (privilege to enter in accord with easement rights).

23. See Restatement § 77 (a) & cmt. d (privilege of landowner applies only when the other has no privilege [or in circumstances explained in subparagraph (C) below]).

24. State v. White, 642 So.2d 842 (Fla. App.1994). The common law "knock and announce" requirement is part of the reasonableness rule of the Fourth Amendment. Wilson v. Arkansas, 514 U.S. 927, 115 S.Ct. 1914, 131 L.Ed.2d 976 (1995).

Protecting third persons. The Restatement recognizes that the defendant may act to protect property interests of others, or at least those of family members. The defendant must reasonably believe that the facts would justify the possessor's use of force and must use force proportioned to the facts as they reasonably appear.[25] It would seem that the privilege to protect family members' property would include the privilege to use reasonable force to remove trespassing chattels under the same conditions that he could do so on his own behalf.[26]

Third person injury. As in the case of self-defense, an energetic defense of property may unintentionally cause injury to an innocent third person who is in no way involved. So long as the force used by the defendant against the intruder is reasonable and privileged force, the defendant is not liable for an intentional tort, even to the innocent bystander who is injured. In such a case, he may be liable for negligence if he creates an unreasonable risk to the bystander,[27] but he is not liable otherwise.[28]

Traps and spring guns and other unattended defenses. May a possessor set a deadly trap or spring gun likely to cause grave bodily harm in order to protect property? The best one-sentence answer is probably no, except to prevent entry into a dwelling place or commission of a serious felony. But more needs to be said on that topic and it is covered in the sections that follow.

§ 77. Deadly Traps in Defense of Property: Spring Guns

Possessors of land sometimes attempt to protect their property by unattended devices capable of producing deadly force, that is, force likely to include either death or grave bodily harm. Such unattended devices can be called deadly traps. One example is the spring gun, a weapon rigged with trip wires to fire upon intruders, sometimes at very close range. Discussion here focuses on that example. Some other cases that might count as deadly traps are mentioned elsewhere,[1] as are some potential qualifications to the rules.[2]

A Summary

The Restatement's general formulation. The Restatement rule is that a spring gun or other deadly trap is permissible, but only when the facts are such that the defendant could have used such force in person.[3] That formulation requires lawyers and judges to determine when the defendant could have exercised deadly force in person.

25. Restatement § 86. According to the Restatement, the defendant must reasonably believe that the facts are such that the possessor would have a privilege to use force in defense of the property.

26. Cf. State v. Patch, 145 Vt. 344, 488 A.2d 755 (1985).

27. E.g., Passovoy v. Nordstrom, Inc., 52 Wash.App. 166, 758 P.2d 524 (1988).

28. Polando v. Vizzini, 97 N.E.2d 59 (Ohio App. 1949); Restatement § 83.

§ 77

1. § 79 below.

2. § 78 below.

3. Restatement § 85. A number of cases make a similar statement. E.g., Allison v. Fiscus, 156 Ohio St. 120, 100 N.E.2d 237, 44 A.L.R.2d 369 (1951).

The rule can be criticized as infeasible or even as logically impossible in some cases. For instance, if the defendant were physically present when the plaintiff attempted to enter the property, the defendant would ordinarily be required to warn the plaintiff off before using force and certainly before using deadly force. No such warning could be given by the traditional spring gun, so the comparison to a situation in which the defendant is personally present will at best provide only partial guidance. However, the Restatement's ideas, when picked out in detail, work out to be somewhat similar to the specific rules set out next.

Formulating particular rules. Lacunae in the cases create uncertainties about the precise rules, but a reasonable approximation of the overall tendency of the courts can be expressed as follows.

(1) Self-defense. The defendant is privileged to use deadly traps to protect the persons of himself and others against deadly force if the use of such traps is otherwise reasonable under the rules for self-defense, but except as stated in the next paragraph, there is no independent privilege to protect property interests by deadly traps.

(2) Protection of dwelling place against felonious entry. (A) Unless criminal statutes provide or imply otherwise, the defendant may protect his dwelling place by deadly traps against intruders who are in fact entering or attempting to enter in the course of a felony or attempted felony, provided deadly traps are otherwise reasonable.[4] In some states, this privilege may be extended to permit protection of other buildings against serious depredation.[5] But it seems that the defendant uses a deadly trap at his peril, so that if the spring gun harms or kills a straying child who is not in fact attempting felonious entry, the privilege is no protection.[6]

(B) Criminal statutes forbidding any use of spring guns or other deadly traps may be construed to modify or eliminate the rule in subparagraph (A).[7]

(C) Criminal statutes permitting or refusing to permit the use of deadly force to repel a felony or entry into a dwelling place may be construed to modify or reinforce the rule stated in (A).[8]

(3) Mere trespassers and non-felonious intruders. The defendant has no privilege to use deadly traps to defend against mere trespassers or those committing minor crimes outside the dwelling place. The defen-

4. This is the implication but not the specific holding in a number of cases. E.g., Scheuerman v. Scharfenberg, 163 Ala. 337, 50 So. 335 (1909); Allison v. Fiscus, 156 Ohio St. 120, 100 N.E.2d 237, 44 A.L.R.2d 369 (1951); cf. Katko v. Briney, 183 N.W.2d 657 (Iowa 1971) (if the trespasser is committing a "felony of violence" or one punishable by death).

5. Scheuermann v. Scharfenberg, 163 Ala. 337, 50 So. 335 (1909).

6. See Allison v. Fiscus, 156 Ohio St. 120, 100 N.E.2d 237, 44 A.L.R.2d 369 (1951) ("[O]ne who sets a spring gun or trap does so at his peril"); Restatement § 85, cmt. d.

7. See § 78 below.

8. E.g., FLA. STAT. ANN. § 782.02.

dant is liable to such trespassers if they are injured by the defendant's deadly trap.[9]

(4) Unintended harm; negligence. When the defendant creates a condition on his land that may be dangerous to trespassers but is not created for the purpose of causing them harm, the defendant is liable if at all only for negligence.[10]

Illustrative Authorities

General disapproval of spring guns and deadly traps. Courts express dislike for and concern at the use of spring guns and other deadly traps or "engines of destruction."[11] But cases that reflect general disapproval of spring guns often do not state precise rules governing their use or misuse. Many of these cases are ordinary negligence cases that do not involve spring guns or even intentional torts. They collaterally condemn the use of spring guns against trespassers only on their way to saying that the landowner is not liable for a negligently inflicted injury to a trespasser.[12] Cases in this group provide little guidance on the question of the possessor's justification for using such force in defense of property, except that they sometimes cite the leading English case with approval.

Bird v. Holbrook. The English case that has influenced American law is *Bird v. Holbrook,*[13] a case decided by an English court in 1828. The defendant set a spring gun in his walled garden because he had previously suffered theft of some of the tulips he raised there. A neighbor's peahen escaped and got into the garden. The plaintiff offered to get it. The plaintiff climbed the wall and called out for the occupant, but, getting no answer, jumped into the garden to retrieve the hen. The spring gun was triggered and the plaintiff was seriously wounded.

The *Bird v. Holbrook* court imposed liability upon the defendant. Distinguishing earlier authority, one of the judges emphasized that the defendant had not only failed to give notice that the gun was there but had tried to keep it secret in order to wound the tulip thief. Another judge emphasized that if the spring gun were justified, it would be justified only at night when the thief might come. *Bird* is clear about the defendant's liability on the facts, but uncertain about the defendant's potential liability to an actual burglar.

9. McKinsey v. Wade, 136 Ga.App. 109, 220 S.E.2d 30 (1975); Katko v. Briney, 183 N.W.2d 657 (Iowa 1971).

10. The rules of negligence law that hold a landowner liable to a trespasser if the landowner's acts, or the condition he tolerates on the land, amounts to willful or wanton misconduct are closely analogous to the rules that hold the landowner has exceeded his privilege if he uses unreasonable force to repel a trespasser. Under one view, a trap would represent "willful and wanton" misconduct on the landowner's part. See, e.g., Harper v. Kampschaefer, 549 N.E.2d 1067 (Ind.App.1990).

11. See J.D. Perovich, Annotation, Use of Set Gun, Trap, or Similar Device on Defendant's Own Property, 47 A.L.R.3d 646 (1973).

12. E.g., Fox v. Warner–Quinlan Asphalt Co., 204 N.Y. 240, 97 N.E. 497 (1912); Weitzmann v. A.L. Barber Asphalt Co., 190 N.Y. 452, 83 N.E. 477 (1908); Gramlich v. Wurst, 86 Pa. 74 (1878).

13. Bird v. Holbrook, 4 Bing. 628, 130 Eng. Repr. 911 (C.P. 1828).

Katko v. Briney. The most famous American case is quite different. In *Katko v. Briney*[14] one of the defendants had inherited an unoccupied farm house. For ten years, a series a housebreaking events repeatedly caused damages. The defendants boarded the windows and posted no trespassing signs. Eventually they set a spring gun, a shotgun rigged with a wire from the doorknob in one of the rooms to the gun's trigger. No signs or other warnings about the gun were given.

The *Katko* plaintiff was a man who was looking for old bottles and jars. He had been there before a shotgun had been set up. This time, however, when he opened the door, the gun was triggered and the blast blew part of his tibia away. He suffered considerable injury and was criminally punished by a fine of $50 and a 60–day jail sentence (from which he was paroled).

Although the plaintiff in this case entered the premises with a minor criminal purpose, he was allowed to recover. The court rejected the defense that spring guns were permissible means of defending property on the ground given in the Restatement, that human life and limb are more important than property interests. The court appeared to approve the Restatement's rule formulation. Some other cases are in accord in allowing recovery by the thief (or his estate), so long as he is not entering a dwelling place.[15]

§ 78. Qualifying and Considering the Deadly Trap Rules

Property vs. Life

Most discussions of deadly force, by traps or otherwise, emphasize the importance of human life. Human life undoubtedly represents the single most important factor to be considered. However, the suggestion that deadly force is invariably unacceptable because property interests are always small in comparison to human life is rhetorically appealing but analytically weak, as is the suggestion that the landowner can always buy insurance to protect property interests.

First, not all property interests are alike. A storehouse of goods is not like a home. Property in the form of a home, for those lucky enough to have such property, represents fundamental human needs and satisfactions, a very personal refuge, the violation of which is harmful not merely to "property" but to human beings. Second, the defense of property by deadly force is usually not a simple exchange of life for

14. Katko v. Briney, 183 N.W.2d 657 (Iowa 1971).

15. McKinsey v. Wade, 136 Ga.App. 109, 220 S.E.2d 30 (1975) (young man breaking into vending machine killed when dynamite bomb went off, liability); cf. Harper v. Kampschaefer, 549 N.E.2d 1067 (Ind.App. 1990) (cable stretched across private road or path to stop ATVs; it caught decedent at the neck and killed him; jury could find wanton misconduct under negligence law and hence could impose liability). In Goldfuss v. Davidson, 79 Ohio St.3d 116, 679 N.E.2d 1099 (1997) a landowner shot in the direction of two thieves who had been planning to steal equipment from his barn; one was struck and died. His estate pursued the claim as a negligence claim and it was defended on that ground. The jury found for the plaintiff but reduced damages for "comparative negligence." Issues of privilege were procedurally sidetracked.

property as the rhetoric suggests, but a risk of life balanced against a certain invasion. Third, if the mentally competent intruder is fully informed of the specific risks that entry is likely to result in a shotgun or dynamite blast but proceeds anyway, human life is surely at risk, but it is the intruder's choice. These considerations suggest that the courts may well be right to imply that defense of a dwelling place by deadly force, including deadly traps, might be justified, although defense of other property is not.

It does not follow, however, that deadly traps are always reasonable, even inside a dwelling place. A trap to impede entrance into a bedroom in the nighttime when people are present might be reasonable if the threat is great, but a stick of dynamite that blows up anyone who rings the front door bell in the daytime is not. Nor is a deadly trap reasonable if the risk of burglars is nill but the risk of a stray child is high.

Warnings

The risk of grave injury or death to relatively innocent intruders suggests that an advance warning, by signs or pictographs or otherwise, should ordinarily be required. The Restatement does not directly require a notice,[1] but some cases may imply that the spring gun might be justified only if such a notice or warning were given and conversely may imply that if a notice is given then the spring gun would be justified.[2] It is true, of course that a locked door warns the trespasser that he is not wanted,[3] but it hardly serves to warn him that he faces death by a dynamite explosion. If the Restatement is right in suggesting that the possessor cannot do indirectly by deadly traps what he cannot do in person, then either an actually communicated warning or at least a good faith and reasonable effort to communicate one would be required. Given the ease and low cost with which a warning can usually be provided, and the added fact that a warning might even further the landowner's interests by dissuading some trespassers, perhaps any privilege should be limited to cases in which the landowner has reasonably and in good faith attempted to provide such a warning.[4] Although this does not sound controversial, some decisions have attributed no significance to a warning and have thus permitted the landowner to create deadly and unexpected conditions on the land to repel trespassers.[5]

§ 78

1. The Restatement seems to say that no warning is required. Restatement § 85, cmt. c. The Restatement does provide that giving a warning is not enough if the force is not otherwise justified.

2. Larmore v. Crown Point Iron Co., 101 N.Y. 391, 394, 4 N.E. 752, 754 (1886) ("he cannot, without giving any warning, place thereon spring-guns or dangerous traps"). Similarly, some cases refer to the "hidden" character of "engines of destruction" like spring guns. Mendelowitz v. Neisner, 258 N.Y. 181, 179 N.E. 378 (1932). See also Bird v. Holbrook, § 77, supra.

3. "A lock on a door is sufficient warning to any prospective thief that he is not to feloniously break that lock and enter the building." Allison v. Fiscus, 156 Ohio St. 120, 128, 100 N.E.2d 237, 241, 44 A.L.R.2d 369 (1951).

4. See Posner, Killing or Wounding to Protect a Property Interest, 14 J. Law & Economics 201, 214 ff. (1971).

5. Doehring v. Wagner, 80 Md.App. 237, 562 A.2d 762 (1989) (cable stretched across private road to deter motorcyclists who had been accustomed to using the road; cyclist killed when he ran into it at night; the

Criminal Statutes

The common law rules for deadly traps, at least in the form of spring guns, may be modified indirectly because a number of statutes proscribe the use of spring guns altogether, with a provision of criminal penalties for a violation.[6] Criminal law rules do not automatically carry over into tort law, but they often do. Criminal statutes against spring guns might be construed to abolish any privilege to use such guns, although that reading might leave other deadly mechanical devices available to the landowner under common law rules.

Suing for One's "Own Wrong"—Forfeiting Rights

Some courts have it that some kind of general principle forecloses recovery by one injured in the course of committing a serious criminal act. So long as his injury can be seen to result from his "own wrong," the criminal forfeits his civil rights in this respect. This principle is supposedly distinct from contributory negligence, assumed risk, or consent.[7]

The principle must be subject to some important limits unless a great deal of tort law has simply been wrong all along, but the limits are not clear.[8] The relevance of this point to spring gun cases is that its application in such a case might bar some claims altogether. It does not

allegation that the defendant did nothing to warn or make the cable visible to a cyclist was of "no significance").

6. 720 Ill.Comp. Stat. 5/24–1(a)(5) "(a) A person commits the offense of unlawful use of weapons when he knowingly: . . . (5) Sets a spring gun . . . ."; Iowa Code Ann. § 708.9. ("Any person who in any place sets a spring gun or a trap which is intended to be sprung by a person and which can cause such person serious injury commits an aggravated misdemeanor"); Mich. Comp. L. Ann. § 750.236 (unattended spring gun, misdemeanor, but manslaughter if anyone is killed); Minn. Stat. Ann. § 609.205 (Person causing death by any of listed means, including setting a spring gun, is guilty of manslaughter).

Cf. Iowa Code Ann. § 704.4 ("A person is justified in the use of reasonable force to prevent or terminate criminal interference with the person's possession or other right in property. Nothing in this section authorizes the use of any spring gun or trap which is left unattended and unsupervised and which is placed for the purpose of preventing or terminating criminal interference with the possession of or other right in property"); Minn. Stat. Ann. § 609.665 (imprisonment and fine for setting spring gun, pitfall, and other traps); S.C. Code § 16–23–450 (unlawful to set spring gun "in any building or in any place within this state").

7. The principle is discussed in § 208.

8. The cases that allow a recovery for injuries or death resulting from a deadly trap are potentially at odds with the "own wrong" rule. See McKinsey v. Wade, 136 Ga.App. 109, 220 S.E.2d 30 (1975). In Oden v. Pepsi Cola Bottling Co. of Decatur, Inc., 621 So.2d 953, 954–55 (Ala.1993) the court reiterated its principle that one "cannot maintain a cause of action if, in order to establish it, he must rely in whole or part on an illegal or immoral act or transaction to which he is a party," but added that this principle "does not foreclose a trespasser's action against a landowner who willfully or wantonly injures him, unless the injuries incurred are a direct result of an injured party's knowing and intentional participation in a crime of moral turpitude. That is, our application of the rule in Hinkle would bar an action by a trespasser injured while attempting to enter an occupied dwelling for the purpose of inflicting bodily injury on the occupant of the dwelling." In Goldfuss v. Davidson, 79 Ohio St.3d 116, 679 N.E.2d 1099 (1997), the landowner in person fired a shot which struck and killed a man who had been about to attempt to steal goods from the barn; the case was conceived as a negligence case, not as an intentional tort case. Even so, the court refused to prohibit recovery by the felon's estate.

seem likely that courts would apply any such forfeiture principle so as to permit the possessor to shoot the felonious intruder intentionally and needlessly. Yet in the state that decided *Katko*,[9] where a thief recovered for injuries sustained in breaking and entering, a court has perhaps suggested that liability would not have been imposed if the defendant had invoked the forfeiture principle.[10] So time continues to add wrinkles to the spring gun rules.

§ 79. Types of "Traps" and Negligence Law

Other deadly traps. The preceding sections have focused on spring guns as the prime example of a deadly trap, but other unattended devices, animate or not, could function in much the same way as a spring gun and could be governed by the same rules. Vicious dogs,[1] or poisonous ponds of toxic waste[2] might be in this category. Conceivably deep pits[3] or electrified objects on the land,[4] or chains or wires that might not be visible to a motorcyclist or snowmobiler[5] might all be deadly traps placed to exclude trespassers, although in most instances they are more likely to represent negligence than intentional harm.[6]

Non-deadly traps. Some unattended devices might count as traps without being deadly or likely to cause serious bodily harm. Some of these are undoubtedly permissible first because they are customary in the community and thus expected, and second because they serve useful purposes for the landowner that have nothing to do with the exclusion of trespassers. A barbed wire fence, for example, would normally be a privileged means of attempting to exclude trespassers as well as a good means for keeping cattle in.[7]

Relation to negligence law. Courts considering injuries to a trespasser will often think of the case as a negligence case rather than as an intentional tort case with a privilege defense. If the landowner digs an

9. § 77, supra.

10. Pappas v. Clark, 494 N.W.2d 245 (Iowa App.1992). Iowa advanced the forfeiture or "own wrong" rule in Cole v. Taylor, 301 N.W.2d 766 (Iowa 1981), a completely different setting. In *Cole,* the plaintiff sued her therapist for failing to prevent her from murdering her husband. The claim was of course denied, the court giving the "own wrong" rule as one reason. The *Pappas* court, wishing to distinguish *Katko* observed that the "own wrong" rule had not been raised there, an observation that presumably is meant to suggest that *Katko* would go the other way if the rule were raised. That seems improbable to this writer, especially in light of the Iowa statutes cited in n. 21.

§ 79

1. See nn. 9 & 10.

2. Cf. Bruister v. Haney, 233 Miss. 527, 102 So.2d 806 (1958) (landowner is liable for intentionally leaving poison to harm trespassing cattle).

3. Gramlich v. Wurst, 86 Pa. 74 (1878) (decedent, attempting to rescue another, was an innocent trespasser who fell in pit and was killed, no recovery, seemingly because the landowner had no intent to harm and was not negligent).

4. Cf. Miller v. General Motors Corp., 207 Ill.App.3d 148, 152 Ill.Dec. 154, 565 N.E.2d 687 (1990) (trespasser injured in touching electrical object on the land, but since his presence could not have been anticipated, the landowner was not liable for negligence).

5. Cf. Harper v. Kampschaefer, 549 N.E.2d 1067 (Ind.App. 1990) (cable caught ATV operator at the neck and killed him).

6. See § 232 below.

7. See Restatement § 84.

excavation in order to construct a building, for example, his purpose is not to trap the trespasser but to exploit his land. In such a case, the question will be resolved under rules of negligence law.

As will be seen in the discussions of landowner negligence,[8] landowners may leave dangerous conditions on their property that may *function* like a trap even if their purpose is not to exclude trespassers. In those cases, too, courts are likely to consider the case under the negligence rules. Those rules correlate closely with the privilege rules. In general, landowner's are not traditionally required to exercise care for the benefit of trespassers, but they are not to willfully injure or entrap them and if they do, they are liable for the harm done.

What counts as a trap or as willful misconduct may thus become central to resolution of many trespasser-injury cases. Although some courts expressly analogize a vicious dog kept to guard the perimeter of a house as a trap like a spring gun,[9] others seemingly do not.[10] Whether the case is regarded as an intentional tort with a privilege defense, a negligence case, or a strict liability case, the most important consideration is whether the court perceives the dog (or other condition) as a trap or as a product of willful behavior.[11]

In *Bramble v. Thompson*,[12] the Maryland Court seemingly did not see a vicious dog kept on the land as a trap, perhaps because the term trap might connote an inanimate contrivance. But the significant features of a trap are that it is unexpected and unknown and that it cannot discriminate between, say, a straying child and a vicious burglar. These are the features that make it an unreasonable form of force to prevent a simple trespass and also the features that make the conduct willful if the case is viewed as a negligence case.

§ 80. Repossession of Land

In Summary

Claimants, squatters, and tenants. Conflicts over possession of land arise in several materially different settings. A person who moves into wrongful possession might be a person who believes she has title; or she might be a squatter or a tenant whose possession is wrongful because her lease has terminated for nonpayment of rent or otherwise. The last

8. Chapter 13.

9. Brewer v. Furtwangler, 171 Wash. 617, 18 P.2d 837 (1933) (inadvertent trespasser could recover for vicious dog attack).

10. See Bramble v. Thompson, 264 Md. 518, 287 A.2d 265, 64 A.L.R.3d 1031 (1972). The *Bramble* court refused to impose liability upon a landowner whose allegedly vicious dog attacked an inadvertent trespasser, on the ground, semble, that keeping vicious dog would not be "wilful or wanton misconduct or entrapment" and because Maryland law seeks to avoid "distinctions or deviations in the law of trespass."

11. Compare Brewer v. Furtwangler, supra n. 9, *with* Bramble v. Thompson, supra n. 10 and Harper v. Kampschaefer, supra n. 5 (deadly cable across private path could be wilful misconduct toward ATV operator who ran into it in the dark) *with* Doehring v. Wagner, 80 Md.App. 237, 562 A.2d 762 (1989) (deadly cable across private roadway was not willful misconduct toward motorcyclist who ran into it in the dark).

12. Bramble v. Thompson, supra n. 10.

is the most common situation. Can the rightful owner of land use reasonable force to oust a title claimant, a mere squatter, or a tenant whose lease has lapsed?

Defense of property vs. recovery of property. Legal rules distinguish between defense of property on the one hand and its recovery or repossession on the other. The owner-possessor of land may use reasonable force to defend possession and other interests in the land. The privilege continues as long as the owner continues to resist the intruder and contest his right to be there, even if, for the moment, the owner is literally off the land. In such a case, the intruder has not acquired a peaceable possession; she is a mere trespasser or has only "scrambling possession."[1] In this situation, the owner is viewed as defending his own possession. In such a case, if he uses no more force than necessary and reasonable,[2] he is privileged and not subject to liability.

Once the owner loses possession to another person, however, the owner has no possession to defend and his self-help privilege is at an end. He may not use force to oust the trespasser who is in peaceable possession. To repossess land in firm possession of another, the owner must ordinarily resort to judicial process. As will be seen, this rule leads to the possibility that if the owner uses force to repossess his own property, the wrongful possessor may have a tort claim.

Forcible Entry Statutes

The underlying rule was developed from a 14th century English statute that forbad forcible repossession by the owner[3] and from American Forcible Entry statutes that do the same.[4] The perception and the policy attributed to these statutes is that forcible repossession creates a risk of a violent response and that the risk of violence should be minimized by forbidding even reasonable force.

Forcible entry and detainer statutes attempt to encourage the owner to use judicial process by offering a carrot and threatening a stick. The carrot is a provision for a relatively speedy and informal trial that will put the owner in possession. The stick is a criminal penalty for resort to force. Many of the statutes are vague about what counts as "forcible" and wholly ambiguous in their implications about a private cause of action in favor of the wrongful possessor.

§ 80

1. See National Garment Co. v. City of Paris, Missouri, 655 S.W.2d 515 (Mo.1983).

2. Schwinn v. Perkins, 79 N.J.L. 515, 78 A. 19 (1910)

3. 5 Richard II c. 7. One edition of the Statutes at Large prints the statute as "Chapter 8," but other editions use "Chapter 7," and the English Parliament in passing amendments to it has three times referred to it as Chapter 7.

4. E.g., CAL. CIV. PROC. CODE § 1159; N.Y. REAL PROP. ACTS § 853. The California statute provides: "Every person is guilty of a forcible entry who either: 1. By breaking open doors, windows, or other parts of a house, or by any kind of violence or circumstance of terror enters upon or into any real property; or, 2. Who, after entering peaceably upon real property, turns out by force, threats, or menacing conduct, the party in possession... ." Many of the statutes are poorly drafted.

Tort Actions against the Rightful Owner for Repossession

Does the statute forbidding forcible reentry mean that the wrongful possessor should have a tort claim against the owner who enters with no more force than required to oust the wrongdoer? No single rule is likely to produce results that are invariably satisfactory.

No action when owner uses reasonable force. In the United States, the courts are divided. Quite a few cases have said that the wrongful possessor has no claim against the repossessing owner, so long as the owner uses no more force than reasonably necessary to evict.[5] This is also the current English view.[6]

Action allowed against owner who uses reasonable force. A large group of courts, usually said to be the majority,[7] permit the wrongful possessor to recover from the owner who violates the statute by using force to reenter, even though the amount of force used is no more than made necessary by the possessor's resistance.[8]

Action allowed against owner for peaceable repossession. Some statutes go further and forbid *any* self-help remedy for the owner out of possession, at least when that owner is a landlord.[9] In line with this,

5. E.g., Watson v. Brown, 67 Haw. 252, 686 P.2d 12 (1984) (commercial lease, statutory summary proceedings are not exclusive remedy); Shorter v. Shelton, 183 Va. 819, 33 S.E.2d 643 (1945).

6. Hemmings v. Stoke Poges Golf Club, Ltd., [1920] 1 K.B. 720, [1918] All.E.R. 798 (C.A. 1919). Commentators believe that this view survives the 1977 Criminal Law Act. See W.V.H. Rogers, Winfield and Jolowicz on Tort (13th ed. 1989). The English statute did not expressly provide anything about civil actions. After centuries of uncertainty, Newton v. Harland, 1 Man. & G. 644, 133 Eng.Rep. 490 (C.P. 1840) held that a landlord who forcibly evicted a holdover tenant would be liable, apparently for the assault and battery on the tenant rather than for dispossession as such. This case was tried three times and ultimately abandoned, but it stood as the law until rejected in 1919 in the *Hemmings* case, supra.

7. See Annotation, Right of Landlord Legally Entitled to Possession to Dispossess Tenant without Legal Process, 6 A.L.R.3d 177 (1966). The majority may be made up at least partly of cases in which actual personal injury or harm to chattels was the result of the entry.

8. Daluiso v. Boone, 71 Cal.2d 484, 455 P.2d 811, 78 Cal.Rptr. 707 (1969); Tatro v. Lehouiller, 147 Vt. 151, 153, 513 A.2d 610, 611 (1986) ("a landlord cannot forcibly evict a tenant at will"); Freeway Park Building, Inc. v. Western States Wholesale Supply, 22 Utah 2d 266, 451 P.2d 778 (1969); People v. Evans, 163 Ill.App.3d 561, 564, 114 Ill.Dec. 662, 516 N.E.2d 817, 819 (1987) ("no person has the right to take possession, by force, of premises occupied or possessed by another, even though such person may be justly entitled to such possession. The forcible entry and detainer statute provides the complete remedy . . . ."; holding that the forcible entry statute supplanted criminal trespass prosecutions). Cases cited in note 10 below also support the text statement by imposing an even broader ground for liability.

Courts taking this view naturally do not focus on the fact that the force was necessitated by the occupant's resistance, since to do so raises the question whether the occupant is in some degree the author, not only of the whole problem, but of the immediate harm as well. The broad statements made in the opinions justify the text statement that, in these cases, liability is imposed even if the force is reasonably proportioned to the need.

9. See Gerchick, No Easy Way Out: Making the Summary Eviction Process a Fairer and More Efficient Alternative to Landlord Self–Help, 41 UCLA L. Rev. 759 (1994); cf. City of Evanston v. O'Leary, 244 Ill.App.3d 190, 184 Ill.Dec. 913, 614 N.E.2d 114 (1993) (city ordinance forbidding peaceful lockouts).

The New York statute was amended so that it is no longer limited to force: "If a person is disseized, ejected, or put out of real property in a forcible or *unlawful* manner, or, after he has been put out, is held

some cases actually impose liability upon the owner who repossesses without using force against the occupant or her goods. One example of liability for a peaceable retaking is the case of a landlord's self-help eviction: the landlord locks the tenant out when the rent is not paid and becomes liable for doing so,[10] at least where a speedy remedy in the courts is available.[11] Many cases involve tenants who wrongfully hold over after the lease has expired for nonpayment of rent or otherwise.

Broad definitions of force. At least as a matter of form, some courts reject the rule that a peaceable repossession is a tort to the occupant, but at the same time define force so broadly that most effective repossessions will be actionable because they are regarded as forcible. North Carolina holds that if a tenant objects to repossession, the landlord is subject to tort liability if he proceeds further, or if he goes beyond repossession and holds the tenant's goods.[12]

Types of Harm To Be Redressed

Liability of the true owner for retaking his own property is complicated further by the fact that at least three distinct kinds of cases can arise. Courts and writers do not always carefully distinguish among them in counting majorities.

First, the owner-defendant's forcible entry could cause actual harm to the wrongful possessor, a physical injury or the like even if he uses only reasonable force.[13] In most cases, physical injury betokens a breach of the peace and in any event it is plausible to say that the owner who wishes to use self-help must accept liability for any actual injuries, intended or not. If he wishes to avoid that risk, he must resort to judicial

and kept out by force or by putting him in fear of personal violence or by unlawful means, he is entitled to recover treble damages in an action therefor against the wrong-doer. [italics added]" N.Y. REAL PROP. ACTS § 853.

Tenants' rights statutes and unfair trade practices statutes may create claims apart from those based on reentry. For example, cutting off electricity to premises after the lease had expired was found by the referee to be an unfair practice under a Connecticut statute. See Gargano v. Heyman, 203 Conn. 616, 525 A.2d 1343 (1987).

10. There are at least two lines of reason for this result. (a) The statutory remedy for the landlord or owner is exclusive, hence he cannot even use peaceable means to repossess. See Mendes v. Johnson, 389 A.2d 781 (D.C.1978). (b) A landlord's lockout of the tenant, although done in the tenant's absence and without violence, is nevertheless defined as "forcible" "in legal contemplation." Ramirez v. Baran, 730 P.2d 515 (Okla.1986). As to commercial leases, however, see n. 19 below. In Serreze v. YWCA of Western Massachusetts, Inc., 30 Mass. App.Ct. 639, 572 N.E.2d 581 (1991) the plaintiffs, who had been given quarters in a transitional home for battered women, were given notice to leave when they refused to continue some of the required counseling; eventually the social agency in charge changed the locks on their doors. This was held to violate the plaintiffs' rights, although they were not tenants and their only "payment" for their apartments was attendance at counseling sessions.

11. Berg v. Wiley, 264 N.W.2d 145, (Minn.1978) (adopting the "modern trend" on this point).

12. Spinks v. Taylor, 303 N.C. 256, 278 S.E.2d 501 (1981). Apparently this would permit a lockout of the tenant so long as her goods were available to her, but a statute subsequently broadened the tenant's rights. See Stanley v. Moore, 339 N.C. 717, 454 S.E.2d 225 (1995).

13. E.g., Daluiso v. Boone, 71 Cal.2d 484, 455 P.2d 811, 78 Cal.Rptr. 707 (1969) (distress and heart problems following confrontation with neighbor who was tearing down the fence and claiming rights of possession).

process. So when the wrongful occupant is actually injured, liability is relatively easy to justify.

Second, the owner's forcible entry could cause harm that would be legally recognizable in the absence of a privilege, such as a technical battery that is merely offensive but not harmful. Neither this claim nor the first one is about the wrongful possessor's rights to possession as such, so in an important way they are not about traditional trespass claims at all.[14]

Third, the wrongful possessor might suffer only injury in the sense that he lost possession of property to which he was not entitled and whatever inconvenience or hardship that might entail.[15] This claim sounds like a claim to a property right because it is based solely upon dispossession. Yet the wrongful possessor has no right to possession, so the claim is hardly a property right in the ordinary sense and it seems unjust if not inane to put him back in possession.[16]

Policy

Danger of violence vs. welfare policy. The policy claim for the rule against forcible repossession by the owner has been that, were the rule otherwise, violent confrontations would be likely and that it is better to preserve the government's "monopoly on force" than to permit this form of self-help. The fact that riotous behavior sometimes results from unpopular arrests suggest that there might be some basis in fact for the claim that retaking property could lead to bloodshed. In fact, however, in the landlord-tenant cases, the holdover tenant is almost always quite vulnerable and seldom in a position to generate an affray. Perhaps the policy today is not based so much upon the fear that widespread violence would occur when the landlord repossesses but upon the humane concern that the tenant would be left homeless.

Limits appropriate to welfare policy. If courts allow a suit by a wrongful occupant out of fear that landlords in particular are in a position to oppress or impose hardships, they must be thinking especially of residential tenants.[17] If the policy is about this kind of welfare rather

14. Hemmings v. Stoke Poges Golf Club, [1920] 1 K.B. 720, [1981] All E.R. 798 (C.A. 1919) (the plaintiff as wrongful occupant was led gently by the hand off the premises; his wife would not budge from her chair, and she and the chair were carried out).

15. Mendes v. Johnson, 389 A.2d 781, 782 (D.C.App.1978) ("He evicted her by packing up and removing all her possessions. Appellee and her daughter had to pay for a motel before finding other lodging"); Freeway Park Building, Inc. v. Western States Wholesale Supply, 22 Utah 2d 266, 451 P.2d 778 (1969) (dispossession of commercial business may have led to lost profits; a case that relies on wrongful eviction as a tort distinct in unspecified ways from the Forcible Entry claim and also relies in part on wrongful attachment).

16. Cf. Schwinn v. Perkins, 79 N.J.L. 515, 516, 78 A. 19 (1910) (courts have observed "the seeming injustice of a judgment restoring the possession of property to one not rightfully entitled thereto").

17. "[T]here is discernible a certain public policy, based upon humane considerations of the wrong, oppression and hardships which might ensue, if families, in any kind of weather, at any time of day or night, might be thus forcibly ejected from their homes with all their effects without notice or warning." City of Evanston v. O'Leary, 244 Ill.App.3d 190, 184 Ill.Dec. 913, 614 N.E.2d 114 (1993) (quoting). One

than about violence, the tort action might appropriately be allowed to, say, residential tenants, but not to commercial tenants or squatters.[18] Courts have sometimes recognized this by allowing the commercial landlord but not the residential landlord to use reasonable self-help remedies to repossess the land peaceably where the lease so provides.[19]

Tenant's process rights. A third policy judgment in support of liability for a peaceable retaking of the land is that the plaintiff-possessor is entitled to be heard in defense of her possession. Her claim is not for the loss of property or possession itself, but for the denial of fair judicial process.

Some judges seem to be leaning toward the view that the possessor is almost always entitled to judicial process and that if the owner uses a self-help remedy he is committing a tort analogous to the denial of due process.[20] Computation of damages for denial of a process right, as distinct from a right to possession, however, is likely to be problematical.[21] In any event, under this analysis, the tort if any to the plaintiff is not an ordinary trespass to real property at all but a highly personal claim to an intangible right.

§ 81. Repossession of Chattels

General Rules

No privilege to use force after possession is lost. As already indicated,[1] the privilege to defend one's possession of chattels by reasonable force[2] does not generally include a privilege to recover possession by force,[3] threats of force,[4] or by an arrest without a warrant.[5] Once

writer also mentioned prevention of homelessness. See Gerchick, No Easy Way Out: Making the Summary Eviction Process a Fairer and More Efficient Alternative to Landlord Self-Help, 41 UCLA L.Rev. 759 (1994).

18. A more radical argument would be that if it is really a policy of achieving tenant welfare by forcing the landlord to accept unpaid occupation until judicial process can be invoked, the state should not require individual citizens to finance the tenant welfare but should pay the rent itself. The opposing view is that even wrongful possession is itself rightful until proven to be wrong and that the tenant should have a right to judicial process. At a minimum, the state should provide a more efficient remedy than the summary eviction process usually proves to be. See the exhaustive analysis of the process in Gerchick, No Easy Way Out: Making the Summary Eviction Process a Fairer and More Efficient Alternative to Landlord Self-Help, 41 UCLA L.Rev. 759 (1994).

19. Rucker v. Wynn, 212 Ga.App. 69, 441 S.E.2d 417 (1994); Craig Wrecking Co. v. S.G. Loewendick & Sons, Inc., 38 Ohio App.3d 79, 526 N.E.2d 321 (1987).

20. Friends of Yelverton, Inc. v. 163rd Street Improvement Council, Inc., 135 Misc.2d 275, 514 N.Y.S.2d 841 (1986) (specific analogy to due process, suggesting that state action might not be required for a due process claim under state constitutions); cf. Mendes v. Johnson, 389 A.2d 781 (D.C.App. 1978) (tenant should have "opportunity to assert various equitable defenses").

21. In Carey v. Piphus, 435 U.S. 247, 98 S.Ct. 1042, 55 L.Ed.2d 252 (1978) a school boy was suspended without a due process hearing, but he would have been suspended had a hearing been held as well. So proper process would have changed nothing in the ultimate result. The Court limited recovery to nominal damages in the absence of any proven harms.

§ 81

1. § 80, supra.

2. Reasonable force and deadly force are considered in § 76 and following sections.

3. Bobb v. Bosworth, 16 Ky. 81 (1808) (violence may be used to defend against a violent taking, but not to regain possession once lost).

possession is clearly lost, the owner must resort to the courts to recover the chattel if a peaceable recovery is not possible. Put otherwise, the law favors the rights of actual possession until the courts can actually determine the rights of the matter.[6]

Defending rightful possession and fresh pursuit. A momentary loss of control during a scuffle is not a loss of possession as long as the parties are still contending for the chattel. As long as the scramble continues, the owner or original possessor can use force in defense of the possession so long as the amount of force is reasonable and the use of force reasonably appears to be necessary to defend possession.[7] The original possessor may even use reasonable force if needed to recover the chattel in the course of or at the end of a fresh pursuit.[8]

Mistake. But the original possessor must be in the right. If the facts did not justify force, or the amount of force used, he has no privilege even if he acted under a reasonable mistake.[9] Thus the seller who mistakenly believes that payments are in arrears and that he has a right to retake the chattel is liable for a conversion if he takes it,[10] the same rule that applies to any other case of conversion.[11]

Fraudulent taking. The usual case is probably one in which the chattel was taken wrongfully, with or without a claim of right, but fresh pursuit followed by the reasonable use of force as needed has been permitted when the plaintiff gained control of the chattel by fraud and the owner-defendant followed immediately, inflicting only such force as needed.[12]

4. Barnes v. Martin, 15 Wis. 240 (1862) (approaching with a knife to regain chattel).

5. A shopkeeper may, however, enjoy a privilege to detain briefly for investigation. See § 84. As to the law of arrest without a warrant, see § 83.

6. See Adams v. Department of Motor Vehicles, 11 Cal.3d 146, 520 P.2d 961, 113 Cal.Rptr. 145, 64 A.L.R.3d 803 (1974).

7. McLean v. Colf, 179 Cal. 237, 176 P. 169 (1918) (defendant had privilege to attempt to regain a paper the plaintiff had snatched from him and inserted in her bodice, but it was a jury question whether the defendant used excessive force; the mere fact that he never succeeded in getting the paper back did not necessarily show that the force was moderate); Spelina v.Sporry, 279 Il. App. 376 (1935) (privilege to recapture lumber the plaintiff was carrying away, but not by use of deadly force).

8. See State v. Elliot, 11 N.H. 540 (1841) (owner of windows caught up with taker 100 rods down the road and wrestled them from her; this was justified); Restatement § 103. The Restatement has it that in this day of speedy travel, one should be permitted to chase down the converter of chattels upon a timely discovery of the wrong, even if that is hours later.

9. See Gortarez v. Smitty's Super Valu, Inc., 140 Ariz. 97, 680 P.2d 807 (1984); Restatement § 100, cmt. d

10. E.g., Binder v. General Motors Acceptance Corp., 222 N.C. 512, 23 S.E.2d 894 (1943).

11. § 62, supra.

12. Hodgeden v. Hubbard, 18 Vt. 504 (1846), overruled on other grounds, Loverin v. Wedge, 102 Vt. 138, 146 A. 248 (1929). The plaintiff misrepresented his assets to a seller who let him have merchandise (a stove). The seller immediately discovered the misrepresentation and set out in hot pursuit, overtaking the plaintiff two miles away. Plaintiff drew a knife and was forcibly held while the defendant took back the stove. The trial judge charged the jury that the plaintiff's misrepresentation did not justify a forcible retaking of the stove, but on appeal this was held error, as the plaintiff had a privilege to retake the property if it was done without a breach of the peace or unnecessary force.

The rules imply that the true owner who has lost possession will be liable for any tort committed in retaking the chattel by force. The more ironic implication of the rules is such an owner may not use force to regain it, but the wrongdoer in possession is privileged to use all the force reasonably necessary to defend the wrongful possession. Juries intent on short-term justice may dislike the irony and disregard the legal rule; but judges intent on long-term peace may in their turn disregard the jury's justice.[13]

The Repossessing Seller

Peaceable repossession. The problem of repossession often arises when chattels are sold on credit, under a conditional sales contract or the like. When the buyer fails to make payments as due, the seller is ordinarily entitled by the terms of the sales documents to repossess the chattel. The Uniform Commercial Code, which governs rights and remedies in chattel sale cases, provides that the seller may retake possession if he does so "without breach of the peace;"[14] but if the seller uses force, he exceeds that privilege and he is liable for harms done.[15]

Repossession against will of the purchaser. "Breach of the peace" as used in the Code and in the pre-Code cases is a vague term. Although some courts find a breach of peace only when the seller uses substantial force, others treat repossession as a breach of the peace when it goes beyond the express or implied consent of the buyer-debtor. So the debtor's actual resistance to repossession is enough to convert the seller's otherwise peaceful efforts into a breach of the peace.[16] The seller is even considered to be in breach of the peace if he continues after a face-to-face demand from the debtor that he desist and depart.[17]

Intrusion in private quarters. Even if the debtor is not physically present and resisting or objecting, the seller may be in breach of the peace because of the intrusive methods of repossession or abusive behavior. For example, a seller who enters the buyer's enclosed areas without consent may be in breach of the peace merely by that entry if

13. See Barnes v. Martin, 15 Wis. 240 (1862) (jury gave a handsome verdict to one Barbara, who came brandishing a knife to the defendant's land to retrieve her wandering cow, but, held, reversed).

14. UCC § 9–503. See 2 James White & Robert Summers, Uniform Commercial Code 574 ff. (3d ed. 1988).

15. Even if the breach of the peace is caused, not by the seller, but by the seller's independent contractor, the seller may be held liable on the theory that peaceable repossession is a nondelegable duty. Nixon v. Halpin, 620 So.2d 796 (Fla.App.1993); MBank El Paso, N.A. v. Sanchez, 836 S.W.2d 151 (Tex.1992). As to liabilities of those who employ independent contractors, see §§ 336 & 337.

16. "A secured party who insists on taking possession after resistance by the debtor faces the consequences of its use of force.... He acts at his peril, and exposes himself to severe potential liability ... ." Nixon v. Halpin, 620 So.2d 796, 798 (Fla. App.1993).

17. Smith v. John Deere Company, 83 Ohio App.3d 398, 614 N.E.2d 1148 (1993). Even if the demand is not made face to face at the time of repossession the creditor may be obliged to honor it. Bloomquist v. First National Bank of Elk River, 378 N.W.2d 81, 84 (Minn.App.1985) ("When a debtor has not consented to repossession and in fact, has specifically revoked any implied right to such repossession, a creditor is not entitled to the self-help remedy but must pursue a judicial remedy").

the quarters are not normally open to the public or casual users.[18] And even more clearly if he breaks or picks locks to enter.[19] Privacy expectations count here, so that even entrance into an open but secluded ranch yard might create a "possibility of immediate violence" that would count as a breach of the peace.[20]

Liability for unprivileged repossession. If the repossessor breaches the peace in repossessing, he becomes liable for harms done. He certainly becomes liable for the physical harm to the plaintiff by way of battery or otherwise,[21] for damages to other property,[22] and even for conversion of the property he repossesses.[23] Punitive damages may be awarded when the creditor's behavior is wrongful in a sufficiently serious way.[24]

Entering Another's Land to Recapture Chattels

Sellers governed by the UCC frequently repossess chattels from defaulting buyers by entering upon the buyer's land to obtain the chattel. Unless the seller breaks in, intrudes in a building, or invades privacy interests, courts often make no special point of the fact that entry upon land was required.[25] The common law rule is in accord. It permits a defendant who is entitled to immediate possession to recover the goods from another's land (a) if the defendant did not cause the intrusion of the goods in the first place and (b) if entry is reasonable as

18. E.g., Bloomquist v. First National Bank of Elk River, 378 N.W.2d 81 (Minn. App.1985) (bank's agents removed broken window to enter garage, then opened garage door from the inside and repossessed the debtor's tools; the debtor was not present but the bank knew that he objected); cf. McLeod v. Jones, 105 Mass. 403 (1870) (mortgagee/purchaser entering into house while owner-mortgagor was away, no privilege).

19. Cf. Berg v. Wiley, 264 N.W.2d 145. (Minn.1978) (landlord's lockout of tenant to repossess premises)

20. Salisbury Livestock Co. v. Colorado Central Credit Union, 793 P.2d 470 (Wyo. 1990).

21. Smith v. John Deere Company, 83 Ohio App.3d 398, 614 N.E.2d 1148 (1993) (repossessor in breach of the peace was a trespasser and thus liable to possessors for any injuries they suffered in the course of repossession of a tractor; no comparative negligence reduction in damages would be appropriate if liability is imposed for the trespass instead of for negligence).

22. E.g., Star Bank, N.A. v. Laker, 637 N.E.2d 805 (Ind.1994) (in moving the debtor's property to reach and repossess one item, the creditor created ruts in the plaintiff's land; in moving the plaintiff's horses to reach another item, the creditor left the horses near some feed, where they ate too much and became ill; in repossessing a third item the creditor mistakenly got a neighbor's property instead and did damage to it); Giese v. NCNB Texas Forney Banking Center, 881 S.W.2d 776 (Tex.App.1994) (creditor had burden of proving it had not damaged other property in repossessing mobile home).

23. Henderson v. Security National Bank, 72 Cal.App.3d 764, 140 Cal.Rptr. 388 (1977); Bloomquist v. First National Bank of Elk River, 378 N.W.2d 81 (Minn.App. 1985) (apparently intending a full recovery of market value of the goods).

24. Star Bank, N.A. v. Laker, 637 N.E.2d 805 (Ind.1994); Bloomquist v. First National Bank of Elk River, 378 N.W.2d 81 (Minn.App.1985)

25. In Salisbury Livestock Co. v. Colorado Central Credit Union, 793 P.2d 470 (Wyo.1990), George had borrowed money on his vehicles and was substantially in arrears. The vehicles were located on land of the Salisbury Livestock Company. The repossessor entered the Livestock Company's land and towed the vehicles. The Livestock Company then sued for trespass to its land. The court recognized that a trespass action might lie in favor of the Livestock Company, but only if the entry could count as a breach of the peace.

to both time and manner.[26]

In some cases, the plaintiff-landowner bears some responsibility for the fact that the goods are on his land, and in such cases the defendant entitled to possession easily has a right to enter, demand the goods, and take them without excessive force.[27] In other cases, the goods have arrived upon the defendant's land through neutral forces, washed up by a flood, for example, or carried upon the land by third persons. Here again, the defendant is privileged to enter and to take the goods, but in these cases the defendant must pay for damage done in the process.[28] Such a case seems indistinguishable from the case of necessity, which requires just such a payment.[29]

Authorities say that if the defendant's chattel comes onto the plaintiff's land by the defendant's own fault, the defendant has no privilege to remove it except by the peaceful agreement of the possessor, unless public or private necessity can be shown.[30] So phrased, the rule might impose liability upon a defendant whose negligently parked car rolls onto the plaintiff's land, not only for the damage done but also for the separate act of "trespass" in recovering the car. Unless the land possessor is entitled to a lien upon the car for some reason, however, it seems useless to suggest that the car owner must pay nominal damages for a peaceable retaking of his car and downright bad policy to suggest that the landowner could properly use force to prevent retrieval of the car. Perhaps it is no problem. The possessor of the land will often agree to a peaceable re-taking of the chattel if no harm has been done, since if he does not agree, he might be held liable for a conversion.[31]

Topic D. Arrest

§ 82. Actions under a Warrant or other Legal Process

Valid warrant. Peace officers are not liable in tort for properly executing a valid, lawfully issued warrant[1] or other judicial process

26. See Arlowski v. Foglio, 105 Conn. 342, 135 A. 397, 53 A.L.R. 481 (1926) (when goods are on land of another without the defendant's act); Shehyn v. United States, 256 A.2d 404 (D.C.App.1969) (one entering land to retrieve his cat is privileged to do so; landowner thus had no privilege to defend his possession and is properly convicted of assault).

27. In Wheelden v. Lowell, 50 Me. 499 (1862), the landowner had fraudulently induced the defendant to sell a horse. Upon discovery of the fraud, the defendant rescinded and entered the land to get the horse. This was held to be no trespass. The court heavily emphasized the fault of the plaintiff landowner.

28. Wippert v. Burlington Northern Inc., 397 F.Supp. 73 (D.Mont.1975) (defendant's railroad train derailed because of high winds; entry upon the plaintiff's property to reclaim the train was not a trespass, but defendant was liable for actual damages caused); Restatement § 198 (2). Cf. Polebitzke v. John Week Lumber Co., 173 Wis. 509, 181 N.W. 730 (1921) (privilege to take logs washed upon the plaintiff's land, no liability for nominal damages that would otherwise be imposed).

29. See § 107 below.

30. Restatement § 200.

31. Restatement § 237 subjects one to liability for failing to surrender possession to one entitled thereto when demand is made.

§ 82

1. A warrant is a writing directing seizure of a person or goods; it must be issued by a court having authority to issue warrants. See Restatement § 113.

according to its terms. They may also enjoy a privilege to arrest even without a warrant in some cases,[2] and a more general qualified immunity to carry out discretionary decisions within the scope of their duties.[3] This section's focus is on the narrow problem of actions taken under the authority of a warrant.

The protective rule does not shield officers from liability for excessive force or other unreasonable means of acting under the warrant; an arrest warrant for traffic violations would not ordinarily justify the use of deadly force.[4] Even a felony charge does not necessarily justify the use of deadly force when the supposed felon presents no physical danger.[5] Unless excused by danger or otherwise, the officer must ordinarily knock and announce his presence and his authority before entering a dwelling house, even though armed with a warrant.[6] Otherwise, however, officers incur no tort liability for proper arrests, searches, or seizures under valid legal process, even if it turns out that the arrested person was innocent.

Warrant fair on its face. Peace officers may receive a warrant that in fact was improperly issued but that is "fair on its face" or "facially valid." At least if the court issuing the warrant has or apparently has jurisdiction,[7] the officer who executes a facially valid warrant in good faith is protected from liability even if the warrant was improperly issued.[8]In other words, the officer need not investigate the wisdom or propriety of the warrant that appears to be valid.[9] Nor need the officer

2. § 83 below.

3. See § 273 below.

4. Restatement § 131 (deadly force authorized if the warrant charges treason or felony and the officer reasonably believes that the arrest cannot be effected without such force).

5. Cf. Tennessee v. Garner, 471 U.S. 1, 105 S.Ct. 1694, 85 L.Ed.2d 1 (1985) (deadly force against a fleeing but nondangerous felon may be constitutionally impermissible); Colorado v. Hutchinson, 9 F.2d 275 (8th Cir.1925) (shooting suspected car thief); § 46. But force that is excessive to effect an arrest may be permissible in self-defense, so that if the arrested person resists in a way that endangers the officer, the officer may be privileged to use great force. Loveless v. Hardy, 201 Ala. 605, 79 So. 37 (1918).

6. Wilson v. Arkansas, 514 U.S. 927, 115 S.Ct. 1914, 131 L.Ed.2d 976 (1995) (Fourth Amendment reasonableness requirement ordinarily requires knock and announce, but not invariably).

7. See e.g., Moody v. McElroy, 513 A.2d 5, 9 (R.I.1986) ("The defendant was entitled to rely on the justice of the peace's representation that he had authority to sign the warrant"); Sell v. Thompson & Coates, Ltd., 163 Wis.2d 765, 472 N.W.2d 834 (Wis. App.1991).

8. Yeager v. Hurt, 433 So.2d 1176, 1179 (Ala.1983) ("A sheriff or other law enforcement officer is privileged to commit acts which would otherwise be a trespass to chattel or conversion when he acts pursuant to a court order which is valid or fair on its face"); Moody v. McElroy, 513 A.2d 5 (R.I.1986); Restatement §§ 122, 124.

9. Torres v. Glasgow, 80 N.M. 412, 417, 456 P.2d 886, 891 (Ct.App.1969) ("The warrant did not evidence on its face a clear absence of jurisdiction of the issuing authority. The officers were not required to question all the language in the writ and determine its legal effect. Nor were they obligated to question the wisdom of Judge McManus in issuing the writ, or the judgment of Mr. Love in initiating its issuance and in requesting their aid in having it executed. In our opinion, the writ would appear valid to an ordinarily intelligent and informed layman. This is all that was required to make the writ valid on its face.") Cf. Baker v. McCollan, 443 U.S. 137, 146, 99 S.Ct. 2689, 2695, 61 L.Ed.2d 433 (1979) (officers infringed no constitutional rights when they failed to discover that a properly arrested prisoner was the "wrong person"; "we do not think a sheriff executing an arrest warrant is required by the Constitution to investigate independently every claim of innocence, whether the claim is

investigate the court's authority to issue the warrant if the court has authority to issue warrants generally, or warrants dealing with the same general kind of conduct and nothing in the warrant gives notice that the court lacks jurisdiction to act or jurisdiction over the person or premises described.[10] The same rule applies to other forms of judicial process. For example, the constable who executes the replevin writ that is facially valid is not liable for seizing the plaintiff's property under the writ's terms[11]in the absence of some notice that the writ is invalid.

Good faith. The rule protecting the officer who properly executes a facially valid warrant is often stated without qualification. However, in at least some cases, the officer is liable if he has actual knowledge that the warrant is invalid or improperly issued even though it is fair on its face. The notable case for liability arises when the officer who executes the warrant was also an officer whose testimony induced the magistrate to issue the warrant in the first place. If the officer misleads the magistrate, or withholds information that would be important in assessing probable cause, he cannot justify his arrest or search merely because the warrant is facially valid.[12]

Losing the protection. The protection is lost if one can determine by reading the warrant that it is invalid. A warrant that authorizes the arrest of the plaintiff for investigation does not charge a crime and is not valid on its face. The officer who arrests the plaintiff on such a warrant will be liable for false arrest. Similarly, if the warrant fails to describe the person to be arrested or the place to be searched with particularity, it is invalid on its face. The officer who executes a warrant to "arrest suspected persons" will be liable for false imprisonment.[13]

based on mistaken identity or a defense such as lack of requisite intent. Nor is the official charged with maintaining custody of the accused named in the warrant required by the Constitution to perform an error-free investigation of such a claim").

10. Restatement § 124.

11. Rock v. Antoine's, Inc., 57 Del. 164, 197 A.2d 737 (1964); Dixie Federal Savings and Loan Ass'n v. Pitre, 498 So.2d 112, 114 (La.App.1986) ("... a sheriff's duty is of a ministerial character; he is without right to question the legality or propriety of orders committed to him officially for execution. A sheriff cannot be held liable in executing a writ where he complies with the terms of the writ. Thus, assuming arguendo that appellant's contentions that the seizure was illegal because of the improper issuance of executory process, his remedy, if any he has, is against the party causing the writ to issue, not the Sheriff or persons acting under his direction who acted in accordance with the directive of the court").

12. Turngren v. King County, 104 Wash.2d 293, 705 P.2d 258 (1985). The Turngren Court said: "When the same officer seeks the warrant and executes it, he should not be allowed to 'cleanse' the transaction by supplying only those facts favorable to the issuance of a warrant. The exception we now announce to the general nonliability rule ... only prevents an officer from asserting the facial validity of a warrant as an absolute defense to a false arrest or false imprisonment action. The officer can still establish a defense to such an action by proving, to the satisfaction of the jury, the existence of probable cause to arrest under the circumstances." Id., 104 Wash.2d at 304, 705 P.2d at 265. If the complaint is not that the officer made an arrest under a warrant but that he instigated the arrest by giving information to the magistrate as a basis for a warrant, the warrant itself cannot provide any defense. See Malley v. Briggs, 475 U.S. 335, 106 S.Ct. 1092, 89 L.Ed.2d 271 (1986).

13. See Moody v. McElroy, 513 A.2d 5, 8 (R.I.1986). The Fourth Amendment to the United States Constitution also requires that warrants must issue only upon probable cause and that the warrants must particularly describe the place to be searched

Departure from the warrant's terms. The valid warrant or one fair on its face operates to protect the defendant who executes it according to its terms. But it may afford no protection for the officer whose conduct is not in accord with the terms of the warrant. If the warrant names John but the officer arrests Jane instead, the rule in some courts and the rule approved by the Restatement is that the warrant provides no protection and the officer is liable, even if he reasonably believed that Jane was John.[14] A different rule relieves the officer who arrests the wrong person if the officer acted reasonably and in good faith after due diligence to ascertain that the plaintiff was the person named.[15]

Harm from manner of seizure or from subsequent acts. A warrant fair on its face protects against tort liability the arrest or seizure it authorizes, but not for the post-arrest or post-seizure torts. For instance, once an arrest is made, the arrested person cannot be held indefinitely without trial; someone, whether the arresting officer or another, must provide a trial or release.[16] Similarly, an officer who seizes the plaintiff's property under a facially valid writ is not liable for the seizure, but may become liable for harm resulting to the property because of his failure to protect it while it is in his custody.[17] In the same way, the officer is liable for improper methods of seizure, for instance, in negligently causing damage to property seized,[18] and of course in going beyond the authority of the writ.

§ 83. Arrest or Detention without a Warrant

The defendant who arrests a person who is in fact guilty of the felony charged, enjoys a complete defense, even though he had no probable cause to make the arrest.[1] Even if the person arrested is not guilty in fact, however, the defendant is privileged in a few instances to make an arrest without a warrant[2] and is not liable for such an arrest if he acts within the limits of that privilege. The privilege may extend not only to police officers but also, in a smaller number of cases, to private individuals. This section summarizes the core common law rules of privilege to arrest or detain without a warrant. Many detailed rules

and the persons or things to be seized. The officer who attempts to justify on a general warrant thus risks not only a false imprisonment or trespass claim, but a federal civil rights claim as well.

14. Restatement § 125.

15. Pierson v. Multnomah County, 301 Or. 48, 718 P.2d 738 (1986) (a kind of Shakespearean mistake-the-twin case).

16. Cf. Baker v. McCollan, 443 U.S. 137, 144, 99 S.Ct. 2689, 2694, 61 L.Ed.2d 433 (1979) (arrested person "could not be detained indefinitely in the face of repeated protests of innocence even though the warrant under which he was arrested and detained met the standards of the Fourth Amendment. For the Constitution likewise guarantees an accused the right to a speedy trial").

17. Yeager v. Hurt, 433 So.2d 1176, 1180 (Ala.1983) ("If the property is lost, damaged, or destroyed the officer, will be liable if the loss is the proximate result of his failure to exercise due care to preserve it").

18. Jeffres v. Countryside Homes of Lincoln, Inc., 214 Neb. 104, 333 N.W.2d 754 (1983) contains a good survey of cases.

§ 83

1. Restatement § 119 (a).

2. As to arrests under a warrant, see § 82.

about arrest and search have been developed in the context of criminal prosecutions. For those details, and for the impact of statutes and constitutional provisions, works on criminal procedure should be consulted[3] as well as statutes in particular states. In addition, the general qualified immunity of officers who act within the scope of their duties may furnish an entirely separate protection. That topic is treated in a later section of this work.[4]

The Nature and Limits of Privileged Arrests and Stops

Purpose. An arrest takes a person into custody for the very particular purpose of bringing the person before a court or similar body administering the law.[5] To claim the privilege of arrest, the defendant must be acting in accord with such a purpose. A confinement for the purpose of extorting a settlement,[6] or for the purpose of holding a witness who is not charged with crime[7] is not an arrest and the privilege to arrest will not protect the defendant. However, some brief stops or detentions, made for the purpose of investigation rather than a charge, may be privileged under separate rules.[8]

Excessive force. Arrests must be effected with no more force than reasonably required to effect the arrest.[9] This means that deadly force is at best only sometimes privileged, as where the arrest is for a serious felony and the defendant reasonably believes the arrest cannot be effected otherwise.[10] Even when deadly force is required to make the arrest effective, it may be impermissible. The common law rule that permitted deadly force as needed to arrest a felon has been subjected to constitutional limitations. In *Tennessee v. Garner*,[11] the Supreme Court held that a statute authorizing deadly force to stop a fleeing felony suspect was unconstitutional under the Fourth/Fourteenth Amendments. In that case, an officer shot a burglary suspect who was attempting to flee the scene and who refused to stop on the officer's demand. Such an officer thus becomes potentially liable. And equally, when the officer's privilege is exceeded by excessive force, the public entity for which he acts may become liable.[12]

Disclosure to the arrested person. The principle of using the minimum force that reasonably appears to be needed also counsels disclosure to the arrested person. The defendant attempting an arrest without a

3. E.g., WAYNE LAFAVE & JEROLD ISRAEL, CRIMINAL PROCEDURE (2d ed. 1992).

4. See Chapter 16.

5. Restatement § 127.

6. Cf. § 438 (liability for abuse of process) .

7. Consult particular statutes for rules governing witnesses.

8. Terry v. Ohio, 392 U.S. 1, 88 S.Ct. 1868, 20 L.Ed.2d 889 (1968).

9. Colorado v. Hutchinson, 9 F.2d 275 (8th Cir.1925).

10. Restatement § 131.

11. Tennessee v. Garner, 471 U.S. 1, 105 S.Ct. 1694, 85 L.Ed.2d 1 (1985).

12. In McCummings v. New York City Transit Authority, 81 N.Y.2d 923, 613 N.E.2d 559, 597 N.Y.S.2d 653 (1993), a mugger, who with two others had attacked a 72-year-old man in a subway, was shot by an officer as he fled. The shots pierced his spinal cord and he was paralyzed from the chest down. The New York Court of Appeals, over two dissents, upheld a jury verdict for the plaintiff against the Transit Authority who had employed the officer.

warrant must normally state his purpose to make an arrest and the grounds for it, although he need not accurately state the precise crime involved.[13] Similarly, one attempting an arrest under a warrant should disclose the warrant.[14] These disclosures are not required if the defendant reasonably believes that such disclosures create dangers to the defendant or to others, or if they are likely to prevent the arrest, or if they are useless because the person to be arrested cannot understand or already knows the charge.[15] Where the disclosure is feasible, however, it is important as tending to reduce the amount of force required to effect the arrest of a plaintiff who might otherwise perceive the arrest as an attack or a misuse of power.

What Arrests Are Privileged

Probable cause. Some of the traditional distinctions in the law of arrest may be somewhat doubtful today,[16] and the exact privileges that justify an arrest without a warrant may vary slightly according to statutes in particular jurisdictions. However, no warrantless arrest is privileged unless the defendant has probable cause, that is, reasonable objective grounds to believe that a crime was committed and that the plaintiff committed it.[17] The defendant who acts in all goods faith but lacks a rational basis for believing that the plaintiff committed the crime is not protected by the privilege.

Private persons. Private persons are privileged to effect an arrest for criminal offenses in limited circumstances. The privilege permits a private defendant to arrest the plaintiff when (1) the plaintiff has in fact committed the felony for which he is arrested, or (2) someone has committed that felony and the defendant reasonably suspects the plaintiff as the person responsible, or (3) the plaintiff has committed a breach of the peace in the presence of the defendant. Beyond this, the private defendant has a limited privilege to effect an arrest to prevent an attempted felony in his presence.[18]

Police officers. Police officers enjoy the same privilege to effect an arrest as private persons and in addition may arrest on reasonable suspicion of a felony even if it turns out that no felony has actually been committed.[19] Officers may be permitted by statute to arrest for misdemeanors committed in their presence even though no breach of the peace is threatened. By statute or by expansion of the common law rule, officers may even be permitted to arrest for misdemeanors that do not risk a breach of the peace and that are not even in their presence.[20]

13. See Bauldock v. Davco Food, Inc., 622 A.2d 28 (D.C.1993).

14. Restatement § 128 (1).

15. Restatement § 128 (2).

16. Cf. Tennessee v. Garner, 471 U.S. 1, 14, 105 S.Ct. 1694, 1703, 85 L.Ed.2d 1 (1985) (the distinction between felonies and misdemeanors "is minor and often arbitrary. Many crimes classified as misdemeanors, or nonexistent, at common law are now felonies").

17. § 85 below.

18. Gortarez v. Smitty's Super Valu, Inc., 140 Ariz. 97, 680 P.2d 807 (1984); Restatement § 119 (summarizing all the situations).

19. Restatement § 121.

20. Torrey v. City of Tukwila, 76 Wash. App. 32, 882 P.2d 799 (1994) (officers acting together, misdemeanor in the presence of one, arrest by the other, no tort).

§ 84. Detention for Investigation: Merchants and the Shoplifting Problem

Investigative stops by officers. As already indicated,[1] officers are constitutionally permitted to stop a person for questioning, so long as the person knows she is free to leave and in addition to make brief investigatory stops based upon a reasonable suspicion.[2] The officer who goes beyond these narrow limits is subject to liability for false arrest or for violation of the Fourth Amendment unless he has a warrant or can justify an arrest by showing probable cause.

Merchants—the traditional common law. The traditional common law recognized no privilege of private persons to detain for investigation. The merchant who suspected shoplifting could make an arrest, but only if the shopper was in fact guilty of a felony, or if a felony has in fact been committed and the shopper was reasonably suspected.[3] These privileges provided little protection, since individual thefts might never reach the felony level and since in any event the merchant might be mistaken about whether a theft took place. The limited privilege to arrest for a misdemeanor would not ordinarily apply, since shoplifting does not normally induce breach of the peace.[4] Nor would the privilege to recapture wrongfully taken chattels help if the merchant was mistaken.[5]

Creating judicial privileges for merchants. As shoplifting has become a major source of losses to merchants,[6] some courts judicially created a privilege more protective than the traditional one. Under this more protective privilege, a merchant who reasonably believes that a person has committed a theft or has attempted a theft may detain the person for a limited period of time and for the limited purpose of investigating the facts.[7] The Restatement endorses this privilege.[8]

Limited scope of the privilege. In the leading case, a detention of twenty minutes was held to be a justified exercise of the privilege.[9] The defendant is "entitled to use a reasonable amount of compulsion in order to effect that restraint."[10] But the defendant loses the privilege if he

§ 84

1. § 83 supra.

2. Terry v. Ohio, 392 U.S. 1, 88 S.Ct. 1868, 20 L.Ed.2d 889 (1968).

3. "The harsh corollary of the common-law rule was that, if the suspicion of theft or interference proved to be erroneous, the detention was per se unreasonable and not warranted by the circumstances." Florida v. Jones, 461 So.2d 97, 99 (Fla.1984).

4. Gortarez v. Smitty's Super Valu, Inc., 140 Ariz. 97, 680 P.2d 807 (1984).

5. Great Atlantic & Pacific Tea Co. v. Paul, 256 Md. 643, 261 A.2d 731 (1970); § 81, supra.

6. Forbes magazine asserted a $30 billion annual loss for shoplifting and employee theft in 1988. Forbes 258 (Nov. 14, 1988). The same source says that retailers spend $250 million annually on protections against shoplifting such as special tags on merchandise that will ring if tagged goods are carried out the door.

7. Collyer v. S.H. Kress Co., 5 Cal.2d 175, 54 P.2d 20 (1936). The privilege was recognized earlier in the exactly analogous case of a restaurant patron suspected of attempting to leave without paying for a meal. Jacques v. Childs Dining Hall Co., 244 Mass. 438, 138 N.E. 843, 26 A.L.R. 1329 (1923) (recognizing privilege but leaving reasonableness of the detention to the jury).

8. Restatement § 120A.

9. Collyer v. S.H. Kress Co., supra n. 7.

10. Collyer v. S.H. Kress Co., supra n. 7.

detains the plaintiff either for an unreasonable time or in an unreasonable manner.[11] In other words, the defendant's probable cause to believe in the plaintiff's guilt does not justify an improper method of questioning and the defendant who unnecessarily handcuffs the plaintiff or makes an exhibit of her in the presence of other customers may lose the privilege.[12]

Statutory privileges for merchants. Most states have enacted statutory versions of the privilege and the contemporary cases are often based on the statute rather than on common law development.[13] Some of the statutes reflect a purpose to protect other repeat-theft victims such as farmers, libraries, museums, and even video rental stores.[14]

Triggering the statutory privilege. The statutory privilege is normally triggered only if the merchant has probable cause to believe a theft has occurred or is being attempted. Since the theft would not normally be completed until the shoplifter has actually passed the checkout counter or left the store, some statutes specifically provide that the privilege to detain for investigation is triggered if the suspect conceals goods[15] or removes anti-theft tags.[16] Others appear to erect the privilege only if the merchant reasonably believes an actual theft has been completed.[17] Some courts have said that the statute must be strictly construed, so that, for example, the merchant may be privileged to detain a suspected thief but not a suspected counterfeiter.[18]

Limiting the statutory privilege. As with the Restatement's privilege, the statutory privilege is usually limited both in duration and in scope. The merchant can investigate, or under some statutes can summon police officers when he has probable cause,[19] but he has no privilege to exact a punishment.[20] And the merchant may detain the suspected

11. Cervantez v. J.C. Penney Company, Inc., 24 Cal.3d 579, 590, 595 P.2d 975, 981, 156 Cal.Rptr. 198, 204 (1979) (the rules strikes a "delicate balance" "between the individual's right to liberty and the property owner's right to protect his property"; "a privilege to arrest a person who had not in fact committed an offense in the merchant's presence solely on the basis of probable cause would constitute a substantial further encroachment on the individual's right to liberty"); Jacques v. Childs Dining Hall Co., 244 Mass. 438, 138 N.E. 843, 26 A.L.R. 1329 (1923).

12. Cf. K–Mart Corporation v. Washington, 109 Nev. 1180, 866 P.2d 274 (1993) (under a statutory privilege).

13. E.g., Gortarez v. Smitty's Super Valu, Inc., 140 Ariz. 97, 680 P.2d 807 (1984); Lerner Shops of Nevada, Inc. v. Marin, 83 Nev. 75, 423 P.2d 398 (1967); Stienbaugh v. Payless Drug Store, Inc., 75 N.M. 118, 401 P.2d 104 (1965);.

14. E.g., Fla. Stat. Ann. § 812.015 (farmers)

15. E.g., Iowa Code Ann. § 808.12.

16. E.g., 11 Del. Code Ann. § 840

17. Md. Cts. & Jud. Pro. Code § 5–402

18. Taylor v. Super Discount Market, Inc., 212 Ga.App. 155, 441 S.E.2d 433 (1994).

19. Ariz. Rev. Stats. § 13–1805; 11 Del. Code Ann. § 840. This is also the conclusion in Melia v. Dillon Companies, Inc., 18 Kan. App.2d 5, 846 P.2d 257 (1993) ("once probable cause exists, the merchant's defense under § 21–3424(3) includes the right to reasonably detain a suspected shoplifter for the sole purpose of investigation by a law enforcement officer"). Of course, summoning the police to make an arrest is not privileged where a detention in the store itself would not be privileged. See Smits v. Wal–Mart Stores, Inc., 525 N.W.2d 554 (Minn.App.1994).

20. Ariz. Rev. Stats. § 13–1805 ("may detain on the premises in a reasonable manner and for a reasonable time any person suspected of shoplifting as defined in subsection A of this section for questioning or summoning a law enforcement officer"); West's Ann.Cal.Penal Code § 490.5 (b) (1)

shoplifter for a reasonable time to accomplish the investigation or perhaps to await the arrival of officers, but may not detain for longer than a brief or "reasonable" period[21] or by improper or unnecessary force.[22] In determining whether the detention was carried out in a reasonable manner, some courts have permitted the plaintiff to introduce evidence of the merchant's own training or policy manuals.[23] However, some statutes, if read literally, appear to authorize an actual arrest by the merchant.

Issues in the merchant detention cases. As this discussion shows, two distinct questions can arise when the merchant claims a privilege to detain, either under common law or statute. In the first place, no arrest or detention of any kind is justified unless the merchant has probable cause. But once probable cause is established, the second question is whether the acts committed by the merchant exceed the privilege. As to this second question, the presence of probable cause matters not at all. These two issues dominate most of the cases, but in some cases, the issue may be seen to be less about the privilege than about the plaintiff's consent to questioning or even more fundamentally to the lack of any real detention. If the defendant merely questions the plaintiff without any implied force or threat, the defendant may not have detained the plaintiff at all and if not, there is no tort.[24]

§ 85. Arrest: Probable Cause

The term probable cause is central in the law of criminal procedure, false arrest, and malicious prosecution. An arrest without a warrant, for example, can only be justified if the persons making the arrest had probable cause for an arrest, that is, if they had reasonably trustworthy information that was sufficient to permit a prudent person's belief that the plaintiff had committed a criminal offense or was in the act of doing so.[1]

("A merchant may detain a person for a reasonable time for the purpose of conducting an investigation in a reasonable manner whenever the merchant has probable cause to believe the person to be detained is attempting to unlawfully take or has unlawfully taken merchandise from the merchant's premises"); Colo. Rev. Stats. § 18–4–407 (may question).

21. E.g., Mass. Gen. L. Ann. 231 § 94B. However, some statutes, if read literally, would appear to authorize a full scale arrest of the suspected shoplifter. Ala. Code § 15–10–14.

22. Wal–Mart Stores, Inc. v. Mitchell, 877 S.W.2d 616, 618 (Ky.App.1994) ("statute does not provide the merchant or its employees with a license to manhandle or browbeat a child in an attempt to discover if he has unlawfully taken merchandise from the premises"); K–Mart Corporation v. Washington, 109 Nev. 1180, 866 P.2d 274 (1993), supra n. 12.

23. K–Mart Corporation v. Washington, supra n. 12; D. A. Johns, Annotation, Admissibility of Defendant's Rules or Instruction for Dealing with Shoplifters, in Action for False Imprisonment or Malicious Prosecution, 31 A.L.R.3d 705 (1970). In K–Mart Corporation v. Washington the court noted that the defendant's manual was not the standard or test of liability but was merely some evidence on the question of reasonableness.

24. See Taylor v. Super Discount Market, Inc., 212 Ga.App. 155, 441 S.E.2d 433 (1994) (questions about suspected counterfeit bill not "unlawful"); Sweeney v. F.W. Woolworth Co., 247 Mass. 277, 142 N.E. 50, 31 A.L.R. 311 (1924); see §§ 36 & 37, supra.

§ 85

1. See Beck v. Ohio, 379 U.S. 89, 85 S.Ct. 223, 13 L.Ed.2d 142 (1964); Wolfe v. Wiener Enterprises, Inc., 648 So.2d 1293 (La.1995); Renk v. City of Pittsburgh, 537 Pa. 68, 641 A.2d 289 (1994).

It is not necessary that the evidence point to guilt beyond a reasonable doubt, only that it would suffice to induce a reasonable belief in guilt.[2] Alternative explanations need not be ruled out. A merchant sees a shopper put merchandise in his pocket then leave the store without paying. The merchant may reasonably entertain a belief in the shopper's guilt although the shopper's conduct could equally be explained on the ground that she forgot to pay and was entirely innocent of any intended theft.[3]

The probable cause requirement does not directly resolve cases. The rule points to a need for analysis of the facts as they appeared at the time of the arrest and of the reasonable inferences to be drawn from them.

Probable cause language is sometimes confusingly carried over to matters that do not involve probable cause at all. It has been said that an arresting officer must ordinarily show he had reasonable grounds to believe that the arrested person committed the crime for which the arrest was made or at least one of the same general kind. Under this view, a reasonable ground to believe that the plaintiff committed some other crime would not justify the arrest.[4] But it has also been said that the validity of an arrest is not affected by the fact that the person making the arrest mischaracterizes the underlying crime.[5]

As ideas about probable cause, these two views may be hard to reconcile, but as rules about the *manner* in which an arrest is to be effected, each view may be justified under some set of facts. One making an arrest should ordinarily disclose his intent to arrest and the factual basis for it, but it is not ordinarily important that he correctly identify the crime of shoplifting rather than, say, petty larceny. Nor is disclosure invariably required because in some cases disclosure may be dangerous. These concerns have little to do with probable cause and much to do with the very different issue whether the manner of the arrest was reasonable.

2. See Bostic v. City of Chicago, 981 F.2d 965, 968–69 (7th Cir.1992) ("Although probable cause requires more than mere suspicion, it does not require that the evidence at the time of arrest be sufficient to prove guilt beyond a reasonable doubt. Rather, probable cause exists if, at the moment of the arrest, the facts and circumstances within the knowledge of the police officers and of which they had reasonably trustworthy information were sufficient to warrant a prudent person in believing that the petitioner had committed or was committing an offense"). Perhaps it would be accurate to say that probable cause exists when one can reasonably believe from the evidence available that the issue of guilt would properly be submitted to a jury. Thus some courts permit a finding of probable cause when the facts would induce a prudent prosecutor "to believe or entertain an honest or strong suspicion that the person arrested is guilty." Lindsey v. Camelot Music, Inc., 628 So.2d 314, 315 (Ala.1993).

3. E.g., Melia v. Dillon Companies, Inc., 18 Kan.App.2d 5, 846 P.2d 257 (1993).

4. Etheredge v. District of Columbia, 635 A.2d 908, 919–20 (D.C.1993) ("Historically, '[a]n arrest for one offense cannot be justified by proof of another, even though intimately connected in time and place'," but in some cases, "no harm, no foul").

5. Bauldock v. Davco Food, Inc., 622 A.2d 28 (D.C.App.1993).

§ 86. Judge and Jury in Probable Cause Determinations

As long as the evidence permits reasonable people to differ, the jury, not the judge, is the trier of fact; but the judge decides whether the facts found by the jury constitute probable cause.[1]

In some courts, the rule that makes judges the decision makers on probable cause issues is applied broadly, so that judges must either get a jury's determination of facts by special verdict and then make their own probable cause decision or must instruct the jury on many precise sets of facts that might constitute probable cause.[2]

In other cases, formulations of the rule are hard to interpret. Some cases say that if the facts are in dispute, the issue of probable cause is for the jury.[3] Sometimes it seems clear that this formulation is merely a shorthand version of the general rule, so that the jury must determine the facts but the judge must still evaluate them to determine whether or not they showed probable cause. But some courts may actually allow the jury to determine not only the disputed facts but also to decide what inferences of guilt the defendant could reasonably draw from them.[4] In addition, the rule that makes the judge the decision maker on probable cause is sometimes applied erratically or is consciously or unconsciously rejected. The result is that in particular cases juries are allowed to be the decision makers.[5] Alabama has made the judge the decision maker in malicious prosecution but not in false arrest cases.[6]

In any event, the rule that assigns the probable cause issue to the judge for decision does not apply to other reasonableness determinations. For instance, even if the judge finds that the defendant had probable cause to believe in the plaintiff's guilt, the defendant might be liable if he uses unreasonable force to effect the arrest, or if he detains the plaintiff for longer than permitted by the merchant's privilege to investi-

§ 86

1. E.g., Bauldock v. Davco Food, Inc., 622 A.2d 28 (D.C.App.1993) (false arrest case; "where the facts are undisputed or clearly established" probable cause is a question of law for the court); Collyer v. S.H. Kress Co., 5 Cal.2d 175, 54 P.2d 20 (1936) (false arrest case); Melia v. Dillon Companies, Inc., 18 Kan.App.2d 5, 846 P.2d 257 (1993) (false arrest case); Best v. Duke University, 337 N.C. 742, 750, 448 S.E.2d 506, 510 (1994) (malicious prosecution case) ("Whether probable cause exists is a mixed question of law and fact, but where the facts are admitted or established, the existence of probable cause is a question of law for the court").

2. See Gustafson v. Payless Drug Stores Northwest, Inc., 269 Or. 354, 525 P.2d 118 (1974).

3. E.g., Thrifty Rent-A-Car v. Jeffrey, 257 Ark. 904, 520 S.W.2d 304 (1975).

4. Parkin v. Cornell University, Inc., 78 N.Y.2d 523, 583 N.E.2d 939, 577 N.Y.S.2d 227 (1991); cf. Greenberg v. Wolfberg, 890 P.2d 895, 903 (Okla.1994) ("Where the facts which relate to the existence or non-existence of probable cause are admitted *and support but a single inference*, whether they constitute probable cause is a question of law for the court's determination." (emphasis added)).

The logic of the rule is that the jury's role as fact-finder must be preserved, but that, disputed or not, once the facts are determined, the judge must evaluate them to determine probable cause. However, the rule is sometimes stated somewhat more cautiously, as if the jury might have a role in the evaluation of probable cause.

5. Holmes v. Nester, 81 Ariz. 372, 306 P.2d 290, 62 A.L.R.2d 1322 (1957).

6. Frison v. Delchamps Store No. 11, 507 So.2d 478 (Ala.1987).

gate shoplifting. Those questions are for the jury, not the judge, provided evidence permits reasonable people to differ.[7]

§ 87. Burden of Proof on Probable Cause and other Issues in Arrest Cases

General rule. So far as the common law of torts goes, the plaintiff who proves he was detained without legal process, has proved a false imprisonment or false arrest case. The defendant has the burden of justifying the arrest without a warrant by proving that the arrest was made on probable cause.[1] That is, the defendant is privileged, and escapes liability, if he can show that he had reasonable grounds to believe that the defendant committed the crime for which the arrest was made. Similarly, if the case is one in which the defendant has a privilege to detain briefly for investigation, that the detention was reasonable.[2] The burden of proof rule can be expressed differently, by saying that an arrest without legal process generates a "presumption" that the arrest was unlawful.[3]

Although the common law burden of proof rule is both clear and well-settled in common law arrest cases, the range of cases to which it applies requires additional explanation.

Burden of proof on probable cause in civil rights cases. An arrested person may sue for violation of federal civil rights if officers make the arrest in violation of the Fourth Amendment's proscription against unreasonable searches and seizures.[4] Fourth Amendment violations also impact criminal prosecutions; if the warrantless arrest is itself without probable cause, evidence obtained incident to the arrest may not be used to convict. In that context, the Supreme Court has treated warrantless arrests as putting the burden upon the officers to justify the arrest by showing probable cause.[5] Presumably this approach would carry over to the civil rights claim for unlawful arrests,[6] but language in some cases may suggest that the plaintiff must prove a want of probable cause in the first instance.[7]

7. E.g., Wal–Mart Stores, Inc. v. Mitchell, 877 S.W.2d 616 (Ky.App.1994) (merchant's privilege claimed, but jury could find defendant exceeded privilege by manhandling minor plaintiff).

§ 87

1. Children v. Burton, 331 N.W.2d 673 (Iowa 1983); Garton v. City of Reno, 102 Nev. 313, 720 P.2d 1227 (1986); Hollender v. Trump Village Cooperative, Inc., 58 N.Y.2d 420, 448 N.E.2d 432, 461 N.Y.S.2d 765 (1983); Terry v. Zions Cooperative Mercantile Institution, 605 P.2d 314 (Utah 1979); Otto v. J. Grant Wallace Ltd., 47 D.L.R.4th 439 (Q.B. Alberta 1988).

2. Foley v. Polaroid Corp., 400 Mass. 82, 508 N.E.2d 72 (1987);

3. E.g., Clarke v. District of Columbia, 311 A.2d 508 (D.C.1973).

4. § 47, supra.

5. Beck v. Ohio, 379 U.S. 89, 97, 85 S.Ct. 223, 229, 13 L.Ed.2d 142 (1964) ("it was incumbent upon the prosecution to show with considerably more specificity than was shown in this case what the informer actually said, and why the officer thought the information was credible"); Recznik v. City of Lorain, 393 U.S. 166, 89 S.Ct. 342, 21 L.Ed.2d 317 (1968).

6. See Washington v. Simpson, 806 F.2d 192 (8th Cir.1986).

7. Cf. Tatro v. Kervin, 41 F.3d 9 (1st Cir.1994) (semble, plaintiff had burden of proof by preponderance of the evidence standard, but not by clear and convincing evidence standard); Moody v. Ungerer, 885 P.2d 200, 202 (Colo.1994) ("In the context

The issue is somewhat confused. The plaintiff clearly has the burden of proving a constitutional or other violation in the first place, but the Supreme Court has characterized the qualified immunity available to officers as an affirmative defense, which ordinarily means the officer would be required to plead and presumably prove the facts necessary to show the immunity. The confusion arises when courts address the affirmative defense without really deciding whether the plaintiff has stated a valid constitutional tort claim in the first place. In such cases the logic of saying that immunity is an affirmative defense requires the defendant to plead[8] and prove[9] that his actions were not reasonably understood to be unconstitutional under the existing law or that the plaintiff's constitutional right was clear under the circumstances. In line with this, some authority has held that when the defendant asserts the federal "qualified immunity," it he has the burden of proving probable cause just as he does under the common law arrest privilege.[10]

Yet a number of federal courts of appeals have held the opposite, putting the burden upon the plaintiff, even when they said they were dealing with the affirmative immunity defense.[11] The reason for this apparent anomaly perhaps lies in the fact that the federal courts have often tended to skip over the issue of constitutional violation in order to decide the immunity issue, and in so doing have conflated the two.[12] Perhaps courts professing to be deciding the immunity issue are at least to some extent actually deciding the constitutional violation issue; if so, they are without dispute correct in putting burden upon the plaintiff to show a Fourth Amendment violation.

Be that as it may, the Supreme Court has sought to separate the two questions, emphasizing that the first issue is whether the plaintiff has proved a constitutional violation at all.[13] Careful separation of the issues

of an allegedly illegal seizure, the plaintiff must not only prove that there was a seizure but that the seizure was unreasonable").

8. Gomez v. Toledo, 446 U.S. 635, 100 S.Ct. 1920, 64 L.Ed.2d 572 (1980).

9. Benigni v. City of Hemet, 879 F.2d 473, 479 (9th Cir.1988); see Harlow v. Fitzgerald, 457 U.S. 800, 819, 102 S.Ct. 2727, 2738, 73 L.Ed.2d 396 (1982) ("if the official pleading the defense claims extraordinary circumstances and can *prove* that he neither knew nor should have known of the relevant legal standard, the defense should be sustained"(emphasis added)).

10. E.g., Dellums v. Powell, 566 F.2d 167 (D.C.Cir.1977) (using the immunity rules and analogy to common law rules in an arrest case, and therefore putting the burden on the defendant).

11. E.g., Sorenson v. Ferrie, 134 F.3d 325 (5th Cir.1998).

12. Thus Omdahl v. Lindholm, 170 F.3d 730, 733 (7th Cir.1999) asserts that "The qualified immunity defense places the burden of establishing the existence of the alleged constitutional violation on the" plaintiffs; but it is not the defense that puts the burden upon the plaintiff; plaintiffs always have the burden of proving their claim, and in a civil rights claim based upon violation of the Fourth Amendment that means the plaintiff must prove a constitutional violation whether a defense is asserted or not. See also Eversole v. Steele, 59 F.3d 710 (7th Cir. 1995); Spurlock v. Satterfield, 167 F.3d 995, 1005 (6th Cir.1999) ("Qualified immunity, like absolute immunity, is also available as an affirmative defense that protects public officials not only from liability, but also from the 'burdens of trial and discovery.' . . . [T]he burden is on the plaintiff to allege and prove that the defendant violated a clearly established constitutional right"); Sorenson v. Ferrie, 134 F.3d 325 (5th Cir. 1998).

13. Siegert v. Gilley, 500 U.S. 226, 111 S.Ct. 1789, 114 L.Ed.2d 277 (1991).

may lead to greater clarity of analysis. But in the arrest cases, the question remains whether the plaintiff proves a Fourth Amendment violation by proving a warrantless arrest or whether the plaintiff must go further and prove a want of probable cause. The Supreme Court may have assumed or tacitly decided that a warrantless arrest, nothing else appearing, is prima facie a violation of the Fourth Amendment.[14] If so, the burden of proving probable cause is upon the arresting officers, just as it is in common law tort cases and in the Fourth Amendment cases involving criminal prosecutions.

Burden of proof in excessive force and subsequent treatment claims. Probable cause for arrest is not an issue in every claim of false arrest or Fourth Amendment violation. If the plaintiff's claim is that the arrest was unlawful only because the force used was excessive or unreasonable, the issue is not about probable cause at all. In that case, many courts hold that the plaintiff has the burden of showing the amount of force and showing that it was excessive.[15]

A single opinion may state two seemingly different burden of proof rules in false arrest cases. The explanation seems to be that one rule applies to excessive force claims and puts the burden on the plaintiff, while the other applies to the want-of-probable-cause kind of case and puts the burden on the defendant to show probable cause.[16]

Similarly, the plaintiff may have claims based upon mistreatment after a warrantless arrest—a failure to take him before a magistrate, for example. The issues and the burden of proof on such claims are not those in determining whether the arrest itself was privileged.

Burden of proof in malicious prosecution claims. Although the burden is upon the defendant to justify an actual detention of the plaintiff—a false arrest or imprisonment—the rule is otherwise when the plaintiff's complaint is not detention but wrongful or malicious prosecu-

14. In Siegert v. Gilley, 500 U.S. 226, 111 S.Ct. 1789, 114 L.Ed.2d 277 (1991), the Court insisted that the first issue is whether a violation of the constitution occurred. Then in Hunter v. Bryant, 502 U.S. 224, 112 S.Ct. 534, 116 L.Ed.2d 589 (1991), a Fourth Amendment case, the Court went straight to the immunity, ignoring the question whether the warrantless arrest was a violation of the constitution. This is no contradiction if the Court believes a warrantless arrest shows a prima facie violation of the Fourth Amendment. See also Peterson v. City of Plymouth, Minnesota, 945 F.2d 1416 (8th Cir.1991) (plaintiffs satisfied the "threshold requirement" that the constitution must have been violated by showing the defendant officers "arrested Mr. Peterson without probable cause"). But some courts require the plaintiff to plead specific facts to negate the immunity. See Breidenbach v. Bolish, 126 F.3d 1288 (10th Cir.1997) and § 276.

15. Edson v. City of Anaheim, 63 Cal. App.4th 1269, 74 Cal.Rptr.2d 614 (1998); Dauffenbach v. City of Wichita, 233 Kan. 1028, 667 P.2d 380 (1983) (officer "presumed" to have acted correctly until plaintiff proves otherwise); Johnson v. Peterson, 358 N.W.2d 484 (Minn.App.1984). Others, however, hold that an officer, like any person who seek to justify a battery, has the burden of proving the justification. E.g., Skinner v. Brooks, 74 Ohio App. 288, 58 N.E.2d 697 (1944).

16. Thus (1) the burden on probable cause is on the defendant but (2) the plaintiff must prove that he was "restrained of his liberty under the probable imminence of force without any legal cause or justification." Garton v. City of Reno, 102 Nev. 313, 720 P.2d 1227 (1986). The quoted clause presumably refers to the plaintiff's burden to show force and its amount in a case where the arrest is otherwise lawful.

tion.[17] In the malicious prosecution cases, the plaintiff bears a heavy burden, because prosecution is the way society normally wishes to resolve issues of guilt and because it should not be discouraged by tort liability that comes too easily. One of the rules that restrict the malicious prosecution claim is that the plaintiff must sustain the burden of proving the *absence* of probable cause for the prosecution, just the reverse of the burden of proof rule when the plaintiff complains of an arrest.

Topic E. Privileges to Enter Land of Another

§ 88. Privileges to Enter Land of Another Generally

To a large extent, the privileges to enter upon land of another person are derived from or represent examples of more general privileges, such as the privilege to recapture chattels under certain circumstances,[1] the privilege to seize property or to make an arrest that itself is privileged,[2] or the privilege to execute legal process or court orders.[3] Necessity, public or private, may also provide a partial or complete privilege to enter land of another, as where one puts a boat ashore on the plaintiff's land to avoid serious risk of life in a storm.[4] Finally, the landowner's consent to use of her land bars recovery for uses consistent with the consent.[5]

Subject to some substantial qualifications, courts have also recognized several privileges that apply only or mainly to entry upon land. The immediately following sections discuss these examples:

(1) In cases of heavily regulated industries such as the liquor industry, regulatory agencies may be permitted to make inspections without a warrant. In the case of other industries, a warrant may be required, but government administrators may be permitted to obtain a warrant without grounds for suspecting a particular crime.[6]

(2) Florida has permitted media employees to enter private property along with officials in some cases.[7]

(3) Places of public accommodation such as restaurants and hotels are under statutory obligations to admit customers without discrimination, and common law rules may impose similar obligations upon common carriers and public utilities.[8]

17. Greenberg v. Wolfberg, 890 P.2d 895 (Okla.1994); § 432.

§ 88

1. See § 81, supra.

2. E.g., Lee v. Greene, 114 N.C.App. 580, 442 S.E.2d 547 (1994); Restatement § 207 & 204. Absent a warrant, only the entry to make an arrest or re-arrest can justify forcible entry of a dwelling, however. See Restatement § 206. See § 106. In addition, even if armed with a warrant, an officer must ordinarily "knock and announce" and this is a constitutional principle as well as a common one. Wilson v. Arkansas, 514 U.S. 927, 115 S.Ct. 1914, 131 L.Ed.2d 976 (1995).

3. See Restatement § 210 (executing court order); Restatement §§ 208, 209 (civil process).

4. See §§ 107 & 108.

5. See § 95.

6. See § 89.

7. See § 96.

8. See § 91.

(4) A few cases permit persons to enter land that is generally open to the public—usually a mall or shopping center—to carry out discussions or protests on social or political issues.[9]

§ 89. Administrative or Regulatory Inspections and other Official Entries

As already indicated, peace officers have no general privilege to enter land of another; except in cases of necessity, they are subject to liability if they do so without warrant, court order, or grounds that furnish a privilege to arrest or search. The older common law view, however, distinguished the case of administrative or regulatory inspections, such as those that might be instituted to enforce health regulations or zoning laws. The common law view held that, as to these, statutes could authorize inspections without a warrant and without probable cause to believe that a crime was being committed.[1]

Issues raised. The regulatory or administrative inspection cases raise two distinct issues, both of which have now been addressed by the Supreme Court under the Fourth Amendment of the United States Constitution in cases involving criminal prosecutions or suits for injunction. The first issue is whether a search warrant is required for administrative searches. The second question is whether a warrant or a search will be justified if it is in some sense "reasonable," even if no there are no grounds to believe that a crime has been committed.

General rule: warrant required. On the first issue, the Supreme Court has now made it clear that in the absence of emergency,[2] the Fourth Amendment's prohibition against unreasonable searches and seizures requires search warrants based upon probable cause to make regulatory inspections without the possessor's consent, whether the premises are used as private homes or commercial buildings.[3]

Exceptions. The Court has recognized an exception permitting warrantless inspections in the case of a few businesses that have historically been subjected to close governmental regulation or supervision. Examples are the liquor[4] and firearms industries.[5] Even an automobile junkyard, with its potential for use in handling stolen automobiles, might

9. See § 92.

§ 89

1. Restatement § 211. In a prescient qualifier, the restaters disclaimed any address to constitutional restrictions on the rule they offered. See Cmt. b.

2. Fighting a fire, for example, and beyond that inspections for arson when evidence has appeared in the course of fighting the fire. Michigan v. Tyler, 436 U.S. 499, 98 S.Ct. 1942, 56 L.Ed.2d 486 (1978). Emergency in this sense is closely analogous to the common law privilege of necessity, covered in §§ 107 & 108.

3. Camara v. Municipal Court of San Francisco, 387 U.S. 523, 87 S.Ct. 1727, 18 L.Ed.2d 930 (1967) (land use regulation under zoning provisions); Marshall v. Barlow's, Inc., 436 U.S. 307, 98 S.Ct. 1816, 56 L.Ed.2d 305 (1978) (inspections under Occupational Safety and Health Act (OSHA)).

4. See Colonnade Catering Corp. v. United States, 397 U.S. 72, 90 S.Ct. 774, 25 L.Ed.2d 60 (1970) (Congress can permit warrantless searches for liquor tax violations but in this case had not permitted agents to break down doors in making a warrantless search).

5. United States v. Biswell, 406 U.S. 311, 92 S.Ct. 1593, 32 L.Ed.2d 87 (1972).

qualify.[6] As to these, statutes may provide for warrantless searches. The reason is said to be that, given the history of governmental oversight of such businesses, an entrepreneur who engages in such a business has "voluntarily chosen to subject himself to a full arsenal of governmental regulation."[7] But the warrantless search is justified only if there is a substantial governmental interest to be protected, the inspection is necessary to further that interest, and the program of inspection is so regulated that it defines the scope of the inspector's discretion and operates to inform the owner of the business about its appropriate scope.[8]

What counts as probable or reasonable cause. The second issue asks what counts as probable or reasonable cause for a search, because such grounds for the search must be shown to obtain a warrant and to justify a search without a warrant where none is required. On this issue, the Court has held that judges may issue a warrant for administrative inspections, at least in some cases, even if there is no evidence of an existing violation of the regulations. The enforcing agency must, however, show at least reasonable general standards for conducting a search that are not arbitrary in selecting the particular target.[9]

§ 90. Trespass Ab Initio

One who enters land under legal authority is not liable for a trespass merely because of the entry. The officer who enters to make a lawful arrest, under a warrant or under the rules for arrest without a warrant, is an example, although civilians often have legal authority or right to enter land, too.[1] But one who enters land under a privilege escapes liability for the entry itself, not for any subsequent tortious misconduct. The officer who uses unnecessary force, or who breaks the flower pots and kicks the puppy, becomes liable for the harm done, though his original entry was privileged. These two points—the privilege and its limit—seem almost tautological and too obvious to mention.

An old common law rule added a crazy wrinkle to this simple and obvious set of rules. It said that by abusing the privilege of legal

6. New York v. Burger, 482 U.S. 691, 107 S.Ct. 2636, 96 L.Ed.2d 601 (1987).

7. Marshall v. Barlow's, Inc., 436 U.S. 307, 98 S.Ct. 1816, 56 L.Ed.2d 305 (1978). Somewhat similarly, some searches outside of homes and businesses may be justified because the plaintiff has no expectation of privacy at all, as might conceivably be the case where a government employee's desk drawers are searched by superiors. The reasonable expectation of privacy of course varies with the facts and social contexts. Even when the employee has an expectation of privacy in the workplace, searches without a warrant may be reasonable in specific instances and if they are, no warrant is required. O'Connor v. Ortega, 480 U.S. 709, 107 S.Ct. 1492, 94 L.Ed.2d 714 (1987).

8. New York v. Burger, 482 U.S. 691, 107 S.Ct. 2636, 96 L.Ed.2d 601 (1987).

9. See Camara v. Municipal Court of San Francisco, supra n.3; Marshall v. Barlow's, Inc., supra n. 7; WAYNE LAFAVE AND JEROLD ISRAEL, CRIMINAL PROCEDURE § 3.9 (2d ed. 1992).

§ 90

1. For example, the right of all citizens to equal access to places of public accommodation is given by law and could be regarded as "legal authority." Something like this was the view in the original case, The Six Carpenter's Case, 8 Co. 146a (K.B. 1610).

authority, an officer became a trespasser *ab initio*, from the beginning.[2] This in turn implied that the defendant was liable for the initial entry and for any harm done, including harm done before he abused the privilege. The doctrine only applied to defendants who entered under an authority of law, but as already indicated, that might include persons besides officers.

Modern law holds that the defendant who enters rightfully but later exceeds his privilege is liable for a "trespass" even though the original entry itself was not trespassory.[3] So far as the *ab initio* doctrine holds the same, it is a harmless if needlessly theoretical doctrine. But so far as the doctrine goes on to permit a recovery for acts that were regarded as innocent or privileged when they were committed, it is not harmless at all.

The officer's liability for acts that were privileged when they were committed might be seen as a primitive means of protecting against abuses by those holding official or practical power,[4] but liability from the time of the wrongdoing seems wholly adequate to that objective, especially when that liability is coupled with liability for extensive attorney fees under the civil rights laws.[5]

The *ab initio* doctrine can also be seen as a covert imposition of punitive damages, because by making the defendant liable for innocently caused harms he is indirectly punished for the later misconduct that did not cause those harms. But there seems no reason to go underground on this point: if punitive damages are justified and permitted, they can be awarded directly. If they are not permitted on the facts, then to obtain punitive results covertly is to subvert the punitive damages rules that courts themselves have made. Beyond that, imposition of punitive liabilities under the *ab initio* rule will only happenstantially inflict the right amount of punishment because the post-entry conduct may deserve heavy punishment even though the liabilities for entry itself would be small.

As a means of assessing appropriate actual damages for the trespass, the *ab initio* doctrine is wildly off base. Although the defendant can appropriately be held for unintended harms resulting from the trespass, he cannot be justly held for the entry itself or for non-tortious caused

2. The Six Carpenter's Case, 8 Co. 146a (K.B. 1610).

3. See Suggs v. Carroll, 76 N.C.App. 420, 333 S.E.2d 510 (1985).

4. See W.V.H. Rogers, Winfield and Jolowicz on Tort 369 (13th ed. 1989). Although the "legal authority" envisioned in the *Six Carpenter's Case* included the simple case of one who has a right to enter the tavern and the case of one who has common use of a field, it also included authority of landlords to seize and hold the tenant's goods until arrears in rent were paid. So it is not implausible to suggest that the rule was triggered in part by potential for abuse by those in power.

5. As to liability for trespass under civil rights legislation, see Monroe v. Pape, 365 U.S. 167, 81 S.Ct. 473, 5 L.Ed.2d 492 (1961), affected as to the standard for a municipality's liability, Monell v. Dept. of Social Services, 436 U.S. 658, 98 S.Ct. 2018, 56 L.Ed.2d 611 (1978). As to attorney fees recoveries in such cases, see 1 Dan B. Dobbs, Law of Remedies § 3.10 (2d ed. 1973).

harms that occur before the trespass any more than he can be held for last week's storm damage to the plaintiff's house.

The Restatement rejects the doctrine, finding few cases since the year 1900 to support it.[6] Occasionally the doctrine is still cited in support of results that appear to have nothing to do with liability for acts that were accounted innocent when they took place.[7]

§ 91. Public Utilities and Public Accommodations

In a few instances, a person has not merely a privilege but also a legal right to enter land (or use the chattels) of another. The legal right to enter or use land carries with it a privilege to do so as well. The privilege may be only a half-privilege, however—a privilege to enter but not a privilege to use force to do so or to resist removal with force.[1]

Public utilities and carriers. Common carriers and public utilities are required to accept all comers as customers. A prospective customer of a utility or carrier has a right to enter upon that part of its premises open to the public and to remain for a reasonable period of time in connection with use of the utility or carrier.[2] For example, a prospective traveler may enter a train station to purchase a ticket and remain for an appropriate time in the waiting room. The privilege is lost or subject to counter-privileges of the landowner if the customer's conduct is unreasonable or disruptive.

Public accommodations. A more contemporary case arises under public accommodations statutes, which require places open to the public

6. Restatement § 214 (2).

7. In Zapata v. Ford Motor Credit Co., 615 S.W.2d 198 (Tex.1981) the court held that a seller-financer's contract with a consumer violated the credit code because it provided for a waiver of the buyer's claim for wrongful detention unless the buyer made a demand within 24 hours. The statute forbad waivers of rights for illegal acts committed "in repossession." Worrying over the "fact that the wrongful detention waived does not occur until at least 24 hours 'after repossession,'" the Texas Court thought that "after" became "in" by virtue of the *ab initio* doctrine. But the court did not hold the defendants liable for repossession; it only held the purported waiver of a claim for wrongful detention to be a violation of statute.

In Williams v. Garnett, 608 S.W.2d 794 (Tex.Civ.App.1980) the defendant contracted to purchase a house from the plaintiff and was allowed to occupy the premises before closing. The parties never closed and the defendant committed certain acts that appeared to be a repudiation. The plaintiff asked the defendant to vacate the premises. The defendant did not, but occupied it for seven months without paying anything. Not surprisingly, the court affirmed a judgment for the rental value of the premises during the defendant's occupancy. It explained this by invoking the *ab initio* doctrine. However, this was a case not merely of harm to the plaintiff but also one of gain to the defendant. That gain was measurable by rental value, so liability for rental value would be appropriate entirely apart from the *ab initio* principle. In any event, traditional *ab initio* had no application because the defendant was not on the premises under a privilege afforded by law.

§ 91

1. See Monnier v. New York Cen. & H.R.R., 175 N.Y. 281, 67 N.E. 569 (1903). Some authority permits a railroad passenger to resist wrongful ejectment with a rather modest amount of force, that sufficient to "denote that he was being removed by compulsion and against his will. . . ." New York, L.E. & W.R. Co. v. Winter's Adm'r, 143 U.S. 60, 73, 12 S.Ct. 356, 360, 36 L.Ed. 71 (1892). The Restatement accepts this view. Restatement § 191, cmt. g.

2. Restatement § 191.

to accept customers without discrimination based on, say, race.[3] These statutes create a right to enter places of public accommodation and a privilege against legal liability for doing so.[4]

§ 92. Free Speech Rights on Another's Land

Landowner's general right to exclude entrant in places otherwise open to the public. When a landowner opens a retail market or a shopping center to the public, people who enter are not ordinarily trespassers at all because they are on the land with the owner's consent. But if no public accommodations statute controls the case, the owner can revoke her consent by asking the entrant to leave the premises. If the entrant does not do so, he becomes a trespasser. That much is the general rule.

The company town exception under the Constitution. Free speech rights intervene to furnish something like a privilege when the private landowner's land is actually a "company town," owned privately but functioning exactly like any other town, with a business block, residential buildings, streets and sewers and other town characteristics open to the public. This was the case in *Marsh v. Alabama.*[1] Marsh distributed religious literature while standing on the street or sidewalk and was arrested when she refused to leave. Her conviction would have been improper had the town belonged to a municipal corporation, since public entities can regulate but cannot wholly bar dissemination of ideas. The Supreme Court held it equally improper when the entire town was privately owned by a company.

Refusing to extend the company town exception. For a period the Supreme Court seemed willing to extend the company town doctrine to ordinary malls or shopping centers. But the Court backed off and in *Hudgens v. National Labor Relations Board,*[2] the Court made it clear that the First Amendment's free speech rights do not protect a trespass on privately owned shopping centers.

Even if the United States Constitution does not operate to protect an entrant on private land such as a mall, state law might do so.[3] Most state law does not. On the contrary, in most states, free speech rights do not trump private property rights, and the landowner can exclude speakers, leafleteers, and others.[4] The cases so holding usually reflect the

3. 42 U.S.C.A. § 2000a.

4. See Georgia v. Rachel, 384 U.S. 780, 86 S.Ct. 1783, 16 L.Ed.2d 925 (1966) (criminal prosecution could not be maintained).

§ 92

1. Marsh v. Alabama, 326 U.S. 501, 66 S.Ct. 276, 90 L.Ed. 265 (1946)

2. Hudgens v. National Labor Relations Board, 424 U.S. 507, 96 S.Ct. 1029, 47 L.Ed.2d 196 (1976).

3. PruneYard Shopping Center v. Robins, 447 U.S. 74, 100 S.Ct. 2035, 64 L.Ed.2d 741 (1980) (state does not violate property owner's due process right by requiring owner to permit speech activities in places otherwise open to the public, nor is state's rule a taking of property that requires compensation).

4. See Cologne v. Westfarms Associates, 192 Conn. 48, 469 A.2d 1201 (1984) (women's group not entitled to an injunction to force mall to permit use for women's literature, petitions); Estes v. Kapiolani Women's and Children's Medical Center, 71 Haw. 190, 787 P.2d 216 (1990) (abortion protes-

rule also applied under the federal Constitution, that free speech guarantees are guarantees against governmental abridgement, not guarantees against private actions.[5] The result is that in most states, one has no privilege to enter or remain on land otherwise open to the public except within the terms of the permission granted expressly or by implication.

State-law cases extending the company town exception. At this writing, two states have created a somewhat general right or privilege to use mall or shopping center space for speech activities where the space in question resembles the public sidewalk or street in traditional town business blocks.[6] Another has recognized a similar right or privilege where the mall is formally owned by a public entity like a city.[7] Three others have recognized a privilege that so far is more limited, namely a privilege to use space in malls or shopping centers for the very narrow purpose of ballot access—obtaining signatures for an initiative or referendum or for placing one's name on a ballot.[8] In a similar vein, some Canadian decisions have established a union's privileges to distribute leaflets at a mall in an attempt to organize an employer located there.[9] And Pennsylvania accepted a privilege to hand out leaflets on the

tors on grounds of private hospital not entitled to injunction to permit their use, federal decisions adopted as state law); People v. DiGuida, 152 Ill.2d 104, 178 Ill.Dec. 80, 604 N.E.2d 336 (1992) (grocery store; criminal prosecution for trespass permissible); Woodland v. Michigan Citizens Lobby, 423 Mich. 188, 378 N.W.2d 337 (1985); City of Helena v. Krautter, 258 Mont. 361, 852 P.2d 636 (1993) (abortion protestors at clinic; criminal prosecution for trespass permissible); SHAD Alliance v. Smith Haven Mall, 66 N.Y.2d 496, 488 N.E.2d 1211, 498 N.Y.S.2d 99 (1985); State v. Felmet, 302 N.C. 173, 273 S.E.2d 708 (1981) (criminal conviction of draft protestor who may have been somewhat intrusive in soliciting signatures); Eastwood Mall, Inc. v. Slanco, 68 Ohio St.3d 221, 626 N.E.2d 59 (1994); Lovejoy Specialty Hosp. v. Advocates, 121 Or. App. 160, 855 P.2d 159 (1993) (abortion protestors liable for trespass damages and punitive damages); Western Pennsylvania Socialist Workers 1982 Campaign v. Connecticut General Life Insurance Company, 512 Pa. 23, 515 A.2d 1331 (1986); Charleston Joint Venture v. McPherson, 308 S.C. 145, 417 S.E.2d 544 (1992) (mall could properly obtain injunction against trespassers who repeatedly parked van carrying large sign; it was not a public forum although it allowed other activities on its premises).

Some of the cases stake out a general denial of any right or privilege to use another's land for speech related activities but actually involve only relatively small private properties that seem distinguishable from large malls or involve intrusive conduct that could be prohibited by rule in any event.

5. E.g., Woodland v. Michigan Citizens Lobby, 423 Mich. 188, 378 N.W.2d 337 (1985); Southcenter Joint Venture v. National Democratic Policy Committee, 113 Wash.2d 413, 780 P.2d 1282 (1989).

6. Robins v. Pruneyard Shopping Center, 23 Cal.3d 899, 592 P.2d 341, 153 Cal. Rptr. 854 (1979); New Jersey Coalition Against War in the Middle East v. J.M.B. Realty Corp., 138 N.J. 326, 650 A.2d 757 (1994).

7. Jamestown v. Beneda, 477 N.W.2d 830 (N.D.1991) (abortion protestors in mall technically owned by city but leased out to mall operators; city ownership of places analogous to public streets and walks was enough to require owners to permit peaceful speech activity).

8. Batchelder v. Allied Stores International, Inc., 388 Mass. 83, 445 N.E.2d 590, 38 A.L.R.4th 1206 (1983) (recognizing a right under a free elections provision but not addressing the broader free speech provision); Lloyd Corporation, Ltd. v. Whiffen, 315 Or. 500, 849 P.2d 446 (1993); see Southcenter Joint Venture v. National Democratic Policy Committee, 113 Wash.2d 413, 780 P.2d 1282 (1989) (explaining an earlier decision on this ground).

9. Cadillac Fairview Corp. Ltd. v. R.W.D.S.U., 64 D.L.R.4th 267 (1989) (relying on labor relations statutes); Regina v. Layton, 38 C.C.C.3d 550 (Provincial Ct. 1986) (relying on freedom of expression or association).

campus of a private university that was otherwise open to the public, at least where the leaflets concerned events on the campus itself,[10] but was unwilling to say that the privilege applied to permit use of shopping malls in a similar way.[11] Even where the privilege has been recognized for malls and places open to the public generally, it has not been extended to cover other private property such as a parking lot or a computer system flooded with "trespassing" email.[12]

Bases. In creating these extensions of the privilege, some courts have read the state's constitution to protect speech or speech-related activities against private as well as against governmental action and hence to protect the activity against exclusion by a private landowner.[13] In other cases, courts have perhaps placed more emphasis on the idea that large malls or shopping centers have displaced traditional business districts with their public streets, walks, and parks, and so functionally operate as public forums subject to free speech guarantees.[14] The Michigan Court observed that "this approach would simply treat the shopping centers as if they were the state for purposes of the state constitution's free speech and petition provisions [but] there is no legal basis to distinguish shopping malls from other places where large numbers of people congregate... .", mentioning sport stadiums, convention halls, theaters, private parks, large office or apartment buildings, factories, supermarkets and department stores as indistinguishable examples.[15]

Limiting the extended speech rights on others' property. The few cases that have extended the company town exception to shopping centers or malls do not support an unlimited right or privilege to enter or remain on land of others.

First, in line with limits expressed in most detail in a New Jersey decision,[16] the cases support only a right or privilege to enter and use premises that are open to the public generally and to do so in ways consistent with normal use of those premises.[17] Private clinics or medical

10. Pennsylvania v. Tate, 495 Pa. 158, 432 A.2d 1382 (1981) (criminal trespass prosecutions reversed). New Jersey extended the privilege to speech activities on a campus that were unrelated to campus affairs in State v. Schmid, 84 N.J. 535, 423 A.2d 615 (1980), then later applied the privilege to shopping malls in New Jersey Coalition Against War in the Middle East v. J.M.B. Realty Corp., supra n. 6.

11. Western Pennsylvania Socialist Workers 1982 Campaign v. Connecticut General Life Insurance Company, 512 Pa. 23, 515 A.2d 1331 (1986).

12. Planned Parenthood of San Diego v. Wilson, 234 Cal.App.3d 1662, 286 Cal.Rptr. 427 (1991) (abortion protesters); CompuServe Inc. v. Cyber Promotions, Inc., 962 F.Supp. 1015 (S.D.Oh.1997) (unsolicited email to Internet company's subscribers);Intel Corp. v. Hamidi, 1999 WL 450944 (App. Dept. Super.Ct. 1999)(not published) (email on plaintiff's computer system to all plaintiff's employees).

13. E.g., Batchelder v. Allied Stores International, Inc., 388 Mass. 83, 445 N.E.2d 590, 38 A.L.R.4th 1206 (1983).

14. See Robins v. Pruneyard Shopping Center, 23 Cal.3d 899, 592 P.2d 341, 153 Cal.Rptr. 854 (1979); New Jersey Coalition Against War in the Middle East v. J.M.B. Realty Corp., 138 N.J. 326, 650 A.2d 757 (1994).

15. Woodland v. Michigan Citizens Lobby, 423 Mich. 188, 378 N.W.2d 337 (1985).

16. New Jersey Coalition Against War in the Middle East v. J.M.B. Realty Corp., 138 N.J. 326, 650 A.2d 757 (1994).

17. This is a non-technical restatement of New Jersey's expressly stated balancing test, but it appears consistent with the rationale applied in other states.

offices, for example, are not open to the public in the same way that a shopping center is, so courts may deny the privilege to enter such premises, even for the purpose of discussing public issues with users.[18] Probably the same would hold true even for small shopping centers that have not substantially displaced the traditional business blocks.

Second, the privilege does not permit uses that would interfere with the landowner's uses and the landowner can prescribe reasonable regulations governing the speech activities on private premises. Bullhorns or loudspeakers[19] could be forbidden, and presumably other distracting or obstructive behavior such as chanting or aggressive pursuit of shoppers. Restrictions on the place used for speech activities, if they are reasonable and do not operate to isolate the speaker from other users of the land, seem to be appropriate.[20] Put differently, the landowner may impose reasonable limits to regulate the time, place, and manner of speech. The landowner might exclude commercial speech altogether as inconsistent with the landowner's purposes and uses of the land.

TOPIC F. DISCIPLINE

§ 93. Use of Force and Confinement in Military Discipline or to Enforce Military Orders

Harms to military personnel. When an officer of the armed forces of the United States, acting incident to service, uses force against or confines another member of the armed forces, the officer is almost invariably protected against tort liability under federal law.[1] The rule excludes liability for harms resulting from intended constitutional violations as well as for more routine injuries.[2] In addition, the Uniform Code of Military Justice[3] governs the internal disciplinary rules of the armed forces, establishing courts martial, and appropriate military punishments for various misbehaviors.[4] The victim of an officer's use of force or confinement as a part of military discipline, therefore, stands little chance of any tort law recovery in civilian courts.

Common law rules would obtain similar results. Although the Restatement couches these rules in terms of common law privilege, they

18. Allred v. Harris, 14 Cal.App.4th 1386, 18 Cal.Rptr.2d 530 (1993).

19. New Jersey Coalition Against War in the Middle East v. J.M.B. Realty Corp., 138 N.J. 326, 650 A.2d 757 (1994).

20. Lloyd Corporation, Ltd. v. Whiffen, 315 Or. 500, 849 P.2d 446 (1993).

§ 93

1. A series of protective barriers has been erected against liability. The *Feres* rule bars suits based on acts of service personnel incident to service. A statute immunizes against claims based upon assault, battery, false imprisonment and some other torts. Another statute relegates the claimant to suits against the government, which may then invoke the immunity rules. See § . Besides these protections, the Supreme Court has recognized a kind of discretionary immunity for acts performed within the "outer perimeter" of official duty and a more or less separate "good faith" immunity in constitutional tort cases. See §§ 273 & 278 below.

2. E.g., United States v. Stanley, 483 U.S. 669, 107 S.Ct. 3054, 97 L.Ed.2d 550 (1987) (serviceman secretly administered dangerous drug in experiment, no liability).

3. 10 U.S.C.A. § 801 et seq.

4. See DAVID A. SCHLUETER, MILITARY CRIMINAL JUSTICE: PRACTICE AND PROCEDURE (3d ed. 1992);

are based in part on a recognition of military jurisdiction over intra-military disputes and federal supremacy in the case of federal military officers.[5]

Harms to civilians. Beyond the matter of intra-military discipline, the Restatement provides that military personnel are privileged to obey a superior's lawful or apparently lawful order.[6] This rule means that even a civilian who was in no way subject to military discipline would have no claim against service personnel who carry out an order to confine the civilian.[7] On the other hand, the privilege to obey an apparently valid order would not itself bar the claim against the officer who issued the illegal order, and such officers have been subjected to liability.[8] Put differently, military personnel could not exceed their power and authority with impunity or rely upon directives that exceeded the limits of an officer's power.[9] However, officers of the United States armed forces may now be immunized by statute. So taken together, these rules effectively deny the plaintiff relief from harm inflicted incident to military service unless that harm counts as a taking of property for which compensation is constitutionally mandated.[10] The limited number of cases in which liability may be imposed upon the United States government itself for torts committed by service personnel is considered in connection with the Federal Tort Claims Act.[11]

5. See Keppleman v. Upston, 84 F.Supp. 478 (N.D.Cal.1949)

6. Trammell v. Bassett, 24 Ark. 499 (1866) (confederate soldiers obeying order to seize goods can plead this as justification); Neu v. McCarthy, 309 Mass. 17, 33 N.E.2d 570 (1941) (soldiers are privileged to obey illegal orders of superiors unless they are "palpably and obviously illegal," so taking convoy through red traffic lights on a captain's orders was privileged); Herlihy v. Donohue, 52 Mont. 601, 161 Pac. 164 (1916) ("the inferior military officer may defend his act against civil liability by reference to the order of his superior, unless such order bears upon its face the marks of its own invalidity or want or authority"); Restatement § 146. The analogy is to the privilege of an arresting officer to execute a warrant fair on its face. See § 83, supra.

7. See Restatement § 146, Ill. 1.

8. Herlihy v. Donohue, 52 Mont. 601, 161 Pac. 164 (1916) (militia commander, called out to deal with a state of insurrection, ordered saloons closed; when the plaintiff violated the order, the commander ordered destruction of the liquor; held, the commander is liable for this illegal order but the officers executing the order were not, since the order was not palpably illegal).

9. In Little v. Barreme, 6 U.S. (2 Cranch) 170, 2 L.Ed. 243 (1804), an officer seized a ship on a directive of the President in time of war to seize ships bound either to or from French ports. However, the statutory authority was explicitly limited to seizure of ships bound *to* French ports. The officer was liable. In Bates v. Clark, 95 U.S. (5 Otto) 204, 24 L.Ed. 471 (1877), officers seized plaintiffs' whiskey and were found liable. They were authorized to seize whiskey in "Indian country," and in good faith believed they had done so. But in fact or law, the whiskey was not in Indian country, so they had no authority to seize it. "[W]hatever may be the rule in time of war and in the presence of actual hostilities, military officers can no more protect themselves than civilians in time of peace by orders emanating from a source which is itself without authority." The Supreme Court later interpreted these cases as meaning that the officers "did not merely mistakenly conclude that the circumstances warranted a particular seizure, but failed to observe the limitations on their authority by making seizures not within the category or type of seizures they were authorized to make." Butz v. Economou, 438 U.S. 478, 98 S.Ct. 2894, 57 L.E.2d 895 (1978).

10. See § 109 below.

11. §§ 264–267 below.

§ 94. Force and Confinement in the Discipline of Children

Parental Privileges

The state has a general duty to protect children and it may remove children from the custody of abusive or neglectful parents. It may also criminally prosecute parents who abuse their children. As to the civil liability of parents under tort law, parents are still generally immune from liability in tort to their children in some states.[1] Where the parental tort immunity has been abolished or limited, parents may still be privileged to carry out specific acts that, but for the privilege, would count as a tort. In particular, parents and those who act in the place of parents, are privileged to apply a degree of force or to impose confinement upon their minor children,[2] a rule largely correlative with the parents' duty to provide for their children.[3]

Although the amount and kind of force that is privileged is obviously limited, it is difficult to formulate a standard describing the limit. An appropriate standard would establish limits but would also recognize the wide cultural and personal differences among parents about methods of child-rearing.[4] The Restatement attempts to solve the problem by saying that the parents may apply the force or impose the confinement that they reasonably believe is necessary for controlling or training their children.[5] Presumably this standard excludes liability for child spanking even though many people oppose such punishment, but at the same time would not exclude liability for burning a child with cigarettes or locking her in a closet for days without food.

Perhaps recognizing that its standard cannot readily be applied, the Restatement adds a series of factors to be considered in determining whether the punishment inflicted is reasonable and administered for the control or training of the child. Factors bearing on the question include the age and condition of the child, the nature of the child's offense, the possibility of an example to other children in the family, whether the punishment inflicted is "necessary and appropriate" to compel obedience, and whether it is disproportionate, unnecessarily degrading or likely to cause serious or permanent harm.[6]

Statutes that permit the state to take custody of an abused child confront a similar problem in setting standards. The strategy of some of these statutes is to provide a general standard followed by a list of

§ 94

1. The general immunity of parents is considered in Chapter 18.

2. Restatement § 147.

3. Cf. R.J.D. v. The Vaughan Clinic, P.C., 572 So.2d 1225 (Ala.1990) (given parental duty to provide for children, mother's consent for detention of 17–year-old daughter in clinic was effective to prevent clinic's liability to the daughter).

4. Cf. Holodook v. Spencer, 36 N.Y.2d 35, 324 N.E.2d 338, 364 N.Y.S.2d 859 (1974) (emphasizing different economic, education, cultural, ethnic and religious attitudes toward child-rearing that make it difficult to judge parental negligence toward a child).

5. Restatement § 147.

6. Restatement § 150.

specific acts that also count as abuse. But these statutes exemplify the problem; they do not solve it. The statute that tells us that a parent is abusive if he acts in a heinous or abhorrent manner or rapes his child tells us only what we already know.[7] Some proposed standards[8] and some statutes[9] attempt to judge child abuse less by judging the parent's act than by judging the result, so that if the child suffers severe emotional damage, physical harm, or disfigurement, the court might conclude that abuse was inflicted. It is apparent that the problem of determining abuse has not been clearly provided for in this context any more than in the context of a tort privilege to discipline children.[10]

Non-parents in Charge of Minors

The parents' privilege to discipline children is extended to persons who are properly in charge of children but who are not actually parents of the children.[11] This may include schools and teachers, school bus drivers, child-care attendants, surrogate parents and others similarly situated. Persons who take the role of parents, temporarily or permanently, are also accorded a privilege to discipline the child. However, in some cases at least, the parent may impose restrictions on the privilege, for example, by forbidding the babysitter to spank a child.[12] In addition, the amount of force that is acceptable when applied by a parent may be found to be unreasonable when applied by a person only temporarily in charge of a child.[13]

School systems today often regulate the power of teachers and administrators to impose corporal punishment. Where the school system itself does not acknowledge the parents' right to forbid such punishment, parents usually have no common law power to restrict it.[14] Thus teachers or school administrators are generally permitted to impose corporal punishment when it is otherwise within the broad "reasonableness" limits, unless a statute or school regulation provides otherwise.[15]

7. See, e.g., ME. REV. STAT. ANN. Title 22 § 4055.

8. See IJA–ABA Joint Commission on Juvenile Justice Standards, Juvenile Justice Standards Project, Standards Relating to Abuse and Neglect, 2.1 B. (1981). See IRA MARK ELLMAN, PAUL M. KURTZ, & ANN M. STANTON, FAMILY LAW 1099 (1986); LYNN WARDLE, WARDLE, CHRISTOPHER BLAKESLEY & JACQUELINE PARKER, CONTEMPORARY FAMILY LAW § 27.04.

9. E.g., 42 U.S.C.A. § 10408 (family violence includes any act that results or threatens to result in physical injury); CAL. WELF. & INST. CODE § 361 (a) (3) (child suffering severe emotional damage); CONN. GEN. STAT. ANN. § 17a–101 (child suffering from physical injury or is in physical danger).

10. Mary J. Cavins, Annotation, Physical Abuse of Child by Parent as Ground for Termination of Parent's Right to Child, 53 A.L.R.3d 605 (1974), reflects a considerable body of case litigation on under the statutes.

11. See Restatement § 147 (2).

12. See Restatement § 153.

13. See Restatement § 150 (a).

14. Ingraham v. Wright, 430 U.S. 651, 662, 97 S.Ct. 1401, 1407, 51 L.Ed.2d 711 (1977) ("the concept of parental delegation has been replaced by the view more consonant with compulsory educational laws that the State itself may impose such corporal punishment as is reasonably necessary . . . ."); Restatement § 153 (2).

15. See Rinehart v. Western Local School Dist. Bd. of Education, 87 Ohio App.3d 214, 621 N.E.2d 1365 (1993) (paddling for privately calling teacher a "dickhead").

Excessive force, wrongful purpose, or a disproportionate response to the problem are all grounds for concluding that the teacher has exceeded the privilege and loses protection.[16]

The result is similar when the claim asserted is not a common law tort claim but a constitutional tort claim under civil rights acts. The Supreme Court has held that a teacher does not violate the constitutional rights of students by applying the kind of force that would be reasonable discipline and would be privileged under the common law rule.[17]

The privilege to discipline a child by corporal punishment was attacked in one striking opinion.[18] A school bus driver slapped an unruly child. The judge found that the slap did not count as excessive force, but nevertheless imposed liability. She thought that "physical violence should never be invoked, least of all against children who are so seriously harmed by it." Referring to studies, she said that "Sanctioning *any* degree of corporal punishment can also heighten the risk of serious child abuse by those in positions of authority.... The tort of battery, which once protected only the bodily integrity of men, must now protect all persons.... ."

Topic G. Consent

§ 95. Consent as a Bar

One who consents or apparently consents to acts that would otherwise count as an intentional tort cannot recover damages for those acts. Among the trespassory and intentional torts, consent defeats the claim for battery,[1] for false imprisonment,[2] and for trespass to land or chattels[3] or conversion.[4] For example, a sexual touching would be a battery if it is not effectively consented to, but if the plaintiff effectively consents to the touching, there is no battery.[5] Similarly, if the plaintiff consents to a friendly wrestling match with the defendant, the plaintiff cannot recover

16. E.g., Thomas v. Bedford, 389 So.2d 405 (La.App.1980);

17. Ingraham v. Wright, 430 U.S. 651, 97 S.Ct. 1401, 51 L.Ed.2d 711 (1977). Although restraint of a child and deliberate infliction of pain implicates the Fourteenth Amendment's protection against deprivation of liberty, the child's "liberty interest" is subject to historical limitations expressed in the common law privilege.

18. Rodriguez v. Johnson, 132 Misc.2d 555, 504 N.Y.S.2d 379 (N.Y. City Civil Ct. 1986).

§ 95

1. Houston v. Kinder–Care Learning Centers, Inc., 208 Ga.App. 235, 430 S.E.2d 24 (1993); see Janelsins v. Button, 102 Md. App. 30, 648 A.2d 1039 (1994)

2. E.g., Lolley v. Charter Woods Hosp. Inc., 572 So.2d 1223 (Ala.1990) (written consent to confinement for treatment).

3. Cf. Florida v. Bostick, 501 U.S. 429, 111 S.Ct. 2382, 115 L.Ed.2d 389 (1991) (Fourth Amendment proscriptions against unreasonable search and seizure are not implicated when search of luggage is consensual; question whether under totality of circumstances the consent was effectively given).

4. See L & W Engineering Co., Inc. v. Hogan, 858 S.W.2d 847 (Mo.App.1993); Michel v. Melgren, 70 Wash.App. 373, 853 P.2d 940 (1993).

5. E.g., Schieffer v. Catholic Archdiocese of Omaha, 244 Neb. 715, 508 N.W.2d 907 (1993).

for injuries sustained in that match.[6] An analogous rule applies in some but not all negligence cases under the name of assumed risk.

The consent principle is general in its scope, firm in its acceptance, and central in its significance. It makes the plaintiff's right of self-determination or autonomy the centerpiece of the law on intentional torts and to some extent other torts as well. Nevertheless, a cluster of subsidiary rules and definitions both enlarge and constrain its application. This section sketches the main rules, which are then illustrated, qualified, and explained in the sections that follow.

(1) Objective, manifested, or apparent consent. The plaintiff effectively consents if appearances created by her words or acts lead the defendant reasonably to believe she consented, even if the plaintiff did not subjectively intend to consent.[7] The plaintiff likewise effectively consents if the she actually or subjectively consents to the defendant's conduct, even if that consent is not expressed or manifested.[8]

(2) Incapacity, mistake, fraud and duress. The plaintiff's consent or apparent consent is ineffective to bar recovery if the plaintiff lacked capacity to give consent due to her minority or mental disability and if the defendant knew or should have known it.[9] Similar rules apply when the plaintiff is induced to profess consent as a result of the defendant's misrepresentation[10] or duress,[11] or as a result of a mistake of which the defendant knew or should have known.[12]

(3) Consent obtained by abuse of power. Some professions of consent are obtained by serious abuses of power. When employers or psychiatrists use their special power or authority to obtain sexual favors from employees or patients, purported consent by the employee or patient may be ineffective even if these abuses of power fall short of duress. The same principle may apply in some degree to others such as lawyers, physicians, or clergy.[13]

(4) Mistake or misrepresentation as to collateral matter. The plaintiff's mistake, including a mistake induced by a misrepresentation, does not vitiate her consent if the mistake is only about a "collateral" matter not going to the essential nature of the transaction.[14]

(5) Informed consent. Mistake in giving consent is usually the result of wrong information. Some defendants, because of their relationship to the plaintiff, are under an affirmative obligation to provide appropriate information to the plaintiff to permit an informed consent and are subject to liability if they fail to do so and harm results.[15]

(6) Consent to conduct, not harm. The plaintiff who has consented or apparently consented to conduct cannot recover damages for harm

6. Cf. Hellriegel v. Tholl, 69 Wash.2d 97, 417 P.2d 362 (1966) (horseplay).

7. § 96 below.

8. § 97 below.

9. § 98 below.

10. § 100 below.

11. § 101 below.

12. § 100 below.

13. § 102 below.

14. § 100 below.

15. § 103 below.

resulting from that conduct, even though the plaintiff did not expect harm to result and did not consent to harm.

(7) Burden of proof. In many cases, consent is not a true affirmative defense but instead marks a deficiency in the plaintiff's prima facie case. For example, the defendant does not intend an offensive battery when he touches the plaintiff in a consented-to way. The plaintiff's consent in such a case negates any tortious intent, so the plaintiff fails in one element of her proof.

§ 96. Manifestation of Consent

The Standard: Manifested or Objectively Determinable Consent

Actual consent to an act is a subjective willingness for the act to occur. Apparent consent is conduct, including words, that are reasonably understood by another as a reflection of consent.[1] Either actual or apparent consent is effective to relieve the actor of responsibility for the acts addressed.[2]

Because the appearance of consent is effective if it leads the defendant reasonably to believe consent is actual, a plaintiff's private and uncommunicated reservation does not subject the defendant to liability. The defendant is entitled to rely in good faith upon the reasonable appearance of consent created by the plaintiff. In a well-known case, the plaintiff was in a line of immigrants on board a ship and awaiting a vaccination needed to enter the country. She held up her arm as others did and received the vaccination. She suffered some harm from it and brought suit, but the court held that even if she did not subjectively consent, her conduct gave the appearance of consent and that the defendant was entitled to rely upon the appearance even if the plaintiff never subjectively meant to consent at all.[3] It might be possible to interpret the facts differently. Perhaps the plaintiff's upraised arm was a protest, not a consent.[4] The question is whether the defendant reason-

§ 96

1. Restatement § 892.

2. E.g., Smith v. VonCannon, 283 N.C. 656, 661, 197 S.E.2d 524, 529 (1973) ("An apparent consent is sufficient if brought about by acts of the [plaintiff]"); Carr v. Mobile Video Tapes, Inc., 893 S.W.2d 613 (Tex.App.1994) (apparent consent by someone with authority to give it); Restatement § 892 (2). In the Restatement's formula, consent is the actual willingness for conduct to occur; effective consent then occurs when the plaintiff either consents or gives the appearance of consenting and has the legal capacity to consent. See §§ 892 & 892A.

3. O'Brien v. Cunard S.S. Co., 154 Mass. 272, 28 N.E. 266 (1891).

4. See Symposium, Five Approaches to Legal Reasoning in the Classroom: Contrasting Perspectives on O'Brien v. Cunard S.S. Co. Ltd., 57 Mo. L. Rev. 346 (1992). Bourne, Ibid., *Introduction*, suggests that perhaps Ms. O'Brien raised her arm in "an act of silent protest or signal of abject resignation in the face of overwhelming intimidation." Some writers have opposed the objective or manifested consent rule altogether, seeing the rule, not as a protection of everyone's autonomy, but as part of a system of force and injustice imposed upon women. See Shalleck, *Feminist Legal Theory and the Reading of O'Brien v. Cunard*, 57 Mo. L. Rev. 371 (1992); Banks, *Teaching Laws with Flaws: Adopting a Pluralistic Approach to Torts*, 57 Mo. L. Rev. 443 (1992). The same author, more mildly, argued that the surrounding circumstances in *O'Brien* created a threatening or coercive situation.

ably believed that the plaintiff's words or conduct reflected a genuine consent.

Implied Consent by Conduct

Effective consent can be manifested by nonverbal conduct of the plaintiff. It can be shown by actions,[5] by a course of conduct,[6] by social conventions applicable to the setting, or by a relationship between the parties.[7] Perhaps most real-life consent is implied rather than expressed. We join a game of tag; we consent to being touched. We engage in a course of practical jokes with a friend over a long period of time; we consent to the kind of touchings or confinements those jokes lead us to expect. Body language communicates many feelings or attitudes, including consents. If you go home after a long hard day and slump in the chair, your partner or friend might take that as a consent to have your neck rubbed. Indeed, your relationship with a partner might itself demonstrate a general consent to friendly touchings.

Many false imprisonment cases require judges and juries to interpret conduct. A customer, suspected of shoplifting, is asked to follow a guard and does so. She is taken to a room and interrogated by several store employees. The nonverbal conduct and demeanor of the store employees may count as an implicit threat to confine the plaintiff if she attempts to leave. On the other hand, her conduct in remaining there without protest may suggest consent. The defendant's meaning is found in his nonverbal conduct and so is the plaintiff's. When the plaintiff merely goes along without protest, courts usually find that the plaintiff was not confined, since she remained voluntarily.[8]

Whether the plaintiff has communicated an apparent consent by conduct rather than by words turns on the interpretation of facts, not on rules. Conduct that might amount to an implied consent must be understood fairly and realistically. Courts are charged with the obligation to reject spurious assertions that the plaintiff consented when she obviously did not. In *Miller v. National Broadcasting Co.*,[9] an NBC producer entered the plaintiff's home along with paramedics who had been called to resuscitate the plaintiff's husband. The producer filmed the events that culminated in the husband's death. In a suit for trespass and other torts, NBC asserted that the plaintiff had impliedly consented

5. See Janelsins v. Button, 102 Md.App. 30, 648 A.2d 1039 (1994); Cardwell v. Bechtol, 724 S.W.2d 739, 67 A.L.R.4th 479 (Tenn. 1987) (by presenting herself to the doctor and then submitting to treatment without resistance, the plaintiff consented to spinal manipulation).

6. Wytupeck v. City of Camden, 25 N.J. 450, 136 A.2d 887 (1957) (landowner's habitual acquiescence in use of land by others may constitute a license); Sumner v. Hebenstreit, 167 Ill.App.3d 881, 118 Ill.Dec. 888, 522 N.E.2d 343 (1988) (same).

7. Prahl v. Brosamle, 98 Wis.2d 130, 295 N.W.2d 768 (1980).

8. E.g., Reicheneder v. Skaggs Drug Center, 421 F.2d 307 (5th Cir.1970); Faniel v. Chesapeake and Potomac Tel. Co. of Maryland, 404 A.2d 147 (D.C.1979); Hardy v. LaBelle's Distributing Co., 203 Mont. 263, 661 P.2d 35 (1983).

9. Miller v. National Broadcasting Co., 187 Cal.App.3d 1463, 232 Cal.Rptr. 668, 69 A.L.R.4th 1027 (1986).

to NBC's entrance by calling the paramedics. The court said simply that this assertion was "devoid of merit" as indeed it was.

Probably no single act, segregated from its social or relational context, can evince consent. Holding your arm up may signify consent to a vaccination if you are standing in the vaccination line, but it signifies no such thing if you are sitting in class and the teacher is asking questions. The act takes its meaning from the context. What is true of actions is also true of silence. If the plaintiff watches the doctor approach with a syringe and says nothing when the doctor says "I'm going to vaccinate you now," silence may suggest consent even if the plaintiff makes no move at all. But a generalization about silence is not warranted, much less a rule, because situations, relationships, social customs and expectations condition the interpretation of acts and silences.

Implied Consent by Custom

A special form of consent by silence arises in the case of social custom, as distinct from overt conduct of the plaintiff. For example, in a given area it may be customary to permit hunting or fishing on unenclosed rural lands, so that unless the landowner posts a notice to the contrary, no one is a trespasser who enters such land to fish.[10]

Qualifications can be illustrated by the door-to-door solicitor case. Suppose social custom permits door-to-door salespersons to knock on your door and offer their wares. Such an entry upon your land is a technical trespass unless you have consented. But if you say nothing to show your dissent from the general custom of the community, your silence might reasonably be taken to import consent that the door-to-door salesperson can enter your land and knock on your door,[11] or even that a driver can turn a car around in your driveway.[12]

The salesperson example reflects three important limits. First, you could reasonably be expected to know of the custom to permit unannounced callers to enter without liability for trespass. Second, you have an opportunity, at low cost, to express your dissent from the custom. You could post a sign forbidding salespeople to enter. Third, a harmless entry that does not include entering your home is in accord with the limits of the apparent consent. In the light of these facts, the salesperson can reasonably believe he has permission to enter for the limited purpose of offering goods for sale.

A unique Florida case seems to ignore the limits of consent by social custom. In *Florida Publishing Co. v. Fletcher*,[13] a fire of undetermined

10. Marsh v. Colby, 39 Mich. 626 (1878).

11. Prior v. White, 132 Fla. 1, 180 So. 347, 116 A.L.R. 1176 (1938) (concluding that such a custom existed and, quoting Cooley, giving the further illustration of a retail business, which implicitly invites people to enter); Smith v. VonCannon, 283 N.C. 656, 663, 197 S.E.2d 524, 529 (1973) ("In the absence of notice to the contrary, a stranger to the occupant of a house is entitled to assume that he may walk to the front door thereof ...without being sued for trespass").

12. Smith v. VonCannon, supra n. 11.

13. Florida Publishing Co. v. Fletcher, 340 So.2d 914 (Fla.1976).

origin did significant damage to the plaintiff's home while she was out of town. The babysitter died. Police and firefighters entered the premises and invited a newspaper photographer to take pictures. The photographer did so and published one in a newspaper. The plaintiff sued for trespass and invasion of privacy. The court held in favor of the newspaper. Affidavits from publishers claimed that there was a long-standing custom to permit media representatives on the property where a matter of great public interest has occurred. Since consent can be implied from custom, the court thought the plaintiff had no claim.

Fletcher seems to violate all the appropriate conditions for finding a genuine implied consent. First, nothing showed the plaintiff knew of the "custom" or was likely to know of it. Indeed, as described in the affidavits submitted by the press, the custom was not a general custom applicable to all individuals but a custom applicable to a few cases of "disaster." Second, the plaintiff had no reasonable opportunity to forestall entry into her home by strangers; she was out of town. Although it might be reasonable to expect that a homeowner would post a sign if she wished to exclude salespeople, it would not similarly be reasonable to expect the homeowner to post a sign about such unlikely entrants as press photographers. Third, the entry was far more intrusive than a knock on the door. Most people would not be understood to consent to a stranger's entry in their home in their absence. So even if there was implied consent, the defendant's conduct was surely outside its scope.

Perhaps *Fletcher* is not really about consent at all but about a rule of law imposed by the court. Some of the court's language seemed to flirt with the idea that the photographer might share the privilege of the public officials on the premises because they had invited his entry. If the photographer was informally deputized to make pictures for official purposes, this line of thought is certainly plausible.[14] But it is not plausible to suggest that the public official has the power to create a privilege that the public official himself did not have, such as a privilege to publish news photos, and the court did not appear to rely on any such idea.[15]

Whatever the explanation of *Fletcher*, it seems to stand alone on its facts. Other courts have not accepted or applied *Fletcher* to permit intrusions into a home[16] and they have refused to recognize a First

14. Restatement § 891 provides that when privileges are not based upon consent, the performance of a privileged act can be delegated to another person if the purpose of the privilege can be served in this way. If the fire marshall could not take photos of the fire scene in *Fletcher*, the marshall could request the newsphotographer to do so. Perhaps that line of thinking was not helpful in *Fletcher* because it would not privilege the later publication of the photos.

15. "Lieutenant Kuenning had no authority to extend a consent to Brosamle to enter the land of another. Although entry by Lieutenant Kuenning was privileged, he committed a trespass by participating in the trespass by Brosamle." Prahl v. Brosamle, 98 Wis.2d 130, 154–55,295 N.W.2d 768, 782 (1980).

16. See Prahl v. Brosamle, 98 Wis.2d 130, 295 N.W.2d 768 (1980); cf. Wilson v. Layne, 526 U.S. 603, 119 S.Ct. 1692, 143 L.Ed.2d 818 (1999) (officers violate the Fourth Amendment by inviting media representatives to enter the plaintiff's home while officers executed a warrant).

Amendment right of the press to enter private property merely because newsworthy events occur there.[17]

Why Manifested Consent Is a Bar

Why should the plaintiff be barred from recovery on the basis of manifested consent when she has not actually consented? In the usual case, the main reason is that the defendant who acts on a reasonable understanding of appearances is simply not a wrongdoer. The consent does not relieve him of liability for a tort; he is not a tortfeasor at all.[18]

To see this point, suppose the plaintiff and defendant are married to each other and the plaintiff manifests a consent to a loving embrace. Neither plaintiff nor defendant is aware that the plaintiff has a particularly fragile vertebrae. When the defendant embraces the plaintiff in an ordinary way, the bone is broken. In this case the defendant has intentionally touched the plaintiff, but not intentionally harmed her. Intentional touching suffices to show a battery if the touching is intended to be offensive. If the defendant had intended an unconsented-to touching, an intent to offend could be inferred. In that case, the defendant would be liable for all actual harm resulting. But in the hug example, the defendant cannot be seen to intend offense by the embrace; given the appearance of consent, the embrace seems unoffensive and therefore not wrongful.

Somewhat more generally, any other rule would oppose the freedom and autonomy of both parties, either by imposing liability or making it more difficult for them to obtain what they both want. Suppose you would like to fish my farm pond and I would like for you to do so because it is woefully overstocked. I manifest a consent. If you can rely on that manifestation, we will both be better off because you'll catch the fish you want and I'll get the stock reduced. A rule that says you cannot rely on the appearance of consent would allow me to sue you after you have taken me at my word and improved my pond. If that were the law you might well refuse to rely on appearances. You would not enjoy fishing and I would not get reduction in my fish population. The objective appearance rule fosters both freedom and autonomy.[19]

The downside of the objective rule is that appearances may be misleading. When the people involved differ in gender, ethnicity, or culture, and especially when the conduct in question touches intimate or

17. Stahl v. State, 665 P.2d 839 (Okla. Crim.App.1983); Anderson v. WROC–TV, 109 Misc.2d 904, 441 N.Y.S.2d 220 (Sup. Ct. 1981), on appeal as to non-media defendants, Anderson v. WHEC–TV, 92 A.D.2d 747, 461 N.Y.S.2d 607 (1983); Middleton, Journalists, Trespass, and Officials: Closing the Door on Florida Publishing Co. v. Fletcher, 16 Pepp. L. Rev. 259 (1989). Conceivably, some of the courts that recognize a First Amendment right of private citizens to use malls or shopping centers that are otherwise open to the public, see § 92, supra, could extend similar privileges to the press on that particular kind of property.

18. E.g., Janelsins v. Button, 102 Md. App. 30, 648 A.2d 1039 (1994); Schieffer v. Catholic Archdiocese of Omaha, 244 Neb. 715, 508 N.W.2d 907 (1993)

19. See, discussing some values of objective approaches in negligence law, Gregory C. Keating, Reasonableness and Rationality in Negligence Theory, 48 Stan. L. Rev. 311, 371 ff. (1996).

sensitive matters such as sexual relations, the defendant must not presume too quickly to interpret conduct, custom, or even words as consent.[20] In particular, defendants who possess power or authority over others must be wary of the possibility that appearance of consent is misleading. For example, employers, psychiatrists, and priests must recognize that employees, patients, and parishioners do not necessarily feel free to reject sexual advances and that the appearance of consent is the result of other forces.[21]

§ 97. Unmanifested Consent

The usual case is one in which the plaintiff manifests consent to the defendant's act, whether or not the manifestation represents the plaintiff's subjective state of mind. In the reverse situation, the plaintiff does not outwardly manifest consent but does in fact subjectively or secretly consent to the defendant's act. The consensus seems to be that a subjective or "real" consent is a bar to recovery even though the defendant was unaware of such consent.[1]

It seems easy enough to see why a defendant is not a wrongdoer when he reasonably believes he is acting in accord with the plaintiff's wishes; that is the case of manifested consent. The plaintiff's private and unexpressed consent, however, gives the defendant no basis for claiming innocence; by hypothesis, he knows nothing of the plaintiff's consent. Suppose the defendant enters upon the plaintiff's land to fish in the plaintiff's pond, but believes he is unwelcome. In such a case, he is prima facie a technical trespasser because he has the intent to enter and he does enter. (He also has an antisocial state of mind, but that is not required to show trespass.) If the plaintiff later brings suit for the trespass and the defendant learns that the plaintiff had in fact written but not mailed a note to say he was welcome, why should the plaintiff's private and unexpressed consent operate to bar the claim?

If such a subjective, unmanifested consent is a bar to the plaintiff's claim it must be because she has suffered no injury when the defendant acted in accordance with her will, even if, later on, she changed her mind about what she wanted. It is not that the defendant is no wrongdoer as it is in the case of manifested consent, but that the plaintiff has suffered no harm when her wishes are met.

While manifested consent indicates that the defendant is not a tortfeasor in the first place, unmanifested consent seems like a true affirmative defense, at least in the pond illustration. Why is that so? It is so because the plaintiff can prove a prima facie case by showing entry and intent to enter. The defendant must then sustain the burden of showing consent.

20. See JUDEE BURGOON AND THOMAS SAINE, THE UNSPOKEN DIALOG: AN INTRODUCTION TO NONVERBAL COMMUNICATION (1978) (discussing gender, cultural and subcultural differences in nonverbal communication).

21. See § 102.

§ 97

1. Restatement § 892 (1).

§ 98. Incapacity to Give Consent

Effects of Incapacity

Incapacity known to the defendant. Minors, intoxicated persons, insane persons and others similarly situated may lack capacity to give actual consent. A professed consent is not effective to bar the plaintiff's claim if the plaintiff lacked capacity to give consent and the defendant knew or should have known of the plaintiff's incapacity.[1] For instance, if the defendant knows he is dealing with a child or an insane person, he must know that the child cannot effectively consent and he is held liable for torts to the child even if the child professed a consent.[2] The rule ultimately turns on appearances to the defendant rather than on the plaintiff's secret status as a legally incompetent person, and is thus merely an example of the objective manifestation requirement.

Incapacity not known to the defendant. If the plaintiff gives the appearance of consent and the defendant reasonably believes the plaintiff has capacity to consent and has consented in fact, the defendant will not have the intent required to establish an intentional tort against the plaintiff. Incapacity negates actual consent[3] but when the plaintiff gives the appearance of capacity and the appearance of consent, the defendant is not acting tortiously at all when he acts in accord with the appearance.[4] It may be, however, that some defendants, because of their relationship to the plaintiff, are under a duty to take extra precautions to be sure that the plaintiff's consent is based upon adequate understanding of the relevant facts[5] and that they may not use duress or fraud

§ 98

1. See Reavis v. Slominski, 250 Neb. 711, 551 N.W.2d 528 (1996). When liability is imposed, courts sometimes emphasize the defendant's knowledge of the plaintiff's incapacity. See McCue v. Klein, 60 Tex. 168 (1883). Sometimes courts do not emphasize the defendant's knowledge but the facts make it clear that the defendant in fact knew of the incapacity, as where the defendant is dealing with a child. See note 4 below. Cf., State v. Lough, 70 Wash.App. 302, 853 P.2d 920 (1993) (state had to prove that victim lacked capacity to consent and that defendant knew it; defendant may negate criminal liability by showing he reasonably believed in victim's mental capacity), aff'd on other grounds, 125 Wash.2d 847, 889 P.2d 487 (1995). Prosser & Keeton took the view stated in this text. See PROSSER & KEETON 114.

2. E.g., United States v. McCabe, 812 F.2d 1060 (8th Cir.1987) (small child could not consent to his own kidnapping); Commonwealth v. Nickerson, 87 Mass. 518 (1862) (similar); Robalina v. Armstrong, 15 Barb. 247 (N.Y.Sup.Gen.Term 1852) (similar).

3. Compare Restatement § 892 ("consent" distinguished from apparent consent) with Restatement § 892A (requiring capacity for [actual] consent to be effective).

4. Except as stated in the next paragraph, the cases cited in the Reporter's Notes to the Restatement imposed liability in spite of the plaintiff's professed consent *only* where the defendant must have known of the plaintiff's incapacity, as where the defendant was dealing with a child and knew it. With the same exception, none of the cases overtly stated or even implied that the defendant would be liable if he could not reasonably be expected to discern the incapacity. Statutes may embody the same standard. E.g. OHIO REV. CODE ANN. § 2907.03 (A) (2) (sexual conduct impermissible when "[t]he offender knows that the other person's ability to appraise the nature of or control his or her own conduct is substantially impaired").

5. Cf. Demers v. Gerety, 85 N.M. 641, 515 P.2d 645 (1973), rev'd on other grounds, 86 N.M. 141, 520 P.2d 869 (1974), on appeal after remand, 92 N.M. 396, 589 P.2d 180 (1978) (first concluding that a patient's consent, obtained by a nurse while

to obtain consent.[6]

Where tort liability is equivalent to avoidance of a contract. In one situation, liability may be imposed upon a defendant even though he believes himself to be dealing with a competent person whose apparent consent is valid. That is the situation in which tort liability functions exactly like a rescission or avoidance of a transaction, that is, to produce restitution on both sides. Suppose the plaintiff is mentally incompetent but does not appear so. She contracts to and does sell her goods to the defendant. Under the normal rules of restitution, an incompetent person may avoid or rescind her purported contracts, even though the defendant was unaware of the incompetence at the time of contracting.[7] On the facts supposed, the plaintiff might instead sue in tort for conversion. The defendant would be liable for the value of the goods less the price he paid.[8] In form this is tort liability, but in fact it works the same financial result as avoidance of the contract. The defendant does not make his expected profit on the deal, but, transaction costs aside, he loses nothing. In this situation, the plaintiff's consent is ineffective even though the plaintiff's incompetence is unknown to the defendant and undiscoverable by him because the formal tort liability is functionally merely a rescission.

Determining Capacity

Adults generally. The competency of adults is a matter of fact to be determined in each case. The plaintiff who wishes to escape the normal consequences of consent must sustain the burden of proving incapacity and that the defendant knew or should have known of the incapacity.[9]

Courts determine mental incapacity in a number of diverse contexts and by somewhat different tests. Capacity is relevant to the validity of a contract or will, to civil commitment, to criminal punishment and to the operation of the statute of limitations. The topic of capacity in criminal law lies in the marches of metaphysics, far beyond the borders of this book.[10] In the law of civil commitment, incapacity is often judged by determining whether a person is a threat to herself or to others.[11] In other situations, courts usually judge capacity of adults by asking wheth-

the patient was affected by Nembutal did not protect the surgeon, but ultimately concluding that the patient was not in fact rendered incompetent and that the surgeon was not liable). As to informed consent, see §§ 250 & 251.

6. § 100, below.

7. Dan B. Dobbs, Law of Remedies § 13.4 (3) (2d ed. 1993).

8. The facts are closely similar to those in Bolton v. Stewart, 191 S.W.2d 798 (Tex. Civ.App.1945), where liability was imposed with credit for the sums the defendant had paid for the goods. The court rejected liability for punitive damages.

9. Demers v. Gerety, 85 N.M. 641, 515 P.2d 645 (1973), reversed on other grounds, 86 N.M. 141, 520 P.2d 869 (1974), on appeal after remand, 92 N.M. 396, 589 P.2d 180 (1978); Grannum v. Berard, 70 Wash.2d 304, 422 P.2d 812 (1967).

10. On the whole topic of responsibility in criminal law see Wayne LaFave and Austin Scott, Jr., Criminal Law 302–403 (2d ed. 1986).

11. See Michael Perlin, Law and Mental Disability § 1.02 (1994) (reflecting this and other tests in the civil commitment setting).

er they can manage their own daily affairs[12] or can understand their rights[13] and the nature and effect of their acts.[14]

This means that mental limitations are not equivalent to incapacity. A person is not necessarily incapable of giving consent merely because he has extremely low intelligence.[15] Even a person who suffers from delusions or other mental disabilities may be competent for some purposes and may thus have the capacity to consent to things unaffected by the delusion.[16] So one's ability to pay bills and obtain daily necessities may show sufficient capacity for at least some decisions.

Patient's refusal of life-saving treatment. When an adult refuses to accept life-saving treatment for herself, some judges may have permitted their decisions about the fact of competency to be influenced by their feelings about policy. Some judges seem to have believed that a patient's rejection of needed medical attention itself shows incompetency. Finding "incompetency," courts can appoint a guardian to give consent in place of a patient who is refusing life-saving treatment, with the effect that treatment is imposed against her will. Some of these decisions may have forced treatment upon competent adults, either because judges were horrified at the possibility that the adult would reject life-saving treatment or because they felt the adult owed the state a duty to live and care for her family.[17]

More recent decisions demonstrate greater respect for individual decisions and less willingness to permit such an intrusion by the power of the state. The Florida Supreme Court has rejected the idea that forced medical procedures are permissible merely because the patient has children who would benefit from her survival.[18] Illinois will abide the

12. Matter of Estate of Frisch, 250 N.J.Super. 438, 594 A.2d 1367 (1991); cf. McCarthy v. Volkswagen of America, 55 N.Y.2d 543, 435 N.E.2d 1072, 450 N.Y.S.2d 457 (1982) (able to "protect their legal rights").

13. The tests may be expressed in more detail and varied in the exact form of words. The statute of limitations may be tolled or held in abeyance when the plaintiff is "insane;" for this purpose, some statutes extend the plaintiff's right to sue when she cannot comprehend rights she is otherwise bound to know. See Meiers–Post v. Schafer, 170 Mich.App. 174, 427 N.W.2d 606 (1988). Testamentary capacity might be determined by asking whether the testator understood the nature of her act in making a will and knew the character of her property and the natural objects of her bounty. E.g., In re Estate of Wagner, 246 Neb. 625, 522 N.W.2d 159 (1994).

14. Landmark Medical Center v. Gauthier, 635 A.2d 1145 (R.I.1994) (mental illness did not negate capacity to contract when a person understands nature and effect of acts). Cf. Reavis v. Slominski, 250 Neb. 711, 551 N.W.2d 528 (1996) (capacity to understand and weigh harm and risks of harm against benefits flowing from proposed conduct (sexual intercourse in this instance)).

15. State v. Singleton, 1994 WL 772861 (Tenn.Crim.App.1995) (IQ of 74, consent to search that turned up body in the freezer was valid).

16. See Matter of Gordy, 658 A.2d 613, 617 (Del.Ch.1994) ("we all have mental incapacities of various types. Some of us are able to learn foreign languages; for others it seems too difficult; for some calculus (or quantum physics) is beyond us. In some sense mental incapacity is simply the human condition"); Matter of Estate of Zielinski, 208 A.D.2d 275, 623 N.Y.S.2d 653 (1995) (discussing testamentary capacity).

17. Application of President and Directors of Georgetown College, Inc., 118 U.S.App.D.C. 80, 331 F.2d 1000, 9 A.L.R.3d 1367 (D.C. Cir. 1964).

18. Matter of Dubreuil, 629 So.2d 819 (Fla.1993)

patient's wishes where the patient had expressed opposition to the treatment before she became incompetent and where her wishes are grounded in her firmly held religious beliefs.[19] Most courts apparently attempt to determine competency as a matter of fact, without attempting to force their own beliefs on the patient. It now seems likely that courts would say, with the Massachusetts Court, that a person is not incompetent merely because she rejects life-saving treatment, even when that treatment would not offend her religious beliefs. That court refused to uphold the appointment of a guardian who would in effect force an amputation upon the patient.[20] The Delaware Chancery Court found a 96–year old woman with Alzheimer's disease to be competent enough to decide against a feeding tube necessary to save her life.[21]

Minors. It is usually said that minors as a class lack legal capacity. Consequently, minors cannot consent to, say, medical procedures. Instead, parents or guardians must consent on their behalf.[22] Nevertheless, minors are obviously competent to make many decisions, and their capacity to do so expands to cover increasingly complex decisions as they mature. In spite of broad language about incapacity, courts do in fact recognize that many minors can consent to some touchings that would be actionable in the absence of consent. Even a small child might effectively consent to a benign handshake, older minors to games that entail touchings,[23] and teenagers or mature minors to at least some medical procedures.[24] In addition, and within limits, mature teenage females have a constitutional right to decide for themselves to have an abortion and hence the power to give or withhold consent to that procedure.[25]

19. In re Brooks' Estate, 32 Ill.2d 361, 205 N.E.2d 435 (1965) (based on deeply held religious beliefs, an allegedly incompetent woman had expressed opposition to blood transfusions long before any incompetency, court erred in appointing guardian to consent to transfusion).

20. Lane v. Candura, 6 Mass.App.Ct. 377, 376 N.E.2d 1232, 93 A.L.R.3d 59 (1978); accord Rodriguez v. Pino, 634 So.2d 681, 685 (Fla.App.1994) ("Obviously, a patient may not be deemed incompetent simply because his decision is not a medically appropriate one").

21. Matter of Gordy, 658 A.2d 613, 618 (Del.Ch.1994) ("I conclude that she has made a rational choice concerning her medical treatment at the end of her very long life that deserves to be respected").

22. § 99 below.

23. Cf. Hellriegel v. Tholl, 69 Wash.2d 97, 417 P.2d 362 (1966) (teen-ager consenting to roughhouse play could not recover for injury). When the plaintiff pursues such claims on a negligence rather than a battery theory, the consent defense becomes an assumed risk defense, and minors may assume the risk exactly as they may consent. Frazier v. Norton, 334 N.W.2d 865 (S.D. 1983).

24. In re E.G., 133 Ill.2d 98, 139 Ill.Dec. 810, 549 N.E.2d 322 (1989) (minor, found to be mature by clear and convincing evidence, was competent to refuse life-saving treatment); Cardwell v. Bechtol, 724 S.W.2d 739, 67 A.L.R.4th 479 (Tenn. 1987) (17–year-old could consent to osteopath's manipulative treatment of her spine, no action for battery when the treatments appeared to produce serious harm). Capacity of a minor to consent depends upon the maturity and understanding of the individual minor, not on a fixed standard for all minors. If the minor understands the risks and benefits and other considerations as well as competent adults, then the minor can give consent.

25. E.g., City of Akron v. Akron Center for Reproductive Health, Inc., 462 U.S. 416, 103 S.Ct. 2481, 76 L.Ed.2d 687 (1983); Ohio v. Akron Center for Reproductive Health, 497 U.S. 502, 110 S.Ct. 2972, 111 L.Ed.2d 405 (1990); Hodgson v. Minnesota, 497 U.S. 417, 110 S.Ct. 2926, 111 L.Ed.2d 344

Statutes traditionally criminalized sexual relations with minors under a stated age, in effect depriving those minors of the power to consent. Courts carried these criminal statutes over into tort law, holding that the seducer of an under-age minor would be liable in tort, since the consent would be ineffective.[26] It is said that these statutes are only sporadically enforced[27] and certainly they have not been the basis for major tort litigation for a long time. A mature minor's right to consent to abortion might seem to imply a right to consent to sexual activity as well. Arguably the case is different, however. Some writers have argued that even explicit professions of consent by minors are in reality coerced.[28]

The problem of consent by minors is partly a factual one, just as it is with arguably incompetent adults. That is, courts want to know whether, as a matter of fact, the individual minor has the experience and intelligence to make the decision in question. The minor's capacity may differ according to the transaction involved. A minor's consent to a touching by another minor might be well within her capacity when consent to touching by an older person might not.[29] Or a child might have capacity to consent to a friendly hug but, even apart from statutes, no capacity to consent to sexual fondling.

Besides the question of capacity as a purely factual matter, the courts are also concerned to preserve a decision-making role for parents or guardians as well. To say that a minor is not legally competent to give consent, then, may be to say either (a) that the minor lacks sufficient seasoning to make rational decisions informed by experience or (b) that whatever the minor's practical wisdom, the parents rather than the minor should have the power to decide the particular question. This point shows up when one parent has custody of the child and the other does not. The non-custodial parent cannot avoid liability for kidnaping on the ground that the child consented, even though we may suspect that the child herself may be wise enough to know what she wants.[30] So

(1990). The Court has emphasized that maturity of the individual minor is an important consideration in determining whether a regulation of the minor's right to abortion is permissible. The exact nature of the right and the forms of permissible regulation continue to be litigated; neither the scope of the right nor the ultimate test by which statutory regulation of abortions is measured, see Planned Parenthood of Southeastern Pennsylvania v. Casey, 505 U.S. 833, 112 S.Ct. 2791, 120 L.Ed.2d 674 (1992), is a topic in this book.

26. E.g., Glover v. Callahan, 299 Mass. 55, 12 N.E.2d 194 (1937).

27. Oberman, Turning Girls into Women: Re–Evaluating Modern Statutory Rape Law, 85 J.Crim. L. & Criminology 15, 36 (1994).

28. Oberman, supra n. 27 at 70 argues that "Even between age-mates in a situation of apparent social equality, power may be so vastly imbalanced that evidence of verbal consent does not reveal the true nature of a teenage sexual encounter."

29. "In some cases consent between minors may be a valid defense where, for example, they are of the same peer group and of equal maturity." Matter of A.B., 556 A.2d 645, 649 (D.C.App.1989). Age of consent statutes now often reflect such thinking because they criminalize sexual activity with mature minors as statutory rape only in the case of an older person who has sexual relations with the minor. E.g., Vernon's Ann. Mo. Stat., § 566.034 (person over 21 years of age having intercourse with a person less than 17 years of age).

30. See Commonwealth v. Nickerson, 87 Mass. 518 (1862).

some consent-by-minors issues are less about protecting minors than about asserting parental rights to govern the minor or about the right of one parent against another.

§ 99. Giving or Refusing Consent on Behalf of Those Lacking Capacity

Parents of minors. When a minor lacks capacity to give consent, parents usually have the power to give consent on the minor's behalf. The common example is that parents are required to consent for a serious or substantial medical procedure to be performed upon a minor,[1] but the rule applies to other invasions of the child's person as well[2] or even to confinement of the child.[3] There are limits, however, to the parent's power to give effective consent. Court approval may be required for seriously invasive procedures like organ donations by an incompetent or for decisions to withdraw life support.

Mentally incompetent persons. An agent or guardian may give consent on behalf of an incapacitated adult when the act in question is arguably for the benefit of the incompetent person. The usual case is one in which an incompetent person may need medical treatment or surgery. In the case of one who is temporarily incapacitated because of anesthetic, courts have suggested that an adult family member could consent to a desirable extension of a medical procedure.[4] In the case of one who is more or less permanently incapacitated, a formal guardian might be appointed to make medical decisions. In some cases the guardian has been permitted to refuse consent to life-saving treatments[5] or to withdraw existing treatments necessary to sustain life,[6] provided the guardian follows the standards set by the court for making that decision.

Standard to be applied by the guardian making a decision on consent—best interests. In general, guardians or parents are expected to act in the best interest of their wards or children. It seems clear that neither parents nor guardians could effectively consent to harvesting organs from children or wards merely to sell to strangers. The best

§ 99

1. Doerr v. Movius, 154 Mont. 346, 463 P.2d 477 (1970); cf. Vandervelden v. Victoria, 177 Wis.2d 243, 502 N.W.2d 276 (1993) (mother's consent to medical procedure that harmed child she was carrying was a bar to action brought by child after birth).

2. Parents may consent on the child's behalf, for example, to forms of discipline in a private kindergarten. Houston v. Kinder–Care Learning Centers, Inc., 208 Ga.App. 235, 239, 430 S.E.2d 24, 27 (1993) ("no evidence here of any touching other than that which had been contracted for when the Houstons placed their infant in the care of Kinder–Care. The use of time-out as a disciplinary tool was within the guidelines of Kinder–Care and was so used with John").

3. R.J.D. v. The Vaughan Clinic, P.C., 572 So.2d 1225 (Ala.1990).

4. See Tabor v. Scobee, 254 S.W.2d 474 (Ky.1951) (20–year old woman under anesthesia, defendants should have obtained consent of mother who was in the hospital before removing fallopian tubes).

5. Matter of Gordy, 658 A.2d 613 (Del. Ch.1994)

6. DeGrella v. Elston, 858 S.W.2d 698 (Ky.1993) uses a substituted judgment test and permits the guardian to terminate feeding and hydration of a person in a persistently vegetative state if clear and convincing evidence shows that would have been the choice of the incompetent. *DeGrella* cites and discusses many of the cases that struggle with this issue.

interests standard asks whether the invasive procedure at issue would be in the best interests of the ward or child. If the answer is no, the procedure may not be used.[7] But when the stakes are highest, as when the guardian proposes to withdraw life support from a comatose ward or a parent proposes to harvest an organ from one child to benefit a sibling, courts have sometimes departed from the best interest test or have interpreted it in unusual ways. In the case of a proposed transplant of an organ from one sibling to another, the courts are somewhat divided when the incompetent actually has a relationship with the other family member.[8] Such an operation could not physically benefit the incompetent, but a court might nevertheless think that an organ donation is in the best interest of the donor because of his emotional relationship with the needful family member.[9]

—substituted judgment. The substituted judgment standard asks what decision the ward or child herself would make were she competent to make it. If the ward were the same person except that she was competent and would consent to the procedure, the procedure would be permissible under the substituted judgment test, but not if the ward would refuse consent.[10] If the ward had clearly stated preferences before she became incompetent, this test might work and work well. In other cases, the substituted judgment standard whimsically invites judges to imagine what the ward would be if she were not herself, an approach that seems wholly unusable at best.[11]

Limits of the tests. On the other hand, the best interests standard may not always be meaningful, either. Perhaps it is not meaningful when the question is whether to terminate extraordinary medical life support for a patient in an irreversible coma.[12] The best interests test could also ignore the ward's known preferences, expressed at a time she was wholly competent.[13] Both tests have the potential for invading the

7. Curran v. Bosze, 141 Ill.2d 473, 153 Ill.Dec. 213, 566 N.E.2d 1319, 4 A.L.R.5th 1163 (1990) (holding that permission to take bone marrow from child under 4 years old would be denied under the best interests standard, even though the bone marrow might save the life of a half-sibling).

8. See Lisa K. Gregory, Annotation, Propriety of Surgically Invading Incompetent or Minor for Benefit of Third Party, 4 A.L.R.5th 1000 (1993)

9. Strunk v. Strunk, 445 S.W.2d 145, 35 A.L.R.3d 683 (Ky. 1969).

10. Strunk v. Strunk, supra n. 9; In re Martin, 450 Mich. 204, 538 N.W.2d 399 (1995) (surrogate decision maker may withhold life-sustaining treatment when it is clear that the particular patient would have refused the treatment under the circumstances involved; the question is not what a reasonable person would have chosen but what this patient would have chosen; but before surrogate can refuse treatment, proof must show patient's preference for refusal by clear and convincing evidence).

11. See William Krais, The Incompetent Developmentally Disabled Person's Right of Self–Determination: Right-to-Die, Sterilization and Institutionalization, 15 Am. J. L. & Med. 333 (1989). Much worse things have been said about it because it "allows the state to invade the bodily integrity of the incompetent without having to justify the invasion." Louise Harmon, Falling Off the Vine: Legal Fictions and the Doctrine of Substituted Judgment, 100 Yale. L. J. 1, 61 (1990).

12. The decision to remove life support represents a different context from the decision to harvest an organ. On the problems of removing life support, see John Hodson, Annotation, Judicial Power to Order Discontinuance of Life Sustaining Treatment, 48 A.L.R.4th 67 (1966).

13. This appeared to be the case in Application of President and Directors of

patient's autonomy interests, but if the patient is indeed incompetent, those interests have scant scope in any event and a truly neutral test that does not assume one choice to be better than another is perhaps impossible to find. These difficult cases, perhaps as much as any others, reflect something of the limits of law's ability to resolve real problems in morally acceptable ways.

§ 100. Mistake Negating Consent

Consent negated by mistake or misrepresentation. The plaintiff's purported consent is ineffective to bar her claim if it is induced by misrepresentation[1] or is given under a material mistake of which the defendant is or should be aware.[2] The mistake is frequently though not always induced by the defendant's fraud or misrepresentation. Many cases decided in many settings summarize the point by saying that "fraud vitiates consent"[3] or that consent is ineffective if given as a result of fraud,[4] meaning that the plaintiff in such a case can recover.

Relation to the manifested consent rule. These rules are often instances of the more general principle that effectiveness of a consent is determined by appearances presented to the defendant.[5] The defendant who misrepresents the nature of the transaction, or who knows that the plaintiff is mistaken about it, knows that the plaintiff is not consenting to the defendant's acts. For instance, suppose the defendant offers the plaintiff a cup of coffee he knows to be contaminated with a poison or a deadly virus. The plaintiff takes the cup with no reason to know it is contaminated. The plaintiff's acceptance of the coffee manifests consent to take the cup and to drink coffee, but not consent to drink poison. Whether this is viewed as a mistake by the plaintiff or a misrepresentation by the defendant, the important point is that the defendant cannot believe the plaintiff is consenting to the poison.

Georgetown College, Inc., 118 U.S.App.D.C. 80, 331 F.2d 1000, 9 A.L.R.3d 1367 (D.C. Cir. 1964).

§ 100

1. Restatement § 892B. The term fraud is often used as well as the term misrepresentation. Fraud is a form of misrepresentation that imports intentional or knowing lies.

2. Restatement §§ 49 & 892B.

3. Neal v. Neal, 125 Idaho 617, 873 P.2d 871 (1994); Slawek v. Stroh, 62 Wis.2d 295, 215 N.W.2d 9 (1974) (consent to injections on the misrepresentation that they would not cause miscarriage is no bar to battery claim). There is a strange statement in Baugh v. CBS, Inc., 828 F.Supp. 745 (N.D.Cal.1993), that fraud does *not* affect the validity of consent; no cases are cited.

4. Janelsins v. Button, 102 Md.App. 30, 648 A.2d 1039 (1994); Micari v. Mann, 126 Misc.2d 422, 481 N.Y.S.2d 967 (1984) (acting teacher represented that students' sexual acts were needed as part of their drama training). Sometimes misrepresentation counts as a separate tort and not merely a means of dissolving the shield of consent. See John Ludington, Annotation, Medical Malpractice: Liability Based on Misrepresentation of the Nature and Hazards of Treatment, 42 A.L.R.4th 543 (1985). Misrepresentation is most commonly an economic tort, not one related to battery, see Chapter 35. So it may be more felicitous to think of the misrepresentation in the present context only as a way of negating consent.

5. § 96 supra.

Types of Mistake that Will Negate Consent

Misrepresentations and mistakes as to collateral matters. The plaintiff's mistake, whether induced by misrepresentation or not, must be material if it is to vitiate consent. More than that, the mistake must be about the nature of the transaction to which the plaintiff purportedly consents, not merely about some collateral matter of such as the transaction's value, cash cost, or method of payment.[6]

Collateral mistakes. To see a collateral mistake, suppose that a professor wishes to conduct experiments to determine whether people can distinguish between different stimuli applied to their shoulders and agrees to pay the plaintiff "the university rate." The plaintiff consents to be part of the experiment in the belief the rate is $20 an hour when in fact it is only $10. The Restatement suggests that this mistake is collateral only and not a ground for ignoring the plaintiff's consent.[7] So the professor would not be liable for battery although the plaintiff might be permitted to rescind the contract.

Mistakes about the nature or character of the transaction. The plaintiff is mistaken about the nature or character of the transaction when she is mistaken about a major feature of the transaction. Battery claims provide good examples. The plaintiff who professes consent to a touching is mistaken about the nature of the touching if her mistake relates to facts that make the touching harmful or offensive or prevent it from being so. For instance, the plaintiff who consents to manipulation of her body in the belief that it is for medical purposes when in fact it is only for the sexual gratification of the defendant, is mistaken about the nature of the touching, not merely about some collateral matter.[8] The same is true if the plaintiff consents to physical violence by her psychiatrist in the belief that "sluggo" treatment was therapeutic.[9] A sexual seduction induced by misrepresentation such as the defendant's assertion of an intent to marry is understandable in the same way, as a battery in which fraud has vitiated the consent.[10]

Other plaintiffs who are mistaken about the nature of the transaction include those who consent to sexual relations in the mistaken belief that the defendant is free of infection or that he cannot cause pregnancy. In such cases, if the defendant knows of the plaintiff's mistake or has induced it by a misrepresentation, he becomes liable for a battery, at

6. Restatement §§ 57 & 892, cmt. g.

7. See Restatement § 892B, Ill. 9 & Restatement § 57, Ill. 1.

8. Bartell v. State, 106 Wis. 342, 82 N.W. 142 (1900) (nude massage by "magnetic healer" ostensibly for medical purposes).

9. Rains v. Superior Court (The Center Foundation), 150 Cal.App.3d 933, 198 Cal. Rptr. 249 (1984).

10. See Piggott v. Miller, 557 S.W.2d 692 (Mo.App.1977). Jane E. Larson, "Women Understand So Little, They Call My Good Nature 'Deceit'": A Feminist Rethinking of Seduction, 93 COLUM. L. REV. 374 (1993), proposes a much expanded liability to be imposed not only when consent is secured by misrepresentation but also when it is secured by manipulation. The original common law tort for seduction was maintainable only by the father of a minor female and was based upon loss of her services resulting from the seduction.

least if disease or pregnancy actually results.[11] On the other hand, and quite apart from the plaintiff's consent, the defendant lacks the intent necessary for a battery if he neither knows nor should know that he is infected.[12]

The point is not limited to battery cases. In *Copeland v. Hubbard Broadcasting, Inc.*,[13] a homeowner consented to the entry of a woman who identified herself as a student but who in fact was there to videotape scenes for a television station. The homeowner's consent to her entrance did not bar the trespass claim. Commonly held values suggest that the transaction consented to—entrance by a student—would be viewed as radically different in nature from the transaction that actually took place—invasion by a journalist with a video camera.

At the borders and fringes of the problem. Some mistakes are not readily classified. Others present problems in adjudication because they become entangled with policy concerns that only happenstantially relate to mistakes.

In a very unusual Idaho case,[14] a divorcing wife sued her husband for battery, claiming that she had consented to sexual intercourse with him without knowing of his sexual relationship with another woman. She essentially claimed that her ignorance should count as a mistake and that the mistake negated her consent. The infidelity of sexual partners is traditionally a matter of great moment, so it was undoubtedly important. Quite possibly, however, its greatest importance was its bearing on other issues such as whether the marriage should continue or whether the parties should seek counseling. It seems far from clear that the wife's mistake was about the nature of acts she consented to. Nevertheless, the Idaho Court thought that it was at least a jury question whether the wife made a "mistake concerning the nature of the contact or the harm to be expected from it" and hence could recover for battery.

11. Kathleen K. v. Robert B., 150 Cal. App.3d 992, 198 Cal.Rptr. 273, 40 A.L.R.4th 1083 (1984) (contracting herpes); Barbara A. v. John G., 145 Cal.App.3d 369, 193 Cal.Rptr. 422 (1983) (lawyer telling client he could get no one pregnant); Hogan v. Tavzel, 660 So.2d 350 (Fla.App.1995) (genital warts not revealed); Crowell v. Crowell, 180 N.C. 516, 105 S.E. 206 (1920) (it was an "assault [battery] for the husband to communicate to his wife, while concealing from her the fact that he was infected therewith, a foul and loathsome disease"); De Vall v. Strunk, 96 S.W.2d 245 (Tex. Civ. App. 1936) (implicitly recognizing that consent of the plaintiff was no bar to claim that she was infected with "crabs" by intercourse with the defendant and expressly holding that participation in an illegal act of intercourse did not bar her claim); Restatement § 892B, Ill. 5; cf. Doe v. Johnson, 817 F.Supp. 1382 (W.D.Mich.1993) (suggesting substantial certainty test). Some cases lace the discussion with references to confidentiality, but the point seems simpler: the defendant caused or knew of the plaintiff's mistake about a basic characteristic of the transaction. One case treated sexual relations outside marriage as illegal and barred the plaintiff because she was an participant in the illegal act. Zysk v. Zysk, 239 Va. 32, 404 S.E.2d 721 (1990). Distinguish cases that assert negligent communication of sexual diseases, e.g., S.A.V. v. K.G.V., 708 S.W.2d 651 (Mo.1986) (spousal immunity abolished as to wife's claim against husband for negligently communicating sexual disease).

12. McPherson v. McPherson, 712 A.2d 1043 (Me.1998).

13. Copeland v. Hubbard Broadcasting, Inc., 526 N.W.2d 402 (Minn.App.1995).

14. Neal v. Neal, 125 Idaho 617, 873 P.2d 871 (1994).

At the other end of the spectrum are the cases in which a patient consents to an invasive medical procedure in ignorance of the fact that the surgeon suffers from AIDS or HIV. If the patient is actually exposed to the virus or becomes infected, she has an action based on the doctor's negligence[15] or failure to provide her with informed consent.[16] If she is not infected or exposed, however, a battery claim might be a major option.[17] She could plausibly argue that consent to an appendectomy is not consent to an appendectomy performed by an HIV infected doctor with sores on his arms, that is, that she was mistaken about the essential nature of the operation she consented to. At this writing there are few cases, most of them hobbled by a concern to avoid allowing emotional distress damages when the plaintiff has suffered no actual exposure to a toxic substance. Perhaps with this concern in mind,[18] one court has held that when the plaintiff did not actually suffer infection, the plaintiff's consent was a bar, even though she knew nothing of the doctor's infection[19] and some other courts have reached similar results.[20]

§ 101. Consent Obtained by Duress or Coercion

Physical and unlawful threats. Duress includes physical coercion and threats of it, that is, force or coercive threats that are intended to and do prevent the plaintiff's free choice.[1] The defendant cannot arrest

15. Cf. B.N. v. K.K., 312 Md. 135, 538 A.2d 1175 (Md. 1988) (negligence, intentional infliction of distress and fraud actions cognizable when sexual partner fails to reveal affirmatively his active case of herpes); cf. R.A.P. v. B.J.P., 428 N.W.2d 103 (Minn.App.1988) (sexual partner was negligent in engaging in sexual activity without disclosing that she had herpes); Long v. Adams, 175 Ga.App. 538, 333 S.E.2d 852 (1985) (disease communicated by sexual partner, negligence claim recognized); cf. Mussivand v. David, 45 Ohio St.3d 314, 544 N.E.2d 265 (1989) (sexual partner had duty to warn partner for benefit of her husband).

16. See Faya v. Almaraz, 329 Md. 435, 620 A.2d 327 (1993) (doctor who has tested HIV positive must disclose that fact to the patient before performing an invasive procedure). Whether fear of future harm from exposure is actionable, and what counts as exposure to a disease are both difficult points considered elsewhere. See § 311.

17. The difference is that a battery is actionable without proof of bodily harm or economic loss; the offensive touching is harm in itself.

18. As to the problems of claims for fear of future harm and of "exposure" in toxic tort cases, see § 311. It is also true that the risk of spreading infection is extremely small if the surgeon wears gloves, in which case infection is likely to occur only if the surgeon nicks himself. However, the battery claim, unlike some other tort claims, is based on the plaintiff's right to make for herself all decisions about her own body, not about seeking the plaintiff's best's interests against her will, or accommodating the interests of the defendant and those of the plaintiff.

19. K.A.C. v. Benson, 527 N.W.2d 553 (Minn.1995). The *K.A.C.* court said: "In medical malpractice claims, battery consists of touching of a substantially different nature and character from that to which the patient consented... .T.M.W. does not allege that Dr. Benson performed a different procedure from that to which she consented. Moreover, because Dr. Benson's conduct did not significantly increase the risk that T.M.W. would contract HIV, it cannot be said that Dr. Benson failed to disclose a material aspect of the nature and character of the procedure performed. Consequently, plaintiff's battery claim must fail." Id. at 560.

20. Kerins v. Hartley, 27 Cal.App.4th 1062, 33 Cal.Rptr.2d 172 (1994) (policy to limit emotional harm claims based on fear of future harm is carried over to battery cases, even though surgeon ignores the limits or conditions of the plaintiff's consent).

§ 101

1. Terms like free will, free choice, genuineness of consent and similar expressions

the plaintiff at gunpoint and then assert that the plaintiff consented to the arrest because the plaintiff voluntarily chose confinement in preference to a bullet. Threats of physical force or confinement are commonly the basis for false imprisonment claims. That is, confinement may be achieved not only by locking the plaintiff in a room but by indicating that she will be physically halted if she attempts to leave or that she will be subjected to worse forms of imprisonment.[2] On the other hand, threats to do acts that are not themselves illegal or tortious seldom render consent ineffective.

Economic threats to produce purely economic gains. Economic threats that induce consent to economic transactions generally do not count as duress or improper coercion.[3] For example, transactions involving buying and selling are based on implicit or express threats. The buyer who refuses to pay more than $25,000 for an automobile is in effect threatening not to buy at all unless the seller lowers the price. If the seller consents to sell at that price even though the car is worth more, the seller cannot later recover for conversion of the chattel on the ground that his consent was produced by duress. Similarly, the employer may threaten to discharge an unproductive employee unless her job performance improves. These threats are economic on both sides—they threaten to impose economic loss in order to obtain economic gain.

Objectively non-coercive threats without abuse of power. The difficult cases of duress or coercion lie in the middle ground between threats of physical force or illegal action on the one hand and simple threats of economic self-interest on the other. Many of the quotidian bargains by which we arrange our relationships are grounded in implicit or explicit threats. In the Restatement's example,[4] a friend says to you, "if you are not still here when I get back, our friendship is over." You remain in confinement because you value the friendship. You cannot recover for false imprisonment on the ground that your consent was obtained by duress or coercion.

Several observations can be made about threats like this. One is that reciprocal demands are part of the give and take of life. If I cannot terminate our friendship, my own freedom is significantly diminished. If I can terminate it but cannot mention the conditions that will lead me to do so, communication between us is significantly diminished or left to murky implication. The threat in this example seems childish but it

are conventional in discussions of duress. They may not be the best terms. What is perhaps objectionable is that the plaintiff is forced to make any choice at all or the choice between the alternatives presented. See John Dalzell, Duress by Economic Pressure, Part I, 20 N.C.L.Rev. 237, 238 (1942).

2. In Marcus v. Liebman, 59 Ill.App.3d 337, 16 Ill.Dec. 613, 375 N.E.2d 486 (1978) the plaintiff was a voluntary patient in a psychiatric facility. When she wanted to leave, the defendant threatened involuntary commitment to a state hospital if she attempted to leave. This was a false imprisonment.

3. This observation is part of the larger one that tort law generally treats economic activity differently from physical activity. However, some forms of economic duress are considered abusive or dangerous and may be important elements in some economic torts. Abuse of legal process and antitrust violations are examples.

4. Restatement § 892B, cmt. j.

represents a way of communicating about things that are important in a relationship. Although threats, express or implied, may not be gracious forms of communication, they do impart useful information and perform an important part of our social quid pro quo that permits cooperative behavior.

Two other observations about the Restatement's example are that the threat, from an objective point of view, is not coercive in any serious way and it involves no abuse of special power or position.

Coercive threats. As the observations above suggest, many threats or implicit threats are legitimate and others simply are not the basis for any legal response. There is a general formula for determining which threats count as sufficiently coercive to negate consent. That formula says that duress is a threat of unlawful conduct that is intended to and does prevent the plaintiff, as a person of ordinary firmness, from exercising free will or choice.[5] The formula seems almost useless in practice and most cases in fact involve contracts or avoidance of transactions rather than claims for trespassory torts like battery or trespass to land.

Aside from threats of physical harm and threats of torts or crime, most threats that negate consent or furnish an independent ground for a tort suit[6] represent serious abuses of power in some form. Some important abuses of this kind include sexual demands by employers and others in special positions of power. These are considered in the next section.

§ 102. Consent Obtained by Abuse of Power or Position

Some threats are viewed either as inherently coercive or as an abuse of power or position or both. If the threats are coercive, the "consent" is not genuine as a matter of fact and must be given no legal effect. If the threats are an abuse of power, the profession of consent, whether genuine or not, might be denied any legal effect as a matter of policy. The possibility that consent should be disregarded for either of these reasons is not limited to any particular group of cases because that possibility turns on the facts of the individual case. This section considers the possibility that the profession of consent to sexual relations with one's employer, psychotherapist, doctor, lawyer, or religious leader is ineffective because of the abuse or potential for abuse of such a special relationship. Other relationships, such as that between student and teacher, could raise the same kind of issue.[1]

5. Restatement § 871, cmt. f.

6. If a public employee is forced by duress to resign from her job, she may have a civil rights claim for deprivation of "property" in the job without due process of law. See Angarita v. St. Louis County, 981 F.2d 1537 (8th Cir.1992). Another example is the abuse of process claim. See § 438.

§ 102

1. Cf. Micari v. Mann, 126 Misc.2d 422, 481 N.Y.S.2d 967 (1984) (acting teacher induced students to engage in a variety of sexual acts as part of their drama training, held actionable); P.L. v. Aubert, 527 N.W.2d 142 (Minn.App.1995)(student sued the school as well as the teacher for battery and intentional infliction of distress based upon sexual touchings but the consent issue was

Job threats and sexual harassment. Demands for sexual favors by employers or supervisors may be implicitly threatening because of the power of employers to affect jobs and job benefits. Such threats present the employee with choices she should not be required to make. Although an employer may properly make implicit or explicit economic threats to gain economic performance, the employer may not suggest that the job or its benefits in any way depend upon the employee's agreement to sexual relations with the employer. To do so counts as quid pro quo sexual harassment under federal job discrimination statutes.[2]

Even a simple invitation by an employer or supervisor to engage in sexually related contact may imply a quid pro quo demand or threat and constitute harassment.[3] The consent professed by the employee in such cases does not bar her claim if the employer's sexual advances were in fact unwelcome.[4] So the employee proves a prima facie case by showing (a) that she was subject to unwelcome sexual conduct and (b) that her reaction to that conduct was used as a basis for decisions affecting compensation, terms, conditions or privileges of employment.[5]

Psychotherapists and counselors. Consent, especially consent to physical touching and sexual activity, is often induced by respect, affection, or dependence. Such a consent is of course perfectly effective and one who consents to sexual activity normally has no claim based on the activity consented to. However, in some cases the defendant owes the plaintiff a duty to avoid a potentially harmful sexual contact even if the plaintiff consents or professes consent. This is most notably the case of psychiatrists and other therapists who routinely confront troubled and vulnerable patients. Such patients often become excessively attached to their therapists and often consent to sexual contact with them. Therapists label this commonly observed phenomenon as "transference" and elaborate a theory to explain it.[6]

not even raised or discussed on appeal; the school was subject to vicarious liability).

2. 42 U.S.C.A. § 2000e ("Title VII"). Quid pro quo sexual harassment is a form of job discrimination that occurs when an employee's superiors either expressly or impliedly make the employee's sexual conduct a condition of job benefits. See Karibian v. Columbia University, 14 F.3d 773 (2d Cir. 1994); Hicks v. Gates Rubber Co., 833 F.2d 1406 (10th Cir.1987). A different form of sexual harassment is the hostile work environment, which does not ordinarily correspond to any of the trespassory torts but does bear some resemblance to, and may encompass, the tort of intentional infliction of emotional distress. See 1 Charles Sullivan, Michael Zimmer, & Richard Richards, Employment Discrimination § 8.7 (2d ed. 1988); Alba Conte, Sexual Harassment in the Workplace: Law and Practice §§ 3.21 & 3.22 (2d ed. 1994). On intentional infliction of distress, see § 303.

3. See Alba Conte, Sexual Harassment in the Workplace: Law and Practice § 3.15 (2d ed. 1994).

4. Meritor Savings Bank, FSB v. Vinson, 477 U.S. 57, 106 S.Ct. 2399, 91 L.Ed.2d 49 (1986). The Supreme Court's comments are consistent with the view that a professed consent by one whose choice is so constrained is likely to be no real consent at all. Hence, "[t]he correct inquiry is whether respondent by her conduct indicated that the alleged sexual advances were unwelcome, not whether her actual participation in sexual intercourse was voluntary." Id. 477 U.S. at 58, 106 S.Ct. at 2401.

5. Karibian v. Columbia University, 14 F.3d 773, 777 (2d Cir.1994).

6. Some therapeutic theories explain the "transference phenomenon" as a displacement of the patient's feelings about some other persons. Those feelings are then redirected at the therapist. See Barry Furrow, Malpractice in Psychotherapy 33 (1980).

The patient's consent in such cases may be the result of diminished capacity or possibly the result of forces outside her control,[7] but even if such a consent is as real as any other, it is usually assumed and always claimed that a patient's sexual behavior with her therapist is ultimately harmful to the patient's recovery and development.[8] If that is in fact so, the therapist who engages in sexual activity with his patient is actually breaching the professional duty of care which includes a duty to avoid the risk of further emotional harm, even if the patient knowingly consents to it. For this reason, and because given the patient's vulnerability, the "consent" is highly suspect, courts[9] and legislatures[10] hold or provide that the therapist is liable in spite of the patient's professed consent.

The plaintiff in these cases often asserts the claim on a theory of negligence, no doubt because the therapist's liability insurance will cover negligence but not intended torts.[11] Some cases have suggested that the therapist is liable for breach of fiduciary duty.[12] In none of these cases is the patient's consent a bar to the claim.

Physicians and attorneys. Medical doctors treating patients for medical conditions ordinarily have little role in providing for the patient's mental health. A physician who engages in sexual activity with a patient

The legal theory is that since this is predictable, therapists should be prepared to deal with it in professional ways and that the therapist is negligent in failing to do so.

7. Cf. Roy v. Hartogs, 81 Misc.2d 350, 366 N.Y.S.2d 297 (1975) (allegations of consent to sexual relations obtained by "coercion by a person in a position of overpowering influence and trust" stated a good claim).

8. Plaintiffs always claim they have been emotionally harmed at the breach of trust, that they feel demeaned, depressive or suicidal and suffer in other ways. Although the American Psychiatric Association condemns sex-with-patients as always unethical, a few therapists have claimed that it can be useful therapy. See MICHAEL PERLIN, LAW AND MENTAL DISABILITY § 3.04 (1994).

9. Simmons v. United States, 805 F.2d 1363 (9th Cir.1986); cf. McNall v. Summers, 25 Cal.App.4th 1300, 30 Cal.Rptr.2d 914 (1994) (psychiatrist's sexual conduct with patient, consent might have resulted from transference phenomenon, semble, and psychiatrist might have induced patient to believe sexual relation was part of therapy); Corgan v. Muehling, 143 Ill.2d 296, 158 Ill.Dec. 489, 574 N.E.2d 602 (1991) (one holding himself out as a registered psychologist allegedly caused harmful emotional reactions in patient as a result of sexual activities together; the claim is actionable if plaintiff proves negligent handling of transference phenomenon); Bunce v. Parkside Lodge of Columbus, 73 Ohio App.3d 253, 596 N.E.2d 1106 (1991) (counselor at drug rehabilitation center and patient, liability under statute); see Linda Jorgenson, Rebecca Randles, and Larry Strasburger, The Furor over Psychotherapist-patient Sexual Contact: New Solutions to an Old Problem, 32 WM. & MARY L. REV. 645 (1991).

10. CAL.CIV.CODE § 43.93 (b) (patient may recover if there is therapeutic deception); ILL.COMP.STAT. 140/2 (patient may recover if the patient was emotionally dependent or the therapist practiced deception); MINN. STAT. § 148A.02 (similar); WIS. STAT. ANN. § 895.70 (patient may recover regardless of emotional dependence or deception).

11. See, e.g., Zipkin v. Freeman, 436 S.W.2d 753 (Mo.1968). In spite of the "negligence" theory, the therapist's decision to have sexual relations with a patient is obviously intentional. Facts and allegations recited in the cases seem to indicate that the therapist is sometimes cruel, sometimes greedy, and always abusive. So the negligence designation fails to capture the nature of the serious wrongs perpetrated by therapists in these situations.

12. Roy v. Hartogs, 81 Misc.2d 350, 351, 366 N.Y.S.2d 297 (1975) ("This case involves a fiduciary relationship between psychiatrist and patient and is analogous to the guardian-ward relationship ... 'Consent obtained under such circumstances is no consent, and should stand for naught' ").

is thus not in the same position as a therapist. Courts have said that a medical doctor, having no duty to protect the patient from her own consent or even to avoid risk of emotional harm that can result from sexual activities, can rely on the patient's consent in the absence of fraud or duress by the physician or known incapacity on the part of the patient.[13] Lawyers are presumably in a similar position. They may find themselves disciplined for violation of ethical rules if they engage in sexual relations with clients, but the clients, not relying upon lawyers for emotional protection from themselves, are free to consent to sexual activities.[14]

The rules about lawyers and medical doctors, however, do not reflect privileges based upon status or profession. They reflect the professional roles undertaken. If a lawyer or medical doctor were to initiate sexual relations as a form of treatment,[15] or to engage in counseling or therapy, then liability would become appropriate.[16] Similarly, if these doctors or lawyers were to demand sexual favors as a condition of providing their best professional services,[17] or to exact a profession of consent by duress,[18] it seems reasonably clear that the professed consent would present no bar to the plaintiff's claim.

Analogies to the federal employment harassment cases suggest that a lawyer's demand for sexual activities with a client could carry an implicit threat that zealous professional services would depend upon compliance.[19] The analogy would also suggest that the "consent" ob-

13. Atienza v. Taub, 194 Cal.App.3d 388, 239 Cal.Rptr. 454 (1987); Odegard v. Finne, 500 N.W.2d 140 (Minn.App.1993).

14. Suppressed v. Suppressed, 206 Ill. App.3d 918, 151 Ill.Dec. 830, 565 N.E.2d 101, 105 (1990) (lawyer, although fiduciary, owed no duty comparable to a therapist's duty to improve patient's emotional well-being); cf. Vallinoto v. DiSandro, 688 A.2d 830 (R.I.1997) (rejecting a malpractice claim on the ground that client was not coerced and emotional harm claim on the ground that emotional harm may not have been caused by sexual relationship with attorney).

15. See Atienza v. Taub, 194 Cal.App.3d 388, 239 Cal.Rptr. 454 (1987) (citing cases imposing liability and distinguishing them on the grounds that in those cases sexual relations were "initiated by the physician purportedly in furtherance of his treatment of the patient").

16. Dillon v. Callaway, 609 N.E.2d 424 (Ind.App.1993) (medical doctor began providing "therapy" for patient, which turned into sadomasochistic sexual activities that eventually triggered severely harmful reactions in the patient; the patient's compensation fund was subject to liability because the doctor was acting as a therapist and the transference phenomenon theories applied).

17. McDaniel v. Gile, 230 Cal.App.3d 363, 281 Cal.Rptr. 242 (1991) (client claimed lawyer reduced or eliminated his representation of her divorce claim when she refused to have sexual relations and that he stated or implied he would represent her zealously if she "played the game the right way"; error to give summary judgment for defendant on the claims for intentional infliction of emotional distress and malpractice); see Doe v. Roe, 756 F.Supp. 353 (N.D.Ill.1991), aff'd, 958 F.2d 763 (7th Cir.1992) (lawyer for divorce-suit plaintiff, caught in sexual situation with his client, lost ability to collect his fee from the client's husband and demanded the fee from the client; the federal racketeering claim failed, but the court noted that the plaintiff might have good state-law claims for breach of fiduciary duty).

18. See Doe v. Roe, supra n. 17 (threats of bodily injury unless fee was paid).

19. In divorce cases in particular, the lawyer who seeks sexual relations with a client may have a conflict of interest, first because he may consciously or unconsciously oppose his client's reconciliation with her spouse, and second because he may delay an expeditious conclusion in order to maintain the sexual status quo. Other possible con-

tained as a result should be suspect as a matter of reality and ineffective as a matter of policy. But an Illinois case has in effect rejected this idea, holding also that the attorney's fiduciary duty to his client does not extend to personal relationships with the client.[20]

It is also possible that as a matter of public policy a patient's or client's consent should be given no effect when consent would give the professional a conflict of interest. In a Canadian case, *Norberg v. Wynrib*,[21] the plaintiff had become addicted to drugs. When her sources dried up, she sought prescriptions from the defendant, supposedly for her pain. The defendant prescribed drugs and also treated other complaints. Eventually he forced her to admit that she was addicted. Thereafter, he refused to prescribe drugs unless she would engage in sexual touchings. After this arrangement was broken up and the plaintiff rehabilitated, she sued the defendant. The Justices of the Supreme Court of Canada agreed that the plaintiff had a claim, but differed about the reasons for it. One group emphasized the power relationships between the parties as affecting either the reality of consent or the policy grounds for giving it legal effect. Another group thought that the doctor was liable in spite of the implied profession of consent because he acted in violation of fiduciary duty. There were other views as well.

It seems clear that at the very least the doctor in *Norberg* put himself in a position of conflict of interest. His professional duty was to heal the patient's addiction if he could, but his personal interest would have been to keep her addicted so he could continue his drug-for-sex arrangement. Even if the consent was "real," it would be very bad policy to permit professionals to deny their patients or clients the treatment they are entitled to or even to put themselves in a position of conflict of interest.

Clergy. Serious sexual abuse by members of the clergy has been widely reported and a number of cases have reached the courts. When pastors or priests abuse minors, courts have sometimes imposed liability,[22] although even in the child abuse cases courts have sometimes

flicts can be seen in Suppressed v. Suppressed, supra n. 14 (allegation that after client's husband caught lawyer in sexual situation with client, husband refused to pay attorney fees, which lawyer then demanded from client). Clouded judgment might be a significant result as well. On conflict of interest, see Margit Livingston, When Libido Subverts Credo: Regulation of Attorney–Client Sexual Relations, 62 FORDHAM L. REV. 5, 15 ff. (1993).

20. Suppressed v. Suppressed, supra n. 14. The opinion is much shaped by the court's view that the claim was a claim for "malpractice" with characteristics of a negligence claim rather than one for an intentional tort. It discusses the requirement that the defendant owe a "duty of care" and proof of actual damages both reflecting negligence thinking. Barbara A. v. John G., 145 Cal.App.3d 369, 193 Cal.Rptr. 422 (1983) held that if the client could prove a "confidential relationship" on the facts of her case, the lawyer would have the burden of showing that the client's consent to sexual acts was fully informed and freely given but refused to recognize that such a relationship is always involved in lawyer-client cases.

21. Norberg v. Wynrib, 92 D.L.R.4th 449 (Can. 1992).

22. See Fontaine v. Roman Catholic Church of Archdiocese of New Orleans, 625 So.2d 548 (La.App.1993) (a priest allegedly sexually abused a 17–year old and later published photographs in a magazine and circulated video tapes; held, these allega-

invoked immunities to protect the religious organization from liability.[23] When a pastor or priest sexually exploits an adult, such as a member of the congregation or parish who seeks religious counseling, courts have sometimes insisted that the adult's consent is a bar,[24] and when the claim is based upon negligence, they have concluded that there is no tort of "clergy malpractice."[25] Such cases obviously reject the analogy to the abusive therapist,[26] even though in most instances the clergy's sexual abuse originates in counseling situations in which confidence is reposed and authority is respected by the victim. However, at this point the cases are not numerous, so they may not represent broadly held views.[27] In any event, some limited authority does support liability of clergy or their religious organization or superiors for battery or for breach of fiduciary duty.[28]

§ 103. Informed Consent: Duty to Provide Information

As already shown, the plaintiff's consent to an invasion is ineffective to bar a claim if the plaintiff is mistaken about the nature of the invasion and the defendant knows it.[1] In some cases, however, the plaintiff is not so much mistaken about the nature of the proposed

tions state a privacy invasion claim); Mrozka v. Archdiocese of St. Paul & Minneapolis, 482 N.W.2d 806 (Minn.App.1992).

23. See Schultz v. Roman Catholic Archdiocese of Newark, 95 N.J. 530, 472 A.2d 531 (1984) (forcible sexual acts against a member of priest's Boy Scout group, resulting in boy's suicide; held, the Archdiocese is a charity and immunity from tort liability for its negligence in failing to prevent such things); cf. Foreign Mission Board of the Southern Baptist Convention v. Wade, 242 Va. 234, 409 S.E.2d 144 (1991) (controlling employer of missionary had no duty to protect children from molestation by their missionary-father, even though employer knew of the sexual abuses).

24. Schieffer v. Catholic Archdiocese of Omaha, 244 Neb. 715, 718, 508 N.W.2d 907, 911 (1993): ("What is involved in this case is conduct between consenting adults. There is no allegation that the defendant used force or fraud to accomplish his sexual relations"); but cf. F.G. v. MacDonell, 150 N.J. 550, 696 A.2d 697 (1997) (clergy sexual abuse of counseling situation is breach of fiduciary duty; "troubled parishioners should be able to seek pastoral counseling free from the fear that the counselors will sexually abuse them. Our decision does no more than extend to the defenseless the same protection that the dissent would extend to infants and incompetents"). When the adult is not in counseling with the minister, the consenting adults rule is clearly applicable. See Bladen v. First Presbyterian Church of Sallisaw, 857 P.2d 789 (Okla.1993).

25. See § 258.

26. See Hertel v. Sullivan, 261 Ill. App.3d 156, 160, 198 Ill.Dec. 574, 633 N.E.2d 36, 39 (1994) ("We reject plaintiff's suggestion that the duties of a priest to his parishioner or of a minister to his congregation should be equated with the duties of a psychologist to his patient. A priest or minister is not required to possess and apply the knowledge and use the skill and care ordinarily used by a reasonably well-qualified psychologist").

27. See John Wagner, Jr., Annotation, Cause of Action for Clergy Malpractice, 75 A.L.R.4th 750 (1990).

28. See Moses v. Diocese of Colorado, 863 P.2d 310 (Colo.1993) (no separate tort of clergy malpractice but church might be liable for negligent hiring, negligent supervision, and breach of fiducial duty when it neither sought to prevent nor to ameliorate the effects of priestly sexual behavior with vulnerable parishioners); Destefano v. Grabrian, 763 P.2d 275 (Colo.1988) (clergyperson giving marriage counseling to husband and wife and having sexual intercourse with one of them); F.G. v. MacDonell, 150 N.J. 550, 696 A.2d 697 (1997) (fiduciary duty).

§ 103

1. § 100 supra.

invasion as ignorant about its potential risks or consequences. In such a case, the mistake rules would not vitiate the plaintiff's consent.

Medical operations and procedures often involve this point. At one time it was thought that when a surgeon operated upon a plaintiff who did not know and had not been informed of the risks of the operation, the plaintiff might have a claim for battery because the consent would be ineffective. Such a claim would be a good one no matter how well the operation was performed or what benefits it conferred. It is clearly right to treat the operation as unconsented to if the plaintiff was mistaken about the nature of the operation and the defendant knew it. But the plaintiff's ignorance of the risks does not necessarily mean the plaintiff was mistaken about the nature of the operation.

Why is it that the plaintiff who is ignorant of the risks of a medical procedure may not be mistaken about its nature? First, the patient is not mistaken at all if she knows that operations have risks and knows also that she does not know what they are. Mistake is a state of mind not in accord with the facts. A person who knows she does not know a fact is not mistaken about that fact at all.[2] Second, the plaintiff might erroneously believe she knows the risks when she does not; in that case, she is indeed mistaken, but not necessarily about the nature of the operation. The risks of a procedure and safer alternatives might not go to the nature of the operation, only to collateral matters of value. These points indicate some of the reasons why ignorance is not always the equivalent of a mistake that will vitiate consent.

Even if the plaintiff is not mistaken, however, her consent to a medical procedure might be ineffective to bar her suit for other reasons. Courts can impose upon the surgeon or physician a duty to use reasonable care to inform the plaintiff of the important or material risks or at least of risks that other doctors would explain to a patient. That is what courts have come to hold under the rules of negligence law and under the specific rubric of informed consent.[3]

The result is that in most courts, battery claims against the surgeon would be entertained only if the surgeon has exceeded the consent by performing an operation not consented to at all[4] or by operating with knowledge that the plaintiff was mistaken (not merely ignorant) about the nature of the operation. If the surgeon's fault is that he failed to provide information that should have been provided, the plaintiff's consent holds good to bar the battery claim. In that case, the surgeon's liability, if any, must be based on a showing that he was negligent, either in failing to disclose material facts or in performing the operation itself. These claims are discussed in the context of medical malpractice claims generally.[5]

2. See 2 DAN B. DOBBS, LAW OF REMEDIES § 11.2 (2d ed. 1993).

3. See §§ 250 & 251 below.

4. E.g., Gerety v. Demers, 92 N.M. 396, 589 P.2d 180 (1978).

5. See Chapter 14.

The distinction between the plaintiff's ignorance of risks and her mistake about the nature of the operation is slippery. The difficulty is now compounded because courts in recent years have begun to use the term "informed consent" both in discussing (a) the doctor's obligation to provide information (the claim usually treated as a negligence claim) and (b) his obligation to operate within the limits of the plaintiff's consent (the claim usually treated as a battery claim).[6] This difficulty requires careful reading of the cases, some of which say the plaintiff did not give informed consent but appear to mean that she did not give any consent at all to the operation or procedure that was performed.

§ 104. Scope and Termination of Consent

Consent does not bar the plaintiff's claim (a) for any tortious conduct that is outside the scope of the consent or apparent consent nor (b) for any tortious conduct occurring after consent has been effectively revoked and the defendant has an opportunity reasonably to avoid that conduct.

Scope of Consent

Liability for exceeding the consent. The plaintiff may limit her consent as she likes, consenting to one act but not another, or to acts at one time but not another, or to acts under some conditions but not others.[1] The scope of the defendant's protection is the scope of the consent. If his conduct would be tortious except for consent and his conduct goes beyond the consent or its conditions, he is subject to liability.[2]

Determining the scope. The scope of the consent may itself be subject to dispute because its scope, like its existence, depends heavily upon implications and the interpretation of circumstances. Consent to shoot rabbits in the landowner's woods is almost certainly not consent to shoot them in the landowner's front yard.[3] Possibly also a consent to operate on the right ear is not consent to operate upon the left one,[4] but it is not impossible to believe that a patient about to undergo an operation consents by implication to extensions of the operation that become

6. For instance, Fox v. Smith, 594 So.2d 596 (Miss.1992) speaks repeatedly of informed consent but appears not to involve a failure to provide information but a medical procedure that simply was not even professedly consented to. Moure v. Raeuchle, 529 Pa. 394, 604 A.2d 1003 (1992) likewise speaks throughout of informed consent, but a major illustration in the opinion suggests the court has in mind, not a failure to provide information, so much as a scope of consent issue. The illustration is Mohr v. Williams, 95 Minn. 261, 104 N.W. 12 (1905), § 130 below—a case involving an operation different from the one consented to.

§ 104

1. See Restatement § 892A (3).

2. E.g., Karl J. Pizzalotto, M.D. v. Wilson, 437 So.2d 859 (La.1983).

3. But in Florida Publishing Co. v. Fletcher, 340 So.2d 914 (Fla.1976) the court ignored the difference between consent-by-custom to enter land and consent for a stranger to enter a dwelling place in the owner's absence.

4. Mohr v. Williams, 95 Minn. 261, 104 N.W. 12 (1905), overruled in part, Genzel v. Halvorson, 248 Minn. 527, 80 N.W.2d 854 (1957).

medically desirable[5] and certainly to extensions needed because of medical emergency.

Consent to act as consent to consequences. Consent to the defendant's acts is not consent to injury resulting from those acts. Nevertheless, the defendant is guilty of no intentional tort so long as his acts are those consented to, even if harmful consequences result.[6] In *Hellriegel v. Tholl,*[7] the plaintiff and other boys were engaged in horseplay. Several boys picked up the plaintiff, and threw him into the water. These acts seem to have been tacitly consented to because they were part of the activities engaged in by all the boys. The plaintiff suffered a terrible and unexpected injury. Although he never consented to injury, he did consent to the acts that caused it and that was enough to bar his claim. Put differently, a consent is not normally interpreted to contain an implicit condition, "I consent provided I am not hurt."

There are express and implicit conditions to consents, however, and they are traditionally effective if communicated or understood.[8] If I present myself to you as a student seeking to learn more about the legal profession, you might admit me to your office on the implicit condition or understanding that I am what I claim to be, and not, say, a television reporter with a hidden camera.[9]

However, California courts have put in question the ability of a patient to condition her consent to an operation on the surgeon's freedom from the HIV or AIDS virus. Under a California decision, a patient who consents only to an operation by an AIDS-free surgeon has no claim for battery and the attendant emotional distress when the surgeon ignores the limitations of her consent unless the patient is actually infected or at least physically exposed to the virus.[10]

Revocation or Termination of Consent

Power to revoke and effect of revocation. A plaintiff who gives consent may terminate or revoke it at any time by communicating the revocation to those who may act upon the consent.[11] A communicated

5. Kennedy v. Parrott, 243 N.C. 355, 90 S.E.2d 754 (1956).

6. "Where the plaintiff consented to the battery itself, the consent extends to ordinary consequences stemming from it." Janelsins v. Button, 102 Md.App. 30, 38, 648 A.2d 1039, 1043 (1994).

7. Hellriegel v. Tholl, 69 Wash.2d 97, 417 P.2d 362 (1966).

8. Ashcraft v. King, 228 Cal.App.3d 604, 610, 278 Cal.Rptr. 900 (1991) ("Ms. Ashcraft's claim of battery rested on the theory that although the operation was consented to, the consent was subject to a specific condition: only family donated blood would be used. If Ms. Ashcraft could establish the existence of this condition and its breach by Dr. King, she would establish a battery").

9. See Copeland v. Hubbard Broadcasting, Inc., 526 N.W.2d 402 (Minn.App.1995).

10. Kerins v. Hartley, 27 Cal.App.4th 1062, 33 Cal.Rptr.2d 172 (1994); cf. K.A.C. v. Benson, 527 N.W.2d 553 (Minn.1995) (no battery claim absent actual exposure where plaintiff consented to the very operation performed, even though she never consented to an operation by an infected surgeon).

11. Restatement § 892A(5) & cmt. i. Mims v. Boland, 110 Ga.App. 477, 138 S.E.2d 902 (1964) purports to require that the plaintiff not only communicate withdrawal of consent but that she do so with such clarity and in such a way "as to leave no room for doubt in the minds of reasonable men that in view of all the circumstances consent was actually withdrawn."

revocation withdraws the defendant's privilege; once the consent is withdrawn he becomes liable for any act that would be tortious without consent. For example, if a patient, about to be operated upon, revokes her consent, the surgeon commits a battery if he proceeds with the operation and becomes liable even if he carried out the operation with skill.[12] If a landowner revokes her consent to a visitor's presence, the visitor becomes a trespasser if he does not leave.[13]

Defendant's reasonable opportunity. The defendant must, however, be permitted a reasonable opportunity to discontinue his conduct. For example, if the plaintiff has permitted the defendant to store his car on the plaintiff's land, the defendant must remove the car when the consent is revoked, but at the same time he is given a reasonable opportunity to do so.[14] Similarly, the physician carrying out a medical procedure when consent to it is revoked must be permitted to discontinue the procedure in a medically safe way.[15]

Automatic termination. A consent may be terminated in accordance with a condition established in the consent itself. Suppose that A gives B permission to move B's house trailer onto A's land and to keep it there for the rest of B's life. By its own conditions, the consent terminates when B dies. B's personal representative becomes a trespasser if he does not remove the trailer within a reasonable time thereafter.[16]

Irrevocable consent. A few almost-unique cases aside,[17] courts have held that a consent could be irrevocable only when it takes the form of a license or consent to use real property that is coupled with a legal interest in that property,[18] or where the licensee has expended large sums in making improvements under the license.[19] This second ground may be referred to as an executed license or more simply as a case of equitable estoppel.[20]

Mims was discussing revocation of consent in the midst of a medical procedure. Such a demanding standard for revocation probably does not apply to, say, consent to sexual contact.

12. Pugsley v. Privette, 220 Va. 892, 263 S.E.2d 69 (1980).

13. Hector v. Metro Centers, Inc., 498 N.W.2d 113 (N.D.1993).

14. Restatement § 177.

15. Mims v. Boland, 110 Ga.App. 477, 138 S.E.2d 902 (1964).

16. Steiger v. Burroughs, 878 P.2d 131 (Colo.App.1994); Restatement § 177.

17. (1) Peterson v. Sorlien, 299 N.W.2d 123, 11 A.L.R.4th 208 (Minn. 1980) (parents, believing that their adult child had lost her volitional capacity because she had been indoctrinated by a "cult," detained her to "deprogram" her; in effect, her consent once given could not be withdrawn until she regained or apparently regained her volitional capacity). (2) Tope v. Howe, 179 Mich.App. 91, 445 N.W.2d 452 (1989) asserted without citation that once police were voluntarily admitted to one's home, the consent to enter "cannot be revoked by a person's later request for a warrant or that the police leave the premises." Perhaps the court meant to say that the revocation was not clearly communicated. The same court later said that although one cannot retroactively revoke consent, it could be revoked prospectively at any time. People v. Powell, 199 Mich.App. 492, 502 N.W.2d 353 (1993).

18. E.g., Bomberger v. McKelvey, 35 Cal.2d 607, 220 P.2d 729 (1950) (consent to place chattels on owner's land is irrevocable license to remove them within the period contemplated by the license); Anchor Stone & Materials Co. v. Carlin, 436 P.2d 650 (Okla.1967).

19. Keystone Copper Mining Co. v. Miller, 63 Ariz. 544, 164 P.2d 603 (1945).

20. Equitable estoppel arises when one party communicates something upon which

§ 105. Consent to Crime

When the plaintiff is injured in the course of a criminal act to which she has consented, courts can seldom find entirely satisfactory rules. Suppose the plaintiff consents to fight in an illegal boxing match with the defendant. The defendant strikes a forceful blow that injures the plaintiff quite seriously. If the plaintiff's consent is a bar to his claim, the defendant is relieved of liability for his illegal acts. Some courts so hold, not only in the case of illegal fights but in the case of other consensual but illegal activities as well.[1] On the other hand, if the plaintiff's consent is not a bar, the plaintiff recovers in spite of her illegal conduct. Furthermore, the defendant is also entitled to recover for blows he receives. This might be viewed as "rewarding" the illegal conduct or at least as failing to punish it, or perhaps as wasting judicial resources to set off the two claims against one another. But some courts have said a recovery by both is permitted, the consent being no bar.[2]

Neither rule is apt. The obvious solution, and the one adopted by the Restatement,[3] is that deterrence and punishment for the illegality is to be left to the criminal law; tort law may thus proceed under its ordinary rules, which means that the plaintiff's consent is a bar just as it is in any other case, subject to two qualifications.

The first qualification is that when the statute makes conduct illegal in order to protect the plaintiff from her own professed consent, her consent is no bar. Age of consent or statutory rape statutes, for example, provide that intercourse with a minor under a specified age is a crime regardless of the minor's consent.[4] Quite possibly such statutes should be regarded as an indirect command to disregard the minor's consent in a tort suit, since they evidently proceed on the theory that under a certain age minors have no capacity to give informed and meaningful consent.[5]

The second qualification should be but is not always recognized. Consent to an illegal act does not ordinarily make the plaintiff an outlaw. The plaintiff's consent should bar a claim for what she consented to, but no more. Consent to an illegal abortion, for example, is not consent to negligent infliction of harm or death. To bar the plaintiff in such a case is not to enforce her consent but to permit infliction of harm

the other reasonably relies and the relying party would be materially prejudiced if the other is permitted to assert something contrary to the original communication. See Dan B. Dobbs, Law of Remedies § 2.3 (5) (2d ed. 1993). Both the license-coupled-with-interest and the executed license theories are applied in estoppel-like situations. See Stillwater Columbia Ass'n, Inc. v. Shepherd, 727 P.2d 596 (Okla.App.1986).

§ 105

1. Goldnamer v. O'Brien, 98 Ky. 569, 33 S.W. 831 (Ky. 1896) (consent to illegal abortion is a bar to recover for inducing the abortion). The plaintiff is sometimes barred on the basis of a wider rule that selectively refuses to permit the plaintiff to recover if she has participated in an illegal act. As to that, see § 208. In Castronovo v. Murawsky, 3 Ill.App.2d 168, 120 N.E.2d 871 (1954) the victim consented to an illegal abortion; she died, not because it was illegal but because it was negligently performed; nevertheless, the court denied recovery.

2. See Brown v. Patterson, 214 Ala. 351, 108 So. 16 (1926); Annotation, 47 A.L.R. 1093 (1927).

3. Restatement § 892C.

4. Vernon's Ann. Mo. Stat., § 566.034.

5. E.g., Glover v. Callahan, 299 Mass. 55, 12 N.E.2d 194 (1937).

she never consented to. The reasons for doing that, if any, are not based upon consent at all.

§ 106. Emergency as a Substitute for Consent

A health care provider may deliver medically indicated emergency care when neither the patient nor an appropriate agent can make the choice pro or con.[1] This might occur, for example, if the patient were unconscious and would die without immediate treatment and if no family member or guardian were on hand to make decisions.

The term emergency implies both that the plaintiff's health is in jeopardy so that immediate medical attention is required and that a person authorized to consent is not available to make the requisite decision.[2] In such cases the physician may take medically indicated steps that do not risk more harm than they are likely to avoid, provided that the physician has no reason to think the plaintiff would refuse consent.[3] The effect of these rules is that a true emergency is ordinarily a substitute for the patient's consent.

It is sometimes suggested that the emergency rules are grounded in some kind of implied consent by the patient.[4] But as the patient is unconscious or mentally compromised when the issue arises, it is more accurate to say that the rule is a rule of law rather than a rule of consent. Although the rule is based upon what judges believe people would generally want to happen, it is not based on implicit communication from the particular patient.

The emergency rule is not intended to permit providers to overrule or avoid confronting the patient's wishes. If the plaintiff is conscious, the physician must inform her of the proposed treatment and its risks.[5] "A physician must respect the refusal of treatment by a patient who is capable of providing consent, even in an emergency."[6] If the patient, while competent, has reliably expressed her opposition to a particular medical procedure, her wishes are not to be overridden when she falls unconscious and death is imminent.[7]

One well-known case may represent a contrary spirit. In *Kennedy v. Parrott*,[8] In *Kennedy*, the doctor obtained consent to do an appendectomy. In the course of the operation he found enlarged cysts on the patient's left ovary and punctured them. In doing so, he allegedly cut a

§ 106

1. E.g., Miller v. Rhode Island Hospital, 625 A.2d 778 (R.I.1993), relying heavily on Canterbury v. Spence, 464 F.2d 772 (D.C.Cir.1972); Restatement § 892D.

2. E.g., Karl J. Pizzalotto, M.D. v. Wilson, 437 So.2d 859 (La.1983).

3. Restatement § 892D.

4. E.g., Traxler v. Varady, 12 Cal. App.4th 1321, 16 Cal.Rptr.2d 297 (1993); Leach v. Shapiro, 13 Ohio App.3d 393, 469 N.E.2d 1047 (1984).

5. Cunningham v. Yankton Clinic, 262 N.W.2d 508 (S.D.1978).

6. Miller v. Rhode Island Hospital, 625 A.2d 778 (R.I.1993).

7. Rodriguez v. Pino, 634 So.2d 681 (Fla.App.1994); Estate of Leach v. Shapiro, 13 Ohio App.3d 393, 469 N.E.2d 1047 (1984).

8. 243 N.C. 355, 90 S.E.2d 754, 56 A.L.R.2d 686 (1956).

blood vessel, which in turn caused the patient some additional problems. The patient claimed battery because she had not consented to treatment of the cysts. The court first dismissed the importance of consent as a "fetish," then said that the patient had impliedly consented to extensions of the operation as appeared necessary in the doctor's medical judgment during the time the patient was incapacitated by anesthesia. If the cysts represented an emergency or the patient truly implied consent, the court's analysis is surely correct. However, if the cysts represented a common or predictable problem, the doctor could have advised the plaintiff in advance of the operation and could have sought her consent. If that was the case, the cysts did not represent an emergency and the effect of the decision is to sidestep the requirement of informed consent.[9]

Topic H. Necessity

§ 107. Private Necessity

In a limited group of situations, partial or complete privileges protect defendants whose acts in emergencies would otherwise count as trespass to land or chattels or as conversion. The emergency and the privilege it generates are both called "necessity." The privilege can be invoked only to avert a public disaster or serious imminent harm to the defendant or to others. The rules recognize two distinct privileges, private necessity considered in this section and public necessity considered in the next.

Rule and example. A commonly cited example of private necessity is the case of a sudden storm on a lake that justifies the defendant in putting his small boat ashore on the plaintiff's property to avoid serious threat to his life or property. He is privileged to enter for such a purpose. That privilege means: (a) he is not liable for damages when no harm is no done, (b) he is under no civil disability that attaches to "trespassers,"[1] and (c) the landowner has no privilege to push him back into the lake.[2] If the emergency or necessity arises from the defendant's own fault, it seems probable that he would lose the immunity from liability,[3] but still retain the privilege of shelter on the land so long as the alternatives were unsafe.[4]

9. Compare Karl J. Pizzalotto, M.D. v. Wilson, 437 So.2d 859 (La.1983). In that case the patient consented to a limited operation but the surgeon removed her reproductive organs. Testimony indicated that removal was medically correct, but as the surgeon had not discussed this possibility with the patient nor obtained her consent, and as there was no life-or-death emergency, the surgeon was liable for battery.

§ 107

1. See Rossi v. DelDuca, 344 Mass. 66, 181 N.E.2d 591 (1962) (child entered defendant's land to escape a dog in the street only to be attacked by the defendant's dog; under the statute she was not entitled to recover if she was a trespasser, but under the necessity privileges she was not a trespasser and could recover).

2. Ploof v. Putnam, 81 Vt. 471, 71 A. 188 (1908) (on facts similar to those in the text).

3. Thus where the defendant knew a danger might arise and could have arranged to avoid it he cannot claim the necessity privilege. Currie v. Silvernale, 142 Minn. 254, 171 N.W. 782 (1919).

4. Cf. Depue v. Flateau, 100 Minn. 299, 111 N.W. 1 (1907) (when supper guest became ill in very cold weather, landowner

Serious and imminent threat required to invoke the privilege. The privilege can only be invoked when the defendant is threatened, or reasonably appears to be threatened, with serious harm and the response is reasonable in the light of the threat.[5] Courts have not suggested that homeless persons could occupy private property on the ground that they have no home of their own.[6] And the harm threatened must not only be imminent but harm that is legally recognizable. For instance, abortion protestors who enter a clinic cannot claim a necessity defense on the ground that their trespasses are necessary to prevent perfectly legal abortions.[7] For the same reason, a homeowner has no privilege to enter the plaintiff's land to stop the perfectly legal drainage of plaintiff's water upon the defendant's land.[8]

Limits of the privilege: liability for actual harm. The private necessity privilege is "incomplete"[9] because it protects against liability for technical trespass and deprives the landowner of his usual counter-privilege to rebuff the trespasser, but it does not protect the defendant against liability for actual harm done.[10] The skier who is lost in a snow storm may enter your cabin for shelter without liability. But if he burns the furniture to stay warm he must pay for its destruction.

The Vincent case. The leading case establishing liability for actual harm is *Vincent v. Lake Erie Transportation Co.*[11] In *Vincent*, a ship had

could not refuse to allow him to stay the night; semble, this would hold true even if the guest was voluntarily intoxicated). Rigby v. Chief Constable of Northamptonshire, [1985] 1 W.L.R. 1242 (Q.B.), not distinguishing among any of the sub-privileges or between public and private necessity took the view that the necessity doctrine could not be invoked by a defendant who was at fault in creating the necessity.

5. Protectus Alpha Navigation Co. v. North Pacific Grain Growers, 585 F.Supp. 1062 (D.Or.1984), aff'd, 767 F.2d 1379 (9th Cir.1985) (not reasonable to unmoor burning boat to protect against remote risk that fire would cause explosion in grain elevator).

6. London Borough of Southwark v. Williams, [1971] 1 Ch. 734, [1971] 2 All. E.R. 175, rejected the necessity defense urged on behalf of homeless persons who entered empty houses. In Tobe v. City of Santa Ana, 9 Cal.4th 1069, 40 Cal.Rptr.2d 402, 892 P.2d 1145 (1995) the court upheld an ordinance against various kinds of "camping" on open public property, but may have suggested that enforcement against people who literally had no alternative but to sleep in a municipal parking lot would raise issues for litigation.

7. Cyr v. State, 887 S.W.2d 203 (Tex. App.1994). Other protestors have also failed in their assertion of necessity and related defenses. E.g., Commonwealth v. Hood, 389 Mass. 581, 452 N.E.2d 188 (1983) (trespassing to distribute leaflets against nuclear arms race).

8. Grant v. Allen, 41 Conn. 156 (1874).

9. Francis Bohlen, Incomplete Privilege to Inflict Intentional Invasions of Interests of Property and Personality, 39 Harv. L. Rev. 307 (1926).

10. Currie v. Silvernale, 142 Minn. 254, 171 N.W. 782 (1919); Vincent v. Lake Erie Transportation Co., 109 Minn. 456, 124 N.W. 221 (1910); Ruiz v. Forman, 514 S.W.2d 817 (Tex.Civ.App.1974); Restatement § 197 (2); cf. Allen v. Camp, 14 Ala. App. 341, 70 So. 290 (1915) (after defendant's child was bitten by dog, defendant killed it for the purpose of determining whether it had rabies, liability); cf. United States v. M/V Miss Beholden, 856 F.Supp. 668 (S.D.Fla.1994) (vessel intentionally grounded on coral reef when it was taking on water and could not make port was strictly liable for damage to coral under the National Marine Sanctuaries Act, 16 U.S.C.A. § 1431 et seq.). Some negligence cases, to which the necessity defense does not directly pertain, have nevertheless asserted the same general idea.

11. Vincent v. Lake Erie Transportation Co., 109 Minn. 456, 124 N.W. 221 (1910).

been tied at the plaintiff's dock unloading goods in Duluth, Minnesota. A violent storm arose. The captain prudently determined that it was unsafe to put out into the lake. He renewed the lines that held the ship at the dock, although this meant that by action of the waves, the ship repeatedly struck the dock and damaged it, a fact of which the captain was aware. Although the dock owner would have no privilege to defend his possession or property by casting the ship off, the dock owner was allowed to recover for actual harm to the dock. The case generates a lot of discussion because the result might be explicable on different grounds and because the scope of the principle is perhaps debatable.[12] But the simplest explanation is that if the captain was a trespasser, he is liable for actual harm done in spite of his incomplete privilege to trespass.

Extending the privilege to battery cases? The limited privilege of private necessity has been recognized by the Restatement and applied by the courts to protect the defendant from liability for technical interference with property; but so far the idea has not been carried over to an interference with the person that is a technical battery but causes no harm. Bohlen suggested that an offensive but not harmful battery would be in the same category as a technical but not harmful trespass.[13] The plaintiff who is offended but not physically harmed by a touching needed to save the defendant from dire harm would have no claim if that suggestion were accepted. Perhaps Bohlen wrote before we had come to know just how offensive some touchings can be.

§ 108. Private Individuals Acting out of Public Necessity

General rule. In the traditional view of public necessity, a defendant who damages, destroys, or uses the plaintiff's property in the reasonable belief that by so doing he can avoid or minimize serious and immediate harm to the public is protected against liability for intentional torts by a

12. One line in the opinion suggests that liability might be imposed as restitution rather than as tort damages because the captain saved the ship at the expense of the dock. But the captain "saved the ship" only if destruction were certain to result when it cast off. Since destruction was not certain, what the captain really saved was the risk or chance of destruction, which might have been quite small. The saved-the-ship idea also suggests, probably wrongly, that the captain would not be liable if, after damaging the dock, the ship sank anyway. A broader possible basis for *Vincent* is that one who acts obtains the benefits of his action and therefore should pay the costs he inflicts upon others as well. See Richard Epstein, A Theory of Strict Liability, 2 J. Legal Stud. 151, 157–160 (1973). Still another possibility is that the rule in *Vincent* proleptically resolves disputes between dockowner and captain by making either actor liable for harm actually done to the other and at the same time supports the best economic result. That is, the dockowner, seeing her dock being damaged, might try to cast the ship off, just as the captain attempts to hold it fast to the dock. The *Vincent* rule tells these two parties which one should give way and provides an incentive to do so. If the threatened damage to the ship is $1,000 and that to the dock is only $500 the dockowner will not risk the liability of $1,000 to save $500, especially since she knows she can recover for the damages.

13. Bohlen, supra n. 9 at 319–324. He went on to say, however, that even though the defendant might (in his view) have a privilege to inflict an offensive touching, the plaintiff would not lose her privilege to resist it.

complete privilege.[1] Sometimes the privilege is claimed by a public official acting in the public interest, but even a private individual enjoys its protection.[2]

To invoke the privilege the actor must show that (a) public rather than private interests are involved, (b) he was reasonable in believing that action was needed, and (c) the action he took was a reasonable response to that need.[3] In contrast to the privilege of private necessity, the public necessity privilege is complete because it protects against liability for actual harm inflicted and not merely against liability for technical trespass.

Examples. A time-honored example of the public necessity privilege is the case of the defendant who destroys the plaintiff's house to prevent the spread of fire that would otherwise engulf a whole city. The defendant who correctly or reasonably perceives the need for such action cannot be held liable, even for the actual harm inflicted.[4] Similarly, the plaintiff's property may be destroyed to prevent the spread of disease[5] or to prevent its use as an agent of destruction by the public enemy such as an invading army.[6]

Private individuals pleading public necessity. The rule of nonliability is easy to understand when it is applied to protect individuals as distinct from public entities that benefit. The individual defendant acting in an emergency is not likely to take action to protect against dire public loss if he will be personally liable for the losses that will certainly be inflicted. His interests in such a case may be largely divorced from those of the public at large, so immunity from liability is perhaps needed to induce his beneficial action. Perhaps more importantly, it would be unjust to make a single individual bear the loss reasonably incurred for the benefit of the entire public. This explains why the rule is otherwise in the usual

§ 108

1. Restatement §§ 196 (land) & 263 (chattels). The Restatement uses the term "imminent public disaster."

2. Restatement § 196, cmt. e.

3. Beach v. Trudgain, 43 Va. 219 (1845) (defendants could not justify destruction of plaintiff's house as a firebreak if spread of fire could have been avoided otherwise).

4. Surocco v. Geary, 3 Cal. 69 (1853); American Print Works v. Lawrence, 23 N.J.L. 9 (1850), aff'd, 23 N.J.L. 590 (1851).

5. Seavey v. Preble, 64 Me. 120 (1874) (removing wallpaper from smallpox sick room justified); South Dakota Dept. of Health v. Heim, 357 N.W.2d 522 (S.D.1984) (destruction of diseased herd justified); State v. Mayor and Aldermen of Knoxville, 80 Tenn. 146 (1883) (nuisance created by smoke from repeated burnings of smallpox tainted goods was justified); cf. McGuire v. Amyx, 317 Mo. 1061, 297 S.W. 968, 54 A.L.R. 644 (1927) (health officer not liable for confining person if he reasonably believed she had smallpox); Preudhomme v. Stebbins, 269 App.Div. 409, 55 N.Y.S.2d 397 (1945); (seizing dogs suspected of rabies); Putnam v. Payne, 13 Johns. 312 (N.Y. 1816) (vicious dog that had been bitten by mad dog was loose in the street; defendant justified in shooting the dog).

6. United States v. Caltex, Inc., 344 U.S. 149, 73 S.Ct. 200, 97 L.Ed. 157 (1952) (destruction of oil and oil terminal as invading troops were entering the city of Manila); Harrison v. Wisdom, 54 Tenn. 99, 116 (1872) (destruction of whiskey in Clarksville, Tennessee as federal troops approached; in determining necessity jury could consider "the rapid advance of a hostile army known to be undisciplined and licentious, and whose occupation of captured places in the line of march was known to be accompanied by acts of besotted vandalism").

case of private necessity, where the actor has incentive enough to protect his own life and needs no immunity to encourage him.[7]

Injustice to the property owner. The public necessity rule recognizes that it would be unjust to impose the costs of saving the city upon its benefactor by making him pay for the destruction of the plaintiff's property. But if it is unjust to make the actor pay the costs of securing the city's safety, is it equally unjust to make the private property owner sacrifice his property for the benefit of other citizens?

In two kinds of cases the uncompensated destruction of the plaintiff's property to protect the public seems fully justified. *First*, the property destroyed for the public benefit might have been lost in any event. To create a firebreak by destroying a house in the path of the fire is only to hasten a loss that seemed inevitable in any event. In a sense, the destruction causes no appreciable loss at all.[8] *Second*, destruction of property without compensation is justified when the property itself threatens others. So a building about to fall upon a city street could be removed or a diseased herd of cattle could be killed[9] or infected bedding burned[10] to prevent contagion.

The next section considers whether, these cases aside, the plaintiff whose property has been damaged to save the public can claim against the public entity who benefitted from the plaintiff's loss.

§ 109. Public Entities: Necessity, Police Power, and Taking of Property

Arguments for public liability. If the destruction of the plaintiff's property actually saves the city, or avoids a substantial risk to it, the plaintiff can plausibly argue that the city should pay for the benefit it received at the plaintiff's expense. Such a claim sounds like one for restitution to prevent unjust enrichment or something very close to it.[1] If

7. One flaw in this scheme of thought is that the private necessity cases as traditionally understood might include those in which the defendant acts altruistically for the benefit of another person and in which he himself has no interest. If that matters, then perhaps it suggests that we have miscast the categories; instead of public necessity vs. private necessity, we should think of defendants acting for others and those acting at least in substantial part for their own interests.

8. In United States v. Caltex, Inc., supra n. 6, if the plaintiff's oil facilities not been destroyed, the enemy army would have seized them, and would probably have destroyed the facilities when the fortunes of war were reversed to prevent the facilities' return to the United States.

9. South Dakota Dept. of Health v. Heim, 357 N.W.2d 522 (S.D.1984).

10. Mayor of Savannah v. Mulligan, 95 Ga. 323, 22 S.E. 621, 622 (1895) ("To destroy property because it is a dangerous nuisance is not to appropriate it to a public use. . . . ," quoting).

§ 109

1. Restitution is measured by the value of what the defendant received, not by the loss of the plaintiff. In this context, however, the value received by the defendant would not be the entire value of all property saved but what reasonable people would pay for the right to destroy the plaintiff's property (under eminent domain or otherwise). See 1 Dan B. Dobbs, Law of Remedies § 4.5 (1) (2d ed. 1993). As a practical matter that would mean in the public necessity cases that the public entity would pay the value of the property destroyed, approximately the same as paying tort damages. The claim itself, however, would not be

the city was not in fact saved but the plaintiff's property was intentionally damaged or destroyed by a city's agent, it is still right that the public as a whole bear the costs of harms inflicted to serve public purposes rather than that the individual be forced to sacrifice his property for the good of others.[2] The Restatement's formulation of the public necessity privilege protects the individual actor but leaves the possibility of public entity liability open.[3]

Constitutional just compensation requirements. Public entities do in fact sometimes provide for public compensation in particular cases of destruction by necessity,[4] although the statute may be given a narrow construction that defeats liability.[5] Regardless of statute, however, public entities are constitutionally required to pay just compensation for property they take.[6] For example, if a city wants to create a park or a firebreak, it can take the land of private landowners for such public purposes, but it must pay for what it takes. Entities may institute formal proceedings—eminent domain or condemnation proceedings—to take private property and to pay appropriate compensation. When they take property without instituting proceedings, the aggrieved owners may bring inverse condemnation suits seeking compensation. Such suits closely resemble tort actions.

Police power/necessity. Although a public entity is liable for a taking of the plaintiff's property, courts have said it is not liable for harms resulting from the exercise of police or regulatory power[7] and not liable

based on a tort theory but on a benefit received theory.

2. "The ... guarantee that private property shall not be taken for a public use without just compensation was designed to bar Government from forcing some people alone to bear public burdens which, in all fairness and justice, should be borne by the public as a whole." Armstrong v. United States, 364 U.S. 40, 49, 80 S.Ct. 1563, 1569, 4 L.Ed.2d 1554 (1960). "[I]f it was an act done by the officers having competent authority ... and especially if the act was done with an honest view to obtain for the public some lawful benefit or advantage, reason and justice obviously require that the city, in its corporate capacity, should be liable to make good the damages sustained by an individual in consequence of the acts thus done." Thayer v. Boston, 36 Mass. 511 (1837). In Owen v. City of Independence, 445 U.S. 622, 100 S.Ct. 1398, 63 L.Ed.2d 673 (1980) the Court quoted the language above from *Thayer* and added that it would be uniquely amiss if government "were permitted to disavow liability for the injury it has begotten." These arguments can be phrased to apply to private defendants: "[I]t seems simply unconscionable to exact that subsidy from the individual victims of serious accidents by depriving them of their right to compensation from the enterprises responsible for their injuries." Gary Schwartz, Tort Law and the Economy in Nineteenth-Century America: A Reinterpretation, 90 YALE L. J. 1717 (1981).

3. Restatement § 196, cmts. e & h.

4. E.g., 21 U.S.C.A. § 114a (authorizing payment for destruction of diseased livestock).

5. Bowditch v. Boston, 101 U.S. (11 Otto) 16, 25 L.Ed. 980 (1879) (statute provided reasonable compensation when city officers consult together and determine that plaintiff's house should be destroyed to prevent spread of fire, but no compensation is due if the officers failed to consult together before destroying the plaintiff's house).

6. U.S. Const. Amend. V ("nor shall private property be taken for public use, without just compensation"); U.S. Const. Amend. XIV ("nor shall any State deprive any person of life, liberty, or property, without due process of law").

7. Farmers Ins. Exchange v. State, 175 Cal.App.3d 494, 221 Cal.Rptr. 225 (1985). The police power locution is likely to be used when the plaintiff's claim is grounded explicitly on the constitutional right to just compensation for taking of property, while the language of necessity is likely to be used

for destruction as a matter of public necessity.[8] When the destroyed property presented no dangers to others and would not have been destroyed anyway, it is hard to see the difference between cases of "taking" for which compensation must be paid and cases of public necessity (or police power) for which no compensation is due.

Law enforcement damaging private property. The problem is presented when law enforcement officers break into the plaintiff's home or business to capture a felon who has barricaded himself there without the plaintiff's connivance or permission. Capturing the felon is surely a public good that is at least analogous to public necessity; certainly one can think of the officer's action in damaging property as "police power." But it is just as easy to say that the officer's action is a kind of taking or damage of property for which the public entity ought to pay. Minnesota, whose constitution requires payment for property "taken, destroyed or damaged for public use," has said that in this kind of case the entity must pay for the harm to private property.[9] There is a little support for the idea in some other states.[10] But other courts have rejected the inverse condemnation or just compensation claim, holding that police entries upon private land are proper law enforcement activities and either privileged under the public necessity rule or protected as an exercise of legitimate police power. Under these holdings, the entity is not liable under the just compensation clause for the damage or destruction done by the officers.[11]

when the plaintiff's claim is grounded in common law tort. Police power may be a much broader conception, but it is grounded in the necessity idea. See McCoy v. Sanders, 113 Ga.App. 565, 148 S.E.2d 902 (1966).

8. In United States v. Caltex, Inc., 344 U.S. 149, 73 S.Ct. 200, 97 L.Ed. 157 (1952), the plaintiff's oil storage facilities and oil in Manila were destroyed by the army to prevent their falling into the hands of the advancing enemy army. The plaintiff claimed compensation under the takings clause of the Fifth Amendment. The Court appeared to distinguish a taking for use and a mere destruction. The property "was destroyed, not appropriated for subsequent use." And its destruction was one of the "necessities of the war." Hence compensation, required for "takings," was denied. In addition, legislatures may codify some version of the public necessity doctrine so long as they do not attempt to authorize an unconstitutional taking. See Marty v. State, 117 Idaho 133, 786 P.2d 524 (1989).

9. Wegner v. Milwaukee Mutual Ins. Co., 479 N.W.2d 38, 23 A.L.R.5th 954 (Minn. 1991) (police SWAT or ERU team attacking house with tear gas and grenades to reach suspected felon); McGovern v. City of Minneapolis, 480 N.W.2d 121 (Minn.App. 1992) (police executed no-knock warrants by entering the house with a front-end loader, knocking out a wall and picture window).

10. Wallace v. City of Atlantic City, 257 N.J.Super. 404, 608 A.2d 480 (1992); Steele v. City of Houston, 603 S.W.2d 786 (Tex. 1980). In *Wallace*, police conducted a narcotics raid aimed at a tenant, causing damage to the landlord's premises in the process. The court found no tort liability but imposed liability for a taking of property. "As an innocent third party he should not bear the sole financial burden of such an undertaking. Since the damage was incurred for the public good, rather than for the benefit of the private individual, the public should bear the cost. The intended beneficiary of the police action was not plaintiff, but society as a whole." In *Steele*, the court said the plaintiff was entitled to compensation under the Texas constitutional provision if the officers attempting to recapture convicts intentionally set the plaintiff's house afire or refused to extinguish the fire after it was set. The court also said that necessity was a defense but that the City of Houston had not adequately demonstrated real necessity.

11. *SWAT team arrest and building damage*: Customer Co. v. City of Sacramento, 10 Cal.4th 368, 895 P.2d 900, 41 Cal.

Necessity vs. other emergencies. The necessity issue in these cases arises only when acts on behalf of a public entity would, if not privileged, amount to an intentional trespassory tort. If the person acting for public benefit does not intend an invasion of the plaintiff's interests, either under the purpose or the substantial certainty test,[12] then the case will be analyzed in terms of negligence or possibly as a violation of civil rights, not as an intentional tort with a potential necessity defense. In such cases any emergency faced by the defendant is quite relevant, but it bears on the question whether the defendant has committed a tort in the first place, that is, whether he was negligent.[13]

Claims against one benefitted by the plaintiff's loss in other settings. The idea that a defendant might be liable for benefits he gained as a result of the losses imposed upon the plaintiff is a broad one, not limited to necessity cases. But the language in which the idea is considered and the particular rules applied to work out the potential liabilities are enormously different when the defendant commits no intentional invasion of the plaintiff's interest. High speed police chases may represent emergencies and may risk harm to innocent bystanders for the public good, but such harm is not normally intended and when it is not, the innocent victim must prove negligence[14] or civil rights violations[15] and

Rptr.2d 658 (1995) (state Constitution requiring compensation for property taken or damaged cannot be read literally to cover law enforcement activities; the law of necessity and corresponding police power confirms that narrow reading of the constitutional provision); cf. Sullivant v. City of Oklahoma City, 940 P.2d 220 (Okla.1997) (entry of tenant's premises under a warrant, landlord could not recover under the takings clause for damage done, but might have a tort recovery if warrant was executed illegally). *Searching for evidence and causing damage*: McCoy v. Sanders, 113 Ga.App. 565, 148 S.E.2d 902 (1966) (damage done in draining pond to search for body on the plaintiff's property, no public entity liability for exercise of police power grounded in necessity); Gillmor v. Salt Lake City, 32 Utah 180, 89 P. 714 (1907) (searching for body in river, officers trampled the plaintiff's property and made access to some of it dangerous; no liability in tort for acts done for public benefit). *Seizing property as evidence and damaging it*: Emery v. State, 297 Or. 755, 688 P.2d 72, 44 A.L.R.4th 341 (1984) (seizing and dismantling truck as evidence on murder charge, no obligation to restore truck; dissents). Cf. Porter v. United States, 473 F.2d 1329 (5th Cir.1973) (Congress authorized a federal taking of property involved in the assassination of President Kennedy, for which the court approved compensation, but the plaintiff was not entitled to recover for harms done to the property in the course of investigation). See Judy Zelin, Annotation, Seizure of Property as Evidence in Criminal Prosecution or Investigation as Compensable Taking, 44 A.L.R.4th 366 (1987).

In Rigby v. Chief Constable of Northamptonshire, [1985] 1 W.L.R. 1242 (Q.B.) a "psychopath" broke into the plaintiff's gun shop, barricaded himself, and began firing. Police eventually fired a tear gas cannister which set fire to the premises. Part of the danger arose from the felon himself, but part of it may have arisen also from the fact that the plaintiff's weapons were on hand. The court held that necessity was a complete defense to the plaintiff's trespass claim. But since the danger contained by the police may have arisen in part by reason of the very property destroyed—the guns—the case may not be the best precedent for invoking the defense when the plaintiff's property poses no threat at all.

12. § 24.

13. § 129.

14. Cairl v. City of St. Paul, 268 N.W.2d 908, 100 A.L.R.3d 807 (1978) rejected strict liability for damage done in high speed chases. A ridiculous, cartoon-like chase is described in City of Pinellas Park v. Brown, 604 So.2d 1222 (Fla.1992) (upholding the plaintiff's allegations of police negligence).

15. E.g., Williams v. Denver, 99 F.3d 1009 (10th Cir.1996).

must face any defenses appropriate to such cases.[16] The concern that innocent individuals should not be made to sacrifice personally for the benefit of others can be reflected in the imposition of strict liability upon a defendant who can force all beneficiaries to share the costs, but as will be seen, such liability is imposed only in special cases and it is not addressed by the necessity rules appropriate to intentional torts.[17]

16. California, for example, provides blanket immunities in this situation. Payne v. City of Perris, 12 Cal.App.4th 1738, 16 Cal.Rptr.2d 143 (1993); Colvin v. City of Gardena, 11 Cal.App.4th 1270, 15 Cal. Rptr.2d 234 (1992).

17. See Lapierre v. Attorney–General of Quebec, 16 D.L.R. 4th 554 (Can. 1985) (victim of idiosyncratic reaction to vaccine in large-scale vaccination program could not force community at large to contribute to her loss on theory that public vaccination was a necessity for public benefit and that public should share in costs the program inevitably imposes). Strict liability can be imposed by common law or statute in such cases as a means of indirectly requiring benefitted persons to share in the idiosyncratic loss, but this does not require any discussion of necessity. See § 399.

Subpart B. Negligent Physical Interference with Person or Property

1. The Negligence Case and Its Defenses

(a) Elements of the Case

Chapter 6

The Negligence Cause of Action

§ 110. Characteristics of the Negligence Case

A person who negligently causes personal injury or property damage is subject to liability in tort. Definitions of negligence and an explanation of the elements of the tort can be briefly postponed while the chief distinguishing characteristics of the negligence case are considered.

Negligence claims represent the great majority of tort claims presented, brought, or tried today. In part, this reflects the large number of injuries resulting from the use of automobiles—which are often used negligently but not so often as instruments of intentional torts. Negligence claims are not, of course, limited to automobile cases. A wide range of human misery is produced by negligence and it is negligence law on the whole that controls suits for injuries suffered by patients, tenants, and customers at the hands of doctors, landlords, and businesses. Negligence law usually controls when injury is inflicted in the course of an active sport, in the course of law enforcement or firefighting activities, or in the course of farming. People are negligently shot, burned, drowned, or poisoned. Although intentional wrongdoing may be found in any of these cases and strict liability in some of them, the overwhelming number turn on a claim that the defendant was negligent. The concept of negligence and the sets of rules that go with that concept dominate the law of torts.

Negligence cases have many important characteristics. They may require intensive preparation and detailed evidence, often complex and scientific evidence, for example. But in terms of broad legal structure, the negligence case can be characterized by a few points:

1. *Open-ended claims.* The structure of the negligence case allows the plaintiff to claim that any given conduct was negligent. The argument is that the defendant should not have indulged in that conduct at all or he should have carried it out more safely. It is not necessary for the plaintiff to show some predetermined act. At least in form, this differs from the rules for the intentional trespassory torts covered in the immediately preceding chapters. The trespassory torts described particu-

lar conduct that counted as a tort—a harm or offensive touching, a confinement, an entry upon land. Negligence law in contrast is open-ended. The plaintiff can assert that *any* conduct counts as negligence.[1] The plaintiff must, of course, convince the trier of fact of her assertions, but no pre-existing rules require her to prove any particular conduct in the way that rules require proof of somewhat specific conduct to show a trespass or a battery.

2. *Jury roles*. There are many important rules governing negligence cases. Nevertheless, because the negligence claim is open-ended and requires evaluation case-by-case, rules do not always have an enormous direct impact on the ultimate result. The decision-maker at trial, on the other hand, has a great impact on the ultimate result of the case. Judge and jury share the role of decision maker. Some of the rules in tort cases bear on allocation of power between the judge, as a trained professional, and the jury, as a representative of the community. Overall, juries are a highly significant force in deciding negligence and are subject to fewer restrictions than in some other kinds of tort cases.

3. *Actual harm requirement*. A third characteristic of negligence cases can be seen in the rule that no claim for negligence will be recognized unless the plaintiff suffers actual harm. The most uncomplicated meaning of the actual harm rule is that there is no such thing as a negligence suit for nominal damages, much less one for presumed damages. Here again, the trespassory torts were quite different. A trespass to land, for example, always justified at least the recovery of nominal damages.[2] Similar rules applied to the other trespassory torts. The negligence claim is different. No matter how offended or distressed the plaintiff might be when the defendant drives at 100 mph in a school zone, the defendant is not liable for negligence if he causes no harm.

4. *Preoccupation with bodily harm and property damage*. The actual harm requirement does not itself exclude the possibility that some purely emotional harms could be actionable against a negligent defendant. And in fact defendants who are guilty of negligently causing serious emotional distress are occasionally held liable for such harm even though they have caused neither bodily injury nor property damage. However, courts almost invariably impose especially restrictive rules on such claims and deny recovery in many of them. Some of the same reluctance carries over to other intangible injuries, such as financial injuries the plaintiff suffers even when no physical harm is done. Here, too, negligence rules are usually adapted to limit the cases in which the plaintiff can recover. The upshot is that the core of negligence law is about injury to persons and property. Other tort rules protect against intangible losses like emotional or financial harm, but negligence alone is often not enough for liability in those cases.

§ 110

1. This characteristic is limited by no-duty and immunity rules. See Chapter 12.

2. E.g., Gross v. Capital Electric Line Builders, Inc., 253 Kan. 798, 861 P.2d 1326 (1993).

5. *Damages when a negligence claim is established.* When the plaintiff succeeds in establishing a negligence claim against the defendant, courts award damages for a wide range of injuries, including damages for emotional harm and financial loss. At first glance, this statement seems to contradict those in the immediately preceding paragraph. But there is no contradiction. The preceding paragraph indicated that there is seldom a tort claim for stand-alone emotional or financial harm based on simple negligence. But once a negligence claim is established by showing that the defendant negligently caused property damage or bodily injury, the victim can recover all damages that are reasonably foreseeable, including damages for such intangibles as pain, a sense of lost enjoyment of life, and emotional distress. Financial loss resulting from injury or property damage, such as lost wages or the costs of medical attention, is likewise recoverable, as are all proven future losses.

§ 111. Negligence: The Common Law Background

Strict liability for trespassory torts? In the law of torts, the word negligence is old but its current content is relatively new. Although the concept of fault was important in the old action on the case, negligence did not appear as a somewhat general system for resolving personal injury and property damage claims until the 19th century, mostly after the American Civil War. The English common law of tort as it stood in the 14th century was very largely the law of trespassory torts.[1] The traditional view is that strict liability was imposed when the writ of Trespass could be used.[2] That included cases of direct and immediate harm from the unauthorized use of physical force. Under this view, the defendant might be liable for an accidental shooting, even if the defendant was not negligent.[3]

Action on the case for indirect harms. By the direct harm test in Trespass cases, an ordinary vehicular collision might result in strict liability. But if that was the logic of the old Trespass action, it was never applied to such facts in America. Instead, negligence law developed from the action on the Case.[4] The action on the Case was proper (a) when the defendant inflicted injury that was not immediate and direct,[5] (b) when

§ 111

1. See S.F.C. Milsom, Historical Foundations of the Common Law 305 (2d ed 1981).

2. See § 14. Some scholars have challenged this view. See Gary Schwartz, Tort Law and the Economy in Nineteenth–Century America: A Reinterpretation, 9 Yale L.J. 1717 (1981); Gary Schwartz, The Character of Early American Tort Law, 26 U.C.L.A. L. Rev. 641 (1989); Stephen Young, Reconceptualizing Accountability in the Early Nineteenth Century: How the Tort of Negligence Appeared, 21 Conn. L. Rev. 197 (1989).

3. Weaver v. Ward, Hob. 134, 80 Eng. Rep. 284 (K.B. 1616).

4. See S.F.C. Milsom, Historical Foundations of the Common Law 283 (2d ed 1981).

5. The classic and much quoted example of the distinction between Trespass and Case: if you throw a log and strike the plaintiff, he has an action in Trespass, but if you leave a log in the road and the plaintiff falls over it in the dark, the plaintiff has an action on the Case. Reynolds v. Clarke, 1 Str. 634, 93 Eng.Rep. 747 (K.B. 1726). The direct-indirect test for distinguishing Trespass and Case is consistent with earlier decisions, but the explicit for-

injury arose out of consented-to invasions that were carried out badly, as where a veterinarian undertakes to cure the plaintiff's horse and fails as a result of his negligence or neglect;[6] and (c) when the defendant's fault lay in his failure to act rather than in some affirmative misconduct.[7] In the action on the Case, the plaintiff was required to prove both the defendant's fault and actual harm. Those requirements apply to the negligence action today.

Relationship of parties in actions on the Case. The action on the Case originally involved parties who had a relationship with each other by contract or status.[8] That setting differed from that found in the action of Trespass, which in contrast often involved strangers whose duties did not depend upon a relationship between the parties. In Case, for example, the defendant would be an innkeeper,[9] the plaintiff a guest; or the defendant a surgeon, the plaintiff a patient.[10]

Significance of parties' relationship. The contract or relationship of the parties was doubly important in such cases. *First*, the relationship of the parties is important because that relationship may require the defendant to take affirmative steps to avoid harm to the plaintiff; hence the word neglect (the root for negligence) appears in these cases in the sense that the defendant should be liable for a failure to act.

Second, the standard of care or duty owed by the defendant was implicitly set by accepted community practices and expectations as incorporated in the contract itself; the defendant who holds himself out as an artificer of any kind implicitly says he will follow the standards of such artificers. The defendant who undertakes to move casks of brandy safely will be liable for spilling the brandy because that is a failure to perform as promised.[11] Equally, the parties' explicit or implicit expecta-

mulation of the test does is not found until around 1700. See M.J. PRICHARD, *Scott v. Shepherd* (1773) AND THE EMERGENCE OF THE TORT OF NEGLIGENCE 5, 13 ff. (1976).

6. Waldon v. Marshall, Y.B. Mich. 43 Ed. 3, f. 33, pl. 38 (1370), *printed and translated in* C.H.S. FIFOOT, HISTORY AND SOURCES OF THE COMMON LAW: TORT AND CONTRACT 81 (1949) .

7. C.H.S. FIFOOT, HISTORY AND SOURCES OF THE COMMON LAW: TORT AND CONTRACT 66 (1949). See Steinson v. Heath, 3 Lev. 400, 83 Eng. Rep. 750 (K.B. 1694) ("case lies for non-feasance, against my shepherd for negligent keeping my sheep, against my carter for negligent keeping my horses, and for not repairing a bridge by which I am to pass.... against a chaplain, for not reading prayers, against an innkeeper, who refuses to lodge me ..."). One writer went so far as to say that the "primary meaning" of negligence in the early American cases was "nonfeasance," that is, neglect of some positive duty imposed by law. MORTON HORWITZ, THE TRANSFORMATION OF AMERICAN LAW, 1780–1860 86 (1977). A late example of this association of Case and nonfeasance or nonaction was Ogle v. Barnes, 8 T.R. 188, 101 Eng.Rep. 1338 (K.B. 1799).

8. See S.F.C. MILSOM, HISTORICAL FOUNDATIONS OF THE COMMON LAW 393 (2d ed. 1981); Percy Winfield, The History of Negligence in the Law of Torts, 42 L. Q. REV. 184 (1926).

9. The Innkeeper's Case, Y.B. Easter 42 Ed. 3, f. 11, pl. 13 (1369), *printed and translated in* C.H.S. FIFOOT, HISTORY AND SOURCES OF THE COMMON LAW: TORT AND CONTRACT (1949); Burgess v. Clements, 4 M. & S. 306, 105 Eng.Rep. 848 (K.B. 1815).

10. Dr. Groenvelt's Case, 1 Ld. Raym. 213, 91 Eng. Rep. 1038 (1697) (dictum that case would lie against a surgeon for "mala praxis," "his ill practice upon the body of J.S.").

11. Coggs v. Bernard, 2 Ld. Raym. 909, 92 Eng.Rep. 107 (1703) (a case actually pleaded as an action on the case with the language of "assumpsit" or undertaking, which was also the language of a contract claim).

tions may relieve the defendant of liability; the guest may undertake to protect his own property and thus relieve the innkeeper of liability when it is stolen.[12]

Particularization of duties in action on the Case. Given that duties in Case tended to find their source in community custom and conduct of the parties, courts naturally did not impose any universal principles of responsibility. They imposed liabilities they thought proportioned to the parties' own contract or expectation. Doctors were to use the care of doctors, farriers the care of farriers and so on. Bailees who without charge accepted temporary custody of the plaintiff's property owed a duty to care for that property that was considerably different from the duty owed by a bailee who was paid to care for the property.[13] In some categories, the duty could be strict at times. Common carriers and innkeepers might be charged with loss of the guest's property even if the innkeeper was not at fault.[14] So defendants might argue that they were not in any recognized category such as a common carrier and hence that they owed no duty of care at all.[15]

Stranger cases. But things were changing by 1700. Defendants who are not in a contractual relation with the plaintiff—strangers they are called—are beginning to cause serious harms. The stranger who causes a collision on the road is still liable in trespass in 1700 and for a long time afterwards,[16] but plaintiffs are beginning to bring suit in Case against strangers who cause indirect or mediate harms.[17] Because the parties are

12. In Burgess v. Clements, 4 M. & S. 306, 105 Eng.Rep. 848 (K.B. 1815), the innkeeper set up the guest in a special show room, giving him a key. The guest left his sample case in the room without locking the door. Lord Ellenborough wanted to bar the guest in part because the property was lost through the guest's own fault. But LeBlanc, J. had a different reason for barring the plaintiff. He thought the parties prescribed their own terms by their conduct, and that in accepting the key, the plaintiff discharged the innkeeper of responsibility. See also Sanders v. Spencer, Dyer 226, 73 Eng. Rep. 591 (K.B. 1556).

13. See Thomas M. Cooley, The Law of Torts 628–633 (1879). Cooley repeated the supposed rule requiring extreme care, ordinary care, or slight care, depending upon whether the bailment was for the benefit of the bailee, mutual benefit, or the benefit of the bailor only, but he also attempts to fit this to the general formula of ordinary care by treating the benefit issue as part of the circumstances, and he recognizes, too, that the understanding of the parties is what ultimately governs.

14. See Calye's Case, 8 Co.Rep. 32a, 77 Eng.Rep. 520 (K.B. 1584) (if the guest's goods are stolen, the innkeeper is liable).

15. Lovett v. Hobbs, 2 Show. 127, 89 Eng.Rep. 836 (K.B. 1680). The actual words were "the action lay not," against a coachman who damaged or lost goods because the coachman was not a common carrier. The argument was rejected because the coachman was like a waterman who carries men and goods as a common carrier.

16. Leame v. Bray, 2 East. 593, 102 Eng.Rep. 724 (K.B. 1803).

17. A master improvidently sends his servant to train ungovernable horses in a crowded place; they cause injury to the plaintiff, who successfully brings an action on the Case. (Harm was considered indirect when the defendant acted through an agent or servant.) Michael v. Alestree, 2 Lev. 172, 83 Eng.Rep. 504 (1676). The classic log-in-the-road example of the distinction between Trespass and Case also envisions a stranger case. See Reynolds v. Clarke, 1 Str. 634, 93 Eng.Rep. 747 (K.B. 1726). Or the defendant leaves a pile of lime in the street; the wind blows the lime, which startles the horse, which breaks the chaise in its frightened dash. Lord Mansfield tells the jury to decide whether the defendant was guilty of "blameable negligence." Flower v. Adam, 2 Taunt. 314, 127 Eng.Rep. 1098 (C.P. 1810). When the parties were neighbors, courts might derive a duty of reasonable care from the maxim that you must enjoy your property in such a way as not to injure others,

strangers, not in a contractual relationship, the defendant's negligence is understood in a general, or at least undefined sense. By the 1800s, there is nothing unusual about suing a stranger in Case rather than Trespass and the negligence standard necessarily ceases to arise from the parties' relationship. At some point, too, the plaintiff is given an option: he can sue in Case even if injury is direct, so long as he can actually prove negligence and actual harm.[18] The net result is that by 1800, plaintiffs sue in Case for road accident injuries. The older connection of Case (and negligence) to particular occupations and particular duties is no longer required. So negligence is already becoming a general idea even though its standards have not been articulated.

Coming to America. A great deal of the common law of tort migrated to America with colonization. Even as the American revolution was being launched, English judges were still debating tort cases by debating the direct vs. indirect distinction.[19] After Independence, the Constitution allocated Admiralty jurisdiction,[20] with its potential for covering maritime torts, to the federal government. Otherwise, tort law was the province of the States, which usually[21] made formal provision for reception of the English common law as the basis of their own legal systems.[22] The sparse American authority on torts in the generation or so after adoption of the Constitution seems to indicate that courts were routinely thinking primarily in terms of fault or negligence.[23] Nevertheless, in the

see Vaughan v. Menlove, 3 Bing. (N.C.) 468, 132 Eng.Rep. 490 (C.P. 1837), which is also used in nuisance cases. See M.J. PRICHARD, *Scott v. Shepherd* (1773) AND THE EMERGENCE OF THE TORT OF NEGLIGENCE 15 ff. (1976) (noting a few "straws in the wind" from earlier times but identifying the late 17th century as the beginning of "non-relationship" negligence cases).

18. Williams v. Holland, 10 Bing. 112, 131 Eng. Rep. 848 (C.P. 1833). This view was also followed in America. Dalton v. Favour, 3 N.H. 465 (1826). See E.F. Roberts, Negligence: Blackstone to Shaw To ? An Intellectual Escapade in a Tort Vein, 50 CORNELL L. REV. 191, 201 (1965).

19. Scott v. Shepard, 2 Wm. Bl. 892, 96 Eng.Rep. 525 (1773) (Blackstone, J. dissenting at the court's allowance of Trespass against a defendant tossed a lighted squib at A, who batted it away towards B, who batted it towards the plaintiff, who lost sight of an eye as a result). If, however, the plaintiff showed both fault and actual harm, at least when harm was not intended, courts sustained the action on the case. Slater v. Baker, 2 Wils. 359, 95 Eng.Rep. 860 (K.B. 1767) (surgeon's treatment of broken leg, plaintiff not required to sue vi et armis).

20. 1 THOMAS SCHOENBAUM, ADMIRALTY AND MARITIME LAW §§ 1–6 & 3–1 (2d ed. 1994).

21. Later, Florida, Louisiana, California and some Southwestern States were brought into the union with varying degrees of Spanish, or Spanish–French civil rather than common law background. See LAWRENCE FRIEDMAN, A HISTORY OF AMERICAN LAW 169, 171–76, 364–65 (2d ed. 1985).

22. E.g., COLO. REV. STATS. ANN. §§ 2–4–211; 5 ILCS 50/1. See LAWRENCE FRIEDMAN, A HISTORY OF AMERICAN LAW 107 ff. (2d ed. 1985). Less obviously but more importantly, what the states really adopted, at least over time, was the common law process, not merely rules of particular cases. The common law process contemplates continued development. See, e.g., Wright v. Grove Sun Newspaper Co., Inc., 873 P.2d 983 (Okla. 1994).

23. See Gary Schwartz, Tort Law and the Economy in Nineteenth-Century America: A Reinterpretation, 9 YALE L.J. 1717 (1981). Many of the early cases seemed to involve indirect injury, so their discussion of negligence is no surprise. E.g., Colt v. M'Mechen, 6 Johns. 160 (N.Y.Sup.Ct.1810) (common carrier's liability for loss of goods except for act of God or the public enemy, considering whether loss resulted from negligence as opposed to Act of God); Foot and Reynolds v. Wiswall, 14 Johns. 304 (N.Y. 1817) (the plaintiff's sloop was damaged by a steamboat on the Hudson River on a dark

early 1800s, negligence seems not to have become a widespread or general system of adjudication.

§ 112. Negligence: Adopting a General Principle of Liability for Fault

Growing into modern tort law. The older tort law, based on a distinction between Trespass with its direct invasion and Case with its indirect invasion, differed from modern tort law in three important ways. *First*, in contrast to contemporary law, strict liability was or may have been imposed in the Trespass/direct harm cases. *Second*, the liabilities imposed in Case, although based on fault of some kind, were not originally adjudicated under a general fault standard applicable to everyone but under standards set by the particular profession or calling of the defendant. *Third*, the lineaments of negligence itself had not been drawn clearly; what would count as fault in any general system of fault was undetermined. All three of these things began to be altered significantly in the 19th century, mostly after 1850.

(1) Eliminating or limiting the role of strict liability. If strict liability was imposed for direct injuries, such liability was limited or eliminated in favor of a fault-based system. By around 1800 lawyers began arguing that a distinction existed between intentional or wilful torts on the one hand and merely negligent torts on the other.[1] The distinction was not immediately developed, but in another generation we find courts beginning to distinguish negligence from intent[2] or at least to show a

night in 1812, a jury charge in terms of negligence with the burden upon the defendant to exonerate himself by proving freedom from fault was seemingly accepted by the parties). In Vincent v. Stinehour, 7 Vt. 62 (1835), the plaintiff alleged what might have been considered a direct and forcible injury except that it may have involved the intervening reaction of an animal: the defendant ran over the plaintiff with a carriage. The court refused to charge on liability without fault and required negligence to sustain a claim. The jury found for the defendant. The Vermont Supreme Court upheld a judgment for the defendant on the ground that "no one can be made responsible, in an action of trespass, for consequences, where he could not have prevented those consequences by prudence and care." For this broad statement, the court relied on cases in which the defendant had done no act at all with reference to the plaintiff, as where his horse simply ran away with him. In some other cases the setting involved indirect injury but the facts might have been thought to suggest strict liability in a later generation; yet liability was limited by the fault principle. In Livingston v. Adams, 8 Cow. 175 (N.Y. 1828) an upper riparian owner's dam broke, leading to damages of the lower owner's property. The court considered the case in terms of negligence, not strict liability. The case may be distinguishable from Rylands v. Fletcher, L.R. 3 H.L. 330 (1868) where strict liability was imposed when a pond's waters flooded the plaintiff's coal mine, but it would not have been bizarre to suggest strict liability in Livingston. In Panton v. Holland, 17 Johns. 92 (N.Y.1819) the defendant excavated his own land, with the result that the plaintiff's nearby house partially collapsed from lack of support. The court held that liability turned solely on negligence, although here again strict liability for removal of lateral or subjacent support would not be inconceivable. See Restatement § 817.

§ 112

1. Ogle v. Barnes, 8 T.R. 188, 101 Eng. Rep. 1338 (K.B. 1799); E.F. Roberts, Negligence: Blackstone to Shaw to ? An Intellectual Escapade in a Tory Vein, 50 CORNELL L. Q. 191, 199 (1965).

2. E.F. Roberts, Negligence: Blackstone to Shaw to ? An Intellectual Escapade in a Tory Vein, 50 CORNELL L. REV. 191, 200 (1965).

dislike of the Trespass rule that imposed liability for non-faulty direct harm.[3]

In 1850, in *Brown v. Kendall,*[4] the Massachusetts Court abolished the rule that a direct physical injury entailed strict liability. The court held that when the defendant who attempted to beat a dog but unintentionally struck the plaintiff instead would not be liable for battery in spite of the direct force applied. Instead, the defendant would be liable only if he intended to strike the plaintiff or if he was at fault in striking him. This would seem to mean that other direct applications of force, such as would occur in railroad accidents or industrial injuries, would not automatically subject the defendant to the threat of liability; instead, the plaintiff would be required to prove fault. The shift or apparent shift from strict liability to fault-based liability is the foundation but not the point of the present section; strict liability itself is considered later.[5]

(2) Creating a principle of general application. In the 19th century, it looks as if courts began to develop general or "universal" principles. They began to feel, in particular, that fault was the general basis for liability and a limit of liability as well. Instead of judging cases by imposing particular duties upon particular callings, courts could simply treat negligence as the basis of liability in all or a large universe of cases. Many observers thought that is what *Brown v. Kendall* did. Intentional invasion, not direct invasion, became the basis for liability in the trespassory tort. Negligence became the basis of liability otherwise. Negligence was no longer focused upon parties who stood in some special or contractual relationship;[6] "neglect," was no longer a matter of a particular duty of a vet to the farmer or innkeeper to a guest, but a general duty of all to all.[7] This generality made it possible for negligence

3. Ever since Weaver v. Ward, Hob. 134, 80 Eng. Rep. 284 (K.B. 1616) which imposed strict liability but left a safety valve, courts had recognized that the defendant was not liable, even for direct harm resulting from some kinds of "inevitable accidents" in which the defendant was "utterly without fault," provided the defendant shouldered the burden of proving that defense. "Utterly without fault" in *Weaver v. Ward* seems to have meant that the defendant did not act at all or perhaps that the immediate cause of harm was an intervening act. The idea that liability was inappropriate if the defendant was "utterly without fault" was gradually transmuted. By 1835, the Vermont Court was saying that the defendant would not be liable if the injury was inevitable, which in turn meant that the defendant was not negligent. Vincent v. Stinehour, 7 Vt. 62 (1835).

4. Brown v. Kendall, 60 Mass. 292 (1850).

5. See Chapter 23.

6. Brown v. Kendall was not the first case to impose a negligence standard among parties who had no contractual relationship. For example, in Livingston v. Adams, 8 Cow. 175 (N.Y. 1828) an upper riparian owner ponded water for his mill, but the dam broke and damaged the plaintiff's mill downstream. The trial judge charged in terms of negligence. The charge was not in issue on appeal and the court did not pass on it, but held the evidence sufficient to warrant a verdict for the defendant under the standard dictated by the unobjected-to instruction. Arguably the parties in Livingston v. Adams had a relationship of sorts as riparian owners sharing the same resources. Vincent v. Stinehour, 7 Vt. 62 (1835), however, involved a road injury; the defendant's horse pulled the carriage over the plaintiff on the road. The parties were in no relationship whatever, but the court used a negligence test of liability.

7. See G. Edward White, Tort Law in America 16 (1980).

law to cover virtually any kind of case not exempted by statute or some special rule.

There were, of course, qualifications, both because some strict liability was retained or developed and because some faulty defendants escaped liability. No duty and immunity rules might protect landowners or governmental entities from liability for negligence, for example. In fact, Professor Rabin has argued that in the light of no duty rules and other limitations on liability, fault did not become a general or comprehensive test of liability at all.[8] It is assuredly true that many negligent defendants escape liability and in that sense the negligence rule of *Brown v. Kendall* did not institute a universal regime. Yet, although no-duty rules seem to eliminate negligence as a criterion of liability, they sometimes only shift the decision-making power to judges, who may speak the language of duty or immunity but who may in fact rest their decisions on judgments about fault or who specify what counts as fault in a particular context.[9] In any event, negligence thinking, though far less than universal, became the dominant or default mode of thinking about tort suits between strangers in the years after the Civil War.

(3) Developing the negligence concept. If negligence was to become a general principle of law, the concept and its limits would require a development and definition that had not been necessary earlier. Before the 19th century, many actions between strangers had fit the Trespass-strict-liability mold. In these actions, there was no occasion to consider any standard of care or what might count as negligence. On the other hand, when the plaintiff and defendant stood in some definite relationship, that relationship itself might define the kind of care the parties should exercise.

Negligence as a general principle that could apply to suits among non-contracting parties or strangers—railroad crossing accidents for example—would require courts to set up some kind of meaningful standard about what would constitute fault or negligence. *Brown v. Kendall* set the general standard for negligence law: the defendant should use ordinary care, or more particularly, the care of a reasonable and prudent person. The actual conduct that would count as ordinary care would vary with circumstances, since a reasonable person would exercise more care when danger is greater.[10]

8. Robert Rabin, The Historical Development of the Fault Principle: A Reinterpretation, 15 GA. L. REV. 925 (1981).

9. It would not be possible to justify all the landowner/no-duty cases on the ground that the landowner is not at fault. But perhaps most of them can be understood as cases in which, at least according to someone's view, the landowner is not faulty at all. Why, for example, should a homeowner be considered faulty for failing to expend funds to keep their properties safe for intruders? The traditional no-duty rule said he was not liable and it is certainly not preposterous to think that the courts announcing such a rule believed themselves to be applying some kind of fault principle.

10. "[W]hat constitutes ordinary care will vary with the circumstances.... In general, is means that kind and degree of care, which prudent and cautious men would use, such as it required by the exigency of the case.... " Brown v. Kendall, 60 Mass. 292 (1850).

Adopting negligence analysis and the fault principle. With the decision in *Brown v. Kendall*, the profession began to perceive torts as a separate subject of the law[11] and came to perceive fault as its core.[12] One species of fault was intentional harm, so where liability had once been imposed for direct invasions, liability was now imposed for intentional invasions. The other major kind of fault was negligence. After the Civil War, jurists began to puzzle out the contours of the negligence action as railroad trains and other machines churned up injuries on a new scale.[13] The ordinary care formula in *Brown v. Kendall* and its minor variations became the basis for an enormous body of modern negligence law.

§ 113. Negligence: After the Fault Principle

Strangers and privies. Brown v. Kendall[1] explicitly adopted a general principle of fault as the basis of tort liability in 1850,[2] but the implications of a general principle of negligence were not immediately apparent. For a period, courts sometimes continued to think of particular duties owed by a defendant in a particular relationship to the plaintiff. The carrier owed one duty; the gratuitous bailee another, and so on. It remains true today that in spite of the broad negligence principle, many decisions focus on the particular duty or standard of care owed by a particular class of defendant rather than by people generally.[3] The general standard of ordinary care is most often seen in suits between strangers. In a substantial way, the old distinction between suits between strangers and those between parties in a contract or status relationship has continued to have its effects.

Fleshing out the negligence concept. Nor was the work of creating negligence law complete with the adoption of a fault system or even with adoption of a general concept of negligence. No one has failed to notice that the reasonable and prudent person standard, though beautifully general in its formulation, is painfully imprecise as a guide for particular cases.[4] It provides a common set of ideals or terms to permit professional discussion, but does not point that discussion in any particular direction.

11. The first torts book was Francis Hilliard, The Law of Torts (1859). See G. Edward White, Tort Law in America 16 (1980). Most of Hilliard's book was devoted to topics other than negligence—libel, malicious prosecution, and nuisance, for example.

12. See O.W. Holmes, The Common Law 77 (1881).

13. Lawrence Friedman, A History of American Law 468 (2d ed. 1985) (in the 19th century, railroad law and tort law "grew up together" and were much the same).

§ 113

1. Brown v. Kendall, 60 Mass. 292 (1850).

2. § 113, supra.

3. See especially Chapters 13–17 below. E.g., Iemma v. Adventure RV Rentals, Inc., 632 N.E.2d 1178, 1182 (Ind.App.1994) ("The bailee must use slight care when the bailment is for the sole benefit of the bailor, great care when the bailment is for the sole benefit of the bailee, and ordinary care when the bailment is for the mutual benefit of the bailor and bailee"). Distinguish the question of party relationship as the ground, or part of a ground, for imposing strict liability.

4. O.W. Holmes, The Common Law 111 (1881) called the standard a "featureless generality" and thought that with experience, statutes and judicial decisions would make it more precise.

It remained for succeeding generations to develop a series of ideas that tended to make the negligence concept more precise.

In his 1881 book, *The Common Law*, Holmes emphasized that the negligence standard was objective, based on abilities of the reasonable person rather than on the actual abilities of the individual defendant.[5] He went on to add something just as important to the simple reasonable person standard. He recognized that there would be no liability for negligence unless the defendant's conduct presented a "threat" of harm, what we would today call a risk. Further than that, liability would not be imposed unless the reasonable person could foresee harm resulting from his conduct.[6] "Reasonable foreseeability" of harm became one of the important ways of evaluating the reasonableness of the defendant's conduct.[7]

By 1915 lawyers were developing the idea that negligence was not only "unreasonable" conduct, but conduct that involves unreasonable risks. Henry Terry proposed to recognize explicitly that unreasonableness of risk turned on a balance of several factors. How risky was the conduct? What values were at risk? What were the hoped-for gains to be derived from the conduct?[8] Terry's ideas of balancing risks of conduct against its utility were to become part of the mainstream of thought about negligence law.

By the 1920s, lawyers and legal scholars were preparing for the First Restatement of Torts. They worked out the physical, mental and "moral" characteristics of the reasonable person whose conduct set the standard of care along lines that are now generally accepted as background.[9] By that time, too, liability insurance had become readily available in its modern and useful form. Details remained to be worked out or altered or given new emphasis—the effect of custom[10] and the effect of statutes[11] and the analysis of risks in a negligence case,[12] for example. But the main conceptions of contemporary negligence law were in place.

5. O.W. HOLMES, THE COMMON LAW 108 (1881) (if "a man is born hasty and awkward, is always having accidents and hurting himself or his neighbors, no doubt his congenital defects will be allowed for in the courts of Heaven, but his slips are no less troublesome to his neighbors than if they sprang from guilty neglect. His neighbors accordingly require him . . . to come up to their standard and the courts which they establish decline to take his personal equation into account").

6. O.W. HOLMES, THE COMMON LAW 96 (1881). Contrast the earlier view stated in THOMAS G. SHEARMAN & AMASA A. REDFIELD, LAW OF NEGLIGENCE § 7 (1869) that "It is not an essential element of culpable negligence that the defendant should have anticipated, or have had reason to anticipate, that his carelessness would injure another person. It is enough that he did not use the care and skill usual in similar circumstances."

7. See Patrick J. Kelley, Who Decides? Community Safety Conventions at the Heart of Tort Liability, 38 CLEV. ST. L. REV. 315, 345 (1990). Kelley concludes that before Holmes, "foreseeability" was only relevant on proximate cause issues or was subordinated to the question what a reasonable person would do.

8. Henry Terry, Negligence, 29 HARV. L. REV. 40 (1915). Terry had his own nomenclature and system of explanation, somewhat more complex than the summary here.

9. See Seavey, Negligence—Subjective or Objective?, 41 HARV. L. REV. 1 (1927).

10. §§ 163–165 below.

11. See §§ 133–142 below.

12. §§ 143–147 below.

Boundaries and exceptions. The new general concept of negligence also required boundaries. Duties of care were limited so as to exclude liability for many purely emotional harms[13] and to limit the care required by, say, landowners to trespassers.[14] Causal rules were worked up; the defendant would not be liable unless he in fact caused actual harm to the plaintiff[15] and even then would not be liable unless the harm was significant or reasonably close.[16] The plaintiff's own fault, now called contributory negligence, had to be worked into the case somehow,[17] and so did the plaintiff's consent to face the risks imposed by the defendant.[18] Courts also had to think out a way to deal with cases in which several different people were at fault.[19] These and other problems were approached mainly in the 20th or the very late 19th century.

Leaving a place for strict liability. Although negligence law came to dominate tort thinking, courts were unwilling to abolish all strict liability after *Brown v. Kendall.* They retained strict liability or semi-strict liability in a number of cases associated with certain nuisances,[20] certain trespassory acts,[21] and certain especially dangerous or abnormal activities.[22] In the 20th century they added strict liability for defective products to the list.[23] Statutes in recent years have gone on to add liabilities for certain environmental harms.[24]

Disenchantments and alternatives. Negligence law does not necessarily work well in all cases. Many plans have been offered or adopted to make special provisions for particular classes of cases, or in some cases, to supplement negligence law. For example, workers' compensation, which has been adopted everywhere, imposes strict liability upon employers for on-the-job injuries to workers, but the compensation is limited. The Keeton–O'Connell no-fault plan, some form of which has been adopted in many states, requires auto owners to provide for their own minor injuries through special insurance, reserving the negligence claim for cases of more serious injury.[25] In addition, defendant-oriented groups have supported many "tort reform" proposals that would not provide a substitute for negligence claims but would limit those claims in various particular ways.[26] In spite of these developments, however,

13. See Chapter 20.

14. See Chapter 13.

15. See Chapter 9.

16. See Chapter 10.

17. See Chapter 11.

18. Id.

19. See §§ 174–176 & Chapter 26.

20. See Chapter 34.

21. Intentional entry upon land in the reasonably mistaken belief that it is one's own land might be considered semi-strict liability. See § 51, supra.

22. See Chapter 23.

23. Chapter 24.

24. E.g., United States v. Northeastern Pharm. & Chem. Co., 810 F.2d 726 (8th Cir.1986) (strict liability under CERCLA statutes); United States v. West of England Ship Owner's Mutual Protection & Indemnity Ass'n, 872 F.2d 1192 (5th Cir.1989) (strict liability under Federal Water Pollution Control Act). See ALLAN J. TOPOL & REBECCA SNOW, SUPERFUND LAW AND PROCEDURE §§ 1.2, 4.4 (1992).

25. ROBERT KEETON AND JEFFREY O'CONNELL, BASIC PROTECTION FOR THE TRAFFIC VICTIM (1965).

26. E.g., § 384 (damages limits); 389 (abolition of joint and several liability).

negligence law remains at the center of personal injury and property damage claims in tort.

§ 114. Elements of the Prima Facie Case for Negligence

Negligence and the Negligence Case

Negligence as risky conduct. In modern law, the term negligence in its primary meaning merely describes conduct. In that sense it has come to mean conduct that is unreasonably risky, such as driving a car at a high speed. A good deal of tort law is devoted to deciding what counts as an unreasonable risk and to deciding as well whether the judge or the jury is the decision maker in particular cases.

Negligence as a type of case. The term negligence is also used in a different way to refer to the claim or cause of action. That is, the term negligence may refer to the bundle of rules and procedures that govern the negligence case or law suit rather than to the defendant's conduct itself.

Elements of the case. The rules for the negligence case require that the plaintiff has the burden of proving all of the following elements in order to establish an actionable claim for negligence.

1. The defendant owed the plaintiff a duty of care, for instance, not to engage in unreasonably risky conduct;
2. the defendant breached that duty by his unreasonably risky conduct;
3. the defendant's conduct in fact caused harm to the plaintiff;
4. the defendant's conduct was not only a cause in fact of the plaintiff's harm but also a proximate cause, meaning that the defendant's conduct is perceived to have a significant relationship to the harm suffered by the plaintiff.
5. the existence and amount of damages, based on actual harm of a legally recognized kind such as physical injury to person or property.

The formula is broad and general. It resolves no cases. Instead, it points to issues and sets the terms in which lawyers will argue the case. The plaintiff must establish each of the elements named by proof or persuasion, but she need not show any others. Each of these elements comes in for substantial discussion in this book. This section attempts only to sketch the elements together before isolating each for extended discussion and to warn of some problems in terminology.

The plaintiff who proves her prima facie case will not necessarily prevail because the defendant may succeed in presenting affirmative defenses that will wholly or partly defeat the plaintiff's claim. Common defenses include the plaintiff's contributory negligence, which in most states today will reduce the plaintiff's damages but not necessarily defeat her claim; assumed risk, and the statute of limitations. In addition to such defenses, whole areas of liability are excluded on the ground that

the defendant is immune or owes no duty to the plaintiff. Discussion of the defenses is reserved for treatment after the prima facie case has been covered.

§ 115. The Elements: Meaning and Terminology

Duty or Standard of Care

It sounds surprising, but there are cases in which the defendant literally owes the plaintiff no duty that bears on the harm suffered. In the ordinary case, however, the defendant does owe a duty of care. The only question about the duty in such cases is whether the care owed is some especially high care or whether it is more modest. This phase of the duty issue is usually discussed in terms of the "standard of care." The duty or standard imposed in most cases is the duty of reasonable care under the circumstances, no more, no less. Equivalent shorthand terms are due care and ordinary care. Judges, not juries, ordinarily determine whether a duty exists and the standard it imposes.

It is also possible to use the term duty in a radically different way by speaking of duties that are not standards at all. Instead of saying that the defendant is under a duty of reasonable care, a judge could say the defendant is under a duty to keep a lookout or to drive so that he could stop within the range of his vision. This kind of usage is almost always a shorthand expression that really refers to something else. In this book, the term duty is used in the first sense, as stating a legal standard by which the defendant's conduct is to be judged, or, in some cases, the absence of any standards that the defendant must meet.

Breach of Duty; Negligence

(1) Negligence as risk. The defendant must have breached his duty of care to the plaintiff. When the defendant owes a duty of reasonable care, the defendant breaches that duty by conduct that falls short of such care, that is, by conduct that is unreasonably risky. Juries, not judges, decide whether the defendant was negligent unless the question is too clear to permit different evaluations by reasonable people.

(2) Negligence as breach of duty. Sometimes jurists define negligence as a breach of the duty of care. In this definition, you are not negligent, or at least not actionably negligent, if you were under no duty of care, no matter how unreasonably risky your conduct might be.[1] At other times lawyers and judges use the term negligence to mean unreasonably risky conduct, regardless whether the defendant is under a duty of care. Judges who define negligence as a breach of duty wrap the duty and the negligence issue together. This leads to ambiguities in judicial opinions.[2] For example, to say "the defendant breached no duty" or "there was no actionable negligence" might mean the defendant was under no duty at

§ 115

1. E.g., Beinhorn v. Griswold, 27 Mont. 79, 69 P. 557, 558 (1902) ("There can be no negligence without breach of duty").

2. Terry said the first way of speaking was "a misconception." Henry Terry, Negligence, 29 Harv. L. Rev. 40 (1915).

all, *or* it might mean the defendant was under a duty of reasonable care but that he did not breach that duty because he acted reasonably. When judges define negligence as unreasonable risk, they reduce ambiguity because such a definition allows people to evaluate the riskiness of the defendant's conduct independent of the duty-of-care issue. The second way is the way preferred in this book.

Cause in Fact

Actual harm requirement. Negligence law grew out of the old common law action on the Case and carried over its requirement that the plaintiff cannot recover without showing actual harm resulting from the defendant's conduct.[3] Put differently, the defendant's acts must cause the harm of which the plaintiff complains. Sometimes this is referred to as a requirement that the plaintiff must prove actual damages and sometimes as a requirement that the plaintiff must prove causation in fact.

Tests of cause in fact. The traditional view is that the plaintiff's injury is caused by the defendant's conduct if, but for the defendant's conduct, the plaintiff would not have suffered the injury. However, causation turns out to be a complex business, and this but-for test is not always suitable. Sometimes courts tweak the test or abandon it in favor of a softer evaluation of causation. Some jurists believe courts have also abandoned the causation requirement altogether in one line of cases. If that is correct—it is more a matter of viewpoint than a matter of fact—then the element that must be proved by the plaintiff here is not necessarily causation but causation or a legally recognized substitute for causation. For the greater majority of cases, however, the plaintiff must prove that the defendant's tortious conduct caused actual harm, even if courts sometimes use clement tests of causation.

Proximate Cause

The requirement. In addition to proving causation in fact, the plaintiff must prove that the defendant's conduct was a proximate cause of the plaintiff's harm. This means at bottom that the plaintiff must persuade the court or jury that the defendant's conduct not only in fact caused the plaintiff's harm but that it was a reasonably significant cause. Making sense of this idea will require a substantial analysis. But it is possible to make do until that analysis can be reached, however, by noticing two ways courts might approach a proximate cause question.

Excluding liability for fortuitous, unrisked harm. In some cases courts might think that the defendant's misconduct is not a proximate cause of the plaintiff's harm because the harm is perceived to be a fortuitous rather than a foreseeable result of the defendant's negligent conduct. Suppose a defendant drives too fast. Because of his speed, he is positioned on the highway miles ahead of the place he would be if he had driven at a normal speed. A plane crashes into the car and injures the

3. See Copeland v. Compton, 914 S.W.2d 378 (Mo.App.1996).

passenger-plaintiff. In such a case, the defendant is negligent and his conduct is a cause in fact of the harm. Nevertheless, his negligence is probably not a proximate cause of the harm. The risks that make us think the defendant was negligent do not include risks that look anything like the risk of being under a crashing airplane.

Excluding liability for a trivial cause among more significant causes. In other cases courts might think the defendant's misconduct is not a proximate cause of the plaintiff's harm because the harm is perceived to be more significantly related to other causes. This usually occurs when some other person besides the defendant is also negligent and is the immediate trigger of harm. Suppose I leave a log in the path, running the risk that you might trip on it in the dark. As you walk along in the dark, a robber pushes you as you approach the log, causing you to fall on it. I was negligent in leaving the log there and you suffered harm as a result. Nevertheless, some courts might well emphasize the greater importance of the robber's acts in causing your harm and conclude that my negligence was not a proximate cause.

Multiple causes. Although courts may use proximate cause doctrine to exclude the liability of some negligent actors in the negligence drama, they may also impose liability upon numerous defendants. Many different defendants may all be actual and proximate causes of the plaintiff's harm and many different defendants may be liable to the plaintiff for that harm. The methods for dividing responsibility when two or more defendants are liable must be considered later, but it is important in understanding elements of the negligence case to know that more than one proximate cause may be recognized for a single harm.

Structuring the proximate cause rule. In stating the elements of a prima facie case for negligence, some courts combine actual and proximate cause into a single element, calling this element proximate cause. These courts might thus abbreviate the list of elements of the prima facie case by saying that the plaintiff must prove duty, breach and proximate cause. Although this statement appears to omit the cause in fact element, in this formula cause in fact is included in the court's definition or understanding of proximate cause.

This form of stating the elements of the case does not differ in substance from the list of elements in the preceding section. However, courts that use the combined cause in fact and proximate cause locution risk considerable ambiguity. Suppose a judicial opinion tells us that the plaintiff must lose her claim because the defendant's conduct was not a proximate cause. In a court that conflates proximate cause and cause in fact, such a statement may mean that the defendant's conduct was not a cause in fact or may mean to say that although his conduct was a cause in fact, it was not a proximate cause. Wrapping the cause in fact and proximate cause issue together clouds the court's message to the bar. In this book the term proximate cause is not intended to refer to cause in fact.

Alternative to proximate cause analysis; duty and scope. The duty and proximate cause issues are always viewed as separate issues when courts list the elements of a negligence case. Nevertheless, in some cases courts can resolve a legal problem either by speaking in terms of duty or in terms of proximate cause. You could say that a social host who serves alcohol to an intoxicated guest is not a proximate cause of injuries inflicted by the guest's later drunken driving. Or you could say that the social host owed no duty to the victim. Whether either locution leads to the correct result is not the point here and indeed it is not a point easy to make without going into more detail than is appropriate to an introductory section. But the illustration warns the reader that the elements of the prima facie case have a dismaying tendency to emulate one another.

*

CHAPTER 7

NEGLIGENCE STANDARDS

TOPIC A. NEGLIGENCE AND THE REASONABLE PERSON STANDARD

§ 116. Negligence: Conduct vs. State of Mind

Negligence as risk. Negligence is conduct that creates or fails to avoid unreasonable risks of foreseeable harm to others.[1] As will be seen, not all risky conduct is negligent, for some risks are entirely justified. And not all negligence is actionable as a tort, for some negligence is permitted and some causes no harm. To determine negligence, then, is to fit only one piece into the jigsaw puzzle of a lawsuit. One other warning is called for. Although negligence is indeed unreasonably risky conduct, that kind of conduct is often referred to by saying that the defendant is negligent if he fails to act as a reasonably prudent person under the circumstances.[2]

Negligence as conduct, not state of mind. Because the emphasis in negligence cases is on unreasonably risky conduct, the concept is not entirely parallel to the case of intent, where liability is based upon a combination of intent and conduct. A bad state of mind is neither necessary nor sufficient to show negligence,[3] and conduct is everything. One who drives at a dangerous speed is negligent even if he is not aware of his speed and is using his best efforts to drive carefully. Conversely, a person who drives without the slightest care for the safety of others is not negligent unless he drives in some way that is unreasonably risky.[4] State of mind, including knowledge and belief, may motivate or shape conduct, but it is not in itself an actionable tort. The legal concept of negligence as unduly risky conduct distinct from state of mind reflects the law's strong commitment to an objective standard of behavior.

§ 116

1. See Henry Terry, Negligence, 29 HARV. L. REV. 40 (1915).

2. Reasonable person terminology is used in definitions and in jury instructions as a simple and general way of conveying the idea, since reasonable persons will not take unjustified risks. Analysis of negligence claims, however, usually moves to the more specific question of unjustified risk. Professor Simons has argued that reasonable person and unjustified risk are at least theoretically distinct conceptions, see Kenneth W. Simons, Negligence, 16 SOCIAL PHILOSOPHY & POLICY 2, 52 (1999). However, courts analyze the justification for risks in appellate decisions and give the reasonable person instruction at trial with no apparent sense of conflict, so the reasonable person test seems to be the simple or shorthand way of talking about unjustified risks.

3. See Restatement § 282.

4. See City of Little Rock v. Cameron, 320 Ark. 444, 897 S.W.2d 562 (1995); Restatement § 283 C, cmt. d.

Conduct including acts or omissions. Conduct is often an affirmative act such as driving too fast. But conduct can include omissions or failures to act. A driver's failure to apply the brakes when a cow wanders into the road is conduct and so is a jailer's failure to prevent a prisoner's suicide. On the other hand, an unconscious person's movement is not conduct even if that movement harms someone. Conduct involves at least a degree of volition.

Intentionally risky conduct: the relation of negligence and intentional torts. How does this conception of negligence as conduct work with the defendant who knows that his conduct is riskier than normal? *First,* Such a defendant is not guilty of an intentional tort merely because he knows of the risk. Intent to commit a battery, for example, requires either a purpose or a substantial certainty that a harmful or offensive contact will be made. Intentionally taking a *risk* of contact is not the same as a purpose or a certainty that such contact will result. So intentional conduct and even intentional risk-taking is analyzed under negligence rules unless the defendant has a purpose to invade the plaintiff's interests or a certainty that such an invasion will occur. *Second,* The defendant who intentionally takes a risk may or may not be negligent; negligence will depend upon the seriousness of the risk and the reasons for taking it.

Examples of intentionally risky conduct. To see these points in an example, suppose the batter in a softball game knows the batted ball might conceivably break a window outside the park and across the street, but also knows that it is unlikely. He is intentionally taking a risk when he attempts to bat; but the risk is small, far short of a substantial certainty. By definition of intent, the batter, though intentionally taking a risk, is not intentionally causing the softball to enter another's land. Intentional risk-taking is not intentional touching required in battery cases or intentional entry upon land required in trespass cases. Is the batter then chargeable with negligence if not intent? That depends upon whether the risk was an unreasonable one. If the house is very close even though outside the park, maybe the batter is negligent, but if the risk of a broken window from a batted ball is a very small risk, batting the ball may not be negligent.

When state of mind is relevant. In spite of the fact that it is conduct and risk, not mental state that determines negligence, the defendant's state of mind is not necessarily irrelevant in a negligence case. The defendant's knowledge of facts that make a given act risky (as distinct from his attitude) is frequently important on the negligence issue. And his socially useful purpose in taking a risk may be evidence that his conduct is not unreasonably risky. Finally, a defendant who is taking an unreasonable risk and knows it may be guilty of reckless or wanton misconduct that would justify punitive damages or other liabilities. None of this, however, departs from the requirement of objectively unreasonable outward conduct.

§ 117. The Objective Reasonable Person Standard

Generality of the reasonable care standard. In the latter half of the 19th century, courts began to develop a general duty or standard of care describing the duty of all persons to exercise ordinary care, meaning the care of a reasonable person, for the benefit of other persons, not merely the particular duties of, say, a veterinarian to a farmer. The standard for determining negligence purports to apply invariantly to all negligence cases.[1]

More specific standards. It may be more accurate to say that the general duty or standard of ordinary care is a default rule, a standard applied when there is no other more specific standard addressed to the particular parties or their particular situation and where the defendant has not undertaken some different level of care. The default standard of reasonable care yields to the law's lesser standard for children, for instance, and in medical malpractice cases the standard yields to the standard implicitly undertaken by the physician and based upon the custom of the medical community.[2] Courts deviate from the reasonable care standard in other cases, too; for example, they may require of landowners very little care toward trespassers.[3] Nevertheless, for a great mass of cases, the general standard of ordinary or reasonable care is the standard courts apply. The reasonable person standard does not by itself resolve negligence issues, but it reflects fundamental conceptions and methodology of resolving negligence issues.

Stating the general standard of care. The duty owed by all people generally—the standard of care—is the duty to exercise the care that would be exercised by a reasonable and prudent person[4] under the same or similar circumstances to avoid or minimize risks of harm to others.[5] Since no one tries to avoid risks that cannot be identified or harms that cannot be foreseen as a possibility, the reasonable person exercises care only about the kinds of harm that are foreseeable to reasonable people[6] and risks that are sufficiently great to require precaution.[7] The standard applies equally when the issue is the plaintiff's contributory negligence.[8]

§ 117

1. E.g., Fox v. City and County of San Francisco, 47 Cal.App.3d 164, 120 Cal.Rptr. 779 (1975) ("the standard of care is always the same—ordinary care under the circumstances"); Stewart v. Motts, 539 Pa. 596, 654 A.2d 535 (Pa. 1995) ("there is but one standard of care to be applied to negligence actions involving dangerous instrumentalities in this Commonwealth. This standard of care is 'reasonable care' ").

2. § 242.

3. § 232 below.

4. Until quite recently, this standard was expressed as the standard of the reasonable man. With the effort to use gender-neutral phrases, that statement of the standard is in the process of being abandoned. In some cases, gender might matter in assessing foreseeable risks and where it does, it can be considered as part of the circumstances.

5. E.g., Mansfield v. Circle K. Corp., 877 P.2d 1130 (Okla.1994) ("the standard of conduct is that of a reasonably prudent person under the same or similar circumstances"); Gossett v. Jackson, 249 Va. 549, 457 S.E.2d 97 (Va. 1995) (negligence is "the failure to exercise 'that degree of care which an ordinarily prudent person would exercise under the same or similar circumstances to avoid injury to another' ").

6. § 143.

7. §§ 144–145.

8. § 199.

The term negligence as used in this book will generally apply equally to contributory negligence of a plaintiff.

Sometimes "prudent person" is given identity as a member of a class. For example, depending on the defendant's occupation, courts will often speak of the prudent physician, engineer, ship captain, plumber, or dog owner.[9] Such formulations combine a statement of the standard with an application of it to the facts. Although the standard for physicians and some other professionals has widely been regarded as a standard that differs from the reasonable person standard,[10] it seems fairly certain that not all such formulations are intended to represent a departure from the reasonable person standard. To speak of the reasonable dog owner is to speak of the reasonable person. One of the circumstances is that the defendant owns a dog with all the risks that dog ownership entails, so it is convenient to speak of the reasonable dog owner, and no harm is done by such a locution as long as no one thinks dog owners are relieved of the reasonable person standard or that canine ownership is the only circumstance of significance.

In the case of the plaintiff's contributory negligence, the standard is generally the same except that the risks to be avoided are risks to the plaintiff herself. The term negligence as used in this book will generally include contributory negligence as well.

The standard is often described as the standard of ordinary care, due care, or reasonable care.[11] It may also be referred to as the reasonable person or prudent person standard. The terms are interchangeable, and they all refer to external conduct that would be dictated by "care" or "prudence," not to the prudent or careful state of mind. These terms are largely the terms of jury instructions and with only slight variations in expression, they are accepted everywhere.[12] The idea is that the jury would be able to say (for example) that 60 mph was faster than a

9. S.K. Whitty & Co. v. Laurence L. Lambert & Associates, 576 So.2d 599 (La. App. 4th Cir. 1991) (engineer); Butcher v. Gay, 29 Cal.App.4th 388, 34 Cal.Rptr.2d 771 (1994) (dog owner); Greenberg v. Giddings, 127 Vt. 242, 246 A.2d 832 (1968) (plumber); Pryal v. Mardesich, 51 Wash.2d 663, 321 P.2d 269 (1958) (captain). Similarly, the reasonable care standard in employment is usually expressed by saying that an employer generally owes employees and contractors a reasonably safe place to work. E.g., Blair v. Campbell, 924 S.W.2d 75 (Tenn.1996).

10. Chapter 14.

11. United Blood Services Etc. v. Quintana, 827 P.2d 509 (Colo.1992); Stewart v. Motts, 539 Pa. 596, 654 A.2d 535 (1995); Furman v. Rural Electric Company, 869 P.2d 136 (Wyo.1994). "Ordinary" care is not a reference to the statistical occurrence but to a value judgment. See Clarence Morris, Custom and Negligence, 42 Colum. L. Rev. 1147, 1157 (1942). That point can be logically verified by noting that custom (the ordinary practice) is not the standard of care. See §§ 163–165.

12. Some judges have charged juries in some variation on the language of Baron Alderson in Blyth v. Birmingham Waterworks Co., 11 Ex. 781, 156 Eng.Rep. 1047 (1856): "Negligence is the omission to do something which a reasonable man, guided upon those considerations which ordinarily regulate the conduct of human affairs, would do, or doing something which a prudent and reasonable man would not do." Frequently this kind of language will be combined with both the reasonable person and due care or ordinary care language in a single instruction. E.g., Caliri v. State Dept. of Transportation, 136 N.H. 606, 620 A.2d 1028 (1993) (quoting New Hampshire's standard negligence instruction).

reasonable prudent person would drive under the particular circumstances and therefore that the defendant who drove that speed was negligent.

Non-technical usages of "standard." The term "standard" sometimes creeps into judicial discussions in a way that is informal at best and potentially confusing. Judges sometimes speak of "proving" a standard of care, for example, but since a standard is by definition set by the judge in the first place, there is never a question of proving the standard itself. Sometimes in locutions like this, judges mean that the plaintiff should prove facts that invoke one standard rather than another as being proper for the case. Or that the plaintiff must prove facts that show a *breach* or *violation* of the standard. It cannot be too often repeated that the standard itself is a general duty prescribed by law.

Relation of reasonable person standard to risk. Courts project the reasonable person as an ideal to help themselves and juries estimate whether the defendant's harm-causing conduct was too risky. Apart from the risk of harms to others, courts are not interested in whether the defendant was unreasonable. The defendant may unreasonably invest in bags of fortune cookies in the belief that they predict the future, but such unreasonable behavior is not negligence because it creates no risks of harm to other people. So the reasonable person standard is always applied to judgments about risky behavior. Unreasonable risk-taking is the central point; the reasonable person standard is only a step in judging whether the harm-causing conduct was unacceptably risky.

Methods for determining risks acceptable to the reasonable person. The reasonable person standard is important, but it does not by itself direct juries or judges to clear conclusions in close cases. The legal system has developed three broad ways to make the reasonable person standard a little more specific. First, courts invest the imaginary reasonable person with certain mental and physical characteristics. The defendant's conduct can thus be compared to the conduct we would expect of a reasonable person having, say, certain knowledge and ability.[13] Second, courts may sidestep the effort to apply general standards by adopting specific rules about specific kinds of conduct such as speeding, condemning that conduct as at least prima facie negligence.[14] Finally, courts may attempt to estimate how the reasonable person would behave more directly. For instance, they might attempt to estimate the magnitude or the risks involved in the defendant's conduct, and to weigh those risks along with the costs and benefits of acting more safely.[15] Or, alternatively, courts might regard customary community behavior, not as a standard, to be sure, but as persuasive evidence of how a reasonable person would behave.[16] The remaining sections in this chapter explain the rules

13. See §§ 119–122 below.

14. See §§ 132–134.

15. §§ 144–147. Some ways of doing this might be regarded as supplanting the reasonable person standard rather than carrying it out.

16. See §§ 163–165 below.

attached to these three general methods for applying the reasonable person standard.

§ 118. Objective and Subjective Features of the Standard

Standard as objective. The reasonable person or due care standard is very largely but not entirely objective. The first clause in the standard demands the safety efforts that a reasonable person would make. The standard is both general and objective. It applies to cases generally, and it demands conduct that might be easy enough for the hypothetical reasonable person but that might be difficult for the real and particular defendant. The standard holds a real and particular defendant mainly to the standards of the ideal reasonable person rather than to the real defendant's own best judgment or ability.

Characteristics of reasonable people. When we ask about the characteristics of the reasonable person against whom the defendant is judged, we find that the standard is not wholly objective. The reasonable person whose standards the defendant must meet is said to have these attributes:

(1) Normal intelligence;[1]

(2) normal perception, memory, and at least a minimum of standard knowledge;[2]

(3) all the additional intelligence, skill, or knowledge actually possessed by the individual actor; and[3]

(4) the physical attributes of the actor himself.[4]

Semi-subjective components. The first two sets of attributes in effect insist on the objective standard. The defendant whose intelligence is less than normal, for instance, is still held to the objective reasonable person standard. He cannot escape liability by doing his own, personal or subjective best. On the other hand, items (3) and (4) could be seen as subjective standards because they refer us to the defendant's own special intelligence or skills and his own special physical characteristics. Even these items, however, call for a kind of objective judgment. The objective reasonable person would surely use any special physical or mental abilities he might have to avoid unreasonable risks to others, and would take into account any physical limitations he might have for the same purposes. So in an important practical sense, all of these attributes of the reasonable person ask us to judge the defendant's conduct by a largely objective standard.

Flexibility: circumstances alter cases. The other clause in the standard emphasizes the particular facts of the particular case—the "circumstances." This is not necessarily a subjective standard; it does not ask

§ 118

1. See § 120 below.
2. See § 122 below.
3. Id.
4. See § 119.

whether the defendant is to be excused because he was having a bad day or held to an especially high standard because he had a good night's sleep. Instead, it tells us that what counts as reasonable care will vary with the risks presented. The reasonable person will exercise care commensurate with the danger.[5] Perhaps, for example, a reasonable person would slow down when driving near a group of playing children.

The circumstances clause also has a forgiving aspect. For example, if the defendant was required to act in an emergency not of his own creation, he might take longer to react than would be reasonable at other times. Measuring the defendant's conduct against that of the hypothetical reasonable person under the circumstances, including the circumstance of emergency, we may think the defendant not negligent, even though such a slow reaction time might be counted as negligence if there were no emergency at all.[6] The circumstances clause brings flexibility and common sense to the standard. In addition, when a plaintiff knows she is dealing with a person of limited capacity, the plaintiff might be expected to care for herself rather than to depend upon a person of known limits.[7] If so, the defendant's subjective limitations of intelligence or judgment do count in an indirect way. Likewise, the plaintiff's own contributory negligence may be forgiven if it was the result of her subjective limitations of which the defendant was aware.[8] So, in effect, a subjective standard does control some of the cases.[9]

All this is very well, but exceedingly abstract. For practical judgments about negligence, judges and jurors need considerably more than to be told to demand reasonableness. A degree of concrete content can be added to the reasonable person formula by specifying the kinds of mental or physical abilities the defendant must use to avoid creating unreasonable risks to others. This is conventionally done by saying that the reasonable person has certain attributes of mind and body and that he uses them in certain ways. The next sections discuss the attributes of the hypothetical reasonable person.

§ 119. Physical Characteristics

Physical disabilities. The reasonable person standard becomes partly subjective when it comes to physical attributes of the defendant. Except in the case of voluntary intoxication,[1] one with physical illness or other

5. E.g., Wilson v. City of Kotzebue, 627 P.2d 623 (Alaska 1981); McCartney v. Pawtucket Mutual Ins. Co., 1994 WL 723056 (Conn.Super.1994); Poluski v. Richardson Transportation, 877 S.W.2d 709 (Mo.App. 1994).

6. See § 129 below.

7. One version of this point is discussed in § 214. This may be explained as an assumed risk, but the effect is the same as using a subjective standard for the defendant in such a case.

8. See § 200.

9. Other mixes of objective and subjective elements are possible. See Helmut Koziol, Liability Based on Fault: Subjective or Objective Yardstick?, Maastrict J. of European and Comp. L. 111 (1998) (discussing the objective vs. subjective standards of various European countries and suggesting that the objective standard is appropriate only when the actor undertakes activities requiring special abilities, undertakes a business enterprise, or uses a dangerous thing).

§ 119

1. § 123 below.

physical disability is held to the standard of a reasonable person having such a disability, not to a standard of some ideal normal physical capacity.[2] A shorter person or an unsighted person is not expected to see and avoid danger that could only be perceived by a taller or sighted person. One with a hearing loss is not expected to hear approaching danger.[3] The same idea applies to other physical disabilities or limitations.[4]

Protective aspects of the rule for disabled persons. (a) Known physical traits. Sometimes this rule is discussed as if it were especially protective of persons with disabilities or physical limitations.[5] Sometimes that is true. The rule says in effect that an unsighted person is not to be considered negligent merely by going out into the world.[6] The rule forestalls the specious argument that an unsighted person would be negligent in crossing the street because the standard reasonable person would not close his eyes while crossing.[7]

(b) Unknown physical traits. The rule also helps protect the defendant who is reasonably unaware of a physical limitation or disability until it results in harm. The defendant who is suddenly and unforeseeably incapacitated while driving, as the result of a heart attack or seizure may lose substantial control of his vehicle and inflict great harm, but even if his movements count as action and not merely as a reflex, he is not in violation of the reasonable person standard and not liable for the harm done, so long as the physical seizure was in fact unforeseeable.[8]

2. Muse v. Page, 125 Conn. 219, 4 A.2d 329 (1939); Memorial Hospital of South Bend, Inc. v. Scott, 261 Ind. 27, 300 N.E.2d 50 (1973); Restatement § 283 C.

3. Fink v. City of New York, 206 Misc. 79, 132 N.Y.S.2d 172 (Sup. Ct. 1954) ("deaf mute" could not hear siren of approaching fire truck, but used his eyes in reliance on a stop light; held, he was not guilty of contributory negligence).

4. Advanced age is not itself a disability, but courts have sometimes treated age as correlative with or evidence of some kinds of physical limitation. See Plunkett v. Brooklyn Heights Railroad Company, 129 App.Div. 572, 114 N.Y.S. 276 (1908), aff'd per curiam, 198 N.Y. 568, 92 N.E. 1098 (1910); cf. Stewart v. Gibson Products Co. of Natchitoches Parish, Louisiana, Inc., 300 So.2d 870 (La.App.1974) (court treated age as correlative with frailty).

5. Prosser saw the rule as reflecting the disabled person's entitlement "to live in the world." Prosser & Keeton § 32, p. 176. That reflects the protective side of the rule, but not the more demanding side. The protective side of the rule should not be confused with the duty of care owed *to* a disabled person. One who knows or should know he is dealing with a person under a physical disability is expected to use reasonable care in the light of that knowledge. See §§ 198 & 200.

6. See Harris v. Uebelhoer, 75 N.Y. 169 (1878) (we are all blind on a dark night; we are not required to stay at home but to exercise reasonable care when we go out); Knoxville Optical Supply, Inc. v. Thomas, 1993 WL 574 (Tenn.App.1993). Other and distinct safety protections for persons with a disability are found in special duties imposed upon defendants generally or those in a special relationship to the disabled person, for example, statutory duties requiring traffic to yield to unsighted persons and common law rules requiring care commensurate with the plaintiff's disability. See, e.g., Wright v. Engum, 124 Wash.2d 343, 878 P.2d 1198 P

7. Seavey, Negligence—Subjective or Objective?, 41 Harv. L. Rev. 1, 14, n. 14 (1927) poses this example. The blindfold example is specious in any event; the suggested comparison is not a parallel case because the blindfolded actor would not be using all the senses reasonably available, while the unsighted person would be.

8. E.g., Freeman v. Martin, 116 Ga.App. 237, 156 S.E.2d 511 (1967); Moore v. Presnell, 38 Md.App. 243, 379 A.2d 1246 (1977); Annotation, Physical Defect, Illness, Drow-

The demanding side of the rule for disabled persons. The physical disability rule is not always protective of disabled persons. First, a disability does not necessarily prevent a person from acting to secure reasonable safety and if it does not, it is irrelevant to the negligence issue.[9]

More importantly, a person with physical disabilities or limitations must still act as a reasonable person with those limitations in mind. To the extent that a reasonable person with similar limitations would do so, a disabled person must adjust for limitations by using other senses or by altering conduct to minimize the risks created by the disability.[10] For example, one who is of small stature and cannot reach the brake pedals, may be negligent in driving a car not equipped with hand controls; a reasonable person of such stature would not drive without being able to stop the car.[11] An unsighted person may be expected to take special precautions to meet the standard of reasonable care.[12]

In the same way, one who knows or can reasonably foresee that he is subject to seizures that prevent safe driving may be negligent in driving at all if those seizures cannot be controlled.[13] One who recognizes the onset of an insulin reaction, drowsiness, or fatigue may be unreasonable in continuing to drive or operate machinery.[14]

The actor's vision is sometimes treated the same way, sometimes somewhat differently. One who has only limited peripheral vision is not expected to see dangers far to one side, but he may be expected to compensate for the loss of vision by turning his head if he is or should be aware of that loss, and certainly he is expected to react to warnings within his vision that suggest peripheral dangers.[15] Courts seem to go beyond this rule in some cases and tend to get results consistent with a

siness, or Falling Asleep of Motor Vehicle Operator as Affecting Liability for Injury, 28 A.L.R.2d 12 (1953).

9. See McCartney v. Pawtucket Mutual Ins. Co., 1994 WL 723056 (Conn.Super.1994) (woman in her mid-eighties, house-bound and in a wheel chair could still have arranged for heating oil to prevent frozen pipes).

10. E.g., Mahan v. State, 172 Md. 373, 191 A. 575 (1937) (driver whose small stature made vision difficult expected to exercise "greater watchfulness"); Rosser v. Smith, 260 N.C. 647, 133 S.E.2d 499 (1963) (semble, hearing impaired person should have compensated for the impairment by wearing her hearing aid or alternatively by keeping better lookout); Mackie v. McGraw, 183 Ore. 204, 191 P.2d 403 (1948) (hearing impaired plaintiff expected to be "more vigilant").

11. Cf. Sanders v. Walden, 214 Ark. 523, 217 S.W.2d 357, 9 A.L.R.2d 1040 (1949) (one entrusting car to man who might not be able to brake it was negligent, inferentially the driver himself was as well).

12. Poyner v. Loftus, 694 A.2d 69 (D.C.App.1997) ("in the exercise of common prudence one of defective eyesight must usually as a matter of general knowledge take more care and employ keener watchfulness in walking upon the streets and avoiding obstructions than the same person with good eyesight, in order to reach the standard established by the law for all persons alike, whether they be weak or strong, sound or deficient").

13. E.g., Goodrich v. Blair, 132 Ariz. 459, 646 P.2d 890 (1982) (driver subject to heart attacks); Lutzkovitz v. Murray, 339 A.2d 64, 93 A.L.R.3d 321 (Del. 1975) (risk of blackout); Storjohn v. Fay, 246 Neb. 454, 519 N.W.2d 521 (1994).

14. Keller v. DeLong, 108 N.H. 212, 231 A.2d 633 (1967); Howle v. PYA/Monarch, Inc., 288 S.C. 586, 344 S.E.2d 157 (1986).

15. Bennett v. State, 503 So.2d 1022 (La.App.1987).

more or less objective standard. This is accomplished by presuming that one could see what was there to be seen,[16] at least in the absence of a distraction[17] or evidence that the actor's vision is defective in a particular way.

Contributory negligence. The same general standards apply when the issue is contributory negligence of the plaintiff instead of negligence of the defendant.[18]

Physical prowess. It seems probable that the defendant will be expected to act reasonably in the light of any special physical abilities he might have. If a strong swimmer attempts to save a drowning person he would almost certainly be expected to use whatever added strength and stamina he has and would not readily be exonerated for giving up the effort merely because he had reached the limits of endurance that could be attributed to the hypothetical reasonable person.

§ 120. Mental and Psychological Capacity

Liability of mentally disabled. It goes almost without saying that a mentally able person is negligent if he unreasonably fails to take medication he knows is necessary to prevent dangerous mental states.[19] The legal rule, however, goes much further than this. Insane adults and others suffering mental disability are liable both for their intentional[20] and negligent torts.[21]

Only limited and somewhat peculiar authority qualifies this general rule. Wisconsin has held that one cannot be liable for acts committed as a result of a sudden onset of an unforeseeable insanity.[22] New York once seemed to hold that liability would not be imposed for harm caused by a person who became insane as a result of extraordinary efforts to protect the plaintiff.[23] Otherwise, however, the rule that mentally impaired persons are liable for their torts seems to be rather fully accepted.

Standard of care. The standard of care applied to an adult suffering mental impairment or psychological disturbance remains the standard of

16. E.g., Mort v. Walter, 98 Ill.2d 391, 75 Ill.Dec. 228, 457 N.E.2d 18 (1983); Dennis v. Bolden, 606 So.2d 111 (Miss.1992); Huntwork v. Voss, 247 Neb. 184, 525 N.W.2d 632 (1995).

17. E.g., Little Creek Investment Corporation v. Hubbard, 249 Va. 258, 455 S.E.2d 244 (1995).

18. E.g., Tomey v. Dyson, 76 Cal.App.2d 212, 172 P.2d 739 (1946); Stewart v. Gibson Products Co. of Natchitoches, 300 So.2d 870 (La.App.1974); Allen v. Boston & M. R.R., 245 Mass. 139, 139 N.E. 511 (1923).

19. See Stuyvesant Associates v. Doe, 221 N.J.Super. 340, 534 A.2d 448 (1987).

20. § 69, supra.

21. Restatement § 895J.

22. See Breunig v. American Family Ins. Co., 45 Wis.2d 536, 173 N.W.2d 619, 49 A.L.R.3d 179 (1970). *Breunig* holds that one who is suddenly overcome by a mental disability without forewarning is to be treated like a person who suffers a sudden heart attack or seizure, which is to say that such a person need not comply with some external standard. The premise seems to be that when insanity is not sudden, the defendant has some kind of reasonable opportunity to do something to prevent himself from inflicting harm. The supposed difference between sudden and long-term insanity may rest on distinctions that cannot be maintained.

23. Williams v. Hays, 157 N.Y. 541, 52 N.E. 589 (1899) (a case difficult to interpret, however).

the reasonable prudent person of normal intelligence, judgment and rationality. Consequently, defendants who suffer from bad judgment or mental deficiency,[24] insanity[25] or antisocial penchants for abusing children[26] are held to the objective or "external" standard of the reasonable prudent person. The same is true with one who is voluntarily intoxicated.[27] Put differently, if the defendant's conduct, carried out by sane or sober people, would count as negligence, the defendant cannot escape liability on the ground that he behaved as a reasonable and prudent person afflicted with insanity or drunkenness.

Contributory negligence. Here as elsewhere, similar rules or standards may apply to the plaintiff who is charged with contributory negligence.[28] But some judges have resisted this view, preferring to apply a subjective standard to plaintiffs who suffer mental limitations,[29] even though the objective test is used for defendants.

There is probably a better explanation for allowing a mentally impaired plaintiff to recover in spite of conduct that objectively appears to count as contributory negligence. In a nutshell, it is that the defendant in many instances is under a duty to protect the plaintiff from her own fault. The defendant's obligation is quite sufficient to explain why the plaintiff's contributory negligence is no bar without positing a subjective standard for the plaintiff. For example, a mental institution cannot subject its impaired patients to unreasonable risks of harm and then escape liability on the ground that they foolishly failed to avoid the risk.[30] A similar approach explains the defendant's liability in the case of jailers who fail to protect intoxicated or suicidal prisoners[31] and in other cases in which the defendant is aware of the plaintiff's disability.[32] So

24. Vaughan v. Menlove, 3 Bing. (N.C.) 468, 132 Eng.Rep. 490 (C.P. 1837) (rejecting the defendant's argument that he should not be liable if he acted honestly and to the best of his own judgment).

25. Johnson v. Lambotte, 147 Colo. 203, 363 P.2d 165 (1961); Anicet v. Gant, 580 So.2d 273 (Fla.App.1991); Sforza v. Green Bus Lines, 150 Misc. 180, 268 N.Y.S. 446 (N.Y.Mun.Ct.1934); Kuhn v. Zabotsky, 9 Ohio St.2d 129, 224 N.E.2d 137 (1967); Restatement §§ 283 B & 895J; see Seidelson, Reasonable Expectations and Subjective Standards in Negligence Law: The Minor, The Mentally Impaired, and the Mentally Incompetent, 50 Geo. Wash. L. Rev. 17 (1981).

26. C.T.W. v. B.C.G. & D.T.G., 809 S.W.2d 788 (Tex.App.1991) (one with "pedophilic disorder" must nevertheless meet the standards of the person of ordinary prudence).

27. § 123.

28. Galindo v. TMT Transport, Inc., 152 Ariz. 434, 733 P.2d 631 (Ct. App. 1986); Fox v. City and County of San Francisco, 47 Cal.App.3d 164, 120 Cal.Rptr. 779 (1975).

29. Mochen v. State, 43 A.D.2d 484, 352 N.Y.S.2d 290 (1974); Stacy v. Jedco Construction, Inc., 119 N.C.App. 115, 457 S.E.2d 875 (1995); Feldman v. Howard, 5 Ohio App.2d 65, 214 N.E.2d 235 (1966), rev'd on other grounds, 10 Ohio St.2d 189, 226 N.E.2d 564 (1967); Birkner v. Salt Lake County, 771 P.2d 1053 (Utah 1989).

30. Bramlette v. Charter–Medical–Columbia, 302 S.C. 68, 393 S.E.2d 914 (1990); cf. Cowan v. Doering, 215 N.J.Super. 484, 522 A.2d 444 (1987), aff'd, 111 N.J. 451, 545 A.2d 159 (1988). See § 200.

31. Wilson v. Kotzebue, 627 P.2d 623 (Alaska 1981) (intoxication of prisoner); Hickey v. Zezulka, 439 Mich. 408, 487 N.W.2d 106 (1992) (suicidal prisoner).

32. E.g., Stacy v. Jedco Construction, Inc., 119 N.C.App. 115, 457 S.E.2d 875 (1995); Higgins v. East Valley School Dist., 41 Wash.App. 281, 704 P.2d 630 (1985).

perhaps the subjective standard for plaintiff cases should be taken with a grain of salt.[33]

§ 121. Bases for and Alternatives to the Mental Capacity Rules

The rule that mentally impaired persons are liable for their torts, and the rule that imposes an objective standard of behavior upon such persons are closely correlated. If an objective standard were not imposed, the rule of liability would be at least partly meaningless. The two rules should perhaps stand or fall together. What is the justification for them?

Civil law alternatives. In a sense courts impose a kind of strict liability when they hold a person responsible for harms he had not the mental capacity to avoid. A different approach would be to regard the mentally incompetent person as a force of nature, like lightning, and leave it to all other individuals to insure themselves or provide their own protection.[1] Some civil law countries in fact have immunized the insane person from tort liability, at least in certain circumstances.[2]

Justifications for the objective standard.[3] *(1) Role of objective standards in judicial process*. One justification for objective standards in law generally is that they are essential if the judicial process is to remain accessible and accountable. Lawyers and litigants cannot evaluate judges or the legal process itself if judges could decide cases by what they feel in their heart or on the basis of messages from the Deity without reference to any standards that lawyers can understand, discuss, and argue. If the standard were subjective, it would be difficult (though not impossible) to adduce evidence that the defendant did or did not do his best, given his impairment, but even more difficult to know whether the judge or jury made a justifiable decision.

(2) Difficulty of distinguishing incapacity from poor capacity. It may be impossible to distinguish insanity that should exonerate an individual from all the other determinants that shape his conduct. No one is responsible for choosing his own genetic makeup, life experience, body chemistry or mental ability. So far as conduct is determined by those things, it can be said that no one is responsible. A person who causes

33. See Seidelson, Reasonable Expectations and Subjective Standards in Negligence Law: The Minor, The Mentally Impaired, and the Mentally Incompetent, 50 GEO. WASH. L. REV. 17 (1981).

§ 121

1. See Yancey v. Maestri, 155 So. 509 (La.App. 1934) (under civil law view, insane person's "acts are looked upon as inevitable accidents").

2. See GERMAN CIVIL CODE § 827 (excluding civil responsibility for one who is unable to exercise free will, except where he brought on temporary disability by use of alcohol or similar means). Not all civil law countries today follow this view. In Mexico, the CÓDIGO CIVIL PARA EL DISTRICTO FEDERAL § 1911 provides that the incompetent person is liable unless some other person such as a guardian is liable ("El incapaz que cause daño debe repararlo, salvo que la responsabilidad recaiga en las personas de él encargadas, conforme lo dispuesto en [otros artículos]."); for others, see Torts—Liability for One's Own Act § 215, in XI INT. ENCYC. COMP. L. (A. TUNC, ed., 1979).

3. See Curran, Tort Liability of the Mentally Ill and Mentally Deficient, 21 OHIO ST. L. J. 52 (1960); Restatement § 283 B.

harm through impatience, awkwardness, or stupidity in this sense is not morally responsible for his actions. But neither law nor society could survive a rule that exonerated every such fault.[4] The immunity suggested by such reasoning could be pared down by drawing a distinction between the stupidity and mental deficiency, but that distinction is difficult to draw as a practical matter and perhaps morally unjustified as well. Similarly, the distinction between mental disability and a propensity for bad behavior may be difficult to maintain. The difference between someone who sexually abuses children and someone who suffers a "pedophilic disorder" is in the mind of the observer, not in the reality of the harm inflicted.[5]

(3) Difficulty of making causal judgments and setting an appropriate subjective standard. Mental impairments do not necessarily prevent safe behavior; even a schizophrenic may drive well. Any rule exonerating insane persons would necessarily force courts not only to decide what counts as insanity but also to determine whether the particular insanity on the particular occasion caused the defendant's negligent conduct. And, since some insane persons can do some things safely, courts would be obliged to impose some kind of standard, so that the defendant would remain liable for those harms he could reasonably avoid. This might come uncomfortably close to saying that an insane person would be held to the standard of a reasonable and prudent insane person with the defendant's particular insanity.[6] At any rate, a meaningful test of liability would not likely represent either practical or moral improvement over the rule imposing objective standards.

(4) Choosing between innocent parties. Tort liability is not a criminal conviction or a badge of infamy. The insane defendant will be obliged to pay a tort judgment, but only if he has the money to do so. The loss must fall somewhere, and as between the injured victim and an insane defendant with insurance or sufficient funds to pay, the loss may appropriately fall upon the defendant who caused the harm.

(5) Incentives. Finally, some authorities have suggested that tort liability will provide proper incentives to those "in charge" of the insane person to control his conduct. This point does not seem quite right. If one in charge is negligent in failing to control the insane person, he will be liable for his own negligence. If incentive is obtainable in the law of negligence, liability of the caretaker for his own negligence should be more effective than liability of the insane person himself. If the caretaker is not negligent but on the contrary has exercised optimum care to

4. Cf. Seidelson, Reasonable Expectations and Subjective Standards in Negligence Law: The Minor, The Mentally Impaired, and the Mentally Incompetent, 50 GEO. WASH. L. REV. 17 (1981) (if doing one's best were the standard, universal immunity would result).

5. In C.T.W. v. B.C.G., 809 S.W.2d 788 (Tex.App.1991) the defendant sexually abused his step grandchildren. He sought to defend against tort liability on the ground that this sexual abuse was the result of a "pedophilic disorder." The court rejected the argument that the defendant should be held only to the standard of "an ordinary prudent person with the mental illness of pedophilia."

6. See n. 5, supra.

control the insane person, there is no reason to give him incentives to do more.

§ 122. Knowledge, Perception, Memory, Experience, and Skills

Reasonable person standard as to knowledge and memory. Ordinary care requires one to act in a way that would be reasonable given the knowledge or information that would be possessed by a reasonable person under the circumstances.[1] Relatedly, one must also exercise senses reasonably for the perception of danger,[2] and to fix and retain significant information in memory for a reasonable period of time.[3] Forgetfulness is usually forgiven only when there is a specific reason for it, such as distraction or emergency.[4]

Knowledge and risk. Knowledge is intimately related to the concept of negligence as conduct entailing an unreasonable risk. If you know that dropped objects fall, you will probably perceive a risk that others might be harmed if you were to drop a torts book off a tall building. In a sense, you do not directly "know" risks; knowledge of facts is not the same as perception of a risk. Nevertheless, knowledge of facts is an essential step in that perception.

Knowledge possessed by a reasonable person. The reasonable person has some general knowledge in common with others in the community. Knowledge in this sense means systematic information capable of generalization and use in various situations. We all know that fire burns, for example. Speaking of knowledge in this sense, the Restatement has it that the knowledge of a reasonable person is the knowledge that is common in the community generally.[5] It includes elemental knowledge about humans, animals, and forces of nature.

The rule means that the defendant is expected to act in a way consistent with knowledge of commonly understood dangers, for example, that dropped objects fall, that high electrical voltages can kill, gas can explode when combined with fire, that children have a propensity for darting into the street, and that a snarling dog can inflict wounds by biting. On the other hand, the defendant is not expected to have specialized knowledge, for example, knowledge that gasoline fumes are heavier than air.[6]

§ 122

1. Restatement § 290.

2. Dobson v. Louisiana Power and Light Co., 567 So.2d 569 (La.1990); Restatement § 289, cmt. e.

3. Restatement § 289, cmt. f.

4. See, e.g., Tomlinson v. Wilson & Toomer Fertilizer Co., 165 So.2d 801 (Fla. App.1964); Conner v. Farmers and Merchants Bank, 243 S.C. 132, 132 S.E.2d 385 (1963). All defendants could defeat claims if they were allowed to argue that even a reasonable person will forget a percentage of information and that the defendant's lifetime percentage of forgetting is within that range. A number of memory cases are analyzed in Grady, Why Are People Negligent? Technology, Non Durable Precautions, and the Medical Malpractice Explosion, 82 Nw. U. L. Rev. 293 (1988).

5. Restatement § 290.

6. Blakes v. Blakes, 517 So.2d 444 (La. App.1987).

These rules and their applications are sometimes seen in explicit statements, but perhaps more often they are seen by the shadows they cast. For instance, the many decisions that refuse to apply the attractive nuisance doctrine to aid a child injured by fires[7] or water[8] attest to the courts' belief that even children can appreciate and avoid such dangers. Many other decisions can be found holding that a person should have known of a specific kind of common danger.[9]

Variation in knowledge over time. The knowledge held by reasonable people changes over time and varies over place. At one time people knew little or nothing about the dangers of tobacco or asbestos. An architect who specified asbestos in a building in the 1930s would not be expected to know that it could cause serious injury, but almost everyone today knows otherwise. Because of this variation in knowledge from time to time and place to place, the question of appropriate knowledge is often submitted to the jury, subsumed in the broader question whether the defendant conducted himself in an unreasonably risky way.

Information. Information, in the sense of isolated facts of transient importance, is different from knowledge that can be generalized. We all know objects fall, but we do not all know the same particular facts. For instance, you know, but others do not, that a pot is on the range and the burner is on. Information of this kind differs from knowledge because this information cannot be generalized; it is both ephemeral and peculiar to circumstances. We might expect everyone in the community to have the knowledge that gunpowder can burn or explode, but we might not expect everyone who sees "sand" in a jar to have the information that the sand is actually gunpowder.[10]

Although we cannot standardize the particular information that a reasonable person will possess, we can say that a reasonable person would always use the information that he has acquired, or should have acquired in particular circumstances. If the defendant knows or should know that his car's brakes have ceased to work he must act on that information. On the issue of information, the lawyer's problem is frequently a matter of proof, that is, of showing what information the defendant actually had or should have had under the circumstances.

Knowledge of one's own ignorance; failure to acquire information. In some instances the actor knows or should know that he is ignorant of facts that might prove important in estimating a risk. If a reasonable person finds herself in a strange place confronted with a bottle that says "Drink Me," she may know nothing about the bottle's contents, but she

7. E.g., Piwowar v. Garrett, 182 Ill. App.3d 411, 130 Ill.Dec. 916, 538 N.E.2d 127 (1989).

8. Gordon v. C.H.C. Corp., 236 So.2d 733 (Miss.1970); cf. Johnson v. Washington County, 518 N.W.2d 594 (Minn.1994).

9. E.g., Riley v. Brasunas, 210 Ga.App. 865, 438 S.E.2d 113 (1993) (falling from heights); Logan v. Old Enterprise Farms, Ltd., 139 Ill.2d 229, 151 Ill.Dec. 323, 564 N.E.2d 778 (1990) (same); Skelton v. Twin County Rural Electric Ass'n, 611 So.2d 931 (Miss.1992) (tree climbing by a child); Harper v. Herman, 499 N.W.2d 472 (Minn. 1993) (diving in shallow water).

10. The example is from Seavey, Negligence—Subjective or Objective?, 41 Harv. L. Rev. 1 (1927).

surely knows of her own ignorance. Reasonable care may require her to find out something about the bottle's contents or provenance before she imbibes. This is not because she is expected to know the bottle's contents but because what she does know tells her that more information should be sought.[11]

Superior or specialized knowledge or skill. A reasonable person will act in the light of (a) knowledge shared by the community generally and also (b) information and knowledge that he himself has that is not generally known and that reasonable people would not ordinarily have. The Restatement puts this by saying that the standard is the standard of the reasonable person with the superior knowledge, skill, and other qualities of the defendant.[12]

The rule has obvious application to professionals like physicians and surgeons, who are held to possess the skill and knowledge of others in good standing in their profession.[13] A physician who knows more than a layman, must use that additional knowledge in the practice of medicine. But the point reaches even further. A physician who knows more than other physicians is also expected to use that special knowledge. Physicians who know more must not stop short of appropriate treatment on the ground that other physicians would have done no better.[14] The principle applies equally to any kind of skill or experience. A person with special knowledge about the operation of earth scrapers is expected to use that knowledge to avoid injury to others.[15]

Reasonable person standard and superior knowledge. The superior knowledge rule can be explained by saying that the actor's superior knowledge is one of the "circumstances" that a reasonable person would take into account[16] or by saying that a reasonable person will use all the knowledge he actually has in dealing with a recognizable risk. Either way, the standard of care, that of the reasonable person under the same or similar circumstances, remains the same.[17] So it is right to tell a jury that a reasonable person will use the relevant special knowledge he has,[18] but not right to tell the jury that he is held to a higher standard of care.[19]

11. See, e.g., Cramer v. Housing Opportunities Com'n of Montgomery County, 304 Md. 705, 501 A.2d 35 (1985); Wilson v. City of Eagan, 297 N.W.2d 146, 8 A.L.R.4th 1277 (Minn. 1980).

12. Restatement § 289 (superior knowledge in recognizing a risk); Restatement § 299, cmt. f (superior competence in both recognizing and dealing with risk); Restatement § 290, cmt. f (similar).

13. On medical malpractice and its standard of care generally see § 242 below.

14. Toth v. Community Hospital at Glen Cove, 22 N.Y.2d 255, 239 N.E.2d 368, 292 N.Y.S.2d 440 (1968).

15. Hill v. Sparks, 546 S.W.2d 473 (Mo. App.1976); cf. Dobson v. Louisiana Power and Light Co., 567 So.2d 569 (La.1990) (tree trimming); Sandella v. Dick Corp., 1995 WL 348192 (Conn.Super.1995) (actor was informed of hazard occurring when catatonic polymers and water were combined and was required to act on that knowledge).

16. See Sinai v. Polinger Co., 498 A.2d 520 (D.C.App.1985).

17. LaVine v. Clear Creek Skiing Corp., 557 F.2d 730 (10th Cir.1977); Cervelli v. Graves, 661 P.2d 1032 (Wyo.1983).

18. Cf. Hill v. Sparks, 546 S.W.2d 473 (Mo.App.1976).

19. Fredericks v. Castora, 241 Pa.Super. 211, 360 A.2d 696 (1976); Cervelli v. Graves, 661 P.2d 1032 (Wyo.1983); see Sinai v. Polinger Co., 498 A.2d 520 (D.C.App. 1985). To avoid confusion, the court may simply refuse to instruct at all on superior knowledge, leaving it to the jury under a

§ 123. Intoxicated Persons

Sober person standard vs. risk of drinking. A voluntarily intoxicated person[1] is in effect held to the standard of a reasonably sober person.[2] This seems to contradict the rule that the reasonable person has the physical attributes of the actor. The seeming contradiction is ameliorated by the fact that the decision to ingest alcohol or drugs itself creates a risk that the actor's physical (as well as mental) capacities will be diminished. One who drinks knowing he will soon drive a car, for example, may be negligent or contributorily negligent in choosing to drink under those circumstances. Liability might then be imposed less because the sober person standard is applied and more because the defendant took unreasonable risks in drinking at all.

When drinking creates no risks. The same cannot be said, however, about one who drinks at bedtime, expecting only to fall asleep in bed. Such a drinker seems to create no risks from his own diminished physical capacity. If he were unforeseeably required to drive at that point and his driving caused injury, liability could not be imposed upon the ground that he was negligent in becoming intoxicated. If he is liable in such a case it looks as if he is being expected to use physical capacities he does not have. If the rule would dictate such a result, then to that extent it is in conflict with the general rule that an actor need use only such physical capacity as he has.

Overt conduct required to establish negligence. Intoxication cases raise another problem. Negligence consists of harm-causing conduct.[3] Neither the defendant's state of mind nor his physical condition are in themselves negligence. Consequently, the mere fact that a driver's mental or physical faculties are affected by alcohol does not necessarily lead to the conclusion that the driver was negligent,[4] not even if he is involved in a collision with a stationary object.[5] If his overt conduct was blameless, intoxication is irrelevant and he is not negligent and not liable. On the other hand, if the driver drove too fast, or failed to keep a lookout, or drove in the wrong lane of traffic, his conduct shows a departure from the reasonable person standard, and liability is appropri-

standard reasonable person instruction to figure that the defendant should use all his knowledge and skill to avoid injury to others. LaVine v. Clear Creek Skiing Corp., supra n. 17.

§ 123

1. One who is involuntarily intoxicated, forcibly drugged by another for example, is not held to an external standard with respect to physical conditions or traits. Davies v. Butler, 95 Nev. 763, 602 P.2d 605 (1979); Restatement § 283 C, cmt. d.

2. Townsend v. Jones, 183 Kan. 543, 331 P.2d 890 (1958); Remmenga v. Selk, 150 Neb. 401, 34 N.W.2d 757, 763 (1948); Restatement § 283 C, cmt. d.

3. § 116, supra.

4. Remmenga v. Selk, 150 Neb. 401, 34 N.W.2d 757, 763–64 (1948); Benoit v. Wilson, 150 Tex. 273, 239 S.W.2d 792 (1951). Courts frequently treat this as a rule about cause in fact or proximate cause rather than a rule about the nature of negligence, saying or implying that the intoxication was not a cause of injury unless it translated into outward conduct. E.g., Lynch v. Clark, 183 Or. 431, 194 P.2d 416, 422 (1948).

5. City of Little Rock v. Cameron, 320 Ark. 444, 897 S.W.2d 562 (1995).

ate, but only because his conduct was faulty, not because he was intoxicated.[6]

Admission of evidence of intoxication. Because it is conduct, not intoxication that counts as negligence, it might be argued that evidence of the defendant's intoxication should be excluded as irrelevant and prejudicial except when punitive damages are in issue. But courts do in fact admit evidence of intoxication where that evidence tends to support an inference that the actor's actual conduct fell short of the reasonable prudent person standard.[7] For instance, proof of intoxication may be evidence tending to show that the defendant's perception of danger was impaired. Even if evidence of intoxication is admissible, however, it may be quite insufficient to prove negligence. Whether evidence of intoxication is *sufficient* to show negligence depends upon the facts.[8]

Statutes. Statutes make intoxication relevant in certain kinds of cases. For example, statutes prohibit driving while intoxicated or under the influence of alcohol. Some courts say that violation of such statutes is negligence per se, that is, negligence in itself.[9] But since the defendant's intoxication must lead to specific negligent conduct such as an improper lookout or driving on the wrong side of the road[10] and in addition, it must be a legal cause of the plaintiff's harm,[11] some states refuse to characterize violation of the statute as negligence per se.[12] Either way, however, these statutes form a basis for admission of evidence on intoxication and instructions that permit the jury to consider it.[13]

Contributory negligence. What's sauce for the goose is sauce for the gander and the intoxicated plaintiff charged with contributory negligence would normally come under the same rules as the intoxicated defendant.[14] But courts have sometimes excused the plaintiff on the theory that at some point drinking may become involuntary or that the plaintiff's drinking was not a proximate cause of her injury.[15] And in

6. See Alan H. McCoid, Intoxication and Its Effect upon Civil Responsibility, 42 Iowa L. Rev. 38 (1956).

7. E.g., Mitchell v. Montgomery County, 88 Md.App. 542, 596 A.2d 93, 100 (1991); Barnes v. Walsh, 130 Or.App. 533, 883 P.2d 234 (1994).

8. See Lynch v. Clark, 183 Or. 431, 194 P.2d 416 (1948); Benoit v. Wilson, 150 Tex. 273, 239 S.W.2d 792 (1951).

9. Anderson v. Morgan, 73 Ariz. 344, 241 P.2d 786 (1952); Hasson v. Hale, 555 So.2d 1014 (Miss.1990); Cook v. Spinnaker's of Rivergate, Inc., 878 S.W.2d 934 (Tenn.1994).

10. See Yost v. Miner, 163 N.W.2d 557 (Iowa 1968).

11. Anderson v. Morgan, 73 Ariz. 344, 241 P.2d 786 (1952); King v. Allred, 309 N.C. 113, 305 S.E.2d 554 (1983).

12. Yost v. Miner, 163 N.W.2d 557 (Iowa 1968); cf. Loevsky v. Carter, 70 Haw. 419, 773 P.2d 1120 (1989) (under Hawaii rule, violation is evidence of negligence only, not negligence per se).

13. E.g., Wade v. City of Chicago Heights, 216 Ill.App.3d 418, 159 Ill.Dec. 228, 575 N.E.2d 1288 (1991).

14. Cf. Del E. Webb Corp. v. Superior Court, 151 Ariz. 164, 726 P.2d 580 (1986) (patron's contributory negligence or assumed risk available as defense in suit against alcohol provider).

15. See, e.g., Davies v. Butler, 95 Nev. 763, 602 P.2d 605 (1979); Ballou v. Sigma Nu General Fraternity, 291 S.C. 140, 352 S.E.2d 488 (1986); Cook v. Spinnaker's of Rivergate, Inc., 878 S.W.2d 934 (Tenn. 1994).

some cases the defendant may be under a duty to protect the plaintiff from her own intoxication or other fault, in which case, the plaintiff's own intoxication, being the very risk the defendant is obliged to guard against, is no defense.[16]

Topic B. The Standard of Care for Children

§ 124. The General Standard of Care for Children

Liability of children. Very young children—usually those under about four or five years of age—are generally thought to be incapable of negligence.[1] Under the "rule of sevens," followed in a few states and discussed in a later section, children up to the age of seven are protected from tort liability. Otherwise, however, children are not immune from tort liability merely by virtue of their status as children.[2] The standard of care expected of them is another matter.

Subjective standard generally. With some exceptions to be mentioned,[3] children are not subjected to the reasonable person standard but are instead held to a standard that is largely subjective. A minor, even an older one, is not required to conduct himself as a reasonable adult or even as a reasonable child of similar age.[4] The minor is instead required to conduct himself only with the care of a minor of his own age, intelligence, and experience in similar circumstances[5] and juries are so instructed.[6] In line with this, a minor's violation of a statute is usually not considered as negligence per se.[7] The logic of the subjective standard

16. See Loeb v. Rasmussen, 822 P.2d 914 (Alaska 1991) (duty to protect minor from her own drinking); McMahon v. New York, N.H. & H.R. Co., 136 Conn. 372, 71 A.2d 557 (1950); § 200.

§ 124

1. Mastland, Inc. v. Evans Furniture, Inc., 498 N.W.2d 682 (Iowa 1993); Thompson v. Wooten, 650 S.W.2d 499 (Tex.App. 1983); Price v. Kitsap Transit, 125 Wash.2d 456, 886 P.2d 556 (1994). See Oscar Gray, The Standard of Care for Children Revisited, 45 Mo. L. Rev. 597 (1980). Georgia, by construction of a statute, has immunized all children under the age of 13 years. Horton v. Hinely, 261 Ga. 863, 413 S.E.2d 199 (1992) (two nine-year-olds poured gasoline on a seven-year-old and set him afire, no liability).

2. § 895I. As to intentional torts, see § 25. Children may usually disaffirm their contracts; so far as tort liability is dependent upon such a contract, liability may at times be inappropriate.

3. § 127, below.

4. There are occasional lapses in which courts may speak of the "average" child or the like. See Fire Insurance Exchange v. Diehl, 206 Mich.App. 108, 520 N.W.2d 675 (1994). It is improbable that these casual statements are intended to alter the usual rule.

5. With minor variations in language, there are many cases. First National Bank of Arizona v. Dupree, 136 Ariz. 296, 665 P.2d 1018 (App. 1983); Lehmuth v. Long Beach Unified School Dist., 53 Cal.2d 544, 348 P.2d 887, 2 Cal.Rptr. 279 (1960). See Restatement § 283A.

6. Frazier v. Norton, 334 N.W.2d 865 (S.D.1983); Bauman v. Crawford, 104 Wash.2d 241, 704 P.2d 1181 (1985). More specific instructions about the child's particular disabilities may not be required if those disabilities are fairly encompassed with the general "age, intelligence, experience" instruction. See Mathis v. Massachusetts Elec. Co., 409 Mass. 256, 565 N.E.2d 1180 (1991) (not necessary to instruct on child's hyperactivity and learning disability, seemingly because the general child standard adequately encompassed the specific disabilities).

7. Alley v. Siepman, 87 S.D. 670, 214 N.W.2d 7 (1974); but cf. Llewellyn v. M & S

is that if a minor has limited mental capacity, he is held only to the care that could be expected of a person with such limited capacity,[8] even though an adult of limited mental capacity is held to the reasonable person standard.[9]

Contributory negligence. Most of the cases articulating the subjective child standard are concerned with the contributory negligence of the child plaintiff. However, negligence of a defendant and contributory negligence of a plaintiff are normally judged under the same standard.[10] So children as defendants may be held liable for negligence in failing to use their own capacity.[11] As plaintiffs, they may have their damages award reduced for the same reason, except when the defendant is under a duty to protect the child from his own immaturity or fault.[12]

Settings for the rule. Although children may be held to the adult standard in the operation of motor vehicles,[13] the child standard is readily invoked to protect children against legal responsibility for their acts in the course of ordinary childhood games[14] and common childhood activities like bicycle riding[15] or dashing for the ice cream truck.[16] But it also protects children from responsibility for injuries resulting from activities that are in no way innocent, such as playing with fire.[17]

Standard objective in form, subjective in fact. The standard is cast in an objective form, referring as it does to some other, hypothetical, child. However, the standard is subjective in that it ultimately refers back to the individual child himself. He is to act as a person with all of his own

Transp., Inc., 1999 WL 452094 (Wis.App. 1999) (instruction that statute against pedestrian darting into street "included" child 7 ½ years old was correct).

8. Sherry v. Asing, 56 Haw. 135, 531 P.2d 648 (1975); Harris v. Indiana General Service Co., 206 Ind. 351, 189 N.E. 410 (1934) (18–year-old allegedly with mental age of 6).

9. § 120 supra.

10. See Camerlinck v. Thomas, 209 Neb. 843, 312 N.W.2d 260, 27 A.L.R.4th 1 (1981); Daniels v. Evans, 107 N.H. 407, 224 A.2d 63 (1966); Charbonneau v. MacRury, 84 N.H. 501, 153 A. 457, 73 A.L.R. 1266 (1931); Goss v. Allen, 70 N.J. 442, 360 A.2d 388 (1976); Standard v. Shine, 278 S.C. 337, 295 S.E.2d 786 (1982).

11. See e.g., McGregor v. Marini, 256 So.2d 542 (Fla.App.1972) (third-grade boys playing with matches in empty house caused a fire, liability potential if capacity is proven); Camerlinck v. Thomas, 209 Neb. 843, 312 N.W.2d 260, 27 A.L.R.4th 1 (1981) (6–year-old boy); Deliso v. Cangialosi, 117 Misc.2d 105, 457 N.Y.S.2d 396 (1982) (11–year-old); cf. Dorais v. Paquin, 113 N.H. 187, 304 A.2d 369 (1973) (no child-standard instruction required where evidence showed adult capacity).

12. Boyer v. Johnson, 360 So.2d 1164 (La.1978); cf. Bexiga v. Havir. Mfg. Corp., 60 N.J. 402, 290 A.2d 281 (1972) (duty to protect machinery operator from negligence in getting hand hurt in machinery). See § 200.

13. § 127 below.

14. First National Bank of Arizona v. Dupree, 136 Ariz. 296, 665 P.2d 1018 (App. 1983); Hoyt v. Rosenberg, 80 Cal.App.2d 500, 182 P.2d 234, 238, 173 A.LR. 883 (1947).

15. Roberts v. Fisher, 169 Colo. 288, 455 P.2d 871 (1969); King v. Casad, 122 Ill.App.3d 566, 78 Ill.Dec. 101, 461 N.E.2d 685 (1984). Contra: Tauranga Electric–Power Board v. Karora Kohu, [1939] N.Z.L.R. 1040 (C.A.) (a 17–year-old is held to an adult standard when riding a bicycle in violation of a traffic regulation).

16. Neal v. Shiels, Inc., 166 Conn. 3, 347 A.2d 102 (1974) (contributory negligence issue).

17. Farm Bureau Insurance Group v. Phillips, 116 Mich.App. 544, 323 N.W.2d 477 (1982). Even a sexual assault by a seven-or eight-year-old was somehow brought under a kind of child standard in Fire Insurance Exchange v. Diehl, 206 Mich.App. 108, 520 N.W.2d 675 (1994).

important qualities, that is, as a person of his age, his experience, and his intelligence. In other words, in spite of its form, the standard is quite literally subjective.

Children with limitations or special abilities. The child with mental limitations is not expected to conduct himself with the care of the ordinary child, but only with the care his mental abilities and experience permit.[18] Conversely, a child whose intelligence and experience give him the capacities of an adult will be expected to act with the same care as a reasonable person.[19] And, since age often correlates with capacity, conduct that is negligent in a 17–year-old may not be negligent in a 14–year-old.[20]

Holding children responsible. In a sense, the child standard is almost no standard at all; it holds the child to whatever he can reasonably do, perhaps best indicated by what he in fact has done. However, if the child appears to have normal capacity for his age, the conduct and capacity of real-life children of the same age may provide evidence as to the child's probable capacity.[21] Courts have thus held in particular cases that evidence was sufficient to make a jury issue on the minor's negligence or contributory negligence.[22] In extreme cases, they have concluded that a minor has violated the standard as a matter of law[23] or that no child-standard instruction need be given to the jury because the facts showed the child to have adult capacities.[24] In the absence of evidence that the child suffers special disabilities or enjoys special talents, perhaps courts and juries are in fact following a kind of reasonable child standard rather than the fully subjective standard that courts articulate.

§ 125. Rationales for the Child Standard

Incapacity. Prosser suggested that the child standard is appropriate because children cannot meet an adult standard.[1] This seems to be no rationale at all. The same could be said of insane persons for whom no similar protection is provided. Prosser also suggested that children differ

18. Sherry v. Asing, 56 Haw. 135, 531 P.2d 648 (1975); see Camerlinck v. Thomas, 209 Neb. 843, 312 N.W.2d 260, 27 A.L.R.4th 1 (1981) (stating that mental limitations as well as special mental powers of a child are taken into account).

19. Dorais v. Paquin, 113 N.H. 187, 304 A.2d 369 (1973).

20. See Dimond v. Kling, 221 N.W.2d 86, 91 (N.D.1974).

21. Oscar Gray, The Standard of Care for Children Revisited, 45 Mo. L. Rev. 597, 602 (1980).

22. Dorrin v. Union Electric Co., 581 S.W.2d 852 (Mo.App.1979); Camerlinck v. Thomas, 209 Neb. 843, 312 N.W.2d 260, 27 A.L.R.4th 1 (1981) (evidence sufficient to permit jury to find a 6–year-old boy negligent in causing the loss of another's child's eye); Deliso v. Cangialosi, 117 Misc.2d 105, 457 N.Y.S.2d 396 (1982) (11–year-old playing Monkey-in-the-Middle and tossing keys, which struck plaintiff's car, negligence found); Kirchoffner v. Quam, 264 N.W.2d 203 (N.D.1978) (15–year-old golfer found negligent under child standard).

23. Harlow v. Connelly, 548 S.W.2d 143 (Ky.App.1977) (17–year-old minor who had been drinking for years, injured while riding with drinking driver was guilty of contributory negligence as a matter of law).

24. Dorais v. Paquin, 113 N.H. 187, 304 A.2d 369 (1973).

§ 125

1. Prosser & Keeton § 32, p. 179.

from adults with limited intelligence because the limitations of children are normal to the whole class.[2] The distinction may be sound, but it does not suggest the subjective standard for children. It suggests instead that the standard should be an objective one based on the reasonable child of a similar age.[3] Perhaps that is in fact how juries interpret the standard.

Protecting children from their contributory negligence. Part of the motivation for adopting a child standard, as distinct from the rationales, no doubt turned on a desire to protect the child from the effects of his own contributory negligence when he was injured by the defendant. Under the original contributory negligence doctrine, a plaintiff guilty of failure to exercise care for her own safety was simply barred, even if the defendant was far more faulty.[4] In the latter half of the 20th century, however, almost all states in the United States had adopted some form of comparative negligence rule under which a plaintiff can recover from the negligent defendant in spite of the plaintiff's own contributory fault, with an appropriate reduction in damages awarded.[5] Perhaps more importantly, however, courts now perceive the possibility that when the plaintiff's minority is known to the defendant, the defendant's duty of reasonable care will require him to protect the plaintiff from his own immaturity so far as that can be done reasonably. This development provides protection for minors without sacrificing either the objective standard or the protection to which others are entitled.[6]

Encouraging child development. What has been called the welfare rationale[7] asserts that children must be permitted to gain experience by acting in the world in order to mature, to learn by doing and to become socialized by interacting with others. The implicit argument of this rationale may be that tort liability would discourage daily activities of children. If that is the argument, it seems unconvincing as a matter of fact to suggest that a child would refuse to play tag because of potential tort liability.[8]

Fairness of protection of child defendants. The welfare rationale may merge with the "fairness" rationale if it is based upon the idea that it would be particularly inappropriate to tax a child defendant with tort liability that might cloud his whole adult life when the child is in fact incapable of taking greater care. It is possible to imagine that a vindictive plaintiff could assert a claim against an impecunious child and renew the judgment until the child is an income-earning adult, then

2. The "normal" statement was made in Charbonneau v. MacRury, 84 N.H. 501, 153 A. 457, 73 A.L.R. 1266 (1931); PROSSER, supra n. 1, treated it as if it were a reason for a special child standard.

3. Prosser & Keeton gave another reason that also suggests an objective child standard, namely that the community has sufficient experience to form a judgment about what could be expected of children. The premise seems correct, but, again, it suggests an objective child standard.

4. § 199 below.

5. § 201 below.

6. Seidelson, Reasonable Expectations and Subjective Standards in Negligence Law: The Minor, The Mentally Impaired, and the Mentally Incompetent, 50 GEO. WASH. L. REV. 17 (1981). See generally § 200 below.

7. Caroline Forell, Reassessing the Negligence Standard of Care for Minors, 15 N.M. L. REV. 485, 498 ff. (1985).

8. Caroline Forell, supra n. 7.

enforce the judgment by periodic garnishments or attachments, perhaps even making it impossible for the defendant to go to college or support a family. But this scenario is improbable for more than one reason. Even if a plaintiff could be found to devote herself to a lifelong effort to enforce such a judgment, it will be hard indeed to find lawyers who will pursue claims that cannot be collected by way of insurance of other existing assets. As a practical matter, then, the child defendant is no more exposed to disastrous liability than anyone else.

Doubt about these rationales had led at least one commentator to suggest a fundamentally different scheme of child liability.[9] In this structure, carefree or childhood activities of children are distinguished from more dangerous ones. The child standard would be used only for the former, presumably, for example, the games of younger children. For activities that are not of the carefree kind needed for child development, that is to say, dangerous activities, an adult standard would apply. Whether the courts move to such an organization of liability remains to be seen, but it is true, as indicated more fully in short order, that they have already imposed an adult standard upon older children for a limited number of "adult activities."[10]

§ 126. Children under the Rule of Sevens

The rule of sevens. A rule sometimes called the Illinois rule and sometimes called the rule of sevens does not formally modify the subjective standard, but it does provide an immunity for some children and some procedural advantages for others. Perhaps as many as ten or twelve states still use the rule of sevens in some form;[1] others have rejected it.[2] In its full fledged version the rule provides:

(a) children under the age of seven years are incapable of negligence;

(b) children from seven to 14 are presumptively incapable of negligence, but the court will permit evidence to show capacity;

9. Caroline Forell, supra n.7.

10. § 127 below.

§ 126

1. Savage Industries, Inc. v. Duke, 598 So.2d 856 (Ala.1992); Savage v. Martin, 256 Ill.App.3d 272, 195 Ill.Dec. 142, 628 N.E.2d 606 (1993); Queen Ins. Co. v. Hammond, 374 Mich. 655, 132 N.W.2d 792 (Mich. 1965); Steele v. Holiday Inns, Inc., 626 So.2d 593 (Miss.1993). Some states accept some parts of the rule but not others. Most of the states using the rule are clustered in the south and in the middlewest.

2. E.g., Patterson v. Cushman, 394 P.2d 657, 6 A.L.R.3d 421 (Alaska 1964) (but adopting a rebuttable presumption that child under seven is incapable of contributory negligence); Grace v. Kumalaa, 47 Haw. 281, 386 P.2d 872 (1963); Peterson v. Taylor, 316 N.W.2d 869 (Iowa 1982); Honeycutt v. City of Wichita, 247 Kan. 250, 796 P.2d 549 (1990); White v. Nicosia, 351 So.2d 234 (La.App.1977); Tenney v. Taylor, 392 A.2d 1092 (Me.1978); Taylor v. Armiger, 277 Md. 638, 358 A.2d 883 (1976) (jury question whether five-year-old was guilty of contributory negligence); Eckhardt v. Hanson, 196 Minn. 270, 264 N.W. 776, 107 A.L.R. 1 (1936); Lester v. Sayles, 850 S.W.2d 858 (Mo.1993); Camerlinck v. Thomas, 209 Neb. 843, 312 N.W.2d 260, 27 A.L.R.4th 1 (1981); Galloway v. McDonalds Restaurants of Nevada, Inc., 102 Nev. 534, 728 P.2d 826 (1986); Hamel v. Crosietier, 109 N.H. 505, 256 A.2d 143 (1969); Standard v. Shine, 278 S.C. 337, 295 S.E.2d 786 (1982). See Shelanie v. National Fireworks Ass'n, 487 S.W.2d 921 (Ky.1972)

(c) over the age of 14 a minor is presumed capable of negligence, but evidence may show to the contrary.

Effect on the standard. Since the standard of care for children is a subjective one in any event, clauses (b) and (c) have a procedural effect by allocating the burdens of showing fault but do not affect the ultimate standard itself.[3] If the child is a defendant, the plaintiff in either case will necessarily be required to show the child's capacity for negligence. Clause (a), is different; it provides an effective immunity for children under seven years of age even if they in fact have the intelligence and experience to conduct themselves more safely in the circumstances. In one sense this can be viewed as a modification of the standard, since the subjective capacity of the child is ignored for children under seven.

Application of the rule of sevens. As already indicated, only about a dozen states apply the clause (a) rule to protect children under seven against all responsibility, but even states that reject such a rule hold that very young children, such as three-or four-year-olds, are incapable of negligence.[4]

So far as clause (b) goes, it normally dictates a jury instruction on the presumption, but in particular cases the court may conclude that the presumption has been overcome so that a child between 7 and 14 years of age can be found negligent on the basis of the usual subjective standard for children.[5] In some cases the court may even conclude that the child was negligent as a matter of law.[6]

§ 127. Holding Children to the Adult Standard

Adult standard of care. Most courts that have considered the question now hold that children engaged in certain activities are held to the adult reasonable person standard of care.[1] Most of the cases have held so when a child was operating a motorized vehicle,[2] boat,[3] plane, snowmobile[4] or machine[5] and most have gone no further.

3. Thus even under the rule of sevens, the court attempts to consider the subjective capacities of any child over seven years of age. See, e.g., Savage Industries, Inc. v. Duke, 598 So.2d 856 (Ala.1992) (stating a rules of sevens and requiring consideration of the child's intelligence and other capacities).

4. See Oscar Gray, The Standard of Care for Children Revisited, 45 Mo. L. Rev. 597 (1980).

5. Smith v. Bradford, 475 So.2d 526 (Ala.1985); Splain v. Hines, 609 So.2d 1234 (Miss.1992).

6. Cates v. Kinnard, 255 Ill.App.3d 952, 193 Ill.Dec. 460, 626 N.E.2d 770 (1994); Norfolk and Portsmouth Belt Line R.R. v. Barker, 221 Va. 924, 275 S.E.2d 613 (1981).

§ 127

1. Connecticut is perhaps the only jurisdiction to reject the adult standard in the last quarter century or so. See Mahon v. Heim, 165 Conn. 251, 332 A.2d 69 (1973); Annotation, Age of minor operator of automobile or other motor-powered vehicle or craft as affecting his primary or contributory negligence, 97 A.L.R.2d 872 (1964).

2. Prichard v. Veterans Cab Co., 63 Cal.2d 727, 408 P.2d 360, 47 Cal.Rptr. 904 (1965); Perricone v. DiBartolo, 14 Ill.App.3d 514, 520, 302 N.E.2d 637 (1973) (gasoline-powered minibike); Thomas v. Settle, 247 Va. 15, 439 S.E.2d 360 (1994). In Ardinger v. Hummell, 982 P.2d 727 (Alaska 1999) a 14-year-old allegedly entrusted her mother's car to a 15-year-old companion. The 15-year-old boy's driving resulted in his death. The 14-year-old was held to an adult standard as to the entrustment itself on the ground that it stemmed from her possession of the car.

3. Dellwo v. Pearson, 259 Minn. 452, 107 N.W.2d 859, 97 A.L.R. 2d 866 (1961).

Perhaps strangely, the adult standard has not been applied in the case of older minors who ride bicycles,[6] although their use is familiar to most children. Nor has it usually been applied to minors who handle firearms,[7] although their use is dangerous. The adult standard has likewise been rejected when it comes to children setting fires.[8] The emphasis on the operation of motorized vehicles leads to some odd results: while a 12–year old is held to an adult standard in operating a motor boat,[9] a 16–year-old is held only to the "child" standard while riding a bicycle or skiing[10] or attempting to climb out the window of a moving truck.[11]

Rejection of a rule of law applying the adult standard, however, does not mean that the child is not negligent in fact or that the jury cannot so find. The subjective child standard may lead to the conclusion that the particular minor had adult capacity as a matter of fact even if such capacity is not attributed to him by a categorical rule of law. So a child riding a bike or playing around dangerous machinery might be found negligent because he had the capacity to act more safely and failed to use it.[12]

Generalizations as to activities covered. The Restatement characterizes those activities as those normally undertaken by only adults, and for which adult qualifications are required.[13] The leading case, *Dellwo v. Pearson*,[14] avoided a general characterization and merely listed the operation of automobiles, airplanes, or powerboats as three activities in which a minor would be held to the the adult standard. Other courts

4. Robinson v. Lindsay, 92 Wash.2d 410, 598 P.2d 392 (1979); Ryan v. Hickson, 55 D.L.R.3d 196 (Ontario H.C. 1974).

5. E.g., Jackson v. McCuiston, 247 Ark. 862, 448 S.W.2d 33 (1969) (tractor propelled bush hog or stalk cutter); Goodfellow v. Coggburn, 98 Idaho 202, 203–04, 560 P.2d 873 (1977) (tractor).

6. E.g., Schomp v. Wilkens, 206 N.J.Super. 95, 501 A.2d 1036 (1985); Bauman v. Crawford, 104 Wash. 2d 241, 704 P.2d 1181 (1985).

7. Purtle v. Shelton, 251 Ark. 519, 474 S.W.2d 123, 47 A.L.R.3d 609 (1971) (deer hunting); LaBarge v. Stewart, 84 N.M. 222, 501 P.2d 666 (N.M.App.1972) (demonstration of Russian roulette by minor who thought he knew where the bullet was); Thomas v. Inman, 282 Or. 279, 578 P.2d 399 (1978). See Caroline Forell, Reassessing the Negligence Standard of Care for Minors, 15 N.M. L. Rev. 485, 487 (1985). But see Goss v. Allen, 70 N.J. 442, 360 A.2d 388 (1976) (dictim that hunting would normally entail an adult standard); Huebner v. Koelfgren, 519 N.W.2d 488 (Minn.App.1994) (14½-year-old boy handling a BB gun, adult standard).

8. Farm Bureau Insurance Group v. Phillips, 116 Mich.App. 544, 323 N.W.2d 477 (1982); Strehlke v. Camenzind, 111 D.L.R. 319 (Q.B.Alberta 1980).

9. Dellwo v. Pearson, 259 Minn. 452, 107 N.W.2d 859, 97 A.L.R.2d 866 (1961).

10. Goss v. Allen, supra n. 7 (17–year-old skiing).

11. Strait v. Crary, 173 Wis.2d 377, 496 N.W.2d 634 (Ct.App.1992) (16–year-old drinking passenger attempting to climb out the window of a moving truck fell out and suffered a broken leg; he was entitled to an instruction on the child standard of care).

12. Cates v. Kinnard, 255 Ill.App.3d 952, 193 Ill.Dec. 460, 626 N.E.2d 770 (1994); Ledbetter v. Ashland Oil & Refining Co., 363 S.W.2d 492 (Tex.Civ.App.1962) .

13. Restatement § 283A.

14. Dellwo v. Pearson, 259 Minn. 452, 107 N.W.2d 859, 97 A.L.R.2d 866 (1961).

have invoked the adult standard when the child engages in "inherently dangerous" activities.[15]

Inadequacy of generalizations. Not surprisingly, the idea of an adult standard for minors has been criticized both because it goes too far[16] and because it does not go far enough to impose responsibility.[17] Certainly the generalizations that attempt to state when an adult standard will be applied appear to be inadequate. The Restatement's "adult activities" test may be inadequate because the Restatement itself recognizes car-driving as one of the activities for which the adult standard is appropriate, although it is hardly one that is normally engaged in only by adults.[18]

The inherent danger test is also of doubtful use. One problem is that inherent danger would surely cover the use of firearms but courts have so far resisted bringing them within the rule. A second problem is that all danger is inherent, which is to say that the term may describe the judge's feelings but does not seem to describe a verifiable attribute of the danger itself. Put differently, inherent danger is like beauty, to be found in the eye of the beholder.

The mere list of activities in *Dellwo v. Pearson*, although perhaps a circumspect beginning, hardly describes for lawyers the other kinds of activities that are indistinguishable in principle. If the list is the thing and not a principle behind it, it will be impossible to know what other activities should be added to the list.

Dubious reasons for limiting use of the adult standard. The absence of a defining principle has led courts to offer a number of dubious reasons for maintaining the child standard in various situations, for example the wholly illogical argument that since motor vehicle cases occur more frequently, the adult standard should be used in those cases but not in cases of other dangerous activities.[19]

Insurance. Courts have probably been moved to apply the adult standard by several different feelings. They are almost certainly influenced by the fact that liability insurance can and usually does cover activities in motorized vehicles, so that if a minor is held liable there is a good chance that he will not find himself saddled with a heavy debt at the beginning of his adult life.

Increased confidence in older minors. Second, courts are undoubtedly more confident than they once were in the ability of young people to drive with competence even if not with restraint or caution, both because of their view of minors and because minors now often have a great deal

15. Robinson v. Lindsay, 92 Wash.2d 410, 598 P.2d 392 (1979).

16. Binchy, The Adult Activities Doctrine in Negligence Law, 11 WM. MITCHELL L. REV. 733 (1985).

17. Caroline Forell, Reassessing the Negligence Standard of Care for Minors, 15 N.M. L. REV. 485 (1985).

18. See Id. at 487.

19. Caroline Forell, supra n. 17, discussing arguments based on frequency of harm, precedent, right to hunt, licensing of cars, and (inevitably) the floodgates argument.

of driving experience. Older minors, at least, can assuredly drive well even if they do not always do so. These two considerations tend to support the application of the adult standard to motor vehicle cases. The second reason may even suggest that older minors should be held to an adult standard in all cases, or at least in many of them.

Reasonable expectations of the other party. (a) There is, however, another reason for extending the adult standard. It is a reason that also suggests limits on the adult standard. The court in *Dellwo v. Pearson* reasoned that while one observing children at play may anticipate risky conduct, those at risk from motor vehicles usually cannot recognize that they are dealing with minors.[20] Their very expectations of an adult level of safety undermine their ability to forestall danger in the case of a minor with whom they do not deal face to face. So when the older minor creates risk to others who cannot identify the actor as a minor or protect themselves, the adult standard seems the most appropriate one for protecting the reasonable expectations of the other party or indeed of the community at large.[21]

(b) The reasonable expectation rationale implies a limitation as well as an expansion of the adult standard. When the plaintiff knows she is dealing with a minor-defendant and has opportunities to protect herself, the reasonable expectation rationale offers no occasion to apply the adult standard.[22] The distinction between minors who are known to the plaintiff and those who are strangers is consistent with some of the results in a number of cases that might otherwise seem puzzling or contradictory. For instance, some firearm cases have refused to hold a minor to an adult standard, but this is entirely explicable on their facts because the victim of injury knew they were dealing with a minor and must have known what quality care they could expect.[23] Similarly, ski advisors working with beginners, some of whom included minors, would know they were dealing with persons of limited experience and control and should not expect the level of safety they would have with more experienced skiers.[24] In such cases, the child standard is justified, not

20. "[O]ne cannot know whether the operator of an approaching automobile, airplane, or powerboat is a minor or an adult, and usually cannot protect himself against youthful imprudence even if warned." Dellwo v. Pearson, 259 Minn. 452, 107 N.W.2d 859, 863, 97 A.L.R. 2d 866 (1961).

21. See Seidelson, Reasonable Expectations and Subjective Standards in Negligence Law: The Minor, The Mentally Impaired, and the Mentally Incompetent, 50 GEO. WASH. L. REV. 17 (1981); ALLEN LINDEN, CANADIAN TORT LAW 132 (5th ed. 1993). Professor Forell supports the use of an adult standard in a different configuration of cases that will often overlap. She supports the child standard only for "carefree" activities but not dangerous ones. See Forell, supra n. 17.

22. Other grounds for applying the adult standard might still apply, of course. Confidence in older minors' ability or a general preference for the adult standard could still dictate its use.

23. See Purtle v. Shelton, 251 Ark. 519, 474 S.W.2d 123, 47 A.L.R.3d 609 (1971) (two teen-aged boys deer hunting together but posted at different stands); LaBarge v. Stewart, 84 N.M. 222, 501 P.2d 666 (N.M.App.1972) (teenager showing another teenager "Russian roulette" but pointing gun at victim instead of himself).

24. This was the situation in Goss v. Allen, 70 N.J. 442, 360 A.2d 388 (1976).

because of the plaintiff's fault, consent, or assumed risk, but because the plaintiff could fairly expect limited safety from the known minor.

Violation of statute. Violation of a specific statutory command is often treated as negligence in itself. In some instances courts hold minors to the statutory standard or command, but in most cases they do not.[25]

TOPIC C. THE EFFECT OF CIRCUMSTANCES. PARTICULARIZING THE ADJUDICATION

SUBTOPIC 1. CONSIDERING SPECIAL CIRCUMSTANCES

§ 128. Effect of Circumstances: Special Danger and Commensurate Care

The invariant standard. In the general negligence case, the defendant's obligation is to use the care of a reasonable person under the circumstances. The standard does not change even if the situation is fraught with danger. The circumstances clause allows for infinite flexibility, but the standard itself, which takes all those circumstances into account, remains the same.[1] Put differently, the standard remains the same in all cases, but the safety-seeking conduct required by the standard will vary with circumstances.[2]

The firearm illustration. Firearm cases illustrate how the reasonable person standard calls for the right amount of care in a dangerous situation. Suppose the defendant is handling a firearm. Instead of saying that because of its deadly potential, the defendant must meet some higher standard of care, courts demand that the defendant act as a reasonable person under the circumstances.[3] One of those circumstances is the fact that weapons can kill and cause grave injury. So the reasonable person handling such a firearm will use a greater *amount* of care than he would use in handling a fish. The *standard* of care is the same in either case, but the amount of attention or energy and the particular physical acts necessary to be reasonable will vary with the circumstance of heightened danger. In short, the meaning of the reasonable person standard is that the defendant must use the care commensurate with the known or reasonably foreseeable danger.[4]

Commensurate care in other cases. The idea of care commensurate with the known or foreseeable danger (and commensurate as well with

25. § 140 below.

§ 128

1. Sansonni v. Jefferson Parish Sch. Board, 344 So.2d 42 (La.App.1977); Stewart v. Motts, 539 Pa. 596, 654 A.2d 535 (Pa. 1995); Restatement § 298 cmt. b.

2. Coburn v. City of Tucson, 143 Ariz. 50, 52, 691 P.2d 1078, 1080 (1984) ("[T]he duty remains constant, while the conduct necessary to fulfill it varies with the circumstances").

3. Purtle v. Shelton, 251 Ark. 519, 474 S.W.2d 123, 47 A.L.R.3d 609 (1971); Tucker v. Lombardo, 47 Cal.2d 457, 303 P.2d 1041 (1956); Mikula v. Duliba, 94 A.D.2d 503, 464 N.Y.S.2d 910 (1983).

4. Anderson v. Nashua Corp., 246 Neb. 420, 519 N.W.2d 275 (1994); Stewart v. Motts, 539 Pa. 596, 654 A.2d 535 (1995).

other circumstances such as the defendant's own safety) applies to all kinds of cases. It most obviously applies in cases of heightened danger, as where the defendant is handling toxic substances[5] or firearms,[6] or supplying gas or electricity.[7] But it is not limited to especially dangerous substances. The driver who sees children playing near the road must exercise care commensurate with the recognized danger that children may dart out into the road,[8] the owner of a dog must act on the possibility that the dog will escape,[9] and the operator of a swimming pool must use care proportioned to the risks that arise when non-swimmers are allowed in the pool.[10]

Expressions requiring extraordinary care. When the defendant confronts heightened danger, it is easier to say that he must exercise the highest care than to explain the full meaning of the reasonable person standard. Perhaps for this reason, courts have often said they required the utmost care, or extraordinary care, or the highest care when it comes to handling a firearm, or supplying gas or electricity.[11] Opinions that speak in such language probably mean only what has already been said, that the defendant must act as a reasonable person under the circumstances and that a reasonable person will normally conduct himself in accordance with the dangers reasonably to be perceived.[12] This is borne out by the fact that when courts actually focus on the issue, they tend to say that the reasonable care standard sufficiently covers the case[13] and that instructions on a higher standard of care would be error.[14]

Most instructions and discussions of commensurate care emphasize the added effort needed when danger is especially prominent, but the underlying point is much broader. Special danger is one, but only one circumstance bearing on the reasonableness of any given risk. The circumstance that safety is especially costly, or that it runs risks to other persons, is also an important circumstance.[15] The relationship of the parties might be another.[16] So the care required is not strictly the care

5. Imperial Distribution Services, Inc. v. Forrest, 741 P.2d 1251 (Colo.1987)

6. Note 3, supra.

7. Schultz v. Consumers Power Co., 443 Mich. 445, 506 N.W.2d 175 (1993).

8. Thomas v. Newman, 262 Ark. 42, 553 S.W.2d 459 (1977); Finch v. Christensen, 84 S.D. 420, 172 N.W.2d 571 (1969); cf. Aycock v. W. & W. R.R., 51 (6 Jones) N.C. 231 (1858) (cattle on or near railroad track, engineer should reduce speed and prepare for an emergency stop).

9. DeRobertis v. Randazzo, 94 N.J. 144, 462 A.2d 1260 (1983).

10. Johnson v. Young Men's Christian Association of Great Falls, 201 Mont. 36, 651 P.2d 1245 (1982).

11. E.g., Lee v. Hartwig, 848 S.W.2d 496 (Mo.App.1992) (firearms); Blueflame Gas, Inc. v. Van Hoose, 679 P.2d 579 (Colo.1984) (propane gas); Valiant Ins. Co. v. City of Lafayette, 574 So.2d 505 (La.App.1991) (electricity).

12. See Tucker v. Lombardo, 47 Cal.2d 457, 303 P.2d 1041 (1956); Mikula v. Duliba, 94 A.D.2d 503, 464 N.Y.S.2d 910 (1983).

13. E.g., Imperial Dist. Services, Inc. v. Forrest, 741 P.2d 1251 (Colo.1987); Laney v. Consumers Power Co., 418 Mich. 180, 341 N.W.2d 106 (1983); Wyrulec Company v. Schutt, 866 P.2d 756 (Wyo.1993).

14. Stewart v. Motts, 539 Pa. 596, 605, 654 A.2d 535, 539 (1995) ("this Commonwealth recognizes only one standard of care in negligence actions involving dangerous instrumentalities—the standard of reasonable care under the circumstances").

15. §§ 144 & 145.

16. The relationship of the parties is often so important that courts have made

commensurate with danger, but care commensurate with all the circumstances.

§ 129. Effect of Circumstances: Emergency and Unavoidable Accident

Emergency as a circumstance to be considered. When an unforeseeable danger arises, when alternative action is possible, and quick judgment is required, courts often refer to the "emergency doctrine."[1] If an actor is confronted with a sudden and unforeseeable emergency not of the actor's own making, the jury is permitted to consider the emergency as one of the circumstances relevant in determining whether the actor behaved reasonably.[2] Put differently, even reasonable persons may conduct themselves in response to an emergency in ways that would not be reasonable if time permitted more thoughtful decision-making.

Although it is convenient to refer to this idea as the emergency doctrine, it is not, properly speaking, a doctrine at all. Neither is it a defense or a lower standard of care. It is instead merely an application of the reasonable person standard, with the emergency as one of the circumstances to be considered in forming a judgment about the actor's fault.[3] Legal issues arise mainly because defendants frequently ask the trial judge to give an instruction specifically authorizing the jury to consider the emergency in determining negligence, or the related instruction that the defendant is not liable for unavoidable accident.[4]

Examples. Although sudden and unforeseen emergencies can arise in almost any context,[5] most of the emergency instruction cases involve motor vehicle collisions. The defendant driver is confronted with a sudden threat from another vehicle—it veers into his lane, or suddenly begins backing toward him, or suddenly blocks the defendant's lane of traffic.[6] Or the defendant encounters unforeseeable ice on the road.[7] There are as many variations as there are unexpected dangers. In each case, the defendant steers his own vehicle to avoid the danger, but in doing so he collides with the plaintiff's car. In retrospect, we can see that a different evasion of the threat would have been more successful.

special rules governing some relationships. Many of these, like the special rules for duties of landowners to licensees, could easily be fit within the reasonable person rule, considering one's status on the land as one circumstances. As to rules for landowners, see Chapter 13.

§ 129

1. See Scott v. Iverson, 120 Or.App. 538, 853 P.2d 302 (1993).

2. Restatement § 296 (1).

3. See e.g., DiCenzo v. Izawa, 68 Haw. 528, 723 P.2d 171 (1986); Weiss v. Bal, 501 N.W.2d 478 (Iowa 1993); Ebach v. Ralston, 510 N.W.2d 604 (N.D.1994).

4. On instructions, see § 131 below.

5. *Aviation*: Bolick v. Sunbird Airlines, Inc., 96 N.C.App. 443, 386 S.E.2d 76 (1989) aff'd per curiam, 327 N.C. 464, 396 S.E.2d 323 (1990); *Medical needs*: Doe v. State, 155 Misc.2d 286, 588 N.Y.S.2d 698 (N.Y.Ct.Cl. 1992). Distinguish medical "emergencies" for which the doctor is prepared by training and foresight. See n. 13.

6. Wilson v. Sibert, 535 P.2d 1034 (Alaska 1975); Thomson v. Littlefield, 319 Ark. 648, 893 S.W.2d 788 (1995); Johnson v. Ray, 206 Ga.App. 262, 424 S.E.2d 892 (1992).

7. E.g., Sullivan v. Fairmont Homes, Inc., 543 N.E.2d 1130 (Ind.App.1989).

Limited time for decision. The emergency doctrine contemplates that the actor has only a limited time for decisions and actions. A few decisions have emphasized that the actor must have time only for instinctive reactions and some have thus focused on whether the actor had more than a very few seconds.[8] But such reasoning seems to miss the point that the emergency doctrine is only an application of the reasonable person rule. The question is not instinct but reasonableness.

Negligence in causing or failing to prevent emergency. Emergency does not, of course, explain the defendant's conduct that occurred before the emergency. The defendant who negligently creates an emergency does not escape liability on the ground that, once the emergency occurred, he behaved reasonably.[9] So the emergency instruction is inappropriate when the emergency is created in whole or part by the defendant's negligence.[10]

Foreseeable dangers. An emergency is by definition unexpected. If a danger is foreseeable and can be prepared for, its arrival is no emergency at all. For example, a driver can anticipate that cars ahead may stop suddenly,[11] and that, near a playground, children may run into the street as the car approaches.[12] If those things happen, the driver cannot claim emergency. He is not necessarily negligent in such a case, but the question of his negligence is to be judged with the expectation that he would be prepared for such events, not with the expectation that he would be unable to cope with them. The same thing is true with a physician or surgeon suddenly confronted with complications in the course of a medical procedure; if they are complications that he should reasonably be prepared for, there is no emergency in the legal sense.[13]

Choosing the lesser of evils. The only logical application of the emergency doctrine occurs when the defendant's conduct would be deemed unreasonable except for the limited reaction time permitted by the emergency. If his conduct would be reasonable even given time to think, he is not negligent, but the emergency doctrine is irrelevant. Suppose that, in an emergency, the defendant is confronted with the option of risking damage to property on the one hand or death of a

8. Cook v. Thomas, 25 Wis.2d 467, 131 N.W.2d 299 (1964) (listing the number of seconds for reaction in numerous cases, ranging from less than two upward to four seconds).

9. Howell v. Cahoon, 236 Va. 3, 372 S.E.2d 363 (1988); Restatement § 296 (2).

10. E.g., Brown v. Spokane County Fire Protection Distr. No. 1, 100 Wash.2d 188, 668 P.2d 571 (1983). Sometimes courts have used a much broader phrase, saying that the doctrine is inapplicable when the peril was brought about by the defendant's own *conduct*, or the emergency was of the defendant's own making. E.g., Mitchell v. Johnson, 641 So.2d 238 (Ala.1994); Tyson v. Brecher, 622 N.Y.S.2d 344, 212 A.D.2d 851 (App.Div. 1995). Read literally, such a statement would imply that the defendant would be deprived of the emergency doctrine if his conduct was an innocent, non-negligent cause of the emergency. That is probably not the courts' intent.

11. E.g., Chodorov v. Eley, 239 Va. 528, 391 S.E.2d 68 (1990).

12. Cf. Weiss v. Bal, 501 N.W.2d 478 (Iowa 1993) (driving through school parking lot after basketball game, appearance of pedestrians crossing the traveled way to reach their cars was not uncommon and not an emergency).

13. Hippocrates Mertsaris v. 73rd Corp., 105 A.D.2d 67, 482 N.Y.S.2d 792 (1984).

human being on the other.[14] If the defendant chooses the lesser of evils—damage to property—he is probably acting exactly as a person would act if given time to think out his actions in advance. In such a case it is right to hold that he is not negligent and not liable, but wrong to suggest that the emergency doctrine has anything to do with the decision.[15]

§ 130. Statutes Creating Emergency Defenses or Immunities

Statutes have created rules for at least two specific situations involving urgent demands that would not necessarily qualify for the emergency doctrine. In addition, these statutes may go far beyond the common law emergency rules by creating immunities, defenses, or lower standards of care.

Emergency vehicles. One kind of statute makes a special provision for emergency vehicles such as ambulances, fire engines, or police vehicles. Some of these statutes speak in one clause of liability for reckless behavior and in another of liability for negligence or failure to exercise due care. Some courts have held that the due care clause dominates or controls.[1] But other courts have chosen to exclude the due care clause, with the result that the operator of an emergency vehicle is not only privileged to disobey traffic rules but also to drive negligently; he is liable only if he goes beyond negligence and acts recklessly.[2] Under these latter decisions, the statutory provisions in effect provide a lower standard of care, and they are thus not at all comparable in their effect to the emergency doctrine at common law.

Medical emergency. The states have adopted statutes providing special protections to doctors and sometimes others who provide care in certain emergencies. The statutes usually eliminate liability for negligence altogether, leaving liability only for reckless or gross derelictions.[3] Sometimes the protection extends only to emergency care outside the doctor's usual place of practice, at a roadside for example. But some statutes have extended the protection to cover in-hospital emergencies as well.[4] Such statutes are discussed in connection with medical malpractice

14. Indiana Consolidated Ins. Co. v. Mathew, 402 N.E.2d 1000 (Ind.App.1980) (defendant chose not to push flaming mower out of garage to avoid fire in the garage, since to do so would create serious risk of injury to himself).

15. See Scott v. Iverson, 120 Or.App. 538, 853 P.2d 302 (1993); Brown v. Spokane County Fire Protection Distr. No. 1, 100 Wash.2d 188, 668 P.2d 571 (1983).

§ 130

1. Torres v. City of Los Angeles, 58 Cal.2d 35, 372 P.2d 906, 22 Cal.Rptr. 866 (1962); Brown v. Spokane County Fire Protection Distr. No. 1, 100 Wash.2d 188, 668 P.2d 571 (1983) (recklessness test applies only to exclude automatic liability that would otherwise result from violation of a traffic law).

2. Saarinen v. Kerr, 84 N.Y.2d 494, 620 N.Y.S.2d 297 644 N.E.2d 988 (1994); Morris v. Leaf, 534 N.W.2d 388 (Iowa 1995); Peak v. Ratliff, 185 W.Va. 548, 408 S.E.2d 300 (1991).

3. E.g., Cal. Bus. & Prof. Code § 1627.5 excuses liability altogether as long as the doctor was in good faith.

4. Gordin v. William Beaumont Hospital, 180 Mich.App. 488, 447 N.W.2d 793 (1989); see Clayton v. Kelly, 183 Ga.App. 45, 357 S.E.2d 865 (1987) (if treatment was not part of doctor's preexisting duty to patient, he could claim immunity of the stat-

liabilities.[5] However, it is important to recognize that these statutes quite literally provide an immunity for negligence, something the emergency doctrine does not do.

§ 131. Jury Instructions on Emergency, Unavoidable Accident, and Commensurate Care

Trial judges normally instruct juries on the legal rules necessary for the jury's appropriate determination of the case. Courts have often given one or more of a quartet of instructions closely related to the standard of care. They have instructed on the emergency doctrine[1] and on its complement, the commensurate care rule.[2] They have also sometimes instructed the jury that the defendant is not liable for an unavoidable accident[3] and that the mere happening of an accident or injury is not itself evidence of negligence.[4]

The legal rules that support these instructions are fully accepted, but many courts are now concerned that the instructions

themselves are both unnecessary and undesirable. A number have consequently held that trial judges should no longer give instructions on emergency,[5] unavoidable accident,[6] or mere happening,[7] or that if such instructions are given, that they should be used rarely or with caution.[8]

The tradition of giving some or all of the instructions probably reflected the view that juries should be channeled as narrowly as

ute even if the emergency and his conduct occurred in the hospital).

5. § 252 below.

§ 131

1. E.g., Nichols v. Elixer Industries, 613 So.2d 1259 (Ala.1993); Young v. Clark, 814 P.2d 364, 10 A.L.R.5th 1074 (Colo. 1991); Harris v. PT Petro Corp., 650 A.2d 1346 (Me.1994). See, *requiring* the instruction, Frito-Lay, Inc. v. Cloud, 569 N.E.2d 983 (Ind. App.1991).

2. Moore v. Rye, 255 Ark. 469, 500 S.W.2d 751 (1973); Clayborne v. Mueller, 266 Md. 30, 291 A.2d 443 (1972); Johnson v. Young Men's Christian Association of Great Falls, 201 Mont. 36, 651 P.2d 1245 (1982). Some states' pattern instructions include at least one on commensurate care. E.g., Cal. BAJI Instruction 3.42 & 6.45 (electricity, railroads).

3. E.g., Athey v. Bingham, 823 P.2d 347 (Okl.1991); Anderson v. Toone, 671 P.2d 170 (Utah 1983).

4. E.g., Stearns v. Plucinski, 482 N.W.2d 496 (Minn.App.1992).

5. Lyons v. Midnight Sun Transportation Services, Inc., 928 P.2d 1202 (Alaska 1996); Wiles v. Webb, 329 Ark. 108, 946 S.W.2d 685 (1997); Knapp v. Stanford, 392 So.2d 196 (Miss.1980); Simonson v. White, 220 Mont. 14, 713 P.2d 983 (1986). See also Fla. Standard Jury Instructions in Civil Cases 4.8 (Comment) Ill. Pattern Jury Instructions (Civ.3d) 12.02.; Mo. Approved Instructions (MAI) 1.04 ("No 'sudden emergency' instructions may be given").

6. Butigan v. Yellow Cab Co., 49 Cal.2d 652, 320 P.2d 500, 65 A.L.R.2d 1 (1958); Tolbert v. Duckworth, 262 Ga. 622, 423 S.E.2d 229, 21 A.L.R.5th 852 (1992).

7. Kennelly v. Burgess, 337 Md. 562, 654 A.2d 1335 (1995). In medical malpractice cases, closely analogous instructions are to the effect that the doctor is not liable for an honest mistake or that he is not a guarantor or insurer of good results. Some courts have rejected such instructions, as in, e.g., Riggins v. Mauriello, D.O., 603 A.2d 827 (Del.1992), but others maintain them, as in, e.g., Nowatske v. Osterloh, 198 Wis.2d 419, 543 N.W.2d 265 (1996).

8. *Emergency:* Myhaver v. Knutson, 189 Ariz. 286, 942 P.2d 445 (1997) (good review of authorities); Merritt v. Simonson, 630 So.2d 428 (Ala.1993); Weiss v. Bal, 501 N.W.2d 478 (Iowa 1993); Gagnon v. Crane, 126 N.H. 781, 498 A.2d 718 (1985). *Unavoidable accident:* Syrcle v. Springer, 239 Ill.App.3d 148, 179 Ill.Dec. 910, 606 N.E.2d 742 (1992); Reinhart v. Young, 906 S.W.2d 471 (Tex.1995).

possible by specific rules. The reluctance some judges now feel about those instructions may reflect the opposite view that juries can work and work fairly with guiding principles and rules.

However that may be, four explicit arguments have been urged against giving the instructions. (1) The instructions are unnecessary because the instruction on the reasonable person standard fully covers the idea. (2) The instructions can confuse the jury by suggesting a different standard or by implying that there is some other issue in the case. (3) The instructions are not neutral; they unduly emphasize the defendant's side of the case. (4) It is difficult for trial judges to write these instructions in a way appropriately worded for the particular case, so they generate added litigation which is acceptable only if the instructions were not adequately covered by the instruction on the reasonable person standard. It has also been suggested that the instruction is somehow incompatible with comparative fault regimes.[9]

The emergency instruction illustrates the argument that the instructions are not necessary. Judges always tell the jury that the defendant is held to the standard of the reasonable person under the circumstances. Emergency, if one exists, is one of the circumstances, and lawyers are free to argue to the jury that the defendant behaved reasonably considering the emergency (or any other circumstance). Perhaps the same thing could be said of the commensurate care instruction.[10] Something similar could be said about the unavoidable accident and mere happening instructions; they merely emphasize particular applications of the general reasonable care standard. Indeed, the unavoidable accident instruction is merely tautological, for if the accident was unavoidable by the exercise of ordinary care, the defendant is simply not negligent.[11]

Of the other arguments, the chief is that the emergency, unavoidable accident, and mere happening instructions unfairly emphasize the defendant's side of the case. The general instruction on negligence tells the jury to consider "the circumstances," but the emergency instruction highlights a single circumstance, the emergency, for special consideration. Since the trial judge could not conceivably instruct on every "circumstance" in the case, the effect is to emphasize one circumstance that favors the defendant. The unavoidable accident and mere happening instructions also run the risk of confusing the jury by suggesting a "a spurious additional issue."[12] They also unduly emphasize the defendant's side of the case in preference to the plaintiff's.

9. Moran v. Atha Trucking, Inc., ___ W.Va. ___, ___ S.E.2d ___, 1997 WL 751960 (1997) (rejecting the suggestion).

10. Purtle v. Shelton, 251 Ark. 519, 474 S.W.2d 123, 47 A.L.R.3d 609 (1971) .

11. But one writer appears to say that at least in the earlier cases, unavoidable accident was one of several "separate dimensions of negligence beyond taking due care." She regards unavoidable accident as a distinct form of analysis, not merely a confusing shorthand. See Barbara Ann White, Risk-utility Analysis and the Learned Hand Formula: A Hand that Helps or a Hand that Hides?, 32 Ariz. L. Rev. 77, 90 (1990).

12. Randle v. Allen, 862 P.2d 1329, 1335 (Utah 1993); see also Butigan, supra n. 6, 49 Cal.2d at 660, 320 P.2d at 505. In a res

The commensurate care instruction is not given so often, but its ideas, too, could be covered adequately in the general instruction on the reasonable person standard.[13]

Subtopic 2. Prescribing Specific Conduct

(a) Common Law Rules

§ 132. Common Law Rules Prescribing Specific Conduct

The objective and universal duty of care, represented by the reasonable person standard, is an ideal. It is not always the reality. Courts depart from the ideal, at least in the way they formulate rules, in two broad groups of cases.

In one group, courts put aside the reasonable person standard. They impose a different and usually lower level of care as the standard for judging liability. For example, courts require recklessness or wanton misconduct before imposing liability in certain kinds of cases, or alternatively say that the defendant owes a duty of slight rather than ordinary care.[1] In these cases, the defendant's failure to behave as a reasonable person is not sufficient for tort liability.[2] The extreme version of this approach

holds that the defendant owes no care at all. Cases in this group usually represent special protections for particular classes of defendants such as landowners, governmental entities and their officers, family members and others. Most of the diverse cases in this large group are considered in later chapters.[3]

In the second group of cases, courts say they adhere to the reasonable person standard of care but they attempt to create specific rules of conduct that they then declare to be the rule the reasonable person will always follow. One result in these cases is that the general standard is left behind and specific rules are put in its place. The insistence that circumstances are important in judging conduct, seen in the emergency or special danger cases, likewise disappears in the face of a specific rule

ipsa loquitur case, the mere happening or negligence-is-not-presumed instruction may be especially confusing as apparently contradicting the res ipsa loquitur inference. See Eaton v. Eaton, 119 N.J. 628, 575 A.2d 858 (1990).

13. See Hampton v. State Highway Com'n, 209 Kan. 565, 498 P.2d 236 (1972) (upholding trial court's refusal to give instruction; the instructions should "not place undue emphasis" on the defendant's arguments).

§ 132

1. Iemma v. Adventure RV Rentals, Inc., 632 N.E.2d 1178 (Ind.App.1994) (bailee who holds goods for benefit of bailor owes only slight care).

2. Some of these cases could be understood to accept the reasonable prudent person standard but to specify particular kinds of conduct that the court considers reasonable as a matter of law. That is not the language of the cases under discussion but it might nevertheless represent some of the underlying feelings.

3. Chapters 14–21.

that brooks no breach. This relatively rigid approach may be less common than once it was, but it still occurs.

Following this practice, courts have said at one time or another that you are always negligent or contributorily negligent if you don't stop, look, and listen when you cross a railroad track,[4] if you cannot stop your car within the range of your headlights or within the assured clear distance ahead,[5] if you cross between intersections without constantly keeping a lookout in all directions,[6] if you are a pedestrian struck by a car while near the curb, although not if you were struck in the middle of the street.[7] The rule that you are presumed to see what was visible[8] and the rule that forgetfulness of a danger is automatically negligence in the absence of some special excuse[9] operate in a similar fashion. But the courts can be very selective in what they condemn in this fashion. Courts do not hold the driver who fails to wear a seat belt to be guilty of contributory negligence as a matter of law.[10]

A rule of law specifying a particular item of conduct is different from an assessment of the evidence in the particular case. Courts frequently assess the evidence to determine whether it warrants submission to the jury. If the evidence is so strong that reasonable people could not differ but would be compelled to find in a particular way on the negligence issue, courts are fully authorized to direct a verdict and thus to exclude any jury decision to the contrary. A rule of law, however, is just the opposite of an assessment of evidence. A rule of law that it is negligent not to stop, look, and listen, forbids any assessment of the evidence to determine whether it was negligent in the particular circumstances or not. A rule of law like this will get the right results in many cases, but it is overinclusive. It will impose liability in some cases when no liability would be imposed under the reasonable person standard.

Many courts now recognize that the problem is usually to assess the evidence in the case, not to make a specific rule of law that covers all cases. So some courts have now said that you are not invariably negligent if you fail to stop, look, and listen,[11] or if you cannot stop your car

4. Baltimore & Ohio R.R. v. Goodman, 275 U.S. 66, 48 S.Ct. 24, 72 L.Ed. 167, 56 A.L.R. 645 (1927).

5. Marshall v. Southern Railway Co., 233 N.C. 38, 62 S.E.2d 489 (1950); see See Annotation, 31 A.L.R.2d 1424 (1953). Statutes may impose the same rule. See Pond v. Leslein, 72 Ohio St.3d 50, 647 N.E.2d 477 (1995).

6. Hennings v. Schufeldt, 222 Neb. 416, 384 N.W.2d 274 (1986).

7. Cf. Bower v. Brannon, 141 W.Va. 435, 90 S.E.2d 342 (1955) (Cases "in which the pedestrian was struck at or near the curb or edge of the street or highway from which he had started to cross to the other side" are almost uniformly cases of contributory negligence as a matter of law).

8. E.g., Carson v. LeBlanc, 245 Va. 135, 427 S.E.2d 189 (1993).

9. Scott v. City of Lynchburg, 241 Va. 64, 399 S.E.2d 809 (1991).

10. In the days before comparative negligence was adopted, most courts made a rule of *no* negligence: failure to wear seat belts was not contributory negligence at all. In the absence of statutory compulsion, some courts continue this approach. See Wright v. Hanley, 182 W.Va. 334, 387 S.E.2d 801 (W.Va. 1989) (where statute did not make wearing a seat belt mandatory).

11. Pokora v. Wabash Railway, 292 U.S. 98, 54 S.Ct. 580, 78 L.Ed. 1149, 91 A.L.R. 1049 (1934), effectively rejecting Baltimore & Ohio R.R. v. Goodman, supra n. 4; Zook v. Norfolk & Western Railway, 268 Ill.

within the range of your headlights,[12] or you are struck as you step off the curb instead of in the middle of the street.[13]

But many cases establishing specific rules of law remain on the books and contemporary decisions continue to assert them.[14] It may be that many of these are really cases in which judges have in fact tried to assess evidence in the particular case but have expressed themselves poorly or have fallen back on the professional habit of presenting their assessment about evidence as if it were a rule of law. In other instances, however, it may be that the generalization into a rule of law represents a real reluctance to let juries make independent evaluations of negligence under the flexible standard of the reasonable person.

(b) Adopting Statutory Rules

§ 133. Effects of Statutes in Tort Law

The term "statute" can include not only the products of state legislatures and Congress, but also ordinances, administrative regulations, and even constitutions. Statutes in this broad sense impact tort law in many ways. They fall initially into two categories. First, some statutes expressly or implicitly address tort law, perhaps by creating a duty or defense or some particular rule of conduct. Second, other statutes do not address tort law at all but instead make rules to be enforced under the criminal law or by administrative regulation.

A statute that addresses tort law is simply enforced by the courts according to its express or implied terms, so long as the statute's provisions are constitutional. On the other hand, when the statute is a criminal statute and says nothing of tort law, courts are not obliged by the statute to consider it at all in tort cases. But, just as important, courts may usually accept the statutory rule of conduct as a judicial rule for tort cases, even though the statute itself does not require it. In other words, courts are free to accept, reject, or modify the rule as applied in tort law, so long as the statute does not state or imply to the contrary.

Because courts are free to adopt or reject some statutory standards but are compelled to apply others, some differences in statutes must be identified as a step in determining the court's appropriate options.

Statutes imposing a duty but not otherwise altering the incidents of a tort claim. One kind of statute imposes a specific duty or a standard of care that would not exist at common law but does not otherwise change the rules for negligence, causation, defenses, and procedures. For instance, statutes may require owners to post a lifeguard at certain

App.3d 157, 205 Ill.Dec. 231, 642 N.E.2d 1348 (1994) (jury question; jury could find it was "not reasonable for a driver not having any indication of an approaching train to stop his truck, get out, and look down the tracks").

12. Chaffin v. Brame, 233 N.C. 377, 64 S.E.2d 276 (1951), effectively rejecting Marshall v. Southern Railway Co., supra n. 5.

13. Sydenstricker v. Vannoy, 151 W.Va. 177, 150 S.E.2d 905 (1966) (clarifying the statement in Bower, supra n. 7, and holding that it is not negligence as a matter of law to be struck by a car near the curb).

14. E.g., Nickell v. Russell, 247 Neb. 112, 525 N.W.2d 203 (1995).

swimming pools, require landowners to cut weeds to enhance visibility at an intersection, or require landlords to equip premises with secure locks as protection against intruders. If a plaintiff is harmed by violation of such a statute, courts think of the plaintiff's case as an ordinary negligence case with the same issues and rules as other negligence cases except that the plaintiff proves negligence by proving violation of the statute. But because it is an ordinary negligence case, the plaintiff must also prove causation and damages, and she will lose if she fails to do so.[1]

Statutes creating a new claim, duty, or defense. A second kind of statute goes further. By express terms or by implication, this kind of statute creates a new claim or cause of action not recognized at common law. Instead of merely adding a specific duty, it creates a set of rules about conduct or about adjudication. The Federal Employers Liability Act (FELA) can be viewed in this light. The FELA creates a federal claim on behalf of railroad workers injured on the job. The statute abolishes the defenses of contributory negligence and assumed risk[2] and is interpreted to impose a liberal view of fault and causation that makes recovery relatively easy.[3] Were there no such statutes, the railroad employees would ordinarily be limited to state tort law claims for workers' compensation payments for on the job injury or would be subject to defenses like contributory negligence and assumed risk. Although FELA cases are still negligence cases in the sense that negligence is an issue, some of the rules of conduct and litigation are different. Many other statutes are like the FELA in providing a new set of rules, even though the case may still fit within the general scheme of negligence law.[4] Even the United States Constitution itself may implicitly create a tort claim.[5]

Statutes limiting a claim or creating defenses. Statutes can restrict as well as expand tort liability. A third kind of statute is like that. It may create new defenses to common law tort claims or enact a lower standard of care for some activities.[6] Statutes can also make procedural demands

§ 133

1. See, e.g., Brock v. Watts Realty Co., Inc., 582 So.2d 438, 43 A.L.R.5th 839 (Ala. 1991) (common law did not recognize a duty of care to protect tenant against intruders, but ordinance created a duty with respect to locks); Haft v. Lone Palm Hotel, 3 Cal.3d 756, 478 P.2d 465, 91 Cal.Rptr. 745 (1970).

2. The Federal Employers Liability Act (FELA) 45 U.S.C.A. § 51.

3. See Kernan v. American Dredging Co., 355 U.S. 426, 78 S.Ct. 394, 2 L.Ed.2d 382 (1958).

4. Some important federal statutes like this include the Jones Act, 46 U.S.C.A. § 688 (some FELA rules applied to injured seafaring employees); Federal Tort Claims Act, 28 U.S.C.A. §§ 2671–2680 (creating rights against government for certain torts); the Emergency Medical Treatment Act, 42 U.S.C.A. § 1395dd (rights to emergency screening and treatment at certain hospitals); various civil rights acts, including 42 U.S.C.A. § 1983 (denial of federal right under of color of law is actionable); 42 U.S.C.A. § 2000e (certain employment discrimination actionable after procedural prerequisites); Americans with Disability Act, 42 U.S.C.A. § 12101 et seq.; Comprehensive Environmental Response, Compensation and Liability Act (CERCLA) (Superfund Act), 42 U. S. C. A. § 9607 et seq. In the states, statutes creating a claim for elder abuse are in this category. See, e.g., WASH. REV. CODE § 74.34.200.

5. Bivens v. Six Unknown Named Agents of Federal Bureau of Narcotics, 403 U.S. 388, 91 S.Ct. 1999, 29 L.Ed.2d 619 (1971) (federal officers can be sued for constitutional violations).

6. Guest statutes, now largely out of fashion and repealed in most states, relieve a host-driver of the duty of ordinary care and make him liable only for gross negli-

on one of the parties, often the plaintiff, that did not exist at common law or under the general rules of procedure. Some even enact immunities or virtual immunities from tort liability. The Constitution itself may be interpreted to create immunities from, or limits on the remedies for tort claims,[7] as may some treaties with foreign countries.[8]

Statutes disclaiming tort law effects. Legislatures sometimes provide that statutory rules or standards are *not* to be given any tort law effects but are to be enforced solely by criminal law or administrative sanctions. The federal and state Occupational Safety and Health Acts (OSHA) and the accompanying regulations provide detailed rules for safety conditions in many industries.[9] But the statute may be read to say that it is to be enforced by regulatory agencies, not by tort law.[10] Since the legislature is supreme so long as it acts within the scope of its constitutional powers, courts are obliged to follow the statutory directive. They are not free to adopt the safety regulations as tort rules or standards if the legislature has said that the safety regulations are not to affect tort law.[11]

Implied disclaimer of tort effects. When a statute provides one remedy, such as a criminal sanction or an administrative remedy, but says nothing about tort remedies, it is often possible to construe the statute as implicitly excluding any tort-law effects.[12] If a statute imposes a new affirmative duty, unfamiliar in tort law, the absence of a provision for tort liability is likely to lead the courts to ignore the statute for tort law purposes, either because they feel compelled by the statute's negative implications or because they think it wiser not to adopt the statute's rules. For example, all states require persons to report reasonably

gence or wanton misconduct. "Good Samaritan" statutes relieve medical doctors and sometimes others of the ordinary care standard when they give treatment in various emergency situations, and recreational use statutes relieve landowners of ordinary care standards towards recreational users of the land. Sometimes statutes are treated as expressing the maximum duty of the defendant, with the effect that the defendant's duty is limited. The same occurs with "preemption" under federal law.

7. Nixon v. Fitzgerald, 457 U.S. 731, 102 S.Ct. 2690, 73 L.Ed.2d 349 (1982).

8. The Warsaw Convention 49 STAT. 3000 (1934); 137 L.N.T.S. 11, No. 3145, printed in note following 49 USCA § 40105 limits damages recoverable for death in international air flights. The low figure it set has been revised upward by agreement of air carriers known as the Montreal Agreement.

9. 29 U.S.C.A. § 651 et seq.

10. The exact provision in the federal statute: "Nothing in this chapter shall be construed to supersede or in any manner affect any workmen's compensation law or to enlarge or diminish or affect in any other manner the common law or statutory rights, duties, or liabilities of employers and employees under any law with respect to injuries, diseases, or death of employees arising out of, or in the course of, employment." 29 U.S.C.A. § 653(b)(4).

11. The statute says in § 653(b)(4) that it is not to "affect" common law rights or liabilities, and accordingly, a number of courts have refused to treat violation of the statute as negligence. Ries v. National Railroad Passenger Corporation, 960 F.2d 1156 (3d Cir.1992); Canape v. Petersen, 897 P.2d 762 (Colo.1995); Hernandez v. Martin Chevrolet, Inc., 72 Ohio St.3d 302, 649 N.E.2d 1215 (1995). Contra, Pratico v. Portland Terminal Co., 783 F.2d 255 (1st Cir. 1985) (reading legislative history to mean that Congress merely intended to preserve workers' compensation remedy). Some have striven for a middle ground, treating violation of the statute as evidence of negligence, but not negligence in itself. Wendland v. Ridgefield Construction Services, Inc., 184 Conn. 173, 439 A.2d 954 (1981). Some of the judicial discussions fail to recognize the statutory limitation.

12. See THOMAS COOLEY, THE LAW OF TORTS 653 (1879).

suspected child abuse. But these statutes do not ordinarily mention tort liability for failure to report. The affirmative duty to protect a child from someone else does not fit the pattern of traditional tort law, so it is no surprise that some courts do not treat violation of the reporting statute as a tort.[13]

Preemptive statutes. A special case of statutes excluding tort law effects is the case of federal preemption. A federal statute may set rules of conduct and create a federal remedy, administrative or otherwise, and at the same time preempt or exclude ordinary state tort law. For instance, federal statutes can specify the warnings to be placed upon poisons or dangerous substances like tobacco products. At the same time, the federal statute may preempt tort law so that if the defendant who sells poisons prints the warning prescribed by the federal statute, state courts, even though they believe the warning is dangerously inadequate, cannot impose tort liability.[14]

The OSHA statute merely provides that its standards have no application to tort claims, but it leaves courts free to administer the ordinary reasonable care standard in tort cases. In contrast, federal preemption can displace tort law altogether. Federal preemption may leave the plaintiff a federal remedy, if one is provided by the federal statute. If one is not provided by the federal statute, it may leave the plaintiff no remedy at all.

Statutes not directed at tort law. Many, many statutes prescribe specific conduct and impose a criminal penalty for violation without mention of tort-law consequences. Courts could interpret such statutes as excluding tort law effects by implication. The provision of one remedy without mention of another may suggest that the remedy mentioned, criminal punishment in this instance, is the only remedy to be administered. In contemporary law, however, courts have seldom taken this route with criminal statutes that prohibit some specific, dangerous or antisocial act. Instead they have adopted the statutory rule, imported it into the common law, and applied it in tort cases as a specific rule of conduct.

Statutes expressly or implicitly creating a tort claim are quite different from the statutes that only impose a criminal remedy and are merely adopted by the courts. First, as a matter of process, the rights and liabilities under the statutes creating a new claim are determined by the statute itself. Second, the statutory claim may not be one for negligence at all; it may be based on intentional wrongdoing or on strict liability, that is, on a non-negligent violation of the statute. Third, the

13. Freehauf v. School Board of Seminole County, 623 So.2d 761 (Fla.App.1993), dism'd, 629 So.2d 132 (1993); Cechman v. Travis, 202 Ga.App. 255, 414 S.E.2d 282 (1991). A little authority supports the potential for liability for failure to report as mandated. See Landeros v. Flood, 17 Cal.3d 399, 131 Cal.Rptr. 69, 551 P.2d 389 (1976).

14. See CSX Transportation, Inc. v. Easterwood, 507 U.S. 658, 113 S.Ct. 1732, 123 L.Ed.2d 387 (1993); Cipollone v. Liggett Group, Inc., 505 U.S. 504, 112 S.Ct. 2608, 120 L.Ed.2d 407 (1992); Pilot Life Ins. Co. v. Dedeaux, 481 U.S. 41, 107 S.Ct. 1549, 95 L.Ed.2d 39 (1987).

claim may not carry the procedural and other incidents of the negligence case; it may impose different procedures, different concepts, and different defenses.

When a criminal law or regulatory statute is adopted by the courts, on the other hand, the court adopts the statute's rule even though the statute made no provision, not even an implied one, for civil liability. As a matter of process, the court has the legal power to adopt or reject the statutory standard, a power it does not have if the statute creates a new cause of action. In federal courts, the difference goes one step further, because, with limited exceptions, there is no federal common law. Outside of general maritime law, federal law is not judge-made law in the way common law is. Hence, federal courts do not develop tort law by adopting or adapting statutes. At least in theory, they must follow the statutory command without either diminishing or enlarging it.

On the second and third counts, the court adopting a criminal law standard for tort cases fits the statutory rule into the ordinary negligence case; it does not create or import special procedures or new standards other than the rule itself.

§ 134. General Rules for Applying Statutes as Tort Standards

Although some statutes expressly create a tort claim or establish some special rule for tort cases, a very large number of statutes provide only a criminal penalty or some form of administrative enforcement. These statutes prescribe nothing at all about tort law, so they can be identified here as nonprescriptive statutes. Although such statutes prescribe no tort-law effects at all, courts are usually free nonetheless to adopt the standards or rules of conduct from such statutes and to apply them to tort cases. For instance, a statute may forbid driving at a speed in excess of a posted limit and may impose a criminal penalty only; but courts are nevertheless likely to use that speed limit as a standard for judging negligence.

This section explains the effect of the nonprescriptive statutory standard when courts adopt it as a standard or as a rule of conduct. Sections that follow state the rules limiting the use of such statutes and excusing violations.

(1) *Initial effect of statute violation. (a) Negligence per se.* When courts apply the standard or rule of conduct from a nonprescriptive statute, the majority do so under the rule of negligence per se. That rule holds that an adult's violation of statute is negligence in itself if it causes harm of the kind the statute was intended to avoid and to a person within the class of persons the statute was intended to protect. In the absence of a valid excuse, violation conclusively shows negligence.[1]

§ 134

1. Rong Yao Zhou v. Jennifer Mall Restaurant, Inc., 534 A.2d 1268 (D.C.1987); Jones v. Blair, 387 N.W.2d 349 (Iowa 1986). The rules may be codified in some statutes. See West's Ann. Cal. Evid. Code § 669.

Violation of statute equally proves the plaintiff's contributory negligence in appropriate cases.[2]

Because certain limited excuses are recognized, some courts describe the rule as a presumption of negligence rule[3] or a prima facie negligence rule[4] to emphasize that the finding of negligence can be rebutted under limited circumstances. Some such courts expressly reject the negligence per se terminology, but they apply essentially the same rule.[5] Although it is possible that a rule described in terms of prima facie or presumptive negligence is a slight variant on the per se rule, the differences, if any, are minor indeed.[6]

The negligence per se rule may apply to any statutory instrument, including ordinances[7] and administrative regulations,[8] although some states treat violation of ordinances and local regulations as merely some evidence of negligence.[9]

(b) *Evidence of negligence*. A few courts reject the per se rule and treat violation as merely some evidence of negligence[10] or as "guidelines

2. E.g., Donaldson v. Indianapolis Public Transportation Corp., 632 N.E.2d 1167 (Ind.App.1994); Adams v. Mills, 312 N.C. 181, 322 S.E.2d 164 (1984).

3. Cal. Evid. Code § 669 specifies that certain statutory violations create a presumption of negligence, rebuttable by a showing, among other things, that "The person violating the statute, ordinance, or regulation did what might reasonably be expected of a person of ordinary prudence, acting under similar circumstances, who desired to comply with the law." Zeni v. Anderson, 397 Mich. 117, 243 N.W.2d 270 (1976) speaks of a presumption, also rebuttable by excuses of the kind recognized in the Restatement.

4. See, e.g., Waugh v. Traxler, 186 W.Va. 355, 412 S.E.2d 756 (1991).

5. Courts that reject the terminology of per se seem to have in mind (a) that excuses are available so that the defendant might not ultimately be liable, and (b) that *negligence* per se is not *liability* per se, because the statute violator is not liable unless his act is a cause and a legal cause of the harm done. Both of these things are true under the negligence per se rule as well, however.

6. For instance, some courts might mean that the defendant could rebut the finding of negligence simply by persuading the jury that his conduct was reasonable in spite of the violation. This would be more favorable to the defendant than the Restatement's rule that rebuts the negligence finding only when specific excuses are presented. See Kalata v. Anheuser-Busch Companies, Inc., 144 Ill.2d 425, 581 N.E.2d 656, 163 Ill.Dec. 502 (1991) ("A violation of a statute or ordinance designed to protect human life or property is prima facie evidence of negligence.... The violation does not constitute negligence per se, however, and therefore the defendant may prevail by showing that he acted reasonably under the circumstances").

7. E.g., Fresno Traction Co. v. Atchison, T. & S. F. Ry., 175 Cal. 358, 165 P. 1013 (1917); Nettleton v. Thompson, 117 Idaho 308, 787 P.2d 294 (1990).

8. Davis v. Marathon Oil Co., 64 Ill.2d 380, 356 N.E.2d 93, 1 Ill.Dec. 93 (1976). Internal policies or rules of a private company may be admissible (for example, to show foreseeability of harm, feasibility of dealing with a risk, or reliance by the plaintiff); but they do not set the standard of care. Mayo v. Publix Super Markets, Inc., 686 So.2d 801 (Fla.App.1997). Internal rules or policies of a governmental agency, such as a police department, may count as "regulations" setting the standard. See Peterson v. City of Long Beach, 24 Cal.3d 238, 155 Cal.Rptr. 360, 594 P.2d 477 (1979); Galapo v. City of New York, 219 A.D.2d 581, 631 N.Y.S.2d 366 (1995); contra, Clark v. District of Columbia,708 A.2d 632 (D.C. 1997). (suicide prevention plan was internal, unpublished policy violation of which was admissible in evidence but insufficient standing alone to show negligence). California now provides that an internal policy or rule is considered as a statute only if it is promulgated as an ordinance or as a formal regulation. Cal. Evid. Code § 669.1.

9. E.g., Griglione v. Martin, 525 N.W.2d 810 (Iowa 1994).

10. Bussell v. Missouri Pacific R.R., 237 Ark. 812, 376 S.W.2d 545 (1964); Ridley v.

for civil liability."[11] This rule permits the jury to conclude that a statute violator behaved in a reasonable way even if he presents no particular excuse.

A number of courts that normally use the negligence per se rule nevertheless apply the evidence of negligence rule selectively. They may use the evidence of negligence rule when they believe the per se rule is too inflexible or too demanding[12] and when they believe that the statute is antagonistic to the per se rule but not antagonistic to the evidence rule.[13] When the per se rule is rejected because the harm suffered is not the kind at which the statute was aimed or the plaintiff is not within the class to be protected, courts may nevertheless treat violation of the statute as some evidence of negligence.[14]

The evidence of negligence rule is flexible and easy to administer. It does not generate litigation over excuses or over questions about what risks and harms were covered by the statute. The per se rule is often justified in part on the ground that it creates more certainty,[15] but it is far from clear that it creates as much certainty as it creates litigation and litigation strategy. If it does create more certainty, it creates it at the price of risking strict liability. So the evidence of negligence rule is a fair contender for support.

(2) Applications of negligence per se. The negligence per se rule is commonly applied in motor vehicle cases. Defendants who violate rules of the road, by speeding or making improper turns, for example, are

Safety Kleen Corp., 693 So.2d 934 (Fla. 1996); Dongo v. Banks, 448 A.2d 885 (Me. 1982); Guinan v. Famous Players–Lasky Corporation, 267 Mass. 501, 167 N.E. 235 (1929); Jones v. Goeden, 232 Neb. 177, 440 N.W.2d 199 (1989); Eaton v. Eaton, 119 N.J. 628, 575 A.2d 858 (1990); Gronneberg v. Hoffart, 466 N.W.2d 809 (N.D.1991). Statutes may prescribe this rule. WASH. REV. CODE § 5.40.050. Cf. Natural Gas Processing Co. v. Hull, 886 P.2d 1181 (Wyo.1994) (evidence of negligence, not specifying whether that is to be the general approach or not).

11. Galloway v. State, 654 So.2d 1345 (La.1995).

12. Ferrell v. Baxter, 484 P.2d 250 (Alaska 1971).

13. Wendland v. Ridgefield Construction Services, Inc., 184 Conn. 173, 439 A.2d 954 (1981) (OSHA statute violation). Legislation sometimes provides that violation of a particular statutes has no effect or at most is evidence of negligence. E.g., CAL. VEHICLE CODE § 27315; N.C. GEN. STAT. § 20–141.

14. Koll v. Manatt's Transportation Co., 253 N.W.2d 265 (Iowa 1977); Manchack v. Willamette Industries, Inc., 621 So.2d 649 (La.App.1993); contra, DiCaprio v. New York Central R.R., 231 N.Y. 94, 131 N.E. 746, 16 A.L.R. 940 (1921) (statute required railroad to fence out cattle, but it was not intended to protect children who might wander onto the track; violation "was [not] the basis for any claim of negligence").

15. A different attempt at justification came from Cardozo. In a line that has forestalled much thought about the subject, he asserted that the evidence of negligence rule could not be used because "the jury has no dispensing power." Martin v. Herzog, 228 N.Y. 164, 126 N.E. 814 (1920). The term suggested the power once held by English monarchs to dispense with or suspend statutes. But it begged the question. In saying nothing of tort law did the statute nevertheless impose a tort rule and if so did it impose the per se rather than the evidence rule? Another torts great argued that the per se rule was needed to control the rogue jury. Clarence Morris, The Relation of Criminal Statutes to Tort Liability, 46 HARV. L. REV. 453, 461 (1933) . Why rogue juries are more a problem when liability is based on statute is not clear. In any event, the judge's usual power to direct verdicts and to grant new trials is ample to control juries. It may also be a mistake to base a rule of law for everyone on the the rare worst-case scenario rather than on the usual well-tried case.

negligent as a matter of law and the jury is not permitted to say otherwise.[16] The rule applies equally to the adult plaintiff so that her violation counts as contributory fault per se.[17]

Although courts refuse to adopt the statutory standard in some cases, and especially when the statute imposes certain affirmative obligations,[18] the negligence per se rule is applied to a wide variety of statutory violations. A statute requires a lifeguard at a pool, lights on a ship, buildings constructed to specific requirements, safety devices for protection of construction workers, smoke detectors for the protection of tenants; violation is negligence per se.[19] Statutes regulating sales or dispensation of dangerous items like guns[20] and alcohol[21] may also sometimes furnish grounds for a negligence claim by persons injured as a result of the sale. Even statutes regulating economic relations of the parties, such as those requiring disclosure of specific information, have been held to be the basis of a negligence per se claim.[22]

(3) *Excused violations.* A violation of statute can be excused on any terms the court sees fit to adopt, but in most instances the excuses available are quite limited and closely similar to the claim that compliance was practically impossible or that the defendant did everything reasonably possible in trying to comply with the law. The excuses are discussed in a separate section.

§ 135. Adopting or Rejecting the Statutory Standard

Many statutes prescribe no tort law effects at all. A highway speed limit statute usually prescribes a criminal penalty, but as to tort liability it prescribes nothing. Early tort thinkers recognized a problem with nonprescriptive statutes like this; the statute's silence about tort-law effects might imply that the legislature intended a criminal punishment and nothing more.[1] Yet courts in fact very often say that violation of

16. E.g., Thomas v. Commerford, 168 Conn. 64, 357 A.2d 476 (1975) (unsignalled turn); Martin v. Herzog, 228 N.Y. 164, 126 N.E. 814 (1920) (lights).

17. E.g., Duphily v. Delaware Electric Cooperative, Inc., 662 A.2d 821 (Del.1995); Thomas v. Commerford, 168 Conn. 64, 357 A.2d 476 (1975). As to violation of statute by minors, see § 140.

18. Courts have been most reluctant to impose a duty upon the defendant to protect the plaintiff from some third person. This reluctance carries over to cases in which statutes impose such a duty.

19. Kernan v. American Dredging Co., 355 U.S. 426, 78 S.Ct. 394, 2 L.Ed.2d 382 (1958) (ship lights) ; Haft v. Lone Palm Hotel, 3 Cal.3d 756, 478 P.2d 465, 91 Cal. Rptr. 745 (1970) (lifeguard); Alderman's Inc. v. Shanks, 536 N.W.2d 4 (Minn.1995) (building, fire door); Barnaby v. A. & C. Properties, 188 A.D.2d 958, 592 N.Y.S.2d 98 (1992) (workers, scaffolding act); Reed v. Phillips, 192 W.Va. 392, 452 S.E.2d 708 (1994).

20. E.g., Coker v. Wal–Mart Stores, Inc., 642 So.2d 774 (Fla.App.1994).

21. E.g., Loeb v. Rasmussen, 822 P.2d 914 (Alaska 1991). Some courts traditionally reject the normal negligence per se rule when it comes to provision of alcohol, effectively immunizing sellers who provide alcohol to intoxicated persons and minors. E.g., Mills v. City of Overland Park, 251 Kan. 434, 837 P.2d 370 (1992). See § 332.

22. Alaface v. National Investment Co., 181 Ariz. 586, 892 P.2d 1375 (Ct.App. 1994).

§ 135

1. See THOMAS COOLEY, THE LAW OF TORTS 653 (1879) ("Where the statute imposes a new duty, where none existed before, and gives a specific remedy for its violation, the

such a statute automatically proves negligence on the part of the violator, subject only to a limited range of excuses or to none at all.

It is not clear how courts came to accept this rule. The history of the negligence per se rule seems not to have been written, but it seems clear that it grew up without careful explicit consideration.[2] Commentators dreamed up some fanciful explanations for the rule. One argument was that the legislature intended to provide for tort liability but forgot to do so. Another was that reasonable people always obey statutes.[3]

These arguments probably convince no one who does not already wish to be convinced. Although there are occasional statutes that genuinely imply that a tort claim will lie for their violation,[4] the argument that the legislature invariably forgets what it was aiming to do, while perhaps tempting to a satirist of the political process, seems to provide no basis for a responsible development of rules by the judiciary.

Contemporary thought has cut through the argument that courts must apply nonprescriptive statutes in tort cases. So far as there is now any recognized theory at all, it is that the statute itself has no tort law effects. Rather, (unless the statute itself provides otherwise) the courts are free to create tort law rules and to adopt and import rules from statutes about other matters if they wish to do so. The statutory rule, as the Wisconsin Court said, is a "judicial transplant."[5] The Restatement advances this adoption theory and a number of courts have supported it

presumption is that this remedy was meant to be exclusive, and the party complaining of a breach is confined to it").

2. The problem runs back as far as the 14th century with the enactment of a statute on repossession of land by forcible entry. 5 Richard II c. 7. Courts have struggled over the years with the question whether that statute created a tort claim and if so what it looked like. See § 80. As late as 1860 the New York Court of Appeals was rejecting the idea that a criminal statute would have tort law effect. Brown v. Buffalo & State Line R.R., 22 N.Y. 191 (1860). Some 19th century statutes did provide expressly for tort liability and some courts may have moved unthinkingly from those statutes to the now-common statutes that provide nothing of the sort. Another line of 19th century cases involved an element of social reform. Important statutes were addressed to nonreciprocal risks and reflected legislative efforts to protect people who neither inflicted risks upon others nor had an opportunity to protect themselves. Early negligence per se cases thus involved railroads, purveyors of dangerously bad food, and unlabeled poisons, and employers of child labor. This background suggests that the per se rule has been much expanded beyond its origins.

3. See Thayer, Public Wrong and Private Action, 27 Harv. L. Rev. 317 (1913); 3 Harper, James and Gray § 3.17; Prosser & Keeton § 36. Note that the legislature might well have been willing to impose criminal liability, especially for a limited fine typical in many traffic ordinances, but not unlimited civil liability; and that it might have been willing to impose liability when guilt is established beyond a reasonable doubt as required in some criminal cases, but not upon merely a preponderance of evidence, the standard in civil cases.

4. Where the statute speaks of amounts recoverable, or specifically refers to tort rules, the implication seems reasonably clear. See, respectively, Key Tronic Corp. v. United States, 511 U.S. 809, 114 S.Ct. 1960, 128 L.Ed.2d 797 (1994); Ross v. Schooley, 257 Fed. 290 (7th Cir.1919). Federal statutes differ from state statutes in that there is no federal common law of tort, only law emanating from the Constitution and the federal statutes. Conceivably, one could more readily find that Congress implicitly created a tort claim in such a system than in the ordinary state-law system.

5. Olson v. Ratzel, 89 Wis.2d 227, 278 N.W.2d 238 (Ct.App.1979).

explicitly[6] or by clear implication.[7] Others simply reflect the theory without mentioning it by applying some statutes in tort cases and not applying others.

Several groups of nonprescriptive statutes are often regarded as unsuitable for use in tort cases. First, courts usually refuse to adopt statutory standards that were not aimed at protecting groups that included the plaintiff and those not aimed at protecting against harms of the kind suffered by the plaintiff.[8] Second, courts often excuse the violation of statutes when judges are convinced that violation does not necessarily bespeak negligence. They routinely refuse to apply the statutory standard to children, for example.[9] Third, courts reject statutes on the somewhat opaque ground that the statute was intended to protect the public without protecting any individual.[10] Each of these grounds is discussed in separate sections.

Courts may also reject nonprescriptive statutes for use in tort cases when the statute is outmoded or absurd.[11] Purely abstract statutes that require reasonableness or the like but that do not specify the particular conduct required can likewise be discarded,[12] although some fairly abstract statutes are sometimes given the negligence per se effect.[13] Many[14] but not all[15] cases discard licensing statutes and some analogues[16] as well.

6. Rong Yao Zhou v. Jennifer Mall Restaurant, Inc., 534 A.2d 1268 (D.C.1987); Ferrell v. Baxter, 484 P.2d 250 (Alaska 1971); Clinkscales v. Carver, 22 Cal.2d 72, 136 P.2d 777 (1943); Mansfield v. Circle K Corp., 877 P.2d 1130 (Okla.1994); Stachniewicz v. Mar–Cam Corp., 259 Or. 583, 488 P.2d 436 (1971); Rudes v. Gottschalk, 159 Tex. 552, 324 S.W.2d 201 (1959).

7. See Marquay v. Eno, 139 N.H. 708, 662 A.2d 272 (1995). A number of courts have implicitly accepted the adoption theory in quoting with approval from Restatement sections that express the theory. E.g., Zeni v. Anderson, 397 Mich. 117, 243 N.W.2d 270 (1976).

8. § 137 below.

9. § 140 below.

10. § 142 below.

11. See Restatement § 286, cmt. d. Prosser argued for this result but recognized some court courts, at least at one time, had felt bound to import the outmoded criminal statute into tort cases. See PROSSER & KEETON, § 36.

12. E.g., Bailey v. Lenord, 625 P.2d 849 (Alaska 1981); Hurst v. Ohio Dept. of Rehabilitation and Correction, 72 Ohio St.3d 325, 650 N.E.2d 104 (1995).

13. Courts sometimes purport to adopt and enforce statutes which merely prescribe a general standard of care (you must drive reasonably) or a desired results (brakes must be in working order) as a workable standard.

14. Brown v. Shyne, 242 N.Y. 176, 151 N.E. 197, 44 A.L.R. 1407 (1926) (one holding himself out to practice medicine but who has no license and who injures the would-be patient is not guilty of negligence per se merely because of his breach of the licensing statute); see Keenan v. Hill, 190 Ga.App. 108, 378 S.E.2d 344 (1989) (rule stated, but contrary instruction was not prejudicial on the facts); Gregory, Breach of Criminal Licensing Statutes in Civil Litigation, 36 CORNELL L. REV. 622 (1951).

15. Duty v. East Coast Tender Service, Inc., 660 F.2d 933 (4th Cir.1981) (operation of vessel without licensed operator required by Coast Guard regulation); Mundy v. Pirie–Slaughter Motor Co., 146 Tex. 314, 206 S.W.2d 587 (1947) (one who knowingly permits another to drive without a license is guilty of negligence per se); cf. Corgan v. Muehling, 143 Ill.2d 296, 574 N.E.2d 602, 158 Ill.Dec. 489 (1991) (violation of statute requiring psychologist's registration creates an implied private right of action in favor of harmed patient). Sometimes the court simply takes no notice of the fact that the statute is a kind of licensing statute, as in Mississippi Power Co. v. Jones, 369 So.2d 1381 (Miss.1979) ("certificate of approval" required, recovery allowed seemingly on the basis of the ordinance's violation).

16. See Horstmeyer v. Golden Eagle Fireworks, 534 N.W.2d 835 (N.D.1995).

Particular statutes might be rejected on the ground that their use in tort cases would be impractical or difficult—for example, because they might raise unwieldy questions of causation.[17] Even if the statute provides a standard suitable for tort cases, courts may conclude that the statute, as properly construed, was not violated at all and hence affects nothing.[18]

A court's rejection of a statutory standard necessarily reflects its attitudes about justice and policy. Courts refused for a long time to impose liability upon sellers of alcohol who sold in violation of statutory restrictions. They simply rejected the statutory standard as inappropriate.[19] As public and judicial attitudes changed, courts began to adopt the statutory standards for liquor sellers and to impose tort liability for their violation, for example, when the seller provides alcohol to an intoxicated person who then causes harm as a result of the intoxication.[20] There are many examples of statutes that are rejected as grounds for tort liability on very broad grounds of policy or attitude, including, for example, statutes that would, if utilized in tort litigation, impose liability upon governmental agencies or officers. So far, however, courts and commentators have not advanced any systematic principles for determining when to adopt and when to reject a nonprescriptive statute.

§ 136. Implications of the Adoption Theory: Adopting Federal Statutes and Expanding State Statutes

The adoption theory explains why courts can utilize criminal or regulatory statutes as tort-law rules and also why courts can refuse to use them. The theory has implications. One implication is that courts could adopt federal statutory standards in some cases. Another is that courts could adopt a statutory standard to govern cases that were not included within its terms.

Adopting federal statutes in state-law torts. If Congress, acting within its Constitutional limits, enacts a statute creating a private right of action, both state and federal courts must recognize such a right. However, since there is no general federal common law of torts, federal courts have no occasion to adopt criminal or regulatory statutes for any purpose except that actually expressed or implied by the Congress. But could state courts (or federal courts sitting in diversity) adopt a federal statute standard for state tort law purposes?

17. Stachniewicz v. Mar–Cam Corp., 259 Or. 583, 488 P.2d 436 (1971); Olson v. Ratzel, 89 Wis.2d 227, 278 N.W.2d 238, 4 A.L.R.4th 313 (Ct.App. 1979).

18. Tedla v. Ellman, 280 N.Y. 124, 19 N.E.2d 987 (1939); McMaster v. Zwicker, 194 Ill.App.3d 923, 141 Ill.Dec. 467, 551 N.E.2d 654 (1990) (construing statute setting standards for automobile brakes as applicable only when the owner had knowledge of the brakes' alleged defect). The operative effect is the same as saying that the violator is excused, but the analytical approach differs in that it purports to construe the statute and to conclude that the violator's act was not covered by the statute.

19. E.g., Stachniewicz v. Mar–Cam Corp., 259 Or. 583, 488 P.2d 436 (1971); Garcia v. Hargrove, 52 Wis.2d 289, 190 N.W.2d 181 (1971).

20. Rong Yao Zhou v. Jennifer Mall Restaurant, Inc., 534 A.2d 1268 (D.C. 1987) ; Sorensen v. Jarvis, 119 Wis.2d 627, 350 N.W.2d 108 (1984); see § 332.

The logical answer is a qualified yes. If state courts are free to make any given common law rule, then they are equally free to adopt that same rule from a statute—or for that matter from a law review article. The rule so adopted is a common law rule, no more, no less. In line with this, courts have not infrequently concluded that a federal statute sets a standard to be incorporated by the state courts into the state's common law.[1]

States cannot adopt a federal statutory rule or standard, however, if the federal statute forbids its use in tort litigation[2] or preempts the field so that state tort suits are utterly foreclosed.[3] Whether a federal statute implicitly or expressly preempts the matter to exclude ordinary state-law tort claims is largely a matter of statutory construction, but no simple matter even so.

Expanding a Statute's Scope

Application of statutes beyond the legislative command. The logic and good sense of the adoption theory is that courts that are free to create judge-made law can adapt as well as adopt statutes. In particular, courts might adopt a statutory rule and give it any scope appropriate under the common law, even if the legislature had a much more restricted scope in mind for the statute's criminal law applications.[4] So even if legislation for factory safety were directed only at protection of employees, a court might logically decide that the factory safety standards should apply for the benefit of all persons who might foreseeably be endangered by the statute's violation, including, say, business visitors in the factory.

§ 136

1. *Federal gun control statutes:* Franco v. Bunyard, 261 Ark. 144, 547 S.W.2d 91 (1977) (violation of federal statute requiring information to be given before selling a gun is evidence of negligence under Arkansas' evidence-of-negligence rule); Coker v. Wal–Mart Stores, Inc., 642 So.2d 774 (Fla.App. 1994) (violation of federal statute against selling ammunition to minors is negligence per se); Rubin v. Johnson, 550 N.E.2d 324 (Ind.App.1990) (one who violates state gun control statute by selling gun to person of unsound mind would be guilty of negligence per se). *Federal safety standard*: Grey's Ex'r v. Mobile Trade Company, 55 Ala. 387 (1876). *Testing required by federal agency*: liability of the federal government, when it is not immune altogether, is determined by state law, which might conceivably adopt a federal statutory standard as the state law rule and then apply it to the federal government. cf. Loge v. United States, 662 F.2d 1268 (8th Cir.1981) (federal regulation for testing polio vaccine not enforced by government, liability potential). *OSHA (Occupational Safety & Health Act)*: The statute itself seems to exclude any use that would "affect" a common law action, but some states have treated violations as negligence per se or evidence of negligence. See § 133.

2. As the Occupational Safety and Health Act appears to do. See § 133. States can adopt statutes of their own, even if they duplicate the federal standard, so long as the federal law does not preempt state law on the point.

3. Hoffman v. Merrell–Dow Pharm., Inc., 857 F.2d 290 (6th Cir.1988) (recognizing that states are free to apply a federal standard unless Congress, preempted the matter; the court suggested that in some cases preemption might be found because Congress chose to set a standard enforceable by administrative action but not by a private right of action).

4. Cf. Rudes v. Gottschalk, 159 Tex. 552, 324 S.W.2d 201 (1959) ("As the power of adopting or rejecting standards rests with the civil courts, we may accept or reject the criminal statute or use such part thereof as may be deemed appropriate for our purpose.... we still retain the test of foreseeability of harm before liability is imposed under the doctrine of negligence per se").

§ 137. Class of Risk and Class of Person Covered by the Statute

Two important limitations commonly constrain the rule that makes violation of a nonprescriptive statute negligence per se. First, violation of statute is not negligence (or contributory negligence) per se unless the statute is construed to protect against the type of risk or type of harm that actually occurred.[1] Second, violation is not negligence or contributory negligence per se unless the statute is construed to protect a class of people that includes the plaintiff.[2]

Traditional discussions of these rules tend to imply that the problem is one of statutory construction rather than one of judicial fairness and policy. That implication may be wrong, since the problem under discussion only arises when the statute itself has not prescribed any tort-law effects. Nevertheless, it is convenient to express the rules in some such language and to use the strange figure of speech that attributes intent to a statute as well. Furthermore, the class of harm/class of person rules can function very well to place sensible limits on liability. Whether those limits come from the statutes themselves or from the good sense of courts can be left for the next section.

Type of Harm, Risk, or Interest

Type of harm. Suppose a statute forbids poisons in restaurant kitchens. The defendant violates the statute by placing rat poison near a stove in the restaurant's kitchen. The poison causes an explosion in which the plaintiff is injured. One reasonable way to analyze the case is to say that the kind of *harm* the statute is intended to avoid is poisoning, not burns or explosive trauma. Not surprisingly, the Oklahoma Court held that violation of such a statute was not negligence per se.[3]

Type of risk, means, or instrumentality. In some cases the statute might be construed as intended to prevent the very kind of *harm* that occurred, but only when the harm is inflicted by certain means. In a case from Illinois,[4] one Allen purchased a small quantity of gasoline from a service station, placing it in a pint-sized insecticide can. The service station made the sale in violation of a statute that required delivery only to containers that were labeled for gasoline and that met certain other conditions. Allen used the gasoline to start a fire at an apartment building. Four people died in the fire. In a tort suit for their death brought against the service station, the plaintiffs argued that the court should use the statute's provision as a basis for liability. The court

§ 137

1. E.g., Busby v. Quail Creek Golf and Country Club, 885 P.2d 1326 (Okla.1994); cf. Rocovich v. Consolidated Edison Co., 78 N.Y.2d 509, 583 N.E.2d 932, 577 N.Y.S.2d 219 (1991) (scaffolding act, requiring safety devices for workers working at an elevation, did not apply when worker merely slipped and fell into a narrow trough of hot oil).

2. Wright v. Brown, 167 Conn. 464, 356 A.2d 176 (1975); Inland Steel v. Pequignot, 608 N.E.2d 1378 (Ind.App.1993); Hite v. Brown, 100 Ohio App.3d 606, 654 N.E.2d 452 (1995); Restatement § 286.

3. Larrimore v. American National Ins. Co., 184 Okl. 614, 89 P.2d 340 (1939).

4. Stafford v. Borden, 252 Ill.App.3d 254, 192 Ill.Dec. 52, 625 N.E.2d 12 (1993).

refused to do so, even though the statute undoubtedly meant to protect people from fire dangers.

One way to view the facts is to say that the statute intended to protect against fire and burning, but only to the extent that labeling proper containers would tend to increase fire safety. The labeling rule would seldom if ever reduce arson risks, so the statute might have been intended to cover the general *type* of harm suffered—fire—but not the risk of harm by means of arson. This kind of analysis suggests that courts need a rule like the type of risk rule that focuses in part on how the injury came about, as well as a type of harm rule that focuses on the end result alone.

Type of risk overlapping type of harm rule. The type of risk and type of harm rules can in fact overlap substantially or totally, depending on how broadly the court defines risk and harm. Because of the overlap and because the rules have the same effect, it is at least arguable that one broadly stated rule would provide more clarity.

Gorris v. Scott[5] is a leading, much-cited case. A statute there required that animals transported by ship had to be penned separately. The purpose was to avoid the spread of disease through close contact. The carrier did not pen the plaintiff's animals separately. Some were washed overboard and lost, a result that would have been avoided if the animals had been penned. The court held that, since the purpose of the pen requirement was to prevent disease, not loss through perils of the sea, the violation of the statute furnished no ground for action.

The Restatement proposes to deal with this kind of case by the scope of risk rule rather than the type of harm rule. That is, the Restatement focuses here on the way harm comes about and concludes that the statute was not intended to prevent harm through forces of the sea. But you can just as easily view *Gorris v. Scott* as a type of harm case. The requirement of pens was not meant to protect against harms like drowning but harms like disease.

Inevitably, to describe the harm is to describe at least a little about how the harm comes about. The ability to shift from type of harm to type of risk by slight shifts in linguistic usages and the inability to describe one without implications about the other suggests that the distinction is not so much one found in nature as it is in courtrooms and classrooms. If the distinction is meaningful in practice, it is not because of its intrinsic merit but because courts can bring to it a sense of justice and balance they do not get from the rule itself.

Different interests. The Restatement subdivides the type of harm/risk rule even further. The Restatement has it that the court will not adopt the statutory rule where the statute was not intended to protect the interest that was in fact harmed.[6] What the American Law Institute had in mind was that tort law can be viewed as protecting several

5. Gorris v. Scott, 1874 L.R. 9 Ex. 125.

6. Restatement § 286 (c).

distinct "interests"—for instance, interests in bodily security, security of property, emotional well-being, and economic opportunity. If the statute is aimed at protecting the interest in bodily security, it may not be aimed at protecting economic opportunity. The Restatement poses a case in which the defendant violates rules about the safety of building structures, with the result that the building collapses. The statute was no doubt intended to protect workers from physical injury, but not intended to protect them from purely economic losses resulting from the fact that they cannot work while the building is being repaired. So the defendant is not liable to workers who are not injured but who lose wages.

Conversely, some statutes represent economic regulation and are not intended as safety statutes. Their protection does not extend to personal injury, which can be considered either a different "interest" or a different type of harm and in either event not within the scope of the statute.[7]

Class of Persons

The class of persons rule is very similar to the type of harm/type of risk rule. The idea is that even if the plaintiff suffers the type of harm covered by the statute, she cannot claim negligence per se unless she is within the class or group of people the statute was intended to protect. But when you describe the risk of harm and the type of harm, you often implicitly describe the class of persons as well. So, in many cases, courts could get the same result whether they used the type of harm/type of risk rule or the class of person rule.

In a Mississippi case,[8] the defendant pulled over and parked on the left side of the street to chat with a friend. When the visit was completed, the defendant looked in all directions, saw no one, and started driving off. She immediately struck a small child, who had not been visible. The court refused to hold that the defendant's violation of the right-side-of-the-street statute was negligence per se, saying that the class of persons to be protected by that traffic rule was pedestrians and drivers acting in reliance upon orderly flow of traffic.

The result seems correct. It would be no less correct if the court had said that the statute was aimed at preventing harms that would be more likely to occur from being on the wrong side of the road. If the defendant had gone around the block so as to face the right direction, the risk to children under a bumper would not have been lessened. So the case can be analyzed either in terms of the class of persons or the class of risk involved.

Class of Harm and Person as Proximate Cause Rules

Proximate cause and class of person/type of risk rules. The thrust of the rules about class of person and type of risk, harm, or interest is

7. Cates v. Albertson's, Inc., 126 Idaho 1030, 895 P.2d 1223 (1995) (statute was economic regulation, and thus addressed different type of harm from personal injury claimed by the plaintiff).

8. Haver v. Hinson, 385 So.2d 605 (Miss.1980).

sometimes expressed by saying that violation of the statute is not negligence per se unless violation is a proximate cause of the harm suffered. Proximate cause is part of the language of common law tort analysis that is often equivalent to the class of person/type of risk or harm analysis in cases of statutory violation. The class of person/type of risk or harm language may be a little more precise, but courts usually appear to have the same ideas in mind when they use the language of proximate cause.[9]

§ 138. Class of Harm and Person: Interpreting the Statutory Purposes

Statutes seldom indicate clearly what class of persons and risks they are intended to protect against. How can courts apply the class of person/risks rules without knowing who the legislature intended to protect and against what? More fundamentally, the nonprescriptive statutes under discussion make no provision at all for tort liability or tort standards, so it seems impossible to determine from the statute itself the appropriate class of harms or persons to be covered.

Given that courts adopt the rules of nonprescriptive statutes as they seem fitted for tort law, one entirely appropriate solution is to treat the statute as encompassing all persons and harms that would foreseeably be safer if the statute were obeyed. Conversely, that solution would treat the statute as encompassing no persons or harms that would not be foreseeably safer if the statute were obeyed.[1]

For example, statutes often regulate driving safety by requiring brakes, limiting speed, or prohibiting intoxicated driving or specific kinds of vehicular movements. Such statutes are obviously for the protection of others using the streets and highways, but since it is foreseeable that bad brakes, excessive speed, intoxicated driving, dangerous vehicular movement, or even overweight vehicles can also cause harms to persons or property off the highway, courts have every reason to say that the statutory rule applies for the benefit of persons off the road as well.[2]

On the other hand, if you park your car in an on-street loading zone created by an ordinance, you are in violation of the statute; but your

9. E.g., in Hack v. Nester, 241 Va. 499, 404 S.E.2d 42 (1990), the court said it was negligence per se for an owner to entrust her car to an unlicensed driver who later drove the car negligently and caused harm; but since the unlicensed driver had been eligible to get a driver's license, lending the car was not a proximate cause of the harm he caused. The idea seems to be identical to the idea that the type of risk or harm the statute was intended to prevent by the licensing statute was harm that would be caused by one who could not qualify for a license and who therefore would represent a risk to others.

§ 138

1. Torres v. State, 119 N.M. 609, 894 P.2d 386 (1995).

2. Castro v. Hernandez–Davila, 694 S.W.2d 575 (Tex.App.1985) (intoxicated driver who drove into apartment building, causing a wall to collapse; negligence per se); Sigrist v. Love, 510 P.2d 456 (Colo.App. 1973) (left turn in violation of statute led to injury off the highway; negligence per se); but cf. Erickson v. Kongsli, 40 Wash.2d 79, 240 P.2d 1209 (1952) (property owners off the road were not within class protected by right of way rules for vehicles).

violation creates no more risk that a child will dart into the street from behind your car than if you had parked to unload goods. If it is a matter of legislative intent, courts can suppose that the legislature never created loading zones as child safety statutes but only as convenience for merchants, so that violation of the statute is irrelevant. If it is a matter of judicial fairness or policy, the same limitation applies because the harm foreseeable from illegal parking in the loading zone is not injury to children but delay of persons making a delivery.

Sometimes, however, courts attempt to give the statute's standard a narrow scope because of narrow words used in the statute itself. A statute that requires covering or fencing elevator shafts in work places might be titled "An Act to Protect Workers." This or similar language could lead a court to say that only workers are within the class protected, so that if a firefighter or a person making a delivery to the premises falls into an open shaft, he enjoys none of the statute's protections. Courts have actually so held.[3]

Cases of this kind classify injured persons to provide unequal protection. The injured firefighter or business visitor on the premises is not a second class citizen. Although the legislature might properly refuse to impose the costs of fencing a shaft solely for the benefit of odd visitors, it costs the factory owner no more to fence for the benefit of all than to fence for the benefit of some. When the class of persons/risk rules are used in this way, they can lead to invidious differences in protection. Since courts are not required to adopt the statutory rule in the first place, they are not required to adopt its limitation either. So courts are free to avoid making unjust distinctions like those in the shaft cases. Courts can take one of at least four approaches:

(1) Adhere to the foreseeability principle: protect all persons who would naturally and foreseeably be injured by a violation of the statute and protect them against risks that are foreseeable from its violation. This is a class of risk and class of person rule, but it judges the scope of the risk and the size of the class by what is foreseeable, not by the preoccupation of the legislature with a particular constituency.

(2) Conceptualize classes of persons and risks in broad rather than specific terms. Categories like "type of harm" and "kind of risk" are not precise and it does not pay to tune them finely. The category in the shaft cases does not have to be "defendant's employees" but could be anyone who is endangered by the open shaft that the legislature has forbidden.

(3) Reject the class of person and class of risk limitations altogether because the statutes under discussion do not address tort suits at all

3. Gibson v. Leonard, 143 Ill. 182, 32 N.E. 182 (1892) (firefighter on the premises); Kelly v. Henry Muhs Co., 71 N.J.L. 358, 59 A. 23 (1904) (firefighter); cf. DiCaprio v. New York Central R.R., 231 N.Y. 94, 131 N.E. 746, 16 A.L.R. 940 (1921) (mandate to railroad to fence out cattle did not protect small child who wandered onto the track).

and are of interest only because courts choose, as a matter of judicial policy, to adopt them.

(4) Courts can reject negligence per se when the statute does not cover persons like the plaintiff or harms like those she suffered, but can nevertheless treat violation of the statute as some evidence of negligence.

Of these choices, the use of a foreseeability based principle to determine scope of risk and appropriate class of persons is probably the best, if for no other reason than that it is intensely familiar to judges and lawyers from the analogous cases of proximate cause.

§ 139. Rejecting the Class of Harm/Person Rules

Imposing liability without the class of risk restriction. When the plaintiff is not within the class of persons the statute was designed to protect, or the injury is not the type of harm covered by the statute, courts sometimes may adopt the statute's standard, but if they do, they are likely to treat a violation as merely evidence of negligence and not negligence per se.[1]

If the per se effect is deemed more suited, courts could treat violation of a statute intended to protect a different class of person from a different class of harm as negligence per se, so long as the statute itself did not explicitly or implicitly provide otherwise. Whether to do so is a question of fairness and policy as determined by the courts.

The point can be illustrated by a case in which the Supreme Court of the United States rejected the limitations imposed by the type of harm/type of risk rules for suits under federal statutes by railroad workers and seafaring employees in order to further the protections provided for those workers. In *Kernan v. American Dredging Co.*,[2] a regulation required lights on scows no less than eight feet above the water. The point was to provide a light visible at a distance for navigation safety. The light provided on the defendant's scow was a kerosine lantern no more than three feet above the water. Petroleum products had accumulated on the river and their vapors were ignited by the low flame. A worker lost his life. Since the purpose of the eight-foot requirement was for navigation safety, not fire safety, the common law rules would surely have held that violation of the regulation was irrelevant. But the Supreme Court held otherwise.

The Court in *Kernan* ignored the limits that would be placed on liability by strict adherence to statutory purposes. The Court may have gone quite a bit beyond that, however, because low lights may not have created a foreseeable risk of igniting the vapors on the waters. The middle position would be that the courts can properly ignore the legisla-

§ 139

1. Melerine v. Avondale Shipyards, Inc., 659 F.2d 706 (5th Cir.1981); Koll v. Manatt's Transportation Co., 253 N.W.2d 265 (Iowa 1977); contra, apparently refusing to give any effect at all to the statute, DiCaprio v. New York Central R.R., 231 N.Y. 94, 131 N.E. 746, 16 A.L.R. 940 (1921).

2. Kernan v. American Dredging Co., 355 U.S. 426, 78 S.Ct. 394, 2 L.Ed.2d 382 (1958).

ture's preoccupation with a narrow issue, but that they can also limit liability to those risks that would foreseeably be greater if the statute is violated.

§ 140. Excused and Unexcused Violations Excused Violation of Statute

Power to excuse violations. The power to excuse violation of a nonprescriptive statute is the logical result of the court's power to adopt or reject the statute as a standard in the first place. Indeed, excused violation is a kind of limited rejection of the statute as a standard for tort law purposes. In the excuse cases, courts accept the statutory rule as the usual standard but reject it for particular cases where the rule appears undesirable or unjust. In these cases, courts say they "excuse" violation of the statute. An excused violation is not negligence.[1]

Categories of excuses. The excuse doctrine helps courts avoid turning statutory commands into a general system of strict liability. Nevertheless, courts retain control of the excuses they believe acceptable. Excuses recognized by the Restatement's non-exclusive list[2] are usually accepted by courts. The actor is generally excused in these cases:

(1) The actor is incapacitated (by minority or by incompetency) and violation is reasonable in light of that incapacity.[3] *For example*, a child runs into the street chasing a ball, violating the statute by failing to look in both directions.[4] In line with this excuse and this example, courts commonly let the jury consider a minor's conduct under the traditional child standard of care or some variation of it rather than under the strict per se rule.[5] Alternatively, courts may hold that the statute itself is aimed at protecting children from their own inexperience or incapacity, with the result that the child's violation is not deemed to be contributory negligence.[6]

(2) The actor does not know and could not reasonably discover the occasion for compliance with the statute.[7] *For example*, the nighttime driver is required by statute to display lights in the rear of his vehicle, but does not know his rear lights have burned out and has no means of anticipating or discovering the

§ 140

1. See, e.g., Gore v. People's Savings Bank, 235 Conn. 360, 665 A.2d 1341 (1995) ("the defendant ordinarily may avoid liability upon proof of a valid excuse or justification").

2. Restatement § 288A.

3. Restatement § 288A (2) (a).

4. Cf. Ranard v. O'Neil, 166 Mont. 177, 531 P.2d 1000 (1975) (contributory negligence of 8–year old dashing into street excused if he lacked capacity for compliance with statute).

5. E.g., Burgbacher v. Lazar, 97 A.D.2d 496, 468 N.Y.S.2d 14 (1983); Alley v. Siepman, 87 S.D. 670, 214 N.W.2d 7 (1974); Rudes v. Gottschalk, 159 Tex. 552, 324 S.W.2d 201 (1959) (child standard of care rather than child's ability to understand the statute). A few courts apply the negligence per se rules to children. D'Ambrosio v. Philadelphia, 354 Pa. 403, 47 A.2d 256, 174 A.L.R. 1166 (1946).

6. See Busby v. Quail Creek Golf and Country Club, 885 P.2d 1326, 1331–32 (Okla.1994).

7. Restatement § 288A (2) (b).

fact.[8] This rule does not excuse ignorance of the law, only a reasonable ignorance of facts that would invoke the law.[9] But ignorance of the facts would not be an excuse if the statute requires investigation and knowledge.[10]

(3) The actor cannot comply with the statute even by diligent effort.[11] *For example,* the defendant's car is struck by another, so that the steering mechanisms are damaged; the defendant cannot prevent his car from moving into another lane in front of an oncoming motorcyclist, the plaintiff.[12]

(4) The actor is faced with an emergency not caused by his own negligence, and in the light of that emergency could not reasonably be expected to achieve compliance with the statute.[13] *For example,* a car ahead suddenly stops on the highway and the driver of the vehicle behind moves his vehicle to the left lane in violation of statute, ultimately causing a collision in that lane.[14]

(5) Violation of statute is safer for the actor or others than compliance.[15] *For example,* a driver swerves into the left lane to avoid a child darting out on his right.[16]

Generalizing the excuses. These excuse categories do not purport to be exclusive. Courts can recognize any excuse that they deem appropriate. Courts can also generalize the excuses as the California Court did long ago by saying that (unless the court decides to impose strict liability) an actor is excused when he shows that notwithstanding the violation, "he did what might reasonably be expected of a person of ordinary prudence, acting under similar circumstances, who desired to comply with the law."[17]

Burden of proof. Behind the categorical and the generalized excuses lies a residue of reasonable-prudent-person thinking. The negligence per se rule is a complicated and roundabout way of requiring due care—a goal that could be satisfied more directly by a rule that violation of statute is evidence of negligence for the jury to consider. Nevertheless, the plaintiff gains at least a procedural advantage from the per se rule, because once the statutory violation is shown, the defendant must carry

8. Leiken v. Wilson, 445 A.2d 993 (D.C.App.1982); Brotherton v. Day & Night Fuel Co., 192 Wash. 362, 73 P.2d 788 (1937).

9. Nettleton v. Thompson, 117 Idaho 308, 787 P.2d 294 (Ct.App.1990); see Juarez v. Wavecrest Management Team, Ltd., 88 N.Y.2d 628, 649 N.Y.S.2d 115, 672 N.E.2d 135 (1996) (statutory duty of landlords to remove lead paint where child lived in premises did not impose a duty to find out whether a child was there).

10. Smith v. Owen, 841 S.W.2d 828 (Tenn.App.1992) (ordinance imposed upon landlord a duty to inspect wiring in leased premises, hence landlord's lack of knowledge of defect is no defense).

11. Restatement § 288A (2) (c).

12. Giancarlo v. Karabanowski, 124 Conn. 223, 198 A. 752 (1938).

13. Restatement § 288A (2) (d).

14. See Jones v. Blair, 387 N.W.2d 349 (Iowa 1986) (recognizing principle).

15. Restatement § 288A (2) (e).

16. A famous example, based on Tedla v. Ellman, 280 N.Y. 124, 19 N.E.2d 987 (1939).

17. Alarid v. Vanier, 50 Cal.2d 617, 624, 327 P.2d 897, 900 (1958); Waugh v. Traxler, 186 W.Va. 355, 412 S.E.2d 756 (1991).

the burden of showing any excuse,[18] if, indeed, an excuse will be accepted.

The trouble from the plaintiff's point of view is that the negligence per se rule also applies to contributory fault, so that the plaintiff may be automatically saddled with contributory negligence if she violates a statute, just as the defendant is automatically saddled with negligence. When the shoe is thus uncomfortably on the other foot, the burden of proving an acceptable excuse is of course on the plaintiff.

Construing the Statute to Eliminate Violation

Excuse is not the only formal way in which the defendant can avoid a negligence per se condemnation. In some cases the defendant can plausibly argue that he simply did not violate the statute at all.

One kind of no-violation decision is a purely factual determination; if the plaintiff claims that the defendant ran a stop light in violation of a statute, the jury must determine whether the defendant in fact ran the light.[19] The appellate courts will have little role in such determinations. They are more involved in the second kind of decision that the statute was not violated. The second kind turns on the meaning of statutory language. For instance, courts may construe the statute to apply only when the defendant has actual knowledge of the relevant conditions to which the statute is addressed.[20] Or particular statutes may be construed to address conditions not involved in the case, as where a statute requiring operators of swimming pools to maintain life-saving equipment is construed to require such equipment only when the pool was open for use and not when it was closed after the season was over.[21] There are many such possibilities, turning on construction of the words of individual statutes.[22] When courts conclude that the actor's conduct is outside the scope of the statutory command, the actor is not in violation and cannot be guilty of negligence per se.

§ 141. Rejecting Excuses: Strict Liability under Statutes

Strict liability; refusing to accept excuses. Courts are not required to recognize excuses. They can choose instead to impose strict liability so that even if the defendant has acted with every possible effort to comply with the statute he could be held liable.[1] When courts recognize this kind of strict liability, they may not

18. Ferrell v. Baxter, 484 P.2d 250 (Alaska 1971); Jones v. Blair, 387 N.W.2d 349 (Iowa 1986).

19. See e.g., Pond v. Leslein, 72 Ohio St.3d 50, 647 N.E.2d 477 (1995).

20. Johnson v. Matlock, 771 F.2d 1432 (10th Cir.1985).

21. Kerns v. G.A.C., Inc., 255 Kan. 264, 875 P.2d 949 (1994).

22. E.g., Musgrave v. Southern Pac. Co., 49 Ariz. 512, 68 P.2d 202 (1937) ("sufficient" fences meant "reasonably sufficient" fences); Thomson v. Littlefield, 319 Ark. 648, 893 S.W.2d 788 (1995). (regulation applied to different kind of trucks); Tedla v. Ellman, 280 N.Y. 124, 19 N.E.2d 987 (1939) (statute construed to include unstated exceptions, including exception to permit pedestrian to walk on the "wrong" side when it was safer to do so).

§ 141

1. O'Donnell v. Elgin, J. & E. Ry., 338 U.S. 384, 70 S.Ct. 200, 94 L.Ed. 187, 16 A.L.R.2d 646 (1949).

only reject excuses but may also import some other strict liability rules favorable to the plaintiff.[2]

An example of strict liability under a statutory standard is *Spalding v. Waxler*.[3] The defendant's brakes simply failed to work. A collision resulted. According to the evidence, the defendant had in fact been quite careful to have the vehicle regularly serviced and brakes had been inspected less than six months earlier. He had no warning that the brakes might fail. Nevertheless, the court held that the defendant was in violation of the adequate brakes statute and guilty of negligence per se. He was not excused by reason of the emergency since he had a statutory duty to maintain the brakes. In other words, the statutory duty was absolute and due care was not sufficient to discharge it.

Most states do not impose strict liability under their adequate braking statutes.[4] However, some states do impose special demands in brake failure cases,[5] and others impose strict liability under different statutes by selectively refusing to accept excuses for particular statutory violations. A few states, for example, hold that a driver is not excused if his vehicle strikes a hidden and unforeseeable patch of ice, goes into a slide that cannot be controlled, and causes a collision on the wrong side of the road,[6] even though it is clear that he is not negligent.[7] In such a case he is said to have violated a statute requiring him to stay on the right side of the road.

Statutes like the adequate brake statutes and the right side of the road statutes do not prescribe conduct, only an ideal result to aim for or achieve. They do not, for example, specify the kind of inspection required for brakes, nor the interval for inspection. If such statutes specified tort liability at all, they would lend themselves to a strict liability construction. But because the statutes do not create a tort cause of action or dictate tort-law results, courts probably should recognize that it is they themselves who are imposing strict liability and spell out their justifications for such liability.

2. For instance, courts may hold that the statute imposes strict liability and that therefore the plaintiff's contributory negligence does not count against her. See Van Gaasbeck v. Webatuck Central School District No. 1, 21 N.Y.2d 239, 287 N.Y.S.2d 77, 234 N.E.2d 243 (1967).

3. Spalding v. Waxler, 2 Ohio St.2d 1, 205 N.E.2d 890 (1965).

4. E.g., Gowins v. Merrell, 541 P.2d 857 (Okla.1975) ("If owner properly maintains brakes, he will not be liable for damages resulting from unexpected brake failure if he acts as a prudent person after failure occurs"); see Allan E. Korpela, Annotation, Automobiles: Liability of Owner or Operator of Motor Vehicle for Injury, Death, or Property Damage Resulting from Defective Brakes, 40 A.L.R.3d 9 (1971).

5. In Maloney v. Rath, 69 Cal.2d 442, 445 P.2d 513, 71 Cal.Rptr. 897 (1968), the court rejected strict liability under an adequate brakes statute and approved excuses based on due care; but it also held that the exercise of due care was nondelegable, so that if the driver's brake mechanic was guilty of negligence, the driver would be responsible for it.

6. E.g., Teply v. Lincoln, 125 Idaho 773, 874 P.2d 584 (Idaho App.1994).

7. He would not be negligent if the ice could not be anticipated and he faced a sudden emergency, which is a reason given in some courts for excusing wrong-side-of-the-road slides on ice. E.g., Young v. Flood, 182 Mich.App. 538, 452 N.W.2d 869 (1990). He would also not be negligent if he found it impossible to steer once he hit the unforeseeable ice.

§ 142. Statutes Creating Duties Only to the Public

Courts do not adopt a statutory standard or rule to govern tort cases if they believe the statute creates only a "public duty." Put differently, violation of a statute that creates a public duty only and not a duty to individuals is not negligence per se.[1] This rule is a part of the public duty doctrine, which comes in for more discussion in connection with the immunities given to public entities.[2]

The results may be correct in many cases, but the arguments are sometimes dubious. The idea is that the legislature may intend without saying so to exclude the tort liability it never mentioned in the first place and that the judge can divine both sets of silences. This is usually formulated by saying that some statutes were intended to impose a duty to the public but not to private individuals who may be injured by its violation. If no tort duty is imposed to private individuals, then they cannot claim violation of the statute as negligence per se.

A Restatement example of the rule is the case of a statute prescribing a very low highway speed limit to conserve gasoline in time of intense shortage. One who violates the 35–mph speed limit so imposed and causes harm in the process is not subject to the negligence per se rule, the Restatement says, because the statute creates obligations only to the state, not to individuals.[3]

The illustration is not very convincing or helpful because courts would get the same result even if there were no public duty doctrine. In the Restatement illustration, a highway accident was not one of the risks the statute was intended to prevent. So the rule that limits per se effects of the statute to harms it was intended to prevent would suffice quite nicely to exclude any per se rule and no public duty analysis is required or helpful on these facts.[4]

But courts may use the public duty doctrine to exclude the statute even when the harm that occurs to the plaintiff is the very kind the statute was intended to prevent. A common example occurs with ordinances that require landowners to remove natural accumulations of snow and ice from abutting public walks. Courts often hold that such ordinances impose a duty to the public but not a duty to individuals injured by the violation. The result is that the landowner is not liable for injuries resulting from his violation of the ordinance.[5]

§ 142

1. Restatement § 288.

2. The public duty doctrine is a part of the system of public entity immunities that protect them against tort liability for their negligence. See § 271. That doctrine does not merely deprive the plaintiff of the per se rule. It goes on to assert that a statute imposing a duty to the public at large has *no* legal effect in a tort suit; it creates no duty to the plaintiff and is thus not even evidence of negligence.

3. Restatement § 288, ill. 1.

4. Cooper v. Hoeglund, 221 Minn. 446, 22 N.W.2d 450 (1946), the case on which the Restatement's illustration is based, actually made the same point—that the risk was not within the statutory purpose.

5. E.g., Lopatkovich v. City of Tiffin, 28 Ohio St.3d 204, 503 N.E.2d 154 (1986) (duty to municipality only, not to those who might be injured; "snow and ice are part of wintertime life in Ohio"); Martin v. Altman, 568 A.2d 1031 (R.I.1990) (public duty

Assertions about public duty are usually made to foster immunity for public entities.[6] So when courts declare that a statute is aimed at protection of private individuals or only aimed at protection of the public, they are usually stating a judicially preferred rule, not a construction of the statute.[7]

TOPIC D. UNREASONABLE RISK AND FORESEEABILITY OF HARM

§ 143. Foreseeability of Harm

Risk and foreseeability. An actor is negligent only if his conduct created an unreasonable risk of harm to others and the actor recognized, or as a reasonable person should have recognized that risk. These rules are commonly stated in terms of foreseeability: conduct is not negligent unless harm was foreseen by the actor or would have been foreseeable to a reasonable person, and the harm could reasonably have been avoided.[1] These forms of statement, one in terms of risk and one in terms of foreseeability, mean the same thing.

The requirement of these rules is two-fold. The risk must be recognized or reasonably recognizable, and it must also be an unreasonable risk because it could be reasonably avoided or reduced. Contributory negligence of a plaintiff is judged in the same way, except that with contributory negligence the plaintiff is risking harm to herself rather than to others.

Intentional torts distinguished. Liability for unreasonably risky conduct that causes harm differs from liability for intent partly in that intentional wrongdoing is based upon conduct that is coupled with either a purpose that is legally wrong or a certainty that legal harm will result. Negligence, in contrast, is based upon a reasonably foreseeable harm, not a certain or intended one. That is to say, negligence entails a recognizable chance or risk, an unreasonable likelihood but not a certainty of harm.

Acceptable risks. Almost all conduct creates some degree of risk that others would be harmed, but not all conduct is unreasonably risky.

only). Some courts get the same result on the basis of other arguments. The best reason for denying liability may be simply that a government entity cannot extract public benefits from particular individuals. The landowner's addition of non-natural dangers such as water that may freeze is another matter; that is a basis for liability. See, e.g., Easton v. The 1738 Partnership, 854 P.2d 1362 (Colo.App.1993).

6. § 271 below.

7. See e.g., Schell v. DuBois, 94 Ohio St. 93, 113 N.E. 664 (1916) (stating without construction that "The [stautory] obligation was imposed upon him for the protection of the public, and for each member of the public"). Reasons given for the rule bear on immunity, not on statutory construction. See, e.g. Ezell v. Cockrell, 902 S.W.2d 394 (Tenn.1995).

§ 143

1. Foreseeable harm, appreciable risk, unreasonable risk and similar locutions all refer to the same general idea. Courts use these expressions constantly in various configurations. E.g., Butler v. Acme Markets, Inc., 177 N.J.Super. 279, 426 A.2d 521 (1981), aff'd 89 N.J. 270, 445 A.2d 1141 (1982); see Restatement § 291.

Multitudes are injured by automobiles and even a small child on a tricycle can harm a pedestrian. If you let a friend drive your car, you take a degree of risk. Harm is foreseeable. The steering may lock, a wheel may come off, injuries to others may ensue. Yet these small risks of foreseeable harm are not in themselves unreasonable, and without more they form no basis for asserting that you are negligent, even if someone is injured.[2] What makes risks or chances of harm unreasonable?

Negligence entails foreseeable harm. First, no risk is unreasonable unless it would be recognized by a reasonable person in similar circumstances as a risk that should be avoided or minimized or the risk was in fact recognized as such by the particular defendant. A person who sees "sand" in a jar, may not recognize the risk that it is not sand at all but an explosive. If, in his belief that he is dealing with sand, he causes an explosion that harms the plaintiff, he is not negligent unless a reasonable person would have recognized a risk of explosion or at least some similar risk.

What the defendant should have foreseen often depends a great deal on the knowledge and information he has or should have. If you have stored your goods with me and I know that a flood is likely to occur, I should recognize a risk to your goods and take appropriate action for their safety. If I do not know that a flood is on its way but merely that my warehouse lies in the flood plain, I may still know enough to require me to listen to weather reports. If I know neither of these things but a reasonable person would know them, I am still required to act on the basis of the risks that would have been recognized by a reasonable person in my position, and I am liable for the flood damage if I do not do so.

Scope of foreseeable harm. Risks or foreseeable harms can be described at different levels of abstraction, that is, broadly or narrowly. If we tried to describe all the particular risks or foreseeable harms that speeding would create, the list would be long, and we might still not think of some particular kinds of harm. But without identifying all the possible versions of speed-related harm, we can surely foresee broad categories of risks and harms to persons and property resulting because the driver might lose control. So if a speeding driver crashes into your living room, the fact that a reasonable person would not have specifically recognized a risk of harm to living room furniture will not assist the driver to avoid liability.[3] It is one of the cluster of harms in a generally foreseeable category, and that is enough.[4]

Foreseeability as a jury question. Foreseeability is seldom if ever a pure fact. You cannot determine whether a reasonable person would

2. See Parsons v. Crown Disposal Co., 15 Cal.4th 456, 936 P.2d 70, 63 Cal.Rptr.2d 291 (1997) (foreseeability alone is not enough; court must determine whether conduct at issue is sufficiently likely to result in the kind of harm experienced).

3. E.g., Castro v. Hernandez–Davila, 694 S.W.2d 575 (Tex.App.1985) (intoxicated driver who drove into apartment building, causing a wall to collapse).

4. For more detail about the problem sketched in this paragraph, see § 189 on "proximate" or "legal" cause.

recognize a risk of harm in the way you can determine whether a traffic signal is red. Reasonable foreseeability of harm is instead a judgment call. In some cases it is a call that is easy to make and so clear that courts will brook no argument. But aside from the easy cases, the question of what is or is not foreseeable to a reasonable person in the position of the defendant is normally a jury question, part of its overall evaluation of the defendant's conduct.

Unreasonableness of the risk. A second element in determining whether risk is unreasonable is usually the more important one. A risk is not unreasonable if a reasonable person in the defendant's shoes would not take action to minimize or avoid the risk. You allow an adult swimmer to use your home swimming pool. A reasonable person can easily recognize a risk of drowning or diving injuries—that is, you can foresee harm—but since you can ordinarily expect the swimmer to take care of himself, that harm is improbable, and you can reasonably share your pool.[5]

Probability of harm; uses of "foreseeability." Courts often use the term "foreseeable" as a shorthand expression. They might say, for example, that a defendant is negligent if harm was foreseeable.[6] Such statements should not ordinarily be taken in a literal way. Harm is a foreseeable consequence of almost all acts but courts definitely do not mean that *all* acts are negligent. Courts are likely to use the term "foreseeable" to mean that harm was not only foreseeable but also too likely to occur to justify risking it without added precautions. Similarly, courts sometimes speak as if foreseeability came in degrees and that some harms were "more foreseeable" than others.[7] Such expressions would be hard to interpret if taken too literally, but they make sense if they are understood to mean that the risk or probability of harm is greater in some cases than others. Along the same lines, when courts say that harm is unforeseeable, they may mean that although harm was actually foreseeable on the facts of the case, a reasonable person would not have taken action to prevent it because the risk of harm was low, and harm was so improbable that a reasonable person would not have taken safety precautions. Put differently, there was a recognizable risk of harm, but the risk was not unreasonable.

So probability of harm or the magnitude of the risk is an important element in judging what a reasonable person would do about the risks. But it is not the only element, because sometimes it is so worthwhile to take serious risks that even the prudent person will take them. The next section considers that possibility.

5. As to other cases in which you are not negligent because you can reasonably expect others to protect themselves, see § 162.

6. Rockweit v. Senecal, 197 Wis.2d 409, 541 N.W.2d 742 (1995) (quoting earlier authority).

7. E.g., Pamela W. v. Millsom, 25 Cal. App.4th 950, 30 Cal.Rptr.2d 690 (1994) (requiring a "high degree of foreseeability" before imposing duty of care upon landlords to protect against intruders).

§ 144. Unstructured Weighing of Reasonableness

Acceptable risks. Foreseeable risk or probability of harm from conduct is only one factor in determining whether that conduct is negligent. Tort law recognizes that risky conduct is not always negligent. One important line of thought when the usefulness of conduct outweighs the risks it imposes upon others is that the conduct is not negligent. Risks of conduct are weighed against its utility, costs against benefits it produces. If the benefits of conduct are enough, some degree of risk or foreseeable harm is acceptable.[1] If maximum safety were desirable, cars might be armor-plated tanks to limit the risk of injuries in collisions; swimming pools and even bathtubs might be forbidden because people drown in both. Anyone can think of endless examples of tolerable risks, for our lives are filled with them. This section and those immediately following focus on approaches that, formally or informally, weigh risks against utilities of the defendant's conduct.

The main factors. In determining whether a jury can reasonably find the defendant's conduct to be negligent, the relationship of the parties is important, but courts most commonly consider relationships on the issue of duty rather than on the issue of negligence.[2] When it comes to negligence, courts routinely[3] engage in an informal assessment of three factors, weighing (1) the magnitude of the risk and (2) the gravity of the risk against (3) the utility of the defendant's conduct and the costs of making it safer.[4] Expressed differently but meaning the same thing, courts consider the *likelihood* that the defendant's conduct will cause harm and the *amount* of harm it will cause if harm indeed results; and they will weigh these considerations against the *usefulness* of the conduct and the cost of making it safer.[5]

§ 144

1. Many cases exemplify or state the point. In Clark v. St. Dominic-Jackson Memorial Hospital, 660 So.2d 970 (Miss.1995) the court stated succinctly that although taking unnecessary chances might be negligence, "[t]aking a 1% chance when necessary might be exemplary. . . . "

2. For instance, courts traditionally said that landowners owed only limited duties to trespassers, such as the duty not to set a trap or wantonly injure them. The limited duty was based upon the landowner-trespasser relationship. Some courts have now said that landowners owe a duty of reasonable care to everyone, including trespassers. Under that rule, it may be that the trespasser-landowner relationship is still important in determining what safety precautions are reasonably required. See Scurti v. City of New York, 40 N.Y.2d 433, 387 N.Y.S.2d 55, 354 N.E.2d 794 (1976) and Chapter 13 generally.

3. Courts do not necessarily follow an economic interpretation of the risk-utility analysis or require explicit proof. Nor do they ordinarily instruct juries on risk-utility analysis.

4. See Gilhooley v. Star Market Co., Inc., 400 Mass. 205, 508 N.E.2d 609 (1987) ("likelihood of injury to others, the seriousness of the injury, and the burden of avoiding the risk"); Restatement § 291(negligence if magnitude or the risk outweighs the utility of the defendant's act). The Louisiana Court put the idea succinctly: "Actionable negligence also results from the creation or maintenance of an unreasonable risk of injury to others. In determining whether the risk is unreasonable, not only the seriousness of the harm that may be caused is relevant, but also the likelihood that harm may be caused." Bass v. Aetna Ins. Co., 370 So.2d 511 (La.1979).

5. The usefulness or utility of conduct actually includes the costs saved by not adopting some other course of conduct, but it is sometimes clearer if utility and cost of greater safety are stated separately.

Not only do appellate courts routinely consider these factors in assessing evidence of negligence, they have done so almost from the beginning of the negligence era.[6] In many instances, courts weigh risks against utilities, costs against benefits, without formally identifying these factors, but, formally or informally, courts do compare costs and benefits or risks and utilities of conduct in evaluating evidence of negligence.[7]

Example. The most ordinary kinds of negligence cases involve such an analysis. Driving cars is risky, as the statistics show, but it is also useful, so you would be negligent for driving a car only if you add to the normal risks of cars by, say, driving fast. But even fast driving is useful on occasion. If you are driving fast because you are transporting a dangerously wounded person to the hospital, there is some extra utility or usefulness in your conduct that justifies some extra risks. If you continue to drive fast although a herd of sheep approach, maybe you are still justified, since the amount of harm you might do to the herd is still small in comparison to the life of your wounded passenger. But if instead of a herd of sheep you encounter a street full of soccer-playing children, the amount of harm threatened by your speed is now so great that you'll probably be negligent if you don't slow down. This kind of reasoned but not necessarily quantified weighing of risks and utilities or costs and benefits of the defendant's conduct is routine.

Probability and amount of harm. The case of the fast driver shows that estimating the importance of a risk involves two things. First you must estimate probability. How *likely* is it that harm will occur?[8] Second, and quite different, how *much* harm will occur if the risk does in fact eventuate in harm?[9] A person who fires a rifle in an apparently empty meadow runs only a small risk of hitting some unseen person, but if that risk eventuates, the harm potential for serious injury or death is great. On the other hand, a person who fires a gun that shoots ping-pong balls into a crowded street creates a very high risk of very small harm. These

6. Many opinions, including contemporary ones, are focused on whichever factor was relevant in the particular dispute, so that some discuss probability, while others discuss the small injury expected or the burden of avoiding it or the advantages of the risky conduct. E.g., Beatty v. Central Iowa Ry. Co., 12 N.W. 332, 58 Iowa 242 (1882) (railroad constructed almost parallel to road created risks that horses would bolt and injure their riders, but "All persons must accept the advantages of this mode of intercommunication with the danger and inconveniences which necessarily attend it"); Chicago, B & Q Ry. Co. v. Krayenbuhl, 65 Neb. 889, 903, 91 N.W. 880, 882 (1902) (weighing danger of machinery against its benefits).

7. Indiana Consolidated Ins. Co. v. Mathew, 402 N.E.2d 1000 (Ind.App.1980) (defendant fled when mower caught fire in the plaintiff's garage, instead of pushing it out; the garage burned, but the defendant was not negligent because the expected harm to the garage was less than the expected harm to the defendant). Courts often discuss the factors or some of them in discussing the special acts of care required when dangers is increased.

8. Courts sometimes speak of harm being more or less foreseeable, but this seems to be at best an infelicitous expression. The point seems to be that harm may be more probable in some instances than others.

9. Dole Food Co., Inc. v. North Carolina Foam Industries, Inc., 188 Ariz. 298, 305, 935 P.2d 876, 883 (App.1996) ("Damage of potentially great severity but lesser likelihood of occurrence may warrant precautions equal to those taken to avoid harm of greater probability but lesser severity").

cases suggest why the trier must consider both the likelihood of harm and its extent.

Utility of defendant's conduct to third persons or society. The risk of harm must be weighed against the usefulness of the defendant's conduct.[10] The defendant's conduct might be useful in several different kinds of ways. In the example of the wounded passenger, the driver seems selfless—the wounded person, not the driver, will benefit from the expedited medical attention. Utility is often like this. The defendant's conduct is a risk to one person but the same conduct has great utility to another or to society at large. In this situation, if the defendant changes his conduct to make things safer for A, B will pay the cost of that change by facing a greater risk. The trier must determine whether increasing the risk to B is reasonable because the same conduct reduces the risk to A.

Utility of defendant's conduct to himself. Frequently, the utility of the defendant's conduct is a utility mainly or most obviously to himself and beneficial to society only because society's well-being is composed (at least in part) of aggregate individual benefits. I operate a factory that occasionally permits escape of gases that cause small damage to your adjacent property. I can avoid occasional leaks only by expending large sums of money. For me, there is some utility in continuing to permit occasional leaks; it saves me the cost of avoiding them. That kind of cost-saving utility is also one basis for risk-utility or cost-benefit comparisons. That is partly because the utility to the defendant is seldom if ever utility to him alone; costs to the defendant will be passed on to customers or workers in the form of higher prices or lower wages. It is also partly because plaintiffs and defendants are treated equally so that the utilities to each are properly considered whether they are important to others or not.[11]

Comparing dollar costs. So far, risk-utility balancing has been presented as an unstructured set of considerations, each of which is important in some not-very-defined way, or as Harper, James & Gray express it, the "tone" of the discussion is "more moral than economic."[12] Indeed, from a moral viewpoint, it may be that risks and utilities should be weighed and offset only in very narrow ways. It has been argued that

10. Cf. Parsons v. Crown Disposal Co., 15 Cal.4th 456, 936 P.2d 70, 63 Cal.Rptr.2d 291 (1997) (noise of a garbage truck frightened nearby horse, which threw its rider; a defendant is not negligent "merely by causing a machine to produce noises or emissions that are necessary to the regular operation of the machine.... there shall be no liability for fright to a horse and consequent damages ... when all that the plaintiff can point to is that a socially beneficial machine ... properly was used in the manner for which it is designed").

11. This statement has now become controversial. Several writers have sought to treat the plaintiff's interests in security as more important than the defendant's interests in freedom to act. See, e.g., Richard Wright, The Standards of Care in Negligence Law in Philosophical Foundations of Tort Law 249 (David G. Owen, ed. 1995). Perhaps also some cases could be read to mean that at the extreme of very low risk, no care at all is required. See Gregory C. Keating, Reasonableness and Rationality in Negligence Theory, 48 Stan. L. Rev. 311 (1996).

12. Harper, James & Gray § 16.9, pp. 477–478.

a money cost of safety should not by itself suffice to justify serious risks of human death, for example. In this view, freedom to act might be weighed against personal security from harm, but not against financial costs alone.[13]

Some important thinkers, however, have shaped the risk-utility analysis into a more rigorous model for decision and one based on economic analysis and dollar comparisons between the costs to the defendant of avoiding harm and the cost to the plaintiff of suffering that harm. In the escaping-gas example, the more structured approach might hold that I am not negligent if it would cost me more to avoid the gas leaks than those leaks cost you and others in property damage. The next section considers this form of analysis.

§ 145. Structured Weighing of Risks against Utilities

Courts routinely apply some form of risk-utility weighing as a means of determining whether conduct was negligent. Some courts[1] have gone further by explicitly approving a form of risk-utility weighing that may be more rigorous or structured[2] than the free-form estimate of risks and costs sketched in the immediately preceding section.

Judge Hand's formula in Carroll Towing. The structured or rigorous model is usually traced to an opinion written by an impressive judge, Judge Learned Hand, and in fact is often referred to as the Hand formula or as the *Carroll Towing* doctrine after the case in which Hand advanced his ideas. *United States v. Carroll Towing*[3] was an admiralty case. A barge in a busy harbor broke loose and caused damage. Harm could have been avoided if a caretaker or bargee had been on board at all times, but he was not. The question was whether it was negligent not to have a 24–hour bargee.

13. Gregory C. Keating, Reasonableness and Rationality in Negligence Theory, 48 Stan. L. Rev. 311, 383 (1996) (offering a detailed theory for measuring "reasonableness", based on ideas of reciprocity and cooperation among free and equality individuals, rather than "rationality", based on maximizing aggregate human values as expressed in dollars). Professor Simons describes a number of ways in which one could weigh risks and utilities, for example, by saying that risk-taking is justified only if the utility of the risk is very much greater than the harm, although he disapproves this approach. See Kenneth W. Simons, Negligence, 16 Social Philosophy & Policy 2, 52, 78–80 (1999).

§ 145

1. Among the cases expressly recognizing a more rigorous approach embodied in the Hand formula discussed below, see, e.g., Levi v. Southwest Louisiana Electric Membership Cooperative, 542 So.2d 1081 (La. 1989); Lowe v. Estate Motors Limited, 428 Mich. 439, 410 N.W.2d 706 (1987). Among the cases that might be viewed as adopting a more rigorous approach but that do not state the explicit relationships between risk and utility, see Crane v. Smith, 23 Cal.2d 288, 144 P.2d 356 (1943) (formula from Restatement § 291). For a report of a survey of cases and citations to many of them, see Stephen G. Gilles, The Invisible Hand Formula, 80 Va. L. Rev. 1015, 1016, n. 4 (1994).

2. Emphasizing the rigor, structure, or form, see Michael D. Green, The Schizophrenia of Risk–Benefit Analysis in Design Defect Litigation, 48 Vand. L. Rev. 609 (1995); Barbara Ann White, Risk-utility Analysis and the Learned Hand Formula: A Hand that Helps or a Hand that Hides?, 32 Ariz. L. Rev. 77 (1990).

3. United States v. Carroll Towing Co., 159 F.2d 169 (2d Cir.1947).

Judge Hand recognized the traditional idea that a weighing of risks and utilities was necessary. He said, "[T]he owner's duty ... to provide against resulting injuries is a function of three variables: (1) The probability that [the barge] will break away; (2) the gravity of the resulting injury, if she does; (3) the burden of adequate precautions." This language summed up the experience of many cases, but Hand then went on. He identified the burden of precaution as B, damages as L, and probability as P, then stated his famous formula:

> [L]iability depends upon whether B is less than L multiplied by P: i.e., whether $B < PL$.

Precaution a burden to third persons or society. The burden of precaution in Judge Hand's formula includes any cost the defendant might have to incur to make things safe enough, but it also includes costs that would be inflicted upon others or upon society at large. For instance, cars often strike telephone or light poles. If the pole gives way and falls on impact, the passengers in the car are safer than if they had collided with an immovable object. On the other hand, falling poles may strike pedestrians or others. To make things safer for pedestrians is to make them riskier for car passengers and vice versa. So if the telephone company installs stronger poles to protect the pedestrian, part of the cost of doing so will be borne by car passengers who suffer injury as a result.[4]

Precaution a burden to defendant. In *Carroll Towing* itself, the burden of precaution was simple: the increased or marginal cost to the defendant of keeping a bargee on board 24 hours a day. Suppose that cost was, say, $30,000 a year in increased wages, and that breakaways averaged one a year with an average damage to other vessels of $20,000. In that scenario, the barge owner would not be negligent in failing to keep a 24-hour bargee because the cost to prevent a $20,000 loss would be a $30,000 expenditure, a result usually condemned as economically "inefficient."[5]

The firm analogy. The Learned Hand test treats the two parties as if they were partners in a firm. It says the firm would be foolish to spend $30,000 in one department to avoid a $20,000 loss in another department. A firm that does that regularly will soon be out of business. Although the plaintiff and defendant are not in fact members of the same private firm, they are members of the same society. That society is a very large firm that will be poorer if one of its citizens must spend $30 to save another $20.

Putting costs and benefits on the same scale. Thinking about the problem in terms of the *Carroll Towing* formula, a judge or juror[6] can

4. See Bernier v. Boston Edison Co., 380 Mass. 372, 403 N.E.2d 391 (1980) (concluding that risks to pedestrians were greater and hence that the defendant was negligent in constructing pole that would fall on slight impact).

5. See Richard Posner, A Theory of Negligence, 1 J. Leg. Stud. 29 (1972). Posner used examples similar to those given here.

6. The formula is mainly used by judges reviewing evidence to determine a directed verdict or motion for summary judgment, and only then when one party makes an argument based on the formula or some

compare benefits with costs because they have now been put on a common scale. Better safety is achieved at a cost of $30,000, but the safety benefit is only $20,000. The same point can be made by saying that the utility or benefit to the defendant in *not* having a bargee is $30,000 a year saved, but that the utility or benefit to injured parties that will result from having a 24–hour bargee is $20,000. By reducing all the costs and benefits to dollar terms, we can make such comparisons, and that is a great advantage. The great disadvantage of reducing the risks, costs, and benefits to dollar terms is that we might be treating quite incommensurate risks alike.[7]

Evidence and arguments suggested by the formula. On the illustrative facts above, the dollar comparison of utilities favors the defendant, but the test can just as easily work the other way around. If the defendant's cost of preventing the harm is less than the expected value of the harm itself, he is definitely negligent and liable under the Hand formula, as was the case in *Carroll Towing* itself. Indeed, one of the most important functions of the formula may be to direct lawyers to helpful kinds of evidence. Plaintiffs' lawyers may be thus led by the Hand formula to claim that the defendant failed to use a cheaper means of achieving safety. For instance, a plaintiff's lawyer might try to prove that the defendant could have avoided the breakaway in *Carroll Towing* by making a one-time capital investment in better tie-down technology that would be far less costly than either the full-time bargee or the potential harm from breakaways.[8] Similarly, the formula suggests and supports jury argument. The plaintiff who can show that by spending $1 the defendant could have avoided serious injury or injuries to many people has a ready-made and appealing jury argument. The Hand formula may not work as well for defendants' jury arguments; they may not wish to argue that it would have been costly to a large corporation to avoid paralyzing the plaintiff. But even defendants may find it possible

part of it. Juries are routinely instructed in the reasonable person standard without explanation about risk-utility balancing. See Stephen G. Gilles, The Invisible Hand Formula, 80 VA. L. REV. 1015 (1994) (concluding that the Hand formula is "underenforced" because of omissions to instruct the jury in its terms). Jury instruction issues always involve conflicts between thinkers who feel the jury should be led by the hand (or in this case by the Hand formula) with detailed instructions and those who feel the jury should be given only broad guidelines. A single person often believes both things about different issues to be decided by the jury. Whether the Hand formula is "underenforced" may depend on how much detailed instruction you believe the jury should have. In any event, juries are instructed on probability (under the rubric of foreseeability) and on commensurate care, a notion that embodies part of the risk-utility weighing. Juries may also hear lawyers' arguments about costs and benefits of the defendant's conduct and understand the relevance of evidence on those issues, such as evidence that the defendant could have achieved safety by a small expenditure.

7. See Gregory C. Keating, Reasonableness and Rationality in Negligence Theory, 48 STAN. L. REV. 311, 342 (1996) (people have "diverse and incommensurable conceptions of the good," and those at risk generally do not value the injurer's aims and benefits as the injurer does, a theme that appears in several places).

8. The cost of a capital investment may be hard to figure not only because it may avoid many injuries during its effective life but also because the defendant's expenditure is a cost for which the defendant receives some compensating gain in the form of increased capital assets.

to introduce evidence and to make arguments based on the Hand formula in appellate courts.

Probability and average. To speak of probability is to speak of foreseeability, but the language of probability is more precise in its structure. We can think of probability in terms of odds or percentages—a probability of .9 or a probability of .5 for example—but it sounds foolish to speak of .9 or 90% foreseeability. In the examples used above, probability is reflected in the averaging. If untended barges break away an average of ten times in a ten year period, doing damage each time, we know something about the probability of breakaways—one a year. If the untended barges break way twenty times in a 10-year period, the average is no longer one a year but two a year, and the probability is correspondingly twice as high as our first estimate. The same kind of thinking applies to the amount of harm factor. Some injuries might be small, while others are large, but it is the average that best expresses the total amount of harm for the time period involved.

Discounting to reflect probability. Part of the impact of Judge Hand's test comes from the fact that it literally discounts the plaintiff's damages as a part of getting the average. Probability can be expressed as a percentage or chance. If a given harm is certain to occur, the probability would be 1.00, but if the chance of its occurrence is only 50–50, the probability would be 0.50. So if the defendant's conduct created a risk of $100 damage, but the probability of harm was 0.50, the Hand formula tells us that we treat the damage in issue as $50 instead of $100 for purposes of comparing the defendant's cost. That is because we discount or multiply probability times harm to get the average. 0.50 x $100 gives us an average $50 damage.

Amount of plaintiff's recovery unaffected by the discount. Although probability is used to discount the damage when the point is to determine the defendant's negligence, probability is not used to reduce the plaintiff's actual recovery. If the defendant is found to be negligent by application of these rules, he is liable for all of the plaintiff's injury, whether it is $50, $100, or many times those amounts. The discount applies only as a way of determining the total risk imposed by the defendant's conduct.

Averaging, or the use of the probability discount, is important if the defendant is to estimate the appropriate overall amount to invest in safety. Any particular injured individual might suffer damages much less than the defendant's cost to avoid the harm but still recover because the average harm would exceed that cost. And vice versa: the injured individual might suffer much greater harm than the defendant's cost of avoidance and yet be denied recovery because the cost of avoidance was too high compared to the average or probable overall harms. Indeed, one of the criticisms of the Hand formula, at least as it might be rigorously applied, is that it may do social good without doing individual justice. The next section summarizes some of the criticisms.

§ 146. Supporting and Criticizing Structured Risk-Utility Assessments

In some negligence claims based on alleged medical malpractice and a few others, courts may bypass the risk-utility assessment altogether. In those cases, the custom of the profession may furnish the standard of care, so that even very risky procedures may not be counted as negligence if the profession customarily engages in

such procedures.[1] Otherwise, however, courts do routinely attempt to weigh risks and utilities to determine whether the defendant was negligent.

The Hand formula discussed in the immediately preceding section is often seen to be more rigorous than a free-form weighing of costs and benefits to determine whether conduct is negligent. Part of the rigor lies in the fact that the Hand formula places risks and utilities on a common scale of dollars so that they can be fully compared. Another part lies in the fact that the formula sets up precise relationships among probability, gravity of harm, and cost of safety. These characteristics represent both strengths and weaknesses of the formula.

Justifications and Limits

Economic justifications. Under an economic interpretation of the Hand formula, the purpose of a rigorous weighing of costs and benefits of the defendant's conduct is to generate a rule of liability that gives actors incentives to invest an appropriate amount in safety. Since virtually all conduct carries some risk, a world of perfect safety would eliminate or fantastically transform almost all conduct. The rigorous model of risk-utility weighing is often supported as an economic analysis intended to impose liability for economically inefficient risk-taking but to protect conduct that is efficient in the sense that the risks involved are worth taking. Risks that are worth taking produce more gains than losses, to the benefit of society as a whole by maximizing wealth (as a measure of human preferences). Judge Posner has provided some of the clearest arguments along these lines.[2]

Other advantages. Although commentators most often discuss economic justifications of the Hand formula, other justifications might be advanced. The rigorous approach may be better at protecting everyone's rights and freedoms to act in the world than a more intuitive approach. At the same time, it sets limits on that right. Moreover, it provides lawyers with a guide that is helpful in knowing what kind of evidence to produce. Finally, it constrains judges to explain their conclusions about negligence, not merely as an unfathomable exercise of power or discretion, but in terms that can be judged by professionals in the field.

§ 146

1. § 242.

2. Writing on this topic by economically oriented thinkers is voluminous. Judge Posner's writings are among the best known. See Richard Posner, A Theory of Negligence, 1 J. Leg. Stud. 29 (1972); Richard Posner, Economic Analysis of Law 163 ff. (4th ed. 1992).

Criticizing the Hand Formula

Incentives. Some criticisms of the Hand approach do not attack the underlying ideas of the formula so much as the claim that it promotes efficiency and appropriate safety incentives. In this group, some criticisms offer more or less technical variations or improvements on the formula.[3] Others deny that tort law provides incentives at all and hence suggest that the Hand formula might be irrelevant unless it serves other purposes.[4]

Inability to provide quantified data. A different kind of criticism is based on a misunderstanding of the formula, and it should be disposed of quickly. That criticism is essentially that the data required by the formula will not be available or that lawyers should not have to be mathematicians. But the formula does not require mathematical proof. For instance, the formula does not require lawyers to introduce evidence of probability expressed in mathematical terms or even evidence about dollar costs of safety precautions.

It is true, of course, that the plaintiff must prove her case somehow, and in some instances she may be unable to make a convincing case without showing some reliable evidence that the defendant's conduct created a substantial probability of harm[5] or that the defendant could have taken safety precautions at a low dollar cost.[6] But the Hand formula does not itself require numerical evidence, although it illuminates the ways in which such evidence is useful. In the great majority of cases, including Hand's own decision in *Carroll Towing*, the formula is applied to rough estimates derived from practical everyday evidence.

Nor is the formula useless for failure to require such proof. Like many other legal rules, it may represent less a guide to conduct than a guide for lawyers about the kind of evidence that will be useful, whether or not that evidence is quantified. A plaintiff's lawyer, for example, can attempt to demonstrate that the defendant could easily have provided better safety without demonstrating the exact cost of doing so, or that harm was highly probable because it had often occurred in similar circumstances, even if the probability cannot be expressed in a percentage. The formula also provides a meaningful model for analysis by

3. See Mark Grady, A New Positive Economic Theory of Negligence, 92 YALE L. J. 799 (1983) (since injurers cannot always know what level of precaution courts will find acceptable, the formula must be applied in a different way).

4. E.g., Daniel Shuman, The Psychology of Deterrence in Tort Law, 42 KAN. L. REV. 115 (1993)

5. E.g, Turpin v. Merrell Dow Pharmaceuticals, Inc., 959 F.2d 1349 (6th Cir.1992) (statistical evidence on probability that Bendectin caused fetal limb-reduction was inadequate).

6. McCarty v. Pheasant Run, Inc., 826 F.2d 1554 (7th Cir.1987) (plaintiff claimed hotel should have provided better locks, but put on no evidence as to costs). In contrast, in Grimshaw v. Ford Motor Co., 119 Cal. App.3d 757, 174 Cal.Rptr. 348 (1981), the plaintiff was able to show exact dollar costs of improvements that would have prevented the Pinto car from engulfing its occupants in flames. The evidence was highly effective and the plaintiffs recovered. In addition to direct cost evidence, the plaintiff's lawyer might be able to produce evidence of customary precautions. Such evidence tends to show both foreseeability of harm and the relative feasibility of a safety precaution. See §§ 163–165.

judges, even if judges must use estimates of probabilities, costs, and benefits.[7]

Individual justice. One of the most fundamental criticisms generated by rigorous application of the *Carroll Towing* test is that it emphasizes social good too much and individual justice or moral choice too little.[8] It makes the rights of the individual plaintiff depend in part upon what is good for society as a whole. In one form or another, this is the most central argument against Hand's formula. Although the Hand formula does not call for use of actual numbers like those used in the illustrations, and a complete set of such numbers could seldom be produced in court, the formula does definitely emphasize the importance of estimating social advantage or wealth maximization in society at large by insisting that no one should be required to spend more on safety than the sums saved by those expenditures. Some thinkers may fear that weighing risks and utilities turns "moral analysis into a bloodless form of calculation" that simply involves plugging in numbers.[9]

Incommensurables. Another characteristic of the more rigorous Hand test has found disfavor in some quarters. At least as it has been developed in economic theory, the Hand test asks us to reduce the utilities of both parties to a common scale of dollars. The common scale is important, because it permits comparison. However, the result is that a broken leg is valued like a commodity; its worth is expressed in the jury's assessment of dollar value based on medical costs, wage loss, and pain—no more, no less. If that total value is only $10,000 but the cost to the defendant to avoid the injury is $15,000, the defendant is not negligent. But if the death of a human being is intractably incommensurate with dollar costs of safer conduct, the common scale, however elegant, is exactly the wrong scale.[10] To some extent, this criticism is meliorated by the fact that the jury is allowed to decide the value of intangibles like pain and loss of enjoyment, even though the jury must

7. Levi v. Southwest Louisiana Electric Membership Cooperative, 542 So.2d 1081 (La.1989); see David G. Owen, Defectiveness Restated: Exploding the "Strict" Products Liability Myth, 1996 U. ILL. L. REV. 743 (1996) ("This type of 'cost-benefit' or 'risk-utility' analysis may be problematic if relied upon excessively as a mechanical device for producing automatic 'right' answers, but it nicely describes the decisional calculus that lies at the heart of products liability law in particular and accident law in general").

8. See, e.g., Bamford v. Turnley, 3 B. & S. 67, 122 Eng.Rep. 27 (Exch. Ch. 1862) (Judgment of Bramwell B.) (arguing that defendant must use the gains from his activities to pay the costs of harms inflicted on others); Gregory C. Keating, Reasonableness and Rationality in Negligence Theory, 48 STAN. L. REV. 311 (1996); George P. Fletcher, Fairness and Utility in Tort Theory, 85 HARV. L. REV. 537 (1972).

9. See Kenneth W. Simons, Negligence, 16 SOCIAL PHILOSOPHY & POLICY 2, 52, 80 (1999) (but suggesting that "qualitative" balancing without using dollar costs would avoid this problem).

10. See Barbara Ann White, Risk-utility Analysis and the Learned Hand Formula: A Hand that Helps or a Hand That Hides?, 32 ARIZ. L. REV. 77, 111, n. 192 (1990); Gregory C. Keating, Reasonableness and Rationality in Negligence Theory, 48 STAN. L. REV. 311, 342 (1996); cf. Michael D. Green, The Schizophrenia of Risk–Benefit Analysis in Design Defect Litigation, 48 VAND. L. REV. 609 (1995) (emphasizing incommensurability and the impracticability of making a jury argument that human lives are worth less than the cost of a safety feature on an automobile); Richard Wright, The Standards of Care in Negligence Law in PHILOSOPHICAL FOUNDATIONS OF TORT LAW 249 (David G. Owen, ed. 1995).

necessarily reduce those values to dollar damages. It might also be meliorated by a "hybrid" approach, as where qualitative values could be considered to constrain the use of a pure dollar scale.[11]

Unworkable in some cases. Still another criticism is that some kinds of cases seem to lend themselves only poorly to a rigorous risk-utility analysis. For instance, when the defendant is charged with a moment's inattention or negligently forgetting to do something necessary for safety, it is quite difficult to analyze the costs to achieve better safety. What are the costs of remembering?[12] One scholar has put the point more strongly by saying that where repeated safety efforts are required—as where a driver must constantly keep a lookout—even reasonable people will occasionally lapse, but that in such cases courts routinely impose liability.[13] The implication is that the risk-utility balance cannot explain this liability and thus that the risk-utility balance applies only to "durable precautions" such as designs, plans, or systems for dealing with hazards.

A different kind of unworkability argument is that in some cases the defendant knows there is some kind of risk but does not know its extent or what will reduce the risk. In such a case, how much money should he spend to get more information? Without knowing the magnitude or severity of the risks, it will be difficult indeed to know how much to invest in getting more information. This is routinely a problem for manufacturers of new drugs, which usually have risks the full extent of which may never be known.[14]

Perspectives for Evaluation

(1) Although the Hand formula in *Carroll Towing* is usually analyzed in economic terms, part of its operation can be viewed as a moral proposition that you should treat others as you would treat yourself.[15] If

11. Kenneth W. Simons, Negligence, 16 Social Philosophy & Policy 2, 52, 86 (1999) (suggesting that under the Hand test, a value must be placed on human life when it is at risk, but that if the risk is death by fire, the trier could also consider whether such a death is particularly dreaded).

12. See Izhak Englard, The System Builders: A Critical Appraisal of Modern American Tort Theory, 9 J. Leg. Stud. 27 (1980); Mark Grady, Why Are People Negligent? Technology, Non–Durable Precautions, and the Medical Malpractice Explosion, 82 Nw. U. L. Rev. 293 (1988). Judge Posner himself may have implied the jury could figure a forgetful (or sleepy) person's cost "of schooling herself to greater vigilance." Wassell v. Adams, 865 F.2d 849 (7th Cir.1989).

13. Grady, Res Ipsa Loquitur and Compliance Error, 142 U. Pa. L. Rev. 887 (1994).

14. Relatedly, a rigorous risk-utility analysis might be acceptable or even appealing where the plaintiff and defendant are engaged in similar activities, potentially imposing similar risks upon each other. That was the situation in *Carroll Towing*, where barges imposed risks to other vessels and vice versa. But, it might be argued, when a defendant systematically imposes risks upon victims who never impose similar risks in return, the formula is less attractive. That might be the case of product manufacturers whose products risk harm to consumers where consumers do not in return risk harms to the manufacturers. David Barnes & Lynn Stout, The Economic Analysis of Tort Law 38 (1992) suggests something like this, reading the Hand formula to mean "victims suffer so that actors may prosper," and suggesting that in nonreciprocal risk cases like the manufacturer-consumer case, using the Hand formula might have "distributional" implications.

15. Cf. Kenneth W. Simons, Deontology, Negligence, Tort, and Crime, 76 B.U. L. Rev. 273 (1996).

you can save $100 of your own by spending $50, you should and would do so. If you can save $100 of your own only by spending $200, you would not make the expenditure. Only if you should treat others better than you would treat yourself is there reason to think you are wrong in failing to take the $200 precaution.[16] Sometimes defendants are indeed under an obligation to treat the plaintiff with special care arising from an undertaking or special relationship. But where the defendant is guilty of no misleading, has no special relationship with the plaintiff, and does not owe more care by custom or his own undertaking, the Hand formula can often be seen in moral rather than economic terms. Indeed, utility itself, whether cast in economic terms or not, can be seen to have a moral quality.[17]

(2) People can reasonably think that both the justifications and the criticisms of the Hand formula are exaggerated. The formula assuredly has its uses in the process of determining negligence, but it may be more useful in some cases than others. Positive statutory law displaces the formula in many cases. Relationships of the parties may dictate duties or defenses in others. Custom may be especially important in still others. The formula can be seen as a default formula, to be used when it is not trumped by something more important.

(3) Judges do in fact use some kind of risk-utility analysis, not necessarily under that name and not necessarily with the rigor that economic analysis would suggest. Most of the objections to the Hand formula seem aimed at its rigorous comparison of dollar costs rather than at the underlying idea that some kind of weighing of costs and benefits is necessary.

(4) If all weighing of costs and benefits, risks and utilities, were discarded, courts might be hard pressed to find any generally applicable way of analyzing negligence. A judge's conclusory statements that the defendant did or did not behave reasonably would not be satisfactory and would not much resemble anything we would like to call law. However, it would be possible to weigh costs and benefits, risks and utilities by appealing to the ideals of a reasonable person who considers something besides dollar costs.[18]

§ 147. Slight and Aggravated Negligence

The risk-utility formula, structured or unstructured, suggests that some negligent acts are in a sense worse than others. If it is unreason-

16. Arguing that because willingness to face risks differs legitimately in a plural society, you should indeed treat others according to some standard of reasonableness, not according to your own preferences or according to an economic valuation, see Gregory C. Keating, Reasonableness and Rationality in Negligence Theory, 48 Stan. L. Rev. 311 (1996). Professor Richard Wright thinks that morally speaking, you need not treat others as yourself and in fact a rule requiring you to do so is to treat no one as a distinct person with her own life to lead. See Richard Wright, supra n. 10.

17. See David G. Owen, The Moral Foundations of Products Liability Law: Toward First Principles, 68 Notre Dame L. Rev. 427 (1993).

18. Gregory C. Keating, Reasonableness and Rationality in Negligence Theory, 48 Stan. L. Rev. 311, 342 (1996).

ably risky to drive at 80 mph under given conditions, then it is more risky to drive at 90, and more risky still to do so when playful children are nearby and likely to dart into the street. That is to say that if the probability or magnitude of harm is higher, we can think of the defendant as "more" negligent. Similarly, if the utility of the defendant's conduct diminishes, even the same risk becomes less justified and his conduct more aggravated. To recognize this point is not to displace the reasonable person standard but to uphold it. The reasonable person recognizes that greater risks call for increased caution, or, as the courts say, care commensurate with the risks.

Slight, ordinary, and extraordinary care. This line of thought suggests that there are many degrees of negligence. It definitely does not suggest that there are merely three degrees of negligence, but in the early 18th century a judge came up with the idea that all negligence could be classified in three degrees—slight, ordinary, and gross.[1] A person might be guilty of slight negligence if he failed to exercise extraordinary care and guilty of gross negligence if he failed to exercise even slight care.

This tripartite division of care happened to fit neatly into the judge's ideas about the kind of care required in bailment cases. He thought you would be obliged to exercise only slight care if you held another's property as a favor, and hence you'd be liable only for gross negligence. On the other hand, if you held another's property for your own benefit, you'd be obliged to exercise extraordinary care and would be liable for slight negligence. If the bailment was for mutual benefit, ordinary care would be required and you would be liable for ordinary negligence. This little schematic picture is still sometimes the basis for decisions in bailment cases.[2] Read literally, it provides standards of care different from the standard of the ordinary prudent person standard—less care in one instance, more in another.

Degrees of negligence generally irrelevant. It is not easy to believe that there are three and only three degrees of fault, since risks imposed by the defendant's conduct range in virtually infinite gradations. But in the great mass of cases there is no occasion at all to distinguish among any degrees of fault at all. In most cases, a defendant is subject to liability for negligence whether his negligence is great or small. He is liable for damages that will compensate the plaintiff for the plaintiff's actual harm, but that liability is not diminished if the defendant's negligence is slight, nor is it increased if the defendant's negligence is gross.[3]

§ 147

1. Coggs v. Bernard, 2 Ld.Raym. 909, 92 Eng.Rep. 107 (1703).

2. E.g., Coachmen Industries, Inc. v. Crown Steel Co., 577 N.E.2d 602 (Ind.App. 1991) ("Because Coachmen, as bailee, received no benefit from this arrangement, it was obligated to exercise only slight care in protecting the material from injury").

3. Distinguish comparative fault issues. "Degrees" of fault may be relevant in determining comparative responsibility, but only in a purely relative way: A's negligence is compared with B's to determine the share of ultimately responsibility. It may be

Practical difficulties. Certainly the division of all negligence into three degrees has not proved helpful and has been generally criticized. The trouble is that it is extremely difficult to use effectively. If you say that in one circumstance the defendant is liable for slight negligence and in another only for gross negligence, you invite a great deal of bootless wrangling over questions that cannot be objectively determined in any event. Was the defendant's negligence more than "ordinary"? Was the case one that required gross negligence or was it one that required only slight negligence? Where courts tried to institute a general scheme of slight, ordinary, and gross negligence, difficulties of this kind made it clear that the scheme was not practical, and it was abandoned.[4] Nothing was lost in leaving the scheme behind because the reasonable prudent person test, with its attention to circumstances, was quite adequate to deal with the cases.

Where degrees of negligence are relevant. Nevertheless, courts and legislatures do provide for limited standards of care in particular cases. In some of these, the defendant is held only to a standard of "slight" care, which is to say he is liable only if he is guilty of "gross" negligence. In others, courts insist on a standard even more protective of the defendant: the defendant is liable only if he is guilty of reckless, willful, or wanton misconduct. For example, statutes often provide that operators of emergency vehicles like fire engines are liable only for reckless or wanton misconduct.[5] Similarly, statutes may limit the liability of public entities to cases of wanton misconduct.[6] Landowners owe a similarly limited duty of care to many persons on the land.[7] The old guest statutes provided that the driver of an automobile was liable to a nonpaying guest only for gross negligence, or, in some jurisdictions, willful, wanton, or reckless conduct.[8] Only slightly different are punitive damages, which may be awarded in negligence cases only upon a finding of "malice" or wanton misconduct or the like.[9] These limited standards of care and the standard for punitive awards make "degrees of negligence" quite relevant in particular cases.

Gross negligence. Gross negligence can be used to mean what it says—a high, though unspecified degree of negligence. Presumably this

that both A and B are only slightly negligent as measured on an absolute scale, but they are nevertheless together responsible for the entire set of damages.

4. See Prosser & Keeton, 210.

5. E.g., Saarinen v. Kerr, 84 N.Y.2d 494, 644 N.E.2d 988, 620 N.Y.S.2d 297 (1994)

6. See Calloway v. Kinkelaar, 168 Ill.2d 312, 213 Ill.Dec. 675, 659 N.E.2d 1322 (1995); cf. Grimm v. Arizona Board of Pardons & Paroles, 115 Ariz. 260, 564 P.2d 1227 (1977) (parole's board's release of dangerous prisoner, gross negligence).

7. See Calvillo–Silva v. Home Grocery, 19 Cal.4th 714, 968 P.2d 65, 80 Cal.Rptr.2d 506 (1998) and Chapter 13 generally.

8. See, e.g., Scott v. Villegas, 723 So.2d 642 (Ala.1998) (quoting and discussing Alabama's guest statute, which requires wanton misconduct, defined to require conscious culpability). Most of these statutes have been repealed or held unconstitutional, as in Brown v. Merlo, 8 Cal.3d 855, 106 Cal.Rptr. 388, 506 P.2d 212 (1973).

9. See e.g., Tackett v. State Farm Fire & Casualty Ins. Co., 653 A.2d 254, 265 (Del.1995) ("Mere inadvertence, mistake or errors of judgment which constitute mere negligence will not suffice. It is not enough that a decision be wrong. It must result from a conscious indifference to the decision's foreseeable effect"). On punitive damages, see §§ 381–383.

means conduct that is appreciably more risky, or less beneficial, than conduct qualifying as ordinary negligence. Used in that way, the term would not require any particular state of mind so long as the conduct itself creates an extremely unjustified risk. A defendant might be grossly negligent in this sense without being aware that his conduct would be so characterized.[10] Many courts, however, have defined gross negligence in particular cases as requiring a bad state of mind as well as extreme fault.[11] When they do so, they usually give gross negligence the same definition as willful and wanton misconduct.

Reckless, willful or wanton conduct. The idea of reckless, willful or wanton misconduct is similar in that the risk-utility balance strongly disfavors the defendant's conduct—the risk was high, or very serious harm was threatened, or the cost of avoiding the danger was very low. But reckless, willful or wanton misconduct also entails a mental element that is not necessarily required to establish gross negligence.

The defendant is guilty of reckless, willful or wanton misconduct only if he was conscious of the risk or had specific reason to know about it[12] and proceeded without concern for the safety of others.[13] The defendant does not intentionally harm another, but he intentionally or consciously runs a very serious risk with no good reason to do so. He is guilty of "conscious indifference" as the courts say. Although reckless, willful, or wanton misconduct is not the same as intentional harm, in extreme cases courts may treat wanton misconduct more like an intentional tort than like negligence.[14]

The state-of-mind requirement is not, of course, related to "degrees of negligence," which is a matter of conduct, not a matter of mental states. However, the defendant's state of mind can ordinarily only be

10. Thus, for example, gross negligence, signifying extreme fault without a bad state of mind, is not a sufficient basis for an award of punitive damages, which requires a state of mind as well. Paiz v. State Farm Fire & Casualty Co., 118 N.M. 203, 880 P.2d 300 (1994).

11. E.g., Wal-Mart Stores, Inc. v. Alexander, 868 S.W.2d 322 (Tex.1993); Hardingham v. United Counseling Service of Bennington County, Inc., 164 Vt. 478, 672 A.2d 480 (1995) ("gross negligence is more than an error of judgment, momentary inattention, or loss of presence of mind; rather, it amounts to a failure to exercise even a slight degree of care and an indifference to the duty owed"; "Gross negligence is substantially and appreciably higher in magnitude and more culpable than ordinary negligence.... It is a heedless and palpable violation of legal duty respecting the rights of others").

12. Reason to know or notice: The defendant has information that would lead directly to an inference of the relevant facts or conditions. Reason to know or notice is not equivalent to "should know." See Restatement § 12. Whether the "reason to know" category is really needed, or for that matter, can really be applied in a principled way, is another matter.

13. E.g., Bader v. Lawson, 320 Ark. 561, 898 S.W.2d 40 (1995) ("utter indifference to, or conscious disregard of, the safety of others"); Doe v. Calumet City, 161 Ill.2d 374, 204 Ill.Dec. 274, 641 N.E.2d 498 (1994) (statutory definition similar); Morris v. Leaf, 534 N.W.2d 388 (Iowa 1995) ("in disregard of a risk known to or so obvious that he must be taken to have been aware of it, and so great as to make it highly probable that harm would follow"); Campbell v. City of Elmira, 84 N.Y.2d 505, 644 N.E.2d 993, 620 N.Y.S.2d 302 (1994) (harm highly probable coupled with conscious indifference to the outcome); Restatement § 500.

14. See Ziarko v. Soo Line R.R., 161 Ill.2d 267, 204 Ill.Dec. 178, 641 N.E.2d 402 (1994) (sometimes more like negligence, sometimes more like intent).

proved by proving the defendant's conduct, so that extreme departure from ordinary care in many cases tends to prove not only gross negligence but a conscious indifference to the rights of others.

Comparative fault distinguished. In a way, degrees of negligence are also implicated in comparative negligence decisions,[15] but both the purpose and the assessment are different. In assessing comparative fault of the plaintiff and defendant for the purpose of reducing the faulty plaintiff's damages recovery, the trier of fact is not concerned with the absolute degree of either party's negligence, but with a comparison of the two. The comparative fault of the plaintiff and the defendant is conventionally expressed in percentage terms, so the plaintiff's negligence might be 10% of the total and the defendant's 90%. But the 90% figure does not mean that the defendant was grossly negligent or reckless; it means only that whatever the "degree" of the defendant's negligence, it was nine times as much as the plaintiff's.

15. See Chapter 11.

Chapter 8

Proving and Evaluating Negligence Claims: Judge, Jury, and Evidence

Topic A. Judge and Jury

§ 148. Roles of the Jury in Negligence Cases

Much of the legal argument in negligence litigation is directed to questions of legal process. The first question for either the plaintiff's or defendant's lawyer is likely to be, will the case get to the jury? Or will the judge intervene to take the case from the jury by summary judgment or directed verdict? Process of course is always important; it is doubly important when, as in negligence cases, the rules of law do not closely constrain the outcome. In that situation, a good decision-making process is the main hope for results that are both fair to the parties and wise in policy.

Juries as fact-deciders. The first major role for juries in negligence cases is determination of the facts. At least some of the factual contentions of the parties are in dispute in almost every negligence case. Frequently the facts bearing on negligence or causation are disputed, but even when the parties agree upon those facts, they are likely to differ about the facts bearing on the extent of the plaintiff's injury. Where evidence shows a dispute about historical facts, the jury is almost invariably the decision-maker. Did the engineer blow the whistle at the crossing? Was the light green? Did the doctor warn the patient of the dangers of a proposed operation? These are decisions for the jury, not the judge, so long as the evidence creates dispute. Even if there is no overt dispute, the jury must still determine whether evidence supporting the plaintiff's claim is true or false; if not convinced by the plaintiff's evidence, the jury must find the facts in favor of the defendant, even when the defendant has introduced no evidence at all.[1]

Credibility of witnesses. In deciding pure facts, juries must often decide the weight of evidence and inferences to be drawn from it. Juries must also decide whether one witness is mistaken or lying, while deciding whether another has told at least part of the truth. The process rule here is that the jury is the sole judge of credibility of witnesses. Judges may not decide which witnesses were telling the truth and which

§ 148

1. § 150.

were lying or mistaken.[2] That means judges cannot direct a verdict for either party based on the judge's view about which witnesses were telling the truth. Moreover, the credibility of witness decision by the jury is qualitative, not quantitative. That is, the jury may believe the one witness who says the defendant was speeding and disbelieve the 32 who say he was not.[3] Judges do, however, instruct juries as to matters to keep in mind in judging credibility. For instance, judges may tell the jury that in determining credibility it should consider the consistency of a witness' testimony and whether the witness has an interest in the outcome of the case.[4]

Juries as conduct evaluators. The second major role for juries in negligence cases is to evaluate the facts to determine whether the defendant was negligent, whether his conduct was a legal cause of the plaintiff's harm, and the amount of damages.[5] The value judgments entailed are quite different from the determination of historical facts. If the plaintiff claims injury resulting when, on a dark night, she bumped into a face-level box attached to a utility pole, the jury must first determine whether defendant attached such a box to the pole, how high it was, and whether the plaintiff in fact bumped into it. Those are questions of historical fact. Once those historical facts are determined, the jury must go further and decide whether the defendant's conduct amounted to the negligent creation of an unreasonable risk. For this there is no conclusive legal guide except the standard of the reasonable and prudent person. It is the jury's job to make a judgment whether the defendant's conduct met that standard.[6] Similarly, juries must make a judgment call in deciding whether the defendant's conduct was a legal cause of the plaintiff's harm, which is usually to say whether it created a risk of the general kind of harm the plaintiff suffered.[7] Finally, the jury makes judgments about the appropriate amount of damages on certain intangible elements like pain and suffering and punitive damages.[8]

Although courts often say that negligence is a fact question for the jury, or a mixed question of law and fact, such expressions are conventional shorthand. They are not intended to deny that the jury's role is to

2. E.g., Young v. Wlazik, 262 N.W.2d 300 (Minn.1977) (judge's instruction that railroad employee was ringing the bell was erroneous because it in effect decided a disputed fact), overruled in part by Perkins v. Nat'l Railroad Passenger Corp., 289 N.W.2d 462 (Minn.1979).

3. See Mazzotta v. Los Angeles Ry. Corp., 25 Cal.2d 165, 153 P.2d 338 (1944).

4. Instructions often given along these lines: "You [the jury] are the sole judges of the facts in this case and must determine which witnesses you will believe and what weight you will give to their testimony. In doing so you may take into account each witness' ability and opportunity to observe, [his/or/her] memory, [his/or/her] manner while testifying, any interest, bias or prejudice [he/or/she] may have, and the reasonableness of his testimony considered in the light of all the evidence in the case." See Michigan Standard Jury Instructions 2.01 & 4.01 (2d ed. 1981).

5. Restatement § 328C.

6. Delmarva Power & Light v. Stout, 380 A.2d 1365 (Del.1977) (jury to decide whether the known conduct violated the reasonable person standard); cf. Kemper v. Builder's Square, 109 Ohio App.3d 127, 671 N.E.2d 1104 (1996) (jury to say whether defendant's method of displaying and securing was negligent).

7. See Chapter 10.

8. See § 377.

evaluate conduct once it has determined what that conduct in fact was.[9] Because part of the jury's role is to make normative decisions or value judgments, courts do not normally grant summary judgment on negligence issues, even if the facts are undisputed. In other words, the jury must still weigh the risks and utilities associated with the facts it has determined to exist.[10]

§ 149. Roles of the Judge in Negligence Cases

Procedural and administrative roles aside, common law judges have several major roles in negligence cases.

1. *Legal duties and standards*. Judges rather than juries determine whether the defendant was under a duty of care at all and if so what standard of care applied. That is to say that the standard of care and existence of a duty to use care are matters of law and are determined by legal rules.

For a great many cases, legal rules have long since made it clear that the defendant owes the plaintiff a duty of reasonable care as judged by the standard of the ordinary prudent person under the circumstances. In some cases, however, judges determine (usually on the basis of appellate precedent) that some other standard applies, so that the defendant owes only some lesser duty, such as a duty not to impose risks wilfully or wantonly. In still others, courts may conclude that the defendant owes no duty at all. All such decisions are to be made by judges, not juries.

If the judge concludes that the defendant owed no duty at all, the judge will grant a motion to dismiss, or a summary judgment, or a directed verdict, whichever is procedurally appropriate. If the judge determines that the defendant owed a duty of care, the judge will instruct the jury as to the proper standard. If the proper standard depends upon which version of facts the jury accepts, the judge will likewise instruct the jury to determine the facts and then apply the appropriate standard.

2. *Sufficiency of the evidence. (a) Insufficient evidence.* Although judges are not empowered to decide the factual disputes in the case, they are definitely empowered to conclude that there is no evidence at all and equally empowered to conclude that the evidence is so weak that reasonable people could not accept it as sufficient to prove the plaintiff's case. If no reasonable person could find the defendant's conduct to be negligent, the judge will direct a verdict for the defendant.[1] On the other

9. See Foster v. South Carolina Dept. of Highways and Pub. Transport., 306 S.C. 519, 413 S.E.2d 31 (1992) ("Negligence being a mixed question of law and fact, it is the court's duty to define negligence, but it is the jury's province to draw the inference from the facts. Only when the evidence supports but one reasonable inference does the question become a matter of law for the court").

10. E.g., Little v. Liquid Air Corp., 952 F.2d 841 (5th Cir.1992).

§ 149

1. The usual test is whether reasonable people may differ. The exact formula may be slightly different in some jurisdictions without changing the essential meaning of the test except perhaps in small degree. E.g., Lowe's Home Centers, Inc. v. Laxson,

hand, if reasonable people, considering the evidence in the light most favorable to the plaintiff,[2] could differ, the issue will be one for the jury to decide. In that case, the judge must leave the issue to the jury for its decision, even if the judge has a strong personal opinion that the defendant is not negligent.[3] The judge has a similar role when it comes to other issues in the plaintiff's case, for example, the issues of actual and legal cause.[4]

(b) Forms of insufficiency: reasonable people cannot differ as to facts. The plaintiff's evidence might be insufficient in two distinct senses. First, the plaintiff may not have sufficient evidence of facts necessary to her case.[5] If she wishes to prove that the defendant was negligent in driving too fast, but cannot prove anything about his speed, the judge must direct a verdict for the defendant on that issue.

(c) Forms of insufficiency: reasonable people cannot differ about whether facts amount to negligence. Second, the plaintiff may prove the historical facts quite clearly, but the facts may fail to show any basis for evaluating those facts as "negligence." That is, the evidence may not permit reasonable persons to conclude that the defendant violated any standard of care.[6] If the plaintiff proves that the defendant was driving at 55 miles an hour on a clear, open highway, the facts are proven but the judge may conclude that reasonable people could not find negligence on the basis of such speed under the circumstances of the case. If so, the judge must again direct a verdict for the defendant. In the same way, reasonable people cannot find that a defendant is negligent in failing to warn of a danger if the defendant neither knew nor should have known of it.[7] Judges may differ among themselves about whether reasonable people could differ. Some judges will leave close cases to the jury, while others prefer to resolve doubts in favor of jury control.[8]

655 So.2d 943 (Ala.1994) ("Whether fair-minded persons, exercising impartial judgment, could reasonably infer from the evidence that Latham was acting reasonably when the accident occurred").

2. E.g., Abebe v. Benitez, 667 A.2d 834 (D.C.App.1995).

3. See District of Columbia v. Coleman, 667 A.2d 811 (D.C.App.1995) ("The absence or presence of contributory negligence is generally a question for the jury.... It is only where the minds of reasonable persons cannot differ that the court is justified in deciding the question as a matter of law"); McHaffie v. Bunch, 891 S.W.2d 822 (Mo. 1995) ("If reasonable minds could differ as to when a driver knew or could have known of a reasonable likelihood of collision, the question of when the duty arises to take evasive action is for the jury"); Franconia Associates v. Clark, 250 Va. 444, 463 S.E.2d 670 (Va. 1995) (contributory negligence, reasonable people could differ).

4. E.g., Morehart v. Dillard Department Stores, 322 Ark. 290, 908 S.W.2d 331 (1995) (plaintiff who fell on defendant's ramp offered no evidence as to cause of the fall, directed verdict proper).

5. See Restatement § 328B (b) (existence or non-existence of facts).

6. Restatement § 328B (d).

7. Scordino v. Hopeman Brothers, Inc., 662 So.2d 640 (Miss.1995) (asbestos dust); cf. Cloonan v. Food–4–Less of 30th and Weber, Inc., 247 Neb. 677, 529 N.W.2d 759 (1995) (jury cannot find negligence of store owner in customer slip-and-fall case where slippery substance could not have been discovered).

8. See Parsons v. Crown Disposal Co., 15 Cal.4th 456, 936 P.2d 70, 63 Cal.Rptr.2d 291 (1997) (majority: garbage truck noise that frightened horse was not negligent, even though truck operated near bridle path and steps could have been taken to reduce the risk; dissent: it was a jury question whether defendant was negligent).

(d) Forms of insufficiency: Inferences of fact. Insufficient evidence issues often arise when the plaintiff must rely upon circumstantial evidence. Circumstantial evidence can be exceptionally strong, perhaps stronger than much unreliable eyewitness testimony. But the circumstances proven by evidence must rationally permit inferences in favor of the plaintiff if it is to assist the plaintiff's case. If the chain of inferences from circumstantial evidence do not rationally support the plaintiff's claim, the judge will not permit the jury to draw those inferences.

For instance, suppose the plaintiff proves that he was crossing a street on foot when he was struck by the defendant's car but he proves nothing else. The plaintiff wishes the jury to infer that the defendant failed to keep a proper lookout or drove too fast, but those inferences are not compelling because one could also infer that the plaintiff walked in front of the defendant's vehicle. If the plaintiff has no other evidence of negligence, the judge is likely to direct a verdict for the defendant in such a case.[9]

(e) Exceptionally strong evidence; directing a verdict for the party with the burden of proof. The judge's power to direct a verdict for the defendant when the plaintiff's evidence is insufficient does not suggest that the judge has equal power to direct a verdict for the plaintiff when the evidence is very strong. In fact, judges are most reluctant to direct a verdict for the party having the burden of proof,[10] as the plaintiff does on the issues of negligence and cause. That is partly because even if the plaintiff's evidence is uncontradicted, the jury would nevertheless be within its powers in disbelieving that evidence. Only in quite rare cases, when the plaintiff's evidence is overwhelmingly strong, or the admitted conduct violates a statute or specific rules of law, do courts direct a verdict for the plaintiff, as where the defendant runs a stop sign and drives into the side of the plaintiff's car which is in plain view but which the defendant never saw.[11]

When the issue is not the defendant's negligence but the plaintiff's contributory negligence, the defendant, not the plaintiff, has the burden proof. In that situation the parties' roles are reversed. So the defendant should seldom be able to persuade a judge to direct a verdict in favor of the defendant on the issue of contributory fault of the plaintiff. Again, however, courts will do so when the plaintiff has admittedly violated a statute or a specific rule of law.[12]

(f) New trial powers. As the paragraphs above indicate, judges can direct verdicts for insufficient evidence and thus remove the jury from

9. Cf. Gift v. Palmer, 392 Pa. 628, 141 A.2d 408 (1958) (small child struck in street; directed verdict even though defendant's view of street and access to it was clear).

10. E.g., Brandt v. Pelican, 856 S.W.2d 658 (Mo.1993). One qualification: the defendant has the burden of proving the plaintiff's contributory negligence or assumed risk as a defense, yet in some periods judges were sometimes rather willing to direct a verdict for the defendant on these issues. E.g., Allison v. Snelling & Snelling, Inc., 425 Pa. 519, 229 A.2d 861 (1967).

11. Floyd v. Worobec, 248 Neb. 605, 537 N.W.2d 512 (1995) .

12. See §§ 132 & 134, supra; and see n. 10, supra.

the decision-maker's role only when reasonable people could not differ on the issue. However, when a judge feels that a jury has done an injustice, the judges has one power in reserve. That is the power to grant a new trial. The judge might grant a new trial for some error in the first trial, but the ground for new trial that is of interest here is different. In some states the judge is empowered to grant a new trial whenever the judge concludes that the jury's verdict was against the weight of the evidence.[13] More cautious jurisdictions may constrain the judge's new trial power somewhat more, but they still permit judges to grant a new trial even where a directed verdict would be improper.[14] Under the more liberal new trial rules, judges are permitted to weigh the evidence and credibility of witnesses in deciding whether to grant a new trial.

Why are judges allowed to weigh the evidence and determine credibility on a motion for new trial when they are not allowed to do so on a motion for directed verdict? Part of the answer is that the judge's decision on a motion for directed verdict would decide the whole case, while a motion for new trial resubmits the case to a new jury. Another part of the answer is that judges are highly motivated not to grant a new trial because of the costs of trial to the judicial system as well as to the parties, and so judges are not likely, even subconsciously, to be overgenerous in granting the motion. For the same reason, however, the losing party will seldom be successful in obtaining a discretionary new trial on these grounds.

3. *Types of harm compensable.* Judges, through legal rules, prescribe the types of harm compensable. When the plaintiff claims emotional harm resulting from the defendant's negligent injury to someone else, for example, courts often impose quite restrictive rules, the effect of which is to deny recovery in many instances.

4. *Evidentiary rulings.* Besides their important administrative and procedural roles, judges in negligence cases carry out two important functions that constrain or shape the jury's participation. First, judges decide what evidence to admit or exclude from the jury's consideration. In general, judges admit all relevant evidence and exclude irrelevant and hearsay evidence. But even some relevant evidence might be excluded and thus not heard by the jury when its relevance is remote and its prejudicial impact is high. In the case of expert testimony, the judge may also exclude the evidence if the expert is deemed not sufficiently quali-

13. Bristow v. Flurry, 320 Ark. 51, 894 S.W.2d 894 (1995) ("when the verdict is clearly against the preponderance of the evidence"); Malmberg v. Lopez, 208 Conn. 675, 546 A.2d 264 (1988) (duty to set aside the verdict when it is manifestly unjust and that includes inadequate award of damages); Carr v. Strode, 79 Hawai'i 475, 904 P.2d 489 (1995) (movant need establish only that "the verdict rendered for its opponent is against the manifest weight of the evidence"); Pocatello Auto Color, Inc. v. Akzo Coatings, Inc., 127 Idaho 41, 896 P.2d 949 (1995) ("Because the trial court evaluates the credibility of the evidence on a motion for a new trial, a trial court may properly grant the motion in cases where there is substantial evidence to support the jury's verdict and a judgment n.o.v. [or directed verdict] would have been inappropriate").

14. See Gaston v. Viclo Realty Co., 215 A.D.2d 174, 626 N.Y.S.2d 131 (App.Div. 1995)

fied or if the testimony does not meet up to standards of the expert's profession.[15]

5. *Instructions.* Beyond this, judges exercise important constraints on the jury by instructing the jury on the legal rules. Instructions must correctly and impartially state the legal rules applicable to the evidence in the case but must equally avoid dealing with claims or defenses not supported by the evidence.[16] The judge's error on any of these points can lead to a reversal on appeal and a new trial.

In some instances, the judge would direct a verdict for the defendant *if* the defendant's version of the facts is taken as true, but the judge must leave it to the jury to say whether that is the case. In that instance, judges use instructions as a kind of conditional directed verdict: they tell the jury that it must find in favor of the defendant if the jury also finds the facts to be as the defendant claimed.[17]

Topic B. Proving Facts to Permit the Negligence Evaluation

§ 150. Burden of Proof[1]

The plaintiff has the burden of proving facts to establish each element of her case. In the negligence case, it is not enough to show that the plaintiff suffered an injury in an accident in which the defendant was in some way involved.[2] The plaintiff must provide evidence of facts from which the judge can determine that the defendant was under a duty of care,[3] and facts from which a jury could reasonably find negligence,[4] cause in fact,[5] and proximate cause[6] by a greater weight of the evidence. The defendant, on the other hand, has the burden of proving facts to support affirmative defenses such as contributory negligence or comparative fault,[7] or the statute of limitations.

15. See Daubert v. Merrell Dow Pharm., Inc., 509 U.S. 579, 113 S.Ct. 2786, 125 L.Ed.2d 469 (1993); Kumho Tire Co., Ltd. v. Carmichael, 526 U.S. 137, 119 S.Ct. 1167, 143 L.Ed.2d 238 (1999).

16. E.g., Nowatske v. Osterloh, 198 Wis.2d 419, 543 N.W.2d 265 (Wis. 1996).

17. E.g., Chisholm v. Hall, 255 N.C. 374, 121 S.E.2d 726 (1961). This is one form of a "peremptory" instruction.

§ 150

1. See generally 2 John W. Strong et al., McCormick on Evidence §§ 336–339 (1992).

2. E.g., Brewster v. United States, 542 N.W.2d 524 (Iowa 1996).

3. See, e.g., Vasquez v. Wal-Mart Stores, Inc., 913 P.2d 441 (Wyo.1996). Judges sometimes speak of "proving" a duty or a standard of care, duties or standards are by definition set by the judge in the first place, there is never a question of proving the standard itself as distinct from facts which provide grounds for invoking the duty or facts that show a breach of the duty or standard.

4. E.g., Anglin v. Kleeman, 140 N.H. 257, 665 A.2d 747 (N.H. 1995).

5. E.g., Miller v. Evangeline Parish Police Jury, 663 So.2d 398 (La.App.1995).

6. E.g., Stewart v. Federated Dept. Stores, Inc., 234 Conn. 597, 662 A.2d 753 (1995) ("the plaintiff must show, by a fair preponderance of the evidence, that harm intentionally caused by a third person is within the scope of the risk created by the defendant's negligent conduct").

7. Hill v. City of Lincoln, 249 Neb. 88, 541 N.W.2d 655 (1996).

The term burden of proof is of fundamental importance in all litigation and often decisive in tort cases. The term has three distinct aspects or meanings. These meanings are most readily illustrated by considering the plaintiff's burdens, but the ideas apply to the defendant's affirmative defenses as well.

(1) *Burden of production and directed verdict.* The plaintiff must produce evidence from which reasonable jurors could find that the elements of the plaintiff's case were proven by a preponderance of the evidence. For instance, in a negligence case, the plaintiff must prove facts that tend to show the defendant was negligent and that the plaintiff suffered legally recognizable harm as a result. If the plaintiff produces no evidence, or produces evidence from which reasonable people could not find negligence or causation, then the judge must direct a verdict or enter a nonsuit against her.[8] Conversely, if she produces such evidence, she has made a prima facie case and it goes to the jury for the jury's determination.[9]

(2) *Burden of persuasion and the jury's findings.* The plaintiff also has the burden of persuading the trier of fact that the elements of her case have been proven. The evidence adduced may be sufficient to satisfy the plaintiff's burden of production without actually convincing the jury. The plaintiff's burden of persuasion is reflected, not in a directed verdict but in an instruction that tells the jury that it must find for the defendant if it is not affirmatively persuaded by the plaintiff's proof.[10] If the jury thinks the defendant might be negligent, but that it is equally likely that he is not, it must find for the defendant, not the plaintiff. So the plaintiff who satisfies her burden of production does not necessarily win; she must also persuade the jury. As this implies, courts do not ordinarily direct a verdict in favor of a party who has the burden of persuasion, even if she has satisfied her burden of production.[11]

(3) *The weight, quantum, or standard of persuasion.* The standard for the great majority of tort cases is that the plaintiff must prove or persuade the trier by a preponderance of the evidence. Preponderance of the evidence means merely the greater weight of the evidence. Contemporary writers and judges often express this mathematically by saying the plaintiff must establish the facts necessary to her case by a probability greater than 0.5 or greater than 50%. That is to say that the facts claimed by the plaintiff must be more likely than not to exist.

A lesser standard of persuasion is almost unheard of.[12] In a few instances, courts require a more demanding standard, such as clear and

8. E.g., Hoffman v. Mogil, 445 Pa.Super. 252, 665 A.2d 478 (Pa.Super. 1995).

9. E.g., Rechenbach v. Haftkowycz, 100 Ohio App.3d 484, 654 N.E.2d 374 (1995).

10. E.g., California Jury Instructions (Book of Approved Jury Instructions) 2.60.

11. A directed verdict for the plaintiff is thus "hen's teeth rare." See De Leon Lopez v. Corporacion Insular de Seguros, 931 F.2d 116 (1st Cir.1991) (directing a verdict for the plaintiff where the hospital switched babies of two mothers).

12. But something like a lesser standard of persuasion as well as a lesser burden of production is permitted in certain cases in which the plaintiff or the decedent has lost a medical chance of survival or improvement, but not a chance of more than 0.5. A

convincing evidence.[13] Sometimes courts, without formally altering the preponderance standard, note special needs to be cautious in some cases,[14] or conversely, that the facts warrant an inference that meets the preponderance burden. In terms of a jury instruction under the usual preponderance standard, judges may warn the jury that it must find for the defendant if its mind is evenly balanced on any fact necessary to establish the plaintiff's claim.

Denials and conflicting testimony. The defendant's testimony frequently conflicts in one or more particulars with the plaintiff's testimony. For instance, the plaintiff's witnesses might testify that the defendant was speeding, while the defendant's might testify that he was driving well within the speed limits. If the plaintiff is attempting to show negligence by showing speed, she has met her burden of production by offering testimony to that effect. That testimony is sufficient to leave the question to the jury under an instruction that the plaintiff must persuade the jury by a preponderance of the evidence. The defendant's assertion that he was not speeding does not ordinarily change the plaintiff's burden or add to the defendant's. When she produces evidence of the defendant's speed, the plaintiff has satisfied her burden of production. Her burden remains to persuade the jury, so the jury will be instructed to find for the defendant unless the plaintiff has convinced it by the greater weight of the evidence. In other words, the defendant's denial that he was speeding does not mean that he has the burden of persuasion about speed; that burden remains with the plaintiff.

Defendant's burden. The defendant does, however, have the burden of proving any affirmative defense. For example, if he wishes to assert that his liability should be reduced because of the plaintiff's contributory fault, he must meet the burden of production by offering evidence that the plaintiff was at fault. On that issue he likewise has the burden of persuasion, meaning that the jury is instructed *not* to find contributory fault in the plaintiff unless the defendant has convinced the jury of such negligence by a preponderance of the evidence.

§ 151. Circumstantial Evidence—Nature and Use

Circumstantial evidence. Circumstantial evidence is evidence of a fact that tends to establish and thus to permit an inference of another fact. Evidence that a car driven by the defendant came to a stop only

better explanation of those cases may be that they merely reflect the defendant's duty, on particular facts, to maximize chances and that they do not involve an issue of causation or lesser proof standards at all. See §§ 178 & 179. To the extent that a presumption is not based on rational probabilities but on some sense of policy or justice, a presumption may have the *effect* of lessening a burden of production or persuasion, although that is not its formal structure. See § 152.

13. Some cases require clear and convincing evidence to support claims for punitive damages, libel, or fraud. See §§ 383, 419, & 470.

14. See Ellis County State Bank v. Keever, 888 S.W.2d 790 (Tex.1994) (malicious prosecution, standard is preponderance of evidence, but because resort to courts is important, trier should be cautious).

after skidding 500 feet and knocking down a tree 12 inches in diameter, for example, tends to establish that the defendant was driving very fast.[1]

General admissibility. Subject to the rules of evidence, circumstantial evidence is admissible at trial. In fact, it is very often used in tort cases. In many instances, circumstantial evidence based on physical facts like skid marks may be more trustworthy than eyewitness testimony.

Judge's role in monitoring circumstantial evidence. The trial judge must decide in the first place whether the circumstantial evidence offered rationally tends to support the inference of any relevant fact and must exclude the evidence if it does not. And at the end of the trial, upon the defendant's motion for a directed verdict, the judge must often decide as well whether the evidence as a whole is sufficient to permit reasonable jurors to draw the inferences necessary to establish a claim.[2]

The judge must exclude, or hold insufficient, any circumstantial evidence that does not rationally support the proposed inference. The judge must treat even rationally supportive evidence in the same way if it is so weak that it is speculative. This latter point is one of probability.[3] The fact that the defendant was driving a powerful car may rationally suggest the possibility that he was speeding, but the possibility is not strong enough to permit jurors to infer speed from the car's power alone, so this kind of speculative circumstantial evidence is usually rejected.[4]

Circumstantial evidence going to the jury. If circumstantial evidence is sufficient to permit reasonable jurors to draw the inference sought, the issue goes to the jury, which assesses its weight. Suppose the plaintiff is injured in a railroad crossing collision. She sues, contending that the train's engineer did not blow the whistle. The engineer testifies that he did, but the plaintiff's testimony is that she heard no whistle. The jury could draw the inference that no whistle was blown by reasoning that the plaintiff probably would have heard the whistle if it were sounded.[5] But of course the jury could also draw a different inference, even if it believes the plaintiff is telling the truth as she

§ 151

1. Johnson v. Yates, 31 N.C.App. 358, 229 S.E.2d 309 (1976) (excluding a trooper's opinion testimony about speed because the facts were quite sufficient to permit a determination of high speed).

2. See, e.g., Blount v. Bordens, Inc., 910 S.W.2d 931 (Tex.1995). The same issue of course may be reached on motion for summary judgment when there is no dispute of material facts. See cases cited in note 3 below.

3. E.g., Hasselbach v. TG Canton, Inc., 209 Mich.App. 475, 531 N.W.2d 715 (1994) (more likely than not standard; hot water in shower might have represented defect or might simply have been set too hot by victim, summary judgment for defendant); Summers v. Fort Crockett Hotel, Ltd., 902 S.W.2d 20 (Tex.App.1995) ("When circumstances are consistent with either of two facts and nothing shows that one is more probable than the other, neither fact can be inferred"; decedent might have fallen over balcony rail because it was too low or might have gone over the side for other reasons, summary judgment for defendant).

4. E.g., Claytor v. Owens-Corning Fiberglas Corp., 662 A.2d 1374 (D.C.App. 1995) (presence at a job-site where asbestos products were used does not permit an inference that the plaintiffs were exposed to asbestos).

5. E.g., South v. National R.R. Passenger Corp., 290 N.W.2d 819 (N.D.1980).

understands it. The jury could infer that the plaintiff was careless or paying no attention, distracted, or possibly suffering from hearing loss.

Effect of circumstantial evidence. Drawing inferences of fact from circumstantial evidence is largely a matter of assessing probability. Given the fact that the plaintiff did not hear a whistle blowing, is it more probable that the whistle was or was not sounded? That probability is likely to vary with many other circumstances in the case and with the jury's assessment of particular individuals involved. The probability that the whistle was not sounded may be low if the jury concludes from the plaintiff's demeanor that she has hearing difficulties. The probability will be strengthened enormously if none of the six people present heard a whistle,[6] and even without six witnesses, evidence that one did not see or hear an event may suffice to establish its nonexistence in some cases.[7]

Since probabilities turn on the facts of each case, including to some extent the personalities of the parties and witnesses, the trier of fact must weigh the proposed inference case by case. So the inference will be accepted as reasonably probable in some cases but not in others. These ideas are expressed in two important ways. First, the inference is ordinarily permissible, but not mandatory. Second, circumstantial evidence of this kind does not create a "presumption" or shift the burden of persuasion. It is evidence for the jury to consider and weigh, nothing more.

Chains of inferences. Some inferences in everyday life probably seem so obvious or compelling that we are likely to reach a conclusion without recognizing that it is based on an inference rather than on direct observation. "The fish aren't biting today" may seem like a direct observation of an angler who has caught no fish, but it is actually an inference that his empty creel reflects piscine anorexia rather than his own deficiency in the angler's art. The same is true in litigation. What sounds like direct observation is often a matter of inference. Inferences are sprinkled throughout trials like salt on french fries.

This is an important observation because lawyers sometimes argue that one cannot pile an inference upon an inference, or even more rhetorically, that one cannot pyramid or chain inferences. But one does and one must. The inference that the engineer did not blow the whistle is in part an inference drawn from the fact that the plaintiff did not hear a whistle. But that inference itself is based on the inference that the plaintiff would have heard the whistle had it been blown. We cannot know that for sure; a decision that she would have heard it is based at

6. Cf. Carruth v. Pittway Corporation, 643 So.2d 1340 (Ala.1994) (fact that all six people in house that burned were found in their beds permits inference that they did not hear smoke alarm and other evidence permitted inference that, if it had sounded, it would have been so loud that they would have heard it, hence the further inference that the alarm did not sound).

7. E.g., Sokolowski v. Medi Mart, Inc., 24 Conn.App. 276, 587 A.2d 1056 (1991) (no one heard bottle break during 15 minute period, permitting inference that break occurred earlier); Thoma v. Cracker Barrel Old Country Store, Inc., 649 So.2d 277 (1995) (no one saw liquid spilled on floor, permitting inference that spill must have occurred earlier).

least in part on an inference about her capacity to hear and absorb information. So of course law courts as well as scientists and ordinary people do pile inferences upon inferences.

Although some courts have purported to condemn stacking, chaining or pyramiding inferences,[8] it is almost certain that courts permit stacking when the inferences are convincing or reflect strong probabilities[9] and also in a great many cases in which inferences seem like direct observation. Certainly many decisions have overtly permitted drawing inferences upon inferences or have expressly said that no rule prohibits such reasoning.[10]

It is true, however, that inferences can be unjustified, even when they stand alone. If a merry-go-round wobbles, there seems no reason to infer that it has been wobbling so long that the city should have discovered its defect and corrected it, but occasionally such implausible inferences have been accepted.[11] It is also true that chains, stacks, or pyramids of inferences add to the problem of weighing probabilities.[12] If the plaintiff proves facts and invites the trier to draw a string of five inferences, the probability that any one inference is correct might be quite high, but the probability that all five are correct is, mathematically speaking, quite a bit lower. Yet even if the math suggests that all five are not likely to be so, the trier must make its own estimates, and the coherence of the plaintiff's story, warts, inferences, and all, is no doubt rightly judged in the light of the alternative explanations. Even a long string of inferences presents a better explanation for a fire than a shrug of the shoulders.[13]

8. E.g., Silver Springs Moose Lodge No. 1199 v. Orman, 631 So.2d 1119 (Fla.App. 1994); cf. Hurt v. Charles J. Rogers Transportation Co., 164 Ohio St. 329, 130 N.E.2d 820 (1955) (reasoning that only speculative inferences were unacceptable, then asserting that "An inference which is based solely and entirely upon another inference and which is unsupported by any additional fact or another inference from other facts is an inference upon an inference and is universally condemned", finding that the multiple inference were permissible after all because some were based on direct factual testimony).

9. Mediq PRN Life Support Services, Inc. v. Abrams, 899 S.W.2d 101 (Mo.App. 1994) ("This rule against stacking or pyramiding inferences is not a general rule applicable to all situations but a rule of reason applied in the trial court's discretion to guard against attenuated reasoning, as where an initial inference is drawn from a fact, and other inferences are built solely and cumulatively upon the first, so that the conclusion reached is too remote and has no sound logical foundation in fact").

10. E.g., Hampton v. Moistner, 654 N.E.2d 1191 (Ind.App.1995).

11. In Flom v. Flom, 291 N.W.2d 914 (Minn.1980) an unwilling wife and mother was coaxed to ride a manually operated merry-go-round in a park in spite of her fear of "rides." Her husband pushed the merry-go-round, carrying her and the children. It allegedly wobbled 3–4 inches after a "chattering sound," which led the husband to attempt to stop it. At that point the wife fell off. The city was held liable on the ground that the jury could infer (a) a substantial wobble could only have been caused by a defect in the mechanical structure, and (b) that such a defect as would cause a wobble must have existed a long time, and (c) a long time was long enough to expect a reasonable city to discover the defect and correct it. If the case is preposterous it is not because there is a chain of inferences but because some of the inferences seem wildly unjustified.

12. See Hampton v. Moistner, 654 N.E.2d 1191 (Ind.App.1995).

13. See, e.g., Voorde Poorte v. Evans, 66 Wash.App. 358, 832 P.2d 105 (1992) (before the defendant's trespass, electrical service had been turned off; the defendant had service restored; defendant's employees,

Expert testimony and circumstantial evidence. Some circumstantial evidence needs no explanation; jurors will rightly understand the evidence and the potential inferences. Five hundred feet of skid marks tell a rather compelling tale. But in many instances, circumstantial evidence must be explained by someone with special knowledge. While most of us might be quite sure that 500–foot skid marks indicate high speed, we are not likely to be sure what 45–foot skid marks mean. In that case the evidence may be rejected unless expert testimony can give a more or less scientific explanation of the circumstantial evidence.[14]

Issues considered to involve scientific matters often require expert interpretation of circumstantial evidence, or expert conclusions in lieu of circumstantial evidence. For instance, if the question is whether a drug manufactured by the defendant could cause birth defects when ingested by a pregnant woman, the plaintiff might introduce evidence that a large number of children suffered birth defects when their mothers used the drug during pregnancy and that when the drug was given to pregnant rats, their offspring suffered birth defects. Since birth defects also occur when no drug is ingested, this evidence is suggestive but assuredly not conclusive. In cases like this, experts on both sides are likely to testify, and the case may become one that is less about circumstantial evidence than about expert opinion and whether the experts are qualified or the opinions they offer are acceptable.[15]

§ 152. Presumptions[1]

Presumptions are usually treated in the law of evidence. They require only a limited discussion here to indicate roughly some of the ways in which circumstantial evidence can affect tort trials and verdicts. The general structure of a presumption is familiar: if Fact A is proved, then Fact B is presumed to be true. Unfortunately, the term presumption itself is used in a variety of ways to mean quite different things.

Usages and Mis-usages of "Presumption"

The term presumption has been applied "to a widely disparate set of decisions,"[2] but it is enough here to list four common usages.

(1) Conclusive or irrebuttable presumptions. Judges may say that proof of Fact A creates a conclusive or irrebuttable presumption of Fact

who were not available to testify, were present when the fire started; all possible causes except an electrical problem were eliminated and no alternative explanation was offered; an inference that the defendant caused the fire (not that he was negligent) was permissible).

14. See Brugh v. Peterson, 183 Neb. 190, 159 N.W.2d 321, 29 A.L.R.3d 236 (1968) (professor of engineering explaining skid marks after first determining "coefficient of friction" on the particular road).

15. See Daubert v. Merrell Dow Pharmaceuticals, Inc., 509 U.S. 579, 113 S.Ct. 2786, 125 L.Ed.2d 469 (1993); see also Kumho Tire Co., Ltd. v. Carmichael 526 U.S. 137, 119 S.Ct. 1167, 143 L.Ed.2d 238 (1999).

§ 152

1. See 2 John W. Strong et al., McCormick on Evidence §§ 342–344 (1992).

2. Ronald J. Allen, Presumptions in Civil Actions Reconsidered, 66 Iowa L. Rev. 843, 845 (1981).

B in some cases. Under some versions of the rule of sevens,[3] for example, a court might conclusively presume that a child under the age of seven is incapable of negligence.[4] It might be far better to avoid the language of presumptions in cases like this; the court has simply made a rule of law that children under seven are immune from liability for negligence.

(2) Presumption as a way of stating the initial burden of production. Judges may also use the term presumption to state, in a semi-literary form, the idea that one party has a burden of producing evidence. "Negligence is not presumed" and "the defendant is presumptively innocent" are two ways of saying nothing more complex than that the plaintiff has the burden of proving negligence.[5] Although the idea can be expressed as a presumption, nothing is added by using the term in this context.

(3) Permissible inference of fact. Judges may say that when Fact A is proved, Fact B is presumed when they only mean that the trier can rationally infer the existence of Fact B. To say that proof of Fact A creates a *presumption* that Fact B is also true usually suggests that the evidence has somehow altered the parties' burdens of proof in one or more ways. But judges sometimes use the term presumption in a kind of literary way, to mean much less than it says, that is, to mean nothing more than Fact A is circumstantial evidence of Fact B.

For example, suppose the plaintiff, in a pharmacy, slips on an oily substance. Upon inspection, a broken bottle of baby oil is found nearby. Evidence is that two customers have been standing nearby for thirty minutes and did not hear any sound of a breaking bottle. A jury might infer that the oil had been on the floor for at least thirty minutes and might then go on to conclude that thirty minutes was plenty of time for the store owner to have discovered the danger and eliminated it.[6] To say that the jury would be *permitted* to draw the 30–minute inference, however, is not to say that the jury *must* draw the inference, or that any kind of proof burden has been shifted. If the court means to say only that the jury is permitted to draw the 30–minute inference, it clouds the issue to speak of presumption.

(4) Presumptions altering a burden. In more careful legal speech, the term presumption is reserved for cases in which proof of Fact A in some manner alters a burden of production or a burden of persuasion or both. In this usage, when the plaintiff proves Fact A, Fact B is taken as provisionally established. Provisionally, because Fact B can be disestablished by some additional evidence. How Fact B can be disestablished

3. See § 126, supra.

4. E.g., Pino v. Szuch, 185 W.Va. 476, 408 S.E.2d 55 (1991).

5. E.g., Gaston v. Hunter, 121 Ariz. 33, 588 P.2d 326 (Ct.App. 1978); Morehart v. Dillard Department Stores, 322 Ark. 290, 908 S.W.2d 331 (1995) ("The burden is always on the party asserting negligence to prove it, as negligence is never presumed"); Wardell v. McMillan, 844 P.2d 1052 (Wyo. 1992).

6. Cf. Sokolowski v. Medi Mart, Inc., 24 Conn.App. 276, 587 A.2d 1056 (1991) (on similar but weaker facts, permitting jury to infer negligence).

and who decides, judge or jury, are issues that raise the complications discussed below.

Potential Effects of a Presumption

The speeding example. An example helps to identify the different potential effects of a presumption. Suppose the plaintiff claims to have been injured by the defendant's negligence in driving an automobile. The plaintiff offers evidence that the applicable speed limit was 40 miles per hour, that the defendant was driving at 45 miles per hour and that as a result of the speed he collided with the plaintiff's car, causing injury. Some courts do not deal with this situation by using presumptions but by a rule that merely permits the jury to consider evidence of statute violation along with other evidence in the case. Suppose, however, that the court wishes to treat violation of statute as a presumption.[7] What are the exact effects of doing so?

Maximum power presumptions. When a presumption is given its maximum effect, it shifts the burden of going forward with the evidence to the opponent and shifts the ultimate burden of persuasion as well. The maximum presumptive effect of the plaintiff's proof of speed in excess of the legal limit is that

(a) the plaintiff will prevail on the negligence issue by directed verdict unless the defendant introduces some evidence of an acceptable excuse, and

(b) even if the defendant introduces such evidence, that the jury would be instructed that the verdict should be for the plaintiff unless the defendant has persuaded the jury by a preponderance of the evidence that he was *not* negligent.

The presumption in the speeding illustration does not mean that the defendant will lose the case. The presumption may establish his negligence, but he might still prevail because his conduct was not an actual or legal cause of harm or because he has a good affirmative defense.

Nor does the presumption bootstrap itself. In the illustrative case, the defendant's *speed* is not what is presumed; on the contrary, the speed is Fact A, the fact that triggers the presumption of something else, negligence. What if the defendant denies that he was speeding? Under the familiar rule, the jury is the sole decision-maker on credibility issues, so the presumption is not generated until the jury finds that the defendant was in fact speeding.

Until the jury finds that the defendant was speeding, there is no presumption to apply. How, then, can the judge direct a verdict against

7. Some courts do treat violation of statute as creating a "presumption" of negligence. The example is not completely satisfactory because the negligence so presumed is not a "fact" like a red stop light but a conclusion based on evaluation of conduct. Nevertheless, the essence of a presumption applies: "a standardized practice, under which certain facts are held to call for uniform treatment with respect to their effect", see 2 JOHN W. STRONG ET AL., MCCORMICK ON EVIDENCE §§ 342, p. 449 (1992), even though the "uniform treatment" is not "proof of other facts" but a report card that says "negligence."

the defendant who denies speeding but offers nothing to rebut the presumption of negligence? The answer is that the judge can "direct a verdict" by a peremptory instruction to the jury to find in favor of the plaintiff *if* the jury also finds that the defendant was guilty of speeding.[8] If the defendant has offered an excuse for his speed, the instruction can go on to tell the jury that if speed is established by a preponderance of the evidence, it must find for the plaintiff unless the defendant has proven an excuse by a preponderance of the evidence. In this way, the presumption is given maximum effect, first by requiring the defendant to produce evidence or lose, and then by shifting the ultimate burden of persuasion to the defendant.

Minimum power presumptions. Courts may adopt a less powerful presumption, in its pure form often said to reflect the "bursting bubble" theory that a presumption disappears once evidence is introduced to rebut it. Under this theory, the effect of a presumption is usually to shift the burden of going forward with the evidence. In the speeding example, the plaintiff's proof of statute violation would mean that the plaintiff would be entitled to a directed verdict (or peremptory instruction) on the negligence issue unless the defendant produced some evidence to rebut the presumed fact. (In the speeding example, rebuttal would be proof of an acceptable excuse.) But if the defendant produces some evidence, the plaintiff will *not* get a directed verdict on the issue and the jury will *not* be told that the burden of proof has shifted. The plaintiff will still be required to persuade the jury by a preponderance of the evidence.

The disappearance of the presumption does not mean that the proponent of the presumption would lose the issue, much less other issues in the case. In many instances, the plaintiff's proof permits an inference even if the presumption has vanished. In the speeding example, if the defendant offers some proof of an acceptable excuse, the presumption would disappear and the burden of proof would not be shifted, but the jury would still be permitted to "infer" negligence, even though the presumption was no longer of importance.[9]

Conclusion. The law is riddled with presumptions on an amazing variety of topics, many of them unrelated to tort law. Some presumptions arise because Fact A makes Fact B a high probability. Others arise for reasons of rightly or wrongly perceived social policy. Some jurists have tried to prescribe a single effect for all presumptions, some favoring the maximum effect, others the minimum or bursting bubble effect. Authorities are in conflict on theory and in application and the confusion

8. See 2 John W. Strong et al., McCormick on Evidence § 344, p. 461 (1992). The term peremptory instruction may be used to cover an instruction that directs a verdict on a particular issue in the case and likewise to cover a conditional instruction in this form: "If you find Fact A to exist by a preponderance of the evidence, then you must find a verdict for the plaintiff." See, e.g., Chisholm v. Hall, 255 N.C. 374, 121 S.E.2d 726 (1961).

9. See 2 John W. Strong et al., McCormick on Evidence § 344, p. 463 (1992). Court may fudge the point by calling the jury's attention to the potential inference or, with perhaps confusing results, referring the jury to a presumption. See Id. at pp. 467–68.

has led one important commentator to suggest that the term itself be abolished.[10]

Uniform treatment of all presumptions may not be feasible or desirable. Cases of all stripes can be found. What is most important for a book on tort law, as distinct from a book on evidence, is not the state of authority on presumptions. What is important is to recognize that circumstantial evidence—Fact A—might result in a range of effects from permissible inference, to a shifted burden of production, to a shifted burden of persuasion. Concomitantly, that range of difficult choices might suggest something of the difficulty the legal system faces in producing a confident justice in really close cases.

§ 153. The Specific Conduct Requirement

Negligence itself is not a historical fact. It cannot be proven in any direct sense because negligence represents an evaluation of facts rather than the facts themselves. Nevertheless, the evaluation rests upon facts about the defendant's conduct.

Facts showing specific conduct. As a practical matter, the facts required to show negligence must ordinarily meet a demanding standard of specificity. They must show precisely what the defendant did or didn't do. The plaintiff must point to a particular way in which that conduct could have been made safer. The plaintiff cannot prevail by saying that the defendant drove his car so negligently that he injured the plaintiff. Although such generalities may suffice for some pleadings, they are too conclusory to count as evidence. Even if such a generality could be admitted as evidence, it would not be evidence about what we need to know to evaluate the defendant's conduct. What we need to know is what precise physical actions the plaintiff claims the defendant should have done differently to present less risk.

Example. For example, suppose the plaintiff falls from a balcony at a hotel. In a suit against the hotel for negligence, it won't do to say that the hotel negligently allowed him to fall. That would be like saying that if an accident occurred, it must be the defendant's fault, a view that courts consistently reject. Instead, the plaintiff must assert a particular way in which the defendant acted or failed to act. Perhaps he would assert that the balcony railing was only 36 inches high when it should have been 42 inches high.

Purpose of specificity requirement. Why the requirement of such specificity? One important reason is that only when you know specific conduct can you estimate the risks and utilities of that conduct, a process normally implicit in finding negligence. It is impossible to estimate either risks or utilities when no particular conduct is identified. If, instead of judging conduct by risks and utilities, you attempt to judge

10. See Ronald J. Allen, Presumptions in Civil Actions Reconsidered, 66 Iowa L. Rev. 843 (1981).

it by community custom or by legislative standards, the same problem arises; you must know the conduct you are judging.

It is, of course, possible for a plaintiff to claim that the defendant is negligent by engaging at all in some general activity like driving cars or running hotels. But it would be almost impossible to successfully contend that reasonable people never ever drive cars or operate hotels, because the utility of such activities is very high. As a practical matter, then, the plaintiff must ordinarily attempt to prove some specific way in which the car was driven or the hotel was maintained that could reasonably have been made safer. When the plaintiff proves that the hotel balcony rail was only 36 inches high and claims that it should have been 42 inches high to prevent a person from losing balance and falling over, it becomes possible to estimate risks and the costs of reducing them and hence possible to judge whether the hotel was or was not negligent.

Other purposes. There are some other reasons why specific conduct must be identified in order to claim negligence, but they will make more sense in connection with chapters on cause in fact and proximate cause. In brief, it will be impossible to conclude that the defendant's conduct was a cause of the plaintiff's harm or that the harm was within the scope of the risk unless you know what the risk was; to know that, you must know the specific conduct claimed to be negligent.

TOPIC C. SUBSTITUTES FOR FACTUAL EVIDENCE. RES IPSA LOQUITUR

§ 154. Res Ipsa Loquitur: General Rules

To prove the defendant negligent, the plaintiff must normally provide evidence of the defendant's specific conduct. Proof that an accident happened or even that the defendant caused an injury is not enough by itself; as courts say, negligence is not presumed.[1] Cases that fit the res ipsa loquitur pattern constitute an exception. The Latin phrase means that the thing speaks for itself, which is to say, the plaintiff's injury and the immediate events surrounding it can by themselves show negligence, even though the plaintiff is unable to prove any specific act that was unreasonably dangerous.

The core rule. The core of the res ipsa loquitur doctrine[2] is simple and straightforward. If the defendant owes the plaintiff a duty of care,[3]

§ 154

1. E.g., Fedorczyk v. Caribbean Cruise Lines, Ltd., 82 F.3d 69 (3d Cir.1996).

2. There is a truly minor dispute about whether it is permissible to speak of a "doctrine." See, e.g., Jackson v. Millar, 59 D.L.R.3d 246, 255 (Can. 1975). The argument is that res ipsa loquitur refers to a rule of circumstantial evidence, which is true enough. On the other hand, it has been saddled with a cluster of putative rules, so that it is a doctrine in the sense that it comprises a body of related rules.

3. When the defendant literally owes no duty to the plaintiff, that means the defendant is free to be negligent, so the inference of negligence is of no assistance. When the defendant owes a reduced duty, such as a duty only to avoid willful misconduct, the facts might justify an inference of negligence but not an inference of willful or reckless behavior. In such cases, res ipsa

the jury is permitted to infer that the defendant was negligent in some unspecified way when, on the evidence adduced, experience indicates (1) that the injury was probably the result of negligence, even though the exact nature of that negligence is unknown, and (2) that it was probably the defendant who was the negligent person.[4] The first requirement, that negligence must be the more probable explanation for the injury, is often expressed somewhat differently, by saying that the injury must be of a kind which ordinarily does not occur in the absence of negligence.[5] Courts apparently mean the same thing by the two formulations—they may use both in the same opinion[6]—but the ultimate point is technically an estimate of probabilities that the defendant was guilty of some unspecified and perhaps unknowable negligence.[7]

The limiting rules. Aside from the fact that courts are especially cautious about using res ipsa loquitur in professional malpractice cases[8] and against defendants whose duty of care is otherwise limited,[9] many cases have added constraining rules in England[10] and Canada[11] as well as in the United States. The American cases frequently say that res ipsa loquitur doctrine cannot apply unless (a) the defendant was in exclusive control of the harm-causing instrumentality at some relevant time and (b) the plaintiff shows that she was not responsible for, or not an active participant in her own injury. Less importantly, some courts have also said that (c) once specific acts of negligence are pleaded or proved, res ipsa loquitur is no longer available; and that (d) res ipsa loquitur is not available at all unless the defendant has superior access to the evidence.

loquitur does not aid the plaintiff. See Restatement Second § 328 D, cmt. j. Conversely, if the defendant owes some especially high duty of care, res ipsa loquitur may apply with special ease. See Irwin v. Pacific Southwest Airlines, 133 Cal.App.3d 709, 184 Cal.Rptr. 228 (1982).

4. E.g., Brewster v. United States, 542 N.W.2d 524 (1996) (evidence should show that on the whole, "it is more likely that the event was caused by negligence than that it was not"); Valley Properties Limited Partnership v. Steadman's Hardware, Inc., 251 Mont. 242, 824 P.2d 250 (Mont. 1992); Kambat v. St. Francis Hospital, 89 N.Y.2d 489, 678 N.E.2d 456, 655 N.Y.S.2d 844 (1997); Restatement § 328D, cmt. e; see Myrlak v. Port Authority of New York and New Jersey, 157 N.J. 84, 95, 723 A.2d 45, 51 (1999).

5. Restatement Second § 328D. Emphasis on the ordinary course of things goes back to Scott v. London and St. Katherine Docks Co., 3 H. & C. 596, 159 Eng.Rep. 665 (1865). Another statement that is no doubt intended to mean the same as the more-probable-than-not version but could be misconstrued is that the defendant's negligence is "the most plausible explanation for the plaintiff's injury." Giles v. City of New Haven, 228 Conn. 441, 636 A.2d 1335 (1994). If A, B, and C are the possible explanations of an injurious event, C being the defendant's negligence, and the likelihood of each is .33, .33 and .34 respectively, the defendant's negligence is the most probable of the three, but the probability that the defendant was *not* negligent is still greater than the probability that he was, though he is a slightly more plausible candidate than the others.

6. The Restatement as well, see § 328D blackletter and cmt. e.

7. See David Kaye, Probability Theory Meets Res Ipsa Loquitur, 77 Mich. L. Rev. 1456, 1476 (1979). Emphasis on the unusualness of the event under the "does not ordinarily happen" phraseology might easily lead to doubtful results. See Calabretta v. National Airlines, Inc., 528 F.Supp. 32 (E.D.N.Y.1981) (airline passenger felt ear pain on landing, ultimately lost her hearing; res ipsa applies because ear problems do not commonly result from flights).

8. See §§ 148 & 249 below.

9. See n. 3, supra.

10. See W. V. H. Rogbers, Winfield & Jolowicz on Tort 139 (14th ed. 1994).

11. See Allen M. Linden, Canadian Tort Law 214 (5th ed. 1993).

Every one of these limiting rules is subject to substantial qualifications treated in later sections.

The leading res ipsa example. The most important ancestor of the res ipsa doctrine is also its best illustration. In *Byrne v. Boadle*,[12] the plaintiff was a pedestrian who was struck by a barrel of flour as he was walking adjacent to the defendant's shop. Although it was a fair inference that the barrel had come from the defendant's shop, the plaintiff was unable to show that the defendant had been negligent in any particular way. Nevertheless, the court thought the happening spoke for itself and that the jury would be permitted to find that the defendant was negligent, albeit in unspecified ways.

Relation to circumstantial evidence and the specific conduct requirement. As courts and commentators often say, res ipsa loquitur cases are circumstantial evidence cases. The statement is true, but it fails to identify the more important point, that res ipsa loquitur cases are also overwhelmingly different from ordinary circumstantial evidence cases. Apart from res ipsa cases, the plaintiff's evidence, circumstantial or direct, must point to specific conduct of the defendant, as where long skid marks circumstantially prove high speed. In contrast, res ipsa loquitur cases permit the jury to infer negligence without knowing any particular misconduct at all.

For instance, in *Byrne*, the plaintiff did not prove, either circumstantially or otherwise, that the barrel had been stored on its side instead of standing up, or that a rope holding the barrel had frayed and broken or any other particular acts that could be counted as negligence because they could be evaluated in terms of their costs, risks, or justifications in customary practices. The claim was only that the circumstances warranted the belief that the defendant was negligent in a wholly mysterious way.

However, res ipsa loquitur is sometimes invoked needlessly and inappropriately. If the trier can infer that the defendant was probably guilty of one of several specific acts of negligence but cannot be sure which act it was, res ipsa is not properly involved. For example, if a car parked at the curb by the defendant begins to roll downhill in the absence of interference by others, a trier might infer that the defendant either failed to set the brakes or failed to cut the wheels properly against the curb, or failed to put the car in parking gear, or some combination. Although the jury might not be sure which of these negligent omissions occurred, if it can conclude that one of them did, then the case is merely one of ordinary circumstantial evidence. Similarly, in rear-end collisions: res ipsa is not needed because the jury can infer specific negligence on the part of the rear driver—he was either not keeping a proper lookout or driving too fast or both. When courts speak of res ipsa loquitur in cases like this perhaps no harm is done,[13] but they risk confusing the

12. Byrne v. Boadle, 2 H. & C. 722, 159 Eng. Rep. 299 (Exch. 1863).

13. See Sullivan v. Snyder, 374 A.2d 866. (D.C.App.1977) (discussing res ipsa lo-

process of inferring specific negligent acts with the process of estimating the probability of unknown acts of negligence.

§ 155. Estimating Probabilities of Negligence

Estimating probabilities: common experience. The jury cannot find negligence by way of res ipsa loquitur doctrine unless the jury concludes that negligence was more probably than not the cause of injury.[1]

"More probable than not" is of course an estimate, not an accurate quantification of probabilities. For this reason, a degree of caution is required in determining whether res ipsa loquitur applies.[2] Perhaps it is a safe bet that the more the defendant must take repeated precautions to obtain safety, the more likely it is that he will fail to take one of them and hence the more likely it is that res ipsa can apply.[3] If the case reaches the jury at all, jurors are usually expected to draw on their knowledge or experience to make the estimate of probabilities. But it is only general experience in life that is required, not experience with the particular accident. So jurors have been permitted to conclude that when a modern airplane crashes without explanation and no other cause appears likely, that the operator of the plane was negligent, even though the jurors themselves are not pilots and have no actual data on the subject of air-crash negligence.[4]

Judicial control. On the other hand, courts refuse to submit cases to the jury on the res ipsa loquitur theory when they conclude that there simply is not enough experience to justify an estimate of probabilities and also when, drawing on their own experience, they conclude that negligence is not in fact more probable than not. For example, if the only evidence is that a tire blows out on a moving vehicle, negligence of the manufacturer does not seem to be a highly probable explanation, since tires are not expected to last forever and many other causes of blowout are readily imaginable.[5] If the plaintiff falls while on an escalator because it made a funny little bump or thrust or stop, the judge may decide that no common knowledge about escalators permits an inference that they do not bump, much less that bumps result from negligence.[6]

quitur in a rear end collision case where an inference of specific negligence seems more plausible).

§ 155

1. See § 154.

2. Hailey v. Otis Elevator Co., 636 A.2d 426 (D.C.App.1994) ("Given the power of res ipsa loquitur ... and the consequent caution with which it should be applied ... [it] must be based upon a widespread consensus of a common understanding").

3. See Mark F. Grady, Res Ipsa Loquitur and Compliance Error, 142 U. Pa. L. Rev. 887 (1994).

4. Permitting res ipsa loquitur in airplane crashes: Dunn v. Grand Canyon Airlines, Inc., 66 F.3d 334 (unpublished), opinion available, 1995 WL 547723 (9th Cir. 1995); Widmyer v. Southeast Skyways, Inc., 584 P.2d 1 (Alaska 1978); Newing v. Cheatham, 15 Cal.3d 351, 540 P.2d 33, 124 Cal. Rptr. 193 (1975). Earlier decisions refused to permit res ipsa in airplane cases, some of which were also private plane cases and are conceivably distinguishable on that ground.

5. Goodyear Tire & Rubber Co. v. Hughes Supply, Inc., 358 So.2d 1339 (Fla. 1978).

6. Hailey v. Otis Elevator Co., 636 A.2d 426 (D.C.App.1994); Barretta v. Otis Elevator Co., 242 Conn. 169, 698 A.2d 810 (1997); Holzhauer v. Saks & Co., 346 Md. 328, 697 A.2d 89 (1997).

Such conclusions are usually limited to the particular evidence in the case and do not exclude res ipsa from all claims of similar injuries. Nevertheless, some fact patterns seem to be generally inappropriate for res ipsa. Courts usually think that the defendant's negligence is not a sufficiently likely explanation of events when the plaintiff, as an invitee in the defendant's place of business, falls on a slippery substance. Without more evidence, the possibilities are too strong that the defendant was not responsible for placing the substance there and that he did not have time to discover it and make it safe, so specific evidence on these points is usually required.[7]

Estimating probabilities: expert testimony. When common knowledge or experience furnishes no basis for estimating probabilities of negligence, courts now allow the plaintiff to introduce expert testimony to establish the probability that negligence is the explanation for injury.[8] For example, an expert may be able to estimate the probability that negligence is the explanation when a surgical operation goes horribly wrong. The expert's estimate of probabilities need not be grounded in statistical studies any more than the estimate jurors themselves make from common knowledge. The expert's estimate, however, may be disputed by other experts.

Illustrative applications. (a) Tangible instruments of harm. Most res ipsa loquitur cases arise when the plaintiff is injured by an identified instrument of harm. Frequently an object that should be contained or stationary in fact escapes, moves, or explodes, becoming an active source of harm. For example, a light fixture falls from the ceiling without apparent cause.[9] There are endless variations—the plaintiff is struck by a falling object,[10] by an unattended car that somehow has broken lose,[11] by a wheel that flies off a moving vehicle;[12] the defendant's grenade explodes prematurely,[13] or its bottle explodes in the plaintiff's hand,[14] or its chair collapses when the plaintiff sits upon it;[15] gas lines explode or catch fire,[16] water bursts from its pipes,[17] cattle escape from their pens.[18]

7. E.g., Riverview Regional Medical Center, Inc. v. Williams, 667 So.2d 46 (Ala. 1995); Brown v. Poway Unified School District, 4 Cal.4th 820, 843 P.2d 624, 15 Cal. Rptr.2d 679 (1993).

8. Morgan v. Children's Hosp., 18 Ohio St.3d 185, 480 N.E.2d 464, 49 A.L.R.4th 51 (1985); Mireles v. Broderick, 117 N.M. 445, 872 P.2d 863 (1994) (listing authorities).

9. E.g., Anderson v. Service Merchandise Co., Inc., 240 Neb. 873, 485 N.W.2d 170 (1992).

10. E.g., Cardina v. Kash N' Karry Food Stores, Inc., 663 So.2d 642 (Fla.App.1995) (case of tomatoes falling from stack).

11. Housing Authority of City of Rolla v. Kimmel, 771 S.W.2d 932 (Mo.App.1989); Hill v. Thompson, 484 P.2d 513, 55 A.L.R.3d 1254 (Okl. 1971). Unattended car cases can become ordinary circumstantial evidence cases if the facts pinpoint the inference of a specific act of negligence, such as failure to set the wheels against a curb.

12. Neace v. Laimans, 951 F.2d 139 (7th Cir.1991).

13. McGonigal v. Gearhart Industries, Inc., 851 F.2d 774 (5th Cir. 1988).

14. Escola v. Coca Cola Bottling Co., 24 Cal.2d 453, 150 P.2d 436 (1944).

15. E.g., Trujeque v. Service Merchandise Co., 117 N.M. 388, 872 P.2d 361 (1994).

16. Harvey v. Metropolitan Utilities District of Omaha, 246 Neb. 780, 523 N.W.2d 372, 34 A.L.R.5th 739 (1994) (gas leak at meter controlled by the defendant utility).

17.–18. See notes 17 and 18 on page 375.

Sometimes the instrument of harm is something that is properly moving or active to begin with, but it takes a course that is so unexpected that negligence remains a strong likelihood, as where a car driven along a safe and clear highway suddenly leaves the road and strikes an unsuspecting tree in a field,[19] or, what is virtually the same thing, an aircraft on a safe flight crashes without explanation.[20] At other times the instrument of harm is almost definitionally negligent, as where food in a sealed container proves to be poisonous or otherwise dangerous to health.[21] Because it is all a matter of appraising evidence, res ipsa loquitur may also be rejected in most of these instances if the facts of a particular case suggest an explanation not based on negligence, or if the defendant was not the negligent person.

(b) Unknown instruments of harm; the caretaker and custodial cases. No formal rule limits res ipsa loquitur to cases in which the instrumentality of harm is known. The doctrine has been applied in some cases where it was not. Suppose the plaintiff suffers an injury while in the defendant's custody. The plaintiff is an infant in a day care center, a patient anesthetized upon an operating table, or a nursing home patient unable to communicate. If the infant is returned from day care with a concussion and damage to the optical nerve that requires surgery,[22] it is not implausible to say that the day care center, with its obligation to supervise and protect, was likely negligent, even though the plaintiff cannot prove that the harm was done by a falling barrel or any other particular tangible item. The same idea applies to others in the custody of caretakers, such as patients in nursing homes[23] and those who are anesthetized.[24]

17. State Farm Fire & Casualty Co. v. Municipality of Anchorage, 788 P.2d 726 (Alaska 1990) (underground water pipe); cf. Pickersgill v. City of New York, 168 Misc.2d 768, 642 N.Y.S.2d 469 (Civ. Ct. N.Y. 1996) (sewer backup).

18. Roberts v. Weber & Sons, Co., 248 Neb. 243, 533 N.W.2d 664 (1995). Some courts categorically refuse to apply res ipsa to cattle-on-the highway cases, but at least some of the cases refusing res ipsa are justified in doing so on their particular facts. See Vanderwater v. Hatch, 835 F.2d 239 (10th Cir. 1987).

19. Eaton v. Eaton, 119 N.J. 628, 575 A.2d 858 (1990); Porterfield v. Brinegar, 719 S.W.2d 558 (Tex.1986).

20. Note 4, supra.

21. E.g., Atlanta Coca–Cola Bottling Co. v. Ergle, 128 Ga.App. 381, 196 S.E.2d 670 (1973). Food contamination cases have long been pursued on theories of strict product liability and breach of warranty as well as on theories of negligence with its res ipsa loquitur inference. Food in sealed containers that is contaminated with foreign objects—mice are commonly claimed—is almost always "defective" under a warranty or strict liability theory, a view entirely consistent with res ipsa loquitur. See e.g., Vamos v. Coca–Cola Bottling Co. of New York, Inc., 165 Misc.2d 388, 627 N.Y.S.2d 265 (1995) (AA batteries in soft drink).

22. Fowler v. Seaton, 61 Cal.2d 681, 394 P.2d 697, 39 Cal.Rptr. 881 (1964) (child 3 years and 10 months, unable to talk about injury, suffering serious head injury and eye damage); cf. Ward v. Forrester Day Care, Inc., 547 So.2d 410 (Ala.1989) (11–week old baby returned from day care with broken arm); Myers v. Moore, 240 Mo.App. 726, 217 S.W.2d 291 (1949) (5–week-old baby, apparently chewed by something, possibly rats, while in defendant's care).

23. Franklin v. Collins Chapel Connectional Hospital, 696 S.W.2d 16 (Tenn.App. 1985).

24. Ybarra v. Spangard, 25 Cal.2d 486, 154 P.2d 687 (1944). Medical res ipsa loquitur presents several special problems. See §§ 248 & 249.

Since res ipsa loquitur almost always depends upon analysis of the particular facts, custodial cases do not invariably require the application of res ipsa loquitur any more than other kinds of cases. The nature and extent of the injury, the age and capacity of the injured person, and the kind of care expected, are all important factors in estimating the probability of negligence. The fact that a child returns from day care with an ordinary bruise of the kind all children might incur in playing and falling, would not prompt an inference that the supervisor was negligent, nor would the fact that the child simply fell down while playing.[25] The same is true with many injuries that are consistent with harms that occur without negligence and those to which common experience can attribute no fault.[26]

Nonreciprocal risks. Almost all the illustrations of res ipsa loquitur given above, whether involving a tangible instrumentality or not, are cases of nonreciprocal risks. That is, the defendant is in a position to negligently harm the plaintiff, but the plaintiff is not in a position to inflict similar harms upon the defendant. It is exemplified by all those cases in which gravity plays a heavy role because the pedestrian on the street is endangered by falling barrels but creates no similar risk to people on the second story. This nonreciprocal feature might be regarded as merely a consequence of the idea that if the defendant was not in exclusive control, one could not readily conclude that the defendant was the negligent actor. However, even where literal control is compromised, the nonreciprocal feature of res ipsa is often very prominent, as where the plaintiff is injured by an exploding soda bottle or a collapsing chair. The defendant may lack literal control in such cases, but the risk is a one way street. The nonreciprocal character of many res ipsa cases is not the function of a rule, but it is a characteristic that often appears and may suggest a moral basis for the inference when otherwise the case might be doubtful.

§ 156. Procedural Effect

Permissible inference rule. In most cases, the effect of the judge's decision that res ipsa loquitur can be applied is only that the jury will be permitted to infer negligence, not that it is required to do so.[1] This means that the plaintiff gets past a summary judgment motion and escapes a directed verdict for the defendant. But the plaintiff still has the burden of persuading the jury to draw the inference of negligence and will lose unless the jury concludes that negligence is more likely than not. So res ipsa loquitur does not ordinarily shift the burden of persua-

25. Ward v. Mount Calvary Lutheran Church, 178 Ariz. 350, 873 P.2d 688 (1994).

26. Helton v. Forest Park Baptist Church, 589 S.W.2d 217 (Ky.App. 1979) appeared to view the facts in this light, although the decision may be arguable. See also Bunn v. Urban Shelters and Health Care Systems, 672 A.2d 1056 (D.C.App. 1996) (nursing home injury, no negligence inferrable).

§ 156

1. E.g., Mobil Chemical Co. v. Bell, 517 S.W.2d 245 (Tex.1974); Roberts v. Weber & Sons, Co., 248 Neb. 243, 533 N.W.2d 664 (1995); Eaton v. Eaton, 119 N.J. 628, 575 A.2d 858 (1990).

sion or even require the defendant to put on any evidence at all.[2] Much less does res ipsa loquitur ordinarily require or even permit the judge to direct a verdict for the plaintiff.[3]

Shifting the burden of going forward. A few courts hold, with California, that when res ipsa applies, the defendant must introduce at least some evidence to rebut the inference, and that the jury must find negligence if the defendant fails to do so.[4]

Strong inferences under the permissible inference rule. Even under the permissible inference rule, rare cases may call for special treatment. The weight of circumstantial evidence is sometimes great, sometimes weak. The same is true with the res ipsa inference. It is possible to imagine that the plaintiff's evidence creates an inference so strong that, unless the evidence is simply not credited, it should carry the case for the plaintiff in the absence of rebuttal.[5]

Effect of rebuttal evidence. Under the permissible inference rule followed in most states, rebutting evidence from the defendant is like the defendant's evidence in any other case. If the defendant offers evidence to show specific injury-causing facts and that evidence excludes negligence of the defendant, the jury may believe the evidence and find in favor of the defendant. In exceptionally strong cases of uncontradicted rebuttal that clearly dispels the inference of negligence, the jury might even be compelled to find for the defendant.[6] If the jury disbelieves the defendant's evidence, it may accept the res ipsa loquitur inference and find for the plaintiff, or it may still find for the defendant because it is still unconvinced that negligence is the most likely explanation.

In some cases, the jury can believe all of the defendant's testimony and still rationally find that the defendant was negligent. For example, if the plaintiff was injured by the malfunctioning equipment at the defendant's factory, the defendant's rebuttal evidence might show that the equipment failed because of manufacturing flaws, but the jury might nevertheless still be permitted to draw the res ipsa inference of negligence because the rebuttal does not exclude the possibility that the defendant should have discovered the flaws.[7] Or the defendant might offer evidence describing all its careful acts, but failing to explain how, given its due care, the injury could occur. In such a case, even if the jury

2. E.g., Brewster v. United States, 542 N.W.2d 524 (Iowa 1996).

3. Wise v. Timmons, 64 Ohio St.3d 113, 592 N.E.2d 840 (1992).

4. See Brown v. Poway Unified School District, 4 Cal.4th 820, 843 P.2d 624, 15 Cal.Rptr.2d 679 (1993); Jackson v. Oklahoma Mem. Hospital, 909 P.2d 765 (1995).

5. De Leon Lopez v. Corporacion Insular de Seguros, 931 F.2d 116 (1st Cir.1991) (hospital mixed newborn babies of two different mothers and did not discover the mistake for over a year); see Imig v. Beck, 115 Ill.2d 18, 104 Ill.Dec. 767, 503 N.E.2d 324 (1986) (recognizing that some inferences may be exceptionally strong and that in exceptional cases so strong as to warrant a directed verdict for the plaintiff, but holding that the facts before the court did not warrant application of such an exceptional rule).

6. E.g., Van Hook v. Anderson, 64 Wash.App. 353, 824 P.2d 509 (1992) (sponge remained in patient's body after operation, doctor showed that nurses had reported to him an erroneous sponge count).

7. Mobil Chemical Co. v. Bell, 517 S.W.2d 245 (Tex.1974).

believes the rebutting testimony as far as it goes, the inference of negligence is not necessarily dissipated, and the jury may again be allowed to draw the inference of negligence.[8]

Defendant's risks in offering rebuttal. The defendant's decision to present or withhold rebuttal evidence may entail a calculated risk. Suppose the defendant proves that he took great care to make the harmful instrumentality safe. Some jurors may react to such evidence with renewed suspicion that the defendant was negligent in some unexplained way, since, after all, something definitely did go wrong and definitely did injure the plaintiff.[9] Or suppose the defendant offers rebuttal evidence that there were other causes of the injury. If the trier thinks these other putative causes were inadequate to cause the harm suffered by the plaintiff, the trier may think the defendant's evidence was false and from that may conclude that the defendant was negligent in some unadmitted way,[10] again reinforcing the possible res ipsa inference. With considerations like these in mind, the defendant in some cases may prefer to offer no rebuttal, but to rely instead upon the argument that the inference of negligence is too weak.

§ 157. Attributing Fault to the Defendant: The Exclusive Control Rule and Its Reform

Sufficiency of exclusive control. Res ipsa loquitur cannot be applied unless the evidence makes it probable that the causal negligence is the defendant's, not that of another person. Evidence that the defendant had exclusive control of the instrumentality of harm at the time of the accident is usually sufficient for this purpose. When a barrel falls on the plaintiff, the probability is that someone is negligent. When it falls from the defendant's warehouse, the probability is that the defendant is that negligent person.

The earlier exclusive control requirement. Courts have often said that the defendant's exclusive control was not only sufficient to show the defendant's probable connection with the accident but also necessary. The exclusive control requirement turned out to be over-inclusive because other kinds of evidence might point to the defendant's responsibility for the injury. For example, a manufacturer who produces foodstuffs in sealed containers which are then sold to consumers through a retailer is not in exclusive control of the food at the time the purchaser eats it.

8. E.g., Reynolds Metals Co. v. Yturbide, 258 F.2d 321 (9th Cir.1958); Escola v. Coca Cola Bottling Co. of Fresno, 24 Cal.2d 453, 150 P.2d 436 (1944); Kambat v. St. Francis Hospital., 89 N.Y.2d 489, 678 N.E.2d 456, 655 N.Y.S.2d 844 (1997) (18–inch towel discovered in patient after hysterectomy, evidence that all the towels were carefully counted does not necessarily dispel inference of negligence by surgeons or hospital); Goldstein v. Levy, 74 Misc. 463, 132 N.Y.S. 373 (App.Term. 1911).

9. Cf. Roberts v. Weber & Sons Co., 248 Neb. 243, 533 N.W.2d 664 (1995) (escaping cattle caused injury; defense evidence that the pens were secure, state-of-the-art enclosures tended to show that cattle would not have escaped without negligence).

10. See, suggesting this line of inference, Fowler v. Seaton, 61 Cal.2d 681, 394 P.2d 697, 39 Cal.Rptr. 881 (1964) .

But if the food is contaminated, the high probability is that the manufacturer, not the retailer, is the responsible person.

Reformulations of the exclusive control requirement. Although there are still decisions that apply the control rule to reject res ipsa loquitur,[1] courts have generally reformulated the rule in one or more ways. They say the control required is control at the time of the negligence or probable negligence rather than the time of the injury,[2] or that it is the right or authority to control, not actual physical control that counts,[3] or that the test ultimately is not so much control per se but "management" or "responsibility."[4] Other courts continue to state the exclusive control test, but determine "control" on the basis of an estimate of probabilities that the defendant rather than another person had control at the relevant time.[5] Overall, it seems safe to say more simply that the plaintiff can point to the defendant as the negligent person by evidence that excludes the possibility that others were negligent[6] or by showing that the defendant was responsible for all of the probable causes of the injury.[7] The best solution, however, is to recognize that the problem is to assess evidence in a particular case, not to promulgate a rule or to increasingly redefine "control."

Multiple actors. A literal application of the exclusive control rule would foreclose the use of res ipsa when two or more persons control the instruments of harm. Even without an exclusive control rule, or with a modified control rule, res ipsa is not available unless the plaintiff can provide some kind of evidence to connect the defendant to the accident. For example, if the plaintiff is injured in an unexplained collision between two moving motor vehicles, res ipsa loquitur will not normally apply.[8] With no evidence of how the collision occurred, it is fair to say that someone is probably negligent, but the probability that Driver A is

§ 157

1. E.g., Contreras v. Vannoy Heating & Air Conditioning, Inc., 270 Mont. 393, 892 P.2d 557 (1995) (defendant did not have exclusive control over exploding boiler); Ebanks v. New York City Transit Authority, 70 N.Y.2d 621, 518 N.Y.S.2d 776, 512 N.E.2d 297 (1987) (escalator injury).

2. Mobil Chemical Co. v. Bell, 517 S.W.2d 245 (Tex.1974); McGuire v. Stein's Gift & Garden Center, Inc., 178 Wis.2d 379, 504 N.W.2d 385 (1993).

3. E.g., McDowell v. Southwestern Bell Tel. Co., 546 S.W.2d 160, 168, 99 A.L.R.3d 604 (1976).

4. Giles v. City of New Haven, 228 Conn. 441, 636 A.2d 1335 (1994).

5. E.g., Anderson v. Service Merchandise Company, Inc., 240 Neb. 873, 485 N.W.2d 170 (1992) (one who worked on lighting fixture earlier excluded as not likely to be the person responsible for its fall much later, leaving operator of premises in "exclusive control").

6. Escola v. Coca Cola Bottling Co., 24 Cal.2d 453, 150 P.2d 436 (1944); Anderson v. Service Merchandise Company, Inc., supra n. 5.

7. See Mireles v. Broderick, 117 N.M. 445, 872 P.2d 863 (1994) ("the meaning of 'exclusive control' in res ipsa loquitur cases is fact specific within any given case"); Dalley v. Utah Valley Regional Medical Center, 791 P.2d 193 (Utah. 1990).

8. See Sheltra v. Rochefort, 667 A.2d 868 (Me.1995); Schofield v. King, 388 Pa. 132, 130 A.2d 93 (1957) (mere happening of two-car accident not sufficient evidence of negligence). Distinguish (a) a passenger's suit against a carrier involved in a two-vehicle collision and (b) a mid-air collision of two aircraft, one of which has been assigned the duty of visual contact by the control tower. See Irwin v. Pacific Southwest Airlines, 133 Cal.App.3d 709, 184 Cal. Rptr. 228 (1982).

negligent is no greater than the probability that it was Driver B, and vice versa.[9] The same is true whenever two or more persons, including the plaintiff herself, participate actively in any event.[10] It is a matter of assessing evidence rationally, however; so res ipsa is not excluded if one motor vehicle strikes a stationary object causing injury to the plaintiff.[11]

Eliminating the fault of some actors; serial control cases. At the same time, additional evidence may raise the probability that it was the defendant and not some other actor who was at fault. In the classic case, probabilities point to the defendant because all other actors are eliminated. In an exploding bottle case, the plaintiff showed that the bottle had not been mishandled or subjected to pressure or temperature change after it left the hands of the defendant bottler. That evidence, if accepted, eliminated negligence of the distributor and retailer, leaving a probability that the defendant and no one else was at fault.[12] In some cases of serial control, the evidence may even warrant the belief that both actors were negligent, the first in causing a defect and the second in failing to discover it.[13]

Due care requiring protection from other actors; public access cases. Many decisions are now consistent with the view that any rational basis for attributing fault will suffice and some have said so explicitly.[14] Many instruments, such as elevators, are made available for public use, so that the manufacturer, owner, or servicer definitely has limited control. But since due care requires that those instruments be made and maintained in a condition safe for use by many people,[15] the fact that the public has access to them does not necessarily mean that the manufacturer, owner,

9. At first blush, a different analysis might seem persuasive. You might argue that both drivers were probably negligent on the ground that in most two-car collisions both drivers are in fact negligent. The premise is not implausible, but courts generally have shied away from remote statistical categories of that kind. For instance, if one driver had blond hair and one had brown hair, and statistical evidence showed that blonds were negligent more often then brunettes, courts would not permit the jury to infer that the blond was probably negligent.

10. E.g., Dillworth v. Gambardella, 970 F.2d 1113 (2d Cir.1992) (two skiers collide); Brown v. Poway Unified School District, 4 Cal.4th 820, 843 P.2d 624, 15 Cal.Rptr.2d 679 (1993) (slip and fall).

11. E.g., Fox v. Dannenberg, 906 F.2d 1253 (8th Cir.1990) (reviewing many Missouri cases); Merchants Fast Motor Lines, Inc. v. State, 917 S.W.2d 518 (Tex.App. 1996) (truck left road and damaged state's guardrails, no sign of evasive action, hence res ipsa loquitur inference permitted).

12. Escola v. Coca Cola Bottling Co., 24 Cal.2d 453, 150 P.2d 436 (1944). Cf. Anderson v. Service Merchandise Company, Inc., 240 Neb. 873, 485 N.W.2d 170 (1992) (one who worked on lighting fixture earlier excluded not likely to be the person responsible for its fall much later, leaving operator of premises in "exclusive control"). The plaintiff is not required to eliminate all possibility that others were at fault, only to show that the probability of others' fault is so low that the defendant emerges as the probable responsible party. See Giles v. City of New Haven, 228 Conn. 441, 636 A.2d 1335 (1994).

13. Cf. Brown v. Racquet Club of Bricktown, 95 N.J. 280, 471 A.2d 25 (1984); Maciag v. Strato Medical Corp., 274 N.J.Super. 447, 644 A.2d 647 (1994) (raising the possibility that one defendant furnished inappropriate material for a medical device, that the manufacturer negligently designed the device, and that doctors negligently used it).

14. E.g., Mireles v. Broderick, 117 N.M. 445, 872 P.2d 863 (1994).

15. Trujeque v. Service Merchandise Co., 117 N.M. 388, 872 P.2d 361 (1994) (chair should be safe for any number of customers).

or servicer is not negligent. Consequently, if a plaintiff is injured when a hospital wheelchair collapses,[16] or an escalator or elevator malfunctions,[17] an automatic door closes on her,[18] or a public telephone shocks her,[19] she may often be permitted to claim res ipsa loquitur negligence, so long as she can exclude herself as the probable cause of the injury. But again, it is a matter of assessing the probabilities in each case, so in particular cases public access to the instrument of harm defeats the use of res ipsa loquitur.[20]

Joint control and plaintiff-participation. The same problem of identifying the defendant as the party who is probably negligent arises when the plaintiff herself is actively involved in the events leading to injury and when a group of persons such as doctors in an operating room share joint control. These two situations are addressed in the following sections.

§ 158. Special Liabilities of Multiple Defendants

Although courts usually insist that res ipsa loquitur must be grounded in some kind of evidence rationally pointing to the defendant as the wrongdoer, there are several kinds of cases in which courts may impose liability for reasons quite different from those associated with res ipsa loquitur and its reasonable inference that the defendant was negligent. In some of the multiple actor cases, courts have not only dropped the exclusive control requirement but have sometimes imposed liability upon defendants who are not likely to have been the wrongdoers. In doing so, they have sometimes said that joint control of those in a whole a group is enough to make all in the group liable for the negligence of some member whose identity is unknown,[1] or that two or more defendants owed a "joint duty" to the plaintiff.[2]

Such broad statements suggest a kind of collective responsibility for fault that would be a form of strict liability for those in the group who are innocent. As will appear, however, a number of the cases that

16. Darrough v. Glendale Heights Community Hospital, 234 Ill.App.3d 1055, 600 N.E.2d 1248, 175 Ill.Dec. 790 (1992). Similarly a chair on business premises open to the public. Trujeque v. Service Merchandise Co., 117 N.M. 388, 872 P.2d 361 (1994).

17. E.g., Cox v. May Department Store Company, 183 Ariz. 361, 903 P.2d 1119 (Ariz.App.1995) (plaintiff's jacket caught in escalator handrail assembly); Qualls v. United States Elevator Corp., 863 P.2d 457 (Okla.1993) (automatic elevator fell from second floor to basement, res ipsa against installer-maintainer; control is in the person who "assumes responsibility for the fitness of an instrumentality").

18. Brewster v. United States, 542 N.W.2d 524 (Iowa 1996).

19. Seeley v. New York Tel. Co., 281 App.Div. 285, 120 N.Y.S.2d 262 (1953).

20. City of New Smyrna Beach Utilities Com'n v. McWhorter, 418 So.2d 261 (Fla. 1982) (sewer main stopped, plaintiff's house flooded by backup, but public access to sewer eliminated res ipsa loquitur); Ebanks v. New York City Transit Authority, 70 N.Y.2d 621, 518 N.Y.S.2d 776, 512 N.E.2d 297 (1987) (escalator, risk of public abuse).

§ 158

1. E.g., Wick v. Henderson, 485 N.W.2d 645 (Iowa 1992).

2. Calabretta v. National Airlines, Inc., 528 F.Supp. 32 (E.D.N.Y.1981) (manufacturer of aircraft and airline operator could be found to owe a common duty to passenger, so res ipsa might apply when passenger felt ear pain and lost hearing).

embrace such broad statements are actually consistent with a much narrower rule.

Caretakers or custodians: the surgery cases. When several health care professionals are all engaged in surgery upon a patient, who in turn is anesthetized and unable to determine what is happening, a number of decisions have held that some or all of the professionals may be subjected to liability for an injury that is not within the risk of the operation, as where the patient recovers from an operation with third degree burns on a part of her body not involved in the operation.[3] The problem in such cases is not to find negligence; negligence is quite likely when a distant and previously healthy part of the body is harmed. The problem is that it is extremely unlikely that every one of the professionals—nurses, anesthesiologists, operating surgeons and their assistants—are negligent. It is sometimes suggested that by holding all of them liable, those with knowledge would be forced to reveal it.[4] That is not, of course, to suggest that an inference of universal negligence is plausible, but it would seem to be a justification for liability on other grounds if there were reason to believe that all those held liable in fact had knowledge of the negligent act. But that, too, is extremely unlikely, so the justification is at least subject to vigorous debate.

Vicarious liability explanations applicable to some cases. There are two or three related doctrines that may have confused some of the cases. One is that (in some states) the chief surgeon is treated as the temporary employer of all the others in the room on the ground that the surgeon can direct their acts. Under this captain-of-the-ship doctrine, the chief surgeon might be held for the negligence of others on a vicarious liability theory, not under res ipsa.[5] The second doctrine is based on the non-delegable duty doctrine. Under that doctrine, the hospital may be liable not only for acts of its employees, such as nurses or nurse-anesthetists, but also for the acts of independent contractors such as surgeons, on the theory that there are some duties that cannot be delegated to others. This would make the hospital vicariously liable for the negligence of all the actors, as if it were an employer of everyone in the operating room.[6]

These two doctrines of vicarious liability would operate quite differently from res ipsa loquitur in one important respect. They would make the chief surgeon or the surgeon and the hospital together liable for the negligence of the unknown actor, but they would not make nurses liable unless there were evidence to show that they were more likely than not the negligent cause of the harm.

3. E.g., Dalley v. Utah Valley Regional Medical Center, 791 P.2d 193 (Utah. 1990). Res ipsa loquitur in the medical setting is further discussed in §§ 248 & 249.

4. See Ybarra v. Spangard, 25 Cal.2d 486, 154 P.2d 687 (1944).

5. See Szabo v. Bryn Mawr Hospital, 432 Pa.Super. 409, 638 A.2d 1004 (1994); Oberzan v. Smith, 254 Kan. 846, 869 P.2d 682 (1994) (stating the doctrine, but refusing to extend outside the operating room to hold an absent doctor liable for a technician's insertion of an enema).

6. See Kolakowski v. Voris, 83 Ill.2d 388, 47 Ill.Dec. 392, 415 N.E.2d 397 (1980).

Spoliation explanation applicable to some cases. A third idea is that a person might be liable in tort for "spoliation of evidence" if he is under a duty to preserve it,[7] but that if he is a party to litigation, the court might more simply shift the burden of proof to a person who has destroyed evidence.[8] Spoliation of evidence liability is a much milder dose than res ipsa loquitur, because it depends first upon a duty to preserve the evidence and second upon knowing or at least negligent destruction. There has been no suggestion that a defendant could first be presumed to have the evidence and then held liable for failing to reveal it.

Commenting on caretaker-custodial cases. The just basis for liability of a hospital or surgeon for injury to a patient that may have been caused by any one of the health care team is easy to identify, at least in part. It is grounded in the idea that those who accept custody of a person who is unable to care for herself are implicitly accepting responsibility to guarantee care, or at least to provide information about the causes of harm inflicted. In a sense this is a kind of strict liability, but it is rooted in the implicit terms of the parties' consensual arrangements.[9] For this reason, the idea might appropriately extend to other custodial cases, such as those in which an institution cares for the infirm aged, or a disabled individual, and those in which day-care centers accept the care of very young children.[10] The vicarious liability theories approximate this just basis of liability. The res ipsa loquitur theory coupled with a joint control rule does not.

Carriers. A special liability has always attached to common carriers. Courts have said repeatedly that they are held to a standard of utmost diligence or some similarly elevated standard of care to their passengers,[11] allowing an injured passenger to get to the jury somewhat readily. Some courts go on to say that when a passenger is injured, the carrier is actually presumed to have been negligent and the burden shifts to the carrier to exculpate itself if it can.[12] This latter idea can be expressed as a rule of res ipsa loquitur. A number of courts have applied the rule even when the passenger's injury is the result of a collision between the

7. See Smith v. Abbott Ford, Inc., 151 Cal.App.3d 491, 198 Cal.Rptr. 829 (1984).

8. See Sweet v. Sisters of Providence in Washington, 895 P.2d 484 (Alaska 1995); cf. Neace v. Laimans, 951 F.2d 139 (7th Cir. 1991) ("destruction supports the application of res ipsa loquitur").

9. Seavey long ago noted the close analogy to the bailment rule that when a bailee cannot return the bailed chattel in good condition, the burden shifts to the bailee to explain the loss or damage. Seavey, Res Ipsa Loquitur: Tabula in Naufragio, 63 Harv. L. Rev. 643, 647 (1950). The idea is now so strongly associated with res ipsa that the bailment rule itself may be explained as a res ipsa rule. E.g., Kinder v. Fantasy Coachworks, Ltd., 762 S.W.2d 533 (Mo.App.1988). The bailment cases of course explain why the person who accepts custody of the chattel should also accept responsibility for proving an explanation, but they do not suggest that mere employees of the bailee would also be saddled with liability in the absence of evidence that they were probably negligent. The bailment analogy suggests that the chief surgeon, or the hospital, or some similar person who is seen to accept custody, should be the person obliged to explain or pay.

10. See § 155.

11. E.g., Nelson v. Flathead Valley Transit, 251 Mont. 269, 824 P.2d 263 (1992).

12. Dean v. Young, 263 Ill.App.3d 964, 201 Ill.Dec. 313, 636 N.E.2d 745 (1994); Smith v. Regional Transit Authority, 559 So.2d 995 (La.App.1990).

carrier and another moving vehicle,[13] a case to which, carriers aside, res ipsa does not apply. It might be easier to perceive the rule as one based on the carrier's virtual custody of the passenger and the expectations that arise when the passenger entrusts herself to the carrier's management. Whatever the rationale, the carrier collision cases represent potential liability of a defendant who is not shown to have been guilty of specific acts of negligence and who necessarily shares control with other drivers involved in the collision.

Other joint control or joint duty cases. Liabilities have been imposed in a variety of other joint control or joint duty cases.[14] Sometimes, as in the custody and carrier cases, the courts appear to be imposing a kind of strict liability, not liability based on rational inferences that all defendants were negligent.[15] At other times, the evidence circumstantially suggests specific acts of negligence on the part of some of the defendants, so that liability of several defendants is quite understandable on that ground, without resort to res ipsa loquitur.[16] In all such cases, analysis would be clarified and policy fostered if courts put aside the doubtful assertion that res ipsa applied and instead identified the duty and its basis in justice or policy.

§ 159. Plaintiff's Participation in Events Leading to Injury

Plaintiff participation and the control issue. Many cases have stated that, to claim the benefits of res ipsa loquitur, the plaintiff must first prove that she herself did not voluntarily or actively participate in causing the injury.[1]

The logic of the supposed rule is that when the plaintiff has actively participated in the events leading to injury, the defendant could not have had exclusive control in any literal way. The plaintiff participation cases

13. Capital Transit Co. v. Jackson, 149 F.2d 839 (D.C. Cir. 1945); Plumb v. Richmond Light & Railroad, 233 N.Y. 285, 135 N.E. 504, 25 A.L.R. 685 (1922).

14. See Joan Teshima, Annotation, Applicability of Res Ipsa Loquitur in Case of Multiple, Nonmedical Defendants—Modern Status, 59 A.L.R.4th 201 (1988).

15. In Corcoran v. Banner Super Market, Inc., 19 N.Y.2d 425, 280 N.Y.S.2d 385, 227 N.E.2d 304 (1967), a board that had been bridging the gap between the roofs of neighboring buildings fell down to Flatbush Avenue and struck the plaintiff. The Court of Appeal held that, as the owners of the two buildings had a "joint duty" of care, res ipsa loquitur would apply to allow the plaintiff to establish negligence. The court thought that each owner had a duty to inspect the premises. It did not suggest that both owners put the board there, or knew it was there, or even had time to find it there. Instead it said the owners had a duty to inspect. If that meant a duty to keep continual watch, it was an amazing change in the law and certainly a demand for more than ordinary care. If it meant only a duty to use care to inspect at reasonable times, res ipsa seems inappropriate for exactly the same reason it is inappropriate in slip and fall cases: the fact of injury does not tend to prove that the condition had been present long enough for the defendant to have discovered it by reasonable care.

16. See § 249.

§ 159

1. E.g., Bunn v. Urban Shelters and Health Care Systems, Inc., 672 A.2d 1056 (D.C.App.1996) ("no voluntary action or contribution on plaintiff's part"). Some apparently do not put the burden of proof upon the plaintiff, merely saying that there must be no indication that plaintiff is responsible. E.g., Fedorczyk v. Caribbean Cruise Lines, Ltd., 82 F.3d 69 (3d Cir.1996)

are thus merely one particular example of the exclusive control problem, which in turn is an effort to determine whether the defendant and not someone else is most probably the negligent actor. Older cases, reading "control" quite literally, sometimes went to extremes to reject res ipsa loquitur. A famous example is the case of a plaintiff who was injured when the defendant's chair, in which the plaintiff was sitting, collapsed. The court rejected res ipsa loquitur in that case on the ground that, since the plaintiff was in the chair, the defendant was not in control.[2] As indicated below, such literal application of control, in the plaintiff participation cases or others, is no longer common.[3]

Plaintiff participation as contributory fault. The plaintiff participation rule, if rule is the right word, is logically not a matter of contributory negligence but of control, bearing upon the question "who was the negligent person?"[4] But some courts have assumed that plaintiff participation is a rule about the plaintiff's contributory negligence. If that were so, the rule would be a strange one. Before comparative fault, contributory negligence was already a bar to the plaintiff's claim, so such a rule was not required. In addition, the plaintiff participation rule as stated in most cases shifts the burden to the plaintiff to prove her own freedom from fault, definitely not the rule used in contributory negligence cases. So it seems incorrect to interpret the rule as one about contributory fault instead of a rule about identification of the probable negligent actor.

Nevertheless, by treating the plaintiff participation rule as some species of contributory fault rule, some courts have been able to initiate a kind of reform. They have been able to say that under comparative fault systems, the plaintiff participation rule simply disappears.[5] This gets the same result that is obtained under the liberalized versions of the control rule, which recognize that res ipsa can appropriately apply if the evidence makes it probable that the defendant was negligent, since the plaintiff's fault does not necessarily negate the defendant's.[6] Some courts have achieved the same result by not discussing plaintiff participation at all.[7]

§ 160. Plaintiff's Access to or Use of Specific Evidence

Defendant's superior access to evidence not required. Courts have sometimes deviated from standard res ipsa loquitur rules both toward

2. Kilgore v. Shepard Co., 52 R.I. 151, 158 A. 720 (1932).

3. On the collapsing seat facts, see, allowing res ipsa, Rose v. Melody Lane of Wilshire, 39 Cal.2d 481, 247 P.2d 335 (1952); Sweet v. Swangel, 166 N.W.2d 776 (Iowa 1969); Trujeque v. Service Merchandise Co., 117 N.M. 388, 872 P.2d 361 (1994).

4. See Sweet v. Swangel, 166 N.W.2d 776 (Iowa 1969) (not to be confused with contributory negligence); Watzig v. Tobin, 292 Or. 645, 642 P.2d 651 (1982).

5. See Cox v. May Department Store Co., 183 Ariz. 361, 903 P.2d 1119 (1995); Giles v. City of New Haven, 228 Conn. 441, 636 A.2d 1335 (1994); Peplinski v. Fobe's Roofing, Inc., 193 Wis.2d 6, 531 N.W.2d 597 (1995).

6. Watzig v. Tobin, 292 Or. 645, 642 P.2d 651 (1982).

7. Khirieh v. State Farm Mut. Auto. Ins. Co., 594 So.2d 1220 (Ala.1992); Sheltra v. Rochefort, 667 A.2d 868 (Me.1995).

more liability and toward less. As already indicated, some courts have extended liability to defendants who are not likely to have been negligent.[1] In the opposite direction, courts have sometimes said that even a rational inference that negligence was probable would not suffice to justify the use of res ipsa loquitur. Instead, the doctrine could be applied only if the defendant had superior access to the relevant evidence.[2] This rule is sometimes repeated, but not so often applied. It is surely not applied in the unqualified form just stated. For example, if a plane or car crashes and kills all aboard, the estate or employer of the deceased pilot or driver may be subjected to res ipsa loquitur even though, as to the immediate cause of the accident, they could not know more than the deceased victims, but res ipsa loquitur may be applied if the facts otherwise justify its use.[3]

Superior knowledge as shorthand for other rules. Most often, the superior knowledge rule is an overstatement or a misstatement. It is an overstatement of the rule that the plaintiff cannot invoke res ipsa loquitur if he has all the facts, so a more moderate statement of the supposed rule would be that res ipsa applies when it is "impossible for the plaintiff to determine the sequence of events, *or* when the defendant has superior knowledge or means of information to determine the cause of the accident."[4]

Beyond that, the putative superior knowledge requirement turns out to be a cardboard defense whenever superior knowledge is attributed to the defendant merely because the defendant is in control of the harmful instrumentality.[5] Since control or some other ground for attributing fault to the defendant is required in any event, a superior knowledge requirement is merely a confusing reiteration of an element the plaintiff must prove anyway.

In other cases, it looks as if the plaintiff's equal knowledge of events is relevant because it speaks of the plaintiff's contributory fault, not of res ipsa loquitur.[6] In such a case, to assert the defendant's lack of superior knowledge bearing on res ipsa loquitur rather than on contributory fault is merely a solecism. Likewise, the landowner who has no knowledge of a danger may be under no duty to warn a licensee or trespasser, but again, the lack of superior knowledge in such a case has nothing to do with res ipsa loquitur. Finally, superior knowledge of the defendant is most definitely relevant as an affirmative ground for

§ 160

1. § 158.

2. Cox v. May Department Store Co., 183 Ariz. 361, 903 P.2d 1119 (1995).

3. E.g., Widmyer v. Southeast Skyways, Inc., 584 P.2d 1 (Alaska 1978) (plane crash); Merchants Fast Motor Lines, Inc., v. State, 917 S.W.2d 518 (1996) (truck going off the road).

4. Jones v. Tarrant Utility Co., 638 S.W.2d 862, 865 (Tex.1982) (emphasis added).

5. See Hale v. American Family Mutual Ins. Co., 927 S.W.2d 522 (Mo.App.1996); Kemper v. Builder's Square, Inc., 109 Ohio App.3d 127, 671 N.E.2d 1104 (Ohio App. 1996).

6. E.g., Zambito v. Southland Recreation Enterprises, Inc., 383 So.2d 989 (Fla. App.1980).

invoking res ipsa loquitur in some cases,[7] but that is to say that the defendant's superior knowledge is sufficient for res ipsa, not that it is necessary.[8]

The plaintiff does not introduce available evidence. Nevertheless, the plaintiff's access to evidence can be important for a different reason. When the plaintiff apparently has access to evidence but does not introduce it, the trier may sometimes infer that the absent evidence was unfavorable to the plaintiff.[9] Even if the evidence would be favorable to the plaintiff, the plaintiff should make a reasonable effort to introduce the evidence before relying upon res ipsa[10] or indeed before relying upon purely statistical circumstantial evidence.[11] These views, however, are quite a bit narrower than a rule that purports to discard res ipsa loquitur when the plaintiff's access to evidence is no worse than the defendant's.

The plaintiff pleads or proves evidence of specific negligence. The notion that res ipsa applied only to assist a plaintiff who could not get the facts got a little support from cases that excluded the res ipsa inference when the plaintiff introduced specific evidence of negligence. Courts now usually say that the plaintiff is not precluded from reliance upon res ipsa loquitur merely because she introduces evidence of specific negligent acts.[12] However, if the plaintiff's specific evidence fully explains all the relevant events, courts continue to exclude res ipsa and in that case the plaintiff must stand or fall on the specific evidence.[13]

7. E.g., Metz v. Central Illinois Electric and Gas Co., 32 Ill.2d 446, 207 N.E.2d 305 (1965).

8. Johnson v. Foster, 202 So.2d 520, 525 (Miss.1967) ("Exclusive knowledge and control of the evidence may be sufficient reason to apply the doctrine, but it does not necessarily follow that the doctrine will not be applied when the evidence is not available to either party").

9. E.g., Tonarelli v. Gibbons, 121 Ill. App.3d 1042, 77 Ill.Dec. 408, 460 N.E.2d 464 (1984) (presumption adverse to railroad when it failed to call only living eyewitness who was apparently in its control); see § 451 on spoliation of evidence. This may explain cases like Warren v. Jeffries, 263 N.C. 531, 139 S.E.2d 718 (1965), where, if the plaintiff's testimony was believed, the defendant's parked car ran away, killing a small boy. Conceivably there was a mechanical defect that would have explained the accident and conceivably it would have been one the defendant could not reasonably have discovered. The plaintiff offered no evidence as to the mechanical condition of the car and hence did not exclude this somewhat remote possibility. The court refused to apply res ipsa loquitur. See Byrd, Proof of Negligence in North Carolina, (Part I), 48 N. C. L. Rev. 452, 456 (1970). Some courts might reject the inference from absent evidence, see Herbert v. Wal–Mart Stores, Inc., 911 F.2d 1044 (5th Cir.1990), but the inference from absent evidence used against a plaintiff who has the burden of proof it is not implausible.

10. Cox v. May Department Store Co., 183 Ariz. 361, 903 P.2d 1119 (1995) first stated the broad rule, then made this narrower statement: "Invocation of res ipsa loquitur is no substitute for reasonable investigation and discovery. The doctrine may benefit a plaintiff unable directly to prove negligence; it does not relieve a plaintiff too uninquisitive to undertake available proof."

11. Cf. Howard v. Wal–Mart Stores, Inc., 160 F.3d 358 (7th Cir.1998) (either A's bus or B's bus struck plaintiff; that A had 51% of the buses in the area is not enough unless plaintiff can show further investigation infeasible; if the plaintiff does not show that, the inference is that she investigated and found facts against her case or that she should not recover because she has invoked expensive judicial processes without doing her share of the work).

12. E.g., Mireles v. Broderick, 117 N.M. 445, 872 P.2d 863 (1994).

13. Peplinski v. Fobe's Roofing, Inc., 193 Wis.2d 6, 531 N.W.2d 597 (1995).

Since the jury might reject the evidence of specific negligence, either because they disbelieved it or because they thought the acts described were not unreasonably risky, the plaintiff might lose the case when she would win with res ipsa loquitur. The question ought to be, not whether specific evidence "fully explains" the events, but whether, if the jury rejects that explanation, a res ipsa inference of negligence rationally remains.

When the plaintiff pleads specific negligent conduct, the legal problems are similar to those that arise when the plaintiff actually puts on evidence of specific negligent conduct. The cases take several different positions. At one end of this lugubrious line of cases, courts simply foreclose any use of res ipsa when specific negligence is pleaded. At the other end, courts hold that pleading specific facts has no effect on res ipsa loquitur if it is otherwise proper in the case.[14] In between are cases that in various ways attempt compromise and provide confusion, permitting res ipsa in some cases where specific negligence has been alleged and rejecting it in others.[15] Under modern pleading, all this is anomalous or worse. Since the plaintiff is not obliged to expound theories of legal liability in her complaint, nor to plead evidence, there is really almost no pleading that should foreclose the use of res ipsa loquitur.[16]

§ 161. Jury Instructions

Permitting the inference under a general negligence instruction. At least in those jurisdictions that treat res ipsa loquitur as only authorizing the jury to draw an inference of negligence, courts could conceivably submit a res ipsa case to the jury without any special instruction on res ipsa loquitur. Under such an approach, the jury would draw its own conclusions from the fact of injury. In a sense this is a neutral approach, one that does not single out the possible inference of negligence from the injury itself. Several courts have played with this idea or partially adopted it.[1]

Giving or requiring instruction on res ipsa loquitur. Most courts, however, assume that if the plaintiff can avoid a directed verdict because her case fits the res ipsa pattern, then an instruction to the jury should also be given. Certainly the res ipsa instruction is required if the trial judge has also given the unfortunate instruction to the effect that the

14. See Holzhauer v. Saks & Co., 346 Md. 328, 697 A.2d 89 (1997).

15. See J. F. Rydstrom, Annotation, Modern Trends as to Pleading a Particular Cause of Injury or Act of Negligence as Waiving or Barring the Right to Rely on Res Ipsa Loquitur, 2 A.L.R.3d 1335 (1966).

16. See Brewster v. United States, 542 N.W.2d 524 (Iowa 1996).

§ 161

1. Zukowsky v. Brown, 79 Wash.2d 586, 488 P.2d 269 (1971). In Mobil Chemical Co. v. Bell, 517 S.W.2d 245 (Tex.1974) the court recognized a measure of discretion in the trial judge on the res ipsa instruction, because the factual development at trial can be widely different. Some cases, without rendering a definitive decision, have raised the possibility that the instruction could be omitted (or covered implicitly by the general negligence instruction). Dover Elevator Co. v. Swann, 334 Md. 231, 638 A.2d 762 (1994).

mere happening of an accident is not negligence, since the mere happening instruction appears to foreclose the very inference permitted by res ipsa.[2] Some courts have gone further by declaring that in any case to which res ipsa loquitur applies, an instruction on its nature and effect must be given.[3] The instruction is usually couched in the language of the rule. The jury is told that if the accident is the kind that does not ordinarily happen without negligence, and if the defendant was in exclusive control of the instrumentality that caused harm, then the jury may infer that the defendant was negligent.[4] In presumption jurisdictions the jury is told that it is required to find for the plaintiff unless the defendant has produced evidence to rebut the inference.[5]

Topic D. Evaluating Conduct

§ 162. The Process of Evaluating the Facts

Evaluating under legal standards of care. As already indicated,[1] the jury's role includes not only a finding of historical facts—what people did and didn't do—but an evaluation of those facts, a normative decision about whether the defendant's conduct amounted to negligence. The parties must structure their evidence and argument accordingly. The jury's value judgment is made on the basis of the reasonable prudent person or due care standard, which in turn requires the jury to consider what was known or should have been known to the defendant, what harms were foreseeable, whether the risk of those harms was justified because the risk was small or the gains expected from the conduct were large in comparison. For these reasons, when the matters at issue are not common knowledge, the parties normally attempt to provide evidence from which the jury can estimate the seriousness of the risk and the costs or feasibility of avoiding it.

Experts and the ultimate evaluation. For the great mass of cases, the jury makes its value judgments without direct evidence about the ultimate issue of negligence. It is true that when the plaintiff claims professional negligence, such as medical malpractice, or negligence that requires technical knowledge to understand, experts may be required as well as permitted to testify about risks and alternatives, or even that the defendant's conduct violated governing standards.[2] Otherwise, however,

2. Eaton v. Eaton, 119 N.J. 628, 575 A.2d 858 (1990) (plain error not to give res ipsa loquitur instruction after a mere happening instruction had been given).

3. E.g., State Farm Fire & Casualty Co. v. Municipality of Anchorage, 788 P.2d 726 (Alaska 1990); Ravin v. Gambrell, 788 P.2d 817 (Colo.1990).

4. E.g., Southern Indiana Gas v. Indiana Ins. Co., 178 Ind.App. 505, 383 N.E.2d 387 (1978); Mireles v. Broderick, 117 N.M. 445, 872 P.2d 863 (1994) (both cases reflecting standard instructions that actually use the term res ipsa loquitur in addressing the jury).

5. California provides for optional instructions, one based upon a permissible inference, the other upon a presumption, the choice being dependent upon the facts of the case. For the presumption instruction, see California Jury Instructions (Book of Approved Jury Instructions), 4.03.

§ 162

1. § 148, supra.

2. See §§ 246 & 247 (expert testimony requirement in medical malpractice cases).

experts are generally not required or even permitted to testify either to matters of common knowledge or to the ultimate conclusion of negligence. The conclusion that a person is negligent is quite different from the conclusion that skid marks on a certain road show the car's speed to be no less than 30 mph.[3] That is an opinion, but mainly one about the probable facts, to which the expert may testify if he is appropriately qualified and if the testimony may assist the jury. In contrast, the expert could not testify that it is negligent to drive 30 mph on that road or under the existing circumstances. That is the rule because the determination of negligence is the normative issue that the jury must decide for itself and because experts must not be allowed to take over the jury's function or unduly influence it.[4]

Testimony bearing on risks. Although witnesses, expert or otherwise, are not ordinarily permitted to testify that the defendant's risky conduct counts as negligence,[5] many witnesses may be able to provide testimony to help show just how risky the conduct was. For example, when a car knocked down a utility's pole, which fell upon the plaintiffs, the jury had to determine whether the pole should have been stronger, to resist impact better. An expert testified that the defendant's pole would fall when struck by a Buick Skylark driving at only 6 miles per hour.[6] This kind of testimony is admissible to help the jury estimate how risky the defendant's pole really was. Sometimes studies about the riskiness of a given activity or product design are admissible, too, if for nothing else than to show that harm was foreseeable.[7]

Evaluation without testimony. The most noticeable thing about the expert testimony just described is that, helpful as it is, it almost always leaves large gaps that the jury must fill from its own experience and estimates. Granted that the pole would fall when struck by a straying Skylark, and that sometimes it might fall upon a pedestrian, the question remained for the jury whether that risk was enough to count as negligence, or whether a reasonable person would have constructed the pole as the defendant did in spite of the risk.

Juries are generally permitted to evaluate negligence on the basis of their own experience and perceptions of the risks involved. Neither expert opinion nor evidence of any special custom is required to permit

3. Brugh v. Peterson, 183 Neb. 190, 159 N.W.2d 321, 29 A.L.R.3d 236 (1968).

4. See Steffensen v. Smith's Management Corporation, 862 P.2d 1342 (Utah 1993) (expert could not offer opinion about relative percentages of fault among parties). Under modern evidence rules, courts may sometimes permit experts to give ultimate opinions, but trial judges may and should exclude expert testimony that either merely tells the jury what result to reach or offer legal conclusions or when it is not helpful to the jury in performing its role, as when the conclusion offered is a matter of common knowledge which the jury can decide for itself. Persinger v. Norfolk & Western Ry., 920 F.2d 1185 (4th Cir.1990) (expert testimony that a given weight was unsafe to lift because that is within the common knowledge of the jurors).

5. Professional malpractice cases are again different in this respect.

6. Bernier v. Boston Edison Co., 380 Mass. 372, 403 N.E.2d 391 (1980).

7. See, e.g., Carol A. Crocca, Annotation, Admissibility of Government Factfinding in Products Liability Actions, 29 A.L.R.5th 534 (1995).

this evaluation, so long as the kinds of risk involved are within the community's general understanding.[8] Only on matters outside that understanding, such as the riskiness of a given chemical[9] or the danger of a given medical procedure,[10] will expert testimony be required to estimate the degree of risk involved.

Jury estimating risks in light of safety efforts of others. Sometimes it is clear that an act is not risky enough to count as negligence because the defendant could reasonably expect that other people would minimize the risk, thus bringing it within tolerable bounds.[11] That seems especially obvious when the defendant attempts to minimize the risk or "shift responsibility" by hiring or relying upon a competent person to eliminate it.[12] But the idea is broader. It turns on nothing more than the defendant's reasonable expectations that others will make safety contributions. A driver may not be negligent in driving through an intersection in accordance with a green light, even if the driver cannot see traffic approaching on side streets. There is a risk, but it is small in light of the reasonable expectation that drivers approaching from a blind side street would themselves exercise due care and follow the traffic signal.[13] A physician who leaves town while a patient still requires care may be creating no risk at all if he arranges for a substitute physician.[14]

Jury estimating risks in the light of the plaintiff's ability to protect herself. Sometimes the defendant's conduct is not risky enough to count as negligence because the defendant can expect the plaintiff herself to avoid the harm and hence foresees no harm from his actions. This is most commonly so when the defendant creates an open and obvious

8. E.g., Delmarva Power & Light v. Stout, 380 A.2d 1365 (Del.1977); Holcombe v. NationsBanc Financial Services Corporation, 248 Va. 445, 450 S.E.2d 158 (1994) (expert not required to establish proper angle for storing partitions that fell on the plaintiff).

9. E.g., Turpin v. Merrell Dow Pharmaceuticals, Inc., 959 F.2d 1349 (6th Cir.1992) (expert testimony, based on studies, was inadequate to show that drug Bendectin was dangerous). See § 151, supra.

10. E.g., Walski v. Tiesenga, 72 Ill.2d 249, 21 Ill.Dec. 201, 381 N.E.2d 279 (1978).

11. Judge Posner addressed the mirror-image of this idea when he observed that a pedestrian-plaintiff would not be guilty of contributory negligence for failing to wear a helmet. "A pedestrian is not required to exercise a level of care ... that would be optimal if there were no sanctions against reckless driving.... The law normally does not require duplicative precautions unless one is likely to fail or the consequences of failure ... would be catastrophic." Greycas, Inc. v. Proud, 826 F.2d 1560, 1566 (7th Cir.1987).

12. E.g., Van Hook v. Anderson, 64 Wash.App. 353, 824 P.2d 509 (1992) (surgeon could rely upon nurses to count sponges and he was not negligent in leaving a sponge in the patient's body when he relied on nurses' assurance that sponges were accounted for); cf. Holger v. Irish, 316 Or. 402, 851 P.2d 1122 (1993) (surgeon not vicariously liable for nurse's negligent sponge count). In some instances, as a matter of conscious policy, courts refuse to permit an actor to delegate responsibility for due care to others; his duty is said to be nondelegable, and in that case he may be held liable for the other's negligence, although he himself is not at fault. E.g., Long v. Hacker, 246 Neb. 547, 520 N.W.2d 195 (1994). See § 337 below.

13. Many cases state some variation on the rule that a defendant can normally assume that others will exercise reasonable care and can shape his own conduct accordingly. E.g., Morgan v. Braasch, 214 Ga.App. 82, 446 S.E.2d 746 (1994) (intersection collision); Sims v. Huntington, 271 Ind. 368, 393 N.E.2d 135 (Ind. 1979).

14. Manno v. McIntosh, 519 N.W.2d 815 (Iowa App.1994) (discussed in terms of "abandonment" of the patient).

danger that people can be expected to see and avoid. The risks of a parked car, or a sprinkler head in the lawn, or other obvious dangers,[15] although representing foreseeable harms, are nevertheless very small risks because most people who might be hurt will avoid danger for themselves. Similarly, the owner of a building who hires someone to repair the roof may create a risk by not furnishing safety nets. Although the owner could easily foresee harm from the repairer's fall, the owner might also expect that the repairer would take steps to provide her own safety equipment or at least to ask for it if it is needed.[16] The jury can properly consider, then, the possibility that the defendant's conduct is not unreasonably risky because others, including the plaintiff herself, may reduce the risk.

Jury estimating risks in the light of risks others will add. It is not true, of course, that one never need anticipate the negligence of others. Sometimes that is the very thing the defendant should foresee and protect against. The defendant who creates an obvious risk cannot always expect that it will be avoided; a distracted customer carrying a package might collide with an obstruction that would ordinarily be obvious and avoidable.[17] The defendant who lends a car to an incompetent driver[18] or who gives alcohol to an intoxicated person or a minor[19] creates a risk, perhaps quite unreasonable, that the driver or the drinker will cause harm to others. If the probability of injury is unreasonably high in the light of the harm that may result and the relatively low cost of avoiding it, liability is entirely appropriate.[20]

Other issues distinguished. Many of the questions about negligence are easily confused with other issues in the case, such as contributory fault of the plaintiff, assumed risk, intervening cause, and even the broad question of duty. Most fundamentally, however, they are first questions of negligence, for if the defendant is not negligent at all in the light of the risks reasonably to be foreseen, there are no other real issues in the case.

Estimation of costs and advantages. Even small risks may be unreasonable and may count as negligence if they can be avoided at little cost. Even large risks might be justified if they carry with them even greater advantages. So the jury must estimate, if it can, something about the costs of greater safety and the advantages of continuing the defendant's conduct as it is. Sometimes evidence can elucidate such issues. Evidence

15. See Pomer v. Schoolman, 875 F.2d 1262 (7th Cir.1989); McFarland v. Kahn, 123 Ariz. 62, 597 P.2d 544 (1979) (sprinkler head).

16. Stinnett v. Buchele, 598 S.W.2d 469 (Ky. App.1980).

17. E.g., Ward v. K mart Corporation, 136 Ill.2d 132, 143 Ill.Dec. 288, 554 N.E.2d 223 (1990) (customer carrying mirror that blocked his view ran into a dangerously placed obstruction); Urban v. Wait's Supermarket, Inc., 294 N.W.2d 793 (S.D.1980) (customer distracted by search for cupcake holders fell on watermelons in aisle).

18. So-called negligent entrustment of a chattel. E.g., Renfro v. Adkins, 323 Ark. 288, 914 S.W.2d 306 (1996). See § 330.

19. E.g., Brigance v. Velvet Dove Restaurant, Inc., 725 P.2d 300 (1986). See § 332.

20. See Ransom v. City of Garden City, 113 Idaho 202, 207, 743 P.2d 70, 75 (1987) (quoting PROSSER AND KEETON).

that the defendant repaired premises or changed his way of conducting business after the plaintiff's injury is not usually admissible to show a standard of care, but if the defendant has argued that a safer practice is not feasible, evidence that the defendant has himself adopted the practice later can fairly be admitted so show that, after all, the practice was indeed feasible.[21]

Here, as with the question of risk, definitive testimony is unlikely and ball park estimates are usually tolerated, perhaps even inevitable. Sometimes it is easy to estimate that costs of greater safety will be low, as where the defendant can make a product safer by including a warning on its label or on a decal.[22] Sometimes it is even possible to obtain rather precise estimates of the cost of greater safety.[23] More commonly, risks cannot be precisely weighed and juries and judges alike are expected to estimate costs in a very broad manner.[24] There are limits: the court's own ball park estimate may convince the court that the case must not be left to the jury at all,[25] or the court may conclude that general experience is not enough to permit a reasonable cost estimate and therefore that the plaintiff must introduce evidence on that subject or suffer a directed verdict.[26] In very many cases, however, the matter of cost, like the matter of risk, is left to the jury's evaluation without a specific requirement of testimony.

The jury may obtain assistance in evaluating the defendant's conduct as a whole, or in estimating foreseeability, the extent of the risk, or even costs, in one special way. Custom may help in the overall evaluation or in providing indirect evidence about subsidiary issues like foreseeability. Custom is considered in the sections that follow.

§ 163. Evidence of Custom or Practice to Assist Evaluation: General Rules

Custom as inconclusive evidence of due care. Evidence of customary practices is normally admissible to help assist the jury in making an evaluation of the facts and in determining the ultimate issue of negligence. Courts today almost always say that the customary practice is not the standard of care—the standard remains that of the reasonable and

21. See Ray v. American National Red Cross, 685 A.2d 411 (D.C.App.1996).

22. E.g., Watson v. Navistar International Transport. Corp., 121 Idaho 643, 827 P.2d 656 (1992).

23. Hunter v. Dept. of Transportation and Dev., 620 So.2d 1149 (La.1993) (costs of making median wider to increase safety for left-turn drivers).

24. Thus in Ann M. v. Pacific Plaza Shopping Center, 6 Cal.4th 666, 863 P.2d 207, 25 Cal.Rptr.2d 137 (1993) the court observed in broad terms that "The monetary costs of security guards is not insignificant" without reference to any evidence or any specific costs.

25. In Ramirez v. Plough, Inc., 6 Cal.4th 539, 863 P.2d 167, 25 Cal.Rptr.2d 97 (1993), the court concluded that product warnings for aspirin need not be given in the Spanish even though the manufacturer advertised in Spanish to Spanish speaking consumers. The case turned on several legal doctrines and policies, but in part on the court's belief, seemingly not based on actual trial evidence, that costs of adding warnings could be very high.

26. See McCarty v. Pheasant Run, Inc., 826 F.2d 1554 (7th Cir.1987).

prudent person.[1] Custom evidence is merely admissible to assist the jury in determining what reasonable care requires in the circumstances.[2] Custom evidence can be introduced either to show that the defendant fell short of the custom and thus might be accounted negligent, or that the defendant complied with custom and thus might be seen as exercising due care.

Constraints on use of custom. When custom is used in this kind of undifferentiated way as bearing generally on the ultimate issue of negligence, or to prove that the defendant should have had knowledge of the customary safety precautions, courts impose limitations on its use, including the following:

(1) Courts often say that to be a custom, the practice must be widespread, notorious, or even that it must be universal.[3] If such demands are too stringent, it is at least true that the practice must be common and not merely a sporadic or occasional practice.[4]

(2) When the plaintiff attempts to prove negligence by proving violation of custom, the custom must be one generated by safety concerns, not one arising for reasons unrelated to safety.

(3) A custom to violate statutory or regulatory requirements is not ordinarily to be admitted to show reasonable care, but such a custom may occasionally bear on the possibility that violation was excused. In addition, minors, who are often not held to statutory standards anyway, may be permitted to claim they were exercising due care while following a custom to violate a statute.[5]

Relevance of practices that do not amount to customs. Practices that are not widespread enough to count as custom, including the defendant's own business practices,[6] may be relevant, not on the ultimate issue of negligence or for an undifferentiated evaluation of it, but to prove some particular points along the way. Such practices, as well as custom itself, can be used, where the facts make it appropriate, to show (1) that the precaution was feasible,[7] (2) that the harm it was intended to avert was foreseeable,[8] or (3) that the plaintiff reasonably relied upon the past

§ 163

1. However, custom, like agreement, may shape the plaintiff's expectations of safety and hence may conceivably impose a duty that does not otherwise exist or immunize a defendant who is otherwise under a duty.

2. Texas & Pacific Railway v. Behymer, 189 U.S. 468, 23 S.Ct. 622, 47 L.Ed. 905 (1903); The T.J. Hooper, 60 F.2d 737 (2d Cir.1932); Restatement Second § 295A.

3. Rentz v. Brown, 219 Ga.App. 187, 464 S.E.2d 617 (1995).

4. Trimarco v. Klein, 56 N.Y.2d 98, 436 N.E.2d 502, 451 N.Y.S.2d 52 (1982) ("fairly well defined").

5. E.g., Alley v. Siepman, 87 S.D. 670, 214 N.W.2d 7 (1974).

6. See e.g., Potter v. Firestone Tire and Rubber Co., 6 Cal.4th 965, 863 P.2d 795, 25 Cal.Rptr.2d 550 (1993). The defendant would not ordinarily be permitted to rely upon its own internal practices as a defense.

7. See Camenzind v. Freeland Furniture Co., 89 Or. 158, 174 P. 139, 144 (1918).

8. See Clarence Morris, Custom and Negligence, 42 Colum. L. Rev. 1147 (1942).

practice, especially one followed in the past by the defendant itself.[9] Indeed, where the plaintiff has reasonably relied upon a customary safety practice or even upon a practice or policy followed only by the defendant, the custom or practice comes very close to operating as a standard of conduct and not merely as evidence bearing on the question of reasonable care.

§ 164. Safety Custom as Evidence or Standard

Customs are specific practices widely used or accepted in a relevant community or culture. In a tort case, the relevant community may be a geographical location such as a city or it may be an industry, trade, profession or sport. Both customs, as widely followed practices, and practices that are not so widely used, may be relevant in tort cases in different ways.

Importance of custom generally. Customs of society at any given time are often important in tort law, and in a variety of ways. For instance, judges know, in a general way, the kind of world we live in and they write opinions and develop rules and policies in accord with their understanding of the world's customs or practices.[1] Custom shapes expectations and creates or reflects social norms and private consensus.[2] Even very specific customs, like the custom of crying "fore" before driving a golf ball, may shape a judge's decision even when there is no evidence about it in the particular case.[3] Custom can reflect social or official policy, too, so that civil rights claims may be asserted on the basis of unconstitutional customs as well as on the basis of unconstitutional legislation.[4] Courts sometimes consciously depart from the community's standards of behavior, as where the Constitution demanded an end to segregated schools. But law follows as often as it leads, so courts sometimes show a strong reluctance to impose rational standards that depart from strong community customs or practices.[5]

9. E.g., Roberts v. Indiana Gas and Water Co., 140 Ind.App. 409, 218 N.E.2d 556 (1966) (where reliance is foreseeable, omission of the customary precaution may be negligence "in itself").

§ 164

1. "In determining whether the defendant had a duty to be careful, we look to existing social values and customs, as well as to appropriate social policy." See, e.g., Davis v. Westwood Group, 420 Mass. 739, 743, 652 N.E.2d 567, 569 (1995).

2. E.g.: (1) Privacy expectations, on which much of the right of privacy turns, are understood partly in terms of custom. Hill v. National Collegiate Athletic Assn., 7 Cal.4th 1, 865 P.2d 633, 26 Cal.Rptr.2d 834 (1994). (2) The current role of custom and consumer expectation in products liability cases is complicated, but at least on occasion, consumer expectations, often generated by or reflecting custom, demonstrate the standard for a product. See Restatement of Products Liability § 2, cmt. g (Tentative Draft No. 2).

3. See McWilliams v. Parham, 269 N.C. 162, 152 S.E.2d 117 (1967).

4. Under 42 U.S.C.A. § 1983 one who acts under color of either law or custom to deprive another of federal rights is subject to a federal civil rights claim. A separate importance of custom occurs when the plaintiff sues a municipality under that statute, because in that case the plaintiff must show that the unconstitutional actions represent a municipal policy, which in turn can be shown by custom or practices of the municipality. See Monell v. Department of Social Services, 436 U.S. 658, 98 S.Ct. 2018, 56 L.Ed.2d 611 (1978).

5. For example, many courts have refused even to permit a jury to consider a plaintiff's failure to wear a seatbelt as con-

Relevance of custom on the negligence issue. On the issue of negligence, a safety custom is often relevant because it reflects the judgment and experience of many people and thus directly suggests how a reasonable person might behave under the circumstances, on the theory that customary behavior is usually not negligent, or on the more specific ground that, under some circumstances, customary behavior tends to prove the proper balance of risks and utilities.[6] A community's custom, or that of an industry, can also bear on the defendant's probable knowledge of the problem. It also suggests at least one solution, the solution provided by the custom itself.

Custom takes on added and different relevance when the plaintiff relies upon the defendant to comply with a safety custom and is injured because the defendant does not do so. Even if due care does not require gas companies to odorize natural gas, a practice of doing so may lead users to rely on the smell as an indication of gas leaks, so that once the custom is in place it will be negligence to drop it.[7] Custom—or even practices that do not rise to the level of custom—might also tend to prove something less global but still important. A custom or a sporadic practice may at least show that the practice is a feasible one or that the danger to which the practice is addressed is foreseeable.[8]

Custom and the standard of care. At least where both the plaintiff and defendant are part of the custom community or have accepted its customary standards,[9] a safety custom in a negligence case is relevant evidence tending to show what does or does not count as reasonable care.[10] Some early cases gave different answers, either banishing custom from the case entirely[11] or on the contrary treating it as the ultimate standard of care.[12] These do not represent contemporary authority.[13]

tributory negligence, and at least one court has held that if the jury does consider that issue, community custom will bear on the question whether failure to wear the belt is negligence, even if a statute requires wearing it. Waterson v. General Motors Corporation, 111 N.J. 238, 544 A.2d 357 (1988).

6. Richard A. Posner, Economic Analysis of Law § 6.3 (4th ed. 1992).

7. See Roberts v. Indiana Gas and Water Co., 140 Ind.App. 409, 218 N.E.2d 556 (1966) (where reliance is foreseeable, omission of the customary precaution may be negligence "in itself").

8. The feasibility point has been recognized at least since publication of the leading article on custom, Clarence Morris, Custom and Negligence, 42 Colum. L. Rev. 1147 (1942).

9. See, distinguishing the effect of custom in consensual and stranger relationships Richard A. Epstein, The Path to the T.J. Hooper: The Theory and History of Custom in the Law of Tort, 21 J. Leg. Studies 1 (1992).

10. Restatement Second § 295A.

11. See Mayhew v. Sullivan Mining Co., 76 Me. 100 (1884) (excluding custom evidence on the facts and suggesting that custom was definitionally irrelevant in all cases).

12. Titus v. Bradford, B. & K. R.R., 136 Pa. 618, 626, 20 A. 517, 518 (1890) ("no jury can be permitted to say that the usual and ordinary way, commonly adopted by those in the same business, is a negligent way").

13. Some contemporary cases hold that no negligence was proven on the facts, and in the course of so holding also state that no custom was violated. These cases probably do not mean to assert that violation of a custom is required to establish negligence or that it is the standard. They seem to mean only that on the facts of the particular case the plaintiff simply has not adduced evidence of negligence, either by evidence of custom or by evidence of high danger that could be feasibly avoided. E.g., Wilbur v. Schweitzer Excavating Co., 181 Neb. 317,

With the exception of professional malpractice cases, the standard of care remains the standard of the reasonable person under the circumstances. Violation of, or compliance with custom is thus relevant and admissible, but not conclusive on the negligence issue; custom merely provides evidence that may or may not persuade the jury on the negligence issue.[14]

The T.J. Hooper illustration. The best-known case, *The T.J. Hooper*,[15] illustrates the general rule. In that case, the defendant's tug, towing a string of barges in the coastal seas, had no radio receiver. Had the tug had one, it could have received a storm warning and could have put into a safe port. Not having one, the tug proceeded at sea and the barges' cargoes were destroyed in a storm. The cargo owners sued the tug. At that time, there was no general custom for tugs to carry receivers, but they were cheap and could obviously contribute to safety of the cargoes. The general practice of the tug industry, however, was not the standard of care. It was admissible as evidence, but not conclusive, so the tug could properly be held responsible in spite of the fact that it had operated in line with industry practice.

Custom as a sword and custom as a shield. Evidence of a custom may be used either as a sword or a shield. As a sword, the plaintiff can show the defendant's violation of a safety custom as some evidence that the defendant failed to act as a reasonable person under the circumstances.[16] In some cases, evidence of the custom is presented by an expert,[17] but the rule is no less applicable if the custom is institutionalized in advisory standards of the relevant industrial association.[18] As a

148 N.W.2d 192 (1967). Occasionally judges use the term "standard" quite loosely, saying, for example, that custom "is admissible to establish a standard of care," as in French v. Ehrenfeld, 180 A.D.2d 895, 579 N.Y.S.2d 480 (1992), but from their citations and other evidence it seems clear that they do not mean to say that custom is the standard or that it supplants the reasonable care standard, only that it is evidence of reasonable feasibly.

14. Texas & Pacific Railway v. Behymer, 189 U.S. 468, 23 S.Ct. 622, 47 L.Ed. 905 (1903); The T.J. Hooper, 60 F.2d 737 (2d Cir.1932); Upham v. Chateau De Ville Dinner Theatre, Inc., 380 Mass. 350, 403 N.E.2d 384, 19 A.L.R.4th 1103 (1980); McWilliams v. Parham, 273 N.C. 592, 160 S.E.2d 692 (1968).

15. The T.J. Hooper, 60 F.2d 737 (2d Cir.1932).

16. McComish v. DeSoi, 42 N.J. 274, 200 A.2d 116 (1964) (testimony based on safety manuals of industry to show what experienced people do as evidence of what should be done); Trimarco v. Klein, 56 N.Y.2d 98, 436 N.E.2d 502, 451 N.Y.S.2d 52 (1982) (custom of landlords to use tempered glass or plastic, not ordinary glass, as shower or tub enclosures was evidence, along with evidence of low cost and other matters, admissible on the issue of landlord's negligence); Besette v. Enderlin School Dist. No. 22, 310 N.W.2d 759 (N.D.1981) (school child injured in fall from slide, evidence that other schools had safer playground surfaces admissible as a custom); Kaiser v. Cook, 67 Wis.2d 460, 227 N.W.2d 50 (1975) (evidence that other race tracks prohibited spectators at the dangerous number 3 and 4 turns sufficient to get the plaintiff to the jury). It should go without saying that the plaintiff must show violation of the custom as well as its existence. Guldy v. Pyramid Corp., 222 A.D.2d 815, 634 N.Y.S.2d 788 (App. Div. 1995).

17. E.g., Doe v. Dominion Bank of Washington, 963 F.2d 1552 (D.C.Cir.1992) (expert testified as to security customs of commercial landlords; this was sufficient to sustain plaintiff's burden in suit against landlord for rape in the building).

18. E.g., Hansen v. Abrasive Eng'g & Manufacturing, Inc., 317 Or. 378, 856 P.2d 625 (1993) (ANSI advisory standard admissible but not conclusive).

shield, the defendant can show his compliance with custom as evidence that his conduct was that of a reasonable person, or, what is the same thing, that the safety precaution demanded by the plaintiff was not customarily used in the relevant community.[19] Similarly, the plaintiff who is charged with contributory fault is permitted to show that what he did was in accordance with custom and hence arguably but not conclusively evidence that he exercised due care.[20]

Community of custom. In many cases, the plaintiff and defendant are members of the same community of custom. For example, they are both part of the same geographical community in which the custom is followed, or they are entering into consensual transactions with each other on the basis of the same industrial custom. In such cases, their reasonable expectations of each other are largely or perhaps wholly dictated by the known custom rather than by reasonable care judged in the abstract. In such cases it may be appropriate to give the custom very great weight. If I ship my goods by way of a barge to be towed by your tug, I might be understood to accept the customary care that goes with towing barges unless you and I contract for a different standard of care. At least that is true where I know the customary standard or where you reasonably believe that I know it or should find it out. Cases like that are in fact very similar to cases in which the defendant's duty of care is limited because the plaintiff assumes the risk.

Great weight might also be given to custom used as a sword when the parties are both members of the same custom community. As Professor Morris argued, one who contracts for the defendant's services is equally entitled to expect those services to be delivered with the customary safety.[21] In the same way, known safety customs in the design or manufacture of products may bear heavily on the question whether those products were defective.[22] Professor Epstein has argued that custom is or ought to be the standard of care and not merely evidence when the parties have bargained against a background of custom.[23] That goes further than the rule stated by the courts, but it is surely true that some consensual relationships may imply an agreed-upon standard that might be something quite different from the standard of the reasonable prudent person.

19. The T.J. Hooper, 60 F.2d 737 (2d Cir.1932); LaVallee v. Vermont Motor Inns, Inc., 153 Vt. 80, 569 A.2d 1073 (1989).

20. E.g., Wanner v. Getter Trucking, 466 N.W.2d 833 (N.D.1991).

21. Clarence Morris, Custom and Negligence, 42 COLUM. L. REV. 1147, 1153 (1942).

22. Consumers are not aware, or expected to be aware, of all safety and risk customs of a manufacturer, so the use of custom by the defendant may be circumscribed. On the other hand, consumers may reasonably assume that the product is made with the customary safety designs or equipment and when it is not, the product may be defective. Industry custom might also show that a reasonable alternative design is possible.

23. Richard A. Epstein, The Path to the T.J. Hooper: The Theory and History of Custom in the Law of Tort, 21 J. LEG. STUDIES 1 (1992); cf. RICHARD A. POSNER, ECONOMIC ANALYSIS OF LAW § 6.3 (4th ed. 1992). (economic analysis suggesting that as between industry and its customers, level of precaution taken by industry is "likely to be efficient" and hence that compliance with that custom should be a defense).

In the context of sports and games, courts have come close to accepting such a view. The plaintiff who is injured while playing a sport assumes the risk of dangers that are inherent in the sport. What if the plaintiff is injured by a player who violates one of the rules of the game? Violation of the rules of the game is not necessarily enough to make a case of liability, because at least some of the rules are customarily violated. The plaintiff who joins the game community takes its customs as a standard, including the customs to violate rules.The final step in these cases should not be permitted to obscure the point that the due care standard is displaced by a preference for custom as a standard. That final step is that courts doubt their ability to delineate the customs of games and so for practical reasons pick the next best standard, holding rule-violating defendants only to a standard based on recklessness.[24]

§ 165. Imposing and Avoiding Constraints on Use of Custom Evidence

Ambiguities in the custom or its scope. Conduct may be clear and certain at the same time that its meaning may be doubtful. Suppose that it is customary to include certain safety features in bridges, all of which were designed for public use. Is the feature a custom about bridges, or a custom only about bridges for public use? The Iowa Court held that the jury should *not* be instructed to consider customs in public bridge design in determining negligence of a private bridge owner, in the absence of testimony that showed the public bridge custom had also become a custom in private bridge cases.[1] Perhaps this is not a subject suited to simple rules. The meaning of some ambiguous conduct, like the meaning of some ambiguous words, can be sorted out by the jury if reasonable people could differ. So in appropriate cases, evidence of the bridge safety custom might be admissible if it were coupled with evidence that the cost of the safety feature was low, or that it was well-known, or otherwise adaptable to privately owned bridges.

Custom in violation of statute. Sometimes an act in accord with settled custom is nevertheless a violation of statute. A custom to provide less care than required by the statute ordinarily cannot be relied upon by the defendant to avoid the statutory standard or to excuse violation.[2] In

24. See the excellent discussion in Crawn v. Campo, 136 N.J. 494, 643 A.2d 600 (1994). The sports cases are discussed generally in § 215. Courts also assert that they wish to encourage sporting activities by applying a recklessness standard. This seems less persuasive a basis for the rule, partly because there is no obvious reason to single out sports as distinct from other leisure activities and partly because courts do not seem to be the agency that society expects to give this particular kind of guidance in the lives of individuals.

§ 165

1. Simon's Feed Store, Inc. v. Leslein, 478 N.W.2d 598 (Iowa 1991). The requirement of a "definite" custom may be addressed to this point. Cf. Rhine v. Duluth, M & I R.R., 210 Minn. 281, 297 N.W. 852 (1941) (witnesses had observed many instances in which railroad had set flares at crossing, but the custom might have been to set flares only when the trains were engaged in switching movements, not when they were proceeding in a straightaway movement).

2. Smith v. Aaron, 256 Ark. 414, 508 S.W.2d 320 (Ark. 1974); Sanchez v. J. Bar-

the case of a minor's violation of statute, however, the courts themselves often reject the statutory standard in favor of the common law protective standard for minors. Consequently courts may permit the minor to rely upon a statute-violating custom.[3] When the custom requires greater care than is required by statute, custom is presumably admissible on the issue of negligence because the statutory standard is usually a minimum, not a maximum.[4]

Custom to provide care different from that dictated by the risk-utility balance. When courts say that custom is not conclusive on the negligence issue, they necessarily mean that custom can be trumped by the ordinary care standard, which in turn is usually assessed by reference to the risk-utility balance. So if a universal custom were highly risky and likely to cause great harm but could be avoided by an expenditure of $1, the jury would be permitted to find negligence in spite of the exculpatory custom.

When a custom clearly calls for more care than would be dictated by the risk-utility balance—calls for inefficient levels of care, some economists might say—the answer is not entirely clear from the cases. Courts do routinely if roughly weigh risks and utilities in determining negligence, but courts can nevertheless analyze negligence by other means as well. At least when custom generates expectations of the parties, it may be that those expectations will demand more or less than would be demanded by a balance of risks and utilities and that courts would permit custom to trump the risk-utility balance in such cases.[5]

Non-safety customs. Not all practices can be used as ultimate evidence of negligence or its absence. First, a custom in the community, no matter how well established, is not necessarily related to safety at all. It may be based upon cultural or other preferences. Many churches do not burn candles, but their reasons for leaving candles out of their services are most likely related to religious and stylistic preferences, not to any fear of burning the church down. Violation of a custom that is not a safety custom is no more relevant to establish the ultimate issue of negligence than violation of a statute that does not set a safety standard.[6]

Practices that are not customs. (a) As a shield. A second constraint on the use of custom to establish the ultimate issue of negligence is that

ron Rice, Inc., 77 N.M. 717, 427 P.2d 240 (1967).

3. Alley v. Siepman, 87 S.D. 670, 214 N.W.2d 7 (1974).

4. See Duncan v. Corbetta, 178 A.D.2d 459, 577 N.Y.S.2d 129 (1991) (custom to use pressure-treated wood in stair construction, although ordinance permitted use of ordinary lumber; trial judge should have admitted evidence of custom).

5. When undertakings or expectations of the parties control, they appear to trump the risk-utility balance, whether or not those expectations are based upon a preexisting custom. The custom of medical practitioners, for example, is ordinarily the standard of care. See § 242 below. Strict liability under the Restatement Second's § 402A, which determined defectiveness of products in part by reference to consumer expectations, was probably also an example. Similarly, informed consent cases are rooted in the patient's expectations. Even more clearly, then, expectations of the parties would trump risk-utility balancing when those expectations are based on custom.

6. See Levine v. Russell Blaine Co., 273 N.Y. 386, 7 N.E.2d 673 (1937).

not every practice counts as a custom. A practice followed by some persons in a business but one that is not widely used is not necessarily a custom at all. Nor is the defendant's own practice or internal rules a custom. Defendants cannot appropriately rely upon such occasional practices or their own practices to justify their risky conduct.[7] Some courts emphasize that custom evidence is not admissible to prove negligence unless the custom is uniform, well-known, widely followed, or notorious.[8] In this context, the idea seems right, even if it is sometimes stated too emphatically.

(b) As a sword.—bearing on reasonable care or defendant's knowledge. When the plaintiff rather than the defendant seeks to rely upon occasional practices that do not count as a custom, the rules remain the same for some but not all purposes. It remains true that one or two examples of a safer practice would not ordinarily count as a custom at all.[9] And if the plaintiff seeks to show that the defendant should have known of the safety methods represented by the custom, the custom or practice must again be well-known and well-defined enough to permit the inference that the defendant should have known about it.[10] If the plaintiff seeks to show that the practice simply represents reasonable care, some courts even require in such cases that the custom be a general one or else a custom of the local vicinity.[11]

—bearing on foreseeability and feasibility. However, the plaintiff may attempt to show a given practice to establish much narrower propositions, none of which require that the practice actually count as a custom. Even an occasional practice may show (1) that the practice is feasible,[12] (2) that the harm addressed by the practice is foreseeable, (3)

7. Ganz v. United States Cycling Federation, 273 Mont. 360, 903 P.2d 212 (1995). A practice followed only by the defendant and not by others in the industry might nevertheless be relevant if the plaintiff was aware of the practice and should have conducted herself in the light of that known practice. In other words, even a practice that does not count as a custom might still bear on the issues of contributory fault and assumed risk.

8. Rentz v. Brown, 219 Ga.App. 187, 464 S.E.2d 617 (1995) (custom must be universal); Braden v. Workman, 146 Mich. App. 287, 380 N.W.2d 84 (1985) ("certain, uniform and notorious"). When such requirements are imposed upon the use of custom as a sword, they may be misplaced, as shown in the next paragraph.

9. Garthe v. Ruppert, 264 N.Y. 290, 190 N.E. 643 (1934).

10. See Rhine v. Duluth, M. & I. R.R., 210 Minn. 281, 297 N.W. 852 (1941) (custom must be uniform and also notorious enough to indicate defendant would know of it); Trimarco v. Klein, 56 N.Y.2d 98, 436 N.E.2d 502, 451 N.Y.S.2d 52 (1982) (need not be "universal. It suffices that it be fairly well defined").

11. Sprecher v. Roberts, 212 Wis. 69, 248 N.W. 795 (Wis. 1933).

12. Camenzind v. Freeland Furniture Co., 89 Or. 158, 174 P. 139 (1918). A custom that develops *after* the plaintiff's injury might also show feasibility. That kind of case resembles the subsequent repair problem. Apart from products liability cases, the rule usually is that subsequent repairs cannot be shown to establish the ultimate conclusion that the defendant was negligent, but this rule is now usually stated as a prelude to a exception. One exception is that subsequent repair can be admitted to show that a safer (repaired) condition was feasible. E.G., Holcombe v. NationsBanc Financial Services Corporation, 248 Va. 445, 450 S.E.2d 158 (1994). Products liability cases are sometimes treated differently, but again subsequent product improvements are admissible at least to show feasibility of a safer product. See Cover v. Cohen, 61 N.Y.2d 261, 461 N.E.2d 864, 473 N.Y.S.2d 378 (1984). Likewise in product actions, some authority supports the admission of

that the plaintiff foreseeably relied upon a practice so that it became negligence for the defendant to omit the practice without warning,[13] or (4) that the plaintiff reasonably relied upon the safety practice and hence was not guilty of assumed risk.[14] In all of these cases, occasional practices that are not necessarily widespread may be relevant to the discrete issues named, even if they are not relevant to establish the ultimate conclusion of negligence itself or the defendant's knowledge of the practice.

Much the same is true about evidence that, after an injury, the defendant took remedial steps to increase safety. Evidence of such subsequent remedial measures is not usually admissible to show a standard of care, but if the defendant has argued that a safer practice is not feasible, evidence that the defendant has himself adopted the practice later can fairly be admitted.[15]

—defendant's internal rules or practices. Similarly, while the defendant's internal rules or procedures, or past practices, cannot be used as a shield for the defendant, those internal rules may be admitted on behalf of the plaintiff to show that a defendant who was under a duty to exercise reasonable care,[16] itself recognized the danger and an appropriate means to avoid it.[17] The defendant's internal rules may even be introduced as bearing on the care a reasonable person would provide.[18]

The defendant's own institutional rules or practices count as evidence, more or less persuasive, bearing on the reasonable care issue, but such rules do not themselves ordinarily count as the standard of care.[19]

subsequently developing custom as bearing on feasibility. D.L. v. Huebner, 110 Wis.2d 581, 329 N.W.2d 890 (1983).

13. Fowler v. Key System Transit Lines, 37 Cal.2d 65, 230 P.2d 339 (1951); Roberts v. Indiana Gas and Water Co., 140 Ind.App. 409, 218 N.E.2d 556 (1966) (where reliance is foreseeable, omission of the customary precaution may be negligence "in itself"); Florence v. Goldberg, 44 N.Y.2d 189, 404 N.Y.S.2d 583, 375 N.E.2d 763 (1978).

14. McWilliams v. Parham, 269 N.C. 162, 152 S.E.2d 117 (1967) (custom to cry a forewarning before driving golf ball indicated plaintiff was not guilty of assumed risk in being on the fairway).

15. See Ray v. American National Red Cross, 685 A.2d 411 (D.C.App.1996).

16. When the defendant is under no legal duty to act at all, the defendant's internal rules requiring action do not create a duty unless the plaintiff has relied upon those rules or is contractually entitled to benefit from them. See Rhodes v. Illinois Central Gulf Railroad, 172 Ill.3d 213, 665 N.Ed.2d 1260 (1996) (no duty to aid trespasser who was injured, but not by the defendant; and internal rules do not create a duty); Buczkowski v. McKay, 441 Mich. 96, 490 N.W.2d 330 (1992) (no duty to protect plaintiff from another person, defendant's internal policies create no such duty).

17. Thropp v. Bache Halsey Stuart Shields, Inc., 650 F.2d 817 (6th Cir.1981); Ganz v. United States Cycling Federation, 273 Mont. 360, 903 P.2d 212 (1995). See Potter v. Firestone Tire and Rubber Co., 6 Cal.4th 965, 863 P.2d 795, 25 Cal.Rptr.2d 550 (1993) (relying in part on violation of internal rules); Fielder v. Stonack, 141 N.J. 101, 661 A.2d 231 (1995) (relying on internal rules of defendant to determine willful misconduct).

18. Calloway v. City of New Orleans, 524 So.2d 182, 6 A.L.R.5th 1108 (La.App. 1988) (sheriff's policies about when to provide medical attention to pregnant women); Briggs v. Morgan, 70 N.C.App. 57, 318 S.E.2d 878 (1984) (city policy to have back-up bells on its garbage trucks admissible in the same way as defendant's voluntarily adopted safety handbook).

19. So a limiting instruction may be required, advising the jury that the rules of the defendant cannot be used to set a higher duty than is required by law. Clarke v.

However, when the defendant's liability is based upon its contract or undertaking to use a given standard of care, as in the case of a hospital treating a patient, the defendant's own rules may reflect the standard of care owed.[20] And the defendant's own rules or practices become a virtual standard when the defendant should foresee that the plaintiff will rely upon continued adherence to those rules and that the plaintiff will be endangered when the rules are ignored.[21] The defendant's past practices may even create contractual expectations that set standards. If the plaintiff contracts to lease premises from a landlord that has provided a security guard in the past, the landlord's withdrawal of that guard may be negligence under the standard impliedly set by the parties themselves.[22]

Strangers to the custom community. If custom should have special importance where the plaintiff and defendant have consensually accepted it, it may be unfair to give any weight at all to custom when one party is a stranger to the custom.[23] A community custom to fire shotguns in the air at midnight on New Year's will hardly assist the defendant who brings down a passing balloonist with the customary blast. On the other hand, if the plaintiff asserts that the defendant violated a safety custom, the violation may be quite relevant, whether or not the plaintiff was a stranger. Suppose the passing balloonist is injured because the defendant's factory explodes when the defendant ignores a customary safety precaution. The balloonist is definitely a stranger, in no consensual or special relationship to the factory owner, but the violation of the safety custom is no less relevant for all that.

New York City Transit Authority, 174 A.D.2d 268, 580 N.Y.S.2d 221 (1992).

20. See Pedroza v. Bryant, 101 Wash.2d 226, 677 P.2d 166 (1984). The customary practice of health care providers is often the standard of care, not merely evidence. See § 242 below.

21. E.g., Florence v. Goldberg, 44 N.Y.2d 189, 404 N.Y.S.2d 583, 375 N.E.2d 763 (1978) (practice of furnishing crossing guard for school children).

22. See Kline v. 1500 Massachusetts Avenue Apartment Corp., 141 U.S.App. D.C. 370, 439 F.2d 477, 43 A.L.R.3d 311 (1970).

23. See Richard A. Epstein , The Path to the T.J. Hooper: The Theory and History of Custom in the Law of Tort, 21 J. LEG. STUDIES 1 (1992).

*

CHAPTER 9

CAUSE IN FACT

TOPIC A. CAUSATION REQUIREMENT AND ITS TERMINOLOGY

§ 166. The Cause-in-Fact Requirement

The plaintiff asserting a claim based upon negligence must prove all the elements summarized in Chapter 7. Although this chapter addresses the actual cause element, proof of that element alone will not suffice any more than proof of negligence will suffice without proving causation.

Cause in fact and damages required. The cause in fact rule requires the plaintiff to prove that the defendant's conduct caused legally recognized damages. In part, this statement means that damages are not presumed as they are in the case of some intentional torts; the plaintiff who is not harmed by negligence cannot even recover nominal damages.[1] More significantly, the statement means that the plaintiff must prove not merely that she suffered harm sometime after the defendant's negligent act occurred but that the harm was caused in fact by the defendant's conduct. As with other factual matters, the plaintiff has the burden of proof and persuasion and hence must prove that the defendant's conduct was more probably than not the cause of the harm suffered.[2]

Four forms of cause in fact issues. The cause in fact requirement is usually viewed as a straightforward issue: did he or didn't he cause harm to the plaintiff? That issue manifests itself for lawyers, however, in at least three or four distinct forms.

Type 1 causation problem: scientific connection. One kind of cause in fact problem centers on scientific doubt, or at least on lay ignorance about the connection between the defendant's acts and the plaintiff's injury, frequently a problem in toxic tort cases. Suppose the plaintiff gets skin cancer after she is in an auto accident.[3] Or that she is born with a

§ 166

1. E.g., Ponder v. Angel Animal Hospital, Inc. 762 S.W.2d 846 (Mo.App.1988) (negligent castration of dog not actionable because castration did not affect dog's market value and actual damages are required to sustain negligence action).

2. Exceptions are discussed in §§ 175–178. The defendant who does not merely deny the plaintiff's causal claim but who attempts to establish a different cause, may be required to shoulder the burden of proving that his proposed alternative cause is more probable than not. See Stinson v. England, 69 Ohio St.3d 451, 633 N.E.2d 532 (1994).

3. See Kramer Service, Inc. v. Wilkins, 184 Miss. 483, 186 So. 625 (1939) (evidence insufficient to show that plaintiff's cancer

birth defect after her mother ingested the defendant's drug during her pregnancy.[4] In such cases the plaintiff must present evidence to prove that auto accidents can cause skin cancer or that the defendant's drug can cause birth defects. She must then go further and present evidence that causation is not merely scientifically possible, but that it existed in her particular case. These are questions of fact in the scientific sense. On this type of causal issue, rules of law describe the issue or the evidence required but do not resolve it.[5] Sometimes the causal issue is so much within common experience that no testimony is required at all. For example, traumas can cause bruises, so we can readily believe that your fall caused the bruise on your arm. But when the causation issue is not within ordinary understanding and experience, these factual questions are resolved by scientific or medical evidence.[6]

Type 2 causation problem: who is the cause? Another kind of cause in fact problem occurs when the plaintiff is definitely injured by someone or something but cannot produce evidence to indicate which person among many was the injurer. In an old New York case, the plaintiff contracted typhoid after exposure to contaminated water for which the defendant was responsible. There were many other sources of typhoid, including the common house fly and infected vegetables. So to show causation, the plaintiff needed evidence to show that the water was more probably the source of the disease than other things. Although medical or scientific evidence is important as background in this kind of case, the critical facts are likely to be more mundane. The plaintiff's repeated drinking of the contaminated water over a period of time no doubt counted heavily in favor of a finding that the water and not some fresh vegetable caused the typhoid.[7] The same is true in modern toxic tort cases. If the plaintiff gets cancer after working around asbestos for many years, the court may have no doubt that asbestos caused the cancer, but to hold a particular producer of asbestos liable the plaintiff must prove exposure to that company's asbestos. If she fails, she has not proved that that company was a cause in fact of her harm.[8] In this kind of case, there are sometimes special rules to aid the plaintiff,[9] but most often the plaintiff will lose her case because she has not proved cause in fact.

was result of trauma for which defendant was responsible).

4. See, e.g., Turpin v. Merrell Dow Pharmaceuticals, Inc., 959 F.2d 1349 (6th Cir.1992).

5. But see Lohrmann v. Pittsburgh Corning Corp. 782 F.2d 1156 (4th Cir.1986), as asbestos exposure case, holding that mere exposure alone was not sufficient, but adding what sounds like a rule of law that exposure must be frequent and close. In Horton v. Harwick Chemical Corp., 73 Ohio St.3d 679, 653 N.E.2d 1196 (1995), *Lohrman* was criticized as imposing a rule of law rather than working from an assessment of evidence.

6. The difficulties of producing acceptable evidence in complex, toxic tort cases, can be substantial. See § 360. Consequently, it has been suggested that as a matter of policy some relief from the burden would be appropriate in special cases. See Margaret A. Berger, Eliminating General Causation: Notes Towards a New Theory of Justice and Toxic Torts,97 Colum. L. Rev. 2117 (1997).

7. Stubbs v. City of Rochester, 226 N.Y. 516, 124 N.E. 137 (1919).

8. E.g., Claytor v. Owens–Corning Fiberglas Corporation, 662 A.2d 1374 (D.C.App.1995).

9. See § 176.

Type 3 causation problem: would safe behavior have avoided injury? A third kind of cause in fact problem is one that generates much academic writing. It cannot be resolved by medical or scientific evidence or by proving which among several defendants was the author of the plaintiff's harm. Suppose the defendant does not check his rear view mirror before backing up and in consequence he backs over a child squatting behind the car. The defendant is negligent—he should have checked the mirror—but the critical point for a cause in fact argument is that he would not have avoided the injury by checking the mirror, since that would not have revealed the squatting child. Courts say in this kind of case that the defendant's negligence was not a cause in fact of the harm and that he is not liable.

As later sections will indicate, this kind of cause in fact question turns heavily not on scientific or medical causation, but upon estimates about what would have happened if the defendant had behaved more carefully and upon the legal tests or standards for judging causation. It is this particular kind of cause in fact problem that has led many serious thinkers to penetrating and puzzling analyses.[10]

Type 4 causation problem: what harm was caused? A final cause in fact problem is to determine what harm was caused by the defendant's negligent conduct. In some instances it is appropriate to apportion harm to causes, that is, to hold a defendant liable for a portion of the plaintiff's harm but not all of it. That is most obviously the case when one defendant breaks the plaintiff's arm and another defendant, acting independently, breaks the plaintiff's leg. Apportionment problems turn both on proof of facts—who caused what?—and also on several kinds of legal policy.[11]

§ 167. Terminology and Structure: Cause in Fact and Proximate Cause

Long but confusing legal tradition has assigned the term "causation" to two entirely different kinds of legal problems. The first issue is about causation in the sense that term is used in every day speech: Did the defendant's negligent conduct cause the plaintiff's harm or not? The second issue is about the appropriate scope of the defendant's legal responsibility for negligent conduct that has in fact caused harm. This scope of responsibility issue often turns on whether the kind of harm the plaintiff suffered was the same kind the defendant risked by his negligence.

10. E.g., Richard Epstein, A Theory of Strict Liability, 2 J. Leg. Stud. 151 (1973), REPRINTED IN Richard Epstein, a Theory of Strict Liability (1980); WEX MALONE, RUMINATIONS ON CAUSE-IN-FACT, 9 Standf. L. Rev. 60 (1956), REPRINTED IN Wex Malone, Essays on Torts 160 (1986); STRASSFELD, IF . . . : COUNTERFACTUALS IN THE LAW, 60 Geo. Wash. L. Rev. 339 (1992); RICHARD WRIGHT, CAUSATION IN TORT LAW, 73 Cal.L.Rev. 1735 (1985); SYMPOSIUM ON CAUSATION IN THE LAW OF TORTS, 63 Chi.-Kent L. Rev. 397 (1987); Arno Becht & Frank Miller, The Test of Factual Causation (1961).

11. See §§ 176–179.

Courts often lump the two issues together under the rubric of "proximate cause."[1] Courts recognize, however, that even if these issues are sometimes called by the same name, they are quite different issues and turn on quite different kinds of analysis, so that they are quick to say that proximate cause questions are composed of cause in fact and scope of responsibility issues.[2] Unfortunately, courts also use a variety of terms to describe scope of responsibility issues.[3] This chapter and the next will use the terms actual cause or causation in fact for the first issue, and the term proximate or legal cause for the second, not because those terms are clear, but because they come closest to professional usage.

Both issues are somewhat misnamed. Cause in fact is certainly not a fact in the sense that it can be identified by the senses like the existence of a tree. Cause in fact is at least to some extent a concept or mental construct, a perception about the relationship of two events. Proximate cause, on the other hand, is not about causation at all but about the significance of the defendant's conduct or the the appropriate scope of liability, an issue that entails heavy elements of moral and policy judgment about the very particular facts of the case. Indeed, some courts, recognizing this, prefer an entirely different set of words to identify this kind of question.[4] Since the two issues represent different legal concerns and are tested by adverting to different legal rules, it is highly important to illustrate their difference, if only in a preliminary way.

Suppose the question is: did Donnie break Margaret's leg when he negligently ran into her, or was her leg already broken? That is one form of a question about the existence of causation; was Donnie's conduct a cause in fact of the harm? The existence of cause—the cause in fact question—is often tested by asking whether, but for the defendant's conduct, the injury would have been avoided.[5]

Now suppose that the question turns on different facts: Dennis negligently left tainted meat in his refrigerator. A thief took the meat and sold it to Penny, who ate it and became ill. Should Dennis be liable for his negligence? That is not a question about the *existence* of causa-

§ 167

1. Fedorczyk v. Caribbean Cruise Lines, Ltd. , 82 F.3d 69 (3d Cir.1996) ("Courts have often conflated cause in fact and legal causation into proximate cause, but the two are conceptually distinct"). In certain instances, however, it is possible to view the legal problem presented by a set of facts either as a cause in fact or a scope of risk problem.

2. See, e.g., Hertog v. City of Seattle, 138 Wash.2d 265, 979 P.2d 400 (1999) ("proximate cause ... consists of cause in fact and legal causation").

3. Including proximate cause, legal cause, scope of risk, scope of duty, and foreseeability, but again, these terms can be used to describe the second issue alone or as umbrella terms for both the first and the second issue.

4. Courts can consider the moral and policy significance—or insignificance—of the defendant's negligent conduct under headings other than proximate cause, specifically by determining whether the defendant was under a duty of care, by determining the scope of that duty, and by determining whether the defendant was negligent with respect to the harm involved. See § 230. Instances of a duty approach appear in Chapters 12–21.

5. See § 168.

tion, for Dennis' conduct surely is one of the causes in fact of Penny's harm. We can see that by asking whether Penny would have been harmed if Dennis had properly disposed of the meat. Penny would not have been, so Dennis's conduct is one cause in fact. The question whether Dennis should escape liability, then, is about the appropriate scope of Dennis' liability, whether Dennis' conduct is important enough to justify imposing liability. Or you could say it is about the legal *significance* of causation, rather than the existence of causation. This kind of question is usually tested by asking whether the general type of harm, or sometimes the intervening force that brought it about, was foreseeable.[6]

The chief reason to mention the scope of liability or proximate cause issue in a chapter on cause in fact is that in judging cause in fact issues, it is important to understand that a finding of causation does not determine liability. The plaintiff must not only prove negligence and causation but also must persuade the judge and jury that liability is morally and practically justified. Whenever this point is forgotten, the tendency is to build moral and practical judgments into the cause in fact question. Those judgments are important, but the law has separate places for them. The causation in fact issue is difficult enough without importing difficulties from proximate cause analysis.

Topic B. Tests of Causation

§ 168. The But–For Test of Cause in Fact

The but-for test. In the great mass of cases, courts apply a but-for test to determine whether the defendant's conduct was a cause in fact of the plaintiff's harm, although there are some important exceptions.[1] Under the but-for test, the defendant's conduct is a cause in fact of the plaintiff's harm if, but-for the defendant's conduct, that harm would not have occurred.[2] The but-for test also implies a negative. If the plaintiff would have suffered the same harm had the defendant not acted negligently, the defendant's conduct is not a cause in fact of the harm.[3] The negative part of the but-for test must sometimes be qualified but it is applied in many, many cases as a routine matter. The but-for test requires the plaintiff to persuade the trier that different, non-negligent conduct by the defendant would have avoided harm to the plaintiff.

6. See §§ 187–189 and Chapter 10 generally. *Some* type of harm must be foreseeable, else the defendant is not negligent at all. The problem, whether denominated as one of proximate cause or as one about the scope of duty, arises when the plaintiff suffers a harm that is arguably quite different in its nature from the kind of harm that was foreseeable.

§ 168

1. § 175–179.

2. E.g., Hagen v. Texaco Refining and Marketing, Inc., 526 N.W.2d 531 (Iowa 1995) ("that a defendant's conduct was a substantial factor in producing the damages and the damages would not have occurred except for the defendant's conduct").

3. More technically expressed, the plaintiff must persuade the trier that she would not have suffered the harm had the defendant acted otherwise and if she fails to persuade the trier, the trier must find that the defendant's conduct was not a cause in fact.

Meeting the but-for test. In most cases, causation seems obvious and presents no obstacle to the plaintiff. The defendant negligently crashes his airplane into the plaintiff's apartment. The defendant's conduct is a but-for cause of the harm done to the apartment; but-for his negligent piloting, the apartment would have remained standing.

Failing the but-for test. In a number of cases, however, the but-for test of cause in fact puts the plaintiff out of court, even though the defendant is clearly negligent. For example, suppose a product manufacturer is negligent in failing to provide an adequate warning in the owner's manual for an automobile that could start a fire. If the plaintiff admits that he never read the owner's manual at all, the manufacturer's failure to provide it is not a but-for cause of the fire started by the car; an unread warning would have changed nothing.[4] In one case[5] the plaintiff was squatting behind a car. The owner backed up without looking in the rear-view mirror and ran over the plaintiff. The problem was that the owner would not have seen the plaintiff by looking in the rear view mirror. Perhaps the most common way to look at such a case is to say that the driver's negligent conduct was not a but-for cause of the plaintiff's harm. Had the driver looked, she would have seen nothing and would have proceeded to back up. The same injury would have resulted. In an analytically very similar case, a sailor fell overboard and sank like a stone. The ship carried a defective lifeboat and the rescue attempt was futile. But even a good lifeboat would have been of no assistance because the sailor was lost immediately.[6] Although courts could look at these cases in other ways,[7] most judges probably feel that the most straightforward analysis disposes of the claim on cause in fact/but-for grounds.

Multiple causes. Nothing is the result of a single cause in fact. The but-for test does not say otherwise. A special problem with multiple causes arises and requires a different test of causation when either of two causes standing alone would suffice to cause the plaintiff's injury,[8] but it is by no means true that the but-for test reduces everything to a single cause. In fact there are always many causes that meet the but-for

4. Bloxom v. Bloxom, 512 So.2d 839 (La. 1987).

5. Jordan v. Jordan, 220 Va. 160, 257 S.E.2d 761 (1979).

6. Ford v. Trident Fisheries Co., 232 Mass. 400, 122 N.E. 389 (1919). However, rescue at sea cases now show a different spirit, demanding that the vessel maximize the sailor's chances and holding it liable for failure to do so. See 179 below.

7. An alternative analysis is to say that the defendant's conduct IS a cause in fact of the plaintiff's harm. In this analysis, the driver would escape liability, if at all, on the ground that the driver's negligence was not a proximate or legal cause of the harm, because the risk created by not checking the rear view mirror was only a risk of harms that could have been avoided by checking the mirror, not a risk of running over a squatter too low to be seen. In terms of formulation, debate boils down to a question whether you focus on the defendant's "conduct" or on the "negligent segment of the defendant's conduct" as a cause in fact. See Thode, The Indefensible Use of the Hypothetical Case to Determine Cause in Fact, 46 Tex. L. Rev. 423 (1968); JAMES HENDERSON, A DEFENSE OF THE USE OF THE HYPOTHETICAL CASE TO RESOLVE THE CAUSATION ISSUE, 47 Tex. L. Rev. 183 (1969) AND THODE, A REPLY TO THE DEFENSE, 47 Tex. L. Rev. 1344 (1969). THE PROXIMATE CAUSE APPROACH IS INTELLECTUALLY PLAUSIBLE ENOUGH, BUT IT MAY TAKE ANALYSIS ON A ROUND ABOUT TRIP BACK TO THE SAME FUNDAMENTAL POINT THAT CAN OFTEN BE HANDLED DIRECTLY UNDER THE BUT-FOR TEST.

8. § 170.

test, some represented by negligent conduct, some not. A negligently fells a tree; to get around it, B walks out into the street; C, driving a car, hits his brake to avoid running into C; D, a passenger, is thrown into the windshield. As a pure matter of cause in fact the conduct of A, B, and C are all causes in fact. Without A's conduct, none of this would have occurred and the same can be said of the conduct of the others. If A or C escape liability, it will not be on the ground that they are not causes in fact. The but-for test shows that they are all causes in fact, and if liability is avoided, it will be on an entirely different ground.

§ 169. The Hypothetical Alternative Case in But-for Analysis

The but-for test of causation can be applied only by comparing what happened with a hypothetical alternative. What would have happened if the defendant had *not* been negligent? Would the plaintiff have been injured in the same way even if the defendant had not been negligent? If so, then the defendant's negligent conduct is not a cause in fact of the harm. The hypothetical alternative never occurred, so any comparison of the hypothetical to the events that actually occurred is only a construction of the intellect and often a speculative one at that, not a fact at all. It is nonetheless a construction required by the rule.

Sometimes judges conclude that they cannot know whether reasonable, non-negligent conduct by the defendant would have avoided injury or not, and hence that the plaintiff has failed to sustain her burden of proof.[1] At other times, judges believe they know that reasonable care by the defendant would not have aided the plaintiff. In *Salinetro v. Nystrom*,[2] the plaintiff, who had been in an automobile accident, presented herself to the doctor for x-rays of her lower back and abdominal area. According to the plaintiff, the doctor negligently failed to ask whether she was pregnant. Later, learning that x-rays might have injured her fetus, she terminated her pregnancy and brought suit for negligence. The cause in fact problem arose because at the time the x-rays were taken, the plaintiff did not know she was pregnant. So the court thought it knew what the hypothetical alternative scenario would have been. It thought that the doctor would have asked the plaintiff "Are you pregnant?" and she would have said "No." That meant the x-rays would have been taken anyway, with the same result. So in the court's view, the doctor's negligent failure to ask was not a but-for cause of the harm.

If the court was right in its vision of the hypothetical alternative, then the *Salinetro* decision is right. But its imagined alternative is not the only plausible one for two kinds of reasons. First, the doctor could have avoided negligent conduct in quite a number of ways. For instance, he might have posted signs or handed patients an explanatory pamphlet,

§ 169

1. Fedorczyk v. Caribbean Cruise Lines, Ltd., 82 F.3d 69 (3d Cir.1996) (defendant negligently attached too few non-slip strips in its bathtub, but plaintiff could not prove added strips would have prevented fall).

2. 341 So.2d 1059 (Fla.App. 1977).

or insisted on a pregnancy test, or an accurate record of menstrual periods. Some of those alternative methods of avoiding negligence would probably have led the patient to avoid the x-rays and the loss of her child.[3]

Second, even if the doctor had merely asked "Are you pregnant," the plaintiff herself might not have responded as the court imagined she would, by saying she was not.[4] She might have said instead "does it matter?"—which in turn might have led her to get full information and to have a pregnancy test before having the x-rays. It is not hard to imagine a patient who is ignorant of x-rays or too trusting of doctors but who would be alert to avoid harm to her fetus if only she is asked the pregnancy question. The truth is that no one knows what would have happened in the imagined world without the defendant's negligence.

The *Salinetro* case is only one of many cases in which the cause in fact determination must be made on the basis of speculation about whether the injury really could have been avoided if the defendant had not been negligent.[5] This speculation undermines the values in the tort system in general and in the causation requirement in particular. These and other difficulties with the but-for test have led many writers to struggle for greater clarity,[6] to say that the test only works well when causation is so clear that no test is needed anyway, to urge abolition of the test altogether,[7] or to work from models or paradigms rather than from rules.[8] Courts have not gone so far as to abolish the but-for test, but they have often found ways to alleviate the plaintiff's problem with the but-for rule and lawyers have some strategies available as well. These adaptations to the but-for rule are discussed in some of the remaining sections.

§ 170. Two or More Persons as Causes: The Joint and Several Liability Rule

Sometimes two tortfeasors are both causes of the plaintiff's harm. (Any number of tortfeasors might be causes, but it is convenient to speak of two.) What are the legal effects of holding two tortfeasors liable to the

3. Conceivably, courts could attempt to set up a principle about the kind of alternative scenario that should be used. A rule could state that courts should envision an alternative scenario that is highly probable, or instead should use one that involves the least cost to the defendant, or one that involves the least change in what actually happened. It does not seem likely that any such rules will ever be imposed.

4. The plaintiff made it easy for the court to select its particular alternative because she herself said she would have told the doctor she was not. That testimony should not preclude careful lawyers from arguing that further information was still possible along the lines suggested in the text.

5. See, e.g., Israel v. Barnell, 1996 WL 365413 (Conn.Super.1996); Thompson v. Tuggle, 486 So.2d 144 (La.App.1986) (no witnesses saw the chain saw sever decedent's jugular; did the saw kickback or did decedent fall on it? Would would a different design have avoided the kickback?).

6. See Arno Becht and Frank Miller, The Test of Factual Causation (1961).

7. See Leon Green, The Causal Relation Issue in Negligence Law, 60 Mich. L. Rev. 543 (1962) (the cause questions asks for judgment that has no component parts).

8. See Richard Epstein, A Theory of Strict Liability, 2 J. Leg. Stud. 151 (1973).

plaintiff? This is a large topic and treated more fully later, but a little information about it is required to make sense of the multiple cause cases discussed in the next sections. When courts impose liability at all in multiple causes cases, they have two basic options.

Apportionment. Courts can hold that a tortfeasor is responsible only for some particular share or portion of the plaintiff's loss, no more. One form of apportionment is causal. That is, apportionment may be made on the ground that one defendant caused a particular loss or an identifiable share of the loss and should be liable for no more.[1] A different apportionment is based on comparative fault. Each defendant is held liable for a percentage of the plaintiff's damages in proportion to that defendant's percentage share of fault.[2] It is easy to confuse fault and causation, but they are quite different. One defendant might be extremely negligent, yet cause only a broken finger, while the second defendant might be guilty of only minor negligence, yet cause a severe head injury. The difference between causal and fault apportionment thus becomes very important.

No apportionment; joint and several liability. In other cases, courts may conclude that no apportionment is rationally possible on the evidence or that apportionment is undesirable. In those cases, the two tortfeasors are held jointly and severally liable to the plaintiff. Today, that antique lawyer's term means mainly that (1) the plaintiff may sue each tortfeasor, A or B, separately; (2) the plaintiff may sue both tortfeasors in a single action; (3) the plaintiff may obtain a judgment against one tortfeasor alone and enforce it against that one; (4) the plaintiff may obtain a judgment against both tortfeasors and enforce it against both; but (5) the plaintiff may not actually collect more than one full compensation. If the plaintiff collects all her damages from one tortfeasor, most states today permit the defendant who paid more than his just share of liability to recover contribution or indemnity from the other tortfeasor.[3]

Grounds for joint and several liability. One group of grounds for imposing joint and several liability are related to vicarious responsibility. The employer is jointly and severally liable along with his employee for torts committed by the employee within the scope of employment. Similarly, partners and joint enterprisers are vicariously liable for the torts of each other committed within the scope of the partnership or enterprise. Finally, persons who act in concert, pursuant to a common plan or design, to commit a crime or tort are true joint tortfeasors; each is liable for harm done by the others involved, though he himself has committed no direct harm. In all these cases, joint and several liability is imposed vicariously.[4] The employer, the enterpriser, the partner, and the joint tortfeasor are not liable because their negligence caused the harm, but because of their legal relationship to another. The effect of the rule

§ 170

1. See § 174.
2. See § 201.
3. See § 386.
4. See § 340.

in these cases is to impose liability upon a person whose negligence has not caused harm.

In this chapter, the most common ground for joint and several liability is that two or more tortfeasors have caused a single injury.[5] However, many states have partly abolished joint and several liability and rely upon an initial apportionment in the first instance.[6] In such states, the apportionment rules, including the causal apportionment rules introduced in this chapter, become most significant.

§ 171. Multiple Causes: Substantial Factor and Conduct Aggregating Tests of Causation in Fact

But-for and Multiple Tortfeasors

Where but-for demonstrates multiple actors are causes in fact: each cause is necessary. Any given event, including an injury, is always the result of many causes. Most causes can be ignored in tort litigation, but quite frequently, courts must focus on two or more causes. The but-for test of causation often permits a finding that the negligent acts of any number of tortfeasors are all causes in fact, as well as a finding that the plaintiff's own negligence is a cause in fact.

—example: A creates risk of harm from B's negligence. For example, suppose that an apartment house manager, A, negligently leaves the plaintiff's door unlocked after checking the apartment. The security guard, B, who is required to check all doors, negligently omits to check this one. The result is that a thief walks in the unlocked door and steals the plaintiff's stereo and jewelry. But-for A's negligence in leaving the door unlocked, the plaintiff would have had no loss.[1] But for B's negligence in failing to check, the plaintiff would have had no loss. Both A and B are but-for causes of the loss and they are traditionally liable jointly and severally.

Where but-for demonstrates that multiple actors are not causes in fact: each cause is sufficient. Two tortfeasors are but-for causes in some cases but not in others. Two kinds of examples create most of the problems and also result in the most concrete changes in the but-for rule.

When each of two or more causes would be sufficient, standing alone, to cause the plaintiff's harm, a literal and simple version of the but-for test holds that neither defendant's act is a cause of the harm. The classic example is the case of two fires being swept by winds towards the plaintiff's property. Either fire is sufficient to burn the property. Before either fire reaches the property, they combine. The combined fire burns the plaintiff's property. If A negligently set one fire and B

5. See § 174.

6. See § 389.

§ 171

1. The trier would be permitted to find but-for causation as long as the burglar took advantage of the unlocked door; the answer would be otherwise if the door had been bashed in.

negligently set the other, each could claim that he is not a cause under the but-for rule, since, even if he had set no fire, the other fire would have burned the property. Since both A and B could make the same argument, a court that applied the unvarnished but-for test here would effectively bar the victim from any recovery from either of the two negligent defendants.

The but-for test in such cases leads to a result that is almost always condemned as violating both an intuitive sense of causation and good legal policy. Cases like the two fire cases have consequently put the simple but-for test in doubt and courts have in fact modified that test to deal with such cases.

Substantial Factor as an Alternative Test of Causation

Substituting the substantial factor test. When two or more tortfeasors actively cause harm, courts usually drop the but-for test. So far as they rely upon any test of causation at all when causal issues are embarrassing, they may invoke the "substantial factor" test.[2] That test says that all defendants who are substantial factors in the harm are causes in fact.[3]

Applied to duplicative causation[4] cases. In the example of the two fires that combine to burn the plaintiff's property, the substantial factor test allows courts to avoid causal analysis and to hold that the two tortfeasors who set the two different fires are both causes of the plaintiff's harm, provided only that each fire was sufficient standing alone to cause the same harm. If one fire was set by a tortfeasor and the other by lightning, the trier of fact can still find that the tortfeasor is a cause in fact and liable for the damage done.[5] The substantial factor approach may also resolve some problems of multiple polluters.[6]

2. Restatement § 432 (2).

3. E.g., Vincent v. Fairbanks Memorial Hospital, 862 P.2d 847 (Alaska, 1993); Mitchell v. Gonzales, 54 Cal.3d 1041, 1 Cal. Rptr.2d 913, 819 P.2d 872 (1991).

4. This is the terminology of Professor Richard Wright, Causation in Tort Law, 73 Cal. L. Rev. 1735 (1985) for cases like the two-fire case.

5. Anderson v. Minneapolis, St. Paul & Sault Ste. Marie Railway, 146 Minn. 430, 179 N.W. 45 (1920) (negligently set fire combined with fire of unknown origin; negligent firesetter is liable for all damage).

6. Cf. Landers v. East Texas Salt Water Disposal Co., 151 Tex. 251, 248 S.W.2d 731 (Tex. 1952) (two polluters, either of which would seemingly have been sufficient to kill fish in the plaintiff's lake; both are liable).

When no one polluter independently releases enough hazardous material into the environment to cause harm, but the entire group of polluters, each acting independently, collectively release an amount sufficient to cause harm, courts may treat each as causal. One of four grounds may be available, depending on the exact facts. These include: (a) the substantial factor approach, (b) the single indivisible injury rule, see § 174 below; (c) but-for causation, which will yield a finding of causation if the entire group of polluters collectively contributes exactly the number of units of pollution to cause harm, since in that case any one polluter would have avoided the harm by withholding his pollution; and (d) the argument that the group of singly insufficient causes is a variation of the duplicative cause or two fire cases where the total pollution is more than enough to cause harm, the extra pollution being compared to the "extra" fire. By statute, a number of persons may be liable for any given "release" of hazardous materials. See, e.g., the Superfund statute, 42 U.S.C. § 9607.

The courts have reached the right result in cases like the two-fires example, where each cause would be sufficient by itself to cause the harm. In fact, in one view, such cases represent the single most justified use for the substantial factor test.[7] If either fire alone was sufficient to burn the plaintiff's property, and if the defendant (or all defendants) were negligent, justice and policy both point to the liability of each tortfeasor. The defendant was negligent; he created a risk of burning the plaintiff's property; the property was in fact burned; and the harm was neither worse than nor different from the harm that would have been suffered if no other fire had been set. It would be a windfall to the negligent defendants if they were to escape liability for the harm merely because another tortfeasor's negligence was also sufficient to cause the same harm. It is also possible to construct a neutral, non-policy definition of causation to achieve the same result, the bottom line of which is that duplicative causes are still causes.[8]

Limits of substantial factor; preemptive causation[9] cases. The substantial factor test does not suggest unlimited liability. If one of the two fires burns the plaintiff's property to the ground before the other spreads to the scene, the second fire is not a cause at all,[10] even though it would have burned the plaintiff's property in the same way. Your acts today cannot in any practical sense cause something that happened in 1939, or even something that happened one second before you acted.

Limits of substantial factor; its intuitive nature. The substantial factor test is not so much a test as an incantation. It points neither to any reasoning nor to any facts that will assist courts or lawyers in resolving the question of causation. Put differently, the substantial factor test requires no particular mental operation.[11] It invites the jury's intuition.[12] In one view, that represents a loss of precision in analysis

7. David W. Robertson, The Common Sense of Cause in Fact, 75 Tex. L. Rev. 1765, 1776 (1997).

8. This woefully under-expresses the elaborate analysis of causation provided by Professor Richard Wright. He argues that cause is established if an event is a necessary element of a set of events sufficient to produce the harm. The two fire case represents two sufficient sets under this test. See Richard W. Wright, Causation, Responsibility, Risk, Probability, Naked Statistics, and Proof: Pruning the Bramble Bush by Clarifying the Concepts, 73 Iowa L. Rev. 1001 (1988).

9. Preemptive cause is Professor Wright's term, contrasting with duplicative cause. See n. 4, supra.

10. Saden v. Kirby, 660 So.2d 423 (La. 1995) (flooding by one entity had already peaked before other entity's acts).

11. David W. Robertson, Williams Powers, Jr., and David A. Anderson, Cases and Materials on Torts 158–159 (1989); see JOSEPH W. GLANNON, THE LAW OF TORTS 127 (1995).

12. An Iowa jury instruction quoted in Foggia v. Des Moines Bowl–O–Mat, Inc., 543 N.W.2d 889 (Iowa 1996) has it that "[t]he conduct of a party is a proximate cause of damage when it is a substantial factor in producing damage and when the damage would not have happened except for the conduct. 'Substantial' means the party's conduct has such an effect in producing damage as to lead a reasonable person to regard it as a cause. There can be more than one proximate cause of an injury or damage." It may be noticed that this is the equivalent, on the causal issue, of the reasonable person instruction on the negligence issue. However, courts and lawyers use detailed analyses to determine whether the evidence suffices to show unreasonably risky conduct; that is the very thing missing from the substantial factor approach to causation.

with no corresponding gain.[13]

Aggregating Conduct of Multiple Actors

Various authors have suggested that instead of using the intuitive substantial factor approach, courts might obtain similar results more forthrightly by applying a variation on the but-for rule. In this variation, the conduct of all defendants as a group is aggregated and considered as a whole.[14] The but-for test is then applied to their conduct taken as a unit or set. If the combined conduct is a but-for cause of the plaintiff's harm, then cause is established. The combined fires, for instance, taken as a whole, undoubtedly burned the plaintiff's property. The Iowa Court has expressly adopted this test for judging causality.[15]

This approach, which groups defendants or their conduct together into a set of relevant conduct, is more satisfying than the amorphous substantial factor test, but it depends on a decision to group various acts of various defendants together, and on a decision about what acts should be treated in this collective manner. At least to some extent, the decision to aggregate conduct of different defendants, and the decision to include or exclude specific acts in that aggregate unit, is likely to be a policy decision, or merely an intuitive selection. In either case, it may generate further legal issues, this time over the criteria for the policy decisions.

Professor Wright, working from suggestions of earlier legal thinkers, has formulated a detailed definition of causation that also works with the idea that conduct or events can be grouped together into a set. But Wright rejects the aggregate but-for test. He proposes to say that if the entire set of events is sufficient to cause the harm and the defendant's act is a necessary element of the set, then causation is established.[16] He attempts to define the appropriate set or cluster without resort to policy or intuitive decisions, by limiting the cluster to causally relevant factors.[17] Since none of this is familiar to jurists and not easily mastered, it may be that courts and lawyers will continue to consider policy and apply intuition in a great many cases.

13. David W. Robertson, The Common Sense of Cause in Fact, 75 Tex. L. Rev. 1765, 1780 (1997).

14. Aggregation is routinely performed in cases of tortfeasors who act in concert and with tortfeasors who, though acting independently, create a single indivisible injury. See § 170. The question is whether aggregation represents a useful tool beyond those situations.

15. Spaur v. Owens–Corning Fiberglas Corp., 510 N.W.2d 854, 858 (Iowa 1994) ("when the conduct of two or more persons is so related to an event that their combined conduct, viewed as a whole, is a but-for cause of the event, and application of the but-for rule to them individually would absolve all of them, the conduct of each is a cause in fact of the event"). The court later said the test had no application to judging causality of the plaintiff's conduct, which should be dealt with as comparative fault. Foggia v. Des Moines Bowl–O–Mat, Inc., 543 N.W.2d 889 (Iowa 1996). That may not quite express the problem, however, because comparative fault reductions are normally based only on the plaintiff's conduct that is causal, at least in part.

16. Wright, Causation in Tort Law, 73 Calif. L. Rev. 1735 (1985).

17. Richard W. Wright, Causation, Responsibility, Risk, Probability, Naked Statistics, and Proof: Pruning the Bramble Bush by Clarifying the Concepts , 73 Iowa L. Rev. 1001 (1988).

In most instances of multiple tortfeasors, the rigors and speculations of the but-for test are ameliorated, but not by any conscious application of the substantial factor test or of tests based upon clustering various acts into sets. Instead, the demands of the but-for rule are evaded in many cases by a series of techniques that include liberal inferences of causation, and by several discrete rules that resolve doubts against the tortfeasor.

Topic C. Problems of Proving Causation

§ 172. Connecting Negligence and Causation

Plaintiffs who encounter difficulties in proving causation can sometimes take advantage of one of the liberalizing rules seen in later sections. Plaintiffs may also find that when the but-for rule is a problem, that problem may be avoided by asserting that some different conduct of the defendant was negligent.

The Specific Act of Negligence and Causation

The specific act of negligence claimed by the plaintiff largely determines the hypothetical alternative conduct to be compared. If the plaintiff alleges that the defendant failed to keep a proper lookout, the hypothetical alternative case to be considered is one in which the defendant does keep a proper lookout and the question becomes whether, had he done so, he would have avoided injuring the plaintiff. On the other hand, if the plaintiff's claim is that the defendant drove too fast, the alternative case to be considered in testing causation is not one in which the defendant keeps a better lookout but one in which he drives more slowly. Because the specific negligence claimed points to the alternative conduct to be considered in assessing causation, the plaintiff's case on the negligence issue directly affects her case on the causal issue. For this reason the plaintiff's lawyer may spend a great deal of effort in structuring the negligence claim in order to get a favorable outcome on the causal issue.

Suppose the plaintiff is injured when a tree on the defendant's land falls during a windstorm. The plaintiff can show that the defendant knew the tree was dangerously likely to fall and that he was negligent in failing to brace the tree. However, the windstorm was so severe that it might have blown down the tree, even if it was braced. On such evidence, the plaintiff's case is in jeopardy; she may be unable to show causation under the but-for rule. By relying on a different claim of negligence, the plaintiff's lawyer can sometimes point to an alternative safer scenario that will meet the but-for rule. Instead of asserting that the defendant should have braced the tree, the plaintiff's lawyer can assert that the defendant should have exercised reasonable care by cutting it down. If the tree had been cut down, it surely would not have blown over on the plaintiff. The failure to cut the tree is thus a cause in fact of the plaintiff's harm.

This example points to an important connection between the claim of negligence and the causal issue. Except in res ipsa loquitur cases, the legal system demands proof of very specific acts of negligence, partly because the hypothetical alternative demanded by the but-for test can only be applied to specific acts. The plaintiff's strategy can take advantage of this point by asserting negligence that points to favorable hypothetical alternative scenarios. That is not always easy to do. In the tree case, the plaintiff is more likely to be successful on the causal issue if she claims a negligent failure to cut, but she might find it easier to prevail on the negligence issue by claiming only a failure to brace. Nevertheless, some causal problems for the plaintiff can be solved by claiming the right act of negligence.

Res Ipsa Loquitur and Causation

A second strategy may be available in some cases. That strategy obscures the causal problem by avoiding any claim of specific negligent acts at all—that is, by relying on res ipsa loquitur. Res ipsa loquitur allows the plaintiff to establish negligence circumstantially without establishing the particular acts of the defendant that caused harm. The doctrine was not intended to establish all causal issues,[1] but it does permit an inference of both negligence and some kinds of causation. Res ipsa loquitur may operate to bypass the but-for rule, simply because the but-for rule cannot be applied with knowing specific acts of negligence.

For example, in the best-known case, *Byrne v. Boadle*,[2] the plaintiff was hurt when a flour barrel fell from the defendant's premises. The plaintiff did not allege any specific act of negligence, but the court thought *res ipsa loquitur,* the thing speaks for itself. So the plaintiff prevailed. But suppose that, in contrast, the defendant's negligence had been identified: he had negligently failed to inspect the ropes securing the barrel. Given a specific claim of negligence, the but-for test could be applied by asking whether a reasonable inspection would have revealed that the ropes were dangerous. If the defect in the rope was hidden and would not have been discovered upon reasonable inspection, the plaintiff would have proved specific negligence but would have lost on the but-for issue.

This example does not suggest that res ipsa loquitur is wrong or that it operates unfairly. After all, it is applied only when both negligence and causation seem probable, as indeed both did in the flour barrel

§ 172

1. Res ipsa loquitur logically establishes that the defendant was negligent in an unknown way and that the defendant's unknown negligence rather than the act of some other person probably caused the plaintiff's harm. But res ipsa loquitur could seldom establish medical or scientific connections. For instance, res ipsa loquitur might establish that a surgeon or hospital was negligent when the plaintiff awoke from an operation with a burn on a part of her body not involved in the operation, but it would not show that the operation or the burn caused the later development of a skin cancer.

2. Byrne v. Boadle, 2 H. & C. 722, 159 Eng.Rep. 299 (Exch. 1863), discussed in § 154, supra.

case. Nonetheless, the plaintiff who can use res ipsa loquitur may be able to dodge the but-for bullet.

Although res ipsa loquitur may assist the plaintiff on causal as well as on negligence issues in some cases, it does not always do so. The flour barrel example suggests how it might help when the hypothetical alternative scenario is a potential problem. But when the cause in fact problem is not about the but-for test but about the scientific or medical connection between act and injury, res ipsa is not likely to help at all. The plaintiff who claims to suffer skin cancer as a result of defendant's one-car accident does not improve her position on the cause in fact issue by asserting res ipsa loquitur instead of excessive speed or failure to keep a lookout. No matter why the accident occurred, car accidents do not generally cause skin cancer.[3]

§ 173. Evidence and Inferences of But-for Causation

Although courts have found it necessary to modify the but-for test in several discrete situations, they have not abandoned the test for most routine cases. Even so, courts have often recognized, implicitly or explicitly, that the jury must be permitted to make causal judgments from its ordinary experience without demanding impossible proof about what would have occurred if the defendant had behaved more safely.[1] Even scientific or medical causation might be proven by circumstantial evidence leading to an inference of causation.[2]

In particular, if the defendant's conduct is deemed negligent for the very reason that it creates a core risk of the kind of harm suffered by the plaintiff, then it is often plausible to infer causation in fact. When we say that the pharmacist is negligent in doubling the dosage of a prescription we are saying that it is too likely that the patient will suffer serious injuries from the drug, and if she does suffer the kind of injury the drug is capable of producing, the trier can infer causation.[3] If we say that the defendant is negligent because his stairs were poorly lighted we are saying that it is all too likely that someone will fall because of the poor lighting. When someone does in fact fall on the poorly lit stairs it is quite plausible to infer that bad lighting had something to do with it.[4]

3. See § 166; cf. King v. Searle Pharmaceuticals, Inc., 832 P.2d 858 (Utah 1992) (fact that the defendant's IUD was inherently dangerous did not prove that its defect was responsible for causing the IUD to be lodged in the abdomen rather than the uterus).

§ 173

1. See Restatement § 433B, cmt. b.

2. E.g., Reynolds Metals Co. v. Yturbide, 258 F.2d 321 (9th Cir.1958) (defendant's plant operations produced fluoride compounds, evidence of heavy amounts of such compounds in the vegetation nearby, with lesser amounts farther away, warranted inference of escape; symptoms of nearby landowners, coupled with lack of other explanations, warranted medical opinion that illness resulted from escape of fluorides from the plant).

3. Zuchowicz v. United States, 140 F.3d 381 (2d Cir.1998). See Liriano v. Hobart Corp., 170 F.3d 264 (2d Cir.1999) ("When a defendant's negligent act is deemed wrongful precisely because it has a strong propensity to cause the type of injury that ensued, that very causal tendency is evidence enough to establish a prima facie case of cause-in-fact").

4. See Zuchowicz v. United States, 140 F.3d 381 (2d Cir.1998) Reynolds v. Texas & Pac. Ry. Co., 37 La.Ann. 694 (1885); Re-

Courts are avowedly liberal with such causation issues[5] and many cases have permitted an inference of causation in fact along these lines. If the defendant is negligent in failing to provide a fire escape in an apartment building,[6] a lifeguard at a hotel swimming pool,[7] or a warning about dangers of a product,[8] the risks are all too great that someone will die in a fire, drown, or suffer product injury, so juries may be permitted in such cases to infer that the defendant's negligent conduct was a cause in fact of the harms suffered in each case, even though it is perfectly possible that the precautions required would have availed nothing in the particular case.

Many examples of this liberal impulse can be found. In a New York case, the plaintiff was shot while he was in the lobby of a building owned by the defendant. Evidence indicated that an attendant in the lobby tends to discourage crime in the area, so the jury was permitted to infer that had the building had an attendant present, the plaintiff in fact would not have been shot.[9] In an Arkansas case, a doctor failed to report facts that would lead people to suspect child abuse. Testimony indicated that had the doctor made the report, an agency would have investigated but would have probably concluded that the complaint was unfounded. Nevertheless, the court thought that a report of suspected abuse and the following investigation would have led the abuser to stop his attacks. Consequently the court thought the jury could find that the failure to report was a partial cause of the child's death.[10]

Although cases like these tend to ameliorate the demands of the but-for rule, they do not repudiate the rule itself, so the plaintiff must ordinarily prove cause in fact by a preponderance of the evidence, circumstantial or otherwise.[11] Assessment of causal evidence requires an

statement § 433B, Ill. 3. But cf. Fedorczyk v. Caribbean Cruise Lines, Ltd., 82 F.3d 69 (3d Cir.1996) (fall in defendant's bathtub, which had inadequate non-slip strips; since plaintiff might have been standing on existing strips when she fell, she could not show that the addition of other strips would have avoided the fall).

5. See Thompson v. Sun City Community Hospital, Inc., 141 Ariz. 597, 688 P.2d 605 (1984).

6. E.g., Higgins Investments, Inc. v. Sturgill, 509 S.W.2d 266 (Ky.1974) (although the fire blocked decedent's exit from his room so that he could not have reached a fire escape outside it, the only place for a fire escape would have been *in* his room, so if one had been provided, he could have escaped; consequently the failure to provide an escape was a cause of his death). See Wex Malone, Ruminations on Cause-in-Fact, 9 Stanf. L. Rev. 60 (1956), reprinted in Wex Malone, Essays on Torts 160 (1986).

7. Haft v. Lone Palm Hotel, 3 Cal.3d 756, 478 P.2d 465, 91 Cal.Rptr. 745 (1970) (hotel pool drowning; hotel was required either to provide guard or post a warning; it did neither, burden of proof shifted to the defendant to absolve itself if it can); cf. Kopera v. Moschella, 400 F.Supp. 131 (S.D.Miss.1975) (no lifeguard at any time, court does not consider whether, had a lifeguard been employed, he would have been on duty when the drowning occurred).

8. E.g., Coffman v. Keene Corporation, 133 N.J. 581, 628 A.2d 710 (1993).

9. Nallan v. Helmsley–Spear, Inc., 50 N.Y.2d 507, 429 N.Y.S.2d 606, 407 N.E.2d 451 (1980).

10. First Commercial Trust Company v. Rank, 323 Ark. 390, 915 S.W.2d 262 (1996)

11. See, e.g., Skinner v. Square D Company, 445 Mich. 153, 516 N.W.2d 475 (1994) ("Nor is it sufficient to submit a causation theory that, while factually supported, is, at best, just as possible as another theory. Rather, the plaintiff must present substantial evidence from which a jury may conclude that more likely than not, but-for the defendant's conduct, the plaintiff's injuries would not have occurred").

estimate of probabilities, for that reason, slight differences in the facts might warrant a finding of causation in some cases and not in other very similar cases. But is is hard to escape the feeling that the but-for rule with its hypothetical alternative case can be applied rigorously in some cases and quite lightly in others.[12] To some extent, therefore, these cases may reflect concerns similar to those in the lost chance cases.[13]

Topic D. Apportioning Liability According to Causes

§ 174. Indivisible Injury: Causal Apportionment vs. Joint and Several Liability

The question whether a defendant caused any harm at all is usually resolved under the but-for rule or under the substantial factor approach. Other causal questions implicate those rules but generate additional concerns. Sometimes the causal question is who, sometimes what. Who among several actors, was a cause of the harm? What loss did the actors cause? In several distinct kinds of negligence cases, courts have to some extent been willing to impose liability for reasons largely dependent upon policy rather than upon causal proof. The following sections show that causal requirements are subordinated to policy concerns, at least in part, in several situations that are not grounded in the principles of vicarious liability.

Apportionment required.—Distinct injuries. When two or more tortfeasors cause separate harms to the plaintiff, as where one negligently injures her arm and another negligently injures her leg, each tortfeasor is normally liable for the harm he caused, no more.[1] One consequence of this rule is that the plaintiff who is injured by more than one tortfeasor must ordinarily prove which part of her injuries are attributable to which tortfeasor. To say that both are causes of harm is not enough; the plaintiff will be required to show which harm was caused by each, although the court may accept somewhat scanty evidence where the nature of the injuries make apportionment of injuries to causes difficult.

—Divisible injuries. The Restatement also requires apportionment when the plaintiff suffers a single injury rather than distinct harms but the single injury is capable of being apportioned in some rational way. For example, if three defendants each negligently allow the escape of irrigation water so that it floods the plaintiff's farm, there is only one injury, but courts could make a causal apportionment by holding each defendant severally liable according to the volume percentage he contrib-

12. Compare Nallan v. Helmsley–Spear, Inc., supra n. 9 (presence of lobby attendant would have deterred shooting) with Shaner v. Tucson Airport Authority Inc., 117 Ariz. 444, 573 P.2d 518 (App. 1977) (lights in parking lot would not have deterred attack on woman); and cases cited in n. 4 supra.

13. § 178.

§ 174

1. Restatement § 433A.

uted.[2]

—Single indivisible injury rule. When the plaintiff presents evidence that she suffered a single or indivisible injury at the hands of two or more tortfeasors, the burden is shifted to the tortfeasors to show that the plaintiff suffered separable injuries and that they can be apportioned or attributed separately to the different tortfeasors.[3] The effect of this rule is that when the plaintiff suffers injuries that are similar in nature or consequences, so that they cannot be separated in any practical way and cannot be attributed separately to the separate tortfeasors, each tortfeasor is treated as a cause of the entire indivisible injury. Under this rule, the defendants are held jointly and severally liable, which is to say that either one may be forced to pay the plaintiff's damages and collect contribution from the other if he can. Joint and several liability, then, is the antithesis of causal apportionment. A variation on the rule occurs when a single injury is caused by a combination of the defendant's negligence and an unforeseeable force of nature. In such cases, the defendant may be held liable, at least where his negligence alone would have sufficed to cause the harm or where the harm was the same kind risked by the defendant's conduct.[4]

Automobile collisions. The indivisible injury rule is routinely applied in automobile collisions cases. If two negligent drivers cause a collision by their separate acts of negligence and the plaintiff suffers a broken nose and a broken toe in the collision, it is not feasible to attempt proof that the broken toe was the result of A's negligence while the broken nose was the result of B's negligence, and courts do not require it. Instead, they hold that the two drivers are concurrent tortfeasors[5] and both are treated as causes of the plaintiff's harm as a whole.

The rule has been applied even where the two defendants acted at wholly different times and caused wholly different impacts upon the plaintiff, so long as the resulting injury is indivisible. For instance, if the plaintiff suffers muscle strain in an collision with A on the way to work and more muscle strain in a collision with B on the way home eight hours later, the muscle injury is likely to be indivisible so that both tortfeasors can be deemed causes of the plaintiff's harm.[6]

2. Restatement § 433A, and ill. 9. If apportionment is an inherently desirable goal, something similar to this idea could be applied in a large number of cases, and in addition, other forms of apportionment, according to relative fault for example, are available. See, favoring widespread use of apportionment based on relative risks inflicted by various defendants, Gerald Boston, Toxic Apportionment: A Causation and Risk Contribution Model, 25 Envtl. L. 549 (1995).

3. Pang v. Minch, 53 Ohio St.3d 186, 559 N.E.2d 1313 (1990); Restatement § 433B.

4. E.g., Heer v. State, 432 N.W.2d 559 (S.D.1988).

5. "Concurrent" once suggested that the tortfeasors had to act together in time, even though they were not acting together under a common purpose or plan. Courts now say that tortfeasors are concurrent tortfeasors if their independent acts lead to an indivisible injury. E.g., Motorists Mutual Ins. Co. v. Huron Road Hospital, 73 Ohio St.3d 391, 653 N.E.2d 235 (1995). Alternatively, courts may formulate the rule by saying that joint and several liability will be applied if the tortfeasors are concurrent in time or if they produce an indivisible injury.

6. Watts v. Smith, 375 Mich. 120, 134 N.W.2d 194 (1965); Piner v. Superior Court, 192 Ariz. 182, 962 P.2d 909 (1998) (similar); Cf. Burke v. 12 Rothschild's Liquor

Medical malpractice. Courts have also applied the single indivisible injury rule in cases of medical negligence allegedly committed by two or more health care providers. For example, if Dr. A and Dr. B both commit acts of negligence that risk brain damage to a newborn, and brain damage in fact results, the court may conclude that brain damage is a single indivisible injury and impose joint and several liability upon the two doctors.[7] A different conclusion would be appropriate if testimony showed that Dr. A caused 80% of the lost brain function and Dr. B only 20%, or if injuries were entirely separate.

Crashworthiness cases. In the two-fire cases discussed in earlier sections, the two fires combined to cause an indivisible injury but each fire alone would have been sufficient to burn the property. One type of indivisible injury case that does not involve two sufficient causes is the crashworthiness case. The plaintiff is injured in a collision with another motorist. Her injuries are worse because her own car was negligently manufactured, perhaps because her seatbelt gives way and she is thrown from the car. When the plaintiff cannot show exactly which part of her injuries are the result of the original crash and which part are the result of the badly made car, a number of courts invoke the indivisible injury rule. That rule allows the plaintiff to get to the jury against the manufacturer as well as the negligent motorist who caused the collision and potentially to recover all her damages from the manufacturer.[8] This kind of case makes it clear that the indivisible injury rule may have the effect of holding one defendant liable for harms it did not in fact cause. At least *some* of the plaintiff's harms would have occurred even if the manufacturer had made a perfect automobile.

Pollution and toxic torts. The older pollution cases held that independent polluters could only be severally liable, that is, that the plaintiff had to show a basis for apportioning causation among various polluters.[9] On the Restatement's view of things, this might be easy enough, since the plaintiff might be able to show how much polluting materials each defendant contributed and apportion causation on that basis, even if the pollution of any one defendant would have alone caused the entire harm. Still, there were cases lost to the plaintiff who could not show dollar damage done by each defendant. More modern cases reject the older rule and permit the plaintiff to hold defendants jointly and severally liable.[10]

Mart, 148 Ill.2d 429, 170 Ill.Dec. 633, 593 N.E.2d 522 (1992) (Rothschild's caused the plaintiff to fall after which he said he could not move; police officers then threw him into a police wagon; at some undetermined point in these events the plaintiff suffered irreversible injury to his spinal cord and became permanently quadriplegic; held, single indivisible injury is established and joint and several liability is proper).

7. Ravo v. Rogatnick, 70 N.Y.2d 305, 514 N.E.2d 1104, 520 N.Y.S.2d 533, 9 A.L.R.5th 1170 (1987).

8. E.g., Polston v. Boomershine Pontiac–GMC Truck, Inc., 262 Ga. 616, 423 S.E.2d 659 (1992) (reviewing authorities); contra, requiring the plaintiff to show grounds for apportionment, Huddell v. Levin, 537 F.2d 726 (3d Cir.1976).

9. See Farley v. Crystal Coal & Coke Co., 85 W.Va. 595, 102 S.E. 265 (1920).

10. Michie v. Great Lakes Steel Division, National Steel Corp., 495 F.2d 213 (6th Cir.1974); Landers v. East Texas Salt Water Disposal Co., 151 Tex. 251, 248 S.W.2d 731 (Tex. 1952).

Similarly, multiple defendants may be held jointly and severally liable in personal toxic tort cases. For example, if the plaintiff suffers substantial exposure to asbestos produced by A and also substantial exposure to asbestos produced by B, both are causes and if negligent can be held jointly and severally liable.[11]

Preexisting disability. The thrust of the indivisible injury principle is that tortfeasors, not victims, should bear the burdens of uncertainty imposed by their tortious behavior. Consequently, the principle is not limited to cases of two tortfeasors, but can apply whenever the injury inflicted by the tortfeasor combines with another condition to produce an indivisible harm. If the tortfeasor aggravates the plaintiff's preexisting disability, the tortfeasor is ideally liable only for the aggravation. But if the tortious harm combines with the existing condition to leave the plaintiff with an indivisible injury, courts may impose liability for the whole injury upon the defendant unless he can show grounds for apportionment.[12] Sometimes, however, a surprising basis for apportionment can be found. One such apportionment is allowed if the defendant causes the death of a person who is already dying from a preexisting disease. In such a case, the defendant is assuredly liable for causing the death, but only to the extent that he hastens it.[13]

Preexisting self-inflicted harm. Even if the plaintiff's pre-existing condition is self-inflicted, as where the plaintiff who suffers lung cancer both from his own smoking and from exposure to the defendant's asbestos, the indivisible injury rule is sometimes invoked to establish the defendant's causal responsibility for the cancer.[14] Such a holding does not in itself rule out a reduction of the plaintiff's damages on comparative negligence or other non-causal grounds,[15] and of course it is also possible that in particular cases, the evidence will provide a good basis for apportionment.[16]

Non-causal types of apportionment. To impose joint and several liability is to reject causal apportionment. However, that does not mean

11. See Tragarz v. Keene Corporation, 980 F.2d 411 (7th Cir.1992); Padgett v. A & M Insulation Company, 266 Ill.App.3d 320, 640 N.E.2d 21, 203 Ill.Dec. 594 (1994).

12. Lovely v. Allstate Ins. Co., 658 A.2d 1091 (Me.1995); David v. DeLeon, 250 Neb. 109, 547 N.W.2d 726 (1996).

13. Follett v. Jones, 252 Ark. 950, 481 S.W.2d 713 (1972); cf. Dillon v. Twin State Gas & Elec. Co., 85 N.H. 449, 163 A. 111 (1932) (boy falling to almost certain death killed by electrocution as he fell). It may be that this form of apportionment is limited to certain conventional situations. See § 177.

14. Borman v. Raymark Industries, Inc., 960 F.2d 327 (3d Cir.1992) (defendant's asbestos, plaintiff's own smoking resulting in cancer which was treated as single indivisible injury); Martin v. Owens–Corning Fiberglas Corporation, 515 Pa. 377, 528 A.2d 947 (1987) (similar). If grounds for apportionment exist, however, apportionment of responsibility to the plaintiff as one cause is perfectly proper. See Restatement § 433 A, cmt. f.

15. As to comparative fault reductions, see §§ 201 & 202; cf. Menne v. Celotex Corp., 861 F.2d 1453 (10th Cir.1988) (plaintiff exposed to asbestos produced by a number of suppliers, each liable for a share, but seemingly not a causally-apportioned share).

16. See Dafler v. Raymark Industries, Inc., 259 N.J.Super. 17, 611 A.2d 136 (1992), affirmed on the basis of the intermediate court's opinion, 132 N.J. 96, 622 A.2d 1305 (1993).

that any given defendant will be ultimately liable for all damages. Aside from the possibility of contribution from co-defendants, a defendant who is jointly and severally liable may nevertheless be able to reduce liability on the basis of the plaintiff's own comparative fault. It is also possible, as it was not a century ago, to use other means of apportioning liability. For example, it would be possible to ignore the causal question altogether and simply hold each defendant liable for a percentage of the plaintiff's damages that is equal to the defendant's percentage of fault,[17] or to use much more complex formulas. Ideas of this kind, together with enhanced possibilities of scientific evidence, may even affect what counts as a divisible injury.[18] Such a possibility, together with questions about the appropriate scope of the joint and several liability rule belong to the chapter on joint and several liability. For the present chapter, it is enough to say that joint and several liability under the indivisible injury rule reflects one of the ways in which courts sometimes aid the plaintiff who finds it difficult or impossible to make causal proof.

§ 175. Alternative Causes and the Shifted Burden of Proof

Alternative causation rule extending indivisible injury cases. Joint and several liability has been extended one further step in alternative causation cases. In the alternative cause cases, both tortfeasors are negligent, but only one of them has caused the plaintiff's harm. The difficulty is that it is impossible to determine which one is the cause.

The rule in Summers v. Tice. The leading case in the United States is *Summers v. Tice*,[1] where two hunters, acting independently of each other, negligently fired their guns at the same time. One piece of shot struck the plaintiff in the eye. Both hunters were negligent in risking harm to the plaintiff. But only one of them could have fired the shot that struck the plaintiff's eye.[2] As a matter of probabilities, it is not more likely that A fired the shot, nor more likely that B did so, so the plaintiff would be left without recourse against either negligent hunter. The court concluded that the burden should shift to each defendant to show

17. This is the result where joint and several liability has been substantially abolished. See § 386. In Piner v. Superior Court, 192 Ariz. 182, 962 P.2d 909 (1998), a statute made each defendant severally liable for his percentage fault share. The court held that the percentage fault share would be a share of the total damages for indivisible injury.

18. See Gerald Boston, Toxic Apportionment: A Causation and Risk Contribution Model, 25 Envtl. L. 549 (1995).

§ 175

1. Summers v. Tice, 33 Cal.2d 80, 199 P.2d 1 (1948).

2. The court treats the case as if only one shot struck the plaintiff and only one tortfeasor could have fired. However, the plaintiff was struck elsewhere by another shot that caused minor harm. That raises the possibility that the case could be handled under an indivisible injury rationale, although Prosser and the Restatement might regard this as a case of two injuries and therefore not to be blessed with the indivisible injury treatment. See Restatement § 433A (1)(a) and Prosser & Keeton § 41. Both those authorities are obviously concerned about the conflict between the traditional requirement of apportionment and the uncertain scope of the indivisible injury and alternative causation rules.

he was not the cause and if he could not make such a showing, then to stand jointly and severally liable to the plaintiff.

Burden shifting and practical effect. Sometimes the burden shifting in *Summers v. Tice* is given prominence in discussions, as if to suggest that the court was not really imposing liability. But the practical effect of the rule is to impose joint and several liability upon each defendant in the numerous cases in which one defendant cannot show that the other defendant was the cause, so that one actor will be held although he caused no harm whatever. For this reason, the common phrase "alternative liability" is misleading. The liability itself is joint and several, not in the alternative. It is rather causation that is in the alternative, because one or the other but not both tortfeasors are causes of the harm.

Rationale. The opinion in *Summers* did not spell out the reasons for this extraordinary liability in any precise way, perhaps because the result, which has sometimes been reached on other grounds,[3] seems so clearly right on the facts. Beyond the dubious suggestion that defendants might know more than plaintiffs,[4] the court seemed to say that each defendant, by his negligent shot, created the doubt about causation or despoiled the evidence that otherwise would have been available to the plaintiff, so that as a matter of policy, the defendants, rather than the innocent plaintiff, should bear the loss.[5] This rationale has been elaborated by the Canadian Supreme Court.[6] Professor Robertson has given a good account of it in connection with another case.[7] The rationale seems sound, but since many acts in life create doubts and confusions about legal rights but are not necessarily actionable for that reason, some limitations must be applied.

Requirement that all defendants be acting wrongfully. The Restatement accepts *Summers*. The Restatement would shift the burden to the defendants to exculpate themselves if they can whenever the conduct of two or more actors is tortious and harm has been caused by one of

3. See McMillan v. Mahoney, 99 N.C.App. 448, 393 S.E.2d 298 (1990), n. 10 below.

4. It seems inherently improbable that either hunter firing at the same target would be able to watch the scattered shot fly through the air to strike the plaintiff. Hymowitz v. Eli Lilly and Company, 73 N.Y.2d 487, 541 N.Y.S.2d 941, 539 N.E.2d 1069 (1989) explicitly stated this rationale, but only for the purpose of finding it inapplicable to a case of many actors.

5. This theme appears in a number of cases that do not necessarily involve the alternative causation but do involve causal doubts. E.g., Gardner v. National Bulk Carriers, Inc., 310 F.2d 284, 91 A.L.R.2d 1023 (4th Cir. 1962) (the defendant's failure to search for a man overboard "obliterated all possibility of evidence to prove whether a search, if undertaken, would have succeeded or failed").

6. Cook v. Lewis, [1952] 1 D.L.R. 1 (1951) was a case similar to *Summers v. Tice*. In *Cook,* Rand, J. reasoned that the negligent defendants had "violated not only the victim's substantive right to security, but.... also culpably impaired the latter's remedial right of establishing liability. By confusing his act with environmental conditions, he has, in effect, destroyed the victim's power of proof." Later, in Dow Corning Corp. v. Hollis, 129 D.L.R.4th 609 (1995) the majority appeared to approve of that reasoning. As to liability for negligent spoliation of evidence, see § 451.

7. David W. Robertson, The Common Sense of Cause in Fact, 75 Tex. L. Rev. 1765, 1787 (1997), using this reasoning to explain Saunders Sys. Birmingham Co. v. Adams, 217 Ala. 621, 117 So. 72 (Ala. 1928), where the lessor provided a car with no brakes and the driver failed to use them.

them.[8] Under this rule, proof that one of the two actors is negligent simply does not aid the plaintiff at all; they must all be wrongdoers before the burden shifts to them to disprove causation.[9] In this respect, the *Summers* alternative causation rule differs from the concert of action rule that sometimes applies to similar facts. If the two defendants are acting in concert, as part of a common plan or design, they are true joint tortfeasors and each is vicariously liable for the other's negligence. In that case, proof that only one is negligent is sufficient to impose liability against the other as well.[10]

Judicial acceptance. The *Summers* rule is well known to the appellate courts. Although one decision forcefully rejected the whole idea on the ground that it did violence to established principles of causation,[11] most courts appear to regard it as established law on its facts. In an Ohio case, the defendants, A and B, allegedly supplied an explosive compound in separate batches to the plaintiff's employer without giving appropriate warnings about its danger. The plaintiff was seriously injured when one batch of the compound caused an explosion, but it was not possible to determine which batch, A's or B's, was actually involved. The court applied the alternative liability rule, holding that the claim should not have been dismissed on causal grounds.[12]

Judicial limitations. But courts have usually been reluctant to extend the alternative causation rule any further. Another decision of the Ohio Court insisted that the rule could not apply unless the defendants created quantitatively similar risks of harm.[13] With the exception of Michigan,[14] courts almost always reject alternative causation when it comes to products liability cases with numerous defendants. In those cases they have said that the *Summers* alternative causation rule should not apply if there are numerous tortfeasors,[15] or if all tortfeasors have

8. Restatement § 433B (3).

9. Pennfield Corp. v. Meadow Valley Elec., Inc., 413 Pa.Super. 187, 604 A.2d 1082 (1992).

10. In McMillan v. Mahoney, 99 N.C.App. 448, 393 S.E.2d 298 (1990) the complaint alleged that two boys were firing air rifles together, that a pellet from one struck the plaintiff causing brain damage, and that one of the boys was negligent. The court appeared to approve the alternative causation theory, but seemingly decided the case on the ground that the boys acted in concert, since that theory would justify liability of both if either one were negligent.

11. Senn v. Merrell–Dow Pharmaceuticals, Inc., 305 Or. 256, 751 P.2d 215 (1988) (a products liability suit in which the only two possible producers of a vaccine that caused encephalopathy were joined, seemingly rejected alternative causation theory for any kind of case).

12. Minnich v. Ashland Oil Co., Inc., 15 Ohio St.3d 396, 473 N.E.2d 1199 (1984); accord, as to two manufacturers of heparin, a drug alleged to be defective, Wysocki v. Reed, 222 Ill.App.3d 268, 164 Ill.Dec. 817, 583 N.E.2d 1139 (1991); Huston v. Konieczny, 52 Ohio St.3d 214, 556 N.E.2d 505 (1990) (several possible suppliers of beer to underage drinker).

13. Horton v. Harwick Chemical Corp., 73 Ohio St.3d 679, 653 N.E.2d 1196 (1995) (in this case, as distinguished from Summers, the "plaintiffs can at least identify which products they were exposed to most, which contained the highest levels of asbestos, and which were used in a manner more likely to release fibers into the air").

14. Abel v. Eli Lilly & Co., 418 Mich. 311, 343 N.W.2d 164 (1984) approved use of alternative liability against many manufacturers of DES, provided all possible defendants were joined in the action.

15. Sindell v. Abbott Laboratories, 26 Cal.3d 588, 163 Cal.Rptr. 132, 607 P.2d 924 (1980). The idea that alternative liability should not be applied if there are more than

not been joined as defendants.[16] Some of them have also taken seriously the unproved suggestion in *Summers* that the hunters knew more about the causation issue than the plaintiff, and held that, since manufacturers of a generic drug knew no more than the plaintiff about which manufacturer's product caused the plaintiff's harm, the alternative causation rule did not apply.[17] Sometimes courts have suggested limitations on the rule that seem to have no essential connection with it. The occasional suggestion that the defendants must have acted simultaneously is in this category,[18] since simultaneous action is only one of the ways in which the defendant's negligence can operate to obfuscate the causal issue.

The litany of limits on the rule has not been fully explained. It derives from a comment in the Restatement,[19] which did not state normative limits on the rule at all, much less a rationale for such limits. The Restatement instead merely observed that in the cases that had been decided when it was written, all the defendants had in fact been joined and their conduct was substantially simultaneous. It may be more important to observe a quite different pattern in the cases. They are usually cases in which the plaintiff's own fault is not an issue, indeed, cases in which the plaintiff is not inflicting reciprocal risks upon the defendant. If the plaintiff herself is at fault and may have been a cause of her own harm, the strong moral basis for treating the negligent defendants as causes in fact of the harm could become quite attenuated.[20]

Distinguishing res ipsa loquitur. A few opinions[21] seem to confuse the whole idea with the doctrine of res ipsa loquitur, under which the

two tortfeasors seems to be based ultimately on the view that alternative liability is linked to the probability that a tortfeasor who is held liable will in fact be the causal agent. But even with two tortfeasors who create identical risks, the probability does not favor liability of either. The implicit argument, then, seems to be that the two-tortfeasor case is an almost-probability, while the three-tortfeasor case doesn't reach the vaunted heights of the almost-probable. *Summers v. Tice* itself, did not suggest that probability was the basis of the liability but rather that policy was.

16. Gaulding v. Celotex Corp., 772 S.W.2d 66 (Tex.1989).

17. See Collins v. Eli Lilly Co., 116 Wis.2d 166, 342 N.W.2d 37 (1984). Similarly in a medical malpractice case involving two doctors, the court rejected alternative liability because one doctor had settled the case, which the court thought meant that the plaintiff would not be faced with a conspiracy of silence among the defendants. Battocchi v. Washington Hospital Center, 581 A.2d 759 (D.C.App.1990).

18. Smith v. Cutter Biological, Inc., 72 Haw. 416, 823 P.2d 717 (1991) (part of the reason for refusing to apply the alternative causation theory to a suit against several manufacturers of a blood clotting agent); Skipworth v. Lead Industries Ass'n, Inc., 547 Pa. 224, 690 A.2d 169 (1997) (part of the reason for refusing to apply alternative causation theory to suit against manufacturers of lead pigment).

19. Restatement § 433B, cmt. h.

20. Distinguish two kinds of plaintiff fault in this respect. First, suppose the plaintiff and two defendants are all firing rifles at a wall and that this is negligent. A bullet, source unknown, ricochets off the wall and strikes the plaintiff. Second, the plaintiff is deer hunting in camouflaged clothing, so that she is not easily identified as a human. She is struck by a bullet fired by one of the two defendant hunters. In this second scenario, the plaintiff's fault can be dealt with under comparative negligence rules and need not impinge on the causal question as between the two defendants. In the first scenario, however, defendants might present a somewhat plausible argument against application of the alternative causation rule, especially if the court accepts the argument that the rule should not apply to larger numbers of defendants.

21. See Leuer v. Johnson, 450 N.W.2d 363 (Minn.App.1990).

jury may be permitted to infer negligence when that seems the most likely explanation of the injury, even if no specific act of negligence can be identified. The confusion is instantly and easily avoidable by recalling the fundamental difference between the negligence issue and the causation issue. Two matters in particular, however, seem to cause difficulty on occasion. The first is that causation, like negligence, can be inferred from circumstantial evidence. However, the inference of negligence drawn from specific circumstantial evidence or on the basis of res ipsa loquitur, is based upon an estimate of probabilities. Only if reasonable people could find that the defendant was more probably negligent than not does res ipsa ordinarily assist the plaintiff. The very opposite is true under the alternative causation rule, which is meant to redress the difficulty that arises for the very reason that neither defendant is more probably the cause.

One res ipsa loquitur case in particular generates confusion with the *Summers* rule of alternative causation. In *Ybarra v. Spangard,*[22] when the plaintiff awoke from surgery with injury to a previously healthy part of his body, the California Court permitted the jury to infer negligence on the part of numerous defendants involved in the operation. It is easy to regard that case as an extreme one because it violates the normal res ipsa rule—it is most assuredly improbable that every one of those who dealt with the plaintiff's hospital stay was negligent. Whether *Ybarra* is justified or not, however, the alternative causation rule differs deeply. The whole point of the alternative causation rule is that defendants have been shown to be negligent and that the negligent defendants rather than the innocent plaintiff should bear the uncertainty created by that negligence. It comes down to saying that you could reject *Ybarra* out of hand and still quite logically approve of *Summers.*

§ 176. Statistical Substitutes for Causation: Market Share Liability

Under the indivisible injury and alternative causation rules, courts, for reasons of justice or policy, impose joint and several liability upon defendants whose causal responsibility for the plaintiff's injury is not established in the way that is ordinarily required. The market share rule also imposes liability upon defendants who are not shown to have caused the plaintiff's harm, but it does so in a radically different manner. Instead of joint and several liability, under which any defendant is potentially liable for all of the plaintiff's damages, market share theory imposes liability upon each defendant only for a percentage represented by that defendant's share of the market in a harmful product.

The market share rule has a specific beginning. It was proposed in a law review comment to deal with DES cases.[1] DES was a prescription

22. Ybarra v. Spangard, 25 Cal.2d 486, 154 P.2d 687 (1944).

§ 176

1. Comment, DES and a Proposed Theory of Enterprise Liability, 46 Fordham L. Rev. 963 (1978).

drug manufactured by hundreds of companies. Every manufacturer's version was like every other manufacturer's version. Many pregnant women ingested the drug to help prevent miscarriages. Years later, when their daughters reached adulthood, they discovered that DES caused cancers in the daughters' female reproductive system. Since these cancers did not appear for many years, almost no one had records that could establish which of the manufacturers had produced the specific drug ingested by the individual mothers. Indeed, many of the manufacturers no longer existed.

The market share idea was that if manufacturer A sold 40% of all the DES marketed, it was highly probable that A's DES caused about the same percentage of overall injuries. Although A's version of the drug may have caused no injury at all to a particular plaintiff—no one could ever know for sure—if it caused 40% of all injuries, then holding it liable for 40% of each individual plaintiff's injury would be no injustice. In fact, the totals of liability should come out to about the same dollar amount as if each mother were accurately matched with each dose of DES. Averaging out seemed likely because the number of potential plaintiffs was quite large so the courts could reasonably expect averaging to work in a way it might not work if there were only ten potential plaintiffs. Averaging out liabilities is quite unusual in the law, although not unique,[2] so it is no surprise that market share theory is controversial.

Several courts have adopted some form or another of the market share idea in DES cases.[3] These courts hold that each manufacturer of the drug is responsible to each plaintiff, but never for the plaintiff's entire damages,[4] only for a percentage of the plaintiff's damages equal to that manufacturer's share of the market in the drug.

Quite a few other courts, worried over the idea of liability based upon statistical rather than literal causation, have rejected the market share theory, even for the DES cases.[5] When it comes to other products

2. Averaging out is a consciously used device in workers' compensation cases to distribute liability among employers when an employee has been subjected to toxic exposures at different places of employment. This form of averaging out simply requires the employer at the place of last injurious exposure to pay all the compensation due. See, e.g., Union Carbide Corp. v. Industrial Commission, 196 Colo. 56, 581 P.2d 734 (1978); Bracke v. Baza'r, Inc., 293 Or. 239, 646 P.2d 1330 (1982). This system is much less likely to represent accurate shares of liability than the market share theory.

3. Sindell v. Abbott Laboratories, 26 Cal.3d 588, 163 Cal.Rptr. 132, 607 P.2d 924 (1980) (the original case); Conley v. Boyle Drug Co., 570 So.2d 275 (Fla.1990); Smith v. Cutter Biological, Inc., 72 Haw. 416, 823 P.2d 717 (1991); Hymowitz v. Eli Lilly and Company, 73 N.Y.2d 487, 541 N.Y.S.2d 941, 539 N.E.2d 1069 (1989); Martin v. Abbott Laboratories, 102 Wash. 2d 581, 689 P.2d 368 (1984); Collins v. Eli Lilly Co., 116 Wis.2d 166, 342 N.W.2d 37 (1984) (liability in proportion to risk imposed, with market share relevant in determining that risk).

4. The California Court, initiating the whole idea in *Sindell,* may have been uncertain about joint and several liability, but later cleared that up. See Brown v. Superior Court, 44 Cal.3d 1049, 751 P.2d 470, 245 Cal.Rptr. 412 (1988). One court rejected market share liability in favor of an alternative causation theory, which of course does use joint and several liability. Abel v. Eli Lilly & Co., 418 Mich. 311, 343 N.W.2d 164 (1984).

5. Smith v. Eli Lilly & Co., 137 Ill.2d 222, 148 Ill.Dec. 22, 560 N.E.2d 324 (1990); Gorman v. Abbott Laboratories, 599 A.2d 1364 (R.I.1991).

besides DES, the theory has been invoked a few times,[6] but even courts that accept market share theories for DES may reject they theory as inappropriate on the facts, often because the product is not uniform and because it is likely to subject victims to different levels of exposure and to present different levels of risk.[7] Thus courts have generally not extended market share theories to asbestos cases, partly because products using asbestos are likely to present quite different exposures, so that a market comparison of hair dryer exposure and shipboard insulation exposure is really not justified.[8]

In the few states that have affirmatively declared for some form of market share liability, a number of collateral rules have been generated, and collateral litigation to go with them. One idea was that the plaintiff should be required to join a substantial percentage of the defendants who produced the product.[9] This was a point that might be important if the defendants would be jointly and severally liable, for joinder would facilitate their potential contribution claims, but it seems misplaced when each defendant's liability is limited to its market share.

A more significant question is whether a defendant's market share is based on its share of the national market or some local market. Since any given manufacturer might have an enormous share of the national market, yet no share at all in Spokane where the consumer purchased the drug, the question has immediate practical significance. It is also significant because, if a local market is to control, litigation over details of local sales, perhaps sales at a particular pharmacy, is likely to be costly and perhaps even trivial. One of the later DES decisions adopted a national market test,[10] but others tended to emphasize local markets.[11] If all courts adopted market share and used a national test, the prospects would be excellent that all producers would ultimately bear liabilities equal to their approximately correct share. However, the use of different market tests in different states tends to defeat the "averaging out" effects. It may be that if market share is a good idea, it should be implemented by uniform standards.

6. See Hamilton v. Accu–Tek, 62 F.Supp.2d 802 (1999) (collective liability for sellers of .25 caliber handguns who negligently marketed so that guns were all too likely to reach illicit teenage users and to be used in crime).

7. Bly v. Tri–Continental Industries, Inc., 663 A.2d 1232 (D.C.App.1995) (different levels of benzene in petroleum products one reason to reject market share theory on the facts).

8. See Blackston v. Shook & Fletcher Insul. Co., 764 F.2d 1480 (11th Cir.1985); Celotex Corp. v. Copeland, 471 So.2d 533 (Fla.1985). If the plaintiff is exposed to asbestos products of different manufacturers, all with the same level of asbestos, however, the market share theory, if otherwise acceptable, is appropriate. Wheeler v. Raybestos–Manhattan, 8 Cal.App.4th 1152, 11 Cal. Rptr.2d 109 (1992).

9. Wood v. Eli Lilly & Co., 38 F.3d 510 (10th Cir.1994).

10. Hymowitz v. Eli Lilly and Company, 73 N.Y.2d 487, 541 N.Y.S.2d 941, 539 N.E.2d 1069 (1989).

11. E.g., Conley v. Boyle Drug Co., 570 So.2d 275 (Fla.1990). Even under this standard, however, national market figures might be admissible when local figures are not available or reliable. See George v. Parke–Davis, 107 Wash.2d 584, 733 P.2d 507 (1987).

§ 177. Preexisting Conditions: Causing Harm to One Already Endangered

Especially difficult problems of causation arise when the defendant is negligent toward a plaintiff who is already suffering from a disease or disability, or is immediately threatened with probable harm. And, as in many other cases that permit or require apportionment, concerns of justice or policy may shape the apportionment rules.

In one group of cases, the defendant negligently causes the death of a decedent who suffered from a preexisting disease or was threatened with a highly probable and almost immediate death. Although the defendant is a cause of the death, it is easy to think that the defendant merely hastened it. In these cases, courts have held that the defendant is liable, but only for the present value of the decedent's life or limb at the time of her death. That is, the defendant is liable only for hastening the death of the plaintiff or, in injury cases, for making matters worse. The effect is a kind of causal apportionment in which most of the harm is attributed to the preexisting disease or condition and only the aggravation of injury or the acceleration of death is attributed to the tortfeasor.

In the most famous case[1] on present value apportionment according to the decedent's chances of survival, a boy fell from a bridge. He would almost certainly suffer death or very serious injury from plunging into the gorge. But in his fall, he reached for the defendant's electrical wires, which were charged and uninsulated. The charge electrocuted him. The defendant was held liable, but only for the value of the boy's life and prospects at the moment of electrocution. Put differently, if death were the certain outcome of the fall, the defendant was liable for hastening the death, perhaps by seconds, but not for more. On the same reasoning, one who negligently kills a person suffering from a terminal disease is liable for the hastened death only.[2]

There are no doubt limits on this kind of apportionment through use of a present value approach. For one thing, it is both impractical and logically improper to devalue the plaintiff's life, limb, or property in the light of subsequent losses from extraneous forces that no one present at the time would have taken into account. For instance, no defendant should escape liability for killing the decedent in a car accident merely because the decedent was on her way to catch a plane that was later blown up by a terrorist.[3]

Another problem with the present value kind of apportionment is that it can very quickly undermine the normal allocations of liability

§ 177

1. Dillon v. Twin State Gas & Elec. Co., 85 N.H. 449, 163 A. 111 (1932).

2. Follett v. Jones, 252 Ark. 950, 481 S.W.2d 713 (1972); cf. Lancaster v. Norfolk & Western Ry. Co., 773 F.2d 807, 822 (7th Cir.1985) ("the damages of the 'eggshell skull' victim must be reduced to reflect the likelihood that he would have been injured anyway, from a nonliable cause, even if the defendant had not injured him"); McCahill v. New York Transportation Co., 201 N.Y. 221, 94 N.E. 616 (1911) (liability for damages resulting from unusual susceptibility, but unusual susceptibility could be considered in fixing damages).

3. See n. 4 below.

when two tortfeasors are at work. If the plaintiff's property is worth very little because it stands in the path of an unstoppable fire, the defendant who negligently destroys the house with explosives would be liable under a present value approach only for the value of a house that was about to be destroyed anyway, while other rules would hold that the defendant who set the second fire would normally be liable for nothing, since the house was destroyed by the time his fire reached it. The plaintiff whose home is destroyed by an admitted tortfeasor would collect only a fraction of her loss from that tortfeasor and none from the author of the second fire.

The result just described is surely undesirable,[4] so it seems certain that there are limits somewhere to the use of the present value approach to apportionment. Professor Robertson says that in evaluating what the defendant caused, we must take into account risks of future harm from other sources only if those risks "are so far advanced and so nearly certain at the time of the accident that any attempt to ignore their functional identity with pre-existing conditions would seem dishonest."[5]

Nevertheless, courts habitually use present value in calculating damages of many kinds, and so inevitably incorporate estimates about the chances the plaintiff or her property had at the time of the injury or damage.[6] That leads to the question whether some explicit quantification of chances might be permitted or required in some cases.

§ 178. Preexisting Conditions: Increasing Risk of Harm and the Lost Chance Rule

The problem facts. Cases discussed in the preceding section involved a defendant who definitely caused harm, albeit to a person who suffered a preexisting disability or danger. In other cases, the defendant risks harm to such a person, but it is not likely, much less certain, that the defendant actually caused the harm. Instead, the harm is more likely to have resulted from the preexisting condition. One kind of case that has been much litigated is that of a doctor who fails to provide a timely diagnosis or treatment of disease, thereby creating a risk that the treatment will come too late. In such cases, however, the evidence may show that even if diagnosis and treatment had been timely, the patient might have had only a 40% chance of living. On those facts, the plaintiff

4. Cf. Spose v. Ragu Foods, Inc., 142 Misc.2d 366, 537 N.Y.S.2d 739 (Sup. Ct. 1989); Baker v. Willoughby, [1970] A.C. 467, [1970] 2 W.L.R. 50, [1969] 3 All. E.R. 1528 (H.L. 1969) (defendant injured leg, much later, thief shot the same leg, which then required amputation; defendant could not take advantage of the thief's act to reduce his liability for permanent impairment); but cf. Jobling v. Associated Dairies, Ltd., [1981] 3 W.L.R. 155, 2 All. E.R. 752 (H.L. 1981) (where later debility, which would have occurred anyway, was not the result of a tort, defendant tortfeasor could show that inevitable debility in reduction of his own liability). The English cases are discussed in W.V.H. Rogers, Winfield & Jolowicz on Tort 152–153 (14th ed. 1994).

5. David W. Robertson, The Common Sense of Cause in Fact, 75 Tex. L. Rev. 1765, 1798 (1997) (distinguishing contingencies from actualities, that is, from harms that actually did befall the plaintiff before suit).

6. Among many reflections of the pervasive use of value, with its reliance on estimates of chances, see 1 Dan B. Dobbs, Law of Remedies § 3.5 (2d ed. 1993).

definitely could not prove by a preponderance of the evidence that the defendant caused the patient's death. Indeed, the heavy preponderance of the evidence is the other way, for the probability is 60% that the defendant did *not* cause the death in spite of his negligence. Such cases are usually described as increased risk or loss of the chance cases.

Denial of all liability. Some courts have insisted that on facts like the delayed treatment example no one can recover for the patient's death, since the plaintiff has failed to establish causation by a preponderance of the evidence.[1] These courts are unmoved by the very real possibility—some 40%—that in some sense the defendant did indeed cause the death, although we cannot know that with certainty. Most courts actually faced with a specific claim that loss of a chance is itself an item of damages for which recovery is appropriate, however, have permitted recovery in one of two ways.

Liability for all harm. When the plaintiff shows loss of a chance, but a chance of only 50% or less, one group of courts permits the jury to find causation and make an award for the whole of the loss, disregarding the fact that the patient was likely to die regardless of the doctor's negligence.[2] Not all the cases that permit a full recovery are explicit about the reasoning.[3] The clearest of them reason somewhat along these lines, with

§ 178

1. Dumas v. Cooney, 235 Cal.App.3d 1593, 1 Cal.Rptr.2d 584 (1991); Gooding v. University Hospital Building, Inc., 445 So.2d 1015 (Fla.1984). Fennell v. Southern Maryland Hosp. Center, Inc., 320 Md. 776, 580 A.2d 206 (1990); Jones v. Owings, 318 S.C. 72, 456 S.E.2d 371 (S.C. 1995) (lost chance doctrine contrary to the most basic standards); Kilpatrick v. Bryant, 868 S.W.2d 594 (Tenn.1993); Kramer v. Lewisville Memorial Hospital, 858 S.W.2d 397 (Tex.1993) (counting authorities 16–8 in favor of some form of relaxed causal rules); Hotson v. East Berkshire Area Health Authority, 2 All E.R. 909 (H.L. 1987). Michigan so provides by statute for medical malpractice cases. Mich. Comp. Laws Ann. § 600.2912a (2). In Weymers v. Khera, 454 Mich. 639, 563 N.W.2d 647 (1997), a case to which the Michigan statute did not apply, the court refused to apply its earlier lost chance rule to any claim for lost chance other than for loss of chance of life. A great many courts have made general statements that the plaintiff must prove medical causation by a preponderance of the evidence (or, as it is often phrased in medical cases, by a reasonable medical certainty), but many of these cases do not involve quantified evidence of lost chance or indeed any claim that lost chance is separately recoverable.

2. Thompson v. Sun City Community Hospital, Inc., 141 Ariz. 597, 688 P.2d 605 (1984); Mayhue v. Sparkman, 653 N.E.2d 1384 Ind. (1995).

3. Hamil v. Bashline, 481 Pa. 256, 392 A.2d 1280 (1978), though following the reasoning described in the text, also introduced the idea, repeated in other cases, that Restatement § 323(a) in some way supported liability for increased risk. Section 323, however, is addressed to an entirely different problem, namely, the usual rule that one who does nothing owes no duty to take affirmative actions for the benefit of others. It probably does not support liability for increased risk without causation. See § 319 below. The Restatement's § 323 recognizes an exception to the no duty rule and imposes a duty of reasonable care upon one who undertakes to render services but does not use reasonable care in carrying them out. Even then, the Restatement imposes no duty unless the failure to act increases the risk to the beneficiary of the undertaking or the beneficiary relies in some way. All this is what is required to trigger a duty of care; it does not purport to address the other elements of the plaintiff's claim and in particular does not address causation requirements, which are specified several chapters later. Nor does § 323 suggest anything about how damages are measured in increased risk cases. In Thompson v. Sun City Community Hospital, Inc., 141 Ariz. 597, 688 P.2d 605 (1984) the court appeared to say that the defendant's duty was to protect the chance, but it also appeared to say that if the defendant negligently deprived the plaintiff of a chance, the jury could find causation of the whole loss.

which other cases are consistent: (i) The defendant doctor's negligence increased the risk of death; (ii) that increased risk combined with the risk from the existing illness to cause a single indivisible injury, much as the negligently set fire combined with the innocent fire in the two-fire case. (iii) Consequently, if the doctor's negligence was a substantial factor in producing harm, the doctor is liable for the entire harm unless he can show a basis for apportionment.[4]

Liability for value of the lost chance. A second method of permitting recovery recognizes that the defendant may not have caused death, but he caused the loss of the plaintiff's chance to live. This view was developed by Professor King in an article that is now invariably cited in all discussions of the topic.[5] A later article makes it clear that the recovery is for reduction in likelihood of a more favorable outcome.[6] The idea is that the plaintiff's chance of survival itself has value. Confronted with a risk of death, a patient would pay for even a small chance to live.[7] Indeed, a patient retains a physician for that very reason, to maximize his chances of health and survival.[8] In this view, if the plaintiff can sustain the burden of proving that the defendant negligently deprived her of a chance,[9] or a substantial chance,[10] of survival, the defendant should be liable for the value of the chance he has negligently destroyed. The result is quite different from the all or nothing approaches described above. Under the value of the chance rule, the plaintiff recovers, but only an amount representing the value of the chance destroyed by the defendant's negligence. Only a relatively small group of courts has so far accepted this approach on the medical malpractice facts, but the number may be growing.[11]

4. Hamil v. Bashline, 481 Pa. 256, 392 A.2d 1280 (1978). If a court perceives a basis for apportionment, the same reasoning supports the more limited value of the chance award. See Scafidi v. Seiler, 119 N.J. 93, 574 A.2d 398 (1990).

5. Joseph H. King, Jr., Causation, Valuation and Chance in Personal Injury Torts, 90 Yale L. J. 1353 (1981).

6. Joseph H. King, Jr., "Reduction of Likelihood" Reformulation and other Retrofitting of the Loss-of-a-Chance Doctrine, 28 Mem. St. U. L. Rev. 492 (1998).

7. See Murrey v. United States, 73 F.3d 1448 (7th Cir.1996) ("No doubt Murrey would have paid a lot (if he had had a lot to pay) for a 5 percent chance of survival if the alternative was a certainty of immediate death. This shows that he lost something by being deprived of that chance"); Wollen v. DePaul Health Center, 828 S.W.2d 681 (Mo. 1992) (a patient "would pay to have a choice between three unmarked doors—behind two of which were death, with life the third option"). Professor King refines the 3–door metaphor in Joseph H. King, Jr., "Reduction of Likelihood" Reformulation and other Retrofitting of the Loss-of-a-Chance Doctrine, 28 mem. St. u. l. rev. 492, 540 (1998).

8. See Falcon v. Memorial Hospital, 436 Mich. 443, 462 N.W.2d 44, 52 (1990).

9. See Holton v. Memorial Hospital, 176 Ill.2d 95, 118, 679 N.E.2d 1202, 1212, 223 Ill.Dec. 429, 439 (1997) ("To the extent a plaintiff's chance of recovery or survival is lessened by the malpractice, he or she should be able to present evidence to a jury that the defendant's malpractice, to a reasonable degree of medical certainty, proximately caused the increased risk of harm or lost chance of recovery").

10. Delaney v. Cade, 255 Kan. 199, 873 P.2d 175 (1994).

11. See cases cited in notes 7, 12, & 13. Lost chance recoveries in medical malpractice cases are not presently acceptable in England, but the House of Lords may have left the door open for some development. See W.V.H. Rogers, Winfield & Jolowicz on Tort 150 (14th ed. 1994).

Valuing the chance. (a) When the plaintiff's chances for survival are quantified by testimony, the easiest calculation is one that discounts total damages by the plaintiff's chance. If the patient had only a 40% chance of living even when given proper medical treatment, and the defendant's negligence deprived her of all that chance, the defendant should be liable for 40% of the the total damages.[12]

(b) The patient's chance for survival can be valued more subjectively even if testimony quantifies the chance by precise numbers. In *Smith v. State,*[13] the Louisiana Court disfavored any automatic use of the quantified chance to discount "full" damages. Justice Lemmon thought that the quantification of the chance was itself an imprecise matter, and that when it was applied to the necessarily imprecise estimate of damages for the death of a person, "the uncertainty progresses geometrically." The jury would consider all the evidence, including the testimony assigning numerical values to the plaintiff's chances, and come up with its own valuation.

Choosing between the full and the limited recovery. Case counting, always a limited way of mapping the law, is especially likely to be misleading in the lost chance cases. In the choice between permitting a full recovery and limiting that recovery to the value of the chance, more courts (at this writing) appear to support the full recovery. But in some of these cases, including the leading ones on which others tend to rely,[14] no evidence quantified the plaintiff's chance of survival as being only 50% or less. The plaintiff's evidence on causation was weak, but there was no basis for apportionment by limiting liability to the value of the chance. The courts in those cases were therefore faced with a choice of excluding the plaintiff's claim, even though the defendant negligently created a risk of the very harm that occurred,[15] or of allowing a full

12. Wendland v. Sparks, 574 N.W.2d 327 (Iowa 1998); Delaney v. Cade, 255 Kan. 199, 873 P.2d 175 (1994) (seemingly requiring, not merely permitting, quantification and discount); Scafidi v. Seiler, 119 N.J. 93, 574 A.2d 398 (1990) (jury to determine chance in percentage terms); Falcon v. Memorial Hospital, 436 Mich. 443, 462 N.W.2d 44, 52 (1990) ("37.5 percent times the damages recoverable for wrongful death"); Perez v. Las Vegas Medical Center, 107 Nev. 1, 805 P.2d 589 (1991); Roberts v. Ohio Permanente Medical Group, Inc., 76 Ohio St.3d 483, 668 N.E.2d 480 (1996); McKellips v. Saint Francis Hospital, Inc., 741 P.2d 467 (Okl.1987) ("The amount of damages recoverable is equal to the percent of chance lost multiplied by the total amount of damages which are ordinarily allowed in a wrongful death action"). Some of the cases appear to lean toward such calculations without actually stating them in so many words. See Aasheim v. Humberger, 215 Mont. 127, 695 P.2d 824 (Mont. 1985); Herskovits v. Group Health Cooperative, 99 Wn.2d 609, 664 P.2d 474 (1983) (damages should be based on the harms "caused directly by premature death"). There may be a conceptual and technical problem in fitting the claim to the wrongful death statute. *Falcon,* supra, at 56, regarded the claim as a survival action, but also spoke of figuring damages by a percentage of the wrongful death recovery.

13. Smith v. State, 676 So.2d 543 (La. 1996).

14. Hicks v. United States, 368 F.2d 626 (4th Cir.1966); Hamil v. Bashline, 481 Pa. 256, 392 A.2d 1280 (1978).

15. See § 173 (where defendant creates a risk of the very harm that occurred, courts often permit inference of causation). Courts may deal with the causal problems in unquantified chance cases without reference to lost chance precedent or preponderance of evidence rules at all, simply by saying that the evidence was sufficient to permit a jury finding of causation. E.g., First Commercial Trust Company v. Rank,

recovery. In those circumstances, the choice of full recovery might not forecast a rejection of the more limited value of the chance recovery in cases where the evidence quantifies the chance and thus permits an apportionment. This line of thought suggests that the problem is not necessarily one to be resolved by a categorical rule of law but by assessment of the evidence to determine whether a basis for apportionment exists.[16] If it does, then liability can be limited accordingly. If not, then the defendant would be fully liable.

§ 179. Scope of Increased Risk Rules

Rationalizing the Scope of Increased Risk Liability

When the chance is not quantified. When courts permit a full recovery for loss of a chance that is not quantified by the evidence, they perhaps do no more than courts have long done in a variety of cases—they let the jury infer causation in fact because there is no basis for apportioning causation.[1] Such cases do not seem different in principle from those which allow a finding of causation when the swimmer drowns in the absence of a required lifeguard. No one knows for sure whether the lifeguard would have saved the swimmer, but the jury can estimate the probabilities.[2] Such cases, then, are capable of generalization and application to a wide variety of situations so long as the preponderance of the evidence shows that the defendant's negligent conduct was a substantial factor.

When the chance is quantified and less than likely. When, however, the chance is quantified by evidence that assigns it a percentage value, decisions allowing either a full recovery or a value of the chance recovery represent a relatively new departure and the question is whether they have any application beyond the doctor-patient situation already discussed. So far, at least, the value of the chance recovery appears permissible in two situations: (1) The plaintiff has in fact suffered an injury and the problem is "how to reflect the presence of a preexisting condition" in assessing damages; (2) the defendant undertook a duty to maximize the plaintiff's best outcomes, or was assigned such a duty by law.[3]

323 Ark. 390, 915 S.W.2d 262 (1996) (jury could conclude that if doctor had reported suspected child abuse, the investigation that would have resulted would have resulted in no official action but would have deterred abuser).

16. See Anderson v. Picciotti, 144 N.J. 195, 676 A.2d 127 (1996) (although New Jersey has adopted value of the chance rules, evidence in the particular case required use of ordinary but-for instruction).

§ 179

1. § 173.

2. This line of cases was expressly relied upon in Thompson v. Sun City Community Hospital, Inc., 141 Ariz. 597, 688 P.2d 605 (1984) even though the chance in that case was quantified.

3. See Joseph H. King, Jr., "Reduction of Likelihood" Reformulation and other Retrofitting of the Loss-of-a-Chance Doctrine, 28 Mem. St. U. L. Rev. 492, 559 (1998).

—Duty to maximize chances. The fundamental issue is the scope of the defendant's duty to use care to maximize the plaintiff's chances.[4] In the doctor-patient cases the duty to maximize chances seems abundantly clear. The patient retains the doctor for the very purpose of maximizing chances at health and survival and the doctor at least implicitly undertakes to do so. It is therefore not surprising that courts have recognized a doctor's duty to use care to maximize chances and consequent liability for negligent failure to do so.[5]

—Stranger cases. The same rationale does not readily apply to, say, ordinary automobile cases. Although some thinkers have advocated widespread or universal use of increased rules and proportional liability,[6] courts have not so far applied the medical value of the chance rules in stranger cases.[7]

—Special relationship cases. On the other hand, the doctor-patient relationship is not the only one in which an actor might be regarded as undertaking to maximize chances. In *Gardner v. National Bulk Carriers, Inc.*,[8] for example, the captain of a ship discovered that at some unknown time in the past five hours, a seaman had been lost overboard. The master of the vessel, regarding a rescue effort as hopeless, did not make one. The trial court thought that a rescue effort would probably not have succeeded. On appeal, Judge Sobeloff held that the issue was one of duty and that the master had a duty to make a "sincere attempt" at rescue, even if success was not likely. Perhaps loss of chance reasoning also explains why courts think that a helpless victim is worse off when a rescuer discontinues his efforts.[9]

—Toxic tort cases. A number of writers have suggested that some form of increased risk or proportional causation—that is, liability in proportion to the risk or causal contribution—would be especially appropriate in many environmental and toxic tort cases. For example, if an industrial plant releases carcinogens, exposing 1000 people to an increased risk of cancer, some of those people would be expected to have cancer in any event. That situation parallels the preexisting condition situation in the doctor-patient cases. If 20 people would normally suffer cancers but 40 people actually do suffer cancers after the release of toxic materials, there is no obvious way to determine whether any one plaintiff would have suffered cancer without the release. A proportional

4. Falcon v. Memorial Hospital, 436 Mich. 443, 462 N.W.2d 44 (1990); see also Thompson v. Sun City Community Hospital, Inc., 141 Ariz. 597, 688 P.2d 605 (1984). Falcon was in effect overruled by statute. Mich. Comp. Laws Ann. § 600.2912a (2).

5. However, perhaps because of legislation affecting the issue, Michigan held that its lost chance rule did not apply to medical malpractice when the chance lost was the chance of retaining kidney function rather than the chance of retaining life itself. Weymers v. Khera, 454 Mich. 639, 563 N.W.2d 647 (1997).

6. See Makdisi, Proportional Liability: A Comprehensive Rule to Apportion Tort Damages Based on Probability, 67 N.C. L. Rev. 1063 (1989).

7. In Hardy v. Southwestern Bell Tel. Co., 910 P.2d 1024 (Okl.1996) the court refused to hold the telephone company liable for phone failure that may have reduced a customer's chances of survival when the 911 number could not be reached.

8. Gardner v. National Bulk Carriers, Inc., 310 F.2d 284, 91 A.L.R.2d 1023 (1962).

9. See § 318.

causation approach might allow all plaintiffs to recover, but only to the extent their risk was increased.[10] Some form of proportional causation can also be used to allocate liabilities among different defendants.[11]

The reasons for using proportional causation or increased risk rules in these cases are not like the reasons for doing so in the doctor-patient cases. It is not the special undertaking or relationship that might justify such rules in toxic tort cases. The emphasis instead is likely to be on the fact that exposure levels are low and that when the figures are less dramatic than those given here, plaintiffs might go uncompensated and defendants might go undeterred. But it has been argued that proportional liability may actually undermine deterrence[12] and it remains to be seen what courts and legislatures will do with proportional causation in toxic tort cases.

The upshot is that courts can impose a duty to maximize chances whenever that is appropriate in the light of legal policy, of the parties' relationship, or of the undertakings of the defendant. Courts know perfectly well both how to expand and contain such duties to the limits of the justice and policy involved in the particular setting.

Increased Risk of Future Harm

One important distinction remains. In the doctor-patient cases the defendant negligently risked harm to the patient and that very harm in fact came about. Those cases are not necessarily good precedent for liability when the defendant creates a risk of future harm that has not yet in fact occurred and that may never do so.[13] Courts have consequently denied claims for proportional recovery based on an increased risk of future harm that is not more probable than not to occur[14] and that is entirely separable from the harm that has already occurred.[15] Some courts have recognized an exception that is extremely limited by allow-

10. See II American Law Institute, The Reporters' Study, Enterprise Responsibility for Personal Injury 370 (1991). Other kind of allocation among plaintiffs is possible. See Daniel Farber, Toxic Causation, 71 Minn. L. Rev. 1219 (1987).

11. See Gerald Boston, Toxic Apportionment: A Causation and Risk Contribution Model, 25 Envtl. L. 549 (1995).

12. David A. Fischer, Proportional Liability: Statistical Evidence and the Probability Paradox, 46 Vand. L. Rev. 1201 (1993).

13. See David A. Fischer, Proportional Liability: Statistical Evidence and the Probability Paradox, 46 Vand. L. Rev. 1201 (1993) (distinguishing proportional damage recovery from proportional risk recovery and both from the creation of a fund proportioned to risks but set aside to be paid only when the risk eventuates); Joseph H. King, Jr., "Reduction of Likelihood" Reformulation and other Retrofitting of the Loss-of-a-Chance Doctrine, 28 Mem. St. U. L. Rev. 492, 560 (1998).

14. Hagerty v. L. & L. Marine Serv. Inc., 788 F.2d 315 (5th Cir.1986); Mauro v. Raymark Industries, Inc., 116 N.J. 126, 138, 561 A.2d 257, 264 (1989). But cf. Petriello v. Kalman, 215 Conn. 377, 576 A.2d 474 (1990) (plaintiff had present injury caused by a doctor, which left the plaintiff an 8–16% risk for further injury; held, the plaintiff can recover for the increased risk). As to present emotional distress arising from fear of future harm, see § 311.

15. Cf. See Joseph H. King, Jr., "Reduction of Likelihood" Reformulation and other Retrofitting of the Loss-of-a-Chance Doctrine, 28 Mem. St. U. L. Rev. 492, 510 (1998) (recovery more likely if future harm is considered part of present injury).

ing the plaintiff who is subjected to a risk of future harm like cancer to recover immediately for costs of medical monitoring.[16]

16. E.g., Simmons v. Pacor, Inc., 543 Pa. 664, 674 A.2d 232 (1996).

*

CHAPTER 10

PROXIMATE CAUSE

TOPIC A. PROXIMATE CAUSE RULES. REASON AND STRUCTURE

§ 180. Introducing the Proximate Cause Requirement

Proximate cause requirement. To prevail in a negligence action, the plaintiff must bear the burden of showing that the defendant's negligent conduct was not only a cause in fact of the plaintiff's harm, but also a proximate or legal cause.[1]

Function in limiting scope of responsibility. Proximate cause rules are among those rules that seek to determine the appropriate scope of a negligent defendant's liability.[2] The central goal of the proximate cause requirement is to limit the defendant's liability to the kinds of harms he risked by his negligent conduct. Judicial decisions about proximate cause rules thus attempt to discern whether, in the particular case before the court, the harm that resulted from the defendant's negligence is so clearly outside the risks he created that it would be unjust or at least impractical to impose liability. The proximate cause issue, in spite of the terminology, is not about causation at all but about the appropriate scope of responsibility.[3] The issue does not arise until negligence and causation in fact have been proven.

§ 180

1. Legal shorthand expressions sometimes refer to the "proximate cause defense," but proximate cause is an element of the plaintiff's case, not an affirmative defense. See Korando v. Uniroyal Goodrich Tire Co., 159 Ill.2d 335, 637 N.E.2d 1020, 202 Ill.Dec. 284 (1994). Cause in fact, discussed in the preceding chapter, is an element separate from proximate cause, as all courts recognize. However, it is quite common for courts to speak as if these two elements are subparts of a larger element, also called legal or proximate cause. E.g., Skinner v. Square D Company, 445 Mich. 153, 516 N.W.2d 475 (1994). On the terminology of proximate cause and cause in fact, see § 167. This book uses proximate cause only to refer to the scope of liability issue, not to cause in fact.

2. Other rules, those limiting the duty owed by defendants, also seek to impose limits on liability for conduct that would otherwise be considered negligent. See § 230. Proximate cause rules exclude liability for damages, either all damages suffered or damages for particular items of loss. Thus, where the plaintiff need not prove damages, as in the case of intentional trespassory torts, proximate cause limitations may not apply, or not apply in the same way. See § 40. For the same reason, however, proximate cause limitations are fundamental and can apply in any kind of case in which damages must be proven, not merely in negligence cases. For example, proximate cause arguments may be raised in defamation cases. In contracts cases a similar idea is raised under the contemplation of the parties rule. See Hadley v. Baxendale, 9 Ex. 341, 156 Eng. Rep. 145 (1854). Proximate cause rules are also invoked in civil rights cases, see Martinez v. California, 444 U.S. 277, 100 S.Ct. 553, 62 L.Ed.2d 481 (1980), and even in purely criminal cases. E.g., Baylor v. United States,

3. § 181 below.

Illustrating the proximate cause issue. Two examples can illustrate the idea that a negligent defendant who is a but-for cause of harm should nevertheless sometimes escape liability. First, suppose that a surgeon negligently performs a vasectomy. Because the surgery was negligently performed, the patient fathers a child. The child, at the age of 13, sets fire to the plaintiff's barn. Is the surgeon liable for the loss of the barn? He was negligent in performing the vasectomy, and his negligence is a cause in fact of the fire and the loss of the barn. Almost everyone will agree, however, that while the surgeon might be liable for something, he is surely not liable for loss of the plaintiff's barn. Courts are likely in such a case to say that the surgeon's negligence is not a proximate cause of the harm done.

Second, suppose that the defendant negligently manufactures a vacuum cleaner so that it does not have good suction. After several frustrating days using the cleaner, the purchaser takes it to the repair shop. On her way to the shop, the purchaser is struck by a car and suffers injury. The manufacturer was negligent. The manufacturer's negligence was one of the many causes in fact leading to the purchaser's harm—but for the manufacturer's negligence, the purchaser would have stayed home safely cleaning carpets and would not have been struck by a car. Yet here again, legal professionals are likely to agree that the manufacturer's conduct in making the poor vacuum was not a proximate cause of the plaintiff's injury in a vehicular collision.

Foreseeability tests of proximate cause. The most general and pervasive approach to proximate cause holds that a negligent defendant is liable for all the general kinds of harms he foreseeably risked by his negligent conduct and to the class of persons he put at risk by that conduct. Conversely, he is not a proximate cause of, and not liable for injuries that were unforeseeable. This does not mean that the defendant must be the sole proximate cause of the plaintiff's injury.[4] On the contrary, several wrongdoers are frequently proximate causes of harm. In that case, are all liable to the plaintiff, either jointly and severally or on the basis of their comparative fault shares.

On the other hand, if a second person or a new force unforeseeably intervenes to trigger the plaintiff's injury after the defendant's act is complete, responsibility for the injury falls solely upon the second actor.[5] The second actor's unforeseeable conduct in such a case will be called a superseding cause. In these intervening cause cases, courts may phrase the foreseeability test somewhat narrowly, by asking whether the intervening cause itself was foreseeable rather than by asking whether the general type of harm was foreseeable. Under either version of the foreseeability test, courts appear to be working toward the same central idea, that the defendant's liability is limited to those harms he risked by

4. Ehrgott v. City of N.Y., 96 N.Y. 264 (1884); Travis v. City of Mesquite, 830 S.W.2d 94 (Tex.1992). Although the point is well-settled and logically inescapable, courts often speak of "the" proximate cause, presumably without meaning to attack the settled rule.

5. §§ 192 & 197.

his negligence so that he escapes liability altogether for those harms that were not reasonably foreseeable at the time he acted.

Remoteness. Courts sometimes use short phrases to express ideas about proximate cause. They may say or imply that a cause of harm is not proximate if it is insignificant, remote, or logically unrelated to the harm that follows. These phrases point in the right direction, but they are incomplete. The word proximate means near or next or most immediate, and taken literally it suggests that only the most immediate trigger of harm can be the proximate cause. That simply is not the law. Several tortfeasors may all be proximate causes of a single harm; the first tortfeasor in a sequence of events as well as the last is often a proximate and responsible cause. And the defendant's misconduct is not too remote for liability merely because time or distance separates the defendant's act from the plaintiff's harm.[6] A manufacturer whose negligent construction leads to the explosion of a space ship is no doubt a proximate cause of the resulting death and destruction even if the explosion occurs millions of miles away. A doctor who negligently withdraws a psychotic patient's medication may be liable for the patient's murderous acts months later.[7] Nor is the defendant's negligent conduct legally insignificant merely because it is not very bad. In countless cases, defendants are held responsible for injuries inflicted in a moment's inattentiveness at the wheel of a car. The test, once again, turns on some version of reasonable foreseeability, not on mechanics.

§ 181. Reasons for Proximate Cause Limitations

Practical concerns. Why is a defendant, whose negligent act has caused harm, allowed to avoid liability under the proximate cause rules? Courts and writers often suggest that the proximate cause limitation is imposed only or mainly for practical reasons.[1] Without a proximate cause limit, liability, they say, would go on forever, one harm leading endlessly to others. The negligently made vacuum requires a trip to the repair shop, which leads the user to an auto accident, which leads to medical attention, which leads to another injury, which leads to loss of a job, and so on, more or less without end. The argument is that the line against liability must be drawn somewhere and that the proximate cause rules reflect the effort courts make to draw that line.

6. See, e.g., Stephenson v. Air Products and Chemicals, Inc., 114 Ill.App.2d 124, 252 N.E.2d 366 (1969) (as a result of injury caused by defendant, plaintiff suffered a second injury five years later).

7. Estates of Morgan v. Fairfield Family Counseling Center, 77 Ohio St.3d 284, 673 N.E.2d 1311 (1997).

§ 181

1. See Andrews, J., dissenting in Palsgraf v. Long Island R.R., 248 N.Y. 339, 162 N.E. 99, 59 A.L.R. 1253 (1928) ("What we do mean by the word 'proximate' is that, because of convenience, of public policy, of a rough sense of justice, the law arbitrarily declines to trace a series of events beyond a certain point. This is not logic. It is practical politics"); Poskus v. Lombardo's of Randolph, Inc., 670 N.E.2d 383, 423 Mass. 637 (1996) ("There must be limits to the scope or definition of reasonable foreseeability based on considerations of policy and pragmatic judgment"); JOHN G. FLEMING, THE LAW OF TORTS 203 (8th ed. 1992).

Principled limitations. The reasons for proximate cause limitations on liability may be principled as well as practical. Judgments about proximate cause are not precise, but, at least roughly speaking, they reflect the ideas of justice as well as practicality.[2] In particular, they attempt to limit liability to the reasons for imposing liability in the first place. For instance, if the defendant is considered to be negligent only because it makes a vacuum cleaner that does not clean well, it should not be held liable when the purchaser is in an automobile accident while taking the cleaner to be repaired. The defendant in such a case negligently created a risk that the cleaner was not worth its price or that carpets would remain dirty. If the defendant is liable at all, those are the kinds of harms to which liability extends. But equally, the defendant's liability should be limited to such harms, for those are the ones that led us to say the defendant was negligent. Proximate cause rules, which may dictate these results, can be seen as limiting liability to its reasons.

As a corollary to negligence rules. Proximate cause concerns are not limited to negligence cases.[3] Where negligence cases are concerned, however, a rule limiting liability for risk to the scope of the risk may be viewed as a corollary to or even a part of the basic rule of negligence.[4] Negligence rules say that the defendant is free to ignore risks (foreseeable harms) that a reasonable person would ignore. This might be the case because the risks are small or because the costs of avoiding the risks are too high. If the scope of liability were not limited to the scope of the risk, the defendant would not, after all, be free to ignore small risks or risks that should be taken.

For example, suppose the defendant parks his car on the street, parallel to the curb, in a no-parking zone. This conduct is negligent because it runs the risk that traffic will be impeded, but leaving a car parked in a no-parking zone does not negligently create a risk of injury to an able bodied pedestrian. Courts are likely to say that the driver is not a proximate cause of the pedestrian's harm from walking into the car, even though other risks made it negligent to park the car in such a way.[5]

2. "[Proximate cause doctrine is] an instrument of fairness and policy, although the conclusion is frequently expressed in the confusing language of causation, foreseeability and natural and probable consequences.... The determination of proximate cause by a court is to be based upon mixed considerations of logic, common sense, justice, policy and precedent." Zaza v. Marquess and Nell, Inc., 144 N.J. 34, 675 A.2d 620 (1996).

3. Proximate cause rules or some close analog may be applied, for example, in some strict liability cases.

4. Cf. Mark F. Grady, Proximate Cause and the Law of Negligence, 69 Iowa L. Rev. 363 (1984).

5. Some readers may be tempted to say that the pedestrian should be barred for an entirely different reason, namely that injury from walking into the car was the pedestrian's own fault. Under the old common law rules of contributory negligence, the pedestrian would be barred for that reason, but that is not necessarily so under modern comparative negligence rules that simply reduce the pedestrian's recovery. The reason to deny all recovery is that injury to the pedestrian in the example is not one of the risks that was foreseeable to a reasonable defendant and hence not within the risk that would lead us to say he is negligent in the first place.

As this illustration suggests, the risk rule of proximate cause and the ordinary rule of negligence are perhaps two aspects of the same underlying idea. With suitable adaptations to the facts of particular cases, this principle, or something very close to it, furnishes a guide to proximate cause limitations on liability.

The language of foreseeability and risk. Professional usage almost always reduces proximate cause issues to the question of foreseeability. The defendant must have been reasonably able to foresee the kind of harm that was actually suffered by the plaintiff (or in some cases to foresee that the harm might come about through intervention of others). For the ordinary case, the principles behind proximate cause limitations can be implemented quite well by use of this language. However, the term foreseeability is itself a kind of shorthand. The defendant is not liable merely because he could foresee harm; the harm must be the kind that he should have avoided by acting more carefully. That is what is meant by saying that the harm suffered by the plaintiff must have been within the scope of the risk the defendant negligently created. Risks that the defendant could foresee but that are risks reasonably taken are no more a basis for finding proximate cause than for finding negligence.

Limited functions and capacities of proximate cause rules. The function of proximate cause rules is to facilitate or express a value judgment about the appropriate scope of liability of a defendant who is negligent and whose negligence in fact causes harm. The rules and definitions are not primarily aimed at guiding the defendant's conduct but at guiding or expressing judgment about that conduct. The proximate cause rules give us the language of argument and direct the thought that is brought to bear when the connection between the defendant's negligence and the plaintiff's injury seems tenuous. The rules call for judgments, not juggernauts of logic. In consequence, no version of the rules can be expected to assure any given answer in a particular case,[6] and proximate cause issues must always be determined by the jury on the particular facts of the case.[7]

§ 182. Relation to Cause in Fact, Negligence, and Duty Issues

Cause in Fact and Proximate Cause

Conflating proximate and actual cause issues. One major source of confusion about proximate cause lies in the fact that many courts so define the term that it has two distinct meanings. In one form or another, courts often say that the plaintiff, to prove proximate cause, must show (a) cause in fact[1] and (b) that the harm or its manner of

6. See §§ 182 & 227 on using duty concepts to exclude liability in whole categories of cases.

7. E.g., Hollingsworth v. Schminkey, 553 N.W.2d 591 (Iowa 1996); Louk v. Isuzu Motors, Inc., 198 W.Va. 250, 479 S.E.2d 911 (1996).

1. This is the meaning of the statement that a cause of harm must lead in continuous or natural sequence to the harm and in addition must be a cause without which the

occurrence was foreseeable.[2] The effect of this definition is that two distinct legal issues can be called by the same name. It is quite correct to say that the plaintiff must normally prove cause in fact and that if the plaintiff fails to do so, she will lose. However, cause in fact has little or nothing to do with the foreseeability or scope of liability issues to which the proximate cause rules are otherwise directed. When courts conflate the two issues or group them together under the rubric of proximate cause, lawyers cannot always be sure whether the judge is talking about cause in fact or scope of liability problems. Indeed, judges sometimes seem to shift the meanings of the term without realizing it.

Proximate cause: not causation but scope of liability. It should be obvious that if the issue of proximate cause is largely an issue of foreseeability or scope of the risk, it has little to do with cause in fact.[3] For greater clarity, some thinkers would prefer to drop the term proximate cause because the term wrongly suggests that the issue is about causation. They are right that the term itself is misleading. Pervasive professional usage, however, makes it difficult to drop the term entirely. To avoid confusing the scope of risk issue with the cause in fact issue, this book does not use the term proximate or legal cause to encompass cause in fact issues. Instead, the term proximate cause as used in this book refers to issues of policy and justice about the scope of the risks and the scope of appropriate liability of a defendant whose negligence has in fact caused the plaintiff's harm.

Negligence and Proximate Cause

Negligence foreseeability vs. proximate cause foreseeability. The issue of proximate cause does not arise at all unless the defendant is negligent in a way that can be identified. If the defendant is negligent, that necessarily means he should have foreseen some harm, of some kind, to some person or property. The foreseeability question left to be determined under the proximate cause rules is whether he should have foreseen the kind of harm that in fact resulted and whether the plaintiff was within the class of persons to whom such harm might foreseeably befall.

Examples: negligence issues only. Although the difference between foreseeability on the negligence issue and foreseeability on the proximate cause issue seems obvious, it is easy to overlook. Keys-in-the-car cases are good examples. If I leave the keys in the ignition of my parked car, I am surely foolish but not necessarily negligent. I would be negligent only if I should foresee that some dangerous use of the car might follow,

injury would not have occurred. See Anderson v. Nebraska Dept. of Social Services, 248 Neb. 651, 538 N.W.2d 732 (1995); Delbrel v. Doenges Bros. Ford, Inc., 913 P.2d 1318 (Okl.1996).

2. The formulas and their interpretation are considered in § 183.

3. See Baltimore Gas & Elec. Co. v. Lane, 338 Md. 34, 656 A.2d 307 (1995) (the question whether conduct is "a legally cognizable cause" "is essentially one of fairness and social policy"). Courts may also limit liability for reasons other than those associated with the scope of the risk or the kinds of harm foreseeable, but these reasons are usually considered under the rubric of duty.

perhaps because a thief takes the car and drives it negligently. If I can foresee negligent driving by the thief, and if a reasonable person keeps his keys to avoid the risks of reckless thieves, then I am negligent in leaving keys in the car. If the plaintiff is injured when a thief speeds from the scene, the trier's decision that I was negligent is a decision that also answers any proximate cause issue, because it means that I should have foreseen the thief and his reckless driving. On the other hand, if a reasonable person could not be expected to foresee a thief's negligent driving, then it is hard to see how I am negligent in leaving the keys in the car at all, since the worst that could happen would be my loss, not injury to another. In cases like this, no substantial issue of proximate cause arises. The issue is instead about negligence.

Example: when proximate cause issue arises. None of this is to deny that proximate cause issues appropriately arise in many cases. If the thief who finds the owner's keys in the car drives safely away, sells the car to a dealer, who sells it to a retired lawyer, the lawyer's negligence in driving the car into the plaintiff is not proximately caused by the defendant who left the keys in the ignition. In that case we can see that the driver might be negligent because he should foresee a risk of a thief's negligent driving at some point in time soon after the theft. But he did not negligently create a risk that a normal driver would cause injury. The defendant who was careless of his keys risked harm, but not this kind of harm or by these means. The foreseeability issue in this example is about proximate cause, not about negligence, and its answer is that the defendant is not a proximate cause of the harm resulting from the lawyer's driving.

Duty and Proximate Cause

Rules limiting the defendant's duty. Courts immunize some defendants from liability, so that in particular cases a defendant who is guilty of unreasonably risky conduct is nevertheless protected from liability, even as to entirely foreseeable harms. When courts so hold, they often say the protected defendant owes no duty to the plaintiff or that the protected defendant owes only a duty not to be grossly or wantonly negligent. These decisions protect negligent defendants. Proximate cause rules also protect negligent defendants, so the limited duty rules and the proximate cause rules have something in common. In fact, some courts will use the language of proximate cause to resolve some cases that other courts might resolve in the language of duty. The duty and proximate cause analyses are not, however, usefully interchangeable, even though either might get the other's result.

Duty or proximate cause: judge and jury. First, the question whether a defendant owes any duty of care and what standard of care is owed is a question of law for judges to decide. For example, courts make rules of law describing the limited duty owed by landowners to trespassers. In contrast, proximate cause issues are for the jury to decide unless the

issue is so clear that reasonable people could not differ.[4]

Duty or proximate cause: categorical vs. fact-specific decisions. Second, duty rules are classically categorical and abstract; they cover a class or category of cases. Special rules of limited duty may apply, for example, to landowners or to parents who injure their children. A court's decision to hold parents to some limited duty rather than to the ordinary duty of reasonable care must be applied, like any other rule, in the light of the facts of particular cases. But the decision to provide a general immunity for parents who negligently supervise their children is purely one for the court and that decision does not turn on facts of individual cases. In contrast, proximate cause decisions are quite fact-specific. Indeed, one of the difficulties with proximate cause cases is that they cannot easily be generalized. Proximate cause issues, then, turn on factual findings and "evaluative conclusions,"[5] primarily about foreseeability, and hence are fact specific rather than categorical.[6]

Duty or proximate cause: type of policy concerns involved. Finally, although policy concerns about liability can often be expressed either in the language of proximate cause or the language of duty, proximate cause is most centrally concerned with one particular policy or justice issue. It is concerned with limiting liability to risks the defendant negligently created. Duty issues are much broader. Courts may have many reasons, good or bad, for limiting liability. Some of those reasons relate not at all to the foreseeability of harm that is central in proximate cause cases. For instance, courts may hold that social hosts may continue to serve alcohol to a guest long after his intoxication is apparent and in spite of the fact that he will foreseeability attempt to drive a car and thus impose risks of harm to others. Because it was foreseeable that the drinker would drive negligently and cause injuries, it seems preposterous to say that the alcohol server was not a proximate cause of the victim's injury. If he is not to be liable, the reason, good or bad, lies elsewhere. Consequently, many decisions once cast in terms of proximate cause are now discussed in terms of duty, where policy concerns completely alien to foreseeability can be analyzed.

Simplification by excluding duty issues. Most issues that can now be seen as issues about the existence of a defendant's duty rather than issues primarily about foreseeability of harm are excluded from this chapter and left for coverage in the chapters on duty. For example, courts treat stand-alone emotional distress quite differently from ordinary physical injuries. In doing so, they have sometimes used the language of proximate cause. In spite of this, their real concerns have

4. E.g., Anselmo v. Tuck, 325 Ark. 211, 924 S.W.2d 798 (1996); McClung v. Delta Square Limited Partnership, 937 S.W.2d 891 (Tenn.1996).

5. Prosser & Keeton on Torts 274 (5th ed. 1985) emphasized that the jury's role, although conventionally described as fact-finding, entailed evaluation more than a determination of facts verifiable through the senses. It might be added that it also entails evaluation about the particular case before the court, not about categories of cases generally.

6. See Buck v. Union Electric Co., 887 S.W.2d 430 (Mo.App.1994).

not been about foreseeability at all but about the appropriate scope of duty or responsibility for emotional conditions. Leaving these and other similar cases to be resolved under the duty concept permits a coherent view of proximate cause presented in this chapter.

The duty vs. proximate cause debate. Is it better to limit liability by saying that the defendant was under no duty, or by saying that the defendant was not a proximate cause of the harm? This is a long-standing and worthwhile question. The distinctions drawn above suggest that when the court wishes to make a categorical rule and one not wholly dependant upon foreseeability, the issue can usefully be characterized as one of duty rather than one of proximate cause. Be that as it may, however, the debate about appropriate terminology is not always the same as the debate about the appropriate substantive limitations on liability. The famous *Palsgraf* case[7] complicated the lives of generations of law students by tying the terminology question to the substantive question. Judge Cardozo and the majority insisted that the issue should be cast in the terminology of duty (or negligence) and that the substantive rule should relieve the defendant of liability if harm to the plaintiff was unforeseeable. Judge Andrews and the dissenters thought that the issue should be cast in the terminology of proximate cause and that as a matter of substantive law, foreseeability should *not* be determinative. In contemporary law, the terminology distinction has become unimportant whenever the court concludes that the harm inflicted was unforeseeable. Most courts today agree that, whether the issue is one of duty or of proximate cause, the defendant is not liable for unforeseeable kinds of harm. The distinction remains important, however, when courts wish to limit liability for reasons unrelated to foreseeability.

§ 183. Patterns and Formal Tests of Proximate Cause

Courts perceive proximate cause issues in two distinct patterns. Although they ultimately concern themselves with foreseeability in both patterns, the formal language of discussion and the kind of foreseeability involved may depend upon which pattern is involved.

Direct harm pattern and example. In the first pattern, the defendant negligently creates a risk of a harm—call it Harm A—but an entirely different harm—Harm B—results. For example, the defendant negligently drops a banana peel on the walk, creating a foreseeable risk that someone will slip on it. The plaintiff does not slip on the banana peel but hurts her back when she bends over to pick it up. In this kind of situation most courts simply ask whether the harm that occurred was foreseeable, that is, whether it was one of the general kind of harm that was unreasonably risked by the defendant's negligence.

Intervening cause pattern and example. In the second situation, the defendant creates a risk of harm but the immediate trigger for the harm

7. Palsgraf v. Long Island Railroad Co., 248 N.Y. 339, 162 N.E. 99 (1928), discussed below, § 184.

is some other force or person. For example, the defendant negligently drops the banana peel and the plaintiff slips on it, but only because a purse snatcher pushes her as he grabs her purse. In this situation courts are also concerned with foreseeability, but they typically use more complicated language to formulate their inquiries by asking whether the purse snatcher may have been a new cause that superseded the negligence of the banana peel dropper.

Substantial identity of issues. In a strictly literal sense, perhaps all cases belong in the intervening cause category. The plaintiff who injured her back in bending over to pick up the banana peel could be viewed as herself an intervening cause. Almost inevitably, something, if only the movement of air, must intervene between the defendant's act and the plaintiff's injury. But it is also true that the intervening cause cases all entail questions about the scope of the risk, so they can be resolved without a mention of intervening or superseding causes.[1] The distinction between direct and indirect causes could very well be abolished, leaving courts merely to ask whether the injury that occurred was within the risk created by the defendant. Indeed, the cases as a whole may have that effect. Nevertheless, in some cases, courts selectively ignore intervening cause analysis while in others they reach out for it. If the result is the same overall, the language of the opinions is not, so the distinction cannot be wholly ignored.

Formal tests: substantial factor, continuing sequence and intervening cause. The term proximate cause by itself explains nothing, not even the kind of evidence to be considered. In an effort to define the term, courts have at various times invoked a litany of equally impenetrable phrases, some of them simply opaque, others actively misleading. Some of those that are not in common use can be left to a footnote.[2]

§ 183

1. E.g., Sharp v. Town of Highland, 665 N.E.2d 610 (Ind.App.1996). Two leading cases, Overseas Tankship (U.K.), Limited v. Morts Dock & Engineering Co., Limited (The Wagon Mound), [1961] A.C. 388 (Privy Council 1961) and Palsgraf v. Long Island Railroad Co., 248 N.Y. 339, 162 N.E. 99 (1928), could have been resolved by discussing intervening causes, but both courts went straight to the foreseeability issue without first discussing intervening cause.

2. At one time, some authorities said that to be a proximate cause, the defendant's conduct must be a substantial factor in causing the plaintiff's harm. That term explains nothing about what to look for and runs the risk of confusing cause in fact issues to which it is sometimes applied in lieu of the but-for test. See David W. Robertson, The Common Sense of Cause in Fact, 75 TEX. L. REV. 1765 (1997).

Another test, the hindsight test, was actually approved by the Restatement in § 435 (2). It asks whether, looking backward at events, it seems "extraordinary" that the defendant's conduct should have caused harm. This approach is no more certain than the foreseeability rule, and it may only be a way of saying that the exact harm or the manner of its occurrence need not be foreseeable. If it is anything different from this, it seems to lack the moral basis of the foreseeability test. A few courts have invoked a hindsight test in connection with superseding cause issues. See Petolicchio v. Santa Cruz County Fair and Rodeo Assn., Inc., 177 Ariz. 256, 263, 866 P.2d 1342, 1349 (1994) ("An event is superseding only if it was both unforeseeable and when with the benefit of 'hindsight' it may be described as abnormal or extraordinary").

Another idea was to say that the defendant's conduct is a proximate cause if the plaintiff's harm is justly attachable to it. Academic ideas in earlier years tended to offer blockbuster principles or a series of mechanical rules. None of these has worked

With slight variations in the words, courts usually instruct juries or begin their own appellate discussions with a formal definition asserting that a proximate cause of an injury is one which, in a natural and continuous sequence, without any efficient intervening cause, produces the injury.[3] Sometimes courts define proximate by saying that the defendant is liable only for the "natural and probable consequences" of his acts,[4] a test that arguably might be read to put slightly less emphasis on the sequence of events because it is quickly reduced nowadays to a foreseeability test.[5] In either case, if the plaintiff's injury is triggered by a new or intervening cause—one arising after the defendant's negligent act—courts may conclude that the new cause is a superseding cause and that the defendant is relieved of liability.

As the test is stated, the emphasis on sequence and intervening causes seems to depart from a foreseeability rule. But analysis, and most actual decisions as well, indicate that the test ultimately asks judges or juries to consider the reasonable foreseeability of the harm caused or the forces involved in causing it. As succeeding sections show, judges considering the first or direct harm pattern of cases usually want to know whether the general type of harm is foreseeable, while judges considering the second or intervening cause pattern may want to know whether the intervening actor or the force he represents is foreseeable.

§ 184. The Direct Cause Pattern: Liability Limited to Foreseeable Harms

The basic issue. In the direct cause pattern, the defendant negligently risks one kind of harm but an entirely different kind of harm befalls the plaintiff. The problem in such cases is not that some new cause supersedes the defendant's liability, although courts often try to impose a superseding cause analysis upon such cases. The only problem is whether to impose liability for unforeseeable kinds of harm.

Liability limited to foreseeable harms. The great majority of cases hold negligent defendants liable only for harm of the same general kind that they should have reasonably foreseen and should have acted to avoid.[1] The same principle holds defendants liable only to plaintiffs who

well. A summary of these tests can be found in PROSSER & KEETON ON TORTS 276–279.

3. Milwaukee & S.P. Ry. v. Kellogg, 94 U.S. (4 Otto) 469, 24 L.Ed. 256 (1876) (the facts must "constitute a continuous succession of events, so linked together as to make a natural whole" without a "new and independent cause intervening between the wrong and the injury"); Anselmo v. Tuck, 325 Ark. 211, 924 S.W.2d 798 (1996); CSX Transportation, Inc. v. Continental Ins. Co., 343 Md. 216, 680 A.2d 1082 (1996) ("cause which, in a natural and continuous sequence, unbroken by any efficient intervening cause, logically and probably produces the injury").

4. E.g., Gilmore v. Shell Oil Co., 613 So.2d 1272 (Ala.1993).

5. See, e.g., Ross v. Nutt, 177 Ohio St. 113, 114, 203 N.E.2d 118, 120 (1964) ("To find that an injury was the natural and probable consequence of an act, it must appear that the injury complained of could have been foreseen or reasonably anticipated from the alleged negligent act").

§ 184

1. Tetro v. Town of Stratford, 189 Conn. 601, 605, 458 A.2d 5, 7–8 (1983) ("The test for finding proximate cause 'is whether the harm which occurred was of the same general nature as the foreseeable

are in the same general class of people who were at risk from his negligence.[2] These rules make liability congruent with risk or foreseeability. Affirmatively, the defendant is liable for the type of harm he unreasonably risked. Negatively, the defendant is not liable for types of harm that he could not reasonably foresee or those that were foreseeable but were risked by non-negligent, reasonably safe conduct.

The foreseeability rule does not allow a negligent defendant to avoid liability merely because a reasonable person would not have foreseen specific details about the injury or how it happened. It is enough for liability that the kinds of risks, harms, or classes of person were foreseeable in a general way.[3] Similarly, the negligent defendant does not avoid liability merely because the extent of injury is far greater than he could reasonably have foreseen.[4]

The Wagon Mound illustration: type of harm risked. Since the 1960s, an English case has provided a basic model for the foreseeability or risk rule. A ship known as the Wagon Mound, which gives its name to the case,[5] was anchored in the harbor at Sydney, Australia. The ship negligently discharged oil into the water, but, strange to say, the oil created no discernible risk of fire because its composition required very high heat to ignite it.[6] Although the oil created no foreseeable risk of fire, it did create some other risks, most notably the risk that docks in the area would be fouled. To everyone's surprise—a phrase that can almost always announce a proximate cause issue—an improbable concatenation of events led to a fire after all. A piece of debris was floating on the water just under the oil. On the debris a piece of cotton was supported, all apparently by chance. A welder's torch gave off sparks that struck the cotton. The cotton smoldered long enough to acquire sufficient heat to ignite the oil, and the plaintiff's dock was burned.

risk created by the defendant's negligence.' . . . The foreseeable risk may include the acts of the plaintiff and of third parties"); Haynes v. Hamilton County, 883 S.W.2d 606, 611 (Tenn.1994) (proximate cause is shown when cause in fact is proved and "the harm giving rise to the action could have reasonably been foreseen or anticipated by a person of ordinary intelligence and prudence"). The foreseeability rule may be stated as a rule that the defendant owes no duty or is not negligent except as to foreseeable risks. Di Ponzio v. Riordan, 89 N.Y.2d 578, 679 N.E.2d 616, 657 N.Y.S.2d 377 (1997). Many, many decisions obtain such scope-of-risk results, but may add extraneous language on the topic of intervening cause or may rely on the old cause-condition catchphrase. E.g., Sheehan v. City of New York, 40 N.Y.2d 496, 387 N.Y.S.2d 92, 354 N.E.2d 832 (1976).

2. E.g., Splendorio v. Bilray Demolition Co., Inc., 682 A.2d 461 (R.I.1996).

3. See § 189. In relatively rare cases, however, the defendant may create a risk that foreseeably will arise only through one mechanism or through one sequence of events. In such a case, a different mechanism of harm, or a different sequence of events, may induce courts to limit liability under the proximate cause rules.

4. § 188.

5. Overseas Tankship (U.K.), Limited v. Morts Dock & Engineering Co., Limited (The Wagon Mound), [1961] A.C. 388 (Privy Council 1961).

6. For purposes of the decision, the House of Lords accepted the finding that fire was not foreseeable. Later evidence might cast the finding in doubt, but for purposes of the case, it must be taken as true.

Under English authority existing up until that time, it would have been possible to reason that the defendant should be liable for the fire because there were no new independent causes of it; the defendant was a direct cause and that would have been enough for liability.[7] But the Privy Council adopted the risk rule instead. It held that liability for negligence was to be coextensive with the negligence. If the defendant negligently created a risk of harm A, but harm B resulted instead, the defendant would not be liable for harm B. The Privy Council thought that since the only harm foreseeable from negligent discharge of the oil was harm in the nature of fouled docks, the defendant should not be liable for the entirely unforeseeable harm caused by fire. One way to express the idea is to say that, as to the fire, the defendant created no unreasonable risk and hence as to the fire, the defendant was not negligent at all. American cases are overwhelmingly consistent with this rule, although their manner of expression is often slightly different.[8]

The *Wagon Mound* case should not be misunderstood. If the risk of fire had been small but foreseeable and the defendant had had a useful purpose in discharging the oil, the balance of risks and utilities might indicate that the defendant was not negligent at all and hence not liable. On the other hand, if the defendant had no good reason for discharging the oil, even a small risk of fire might be enough to justify a finding that the defendant was negligent. In that case, the fact that fire was foreseeable would indicate that the defendant should be liable for fire damage, even though the risk was small.[9]

The Palsgraf illustration: class of persons at risk. The most famous American case on proximate cause (or almost anything) is grounded in the same basic idea that liability should be limited to risks created by the defendant's negligent conduct. In *Palsgraf v. Long Island Railroad Co.*,[10] railroad employees helping a passenger onto a moving train may have negligently jostled his arm, causing him to drop a package. If the employees were negligent at all, it must have been because they created a risk of harm to the passenger, to his package, or by a stretch of imagination to someone very close by. What happened in fact was that the innocent looking package contained fireworks, which exploded when the package fell. As a result of the explosion, some scales at the other end of the platform fell on Mrs. Palsgraf.

Since the unreasonable risk created by the defendant was a risk to the passenger, or at most to a very small circle of persons who might have been close enough to be injured if he fell, it created no recognizable risk at all to Mrs. Palsgraf. As Judge Cardozo said, "Relatively to her it

7. See § 185 below.

8. See n. 1, supra.

9. This was essentially the proof in another round of the same case, Wagon Mound II, Overseas Tankship (U.K.), Ltd. v. Miller Steamship Co., [1967] 1 A.C. 617 (Privy Council 1966). Prosser saw this as a retreat from *Wagon Mound*, but it seems to be nothing more than a perfectly logical application of the rules of negligence and the foreseeability rule of proximate cause.

10. Palsgraf v. Long Island Railroad, 248 N.Y. 339, 162 N.E. 99 (1928).

was not negligence at all,"[11] so the defendant was not liable. Although Cardozo did not express this result as a rule of proximate cause, the outcome it dictates is the outcome of a proximate cause rule based on risk or foreseeability rule. "[T]he orbit of the danger as disclosed to the eye of reasonable vigilance" marked the scope of liability.[12]

Rescuers. Rescuer cases raise issues about the scope of the *Palsgraf* class-of-persons rule. In a leading case, *Wagner v. International Ry.*,[13] the defendant caused A to fall from a train into a gorge. B went in search of the body. Then B himself fell into the chasm. The trial court held that the defendant's negligence toward A would not support a claim for injury to B. This sounds like the *Palsgraf* rule, but on appeal, Judge Cardozo held that B could recover. Unfortunately, Judge Cardozo did not make it clear whether he regarded liability as an exception to *Palsgraf* or whether he believed that, since "[d]anger invites rescue," the rescue and hence the rescuer was within the scope of the foreseeable risk.

In any event, courts usually recognize that the defendant who is negligent to A may be liable to an injured rescuer,[14] B, so long as B's actions are not wholly abnormal or hopeless.[15] The rescue need not be spontaneous or immediate.[16] It has been held that B may recover for injury incurred in a reasonable rescue attempt if the defendant negligently created an appearance that rescue was needed when it was not.[17] Even when the defendant puts only himself in danger, courts have held him liable for injury to his own rescuer suffered in the course of a rescue attempt.[18] Professional rescuers like firefighters and police officers, how-

11. Palsgraf v. Long Island Railroad, 248 N.Y. 339, 162 N.E. 99, 100 (1928). Others have also observed this way of looking at proximate cause under the risk rule. E.g., Gavagan v. United States, 955 F.2d 1016 (5th Cir.1992).

12. Cardozo expressed the rule as a rule that the defendant was not negligent toward Mrs. Palsgraf and also as a rule that it owed her no duty. The dissent by Judge Andrews insisted that the issue was not about negligence or scope of duty but about proximate cause. On their different views and on the "duty" approach to scope of liability issues, see § 182. For present purposes, nomenclature is not the point.

13. Wagner v. International Ry., 232 N.Y. 176, 133 N.E. 437 (1921).

14. E.g., Thomas v. Garner, 284 Ill. App.3d 90, 672 N.E.2d 52, 219 Ill.Dec. 737 (1996) (policy favors rescue, which negates the "presumption that his intentional act of rescue is the superseding cause of his injuries, thereby allowing him to prove that defendant's negligence is the proximate cause of his injuries"); Solomon v. Shuell, 435 Mich. 104, 457 N.W.2d 669 (1990) (rescuers as a class are foreseeable); Tri–State Wholesale Associated Grocers, Inc. v. Barrera, 917 S.W.2d 391(Tex.App.1996) ("Our jurisprudence is well-settled that the acts of rescuers are generally the foreseeable results of negligent activity"); Restatement § 445. Some courts have excluded the plaintiff's claim by defining the plaintiff out of the rescuer category without discussing the basis in foreseeability or other policy. Cf. Lambert v. Parrish, 492 N.E.2d 289 (Ind. 1986) (injury of relative on the way to the scene of injury, original tortfeasor not liable); Snellenberger v. Rodriguez, 760 S.W.2d 237 (Tex.1988) (police officer at scene collapsed, no peril remaining, not a rescuer).

15. The rescuer's contributory fault is another matter. Since rescue is socially useful, some degree of risk-taking by rescuers is reasonable and not at all negligent. So the risks of rescue are not necessarily counted against the rescuer under comparative negligence rules. See § 199.

16. See Hollingsworth v. Schminkey, 553 N.W.2d 591, 598 (Iowa 1996).

17. See Solomon v. Shuell, 435 Mich. 104, 457 N.W.2d 669 (1990).

18. E.g., Hollingsworth v. Schminkey, 553 N.W.2d 591 (Iowa 1996); Ouellette v.

ever, may be barred from recovery under special rules often applied to them.[19]

Classes of persons and classes of risks. Palsgraf differs from *Wagon Mound* in detail but not in fundamental thrust. The fundamental thrust is that liability for negligence is limited to the risks negligently created by the defendant. The difference in detail is that the risk at issue in *Wagon Mound* could be described as a risk of a certain type or class of harm, while the risk at issue in *Palsgraf* could be described as a risk to a certain class of persons. Many, many common law cases are consistent with the scope of risk rules both in the language of foreseeability[20] and in their results.[21]

Statute violation cases. The rule limiting liability to the scope of the negligently created risk is parallel to the rule invoked in violation of statute cases. As already shown,[22] violation of a statute is negligence per se, but only as to the kinds of risks the statute aimed to avoid and the class of persons the statute aimed to protect. As the next section shows, the language of the courts in common law cases is sometimes more complicated, but both purpose and results are largely the same whether a statute is violated or not.

Risks to particular interests. It is possible to conceptualize different categories of legal interests or entitlements, such as one's interest in personal security as contrasted with the interest in security of one's property. With categories like this in mind, it would be possible to say that under the foreseeability or risk rules, a defendant who negligently risks harm to the plaintiff's property should not be liable if his negligent acts result in harm to the person instead.[23] In fact, however, courts have not drawn a distinction between interests in bodily security and security of one's property.[24] Physical risks of harm to property are in the same general category as risks of physical harm to persons. If I negligently set

Carde, 612 A.2d 687 (R.I.1992); Thompson v. Summers, 567 N.W.2d 387 (S.D.1997). Such cases might also be explained on the very different ground that the defendant, whether tortious or not, benefits from the rescue and should pay its reasonable costs.

19. See Chapter 18.

20. E.g., Hammerstein v. Jean Development West, 111 Nev. 1471, 907 P.2d 975 (1995) (fire alarm going off without cause in a hotel; hotel could foresee that escaping guests might fall or injure an ankle trying to get out). Courts often attempt to adapt the formula definition that focuses on sequence and intervening causes, but in the end tend to get results consistent with a scope of risk. Sometimes courts will emphasize intervening cause reasoning and then explain it in terms of foreseeability or scope of risk as in Concord Florida, Inc. v. Lewin, 341 So.2d 242 (Fla.App.1976).

21. E.g., Horn v. B.A.S.S., 92 F.3d 609 (8th Cir.1996) (if defendant negligently created a risk of harm to boaters by encouraging high speed use of boats on a lake, it is nevertheless not liable for harm resulting from poor lookout rather than high speed); Di Ponzio v. Riordan, 89 N.Y.2d 578, 679 N.E.2d 616, 657 N.Y.S.2d 377 (1997) (gas station negligently allowed motorist to pump gas with engine running, but was not liable when the car rolled backward and injured the plaintiff; running the engine created a fire risk, not a risk of rolling).

22. §§ 137 & 138.

23. Cardozo recognized the possibility but did not embrace it in *Palsgraf*.

24. A prominent example of the fact that courts treat these interests as identical is found in the products liability rule that applies strict liability to physical harms of either person or property but does not apply it as to stand-alone economic harm. E.g., Moorman Manufacturing Co. v. National Tank Co., 91 Ill.2d 69, 61 Ill.Dec. 746, 435 N.E.2d 443 (1982).

fire to your house, I am properly held liable for harm to its occupants, even if I had every assurance that the house was empty at the time.[25] Put differently, injury to persons by forces negligently unleashed is not a different kind of injury from injury to property.[26]

§ 185. The Direct Cause Pattern: Liability for Unforeseeable Harms

Purported liability for unforeseeable harms. Language used by a few courts suggests they will impose liability upon a negligent defendant for harms that are different in kind from the harms he could have reasonably foreseen.[1] Those courts sometimes seem to say that, given duty, negligence, and cause in fact, it is enough that the harm occurred directly, without the intervention of a new actor. It is very doubtful that liability unlimited by foreseeability has much contemporary support.

The Polemis Case. Polemis[2] was a leading case for the rule that the defendant would be liable for all harms directly caused, whether they were foreseeable or not. A stevedore aboard a vessel placed planks across a hatchway. A sling dislodged one of the planks; it fell into the ship's hold. Flames immediately erupted and consumed the ship. The sling operator could surely foresee that if the plank were dislodged, someone below might be struck by it, but no one who has tried making a fire by rubbing pieces of wood together could expect a flame. It was an entirely unexpected result, but because it was "direct," the English Court of Appeal held that the defendants responsible for the plank's fall were liable.

Three groups of cases. Polemis itself was effectively overruled by the *Wagon Mound* decision.[3] Three narrow groups of cases might be understood to support a kind of *Polemis*/direct harm liability unlimited by foreseeability rules. *(1)* In the rescue cases, the defendant creates a risk to A; he is held liable not only to A for any harm done to him but also to rescuers who come to his aid.[4] These cases do not seem necessarily counter to the foreseeability rule. Injury to a rescuer from the forces set in motion by the defendant's negligence seems to fall easily enough

25. Cf. Railway Express Agency, Inc. v. Brabham, 62 So.2d 713 (Fla.1952) (truck running over a box; issue avoided by saying that driver could have reasonably foreseen that a small boy would be in the box); Restatement § 281, cmt. j, posing a case in which the defendant negligently shoots a dog, who, in his pain, knocks down and injures its owner. The defendant would be liable both for injury to dog and to owner. This is not, of course, to say that any negligence whatever toward property is also negligence toward a person.

26. However, for reasons not necessarily associated with foreseeability or proximate cause, courts do treat certain other interests differently when harm is not physical in nature. The interests in emotional and in economic security are fully protected against physical harms, but when those interests are harmed by non-physical means (words for example), courts usually invoke a special set of rules. See Note to Part IV.

§ 185

1. Busta v. Columbus Hospital Corp., 276 Mont. 342, 916 P.2d 122 (1996); Rockweit v. Senecal, 197 Wis.2d 409, 541 N.W.2d 742 (1995).

2. In re Arbitration between Polemis and Furness, Withy & Co., Ltd., [1921] 3 K.B. 560 (C.A. 1921).

3. § 184, supra.

4. § 184, supra.

within the scope of the risks created by the defendant. *(2)* The second group of cases involves a plaintiff who is unusually susceptible to injury and who, for that reason, suffers more harm than an ordinary person as a result of the defendant's negligence. Consistent with the foreseeability or scope of risk approach, these cases can be understood to reflect the general rule that the defendant is liable for the general type of harm he foreseeably put at risk, even if that harm is greater in degree than could be expected.[5] *(3)* A third group of cases once held that if a carrier of goods negligently delayed delivery to the consignee, it would be liable for any harm that befell the delayed goods, even if that harm resulted from an unforeseeable force of nature over which the carrier had no control. As explained elsewhere, these cases probably have little contemporary effect.[6] In addition, both the rescue and susceptible plaintiff cases are generally accepted in jurisdictions that clearly limit liability to foreseeable harms.

Reasons to doubt that liability is imposed beyond the risk. Several reasons suggest caution in interpreting cases that purport to impose liability beyond foreseeable harms. Some cases that verbally reject foreseeability as a test of proximate cause in fact limit liability to foreseeable harms under a duty or negligence analysis. In other words, they do not reject the use of foreseeability to limit liability but merely insist that it is to be considered under the heading of duty rather than proximate cause.[7] Wisconsin, perhaps the chief contemporary exponent of the view that the defendant's acts may be proximate causes of unforeseeable harms, may nevertheless allow the defendant to escape liability because it would be against public policy.[8] Louisiana, listed by Prosser as a state rejecting a foreseeability test of proximate cause,[9] has in fact long since abandoned the proximate cause language altogether in favor of covering the problem by a duty analysis, the point of which is to limit liability to harms that were within the risk created by the defendant's negligence.[10] A third state, Minnesota, has a decidedly checkered history on the question, but at this writing appears to use the general foreseeability rule.[11] The other

5. § 188 below.

6. § 191.

7. Busta v. Columbus Hospital Corp., 276 Mont. 342, 916 P.2d 122 (1996) (using a direct cause test of proximate cause but invoking foreseeability to limit liability because the duty owed is only "with respect to those risks or hazards whose likelihood made the conduct unreasonably dangerous, and hence negligent in the first instance"). In Dahlstrom v. Shrum, 368 Pa. 423, 428–29, 84 A.2d 289, 292 (1951) the court declared that "foreseeability has no place when we are considering proximate or legal cause" but nevertheless applied the foreseeability rule to limit liability on the ground that "no negligence existed as to the plaintiff" because it could not be foreseen that deceased's body would strike plaintiff. This is an excellent statement of the risk rule. If it is given that the plaintiff's injury was unforeseeable, the result is also precisely the result that would be obtained under the foreseeability test of proximate cause.

8. Rockweit v. Senecal, 197 Wis.2d 409, 541 N.W.2d 742 (1995) (public policy).

9. Prosser & Keeton 293.

10. E.g., Younger v. Marshall Industries, Inc., 618 So.2d 866 (La.1993).

11. Ponticas v. K.M.S. Investments, 331 N.W.2d 907, 38 A.L.R.4th 225 (Minn. 1983); Wartnick v. Moss & Barnett, 490 N.W.2d 108 (Minn.1992). Arguably contrary language in an intervening case, Alholm v. Wilt, 394 N.W.2d 488, 491, n. 5 (Minn. 1986), is probably explicable as addressed to a duty issue.

state listed by Prosser, Vermont, does indeed insist that foreseeability is relevant only to negligence,[12] not to proximate cause, although even here liability may be limited by foreseeability when it comes to the duty issue.[13]

Still another reason for uncertainty about cases purporting to impose liability beyond the risk is that, in some formulations, they may stand for no more than the accepted rule that the defendant does not escape liability merely because he could not see the exact manner or extent of harm.[14] If they mean no more than this, they are not minority cases at all, but firmly within the mainstream of the foreseeability rule.[15]

Finally, courts that purport to ignore foreseeability on the proximate cause issue are quite willing, like other courts, to make foreseeability controlling as soon as an intervening cause is perceived.[16] The upshot is that less than a handful of courts purport to apply the kind of strict liability entailed in imposing liability beyond the risk the defendant unreasonably created, and even those may covertly or sporadically introduce foreseeability into the liability equation.

§ 186. The Intervening Cause Pattern and Superseding Cause Analysis

The intervening cause subset of problems. In the intervening cause cases, the defendant negligently creates risks of harm, but the immediate trigger of the harm is another person or a force of nature. That by itself presents no impediment to relief. If the first actor negligently creates a risk of harm and the second actor negligently triggers the risk, both actors are tortfeasors, both are causes in fact of the harm, and both are commonly held liable to the plaintiff under the rules of joint and several liability or comparative fault shares.[1] However, in some instances, the second actor causes a harm that may be outside the scope of the risk originally created by the first. Such cases are simply subsets or particular examples of the basic scope of the risk problem and can be resolved under ordinary foreseeability rules. The cases, however, often obscure this point because courts tend to use somewhat specialized legal language.

Identifying intervening acts and forces. The courts' verbal approach in these cases is built on a rickety scaffold of terms and definitions. First,

12. E.g., Dodge v. McArthur, 126 Vt. 81, 223 A.2d 453 (1966).

13. See Thompson v. Green Mountain Power Corp., 120 Vt. 478, 144 A.2d 786 (1958).

14. See §§ 188 & 189.

15. See Petition of Kinsman Transit Co., 338 F.2d 708 (2d Cir.1964), where Judge Friendly appeared to assert that it would be a rejection of foreseeability and the *Wagon Mound* risk rule if a court tested liability by foreseeability of general kind of damage rather than by foreseeability of specific events. "This comes very close to saying that where the damage was of the sort that was risked, foreseeability is not required." On the contrary, since the defendant is only negligent as to harms foreseeably risked, the only relevant "damages risked" in these cases are those that are foreseeable.

16. E.g., LaFaso v. LaFaso, 126 Vt. 90, 223 A.2d 814 (1966)

§ 186

1. § 170 & Chapter 26 generally.

the issue does not arise at all unless a new force qualifies as an intervening cause. An intervening cause is a new cause that comes into play after the defendant's negligent conduct. If the intervening force is in operation at the time the defendant acted, it is not an intervening cause at all. For instance, if the defendant sets a fire when the wind is blowing, he cannot avoid liability when the wind carries the fire to the plaintiff's house. The wind, as a force in operation when the defendant acted, is not an intervening cause.[2] In many routine cases, causes are deemed legally concurrent rather than intervening. Suppose drivers of two cars both negligently contribute to a collision or a series of collisions that harm the plaintiff. Such cases are almost always treated as cases of concurring negligence, even if the negligence of one driver occurred later than the negligence of the other.[3] The effect is that both are liable for at least a share of the plaintiff's damages and neither can claim the other as a superseding cause.

Superseding causes. If courts perceive an intervening act or force as triggering injury, the defendant's original negligence is still one of the proximate causes of harm if the defendant's conduct led to the plaintiff's injury in a continuous sequence, uninterrupted by an efficient or independent intervening cause.[4] On the other hand, if the judge or the trier of fact believes that the intervening cause is the only proximate cause because it is the efficient or immediate cause, then the intervening cause will be called a superseding cause and the defendant will not be liable.

For example, if the defendant left a dangerous open cellar or excavation and an intervening actor pushed the plaintiff into it, some courts, at least at one time, concluded that the intervening actor was an efficient, independent, or superseding cause of the plaintiff's harm. The result was that the defendant, who made the danger available in the first place, was not liable at all.[5] Sometimes the idea is expressed by saying, somewhat argumentatively, that the defendant only passively created a condition or occasion that made harm possible but that he was not a cause.[6] All of these statements express conclusions, but none of them offers either reasons or guidance to lawyers. Such statements add one more layer of confusion to the analysis.[7] In any event, the propriety of

2. See Restatement § 441 (force is an intervening force, no matter when it originated, if it first operates after defendant has lost control of the danger).

3. See, e.g., Watts v. Smith, 375 Mich. 120, 134 N.W.2d 194 (1965) (plaintiff suffered an indivisible injury in separate collisions, once on the way to work, once on the way home; joint and several liability).

4. § 183 (stating formal rule).

5. See, e.g., Loftus v. Dehail, 133 Cal. 214, 65 P. 379 (1901); Miller v. Bahmmuller, 124 App.Div. 558, 108 N.Y.S. 924 (1908), cases relied upon by the Restatement § 442B in support of its illustration 7.

6. E.g., Graham v. Keuchel, 847 P.2d 342 (Okl.1993). This form of stating a conclusion is especially unfortunate, since it suggests that conditions cannot be causes, which is neither factually nor legally the case. A property owner who negligently permits a gasoline leak to saturate the premises may "passively" permit a condition of the premises which is extremely dangerous. He is no less a cause of harm than the negligent smoker who tosses a match into the gasoline.

7. See Marshall v. Nugent, 222 F.2d 604 (1st Cir.1955); Duncavage v. Allen, 147 Ill. App.3d 88, 497 N.E.2d 433, 100 Ill.Dec. 455 (1986) (noting that the cause-condition distinction has been discredited).

the result in cases like these depends first upon the facts of each case, second upon judicial ideas about the appropriate scope of liability (ideas that have arguably changed over the years), and third upon available alternatives, which now include joint and several liability and comparative fault shares of liability.[8]

Foreseeable intervening causes. A ruling that an intervening actor is a superseding cause embodies the dual conclusion that the intervening actor should be responsible and that the original actor, in spite of his causal negligence, should not. The intervening cause terminology makes the issue look as if it were only concerned about the sequence of events and unrelated to issues of responsibility, foreseeability, or scope of risk. But in contemporary law, when courts then ask what counts as a superseding cause, they return to some form of the foreseeability inquiry. The rule is that if the intervening cause itself is part of the risk negligently created by the defendant,[9] or if it is reasonably foreseeable at the time of the defendant's negligent conduct,[10] then it is not a superseding cause at all. In that case, the defendant is not relieved of liability merely because some other person or force triggered the injury. The wordy labels—superseding, intervening, efficient, independent—although almost always invoked, turn out to be surplusage. The ultimate inquiry is merely whether the intervening cause is foreseeable or whether the injury is within the scope of the risk negligently created by the defendant.

Example. In a leading New York case,[11] the plaintiff was working for a company that sealed gas mains with boiling enamel. The contractor responsible for the project required the plaintiff to work at one end of a street excavation where he was exposed to oncoming traffic and protected only by a quite inadequate barricade. This put the plaintiff at risk that the plaintiff or the boiling enamel or both might be struck by a negligent driver. A driver who suffered a seizure ran through the barricade and into the excavation, causing severe injury to the plaintiff. Because the driver had failed to take his anti-seizure medication, the contractor argued that the driver was a superseding cause of the plaintiff's injury. The argument failed. One reason was that the main outlines of the risk to the plaintiff through intervening negligence were foreseeable, even if the driver's seizure itself was not. Put more generally, an intervening cause does not supersede the defendant's negligence when it reflects the same general kind of risk which rendered the defendant negligent.

8. As to the intervening criminal acts vs. intervening negligent acts, see § 190; as to special features that tend to warrant the superseding cause conclusion, see § 189.

9. Restatement §§ 442A & 442B (creating risk of intervening act itself and creating risk of same type of harm as inflicted through intervening act).

10. Derdiarian v. Felix Contracting Corp., 51 N.Y.2d 308, 434 N.Y.S.2d 166, 414 N.E.2d 666 (1980); Tise v. Yates Construction Co., Inc., 345 N.C. 456, 480 S.E.2d 677 (1997).

11. Derdiarian v. Felix Contracting Corp., 51 N.Y.2d 308, 434 N.Y.S.2d 166, 414 N.E.2d 666 (1980).

Unforeseeable intervening causes outside the scope of the risk. Courts usually say that if an intervening act (or force) is not reasonably foreseeable, then the intervening event is a superseding cause and the defendant as the original actor is relieved of liability.[12] This statement seems to imply that the intervening force itself, not merely the general kind of harm, must have been reasonably foreseeable when the defendant acted. However, that is not invariably true as the succeeding sections show.

Topic B. The General Rules of Foreseeability

§ 187. Foreseeability Terminology: Scope of Risk

As the preceding sections show, courts usually reduce the tests of proximate cause, both in direct and in intervening cause cases, to a question of foreseeability. To some extent, the language of foreseeability is a short hand expression intended to say that the scope of the defendant's liability is determined by the scope of the risk he negligently created. Foreseeability correlates with this idea in most cases, but it can be misleading in others. Some harms that are entirely foreseeable are nevertheless not harms a reasonable and prudent person would seek to avoid. The point of limiting the defendant's liability under proximate cause rules is to make the defendant's liability coextensive with his negligence. Consequently, the defendant is not liable even for foreseeable harms if he was not negligent in failing to minimize those harms.[1]

Perhaps the easiest illustration is the kind of case in which the defendant is negligent in driving a vehicle at high speed and because of the speed arrives at a spot just in time to be struck by a large tree that falls or an airplane that crashes. An injured passenger can certainly assert that falling trees or crashing airplanes are foreseeable. Nevertheless, the defendant's speed does nothing to create or increase the risk of such an incident. Falling trees are foreseeable, but not a greater risk to those who drive fast than to those who drive slowly. Consequently, the defendant is not liable for injuries resulting in this manner.[2] When

12. E.g., Duphily v. Delaware Electric Cooperative, Inc., 662 A.2d 821, 829 (Del. 1995) ("If the intervening negligence of a third party was reasonably foreseeable, the original tortfeasor is liable for his negligence because the causal connection between the original tortious act and the resulting injury remains unbroken. If, however, the intervening negligence was not reasonably foreseeable, the intervening act supersedes and becomes the sole proximate cause of the plaintiff's injuries, thus relieving the original tortfeasor of liability").

§ 187

1. A more accurate statement would be that the defendant is not liable for foreseeable harms unless the risk of such harms was one of the reasons for judging him to be negligent in the first place.

2. Berry v. Sugar Notch Borough, 191 Pa. 345, 43 A. 240 (1899); cf. Doss v. Town of Big Stone Gap, 145 Va. 520, 134 S.E. 563 (1926) (city's alleged negligence made road impassable so that detour was required; decedent was struck by an airplane while on the detour, no liability). The *Berry* court rightly pointed out that if the defendant had struck a tree that had already fallen, the case would have been different. In that case, the defendant's high speed created the risk, among others, that he would be unable to avoid an obstruction in time. (Similarly, *Doss* would presumably be a case for liability if the city constructed a detour that put

courts say that such a risk is unforeseeable what they mean is that it is not a risk enhanced or created by the defendant's conduct.

A carrier's delay in delivering goods can create exactly the same kind of problem. The delay may be negligent because it runs the risk that the shipper or the consignee will suffer economic losses if the goods are not delivered on time. If, because of the delay, the goods aboard a carrier are subjected to an unforeseeable flood or other force of nature, loss of or damage to the goods is fortuitous. Although we all know that floods occur and are in that sense foreseeable, reasonable persons do not act on the remote possibility of flooding. For that reason, a carrier does not create an unreasonable risk of flood damage to goods by its delay unless some immediate danger would be apparent. The carrier in such a case is negligent, but not negligent with respect to risks of flooding, so the carrier's negligence is not a proximate cause of the flood damage. That is all that courts mean by saying that the flood was unforeseeable or that it was an intervening act of God.[3]

§ 188. Foreseeability Required: Extent of Harm

General rule. Courts assume a radical distinction between the *nature* of a harm and its *extent.* The foreseeability or risk rule holds the defendant subject to liability if he could reasonably foresee the nature of the harm done, even if the total amount of harm turned out to be quite unforeseeably large.[1] For example, suppose the defendant negligently operates his power boat so that he could foresee that the plaintiff's stamp collection is washed overboard and lost or ruined. If that happens, the defendant is liable for the loss of the collection, even if the defendant thought it was worth only $100 when in fact it was worth $1 million. The defendant was negligent in creating a risk of loss of the collection; he knew or should have known the nature of the risk, even if he could not have guessed the value of the collection.[2]

The thin skull or eggshell skull rule. The rule that holds the defendant liable for foreseeable harms even when the amount of harm is not foreseeable finds a special expression in the thin skull or eggshell skull rule, as it is usually known. The label derives from an imagined case in which the plaintiff has an unusually thin skull. The defendant, having no reason to know of the plaintiff's peculiar susceptibility, negligently injures the plaintiff's head. The blow would be uncomfortable to normal people, but to the plaintiff it causes a fractured skull and

drivers in a dangerous position from landing airplanes).

3. See § 191.

§ 188

1. Restatement Second § 435 (1) (liability not avoided merely because extent or manner of harm was unforeseeable).

2. The case could be different if the defendant had a very good reason for operating his vessel as he did, for example, to take a seriously injured person ashore for medical help. In that case, if he reasonably believed the stamp collection to be worth only $100, the risk of losing it might be a reasonable risk to take to help a seriously injured person. If so, the defendant was not negligent at all. In that case, the proximate cause issue vanishes, since it comes into play only if the defendant is negligent (or otherwise subject to liability).

serious injury. It seems to be agreed that the plaintiff is entitled to recover for all the harm done, even though a fractured skull was definitely not foreseeable.[3] The defendant, courts say, takes the plaintiff as he finds her.[4] The rule is sometimes put differently by saying that the defendant is liable for aggravation of preexisting injuries or conditions.[5]

It is easy to misunderstand the thin skull rule. First, it does not make the defendant liable for the plaintiff's preexisting condition itself. The defendant's negligence today is not a cause in fact of a condition the plaintiff had yesterday. The thin skull rule merely holds that the defendant is liable for the unforeseeable aggravation of that preexisting condition, not the condition itself.[6] Second, the thin skull rule applies only to the proximate cause issue, not to the negligence issue. It does not require the defendant to exercise special care for an unforeseeably vulnerable plaintiff. The defendant only need exercise ordinary care to prevent foreseeable harms. The thin skull rule comes into play only when the defendant's conduct would put normal people at risk.[7] Once the defendant does that, the thin skull rule provides that he is liable for all the personal injuries actually caused, although they may be greater than those that would be suffered by a normal person.[8]

The fire cases. When the defendant negligently sets a fire that spreads to the plaintiff's property, New York courts developed a unique rule that permitted recovery only by the first person to whose property the fire spread.[9] Other courts have allowed recovery even though the fire has spread substantial distances, or jumped creeks and ridges to reach the plaintiff's property. Perhaps these cases can be explained on the ground that the spread of fire is foreseeable and that no one can count on fires to stop at obvious barriers. However, at least some of the cases seem to illustrate and support the rule that the defendant does not escape liability merely because the harm done is more extensive than the defendant could have foreseen. The defendant who negligently sets a fire might reasonably believe beforehand that if it spread, it would certainly

3. Chicago City Ry. Co. v. Saxby, 213 Ill. 274, 72 N.E. 755 (1904); Cf. Hammerstein v. Jean Development West, 111 Nev. 1471, 907 P.2d 975 (1995) (plaintiff suffered diabetes and was thus more susceptible to gangrene in case of injury to extremity; negligent fire alarm company was liable for that when the plaintiff turned his ankle attempting to escape a hotel when the alarm falsely signaled a fire).

4. E.g., David v. DeLeon, 250 Neb. 109, 547 N.W.2d 726 (1996).

5. See §§ 177 & 178.

6. When the defendant is held liable for the preexisting condition itself and not merely for aggravation of it, it is not because of the thin skull rule but the indivisible injury rule discussed in § 174.

7. If the defendant knows or should know of the plaintiff's peculiar susceptibility, he is of course obliged to exercise ordinary care with that susceptibility in mind and is liable for injuries caused if he does not. But that liability does not invoke the thin skull rule, which deals with injuries of an unforeseeable extent.

8. "The tortfeasor's duty of care is measured by the ordinary person, but the plaintiff's injuries may not be. In short, if [defendant] breached its objective duty of care, it must take its victim as it finds her." Vaughn v. Nissan Motor Corporation in U.S.A., Inc., 77 F.3d 736, 738 (4th Cir. 1996).

9. See Homac Corporation v. Sun Oil Co., 258 N.Y. 462, 180 N.E. 172 (1932) (reviewing earlier decisions, some of which even denied compensation to the first owner).

go no farther than the nearest road. If it somehow leaps the road, however, and continues to burn the other side, some cases hold that the defendant is nevertheless liable.[10]

§ 189. Foreseeability Required: Manner of Harm

Manner of Injury Generally

Manner of injury rule. The defendant is liable for harms he negligently caused so long as a reasonable person in his position should have recognized or foreseen the general kind of harm the plaintiff suffered. He is not ordinarily relieved of liability merely because the manner of injury or its details were unforeseeable.[1]

Examples. If the defendant negligently leaves kerosene where it might be ignited and burn the plaintiff, the fact that ignition unforeseeably triggered an explosion rather than a burning is of no consequence. The general type of accident was foreseeable, and from a known source of harm; the explosion is a mere "variant of the foreseeable."[2] Similarly, the defendant who negligently drives a bus onto a railroad track as the train approaches puts passengers at risk if for any reason the bus is delayed in clearing the track. When the train strikes the bus, the bus driver does not escape liability merely because the delay in getting the bus off the track arose from an unforeseeable obstruction, since, again, some kind of delay and the general type of accident were foreseeable even if the particular obstruction was not.[3]

Risks from forces likely to cause unpredictable and diverse harms. The manner of injury rule is especially applicable when the defendant

10. Atchison, T. & S. F. R. Co. v. Stanford, 12 Kan. 354 (1874) (three and one-half to four miles); Silver Falls Timber Co. v. Eastern & Western Lumber Co., 149 Or. 126, 40 P.2d 703 (1935) (apparently burning for miles, crossing two creeks and a green ridge of timber); Smith v. London and South Western Railway, 6 L.R. 14 (C.P. 1870). One judge in *Smith* gave an additional illustration: "[I]f a person fires across a road when it is dangerous to do so and kills a man who is in the receipt of a large income, he will be liable for the whole damage, however great,.... and cannot set up that he could not have reasonably expected to have injured any one but a labourer." But cf. Milwaukee & S.P. Ry. v. Kellogg, 94 U.S. (4 Otto) 469, 24 L.Ed. 256 (1876) (imposing liability for spread of fire under foreseeability rule).

§ 189

1. E.g., Stodola v. Grunwald Mechanical Contractors, Inc., 228 Neb. 301, 305, 422 N.W.2d 341, 344 (1988) ("The law does not require precision in foreseeing the exact hazard or consequence which happens. It is sufficient if what occurs is one of the kind of consequences which might reasonably be foreseen"); Restatement § 435. Some judges seem to have viewed this well-accepted rule as a rejection of the foreseeability test. See Petition of Kinsman Transit Co., 338 F.2d 708, 723–24 (2d Cir.1964). However, the principle does not seem to be a rejection of the foreseeability test but an indispensable part of it.

2. Hughes v. Lord Advocate, [1963] A.C. 837 (H.L. 1963) (Lord Reid emphasizing "known source" among other things; Lord Guest emphasizing "same type of accident" and Lord Pearce using the "variant" language).

3. Cf. Washington & G. R. Co. v. Hickey, 166 U.S. 521, 17 S.Ct. 661, 41 L.Ed. 1101 (1897) (defendant drove its horse-car onto the track of a steam railroad, then was caught with the train approaching when the gates came down; when the plaintiff passenger was injured in the commotion among the passengers; "it was not material that the driver had no ground to expect the [railroad's] particular negligent act of lowering the gates" since he could foresee that delay from any cause would be dangerous).

negligently creates risks of harm that are quite definite in their results but tend to come about in unpredictable ways. When the defendant unleashes large physical forces such as those associated with automobiles, trains, large ships broken loose from their moorings and other powerful instruments, he creates risks that injury could be caused in diverse ways, too numerous and particular to foresee in detail. For example, if I drive too fast, I create the general risk of causing personal injury and property damage to those on the road and sometimes even to those who are off the road. I probably cannot foresee all the ways in which that general risk might actually come about, but I do know that injury might come about in many particular ways resulting from my speed, including some so bizarre that I might not ever be able to imagine them in advance.[4] In this kind of case, the risk rule does not readily relieve me of liability. The case calls for the rule that if I foresee the risk in general, I need not foresee the details. Consequently, if my speeding causes me to lose control and drive my car into someone's living room, I am liable for the damage done, even if no one would have ever said in advance that the risk of living room damage is a reason not to speed.[5]

Chain collision cases and many others attest to the foreseeability of a billiard ball effect when powerful forces operating at great speed strike objects. It is certainly not unforeseeable that the first object struck is sometimes propelled into another. The billiard ball effect is more dramatic or bizarre if a train strikes a horse which is then propelled through the air until it strikes a person, but the general kind of harm from the same kinds of forces is entirely foreseeable even if the details are not. So here again a rule of law against liability is inappropriate.[6] Equally, when a large ship is allowed to break loose from its moorings in a fast-running river, a variety of harms associated with such a large force can be classed together, so that even if no one would have considered that a loose ship might cause upstream flooding because it could crash into a bridge and dam the river, such harm is nevertheless closely

4. See Washington & G. R. Co. v. Hickey, 166 U.S. 521, 17 S.Ct. 661, 41 L.Ed. 1101 (1897) (a delay was to be foreseen as a danger, and a "delay might be occasioned ... by an almost infinite number of causes. The horses might stumble. The harness might give way. The car might jump the track. A hundred different things might happen which would lead to a delay, and hence to the probability of an accident. It was not necessary that the driver should foresee the very thing itself which did cause the delay").

5. See Castro v. Hernandez–Davila, 694 S.W.2d 575 (Tex.App.1985) (intoxicated driver who drove into apartment building, causing a wall to collapse).

6. Kommerstad v. Great Northern Ry. Co., 120 Minn. 376, 139 N.W. 713 (1913). Contrariwise, Pennsylvania ruled against the plaintiff as a matter of law in Dahlstrom v. Shrum, 368 Pa. 423, 84 A.2d 289 (1951) where the defendant struck and killed one person, knocking his body into the plaintiff. The primary holding was that the defendant was not negligent in striking the first person. The court then attempted to bolster its decision by adding that even if the defendant was negligent in running down the first person, he could not have foreseen injury to another. The second holding sounds almost absurd, either as a factual description or a rule of policy, but it was probably colored by the court's primary holding that the defendant was not negligent at all. The court may have implicitly made an inappropriate analogy to *Palsgraf,* which it cited twice. The analogy would be inappropriate because in *Palsgraf* the physical force used by the train guard had no apparent capacity to harm others at a distance. The physical force of a moving automobile, however, has exactly that capacity.

associated with the foreseeable forces—ships and heavy waters—so that liability is again an appropriate question for the trier of fact and not to be precluded by a rule of law.[7]

Where manner of harm is integral part of the risk. In contrast to the case of many diverse risks that might result from large forces, defendants sometimes create narrow risks that can foreseeably occur in a limited number of ways. If liability is to be limited to the risks the defendant unreasonably created, in such a case the defendant would not be liable when the injury comes about in an unforeseeable way. In the *Derdiarian* case, already discussed in another connection,[8] the defendant posted the plaintiff in a position of danger from oncoming traffic. The plaintiff was struck by an oncoming car. Such an injury was foreseeable even though it was not foreseeable that the driver would lose control because he had a seizure. The details, the manner of occurrence, did not matter in that case. But if the plaintiff had been struck by a falling aircraft, the manner of occurrence would have been very important indeed. The defendant created a risk of injury from surface traffic only. Posting the plaintiff at a different location would not have created any predictable risk of aircraft injury. Most often courts can rightly ignore the details about the manner of injury, because the defendant's negligence is broad enough to cover a variety of sequences, motives and events. However, the problem is not resolvable by a rule of law. If the facts of a particular case show that the risk of harm was limited to a very specific kind of accident, the manner in which harm was inflicted will be relevant.

Whether the risk negligently created by the defendant is a narrow one and focused on a particular manner of occurrence, requires adjudication rather than rules. In one case,[9] the plaintiff and others were working around a vat of molten liquid at 800° centigrade. A worker knocked a cover into the vat, risking the possibility of a splash of molten metal on the plaintiff. That did not happen, but a few moments later, the vat cover, then immersed in the liquid, underwent a chemical change as a result of the intense heat. The chemical change produced a drop of water, which immediately turned to steam and caused an eruption of the molten liquid. The molten liquid struck and injured the plaintiff. The chemical reaction had been completely unknown up until that time, so the eruption by this means was entirely unforeseeable.

As a matter of argumentation, it always serves the defendant to describe the risk as precisely as possible and the plaintiff to describe it as abstractly as possible. The plaintiff can argue that eruption of the

7. Cf. Petition of Kinsman Transit Co., 338 F.2d 708 (2d Cir.1964). In *Kinsman,* Judge Friendly appeared to argue in favor of liability for unforeseeable harms. However, that argument seems to have been based on the view that a harm was unforeseeable if the details of its occurrence were unforeseeable. However, the result in the case is, as the text suggests, consistent with the accepted view that foreseeability refers to the general outlines of the picture, not to the finely etched details.

8. § 186.

9. Doughty v. Turner Manufacturing Co., Limited, [1964] 1 Q.B. 518 (C.A. 1963).

molten metal was foreseeable; it was the risk the defendant created. Such an abstract description of the risk includes eruption from chemical reactions as well as from mechanical action of the lid. If accepted, this description of the risk would show proximate cause. The defendant's technique is to characterize the risk at a lower level of abstraction, as a risk of splashing, which implies that the risk was only a risk of mechanical action of the lid's striking the metal, not a risk of chemical reaction at all. If this description of the risk is accepted, then the injury suffered was outside the risk.

It is not usually possible to say that only one description of the risk is the right one, so the question calls for judgment. Although that judgment is ordinarily left to the jury, sometimes judges feel that the matter is too clear for debate. In the case of the lid falling into the vat of molten metal, the court thought the risk of eruption from a totally unforeseeable chemical change was not anything like the known risk of mechanical action that was risked by knocking the lid into the vat. So, as a matter of law, the plaintiff could not prevail. This result seems understandable when the only foreseeable risk is specifically related to a particular mechanism and that mechanism is not known to create unpredictable results.

Intervening Act Cases

Conflict between intervening act rules and manner of injury rules. Although the courts have often shown that liability is not to be avoided merely because the defendant could not reasonably have foreseen the manner in which injury comes about, they have also said that the defendant will escape liability if the injury comes about through an unforeseeable intervening cause. The two statements seem to be in conflict. If courts relieve the defendant of liability for foreseeable types of harm merely because he could not reasonably have foreseen that the harm would be triggered by an intervening actor, they are in fact saying that the manner of harm (by way of an intervening act) must be foreseeable.

Resolving the conflict. Two approaches are available that help harmonize the manner of harm rules with the tendency to focus on intervening causes. First, courts may hold, with the Restatement,[10] that intervening causes are not superseding causes if the defendant should have foreseen and avoided the general type of harm that resulted, even though the intervening causes were themselves unforeseeable. Second, courts may declare that an intervening cause is foreseeable if it represents a general type of foreseeable intervention, even though it could not have been specifically anticipated.

Johnson v. Kosmos Portland Cement Co.,[11] is a striking and well-known example of the first approach. The defendants negligently failed to clean the hold of a barge to eliminate the possibility of gases

10. Restatement § 442B.

11. Johnson v. Kosmos Portland Cement Co., 64 F.2d 193 (6th Cir.1933).

accumulating there from the residue of petroleum cargoes. Accumulated gases could explode if an acetylene torch were used or a match inadvertently lit. Neither of these events occurred but lightning struck the barge instead. That caused an explosion of the gases and killed two men. Considering the lightning strike to be an unforeseeable intervening cause, the court nevertheless held that the defendant could appropriately be held responsible because the result or type of harm that occurred—explosion and death or injury by explosion—was foreseeable and that foreseeability of the general type of harm or result was enough.

The second approach can also be illustrated by the *Johnson* facts. Although it might not be foreseeable that lightning would strike the barge and ignite the gases, it was foreseeable that some intervening incendiary force could ignite them. Lightning is merely a particular instance of incendiary forces that could do so. It is enough that the defendant should recognize danger from a set or category of forces to which lightning belongs, without identifying all the possible forces in the set. If the defendant should have foreseen dangers from one of the forces in the category or from the same general kinds of forces, the liability is appropriate even if the particular intervening cause was not foreseeable.[12]

Courts do not always follow either approach. In some contemporary cases, judges simply declare that an intervening act was a superseding cause without discussing either of the harmonizing approaches. Occasionally courts still seem to say that the intervening act is a superseding cause if it is not specifically foreseeable.[13]

Effects

The manner of harm rules reflect the general risk rule: the defendant should be liable for the general types of harms he negligently risked, that is, for the general type of harms that were foreseeable, even if those harms result from intervening causes. The result is that in the absence of some special factor, the intervening negligence of a second actor is not often a superseding cause, but intervening criminal acts may be another matter. The next sections consider these two points.

Topic C. Intervening Acts or Forces

§ 190. Intervening Intentional and Criminal Acts

General rule. If an intervening and unforeseeable intentional harm or criminal act triggers the injury to the plaintiff, the criminal act is

12. See Gibson v. Garcia, 96 Cal.App.2d 681, 216 P.2d 119 (1950) (precise form of intervening force need not be foreseeable); Restatement § 435.

13. McKethean v. Washington Metropolitan Area Transit Authority, 588 A.2d 708 (D.C.App.1991) requires specific foreseeability when criminal acts intervene. Some cases that seem to require specific foreseeability of the intervening cause may cloak a concern about negligence or cause in fact. Cf. D'Ambra v. Peak Building Corp., 680 A.2d 939 (R.I.1996) (plaintiff, swerving to avoid being struck by another car, ran into the defendant's dumpster placed in the parking lane; defendant "was not bound to

ordinarily called a superseding cause, with the result that the defendant who negligently creates the opportunity for such acts escapes liability.[1]

As in other superseding cause cases, the real reason to relieve the defendant of liability is not merely that a new cause has intervened but rather that the risk represented is not one that the defendant negligently created. Suppose the lessor of an automobile would be negligent if it failed to check the driving records of a prospective lessee and that it in fact leases a car to A without checking his records. A properly loans the car to B who improperly loans it to C, who has a bad record for driving while intoxicated and who injures the plaintiff by his intoxicated driving of the leased car. Courts find it very easy to say that C's criminal act is a superseding cause and that the lessor is not liable,[2] but the result is more simply understood as a product of the general rule that the defendant is liable only for injuries that were within the scope of the risk he negligently created. The lessor's failure to inquire of A's driving record was negligent because that failure ran the risk that A would prove to be a dangerous driver; it was not negligent at all about the danger that C, of whom the lessor knew nothing, would drive badly. If the harm caused by an intervening actor's criminal act is within the risk negligently created by the defendant, foreseeability of the criminal act itself seems unimportant.[3]

The backside of the general rule that insulates the defendant from liability in cases of unforeseeable intervening criminal acts is that if a criminal or intentional intervening act is foreseeable,[4] or is part of the original risk negligently created by the defendant in the first place, then it is not a superseding cause.[5] That rule has been applied in civil rights claims as well as in common law tort claims.[6]

Older authorities; unforeseeability as a matter of law. In an earlier era, courts tended to hold that intervening criminal acts were unforeseeable as a matter of law. For example, the defendant negligently spills a tank car full of gasoline, into which the intervening actor throws a

anticipate mischievous or wrongful acts on the part of others, and hence was not bound to guard against them," so the driver of the other car was a superseding cause).

§ 190

1. E.g., Phan Son Van v. Pena, 990 S.W.2d 751 (Tex.1999).

2. See Alamo Rent–A–Car, Inc. v. Hamilton, 216 Ga.App. 659, 455 S.E.2d 366 (1995).

3. See Restatement § 449. Suppose the defendant negligently fails to close flood gates that would protect his property, on which by agreement the plaintiff has stored his goods. The danger of flooding is high because the levee might break. The levee does break, but only because a criminal dynamites it. The plaintiff's property is flooded. Since this is the very risk created by the defendant's negligence, and from many of the same forces, there is no very obvious reason why the defendant should escape liability merely because a criminal act intervened.

4. Poskus v. Lombardo's of Randolph, Inc., 423 Mass. 637, 670 N.E.2d 383 (1996); Restatement § 448 (where actor should have realized that a third person might avail himself of an opportunity created by the defendant's negligence).

5. Tenney v. Atlantic Associates, 594 N.W.2d 11 (Iowa 1999); Restatement § 449.

6. See Harris v. Roderick, 126 F.3d 1189 (9th Cir.1997).

lighted match, injuring the plaintiff in the explosion.[7] Or the defendant leaves unguarded a dangerous excavation into which the intervening actor pushes the plaintiff.[8] Or the defendant negligently leaves dynamite where boys might find and steal it. Boys do so; another boy is killed in the explosion that follows.[9]

The earlier cases were prone to declare, contrary to human experience, that criminal acts could not be anticipated or at least that the defendant was under no obligation to anticipate them. Some contemporary cases come close to saying the same thing.[10] This attitude explains why courts at one time held that negligent sellers of alcohol to intoxicated drivers were never responsible; in spite of the fact that there can be many proximate causes, they said it was the drinker, not the seller who was "the" proximate cause.[11] In the same way, no matter what a defendant did to drive someone to suicide, suicide was the responsibility of the victim, not the defendant.[12] In the most extreme form, the idea was that the last human wrongdoer or last culpable will counts as the sole proximate cause,[13] so that intervening criminal acts would always relieve the defendant of liability.

Rejection of the older rule; jury questions. "This archaic doctrine has been rejected everywhere."[14] Today's courts usually recognize that foreseeability, in the nature of things, is fact-specific, so they now often permit juries to find that a criminal act was foreseeable and not a superseding cause.[15] There are, of course, cases that declare a particular criminal act in a particular case to have been unforeseeable as a matter of law. Some of these matter-of-law holdings seem to be out of step and dubious at best,[16] but in any event courts have increasingly recognized

7. Watson v. Kentucky & Indiana Bridge & Railroad Co., 137 Ky. 619, 126 S.W. 146 (1910).

8. See, e.g., Loftus v. Dehail, 133 Cal. 214, 65 P. 379 (1901); Miller v. Bahmmuller, 124 App.Div. 558, 108 N.Y.S. 924 (1908).

9. Perry v. Rochester Lime Co., 219 N.Y. 60, 113 N.E. 529 (1916).

10. See Estate of Strever v. Cline, 278 Mont. 165, 924 P.2d 666 (1996); Doe v. Linder Construction Co., 845 S.W.2d 173 (Tenn.1992), summarized below, note 16.

11. See §§ 195 & 332 below.

12. See § 195 below and Chapter 26 generally.

13. See Patrick J. Kelley, Proximate Cause in Negligence Law: History, Theory, and the Present Darkness, 69 Wash. U. L. Q. 49, 78–81 (1991).

14. Britton v. Wooten, 817 S.W.2d 443, 449 (Ky.1991). See Petition of Kinsman Transit Co., 338 F.2d 708, 719 (2d Cir.1964) ("the discredited notion that only the last wrongful act can be a cause [is] a notion as faulty in logic as it is wanting in fairness").

15. Carlisle v. Ulysses Line Ltd., S.A., 475 So.2d 248 (Fla.App.1985) (cruise line failed to warn or protect against masked gunman in port); McLean v. Kirby Company, a Division of Scott Fetzer Company, 490 N.W.2d 229 (N.D.1992) (employer hired door-to-door salesman without investigating his character; a check would have shown a criminal record and the salesman in fact raped a potential buyer in her apartment; held, the employer is liable, the risk is foreseeable); Travis v. City of Mesquite, 830 S.W.2d 94, 98 (Tex.1992) ("the actor's negligence is not superseded and will not be excused when the criminal conduct is a foreseeable result of such negligence"); Cruz v. Middlekauff Lincoln–Mercury, Inc., 909 P.2d 1252 (Utah 1996) (keys left in car where theft was especially likely, defendant may be a proximate cause of harms done by thief while trying to elude police pursuit).

16. Doe v. Linder Construction Co., 845 S.W.2d 173 (Tenn.1992) is a striking case. A developer in a partially completed large housing project left keys to the plaintiff's home in a central place available to all workmen. The keys identified the owner

that the question is not to be decided categorically but on the facts of each case. In one group of cases, a driver leaves keys in the ignition of the car. A thief steals the car and causes injury in making his escape. Courts have had difficulty with this one. A number of older cases held as a matter of law that the driver's act of leaving the key available was not a proximate cause of the harm because theft was not foreseeable, or that if it was, then negligence of the thief was not.[17] But circumstances vary and times change. Courts have sometimes had to say that in particular cases the car theft and the thief's negligence were both all too foreseeable in particular cases, or that a jury could so find.[18] In general, the courts have moved away from rule-of-law decisions about broad categories of cases like these and have examined the facts of particular cases to determine whether intervening criminal acts are foreseeable.

Unforeseeable intervening act causing a foreseeable result. Even if the intervening cause is not foreseeable, the intervening actor may trigger the very kind of harm the defendant's negligence risked. In that case, the general rule of foreseeability would seem to call for liability. In a number of cases the defendant has negligently created a danger of fire, or a danger that if fire occurred, victims would not be able to escape promptly. Danger of fire is what makes the defendant negligent. If fire does occur and people are injured by it, courts appropriately hold the defendant liable. His liability in such a case is coextensive with negligence because foreseeability of fire is an ingredient in his negligence. Even if arson is not itself foreseeable, injury from fire is, and that should be enough. Some of the arson cases seem to support this view,[19] and

and her premises. Workmen stole the keys, used them to enter the plaintiff's house and raped her. The court held as a matter of law that the acts of rape were superseding causes. The case looks wrong because, given the purpose of locks and keys, it seems clearly foreseeable that the keys could be used for some kind of criminal purpose and there seems no reason to require specific foreseeability of rape, although even that doesn't seem too difficult. The case was criticized in Leslie Bender, Is Tort Law Male?: Foreseeability Analysis and Property Mangers' Liability for Third Party Rapes of Residents, 69 CHI.-KENT L. REV. 313 (1993). See also Estate of Strever v. Cline, 278 Mont. 165, 924 P.2d 666 (1996) (unlocked pickup truck left overnight with Spectrum radar detector, keys, a micro cassette recorder, jumper cables, a Black & Decker car light, Bushnell binoculars, a Shakespeare fishing rod and case, a tape case with 30 cassette tapes, a small tool box, and a Fujica camera in the cab, together with a loaded gun; although it was negligent to leave the gun there because harm was foreseeable, it was not foreseeable that teen-aged boys—thieves—would take the gun and cause a death).

17. E.g., Ross v. Nutt, 177 Ohio St. 113, 203 N.E.2d 118 (1964). If the thief's negligence is not foreseeable, it would seem that the issue is one of negligence, not proximate cause; no harm to others being foreseeable, the defendant simply is not negligent at all. There is a good, supplemented annotation. William H. Danne, Jr., Annotation, Liability of Motorist Who Left Key in Ignition for Damage or Injury Caused by Stranger Operating the Vehicle, 45 A.L.R.3d 787 (1972).

18. See Palma v. U.S. Industrial Fasteners, Inc., 36 Cal.3d 171, 681 P.2d 893, 203 Cal.Rptr. 626 (1984) (foreseeability not necessarily linked to case of parking in a crime-ridden district); Poskus v. Lombardo's of Randolph, Inc., 423 Mass. 637, 670 N.E.2d 383 (1996) (rejecting older authority in favor of a case-by-case adjudication); McClenahan v. Cooley, 806 S.W.2d 767 (Tenn.1991) (accepting trend of growing number of cases to adjudicate foreseeability of criminal act on case-by-case basis).

19. Concord Florida, Inc. v. Lewin, 341 So.2d 242, 245 (Fla.App. 1976) ("the risk created here was not that of an arsonist or madman setting fire to a building, per se, but rather, the risk of fire, itself").

others are at least are consistent with it in subjecting the defendant to liability.[20]

The no-duty rules. The problem of intervening criminal acts is largely a problem of duty, not proximate cause. Courts have said in many contemporary cases that in the absence of a special relationship, the defendant simply owes no duty to take affirmative action to protect the plaintiff from a third person.[21] In the older cases, courts enforced that idea by asserting that, as a matter of law, intervening criminal conduct was not foreseeable. Because intervening criminal acts are quite often entirely foreseeable, that assertion seems strange, but it can now be understood as less about foreseeability itself than about the courts' notion about the appropriate scope of duty, which may turn largely on other matters altogether. Today, once courts decide that a defendant should use reasonable care to protect the plaintiff from crimes, foreseeability of crime has become an issue of fact, not a rule of law. Thus, if a duty of care is owed, taverns providing the alcohol that fuels criminal automobile driving, institutions releasing dangerous persons into the community, landlords leaving locks in disrepair, schools failing to protect students from attackers, and many others are now potentially subject to liability for harmful criminal behavior. But there is no blanket duty any more than there is a blanket immunity. Consequently, such cases must be considered in connection with the rules limiting duty.[22]

§ 191. Intervening Forces of Nature

Forces of nature play a role in many negligence cases. Unforeseeable natural forces are still sometimes called acts of God.[1] Courts often speak of natural forces as if special rules are needed in those cases, but with the exception of certain statutory claims and a few common law cases now of little significance, the decisions comport with the general rules of negligence and proximate cause. It is thus entirely possible to drop terms like "act of God" altogether.[2] And again with one exception, natural

20. d'Hedouville v. Pioneer Hotel Co., 552 F.2d 886 (9th Cir.1977); Hodge v. Nor-Cen, Inc. 527 N.E.2d 1157 (Ind.App.1988); Britton v. Wooten, 817 S.W.2d 443 (Ky. 1991); Kilventon v. United Missouri Bank, 865 S.W.2d 741 (Mo.App.1993) (if defendant was negligent in storing explosives in unmarked trailers, it would be liable for deaths resulting from explosion, even though the explosion was triggered by an arsonist); Ohio Fair Plan Underwriting Ass'n. v. Arcara, 65 Ohio App.2d 169, 417 N.E.2d 115 (1979).

21. See § 322.

22. See Chapter 21.

§ 191

1. Courts sometimes speak of the act of God "defense," e.g., Lang v. Wonnenberg, 455 N.W.2d 832 (N.D.1990), but in common law negligence cases it is not a matter of affirmative defense unless the burden of proof has been shifted to the defendant, as in cases where carriers were entrusted with a shipper's goods. Otherwise, an "act of God," if it works to prevent liability, is a roundabout way of saying that the defendant was not negligent, a point that goes to negate the plaintiff's prima facie case but that is not a matter on which the defendant must carry the burden of proof. However, when statutes put the burden on the defendant to justify a loss, act of God may be a true affirmative defense.

2. See the explication below; also Denis Binder, Act of God? Or Act of Man?: A Reappraisal of the Act of God Defense in Tort Law, 15 Rev. Litig. 1 (1996).

forces almost never create issues of proximate cause as distinct from issues of cause in fact.[3]

Natural force present when defendant acts. First, the defendant who acts in the presence of a natural force such as a high wind, cannot plausibly claim that the wind is an intervening cause at all; it does not intervene if it is already in operation when the defendant acts.

Natural force foreseeable. Second, the defendant who can reasonably be expected to foresee and act upon the danger of a natural force is negligent if he fails to take that force into account. I should not negligently destroy all the boats when heavy flooding is forecast because I can reasonably foresee that they will be needed. By the same token, I cannot claim that the flood, when it arrives, is a superseding cause of the harm that results because boats are not available. The prospect of natural disaster is the very special reason why I should have cared for the boats. I would be liable for my negligence in such a case, just as in other cases of foreseeable harms.[4]

Natural force unforeseeable. Third, the defendant who cannot reasonably be expected to foresee that a dangerous natural force will appear is usually simply not negligent at all because no harm of any kind is a foreseeable result of his acts. If no flood is foreseeable, the defendant is not negligent in failing to sandbag the river.[5] Such a result has nothing whatever to do with proximate cause, which is an issue that can only arise when the defendant is negligent and that negligence can be identified as creating specified risks.

Negligence concurring with unforeseeable force of nature to produce foreseeable harm. Two remaining groups of natural force cases are a little different. Sometimes the defendant negligently creates a risk of harm that is then actually inflicted by an unforeseeable natural force. For example, the defendant's release of waters may risk flooding his neighbor. If the neighbor is in fact flooded, but solely as a result of an unforeseeable rainfall, the defendant is not liable. On the other hand, if the neighbor is flooded as a result of both the extraordinary and unforeseeable rainfall and the defendant's release of waters, courts say that the defendant's negligence "concurs" with the natural force and the

3. "Act of God" often turns out to be about cause in fact rather than about intervening forces or legal cause. Thus intervening forces of nature are said to bar the plaintiff's claim only when the injury would have occurred even without the defendant's activity. See Trotter v. Callens, 89 N.M. 19, 546 P.2d 867 (Ct.App.1976). That means the defendant's activity was not a cause in fact under the but-for rule.

4. See Bradford v. Universal Construction Co., Inc., 644 So.2d 864 (Ala.1994) (if high winds were foreseeable, defendant might have been negligent in leaving unweighted plywood sheets where wind might blow them into the plaintiff); Lanz v. Pearson, 475 N.W.2d 601 (Iowa 1991) (icy or obscured condition on highway); Maussner v. Atlantic City Country Club, Inc., 299 N.J.Super. 535, 691 A.2d 826 (1997) (golf course operator would be subject to liability if it could foresee lightning injuries to patrons and had a duty, or had undertaken one, to protect them).

5. E.g., Rocky Mountain Thrift Stores, Inc. v. Salt Lake City Corporation, 887 P.2d 848 (Utah 1994) ("no duty" to protect against unforeseeable flooding, hence no negligence).

defendant remains liable for the harm done.[6] This is correct on the facts supposed because the type of harm that resulted was of the same general kind risked by the defendant in the first place, so liability is not only consistent with the foreseeability rule but also demanded by it.

Negligence concurring with unforeseeable force of nature to produce unforeseeable harm. A few old cases went beyond this kind of liability. These cases held that a carrier who negligently delayed delivery of a shipment would be liable if, during the delay period, the goods were damaged or destroyed by an unforeseeable natural force such as a flood.[7] Since the defendant's delay was negligent, but not because of the danger of flooding, imposition of liability for physical damage to the goods by an unforeseeable flood conflicts with the foreseeability or scope of risk rule.[8] Other courts, including the United States Supreme Court, have rejected liability for harm resulting from an unforeseeable force of nature where the harm caused was not the kind risked by the defendant.[9] So far as the issue arises with common carriers, liabilities are heavily regulated by federal law with its preemptive power.

The result is that for the overwhelming number of common law cases, ordinary rules of negligence and proximate cause—including scope of risk rules—apply to intervening natural forces and that no special rules attach to such cases.

§ 192. Foreseeable Intervening Negligent Acts

General Rule

Although older cases sometimes took a narrower view, the defendant's responsibility for negligence today is not ordinarily superseded by an intervening cause if he could foresee such an intervening cause or a similar one.[1] Because precise foreseeability is not the test, and because negligence of others is often readily foreseeable, intervening negligent acts can seldom properly count as superseding causes. The result is that, for the great majority of cases, both the negligent original defendant and the negligent intervening actor are both liable for the harm they have together inflicted under the rules for joint and several liability or comparative fault.

When Intervening Act or Force is the Risk Defendant Negligently Created

Principle. The most obvious case for rejecting a superseding cause argument is one in which the trier's finding of negligence logically

6. E.g., Lang v. Wonnenberg, 455 N.W.2d 832 (N.D.1990). The defendant is of course also liable if the rainfall was foreseeable.

7. E.g., Green–Wheeler Shoe Co. v. Chicago, Rock Island & Pacific Ry. Co., 130 Iowa 123, 106 N.W. 498 (1906).

8. See the illustration in § 187 involving a driver whose speed is such that he happens to be under a tree just as it falls.

9. Memphis & Charleston Railroad Co. v. Reeves, 77 U.S. (10 Wall.) 176, 19 L.Ed. 909 (1869).

§ 192

1. § 186.

includes a finding that an intervening cause was foreseeable. Put otherwise, "intervening causes which lie within the scope of the foreseeable risk ... are not superseding causes which relieve the initial tortfeasor from liability."[2]

Applications: injury in minimizing or escaping risk defendant created. When the defendant creates a risk of harm to the plaintiff or others, the risk often includes a risk of injury to those attempting to escape or minimize harm. Consequently, the plaintiff who escapes injury from the defendant's negligently driven truck may recover for injuries incurred in the attempt to escape or to minimize risks to others. For instance, if her car is forced off the road by a negligent defendant, she can recover from that defendant for injury suffered when she is struck by another motorist while trying to minimize risks by flagging other motorists.[3] In such cases, the analogy to the rescue doctrine is sufficiently clear.[4]

Applications: foreseeable intervening natural forces. The intervention of natural forces is the simplest illustration. I start a fire in my field. The wind rises and spreads the fire to a house. If I was negligent at all, it must have been because I could foresee a spread of the fire. A jury's finding that I am negligent must entail a finding that the wind and the spread of fire was foreseeable. That being so, the intervention of the wind is of no consequence whatever; I am liable for harm done by the wind-spread fire.[5] Similarly, if I as a physician fail to warn my patient that his disease is contagious, I can foresee that the disease may spread to others, and I cannot avoid liability to those others on the ground that the intervening growth of virus or bacteria is a superseding cause.[6]

Applications: static conditions and intervening acts. A defendant who creates or maintains any kind of static condition is simply not negligent unless he can foresee some intervening act or force that would tend to cause injury. A slippery floor in an empty world presents no risks

2. Morris v. Farley Enterprises, Inc., 661 P.2d 167, 170 (Alaska 1983). The point is well illustrated in Parvi v. City of Kingston, 41 N.Y.2d 553, 362 N.E.2d 960, 394 N.Y.S.2d 161 (1977), where officers took charge of an intoxicated person, then deposited him near a dangerous highway. Struggling to get back home, he entered upon the highway and was struck. The court said: "To accept the defendant's argument, that the intoxication was itself the proximate cause of Parvi's injury as a matter of law, would be to negate the very duty imposed on the police officers when they took Parvi and Dugan into custody.... it is the very fact of plaintiff's drunkenness which precipitated the duty once the officers made the decision to act." Id. At 560.

3. Marshall v. Nugent, 222 F.2d 604 (1st Cir.1955) (plaintiff's vehicle went off the road to avoid defendant's truck; plaintiff was struck by another motorist while attempting to reach a point at which he could flag traffic; the defendant could not avoid liability on proximate cause grounds). Note that if the plaintiff were injured from forces not risked by the defendant, say the fortuitous crash of an airplane, the defendant would not be subject to liability. See § 189.

4. § 185.

5. New York's rule is uniquely different. See § 188.

6. See DiMarco v. Lynch Homes–Chester County, Inc., 525 Pa. 558, 583 A.2d 422 (1990); Bradshaw v. Daniel, 854 S.W.2d 865 (Tenn.1993); cf. Pate v. Threlkel, 661 So.2d 278 (Fla.1995) (genetically caused condition, duty to warn patient's daughter). In some spread of disease cases, a court might deny liability because of the court's conception of policy, not because of foreseeability. See Zysk v. Zysk, 239 Va. 32, 404 S.E.2d 721 (1990).

at all; only if the defendant can foresee that someone may attempt to walk on the floor will he be negligent. Consequently, if the defendant who maintains a slippery floor, a dangerous step, an unguarded shaft or excavation, or an obstruction that blocks vision at an intersection, is negligent, he cannot reasonably argue that the victim's own act was an unforeseeable superseding cause.[7] The victim might be chargeable with contributory negligence in some cases and might for that reason find her damages reduced, but the negligent defendant will not be able to invoke superseding cause rules to escape liability altogether.[8]

It is of course possible that the defendant, foreseeing no harm, is not negligent at all and will escape liability for that reason. In addition, a third person may sometimes substantially enhance the risk of harm from a static condition. If so, and if such enhanced risk is not foreseeable and not part of the original risk, the enhanced risk may count as a superseding cause.[9] If enhancement of the risk by third persons is itself foreseeable or is the very danger created by the defendant in the first place, the defendant remains liable. For instance, if the defendant negligently leaves a hole in the roadway and the plaintiff's car, striking it, is immobilized, it is foreseeable that the plaintiff may be struck by another motorist, and the defendant cannot avoid liability on the ground that the motorist is a superseding cause.[10]

7. See, e.g., McKenna v. Volkswagenwerk Aktiengesellschaft, 57 Haw. 460, 558 P.2d 1018 (1977) (car ran off onto negligently maintained shoulder then went out of control, causing collision; jury could find that negligence of driver was foreseeable, so that city could not escape liability on proximate cause argument); Atlantic Mutual Ins. Co. v. Kenney, 323 Md. 116, 591 A.2d 507 (1991) (truck parked so as to obstruct drivers' view at intersection); Landy v. Olson & Serley Sash & Door Co., 171 Minn. 440, 214 N.W. 659 (1927) (shaft); Harvey v. Hansen, 299 Pa.Super. 474, 445 A.2d 1228 (1982) (visual obstruction). Cf. Fox v. Travis Realty Co., 262 Ill.App.3d 1071, 635 N.E.2d 538, 200 Ill.Dec. 199 (1994) (plaintiff, attempting to lower himself from an elevator stalled between floors, fell into the shaft when his feet missed the floor and he lost his grip on the elevator's bottom; error for trial court to grant summary judgment for defendant on proximate cause grounds).

8. See Ward v. K mart Corp., 136 Ill.2d 132, 143 Ill.Dec. 288, 554 N.E.2d 223 (1990); Simmers v. Bentley Construction Co., 64 Ohio St.3d 642, 597 N.E.2d 504 (1992). On the plaintiff's fault as a proximate cause rather than comparative fault issue, see § 196.

9. Cf. Bryant v. Glastetter, 32 Cal. App.4th 770, 38 Cal.Rptr.2d 291 (1995) (allegedly intoxicated driver arrested; tow truck driver, removing a car at the insistence of police, was injured by another vehicle; held, no claim against the allegedly intoxicated driver).

10. Cruz v. City of New York, 218 A.D.2d 546, 630 N.Y.S.2d 523 (1995); cf. Bigbee v. Pac. Tel. & Tel. Co., 34 Cal.3d 49, 665 P.2d 947, 192 Cal.Rptr. 857 (1983) (defective telephone booth at an intersection; plaintiff could not get out when he saw a car coming at him; a jury question whether the telephone company can escape liability on superseding cause grounds); Derdiarian v. Felix Contracting Corp., 51 N.Y.2d 308, 434 N.Y.S.2d 166, 414 N.E.2d 666 (1980) (contractor stationed worker at end of an excavation exposed to approaching motorists, one of whom crashed into the excavation). *Obstructions forcing dangerous detour*: When the defendant is responsible for an obstruction that forces the plaintiff into a dangerous detour, some courts regard the plaintiff's injury from dangers of the detour to be either foreseeable or a part of the original risk. In that case, liability is imposed. See O'Neill v. City of Port Jervis, 253 N.Y. 423, 171 N.E. 694 (1930). Other courts believe that if the plaintiff is injured by a negligent driver while she is detouring the defendant's obstruction, the driver is a superseding cause. Newell v. Darnell, 209 N.C. 254, 183 S.E. 374 (1936).

Applications: intervening active negligence; negligent entrustment. The very reason for holding a defendant responsible for entrusting a vehicle to an incompetent driver or a gun to a mentally disturbed person is that the driver may drive dangerously or the disturbed person may fire upon others. If the driver causes an injury without driving dangerously, the entrusting defendant would not be responsible, since the risk he unreasonably created was the risk of dangerous driving, not the risk of safe driving.[11] On the other hand, if the driver's dangerous management of the vehicle causes harm, the defendant who entrusted the vehicle to a foreseeably dangerous driver cannot escape liability on the ground that the driver's negligence intervened to cause the harm, because the driver's negligence is the very danger he should have foreseen.[12]

The same is true when it comes to entrustment of a dangerous weapon.[13] And negligently permitting an unsafe user to have access to a dangerous instrumentality is obviously just a variation on the same point.[14] In that case, too, the defendant's negligence consists in creating the foreseeable danger that another person will intervene to misuse the instrumentality in a dangerous way.[15]

Applications: intervening active negligence; high speed police chases. Contemporary cases involving high speed police chases also illustrate the principle that when the intervening acts are themselves within the risk created by the defendant, they are not superseding causes. Police in pursuit of a law violator may enjoy an immunity from liability or they may not be negligent at all.[16] But if they have no immunity and they are in fact negligent, the risk they create is that some person will be harmed by the negligent high-speed driving of the police or their quarry. If the

11. See, e.g., Keller v. Kiedinger, 389 So.2d 129, 12 A.L.R.4th 1048 (Ala. 1980) (noting that the bad driving must be incompetent in some dangerous respect, but not necessarily actionably negligent, as where the driver is a child not chargeable with negligence).

12. E.g., Jamar v. Patterson, 910 S.W.2d 118 (Tex.App.1995) ("Jamar's negligence in entrusting the motor vehicle to an unlicenced driver was proved to be a proximate cause of her injury by showing that Istre operated the vehicle negligently and that her negligence was a proximate cause of the accident"). Sometimes the person to whom the vehicle is entrusted is the one injured, but that, too, is often foreseeable. See Greenwood v. Gardner, 189 Kan. 68, 366 P.2d 780 (1961) (10–year-old child, himself injured while driving defendant's car at defendant's invitation, jury questions on all issues). A finding of no proximate cause is appropriate, however, when the driver's negligence is not the kind that was foreseeable and when the driver's lack of a license is not proximately related to his bad driving. Hack v. Nester, 241 Va. 499, 404 S.E.2d 42 (1990) (borrower's license had been suspended but he was eligible for reinstatement)

13. See Williams v. Bumpass, 568 So.2d 979 (Fla.App.1990) (defendant negligent to retrieve the owner's gun for him because it was foreseeable that owner would fire it at the plaintiff, intervening act issue not specifically raised); Ross v. Glaser, 220 Mich. App. 183, 559 N.W.2d 331 (1996) (discussing foreseeability mostly in terms of duty of the entrustor).

14. Kuhns v. Brugger, 390 Pa. 331, 135 A.2d 395, 68 A.L.R.2d 761 (1957); Annotation, Liability of Person Permitting Child to Have Gun, or Leaving Gun Accessible to Child, for Injury Inflicted by the Latter, 68 A.L.R.2d 782 (1959).

15. The same is logically true if the gun is taken by theft or fraud and used to rob or kill. See Franco v. Bunyard, 261 Ark. 144, 547 S.W.2d 91 (1977). However, in spite of the constant presence of crime, courts sometimes conclude that criminal acts are unforeseeable and that the defendant is not responsible. See § 190.

16. See § 272.

quarry collides with bystanders, the quarry's negligence cannot logically count as a superseding cause, since, by hypothesis, the police, if negligent at all, must have been negligent because they could foresee that the high speed chase might injure someone. The quarry's negligence was not only foreseeable, but was the very risk that made the officers negligent. Most courts therefore hold that when injury occurs before the chase is called off,[17] it is for the jury to determine whether the quarry's negligence is a superseding cause.[18]

A few cases that reach the opposite result seem to have used proximate cause language to reach entirely different issues of immunity,[19] negligence,[20] or assumed risk.[21]

Other applications. In many other cases, the finding of negligence implies that an intervening act is foreseeable and thus eliminates the superseding cause argument. Suppose the state builds a road with a sharp and deep drop at the edge. If this is negligent, it must be because a driver may foreseeably go off the road and lose control with ensuing harm. To find negligence in such a case is to find that a negligent driver's "intervening" act is foreseeable, so once again, that driver's

17. Kimber v. City of Warrenville, 248 Ill.App.3d 361, 617 N.E.2d 1263, 187 Ill. Dec. 542 (1993).

18. Estate of Aten v. City of Tucson, 169 Ariz. 147, 817 P.2d 951 (Ct.App. 1991); Tetro v. Town of Stratford, 189 Conn. 601, 458 A.2d 5 (1983); Fiser v. City of Ann Arbor, 417 Mich. 461, 339 N.W.2d 413 (1983) (jury question whether officers' negligence was too remote or insignificant); Jones v. Ahlberg, 489 N.W.2d 576 (N.D. 1992); Haynes v. Hamilton County, 883 S.W.2d 606 (Tenn.1994) (overruling a contrary case only six years old); Mason v. Bitton, 85 Wash.2d 321, 534 P.2d 1360 (1975); Peak v. Ratliff, 185 W.Va. 548, 408 S.E.2d 300 (1991) (more than one proximate cause, but concluding that the facts did not show recklessness required under a statute); DeWald v. State, 719 P.2d 643 (Wyo.1986). Some cases that approve liability for police chase injuries simply have not discussed the proximate cause argument at all. Selkowitz v. County of Nassau, 45 N.Y.2d 97, 379 N.E.2d 1140, 408 N.Y.S.2d 10 (1978).

19. Some states simply enact an immunity, which of course has nothing to do with proximate cause but with a policy independent of foreseeability. But some cases invoke the immunity and also use proximate cause language. See Dennis v. City of Philadelphia, 153 Pa.Commw. 81, 620 A.2d 625 (1993).

20. See Chambers v. Ideal Pure Milk Co., 245 S.W.2d 589 (Ky.1952) ("Charged as they were with the obligation to enforce the law, the traffic laws included, they would have been derelict in their duty had they not pursued him"); Oberkramer v. City of Ellisville, 706 S.W.2d 440 (Mo.1986) ("The plaintiffs have pleaded no acts of negligence on the part of the police officers. The proximate cause of the accident was not the manner in which Officer Franey drove his police vehicle but rather the manner in which the pursued traffic violator drove his vehicle. Officer Franey was not careless or reckless and he acted as a prudent police officer performing his duty in an emergency situation"). In DeWald v. State, 719 P.2d 643 (Wyo.1986), the court set a low standard of care for officers in a chase, holding that they would be liable only for outrageous misconduct. It then expressed this idea by saying that merely negligent conduct would not be a proximate cause of injury, though outrageous conduct would be.

21. Blair v. City of Rainbow City, 542 So.2d 275 (Ala.1989) (where pursued driver was the victim, "choice to speed and drive recklessly to evade capture was Ricky's alone"); Kimber v. City of Warrenville, 248 Ill.App.3d 361, 617 N.E.2d 1263, 187 Ill. Dec. 542 (1993) (officer's pursuit might be a proximate cause of bystander injury but not of injury to the pursued driver); cf. Estate of Day v. Willis, 897 P.2d 78 (Alaska 1995) (duty of care to third persons but not to the quarry and the claim might also be barred by the rule that plaintiffs cannot found a claim on their own illegal acts).

negligence is not a superseding cause.[22] Or a defendant leaves a large industrial cable spool weighing half a ton near a school yard. Children find it, try to ride it and are crushed when they fall under it. The children's play with the spool is not a superseding cause.[23] Indeed, if their play and danger is not foreseeable, it is hard to imagine in what way the defendant was negligent in leaving the spool available.

Similarly, when someone is injured by a product whose manufacturer negligently omitted safety devices, the manufacturer cannot automatically escape liability on the ground that the purchaser's negligence in using the product without the safety device was a superseding cause.[24] If you are negligent in failing to provide safety devices, you must necessarily foresee that injury could result; otherwise, no safety device would be needed, and you would not be negligent at all.

When Intervening Act or Force is Foreseeable—Aggravated and Second Injuries

Intervening negligent act foreseeable. In many other cases, the intervening negligence does not seem to be so much a part of the original risk but it is deemed foreseeable or at least arguable enough to permit a jury to so find. Under the approaches already discussed, the defendant today does not usually escape liability merely because he could not foresee the specific manner of injury or the specific kind of intervening act that occurred.[25] Juries are allowed to find that intervening causes are foreseeable and thus to hold the original actor responsible even when the intervening act occurs much later in time. The original actor may be liable, for example, not only for the harm he directly causes, but also for the additional harm inflicted when the injury is aggravated by negligent medical treatment.[26] Somewhat similarly, if the plaintiff suffers a second injury in part because he still operates under a residual disability of the first, the jury may find that the second injury was foreseeable, and the defendant who caused the original harm may be liable.[27]

22. Maresh v. State, 241 Neb. 496, 489 N.W.2d 298 (1992) (rejecting state's superseding cause argument); cf. Rue v. State Dept. of Highways, 372 So.2d 1197 (La. 1979) (similar view on contributory negligence issue).

23. Baltimore Gas & Elec. Co. v. Lane, 338 Md. 34, 656 A.2d 307 (1995), overruled in part, Baltimore Gas & Elec. Co. v. Flippo, 348 Md. 680, 705 A.2d 1144 (1998).

24. Leibreich v. A.J. Refrigeration, Inc., 67 Ohio St.3d 266, 617 N.E.2d 1068 (1993).

25. § 189 supra.

26. Smith v. Hardy, 144 Ga.App. 168, 240 S.E.2d 714 (1977) (jury could find original actor to be proximate cause of subsequent medical negligence); Lujan v. Healthsouth Rehabilitation Corp., 120 N.M. 422, 902 P.2d 1025 (1995); see Annotation, Civil liability of one causing personal injury for consequences of negligence, mistake, or lack of skill of physician or surgeon, 100 A.L.R.2d 808 (1965). If the medical negligence is deemed foreseeable, the traditional rule held that the original actor was jointly and severally liable with the health care provider for the entire injury, but the health care provider was liable only for the injuries he separately caused and jointly and severally liable only to that extent.

27. E.g., Gibo v. City and County of Honolulu, 51 Haw. 299, 459 P.2d 198 (1969); Stephenson v. Air Products and Chemicals, Inc., 114 Ill.App.2d 124, 252 N.E.2d 366 (1969); see Bowyer v. Te–Co., Inc., 310 S.W.2d 892 (Mo.1958); Ferrante v. August, 248 Or. 16, 432 P.2d 167 (1967); Restatement Second of Torts § 460 (1965); Joslyn, Annotation, Proximate Cause: Liability of Tortfeasor for Injured Person's Subsequent Injury or Reinjury, 31 A.L.R.3d 1000 (1970). Under the usual practice, how-

§ 193. Unforeseeable Intervening Acts

Injury Outside the Risk

Intervening negligent act as superseding cause. An intervening act is regarded as a superseding cause when it is outside the scope of the risk the defendant negligently created. This idea is usually expressed in shorthand by saying that if the intervening act is itself unforeseeable, then it may become a superseding cause.[1] The shorthand is misleading when the defendant negligently creates a broad risk of harm that may come about through a variety of means. In those cases, foreseeability of the precise intervening act itself is not important.[2] On the other hand, when the defendant creates a narrow risk likely to come about only through a particular kind of intervening act or in a particular sequence, injury that comes about through any other means is not within the risk. These are the unforeseeable intervening act cases, and in these cases liability is inappropriate whether or not the superseding cause language is used.

Examples. An example is *Sheehan v. City of New York.*[3] In that case, a bus stopped at an intersection to permit passengers to board or alight, but, in violation of traffic regulations, did not pull over to the curb. While the bus was stopped, it was struck from behind by a sanitation truck in which the brakes had failed. A passenger on the bus was injured. Although the bus driver, by stopping at the intersection in a lane of traffic and not at the curb, created risks of injury to passengers who might be boarding or alighting, he did not create any special risk to passengers on board the bus; vehicles must frequently stop in traffic lanes, and especially at intersections. The general risk rule would exclude liability. The result can also be expressed by saying that the operation of the sanitation truck was a superseding cause.

In a South Carolina case,[4] a signal at a railroad crossing was out of order, constantly signaling the imminent arrival of a train that was not approaching. The defendant, responsible for maintaining the signal, was negligent in allowing this condition to persist because it was foreseeable that some individuals would learn of the malfunction and ignore the signal at a time when a train really was approaching. That did not happen. Instead, the plaintiff, a driver who did not know of the malfunction, came to a stop at the crossing. The driver behind her failed to stop

ever, the question is one for the trier, and the trier may conclude that the second injury was independent of the first and thus not caused by it. E.g., Buckland v. Reed, 629 N.E.2d 1241 (Ind.App.1994). Occasionally courts take the issue from the jury and decide for the defendant. Skollingsberg v. Brookover, 26 Utah 2d 45, 484 P.2d 1177 (1971).

§ 193

1. E.g., Duphily v. Delaware Electric Cooperative, Inc., 662 A.2d 821 (Del.1995) quoted in § 186 supra.

2. See § 189.

3. Sheehan v. City of New York, 40 N.Y.2d 496, 387 N.Y.S.2d 92, 354 N.E.2d 832 (1976).

4. Newton v. South Carolina Public Railways Comm'n., 319 S.C. 430, 462 S.E.2d 266 (1995).

and the plaintiff was seriously injured. As the court saw it, nothing like this was within the scope of the risk, which was focused on one particular kind of event, a driver's injury from a train resulting because he discounted the signal. Given that view, the defendant should not be liable and that was the court's holding. However, the outcome was expressed, as it usually is, as a product of the superseding cause rules: the second driver's negligence was a superseding cause.

As these cases show, the superseding cause determination is quite often merely a specific instance of and a way of talking about the fundamental rule that liability is limited to the risks that the defendant has negligently imposed.

Termination of the Risk

The same fundamental idea applies when the defendant creates a risk from particular forces and those forces have been spent, so that the risk has "terminated" and the plaintiff's injury results from a new force that is outside the original risk.

For example, suppose that the defendant negligently drives into the plaintiff's vehicle, leaving it disabled in the eastbound lane of traffic. One risk of the defendant's negligence—impact with the plaintiff's car—has actually eventuated. But other risks remain. In particular, the disabled car might be in danger of being struck from behind by a car traveling in the same direction. If that happens, the defendant will not escape liability merely because some of the injury he risked has already come about.[5] But if the plaintiff's disabled car is struck by a falling airplane, or a car proceeding in the opposite direction and that crosses the center line to strike the plaintiff's car, the injury resulting from *that* impact is unforeseeable and not one of the risks the defendant negligently created. In that case, the plaintiff's stopped car is no more at risk from a sudden chance movement of an oncoming car than if the plaintiff had been driving her car in the same lane, and liability is inappropriate.[6] Similarly, as Judge Magruder suggested, once the impact is over and the plaintiff drives on down the highway, it is possible to think of the risk as being terminated and the situation stabilized.[7]

5. Hairston v. Alexander Tank & Equipment Co., 310 N.C. 227, 311 S.E.2d 559 (1984) (defendant improperly installed wheel on a customer's car; it came off and the customer brought the car to a stop on a bridge, where another driver ran into and killed the customer; the intervening negligence was inexcusable but not improbable).

6. Copple v. Warner, 260 N.C. 727, 133 S.E.2d 641 (1963).

7. Marshall v. Nugent, 222 F.2d 604 (1st Cir.1955). See Exxon Company, U.S.A. v. Sofec, Inc., 517 U.S. 830, 116 S.Ct. 1813, 135 L.Ed.2d 113 (1996), discussed in § 196. In O'Connor v. Nigg, 254 Mont. 416, 838 P.2d 422 (1992), the allegations were that Nigg negligently lost control of his vehicle on an interstate highway, went off the road and turned over. A car behind Nigg stopped, completely off the roadway. Its occupants assisted Nigg into a third car. Five minutes later Officer Cousineau arrived and pulled his car off the road and put on his flashing lights. Another five minutes elapsed before O'Connor approached in his car and slowed. Officer Cousineau motioned him to keep going, but O'Connor slowed almost to a stop, looking back at the scene. At that point, undeterred by the flashing lights, the activity at the scene, or O'Connor's slow or stopped car in the highway, one Drapella drove her car into the rear of O'Connor's car at high speed, failing to apply her brakes. The injured O'Connor

The terminology of risk termination, like a good deal of terminology in proximate cause cases, is superfluous. The underlying idea is that the injury that occurred—a second impact not made more likely by the first—is outside the risk negligently created by the defendant. This is not a mechanical rule. In some cases, the first impact very definitely does create risks of further injuries, and the tortfeasor is liable for them if they occur. For example, a tortfeasor may be liable for injuries inflicted by a health care provider in treating the first injury and also for second injuries resulting because of weakness caused by the first injury.[8]

§ 194. Shifting Responsibility to the Intervening Actor by Contract or Otherwise

Express or implied assumption of responsibility by second actor. Another special category of "superseding cause" cases actually involve shifted responsibility or shifted duty of care. Actor A creates a risk or potential risk of harm to the plaintiff, but B, by contract, tacit understanding, or otherwise, assumes control of the risk and can reasonably be expected to provide adequate safety. Unless such an arrangement violates a contractual obligation to the plaintiff or a public policy,[1] responsibility may be shifted to B, thus relieving A of liability as a matter of law. The general principle, in one form or another, has been recognized explicitly by the Restatement[2] and a number of cases.[3] Many other cases seem to be based on the idea without actually using its terminology.[4]

For example, suppose that Doctor A, believing that he may have made an error in diagnosis, arranges for Doctor B, a specialist, to examine the patient with a view to correcting any error. Doctor B finds the error, but fails to notify the patient, with the result that the disease becomes irreversible. The ordinary rules of superseding cause might

sued Nigg on the theory that he started it all by negligently overturning his car. The court held for the defendant as a matter of law. The result is consistent with a terminated risk view. The likelihood of gawking drivers and impatient speedsters long after the car went off the road may well be outside the risk that Nigg should have had in mind when he overturned.

8. See § 192.

§ 194

1. As in the case of a nondelegable duty. See § 337.

2. Restatement § 452 (2).

3. See e.g., Siggers v. Barlow, 906 F.2d 241 (6th Cir.1990); McCleaf v. State, 190 Ariz. 167, 945 P.2d 1298 (Ariz.App.1997). Some courts have recognized the point but not elucidated it. E.g., Farwell v. Un, 902 F.2d 282 (4th Cir.1990); Kulingoski v. Liquid Transporters, Inc., 39 F.3d 1166 (Table, Text in Westlaw, No. 94–1521) (1st Cir. 1994).

4. See Straley v. Kimberly, 687 N.E.2d 360 (Ind. App. 1997) (A negligently caused break in a gas line; B, the gas company, assumed control, and an hour later caused an explosion that injured P; A is not liable); Freeze v. Congleton, 276 N.C. 178, 171 S.E.2d 424 (1970) (when a small child on the defendant's land is accompanied by parents who know of its dangers, the landowner has limited or no responsibility for the child's safety; responsibility falls upon the parents). Another form of shifted responsibility transfers responsibility to the plaintiff herself. This is the case of assumed risk in the sense of consent to accept the risk. A building contractor who undertakes to make repairs to a building in spite of dangers to herself, for example, is accepting responsibility for her own safety as well as the safety of others. This is a case of shifted responsibility, though not normally one of superseding cause.

treat A and B as joint or concurrent tortfeasors,[5] but if B's promise or undertaking is to be given effect, A may be entitled to avoid liability on the ground that his duty of care terminated and was shifted to B.[6]

The idea that responsibility can be shifted by voluntary transactions between the first and second actor is not limited to cases of express contract. Sometimes a voluntary transfer of control of dangerous property will carry with it an implicit understanding that the second actor will take responsibility.[7] Because voluntary, intended shifting of responsibility in whatever form is easily understood as a shift or transfer of the duty of care, the problem of transferring duties by contract or agreement also appears in cases dealing with "assumed risk"[8] and various settings involving "duty" issues.[9]

Discovery and control without voluntary shift of duty. Some older cases permitted the negligent actor to shift responsibility merely because the second actor discovered the danger and had control of it, even though the second actor had not undertaken, much less promised, to make matters safe. Courts once held that a defendant who leaves dangerous instruments like dynamite where a child can find it and be hurt has no liability once a parent knows that the child is in possession of the dynamite. The parent's discovery and control were treated as sufficient grounds for relieving the negligent defendant, although the defendant never knew of the discovery and did not rely upon it.[10]

In the same vein, courts once held that the manufacturer of a defective product could escape liability to a third person injured by the product's defect if the buyer had discovered its defect and failed to make the product safe. The lumber dealer who sold dangerously defective boards for scaffolding would not be liable to a worker ruined in a scaffold's collapse if the buyer of the lumber had discovered the defect.[11] Similarly, the contractor who constructed a dangerously defective building was to be protected from liability as soon as the landowner accepted the work.[12]

5. Because medical negligence after an injury is inflicted is foreseeable, medical negligence is also presumably foreseeable here.

6. Cf. Siggers v. Barlow, 906 F.2d 241 (6th Cir.1990) (on slightly different facts, hospital rules called for review and action by second doctor; responsibility shifted).

7. Thus in the absence of contract, warranty, or statute, the buyer of land becomes the responsible party for defects. See § 239. With similar limitations, similar rules apply to tenants injured by conditions on the premises.

Although courts have discussed the caveat emptor rule in the land purchase cases, and rule that the deed expresses the whole agreement, the real reason for nonliability of the vendor seems to be that he has parted with control, as is sometimes recognized. See Copfer v. Golden, 135 Cal.App.2d 623, 288 P.2d 90 (1955). That explains the exceptions to the rule as well. If he retains control after title has passed, he remains liable.

8. See §§ 213 & 214.

9. See, e.g., § 321. In products liability cases, the manufacturer can sometimes shift of responsibility for warning product users of dangers to the users' employer, see § 366.

10. Pittsburg Reduction Co. v. Horton, 87 Ark. 576, 113 S.W. 647 (1908).

11. Stultz v. Benson Lumber Co., 6 Cal.2d 688, 59 P.2d 100 (1936).

12. See Blake v. Calumet Construction Corp., 674 N.E.2d 167 (Ind.1996) (stating

The premises of modern products liability rules have to a large extent rendered these old rules obsolete. It is no longer the unalterable rule that responsibility is shifted merely because a dealer or purchaser discovers a product's danger[13] or because a landowner accepts a contractor's work.[14] In line with the fundamental rule of foreseeability, the courts have largely abandoned the effort to construct a rule of law that exculpates the first actor merely because a second actor has discovered the danger and could avoid it. Cases like the dynamite cap cases are probably obsolete for other reasons. Courts today presumably regard children with somewhat more concern than the dynamite cap cases evince, but even if they do not, courts today have much less need to resort to all-or-nothing rules of superseding cause; they can use the rules of joint and several liability or even the rule of limited comparative fault liability to hold the dynamite distributor at least partly liable.

If these observations are correct, then shifting responsibility as a rule of law is most appropriately left to cases of express or implied assumption of responsibility. It remains, of course, appropriate for a jury to conclude in particular cases that the second actor is also a tortfeasor along with the first, or even that the second actor is a superseding cause.[15]

§ 195. Intervening Acts as Superseding Causes Regardless of Foreseeability—Using Proximate Cause as a No Duty Rule to Disallow Categories of Claims

Courts today agree that proximate cause, with its subset of superseding cause problems, is to be determined on a case by case analysis, that it is a jury question in all but the most extreme cases, and that it turns on foreseeability in some form. Yet at times courts have disregarded all three of these rules in several kinds of cases as a matter of law excluding liability for certain categories of injuries. The anomaly is gradually being resolved as courts come to treat the problems raised in these cases as duty problems rather than proximate cause problems. They will be discussed in this book as duty problems, but because of the traditional proximate cause language, some of the main examples are identified here.

the old rule but not necessarily supporting it); Pickens v. Tulsa Metropolitan Ministry, 951 P.2d 1079 (Okla.1997) (stating the old rule without deciding whether to retain it except to bar recovery for open and obvious dangers).

13. See e.g., Finnegan v. Havir Manufacturing Corp., 60 N.J. 413, 290 A.2d 286 (1972) (jury question whether manufacturer could expect that buyer would make obvious danger of punch press safe); Holmes v. Wegman Oil Co., 492 N.W.2d 107 (S.D. 1992) (manufacturer's notice to dealer and active recall program did not automatically shift responsibility to dealer; jury question as to superseding cause). See §§ 366 & 370 below.

14. When the accepted work doctrine comes up today, it is usually abolished, e.g., Kragel v. Wal-Mart Stores, Inc., 537 N.W.2d 699 (Iowa 1995), or modified by the injection of ordinary foreseeability rules, see Bush v. SECO Electric Co., 118 F.3d 519 (7th Cir.1997). See §§ 366 & 376 below.

15. See Carroll Electric Cooperative Corporation v. Lytle Carlton, 319 Ark. 555, 892 S.W.2d 496 (1995).

(1) Alcohol providers. Courts once said that, in the absence of a statute specifically imposing tort liability,[1] a bartender who continues to serve alcohol to a minor or to an intoxicated drinker is not liable to the drinker's victims when he drunkenly runs down innocent people, not even if the bartender knows the drinker will drive. The drinker, not the seller of the alcohol, was regarded as the sole proximate cause of the death or injury to others.[2] This could hardly be an application of the proximate cause rules as understood in contemporary thought, since if any harm is foreseeable it is intoxicated driving and its frequent and terrible results.[3] The rule also departed from the usual practice of examining facts of each case to determine foreseeability. Instead, courts made a categorical rule of non-liability for all alcohol providers. To a substantial extent, these rules have changed as courts have come to recognize that the issue is not one of proximate cause at all, but one of duty. The contemporary alcohol cases are considered further in a later chapter.

(2) Suicide/failure to protect the plaintiff from herself. Courts also once held that one who committed suicide was the sole proximate cause of his own death, and that a defendant whose negligence led to the suicide was categorically excused from any liability. Here again, the rule did not resemble the usual proximate cause rule, since at least some suicides would be the foreseeable result of the defendant's negligence, as for example, where the defendant provided heavy doses of depressing drugs.[4] Courts did apply an exception: the negligent defendant would be liable for suicide if the decedent committed the deed while insane.[5] Courts now recognize that at least in some cases a person may have a duty to help prevent suicide, as in the case of a hospital or jail with a known suicidal patient or prisoners.[6] So the most fundamental issue is

§ 195

1. Mere violation of a statute against selling alcohol to minors or intoxicated persons was not sufficient under this regime. Courts imposed liability only if the statute actually created a cause of action.

2. Fleckner v. Dionne, 94 Cal.App.2d 246, 210 P.2d 530 (1949); Parsons v. Jow, 480 P.2d 396. (Wyo.1971).

3. Courts often did not attempt to justify the rule. They could simply declare that "the proximate cause of injury was deemed to be the patron's consumption of liquor and not its sale" without a word about foreseeability or even about superseding cause. And it was plain that when a provider knew that the drinker would drive, danger was foreseeable, because the same courts held that providing a vehicle to an intoxicated person created a foreseeable risk of harm to others.

4. Cf. Runyon v. Reid, 510 P.2d 943, 58 A.L.R.3d 814 (Okla. 1973) (providing drugs without a prescription in violation of statute, suicide an independent intervening act); Scott v. Greenville Pharmacy, 212 S.C. 485, 48 S.E.2d 324 (1948) (allegations that pharmacy illegally provided drugs without prescription and that the decedent committed suicide under their influence; addiction but not suicide was foreseeable); Lancaster v. Montesi, 216 Tenn. 50, 390 S.W.2d 217 (1965) (allegations that woman committed suicide as a result of defendant's long-term sadistic abuse were insufficient; her act was superseding cause).

5. McLaughlin v. Sullivan, 123 N.H. 335, 461 A.2d 123 (1983); Clift v. Narragansett Television L.P., 688 A.2d 805 (R.I. 1996). See Annotation, Gregory G. Sarno, Liability of One Causing Physical Injuries as a Result of which Injured Party Attempts or Commits Suicide, 77 A.L.R.3d 311 (1977).

6. See Hickey v. Zezulka, 439 Mich. 408, 487 N.W.2d 106 (1992) (jailer must use care to protect one in custody from suicide); Cowan v. Doering, 111 N.J. 451, 545 A.2d 159 (1988) (comparative negligence and superseding cause arguments both misplaced

one of duty; suicide cases are considered primarily in connection with that topic.[7] This means that where a duty of care exists, the old categorical rule against liability disappears and the courts consider negligence and proximate cause in the light of the facts of the particular case. This shift does not mean that liability is inevitable, even if negligence is proved. In some cases, suicide is truly unforeseeable or outside the risk created by the defendant, as in the case of a client who commits suicide because his lawyer negligently lost a case.[8]

(3) Emotional harm. Courts have long treated stand-alone emotional harm claims quite differently from physical injury claims. The difference has frequently been explained on the grounds that emotional harm is not a proximate result of the defendant's negligence. It may be true that different rules of liability ought to be employed when the plaintiff claims emotional harm independent of physical injury, but it is most definitely not true that there is anything unforeseeable about the emotional harm of a mother who sees her child seriously and continuously hurt by the defendant's negligence. Nor could proximate cause rules explain a categorical rule circumscribing emotional harm recoveries. So the older proximate cause explanations have been gradually giving way to the understanding that if liability for emotional harm is to be limited, the limits turn on issues of practicality, policy, and justice and not on bare foreseeability alone. These rules, too, must be treated outside the framework of proximate cause.[9]

(4) Economic harm. Stand-alone economic harm, like stand-alone emotional harm, has often been subjected to special rules of liability and immunity. For instance, the defendant might negligently cut off a supply of electricity to a factory, with the result that workers there lose a day's wages while the electricity is restored.[10] Courts frequently conclude that negligence is no basis at all for recovery when the plaintiff suffers such economic harm and no personal injury or property damage. Sometimes they have explained this result in the language of proximate cause—the injury is too remote or indirect. That is no longer the usual explanation, nor should it be. Courts today more commonly recognize that in many

where defendant owes a caretaker duty). Frequently the cases imposing liability upon institutional caretakers do not even discuss the proximate or superseding cause rules. See Meier v. Ross General Hospital, 69 Cal.2d 420, 445 P.2d 519, 71 Cal.Rptr. 903 (1968).

7. See Chapter 21 generally. The issue also arises in particular instances, as where clergy malpractice leads to a parishioner's suicide, see § 258,

8. McLaughlin v. Sullivan, 123 N.H. 335, 461 A.2d 123 (1983) (alleged lawyer malpractice led to conviction and ultimate suicide, lawyer was under no duty to guard against suicide and the connection between negligence and harm was too attenuated in any event). In addition, some of the cases seem to mean only that the defendant was simply not negligent, in spite of the courts' discussions of proximate cause. For example, a defendant who leaves a gun under the counter may not be negligent at all unless there is a reason to think someone would misuse it. The defendant should escape liability for the decedent's suicide in that case because the defendant is not negligent at all, not because he is negligent but protected by superseding cause rules. See Gilmore v. Shell Oil Co., 613 So.2d 1272 (Ala.1993).

9. See Chapter 21.

10. See Stevenson v. East Ohio Gas Co., 73 N.E.2d 200 (Ohio App.1946). Some of the other kinds of cases are considered in connection with negligent interference with contract. See § 452.

situations the defendant owes no duty to use care to prevent pure economic harm, as distinct from personal injury or property damage. The rule is not universal, but where it applies it bars recovery for reasons quite unrelated to foreseeability.

§ 196. Plaintiff's Own Acts as a Superseding Cause

Plaintiff-fault as superseding cause. When the defendant negligently injures the plaintiff, the plaintiff's own fault is normally relevant only under the rules of contributory negligence or comparative fault. In many instances, the plaintiff's fault would be ground for reducing the recovery of damages, but would not exclude recovery altogether. On the other hand, some cases hold that the plaintiff's fault may sometimes count as a superseding cause,[1] or, as courts often say, the sole proximate cause[2] of the plaintiff's own harm. If so, the plaintiff does not merely suffer a reduction in damages but is barred completely. Similarly, under the avoidable consequences rules for minimizing damages, the plaintiff is regarded as the sole proximate cause of damages suffered because she failed to mitigate damages once injury occurred.[3] As to those damages, the plaintiff cannot recover at all.

Rejecting superseding cause analysis for plaintiff fault. This line of reasoning must be accepted with caution; if widely applied it would undermine the comparative negligence system of fault allocation.[4] It may

§ 196

1. Exxon Company, U.S.A. v. Sofec, Inc., 517 U.S. 830, 116 S.Ct. 1813, 135 L.Ed.2d 113 (1996); Gilmore v. Shell Oil Co., 613 So.2d 1272 (Ala.1993); General Motors Corp. v. Wolhar, 686 A.2d 170 (Del.1996) (seat belt non-use admissible to show non-use as supervening cause of injury); Standard Havens Products, Inc. v. Benitez, 648 So.2d 1192 (Fla.1994); Boltax v. Joy Day Camp, 67 N.Y.2d 617, 499 N.Y.S.2d 660, 490 N.E.2d 527 (1986) (plaintiff's act of diving into shallow pool was an "unforeseeable superseding event that absolves defendants of liability"); George v. Rebbe Excavating & Equipment Co., Inc., 236 A.D.2d 442, 653 N.Y.S.2d 663 (1997); Buckley v. Bell, 703 P.2d 1089 (Wyo.1985). See, also recognizing the possibility of plaintiff-fault as a sole proximate cause, Herzog v. Lexington Township, 167 Ill.2d 288, 657 N.E.2d 926, 212 Ill.Dec. 581 (1995); Eady v. Ridgeway, 1996 WL 539791 (Ohio App. 1 Dist.). Cases advancing the superseding cause theory to bar the plaintiff before the adoption of comparative fault, e.g., Sporna v. Kalina, 184 Minn. 89, 237 N.W. 841 (1931), do not seem to be helpful on the issue today, since under the old pre-comparative-fault regime, a superseding cause analysis and a contributory negligence analysis would both result in a judgment for the defendant.

2. The phrase is defense rhetoric and may cloud the court's holding with ambiguity. On its face the phrase seems to mean that the plaintiff's negligence was a superseding cause so that a negligent defendant is not liable. However, at least in some of the cases, courts appear to use the phrase to mean that the defendant was not negligent at all. See, e.g. Strantz v. Pinion, 652 So.2d 738 (Miss.1995); cf. Gilmore v. Shell Oil Co., 613 So.2d 1272 (Ala.1993) (discussing superseding cause, but concluding that decedent's suicide was unforeseeable to the defendant, seemingly meaning that the defendant was not negligent in leaving gun available).

3. See §§ 203 & 204. The rule could be invoked without reference to proximate cause, but the proximate cause rationale is often used. Whether the rule is limited to cases of post-injury failure of care may be debated.

4. In Wright v. New York City Transit Authority, 221 A.D.2d 431, 633 N.Y.S.2d 393 (1995), a passenger was injured when he entered an unlocked subway motorman's cab and stuck his head outside the cab window of the moving train. The court held as a matter of law that the plaintiff passenger's conduct was a superseding cause that broke the causal connection between his injuries and the Transit Authority's assert-

also permit introduction of evidence that would be forbidden on the comparative fault issue.[5] For this reason, some courts reject the possibility that the plaintiff's fault can be a supervening cause.[6]

Middle ground. If the rhetoric of sole cause and superseding cause is dropped, a middle ground becomes apparent. In some cases, the defendant's negligence simply does not create a risk of the kind of harm that the plaintiff suffered. In such a case, the important thing is not that the plaintiff is at fault, or that the plaintiff's fault was a superseding cause, but rather that the harm was outside the scope of the defendant's negligence, or, what is the same thing, that the risk created by the defendant had terminated. In *Exxon Company, U.S.A. v. Sofec, Inc.*,[7] a tanker ship broke away from the defendants' moorings. The defendants may have been responsible. The ship's captain managed to get the breakaway tanker past a number of perils and safely out to sea. Once he reached safety, however, he neglected to get a fix on his position and he ran aground. Exxon was denied a recovery against the defendants. The Court reasoned that the captain's negligence was a superseding cause.

The superseding cause language might suggest heavy reliance on the captain's fault, and if that were the case, it would be plausible to argue that the decision undermines the comparative fault system. But as often is the case, the superseding cause language merely obscures the important point that the harm that befell the tanker was simply not one of the risks of negligently managed moorings.

The upshot is that if the harm done is outside the risk negligently created by the defendant, then of course the defendant is not to be held liable. On the other hand, if the court focuses on the plaintiff's fault rather than the scope of the risk, the case looks like one for comparative fault rules rather than the Draconian proximate cause rules.

In addition, there is one small class of cases in which the defendant's responsibility is to protect the plaintiff from his own actions. If police officers, having an intoxicated person in custody, haul him to the edge of town and deposit him on a dangerous highway where he is struck

ed negligence in leaving the cab unlocked. This is arguably the very kind of case that ought to be left to comparative fault allocation, because the case must rely on the plaintiff's fault rather than on the limited scope of the risk created by the defendant.

5. On the comparative fault issue, some statutes prohibit introduction of evidence that the plaintiff, injured in an automobile upset or collision, failed to wear a seat belt. But if the defendant can plausibly claim that the plaintiff's failure to wear a seat belt was a supervening cause, the evidence may be admitted on the supervening cause issue, though it must be excluded on the comparative fault issue. E.g., General Motors Corp. v. Wolhar, 686 A.2d 170 (Del. 1996).

6. Beirne v. Security Heating–Clearwater Pools, Inc., 759 F.Supp. 1120 (M.D.Pa.1991); Sumpter v. City of Moulton, 519 N.W.2d 427 (Iowa App.1994). Some decisions have defined intervening cause as an act of a third person or outside force. Cf. Hickey v. Zezulka, 439 Mich. 408, 487 N.W.2d 106 (1992); Vilas v. Steavenson, 242 Neb. 801, 496 N.W.2d 543 (1993). If that definition is adhered to, the plaintiff's own conduct would never count as a superseding cause. If that is the right result, it probably should be achieved through policy analysis rather than through the accident of a definition.

7. Exxon Company, U.S.A. v. Sofec, Inc., 517 U.S. 830, 116 S.Ct. 1813, 135 L.Ed.2d 113 (1996).

by a car, they cannot defend a suit on the ground that his intoxication was an intervening cause. To countenance that argument "would be to negate the very duty imposed on the police officers when they took Parvi and Dugan into custody. It would be to march up the hill only to march down again."[8]

Topic D. Alternatives

§ 197. Joint and Several Liability and Comparative Fault Alternatives to Proximate Cause

Proximate cause rules allocate responsibility among tortfeasors. In intervening cause cases, the all-or-nothing proximate cause rule is no longer the only method for allocating responsibility among the various negligent actors. Another method already discussed is to limit the duty of care owed by defendants in special categories of cases.[1] Even more flexibly, it is now possible and even common to impose joint and several liability upon all the actors in a sequence of wrongdoing that culminates in the plaintiff's harm.[2] Modern procedures for contribution and indemnity permit courts to allocate a portion of responsibility to each of several defendants.[3] With the advent of comparative fault, responsibility can be allocated in different percentages to each defendant. And, where joint and several liability is deemed offensive, each defendant can be held liable for his share of the total fault and no more.[4]

These modern procedures were not all widely available until the latter half of the 20th century, some not until its last quarter. Now that they are in place, they show intervening cause issues in a new light. Before these procedures were available, a judge might perceive that relatively little fault was attributable to A, while much fault was attributable to B. Sometimes the only method for obtaining some kind of rough justice as between A and B was to invoke the all-or-nothing proximate cause rule, letting A go without any liability and imposing all liability upon B. This result was not necessarily justified, because, while it might achieve a rough justice between A and B, it did so at the expense of the innocent plaintiff. Such extremes are no longer necessary. A court can now say, as courts often do, that both tortfeasor A and tortfeasor B are proximate causes and impose liability, either jointly and severally or according to their comparative fault share.

Something similar is true in those cases in which the defendant argues that the plaintiff's fault was the "sole proximate cause." In the days when states almost always barred the plaintiff for even slight

8. Parvi v. City of Kingston, 41 N.Y.2d 553, 560, 362 N.E.2d 960, 965, 394 N.Y.S.2d 161, 166 (1977). Compare Bexiga v. Havir Manufacturing Corp., 60 N.J. 402, 290 A.2d 281 (1972), discussed in § 200.

§ 197

1. § 195 above.

2. See § 174.

3. §§ 386 & 387 below.

4. See § 389. Thus, even in that system of apportionment, the all or nothing conclusion that the first actor is not a proximate cause is no longer so common.

contributory fault, it made little difference whether courts said the plaintiff was guilty of contributory negligence or that her negligence was the sole proximate cause. Either way, the plaintiff would be barred. Now that comparative fault rules have been adopted in most states, the plaintiff who is guilty of comparative fault is not necessarily barred; she may simply find her damages award against the defendant reduced to reflect her fault. Under this system, courts will seldom be justified in resorting to all or nothing proximate cause rules that would bar the plaintiff on the ground that her fault was the sole proximate cause.[5]

5. See Godesky v. Provo City Corp., 690 P.2d 541 (Utah 1984) (noting comparative fault options) & § 196 above.

(b) The Defenses

CHAPTER 11

DEFENSES TO THE NEGLIGENCE CLAIM

TOPIC A. AFFIRMATIVE DEFENSES

§ 198. The Nature of Affirmative Defenses

The immediately preceding chapters set out the elements of the plaintiff's prima facie case. The plaintiff who fails to prove or persuade about any one of those elements must lose her case. But it does not follow that the plaintiff will prevail if she proves all the elements. It remains possible for the defendant to prevail by asserting an affirmative defense such as contributory fault, assumed risk, or the statute of limitations.

The outcome of the case may be determined by the plaintiff's failure to prove or persuade the trier on essential elements like negligence or causation. The outcome may equally be determined by the defendant's failure to prove or persuade the trier that a good affirmative defense exists. The difference, of course, is that the plaintiff has the burden of proof when it comes to elements of the case—negligence, legally recognized harm, cause in fact, proximate, cause, and duty. In contrast, the defendant has the burden of producing evidence about defenses like contributory fault and likewise the burden of persuading the trier of fact about what the evidence shows.[1]

Students are sometimes confused on one point. To say that the defendant has the burden of proving an affirmative defense like contributory fault, is not to say that the evidence on that topic must originate with the defendant. The plaintiff's own evidence or admissions may suffice to show such fault. To say that the defendant has the burden is to say that the defendant will be the party who suffers if the evidence is not forthcoming, so that the defendant must be sure that, from whatever source, evidence on the issue does in fact appear.

Real-world outcomes do actually turn on the burden of proof, both in the sense that the judge may direct a verdict against the party who has the burden of proof if the evidence is insufficient and in the sense that even if a given issue goes to the jury, the jury itself may resolve doubts against the party who has the burden. It is therefore important

§ 198

1. Poyner v. Loftus, 694 A.2d 69 (D.C.App.1997) (nevertheless directing a verdict for the party with the burden of proof); Wyser v. Ray Sumlin Construction Co., Inc., 680 So.2d 235 (Ala.1996). On the two senses of "burden of proof," see § 150.

to bear in mind that the burden falls squarely upon the defendant to show such defenses as contributory fault, assumed risk, or the bar of a statute of limitations. Equally, it should be clear that occasional judicial locutions such as "the proximate cause defense" are merely shorthand expressions and definitely not to be taken literally.

TOPIC B. CONTRIBUTORY NEGLIGENCE AND COMPARATIVE FAULT

§ 199. Traditional Rules of Contributory Negligence

Traditional Rule

The traditional rule, subject to some exceptions[1] and now somewhat modified in many states,[2] held that contributory negligence of a plaintiff, or the person from whom the plaintiff derived her claim,[3] was a complete bar to the claim.[4] Contributory negligence was an affirmative defense, so the defendant had the burden of proof on that issue,[5] but once proved, the plaintiff's causal contributory negligence immunized the negligent defendant.

The rule was extreme. The plaintiff who was guilty of only slight or trivial negligence was barred completely, even if the defendant was guilty of quite serious negligence, as contemporary courts have had occasion to observe in criticizing the rule.[6] The traditional contributory negligence rule was extreme not merely in results but in principle. No satisfactory reasoning has ever explained the rule.[7] It departed seriously from ideals of accountability and deterrence because it completely relieved the defendant from liability even if he was by far the most negligent actor. A regime of accountability would, in contrast, hold the

§ 199

1. § 200.

2. § 201.

3. See Restatement § 494. The spouse of an injured person, for example, may have a claim for loss of consortium or society, but it is commonly regarded as derivative and barred to the extent the injured person herself would be barred. See § 310. As to death actions, see § 297.

4. Butterfield v. Forrester, 11 East. 59, 103 Eng.Rep. 926 (1809), decided long before the main growth stages of negligence, might have been interpreted differently, to mean only that, on the facts of the case, the defendant was not negligent at all because he could not have foreseen the plaintiff's conduct and the need to protect against it. See, explaining some interpretations, Malone, Comment on Maki v. Frelk, 21 VAND. L. REV. 930 (1968); Dobbs, Accountability and Comparative Fault, 47 LA. L. REV. 939 (1987).

5. At one time some courts put the burden upon the plaintiff to prove the absence of contributory fault, but this rule is now obsolete.

6. E.g., Dunleavy v. Miller, 116 N.M. 353, 862 P.2d 1212 (1993)

7. Sometimes it was suggested that contributory negligence was a bar because the plaintiff's negligence was a superseding cause and the defendant's negligence no longer a proximate cause. The plaintiff's negligence may supersede the defendant's in particular cases, but certainly not in all. If A and B drive their respective cars negligently, causing injury to T, a pedestrian, B's negligence does not supersede A's. Instead, both are liable to T. By parity of reasoning, if B is injured and sues A, B's contributory negligence could not supersede A's. Other explanations were equally inappropriate.

defendant liable for a proportionate share of the harm.[8]

Parallels to Negligence Analysis

Contributory negligence is a term of art. It is negligence of a plaintiff in failing to exercise care for herself that is one of the causes of her harm.[9] Under this definition, contributory negligence differs from negligence, which is a failure to exercise reasonable care for others.

Nevertheless, to a very large extent contributory negligence analysis parallels negligence analysis.[10] Although it may be awkward to say that the plaintiff owes the defendant a duty to take reasonable care of herself,[11] contributory negligence, like negligence, definitely entails unreasonably risky conduct.[12] The reasonable person standards and the balance of risks and utilities apply to contributory negligence as well as to negligence.[13] For instance, the plaintiff is not necessarily guilty of contributory negligence when she subjects herself to risks in the course of rescuing another person, because the value of saving another makes the risks reasonable.[14] Such holdings are referred to as the second version of the rescue doctrine,[15] but they don't reflect an independent rule, only the ordinary balance of risks and utilities familiar in negligence cases. In the same way, the balance of risks and utilities suggests that the landowner plaintiff is not necessarily guilty of contributory negligence for failing to close up her business merely because the defendant's business on adjoining land runs a risk of fire.[16] Other features of the negligence analysis, such as the emergency doctrine[17] and

8. See Dobbs, Accountability and Comparative Fault, 47 La. L. Rev. 939, 943 (1987).

9. Restatement § 463.

10. See Restatement of Apportionment of Liability § 3, cmt. a. (Proposed Final Draft 1998).

11. Traditionally a duty is enforceable by a legal action. The defendant has no legal action for breach of a plaintiff's duty to care for herself. Nevertheless, it may be convenient to use the duty locution. You can say (a) that in general, the plaintiff owes a duty to use reasonable care for her own safety, a duty enforceable by a reduction in or bar to her damages recovery; and (b) in some cases, parallel to negligence analysis, the plaintiff owes "no duty" to protect herself. The latter cases can be addressed by saying that the plaintiff has a right or liberty to rely entirely upon the defendant for care in some instances. Plaintiff "no duty" can be seen as a way of talking about the scope of the defendant's duty to protect the plaintiff against her own risky conduct or a way of asserting that the plaintiff has a correspondingly broad right. These cases are discussed in § 200 below.

12. Intended harm is of course not a matter of negligence at all. But unless harm is intended, the *risk* of harm may be either inadvertent or intentional. See § 116.

13. Some scholars believe that the plaintiff's contributory negligence should be judged under a "semi-subjective" standard. See Richard Wright, *The Standards of Care in Negligence Law* in Philosophical Foundations of Tort Law 249 (David G. Owen, ed. 1995). Plaintiffs are sometimes allowed to recover in spite of their apparent negligence, but this is most often because the defendant owes a duty to protect them from their own inadequacies. See § 200 below.

14. Brock v. Peabody Co-operative Equity Exchange, 186 Kan. 657, 352 P.2d 37 (1960).

15. The other version holds that the defendant who negligently endangers A is also liable for injury to A's rescuer. See § 184.

16. Cf. LeRoy Fibre Co. v. Chicago, Milwaukee & St. Paul Railway Co., 232 U.S. 340, 34 S.Ct. 415, 58 L.Ed. 631 (1914); Hennessey v. Pyne, 694 A.2d 691 (R.I.1997) (homeowner near golf course did not assume risk of errant golf balls by being in her yard).

17. See Lyons v. Midnight Sun Transportation Services, Inc., 928 P.2d 1202

the negligence per se rules,[18] also apply to the contributory negligence issue.

Contributory negligence is also like negligence in that the issue is one for the trier of fact unless the matter is so clear that reasonable persons could not differ.[19] Jury instructions understandably make little of the distinction between care for oneself and care for another—understandably because as a practical matter, it would be very difficult to apply in many routine cases. Consequently, the distinction between care for one's self and care for others is seldom controlling in assessing the plaintiff's fault.

Parallels to Cause in Fact and Value of the Chance Analysis

The normal rules of cause in fact[20] likewise apply to contributory negligence. The plaintiff's contributory negligence has no legal effect unless it is one of the but-for causes of the plaintiff's harm or a substantial factor in causing that harm.[21]

It remains to be seen whether courts will apply the loss-of-a-chance rules[22] to fault of a plaintiff.[23] Suppose a patient is likely to die regardless of medical treatment. Her doctor, under a duty to maximize her chances for survival, should administer certain treatment, but negligently fails to do so. Since death is more likely than not, the failure to administer treatment is not a conventional but-for cause of the patient's death. Yet the doctor's negligence reduced the patient's chances of life—and even a chance is worth something. On this reasoning, courts often allow recovery proportionate to the value of the chance.[24] If applied in plaintiff fault cases, the patient's own negligent delay in taking medication might combine with the doctor's negligence to cause an indivisible loss of

(Alaska 1996) (arguing that emergency doctrine originated to ameliorate the contributory negligence rule).

18. E.g., Russell v. Mathis, 686 So.2d 241 (Ala.1996) (plaintiff's violation of statute contributory negligence per se). There are exceptions. E.g., Waterson v. General Motors Corporation, 111 N.J. 238, 544 A.2d 357 (1988) (seatbelt statute). Contributory negligence ordinarily remains a defense even if the *defendant* violates a statute. See Comment Note, Contributory Negligence as a Defense to a Cause of Action Based upon Violation of Statute, 10 A.L.R.2d 853 (1950). There are exceptions to this, too. See Van Gaasbeck v. Webatuck Central School Dist. No. 1, 21 N.Y.2d 239, 287 N.Y.S.2d 77, 234 N.E.2d 243 (1967).

19. E.g., Louk v. Isuzu Motors, Inc., 198 W.Va. 250, 479 S.E.2d 911 (1996). Similarly under the modern comparative negligence approaches. Gordon v. Benson, 925 P.2d 775 (Colo.1996). One difference: Courts direct verdicts or give summary judgments for defendants when they believe that contributory negligence is established as a matter of law because reasonable people could not differ. E.g., Humphrey v. Burlington Northern Railroad Co., 251 Neb. 736, 559 N.W.2d 749 (1997). This entails directing a verdict in favor of the party with the burden of proof, something courts seldom do when the issue is negligence.

20. See Chapter 10.

21. Restatement § 465. Some courts once said that the plaintiff's contributory negligence will bar her if it makes the "slightest contribution" to the resulting harm. E.g., Crane v. Neal, 389 Pa. 329, 132 A.2d 675 (1957). If that language meant to ignore the usual causal rules, it has now been rejected. See McCay v. Philadelphia Electric Co., 447 Pa. 490, 291 A.2d 759 (1972).

22. §§ 178 & 179.

23. Restatement of Apportionment § 4, cmt. f provides for reduced recovery if the plaintiff is chargeable with contributory negligence in reducing the chance.

24. See § 178.

chance, even if death was more likely than not. In that case, the wrongful death recovery would be limited to the value of the lost chance as further reduced by the patient's comparative fault.

Parallels to Proximate Cause Analysis

The same rules of proximate cause that apply on the issue of negligence[25] also apply on the issue of contributory negligence.[26] For example, if the plaintiff is thought to be contributorily negligent in mounting a slippery platform because she risks a slip and a fall, that negligence does not bar recovery when the defendant negligently causes a brick wall to fall on the plaintiff.[27] The risk created by the plaintiff in such a case is not the risk that led us to think her chargeable with contributory negligence, and therefore her fault is no proximate cause and no bar. And vice versa: the plaintiff's own negligence may become a superseding cause so that the defendant is not liable at all, even in a comparative negligence system.[28]

Departing from the Parallels

Although the issue of contributory negligence is ordinarily parallel to the issue of negligence, in a few cases the differences between the two issues may be important. One who exposes himself to risks does not necessarily stand in the same moral position as one who exposes others to the same risks. On a more mundane level, it is possible that a reasonable person would expose himself to risks that he could not reasonably inflict upon others. You might be reasonable, for example, if you dropped into a vat of poison gas to save your child, in spite of the terrible risks;[29] but you could not reasonably push another person into the vat for the same purposes. Sometimes, too, reasonable care on the part of the defendant requires him to protect the plaintiff from the plaintiff's own fault.[30] Even when that is not the case, the defendant may be in a better position than the plaintiff to foresee and avoid particular risks. Consequently, the plaintiff is not guilty of contributory fault merely because she engages in the same conduct as the defendant.[31] Even more obviously, the plaintiff is not guilty of either negligence or contributory negligence if responsibility has been allocated solely to the defendant, which is usually the case with the driver of a car, whose passenger is not expected to keep a lookout at all or exercise control over the driving.[32]

25. See Chapter 11, supra.

26. See Restatement § 468.

27. Smithwick v. Hall & Upson Co., 59 Conn. 261, 21 A. 924 (1890).

28. See Exxon Company, U.S.A. v. Sofec, Inc., 517 U.S. 830, 116 S.Ct. 1813, 135 L.Ed.2d 113 (1996); § 196.

29. Cf. Brock v. Peabody Co-operative Equity Exchange, 186 Kan. 657, 352 P.2d 37 (1960) (mother attempting to enter vat-like warehouse filled with cyanide to rescue child was not necessarily guilty of contributory fault).

30. See § 200 below.

31. See Stubbs v. Pancake Corner of Salem, Inc., 254 Or. 220, 458 P.2d 676 (1969).

32. E.g., Brawner v. Richardson, 57 Or. App. 178, 643 P.2d 1365 (1982); cf. Greycas, Inc. v. Proud, 826 F.2d 1560, 1566 (7th Cir.1987) (Posner, J.: "Due care is the care that is optimal given that the other party is

Cases involving negligence or contributory negligence of children also suggest that there are occasional practical differences between the two concepts. Many of the cases that give children the benefit of a more forgiving standard of care are in fact decisions in which the allegedly negligent child is a plaintiff and the issue is one of contributory negligence.[33] This fact suggests that at least in some cases, the difference between exercising care for one's self and exercising care for others might be important. Some other cases can be interpreted in the same way, as imposing a less demanding standard upon plaintiffs who put themselves but not others at risk.[34]

§ 200. Traditional Exceptions to the Contributory Negligence Rule

The risk-taking plaintiff was not always barred by contributory negligence rules. Under today's comparative fault regimes, the risk-taking plaintiff does not always suffer a reduction in damages, either. Sometimes risk-taking is reasonable; at other times the plaintiff's risky behavior is not a cause of her harm. Even when the plaintiff's conduct counts as contributory fault and when it contributes causally to the plaintiff's injury, courts recognize three major exceptions to the rule barring recovery. If an exception applies, the contributorily negligent plaintiff recovers fully, without any reduction of damages. Under the traditional regime of contributory negligence, the exceptions permitted the contributorily negligent plaintiff a full recovery against (1) a defendant who was guilty of intentional, wanton, or reckless harm, (2) a defendant who had the last clear chance to avoid injury, and (3) a defendant whose duty, under statute or otherwise, was to protect the plaintiff from her own risky conduct.

Intentional, Wanton or Reckless Defendant

Contributory negligence of a plaintiff was never a defense to claims for intentionally inflicted harm. By extension, courts came to hold[1] that it was no defense if the defendant was guilty of willful or wanton or reckless misconduct,[2] such as driving while intoxicated.[3] There was, however, an element of comparative fault; if the plaintiff as well as the defendant was guilty of reckless or wanton misconduct, the rule of contributory negligence applied after all and the plaintiff would be barred.[4]

exercising due care ... It is not the higher level of care that would be optimal if potential tort victims were required to assume that the rest of the world was negligent").

33. See § 124.

34. Notably the seatbelt cases. See § 205.

§ 200

1. E.g., Sparks v. Alabama Power Co., 679 So.2d 678 (Ala.1996); Wolfe v. Baube, 241 Va. 462, 403 S.E.2d 338 (1991).

2. On wanton misconduct, see §§ 27 & 147.

3. E.g., Booker, Inc. v. Morrill, 639 N.E.2d 358 (Ind.App.1994).

4. Harlow v. Connelly, 548 S.W.2d 143 (Ky.App.1977); Sorrells v. M.Y.B. Hospitality Ventures of Asheville, 332 N.C. 645, 423 S.E.2d 72 (1992)

Last Clear Chance

A complicated exception to the contributory negligence defense was called the last clear chance doctrine. In these cases the plaintiff negligently put herself in danger from which she could not escape. The defendant then negligently caused harm to the helpless plaintiff. The salient fact was that the plaintiff could do nothing to save herself once she had put herself in danger, but that the defendant could have avoided injury by ordinary care.[5] In such cases, the plaintiff's earlier contributory negligence would be no bar.[6] The original case involved a plaintiff who had tied his donkey in the road, where it stood eating grass when the defendant negligently ran into it. The plaintiff was not on hand to free the animal and it could not escape. The plaintiff's negligence was no bar to recovery because the defendant had the "last clear chance."[7]

The exception was frequently at issue in railroad cases. If the plaintiff is unconscious or otherwise helpless on the track and the engineer should have discovered his danger and his helpless condition in time to avoid running him down, the plaintiff's negligence in getting on the track in the first place becomes irrelevant and he is allowed to recover against the railroad. The timing was critical, however. The railroad was not liable for its antecedent negligence—operating the train with poor brakes, for example—but only for its negligence after it discovered or should have discovered the plaintiff's plight[8] and only for harms that could then have been avoided by reasonable care.[9]

Discovered peril. Some jurisdictions modified the last clear chance exception, applying a version known as the discovered peril rule. The discovered peril rule held that the exception would not apply unless the defendant actually discovered the plaintiff's helpless condition and was negligent thereafter in failing to avoid injury.[10] The difference between this rule and the last clear chance version is that under the latter, the exception can be invoked not only when the defendant actually discovered the danger but also when he should have done so.

Inattentive plaintiff. The core case for either version of the exception was the case of a helpless plaintiff. However, even the inattentive plaintiff, who was not in fact helpless, might claim the benefit of the rule where the defendant actually discovered his danger in time to avoid harm and negligently failed to do so. Conversely, if the defendant sees a plaintiff who is apparently conscious and able to protect himself by

5. Dominguez v. Manhattan and Bronx Surface Transit Operating Authority, 46 N.Y.2d 528, 388 N.E.2d 1221, 415 N.Y.S.2d 634 (1979); Restatement § 479.

6. E.g., Robinson v. District of Columbia, 580 A.2d 1255 (D.C.App.1990).

7. Davies v. Mann, 10 M. & W. 547, 152 Eng. Rep. 588 (Exch. 1842).

8. Noe v. Chicago Great Western Ry. Co., 130 Ill.App.2d 36, 263 N.E.2d 889 (1969); Robinson v. District of Columbia, 580 A.2d 1255 (D.C.App.1990); Restatement § 479, cmt. h.

9. Restatement § 479.

10. E.g., Walker v. Spokane, Portland and Seattle Ry., 262 Or. 606, 500 P.2d 1039 (1972).

moving, the exception does not apply and contributory negligence remains a bar.[11]

Defendant under a Duty to Protect against Plaintiff's Risky Conduct

In a few cases, the defendant is under a duty to use reasonable care to protect the plaintiff from her own weakness, incapacity, or fault. When the plaintiff is harmed because the defendant breaches that duty of care, the defendant cannot defend on the ground of contributory negligence, since that was the very thing he was obliged to prevent. Another way to state essentially the same idea is to say that what counts as contributory negligence is determined largely by the scope of the defendant's duty.

(1) Statutes. One group of cases derives from a statutory duty to protect the plaintiff. Although contributory negligence is ordinarily a defense, even when the defendant's negligence is proved by showing that he violated a statute,[12] it is no defense at all if the defendant violates a statute intended to protect the plaintiff from his own negligence or incapacity. Courts sometimes say that such statutes impose strict liability.[13] Child labor acts are good examples. If a minor is injured while employed in violation of such a statute, his claim is not to be defeated by his contributory negligence, since the purpose of the statute is to protect him from the risks of his own incapacity and negligence.[14]

The rule depends upon construction of individual statutes as intended to protect "persons from their own inexperience, lack of judgment, inability to protect themselves or to resist pressure, or tendency toward negligence." The most likely candidates are perhaps those statutes aimed at protecting children and others under a disability[15] and those aimed at protecting workers from on the job risks they cannot avoid.[16] Statutes prohibiting the sale of dangerous articles like guns,[17] alcohol,[18] or drugs[19] have sometimes been treated in the same way, so that the

11. See, e.g., Louisville & Nashville R. Co. v. Vanderpool, 496 S.W.2d 349 (Ky. 1973); First Northwestern Trust Co. of South Dakota v. Schnable, 334 N.W.2d 16 (S.D.1983) (actual discovery required in case of inattentive but not helpless plaintiff); Restatement § 480.

12. See Restatement § 483.

13. E.g., Van Gaasbeck v. Webatuck Central School District Number 1, 21 N.Y.2d 239, 287 N.Y.S.2d 77, 234 N.E.2d 243 (1967).

14. E.g., Strain v. Christians, 483 N.W.2d 783 (S.D.1992); D.L. by Friederichs v. Huebner, 110 Wis.2d 581, 329 N.W.2d 890 (1983).

15. Del E. Webb Corporation v. Superior Court, 151 Ariz. 164, 726 P.2d 580 (1986); Van Gaasbeck v. Webatuck Central School District Number 1, 21 N.Y.2d 239, 287 N.Y.S.2d 77, 234 N.E.2d 243 (1967).

16. Wilson v. Vukasin, 277 Mont. 423, 922 P.2d 531 (1996) (under version of statute in effect at the time of injury); Gordon v. Eastern Ry. Supply, Inc., 82 N.Y.2d 555, 626 N.E.2d 912, 606 N.Y.S.2d 127 (1993).

17. Tamiami Gun Shop v. Klein, 116 So.2d 421 (Fla.1959)

18. Loeb v. Rasmussen, 822 P.2d 914 (Alaska 1991). The cases are divided. See, refusing to set aside contributory or comparative negligence rules, Lee v. Kiku Restaurant, 127 N.J. 170, 603 A.2d 503 (1992).

19. Zerby v. Warren, 297 Minn. 134, 210 N.W.2d 58 (1973) (glue sold to minor who died after sniffing)

buyer may be allowed in some instances to recover from the seller in spite of the buyer's own contributory fault.

(2) Common law. In the absence of statute, courts are of course free to impose duties that require defendants to protect vulnerable, incapacitated, or minor plaintiffs from their own inability to protect themselves. One excellent example is the case of a plaintiff who, because of mental or physical disability is under the defendant's care. A hospital or a mental hospital that accepts a suicidal patient suffering from emotional or mental problems should exercise care to prevent suicide, and if it does not, it cannot defeat a claim for the patient's death by suicide by asserting that the patient was contributorily negligent.[20] The rule is not based upon statute, or upon strict liability, but upon the principle that the defendant has a duty to protect the plaintiff from her own dangerous propensities.

The result could be explained quite differently, by saying that the standard of care in the case of contributory negligence is purely subjective, so that the minor or mental patient need only exercise the care of which he is personally capable. That explanation is contrary to the usually stated rules and suffers as well from a dangerous reliance upon subjective standards.[21] The idea that defendants sometimes owe special duties of care to protect the plaintiff from her own disability makes a good deal of sense. Such a duty, which reflects judicial policy or sense of justice, would presumably be recognized only when the defendant knows or should know of the plaintiff's disability and when the defendant by agreement, conduct, or status, has accepted responsibility.

For example, one in the role of a parent, if he owes a duty of care at all, should owe a duty to protect the child against dangers arising from his own foolishness or mental limitations.[22] Similarly, a jailer having custody of prisoners owes them a duty to protect against suicide as well as against others harms.[23] A common carrier might owe a special duty of care to protect a passenger from the effects of her own known disabilities.[24] Manufacturers of machines like punch presses may be negligent in failing to provide safety devices to prevent workers from carelessly

20. E.g., McNamara v. Honeyman, 406 Mass. 43, 546 N.E.2d 139 (1989); cf. Argus v. Scheppegrell, 472 So.2d 573 (La.1985) (doctor under a duty not to prescribe drugs for addicted teenager could not rely upon her contributory negligence to defeat a claim for her death from overdose). Hobart v. Shin, 185 Ill.2d 283, 705 N.E.2d 907, 235 Ill.Dec. 724 (1998) reaches the opposite result, but probably is not contrary. The patient there was apparently fully recovered and did not seem suicidal. Given that, it seems doubt that the doctor was negligent at all.

21. See § 118 on objective standards of negligence. Richard Wright has argued for a "semi-subjective" standard of contributory negligence. See Richard Wright, The Standards of Care in Negligence Law in PHILOSOPHICAL FOUNDATIONS OF TORT LAW 249 (David G. Owen, ed. 1995).

22. Cf. Lynch v. Rosenthal, 396 S.W.2d 272 (Mo.App.1965) (adult plaintiff of very low mental ability injured in farm machinery while living with farmer; plaintiff not necessarily chargeable with contributory fault).

23. Hickey v. Zezulka, 439 Mich. 408, 487 N.W.2d 106 (1992).

24. See McMahon v. New York, N.H. & H. R.R., 136 Conn. 372, 71 A.2d 557 (1950) (intoxicated passenger); Vaughn v. Northwest Airlines, Inc., 558 N.W.2d 736 (Minn. 1997) (passenger injured in handling own luggage).

getting their hands under the press as it descends. Since workers' predictable negligence in carrying out repetitive tasks is the very thing the manufacturer should have protected against, to apply the contributory negligence bar would be to negate the manufacturer's duty. Hence, some courts removed the contributory negligence bar in such cases.[25]

Risks Allocated to Defendant

A similar idea generates a similar result even when the plaintiff suffers no peculiar disability. The idea is that customary practices, the relationship of the parties, or their implicit understandings, may operate to allocate some risks entirely to the defendant, and that as to those, the plaintiff is not responsible and not chargeable with contributory fault. A pedestrian is not expected to wear a helmet against the possibility that a driver may run him down. "The law normally does not require duplicative precautions" in such a case[26] but instead expects drivers to keep their vehicles off the sidewalk. Likewise, if an employer owes a duty to provide a safe place to work, the employee's conduct should be evaluated in the light of that expectation.[27] More pointedly, a doctors may owe a duty to provide patients with material information about the need for and risks of proposed operations. Given the doctor's duty and the patient's corresponding right to rely upon his care, the doctor who advises a mastectomy can hardly be permitted to defend his actions on the ground that his patient was unreasonable in relying upon his advice.[28] In such cases, the defendant's duty determines whether the plaintiff can be charged with contributory negligence or comparative fault.

A slightly different version of the same idea is that even if the defendant has no special duty to the plaintiff beyond the duty of ordinary care, the plaintiff is not to be charged with contributory fault for being where she has a right to be or doing what she has a right to do. In the leading case, the plaintiff was a landowner who stacked goods on his land near a railroad track. The railroad negligently caused a fire and when sued for damage argued that the plaintiff should be barred because he could have stacked his goods farther from the track. This argument was of no avail because the plaintiff's risky conduct was conduct he had a right to pursue.[29]

25. Tulkku v. Mackworth Rees Div. of Avis Industries, Inc., 406 Mich. 615, 281 N.W.2d 291 (1979); Bexiga v. Havir Manufacturing Corp., 60 N.J. 402, 290 A.2d 281 (1972).

26. Greycas, Inc. v. Proud, 826 F.2d 1560, 1566 (7th Cir.1987).

27. See Vendetto v. Sonat Offshore Drilling Co., 725 So.2d 474, 479 (La.1999) ("since the duty to provide a safe place to work allocates substantial risks of maritime employment to the employer, identical conduct is not demanded of the employer and the employee. The law allocates different risks to different parties, and that allocation forms parts of the reasonableness equation in the negligence determination").

28. Cf. Brown v. Dibbell, 221 Wis.2d 653, 588 N.W.2d 631(1998) (patient claimed doctor failed to advise fully on whether mastectomy was needed; if true, contributory negligence of patient in undergoing operation would be no defense).

29. Leroy Fibre Co. v. Chicago, Milwaukee & St. Paul Railway Co, 232 U.S. 340, 34 S.Ct. 415, 58 L.Ed. 631 (1914).

Such cases can be viewed as plaintiff no-duty cases, that is, cases in which the plaintiff has no duty to protect herself from the defendant's negligence. Put differently, they are cases in which the plaintiff has a liberty (or right) to be free from constraints imposed by the defendant. There are probably not many such cases in which the plaintiff's autonomy or citizenship rights permit her to ignore reasonable self-care. As Professor Epstein points out, loss prevention efforts on both sides are now commonly required.[30] But some cases warrant a recognition of the plaintiff's overriding rights. It is surely unacceptable to say that women are guilty of contributory negligence if they venture out at night because they might be raped,[31] or that a homeowner is at fault if he lives near a golf course where a negligent duffer can slice a ball into his eye.[32]

§ 201. Comparative Fault

Development of Comparative Fault

The traditional rule barred all recovery by the plaintiff who was guilty of contributory negligence. Under a pure comparative fault regime, the rule merely reduces the amount of the award to a plaintiff who is chargeable with contributory fault. The plaintiff's conduct is not necessarily different in the two cases. In a comparative fault regime, the conduct may still be called contributory negligence, but the legal effect of that contributory negligence is different. Some lawyers and judges, however, have begun to use the term "contributory negligence" and "comparative negligence" to refer to the legal effects of the plaintiff's faulty conduct as well as to the conduct itself.

Some kinds of comparative fault have been around on a limited scale for a long time. One earlier experiment allowed the negligent plaintiff to recover if the plaintiff's negligence was slight and the defendant's gross.[1] Admiralty law, in ship collision cases, at one time divided damages fifty-fifty.[2]

Modern comparative negligence law works differently, reducing the plaintiff's recovery in proportion to the plaintiff's fault. The idea got its start in 1908 with the Federal Employers Liability Act, which governs suits by railroad employees against their employers.[3] A few other federal statutes made similar provisions for limited groups of plaintiffs.[4] In 1910

30. Richard A. Epstein, Torts § 8.2.1 (1999).

31. See Ellen Bublick, Citizen No–Duty Rules: Rape Victims and Comparative Fault, 99 Colum. L. Rev. 1413 (1999).

32. Hennessey v. Pyne, 694 A.2d 691 (R.I.1997) (homeowner does not assume the risk by living near golf course); cf. William K. Jones, Strict Liability for Hazardous Enterprise, 92 Colum. L. Rev. 1705, 1757 (1992) (discussing arguments and cases that sometimes center around strict liability).

§ 201

1. See Henry Woods & Beth Deere, Comparative Fault § 4.5 (3d ed. 1996). South Dakota still has a statutory variation on this scheme.

2. Get See Thomas J. Schoenbaum, Admiralty and Maritime Law, § 12–4 (2d ed. 1994). Admiralty now allocates liability in proportion to fault. United States v. Reliable Transfer Co., Inc., 421 U.S. 397, 95 S.Ct. 1708, 44 L.Ed.2d 251 (1975).

3. 45 U.S.C.A. § 53.

4. E.g., the Jones Act, 46 U.S.C.A. § 688 (adopting rule of FELA for seamen).

Mississippi enacted a general comparative negligence statute, followed by Wisconsin in 1931 and Arkansas in 1955.[5] After this slow beginning, change came rather quickly in the 1960s and 1970s. Most of the change came through legislation, but after 1973, a number of states followed Florida's lead[6] by judicially adopting comparative negligence. By the 1980s, only four states—Alabama, Maryland, North Carolina and Virginia—had failed to adopt comparative negligence rules.[7] The overwhelming majority of American states thus now follows the general system adopted in other common law[8] and in the major civil law countries.[9]

Proportionate Reduction of Damages Awarded

Almost all the American systems of comparative fault reduce the plaintiff's recovery in proportion to the plaintiff's relevant fault. The plaintiff's fault is not relevant if it is not one of the causes in fact of the plaintiff's harm. Nor is it relevant if it is not a proximate cause.[10] In the usual case, all of the plaintiff's fault is relevant and to be compared with the defendant's fault.

Although the fault is not relevant if it is not a cause of the harm, courts in negligence cases ordinarily compare fault, not causation.[11] Causation usually remains an all or nothing issue. Once it is established, the causal fault of the plaintiff is compared with the causal fault of the defendant. To say that the defendant is guilty of 75% of the negligence is to make a comparative statement. It is not to say that the defendant necessarily took enormous risks, only that the risks he did take were much greater than the risks taken by the plaintiff.

If the defendant's fault is, say, 75% of all the relevant fault and the plaintiff's fault is 25%, then the plaintiff's damages must be reduced by 25%. Suppose the plaintiff's damages are assessed at $10,000. The 25% reduction will allow the plaintiff to recover only $7500. So the defendant is liable for a share of the damages equal to his share of the fault. In exactly the same way, the plaintiff bears a share of her damages equal to her share of the fault. The same principle applies when two or more defendants are negligent, although multi-party cases do raise other issues that are more complex.[12]

5. See Victor E. Schwartz, Comparative Negligence §§ 1–4(b) (3d ed. 1994).

6. Hoffman v. Jones, 280 So.2d 431, 78 A.L.R.3d 321 (Fla. 1973).

7. See Victor E. Schwartz, Comparative Negligence §§ 1–5(e) (3d ed. 1994).

8. Australia & New Zealand: John G. Fleming, The Law of Torts 271–72 (8th ed. 1992); Canada: Allen M. Linden, Canadian Tort Law, 441–42 (5th ed. 1993); England: See W.V.H. Rogers, Winfield & Jolowicz on Tort 184–87 (14th ed. 1994).

9. A.M. Honoré, Causation and Remoteness of Damage, XI Int. Enc. Comp. L., Torts, ch. 7, § 146 (1985) reflects variations. A few countries still use rather crude forms of comparative fault judgments.

10. See Restatement of Apportionment of Liability § 4.

11. In strict liability cases, the apportionment may be described as comparative causation. See § 369. In spite of the orthodoxy expressed in the text, courts sometimes seem to imply that causation might somehow have a role in weighing culpability. See § 202.

12. See § 210.

Pure and Modified Systems of Comparative Fault

The pure or complete system. Two different and mutually exclusive systems of comparative fault are in use. The first, called the complete or pure comparative fault system, applies comparative fault to all plaintiffs in all negligence cases.[13] Under this system, no plaintiff is completely barred from recovery because of her contributory negligence. Around a dozen states as well as the major federal statutes adopt this system.[14]

The two incomplete systems. The second system of comparative fault, called the incomplete or modified system, continues to use the traditional complete bar rule when the plaintiff's fault reaches a specified breakpoint. The incomplete system itself has two slightly variant versions. In one, the "greater-than" version, the plaintiff is completely barred if her fault exceeds that of the defendant.[15] Something like 20 states follow this version.[16] In the other, the "equal to" version, the plaintiff is completely barred if her fault, though not exceeding the defendant's, is at least equal to it.[17] About a dozen states apply this most limited version of comparative fault.[18]

Examples. In simple two-party cases, the examples are straightforward. Suppose the jury finds the plaintiff to be chargeable with 60% of the negligence, the defendant 40%. The plaintiff's damages are $10,000. The defendant is liable for only 40% or $4,000. The plaintiff must bear $6,000 of her own loss. Under either of the incomplete versions, however, the plaintiff would recover nothing whatever; the traditional rules of contributory negligence would bar all recovery because her negligence is not only equal to but also greater than the defendant's. On the same facts, if the trier pegged the plaintiff's negligence at 50% the plaintiff would recover $5,000 or 50% of her damages both in the complete comparative negligence states and in the greater-than states, because the plaintiff's negligence would not be greater than the defendant's. On the other hand, in the "equal to" states, the plaintiff guilty of 50% of the negligence would be barred altogether.

Evaluating the systems. The pure or complete system has been favored by thoughtful commentators,[19] by a number of courts,[20] and in

13. As to other torts, see § 206.

14. This group includes Alaska, California, Florida, Kentucky, Louisiana, Michigan, Mississippi, Missouri, New Mexico, New York, Rhode Island, and Washington as well as Puerto Rico. For complete compilations of statutes see Victor E. Schwartz, Comparative Negligence §§ §§ 2–1(a) (3d ed. 1994); Henry Woods & Beth Deere, Comparative Fault § 1.11 (3d ed. 1996).

15. E.g., N.H. Stats. Ann. § 507:7–d (plaintiff can recover if her negligence is "not greater than the fault of the defendant").

16. These states currently appear to include Connecticut, Delaware, Hawaii, Illinois, Indiana, Iowa, Massachusetts, Minnesota, Montana, Nevada, New Hampshire, New Jersey, Ohio, Oklahoma, Oregon, Pennsylvania, South Carolina, Texas, Vermont, Wisconsin and Wyoming. See Henry Woods & Beth Deere, Comparative Fault supra n. 1 § 1:11.

17. E.g., Ark. Code Ann. § 16–64–122.

18. These states currently include Arizona, Arkansas, Colorado, Georgia, Idaho, Kansas, Maine, Nebraska, North Dakota, Tennessee, Utah and West Virginia. See the compilation in Henry Woods & Beth Deere, Comparative Fault supra n. 1, § 1:11.

19. William L. Prosser, Comparative Negligence, 41 Cal. L. Rev. 1, 25 (1953).

the federal statutes such as the FELA.[21] Legislators on the other hand have tended to favor the incomplete system. The complete system of comparative fault often strikes casual observers as unfair because in that system, a plaintiff guilty of 90% of the negligence could recover damages from the defendant who is guilty of only 10% of the negligence.[22] In evaluating the complete system of comparative negligence, however, it is important to remember that each party bears exactly his or her proportionate share of the damages. The plaintiff guilty of 90% of the negligence would, after all, bear 90% of her loss. It is also important to remember that if the defendant is also injured, as often is the case in automobile collisions, the same plaintiff would bear 90% of the defendant's loss.

Moreover, under the incomplete systems, the plaintiff who is charged with 49% of the negligence would recover 51% of her damages, while the plaintiff charged with 51% would recover nothing at all. Yet it is hard to justify absolving a defendant of all liability when he was guilty of 49% of the negligence.[23] As the Michigan Court said, the incomplete systems do not eliminate the traditional bar of contributory negligence, they only "lower the barrier."[24] Not only is proportionate fault a just way to share the jointly caused losses, it avoids some issues and litigation created by incomplete systems[25] and some of the temptations to resort once again to the all-or-nothing exceptions.

§ 202. Assigning Shares of Responsibility

Comparing Unjustified Risks

Comparing unjustified risks. It would be wrong as well as impossible to compare the plaintiff's general moral worth with the defendant's. In the most straightforward systems of comparative negligence no such comparison is required. Juries comparing negligence of the plaintiff and defendant can consider the plaintiff's causally related negligence with the defendant's causally related negligence.[1] That is, juries can compare

20. Some major decisions include Kaatz v. State, 540 P.2d 1037 (Alaska 1975); Li v. Yellow Cab Co. of California, 13 Cal.3d 804, 532 P.2d 1226, 119 Cal.Rptr. 858, 78 A.L.R.3d 393 (1975); Hoffman v. Jones, 280 So.2d 431, 78 A.L.R.3d 321 (Fla. 1973); Alvis v. Ribar, 85 Ill.2d 1, 421 N.E.2d 886, 52 Ill.Dec. 23 (1981) (later supplanted by legislative intervention); Placek v. City of Sterling Heights, 405 Mich. 638, 275 N.W.2d 511 (1979). See also United States v. Reliable Transfer Co., Inc., 421 U.S. 397, 95 S.Ct. 1708, 44 L.Ed.2d 251 (1975) (admiralty damages to be allocated in proportion to fault).

21. 45 U.S.C.A. § 53.

22. Such extreme findings are rare, but in Wassell v. Adams, 865 F.2d 849 (7th Cir.1989) the jury attributed 97% of the negligence to the plaintiff. Under the complete comparative negligence system then controlling in Illinois, the plaintiff recovered $25,500 out of her $850,000 damages.

23. See Alvis v. Ribar, 85 Ill.2d 1, 421 N.E.2d 886, 52 Ill.Dec. 23 (1981) (advocating a pure system).

24. Placek v. City of Sterling Heights, 405 Mich. 638, 661, 275 N.W.2d 511, 519 (1979). See also Li v. Yellow Cab Co. of California, 13 Cal.3d 804, 827, 532 P.2d 1226, 1242, 119 Cal.Rptr. 858, 875, 78 A.L.R.3d 393 (1975) (similar).

25. See § 210.

§ 202

1. Arguing contra, Richard A. Epstein, Plaintiff's Conduct in Products Liability Actions: Comparative Negligence, Automatic Division and Multiple Parties, 45 J. Air L. & Com. 87 (1979).

the relevant unjustified risks taken by the defendant with the relevant unjustified risks taken by the plaintiff. As in all negligence cases, juries must estimate whether the risks taken by the defendant were unreasonably high. Comparative negligence systems ask the jury to make the same estimate about risks taken by the plaintiff. This should ordinarily be well within the traditional capacities of the jury.

Example. Suppose a collision between a vehicle operated by the defendant at 100 mph and a vehicle operated by the plaintiff at 70 mph. The trier concludes that both drivers were negligent in that speeding unreasonably increased the risk of collision and serious damages. Possibly the risk of collision created by the two drivers would be similar, but the defendant almost certainly created a greater likelihood of greater harm by driving at 100 mph. If the defendant created unjustified risks of collision that far exceeded the unjustified risks created by the plaintiff, it becomes easy to say he was comparatively "more negligent" than the plaintiff. How much more is an estimate, but the degree of risk, which is always essential to the idea of negligence, is an estimate that must be made whether you are comparing negligence or merely determining the defendant's own fault. If the trier believes that driving 100 mph created about three times the risk of driving negligently at 70 mph, the apportionment will be 75–25%. The 75–25 apportionment is only a rough estimate of comparative fault, but it has usually seemed better than no effort to estimate it at all.[2]

Excluding justified and irrelevant risks. A comparison of negligence is a comparison of unjustified risks. No comparison is to be made of risks that are justified, that is, of non-negligent conduct. Suppose the plaintiff speeds at 75 mph in a 55 mph zone because she is rushing her injured child to the hospital. She may not be negligent at all, because the risk may be justified by the prospect of aiding the child. Suppose, however, the jury believes that, considering the nature of the child's injury, 75 mph is much too fast, and that, given the risk to others and to herself, the plaintiff should not have driven more than 65 mph. Some of the risk created by the plaintiff in that case would be justified, that is, non-negligent. The jury would compare only the risk created by increasing the speed from 65 to 75. The point is not that the jury knows how much risk is created by the added speed but that its estimate should be about that risk and not about another. Similarly, risks of harms to different classes of people and risks of radically different kinds of harm should be excluded from the comparison. If the defendant's speed not only ran the risk of collision but also the risk that the engine would be damaged, the engine-damage risk probably should not be piled on top of the collision risk in estimating the defendant's percentage of fault.[3]

2. See Kaatz v. State, 540 P.2d 1037, 1048 (Alaska 1975) (allocations under comparative fault more accurate than the traditional all or nothing rule). Maine, however, has adopted a radically different system, which essentially tells the jury to do justice without regard to relative degree of fault, so a defendant whose fault was more than 50% might pay only a small fraction, say 20% of the damages. See Pelletier v. Fort Kent Golf Club, 662 A.2d 220 (Me.1995).

3. This is not to say that the trier should not consider all risks of the same general kind, whether to self or others. See

"Factors" Bearing on Comparison of Fault

Specifying factors bearing on the negligence issue. Some authorities suggest that relative fault judgments will be improved or at least better controlled if a number of important "factors" guide the assignment of relative fault. For example, it has been suggested that the jury should be told to consider the reasonableness of a party's conduct in confronting a risk, the existence of a sudden emergency, and whether the conduct might be justified because it was aimed at saving a life.[4]

These particular factors are merely familiar instances of the fundamental negligence analysis. Whether conduct is unreasonably risky depends largely on the probability that harm will result, the amount of that harm, and the costs of avoiding the risk. Instructions that specify particular instances of the general principle may run risks of overemphasizing particular facets of the negligence issue, which has not changed its nature merely because the issue arises with respect to both parties.[5] If those instructions are not needed when the issue is simply the negligence of a defendant, they are not needed when the issue is the negligence of both parties.

State of mind. The orthodox view is that negligence is conduct, not a state of mind.[6] That view comports with the equally orthodox holding that conduct is judged by the standard of the reasonable and prudent person, not by the subjective capacities of the individual actor.[7] However, the actor's state of mind is relevant in judging the unreasonable risks created by his conduct when his state of mind bears upon the utility of his conduct. His purpose in speeding to save a child's life may show that his speeding has some utility. His purpose to gratify his own ill-will and spite by frightening others shows just the contrary.[8] The Restatement of Apportionment proposes to take into account "each person's actual awareness, intent, or indifference with respect to the risks created by the conduct."[9] These considerations are difficult to formulate, but presum-

Kenneth W. Simons, The Puzzling Doctrine of Contributory Negligence, 16 CARDOZO L. REV. 1693, 1725–26 (1995).

4. Eaton v. McLain, 891 S.W.2d 587, 592 (Tenn.1994). The Eaton Court listed these factors: "(1) the relative closeness of the causal relationship between the conduct of the defendant and the injury to the plaintiff; (2) the reasonableness of the party's conduct in confronting a risk, such as whether the party knew of the risk, or should have known of it; (3) the extent to which the defendant failed to reasonably utilize an existing opportunity to avoid the injury to the plaintiff; (4) the existence of a sudden emergency requiring a hasty decision; (5) the significance of what the party was attempting to accomplish by the conduct, such as an attempt to save another's life; and (6) the party's particular capacities, such as age, maturity, training, education, and so forth."

5. Thus courts have increasingly recognized objections to instructions on emergency, since the point is already covered by the general instruction on the standard of care and the emergency instruction may unduly emphasize the point of view of one party. See § 131.

6. § 116.

7. §§ 117 & 118. Children may be given the benefit of a special and lower standard of care.

8. See Gregory C. Keating, Reasonableness and Rationality in Negligence Theory, 48 STAN. L. REV. 311, 369 (1996).

9. Restatement of Apportionment of Liability § 8 (d). Discussion at the annual meeting in 1999 indicated that this section may be redrafted in some respects.

ably they do not justify liability that turns on evaluations of the actor's moral worth rather than upon unreasonable risky conduct. Undue emphasis upon mental capacity in comparing fault may also undermine substantive rules. One case[10] suggested that personal capacities of the actor, including age, maturity, and education should be considered in allocating fault. These are indeed factors that might traditionally be considered for child actors,[11] but not adults. If they are considered for adults, the result would be that the substantive rule of tort law holds an adult liable for risky behavior even if he is mentally subnormal, but that the apportionment rule could allow a trier of fact to excuse him.

Comparing Causation

Comparing proximate causation. The orthodox view in negligence cases is that comparative negligence is just what it sounds like—a comparison of the negligence or culpability of each party, an idea easily understood as a comparison of the unjustified risks taken by each. The only negligence to be compared is negligence that is a cause in fact and also a proximate cause in the sense that the harm caused was the kind of harm put at risk. But this does not mean that causation itself is somehow put on the scales and weighed. Instead, cause in fact and proximate cause concepts are gatekeeping concepts, excluding some negligence from consideration when it is not causal in fact and when it is too remote.

Some cases[12] and statutes,[13] however, use terminology that at least flirts with the possibility of adding another layer of complexity and uncertainty by suggesting that the trier of fact, after weighing comparative fault, could also by some unspecified method weigh the causal importance of the parties's respective fault.[14] Suppose a court says that the jury coming up with a comparative negligence figure should consider "the relative closeness of the causal relationship between the conduct of the defendant and the injury to the plaintiff."[15] That sounds like an invitation to make some kind of judgments about comparative proximate cause, perhaps an invitation to conclude that although both parties negligently contributed to an indivisible injury, and both were equally at fault, the negligence of one was somehow more proximate or more important that the other. Possibly the quoted statement is intended, in

10. Eaton v. McLain, 891 S.W.2d 587 (Tenn.1994).

11. See § 124. Some authority favors considering the child's age, experience, and intelligence not only on the issue of liability but also on the issue of apportionment. See Hanson v. Binder, 260 Wis. 464, 50 N.W.2d 676 (1952). Judge Woods concluded that most other decisions assumed that these subjective factors bore on liability but had no effect upon apportionment. See Henry Woods and Beth Deere, Comparative Fault 12:3–12:4 (3d ed. 1996).

12. See Eaton v. McLain, 891 S.W.2d 587, 592 (Tenn.1994) ("the relative closeness of the causal relationship between the conduct of the defendant and the injury to the plaintiff" is one factor in assessing fault percentages). Perhaps some of the language in Steele v. Kerrigan, 148 N.J. 1, 689 A.2d 685 (1997) could be read that way.

13. Uniform Comparative Fault Act § 2 (extent of causal relation).

14. See the excellent discussion in Victor Schwartz, Comparative Negligence § 17–1 (a) (3d ed. 1994).

15. Eaton v. McLain, 891 S.W.2d 587 (Tenn.1994).

spite of its causal language, only to suggest that sometimes a party who has the last chance to avoid harm may be more at fault than a party whose negligence occurred earlier.[16] If it is intended to add a comparison of causal significance to the ordinary negligence case, however, it looks very much as if a whole new conceptual apparatus will be needed. And it may be doubted whether the added complexity will produce better justice.

§ 203. Distinguishing Avoidable Consequences and Comparative Negligence

The avoidable consequences/mitigation of damages rule. The first rule[1] of avoidable consequences denies the plaintiff a recovery for negligently inflicted damages that she could have avoided or minimized by reasonable care or expenditure.[2] For example, the plaintiff who unreasonably delays in obtaining medical attention for her injury, or who unreasonably refuses to follow medical advice, cannot recover for exacerbation of the injury resulting from her own delay or refusal.[3] The effect is to reduce the plaintiff's recovery but not to bar the plaintiff entirely. In that respect, the avoidable consequences or mitigation of damages rule was obviously different from the old rule of contributory negligence.

Distinguishing comparative negligence regimes: fault apportionment vs. causal apportionment. The comparative fault and avoidable consequences rules represent two radically different systems for reducing the plaintiff's award. In the ordinary comparative negligence case, each party's fault has contributed to the whole harm. In the old language, both plaintiff and defendant are concurrent causes of an indivisible harm. Because the plaintiff has suffered but one harm that cannot be divided into parts, courts in a comparative negligence system apportion liability between the plaintiff and defendant in proportion to their fault in causing the loss as a whole.

In contrast, the avoidable consequences rule traditionally applied when courts could identify and isolate two or more distinct items of harm resulting from two or more distinct acts or causes.[4] When courts deemed it just, they could allocate the entire responsibility for one item of harm to the plaintiff as the responsible cause of that particular harm. The allocation of responsibility was not based upon a percentage of fault but upon the fact that a specific item of harm could be identified as the plaintiff's entire responsibility. For example, if the plaintiff unreasonably failed to take antibiotics after the defendant caused her an injury, and her failure to do so necessitated four weeks of hospital care that

16. See § 207.

§ 203

1. For subsidiary rules see 1 DAN B. DOBBS, LAW OF REMEDIES § 3.9 (2d ed. 1993).

2. See, e.g., James Hardie Gypsum (Nevada) Inc. v. Inquipco., 112 Nev. 1397, 929 P.2d 903 (1996) (property damage). The rule is not limited to tort cases. See 3 DAN B. DOBBS, Law of Remedies § 12.6 (2d ed. 1993).

3. Preston v. Keith, 217 Conn. 12, 584 A.2d 439 (1991); Bryant v. Calantone, 286 N.J.Super. 362, 669 A.2d 286 (1996).

4. See Restatement § 465.

otherwise would not have been required, the avoidable consequences rule would relieve the defendant of all liability for the added hospitalization.[5] The plaintiff would be deemed to be the sole proximate cause of the costs associated with those additional weeks of care.[6]

The avoidable consequences or mitigation of damage rule can be called a rule of *causal* apportionment, in contrast to the rule of *fault* apportionment applied in comparative fault cases.[7] Sometimes courts address this kind of apportionment in terms of percentages, but that is misleading. The added cost of hospital care in the example is not a percentage; it is an item of damage that can fairly be attributed solely to the plaintiff. The language of percentage, on the other hand, is exactly the right language for fault apportionment under comparative fault rules where no particular item of harm can be distinctly allocated to the plaintiff.

Application of the two systems. The avoidable consequences approach to apportionment does not yield the same results as the comparative negligence apportionment except by happenstance. Suppose that the plaintiff's damages were $100,000 and that the plaintiff's fault was 5% of the total. Under a comparative fault approach, the plaintiff's award would be reduced by 5% so that she would recover $95,000. Now suppose that the plaintiff's only fault was her failure to take antibiotics after the injury was inflicted and that this failure aggravated her injury and necessitated additional hospitalization costing $10,000. If we think of the plaintiff's fault as comparative negligence amounting to 5%, she will recover $95,000. But if we think of it as a failure to minimize damages, the avoidable consequences rule will allow her to recover only $90,000.

§ 204. The Role of Avoidable Consequences in Comparative Fault Regimes

Which rule applies? With the adoption of comparative fault regimes in most states, the remaining role of the avoidable consequences or mitigation of damages approach to apportionment of responsibility between the plaintiff and defendant has been called into question. In many instances the issue does not arise because no causal apportionment is possible, so that comparative fault represents the only possible method for apportionment. For example, it is seldom possible in highway accidents to say that the plaintiff's broken leg is a result of the defendant's

5. See Keans v. Bottiarelli, 35 Conn. App. 239, 645 A.2d 1029 (1994).

6. Judges who attempt to provide a rational basis for understanding avoidable consequences rules usually explain or imply that it is merely a proximate cause rule. See, e.g., Preston v. Keith, 217 Conn. 12, 584 A.2d 439 (1991); Moulton v. Alamo Ambulance Service, Inc., 414 S.W.2d 444 (Tex.1967).

7. "Causal" in the sense that one entire item of harm is legally attributed to one "cause," meaning the conduct of one person. "Causal" also in the sense that the basis for attributing responsibility entirely to one person is found in proximate cause theory. Hence the term causal apportionment has the same deficits as any reference to proximate cause. It does not refer to cause in fact; the defendant's conduct as well as the plaintiff's is one of the causes in fact of the added harm. However, the apportionment is entirely in accord with judicial ideas about superseding cause or shifted responsibility.

fault but that the plaintiff alone is responsible for her broken arm. Comparative fault apportionment is particularly well suited when causal apportionment is not possible.

The options. When causal apportionment is possible, as where the plaintiff's failure to follow medical advice makes her injuries worse, adoption of comparative fault rules leaves courts with several basic options, on which complex variations can be imagined.

(1) Comparative negligence principles absorb the avoidable consequences rule. If the plaintiff and defendant are both culpable causes of the plaintiff's injury,[1] apportionment of responsibility is made entirely under comparative fault rules; mitigation or avoidable consequences rules are dropped altogether. Some courts may have this in mind.[2] Statutes,[3] including the Uniform Comparative Fault Act[4] may lend support for this approach by defining fault to include failure to minimize damages.

The total comparative fault approach is the easiest to state, but it does have some problems. If the plaintiff unreasonably caused herself a discrete item of harm in the sum of $10,000, the jury could still set a percentage of overall fault that would force the defendant to bear a portion of that harm. Conversely, if the plaintiff's only fault caused her $10,000 in added harm, the jury might set a percentage of overall fault that reduced the plaintiff's damages by $50,000 instead. When the plaintiff is chargeable with fault in causing an indivisible harm and also with fault in causing some divisible and isolated item of harm, the complexities become quite difficult.[5] A third possible problem results from the fact that by combining the plaintiff's fault in causing the accident with her fault in failing to minimize damages, the court may be required to bar the plaintiff's claim altogether under the incomplete systems of comparative fault.

(2) Applying avoidable consequences rule to post-injury conduct. Some courts hold that the plaintiff's negligence is counted as contributory negligence if it contributed to the initial injury and is to thus be apportioned under comparative negligence statutes where they are

§ 204

1. See Baker v. Morrison, 309 Ark. 457, 829 S.W.2d 421 (1992) (requiring causation to invoke comparative negligence apportionment in failure to minimize cases); Waterson v. General Motors Corporation, 111 N.J. 238, 544 A.2d 357 (1988).

2. E.g., Ridley v. Safety Kleen Corp., 693 So.2d 934 (Fla.1996); McDonnell v. Chally, 529 N.W.2d 611 (Iowa 1994); McKay's Family Dodge v. Hardrives, 480 N.W.2d 141 (Minn.App.1992); Business Men's Assurance Company of American v. Graham, 891 S.W.2d 438 (Mo.App.1994).

3. E.g., Minn. Stat. Ann. § 604.01 (" 'Fault' includes ... unreasonable failure to avoid an injury or to mitigate damages").

4. Uniform Comparative Fault Act § 1.

5. See Paul A. LeBel, Reducing the Recovery of Avoidable "Seat-belt Damages": a Cure for The Defects of Waterson v. General Motors Corporation, 22 Seton Hall L. Rev. 4 (1991). In Ridley v. Safety Kleen Corp., 693 So.2d 934 (Fla.1996), the court attempted to simplify the computation by requiring the jury to make a single finding of fault that included both the plaintiff's negligence that contributed to impact and her negligence that merely aggravated injury, but it remains to be seen whether that simplification generates difficulties of its own.

adopted. But these courts go on to hold that the plaintiff's failure to minimize damages *after* the injury has occurred is a matter of the avoidable consequences rule, to be causally apportioned where possible.[6] Under this rule, the plaintiff who fails to use a safety device like a seatbelt is not chargeable with contributory negligence, since failure to use the seatbelt did not cause the accident. Equally, she is not subject to the mitigation rules because the failure to use the seatbelt occurred before rather than after injury.[7]

This solution may be criticized on the ground that at least on some occasions the plaintiff's pre-injury fault can cause a separate and identifiable element of harm. If so, the question should be whether that item can fairly be laid at the plaintiff's door and whether she should bear the entire responsibility for it. The question whether the plaintiff's fault occurred before rather than after injury should not invariably be dispositive. Indeed, when continuing conduct is involved, it may not even be reasonably possible to know what is "before" and what is "after."[8]

(3) Applying avoidable consequences rule to discrete items of harm. Some courts reject the first two approaches. They apply comparative fault apportionment unless the plaintiff's pre-injury fault caused some particular item of damage to which causal apportionment principles could be applied.[9] Under the view of these cases, if the plaintiff suffers added injury in an auto collision because she failed to wear a seatbelt, these courts invoke the avoidable consequences or mitigation of damages rule to bar recovery for the added injuries. They do so even though the plaintiff's fault occurred before rather than after the injury. In such cases, the defendant must prove that the plaintiff was at fault and that some identifiable items or amounts of harm resulted from that fault. In addition, it must appear that the separate items of harm should justly be borne entirely by the plaintiff rather than apportioned between the parties. If the defendant cannot identify separate items of harm, then the avoidable consequences rule is inappropriate.[10]

6. Russo Farms, Inc. v. Vineland Board of Education, 144 N.J. 84, 675 A.2d 1077 (1996); Ostrowski v. Azzara, 111 N.J. 429, 545 A.2d 148 (1988); see Restatement § 918 ("after the commission of a tort"); but cf. Waterson v. General Motors Corporation, 111 N.J. 238, 544 A.2d 357 (1988) (applying a separate kind of comparative negligence apportionment to damages that could have been avoided by plaintiff's reasonable use of a seatbelt).

7. See § 205.

8. See the court's struggle in Cipollone v. Liggett Group, Inc., 893 F.2d 541 (3d Cir.1990). When nonaction is negligent, it may "begin" before the defendant's negligence and continue afterwards. See Del Tufo v. Township of Old Bridge, 147 N.J. 90, 685 A.2d 1267 (1996) (arrestee's continuing negligence in failing to inform police that he had taken overdose of cocaine treated as contributory negligence, not avoidable consequences).

9. Spier v. Barker, 35 N.Y.2d 444, 323 N.E.2d 164, 363 N.Y.S.2d 916, 80 A.L.R.3d 1025 (1974) (failure to wear seatbelt); Halvorson v. Voeller, 336 N.W.2d 118 (N.D. 1983) (cyclist's failure to wear helmet).

10. The defendant generally bears the burden of proving the amount of harm that would have been avoided. See Caiazzo v. Volkswagenwerk, 647 F.2d 241 (2d Cir. 1981) (defendant had burden of proving the "consequences of the Caiazzos' failure to wear seat belts"); Business Men's Assurance Company of American v. Graham, 891 S.W.2d 438 (Mo.App.1994).

(4) Restatement of Apportionment. The Restatement of Apportionment supports a combination rule. First, the defendant is fully liable without reduction for all injuries that he alone caused. Second, injury resulting both from the defendant's negligence and the plaintiff's failure to mitigate is seen to be itself an indivisible injury which must be apportioned on the rules of comparative fault rather than the rules of avoidable consequences.[11] For example, the defendant negligently breaks the plaintiff's leg without any fault of the plaintiff. For that, the defendant is fully responsible. If the plaintiff then has additional medical expense because she failed to take antibiotics prescribed, that additional expense is a result of the combined fault of the defendant, whose negligence created the need for antibiotics, and the plaintiff. As to the additional medical expense, comparative fault apportionment is used.[12] The seatbelt cases discussed in the next section raise similar possibilities.

§ 205. Comparative Negligence or Avoidable Consequences in Seatbelt and Other Safety Precaution Cases

Contributory negligence. In the light of safety factors involved, the plaintiff's failure to wear an available seatbelt or safety harness may be quite unreasonable. Nevertheless, failure to use the seatbelt does not normally cause injuries in the initial impact, only injury from a "second collision" when the unbelted plaintiff is thrown out of the car or against an object in the car. Consequently, courts have mostly held that failure to wear a seatbelt cannot count as contributory negligence to bar the entire claim.[1]

Avoidable consequences and comparative negligence. The same argument does not apply to methods for reducing the plaintiff's damages. One method for reduction is to use the avoidable consequences or mitigation of damages rule, eliminating altogether the portion of the plaintiff's damages that the defendant proves could reasonably have been avoided by use of a seatbelt but otherwise allowing the plaintiff's claim. A fair number of courts have authorized such reductions in the plaintiff's damages[2] based upon the avoidable consequences[3] or comparative fault rules.[4]

11. See Restatement of Apportionment §§ 3, 8 & 50.

12. See Id. § 3, Ill. 4.

§ 205

1. See Leonard Schwartz, The Seat Belt Defense and Mandatory Seat Belt Usage: Law, Ethics, and Economics, 24 Idaho L. Rev. 275 (1988).

2. See Christopher Hall, Annotation, Nonuse of Seatbelt as Reducing Amount of Damages Recoverable, 62 A.L.R.5th 537 (1998).

3. Spier v. Barker, 35 N.Y.2d 444, 323 N.E.2d 164, 363 N.Y.S.2d 916, 80 A.L.R.3d 1025 (1974) (failure to wear seat belt); Halvorson v. Voeller, 336 N.W.2d 118 (N.D. 1983) (cyclist's failure to wear helmet).

4. Hutchins v. Schwartz, 724 P.2d 1194 (Alaska 1986); Ridley v. Safety Kleen Corp., 693 So.2d 934 (Fla.1996); Waterson v. General Motors Corporation, 111 N.J. 238, 544 A.2d 357 (1988); Some statutes authorize the reduction. E.g., Cal.Veh. Code § 27315 (j); Oh. Rev. Code Ann. § 4513.263 (F) ("shall be considered by the trier ... as contributory negligence" and may diminish the recovery). Some do so but impose a cap. See n.6 below.

Example. Suppose the plaintiff's total damages are $100,000, $10,-000 of which resulted because she failed to use an available seatbelt. A court rejecting the causal approach of the avoidable consequence rule is in effect refusing to make a simple deduction of $10,000 additional damages caused by failure to wear the restraint. If the court turns to the fault apportionment system of comparative negligence, it might find the plaintiff's fault is 10% in causing the accident and another 5% in failing to wear the seatbelt. Instead of reducing the plaintiff's total damages by 15% for her seatbelt fault plus her accident-fault, the court might first reduce the damages to $90,000 for her accident-fault, then identify the harms caused by failure to wear a seatbelt and reduce damages for those harms alone by 5%.[5]

Capped reduction. One solution to the comparative negligence complexities might be an arbitrary statutory reduction at a fixed percentage. Apparently no state has tried this, but several states have authorized a comparative negligence reduction with an arbitrary limit providing that the reduction may not exceed a specified small percentage figure, such as 5%.[6] Another legislative approach admits seatbelt non-use evidence to mitigate pain and suffering damages but not others.[7]

Barring all reduction. Judges have held in many states that the award is not to be reduced either under comparative negligence or avoidable consequences rules[8] and legislation now so provides in most states. Indeed, some of the statutes broadly exclude admission of evidence about seatbelt nonuse for any purpose,[9] and some even relieve adults of liability to a child when the adult negligently fails to utilize child restraint systems.[10]

5. See Restatement of Apportionment § 50 (Proposed Final Draft 1999). More complex formulas are possible. See Waterson v. General Motors Corporation, 111 N.J. 238, 544 A.2d 357 (1988). The case is fully explicated in Paul A. LeBel, Reducing the Recovery of Avoidable "Seat-belt Damages": A Cure for The Defects of Waterson v. General Motors Corporation, 22 Seton Hall L. Rev. 4 (1991).

6. E.g., Mich. Comp. L. § 257.710e (6); Mo. Rev. Stat. § 307.178 (4) (not to exceed 1%).

7. See Anderson v. Watson, 953 P.2d 1284, 62 A.L.R.5th 877 (Colo. 1998) (applying the Colorado statute to this effect).

8. E.g., Amend v. Bell, 89 Wash.2d 124, 570 P.2d 138 (1977); see Christopher Hall, Annotation, Nonuse of Seatbelt as Reducing Amount of Damages Recoverable, 62 A.L.R.5th 537 (1998).

9. About 30 statutes in three groups provide that evidence of failure to wear a seatbelt (1) is not evidence of contributory negligence, or (2) "shall not be admissible into evidence in a civil action," with specified exceptions, (3) is not admissible and no exceptions are recognized. See Olson v. Ford Motor Co., 558 N.W.2d 491 (Minn. 1997) (plaintiff could not prove that defective seatbelt caused his injury); contra: Bridgestone/Firestone, Inc. v. Glyn–Jones, 878 S.W.2d 132 (Tex.1994). Cf. General Motors Corp. v. Wolhar, 686 A.2d 170 (Del. 1996) (failure to wear seatbelt cannot show comparative fault but can show superseding cause).

10. E.g., Iowa Code, § 321–446 (operator's failure to comply with requirements for use of a child restraint system "does not constitute negligence"); cf. Gaertner v. Holcka, 219 Wis.2d 436, 580 N.W.2d 271 (1998) (no contribution claim will lie against person who violated statute requiring children be secured with seatbelts); but cf. Dellapenta v. Dellapenta, 838 P.2d 1153 (Wyo.1992) (adult's failure to secure a child with appropriate seat restraints can constitute negligence) .

Other pre-injury safety precautions. Although statutes in many states resolve the specific issue of seatbelt use, many non-seatbelt cases fit the seatbelt pattern and may involve similar issues. In fact, the virtually identical problem of the cyclist who fails to wear a helmet has already arisen, and been treated to the same split of common law authority that governs seatbelts.[11] Many other cases could exhibit the same essential characteristics of a pre-injury failure of care that causes discrete, divisible harm. For example, a pilot's failure to take a working parachute might be unreasonable on some occasions, although the absence of a parachute would not cause a plane's malfunction. A vacationer's failure to wear a life vest in a boat, a factory's failure to have a working fire extinguisher or sprinkler system,[12] and a building owner's failure to maintain the safety of heavy marble panels[13] could all add to the harm done when and if a harmful event occurs. In fact, pre-injury precautions are a regular feature of reasonable care, ranging from protective clothing for cold weather to canteens of water for desert hikers. The seatbelt cases raise the question whether the plaintiff's failure to take pre-injury self-protective measures is always to be taken from the jury under the rule adopted by many courts, or whether some reduction in damages is appropriate. Consequently, it remains important to notice the judicial reasons for refusing to count seatbelt negligence.

Judicial arguments against counting seatbelt negligence. Most of the reasons for refusing to charge the plaintiff with any responsibility for failure to wear protective devices might not be applied in cases generally. Courts have said that there was no statutory obligation to wear seatbelts and therefore a jury would not be allowed to find a failure to do so to be negligence;[14] that the plaintiff need not anticipate the negligence of others[15] and therefore is not negligent in failing to protect herself by a seatbelt; that a tortfeasor would get a windfall if the plaintiff's recovery were reduced to reflect her own fault although plaintiff's damages are proportioned to her fault in other cases; or that the defendant must accept the plaintiff as he finds her, although this rule does not otherwise protect the plaintiff against her own negligence. The strangest argument is that the plaintiff's pre-injury fault did not cause the accident and therefore should not be allowed to reduce damages it did cause.[16] This

11. E.g., Dare v. Sobule, 674 P.2d 960 (Colo.1984) (evidence of failure to wear helmet inadmissible to show negligence or reduce damages under mitigation doctrine); Halvorson v. Voeller, 336 N.W.2d 118 (N.D. 1983) (failure to wear helmet goes to reduce damages caused by that failure).

12. See Acculog, Inc. v. Peterson, 692 P.2d 728 (Utah 1984) (failure to have fire extinguisher to protect valuable equipment could not be considered as contributory fault, withholding a ruling on avoidable consequences).

13. Business Men's Assurance Company of American v. Graham, 891 S.W.2d 438 (Mo.App.1994).

14. As a result of federal financial incentives, statutes now usually require at least the front seat occupants to wear seatbelts. E.g., CONN. GEN. STAT. § 14–100a(c).

15. This is an old saying that simply is not true. At best it can be applied in some particular instances, not in a entire category of cases. See § 162.

16. When the shoe is on the other foot, defendants are readily held liable for the damage they did in fact cause or the damage they made worse, even if they did not cause the accident or initial injury. This is true, for example, in products liability cases, where the manufacturer is held liable

argument was coupled with the mechanical argument that the failure to wear a seatbelt occurred before injury and that only post-injury negligence could be used to invoke the avoidable consequences rule.

With the passage of time, the weaknesses in the arguments seem sufficiently apparent.[17] Why, then, did courts (and then legislatures) adopt a rule relieving the plaintiff from responsibility for unreasonable failure to protect herself? Probably less for any of the stated reasons than because courts in earlier days were themselves unsure that reasonable care required a seatbelt. Besides that, courts are aware that they must follow society at least as often as they lead it, and they were probably well aware that a very large number of people simply refused to wear safety belts.[18]

In any event, the reasons for refusing to permit a jury to reduce the plaintiff's damages for seatbelt negligence are not necessarily appealing when the plaintiff is in fact arguably at fault in failing to take pre-injury precautions. Suppose the plaintiff stores a large quantity of flammable materials that do not themselves create a risk of igniting a fire but that will cause a fire to burn quickly and spread if one occurs. Reasonable care might require a sprinkler system. That will depend upon facts about the degree of risk and the costs involved. But if the plaintiff is in fact at fault in failing to take this pre-injury precaution, perhaps courts should be willing to permit the jury to apply the avoidable consequences rule or to make a comparative negligence reduction in damages.[19] In some ways, the plaintiff who risks the spread of fire is an especially good candidate for a damage reduction. That plaintiff has not only risked harm to himself like the seatbelt scoffer or the boater who refuses to wear a life vest; he has also risked harm to others. Even if the seatbelt cases protecting the plaintiff from responsibility are right on their facts, they do not necessarily control other pre-injury safety precaution cases.

§ 206. Intentional or Reckless Torts after Comparative Negligence

Intentional Torts

Traditional rule. Before adoption of comparative negligence rules, contributory negligence was never a defense to intentional torts. Nor

for defects in a car that make injuries worse when those injuries are caused by other drivers. See, e.g., Caiazzo v. Volkswagenwerk, A.G., 647 F.2d 241 (2d Cir.1981).

17. A good answer to each argument was presented by Justice Feldman in Law v. Superior Court, 157 Ariz. 147, 755 P.2d 1135 (1988).

18. Leaving the issue to the jury would not have been an appealing answer in the early days of seatbelts, either, since many juries would have voted their biases against seatbelts, with the result that seatbelt negligence might work to discriminate against unpopular plaintiffs and those unlucky enough to get a jury that understood the safety issue.

19. See Desco Corporation v. Harry W. Trushel Construction Co., 186 W.Va. 430, 413 S.E.2d 85 (1991) (plaintiff who moved goods into his warehouse before sprinkler system was operative assumed the risk [treated as a form of comparative fault]); accord, Skarpness v. Port of Seattle, 52 Wash.2d 490, 326 P.2d 747 (1958); Waterway Terminals Co. v. P.S. Lord Mechanical Contractors, 256 Or. 361, 474 P.2d 309 (1970).

was it a defense to reckless, wanton or wilful torts, which courts considered to be substantially equivalent to intentional torts. Most courts dealing with the question have carried these rules over to the regime of comparative negligence, holding or assuming that the plaintiff's comparative fault cannot be used to reduce the liability of an intentional tortfeasor.[1] Sometimes the governing comparative negligence statute so provides.[2] Under this view, if the defendant batters the plaintiff, the plaintiff's negligence in taunting the defendant does not reduce the plaintiff's damages.[3]

Applying comparative fault to defendants' intentional torts or intentional harms.[4] A few courts have held that some kind of comparative fault principles can apply in apportioning liability to intentional tortfeasors in at least some kinds of cases.[5] This view is also supported by the Restatement of Apportionment of Liability[6] and by commentary.[7] Some comparative fault statutes impliedly [8]or expressly enact the same rule.[9] The moral basis for this view is that the plaintiff as well as the defendant should bear responsibility for her harmful and faulty acts.

The issue does not ordinarily arise merely because the tortfeasor commits an intentional *act.* Many intentional acts, such as driving a vehicle, are not tortious in any way at all. Some are tortious because they create unreasonable risks. Driving a car a high speed is like this, but intentionally driving at high speed is still not an intentional tort unless the defendant either intends to inflict harm or is certain to do so.[10]

§ 206

1. E.g., Cartwright v. Equitable Life Assurance Soc'y, 276 Mont. 1, 914 P.2d 976 (1996); see Morgan v. Johnson, 137 Wash.2d 887, 976 P.2d 619, 623 (1999) Henry Woods & Beth Deere, Comparative Fault § 7.1 (3d ed. 1996); Allan L. Schwartz, Annotation, Applicability of Comparative Negligence Principles to Intentional Torts, 18 A.L.R.5th 525 (1995). The Uniform Comparative Fault Act did not purport to change this traditional rule. See the Comment to § 1.

2. La. Stat. Ann. Civ. Code Art. 2323 (C). Cf. Fla. Stat. Ann. § 768.81 (4) (a) ("This section applies to negligence cases"; no mention of intentional torts). Similarly, a statute that only applies to actions based on "fault" does not affect strict liability claims. See Irvine v. Rare Feline Breeding Center, Inc., 685 N.E.2d 120 (Ind.App.1997).

3. Whitlock v. Smith, 297 Ark. 399, 762 S.W.2d 782 (1989).

4. Some intentional torts are artificially defined to impose liability even though harm is not intended.

5. See nn. 17 & 18 below.

6. See Restatement of Apportionment of Liability § 1, cmt. b. The view is qualified by recognizing that in some instances the plaintiff has no duty to act with care for his own safety, as where to do so might require the plaintiff to give up an important right. See Id. § 3, cmt. d.

7. See Gail D. Hollister, Using Comparative Fault to Replace the All-or-Nothing Lottery Imposed in Intentional Torts Suits in Which Both Plaintiff and Defendant Are at Fault, 46 Vand. L. Rev. 121 (1993).

8. If comparative negligence is governed exclusively by statute and the statute covers "any civil action," or "actions for personal injury," intentional and strict liability torts appear to be covered. If the statute only addresses "actions for negligence," it seems to exclude actions for intentional torts. Some statutes, cobbled up for various purposes, send mixed messages.

9. Ind. Stat. § 34–6–2–45 ("'Fault' includes any act or omission that is negligent, willful, wanton, reckless, or intentional toward the person or property of others").

10. See § 116. Thus a jailer may intentionally refuse to provide medical attention to a prisoner, but unless the assertion is that he intended harm or that harm was certain, the claim is one for negligence, so

On the other hand, intentional torts are not all alike and in a few instances a morally innocent person may intend an act that turns out to be tortious, as where the hunter intends to kill an animal he reasonably believes to be a wolf but which in fact is the plaintiff's dog.[11] If the plaintiff is chargeable with negligence in this kind of case, it would present an especially strong case for invoking comparative fault because the plaintiff is guilty of negligence and the defendant is (morally) guilty of nothing.[12] Yet the argument might be read as merely saying that the rule of liability itself is wrong. If it is true that the defendant is morally innocent, perhaps there should be no liability at all. If liability is rightly imposed upon the morally innocent because of some legal policy, the scope of that policy should determine whether comparative fault principles should reduce damages, not a universal rule about using comparative fault. Other configurations of intentional torts might call for different answers.[13]

Beyond this, however, negligence and contributory negligence take their ultimate meanings from each other and from the relationships involved. It may be contributory negligence to allow a dog to roam the interstate highway, but in spite of risks of hunters, we should not assume that the plaintiff is chargeable with fault in allowing a dog to roam the woods. Perhaps instead, the plaintiff is merely exercising a public right or privilege to use the woods.[14] If so, we should not lightly transmute the plaintiff's right into some species of fault.

In still other intentional tort cases the defendant's assertion of a privilege may turn the issue into one that often seems indistinguishable from the negligence issue. For example, the self-defense plea quickly converts the intentional battery case into an issue about the reasonableness of the defendant's perception that force was needed and the

the prisoner's contributory negligence can appropriately reduce the defendant's liability. Del Tufo v. Township of Old Bridge, 147 N.J. 90, 685 A.2d 1267 (1996).

11. See Ranson v. Kitner, 31 Ill.App. 241 (1889); § 69 supra; cf. Wiseman v. Schaffer, 115 Idaho 537, 768 P.2d 800 (Idaho App.1989) (towing vehicle under reasonable mistake, summarized in § 62, supra).

12. See Gail D. Hollister, Using Comparative Fault to Replace the All-or-Nothing Lottery Imposed in Intentional Torts Suits in Which Both Plaintiff and Defendant Are at Fault, 46 Vand. L. Rev. 121 (1993).

13. Gail D. Hollister, Using Comparative Fault to Replace the All-or-Nothing Lottery Imposed in Intentional Torts Suits in Which Both Plaintiff and Defendant Are at Fault, 46 Vand. L. Rev. 121, 150–166 (1993) identifies four categories: (1) defendant reasonably believed the facts to be such that his acts were not wrongful or harmful; (2) defendant believed that his conduct would be harmful but that he nevertheless had a right to pursue it (as in self defense); (3) defendant intended a tortious injury but different from the one actually inflicted; (4) defendant intended the injury caused and did not believe he had a privilege. Hollister argued that defendants should not be able to claim the plaintiff's comparative fault when the defendant wanted to inflict the harm done and knew there was no privilege to inflict it and also when the defendant took advantage of that fault to commit his tort. On the other hand, Hollister thought that provocation should be considered as comparative fault.

14. Cf. Leroy Fibre Co. v. Chicago, Milwaukee & St. Paul Railway Co, 232 U.S. 340, 34 S.Ct. 415, 58 L.Ed. 631 (1914) (plaintiff could have avoided risk of fire from defendant's trains by moving plaintiff's goods farther from the track, but plaintiff had a right to use the property and was not barred).

reasonableness of the amount of force used.[15] In this kind of case, at least as between two persons committing intentional harms, comparative fault may work reasonably well.

Not only are intentional torts themselves different from one another, comparative fault can be applied to such torts in at least four quite different settings with potentially quite different impacts: (1) Plaintiff and defendant are both intentional tortfeasors. (2) The plaintiff is an intentional tortfeasor injured by the negligent defendant.[16] (3) The defendant is an intentional tortfeasor and the plaintiff is merely negligent to himself or others. (4) One of two defendants is negligent, the other intentional. Subcategories of this one might include (a) defendants acting independently but causing a single indivisible injury and (b) a negligent defendant who creates a risk of an intentional tort by another.

The difference in various intentional torts and their potential application perhaps counsels caution in making a category-wide rule that always or never applies comparative fault.

In fact, few cases so far seem to have reduced a personal injury defendant's liability for his own intentional wrongdoing merely because the plaintiff was guilty of contributory negligence.[17] Most of the cases instead involve a comparison of one defendant's negligence with another defendant's intentional wrongdoing,[18] an approach that might be justified in some claims between defendants for contribution. It may turn out that intentional torts should be weighed on the comparative negligence scale in some case patterns but not others.[19]

The principles are at odds with one another. It is morally appealing to think that each person should bear some accountability for his or her own fault, whether that fault is grounded in intent or in negligence. Yet the measure of liability should not be divorced from the basis for that

15. See § 70.

16. In some cases in this pattern, the intentionally wrongdoing plaintiff is barred completely, in others allowed a full recovery, depending, evidently, upon the strength of the policies involved. See § 208.

17. Comeau v. Lucas, 90 A.D.2d 674, 455 N.Y.S.2d 871 (1982) may have been such a case. The court approved a comparative negligence instruction, but whether it went only to the claim of negligent supervision or to the claim against the intentional tortfeasor is unclear from the report. At least part of the reason for applying comparative fault principles in Bonpua v. Fagan, 253 N.J.Super. 475, 602 A.2d 287 (1992) was that there were intentional physical attacks by both plaintiff and defendant. Louisiana has long considered the plaintiff's provocation (by verbal abuse, for example) as grounds for limiting the damages recovery in a battery case, and with the adoption of comparative negligence, its courts applied that rule as an aspect of comparative fault. See Jones v. Thomas, 557 So.2d 1015 (La.App.1990). As to provocation in battery cases, see § 73. However, in 1996 the Louisiana Civil Code was amended to eliminate comparative negligence defenses against intentional torts, La. Stat. Ann. Civ. Code Art. 2323 (C).

18. E.g., Hutcherson v. City of Phoenix, 192 Ariz. 51, 961 P.2d 449 (1998); Thomas v. First Interstate Bank of Arizona, 187 Ariz. 488, 930 P.2d 1002, 54 A.L.R.5th 827 (1996); Weidenfeller v. Star and Garter, 1 Cal.App.4th 1, 2 Cal.Rptr.2d 14 (1991); Blazovic v. Andrich, 124 N.J. 90, 590 A.2d 222, 18 A.L.R.5th 1031 (1991); Reichert v. Atler, 117 N.M. 623, 875 P.2d 379 (1994); Torres v. State, 119 N.M. 609, 894 P.2d 386 (1995).

19. See § 390 on apportionment problems in multiple tortfeasor cases and in particular in the kind of case in which A negligently risks B's intentional wrongdoing.

liability and the rules must apply the fault comparison in ways that can be rationally evaluated by reviewing judges. Although it has been argued that negligence and other kinds of fault are not truly different except in degree and that negligence can thus be compared with other kinds of fault,[20] the similarity between negligence and intentional wrongdoing seems to appear mainly at high levels of abstraction. In negligence claims, risks and utilities may be difficult to estimate, but we know what we are estimating. Intent—its clarity and intensity, its moral quality, its roots in personal failure, tragedy, misapprehensions, or cultural ideals—would be very hard to weigh on a scale comparable to the risk-utility scale in negligence cases. Such difficulties open the door to highly subjective judgments about an individual's moral worth rather than about an individual's conduct. Biased judgments would be difficult or impossible to detect and review on appeal in the absence of a firm standard for comparison.

Whatever the difficulties with the minority view, however, it does not mean that the plaintiff would always suffer a reduction in damages in a suit against a single intentional tortfeasor. Courts may find that the plaintiff in particular cases had no duty to protect herself by giving up an important right. The plaintiff has a right to walk on the street, even if there is a constant danger that she will be attacked by an intentional wrongdoer. In such cases, an attacker could scarcely hope to reduce the plaintiff's recovery on the ground that she should have remained locked in her house.[21]

Reckless, Wilful or Wanton Torts

Reckless, wilful or wanton torts. The old contributory negligence regime often lumped reckless or wanton torts together with intentional torts. Reckless or wanton torts are usually characterized by extreme risk coupled with an attitude of conscious indifference. In contributory negligence cases, that meant that the plaintiff could recover fully, without reduction in damages, if the defendant's conduct could be characterized as wilful, reckless, or wanton.[22] The Uniform Comparative Fault Act requires the comparison of the plaintiff's negligence with the defendant's reckless or wanton misconduct, so long as that misconduct falls short of an intentional tort.[23] A number of the cases are in accord,[24] at least where the facts of the particular case make the reckless conduct more like negligence than intent.[25] A few go the other way, allowing an

20. Gail D. Hollister, Using Comparative Fault to Replace the All-or-Nothing Lottery Imposed in Intentional Torts Suits in Which Both Plaintiff and Defendant Are at Fault, 46 VAND. L. REV. 121 (1993).

21. See Restatement of Apportionment § 3, cmt. d, Ill. 8.

22. § 206.

23. Uniform Comparative Fault Act, § 1 (" 'Fault' includes acts or omissions that are in any measure negligent or reckless toward the person or property of the actor or others").

24. E.g., Yerkes v. Asberry, 938 S.W.2d 307 (Mo.App.1997); Cartwright v. Equitable Life Assurance Soc'y, 276 Mont. 1, 914 P.2d 976 (1996).

25. Poole v. City of Rolling Meadows, 167 Ill.2d 41, 656 N.E.2d 768, 212 Ill.Dec. 171 (1995); see Annotation, Application of Comparative Negligence in Action Based on Gross Negligence, Recklessness, or The Like, 10 A.L.R.4th 946 (1981).

unreduced recovery when the defendant is chargeable with reckless or wanton misconduct.[26]

§ 207. Last Clear Chance after Comparative Negligence

Under the traditional rules, the plaintiff chargeable with contributory negligence could recover all her damages without reduction if the defendant had the last clear chance to avoid injury to the plaintiff at a time when the plaintiff could no longer save herself.[1] This exception, and its discovered peril version, was an all or nothing rule like the contributory negligence rule itself. It did not merely reduce the plaintiff's recovery; it allowed a full recovery in spite of the plaintiff's fault.

The only thing like a logical explanation for this exception to the rule of contributory negligence was that when the defendant had the last clear chance, the plaintiff's negligence was not a proximate cause of her own harm and should therefore not be considered at all. The explanation could not possibly be correct in all cases to which the rule applied, for on a great many occasions when the negligence of two or more persons combines to cause a single injury, the conduct of both is regarded as a proximate cause and both are responsible.

As a result, the last clear chance doctrine has been widely regarded as merely a judicial effort to ameliorate the rigors of the complete bar at a time when courts uniformly felt they could not themselves institute a regime of comparative fault. Given that view, it is no surprise that once comparative negligence systems were adopted, last clear chance doctrine was almost always discarded,[2] either legislatively[3] or judicially.[4] Some states have not clearly passed on the issue, but the doctrine does not survive in more than a handful of states at most.[5]

In incomplete or modified systems of comparative negligence, the plaintiff is barred in most states if her negligence is greater than the defendant's, and sometimes even when it is only equal to the defendant's. To the extent that contributory negligence remains a bar to the highly faulty plaintiff, it might be argued that last clear chance rules should continue in effect. This was firmly rejected in Wyoming[6] and seems to have no support in mainstream comparative negligence law.[7]

26. E.g., Davies v. Butler, 95 Nev. 763, 602 P.2d 605 (1979). But even these courts might accept the view that a comparative fault approach is better when the reckless or wanton conduct is more like negligence than intent. Cf. Ziarko v. Soo Line R.R., 161 Ill.2d 267, 204 Ill.Dec. 178, 641 N.E.2d 402 (1994).

§ 207

1. § 200.

2. HENRY WOODS & BETH DEERE, COMPARATIVE FAULT § 8.3 (3d ed. 1996).

3. E.g., CONN. GEN. STAT. ANN. § 52–572h (*l*); MINN. STAT. ANN. § 604.01; ORE. REV. STAT. § 18.475.

4. E.g., Spahn v. Town of Port Royal, 330 S.C. 168, 499 S.E.2d 205 (1998).

5. See, e.g., Fouts v. Builders Transport, Inc., 222 Ga.App. 568, 474 S.E.2d 746 (1996).

6. Danculovich v. Brown, 593 P.2d 187 (Wyo.1979).

7. See VICTOR E. SCHWARTZ, COMPARATIVE NEGLIGENCE § 7–2 (g) (3d ed. 1994).

Although last clear chance and discovered peril doctrines retain none of their original legal force in most states, the facts upon which those doctrines were based are still relevant in determining negligence and comparing fault. In many negligence cases, the defendant creates risks of harm, but harm that might be avoided by any one of several means, including the plaintiff's own efforts to avoid harm. In last chance cases, however, the defendant by definition creates a risk of harm that others cannot avoid. One who unreasonably imposes a great risk of harm is properly considered to be more at fault than one who imposes a smaller risk. So last clear chance and discovered peril facts suggest greater negligence on the part of the defendant, with the result that the trier can appropriately assign a higher percentage of fault to him.[8]

The proximate cause rationale for last clear chance rules did not justify a rule of law that always forgave the plaintiff's fault when the defendant had the last chance. However, to abolish the last clear chance/discovered peril doctrines is not to abolish the concept of proximate cause. In some cases the plaintiff's negligence simply is not a cause in fact or a proximate cause of the harm. When it is not, it has no effect as comparative negligence.

§ 208. Effect of Plaintiff's Illegal Acts

People should not profit from their own wrongs. Courts in scores and scores of cases have said that this is a basic principle of law. Although its roots reach into restitutionary law, its principle also stands behind many property and economic torts. If I convert your goods, I should not be allowed to keep them without paying; the law must not allow me to profit from my own wrong.

The principle has been invoked in a variety of cases, but selectively. Sometimes it is extended to trump well-established rules or even statutes;[1] sometimes vice versa, other rules trump the principle;[2] sometimes the principle is rejected,[3] or is ignored where discussion might be

8. McIntyre v. Balentine, 833 S.W.2d 52 (Tenn.1992); Danculovich v. Brown, 593 P.2d 187 (Wyo.1979); see Restatement of Apportionment of Liability § 8, cmt. c (timing of each party's conduct relevant in fixing percentages of fault).

§ 208

1. See Barker v. Kallash, 63 N.Y.2d 19, 479 N.Y.S.2d 201, 468 N.E.2d 39 (1984); Riggs v. Palmer, 115 N.Y. 506, 511, 22 N.E. 188, 190 (1889) ("all laws, as well as all contracts, may be controlled in their operation and effect by general, fundamental maxims of the common law. No one shall be permitted to profit by his own fraud, or to take advantage of his own wrong, or to found any claim upon his own iniquity, or to acquire property by his own crime").

2. Simon & Schuster, Inc. v. Members of the New York State Crime Victims Board, 502 U.S. 105, 112 S.Ct. 501, 116 L.Ed.2d 476 (1991) (statutes depriving criminals of profits made from writing about their crimes are unconstitutional). *Compare* McCummings v. New York City Transit Authority, 81 N.Y.2d 923, 613 N.E.2d 559, 597 N.Y.S.2d 653 (1993) (police officer negligently injured a mugger who was either in the act of attacking or running away, mugger can recover) *with* Barker v. Kallash, supra n. 1(boy injured while making a pipe bomb is committing seriously immoral act and cannot recover from one who provided the materials).

3. Goldfuss v. Davidson, 79 Ohio St.3d 116, 679 N.E.2d 1099 (1997) (decedent, intending to steal from landowner, was killed by landowner's shot; public policy did not preclude recovery for injuries sustained in commission of a felony because "The law

expected.[4] Many cases that invoke the principle would be decided the same way even if no such principle existed. The doctor who conceals his negligence from the patient, for example, may be denied the statute of limitations as a defense to bar claims for his concealed wrongdoing.[5] The robber and the burglar cannot complain if he is harmed when the victim reasonably defends himself, but the victim's privilege suffices to explain that result without resort to any special privilege or immunity.[6]

In most of these cases, the principle has nothing whatever to do with comparative negligence. Much less does it always conflict with apportionment goals of the comparative negligence system. For example, the principle is invoked to hold that the wilful slayer cannot claim to inherit from his victim.[7] Likewise, if the plaintiff commits a felony and then suffers imprisonment as a punishment, he cannot often hope to recover in tort from a defendant who encouraged the crime or negligently made it possible.[8] The same result is imposed even when the defendant as a lawyer for an accused person owes that person a very considerable duty of care. A felon who is in fact guilty of the crime on which he is convicted has no claim for negligent malpractice against his attorney: he must not profit from his own wrong or found his claim on his own illegal act.[9] The defendant in such a case owes the plaintiff no duty to protect him against his own criminal proclivities. In such settings, the principle has virtually no connection with contributory negligence. The point is less about profiting from your own acts than about taking responsibility for them.

However, in some cases courts have extended the principle to mean that a plaintiff who suffers a tortious injury as a result of her own seriously[10] illegal or immoral act simply cannot recover from the tortfea-

should not encourage vigilantism", even though the case was conceptualized as a negligence case and recovery allowed on that ground, not on intentional tort ground).

4. E.g., Katko v. Briney, 183 N.W.2d 657 (Iowa 1971) (plaintiff breaking into empty farm house injured by spring gun can recover); McCummings v. New York City Transit Authority, supra n. 2 (mugger can recover when injured by police negligence).

5. See, e.g., Geisz v. Greater Baltimore Medical Center, 313 Md. 301, 545 A.2d 658 (1988).

6. Cf. Calvillo–Silva v. Home Grocery, 19 Cal.4th 714, 968 P.2d 65, 80 Cal.Rptr.2d 506 (1998) (statutory immunity from liability to one injured in the commission of a felony, but immunity for use of deadly force ultimately turned on common law justification).

7. Riggs v. Palmer, 115 N.Y. 506, 511, 22 N.E. 188, 190 (1889).

8. Adkinson v. Rossi Arms, 659 P.2d 1236 (Alaska 1983) (convicted killer sued gun manufacturer, claiming gun's defect caused its discharge and led to his prison sentence; "allowance of the action sought to be maintained by the Adkinsons would erode the societal norms"); Cole v. Taylor, 301 N.W.2d 766 (Iowa 1981) (therapist who negligently fails to deter patient's murder of her husband is not liable); Feltner v. Casey Family Program, 902 P.2d 206 (Wyo. 1995) (placement of young, seductive foster-care female in family without warning led to sexual encounter with family's teen-aged male and to male's conviction, no liability). But cf. Meah v. McCreamer, [1985] 1 All. E.R. 367 (Q.B. 1984) (defendant negligently caused auto collision which caused plaintiff's brain injury which caused plaintiff to commit rapes, which led to plaintiff's imprisonment; plaintiff can recover for the imprisonment).

9. Adkins v. Dixon, 253 Va. 275, 482 S.E.2d 797 (1997).

10. See Ardinger v. Hummell, 982 P.2d 727 (Alaska 1999) [1999 WL 521701] (public policy rational for barring all recovery in a comparative fault system is limited to

sor who owes her a duty of care.[11] Before the adoption of comparative negligence systems it would not have mattered whether the court invoked the contributory negligence bar or the immoral plaintiff principle, since both would have barred the plaintiff. After the adoption of comparative negligence, however, a rule that bars the claim of the immoral plaintiff potentially conflicts with the comparative negligence system of apportionment, which would only reduce damages.

In *Barker v. Kallash*,[12] the New York Court of Appeals invoked the principle that one should not be permitted to profit from his own wrong to bar an injured person's claim against another wrongdoer. In that case, the 15–year-old plaintiff was making a pipe bomb with ingredients furnished by the defendant. The bomb exploded, causing injury to the plaintiff. Instead of reducing the plaintiff's recovery under comparative negligence rules, the court denied recovery altogether. It concluded that when "the plaintiff's injury is a direct result of his knowing and intentional participation in a criminal act he cannot seek compensation for the loss, if the criminal act is judged to be so serious an offense as to warrant denial of recovery.... Thus a burglar who breaks his leg while descending the cellar stairs, due to the failure of the owner to replace a missing step cannot recover compensation from his victims." Although the comparative negligence statute on its face seemed to govern and to permit the plaintiff to proceed subject to a reduction in damages, the court thought that the immoral plaintiff principle required dismissal of the claim altogether.

As *Barker* shows, the principle that denies relief to a plaintiff who had committed serious wrongdoing can bar a plaintiff who was not committing an intentional wrong to the defendant and who was not even negligent toward him. The same is true when both the plaintiff and the defendant engage in an immoral or illegal act the court regards as especially serious. In a Virginia case, the plaintiff was a woman who engaged in premarital sexual intercourse with a man who knew he had herpes but who provided neither protection nor a warning. As a result of the intercourse, the plaintiff contracted herpes. But such premarital intercourse violated Virginia's fornication statute. When the woman sued the man for the injury he had inflicted, the Virginia Court denied

"cases involving serious criminal conduct that intentionally threatened the safety of others, such as homicide, rape, and arson"). Some courts have been less cautious, however. See Zysk v. Zysk, 239 Va. 32, 404 S.E.2d 721 (1990) (premarital sexual activity enough to bar the plaintiff).

11. Courts have phrased the idea in various terms. One formulation is that "a person cannot maintain an action if, in order to establish his cause of action, he must rely, in whole or in part, on an illegal or immoral act or transaction to which he is a party, or to maintain a claim for damages based on his own wrong or caused by his own neglect, ... or where he must base his cause of action, in whole or in part, on a violation by himself of the criminal or penal laws." Cole v. Taylor, 301 N.W.2d 766, 768 (Iowa 1981).

12. Barker v. Kallash, 63 N.Y.2d 19, 479 N.Y.S.2d 201, 468 N.E.2d 39 (1984). The case was not a sympathetic one for the plaintiff: the defendant was a nine-year-old boy who had furnished firecracker powder. The court's language and the principle it invokes, however, would seem to apply equally if a terrorist had paid the plaintiff to make bombs. In that case, the principle would seem to benefit a party whose acts are probably morally more reprehensible.

all recovery on the ground that the plaintiff had consented to or participated in an immoral or illegal act, although she had not put the man at risk either intentionally or negligently.[13]

Similarly, Michigan has held that one injured by drugs obtained from a pharmacist without a valid prescription has no claim against the pharmacist for injuries that follow.[14] Sometimes the immoral plaintiff principle seems to trump all other rules. Although the custodian of a suicidal person owes a duty of care to prevent suicide, suicide of a sane person was traditionally regarded as an immoral act, so that even some contemporary courts may immunize the custodian who fails to protect a suicidal (and therefore putatively immoral) person from herself.[15]

These cases are not explained by the fact that the plaintiff is guilty of some intentional tort. Although it is possible to foreclose recovery by an intentional tortfeasor against his victim,[16] in none of the cases just described was the plaintiff a tortfeasor at all; in none did he create risks to the defendant. And the rule may be invoked against a plaintiff who is guilty only of negligence, not intentional wrongdoing.[17] Nor are these cases to be explained on the ground that the plaintiff has violated a statute. The plaintiff's violation of statute is ordinarily relevant, of course, as showing contributory negligence, but not as forbidding the claim entirely.[18] Moreover, as these same cases show, the plaintiff may be barred even though the statute she violates is not aimed at her protection or even at the defendant's. The cases rest on the idea that courts can identify some especially reprehensible conduct that ought to outlaw the plaintiff who commits it, even if such a ruling protects a person who has negligently harmed the plaintiff and even if it discards the comparative fault apportionment system.

13. Zysk v. Zysk, 239 Va. 32, 404 S.E.2d 721 (1990). But in Hernandez v. Yoon, 173 Misc.2d 429, 661 N.Y.S.2d 753 (Sup. Ct. 1997) a male plaintiff, complained against his doctor that a vasectomy was negligently performed, resulting, through the plaintiff's adultery, in an unwanted pregnancy of a woman not his wife; his suit was allowed to go forward.

14. Orzel v. Scott Drug Co., 449 Mich. 550, 537 N.W.2d 208 (1995).

15. Hill v. Nicodemus, 979 F.2d 987 (4th Cir.1992) (Virginia law).

16. See Williams v. Thude, 188 Ariz. 257, 934 P.2d 1349 (Ariz. 1997). Some cases that deny all recovery to the immoral plaintiff can be understood merely as cases in which, as a matter of law, the plaintiff's fault exceeded the defendant's. Cf. Oden v. Pepsi Cola Bottling Co. of Decatur, Inc., 621 So.2d 953 (Ala.1993), (a young man trying to steal soft drinks from the defendant's machine by tilting it over was killed when the machine fell and crushed him, recovery denied on immoral plaintiff grounds).

17. As in Aetna Casualty & Surety Co. v. Curley, 585 A.2d 640 (R.I.1991) (person who was negligent in causing death of decedent, although not a formal party to wrongful death and survival actions, could not take as beneficiary, so the action was barred).

18. The fact that the plaintiff is guilty of contributory negligence per se in violating a statute shows negligence but it does not show how much, so a comparison of the plaintiff's per se fault and the defendant's negligence is still appropriate, as in Illinois Central R.R. v. White, 610 So.2d 308 (Miss. 1992). It is thus not plausible to say that the plaintiff's violation of statute shows that her negligence exceeds the defendant's. So to hold would defeat any real comparison of fault and courts seem generally to have resisted this kind of programming of the negligence issue. See Victor E. Schwartz, Comparative Negligence § 6–3 (3d ed. 1994).

In the restitution cases, the wrongdoer takes or holds something, tangible or intangible, that belongs to the plaintiff. It may be difficult to say what belongs to the plaintiff in some cases, but it is not difficult to say that if the defendant has it, he must give it up. When the principle is broadened to bar a plaintiff's suit against a defendant who took part in the same wrong and negligently injured the plaintiff as well, it loses its hard edge and its moral certainty. Indeed, the normal rule of *pari delicto*, under which wrongdoers in equal fault lose their claims against each other, is a rule of comparative responsibility; only if the plaintiff's fault is equal to or greater than the defendant's is she barred under that rule.[19] Yet the cases just described do not weigh comparative fault at all, nor do they attempt to discern whether imposing liability upon the defendant might tend better to enforce the underlying policy.

Consider a New York case[20] in which the twelve-year-old plaintiff had been raped. When she discovered that she was pregnant as a result of the rape, she obtained an abortion without delay. In that procedure, she suffered neurological damage, allegedly as a result of medical malpractice. She never got to trial on the medical negligence issue because by the time she discovered her pregnancy, it was so far advanced that the abortion was illegal. The court invoked the immoral plaintiff principle with the result that the plaintiff was denied the protection of reasonably safe medical care; and the defendants, who participated in the same abortion, avoided all potential liability for negligence. As one court said, some of these holdings run the risk of rating the plaintiff's wrong too highly and at the same time protecting the wrongdoer too much.[21]

As already indicated, courts may bar the plaintiff completely and refuse to use comparative fault apportionment when they regard the plaintiff's own acts as the sole proximate cause of her harm.[22] In this respect, the sole proximate cause cases resemble the immoral plaintiff cases. Both lines of reasoning can remove cases from the comparative fault apportionment system and deal with them, as courts did in the old regime of contributory negligence, on an all or nothing basis. Some cases deserve to be dealt with in that way, but perhaps not cases in which the defendant is as much at fault as the plaintiff.

19. See General Car & Truck Leasing System, Inc. v. Lane & Waterman, 557 N.W.2d 274 (Iowa 1996).

20. Symone T. v. Lieber, 205 A.D.2d 609, 613 N.Y.S.2d 404 (1994).

21. Doe v. Roe, 841 F.Supp. 444 (D.C. App. 1994) (criticizing Virginia's refusal to redress the negligent spread of disease to a woman whose crime was premarital sexual intercourse; the holding "essentially immunizes from all possible liability those who consciously or unconsciously spread infectious and incurable disease. Concern over the spread of such disease is undoubtedly a pressing social concern in its own right"); Flanagan v. Baker, 35 Mass.App.Ct. 444, 621 N.E.2d 1190 (1993) (bomb-making boy injured, the public policy to emphasize is not that all criminal wrongdoers should be denied recovery against injurers, but that the persons who allegedly furnished the firecrackers to the plaintiff should not be shielded from possible liability when the welfare of the general public is potentially threatened by such misconduct); cf. DiMarco v. Lynch Homes–Chester County, Inc., 525 Pa. 558, 583 A.2d 422 (1990) (condemnation of casual sex exalts "an unheeded morality over reality").

22. § 196.

§ 209. Duty and Negligence Issues after Comparative Negligence

Distinguishing Cases of No Negligence

The old regime of contributory negligence as a complete bar began with a looming ambiguity. Was the defendant relieved of liability because some separate principle barred the plaintiff who was at fault? Or only because the defendant could reasonably rely upon the plaintiff to protect herself and was thus simply not negligent? The ambiguity had little practical significance in the old system, because, either way, the defendant escaped liability. Comparative negligence changes that. If the plaintiff's fault establishes contributory negligence, she may still recover with reduced damages. On the other hand, if the defendant owes no duty or care or if he is not negligent because he could reasonably expect the plaintiff to protect herself, he is not liable at all.[1]

Contributory negligence on the part of the plaintiff and lack of negligence on the part of the defendant are easily confused in these circumstances. The issue often arises in "open and obvious danger" cases—when the defendant creates a condition that will be dangerous to anyone who ignores it but that is safe enough when people pay reasonable attention. For instance, an automobile legally parked at the curb is an obstruction in the street, but not ordinarily dangerous. The owner who parks it there can expect that people will see it and avoid it. If the plaintiff runs into the parked automobile, it is ordinarily the owner of that car who can recover, not the plaintiff who ran into it. Nothing else appearing, the trier may conclude that one who parks a car is not negligent and hence that he is not liable at all.[2] Such a finding is probable, perhaps even compelled in some cases, because the defendant can reasonably expect no harm. It is not a question of contributory negligence with a reduction in damages. Many cases, although on different facts, resemble this one in its analysis.[3]

§ 209

1. See Wex S. Malone, Comment on Maki v. Frelk, 21 VAN. L. REV. 930 (1968); Wex S. Malone, Some Ruminations on Contributory Negligence, 1981 UTAH L. REV. 91, reprinted in WEX S. MALONE, ESSAYS ON TORTS 197 (1986).

2. Thus, in the absence of statute or hidden danger, if the car is damaged, its owner has a claim, not the other way around. See Dan B. Dobbs, Accountability and Comparative Fault, 47 LA. L. REV. 939, 950 (1987).

3. E.g., McFarland v. Kahn, 123 Ariz. 62, 597 P.2d 544 (1979) (sprinkler head in lawn not unreasonably dangerous because defendant could expect those nearby to take care of themselves); Stinnett v. Buchele, 598 S.W.2d 469 (Ky. 1980) (employer failed to furnish roof worker a safety device, but, semble, could expect worker to protect himself so as a matter of law employer not negligent; worker could recover nothing); Blair v. Ohio Dept. of Rehabilitation and Correction, 61 Ohio Misc.2d 649, 582 N.E.2d 673 (1989) (visitor knew of danger and could have avoided it, so defendant's need for care reduced). A number of annotations deal with various similar situations, e.g., Linda A. Sharp, Annotation, Liability for Injury to Customer from Object Projecting into Aisle or Passageway in Store, 40 A.L.R.5th 135 (1996).

The same point is sometimes made in different language. Instead of saying that the defendant simply is not negligent, courts may say (1) the defendant had no duty to protect against obvious dangers or (2) the plaintiff assumed the risk of such dangers.

Products liability cases raise more complex issues, but in some special products

On the other hand, when the defendant can reasonably foresee that the some people will *not* observe an open danger or will not be able to protect themselves from it, the answer is different. Suppose the defendant owes the plaintiff a duty of reasonable care and knows that the plaintiff, who is carrying a large carton, might be blinded to a narrow hole, but does nothing to assist the plaintiff, to warn her, or to cover the hole. It would be entirely foreseeable that the plaintiff would step into the hole and fall. In that case, the trier could find the defendant to be negligent.[4] Whenever the defendant can expect that the danger might not be avoided by a reasonably careful person, he cannot avoid liability for negligence on the ground that the danger would often be obvious. In that case, the defendant may still have a comparative negligence defense that would reduce the plaintiff's damages, but he would not avoid all liability.

Expectations of the parties condition these cases. People expect and watch for obstructions like cars in the road. They don't expect holes in the floor of a department store. Consequently, car owners can usually park their cars on the street with the reasonable expectation of safety. Department store owners cannot reasonably leave holes in the floors with the same expectation, no matter how obvious the hole would be if the shopper were not looking at merchandise. For all cases like the car-parked-in-the-road case, the adoption of comparative negligence changes reasons but not results: the defendant, not being negligent, is not liable, not even for a small percentage. For all cases like the hole-in-the-department-store-floor case, the adoption of comparative negligence can change everything: the negligent defendant is liable, but may get a reduction in his liability if the plaintiff is also negligent. What these cases show is that comparative negligence rules are of no assistance to the plaintiff unless the defendant is actually negligent.

Distinguishing Cases of No Duty

Comparative negligence rules are likewise of no assistance to the plaintiff when the defendant is under no duty to the plaintiff, or, what is often the same thing, when the plaintiff's conduct is the sole proximate cause of her harm.[5]

The orthodox view is that adoption of comparative negligence does not impose new duties or alter old ones.[6] If the defendant was under no

cases, the fact that the danger is obvious will tend to show that the product is not defective. See House v. Armour of America, Inc., 929 P.2d 340 (Utah 1996); § 360.

4. Cf. Ward v. K mart Corporation, 136 Ill.2d 132, 143 Ill.Dec. 288, 554 N.E.2d 223 (1990) (customer carrying large mirror walked into a post, view of which was blocked by his package).

5. Some of the cases discussed in § 208 are explicable in these terms. See, e.g., Feltner v. Casey Family Program, 902 P.2d 206 (Wyo.1995). As to cases in which the plaintiff is barred entirely because her own act is the sole proximate cause, see § 196. As to rules limiting the duty owed to the plaintiff, see Chapters 12–21.

6. E.g., Rhubright v. Wigest Corporation, 1997 WL 72109 (Ohio App. 1997); Hansen v. Washington Natural Gas Co., 95 Wash.2d 773, 632 P.2d 504 (1981); see Richards v. Owens–Illinois, Inc., 14 Cal.4th 985, 928 P.2d 1181, 60 Cal.Rptr.2d 103 (1997); Blair v. Campbell, 924 S.W.2d 75 (Tenn. 1996).

duty of care to the plaintiff, comparative negligence does not change that. For example, the traditional view is that the landowner owes no duty to a trespasser or mere licensee in most circumstances.[7] In such a case, the trespasser who is injured by a dangerous condition on the land does not recover damages reduced by her comparative fault; she recovers nothing.[8] Comparative fault is not an issue in such cases because the defendant is not subject to liability in the first place.

§ 210. Comparative Negligence When Multiple Actors Cause Harm

This section summarizes some of the main comparative fault problems that occur when fault is assessed against several actors. Ultimate apportionment of all responsibilities, especially as affected by tort reform, is discussed in Chapter 26.

Defendant's Counterclaim—The Setoff Rule

In many personal injury cases—notably those arising from vehicular collisions—both the plaintiff and defendant are injured. If one sues the other, compulsory counterclaim rules usually require the other to present his counterclaim or lose it. If the trier of fact finds that both parties are at fault and that both are injured, at least one additional step in calculation of damages is required.

Suppose that in a "pure" or complete comparative negligence system the jury finds: (a) the plaintiff was guilty of 40% of the negligence and suffered $100,000, and (b) the defendant was guilty of 60% of the negligence and suffered $14,000 in damages. In the first step, common to all comparative negligence reductions, the judge or jury would reduce the plaintiff's recovery by 40%. That would, provisionally at least, leave her with a potential for judgment of $60,000.

In the counterclaim case, the same step must be repeated for the defendant. That would reduce the defendant's counterclaim by 60%, leaving him a potential judgment for 40% of $14,000 or $5600. In many states, the defendant's counterclaim on these facts would fail, since the defendant's negligence is greater than the plaintiff's, but a counterclaim could succeed not only in pure comparative negligence system but in some circumstances under the incomplete systems. Given a successful counterclaim, for a net of $5600, should that sum be set off against the plaintiff's negligence-reduced recovery of $60,000? If so, the plaintiff would recover a net of $54,400, representing the plaintiff's claim as reduced by her comparative fault, minus the defendant's claim reduced by his comparative fault.

Although the setoff looks reasonable at first glance, the operation of the setoff is a problem when the judgments will be paid by the parties'

7. §§ 232 & 233 below.

8. E.g., Olson v. Sanitary & Improvement Distr. No. 177, 251 Neb. 380, 557 N.W.2d 651 (1997) (licensee, no duty on the facts, summary judgment for defendant); § 232.

liability insurers. An award to the plaintiff represents a correct accounting for her fault; given that award, she will absorb 40% of her own loss. A setoff would reduce her recovery more than appropriate to reflect her fault. The beneficiary of the setoff would be the defendant's liability insurer, which would pay $5600 less than its insured's comparative fault share. With this in mind, some courts have held that, when there is full liability insurance on both sides, no setoff should be allowed.[1] When liability insurance is not in the picture, on the other hand, this view holds that the setoff should be allowed to prevent dislocations that might arise if one party is partially insolvent. Some statutes forbid the setoff in comparative negligence cases, without limiting the statutory rule to cases covered by insurance.[2] The Uniform Act provides for setoff only by agreement of the parties.[3]

Comparing the Plaintiff's Fault with Multiple Defendants—The Aggregation Problem

In pure or complete comparative fault systems, the plaintiff is entitled to recover against all defendants who are found to be negligent, regardless whether the plaintiff's negligence exceeded that of the defendants or not. Traditionally, joint and several liability rules then allowed the plaintiff to recover the entire judgment against any one defendant or group of defendants. If one defendant paid more than his appropriate share, he could seek contribution from the others.

Incomplete systems of comparative fault limit the plaintiff's right to recover to cases in which the plaintiff's negligence is less than, or at least not more than, the tortfeasors' negligence. The question in those states is whether the plaintiff's negligence is compared to each individual defendant's negligence or whether the defendants' negligence is aggregated. For instance, suppose the plaintiff's fault is 40%, and the fault of each defendant, A and B, is 30%. If the defendants cannot be treated as a unit so that their fault is aggregated, then the plaintiff will be denied recovery against each, since her fault is greater than either standing alone . . Several courts taken that view.[4] They would deny the plaintiff recovery from anyone in the example. Most states, by judicial decision or by provision of statute, have allowed the plaintiff to aggregate the negligence of all defendants and to recover if her negligence is less than, or does not exceed that aggregate.[5] This approach seems especially consistent with the rule of joint and several liability, which, subject to

§ 210

1. Jess v. Herrmann, 26 Cal.3d 131, 161 Cal.Rptr. 87, 604 P.2d 208 (1979); Stuyvesant Ins. Co. v. Bournazian, 342 So.2d 471 (Fla.1976); accord, Miller v. Amundson, 117 Wis.2d 425, 345 N.W.2d 494 (1984).

2. Ore. Rev. Stats. § 18.490; R.I. Gen. Laws § 9–20–4.1.

3. Uniform Comparative Fault Act § 3.

4. E.g., Reiter v. Dyken, 95 Wis.2d 461, 290 N.W.2d 510 (1980).

5. Walton v. Tull, 234 Ark. 882, 356 S.W.2d 20, 8 A.L.R.3d 708 (1962); Mass. Gen. Laws Ann. ch. 231 § 85 (comparative negligence rules apply if plaintiff's negligence "was not greater than the total amount of negligence attributable to the person or persons against whom recovery is sought"); Restatement of Apportionment § 7, cmt. n; Henry Woods & Beth Deere, Comparative Fault § 13.1 (3d ed. 1996).

contribution rights, holds each defendant initially liable for the aggregate harm.

Whose Fault is Counted

Effect of counting fault of many persons. A number of states have abolished or partially abolished joint and several liability, leaving each tortfeasor liable for his comparative fault share of an indivisible injury, no more, no less.[6] Where that is the case, the plaintiff's recovery is directly affected by the number of actors whose fault can be counted. One hundred percent is the maximum fault available to share among all the negligent actors, whether there are two or twenty. When only two actors are negligent, the average fault of each tortfeasor is 50%; when twenty actors are negligent, the average fault is 5%. In the absence of joint and several liability, defendants will do better if they can find additional negligent actors to share in the blame. If defendant A can get the court to count the fault of B and C, A's own percentage of fault and therefore percentage of liability is likely to be less. That is true, as the Arkansas Court long ago pointed out,[7] even though A's own fault remains exactly what it was before other tortfeasors were discovered.[8]

Settings for the "whose fault" issue. One limited version of the whose fault issue arises when the plaintiff is not herself at fault but derives her claim from someone who is. When the plaintiff claims loss of consortium resulting from injury to a spouse, for example, courts usually reduce the plaintiff's lost consortium recovery by the negligence of the injured spouse.[9] The issue arises more significantly in at least four major and distinct settings. Should juries compare fault of (1) a person who is not joined as a party because he cannot be found or is insolvent? (2) a person who is not a party at the time of the verdict because he has settled the plaintiff's claim?[10] (3) a person who is in some sense at fault but who is not liable because of a formally recognized immunity or otherwise? A later chapter considers the fourth setting, in which A negligently gives B an opportunity to cause intentional harm to the plaintiff and the issue is whether or how to compare negligence of the two defendants.[11]

Only parties' fault compared. Statutes may answer at least some of these questions by limiting the comparison of the negligence to "parties" or "defendants."[12] Sometimes statutes expressly state that the negli-

6. See Chapter 26.

7. Walton v. Tull, 234 Ark. 882, 356 S.W.2d 20, 8 A.L.R.3d 708 (1962).

8. But cf. Lyon v. Ranger III, 858 F.2d 22, 25 (1st Cir.1988) (" We are aware of no legal principle that requires a district court to reduce, perhaps to inconsequential levels, such serious fault, simply because two (or three, or thirty) colleagues also failed to take proper care.").

9. See Restatement § 494; Michael A. DiSabatino, Annotation, Negligence of Spouse or Child as Barring or Reducing Recovery For Loss of Consortium by Other Spouse or Parent, 25 A.L.R.4th 118 (1981). See § 336.

10. Relatedly, crediting the nonsettling tortfeasor in the light of the settling tortfeasor's payment is considered with other apportionment materials in § 388.

11. See § 390.

12. See Davis v. O'Brien, 320 Or. 729, 891 P.2d 1307 (1995) (construing statute to this effect).

gence of non-parties is definitely not to be compared.[13] This approach has been supported on the ground that, where joint and several liability is abolished, comparing the fault of non-parties forces the plaintiff to join large numbers of defendants whose liability is doubtful, lest the trier conclude that not all of the negligence is attributable to joined parties.[14] Some states allow the trier to compare the negligence of nonparties, but only those nonparties the plaintiff has a legal right to sue.[15]

Non-parties' fault compared. The disadvantage of the approach that only considers the negligence of parties, especially if it also prevents the jury from assessing the negligence of settling tortfeasors,[16] is that it asks for a woefully distorted picture of the fault fairly attributable to each person. By express statutory requirement,[17] or by judicial construction in a number of states,[18] the trier is to compare of all fault that is a proximate cause of the harm, whether it is the fault of parties or not. Statutes may also provide specially for considering and comparing the fault of settling tortfeasors.[19]

Third persons who are legally or practically immune. In many situations, a person who might be considered "at fault" in causing harm is formally or practically immune from tort liability.[20] From the plaintiff's point of view, that is of no concern in a joint and several liability system if other tortfeasors are solvent. However, where the rule of joint and several liability has been abolished and each defendant is liable only for his comparative fault share, plaintiffs stand to lose significantly if an immune actor's fault is considered, for it will reduce the amount of fault that can be assigned to the defendant and hence will usually reduce the defendant's liability.

The courts are divided. Some have held that the fault of an employer who is immune from liability under workers' compensation laws, must be considered in assessing the fault of the defendant,[21] with the expected

13. E.g., CONN. GEN. STAT. § 52–572h (negligence compared is that of "parties" and "released persons," but defendant may implead others not originally joined)

14. See Donner v. Kearse, 234 Conn. 660, 662 A.2d 1269 (1995) ("fostering marginal and costly litigation in our courts").

15. Pepper v. Star Equipment, Ltd., 484 N.W.2d 156 (Iowa 1992); Ridings v. Ralph M. Parsons Co., 914 S.W.2d 79 (Tenn.1996).

16. As in Davis v. O'Brien, 320 Or. 729, 891 P.2d 1307 (1995).

17. COLO. REV. STAT. ANN. § 13–21–111.5 (3)(b) permits the defendant to give formal notice claiming that a nonparty is negligent within 90 days of the suit's commencement, presumably to permit the plaintiff to join that person.

18. See Wells v. Tallahassee Memorial Regional Medical Center, Inc., 659 So.2d 249 (Fla.1995); Bode v. Clark Equipment Co., 719 P.2d 824 (Okla.1986) (in aggregating negligence of tortfeasors to compare with the plaintiff's negligence, trier must consider negligence of immune nonparty tortfeasors as well as negligence of defendant); accord as to identified persons where several liability prevails, Restatement of Apportionment § 29B, cmts. d & e. Tennessee compares the negligence of nonparties whom the plaintiff has the right to sue and join. Ridings v. Ralph M. Parsons Co., 914 S.W.2d 79 (Tenn.1996).

19. COLO. REV. STAT. ANN. § 13–21–111.5 (3)(b); CONN. GEN. STAT. § 52–572h.

20. See Chapter 12 on no-duty and immunity rules generally.

21. DaFonte v. Up–Right, Inc., 2 Cal.4th 593, 828 P.2d 140, 7 Cal.Rptr.2d 238 (1992); Dietz v. General Electric Co., 169 Ariz. 505, 821 P.2d 166 (1991); Cf. Bode v. Clark Equipment Co., 719 P.2d 824 (Okla.1986) (fault of immune employer considered to

result that defendant's percentage share of fault will be less than it would be if only the defendant's fault were considered. In most instances, such courts will presumably reach the same result with when a defendant is immune for other reasons.[22] As the Restatement of Apportionment notes, however, some cases that are theorized as "immunity" cases are actually cases in which the particular defendant is under no legal duty, so that there is no legal fault at all and none to be compared.[23] Similarly, the Washington Supreme Court has held that the putative fault of a child should not be considered when the child, though causing harm, was simply too young to be legally at fault.[24] Similarly, California has held that in a strict products liability case where the defendant tobacco manufacturer is immunized by statute on the ground that liability is inappropriate, the tobacco manufacturer's role in causing lung disease is not to be considered in assigning fault.[25]

A few courts, most notably the Supreme Court of Iowa, have held that the immune defendant's fault is to be ignored in the case of an employer immune under workers' compensation statutes[26] and in the case of other immunities as well.[27] Even the negligence of an insolvent person might be excluded under this view. The Iowa Court said that, to prevent "fault siphoning", the negligence of a nonparty is not to be considered if the plaintiff "has no possibility of obtaining an enforceable judgment" against him.[28]

Topic C. Reducing Damages or Shifting Responsibility by Assumed Risk

§ 211. Assumed Risk

Assumed risk today is increasingly discarded as a separate defense. Cases formerly resolved under assumed risk rationales can now be resolved by (1) applying the comparative fault rules, (2) holding that the defendant had no duty of care, or (3) holding that the defendant did not breach a duty. Which resolution is appropriate depends upon the facts of the case.

determine whether the fault of all persons exceeded the plaintiff's fault).

22. Y.H. Investments, Inc. v. Godales, 690 So.2d 1273 (Fla.1997) (on the facts, parent was immune to a claim by her child, but her fault is considered in assessing the defendant's fault and defendant is liable only for his share).

23. Restatement of Apportionment § 29B, cmt. e.

24. Price v. Kitsap Transit, 125 Wash.2d 456, 886 P.2d 556 (1994).

25. Richards v. Owens–Illinois, Inc., 14 Cal.4th 985, 928 P.2d 1181, 60 Cal.Rptr.2d 103 (1997).

26. Peterson v. Pittman, 391 N.W.2d 235 (Iowa 1986); Ridings v. Ralph M. Parsons Co., 914 S.W.2d 79 (Tenn.1996) ("fault may be attributed only to those persons against whom the plaintiff has a cause of action in tort").

27. Pepper v. Star Equipment, Ltd., 484 N.W.2d 156 (Iowa 1992) (bankrupt's immunity); Schwennen v. Abell, 430 N.W.2d 98 (Iowa 1988) (wife could not recover against husband for husband's negligence in causing injury to himself; in wife's suit against third person for loss of consortium, husband's negligence is not to be considered).

28. Pepper v. Star Equipment, Ltd., 484 N.W.2d 156, 158 (Iowa 1992)

The Traditional Rule and Its Basis in Consent

Traditional rule. Courts traditionally held that a plaintiff who assumed the risk of the defendant's negligence could not recover. Children as well as adults could assume the risk and if they did, their claims would be barred.[1] Although this rule had the same legal effect as the traditional rule of contributory negligence, courts thought of the two rules as entirely distinct.

Assumed risk as consent, express or implied. The assumed risk rule was sometimes expressed in terms of the maxim, *volenti non fit injuria* or under the name of incurred risk. However formulated, the essential idea was that the plaintiff assumed the risk whenever she expressly agreed to do so by contract or otherwise,[2] and also when she impliedly did so by words or conduct.[3] Courts began to think that conduct implied consent whenever the plaintiff had specific knowledge of the risk posed by the defendant's negligence, appreciated its nature,[4] and proceeded voluntarily[5] to encounter it nonetheless. The Restatement and more modern theory added that the risk was assumed only if the plaintiff's conduct in encountering the risk manifested the plaintiff's willingness to accept responsibility for the risk.[6]

The Contributory Negligence Connection

Slouching toward contributory negligence. In spite of the doctrine's grounding in the plaintiff's actual or apparent consent to accept responsibility for a risk, courts often applied the doctrine without inquiring whether the plaintiff's conduct could reasonably be interpreted as any kind of consent at all.[7] Instead, they treated the plaintiff's voluntary encounter with the risk as sufficient to raise the bar of assumed risk, even though in many instances such conduct would not bespeak consent at all. In a South Carolina case, the plaintiff attempted to move a boat that had fallen onto the highway. While holding one end of the boat, he

§ 211

1. Tucker v. Lombardo, 47 Cal.2d 457, 303 P.2d 1041 (1956) (12–year-old working on skeet shooting range); Greaves v. Galchutt, 289 Minn. 335, 184 N.W.2d 26 (1971) (11– and 12–year-old boys playing with gun they thought unloaded).

2. Restatement § 496A.

3. § 214.

4. See Haynes v. Hoffman, 164 Ga.App. 236, 296 S.E.2d 216, 33 A.L.R.4th 785 (1982); Goepfert v. Filler, 563 N.W.2d 140 (S.D.1997) (using a quasi-objective test); Shorter v. Drury, 103 Wash.2d 645, 695 P.2d 116 (1985) (using a subjective test); Restatement §§ 496A, 496C–496E. Under subjective tests for the plaintiff's knowledge or appreciation of the risk, the question would often be for the jury, as in Salmeron v. Nava, 694 A.2d 709 (R.I.1997).

5. See § 214.

6. Restatement § 496C.

7. Plaintiff's encounter with a dangerous condition created or tolerated by the defendant would often be treated as an assumed risk as a matter of law without further inquiry into consent, either subjectively or objectively. For example, in Curtis v. Traders Nat. Bank, 314 Ky. 765, 237 S.W.2d 76 (1951) a customer entering bank during rain tried to walk carefully through water accumulated on the marble floor but slipped. The court held that she assumed the risk. The case illustrates the fact that courts did not always insist on actual consent or even manifested consent. However, the contemporary view is that if the bank could reasonably foresee that the plaintiff might enter in spite of water on the floor, the bank owes ordinary care and the plaintiff has not consented to assume the risk. See, among others, § 235 (foreseeable encounter with obvious danger).

saw the defendant's car coming, but remained in the road with the boat. The car struck the plaintiff. The trial court believed that the jury should have been instructed on assumed risk,[8] although it is clear that the plaintiff was not consenting to the driver's negligence. On facts like these, however, assumed risk has general become a version of contributory negligence.

The purported distinction based on venturesome spirit. With the application of assumed risk to cases that looked like ordinary contributory negligence, courts attempted to distinguish the two doctrines. Instead of pointing to the difference between consent and culpability, however, they said that assumed risk, since it involved a known risk, entailed a plaintiff guilty of venturesomeness rather than inadvertence or carelessness.[9]

The distinction was a convenient item of rhetoric but unsound as analysis. The fact that the plaintiff confronted a known risk would not invariably show consent, nor would it suggest a qualitatively different kind of contributory negligence. Defendants, like plaintiffs, are often negligent in creating or maintaining known risks, but since some known risks are reasonable, defendants are not necessarily negligent for doing so, much less are they guilty of any kind of super-negligence. The distinction is also unsound in suggesting that negligence was to be equated with carelessness or inadvertence rather than unreasonable risk-taking.[10] Nevertheless, in this group of cases, courts had moved from consent to something that seemed logically indistinguishable from contributory negligence.

Reasonable confrontation of known risks. When the plaintiff's conduct in confronting a known risk was in fact unreasonably risky, it did not much matter in the days before comparative negligence whether the courts thought of it as assumed risk or contributory negligence. The plaintiff was barred either way. However, in some of the cases the plaintiff's conduct may have been entirely reasonable, so that her conduct should not have barred her claim unless she had actually consented to accept responsibility or had manifested such a consent to the defendant. By treating any confrontation of a known risk as if it were a consent to accept the risks, courts in fact departed from the underlying reasons for the doctrine. Assumed risk took on a life of its own, reflecting policies or biases of the time rather than the plaintiff's actual or apparent consent.[11]

8. Spahn v. Town of Port Royal, 326 S.C. 632, 486 S.E.2d 507 (S.C.App.1997), aff'd on other grounds, 330 S.C. 168, 499 S.E.2d 205 (1998).

9. Ball v. Hilton Hotels, Inc., 32 Ohio App.2d 293, 295, 290 N.E.2d 859, 861 (1972) ("contributory negligence is based upon carelessness whereas assumption of risk is based upon venturousness") This aphorism came to be a kind of new test of assumed risk in some courts, who ceased to inquire whether the plaintiff consented or confronted a known risk but whether the plaintiff evinced a venturesome spirit. See Thibodeau v. Vandermark, 234 Va. 15, 360 S.E.2d 171 (1987). Courts also distinguished the two doctrines by insisting that assumed risk entailed a subjective state of mind.

10. See § 116.

11. See Peter H. Schuck, Rethinking Informed Consent, 103 Yale L.J. 899, 912 (1994) (assumed risk as a "culturally con-

The No Duty or No Negligence Connection

In a third group of cases, courts used the term assumed risk to express the view that the defendant should not be liable, but the reasons for nonliability did not lie in the plaintiff's consent or in her culpability. These were cases in which courts themselves, for reasons not much connected to the plaintiff's conduct or consent,[12] narrowed or eliminated the defendant's duty, or else concluded that the defendant simply was not negligent.

For instance, courts often hold that landowners are free to leave dangerous conditions on their land, so long as those conditions are not hidden. If someone is injured by a dangerous but obvious condition on the land, the landowner is frequently not liable because he is under no duty of care with respect to conditions on his own land.[13] Courts have often expressed this and similar rules by saying that the plaintiff assumed the risk of open dangers on the land or those of which she knew.[14] To use assumed risk terminology in such cases added greatly to the existing confusion, because in these cases assumed risk did not mean either consent or contributory negligence. Ultimately, it was not even based on the plaintiff's conduct, but upon judicial policy to give the landowner freedom from care. In other cases courts might invoke "assumed risk" when the defendant simply is not negligent because he can reasonably expect the plaintiff to care for her own well-being.[15] Again, the terminology of assumed risk merely confuses the issue.

The early law of assumed risk was devoted to liabilities of employers for injury to employees. Courts seldom inquired about the employee's real or even apparent consent to accept employment risks. Instead, courts conclusively "presumed" that, by accepting employment, the employee assumed the ordinary risks of employment and in addition assumed risks of specific employer negligence when he was made aware

structed and highly normative doctrine" rather than a "fact").

12. These cases usually entail a "voluntary association" of the parties, as explained in the classic and much more detailed treatment of this topic in 4 Harper, James & Gray, § 21.1. The voluntary association, however, did not suggest consent, only that the defendant was free from obligation to someone who was in a position to take it or leave it.

13. The details and qualifications to this idea are covered in Chapter 13.

14. E.g., in DeAmiches v. Popczun, 35 Ohio St.2d 180, 299 N.E.2d 265 (1973) the plaintiff was returning to her rented home in icy weather. She knew landlord-defendant had failed to repair a hole. She could not see the hole under snow. In trying to avoid it, she slipped and fell. The court found no liability and expressed itself in terms of the plaintiff's assumed risk. But it was not unreasonable to return home, hole or no hole, so it was not a case of contributory negligence masquerading as assumed risk. Nor would anything in the plaintiff's conduct suggest an actual or apparent consent to face the risk. The terminology in cases like this, then, seems to be an alternate expression for the conclusion that the defendant was not negligent or owed no duty of care. The assumed risk terminology tends to distract courts from considering whether the defendant *should* owe a duty of care.

15. E.g. Green v. City of New York, 693 N.Y.S.2d 43 (App. Div. 1999) (plaintiff playing basketball on a court as a city correctional facility slipped and fell on defect of which he was aware, after discussing "consent," the court concludes that since the plaintiff was in a position to protect himself, the defendant did not breach a duty of care).

of those risks.[16] Since accepting employment could hardly count as contributory negligence and since it would seldom reflect either actual or apparent consent to employer negligence, these cases seem in reality to reflect a judicial policy or bias, not a decision about the plaintiff's conduct at all.

The earliest employment cases developed the fellow servant rule, which asserted that a worker always assumed the risk of the negligence of fellow employees. An employee of a railroad, for example, could not recover from the railroad when the railroad's engineer negligently derailed a train and caused injury to other employees.[17] Twentieth century statutes abolished[18] or limited assumed risk defenses[19] in the employment context, but not before the doctrine had spread beyond the employer-employee setting in most states. And where the doctrine survives at all, it continues to apply to a few employees not covered by the statutes.[20] In addition, courts often bar public employees like firefighters and police officers from recovering against negligent citizens whose fires or law violations cause harm, and often explain this result on assumed risk grounds.[21]

Abolishing Assumed Risk or Merging It with Contributory Negligence

Abolishing assumed risk doctrine. "[W]hen we are tempted to say 'assumption of risk' we should instead say something else."[22] As early as the 1950s, some courts began to recognize that assumed risk rules had no separate status or function and could be usefully abolished.[23] Since assumed risk always seemed to be a way of talking about some other

16. See, e.g., Wilson v. Lindamood Farms, Inc., 675 S.W.2d 187 (1984) ("ordinary risks are assumed by an employee whether he is actually aware of them or not; for the dangers and risks that are normally or necessarily incident to his occupation are presumably taken into account in fixing his rate of wages"). But see § 214 (risk of inherent dangers, but not employer negligence is assumed).

17. E.g., Murray v. South Carolina Railroad, 26 S.C.L. (1 McMul. 385) (S.C. 1841). This specific form of assumed risk is the "fellow servant rule". The idea originated in Priestly v. Fowler, 3 M. & W. 1 (Exch. 1837), where Lord Abinger argued that the employee was in the best position to protect himself from co-workers and should bear the risk for that reason.

18. Assumed risk as a complete defense was abrogated by the Federal Employers' Liability Act (FELA) as to interstate railroad employees. 45 U.S.C.A. § 53.

19. Workers' compensation statutes enacted everywhere by 1940 substituted workers' compensation benefits in many cases, leaving the doctrine obsolete as to those. The compensation statutes often abolished assumed risk directly if the employer rejected the workers' compensation system.

20. As in Rickey v. Boden, 421 A.2d 539 (R.I.1980) (employee had to climb a stair she knew was dangerous in order to reach the designated coffee room for a break).

21. See Chapter 17.

22. Stephen D. Sugarman, Assumption of Risk, 31 VAL. U. L. REV. 833, 835 (1997).

23. See, e.g., Arnold v. City of Cedar Rapids, Iowa, 443 N.W.2d 332 (Iowa 1989); Perez v. McConkey, 872 S.W.2d 897 (Tenn. 1994). Meistrich v. Casino Arena Attractions, Inc., 31 N.J. 44, 155 A.2d 90, 82 A.L.R.2d 1208 (1959) initiated the trend towards this view. The arguments for this position are thrashed out in a Symposium, 22 LA. L. REV. 1 (1961). John Diamond, Assumption of Risk after Comparative Negligence: Integrating Contract Theory into Tort Doctrine, 52 OHIO ST. L. J. 717 (1991) is very helpful on the translation of old assumed risk into contemporary doctrines of limited duty and comparative fault.

established legal doctrine, a number of courts found that assumed risk could be better expressed by discussing the basic concepts of duty, negligence, or contributory negligence. Confusingly, however, some courts receptive to the idea that assumed risk is merely an alternative expression for other concepts, may nevertheless still use the language of assumed risk from time to time.[24]

Absorbing assumed risk into comparative negligence practice. After the advent of comparative negligence, courts found it logically or morally difficult to maintain a dual system in which the plaintiff's fault only reduced damages if it was called contributory negligence, while it barred the plaintiff entirely if it was called assumed risk. Consequently, most comparative negligence states, by statutory provision[25] or judicial decision,[26] simply "merge" assumed risk into comparative negligence in many routine cases.

Many cases are appropriate to resolution under the comparative negligence rules. The hitchhiker who falls asleep on the highway's edge is not assuming the risk of being run over by a negligent driver; he is merely negligent and accordingly may suffer a defeat or a reduction in damages under comparative negligence rules.[27] The same is true for the worker who injures himself in a task he recognized as dangerous,[28] or the customer who falls in her attempt to enter a business in spite of water on its floor.[29]

Retaining assumed risk/consent as a complete bar. The comparative negligence system could not absorb and control all the cases that once went under the livery of assumed risk. Where assumed risk was a matter of the plaintiff's apparent consent to accept risks generated by the defendant or a poor expression for a judicially created no-duty rule, legal responsibility was shifted to the plaintiff. In these cases, the defendant would not liable at all, even after comparative negligence was adopted. The reasons for barring the plaintiff entirely can now be divorced from the old law and terminology of assumed risk and can be stated as cases of no duty or no negligence. The cases themselves, however, remain. Consent as a bar to the plaintiff's claim is considered in the next section.

24. See Morgan v. State, 90 N.Y.2d 471, 662 N.Y.S.2d 421, 685 N.E.2d 202 (1997) (using both assumed risk and limited duty language).

25. IND. CODE § 34–4–33–2 (fault defined to include certain types of assumed risk); MASS GEN. L. ANN. ch. 231, § 85 (defense abolished).

26. See, e.g., Knight v. Jewett, 3 Cal.4th 296, 11 Cal.Rptr.2d 2, 834 P.2d 696 (1992); King v. Kayak Manufacturing Corp., 182 W.Va. 276, 387 S.E.2d 511 (1989). At this writing, as many as five comparative negligence states may still hold out for the old complete bar.

27. Simmons v. Frazier, 277 Ark. 452, 642 S.W.2d 314 (1982).

28. Capiello v. Exxon Corporation, 695 So.2d 1097 (La.App.1997); Brittain v. Booth, 601 P.2d 532 (Wyo.1979).

29. Cf. Wieseler v. Sisters of Mercy Health Corp., 540 N.W.2d 445 (Iowa 1995) (although frost on walk was visible, defendant hospital was under a duty of care, so that plaintiff's recovery might be reduced for comparative fault but not barred), overruled on other grounds, Sheets v. Ritt, Ritt, & Ritt, Inc., 581 N.W.2d 602 (Iowa 1998).

§ 212. Plaintiff's Consent Altering Defendant's Duty

As already indicated, some instances of "assumed risk" represent the plaintiff's consent or apparent consent to accept a risk created by the defendant. The effect of the plaintiff's consent to accept the risk is that the defendant has no duty to the plaintiff with respect to that risk. By agreement, responsibility has been shifted to the plaintiff. The plaintiff's consent to the defendant's conduct and the risk it entails is not about contributory negligence or the plaintiff's culpable conduct at all, but about consent, agreement, important information, or relationships that shift responsibility. Thus even after the adoption of comparative negligence, a consent of this kind operates to bar the plaintiff's claim in its entirely because it qualifies or limits the defendant's duty of care.[1]

It is also possible, of course, to bar the plaintiff's claim even if the plaintiff has not consented to accept the risk. Courts are free to shift responsibility to the plaintiff for reasons that have nothing to do with any actual consent, simply because they believe the defendant should not have the burden of acting with care. The idea in such cases is that the defendant is under no duty to the plaintiff, although the court may explain such cases on the inaccurate ground that the plaintiff assumed the risk. Sometimes it is said the "primary meaning" of assumed risk is nothing more than this, that the defendant is under no duty to the plaintiff.

In some cases the plaintiff's consent to accept a risk does not entirely eliminate the defendant's duty but alters the standard by which that duty is met. For example, suppose a seriously ill patient, losing confidence in ordinary medical treatment, asks her doctor for an experimental treatment that is also dangerous. When the risky experimental treatment causes harm or fails to cure, the patient cannot claim that the doctor was negligent in providing an experimental treatment if her choice was fully informed. The result can be explained on the ground that the patient assumed the risk in the sense of consent.[2] The relevance of the patient's choice in such a case is not that the plaintiff was foolish or unreasonable but that her consent relieved the defendant of responsibility he might otherwise have had. In the light of her consent (and the choice or preference it reflected), the doctor was not negligent in providing the experimental treatment. Put in the language of duty, he was under no duty to provide standard medical treatment.

In some cases it is less a matter of consent than information passed to the defendant which leads the defendant to believe, quite reasonably, that the plaintiff can adequately care for herself. If the plaintiff assures

§ 212

1. See, e.g., Turcotte v. Fell, 68 N.Y.2d 432, 510 N.Y.S.2d 49, 502 N.E.2d 964 (1986); King v. Kayak Manufacturing Corp., 182 W.Va. 276, 387 S.E.2d 511 (1989).

2. Cf. Boyle v. Revici, 961 F.2d 1060 (2d Cir.1992) (on very similar facts, jury could find assumed risk). The rule mimics the general rule in medical malpractice claims that the physician owes only the duty of care customarily provided by other physicians in the same school of medicine, so that, for example, a chiropractor need not follow the practices or methods deemed essential by a medical doctor. See § 245.

the defendant that the plaintiff is an experienced electrician, the defendant may reasonably expect the plaintiff to be able to recognize electrical dangers on the defendant's premises. In that case, the risks of harm may be so small that the defendant is not negligent in having electrical apparatus that would be too risky for untrained people.[3]

If the defendant has no duty of care, or is not negligent, an element necessary to the plaintiff's prima facie case is missing. When assumed risk means that the plaintiff's consent has shifted responsibility in this way, then it does not look much like an orthodox affirmative defense. It is rather an assertion that the plaintiff has not proved duty or negligence.[4]

The difficulty is to determine in which case the plaintiff's conduct is merely negligent and is covered by comparative fault rules and in which case it manifests a consent to accept the entire risk and is a complete bar to the claim. This problem remains regardless whether the issue is framed in the old terminology of assumed risk or framed directly as a question of consent and the resulting limits on the defendant's responsibility.

§ 213. Express Consent Shifting Responsibility

Express consent (express assumed risk). The plaintiff may expressly assume a risk by accepting the defendant's disclaimer of responsibility or by giving a release or other exculpatory agreement in advance of injury, unless, on the facts, some policy is opposed to such a consensual arrangement. The plaintiff can expressly assume the risk either orally or in writing. If the effect of the agreement is clear and untainted by deceptive behavior or the like,[1] an express assumed risk ordinarily will relieve the defendant of the duty that otherwise existed.[2] Alternatively, it will establish a standard of care that shows he has breached no duty.

Examples. For example, those who contract for the privilege of engaging in dangerous activities like racing or sky-diving are often required to release the provider from all liability in advance.[3] Likewise, a patient might demand (and therefore consent to) surgery to be per-

3. Thus courts hold that a landowner has no duty to protect a contractor from risks incidental to, or part of, the very work the contractor was hired to perform. Dawson v. Bunker Hill Plaza Associates, 289 N.J.Super. 309, 673 A.2d 847 (1996); Jones v. Chevron U.S.A., Inc., 718 P.2d 890 (Wyo. 1986). Cf. Stinnett v. Buchele, 598 S.W.2d 469 (Ky. 1980) (experienced roof worker). The *Stinnett* court held as a matter of law that the defendant was not negligent in failing to provide safety devices. Whether that holding is correct or not, the idea that the risk created by the defendant must be judged in the light of the plaintiff's apparent capacity to deal with it is correct.

4. Presumably, however, if the facts are such that the defendant would ordinarily be under a duty of care, the defendant will have the burden of showing the consent that alters his duty.

§ 213

1. Some authority holds that exculpatory provisions must be expressed in unmistakable language. Gross v. Sweet, 49 N.Y.2d 102, 424 N.Y.S.2d 365, 400 N.E.2d 306 (1979).

2. E.g., Boyle v. Revici, 961 F.2d 1060 (2d Cir.1992); Restatement of Apportionment § 2.

3. E.g., Jones v. Dressel, 623 P.2d 370 (Colo.1981) (sky-diving). The scope of some of these releases might be doubtful.

formed without blood transfusions.[4] In such a case, the physician has no duty to administer blood transfusions. In fact, the physician would violate the patient's rights if he administered transfusions after agreeing not to do so. His compliance with the patient's wishes is not negligent.

Public policy limits on consent. Sometimes courts find it important to impose a duty of reasonable care even when the plaintiff has expressly agreed to relieve the defendant of responsibility. For instance, products manufacturers and distributors cannot use disclaimers or exculpatory agreements to avoid liability for personal injury resulting from dangerous products.[5] In a leading case outside the products field,[6] the defendant hospital would admit patients only if they signed a release relieving the hospital of all liability. The California Court believed that such a release was void as against public policy, partly because the patients did not acquiesce voluntarily and partly because medical services were themselves so important. Similarly, releases in cases of medical research upon human beings—experimentation as distinct from treatment—may be void.[7] Possibly public agencies like schools should not be allowed to condition a student's participation rights on a general release of all liability for negligence.[8] Historically, businesses affected with a public interest, including some professional bailees,[9] carriers,[10] and public utilities[11] could not contractually avoid liability for their own negligence. Some courts have extended this kind of thinking even to nonessential private services.[12] And courts have declared it against public policy for

4. Shorter v. Drury, 103 Wash.2d 645, 695 P.2d 116 (1985) (patient religiously opposed to blood transfusions specifically released surgeon in advance of operation).

5. § 371.

6. Tunkl v. Regents of University of California, 60 Cal.2d 92, 32 Cal.Rptr. 33, 383 P.2d 441, 6 A.L.R.3d 693 (1963).

7. Vodopest v. MacGregor, 128 Wash.2d 840, 913 P.2d 779 (1996). Federal regulations governing research on human subjects require informed consent without either exculpatory language or a release of the researcher. C.F.R. § 46.116.

8. Wagenblast v. Odessa School Dist. No. 105–157–166J, 110 Wash.2d 845, 758 P.2d 968 (1988); but cf. Joseph H. King, Jr., Exculpatory Agreements for Volunteers in Youth Activities—The Alternative to "Nerf®" Tiddlywinks, 53 OHIO ST. L. J. 683 (1992) (favoring effective exculpatory agreement for volunteers and sponsoring entities in youth activities). Contrast a provision that simply allocates responsibility to a student for a particular item contributing to safety. For example, a release might provide that the student was to bring her own food and water on a field trip or hike and that the school board would not be liable for failing to provide such items. In that kind of case, the school may not be negligent in failing to provide water or food, a result that would also be reached without reference to consent if the school had simply issued clear instructions about responsibility for food and water.

9. E.g., Berrios v. United Parcel Service, 265 N.J.Super. 436, 627 A.2d 701 (1992), aff'd per curiam, 265 N.J.Super. 368, 627 A.2d 665 (following majority rule that parking lot owners cannot exempt themselves from liability for negligence care where vehicle owner was not aware of the exculpatory clause; dictum that the clause would be void even if the owner was aware, with emphasis on public duty and unequal bargaining power).

10. Interstate carriers subject to federal control are permitted to limit liability under specified circumstances. See, e.g., 49 U.S.C.A. § 11706 (c) (provisions for limits by rail carriers).

11. E.g., Southwestern Public Service Co. v. Artesia Alfalfa Growers' Ass'n, 67 N.M. 108, 353 P.2d 62 (1960).

12. Dalury v. S–K–I, Ltd., 164 Vt. 329, 670 A.2d 795 (1995) (ski resort's general exculpatory agreement invalid).

employers to use the contract of employment to extract a release of liability for their own negligence.[13]

Express assumed risk by way of releases in advance or exculpatory clauses of any kind may thus be rendered ineffective when it violates public policy. Otherwise, however, its effect is to shift the entire responsibility from the defendant to the plaintiff, so that the plaintiff will not recover at all.

§ 214. Implied Consent Shifting Responsibility

Implied consent (implied assumed risk). Most agreements in everyday life are tacit, not expressed. No logical reason prevents parties from tacitly or impliedly consenting or agreeing to a shift of responsibility to the plaintiff. The traditional assumed risk rules found such tacit consent when the plaintiff, knowing of the risk and appreciating its quality, voluntarily chose to confront it. For instance, if the plaintiff accepted dangerous employment, he was once held to have assumed the risk of employment dangers, including the employer's negligence. Holdings like this gave the doctrine of implied assumption of risk a bad name, and courts gradually modified such holdings.[1]

Voluntary assumption. To avoid the harsh applications of assumed risk, courts developed some constraining rules. One of them was that the plaintiff's confrontation of the risk had to be voluntary, which was to say that the plaintiff had to have a reasonable alternative course of action. For example, if passengers in a car discover that their driver is dangerous and voluntarily remain in the car, they assume the risk of the dangers they have discovered. But if they are by then in an unfamiliar area, on a cold night, without any alternative transport to their homes or jobs, their continued exposure to the risk "is not in a true sense voluntary" and their claim for injury at the driver's

hands is not barred.[2] On the same understanding of what counts as voluntary, a tenant does not assume the risk by using the only privy provided by the landlord, even if she knows the privy is dangerous.[3] Further, if the plaintiff had no real choice except to face the risk created by the defendant or to give up a significant right, such as a right to use the plaintiff's own property, the plaintiff's decision to confront the risk would not be a bar.[4]

Knowledge of the risk and subjective consent. Another rule to avoid the harsh results of the implied assumed risk doctrine held that the

13. See Lakube v. Cohen, 304 Mass. 156, 23 N.E.2d 144 (1939); Pittsburgh, C. C. & St. L. Ry. v. Kinney, 95 Ohio St. 64, 115 N.E. 505 (1916).

§ 214

1. See Siragusa v. Swedish Hospital, 60 Wash.2d 310, 373 P.2d 767 (1962).

2. Ridgway v. Yenny, 223 Ind. 16, 57 N.E.2d 581

3. Rush v. Commercial Realty Co., 7 N.J.Misc. 337, 145 A. 476 (1929).

4. See Leroy Fibre Co. v. Chicago, Milwaukee & St. Paul Railway Co, 232 U.S. 340, 34 S.Ct. 415, 58 L.Ed. 631 (1914); Hennessey v. Pyne, 694 A.2d 691 (R.I.1997) (homeowner not required to stay indoors to avoid perils of living near a golf course).

plaintiff did not assume the risk unless she knew of the risk itself as well as the facts that gave rise to it and "really" assumed the risk. This kind of statement implied what many cases substantiated, that the plaintiff's subjective consent was required.[5]

Yet a subjective test made no logical sense. If the plaintiff's conduct was to be considered as a potential bar because it was a species of contributory negligence, the objective negligence test would be right for the plaintiff as well as for the defendant. On the other hand, if the plaintiff's conduct was to be considered as a potential bar because it relieved the defendant of a duty, then an objective manifestation to the defendant would suffice, and the defendant would not be required to fathom the plaintiff's subjective mental state. Perhaps courts obtained results largely consistent with an objective standard by saying that the plaintiff who denied her appreciation of a risk was simply not to be believed if a reasonable person in her position would have appreciated it.[6] In any event, as courts come to perceive the issue in terms of the defendant's limited duty, they implicitly or sometimes expressly reject a subjective test of consent.[7]

Implication of consent from conduct. The real problem in these cases is not reached by rules about voluntariness or subjective consent. The problem lies in the courts' tendency to equate confrontation of known risks with a manifestation of consent. A plaintiff who knows of a risk, understands it, and decides to take it anyway may be negligent in some cases, but a defendant could seldom reasonably understand the plaintiff's conduct to mean that she agreed to accept all risks of the defendant's negligence. As Prosser pointed out, the driver of an automobile cannot reasonably believe that the jaywalking plaintiff is consenting to the driver's negligence.[8] The jaywalker assuredly confronts a known risk and does so voluntarily, but voluntary confrontation of the risk does not communicate any release of the driver from the duties of ordinary care. Instead, the jaywalker is simply negligent. His negligence is to be judged under comparative fault rules.

Prosser's jaywalker example makes the point well, but there is more to it. The court that finds consent when the plaintiff is confronting a known risk in a reasonable way is limiting the plaintiff's freedom to act reasonably. An investor buys property knowing that the defendant next door has contaminated it with gasoline. Certainly he must know there is

5. See Get–N–Go, Inc. v. Markins, 544 N.E.2d 484 (Ind.1989) ("the defense demands a subjective analysis focusing on the plaintiff's actual knowledge and appreciation of the specific risk involved and voluntary acceptance of that risk").

6. E.g., Benjamin v. Deffet Rentals, Inc., 66 Ohio St.2d 86, 419 N.E.2d 883 (1981) (risks of diving into shallow water; "it may be assumed that a person of whatever age is able to appreciate the obvious risks incident to any sport or activity in which he may be able to engage with intelligence and proficiency, and must act accordingly").

7. See Neighbarger v. Irwin Industries, Inc., 8 Cal.4th 532, 34 Cal.Rptr.2d 630, 882 P.2d 347 (1994) (expressly rejecting subjective consent test in certain cases, but also holding that the limited duty conclusion results from the court's perception of policy, perhaps policy not necessarily fixed by the parties' consent).

8. Prosser and Keeton, § 68, p. 490.

a risk that contamination will continue or be worse than expected, but someone must deal with contaminated property and it is not unreasonable to buy and plan a cleanup. If his claim against the polluter is barred by assumed risk, his freedom to carry on reasonable and desirable economic activity is seriously diminished while the tortfeasor, who never bargained for or expected his consent, will not pay for the harms he has done. The Maryland Court dealt with facts like these by firmly declaring that assumed risk was not a defense to intentional tort claims like trespass,[9] but one could say even more directly that a reasonable sale and purchase between A and B evinces no assumption of C's tort.

Allocating cases between comparative negligence and complete bar systems. Perhaps because implications of consent are often so uncertain, contemporary courts usually say that implied assumed risk does not survive the adoption of comparative negligence, meaning that implied assumed risk will be treated as contributory negligence.[10] Conversely, they sometimes say that express assumption of the risk survives the adoption of comparative negligence rules.[11] The logical distinction, however, is not between implied and expressed assumed risk but between the plaintiff's fault and the plaintiff's apparent consent. At least in a few cases, defendants can reasonably understand the plaintiff's conduct as a consent to shift responsibility to the plaintiff. So unless public policy counsels otherwise on particular facts, it would seem that the plaintiff could tacitly or impliedly agree to relieve the defendant of a duty, or consent to negligence in the same way that she can expressly do so. Perhaps some courts do not really mean to categorically cast all implied consent cases into the comparative negligence system. One case defined express assumption of the risk to include any "actual consent," such as the consent that could be found if the plaintiff voluntarily participated in a contact sport.[12] Under that definition, almost any implied consent would count as an express one.

Implied consent cases as a bar after comparative negligence. In fact, courts have concluded in a number of post-comparative fault cases that the defendant was relieved of a duty of care to an apparently consenting plaintiff. In such cases, the plaintiff is barred completely because the defendant's duty of care is limited. Courts may, of course, limit the duty owed for policy reasons that are independent of the plaintiff's manifested consent.[13] But in the absence of special reasons to hold otherwise, the

9. JBG/Twinbrook Metro Limited Partnership v. Wheeler, 346 Md. 601, 697 A.2d 898 (1997).

10. Cf. Gallagher v. Cleveland Browns Football Company, 74 Ohio St.3d 427, 659 N.E.2d 1232 (1996) (distinguishing implied assumed risk from primary assumed risk). As the terms are used in this section, a plaintiff could impliedly or tacitly consent to a risk and thus relieve the defendant of a duty. Such an implied assumed risk would also be assumed risk in the primary sense. In other words, implied and express are parallel terms, while primary and secondary constitute a separate set of parallels.

11. E.g., Shorter v. Drury, 103 Wash.2d 645, 695 P.2d 116 (1985).

12. Kuehner v. Green, 436 So.2d 78, 47 A.L.R.4th 395 (Fla. 1983).

13. Some opinions seem to suggest that the defendant's limited duty in these cases stems somewhat vague policy factors associated with the "nature of the activity involved and the relationship of the parties." See Neighbarger v. Irwin Industries, Inc., 8

plaintiff's apparent consent is by itself ample ground for concluding that the defendant's duty is limited or that the defendant is simply not negligent at all.

So it is no surprise to find that the nurse hired to care for and restrain combative Alzheimer's patients impliedly assumes the risk that one of her patients will harm her, or put otherwise, the patient is not liable for harm to the nurse even though he may be liable if he harms strangers.[14] A quite familiar example discussed in the next section is the case of the spectator at a sporting event who is denied all recovery because she has impliedly consented to the dangers of the game, including, say, the danger of being struck by a wayward ball. On the other hand, if doubt remains whether the plaintiff impliedly consented to accept the risk, the plaintiff's conduct should be considered under the rules for comparative negligence and not as a consent that bars the action entirely.

Scope of apparent consent. Although the plaintiff may consent to accept a risk of the defendant's conduct either by express agreement or by implication—the so-called primary sense of assumed risk—the conclusion that she relieves the defendant of a duty does not necessarily mean that she has consented to relieve the defendant of all possible duties of care. In fact, when a plaintiff enters into a dangerous activity with the defendant—dangerous employment, for example—it looks as if the plaintiff might be consenting to the known existing risks, and to the normal, expected, or inherent danger of the activity. By definition, the defendant's negligence is not an inherent risk. On the contrary, negligently created risks are avoidable by ordinary care. So modern cases sometimes recognize that the plaintiff might assume the ordinary employment risks, but does not assume the risk of the defendant's negligence at all.[15] This idea, too, is illustrated in the sports cases discussed in the next section.

Cal.4th 532, 34 Cal.Rptr.2d 630, 882 P.2d 347 (1994). In the sports cases, courts seem to be going directly to a rule of limited duty for reasons of perceived policy not necessarily based upon the plaintiff's apparent consent. See § 215. In some other cases the language of assumed risk continues to be used although the cases themselves seem to reflect judicial policy more than consent. That is probably the best explanation of the firefighter's rule, under which firefighters are barred from suing negligent firesetters. See Chapter 17.

14. See Herrle v. Estate of Marshall, 45 Cal.App.4th 1761, 53 Cal.Rptr.2d 713 (1996); Anicet v. Gant, 580 So.2d 273 (Fla. App.1991); Gould v. American Family Mut. Ins. Co., 198 Wis.2d 450, 543 N.W.2d 282 (Wis. 1996).

15. See, e.g., Burnett v. Caho, 7 Ill. App.3d 266, 285 N.E.2d 619 (1972); Morgan v. Roper, 250 S.C. 280, 157 S.E.2d 572, 575 (1967) ("The general rule is that a servant assumes the risk ordinarily incident to his employment, but not those due to the master's negligence"); Barnette v. Doyle, 622 P.2d 1349 (Wyo.1981). The plaintiff might assume some additional risks by agreement or by specific conduct in confronting a specific identified risk. However, logically speaking, the rule that voids an express assumed risk that absolves an employer of future negligence, see Pittsburgh, C. C. & St. L. Ry. v. Kinney, 95 Ohio St. 64, 115 N.E. 505 (1916), ought to apply equally to the implied assumed risk except where "implied assumed risk" means that the defendant was not negligent. Public employees like firefighters and police officers are said to assume risks inherent in or normal to their work, but not risks disassociated from the reasons that brought the officer to the scene of danger. E.g., Wiley v. Redd, 110 Nev. 1310, 885 P.2d 592 (1994). See § 286.

§ 215. Assumed Risk in Sports Cases

Spectators

Before the adoption of comparative negligence, courts found that spectators at sporting events such as baseball games assumed the risk of being struck by wayward balls or the like, at least where the spectator chose an unscreened seat when a safer seat was available. Although many cases formerly classed as assumed risk cases are now treated as cases of contributory negligence and therefore subjected to comparative negligence rules, the spectator cases of this kind are not treated as comparative negligence cases. Instead, they are treated as instances of assumed risk in the primary sense, which is to say they are treated as cases in which the defendant owed no duty or was not negligent. The term assumed risk can be dropped out in such cases and often is.

Given the plaintiff's awareness of danger and choice of seat, the sports operator's only duty is to provide some reasonably safe accommodations.

That is often defined as an obligation to provide screening in the most dangerous areas sufficient to protect the number of people who can be expected to wish the protection on ordinary occasions.[1] Consequently, the plaintiff who is injured by a foul or misthrown ball or an errant hockey puck while she is sitting in an unprotected area simply has no claim.[2] Put more broadly, the operator of sports enterprises "has no duty to protect an invitee against the ordinary hazards of the sports activity."[3]

These rules do not mean that the sports enterprise never owes a duty of care, much less that it never breaches the duty. For instance, the enterprise might provide a defective screen behind home plate, or bleachers that collapse. If so, it is quite likely to be held liable for its negligence.[4] Similarly, these rules do not mean that assumed risk is invariably the equivalent of no duty. Sometimes plaintiffs are merely contributorily negligent in knowingly facing a danger.[5] The plaintiff who

§ 215

1. Arnold v. City of Cedar Rapids, Iowa, 443 N.W.2d 332 (Iowa 1989); Akins v. Glens Falls City School District, 53 N.Y.2d 325, 424 N.E.2d 531, 441 N.Y.S.2d 644 (1981); Lawson v. Salt Lake Trappers, Inc., 901 P.2d 1013 (Utah 1995).

2. Lawson v. Salt Lake Trappers, Inc., 901 P.2d 1013 (Utah 1995) (foul ball); Gilchrist v. City of Troy, 67 N.Y.2d 1034, 494 N.E.2d 1382, 503 N.Y.S.2d 717 (1986) (puck).

3. King v. Kayak Manufacturing Corp., 182 W.Va. 276, 387 S.E.2d 511 (1989).

4. As in, e.g., Boyer v. Iowa High School Athletic Ass'n, 260 Iowa 1061, 152 N.W.2d 293 (1967) (collapsing bleachers, res ipsa loquitur applicable). Cf. Jones v. Three Rivers Management Corp., 483 Pa. 75, 394 A.2d 546 (1978) (baseball stadium so designed that patron was at risk from batted balls while she was walking on an interior concourse; this design is not an inherent, ordinary, or expected risk of baseball, so the no-duty rule did not apply).

5. In many cases of open or obvious danger, the defendant owes a duty of care so long as he can reasonably foresee that injury may occur in spite of the fact that the danger is obvious. In such cases the plaintiff may not be at fault at all. If she is at fault, it is fault, not consent. Thus the plaintiff in such cases is not barred, although her damages may be reduced. E.g., Urban v. Wait's Supermarket, Inc., 294 N.W.2d 793 (S.D.1980) (grocery store shopper forgot watermelons in aisle and fell over one while looking for cupcake holders).

remains in the bleachers after one end collapses is surely owed a duty of care, but she is also probably guilty of negligence in remaining seated as the bleachers go down.

The difference between assumed risk in the sense of no duty and assumed risk in the sense of contributory negligence becomes easy to recognize if the assumed risk terminology is dropped. In the collapsing bleachers example, it would be hard to assert that the sports enterprise owed no duty of care to provide reasonably safe bleachers. Given the duty of reasonable care, the plaintiff's conduct becomes legally relevant, not because it shows consent, but only because it shows risk.

Participants

Risks of negligence not assumed; risks inherent in the sport. Similar ideas apply to participants in organized sports. In the old language of assumed risk, participants impliedly "assume the risk" of all the dangers inherent in the sport. In many sporting activities, dangers inherent in the sport would never include another person's negligence. If a skier impliedly assumes only the risks of dangers inherent in skiing, she does not assume the risks of dangers hidden below the snow as a result of the slope operator's negligence, since the operator's negligence is by no means inherent in the sport.[6] Similarly, a horseback rider assumes the risk of being thrown, but only the inherent risk, not the added risk incurred by reason of the stables' negligence.[7]

Risks of negligence assumed or defendant's duty limited. Participants in active, competitive sporting contests—football, for example—often must expect negligently caused physical injury. A number of courts, now usually dropping the old assumed risk terminology,[8] have accordingly held that in such cases the duty of other participants is only a duty to avoid intentional or reckless injury.[9] This limited duty or standard of care is derived directly from the plaintiff's limited expectations of safety.[10] The limited duty rule is another way of saying that negligence of excited players is an inherent risk of the game[11] even

6. See Sunday v. Stratton, 136 Vt. 293, 390 A.2d 398 (1978). The ski industry has prevailed upon legislatures to enact protective statutes which, in some states, provide that the skier assumes risks inherent in the sport. They may offer less protection than intended, since "an inherent risk is one that cannot be removed through the exercise of due care." Brett v. Great American Recreations, Inc., 144 N.J. 479, 499, 677 A.2d 705, 715 (1996). But some statutes appear to force individuals to assume risks of hidden dangers that could have been corrected by the operators' reasonable care. See UTAH CODE ANN. § 78–27–51.

7. Halpern v. Wheeldon, 890 P.2d 562 (Wyo.1995). A number of states have now passed equine recreation statutes which, like the ski statutes, are aimed at limiting liability.

8. The traditional implied assumption of the risk, not based on actual consent, seems to have been resurrected in Morgan v. State, 90 N.Y.2d 471, 662 N.Y.S.2d 421, 685 N.E.2d 202 (1997).

9. Knight v. Jewett, 3 Cal.4th 296, 11 Cal.Rptr.2d 2, 834 P.2d 696 (1992) (conduct must be so reckless "as to be totally outside the range of the ordinary activity involved in the sport"); Nabozny v. Barnhill, 31 Ill. App.3d 212, 334 N.E.2d 258, 77 A.L.R.3d 1294 (1975) (soccer; deliberate prohibited kick could be actionable on this standard).

10. See Turcotte v. Fell, 68 N.Y.2d 432, 510 N.Y.S.2d 49, 502 N.E.2d 964 (1986).

11. See Knight v. Jewett, 3 Cal.4th 296, 11 Cal.Rptr.2d 2, 834 P.2d 696 (1992).

though negligence is not an inherent risk as to spectators. The limited duty approach makes it clear that even violation of a rule of the game does not in itself result in liability; if the violation is one that is ordinary to the way the game is played, the defendant will be liable only if he is reckless or intends harm.[12]

The limited duty rule has been applied to professional games like football[13] and hockey,[14] and to professional horse racing[15] and quite arguably is best confined to professional sports.[16] But the limited duty rule has also been applied to recreational games of football,[17] soccer,[18] softball,[19] and even to games that seem to be little more than horseplay in which the rules are constructed on the fly.[20]

Some courts have formulated the rule broadly, as if it covered all sporting activities. If the underlying point is the one rooted in the consent type of implied assumed risk, that is, the reasonable expectations of the parties involved, a more cautious formulation is required. To say that professional football players must expect some rather serious misbehavior is not to say that ping pong players should expect to be blinded by a thrown paddle.[21] If the limited duty rule is true to its consensual heritage, the reasonable expectations of the parties must be taken into account, so that the particular facts of the cases and the particular kind of sporting activity will be important. Hunters, for example, presumably know that they are at risk from other hunters, but given the seriousness of potential injury, those who participate should not be viewed as consenting to being shot. Consequently, the cases so far have required hunters to exercise the care of reasonable and prudent persons.[22]

However, some courts have extended the limited duty rule to games like golf[23] and tennis,[24] in which players might expect slightly more

12. Gauvin v. Clark, 404 Mass. 450, 537 N.E.2d 94 (1989); Turcotte v. Fell, 68 N.Y.2d 432, 510 N.Y.S.2d 49, 502 N.E.2d 964 (1986).

13. Hackbart v. Cincinnati Bengals, Inc., 601 F.2d 516 (10th Cir.1979).

14. Gauvin v. Clark, 404 Mass. 450, 537 N.E.2d 94 (1989).

15. Turcotte v. Fell, 68 N.Y.2d 432, 510 N.Y.S.2d 49, 502 N.E.2d 964 (1986).

16. See Stephen D. Sugarman, Assumption of the Risk, 31 Val. U. L. Rev. 833 (1997).

17. Knight v. Jewett, 3 Cal.4th 296, 11 Cal.Rptr.2d 2, 834 P.2d 696 (1992).

18. Jaworski v. Kiernan, 241 Conn. 399, 696 A.2d 332 (1997).

19. Crawn v. Campo, 136 N.J. 494, 643 A.2d 600 (1994).

20. Pfister v. Shusta, 167 Ill.2d 417, 657 N.E.2d 1013, 212 Ill.Dec. 668 (1995) (kicking a crushed can in dormitory lobby); but cf. Yount v. Johnson, 121 N.M. 585, 915 P.2d 341 (Ct.App.1996) (limited duty rule not to be applied to horseplay between teenaged young men).

21. See Bangert v. Shaffner, 848 S.W.2d 353 (Tex. Ct. App. 1993) (parasail harnessed upside down with disastrous results, ordinary care standard applied).

22. See Hendricks v. Broderick, 284 N.W.2d 209 (Iowa 1979) (decided when Iowa was still using the assumed risk terminology; no assumption of the risk of another hunter's negligence); Knight v. Jewett, 3 Cal.4th 296, 11 Cal.Rptr.2d 2, 834 P.2d 696 (1992) (cautioning that the sports rule might not apply to less active sports and pointing out that the reasonable care standard was routinely applied to hunters).

23. Thompson v. McNeill, 53 Ohio St.3d 102, 559 N.E.2d 705 (1990); Mangone v. Pickering, 1997 WL 197232 (Mass.Super.) (applying the limited duty even to a golfer's practice swing, in which the club struck the

civilized behavior, and to playful but noncompetitive activities, in which the enthusiasm of competition does not seem to make negligent or violent behavior the norm.[25] It may be that some courts are in the process of creating a freestanding limited duty rule, divorced from its foundation in the parties' expectations.[26] The opinions suggest that the duty should be limited because of the danger of a flood of litigation, and because of a supposed policy of encouraging vigorous physical competition.[27] Both these reasons, as distinct from the parties' reasonable expectations, may be doubted. In any event, they are potentially at odds with the parties' expectations. Where the parties reasonably expect that a game rule will be followed by other players, it would seem that the parties' expectations should control. Ordinary care under the circumstances should be the standard unless the plaintiff has clear notice that she is entitled to lesser protection.

A few courts in recent years have insisted on the ordinary negligence standard for sports participants.[28] Quite possibly that standard would yield the same results in most cases, since reasonable care takes circumstances, including the customs and expectations of the parties, into account.

Topic D. Limitations of Action

§ 216. Statutes of Limitation

The statutory bar. Statutes of limitation almost invariably prescribe the period of time in which the plaintiff must bring a given kind of claim or counterclaim.[1] The structure of statutes, and the periods they prescribe, vary from state to state and vary as well according to the kind of claim asserted. In negligence cases, statutes often require the plaintiff to commence her action within two or three years. Federal legislation often fails to provide a statute of limitations,[2] but the void is filled by the

plaintiff's jaw). Contra: Zurla v. Hydel, 289 Ill.App.3d 215, 224 Ill.Dec. 166, 681 N.E.2d 148 (1997).

24. Hoke v. Cullinan, 914 S.W.2d 335 (Ky.1995).

25. See Ford v. Gouin, 3 Cal.4th 339, 11 Cal.Rptr.2d 30, 834 P.2d 724 (1992) (water skiing boat operator allegedly negligent in towing skier under a low, overhanging branch).

26. Pfister v. Shusta, 167 Ill.2d 417, 657 N.E.2d 1013, 212 Ill.Dec. 668 (1995) (applying the limited duty rule and rejecting, semble, inquiry into scope of plaintiff's consent in a spontaneous game without rules).

27. Jaworski v. Kiernan, 241 Conn. 399, 696 A.2d 332 (1997).

28. Auckenthaler v. Grundmeyer, 110 Nev. 682, 877 P.2d 1039 (1994) (horse and dog event); Lestina v. West Bend Mutual Ins. Co., 176 Wis.2d 901, 501 N.W.2d 28 (1993) (recreational soccer).

§ 216

1. The statute of limitations generally bars as a counterclaim what it would bar as a claim. Exceptions often applied: (a) the statute does not bar a claim for recoupment, that is one that is merely asserted to reduce liability; see Ed Miller & Sons, Inc. v. Earl, 243 Neb. 708, 502 N.W.2d 444 (1993); (b) the statute does not bar compulsory counterclaims, those arising from the same transaction. Stein v. Feingold, 629 So.2d 998 (Fla.App.1993); 2 Calvin Corman, Limitation of Actions § 13.5 (1991 & Supp.); Annotation, Claim barred by limitation as subject of setoff, counterclaim, recoupment, cross bill, or cross action, 1 A.L.R.2d 630 (1948).

2. See Board of Regents of University of State of New York v. Tomanio, 446 U.S.

courts, which must concoct a time limit out of analogous state statutes.[3] The federal legislative failures aside, statutes of limitations appear to be a part of all legal systems.[4] Doctrines like laches and estoppel sometimes deny the plaintiff access to court on the basis of equities in the particular case, as where the plaintiff's delay in suing has caused prejudice to the defendant.[5] The statute of limitations, in contrast, attempts to state a bright-line rule barring claims within the named class after the period specified in the statute.

As an affirmative defense. In rare cases, particular statutes may be construed as an elimination of the cause of action altogether, as a condition precedent to suit,[6] or as a limit on the courts' jurisdiction,[7] so that the time bar cannot be waived by the defendant's failure to plead it and the normal rules for tolling a statute of limitations do not apply.[8] In most instances, however, the defendant has the burden of pleading the statute as a defense and the burden of proving facts that show it has run.[9] If he does not plead the statute in a timely way, the defense is waived.[10]

Reasons for adopting a limitation system. Courts and writers usually give a variety of reasons for the statute of limitations.[11] Sometimes courts suggest that the plaintiff might have "waived" her claim by her delay in bringing suit,[12] but more often they emphasize justice and process concerns, including those that follow:

478, 100 S.Ct. 1790, 64 L.Ed.2d 440 (1980) (Congressional failure to provide statute of limitations for federal claims is "a void which is commonplace in federal statutory law.")

3. Owens v. Okure, 488 U.S. 235, 109 S.Ct. 573, 102 L.Ed.2d 594 (1989) (where state has several statute of limitations sections that might apply, federal courts in § 1983 civil rights actions should borrow the general or residual personal injury statute, not the narrower assault and battery statute); Wilson v. Garcia, 471 U.S. 261, 105 S.Ct. 1938, 85 L.Ed.2d 254 (1985).

4. E.g., ALTA. REV. STAT. ch. L–15.; ONT. REV. STAT. ch. 240; THE MEXICAN CIVIL CODE arts. 1135–1294 (Michael Wallace Gordon, Translator, revised version Tr. by Otto Schoenrich) ("prescription"); see J.A. JOLOWICZ, Procedural Questions, XI INT. ENC. COMP. L. Torts ch. 13 § 61 (Andre Tunc ed. 1986).

5. See 1 DAN B. DOBBS, LAW OF REMEDIES § 2.4 (4) (2d ed. 1999).

6. E.g., National Railroad Passenger Corp. v. Krouse, 627 A.2d 489 (D.C.App. 1993) (FELA cases).

7. Some Federal Tort Claims Act cases construe the FTCA limitation as a jurisdictional limitation. See Caton v. United States, 495 F.2d 635 (9th Cir.1974); David Abney, For Whom the Statute Tolls: Medical Malpractice under the Federal Tort Claims Act, 61 NOTRE DAME L. REV. 696 (1986). Contra, the statute is subject to equitable tolling and is therefore not jurisdictional, Krueger v. Saiki, 19 F.3d 1285 (8th Cir.1994).

8. Carlson v. Independent School District No. 623, 392 N.W.2d 216 (Minn.1986); In the Interest of M.J.Z., 874 S.W.2d 724 (Tex.App.1994); See In re Joseph B., 258 Ill.App.3d 954, 197 Ill.Dec. 56, 630 N.E.2d 1180 (1994) (no tolling).

9. Public Service Co. of Oklahoma v. Allen, 876 P.2d 680 (Okla.1994). Because the defendant must plead and prove the defense, it cannot be raised by motion to dismiss unless the time bar appears on the face of the complaint or prior pleading by which the plaintiff is bound. Pontier v. Wolfson, 637 So.2d 39 (Fla.App.1994).

10. E.g., Feldman v. Gogos, 628 A.2d 103 (D.C.App.1993).

11. An excellent statement of the reasons for statutes of limitations is found in Institute of Law Research and Reform, Limitations (Report Discussion No. 4, Edmonton, 1986).

12. E.g., Lee v. Gaufin, 867 P.2d 572 (Utah 1993).

(1) Evidence will deteriorate as memories fade or even become distorted in ways that cannot be convincingly tested, so "stale claims" should be barred.

(2) Renewal of an ancient grievance in court may initiate more conflicts than it resolves; and in any event society should not use its judicial resources to reignite a conflict that had been quieted by time.

(3) The defendant, who may not in fact have been a wrongdoer, is entitled at some point in time to peace of mind that comes from knowing the potential conflict has burned out.

(4) The defendant's ability to manage business or personal affairs is clouded by a potential law suit; for instance, he may be unable to borrow money or make business commitments until claims are resolved; if he does not in fact know of the potential claims, he may make financial commitments that prove disastrous in the light of a late-asserted claim.

(5) For similar reasons, insurers find it costly to insure against a defendant's liability for an indefinite time into the future; these costs represent real costs to society (in the form of increased premiums for insurance or increased costs of goods); if these costs can reasonably be avoided by requiring prompt suit, society in general is better off.

(6) In some cases, stability of transactions or relationships has other important social values; a consent to adoption of a child should not be subject to revocation or attack long after the child has established a relationship with adoptive parents, for example.[13] In greater or lesser degree the same stability or security interests affect many other potential litigations as well.

(7) Over time, society's expectations and standards change, sometimes in ways that society itself does not perceive immediately; without a limitation, judges or juries might unjustly impose today's standards on events that took place twenty, thirty or fifty years ago.

Inflexibilities. Although these reasons are convincing, none of them points to any particular time limit. In fact it might be argued that none of the reasons necessarily points to a bright-line time limit at all. It would be possible to imagine a system in which judges attempt to estimate in each case whether the plaintiff had waited too long to bring suit. Other alternatives could include financial disincentives for delayed filings. For example, a statute might require the court to reduce the plaintiff's damages by a percentage for each year of unseasonable delay, or to limit the damages to actual pecuniary losses in the case of late suit. In some "equity" cases courts do attempt to estimate whether the plaintiff has delayed "too long" without following any bright-line time

13. See In re Joseph B., 258 Ill.App.3d 954, 197 Ill.Dec. 56, 630 N.E.2d 1180 (1994).

period rule. But such a process would be expensive. And by making the defendant litigate the merits of a limitation, it would deprive the defendant of some of the important privileges the statute seeks to assure. Part of the value of the statute is that it provides a bright-line rule.[14] Such a rule excludes a suit brought one day late as well as a claim that is twenty years old.[15] So in spite of its value, the application of the statute can seem arbitrary or unjust at times.

Flexibilities. Although old claims may be unjust claims, the general policy of courts is to decide cases on their merits; courts, not time, should generally decide whether the claim is unjust or not. Courts infuse a degree of flexibility in applying statutes of limitation, principally but not exclusively by their control over the starting time for the statutory clock and by their control over time-outs or tolling. Sometimes courts can also choose which of several statutes applies to the case.

§ 217. Starting the Clock in Negligence Claims—The Accrual Rule

Starting the clock: accrual of the claim. The prescriptive period traditionally began—the statutory clock started to run—when the plaintiff's claim accrued. In negligence claims, unlike some others, the claim does not accrue until (a) the defendant had committed a negligent act and (b) it had caused legally cognizable harm.[1]

Act vs. harm. Sometimes, contrary to the rule stated above, courts say that the claim accrues when the defendant commits the negligent act. Special statutes aimed at protecting particular groups may so provide.[2] Such a provision could bar the claim before the plaintiff could sue. If the defendant negligently gives the plaintiff a dangerous medication in January, but it does not cause harm until three years later, a two year statute that begins to run at the time of the defendant's act rather than at the time of the plaintiff's harm would have run long before the plaintiff had a cause of action. The traditional view avoids

14. Laches, the old defense originating in the once-separate equity courts and still applied mainly in cases where equitable relief is sought, was not a bright-line approach to the bar. Laches allowed judges to decide in each case whether the plaintiff had unreasonably delayed in bringing suit and whether the defendant was prejudiced by the delay. See 1 Dan B. Dobbs, Law of Remedies § 2.4 (4) (2d ed. 1993). The ordinary statute of limitations approach is not comparable. However, courts occasionally do suggest that the trial court has a range of discretion in determining when the claim accrues in doubtful cases. See Lindsay Mfg. Co. v. Universal Surety Co., 246 Neb. 495, 519 N.W.2d 530 (1994).

15. E.g., State v. Johnson, 19 Kan. App.2d 315, 868 P.2d 555 (1994)

§ 217

1. Restatement § 899, cmt. c; Kronos, Inc. v. AVX Corp., 81 N.Y.2d 90, 612 N.E.2d 289, 595 N.Y.S.2d 931 (1993).

2. In LaBello v. Albany Medical Center Hospital, 85 N.Y.2d 701, 628 N.Y.S.2d 40, 651 N.E.2d 908 (1995) a child claimed against the mother's physician for injury allegedly inflicted before he was born. The statute explicitly provided that malpractice claims accrued at the time of act or omission of the physician. However, the court thought the statute silently assumed the existence of a person with "juridical capacity to sue," and concluded that no suit could be commenced until the plaintiff was born alive. At that point and only at that point did the tort claim accrue. The statute of limitations began to run at that point.

that result by holding that the claim accrues when damage is done and the plaintiff can sue.

§ 218. Starting the Clock in Negligence Claims—The Discovery Rule

Undiscovered injury. Under the accrual rule, the plaintiff's claim was barred unless she commenced suit within the statutory time period, even if she was not aware of either harm or negligence during that period.[1] The problem of undiscovered harm is especially acute when the plaintiff is subjected to toxins that cause harm slowly over long periods of time. Accordingly, many modern statutes[2] and case decisions[3] postpone the accrual date until the plaintiff discovers or should discover some of the relevant facts. A few medical malpractice statutes limit the discovery rule to cases in which the

defendant surgeon has left a foreign object in the patient's body.[4] Statutes in some states make special provision for delayed suits claiming childhood sexual abuse by the defendant.[5]

Facts that must be discovered to start the clock. So far, formulations of the discovery rule have often been casual rather than definitive. Given some latitude for differences in the exact wording, the usual idea seems to be that the statute will not begin to run until

(a) all the elements of the tort are present *and*

(b) the plaintiff discovers, or as a reasonable person should have discovered,

(i) that she is injured and

(ii) that the defendant, or the defendant's product or instrumentality, had a causal role in the injury, or that there was enough chance that defendant was connected with the injury to require further investigation that in turn would have revealed the defendant's connection.[6]

§ 218

1. E.g., Shearin v. Lloyd, 246 N.C. 363, 98 S.E.2d 508 (1957).

2. E.g., 42 U.S.C.A. § 9658 (certain toxic torts cases); Ill. Comp. Stats. Ann. § 13–212 (a).

3. United States v. Kubrick, 444 U.S. 111, 100 S.Ct. 352, 62 L.Ed.2d 259 (1979) (Federal Tort Claims Act); Urie v. Thompson, 337 U.S. 163, 69 S.Ct. 1018, 93 L.Ed. 1282, 11 A.L.R.2d 252 (1949); Liddell v. SCA Services of Ohio, Inc., 70 Ohio St.3d 6, 635 N.E.2d 1233 (1994); Chase v. Sabin, 445 Mich. 190, 516 N.W.2d 60 (1994). As to the Federal Tort Claims Act cases under the *Kubrick* rule, supra, see David Abney, for Whom the Statute Tolls: Medical Malpractice under the Federal Tort Claims Act, 61 Notre Dame L. Rev. 696 (1986).

4. A little authority holds this parsimonious use of the discovery rule to be unconstitutional. See Comstock v. Collier, 737 P.2d 845 (Colo.1987). Where the statutes are constitutional, litigation erupts over what counts as a foreign body. E.g., Rockefeller v. Moront, 81 N.Y.2d 560, 618 N.E.2d 119, 601 N.Y.S.2d 86 (1993) (suture improperly affixed to an organ not involved in the operation is not a foreign object); See Annotation, Medical Malpractice: Applicability of "Foreign Object" Exception in Medical Malpractice Statutes of Limitations, 50 A.L.R.4th 250 (1987).

5. § 222 below.

6. E.g., Moll v. Abbott Laboratories, 444 Mich. 1, 506 N.W.2d 816 (1993); Grunwald v. Bronkesh, 131 N.J. 483, 621 A.2d 459 (1993); Schiele v. Hobart Corp., 284 Or.

Discovery of negligence or evidence of negligence, as distinct from a causal connection, is not required to start the statute running.[7]

A little authority is more favorable to the plaintiff than the rule just stated and a little is less so. In the more favorable category, some courts have said that the statute will not begin to run until the plaintiff actually knows, not only that she is injured and that the defendant has some causal role, but also that the defendant has committed some wrong or default. At least they have said so in drug product liability cases.[8] Some courts have also said that discovery of temporary injury is not enough to start the statute if in fact the injury is permanent.[9] One court may have implied that the statute is not triggered until the plaintiff has discovered useful evidence and has some "incentive" to sue.[10]

In the less favorable category, some cases say, or could be read to say, that the statute begins to run when the plaintiff discovers her injury, even if she discovers neither a wrong by the defendant nor even a causal connection to the defendant.[11]

In any event, the discovery rule does not depend upon discovery of legal rights as distinct from discovery of facts. If the plaintiff discovers the facts, her ignorance of legal rules that give her a claim has no effect to postpone running of the statute.[12] Nor does the rule depend upon discovery of all the consequences of the injury. If the plaintiff discovers the injury and its connection to the defendant, the statute begins to run

483, 587 P.2d 1010 (1978); Pocono International Raceway, Inc. v. Pocono Produce, Inc. 503 Pa. 80, 468 A.2d 468 (1983); C. v. C., 114 D.L.R.4th 151 (Ont. Ct. 1994). In the case of lawyers and clients or physicians and patients, it may be that discovery of the "connection" between the defendant's conduct and injury would not be enough. If the plaintiff loses her case, she necessarily knows that the lawyer is connected with the loss, but does not necessarily have reason to suspect anything wrong. So discovery of grounds for suspicion might be a better test in those cases.

7. See United States v. Kubrick, 444 U.S. 111, 100 S.Ct. 352, 62 L.Ed.2d 259 (1979).

8. Anthony v. Abbott Laboratories, 490 A.2d 43 (R.I.1985); cf. Lopez v. Swyer 62 N.J. 267, 300 A.2d 563 (1973); Roe v. Jefferson, 875 S.W.2d 653 (Tenn.1994).

9. Schiele v. Hobart Corp., 284 Or. 483, 587 P.2d 1010 (1978). Other courts have said that while discovery of de minimis harm will not start the statute, if the discovered harm is more than de minimis the statute begins to run even if the plaintiff discovers that her injuries are much more serious. See, e.g., Hicks v. Hines, 826 F.2d 1543, 88 A.L.R.Fed. 501 (6th Cir.1987).

10. Allred v. Chynoweth, 990 F.2d 527 (10th Cir.1993).

11. Langner v. Simpson, 533 N.W.2d 511 (Iowa 1995) (medical malpractice statute begins to run when patient knew or should have known of the injury, even though the patient did not know the physician had negligently caused the injury). See Renaud v. Sigma–Aldrich Corp., 662 A.2d 711 (R.I.1995) (plaintiff brought timely suit against A, but discovered after the statute had run that B was the proper defendant; the discovery rule does not aid the plaintiff).

12. See United States v. Kubrick, 444 U.S. 111, 100 S.Ct. 352, 62 L.Ed.2d 259 (1979); Jolly v. Eli Lilly & Co., 44 Cal.3d 1103, 751 P.2d 923, 245 Cal.Rptr. 658 (1988). Casual formulations might leave some doubts. In Madlem v. Arko, 592 N.E.2d 686 (Ind.1992) said "a tort claim accrues and the statute of limitations begins to run when the plaintiff knew or, in the exercise of ordinary diligence, could have discovered that an injury had been sustained as a result of the tortious act of another." Whether this means the plaintiff must discover the defendant's conduct or the legal quality of a tort is perhaps uncertain.

even if some of its injurious consequences are not discovered until much later.[13]

When reasonable people may differ as to whether or when the plaintiff actually discovered relevant facts or should have discovered them, the question may be left to the jury to determine.[14] In that kind of case, the statute of limitations defense is not a threshold defense at all, but instead is tried along with the merits of the case. There are, however, a number of cases in which the undisputed facts allow the court to say as a matter of law that the plaintiff actually discovered the relevant facts or that reasonable people could only conclude that she should have done so.[15]

Discovering evidence or symptoms. The "should have discovered" portion of the rule is important. The test seems to be objective, that is, what a reasonable person in the plaintiff's position would have discovered.[16] Symptoms might be enough to require a reasonable person to seek diagnosis that in turn would reveal the injury. In such a case, the claim should not accrue under the discovery rule from the onset of symptoms. Symptoms are important only because they are evidence that the plaintiff should have discovered injury at some *later* time by investigating the symptoms further.[17] The question is when the plaintiff would have discovered injury, not when symptoms began to appear. There are of course cases in which the symptom *is* the injury, and its discovery triggers the statute.[18] In addition, some courts have used quite broad language suggesting that discovery of any "problem" might be enough to start the statute.[19]

Trivial symptoms, or those consistent with a temporary or minor injury, might not suggest a serious or permanent injury that would lead the plaintiff to investigate further. Perhaps it is arguable that the plaintiff who suffers a major or permanent injury should not be barred by a long-ago discovery of transient or trivial symptoms.[20]

Discovering defendant's connection. If the plaintiff reasonably believes the injury is not caused by the defendant, mere knowledge of the

13. Moll v. Abbott Laboratories, 444 Mich. 1, 506 N.W.2d 816 (1993). However, if the plaintiff suffered two distinct injuries, discovery of one does not start the statute running on the other. See Larson v. Johns–Manville Sales Corp., 427 Mich. 301, 399 N.W.2d 1 (1986) & § 223. As to "repression" of knowledge in the sexual abuse cases, see § 222.

14. E.g., Mohr v. Commonwealth, 421 Mass. 147, 653 N.E.2d 1104 (1995).

15. E.g., Alaface v. National Investment Co., 181 Ariz. 586, 892 P.2d 1375 (Ariz.Ct. App.1994).

16. BASF Corp. v. Symington, 512 N.W.2d 692 (N.D.1994) (test is objective even if the plaintiff is mentally disabled).

17. Cf. Burgess v. Eli Lilly and Company, 66 Ohio St.3d 59, 609 N.E.2d 140 (1993) (statute providing for accrual when the plaintiff learns she has injury that "may" be related to toxic exposure is unconstitutional; learning that one *may* have an injury is not equivalent to either the learned or should have learned test).

18. See Caughell v. Group Health Cooperative of Puget Sound, 124 Wash.2d 217, 876 P.2d 898 (1994) (plaintiff's discovery that she was addicted to drugs prescribed by doctor would be discovery of injury).

19. Economy Housing Co., Inc. v. Rosenberg, 239 Neb. 267, 475 N.W.2d 899 (Neb. 1991) (lawyer malpractice case).

20. See Schiele v. Hobart Corp., 284 Or. 483, 587 P.2d 1010 (1978).

injury alone is not enough to start the clock.[21] In *Browning v. Burt*,[22] the plaintiff discovered her medical condition resulting from a surgeon's allegedly negligent operations but had no occasion to know that the hospital had been negligent in permitting the surgeon to operate. The statute of limitations did not begin to run on her claim against the hospital until she learned that other patients of the same surgeon had similar complaints. But ordinarily at least, it is the defendant's connection with harm, not the defendant's negligence, that must be discovered.[23]

Toxic tort cases. The discovery rule is especially appealing for victims of toxic torts, the effects of which may not appear for many, many years or even for generations. A federal environmental statute that creates certain liabilities in connection with disposal or release of hazardous substances superimposes several rules on state law dealing with personal injury or property damage in that setting. Under this statute, the state must give the plaintiff the benefit of the discovery rule. The state must also toll the statute of limitations for minors until they reach majority, and toll the statute for incompetents until they become competent or have a guardian appointed.[24]

§ 219. Starting the Clock in Negligence Claims—"Statutes of Repose"

Statutes of ultimate repose. Statutes of ultimate repose provide a counter rule to the accrual-discovery rule by adding an alternative prescriptive period which begins running at the time of the defendant's act rather than at the time harm was inflicted or discovered. For example, the traditional accrual statute might provide that suits must be brought within three years from the time harm occurred or should have been discovered. The repose statute might add that in no event could suits be commenced more than ten years after the defendant's negligent act. In the case of injury by a manufactured product, the repose statute might provide that suit must be brought no more than ten years after the product was sold by the defendant.[1] In such a case, the plaintiff gets the benefit of the accrual and discovery rules, but only during the first ten years after the defendant sold the product.

Affected groups. These statutes, usually considered to be a part of the "tort reform" legislation of the 1970s and 1980s,[2] were constructed

21. Chase v. Sabin, 445 Mich. 190, 516 N.W.2d 60 (1994).

22. Browning v. Burt, 66 Ohio St.3d 544, 613 N.E.2d 993 (1993).

23. United States v. Kubrick, 444 U.S. 111, 100 S.Ct. 352, 62 L.Ed.2d 259 (1979); Caughell v. Group Health Cooperative of Puget Sound, 124 Wash.2d 217, 876 P.2d 898 (1994).

24. 42 U.S.C.A. § 9658.

§ 219

1. E.g., Conn. Gen. Stats. § 52–577a (ten years from date defendant parted with possession of the product); Ill. Comp. Stats. § 13–213 (12 years from first sale or ten years from sale to first purchaser, whichever is shorter, in strict product liability actions); cf. See Colo. Rev. Stats. Ann. § 13–21–403 ("rebuttable presumption" that after the outer limit period, the product is non-defective).

2. Other tort reform legislation limited damages, see § 384, and altered rules of

for the protection of particular groups that have lobbied for them,[3] notably products manufacturers, architects and builders, health care professionals, and governmental entities. Until the middle of the twentieth century or even later, all these groups enjoyed the protection of special substantive rules or practices, such as the privity rule that protected manufacturers and builders. So to some extent, the statutes of repose substitute some new special protections that courts had removed.

In the case of architects, engineers, and builders on real property, the trigger date for starting the repose period is usually the date the improvements on real property were "completed."[4] Health care providers' repose statutes begin to run with the doctor's last act or completion of the treatment, even if harm does not occur or become apparent until later.[5] Government entities have always obtained highly preferential treatment in tort law, and frequently enjoy special statutes of repose.[6] In addition, governmental entities often benefit from special notice-of-claim statutes requiring the plaintiff to assert a claim administratively or give notice of the claim within a relatively short time of its accrual.[7]

Construction of statutes. Statutes of repose that protect architects and builders usually provide that the statute begins to run when the improvement on land is substantially completed. Such statutes can promote litigation over what counts as substantial completion and what counts as an improvement.[8] They also raise the question whether a supplier of components used in the construction is one of the defendants given special protection by the statute.[9]

liability apportionment, see §§ 389 & 390.

3. See Branch v. Willis–Knighton Medical Center, 636 So.2d 211 (La.1994); Noll v. Harrisburg Area YMCA, 537 Pa. 274, 643 A.2d 81 (1994). Some rules of ultimate repose antedated the tort reform era. See Zenith Radio Corp. v. Hazeltine Research Inc., 401 U.S. 321, 91 S.Ct. 795, 28 L.Ed.2d 77 (1971).

4. E.g., Cal. Code Civ. Pro. § 337.15 (10 years after the substantial completion of the development or improvement); Vernon's Ann. Mo. Stat. § 516.097 (10 years after improvement is completed); cf. Ala. Code § 6–5–221 (13 years after action accrue or would have accrued). See e.g., Noll v. Harrisburg Area YMCA, 537 Pa. 274, 643 A.2d 81 (1994).

5. See Fla. Stats. Ann., § 95.11 (4); Mich. Comp. L. Ann. § 600.5838a; Vernon's Ann. Mo. Stat. § 516.105.

6. See, e.g., Whitlow v. Bd. of Education of Kanawha County, 190 W.Va. 223, 438 S.E.2d 15 (1993) (but holding the preference for governmental defendants to be unconstitutional as applied to claims of minors).

7. E.g., Rev. Code. Wash. § 4.92.110. Similar notice-bar statutes sometimes apply to other protected groups. E.g., Cal. Code Civ. Pro. § 364 (health care providers). If the notice is not timely given, the suit is barred even if it is commenced within the prescription period. See McNeil v. United States, 508 U.S. 106, 113 S.Ct. 1980, 124 L.Ed.2d 21 (1993) (notice to federal agency before filing tort claim required by statute and suit is to be dismissed if filed before notice is given, even though notice is given later).

8. Noll v. Harrisburg Area YMCA, 537 Pa. 274, 643 A.2d 81 (1994) (with chattels added, permanent addition is the test, taking into account the law of fixtures plus objective intent of parties controls; easily removable diving blocks were not fixtures, hence not covered by the statute).

9. Supplier does not come under the improvements statute: McConnaughey v. Building Components, Inc., 536 Pa. 95, 637 A.2d 1331 (1994); supplier does come under the improvements statute: Forsyth Memorial Hospital, Inc. v. Armstrong World Industries, Inc., 336 N.C. 438, 444 S.E.2d 423 (1994).

The medical malpractice statutes likewise require construction. The courts may not be entirely sure whether they wish to focus on status of the defendant or the conduct charged against him to determine whether the claim is a malpractice claim or not. For instance, some courts confer the protections of the malpractice repose statutes upon suppliers of allegedly defective blood[10] products, while other courts do not.[11] One court has held that a claim against a physician for sexual harassment or battery during a medical exam is a claim of medical malpractice so that the medical statute applied to protect the physician.[12] But another held that a hospital's negligent credentialing of an incompetent surgeon was not protected by the special malpractice statute.[13]

Where the repose statute calculates the period from the defendant's last act or omission, the courts may be compelled to decide what segment of compound activities are to be considered to be the relevant act: was it the pathologists' erroneous diagnosis, completed on one day, or the "act" of diagnosing and communicating the diagnosis to the attending physician, completed days later?[14]

Statute of repose effects. When a statute of repose governs the case, the plaintiff might be barred before she discovers her injury. Beyond that, the plaintiff might be barred before any harm at all has occurred.[15] For instance, if the statute of repose uses a twelve-year period of time and the plaintiff suffers injury from a product that was sold in defective condition thirteen years earlier, the statute of repose would have barred her claim a year before she was injured at all. This was never possible under the traditional statute of limitation.

A particularly stringent form of "repose" bars a young minor's claim before majority and possibly before the claim accrues.[16] Other extraordinary effects are possible under some statutes. At least one court has held that the repose statute bars a medical malpractice claim even if the claim was fraudulently concealed by the surgeon-defendant.[17] In

10. Smith v. Paslode Corp., 7 F.3d 116 (8th Cir.1993) (Red Cross was health care provider for statute of limitations purposes); Bradway v. American National Red Cross, 263 Ga. 19, 426 S.E.2d 849 (1993).

11. Silva v. Southwest Florida Blood Bank, Inc., 601 So.2d 1184 (Fla.1992) (supplier of blood contaminated with HIV virus was not engaged in diagnosis, treatment or care and hence did not get the protection of the medical statute); Branch v. Willis–Knighton Medical Center, 636 So.2d 211 (La.1994) (similar); Swanigan v. American National Red Cross, 313 S.C. 416, 438 S.E.2d 251 (1993); Doe v. American National Red Cross, 176 Wis.2d 610, 500 N.W.2d 264 (1993) (similar).

12. Hagan v. Antonio, 240 Va. 347, 397 S.E.2d 810 (1990) (allegation by female plaintiff that male doctor improperly played with her breasts and made sexual remarks was a "medical malpractice" claim based on performance of professional services, hence the claim was subject to the special limitations of the malpractice statute).

13. Browning v. Burt, 66 Ohio St.3d 544, 613 N.E.2d 993 (1993).

14. Green v. National Health Laboratories, Inc., 316 Ark. 5, 870 S.W.2d 707 (1994) (the compound act of diagnosing and communicating was considered to be the relevant act).

15. See First Maryland Leasecorp v. Rothstein, 72 Wash.App. 278, 864 P.2d 17 (1993).

16. See Lee v. Gaufin, 867 P.2d 572 (Utah 1993) (holding the statute treating minor medical malpractice victims differently was unconstitutional under the state constitution).

17. Horn v. Citizens Hospital, 425 So.2d 1065 (Ala.1982).

products cases, the defendant manufacturer is sometimes protected because it sold the product long ago even though its failure to correct a defect might seem to be a continuing tort.[18]

Constitutionality. Most of the decided cases have upheld the constitutionality of statutes of repose against attacks by adult plaintiffs based on the claim that the statutes violate due process, equal protection, or state constitutional guarantees.[19] The cases taken as a whole present a relatively firm picture of general support for the statutes, but in some instances the arguments presented are narrow or poorly articulated, so that a decision favoring constitutionality does not necessarily preclude a different decision in a later case when a different constitutional argument is presented.

A different and substantial group of jurists have roundly condemned the statutes for barring the claim before it accrues.[20] A number of courts have held some version of the statutes to be unconstitutional, frequently under state constitutional provisions that require open courts or that guarantee a remedy.[21] Professor McGovern found no less than 17 different types of state constitutional provisions involved in the constitutional arguments.[22] Some of the major arguments included these elements: (1) Victims of the statute's preferred defendants are treated differently from victims of other defendants. (2) The repose statute denies due process of law by a rule that potentially bars a claim before it arises. (3) The statutes are designed to provide a benefit to one group at the expense of another. They benefit the preferred defendants by reducing their exposure to liability and thus indirectly reducing their insurance costs.

18. See Spilker v. City of Lincoln, 238 Neb. 188, 469 N.W.2d 546 (1991) (Westinghouse sold electrical switchgear with an instruction book that directed workers making a repair to use a specified receptacle, an action that in fact would subject the victim to high voltage burns and ultimate death; the product and deadly instruction had been delivered 22 years earlier, so the statute barred the claim). Whether the manufacturer's failure to correct a deadly instruction is a continuing tort would depend upon whether the manufacturer was under a duty to give a post-sale warning. See Patton v. Hutchinson Wil-Rich Manufacturing Co., 253 Kan. 741, 861 P.2d 1299 (1993).

19. E.g., Mayo v. Rouselle Corp., 375 So.2d 449 (Ala.1979) (equal protection); Yarbro v. Hilton Hotels Corp., 655 P.2d 822 (Colo.1982) (equal protection, due process, and state constitutional attacks); Zapata v. Burns, 207 Conn. 496, 542 A.2d 700 (1988) (equal protection attack); Josephine Herring Hicks, The Constitutionality of Statutes of Repose: Federalism Reigns, 38 VAND. L. REV. 627 (1985).

20. "Except in topsy-turvy land you can't die before you are conceived, or be divorced before ever you marry, or harvest a crop never planted, or burn down a house never built, or miss a train running on a non-existent railroad. For substantially similar reasons, it has always heretofore been accepted, as a sort of legal 'axiom,' that a statute of limitations does not begin to run against a cause of action before that cause of action exists, i. e., before a judicial remedy is available to the plaintiff." Frank, J., dissenting in Dincher v. Marlin Firearms Co., 198 F.2d 821, 823 (2d Cir.1952). Another locution of some popularity is that the legislatures which pass such statutes are attempting to declare the bread stale before it is baked. See, e.g, Chase v. Sabin, 445 Mich. 190, 516 N.W.2d 60 (1994).

21. E.g., Hazine v. Montgomery Elevator Co., 176 Ariz. 340, 861 P.2d 625 (1993); Perkins v. Northeastern Log Homes, 808 S.W.2d 809 (Ky.1991); Carson v. Maurer, 120 N.H. 925, 424 A.2d 825, 12 A.L.R.4th 1 (1980); Hardy v. VerMeulen, 32 Ohio St.3d 45, 512 N.E.2d 626 (1987).

22. See Francis McGovern, The Variety, Policy and Constitutionality of Product Liability Statutes of Repose, AM. U. L. REV. 579, 600 ff. (1981).

Similarly they may benefit the public by reducing costs of services or goods from the preferred defendants. Yet these benefits are not paid for by those who receive them but by their victims. (4) The statutes deny a remedy to one who has suffered a wrong or close the doors of courts in violation of a state constitutional provision.

When the statutes seek to abrogate the rights of minors for the benefit of the preferred defendants, courts have frequently found the statutes to be unconstitutional on the ground that they denied equal protection or analogous provisions of state constitution.[23]

§ 220. Starting the Clock in Negligence Claims—Continuing Negligence

When the defendant's act rather than the plaintiff's discovery starts the statute running, the defendant's continuing intentional harms[1] and continuing negligence present a difficult problem. His continuing failure to act can be even more puzzling. For example, suppose that the defendant, by polluting ground water or air, may subject the plaintiff to toxic exposures every day over a long period of time. His original act of dumping toxic materials may have been completed long ago, but in a sense he continues to be at fault because he could clean up the pollution at any time, as recently as yesterday.

A different example involves a relationship between plaintiff and defendant, with the added possibility here that the statute should not begin to

run before the relationship is terminated. The case of the physician who negligently fails to diagnose or treat the patient is in this category, as are lawyer malpractice cases.[2] As long as the patient remains in his care, she could reasonably expect a correction of the diagnosis or treatment, so again, the defendant in a sense continues to be negligent. In such cases it is sometimes possible to say that the statute should not begin to run until the negligent conduct has ceased.

To say the statute should not begin running before the negligent conduct has ceased is not the same as saying that the statute begins running at that point or at the termination of, say, a physician-patient relationship. Fairness dictates that the statute should be tolled until the relationship is terminated, but it does not suggest that termination itself

23. See Green v. Lewis Truck Lines, 315 S.C. 253, 433 S.E.2d 844 (S.C. 1993); Lee v. Gaufin, 867 P.2d 572 (Utah 1993); Whitlow v. Bd. of Education of Kanawha County, 190 W.Va. 223, 438 S.E.2d 15 (1993); but cf., Kumar v. Hall, 262 Ga. 639, 423 S.E.2d 653 (1992) (comatose, brain damaged person had no "standing" to assert unconstitutionality of repose statute because he was in fact represented by a guardian).

§ 220

1. See Cusseaux v. Pickett, 279 N.J.Super. 335, 652 A.2d 789 (1994) (regarding "battered woman syndrome" a tort separate from battery or outrage, seemingly as a means to saying that the attacks counted as a continuing tort so that plaintiff recovers all damages, including damages that accrued from beatings outside the statutory period).

2. § 491 below.

should start the statute running when the plaintiff does not and could not discover the injury until some time after termination.

Major variables. The cases are not obviously consistent with one another. At least two variables seem important. First, the continuing negligence might produce either a series of separately identifiable harms or it might produce only a single indivisible injury. Second, defendants may owe a duty to take affirmative steps to minimize harm to the plaintiff or they may not. It is at least logical to say that when the defendant owes a duty to the plaintiff to act affirmatively and fails to do so, and when that failure produces a single harm, or a series of harms that cannot be segregated one from another, the defendant's negligence is continuing and the statute does not begin to run until some definitive event occurs.[3] Termination of toxic exposure or termination of treatment, or the patient's discovery of the relevant facts, would be examples of such a definitive event. On the other hand, if the continuing negligence causes a series of separate harms, each one actionable, the statute of limitations may begin on each harm separately, so that the plaintiff might be barred as to earlier acts of negligence but not as to later ones.[4]

Continuing treatment rule in medical malpractice. Some courts in medical malpractice cases emphasize continuing treatment of the patient rather than continuing negligence. New York's judicial doctrine of continuous treatment has it that when a physician commits wrongful acts or omissions in the course of a continuous treatment for an original complaint, the plaintiff's claim does not accrue for statute of limitations purposes until the treatment comes to an end.[5] Some other courts have spoken of a continuing relationship rather than continuing treatment, but seemingly with about the same thing in mind.[6]

Some decisions skip the logic and the policy and focus on the words. The Minnesota Court held that when a physician repeatedly found a lump in the patient in examinations over a period of years, but failed to find a malignancy, the patient—who had to undergo a radical mastectomy when the malignancy was finally found—could not rely upon the continuous treatment doctrine. The court seemed to feel that there was

3. Page v. United States, 729 F.2d 818, 822–23 (D.C.Cir.1984) ("it seems unrealistic to regard each prescription of drugs as the cause of a separate injury, or as a separate tortious act triggering a new limitation period"); Meadows v. Union Carbide Corp., 710 F.Supp. 1163 (N.D.Ill.1989).

4. See Hegg v. Hawkeye Tri–County REC, 512 N.W.2d 558 (Iowa 1994) (dangerous stray voltage interfering with dairy herd was a "recurring" tort, damages inflicted during statute of limitations period recoverable but not earlier damages).

5. Borgia v. City of New York, 12 N.Y.2d 151, 237 N.Y.S.2d 319, 187 N.E.2d 777 (1962), aff'd, 15 N.Y.2d 665, 204 N.E.2d 207, 255 N.Y.S.2d 878.

6. Gillette v. Tucker, 67 Ohio St. 106, 65 N.E. 865 (1902) (closely associated with the court's contract or implied contract approach to medical malpractice), overruled, Oliver v. Kaiser Community Health Foundation, 5 Ohio St.3d 111, 449 N.E.2d 438 (1983) (adopting the discovery rule as opposed to termination rule, but not considering whether termination would be more appropriate when discovery occurred during treatment). The termination of the professional relationship might also be be treated as the time for starting the statute when the defendant has been guilty of fraudulent concealment. See Weinberg v. Bess, 638 N.E.2d 841 (Ind.App.1994).

no continuing treatment because the doctor had terminated treatment by telling the patient that there was nothing to treat.[7] A very similar case went the other way in Connecticut. Justice Peters' opinion emphasized that the continuing nature of the professional treatment or relationship was determined by a number of factors, including the subjective understandings of the parties, not merely the doctor's conclusion that no further treatment was needed.[8]

Continuing negligence or tort in medical malpractice. A different version of the general idea puts the emphasis on the professional's continuing negligence rather than continuing treatment. If the physician is under no duty to the plaintiff after his original negligence, or if he is under a duty of care but has not breached it, the date of his original negligence, not the treatment termination date, furnishes the starting date for the statute.[9] As the Illinois Court put it,[10] this doctrine is invoked only upon a showing "(1) that there was a continuous and unbroken course of *negligent* treatment, and (2) that the treatment was so related as to constitute one continuing wrong."[11] The continuing negligence doctrine, articulately or not, assumes a duty to act affirmatively for the benefit of the plaintiff.

Single acts of malpractice. Some courts have said that there is a "single act" exception to the continuing treatment doctrine, but the exception seems logically related to the continuing negligence rather than the continuing treatment doctrine. The exception is said to be that when the defendant commits a single, isolated act of malpractice, as distinct from a course of treatment that counts as malpractice, the doctor's subsequent effort to cure the malpractice does not toll the statute of limitations.[12]

§ 221. Tolling, Grace Periods, and Postponed Accrual

Grounds for tolling or time out. In the case of a true statute of limitations, as distinct from a condition precedent to suit, the statute is tolled or under certain conditions stated in the statute itself or judicially imposed by courts. Typically the statute is tolled because of some

7. Fabio v. Bellomo, 504 N.W.2d 758 (Minn.1993).

8. Factors included "the subjective views of the parties as to whether their relationship had terminated; the length of their relationship; the frequency of their interactions; the nature of the physician's practice; whether the physician had prescribed a course of treatment for or was monitoring the condition of the patient; whether the patient was relying upon the opinion and advice of the physician with regard to a particular injury, illness or medical condition; and whether the patient had begun to consult with another physician concerning the same injury, illness or medical condition." Blanchette v. Barrett, 229 Conn. at 278, 640 A.2d at 85 (1994).

9. E.g., Hoemke v. New York Blood Center, 912 F.2d 550 (2d Cir.1990) (no duty of physician to warn patient that transfused blood might be AIDS-virus tainted, hence the statute of limitations was not "tolled").

10. Cunningham v. Huffman, 154 Ill.2d 398, 182 Ill.Dec. 18, 609 N.E.2d 321 (1993). See Langner v. Simpson, 533 N.W.2d 511 (Iowa 1995) (finding treatment was not a continuous course of negligent treatment in psychiatric malpractice case).

11. Emphasis added.

12. Langner v. Simpson, 533 N.W.2d 511 (Iowa 1995).

supposed impediment to the plaintiff's pursuit of her claim—she is a minor;[1] she is mentally disabled;[2] she is in prison[3] or in the armed forces;[4] some other suit or claim is pending on the same subject matter;[5] or she was compelled to use part of the period in an administrative proceeding as a prerequisite to suit.[6]

Grace periods. Tolling can be thought of as a stay or suspension of the statute, a kind of time-out in which the statutory clock is stopped. Statutes sometimes provide grace periods or time extensions instead. For example, a statute might provide that the clock is not stopped while the plaintiff is a minor, but that she does have additional time for suit or a grace period not granted to adults. Many statutes are now phrased to grant this kind of time extension rather than to recognize true tolling. The time or grace period is specified in the statute.[7]

Postponed accrual. A third form of the general idea is that courts might postpone accrual of the claim or the start of the prescriptive period. This type of added time rule is likely to be highly fact-specific. For example, some courts say they postpone accrual of the claim by a client against a lawyer until the lawyer-client relationship is terminated.[8] The postponed accrual approach, taken literally, not only adds time for the plaintiff but postpones her ability to sue until the claim has accrued; but perhaps courts mean to invoke a tolling rather than a postponed accrual in some of the cases.

Contemporary statutory schemes. Legislatures have now written complex tolling statutes in line with the statutes of repose. Many limitations are severe and include one or more of these provisions:

(1) Tolling for some disabilities may be eliminated altogether. For example, Michigan provides that for medical malpractice injuries to the reproductive systems of a child under thirteen years of age, suit must be brought before the child's fifteenth birthday.[9]

§ 221

1. E.g., N.Y. CPLR § 208.

2. E.g., VA. CODE § 8.01–229. Courts emphasize that practical ability to manage one's affairs precludes a finding of mental disability or "unsound mind." E.g., Helton v. Clements, 832 F.2d 332 (5th Cir.1987).

3. ALA. CODE § 6–2–8; VT. STAT. ANN. § 551 (a) (at the time the cause of action accrues).

4. 50 App. U.S.C.A. § 525 provides in part: "The period of military service shall not be included in computing any period now or hereafter to be limited by any law, regulation, or order for the bringing of any action or proceeding in any court, board, bureau, commission, department, or other agency of government by or against any person in military service or by or against his heirs, executors, administrators, or assigns, whether such cause of action or the right or privilege to institute such action or proceeding shall have accrued prior to or during the period of such service. . . . "

5. Norris v. Bell Helicopter–Textron, Inc., 712 F.2d 171 (5th Cir.1983).

6. New Hampshire Division of Human Services v. Allard, 138 N.H. 604, 644 A.2d 70 (1994).

7. E.g., NY CPLR § 208, providing that one who is an infant or insane when the claim accrues is granted extended times for bringing suit. The amount of extension varies according to factors unrelated to the disability.

8. O'Neill v. Tichy, 19 Cal.App.4th 114, 25 Cal.Rptr.2d 162 (1993); Murphy v. Smith, 411 Mass. 133, 579 N.E.2d 165 (1991); Bjorgen v. Kinsey, 466 N.W.2d 553 (N.D.1991).

9. MICH.COMP.L.ANN. § 600.5851 (8).

(2) Instead of truly tolling the statute of limitations, legislatures may now afford the plaintiff only a short grace period for suit after her disability has terminated. Instead of having two or three years in which to bring suit as provided under a basic limitation period, the minor plaintiff may be allowed only six months or a year to sue after reaching majority.[10]

(3) Legislatures have now often provided that there is an outer limit to tolling just as there is an outer limit to the discovery rule. That means that plaintiffs who suffer injury as very young minors might be barred by the outer limit or repose provision long before they reach maturity.[11]

(4) Legislatures have sometimes set up tolling-repose rules that vary, depending upon the point in the tolling period when injury is inflicted or discovered. For instance, Michigan's provision for reproductive injury to children by medical malpractice provides that for younger minors suit must be brought no later than before the 15th birthday, while for older minors suffering the same injury, the general malpractice statute applies.[12]

Tolling rules have thus become quite complex. Within whatever constitutional constraints courts are willing to impose, legislatures are free to limit tolling as they wish, so statutes of individual states must be consulted.

When the plaintiff claims some form of mental or emotional disability, the questions are likely to be different—what counts as a showing of "unsound mind" or mental disability under the statute. The cases of long-delayed suits for childhood sexual abuse raise the most difficult issues of this kind. They are discussed in a separate section.[13]

Judicial or "equitable" tolling. Courts can impose tolling rules of their own if they are not in conflict with the statutory rules. Due process or equal protection principles may indeed require the court to impose a tolling rule when the statute fails to provide one.[14] In particular cases, courts may also allow the plaintiff to pursue an untimely claim because the defendant in negotiating for a settlement has led the plaintiff to believe that the limitation will not be pleaded as a bar.[15] In such cases courts may say that the defendant is estopped to plead the statute of limitations defense. Estoppel applies only if the plaintiff delayed filing

10. See Mich.Comp.L.Ann. § 600.5851 (1).

11. In Barrio v. San Manuel Div. Hosp. For Magma Copper Co., 143 Ariz. 101, 692 P.2d 280 (1984), a statute barred small children from suits for medical malpractice by the time they were ten years old. This was held unconstitutional under a state constitutional provision. Mich.Comp.L.Ann. § 600.5851 (8) refers the case of a minor above the age of thirteen who suffers reproduction organ injury by medical malpractice to the tender mercies of § 600.5838a, which in turn imposes the special medical malpractice limits and provides that "the claim shall not be commenced later than 6 years after the date of the act or omission that is the basis for the claim," except as provided in 5851(8).

12. Mich.Comp.L.Ann. § 600.5851 (8).

13. § 222.

14. Adamsky v. Buckeye Local School District, 73 Ohio St.3d 360, 653 N.E.2d 212 (1995) held that a two year statute of limitations with no tolling provision discriminated against minors and in so doing violated the state's equal protection provision.

15. E.g., Brown Transport Corp. v. James, 243 Ga. 701, 257 S.E.2d 242 (1979).

suit in reliance upon the defendant's acts or representations.[16] Even without an estoppel, however, courts may decide that, as a matter of equity, the statute should be tolled because of the defendant's unfair conduct that prejudiced the plaintiff's timely suit,[17] or for other equitable reasons.[18]

Fraudulent concealment. The defendant's fraudulent concealment of facts that would reveal plaintiff's injury or her rights can be considered as grounds for equitable tolling of the statute[19] or can be viewed as merely an appealing instance for treating the claim as accruing upon discovery. Either way, if established, the concealment furnishes grounds for extending the plaintiff's time for bringing suit.[20] If fraudulent concealment is viewed as an independent ground for tolling the statute, some courts say the plaintiff must ordinarily prove affirmative acts other than the original negligence itself.[21]

§ 222. Childhood Sexual Abuse Claims

Claims for childhood sexual abuse. After about 1980 the courts began to see a number of claims[1] for childhood[2] sexual abuse. The claims are typically brought by mature adults, thirty or forty years of age or even older. They usually allege that a family member,[3] a pastor or a

16. E.g., Stalberg v. Western Title Insurance Company, 27 Cal.App.4th 925, 32 Cal.Rptr.2d 750 (1994); Witherell v. Weimer, 85 Ill.2d 146, 52 Ill.Dec. 6, 421 N.E.2d 869 (1981). Under the discovery rule, the defendant's misrepresentations may delay discovery, so that, unless the plaintiff is utterly unreasonable in relying upon those representations, the reasonable time for discovery may be postponed on an estoppel theory. See Waage v. Cutter Biological Division of Miles Laboratories, Inc., 926 P.2d 1145 (Alaska 1996).

17. Thus in Bowen v. City of New York, 476 U.S. 467, 106 S.Ct. 2022, 90 L.Ed.2d 462 (1986) a federal limitation period was tolled because the very policy being attacked by the class-action plaintiffs had been a secret policy as well as an illegal one.

18. See Stalberg v. Western Title Insurance Company, 27 Cal.App.4th 925, 32 Cal. Rptr.2d 750 (1994).

19. See Bowen v. City of New York, 476 U.S. 467, 106 S.Ct. 2022, 90 L.Ed.2d 462 (1986); Detwiler v. Bristol–Myers Squibb Co., 884 F.Supp. 117 (S.D.N.Y.1995).

20. See Woods v. Schmitt, 439 N.W.2d 855 (Iowa 1989) (distinguishing fraudulent concealment from discovery because the former requires active misconduct, although silence will suffice in the case of a fiduciary); Logerquist v. Danforth, 188 Ariz. 16, 932 P.2d 281 (Ct.App. 1996) (emphasizing that concealment and discovery are separate bases for delaying the start of the clock, but recognizing that "evidence of fraudulent concealment may affect analysis and application of the discovery rule").

21. Langner v. Simpson, 533 N.W.2d 511 (Iowa 1995).

§ 222

1. Most of the claims appear to fit within the definition of a battery. The "consent" of the minor would not ordinarily furnish any defense for several more than sufficient reasons. Occasionally the claim is pursued, at least in part, as a claim of infliction of emotional distress.

2. Adult claims for sexual harassment or discrimination coupled with a post traumatic stress syndrome or other effects that prevent immediate presentation of a claim are not considered in this section. See Ulibarri v. Gerstenberger, 178 Ariz. 151, 871 P.2d 698 (Ct.App. 1993) (claim that psychiatrist indulged in sexual relations with patient, then hypnotically removed her memory, analogy drawn to child sexual exploitation); Wilson v. Zapata Off–Shore Co., 939 F.2d 260 (5th Cir.1991) (rejecting the claim; "If Wilson was harassed, she was certainly aware of it").

3. E.g., Fager v. Hundt, 610 N.E.2d 246 (Ind.1993) (father charged with abusing female child); Leonard v. England, 115 N.C.App. 103, 445 S.E.2d 50 (1994) (grandmother, uncle charged with abusing female child); Ault v. Jasko, 70 Ohio St.3d 114, 637

priest,[4] a physician[5] or therapist,[6] a teacher[7] or other person in a position that combined authority and trust[8] sexually abused the plaintiff when the plaintiff was quite young. Sometimes the victim is abused in an institution.[9] Women are predominantly the claimants, but men have also sued.[10]

The abuse is frequently alleged to have terminated many years earlier. Suit has been delayed so long in these cases that the tolling provisions for minors are often of no aid to the plaintiff. Consequently, nothing else appearing, such suits are dismissed on orthodox grounds.[11]

Repressed memory and the discovery rule. In many cases the claim is that the plaintiff's suffering leads to repression or other psychological reaction that causes her to lose all conscious memory of the abuse before she has become an adult. Although "repression" is controversial among psychologists,[12] when the claim of repression is accepted as a fact, the plaintiff's recovery of memory at a much later time can be analogized to discovery of an injury. A few courts have rejected any such analysis,[13] but most of the courts that have considered it have thought the discovery rule could be applied,[14] provided the proven facts warranted it.[15]

This liberal view may be undercut in some cases, however. Occasion-

N.E.2d 870 (1994) (father charged with abusing female child); C. v. C., 114 D.L.R.4th 1512 (Ont. Ct. 1994) (same).

4. Lovelace v. Keohane, 831 P.2d 624 (Okl.1992); Fontaine v. Roman Catholic Church of Archdiocese of New Orleans, 625 So.2d 548 (La.App.1993)

5. Doe v. Cherwitz, 518 N.W.2d 362 (Iowa 1994).

6. Riley v. Presnell, 409 Mass. 239, 565 N.E.2d 780 (1991) (adult victim, discovery rule applied).

7. Meiers–Post v. Schafer, 170 Mich. App. 174, 427 N.W.2d 606 (1988).

8. Snyder v. Boy Scouts of America, Inc., 205 Cal.App.3d 1318, 253 Cal.Rptr. 156 (1988) (boy scout leader, facts alleged now covered by statute); Doe v. First United Methodist Church, 68 Ohio St.3d 531, 629 N.E.2d 402 (1994) (choir director associated with school and church).

9. Callahan v. State, 464 N.W.2d 268 (Iowa 1990) (small child, "deaf and cerebral palsied" abused in state school over period of years).

10. E.g., O'Neal v. Division of Family Services, 821 P.2d 1139 (Utah 1991).

11. E.g., Snyder v. Boy Scouts of America, Inc., 205 Cal.App.3d 1318, 253 Cal.Rptr. 156 (1988) (now covered by statute); McAfee v. Cole, 637 A.2d 463 (Me.1994); Doe v. First United Methodist Church, 68 Ohio St.3d 531, 629 N.E.2d 402 (1994).

12. See ELIZABETH LOFTUS AND KATHERINE KETCHAM, THE MYTH OF REPRESSED MEMORY: FALSE MEMORIES AND ALLEGATIONS OF SEXUAL ABUSE (1994); Elizabeth Loftus, The Reality of Repressed Memories, 48 AM. PSYCHOLOGIST 518 (May 1993).

13. Doe v. Doe, 973 F.2d 237 (4th Cir. 1992) (forecasting North Carolina law); Lemmerman v. Fealk, 449 Mich. 56, 534 N.W.2d 695 (1995); Shippen v. Parrott, 506 N.W.2d 82 (S.D.1993) (rejecting discovery rule).

14. Johnson v. Johnson, 701 F.Supp. 1363 (N.D.Ill.1988); Logerquist v. Danforth, 188 Ariz. 16, 932 P.2d 281 (1996); Mary D. v. John D., 216 Cal.App.3d 285, 264 Cal. Rptr. 633, (Cal. App. 1989), remanded, 275 Cal.Rptr. 380, 800 P.2d 858 (1990); McCollum v. D'Arcy, 138 N.H. 285, 638 A.2d 797 (1994); Ault v. Jasko, 70 Ohio St.3d 114, 637 N.E.2d 870 (1994); Olsen v. Hooley, 865 P.2d 1345 (Utah 1993); cf. Tyson v. Tyson, 107 Wash.2d 72, 727 P.2d 226 (1986) (no memory is not enough by itself, but might be if there is corroborating evidence, now governed by a Washington statute). Some courts apply the discovery rule without stating the exact facts required for its use. Osland v. Osland, 442 N.W.2d 907 (N.D. 1989).

15. Cf. Rigazio v. Archdiocese of Louisville, 853 S.W.2d 295 (Ky.Ct.App.1993) (plaintiff knew of abuse, then repressed his knowledge, then recovered it; discovery rule did not assist him).

ally courts adopt a narrower variation in the discovery rule[16] or impose a special proof requirement, as when they demand special corroborating evidence that the sexual abuse took place.[17] The renewed scrutiny of expert testimony since 1993[18] suggests that some courts may reject the whole idea of repression unless experts in the field come to some better agreement about its existence.[19]

Memory intact but other psychological impediments to suit. Sometimes plaintiffs have admitted that they had always retained the memory of the defendant's course of abuse, but have argued that they had not been aware that the abuse was a cause of their present emotional problems until some recent discovery. Although some judicial decisions[20] and some statutes[21] would apply the discovery rule when the plaintiff is aware of the abuse but not aware of its connection to her emotional injury, others have held if memory is retained, the discovery rule has no application.[22] A similar case is one in which the plaintiff retained full memory of the abuse and also knew it caused emotional harm, but was psychologically unable to bring suit. In that case, too, the court refused

16. Fager v. Hundt, 610 N.E.2d 246 (Ind.1993) adopts a complicated rule. First, the victim of childhood sexual abuse is deemed to discover whatever her parent or guardian discovered or should have discovered. Second, the first rule does not apply when the action is brought against a parent or guardian who has "fraudulently concealed" the abuse. So the plaintiff must first establish the concealment, then establish that she brought suit within the period allowed after she discovered or should have discovered the injury.

17. Olsen v. Hooley, 865 P.2d 1345 (Utah 1993) (similar acts committed by the defendant would be one example).

18. See Daubert v. Merrell Dow Pharmaceuticals, Inc., 509 U.S. 579, 113 S.Ct. 2786, 125 L.Ed.2d 469 (1993); Kumho Tire Co., Ltd. v. Carmichael, 526 U.S. 137, 119 S.Ct. 1167, 143 L.Ed.2d 238 (1999) . .

19. Cf. Doe v. Maskell, 342 Md. 684, 679 A.2d 1087 (1996) (rejecting the idea of repression on the basis of scientific testimony in the particular case). In Borawick v. Shay, 68 F.3d 597 (2d Cir.1995) the court excluded the proposed testimony of hypnotically induced "memories", thereby undercutting the plaintiff's claim.

20. Dunlea v. Dappen, 83 Hawai'i 28, 924 P.2d 196 (1996); Hammer v. Hammer, 142 Wis.2d 257, 418 N.W.2d 23 (Wis.App. 1987); C. v. C., 114 D.L.R.4th 1512 (Ont. Ct. 1994) (plaintiff had not "made a connection between [her father's] abuse and her injuries, until a time within the prescriptive period; action permitted); cf. Riley v. Presnell, 409 Mass. 239, 565 N.E.2d 780 (1991) (patient of therapist did not realize for years that his emotional difficulties were the result of inappropriate treated that involved sexual activity with the therapist and use of drugs). See also Held v. State Farm Insurance Co., 610 So.2d 1017 (La. App.1992) (claim by a sexually abused daughter whose post traumatic stress syndrome "prevented her from acting [to sue] until she knew [from therapy] she was completely innocent and her father was solely responsible" was not barred).

21. N.J. Stat. Ann. § 2A:61B–1 ("the cause of action shall accrue at the time of reasonable discovery of the injury and its causal relationship to the act of sexual abuse"); N.M. Stats. Ann. § 37–1–30 ("knew or had reason to know, as established by competent medical or psychological testimony, that an injury was caused by childhood sexual abuse").

22. DeRose v. Carswell, 196 Cal.App.3d 1011, 242 Cal.Rptr. 368 (1987); E.W. v. D.C.H., 231 Mont. 481, 754 P.2d 817 (1988); Doe v. First United Methodist Church, 68 Ohio St.3d 531, 539, 629 N.E.2d 402, 409 (1994) ("Although appellant may not have discovered the full extent of his psychological injuries until September 1989, the fact that appellant was aware upon reaching the age of majority that he had been sexually abused by Masten was sufficient to trigger the commencement of the statute of limitations for assault and battery"). Subsequent statutes probably affect some of these deci-

to use the discovery rule to permit suit.[23]

Tolling for unsound mind or mental disability. Statutes of limitation are usually tolled when the plaintiff suffers a mental disability, variously described in the statutes as insanity, unsound mind, or incompetence. When the plaintiff is able to show that she was mentally disabled as a result of the alleged sexual abuse or otherwise, the tolling provision may permit her to proceed with the suit.[24] But courts have often insisted that the statute cannot be tolled under the mental disability provision merely because the plaintiff has repressed painful memories or suffered post-traumatic stress disorder.[25] Instead, the statute is usually tolled for mental disability only when the plaintiff was unable to manage her own affairs. If she managed her life acceptably before discovery of the childhood abuse, she was not mentally incompetent and the statute is not tolled for the mental disability.[26]

Statutory provisions. A number of states have now enacted statutes addressed to delayed claims of childhood sexual abuse, permitting the victim to sue within a specified time after "discovery" of the abuse or the injury or emotional condition resulting from it.[27] At the same time the statutes impose limits. For instance, the statute may be limited to cases of childhood sexual abuse[28] and may thus deny relief to an adult victim who suffers the same psychological loss of memory.[29] The legislature's adoption of a statute covering the subject might also operate to bar or limit common law development, although Iowa has held that its common law discovery rule can be applied to relieve the alleged victim of sexual abuse even though she does not meet the statutory rules.[30]

sions. See CA. CODE CIV. PRO. § 340.1; MONT. CODE ANN. § 27–2–216.

23. O'Neal v. Division of Family Services, 821 P.2d 1139 (Utah 1991).

24. See Leonard v. England, 115 N.C.App. 103, 445 S.E.2d 50 (1994) (where a physician provided an affidavit that the plaintiff had lacked sufficient capacity to make decisions about her legal rights until a time within the limitations period).; Kelly v. Marcantonio, 678 A.2d 873 (R.I.1996) (insanity based upon repressed memory is a factual question, not a question of law; the trial judge must determine "whether the alleged repressed recollection in a particular case is sufficiently relevant, reliable, and scientifically and/or medically established so as to constitute "unsound mind," thereby tolling the action limitation period").

25. Smith v. Smith, 830 F.2d 11 (2d Cir.1987) (N.Y. law, post traumatic stress is not "insanity" under tolling provisions); Florez v. Sargeant, 185 Ariz. 521, 917 P.2d 250 (1996) (ability to manage own affairs standard); Doe v. Maskell, 342 Md. 684, 679 A.2d 1087 (1996) (ability to manage own affairs standard); Travis v. Ziter, 681 So.2d 1348 (Ala.1996) (repressed memory is not insanity).

26. Florez v. Sargeant, 185 Ariz. 521, 917 P.2d 250 (1996); Olsen v. Hooley, 865 P.2d 1345 (Utah 1993).

27. ALASKA STATS. § 09.55.650; CAL CODE OF CIV. PROC. § 340.1; CONN. GEN. STATS. ANN. § 52–577d (17 years from age of majority is maximum time); IOWA CODE ANN. § 614.8A; KAN. STAT. ANN. § 60–523; MASS. GEN. L. ANN. c. 260, § 4C; 14 ME. REV. STAT. ANN. § 752–C; MONT. CODE ANN. § 27–2–216; N.J. STAT. ANN. § 2A:61B–1; N.M. STATS. ANN. § 37–1–30; Ore. Rev. Stats. § 12.117 (child abuse, including sexual abuse of child); R.I. GEN. L. ANN. § 9–1–51; REV. CODE WASH. ANN. § 4.16.340. Distinguish statutes addressed to sexual abuse by therapists, which may also cover some child abuse cases. See, e.g., WIS. STATS. ANN. § 893.585.

28. All of the statutes cited in n. 27 apply only to childhood sexual abuse.

29. Courts have regarded the discovery rule appropriate in the case of adult victims if the fact support the claim that memory was repressed. Olsen v. Hooley, 865 P.2d 1345 (Utah 1993); Riley v. Presnell, 409 Mass. 239, 565 N.E.2d 780 (1991).

30. Doe v. Cherwitz, 518 N.W.2d 362 (Iowa 1994).

The memory problem. One of the usual arguments in favor of a statute of limitations is that it is needed because evidence grows "stale" over time, to the possible prejudice of the defendant. The child sexual abuse cases, however, present different problems of memory, ones that the statute of limitations does not deal with very well. Although every plaintiff may sue in good faith, not every memory is necessarily accurate. It is not so much that the evidence for the defendant is stale as that the plaintiff's evidence may itself be untrustworthy for reasons not associated with the lapse of time.

The statute of limitations copes only with extreme cases of delay. To keep courts open to the victimized plaintiffs while protecting innocent defendants, it might be better to require a preliminary screening. The literature and press reports suggest that some therapists actually plant false memories.[31] On the other hand, it may be that experts can be found to trivialize what is in fact a serious social problem and a grave personal injustice to the victims.[32] A preliminary procedure to screen out some cases, or at least a vigilant judge who uses pre-trial procedures with care, might furnish a better solution than the automatic bar of the statute of limitations.

§ 223. Accrued Claims with Latent Harm

When the plaintiff is exposed to a toxin that causes small harm but that may cause very serious harm in the future, the statute of limitations is a potential problem. The plaintiff must sue within the statutory period for the small harm done and also (under rules against splitting a cause of action) for all future harm. The trouble is that the plaintiff may be unable to show a likelihood of future damages. If she sues at all, res judicata rules traditionally prevented a later suit brought after injury actually resulted. If she did not sue, the statute of limitations would eventually run because once she suffered some degree of harm, her cause of action accrued.

In *Hagerty v. L & L Marine Services, Inc.*,[1] the plaintiff was thoroughly drenched with a known carcinogen, dripolene. He knew that the substance was carcinogenic and he showered off, but he had some immediate symptoms including cramping, dizziness, and stinging in his extremities. His claim for tort was complete because he suffered damages. But, although cancer was a distinct possibility in his future, he did

31. Elizabeth F. Loftus, The Reality of Repressed Memories, 48 AM.PSYCHOLOGIST 518 (May 1993) is a balanced, knowledgeable, and concerned presentation by one of the foremost scientific students of memory (and testimony). Loftus insists that child sexual abuse is real and prevalent, but that allegations cannot be properly accepted uncritically. She documents some forms of "therapy" in which the therapist actually "plants" the whole idea of sexual abuse and some cases that will strike lawyers as based on almost childlike naiveté on the part of therapists.

32. At least some victim-advocates think so. See Underwager v. Salter, 22 F.3d 730 (7th Cir.1994).

§ 223

1. Hagerty v. L & L Marine Services, Inc., 788 F.2d 315 (5th Cir.1986), modified on other grounds, 797 F.2d 256 (1986).

not have cancer at that time. He could not postpone suit to await events, since his claim had accrued.

In situations like this, several possible options are available, perhaps none very satisfactory. One might be to permit the plaintiff to sue within the time permitted by the statute of limitations and to retain jurisdiction over the case for a long period, with or without medical monitoring damages.[2] This solution runs counter to established habits and might defeat the purpose of the statute of limitations.

A second option is to allow the plaintiff damages for his fear of future cancer, but nothing for the cancer itself should it occur because only one claim arises from a single set of facts.[3]

A third option is to allow the plaintiff to recover for the increased risk of harm, or put the other way around, for the value of his lost chance of a healthy life. If he had a 40% chance of getting cancer, this approach might allow him to recover 40% of the damages that would be appropriate if he actually suffered cancer. Although some courts have approved lost chance recoveries in certain cases,[4] Hagerty's case is different from the typical lost chance case. In most of the lost chance cases, no future event can make causation or loss clear.[5] In Hagerty's case, however, the future will tell whether Hagerty suffers from cancer. For this reason, it would be possible to purchase insurance against the risk of future cancer and one court suggested that the best solution might be to award an insurance policy to the plaintiff in such cases.[6]

To the *Hagerty* court it seemed wrong to bar the plaintiff from recovery for a devastating disease caused by the defendant merely because he has suffered some minor harm much earlier. It also seemed wrong to allow a recovery for a cancer he might never have.[7] So the court concluded that Hagerty could recover now for injuries suffered so far and for his emotional harm based on fear of the cancer but that if cancer occurred later, he should be permitted to bring a separate suit for that.[8]

Hagerty's proposed solution is not unique. Something like the *Hagerty* approach has even been sanctioned by the Supreme Court in antitrust cases.[9] In the toxic torts setting, some courts have endorsed it

2. On medical monitoring damages and funds, see § 377.

3. Fear of future harm is a recoverable element of damages once a tort is established. See § 311.

4. See §§ 178 & 179.

5. For instance, if the defendant physician fails to correctly diagnose cancer in January but does diagnose it in September, the delay is likely to reduce the patient's chances of survival, but if the patient dies, no one can be sure whether the physician's failure actually made a difference or not.

6. Hicks v. Hines, 826 F.2d 1543, 1545, 88 A.L.R.Fed. 501 (6th Cir. 1987).

7. See also Eagle–Picher Industries, Inc. v. Cox, 481 So.2d 517, 525 (Fla.App.1985).

8. "[T]he disease of cancer should be treated as a separate cause of action for all purposes. .... A prior but distinct disease, though the tortfeasor may have paid reparations, should not affect the cause of action and damages for the subsequent disease." 788 F.2d at 320.

9. "In antitrust and treble-damage actions, refusal to award future profits as too speculative is equivalent to holding that no cause of action has yet accrued for any but those damages already suffered. In these instances, the cause of action for future damages, if they ever occur, will accrue only on the date they are suffered; thereafter the

with enthusiasm.[10] A much-cited Florida decision took a similar view, saying that if the plaintiff's exposure to asbestos had not yet caused cancer, the plaintiff would be permitted to sue later when and if cancer occurred.[11] The idea is that the plaintiff suffers two distinct injuries from the defendant's wrongdoing, not merely one injury with latent or late-developing harm. In such a case, the claim for the second injury will not be barred either by a judgment in the first suit or by the plaintiff's failure to sue on the first injury within the limitation period.[12] Although some courts might reject such a view,[13] it follows the approach generally taken in release cases. In those cases the courts hold that a broadly worded release bars claims for unknown damages resulting from a known injury but not claims for an unknown injury that neither the plaintiff nor the defendant believed was involved.[14]

TOPIC E. COMPLIANCE WITH STATUTE

§ 224. Compliance with Statute

General rule: not a defense. The fact that the defendant has complied with a statute is not ordinarily in itself a defense. The trier of fact may find that, although the defendant complied with the statutory directives, he should have done even more to attain reasonable levels of safety.[1] The point is easy to see when it comes to speed limits. Although the speed limit may be 60 mph, under some circumstances reasonable care requires a speed of no more than 30 mph.

Admissible as evidence. On the other hand, the defendant's compliance with a statute that thoroughly regulates the behavior in question tends to support the defendant's argument that he is not negligent. So the defendant's compliance may be evidence for the trier to consider on the negligence issue even though it is not a defense.[2]

plaintiff may sue to recover them at any time within four years from the date they were inflicted." Zenith Radio Corp. v. Hazeltine Research Inc., 401 U.S. 321, 339, 91 S.Ct. 795, 806, 28 L.Ed.2d 77 (1971)

10. Ayers v. Township of Jackson, 106 N.J. 557, 525 A.2d 287

11. Eagle–Picher Industries, Inc. v. Cox, 481 So.2d 517 (Fla.App.1985). The court noted that the rule against splitting a cause of action was correlative with the rule that allowed the plaintiff to recover all (future) damages in one suit. If the plaintiff could not recover the future harm damages, then the rule against splitting the cause of action had no application.

12. Miller v. Armstrong World Industries, Inc., 817 P.2d 111 (Colo.1991) (discovery of pleural thickening from asbestos exposure does not trigger the statute as to a claim for asbestosis if asbestosis is a distinct disease; whether the two are distinct diseases are questions of fact); Wilber v. Owens-Corning Fiberglass Corporation, 476 N.W.2d 74, 78 (Iowa 1991); Smith v. Bethlehem Steel Corp., 303 Md. 213, 492 A.2d 1286 (1985); Marinari v. Asbestos Corporation, Ltd., 417 Pa.Super. 440, 445, 612 A.2d 1021, 1023 (1992); cf. Capital Holding Corporation v. Bailey, 873 S.W.2d 187 (Ky. 1994) (claim for distress resulting from exposure to toxic substance would not prevent a later suit for negligently causing asbestos injury should such an injury eventuate); Larson v. Johns–Manville Sales Corp., 427 Moch. 301, 399 N.W.2d 1 (1987) (separate start for asbestosis and cancer resulting from asbestosis).

13. Pecorino v. Raymark Industries, 763 S.W.2d 561 (Tex.App.1988). Note, Claim Preclusion in Modern Latent Disease Cases: A Proposal for Allowing Second Suits. 103 HARV. L. REV. 1989 (1990) approves the general idea but proposes some limits on damages that would benefit defendants.

14. 2 DAN B. DOBBS, LAW OF REMEDIES § 11.9 (2d ed. 1993).

§ 224

1. Restatement § 288 C.

Bases for the rules. These rules are a product of our understanding about how statutes work and how they are meant to work. Most statutes and even regulations are relatively permanent and relatively abstract; they cannot take into account the particular concerns of individual cases. They aim at minimum standards but are not meant to establish the outer limits of the defendant's safety responsibilities. When it comes to technological standards, they are quickly outdated with no guarantee that the legislature or regulators will have time or information necessary to update them. Beyond that, many statutes are written in response to lobbying efforts of the industry they purport to regulate, and they are not likely to represent a balanced attempt by neutral parties to achieve appropriate safety. For these reasons and many others, including the practical problems of interpreting and applying statutes, compliance with statute cannot ordinarily count as a defense.[3]

Exceptional cases. Even so, legislators or regulators can expressly provide that the compliance with a particular statute is a complete defense. And what legislators could provide in express terms, they can also imply. In rare cases, courts may conclude that in spite of the general rule to the contrary, compliance with statutory standards is a complete defense, either because the statute itself so implies or because the court concludes as a matter of law that on the facts of the case compliance necessarily shows reasonable care.[4]

Federal preemption. In addition, federal statutes are sometimes construed to preempt or displace state law, including state tort law. When this occurs, the defendant's compliance with a preemptive federal statute leaves the plaintiff nowhere to turn. The effect is that compliance with a federal preemptive statute is a complete defense. For example, federal regulations govern the speed of railroad trains under some circumstances. These regulations have been construed to preempt state law. So the plaintiff injured by a fast-moving train is defeated when the railroad can show that the speed of the train complied with the limits set by the federal government, regardless whether the speed was unreasonable in the given locality.[5] Preemption has often been a major issue in the field of products liability.[6]

2. Ake v. General Motors Corp., 942 F.Supp. 869 (W.D.N.Y.1996); Miner v. Long Island Lighting Co., 40 N.Y.2d 372, 353 N.E.2d 805, 386 N.Y.S.2d 842 (1976); Zacher v. Budd Company, 396 N.W.2d 122 (S.D. 1986).

3. See Teresa Moran Schwartz, The Role of Federal Safety Regulations in Products Liability Actions, 41 Vand. L. Rev. 1121 (1988).

4. Ramirez v. Plough, Inc., 6 Cal.4th 539, 25 Cal.Rptr.2d 97, 863 P.2d 167 (1993) (statute requiring product warnings in English implied that warnings need not be in Spanish); Montgomery v. Royal Motel, 98 Nev. 240, 645 P.2d 968 (1982).

5. See CSX Transportation v. Easterwood, 507 U.S. 658, 113 S.Ct. 1732, 123 L.Ed.2d 387 (1993).

6. For example, a federal statute requires that cigarette packages must contain a specified health warning. The statute also provides that states may not impose any additional requirement about how cigarettes are advertised or promoted. A plaintiff who claimed that the warning was inadequate because it failed to warn of addiction found that claim preempted because the

When the federal statute does not preempt state law, then it furnishes no automatic defense, but as in other cases, the defendant's compliance is admissible as some evidence tending to show that he is not negligent.[7]

tobacco companies had complied with the federal warning requirement. Cipollone v. Liggett Group, Inc., 505 U.S. 504, 112 S.Ct. 2608, 120 L.Ed.2d 407 (1992). The plaintiff in that case could claim negligent testing as opposed to a negligent warning, however. On products preemption, see § 373.

7. See Doyle v. Volkswagenwerk Aktiengesellschaft, 267 Ga. 574, 481 S.E.2d 518 (1997).

2. Immunities and Limited or Special Duties Affecting Liability for Negligence

a. The Concepts

CHAPTER 12

IMMUNITIES AND LIMITED DUTIES: THE CONCEPTS

§ 225. Immunity and Limited Duty

The chapters immediately following this one deal with a number of situations in which courts have protected defendants from liability in spite of the defendants' unreasonably risky behavior that has caused physical harm[1] to the plaintiff. In these cases, courts use one of two closely related concepts to shield defendants.

Limited or no duty. One concept is that the defendant owed the plaintiff no duty of care, or, more commonly, that the defendant owed a duty measured by such an undemanding standard that the defendant simply did not breach the duty by his risky behavior. For example, in some cases, the defendant's only duty is not to cause harm by willful or reckless behavior.[2] That means that the defendant's ordinary negligence is not a tort at all. And if the defendant owed no duty, he is assuredly not liable.

Immunity. The second concept is that the defendant in some cases is immune from suit or alternatively immune from tort liability. The term immunity is commonly used to refer to the special protections sometimes accorded to public entities and officers,[3] to family members,[4] and to charities.[5] Lawyers and judges almost always believe that if there are two legal words in the vocabulary, they mean two different things, so they believe that no-duty rules and immunity rules are different in some important way.[6] Sometimes, however, the difference between the two lies in how we are likely to feel about the rules rather than in their ultimate

§ 225

1. Emotional harm is separately treated in Chapter 20.

2. § 232.

3. Chapter 15.

4. §§ 279 & 280.

5. § 282.

6. With some immunities, the burden is formally upon the defendant to establish the immunity, while the burden is upon the plaintiff to establish a duty of care. See Frank L. Maraist and Thomas C. Galligan, Jr., The Employer's Tort Immunity: A Case Study in Post-modern Immunity, 57 LA. L. REV. 467 (1997). But that difference breaks down when the immunity is regarded as jurisdictional, as it is when the federal government is sued, and also when the immunity is established by a simple undisputed fact, such as the defendant's status as a charity or other protected class.

legal effect on the plaintiff's claim. The plaintiff cannot prevail against a defendant who is under no duty and equally cannot prevail against a defendant who is immune and to that extent the two concepts are the same.[7]

Immunities vs. privileges; immunities as bright-line rules. Immunities do differ from no-duty rules in degree. They tend to be—or at least judges want them to be—bright line rules that can intercept the claim early in the litigation and without evaluation of many facts or adjudications on the merits. Immunities also differ from privileges. Immunities tend to shield defendants because of their legal status, while privileges tend to shield defendants because their actions were justified in the particular case. Privileges raise fault issues and go to the merits of the case, while immunities may be accorded even to wrongdoers. The line between status and justification is blurred, however, when immunity turns on the defendant's power to exercise discretion and when it turns on the defendant's good faith.

Examples. When a governmental entity or its officers are protected from liability because the officer's act was "discretionary," judges speak of immunity. However, in some such cases the exercise of discretion bears a resemblance to a defendant's use of force in self-defense. We might in retrospect think the occasion called for no defense, but we also think that the defendant is justified in acting in defense if he reasonably believed he was attacked. We relieve such a defendant of liability because in an important way we think he is justified. The discretionary immunity sometimes looks more like this kind of justification or privilege than a true immunity. In contrast, charitable immunity is a good example of a true immunity that does not resemble privilege at all. Where the rule of charitable immunity still applies, it simply bars suit against a negligent charity. It does not resemble a defense based upon justification, because we do not think charities are justified in negligently fostering child abusers or operating upon the wrong patients.

Immunity from suit. Courts sometimes emphasize the bright-line quality of immunity by saying that an immunity is an immunity from suit, not merely an immunity from liability. The point of that saying is to assert that the value of the immunity is to save the defendant from the costs and uncertainties of a trial and hence to claim that courts can rightly avoid considering the merits of the individual case. Some immunities are even considered to be "jurisdictional," perhaps meaning that the judge should raise the immunity issue even if the defendant failed to do so.[8]

Role of judges. No-duty rules, like immunities, tend to avoid the adjudication of particular cases in favor of broad rules covering large

7. See Weinberg v. Dinger, 106 N.J. 469, 524 A.2d 366 (1987) (a determination that the defendant owes no duty of care "is a judicially-created tort immunity").

8. E.g., Carlyle v. United States, Dept. of the Army, 674 F.2d 554 (6th Cir.1982) (under Federal Tort Claims Act, a function of statutory language and the convention that federal court jurisdiction is in a sense limited).

classes of cases. The similarities between no-duty rules and immunity rules are so great that the two terms can often be used interchangeably and this book will use the term duty to include immunities in many instances. The most significant identity of limited or no-duty rules and immunity rules is that they are determined by judges or legislatures, not by juries. That is an enormous contrast with the negligence issue, which is a jury determination whenever reasonable people can differ.

§ 226. Duty: The Role of Judges

Duty required. Lawyers and judges agree that duty is the foundation of all liability for negligence. The defendant is not liable to the plaintiff unless the defendant owed the plaintiff a duty and breached it, causing harm. Yet lawyers and judges use the term duty in a variety of different ways, not always with the same meaning. Sometimes they use duty to refer to a general standard or obligation. At other times they use duty as a conclusion about whether the defendant's particular act or omission should be actionable, irrespective of any general standard.

Duty as dealing with rules capable of general application. The most coherent way of using the term duty states a rule of law rather than an analysis of the facts of particular cases. For example, when a court says that people in general are under no duty to take affirmative actions to help others,[1] the court is stating a rule of law that is capable of being applied in a wide variety of reasonably identifiable cases. When a court says that landowners owe to trespassers only the duty to avoid wilful injury, it is stating a general standard that is a rule of law. The rules so stated may or may not be good rules, and they may or may not have exceptions, but they are clearly rules; they do not turn on analysis of the facts of particular cases.

Distinguishing the issue of breach or negligence. In contrast, courts could state an infinite number of duties if they spoke in highly particular terms–a duty to watch out of for children, a duty to look when you back your car, a duty to suture the incision after a medical operation, and so on without limit. All such statements are readily comprehensible but they use the term duty to state conclusions about the facts of particular cases, not as a general standard. The general standard or duty, varied in some relationships, is the duty of reasonable care. When a court says there is a duty to look when you back your car, it is applying the general reasonable care duty, not creating a new and different duty. Similarly, if a court says that the owner of a barge in a crowded and busy harbor has a duty to keep someone on board to deal with dangers, the court seems to be deciding something much more specific than a general duty or obligation. It seems to be deciding the negligence or breach of duty issue.[2] The judge's conclusion that a bargee should be kept on board at a particular time and place is the product of reasoning from legal rules but is not itself a rule of law capable of legitimate generalization; it is an

§ 226

1. Chapter 21.

2. United States v. Carroll Towing Co., 159 F.2d 169 (2nd Cir.1947).

adjudication of fault in a particular case, an adjudication of the breach or negligence issue.

The same is true when the judge's conclusion is reversed. A statement that defendant owed no duty to keep a lookout for pet mice in the roadway could of course be generalized after a fashion to cover all other cases of small pets in the highway. But the point such a statement makes is less about rules than about analysis of the facts. That analysis leads to the conclusion that ordinary care does not require a driver to spot small pets on the highway. In such a case, the words may be the words of duty but the process of decision is the process of determining what counts as ordinary care under the circumstances.

Judge-jury roles. A part of the problem with "duty" is that it masks a serious legal process issue. It is usually said that judges decide duty issues, while juries decide the facts and make the evaluations necessary to determine whether or not the defendant was negligent. Yet all the issues in a negligence case—negligence itself,[3] cause in fact,[4] and proximate cause,[5] even contributory negligence[6]—can be phrased as questions of duty. The judge who wishes to take over the case from the jury can easily express the issue as one of duty. Ideally, therefore, a duty can be cast as a rule of law rather than as a decision about whether the particular actions of a particular defendant should be actionable.

Duty issues. The main issues about duty go to its existence, its measure, and its scope.[7] Did the defendant owe any duty to the plaintiff? If defendant owed a duty, what was that duty? Put differently, what standard of care does that duty demand or what interest is the defendant obliged to protect? And finally, a question that is often addressed as one of proximate cause, what was the scope of the duty? Did it include the risks involved in the case before the court?

§ 227. Existence of a Duty

Among strangers—those who are in no special relationship that may affect duties owed—the default rule is that everyone owes a duty of reasonable care to others to avoid physical harms.[1] This rule is displaced in favor or more limited duties in a number of instances. Beyond that, judges may even say that the defendant in some cases owes "no duty" at all. "No duty" is a convenient expression, but defendants almost always owe some kind of duty, although not necessarily a duty of due care.

3. See below, this section.

4. See § 179 (discussing duty to maximize plaintiff's chances of survival leading to liability for loss of a chance without proving ordinary but-for causation).

5. See § 253 below.

6. As where the defendant owes the plaintiff a duty to protect her from her own fault, thus eliminating the bar of contributory negligence. See § 200.

7. Prosser used the term a little differently. He wanted to use the term duty to raise the existence question, but not the question of "what duty" or its measure. See PROSSER & KEETON § 53, p. 356.

§ 227

1. Thus "[i]n the usual run of cases, a general duty to avoid negligence is assumed, and there is no need for the court to undertake detailed analysis of precedent and policy." Hamilton v. Accu-Tek, 62 F.Supp.2d 802 (1999).

When courts say the defendant owed no duty, they usually mean only that the defendant owed no duty *that was breached* or that he owed no duty *that was relevant on the facts*.

For example, the orthodox view is that the defendant is free to watch an unsighted person step in front of a car, even if, with no inconvenience or danger to himself, the defendant could have called out a warning.[2] The defendant, it is said, has no duty to act affirmatively for the benefit of others in the absence of some special relationship. Whether this is a good rule or not, it does not literally mean that the defendant owed *no* duty whatever to the unsighted person. It means only that he owed no duty to do a particular thing, to act affirmatively. The defendant would still owe the unsighted person a duty not to negligently run her down.

Nevertheless, within its realm, "no duty" is the right expression . The rule of no duty to affirmatively assist others applies to a whole category of cases and is very largely divorced from the analysis of particular facts of particular cases. It is a rule that can be applied to a wide variety of cases in which the defendant took no action at all. Such a rule is thus a rule of law; it is within the province of judges to determine, not juries. Whether or not the rule is a good one, it can be appropriately expressed as a rule that, when no exception applies, the defendant is under no duty to take affirmative steps to protect the plaintiff.

Rules declaring that no duty exists can easily be made too broad or too narrow. Because they are rules of law, not decisions about particular cases, they cover all cases in the category to which they are addressed. They are expressions of "global" policy rather than evaluations of specific facts of the case.[3] Consequently, no-duty rules should be invoked only when all cases they cover fall substantially within the policy that frees the defendant of liability. On the other hand, no-duty rules should be rules of law having the quality of generality. Consequently they should not be merely masks for decisions in particular cases. If the court means to say that the defendant was not negligent under the facts of the case, the no-duty language is apt to create confusion.

An example of the difficulty of over- and under-breadth arises in a number of cases involving landowners who fail to trim too-exuberant foliage at the edges of their land. In these cases, drivers are injured in intersection collisions because the intersection is hidden or obscured by the landowner's vegetation. Many of the cases say that the landowner owes no duty to trim the foliage.[4] Quite possibly many courts mean just what they say: regardless how dangerous the intersection, regardless how cheap and easy it is to trim the foliage, the owner simply does not owe a duty of reasonable care and is thus free to be negligent. If this is

2. § 314.

3. See Stephen D. Sugarman, 31 VALPARAISO U. L. REV. 833, 843 (1997) (a clear and lively explanation of the difference between no duty and no breach analyses).

4. See William J. Appel, Annotation, Liability of Private Landowner for Vegetation Obscuring View at Highway or Street Intersection, 69 A.L.R.4th 1092 (1990).

what courts mean, the rule may be a true no-duty rule, but it may be too broad because in some cases it would relieve a landowner of an almost cost-free task even when, quite foreseeably, lives are at stake.

Possibly some courts are really using the no-duty locution as a convenient but misleading way to decide the *breach* of duty issue—the negligence issue—instead of leaving that issue to the jury. They may think that, at least on the facts of the case, the burden on the landowners would outweigh the safety benefits for drivers. But if this is what courts are doing in the foliage cases, it looks as if they might be deciding issues about costs, benefits, and foreseeability that are normally jury questions. Worse, they might be deciding those cases without the benefit of appropriate evidence about the costs and benefits.

Two thoughtful judges who addressed this problem rejected the no-duty rule. They said defendants owed a duty of ordinary care and the question was whether the duty was breached. Justice Feldman in effect refused to let trial judges make rules of law that defined specific duties (or freedoms) to act in particular ways. Instead, he insisted that judges must follow the general rule of law that imposed a due care standard. Juries would evaluate particular conduct like "not cutting bushes" against the reasonable prudent person standard of care.[5] Justice Linde similarly rejected the idea that you could make any general rule of law more specific than the reasonable person standard. You need facts or data to determine how risky the intersection might be and similarly to determine costs of clearing it. These facts will differ from case to case, and consequently the issue is not to be decided by a rule of law covering all intersections, at all times, and at all costs.[6] These cases do not impose liability; they impose the ordinary prudent person standard for determining liability.

Courts often find it useful or necessary to limit or eliminate the defendant's duty of care by a rule of law. But in many cases, courts may be using the language of duty with all its breadth for what is or should be essentially a negligence question to be decided case by case rather than by a rule of law.

§ 228. The Nature, Measure or Standard of the Duty

As already suggested, it is convenient in many cases to say that the defendant owed no duty of care, although in most cases the defendant definitely owes a duty of some kind and the question is whether about the measure of the duty, its scope, and its application to the facts.

The general duty of care, the duty of the reasonable person under the circumstances, could conceivably be applied in all cases, leaving it to

5. Coburn v. City of Tucson, 143 Ariz. 50, 691 P.2d 1078 (1984). See also Martinez v. Woodmar IV Condominiums Homeowners Association, Inc., 189 Ariz. 206, 941 P.2d 218 (1997) ("danger neither creates nor eradicates duty; it only indicates what conduct may be reasonable to fulfill the duty" and "we disapprove of attempts to equate the concepts of duty with specific details of conduct").

6. Donaca v. Curry County, 303 Or. 30, 734 P.2d 1339 (1987).

the jury to determine whether, on the facts, the defendant breached that duty by his negligence. However, courts in fact impose different standards of duty, ranging from almost no duty at all—a duty to avoid intentional or wanton injury, for example—to a very strict duty—a duty to use the utmost care,[1] or even to avoid injury altogether.[2]

The general duty of reasonable care arises when the harm complained of is physical harm to person or property and the parties are strangers, that is, when the parties are not in a special relationship and they have not undertaken special obligations. When the harm is different, when the parties are in a special relationship, or when they have tacitly agreed or been led to expect a different kind or level of duty, however, courts may prescribe or recognize different obligations. Focusing on the status, relationship or undertakings of the parties, courts traditionally held that landowners owed only the duty to not wantonly or intentionally injure trespassers and licensees;[3] that health care providers owed the duty of care established by their peers, which was sometimes of the highest quality but sometimes woefully unsafe[4]; that governmental entities,[5] charities,[6] and parents[7] were immune to suits by citizens, beneficiaries, or children. They also held that no one owed a duty of care to a fetus[8] or a duty of care to avoid killing a person[9] or causing her emotional harm.[10] Nor was a duty of reasonable care owed to take any affirmative steps to aid a person in danger.[11] Courts have gradually altered the limited duty rules in most of these categories, but they have not abolished them in favor of a duty of reasonable care.

The task in most of the instances named above has become to formulate the duty, its measure, standard, or scope. Sometimes it is expressed as a lowered standard of care, as where the defendant need only avoid wanton injury. Sometimes the limited duty is structured as a no-duty rule coupled with a duty of ordinary care on very specific facts. Sometimes the limited duty appears in a whole set of rules. In the case of emotional harms negligently inflicted without accompanying physical injury, for instance, courts often specify in detail the kind of harm that is actionable and the specific facts necessary before liability will be imposed. In almost no instance, not even in the case of government immunities, is the defendant without some residual obligation of care,

§ 228

1. Common carriers such as public busses, railroads and even elevators traditionally owed the duty of utmost care, Markwell v. Whinery's Real Estate, Inc., 869 P.2d 840 (Okla.1994), or highest care to their passengers. Doser v. Interstate Power Co., 173 N.W.2d 556 (Iowa 1970). Some jurisdictions have rejected this old rule in favor of a reasonable care standard. Pazmino v. Washington Metropolitan Area Transit Authority, 638 A.2d 677 (D.C.App.1994).

2. On strict liability, see Chapters 23–25. Traditional libel law could also impose strict liability. See Chapter 34.

3. §§ 232 & 233.

4. Chapter 14.

5. Chapter 15.

6. § 282.

7. Chapter 16.

8. Chapter 19.

9. Chapter 20.

10. Chapter 26.

11. Chapter 21.

however circumscribed it may be. However, as already indicated, courts nevertheless address negligence issues by speaking of duty in some cases.

§ 229. Determining the Existence and Measure of Duty

How do courts go about determining whether to impose a duty of care and when one is imposed, how do they decide on its measure or scope? As courts have said, the existence of a duty is not a discoverable fact of nature.[1] No legal concept is. To say that the defendant is under a legal duty is merely a conclusion that the defendant should be subject to liability in the type of case in question. One of Prosser's most quoted passages had it that "duty is not sacrosanct in itself, but is only an expression of the sum total of those considerations of policy which lead the law to say that the plaintiff is entitled to protection."[2] Or as the Colorado Court put it, "the question of whether a duty should be imposed in a particular case is essentially one of fairness under contemporary standards—whether reasonable persons would recognize a duty and agree that it exists."[3] These are not assertions that duty is unimportant. They are assertions that duty should be constructed by courts from building blocks of policy and justice.[4]

By about 1960 courts were beginning to formulate some considerations of policy relevant to establishing or rejecting a duty of care. The California Court said it would consider (1) the extent to which the transaction was intended to affect the plaintiff, (2) the foreseeability of harm to him, (3) the degree of certainty that the plaintiff suffered injury, (4) the closeness of the connection between the defendant's conduct and the injury suffered, (5) the moral blame attached to the defendant's conduct, (6) the policy of preventing future harm by deterrence, and (7) administrative factors, including the feasibility of administering a rule that imposed a duty.[5] To this list can be added (8) the relationship of the parties[6] and the customs to which they jointly subscribe.[7]

§ 229

1. See Tarasoff v. Regents of the University of California, 17 Cal.3d 425, 434, 551 P.2d 334, 342, 131 Cal.Rptr. 14, 22, 83 A.L.R.3d 1166 (1976) ("legal duties are not discoverable facts of nature, but merely conclusory expressions that, in cases of a particular type, liability should be imposed for damage done").

2. Prosser & Keeton, § 54, p. 358.

3. Casebolt v. Cowan, 829 P.2d 352, 356 (Colo.1992) (quoting).

4. If Prosser's language is taken to mean that duty is constructed merely from policy rather than from justice or conceptions of rights, that is too narrow. Cf. John C.P. Goldberg & Benjamin C. Zipursky, The Moral of McPherson, 146 U. of Pa. L. Rev. 1733 (1998) (a sustained attack on Prosser's views).

5. Amaya v. Home Ice, Fuel & Supply Co., 59 Cal.2d 295, 379 P.2d 513, 29 Cal. Rptr. 33 (1963), overruled in Dillon v. Legg, 68 Cal.2d 728, 441 P.2d 912, 69 Cal.Rptr. 72, 29 A.L.R.3d 1316 (1968) on its precise holding but not on its methodology. *Dillon* itself has been modified on its substantive point, without affecting the *Amaya* factors. Most of the *Amaya* factors were derived from Biakanja v. Irving, 49 Cal.2d 647, 320 P.2d 16, 65 A.L.R.2d 1358 (1958), not a personal injury case. Biakanja in turn derived them from treatises by Prosser and Harper & James.

6. See, e.g., Lough by Lough v. Rolla Women's Clinic, Inc., 866 S.W.2d 851 (Mo. 1993). Relationship of the parties is so pervasively important in determining existence and measure of duty that it often goes unmentioned, but it appears in most of the chapters immediately following.

7. See Richard Epstein, The Path to the T.J. Hooper: The Theory and History of

These factors are so numerous and so broadly stated that they can lead to almost any conclusion. They have now become somewhat mechanical bases for structuring judicial opinions in the direction judges feel appropriate. More importantly, however, they are mainly the very same factors that determine the negligence question. Yet when the question is phrased as a question of duty, the judge, not the jury, will be the decision maker, even on such quintessential jury issues as foreseeability.[8]

The first factor—the extent to which the transaction was intended to affect the plaintiff—made sense where it first arose, a case in which the plaintiff suffered a purely financial injury as a result of dealings between two other people.[9] That factor has been carried forward without much care into personal injury litigation. The seventh factor, which appeals to the judgment of courts about feasibility and convenience in the legal system, is also quite distinct from ordinary concerns of juries. The remaining factors, however, are matters a jury would normally consider in determining negligence. Foreseeability of harm, of course, is critical on the negligence issue as well as on the proximate cause issue. Closeness of connection seems to be a variation on the foreseeability factor. Moral blame is a very broad term, but it must surely include the kind of blame fixed in finding that the defendant was negligent.

Given the similarity between the duty factors decided by the judge and the negligence factors decided by the jury, it may be appropriate to wonder whether judges are in a position to shape refined limited duty rules without taking over the jury role.

Part of the problem is that courts rightly want to have rules of law, such as the duty rules, but also rightly want to leave room for adjudication of each case on its own merits. One of those goals is sacrificed when duty rules describe highly specific obligations rather than general standards of care. Rules of law, because they necessarily cover whole categories of cases, may wrongly treat a lot of diverse cases alike, as where all landowners are exempted from reasonable care in cutting back obstructive foliage when only a few would find it burdensome to do so.[10] The reasonable, prudent person standard, on the other hand, is broad enough to permit the trier to take many unique details into account, so triers can thus avoid treating different cases as if they were the same. But that standard is also broad enough to permit different juries to obtain radically different results in similar or identical cases.

No doubt courts hope that some limited duty rules would promote more appropriate uniformity of treatment for similar cases. Perhaps that

Custom in the Law of Tort, 21 J. Leg. Studies 1 (1992) (especially helpful on the question of who is to be bound by a custom).

8. Thus the California Court flatly announced that "Foreseeability, when analyzed to determine the existence or scope of a duty, is a question of law to be decided by the court." Ann M. v. Pacific Plaza Shopping Center, 6 Cal.4th 666, 678, 25 Cal. Rptr.2d 137, 145, 863 P.2d 207, 215 (1993).

9. Biakanja v. Irving, 49 Cal.2d 647, 320 P.2d 16, 65 A.L.R.2d 1358 (1958).

10. Discussed in § 227.

is what courts had in mind when they held, in effect, that the plaintiff was under no duty to wear a seatbelt and could not, therefore, be charged with contributory negligence in failing to do so. Given a population resistant to wearing restraints, most juries probably would have found no contributory negligence anyway. But those that did find contributory negligence might have done so, not because the merits of seatbelts were different in the particular cases, but because of bias or extraneous factors.[11] A rule of law on the specific point, even a wrong rule, might avoid occasional discriminatory treatment that could result from case by case adjudication under the rubric of comparative negligence.

Nevertheless, specific rules of law that narrow the defendant's duty give the defendant freedom to be negligent in the sense that he can take unreasonable risks. The general duty of reasonable care under the circumstances suffices in the great majority of instances and preserves an appropriate arena for adjudication of individual cases. Such a general duty of reasonable care is by definition not burdensome. Nor does it leave juries free to bring in irrational verdicts, because the judge remains free to direct a verdict when, on the facts of a particular case, reasonable people could not differ. In the great majority of injury cases, the elaborate efforts to describe particular duties are both unnecessary and undesirable.

§ 230. Scope of Duty

Almost every issue in a negligence case could be decided by judges under the rubric of duty. When courts decide that the negligent defendant's conduct was a cause in fact but not a proximate cause of the plaintiff's harm, an alternative approach would be to say that the defendant owed the plaintiff no duty with respect to the risk involved. (It would be just as plausible and maybe more enlightening to say that the defendant was not negligent toward the plaintiff with respect to the risk involved.)

Many writers and some courts favor approaching scope of risk issues involved in proximate or legal cause decisions through the language of duty. The great advantage of doing so is that the confusions engendered by the use of causal language might be avoided. Among highly knowledgeable legal professionals, the causal language is quickly shrugged off once it is recognized that the problem is about the scope of foreseeable risk, not about causation. However, few if any judges can specialize in the diverse legal issues that confront them. They cannot all be up-to-date experts in tort theory. Consequently, when judges confront a problem already labeled as a proximate cause problem, the label alone is likely to have at least some subliminal effects that steer analysis in the wrong direction.

But as the preceding sections have suggested, duty issues themselves are slippery chameleons. Moreover, to cast an issue in terms of duty is to

11. See § 205.

provide another subliminal suggestion—namely that the decision is to be made by judges rather than juries.

The famous debate between Judges Cardozo and Andrews in *Palsgraf v. Long Island Railroad*[1] touched this point. Mrs. Palsgraf was unexpectedly injured when the defendant knocked a package from the hands of an intending passenger on its railroad. To everyone's surprise, the package contained fireworks, which exploded and toppled a scale some distance away, injuring Mrs. Palsgraf in the process. Judge Andrews argued that the railroad owed a duty to everyone and that the issue was one of proximate cause. Cardozo argued that duties are relative and that a duty was owed only to those who are foreseeably at risk. Since Mrs. Palsgraf was not foreseeably at risk by reason of the railroad's acts, it owed no duty to her. Ever since that time, it has been possible to think of scope of risk problems as problems about the scope of the duty rather than as problems of proximate cause.

However, the same idea could be understood in terms of negligence or breach of duty rather than in terms of the existence of a duty. The railroad was not negligent toward Mrs. Palsgraf at all; that is so clear that reasonable people could not differ. Cardozo himself made the same point: "Relatively to her it was not negligence at all."

Because many proximate cause issues (under whatever name) are fact-specific and do not lend themselves to category-wide rules, it may be reasonable to continue the usual professional terminology. Nevertheless, it must be recognized that in some decisions, courts do make rules of law about the scope of the defendant's duty, rules that have nothing to do with the foreseeability issue in proximate cause cases. The approach taken in this book, then, is to consider scope of liability issues under the traditional proximate cause terminology when the issue turns on the scope of the foreseeable risk. In that kind of case, the issue is for the jury whenever reasonable people can differ. On the other hand, when the court attempts to generate a categorical rule not based primarily upon foreseeability in the particular case, the topic is considered with the limited duty cases in the following chapters.

§ 230

1. Palsgraf v. Long Island Railroad, 248 N.Y. 339, 162 N.E. 99 (1928). See §§ 182 & 184.

*

b. Status or Relationship of the Parties Affecting Duties

Chapter 13

Owners and Occupiers of Land

Topic A. Duties to Those Outside the Premises

§ 231. Duties to Those Outside the Premises

Landowners—a term used in this chapter to include possessors and those who act in their right—owe a duty to neighboring landowners not to create what the law calls a nuisance, that is, a serious interference with their use and enjoyment of land by pollution or the like. Similarly, owners and occupiers must not create a public nuisance by blocking or interfering with use of public streets or ways. On the whole, nuisance law addresses risks to the use and enjoyment and economic rights rather than risks of physical harm to individuals, and it is considered in a later chapter.[1]

Natural Conditions on the Land

General rule. Courts traditionally drew a major distinction between natural and artificial conditions on the land. The usual statement is that occupiers of land are under no duty to use care to alter the land's natural condition, even when those conditions are dangerous to persons on public ways.[2] So for example, if naturally occurring surface waters[3] or insects escape[4] from the land and cause harm, the landowner is not responsible unless his affirmative acts caused or contributed to those evils.

Even more clearly, the landowner ordinarily has no obligation to remove or make safe naturally occurring snow or ice from sidewalks adjacent to but not a part of his land,[5] although he may be subject to

§ 231

1. Chapter 38.

2. Restatement § 363.

3. Ken Cowden Chevrolet, Inc. v. Corts, 112 Mich.App. 570, 316 N.W.2d 259 (1982) (land in natural condition blocked view and caused erosion, no liability for nuisance). The landowner who does nothing about surface waters that flow from his land and potentially cause harm seems to be protected under any of the three rules carried in the muddied currents of water law. Justice Mosk succinctly described the three water law rules in Keys v. Romley, 64 Cal.2d 396, 412 P.2d 529, 50 Cal.Rptr. 273 (1966). Water law, with its distinctions among surface waters, stream waters, percolating waters, and ponded waters, is a specialized subject.

4. Merriam v. McConnell, 31 Ill.App.2d 241, 175 N.E.2d 293, 83 A.L.R.2d 931 (1961) (trees that hosted insects that then migrated to plaintiff's land not a nuisance).

5. Even when an ordinance compels removal, it is usually interpreted as imposing a duty to assist the city, not a duty to individuals who may be injured. E.g., Lopatkovich v. City of Tiffin, 28 Ohio St.3d 204, 503 N.E.2d 154 (1986).

liability for actively making matters worse, for example by artificially and unreasonably draining harmful waters from his own land. It seems to follow that the landowner need not alter existing conditions on roads or lands around his own, even to make entrance to his own business safer for customers.[6]

Falling trees. A number of cases have arisen in which naturally growing[7] trees have become rotten and have fallen upon persons using the adjacent highway. Some writers view the no-duty rule as overkill. Their idea is that courts made a broad no-duty ruling against all liability when in reality they were motivated by narrower concerns: the burden of inspecting trees and other natural conditions was too great for absent landowners and those with large rural holdings.[8] The logic of this view is that the no-duty rule might have yielded sound results as late at the 18th century or so when vast tracts of land were held, but should be exchanged for a duty of reasonable care today. Indeed, a rule of reasonable care would work well, because it would not demand inspections of thousands of potentially falling trees, and perhaps would require no inspection of any tree at all until there was some reason to believe it might become a danger.[9]

Those who adopted the overkill view, however, did not propose a reasonable care alternative. Instead, as reflected in the Restatement,[10] they proposed to say that in urban but only in urban areas, landowners owed a duty to use reasonable care to prevent harm to users of the highway from trees on the land. Because some rural landowners might actually have only a few trees and some urban landowners many, this position also suffered from generalization when evaluation of the facts would have done very well instead.[11]

6. See Davis v. Westwood Group, 420 Mass. 739, 652 N.E.2d 567 (1995) (placement of parking lot for business across a dangerous highway; not actionable); cf. Ferreira v. Strack, 636 A.2d 682 (R.I.1994) (church had no duty to control dangerous highway between parking lot and church building). A landowner may have some special relationship to the plaintiff, however, that generates some duty of protection outside the land. See Chapter 21.

7. If the trees have been planted, they may come under the rule for artificial rather than natural conditions. See Carver v. Salt River Valley Water Users' Assn., 104 Ariz. 513, 456 P.2d 371 (1969)

8. See Prosser & Keeton § 57, p. 390.

9. See Restatement § 363, cmt. e.

10. Restatement § 363 (2).

11. See Taylor v. Olsen, 282 Or. 343, 578 P.2d 779 (1978) ("The extent of his responsibility either to inspect his trees ... cannot be defined simply by categorizing his land as 'urban' or 'rural.' " ... "[I]t is not a matter of zoning or of city boundaries but of actual conditions"). Carver v. Salt River Valley Water Users' Assn., 8 Ariz. App. 386, 446 P.2d 492 (1968), reversed on other grounds and with a contrary dictum, 104 Ariz. 513, 456 P.2d 371 (1969) ("[W]e see little reason why a possessor of land with a row of trees adjacent to a heavily traveled highway should be automatically relieved of liability merely because the locality is to be labeled as 'rural,' regardless of how great the risk and how small the effort needed to eliminate it. Where reasonable men can differ as to whether the risk is unreasonable in the light of the utility of the use being served by the risk, then the question of whether a possessor has exercised reasonable care should be left to a jury'). In addition, the landowner's own business operations as a logger or otherwise might entail inspection so that the marginal cost of that operation for safety purposes would approach zero. See Taylor v. Olsen, supra."

A little authority follows this line of thought by imposing a duty of reasonable care in all cases, in effect rejecting the distinction between artificial and natural conditions.[12] The California Court also took this view with respect to the danger of landslides that might harm neighbors.[13] The duty of reasonable care does not imply extensive liability. Even if his land is not heavily wooded, a landowner may have no reason at all to suspect that a tree is dangerous and no reason to inspect for rot.[14] And of course he would not be liable for failure to inspect if inspection would have revealed nothing.[15]

Much more authority has followed the urban-rural distinction.[16] In this view, the landowner who is not on notice that the tree is dangerous is under no duty to use care with respect to natural rural trees but must use care with respect to natural urban trees. This view turns the courts' attention to the classification of lands as urban or rural rather than to an adjudication of actual negligence.[17]

The debate about falling trees and limbs is mostly about a duty of inspection. If the landowner actually knows that a tree has become a danger to those on the highway, he is obliged to use reasonable care to deal with the risk whether he is urban, rural, or in-between.[18] The debate itself is not always on target, however, because a duty of reasonable care would not invariably require inspection in any event.

Vegetation obscuring vision of highway users. In the case of vegetation on the land that obscures highway dangers and thus indirectly contributes to a collision and injury, awareness of risk has not been a serious consideration. A number of courts have simply said the landowner has no duty to cut vegetation that is dangerous as an impediment to highway users' clear vision.[19] The other view is that no reason counsels departure from the duty of ordinary care, so that the question of the landowner's negligence will go to the jury if reasonable people can differ.[20]

12. The best discussion is Justice Linde's in Taylor v. Olsen, 282 Or. 343, 578 P.2d 779 (1978); cf. Carver v. Salt River Valley Water Users' Assn., 8 Ariz.App. 386, 446 P.2d 492 (1968), reversed on other grounds, 104 Ariz. 513, 456 P.2d 371 (1969). Statutes or ordinances may also impose the duty. See Harris v. Village of East Hills, 41 N.Y.2d 446, 362 N.E.2d 243, 393 N.Y.S.2d 691, 95 A.L.R.3d 772 (1977).

13. Sprecher v. Adamson Companies, 30 Cal.3d 358, 178 Cal.Rptr. 783, 636 P.2d 1121 (1981).

14. See Restatement § 363, cmt. e.

15. Carver v. Salt River Valley Water Users' Assn., 104 Ariz. 513, 456 P.2d 371 (1969); Taylor v. Olsen, 282 Or. 343, 578 P.2d 779 (1978).

16. E.g., Valinet v. Eskew, 574 N.E.2d 283 (Ind.1991);Staples v. Duell, 494 S.E.2d 639, 329 S.C. 503 (Ct.App.1997).

17. Hensley v. Montgomery County, 25 Md.App. 361, 334 A.2d 542, 94 A.L.R.3d 1148 (1975) (concluding that suburban forest land was more like rural land).

18. See Lemon v. Edwards, 344 S.W.2d 822 (Ky.1961).

19. E.g., Driggers v. Locke, 323 Ark. 63, 913 S.W.2d 269 (1996); see William J. Appel, Annotation, Liability of Private Landowner for Vegetation Obscuring View at Highway or Street Intersection, 69 A.L.R.4th 1092 (1990).

20. See the opinions in Coburn v. City of Tucson, 143 Ariz. 50, 691 P.2d 1078 (1984); Donaca v. Curry County, 303 Or. 30, 734 P.2d 1339 (1987), discussed in § 227.

Active Conduct and Artificial Conditions

Reasonable care owed to those outside the land. Nuisance aside, the occupier of land must use reasonable care for the safety of those outside the land to prevent direct harm resulting from his affirmative activities on the land.[21] For instance, if he negligently allows building materials to fall on persons outside the land, he is subject to liability.[22] The same applies to those persons such as building contractors who are on the land in the right of an occupier. Similarly, except under open range rules, the owner must use care to prevent horses or cattle from escaping onto the highway where they might cause collisions.[23] The occupier must also use care with respect to artificial conditions on the land that risk injury to those outside it. If structures on his land cause water to accumulate on the walk, he must use reasonable care to avoid injury to pedestrians who may slip on the ice it forms.[24] When legitimate activity on the land does not itself cause immediate physical harm but merely distracts motorists on nearby highways with resulting collisions and injuries, courts may assign the entire responsibility to the motorists and none of the landowner.[25]

Reasonable care owed to foreseeable strays from the highway. The land occupier owes not only a duty of reasonable care to protect those on the public way from activities and condition on his land, but also a duty of care to those who foreseeably stray from the road onto the land itself and are injured by a condition such as an excavation that was put there after the road was built. The duty of care is owed if the landowner should foresee that a highway user would inadvertently enter the land even if she is exercising due care.[26]

What this says is that the risk must be one to travelers who are reasonably careful. It does not say that the plaintiff must herself be without fault in the particular instance if the risk would also be one to reasonably careful people. The fault of the actual plaintiff would thus become a matter of contributory negligence, not a matter of the defendant's duty.[27] It is easy to miss the distinction, and some authority holds

21. Restatement § 371.

22. Cf. Bradford v. Universal Construction Co., Inc., 644 So.2d 864 (Ala.1994) (plywood sheet blown by heavy wind).

23. Roberts v. Weber & Sons, Co., 248 Neb. 243, 533 N.W.2d 664 (1995) (applying res ipsa loquitur).

24. Pritchard v. Mabrey, 358 Mass. 137, 260 N.E.2d 712 (1970).

25. See Largosa v. Ford Motor Co., 303 Ill.App.3d 751, 237 Ill.Dec. 179, 708 N.E.2d 1219 (1999) (landowner-operating of commercial bungee jumping business adjacent to the highway not responsible for accidents resulting when motorists gaped at jumpers).

26. Restatement § 368. Cf. Indiana Limestone Co. v. Staggs, 672 N.E.2d 1377 (Ind.App.1996) ("The foreseeability of a deviation from the roadway depends not upon whether the deviation is intentional or inadvertent, but whether the deviation is a normal incident of travel—that is, whether the condition of the roadway is such that a vehicle is likely to deviate from it in the ordinary course of travel and come in contact with the excavation")

27. Cf. Lee v. Chicago Transit Authority, 152 Ill.2d 432, 605 N.E.2d 493, 178 Ill.Dec. 699 (1992) (electrified third rail at level crossing 6.5 feet from sidewalk; defendant owed a duty of reasonable care to foreseeable trespassers, purportedly under Restatement § 337, and the fact that the decedent was severely intoxicated went only to the issue of contributory negligence, not duty).

that the defendant is under no duty to one who is actually at fault, even if the land's condition was a threat to persons who were faultless as well.[28] But no matter what, harm to someone must be foreseeable and on that point the danger's distance from the road is highly relevant. A utility pole at the road's edge is a great danger even when it is obvious, while a hidden excavation 100 yards from the road is not.[29]

The occupier's duty of care may extend in some cases to persons who intentionally enter the land either out of necessity[30] or because the land appears to be a part of the public way, so long as risk to such persons is foreseeable.[31]

Topic B. Duties to Those on the Premises

§ 232. Duties to Trespassers

The Trespasser Category

Categories. Traditional common law reasoned extensively through classification and categories. All entrants upon land were classified as trespasser, licensees, or invitees, classifications that abounded with subtleties and subclassifications.[1]The possessor of land and those who stood in his shoes[2] owed different duties to each class, although the duty to trespassers and licensees was closely similar. Similar rules were applied to those who used the defendant's personal property.[3] Most courts

28. See City of McAllen v. De La Garza, 898 S.W.2d 809 (Tex.1995).

29. See Restatement § 368, cmt. h. In many of the utility pole cases, the pole may in fact have been placed within the highway right of way, although at a distance from the paved portion of the highway. Cases are often unclear on this point. Cf. Memphis Light, Gas and Water Div. v. Goss, 494 S.W.2d 766 (1973) (nine inches outside the paved portion). The pole cases, as distinct from most excavation cases, may be affected by governmental regulations.

30. See Restatement § 368, cmt f. (detour necessitated by obstruction in the road, provided the detour is to be expected as ordinary travel).

31. Aluminum Company of American v. Walden, 230 Ark. 337, 322 S.W.2d 696 (1959); Jasper v. Chicago Great Western Ry. 248 Iowa 1286, 84 N.W.2d 21 (1957) (plaintiff on railroad track at what appeared to be a public crossing); Restatement § 367.

§ 232

1. Some courts subdivide the traditional categories. E.g., Ryals v. United States Steel Corporation, 562 So.2d 192 (Ala.1990) ("mere" trespassers and those who enter with intent to commit a crime); Baltimore Gas and Elec. Co. v. Flippo, 348 Md. 680, 705 A.2d 1144 (1998) (noting licensee by invitation and bare licensee subcategories).

2. A possessor of land who could take advantage of the limited duty rules included persons in actual occupancy and exercising control, see Restatement § 328 E. Contractors creating conditions on the land on behalf of the landowner enjoyed the same benefits, see Restatement §§ 383–384, as did members of the possessor's household. Restatement § 382. Persons with nonpossessory interests in the land, like easement holders, have sometimes been brought under the same rules, sometimes not. Acton v. Wilmington & N.R.R., 407 A.2d 204 (Del. 1979) (easement holder shares possessor's immunity); Humphrey v. Twin States Gas & Elec. Co., 100 Vt. 414, 139 A. 440 (1927) (does not). A trespasser who injures another trespasser does not enjoy the immunity, either. Mt. Zion State Bank & Trust v. Consolidated Communications, Inc., 169 Ill.2d 110, 214 Ill.Dec. 156, 660 N.E.2d 863 (1995).

3. Payne v. M. Greenberg Const., 130 Ariz. 338, 636 P.2d 116 (Ariz.App.1981); Olivier v. Snowden, 426 S.W.2d 545 (Tex. 1968). The protective rules do not apply when the possessor of a chattel abandons it.

continue to apply this schematic approach to adjudication, but a substantial number have now rejected it in favor of the duty of ordinary care, at least in some of the categories.[4]

Who is within the trespasser category. The trespassers category excluded some children under limited circumstances,[5] but otherwise included all those who might be sued for trespass because they intentionally entered the land. The category was even broader: it included any person entering the land without the owner's express or implied consent.[6] So a person who was carried unconscious onto the land by others might be a trespasser for the purpose of determining the landowner's duty of care.[7] Persons who were invitees or licensees in one portion of the premises might become trespassers when they entered areas to which no permission extended.[8]

Under these rules, trespassers could be quite different one from another. One might be a burglar, vandal, or a helpless drunk; another might be a boy walking on a railroad trestle, a motorcyclist who strikes a hidden cable, or a neighbor who takes an uninvited shortcut across the lawn.

The "General Rule"

No duty of reasonable care to trespassers. The landowner owed no duty of reasonable care to trespassers.[9] Instead, the duty was merely not to cause intentional injury, to set a trap, or to cause wanton injury.[10] The landowner was thus free to maintain dangerous conditions like excavations and also free to carry on dangerous operations such as high speed trains. When a trespasser was harmed, adjudication did not require a

Baltimore Gas & Elec. Co. v. Flippo, 348 Md. 680, 705 A.2d 1144 (1998) refused to apply trespasser rules to a boy climbing a tree where he had a right to be and whose only alleged trespass was that he touched the defendant's electrical wire, which caused his injury. The court distinguished cases in which the plaintiff trespassed upon the defendant's pole and was then shocked by touching a wire, since in that case the plaintiff had no right to be upon pole. Where the categories have been abolished for real property, they are presumably abolished for personal property as well. Estate of Strever v. Cline, 278 Mont. 165, 924 P.2d 666 (1996). *Guest statutes*: at one time many states passed statutes limiting the duty of care owed by a vehicle driver to "guests" in the car, so that the driver was liable only for wanton misconduct or in some states gross negligence. As with the analogous rules for landowners, this limited duty generated much litigation over status, in contrast to litigation over the driver's fault. Some states held the statutes unconstitutional; others repealed them. Few remain.

4. § 237.

5. § 236.

6. See, e.g., Lacy v. Sutton Place Condominium Association, Inc., 684 A.2d 390 (D.C.App.1996).

7. Copeland v. Baltimore & O.R.R., 416 A.2d 1 (D.C.App.1980); cf. Frederick v. Philadelphia Rapid Transit Co., 337 Pa. 136, 10 A.2d 576 (1940) (one who fell on track was treated as if he were a trespasser).

8. Boyette v. Trans World Airlines, Inc., 954 S.W.2d 350 (Mo.App.1997) (passenger in airport terminal building became a trespasser when he entered a trash compactor).

9. Sometimes expressed in the saying that trespassers take the land at their own risk and as they find it. See Gaboury v. Ireland Road Grace Brethern, Inc., 446 N.E.2d 1310 (Ind.1983).

10. E.g., Ryals v. United States Steel Corporation, 562 So.2d 192 (Ala.1990); Lacy v. Sutton Place Condominium Association, Inc., 684 A.2d 390 (D.C.App.1996); Morrell v. Peed Brothers, Inc., 218 Ga.App. 656, 462 S.E.2d 798 (1995); Gladon v. Greater Cleveland Regional Transit Authority, 75 Ohio St.3d 312, 662 N.E.2d 287 (1996).

balance of risks and utilities, since the possessor was under no duty. Unless an exception applied, he was not even required to keep a lookout while he was carrying on dangerous activities on the land.[11]

The rule severely limiting duties of care to trespassers was slightly less harsh that it might sound because in many cases to which it would apply, the landowner probably was not negligent even under an ordinary care standard. In addition, the rule has been moderated substantially both by way of definitions and by way of exceptions.

Discovered or Known Trespasser Exception

Duty to known trespasser. Even a trespasser, however, is not an outlaw.[12] In most states, once the landowner has discovered the trespasser's presence on the land in circumstances that suggest he might encounter danger, the landowner comes under a duty of ordinary care.[13] Under the Restatement's view, foreseeability of a trespasser is not enough; the landowner must know or have reason to know that he is actually present.[14]

Some jurists regard the known trespasser rule as an exception to the general willful-wanton standard.[15] Others think that it is an application of the general willful and wanton test because failure to exercise ordinary care after discovery of a human being in danger is regarded as willful and wanton misconduct for which landowners are always liable.[16] Either way, the possessor is under a duty of reasonable care once he knows or is on notice of both the trespasser's presence and the impending danger.

Breach of the duty. With the duty of care so established, the plaintiff still has the burden of showing that it was violated by failure to act as a reasonable person under the circumstances. In many cases a warning from the landowner that the trespasser is about to walk into danger suffices to fulfill his duty of care. If the danger is one that the trespasser could reasonably be expected to see and avoid, even a warning may not be required.

11. See Wolf v. National Railroad Passenger Corp., 697 A.2d 1082 (R.I.1997).

12. See Antoniewicz v. Reszcynski, 70 Wis.2d 836, 236 N.W.2d 1 (1975) (unless he is in fact on the premises for illegal purposes). Some states provide landowners an immunity from claims by persons injured in the act of committing a felony. See Calvillo–Silva v. Home Grocery, 19 Cal.4th 714, 968 P.2d 65, 80 Cal.Rptr.2d 506 (1998). As to others injured as a result of their own wrongdoing see § 208.

13. See Aluminum Company of American v. Guthrie, 303 Ark. 177, 793 S.W.2d 785 (1990) (duty "to exercise ordinary care under the circumstances to avoid injury to him after discovering his peril"); Lee v. Chicago Transit Authority, 152 Ill.2d 432, 605 N.E.2d 493, 178 Ill.Dec. 699 (1992).

14. Restatement §§ 337–338. As to reason to know, see 25 below. For cases departing from this limitations, see n. 26 below.

15. McVicar v. W.R. Arthur & Co., 312 S.W.2d 805, 65 A.L.R.2d 785 (1958)

16. Frederick v. Philadelphia Rapid Transit Co., 337 Pa. 136, 10 A.2d 576 (1940) ("it is wanton negligence, within the meaning of the law, to fail to use ordinary and reasonable care to avoid injury to a trespasser after his presence has been ascertained"); see Ryals v. United States Steel Corporation, 562 So.2d 192 (Ala.1990) ("Wantonness may arise after discovery of actual peril, by conscious failure to use preventive means at hand").

Rejecting the duty. A few courts may continue to reject the discovered trespassers rule, making liability depend upon proof that the landowner was guilty of some wilful or wanton misconduct and by refusing to treat ordinary negligence after discovery of the trespasser's peril as willful misconduct.[17]

Affirmative action to save trapped trespasser. If the landowner has breached no duty to a trespasser, but discovers that the trespasser is trapped, or is injured and helpless, it would seem that the landowner must then exercise reasonable care to provide affirmative assistance, even though the landowner did not cause harm in the first place.[18] This is in line with the rule in other circumstances that requires reasonable care when the defendant's instrumentality innocently causes harm.[19]

Foreseeable Trespassers

Qualified duty to reasonably anticipated trespassers. Even when the particular trespasser is not known or discovered, the landowner may come under a duty not merely to avoid wilful or wanton harm but also to conduct his affirmative activities with reasonable care for their safety. The Restatement so provides for cases in which the landowner knew or should know that trespassers "constantly" trespassed within a "limited area."[20]

The constant or frequent trespassers rules grew out of cases in which trespassers crossed the defendant's railroad track at a given point, establishing a visible beaten path as an indication of their presence. On those facts, railroads were expected to keep reasonable lookout for trespassers at that spot,[21] an obligation that otherwise existed only for public crossings or heavily traveled places.[22] This obligation of reasonable care applied to conditions on the land as well as to activities, so if a foreseeable trespasser on an apparently safe private road sank into it and found himself covered with burning embers, he could recover if the landowner had failed to provide a reasonable warning.[23]

17. Carroll v. Spencer, 204 Md. 387, 104 A.2d 628, 44 A.L.R.2d 1247 (1954) (but apparently assume that if the trespasser's peril was great enough and immediate enough, a warning might be required).

18. Pridgen v. Boston Housing Authority, 364 Mass. 696, 308 N.E.2d 467, 70 A.L.R.3d 1106 (1974); contra: Boyette v. Trans World Airlines, Inc., 954 S.W.2d 350 (Mo.App.1997) (also perhaps contrary to authority it cites, which imposes a duty of affirmative care after discovery). Distinguish Rhodes v. Illinois Central Gulf Railroad, 172 Ill.2d 213, 665 N.E.2d 1260, 216 Ill.Dec. 703 (1996) (injured intoxicated person on premises, but injury did not result from landowner's premises or acts, no duty). Liability, if any, is of course limited to harms resulting from the landowner's negligent failure to provide assistance.

19. § 316.

20. Restatement §§ 334, 335.

21. E.g., First National Bank of Fort Smith v. Kansas City Southern Railway Co., 865 S.W.2d 719 (Mo.App.1993) (called the public user doctrine in Missouri).

22. Joy v. Chicago, B. & Q. R. R., 263 Ill. 465, 105 N.E. 330 (1914) ("no duty upon a railroad company to keep a lookout for trespassers on its track in the open country, remote from public crossings, cities, and towns"); Martin v. Midsouth Rail Corp., 584 So.2d 1282 (Miss.1991) ("no duty to keep a lookout for trespassers on the railroad track"). Statutes sometimes imposed a duty to keep a lookout.

23. Imre v. Riegel Paper Corp., 24 N.J. 438, 132 A.2d 505 (1957); Restatement § 335.

Limited use of foreseeability tests. Courts sometimes suggested that the basis for liability was only the landowner's implied invitation or license. Likewise, commentators at first emphasized limits on these rules by saying that they applied only to specific or limited areas of land and to cases of many trespassers who left their spoor in the form of a path.[24] However, the emphasis on numbers, paths, and limited areas may now be seen as matters of evidence tending to show that trespassers are foreseeable, not as rules of law and not because an implied invitation or license is required.

Expanded use of foreseeability tests. For the Restatement, foreseeability of trespassers was enough to trigger a duty only if the trespassers were "constantly" trespassing on a limited area. Otherwise, the duty to trespassers would be triggered only if the landowner actually knew or had reason to know that the trespasser was about to encounter a danger. "Have reason to know" was a term of art. It did not mean foreseeability but specific knowledge that leads to the inference that the trespasser is actually present.[25] However, some courts are now departing from the Restatement's scheme by treating foreseeable trespassers as if they were "known" trespassers.

The result for these courts is that if a trespasser's presence and encounter with danger is reasonably foreseeable, the landowner after all comes under a duty of reasonable care. For example, where a landowner constructs an unmarked cable in a wooded area where horseback riders, snowmobilers, motorcyclists and others foreseeably would be harmed, the landowner cannot escape under the no duty rule; he owes a duty of reasonable care.[26] Some courts get the same results on the theory that the landowner, by failing to make the cable reasonably visible, has acted wilfully or wantonly.[27] Either way, the total picture of duties to trespassers is very different from the one presented by the general no duty rule.

On the other hand, it is always important to recognize that when courts impose a duty they do not necessarily impose liability. The landowner is not liable for harm to the trespasser unless the landowner has failed to act as a reasonable person under the circumstances. For

24. See Prosser & Keeton, § 58, p. 395 (frequent trespassers on limited area); Restatement §§ 334–335 ("constant trespassers").

25. Restatement § 12 defines reason to know to mean that the actor had information that would lead a reasonable person to infer the existence of the fact in issue. This is definitely not the same as recognizing a risk or probability that the fact exists. The same section contrasts the usual "should know".

26. E.g., Webster v. Culbertson, 158 Ariz. 159, 761 P.2d 1063 (1988) (relying in part on Restatement § 337 as to known trespassers, but applying it, in line with § 335 to a case of a trespasser who was merely foreseeable). Accord, Lee v. Chicago Transit Authority, 152 Ill.2d 432, 605 N.E.2d 493, 178 Ill.Dec. 699 (1992) ("third rail" at a level crossing electrocuted a man; foreseeability, semble, is equivalent to reason to know; it is not necessary to show that the defendant foresee anyone "about" to encounter danger). "Constancy" of the trespass, beaten paths, and limited areas of trespass do not appear significant in cases like this.

27. Seeholzer v. Kellstone, Inc., 80 Ohio App.3d 726, 610 N.E.2d 594 (1992) (landowner knew trespassers used land, but strung a cable in a wooded area; it was struck by the trespasser's all-terrain vehicle).

example, if the landowner blocks access to the land by steel cables that are well marked, the landowner has not breached his duty of care.

§ 233. Licensees

Licensees defined. In states that retain the system of adjudicating landowner liability by classifying entrants upon the land,[1] courts set up limited duties to licensees. Licensees are those on the land by the landowner's express or implied consent[2] but who are there for their own purposes.[3] They do not qualify for invitee status because they are not on land open to the public generally and not present for any potential economic transaction with or benefit to the landowner. One who is an invitee on one portion of the land, may be a licensee only on another part.[4]

Who is included in the category. The traditional definition of licensees has the effect of saying that even social guests are licensees, not invitees, because, although the owner's invitation is a consent to their presence, they are not potentially engaged in direct economic transactions with the owner.[5] Quite a few other people fit the definition of a licensee. For examples, people who are hunting or fishing on the land with at least the tacit or implied permission of the landowner are licensees,[6] as are those permissibly on the land to look for their pet,[7] take a short cut,[8] sell goods or distribute advertising[9] or religious literature[10] or to solicit contributions.[11] So are people who are on the premises to help friends or relatives with work around the house[12] or to help with a Girl Scout troop[13] or to study the Bible with an owner who does not make a business of such things.[14]

§ 233

1. See § 237as to abolishing the categories and adopting a reasonable care standard.

2. Restatement § 330. Those privileged to be on the land for reasons other than the occupier's consent—notably firefighters and police officers—do not fit this definition. They are covered in Chapter 17.

3. Newton v. New Hanover County Bd. of Education, 342 N.C. 554, 467 S.E.2d 58 (1996).

4. See § 234.

5. Scifres v. Kraft, 916 S.W.2d 779 (Ky. App.1996); Carter v. Kinney, 896 S.W.2d 926 (Mo.1995).

6. Douglas v. Bergland, 216 Mich. 380, 185 N.W. 819 (1921) (fisher); Waller v. Smith, 116 Wash. 645, 200 P. 95 (1921) (hunter), overruled on other grounds, Laudermilk v. Carpenter, 78 Wash.2d 92, 457 P.2d 1004 (1969).

7. French v. Sunburst Properties, 521 N.E.2d 1355 (Ind.App.1988).

8. Cochran v. Burger King Corp., 937 S.W.2d 358 (Mo.App.1996) ("gratuitous licensee").

9. E.g., Malatesta v. Lowry, 130 So.2d 785 (1961); Stacy v. Shapiro, 212 A.D. 723, 209 N.Y.S. 305 (1925).

10. Perry v. Williamson, 824 S.W.2d 869 (Ky.1992); Singleton v. Jackson, 85 Wash. App. 835, 935 P.2d 644 (1997) (Jehovah's Witness, on premises to make "religious solicitation" was implicitly permitted to make contact by way of front door, but was not an invitee).

11. See Reilly v. Spiegelhalter, 100 N.J.Super. 276, 241 A.2d 665 (1968) (conceded to be at least a licensee); Singleton v. Jackson, 85 Wash.App. 835, 935 P.2d 644 (1997) ("religious solicitation").

12. Young v. Paxton, 316 Ark. 655, 873 S.W.2d 546 (1994).

13. Zuther v. Schild, 224 Kan. 528, 581 P.2d 385 (1978). The classification in *Zuther* is now obsolete in Kansas with its adoption of a general reasonable care standard. See § 237.

14. Carter v. Kinney, 896 S.W.2d 926 (Mo.1995). Even worshipers in a church held open for such a purpose have been held to be licensees in some cases. See Au-

Duty to licensee. Courts have repeatedly said that the duty to licensees is the same or substantially the same as the duty to trespassers.[15] In the absence of special circumstances, courts do not regard the landowner's permission to enter or even his invitation to a social guest as an assurance that the premises will be made safe.[16] Hence, the landowner is under no general duty of reasonable care with respect to conditions on the land, but owes only the duty not to intentionally, willfully, or wantonly injure the licensee.[17] This means, subject to the exceptions below, that the landowner need not inspect the land or correct unsafe conditions for the benefit of the licensee. As with trespassers, a duty of reasonable care is imposed once the landowner actually knows or has notice of the licensee's presence and knows or has notice of the danger the licensee is about to encounter.[18]

Conditions on the land. (a) Knowledge or foreseeability of danger. The duty to licensees may go beyond the duty to trespassers both as to passive conditions on the land and as to active negligence. As to conditions, the landowner is under a duty at least to warn when he knows, or has reason to know[19] both (1) the existence of a danger and (2) the plaintiff's presence in a place where she might encounter it. This is the same rule used for trespassers. The question is whether, in the case of licensees, the duty is imposed more readily.

It would be possible to say that a *should have known* test is applied to both factors. Alternatively, it would be possible to say that a *should have known* test is applied to one factor but that as to the other the landowner must have actually known or had reason to know. The Restatement says the defendant must either know or "have reason to know" of the first factor, danger.[20] This means that the landowner who should have known the danger but did not, would have no duty to a licensee whose presence was known. Sometimes, however, courts say that the landowner must make the premises as safe as they appear to be, a statement that can be read abstractly to imply that the landowner is responsible even if he did not actually know of the danger.[21] Harper,

try v. Roebuck Park Baptist Church, 285 Ala. 76, 229 So.2d 469 (1969). This result seems inconsistent with the public invitee test and many other church cases go the other way or else are decided upon other issues. See Claudia G. Catalano, Annotation, Liability for Personal Injury or Death Allegedly Caused by Defect in Church Premises, 8 A.L.R.5th 1 (1993).

15. E.g., Waddell v. New River Co., 141 W.Va. 880, 93 S.E.2d 473 (1956).

16. See, e.g., Landry v. Hilton Head Plantation Property Owners Association, Inc., 317 S.C. 200, 452 S.E.2d 619

17. E.g., Illinois Central R.R. v. White, 610 So.2d 308, 316 (Miss.1992) ("The duty owed to a licensee and trespasser is the same, i.e., not to willfully or wantonly injure him").

18. See Illinois Central R.R. v. White, 610 So.2d 308 (Miss.1992). As with trespassers, courts sometimes say that it is willful or wanton not to use reasonable care after the licensee's presence is or should be known. Cooper v. Corporate Property Investors, 220 Ga.App. 889, 470 S.E.2d 689 (1996).

19. See § 232, n. 25.

20. Restatement § 342.

21. Holzheimer v. Johannesen, 125 Idaho 397, 871 P.2d 814 (1994) ("A landowner is only required to share with the licensee knowledge of dangerous conditions or activities on the land"); Scifres v. Kraft, 916 S.W.2d 779, 781 (Ky.App.1996) ("A possessor of land owes a licensee the duty of reasonable care either to make the land as

James and Gray suggests that increasingly the likelihood of the licensee's presence and the consequent likelihood of harm is becoming the touchstone.[22]

(b) Knowledge or foreseeability of the licensee's presence. As to the second factor, the licensee's presence, the Restatement makes no clear and explicit statement. Perhaps it is enough that the presence of the licensee could be reasonably foreseen, that is, that the landowner should have known the licensee was or might be present. Some cases seem to take this view.[23] For instance, in an Arkansas case, the owner knew that friends of farm employees sometimes came to the farm and shared the employees' work until their work day was done. Knowing that and also knowing the dangers of specialized machinery, the landowner owed a duty of reasonable warning to the licensee-visitors.[24]

Activities on the land. Courts have imposed duties of reasonable care with respect to activities as distinct from mere conditions on the land[25] when the landowner should foresee the risk of harm. So if a landowner is engaged in active operations on the land, for example by driving vehicles, operating cranes, or constructing buildings, he must keep a reasonable lookout for licensees who have permission to be present and must govern his operations by the standards of reasonable care.[26]

The remaining negligence issue. The warning required in all duty cases applies here: to establish a duty of care is not to prove its breach. The landowner who is required to keep a reasonable lookout is not necessarily required to keep a constant lookout for a licensee who is unlikely to appear.

Equally, if the landowner reasonably believes that the licensee knows of the danger or would discover the danger and protect herself, the landowner is not negligent, although courts may express this notion by saying that the landowner is under no duty of care with respect to such dangers.[27] This is not a question of the licensee's contributory

safe as it appears, or to disclose the fact that it is as dangerous as he knows it to be").

22. 5 Harper, James & Gray § 27.8, p. 204.

23. Cooper v. Corporate Property Investors, 220 Ga.App. 889, 891, 470 S.E.2d 689, 691 (1996) ("ordinary care and diligence must be used to prevent injuring him after his presence is known or reasonably should be anticipated.").

24. Dorton v. Francisco, 309 Ark. 472, 833 S.W.2d 362 (1992).

25. Lipham v. Federated Department Stores, Inc., 263 Ga. 865, 440 S.E.2d 193 (1994) (host negligently bumped into guest); Hoffman v. Planters Gin Co., Inc., 358 So.2d 1008 (Miss.1978) (plaintiff's leg amputated by operating auger in a cotton gin).

26. Jeffries v. Potomac Development Corp., 822 F.2d 87 (D.C.Cir.1987) (licensee by invitation, duty of reasonable care as to affirmative acts); Silver v. Navarette, 350 S.W.2d 878 (Tex.Civ.App.1961) (crane operation in salvage yard); see Jenkins v. Lake Montonia Club, Inc., 125 N.C.App. 102, 105, 479 S.E.2d 259, 262 (1997) (dictum).

27. Young v. Paxton, 316 Ark. 655, 873 S.W.2d 546 (1994); Dorr v. Big Creek Wood Products, Inc., 84 Wash.App. 420, 927 P.2d 1148 (1996); see Restatement §§ 341–342. Restatement § 342 puts both an objective and a subjective test. The landowner is not liable if he reasonably believes that the licensee will discover the danger and protect herself. § 342 (a). The landowner is also not liable if the licensee does in fact know or have reason to know of the danger. § 342 (c). This second or subjective test seems to be an inappropriate importation of

negligence in failing to avoid the danger, which is a matter entirely distinct from the question of the landowner's duty and breach. Courts typically speak as if the fact that the danger is obvious or open is enough in itself to eliminate any duty by the landowner to warn of the danger. However, the fact that a danger is obvious is good but not necessarily conclusive evidence that the licensee can be expected to avoid it without a warning by the landowner.[28]

§ 234. Classification of Invitees

Invitees defined. Landowners ordinarily owe a duty of reasonable care to their invitees.[1] Invitees are either (a) "public invitees" who are invited to enter the land as a member of the public, or (b) business visitors, invited to enter the land in connection with some business dealing with the possessor.[2]

At one time, courts often failed to recognize the public invitee category. Those courts tended to emphasize the potential economic benefit to the landowner as the basis the plaintiff's status as an invitee. As a result of this earlier emphasis on supposed financial benefits to the landowner, courts sometimes came up with peculiar decisions, such as those holding a church member entering a church for its services or meetings was not entitled to ordinary care because her presence was not a financial benefit to the church; the worshiper was only a licensee, not an invitee.[3] The cases today are mostly consistent with the Restatement's tests.[4]

An "invitation" is an essential element under both the public invitee and business invitee tests. A person who is on the land under an official privilege—a firefighter, for example—is not an invitee at all.[5] The word "invitation" is itself a term of art. In few cases does the invitee have a personal, formal, and express invitation. The invitation is found in the fact that the premises are held open to the public as in the case of retail stores, airports, and public parks, or in the fact that the landowner has

contributory negligence rules. So far as duty and negligence are concerned, the test is logically about what the landowner could reasonably expect of the licensee.

28. Cf. Tincani v. Inland Empire Zoological So'cy, 124 Wash.2d 121, 875 P.2d 621 (1994) (defining open and apparent danger as one of which the licensee knows or has reason to know)

§ 234

1. See § 235.

2. Restatement § 332.

3. Autry v. Roebuck Park Baptist Church, 285 Ala. 76, 229 So.2d 469 (1969); Coolbaugh v. St. Peter's Roman Catholic Church of Bridgeport, 142 Conn. 536, 115 A.2d 662 (1955). These cases may be influenced in some degree by the rules granting tort immunity to charitable organizations. As to that immunity, see § 282.

4. E.g., Young v. Paxton, 316 Ark. 655, 873 S.W.2d 546 (1994); Jump v. Bank of Versailles, 586 N.E.2d 873 (Ind.App.1992); Martin v. City of Washington, Mo., 848 S.W.2d 487 (Mo. 1993); Morris v. Krauszer's Food Stores, Inc., 300 N.J.Super. 529, 693 A.2d 510 (1997) (employee on portion of employer's premises open to the public was public invitee); Cole v. Fairchild, 198 W.Va. 736, 482 S.E.2d 913 (1996) (recognizing test but not recognizing that "public" might include a large group less than all human individuals).

5. The upshot is that firefighters and police officers are treated more or less like licensees in many cases, although the theory has become more complicated. See Chapter 17.

arranged for the plaintiff to be on the land, as in the case of a contractor hired to haul out garbage. Any conduct that communicates the idea that the entrant's presence is desired will do.[6] On the other hand, the landowner who merely permits a hunter to use his land has not issued any invitation at all, even implicitly.

Perhaps the focus should be less on invitation than on the underlying principle. The real point is that anyone who receives implicit or explicit assurance of safety is entitled to the invitee status and the reasonable care that goes with it.[7] The public invitee and business visitor categories only represent efforts to find objective correlatives to this underlying principle.

Who is included in the invitee category. Customers and prospective customers on the premises of any business open to sell goods,[8] provide services,[9] entertainment[10] or recreation[11] are easily invitees by any definition. So are employees,[12] independent contractors,[13] and the employees of independent contractors[14] who have been expressly or impliedly invited to the land. So are people who are invited to private portions of the premises, if they are invited for potential economic benefit of the

6. Cole v. Fairchild, 198 W.Va. 736, 482 S.E.2d 913 (1996) ("An 'invitation' occurs when a possessor of certain premises exhibits conduct which makes others believe the possessor wants them to be on the premises").

7. "[T]he basis for invitee status is the implied assurance of safety conveyed to the visitor.... " Blair v. Ohio Dept. of Rehabilitation and Correction, 61 Ohio Misc.2d 649, 582 N.E.2d 673 (1989). Scores of cases have quoted or paraphrased the assertion that the invitee enters upon the representation or assurance that the land has been prepared and made safe for his reception. See Restatement § 343, cmt. b. That statement implies something about the nature of the landowner duty, but also something about who counts as an invitee—one who receives assurances, often implicit, that the land is reasonably safe for her entry.

8. E.g., Hose v. Winn–Dixie Montgomery, Inc., 658 So.2d 403 (Ala.1995); Clohesy v. Food Circus Supermarkets, Inc. 149 N.J. 496, 694 A.2d 1017 (1997); Hoover v. Broome, 324 S.C. 531, 479 S.E.2d 62 (S.C.App.1996).

9. Branks v. Kern, 320 N.C. 621, 359 S.E.2d 780, 68 A.L.R.4th 817 (1987) (veterinarian); see Boren v. Worthen National Bank of Arkansas, 324 Ark. 416, 921 S.W.2d 934 (1996) (bank customer would be invitee). When the service itself rather than a condition of the land is the source of harm, the service provider may be held to a duty appropriate to the type of service, e.g., health care.

10. Martin v. City of Washington, Mo., 848 S.W.2d 487 (Mo. 1993) (high school football game, bleacher gave way with the plaintiff, who was classed a public invitee); Mostert v. CBL & Associates, 741 P.2d 1090 (Wyo.1987) (movie patron invitee and entitled to warning of off-premises flash flooding due to storms during movie).

11. E.g., Hylazewski v. Wet 'N Wild, Inc., 432 So.2d 1371 (Fla.App.1983) (swimming pool, artificial waves); Peterson v. Summit Fitness, Inc., 920 S.W.2d 928 (Mo. App.1996) (fitness center, swimming pool).

12. Morris v. Krauszer's Food Stores, Inc., 300 N.J.Super. 529, 693 A.2d 510 (1997) (on portion of premises open to public). The employer's duty to employees is independent of his status as landowner but is congruent with his duty as landowner to an invitee. The employer's duty includes a duty to provide a reasonably safe place in which to work.

13. See Lane v. Groetz, 108 N.H. 173, 230 A.2d 741 (1967); Dawson v. Bunker Hill Plaza Associates, 289 N.J.Super. 309, 673 A.2d 847 (1996). This category includes those who by invitation make delivery of goods, e.g., Busy Bee Buffet v. Ferrell, 82 Ariz. 192, 310 P.2d 817 (1957), and those who haul trash or garbage out. Hull v. Bishop–Stoddard Cafeteria, 238 Iowa 650, 26 N.W.2d 429 (1946).

14. Montes v. Indian Cliffs Ranch, Inc., 946 S.W.2d 103 (Tex.App.1997).

landowner. When consistent with the purpose for which the invitation is implicitly or explicitly issued, those who accompany the invitee are themselves invitees.[15] Visitors to invitees are also invitees in some cases. For example, visitors to patients in a hospital[16] and visitors to inmates in a correctional institution[17] are invitees, as are those who enter a cemetery to visit a grave.[18]

At a time when courts thought of invitees solely as "business visitors," it was hard to explain many of the actual decisions, which are now entirely understandable on the ground that invitees include every person on land open to the public, as long as his presence is consistent with the public invitation. So you are an invitee in a store even if you enter only to kill time between airplanes and intend to buy nothing.[19] If you have children in tow, they, too are invitees.[20] If you are at the airport to see a friend off, you are still an invitee, and so is the photographer making pictures of deplaning passengers.[21] It is no longer necessary to justify such holdings with farfetched suggestions that the visitor who buys nothing today might do so at some indefinite time in the future. The public invitee category can cover these examples quite easily, as well as the case in which you enter a public park or national forest where no economic transaction is even possible.[22]

The tests also explain why salespersons calling at a residence can be classified in different ways. A salesperson who comes uninvited to your home is not an invitee, for she has no invitation of any kind.[23] The salesperson who comes in response to an implicit or explicit invitation is a business invitee, for that person has an invitation to be there and is dealing with you in a potential economic exchange.[24] Finally, the sales

15. Children for example, see n. 20 below.

16. Wieseler v. Sisters of Mercy Health Corporation, 540 N.W.2d 445 (Iowa 1995); Sutherland v. Saint Francis Hospital, Inc., 595 P.2d 780 (Okla.1979).

17. Blair v. Ohio Dept. of Rehabilitation and Correction, 61 Ohio Misc.2d 649, 582 N.E.2d 673 (1989),

18. See Thomas J. Goger, Annotation, Liability in Action Based upon Negligence, for Injury to, or Death of, Person Going upon Cemetery Premises, 63 A.L.R.3d 1252 (1975) (also reflecting some cases holding visitors to be licensees).

19. Cf. Hoover v. Broome, 324 S.C. 531, 479 S.E.2d 62 (S.C.App.1996) (entering service station to ask directions).

20. E.g., Orr v. First National Stores, Inc., 280 A.2d 785, 50 A.L.R.3d 1202 (Me. 1971); Wal–Mart Stores, Inc. v. Lerma, 749 S.W.2d 572 (Tex.App.1988).

21. Cf. Mathias v. Denver Union Terminal Ry., 137 Colo. 224, 323 P.2d 624 (1958) (photographer making photographs at train station was invitee so long as he was in area intended for public use).

22. Smith v. United States, 117 F.Supp. 525 (D. N.D. Cal. 1953) (public campground in National Forest owned by United States).

23. Stacy v. Shapiro, 212 A.D. 723, 209 N.Y.S. 305 (1925); Bidiman v. Gehrts, 133 Or.App. 145, 890 P.2d 436 (1995) (insurance agent had previously contacted the defendant for policy renewal at defendant's business, not at home; no implicit invitation); cf. Edmunds v. Copeland, 197 Ga. App. 292, 398 S.E.2d 280 (1990) (invitation not established, insurance sales agent was a licensee only); Singleton v. Jackson, 85 Wash.App. 835, 935 P.2d 644 (1997) (entrance to make religious solicitation was by implicit permission, but not by invitation, hence solicitor was licensee only).

24. Handleman v. Cox, 39 N.J. 95, 187 A.2d 708 (1963) (salespersons on portion of premises not open to the public, but prior dealings of the parties would support a jury finding of invitation to be there).

person who enters a place open to the public should qualify as a public invitee.[25]

Scope of invitation. The scope of the invitation or assurance of safety may be limited. For this reason, a person may be an invitee on one portion of the premises but not on another.[26] For instance, the plaintiff at a shopping mall may be an invitee on the parking lot, but not while taking a shortcut through the flower bed.[27] And a person may be an invitee at one time but not another.[28] For instance, a restaurant customer is an invitee when she parks and retrieves her car during serving hours, but not when she leaves her car there and returns for it after the restaurant is closed.[29] The nature of the invitation and its purposes, custom, and reasonable expectations of the invitee are usually a clear guide. The layout of the premises may also be instructive. A customer in search of a public restroom on the premises is still an invitee if she reasonably enters a storeroom by mistake.[30]

Courts have also held that an invitation to enter for one purpose may not carry with it an assurance of safety when the entrant uses the land for an inconsistent purpose.[31]

§ 235. Duty Owed Invitees

General duties of care. The landowner owes to the invitee a duty of care to make conditions on the land reasonably safe[1] and to conduct his active operations with reasonable care for the invitee whose presence is known or reasonably foreseeable.[2] In some cases but not in all, reasonable care under the circumstances requires an inspection of the premises and active steps to make them safe.[3] In other cases, the landowner may satisfy his duty of reasonable care by providing a warning. Under limited

25. Austin v. Buettner, 211 Md. 61, 124 A.2d 793 (1956) is consistent with this view but was decided before the Restatement Second established the public invitee category. There a salesperson entered a tavern open to the public and fell down a hidden flight of stairs before making any sales contact.

26. E.g., Mathias v. Denver Union Terminal Ry., 137 Colo. 224, 323 P.2d 624 (1958); Gladon v. Greater Cleveland Regional Transit Authority, 75 Ohio St.3d 312, 662 N.E.2d 287 (1996) (railroad passenger not an invitee on the track).

27. Cf. Nicoletti v. Westcor, Inc., 131 Ariz. 140, 639 P.2d 330 (1982); (short cut through plantings).

28. Restatement § 332, cmt. l.

29. Savage v. Flagler Company, 185 Ga. App. 334, 364 S.E.2d 52 (1987), modified on other grounds, Flagler Company v. Savage, 258 Ga. 335, 368 S.E.2d 504 (1988).

30. Miniken v. Carr, 71 Wash.2d 325, 428 P.2d 716 (1967).

31. Markle v. Hacienda Mexican Restaurant, 570 N.E.2d 969 (Ind.App. 1991) (plaintiff drove into shopping center to eat at a restaurant there, saw a friend, and was transferring an item from his vehicle to his friend's when he fell in a pothole; jury question whether this was within the scope of the invitation to use the parking lot).

§ 235

1. Mensink v. American Grain, 564 N.W.2d 376 (Iowa 1997); Adkins v. Chevron, USA, Inc., 199 W.Va. 518, 485 S.E.2d 687 (1997); Restatement § 343.

2. E.g., New York Central R.R. v. Wyatt, 135 Ind.App. 205, 184 N.E.2d 657 (1962). See Joseph A. Page, The Law of Premises Liability § 4.10 (2d ed. 1988 & Supp.). When active operations or negligent delivery of services are involved, courts often proceed directly to discussion of ordinary negligence without classifying the plaintiff.

3. See Mensink v. American Grain, 564 N.W.2d 376 (Iowa 1997)

circumstances, the landowner also owes a duty of care to protect the invitee from others persons or from animals.[4] Given the duty of reasonable care, the invitee's suit is an ordinary negligence case and the ordinary rules of negligence apply, so that the plaintiff must prove actual and proximate cause as well as negligence by the defendant in creating or maintaining an unreasonably dangerous condition.

Slip and fall cases. Slip and fall cases and their variants[5] are quite common.[6] The duty of reasonable care is routinely played out in three ways:

(a) If the defendant negligently creates the dangerous condition, as where a grocery clerk spills a slippery substance on the floor, or the defendant negligently waxes the floor, the defendant will be subject to liability for injuries suffered in the invitee's fall.[7]

(b) If the landowner negligently markets goods in such a way that they are likely to be dislodged by other customers with resulting injury to the plaintiff, the trier can find negligence.[8]

(c) Finally, if some unknown person creates a condition of danger, by dropping a substance on the floor for example, the store defendant is not negligent in creating the danger but may be negligent in failing to inspect periodically for such mishaps.[9]

In this last scenario, courts tend to say that if the dangerous substance has been present for a long period of time, the trier can infer that the store was negligent in failing to inspect or discover.[10] Sometimes the reasoning is so stylized that the results look almost like a kind of strict liability.[11] On the other hand, courts refuse to apply res ipsa

4. Restatement § 344. Protection from third persons generally is considered in Chapter 21.

5. As where merchandise falls upon a customer, or a customer carrying parcels collides with an object in the aisle. See Linda A. Sharp, Annotation, Liability for Injury to Customer from Object Projecting into Aisle or Passageway in Store, 40 A.L.R.5th 135 (1996); Michael P. Sullivan, Annotation, Liability for Injury to Customer or Other Invitee of Retail Store by Falling of Displayed, Stored, or Piled Objects, 61 A.L.R.4th 27 (1989).

6. Many are reviewed in annotations. See, e.g., Sonja A. Soehnel, Annotation, Liability of Operator of Grocery Store to Invitee Slipping on Spilled Liquid or Semiliquid Substance, 24 A.L.R.4th 696 (1981)

7. Finan v. Atria East Associates, 230 A.D.2d 707, 646 N.Y.S.2d 164 (1996) (claim of negligently waxed floor); Smith v. Wal–Mart Stores, Inc., 314 S.C. 248, 442 S.E.2d 606 (1994).

8. E.g., Owens v. Redd, 215 Va. 13, 205 S.E.2d 669 (1974) (jury could find that bottles were negligently stacked); JOSEPH A. PAGE, THE LAW OF PREMISES LIABILITY § 7.12 (2d ed. 1988 & David A. Elder, Supp.).

9. Courts often say that the defendant must have actual or constructive knowledge of the danger. This expression is merely another way of saying alluding the negligence standard: the plaintiff must prove that the defendant either knew or should have known of the danger. See, e.g, Thoma v. Cracker Barrel Old Country Store, Inc., 649 So.2d 277 (Fla.App.1995) (jury could find that the defendant's employees, standing nearby, should have seen a spill on the floor).

10. E.g., J. Weingarten, Inc. v. Thompson, 251 Ark. 914, 475 S.W.2d 697 (1972) (from discoloration of old, black-looking leaf, far from vegetable display, an inference that it had been present two days in spite of regular cleanups). See also n. 11.

11. In Sokolowski v. Medi Mart, Inc., 24 Conn.App. 276, 587 A.2d 1056 (1991) the plaintiff slipped on a substance on the floor, perhaps a lotion. Workers were standing nearby for 15 minutes and had not heard a bottle break. Hence, the court reasoned, the substance might have been on the floor

loquitur to slip and fall cases, and if no evidence supports an inference that the condition has been present for a substantial period, the jury has no basis for concluding that the defendant was negligent.[12]

Traditional rule of obvious dangers and natural accumulations. Following the First Restatement, courts often said that the landowner owed no duty to his invitees to make the premises safe or to warn of dangers known or obvious to invitees. That was equivalent to saying that if the danger was open or obvious, then the defendant was under no duty at all, even if he could expect that invitees will not learn enough to protect themselves.[13] Courts also sometimes said that the landowner was not liable to invitees for injuries resulting from natural accumulations of snow or ice. But some of the cases cited for this proposition seem to involve injuries on the public sidewalk adjacent to the land rather than on the land itself and others seem only to be instances of the open and obvious danger rule.[14] The accumulations rule, as applied on the land itself, would therefore presumably be modified when the open and obvious danger rule is modified.[15]

The Restatement rule for obvious dangers. The Restatement Second, in line with general negligence law, took a more cautious view. It provided that when the allegedly dangerous condition is open and obvious, the landowner is not liable to invitees for harm from known or obvious dangers except where the landowner should anticipate harm in spite of the knowledge or obviousness.[16] Put the other way around, the landowner is subject to liability if he can foresee harm in spite of the fact that the danger was obvious. In recent years, this view has commanded almost complete acceptance where it has been expressly considered.[17]

more than 15 minutes and that was sufficient time for a reasonable store to discover the condition and make it safe. Similarly, in Kenney v. Kroger Company, 569 So.2d 357 (Ala.1990) the fact that a bottle of liquid was open on the shelf and a large amount of liquid had spilled or dripped to the floor was said to support an inference that the condition had been present a long time.

12. E.g., Gulycz v. Stop and Shop Cos., Inc., 29 Conn.App. 519, 615 A.2d 1087 (1992).

13. Duke v. Gold Kist, Inc., 686 So.2d 262 (Ala.1996) (specifically rejecting Restatement § 343 A); Griebler v. Doughboy Recreational, Inc., 160 Wis.2d 547, 466 N.W.2d 897 (1991) (guest diving into pool of unknown depth; landowner is not responsible even if a reasonable person would not have appreciated the gravity of the risk). Griebler is criticized succinctly in Joseph A. Page, The Law of Premises Liability § 4.06, 1996–97 Supp. p. 33 (by David A. Elder). Cf. Perry v. Williamson, 824 S.W.2d 869 (Ky. 1992) ("If the hazard is obvious then it does not involve an unreasonable risk of harm to the licensee").

14. See Brandert v. Scottsbluff Nat. Bank & Trust Co., 194 Neb. 777, 235 N.W.2d 864 (1975).

15. See Iwai v. State, 129 Wash.2d 84, 915 P.2d 1089 (1996).

16. Restatement § 343 A (1).

17. See Ward v. K mart Corporation, 136 Ill.2d 132, 143 Ill.Dec. 288, 554 N.E.2d 223 (1990); Douglass v. Irvin, 549 N.E.2d 368 (Ind.1990); Wieseler v. Sisters of Mercy Health Corp., 540 N.W.2d 445 (Ia. 1995) Colvin v. A R Cable Services–ME, Inc., 697 A.2d 1289 (Me. 1997); Bertrand v. Alan Ford, Inc., 449 Mich. 606, 537 N.W.2d 185 (1995); Tharp v. Bunge Corporation, 641 So.2d 20 (Miss.1994) ("We now abolish the so-called 'open and obvious' defense and apply our true comparative negligence doctrine"); Harris v. Niehaus, 857 S.W.2d 222 (Mo.1993); Welton v. Lucas, 283 Mont. 202, 940 P.2d 112 (1997); Hamernick v. Essex Dodge Ltd., 247 Neb. 392, 527 N.W.2d 196 (1995); Dawson v. Payless For Drugs, 248 Or. 334, 433 P.2d 1019 (1967); Callander v. Charleston Doughnut Corp., 305 S.C. 123, 406 S.E.2d 361 (1991); Parker v. Highland

Basis for the Restatement Second rule. For the Restatement and its adherents, the basis of the rule is that the landowner is not negligent at all if he can foresee no harm, and that is the case if he can reasonably believe that the invitee will (a) know or see the danger and (b) avoid it. On the other hand, he is indeed negligent if he can foresee that the plaintiff will encounter the danger in spite of its obvious character.

Where plaintiff's encounter with obvious danger is foreseeable. Landowners can foresee that the invitee will encounter an obvious danger for at least two reasons. First, in some cases the plaintiff's only reasonable choice is to encounter the danger. A tenant in an apartment building, for example, may be required to cross a floor maintained by the landlord that has become dangerously slippery from waxing, or to cross ice on the steps in order to reach her apartment. Even if she knows the danger, a decision to encounter it is more reasonable than a decision to never enter her apartment. The plaintiff's decision to encounter a known danger will often be reasonable when the plaintiff is exercising a right like the tenant's right to reach her own apartment through a common passageway or the right[18] of a member of the public to use public land or to reach a public utility.[19] Similarly, the plaintiff's decision to encounter a known risk is sometimes reasonable when the plaintiff must take the risk to fulfill an obligation or to carry out employment obligations.[20] Because such decisions will be reasonable or rightful under the circum-

Park, Inc., 565 S.W.2d 512 (Tex.1978) ("We now expressly abolish the so-called no-duty concept in this case.... The reasonableness of an [plaintiff's] conduct under the circumstances will be determined under principles of contributory negligence"); Iwai v. State, 129 Wash.2d 84, 915 P.2d 1089 (1996). See Joseph A. Page, The Law of Premises Liability § 4.6 (2d ed. 1988 & Supp.); Ernest H. Schopler, Annotation, Modern Status of The Rule Absolving a Possessor of Land of Liability to Those Coming Thereon For Harm Caused by Dangerous Physical Conditions of Which The Injured Party Knew And Realized The Risk, 35 A.L.R.3d 230 (1971).

After *Ward*, the Illinois legislature enacted a statute providing that: "The duty of reasonable care under the circumstances which an owner or occupier of land owes to such entrants does not include any of the following: a duty to warn of or otherwise take reasonable steps to protect such entrants from conditions on the premises that are known to the entrant, are open and obvious, or can reasonably be expected to be discovered by the entrant; a duty to warn of latent defects or dangers or defects or dangers unknown to the owner or occupier of the premises; a duty to warn such entrants of any dangers resulting from misuse by the entrants of the premises or anything affixed to or located on the premises; or a duty to protect such entrants from their own misuse of the premises or anything affixed to or located on the premises." 740 ILCS 130/2.

18. This same point has been made when the question is one of contributory negligence or assumed risk. See, e.g., Leroy Fibre Co. v. Chicago, Milwaukee & St. Paul Railway Co, 232 U.S. 340, 34 S.Ct. 415, 58 L.Ed. 631 (1914) (not an assumed risk to store flammables on property in spite of the danger that defendant would negligently set them afire). See § 214. Some courts have overlooked this point. See DeAmiches v. Popczun, 35 Ohio St.2d 180, 299 N.E.2d 265 (1973), discussed in § 211.

19. Iwai v. State, 129 Wash.2d 84, 915 P.2d 1089 (1996); Restatement § 343 A (2).

20. See Osborn v. Mission Ready Mix, 224 Cal.App.3d 104, 273 Cal.Rptr. 457 (1990) ("It is ... the law that a workman on the job, doing the job he was hired to do, is not required to exercise the same quantum of care that may be required of other invitees ..... it is foreseeable that even an obvious danger may cause injury, if the practical necessity of encountering the danger, when weighed against the apparent risk involved, is such that under the circumstances, a person might choose to encounter the danger").

stances, the landowner will often be able to foresee resulting harm in cases of this sort.

A second kind of case in which the plaintiff's encounter with obvious danger is foreseeable is one in which the plaintiff is foreseeably distracted, or acts under emergency or pressing need. A grocery store owner who lays watermelons in a crowded aisle may be able to foresee that a distracted shopper will take a step backward and fall.[21] The operator of a pharmacy that remains open in spite of ice covering its parking lot and entrance must surely hope and foresee that people will attempt to enter and may be injured in a fall.[22] In cases likes these, the result would turn on the plaintiff's possible contributory negligence, not on the defendant's lack of duty.

Distinguishing contributory negligence. In spite of the relative clarity of the Restatement, good analysis of obvious danger cases is prey to at least two levels of confusion. One level of potential confusion arises because evidence that a condition is open or obvious to observers is good evidence about two distinct things. First it might suggest that the plaintiff was chargeable with contributory negligence. Second, it might suggest that the defendant was not negligent—he could perhaps rely on the plaintiff to avoid obvious danger and thus avoid injury.[23] These two points are entirely different. In most courts, if the jury concluded that the plaintiff was guilty of contributory negligence in failing to avoid an obvious danger, the result might be merely to reduce the damages award under the rules of comparative negligence. If the jury found the defendant not negligent on the ground that, since the plaintiff could be expected to avoid the danger, harm was not foreseeable, the plaintiff could not recover at all.

The contributory negligence inquiry balances the foreseeable risks and utilities as they would be perceived by a reasonable person in the plaintiff's situation. The inquiry into the defendant's negligence balances the foreseeable risks and utilities as a reasonable person in the defendant's situation would perceive them. Both tests are objective, but they may apply in slightly different circumstances or at different times. Consequently, the result of one test is not necessarily congruent with the

21. Urban v. Wait's Supermarket, Inc., 294 N.W.2d 793 (S.D.1980). In Tennant v. Shoppers Food Warehouse Md. Corp., 115 Md.App. 381, 693 A.2d 370 (1997) the court, quoting earlier authority, said: "The storekeeper expects and intends that his customers shall look not at the floor but at the goods which he displays to attract their attention and which he hopes they will buy. He at least ought not to complain, if they look at the goods displayed instead of at the floor to discover possible pitfalls, obstructions, or other dangers, or if their purchases so encumber them as to prevent them from seeing dangers which might otherwise be apparent. Patrons are entitled therefore to rely to some extent at least upon the presumption that the proprietor will see that the passage ways provided for their use are unobstructed and reasonably safe."

22. Dawson v. Payless For Drugs, 248 Or. 334, 433 P.2d 1019 (1967).

23. In many states today, assumed risk need not be a third complication, because it would be covered either in the contributory negligence analysis or in the no-negligence analysis. See §§ 211–214. Where assumed risk remains as a theoretically separate concept, the confusion is formidable and depressing. See the discussion of the problem in Parker v. Highland Park, Inc., 565 S.W.2d 512 (Tex.1978).

result of the other. Sometimes the plaintiff's encounter with an obviously dangerous condition is reasonable under the circumstances, but a reasonable defendant would not necessarily have foreseen such circumstances. In that case, the defendant is not liable because he is not negligent. At other times, the answer is reversed: the plaintiff is guilty of contributory negligence but the defendant should have foreseen her negligent behavior and consequent injury. In that case the defendant is liable but the plaintiff's recovery would be reduced in a comparative negligence state. In still other cases, the plaintiff would be acting quite reasonably in confronting a known danger and should not even suffer a reduction in damages.[24]

Case analysis vs. rule of law. Another level of potential confusion in open and obvious danger cases arises because it is all too easy to confuse a finding for the defendant on the facts of a particular case with a rule of law for all cases. In some particular cases, the obviousness of danger is compelling, so that the court might take the case from the jury by directed verdict or summary judgment. The court might conclude that the defendant was not negligent at all because he could expect the plaintiff to avoid the danger and thus avoid injury, and further that reasonable jurors could not reach a contrary conclusion. Such a conclusion would be plausible if, for example, the plaintiff injured herself by walking into the checkout counter at a grocery store. Holding that the particular defendant was not negligent would not be a rule of law but an analysis of the evidence in the particular case.

Analysis of the facts of particular cases is very different from a rule of law that obvious dangers always bar recovery. The rule of the first Restatement and the one still followed in some cases[25] is not a judgment about the evidence or the facts of the particular case but a rule of law. These cases treat obvious danger as the ultimate issue rather than as evidence to be assessed.

Such cases may also lead to mechanical treatment of the contributory negligence issue. For example, if a court uses obviousness as the ultimate test rather than foreseeability of harm on the facts, it may go on to say that a finding of negligence on the part of the defendant precludes a finding of contributory negligence on the part of the plaintiff. The reasoning is that a finding of negligence means a finding that the danger was not obvious and that if it was not obvious then the plaintiff could not be charged with contributory negligence.[26] As already observed, this is not necessarily so. What is reasonable to the plaintiff at the

24. Suppose that a guest of a tenant in a large high-rise apartment building is present in the tenant's apartment when the landowner negligently causes the loss of electricity. After two days without water or food, the guest attempts to make her way down the stairs, on which she is an invitee and falls in the dark. It seems preposterous to say that the guest-invitee should prefer to starve or die of dehydration, so her conduct in choosing the dark stairs is entirely reasonable.

25. See n. 13.

26. Perry v. Williamson, 824 S.W.2d 869 (Ky.1992).

moment she confronts danger is not invariably what is foreseeable to a defendant at the time a condition is created or maintained.

§ 236. Children on the Land

Invitees and Licensees

Where landowners' liability is still determined by categorizing entrants upon the land as trespassers, licensees, and invitees, children as well as adults are subject to the classification scheme. Except as explained below, their rights are determined by the classification in the same way as adults' rights.

When adults are classed as invitees, the children who accompany them are properly categorized in the same way unless the entrance of children is inconsistent with the express or implied limits of the invitation.[1] Children can of course also be invitees in their own right, as where they enter a retail store.[2] The duty owed to child invitees is of course the same as that owed the adult invitee, namely, the duty of reasonable care. However, what counts as reasonable care with a child invitee may be different, since children may overlook dangers that adults would avoid.[3]

Children, like adults, may be licensees, as for example where they are social guests or with adults who are social guests.[4] In such cases, they are ordinarily owed only the care owed to adult licensees.[5] However, where the defendant owes a duty of care to child trespassers under the rules stated below, he owes the same duty to child licensees.[6] In addition to the limitation on duty implied in the licensee category, some authority holds that with children of tender years who are accompanied by parents, responsibility for their safety shifts to the parents, at least if the parents know of the danger.[7] On the other hand, if the landowner (or anyone else) has been entrusted with and accepted responsibility for supervising a child, he owes a duty of reasonable care to provide supervision regardless of the child's status on the land.[8]

Child Trespassers

The problem. Children may be and often are trespassers to whom the landowner owes no more duties than he owes to adult trespassers.

§ 236

1. E.g.,Wal–Mart Stores, Inc. v. Lerma, 749 S.W.2d 572 (Tex.App.1988).

2. Orr v. First National Stores, Inc., 280 A.2d 785, 50 A.L.R.3d 1202 (Me. 1971).

3. See Johnson v. Pettigrew, 595 N.E.2d 747 (Ind.App.1992).

4. E.g., Bradford v. Feeback, 149 Mich. App. 67, 385 N.W.2d 729 (1986).

5. Robles v. Severyn, 19 Ariz.App. 61, 504 P.2d 1284 (1973).

6. Restatement § 343B.

7. Freeze v. Congleton, 276 N.C. 178, 171 S.E.2d 424 (1970). Illinois has come up with a stringent rule that appears to allow the defendant to invariably shift responsibility for the trespassing child to the parents who "bear the primary responsibility for safety of their children" whenever the danger is "obvious." In effect the defendant is allowed to assume that if the child is out alone, he has capacity to appreciate dangers. Mt. Zion State Bank & Trust v. Consolidated Communications, Inc., 169 Ill.2d 110, 214 Ill.Dec. 156, 660 N.E.2d 863 (1995).

8. Johnson v. Pettigrew, 595 N.E.2d 747 (Ind.App.1992).

But child trespassers are not for that reason alone evil-doers or even negligent actors and they are almost always more vulnerable to harm because they fail to understand danger or its seriousness. Many of these trespassers are small children, sometimes two or three years old. A three-year-old trespasser wanders into a neighbor's backyard, falls into the unfenced pool and drowns.[9] Some of the older children seem to have devoted no time to meditation on the rights of property owners, but they are not vandals. A seven-year-old deliberately enters a garbage dump to look for comic books and is horribly burned when the crust gives way and he sinks into burning embers.[10]

Contemporary general rule. If the landowner in such cases could foresee that children might enter and be harmed because, given their age and experience, they might fail to appreciate the danger, and if the landowner could have avoided such serious risks with a relatively small expense, courts today generally recognize a duty of care to the child and liability for negligence.[11] Where the landowner owes such a duty to a trespassing child, he owes no less to the child licensee or invitee.[12] The rule is subject to some qualification or at least explanation, and a few courts reject it altogether, treating the child trespasser like any other.[13]

Origin of the special rule. The idea originated around 1875. A seven-year-old child played on a revolving turntable, a heavy piece of machinery used to rotate railroad engines. Caught between the surface and the wall, he lost a leg. The railroad asserted that it owed no duties to this trespasser. The Minnesota Court, noting the turntable appealed to the "natural instincts" of children and at the same time was highly dangerous to them, argued that the child was "induced" to use the turntable by its very attractiveness. The court compared the allure of the turntable to strong-scented meat used to attract and trap dogs.[14] For this reason the trespass was to be forgiven[15] and the child treated as an invitee.

9. Giacona v. Tapley, 5 Ariz.App. 494, 428 P.2d 439 (1967) (five-year-old, liability recognized); Goodwin v. Jackson, 484 So.2d 1041 (Miss.1986) (three-year-old, liability denied).

10. Rush v. Plains Tp., 371 Pa. 117, 89 A.2d 200 (1952) (no liability); cf. Dehn v. S. Brand Coal & Oil Co., 241 Minn. 237, 63 N.W.2d 6 (1954) (similar facts but stronger evidence that landowner knew of fires, liability).

11. See cases cited in nn. 22–24 below; JOSEPH A. PAGE, THE LAW OF PREMISES LIABILITY § 2-8_2.13 (2d ed. 1988 & Supp.). The liability is essentially liability for negligence. See, e.g., Gregory v. Johnson, 249 Ga. 151, 289 S.E.2d 232 (1982). But some qualifications are stated below.

12. See Rosenau v. City of Estherville, 199 N.W.2d 125, 136 (Iowa 1972).

13. E.g., Osterman v. Peters, 260 Md. 313, 272 A.2d 21 (1971); Elliott v. Nagy, 22 Ohio St.3d 58, 488 N.E.2d 853 (1986).

14. Keffe v. Milwaukee & St. Paul Ry., 21 Minn. 207 (1875). The Supreme Court had held for the plaintiff in a similar case two years earlier in Sioux City & Pacific R.R. v. Stout, 84 U.S. (17 Wall.) 657, 21 L.Ed. 745 (1873).

15. The function of the child trespasser rules is to take the child out of the trespasser category and to place the landowner under a duty of reasonable care. It has no logical application to harms occurring outside the land. It is unrelated for example to the so-called Pied Piper cases in which a street vendor attracts small children to cross the street and thus subjects them to traffic hazards. See Neal v. Shiels, Inc., 166 Conn. 3, 347 A.2d 102 (1974). But courts occasionally use the attractive nuisance terminology even when injury does not occur on the land and sometimes as if were a theory of recovery in itself. Such decisions can add confusion.

"Attractive nuisance" vs. foreseeability. The earliest cases were based on the theory that the child was lured to the land by some special attraction like the railroad's turntable. For this reason, courts often called the special rule for child trespasses the attractive nuisance doctrine. The idea that the child had to be lured to the land by something attractive to children led Justice Holmes to hold that the doctrine had no application unless the child was attracted to the land by the very thing that injured her.[16] Technically, Holmes may not have been overruled,[17] but in any event his view is now usually rejected in mainstream tort law. What is now required instead of allure is that the landowner must know or have reason to know, or at least foresee, that children are likely to trespass and because of their youth will be at unreasonable risk for serious injury.[18] For this reason, "attractive nuisance" is no longer a good description of the doctrine.

"Foreseeability "vs. "reason to know". The Restatement Second says the landowner must *know or have reason to know*[19] that child trespassers are likely and that a condition on his land may endanger them. That seems to be an obscure way of saying that the landowner need not investigate to discover the condition or the possibility of trespassers.[20] If the point were reformulated to say that the landowner owes reasonable care to foreseeable child trespassers, the outcome of cases would ordinarily be the same, because ordinary care would not require investigation about the prospect of trespassers unless some fact suggested the need to inspect or investigate.

Yet a small effort toward investigation or inspection is warranted in some cases. It would not be fearsomely burdensome to hold that if a railroad is going to install a turntable it might inquire whether children play near about. If the Restatement's formula rejects liability on such facts, it is questionable at best. If the formula accepts liability on such facts, it would be simpler to say that the landowner owes a duty or reasonable care under the circumstances.[21] Some of the decisions approve

16. United Zinc & Chemical Co. v. Britt, 258 U.S. 268, 42 S.Ct. 299, 66 L.Ed. 615 (1922).

17. See McGettigan v. National Bank of Washington, 320 F.2d 703, 706 (D.C.Cir. 1963). Holmes' decision in *Britt* was rendered in the days before Erie R.R. v. Tompkins, 304 U.S. 64, 58 S.Ct. 817, 82 L.Ed. 1188 (1938)., After the decision in *Erie,* the federal common law of torts more or less ceased to exist, so it would now be difficult for the Court directly to overrule the *Britt* case.

18. E.g., Kahn v. James Burton Company, 5 Ill.2d 614, 126 N.E.2d 836 (1955) ("The element of attraction is significant only in so far as it indicates that the trespass should be anticipated, the true basis of liability being the foreseeability of harm to the child"); Banker v. McLaughlin, 146 Tex. 434, 208 S.W.2d 843, 8 A.L.R.2d 1231 (1948) ("The element of attraction is important only in so far as it may mean that the presence of children was to be anticipated"). Contra: Nelson v. City of Rupert, 128 Idaho 199, 911 P.2d 1111 (Idaho 1996) (child trespasser must be attracted by the injury-causing condition).

19. Restatement § 339. "Reason to know" is not necessarily actual knowledge of the fact in question, but it is knowledge of specific facts that would lead to an inference of such a fact. See Restatement § 12. The original Restatement used "should have known," which is to say a straight negligence or foreseeability approach.

20. See Restatement § 339, cmts. g & h.

21. Mathis v. Massachusetts Electric Co., 409 Mass. 256, 565 N.E.2d 1180 (1991) (child trespasser rules reflect national trend toward uniform standard of care); McGetti-

the Restatement's six-paragraph rule in toto without necessarily focusing on the reason to know formula.[22] Other courts have definitely used a *should know* or foreseeability formulation in place of the *reason to know* phrase.[23] Sometimes the same court will use both terms,[24] a fact that may suggest the difference in practice between the two formulations is minuscule.

Harmful potential. To a large extent, the attractive nuisance doctrine becomes merely an application of ordinary negligence law. This means in part that the defendant who is under a duty of care is nevertheless not liable for harms done to anyone on his land, trespasser or not, unless he fails to act with ordinary care. If, on the facts, a reasonable person would perceive no unreasonable risk, then the landowner is not negligent and not liable. The landowner must be on notice of (or be able as a reasonable person to foresee) both the dangerous condition[25] on the land and the likelihood of child trespassers[26] who because of their youth and inexperience will not protect themselves.[27]

Balance of risks and utilities. Even if harm is foreseeable, the risk may be small compared with the cost of removing it. The ordinary negligence rule invites juries to compare the risks of injury with the utility to the defendant of keeping the risks as they are. So if the cost or burden of eliminating or reducing the risk is great, and the foreseeable risk is small, the defendant is not negligent and not liable at all. The same rule is applied in the trespassing child case.[28] A large rotating auger that could dismember a human being may have great utility in unloading

gan v. National Bank of Washington, 320 F.2d 703 (D.C.Cir.1963) (favoring an ordinary negligence approach); HARPER, JAMES AND GRAY § 27.5 at nn. 6 & 25 (favoring a simple negligence approach and criticizing the Second Restatement's departure from it).

22. Porter v. Delmarva Power & Light Co., 547 A.2d 124 (Del.1988); Hofer v. Meyer, 295 N.W.2d 333 (S.D.1980); Texas Utilities Electric Co. v. Timmons, 947 S.W.2d 191 (Tex.1997) (quoting the formula; seemingly not recognizing that Texas had stated a foreseeability test in Banker v. McLaughlin, n. 23 below); Thunder Hawk, v. Union Pacific R.R., 844 P.2d 1045 (Wyo.1992).

23. E.g., Gregory v. Johnson, 249 Ga. 151, 289 S.E.2d 232 (1982) (reasonable foreseeability); Mt. Zion State Bank & Trust v. Consolidated Communications, Inc., 169 Ill.2d 110, 214 Ill.Dec. 156, 660 N.E.2d 863 (1995) (but holding that harm from obvious danger was not foreseeable); Mathis v. Massachusetts Electric Co., 409 Mass. 256, 565 N.E.2d 1180 (1991) (foreseeable child trespassers); Banker v. McLaughlin, 146 Tex. 434, 208 S.W.2d 843, 8 A.L.R.2d 1231 (1948). In Louisville Trust Co. v. Nutting, 437 S.W.2d 484 (Ky.1968) the court purported to paraphrase the Restatement, but changed the "have reason to know" language to "should know." In Spur Feeding Co. v. Fernandez, 106 Ariz. 143, 472 P.2d 12, 49 A.L.R.3d 925 (1970) the court quoted the Restatement's "have reason to know" test, but appeared to apply a simple foreseeability test. The area was remote from habitation and no children had been there before. But the court thought the fact that the operation was visible from the highway.

24. Anderson v. Cahill, 485 S.W.2d 76 (Mo.1972); Bateman v. Mello, 617 A.2d 877 (R.I.1992).

25. Restatement § 339 (b).

26. Restatement § 339 (a).

27. Restatement § 339 cmt. i.

28. Bateman v. Mello, 617 A.2d 877 (R.I.1992) (liability on the facts would pose "devastating implications for landowners"); Banker v. McLaughlin, 146 Tex. 434, 208 S.W.2d 843, 8 A.L.R.2d 1231 (1948) (dangerous pit was easily filled and served no useful purpose); Restatement § 339 (d) (the special rule for trespassing children does not apply unless "the utility to the possessor of maintaining the condition and the burden of eliminating the danger are slight as compared with the risk to children").

a railroad car, but at relatively small cost, it can be covered to protect children, so a jury could appropriately find negligence if the landowner could foresee that children may play nearby.[29]

Specific rules or guidelines. Although the principle is the principle of ordinary care, courts, with some support from the Restatement,[30] added some specific rules or guidelines about what the landowner can reasonably expect of child trespassers. All of these should be taken with a grain of salt. They run somewhat along these lines:

(1) Older children. Older children, roughly beginning with the teen-aged years, can generally recognize dangers and protect themselves. Hence as to them, the risks of conditions on the land are reasonable,[31] provided that they do not amount to hidden dangers.[32] The real question about the landowner's duty, however, is not the child's age as such but whether such a child was at risk because he might fail to appreciate the dangers on the land. Age is strong evidence, but most courts reject a hard and fast rule about it.[33]

(2) Common hazards. The landowner is not ordinarily responsible for common hazards such as those associated with heights,[34] fire,[35] and bodies of water,[36] at least where those hazards are natural to the locality.[37] This list is particularly suspect. Whether a child should be expected to recognize and appreciate dangers of fire or water depends on the facts—the age of the child, for example. Whether the burden on the landowner is too great also depends on the facts. The burden of keeping a fence around a pool in repair is small compared to human life,[38] but in the case of a large irrigation canal miles in length, the burden of fencing might be too great.[39] To make rules about bodies of water or fire in these

29. Spur Feeding Co. v. Fernandez, 106 Ariz. 143, 472 P.2d 12, 49 A.L.R.3d 925 (1970).

30. Restatement § 339 cmt. j, listing fire, water, and falling from a height as dangers that children "under ordinary conditions" may be expected to appreciate and avoid unless the condition is hidden or some other special factor exists.

31. Restatement § 339, cmt. c.

32. If the risk amounts to a hidden danger of which the landowner knows, and if the child trespasser's coming is foreseeable, the duties owed to an adult trespasser would protect the child.

33. See Ricketts v. Norfolk Southern Ry. Co., 686 So.2d 1100 (Ala.1996) (rejecting the age of 14 as a standard demarcation); Texas Utilities Electric Co. v. Timmons, 947 S.W.2d 191 (Tex.1997) ("Like most courts, we decline to put an age limit on the beneficiaries of the attractive nuisance doctrine").

34. E.g., Logan v.Old Enterprise Farms, Ltd., 139 Ill.2d 229, 564 N.E.2d 778, 151 Ill.Dec. 323 (1990) (risk of falling from tree was obvious to child of 15).

35. Sampson v. Zimmerman, 151 Ill. App.3d 396, 502 N.E.2d 846, 104 Ill.Dec. 349 (1986) (asserting that even a four-year-old would appreciate the danger of a lighted candle).

36. Goodwin v. Jackson, 484 So.2d 1041 (Miss.1986). Swimming pools: conceivably a fencing ordinance will create a duty even to trespassers. Bell v. Page, 271 N.C. 396, 156 S.E.2d 711 (1967).

37. Some cases seem to have natural conditions in mind. See Lohrenz v. Lane, 787 P.2d 1274, 1278 (Okl.1990) ("A body of water—either standing, as in ponds and lakes, or running, as in rivers and creeks, or ebbing and flowing, as on the shores of seas and bays—is a natural object incident to all countries which are not deserts").

38. Giacona v. Tapley, 5 Ariz.App. 494, 428 P.2d 439 (1967).

39. See Dombrowski v. Maricopa County Municipal Water Conservation Dist., 108 Ariz. 275, 496 P.2d 136 (1972).

cases is to reject the important facts bearing on foreseeability and burden. Consequently, courts do in fact impose a duty of reasonable care to prevent a child's drowning in a swimming pool[40] or being burned in a fire.[41] Whether the duty was breached in a particular case, depends upon the amount of risk and the costs of avoiding it.

(3) Moving trains. Children ordinarily understand the danger of large moving trains or other items set in motions by adults, so they present no special risk to child trespassers.[42] It is true that trains in motion, by their bulk and their noise, give their own fearsome warnings, but of course none of the children who attempt to ride or play on them think they can be thrown under the grinding and cutting wheels. The highest tradition of the common law requires justice according to the facts of the case, not according to a model of cases in general, and it is not beyond conception that some children would foreseeably be unable to appreciate the risk of moving trains, just as they are unable to appreciate the risk of other moving machinery. The real reason railroads are not usually liable is that it is seldom negligent to move trains; it is the nature of railroads to move them and the goods and passengers they carry. But if the railroad could ensure safety for foreseeable child trespassers by, say, locking boxcar doors, there is no real reason to immunize the railroad that refuses to do so.

Balance of risks and utilities; artificial conditions. The cases mostly involve artificial conditions on the land,[43] not natural conditions. The Restatement issues a caveat expressing uncertainty whether the rules could cover natural conditions on the land, such as natural ponds of water or a natural precipice. On the other hand, if the condition was created by a human agency, the child trespasser rules apply to impose a duty of care. So even if the dangerous condition was not created by the

40. E.g., King v. Lennen, 53 Cal.2d 340, 1 Cal.Rptr. 665, 348 P.2d 98 (1959) (a child is more likely to be aware of and avoid a common hazard, but the ultimate question is whether the hazard could be understood by children, not whether it was common); Giacona v. Tapley, 5 Ariz.App. 494, 428 P.2d 439 (1967); Gregory v. Johnson, 249 Ga. 151, 289 S.E.2d 232 (1982) (applying attractive nuisance to a swimming pool although earlier authority had flatly stated that the doctrine did not apply to bodies of water); see Thomas R. Trenker, Annotation, Liability of Swimming Facility Operator for Injury to or Death of Trespassing Child, 88 A.L.R.3d 1197 (1978); cf. Banker v. McLaughlin, 146 Tex. 434, 208 S.W.2d 843, 8 A.L.R.2d 1231 (1948) (child drowning in pit created by developer; pit was easily filled and served no useful purpose). Courts that treat child trespassers like adults, of course, bar the claim. See Osterman v. Peters, 260 Md. 313, 272 A.2d 21 (1971), as do those which treat the body-of-water guideline as a rule rather than as evidence. See Goodwin v. Jackson, 484 So.2d 1041 (1986).

41. Louisville Trust Co. v. Nutting, 437 S.W.2d 484 (Ky.1968) (fire; the nature of the danger and its risk are variables that must be considered in each case); Dehn v. S. Brand Coal & Oil Co., 241 Minn. 237, 63 N.W.2d 6 (1954).

42. Holland v. Baltimore & Ohio R.R., 431 A.2d 597 (D.C.App.1981); Honeycutt v. City of Wichita, 247 Kan. 250, 796 P.2d 549 (1990). See Wade R. Habeeb, Annotation, Railroad's Liability for Injury to or Death of Child on Moving Train Other than as Paying or Proper Passenger, 35 A.L.R.3d 9 (1971). In Thunder Hawk, v. Union Pacific R.R., 844 P.2d 1045 (Wyo.1992) the court held that the moving train rule did not apply to stationary trains that start up after the child is on board.

43. The Restatement applies its child trespasser rules to artificial conditions only, but defines that to include "controllable forces already in operation" such as machinery; but it excludes "activities" on the land. Restatement § 339, cmt. a.

landowner but by some third person such as a trespasser, the landowner will be obliged to use reasonable care.[44]

The comments already made about the specific guidelines apply to the distinction between artificial and natural conditions. In most cases, it might be an unreasonable burden upon the landowner to alter a natural condition on the land to make it safe, but whether that is so depends upon the facts of the particular case. Conversely, it is not always cheap to make an artificial condition safe. Most artificial conditions are structures of some kind and most of them cost money and serve useful purposes. The real point with either kind of condition is to determine whether the burden of making it safe outweighs the risks of harm. This is the determination made under the ordinary negligence rules.

Child trespasser rules and comparative fault. One clause in the Restatement's formulation of rules seems misleading and certainly maladapted to a regime of comparative negligence. Section 339 (c) provides that the landowner is subject to liability only if "the children because of their youth do not discover the condition or realize the risk involved in intermeddling with it.... " This clause says or implies that the child who discovers danger and confronts it is completely barred from all recovery. In a system of comparative negligence, the child's discovery of danger could undoubtedly count as contributory negligence, but whether that negligence was great, small, or nonexistent would depend upon the facts of the case, not upon a rule of law. In a comparative negligence system, this rule is inappropriate because it seems to bar the negligent plaintiff completely.

On the other hand, a court could reason exactly in the opposite way to relieve the trespassing child of all responsibility. It could say that if a jury finds liability under the Restatement's child trespasser rules that is equivalent to a finding that the child was not in fact guilty of contributory negligence. That is so, the court could argue, because liability can be imposed only if the actual child before the court did not in fact discover the condition or realize the risk because of his age and inexperience. This would necessarily mean that, under the child standard of care, the child was not guilty of contributory negligence. Given such reasoning, a trespassing child would never be subject to a comparative negligence reduction in the award.[45] It is conceivable that in some cases landowners ought to be required to protect a child against her own negligence.[46] Such a policy is sparingly applied, but even if it should apply in some landowner cases, it seems surprising at best to suggest that it applies only to trespassing children.

The Restatement requires courts to handle a double edged sword, which either bars all negligent trespassing children in spite of compara-

44. McGettigan v. National Bank of Washington, 320 F.2d 703 (D.C.Cir.1963); Restatement § 339, cmt. c.

45. Florida seems to have had something like this in mind. See Larnel Builders, Inc. v. Martin, 110 So.2d 649, 650 (1959). This has led to a somewhat baroque embellishment of the doctrine. See Martinello v. B & P USA, Inc., 566 So.2d 761 (Fla.1990).

46. See § 200.

tive negligence rules or allows full recovery in spite of those rules, depending on which edge of the sword the court presents to the issue. A better approach would say that Restatement § 339 (c) is obsolete in comparative negligence states. The child's actual discovery of the danger should be assessed under contributory negligence rules.

That is not quite the end of the matter, however. The fault of the child-plaintiff or her discovery-in-fact of the danger is a matter quite different from the negligence of the landowner. The landowner breaches no duty of care unless he should reasonably foresee harm to the child. If he can foresee a trespass only by children old enough to see, appreciate, and avoid the danger, he is not negligent and not liable at all. That point is not a matter of what the particular child knew or discovered, or of comparative fault. It is rather that the landowner is simply not negligent.[47]

§ 237. Abolishing the Categories and Requiring Reasonable Care

At least as a matter of form, the landowners' rules, relying on categories of trespasser, licensee, and invitee, reject the general duty of reasonable care under the circumstances. As a matter of substance, however, it is quite possible that courts intend by these classifications to enforce a duty of reasonable care, but to displace the jury's role in favor of tight control by the judges. By manipulating the classifications and by taking from the jury issues about what counts as willful or wanton or foreseeable, judges may be doing little more in most cases than deciding the negligence issue. The price of such control has been high, however. Injustice is probably done in some cases, and when it is avoided, the judiciary must be involved in an added layer of litigation (the classification process and its almost interminable ramifications).

Abolishing the categories and substituting the standard of reasonable care. The system of categories and limited duties suffered its first attack in England, which had originated the rule. In 1957 Parliament passed the Occupiers' Liability Act, which imposed a single common duty of care for all visitors.[1] About the same time, the United States Supreme Court rejected the common law classification approach when it came to Admiralty cases.[2]

47. See, e.g., Holland v. Baltimore & Ohio R.R., 431 A.2d 597 (D.C.App.1981); Lister v. Campbell, 371 So.2d 133 (Fla.App. 1979) (15 Mt. Zion State Bank & Trust v. Consolidated Communications, Inc.), 169 Ill.2d 110, 214 Ill.Dec. 156, 660 N.E.2d 863 (1995); Restatement § 339, cmt. i. Some of the cases that make this point also hold that the child can appreciate a wide number of "obvious" risks, a view that led Justice Harrison dissenting in a suit against a telephone company to say: "The majority opinion confirms something that we should have known already: in Illinois, it is better to be a telephone company than to be a little boy." The perception that the defendant can expect some children to protect themselves, however, is a valid point even if courts apply it too stringently in some cases.

§ 237

1. Occupiers' Liability Act, 5 & 6 Eliz. 2, c. 31 (1957). The act is discussed in W.V.H. Rogers, Winfield & Jolowicz on Tort 225 ff (14th ed. 1994).

2. Kermarec v. Compagnie Generale Transatlantique, 358 U.S. 625, 79 S.Ct. 406, 3 L.Ed.2d 550 (1959).

Beginning in 1968 with a California decision,[3] American state courts began to abolish the categories and to substitute the general reasonable care standard. One group applied the reasonable care rule to any entrant upon land, including trespassers.[4] Another group retained the trespasser category with its special rules, but applied the reasonable care standard to all other entrants.[5]

Reasonable care does not require actions to protect or warn visitors whose coming is not known or reasonably foreseeable.[6] Since trespassers and licensees are often unforeseeable visitors,[7] the standard of reasonable care under the circumstances will not often result in any new liability. In any event, the reasonable care rule of ordinary negligence law recognizes that the burdens or costs to the defendant in making the land safe must be considered along with the risk to the plaintiff, so that many risks are entirely justified under that rule.[8]

Reasons for the change. The most obvious reason for change was that the common law categories did not correlate with the rights and wrongs of the cases or with the legal principles that would normally be determinative.[9] For instance, whether you are a licensee or invitee says nothing whatever about the amount of burden that would be imposed

3. Rowland v. Christian, 69 Cal.2d 108, 70 Cal.Rptr. 97, 443 P.2d 561 (1968).

4. District of Columbia, Alaska, California, Colorado, Hawaii, Louisiana, Nevada, New Hampshire, New York. Legislation in Colorado has since intervened. Colo. Rev. Stats. § 13–21–115.

5. Kansas, Maine, Massachusetts, Minnesota, Nebraska, North Carolina, North Dakota, Rhode Island, Tennessee, Wisconsin, and Wyoming. Illinois abolished the licensee-invitee distinction by statute. See 740 ILCS § 130/2.

6. See Webb v. City and Borough of Sitka, 561 P.2d 731 (Alaska 1977) ("the foreseeability of her presence determines in part (a) the likelihood of injury to her, and (b) the extent to which the City must take action or the interest it must sacrifice to avoid the risk of injury"); Marioenzi v. DiPonte, Inc., 114 R.I. 294, 333 A.2d 127 (1975), overruled on other grounds, Tantimonico v. Allendale Mutual Ins. Co., 637 A.2d 1056 (R.I.1994); Hudson v. Gaitan, 675 S.W.2d 699 (Tenn.1984) ("foreseeability of the presence of the visitor and the likelihood of harm to him being one of the principal factors in assessing liability").

7. Courts sometimes say the status of the visitor is still relevant as bearing on the landowner's foreseeability or reasonable expectations. See Peterson v. Balach, 294 Minn. 161, 199 N.W.2d 639 (1972); Scurti v. City of New York, 40 N.Y.2d 433, 387 N.Y.S.2d 55, 354 N.E.2d 794 (1976). That is a shorthand expression; it is not the status itself that is relevant but some of the facts that are that establish status. "Foreseeability of the visitor's presence determines in part the likelihood of injury to him, and the extent of the interest which must be sacrificed to avoid the risk of injury." Smith v. Arbaugh's Restaurant, Inc., 469 F.2d 97 (D.C.Cir.1972). See also O'Leary v. Coenen, 251 N.W.2d 746 (N.D.1977).

8. See, e.g., Webb v. City and Borough of Sitka, 561 P.2d 731 (Alaska 1977) ("A landowner or owner of other property must act as a reasonable person in maintaining his property in a reasonably safe condition in view of all the circumstances, including the likelihood of injury to others, the seriousness of the injury, and the burden on the respective parties of avoiding the risk").

9. Smith v. Arbaugh's Restaurant, Inc., 469 F.2d 97 (D.C.Cir.1972) ("If immunities from liability are to exist, they should be based on consideration of factors which are relevant in modern society and unrelated to classifications of trespassers, licensees and invitees"). Pickard v. City and County of Honolulu, 51 Haw. 134, 452 P.2d 445 (1969) ("We believe that the common law distinctions between classes of persons have no logical relationship to the exercise of reasonable care for the safety of others"); Basso v. Miller, 40 N.Y.2d 233, 352 N.E.2d 868, 386 N.Y.S.2d 564 (1976) (courts should "correlate the duty of care owed plaintiff with the risk of harm reasonably to be perceived" not with status).

upon the landowner to make conditions reasonably safe, nor about the degree of risk his carelessness imposed upon others.[10]

As the reform courts said, the adjudication-by-classification procedure in premises liability cases was sometimes harsh or unjust.[11] The system left the landowner free to impose unreasonable risks of harm upon others without responsibility.[12] The reform courts were also concerned about what seemed to be the almost-feudal privilege the rules accorded to landowners.[13] Most of all, these courts emphasized that the traditional categories promoted complexity, confusion,[14] and a misuse of judicial time[15] as courts manipulated the doctrines and added distinctions to prevent the most serious injustices.

The perception of occasional injustice and common confusion was coupled with the perception that it was not needed either for the purpose of getting justice or the purpose of imposing appropriate controls on juries. "Not needed" was too mild. Although the traditional rules were almost Byzantine in their elaboration, they nevertheless produced a simplistic system that could not appropriately "allocate costs and risks of human injury", especially where the status question prevented the court from reaching "the fundamental questions whether the defendant had acted reasonably in light of all the circumstances in the particular case."[16]

10. "[T]he closeness of the connection between the injury and the defendant's conduct, the moral blame attached to the defendant's conduct, the policy of preventing future harm, and the prevalence and availability of insurance bear little if any relationship to the classification.... " Rowland v. Christian, 69 Cal.2d 108, 70 Cal.Rptr. 97, 443 P.2d 561 (1968). Cf. Limberhand v. Big Ditch Co., 218 Mont. 132, 706 P.2d 491 (1985) (test is always reasonable care, not status).

11. E.g., Jones v. Hansen, 254 Kan. 499, 867 P.2d 303 (1994); See Peterson v. Balach, 294 Minn. 161, 199 N.W.2d 639 (1972) (guest in the owner's home subject to lesser standard of care than guest in the owner's car); Ford v. Board of County Comn'rs, 118 N.M. 134, 879 P.2d 766 (1994) (recovery a matter of chance, depending on category pigeonhole).

12. For instance, the *Rowland* court argued that status, as opposed to individual merits, would not be an immutable indicator of the landowner's moral blame, the foreseeability of harm, or the burden that would be imposed by requiring reasonable care. See Rowland v. Christian, 69 Cal.2d 108, 70 Cal.Rptr. 97, 443 P.2d 561 (1968). See also Cates v. Beauregard Electric Co–operative, Inc., 328 So.2d 367 (La.1976); O'Leary v. Coenen, 251 N.W.2d 746 (N.D. 1977) ("the common law categories have no logical relationship to the exercise of reasonable care for the safety of others").

13. Smith v. Arbaugh's Restaurant, Inc., 469 F.2d 97 (D.C.Cir.1972) (landowner privilege and the felt importance of exploiting land); Antoniewicz v. Reszcynski, 70 Wis.2d 836, 236 N.W.2d 1 (1975) (both courts cited the first edition of Harper, James & Gray).

14. See Kermarec v. Compagnie Generale Transatlantique, 358 U.S. 625, 79 S.Ct. 406, 3 L.Ed.2d 550 (1959); Rowland v. Christian, 69 Cal.2d 108, 70 Cal.Rptr. 97, 443 P.2d 561 (1968); Jones v. Hansen, 254 Kan. 499, 867 P.2d 303 (1994); Peterson v. Balach, 294 Minn. 161, 199 N.W.2d 639 (1972).

15. Mile High Fence Co. v. Radovich, 175 Colo. 537, 489 P.2d 308 (1971).

16. Mounsey v. Ellard, 363 Mass. 693, 707, 297 N.E.2d 43, 51 (1973). Cf. Smith v. Arbaugh's Restaurant, Inc., 469 F.2d 97 (D.C.Cir.1972) ("We do not believe ... that the problem of allocating the costs and risks of human injury is a simple one. Nor do we believe that one value-human safety-should be advanced above all others. We recognize that the allocation of costs requires the resolution of a complex equation, one for which society has not as yet provided a computer. Rather, for centuries the costs of personal negligence have been allocated by

In addition, the system of classification was closely similar to the old guest statutes, which had been held unconstitutional in some states[17] and repealed in most others on the ground that they made invidious distinctions.[18]

One assertion on behalf of the category-based rules was that they had been around hundreds of years and that courts have devoted time and effort to construct them.[19] That point does not seem to address the merits of the categories, however. Another point is that the categories promote certainty and predictability in the law.[20] The reform courts have rejected this view. Indeed, the reform courts saw the application of traditional rules as confusing, uncertain, and changing,[21] so that far from making the law predictable, they made it uncertain.[22] In any event, the reasonable care rule, created by courts and used by them in vast numbers of negligence cases, does not seem to sponsor especially unpredictable results in landowner cases.[23]

Perhaps the expressed concern with predictability sometimes represented a somewhat different feeling that juries were not capable of deciding these cases,[24] or that rogue juries might improperly impose liabilities. Such concerns seem misplaced. Most premises liability cases are rather simple on their facts, certainly simple as compared to major products liability suits. And it is unlikely that juries will be more roguish in suits against landowners than in others, such as suits against large corporations that have manufactured and distributed dangerous goods. Yet courts were willing to impose not merely a duty of reasonable care but strict liability in the case of manufacturers of defective goods. There are certainly differences in the two kinds of cases, but the differences do not suggest that jury antipathy to defendants should or does lead courts to adopt protective rules in other instances.

Even if the rogue jury were somehow a unique concern in premises cases, judges do not need a categorical rule of law based on status of entrants to fulfill this function. If the landowner's lack of negligence is

a jury according to the standard of reasonable care under all the circumstances").

17. E.g., Bierkamp v. Rogers, 293 N.W.2d 577 (Iowa 1980).

18. Antoniewicz v. Reszcynski, 70 Wis.2d 836, 236 N.W.2d 1 (1975), abolishing the licensee category, expressly argued that the court's earlier abolition of similar rules for automobile guests was analogous.

19. Gerchberg v. Loney, 223 Kan. 446, 576 P.2d 593 (1978); Carter v. Kinney, 896 S.W.2d 926 (Mo.1995). Kansas, which asserted this argument in *Gerchberg,* later adopted the reform view.

20. Carter v. Kinney, 896 S.W.2d 926 (Mo.1995).

21. Ouellette v. Blanchard, 116 N.H. 552, 364 A.2d 631 (1976) is an especially good discussion of the continual changes courts have made in trying to avoid injustice in application of the categories.

22. See Heins v. Webster County, 250 Neb. 750, 758, 552 N.W.2d 51, 56 (1996).

23. Most tort law rules do not provide high predictability to the actors, although they may do so for lawyers. Most tort law rules instead frame the nature of the debate and guide lawyers about the kind of evidence to produce.

24. See Gerchberg v. Loney, 223 Kan. 446, 576 P.2d 593 (1978) (suggesting a choice between unusually detailed instructions and a free hand to decide liability on any standard; "Can a lay jury reasonably be expected to consider the proper relative effect of natural and artificial conditions on the premises.... ").

so clear that reasonable people could not differ, judges can take the case from the jury by directed verdict or otherwise without making a rule for all cases involving licensees or trespassers. In fact, a straightforward negligence rule for landowners is likely to induce better evidence about the costs and benefits of the landowner's conduct and about the degree of risk involved, all of which would give the landowner full protection for productive work.

Trespassers. At this writing, a slight majority of the reform courts retain the trespasser category, limiting the landowner's duty to trespassers under the traditional rules. As always, however, trespassers appear in many forms, including toddler children whose presence is entirely foreseeable, so this group of reform courts will presumably retain the complications of attractive nuisance rules, "known" trespassers, and frequent trespassers.

In the remaining reform jurisdictions, the reasonable care standard governs even in the case of trespassers. However, the foreseeability of the trespasser, the degree of risk, and the cost or inconvenience of steps needed to make the premises safe would be considered. Consequently, the trespasser's status has a residual importance as evidence for the jury.[25] Indeed, in some cases courts could hold that the trespasser's coming was unforeseeable, so that juries would not be allowed to find negligence at all: if there is no one coming, you can leave the child's toy on the floor because no one will be injured by it. For these reasons and at least two others, the fear that a burglar could recover is highly improbable.[26]

Exceptions or limits to the rule of reasonable care. As indicated in the next section, recreational use statutes to some extent reinstitute a scheme of limited duties for certain entrants upon land. In addition, most courts limit the rights of professional risk-takers like firefighters and police officers.

Prospects. Some courts that initially resisted the change, have now accepted the reform.[27] On the other hand, the District of Columbia and Rhode Island, both of which had eliminated all categories in earlier decisions, have now restored the trespasser classification.[28] Both contin-

25. Scurti v. City of New York, 40 N.Y.2d 433, 387 N.Y.S.2d 55, 354 N.E.2d 794 (1976).

26. First, a burglar might recover in the case of an intentional tort that exceeds the homeowner's privilege, as in the case of a spring gun that mutilates the burglar. See §§ 76–80. However, the landowner presumably can do negligently everything he would be permitted to do intentionally in pursuit of a privilege. So short of setting a trap, the landowner is likely to be fully protected against the imaginary burglar suits. Second, the burglar, at least in some jurisdictions, might be faced with the rule that he cannot recover for harms arising from his own wrongdoing. See § 208. Third, although probably unnecessary, specific statutes forbid recovery for injuries sustained in the commission of a felony. See Calvillo–Silva v. Home Grocery, 19 Cal.4th 714, 968 P.2d 65, 80 Cal.Rptr.2d 506 (1998) (applying such a statute).

27. Kansas withstood repeated assaults on traditional rules until it abolished the licensee-invitee categories in Jones v. Hansen, 254 Kan. 499, 867 P.2d 303 (1994).

28. Holland v. Baltimore & Ohio R.R., 431 A.2d 597 (D.C.App.1981); Tantimonico v. Allendale Mutual Ins. Co., 637 A.2d 1056 (R.I.1994).

ue to use the reasonable care standard for licensees and invitees, however.[29] The only state to resume something like the common law categories is Colorado, where stringent legislation was been passed to restore the categories and add additional protections for some landowners.[30] In 1998, the North Carolina Supreme Court counted 11 jurisdictions that had adopted the reasonable care standard across the board and 14 more that had done so for licensees and invitees.[31] That list includes some states that merely shifted social guests from the licensee to the invitee category,[32] but in any event something close to half the states have now modified the traditional rule in favor of a reasonable care standard for most cases. No less than five of the reform decisions were handed down between 1993 and 1998, so it may be that the earlier announcements that reform had been halted were premature.

§ 238. Recreational Use Statutes

Statutory Protections

The statutory gist. All or virtually all states have enacted recreational use statutes.[1] The gist of these statutes is to immunize landowners or occupiers from liability for most non-willful harms to persons who are permitted to use the land for recreational purposes without a fee or charge. The stated purpose of the statutes is to encourage landowners to open private lands for recreational use in an increasingly crowded society with inadequate public recreational space.[2] Some states tack on various additional provisions, such as special protections for farmer-landowners[3] or educational uses.[4]

Converting invitees to trespassers. The statutes are couched in stringent terms. For instance, they may say that the permitted but non-paying user has neither invitee nor licensee status[5] or that he is to be treated as a trespasser.[6] The statutes commonly provide that no duty of care is owed to make the premises safe for the non-paying recreational users. Such provisions have the effect of restoring the common trespasser or licensee categories. They sometimes grant landowners even broader protections that they would obtain under contemporary common law categories. That is certainly the case with the recreational user who is on

29. See Sandoe v. Lefta Associates, 559 A.2d 732 (D.C.App.1988); Labrie v. Pace Membership Warehouse, 678 A.2d 867, 869 (R.I.1996).

30. Colo. Rev. Stats. § 13–21–115.

31. Nelson v. Freeland, 349 N.C. 615, 507 S.E.2d 882 (1998).

32. See Wood v. Camp, 284 So.2d 691 (Fla.1973) (licensees by invitation treated as invitees); Burrell v. Meads, 569 N.E.2d 637 (Ind.1991).

§ 238

1. See Joseph A. Page, The Law of Premises Liability § 5.13 (2d ed. 1988 & David A. Elder Supp.); Robin Cheryl Miller, Annotation, Effect of Statute Limiting Landowner's Liability For Personal Injury to Recreational User, 47 A.L.R.4th 262 (1987).

2. Often expressed in the statute itself. E.g., Fla. Stat. Ann. § 375.251.

3. Mich. Comp. L. Ann. § 324.73301.

4. N.C. Gen. Stats. § 38A–4.

5. E.g., Cal. Civ. Code § 846.

6. N.C. Gen. Stat. § 38A–4.

land open to the public. The common law rule would treat such a person as a public invitee, to whom the landowner owes a duty or reasonable care.[7] Under the recreational use statute, however, the landowner owes only the duty to avoid willful or malicious injury, or sometimes gross negligence.[8]

Known dangers. Some of the statutes affirmatively provide that liability may be imposed when the landowner actually knows of a danger.[9] However, other statutes make no such provision. Most do not directly recognize the common law distinctions between known and unknown dangers, between known and unknown users, or between natural and artificial conditions. Such statutes raise the possibility that the landowner would be immune from liability even when he fails to warn a known user who is about to encounter a known danger.[10] It seems quite possible that such statutes would actually leave the permissive land user worse off than she would be under the contemporary liberal rules for liability to known or foreseeable trespassers.

However, many of the statutes also provide for liability for willful or malicious failure to guard or warn[11] or sometimes for "gross negligence."[12] As shown in earlier sections, failure to warn about a known hazardous condition can be equated with willful or wanton misconduct,[13] so it may be that many of the statutes come out on recreational users about where the common law came out on the same facts.

Activities. The statutes may also affect liability for negligent activities. Some statutes provide that the owner owes no duty to warn as to dangerous activities,[14] which could conceivably mean that the owner is not liable for an activity negligently carried on.

Attractive nuisance. The statutes may also relieve the landowner of common law duties recognized under the attractive nuisance or child trespasser rules. Although some statutes specifically recognize the ongoing validity of the attractive nuisance rules,[15] others say nothing at all about the child trespasser. When the statute says nothing on the subject, some courts have read in an exception so that the landowner remains responsible for his negligent harm to foreseeable child trespassers who could not be expected to discover the dangers on the land for themselves.[16] But some courts have held that the recreational use statutes,

7. See § 234.

8. E.g., Brooks v. Northwood Little League, Inc., 327 S.C. 400, 489 S.E.2d 647 (Ct.App.1997).

9. Ala. Code § 35–15–24 (landowner knows of danger and of user's presence); Rev. Code Wash. Ann. § 4.24.210 ("known dangerous artificial latent condition for which warning signs have not been conspicuously posted").

10. For example, where the defendant strings a steel cable across a trail, knowing that cyclists ride there. See Wirth v. Ehly, 93 Wis.2d 433, 287 N.W.2d 140 (1980) (denying recovery under a predecessor of the current statute).

11. Cal. Civ. Code § 846 ("willful or malicious" failure to guard or warn); N.Y. Gen. Oblig. L. § 9–103.

12. Mich. Comp. L. Ann. § 324.73301.

13. E.g., § 232.

14. E.g., Idaho Code § 36–1604.

15. E.g., Ariz. Rev. Stat. § 33–1551; Rev. Code Wash. Ann. § 4.24.210.

16. Smith v. Crown–Zellerbach, Inc., 638 F.2d 883 (5th Cir.1981).

giving landowners special benefits without exception, in effect superseded the attractive nuisance rules.[17] This puts the child who is subjected to foreseeable dangers in a worse position than many adult trespassers under the common law rules.[18]

Statutory Coverage

Owners; recreational use. Much of the litigation under recreational use statutes deals with their coverage. The statutes do not apply at all unless the defendant is an owner or occupant as defined in the statute. Nor do they apply when the plaintiff's use of the land is not for a recreational purpose as defined in the statute. Some statutes define recreational purpose in general terms,[19] but others present a catalog of recreational activities that might include skateboarding, spelunking, and parachuting and many other specific activities.[20]

Open to the public. The statutes' stated purpose is to encourage use of private land for recreation. However, the landowner need take no steps to qualify for the special protections of the statute. The statutes do not require the landowner to dedicate an easement for public use, to register the land, or even to inform the public by signs or otherwise that it is available. Even the statutes that require that the land be open for public recreational use,[21] do not require the landowner to mention the fact to anyone.[22]

Some of the statutes do not even require that the land be open to the public, only that the landowner permit or invite a person to use the land.[23] Such statutes may protect the landowner even if he has tried to exclude all users by erecting barriers and posting No Trespassing signs.[24]

17. E.g., Coursey v. Westvaco Corporation, 790 S.W.2d 229 (Ky.1990).

18. See § 232.

19. E.g., N.C. Gen. Stats. § 38A–2.

20. E.g., Cal. Civ. Code § 846 (listing 20 activities, some of which overlap, but not including skateboarding); Rev. Code Wash. Ann. § 4.24.210 (amended to include skateboarding). Both subjective purpose of the plaintiff and the nature of the activity may be considered in determining whether the statute applies. Kosky v. International Ass'n of Lions Clubs, 210 Wis.2d 463, 565 N.W.2d 260 (Wis.App.1997). Cf. Farnham v. Kittinger, 83 N.Y.2d 520, 634 N.E.2d 162, 611 N.Y.S.2d 790 (1994) (enter the land in a four-wheel drive vehicle capable of recreational use, not necessarily recreational if the purpose was only to urinate). Presumably, the injury must be connected with the recreational uses or purposes in some manner; the immunity does not extend to the landowner who acts in some capacity other than landowners. See Id.

21. E.g., Fla. Stat. Ann. § 375.251; Rev. Code Wash. Ann. § 4.24.210.

22. See Coursey v. Westvaco Corporation, 790 S.W.2d 229 (Ky.1990) ("a landowner must show he knew and condoned the public making recreational use of his property, and by the landowner's words, actions or lack of action it must be able to be reasonably inferred the landowner intended to permit such use"),

23. New York, for example, provides that the owner "owes no duty to keep the premises safe for entry or use by others for [stated recreational activities] or to give warning of any hazardous condition or use of or structure or activity on such premises to persons entering for such purposes. . . . " N.Y. Gen. Oblig. L. § 9–103.

24. E.g., Larini v. Biomass Industries, Inc., 918 F.2d 1046 (2d Cir.1990); cf. Verdoljak v. Mosinee Paper Corporation, 200 Wis.2d 624, 547 N.W.2d 602 (1996) (gate barred entrance; motorcyclist injured in running into the gate, a bar suspended from chains; held, the statute "does not purport to condition that limit to owners who open their land to those who use it for recreational activities."). Note that if the statutory protections were denied, the un-

In consequence, the statutes sometimes reduce the landowner's duty to something considerably less than reasonable care even when the landowner withholds the recreational benefits the statute purports to seek. Some authority goes the other way, withholding the statutory protections when the landowner in fact excludes users.[25] That result that seems compelled where the statute actually requires that the land be opened to the public.

Suitability for recreation. The statutes do not by their terms require that the land be suitable for recreation.[26] The landowner gets the protection of the statute even if the land is not suited for recreation. In a California case, the plaintiff child was sitting to one side while other children played on stacked pipes. The pipes dislodged and fell on the child. The court thought that the child was a recreational user, even if she was not engaged in playing on the pipes and even if the land was not suited to recreation.[27]

Public land, urban land. Given a purpose to encourage owners to open private lands to the public for recreation, it seems unlikely that the statute would apply to lands already owned by the public, to lands such as parks that are already open to the public, or indeed to urban land generally. Some statutes specifically answer one or more of these questions, for example, by granting the statutory immunities to urban[28] and public lands[29] or sometimes by limiting the statutory favors to private or rural owners.[30]

When the statute is not explicit, courts have divided on such issues. Most courts appear to give public entities[31] and urban landowners[32] the benefit of the statutory protections, but some hold that the statute, intended to encourage opening of private lands, could hardly have been meant to apply to municipalities.[33] Likewise, a few apply the statute only

permitted plaintiff would be a trespasser. Whether he would be entitled to a duty of care would depend, at least in some states, upon whether he were a discovered or foreseeable trespasser and whether the danger was one he was unlikely to discover.

25. See Crawford v. Tilley, 780 P.2d 1248 (Utah 1989).

26. Although the statutes do not impose a suitability test, the plurality in Iannotti v. Consolidated Rail Corp.,74 N.Y.2d 39, 542 N.E.2d 621, 544 N.Y.S.2d 308 (1989), argued that suitability to a recreational purpose was required because "(1) there could be no public interest in inducing the owners of such unsuitable properties to make them available for public recreation; and (2) that being so, offering immunity as the quid pro quo to such owners would be pointless and would not further the underlying statutory purpose." The exact status of this idea in New York is presently uncertain. Farnham v. Kittinger, 83 N.Y.2d 520, 634 N.E.2d 162, 611 N.Y.S.2d 790 (1994).

27. Ornelas v. Randolph, 4 Cal.4th 1095, 847 P.2d 560, 17 Cal.Rptr.2d 594 (1993).

28. E.g., Rev. Code Wash. Ann. § 4.24.210.

29. Ariz. Rev. Stat. § 33–1551 (a public or private owner).

30. N.C. Gen. Stats. § 38A–2 (defining owner to exclude governmental entities).

31. E.g., Watson v. City of Omaha, 209 Neb. 835, 312 N.W.2d 256 (1981) (public entities liable only when private individual would be, and since private individual would be protected, so is the public entity); Sega v. State, 60 N.Y.2d 183, 456 N.E.2d 1174, 469 N.Y.S.2d 51 (1983).

32. E.g., Gallagher v. Omaha Public Power District, 225 Neb. 354, 405 N.W.2d 571 (1987).

33. E.g., Delta Farms Reclamation Dist. v. Superior Court of San Joaquin County, 33 Cal.3d 699, 660 P.2d 1168, 190 Cal.Rptr.

to rural or undeveloped lands.[34]

The strange case of swimming pools. None of the statutes apply to protect landowners who accept a fee for the plaintiff's use of the land. Otherwise, however, the statutes as broadly construed cover a wide range of recreational possibilities when they include urban land. When the statute does not by its terms require as a condition of protection that the land be opened to the public generally, it would seem that it would cover even an urban landowner who invites a neighbor to swim in a backyard pool. Some courts have looked at the policy of the statute rather than the words. Since the statute is aimed at opening land to the public for recreation, and since the backyard pool is not open to the public, the common law, not the statute, applies to such a case.[35] Beyond this, some courts have tried to limit the broad sweep of the statutes by saying that they do not cover indoor pools, either.[36] Perhaps such decisions mean that at some point courts must circumscribe such statutes written with a brush so broad as used in these recreational use statutes.

Topic C. Duties of Vendors and Lessors

§ 239. Vendors of Land

Once the landowner sells the land or leases it to a tenant, his duties to make conditions on the land reasonably safe are limited or nonexistent. The reasons for and effects of the limitation are not like those in landowner cases already covered. In other landowner cases, the question was whether anyone owed a duty of any kind. In cases of vendors and landlords, however, the question is not so much whether a duty is owed but who owes it. It is not the existence of responsibility but the allocation of it. Subject to some qualifications, the traditional common law regarded the transfer of land title as a shift of responsibility[1] for conditions that might cause physical harm to others on the land.

Once the purchaser of land takes title and possession, he becomes responsible for dangers to himself or others on the land; and correspondingly the vendor is freed from responsibility.[2] If the vendor knew of a danger on the land and concealed it, he would remain responsible for harms resulting after transfer to the purchaser, but then only until the

494 (1983); Conway v. Town of Wilton, 238 Conn. 653, 680 A.2d 242 (1996).

34. See Harrison v. Middlesex Water Co., 80 N.J. 391, 403 A.2d 910 (1979).

35. Loyer v. Buchholz, 38 Ohio St.3d 65, 526 N.E.2d 300 (1988).

36. E.g., Cassio v. Creighton University, 233 Neb. 160, 446 N.W.2d 704 (1989).

§ 239

1. Shifting responsibility: see § 194. The rules are commonly explained by the maxim caveat emptor, let the buyer beware, but so far as liability to third persons is concerned, they seem to represent the expectations of the parties to the sale or lease.

2. See, e.g., O'Connor v. Altus, 67 N.J. 106, 335 A.2d 545 (1975) (distinguishing a former owner from a former owner who was also a builder); Restatement § 352; Emile F. Short, Annotation, Liability of Vendor or Grantor of Real Estate for Personal Injury to Purchaser or Third Person Due to Defective Condition of Premises, 48 A.L.R.3d 1027 (1973).

purchaser discovered the danger or had reason to know of it, or perhaps until the purchaser has time to make it reasonably safe.[3] The vendor would also escape liability if the purchaser knew of the danger or had reason to know of it.

When the condition creates a danger which causes harms to persons outside the land, the vendor remains responsible for his negligence in creating or maintaining the condition, but again the responsibility would terminate when the purchaser discovers the danger and perhaps until he has reasonable opportunity to make it reasonably safe.[4]

§ 240. Traditional Common Law Duties of Lessors[1]

Relevance of the common law framework. This section discusses the traditional common law duties of landlords. Those duties may be modified in some instances when the landlord is charged with negligence in failing to protect a tenant from an attacker and when the landlord is charged with breaching a "warranty" of habitability. The duty to protect the plaintiff from others is a large subject not limited to landlords and it is considered in another chapter.[2] The so-called warranty of habitability is considered in the next section. This modification may require repairs by a landlord that would not be required by the common law rules. On the other hand, some common law rules will require an inspection that would not be required under the warranty of habitability. Further, the habitability warranty does not apply to all cases. Consequently, the common law rules remain important not only as the starting place for the habitability warranty but also because in a number of instances they are controlling.

Responsibility shifted to tenant. With respect to dangerous conditions of leased premises, lessors ordinarily[3] owed the same duties to the tenant and the tenant's guests or others on the premises with the tenant's consent.[4] That was frequently no duty at all. The traditional

3. Restatement § 353(2) would hold the vendor responsible until the purchaser actually discovers the danger and has a reasonable opportunity to take effective precautions if the vendor actively concealed the danger. If the vendor merely fails to disclose, the Restatement would terminate the vendor's responsibility when the purchaser discovers or has reason to know of the condition. § 353 (1). The distinction between the two cases does not seem worth preserving.

4. Restatement § 373. The Restatement again draws a distinction: if the vendor creates or conceals the condition, his responsibility continues until the purchaser both discovers and has opportunity to make the condition safe. If he merely permits a dangerous condition to remain, his responsibility terminates when the purchaser has reasonable opportunity to discover the danger.

§ 240

1. On the whole topic, see Jean C. Love, Landlord's Liability for Defective Premises: Caveat Lessee, Negligence, or Strict Liability?, 1975 Wis. L. Rev. 19.

2. Chapter 21.

3. At least one duty may be peculiar to tenants: the duty to protect the tenant from a danger of which the tenant knows, when the tenant must confront that danger to obtain use of the premises she has leased. See Hallberg v. Flat Creek Animal Clinic, 225 Ga.App. 212, 483 S.E.2d 671 (1997).

4. Shump v. First Continental–Robinwood Associates, 71 Ohio St.3d 414, 644 N.E.2d 291 (1994) (breach of duty to tenant would be breach to tenant's guest); Ortega v. Flaim, 902 P.2d 199 (Wyo.1995) (no duty to tenant, no duty to tenant's guest).

common law viewed a lease as a sale of land for a period of time. Consequently, when the landowner leased land to a tenant, the tenant was in the role of a land buyer. Like other land buyers, the tenant became responsible for the harms caused by negligently created or maintained conditions of the leased premises; concomitantly, the landlord ceased to be responsible for it. In the absence of an exception, the landlord was not legally responsible for conditions that arose on the land after he leased it[5] or even for those that existed at the time of the lease.[6]

Concealed or undisclosed conditions. As an exception to the general rule, the landlord remained liable for harms done by an unreasonably dangerous condition of which he knew or had reason to know and which he concealed or failed to disclose, provided it is also a condition that the tenant was not likely to discover and does not in fact discover.[7] The proviso is often expressed by saying that the landlord's responsibility for conditions existing at the time of the lease extends only to latent defects, not patent ones.[8] Once the tenant discovered the danger and had opportunity to remedy it, the landlord's responsibility for concealment terminated; perhaps in some cases it terminated as soon as the tenant *should* have discovered the danger and taken precautions.[9]

Contract to make repairs. The landlord was responsible for unreasonably dangerous conditions if he has contracted to repair them and negligently fails to do so after he knows or should know of the danger.[10] At one time this was viewed as a purely contractual matter, so that the landlord would be liable for the cost of making repairs or some similar measure of damages but would not be liable for the injury caused by the disrepair.[11] Today, however, the landlord's contract to repair is treated as creating a duty of reasonable care as well. If he negligently fails to repair an unreasonably dangerous condition, he becomes liable for negligence, so that he is liable for the harms caused by disrepair as well as for the cost of bringing the premises up to the promised standard.[12] Since the landlord is liable only for a negligent failure to comply with the contractual duty, he is not responsible for repairs under this exception unless he is put on notice that they are needed and he has a reasonable opportunity to make them.[13]

5. Restatement § 355.

6. Restatement § 356.

7. Restatement § 358. Courts often say, that the dangerous condition must have been actually known by the landlord. E.g., Ortega v. Flaim, 902 P.2d 199 (Wyo.1995). If this is to be taken literally, the landlord's "reason to know" will not be enough.

8. See, e.g., Dowler v. Boczkowski, 148 N.J. 512, 691 A.2d 314 (1997); Munzi v. Kennedy, 538 A.2d 1015 (R.I.1988).

9. Restatement § 358. The Restatement provides that if the landlord does not actively conceal the condition, his responsibility terminates when the tenant has reasonable opportunity to discover the condition.

10. Restatement § 357.

11. E.g., Leavitt v. Twin County Rental Co., 222 N.C. 81, 21 S.E.2d 890 (1942).

12. Restatement § 375.

13. See McKenzie v. Egge, 207 Md. 1, 113 A.2d 95 (1955); Juarez v. Wavecrest Management Team Ltd., 88 N.Y.2d 628, 649 N.Y.S.2d 115, 672 N.E.2d 135 (1996) (lead-based paint; stating notice requirement both for contractual and statutory duty of repair).

Repairs negligently made. Even if not contractually obliged to make repairs, the landlord was under a duty to use reasonable care when he voluntarily made repairs on the leased premises after the tenant had taken possession.[14]He was thus subject to liability for actual harm if he negligently repaired a condition so that it was more dangerous, provided the tenant neither knew nor should have known of the increased danger.[15] The condition might be more dangerous either because alterations made it more infirm than before[16] or because the purported alterations gave an appearance of safety upon which the tenant relied.[17]

Land leased for public admission. The lessor who leases the premises for admission of the public owes a duty of reasonable care to discover dangers to the public and to correct them if he has reason to think that the lessee will admit the public before putting the premises in reasonably safe condition.[18] Even when this rule applies, it does not impose strict liability; the lessor's duty is to exercise reasonable care, no more.[19]

Portions of premises over which lessor retains control. In many instances, the lessor retains control over some portion of the premises that various tenants have a right to use. For instance, the landlord controls halls, stairways, and sidewalks that are part of an apartment building or complex of buildings. At the same time, those portions of the premises are intended for the tenants' use. As to such portions, the lessor owes a duty of reasonable care to make the premises safe for the benefit of the tenants and others lawfully upon the land.[20] Reasonable care will required inspection from time to time and reasonable effort to make dangerous situations safe. The proviso seen in some other instances does not apply here; the tenant's actual knowledge of the danger does not relieve the lessor of a duty of care. The tenant's property rights—to enter her apartment, for example, even if the only stairs to it are in dangerous condition—are trumps in this instance.

The rules just discussed are often referred to as the common passageway rules. However, the point is not that tenants are entitled to use of the defective premises but that the landlord has retained control. For that reason, similar rules apply to other portions of the land that are not intended for the tenants' use but that must be safe if the leased

14. Repairs negligently completed before the lease will not bring the landlord under this rule. Casey v. Estes, 657 So.2d 845 (Ala.1995).

15. See Restatement § 362.

16. E.g., Durkin v. Hansen, 313 S.C. 343, 437 S.E.2d 550 (Ct.App.1993) where the landlord's carpet cleaning left slippery soap on the kitchen tile floor with predictable results.

17. E.g., Ginsberg v. Wineman, 314 Mich. 1, 22 N.W.2d 49 (1946) where the landlord's agent purported to make a stair safe but (as the trier could find) actually only reinserted nails in holes that were loose, then told the tenant the stair was repaired. The tenant's employee, who was badly injured when the stair gave way, was allowed to recover.

18. Restatement § 359; see Lopez v. Friedman Brothers Investment Co., 106 Md.App. 774, 106 Md.App. 779 (1995)

19. See Johnson County Sheriff's Posse, Inc., v. Endsley, 926 S.W.2d 284 (Tex.1996) (lessor of rodeo arena was not negligent in failing to pick all rocks on its dirt floor).

20. Rodrigue v. Rodrigue, 694 A.2d 924 (Me.1997); Restatement § 360.

premises are to be safe.[21] For example, the lessor must not negligently allow the roof to collapse[22] or wiring within the walls or ceilings to become a fire hazard.[23]

§ 241. The Lessor's Warranty of Habitability or Continuing Duty to Repair

"Implied warranty." Most states, by statute or judicial decision, have now recognized an implied warranty of habitability in residential leases,[1] but not commercial ones.[2] Courts say that by leasing the property, the lessor implicitly guarantees that there are no defects, or at least no latent defects, and no housing law violations in facilities vital to the use of the premises, and, in many states, that essential features will remain in such condition during the lease, and that it will remain "habitable."[3] A number of courts take the position that the warranty cannot be "waived"[4] except perhaps in the case of a single-family dwelling.[5]

Strict liability rejected. The implied warranty originally served to give the tenant leverage to insist upon repairs. The tenant might, for example, withhold rent or make repairs and deduct the cost from her

21. See Restatement § 361; Restatement Second of Property § 17.4 (1976).

22. Restatement § 361.

23. Leavitt v. Glick Realty Corp., 362 Mass. 370, 285 N.E.2d 786 (1972) (subtenant died of smoke inhalation from fire caused by wiring in the ceiling of the apartment). Cf. Coleman v. Steinberg, 54 N.J. 58, 253 A.2d 167 (1969) (heating system for all tenants caused harm to child in one apartment).

§ 241

1. E.g., Pole Realty Co. v. Sorrells, 84 Ill.2d 178, 417 N.E.2d 1297, 49 Ill.Dec. 283 (1981) (warranty applies to single-family dwellings as well as to multiple-unit dwelling structures); Kline v. Burns, 111 N.H. 87, 276 A.2d 248 (1971) (implied warranty of habitability in an apartment rental); see Robert S. Schoshinski, American Law of Landlord and Tenant § 3.16 (Supp. 1997) (describing the historical development and listing many cases); Jonathan M. Purver, Annotation, Modern Status of Rules as to Existence of Implied Warranty of Habitability or Fitness for Use of Leased Premises, 40 A.L.R.3d 646 (1972). Several states have refused to recognize the warranty. E.g., Ortega v. Flaim, 902 P.2d 199 (Wyo.1995).

2. See Thomas M. Fleming, Annotation, Implied Warranty of Fitness or Suitability in Commercial Leases—Modern Status, 76 A.L.R.4th 928 (1990). Statutes originate the warranty in many instances, and some of these appear to exclude the warranty for commercial leases. E.g., 9 Vt. Stat. Ann. § 4457. See also the Uniform Residential Landlord & Tenant Act. Courts themselves also formulate the rule as one for residential leases. Johnson v. Scandia Associates, 641 N.E.2d 51 (Ind.App.1994). A few cases do recognize an implied warranty of suitability for the commercial purpose. E.g., Richard Barton Enterprises, Inc., v. Tsern, 928 P.2d 368 (Utah 1996); Davidow v. Inwood North Professional Group, 747 S.W.2d 373, 76 A.L.R.4th 919 (1988). However, many of these, like many of the residential lease cases, are not about injury but about the tenant's right to withhold rent or to defend against a suit for rent on the ground that the premises were defective.

3. Estate of Vazquez v. Hepner, 564 N.W.2d 426 (Iowa 1997).

4. E.g., Green v. Superior Court, 10 Cal.3d 616, 111 Cal.Rptr. 704, 517 P.2d 1168 (1974).

5. Restatement Second of Property § 5.6 (1976) leaves the parties free to bargain, although courts have emphasized that this only means tenant loses in most urban apartment house leases. However, the Restatement would strike any agreement for reducing the landlord's obligations if it is unconscionable. One reason why it might not be unconscionable to reduce the landlord's duties would be that the premises are for single-family or commercial use. See id. at cmt. e.

rental obligations. Yet the language of implied warranty, long associated with strict liability, suggested that the landlord would be liable without fault for personal injuries resulting from dangers on the leased premises. As courts began to consider the implied warranty theory in personal injury claims, however, it has turned out that the landlord was not strictly liable at all.[6] The "warranty" requires only that the landlord keep the premises in reasonable repair when the landlord knows or should know of the defect.[7] The warranty is not a warranty that the lessor has implicitly made[8] but a rule of law imposed by the court.

Statutes. Legislative enactments in the form of statutes or ordinances often establish a warranty of habitability or some specific requirement for safety and habitability of the premises. These instruments may make it clear by their own terms that the landlord's obligation arises only when he has notice of the defect.[9] In any event, courts have generally interpreted these statutes as demanding only reasonable care, requiring the landlord to remedy a defect only when he knows or should know of its existence.[10] If the landlord does in fact violate the ordinance or statute, however, that violation is negligence per se.[11]

Reasons for and against. Commentators and courts have given several reasons for imposing the "implied warranty." Today's tenants—perhaps more accurately, today's tenants in multifamily dwelling units—use rental payments to buy a whole package of goods and services, not merely land. And the tenants lack equal bargaining power, so unfair terms and performance are likely. In addition, landlords are seen to be in better position to make repairs. None of these reasons applies to all tenancies or tenants and none leads inexorably to the implied warranty in all cases, and certainly not in all cases involving injury. But there are public concerns that housing should not breed filth, pestilence, or crime with their spreading effects. Moreover, many tenants are children who cannot protect themselves at the wholly hypothetical bargaining table where the lease is made. To require that no apartment contain lead paint that could destroy brain cells and ruin children, or unprotected windows on upper floors from which child could easily fall, does not seem excessive.

6. Peterson v. Superior Court, 10 Cal.4th 1185, 899 P.2d 905, 43 Cal.Rptr.2d 836 (1995), overruling Becker v. IRM Corp., 38 Cal.3d 454, 213 Cal.Rptr. 213, 698 P.2d 116 (1985).

7. Peterson v. Superior Court, 10 Cal.4th 1185, 899 P.2d 905, 43 Cal.Rptr.2d 836 (1995); Estate of Vazquez v. Hepner, 564 N.W.2d 426 (Iowa 1997).

8. Eric T. Freyfogle, The Installment Land Contract as Lease: Habitability Protections And the Low-income Purchaser, 62 NYULR 293 (1987) said it was a covenant not a warranty, but as he goes on to recognize, it is imposed upon the landlord by a rule of law, not something the landlord voluntarily covenants or agrees to do.

9. E.g., 14 Me. Rev. Stats. Ann. § 6021, providing for notice by the tenant to the landlord.

10. Gore v. People's Savings Bank, 235 Conn. 360, 665 A.2d 1341 (1995); Richwind Joint Venture v. Brunson, 335 Md. 661, 645 A.2d 1147 (1994) (both dealing with obligations of the landlord to remove lead-based paint).

11. E.g., Gore v. People's Savings Bank, supra n. 10.

On the other hand it is not so clear that commercial tenants need to do more than use the market. With commercial tenants it seems simplest to let the parties bargain for a warranty or against one.

CHAPTER 14

HEALTH CARE PROVIDERS AND OTHER PROFESSIONALS

TOPIC A. TRADITIONAL DUTIES OF HEALTH CARE PROFESSIONALS

§ 242. The Traditional Medical Standard of Care

As a negligence action with special duty. The tort action for medical malpractice is a negligence action, accompanied by the usual rules attendant to such actions. The plaintiff must prove negligence, causation, and damages, for example, and the defendant may defend in a proper case by asserting contributory fault,[1] the avoidable consequences rules,[2] or consent of the patient.[3] However, professional persons such as medical doctors and lawyers traditionally stand in a special relationship to their patients or clients. If their relationship is not necessarily contractual, it is nevertheless based upon the professional's implicit undertaking or commitment to provide professional services that at least met the standard of care of other professionals in the same field.[4] As a result, the duty of care owed by medical and other professionals is usually expressed in and applied in a special way.

The professional-peer standard. Most courts recognize that professional persons can undertake to provide some specific service or some specific level of care.[5] In the absence of some specific undertaking, the

§ 242

1. Harlow v. Chin, 405 Mass. 697, 545 N.E.2d 602 (1989) (if doctor told patient to return if pain intensified, patient could be charged with comparative fault in not returning for an extended period); Elkins v. Ferencz, 694 N.Y.S.2d 27 (App. Div. 1999) (patient's use of drugs, failure to furnish accurate medical history, and delay of treatment). However, what counts as contributory fault chargeable against the plaintiff may be limited by the doctor's duty. The act the doctor has a duty to prevent cannot be asserted as contributory fault. Thus in Argus v. Scheppegrell, 472 So.2d 573 (La. 1985) the doctor was under a duty not to prescribe drugs for an addicted teenager. He breached his duty by prescribing and the teenager died of an overdose. He could not assert her contributory fault in taking the drugs; that was the foreseeable act he was under a duty to prevent by refusing a prescription. An Illinois decision permits the jury to consider the contributory negligence of a patient who commits suicide, but there the argument centered on the patient's capacity rather than the doctor's duty, and the court's reasoning on contributory negligence seemed to indicate that the doctor was not negligent in the first place. See Hobart v. Shin, 185 Ill.2d 283, 705 N.E.2d 907, 235 Ill.Dec. 724 (1998).

2. Keans v. Bottiarelli, 35 Conn.App. 239, 645 A.2d 1029 (1994).

3. Boyle v. Revici, 961 F.2d 1060 (2d Cir.1992) (fully informed patient who sought non-standard treatment assumed the risk).

4. Restatement § 299A.

5. A professional like a doctor might be held on a misrepresentation or a contract theory. Hull v. Ratino, 1989 WL 128492

patient normally understands and expects that physicians acting within the ambit of their professional work[6] will exercise the skill, knowledge, and care normally possessed and exercised by other members of their profession[7] of the same school of practice in the relevant medical community. Similarly, the physician implicitly undertakes to meet at least such a standard.

Because this principle imports the standards of the defendant's own profession or school of practice, it can apply equally to dentists,[8] mental health professionals[9] and to licensed practitioners like chiropractors and podiatrists who are not medical doctors.[10] Something of the same idea applies to nurses.[11] In fact, it applies to professionals generally, not

(Tenn.App.1989); (contract specified type of operation; deviation was a breach of contract without regard to medical customs); Clark v. St. Dominic–Jackson Memorial Hospital, 660 So.2d 970 (Miss.1995) (misrepresentation by hospital that he had appropriate facilities). Nothing elaborate is required to say that he must exercise the care appropriate to his undertaking as reasonably understood by his patient.

6. The professional standard is irrelevant to non-professional activities, for example, to slippery floors in a hospital. Self v. Exec. Comm. Georgia Baptist Convention, 245 Ga. 548, 266 S.E.2d 168 (1980). Sometimes it is difficult to differentiate bad housekeeping and bad medical care, as where rats in a hospital repeatedly bit a comatose patient. See Lejeune v. Rayne Branch Hospital, 556 So.2d 559 (La.1990) (court was untroubled by lack of expert testimony).

7. E.g., Keebler v. Winfield Carraway Hospital, 531 So.2d 841, 845 (Ala.1988) (physicians must "exercise such reasonable care, diligence, and skill as reasonably competent physicians" in the relevant medical community would exercise in the same or similar circumstances); Purtill v. Hess, 111 Ill.2d 229, 489 N.E.2d 867, 95 Ill.Dec. 305 (1986) (physician must possess and apply the knowledge, skill, and care of a reasonably well-qualified physician in the relevant medical community). Courts and writers have often referred to the "average" skill in the profession, but that seems to be only a loose synonym for "ordinary" skill. "Half of the physicians of America do not automatically become negligent ... merely because their skill is less than the professional average." Restatement § 299A, cmt. e. See also, criticizing the "average" term, Nowatske v. Osterloh, 198 Wis.2d 419, 543 N.W.2d 265 (1996).

8. Douglas v. Freeman, 117 Wash.2d 242, 814 P.2d 1160 (1991) (dental clinic).

9. Stone v. Proctor, 259 N.C. 633, 131 S.E.2d 297, 99 A.L.R.2d 593 (1963) (psychiatrist, electroshock treatments); Michael L. Perlin, Law and Mental Disability § 3.02 (1994); see Vilcinskas v. Johnson, 252 Neb. 292, 562 N.W.2d 57 (1997) (by implication). The most prominent therapist cases have been those in which the therapist might have prevented a dangerous patient from causing injury to a third person or committing suicide and those in which the therapist is guilty of sexual misconduct with a patient. See §§ 102, 329 & 331. For analysis of all kinds of psychiatric malpractice claims, see Steven R. Smith, Mental Health Malpractice in the 1990s, 28 Hous. L. Rev. 209 (1991).

10. See § 245.

11. At one time courts may not have regarded nurses at medical professionals. In addition, the undertaking of hospital nurses to the patient is indirect. Contemporary courts have imposed a nursing standard of care, however, see Planned Parenthood of Northwest Indiana, Inc. v. Vines, 543 N.E.2d 654 (1989) or have expected nurses to meet all the standards imposed upon them by extraneous guidelines or hospital rules. So expert testimony is normally required to establish a professional negligence claim against a nurse. Boccasile v. Cajun Music Limited, 694 A.2d 686 (R.I.1997). Even so, courts may phrase the standard without clear reference to the practice of the community of nursing professionals, for instance by saying that the standard is that of a reasonably prudent nurse. See Fein v. Permanente Medical Group, 38 Cal.3d 137, 211 Cal.Rptr. 368, 695 P.2d 665 (1985). In a very large number of cases, courts seem to assume a professional-reasonable person standard of care, but simply say that testimony showed the "standard of care" for the nurse was some specific act, such as rolling the patient to prevent bedsores, without indicating whether this "standard" was derived from the practice of other nursing

merely those in the health care field.[12] The architect,[13] engineer,[14] lawyer,[15] and auditor,[16] for example, owe their clients the standard of qualified practitioners in the same profession, or other practitioners in the same general geographical area.[17]

Reasonable person standard distinguished. The professional standard of care is not the reasonable person standard used in most negligence cases.[18] The reasonable person standard asks the trier to weigh the reasonableness, that is at least in part to weigh the risks and utilities of the defendant's conduct;[19] but the professional standard asks the trier only to determine whether the defendant's conduct conformed to the medical standard or medical custom in the relevant community. Thus under the traditional rule, as long as a doctor follows the medical standard or custom, he is not negligent, regardless of how risky the custom or how unnecessary.[20] The professional standard differs from the reasonable care standard also in that courts traditionally require the malpractice plaintiff to establish the professional standard by expert testimony.[21] No such category-wide rule applies in ordinary negligence cases. In spite of these profound differences, courts seem increasingly to blend the language of reasonable person with the language of professional standards in an uncertain mixture with uncertain effects.[22]

Custom as standard; more than one accepted practice. The term "standard" itself may be misleading in this context. Courts judge the defendant's medical conduct, not under a general standard like reasonable care or good medical practice, but by asking medical experts whether that particular procedure is medically acceptable in the relevant

professionals or from hospital rules or elsewhere. A number of special problems arise for nurses, such as the question whether to exercise independent judgment and to disobey a doctor's orders. See Elizabeth J. Armstrong, Nurse Malpractice in North Carolina: The Standard of Care, 65 N.C. L. Rev. 579 (1987). For a review of a number of types of nursing negligence see Frank J. Cavico and Nancy M. Cavico, The Nursing Profession in the 1990's: Negligence and Malpractice Liability, 43 Clev. St. L. Rev. 557 (1995). The topic is important partly because nurse negligence is often the predicate for a hospital's vicarious liability.

12. District of Columbia v. Hampton, 666 A.2d 30 (D.C.App.1995) (applied to social workers, on the theory that their decisions in placing a child in a foster home were too exotic for a jury to understand); Advincula v. United Blood Services, 176 Ill.2d 1, 678 N.E.2d 1009, 223 Ill.Dec. 1 (1996).

13. E.g., Simon v. Drake Construction Co., 87 Ohio App.3d 23, 621 N.E.2d 837 (1993) (worker injured, allegedly due to architect's design failure, no claim without expert testimony).

14. Rogers v. Price, 698 So.2d 723 (La. App.1997).

15. See Chapter 36. As reflected there, the local standard is seldom applied to lawyers.

16. Usually applied in misrepresentation cases, as to which see Chapter 35.

17. Rogers v. Price, 698 So.2d 723 (La. App.1997).

18. See Harris v. Groth, 99 Wash.2d 438, 663 P.2d 113 (1983).

19. See §§ 144–146.

20. The difference is shown dramatically in Helling v. Carey, 83 Wash.2d 514, 519 P.2d 981, 67 A.L.R.3d 175 (1974), discussed in § 247.

21. See § 246.

22. E.g., Starcher v. Byrne, 687 So.2d 737, 740 (Miss.1997) (court states the standard as one of "reasonable and ordinary care" but then restates it as an obligation to treat patients with the skill and other qualities practiced "by minimally competent physicians in the same specialty or general field of practice.... ").

community. Except in cases of res ipsa loquitur or obvious negligence, the "standard" is usually any medical custom or practice of that community in the way the particular procedure is used.[23] When there are two schools of thought or custom in the medical community about a given procedure, the defendant is free to follow either custom without liability.[24]

§ 243. Jury Instructions under the Medical Standard

The usual jury instructions state the medical standard of care, incorporating the locality rule where that is still appropriate, and they make due reference to the defendant's speciality or school of practice. The jury is thus told that the physician must "possess and use the care, skill and knowledge ordinarily possessed and used under like circumstances"[1] and that the physician is negligent only if he failed to follow the medical conduct of other physicians in similar circumstances.[2] Sometimes courts add that the physician must use ordinary care in applying the professional skills, knowledge and training.[3]

However, courts very often add a good deal of rhetoric the effect of which is to repeatedly emphasize instances of non-liability. Such instructions are common even where the plaintiff has never asserted the liabilities the court negates. Trial judges often say that the doctor-defendant is not required to exercise the highest care, only the ordinary care of his profession,[4] that the physician is not liable for a bad result, nor for a mistake or error of judgment where he acted in good faith, that medicine is an inexact science and that the physician was not an insurer of the plaintiff's health nor a guarantor of her recovery.[5]

Broadly speaking, such instructions raise two kinds of objections. When juries are instructed with these rhetorical flourishes, the plaintiff's burden is emphasized several times—first in the more straightforward

23. As to published guidelines as standards or quasi-standards, see § 247.

24. Katsetos v. Nolan, 170 Conn. 637, 368 A.2d 172 (1976);Sinclair v. Block, 534 Pa. 563, 633 A.2d 1137 (1993).

§ 243

1. Vergara v. Doan, 593 N.E.2d 185 (Ind.1992); Burns v. Metz, 245 Neb. 428, 432, 513 N.W.2d 505, 508 (1994)

2. McLaughlin v. Sy, 589 A.2d 448 (Me. 1991).

3. See Boyanton v. Reif, 798 P.2d 603 (Okl.1990).

4. See Tennant v. Marion Health Care Foundation, Inc., 194 W.Va. 97, 459 S.E.2d 374 (1995).

5. See Dotson v. Hammerman, 932 S.W.2d 880 (Mo.App.1996) ("An honest error of judgment in making a diagnosis is insufficient to support liability unless that mistake constitutes negligence"); Donaldson v. Maffucci, 397 Pa. 548, 156 A.2d 835 (1959); Bryan v. Burt, 254 Va. 28, 486 S.E.2d 536 (Va. 1997) ("A physician is neither an insurer of diagnosis and treatment nor is the physician held to the highest degree of care known to the profession. The mere fact that the physician has failed to effect a cure or that the diagnosis and treatment have been detrimental to the patient's health does not raise a presumption of negligence"); Gerard v. Sacred Heart Medical Center, 86 Wash.App. 387, 937 P.2d 1104 (1997) ("medicine is an inexact science where the desired results cannot be guaranteed, and where professional judgment may reasonably differ as to what constitutes proper treatment"). Statutes may make announce similar rules. E.g., 40 PA.STAT. § 1301.606 ("In the absence of a special contract in writing, a health care provider is neither a warrantor nor a guarantor of a cure").

instruction on the standard of professional care and then again and again with the rhetorical and more emphatic versions. If this is not bad enough, some trial judges not only indulge in the rhetorical emphasis, but even repeat the repetition itself several times.[6] Because repetition of the same idea in varied forms is likely to predispose the jury to a defense finding, all such instructions are suspect.

A second line of objection has been that the instructions are affirmatively misleading. An instruction that tells the jury that the physician is not liable for honest error or good faith mistake injects subjective, good faith issues into the objective negligence test and may lead the jury to think that bad faith, not a departure from professional standards, is the test of liability. This kind of instruction is now very widely condemned by the appellate courts.[7] Some courts have begun to reconsider the no-guarantee instruction as well, holding that it should not be given when the plaintiff has not, after all, asserted a guarantee,[8] or that some constraints should be imposed upon its use.[9] Other courts, however, continue to approve instructions containing some of the locutions listed above.[10]

§ 244. The Relevant Geographical Community

At one time, courts held that the professional standard of care for medical doctors was the standard in the very same locality where the doctor practiced.[1] If a town's six doctors all ignored helpful new drugs for treatment of the plaintiff's condition, none of them would be guilty of medical malpractice for failing to prescribe such a drug when it was needed. One theory sometimes advanced for this result was that small-town doctors might not have the latest equipment or training and should

6. See Wall v. Stout, 310 N.C. 184, 311 S.E.2d 571 (1984) (jury instructed at least three times that doctor was not a guarantor or insurer).

7. Day v. Morrison, 657 So.2d 808 (Miss. 1995); Parodi v. Washoe Medical Center, Inc., 111 Nev. 365, 892 P.2d 588 (1995); Wall v. Stout, 310 N.C. 184, 311 S.E.2d 571 (1984); DiFranco v. Klein, 657 A.2d 145 (R.I.1995); cf. Kennelly v. Burgess, 337 Md. 562, 654 A.2d 1335 (1995) (detailed criticism of instructions that mere happening of injury does not prove negligence). On other misleading and one-sided instructions generally, see § 131.

8. Bratton v. Bond, 408 N.W.2d 39 (Iowa 1987) (unless, perhaps, the plaintiff asserts a warranty claim); Wall v. Stout, 310 N.C. 184, 197, 311 S.E.2d 571, 579 (1984) (" an instruction to the effect that a physician is 'not an insurer of results' should not be given when no issue concerning a guarantee has been raised").

9. Jones v. Porretta, 428 Mich. 132, 405 N.W.2d 863 (1987) (at least when coupled with charge that adverse results are no evidence of negligence in a res ipsa loquitur case; also addressing need for unslanted instructions); Christensen v. Munsen, 123 Wash.2d 234, 867 P.2d 626, 30 A.L.R.5th 822 (1994) (evidence must warrant the instruction and it must be a supplement to a proper charge on the standard of care).

10. E.g., Dupuy v. Allara, 193 W.Va. 557, 457 S.E.2d 494 (1995).

§ 244

1. The idea seems to have originated in Small v. Howard, 128 Mass. 131 (1880), but courts might have read too much into that case. The defendant there was a village doctor and not a surgeon, but was required to do surgery for the plaintiff. The court emphasized that the village doctor should not be expected to practice at the level of "eminent surgeons" in large cities. The point seems to have been as much that the defendant was not a specialist in surgery as that he was practicing in a village.

not be liable merely for that reason. This locality rule did not necessarily apply to other professionals,[2] and in any event the reason given for it was spurious.

Even without a locality rule, the jury could have considered all the circumstances, including limitations on equipment.[3] A physician who lacks equipment or training to treat a given patient need only refer the patient to a more appropriate provider. Under none of the standards is the physician or surgeon held to any level of care he has not undertaken to give. Albert Schweitzer was not committing a tort when he exercised reasonable care in a primitive clinic in equatorial Africa. The rural general practitioner confronted with an emergency requiring the skill of an orthopedic surgeon is not held to the orthopedist's standard of care, but that is not because he practices in a rural rather than an urban community. It is because, like all others, he is held to the standard he professes, not some other.

Besides the faulty rationale for the same locality rule, courts and writers often point out that today's mainstream medical doctors are all trained in the same basic way throughout the country and all have access to continuing education and even to instant computer guidance.[4] Medical and scientific facts are the same everywhere. These considerations, and perhaps a moral revulsion at the idea that a small group of bad practitioners can inflict substandard care on rural communities,[5] have led most states by statute or judicial decision to discard the same locality test of the standard of care,[6] although a few states continue to use that test in some form.[7]

Most courts now look to the medical community in the same or similar localities,[8] in the state,[9] or in the nation as a whole[10] for

2. See Pederson v. Dumouchel, 72 Wash.2d 73, 431 P.2d 973, 31 A.L.R.3d 1100 (1967) (noting that the locality rule had not been adopted for lawyers).

3. Courts adopting a similar or national community rule often point out that the local conditions are among the circumstances to be taken into account. E.g., Brune v. Belinkoff, 354 Mass. 102, 235 N.E.2d 793 (1968).

4. See 1 Barry R. Furrow, Thomas L. Greaney, Sandra H. Johnson, Timothy S. Jost, & Robert L. Schwartz, Health Law 362–63 (1995).

5. "The 'locality rule' had two practical difficulties: first, the scarcity of professional men in the community who were qualified or willing to testify about the local standard of care; and second, the possibility of a small group, who, by their laxness or carelessness, could establish a local standard of care that was below that which the law requires. The fact that several careless practitioners might settle in the same place cannot affect the standard of diligence and skill which local patients have a right to expect. Negligence cannot be excused on the ground that others in the same locality practice the same kind of negligence. No degree of antiquity can give sanction to usage bad in itself." Pederson v. Dumouchel, 72 Wash.2d 73, 78, 431 P.2d 973, 977, 31 A.L.R.3d 1100 (1967).

6. See cases cited nn. 8–10 below; James O. Pearson, Jr., Annotation, Modern Status of "Locality Rule" in Malpractice Action Against Physician Who Is Not a Specialist, 99 A.L.R.3d 1133 (1980).

7. See Trindle v. Wheeler, 23 Cal.2d 330, 143 P.2d 932 (1943); Morris v. Thomson, 130 Idaho 138, 937 P.2d 1212 (Idaho 1997) (same locality standard by statute except when local standard cannot be ascertained).

8. E.g., Bahr v. Harper–Grace Hospitals, 448 Mich. 135, 528 N.W.2d 170 (1995); Purtill v. Hess, 111 Ill.2d 229, 489 N.E.2d 867, 95 Ill.Dec. 305 (1986); Chapel v. Allison, 241 Mont. 83, 785 P.2d 204 (1990); Donaldson v. Maffucci, 397 Pa. 548, 156 A.2d 835 (1959); see DiFranco v. Klein, 657 A.2d 145

appropriate standards. In the last category, some courts do not mention geography, national or local, except to say that the locality might be relevant as a circumstance to be considered in determining whether the doctor exercised reasonable care.[11] For board-certified medical specialists, the standard is usually said to be a single national standard of the specialty involved.[12]

§ 245. Schools of Practice and Their Interaction

Standards for Different Schools

Many medical doctors are specialists who have added training and experience and who have been examined by a specialty board.[1] Besides the many different specialties among medical doctors, there are many kinds of licensed practitioners who are not medical doctors at all. That is of course the usual case with nurses, who are closely identified with medical practice. It is also the case with many practitioners whose practice is quite different from medical practice. These include most notably podiatrists, chiropractors, and various other drugless practitioners.

Although the specialists and the other practitioners are quite different, all fall under the same general legal principle. Each is held to the standard he has implicitly professed as his own. If he holds himself out as a medical doctor, or as having the skills of a medical doctor, he is held to the medical standard.[2] If he holds himself out as a podiatrist[3] or

(R.I.1995). Statutes so provide in some states. E.g., La. Rev. Stat. § 2794; Md. Cts. & Jud. Pro. Code § 3–2A–02; N.C. Gen. Stat. § 90–21.12; Tenn. Code Ann. § 29–26–115. Cf. Jordan v. Bogner, 844 P.2d 664 (Colo.1993) ("same or similar locality," but also referring to standards "in the community" where physician practices). Similar locality seems to mean mainly similar in size or medical facilities. Exact similarity is not required. See First Commercial Trust Co. v. Rank, 323 Ark. 390, 915 S.W.2d 262 (1996) (Panama City, Florida is similar enough to Hot Springs, Arkansas, although the former is three times the size of the latter).

9. Fitzmaurice v. Flynn, 167 Conn. 609, 617, 356 A.2d 887, 892 (1975) (in Connecticut, the "general neighborhood" standard means the whole state).

10. Rolon–Alvarado v. Municipality of San Juan, 1 F.3d 74 (1st Cir.1993) (Puerto Rico law); Travers v. District of Columbia, 672 A.2d 566 (D.C.App.1996) (applied negatively to defeat the plaintiff whose expert witness testified to a standard but failed to say it was a national one); Keebler v. Winfield Carraway Hospital, 531 So.2d 841 (Ala.1988); Hall v. Hilbun, 466 So.2d 856 (Miss.1985).

11. Vergara v. Doan, 593 N.E.2d 185 (Ind.1992); Brune v. Belinkoff, 354 Mass. 102, 235 N.E.2d 793 (1968) ("the degree of care and skill of the average qualified practitioner, taking into account the advances in the profession. In applying this standard it is permissible to consider the medical resources available to the physician as one circumstance in determining the skill and care required. Under this standard some allowance is thus made for the type of community in which the physician carries on his practice"); Pederson v. Dumouchel, 72 Wash.2d 73, 431 P.2d 973, 31 A.L.R.3d 1100 (1967).

12. See Jordan v. Bogner, 844 P.2d 664 (Colo.1993)

§ 245

1. See Steven E. Pegalis and Harvey F. Wachsman, American Law of Medical Malpractice 2d § 3.2 (1992) (describing training and specialties).

2. Brown v. Shyne, 242 N.Y. 176, 151 N.E. 197, 44 A.L.R. 1407 (1926) (chiropractor who held himself out as having medical skills would be held to medical standard of care). On the other hand, the absence of a license by itself does not show that the

chiropractor,[4] however, he is held to the standards followed in those pursuits, not to the medical standard.

Licensing laws appear to impose one external constraint upon practitioners like chiropractors. They may be licensed to carry out specific techniques but not licensed to administer drugs, to perform surgery, or to treat infectious diseases, malignancies, and other medical problems.[5] When the practitioner recognizes that the patient's condition cannot be properly or effectively treated within the limits imposed by his license, he must not attempt treatment.

Duty to Refer

While a chiropractor or other non-medical practitioner might be expected to recognize the boundaries imposed by his own license and school of practice, it is not so obvious that he is to be expected to recognize a medical problem. In a New Jersey case, the chiropractor took x-rays, as was permitted by the licensing statute for the purpose of determining whether the spine was aligned as chiropractors think it should be. The x-rays clearly showed soft tissue abnormalities that turned out to be a serious disease. Because the chiropractor did not recognize the abnormalities, he did not refer to a medical doctor. The result was that the patient's treatment for his Hodgkin's disease was much delayed. The New Jersey Court held the evidence sufficient to support a finding of negligence in failing to recognize and refer the patient to a medical doctor.[6]

On the other hand, Wisconsin has taken the view that while a non-medical practitioner like a chiropractor should limit his treatment to the scope of his license when a reasonable practitioner in the field would recognize that the patient's condition will not be responsive to further treatment, he need not go further and make a referral. That court thought that a duty to refer would improperly impose upon the chiropractor a duty to make a medical decision.[7] The absolute form of that decision seems to leave no room for testimony that the chiropractic standard itself would require, not a diagnosis, but a referral.

Religious Practice and Duty to Refer

Religious beliefs of either a medical or non-medical practitioner are conceivably relevant in determining the health-care practitioner's duty to refer or treat. A California case held that church counselors, offering religious, not secular counseling, had no duty to refer a suicidal young man to professional counselors.[8] But in another case, a court in a dictum

medical procedure was performed negligently. See Turek v. Saint Elizabeth Community Health Center, 241 Neb. 467, 488 N.W.2d 567 (1992).

3. E.g., Creasey v. Hogan, 292 Or. 154, 637 P.2d 114 (1981).

4. E.g., Piazza v. Behrman Chiropractice Clinic, Inc., 601 So.2d 1378 (La.1992).

5. See, e.g., N.Y. Educ. L. § 6551.

6. Rosenberg v. Cahill, 99 N.J. 318, 492 A.2d 371 (1985).

7. Kerkman v. Hintz, 142 Wis.2d 404, 418 N.W.2d 795 (1988).

8. Nally v. Grace Community Church of the Valley, 47 Cal.3d 278, 253 Cal.Rptr. 97, 763 P.2d 948 (1988). See § 258.

supported a duty of a Catholic hospital to refer a rape victim to a hospital that would counsel on pregnancy prevention.[9]

The Christian Scientist practitioner, who professes to heal by spiritual treatment as a part of his religious belief, has the advantage of the general principle that holds him only to the standards he professes to follow.[10] He may also avoid being tested even by his own standards on the ground that in the interest of religious freedom courts will not attempt to interpret the teachings of a church.[11] In cases like this, a duty to refer that is not recognized by the Christian Science standard itself would raise the objection that it interferes with religious freedom.

§ 246. The Expert Testimony Requirement

The requirement of expert opinion to establish the medical "standard." In medical malpractice claims, cause in fact must sometimes be established by experts.[1] The more significant problem for most plaintiffs, however, is that, unless res ipsa loquitur applies or negligence is obvious, courts require the plaintiff to establish the medical "standard" itself by expert testimony.[2] Similar statements are sometimes made about other professionals.[3]

To establish a medical standard, the expert testimony must ordinarily be specific rather than general. It does not state that the medical standard is "high care" or "reasonable care" or "good medical care." It rather must state that the particular diagnosis, treatment, or procedure in question did or did not meet the "standards" of the medical community. The testimony might state, for example, that the medical communi-

9. Brownfield v. Daniel Freeman Marina Hospital, 208 Cal.App.3d 405, 256 Cal. Rptr. 240 (1989).

10. Spead v. Tomlinson, 73 N.H. 46, 59 A. 376 (1904) ("the duty the law imposes ... on the person who undertakes to do anything for the benefit of his employer, is that of using ordinary care to do what he has agreed to do in the way he agreed to do it"; Christian Science practitioner not held to standard of a physician).

11. Baumgartner v. First Church of Christ, Scientist, 141 Ill.App.3d 898, 490 N.E.2d 1319, 96 Ill.Dec. 114 (1986). In Lundman v. McKown, 530 N.W.2d 807 (Minn.App.1995) a very sick child died a painful and lingering death when his mother and Christian Science personnel gave him treatment by prayer and readings. Testimony indicated that he could have been saved by medical treatment. In a suit for wrongful death, the court recognized that with a competent adult, the standard would be that of a reasonable Christian Science practitioner, but that in spite of important religious freedom principles, the state's obligation to protect children demanded a rule of liability in the case of children, or at least children in such dire medical straits.

§ 246

1. E.g., Smith v. Knowles, 281 N.W.2d 653 (1979).

2. The requirement may be too broad. Expert testimony might be required in any case in which technical explanation is needed, regardless whether the defendant undertook a professional relationship with the plaintiff or not, but the testimony might related to technical matters rather than to the conclusory "standard of care." See, e.g., Tillman v. Washington Metropolitan Area Transit Authority, 695 A.2d 94 (D.C.App. 1997) (experts needed to testify whether police officers handcuffed arrestee too tightly).

3. E.g., District of Columbia v. Hampton, 666 A.2d 30 (D.C.App.1995) (standard for social worker must be proven; a case that could possibly be understood as meaning only that the plaintiff was required to prove breach of the due care standard by showing risks were unreasonably great).

ty's "standard" called for a diagnostic test that was not administered, or administration of a smaller dosage of an anesthetic than was given.

Qualifying a medical expert. In some cases, the physician-defendant himself testifies to or admits the standard of care claimed by the plaintiff.[4] When he does not, the plaintiff's lawyer must show that her medical expert is qualified to give an opinion about the medical standard. Under the same-locality rule, if the defendant doctor practiced in Nantucket, any qualified medical expert could testify about medical causation,[5] but only an expert who could state the standard or custom in Nantucket could testify that the defendant's conduct fell short of that standard. The effect of this rule was that the plaintiff suing a Nantucket doctor would usually be required to find another Nantucket doctor who would testify against the defendant. In many instances, the plaintiff could obtain quite good evidence, but only from "outsiders" who were not allowed to testify.[6] The effect was that the plaintiff's claim was defeated.

When courts began to hold that the relevant medical community included similar localities or even the nation as a whole, the most immediate practical effect was that physicians from other localities were allowed to testify about the proper standard.

Content of the expert medical testimony. When courts adopt either the similar locality or the national community standard, they open the door to testimony from doctors outside the defendant's community. But the content of that testimony must still establish the medical standard, not merely an expert's own judgment. The physician-witness who testifies that the defendant failed to meet professional standards cannot simply say that what the defendant did was dangerous and that the danger outweighed the hope of saving the patient. He must say that the medical standard was violated. Yet in many cases of bad medical judgment it is difficult to say that there is a customary standard or that any one knows what it is. If the physician witness can only testify that he was medically trained not to use the procedure used by the defendant, or that by his own judgment the defendant's treatment was wrong,[7] that he himself would not have used the procedure or used a better one,[8] that all the doctors he knows agree that the treatment was wrong,[9] his testimony has not necessarily established a standard. In that case, the plaintiff will find her case dismissed.

4. E.g., Douglas v. Freeman, 117 Wash.2d 242, 814 P.2d 1160 (1991).

5. See Scott v. Calia, 1997 WL 367234 (Tenn.App.1997).

6. See, e,g, Holmes v. Elliott, 443 So.2d 825 (Miss.1983). Mississippi has gone to a national standard since this case was decided.

7. Walski v. Tiesenga, 72 Ill.2d 249, 21 Ill.Dec. 201, 381 N.E.2d 279 (1978).

8. See Clark v. District of Columbia, 700 A.2d 235 (D.C.1997).

9. Travers v. District of Columbia, 672 A.2d 566, 569 (D.C.App.1996) ("It is the consensus of opinion of all the surgeons with which I have worked with and taught with that we do use aspirin when it reaches about two times normal", did not establish standard).

Beyond that, even if the physician-witness testifies firmly to a standard of care, his testimony is not necessarily enough. The plaintiff must show that the violated standard is one that applies to the defendant physician. In *Travers v. District of Columbia,*[10] the court had adopted the national standard rather than the same or similar communities standard. An expert witness testified to a standard, but failed to identify it as a *national* standard. The court in effect assumed that the testimony could have referred to a local rather than a national standard and that the two were different. So the plaintiff's case was dismissed for lack of proof of the *national* standard.

Testimony by a witness belonging to a different specialty or school of medicine. Can an expert witness testify about the standard of care appropriate to a defendant who (a) practices in a different locality, or (b) practices a different specialty, or even (c) an entirely different kind of school of healing? For example, could a medical doctor testify against a podiatrist, or, with the shoe on the other foot, vice versa?

It is clear that the standard governing the defendant is his own standard as a specialist or a licensed practitioner. The chiropractor may not be held to the standard of the orthopedic surgeon. However, as a matter of logic, any person who knows the relevant standard for chiropractors could testify about that standard. It might be possible for obstetricians to testify about the standards for radiology or even for a Ph.D in chemistry to state something about the standard of care to be used in prescribing certain drugs. Some courts have stated a hard line against such testimony, however. One view requires the expert witness not merely to know the standard applicable to the defendant but to be in a specialty or kind of practice that uses substantially the same standard. Taken literally, this view means that an orthopedic surgeon who says he knows the standard of care for podiatric surgery may not be heard in court.[11]

Some other courts have tried to find a rationale for a more liberal view but one that still exerts a great deal of control over the testimony that goes to the jury. Thus some courts allow a medical doctor to testify as to the standards governing another school of practice when the standards are the same as to the particular procedure in issue,[12] or, more vaguely, when the standards turn on matters that each of the two schools "share in common in terms of education, training and licensure".[13] In the same way, if the witness can show that the standards in

10. Travers v. District of Columbia, 672 A.2d 566 (D.C.App.1996).

11. See Dolan v. Galluzzo, 77 Ill.2d 279, 396 N.E.2d 13, 32 Ill.Dec. 900 (1979) (stating that to testify about podiatry standards, the witness would have to be a licensed podiatrist, but it was not clear that the proffered witness could have testified to the standards of a podiatrist).

12. Pollard v. Goldsmith, 117 Ariz. 363, 572 P.2d 1201 (1977); Marshall v. Yale Podiatry Group, 5 Conn.App. 5, 496 A.2d 529 (1985); Faulkner v. Pezeshki, 44 Ohio App.2d 186, 337 N.E.2d 158 (1975) ("minimum standards applicable wherever medicine is practiced"); Creasey v. Hogan, 292 Or. 154, 637 P.2d 114 (1981).

13. Rosenberg v. Cahill, 99 N.J. 318, 334, 492 A.2d 371, 379 (1985).

his community are the same as those in the defendant's community, the locality rule will not exclude his testimony.[14]

The least controlling view permits the expert to testify about the standard in a different specialty or different community once the expert establishes his knowledge of that standard.[15] At least the trial judge is given discretion, under this view, either to admit[16] or exclude[17] the expert testimony.

§ 247. Exceptions and Departures from the Professional Standard or from the Expert Opinion Requirement

Although expert medical testimony is usually required to establish the relevant medical standard of care, courts have recognized exceptions. Occasionally courts impose some specific duty independent of the medical standard, as where a court simply adopts a rule of law that the surgeon must remove foreign objects from the patient's body before closing the incision, in which case, a medical standard that permits the surgeon to delegate this task does not govern at all.[1] A more general exception, recognized in the res ipsa loquitur rule and in the similar idea of obvious negligence, is discussed in a separate section.

Liberal Elaborations on the Medical Testimony Requirement

Two rather minor elaborations on the medical testimony requirement can affect the practical operation of the expert testimony requirement. First, the plaintiff who lacks independent expert testimony may nevertheless establish the standard of care by relying upon the defendant physician's own testimony or admission.[2]

Second, most states follow liberal evidence rules like those used in the Federal Courts. These rules permit the plaintiff to introduce learned medical treatises in evidence to establish the medical standard, provided they are shown to be reliable and accepted in the profession.[3] The

14. Hundley v. Martinez, 151 W.Va. 977, 158 S.E.2d 159 (1967).

15. See Bodiford v. Lubitz, 564 So.2d 1390 (Ala.1990) ("orthopedic surgeon who is familiar with the standard of care for podiatrists may be considered an expert in the area of podiatry"); Melville v. Southward, 791 P.2d 383 (Colo.1990); Creasey v. Hogan, 292 Or. 154, 637 P.2d 114 (1981) (as to different community; possibly a tighter standard as to different specialty); Bahr v. Harper–Grace Hospitals, 448 Mich. 135, 528 N.W.2d 170 (1995).

16. McMillan v. Durant, 312 S.C. 200, 439 S.E.2d 829 (1993) (approving trial judge's decision to permit doctor-teacher to testify as to nursing standards with which he was familiar).

17. See Swanson v. Chatterton, 281 Minn. 129, 160 N.W.2d 662, 31 A.L.R.3d 1152 (1968) (upholding the trial judge's exclusion of an internist's proposed testimony about orthopedic standards).

§ 247

1. Ravi v. Coates, 662 So.2d 218 (Ala. 1995) (duty to remove even if customary standard leaves sponge count responsibility to nurses).

2. Trindle v. Wheeler, 23 Cal.2d 330, 143 P.2d 932 (1943) ("[The plaintiff] was entitled to rely upon the expert testimony which had been introduced by the defendant; and in the absence of any such testimony offered by the plaintiff the court, on the motion for a directed verdict, was required to consider the evidence favorable to the plaintiff introduced by the defendant").

3. See, e.g., Jacober v. St. Peter's Medical Center, 128 N.J. 475, 608 A.2d 304 (1992) (excellent explication of the ins and outs of the rule and its predecessor).

plaintiff will not necessarily prevail by using the defendant's own testimony or by using learned treatises. Even if a standard of care is established by such means, the plaintiff will still be required to establish that the standard of care was breached and that the breach caused harm to the plaintiff. The medical defendant who admits to the standard of care urged by the plaintiff will presumably not admit that he breached it, and treatises may not be sufficiently specific to show a breach or to show causation on the particular facts of the case.[4]

Exceptions to the Professional Standard or the Expert Testimony Requirement

Liberal elaborations of the medical testimony rule continue to rely upon the medical profession's own standards. Exceptions to the medical testimony requirement differ significantly because they may allow the plaintiff to get to the jury on the basis of a standard that is extraneous to the medical custom. Perhaps the extraneous standard in reality often coincides with the actual medical custom or standard, but if so, the plaintiff is not required to prove it. For that reason, the exceptions call into question the underlying standard of care itself.

Manufacturer's instructions or warnings. When a physician prescribes a drug,[5] administers an anesthetic,[6] or uses medical equipment or supplies[7] without heeding the manufacturer's warnings or instructions, courts usually permit the plaintiff to introduce the manufacturer's clear and explicit instructions or warnings. Such instructions, which in the case of drugs are included in the package insert and printed in the Physicians' Desk Reference, are treated as evidence of the appropriate standard of care[8] or even as prima facie proof of the standard.[9] The plaintiff would prefer the latter version, but both versions look to standards that arise in the first instance outside of medical practice.

Judicial assessment of risks independent of medical standards or testimony. In a few cases, courts have themselves directly assessed risks

4. E.g, Smith v. Knowles, 281 N.W.2d 653 (Minn.1979) (if plaintiff established that early diagnosis should have been made, plaintiff still failed to show that physician departed from standard or that if he did that his negligence was a cause of the decedent's death).

5. E.g., Ohligschlager v. Proctor Community Hospital, 55 Ill.2d 411, 303 N.E.2d 392 (1973).

6. Julien v. Barker, 75 Idaho 413, 272 P.2d 718 (1954)

7. Simers v. Bickers, 260 Ill.App.3d 406, 632 N.E.2d 219, 198 Ill.Dec. 160 (1994) (appellate court reversed a jury finding for defendant, concluding for itself that defendant, who was not an optometrist, was negligent in failing to follow manufacturer's directions in fitting contact lenses); cf. Craft v. Peebles, 78 Hawai'i 287, 893 P.2d 138 (1995) (doctor, with knowledge of the patient's breast implant, performed a procedure upon patient's breast against which manufacturer of implant had warned).

8. Bowman v. Songer, 820 P.2d 1110, 19 A.L.R.5th 1032 (Colo. 1991); Craft v. Peebles, 78 Hawai'i 287, 893 P.2d 138 (1995); Thompson v. Carter, 518 So.2d 609 (Miss. 1987) (evidence of the standard, shifts burden of persuasion to physician to explain departure from it); Ramon v. Farr, 770 P.2d 131, 82 A.L.R.4th 155 (Utah 1989). See Salgo v. Leland Stanford Jr. University Bd. of Trustees, 154 Cal.App.2d 560, 317 P.2d 170 (1957).

9. Ohligschlager v. Proctor Community Hospital, 55 Ill.2d 411, 303 N.E.2d 392 (1973); Mulder v. Parke Davis & Company, 288 Minn. 332, 181 N.W.2d 882, 45 A.L.R.3d 920 (1970); Armstrong v. State, 214 A.D.2d 812, 625 N.Y.S.2d 317 (1995).

of a medical procedure, either finding the procedure to be negligent or allowing the trier of fact to do so. *Helling v. Carey*[10] is a leading case. The patient of an ophthalmologist lost most of her vision because no pressure test for glaucoma was administered. The test itself cost very little, took very little time, and presented no risks. The risk of glaucoma was not large, but devastating when it eventuated. In spite of the test's utility, the standard practice of ophthalmologists was not to administer it except to high-risk groups. Under the traditional rules, then, an ordinary patient would have no claim against the ophthalmologist, since he did not breach the medical custom standard by failing to administer the test. The Washington Court, however, held that "irrespective of its disregard by the standards of the opthalmology profession, it is the duty of the courts to say what is required to protect patients under 40 from the damaging results of glaucoma."[11]

Helling was using an ordinary negligence or reasonable person test rather than the medical test. That permitted the court to make a risk-utility assessment under the negligence rules. That alone would have been a radical departure from the medical community's standard. The court went further, however, by applying the negligence test itself rather than leaving the risk-utility balance to the jury: the defendant was negligent as a matter of law.[12] A matter of law ruling of this kind will no doubt be rare, and if weighing risks and utilities are to be permitted, the jury will normally be the weighmaster.[13]

On the other hand, *Helling's* decision to consider information about risks and usefulness of the medical procedure in question is essentially an adoption of the ordinary negligence tests. If risks and utilities of the pressure test can be taken into account in glaucoma cases, risks and utilities are equally relevant in other cases, provided the plaintiff adduces reliable testimony to support an assessment. The *Helling* Court has in fact subsequently said that reasonable prudence is now the test of medical negligence, and that risk and utility evidence can be introduced to support a finding of medical negligence, as long as the costs and probabilities can be expressed in relatively exact terms and judgment factors are eliminated.[14] The adoption of a negligence test also implies that while medical experts might be required to establish medical facts such as the probability of harm from any given procedure, they would not necessarily be experts in the same specialty as the defendant and they would not be required to show a medical standard of care.

10. Helling v. Carey, 83 Wash.2d 514, 519 P.2d 981, 67 A.L.R.3d 175 (1974).

11. 83 Wash.2d at 519, 519 P.2d at 983.

12. Similarly in Pederson v. Dumouchel, 72 Wash.2d 73, 431 P.2d 973, 31 A.L.R.3d 1100 (1967) the court concluded that "it is negligence as a matter of law for a hospital to permit a surgical operation upon a patient under general anesthetic without the presence and supervision of a medical doctor in the operating room, in the absence of extraordinary and emergent circumstances."

13. See Christensen v. Munsen, 123 Wash.2d 234, 867 P.2d 626, 30 A.L.R.5th 822 (1994) (noting that "unlike the plaintiff in Helling, the plaintiff here was able to argue her theory of the case to the jury under the instructions given" and affirming judgment for the defendant).

14. Harris v. Groth, 99 Wash.2d 438, 663 P.2d 113 (1983).

The issues raised in *Helling* have not been raised often since that case was decided, but some courts have allowed risk-utility proof to override the excessively risky medical custom standard. In two cases, plaintiffs claimed to have been infected with the AIDS virus through blood transfusions. The blood was supplied by blood banks who had followed professional practice by accepting blood without using readily available means to minimize the AIDS risk. The plaintiffs would have been defeated under the traditional professional standard rule. Nevertheless, the plaintiff was allowed to get to the jury in both cases. The Colorado Court recognized that the standard itself might be impugned by evidence showing the devastating risks, the defendants' knowledge of the risks, and the relatively small cost of greater safety.[15] The New Jersey Court similarly entertained testimony about risks and foreseeability, although that testimony was presented by experts who were not in the blood banking business.[16]

In addition, the language of courts seems to be gradually shifting to recognize that the professional standard must incorporate a minimum reasonable care standard as well. The Supreme Court of Wisconsin adopted a reasonable care standard by name.[17] The Supreme Court of Illinois has said even under the professional standard, the medical practitioner must exercise "due care or ordinary care, commensurate with the apparent risk."[18]

The Medical Guidelines Approach

Another way to set standards looks neither to ordinary negligence analysis nor on medical custom. Practice guidelines can provide an authoritative list of effective and appropriate procedures for all or a large number of medical problems.[19] Any organization from a local medical society or hospital or national associations of medical specialists to state-organized commissions can publish protocols or guidelines. A number of sets, with varying scope, are in existence.[20] Quite apart from statute, courts have accepted evidence of such guidelines as sufficient to establish the standard of care in favor of the plaintiff.[21]

15. United Blood Services, Div. of Blood Systems, Inc. v. Quintana, 827 P.2d 509 (Colo.1992). The court expressed the rule somewhat indirectly by saying that the plaintiff could introduce expert testimony that the medical standard itself was "unreasonably deficient by not incorporating readily available practices and procedures substantially more protective". Accord, Advincula v. United Blood Services, 176 Ill.2d 1, 38, 678 N.E.2d 1009, 1027, 223 Ill.Dec. 1, 19 (1996) (evidence that "the prevailing professional standard of care, itself, constitutes negligence" could overcome professional standard).

16. Snyder v. American Ass'n of Blood Banks, 144 N.J. 269, 676 A.2d 1036 (1996) (blood banks' trade association prescribed arguably lax standards; held it was under a duty to the plaintiff, considering foreseeability and risk testimony).

17. Nowatske v. Osterloh, 198 Wis.2d 419, 543 N.W.2d 265 (1996).

18. Advincula v. United Blood Services, 176 Ill.2d 1, 25, 678 N.E.2d 1009, 1021, 223 Ill.Dec. 1, 13 (1996).

19. See Clark Havighurst, Practice Guidelines as Legal Standards Governing Physician Liability, 54 L. & Contemp. Probs. 87 (1991).

20. See 1 Barry R. Furrow, Thomas L. Greaney, Sandra H. Johnson, Timothy S. Jost, & Robert L. Schwartz, Health Law 363 (1995).

21. See Bradford v. McGee, 534 So.2d 1076 (Ala.1988) (treating standard as estab-

Several states have actively sponsored the development of practice guidelines and have provided for their legal effect. Maine's statute provides that physicians (but not patients) may elect whether to be covered by the practice guidelines. The statute also provides that physician compliance with the guideline can be used by the defendant as a shield, but his noncompliance cannot be used by the plaintiff as a sword.[22] Kentucky, on the other hand, merely provides that compliance with practice guidelines developed or approved by a state official only gives rise to a presumption that the physician had met the appropriate standard of care.[23] Maryland simply provides that practice parameters are not admissible in evidence to show a standard of care either way.[24] At this writing, most states have not officially made provisions for practice guidelines.

Courtroom use of standards prescribed in advance to establish limits on liability of defendants presents some inherent problems. As a means of limiting a patient's rights, standards might have the most legitimacy if they were generated by governmental agencies with public representatives. But such standards are likely to be politically driven, for example, by cost-cutting motives, and may not reflect good assessment of responsible medical care. On the other hand, if standards-in-advance are generated purely by medical professionals, perhaps with an eye to potential liability, medical professionals and not the public processes of courts or legislatures would be deciding the patient's rights.[25]

Other less serious problems are nevertheless of immediate practical importance. At the very least it will be a challenge to keep standards up to date and to make them specific enough to be more useful than risk-utility evidence without at the same time producing a kind of medical Code of Federal Regulations.[26] Unless guidelines are highly specific—"one cubic centimeter administered every four hours plus or minus one minute" would be a specific guideline—issues of compliance and non-compliance may raise the same problems of expert testimony and technical evidence that are now raised in discussions about the "standard of

lished by testimony showing a recommendation of the American College of Obstetrics and Gynecology); cf. Pollard v. Goldsmith, 117 Ariz. 363, 572 P.2d 1201 (App. 1977) (defendant admitted that American College of Surgeons guideline was authoritative and, so admitted, it established the standard of care).

22. 24 Me. Rev. Stats. Ann. § 2975. A somewhat less one-sided approach is to make compliance with the guideline conclusive evidence that the doctor used reasonable care, but that non-compliance would only amount to some inconclusive evidence that due care was not used. See Sam A. McConkey IV, Simplifying the Law in Medical Malpractice: The Use of Practice Guidelines as the Standard of Care in Medical Malpractice Litigation, 97 W. Va. L. Rev. 491 (1995).

23. Ky. Rev. Stat. § 342.035. Since the plaintiff already has the burden of proving negligence, it is not clear what the presumption adds.

24. Ann. Code Md., Health-Gen. § 19-1606.

25. See, discussing who has the right to set standards, especially where there is no market in which consumers can choose an alternative, Clark Havighurst, Practice Guidelines as Legal Standards Governing Physician Liability, 54 L. & CONTEMP. PROBS. 87 (1991).

26. See Lori Rinella, The Use of Medical Practice Guidelines in Medical Malpractice Litigation—Should Practice Guidelines Define the Standard of Care?, 64 U.M.K.C. L. Rev. 337 (1995).

care." In addition, the reasons to say that compliance with statutes and regulations should not be taken to show conclusively that the defendant exercised due care apply as well to compliance with medical protocols.[27] There is room to hope medical guidelines would be quite useful in reducing the cost of unnecessary tests, procedures, and medications,[28] but also room for healthy scepticism about their value as ultimate tests of liability or non-liability.

§ 248. Standard Res Ipsa Loquitur in Medical Cases

Applicability to medical cases. Courts and writers sometimes say that res ipsa loquitur does not generally apply to medical malpractice claims. That is true in the sense that the res ipsa loquitur rules applied to the facts of medical malpractice claims seldom warrant submission of the claim to the jury. But in most states there is no independent rule of law that excludes res ipsa loquitur in medical cases.[1] When the rules of res ipsa loquitur permit an inference of negligence, then no expert testimony is required to establish the standard of care.

General rule of res ipsa loquitur. The general rule of res ipsa loquitur merely permits the trier of fact to infer negligence as the cause of harm without proof of specific acts of negligence when the facts fairly analyzed show that, more likely than not, (a) the plaintiff's harm was caused by negligence, even though the specific act of negligence is not identified, and (b) the defendant was the author of that negligence. Courts usually list three or four or more elements to this guide to analysis, but the additional elements are logically only evidence about one of the two items listed here.[2]

27. See Teresa Moran Schwartz, The Role of Federal Safety Regulations in Products Liability Actions, 41 VAND. L. REV. 1121 (1988); § 224.

28. One stated rationale is that guidelines will eliminate the overuse of costly tests and medication now being prescribed by some doctors in the hope that by so doing they will avoid lawsuits.

§ 248

1. Georgia still insists that res ipsa loquitur simply cannot be applied in medical malpractice cases. Kapsch v. Stowers, 209 Ga.App. 767, 434 S.E.2d 539 (1993). But, without using the term, Georgia acknowledges one pattern of res ipsa cases based on common knowledge, obvious or gross negligence. See Killingsworth v. Poon, 167 Ga. App. 653, 307 S.E.2d 123 (1983); Thomas A. Eaton, Res Ipsa Loquitur and Medical Malpractice in Georgia: a Reassessment, 17 GA. L. REV. 33 (1982). The factual patterns considered sufficient to invoke res ipsa loquitur may be somewhat narrow in some other states as well. In Jones v. Porretta, 428 Mich. 132, 405 N.W.2d 863 (1987), Michigan's doubts were resolved in favor of permitting res ipsa loquitur where the facts warrant it.

2. Courts and writers frequently state res ipsa rules in three or four parts, requiring exclusive control in the defendant and sometimes requiring the plaintiff to negate her own contribution to the injury. These supposed elements are logically important only because they are among the ways in which the defendant can be identified as the wrongdoer or wrongdoing itself can be shown to be more probable than not. In addition, some courts say that res ipsa loquitur will not be applied unless the defendant has better access to the evidence than the plaintiff. See Jones v. Porretta, 428 Mich. 132, 405 N.W.2d 863 (1987). That idea seems to be based, not on contributory negligence rules, but on an earlier notion that res ipsa loquitur was an invention to assist the plaintiff rather than a way of estimating the probable truth of the case. On all this, see §§ 154–161.

Plaintiffs usually identify the defendant as the author of the harm by showing that he was in exclusive control of the instrumentality that caused harm, but it is probably fair to say that for most courts today, any form of evidence that points to the defendant as the most likely author of the harm will suffice.

Plaintiffs usually adduce no evidence at all that negligence was more likely than not. Instead, they attempt to persuade the judge and jury that common experience shows the injury to be of a kind that ordinarily does not occur in the absence of negligence. If that argument is persuasive, then negligence was probably the explanation in this particular case. The idea is that common knowledge and experience are quite sufficient to show that if a barrel falls from the defendant's building and strikes a pedestrian on the public walk, someone is probably negligent. If the judge thought that common experience failed to indicate negligence as the most likely explanation for the injury, the plaintiff would not get to the jury on the res ipsa loquitur theory.[3]

When res ipsa does not apply. These same essential rules apply in medical malpractice cases. Res ipsa loquitur cannot be applied to get the plaintiff to the jury if injury or a bad result is one of the risks of the medical procedure. If well-performed sterilization procedures are not always effective to prevent pregnancy, the fact that the plaintiff became pregnant after such a procedure does not bespeak negligence.[4] Commonly enough, an injury occurs at the site of an invasive procedure, but such an injury may reflect an inherent risk of the procedure, not negligence. If proper administration of anesthesia by way of an endotracheal tube creates an risk of injury to teeth, the fact that teeth are injured in the procedure does not by itself prove negligence.[5] If a patient has a history of anal diseases, a bruise from an hospital administered enema is just as likely attributable to the patient's condition as to hospital negligence.[6] There are many variations on the essential theme.[7]

The analysis is not a mechanical one, however. Some injuries, even though they occur at the site of a medical procedure, nevertheless indicate the probability of negligence. If the plaintiff can establish that, then res ipsa loquitur may be appropriate.[8]

Res ipsa loquitur in obvious or gross negligence cases. In a few cases, courts have considered the negligence of a physician or surgeon to be so

3. On res ipsa loquitur generally, see §§ 154–161.

4. Farley v. Meadows, 185 W.Va. 48, 404 S.E.2d 537 (1991).

5. Chism v. Campbell, 250 Neb. 921, 553 N.W.2d 741 (1996).

6. Kelly v. Hartford Casualty Ins. Co., 86 Wis.2d 129, 271 N.W.2d 676 (1978).

7. See e.g., Walker v. Skiwski, 529 So.2d 184 (Miss.1988) (fact that an infant's penis was deformed and that he suffered pain in urination does not show negligent circumcision).

8. See Higdon v. Carlebach, 348 Mich. 363, 83 N.W.2d 296 (1957) (dentist cut patient's tongue with rotating disk attached to electric drill; no expert testimony required); Killingsworth v. Poon, 167 Ga.App. 653, 307 S.E.2d 123 (1983) (injection in shoulder for pain punctured patient's lung; Georgia obvious negligence doctrine applied). Perhaps in on-site injuries, the best res ipsa case is made out by expert testimony indicating that such an injury is ordinarily avoidable by reasonable care.

obvious or gross that a jury should be allowed to find negligence even without expert medical testimony, either because gross and obvious negligence is an independent exception or because res ipsa loquitur can be invoked in such cases. These are classically cases in which a surgeon operates on the wrong organ or body part,[9] leaves foreign objects in the patient's body,[10] misconnects a machine so that gas is pumped into the patient's uterus,[11] or causes injury to a healthy part of the body not involved in the operation.[12] In such cases, the jury is authorized to apply common knowledge and experience and to conclude that the results are a sign of negligence.

Res ipsa loquitur in non-obvious cases coupled with testimony of medical likelihood. The fact that the plaintiff's injury does not ordinarily occur without negligence can be shown by expert medical testimony even when it cannot be shown by common knowledge or experience. The fact that a surgery goes wrong, even hideously wrong, might often be one of the unavoidable risks and not proof of negligence at all. Nevertheless, a medical witness might show that the particular harm is usually avoidable by reasonable care, even when that witness cannot identify any particular act of negligence. In such a case, the medical testimony supplies the same understanding that common knowledge provides in the cases of obvious negligence. If such testimony is believed, it suffices to permit an inference that negligence is more probable than not and thus to permit a finding for the plaintiff if the other elements of the case are proved.[13]

It is easy to mistake what testimony is needed in such cases. Sometimes courts have treated testimony that the injury was "not an ordinary risk of the surgery" as if it were testimony that the injury would not ordinarily occur without negligence.[14] But the two statements

9. Long v. Hacker, 246 Neb. 547, 520 N.W.2d 195 (1994) (wrong vertebra); Manax v. Ballew, 797 S.W.2d 71 (Tex.App. 1990) (wrong part of back).

10. Tiller v. Von Pohle, 72 Ariz. 11, 230 P.2d 213 (1951) (large cloth sack lodged in plaintiff's bowel after abdominal operation, inference that it was a result of the operation would be permitted); Kambat v. St. Francis Hospital., 89 N.Y.2d 489, 678 N.E.2d 456, 655 N.Y.S.2d 844 (1997) (18 x 18–inch towel or laparotomy pack). The duty of counting sponges or the like is usually assigned to a nurse. In that case, the rational inference may be that the nurse, not the doctor, was negligent. However, as a matter of policy, courts may hold the surgeon liable. See Ravi v. Coates, 662 So.2d 218 (Ala.1995).

11. Chin v. St. Barnabas Medical Center, 160 N.J. 454, 734 A.2d 778 (1999).

12. Wick v. Henderson, 485 N.W.2d 645 (Iowa 1992) (operation for gallbladder, injury to left arm); Dalley v. Utah Valley Regional Medical Center, 791 P.2d 193 (Utah 1990) (Caesarean, burn on calf); Beaudoin v. Watertown Memorial Hospital, 32 Wis.2d 132, 145 N.W.2d 166 (1966) (vaginal polyp removed, burns on buttocks).

13. Kennelly v. Burgess, 337 Md. 562, 654 A.2d 1335 (1995); Hightower–Warren v. Silk, 548 Pa. 459, 698 A.2d 52 (1997); Mireles v. Broderick, 117 N.M. 445, 872 P.2d 863 (1994); Morgan v. Children's Hosp., 18 Ohio St.3d 185, 480 N.E.2d 464, 49 A.L.R.4th 51 (1985); Restatement § 328D, cmt. d. Statutory protections for health care providers, however, may close this route. In Larsen v. Zarrett, 498 N.W.2d 191 (N.D. 1993) the court thought a statute foreclosed use of res ipsa loquitur in all except obvious cases of negligence.

14. See Perkins v. Hausladen, 828 S.W.2d 652 (Ky.1992), where in the course of an ear operation the doctor's drill struck a vein and where the court appeared to think that infrequence of such an occurrence established that it was not an inherent risk of the operation.

are not the same. An injury resulting from a medical procedure might be quite rare; yet when it occurs, it might most often occur without negligence. The ultimate issue is the probability of negligence as the cause of harm and except in the "obvious" cases, expert testimony should tend to establish something about probability, not merely something about frequency.[15]

Expert factual testimony to make negligence potentially obvious. The usual medical expert testimony used as a predicate for res ipsa loquitur is conclusory: the expert testifies that the injury suffered ordinarily does not occur without negligence. However, experts may also testify as to medical facts. In a few cases, non-conclusory testimony about facts may make negligence sufficiently "obvious" to permit a finding of negligence without expert testimony on the standard of care. In one case,[16] the defendant operating on the patient's ear, cut a nerve that controlled one side of the patient's face, with the result that the patient could not close her eye or control that side of the face. The nerve was at the site of the operation, but medical testimony demonstrated that it was "almost impossible" to cut it because it was encased in hard bone and because four specific procedures worked as safeguards against cutting. Extreme rarity of a cut, plus these medical facts, would warrant the jury in drawing an inference of negligence.

§ 249. Ybarra v. Spangard: Multiple Defendant Res Ipsa Loquitur

The plaintiff who claims the benefit of res ipsa loquitur must not only show that negligence is more likely than not; she must also show that the defendant was more likely than not the negligent person. Such a showing is often accomplished by evidence that the defendant was in exclusive control of the instrumentality causing the plaintiff's harm. When a number of defendants are likely suspects, the guilt cannot be laid at any one defendant's door and res ipsa loquitur cannot apply. It is possible to imagine in the abstract that every single one of five defendants was negligent, in which case it would be appropriate to apply res ipsa loquitur to all five; but such cases are rare.

Yet in the famous case of *Ybarra v. Spangard*[1] the California Supreme Court held that res ipsa loquitur—or what it called by that name—would apply against a number of defendants. The plaintiff in that case had a simple operation for appendicitis but awoke with pain in his arm. The arm was ultimately paralyzed. An unnamed person had given him an injection before the operation and at least three nurses attended him before, after, or during the operation. At least two doctors and an

15. See David Kaye, Probability Theory Meets Res Ipsa Loquitur, 77 MICH L. REV. 1456, 1476 (1979).

16. Cho v. Kempler, 177 Cal.App.2d 342, 2 Cal.Rptr. 167, 76 A.L.R.2d 774 (1960).

§ 249

1. Ybarra v. Spangard, 25 Cal.2d 486, 154 P.2d 687 (1944).

anesthetist, besides nurses, attended him during the operation and two other doctors were involved as employers of those present.

Because the patient suffered an injury to a part of his body not involved in the operation, it was plausible to infer that someone involved was causally negligent, but hardly conceivable that all those present contributed to his injury. The court did not appear to argue that the facts justified a rational inference that all actors were negligent. It rather emphasized what might be called their custodial role towards an anesthetized patient and the patient's inevitable lack of information. The court went on to suggest that it was really only holding all of the doctors and nurses as financial hostages so that the guilty would confess or the innocent would point the finger at the responsible person.[2]

Holding all the defendants hostage would itself be a justified response if evidence showed that all of them had knowledge of the facts. But that was not the case and it is inherently improbable that everyone in an operating room knows exactly what everyone else is doing every second of the time; at least one person's eyes should be on the scalpel. Consequently, Seavey saw the case as "inequitable,"[3] which would be a rather mild description if there were no more to it.

On the other hand, if the inappropriate res ipsa loquitur terminology is dropped, the question can be reconsidered in terms of duty. It is reasonable to say that one or more primary caregivers—the surgeon and the hospital, for example—implicitly undertake a special responsibility to the helpless patient whose custody they have accepted. They should guarantee either due care or information about those who were negligent. In addition, all those in the operating room shown to have actual knowledge of the facts should be held responsible for divulging them. Professor Thode's version of this idea came out about where *Ybarra* itself came out—everyone is liable.[4] A more palatable version would limit such duties to those who contracted with the patient or undertook special custodial duties. There seems no reason in fact or in justice to think that all nurses, orderlies, janitors and others who may have touched the patient are undertaking to guarantee either results or information.

A revised version of *Ybarra* would drop the res ipsa loquitur language and simply impose a duty upon primary caretakers of incapacitated patients to guarantee either (a) that no harm would be negligently inflicted or (b) if harm resulted, that full information about the negligent actor would be provided. This, like *Ybarra* itself, is potentially a narrow form of strict liability, but it is strict liability that falls only upon the main actors.

2. Cf. Saul Levmore, Gomorrah to Ybarra and More: Overextraction and the Puzzle of Immoderate Group Liability, 81 Va. L. Rev. 1561 (1995) (discussing varied possibilities of getting information this way).

3. Seavey, Res Ipsa Loquitur: Tabula in Naufragio, 63 Harv. L. Rev. 643 (1950).

4. Thode, The Unconscious Patient: Who Should Bear the Risk of Unexplained Injuries to a Healthy Part of his Body?, 1969 Utah L. Rev. 1.

A number of courts have cited and verbally approved *Ybarra*, but only rarely going as far as *Ybarra* went.[5] Other cases that have verbally approved *Ybarra,* or have been listed by writers as following that decision,[6] actually impose liability only upon those in charge and in a way consistent with the captain of the ship doctrine[7] or a nondelegable duty.[8] The purported follower of *Ybarra* may turn out on examination to be supported by quite adequate proof of specific negligence, so that res ipsa loquitur is not necessary or relevant at all.[9] In some cases, several different defendants were held potentially liable, but the facts would perhaps warrant a conclusion that could not be believed in *Ybarra*—that all defendants were in fact negligent.[10] Many of these cases seem to have little enough to do with res ipsa loquitur, and none of them suggests by their facts that liability should be imposed upon every nurse in the operating room.

§ 250. Informed Consent

Unconsented-to operations. On principles of autonomy and self-determination, human beings have the right to determine what can be done to their own bodies.[1] Patients have a right to refuse a recommended

5. See Dalley v. Utah Valley Regional Medical Center, 791 P.2d 193 (Utah. 1990).

6. Horner v. Northern Pacific Beneficial Association Hospitals, 62 Wash.2d 351, 382 P.2d 518 (1963) was cited by Prosser as following *Ybarra* but in fact the court merely held the hospital employer liable. Res ipsa loquitur was involved, but merely to establish that someone employed by the hospital was at fault, not to establish liability of individuals.

7. See Swierczek v. Lynch, 237 Neb. 469, 466 N.W.2d 512 (1991) where the court combined a discussion of res ipsa loquitur with discussions of the chief surgeon's liability for negligence of borrowed servants and the hospital's nondelegable duty of care.

8. See Kolakowski v. Voris, 83 Ill.2d 388, 415 N.E.2d 397, 47 Ill.Dec. 392 (1980); Beaudoin v. Watertown Memorial Hospital, 32 Wis.2d 132, 145 N.W.2d 166 (1966).

9. See Wick v. Henderson, 485 N.W.2d 645 (Iowa 1992); Chin v. St. Barnabas Medical Center, 160 N.J. 454, 734 A.2d 778 (1999) (three individuals all had something to do with wrongly connecting machine that caused patient's death); Becker v. Lake County Memorial Hospital West, 53 Ohio St.3d 202, 560 N.E.2d 165 (1990) (the plaintiff was improperly restrained during a surgical operation; the nurses present should have fastened the restraints and the surgeon should have told them to do so).

10. In Chin v. St. Barnabas Medical Center, 160 N.J. 454, 734 A.2d 778 (1999) the court shifted the ultimate burden of proof to medical defendants to exculpate themselves, but there was evidence that each of the individuals held liable had participated, as supervisor or otherwise, in connecting the wrong tubes to a machine, which then pumped nitrogen into a patient's body. In Maciag v. Strato Medical Corp., 274 N.J.Super. 447, 644 A.2d 647 (1994) doctors inserted a catheter into the plaintiff's body to be left there permanently. The tubing disintegrated into pieces, some large, some too small to be removed by surgery. These were lodged in or near the patient's pulmonary artery. Evidence indicated that Dow Corning may have supplied inappropriate material for the tubing as a component part, knowing its intended use; that the manufacturer of the device may have negligently designed or made the device; and that doctors may have negligently inserted or monitored it. An earlier New Jersey case, sidestepping the res ipsa terminology, imposed liability upon the operating surgeon and suppliers of equipment that broke off in the plaintiff's spinal canal, but not upon nurses in the operating room. Anderson v. Somberg, 67 N.J. 291, 338 A.2d 1 (1975).

§ 250

1. Schloendorff v. Society of New York Hospital, 211 N.Y. 125, 105 N.E. 92 (1914) overruled in part by Bing v. Thunig, 2 N.Y.2d 656, 163 N.Y.S.2d 3, 143 N.E.2d 3(1957).

medical procedure,[2] even if it is necessary to save the patient's life.[3] Thus a surgeon who operates without the appearance of express, implied, or substituted consent[4] is by definition prima facie guilty of a battery.[5] Consent procured by misrepresentation of material facts[6] or duress[7] is also ineffective and a medical procedure performed on the basis of such a consent would also be a battery. The same idea applies when the plaintiff consents only to an operation by Dr. A, but it is performed in fact by Dr. B.[8]

The informed consent principle. Courts have recognized that these principles also imply another: unless patients are incapacitated, they are entitled to material information about the nature of any proposed medical procedure. For example, patients are entitled to information about the risks of the procedure, its necessity, and alternative procedures that might be preferable. This is the general principle of informed consent, the "bedrock of . . . respect for the individual's right."[9]

Although the principle seems to express fundamental American values,[10] is supported by explicit principles of medical ethics,[11] and hardly seems to represent an enormous burden to anyone,[12] it has generated much literature,[13] some of which is unfriendly to informed consent rights, at least in part.[14] Courts themselves are divided on approaches,

2. See Miller v. Rhode Island Hospital, 625 A.2d 778 (R.I.1993).

3. See In re A.C., 573 A.2d 1235 (D.C.App.1990); In re Dubreuil, 629 So.2d 819 (Fla.1993); cf. Anderson v. St. Francis–St. George Hospital, Inc., 77 Ohio St.3d 82, 671 N.E.2d 225 (1996) (hospital prolonging life against patient's wishes liable for battery, but not for the prolonged life itself).

4. See §§ 100 & 106 (consent for those lacking capacity and emergency as a substitute for consent).

5. E.g., Gragg v. Calandra, 297 Ill. App.3d 639, 696 N.E.2d 1282, 231 Ill.Dec. 711 (1998); see § 28. If there is a potential privilege, good motive may matter, but good motive alone does not justify the battery. See § 25.

6. See Bloskas v. Murray, 646 P.2d 907, 913, 42 A.L.R.4th 527 (Colo. 1982); cf. Rains v. Superior Court, 198 Cal.Rptr. 249, 150 Cal.App.3d 933 (1984) (misrepresentations and assorted misdoings treated as battery); §§ 100–103.

7. § 101.

8. Perna v. Pirozzi, 92 N.J. 446, 457 A.2d 431 (1983); see Guebard v. Jabaay, 117 Ill.App.3d 1, 452 N.E.2d 751, 72 Ill.Dec. 498 (1983).

9. Fox v. Smith, 594 So.2d 596, 604 (Miss.1992).

10. See Peter H. Schuck, Rethinking Informed Consent, 103 YALE L.J. 899 (1994) (autonomy, economic efficiency, and anti-statism).

11. See Anthony Szczgiel, Beyond Informed Consent, 21 OHIO N. U. L. REV. 171, 217–230 (1994).

12. But Peter H. Schuck, supra n. 10, thinks that, because physicians are compensated at such a high rate, every minute of their time is worth counting in the costs, so that the burden could in this sense be "onerous." He calls for extensive cost-benefit studies.

13. Katz, Informed Consent—A Fairy Tale? Law's Vision, 39 U. PITT. L. REV. 137 (1977); Peter H. Schuck, Rethinking Informed Consent, 103 Yale L.J. 899 (1994); Jon R. Waltz and and Thomas W. Scheuneman, Informed Consent to Therapy, 64 NW. U. L. REV. 628 (1970) (a very helpful analysis undimmed by the passing years); Textbook treatments include 1 BARRY R. FURROW, THOMAS L. GREANEY, SANDRA H. JOHNSON, TIMOTHY STOLZFUS JOST AND ROBERT L. SCHWARTZ, HEALTH LAW § 6–10 (1995); 3 DAVID W. LOUISELL & HAROLD WILLIAMS, MEDICAL MALPRACTICE Ch. 22 (various dates); STEVEN E. PEGALIS, & HARVEY F. WACHSMAN, 1 AMERICAN LAW OF MEDICAL MALPRACTICE 2d Ch. 4 (1992).

14. See Richard Epstein, Medical Malpractice: The Case for Contract, [1976] AM. BAR FOUND. J. 87 at 127 ("The root problem with the informed consent doctrine is that it is forever at war with the mutual

and some courts, as well as a number of legislatures, have erected substantial limitations on application of the principle.

Battery vs. negligence approaches. On the basis of the informed consent principle, some courts hold that a physician who performs a procedure upon the patient's body without first providing adequate information is subject to liability for battery.[15] Most courts now take a view more favorable to the health care provider. They say that the patient's claim is not for battery but for negligence, and that the battery claim will be reserved for cases in which the operation performed was different from the one to which the patient consented.[16] Thus under the view currently prevailing, the patient who consents to an operation on his right toe has a battery action if the surgeon operates on the left toe instead. But the patient who consents to an operation on his right toe without being informed that the operation entails a serious risk that he will lose his leg must make out a claim for negligent nondisclosure.

Under neither view, however, is the plaintiff required to prove negligence in conducting the operation. If the elements of an informed consent claim are proved under the applicable theory, the surgeon is liable for the harm resulting even if he operated with consummate skill. The wrong done is not a negligent operation but a failure to respect the patient's right of choice.

Elements of the claim. For many courts, the shift to negligence theory meant that the plaintiff would be required to prove five things: (1) nondisclosure of required information; (2) actual damage such as loss of a leg, (3) resulting from the risks of which the patient was not informed;[17] (4) cause in fact, which is to say that the plaintiff would have rejected the medical treatment if she had known the risk; and (5) that reasonable persons, if properly informed, would have rejected the proposed treatment.[18] Louisiana has accepted this view of informed consent as a negligence rather than a battery claim, but permits the plaintiff nevertheless to recover damages like those in battery cases—in this

expectations of the parties"); Schuck, supra n. 10 (unfavorable to the view that patient autonomy is a value itself and favoring a cost-benefit analysis); Aaron Twerski & Neil Cohen, Informed Decision Making and the Law of Torts: The Myth of Justiciable Causation, 1988 U. Ill. L. Rev. 607.

15. Fox v. Smith, 594 So.2d 596 (Miss. 1992); Friter v. Iolab Corp., 414 Pa.Super. 622, 607 A.2d 1111 (1992) (hospital participating in clinical study of experimental device failed to provide information required by FDA).

16. E.g., Cobbs v. Grant, 8 Cal.3d 229, 502 P.2d 1, 104 Cal.Rptr. 505 (1972); Kennis v. Mercy Hospital Medical Center, 491 N.W.2d 161 (Iowa 1992).

17. For example, a surgeon fails to inform his patient that a proposed operation may result in loss of tongue function. After the operation the patient in fact has lost tongue function, but that is because of side effects of anesthesia that the doctor could not have known about. Some authority says that in such a case the plaintiff has not proved "medical causation" and that she cannot recovery on an informed consent theory. See Canesi v. Wilson, 158 N.J. 490, 730 A.2d 805 (1999). The point seems to be a scope of the risk or proximate cause point.

18. See Aronson v. Harriman, 321 Ark. 359, 901 S.W.2d 832 (1995) (but treating third element as a "factor" to consider); Woolley v. Henderson, 418 A.2d 1123 (Me. 1980).

instance, for a loss of self-determination rights, even if no physical harm is done.[19]

The medical standard of disclosure. On the question of what must be disclosed, the courts are divided into roughly two camps. The older cases and a large group of statutes require the plaintiff to prove the medical standard of disclosure. If medical custom or standard requires no disclosure, the doctor, though a fiduciary, owes no duty to divulge information, no matter how critical it might be to the patient. If the medical standard requires disclosure of one risk but not another equally great, the rule entitles the plaintiff to half the relevant information, not all of it.[20] The medical standard requires expert testimony to establish the standard.[21] Tabulating the position of different states is inherently imprecise and may be even more so when, as here, legislatures have intervened to enact specific requirements.[22] For what it is worth, however, a little more than half the states, many under the command of a statute,[23] appear to adopt the medical standard of disclosure rather than the patient or materiality standard as a general rule.[24]

The patient or materiality standard of disclosure. Beginning in 1972 when three leading decisions broke with the earlier decisions,[25] the new cases deciding the issue on first impression and independent of statutory commands have tended to favor a duty to disclose all material information, that is, information the physician can reasonably expect a patient would want to consider in determining whether to undergo the medical procedure.[26]

19. Lugenbuhl v. Dowling, 701 So.2d 447 (La.1997); cf. Provenzano v. Integrated Genetics, 22 F.Supp.2d 406 (D.N.J.1998) (laboratory failed to recognize genetic problem with fetus, parent can recover even if she would not have terminated the pregnancy, since she lost right to decide).

20. But revealing one risk and not the other might count as a misrepresentation and might be actionable on that ground under the rule that an half-truth is a half-lie and as such is actionable, at least in economic transactions. See § 481.

21. E.g., Woolley v. Henderson, 418 A.2d 1123 (Me.1980). The testimony may, of course, come from defense witnesses, as in Davis v. Caldwell, 54 N.Y.2d 176, 429 N.E.2d 741, 445 N.Y.S.2d 63 (1981).

22. See Anthony Szczgiel, Beyond Informed Consent, 21 Ohio N. U. L. Rev. 171, 212 (1994).

23. E.g., N.Y. CPLR 4401–a & N.Y. Pub. Health L. § 2805–d; N.C. Gen. Stat. § 90–21.13.

24. E.g., Davis v. Caldwell, 54 N.Y.2d 176, 429 N.E.2d 741, 445 N.Y.S.2d 63 (1981). See 1 Barry R. Furrow, Thomas L. Greaney, Sandra H. Johnson, Timothy Stolzfus Jost and Robert L. Schwartz, Health Law § 6–10 (1995) (listing cases and statutes). As to cases, see Laurent B. Frantz, Annotation, Modern Status of Views as to General Measure of Physician's Duty to Inform Patient of Risks of Proposed Treatment, 88 A.L.R.3d 1008 (1978). Some cases may have stated both the medical and the patient rule. See Bloskas v. Murray, 646 P.2d 907, 913, 42 A.L.R.4th 527 (Colo. 1982).

25. Canterbury v. Spence, 464 F.2d 772, 150 U.S.App.D.C. 263 (1972); Cobbs v. Grant, 8 Cal.3d 229, 502 P.2d 1, 104 Cal. Rptr. 505, (1972); Wilkinson v. Vesey, 110 R.I. 606, 295 A.2d 676, 69 A.L.R.3d 1202 (1972).

26. Carr v. Strode, 79 Hawai'i 475, 904 P.2d 489 (1995); Cowman v. Hornaday, 329 N.W.2d 422 (Iowa 1983); Harnish v. Children's Hospital Medical Center, 387 Mass. 152, 439 N.E.2d 240 (1982); Largey v. Rothman, 110 N.J. 204, 540 A.2d 504 (1988); Scott v. Bradford, 606 P.2d 554 (Okl.1979); Moure v. Raeuchle, 529 Pa. 394, 604 A.2d 1003 (1992). As to the information to be disclosed, see § 251.

These courts have insisted that "[r]espect for the patient's right of self-determination ... demands a standard set by law for physicians rather than one which physicians may or may not impose upon themselves."[27] Further, the patient's right to weigh her subjective fears against the risks disclosed is a personal, not a medical question, and it is "reserved to the patient alone."[28]

Since a medical standard is not involved in the materiality test, expert testimony is not required. Disclosure is to be made when the information is material to a decision. However, experts may be required to show both that material information existed and that the defendant should reasonably have known about it.[29]

A few states do not directly use a physician standard, yet may not be completely within the materiality regime, for example because they may provide specific lists of risks or treatments to which the patient's right of information attaches.[30]

The therapeutic exception. Sometimes jurists list "exceptions" to the right of informed consent. Many of these are not exceptions but merely applications of the rule according to its own terms. For example, it is not an exception to the rule to say that the doctor is not liable without negligence; that *is* the rule. Supposed exceptions for emergencies and incompetent patients are in the same category; the right of informed consent is aimed at adults who are not incapacitated by nature or by emergency, although in that case consent by a guardian or relative, if feasible, may be required. One exception that courts have verbally acknowledged would truly count as an exception to the principle. That is the putative privilege to withhold information for therapeutic reasons. The idea is that in some instances, if a physician told the patient of the risk, the knowledge itself would harm the patient. Courts have warned themselves to be cautious should such a case actually be argued. They have said that the supposed privilege should not be recognized merely because a physician fears that disclosure of risks will lead the patient to make a bad decision. And even if disclosure by itself could seem to

27. Canterbury v. Spence, 464 F.2d 772, 784, 150 U.S.App.D.C. 263, 275 (1972).

28. Cobbs v. Grant, 8 Cal.3d 229, 502 P.2d 1, 104 Cal.Rptr. 505, (1972).

29. Harnish v. Children's Hospital Medical Center, 387 Mass. 152, 439 N.E.2d 240 (1982); see Marchione v. State, 194 A.D.2d 851, 598 N.Y.S.2d 592 (1993) (priapism was not definitely established as a result of medication at the time physician prescribed it; no warning due); Waltz and Scheuneman, Informed Consent to Therapy, 64 N.W. L. REV. 628 (1970).

30. The Georgia statute requires disclosure of "material" risks, but lists them specifically and perhaps exclusively. GA. CODE § 31–9–6.1. Texas uses a "reasonable person" test but operates under a statute requiring a panel to list all medical procedures that require disclosure and makes the patient's rights depend somewhat on that. See Peterson v. Shields, 652 S.W.2d 929 (Tex.1983). Oregon's statute requires the physician to specify certain information and then specifically ask the patient if she wants to know more. A failure to ask that question can support an informed consent claim. Zacher v. Petty, 312 Or. 590, 826 P.2d 619 (1992). Some states, in addition to whatever general rule is followed, prescribe information to be given patients about specific medical procedures. E.g., N.Y. PUB. HLTH. L. §§ 2404, 2496 (breast cancer and hysterectomies respectively); See, e.g., MO. STAT. ANN. § 188.039 (abortion). See Anthony Szczgiel, Beyond Informed Consent, 21 OHIO N. U. L. REV. 171, 212 ff. (1994).

menace the patient's health, the physician may be obliged to make the disclosure to a relative.[31]

The double test of "causation." Even if the defendant breaches his duty to disclose information that is material or is to be disclosed under the community medical standard, he is not subject to liability unless both the plaintiff herself and a reasonable person would have rejected the operation had full information been provided.[32] The first half of this rule is a concomitant of the decision to treat the claim as one for negligence rather than one for battery. Damages must be proven in negligence and that implies that the tort must have caused them. So if the missing information would have changed nothing, the plaintiff has no claim. This is not so controversial, even though, in product liability cases, courts use a quite different technique, presuming that if a material warning had been given the victim would have read and acted upon it.[33]

The second half of the rule—denying recovery unless reasonable people would have refused the operation—is more or less unique to the medical informed consent cases, but seems to be followed in all but two states.[34] It has been called an objective test of causation, but if the full disclosure would have led the plaintiff to refuse the operation, both the defendant's breach and its causal role is clearly established,[35] so the rule does not reflect the causation requirement but imposes some additional and most unusual obstacle.

The real effect of the rule is to limit the defendant's duty of disclosure for the protection of patients who have the same feelings about the risks and advantages of the operation that the mainstream of reasonable people would have. The special concerns of an individual get no protection under this rule and "a patient's right of self-determination is irrevocably lost".[36] The underlying right of the patient to decide for herself becomes a right to decide only so long as people in general would think her decisions reasonable. This rule is controversial and again, in the comparable case of product warnings, courts impose no such demand.

People who hold strong feelings against specific medical procedures and know exactly what they want to avoid may obtain some protection by way of contract limits. Such a patient might, for instance, contract with the doctor that no blood transfusion would be administered. Those who are more vulnerable, ignorant, or afraid are not likely to be able to take this route, for they will not know exactly what to prohibit.

31. Canterbury v. Spence, 464 F.2d 772, 784, 150 U.S.App.D.C. 263, 275 (1972).

32. E.g., Canterbury v. Spence, 464 F.2d 772 (D.C.Cir.1972); Harnish v. Children's Hospital Medical Center, 387 Mass. 152, 439 N.E.2d 240 (1982).

33. See § 367 on product warnings.

34. Arena v. Gingrich, 305 Or. 1, 748 P.2d 547 (Or. 1988)

35. Scott v. Bradford, 606 P.2d 554, 559 (Okl.1979); Arena v. Gingrich, 305 Or. 1, 748 P.2d 547 (1988).

36. Scott v. Bradford, 606 P.2d 554, 559 (Okl.1979). McPherson v. Ellis, 305 N.C. 266, 287 S.E.2d 892 (1982) takes the same view, spelling out more detail, but a statute has now set that case aside.

However, the patient's obligation to take reasonable care for herself is the complement of the doctor's duty to disclose. Consequently, if the doctor is under a legal duty of disclosure, he cannot justify his failure to do so on the ground that the patient was chargeable with contributory fault because she should have ascertained the risks or needs from some other source. On the contrary, his duty to disclose, when it exists, demonstrates the plaintiff's right to rely upon his disclosure.[37]

§ 251. Informed Consent—What Must Be Disclosed

The medical standard. Under the medical standard, the information to be disclosed is wholly dependent upon whether doctors in the relevant community testify that disclosure is required by a "medical" standard or practice, although some courts put the burden upon the defendant to show the standard of disclosure.[1] No matter who has the burden of introducing evidence on the issue, a medical standard of disclosure, as distinct from treatment, frequently may be hard to find or may not exist at all.[2]

Officially identified risks. In some states, statutes require a panel or a state official to identify particular risks that accompany particular medical procedures.[3] Statutes themselves may describe the risks to be disclosed.[4] If the risks specified by a panel or by the statute are disclosed, the doctor's duty is presumptively fulfilled.[5]

The materiality standard. The materiality standard does not rely upon prepared lists or upon the disclosure conventions of the medical community. Under the materiality standard, the doctor must disclose material information of which he knows or should know. What the doctor should know is a medical question and unless admitted must ordinarily be established by expert testimony or at least by medical information such as textbooks.[6] Given that he should know of a particu-

37. Brown v. Dibbell, 227 Wis.2d 28, 595 N.W.2d 358 (1999) (but nothing that the patient might be chargeable with fault in failing to accurately give her medical history).

§ 251

1. Gorab v. Zook, 943 P.2d 423, 427 (Colo.1997) (once the plaintiff proves nondisclosure, "the burden then shifts to the physician to go forward with expert testimony showing that the nondisclosure conformed" with medical standards). The burden in *Gorab* is only to produce some evidence. When the doctor does that, the plaintiff will lose unless she produces contradictory evidence.

2. See Canterbury v. Spence, 464 F.2d 772, 783–84, 150 U.S.App.D.C. 263, 274–75 (D.C.Cir.1972) (doubting the "reality of any discernible custom" as to communication and recognizing "danger that what is in fact no custom at all may be taken as an affirmative custom to maintain silence"); Cobbs v. Grant, 8 Cal.3d 229, 243, 502 P.2d 1, 10, 104 Cal.Rptr. 505, 514 (1972) (standards of disclosure so nebulous that doctors would be vested with "virtual absolute discretion").

3. N.Y. Pub. Health Law § 2404 (official to prepare a written statement indicating alternatives to surgery for breast cancer and some of the potential complications; doctors must provide this official statement to patients).

4. E.g., Iowa Code Ann. § 147.137.

5. Tex. Civ. Stat. Art. 4590i §§ 6.06 & 6.07.

6. See Harnish v. Children's Hospital Medical Center, 387 Mass. 152, 439 N.E.2d 240 (1982).

lar risk or other medical information, the duty to disclose turns entirely on materiality of the information.

Objective/subjective tests of materiality. If the patient attaches special importance to some particular matter and the doctor knows or should know it, that matter is material even if most other people would not be concerned about it.[7] For example, relatively few people object to blood transfusions, but some do, and if the doctor knows that the patient is one of the few, the matter is clearly material. When the doctor could not be reasonably expected to know of any special concerns the patient might have, materiality is judged by an objective standard. Material information is that which "a reasonable patient would consider in deciding whether to undergo the medical procedure."[8] This test of materiality recognizes that many items of information may be material because they are important in the decision-making process, even though they are not decisive.[9]

Immaterial items. Medical doctors sometimes caricature the informed consent rules by suggesting that they impose preposterous obligations, such as an explanation about the size of thread used in sutures. But the materiality rule does not require detailed disclosure of methods unless they are unusual or affect the risks.[10] Certainly the physician owes no obligation to provide the patient a general medical education.[11] Nor need he disclose matters that the patient already knows, nor those that the physician reasonably believes she knows.[12]

Items generally to be disclosed. It is sometimes said that the physician should disclose the diagnosis, the general nature of the contemplated procedure, the material risks involved in the procedure, the probability of success associated with the procedure, the prognosis if the procedure is not carried out, and the existence and risks of any alternatives to the procedure.[13]

But the list is obviously not exclusive. If a surgeon merely advises a woman of a cancer diagnosis and performs a mastectomy without first

7. See Restatement § 538 (2) (b) (knows or has reason to know that the recipient regards the material as important).

8. Moure v. Raeuchle, 529 Pa. 394, 405, 604 A.2d 1003, 1008 (1992). Variations in wording appear to be aimed at the same idea. See Hondroulis v. Schuhmacher, 553 So.2d 398 (La.1988) (material information would be an influence on the decision); Phillips v. Hull, 516 So.2d 488 (Miss.1987) ("whether a reasonable person in the patient's position would have considered the risk significant in making his or her decision"); Restatement § 538 (2) (a). (material information would be important in making a choice).

9. See generally, Jon R. Waltz and Thomas W. Scheuneman, Informed Consent to Therapy, 64 Nw. L. Rev. 628, 638 (1970). In some circumstances, the physician must disclose alternative medical procedures, even if they are more risky than the one proposed. The patient would presumably reject most riskier alternatives, but the information still may be material in the decision making process. See Logan v. Greenwich Hosp. Assn., 191 Conn. 282, 465 A.2d 294 (1983).

10. Masquat v. Maguire, 638 P.2d 1105 (Okl.1981) (different methods of performing a tubal ligation, no disclosure required).

11. See Cobbs v. Grant, 8 Cal.3d 229, 502 P.2d 1, 104 Cal.Rptr. 505 (1972).

12. See, e.g., Sard v. Hardy, 281 Md. 432, 445, 379 A.2d 1014, 1022 (1977).

13. E.g., Phillips v. Hull, 516 So.2d 488 (Miss.1987); Tisdale v. Pruitt, 302 S.C. 238, 394 S.E.2d 857 (1990).

performing a biopsy to be sure the operation is needed, the surgeon may have been guilty of malpractice, and if the patient was not advised that the diagnosis was made without a biopsy, the surgeon surely has deprived the patient of material information.[14] It is also material to know whether the malady itself is serious and the prognosis if treatment is accepted. A patient might prefer not to undergo an invasive and painful operation that would only extend her lifetime by a matter of a month or two.

Material risk. Whether a risk is material depends upon its severity and its likelihood of occurrence.[15] "A very small chance of death or serious disablement may well be significant; a potential disability which dramatically outweighs the potential benefit of therapy or the detriments of the existing malady" may require discussion.[16] The materiality of a risk is ordinarily for the jury,[17] but in some cases the risk is so remote or negligible that a directed verdict or summary judgment is appropriate.[18]

Prognosis if treatment is accepted. As already indicated, the prognosis or probability of the proposed treatment's success is highly material in almost any imaginable case. In *Arato v. Avedon*,[19] the California Court recognized that and left the issue to the jury under a materiality instruction. However, the court also held that the materiality standard would not govern the duty to reveal information that was not about risks of the medical procedure itself. For all other information—life expectancy information was in issue in *Arato*—the medical standard of disclosure would govern, not the materiality standard. So when doctors recommended a painful course of treatment that had no known chance of significantly prolonging the patient's life, the California view held that the materiality standard did not control at all. An informed consent claim could be pursued only if the medical standard required doctors to reveal the improbability of success or the fact that it might extend life only for several months. Since the medical standard was nondisclosure rather than disclosure, the doctors were not subject to liability. Even the patient's answer to the doctor's questionnaire that he wished to be told the truth did not "heighten the duty of disclosure".[20]

Experience and success rate of the physician or surgeon. Experience and success rate of the physician or surgeon are relevant, not to the decision to accept treatment, but to the decision to accept it at the hands of the defendant. A little authority has specifically declared that the

14. Davis v. Caldwell, 54 N.Y.2d 176, 429 N.E.2d 741, 445 N.Y.S.2d 63 (1981).

15. Feeley v. Baer, 424 Mass. 875, 876, 679 N.E.2d 180, 181 (1997) ("materiality of information about a potential injury is a function not only of the severity of the injury, but also of the likelihood that it will occur").

16. Wilkinson v. Vesey, 110 R.I. 606, 295 A.2d 676, 689, 69 A.L.R.3d 1202 (1972).

17. Moure v. Raeuchle, 529 Pa. 394, 405, 604 A.2d 1003, 1008 (1992).

18. Feeley v. Baer, 424 Mass. 875, 679 N.E.2d 180 (1997).

19. Arato v. Avedon, 5 Cal.4th 1172, 23 Cal.Rptr.2d 131, 858 P.2d 598 (1993).

20. Arato v. Avedon, 5 Cal.4th at 1189, 23 Cal.Rptr.2d at 142, 858 P.2d at 609; but cf. Hales v. Pittman, 118 Ariz. 305, 309, 576 P.2d 493, 497 (1978) ("because of the fiduciary relationship between physician and patient, the scope of the disclosure required can be expanded by the patient's instructions to the physician").

patient is "entitled to information concerning the treating physician's experience with the particular procedure"[21] or at least that the plaintiff was entitled to such information under the particular circumstances.[22] The profession itself is increasingly studying and sometimes publishing outcome records, so it is possible that, even under restrictive medical standards of disclosure, doctors may be obliged to reveal some information of this kind.[23]

Disclosure of surgeon's disease, drug use or the like. A surgeon who is addicted to alcohol or other drugs may present special risks of inept surgery. A surgeon who has a contagious disease—AIDS is prominent in the discussions—might perform competent or excellent surgery, yet might present a risk of contagion. In the case of AIDS, a properly gloved and gowned surgeon presents only a very small risk, but it is a fair bet that almost all patients want to consider whether to accept invasive medical procedures to be performed by addicts or AIDS victims. Consequently, if the materiality test is to be applied, the patient's consent would not be informed if she were denied information about either addiction or serious disease. The Maryland Court held that a doctor who had tested HIV positive would be required to disclose this fact before performing invasive surgery,[24] and a New Jersey court held that hospitals had similar duties before permitting HIV positive surgeons to operate.[25] A Louisiana court has held that a surgeon's chronic alcohol abuse is material and must be disclosed,[26] but a Pennsylvania court has gone the other way on the view that only information about the medical procedure itself need be disclosed.[27]

It should be remembered that when a patient does not suffer a harmful outcome as a result of the nondisclosure, the negligence theory denies recovery on the ground that no damages have occurred. Plaintiffs might conceivably show actual damages by showing emotional harm—fear of contracting AIDS, for example—but courts so far have been quite negative about permitting recovery based on fear of AIDS unless the plaintiff shows a physical channel of exposure or a substantial possibility

21. Hales v. Pittman, 118 Ariz. 305, 312, 576 P.2d 493, 500 (1978); cf. Bloskas v. Murray, 646 P.2d 907, 42 A.L.R.4th 527 (Colo. 1982) (in misrepresentation claim analogous to informed consent claim, evidence that surgeon had represented that he had performed ankle replacements when he had not was sufficient). Foard v. Jarman, 326 N.C. 24, 387 S.E.2d 162 (1990) stated that the court would not impose upon a surgeon an affirmative duty to discuss his experience, but the statement seems to have been limited to the facts of the case. The surgeon in that case in fact had had substantial experience and his statement to the patient was no exaggeration.

22. Johnson v. Kokemoor, 199 Wis.2d 615, 545 N.W.2d 495 (1996) (brain surgeon had little experience in an unusually complicated and dangerous operation, and evidence indicated that inexperience of the surgeon dramatically increased risks of serious harm, which in fact occurred; evidence admissible on informed consent issue).

23. See 1 Barry R. Furrow, Thomas L. Greaney, Sandra H. Johnson, Timothy Stolzfus Jost and Robert L. Schwartz, Health Law § 6–11, p. 418 (1995).

24. Faya v. Almaraz, 329 Md. 435, 620 A.2d 327 (1993).

25. Behringer v. The Medical Center at Princeton, 249 N.J.Super. 597, 592 A.2d 1251 (N.J. Super. 1991).

26. Hidding v. Williams, 578 So.2d 1192 (La.App.1991).

27. Kaskie v. Wright, 403 Pa.Super. 334, 589 A.2d 213 (1991).

of contracting the disease.[28] In those states that still recognize a battery theory for nondisclosure of material facts, however, recovery without proof of actual physical harm would still be theoretically possible.

Disclosure of physician's financial interests and incentives. In *Moore v. The Regents of the University of California,*[29] the patient claimed that the physicians and the hospital had discovered special qualities in his blood cells and withdrew blood ostensibly in the course of treatment but in reality to develop a commercial cell line of great value. The patient was not informed. The California Court refused to permit a conversion claim, but said the physician was under a fiduciary duty to disclose some of the facts to the patient. The case differs from the usual informed consent case in that the information withheld would not be material to medical decisions, only to financial ones. The patient who is informed of such intent would thereby learn financial plans of his physicians and could withhold consent in order to bargain for a share of their commercial venture. On the other hand, when the physician's financial interest is to forgo or limit medical tests or appropriate treatment, as is the case in many managed care plans, he has a conflict of interest that is material to purely medical decisions. An Illinois court has held that a failure to reveal such interests can be a breach of fiduciary duty and that in any event the physician's adverse financial interests may be admissible in evidence as bearing on his credibility.[30]

Other information required of a physician. The law of informed consent traces its origin to battery cases, which necessarily involve a bodily contact. However, with the recognition of the law's autonomy-respecting principle, courts may impose liability for failure to provide certain kinds of information even when no bodily contact results. In particular, physicians may be obliged to properly explain fetal genetic defects to pregnant patients[31] and if a patient refuses to undergo a diagnostic procedure or operation, then to explain to the patient the risks of the refusal.[32] The point in both cases is that the decision belongs to the patient and the doctor is liable for harm done in depriving the patient of that decision, even though no bodily contact has resulted. This suggests that other professionals, such as lawyers, may also be obliged to provide certain information to clients, even though no touching of the plaintiff's body is involved.[33]

Manner of disclosure. Discussions of the disclosure required by informed consent rules usually seems to assume that the doctor holds a face-to-face conversation with the patient. No doubt that has often been true, but there has long been some tendency to formalize the process.

28. See § 311.

29. Moore v. The Regents of the University of California, 51 Cal.3d 120, 271 Cal. Rptr. 146, 793 P.2d 479 (1990).

30. Neade v. Portes, 303 Ill.App.3d 799, 237 Ill.Dec. 788, 710 N.E.2d 418 (1999). Both in medical and legal malpractice claims, courts differ as to whether breach of fiduciary duty represents a tort separate from malpractice.

31. § 291.

32. Truman v. Thomas, 27 Cal.3d 285, 165 Cal.Rptr. 308, 611 P.2d 902 (1980).

33. See § 487.

There are now on the books a number of informed consent statutes that encourage the doctor to list risks in a written consent form and that provide at least a presumption that full disclosure has been made once the patient signs the form.[34] As with boilerplate in commercial documents, extensive explanation may defeat the informative purpose. Besides the statutes, other forces are at work to mechanize or formalize the disclosure process. Managed care organizations and even individual physicians provide patients with booklets or pamphlets, monthly health magazines, and even night classes in various aspects of health.[35] The efficiency of such organizations may mean that the patient is informed casually of risks by a staff member but not by the doctor. These changes in the practice of medicine are likely to raise new issues about the effectiveness of disclosures through video tapes, pamphlets, or lengthy consent forms.

Topic B. Statutory Limits on Liability

§ 252. Statutory Limitations: Good Samaritan Statutes

All states, following California's lead, have now adopted a Good Samaritan statute that reduces the duty of care otherwise owed by licensed health care providers when they are rendering certain professional assistance at the scene of an emergency occurring outside the professional's regular practice.[1] Under none of the statutes is the provider liable for medical negligence. Some of California's statutes literally eliminate liability even for gross or wanton negligence, so long as the practitioner acts in good faith.[2] "[T]he goodness of the Samaritan is a description of the quality of his or her intention, not the quality of the aid delivered."[3] Other statutes do not go quite so far; they eliminate liability for ordinary negligence, but preserve a duty not to act wantonly or intentionally.[4]

Some statutes apply only if the defendant renders assistance without payment or expectation of payment, and then only he does so at the "scene of an emergency" or outside his ordinary employment or practice.[5] However, unusual decisions have extended statutes to protect surgeons operating in a regular hospital operating room[6] and even to

34. See Iowa Code Ann. § 147.137; Tex. Civ. Stat. Art. 4590i §§ 6.06 & 6.07.

35. A booklet was the means of disclosure in Foard v. Jarman, 326 N.C. 24, 387 S.E.2d 162 (1990). The patient read and understood it and was barred. In Cary v. Arrowsmith, 777 S.W.2d 8 (Tenn.App.1989) a 35–minute "informational lecture" video tape and a four-page consent form were used as the means of disclosure.

§ 252

1. 3 Louisell & Williams, Medical Malpractice § 21.01 (1996). See Danny R. Veilleux, Annotation, Construction and Application of "Good Samaritan" Statutes, 68 A.L.R.4th 294 (1989).

2. E.g., Cal. Bus. & Prof. Code § 1627.5 (dentists).

3. Perkins v. Howard, 232 Cal.App.3d 708, 714, 283 Cal.Rptr. 764, 767 (1991).

4. E.g., N.C. Gen. Stat. § 20–166(d).

5. E.g., Conn. Gen. Stat. Ann. § 52–557b.

6. Perkins v. Howard, 232 Cal.App.3d 708, 714, 283 Cal.Rptr. 764, 767 (1991).

operating room cases where no emergency exists and the surgeon only mistakenly believes that it does.[7] Some states extend the statute or a similar one to any person who renders emergency assistance, or to other specified persons such as ambulance personnel or teachers on the school grounds. Some go on to apply the special protection to medical professionals who volunteer to provide medical services at sports events and who are thus prepared for the emergency that arises but who are not paid for their services.[8]

The purported basis for these statutes was that they were needed to encourage physicians to render voluntary assistance in roadside emergencies. The idea was that without the statute's immunity, physicians would refuse to provide medical care for fear of legal liability. In fact, however, suits for negligent medical care rendered in such emergencies are practically non-existent. When such suits are brought, the due care standard or the traditional standard for physicians would afford full protection. Those standards would take account of the fact that one acting in an emergency is not necessarily at his best and that equipment and professional assistance may be lacking.

§ 253. Statutory Limitations: Introducing The Malpractice Crisis Statutes

Respected studies show that only a small fraction of people who are negligently injured by health care providers actually make claims.[1] Nevertheless, apparent increase in malpractice litigation has been almost the constant story of medical malpractice since 1840.[2] Many observers have thought that malpractice litigation increased in particular sometime after World War II. By about 1970 the perception of increased litigation was raising concerns among health care professionals to new levels. One undisputed reality was that premiums for medical malpractice insurance rose, probably in part because insurers invest premium

7. Pemberton v. Dharmani, 207 Mich. App. 522, 525 N.W.2d 497 (1994).

8. Ariz. Rev. Stat. § 32–1472. In these statutes and some others, the theme of the now-discredited guest statutes seems prominent, namely that one who is not paid owes no duty of reasonable care.

§ 253

1. See Paul C. Weiler, Howard H. Hiatt, Joseph P. Newhouse, William G. Johnson, Troyen A. Brennan, & Lucian L. Leape, A Measure of Malpractice (1993) (reflecting, in one study, 27,179 negligent medical injuries with only 3,682 claims). Persons with the best claims often do not sue. See Localio, Lawthers, Brennan, Laird, Hebert, Peterson, Newhouse, Weiler & Hiatt, Relation between Malpractice Claims and Adverse Events Due to Negligence, 325 N. ENG. J. MED. 245 (July 25, 1991).

2. See Kenneth Allen de Ville, Medical Malpractice in Nineteenth-Century American: Origins and Legacy 3 (1990). The "increase" here, however, is an increase in appellate litigation compared to general population growth. Perhaps a different figure is needed: the amount of litigation compared to the growing number of physicians. Technology is partly to blame, too. No one seems to have sued because the medical profession applied leaches and other counterproductive treatments, but new technology can raise more hopes and do more harm too. Cf. Mark Grady, Why Are People Negligent? Technology, Nondurable Precautions, and the Medical Malpractice Explosion, 82 Nw. U. L. Rev. 293 (1988) (discussing effects of better medical technology).

income and because investments were not producing well. In some places, malpractice insurance was difficult to procure at all.

Medical professionals and their representatives called this a malpractice crisis (for which lawyers were generally blamed). In a few states, the term crisis might not have been hyperbole; but considered overall, doctors' incomes increased more in the critical period than the cost of insurance, so that they were actually paying a smaller percentage of their income on premiums.[3] If the crisis was not as clear as it seemed, the effect of litigation in producing it was just as uncertain.[4] Nevertheless, the health care profession demanded relief from the threat of excessive responsibility in tort and many legislatures responded. Besides statutory provisions intended to guarantee that insurance would be available, legislation, which differed from state to state, often introduced substantive, remedial, or procedural changes.

Substantive changes. In varying combinations, substantive changes at the state level included the following: (1) The standard of care was narrowed to the defendant's own local community in contrast to the increasing common law acceptance of a similar community or national community standard.[5] (2) Informed consent claims were limited or discouraged, for instance, by adopting a medical rather than a materiality standard.[6] (3) Res ipsa loquitur was eliminated altogether from medical negligence claims;[7] or res ipsa loquitur was limited to specific lists of cases such as those in which surgical instruments were left within the patient's body.[8] (4) The statute of limitations defense was promoted in several ways, for example, by restricting the discovery rule and by enacting statutes of repose which could bar some claims before the patient could discover the harm done.[9]

Remedial changes. The most striking crisis legislation capped the damages recoverable in malpractice suits, either by limiting pain and suffering recovery or by limiting the total that could be recovered even for actual money costs of a serious injury.[10] Other provisions tinkered

3. See 1 Barry R. Furrow, Thomas L. Greaney, Sandra H. Johnson, Timothy S. Jost, & Robert L. Schwartz, Health Law 517 (1995). Professor Hubbard argues that insurance premiums were not the real reason for the vehemence of health care professionals in their demand for protection; instead, tort reform functions as a symbol to register protest against a broad range of changes in health care. F. Patrick Hubbard, The Physicians' Point of View Concerning Medical Malpractice: A Sociological Perspective on the Symbolic Importance of "Tort Reform," 23 Ga. L. Rev. 295 (1989).

4. See 1 Barry R. Furrow, Thomas L. Greaney, Sandra H. Johnson, Timothy S. Jost, & Robert L. Schwartz, Health Law 516–517 (1995).

5. Idaho Code § 6–1012.

6. E.g., N.C. Gen. Stat. § 90–21.13.

7. Idaho Code § 6–1012 (in malpractice action, claimant must prove breach of community standard by direct expert testimony); N.H. Rev. Stat. Ann. § 507–C:2 ("In any action for medical injury, the doctrine of res ipsa loquitur shall not apply").

8. Nev. Rev. Stat. § 41A.100 (five exceptions which codify the pattern of cases, but which leave no room for cases the drafters had not considered).

9. See § 219.

10. See § 384 on damages caps.

with special damages rules like the collateral source rule, or permitted periodic payment of judgments.[11]

Procedural changes. Other provisions set various procedural impediments along the road to suit, including requirements that medical malpractice claims be screened by a panel which may include health care providers. Panel decisions on the merits may lead the parties to a settlement, but if not, the panel decision may be introduced in evidence at trial. Other statutes promoted binding arbitration.[12] Plaintiffs were sometimes required to file special notices before suit could be brought and attorneys were required to personally certify the quality of the claim.

Tort reform. Many of the provisions in the crisis statutes on medical malpractice became models for similar protections of other industries, so that the they are now subsumed in the larger topic now called "tort reform." Constitutional and normative issues as well as strategic effects of such provisions are discussed in connection with that topic.[13]

Negligence unrelated to diagnosis, treatment, or care. Because the malpractice crisis statutes may eliminate a claim altogether (under a stringent statute of limitations, for example) or prevent recovery of all the plaintiff's actual damages (under a cap), it is often to the plaintiff's interest to claim that the provider's tort was not "malpractice," but some other kind of negligence. Presumably a slip and fall on a hospital floor is purely mechanical, not malpractice at all. If the test is whether the act involves diagnosis, treatment, or care, the slip and fall case is outside the statutory constraints. Less certain is the case of a blood bank supplying HIV infected blood for transfusion. Florida has held that this is not treatment or care and the blood bank cannot get the benefit of the statutory restrictions.[14] On the other hand, Colorado treats a blood bank as a health care provider.[15] Ohio applied its crisis statute to a case in which the plaintiff's wheelchair collapsed,[16] no doubt a little more "medical" than the slip and fall case but highly mechanical nonetheless.

Sexual misbehavior of professionals. Does a claim of sexual misbehavior of a professional toward a patient fall within the special limits of the crisis statutes? In a Virginia case,[17] the female plaintiff alleged that the male doctor-defendant had improperly played with her breasts and made sexual remarks during a physical examination. If the Virginia crisis legislation applied, the plaintiff would be barred because she had not provided a timely pre-suit notice as required by the statute. The plaintiff argued that she was required to meet only the rules for ordinary

11. See § 380.

12. See 1 Barry R. Furrow, Thomas L. Greaney, Sandra H. Johnson, Timothy S. Jost, & Robert L. Schwartz, Health Law 524 (1995).

13. §§ 219 (statutes of limitation), 380 & 384 (damages issues).

14. Silva v. Southwest Florida Blood Bank, Inc., 601 So.2d 1184 (Fla.1992).

15. United Blood Services Div. of Blood Systems, Inc., v. Quintana, 827 P.2d 509 (Colo.1992).

16. Rome v. Flower Memorial Hospital, 70 Ohio St.3d 14, 635 N.E.2d 1239 (1994) (claim was medical and thus had to be brought within one year).

17. Hagen v. Antonio, 240 Va. 347, 397 S.E.2d 810 (1990).

negligence cases because the physician's acts could not count as professional services or health care. The Virginia Court, however, held that the alleged acts "stemmed from" a physical examination and as such was covered by the malpractice crisis statute. It said, however, that rape would be distinguishable, even if it stemmed from a physical exam. An Arkansas case reached the opposite result, holding that sexual fondling during a medical examination was actionable as an intentional infliction of emotional harm and not governed by the medical malpractice statutes.[18] Sexual exploitation by nominally consenting patients has been considered in another section.[19]

TOPIC C. HOSPITALS AND MANAGED CARE ORGANIZATIONS

§ 254. Common Law Responsibility of Hospitals

National or reasonable person standard of care. The conflict between local and national standards of care has never been so intense in the case of hospitals as it was with individual physicians. The consensus seems to be that, except when the hospital's liability is vicarious and premised on the negligence of a physician or surgeon,[1] the duty of hospitals toward patients is to act with reasonable care under all the circumstances,[2] or in accordance with the national standard of care for hospitals.[3] One basis for this view is that all hospitals accredited by the Joint Commission on Accreditation of Hospitals must follow national standards set by the JCAH to receive accreditation at all. JCAH standards,[4] the hospital's own bylaws based on national standards,[5] and any statutory requirements are at least evidence of a minimal standard of care.

Immunity. Hospital liability, although now accepted, did not come easily. First, under traditional rules, charitable hospitals, like other charities,[6] were immune to suit for their tortious activities. Similarly, governmentally operated hospitals once shared in governmental immunities.[7] Both the charitable and governmental immunity have generally

18. McQuay v. Guntharp, 336 Ark. 534, 986 S.W.2d 850 (1999).

19. § 102.

§ 254

1. See Advincula v. United Blood Services, 176 Ill.2d 1, 678 N.E.2d 1009, 223 Ill.Dec. 1 (1996).

2. Shilkret v. Annapolis Emergency Hospital Ass'n, 276 Md. 187, 202, 349 A.2d 245, 254, 99 A.L.R.3d 1119 (1975) ("a hospital is required to use that degree of care and skill which is expected of a reasonably competent hospital in the same or similar circumstances"; on the evidence, the standards were national standards of accredited hospitals); Duling v. Bluefield Sanitarium, Inc., 149 W.Va. 567, 142 S.E.2d 754 (1965); see Pederson v. Dumouchel, 72 Wash.2d 73, 431 P.2d 973, 31 A.L.R.3d 1100 (1967).

3. Wickliffe v. Sunrise Hospital, Inc., 104 Nev. 777, 766 P.2d 1322 (1988) (national standard of hospital care under the circumstances in which the defendant operates); 1 DAVID W. LOUISELL AND HAROLD WILLIAMS, MEDICAL MALPRACTICE ¶ 15.02 (various dates and editors, with Supp.).

4. E.g., HealthTrust, Inc. v. Cantrell, 689 So.2d 822, 827 (Ala.1997); Pedroza v. Bryant, 101 Wash.2d 226, 234, 677 P.2d 166, 171 (1984).

5. Pedroza v. Bryant, 101 Wash.2d 226, 234, 677 P.2d 166, 171 (1984).

6. § 305.

7. As to governmental immunities, see §§ 260–272.

been abolished or modified, but vestiges remain. In some states, new immunities have been erected[8] or recovery of damages limited,[9] often as part of widespread efforts to reduce legal responsibility for negligence generally.

Practice of medicine. Second, courts once held that corporations—hospitals—could not legally practice medicine and therefore could not control physicians working in the hospital. For that reason, some of the older cases held that, contrary to the ordinary rules of agency law, hospitals could not be vicariously liable for the negligence of physicians, even those actually employed by the hospital.[10] This view has radically changed. Hospitals that do not enjoy an immunity on other grounds are now generally subjected to liability for the medical negligence of their employees.[11]

Vicarious liability for hospital employees. Private physicians who attend their own patients in a hospital are independent contractors, not employees of the hospital.[12] The hospital is not vicariously responsible for the negligence of such a physician.[13] But the hospital is vicariously liable under agency principles for the negligent acts of its own employees if those acts are committed within the scope of employment. For instance, a hospital is subject to liability for the negligence of its paramedics or emergency medical technicians,[14] its paid resident physicians,[15] and the nurses it employs.[16]

A potential exception to hospital vicarious liability: "captain of the ship." Courts sometimes hold that during the course of a medical operation, the surgeon is "captain of the ship" and becomes responsible for the negligence of all those who are under his immediate control, including hospital employees such as nurses.[17] The rule does not merely hold the surgeon responsible for his own employees, or for his own negligence in supervising hospital employees, but holds him vicariously

8. See St. Luke's Episcopal Hospital v. Agbor, 952 S.W.2d 503 (Tex.1997).

9. See § 384.

10. Rosane v. Senger, 112 Colo. 363, 149 P.2d 372 (1944).

11. See e.g., Bing v. Thunig, 2 N.Y.2d 656, 143 N.E.2d 3, 163 N.Y.S.2d 3 (1957) (overruling cases supporting the earlier view); see Clark C. Havighurst, Making Health Plans Accountable for the Quality of Care, 31 Ga. L. Rev. 587 (1997).

12. See Clark v. St. Dominic–Jackson Memorial Hospital, 660 So.2d 970 (Miss. 1995); Pedroza v. Bryant, 101 Wash.2d 226, 677 P.2d 166 (1984).

13. Oehler v. Humana Inc., 105 Nev. 348, 775 P.2d 1271 (1989).

14. Cf. Calloway v. City of New Orleans, 524 So.2d 182, 6 A.L.R.5th 1108 (La. App. 1988) ("corpsman" trained like ambulance attendant).

15. Register v. Wilmington Medical Center, Inc., 377 A.2d 8. (Del.1977); Moeller v. Hauser, 237 Minn. 368, 54 N.W.2d 639, 57 A.L.R.2d 364 (1952).

16. See McMillan v. Durant, 312 S.C. 200, 439 S.E.2d 829 (1993).

17. McCullough v. Bethany Medical Center, 235 Kan. 732, 683 P.2d 1258 (1984); Long v. Hacker, 246 Neb. 547, 520 N.W.2d 195 (1994). In Harris v. Miller, 335 N.C. 379, 438 S.E.2d 731 (1994) the court held that the ordinary borrowed servant rules apply to a surgeon using a hospital-employed nurse. The usual presumption that the servant remains in his general employment obtains; on the other hand, if it is demonstrated that the surgeon has right of control over the nurse (nurse-anesthetist in this case), then he is the temporary employer and vicariously liable for the nurse's negligence. The fact that the nurse anesthetist may be more expert on particular procedures does not change this rule.

liable even when he is not personally at fault. The rule is rooted in the borrowed servant principles of agency law.[18] Nevertheless, the rule is usually viewed as a judicial effort to assist the plaintiff who would be denied recovery against the hospital under the old charitable immunity doctrine or under the view that hospitals were not liable for medical errors of their own employees.

Courts applying the rule usually do so to hold the doctor liable without necessarily addressing the liability of the hospital. Conceivably, the rule would permit a plaintiff to recover against both the hospital and the doctor on the ground that although the nurse was a temporary employee of the operating surgeon, the nurse was also an employee of the hospital.[19] However, some courts have assumed that if the doctor becomes liable for the negligence of a hospital employee, then the hospital is not liable.[20] The captain of the ship doctrine itself is now widely discredited or at least disliked,[21] and it runs counter to the contemporary view that liability should be borne by hospitals rather than individual doctors.[22]

The ostensible agency addition to vicarious liability. By estoppel or ostensible agency, the hospital may also be liable when it creates or sustains the appearance that an independent physician or surgeon is its employee.[23] So if the hospital contracts with independent physicians for its emergency room work,[24] or X-ray lab, or anesthesia services,[25] but presents those services as part of the routine hospital work, juries are allowed to find that the independent contractor/physician was the ostensible agent of the hospital so that the hospital becomes liable for his negligence. And of course a hospital may actually employ physicians to carry out medical duties, and if so, it is subject to vicarious liability for their torts committed within the scope of their employment.[26]

"Corporate negligence." The claim of corporate negligence is not based upon vicarious liability of the hospital for acts of a physician or surgeon. The leading case is *Darling v. Charleston Community Memorial*

18. See § 339.

19. The court in McConnell v. Williams, 361 Pa. 355, 65 A.2d 243 (1949), which seems to have originated the unlikely comparison to a ship's captain, emphasized that in holding the doctor responsible, it was not eliminating the hospital's liability.

20. E.g., Synnott v. Midway Hospital, 287 Minn. 270, 178 N.W.2d 211 (1970).

21. See Holger v. Irish, 316 Or. 402, 851 P.2d 1122 (1993) (rejecting the effort to impose liability upon the surgeon rather than the hospital); Ellis v. Niles, 324 S.C. 223, 479 S.E.2d 47 (1996) (captain of ship doctrine now discredited and rejected on the facts).

22. See Clark C. Havighurst, Making Health Plans Accountable for the Quality of Care, 31 GA. L. REV. 587 (1997). See the paragraph, *Changes* below this section.

23. Clark v. Southview Hospital & Family Health Center, 68 Ohio St.3d 435, 628 N.E.2d 46, 58 A.L.R.5th 929 (1994) ("[T]he element of representation is satisfied when the hospital holds itself out to the public as a provider of medical services, and the element of reliance is satisfied if the patient looks to the hospital, rather than a specific physician, to provide her with medical care").

24. E.g., Jackson v. Power, 743 P.2d 1376 (Alaska 1987).

25. See Seneris v. Haas, 45 Cal.2d 811, 291 P.2d 915, 53 A.L.R.2d 124 (1955).

26. See Biddle v. Sartori Memorial Hospital, 518 N.W.2d 795 (Iowa 1994).

Hospital,[27] where a doctor's treatment of a broken leg in the defendant hospital led to gangrene and amputation of the leg. The plaintiff claimed that the hospital (1) should have provided nurses sufficiently trained to recognize the signs of gangrene or its dangers early enough to have avoided the need for amputation, and (2) should have provided some kind of supervision or review of the doctor's treatment. The court thought that both claims were tenable and supported by the evidence.

In line with *Darling*, the cases now generally[28] recognize that the hospital itself owes the patient a nondelegable duty of care and causes harm to the patient by failing to provide appropriate facilities, equipment, and staff support,[29] or in negligently selecting, training,[30] reviewing, or supervising[31] physicians who are permitted to use the hospital's resources.

Given these independent duties, the hospital might be liable for harm done by its negligence even though the physician has acted with complete professional care. For example, the hospital might cause harm to the patient by failing to provide competent assistance or suitable equipment to a surgeon in the operating room.[32] On the other hand, when the claim is that the hospital was negligent in giving staff privileges to an incompetent physician, or in failing to supervise his work, the hospital's negligence does not seem to be a proximate cause of any harm unless the physician himself acted negligently. In cases of that kind, the hospital's negligence in permitting a poor surgeon to operate is like the negligence of a car owner who lends a car to a bad driver. If the bad driver caused harm while he was in fact driving carefully, the lender's negligence is not a proximate cause.[33] If the surgeon who should have been supervised in fact operated with great skill, the hospital's failure to supervise is not a proximate cause.

Changes. Although the common law development of hospital liability is somewhat uneven, its general direction seems clear. From the earlier no-liability rules, courts have increasingly recognized that hospitals may

27. 33 Ill.2d 326, 211 N.E.2d 253 (1965).

28. Texas has erected an immunity that covers at least some of these cases, based on a statute that immunized decisions of a hospital's peer review committee to deny or grant hospital privileges to physicians. St. Luke's Episcopal Hospital v. Agbor, 952 S.W.2d 503 (Tex.1997).

29. Register v. Wilmington Medical Center, Inc., 377 A.2d 8. (Del.1977) (hospitals must provide interns and doctors who measure up to the medical community standard); Douglas v. Freeman, 117 Wash.2d 242, 814 P.2d 1160 (1991) (dental assistant not provided). See Edward L. Raymond, Jr., Annotation, Medical Malpractice: Hospital's Liability For Injury Allegedly Caused by Failure to Have Properly Qualified Staff, 62 A.L.R.4th 692 (1989). One case has imposed liability upon a hospital whose policy requiring discharge of a patient when insurance expired interfered with the physician's medical care. Muse v. Charter Hospital of Winston–Salem, Inc., 117 N.C.App. 468, 452 S.E.2d 589 (1995). See also § 255.

30. HealthTrust, Inc. v. Cantrell, 689 So.2d 822 (Ala.1997).

31. Oehler v. Humana Inc., 105 Nev. 348, 775 P.2d 1271 (1989).

32. See Douglas v. Freeman, 117 Wash.2d 242, 814 P.2d 1160 (1991) (failure to provide dental assistant in wisdom tooth extraction was negligent even if dentist performing the extraction was not negligent). It seems possible, however, that a surgeon in a non-emergency operation who undertakes an operation knowing that the equipment or assistance is not available would himself be negligent.

33. See § 192.

be liable for the negligence of their own medical employees, for that of independent contractor-physicians who are identified with the hospital in the public mind, and even for failure to supervise or exclude physicians whose skill is not to be trusted.[34] The directions suggested by these changes perhaps forecast others, such as the studied proposal to impose strict liability[35] and the federal statute prohibiting "patient dumping."[36]

§ 255. Mandatory Hospital Screening and Treatment

Common law. The usual common law view is that, subject only to the most limited kinds of exceptions, no individual or entity is legally obliged to aid a person who is ill or injured.[1] Neither hospitals nor doctors could abandon a person who had been accepted as a patient,[2] but neither would be required to accept a patient in the first place. For example, a hospital could refuse patients who were unable to pay for its services.[3] Some courts developed a limited exception, requiring a hospital to give at least some treatment to a patient who presented an unmistakable medical emergency.[4]

EMTALA statute. Protected by the common law rules, some hospitals engaged in "patient dumping," refusing treatment for the impecunious and uninsured. Congress enacted the Emergency Medical Treatment and Active Labor Act (EMTALA) in 1986 to alleviate that problem.[5] That statute requires hospitals who are part of the Medicare program to provide medical screening and emergency treatment under specified conditions, but not merely to Medicare patients. The statute specifically provides that a civil action may be brought for its violation.

Duties to screen and stabilize. The statute applies only to hospitals having emergency departments. If an individual "comes to the emergency department" with a medical request, the hospital is potentially subjected to two duties. First, it must provide "appropriate" medical screening within the limits of the hospital's capability.[6] Second, if the individual has an emergency medical condition—which is defined to include active labor[7]—the hospital must ordinarily provide medical attention to stabilize that condition.[8] Liability for failure to stabilize does not

34. See, emphasizing the general historical movement toward increased hospital liability, Clark C. Havighurst, Making Health Plans Accountable for the Quality of Care, 31 GA. L. REV. 587 (1997).

35. See 2 AMERICAN LAW INSTITUTE, REPORTER'S STUDY OF ENTERPRISE LIABILITY FOR PERSONAL INJURY 515 (1991); PAUL WEILER, MEDICAL MALPRACTICE ON TRIAL 132–158 (1991).

36. See § 255.

§ 255

1. § 314.

2. See Lyons v. Grether, 218 Va. 630, 239 S.E.2d 103 (1977); cf. Muse v. Charter Hospital of Winston–Salem, Inc., 117 N.C.App. 468, 452 S.E.2d 589 (1995) (hospital could not discharge patient against physician's medical judgment on the ground that insurance had expired).

3. See Harper v. Baptist Medical Center–Princeton, 341 So.2d 133 (Ala.1976) (hospital had no duty to admit injured man who had no insurance).

4. See Walling v. Allstate Ins. Co., 183 Mich.App. 731, 455 N.W.2d 736 (1990).

5. 42 U.S.C.A. § 1395dd.

6. § 1395dd (a).

7. § 1395dd (e) (1) (B).

8. § 1395dd (b).

require proof that the hospital had a discriminatory or other bad motive.[9]

Transfer of patient to another facility. The hospital cannot avoid its obligation to stabilize the condition by routinely transferring the patient to another hospital. Transfer to another hospital is permitted only when the patient has been stabilized or a physician certifies that medical benefits of transfer will outweigh any increased risks[10] and some other conditions are met as well. A patient who is harmed by violation of any provision is entitled to recover damages.[11] However, courts have held that the hospital is free to transfer until it has made a determination that a medical emergency exists, perhaps after presentation in the emergency department.[12]

Patient must come to the hospital. The statute only applies when a patient "comes to" a hospital or emergency department. In some cases, hospitals have forestalled the patient's arrival by announcing in advance that the patient would not be accepted. If the patient is diverted to another hospital by such means, the statute cannot be invoked because the patient did not "come to" the hospital.[13]

Role of state-law malpractice. EMTALA is not a general malpractice statute and it does not preempt state tort law claims. A hospital that abandons an accepted patient might thus be liable under state law, even if it is not responsible under the federal statute.[14]

Screening duty. The statute does not directly prohibit discrimination against impecunious patients.[15] Nor does it set up a standard of care or prohibit negligent medical acts. Instead, it works through specific commands to provide appropriate medical screening and to provide medical treatment needed to assure that the condition is stabilized. Federal courts have striven to constrain the statute so that it does not become a substitute for state malpractice law. Consequently, they have held that the statute's requirement of "appropriate" screening does not mean negligent screening at all, but only screening that the hospital would provide to a paying patient.[16]

9. Roberts v. Galen of Virginia, Inc., 525 U.S. 249, 119 S.Ct. 685, 142 L.Ed.2d 648(1999).

10. § 1395dd (c) (1)(A)(ii).

11. § 1395dd (d)(2)(A).

12. James v. Sunrise Hospital, 86 F.3d 885 (9th Cir.1996); contra, Smith v. Richmond Memorial Hospital, 243 Va. 445, 416 S.E.2d 689 (1992) (patient need not initially arrive at emergency department but may develop a covered emergency after hospitalization).

13. Miller v. Medical Center of Southwest Louisiana, 22 F.3d 626 (5thCir.1994).

14. See Bryan v. Rectors and Visitors of the University of Virginia, 95 F.3d 349 (4th Cir.1996) (emphasizing limited role of the statute and the possibility of state tort liability).

15. Noting that the problem addressed by the statute arose because hospitals did not want the financial burden of caring for indigent patients, some courts, especially in earlier decisions under the statute, held that the statute only applied to indigents, but "Congress wrote a statute that plainly has no such limitation on its coverage." Cleland v. Bronson Health Care Group, Inc., 917 F.2d 266, 269 (6th Cir.1990).

16. See Summers v. Baptist Medical Center Arkadelphia, 91 F.3d 1132, 1138 (8th Cir.1996) ("Patients are entitled under EMTALA, not to correct or non-negligent treatment in all circumstances, but to be treated as other similarly situated patients

Most courts have implicitly or explicitly rejected the view that the hospital's liability depends upon a subjective discriminatory motive as opposed to disparate treatment in fact.[17] The Sixth Circuit, however, has insisted motive is the test of appropriate screening and that the hospital is not liable unless has an improper discriminatory motive.[18]

Outside the Sixth Circuit, at least, it would seem that the appropriate screening requirement also implies an obligation to provide at least some minimum medical check and that it must be calculated to identify medical emergencies. If the hospital does not screen at all or its acts are not calculated to reveal medical emergencies, liability follows.[19]

Stabilization duty. The statute requires stabilization of the patient's condition if an emergency exists.[20] In the case of active labor, stabilization means complete delivery. Otherwise stabilization requires treatment that reasonably assures that no deterioration of the condition would result from transfer to another facility.[21] Patients with no prospect of recovery and patients requiring long-term treatment, however, have posed challenging problems, as Baby K's case shows. Baby K. was born without a cerebrum. She had a brain stem that kept her breathing, but she was permanently unconscious and could not see, hear, or interact with others. In the normal course of events, anencephalics like Baby K die in short time. The Fourth Circuit, however, held that the hospital would be obliged to provide respiration by artificial means, because respiratory failure would be an emergency which required stabilization.[22] Later, the same circuit appeared to say that the duty to stabilize would not require long term treatment, apparently even if the patient's condition had not been secured against deterioration. Once again, the court was concerned to avoid creating a general malpractice claim under the statute. It held that a hospital that issued a do not resuscitate order

are treated, within the hospital's capabilities"); Cleland v. Bronson Health Care Group, Inc., 917 F.2d 266 (6th Cir.1990); Power v. Arlington Hospital Ass'n, 42 F.3d 851 (4th Cir.1994). But cf. James A. Henderson, Jr. and John A. Siliciano, Universal Health Care and the Continued Reliance on Custom in Determining Medical Malpractice, 79 Cornell L. Rev. 1382 (1994) (arguing against a "unitary, wealth-blind standard of care" in medical malpractice actions).

17. Correa v. Hospital San Francisco, 69 F.3d 1184 (1st Cir.1995); Summers v. Baptist Medical Center Arkadelphia, 91 F.3d 1132 (8th Cir.1996).

18. Cleland v. Bronson Health Care Group, Inc., 917 F.2d 266 (6th Cir.1990). However, when the Sixth Circuit carried over this motive requirement to the duty of stabilization, the Supreme Court promptly reversed, holding that the duty to stabilize did not depend upon motive. Roberts v. Galen of Virginia, Inc.,525 U.S. 249, 119 S.Ct. 685, 142 L.Ed.2d 648 (1999). Discrimination in delivery of medical care is important, however, under disability statutes, for instance, discrimination against persons with AIDS. See D.B. v. Bloom, 896 F.Supp. 166 (D.N.J.1995).

19. Correa v. Hospital San Francisco, 69 F.3d 1184 (1st Cir.1995) (delay so egregious that it amounted to a denial of screening).

20. Thornton v. Southwest Detroit Hospital, 895 F.2d 1131, 1134 (6th Cir.1990) ("once a patient is found to suffer from an emergency medical condition in the emergency room, she cannot be discharged until the condition is stabilized, regardless of whether the patient stays in the emergency room").

21. § 1395dd (e)(3)(A).

22. In the Matter of Baby "K.," 16 F.3d 590 (4th Cir.1994).

against the wishes of the patient's family could be liable, if at all, only under state tort law.[23]

§ 256. Managed Care Organizations

The Managed Care Structure vs. Fee-for-Service

The traditional rules of professional liability originated in a fee-for-service system. Patients paid health care professionals for a service. If patients were insured or covered by statutory programs like Medicare or Medicaid, the insurer or the program paid for the service agreed upon by doctor and patient. Under this system, doctors might prefer to recommend more than optimum diagnosis or treatment, say an X-ray "just to be sure." If they were covered by programs or insurance, patients might insist on more. Whether entirely for these reasons or not, costs soared.

Managed care systems, well on their way to replacing the fee-for-service approach, attempt to achieve cost-effective medical care. The idea is to minimize total costs without reducing overall good medical outcomes, although marginally effective medical procedures will be denied. Managed care operates by interposing a third force between doctor and patient, a kind of economically efficient medical conscience that says no to some diagnoses or treatments.

The term Managed Care Organization or MCO refers to any form of managed care structure. A familiar version is the Health Maintenance Organization or HMO. Employers might contract with an HMO to provide comprehensive health care services for all employees, who might in turn contribute to the costs through payroll deductions. The HMO in turn either hires physicians or contracts with organizations of physicians to provide care. The HMO is not merely an insurer; it is actively engaged in managing health care costs by limiting the delivery of medical services unlikely to be helpful.

The amount and perhaps quality of care provided by an HMO is limited by several factors. (1) The contract itself may exclude certain care items such as experimental treatments. (2) The primary physician is usually the first physician to be seen by the patient; that physician acts as a gatekeeper who may have motives besides purely medical ones to limit the patient's access to some kinds of care by refusing a referral to the expensive specialized treatment or hospitalization. The non-medical motives arise from the HMO system for compensating physicians, under which physicians who refer less may be compensated more. (3) The physician is usually paid per capita, which is a specified fee for each patient seen during the coverage period. Repeat visits thus represent a cost to the physician without any increase in income from the HMO.

Inside a hospital, managed care may take the form of utilization review. Utilization review is a system of monitoring hospitalization time

23. Bryan v. Rectors and Visitors of the University of Virginia, 95 F.3d 349 (4th Cir.1996).

and notifying the hospital that the HMO or health care insurer will pay only for a specified hospital stay for a given illness or surgery. In the case of publicly funded hospital stays, regulations may perform the same function.

The arrival of MCOs of various stripes raises the question whether they are themselves liable for any form of bad medical care delivered to the patient. The managed care structure raises several possibilities.

Potential Liability of MCOs

Vicarious responsibility. (a) Staff model. The HMO is a fiscal and management organization. It does not itself practice medicine. For this reason, some statutes provide complete immunity to the HMO against liability based upon negligence of the person rendering services.[1] However, when the HMO is organized on the "staff model," it actually employs physicians, so that under ordinary agency principles, it would be legally responsible for their negligence within the scope of employment. At one time courts took the view that corporations could not practice medicine so that even if a physician were a corporate employee, the corporation could not exercise significant control and could not be vicariously liable. This view has now been largely repudiated in the case of hospitals,[2] but one or two decisions may have given it a degree of approval in the case of HMOs, relieving the organization of liability for the negligence of its own employee physician.[3] If the cases actually followed the older view, they are out of step and it seems likely that most courts will follow those cases that apply ordinary vicarious liability rules.[4]

(b) Independent Provider Model or independent contractors. The Independent Provider Association or IPA model for MCOs is structurally different. Here the MCO contracts with still another organization to provide physicians, or in a variation on that, contracts directly with independent physicians who would traditionally be seen as independent contractors, not employees of the HMO. Because the physicians in this situation usually appear to be independent contractors, the HMO is not vicariously responsible for their acts unless the plaintiff can show an exception to the rule.[5]

§ 256

1. 215 Ill. Comp. Stats, 165/26; Vernon's Ann. Mo. Stats. § 354.125. A statute in this form does not appear to address the question of liability for cost-savings decisions.

2. § 254.

3. Mitts v. H.I.P. of Greater New York, 104 A.D.2d 318, 478 N.Y.S.2d 910 (1984) viewed the HMO as merely an insurer; if that were the case, nonliability would easily be the proper result. Williams v. Good Health Plus, Inc.-HealthAmerican Corporation of Texas, 743 S.W.2d 373 (Tex.App. 1987) may have invoked the corporate inability to practice rule, but perhaps more fundamentally merely held that the IPA model HMO would not be liable for acts of an independent physician who was not an HMO employee.

4. E.g., Sloan v. Metropolitan Health Council of Indianapolis, Inc., 516 N.E.2d 1104 (Ind.App.1987)

5. Raglin v. HMO Illinois, Inc., 230 Ill. App.3d 642, 595 N.E.2d 153, 172 Ill.Dec. 90 (1992); Chase v. Independent Practice Ass'n, Inc., 31 Mass.App.Ct. 661, 583 N.E.2d 251 (1991). As to independent contractors and ostensible agency rules, see § 338.

One set of exceptions holds the employer of independent contractors vicariously liable on an ostensible agency, apparent authority, or agency by estoppel theory.[6] In the case of hospitals, for example, the hospital may be liable for independent contractors who operate the hospital emergency room, since patients reasonably think that going to the emergency room is "going to the hospital;" they do not think they are consulting an unnamed independent contractor.[7] Although authority is sparse, some cases have already carried over this idea to impose vicarious liability upon an IPA-type MCO[8] or upon a staff type MCO who employs an independent consultant.[9]

The second exception is really an assertion that, in spite of appearance to the contrary, the physician is not an independent contractor because the MCO exercises pervasive control over his work and is thus in the role of a "master" who is vicariously liable. MCOs do in fact exercise a good deal of control—that is how cost containment works—but it is more likely to relate to the the provision of expensive services rather than, say, a simple bad diagnosis. Not surprisingly, then, some courts have found the control not to be extensive enough to warrant vicarious liability.[10] But the question turns heavily upon details of evidence as well as argumentation in particular cases, and some authority has recognized that vicarious liability may be imposed under this exception.[11]

Direct liability. (a) Negligent selection or retention of physicians. Unless federal law preempts the claims, at least two kinds of claims might plausibly be asserted against an MCO that are not based on vicarious liability but on its own negligence. First, the analogy to hospital liability suggests that MCOs might well owe a duty of care in selecting and monitoring physicians and hospitals. If so, the MCO would be liable directly for its negligence in selecting or retaining an unsuitable physician, even when it would not be vicariously liable and some cases have so held.[12]

(b) Cost containment devices creating risks. Second, the cost containment methods used by MCOs may themselves undercut appropriate care in particular instances. If a cost containment method such as utilization review effectively denies the patient her rights under the insurance or MCO plan and also counts as bad medical care, liability in tort or contract or both seems entirely appropriate.[13] The design of contractually

6. On the distinctions, see § 338.

7. § 254.

8. Boyd v. Albert Einstein Medical Center, 377 Pa.Super. 609, 547 A.2d 1229 (1988)

9. See Schleier v. Kaiser Foundation Health Plan of the Mid-Atlantic States, Inc., 876 F.2d 174, 277 U.S.App.D.C. 415 (1989).

10. E.g., Raglin v. HMO Illinois, Inc., 230 Ill.App.3d 642, 595 N.E.2d 153, 172 Ill.Dec. 90 (1992).

11. Schleier v. Kaiser Foundation Health Plan of the Mid-Atlantic States, Inc., 876 F.2d 174, 277 U.S.App.D.C. 415 (1989) (staff model HMO hiring independent consultant); see Woolfolk v. Duncan, 872 F.Supp. 1381 (E.D. Pa. 1995) (summary judgment for HMO denied because in light of HMO's right to control independent physician, he may be treated as a servant).

12. McClellan v. Health Maintenance Organization of Pennsylvania, 413 Pa.Super. 128, 604 A.2d 1053 (1992).

13. See Wilson v. Blue Cross of Southern California, 222 Cal.App.3d 660, 271 Cal. Rptr. 876 (1990); McEvoy v. Group Health Co-operative of Eau Claire, 213 Wis.2d 507,

valid cost containment systems itself may create undue risks. The incentive system created by the compensation plans often provides the physician with more compensation if he uses fewer expensive tests and referrals. This may actually put the physician in a conflict of interest when medical needs might dictate a referral but a referral will represent a dollar cost to the physician.[14] Other cost containment features may involve the MCOs dictation of drug and hospital choices that could conceivably be against the patient's interests. Many commentators have addressed these possibilities, directly or indirectly,[15] and such claims have been asserted by patients, but so far, the courts have usually been forced away from the merits of these claims in order to deal with the preemption defense.[16]

(c) Warranty. It has recently been argued that MCOs should be held directly responsible for physician negligence on the ground that they impliedly warrant the quality of services.[17] This theory would not hold the MCO strictly liable. Instead it would impose liability for the negligent acts and omissions of its affiliated health care providers, that is, to stand behind the services it delivers.

ERISA Preemption. The most serious impediment for many patients injured by managed care systems is the prospect of federal preemption, the effect of which is to leave the plaintiff without redress for tortious harms. The problem arises under the Employee Retirement Income Security Act (ERISA),[18] a federal statute intended to set uniform standards for employee benefit and retirement plans. The statute covers medical benefits provided through employment and hence covers a very high percentage of all managed care systems. By its terms, it "supersedes" state laws and decisions that may "relate to any employee benefit plan" covered.[19] Where this provision applies, the covered employee—a patient in the context of medical benefits—may sue under the federal statute itself to recover benefits denied but may not sue on an ordinary

570 N.W.2d 397 (1997) (HMO that refused, for cost containment reasons, to approve continued "out of network" treatment needed by a patient and to which patient was entitled liable for bad faith brech of contract); Kathleen J. McKee, Annotation, Liability of Third-party Health-care Payor for Injury Arising from Failure to Authorize Required Treatment, 56 A.L.R.5th 737 (1998). The *Wilson* court reversed summary judgments for defendants, some of whom had made a utilization review decision denying further hospitalization coverage called for by the physician's treatment plan. Evidence indicated that the patient was entitled to the hospitalization under the underlying insurance policy and that it was medically necessary. Evidence also indicated that the policy did not create any right in the insurer to engage in utilization review. The patient, having no funds, was discharged, and committed suicide, a risk that was probably predictable on the facts.

14. See Neade v. Portes, 303 Ill.App.3d 799, 237 Ill.Dec. 788, 710 N.E.2d 418 (1999) (fiduciary duty to disclose the financial incentives that are adverse to patient health).

15. E.g., Barry R. Furrow, Managed Care Organizations And Patient Injury: Rethinking Liability, 31 GA. L. REV. 419 (1997).

16. E.g., Dykema v. King, 959 F.Supp. 736 (D.S.C.1997).

17. William S. Brewbaker, III, Medical Malpractice and Managed Care Organizations: The Implied Warranty of Quality, 60 L. & CONTEMP. PROBS. 117 (Spring 1997).

18. 29 U.S.C.A. 1001–1461.

19. 29 U.S.C.A. § 1144(a). State laws includes "decisions" as well as rules. 29 U.S.C.A. § 1144(c).

state-law negligence claim.[20] It seems to be generally assumed that a recovery of benefits denied would not include damages for injury that proper benefits would have prevented.[21]

Exactly what claims may be preempted and therefore defeated by ERISA is a matter not authoritatively decided by the Supreme Court at this writing. The cases leave large and sometimes uncertain areas in which the patient is apparently not protected either by a right to sue under the statute or a right to sue under state tort law. The problem could be entirely avoided if the right to sue under ERISA and the right to sue under state tort law were construed to be complementary, so that one right began where the other left off. In that case, plaintiff could either sue under ERISA for damages for negligent harm on the theory that damages are a substitute for benefits, or else the plaintiff would be allowed to sue for tort law damages on the theory that they are not related to the benefits, but in no event would the plaintiff be denied her day in court altogether. That, however, is not the way courts have seen the statute.[22]

Some courts have used preemption as a deadly vacuum, leaving the injured patient nothing. Others have tried to draw distinctions. A leading case held that the claim for malpractice was not always "completely preempted."[23] The Tenth Circuit has held that a claim against an HMO based on the assertion of ordinary malpractice and vicarious liability, not intertwined with the denial of benefits, is simply not preempted.[24] On the other hand, if the claim is that the plan wrongly denied benefits such as hospitalization, that would be a benefits-denied case and preempted.[25]

Enterprise liability and less. Long-time and respected scholars of health care law have concluded that tort liability of managed care

20. "A civil action may be brought (1) by a participant or beneficiary ... to recover benefits due to him under the terms of his plan, to enforce his rights under the terms of the plan, or to clarify his rights to future benefits under the terms of the plan.... " 29 U.S.C.A. § 1132 (a).

21. Cf. Bittner v. Sadoff & Rudoy Industries, 728 F.2d 820 (7th Cir.1984) (the suit for benefits permitted by the statute would not permit a suit for emotional distress based on denial of the benefits).

22. Thus courts see both the section giving a right to sue for federal benefits and the express preemption section as creating different types of preemption. See Jass v. Prudential Health Care Plan, Inc., 88 F.3d 1482, 1487 (7th Cir.1996). Even that, however, does not logically preclude a rule that would allow the plaintiff to sue under ERISA to recover damages for medical injury as a substitute or replacement for the benefits wrongfully denied.

23. Dukes v. U.S. Healthcare, Inc., 57 F.3d 350 (3d Cir.1995). The whole ERISA preemption picture is clouded further by the fact that some decisions arise in the context of a removal by defendants from state court, and by the rule that federal defenses do not justify removal but that "complete preemption" does. The holding that complete preemption does not apply thus sends the case back to state court, but the state court may be compelled to find that the claim, though not "completely preempted," is nevertheless preempted in some plain vanilla way and thus barred. Skirmishes of this kind have dominated a number of the decisions.

24. Pacificare of Oklahoma, Inc. v. Burrage, 59 F.3d 151 (10th Cir.1995) (also reflecting the split of authority on this point among lower courts).

25. See Corcoran v. United HealthCare, Inc., 965 F.2d 1321 (5th Cir.1992); Jass v. Prudential Health Care Plan, Inc., 88 F.3d 1482 (7th Cir.1996).

organizations represents an important need. Professor Furrow suggests that tort liability adds the right amount of pressure to provide incentives to avoid preventable injury.[26] Professor Havighurst, matching a similar suggestion made by others for medical injuries in hospitals, adds the argument that MCOs should the bear the exclusive responsibility for negligence of physicians treating their subscribers.[27] Although cost containment devices work an overall good, they run known risks. When they go wrong because benefits are wrongly denied, the cost containment efforts should not be condemned. But the savings they effect should probably be devoted in part to payment of the harms they cause. Not the least of the advantages of such a solution would be that it would necessarily obliterate the crabbed jurisprudence of preemption.

Topic D. Other Professionals

§ 257. Pharmacists

Although courts say that pharmacists owe their clients the care of other professionals, a good many have undercut this standard by ruling as a matter of law that where the pharmacist accurately fills a physician's prescription, he has no duty to warn the patient that the dosage is too high, or likely to be addictive, or that the drug has special dangers for the plaintiff's condition.[1] Under this no duty rule, the question of reasonable care is not adjudicated at all. Courts do recognize an exception for obvious errors in the prescription or "on the face of the prescription"[2] but not for obvious or even known risks of the drug itself[3] or its addictive propensities.[4]

The reasons for this refusal to adjudicate the issue of negligence are puzzling. Courts sometimes say that it is the physician who has the duty to warn or to prescribe more carefully, but this argument suggests, quite wrongly, that only one person could owe a duty to the patient. Sometimes courts also confuse the learned intermediary doctrine, which deals with responsibility as between the drug manufacturer and the physician, by saying that it is "only the physician who can relate the propensities of

26. Barry R. Furrow, Managed Care Organizations And Patient Injury: Rethinking Liability, 31 Ga. L. Rev. 419 (1997).

27. Clark C. Havighurst, Making Health Plans Accountable for the Quality of Care, 31 Ga. L. Rev. 587 (1997).

§ 257

1. Jones v. Irvin, 602 F.Supp. 399 (S.D.Ill.1985); Nichols v. Central Merchandise, Inc., 16 Kan.App.2d 65, 817 P.2d 1131 (1991); Kampe v. Howard Stark Professional Pharmacy, Inc., 841 S.W.2d 223, 44 A.L.R.5th 829 (Mo. App. 1992). See David J. Marchitelli, Annotation, Liability of Pharmacist Who Accurately Fills Prescription For Harm Resulting to User, 44 A.L.R.5th 393 (1996).

2. Guillory v. Dr. X and ABC Pharmacy, 679 So.2d 1004 (La.App.1996) (duty "to warn the patient or to notify the prescribing physician of an excessive dosage or of obvious inadequacies on the face of the prescription which create a substantial risk of harm to the patient" but no duty "to question a judgment made by the physician . . . or to warn customers of the hazardous side effects associated with a drug").

3. E.g., Johnson v. Walgreen Co., 675 So.2d 1036 (Fla.App.1996).

4. E.g., Pysz v. Henry's Drug Store, 457 So.2d 561 (Fla.App.1984).

the drug to the physical idiosyncrasies of the patient."[5] Such a statement may often be true, especially as between the manufacturer and the physician, but it is not invariably true when a pharmacist knows the patient and should recognize an addictive prescription or serious side effects and when no reason appears why evidence cannot be submitted on that issue as on other factual matters.

Finally, courts say that the pharmacist should not be placed in a position of conflict with the prescribing physician, but when the pharmacist observes addictive use or a prescription of a drug that is contraindicated by the patient's symptoms, the pharmacist is likely to be assisting the physician by conveying that information, either to the patient or to the physician himself. In any event, it is hard to see why courts think the concern is so overwhelming that it should overrule the professional standard of pharmacists themselves. Perhaps they believe that in many cases a breach of the professional standard could not be proven, but that is a question which requires evidence, not a no duty rule that excludes evidence.

A few recent decisions have made inroads on the exculpatory tendency. The Supreme Court of Indiana distinguished between warnings about side effects, which it regarded as exclusively the physician's duty, and warnings about excessive rates of consumption, which it regarded as the appropriate subject of warnings by the pharmacist.[6] Some authority supports a duty when the pharmacist actually knows that the drug prescribed is contraindicated and there is no room for discretion.[7] An Arizona Court favored general use of the professional care standard, so that if professional care required a warning, the pharmacist would be subject to liability for failing to provide one.[8] One pharmacy was held to have undertaken a duty of care because it advertized that its computer could alert the pharmacist if the patient's drugs had negative interactions.[9]

A medicare statute followed in various forms by state statutes attempts to require drug use reviews to assure that the patient does not receive drugs that are contraindicated, that entail negative drug-drug interactions, or that are otherwise inappropriate. The pharmacist must offer counseling to each patient and meet a number of specific standards.[10] States have adopted similar statutes. These statutes may explicitly impose a duty upon pharmacists to review prescriptions before filling

5. McKee v. American Home Products Corporation, 113 Wash.2d 701, 711, 782 P.2d 1045, 1050 (1989).

6. Hooks SuperX, Inc. v. McLaughlin, 642 N.E.2d 514 (Ind.1994).

7. Hand v. Krakowski, 89 A.D.2d 650, 453 N.Y.S.2d 121 (1982), defining contraindicated to mean that for one in the patient's condition, "the drug must never be given" and that the rule against administration of the drug under the circumstances "is absolute and admits of no exceptions". In Hand, the pharmacist knew of the patient's condition and of the medical fact of contraindication.

8. Lasley v. Shrake's Country Club Pharmacy, Inc., 179 Ariz. 583, 880 P.2d 1129 (App. 1994).

9. Baker v. Arbor Drugs, Inc., 215 Mich. App. 198, 544 N.W.2d 727 (1996).

10. See 42 U.S.C.A. § 1396r–8.

them in order to avoid drug-drug interactions and other dangers.[11] Presumably the duty so established would be actionable in a common law negligence action.

§ 258. Clergy Malpractice

Clergy and Church Liability in Tort Generally

Charitable immunity has been largely[1] although not completely[2] abolished, so with few exceptions churches and clergy enjoy no automatic immunity from liability. However, the First Amendment protects the free exercise of religion and, indirectly, any excessive entanglement with religion. Courts are not permitted to investigate or pass judgment on religious doctrine or practice in the absence of a compelling governmental interest. At the same time, the First Amendment grants no blanket immunity for torts and crimes of the clergy if the litigation can proceed without passing on religious doctrine, interfering with, or becoming entangle in religion.

Churches and clergy may of course escape liability when they are under no tort duty and perhaps courts sometimes apply standard legal doctrines in ways somewhat favorable to the clergy or the churches.[3] Virginia once carried this so far as to hold that a missionary institution had no duty to do anything about the known fact that its missionary was sexually abusing his own children.[4]

Given a tort duty, however, courts have recognized that civil or criminal liability may be imposed upon priests, ministers or churches. They have recognized liability or potential liability when a minister negligently drives a vehicle on church business,[5] a priest commits a burglary in furtherance of his religious conviction,[6] or a church causes injury through negligently maintained conditions on its land.[7] They also have also recognized that clergy may be held responsible for libel or slander,[8] even if committed from the pulpit,[9] and for invasion of priva-

11. E.g., N.J.S.A. § 45:14–15.1.

§ 258

1. E.g., Widell v. Holy Trinity Catholic Church, 19 Wis.2d 648, 121 N.W.2d 249 (1963). See § 282.

2. See Schultz v. Roman Catholic Archdiocese of Newark, 95 N.J. 530, 472 A.2d 531 (1984) (allegations that Brother Edmund forced one of his charges into certain sexual acts that led to boy's suicide; church is immune by statute). See § 282.

3. Carini v. Beaven, 219 Mass. 117, 106 N.E. 589 (1914) held that allegations by a young female parishioner that a priest had raped her and that the diocese knew of the priest's gross sexual proclivities failed to state a claim since rape, especially rape in the church, would be unforeseeable.

4. Foreign Mission Board of the Southern Baptist Convention v. Wade, 242 Va. 234, 409 S.E.2d 144 (1991). But cf. J.A.W. v. Roberts, 627 N.E.2d 802 (1994) (defendant, upon whom boy depended for spiritual advice, did not report that boy's father was sexually abusing him; a tort duty might be found to exist.)

5. E.g., Garber v. Scott, 525 S.W.2d 114 (Mo.App.1975).

6. Markley v. State, 507 So.2d 1043 (Ala.Crim.App.1987).

7. Friend v. Cove Methodist Church, Inc., 65 Wash.2d 174, 396 P.2d 546 (1964).

8. Murphy v. Harty, 238 Or. 228, 393 P.2d 206 (1964) (libel).

9. Hester v. Barnett, 723 S.W.2d 544 (Mo.App.1987) (defamation, privacy invasion, alienation of affections).

cy,[10] battery,[11] false imprisonment[12] and the statutory discrimination torts involving sexual harassment of employees.[13] In one long-running case, a church was liable for intentional infliction of emotional distress caused by carrying out its own religious practices against a non-member.[14]

Members of a religious group impliedly assent to its doctrine and established practices. For that reason, a minister might be free to make public accusations against a church member in accord with church doctrine, but fully responsible in tort if the accusations are against strangers to the church or those who have withdrawn from the religious community.[15] But church members do not consent to all forms of negligence and a church may be liable to a member for negligently hiring sexually abusive janitors,[16] or accepting a sexually abusive volunteer to operate its children's nursery,[17] or even for negligently conducting a service in such a way that worshipers at prayer are knocked down and injured.[18] And as Judge Ripple said, a religiously founded hospital would still be expected to follow professional medical standards in spite of its religious aims.[19]

It should also go without saying that the members of the religious group do not consent to financial fraud, and that ministers who defraud their congregations, or who convert goods and monies as well as sinners are fully liable for their misconduct.[20] The minister and his prophets who secure funds by threats of everlasting damnation, if not necessarily liable in tort, may be forced to disgorge the gains they received by undue influence.[21]

10. Guinn v. Church of Christ of Collinsville, 775 P.2d 766 (Okla.1989).

11. Mutual Service Casualty Ins. Co. v. Puhl, 354 N.W.2d 900 (Minn.App.1984) (referred to as an assault in the opinion, but the opinion makes it clear that there was a unconsented to touching).

12. Whittaker v. Sandford, 110 Me. 77, 85 A. 399 (1912).

13. Black v. Snyder, 471 N.W.2d 715 (Minn.App.1991); Davis v. Black, 70 Ohio App.3d 359, 591 N.E.2d 11 (1991).

14. Some of the practices are summarized in Wollersheim v. Church of Scientology of California, 212 Cal.App.3d 872, 66 Cal.Rptr.2d 1 (1989). The tortured path of this litigation, which resulted in a judgment for $2.5 million, is summarized in Church of Scientology of California v. Wollersheim, 42 Cal.App.4th 628, 49 Cal.Rptr.2d 620 (1996).

15. Hester v. Barnett, 723 S.W.2d 544 (Mo.App.1987); Guinn v. Church of Christ of Collinsville, 775 P.2d 766 (Okla.1989).

16. J. v. Victory Tabernacle Baptist Church, 236 Va. 206, 372 S.E.2d 391 (1988) (complaint stated claim for negligent hiring).

17. Broderick v. King's Way Assembly of God Church, 808 P.2d 1211 (Alaska 1991).

18. Bass v. Aetna Ins. Co., 370 So.2d 511 (La.1979) (trotting in the aisles under the Spirit of the Lord although people were in the aisle praying).

19. Dausch v. Rykse, 52 F.3d 1425 (7th Cir.1994).

20. Libhart v. Copeland, 949 S.W.2d 783 (Tex.App.1997) (affirming jury findings on both fraud and conversion with respect to church property).

21. Nelson v. Dodge, 76 R.I. 1, 68 A.2d 51, 14 A.L.R.2d 638 (1949) (minister and his prophet-wife repeatedly told a member of the religious community that God had sent a message requiring him to strip himself of his worldly goods and give them to the minister and prophet). As to coercive indoctrination and proselytizing, see Paul T. Hayden, Religiously Motivated "Outrageous" Conduct: Intentional Infliction of Emotional Distress as a Weapon against "Other People's Faiths," 34 Wm. & Mary L. Rev. 579 (1993).

Clergy Malpractice

Clergy malpractice excluded. When the plaintiff has complained of emotional harm resulting from negligent counseling by a minister or priest, courts have very often refused to allow recovery, usually stating that a cause of action for clergy malpractice is not recognized.[22] The plaintiff who voluntarily accepts religious counseling impliedly assents to be counseled in accordance with religious, not secular tenets and practices. The main concern in such cases, however, is that if such a claim were entertained, the court would be entangled in an investigation of religious doctrine in violation of the First Amendment's protection for the free exercise of religion and prohibition against establishing religion. That concern is broader than this section, because it can implicate a range of cases that do not necessarily involve negligence or for other reasons would not ordinarily be considered malpractice cases at all.[23]

Malpractice characterized. The clergy malpractice claim has been exclusively a problem with religious counseling cases. The term malpractice implies negligence rather than intentional torts and it implies negligence in carrying out a professional duty to someone in the role of a client. Courts seldom offer a definition of clergy malpractice, but they usually appear to have in mind (1) negligent conduct that does not qualify as an intentional tort (2) in carrying out a religious act or duty[24] (3) by one in a religious calling,[25] (4) directed toward a "client" who has voluntarily accepted the authority or services of the religious actor as being religious in character,[26] and (5) of such a nature that legal adjudication would require consideration of religious doctrine or at least religious practices or would otherwise burden free exercise of religion.[27] The exclusion of liability for clergy malpractice, then, does not necessarily exclude liability for other torts, even in the counseling setting.

The Nally case. The furor over the topic began with a California case, *Nally v. Grace Community Church of the Valley*.[28] A young man was

22. Cherepski v. Walker, 323 Ark. 43, 913 S.W.2d 761 (1996); Schieffer v. Catholic Archdiocese of Omaha, 244 Neb. 715, 508 N.W.2d 907 (1993); See John F. Wagner, Jr., Annotation, Cause of Action for Clergy Malpractice, 75 A.L.R.4th 750 (1990).

23. Paul T. Hayden, Religiously Motivated "Outrageous" Conduct: Intentional Infliction of Emotional Distress as a Weapon against "Other People's Faiths," 34 Wm. & Mary L. Rev. 579 (1993) examines indoctrination and discipline cases as well as counseling cases.

24. Bear Valley Church of Christ v. DeBose, 928 P.2d 1315, 1320 (Colo.1996) ("[T]he threshold question is whether the conduct of the defendant is religious" (quoting other cases)).

25. On elements (1), (2) and (3), see Byrd v. Faber, 57 Ohio St.3d 56, 57, 565 N.E.2d 584, 586, 5 A.L.R.5th 1115 (1991) (the term does not include torts like battery or fraud, only "failure to exercise the degree of care and skill normally exercised by members of the clergy in carrying out their professional duties").

26. Courts have not directly mentioned this element, but it is a part of the normal meaning of "malpractice," which is directed toward a client or patient, not toward a stranger.

27. Free exercise of religion is the almost invariable concern in the malpractice/sexual exploitation cases. When courts find that adjudication of the case would not impair free exercise of religion, they proceed on the merits. E.g., F.G. v. MacDonell, 150 N.J. 550, 696 A.2d 697 (1997). Vice versa if they conclude the contrary.

28. Nally v. Grace Community Church of the Valley. 47 Cal.3d 278, 763 P.2d 948, 253 Cal.Rptr. 97 (1988).

suicidal. He was counseled by pastors in his church, who did not hold themselves out as therapists but only as spiritual counselors. After the young man had been seen by a number of medical doctors and a psychiatrist, and after he and his parents had refused to consider commitment to a psychiatric hospital, he committed suicide. His parents sued for clergy malpractice. The California Court refused to recognize a tort duty on the part of non-therapist counselors to refer to therapists. The point was decided partly on the basis of the general principle that absent a special relationship, no one owes a duty to protect others, and partly on the ground it would be impossible to formulate a duty of care applicable to a religious leader providing pastoral counseling. However, it may be that even a purely religious counselor would be subject to liability for malpractice in making a disclosure of information gained in confidence.[29]

Clergy Malpractice by Sexual Exploitation in Counseling

Clergy sexual exploitation within the religious community. Since *Nally,* clergy malpractice has taken on new meanings. It is no longer merely bad spiritual counseling. The problem of clergy sexual abuse has risen to serious proportions, and along with it, the problem of sexual exploitation in the counseling setting.[30]

In the exploitation case (as distinguished from the abuse or molestation case), the clergyman counseling a vulnerable member of the religious community takes advantage of the clergy's authority, standing, and emotional leverage. He uses the special confidence induced in counseling to engage in sexual activity, often adulterous, with the person being counseled. Perhaps in some cases no harm is done, but in others the results are fearful, perhaps permanently ruinous for the vulnerable parishioner.[31] Courts have nevertheless applied the rule against recovery for clergy malpractice in these sexual exploitation situations, sometimes rightly and sometimes perhaps debatably.

In the criminal conversation or alienation of affections situation. One form of the clergy malpractice claim is only a new version of the old tort of criminal conversation or alienation of affections. That is, it is a claim against the minister, not by the person who has an in-counseling affair, but by her husband. Where the old torts of criminal conversation and

29. See Barnes v. Outlaw, 188 Ariz. 401, 937 P.2d 323 (App. 1996) vacated in part, 192 Ariz. 283, 964 P.2d 484 (1998) . .

30. Some church spokespeople try to minimize the injury or the number of occurrences. But one apologist, focusing on the Roman Catholic Church alone and then only on child molestation allegations, asserted that over 400 priests have been accused in recent years and that the Church has paid out over $400 million in settlements. John Patrick Hamm, Note, In Defense of the Church, 33 U. LOUISVILLE J. FAM. L. 705 (1995).

31. For cool professional and scientific assessments, see STEVEN B. BISBING, LINDA MABUS JORGENSON, & PAMELA K. SUTHERLAND, SEXUAL ABUSE BY PROFESSIONALS: A LEGAL GUIDE § 13–3(b) (1995). A number of commentators have said the effects can be similar to those of rape and incest. See Carol C. Nadelson, Afterword, in GLEN O. GABBARD (ED.), SEXUAL EXPLOITATION IN PROFESSIONAL RELATIONSHIPS 230 (1989); accord, Doe v. Lichtenstein, 657 So.2d 628 (La.App.1995) (psychiatrist).

alienation of affections have been abolished, as they have in many states,[32] the claims of a spouse who is not himself a direct victim of sexual abuse or exploitation cannot be entertained because no legal wrong has been done to him, whether the seducer of his spouse is a clergyman or not. A number of the clergy malpractice cases are in this pattern.[33] The court seems exactly right in dismissing them because the tort of criminal conversation has been abolished, not because the claim entails clergy malpractice.

Negligence or malpractice toward the person in counseling. To the extent that the victim of clergy sexual exploitation theorizes her claim as negligence or malpractice, courts have almost always dismissed the claim.[34] The basis for this result is rather formal: the plaintiff would be required to prove a standard of care, which would necessarily be a religious one unless the clergyman had held himself out as having qualification of a secular therapist. According to this view, adjudication of the religious standard or its breach would unconstitutionally entangle the court in religious questions,[35] even though the clergyman's sexual acts are fundamentally opposed to religious doctrine.

If the only claim is that the clergyman's spiritual counseling was of poor quality, this First Amendment argument would be hard to answer. However, the case of sexual exploitation offers three roads to a different answer. First, sexual exploitation in counseling probably is not a religious act at all. Unless some claim is made that the basis for the act is religious, courts may not be constrained by the First Amendment at all.[36] A minister who counsels boys by massaging them is not engaged in religious conduct or explicating religious doctrine.[37]

Second, because liability is imposed for obvious negligence in other professions, including medicine,[38] rational people may conclude that it must be negligent for a counselor to engage in sexual activity with a person he is counseling, since the harmful effects are well-known. That would satisfy the plaintiff's initial burden[39] without reference to religious

32. See § 442.

33. See, rejecting such claims against clergymen, Cherepski v. Walker, 323 Ark. 43, 913 S.W.2d 761 (1996); Amato v. Greenquist, 287 Ill.App.3d 921, 679 N.E.2d 446, 223 Ill.Dec. 261 (1997); Strock v. Pressnell, 38 Ohio St.3d 207, 527 N.E.2d 1235, 75 A.L.R.4th 729 (1988); Bladen v. First Presbyterian Church of Sallisaw, Okla., 857 P.2d 789 (Okl.1993) .

34. Destefano v. Grabrian, 763 P.2d 275 (Co.1988) (but allowing claim for breach of fiduciary duty); Schieffer v. Catholic Archdiocese of Omaha, 244 Neb. 715, 508 N.W.2d 907 (1993) (dismissing claim but largely on the grounds that the plaintiff consented to sexual activity without exploring the quality of consent induced by a religious counselor).

35. The argument, stated in various forms, appears in the great majority of the cases. E.g., Gibson v. Brewer, 952 S.W.2d 239 (Mo.1997).

36. See Sanders v. Casa View Baptist Church, 134 F.3d 331 (5th Cir.1998); Bivin v. Wright, 275 Ill.App.3d 899, 904, 656 N.E.2d 1121, 1124, 212 Ill.Dec. 287, 290 (1995) ("the minister's sexual misconduct was not rooted in the church's religious beliefs").

37. Bear Valley Church of Christ v. DeBose, 928 P.2d 1315 (Colo.1996).

38. § 248.

39. Some cases speak of a "defense" based on the First Amendment or else appear to place the burden of proving religious content upon the defendant. E.g., Strock v. Pressnell, 38 Ohio St.3d 207, 527

standards that might differ from secular ones. Nor does the religious standards issue arise defensively because none of these defendants attempts to defend on the ground that religious doctrine favors his conduct.[40]

Third, a degree of interference with free exercise of religion may be justified if there is a compelling governmental interest in protecting others.[41] Protection of children from the abuse of clergy might count on that score; indeed, protection of troubled adults who can be seriously hurt might count as well. Neither this nor the second argument seems to have been advanced in the cases so far.

Church liability: negligent hiring or supervision. The usual view is that the church or religious entity itself is not vicariously liable for the clergyman's frolic, even though it is a frolic that takes place in the course of a church-sponsored program and is accorded protection as an exercise of religion. Faced with this roadblock, plaintiffs sometimes attempt to allege that the church should be liable for sexual exploitation in counseling because it negligently hired, retained or supervised a clergyman who was or should have been identified as a sexual predator. Hiring and retention might implicate many religious doctrines such as those related to forgiveness, redemption, and faith. The failure to supervise a dangerous clergyman, however, is quite possibly in a different category.

Some courts have been willing to sustain claims against the church for negligent supervision, or for negligent failure to alleviate the harm once it was done.[42] Others, however, insist that any such claims automatically raise issues of church doctrine that courts are forbidden to consider.[43] Missouri has drawn a distinction that permits liability for intention-

N.E.2d 1235, 75 A.L.R.4th 729 (1988). It may be sounder to place the burden upon the plaintiff, but if so that burden is met by proving obvious negligence in the same way it is met in other malpractice cases.

40. As courts sometimes explicitly note. Bivin v. Wright, 275 Ill.App.3d 899, 656 N.E.2d 1121, 212 Ill.Dec. 287 (1995). Cf. Kenneth R. v. Roman Catholic Diocese of Brooklyn, 229 A.D.2d 159, 654 N.Y.S.2d 791 (1997) (claim that church negligently supervised priest when it knew or should have known he had a propensity for sexually abusing children; religious doctrine not involved in decision as to level of supervision, so claim could proceed).

41. This is the statutory rule under 42 U.S.C.A. § 2000bb–1 (the Religious Freedom Restoration Act), a rule that is more restrictive than the constitutional rule. See, providing some of the case and statutory history, Margaret Ann Burton, Nally v. Grace Community Church: Is There a Future for Clergy Malpractice Claims?, 37 Santa Clara L. Rev. 467 (1997).

42. Moses v. Diocese of Colorado, 863 P.2d 310 (Colo.1993) (Bishop, informed of devastating effects of clergyman's sexual activities with victim of childhood incest, attempted to hush it up and did not seek to ameliorate the effects on vulnerable parishioners); Kenneth R. v. Roman Catholic Diocese of Brooklyn, 229 A.D.2d 159, 654 N.Y.S.2d 791 (1997) (negligent supervision of a priest when the church knew or should have known of his propensity to sexually abuse children); Byrd v. Faber, 57 Ohio St.3d 56, 565 N.E.2d 584, 5 A.L.R.5th 1115 (1991) (recognizing possibility but holding pleading not specific enough). In Broderick v. King's Way Assembly of God Church, 808 P.2d 1211 (Alaska 1991) the court refused to dismiss a claim against the church for employment of a sexually dangerous volunteer supervisor for the church's nursery, but no constitutional concern was raised.

43. Swanson v. Roman Catholic Bishop of Portland, 692 A.2d 441 (Me.1997); Gibson v. Brewer, 952 S.W.2d 239 (Mo.1997); Pritzlaff v. Archdiocese of Milwaukee, 194

al failure to supervise a known dangerous clergyman.[44]

Alternatives to Malpractice Claim for Sexual Exploitation

Counselor held out as therapist. At least three types of claims for harms done by clergy sexual exploitation do not appear to raise the clergy malpractice rule. In the first, the clergyman holds himself out as a therapist or professional counselor and not merely a religious counselor or spiritual guide. The usual rule is that one is held to the standard of the profession he claims to follow,[45] so the clergyman in that case can be held to the ordinary secular standard without investigating church doctrine standards.[46]

Intentional torts. In the second, the plaintiff can frame her complaint as one for an intentional tort such as battery or intentional infliction of emotional distress. Such a claim is not formally a malpractice claim. It does not turn on negligence and hence not on any religious standard of counseling. For this reason, the objections lodged against the malpractice claim, that it is redundant[47] and that courts must not adjudicate religious matters, seem quite inapplicable to an ordinary battery claim.

An intentional tort claim like battery would be defeated by an effective consent, but quite possibly consent procured by a clergyman from a vulnerable parishioner in counseling could not be regarded as genuine and would not be effective.[48] Battery and other intentional tort theories may be unattractive, however, because the defendant's liability insurance may exclude such cases. However, for what it is worth, courts have recognized that battery[49] or even intentional infliction suits may be

Wis.2d 302, 533 N.W.2d 780 (1995) (negligent hiring or retention claims could not proceed against church because "the First Amendment . . . prevents the courts of this state from determining what makes one competent to serve as a Catholic priest since such a determination would require interpretation of church canons and internal church policies and practices").

44. "A cause of action for intentional failure to supervise clergy is stated if (1) a supervisor (or supervisors) exists (2) the supervisor (or supervisors) knew that harm was certain or substantially certain to result, (3) the supervisor (or supervisors) disregarded this known risk, (4) the supervisor's inaction caused damage, and (5) the other requirements of the Restatement (Second) of Torts, § 317 are met. This cause of action requires a supervisor. The First Amendment does not, however, allow a court to decide issues of church government—whether or not a cleric should have a supervisor." Gibson v. Brewer, supra n.43.

45. See § 245.

46. Sanders v. Casa View Baptist Church, 134 F.3d 331 (5thCir.1998); Dausch v. Rykse, 52 F.3d 1425 (7th Cir. 1994) (liability for malpractice appropriate if counselor held himself out as having qualifications of secular counselor); cf. Barnes v. Outlaw, 188 Ariz. 401, 937 P.2d 323 (App. 1996) vacated in part, 192 Ariz. 283, 964 P.2d 484 (1998) (unauthorized disclosure and misuse of information given in pastor's counseling session; the "claim arose, not out of any duty Outlaw owed them in his capacity as their pastor, but rather out of his duty as a therapist or counselor to refrain from acting in a manner that carried a foreseeable and unreasonable risk of harm to the person being counseled").

47. Strock v. Pressnell, 38 Ohio St.3d 207, 527 N.E.2d 1235, 75 A.L.R.4th 729 (1988).

48. See § 102.

49. See Byrd v. Faber, 57 Ohio St.3d 56, 565 N.E.2d 584, 5 A.L.R.5th 1115 (1991) (where the plaintiff alleged she was forced

brought[50] when consent does not bar the claim.[51]

Breach of fiduciary duty. In the third type of potentially viable claim, the plaintiff frames her complaint by asserting that the clergyman was a fiduciary. The claim of fiduciary status rests upon the fact that the clergyman sought and the plaintiff reposed trust and confidence. The most constant mark of a fiduciary duty is that the fiduciary must act in the interest of the beneficiary, not in his own interest.[52] Sexual exploitation by a fiduciary is thus a breach of fiduciary duty to act in the beneficiary's interest and not in his own. Such a claim arguably does not require examination of religious standards. Several courts have accepted this theory and concluded that it did not interfere with religious freedom of the defendants because it entails no assessment of doctrine, practice, or ritual.[53]

Other courts have insisted that the Constitution forbids even an examination of fiduciary breach. One said that the clergyman's fiduciary relationship to his victim is "premised" on the "cleric's status as an expert in theological and spiritual matters,"[54] apparently meaning that judicial examination of responsibility for his sexual exploitations would impair his free exercise of religion. Another, involving a claim that the church was negligent in supervising a clergyman, said that the mere comparison of a religious institution's relationship to its clergy with the relationships of the business world runs the risk of constitutional violation.[55]

to have sexual relations with the minister); M.L. v. Magnuson, 531 N.W.2d 849 (Minn. App.1995) (battery claim recognized but case remanded for new trial for error in instruction). Some cases allow the battery action without making it clear whether the battery was upon a stranger or upon a member of the religious community. Mutual Service Casualty Ins. Co. v. Puhl, 354 N.W.2d 900 (Minn.App.1984) (sexual battery).

50. See Amato v. Greenquist, 287 Ill. App.3d 921, 679 N.E.2d 446, 223 Ill.Dec. 261 (1997) (clergyman having an affair with plaintiff's wife allegedly accepted plaintiff in counseling, then used confidential information from counseling sessions to covertly undermine the marriage and further his own relationship with the plaintiff's wife); Gibson v. Brewer, 952 S.W.2d 239 (Mo. 1997) (intentional infliction would not be protected but allegations failed to support the claim). Intentional infliction or outrage claims may be more vulnerable than battery claims to the charge that any decision would entangle courts in religious matters. See Paul T. Hayden, Religiously Motivated "Outrageous" Conduct: Intentional Infliction of Emotional Distress as a Weapon against "Other People's Faiths," 34 Wm. & Mary L. Rev. 579 (1993).

51. In Schieffer v. Catholic Archdiocese of Omaha, 244 Neb. 715, 508 N.W.2d 907 (1993) the court thought the intentional infliction of emotional distress claim would be barred because consenting sexual activity is not outrageous.

52. See Restatement (Third) of Trusts § 2, cmt. b (Tentative Draft No. 1, 1996). Breach of a fiduciary duty is a tort. See Restatement § 874.

53. Sanders v. Casa View Baptist Church, 134 F.3d 331 (5th Cir.1998); Destefano v. Grabrian, 763 P.2d 275 (Colo.1988); Moses v. Diocese of Colorado, 863 P.2d 310 (Colo.1993); F.G. v. MacDonell, 150 N.J. 550, 696 A.2d 697 (1997). A fiduciary relationship may be found between church and member even outside the counseling-sexual exploitation setting. See Davis v. Church of Jesus Christ of Latter Day Saints, 258 Mont. 286, 852 P.2d 640 (1993).

54. Amato v. Greenquist, 287 Ill.App.3d 921, 932, 679 N.E.2d 446, 454, 223 Ill.Dec. 261, 269 (1997).

55. Swanson v. Roman Catholic Bishop of Portland, 692 A.2d 441, 444 (Me.1997). The *Swanson* Court continued: "The imposition of secular duties and liability on the church as a 'principal' will infringe upon its right to determine the standards governing

§ 259. Educational Malpractice

Tort liability generally. In the absence of an immunity,[1] teachers and schools are generally subject to a duty of reasonable care and hence to liability for negligence. For example, schools or teachers are subject to liability for injuries caused by negligently maintained premises,[2] a negligently conducted chemistry lab,[3] and for dangerous playground equipment or negligent supervision.[4] In such cases, schools and teachers are under a duty to exercise the care of the reasonable prudent person under all the circumstances.

Schools sometimes owe affirmative duties to protect students from themselves[5] or others.[6] Possibly teachers or others in a school system would also have obligations apart from statute to report suspected abuse of students by other teachers or by parents, and a school system might be subject to liability for negligently hiring personnel.[7] Negligence aside, teachers may also be liable for intentional torts, as in the case of sexual assault.[8] None of these things is burdened with the malpractice label.

The United States Constitution places some constraints on public educational practices. A state cannot use public schools to manipulate or support one particular religious belief, for example.[9] Federal statutes affecting many schools also have an impact, particularly by forbidding discrimination of various kinds. Under statutes, schools may be responsible for discrimination and hence for sexual harassment.[10] Statutes creating rights for disabled persons also make demands on school systems and impose liabilities when those demands are not met.[11] All of the vast

the relationship between the church, its bishop, and the parish priest." Id. at 445.

§ 259

1. Illinois has extended parental immunity to protect certain decisions of teachers, on the theory that teachers stand in loco parentis. See Palmer v. Mt. Vernon Township High School Dist. 201, 169 Ill.2d 551, 215 Ill.Dec. 120, 662 N.E.2d 1260 (1996)

2. See Howard County Board of Education v. Cheyne, 99 Md.App. 150, 636 A.2d 22 (1994).

3. Connett v. Fremont County School Dist. No. 6, Fremont County , 581 P.2d 1097 (Wyo.1978).

4. Vonungern v. Morris Central School, 240 A.D.2d 926, 658 N.Y.S.2d 760 (App. Div. 1997).

5. Eisel v. Board of Education of Montgomery County, 324 Md. 376, 597 A.2d 447, 17 A.L.R5th 957 (1991) (suicide).

6. Mirand v. City of New York, 84 N.Y.2d 44, 614 N.Y.S.2d 372, 637 N.E.2d 263 (1994); Fazzolari v. Portland School Dist. No. 1J, 303 Or. 1, 734 P.2d 1326 (1987).

7. Marquay v. Eno, 139 N.H. 708, 662 A.2d 272 (N.H. 1995). See § 326.

8. Galli v. Kirkeby, 398 Mich. 527, 248 N.W.2d 149 (1976).

9. Epperson v. Arkansas, 393 U.S. 97, 89 S.Ct. 266, 21 L.Ed.2d 228 (1968) (statute forbidding teaching of evolution unconstitutional as First Amendment violation).

10. See Davis v. Monroe County Bd. of Educ., ___ U.S. ___, 119 S.Ct. 1661, 143 L.Ed.2d 839 (1999); Franklin v. Gwinnett County Public Schools, 503 U.S. 60, 112 S.Ct. 1028, 117 L.Ed.2d 208 (1992).

11. Liability for intentional discrimination against disabled under the Rehabilitation Act: Whitehead v. School Board for Hillsborough County, Fla., 918 F.Supp. 1515 (M.D.Fla.1996). Some statutes do not contemplate a tort action for damages, but even so, money reimbursement may be ordered when a disabled child must seek private education elsewhere. See School Committee of Town of Burlington, Massachusetts v. Dept. of Education of Massachusetts, 471 U.S. 359, 105 S.Ct. 1996, 85 L.Ed.2d 385 (1985).

Constitutional and statutory law of this kind must be left for coverage in more specialized treatises.

Malpractice: textbooks, teaching, and testing. Courts have not defined educational malpractice, but they firmly state that no cause of action for it exists. Presumably an educational malpractice claim arises only when teachers deal professionally with students. In carrying out teaching functions, the teacher is a professional and the student is in a role that can be assimilated to that of a client.

Textbooks. Courts are unlikely to censor a textbook merely because some parents object to the subject matter or believe it to be emotionally harmful.[12] Selection of curriculum is likely to be in the same category.[13]

Teaching. The claim that teachers have taught a student badly so that he graduates without being able to read, for example, is on a different footing, for it can be adjudicated without invoking content censorship and it fits the normal model for professional malpractice. However, the handful of decisions on point hold that, in the absence of discrimination, professional negligence in teaching is not actionable in tort, either in public[14] or in private schools.[15] Perhaps the most persuasive reasons, at least in the case of public schools, lie in the courts' deference to the educational establishment for carrying out its assigned functions under state law, the supposed ability of students to get redress within the system, the courts' unwillingness to impose their own judgment about broad educational policies and their fear of involvement in day-to-day administration of the schools.[16] The argument in some cases that there is no appropriate standard of care,[17] however, depends upon the evidence offered, and it is hard to see why courts should rule out the

12. See Aubrey v. Sch. Dist. of Philadelphia, 63 Pa. Commw. 330, 437 A.2d 1306 (1981) (claim of emotional harm from reading textbooks denied); cf. Carroll v. Lucas, 39 Ohio Misc. 5, 313 N.E.2d 864 (1974) (same, but claim denied on the basis of immunity and the rule that emotional harm claims at that time required intent or contemporaneous physical injury); Contrast Epperson v. Arkansas, supra n. 9 (ban on teaching evolution not permissible).

13. See Wilson v. Continental Insurance Companies, 87 Wis.2d 310, 324, 274 N.W.2d 679, 686 (1979) (dictum).

14. Peter W. v. San Francisco Unified School District, 60 Cal.App.3d 814, 131 Cal. Rptr. 854 (1976); Donohue v. Copiague Union Free School District, 47 N.Y.2d 440, 391 N.E.2d 1352, 418 N.Y.S.2d 375, 1 A.L.R.4th 1133 (1979); see also Hunter v. Bd. of Education of Montgomery County, 292 Md. 481, 439 A.2d 582 (1982). Sometimes Wickstrom v. North Idaho College, 111 Idaho 450, 725 P.2d 155 (1986) is misleadingly cited with this group, but it holds only that the plaintiff failed to give the special notice required for suing a public entity.

15. Blane v. Alabama Commercial College, Inc., 585 So.2d 866 (Ala.1991) (stating only the conclusion that no educational malpractice claim would be recognized on the facts); Rich v. Kentucky Country Day, Inc., 793 S.W.2d 832 (Ky.App.1990); cf. Wilson v. Continental Insurance Companies, 87 Wis.2d 310, 274 N.W.2d 679 (1979) (decided on other grounds and arguably not an educational malpractice case at all, but stating in a dictum that courts would not interfere with teaching methods); Ross v. Creighton University, 957 F.2d 410 (7th Cir.1992) (allegations: academically under-qualified college basketball player badly used by university in a program not designed to provide education).

16. Originally set forth in Donohue v. Copiague Union Free School District, supra n. 14.

17. In Peter W. v. San Francisco Unified School District, supra n. 14, 60 Cal. App.3d at 824, 131 Cal.Rptr. at 860, the court reasoned that "classroom methodology affords no readily acceptable standards of care, or cause, or injury." That court also reasoned that given the prevalent discon-

possibility of evidence they have not seen. It is even harder to see why this argument is deemed persuasive when the complaint is that a university did not provide education for an athlete but instead prepared his assignments for him so that he could continue to use his athletic prowess for the university.[18]

Testing/placement. Testing and placement of students is arguably different, and negligent placement of a young child can have devastating effects that impair a child forever.[19] Most of the cases have treated negligent testing and placement cases like claims for teaching malpractice, denying recovery for similar reasons.[20] Perhaps if the claims pinpointed specific acts of measurable negligence courts would be more open to them. It would be a very bad idea indeed if courts were to regrade a student's essay, but selection of a demonstrably wrong kind of standardized multiple-choice exam for placement might involve a clear standard and provable harm. However, the District of Columbia Court refused to recognize a claim even when the school district allegedly lost the child's records, forced her to stay in the second grade three years instead of providing appropriate special needs education, and attempted to cover up some of its violations of law by altering records of the parent's demand for evaluation.[21] Only one state, by a divided court, has approached the issue as a straightforward tort claim. Montana announced that it simply had "no difficulty in finding a duty of care owed to special education students."[22] So far as placement is discriminatory or fails to provide for special needs, federal statutes may now provide some kind of relief.[23]

Teaching that creates risks of physical harm to third persons. Two cases have utilized the rule against liability for educational malpractice

tent with education, a ruinous number of suits would be brought if the action were entertained. There may be a wide range of teaching methodologies that are acceptable, but evidence might show that some are not. In addition, negligent teaching might not involve a choice of methodology at all but negligence in carrying it out, as for example, by failing to read students' papers, losing their records, or automatically passing them.

18. Ross v. Creighton University, 957 F.2d 410 (7th Cir.1992). The allegation was that Ross was recruited as a basketball player, though academically disadvantaged and woefully short of the average qualifications possessed by other students. He was advised to take courses such as Marksmanship and Theory of Basketball, but they did not count toward a degree. A secretary was assigned to read his assignments and prepare his papers.

19. Hoffman v. Bd. of Education of New York, 49 N.Y.2d 121, 424 N.Y.S.2d 376, 400 N.E.2d 317 (1979) (detailing some of the destruction wreaked upon a new immigrant child).

20. Brantley v. District of Columbia, 640 A.2d 181 (D.C.App.1994); Tubell v. Dade County Public Schools, 419 So.2d 388 (Fla.App.1982) (without discussion); Hoffman v. Bd. of Education of New York, 49 N.Y.2d 121, 424 N.Y.S.2d 376, 400 N.E.2d 317 (1979). Cf. D.S.W. v. Fairbanks North Star Borough School District, 628 P.2d 554 (Alaska 1981) (failure to provide special help for dyslexic students not actionable). Smith v. Alameda County Social Services Agency, 90 Cal.App.3d 929, 153 Cal.Rptr. 712 (1979) is another case misleadingly cited on testing/placement educational malpractice. The court there held that a social service agency that failed to get a boy adopted by foster parents was not subject to a claim.

21. Brantley v. District of Columbia, 640 A.2d 181 (D.C.App.1994).

22. B.M. v. State, 200 Mont. 58, 649 P.2d 425, 33 A.L.R.4th 1157 (1982).

23. See, e.g., 29 U.S.C.A. § 794; 20 U.S.C.A. § 1400 et seq. See n. 11.

as one ground of several for protecting technical schools whose graduates cause harm to others, allegedly as a result of defective education. In the first, a chiropractor's manipulations allegedly contributed to his patient's stroke. The patient claimed that the chiropractic school had inadequately instructed the chiropractor on this risk.[24] In the other, a driving school for people with disabilities graduated a young man whose driving later caused a death.[25] In both cases, the courts categorized the claim as one for educational malpractice and denied recovery. Both advanced other grounds, emphasizing independent state licensing of the school's graduates in each case and the unusual fact that a third person was injured. Neither considered the fact that the school's alleged negligence would have created physical risks to others which might call for a different policy assessment.

A third case alleged that a physician should have supervised a new resident physician and that failure to do so led to a child's brain damage. The court denied all relief for negligent supervision as if it were in the same category as negligent teaching or testing.[26]

Intentional torts. Since malpractice implies a claim for negligence, the decisions do not exclude the possibility that a teacher or school will be held liable for intentional torts to a child that impair his education or placement.[27]

Comment. Most of the teaching malpractice claims presented so far are not very attractive claims. They would probably fail even if courts recognized educational negligence as a tort because they do not assert any acts of negligence. Instead, they usually assert only that the student did not acquire the expected skills, a kind of implicit res ipsa loquitur claim. Such a claim is hardly justified in light of the fact that acquisition of knowledge and intellectual skills requires an effort to learn as well as an effort to teach.

It is not so clear, however, that courts should embrace a broad generalization against any educational malpractice. Although courts have given some reasons for a rule against educational malpractice claims, those reasons present two deficits. First, the reasons do not apply equally to every set of facts that can be classified as educational malpractice. Second, the reasons themselves assert concerns that are not validated in the opinions. Courts are right to avoid day-to-day supervision of schools, but they have not explained why legal liability for breach of a specific standard of care would entail supervision of schools any more than a physician's liability would entail supervision of the medical profession. The testing and placement cases are even more likely to be justiciable on the basis of clear standards, so the same comments apply.

24. Moore v. Vanderloo, 386 N.W.2d 108 (Iowa 1986).

25. Moss Rehab. v. White, 692 A.2d 902 (Del.1997).

26. Swidryk v. Saint Michael's Medical Center, 201 N.J.Super. 601, 493 A.2d 641 (1985).

27. See, so recognizing, Hunter v. Bd. of Education of Montgomery County, 292 Md. 481, 439 A.2d 582 (1982).

Chapter 15

Public Entities and Officers

Topic A. Liabilities of Governmental Entities

Subtopic 1. Traditional Immunities

§ 260. Traditional Immunities and Their Passing

Sovereign immunity. As a matter of sheer power, the medieval kings of England simply did not permit suits against themselves in their own courts, much less in the courts of feudal barons. Eventually, this power was cloaked with a theory or ideal: kings could not be sued because kings were governed by "divine right" and because "The King can do no wrong." As the state took over functions of the monarch, it inherited the monarch's immunity.

These thoroughly undemocratic ideas continued to prosper after the American Revolution,[1] so that both federal and state governments enjoyed a complete immunity from suit except so far as they consented to suit or waived the immunity. The position of Indian Tribes, described as quasi-sovereigns, must be left to more specialized materials.[2] The state and federal immunity covered all the departments and agencies of the respective governments. Constitutions created one partial exception to the general immunity by providing that governments could not take private property for public use without paying just compensation.[3] Such takings are redressed, although not on a tort theory, even when the governmental immunity is otherwise maintained.

Municipal immunity. Municipalities and local public entities also enjoyed governmental immunities, but municipalities were not sovereigns and their immunity historically grew out of an entirely different idea. In *Russell v. Men of Devon*,[4] the supposed municipality was not an entity at all, simply an aggregation of many people; consequently no suit could be entertained. Municipalities have long since been chartered by the state and are usually recognized as corporate entities today. Nevertheless, the immunity remained long after the historical reason disappeared.

§ 260

1. See Osborn v. Bank of United States, 22 U.S. (9 Wheat.) 738, 6 L.Ed. 204 (1824).

2. See Felix S. Cohen et al., Felix S. Cohen's Handbook of Federal Indian Law 324 (1982 ed.).

3. See U.S. Const. Amend. V (just compensation required) and Amendment XIV § 1 (property not to be taken without due process).

4. Russell v. Men of Devon, 2 Term Rep. 667, 100 Eng.Rep. 359 (1798).

The Eleventh Amendment immunity. The Eleventh Amendment of the United States Constitution provides a jurisdictional immunity to the states by forbidding suits against states in federal courts.[5] This immunity does not prohibit such suits in state courts, nor does it prohibit suits against state officers, so long as the state's treasury would not be subject to the judgment. The federal courts may also entertain suits against the states under the aegis of the Fourteenth Amendment where Congress has so provided.[6]

Officers and employees. The immunity of sovereigns and municipalities did not extend to officers or employees of public entities. At one time, it was said that public officers were in fact generally liable for their torts, even if the public entity they served was immune. Today, however, a web of immunities, some absolute, some qualified, may protect public officers in many instances.[7]

Abolishing immunities. Over the years, legislators found reasons, not for the blanket protection of government wrongdoing, but for limited immunities. First and most broadly, some kind of immunity was required to preserve the independence of each branch of government, so that the judicial branch could not intrude upon the appropriate functions of the legislative and executive branch by adjudicating tort suits. Second, some governmental decisions could not be measured against a standard of care. Otherwise, it is now usually accepted that government, instituted to protect and foster the well-being of citizens, should be obliged to make good on the losses it causes by misconduct.

Although all members of the public suffer a cost in some theoretical sense when governmental funds are paid to injured individuals, other members of the public—the injured persons—will suffer in the same amount if the public takes the benefits of governmental activity without also paying its costs. Even if governmental liability does not expose wrongdoing or provide incentives for better and less wrongful government, at least some liabilities have come to seem appropriate on these grounds and others like them.

Consequently, the traditional blanket immunities of sovereigns and municipalities have been abolished or substantially modified both at the federal and at the state level. Nevertheless, some kind of immunity, or unique constraints on duties of governmental entities, remains everywhere. The sections below sketch the main patterns of liability and

5. "The judicial power of the United States shall not be construed to extend to any suit in law or equity, commenced or prosecuted against one of the United States by citizens of another state, or by citizens or subjects of any foreign state." U.S. Const. Amend. XI. The Court construed this language to forbid a federal court suit against a state even by its own citizens. Hans v. Louisiana, 134 U.S. 1, 10 S.Ct. 504, 33 L.Ed. 842 (1890).

6. Quern v. Jordan, 440 U.S. 332, 99 S.Ct. 1139, 59 L.Ed.2d 358 (1979). A federal court injunction may run against individual officers even if that will ultimately compel costly state action; but the injunction may not be used to effect direct payment of state funds. See Edelman v. Jordan, 415 U.S. 651, 94 S.Ct. 1347, 39 L.Ed.2d 662 (1974).

7. § 273 below.

protection for the federal and state governments, municipalities, and officers of public entities.

SUBTOPIC 2. FEDERAL LIABILITY UNDER THE FTCA

§ 261. The Plan of Federal Government Tort Liability

Advent of the Federal Torts Claims Act. In 1887, Congress authorized courts to entertain contract but not tort suits against the United States.[1] At various times, however, Congress has consented to tort suits against the government in particular instances, sometimes simply by providing that a federal agency could sue or be sued.[2] In addition, Congress has dealt with many individual cases by private legislation that appropriated funds directly to the victim.[3] Such a procedure became a burden to Congress. Finally, in 1946, it enacted the Federal Tort Claims Act (FTCA), which gave a general consent to suit against the United States in federal courts, subject to a number of specific limitations.[4]

Procedural requirements. Procedurally, no suit may be brought until a claim has been presented to the appropriate federal agency.[5] After the agency has denied the claim, or has delayed more than six months in determining the claim, the plaintiff may sue. Suit must be brought in federal court.[6] No jury trial is permitted in FTCA claims.[7] Under the statute as it now stands, the only proper party is the government, or the agency involved; governmental employees who commit torts in the scope of their employment are not liable at all.[8]

Governing substantive law. Although the claim must be brought in federal court, state tort law governs the rights and duties of the parties. The statute requires the court to follow the law of the state in which the government's negligent act or omission occurred.[9] The statute makes it clear that liability for a negligent act or omission depends upon a showing that the employee was acting within the scope of his government employment.[10] Federal law governs the question whether the entity

§ 261

1. 24 STAT. 505. Jurisdiction for most contract disputes is in the United States Court of Federal Claims. 28 U.S.C.A. § 1491.

2. E.g., Federal Deposit Insurance Corp. v. Meyer, 510 U.S. 471, 114 S.Ct. 996, 127 L.Ed.2d 308 (1994).

3. See Dalehite v. United States, 346 U.S. 15, 24–25, 73 S.Ct. 956, 962, 97 L.Ed. 1427 (1953) ("the private bill device was notoriously clumsy" so Congress substituted simple access to federal courts).

4. 60 STAT. 843. The provisions are scattered through the United States Code. Jurisdiction is granted in 28 U.S.C.A. § 1346. The main substantive provisions are cited in discussion of particular provisions.

5. 28 U.S.C.A. § 2875.

6. 28 U.S.C.A. § 1346 (b) (exclusive jurisdiction in federal court).

7. 28 U.S.C.A. § 2402.

8. See § 273. As to civil rights violations, see § 278.

9. 28 U.S.C.A. § 1346(b)(1). If government negligence occurs in State A but harm results in State B, State A's law controls; but that includes State A's choice of law rule, which is likely to refer to the law of State B, where harm occurred. If so, the FTCA claim ultimately looks to State B's law. Richards v. United States, 369 U.S. 1, 82 S.Ct. 585, 7 L.Ed.2d 492 (1962).

10. 28 U.S.C.A. § 1346(b).

in question is a federal agency, but the law of the appropriate state determines whether the employee is acting within the scope of his government employment. State law also governs the ordinary substantive tort law questions—the rules of negligence, causation, and comparative fault, for example, and all the rules limiting duties, such as those governing suits against health care providers or landowners. In some instances, state law might recognize a state-law tort duty arising out of a federal statute and if so, the government's violation of such a statute may furnish the basis for federal governmental liability.[11]

Governing remedial law. Since state law control the rights and duties of the parties, it also controls the determination of damages, which is a practical reflection of the state law right.[12] The FTCA itself, however, limits that general rule in two respects. First, the plaintiff in an FTCA case cannot recover punitive damages, and second, interest on the amounts due does not begin to accrue until judgment is entered.[13]

Comparable private person liability. The main substantive directive of the statute provides that the government is to be liable under the appropriate state law when a private person would be liable under like circumstances.[14] The thrust of this provision is simply to apply the substantive law of the appropriate state without regard to the government's historic immunity. The private person rule does not require the plaintiff to show that private persons carry on activities like those of the government. It requires that legal principles applied to the facts would dictate liability[15] or its limits.[16] If a private individual carrying out the activity would be liable for the plaintiff's injury, then the government, too, will be liable unless some residual immunity applies.

Limitations. Although the FTCA begins with a general rule that government is liable for torts in much the same way a private person would be liable, the act then carves out exceptions, withholding jurisdiction from courts when the government's alleged tort is the enforcement of a statute or the exercise of a discretionary function, and also in a number of very particular instances listed in the statute.[17] Beyond this,

11. Cf. Loge v. United States, 662 F.2d 1268 (8th Cir.1981) (government may be held for violation of its own statute or regulation); see § 136 supra.

12. E.g., Williams v. United States, 435 F.2d 804 (1st Cir.1970) (wrongful death damages measures); Trevino v. United States, 804 F.2d 1512 (9th Cir.1986) (issue of excessiveness).

13. 28 U.S.C.A. § 2674.

14. 28 U.S.C.A. § 2674.

15. Thus in Indian Towing Co. v. United States, 350 U.S. 61, 76 S.Ct. 122, 100 L.Ed. 48 (1955), the government's negligent operation of a lighthouse was actionable although private persons do not operate lighthouses. Likewise, the government could not claim the immunity of municipalities operating lighthouses, but was liable as if it were a private person. The effect of *Indian Towing* was to reject the earlier reasoning in Feres v. United States, 340 U.S. 135, 71 S.Ct. 153, 95 L.Ed. 152 (1950), where Justice Jackson had argued that since private persons did not conscript soldiers and operate armies, the army negligence there was not actionable.

16. Courts have given the government the benefit of state-law caps on liability, even when those caps depend upon a scheme of fees to which the government has not contributed. See Carter v. United States, 982 F.2d 1141 (7th Cir.1992).

17. 28 U.S.C.A. § 2680. See also the remedial limitations, supra nn. 12–13.

the Supreme Court itself has concluded that the government cannot be held strictly liable[18] and that the government cannot be liable for its torts to members of the armed forces.[19] The major exceptions to liability are considered further in the sections that follow.

Federal Constitutional claims against the federal government. The FTCA scheme of liability relies, at least formally, upon the state's law of torts. It does not authorize a suit against the federal government for violation of constitutional or other federally guaranteed rights. Constitutional civil rights claims based upon federal actions must be asserted, if at all, against the individual officers responsible, not against the government.[20]

§ 262. The Discretionary Immunity

Protecting Discretion

Enforcement or nonenforcement of statutes. The FTCA retains the sovereign immunity in two major and related instances. The courts have no jurisdiction to hear claims based simply upon the government's enforcement of a statute or regulation, even if the statute or regulation turns out to be invalid.[1] This is a corollary to the idea that under the separation of powers principle, courts could not force Congress to pass a statute or to repeal one, because the power to adopt or reject a statute is legislative in nature, not judicial.[2] The FTCA recognizes that the government may be liable for negligent acts committed while enforcing a statute—an agent's negligent driving while enforcing a statute, for example—but not for the mere fact of enforcement itself.

Enactment or failure to enact statute or regulation. Even more clearly, the government cannot be held for failing to enact a statute or a set of regulations or for adopting a statute or regulations that cause harm. The fact that the plaintiff's injury could have been avoided if a government agency had adopted a reasonable set of regulations establishes no claim at all.[3] Equally, the government is free to adopt a public works project such as a flood control program that causes the plaintiff harm without liability in tort.[4]

18. Laird v. Nelms, 406 U.S. 797, 92 S.Ct. 1899, 32 L.Ed.2d 499 (sonic boom). The private person standard of liability would seem to permit strict liability, but the jurisdictional section of the statute, 28 U.S.C.A. § 1346 speaks of an act that is "negligent or wrongful." The Court thought the latter excluded strict liability.

19. § 263 below.

20. See § 278 below.

§ 262

1. "The provisions of this chapter and section 1346(b) of this title shall not apply to—(a) Any claim based upon an act or omission of an employee of the Government, exercising due care, in the execution of a statute or regulation, whether or not such statute or regulation be valid. . . ." 28 U.S.C.A. § 2680(a).

2. See Dalehite v. United States, 346 U.S. 15, 43, 73 S.Ct. 956, 971, 97 L.Ed. 1427(1953).

3. E.g., Loge v. United States, 662 F.2d 1268 (8th Cir.1981).

4. Coates v. United States, 181 F.2d 816 (8th Cir.1950); see J. D. Perovich, Liability of United States under Federal Tort Claims Act for Damage from Flooding, 4 A.L.R. Fed. 723 (1970). Distinguish: (1) a taking of property for public purposes, with attendant liability under the taking clause; and (2) negligence in carrying out a public works program.

Discretionary immunity. The statute likewise retains sovereign immunity for governmental performance or nonperformance of a discretionary function.[5] For instance, an agency's decision to regulate a financial institution,[6] to carry out safety inspections,[7] to interdict foreign fruit suspected of containing poisons,[8] to issue or deny a grazing permit,[9] to delegate hazardous waste disposal to an independent contractor,[10] or to parole a prisoner,[11] are all protected activities for which liability cannot be imposed, so long as the activities are generally or specifically authorized by statute.[12] In such cases, the fact that the governmental agency has acted negligently or even abused its discretion is irrelevant, for the government is immune.[13]

Justification. The chief justification for this hiatus in governmental responsibility lies in the separation of powers concept.[14] If Congress has constitutionally left discretion in the hands of an agency of the government, the judicial branch must not assume the role allocated to the agency or interfere by imposing tort liability. Other reasons support a degree of protection in particular cases. Many administrative decisions cannot be measured against a standard of care.[15] Others may be like judicial decisions, best left to be redressed by internal review rather than by liability. The problem in all cases has been to determine what counts

5. "The provisions of this chapter and section 1346(b) of this title shall not apply to—(a) Any claim ... based upon the exercise or performance or the failure to exercise or perform a discretionary function or duty on the part of a federal agency or an employee of the Government, whether or not the discretion involved be abused." 28 U.S.C.A. § 2680(a). See generally, Donald N. Zillman, Protecting Discretion: Judicial Interpretation of the Discretionary Function Exception to the Federal Tort Claims Act, 47 Me. L. Rev. 365 (1995); 2 Lester S. Jayson and Robert C. Longstreth, Handling Federal Tort Claims Chapter 12.

6. United States v. Gaubert, 499 U.S. 315, 111 S.Ct. 1267, 1274, 113 L.Ed.2d 335 (1991).

7. United States v. S.A. Empresa de Viacao Aerea Rio Grandense, 467 U.S. 797, 104 S.Ct. 2755, 81 L.Ed.2d 660 (1984).

8. Fisher Bros. Sales, Inc. v. United States, 46 F.3d 279 (3d Cir.1995).

9. See United States v. Morrell, 331 F.2d 498 (10th Cir.1964).

10. Andrews v. United States, 121 F.3d 1430 (11th Cir.1997).

11. Payton v. United States, 679 F.2d 475 (5th Cir.1982) (decision to parole protected as discretionary under statute but prison's failure to provide records showing parolee was dangerous was not protected). Similarly, to admit a dangerous foreign national with a criminal record, to release him within the United States, and to do so without notice to police. Flammia v. United States, 739 F.2d 202, 78 A.L.R. Fed. 677 (5th Cir. 1984).

12. In each example, the discretion is lost if a statute mandates a different action. For instance, issuance of a license or permit may be authorized and thus discretionary in some cases, but in others regulations may mandate a refusal of a license until specified conditions are met. In such a case, the regulation removes the discretion. See Berkovitz by Berkovitz v. United States, 486 U.S. 531, 108 S.Ct. 1954, 100 L.Ed.2d 531 (1988).

13. As the federal courts see it, they have no jurisdiction to hear the claim once it is shown that the immunity is retained. That is because the discretionary immunity in § 2680 (a) is framed as an exception to the grant of jurisdiction in § 1346.

14. See Harold J. Krent, Preserving Discretion without Sacrificing Deterrence: Federal Governmental Liability in Tort, 38 UCLA L. Rev. 871 (1991).

15. Cf. Bruce A. Peterson and Mark E. Van der Weide, Susceptible to Faulty Analysis: United States v. Gaubert and the Resurrection of Federal Sovereign Immunity, 72 Notre Dame L. Rev. 447, 479–480 (1997) (suggesting that fault cannot be assessed when unquantifiable policy variables are involved).

as a discretionary decision that must not be reviewed by courts and what, on the contrary, counts as simply tortious conduct.

Operational-planning distinction. In the first generation after the enactment of the FTCA, the Court worked with a distinction between planning decisions and operational decisions. The first case referred to the "level" of the decision,[16] but later cases seemed more concerned with the nature of the decision.[17] If it was a planning decision, involving a broad issue of social or political policy, it was discretionary. The Coast Guard's decision to operate a lighthouse might be a planning decision and protected, but its failure to maintain the light, with a resulting shipwreck, would be merely operational negligence for which liability would be appropriate.[18] Later decisions of the Supreme Court, however, have shifted focus and perhaps have eliminated the planning-operational distinction.

The Berkovitz case: room for choice and a decision grounded in social or political policy. In the *Berkovitz* case,[19] one of the plaintiff's allegations was that a government agency licensed the manufacture of a polio vaccine. The vaccine caused harm to the plaintiff. The government agency allegedly issued the license without receiving data required by regulation to show that the manufacturer's product was safe. The agency had no rightful choice about this matter. It could not rightfully violate the statute or regulation. For this reason it had no discretion and no discretionary immunity.

The Court in *Berkovitz* envisioned a kind of two-part test for the discretionary immunity. (1) Did the government have room for choice? (2) If so, did the choice depend upon "decisions grounded in social, economic, and political policy"? If the answer to either question is "no," the discretionary immunity does not protect the government (although some other rule may do so). The first part of the test asks whether any discretion at all is involved. If the government had no choice because constitutional, statutory, or regulatory rules compelled a given decision, no discretion was involved at all. The second part of the test asks whether the discretion is the kind that is protected—discretion in decision making that involves social, economic, or political "policy judgment".

A different allegation in *Berkovitz* could be read to assert that the agency did in fact make a determination that the vaccine complied with governmental standards, but that such a determination was incorrect. This claim might or might not involve the discretionary immunity. If it were merely an objective, scientific determination, it would not be protected. On the other hand, if approval involved some kind of policy

16. Dalehite v. United States, 346 U.S. 15, 43, 73 S.Ct. 956, 971, 97 L.Ed. 1427(1953).

17. See United States v. S. A. Empresa de Viacao Aerea Rio Grandense, 467 U.S. 797, 104 S.Ct. 2755, 81 L.Ed.2d 660 (1984).

18. Indian Towing Co. v. United States, 350 U.S. 61, 76 S.Ct. 122, 100 L.Ed. 48 (1955) (government conceding operational character of the Coast Guard's negligence).

19. Berkovitz by Berkovitz v. United States, 486 U.S. 531, 108 S.Ct. 1954, 100 L.Ed.2d 531 (1988).

judgment, the discretionary immunity would protect against liability under this allegation. On that issue, factual development would be required.

United States v. Gaubert: low-level decisions susceptible of policy analysis. Although the Supreme Court clearly adopted the principle that a decision on social, economic, or political issues is required to establish discretionary immunity, the Court in *United States v. Gaubert*[20] also established some rules that tend to undermine that principle. First, *Gaubert* held that a discretionary decision can be made at any level of the governmental process. Even a decision at the operational level might be discretionary if it entailed the kind of judgment the Court had in mind.[21]

Gaubert also held that the immunity for discretion stands to bar a claim even if the government did not actually consider any policy issues at all. "The focus of the inquiry is not on the agent's subjective intent in exercising the discretion conferred by statute or regulation, but on the nature of the actions taken and on whether they are susceptible to policy analysis." At least this is the case when the discretion finds its source in "established governmental policy, as expressed or implied by statute, regulation, or agency guidelines."

Criticisms of Gaubert. Both rules have been criticized as providing excessive protection for negligent governmental decisions that cause harm. Some authors have argued that only actual decisions about policy matters should be protected and then only when the decision is made by a person to whom policy making authority has been delegated and when it is within the scope of his policy-making authority.[22]

Indeed, it does seem strange to say that the government is exercising a discretionary function in constructing a mountainous, curving park road without a guardrail at a precipitous 90–foot drop merely because the court can speculate that preservation of natural beauty might be one of the motives. Yet that speculative possibility shows that even the decision to omit standard safety devices could be "susceptible to policy analysis" in the minds of some judges and could thus be protected under the *Gaubert* formulation, although simple negligence is more likely than a policy determination.[23] Even basic rights can be lost in this line of reasoning. The Eleventh Circuit held that when a drug agency executed a warrant on the wrong man, that was a decision susceptible of policy analysis because the agency may have been concerned that taking time

20. United States v. Gaubert, 499 U.S. 315, 111 S.Ct. 1267, 1274, 113 L.Ed.2d 335 (1991).

21. Gaubert, 499 U.S. at 325, 111 S.Ct. at 1275.

22. Bruce A. Peterson and Mark E. Van der Weide, Susceptible to Faulty Analysis: United States v. Gaubert and the Resurrection of Federal Sovereign Immunity, 72 Notre Dame L. Rev. 447, 486 ff. (1997); cf. Harold J. Krent, Preserving Discretion without Sacrificing Deterrence: Federal Governmental Liability in Tort, 38 UCLA L. Rev. 871 (1991) (pre-Gaubert, distinguishing deliberative and nondeliberative decisions).

23. Bowman v. United States, 820 F.2d 1393 (4th Cir.1987) (actually decided before *Gaubert*).

to get the right man would lead to loss of evidence.[24] The "susceptible" approach allows the court to reach such a result even if the agency in fact was merely flouting rights of citizens and could easily have identified the correct suspect.

However, courts and writers may have overgeneralized *Gaubert*. The claim in *Gaubert* was based solely on the government's regulation of a business in which the plaintiff was interested and on economic harm. It did not involve government construction or maintenance or government safety projects, much less arrests of persons.

Applications and Examples

Regulatory activity and public benefit programs. Regulatory activity—or inactivity, as it sometimes is—may be the obvious case for protection under the discretionary immunity. Even if the FAA is required to inspect airplanes for safety, it may decide on spot checks rather than complete strip-down inspections of all planes.[25] Regulation of financial institutions may in the end cost investors millions, but it is no surprise to find that such regulation, even in its details, is discretionary and protected.[26] Governmental decisions involving distribution of benefits through large public programs are presumably in the same category. For instance, a governmental decision to implement or reject flood control programs may affect lives and property of many persons, but unless statute or regulation is violated, such decisions are at the core of discretionary immunity.[27] Even without the discretionary immunity, courts might be forced to reach the same result because the government would ordinarily have no duty to disburse public benefits and it is hard to imagine a standard of care that could be applied to many regulatory decisions apart from statutory directives themselves.

Nondeliberative decisions. Governmental decisions that are not in fact based on deliberation or consideration of policy do not sound like policy decisions. As already indicated, *Gaubert* held that a decision might be discretionary and protected even if government agents made the decision without considering policy, as long as the decision was "susceptible to policy analysis." However, even if *Gaubert* applies outside the regulatory case, the discretionary immunity only protects policy decisions "based on the purposes that the regulatory regime seeks to accomplish." Driving a motor vehicle "requires the constant exercise of

24. Mesa v. United States, 123 F.3d 1435 (11th Cir.1997).

25. United States v. S.A. Empresa de Viacao Aerea Rio Grandense, 467 U.S. 797, 104 S.Ct. 2755, 81 L.Ed.2d 660 (1984).

26. United States v. Gaubert, 499 U.S. 315, 111 S.Ct. 1267, 1274, 113 L.Ed.2d 335 (1991).

27. See National Union Fire Ins. v. United States, 115 F.3d 1415 (9th Cir.1997) (decision to postpone raising breakwater in a harbor while the corps studied even larger improvements led to millions in flood damage but was discretionary). There is also a specific statute. "No liability of any kind shall attach to or rest upon the United States for any damage from or by floods or flood waters at any place.... " 33 U.S.C.A. § 702c.

discretion'' but negligent driving is not protected because the discretion in driving is not ''grounded in regulatory policy.''[28]

Policy choices made pursuant to standards. Beyond this, a discretionary decision must be one that is potentially based on something that could be called policy, and it must be a policy about social, economic, or political issues. Many choices involving balancing of costs and benefits might not be *policy* choices at all because they are choices made pursuant to safety standards or goals. So the government has rightly been held subject to liability for negligent operation of motor vehicles,[29] airport control towers,[30] and lighthouses,[31] as well as for negligence in treatment of prisoners[32] and in maintenance of government property.[33] Indeed, in most of these cases the discretionary immunity is not even asserted.

Professional, scientific, or technical decisions. Similarly, when the objective is to follow a scientific, technical, or safety standard, the government agent may have many choices. The agent may be required to balance many diverse considerations, but the choices are not choices of policy. Medical decisions by government doctors are in this category. Even if regulations provide that the Veterans' Administration ''may'' admit or reject a patient, when the VA refuses admission on the basis of a negligent medical judgment, the government may be liable for the harm done.[34] An agency's negligence in releasing a dangerous vaccine is in the same category if the decision is scientific or technical rather than governmental.[35] Indeed, as Prosser and Keeton said, the presence of a preexisting safety standard, or any appropriate standard governing the activity, should tend to displace discretion.[36] Conceivably, then, any negligent activity that can be gauged against a known standard of care could be the basis for liability.[37]

Expansive reading of the immunity. In spite of the cases just mentioned, federal courts have tended to read the discretionary immunity quite broadly. Sometimes they treat routine governmental decisions as decisions of ''policy.'' Sometimes they ignore the policy element and

28. Gaubert, 499 U.S. at 325, 111 S.Ct. at 1275, n. 7.

29. E.g., Hetzel v. United States, 310 U.S.App.D.C. 75, 43 F.3d 1500 (D.C.Cir. 1995) (DEA officers' high-speed chase of suspect in the city of Washington, D.C. was negligent and actionable).

30. E.g., Daley v. United States, 792 F.2d 1081 (11th Cir.1986).

31. Indian Towing Co. v. United States, 350 U.S. 61, 76 S.Ct. 122, 100 L.Ed. 48 (1955).

32. See United States v. Muniz, 374 U.S. 150, 83 S.Ct. 1850, 10 L.Ed.2d 805 (1963).

33. See, e.g., Buscaglia v. United States, 25 F.3d 530 (7th Cir.1994) (slip and fall in post office).

34. Collazo v. United States, 850 F.2d 1 (1st Cir.1988).

35. E.g., Deasy v. United States, 99 F.3d 354 (10th Cir.1996); cf. Griffin v. United States, 500 F.2d 1059 (3d Cir.1974) (government acting as a medical or science professional, not as a policymaker, in releasing dangerous vaccine; professional decisions are not political decisions).

36. Prosser & Keeton § 131, p. 1042 (5th ed. 1984).

37. Cf. Rayonier Incorporated v. United States, 352 U.S. 315, 77 S.Ct. 374, 1 L.Ed.2d 354 (1957) (government negligence in firefighting was actionable; the government argued the discretionary immunity only indirectly by asserting that uniquely governmental activities like firefighting were not actionable).

treat any choice as sufficient without considering whether it involves a policy choice on a social or economic matter.

For example, it would seem that decisions of an army medical doctor would not be policy decisions even though they involve judgment. Such decisions are presumably to be guided by professional standards, not by political policy. Yet the Eighth Circuit denounced such a distinction and held that the army's negligent screening of blood donations entailed a "policy" judgment so that the government was not responsible for the army's communication of AIDS to soldiers through transfusion of contaminated blood.[38]

Similarly, no policy judgment is entailed when a government driver operates a vehicle in a way to cause a deadly accident. Yet, without finding any policy element at all, the Tenth Circuit invoked the discretionary immunity in such a case.[39] Another Tenth Circuit case expressly found that a park ranger's actions in unsuccessfully guiding a park visitor around a hostile moose were matters of government "policy."[40]

A government investigation into a colonel's death by shotgun blast would seemingly be a professional search for facts, but the Ninth Circuit has held such an investigation is intertwined with political judgments and thus even if government investigators showed "a general disregard for sound investigative procedure," such procedure is discretionary.[41]

Building bridges with defective rather than safe guardrails seems even less a matter of policy. But the Fourth Circuit, by no means alone, thinks it is a matter of policy because it is likely to entail an allocation of resources.[42] Such a conception of policy encompasses virtually all human acts and certainly all safety measures, few of which can be cost-free.

38. C.R.S. v. United States, 11 F.3d 791, 797 (8th Cir.1993) ("there is no bright line removing 'professional' or 'technical' judgments, whatever these may be, from the scope of the exception"). Cf. Fisher Bros. Sales, Inc. v. United States, 46 F.3d 279 (3d Cir.1995) (claim that government negligently tested imported fruit suspected of being poisoned was in "reality" a claim that the commissioner should not have interdicted fruit and commissioner's decision was discretionary; substantial dissents). A commentator, formerly representing the government, has proposed to extend protection along the lines in *Fisher* by saying that even technical and professional negligence, though not discretionary, should receive the discretionary function protection if the plaintiff 's claim is that it influenced an agency's discretionary decision. Richard H. Seamon, Causation and the Discretionary Function Exception to the Federal Tort Claims Act, 30 U.C. Davis L. Rev. 691 (1997).

39. Flynn v. United States, 902 F.2d 1524 (10 Cir.1990) (accident allegedly resulting from Park Service driver's negligent use of flashing light in a way that led another driver to run down three women; a regulation allowed use of the flashing light in emergencies but gave no standards for decision, so the court concluded that the matter was discretionary).

40. Tippett v. United States, 108 F.3d 1194 (10th Cir.1997)

41. Sabow v. United States, 93 F.3d 1445 (9th Cir.1996).

42. Baum v. United States, 986 F.2d 716 (4th Cir.1993) ("The question of what materials to use in such a project is also fundamentally described as a question of how to allocate limited resources among competing needs. Considered in this light, ... the Park Service's decision in this regard plainly was one bound up in economic and political policy considerations"); Rich v. United States, 119 F.3d 447 (6th Cir.1997) (similar); accord, that the court will protect "resource allocation decisions," Hughes v. United States, 110 F.3d 765 (11th Cir.1997) (postal service's decision to provide inadequate lighting of parking lot, coupled with

Comments

(1) The conclusion that a person is negligent always or almost always entails an assessment of costs and benefits of the conduct in question. Conduct is negligent when greater safety would cost little in comparison to the harm that may be inflicted. Conduct is not negligent when costs of safety clearly outweigh the harm threatened. Although this point is articulated in different ways, it is routinely applied in ordinary negligence cases.[43] When federal courts use the discretionary immunity to protect all governmental decisions involving costs and benefits or allocation of resources, their logic would foreclose all possibility of governmental liability for negligence. That is so because negligence invariably entails some estimate about the reasonableness of cost and benefits of the defendant's conduct. It seems plain, then, that some courts have too quickly equated cost-benefit decisions with the discretionary immunity.

(2) Excessive reliance on the discretionary immunity to resolve FTCA cases is also tending to displace state tort law, which, by statute, is controlling on the substantive issues. It is true that discretion itself is a federal, not a state issue. But as courts increasingly rely on federal statutes and regulations defining employee's duties, they increasingly displace state tort law, using their analysis of discretion as a substitute for analysis of duty or negligence issues. When the army negligently screened blood donors, with the result that AIDS infected blood was given by transfusion to a member of the National Guard, the court invoked an army "directive" which said that the Military Blood Program Office was to develop policies concerning collection, processing and distribution of blood. This simple directive was thought sufficient to grant discretion to the army to act negligently in screening blood for AIDS.[44] Even the *absence* of a federal regulation may suffice to convince a court that the government agency had discretion so that the state law negligence issue is never reached.[45]

(3) It is hard to believe that the government can be much moved by liability for negligence. Nevertheless, the legal incentives should not be set perversely to discourage governmental concern with the kind of safety that other institutions are expected to consider. If the Ford Motor Company produces a dangerous car that tends to explode upon a rear impact, consumers will sooner or later get the information and seek alternatives. In addition, Ford is encouraged to avoid such designs by tort rules that allow victims to recover. But if the federal government chooses dangerously bad materials for bridge railings, highway users will be unlikely to hear of it—and even if they do they cannot turn to another government for safer highways. A more circumspect application

hedges and other hiding places and a lack of security guards allegedly made the lot dangerous for those rightfully obtaining mail and led to attack on the plaintiff, but these were decisions about resources).

43. See §§ 144 & 145 supra.

44. C.R.S. v. United States, 11 F.3d 791 (8th Cir.1993)

45. See Grammatico v. United States, 109 F.3d 1198, 1201 (7th Cir.1997).

of the discretionary immunity would help ensure that the government is held to reasonable safety standards analogous to those found in the private sector.

§ 263. Military Tortfeasors and Victims

Statutory Exceptions to Military Liability

Combatant activity, foreign country claims. The FTCA provides a number of specific exceptions to the waiver of immunity, one of which retains the immunity for all claims "arising out of the combatant activities of the military or naval forces, or the Coast Guard, during time of war."[1] Another exception that can apply even to protect non-combatant military operations is the immunity for claims "arising in a foreign country."[2] Other particular exceptions may also apply if the military action comes within their terms.[3]

The Feres Rule

The Feres "incident to service" rule. The largest protection against liability for torts of a military origin is not to be found in the statute but was created entirely by the Supreme Court in *Feres v. United States*.[4] In that case, a soldier on active duty perished in a barracks fire, allegedly because of the army's negligence. The soldier's executrix sued. In companion cases, soldiers sued for army negligence in performing surgery. The Court concluded that, although the statute contained no language protecting the government from such liabilities, the government should nevertheless be protected against suits "for injuries to servicemen where the injuries arise out of or are in the course of activity incident to service." The *Feres* rule, initially applied to suits against the government under the FTCA, has been carried over to civil rights cases against government agents.[5]

By ordinary standards of statutory construction, the decision has seemed wrong to most observers[6] and the Supreme Court's applications of it have created a "troubled doctrine,"[7] the meaning of which is uncertain after half a century.[8]

Rationales for the Feres rule. Most of the original rationales for the *Feres* rule have been undermined, altered, or applied erratically in later decisions of the Supreme Court.[9]

§ 263

1. 28 U.S.C.A. § 2680(j).

2. 28 U.S.C.A. § 2680(k).

3. See § 261.

4. Feres v. United States, 340 U.S. 135, 71 S.Ct. 153, 95 L.Ed. 152 (1950).

5. As to suits against individual tortfeasors instead of the government, see §§ 273 & 274; and on civil rights grounds, §§ 275–278.

6. See, e.g., United States v. Johnson, 481 U.S. 681, 107 S.Ct. 2063, 95 L.Ed.2d 648 (1987) (Scalia, J., dissenting); Taber v. Maine, 67 F.3d 1029, 1032, 1039 (2d Cir. 1995) (*Feres* willfully ignored language and history of the statute as well as appropriate judicial process (Calabresi, J.)).

7. McAllister v. United States, 942 F.2d 1473, 1480 (9th Cir.1991).

8. Taber v. Maine, 67 F.3d 1029, 1032 (2d Cir.1995).

9. Logically undermined but sometimes converted to "factors" that can be rehabilitated at will for temporary duty. Compare

The *Feres* Court's first rationale, that there are no comparable private liabilities because private persons do not have armies and because the army was not historically liable for torts, has been quietly shelved.[10] The second was that military service members should not recover in tort because they are entitled to military benefits for injury or death, analogous to workers' compensation benefits.[11] That reasoning has been undermined by decisions that grant recovery to others in the same position, including discharged veterans,[12] and by decisions that deny recovery even to those who have no such benefits.[13] The alternate compensation rationale has reappeared, however, as a "factor" to be used in determining whether injury occurred "incident to service,"[14] and Judge Calabresi has ventured an interpretation of the alternate compensation rationale that can explain many cases.[15]

The last *Feres* rationale was that service members stand in distinctive relationship to the government so that federal law should control and that no federal law permits a recovery by service members. This was at best a strange argument to raise against a statute that neither exempted military negligence nor provided for federal law.[16] The Court incrementally altered this rationale over a series of cases. It now appears

United States v. Shearer, 473 U.S. 52, 58, 105 S.Ct. 3039, 3043, 87 L.Ed.2d 38, fn. 4, (1985) (only military discipline rationale controlling) with United States v. Johnson, 481 U.S. 681, 107 S.Ct. 2063, 95 L.Ed.2d 648 (1987) (considering several rationales as factors). But cf. United States v. Stanley, 483 U.S. 669, 107 S.Ct. 3054, 97 L.Ed.2d 550 (1987) (Court must not look to see how factors would operate in particular case).

10. See Indian Towing Co. v. United States, 350 U.S. 61, 76 S.Ct. 122, 100 L.Ed. 48 (1955) (government liability for negligent management of lighthouse, although a municipality would be immune); United States v. Brown, 348 U.S. 110, 75 S.Ct. 141, 99 L.Ed. 139 (1954) (government liability to discharged veteran for medical negligence); United States v. Muniz, 374 U.S. 150, 83 S.Ct. 1850, 10 L.Ed.2d 805 (1963) (government liability for negligent injury to federal prisoner; *Feres* is inapplicable partly because "the Government's liability is no longer restricted to circumstances in which government bodies have traditionally been responsible for misconduct of their employees").

11. Where a workers' compensation statute applies, the benefits provided are ordinarily exclusive, so that the injured worker has no tort claim. This is the rule for federal as well as for private employees. See 5 U.S.C.A. § 8116.

12. United States v. Brown, 348 U.S. 110, 75 S.Ct. 141, 99 L.Ed. 139 (1954); United States v. Muniz, 374 U.S. 150, 83 S.Ct. 1850, 10 L.Ed.2d 805 (1963).

13. Stencel Aero Eng'g Corp. v. United States, 431 U.S. 666, 672–73, 97 S.Ct. 2054, 2058–59, 52 L.Ed.2d 665 (1977); see also Maas v. United States, 94 F.3d 291 (7th Cir.1996) ("Application of the Feres doctrine does not depend on the extent to which its rationales are present in a particular case"; recovery for injury from exposure to radioactive material denied though no benefits are available); Monaco v. United States, 661 F.2d 129 (9th Cir.1981) (family members injured through genetic injury to serviceman; no benefits, but no recovery).

14. See, e.g., Schoemer v. United States, 59 F.3d 26 (5th Cir.1995).

15. See § 266 below.

16. Apparently as a subsidiary argument, the Court suggested that soldiers ought to be subjected to a uniform law, rather than to the differing laws of various states provided for in the FTCA and implied that it would be unfair to soldiers to hold otherwise, since their assignment to bases in one state or another was outside their control. On this aspect of the argument, Justice Scalia commented in a dissent: "The unfairness to servicemen of geographically varied recovery is, to speak bluntly, an absurd justification, given that, as we have pointed out in another context, nonuniform recovery cannot possibly be worse than (what Feres provides) uniform nonrecovery." United States v. Johnson, 481 U.S. 681, 696, 107 S.Ct. 2063, 2072, 95 L.Ed.2d 648 (1987) (Scalia, J., dissenting).

as an entirely different idea: the courts must not adjudicate tort claims because to do so "might" interfere with military discipline.[17] Although the military discipline rationale has some affinity with the discretionary immunity,[18] the *Feres* rule it is intended to support is far, far broader, because the rule excludes liability for all injuries incident to service whether command or discretionary decisions are involved or not.[19]

Extending the Feres Rule under a Military Discipline Rationale

Including off-duty service members. Under the military discipline rationale, the *Feres* rule has been extended. Although the rule does not ordinarily bar claims of service members who are injured while they are on furlough,[20] the Supreme Court ruled out a claim for death of a furloughed soldier who was kidnaped and murdered by another service man, allegedly because the army failed to control the killer, whose propensity for violence was known. To permit such a suit, the Court thought, would implicate military discipline in the sense that commanding officers would have to defend their decisions to a civilian court.[21] The *Feres* incident-to-service rule was thus subordinated to the concern over military discipline,[22] which in turn has become a concern to avoid judicial intrusion on decisions of the armed services.[23]

Including claims based on civilian negligence. The Court also expanded its concept of military discipline. In *United States v. Johnson,*[24] a U.S. Coast Guard pilot died in a crash allegedly caused by the negligence of a civilian FAA controller. Although the plaintiff did not charge negligence against any branch of the armed forces, Justice Powell argued that military discipline included "duty and loyalty to one's service and to one's country." He thought that suits by service members against the government for negligence in any branch "could undermine the commitment essential to effective service and thus have the potential to disrupt military discipline in the broadest sense of the word." The court has also held that whether the particular suit would undermine discipline was irrelevant. If injury was incident to service, no suit would be permitted.[25]

17. United States v. Brown, 348 U.S. 110, 75 S.Ct. 141, 99 L.Ed. 139 (1954); United States v. Muniz, 374 U.S. 150, 83 S.Ct. 1850, 10 L.Ed.2d 805 (1963) ("Feres seems best explained" by the discipline rationale); Stencel Aero Eng'g Corp. v. United States, 431 U.S. 666, 97 S.Ct. 2054, 52 L.Ed.2d 665 (1977); United States v. Shearer, 473 U.S. 52, 105 S.Ct. 3039, 87 L.Ed.2d 38 (1985).

18. See Chappell v. Wallace, 462 U.S. 296, 302, 103 S.Ct. 2362, 2366, 76 L.Ed.2d 586 (1983) ("complex, subtle, and professional decisions ... are essentially professional military judgments").

19. See United States v. Stanley, supra n. 9. Thus for example, an ordinary case of medical malpractice, such as negligent prenatal care for a soldier, does not usually invoke the discretionary immunity but does invoke the *Feres* immunity.

20. Brooks v. United States, 337 U.S. 49, 69 S.Ct. 918, 93 L.Ed. 1200 (1949).

21. United States v. Shearer, 473 U.S. 52, 58, 105 S.Ct. 3039, 3043, 87 L.Ed.2d 38 (1985).

22. However, the Court later, without explaining *Shearer*, insisted that incident-to-service remained the test and that the military status of the plaintiff, not the tortfeasor, was the critical issue. United States v. Johnson, 481 U.S. 681, 687, 107 S.Ct. 2063, 2067, 95 L.Ed.2d 648 (1987).

23. See n. 25, below.

24. United States v. Johnson, 481 U.S. 681, 107 S.Ct. 2063, 95 L.Ed.2d 648 (1987).

25. See United States v. Stanley, 483 U.S. 669, 682–83, 107 S.Ct. 3054, 3063, 97 L.Ed.2d 550 (1987) (a civil rights claim subject to *Feres* rules; held, judicial inquiry

§ 264. Injuries "In Service" under the Feres Rule

Injury after discharge, or during furloughs. The *Feres* rule bars claims by members of the armed services, including reservists on active duty,[1] but only those claims that arise incident to service. If government negligence occurs when the plaintiff has no active connection with the military, the *Feres* rule does not protect the government against liability. A soldier on furlough struck by a jeep on a civilian highway,[2] an air force sergeant on a weekend pass injured when an air force plane crashed into his house,[3] a discharged veteran who is given negligent treatment at a VA hospital[4]—none has sustained injury incident to service. Accordingly, each may proceed with suit. As already noted,[5] however, the Supreme Court in *United States v. Shearer*[6] applied *Feres* to bar a claim by a furloughed service member where the negligence charged was command negligence and the Court considered military discipline peculiarly implicated.

Military negligence both before and after discharge. In a few cases plaintiffs have been able to segregate negligence that occurred during their active service from later negligence that occurred after discharge. In these cases, the government causes latent harm to one on active service, by exposure to radioactive materials, for example. If the government does not discover the danger until after discharge, its negligence in failing to warn or take other appropriate steps to minimize the harm can be viewed as negligence occurring entirely after discharge. In such a case, *Feres* would not bar recovery.[7] On the other hand, if government negligence occurs during the plaintiff's period of service, the mere fact that the injury does not occur until after discharge does not assist the plaintiff.[8]

On active service but off duty. Courts have usually thought that a service member injured while on active duty is barred by *Feres* even if she is in a sense "off duty" at the moment of injury.[9] Nevertheless,

into extent of disruption of discipline would itself be too intrusive; no suit permissible for human experiments on unknowing members of the service, even if chain of command was not implicated).

§ 264

1. Jackson v. United States, 110 F.3d 1484 (9th Cir.1997).

2. Brooks v. United States, 337 U.S. 49, 69 S.Ct. 918, 93 L.Ed. 1200 (1949).

3. Snyder v. United States, 118 F.Supp. 585 (D.Md.1953), judgment reinstated, 350 U.S. 906, 76 S.Ct. 191, 100 L.Ed. 796 (1955); cf. Taber v. Maine, 67 F.3d 1029 (2d Cir.1995) (Seabee on weekend liberty).

4. United States v. Brown, 348 U.S. 110, 75 S.Ct. 141, 99 L.Ed. 139 (1954).

5. See § 263, supra.

6. United States v. Shearer, 473 U.S. 52, 105 S.Ct. 3039, 87 L.Ed.2d 38 (1985).

7. Cole v. United States, 755 F.2d 873 (11th Cir.1985); Molsbergen v. United States, 757 F.2d 1016 (9th Cir.1985). See M.M.H. v. United States, 966 F.2d 285 (7th Cir.1992) (army negligently told plaintiff she had AIDS, discovered error after discharge but failed to disclose its error; claim held actionable).

8. Lombard v. United States, 690 F.2d 215, 69 A.L.R.Fed. 921, 223 U.S.App.D.C. 102 (D.C.Cir.1982) (act of "failing to warn" of potential subsequent harm to children began during service); Monaco v. United States, 661 F.2d 129 (9th Cir.1981) (service exposure to atomic radiation caused cancer that did not occur until after discharge; *Feres* barred claim).

9. Skees v. United States, 107 F.3d 421 (6th Cir.1997) (suicide by off-duty member of the service, allegedly as a result of medical negligence, is incident to service); Jones

courts may be reluctant to extend the *Feres* rule to bar a claim by an off-duty service member who is not involved in any military errand, and is injured off the base.[10]

Considering factors. In *Dreier v. United States,*[11] an enlisted man who had the afternoon off went to his home in Tacoma, then to a recreational area on base for sunbathing and drinking. He was killed there, allegedly as the result of army negligence in failing to make the premises reasonably safe or to warn. The Ninth Circuit, concluding that the injury was not incident to service, felt free to weigh a number of factors in making that determination. The place of the injury, the duty status of the service member, the non-tort benefits that might be payable, and the nature of the plaintiff's activities at the time were all relevant, as were analogous cases.

Because these factors were considered to decide the incident to service issue, which in turn was used to determine whether liability would implicate military discipline and other interests,[12] such an approach arguably conflicts with Supreme Court decisions[13] that oppose any effort to weigh the interference with military discipline on a case by case basis. Yet, the incident to service issue must be determined somehow, and the Ninth Circuit is not alone is resorting to a weighing of various factors. Most commonly, however, that weighing results in the conclusion that the *Feres* rule applied to bar the claim.[14]

Broad interpretation of incident to service test. In any event, courts have usually interpreted "incident to service" quite broadly.[15] Although peacetime medical treatment does not seem particularly military, the

v. United States, 112 F.3d 299 (7th Cir. 1997) (serviceman trying out for Military Olympics allegedly injured by medical negligence; injury was incident to service). Some courts reach this result by weighing various factors. Post-service negligence in treating an in-service injury has also been held subject to the *Feres* bar. Jackson v. United States, 110 F.3d 1484 (9th Cir.1997). The rule was otherwise for a plaintiff injured in service, then negligently treated after discharge. United States v. Brown, 348 U.S. 110, 75 S.Ct. 141, 99 L.Ed. 139 (1954), a case not discussed in Jackson.

10. See Taber v. Maine, 67 F.3d 1029 (2d Cir.1995).

11. Dreier v. United States, 106 F.3d 844 (9th Cir.1996).

12. 106 F.3d at 849. Weighing the impact on military discipline was also done explicitly. Id. at 953.

13. United States v. Stanley, 483 U.S. 669, 682–83, 107 S.Ct. 3054, 3063, 97 L.Ed.2d 550 (1987); cf. United States v. Johnson, 481 U.S. 681, 107 S.Ct. 2063, 95 L.Ed.2d 648 (1987) (non-military identity of tortfeasor not to be considered a factor, at least in the case before the court). *Stanley* was a civil rights case, not an FTCA case, so arguably it does not apply. However, the Court carried the *Feres* rule over to the civil rights claim and applied it there. If the factor or balancing approach is in tension with these cases, it may have been invited by Chief Justice Burger's declaration in United States v. Shearer, 473 U.S. 52, 57, 105 S.Ct. 3039, 3043, 87 L.Ed.2d 38 (1985) that "The Feres doctrine cannot be reduced to a few bright-line rules," and his seeming willingness to attach great weight to military discipline concerns.

14. See Schoemer v. United States, 59 F.3d 26 (5th Cir.1995) (emphasizing location where injury occurred and the service member's activities at the time; also drawing some detailed distinctions).

15. See Major v. United States, 835 F.2d 641, 644–45 (6th Cir.1987) ("the Court has embarked on a course dedicated to broadening the Feres doctrine to encompass, at a minimum, all injuries suffered by military personnel that are even remotely related to the individual's status as a member of the military.... ").

service member who is injured or killed by military surgery[16] or misdiagnosis[17] or negligent prenatal care[18] is barred by *Feres*. So is one who dies in a barracks fire although the connection to military discipline is only that the dead soldier was sleeping in assigned quarters.[19] An enlisted woman who suffers sexual harassment has no claim because such harassment is incident to service.[20] A recruit who dies because a brutal "trainer" holds his head under water dies incident to service.[21] Enlisted men who are victims of damaging human experimentation by the armed forces are suffering "incident to service" and are *Feres* barred,[22] as are obedient soldiers who suffer genetic damage because they were deliberately exposed to dangerous doses of radioactivity.[23]

§ 265. Servicemember's Family under Feres

Derivative claims. A survivor's claim for wrongful death of a service member killed incident to service is treated as a derivative claim and stands on no better ground than a direct claim by the service member had she lived.[1] Similarly, a spouse's loss of consortium claim based upon a service member's injury incident to service is barred along with the main claim for the injury itself.[2] The same is true if the claim is for emotional injury to the spouse; that, too, has its genesis in the service-connected injury.[3]

Potentially independent claims of family members. On the other hand, family members may conceivably have independent claims of their own. When dependents of service members are directly injured, as by negligent medical treatment, *Feres* does not bar their claims and is often not even mentioned in the decisions.[4]

When a service member is negligently exposed to the AIDS virus, to radiation, or to chemical toxins, harm may result to family members, either because the virus or toxin is spread to them or because alteration of the service member's genetic structure results in harm in the next generation. If common law rules would recognize liability for a foreseeable genetic harm or spread of disease-causing agents, it would seem that family members would have an independent action in no way based on harm to the service member and not derived from the service member's

16. Feres v. United States, 340 U.S. 135, 71 S.Ct. 153, 95 L.Ed. 152 (1950).

17. Cutshall v. United States, 75 F.3d 426 (8th Cir.1996).

18. Del Rio v. United States, 833 F.2d 282 (11th Cir.1987).

19. See Feres v. United States, 340 U.S. 135, 71 S.Ct. 153, 95 L.Ed. 152 (1950) (death in a barracks fire).

20. Stubbs v. United States, 744 F.2d 58 (8th Cir.1984).

21. Kitowski v. United States, 931 F.2d 1526 (11th Cir.1991).

22. United States v. Stanley, 483 U.S. 669, 107 S.Ct. 3054, 97 L.Ed.2d 550 (1987).

23. See Hinkie v. United States, 715 F.2d 96 (3d Cir.1983).

§ 265

1. *Feres* itself, supra § 263, was a wrongful death claim.

2. E.g., Skees v. United States, 107 F.3d 421 (6th Cir.1997).

3. Lombard v. United States, 223 U.S.App.D.C. 102, 690 F.2d 215, 69 A.L.R.Red. 921 (D.C. Cir. 1982).

4. E.g., Williams v. United States, 435 F.2d 804 (1st Cir.1970); see 1 Lester S. Jayson and Robert C. Longstreth, Handling Federal Tort Claims § 5A.09.

rights. Unlike the claim for loss of consortium, the family member's claim for genetic harm would not require proof of injury to the service member.

However, a number of cases have held that if the service member was exposed incident to service, the family member who suffers injury through the gene damage to the parent has no claim, often on the argument that military discipline would be disrupted even though the claim does not depend upon injury to the service member.[5] In the analogous case of medical malpractice in pre-natal care of a military mother, a little authority has held that the mother is *Feres*-barred but that the child is not.[6] But even on those facts the injured child was denied recovery in the Fifth Circuit.[7]

§ 266. Feres: Criticism and Reform

Substantive criticism. Some in-service injuries are arguably remedied by benefits provided by the government, much as workers' compensation may provide the exclusive remedy for employers' torts. Nevertheless, criticisms of the results say the *Feres* rules goes too far by foreclosing the possibility of appropriate deterrence of wrongdoing. Some criticisms have implicitly accepted *Feres* for some cases but propose exceptions to the *Feres* doctrine for particular kinds of torts. One proposal is to abolish *Feres* when intentional or constitutional torts are asserted;[1] another is to do so in medical malpractice cases, since medical malpractice does not involve a military decision but a professional one;[2] still another would abolish *Feres* in sexual harassment claims.[3] Some critics have pointed especially to decisions[4] providing tort immunity to military actors carrying out human experiments without informed consent.[5] More broadly, *Feres* forecloses all possibility of deterrence under

5. Lombard v. United States, 223 U.S.App.D.C. 102, 690 F.2d 215, 69 A.L.R.Fed. 921 (D.C. Cir. 1982); Hinkie v. United States, 715 F.2d 96 (3d Cir.1983) (exposure to radioactivity); Mondelli v. United States, 711 F.2d 567 (3d Cir., 1983) (genetic damage by service member's exposure to nuclear explosion causing cancer to child); Monaco v. United States, 661 F.2d 129 (9th Cir.1981); Minns v. United States, 974 F.Supp. 500 (D.Md.1997) (gulf war toxins, family members have no claim). Contrast the result in the analogous case of a civilian employee whose on-the-job injury causes harm to the child she is carrying. Snyder v. Michael's Stores, Inc., 16 Cal.4th 991, 945 P.2d 781, 68 Cal.Rptr.2d 476 (Cal. 1997) (although mother is limited to the workers' compensation remedy, the child suing for her own injury is not).

6. Romero v. United States, 954 F.2d 223 (4th Cir.1992); Del Rio v. United States, 833 F.2d 282 (11th Cir.1987).

7. Scales v. United States, 685 F.2d 970 (5th Cir.1982).

§ 266

1. See David Saul Schwartz, Note, Making Intramilitary Tort Laws More Civil: A Proposed Reform of the Feres Doctrine, 95 Yale L.J. 992 (1986) (proposing liability for intentional and constitutional torts).

2. Keith B. Sieczkowski, Comment, Service Member Recovery for Military Medical Malpractice under the Federal Tort Claims Act: A Judicial Response, 19 St. Mary's L.J. 203 (1987); see also William Brook Lafferty, Comment, The Persian Gulf War Syndrome: Rethinking Government Tort Liability, 25 Stetson L. Rev. 137 (1995).

3. Testimony of Nancy Duff Campbell, House of Representatives Armed Services Committee, 1994 WL 223316 (March 9, 1994).

4. United States v. Stanley, 483 U.S. 669, 107 S.Ct. 3054, 97 L.Ed.2d 550 (1987).

5. See Jonathan P. Tomes, Feres to Chappell to Stanley: Three Strikes and Servicemembers Are Out, 25 U. Rich. L. Rev. 93

neutrally administered rules.[6]

Process criticism. A different line of criticism has pointed out flaws in *Feres'* original reasoning[7] and inconsistencies generated in the Court's development of it,[8] all of which have made *Feres* a "troubled doctrine" and difficult to apply. More than one Court of Appeals has expressed frustration with the development of the doctrine and the virtual impossibility of applying it consistently and fairly.[9] Apart from the practical difficulties, it has been argued that *Feres* is an abdication of the Court's important role in maintaining the traditional checks and balances.[10]

Judge Calabresi's rationalization. Although legislative reform has so far gone nowhere, it may be possible to make the existing doctrine more workable and more rational. In *Taber v. Maine,*[11] Judge Calabresi suggested that most cases can be explained and adjudicated on the ground that alternate compensation systems provide the exclusive remedy, as they do under workers' compensation statutes. But in his view, alternate compensation provided by the military is the exclusive remedy only when injury is truly within the scope of employment. If injury occurs outside of employment duties—say on furlough—alternate compensation may still be payable, but in that case it is not analogous to workers' compensation benefits. Instead it is analogous to an employer-provided fringe benefit, which does not bar the tort claim but only credits the employer for payments actually made.

By focusing on scope of employment, courts would bar all tort claims analogous to on-the-job injuries, just as such tort claims would be barred under workers' compensation statutes in civilian life. It is unnecessary in such cases to allude to military discipline. Similarly, when the injured servicemember is *not* acting in the scope of employment when injury occurs, military discipline is not ordinarily involved at all.

Judge Calabresi recognized, however, that in some cases the military discipline concern arises because of the connection between the tortfeasor and the military, not because of the plaintiff's connection. That might be so, for example, where the claim is based on the military's failure to control a dangerous servicemember. Yet suppose that the military negligently allowed a known dangerous servicemember to take assault rifles and kill a dozen civilians and one marine on furlough in a civilian restaurant. Military discipline concerns do not counsel a rule that bars recovery by the marine, because those identical concerns with

(1990); cf. Claire Alida Milner, Comment, Gulf War Guinea Pigs: Is Informed Consent Optional During War?, 13 J. Contemp. Health L. & Pol'y 199 (1996); Elliott J. Schuchardt, Walking a Thin Line: Distinguishing Between Research and Medical Practice During Operation Desert Storm, 26 Colum. J.L. & Soc. Probs. 77 (1992).

6. See Jonathan P. Tomes, supra n. 5.

7. See United States v. Johnson, 481 U.S. 681, 107 S.Ct. 2063, 95 L.Ed.2d 648 (1987) (Scalia, J., dissenting).

8. See § 263, supra.

9. E.g., Taber v. Maine, 67 F.3d 1029 (2d Cir.1995); McAllister v. United States, 942 F.2d 1473 (9th Cir.1991).

10. Barry Kellman, Judicial Abdication of Military Tort Accountability: But Who Is To Guard the Guards Themselves, 1989 Duke L.J. 1597 (1989).

11. Taber v. Maine, 67 F.3d 1029 (2d Cir.1995).

the identical act do not bar suits by the civilians or their estates.[12] The result of this reasoning is that the focus becomes much like the focus in civilian on-the-job injuries. If the injury is on the job, the government benefits analogous to workers' compensation form the exclusive remedy. If injury is not suffered incident to service—within the scope of employment, as it were—the government should be liable for its negligence.

§ 267. Other Exceptions to FTCA Liability

Specific conduct excepted. Besides the very broad discretionary immunity, the statute creates a number of very specific exceptions to governmental liability. For example, no claim will be recognized for negligent transmission or loss of mail,[1] tax assessments or collections,[2] or claims arising in foreign countries.[3] A number of others are in the statutory list.

Specific torts excepted. One group of exceptions deals with specific torts. Subject to some qualification, § 2680(h) exempts the government from liability if the claim "arises out of" (1) assault, (2) battery, (3) false imprisonment and false arrest, (4) malicious prosecution, (5) abuse of process, (6) libel and slander, (7) misrepresentation and deceit, and (8) interference with contract rights.[4]

Scope of the exceptions. Sometimes writers refer to this statutory list as creating an intentional tort exception, but that is inaccurate, for not all intentional torts are named in the list and some torts named are not necessarily based upon intent. The list notably omits such traditional intentional torts as trespass to land[5] and conversion of personal property,[6] and such newer torts as intentional infliction of emotional distress[7] and privacy.[8] Consequently, the statute does not preclude suit for those torts unless the conduct relied upon to establish them amounts to one of the excepted torts or falls within another area of retained immunity. For

12. Cf. Sheridan v. United States, 487 U.S. 392, 108 S.Ct. 2449, 101 L.Ed.2d 352 (1988) (potential liability when servicemember was negligently permitted to shoot civilian).

§ 267

1. 28 U.S.C.A. § 2680 (b).

2. 28 U.S.C.A. § 2680 (c). Other statutes, however, regulate suits to recover overpayment of taxes.

3. 28 U.S.C.A. § 2680 (k).

4. 28 U.S.C.A. § 2680 (h).

5. See Hatahley v. United States, 351 U.S. 173, 76 S.Ct. 745, 100 L.Ed. 1065 (1956); United States v. Gaidys, 194 F.2d 762 (10th Cir.1952).

6. See CHoPP Computer Corporation, Inc. v. United States, 5 F.3d 1344 (9th Cir.1993). The Supreme Court has held that the government will not be strictly liable under the FTCA. Laird v. Nelms, 406 U.S. 797, 92 S.Ct. 1899, 32 L.Ed.2d 499 (1972) (damage from sonic boom). Liability in some conversion cases might be viewed as a form of strict liability. That is not what is usually meant by the term, and in any event, converters differ from those who merely cause damage in that they usually obtain the converted item. There is thus an element of unjust enrichment in many conversions. It is unlikely that the comparison to strict liability will often be accurate.

7. See Truman v. United States, 26 F.3d 592 (5th Cir.1994) (civilian privately employed but working on a military base could sue for emotional distress resulting from sexual harassment); Sheehan v. United States, 896 F.2d 1168, 107 A.L.R.Fed 297 (9th Cir. 1990) (similar, federal employee not covered by federal compensation act).

8. Birnbaum v. United States, 588 F.2d 319, 47 A.L.R. Fed. 259 (2d Cir. 1978).

example, a plaintiff may recover for intentional infliction of emotional distress accomplished by way of sexual harassment if the harassment was carried out without a bodily touching that would count as a battery. But the battery exception will bar her claim if it is based on a bodily touching.[9] In the same way, if the facts the plaintiff must rely upon amount to a false imprisonment, the plaintiff is barred, even though the facts also show an invasion of privacy or an intentional infliction of emotional harm.[10]

Exceptions to the exceptions. The main statutory qualification is that, after all, the government is liable for assault, battery, false imprisonment, false arrest, abuse of process, or malicious prosecution where the tort is committed by investigative or law enforcement officers of the United States. So a battery, say, would be actionable against the government if it were committed by an officer who is "empowered by law to execute searches, to seize evidence, or to make arrests for violations of Federal law."[11] Separate statutes have also provided that military and VA medical batteries—operations without consent—remain actionable.[12] A battery by other federal employees, on the other hand, is not ordinarily actionable.

Negligently permitting a battery by non-employees. In one group of cases, the plaintiff is injured by a battery that the government could have prevented by the exercise of reasonable care. For instance, prison authorities may be negligent in failing to prevent a group of prisoners from beating another prisoner. The Supreme Court has recognized liability in such a case.[13] As later explained, the statutory exceptions to liability could apply only if there were a basis for liability in the first place. Because the United States would not be liable for batteries of non-employees (or off-duty employees), the exception applies only to batteries committed by employees of the government acting within the scope of employment.[14] Batteries by prisoners or off-duty service members are not within the exception. So if the plaintiff can prove negligence of the government in permitting or risking a battery by non-employees or off-duty employees, the battery exception is irrelevant and the claim may proceed as a simple negligence claim.

Negligently permitting a battery by federal employees. That leaves a major group of cases in which the government negligently permits a battery by federal employees. For instance, the government may negligently hire or supervise a dangerous child molester or a violent worker. If the worker molests children or attacks citizens with acid, the plaintiff's claim is based on the government's negligence. Nevertheless, the

9. Truman v. United States, 26 F.3d 592 (5th Cir.1994).

10. Metz v. United States, 788 F.2d 1528 (11th Cir.1986).

11. 28 U.S.C.A. § 2680(h).

12. 10 U.S.C.A. § 1089(e) (armed forces); 38 U.S.C.A. § 7316 (Veterans' Administration); see Franklin v. United States, 992 F.2d 1492 (10th Cir.1993) (explaining purpose, technical issues, and authorities).

13. United States v. Muniz, 374 U.S. 150, 83 S.Ct. 1850, 10 L.Ed.2d 805 (1963).

14. Sheridan v. United States, 487 U.S. 392, 108 S.Ct. 2449, 101 L.Ed.2d 352 (1988).

plaintiff must ultimately prove the battery in order to show damages. For this reason, some courts have held that the battery exception applies to bar the plaintiff's claims.[15] However, the Ninth Circuit has held that the exception does not relieve the government when its negligence is a proximate cause of a battery, in that case a kidnaping and rape of children by a person hired by the government to teach them.[16] So far, the Supreme Court has not yet determined whether the government could be liable for negligently fostering employee batteries.[17]

Misrepresentation. When the misrepresentation exception is the issue, however, the Supreme Court appears to hold that a claim "arises out of" one of the excepted torts if the underlying facts would support a claim for that tort. In that event, the claim is barred, even if the underlying facts also support some claim that is not excepted. In one case, the government's negligent inspection of a house led it to appraise its value too highly. That in turn led the buyers, relying on the appraisal, to pay too much for the house. The buyers formulated their claim against the government as a claim for negligent inspection. But it would not suffice for the buyers to prove negligent inspection; they would also need to show the misrepresentation and their reliance on it. Consequently, the buyers' case arose out of a misrepresentation and was barred by the exception.[18] Presumably, however, misrepresentation deals only with economic torts; the automobile driver who gives a wrong signal misrepresents his intentions, but it is most unlikely that the statute intended to cover misrepresentations that create physical risks and harms.[19]

SUBTOPIC 3. IMMUNITIES AND LIABILITIES OF STATE AND LOCAL ENTITIES

§ 268. State Sovereign Immunity and Its Waiver

Traditional immunity. Subject to limits imposed by the federal constitution, the American states are sovereigns. The states and their

15. See Johnson v. United States, 788 F.2d 845 (2d Cir.1986) (letter carrier, molestation); Miele v. United States, 800 F.2d 50 (2d Cir.1986); Satterfield v. United States, 788 F.2d 395 (6th Cir.1986) (beating by serviceman).

16. Bennett v. United States, 803 F.2d 1502 (9th Cir.1986). Cf. Gess v. United States, 952 F.Supp. 1529 (M.D.Ala.1996) (trier found that 12 infants in a government hospital were poisoned by a government employee, but battery exception did not bar claim because the defendant had a duty to use care to protect the infants regardless of the poisoner's employment status).

17. A plurality in United States v. Shearer, 473 U.S. 52, 55, 105 S.Ct. 3039, 3041, 87 L.Ed.2d 38 (1985), supported the view that antecedent negligence of the government resulting in a battery would not be actionable. But Sheridan v. United States, 487 U.S. 392, 108 S.Ct. 2449, 101 L.Ed.2d 352 (1988), made a more detailed analysis and left the question open.

18. United States v. Neustadt, 366 U.S. 696, 81 S.Ct. 1294, 6 L.Ed.2d 614 (1961). If the negligent inspection does not lead to a misrepresentation upon which the plaintiff must rely, but instead leads the government to permit defective construction, the plaintiff would have a claim. Block v. Neal, 460 U.S. 289, 103 S.Ct. 1089, 75 L.Ed.2d 67 (1983).

19. See Johnson v. State, 69 Cal.2d 782, 447 P.2d 352, 73 Cal.Rptr. 240 (1968) (under a state statute's misrepresentation exception).

departments and agencies are constitutionally obliged to pay for property taken for public purposes.[1] Otherwise, the state public entities can claim the traditional sovereign immunity from suit. States also enjoy a kind of jurisdictional immunity, because under the Eleventh Amendment to the United States Constitution they ordinarily cannot be sued for damages in federal court.[2] The immunity of the states and their agencies as sovereigns differs from the immunity enjoyed by state officers and that enjoyed by purely local governments like municipalities. Those immunities are considered in later sections.

Abolition of the blanket immunity. Almost all states have now enacted tort claims statutes waiving the blanket common law immunity of the state and its agencies. Besides these general statutes, other statutes may affect immunities in particular cases, and of course both kinds of statutes must be consulted for details. As a matter of structure, about thirty states abolish the tort immunity generally, but retain it in specified circumstances.[3] A second group works in reverse, retaining the immunity generally, but abolishing it for a list of cases in which liability is permitted.[4] In several states, a tort claim against the state must be presented to an administrative body instead of to a court.[5] Some states set up a separate court of claims for hearing tort claims against the state.[6] About three states appear to retain a very broad sovereign immunity.[7]

§ 268

1. See Chicago, Burlington & Quincy R.R. Co. v. Chicago, 166 U.S. 226, 17 S.Ct. 581, 41 L.Ed. 979 (1897).

2. See Hans v. Louisiana, 134 U.S. 1, 10 S.Ct. 504, 33 L.Ed. 842 (1890). Federal courts may issue injunctions against state officials but may not use such injunctions to reach the state's treasury for past obligations. See Edelman v. Jordan, 415 U.S. 651, 94 S.Ct. 1347, 39 L.Ed.2d 662 (1974). States may also be sued in federal court under the Fourteenth Amendment where Congress has so provided. See Quern v. Jordan, 440 U.S. 332, 99 S.Ct. 1139, 59 L.Ed.2d 358 (1979).

3. E.g., ALASKA STATS. § 09.50.250; GA. CODE § 50–21–23.

4. E.g., COLO. REV. STATS. ANN. § 24–10–106; TEX. CIV. PRAC. & REM. CODE § 101.021. This form of immunity waiver probably operates to impose governmental responsibility in fewer cases. For example, it may automatically leave all common law immunity-related doctrines, such as the public duty doctrine, standing as a bar. See Ezell v. Cockrell, 902 S.W.2d 394 (Tenn.1995).

5. ARK. CODE ANN. § 19–10–204; KY. REV. STAT. § 44.073. In Connecticut, the claimant must obtain permission of a commissioners to file suit. See CONN. GEN. STAT. § 4–160. In North Carolina, the Industrial Commission, an administrative agency, is constituted a court for the purpose of hearing claims against the state. N.C. GEN. STAT. § 143–291. Some states set up a system in which liability may be imposed to the extent that liability insurance coverage protects the entity.

6. E.g., ILCS 505/8. In Illinois, this has led to jurisdictional disputes.

7. Alabama, South Dakota, and Wisconsin. See ALA. CONST. ART I, § 14 (the state "shall never be made a defendant in any court of law or equity"); S.D. COD. L. § 21–32–16 (but liability insurance coverage waives immunity); see e.g., Anderson v. City of Milwaukee, 208 Wis.2d 18, 559 N.W.2d 563 (1997) (explaining sovereign, governmental, and discretionary immunities). In the Wisconsin system, the immunity may be indirectly circumvented when the tortious state officer is held liable, for in that case the state may indemnify the officer and pay the costs of defending him. WIS. STAT. ANN. § 895.104. North Dakota judicially abolished immunity in Bulman v. Hulstrand Construction Co., Inc., 521 N.W.2d 632 (N.D.1994), but subsequent legislative activity may affect that decision.

Cases for liability. States in the second group list specific instances in which liability is permitted. They usually include motor vehicle accidents and injuries on negligently maintained state property, dangerous roads and highways,[8] but the list may include other instances, such as medical malpractice in state schools or hospitals.[9]

Cases for no-liability—exceptions to the waiver of immunity. In the largest group of states, the state waives immunity generally, but retains it or otherwise excludes liability in a number of specified instances. Many of these statutes are similar to the Federal Tort Claims Act in providing for liability like that of a private person in similar circumstances,[10] then carving out an immunity for discretionary decisions[11] together with a number of rather specific exclusions from liability. Some statutes are phrased to waive immunity only for cases of personal injury, property damage, or death, thus impliedly retaining the immunity for economic and dignitary torts that do not fall in one of these categories.[12] Strict liability is routinely excluded.[13]

Not infrequently, the pattern of retained immunity or excluded liability is much like that in the FTCA. For instance, statutes may exclude liability for intentional torts like assault, battery, and false imprisonment[14] and for claims resulting from tax assessment or collection.[15] No summary can capture all the exceptions, some of which are quite narrow. Several states, for example, exempt the state from liability for certain injuries resulting from snow and ice conditions.[16] Some specific immunities may be waived to the extent that the public entity is covered by liability insurance.[17]

Very substantial areas of immunity remain even under the most liberal statutes. But even that is not the whole picture. In some states, the plaintiff whose claim against the state is defeated by immunity may nevertheless be able to recover against the tortious officer. The state may then indirectly pay by indemnifying the officer and providing for the costs of his defense.[18]

Procedural and remedial limitations. Statutes almost always impose some special procedural rules for claims against the state, for example, a

8. See, e.g., 14 Me. Rev. Stats. Ann. § 8104–A; Mich. Comp. L. Ann. § 691.1407; Utah Code Ann. §§ 63–30–6; Wyo. Stats. § 1–39–104.

9. See Pa. Consol. Stats. Ann. § 8522; Tenn. Code Ann. § 9–8–307 (perhaps the most detailed list).

10. E.g., Kan. Stat. Ann. § 75–6103; Mass. Gen. L. Ann. ch. 158, § 2.

11. E.g., Iowa Code Ann. § 669.14; Mass. Gen. L. Ann. ch. 258, § 10; Nev. Rev. Stats. § 41.032. New Jersey is a little more detailed on this. N.J. Stats. Ann. § 59:2–3. Several states do not rely upon the discretionary immunity concept, substituting traditional tort rules about duty limitations instead. See N.M. Stats. Ann. § 41–4–2 B.

12. E.g., Fla. Stat. Ann. § 768.28 (1) (personal injury, property damage, death); Texas Civ. Prac. & Rem. Code § 101.021 (1).

13. E.g., Colo. Rev. Stats. Ann. § 24–10–106.5. That may be the implication of statutes requiring a negligence or wrongful act, too. E.g., Idaho Code § 6–903.

14. E.g., Idaho Code § 6–904; Hawai'i Rev. Code § 662–15.

15. E.g., Minn. Stat. Ann. § 3.736; Ore. Rev. Stats. § 30.265.

16. E.g., 51 Okla. Stats. Ann. § 155.

17. See 12 Vt. Stats. Ann. § 5601.

18. See, §§ 273 & 278.

requirement of notice before suit. Many states cap recovery for compensatory damages[19] and punitive damages are denied altogether.[20] Very commonly, interest is not to accrue until judgment is entered.[21]

§ 269. Local Public Entity Immunity and Its Waiver

Common law rule of immunity and exceptions. Municipalities are not sovereigns. They are corporations chartered by the state. Nevertheless, a peculiar history[1] led courts to recognize a distinct municipal immunity, which followed a course of its own. Although states varied somewhat in their approach, they held that municipalities were immune to tort liability, except in cases of (1) torts committed in a proprietary rather than governmental capacity, and (2) nuisance committed by the municipality.[2] Sometimes liability was also extended to cases of (3) negligently maintained municipal property[3] and (4) negligently maintained roads, streets, and sewers.[4]

Governmental vs. proprietary. Courts conceived of the municipal government as operating in several different capacities. If it caused harm while acting in a purely governmental capacity, say in police activities,[5] it enjoyed the immunity. But the municipality had no immunity for its torts when it operated in a corporate or proprietary capacity. For example, a municipality would be subject to liability for torts inflicted in the operation of a municipal electric or water utility.[6]

Tests of governmental or proprietary. Courts do not agree on a test for determining whether an activity is proprietary. Courts have variously held that an activity is or tends to be proprietary (1) if it is carried on for

19. Fla. Stat. Ann. § 768.28 (5) ($100,000 per person); Kan. Stat. Ann. § 75–6105 ($500,000); 14 Me. Rev. Stats. Ann. § 8105 ($300,000); Pa. Consol. Stat. Ann. § 8528 ($250,000 per person).

20. E.g., Cal. Gov. Code § 818; Fla. Stat. Ann. § 768.28 (5); Hawai'i Rev. Stats. § 662–2.

21. E.g., Mass. Gen. L. Ann. ch. 158, § 2.

§ 269

1. See Borchard, Government Liability in Tort, 34 Yale L. J. 129, 132–133 (1924). The immunity originated with Russell v. Men of Devon, 2 Term. Rep. 667, 100 Eng. Rep. 359 (1798), where there was no municipal entity at all and no treasure from which to pay the claim, which, in effect, was against the population as individuals.

2. Murphy v. Town of Chatham, 41 Mass.App.Ct. 821, 676 N.E.2d 473 (1996) (no common law nuisance immunity, so tort claims act limitations did not apply to nuisance claims); Bible Baptist Church v. City of Cleburne, 848 S.W.2d 826 (Tex.App. 1993) (some nuisances not immune).

3. The result was derived from the governmental-proprietary distinction in some cases. E.g., Cooper v. City of Reading, 392 Pa. 452, 140 A.2d 792 (1958). When the city's property is allegedly defective, courts invoke the ordinary tort rules, for example those excluding duties to trespassers. See, e.g., Brindamour v. City of Warwick, 697 A.2d 1075 (R.I.1997) (plaintiff a trespasser, no duty to light her way on public property).

4. Kizer v. City of Raleigh, 121 N.C.App. 526, 466 S.E.2d 336 (1996) (storm sewer); Woods v. Town of Marion, 245 Va. 44, 425 S.E.2d 487 (1993) (ice on street).

5. See § 272 below.

6. E.g., Ranells v. City of Cleveland, 41 Ohio St.2d 1, 321 N.E.2d 885 (1975) (escape of chlorine gas in a water department operation was proprietary, no immunity); Hill v. City of Urbana, 79 Ohio St.3d 130, 679 N.E.2d 1109 (1997) (similar rule after statutory scheme enacted).

profit,[7] (2) if a fee is paid,[8] (3) if the activity relates to public service, whether or not a fee is paid,[9] (4) if the city is under no duty to carry it out,[10] or (5) if the activity is historically one carried out by private enterprise.[11]

Application of the governmental-proprietary test. The governmental-proprietary distinction can produce some surprising case outcomes. A city's operation of an automotive repair garage for its police vehicles has been considered proprietary, for example.[12] On the other hand, some courts treat public parks or swimming pools as proprietary[13] while others do not.[14]

Abrogation and statutory reshaping of immunity. In some states, the common law scheme of municipal immunity and liability remains generally intact.[15] In a great many, legislation has created a new and usually somewhat different scheme of liability and immunity.

Statutory structures. Many legislatures have replaced the blanket immunity with a list of very specific immunities[16] or with a list of instances in which public entities may be subjected to tort rules. Immunity may be waived to the extent that the public entity is covered by liability insurance.[17] Nevertheless, extensive protection may remain by way of affirmative defenses or otherwise.[18] As a matter of legislature structure, some states subject all public entities to more or less the same rules of immunity and liability, so that one statute applies both to states and other public entities such as municipal corporations. Other states treat local public entities under separate statutes.[19]

7. See Town of Brunswick v. Hyatt, 91 Md.App. 555, 605 A.2d 620 (1992) (struggling with cases that seemed to say so).

8. Schulz v. City of Brentwood, 725 S.W.2d 157 (Mo.App.1987) (city day care center).

9. See City of Atlanta v. Chambers, 205 Ga.App. 834, 424 S.E.2d 19 (1992) ("If public service is primary and profit only incidental, the City has municipal immunity").

10. E.g., Blue Fox Bar, Inc. v. City of Yankton, 424 N.W.2d 915 (S.D.1988).

11. Waters v. Biesecker, 60 N.C.App. 253, 298 S.E.2d 746 (1983) (Board's operation of alcoholic beverage store).

12. E.g., Thomas v. Hilburn, 654 So.2d 898 (Miss.1995).

13. Morgan v. City of Ruleville, 627 So.2d 275 (Miss.1993) (using a very broad definition of proprietary: "Proprietary activities are those which, while beneficial to the community and very important, are not vital to a City's functioning). (Zoo, football stadium.)" Cf. Douglas v. York, 445 P.2d 760 (Wyo.1968) (garbage dump proprietary where citizens paid fee for garbage removal; city was liable for spread of fire).

14. E.g., Town of Brunswick v. Hyatt, 91 Md.App. 555, 605 A.2d 620 (1992).

15. E.g., Ark. Code Ann. § 21–9–301 (immunity except for to the extent insured).

16. § 268, supra.

17. E.g., N.C. Gen. Stat. § 153A–435.

18. The FTCA cases, following the implication of the statutory structure, treat the discretionary immunity as jurisdictional and not merely as an affirmative defense. See § 262, supra. A number of cases applying the state-law discretionary immunity, however, treat it as an affirmative defense. See McCummings v. Hurley Medical Center, 433 Mich. 404, 446 N.W.2d 114 (1989); Thompson v. Newark Housing Authority, 108 N.J. 525, 531 A.2d 734 (1987); Creech v. South Carolina Wildlife and Marine Resources Dept., 328 S.C. 24, 491 S.E.2d 571 (S.C. 1997).

19. For example, Chapter 745 of the Illinois statutes contains separate subdivisions for states, local entities, schools, officers and a number of other immunities.

Another structural difference in approaches can be seen in the way public officers and employees are treated. In some instances, the immunity of the employee and the municipality are coextensive, so that if the employee is immune, the municipality is likewise protected.[20] In others, the employee may be exposed to liability when the municipality is not. In either case, the employee who is held liable to the plaintiff may have a right of indemnity against the municipality.[21] The effect of the indemnity is that whether the municipality is formally immune or not, it ultimately pays. becomes liable through its obligation to indemnify the individual employee.

Finally, some statutes create an entirely new scheme of liability and immunity, while others adopt one or more of the common law rules, such as the rule based upon the governmental-proprietary distinction, for particular situations.[22] The recovery of damages and prejudgment interest is limited in many states, and punitive damages barred altogether.[23]

Under any of these systems, lawyers must consult the general statutory provisions for immunity and liability and frequently must also find narrowly drawn statutes providing immunities for very particular activities such as the system for 911 emergency calls[24] or the operation of airports.[25] It is impossible to summarize all these diverse provisions, but some common patterns of liability and non-liability can be discerned. Some of these are described in the next section.

§ 270. Remaining Protections for State and Local Entities: Discretionary Decisions

Policy of the discretionary immunity. Perhaps the chief immunity or defense remaining after statutory restructuring of state and local entity liability is the immunity for decisions of discretion or basic policy.[1] Judicial and legislative decisions are easily included in this category, but so are some executive-branch decisions and action. As explained in connection with the FTCA, the idea is that social and economic policy is to be fixed by legislative and executive branches of the government, not the judiciary, and that the judicial branch must not intrude on those basic decisions.[2] In some instances, this same policy is advanced by the separate rule called the public duty doctrine.[3] The policy dictates that public entities must not be held liable for passing or failing to pass

20. E.g., IL ST CH 745 § 10/2–109 ("A local public entity is not liable for an injury resulting from an act or omission of its employee where the employee is not liable"); see Thomas v. City of Richmond, 9 Cal.4th 1154, 892 P.2d 1185, 40 Cal.Rptr.2d 442 (1995) (recognizing California's general statutory rule with limited exceptions).

21. E.g., Wiehagen v. Borough of North Braddock, 527 Pa. 517, 594 A.2d 303 (1991).

22. Ohio Rev. Code § 2744.02 (B) (3).

23. E.g., ORE. REV. STATS. § 30.270.

24. ALASKA STATS. § 29.35.133.

25. ALA. CODE § 4–4–4.

§ 270

1. Often by statute, as in e.g., KAN. STAT. ANN. § 75–6104.

2. See, e.g., Terwilliger v. Hennepin County, 561 N.W.2d 909 (Minn.1997). The federal cases on the same general rule under the Federal Tort Claims Act are discussed in § 262, supra.

3. See § 271 below.

legislation, even if that legislation is wise and would have avoided injury to the plaintiff.[4] Judicial decisions and some executive branch decisions, such as decisions about the level of security for juvenile detainees,[5] are sufficiently analogous to come within the same immunity.

Limits of the discretionary immunity. The policy behind the discretionary immunity is sound, but it has limits. To hold a public entity liable for a negligent course of conduct in the administration of programs by the executive branch is not invariably an inappropriate intrusion. Liability for negligent operation of a city bus or even of a police department does not mean that the negligent conduct is forbidden. Liability only means that if the entity chooses a dangerous course of conduct, it should pay its way, just as private businesses must do. Besides that, since costs of many governmental decisions and actions represent a real loss or expense to someone in the polity—either the individual victim or the public entity—judges must not defer too readily to misconduct in another branch of government.

Where governmental function is to exercise care. Application of the discretionary immunity is largely a matter of policy perceptions. The immunity is defined by the courts' "pragmatic assessment" of the need for it.[6] Perhaps the immunity is not needed when the entity undertakes activities that can be judged under ordinary standards of care. The function of a public entity's officer is frequently to use due care. A child care worker exercises discretion at almost every moment, but his function is ultimately to exercise due care for the children. Judges do not intrude upon the executive branch if they hold him to the care his function requires.[7] A therapist assuredly exercises professional judgment and in that sense exercises discretion, but his function as a doctor provided by a public entity is to professionally treat patients. If the professional standard of care constrains his choice of treatment or diagnosis, there is no logical occasion to immunize his unprofessional decisions.[8] Essentially the same idea is expressed by saying that the discretionary immunity only applies when a high degree of discretion is required and when it is applied, not merely to routine matters but to "basic policy decisions."[9]

Conscious choice. Be that as it may, courts' perceptions of the need for immunity differ by shades, so the line between immunity and

4. Cf. Hill v. Aldermen of City of Charlotte, 72 N.C. 55 (1875) (injury when city suspended anti-fireworks ordinance, no liability).

5. Jarboe v. Board of County Comn'rs of Sedgwick County, 262 Kan. 615, 938 P.2d 1293 (1997).

6. Defoor v. Evesque, 694 So.2d 1302, 1305 (Ala.1997) (quoting).

7. See Bell v. Chisom, 421 So.2d 1239, 1241 (Ala.1982) (describing court's earlier rejection of immunity for "an aide at the University day care center who allegedly allowed the plaintiff's child to fall off playground equipment. This defendant's function clearly required due care. . . . ").

8. See Terwilliger v. Hennepin County, 561 N.W.2d 909 (Minn.1997). This view was explicitly adopted by the intermediate court, then explicitly rejected in Canon v. Thumudo, 430 Mich. 326, 422 N.W.2d 688 (1988).

9. See, e.g., Mahan v. New Hampshire Dept. of Admin. Services, 141 N.H. 747, 693 A.2d 79, 82 (1997).

responsibility is one of the law's ghostlier demarcations. Some state cases refuse to grant the immunity unless the governmental entity made a conscious choice of conduct.[10] In some cases the conscious choice must also be based upon professional standards[11] or made in good faith.[12] The alternative would be to follow the federal approach.[13] Courts applying that approach immunize the public entity if there was room for policy choice, even if the entity did not actually make a choice but merely did a poor job.[14]

Example of conscious choice rule. For example, under the conscious choice rule, if the public entity fails to erect a guardrail on public property where ordinary care would require one, the entity may be liable to an injured person under ordinary negligence rules unless it chose to omit the rail for some reason of policy.[15] Under the "room for choice" approach, the immunity will protect the entity if the court can imagine policy choices that could have been made, even if the entity did not act for any of the imagined policy reasons or make any conscious choice at all.[16]

Planning vs. operational. Some states also utilize the distinction between planning and operational decisions, limiting the immunity to cases of "planning" and excluding it for actual operations or execution of decisions.[17] Similarly, state cases have often drawn a distinction between discretionary, legislative, or judicial acts on the one hand, and ministerial acts on the other, with immunity for the former only.[18] These distinctions are phrased as if they were tools used to discover the answer to immunity questions. In fact, however, they are usually labels applied

10. Johnson v. State, 69 Cal.2d 782, 795, 447 P.2d 352, 361, 73 Cal.Rptr. 240, 249 (1968) ("to be entitled to immunity the state must make a showing that such a policy decision, consciously balancing risks and advantages, took place. The fact that an employee normally engages in 'discretionary activity' is irrelevant if, in a given case, the employee did not render a considered decision"); Thompson v. Newark Housing Authority, 108 N.J. 525, 531 A.2d 734 (1987) (discretion must have been actually exercised; and in plan or design immunity, feature in issue must have been addressed by planners); Creech v. South Carolina Wildlife and Marine Resources Dept., 328 S.C. 24, 491 S.E.2d 571 (S.C. 1997); Chambers–Castanes v. King County, 100 Wash. 2d 275, 669 P.2d 451, 39 A.L.R.4th 671 (1983).

11. Creech v. South Carolina Wildlife and Marine Resources Dept., 328 S.C. 24, 491 S.E.2d 571 (S.C. 1997).

12. Sabia v. Neville, 165 Vt. 515, 687 A.2d 469 (1996).

13. § 262, supra.

14. Cf. Aguehounde v. District of Columbia, 666 A.2d 443, 449–50 (D.C.App. 1995) (whether or not policy concerns were actually considered in determining component issues, timing of yellow traffic signals was discretionary).

15. Creech v. South Carolina Wildlife and Marine Resources Dept., 328 S.C. 24, 491 S.E.2d 571 (S.C. 1997). On similar facts, the same result seems probable under the view that "operational" decisions are not protected by the immunity. Arnesano v. State, 113 Nev. 815, 942 P.2d 139 (1997).

16. See, e.g., Bowman v. United States, 820 F.2d 1393 (4th Cir.1987) and § 262, supra.

17. Lee v. Department of Health and Rehab. Services, 698 So.2d 1194 (Fla.1997); Canon v. Thumudo, 430 Mich. 326, 422 N.W.2d 688 (1988); Arnesano v. State, 113 Nev. 815, 942 P.2d 139 (1997); Costa v. Josey, 83 N.J. 49, 55, 415 A.2d 337, 340 (1980) ("Once it is determined that a ... program ... will be undertaken ... the government will ordinarily be held to the [statutory] standard of care").

18. See Defoor v. Evesque, 694 So.2d 1302 (Ala.1997).

after the decision on immunity is reached, so they have not been immensely helpful.

§ 271. Remaining Protections for State and Local Entities: The Public Duty Doctrine

Public duty rule. Even if no immunity protects a public entity, the entity may escape liability because it owes no duty that would have avoided injury to the plaintiff. If a fire safety ordinance requires smoke alarms in all new housing but does not require the city to inspect for compliance, ordinary tort rules place no responsibility upon the public entity.[1] Most courts go much further by holding that when a statute imposes upon a public entity a duty to the public at large, and not a duty to a particular class of individuals, the duty is not one enforceable in tort.[2] Under this view, as the saying is, a duty to all is a duty to none.[3] In the classic case for invoking the public duty doctrine, the duty is imposed by statute, but it is possible that the common law would impose a duty that is not enforceable by a tort action.[4]

Examples. The traditional examples of the public duty rule are all cases of non-performance of a statutory duty, not cases of affirmative conduct. A police officer is free to ignore dangerous and illegal conduct committed in his presence; victims injured by such conduct have no claim.[5] In particular, most courts refuse to impose liability for an officer's refusal to arrest a drunk driver, whose drunkenness at the wheel later causes death or serious injury to others.[6] A statute may require prompt report to police when parole violators have escaped from supervision, but the court may conclude that such a statute creates no duty to individuals who may be injured because a dangerous violator is

§ 271

1. See § 337 below. Courts may invoke the public duty doctrine in such a situation even though a simple holding that the statute imposed no duty at all might seem less complicated. E.g., Benson v. Kutsch, 181 W.Va. 1, 7, 380 S.E.2d 36, 42 (1989).

2. See also § 142, supra. Federal courts pursue a somewhat similar idea, refusing to recognize a privately enforceable statutory duty when the statute is not specific. See Suter v. Artist M., 503 U.S. 347, 112 S.Ct. 1360, 118 L.Ed.2d 1(1992). Occasionally judges use the term public duty as merely another way of discussing immunity for governmental decisions. See L. A. Ray Realty v. Town Council of Town of Cumberland, 698 A.2d 202 (R.I.1997) (the doctrine "protects the state and its political subdivisions from tort liability arising out of the performance of governmental functions not commonly undertaken by private entities").

3. See Division of Corrections v. Neakok, 721 P.2d 1121, 1128, n. 9 (Alaska 1986) (rejecting the duty to all, duty to none rule). Cf. Williams v. City of Tuscumbia, 426 So.2d 824 (Ala.1983) ("Tuscumbia contends that a duty imposed upon a municipal fire department is owed to the general public—not to an individual. Does this mean that the whole town has to be on fire before the fire department responds to a call?").

4. See South v. Maryland, 59 U.S. (18 How.) 396, 15 L.Ed. 433 (1855) (sheriff's common law duty to preserve peace analyzed; it is a public duty only and individual injured by sheriff's failure has no claim).

5. Massengill v. Yuma County, 104 Ariz. 518, 456 P.2d 376, 41 A.L.R.3d 692 (1969), overruled, along with the public duty doctrine itself, in Ryan v. State, 134 Ariz. 308, 656 P.2d 597, 35 A.L.R.4th 1188 (1982). Caveat: subsequently enacted statutes may impose similar results in some cases.

6. E.g., Ezell v. Cockrell, 902 S.W.2d 394 (Tenn.1995); see James L. Isham, Annotation, Failure to Restrain Drunk Driver as Ground of Liability of State or Local Government Unit or Officer, 48 A.L.R.4th 320 (1987).

free.[7] City inspectors can ignore inspection and such matters as fire safety standards.[8]

Scope; special duty created by statute. The public duty doctrine has no application when the court concludes that a statute or court order has created a special duty or specific obligation to a particular class of persons rather than to the public at large. A child who is injured as a result of a governmental agency's failure to enforce a court's protective order,[9] or its breach of a statutory duty to investigate[10] or report[11] child abuse, may be permitted to present evidence of negligence and to recover if negligence and causation is proven, provided the court thinks the statute sufficiently narrows the duty to a particular class.[12] But whether the statutory duty is public or special is largely in the eye of the beholder; some courts permit the agency charged with protecting children to ignore inspection requirements and leave the injured child without a claim.[13]

Exceptions and qualifications to the public duty doctrine. Some courts have said that the public duty doctrine will not apply to protect the entity when it is guilty of egregious misconduct,[14] intentional wrongdoing, malice, or recklessness.[15] More significantly, the public duty

7. Hurst v. Ohio Department of Rehabilitation and Correction, 72 Ohio St.3d 325, 650 N.E.2d 104 (1995) ("If the duty owed is general in nature, the wrong created by its breach is to the public in general and, therefore, not individually actionable").

8. E.g., Cracraft v. City of St. Louis Park, 279 N.W.2d 801 (Minn.1979).

9. Sorichetti v. City of New York, 65 N.Y.2d 461, 492 N.Y.S.2d 591, 482 N.E.2d 70 (1985) (court protective order authorizing police to take into custody a violent husband if he violated terms of the order); Nearing v. Weaver, 295 Or. 702, 670 P.2d 137 (1983); cf. Calloway v. Kinkelaar, 168 Ill.2d 312, 659 N.E.2d 1322, 213 Ill.Dec. 675 (1995) (domestic violence statute created duty).

10. Mammo v. State, 138 Ariz. 528, 675 P.2d 1347 (Ct. App. 1983) Brodie v. Summit County Children Services Board, 51 Ohio St.3d 112, 554 N.E.2d 1301 (1990); Gagnon v. State, 570 A.2d 656 (R.I.1990); Sabia v. State, 164 Vt. 293, 669 A.2d 1187 (1995).

11. Landeros v. Flood, 17 Cal.3d 399, 131 Cal.Rptr. 69, 551 P.2d 389, 97 A.L.R.3d 324 (1976).

12. Some authority seems to say that the plaintiff must show a combination of factors, such as the plaintiff's reliance, in addition to a statute that narrowed the duty to a particular class. See Tipton v. Town of Tabor, 567 N.W.2d 351 (1997).

13. See P.W. and R.W. v. Kansas Dept. of Social and Rehabilitation Services, 255 Kan. 827, 877 P.2d 430 (1994) (failure to investigate licensed day-care centers as required by statute); Jamierson v. Dale, 670 S.W.2d 195 (Mo.App.1984); but see Gagnon v. State, 570 A.2d 656 (R.I.1990) (failure to investigate was more than a mere licensing failure; statute created a special duty). See Danny R. Veilleux, Annotation, Governmental Liability For Negligence in Licensing, Regulating, or Supervising Private Day-care Home in Which Child Is Injured, 68 A.L.R.4th 266 (1989).

Distinguish child abuse reporting statutes. Whether reporting statutes may be a basis of liability for public entities and employees is perhaps not yet clear. See Danny R. Veilleux, Annotation, Validity, Construction, and Application of State Statute Requiring Doctor or Other Person to Report Child Abuse, 73 A.L.R.4th 782 (1990). Marquay v. Eno, 139 N.H. 708, 662 A.2d 272 (1995) rejected the statute as a basis for liability of school personnel but was willing to impose liability on common law special relationship grounds.

14. L. A. Ray Realty v. Town Council of Town of Cumberland, 698 A.2d 202 (R.I. 1997).

15. Ezell v. Cockrell, 902 S.W.2d 394 (Tenn.1995); cf. Calloway v. Kinkelaar, 168 Ill.2d 312, 659 N.E.2d 1322, 213 Ill.Dec. 675 (1995) (domestic violence statute created a civil claim but only when police were guilty of willful or wanton negligence in failing to protect).

doctrine eliminates the tort claim based upon a statutory duty but it does not necessarily forbid an action based upon common law duties.[16]

Although some states impose special conditions limiting the public entity's duty of care,[17] the public entity ordinarily has a duty to take reasonable affirmative steps to protect the plaintiff in any of the following instances: (1) the public entity by promise or conduct induces the plaintiff to rely upon action by the public entity; (2) the public entity stands in a special relationship either to the plaintiff or to a person causing harm; or (3) the public entity is guilty of negligent action rather than inaction.

An example of conduct that induces reliance is the case of a city that provides crossing guards for children walking to school. If such conduct induces parents to rely on such guards, the city owes reasonable care to continue the guards and is consequently subject to liability for the death of a child in an unprotected crossing when it unilaterally withdraws guards without notice.[18] The public entity's promise can work in the same way, but the promise must be one on which the plaintiff can reasonably rely.[19] In the special relationship category, police may owe a duty of care to an informant endangered because he responded to a police plea for help in locating a criminal.[20] Likewise, a public entity having custody of the plaintiff owes the plaintiff a positive duty of care because of the special relationship.[21] A public entity's special relationship with a dangerous person may also require reasonable care.[22] When the public entity acts affirmatively, as in the case of a high-speed police chase, courts may or may not recognize an immunity, but the public duty doctrine as such has no application.

Rejection of the doctrine. In a few states, contemporary courts have rejected the public duty doctrine altogether.[23] Some have restricted it to

16. See Marquay v. Eno, 139 N.H. 708, 662 A.2d 272 (1995) (common law duty based on relationship of parties); Benson v. Kutsch, 181 W.Va. 1, 7, 380 S.E.2d 36, 42 (1989) (local public entity would still be liable for negligent conduct in its proprietary capacity). Common law duties to take affirmative action are considered principally in Chapters 21 and 22.

17. See Gleason v. Peters, 568 N.W.2d 482 (S.D.1997) (plaintiff must show some combination of "(1) actual knowledge of the dangerous condition; (2) reasonable reliance by persons on official representations and conduct; (3) an ordinance or statute setting forth mandatory acts clearly for the protection of a particular class of persons rather than the general public; and (4) failure to use due care to avoid increasing the risk of harm").

18. Florence v. Goldberg, 44 N.Y.2d 189, 404 N.Y.S.2d 583, 375 N.E.2d 763 (1978).

19. See Braswell v. Braswell, 330 N.C. 363, 410 S.E.2d 897 (1991) (sheriff's general assurances of safety not sufficient).

20. Schuster v. City of New York, 5 N.Y.2d 75, 154 N.E.2d 534, 180 N.Y.S.2d 265 (1958).

21. E.g., Jackson v. City of Kansas City, 263 Kan. 143, 947 P.2d 31(1997) (police handcuffed man; his girlfriend saw her chance and cut him; a duty of care was owed). See § 326.

22. See Murdock v. Higgins, 454 Mich. 46, 56, 559 N.W.2d 639, 643 (1997).

23. Busby v. Municipality of Anchorage, 741 P.2d 230 (Alaska 1987) (repeating earlier rejections of the doctrine; ordinary tort rules determine whether statute created a duty); Ryan v. State, 134 Ariz. 308, 656 P.2d 597, 38 A.L.R.4th 1188 (1982); Leake v. Cain, 720 P.2d 152 (Co.1986) (ordinary tort rules for determining existence of duty apply to public entities; on the facts, no

special cases. For example, Georgia uses the public duty doctrine only to exclude liability for failure of police protection.[24] In Rhode Island, the rule seems to be only a way of describing the discretionary immunity.[25] Where the common law public duty doctrine is rejected or limited by judicial decision, statutes sometimes provide for similar results in particular cases. For instance, the statute may exclude liability for failure to make an arrest.[26] Even without such statutes, rejection of the doctrine does not automatically result in liability. The plaintiff must establish a duty under ordinary tort principles, and then prove negligence, cause in fact, and proximate cause, as in all other negligence cases.

Rationale and comment. The logic of the public duty rule is formally different from the logic of immunity. It is that the statute creates no duty to act and hence, regardless of immunity, the public entity cannot be liable. Which statutes create a tort duty and which do not? Courts talk as if the answer lay in statutory construction. If the statutory duty is narrowed to protect a particular class of persons, it may create a tort duty, otherwise not. Little statutory construction is possible in most cases and courts sometimes implicitly admit that it is less a matter of construction than a matter of judicial policy. They have thus suggested numerous reasons to exempt public entities from the obligations apparently imposed by statutes.

One minor argument offered in support of the public duty rule is that non-tort mechanisms exist to deal with official negligence.[27] For example, a negligent officer might be suspended. Another minor argument that could only be applied to a case of police failure to arrest or otherwise protect against a dangerous person is that the offender, not the public entity, should be accountable.[28] Neither argument offers comfort to the victim. More importantly, both arguments are dependent upon the assumption of what is in issue—whether public entities are entitled to some special exemption from tort rules applied to private defendants. That assumption can be seen by noticing that such argu-

duty existed); Commercial Carrier Corp. v. Indian River County, 371 So.2d 1010 (Fla. 1979) (public duty rule is essentially an immunity rule and does not survive abrogation of immunity); Stewart v. Schmieder, 386 So.2d 1351 (La.1980); Jean W. v. Commonwealth, 414 Mass. 496, 610 N.E.2d 305 (1993) (prospectively overruled); Maple v. City of Omaha, 222 Neb. 293, 384 N.W.2d 254 (1986) (disapproving the doctrine but holding in favor of the public entity on other grounds); Schear v. Board of County Comn'rs., 101 N.M. 671, 687 P.2d 728 (1984) (rule is a "ghost of sovereign immunity"); Brennen v. City of Eugene, 285 Or. 401, 591 P.2d 719 (1979) (rule is inconsistent with waiver of sovereign immunity); see Coffey v. City of Milwaukee, 74 Wis.2d 526, 247 N.W.2d 132 (1976) ("Any duty owed to the public generally is a duty owed to individual members of the public.") The public duty rule was criticized in Wilson v. Nepstad, 282 N.W.2d 664 (Iowa 1979), but the court actually decided the case by finding a special duty. In some states, statutory schemes of immunity have affected these holdings.

24. Hamilton v. Cannon, 267 Ga. 655, 482 S.E.2d 370 (1997).

25. O'Gara v. Ferrante, 690 A.2d 1354 (R.I.1997) (doctrine "shields the state and its political subdivisions from tort liability arising out of discretionary governmental actions that by their nature are not ordinarily performed by private persons").

26. E.g., ARIZ. REV. STATS. § 12–820.02 A 1 (unless grossly negligent); MASS. GEN. L. ANN. ch. 258 § 10(h).

27. Ezell v. Cockrell, 902 S.W.2d 394 (Tenn.1995).

28. Gleason v. Peters, 568 N.W.2d 482 (S.D.1997).

ments do not relieve private enterprise. No matter how confident judges might be that a private company would discharge an employee who failed to comply with a statute, judges do not relieve companies of their obligations.

A much more serious argument is essentially the same argument presented for the discretionary immunity. Expressed in various ways, the core proposition is that courts should leave allocation of resources to the legislature or to the executive.[29] The argument is persuasive in some cases, but not all cases involve allocation of substantial resources. Some involve simply bad mistakes or horrendous negligence. The officer who simply watches a drunk driver go through dangerous antics for a substantial period without attempting to deal with the situation is not allocating resources; he is behaving very negligently indeed. The resources argument is puzzling, too, when compared to the same argument on the issue of discretionary immunity. A statutory directive to act in a particular way—to investigate reports of child abuse, for example—seems to remove all discretion. Yet the public duty doctrine is intended to foster and protect discretion in the very case where statutes seem to have removed it.

A third argument seems to be predicated upon a deep distrust of the judicial system itself. The argument implicitly asserts that courts cannot formulate and administer an appropriate rule about the scope of liability. An officer should have no duty to arrest a drunk driver he encounters, one court said, because if he tries "to avoid liability by removing from the road all persons who pose any potential hazard, he may find himself liable in many instances for false arrest."[30] It is hard to believe that courts would administer the reasonable care rule of negligence law to require the arrest of every hazardous driver from the road in the first place. If courts did such an unprecedented thing, they could hardly impose liability for doing what they required.

Although the arguments do not seem broad enough to support a public duty rule, they rightly point to particular instances in which liability is inappropriate. For instance, if an officer must choose when to arrest a dangerous person, appropriate caution may counsel delay. If so, he cannot be found negligent. In the same way, a busy precinct may have no officers to spare for the protection of every person within its jurisdiction. If not, it cannot be found negligent. Ordinary negligence rules appropriately exclude liability in such cases, but they leave open the possibility of liability when police officers unprofessionally shirk their duty and when administrative bumbling sends officers to the wrong place. The public duty doctrine, in contrast, excludes liability in all cases in which agencies fail to enforce or obey a statutory directive that is deemed to create a duty to the public at large.

29. E.g., Tipton v. Town of Tabor, 567 N.W.2d 351 (1997).

30. Shore v. Town of Stonington, 187 Conn. 147, 156, 444 A.2d 1379, 1383 (1982). *Shore* considered this argument in connection with the question whether a special duty was owed.

§ 272. Remaining Protections for State and Local Entities: Specific Exclusions of Liability

Contemporary statutes often determine the liabilities and immunities to be accorded state and local public entities. At the same time, courts may intervene to add non-statutory protections. Looking at this somewhat confusing picture in another way, it is possible to see that public entities can often avoid liability for several of their most important activities, either because statutory provisions specifically retain immunity or because those activities come under discretionary immunities or public duty doctrines.

For instance, statutes and court decisions tend to bar claims for injuries resulting from an entity's negligent inspections or licensing, although particular cases in particular jurisdictions may escape that bar.[1] In some jurisdictions and under some conditions, the public entity is protected from liability for its negligence in highway or road design[2] and even for its failure to erect appropriate warning signs or stop lights.[3] The same can be said about a number of intentional torts.[4] Two other general activities, both associated with government's role in protecting against crime, warrant the lengthier discussion below.

Police and Fire Protection

Failure to furnish police and fire protection. The usual rule is that

§ 272

1. Cal. Govt. Code § 818.4; Ga. Code § 50-21-24; Island Shores Estates Condominium Ass'n v. Concord, 136 N.H. 300, 615 A.2d 629, 24 A.L.R.5th 845 (1992) (as to purely economic harms without personal injury or property damage). But Boland v. Town of Tiverton, 670 A.2d 1245 (R.I.1996) takes the view that only the public duty doctrine defeats such a licensing-inspection claim and that the plaintiff can prevail if she establishes an exception to the public duty rule, such as a special relationship or egregious misconduct in the inspection. When the plaintiff suffers personal injury and not merely financial harm from negligently licensing, it may be easier to make the case for liability. See Fowler v. Roberts, 556 So.2d 1 (La.1989) (licensing dangerous driver without imposing medical restriction, no immunity). See Annotations, Thomas M. Fleming, Municipal Liability For Negligent Performance of Building Inspector's Duties, 24 A.L.R.5th 200 (1995); Danny R. Veilleux, Governmental Liability For Negligence in Licensing, Regulating, or Supervising Private Day-care Home in Which Child Is Injured, 68 A.L.R.4th 266 (1989).

2. E.g., Ga. Code § 50-21-24; Arrowwood v. State, 894 P.2d 642 (Alaska 1995) (decision to leave icy road open is discretionary); but see Nusbaum v. Blue Earth County, 422 N.W.2d 713 (Minn.1988) (negligently posting slow-down signs in wrong place actionable).

3. See McLain v. State, 563 N.W.2d 600 (Iowa 1997)

4. The immunity is often retained for claims arising out of assault, battery, and false arrest as well as for those involving no physical interference such as malicious prosecution, defamation, and misrepresentation. See, e.g., Ga. Code § 50-21-24 (7); Mass. Gen. L. Ann. ch. 258 § 10 (c). Some states achieve this by limiting liability to claims for negligence and by limiting liability to a list of specified activities. E.g., 42 Pa. Consol. Stat. Ann. § 8542 (liability limited to claims for negligence; listing liability only in certain cases involving motor vehicles, care of property, and certain streets and other public ways). For some torts, notably false imprisonment, individual officers were traditionally liable and may remain so even when the public entity enjoys an immunity. In California, where officer and entity liability ordinarily go hand in hand, neither is immune from liability for false imprisonment. See Asgari v. City of Los Angeles, 15 Cal.4th 744, 16 Cal.4th 89B, 937 P.2d 273, 63 Cal.Rptr.2d 842 (1997).

public entities are free of all liability for failure to provide police[5] or fire[6] protection, even if that failure is negligent. Similarly, statutes and judicial decisions usually exclude liability for failure to arrest a dangerous person who later harms or kills others.[7] However, unless statutes dictate otherwise, liability may be imposed for failure to protect a specific person if the police establish a special relationship with that person by actively undertaking protection and then carrying it out negligently.

For example, if police attempt to answer a 911 call but negligently go to the wrong address, liability may be imposed because the police have themselves allocated resources.[8] Similarly, unless a statute specifically provides otherwise, courts have imposed liability when a fire department negligently uses dangerous or inadequate methods of fighting a fire.[9] But when the city does nothing to address the particular crime or fire, no liability is the usual rule. The city is not liable if a police officer does nothing at all upon learning that a woman has been kidnaped, even though the officer could have saved her by a phone call.[10] Nor is it liable when it fails to respond to a fire call,[11] fails to enforce fire-safety regulations,[12] or fails to provide adequate water,[13] although there are a

5. E.g., Cal. Gov. Code § 845. See also Id., § 846; see Riss v. City of New York, 22 N.Y.2d 579, 293 N.Y.S.2d 897, 240 N.E.2d 860 (1968). If the claim can be asserted as a civil rights claim, the plaintiff may have better luck, but if the claim rests upon police inaction, the plaintiff will also have serious difficulties in the civil rights claim, too. See §§ 322 & 327 below.

6. Ga. Code § 45–9–40 (6).

7. South v. Maryland, 59 U.S. (18 How.) 396, 15 L.Ed. 433 (1855); Ezell v. Cockrell, 902 S.W.2d 394 (Tenn.1995).

8. De Long v. County of Erie, 60 N.Y.2d 296, 469 N.Y.S.2d 611, 457 N.E.2d 717 (1983); cf. Torres v. State, 119 N.M. 609, 894 P.2d 386 (1995) (police began work on a triple murder but lost the chance to arrest the suspect, who then killed the plaintiff's decedent; liability may be imposed); but cf. Frye v. Clark County, 97 Nev. 632, 637 P.2d 1215 (1981) (fire department response to wrong address no basis for liability, since no special relationship had been established).

9. Harry Stoller and Co., Inc. v. City of Lowell, 412 Mass. 139, 587 N.E.2d 780 (1992); Invest Cast, Inc. v. City of Blaine, 471 N.W.2d 368 (Minn.App.1991). Contra: City of Daytona Beach v. Palmer, 469 So.2d 121 (Fla.1985). City of Daytona Beach v. Palmer cited a number of cases in support, but some of those cases did not deal with negligence in the actual conduct of firefighting. For example, one of the cases cited involved a wise delay in approaching the fires set in a civil disturbance, not the use of inappropriate firefighting technique. This was Biloon's Electrical Service, Inc. v. City of Wilmington, 417 A.2d 371 (Del.1980). Older decisions on liability for negligent handling of fires may be superseded by statutes dealing specifically with that problem.

10. See Kircher v. City of Jamestown, 74 N.Y.2d 251, 544 N.Y.S.2d 995, 543 N.E.2d 443 (1989) (special relationship requires a direct contact with victim, so mere report by witnesses of the kidnapping established no duty).

11. Frye v. Clark County, 97 Nev. 632, 637 P.2d 1215 (1981) (regarding a response to a wrong address as a failure to respond).

12. Motyka v. City of Amsterdam, 15 N.Y.2d 134, 204 N.E.2d 635, 256 N.Y.S.2d 595 (1965) (city under no duty to enforce regulations for fire safety, even after a specific danger was discovered). Statutes offering immunity may be broadly worded and may even include negligent firefighting itself. See Kan. Stats. Ann. 75–6104(n); Mass. Gen. L. Ann. ch. 258 § 10(g); but cf. Harry Stoller and Co., Inc. v. City of Lowell, 412 Mass. 139, 587 N.E.2d 780 (1992) (liability for negligent firefighting as against a general discretionary immunity defense).

13. E.g., Westbrook v. City of Jackson, 665 So.2d 833 (Miss.1995) (failure to supply water for firefighting is governmental and immune, though drinking water supply is proprietary and unprotected by immunity).

few decisions to the contrary.[14] Even when a special relationship is established by police investigation and promises of protection, liability is sometimes rejected.[15]

Negligent police chases. One special category of police activity is the high-speed chase that ends in injury or death, sometimes because the person pursued runs down a bystander, sometimes because the police driver does so, and sometimes because the pursued person is himself killed or injured. These cases are not like those in which the police simply fail to act at all.[16] Rather, they involve affirmatively dangerous conduct that creates risks to the plaintiff. So it is possible to resolve such cases under ordinary negligence rules, holding the public entity subject to liability when the dangers of the chase outweigh the advantages of capturing a suspect, as where as many as twenty police vehicles pursued a traffic violator for 25 miles through densely populated urban areas, with resulting death to bystanders.[17] Such decisions, like many other negligence cases, call for a balancing of risks and utilities, so if the pursuer is a dangerous criminal and the risks to innocent people are low, the chase may not be negligent at all. A variation on this approach might reduce the standard of care for emergency vehicles[18] or might limit the care owed to the person being pursued while maintaining the negligence standard for bystanders.[19]

Some courts, however, tend to think that balancing risks and utilities requires an immunity rather than a simple negligence analysis. Thus some courts resolve the high-speed chase cases on immunity grounds because risks must be weighed.[20] The result of the immunity approach is that it eliminates the capacity to distinguish good cases for liability from bad ones; all chase claims are treated substantially the same. So pursuit of a known violent criminal and pursuit of a traffic violator can equally call for intense risks to the public.

A third approach demands that the public entity itself prescribe a balancing of risks and utilities in its policies for police officers. If the

14. Ziegler v. City of Millbrook, 514 So.2d 1275 (1987); Adams v. State, 555 P.2d 235 (Alaska 1976) (fire hazards actually discovered in hotel). These cases implicate the public duty doctrine, discussed below. Caveat: subsequently enacted statutes bear on the current authority of many immunity cases.

15. Barillari v. City of Milwaukee, 194 Wis.2d 247, 533 N.W.2d 759 (1995).

16. On the traditional distinction between action and nonaction, see Chapter 22.

17. See City of Pinellas Park v. Brown, 604 So.2d 1222 (Fla.1992) (chase partly in densely populated area, up to 120 mph over a course of 25 miles and joined by as many as twenty separate police vehicles—all in pursuit of a driver who had run a red light); accord in adjudicating chase cases under negligence rules, Haynes v. Hamilton County, 883 S.W.2d 606 (Tenn.1994).

18. Statutes are sometimes construed to limit the standard of care for emergency vehicles so that liability is imposed only for reckless or similar exaggerated fault. See, e.g., Saarinen v. Kerr, 84 N.Y.2d 494, 620 N.Y.S.2d 297, 644 N.E.2d 988 (1994).

19. See Day v. Willis, 897 P.2d 78 (Alaska 1995).

20. E.g., Pletan v. Gaines, 494 N.W.2d 38 (Minn.1992); Fielder v. Stonack, 141 N.J. 101, 661 A.2d 231 (1995) (under statute).

entity provides an adequate policy, then it is immune. If not, liability is imposed for negligence in failing to prescribe the policy.[21]

Negligent Release of Dangerous Persons

Courts tend to deny recovery by victims of dangerous prisoners, mental patients, and others who have been negligently released from custody[22] or who have escaped. Although public entities owe a duty of reasonable care to those in custody, and also a duty of reasonable care to control dangerous persons in custody,[23] public entities often avoid responsibility for their negligence in permitting parole or escape,[24] either because statutes specifically say so,[25] because courts invoke discretionary immunity[26] or because they apply the public duty rule[27] or some other immunity.[28] But the tendency is not universal; a few cases have imposed responsibility upon public entities for negligently permitting a prisoner's escape[29] or for the release of dangerous persons[30] and a few statutes contemplate liability for gross negligence in releasing a dangerous person.[31]

The decision to release may be distinguished from negligent supervision by a parole officer,[32] and from a failure to warn persons endangered by the release. Liability may be imposed for failure to warn individuals

21. See Payne v. City of Perris, 12 Cal. App.4th 1738, 16 Cal.Rptr.2d 143 (1993) (immunity attaches even if officer does not follow the public entity's policy or guidelines, but the policy itself must be specific in detailing what is permitted in a chase); Estate of Cavanaugh v. Andrade, 202 Wis.2d 290, 550 N.W.2d 103 (1996) (statutory obligation was to create policy that directed officers to consider seriousness of crime and necessity of pursuit; statute created ministerial, not discretionary duty). Potential federal civil rights liability of the public entity for failure to train may have similar results. See § 277 below.

22. See generally Janet Boeth Jones, Annotation, Governmental Tort Liability For Injuries Caused by Negligently Released Individual, 6 A.L.R.4th 1155 (1981).

23. See § 329 below.

24. See, e.g., S.C. Code § 15–78–60 (21); Don F. Vaccaro, Annotation, Liability of Public Officer or Body For Harm Done by Prisoner Permitted to Escape, 44 A.L.R.3d 899 (1973).

25. E.g., N.J. Stats. Ann. § 59:5–2 (parole or escape); 51 Okl. St. Ann. § 155; S.C. Code § 15–78–60. In states that specify the particular cases for liability rather than specifying exceptions, the lists usually do not seem to include liability for parole or similar decisions. See, e.g., 42 Pa. Consol. Stats. Ann. § 8522.

26. E.g., Beck v. Kansas Adult Authority, 241 Kan. 13, 735 P.2d 222 (1987); Collins v. North Carolina Parole Com'n, 344 N.C. 179, 473 S.E.2d 1 (1996) (official discretion); cf. Goss v. City of Manchester, 140 N.H. 449, 669 A.2d 785 (1995) (police and prosecutors had discretion whether to report parole violation, hence city would not be liable when parole violator later raped and murdered).

27. See Parkulo v. West Virginia Board of Probation and Parole, 199 W.Va. 161, 483 S.E.2d 507 (1996) (public duty rule and discretionary immunity).

28. Board of Regents of the University System of Georgia v. Riddle, 229 Ga.App. 15, 493 S.E.2d 208 (1997) (undermedicated and dangerous mental patient committed murder when he was released; entity was immune under statutory assault and battery immunity).

29. E.g., State v. Silva, 86 Nev. 911, 478 P.2d 591, 44 A.L.R.3d 891 (1970).

30. See Grimm v. Arizona Board of Pardons & Paroles, 115 Ariz. 260, 564 P.2d 1227, 5 A.L.R.4th 757 (1977)

31. Mass. Gen. L. Ann. ch. 258 § 10(i) (gross negligence standard); see Ariz. Rev. Stats. §§ 12–820.02.

32. Hertog v. City of Seattle, 138 Wash.2d 265, 979 P.2d 400 (1999) (imposing duty of reasonable supervision by probation and pre-trial release officers). But some authorities immunize negligent supervision as well. See Johnson v. State, 553 N.W.2d 40 (Minn.1996).

who are known to be in danger. When a California youth authority placed a juvenile in a foster home without warning that he had homicidal tendencies, the court imposed responsibility to exercise reasonable care.[33] Even when a state-employed therapist did not have physical custody of a dangerous person but knew of his threats to a specific individual, the state could be liable if he unreasonably failed either to seek commitment or to provide a warning to the potential victim.[34]

However, the same court took the view that no warning was required when the authorities released a young man known to have violent propensities toward young children. The young man had announced that if released he would molest and murder a child. Once released, he sexually attacked a five year old and murdered him. In the family's wrongful death action, the court concluded that the authorities releasing the young man did not create a specific threat to a particular child. Hence, the court reasoned, the authorities had no duty to warn anyone.[35]

Some courts have rejected such a stringent view. They impose a duty to warn whenever a reasonable person would provide a warning.[36] Perhaps the question ought to be, not whether the victim is identifiable, but whether an effective warning could reasonably have been given to someone who would have prevented the harm. For instance, a warning to foster parents that a juvenile being placed with them was a sexual threat to others might serve not only to protect the family members who were identifiable victims, but also neighbors who were foreseeable but not identifiable.[37]

TOPIC B. IMMUNITIES AND LIABILITIES OF INDIVIDUAL GOVERNMENTAL AGENTS

§ 273. Liability and Immunity of Officers and Employees

State and Local Officers and Employees

Employee immunity and indemnity. Employees and officers of public entities are often immune from liability for harms they cause in the

33. Johnson v. State, 69 Cal.2d 782, 447 P.2d 352, 73 Cal.Rptr. 240 (1968); accord: Onofrio v. Department of Mental Health, 408 Mass. 605, 562 N.E.2d 1341 (1990); Anderson v. Nebraska Dept. of Social Services, 248 Neb. 651, 538 N.W.2d 732 (1995).

34. Tarasoff v. Regents of University of California, 17 Cal.3d 425, 131 Cal.Rptr. 14, 551 P.2d 334, 83 A.L.R.3d 1166 (1976). See § 331 below.

35. Thompson v. County of Alameda, 27 Cal.3d 741, 167 Cal.Rptr. 70, 614 P.2d 728, 12 A.L.R.4th 701 (1980). Cf. Martinez v. California, 444 U.S. 277, 100 S.Ct. 553, 62 L.Ed.2d 481 (1980) ("the parole board was not aware that appellants' decedent, as distinguished from the public at large, faced any special danger").

36. Division of Corrections v. Neakok, 721 P.2d 1121 (Alaska 1986); Hamman v. County of Maricopa, 161 Ariz. 58, 775 P.2d 1122 (1989); Schuster v. Altenberg, 144 Wis.2d 223, 424 N.W.2d 159 (1988). When the plaintiff claims negligence on some ground other than failure to warn, the absence of an identifiable victim is not controlling. See Estates of Morgan v. Fairfield Family Counseling Center, 77 Ohio St.3d 284, 673 N.E.2d 1311 (1997).

37. See Anderson v. Nebraska Dept. of Social Services, supra n. 33.

scope of their public employment. Although civil rights cases are discussed in separate sections,[1] they, too, allow for immunities. The supposition is that immunity is required in at least some cases to assure that the ardor of public officials for performing their tasks will not be dampened.[2] Courts usually assume that official ardor is desirable. They also assume it can be dampened unduly. The first point is a question of values; the second is a question of data. Neither point is demonstrated in most of the case discussions. The Supreme Court has also suggested that unfounded lawsuits entail social costs, including expenses of litigation and diversion of official energies.[3] That argument, however, seems wide of the mark, since the result of immunity is to avoid the trial that could tell us whether the suit was unfounded or not. Not surprisingly in this state of affairs, exact agreement on the application of immunities is not to be found.

The justifications advanced for employee immunity show that it is distinct from the immunity of public entities. In fact, some plaintiffs who would be defeated by the entity's immunity might prevail in a suit against an individual officer.[4] In some states, however, statutes provide that the public entity's liability depends upon the liability of the employee whose acts caused harm. In those states, the plaintiff can recover against both the officer and the entity or against neither.[5]

Employee indemnity. By statute in some states, the public entity must or may defend the employee who is sued for acts committed within the scope of his employment. Likewise, the public entity may be permitted or required to indemnify the employee if he is held liable.[6] When that procedure is applied, it effectively circumvents the entity's immunity and also absolves the employee of any personal responsibility, much as if the employee were covered by liability insurance. From the public employee's point of view, immunity and a right or likelihood of indemnity are both protective devices. From the victim's point of view, any immunity will operate to bar the claim, while existence of indemnity for the employee is often desirable as an indirect contribution to payment of the claim.

§ 273

1. §§ 275–278 below.

2. See, e.g., Harlow v. Fitzgerald, 457 U.S. 800, 814, 102 S.Ct. 2727, 2736, 73 L.Ed.2d 396 (1982).

3. Harlow v. Fitzgerald, supra, n 2.

4. Thus in Pennsylvania, local public entities may be immune to suits for false arrest of their officers, see Burger v. Borough of Ingram, 697 A.2d 1037 (Pa.Cmwlth. 1997), but individual officers may be personally liable for that and other intentional torts. See Renk v. City of Pittsburgh, 537 Pa. 68, 76, 641 A.2d 289, 294 (1994).

5. Cal. Govt. Code § 815.2 ("Except as otherwise provided by statute, a public entity is not liable for an injury resulting from an act or omission of an employee of the public entity where the employee is immune from liability"). See Thomas v. City of Richmond, 9 Cal.4th 1154, 892 P.2d 1185, 40 Cal.Rptr.2d 442 (1995) (recognizing limited exceptions).

6. E.g., Me. Rev. Stats. Ann. § 8112 ("A governmental entity, with the consent of the employee, shall assume the defense of and, in its discretion, may indemnify any employee against a claim which arises out of an act or omission occurring within the course and scope of employment and for which the governmental entity is not liable"); Minn. Stat. Ann. § 3.736, subd. 9.

Judicial, legislative, and quasi-judicial functions. Judges and legislators are usually said to be "absolutely privileged" or absolutely immune from suit based on acts that are within the scope of their judicial or legislative duties. The term absolute immunity reflects the rule that immunity will not be lost even if the defendant acted maliciously, in bad faith, or recklessly. A judge acting within his subject matter jurisdiction, for example, is not liable to a litigant for a malicious ruling.[7]

The immunity embraces all those appropriately engaged in the task. It is most obviously applied, not to personal injury suits, but to defamation claims and other economic harm claims.[8] So witnesses and lawyers as well as judges are immune from suit based on their words in court.[9] Prosecutors share the absolute judicial immunity from suit based on prosecutorial decisions within the scope of their jurisdiction and traditional powers,[10] and so do administrative law judges[11] and experts appointed by the judge to render quasi-judicial evaluations.[12] Nonjudicial work of the same persons, however, is another matter. In hiring and discharging employees, for example, a judge is performing executive rather than judicial functions and in that case loses the absolute privilege.[13]

Legislators, too, are immune from suit based upon their official votes[14] and those based upon speech in the legislature and on related matters,[15] although not upon statements made outside the legislative function.[16]

Executive officers and employees. Public employees of the executive branch—everyone who is not in the legislative or judicial branches—were originally liable for their torts[17] and certainly for those committed

7. See, e.g., K.D. v. Bozarth, 313 N.J.Super. 561, 568, 713 A.2d 546, 549 (1998).

8. See Chapter 28.

9. See, e.g., Hawkins v. Harris, 141 N.J. 207, 661 A.2d 284 (1995); Restatement § 589.

10. See Imbler v. Pachtman, 424 U.S. 409, 96 S.Ct. 984, 47 L.Ed.2d 128 (1976) (absolute immunity protects against § 1983 civil rights claim that prosecutor unconstitutionally suppressed evidence). If the prosecutor goes beyond the traditional role, he may lose his immunity. See Doe v. Phillips, 81 F.3d 1204 (2d Cir.1996) (prosecutor demanded that criminal defendant swear an oath on the Bible in church as a condition to dismissal of charge; no immunity). Some states have extended the absolute immunity to public defenders. See Bradshaw v. Joseph, 164 Vt. 154, 666 A.2d 1175 (1995) (reviewing cases, but basing the decision on a statutory immunity for all state employees). The United States Supreme Court, however, does not extend the immunity to public defenders. Ferri v. Ackerman, 444 U.S. 193, 100 S.Ct. 402, 62 L.Ed.2d 355 (1979).

11. See Butz v. Economou, 438 U.S. 478, 98 S.Ct. 2894, 57 L.Ed.2d 895 (1978).

12. See LaLonde v. Eissner, 405 Mass. 207, 539 N.E.2d 538 (1989).

13. See Forrester v. White, 484 U.S. 219, 108 S.Ct. 538, 98 L.Ed.2d 555 (1988).

14. See Bogan v. Scott–Harris, 523 U.S. 44, 118 S.Ct. 966, 140 L.Ed.2d 79 (1998) (in a federal civil rights claim).

15. " . . .for any Speech or Debate in either House, they shall not be questioned in any other Place." United States Constitution Art. I, § 6. As to local legislators, that is a matter of state law, but some states extend the absolute privilege or immunity even to city councils. See Sanchez v. Coxon, 175 Ariz. 93, 854 P.2d 126 (1993).

16. See Hutchinson v. Proxmire, 443 U.S. 111, 99 S.Ct. 2675, 61 L.Ed.2d 411 (1979) (Senator was subject to suit for defamation based on newsletters and news releases).

17. See 5 Harper, James and Gray, The Law of Torts § 29.8 (2d ed. 1986); Restatement § 895D, cmt. a.

in excess of their authority.[18] In the twentieth century, state courts developed immunities for officers and employees of public entities. A little authority even provides an absolute immunity to higher level state officers, at least as to defamation[19] or as to matters in which it is especially important for high level officers to feel unhampered by possible legal actions.[20] More generally, officers and employees are said to enjoy qualified immunity for discretionary acts, but not for ministerial acts.[21] The discretionary immunity is qualified or conditional because it is usually lost if the officer is guilty of bad faith, malice, corruption, wanton misconduct or the like.[22]

Whether an act is treated as ministerial or discretionary probably depends in part on the how the court feels about the risks of error in the judicial decision. Since application of immunity tends to foreclose trial on the merits, it risks excluding some claims that are meritorious and would

18. A statute might authorize specific acts that otherwise would be actionable, but the early view of this made the officer liable unless he complied quite precisely with the statute's condition. See Little v. Barreme, 6 U.S. (2 Cranch) 170, 2 L.Ed. 243 (1804) (officer liable for seizing a ship proceeding from French port when statute only authorized seizing ships proceeding to French ports).

19. Bauer v. State, 511 N.W.2d 447 (Minn.1994); Restatement § 591 (b).

20. See Thoma v. Hickel, 947 P.2d 816 (Alaska 1997) (on the facts limiting governor to qualified immunity destructible by bad faith, but recognizing that absolute immunity would be available to the governor in some instances). The President of the United States enjoys absolute immunity by virtue of the status. See Nixon v. Fitzgerald, 457 U.S. 731, 102 S.Ct. 2690, 73 L.Ed.2d 349 (1982).

21. Merrow v. Hawkins, 266 Ga. 390, 467 S.E.2d 336 (1996); E.g., Town of Port Deposit v. Petetit, 113 Md.App. 401, 688 A.2d 54 (1997); Davis–Bey v. Missouri Dept. of Correction, 944 S.W.2d 294 (Mo.App. 1997); Meyer v. Walls, 347 N.C. 97, 489 S.E.2d 880 (1997); Miller v. Niblack, 942 S.W.2d 533 (Tenn.App.1996). Ministerial acts are nondiscretionary acts, so the term does not much help. "The important point is that certain types of activity, such as driving cars, posting warning signs, or moving office furniture are the types of activity for which immunity serves no worthwhile purpose; other types of activity, such as evaluating reports of employees' performances or deciding upon parole release warrant at least qualified immunity in order to advance important public objectives: effective government administered by skilled government officials." Chamberlain v. Mathis, 151 Ariz. 551, 556, 729 P.2d 905, 910 (1986). As with the discretionary immunity for state and federal public entities, some courts may treat almost any choice as "discretionary," while others may emphasize that only policy choices are protected. Compare Merrow v. Hawkins, supra, (jailer's decision to give car keys to inmate so he could wash a car led to theft of the car and damage to others; giving the keys is "discretionary") with Davis–Bey v. Missouri Dept. of Correction, supra, (negligent driving of prison bus; driving inmates is not discretionary because it involves no decisions of *policy).*

Some courts apply the discretionary-ministerial rule in a roundabout way by classifying public servants as either officers or employees, and, at least prima facie, attributing discretion to officers and ministerial duties to employees, with the result that officers are immune and employees are not. E.g., Meyer v. Walls, supra. Since some employees might occasionally have discretionary duties and some officers might have ministerial ones, courts using this approach may be compelled to make fine and confusing distinctions to achieve justice.

See generally, Chester James Antieau & Milo R. Mecham, Tort Liability of Government Officers and Employees §§ 2.4–2.9 (1990 & Supp.).

22. See City of Lancaster v. Chambers, 883 S.W.2d 650 (Tex.1994) (defining good faith "objectively"; in a high-speed police chase, the officer acts in good faith if "a reasonably prudent officer, under the same or similar circumstances, could have believed that the need to immediately apprehend the suspect outweighed a clear risk of harm to the public in continuing the pursuit").

be allowed if judges had a fully developed record of the facts. Judicial preference may be either to minimize the risk of error that may harm officials or to minimize the risk of error that may harm citizens. If it is the latter, the immunity will be applied more narrowly and more acts recognized as ministerial. The Restatement has suggested various factors that judges are likely to consider in characterizing the actions of officials as ministerial or discretionary. These include the nature of the injury claimed, the availability of alternative remedies, the ability of courts to judge fault without unduly invading the executive officer's function, and the importance of protecting particular kinds of official acts.[23]

The wave of statutes passed in the latter half of the twentieth century generally confirmed, altered, and sometimes expanded the immunities. One statutory technique provides detailed immunities and extensive protection for governmental employees, or simply lists a few cases in which liability is permissible. Within this framework, the varied local statutes and decisions must always be consulted with care, but the protections provided by local statutes may be overridden by federal civil rights liability.[24]

Another statutory technique is like that now employed for suits against federal employees; the employee is simply immune to claims for negligence committed within the scope of his employment. In such states, the suit must be against the public entity, to stand or fall as the rules for public entities dictate.[25]

Federal Employees

The Federal Tort Claims Act did not originally immunize all federal employees. Congress has now provided that the claim against the government authorized by the Federal Tort Claims Act is the exclusive remedy for anyone injured by a federal tort.[26] Except for constitutional and specific statutory violations by the employee,[27] he is granted complete immunity for torts committed within the scope of his employment. If suit is brought against a federal employee, the Attorney General may certify that he was acting within the scope of his employment. Unless the Attorney General's certification is overturned,[28] the court must substitute the government as defendant and dismiss the claim against the individual government employee.[29]

23. Restatement § 895D, cmt. f. Each of these factors is discussed in the last edition of Prosser, PROSSER & KEETON, § 132 (5th ed. 1984).

24. See §§ 275–278.

25. S.C. CODE § 15–78–70; 12 VT.STATS. ANN. § 5602.

26. 28 U.S.C.A. § 2679. The statute which is the basis of this code section was enacted in response to Westfall v. Erwin, 484 U.S. 292, 108 S.Ct. 580, 98 L.Ed.2d 619 (1988) and is consequently often referred to as the Westfall Act.

27. The statute leaves a remedy against the employee in claims for violation of the constitution or a federal statute "under which such action against an individual is otherwise authorized." 28 U.S.C.A. § 2679 (b)(2) (A) & (B). As to civil rights claims against federal officers, see § 278.

28. Gutierrez de Martinez v. Lamagno, 515 U.S. 417, 115 S.Ct. 2227, 132 L.Ed.2d 375 (1995) permits judicial review of the attorney general's certification.

29. 28 U.S.C.A. § 2679 (d). The statute provides that the attorney general's certification is "conclusive," but the Court has held that it is judicially reviewable.

Under this provision, the plaintiff may have no remedy even for an admitted wrong. In *United States v. Smith,*[30] Mrs. Smith's husband was in the armed forces stationed in Italy. Her child was born there with massive brain damage, allegedly as a result of medical negligence. The Smiths' suit against the allegedly negligent individual doctors was barred by the exclusive remedy provision. The government itself was immune because the Federal Tort Claims Act did not waive immunity of the government for claims arising in foreign countries.[31] The exclusive remedy provision thus immunizes federal employees generally, even if the exclusive remedy is no remedy at all.

Immunities and Substantive Defenses

Statutes prescribing immunities and federal civil rights cases may have popularized the immunity concept. Many of the cases decided today on immunity grounds would probably be decided the same way on the merits of the case. For example, officers are privileged to make an arrest under a warrant valid on its face, and likewise to make an arrest based upon probable cause to believe the arrested person has committed a felony.[32] It may confuse and complicate matters to analyze the officer's discretion in making an arrest and to say he enjoys a discretionary immunity.[33]

§ 274. Liability and Immunity of Government Contractors

As just seen, employees of public entities are sometimes but not always entitled to immunities protecting them from liability that would otherwise attach. Are independent contractors, hired to provide some particular product or service,[1] also entitled to immunities?

The Boyle rule. The Supreme Court has given a conditional yes answer. In *Boyle v. United Technologies Corporation,*[2] the Court has said that a contractor would share the government's immunity whenever "(1) the United States approved reasonably precise specifications; (2) the equipment conformed to those specifications; and (3) the supplier warned the United States about the dangers in the use of the equipment that were known to the supplier but not to the United States." Courts have described this immunity as an affirmative defense, to be proven by the contractor.[3]

Preemption-discretionary immunity basis for Boyle. In *Boyle,* a Marine pilot drowned when his helicopter, supplied by the defendant, went down in water and he could not open the escape hatch. The hatch design

30. United States v. Smith, 499 U.S. 160, 111 S.Ct. 1180, 113 L.Ed.2d 134 (1991)

31. 28 U.S.C.A. § 2680(k).

32. See §§ 82 & 83 supra.

33. As in, e.g., Wright v. Wynn, 682 So.2d 1 (Ala.1996).

1. The distinction between independent contractors and "servants" is considered in § 336.

2. Boyle v. United Technologies Corporation, 487 U.S. 500, 108 S.Ct. 2510, 101 L.Ed.2d 442 (1988).

3. Snell v. Bell Helicopter Textron, Inc., 107 F.3d 744 (9th Cir.1997).

was allegedly defective because it could not open outward against the water pressure. Suit was brought against the supplier under ordinary state tort law. But the Supreme Court reasoned that when unique federal interests were involved, federal law would preempt any conflicting state law rule. Tort law liability would conflict with the government's approval of the escape hatch design. Selection of the design—at least in this case—was a discretionary activity, so if suit had been against the government, it would have been immune on that ground.[4] Although suit was against the contractor, not the government, the Court thought that if contractors were liable for following discretionary specifications of the government, they would necessarily pass the costs of liability on to the government in the form of higher prices. That would, albeit indirectly, defeat the government's discretionary immunity. Hence the contractor was equally protected.

Rejecting Feres as basis for immunity. The *Boyle* Court was most particular in rejecting the rationale for contractor immunity that had been adopted in some Courts of Appeal. Those courts had said that the contractor shared the government's *Feres* defense. The *Feres* rule eliminates government liability for injuries to members of the armed forces while they are on duty.[5] Thus those courts saw the rule as a "military contractor defense." The Supreme Court rejected this rationale. The logic of *Boyle* is that its rules apply to give the contractor the government's immunity when the government approval's of specifications could count as a discretionary decision. Perhaps it implies as well that in no other case does an immunity pass to the contractor. Some courts, however, still refer to the defense as a "military contractor" defense.[6]

Limits to Boyle. The Court's reasoning in *Boyle* set some limits and conditions to the contractor's immunity. First, and most explicitly, the contractor would not be immune if it failed to warn of defects of which it knew and the government did not. Second, the contractor must have complied with the specification,[7] which must have been reasonably

4. See § 262, supra.

5. § 263 supra.

6. The Ninth Circuit appears to hold that the defense only applies to military contractors. See Nielsen v. George Diamond Vogel Paint Co., 892 F.2d 1450 (9th Cir. 1990). This attitude has forced the Ninth Circuit to characterize a ladder on a ship as military equipment. Butler v. Ingalls Shipbuilding, Inc., 89 F.3d 582 (9th Cir.1996). Some other courts have used the term "military contractor defense" where nothing turned on the characterization. E.g., Gray v. Lockheed Aeronautical Systems Co., 125 F.3d 1371 (11th Cir.1997) reversed in part and on other grounds, Gray v. Lockheed Aeronautical Systems, 155 F.3d 1343 (11th Cir.1998). The Court's rationale in *Boyle* seems much broader because the government might have discretionary immunity in many cases not involving military procurement. See Carley v. Wheeled Coach, 991 F.2d 1117 (3d Cir.1993); cf. Yearsley v.W.A. Ross Construction Co., 309 U.S. 18, 60 S.Ct. 413, 84 L.Ed. 554 (1940) (construction contractor immunity in a case antedating *Boyle*).

7. A manufacturing flaw that brings the product out of conformity with the specifications seems to violate this requirement, so most manufacturing flaw cases—as distinguished from design defect cases—seem to be actionable. The cases seem to recognize that if the product does not conform to government specifications, the defense will not apply. See Snell v. Bell Helicopter Textron, Inc., 107 F.3d 744, 749 (9th Cir.1997); Bailey v. McDonnell Douglas Corp., 989 F.2d 794 (5th Cir.1993). At the same time, these cases have been reluctant to accept a broad statement that manufacturing defects are not covered by the defense.

precise.[8] Third, the contractor would not obtain immunity when the government bought goods without specification out of the seller's commercial stock. If the government merely bought a manufacturer's standard can of paint, the seller of paint could not escape liability for chemical burns resulting because the paint was badly formulated.

Government approval of specifications. The *Boyle* immunity for contractors is not limited to cases in which the government provides the specifications. On the contrary, contractors enjoy the defense even when the contractor itself drew up the specifications. However, the immunity is still conditioned on government "approval" of those the specifications in the end. Some of the Courts of Appeal have said that approval requires more than a rubber stamp acceptance of the contractor's specifications, perhaps some kind of substantive review by the government.[9] Similarly, government approval of the overall design is not relevant; the government must approve the design feature that was allegedly defective and the specification must be reasonably precise. A specification that suitable mountings be provided is not enough to transmit the immunity to the contractor.[10]

Contractor's failure to warn. Under the terms of *Boyle* itself, the contractor can claim the immunity only if the contractor has warned the government of dangers that the contractor knows and the government does not.[11] If the contractor has duly warned the government or the government already knows the danger, it is still possible that the contractor should address a separate warning to users of the dangerous product, in instruction manuals or in warnings printed on the product itself.[12]

Under *Boyle,* it would seem that if the government had made a discretionary judgment that warnings were undesirable and had explicitly (or perhaps implicitly) specified "no warning", the contractor would be immune as to any failure-to-warn claim.[13] But if the transactions between contractor and government did not imply government-approved

8. Gray v. Lockheed Aeronautical Systems Co., 125 F.3d 1371 (11th Cir.1997) reversed in part and on other grounds, Gray v. Lockheed Aeronautical Systems, 155 F.3d 1343 (11th Cir.1998)(a general as distinct from a precise specification leaves discretion in the contractor, not the government, so that the discretionary immunity is not involved).

9. Some Courts of Appeals have said that the approval must entail some kind of governmental review and that a rubber stamp approval by the government would not suffice to provide immunity for the contractor. See Trevino v. General Dynamics Corp., 865 F.2d 1474 (5th Cir.1989) (if government delegates its design discretion to the contractor, and merely accepts the ultimate design without approval based on substantive review, the contractor does not obtain the immunity).

10. Snell v. Bell Helicopter Textron, Inc., 107 F.3d 744 (9th Cir.1997).

11. See Gray v. Lockheed Aeronautical Systems Co., 125 F.3d 1371 (11th Cir.1997) reversed in part and on other grounds, Gray v. Lockheed Aeronautical Systems, 155 F.3d 1343 (11th Cir.1998), rejecting immunity in part because no appropriate warning was given to the government itself.

12. Cf. Timberline Air Service, Inc. v. Bell Helicopter–Textron, Inc., 125 Wash.2d 305, 884 P.2d 920 (1994) (government contractor defense does not preclude postmanufacturer duty to warn known users who purchased used military equipment).

13. See Oliver v. Oshkosh Truck Corp. 96 F.3d 992 (7th Cir.1996); Tate v. Boeing Helicopters, 55 F.3d 1150 (6th Cir.1995).

silence when warning was needed, then the case is not one in which a reasonably precise specification has been made about warnings, so presumably the contractor would not be immune. Put more simply, the contractor gets no immunity unless his decision not to warn was prompted by government specifications.[14] Some courts, however, seem to relieve the contractor of any obligation to warn unless warning was required by the contract.[15]

Contractors with state public entities. The *Boyle* rule of course applies whether the contractor is sued in federal or in state court.[16] A very different question is whether a similar rule applies to those who contract with states or local public entities. States have applied some kind of immunity in such cases where the claim is that the contractor's fault was doing the job at all[17] and some authority may go further and adopt an immunity much like *Boyle's*.[18] State tort claims acts may have some effects not yet fully determined.[19] Some of the state cases involve building contractors who do not participate in developing specifications

14. Butler v. Ingalls Shipbuilding, Inc., 89 F.3d 582, 586 (9th Cir.1996) (*Boyle* defense "is inapplicable to a failure to warn claim in the absence of evidence that in making its decision whether to provide a warning" the contractor was acting in compliance with reasonably precise specifications). Distinguish the potential defense that the contractor could rely upon the government to provide appropriate warnings to users. See § 366 below (warnings to sophisticated users); see Miller v. United Technologies Corp., 233 Conn. 732, 660 A.2d 810 (1995).

15. See Hazel Glenn Beh, The Government Contractor Defense: When Do Governmental Interests Justify Excusing a Manufacturer's Liability for Defective Products?, 28 Seton Hall L. Rev. 430 (1997); cf. Perez v. Lockheed Corp., 88 F.3d 340 (5th Cir.1996) (semble, if the claim is for a warning defect in product, the rules of *Boyle* govern, period). When the specifications simply do not speak one way or another about either warning or a safety device, some might conclude that no reasonably precise specification is in issue and hence that the contractor cannot have an immunity. Others might conclude that by omitting reference to a safety device, the specifications are providing that it need not be included. See the divergent opinions in Anzalone v. Westech Gear Corp., 141 N.J. 256, 661 A.2d 796 (1995).

16. See, e.g., Miller v. United Technologies Corporation, 233 Conn. 732, 660 A.2d 810 (1995); Anzalone v. Westech Gear Corp., 141 N.J. 256, 661 A.2d 796 (1995) (equally divided court on how to apply the rule to the facts).

17. Vanchieri v. New Jersey Sports and Exposition Authority, 104 N.J. 80, 514 A.2d 1323 (1986) (plaintiff was injured, allegedly because of inadequate security at a state facility; the independent security service hired by the state would share state's immunity if the state had provided relevant specifications such as number of security guards to be posted); see A. E. Korpela, Annotation, Right of Contractor with Federal, State, or Local Public Body to Latter's Immunity from Tort Liability, 9 A.L.R.3d 382 (1967).

18. See Estate of Lyons v. CNA Insurance Companies, 207 Wis.2d 446, 558 N.W.2d 658 (Ct.App.1996) (architect's allegedly dangerous plans for a bridge, not in conformity with appropriate standards, were approved by state; architect is immune).

19. Some state statutes may directly exclude independent contractors from the enacted immunity. See Ariz. Rev. Stats. § 12–820.02 B. Others define employee to exclude independent contractors. Depending on how the term employee is used, that might imply that contractors are not to share any statutory immunity. See, e.g., Ga. Code § 50–21–22. But Vanchieri v. New Jersey Sports and Exposition Authority, supra n. 17, glossed over any such reading of the New Jersey statute. Where indemnity of employees (or independent contractors) is an important feature of the state's tort claims act, a provision including contractors in the indemnity scheme, as in Kan. Stat. Ann. § 75–6116 (h), might imply that they do not have an immunity in the absence of other statutory provisions.

as military suppliers often do. In these cases, the contractor may defeat the plaintiff's claim less because of immunity than because the contractor is not negligent in complying with the specifications[20] or because in some circumstances the owner's acceptance of the performance rendered terminates the contractor's duty of care.[21]

In the special case of a private contractor who contracts to take over state functions, as where prisons are privatized, they may become state actors who are subject to claims for civil rights violations, but without the protection of the good faith immunity that is provided to state employees.[22]

Carriers under a duty to transport goods. Common carriers are usually obligated to accept and transport goods. In some cases, strict liability is imposed for mishaps resulting from high explosives and similar especially dangerous items. When the mishap occurs while the explosives are in the hands of the common carrier, but without its fault, carriers argue that they should be immune because they are compelled by public laws to accept all goods. On this point the cases are somewhat divided, some imposing strict liability in spite of the carrier's "public duty" and others denying it.[23]

Topic C. Civil Rights Claims

§ 275. Federal Civil Rights Claims Generally

Civil rights litigation covers a broad spectrum. Much of it deals with discrimination that does not directly produce physical harms. For instance, officials or public entities might deprive a person of First Amendment free speech rights without causing physical harm.[1] Or officials might interfere with a family's custody of a child without due process.[2] Special federal and state statutes deal with job, housing, and educational

20. Some cases expressly state the rule as protection for the contractor who complies with the statute and is not negligent in performing the work. See McLain v. State, 563 N.W.2d 600 (Iowa 1997). Compare Valley Forge Gardens, Inc. v. James D. Morrissey, Inc., 385 Pa. 477, 123 A.2d 888 (1956) (the contractor shares the state's privilege "except for negligence or wilful tort") with Lobozzo v. Adam Eidemiller, Inc., 437 Pa. 360, 263 A.2d 432 (1970) (contractor strictly liable for blasting even though blasting was required by specifications).

21. The rules once automatically terminated the building contractor's duty when the landowner accepted the work. Under some circumstances that rule may be applied even now. E.g., Rogers v. Frank C. Mitchell Co., 908 S.W.2d 387 (Mo.App. 1995). On the shifting responsibility to the landowner, see § 194, supra.

22. Richardson v. McKnight, 521 U.S. 399, 117 S.Ct. 2100, 138 L.Ed.2d 540 (1997). In *Boyle,* the Court provided immunity to the contractor out of concern that if the contractor were held liable, the costs would eventually be passed on to the government. In contrast, the Court in *Richardson* thought that liability of the contractor needed no immunity for the very reason that he is subject to market pressures, which would provide "incentives to avoid overly timid, insufficiently vigorous, unduly fearful" operations.

23. This topic is discussed in § 350 below.

§ 275

1. See, e.g., Bernheim v. Litt, 79 F.3d 318 (2d Cir.1996).

2. Whisman v. Rinehart, 119 F.3d 1303 (8th Cir.1997).

discrimination, as well as with forms of discrimination against persons suffering disabilities—the kind of harms considered in Part IV. The present Part, however, focuses on injury, detention, and property damage torts. Most of those cases have arisen since about 1960[3] and under a single federal statute, 42 U.S.C.A. § 1983.

The thrust of § 1983 is to permit recovery of damages as well as injunctive relief for the violation of the plaintiff's federal statutory[4] and constitutional rights under color of state law.[5] For instance, the Fourth Amendment prohibits unreasonable searches and seizures under color of law. An officer who shoots a citizen in the back of the head may be committing the ultimate unreasonable seizure, and if so, § 1983 permits a suit.[6] When a plaintiff claims physical harm or an invasion of property rights under § 1983, the allegations usually assert police or prison misconduct. However, any act under color of state law that deprives a person of a constitutional or other federal right will suffice for the claim. A hospital,[7] mental institution,[8] school or teacher,[9] social worker or welfare department,[10] or other person acting under color of law are all

3. 42 U.S.C.A. § 1983 was enacted in 1871, but has been a mainstay of civil rights torts litigation only since Monroe v. Pape, 365 U.S. 167, 81 S.Ct. 473, 5 L.Ed.2d 492 (1961) overruled on other grounds by Monell v. Dept. of Soc. Svcs. of New York, 436 U.S. 658, 98 S.Ct. 2018, 56 L.Ed.2d 611 (1978). Many of the claims covered by § 1983 are directly comparable to common law trespassory torts such as battery and false imprisonment. See §§ 44–48 supra. Others, like those based on the First Amendment's free speech guarantee, deal with dignitary and economic torts covered in Part IV of this book. See, e.g., § 417.

4. Although violation of federal statutory rights is actionable under § 1983, not every federal statute creates an enforceable right; indeed, not every constitutional provision does so. The statute (or constitutional provision) must be one intended to create a right in the plaintiff and must place a specific obligation placed upon state actors. Statutes may provide elaborate remedial schemes intended to be exclusive and may thus foreclose § 1983 suits. There is a somewhat elaborate jurisprudence. See, discussing some of the major Supreme Court decisions, Harris v. James, 127 F.3d 993 (11th Cir.1997).

5. 42 U.S.C.A. § 1983 provides: "Every person who, under color of any statute, ordinance, regulation, custom, or usage, of any State or Territory or the District of Columbia, subjects, or causes to be subjected, any citizen of the United States or other persons within the jurisdiction thereof to the deprivation of any rights, privileges, or immunities secured by the Constitution and laws, shall be liable to the party injured in an action at law, suit in equity, or other proper proceeding for redress."

6. E.g., Gardner v. Buerger, 82 F.3d 248 (8th Cir.1996).

7. See Morrison v. Washington County, Alabama, 700 F.2d 678 (11th Cir. 1983) (claim against hospital which asked officers to remove delirious patient who needed medical attention could go forward).

8. Youngberg v. Romeo, 457 U.S. 307, 102 S.Ct. 2452, 73 L.Ed.2d 28 (1982) (freedom from unreasonable restraints and minimal training); Shaw v. Strackhouse, 920 F.2d 1135, 118 A.L.R. Fed. 755 (3d Cir. 1990) (failure to protect from foreseeable sexual attacks).

9. See Doe v. Claiborne County, Tennessee, 103 F.3d 495 (6th Cir.1996) (constitutional right to substantive due process violated by teacher's sexual harassment, but school board members had no supervisory duty and are not liable). A different statute, 20 U.S.C.A. § 1681 ("Title IX"), deals with discrimination in federally funded educational programs. Sexual harassment by school teachers is actionable under that statute, See Franklin v. Gwinnett County Public Schools, 503 U.S. 60, 112 S.Ct. 1028, 117 L.Ed.2d 208 (1992), but the school district itself is liable only if a person with coercive power to remedy discrimination has notice of the harassment and is deliberately indifferent to it. Alida Star Gebser v. Lago Vista Independent School Dist., 524 U.S. 274, 118 S.Ct. 1989, 141 L.Ed.2d 277 (1998).

10. Doe v. New York City Dept. of Social Services, 649 F.2d 134 (2d Cir.1981)

subject to liability for unconstitutional acts or policies that foster or permit injury.

Analysis of § 1983 actions tends to use familiar tort ideas. Courts emphasize the importance of actual and proximate cause in § 1983 cases, for example. Many of the rules under § 1983 as well as some of the advantages it offers for the plaintiff have already been summarized.[11] In this chapter, it is important to notice how § 1983 actions affect liabilities and immunities of entities and employees.

§ 276. Civil Rights: State and Local Employees and Other Individuals

Potential for liability and immunity under § 1983. In no case is a defendant subject to § 1983 liability unless he has acted under color of state law or custom. Sometimes private individuals act under color of state law,[1] but the ordinary case is one against a state or local employee who carries out his function in a way that allegedly violates the constitution—a seizure of a person or search of her property without probable cause, for example.[2] Many of the cases discussed in this section involve claims of police misconduct or prisoner abuse, but any violation of federal rights under color of law will suffice for a claim.

The plaintiff may sue officers in their individual or personal capacity[3] for actions under color of state law, in which case the officer is personally liable for his own unconstitutional actions and for his unconstitutional failure to supervise or control subordinates.[4] One advantage the plaintiff enjoys in making § 1983 claims against a state or local employee is that state-law immunities do not protect the officer. On the other hand, officers may plead a federal immunity as an affirmative defense.[5]

(inadequate monitoring of foster home environment); Yvonne L. v. New Mexico Dept. of Human Services, 959 F.2d 883 (10th Cir.1992) (placement in dangerous foster care).

11. See §§ 44–48 supra.

§ 276

1. See Adickes v. S.H. Kress & Co., 398 U.S. 144, 90 S.Ct. 1598, 26 L.Ed.2d 142 (1970) (conspiracy with state officers to enforce custom of segregation).

2. E.g., Yang v. Hardin, 37 F.3d 282 (7th Cir.1994). Describing the main constitutional claims, see §§ 45–48 supra.

3. If the officer is sued in his "official capacity", the suit is treated as one against the entity. If he is sued in his individual capacity, the suit aims to recover against the officer personally, albeit for actions that were in a sense official. The distinction has created pitfalls. See Kentucky v. Graham, 473 U.S. 159, 105 S.Ct. 3099, 87 L.Ed.2d 114 (1985).

4. See Clay v. Conlee, 815 F.2d 1164 (8th Cir.1987) (recognizing supervisory liability of officer and distinguishing the problem of a public entity's liability for failure to supervise or train); cf. Yang v. Hardin, 37 F.3d 282 (7th Cir.1994) (failure to attempt control of fellow officer's unconstitutional conduct was actionable). Such cases do not turn on vicarious or respondeat superior liability; they turn on the officer's own fault in failing to act appropriately to prevent another's misconduct.

5. Harlow v. Fitzgerald, 457 U.S. 800, 102 S.Ct. 2727, 73 L.Ed.2d 396 (1982). Confusion about what is part of the plaintiff's prima facie case and what is part of the affirmative defense has been previously mentioned in connection with Fourth Amendment litigation. See § 87. The Supreme Court has said that no heightened pleading requirement applies to civil rights cases to require pleading specific facts. Leatherman v. Tarrant County Narcotics Intelligence and Coordination Unit, 507

Absolute immunity. The absolute immunity for legislative and judicial acts seen in the common law cases carries over to § 1983 claims as well.[6] The President of the United States is likewise absolutely immune even to suits for constitutional violations.[7]

Executive branch employees. When it comes to the usual case of claims against executive branch employees, the immunity is sometimes described as a good faith immunity, but the term is misleading because it does not turn on subjective good faith and is not lost by subjective malice.[8] Instead, "government officials performing discretionary functions generally are shielded from liability for civil damages insofar as their conduct does not violate clearly established statutory or constitutional rights of which a reasonable person would have known."[9]

The second element has gained most of the attention. The problem is that at a high level of generality, constitutional rights such as the right to due process have been established for generations, while at the most specific level possible, no right is established until it is litigated.[10] The Supreme Court's approach is to say that even if reasonable officers would know that the constitutional right is established, the defendant retains the immunity unless established law makes it apparent that his particular conduct is unconstitutional. For example, a warrantless search of a home is established as unconstitutional unless the officer has probable cause and there are exigent circumstances requiring a search. A reasonable officer should know the rule about warrantless searches, but a reasonable officer would not necessarily know whether information he holds counts as probable cause and whether the circumstances are sufficiently pressing to justify the search. If a reasonable officer could

U.S. 163, 113 S.Ct. 1160, 122 L.Ed.2d 517 (1993). But the Courts of Appeals have forecast an exception. They hold that when immunity is pleaded the plaintiff must in the first instance negate the immunity by pleading (not merely proving) specific facts that show the office should have known that his conduct was unconstitutional. See Breidenbach v. Bolish, 126 F.3d 1288 (10th Cir.1997).

6. See e.g., Butz v. Economou, 438 U.S. 478, 98 S.Ct. 2894, 57 L.Ed.2d 895 (1978) (administrative law judge carrying out judicial function); Bogan v. Scott-Harris, 523 U.S. 44, 118 S.Ct. 966, 140 L.Ed.2d 79 (1998). See § 273.

7. Nixon v. Fitzgerald, 457 U.S. 731, 102 S.Ct. 2690, 73 L.Ed.2d 349 (1982).

8. It is possible, however, that some violations of the constitution are violations only when a bad subjective motive is established. In that event, evidence of a bad motive may be admissible on the issue of violation even though it will be excluded on the issue of immunity. See Grant v. City of Pittsburgh, 98 F.3d 116 (3d Cir.1996).

9. Harlow v. Fitzgerald, 457 U.S. 800, 818, 102 S.Ct. 2727, 2738, 73 L.Ed.2d 396 (1982).

10. The problem was summarized in K.H. v. Morgan, 914 F.2d 846, 851 (7th Cir.1990) as follows: "[I]t would be improper to deny immunity to a particular defendant on the ground that his conduct could be subsumed under some principle of liability in force when he acted. That approach would shrink immunity to trivial dimensions, since it is always possible to find a principle of comprehensive generality (such as 'due process of law') ... Liability in that particular set must have been established at the time the defendant acted. It begins to seem as if to survive a motion to dismiss a suit on grounds of immunity the plaintiff must be able to point to a previous case that differs only trivially from his case. But this cannot be right. The easiest cases don't even arise. There has never been a section 1983 case accusing welfare officials of selling foster children into slavery; it does not follow that if such a case arose, the officials would be immune from damages liability because no previous case had found liability in those circumstances".

believe that the search was permissible in spite of the general rule, the immunity remains.[11] As Justice White once said, the objective immunity "provides ample protection to all but the plainly incompetent or those who knowingly violate the law."[12]

§ 277. Civil Rights: State and Local Public Entities

States. Section 1983[1] imposes liability upon "every person" who violates the plaintiff's constitutional or other federal rights. As a matter of historical analysis, the Supreme Court has concluded that states were not considered "persons" and hence could not be sued at all under § 1983,[2] although they might fall within the proscriptions of some other statutes.

Local public entities subject to liability without immunity. Local public entities are treated as "persons" covered by § 1983, but subject to some special rules. First, the local entity cannot claim the "good faith" immunity of its officer and it has no discretion to violate the constitution.[3] The entity may escape liability, but it cannot interpose the immunity bar.[4]

Requirement of policy, custom, or official decision. Second, local entities are not liable for every constitutional violation, only those that result from a policy, custom, or official decision of the entity.[5] The fact that a police officer used excessive force in making an arrest and thus violated the Fourth Amendment, for example, is enough to make the officer liable but not the entity. On the contrary, the entity will not be responsible unless its policy, custom, or official decision caused the constitutional violation.[6] The Court sometimes expresses this rule by saying that the entity is not to be held vicariously liable, only liable for its own acts. That is a convenient expression but not a literal one; more accurately, the entity is held vicariously liable for official and policy decisions of policymaking officials.

Single act or decision at policymaking level. Plaintiffs can implicate a public entity in constitutional violations in two basic ways. First, they can prove an ongoing plan, program or practice that is unconstitutional or fosters unconstitutional action. Second, they can prove a single

11. Anderson v. Creighton, 483 U.S. 635, 107 S.Ct. 3034, 97 L.Ed.2d 523 (1987).

12. Malley v. Briggs, 475 U.S. 335, 341, 106 S.Ct. 1092, 1096, 89 L.Ed.2d 271 (1986).

§ 277

1. 42 U.S.C.A. § 1983, summarized in § 275, supra.

2. Will v. Michigan Dept. of State Police, 491 U.S. 58, 109 S.Ct. 2304, 105 L.Ed.2d 45 (1989). Similarly, a judgment against an individual officer of the state cannot serve as a basis for reaching state funds. See Hafer v. Melo, 502 U.S. 21, 112 S.Ct. 358, 116 L.Ed.2d 301 (1991).

3. Owen v. City of Independence, Mo., 445 U.S. 622, 100 S.Ct. 1398, 63 L.Ed.2d 673 (1980).

4. Leatherman v. Tarrant County Narcotics Intelligence and Coordination Unit, 507 U.S. 163, 113 S.Ct. 1160, 122 L.Ed.2d 517 (1993).

5. Monell v. Dept. of Social Services, 436 U.S. 658, 98 S.Ct. 2018, 56 L.Ed.2d 611 (1978).

6. E.g., Board of County Comn'rs of Bryan County v. Brown, 520 U.S. 397, 117 S.Ct. 1382, 137 L.Ed.2d 626 (1997).

"official decision" that is unconstitutional or fosters unconstitutionality. When the plaintiff claims that a single decision rather than an ongoing plan, practice, or program has violated her constitutional rights, she must show that the decision was made by the public entity's policy maker for that issue. For example, if a city council votes to discharge a police chief without a hearing, it denies him due process, and since the city council is the policy making authority, such a vote counts as an official decision, so that the city may be subjected to liability.[7] The same rule can apply to any single decision as long as it is made by the policymaking official for the issue involved. Thus where a county attorney made decisions that led officers to break in private premises without a warrant, his decision was official and the county could be subjected to liability.[8]

Ongoing plan, practice or custom. When the plaintiff claims that an ongoing plan, policy, or custom of the entity is unconstitutional, the policy might be formalized and written, but perhaps more often is not. The rule is that no formal policy is required; a custom or practice is sufficient.[9] For example, if a city refuses to train its police officers in the proper use of force, or regularly delays investigation of complaints about excessive force, the city's practice coupled with the city's notice of the problem may be viewed as a custom or even a policy, even though poor training or delay is not a formal or written part of the system.[10] In other words, policy is as policy does. But perhaps the terms policy and custom are inadequate in this setting. Maybe the important thing is that the custom or practice is carried on over time so that the entity or its policymaker has a fair chance to review and decide whether to alter the practice.[11] A custom or practice that is strong and persistent proves its own acceptance at the policymaking level.

Policies and decisions that only risk constitutional violations by others. In some cases a policy or decision is itself unconstitutional. A policy that directs police officers to break into homes without warrants is an example. So is an official decision to stigmatize and then fire a public employee without a hearing. However, many official decisions and policies of a public entity are not themselves unconstitutional; they merely create a risk of unconstitutional action by others. For example, a city

7. Cf. Owen v. City of Independence, Mo., 445 U.S. 622, 100 S.Ct. 1398, 63 L.Ed.2d 673 (1980) (some council members and city manager published accusations, then discharged police chief without a hearing).

8. Pembaur v. City of Cincinnati, 475 U.S. 469, 106 S.Ct. 1292, 89 L.Ed.2d 452 (1986).

9. See, e.g., Monell v. Department of Social Services of City of New York, 436 U.S. 658, 690, 98 S.Ct. 2018, 2036, 56 L.Ed.2d 611 (1978).

10. See, e.g., Allen v. Muskogee, Oklahoma, 119 F.3d 837 (10th Cir.1997) (officers inadequately training in dealing with persons who are both armed and emotionally upset, jury questions).

11. Cf. Board of County Com'rs of Bryan County v. Brown, 520 U.S. 397, 117 S.Ct. 1382, 137 L.Ed.2d 626 (1997) ("If a program does not prevent constitutional violations, municipal decisionmakers may eventually be put on notice that a new program is called for. Their continued adherence to an approach that they know or should know has failed to prevent tortious conduct by employees may establish the conscious disregard for the consequences of their action").

that inadequately trains new police officers runs a risk that some individual officers, lacking training, will act unconstitutionally, perhaps by using excessive and even deadly force, but it is not a certainty and probably not the purpose of a custom not to train.

The problem for the plaintiff in such cases may be three-fold. First, negligence by itself, even official negligence, is ordinarily not sufficient to show a violation of due process or equal protection rights when the official rule or policy is not unconstitutional on its face.[12] A policy that *risks* unconstitutional violations but does not dictate or approve them sounds like a policy that is negligent only, so it might be argued that such a policy does not violate the constitution at all. Second, a practice that risks unconstitutional violations by others might not be considered a custom or policy at all unless the entity's acquiescence in that practice shows deliberate indifference.[13] Third, a policy that is not itself unconstitutional but merely risks constitutional harm by others might be deemed an insufficient basis for liability, either because it does not reflect sufficient fault or because it is causally remote.[14] With some of these considerations in mind, the Court has said that the plaintiff in these cases must prove that the entity was guilty of willful indifference.[15]

Willful indifference might be found in some cases of ongoing policies or programs, even in ongoing failures to act, because sooner or later the entity must become aware of the effects and because the unconstitution-

12. Daniels v. Williams, 474 U.S. 327, 106 S.Ct. 662, 88 L.Ed.2d 662 (1986) (due process); Washington v. Davis, 426 U.S. 229, 96 S.Ct. 2040, 48 L.Ed.2d 597 (1976) (equal protection). However, even a facially neutral policy that discriminates in fact must have rational basis. See Navarro v. Block, 72 F.3d 712 (9th Cir.1995). Distinguish Fourth and Eighth Amendment cases, which turn on reasonableness of searches and seizures, and on cruel punishment respectively. Persons involuntarily committed to mental institutions are also entitled to professional care, which comes close to stating a negligence standard. See Youngberg v. Romeo, 457 U.S. 307, 102 S.Ct. 2452, 73 L.Ed.2d 28 (1982). The same has been held with respect to children placed by the state in foster homes. Kara B. v. Dane County, 205 Wis.2d 140, 555 N.W.2d 630 (1996).

13. See City of Canton, Ohio v. Harris, 489 U.S. 378, 389, 109 S.Ct. 1197, 1205, 103 L.Ed.2d 412 (1989) ("Only where a municipality's failure to train its employees in a relevant respect evidences a 'deliberate indifference' to the rights of its inhabitants can such a shortcoming be properly thought of as a city 'policy or custom' that is actionable under § 1983.... Only where a failure to train reflects a 'deliberate' or 'conscious' choice by a municipality—a 'policy' as defined by our prior cases—can a city be liable for such a failure under § 1983").

14. See Collins v. City of Harker Heights, Texas, 503 U.S. 115, 123–24, 112 S.Ct. 1061, 1068, 117 L.Ed.2d 261 (1992) (inadequate training of officers can be "characterized as the cause of the constitutional tort if—and only if—the failure to train amounted to 'deliberate indifference' "); Board of County Com'rs of Bryan County v. Brown, 520 U.S. 397, 117 S.Ct. 1382, 1390, 137 L.Ed.2d 626 (1997) ("Existence of a 'program' makes proof of fault and causation at least possible in an inadequate training case").

15. City of Canton, Ohio v. Harris, 489 U.S. 378, 109 S.Ct. 1197, 103 L.Ed.2d 412 (1989). The phrase is unfortunate. "Deliberate" indifference is a constitutional requirement in Eighth Amendment claims for cruel and unusual punishment. See § 48. "Deliberate" indifference is sometimes but not always enough to show that official action "shocks the conscience" and hence violates substantive due process. See County of Sacramento v. Lewis, 523 U.S. 833, 118 S.Ct. 1708, 140 L.Ed.2d 1043 (1998). "Willful" indifference here, however, is a court-developed notion that stems from the policy-or-official-decision requirement, which in turn is derived from the statute, not the constitution.

al action is highly likely over time. Hence, a number of courts have recognized that an entity's failure to train police officers might subject the entity to liability for the untrained officers' use of excessive force[16] or denial of medical attention.[17] A little authority supports liability as well for denial of equal protection by police policies that deny appropriate protection to potential victims of domestic violence,[18] but in all of these cases, the plaintiff is more likely to lose because deliberate indifference or other quasi-intentional wrongdoing will be difficult to prove.[19]

On the other hand, when a single decision is made that does not set a standard for the future, the policy decision does not reflect intent to harm. It reflects instead only an unreasonable risk of harm, which is to say negligence. So the Court has held that a policymaker's one-time failure to check the background of an officer, although a policy decision, was not one that showed deliberate indifference.[20]

Constitutional violation. A clear policy of deliberate indifference is not by itself sufficient to show a valid § 1983 claim. The plaintiff must also show a violation of a constitutional or other federal right. A city might be deliberately indifferent to the nutritional needs of its residents, but unless the residents have a right to the city's nutritional beneficence, they have no constitutional claim. With limited exceptions, public entities do not owe affirmative duties of protection.[21] Consequently, a public school is not liable under § 1983 when it is deliberately indifferent to the probability that a student will commit suicide, because the school owes no constitutional obligation to protect the student.[22]

Even affirmative acts that are in some sense deliberately indifferent may be justified by exigencies. The Court has held that the Constitution is not violated at all by a police officer's willful indifference to the possibility of injuring a bystander in the course of a high speed chase. In that case, the needs of law enforcement show that the indifference to

16. E.g., Atchinson v. District of Columbia, 73 F.3d 418, 315 U.S.App.D.C. 318 (D.C.Cir.1996) (reversing dismissal of claim); Flores v. Cameron County, Texas, 92 F.3d 258 (5th Cir.1996) (remand to determine deliberate indifference after verdict for the plaintiff).

17. City of Canton, Ohio v. Harris, supra n. 15.

18. Navarro v. Block, 72 F.3d 712 (9th Cir.1995); Doe v. Calumet City, 161 Ill.2d 374, 641 N.E.2d 498, 204 Ill.Dec. 274 (1994)

19. E.g., Soto v. Flores, 103 F.3d 1056 (1st Cir.1997) (although police officer knew that wife was at risk if he revealed that she had sought police protection from husband's abuse, he told husband, who then killed wife's children and himself, but neither this nor a climate of police disapproval of domestic violence rights sufficed to show discriminatory intent necessary for equal protection claim); cf. West v. Waymire, 114 F.3d 646 (7th Cir.1997) (focusing on the risk of the specific harm—an officer's sexual molestation of a minor—rather than on general risks from an officer known to abuse his powers). See, summarizing some of the cases, Susanne M. Browne, Note, Due Process and Equal Protection Challenges to the Inadequate Response of the Police in Domestic Violence Situations, 68 S. Cal. L. Rev. 1295 (1995).

20. Board of County Com'rs of Bryan County v. Brown, 520 U.S. 397, 117 S.Ct. 1382, 137 L.Ed.2d 626 (1997).

21. DeShaney v. Winnebago County Dept. of Social Services, 489 U.S. 189, 109 S.Ct. 998, 103 L.Ed.2d 249 (1989). On the lack of duty to take affirmative action for the protection of others, see Chapter 22.

22. Wyke v. Polk County School Board, 129 F.3d 560 (11th Cir.1997).

injury does not shock the conscience and consequently that the due process clause has not been violated.[23]

§ 278. Civil Rights: Federal Government and Its Employees

Section 1983[1] addresses violations of federal rights inflicted under color of state law or custom. Consequently, those who act under federal law are not subjected to liability under § 1983. However, the Supreme Court has held that federal agents who violate constitutional rights can be sued directly under the constitution. Such a claim is usually called a *Bivens* action.[2] The result is a right against federal officers that is largely analogous to the statutory § 1983 claim available against state officers and subject to the same immunities.[3]

The federal government itself, however, is not responsible in tort for violation of the federal constitution. Claims against the federal government are governed generally by the Federal Tort Claims Act, which, perhaps anomalously, applies state law only.[4] The effect is that in tort claims under the FTCA applying state tort law, only the government could be liable; its officers cannot be.[5] In tort claims based upon federal constitutional violations, only the officers can be liable; the government cannot be.

23. County of Sacramento v. Lewis, 523 U.S. 833, 118 S.Ct. 1708, 140 L.Ed.2d 1043 (1998).

§ 278

1. 42 U.S.C.A. § 1983, summarized in § 275, supra.

2. Bivens v. Six Unknown Named Agents of Federal Bureau of Narcotics, 403 U.S. 388, 91 S.Ct. 1999, 29 L.Ed.2d 619 (1971).

3. Breidenbach v. Bolish, 126 F.3d 1288 (10th Cir.1997). But the Westfall Act, which immunizes federal employees against state-law tort claims, does not do so with respect to violations of the constitution or a federal statute. See 28 U.S.C.A. § 2679 (b) (2).

4. § 261.

5. § 273, supra.

*

Chapter 16

Family Members and Charities

§ 279. Spousal Immunity

Wives' disabilities at earlier common law. Although a spouse might have claims against an outsider for interference with marital rights,[1] claims against the other spouse were almost nonexistent. The earlier common law subjugated wives to their husbands by viewing the marital couple as a single entity. In the legal unity of husband and wife, the husband was in charge. He was entitled to possess and draw the profits from his wife's properties, for example, and even to "discipline" her. In the formal, hobbled reasoning of some common law periods, the couple were regarded as one legal entity, with the result that neither individual could sue the other.[2]

Married Women's Property Acts. Common law rules were improved somewhat in the 19th century by statutes called the Married Women's Property Acts. These allowed the wife to maintain a legal action against her husband to vindicate her property interests. For example, she could sue her husband for negligent injury to her property or for its conversion. Courts held that the statutes destroyed the legal identity of the two persons so that wife and husband could sue each other.

Immunities remaining after the statutes. For a long time, however, personal torts fell under the old rule, so that neither spouse could sue the other for negligent or even intentional injury. Courts argued that even though the Married Women's Act had individualized the rights of the two parties to the marriage, immunity stood intact, mainly on the theory that suits between husband and wife would be fictitious and fraudulent and that in any event they would destroy the peace and harmony of the home.[3] Translated into today's language, courts argued that a husband could not be challenged in court for beating his wife because the marriage was entitled to "privacy" and freedom from judicial scrutiny.[4]

§ 279

1. As to claims against third persons for interference with family relationships, see § 310 (loss of consortium) and §§ 442–444 (alienation of affection and the like).

2. There are many good brief summaries of this abysmal history. See Price v. Price, 732 S.W.2d 316 (Tex.1987); Restatement § 895F, cmts. b and c.

3. See Carl Tobias, Interspousal Tort Immunity in America, 23 Ga. L. Rev. 359, 441 (1989) (listing judicial concerns over (1) marital harmony, (2) fraud and collusion, (3) the need to defer to the legislature, (4) excessive and frivolous claims, and (5) the availability of alternative remedies).

4. See Reva B. Siegel, "The Rule of Love": Wife Beating as Prerogative And Privacy, 105 Yale L.J. 2117 (1996).

Rejecting the fraud and family harmony arguments. Courts have now widely rejected or discounted the arguments for immunity. Although some claims between spouses might be fraudulent, fraud is also a possibility with suits among friends. Even strangers on a train could cook up a fictitious claim. So courts gradually recognized that the way to deal with fraudulent spousal claims may be to expose the fraud rather than to bar good claims along with bad ones. The family disruption argument has never seemed very persuasive. Since the time of the Married Women's Acts, the wife was allowed to sue for conversion of her property; a suit for negligently breaking her spine seems no more disruptive. Indeed, in many cases, the peace and harmony of the home that courts sought to protect seems not to have existed, or if it did, was destroyed by the tortious behavior for which the wife sued.

Abolishing the blanket immunity. In the latter half of the 20th century, most courts removed the blanket immunity for spousal suits. A large number of these courts have simply abolished the immunity. They apply ordinary tort rules to suits between spouses, at least in personal injury cases and frequently in all cases.[5] The Restatement reflects this approach in its simple provision that no spousal immunity remains.[6]

Some courts have replaced the blanket immunity with a screen that filters out some but not all claims for spousal torts. For instance, some courts initially abolished the immunity only for injuries inflicted by the use of automobiles.[7] But it is hard to draw a rational line at automobile cases, and as the decisions came down, courts gradually moved to a more general abolition of the immunity, so that ordinary tort rules increasingly apply.[8] Thus courts have said that one spouse might be subject to liability to the other for invasion of privacy[9] or for negligent transmission of a venereal disease[10] or for negligently caused falls[11] as well as for vehicular injuries.

Domestic violence torts. Intentional torts of a spouse, often in the form of domestic violence, easily seem to call for liability.[12] The Seventh

5. E.g., Leach v. Leach, 227 Ark. 599, 300 S.W.2d 15 (1957) (relying on Married Women's Property Act); Klein v. Klein, 58 Cal.2d 692, 376 P.2d 70, 26 Cal.Rptr. 102 (1962) (compensation for tort is the fundamental principle in the absence of compelling policy against it); Waite v. Waite, 618 So.2d 1360 (Fla.1993); Burns v. Burns, 518 So.2d 1205 (Miss.1988); Price v. Price, 732 S.W.2d 316 (Tex.1987). Statutes abolish the immunity in some states. E.g., Haw. Rev. Stats. Ann. § 572–28; 750 ILCS 65/1; N.C. Gen. Stat. § 52–5. For lists of cases, see Wayne F. Foster, Annotation, Modern Status of Interspousal Tort Immunity in Personal Injury And Wrongful Death Actions, 92 A.L.R.3d 901 (1980).

6. Restatement § 895F(1).

7. E.g., Fernandez v. Romo, 132 Ariz. 447, 646 P.2d 878 (1982).

8. See Brown v. Brown, 381 Mass. 231, 409 N.E.2d 717 (1980); Merenoff v. Merenoff, 76 N.J. 535, 388 A.2d 951 (1978).

9. Miller v. Brooks, 123 N.C.App. 20, 472 S.E.2d 350 (1996).

10. S.A.V. v. K.G.V., 708 S.W.2d 651 (Mo.1986) (negligent transmission of herpes to wife). See Kristyn J. Krohse, Note, No Longer Following the Rule of Thumb—What to Do with Domestic Torts and Divorce Claims, 1997 U. Ill. L. Rev. 923, 929 (1997).

11. Klein v. Klein, 58 Cal.2d 692, 376 P.2d 70, 26 Cal.Rptr. 102 (1962).

12. See generally Scherer, Tort Remedies for Victims of Domestic Abuse, 43 S. C. L. Rev. 543 (1992).

Circuit even held that an earlier Illinois immunity for intentional torts was unconstitutional since it could not rationally serve the purpose of protecting family harmony to immunize.[13] A reluctant Congress created a civil rights action that in form permits a claim for victims who suffer domestic violence,[14] but only when the violence is "motivated by gender." The restriction may prevent effective use of the statute by women victims, since proving the required "animus based on the victim's gender" may make the outcome so uncertain that litigation will not be worthwhile. Meanwhile, when the issue has been presented in recent years, state courts have usually abolished the immunity for intentional torts,[15] sometimes recognizing the special problem of domestic violence and the fact that women are usually the victims. State domestic violence statutes also sometimes support a claim,[16] but it remains to be seen whether litigation under the statute will redeem the judicial past.

§ 280. Parental Immunity

Rise and Decline of the Parental Immunity

Parental immunity. The early common law metaphysics ascribed a single legal identity to husband and wife. This view supposedly required spousal immunity, but it had no application to suits between parents and children. Consequently writers have supposed that children could sue parents, at least for torts to property. In 1891, however, Mississippi decided *Hewlett v. George*,[1] which spawned a general rule in American law that parents and those in *loco parentis*[2] could not be held liable for either intentional or negligent torts to their minor, unemancipated children. The blanket immunity has now been discarded in the state of its origin and in most others, but remnants of it remain in many states.

Confusion of immunity and privilege; exceptions. The blanket immunity may have gained its standing from the confusion of immunities with

13. Moran v. Beyer, 734 F.2d 1245 (7th Cir.1984). The Illinois statute now abolishes the immunity. See n. 5, supra.

14. 42 U.S.C.A. § 13981.

15. E.g., Stevens v. Stevens, 231 Kan. 726, 647 P.2d 1346 (1982); Lusby v. Lusby, 283 Md. 334, 390 A.2d 77 (1978). A general abolition of the immunity also covers intentional torts. See, e.g., Giovine v. Giovine, 284 N.J.Super. 3, 663 A.2d 109 (1995), overruled as to jury trial rights when the issue is presented in a divorce case, Brennan v. Orban, 145 N.J. 282, 678 A.2d 667 (1996).

16. See N.J. Stats. Ann. § 2C:25–29 (b) (4). As to actions based on police refusals to protect domestic victims, see § 277, supra. Conceivably statutes requiring reports of abuse by medical personnel could support an action for non-reporting. See James T. R. Jones, Battered Spouses' Damage Actions Against Non-reporting Physicians, 45 DePaul L. Rev. 191 (1996).

§ 280

1. Hewlett v. George, 68 Miss. 703, 9 So. 885 (1891), also styled Hewellette v. George, 68 Miss. 703, 9 So. 885 (1891), overruled in Glaskox v. Glaskox, 614 So.2d 906 (Miss.1992).

2. Typically full-time caretakers who act in the role of parents. See Queen v. Carey, 210 Ga.App. 41, 435 S.E.2d 264 (Ga.App. 1993) (grandparent); McGee v. McGee, 936 S.W.2d 360 (1996) (step parent); but cf. Warren v. Warren, 336 Md. 618, 650 A.2d 252 (1994) (no parental immunity for step-parents). Some courts have denied loco parentis status to foster parents who take children under a contract with the state. See Annotation, Foster Parent's Right to Immunity from Foster Child's Negligence Claims, 55 A.L.R.4th 778 (1987).

privileges. Immunity depends only upon the status of the parties; privilege depends upon justifications for the defendant's actions. Parents are undoubtedly privileged to discipline their children,[3] for example, but that is hardly a reason to say that parents are free to beat or rape their children.[4] Over the half century or so after the immunity was introduced, courts gradually seemed to have recognized the distinction, because they created a number of exceptions to the immunity.[5] For example, courts allowed the action when the child was injured in the course of the parent's business activity[6] or by acts that were tortious to people generally and not merely to the child.[7] Courts also allowed recovery for intentional or wilful torts, and where the immunity otherwise remains, they still do.[8]

Partial abrogation of immunity. In the second half of the twentieth century, most states removed the blanket immunity of parents and children. Some of them addressed only or mainly automobile cases,[9] but others attempted a more general and principled approach. The trend was led by Wisconsin's 1963 decision in *Goller v. White*.[10] The Wisconsin court's abrogation of immunity, however, left immunity standing in two situations. First, parents would be immune whenever the alleged negligent act involved an exercise of parental authority over the child. Second, the immunity would remain where the alleged negligent act involved an exercise of parental discretion with respect to the provision of food, clothing, housing and other care.

A number of other courts adopted the Wisconsin formula retaining the immunity when issues of parental authority and discretion were involved[11] or, as sometimes said, for acts that are inherent in the parent-child relationship.[12] A variation on that rule, especially associated with

3. § 94, supra.

4. Roller v. Roller, 37 Wash. 242, 79 P. 788 (1905), overruled in part, Borst v. Borst, 41 Wash.2d 642, 251 P.2d 149 (1952) (rejecting *Roller's* "absolute" immunity; no immunity as to nonparental transactions).

5. See Romualdo P. Eclavea, Annotation, Liability of Parent for Injury to Unemancipated Child Caused by Parent's Negligence—Modern Cases, 6 A.L.R.4th 1066 (1981).

6. E.g., Dzenutis v. Dzenutis, 200 Conn. 290, 512 A.2d 130 (1986) (business activity conducted away from home).

7. See Dzenutis v. Dzenutis, supra n. 6; Grivas v. Grivas, 113 A.D.2d 264, 496 N.Y.S.2d 757 (1985).

8. Herzfeld v. Herzfeld, 732 So.2d 1102 (Fla.Dist.Ct.App.1999) (allegation of parental sexual abuse); Fager v. Hundt, 610 N.E.2d 246 (Ind.1993) (a parent has no immunity for sexual abuse of his child under the "intentional felonious conduct" standard); Foldi v. Jeffries, 93 N.J. 533, 461 A.2d 1145 (1983); Doe By Connolly v. Holt, 332 N.C. 90, 418 S.E.2d 511 (1992) (repeated rapes and sexual molestation); Pavlick v. Pavlick, 254 Va. 176, 491 S.E.2d 602 (Va. 1997); see Henderson v. Woolley, 230 Conn. 472, 644 A.2d 1303 (1994) (no immunity for sexual abuse).

9. See cases cited n. 20 below.

10. Goller v. White, 20 Wis.2d 402, 122 N.W.2d 193 (Wis.1963).

11. Sears, Roebuck & Co. v. Huang, 652 A.2d 568 (Del.1995); Bonin v. Vannaman, 261 Kan. 199, 929 P.2d 754 (1996); Wagner v. Smith, 340 N.W.2d 255 (Iowa 1983); Broadwell v. Holmes, 871 S.W.2d 471 (Tenn.1994); Jilani v. Jilani, 767 S.W.2d 671 (Tex.1988) (applying the test to allow claim for automobile negligence on family vacation). But cf. Caniglia v. Lary, 366 N.W.2d 548 (Iowa 1985) (a 4-year-old child allegedly suffocated as a result of his father's negligent grain-loading operations; claim held actionable).

12. Cates v. Cates, 156 Ill.2d 76, 189 Ill.Dec. 14, 619 N.E.2d 715 (1993) ("[W]e conclude that the immunity should afford

New York cases, retains immunity for injuries resulting from parental "supervision" or its absence.[13]

These formulas have immunized parents in some fairly horrible cases. A parent who allowed his four-year-old to play near a giant grain auger, which amputated his leg at the hip, was immune from liability. A parent who gave a motorcycle to his teenaged son, who had no vision in one eye and impaired vision in the other, was merely "supervising" the boy and not to be held responsible for the resulting and quite predictable injuries.[14] An Illinois case, still law at this writing, held that foster parents' decision to place a three-year-old child in the "upper half of a divided shelf of a wooden cabinet inside a bedroom closet at [their] home with the door closed" with inadequate ventilation and heat fell within the immunity so that there was no liability for the child's death.[15] These interpretations of the Wisconsin-type rules leave an enormous fortress of immunity in place.

Complete abrogation of immunity. A number of courts abrogating the immunity have rejected the reserved immunity and adopted an ordinary negligence test.[16] They take the position that ordinary negligence rules will provide protections for the parents' rightful authority and discretion because appropriate latitude for parental judgment and authority is built into the reasonable person standard. They say that the supervision immunity and the Wisconsin exceptions are vague and protect arbitrary and harmful parental conduct. In contrast, the "standard of reasonable care under the circumstances is well understood in tort law."[17] Under the ordinary negligence rule, a parent might be liable for brain damage to an infant child left alone in a swimming pool, even though the negligence involved "supervision."[18] Since minor children have no authority, discretion, or supervisory power over their parents, the reasonable person standard or something similar must necessarily be used when the parent sues the child for negligence.[19]

As with spousal immunities, courts[20] and legislatures[21] have sometimes completely abolished the immunity only for specified cases, notably

protection to conduct inherent to the parent-child relationship; such conduct constitutes an exercise of parental authority and supervision over the child or an exercise of discretion in the provision of care to the child").

13. See Holodook v. Spencer, 36 N.Y.2d 35, 364 N.Y.S.2d 859, 324 N.E.2d 338 (1974).

14. Nolechek v. Gesuale, 46 N.Y.2d 332, 413 N.Y.S.2d 340, 385 N.E.2d 1268 (1978).

15. Commerce Bank v. Augsburger, 288 Ill.App.3d 510, 680 N.E.2d 822, 223 Ill.Dec. 872 (1997).

16. Broadbent v. Broadbent, 184 Ariz. 74, 907 P.2d 43 (1995); Gibson v. Gibson, 3 Cal.3d 914, 92 Cal.Rptr. 288, 293, 479 P.2d 648 (1971); Anderson v. Stream, 295 N.W.2d 595 (Minn.1980); Hartman v. Hartman, 821 S.W.2d 852 (Mo.1991); Kirchner v. Crystal, 15 Ohio St.3d 326, 474 N.E.2d 275 (1984); Winn v. Gilroy, 296 Or. 718, 681 P.2d 776 (1984). When a court abolishes the immunity without stating a formula of any kind, as in Glaskox v. Glaskox, 614 So.2d 906 (Miss.1992), they presumably have in mind the ordinary negligence rules.

17. E.g., Hartman v. Hartman, supra n. 16 at 857.

18. Broadbent v. Broadbent, supra n. 16.

19. As where a teenaged driver negligently injures a parent. Ales v. Ales, 650 So.2d 482 (Miss.1995) (parent's suit against child permitted).

20. E.g., Nocktonick v. Nocktonick, 227 Kan. 758, 611 P.2d 135 (1980); Transamerica Ins. Co. v. Royle, 202 Mont. 173, 656 P.2d 820 (1983).

those involving automobile injuries, although a handful retain the parental immunity even there.[22]

Rationales

The original rationale for the parental immunity was that parents were to control and children to obey, a state of reciprocity that would lead to domestic tranquility. A legal action by the child would destroy the tranquility of the home and thus violate public policy.[23] Later, courts also argued that without the immunity, fraudulent and collusive suits would be brought. Both of these arguments have been answered by the courts many times.

Fraud is possible in all cases and it is, after all, the function of courts to weed out bad claims, not to dismiss all claims because some may be tainted. In the case of the parental immunity, the fraud and collusion rationale seems especially weak in the light of the fact that adult children, just as disposed to fraud as minors, can sue parents without any artificial restriction.

The family harmony argument now usually seems preposterous. The suggestion that a father convicted of raping his daughter should be protected by considerations of family harmony[24] refutes itself and casts doubt on the integrity of the judicial system as well.

Courts that still retain a substantial immunity for parents have also said that the immunity is needed to prevent subversion of parental authority or discipline.[25] Most of the cases, however, seem to fall into two categories—cases like automobile cases in which insurance is likely, and cases in which a parent abuses a child sexually or otherwise. Parental discipline, like family harmony, is unlikely to be at risk when the parent is insured. Where the parent is guilty of an intentional tort, the courts agree that the immunity is no defense. So parental discipline is unlikely to be compromised if the immunity is abolished. Draconian rules of law like the immunity rules may be needed occasionally, but perhaps they should be applied only when the concerns they represent are very likely to arise in the litigated cases.

Courts have also suggested that without the immunity the negligent parent liable for the child's injury might later inherit the child's recovery and that parental liability might deplete family funds needed to foster other interests of the family. Since most suits will be brought when the parent is insured, the depletion of funds may not be so likely,[26] and in

21. E.g., CONN. GEN. STAT. ANN. § 52–572c; N.C. GEN. STAT. § 1–539–21.

22. E.g.,Warren v. Warren, 336 Md. 618, 650 A.2d 252 (Md. 1994).

23. Hewlett v. George, supra n. 1.

24. See Roller v. Roller, supra n. 4.

25. See Renko v. McLean, 346 Md. 464, 697 A.2d 468 (1997) (reiterating the discipline argument). Compare the military discipline argument for governmental immunity to service personnel suits, § 263, supra.

26. A joint tortfeasor might implead an uninsured parent for contribution and thus indirectly deplete family coffers. See Holodook v. Spencer, 36 N.Y.2d 35, 364 N.Y.S.2d 859, 324 N.E.2d 338 (1974). But a similar effect may be generated even when the parent's liability is not in issue, as where the defendant points to the parent as the sole proximate cause, which he may be allowed

any event both that problem and the possible inheritance of the child's recovery seem almost without weight when compared to the principle that liability for wrong is the norm and immunity the exception.[27]

The last[28] argument for immunity—or for some kind of legal buffer—is that courts must protect parental freedom to rear children in accordance with their own beliefs and attitudes. This view has led to the partial retention of immunity under the Wisconsin and New York rules, but in fact all courts, including those that have flatly abolished the immunity, agree with the aim. The only question is whether categories like "supervision" or "parental discretion" will help judges focus on relevant policies better than the ordinary negligence rules. The negligence rules have the advantage of doing what courts do best by focusing on the facts and the justice of the particular case.

§ 281. Liabilities and Limited Duties of Family Members

Parents owe affirmative duties of care to their minor children that the same parents do not owe to strangers.[1] However, in other instances, substantive tort rules may forgive family harms even though immunity is abolished.

Why non-immune family members may not be liable. Non-immune family members may of course escape liability on the same grounds that strangers do so, for instance, because negligence has not been proven. More significantly, family members may escape liability because tort law often takes account of relationships of the parties in determining what counts as tortious wrongdoing and in determining defenses like consent.[2] They may escape liability also because alternative legal processes like divorce affect tort liability.

Reasonable expectations of safety affected by relationship. Under the first heading, the very issue of negligence itself often depends upon the fact that the plaintiff is reasonably relying upon the defendant to provide safety precautions and that the defendant knows or should know of that reliance.[3] The plaintiff's reasonable expectations of safety in turn may be formed by the family or other long-term intimate relationship and its

to do even though the parent is immune. Sears, Roebuck & Co. v. Huang, 652 A.2d 568 (Del.1995). Cf. Johnson v. Knoxville Community School District, 570 N.W.2d 633 (Iowa 1997). Comparative fault rules and the abolition of joint and several liability in some states may also affect this point.

27. "For negligent or tortious conduct liability is the rule. Immunity is the exception." President and Directors of Georgetown College v. Hughes, 130 F.2d 810, 812 (App.D.C.1942). The language has been much-quoted.

28. Courts have generated longer lists, as in Wagner v. A.O. Smith, 340 N.W.2d 255 (Iowa 1983), but they appear merely to offer alternate labels for essentially similar arguments.

§ 281

1. E.g., Hite v. Brown, 100 Ohio App.3d 606, 654 N.E.2d 452 (1995) (duty to protect); see § 317 below.

2. See Restatement §§ 895F (2).

3. This is a pervasive idea that runs throughout the law of torts and takes many forms. Some aspects of it can be seen in §§ 162–164 among many others.

accretion of custom. For this and similar reasons, conduct that counts as a tort against strangers does not necessarily count as a tort in a family relationship. This is a point that has nothing to do with immunity; it is a matter of substantive tort law. Relatedly, some cases raise policies against liability that do not directly turn on family status.

Emotional harms in marriage; adultery. Most long-term relationships involve emotional hurts and disappointments, but the expectation of mutual give and take in long-term relationships counsels caution about easy liability for emotional harm. What counts as an outrageous infliction of emotional distress must be considered in the light of the parties' relationship and long-term commitments,[4] and in the light, too, of available divorce remedies.[5] Adultery of a spouse is usually painful to the faithful spouse, but if it is painful enough to justify legal intervention, divorce may be a better solution than a tort action combined with a continued marriage. Consequently, courts have tended to deny emotional harm claims based on a spouse's adultery.[6] Some courts have even gone further, saying that the claim for emotional distress based on conduct during marriage would not lie at all.[7] A few, however, have upheld awards of emotional distress damages[8] or permitted such claims to go to the jury.[9]

4. See Henriksen v. Cameron, 622 A.2d 1135 (Me.1993); Hakkila v. Hakkila, 112 N.M. 172, 812 P.2d 1320 (Ct.App.1991).

5. The principle of no-fault divorce is arguably opposed to any general liability for emotional distress. See Ira Mark Ellman and Stephen D. Sugarman, Spousal Emotional Abuse as a Tort?, 55 Md. L. Rev. 1268 (1996); cf. Wiener v. Wiener, 84 A.D.2d 814, 444 N.Y.S.2d 130 (1981). (if husband was guilty of loud abusive language, told wife that the family had lost its love for her, removed her from control of the family budget, and stayed away from the marital home, such acts were "garden-variety disputes best resolved by" a divorce suit or the like).

6. See Whittington v. Whittington, 766 S.W.2d 73 (Ky.App.1989) (adulterous and financially unfair conduct is insufficiently outrageous to meet rules of the emotional distress claim); Ruprecht v. Ruprecht, 252 N.J.Super. 230, 599 A.2d 604 (1991) (similar); Poston v. Poston, 112 N.C.App. 849, 436 S.E.2d 854 (1993) (similar). Some courts have found different grounds for refusing to entertain an emotional distress claim by a faithful spouse based on the other's adultery. See Nagy v. Nagy, 210 Cal.App.3d 1262, 258 Cal.Rptr. 787 (1989) (adultery not a proximate cause of distress).

7. Weicker v. Weicker, 22 N.Y.2d 8, 237 N.E.2d 876, 290 N.Y.S.2d 732 (1968); Pickering v. Pickering, 434 N.W.2d 758 (S.D. 1989) (wife allegedly bore two children fathered by third persons, but for a long period allowed the husband to believe the children were his; he allegedly formed a father's bond with the children before he discovered the truth, but held, court would not entertain domestic emotional distress claims). The scope of *Pickering* seems doubtful since Henry v. Henry, 534 N.W.2d 844 (S.D.1995) (claim for distress resulting from threats during marriage would be actionable but for release of the claims).

8. Massey v. Massey, 807 S.W.2d 391 (Tex. Ct. App. 1991), aff'd, 867 S.W.2d 766 (Tex.1993) (permitting recovery of $362,000 in a divorce suit).

9. Whelan v. Whelan, 41 Conn.Supp. 519, 588 A.2d 251 (Conn.Super.Ct.1991) (allegation that husband falsely told wife he was dying of AIDS, suggesting that wife herself might have been infected); Koepke v. Koepke, 52 Ohio App.3d 47, 556 N.E.2d 1198 (1989) (in filing for divorce, wife revealed that husband was not the father of his putative child, husband's claim for distress could proceed as a separate suit); cf. C.M. v. J.M., 320 N.J.Super. 119, 726 A.2d 998 (1999) (allegations that wife and her paramour concealed the fact that children husband supposed were his own were actually paramour's children, splintering husband's long-term relationship with children; claim stated against paramour). As to liability of an outsider for alienation of affections or the like, see §§ 442 & 444.

Privacy. Privacy invasions raise similar possibilities. There is no doubt that spouses can retain some expectation of privacy even in marriage and that an invasion of privacy is actionable where immunity is abolished.[10] Nevertheless, courts have recognized that the "mutual concessions implied in the marital relationship,"[11] and the "subtle ebb and flow of married life"[12] can affect the parties expectations and their rights. What is a tolerable adjustment in marriage should not retroactively become grounds for a tort claim once a divorce suit is instituted.

Relation to divorce. Besides the argument that divorce should be the only remedy for some torts, even the recognized tort claim may be disadvantaged by entanglement with divorce proceedings. One issue is whether the tort claim can or should be joined or included in the divorce proceeding.[13] Some courts like the joinder and encourage it,[14] while others hold that it is legally impermissible.[15] When joinder is allowed or required, the plaintiff may be denied a jury trial on the tort claim because juries are not ordinarily available in divorce proceedings and because the divorce court is not even equipped to seat them.[16] When joinder is not allowed, courts must seek to avoid duplicative liabilities—once when the divorce court takes his misconduct into account in fixing his financial responsibilities and again when another court adjudicates his tort liability for the same misconduct.[17] These scenarios raise the question whether fault is creeping back into the divorce suit and whether, if so, fault is properly defined in that context.[18]

When a separate tort claim is properly brought for marital misconduct that was also in issue in the earlier divorce case, the divorce case is not ordinarily res judicata.[19] However, findings of fact on issues actually adjudicated in the earlier divorce suit may be treated as conclusive in the tort claim and thus may determine its outcome.[20] In any event, the plaintiff who comes to a property settlement with the defendant in the

10. Burgess v. Burgess, 447 So.2d 220 (Fla.1984) (electronic eavesdropping by estranged spouse); Miller v. Brooks, 123 N.C.App. 20, 472 S.E.2d 350 (1996) (similar).

11. Lewis v. Lewis, 370 Mass. 619, 351 N.E.2d 526 (1976).

12. Merenoff v. Merenoff, 76 N.J. 535, 388 A.2d 951 (1978).

13. See Steven J. Gaynor, Annotation, Joinder of Tort Actions Between Spouses With Proceeding For Dissolution of Marriage, 4 A.L.R.5th 972 (1993).

14. E.g., Twyman v. Twyman, 855 S.W.2d 619 (Tex.1993).

15. E.g., Ward v. Ward, 155 Vt. 242, 583 A.2d 577, 4 A.L.R.5th 1152 (1990).

16. Brennan v. Orban, 145 N.J. 282, 678 A.2d 667 (1996).

17. Cf. Twyman v. Twyman, 855 S.W.2d 619, 625 (Tex.1993) ("a spouse should not be allowed to recover tort damages and a disproportionate division of the community estate based on the same conduct"); Noble v. Noble, 761 P.2d 1369 (Utah. 1988) (divorce judge to consider wife's injuries from husband's tort and make clear findings so judge in tort suit can avoid duplicative award).

18. See Harry D. Krause, on The Danger of Allowing Marital Fault to Re-emerge in The Guise of Torts, 73 NOTRE DAME L. REV. 1355 (1998).

19. E.g., Vance v. Chandler, 231 Ill. App.3d 747, 173 Ill.Dec. 525, 597 N.E.2d 233 (1992); see LEONARD KARP AND CHERYL L. KARP, DOMESTIC TORTS: FAMILY VIOLENCE, CONFLICT AND SEXUAL ABUSE, § 1.36 (1988 & 1998 Supp.).

20. Thus if the divorce court finds that the husband shot the wife in the head, that finding may not be relitigated in the subsequent tort suit. Noble v. Noble, 761 P.2d 1369, 1371 (Utah. 1988).

divorce suit may find that the settlement is interpreted to bar all claims, including the tort claim.[21]

Parental privilege to discipline. The parental privilege to discipline children, usually discussed in connection with physical torts like battery,[23] presumably applies as well to emotional harm claims. A child not allowed to attend a party may in fact be emotionally harmed, but one can feel sure that even in the unlikely event that a child would bring such a claim, it is doomed to failure. Once again, the point is not immunity, but that the substantive rules of tort, as applied in the family situation, simply would not countenance the claim.

Limited duties. Abolition of immunity does not reduce the courts' role in describing appropriate duties for defendants. One court has found policies against imposing liability upon parents for failing to pursue a child's malpractice claim,[24] a view that can be expressed as an immunity but that might be profitably viewed as a limited duty instead.[25] Another court considered liability of a mother who ingested cocaine and alcohol during pregnancy with disastrous results for her child. The court refused to impose liability upon the mother.[26] If the mother's autonomy is paramount,[27] the child's claim might be barred by considerations that have nothing to do with parental immunity.

§ 282. Charities

General principle. General principles of tort law hold that each person is responsible for the harm he negligently causes. He is not relieved of liability for negligence merely because on other occasions he has behaved with charity and generosity towards others. From time to time, however, courts or legislatures appear to forget these principles and to relieve certain defendants of liability for negligently caused harm on the ground that, although their conduct was negligent, the injury was inflicted in the course of kindness or charity. For example, guest statutes once relieved the negligent automobile driver of all liability to his guest. The guest was expected to be so grateful for the ride that the little matter of negligent injury should be forgotten.

Risk-utility balance distinguished. Perhaps the impulse to relieve the good-hearted defendant results from an inadequate understanding of the reasonable person standard. That standard itself gives the defendant

21. As in Henry v. Henry, 534 N.W.2d 844 (S.D.1995).

23. § 94.

24. Bonin v. Vannaman, 261 Kan. 199, 929 P.2d 754 (1996)

25. For example, instead of immunity, the parent might be held to a very low standard of care, or even held liable only for wilful disregard of the child's rights.

26. Stallman v. Youngquist, 125 Ill.2d 267, 126 Ill.Dec. 60, 531 N.E.2d 355 (1988). Similarly, allegations that a mother deserted her child, with emotional trauma for the child, were insufficient in Burnette v. Wahl, 284 Or. 705, 588 P.2d 1105 (1978).

27. As was the case in In re A.C., 573 A.2d 1235 (D.C.App.1990), where the dying mother wanted to avoid a Caesarean although it would have improved chances that her fetus would survive. On the other hand, autonomy interests are nonexistent or insignificant when the mother to be is merely negligent in driving or crossing the street, and in that case liability may be imposed. Bonte v. Bonte, 136 N.H. 286, 616 A.2d 464 (N.H. 1992).

full credit for the usefulness of the act that causes harm by providing that he is not at fault at all (and hence not liable) when his harm-causing act would be overall more useful than harmful. He should not be deterred merely because his act entails small and unavoidable risks.[1] But that is not the same as saying that the defendant should be relieved of responsibility for reasonably avoidable risks resulting from unreasonable and harmful acts, or that his merit as a good citizen should exempt him from the legal rules. In fact, the risk-utility balance assesses the merits of the case, while the immunity prevents a consideration of the merits. Nevertheless, the idea of affording special privileges to benevolent people for unreasonable behavior becomes law from time to time. The old guest statutes represent one example. The immunities of charities represent another.

Charitable immunity once recognized. The immunity of charitable organizations was recognized in a 19th century English dictum,[2] then discarded by the House of Lords.[3] The original case did not even involve personal injury, only a claim by a beneficiary of the charity to share in the charity's program. Its logic had no application to corporate charities, as distinct from trusts, but neither its repudiation in England, nor its origin outside the realm of injury law, nor its irrelevance to corporate charities prevented its adoption in America.[4] As a result, a wide range of charities were allowed to pursue their work without reasonable care and without responsibility for the harms caused by their negligence. At various times the protection has extended to the Boy Scouts,[5] museums of various kinds,[6] a Jewish Community Center,[7] a Confederate Memorial Association,[8] a Little League Baseball organization,[9] and to churches,[10] private schools,[11] and hospitals.[12]

Rationales. Courts gave different reasons, or combinations of reasons, for the immunity. They said variously that liability would divert trust funds for purposes inconsistent with the charity and its donor's intent; that ordinary rules of vicarious liability should not apply to impose liability for the acts of employees; that beneficiaries of a charity

§ 282

1. For a more complete expression of the risk-utility balance, see §§ 144–146.

2. Feoffees of Heriot's Hospital v. Ross, 8 Eng. Rep. 1508 (H.L. 1846), relying in part on an earlier case.

3. Mersey Docks & Harbour Board of Trustees v. Gibbs, 111 Eng. Rep. 1500 (1866).

4. Beginning with McDonald v. Massachusetts General Hospital, 120 Mass. 432 (1876).

5. Schultz v. Boy Scouts of America, Inc., 65 N.Y.2d 189, 480 N.E.2d 679, 491 N.Y.S.2d 90 (1985) (New Jersey law).

6. Morales v. New Jersey Academy of Aquatic Sciences, 302 N.J.Super. 50, 694 A.2d 600 (1997) (aquarium).

7. Abramson v. Reiss, 334 Md. 193, 638 A.2d 743 (1994).

8. Bodenheimer v. Confederate Memorial Ass'n, 5 F.Supp. 526 (1932).

9. Pomeroy v. Little League Baseball of Collingswood, 142 N.J.Super. 471, 362 A.2d 39 (1976).

10. E.g., Watkins v. Southcrest Baptist Church, 399 S.W.2d 530 (Tex.1966).

11. E.g., Ettlinger v. Trustees of Randolph–Macon College, 31 F.2d 869 (4th Cir. 1929).

12. E.g., Howard v. South Baltimore General Hospital, 191 Md. 617, 62 A.2d 574 (1948).

should not recover from it because they must waive their claims or assume the risk of negligence; and that donations to charities should not be discouraged by imposing liability for fault; and that liabilities might terminate a charity's good works.

Rationales attacked. These reasons were individually deficient, as many judges and other critics have pointed out repeatedly.[13] As to the trust fund argument, most charities are corporations, not trusts. More importantly, two people by contract (or donation in trust) cannot dictate their responsibility for torts to those not a party to their arrangement. The argument that charities were not liable under the doctrine of respondeat superior, on the ground that its employees were working for public good rather than for the charity, seems spurious on its face and certainly illogical in the light of the charity's vicarious liability to strangers.[14] The waiver or assumed risk argument was at best fictional. Worse, it operated to remove protection for those who most needed reasonable care. But even then it did not explain all the cases, because beneficiaries of an individual charity (as opposed to a corporate charity) were allowed to recover for negligence, although they assumed the risk as much as beneficiaries of corporations. Further, the immunity applied even to infants who could not possibly have assumed the risk. The "public policy" argument that charities might go out of business if held liable was answered by observing that only the cost of reasonable behavior was entailed. After all, nothing requires a charitable hospital to inflict burns upon a newborn infant in her bassinet.[15] If reasonable care is too much to ask of charities, the cost of insurance is not. Perhaps a more important answer was that if a charity causes so much harm by its negligence that a requirement of reasonable care would drive it out of business, then perhaps it should not be in business at all for in that case it is doing more harm than good.[16]

Beyond the individual defect of each supposed reason for the immunity, all of the reasons were founded directly or indirectly on the policy of subsidizing organizations denominated as charities. Courts accomplished the subsidy by allowing charities to avoid financial responsibility for unreasonable and harmful acts. But these subsidies were not paid by the state; they were paid by the victims whose recovery was denied—through a "coerced donation" of their right of recovery.[17] Not surprisingly, courts ultimately refuted each of the various rationales for the immunity.[18]

13. See e.g., cases cited nn. 17 & 18 below.

14. See Mississippi Baptist Hospital v. Holmes, 214 Miss. 906, 933, 55 So.2d 142, 153, 25 A.L.R.2d 12 (1951).

15. Durney v. St. Francis Hospital, Inc., 46 Del. 350, 83 A.2d 753 (1951).

16. See §§ 143–145, supra.

17. Albritton v. Neighborhood Centers Ass'n for Child Development, 12 Ohio St.3d 210, 466 N.E.2d 867, 871 (1984).

18. The classic criticism, which more or less turned immunity thinking around, is President and Directors of Georgetown College v. Hughes, 130 F.2d 810 (D.C.Cir. 1942). One of the best summaries of major arguments against immunity is Note, The Quality of Mercy: 'Charitable Torts' and Their Continuing Immunity, 100 HARV. L. REV. 1382 (1987).

Modifications or exceptions to the immunity. Not surprisingly, courts first developed a large number of exceptions or modifications that varied from state to state. Most adopted one or more of the following rules. They said that charities would be liable (1) to the extent they have assets that form no part of the charitable trust assets, for example, to the extent that liability was covered by insurance or had assets not part of the charitable funds;[19] (2) for their torts to strangers, that is, to persons who do not receive the benefactions of the charity;[20] (3) for the torts of upper level management, including negligence in hiring or retaining dangerous employees;[21] (4) to beneficiaries of the charity who actually pay for the services that cause harm, at least to the extent that a judgment can be enforced against non-charitable assets.[22]

Rejecting the immunity. Most American courts[23] or legislatures[24] have now rejected the immunity. The Restatement simply says no such immunity exists.[25] Many of the decisions arose out of suits against charitable hospitals, but the reasoning was broad enough to eliminate the immunity for other charitable organizations as well.[26] In addition, some of the states that retain the immunity limit its effect by defining charities with increasing rigor[27] and by removing the immunity to the

19. See, e.g., 14 Me.Rev.Stat.Ann. § 158 (insurance coverage is a waiver of immunity); James v. Prince George's County, 288 Md. 315, 418 A.2d 1173 (1980); cf. Md. Ins. Code, § 19–103. The immunity might be lost if the charity had assets not devoted exclusively to charity. Spivey v. St. Thomas Hospital, 31 Tenn.App. 12, 211 S.W.2d 450 (1947). But self-insurance, or a reserve for contingencies, does not qualify as insurance that waives immunity. Ponder v. Fulton–DeKalb Hospital Authority, 256 Ga. 833, 353 S.E.2d 515 (1987).

20. E.g., Alabama Baptist Hospital Board v. Carter, 226 Ala. 109, 145 So. 443 (1932).

21. Harrell v. Louis Smith Memorial Hospital, 197 Ga.App. 189, 397 S.E.2d 746 (1990) (not liable "unless it fails to exercise ordinary care in the selection of competent officers and servants, or fails to exercise ordinary care in retaining such officers and employees" or in providing adequate number of staff); J. v. Victory Tabernacle Baptist Church, 236 Va. 206, 372 S.E.2d 391 (1988).

22. Ponder v. Fulton–DeKalb Hospital Authority, 256 Ga. 833, 353 S.E.2d 515 (1987).

23. E.g., President and Directors of Georgetown College v. Hughes, 130 F.2d 810 (D.C.Cir.1942) (the leading case); Albritton v. Neighborhood Centers Ass'n for Child Development, 12 Ohio St.3d 210, 466 N.E.2d 867 (1984) (neighborhood center Head Start program for children). Janet Fairchild, Annotation, Tort Immunity of Nongovernmental Charities—Modern Status, 25 A.L.R.4th 517 (1981).

24. Conn. Gen. Stat. Ann. § 52–557d; Mass. Gen. L. Ann. ch. 231, § 85K; Nev. Rev. Stat. § 41.480.

25. Restatement § 895E.

26. See Friend v. Cove Methodist Church, Inc., 65 Wash.2d 174, 396 P.2d 546 (1964); Widell v. Holy Trinity Catholic Church, 19 Wis.2d 648, 121 N.W.2d 249 (1963).

27. The organization may not get the immunity if its articles of incorporation fail to reflect a charitable purpose, perhaps even an exclusive one. See Snyder v. American Association of Blood Banks, 144 N.J. 269, 676 A.2d 1036 (1996). Likewise, in some states if the charity receives income from sources other than charitable donations. Ouachita Wilderness Institute, Inc. v. Mergen, 329 Ark. 405, 947 S.W.2d 780 (1997) (organization for rehabilitation of juvenile offenders was not a charitable organization in part because it received state funds, hence was not a charity dependent upon donations); Lutheran Hospitals and Homes Soc'y of American v. Yepsen, 469 P.2d 409 (Wyo.1970) (hospital not entitled to immunity in part because it received government funds); cf. Child v. Central Maine Medical Center, 575 A.2d 318 (Me. 1990) (no immunity when defendant did not receive its funds mainly from charitable donations); contra, under New Jersey's broad immunity statute, Morales v. New

extent that insurance protects the charity.[28]

Immunity remnants. Once the courts abolished or rejected the immunity, however, legislatures sometimes reinstated the immunity or some remnant of it for particular cases.[29] Legislatures in a number of states impose a cap on damages recoverable against charitable organizations.[30] In addition, several states retain the immunity with whatever modifications or exceptions have been applied in those states. These include Colorado[31] and a string of eastern seaboard states, notably Virginia, Maryland, and New Jersey.[32] However, the rules are so deeply wrinkled that classification is unreliable. Massachusetts, for example, permits a recovery, but it is capped at such a low level that for most purposes Massachusetts could be classified realistically as a state retaining the immunity.[33] On the other hand, Maine purports to retain the immunity but defines charities narrowly.[34]

Where the immunity is retained, it can be applied stringently. In a New Jersey case,[35] the claim was that one Brother Edmund, employed by the defendant Archdiocese, forced some of his Boy Scout charges into sexual acts, after which one boy committed suicide at the age of 12. Since the church was a charity, it was immune. Even New Jersey's stringent statute, however, provides no immunity for claims by victims who are "outside the benefactions" of the charity.[36]

De facto immunities. Besides the fact that some states have retained immunities in some form, de facto immunities may remain even in the

Jersey Academy of Aquatic Sciences, 302 N.J.Super. 50, 694 A.2d 600 (1997). Arkansas adopted a flexible definition of charities, using a number of factors. Masterson v. Stambuck, 321 Ark. 391, 902 S.W.2d 803 (1995) ("(1) whether the organization's charter limits it to charitable or eleemosynary purposes; (2) whether the organization's charter contains a 'not-for-profit' limitation; (3) whether the organization's goal is to break even; (4) whether the organization earned a profit; (5) whether any profit or surplus must be used for charitable or eleemosynary purposes; (6) whether the organization depends on contributions and donations for its existence; (7) whether the organization provides its services free of charge to those unable to pay; and (8) whether the directors and officers receive compensation"). Whether a charity loses its protected status because it pays most of its income to its directors or managers or incurs other expenses that leave little for its ostensible purposes apparently has not been litigated.

28. E.g., 14 Me. Rev. Stats. Ann. § 158.

29. For instance, Rhode Island rejected the immunity early on, but the legislature enacted a statutory immunity for charitable hospitals. Later still, however, the legislature recanted and provided for ordinary liability. See, reflecting this history, Hodge v. Osteopathic General Hospital of Rhode Island, 107 R.I. 135, 265 A.2d 733 (1970); R.I. Gen. Laws § 9–1–26. See also § 283.

30. The immunity appears to be abolished so far as capping statutes apply. Such statutes may be accompanied by provisions for voluntary or mandatory insurance coverage. See Md. Cts. & Jud. Pro. Code § 5–632 (as to hospitals carrying insurance of at least $100,000, that sum is the cap on liability); Mass. Gen. L. Ann. ch. 231, § 85K ($20,000); S.C. Code § 33–56–180 ($250,000); Tex. Civil Practice & Remedies Code § 84.006 ($500,000/$1,000,000). The caps do not apply in all cases.

31. Hemenway v. Presbyterian Hospital Ass'n, 161 Colo. 42, 419 P.2d 312 (1966).

32. See cases cited in nn. 9, 12, & 19.

33. Mass. Gen. L. Ann. Ch. 231, § 85 ($20,000).

34. Child v. Central Maine Medical Center, 575 A.2d 318 (Me.1990).

35. Schultz v. Roman Catholic Archdiocese of Newark, 95 N.J. 530, 472 A.2d 531 (1984).

36. N.J.S.A. § 2A:53A–7.

states that have now abolished the formal immunity. First, asset-weak charities may be unable to pay because they carry no insurance. Second, charities may extract waivers of liability from needy beneficiaries or volunteers, so that suits are barred if these exculpatory agreements are to be upheld.[37]

§ 283. Individual Immunities

The traditional charitable immunity protected trusts and then charitable or nonprofit corporations. Individuals, however, have never enjoyed general protection from liability merely because they were engaged in charitable work when they negligently caused harm.[1] However, legislatures have often been prevailed upon to enact immunities or privileges for particular classes of persons. One thread that runs through many statutes is that persons who act in specified charitable ways either deserve protection against legal responsibility or should be given that protection to encourage their charity.

These statutes differ from the traditional common law charitable immunity in several important ways. First, many of them cover particular charities or acts of charity, not all. Second, they often apply to individuals. Third, not all of the statutes enact a flat immunity; some merely lower the standard of care owed by a charitable individual or organization.

Two prominent groups of statutes have already been discussed in earlier chapters. The medical Good Samaritan statutes relieve medical personnel and sometimes others of any obligation of due care in medical emergencies.[2] Recreational use statutes, limiting a landowner's standard of care to those who use the land without charge, have been enacted almost everywhere.[3]

More recently, statutes have either enacted immunities or lowered standards of care for those who cause harm while acting as a volunteer for a charity or for a particular activity favored by the legislature. Volunteers to assist baseball[4] and horseback riding programs[5] are examples. Donors of food to non-profits organizations are now receiving protections from liability,[6] and the non-profit organization that distributes food may be similarly protected.[7] Again, however, the statutes may lower standards of care without conferring a complete immunity.

37. See Note, The Quality of Mercy: 'Charitable Torts' and Their Continuing Immunity, 100 Harv. L. Rev. 1382 (1987).

§ 283

1. See President and Directors of Georgetown College v. Hughes, 130 F.2d 810, 814 (D.C.Cir.1942).

2. Discussed in § 252, supra.

3. See § 238, supra.

4. The statutes can be quite narrow. One might be directed at volunteers who coach or umpire in non-profit sports programs. 745 Il. Comp. Stats. § 80/1 (standard of care lowered so that no liability is imposed unless conduct falls "substantially below" standard).

5. See Jones v. Westernaires, 876 P.2d 50 (Colo.Ct.App.1993).

6. Cal. Civil Code § 1714.25 (addressing the standard of care)

7. 745 Ill. Comp. Stats. Ann. 50/4.

One recent type of legislation is much broader. It protects virtually all volunteers for work in non-profit activities, and sometimes boards of directors as well.[8] Courts may be recognizing similar immunities for individuals.[9] In 1997, Congress enacted a volunteer protection statute that eliminates most potential liability of volunteers for "nonprofit" organizations unless the volunteer is wilfully or grossly negligent. The term nonprofit may include a number of organizations such as the Chamber of Commerce that would not necessarily have been regarded as charitable.[10] As broad as this shield is, however, liability remains for most ordinary motor vehicle negligence and for wilful misconduct or gross negligence.[11] Congress actually enacted an argument for this statute, asserting that without its protection, volunteers would be discouraged from providing their services to nonprofit organizations because of "unwarranted litigation costs" and other concerns.[12] The statute is thus one of a number that come under the general heading of "tort reform," aimed at overall reduction in liabilities.[13]

8. Colo. Rev. Stats. § 13-21-116; 76 Okl.St.Ann. § 31.

9. Moore v. Warren, 250 Va. 421, 463 S.E.2d 459 (1995).

10. See 26 U.S.C.A. § 501(c).

11. 42 U.S.C.A. § 14503. Although the statute preempts state law, states are permitted to opt out of the statute under certain circumstances.

12. 42 U.S.C.A. § 14501 (a) (6).

13. See §§ 384 & 414.

Chapter 17

Professional Risk-Takers

§ 284. Shifting Responsibility to Professional Risk-Takers

General Rule

An employer ordinarily owes a duty of reasonable care to provide workers and contractors a reasonably safe place in which to work.[1] However, the employer's responsibility for premises safety is ordinarily only to warn of hidden dangers of which the employer knew or should have known.[2] So if the employer retains a worker or contractor to repair a dangerous condition, the employer is not liable merely because he created the danger in the first place. The parties have implicitly or explicitly shifted responsibility for the dangerous condition to the contractor, who has no complaint if the danger he undertook to repair causes him harm.[3] By its own terms, however, the rule does not preclude recovery for injury resulting from hidden dangers of which the employee does not know, or those that arose after the work was undertaken.[4]

A Tennessee case illustrates the idea. The defendant property owner had allowed a roof to become rotten and to leak. The defendant retained a contractor to remove the rotten roof and install a new one. Although the contractor did not know the extent of the rot, he knew he was

§ 284

1. As to employees, the duty of the employer is to provide not only a reasonably safe place in which to work and to warn of hidden dangers, but to provide safe appliances and equipment and a sufficient number of competent fellow workers and to enforce rules for safety. See Hastings v. Mechalske, 336 Md. 663, 650 A.2d 274 (1994).

2. E.g., Chance v. Dallas County, Alabama, 456 So.2d 295 (Ala.1984); Hannon v. Hayes-Bickford Lunch Sys., Inc., 336 Mass. 268, 145 N.E.2d 191 (1957). Responsibility to seamen may differ.

3. Hammond v. City of El Dorado Springs, 362 Mo. 530, 242 S.W.2d 479, 31 A.L.R.2d 1367 (1951); Kowalsky v. Conreco Co., Inc., 264 N.Y. 125, 190 N.E. 206 (1934); cf. Dyer v. Superior Court, 56 Cal. App.4th 61, 65 Cal.Rptr.2d 85 (1997) (tow truck driver injured on the highway while responding to call assumed the risks of highway injury and could not recover against driver who failed to maintain his car and thus necessitated the call for a tow). This was sometimes called "contractual assumed risk." Courts once applied the idea to virtually any job risks, including those that could have been eliminated by reasonable care or providing a reasonably safe place. E.g., Comer v. Texaco, Inc., 514 F.2d 1243 (5th Cir.1975) (worker who needed job assumed risk of attack by working in a high crime area even if he could not get a job elsewhere; consequently the employer was not liable); Smith v. Officers and Directors of Kart-N-Karry, Inc., 346 So.2d 313 (La.Ct.App.1977) (similar). This broad approach to assumed risk has largely passed from the picture.

4. See e.g., Chance v. Dallas County, Alabama, 456 So.2d 295 (Ala.1984).

removing and replacing a roof that was not worth keeping. When it collapsed with him, he had no claim against the owner.[5]

Effect on Third Persons

Shifting responsibility for injuries to third persons. An arrangement under which the contractor assumes the risks of dangers inherent in a job might conceivably affect rights of or against third persons. If the contractor in control of the dangerous instrument makes repairs negligently, or fails to make them, or fails to warn those who are in danger, with resulting injury to some third person, the contractor is subject to liability to the injured person. But in at least some cases, the employer who reasonably relies upon the contractor for safety can escape liability to the victim. The employer may be viewed as having shifted responsibility to the contractor[6] unless the rules of nondelegable duty make him liable along with the contractor.[7] Courts have taken such an approach when the contractor's employee or subcontractor is injured by a condition the contractor was hired to make safe.[8] If the employee was fully informed, he is in the same position as the contractor. If he was not informed, the employer may nevertheless be reasonable in relying upon the contractor to inform the contractor's employee. In either event, the injured contractor's employee has a claim against the contractor, but not against the employer.

Barring the contractor's claim against third persons. The idea of the repair contractor rule is that the contractor accepts the inherent risks of a dangerous condition when he agrees to repair it. The rule is thus a function of the parties' implicit agreement or express understanding. On its face, that understanding protects the employer but does not speak to duties or liabilities of other persons who might create risks to the contractor. The question of a third person's duty may arise in at least two distinct kinds of cases.

First, a contractor might agree to repair an existing condition of static danger on the employer's land. For example, the contractor might agree to repair or replace the employer's utility pole because the pole had been dangerously weakened when T negligently drove his truck into it.

Second, a contractor might agree to deal with prospective dangers as they arise. For example, the contractor or employee might agree to clean up toxic spills that occur in the employer's plant, even though none have yet occurred. The contractor might then be injured later in coping with dangerous toxins spilled through T's negligence. At least in this second situation, it appears that the contractor's agreement with the employer

5. Blair v. Campbell, 924 S.W.2d 75 (Tenn.1996).

6. See § 194, supra.

7. § 337 below.

8. E.g., Whitlow v. Seaboard Air Line R.R. Co., 222 F.2d 57 (4th Cir.1955); Kowalsky v. Conreco Co., Inc., 264 N.Y. 125, 190 N.E. 206 (1934).

to accept the risks of toxins does not inure to the benefit of a third person who negligently exposes the contractor.[9]

The succeeding sections, however, show that when the contractor or employee is a publicly employed risk-taker such as a firefighter or police officer, the answer is different.

§ 285. Limited Duties to Professional Risk-Takers: The Firefighters' Rule

General rule. When firefighters[1] or police officers[2] are injured by perils that they have been employed to confront, they ordinarily have no claim against the person who created those perils. For example, if a landowner negligently causes a fire, the firefighter injured by risks inherent in firefighting has no claim against the landowner. The same is true if the fire is caused by a strict liability activity.[3] In some states the rule may also bar other professional risk-takers. It is known both as the professional rescuers doctrine, and, in spite of its expansion, as the firefighters' rule.[4] This chapter also uses the term public safety officer to include all those to whom the rule applies. Phrased in terms of duty, the rule in effect says that one has no duty to safety officers to avoid creating the danger that requires their services or to protect them from associated dangers of which the defendant has no actual knowledge.[5] Qualifications almost always follow such Draconian rules, and that is certainly the case with the firefighters' rule.

Landowner cases. The firefighters' rule was originally a product of and justified by the special premises liability rules,[6] and perhaps in some states it would still be confined to suits against the occupant of premises.[7] In the premises cases, courts usually treated firefighters as licensees or at least as something closely analogous,[8] holding that they took the

9. Cf. Neighbarger v. Irwin Indus., Inc., 8 Cal.4th 532, 882 P.2d 347, 34 Cal.Rptr.2d 630 (1994) (plant safety officer).

§ 285

1. E.g., Krauth v. Geller, 31 N.J. 270, 157 A.2d 129 (1960) (a leading case on the "firefighters' rule").

2. E.g., Berko v. Freda, 93 N.J. 81, 459 A.2d 663 (1983). The rule originated with and is still sometimes stated in terms of firefighters. The firefighters formulations does not necessarily imply that other officers are excluded.

3. See Lipson v. Superior Court of Orange County (Berger), 31 Cal.3d 362, 644 P.2d 822, 182 Cal.Rptr. 629 (1982).

4. Older cases called it the fireman's rule and must be searched under that term. It is also sometimes referred to as the professional rescuer's doctrine.

5. Carson v. Headrick, 900 S.W.2d 685, 690 (Tenn.1995) (using a variant formulation: "a citizen owes no duty of reasonable care to police officers responding to that citizen's call for assistance"). As to the range of associated dangers see § 286 below.

6. For a collection of the landowners' cases, see Larry D. Scheafer, Annotation, Liability of Owner or Occupant of Premises to Fireman Coming Thereon in Discharge of His Duty, 11 A.L.R.4th 597 (1981); Richard C. Tinney, Annotation, Liability of Owner or Occupant of Premises to Police Officer Coming Thereon in Discharge of Officer's Duty, 30 A.L.R.4th 81 (1981).

7. See Court v. Grzelinski, 72 Ill.2d 141, 379 N.E.2d 281, 19 Ill.Dec. 617 (1978).

8. Some courts concluded that the categories could not apply to firefighters at all because, being on the premises in the public right they were not trespassers, for the same reason they were not permittees or invitees of the landowner. See Krauth v. Geller, 31 N.J. 270, 157 A.2d 129 (1960).

premises as they found them, so the landowner would not be liable for negligently setting the fire that injured the firefighter, or even for leaving a dangerous condition on the premises.[9] Under the premises liability rules, the injured firefighter could recover in several specific kinds of cases—when the landowner is guilty of active negligence, as distinguished from conditions of the property itself,[10] when the landowner has violated an ordinance or safety statute aimed at protecting firefighters or officers,[11] when the firefighter's presence is known and the landowner fails to warn of known dangers,[12] and when injury occurs on premises open to the public.[13] But if the safety officer was in a private residence, or on business premises at a place not open to the public, the courts otherwise barred recovery.

Extension beyond landowners. The courts eventually began to divorce the rule from its connection to landowner cases. They began to say that public safety officers in the course of their employment should be denied recovery for injuries inflicted by the defendant's negligence even when injury occurred outside the defendant's land and even when the defendant was not a landowner at all. For example, in a California case, a police officer was injured while attempting to stop a highway speeder. The rule applied to bar the officer's claim against the speeder. That could not represent a landowner's rule.[14] At the same time, a fair number of courts abolished the special landowner rules and applied ordinary negligence rules to persons who were injured on the land.[15] These changes and other perceptions required reconsideration of the rationales.[16]

Rationales. Sometimes it is suggested that if landowners were liable for negligence in setting fires, they would delay calling for professional help with potential for the spread of fire to neighbors.[17] Prosser thought this was a preposterous suggestion, but no behavioral data has been offered either for or against that view. Such a rationale would limit the rule to a narrow group of cases. A wrongdoer whose misconduct leads a

Hence the shift to an independent "firefighters' rule."

9. E.g., Lee v. Luigi, Inc., 696 A.2d 1371 (D.C.1997) (police officer responding to burglar alarm in the absence of owner slipped on dangerous substance).

10. See Buren v. Midwest Indus., Inc., 380 S.W.2d 96 (Ky.1964).

11. E.g., Dini v. Naiditch, 20 Ill.2d 406, 170 N.E.2d 881, 86 A.L.R.2d 1184 (1960).

12. See Wright v. Coleman, 148 Wis.2d 897, 436 N.W.2d 864 (1989) (emphasizing that the question is one of reasonable care and that not all failures to warn, even of known dangers, would count as negligence).

13. See Meiers v. Fred Koch Brewery, 229 N.Y. 10, 127 N.E. 491, 13 A.L.R. 633 (1920); Cameron v. Abatiell, 127 Vt. 111, 241 A.2d 310 (1968). The public invitation tests would make the firefighter an invitee as to conditions found on portions of the premises open to the public, although that test might not affect liability for the fire itself.

14. Hubbard v. Boelt, 28 Cal.3d 480, 620 P.2d 156, 169 Cal.Rptr. 706 (1980). The result may have been affected by CAL. CIV. CODE § 1714.9, which recognizes a number of exceptions to the rule.

15. See § 237, supra.

16. In some cases the shift is explicit, as in Hack v. Gillespie, 74 Ohio St.3d 362, 365–66, 658 N.E.2d 1046, 1049 (1996).

17. See e.g., Sallee v. GTE South, Inc., 839 S.W.2d 277 (Ky.1992).

police officer into danger and injury would not find himself protected under this rationale.

Prosser suggested that the "most legitimate" basis for the firefighters' rule was that public safety officers were likely to enter the premises at unforeseeable times and places.[18] If this is the most legitimate rationale for the rule, then the rule has little support indeed. First, it cannot explain use of the rule outside the landowner's cases, as where a police officer is injured in pursuing a criminal. Second, unforeseeability of the officer's presence is a question of fact that differs from case to case; it is not something you can make a rule about. It is true that in the landowner cases, courts that still apply the licensee-invitee categories could invoke the premises liability rules or some reasonably close analogy to deny recovery, but even if firefighters are not invitees and should lose because of their licensee status,[19] the feeling persists that the reason for barring a safety officer in the landowner cases could not really be so different from the reason for barring the same officer when she was injured outside the land.

Some courts suggested that the safety officer would collect workers' compensation or similar benefits from the public employer and that if the negligent defendant were required to pay tort damages, the defendant would pay twice, once indirectly as a taxpayer and again as a tortfeasor. One difficulty with this argument is that it was not applied in other instances of public employee injury. Even in its own terms, it did not work. The public employer who paid compensation benefits to the injured firefighter would in fact recoup some or all of the payments from the tort recovery against the negligent defendant.[20] Consequently, if the individual taxpayer-defendant could be identified with the city government for this purpose, it could not be said that he paid twice. The taxpayer's putative payment (by way of the city's compensation payments) would be recouped from his actual payment as a tortfeasor. In fact, in foreclosing the firefighter's recovery, the courts have eliminated the possibility that the city would recoup any of the monies it has paid in compensation.

If firefighters and police officers were to be denied recovery whether injury occurred on the defendant's land or not, the most plausible explanation was grounded, not in the landowners' rules, but in a public policy which in turn was based primarily on arguments from assumed risk in the no-duty sense.[21] The argument is that firefighters and police

18. Prosser & Keeton § 61, pp. 431–32.

19. A disputed point. See Prosser & Keeton, p. 432. In addition, many states have now abolished the licensee-invitee categories.

20. See § 395 below.

21. See, e.g., Hack v. Gillespie, 74 Ohio St.3d 362, 658 N.E.2d 1046 (1996). Some opinions have sought to avoid the assumed risk expression, but they nevertheless raise the same kind of arguments. See Flowers v. Rock Creek Terrace Ltd. Partnership, 308 Md. 432, 520 A.2d 361 (1987) (public policy derived from fact that firefighters are employed for the very purpose of confronting such risks); Kreski v. Modern Wholesale Elec. Supply Co., 429 Mich. 347, 415 N.W.2d 178 (1987). In at least one case, Indiana treated a safety officer's assumed risk as comparative negligence rather than no-duty. Heck v. Robey, 659 N.E.2d 498

officers are paid to face risks inherent in their work, including, evidently, the risks of negligence by third persons. If salaries of these employees do or should reflect advance payment for taking risks, no other payment is due when injury occurs.[22] So the defendant owes no duty to protect safety officers from risks they are employed to confront. Under this rationale, courts currently tend to analyze the cases by considering the risks which were, or were not, inherent in the professional's work or risks the safety officer was paid to deal with.[23]

Rejections and limitations. Besides the limits implicit in the rule itself,[24] some courts have begun to reject any special rule for firefighters, officers, and others who must confront danger. Where assumed risk has been abolished as a separate doctrine,[25] and where the special landowners' rules have been abolished as well,[26] the formal supports for the doctrine are shaky. Even where the landowners' rules are retained, they offer no support for the firefighter's rule as applied to injuries outside the land. For reasons like these, the Supreme Court of Oregon abolished the rule,[27] while others have never accepted it,[28] or counseled a cautious or narrow use of the rule.[29] The English House of Lords noted the American adoption of the rule and summarily dismissed the whole idea.[30] In some states, the rule does not apply to bar recovery when the defendant violated a fire-safety statute or ordinance.[31] And legislatures have abolished the rule[32] or limited it[33] in some states.

§ 286. Risks Covered by the Risk-Takers Rule

Risks associated with professional employment. Perhaps some states

(Ind.1995). On the difference, see §§ 211–214 supra.

22. See Krauth v. Geller, 31 N.J. 270, 274, 157 A.2d 129, 131 (1960) ("Hence, for that risk, the fireman should receive appropriate compensation from the public he serves, both in pay which reflects the hazard and in workmen's compensation benefits.... ").

23. Risks inherent are not necessarily those the officer is paid to confront. See Neighbarger v. Irwin Indus., Inc., 8 Cal.4th 532, 543, 882 P.2d 347, 34 Cal.Rptr.2d 630, 637 (1994) (public employer is using salary and compensation benefits to purchase exoneration of negligent citizens, but private employer of a safety officer might not be buying the same protection for those who injured its safety employees).

24. See §§ 286 & 287 below.

25. See § 211 supra.

26. See § 237 supra.

27. Christensen v. Murphy, 296 Or. 610, 620, 678 P.2d 1210, 1217 (1984).

28. See Mull v. Kerstetter, 373 Pa.Super. 228, 540 A.2d 951 (1988).

29. See Sallee v. GTE South, Inc., 839 S.W.2d 277, 278 (Ky.1992) ("We narrowly circumscribe the application of such exceptions so as to protect no one from responsibility for the consequences of their wrongdoing except where protecting the public makes it essential to do so"); Labrie v. Pace Membership Warehouse, Inc., 678 A.2d 867 (R.I.1996) (expressly avowing a cautious approach); Wright v. Coleman, 148 Wis.2d 897, 436 N.W.2d 864 (1989) (limiting the rule to immunize the landowner only for negligence in causing fire or failing to prevent its spread).

30. Ogwo v. Taylor, 1 A.C. 431 (1987).

31. See N.Y. Gen. Mun. L. § 205–a.

32. E.g., Fla. Stat. Ann. § 112.182 (as to property owners; firefighters and police officers classified as invitees when lawfully on the property); Minn. Stats. Ann. § 604.06; N.J. Stat. Ann. § 2A:62A–21; N.Y. Gen. Oblig. L. § 11–106.

33. Cal.Civ.Code § 1714.9; Nev. Rev. Stats. § 41.139.

still limit the firefighters' rule to premises liability cases.[1] Those cases aside, courts may express the firefighters' rule by saying that it prohibits recovery by a professional risk-taker for injuries from "the negligently created risk that was the very reason for his presence on the scene."[2] Put negatively, they sometimes say that the rule does not bar recovery when the defendant's negligence is "independent" of the circumstances that occasioned the professional's presence.[3] These two ways of stating the point may not be equally revealing, but they appear to aim at the same essential idea. A broader formulation bars the claim for injuries resulting from coping with risks that were unique or special to the professional work in question.[4]

To say that the officer is barred only when injury results from risks that produced the officer's presence may be to permit recovery in an assortment of cases. One case held that a firefighter could not recover for injuries resulting from a negligently set fire, but could recover for injuries inflicted by the owner's attack dogs, since the officer was responding to the fire but not to attack dogs.[5] A number of cases reflect a similar approach. A firefighter might be denied recovery for burns in an electrical fire for which she was summoned, but she could recover for injuries from the explosion of a gasoline tank on the premises[6] or for injuries from other dangerous conditions on the premises.[7] A police officer might be denied recovery for injuries incurred in making an arrest, but not for injuries resulting from the arrested person's hostility two years later.[8] A police officer injured in a high speed chase of an intoxicated person may be denied recovery against the intoxicated person but not against someone who illegally sold him alcohol.[9]

However, a number of decisions under the same formula are not so favorable to the safety officer. These appear to protect defendants not

§ 286

1. Where the rationale is exclusively based on the premises liability rules, off-premises injury is not subjected to the bar of the firefighters' rule and hence the rule formulas in the text do not apply. See Duncan v. Rzonca, 133 Ill.App.3d 184, 478 N.E.2d 603, 88 Ill.Dec. 288 (1985) (police officer injured on the way to respond to a bank alarm that turned out to be a negligently set false alarm).

2. Flowers v. Rock Creek Terrace Ltd. Partnership, 308 Md. 432, 449, 520 A.2d 361, 368 (1987); Wiley v. Redd, 110 Nev. 1310, 885 P.2d 592 (1994) (act of negligence that caused harm must be the same act that required officer's presence); Labrie v. Pace Membership Warehouse, Inc., 678 A.2d 867, 869 (1996) (firefighter's rule applies only when officer "is injured by a risk typically associated with" the crisis created by defendant's negligence).

3. Lipson v. Superior Court of Orange County (Berger), 31 Cal.3d 362, 644 P.2d 822, 182 Cal.Rptr. 629 (1982).

4. See the paragraph *Risks not inherent in the dangerous work or heightened by it* below.

5. Cf. Wiley v. Redd, 110 Nev. 1310, 885 P.2d 592 (1994) (police officer was present because alarm activated; the rule did not bar claim for dog-bite injuries, since failure to warn of the dog was not a reason for her presence).

6. See Lipson v. Superior Court of Orange County (Berger), 31 Cal.3d 362, 377, 644 P.2d 822, 832, 182 Cal.Rptr. 629, 639 (1982).

7. Rennenger v. Pacesetter Co., 558 N.W.2d 419 (Iowa 1997); cf. Paul v. Luigi's, Inc., 557 N.W.2d 895 (Iowa 1997) (similar, police); Newton v. New Hanover County Bd. of Educ., 342 N.C. 554, 467 S.E.2d 58 (1996) (similar, police).

8. Gibbons v. Caraway, 455 Mich. 314, 565 N.W.2d 663 (1997).

9. Gail v. Clark, 410 N.W.2d 662 (Iowa 1987).

only when the officer is injured by the very risk that necessitated the officer's presence, but also a range of associated risks. Such decisions have denied recovery to a firefighter who falls in an unguarded elevator shaft,[10] to a firefighter injured by an explosion of the defendant's car that occurred after the fire was in progress,[11] and to a police officer who slips on oil while investigating premises for a suspected burglary.[12] The professional's presence was not required by the elevator shaft, the car that exploded, or the slippery oil, but recovery was nevertheless denied. Although these risks did not occasion the officer's presence, they were a part of the bundle of risks associated with the particular operation and that was enough. In particular, when the injury occurs on the defendant's land, the officer assumes the risks that portions of the premises not open to the public may be in dangerous condition.

Risks not inherent in the dangerous work or heightened by it. The other side of the coin is that the professional risk-taker assumes only those risks that are inherent in the occupation or in the particular operation[13] and perhaps only risks that are unique[14] to the occupation or in some significant manner heightened by it.[15] Even then, the worker is not barred unless it is plausible to think that the public employer has paid the worker to relieve negligent persons from liability; the garbage worker may face risks of street injury more than an office worker, but the garbage worker is not paid to assume the risks of injury on the street.[16] In the same vein, a firefighter does not assume the risk that the landowner will fraudulently conceal dangers,[17] or fail to warn of dangers when the landowner knows the firefighter is about to encounter them.[18] The defendant does not escape when the negligence occurs after the firefighter's presence was or should have been discovered,[19] or in any

10. Flowers v. Rock Creek Terrace Ltd. Partnership, 308 Md. 432, 520 A.2d 361 (1987).

11. White v. Edmond, 971 F.2d 681 (11th Cir.1992).

12. Lee v. Luigi, Inc., 696 A.2d 1371 (D.C.1997); cf. Rosa v. Dunkin' Donuts of Passaic, 122 N.J. 66, 583 A.2d 1129 (1991) (officer providing emergency medical assistance in defendant's kitchen slipped on powdered sugar, firefighter's rule applies to bar); Kelhi v. Fitzpatrick, 25 Cal.App.4th 1149, 31 Cal.Rptr.2d 182 (1994) (officer, only fortuitously present on the highway, trying to cope with dangers to traffic from wheels that came off a truck; no recovery).

13. See Maltman v. Sauer, 84 Wash.2d 975, 979, 530 P.2d 254, 257 (1975) (was the risk causing injury "inherently within the ambit of those dangers which are unique to and generally associated with the particular rescue activity").

14. See Maltman v. Sauer, 84 Wash.2d 975, 979, 530 P.2d 254, 257 (1975) (unique). The policy rationale seems to support only risks that are peculiar to or of a demonstrably greater magnitude in the plaintiff's professional work. However, in Woods v. City of Warren, 439 Mich. 186, 193, 482 N.W.2d 696, 699 (1992), where a police officer was injured when ice caused him to lose control during pursuit of a thief, the court said that "Although the danger from slippery roads is not unique to police officers, Sergeant Woods' injury flows directly from his performance of his police duties and from a specific risk which, under the circumstances, was increased by his performance of those duties".

15. Ciervo v. City of New York, 240 A.D.2d 693, 659 N.Y.S.2d 320 (App. Div. 1997) (heightened, not inherent is the test).

16. Ciervo v. City of New York, 240 A.D.2d 693, 659 N.Y.S.2d 320 (App. Div. 1997).

17. Lipson v. Superior Court, 31 Cal.3d 362, 644 P.2d 822, 182 Cal.Rptr. 629 (1982).

18. Hack v. Gillespie, 74 Ohio St.3d 362, 658 N.E.2d 1046 (1996).

19. A rule codified in Cal. Civ. Code § 1714.9. Cf. Garcia v. City of South Tucson, 131 Ariz. 315, 640 P.2d 1117 (Ariz.App.

case when he negligently injures the plaintiff through a risk not inherent in the plaintiff's professional work.[20]

Intentional or reckless torts that occasion the officer's presence. The defendant is liable for certain intentional, reckless or willful torts to the safety officer, but quite possibly not for all. When the defendant's reckless misconduct simply causes a fire, for example, a court may protect the defendant on the ground that the firefighter assumed the risk of fire whether it was set recklessly or negligently.[21] Other courts have taken the opposite view, holding that assumed risk is only one element in the public policy behind the firefighter's rule and that moral culpability of the defendant who willfully or recklessly causes a fire weighs so heavily that recovery should be allowed.[22]

Intentional or reckless torts after the officer's presence is needed. When the defendant's willful, wanton, or reckless conduct occurs after the occasion has arisen for the safety officer's presence, the case for recovery is much stronger. The firefighter, for example, assumes the risks associated with fire, but not the risks added by the defendant's subsequent misconduct. This explains why the firefighter can recover for injuries resulting from the defendant's misleading conduct, concealment of dangers, and even for ordinary active negligence that occurs after the firefighter's presence is known.[23]

§ 287. Persons Covered by the Risk–Takers Rule

Generally. As already indicated,[1] courts now extend the firefighters' rule to police officers, with the effect that both firefighters' and police officers are denied recovery for injuries that fall within the inherent special risks of their professions. Although the rule may not include private persons who engage in various forms of rescue work,[2] it has been extended to volunteer firefighters, who are barred along with others.[3]

1981) (police officer accidentally shot by fellow officer at scene of a gun battle).

20. See Lipson v. Superior Court, supra n. 17; Sallee v. GTE South, Inc., 839 S.W.2d 277 (Ky.1992) (not barred as to injury resulting from risk "different in both kind and character"); Flowers v. Rock Creek Terrace Ltd. Partnership, 308 Md. 432, 520 A.2d 361 (1987) (rule does not apply as to perils not reasonably foreseeable as part of the occupational risk); cf. Wright v. Coleman, 148 Wis.2d 897, 436 N.W.2d 864 (1989) (perhaps limiting the firefighters' rule to cases of negligence in causing the fire or failing to prevent its spread, leaving all else to the reasonable care standard).

21. Cf. Hubbard v. Boelt, 28 Cal.3d 480, 620 P.2d 156, 169 Cal.Rptr. 706 (1980) (driver whose speed prompted an officer to give chase was not liable for injuries incurred by the officer in the crash that ensued, a result that may be affected by CAL. CIV. CODE § 1714.9); Young v. Sherwin–Williams Co., 569 A.2d 1173 (D.C.1990) (driver's recklessness left him in great danger, firefighter injured in rescue could not recover since the doctrine is based on assumed risk, not culpability of the defendant).

22. Mahoney v. Carus Chem. Co., Inc., 102 N.J. 564, 510 A.2d 4, 62 A.L.R.4th 703 (1986); cf. Berko v. Freda, 93 N.J. 81, 459 A.2d 663 (1983) (police officer).

23. Supra nn. 17–20.

§ 287

1. § 285 supra.

2. See n. 17 below.

3. E.g., Waggoner v. Troutman Oil Co., Inc., 320 Ark. 56, 894 S.W.2d 913 (1995); Baker v. Superior Court (Leach), 129 Cal. App.3d 710, 181 Cal.Rptr. 311 (1982); Carpenter v. O'Day, 562 A.2d 595, aff'd 553 A.2d 638 (Del.1988); Roberts v. Vaughn,

Public building inspectors and others not employed to face risks. The special rule for public safety officers does not apply to many other public officers or employees who are injured by a defendant's negligence. For example, it does not apply to a public sanitation worker[4] or a publicly employed building inspector or postal worker[5] who is injured by the defendant's negligence, even though, like the firefighter and police officer, the inspector will have compensation from public funds. This apparent discrepancy in the treatment of the two classes of employees is formally avoided by dropping the assumed risk/no duty rationale and returning to premises liability rules, then classifying the building inspector as an invitee.[6]

The classification is no doubt correct in many cases because the inspector is on the premises at a time and place when they are open to the public and thus comes within the public invitation test. Where the old categories like invitee and licensee have been abolished or injury occurs off premises, however, the invitee classification hardly explains why officers like inspectors are treated differently. Rhode Island has said that they should be treated differently because the firefighters' rule should be limited to officers dealing with a crisis or emergency.[7] Perhaps in line with the assumed risk/no duty analysis, it could be said that they have not been paid to assume any special, identifiable risks, or at least not the risk that caused injury.[8] In other words, a building inspector at a place open to the public or where the landowner expects her to be, is assuming no risks of defective premises.[9] Such a view, broader than Rhode Island's limit to emergencies, would also explain why other public employees are not barred wholesale from suing tortfeasors who injured them.[10]

214 Mich.App. 625, 543 N.W.2d 79 (1995) (public policy rationale applies equally to volunteer firefighter and rescue worker). In some instances, at least, the volunteer firefighter is paid a meager sum for each fire, may be entitled to receive workers' compensation benefits, and may have special training.

4. Ciervo v. City of New York, 93 N.Y.2d 465, 693 N.Y.S.2d 63, 715 N.E.2d 91 (1999)

5. See J. D. Perovich, Annotation, Liability of Owner or Occupant of Premises to Building or Construction Inspector Coming upon Premises in Discharge of Duty, 28 A.L.R.3d 891 (1970); cf. J. D. Perovich., Annotation, Liability of Owner or Operator of Premises for Injury to Meter Reader or Similar Employee of Public Service Corporation Coming to Premises in Course of Duties, 28 A.L.R.3d 1344 (1970).

6. E.g., Swift & Co. v. Schuster, 192 F.2d 615 (10th Cir.1951) (government meat inspector in slaughterhouse); Fred Howland, Inc. v. Morris, 143 Fla. 189, 196 So. 472, 128 A.L.R. 1013 (1940) (purporting to view a building inspection as arising out of implied contract between the owner and the city).

7. Labrie v. Pace Membership Warehouse, Inc., 678 A.2d 867 (R.I.1996).

8. See Ciervo v. City of New York, 93 N.Y.2d 465, 693 N.Y.S.2d 63, 715 N.E.2d 91 (1999)

9. See Boyer v. Anchor Disposal, 135 N.J. 86, 638 A.2d 135 (1994) (fire inspector did not assume risk of hidden slippery substance).

10. See Bath Excavating & Const. Co. v. Wills, 847 P.2d 1141 (Colo.1993) (a city water department employee was called to deal with a pipe ruptured by the defendant's negligence, then injured by a mudslide while he was attempting to plug the leak; firefighters' rule does not bar his claim); Ciervo v. City of New York, 93 N.Y.2d 465, 693 N.Y.S.2d 63, 715 N.E.2d 91 (1999) (sanitation worker injured in hole in street, not barred).

Public employees dealing with emergencies or trained to deal with risks. If building inspectors and similar employees are not expected to face special risks, a number of other public employees are. A water department worker may be required to deal with dangerous emergencies created by ruptured pipes; EMTs, paramedics, ambulance drivers or other rescue workers may be confronted with poisonous smoke or any number of other dangers.

In a limited number of cases involving paramedics and the like, courts have applied the firefighters' rule in some and not in others.[11] Some courts tend to assume that a categorical rule is required for such cases rather than an evaluation of the facts bearing on whether the worker was paid to assume the risk in question. Several have said that EMTs, paramedics, or ambulance drivers and the like are not included in the firefighters' rule,[12] or even that the firefighters' rule is limited to firefighters' and police officers and hence automatically excludes all others.[13]

On the other hand, courts can treat the question of the paramedic's assumption of risk as a fact question to be decided like other fact questions, case by case.[14] A court might, for example, conclude that the particular risk encountered by a rescue worker was not inherent in the work and hence not a risk the worker assumed, while leaving it open to conclude that some other risk was one the worker was paid to encounter. Under such a case-specific approach, a court might conclude that a paramedic was not employed to confront toxic fumes generated by the defendant,[15] but that an attendant in a mental health facility for dangerous patients was definitely employed to assume the risks of violent patients[16] or a helicopter rescue crew was employed to face the risk, among others, that the helicopter would crash.[17]

Privately employed safety workers. Police, firefighting, and other safety efforts can be thought of in terms of the rescue doctrine. The rescue doctrine has it that a defendant who negligently creates risks to A may be liable to B who is injured in coming to A's rescue. The doctrine applies even if the defendant is the person being rescued.[18] The rescue doctrine most clearly applies to spontaneous rescuers who have no professional stake or duty in effecting a rescue. When the rescuer is a publicly paid professional whose duty includes such a rescue, states that

11. See Joseph B. Conder, Application of "Firemen's Rule" to Bar Recovery by Emergency Medical Personnel Injured in Responding to, or at Scene of, Emergency, 89 A.L.R.4th 1079 (1992).

12. Kowalski v. Gratopp, 177 Mich.App. 448, 442 N.W.2d 682 (1989) (paramedic or EMT); Krause v. U.S. Truck Co., Inc., 787 S.W.2d 708 (Mo.1990) (ambulance driver killed at scene of multi-vehicle collisions on Interstate 70).

13. Lees v. Lobosco, 265 N.J.Super. 95, 625 A.2d 573 (1993).

14. See Heck v. Robey, 659 N.E.2d 498 (Ind.1995).

15. See Philip Morris, Inc. v. Emerson, 235 Va. 380, 368 S.E.2d 268 (1988).

16. Anicet v. Gant, 580 So.2d 273 (Fla. Dist.Ct.App.1991).

17. Maltman v. Sauer, 84 Wash.2d 975, 530 P.2d 254 (1975).

18. § 184 supra.

apply the firefighters' rule are in effect saying that the rescue doctrine is inapplicable.

The privately employed risk-taker is neither a spontaneous good citizen nor a public employee, so the question arises whether to apply the firefighters' rule or something closer to the rescue doctrine. The assumed risk/public policy rationale of the firefighters' rule is based on the somewhat plausible view that the public employer is paying wages and compensation benefits to the firefighter to protect citizens from firefighter suits because by so doing the public employer exonerates citizens who are also taxpayers-constituents of that public entity. But it is not equally persuasive to construct such a vision of the private employer's relation to third persons who may be negligent toward its employees. While a privately employed safety officer may know of risks to be confronted, it is quite unlikely that the private employer is paying the officer to forego claims against others. Consequently, courts have refused to apply the firefighter's rule to privately employed professional risk-takers, with the result that the ordinary claims and defenses will determine the case.[19]

Manufacturers of products, suppliers of services. Manufacturers of defective or negligently made or designed products are normally responsible for the harms inflicted by those products.[20] When the product causes a fire or makes it worse, however, several courts have held that the firefighters' rule bars recovery by the injured firefighter.[21] The Kentucky Court refused to bar the firefighter, however, saying that landowners, not others, were the beneficiaries of the policy behind the rule.[22] And when the defective product does not cause the fire but is instead provided to the firefighter as a professional tool or a safety device, the firefighters' rule has no application and does not bar recovery.[23] The firefighter may also proceed against the manufacturer who is not the landowner if the product is defective but its danger is not reasonably apparent or to be anticipated.[24] Suppliers of services may

19. Neighbarger v. Irwin Indus., Inc., 8 Cal.4th 532, 34 Cal.Rptr.2d 630, 882 P.2d 347 (1994); Kowalski v. Gratopp, 177 Mich. App. 448, 442 N.W.2d 682 (1989).

20. Chapter 24.

21. White v. Edmond, 971 F.2d 681 (11th Cir.1992) (Volvo allegedly exploded at scene of fire, causing injuries, manufacturer not liable); Flowers v. Rock Creek Terrace Ltd. Partnership,. 308 Md. 432, 520 A.2d 361 (1987) (manufacturer of elevator not liable when firefighter fell twelve stories while fighting fire; such an injury is within the range of anticipated risks); Austin v. City of Buffalo, 179 A.D.2d 1075, 580 N.Y.S.2d 604 (1992); Mahoney v. Carus Chem. Co., Inc., 102 N.J. 564, 510 A.2d 4, 62 A.L.R.4th 703 (1986); Mignone v. Fieldcrest Mills, 556 A.2d 35 (R.I.1989).

22. Hawkins v. Sunmark Indus., Inc., 727 S.W.2d 397 (Ky.1986) (manufacturer of allegedly defective gas pump at service station could not have the protection of the firefighters' rule when firefighter was injured in dealing with fire at the pump). To the extent that a court applies the firefighters' rule only in premises liability cases, the rule would not protect the product manufacturers. See Court v. Grzelinski, 72 Ill.2d 141, 379 N.E.2d 281, 19 Ill.Dec. 617 (1978).

23. E.g., Wright v. Stang Mfg. Co., 54 Cal.App.4th 1218, 63 Cal.Rptr.2d 422 (1997) (water gun broke loose under pressure and caused injury); Shepard v. Morning Pride Mfg. Inc., 217 A.D.2d 308, 636 N.Y.S.2d 173 (1996) (safety equipment).

24. Hauboldt v. Union Carbide Corp., 160 Wis.2d 662, 467 N.W.2d 508 (1991).

create special dangers for safety officers. A fire alarm service may negligently delay in calling the fire department with the result that by the time firefighters enter the building, the floor collapses under them. Without relying on the firefighters' rule, however, Judge Posner held that the alarm company owed no duty to the firefighters.[25]

25. Edwards v. Honeywell, Inc., 50 F.3d 484 (7th Cir.1995) (harm unforeseeable in the sense that alarm company would find it difficult to determine what care to provide or how much to charge subscribers to cover contingent liability to safety officers).

*

c. Type of Harm Affecting Duties

CHAPTER 18

PRENATAL AND BIRTH-RELATED INJURY

§ 288. Prenatal Injury

The Traditional Rule and Its Passing

The early no-duty rule. Until about the middle of the 20th century, a tortfeasor whose impact upon a pregnant woman resulted in harm to the later-born child was protected against liability in the United States. Expressed in terms of duty, the tortfeasor owed a duty to the mother but not to the child. One reason was that the causal connection was difficult to trace. The other was the purely formal argument that the fetus was not a person to whom any duty could be owed.[1]

Rejection of the rule. The causal argument justifies scrutiny of causal proof, which depends upon facts and evidence; but it does not justify a flat rule that prohibits the very proof that would establish causation in particular cases. The formal argument, bereft of either policy or human concern, was just as inadequate if not worse. Both arguments were rejected in 1946 in *Bonbrest v. Kotz*,[2] after which courts reversed course. They now universally hold that no one is to be denied compensation for injury merely because the harm was inflicted before that person's birth.[3] A few courts at one time may have implied that the action for prenatal injury would not be entertained if injury was inflicted before the fetus was viable. But courts have not adopted that rule. So long as the living plaintiff can prove the elements of a tort claim, the fact that the harm was initially done to a pre-viable fetus does not defeat the claim.[4] Wrongful death cases are another matter.

§ 288

1. Dietrich v. Northhampton, 138 Mass. 14 (1884) (emphasizing lack of personhood at the time of injury).

2. Bonbrest v. Kotz, 65 F.Supp. 138 (D.D.C.1946). The dissent of Justice Boggs in Allaire v. St. Luke's Hospital, 184 Ill. 359, 56 N.E. 638 (1900) presaged this shift, as did the Canadian decision in Montreal Tramways v. Leveille, [1933] 4 D.L.R. 337 (Sup. Ct. 1933).

3. E.g., Amann v. Faidy, 415 Ill. 422, 114 N.E.2d 412 (1953); Woods v. Lancet, 303 N.Y. 349, 102 N.E.2d 691, 27 A.L.R.2d 1250 (1951); Sinkler v. Kneale, 401 Pa. 267, 164 A.2d 93 (1960); Restatement § 869 (1). The reversal was complete by about 1972. See Huskey v. Smith, 289 Ala. 52, 265 So.2d 596 (1972); Roland F. Chase, Annotation, Liability for Prenatal Injuries, 40 A.L.R.3d 1222 (1972). As to harm inflicted before conception, however, see § 290 below.

4. Sylvia v. Gobeille, 101 R.I. 76, 220 A.2d 222 (1966) ("we are unable logically to conclude that a claim for an injury inflicted prior to viability is any less meritorious than one sustained after.... With us the test will not be viability but causation")

Wrongful Death Cases

Death claim issues. Death claims for loss of a fetus or a child injured before birth are more complicated, partly because of the way damages are calculated in death actions,[5] partly because death statutes require the "death" of a "person," and partly because other means may be available to redress the loss to parents. In determining whether injury to a fetus was followed by "death of a person"[6] as required by statute, courts have considered separately or together two potentially critical questions: (1) Was the fetus viable at the time of injury? (2) Was the child born alive, with death occurring at some moment after birth?

Fetus not born alive. Some states reject the action altogether in the absence of a live birth.[7] The effect of this rule is that if the defendant does enough damage to terminate life of the fetus before birth, he simply is not liable. Another group of states reject the wrongful death action in the absence of a live birth but permit the mother or parents to recover for mental anguish or emotional harm.[8] Most courts, however, now recognize that an action lies for wrongful death of a stillborn infant or of a fetus not born alive, at least where injury occurred when the fetus was viable.[9] In such cases, a real loss has occurred as a result of the defendant's tort even though death occurred before birth.

Born alive after pre-viable injury. A different pattern occurs if the fetus is injured before viability, but the child is then born alive. In that case, the child could maintain a personal injury action if it lived, so there seems no objection to a wrongful death claim if the born-alive child dies, although a few courts have insisted that viability at injury is essential to any action.[10] If the reality of a tort-caused loss is the essential question, then this view may be too restrictive. Perhaps, as some authority holds, *either* (a) viability at time of injury *or* (b) live birth (with later death) should suffice as a basis for liability.[11] Consistent with this view, some

5. See § 296 below.

6. E.g., Miccolis v. AMICA Mutual Ins. Co., 587 A.2d 67 (R.I.1991).

7. Chatelain v. Kelley, 322 Ark. 517, 910 S.W.2d 215 (1995); Peters v. Hospital Authority of Elbert County, 265 Ga. 487, 458 S.E.2d 628 (1995) (stating rule without reference to viability that live birth is required; facts recited by the court did not reveal whether fetus was viable or not).

8. Tanner v. Hartog, 696 So.2d 705 (Fla. 1997); Giardina v. Bennett, 111 N.J. 412, 545 A.2d 139 (1988); Krishnan v. Sepulveda, 916 S.W.2d 478 (Tex.1995). The father as bystander who is not himself a victim of medical malpractice or other tort, may be denied any emotional harm recovery unless he witnessed the malpractice and the resulting injury under the rule applied in some states. See Carey v. Lovett, 132 N.J. 44, 622 A.2d 1279 (1993); § 312 below.

9. Summerfield v. Superior Court, 144 Ariz. 467, 698 P.2d 712 (1985); Moen v. Hanson, 85 Wash.2d 597, 537 P.2d 266 (1975) (death action); Cavazos v. Franklin, 73 Wash.App. 116, 867 P.2d 674 (1994) (survival action permitted). See Sheldon R. Shapiro, Annotation, Right to Maintain Action or to Recover Damages For Death of Unborn Child, 84 A.L.R.3d 411 (1978).

10. Miller v. Kirk, 120 N.M. 654, 905 P.2d 194 (1995).

11. McKinstry v. Valley Obstetrics–Gynecology Clinic, 428 Mich. 167, 405 N.W.2d 88 (1987) (claim may proceed "if the fetus is born alive, subsequent to the claimed injury, or if the fetus was viable at the time of the alleged injury"); Hudak v. Georgy, 535 Pa. 152, 634 A.2d 600 (1993).

courts have allowed the claim to proceed if the child is born alive, even if injury occurred before the fetus was viable.[12]

Neither viability at injury nor live birth. The most extreme case occurs when injury is inflicted before viability and no live birth occurs. From one viewpoint, the defendant should not escape liability merely because his acts occurred early rather than late in fetal development, much less because the harm was sufficient to terminate life before birth occurred. With some such view in mind, a few recent decisions have allowed recovery in this situation.[13] This opens the door to wrongful death claims when the mother was pregnant for only a week or a day, or possibly even for a claim of death if an egg fertilized *in vitro* is destroyed before it is ever implanted in the mother.

These possibilities suggest that some degree of caution might be appropriate. Although the stage of fetal development at injury seems irrelevant, courts might plausibly require that, regardless when injury was inflicted, either live birth or some substantial fetal development in the mother's womb would be a prerequisite to the wrongful death action. On the other hand, without resorting to a wrongful death action at all, courts could appropriately redress the mother's own claim for emotional injury without restrictions as to live birth or the stage of fetal development.

What is and is not important. Courts have sometimes emphasized viability of the fetus for purely formal or conceptual reasons that are quite divorced from the purposes of tort law. The idea is that until the fetus is viable, there is no "person" apart from the mother. Any harm done is harm to the mother. In personal injury cases, however, that argument misses the point entirely. Whatever may have been the case when injury was inflicted, it set in motion a chain of events that caused injury to a living and suffering human being. Both compensation and deterrence goals of tort law counsel a rule allowing the child to recover for the tort in personal injury cases and one allowing the parents, or at least the mother to recover when the fetus does not survive or the child dies of the injury. The status of the fetus at the time of injury has no bearing on the status of the plaintiff, who is a living human being, harmed by the defendant's torts.

It is not necessarily so, however, that wrongful death actions represent the best way to redress the real loss suffered by the parents. The losses are not much like those at which the traditional death statute was aimed—the loss of pecuniary advantage. Instead, the losses are usually emotional and intangible. An action for emotional harm to parents, or at

12. Kalafut v. Gruver, 239 Va. 278, 389 S.E.2d 681 (1990); see Miccolis v. AMICA Mutual Ins. Co., 587 A.2d 67 (R.I.1991).

13. Wiersma v. Maple Leaf Farms, 543 N.W.2d 787 (S.D.1996); Farley v. Sartin, 195 W.Va. 671, 466 S.E.2d 522 (W.Va. 1995) (emphasizing, however, that the decision did not necessarily apply to cases of conception outside the mother's body). Some of the cases are based upon construction of the statute.

least to the mother, may be a more manageable and suitable form of redress and may also provide a better vehicle for deterrence.[14]

§ 289. Toxic Fetal Injuries and Parental Liability

Fetal Toxic Harm Cases

Toxic torts and mass torts often go together. Separately or together, they represent large topics that require specialized books. While traditional fetal injury claims were usually based on physical impact upon the mother, as in automobile collision cases and simple falls,[1] most fetal harms today are likely to be the results of licit and illicit drugs, environmental toxins, workplace exposures, or contaminants in water or food. Courts are now facing claims of fetal injury from some such exposures and no doubt more will follow.

Yet toxic torts frequently involve low dosages over time, often with a long latency period before harm appears. Unlike an automobile accident, a medical mishap, or a punch in the nose, no one can see the toxic tort happen. A fetus may be peculiarly susceptible to some toxins which can pass from the mother directly to the fetus.[2] But in the case of toxic fetal injuries, many toxic fetal injuries can be inflicted that are not dramatic enough to be identified immediately or with certainty by the use of existing technology. Studies may show, for example, that carbon monoxide, a well-known danger, is harmful to the fetus, but they may be inconclusive about the nature of the harms when exposure is not great.[3] Some effects remain hidden because they operate on the central nervous system of the fetus and leave behind intelligence and learning ability deficits rather than distorted appendages or chemicals in the urine. For instance, even a mother's moderate ingestion of alcohol during pregnancy may lead to substantial deficits in learning ability of her child,[4] but unless the child is a part of a scientific study, her lifelong learning

14. Emotional distress claims, at least when asserted by those to whom no direct duty is owed, do present problems. See § 312 below.

§ 289

1. E.g., Cushing v. Time Savers Stores, Inc., 552 So.2d 730 (La.App.1989) (brain damages to child resulting from fetal impact that caused abruption of the placenta).

2. A good introduction to the methods by which prenatal toxic harm can occur is Steven S. Paskal, Liability for Prenatal Harm in the Workplace: the Need for Reform, 17 U. Puget Sound L. Rev. 283 (1994). Many potential toxic agents are described in various articles in Gideon Koren (Ed.), Maternal-Fetal Toxicology: A Clinician's Guide (2d ed. 1994); see also Sam Kacew and George H. Lambert, Environmental Toxicology and Pharmacology of Human Development (1997).

3. The difficulties of producing a conclusive carbon monoxide study are summarized, along with limited conclusions, in Gideon Koren, Teresa Sharav, and Anne Pastuszak, A Multicenter, Prospective Study of Fetal Outcome Following Accidental Carbon Monoxide Poisoning in Pregnancy,in Gideon Koren, supra n. 2 at 253.

4. See Ann Pytkowicz Streissguth, Paul D. Sampson, Helen M. Barr, Fred L. Bookstein, Heather Carmichael Olson, The Effects of Prenatal Exposure to Alcohol and Tobacco: Contributions from the Seattle Longitudianl Prospective Student and Implications for Public Policy, in Herbert L. Needleman and David Belligener, Prenatal Exposure to Toxicants—Developmental Consequences 148 (1994). Possibly the father's use of alcohol, too. See Gladys Friedler, Developmental Toxicology: Male-mediated Effects, in Maureen Paul, Occupational and Environmental Reproductive Hazards, a Guide for Clinicians 52 (1993).

difficulties may never be understood, much less attributed to her mother's drinking. The same seems to be true if the mother is exposed to lead.[5] For these and associated reasons, lawyers will find it quite difficult—and very expensive—to prove scientific causation.[6]

Quite possibly an enormous number of fetal injuries result in destruction of the fetus at such an early date that the mother is unaware of pregnancy or miscarriage.[7] Even toxic injuries that are recognized because they are dramatic may go unredressed because of doubts about causation and because of the difficulties and expense of securing evidence. These difficulties with toxic torts generally have led many authors to propose rules to make the road easier for the toxic plaintiff,[8] even as others propose to tighten causal rules to provide more protection for defendants.[9] Whatever course the law takes on those issues, however, the number of children damaged in the womb and the even greater number of fetal demise cases appears to be very large indeed, with a corresponding potential for legal response.

Workplace Injury to Fetus and the Workers' Compensation Limit

When the fetus is exposed to hazardous materials because of the mother's or father's exposure in the workplace, workers' compensation laws are potentially implicated. Those laws generally provide for standardized compensation to workers injured on the job as the exclusive remedy; tort claims are forbidden.[10] When a child asserts a claim that she was injured in utero by her mother's exposure to hazardous materials on the mother's job, the question is whether the child's claim in tort should

5. See David Bellinger and Herbert L. Needleman, The Neurotoxicity of Prenatal Exposures to Lead: Kinetics, Mechanisms and Expressions, in HERBERT L. NEEDLEMAN AND DAVID BELLINGER, PRENATAL EXPOSURE TO TOXICANTS—DEVELOPMENTAL CONSEQUENCES 89 (1994) (noting, however, that although the most statistically important study provided evidence that prenatal exposure to lead affects a child's development, other studies do not provide such evidence).

6. Mass studies showing an increased risk of harm to fetuses from particular substances may still fall short. A good illustration is Turpin v. Merrell Dow Pharmaceuticals, Inc., 959 F.2d 1349 (6th Cir.1992). Limitations imposed upon "scientific" testimony in Daubert v. Merrell Dow Pharmaceuticals, Inc., 509 U.S. 579, 113 S.Ct. 2786, 125 L.Ed.2d 469 (1993) may add to the difficulty. See generally, Michael Green, Expert Witnesses and Sufficiency of Evidence in Toxic Substances Litigation: The Legacy of Agent Orange and Bendectin Litigation, 86 NW. U. L. REV. 643 (1992). Kaye, Is Proof of Statistical Significance Relevant?, 61 WASH. L. REV. 1333 (1986); Cohen, Confidence in Probability: Burdens of Persuasion in a World of Imperfect Knowledge, 60 N.Y.U. L. REV. 385 (1985).

7. See Steven S. Paskal, Liability for Prenatal Harm in the Workplace: the Need for Reform, 17 U. PUGET SOUND L. REV. 283 (1994). Some estimate that one fetus is aborted for every child born. See GIDEON KOREN, supra n. 2 at vii.

8. Thus some advocate changes in the requirements of causal evidence in toxic tort cases, see Margaret A. Berger, Eliminating General Causation: Notes Towards a New Theory of Justice and Toxic Torts, COLUM. L. REV. 2117 (1997), while others advocate changes in regulation and compensation systems. See Anita Bernstein, Formed by Thalidomide: Mass Torts as a False Cure For Toxic Exposure, 97 COLUM. L. REV. 2153 (1997).

9. See Eisenberg & Henderson, The Quiet Revolution in Products Liability: An Empirical Study of Legal Change, 37 UCLA L. REV. 479 (1990). Professor Boston proposed a demanding standard for mass tort cases, less for individualized injuries. Gerald W. Boston, A Mass-exposure Model of Toxic Causation: the Content of Scientific Proof and the Regulatory Experience, 18 COLUM. J. ENVTL. L. 181 (1993).

10. See § 395 below.

be barred by the workers' compensation rules. The answer in the handful of cases on point has uniformly been that the claim is not barred by the workers' compensation exclusive remedy rules.[11]

To eliminate the exclusive remedy rule is not to impose liability upon employers for fetal injury. The child, like anyone else claiming tort damages against the employer, will be required to show negligence or, possibly, abnormally dangerous activities. The fact that an employer's business uses dangerous chemicals does not necessarily mean that the employer is negligent. Only if dangerous chemicals are unnecessary or feasible precautions against injury are ignored, is negligence established. In addition, federal antidiscrimination law requires employers to allow women equal access to jobs, including jobs that may endanger a fetus.[12] If the employer's only supposed negligence is in permitting a fully informed pregnant woman to work around dangerous materials, the federal anti-discrimination rule probably protects the employer against tort liability.[13]

Workplace exposure of the father may also cause fetal harm. Besides the possibility of chromosome damage by radiation,[14] some studies, still at the early stage, indicate that fetal harm of anomalies are often associated positively with the father's occupation.[15] The hypothesis is that toxic agents associated with particular occupations may affect chromosome structure, or that the father may inadvertently carry home toxins on his body or in this clothes, exposing the mother during pregnancy. As with so many potential claims of toxic harm, however, proof of causation may have to await generations of study.

Product and Environmental Injuries to Fetus

A number of substances in the environment or in products may cause fetal harm. Lead is famously dangerous to the developing fetus as well as to children.[16] Second-hand smoke is probably a toxin to the fetus.[17] So are some products used by pregnant women. In such a case, if

11. Namislo v. Akzo Chemicals, Inc., 620 So.2d 573 (Ala.1993); Snyder v. Michael's Stores, Inc., 16 Cal.4th 991, 945 P.2d 781, 68 Cal.Rptr.2d 476 (1997); Pizza Hut of America, Inc. v. Keefe, 900 P.2d 97 (Colo.1995) (wrongful death claim); Hitachi Chemical Electro-Products, Inc. v. Gurley, 219 Ga.App. 675, 466 S.E.2d 867 (1995) (alleging that both parents were exposed to dangerous workplace materials). In all the cited cases, the children were born alive.

12. International Union, United Automobile Workers v. Johnson Controls, Inc., 499 U.S. 187, 111 S.Ct. 1196, 113 L.Ed.2d 158 (1991).

13. See 499 U.S. at 208, 111 S.Ct. At 1208.

14. As claimed in cases like Hinkie v. United States, 715 F.2d 96 (3d Cir.1983) (exposure to radioactivity); Mondelli v. United States, 711 F.2d 567 (3d Cir., 1983) (genetic damage by service member's exposure to nuclear explosion causing cancer to child); Monaco v. United States, 661 F.2d 129 (9th Cir.1981). See § 265.

15. Andrew F. Olshan, Kay Teschke, and Patricia A. Baird, Paternal Occupation and Congenital Anomalies in Offspring, 20 AM. J. OF INDUS. MED. 447 (1991).

16. E.g., Kim N. Dietrich, Kathleen M. Kraft, Robert L. Bornschein, Paul B. Hammond, Omer Berger, Paul A. Succop and Mariana Bier, Low-Level Lead Exposure Effect on Neurobehavioral Development in Early Infancy, 80 PEDIATRICS 721 (1987).

17. See H. Westley Clark & Meryle Weinstein, Chemical Dependency in MAUREEN PAUL, OCCUPATION AND ENVIRONMENTAL REPRODUCTIVE HAZARDS 344, 347–48 (1993); see also Julie E. Lippert, Comment, Prenatal Injuries from Passive Tobacco Smoke:

exposure is demonstrated and harm results, liability may be established.[18] As already indicated, however, proof of causation has failed in many claims for prenatal injury against pharmaceutical manufacturers, either on the ground that the evidence of experts was insufficient or on the ground that it was inadmissible altogether as insufficiently accepted among scientists.[19]

The problem of mass exposure—including fetal exposure—to hazardous substances is sometimes addressed through regulation or even through injunctions. For example, a New York court enjoined sandblasting of a bridge to remove lead paint because the resulting dust created substantial risks of exposure to lead, which in turn could lead to limitations on cognitive development and disorders of the nervous and reproductive systems.[20]

Parents' Duty to Fetus

A father whose genetic material is injured may pass along serious birth defects from the moment of conception. A mother may intentionally or unintentionally ingest alcohol—the "teratogen of choice" one authority called it[21]—or harmful agents such as cocaine, alcohol, or lead. Use of these and other drugs in pregnancy is quite common and cuts across social and racial lines.[22] Some, perhaps all of those and other ingested substances may harm the fetus and permanently damage the child. If parents are not protected by an immunity,[23] the question is whether a child has a good claim against her own mother or father for fetal injuries of this kind.

Few cases deal with the parents' duty to the fetus. In non-toxic cases, one claim consistently denied is the claim for dissatisfied life brought by a child against a parent for causing his birth as an illegitimate child.[24] Illinois, in an automobile accident case, refused to entertain a child's action against the mother based upon the mother's negligence during pregnancy;[25] New Hampshire, also in an auto case, thought if the mother owed reasonable care to a child once it was born, a duty of care should be imposed for the fetus as well.[26] Although neither case was a toxic tort case, the Illinois Court's reasoning seemed most significantly

Establishing a Cause of Action for Negligence, 78 Ky. L. J. 865 (1989/90).

18. Hogle v. Hall, 112 Nev. 599, 916 P.2d 814 (1996) (product Accutane, known to be teratogenic if used during pregnancy, physician liable for prescription).

19. See, e.g., Merrell Dow Pharmaceuticals, Inc. v. Havner, 953 S.W.2d 706 (Tex. 1997) (reviewing the sufficiency and admissibility holdings in the Bendectin cases where plaintiffs asserted that children suffered limb reduction defects because of fetal exposure through mothers' ingestion of Bendectin).

20. Williamsburg Around the Bridge Block Association v. Giuliani, 223 A.D.2d 64, 644 N.Y.S.2d 252 (1996).

21. See Ann Pytkowicz Streissguth, et al. supra n. 4 at 174.

22. See Ira J. Chasnoff, Harvey J. Landress, and Mark E. Barrett, The Prevalence of Illicit Drug or Alcohol Use During Pregnancy, 322 New Eng. J. Med. 1202 (1990).

23. See § 280 supra.

24. E.g., Slawek v. Stroh, 62 Wis.2d 295, 215 N.W.2d 9 (1974).

25. Stallman v. Youngquist, 125 Ill.2d 267, 531 N.E.2d 355, 126 Ill.Dec. 60, 78 A.L.R.4th 1071 (1988).

26. Bonte v. Bonte, 136 N.H. 286, 616 A.2d 464 (1992).

addressed to cases involving the mother's use of substances that could harm the fetus. It reasoned that the mother's right of autonomy, bodily integrity, and privacy would make it inappropriate for courts to require a duty of reasonable care. The court left open the possibility for liability based on intentional tort theories. A Texas court has also rejected any duty by a pregnant woman that would impose liability for ingesting cocaine during pregnancy.[27] So far only one mother-ingestion case has actually recognized a potential liability, but it did not discuss the central issue of the mother's own rights, and its authority is clouded by later decisions.[28]

The problem of a mother's potential responsibility for treatment of her own body, or her fetus, depending on the viewpoint adopted, mirrors the problem much-debated in the criminal field, whether it is just or permissible to punish a mother whose drug or alcohol abuse during pregnancy permanently damages or kills the fetus or the later-born child.[29] In addition, the lifestyle of both parents may contribute to toxic and other harms to children in many ways. From the social service viewpoint that is so much of family law, responsibility in tort may be the least desirable of all approaches to a massive problem.[30]

§ 290. Harm from Preconception Negligence

When the plaintiff is injured by negligent acts that occur before the plaintiff was conceived, courts are somewhat divided.[1] Such injuries have occurred in several ways. For example the defendant might damage genetic material of either parent before the plaintiff was conceived, with resulting genetic defects in the plaintiff once conception and birth took place.[2] Or the defendant may negligently harm the mother before conception, resulting in oxygen deprivation of the fetus much later[3] or early termination of pregnancy and damage to the child.[4] Or health care providers, acting before the plaintiff's conception, may negligently fail to

27. Chenault v. Huie, 989 S.W.2d 474 (Tex.App.1999) (doubting whether a workable standard of care could be developed; "The 'reasonable person' standard ... is simply not design to apply to matters involving intimate, private, and personal decisions").

28. Grodin v. Grodin, 102 Mich.App. 396, 301 N.W.2d 869 (1980).

29. Whitner v. State, 492 S.E.2d 777, 328 S.C. 1 (1997) authorizes criminal conviction of a mother who used crack cocaine to the injury of the fetus in the third trimester.

30. Cf. Ira J. Chasnoff (ed), Drugs, Alcohol, Pregnancy and Parenting (1988).

§ 290

1. See generally, Julie A. Greenberg, Reconceptualizing Preconception Torts, 64 TENN. L. REV. 315, 349 ff. (1997); Annotation, Liability for Child's Personal Injuries or Death Resulting from Tort Committed Against Child's Mother Before Child Was Conceived, 91 A.L.R.3d 316 (1980).

2. Some such claims against the government for harms resulting from exposure to nuclear radiation have been dismissed under the *Feres* rule. See § 265, supra.

3. Albala v. City of New York, 54 N.Y.2d 269, 445 N.Y.S.2d 108, 429 N.E.2d 786 (1981).

4. Hegyes v. Unjian Enterprises, Inc., 234 Cal.App.3d 1103, 286 Cal.Rptr. 85 (1991).

prevent development of antibodies in the mother that would damage the fetus once conception occurs.[5]

About a dozen cases have passed on the defendant's duty when the plaintiff had not been conceived at the time the defendant acted. Most of them expressly or implicitly recognize that the ordinary duty of care does not disappear merely because the child was not conceived at the time of the defendant's negligent conduct. The result is that unless some other fact dispels a duty of care, the defendant will be held liable for foreseeable harms he causes to the later-conceived child.[6] Some other courts, seemingly receptive to the claim, have left the matter open .[7] Most of these cases recognizing a duty of care to an unconceived child are in fact suits against health care professionals who are engaged in treating the mother and who at least implicitly undertake to provide appropriate care for the child as well.

A little authority suggests that the duty would extend only to health care defendants or those similarly situated,[8] and a few cases have rejected a duty on the facts of the particular case and on grounds neutral to the preconception issue. For example, a doctor who is only giving birth control counseling would not be expected to test the patient's blood type as a step in protection of an unconceived child,[9] and a drug manufacturer may not be expected to foresee that its product would cause harm to the grandchild of the person who uses the drug.[10] In particular cases, injury to an unconceived child may be regarded as unforeseeable and hence not actionable.[11] Such cases do not exclude liability for preconception negligence when the claim is otherwise actionable.

5. E.g., Walker v. Rinck, 604 N.E.2d 591 (Ind.1992). Several versions of such cases arise, but all essentially turn on the fact that health care providers either trigger antibodies in the mother's blood by transfusion of incompatible blood or fail to test the mother's blood and administer RhoGAM once the blood has been sensitized. In all these cases, injury to the fetus can be avoided only by preconception care.

6. Bergstreser v. Mitchell, 577 F.2d 22 (8th Cir.1978); Jorgensen v. Meade Johnson Laboratories, Inc., 483 F.2d 237 (10th Cir. 1973); Empire Casualty Co. v. St. Paul Fire and Marine Ins. Co., 764 P.2d 1191 (Colo. 1988); Renslow v. Mennonite Hospital, 67 Ill.2d 348, 10 Ill.Dec. 484, 367 N.E.2d 1250, 91 A.L.R.3d 291 (1977); Walker v. Rinck, 604 N.E.2d 591 (Ind.1992); Lough v. Rolla Women's Clinic, Inc., 866 S.W.2d 851 (Mo. 1993); Graham v. Keuchel, 847 P.2d 342 (Okl.1993); Sweeney v. Preston, 642 So.2d 332 (Miss.1994) (without separate discussion of the preconception issue). Michigan cases go both ways. See n. 43 below.

7. Grover v. Eli Lilly and Company, 63 Ohio St.3d 756, 591 N.E.2d 696 (1992) (child could not recover for injury ultimately due to his grandmother's ingestion of DES 28 years earlier, blanket rule against preconception tort liability not required).

8. Hegyes v. Unjian Enterprises, Inc., 234 Cal.App.3d 1103, 286 Cal.Rptr. 85 (1991) (duty might be recognized in professional negligence cases but not in car accident cases three years before conception); Taylor v. Cutler, 306 N.J.Super. 37, 703 A.2d 294 (1997) aff'd without opinion as to this point, 157 N.J. 525, 724 A.2d 793 (1999) . Courts have distinguished the "wrongful life" claim. See McNulty v. McDowell, 415 Mass. 369, 613 N.E.2d 904 (1993). That claim is discussed in § 291 below.

9. McNulty v. McDowell, 415 Mass. 369, 613 N.E.2d 904 (1993).

10. Grover v. Eli Lilly and Company, 63 Ohio St.3d 756, 591 N.E.2d 696 (1992).

11. McAuley v. Wills, 251 Ga. 3, 303 S.E.2d 258 (1983).

New York, however, has issued a blanket rejection of any duty of care for the benefit of an unconceived child.[12] New York stands virtually alone as a clear authority for the complete rejection of a duty of care.[13]

People ordinarily owe a duty of reasonable care. On the face of things, such a duty would be owed in the preconception tort case. The arguments against liability begin with a metaphysical abstraction: the plaintiff was not a person in existence when the defendant was negligent; hence the defendant could owe no duty. This is the argument that is now rejected in the other prenatal tort cases when the plaintiff was born alive and suffers foreseeable harm as a result of the defendant's tort. Its thrust is also rejected or ignored in other kinds of cases. If the defendant negligently manufactures a dangerous product, no one asks whether the harm it causes was done to a person who was in existence when the product was manufactured. If the defendant negligently constructs a balcony so that two years later it falls upon a one-year old child, no one believes that the child should be denied recovery on the ground that she was not in existence when the defendant's negligent acts took place.[14]

A quite different argument against the preconception duty is that as applied to health care professionals, it might present them with a conflict of interest because due care for the unconceived child might be harmful to the mother. The facts do not support the argument in any of the cases brought so far because the mother's well-being and the prospective child's well-being call for identical treatment. It is possible to imagine that a drug needed by the mother might be harmful to either a fetus already carrier or one that might be carried in the future, but a conflict like that is not limited to preconception duties and in any event is usually resolved by giving the mother full information and allowing her to make the choice.[15]

12. Albala v. City of New York, 54 N.Y.2d 269, 445 N.Y.S.2d 108, 429 N.E.2d 786 (1981); cf. Park v. Chessin, 46 N.Y.2d 401, 413 N.Y.S.2d 895, 386 N.E.2d 807 (1978) (preconception genetic counseling not actionable by child born with genetic defects).

13. On the basis of a one-line per curiam order of a divided court in Loerch v. Eli Lilly & Co., 445 N.W.2d 560 (Minn. 1989), Minnesota is said to oppose the duty, but as no facts are given in the opinion it seems impossible to guess at the scope of the Minnesota rule from that case alone. The few remaining cases are not in courts of last resort and their authority is uncertain for various reasons. Sorrells v. Eli Lilly and Company, 737 F.Supp. 678 (D.D.C. 1990) attempted to apply Maryland law to a DES grandchild case in a single, conclusory sentence, but as DES grandchildren would probably be denied relief in any case, the decision may not mean much about preconception torts in general. Morgan v. United States, 143 F.Supp. 580 (D.N.J.1956) rejected a duty on viability rules under Pennsylvania law; but Pennsylvania thereafter eliminated the viability requirement in Sinkler v. Kneale, 401 Pa. 267, 164 A.2d 93 (1960), leaving *Morgan* dangling from a premise that has been removed. Michigan cases have gone both ways. See Carr v. Wittingen, 182 Mich.App. 275, 451 N.W.2d 584 (1990) (rejecting the duty, relying on general viability/born alive rules rather than on any specific rule about preconception torts) rev'd on other grounds, 435 Mich. 856, 456 N.W.2d 713 (1990); Monusko v. Postle, 175 Mich.App. 269, 437 N.W.2d 367 (1989) (recognizing a duty).

14. See Lough v. Rolla Women's Clinic, Inc., 866 S.W.2d 851 (Mo.1993) (giving a version of this hypothetical).

15. See Julie A. Greenberg, Reconceptualizing Preconception Torts, 64 Tenn. L. Rev. 315, 347 ff. (1997).

The final argument against a duty of care derives from the non-specific fear of liability in general or the specific fear of unlimited liability that would result if injury caused genetic damage that might be perpetuated from generation to generation throughout all time. This argument cannot logically lead to a blanket rule against a duty. By its own terms the argument should not eliminate most claims because those claims show no potential for perpetuated harm throughout the generations. Nor is it necessary to bar all claims in order to bar the claim for infinitely perpetuated harm. Where the defendant's conduct does in fact create a potential for harm that will pass on to each generation, the court can eliminate that particular claim, as Ohio did, without barring all preconception torts.[16]

These comments suggest that the blanket rule is inappropriate because it obscures differences among preconception cases. Even on a purely formal analysis without concerns of policy, it is possible to distinguish preconception tort cases according to the time of injury—whether it is after birth, at the moment of birth, injury in utero, or injury before conception.[17] It is also possible to distinguish between those preconception injuries that could be reproduced indefinitely in succeeding generations and those that could not. Because duties most significantly vary with the relationships and undertakings of the parties, another line of distinction is between the duty of care owed by health care workers who undertake to protect the well-being of mother and child and the duty owed by strangers driving automobiles. All these distinctions point to the conclusion that a blanket rule against the duty treats too many disparate cases as if they were alike. They also suggest that while a blanket rule in favor of a duty of care fits well with the usual tort rules—liability for negligence is the norm—courts can find plenty of room to shape duties to their sense of policy and justice without barring all cases.

§ 291. Liability for Interfering with Mother's Opportunity to Avoid or Terminate a Pregnancy

Claims for interference with a mother's opportunity to avoid pregnancy, or to terminate it, have taken three distinct forms. All three forms have in common the assertion that, but for the defendant's negligence, the mother could have avoided giving birth to a child who is either unwanted or who suffers terrible birth defects. The claim is typically brought against a physician with the allegation that he negligently failed to perform a birth control surgery, or that he negligently failed to inform the mother that she was carrying a child with genetic defects, and that, but for the physician's negligence, the mother would have avoided giving birth to the child.

16. Grover v. Eli Lilly and Company, 63 Ohio St.3d 756, 591 N.E.2d 696 (1992).

17. See Julie A. Greenberg, Reconceptualizing Preconception Torts, 64 Tenn. L. Rev. 315, 349 ff. (1997).

Wrongful life. The three kinds of claims are usually labeled differently. The wrongful life claim is one asserted by a child suffering birth defects such as a painful and debilitating disease. The claim is definitely not that the physician caused the disease or defect. It is rather that the physician negligently allowed the child to be born at all and that the child has a claim for the suffering he must undergo as a result. Most courts reject this claim altogether,[1] partly because they are unwilling to say that life itself is harm, or that compensation can be measured for the harm of living as compared to never having lived at all.[2]

A few courts, however, have allowed the child to recover. These have largely limited the child to recovery for medical expenses that otherwise would have been recovered by the parent in the wrongful birth claim discussed below.[3] But there is one difference. Allowing the wrongful life claim logically permits recovery of the extraordinary expenses for the child's entire life expectancy; if the claim is allocated to the parent, some courts limit the expense recovered to the period of the child's minority, leaving uncompensated expense for the remainder of the child's life.[4] Allocation of the medical costs recovery to the child herself may also provide the child slightly better protection against waste or misuse of the recovery, since the recovery will be in the child's name and some formal supervision of the recovery may be required.

Wrongful birth. The wrongful birth claim is asserted by the mother, not the child. The mother typically claims that, but for the defendant's negligence in testing or counseling, the mother would have terminated a pregnancy to avoid birth of a child with serious genetic defects. The claim was initially rejected in 1967,[5] but since a mother's constitutional right to an early-pregnancy abortion was recognized,[6] almost all of the courts considering the question have allowed some kind of recovery in these cases.[7] A closely analogous case arises when an adoption agency negligently or fraudulently places a genetically defective child with adoptive parents, who learn only much later of the difficulty and the

§ 291

1. E.g., Walker v. Mart, 164 Ariz. 37, 790 P.2d 735 (1990); Cowe v. Forum Group, Inc., 575 N.E.2d 630 (Ind.1991).

2. Berman v. Allan, 80 N.J. 421, 404 A.2d 8 (1979). The same view has been taken when a living adult with the right to die has been resuscitated against his express will. Anderson v. St. Francis–St. George Hospital, Inc., 77 Ohio St.3d 82, 671 N.E.2d 225 (1996)

3. Turpin v. Sortini, 31 Cal.3d 220, 182 Cal.Rptr. 337, 643 P.2d 954 (1982); Harbeson v. Parke–Davis, Inc., 98 Wash. 2d 460, 656 P.2d 483 (1983).

4. See, e.g., Arche v. United States, 247 Kan. 276, 798 P.2d 477 (1990) (limiting the parents' recovery of damages to the period of the child's minority). Most courts apparently would not impose such a limit. See Smith v. Cote, 128 N.H. 231, 513 A.2d 341 (1986).

5. Gleitman v. Cosgrove, 49 N.J. 22, 227 A.2d 689, 22 A.L.R.3d 1411 (1967).

6. Roe v. Wade, 410 U.S. 113, 93 S.Ct. 705, 35 L.Ed.2d 147 (1973).

7. E.g., Lininger v. Eisenbaum, 764 P.2d 1202 (Colo.1988); Berman v. Allan, 80 N.J. 421, 404 A.2d 8 (1979); Becker v. Schwartz, 46 N.Y.2d 401, 413 N.Y.S.2d 895, 386 N.E.2d 807 (1978); see Thibeault v. Larson, 666 A.2d 112 (Me.1995) (under a statute); cf. Arche v. United States, 247 Kan. 276, 798 P.2d 477 (1990) (claim is cognizable only when the "child has such gross deformities, not medically correctable, that the child will never be able to function as a normal human being").

expense. Consistently with the wrongful birth cases, courts here again allow parental recovery.[8]

The wrongful birth claim can be viewed as a species of informed consent claim, protecting essential values of individual choice, autonomy, and self-determination. But there is difference of sorts. The wrongful birth plaintiff does not recover for the genetic defect itself but for the loss of the choice to terminate the pregnancy and the damages that flow from that loss. It has been held enough, therefore, if she proves that, given appropriate testing and information, she would have terminated the pregnancy, even if the genetic harm to the child arose from risks separate from those of which she should have been warned.[9]

A small number of courts has denied the wrongful birth claim on the assertion that existence of human life cannot be permitted to count as legal damages, or on the ground that parents would be tempted to perjure themselves to establish their willingness to terminate the pregnancy.[10] In addition, some states, a handful at this writing, have passed statutes as anti-abortion legislation.[11] These statutes, if constitutional,[12] will curtail or eliminate the wrongful birth action. Some advocates for the disabled also dislike the wrongful birth action because they believe that it perpetuates the "disability hierarchy" of values in which the disabled are regarded as worth less.[13]

Wrongful conception or pregnancy. The claim for wrongful pregnancy or conception typically asserts that the defendant physician was negligent in performing a medical procedure to prevent conception and that as a result the mother bore a child, with the added expense of child rearing. The claim differs from the wrongful birth in two important respects. First, it does not rest on a claim that the mother had a right to terminate her pregnancy. The claim thus escapes the bar of those statutes that prohibit suits based upon the mother's loss of opportunity for an abortion.[14] Perhaps partly for this reason, some of the few courts

8. See Meracle v. Children's Serv. Soc. of Wis., 149 Wis.2d 19, 437 N.W.2d 532 (1989); Burr v. Board of County Comn'rs of Stark County, 23 Ohio St.3d 69, 491 N.E.2d 1101, 56 A.L.R.4th 357 (1986).

9. Canesi v. Wilson, 158 N.J. 490, 730 A.2d 805 (1999).

10. See Wilson v. Kuenzi, 751 S.W.2d 741 (Mo.1988); Azzolino v. Dingfelder, 315 N.C. 103, 337 S.E.2d 528 (1985).

11. E.g., Idaho Code § 145.424; Minn. Stat. § 5–334.

12. See Note, Wrongful Birth Actions: The Case against Legislative Curtailment, 100 Harv. L. Rev. 2017 (1987); Julie F. Kowitz, Note, Not Your Garden Variety Tort Reform: Statutes Barring Claims For Wrongful Life And Wrongful Birth Are Unconstitutional Under The Purpose Prong of Planned Parenthood V. Casey, 61 Brook. L. Rev. 235 (1995) (arguing that statutes deny the constitutional rights recognized in Roe v. Wade and later cases); Stephanie S. Gold, an Equality Approach to Wrongful Birth Statutes, 65 Fordham L. Rev. 1005 (1996) (arguing the statutes engage in gender discrimination); Julie Gantz, State Statutory Preclusion of Wrongful Birth Relief: a Troubling Re–Writing of a Woman's Right to Choose And The Doctor-patient Relationship, 4 Va. J. Soc. Pol'y & L. 795 (1997).

13. See Allan H. Macurdy, Disability Ideology And The Law School Curriculum, 4 B.U. Pub. Int. L.J. 443 (1995).

14. E.g., Minn. Stat. Ann. § 145.424 ("No person shall maintain a cause of action or receive an award of damages on the claim that but for the negligent conduct of another, a child would have been aborted", also specifically preserving the wrongful pregnancy claim).

that reject the wrongful birth action actively support the wrongful pregnancy claim.[15]

The wrongful pregnancy claim also differs from the wrongful birth claim because does not necessarily involve an unhealthy or genetically damaged child. Instead, the mother or the parents had decided against enlarging the family for personal or economic reasons. One or two states reject the wrongful pregnancy action altogether.[16] The great majority now recognize the claim,[17] but subject it to some unusual limitations on damages recoverable discussed in the next section.

§ 292. Limiting the Wrongful Birth and Pregnancy Claims by Special Damages Rules

Although wrongful birth and wrongful pregnancy claims are accepted in most courts, they are often undermined by unusual damages rules. The normal compensatory damages rules would award damages for emotional harm and economic costs inflicted by the tort. In the case of wrongful birth or pregnancy, that would mean a recovery for emotional harm to the mother and perhaps to the father and also the costs of rearing the child—two harms that would have been avoided if the physician had not been negligent. Courts have been struck, however, by the idea that a child, healthy or not, would give the parents pleasure and that the parents' putative pleasure should somehow be taken into account.[1] The result has been not only the usual variation among judicial approaches but a series of special rules that do not appear to comport with ordinary rules of damages or evidence.

Damages in Wrongful Birth Claims Generally

Expenses of child rearing. Where the claim for wrongful birth is recognized, most courts allow recovery of some, but usually not all the child-rearing expenses that would have been avoided by a timely termination of the pregnancy.[2] The same rule has been applied to claims based upon an adoption agency's misrepresentations of a prospective adoptive child's health.[3] The cases usually permit recovery of less than all of the costs inflicted by the tort by limiting the recovery to the "extraordinary" expenses, those over and above the ordinary expenses of child rearing.[4] A

15. E.g., Jackson v. Bumgardner, 318 N.C. 172, 347 S.E.2d 743 (1986).

16. See Schork v. Huber, 648 S.W.2d 861 (Ky.1983) (healthy child is not an injury); Thibeault v. Larson, 666 A.2d 112 (Me. 1995).

17. E.g., Emerson v. Magendantz, 689 A.2d 409 (R.I.1997) (reviewing the cases).

§ 292

1. § 293 below.

2. Phillips v. United States, 575 F.Supp. 1309 (D.S.C.1983); Smith v. Cote, 128 N.H. 231, 513 A.2d 341 (N.H. 1986); Schroeder v. Perkel, 87 N.J. 53, 432 A.2d 834 (1981); Becker v. Schwartz, 46 N.Y.2d 401, 413 N.Y.S.2d 895, 386 N.E.2d 807 (1978); Speck v. Finegold, 497 Pa. 77, 439 A.2d 110 (1981); Naccash v. Burger, 223 Va. 406, 290 S.E.2d 825 (1982); Harbeson v. Parke–Davis, Inc., 98 Wn.2d 460, 656 P.2d 483 (1983); James G. v. Caserta, 175 W.Va. 406, 332 S.E.2d 872 (W.Va.1985). See Proffitt v. Bartolo, 162 Mich.App. 35, 412 N.W.2d 232, 236 (1987) ("medical expenses").

3. Meracle v. Children's Serv. Soc. of Wis., 149 Wis.2d 19, 437 N.W.2d 532 (1989).

4. E.g., Phillips v. United States, 575 F.Supp. 1309 (D.S.C.1983); Keel v. Banach, 624 So.2d 1022 (Ala.1993); Siemieniec v.

few have rejected this limitation.[5] A few courts have also limited the recovery to the costs of rearing the child to the age of majority, leaving uncompensated the period of time from majority to the child's death.[6]

Emotional harm. The normal damages rules permit the victim of personal injury tort to recover the attendant emotional harm as a normal element of damages. Emotional harm claims may be rejected or limited, however, in two particular situations. First, emotional harm claims may be denied when the courts wish to treat the tort as primarily an economic tort. Misrepresentation cases are ordinarily like this. Second, emotional harm claims may be subjected to special conditions when emotional harm is asserted as a stand-alone tort rather than as an element of damages flowing from some other tort.[7]

The tort to the mother in the wrongful birth claim inescapably involves the mother's body and intimate rights of autonomy. When the suit is against the mother's physician, it also involves a direct duty on the part of the defendant to the mother herself.[8] For these reasons, the tort probably should be treated as a personal injury tort, so that emotional harms resulting from it should be recoverable as a part of the total damages as they are in other personal injury cases. Some courts take this rather straightforward view, allowing recovery of emotional harm for both parents, or at least for the mother.[9]

However, other courts have been unwilling to permit emotional harm damages at all,[10] and still others have limited the recovery, not only under the offset rules[11] but also by invoking the special bystander rules often applied to the rather different case of stand-alone emotional harms. The stand-alone emotional harm claim typically arises when a child is injured and the parent claims emotional harm. The special bystander rule applied in those cases rejects the emotional harm claim unless the parent actually witnessed the child's injury. But that rule only

Lutheran General Hosp., 117 Ill.2d 230, 111 Ill.Dec. 302, 512 N.E.2d 691 (1987); Arche v. United States, 247 Kan. 276, 798 P.2d 477 (1990); Smith v. Cote, 128 N.H. 231, 513 A.2d 341, 348–49 (N.H. 1986) (including the need for added maternal care as one of the extraordinary costs).

5. Contra: Robak v. United States, 658 F.2d 471 (7th Cir.1981).

6. Arche v. United States, 247 Kan. 276, 798 P.2d 477 (1990) (but noting that the state would be responsible for the disabled child after the child reached adulthood); Bani–Esraili v. Lerman, 69 N.Y.2d 807, 505 N.E.2d 947, 513 N.Y.S.2d 382 (1987). Contra: Greco v. United States, 111 Nev. 405, 893 P.2d 345 (1995).

7. See § 302 below.

8. See § 312 below.

9. Phillips v. United States, 575 F.Supp. 1309 (D.S.C.1983); Keel v. Banach, 624 So.2d 1022 (Ala.1993); Berman v. Allan, 80 N.J. 421, 404 A.2d 8 (1979); Eisbrenner v. Stanley, 106 Mich.App. 357, 308 N.W.2d 209 (1981); Greco v. United States, 111 Nev. 405, 893 P.2d 345 (1995). Cf. Gallagher v. Duke University, 852 F.2d 773 (4th Cir.1988) (handicapped child, but court analyzed case as wrongful conception or wrongful pregnancy case on the facts; emotional distress damages allowed based on distress at having handicapped child). See Annotation, Recoverability of Compensatory Damages for Mental Anguish or Emotional Distress for Tortiously Causing Another's Birth, 74 A.L.R.4th 798 (1989).

10. Siemieniec v. Lutheran General Hosp., 117 Ill.2d 230, 111 Ill.Dec. 302, 512 N.E.2d 691 (1987); Smith v. Cote, 128 N.H. 231, 513 A.2d 341, 348–49 (N.H. 1986); Becker v. Schwartz, 46 N.Y.2d 401, 413 N.Y.S.2d 895, 386 N.E.2d 807 (1978).

11. § 293 below.

applies to bystanders; it has no logical application when the parent herself is a victim of the defendant's tort. When the parent (or anyone) is herself a victim, she recovers emotional harm damages "parasitically," as merely one element of damages for the tort done to her.[12] Nevertheless, some courts have, mistakenly or not, applied the bystander rule to deny the emotional harm claim to the mother, who was a direct victim of the physician's tort.[13]

Damages in Wrongful Pregnancy or Conception Generally

Child rearing expenses. Wrongful pregnancy cases are usually based upon failed sterilization procedures intended to prevent conception. The parents in such cases may face many years of expense in child rearing. Nevertheless, most courts have disallowed recovery for cost of rearing a healthy child.[14] Some say it is no injury at all, although anyone who has reared a child knows that the financial and sometimes the emotional costs can be enormous. Certainly they are the costs the parents sought to avoid by employing the defendant.[15] The "no injury" assertion is, then, in reality a way of asserting a judicial policy, not a fact.[16] Other courts assert that the claim is speculative. Almost all of the decisions are influenced in part by the idea that some kind of offset should apply because the parents will enjoy the child, even if the child is also an expense.[17]

A few courts in important decisions have allowed the jury to award child-rearing costs, at least where the parents sought to avoid having children in part for economic reasons.[18] However, even many of these more liberal courts may reduce the award by imposing offsets.

Emotional and other damages. In the wrongful pregnancy or conception cases, courts have allowed recovery for the mother's pain in delivery

12. Thus emotional harm damages are routinely recovered by the personal injury plaintiff. Except for loss of consortium claims, however, the father is not usually a direct victim of medical malpractice committed against the mother. Consequently, some courts deny the father's claim for emotional harm resulting from death of or injury to a fetus. See Edinburg Hospital Authority v. Trevino, 941 S.W.2d 76 (1997). Cf. Tanner v. Hartog, 696 So.2d 705 (Fla. 1997) (Florida, still requiring an actual "impact" to the emotional harm claimant, does not apply that requirement to emotional harm claims resulting from an independent tort to the mother).

13. Cauman v. George Washington University, 630 A.2d 1104 (D.C.App.1993).

14. See Cockrum v. Baumgartner, 95 Ill.2d 193, 69 Ill.Dec. 168, 447 N.E.2d 385 (1983); Schork v. Huber, 648 S.W.2d 861 (Ky.1983); O'Toole v. Greenberg, 64 N.Y.2d 427, 477 N.E.2d 445, 488 N.Y.S.2d 143 (1985); Johnson v. University Hospitals of Cleveland, 44 Ohio St.3d 49, 540 N.E.2d 1370 (1989); Smith v. Gore, 728 S.W.2d 738, 751 (Tenn.1987); Miller v. Johnson, 231 Va. 177, 343 S.E.2d 301 (1986); James G. v. Caserta, 175 W.Va. 406, 332 S.E.2d 872 (W.Va.1985); Beardsley v. Wierdsma, 650 P.2d 288 (Wyo.1982).

15. See Burke v. Rivo, 406 Mass. 764, 551 N.E.2d 1 (1990).

16. See Cf. Kelly, The Rightful Position in "Wrongful Life" Actions, 42 Hast. L. J. 505, 525–535 (1991).

17. § 293 below.

18. University of Arizona Health Sciences Center v. Superior Court, 136 Ariz. 579, 667 P.2d 1294 (1983); Ochs v. Borrelli, 187 Conn. 253, 445 A.2d 883 (1982); Jones v. Malinowski, 299 Md. 257, 473 A.2d 429 (1984); Burke v. Rivo, 406 Mass. 764, 551 N.E.2d 1 (1990); Lovelace Medical Center v. Mendez, 111 N.M. 336, 805 P.2d 603 (1991); Zehr v. Haugen, 318 Or. 647, 871 P.2d 1006 (1994); Marciniak v. Lundborg, 153 Wis.2d 59, 450 N.W.2d 243 (1990).

of the child and emotional distress at having an unplanned, unwanted, or unaffordable child,[19] the expenses of the negligently performed pregnancy-avoidance procedure,[20] or the cost of repeating the procedure later,[21] pregnancy-related medical expenses, including wages lost because of pregnancy or delivery,[22] and expenses or wage lost in the post-natal period in appropriate cases.[23] The father is entitled to recover for loss of consortium.[24] Perhaps most courts allow recovery of emotional distress damages,[25] but predictably enough, some courts have refused to permit any emotional distress recovery at all,[26] or have limited the recovery of all forms of pain and suffering, including emotional harm, to the period of time from discovery of pregnancy until recovery from childbirth.[27]

Genetic defects in wrongful pregnancy cases. In contrast to the wrongful birth claim, wrongful pregnancy claims usually involves birth of a normal, healthy child, albeit one that the mother sought to avoid bearing. The defendant's negligent failure to prevent the plaintiff's pregnancy may, however, lead happenstantially to the birth of a child suffering genetic defects. If the reason for seeking to prevent pregnancy in the first place was a risk of genetic defects, there seems no reason to deny recovery for the extraordinary expense of rearing the child.[28] On the other hand, if the reasons for preventing pregnancy were not based on genetic risks but on financial, emotional or personal considerations of the parents, the risk the doctor creates by a negligent sterilization procedure is the risk of a normal pregnancy and a healthy child, not the risk of a child suffering genetic defects. In that kind of case, the defendant may not be regarded as a legal or proximate cause of the damages resulting from the genetic problems, even though he is a legal cause of other harms. Some courts have taken this view.[29] Although this approach sounds like a normal application of proximate cause or scope-of-risk rules, that is not clearly the case. The parents sought to avoid having *any* child and the defendant's obligation was to use reasonable care to prevent conception that would lead to birth of any child. No greater care is required to perform the sterilization procedure when its purpose is to prevent a genetically damaged child. This line of reasoning

19. Pitre v. Opelousas General Hosp., 530 So.2d 1151 (La.1988); Burke v. Rivo, 406 Mass. 764, 551 N.E.2d 1 (1990).

20. Smith v. Gore, 728 S.W.2d 738, 751 (Tenn.1987).

21. Lovelace Medical Center v. Mendez, 111 N.M. 336, 805 P.2d 603 (1991).

22. Pitre v. Opelousas General Hosp., 530 So.2d 1151 (La.1988) (expenses of pregnancy and delivery).

23. Smith v. Gore, 728 S.W.2d 738, 751 (Tenn.1987).

24. Pitre v. Opelousas General Hosp., 530 So.2d 1151, 1161–62 (La.1988); Burke v. Rivo, 406 Mass. 764, 551 N.E.2d 1 (1990); Smith v. Gore, 728 S.W.2d 738, 751 (Tenn. 1987).

25. Jackson v. Bumgardner, 318 N.C. 172, 347 S.E.2d 743 (1986)

26. Lovelace Medical Center v. Mendez, 111 N.M. 336, 805 P.2d 603 (1991); Emerson v. Magendantz, 689 A.2d 409 (R.I.1997).

27. Smith v. Gore, 728 S.W.2d 738, 751 (Tenn.1987).

28. Cf. Gallagher v. Duke University, 852 F.2d 773 (4th Cir.1988) (pregnancy would have been prevented if doctor had correctly diagnosed genetic problem, extraordinary costs recoverable).

29. Williams v. University of Chicago Hospitals, 179 Ill.2d 80, 227 Ill.Dec. 793, 688 N.E.2d 130 (1997); Pitre v. Opelousas General Hosp., 530 So.2d 1151, 1161–62 (La.1988).

suggests that the limitation is not appropriate. At least when the physician is on notice that genetic defects are possible, liability for the extraordinary expenses of child-rearing has been permitted.[30]

§ 293. Offsets and Offset Reasoning in Wrongful Pregnancy

Offset for Parents' Emotional Benefits

The benefits rule generally. Benefits to the plaintiff that result directly from a tort must be offset against the damages otherwise due.[1] Almost all of the limitations on the damages recovery in wrongful birth and wrongful pregnancy actions[2] are derived in part from the idea that if the parents suffer economic and emotional harm as a result of having a child, they also gain benefits which should somehow be taken into account. Frequently, the judges assume or declare that benefits must exist and then use the supposed benefits as ground for denying some of the damages altogether.

Wrongful pregnancy and benefit offsetting child-rearing costs as a matter of law. In wrongful pregnancy cases, a number of courts simply declare as a matter of law that the parents' emotional benefits in having an unwanted child is necessarily in excess of all child-rearing costs.[3] The effect is to say that, except in very few states,[4] the cost of rearing the child cannot be recovered in wrongful pregnancy cases.[5] The offsets reasoning and the rule against recovery produced by that reasoning is peculiar for several reasons. First the rule determines the supposed benefit as a matter of law rather than through assessment of the facts. Second, the benefit offset is applied to bar recovery of child-rearing costs but not applied to bar recovery of the costs of pregnancy and delivery.[6] Third, the rule uses one kind of supposed benefit to reduce or bar

30. E.g., Emerson v. Magendantz, 689 A.2d 409 (R.I.1997).

§ 293

1. See 1 DAN B. DOBBS, REMEDIES § 3.8 (2) and 2 Id. § 8.6 (2).

2. § 292 supra.

3. This may be coupled with arguments that the amount of the benefit is unknowable because the child may turn out to be an infamous criminal or President of the United States. See McKernan v. Aasheim, 102 Wash.2d 411, 419–420, 687 P.2d 850, 855 (1984). If the burden is on the defendant to support the offset, however, this argument suggests that no offset should be entertained. Further, unknowable changes that might affect future subjective values would presumably be altogether unimportant in other kinds of cases. For example, it is difficult to imagine that a court would speculate that when a seller reneges on a promise to sell you a house, that you should not recover on the contract because the different house you find as a substitute might turn out to be even more satisfactory.

4. E.g., Lovelace Medical Center v. Mendez, 111 N.M. 336, 805 P.2d 603 (1991); Marciniak v. Lundborg, 153 Wis.2d 59, 450 N.W.2d 243, 249 (1990) ("It was precisely to avoid that 'benefit' that the parents went to the physician in the first place".... it hardly seems equitable to not only force this benefit upon them but to tell them they must pay for it as well as by offsetting it against their proven emotional damages).

5. See Schork v. Huber, 648 S.W.2d 861, 862 (Ky.1983) ("The benefits conferred by the child's existence clearly outweigh any economic burden involved"); Pitre v. Opelousas General Hosp., 530 So.2d 1151, 1162 (La.1988); Emerson v. Magendantz, 689 A.2d 409 (R.I.1997).

6. Pitre v. Opelousas General Hosp., 530 So.2d 1151, 1161–62 (La.1988).

recovery for an entirely different kind of loss. The legal rule that benefits must be ascribed to having an unwanted child, coupled with the compulsory offset reflect a policy decision, not a measurement of damages.

Wrongful pregnancy and assessment of actual benefits to offset against child-rearing costs. A few courts have allowed child-rearing costs.[7] In those courts, no presumption is indulged that benefits of having an unwanted child exceed the costs of rearing the child. Instead, the trier may reduce that recovery by the amount of emotional benefits the trier estimates will actually accrue to the parents. In these cases the trier must estimate the intangible benefits on the basis of the facts of the case, and similarly must estimate the intangible costs in the form of mental distress.

Wrongful pregnancy and the offset of emotional benefits against economic loss? The supposed benefits used to bar the claim for child-rearing costs are intangible benefits such as the emotional pleasure of having the (unwanted) child. This approach seemingly violates the normal rules that benefits from a tort are to be offset only against losses to the same "interest."[8] The idea of the normal rule is that if the defendant negligently burns down your trees, reducing the value of your land, he does not get any credit for the pleasures you might get because your view is enhanced at the same time your shade is lost. Although those pleasures might be real, they do not diminish the economic loss. Yet in the wrongful pregnancy cases, the decisions have usually concluded that the economic losses and the emotional harm were "inextricably related to each other," and that the trier should be allowed to offset emotional benefits against both emotional distress and economic costs.[9] New Mexico has cut across the grain of these decisions, applying the offset for emotional benefits only to the claim for emotional harm, with the result that child-rearing expenses are allowed but emotional harm claims are not.[10]

Wrongful birth. In wrongful birth cases and even in wrongful pregnancy cases resulting in the birth of a genetically damaged child,[11] the courts appear to be more willing to award the extraordinary costs of child-rearing without an automatic and total offset for the parents'

7. See note 18.

8. Restatement § 920 & Comments a & b (1979) ("benefit to the interest of the plaintiff that was harmed"). The offset itself, in any form, is to some extent a violation of or exception to the rule that one person may not force benefits upon another.

9. University of Ariz. Health Sciences Center v. Superior Court (Heimann), 136 Ariz. 579, 667 P.2d 1294, 1299 n. 4 (1983); Jones v. Malinowski, 299 Md. 257, 473 A.2d 429, 435 (1984) (child rearing costs to the age of the child's majority, offset by the benefits derived from the child's aid, society and comfort). Cf. Ochs v. Borrelli, 187 Conn. 253, 445 A.2d 883 (1982) (trial court so instructed with concurrence of plaintiff, perhaps with tacit approval on appeal). See Note, One More Mouth To Feed, 25 Ariz. L. Rev. 1069 (1983).

10. Lovelace Medical Center v. Mendez, 111 N.M. 336, 805 P.2d 603 (1991).

11. Emerson v. Magendantz, 689 A.2d 409 (R.I.1997). But some courts hold that genetic harm is outside the risk and therefore not compensable in wrongful pregnancy cases. Williams v. University of Chicago Hospitals, 179 Ill.2d 80, 227 Ill.Dec. 793, 688 N.E.2d 130 (1997).

supposed emotional benefits.[12] Put differently, some authority in damaged child cases might reject any offset altogether;[13] at most the offset of supposed emotional benefits applies only against emotional harms, not against child-rearing costs. That result seems correct. It is in line with the general rule that offsetting gains must be of the same general kind as the losses they reduce.[14] If the rule were otherwise, the expense recovery aimed primarily at providing medical and related attention for the child would be absorbed by the purely non-economic "benefit" to the parents.[15]

Avoidable Consequences—"Mitigation" of Damages

The avoidable consequences rule excludes recovery for any damages that could have been reasonably avoided by the plaintiff.[16] This rule has raised the question whether a plaintiff suffering from an unwanted pregnancy as the result of the defendant's negligence must seek an abortion to minimize damages. Although courts have sometimes played with the idea as an argument for severely limiting the claim or denying it altogether, almost no court seems to have actually applied such an idea.[17] As the Tennessee Court observed, any such requirement might "infringe upon Constitutional rights to privacy in these matters," and in addition would fail the reasonableness test which is built into the avoidable consequences rule.[18]

In wrongful birth cases, the nature of the case is that there is no opportunity for terminating the pregnancy, but there remains the possi-

12. Phillips v. United States, 575 F.Supp. 1309 (D.S.C.1983) (wrongful birth, judge as trier of fact offset emotional benefits only against emotional distress damages); Blake v. Cruz, 108 Idaho 253, 698 P.2d 315 (1984) ("In determining damages for emotional injury, countervailing emotional benefits attributable to the birth of the child should also be considered and the award adjusted accordingly"); Greco v. United States, 111 Nev. 405, 893 P.2d 345 (1995).

13. See Greco v. United States, 111 Nev. 405, 893 P.2d 345 (1995).

14. Note 8, supra.

15. Where "wrongful life" claims have been recognized, this error is automatically avoided because the child would recover the extraordinary economic costs in his own name; the parents' joys could not, presumably, be offset against the child's loss.

16. See 1 Dan B. Dobbs, Remedies § 3.9 and 2 Id. § 8.7.

17. The possibility of abortion to minimize damages has been suggested as a ground for denying recovery of normal child-rearing expenses. See Robak v. United States, 658 F.2d 471, 479, n. 23 (7th Cir. 1981) ("Because they freely chose not to have an abortion, they should be responsible for the costs of a normal child"); Sorkin v. Lee, 78 A.D.2d 180, 434 N.Y.S.2d 300 (1980) (normal child-rearing expenses were avoidable because abortion was possible, but "We do not suggest that the mother was obliged to terminate the pregnancy"). These cases appear to adopt a rule of damages that excludes the normal costs of child-rearing for the very purpose of *avoiding* the issue of minimizing damages and some of the decisions have spelled this point out in detail. See Flowers v. District of Columbia, 478 A.2d 1073 (D.C.App.1984). In Cowe by Cowe v. Forum Group, Inc., 541 N.E.2d 962 (Ind.App.1989) the child-plaintiff had in fact been adopted. His wrongful life claim for support was denied from the time of adoption on the ground that the adoptive parents assumed the liability; but the adoptive parents were not parties and were not themselves asserting a claim.

18. Smith v. Gore, 728 S.W.2d 738, 751–52 (Tenn.1987). See also Ochs v. Borrelli, 187 Conn. 253, 445 A.2d 883, 885 (1982) (constitutional rights of mother require allowance of child-rearing costs, too); Marciniak v. Lundborg, 153 Wis.2d 59, 450 N.W.2d 243, 247 (1990) (not reasonable under ordinary rules to require abortion to minimize damages)

bility, also open in wrongful pregnancy cases, that damages could be minimized by relinquishing the child for adoption. Relinquishment might indeed work a sound economic result, but the tort is not in the exclusively an economic tort. The defendant, having deprived the mother of one choice, has no right to force upon her another choice she does not want to make. With these ideas in mind, it seems unlikely that courts will require a mother to give up her legitimate claim or her child, one or the other.[19]

19. Courts have sometimes emphasized the plaintiff's probable pleasure in keeping the normal child, and that it would outweigh the costs of rearing, by pointing out that the parents had not or would not put the child up for adoption, even though there would be many available adoptive parents. E.g., Rieck v. Medical Protective Co. of Fort Wayne, Ind., 64 Wis.2d 514, 219 N.W.2d 242, 245 (1974); Ball v. Mudge, 64 Wash.2d 247, 391 P.2d 201, 204 (1964). Those cases seem only to use the usual rule that the "benefits" of the unwanted child outweigh the doctor's potential liability; adoption or lack of adoption is mentioned only a means of demonstrating a basis for that conclusion.

*

CHAPTER 19

WRONGFUL DEATH AND SURVIVAL

§ 294. Wrongful Death and Survival Actions

Common law rules. According to a Latin maxim, personal actions die with the person. The common law followed that maxim, holding that the death of either the tortfeasor or the victim eliminated all tort claims. In particular: (1) If the tort victim died, his cause of action was at an end. His estate had no cause of action.[1] (2) If the tortfeasor himself died after committing a tort against his victim, the victim's claim died as well.[2] (3) If the victim died, her survivors had no independent claim of their own against the tortfeasor for the loss of their support or for their grief and sorrow.[3] There has never been any good explanation for all these rules. For a brief period, some American authority reversed the English common law rule,[4] but by the middle of the 19th century, American courts had returned to the common law fold.[5]

Adoption of statutes. Thereafter, the American courts repeatedly rejected judge-made wrongful death claims except in Admiralty.[6] In the latter half of the 19th century, following the lead of English legislation often known as Lord Campbell's Act,[7] the American states addressed the problem by legislation, sometimes narrowly construed,[8] which remains the source of almost all rights arising out of a person's death.

§ 294

1. See Higgins v. Butcher, Yelv. 89, 80 Eng. Rep. 61 (K.B. 1607). Torts to personal property did survive, however. See Winfield, Death as Affecting Liability in Tort, 29 COLUM. L. REV. 237, 242–43 (1929).

2. See Winfield, supra note 1 at 242; Smedley, Wrongful Death—Bases of the Common Law Rules, 13 VAND. L. REV. 605 (1960).

3. Baker v. Bolton, 1 Camp. 493, 170 Eng. Rep. 1033 (Nisi Prius 1808).

4. See Malone, The Genesis of Wrongful Death, 17 STAN. L. REV. 1043 (1965).

5. Carey v. Berkshire R.R., 55 Mass. (1 Cush.) 475, 48 Am. Dec. 616 (1848). This decision may have been influenced by the fact that the Massachusetts legislature had much earlier created certain rights to recover for death on badly maintained bridges and death caused by boat or railroad. Only limited damages were allowed railroad passengers under these statutes. In the face of these statutes, the Massachusetts Court may have been reluctant to create a general common law right to recover for death without limitation. See Malone, supra note 4 at 1070.

6. Moragne v. States Marine Lines, Inc., 398 U.S. 375, 90 S.Ct. 1772, 26 L.Ed.2d 339 (1970) recognized a judge-made death claim in admiralty, reversing The Harrisburg, 119 U.S. 199, 7 S.Ct. 140, 30 L.Ed. 358 (1886).

7. 9 & 10 Vict. Ch. 93 (1846).

8. Courts often choose between somewhat contradictory maxims of statutory construction. Some courts treat wrongful death statutes as being "in derogation of common law" and hence to be constructed narrowly. Others adopt the opposite maxim, saying the statutes are remedial and hence to be construed liberally. If the derogation approach is applied only to statutes that are in derogation of a common law *right,* that approach can be consistent with the remedial approach. However, such a resolution would mean that wrongful death and sur-

Federal statutes. Tort law is usually state law, not federal law, and that is also true with wrongful death statutes. However, a number of important federal statutes have been enacted, among them the Federal Employers' Liability Act[9] and the Jones Act,[10] providing rights for railroad workers and seamen respectively. A complex mixture of statutes and decisional law of Admiralty covers some maritime cases[11] and treaties and protocols deal with death on international air flights.[12]

Wrongful death and survival statutes. Almost all this legislation deals with death claims in two basic ways or in some combination of those two ways. Wrongful death statutes create a new action in favor of certain beneficiaries who suffer from another's death as a result of a tort. States differ somewhat in measurement of the damages, but all states recognize some kind of claim. Because the statute creates a new cause of action and vests it in the survivors (or their representative), the wrongful death recovery does not go to the deceased's estate and is not subject to claims of the deceased's creditors. The other basic statute is the survival statute.

Survival statutes do not provide for an independent action in favor of the deceased's dependents. Instead, they address the common law rule that a tort cause of action abated with the death of either party. They provide for the survival of whatever action the deceased herself would have had if she had been able to sue at the moment of her death—for example, for his pain and suffering, loss of wages, and medical expenses between the time of injury and death. The right to sue under the survival statute is vested in the deceased person's estate and is subject to claims of the deceased's creditors. In most states both the wrongful death and the survival claim can be made because they do not duplicate items of damages. Some states combine the features of both kinds of statute in a single statute. Such hybrid statutes may produce different approaches to damages or defenses.

Issues. The underlying substance of the claims in death cases is much the same as in other tort cases. The claimants in death actions must show that the defendant would have been liable if the deceased herself had lived. Consequently the familiar issues of duty, breach, causation, and proximate cause are basic to all death and survival actions. Likewise, the special problems associated with fetal harm, federal preemption, medical practice and many others arise in death actions. The main problems to be addressed here concern the distinction that must be drawn between survival and death actions, the statutory scheme

vival statutes are remedial, since they remedy a perceived defect in the common law and do not derogate any common law right.

9. 45 U.S.C.A. § 51.

10. 46 U.S.C.A. App. § 688.

11. The Death on the High Seas Act, 46 App. U.S.C.A. § 761 covers death from injury one maritime league from shore, but when seamen or longshoremen are the victims, the judge-made law of Admiralty or other statutes may apply. See Miles v. Apex Marine Corp., 498 U.S. 19, 111 S.Ct. 317, 112 L.Ed.2d 275 (1990).

12. See Warsaw Convention 49 Stat. 3000 (1934); 137 L.N.T.S. 11, No. 3145, printed in note following 49 USCA § 40105 (limiting damages, a figure revised upwards by an agreement of air carriers known as the Montreal Agreement).

of damages and their distribution, and the special rules for some defenses.

§ 295. Survival Actions—Damages and Scope

Nature and purpose of the survival action. In contrast to the wrongful death action, the survival action does not create a new claim for the benefit of survivors. Instead, it merely reverses the common law rule that a cause of action abates with the death of either party. In its usual form, it allows the deceased's cause of action to continue or survive after his death with damages that he could have recovered if he had been able to sue at the moment of his death.

Cause and manner of death immaterial. If the defendant negligently breaks the victim's leg, resulting in wage loss and medical costs, damages for those items could be recovered by the victim in his lifetime. If the victim dies six months later from other causes without having settled or recovered , the survival statutes permit recovery of the same damages by the victim's estate. A few statutory systems permit survival only in cases like this example, that is, when death does *not* result from the tort.[1] Another group allows the survival action only if death is *not* instantaneous.[2] Since the ordinary survival statute is intended to recoup the losses suffered by the decedent up to the time of his death, however, the usual rule permits the survival action regardless of the cause of death and regardless whether death was instantaneous,[3]

Damages. Damages in the survival action are often quite limited in amount. They reflect only the damages the decedent herself could have claimed at the moment of her death. In the absence of a statutory exclusion, recovery in the survival action may include damages for the decedent's medical expenses resulting from the injury,[4] her conscious[5]

§ 295

1. E.g., VERNON'S ANN. MO. STAT. § 537.020.

2. Starkenburg v. State, 282 Mont. 1, 934 P.2d 1018 (Mont. 1997) (on the ground that there could be no damages for which the decedent could have sued if she died instantly).

3. See Cal. Civ. Proc. Code § 377.20. At one time, the question of what counted as instantaneous death was much litigated in Michigan, but that is no longer an issue. See Hardy v. Maxheimer, 429 Mich. 422, 416 N.W.2d 299 (1987). The fact that death was instant precludes a recovery of post-injury pain and suffering damages, but not necessarily damages for pre-injury fear. See Nelson v. Dolan, 230 Neb. 848, 434 N.W.2d 25 (1989).

4. Warner v. McCaughan, 77 Wash.2d 178, 460 P.2d 272 (1969). Statutes may provide the same. E.g., ANN. L. MASS. c. 228 § 1. In some states medical expense is recoverable in the wrongful death action, in which case it should be excluded from the survival action recovery.

5. Proof must show that there was in fact pain and suffering, which in turn requires consciousness for at least a short interval. See, e.g., Royal Indemnity Co. v. Pittsfield Elec. Co., 293 Mass. 4, 199 N.E. 69 (1935). Evidence about the nature and extent of pain may also be required, which may exclude the recovery in many cases when there are no witnesses. See Bart v. Union Oil Co. of California, 185 Ill.App.3d 64, 132 Ill.Dec. 848, 540 N.E.2d 770, 773 (1989). In St. Clair v. Denny, 245 Kan. 414, 781 P.2d 1043 (Kan. 1989) the court thought that damages could not be recovered for the decedent's pre-impact distress, when decedent was killed immediately upon impact and the only evidence was that decedent was trying to avoid the collision for 60 feet before it happened. But in Nelson v. Dolan, 230 Neb. 848, 434 N.W.2d 25 (1989) the decedent's motorcycle was locked to the defendant's car at high speeds for five sec-

pain and suffering resulting from the injury,[6] any earnings lost between the time of injury and the death,[7] punitive damages against a living tortfeasor,[8] and funeral expenses,[9] provided such expenses have not been allocated to[10] or actually recovered in the wrongful death action.[11]

Excluded and limited damages. Particular statutes, however, may exclude some of the listed items of damage. For example, some exclude pain and suffering recoveries.[12] Some exclude punitive damages.[13] Exclusion of punitive damages may be desirable to prevent repeated punishments where such damages are recoverable in the wrongful death action. Because the survival statutes were intended to reverse the common law rule abating personal actions at the death of either party, they may have no application to actions that were not abated by that rule. The common law rule did not abate actions for property torts or for contract breach; nor did it abate actions if judgment was rendered before death of the party. Unless the statute provides otherwise, then, its exclusions of damages items would not seem to apply when the claim can be characterized as one for property damage, or breach of contract, nor when judgment was rendered before death.[14]

onds before the final impact that caused death. Pre-impact fear was a recoverable item. See also Yowell v. Piper Aircraft Corp., 703 S.W.2d 630 (Tex.1986) (recovery for pre-impact distress was allowed when decedents' plane broke up and they fell 10,000 feet to an immediate death).

6. E.g., Campbell v. Romanos, 346 Mass. 361, 191 N.E.2d 764 (1963); Small v. McKennan Hosp.,, 437 N.W.2d 194 (S.D. 1989). Pain and suffering may include the suffering arising from the deceased's awareness that he will soon die. Nelson v. Dolan, 230 Neb. 848, 434 N.W.2d 25 (1989) (reviewing cases); Yowell v. Piper Aircraft Corp., 703 S.W.2d 630 (Tex.1986) (pre-impact distress damages allowed when decedents' plane broke up and they fell 10,000 feet to an immediate death). In Bowen v. Lumbermens Mutual Casualty Co., 183 Wis.2d 627, 517 N.W.2d 432 (1994) the estate claimed such damages under the theory of negligent infliction of emotional distress, but the court thought there was no evidence that the deceased had ever been aware that he was about to be struck down and denied the claim.

7. Miles v. Apex Marine Corp., 498 U.S. 19, 111 S.Ct. 317, 112 L.Ed.2d 275 (1990) (under Admiralty powers, Court would limit recovery to losses incurred during the decedent's lifetime); Prunty v. Schwantes, 40 Wis.2d 418, 162 N.W.2d 34 (1968); of'. Annotation, Recovery, in Action for Benefit of Decedent's Estate in Jurisdiction Which Has Both Wrongful Death and Survival Statutes, of Value of Earnings Decedent Would Have Made after Death, 76 A.L.R.3d 125 (1977). A few courts have allowed recovery of future lost earnings in the survival action. E.g., Balmer v. Dilley, 81 Wash.2d 367, 502 P.2d 456 (1972). This is the statutory rule in Hawaii under Hawaii Rev. Stats. § 663–8. It has been suggested that where the state also permits a suit under the wrongful death statute, future earnings recoveries in the survival action runs the risk of duplicated recoveries. See 2 DAN B. DOBBS, REMEDIES § 8.3 (2) (2d ed. 1993).

8. E.g., Berenger v. Frink, 314 N.W.2d 388 (Iowa 1982).

9. E.g., Estate of Kronemeyer v. Meinig, 948 P.2d 119 (Colo.App.1997).

10. MO. STAT. § 537.090. specifically lists funeral expenses as recoverable in the death action.

11. In some instances such expenses are allowed on an either/or basis, with recovery permitted in either the survival or the death action but not in both. E.g., S.C. CODE § 15–5–100.

12. E.g., ARIZ. REV. STATS. § 14–3110; WASH. REV. STAT. § 4.20.046. As to "hedonic damages," the decedent's own loss of the pleasure of life, of which he can no longer be aware, see § 377 below.

13. E.g., N.Y. ESTATES, POWERS AND TRUSTS LAW § 11–3.2 (b).

14. Sullivan v. Delta Air Lines, Inc., 15 Cal.4th 288, 63 Cal.Rptr.2d 74, 935 P.2d 781 (1997) (involving only a judgment rendered before death of the victim).

Actions that survive or do not. Some survival statutes expressly provide for survival of a wrongful death claim. Suppose the defendant negligently causes A's death. A's daughter, B, has a potential wrongful death claim against the defendant, but B herself dies before the claim is brought. Some survival statutes are broad enough to allow B's wrongful death claim to survive, so that B's estate can then recover from the defendant for A's death.[15]

In other respects, however, many survival statutes are somewhat narrow because they expressly exclude a number of economic and dignitary torts such as libel, slander, malicious prosecution and the like, leaving those actions to abate upon death,of either party under the common law rule.[16] When the scope of the statute is not clear, courts have sometimes interpreted it generously in favor of survival.[17] A few decisions have held that the statute's exclusion of particular causes of action, such as those for defamation, is unwarranted and unconstitutional, with the result that that in such a state the libel action survives along with ordinary personal injury claims.[18]

Surviving the tortfeasor's death. The usual case for invoking a survival statute involves the death of the tortfeasor's victim and survival of the claim. However, the common law rule also abated the claim if the tortfeasor himself died before judgment. Most survival now acts appear to be worded broadly enough to permit a suit not only when the tort victim has died but also when the tortfeasor himself has died.[19] When the tortfeasor has died, the survival action is brought against the his estate. In that kind of survival action, punitive damages are frequently denied[20]

§ 296. Pecuniary Loss Damages in Wrongful Death Actions[1]

The traditional wrongful death statutes created a whole new cause of action for the benefit of the decedent's survivors. Except in Alabama, which has used a punitive measure of damages,[2] recovery was limited to pecuniary harm of the survivors and thus did not originally include any

15. E.g., Vernon's Ann. Mo. Stat. § 537.020, This may present problems in fair distribution if the recovery. See § 298 below.

16. E.g., N.M. Stats. Ann. § 37–2–4; Ohio Rev. Code Ann. § 2311.21.

17. E.g., Harrison v. Loyal Protective Life Ins. Co., 379 Mass. 212, 396 N.E.2d 987 (1979), (infliction of mental distress is harm to person which survives).

18. Moyer v. Phillips, 462 Pa. 395, 341 A.2d 441, 77 A.L.R.3d 1339 (1975)(libel); Thompson v. Estate of Petroff, 319 N.W.2d 400 (Minn.1982) (intentional tort).

19. E.g., Blakeley v. Shortal's Estate, 236 Iowa 787, 20 N.W.2d 28 (1945) (deceased's tort was that he committed suicide by slitting his throat in the plaintiff's home, causing her emotional distress; the claim survived the deceased's death even harm was not done until after death).

20. E.g., Doe v. Colligan, 753 P.2d 144 (Alaska 1988). Statutes may so provide. See Cal. Civ. Proc. Code § 377.42.

§ 296

1. For more detail and additional citations on several points, see 2 Dan B. Dobbs, Law of Remedies § 8.2 (4) (2d ed. 1993).

2. See Tatum v. Schering Corp., 523 So.2d 1042 (Ala.1988). However, Alabama says that is wrongful death damages are punitive in nature but "nonpenal in effect" because the purpose is to preserve life. See Industrial Chemical v. Chandler, 547 So.2d 812 (1988). Massachusetts formerly applied a punitive measure in death actions.

recovery for, say, the emotional distress of a bereaved spouse. Under the influence of statutory language, courts have estimated pecuniary harm in two quite different ways. Both main approaches to pecuniary loss may be varied by statutory detail. For example, some statutes might add reasonable funeral expenses as an item of recovery[3] And since any but a punitive measure of death damages represents future loss, reduction to present value or an alternative adjustment is required regardless of the way the damages are measured.[4]

Loss to Dependents Measure

Loss of support as measure of pecuniary loss. Courts have mainly interpreted both state[5] and federal[6] wrongful death statutes to allow recovery of sums necessary to replace the direct or indirect financial support lost by the decedent's dependents. Contributions by the decedent to the dependent's support might take the form of carl% but perhaps more often they take the form of provisions for shelter, food, or services rendered.

Forms of evidence. As a matter of proof, dependents might adduce evidence of the reasonable value of, say, benefits provided by the decedent, such as living quarters furnished. Or the dependents might show the decedent's total income together with evidence about the mounts decedent would probably spend for his own maintenance and other items that did not go toward support. The difference would reflect an estimate of support provided.[7]

Prospects of continued support and time period The fact that support has been provided in the past does not necessarily show that it will continue in the future, so courts admit evidence of the decedent's affection for the dependents, or the lack of it, as bearing on future probable contributions.[8] Likewise, the decedent's prospects of gaining greater income in the future is to be considered.[9] Finally, the time period

3. E.g., New York Estates, Powers and Trusts L. § 5–4.3 (reasonable funeral expenses of the decedent if distributee has paid or has become liable to pay them).

4. See 2 Dan B. Dobbs, Law of Remedies § 8.4 (2d ed. 1993).

5. E.g., Freeman v. Davidson, 105 Nev. 13, 768 P.2d 885 (Nev. 1989); see Comment, 44 N.C.L. Rev. 402 (1966).

6. E.g., *Death on High Seas Act:* Moore–McCormack Lines, Inc. v. Richardson, 295 F.2d 583, 96 A.L.R.2d 1085 (1961); *FELA:* Allendorf v. Elgin, Joliet & Eastern Ry. Co., 8 Ill.2d 164, 133 N.E.2d 288, 79 A.L.R.2d 241(1956); *Jones Act:* Van Beeck v. Sabine Towing Co., 300 U.S. 342, 57 S.Ct. 452, 81 L.Ed. 685 (1937).

7. See Lorenz v. Air Illinois, Inc., 168 Ill.App.3d 1060, 119 Ill.Dec. 493, 522 N.E.2d 1352 (1988) (considering a standard instruction allowing the jury to consider the amount of "money, goods and services the decedent customarily contributed in the past" and "was likely to have contributed in the future," as well as what he "spent for customary personal expenses"); Johnson v. Manhattan & Bronx Surface Transit Operating Authority, 71 N.Y.2d 198, 524 N.Y.S.2d 415, 519 N.E.2d 326 (1988) (gross income is an admissible beginning even though decedent would have paid taxes).

8. McDonald v. Price, 80 Cal.App.2d 150, 181 P.2d 115 (1947); McCormick v. Kopmann, 23 Ill.App.2d 189, 161 N.E.2d 720 (1959) ("habits of industry and sobriety").

9. E.g., United States v. Furumizo, 381 F.2d 965 (9th Cir.1967).

Similarly, the decedent's character or conduct may suggest that support would not continue. See Dollarhide v. Gunstream,

during which support would probably be provided must be proven. If support could be expected during the decedent's entire working life, then evidence of the decedent's life expectancy or working life expectancy can be presented. When minors are among the dependents, expectation of support usually terminates at their majority.

Collateral losses. Although dependents are entitled to recover for loss of indirect contributions like the home provided for members of the family, they are not entitled to recover collateral losses resulting from the decedent's death. For instance, they are probably not entitled to recover financial setback that results because they lose a favorable tax status when the decedent dies.[10] On the other hand, the dependent's recovery for loss is not to be reduced by the fact that the decedent's life insurance was payable to the dependent or the decedent's death generated social security payments to the dependent.[11] Some states may cap or limit the total amount of wrongful death damages payable.[12]

Decedents not earning or contributing. Measuring loss to dependents may present serious problems when the decedent is a child, a homemaker, or a retired person with no dependents, especially where non-pecuniary damages are not recoverable. In the case of a child or retired person, the loss to dependents is likely to be zero or very little at most. In the case of a homemaker, services in the home can be valued as a pecuniary contribution, but the sums represented by such services are likely to be relatively small. In the case of a retired person, substantial recovery is also confounded by the limited life expectancy of older persons. These limits on recovery in the case of people whose lives are valuable but who do not earn money in the labor market can be avoided by permitting awards for mental anguish or the like or, to some extent, by adopting the loss to the estate measure of pecuniary loss.

Loss to Estate Measure

The second approach to measuring pecuniary loss figures a recovery on the basis accumulations or savings cut short by the decedent's untimely death. Damages under this approach might be measured in slightly different ways, but the main idea is to add up what the decedent would probably have earned[13] in a normal lifetime and award that sum

55 N.M. 353, 233 P.2d 1042 (1951) (husband drank, attacked wife) or that the decedent was ofno value to the dependent. See Quinonez v. Andersen,144 Ariz. 193, 696 P.2d 1342 (Ct. App. 1984) (death of wife, evidence that surviving husband beat her admitted, "... all that Mr. Quinonez lost was a punching bag and a just and fair award for this loss was zero").

10. See Farrar v. Brooklyn Union Gas Co., 73 N.Y.2d 802, 537 N.Y.S.2d 26, 533 N.E.2d 1055 (1988) (tax status).

11. Cunningham v. Rederiet Vindeggen, 333 F.2d 308 (2d Cir.1964) (death benefit); Bagley v. Blue Flame Propane Co., 418 P.2d 333 (Okl.1966) (evidence of social security benefits to minor children upon death of father inadmissible). These holdings are consistent with the collateral source rules.

12. E.g., Colo. Rev. Stat. § 13–21–203.

13. The decedent's savings from non-earned income such as inheritance or investments are disregarded in most formulas. E.g., State v. Mayberry, 415 N.W.2d 644 (Iowa 1987) ("present worth or value of the estate which the decedent would reasonably be expected to have saved and accumulated as the result of her efforts between the time other death and the end of her natural life had she lived.")

after subtracting something for the costs the decedent would have had to maintain himself.[14] This measure is sometimes called the loss to the estate measure. It ignores loss of support to survivors and concentrates on the potential property loss someone would have had if the decedent had lived out a full lifetime. Inevitably, a certain amount of speculation is permitted in death claims, because the alternative in most instances would be to deny all compensation.[15]

Lost Inheritance Claims

Adding loss of inheritance to the loss to dependents approach. Some courts have allowed dependents to claim both loss to dependents and loss of inheritance of heirs or presumptive heirs. In *Martin v. Atlantic Coast Line R.R.*,[16] the proof at trial tended to show that at the time of his death, the decedent was making contributions to his spouse, and that he would have increased earnings which would probably have been saved. Under the loss to dependents rule, the spousal contributions would be recoverable; under the loss to the estate measure the provable lifetime savings would be recoverable. The *Martin* court allowed recovery of both elements, in effect holding the tortfeasor liable for all losses caused. The *Martin* approach, or something similar, has been adopted by statute[17] and by judicial decision[18] in a number of cases, and when not available under the wrongful death act, is nevertheless sometimes allowed under the survival act.[19] Some such approach might be the only method by

14. E.g., State v. Mayberry, 415 N.W.2d 644 (Iowa 1987).

"That measure is the present worth or value of the estate which the decedent would reasonably be expected to have saved and accumulated as the result of her efforts between the time of her death and the end of her natural life had she lived. Relevant factors in this determination are the 'decedent's age and life expectancy, characteristics and habits, health, education or opportunity for education, general ability, other occupational qualifications, industriousness, intelligence, manner of living, sobriety or intemperance, frugality or lavishness, and other personal characteristics that are of assistance in securing business or earning money.' " See Corlett v. Smith, 107 N.M. 707, 763 P.2d 1172 (Ct.App.1988); Wallace v. Couch, 642 S.W.2d 141 (Tenn.1982). Kentucky makes no deduction for personal maintenance. Charlton v. Jacobs, 619 S.W.2d 498 (Ky.App. 1981).

15. See State v. Mayberry, 415 N.W.2d 644 (Iowa 1987).

16. Martin v. Atlantic Coast Line R.R., 268 F.2d 397, 91 A.L.R.2d 472 (5th Cir. 1959).

17. Fla. Stat. Ann. § 768.21 provides for a loss to survivors recovery and in addition for the "Loss of the prospective net accumulations of an estate" if there is a surviving spouse or lineal descendant, and also in some cases where there is no recovery for loss to survivors; Ohio Rev. Code Ann. § 2125.02(B) (Loss of support, plus loss of prospective inheritance to heirs at law).

18. E.g., Martin v. Atlantic Coast Line R.R., 268 F.2d 397 (5th Cir. 1959) (Federal Employers Liability Act); National Airlines, Inc. v. Stiles, 268 F.2d 400 (5th Cir.1959), cert. denied, 361 U.S. 885, 80 S.Ct. 157, 4 L.Ed.2d 121 (1959) (Death on High Seas Act); Yowell v. Piper Aircraft Corp., 703 S.W.2d 630 (Tex.1986); James T. Tucker, Annotation, Wrongful Death Damages For Loss of Expectancy of Inheritance From Decedent, 42 A.L.R. 5th 465 (1996).

19. See Weil v. Seltzer, 873 F.2d 1453 (D.C.Cir.1989); Evich v. Morris, 819 F.2d 256 (9th Cir.), cert. denied, 484 U.S. 914, 108 S.Ct. 261, 98 L.Ed.2d 218 (1987); McClinton v. White, 497 Pa. 610, 444 A.2d 85 (1982); Criscuola v. Andrews, 82 Wn.2d 68, 507 P.2d 149 (1973); Annot., Recovery, in action for benefit of decedent's estate in jurisdiction which has both wrongful death and survival statutes, of value of earnings decedent would have made after death, 76 A.L.R.3d 125 (1977).

which recovery could be allowed to survivors like adult children who received no current contributions from the deceased.[20]

The lost inheritance claim, when added to the loss of support, makes the tortfeasor responsible for all rather than only some of the losses, so, if permitted by the governing statute, the result seems prima facie right. Some scepticism may be justified, however. Apart from the particular limits in any given statute, future lost inheritance is even less certain than many other future damages, partly because the deceased, had he lived, might have left her estate to different beneficiaries, or might consumed it all in the costs of nursing homes or otherwise.

Caps on Pecuniary Damages

At one time a number of states imposed caps or arbitrary dollar limits on wrongful death recoveries[21] and the Warsaw Convention imposes limits on recovery for the death of international airline passengers[22] There is little reason to fear excessive verdicts in death cases more than in others. Over time, the arbitrary limits were repealed in most states, so few if any general caps remained by the time the "tort reform" movement began to generate statutory changes in tort law in the 1980s. Tort reform legislation, however, has instituted caps in particular kinds of cases such as those involving medical malpractice.

§ 297. Non-Pecuniary Damages in Wrongful Death Cases

Traditional rule. The traditional death statute protected only the pecuniary interests of survivors. For this reason nothing was recovered for the survivor's mental anguish or the loss of love and affection resulting from the death.[1] In the most stringent view, nothing could be recovered for loss of society either, unless that loss of society could be expressed in money terms.[2] The rule was applied both in loss to survivors[3] and in loss to the estate jurisdictions.[4]

Problems when decedent is not a wage earner. As already noted, a limitation of damages to pecuniary losses results in virtual denial of

20. See Schaefer v. American Family Mutual Ins. Co., 192 Wis.2d 768, 531 N.W.2d 585 (1995).

21. See S. Speiser, Recovery for Wrongful Death 2d §§ 7:1—7:4 (1975).

22. 49 Stat. 3000 (1934); 137 L.N.T.S. 11, No. 3145, printed in note following 49 U.S.C.A. § 1502. Carriers have voluntarily agreed to a higher sum than the $8,000 provided by the old treaty, but it is still widely out of line with American tort judgments. The limit does not apply to intentional or reckless harms. See Piamba Cortes v. American Airlines, Inc., 177 F.3d 1272 (11th Cir. 1999) (also reviewing history and the subsequent protocols raising the cap on damages to $75,000).

§ 297

1. E.g., Miller v. Mayberry, 506 N.E.2d 7 (Ind.1987); Nelson v. Dolan, 230 Neb. 848, 434 N.W.2d 25 (1989).

2. Miles v. Apex Marine Corp., 498 U.S. 19, 111 S.Ct. 317, 112 L.Ed.2d 275 (1990) (statutory beneficiaries in FELA, Jones Act, and general maritime claims can recover pecuniary harms only).

3. E.g., Lehrer v. Lorenzen, 124 Colo. 17, 233 P.2d 382 (1951).

4. E.g., Scriven v. McDonald, 264 N.C. 727, 142 S.E.2d 585 (1965) (at that time a loss to estate jurisdiction).

recovery when the decedent is a child, a retired person or any person not in the labor market.[5] In the case of the child and the retired person, death might actually represent an economic gain to survivors because the expense of maintenance could readily exceed any financial contributions.[6] In fact, the traditional measure for a child-death was the value of the child's services minus the cost of rearing the child.[7]

Companionship, society, love, advice, and guidance. The rule against nonpecuniary recovery may be circumvented in particular cases, as Illinois has done by presuming that a pecuniary loss is suffered in the ease of a child's wrongful death.[8] Most states have now gone further by allowing a recovery for the survivor's loss of companionship, society, advice and guidance,[9] sometimes on the theory that such elements have a pecuniary value.[10]

Anguish or emotional harm recoverable. Loss of companionship, society and the like—consortium rights—are usually viewed as something distinct from anguish or grief, so to allow the consortium recovery is not necessarily to allow a recovery for the grief or anguish of survivors. However, by the 1990s many states were permitting recovery for emotional harm or anguish in wrongful death actions. Some of the statutes now provide for it directly, usually in addition to the claims for lost companionship, society, guidance and the like[11] Elsewhere, some courts have expanded liability to include mental anguish recovery under statutes that do not specifically authorize it.[12]

Punitive damages. Alabama has a unique approach to wrongful death damages, basing recovery on a purely punitive measure[13] But traditional death statutes, by limiting damages to pecuniary losses, might appear to exclude punitive damages altogether in the death (but

5. In each case, but especially in the case of a homemaker, the value of the service rendered would have pecuniary value and would be recoverable, E.g., Missouri Pac. R.R. Co. v. Maxwell, 194 Ark. 938, 109 S.W.2d 1254 (1937); Siebeking v. Ford, 128 Ind.App. 475, 148 N.E.2d 194 (1958); Oliver v. Morgan, 73 S.W.2d 993 (Mo.1934). But the sums recovered are not likely to reflect real values or the value of human life.

6. See Sanchez v. Schindler, 651 S.W.2d 249, 251 (Tex.1983) ("If the rule were literally followed, the average child would have a negative worth").

7. E.g., Missouri Pac. R.R.v. Maxwell, 194 Ark. 938, 109 S.W.2d 1254 (1937).

8. E.g., Bullard v. Barnes, 102 I!l.2d 505, 82 Ill.Dec. 448, 468 N.E.2d 1228 (1984).

9. Statutes now often so provide. E.g., E.g., ALASKA STAT. § 09.55.580 (C) ("loss of consortium" and also "loss of assistance or services"); MASS. ANN. LAWS ch. 229, § 2 ("services, protection, care, assistance, society, companionship, comfort, guidance, counsel and advice"). In others cases, courts may regard loss of consortium as being distinct from anguish or grief and may attribute pecuniary value to it. E.g., Krouse v. Graham, 19 Cal.3d 59, 68, 137 Cal.Rptr. 863, 867, 562 P.2d 1022, 1026 (1977); Green v. Bittner, 85 N.J. 1, 424 A.2d 210 (1980).

10. See Nelson v. Dolan, 230 Neb. 848, 434 N.W.2d 25 (1989).

11. E.g., ARK. CODE ANN. § 16–62–102; DEL. CODE ANN. tit. 10, § 3724; OHIO REV. CODE ANN. § 2125.02(b).

12. E.g., City of Tucson v. Wondergem, 105 Ariz. 429, 466 P.2d 383 (1970); Sanchez v. Schindler, 651 S.W.2d 249, 251 (Tex. 1983); See Annotation, Recovery of Damages for Grief or Mental Anguish Resulting from Death of a Child—Modern Cases, 45 A.L.R.4th 234 (1986).

13. See, e.g., Killough v. Jahandarfard, 578 So.2d 1041 (Ala. 1991).

not necessarily the survival) action.[14] Punitive damages could also be excluded on the ground that because the action was statutory, no award could be made unless explicitly authorized by the statute.[15]

However, the policies supporting punitive damages apply as much or more in death actions as any other. For this and similar reasons, some courts have allowed punitive damages in spite of the statute's pecuniary loss requirement.[16] In addition, some statutes can be construed to permit punitive damages because they authorize damages that are fair and just,[17] or because they allow modification of the basic damages award for aggravating or mitigating circumstances.[18] Other statutes now explicitly provide for the award of punitive damages.[19] Besides the statutes themselves, a sizeable number of decisions have now allowed a recovery of punitive damages in death actions or have approved them in principle?[20]

§ 298. Procedure and Distribution of Death Damages

Parties plaintiff. Some statutes permit direct death action suits by beneficiaries; others provide that the wrongful death suit is to be brought by a representative on their behalf. Sometimes the representative is the personal representative of the estate—the same person who sues under the survival act. However, monies recovered under the survival act are payable to the estate and generally subject to claims of the estate's creditors, while damages recovered for the beneficiaries are payable to the beneficiaries without going through the estate and the death action recovery is typically not subject to claims the creditors might have against the estate itself.

Distribution of wrongful death damages. The distribution of damages differs from state to state and the governing statutes must always be consulted for determinative detail. It can be said, however, that many statutes risk serious maldistribution of the damage award. An observer would expect that wrongful death damages to be calculated on the basis of each survivor's loss and that the damages so calculated would then be distributed to the person who suffered that loss. Although some statutes adopt such a principle,[1] many others defeat that principle in one of several ways.

14. See Rubeck v. Huffman, 54 Ohio St.2d 20, 374 N.E.2d 411 (1978).

15. See Alsenz v. Clark County School District, 109 Nev. 1062, 864 P.2d 285 (1993).

16. Portwood v. Copper Valley Elec. Ass'n, *Inc.,* 785 P.2d 541 (Alaska 1990) (pecuniary injury requirement applies only to compensatory damages); Bond v. City of Huntington, 166 W.Va. 581, 276 S.E.2d 539 (1981) (policy behind punitive damages demands award in appropriate death cases).

17. See Boies v. Cole, 99 Ariz. 198, 407 P.2d 917 (1965); Vickery v. Ballentine, 293 Ark. 54, 732 S.W.2d 160 (1987).

18. E.g., Mo. Stat. Ann. § 537.090.

19. N.Y. Estates, Powers and Trusts Law § 5–4.3(b); N.C. Gen. Stat. § 28A–18–2(b):

20. Portwood v. Copper Valley Elec. Ass'n, Inc., 785 P.2d 541 (Alaska 1990); Lewis v. Hiatt, 683 So.2d 937 (Miss.1996); Roach v. Jimmy D. Enterprises, Ltd., 912 P.2d 852 (Okla.1996); McCourt v. Abernathy, 318 S.C. 301, 457 S.E.2d 603 (1995); Behrens v. Raleigh Hills Hospital, Inc., 675 P.2d 1179 (Utah 1983) (suggesting that allowance represents a trend); Clymer v. Webster, 156 Vt. 614, 596 A.2d 905 (1991)

§ 298

1. Ariz. Rev. Stat. § 12–612 C (distribution "in proportion to their damages"); see Chang v. State Farm Mutual Automobile

(1) All statutes limit the beneficiaries in some way, usually to specified family members such as spouses, children, parents, or heirs.[2]

This is underinclusive because many who receive support or who suffer grief at the deceased's loss may not count as "heirs" or children.[3] Indeed, at one time illegitimate children were excluded. That is now unconstitutional,[4] but it is still possible to exclude stepchildren who were fully supported by the deceased[5] unless the statute is broadened to include them.[6]In a Utah case, foster parents who had reared a child after he was removed from his mother's custody were not allowed to recover for his death, apparently not even their medical expenses incurred after his injury; they were not "parents" or heirs and the mother who had lost custody was.[7]

(2) Some statutes appear to contemplate that courts will calculate recovery on the basis of losses incurred by various individuals, but distribute the recovery without regard to losses suffered and even to persons who have no recognizable loss at all.[8]

Under this approach, the recovery for grief, lost support, and loss of inheritance may be totaled and then distributed to each beneficiary without regard to her particular loss. For instance, at least one court held that the recovery of spouses for the death of a child must be equal, even though one spouse had been deprived of the child's custody.[9] An Illinois statute requires distribution in proportion to "dependency," which should produce fight results when the damages are awarded for

Ins. Co., 182 Wis.2d 549, 514 N.W.2d 399 (1994).

2. E.g., KAN. STAT. ANN. § 60–1902 (heirs).

3. See, e.g., Ablin v. Richard O'Brien Plastering Co., 885 P.2d 289 (Colo.App. 1994) (only surviving relatives were siblings, but siblings were not "heirs" as Colorado understands that term).

4. As a matter of equal protection, states can no longer refuse a child's recovery merely because the child is illegitimate. Levy v. Louisiana, 391 U.S. 68, 88 S.Ct. 1509, 20 L.Ed.2d 436 (1968). Equally, a parent of an illegitimate child can recover for the child's death. Glona v. American Guarantee & Liability Ins. Co., 391 U.S. 73, 88 S.Ct., 1515, 20 L.Ed.2d 441 (1968).

5. Steed v. Imperial Airlines, 12 Cal.3d 115, 115 Cal.Rptr. 329, 524 P.2d 801 (1974)(now superseded by statute); Klossner v. San Juan County, 93 Wash.2d 42, 605 P.2d 330 (1980). To avoid a similar problem, the court in Lawson v. Atwood, 42 Ohio St.3d 69, 536 N.E.2d 1167 (1989) came up with the conclusion that the deceased had become the child's parent, event though he had not adopted the child.

6. E.g., CAL. CIV. PROC. CODE § 377.60(b).

7. Moreno v. Bd. of Education of the Jordan School Dist., 926 P.2d 886 (Utah 1996).

8. See, e.g., Arnold v. Turek, 185 W.Va. 400, 407 S.E.2d 706 (1991) (under then existing statute, damages were to include sums for loss of support of various persons but were to be distributed according to the laws of descent and distribution); of. Johnson v. Smith, 241 Va. 396, 403 S.E.2d 685 (1991) (awards for all elements are to be aggregated in a lump sum, then distributed to the list of beneficiaries).

9. Mangrum v. Owens, 917 S.W.2d 244 (Tenn.App.1995). Contra, distributing damages more or less in proportion to court-determined losses, Estate of Williams, 223 Ill.App.3d 505, 585 N.E.2d 235, 165 Ill.Dec. 839 (1992) (on the basis of considerable evidence that the father as custodial parent spent devoted many hours to education and happiness of deceased daughter, the award was distributed about 70% to the father and only 30% to the noncustodial mother); Jones v. Jones, 641 N.E.2d 98 (Ind.App. 1994).

loss of support, but degree of dependency might be the wrong way to distribute damages for grief or loss of consortium.

> (3) Some statutes, like the FELA, have set up classes of beneficiaries, with the direction or implication that none of the recovery goes to the second class if members of the first class survive the deceased.[10] Statutes directing distribution according to the laws of descent and distribution may accomplish the a similar classificatory effect.[11]

The difficulty with this plan is that beneficiaries in the second class may have extensive losses, including loss of support and anguish at the deceased's death. But their losses are not counted at all, or if counted, are then distributed to the first class of beneficiaries. For example, In a Washington case, the parents whose adult son was killed could recover nothing, partly because they were not financially dependent and partly because the deceased son left a child who was entitled to the entire recovery,[12] If damages were award for the parents' loss of their son's service but were distributed to the son's child, that child received a windfall. If the damages never included the parents' loss, the tortfeasor received the windfall.

Some of the anomalous results are no doubt intended. Others, however, seems to result from the fact that at various times the focus is on lost inheritance, while at other times it is on lost support or on anguish and grief. All three kinds of damages are real and it would require all three to approve compensation, but until statutes recognize that different beneficiaries may suffer different losses and should be compensated for those losses, unhappy results will continue to compromise the death statutes' essential purpose.

§ 299. Contributory Negligence and Similar Defenses

Negligence of the Decedent

In wrongful death claims. Wrongful death statutes create a new cause of action for the benefit of survivors; it is not merely a continuance of the deceased's own claim. At the same they provide or have been interpreted to mean that no new cause of action is created unless the deceased himself would have been able to sue had he lived. The effect in most instances is that a defense that would have defeated the deceased's

10. Under the FELA, recovery is for the benefit of "the surviving widow or husband and children of such employee; and, if none, then of such employee's parents; and, if none, then of the next of kin dependent upon such employee." 45 U.S.C.A. § 51. Some state statutes follow a similar plan, allowing to recovery to class 2 beneficiaries if class 1 beneficiaries can take. See, e,g., State ex rel. Griffin v. Belt, 941 S.W.2d 570 (Mo.App.1997).

11. "Heirs" may be defined as those permitted to take under intestacy statutes. Under those statutes, a brother may not be an heir (regardless of the support he received from the deceased) if a parent or child of the deceased is living. See Kelson v. Salt Lake County, 784 P.2d 1152 (Utah 1989). The effect is to say that all damages must be distributed to the parent or child, even if another relative and potential heir has lost support.

12. Masunaga v. Gapasin, 57 Wash. App. 624, 790 P.2d 171 (1990).

claim had he lived will also defeat the wrongful death suit.[1] Consequently, before the adoption of comparative negligence rules, contributory negligence of the deceased was a bar to the wrongful death action[2] whenever it would have barred the deceased's own claim had he lived.[3]

In comparative fault systems. These principles are adapted to the comparative fault regimes now adopted in most states. They require a comparison of the deceased's fault with that of the defendant.[4] The result is that the wrongful recovery will be diminished to reflect the percentage of the deceased's fault,[5] or, if his fault exceeded the breakpoint in a modified comparative fault system, the action will be barred altogether.[6]

Survival claims. Since survival statutes merely perpetuated the cause of action the decedent himself would have had and did not purport to create a "new" cause of action for the benefit of others, a defense that would bar or reduce damages of the deceased would have the same effect on the estate's claim under the survival act.[7]

Negligence of a Beneficiary

Wrongful death actions. In wrongful death suits, a statutory beneficiary whose negligence contributed to the deceased's death is usually subjected to the contributory or comparative negligence rules.[8] Unless the beneficiary's negligence exceeds the breakpoint in a modified comparative fault system, that would normally mean that her recovery would be reduced in proportion to her negligence.[9] However, a few courts have dealt with the beneficiary's negligence in a different manner. In *Teeter v. Missouri Highway* and *Transportation Com'n,*[10] the Missouri Court held that no reduction could be made for the negligence of one of

§ 299

1. See Smith v. Gross, 319 Md. 138, 571 A.2d 1219 (1990) (parental immunity). As to special rules for the statute of limitations defense, see § 300 below.

2. E.g., Wilson v. Iowa Power & Light Co., 280 N.W.2d 372 (Iowa 1979) ("In keeping with the derivative nature of a wrongful death action, we have held that a defense which would have been available against the decedent if he had survived is good against his personal representative"); Restatement § 494.

3. And not a bar, of course, when the deceased was exempt from the contributory negligence rule under any of the recognized exceptions, as where the deceased was a child employed in violation of child labor statutes. Strain v. Christians, 483 N.W.2d 783 (S.D.1992).

4. Henry Woods and Beth Deere, Comparative Fault 9:2 (3d ed. 1996).

5. Champagne v. United States, 513 N.W.2d 75 (N.D.1994); Ginochio v. Hesston Corp., 46 Wash. App. 843, 733 P.2d 551 (1987);.

6. See Kelson v. Salt Lake County, 784 P.2d 1152 (Utah 1989).

7. E.g., Allison v. Snelling & Snelling, Inc., 425 Pa. 519, 229 A.2d 861 (1967) (barring both wrongful death and survival claims).

8. Winding River Village Condominium Ass'n, Inc. v. Barnett, 218 Ga.App. 35, 459 S.E.2d 569 (1995) (beneficiary's contributory negligence would reduce her share of award).

9. Frazier v. Metropolitan Dade County, 701 So.2d 418 (Fla.App.1997) (also reflecting the adjustments made when joint and several liability is abolished and each defendant is liable for his proportionate share only).

10. Teeter v. Missouri Highway and Transportation Com'n, 891 S.W.2d 817 (Mo. 1995).

two beneficiaries. Instead, the primary defendant could achieve a similar result by claiming contribution from the negligent beneficiary as a joint tortfeasor. New Hampshire also refused to reduce recovery for the negligence of a beneficiary where the statute had some attributes of a survival statute.[11]

Survival actions. The survival action is prosecuted by the deceased's personal representative and recoveries are paid to the estate. Consequently, in a formal sense, the negligence of an person who inherits from the estate might seem irrelevant. In line with this, a number of courts have held that the heir's contributory negligence does not bar the survival claim or reduce damages recoverable.[12] Such a rule does not necessarily preclude the defendant from asserting a contribution claim against the same negligent heir, recouping the heir's proportionate share through contribution rather than by way of a comparative fault reduction.[13]

Some authority does not accept the formal view of the survival action but instead treats such actions more like a wrongful death action by recognizing that the negligent heir is in a sense the real plaintiff. As the Rhode Island Court said of the sole heir, "she was, for all intents and purposes, both plaintiff and defendant in the wrongful death action;" public policy would forbid her recovery.[14] Perhaps this reasoning would not apply when there are multiple defendants or multiple heirs. In that case, the same realistic approach—recognizing the culpable heir as a real plaintiff—would presumably warrant a comparative negligence reduction of her claim but would not bar all recovery.

Assumed risk. In contemporary thinking assumed risk is quite often merely a form of contributory negligence and for that reason to be compared with the negligence of the defendant under most comparative fault systems.[15] When assumed risk is so treated, the court's rules for contributory negligence may be expected to apply in the same way. In a few cases, assumed risk is not merely contributory negligence but is instead a true shift of full responsibility for injury. In those cases, the plaintiff in a personal injury case is barred completely.[16] Again, it may be expected that courts in wrongful death cases will treat the bar in the same way they treat other defenses.

11. In re Estate of Infant Fontaine, 128 N.H. 695, 519 A.2d 227 (1986).

12. See Byrne v. Schneider's Iron & Metal, Inc., 190 Mich.App. 176, 475 N.W.2d 854 (1991); cf. In re Estate of Infant Fontaine, 128 N.H. 695, 519 A.2d 227 (1986) (death action with survival attributes). It is usually said that this is the majority rule. See Henry Woods and Beth Deere, Comparative Fault 9:4 (3d ed. 1996); 2 Stuart M. Speiser, Charles F. Krause & Juanita M. Madole, (Recovery for Wrongful Death and Injury 5:10 3d ed. Looseleaf).

13. See Chinski v. New Castle County Vocational and Technical School Dist., 1995 WL 790997 (Del.Super.1995). Or possibly anyone with standing in probate could object to distribution to the heir. That approach would leave the negligent heir's share in the estate for distribution to others.

14. Aetna Casualty and Surety Co. v. Curley, 585 A.2d 640 (R.I.1991).

15. See § 211 supra.

16. See §§ 212–214 supra.

§ 300. Statutes of Limitation

Accrual at injury or at death? Statutes of limitations questions in wrongful death actions are parallel to those in ordinary personal injury actions, but the answers to the questions are sometimes different, not least because the statutes themselves, which are by no means alike, may call for different constructions. One of the central questions arises when the tort victim dies long after the injury was inflicted. During the victim's lifetime, the personal injury statute of limitations would govern her rights, so that if she does not commence an action within the statutory period, her rights are ordinarily barred. If she dies after her personal injury claim is barred, can a wrongful death action be brought?

The argument for allowing the claim is that the wrongful death action creates a new cause of action in favor of the survivors, and that the survivors or their representative could not bring the action until death occurred, so that the statute of limitations should begin to run at death, not sooner. For this reason, or because the death statute specifically provides for accrual at the time of death,[1] a good many courts who are not constrained by specific statutory commands have held that the wrongful death suit may be maintained even after the personal injury action on which it is based has expired.[2]

The other major view is that, although the wrongful death statute creates a new cause of action for survivors, the claim is to some extent derivative of the deceased's own rights. If he would have had no right to sue had he lived, then the survivors would have no rights. In the same way, if his once-existing right had expired, then the survivors's rights have expired, too. In a Texas case, the wrongful death statute of limitation required that suit for death be brought within two years of death. Even so, the Texas Court concluded that the wrongful death action is "entirely derivative" of the decedent's rights, and that since the decedent was barred before his death, no wrongful death action would lie. The wrongful death statute's explicit provision of a two-year period running from the time of death referred only to the time of accrual of the action, not whether an action existed to accrue.[3]

Discovery. The discovery rule is now familiar in personal injury statute of limitations cases.[4] It logically applies as well in survival

§ 300

1. E.g., Ariz. Rev. Stats. § 12–542.

2. Chapman v. Cardiac Pacemakers, Inc., 105 Idaho 785, 673 P.2d 385 (1983); Carroll v. W.R. Grace and Company, 252 Mont. 485, 830 P.2d 1253 (1992); Fernandez v. Kozar, 107 Nev. 446, 814 P.2d 68 (1991). Accord, Restatement § 899, cmt. c; see also 2 Stuart M. Speiser, Charles F. Krause & Juanita M. Madole, Recovery for Wrongful Death and Injury §§ 11:10, 11:13 (statutes not providing when period begins and statutes providing that period begins at accrual, respectively) (3d ed. Looseleaf). The rule is even easier to accept when the personal injury action was still viable at the time of the deceased's death and putatively expired afterward, as in Gentry v. Wallace, 606 So.2d 1117 (Miss.1992).

3. Nelson v. American National Red Cross, 26 F.3d 193 (D.C.Cir.1994); Russell v. Ingersoll–Rand Company, 841 S.W.2d 343 (Tex.1992) (asserting that this is the more authoritative position).

4. See § 218, supra.

actions, which are merely continuations of the personal injury claim,[5] although there is some dissent.[6] In the survival context, the main question is whether suit was brought within the prescriptive period after the decedent discovered or should have discovered the facts considered relevant in the particular jurisdiction.

In the wrongful death setting, use of the discovery rule is more controversial and less certain. Discovery may refer to the decedent's own discovery or lack of discovery during her lifetime; or it may refer to the survivor's discovery or lack of discovery that death may have been caused by the defendant's conduct. A number of cases fall on both sides of the issue.[7] Some authorities flatly reject the discovery rule for death actions,[8] while others apply the discovery rule to postpone accrual of the death action until survivors discovered or should have discovered the relevant facts.[9] It does not seem to be accurate to say that the discovery rule would subject defendants to infinite liability in death actions, but it may be that particular statutory wording leaves courts little room to apply the rule.

When the discovery rule applies in death actions, it may be subject to the rule adopted in some states that no action lies if the decedent's claim expired during her lifetime. Some statutes may incorporate a discovery rule, but little has been decided about how the rule is to be applied in wrongful death cases.[10]

§ 301. Prior Judgment or Release

When an injured victim pursues her claim against the tortfeasor to judgment or settles and releases her claim with him, the victim's claim is terminated. Consequently, there is no personal injury claim to survive and no survival action may be brought.[1]

5. Nelson v. American National Red Cross, 26 F.3d 193 (D.C.Cir.1994); White v. Johns–Manville Corp., 103 Wash. 2d 344, 693 P.2d 687, 49 A.L.R.4th 955 (1985).

6. Anthony v. Koppers Co., Inc., 496 Pa. 119, 436 A.2d 181 (1981). The *Anthony* court reasoned that "by arguing that their decedents were not 'injured' until some time after their deaths [when survivors discovered the alleged tort] appellees concede that no valid cause of action existed at the time of death which could be preserved under the survival statutes." This reasoning seems to misconceive the discovery rule, which does not deny the validity of a claim but only postpones the time for starting the statutory clock.

7. See Judy E. Zelin, Annotation, Time of Discovery as Affecting Running of Statute of Limitations in Wrongful Death Action 49 A.L.R.4th 972 (1987).

8. Miles v. Ashland Chemical Co., 261 Ga. 726, 410 S.E.2d 290 (1991) (on the ground that "infinite" liability would otherwise result); Anthony v. Koppers Co., Inc., 496 Pa. 119, 436 A.2d 181 (1981) (on the ground that "one year after the death, and not thereafter" could not mean one year after discovery).

9. Sweeney v. Preston, 642 So.2d 332 (Miss.1994) (fetal death case, hence no issue of deceased's potential discovery of injury); White v. Johns–Manville Corp., 103 Wash.2d 344, 693 P.2d 687, 49 A.L.R.4th 955 (1985).

10. See Davidson v. Denning, 259 Kan. 659, 914 P.2d 936 (1996).

§ 301

1. Cf. Kronemeyer v. Meinig, 948 P.2d 119 (Colo.App.1997) (earlier wrongful death suit and settlement did not bar survival claim).

The question that has produced division is whether the wrongful death claim is also terminated by the victim's inter vivos settlement or by litigation that goes to judgment. The answer of most courts—in which some legislatures have joined[2]—is that either a settlement by the victim or a judgment for or against him will preclude the wrongful death action where death resulted from the original injury and not from its later aggravation.[3] The argument for this position is summed up by describing the wrongful death suit as derivative of the deceased's own rights. If the deceased had no right to sue at her death, or would have had none had she survived, then survivors have no wrongful death claim.

A few courts have taken the opposite view.[4] They treat the wrongful death suit as a completely independent right of survivors to be protected from the death of the deceased. Because the right of survivors is viewed as an independent right, it is not lost if the deceased releases her claim or recovers damages.

This approach may entail some practical difficulties. Collateral estoppel rules may make it necessary to review in detail the ante-mortem litigation. Unless the risk that the defendant will pay twice for some elements of damages is to be dismissed, some estimate must be made as to what elements of damage already paid by the defendant should he credited against the wrongful death claim. Settlement with an injured person is itself presumably more difficult to accomplish if the defendant cannot know what other potential claims, possibly by unknown persons, may lie ahead. Indeed, some defendants have made efforts to settle not only with the injured victim but with relatives who might bring a death action if the victim dies.[5]

2. 740 Il. Comp. Stats. Ann. § 180/1, § 1 (foreclosing death claim if judgment was rendered or settlement made in decedent's lifetime); cf. D.C. Code § 16–2701 (barring suit if victim "recovered damages" in her lifetime).

3. Hutton v. Davis, 26 Ariz.App. 215, 547 P.2d 486 (1976) (covenant not to sue in deceased's lifetime bars wrongful death action by minor children); Simmons First National Bank v. Abbott, 288 Ark. 304, 705 S.W.2d 3 (1986) (even though survivors' anguish is an element of damages in wrongful death claims, prior judgment in favor of the deceased during her lifetime barred death claim); Varelis v. Northwestern Memorial Hospital, 167 Ill.2d 449, 657 N.E.2d 997, 212 Ill.Dec. 652 (1995) (judgment during deceased's lifetime is a bar); see Vitauts M. Gulbis, Annotation, Judgment in Favor Of, or Adverse To, Person Injured as Barring Action For His Death, 26 A.L.R.4th 1264 (1981).

4. Alfone v. Sarno, 87 N.J. 99, 432 A.2d 857 (1981) (the leading case); Thompson v. Wing, 70 Ohio St.3d 176, 637 N.E.2d 917 (1994). The Supreme Court has approved this approach for a narrow band of Admiralty cases. Sea–Land Services v. Gaudet, 414 U.S. 573, 94 S.Ct. 806, 39 L.Ed.2d 9 (1974), but it does not apply in other federal maritime torts. See Mobil Oil Co. v. Higginbotham, 436 U.S. 618, 98 S.Ct. 2010, 56 L.Ed.2d 581 (1978).

5. This additional cost has proved ineffective to settle the death claim in some cases. See Schiffman v. Service Truck Lines, Inc., 308 So.2d 824, 92 A.L.R.3d 1224 (1975).

CHAPTER 20

EMOTIONAL HARM

TOPIC A. INTRODUCTION TO EMOTIONAL HARM

§ 302. Distress and Emotional Harm in Tort Law

Courts have long recognized that tortfeasors should be responsible for causing distress, emotional harm, anxiety, diminished enjoyment, losses of autonomy, and similar intangible harms. The exact form of the intangible harm, so long as it is real, seldom matters. All such harms can be referred to as distress or as emotional harm. Such harms are real. They represent the antithesis of happiness or enjoyment of life which everyone pursues. One indicator of the importance of this subject lies in the fact that people spend a great deal of time and money to promote happiness and to avoid distress.

Some torts are constructed mainly or exclusively to deal with economic loss. Courts seldom allow emotional harm or distress damages with torts like that. For example, economic fraud and interference with contract usually do not warrant distress damages.

On the other hand, a number of other torts are constructed mainly for the very purpose of permitting recovery for distress. The tort of assault, for example, involves nothing more than a threat of immediate use of force that puts the plaintiff in reasonable apprehension of an unconsented-to bodily touching. By definition, no physical harm is required. The recovery for assault is a recovery for that unpleasant apprehension.

Other torts permit recovery of distress as a major element in the tort, as in the case of libel or slander when the plaintiff's good name is put in doubt by false statements, and in right of privacy cases, which address the distress resulting from the plaintiff's loss of seclusion, or subjection to publicity. The obscure torts of alienation of affections and criminal conversation once allowed one spouse to recover damages against the other spouse's lover, and may still have some life today when therapists induce children to believe their parents abused them.[1] Courts often spoke as if the aggrieved spouse had suffered losses of things and ownership rights, emotional harm or loss lay at the core of these torts. Even denial of informed consent carries with it an element of distress or emotional harm. Many torts of relatively recent vintage are also in this category. These include statutory or common law torts based on some

§ 302

1. See § 444.

form of discrimination, torts like wrongful discharge, and torts based on an insurer's bad faith.

Far and away the most common claims of emotional distress, however, are those associated with personal injury actions. When the plaintiff has suffered a tortious injury, as in an every-day automobile accident, medical malpractice, or product injury, she is entitled to recover for pain and suffering in addition to other losses. Pain and suffering include distress and emotional pain as well as painful sensations. Loss of enjoyment of life is included in the recovery, either as a part of the pain and suffering or as a separate element. The plaintiff must of course present evidence that she has suffered, but otherwise her emotional distress claims, in whatever form, are fully recoverable. In all such cases, emotional harm merely represents one element of damage for the tort. Not very accurately, they are called "parasitic damages" in such cases, meaning only that once a personal injury tort is established, all proximate damages are recoverable, including emotional harm damages.

The difficult case for emotional distress recovery, the case that requires this chapter, is quite different. In the difficult case, the plaintiff does not suffer emotional distress from an assault or a libel, or even from personal injury. Instead, the plaintiff claims stand-alone emotional distress. She asserts that although the defendant did not inflict physical harm, the defendant negligently or intentionally inflicted emotional harm by itself. She might be frightened by the defendant's conduct that does not amount to an assault, for example, or deeply distressed at words used by the defendant that do not amount to a libel or slander.

The problem of stand-alone emotional distress has fascinated many lawyers and judges, who have written at length on it.[2] Legal professionals differ very considerably in their attitude toward recovery for emotional distress. Some see the claim as trivial, as a disruption of the judicial process, or even as presenting risks of outright fakery.[3] Others, on the contrary, contend that courts, perhaps reflecting society at large, have not only perpetuated an outmoded dualism but have devalued the importance of emotional life by their caution in granting recovery.[4]

It is certainly true that on the whole, courts have been extremely cautious in allowing claims for stand-alone emotional harm. In the past, at least, courts have often expressed concerns about the reality of emotional distress, but in most cases the reality or existence of the

2. E.g., Nancy Levit, Ethereal Torts, 61 Geo. Wash. L. Rev. 136 (1992); Stanley Ingber, Rethinking Intangible Injuries: A Focus on Remedy, 73 Calif. L. Rev. 772 (1985); Richard N. Pearson, Liability to Bystanders for Negligently Inflicted Emotional Harm—A Comment on the Nature of Arbitrary Rules, 34 U. Fla. L. Rev. 477 (1982); Fowler V. Harper and Mary Coate McNeely, A Re-Examination of the Basis for Liability for Emotional Distress, 1938 Wis. L. Rev. 426 (1938); Calvert Magruder, Mental and Emotional Disturbance in the Law of Torts, 49 Harv. L. Rev. 1033 (1936); Francis H. Bohlen, Right to Recover for Injury Resulting from Negligence without Impact, 41 Am. L. Reg., N.S. 141 (1902).

3. E.g., Richard N. Pearson, supra n. 2.

4. E.g., Leslie Bender, Feminist (Re)torts: Thoughts on the Liability Crisis, Mass Torts, Power, and Responsibilities, 1990 Duke L.J. 848 (1990); Nancy Levit, supra n. 2.

distress is not in doubt. If you are seriously threatened with future harm by a hostile group of masked men who gather around you in a circle, the rest of us should not doubt that you suffered fear. If your child is crushed by a car, we can believe you suffered anguish.

Although stand-alone emotional harm is real and an important concern, and many cases leave us in no doubt about the reality of the distress, emotional harm does have some special characteristics that call for a degree of caution.

First, emotional harm, as distinct from the financial costs of treatment, cannot ordinarily be represented in dollar awards. We may be confident that the plaintiff suffers distress or some other form of diminished enjoyment in life, but seldom can we give reasons why the distress is worth $100,000 rather than one-tenth as much or ten times as much. That makes us uncertain about the justice of awards. Judicial review is correspondingly difficult or impossible. The same difficulty increases risks that the trier will be more influenced by personal feelings or biases for or against the defendant or the plaintiff than by any good estimate of the harm. Problems of this ilk create problems in justice and also in trial strategy and settlement. A defendant who estimates the chance of losing at 50% may offer to settle for something like 50% of the plaintiff's damages. If damages awards for emotional harm are erratic because they have no objective measurement, settlement will be erratic, too, or will depend on extraneous factors. The same point, however, applies to awards for physical pain and suffering, so perhaps it should have little weight as long as courts are willing to award damages for physical pain.

Second, we may be confident that distress is real but quite uncertain how deep-seated it is and what to expect of the plaintiff herself by way of mitigation. The law is usually compelled to attribute a degree of free will to competent actors. An injured person cannot heal a broken leg by acquiring a better attitude about it. But some persons cope with distress better than others; everyone suffers distress in some measure and most people learn to get over or at least to minimize distress over a period of time. Others nurse their distress and build it up. Even under a thin skull rule, the defendant probably should not be liable for the plaintiff's maladaptive attitudes about distress.

Third, we cannot at this juncture be confident about whether awards for distress accomplish compensation. Awards are not likely to approximate what the plaintiff would have paid to avoid the injury or would have accepted to suffer the injury. No matter what the award for emotional distress, the plaintiff may remain distressed. Indeed, it is possible that awarding a person substantial sums for distress will confirm and reinforce the distress and so perpetuate it. Whether this is true or not, it is easy to see that if you recover damages for lost wages, they replace your wage loss, while if you recover damages for pure emotional harm they don't replace your peace of mind.

A more subtle variation on this problem is that if a recovery of damages does in fact provide some solace to the victim, the solace may be small compared to the harm done the defendant. It is true that the defendant was by hypothesis the guilty party and that an award can at least demonstrate society's support for the victim; but an ounce of solace to the plaintiff that costs a pound of pain to the defendant reduces the total happiness in an unhappy world. Perhaps punitive damages would work better than awards for distress if the defendant is truly deserving of punishment, for punitive damages would focus on the defendant's misconduct and guide damages proportionately.

Finally, in some situations (but not all) courts do not see any reasonable limit on the number of emotional harm claims that can be brought as the result of a single tort. Not only may some plaintiffs pursue trivial affronts, but a large number of people might suffer some degree of distress as a result of a single tort. A negligent or intentional killing or beating might shock millions who watch it on television or read about it.

The reasons for caution about emotional distress claims are not reasons to ignore or reject all such claims. Indeed, they provide some guidance for allowing some claims. When common experience tells us that the injury is real and tortiously produced, the reasons for caution suggest that judges can focus on careful assessment of damages rather than on blanket exclusions of stand-alone emotional harm. More radically, it may be suggested that the focus on sudden, shocking events[5] and the dramatic emotional injury that results has distracted attention from chronic emotional harm that may be more devastating—the grief and absence from loss of a loved one rather than the shock at seeing his death.[6]

Topic B. Intentional Infliction of Emotional Harm

§ 303. Rules of Liability for Intentional Infliction of Emotional Harm

Developing Liability for Intentional Infliction of Distress

Carriers, innkeepers, interference with bodies. In the earlier law, damages could not be recovered for stand-alone emotional harm, but courts recognized an exception by imposing a special duty upon common carriers[1] and innkeepers[2] to exercise civility toward passengers. Some courts applied the same rule to telegraph companies, who might, for

5. See § 311.

6. See § 310.

§ 303

1. See Cole v. Atlanta & W.P.R.R., 102 Ga. 474, 31 S.E. 107 (1897); Lipman v. Atlantic Coast Line R.R., 108 S.C. 151, 93 S.E. 714 (1917). Some of the cases, including the two cited in this note, contain elements of slander, but countenance a recovery without the evidence of pecuniary damages that many slander claims would require.

2. See DeWolf v. Ford, 193 N.Y. 397, 86 N.E. 527 (1908).

instance, be held liable for emotional distress caused by failing to deliver a death notice or the like.[3] This rule went far beyond a duty to avoid severe emotional harm; it imposed liability for such minor misconduct as insulting or profane language. The special liability of carriers was somewhat peculiar and courts today might well conclude that liability for a carrier's insult alone is no longer justified because more finely tuned rules now apply to all defendants.[4] However, the liability of carriers and innkeepers probably played a role in developing a degree of responsibility for emotional harm. Courts also allowed recovery of emotional distress in another class of cases—those involving some kind of mishandling of dead bodies.[5] Here they purported to find a property or quasi-property interest in the body,[6] but in reality they were entertaining claims for emotional distress.[7]

Generalizing liability. Over time, still other cases seemed to demand relief. Courts would sometimes find a battery or other tort so that emotional harm damages could be recovered, if need be by stretching rules to find a physical touching or at least physical harm. In a well-known English case, the defendant deliberately told the plaintiff that her husband had been "smashed up" in an accident and that she must go to him immediately. The victim of this atrocious behavior was seriously distressed and suffered some physical consequences of that distress. The court appeared to think that the physical harm as well as the emotional distress must have been intended and partly on that ground recognized liability.[8]

As the exceptions to the rule against liability accumulated, courts and lawyers gradually began to realize that the traditional rule against liability for emotional harm alone no longer accurately stated what courts were doing in fact. In a 1948 Supplement to the First Restatement of Torts, the American Law Institute for the first time recognized a separate tort for intentional infliction of emotional distress. The special rules and exceptional cases are now largely subsumed in this newly recognized tort.

3. Stuart v. Western Union Tel. Co., 66 Tex. 580, 18 S.W. 351 (1885).

4. Cf. Adams v. New York City Transit Auth., 88 N.Y.2d 116, 666 N.E.2d 216, 643 N.Y.S.2d 511 (1996) (abolishing carrier's special liability for acts of employees not in the scope of employment).

5. E.g., Rollins v. Phillips, 554 So.2d 1006 (Ala.1989) (allegedly unauthorized and unneeded autopsy); see Restatement § 868 (also, against much authority, allowing a claim for mere negligence in mishandling a dead body).

6. Some courts still use quasi-property reasoning, e.g., Smialek v. Begay, 104 N.M. 375, 721 P.2d 1306 (1986).

7. The property theory has been generally dismissed as a fiction and displaced in favor of analyzing the claim in terms of emotional distress. See, e.g., Culpepper v. Pearl St. Bldg., Inc., 877 P.2d 877 (Colo. 1994) (requiring, with most courts, intent). All these traditional exceptions, however, often involved a contractual relationship between the plaintiff and the defendant and some of the early carrier and innkeeper cases purported to find an implied contract of courteous treatment. E.g., Chamberlain v. Chandler, 3 Mason. 242, 5 F.Cas. 413 (Cir. Ct. D. Mass. 1823).

8. Wilkinson v. Downton, [1897] 2 Q.B. 57.

The Contemporary Restatement Rule

As revised in the Restatement Second, the Institute recognized a cause of action only when (1) the defendant causes severe emotional distress, (2) intentionally or recklessly, (3) by extreme and outrageous conduct.

Under this formula, the defendant must intend severe emotional harm (or recklessly risk it) and such harm must in fact result. Intent, as elsewhere in the law of torts,[9] can be shown either by evidence that the defendant acted with a desire or purpose to accomplish the harm, or by evidence that such harm was substantially certain to occur.[10] The Restatement says that a reckless or willful attitude will also suffice to meet the requirement.

Neither intent nor recklessness alone suffice to make out the case; the conduct itself must be outrageous. The requirement of outrageous conduct serves to limit the tort, but the same requirement also serves to provide strong evidence of intent and strong evidence that severe harm in fact resulted.[11]

Given evidence of severe distress, the plaintiff is not required to show that she suffers physical symptoms.[12] Almost all courts recognize the tort and apply these basic rules.

§ 304. Common Characteristics of Outrageous Conduct

Excluding insult, offense, and economic information. Misrepresentation of economic facts is in a sense outrageous in some cases and economic loss to the plaintiff is always distressing. Nevertheless, economic representations are usually redressed only by damages for economic loss, not by damages for emotional distress.[1] On the personal rather than the economic level, insult, affront, indignity, trivial annoyance, or the like, are likewise excluded from the outrage category (although perhaps still sufficient in some common carrier cases).[2] An unfair evaluation and discharge from employment may subject the employee to humiliation, but while the evaluation may be offensive, it is not actionable.[3] If the dean loses his temper and refers to the plaintiff

9. On the requirements of intent, see § 24.

10. E.g., Kjerstad v. Ravellette Publications, Inc., 517 N.W.2d 419 (S.D.1994); see Jackson v. Sun Oil Co. of Pennsylvania, 361 Pa.Super. 54, 521 A.2d 469 (1987).

11. See Traynor, J. in State Rubbish Collectors Ass'n v. Siliznoff, 38 Cal.2d 330, 240 P.2d 282 (1952) (plaintiff was surrounded by rubbish collectors who threatened him with quite credible violence if he continued to compete). In Dickens v. Puryear, 302 N.C. 437, 276 S.E.2d 325 (1981) the plaintiff claimed that he had seduced the defendant's daughter and that the defendant responded by handcuffing the plaintiff to farm machinery in an isolated spot and producing four masked men with nightsticks who in turn threatened to castrate the plaintiff. Evidence of physical symptoms would seem redundant.

12. See § 306.

§ 304

1. See Brogan v. Mitchell Int'l, Inc., 181 Ill.2d 178, 692 N.E.2d 276, 229 Ill.Dec. 503 (1998); § 483.

2. See Tetrault v. Mahoney, Hawkes & Goldings, 425 Mass. 456, 681 N.E.2d 1189 (1997).

3. Crowley v. North Am. Telecomms. Ass'n, 691 A.2d 1169 (D.C.App.1997).

faculty member in a "sexist and condescending manner" as a "young woman," his conduct is not actionable, even considering the disparity between the parties and the reality of the distress inflicted.[4] To emphasize the point, courts often join the Restatement in saying that misconduct causing emotional harm alone is actionable only when it is utterly intolerable and goes beyond all bounds of civilized society.[5]

Four markers of outrage. A finding of outrage obviously depends upon the degree of misconduct and the relationship of the parties. However, four important markers tend to support a finding of outrage when the defendant intentionally inflicts emotional harm by (1) abusing his power or position, that is, by using a position of dominance;[6] (2) taking advantage of or emotionally harming a plaintiff he knows to be especially vulnerable;[7] (3) repeating or continuing acts that may be merely offensive and thus tolerable when committed only once,[8] when the plaintiff cannot avoid the defendant's behavior by leaving;[9] (4) committing acts of physical violence or threatening violence of serious economic harm to a person or property in which the plaintiff is known to have a special interest.[10] In none of these instances are the parties in a position of equality; in each of these instances the defendant uses the inequality to inflict emotional harm without regard for the plaintiff's interests.[11]

It should go without saying that not every exercise of power or authority is wrongful. Sometimes it is fully privileged and desirable, even though the person in authority knows that distress will follow. Plaintiffs may be deeply distressed when they are charged with crime or sentenced for it, for example, but the sentencing judge is not liable in tort for inflicting the sentence, nor is the officer for investigating allegations of crime.[12]

4. Taggart v. Drake Univ., 549 N.W.2d 796 (Iowa 1996).

5. E.g., Taylor v. Metzger, 152 N.J. 490, 706 A.2d 685 (1998); cf. Retherford v. AT & T Communications of Mountain States, Inc., 844 P.2d 949 (Utah 1992) (must be "outrageous and intolerable in that it offended against the generally accepted standards of decency and morality," a requirement perhaps addressed to the particular facts of the case).

6. Restatement § 46, cmt. e.

7. Restatement § 46, cmt. f.

8. See Samms v. Eccles, 11 Utah 2d 289, 358 P.2d 344 (1961), modified, Johnson v. Rogers, 763 P.2d 771 (Utah 1988); Kanzler v. Renner, 937 P.2d 1337 (Wyo.1997). Federal and state antidiscrimination law recognizes a similar point; a work environment may be hostile and discriminatory if the harassing conduct is "pervasive" as well as when it is "severe." See Meritor Sav. Bank, FSB v. Vinson, 477 U.S. 57, 67, 106 S.Ct. 2399, 2405, 91 L.Ed.2d 49 (1986).

9. Contreras v. Crown Zellerbach Corp., 88 Wash.2d 735, 565 P.2d 1173 (1977) (workplace harassment).

10. E.g., LaPorte v. Associated Indeps., Inc., 163 So.2d 267, 1 A.L.R.3d 992 (Fla. 1964) (malicious destruction of plaintiff's dog in her presence by throwing a garbage can at the animal).

11. See Daniel Givelber, The Right to Minimum Social Decency and the Limits of Evenhandedness: Intentional Infliction of Emotional Distress by Outrageous Conduct, 82 COLUM. L. REV. 42, 43 (1982) (a kind of private due process in dealings among unequals).

12. Thus the rules of malicious prosecution permit recovery against those who instigate prosecution only under quite limited circumstances. See §§ 429 & 430. Cf. Mantis v. United Cerebral Palsy Ass'n of Nassau County, Inc., 173 Misc.2d 778, 662 N.Y.S.2d 698 (Sup. Ct. 1997) (agency report of suspected abuse of disabled person).

Adverse persons in positions of power. On the other hand, when creditors, insurers, employers, and landlords intentionally inflict distress by abusing their power over others, the abuse itself may show that the conduct is outrageous. Defendants like these are expected to be somewhat adverse to the interests of debtors, employees, and tenants. Creditors, for example, clearly have every right to demand payment. At the same time, their practical power requires a degree of constraint; harassment by repeated demands and threats of illegal enforcement of the debt, if extreme enough, will permit a common law recovery for distress[13] and sometimes a recovery under federal and state statutes as well.[14]

Likewise, insurance adjusters have every right to engage in hard bargaining and to refuse settlements, but not to threaten bodily harm or racial attacks.[15] Landlords need not love their tenants, but to deprive them of electricity in the winter or refuse for weeks to repair a toilet can be an actionable infliction of distress.[16] Employers may place many demands upon employees, but the employer is not free to threaten the employee [17]or to discharge an aging employee and then send him to an utterly fictitious job in another state.[18] Similar things can be said about others in positions of power or authority.[19]

Caretakers and allies in a position of power. Outrage is not, of course, limited to cases of misconduct by a person in an adverse relationship. On the contrary, the misuse of his position by a trusted physician who improperly fondles a patient, for example, may create a sense of outrage partly because the patient expects the physician to protect her interests rather than to act for his own gratification.[20] Some of the outrage in a District of Columbia case derived from the allegation that a police officer, who could be expected to side with the victim of

13. Cadle Co. v. Hobbs, 673 So.2d 1363 (La.Ct.App.1996) (threats to enforce debt in illegal ways, coupled with suggestion that white people like the debt collector could successfully lie about the African-American debtor).

14. See, e.g., Belile v. Allied Med. Accounts Control Associated Bureaus, Inc., 209 B.R. 658 (Bankr.E.D.Pa.1997) (recovery under federal and Pennsylvania debt collection statutes, partly for threatening actions the collector could not or did not intend to take).

15. Brown v. Manning, 764 F.Supp. 183 (M.D.Ga.1991) (obscene words and racial hostility). Outrage and emotional distress may be important as well in bad faith claims against insurers. See William J. Appel, Annotation, Emotional or Mental Distress as Element of Damages For Liability Insurer's Wrongful Refusal to Settle, 57 A.L.R.4th 801 (1988); Gregory G. Sarno, Annotation, Liability of Insurer, or Insurance Agent or Adjuster, For Infliction of Emotional Distress, 6 A.L.R.5th 297 (1993).

16. See Birkenhead v. Coombs, 143 Vt. 167, 465 A.2d 244 (1983); Simon v. Solomon, 385 Mass. 91, 431 N.E.2d 556 (1982).

17. See LaBrier v. Anheuser Ford, Inc., 612 S.W.2d 790 (Mo.Ct.App.1981) (threats to wife of employee to have that an "all points bulletin" would be put out for the employee).

18. Kroger Co. v. Willgruber, 920 S.W.2d 61 (Ky.1996) (claim that employee of 32 years was discharged for refusal to violate ethical rules, sent to a nonexistent job in South Carolina; both breach of contract and emotional distress claims recognized).

19. For example, even one investigating the death of an infant must exercise some restraint. Dunbar v. Strimas, 632 S.W.2d 558, 34 A.L.R.4th 681 (Tenn. Ct. App. 1981) (without scientific basis, investigator told mother of infant who had just died that there was evidence of sexual abuse and all family members would have to be interrogated).

20. See McQuay v. Guntharp, 331 Ark. 466, 963 S.W.2d 583 (1998).

rape, instead allegedly belittled it, joking about the plaintiff's "marital hymen" half an hour after the rape.[21] A spouse who inflicts emotional harm by misusing his position of confidence and emotional alliance with the other spouse might be in the same category, but to a large extent spousal abuse that is neither criminal in nature nor physically harmful has so far been remedied primarily by divorce, not by tort law.[22]

§ 305. Discrimination and Words Causing Emotional Harm

In earlier days of the outrage tort, the defendant's conduct was sometimes an act of violence that shocked or frightened a witness, or was an exceedingly cruel prank aimed as a single vulnerable individual such as a delusional older person.[1] Contemporary cases reach beyond patterns of that kind.[2] They often touch difficult and sensitive issues and matters of policy as well as matters of individual emotional harm, sometimes dealing with distress resulting from discrimination, which may take many forms, including the use of words.

Antidiscrimination statutes. Quite a few state and federal statutes addressed to discrimination on the basis of race, gender, or disability permit recovery of emotional distress damages, sometimes as the only substantial ingredient in the claim. Detailed treatment is quite beyond the scope of this work, but illustrations are in order. A refusal to rent to African Americans or to tenants with children, for example, may require an emotional distress award, although no physical harm is inflicted.[3] Discriminatory denial of medical or dental treatment to those under a disability may be actionable under some state statutes[4] and possibly under the common law outrage cases.[5] The main federal statute on employment discrimination, Title VII, is a little different because job discrimination is likely to entail economic loss, which was the original focus of the statute. However, even under Title VII, some compensation for emotional distress is now recoverable,[6] and in addition, some job discrimination—notably sexual harassment—may also warrant a common law outrage claim.[7] Some statutes, however, are limited to injunctive or other non-damages remedies.

Words: religious freedom. Distress often results from the defendant's threats or other use of words to the plaintiff about the plaintiff or her direct interests.[8] At least when the words are used to others as well as to

21. Drejza v. Vaccaro, 650 A.2d 1308 (D.C.1994).

22. See § 281.

§ 305

1. See Restatement § 46, Ill. 9.

2. Emotional distress is the main, or perhaps the only ingredient in a number of torts named in § 302.

3. Johnson v. Hale, 940 F.2d 1192 (9th Cir.1991) (under federal statute); Human Rights Commission v. LaBrie, Inc., 164 Vt. 237, 668 A.2d 659 (1995) (under state statute).

4. As in D.B. v. Bloom, 896 F.Supp. 166 (D.N.J.1995).

5. Woolfolk v. Duncan, 872 F.Supp. 1381 (E.D. Pa. 1995).

6. E.g., Smith v. Norwest Fin. Acceptance, Inc., 129 F.3d 1408 (10th Cir.1997).

7. See cases cited n. 20.

8. E.g., Dunbar v. Strimas, 632 S.W.2d 558, 34 A.L.R.4th 681 (Tenn. Ct. App. 1981)

the plaintiff, and when the words do not assert falsehoods, liability for use of words alone raises serious problems. The rules for defamation cases limit the occasions for liability based upon publication. Courts could hardly have any reason to erect barriers in defamation law, only to tear them down when the claim is labeled as one for emotional distress. So far as distress results only from publication of false information to others, then, the law of libel or slander is more appropriate than the claim of outrage. At other times, publication of words may be protected by the First Amendment's guarantee of free speech or freedom of religion.[9] California has held that a threat of divine retribution, no doubt distressing to a believer, is not actionable, although fraud that puts the target of religious persuasion in a coercive atmosphere might be.[10] Massachusetts has held that a religious group's teaching that women are inferior to men and that the "female form is the form of evil," though perhaps seriously distressing to a teen-aged female, could not be the basis of a suit because it represented protected religious doctrine.[11]

Words: racial slurs. Conceivably the First Amendment's protection of free speech could impose a degree of constraint on liability for verbal infliction of emotional harm. The Supreme Court has held that a cruel satire of a public figure cannot be actionable unless it could be considered false.[12] The question has been considered in connection with statutory anti-discriminations laws,[13] which to some extent parallel the tort of intentional infliction of distress; but the answer has not identified itself. Courts are clearly reluctant to impose liability for epithets, racial or otherwise, in the absence of repetition or aggravating factors.[14] On the

(words to mother of deceased infant stating that infant may have been sexually abused); cf. Chuy v. Philadelphia Eagles Football Club, 595 F.2d 1265 (3d Cir.1979) (although the plaintiff knew better from his own doctor, defendant released statement to the press that the plaintiff had an incurable disease; this was actionable, although the instructions do not appear to have required intentional falsehood). Many cases cited in § 304 turn mainly on the use of words.

9. See generally, Paul T. Hayden, Religiously Motivated "Outrageous" Conduct: Intentional Infliction of Emotional Distress as a Weapon against "Other People's Faiths," 34 Wm. & Mary L. Rev. 579 (1993).

10. Molko v. Holy Spirit Ass'n for the Unification of World Christianity, 46 Cal.3d 1092, 252 Cal.Rptr. 122, 762 P.2d 46 (1988).

11. Murphy v. I.S.K. Con. of New England, Inc., 409 Mass. 842, 571 N.E.2d 340 (1991).

12. Hustler Magazine v. Falwell, 485 U.S. 46, 108 S.Ct. 876, 99 L.Ed.2d 41 (1988). See § 420.

13. See DeAngelis v. El Paso Mun. Police Officers Ass'n, 51 F.3d 591 (5th Cir. 1995). Among the many articles, two brief ones, representing different views are Deborah Epstein, Free Speech at Work: Verbal Harassment as Gender-based Discriminatory (Mis) Treatment, 85 Geo. L.J. 649 (1997) and Eugene Volokh, Comment, Freedom of Speech and Workplace Harassment, 39 UCLA L. Rev. 1791 (1992).

14. Weller v. Citation Oil & Gas Corp., 84 F.3d 191 (5th Cir.1996) ("Jezebel," with elaborations, of a woman); Ugalde v. W.A. McKenzie Asphalt Co., 990 F.2d 239 (5th Cir.1993) ("Mexican" and "wetback," applied to Hispanic male; offensive but not outrageous enough); Lay v. Roux Labs., Inc., 379 So.2d 451 (Fla.App.1980) (even "nigger" was not enough, apparently because the slur was spoken only once in a co-employee argument over a parking space); Harville v. Lowville Central School Dist., 245 A.D.2d 1106, 667 N.Y.S.2d 175 (App. Div. 1997) ("Polish Nazi" by a teacher about a student not actionable). In Title VII job discrimination cases, courts have said that mere epithets are not enough standing alone; the plaintiff must demonstrate severe or pervasive conditions. See Meritor Savings Bank, FSB v. Vinson, 477 U.S. 57, 67, 106 S.Ct. 2399, 2405, 91 L.Ed.2d 49, 59 (1986) (sexual harassment); Ugalde v. W.A. McKenzie Asphalt Co., supra (racial slurs).

other hand, racial epithets and the like have surely played a part in liability, and may have been decisive, when the defendant's conduct is also arguably outrageous for other reasons as well.[15] At least in some cases, racial slurs or epithets uttered by an employer or supervisor, or by a public officer, may create a hostile and discriminatory work environment that violates anti-discrimination statutes[16] and may also warrant submission of the outrage question to the jury on a common law claim for intentional infliction of distress.[17]

Sexual harassment. So far as sexual harassment involves an unconsented-to bodily touching, it fits the definition of battery and should easily be actionable as such. Damages for the battery include damages for emotional distress. When sexual harassment does not involve a touching, it may take the form of demands for sexual favors, sexual exposure by the defendant, or the like. The defendant who knows his attentions are unwelcome, but who telephones and calls on the plaintiff persistently for months to request sexual contact, is rightly held liable for infliction of emotional distress.[18] The more common case of sexual harassment occurs in the employment context. Sometimes sexual harassment is inflicted by co-workers,[19] but the classic case of abusing power or position occurs when a supervisor or employer engages in or refuses to halt such indignities.

A number of courts have recognized that sexual harassment (at work or elsewhere) justifies a recovery for intentional infliction of distress.[20] The victim may have federal Title VII[21] employment discrimination claims as well as, or instead of, the common law tort claim, but she can ignore those claims and sue in tort if she is so advised. However, state statutes on employment discrimination[22] or on workers' compensa-

15. See Brown v. Manning,764 F.Supp. 183 (M.D.Ga.1991) (adjuster's obscene and racial hostility).

16. Taylor v. Metzger, 152 N.J. 490, 706 A.2d 685 (1998).

17. Alcorn v. Anbro Eng'g, Inc., 2 Cal.3d 493, 86 Cal.Rptr. 88, 468 P.2d 216 (1970) (white foreman firing African–American, calling him a "goddam nigger" in a loud voice); Gomez v. Hug, 7 Kan.App.2d 603, 645 P.2d 916 (1982) (County Commissioner referring to county employee as a "fucking spic" and "fucking Mexican greaser ... a pile of shit"); Taylor v. Metzger, 152 N.J. 490, 706 A.2d 685 (1998) (both a state statutory claim under an antidiscrimination statute and an intentional infliction or outrage claim is made out when a sheriff for whose department she worked referred to the African–American plaintiff in the presence of another officer as a "jungle bunny," an epithet regarded as particularly offensive); see Contreras v. Crown Zellerbach Corp., 88 Wash.2d 735, 565 P.2d 1173 (1977) (racial epithets, little detail provided).

18. Samms v. Eccles, 11 Utah 2d 289, 358 P.2d 344 (1961).

19. E.g., Kanzler v. Renner, 937 P.2d 1337 (Wyo.1997).

20. Ford v. Revlon, Inc., 153 Ariz. 38, 734 P.2d 580 (1987); McQuay v. Guntharp, 336 Ark. 534, 986 S.W.2d 850 (1999) (doctor allegedly fondling patients during physical examination); Kanzler v. Renner, 937 P.2d 1337 (Wyo.1997); see Fisher v. San Pedro Peninsula Hosp., 214 Cal.App.3d 590, 262 Cal.Rptr. 842 (1989) ("by its very nature, sexual harassment in the work place is outrageous conduct"); Kerans v. Porter Paint Co., 61 Ohio St.3d 486, 575 N.E.2d 428 (1991) (employer did not act to deter store manager's harassment, which included some touchings but also included manager's self-exposure and sexual requests; held, claims not barred by workers' compensation exclusive remedy provision).

21. 42 U.S.C.A. § 2000e.

22. See, e.g., Guzman v. Lowinger, 422 Mass. 570, 664 N.E.2d 820 (1996); Fandrich v. Capital Ford Lincoln Mercury, 272 Mont.

tion[23] may preempt the claim for outrage based on sexual harassment.

§ 306. The Severe Distress Requirement

Severe harm required. The tort for intentional infliction of emotional distress requires not only that the defendant intend severe distress, but also that such distress results in fact from the defendant's outrageous conduct. The point is often put emphatically by saying that the distress must be so severe that no reasonable person should be expected to endure it.[1]

Medical evidence. Although severe distress must be demonstrated, and must be caused in fact by the defendant's tortious conduct, medical testimony is not ordinarily required to demonstrate either the severity of the distress or its cause.[2] Part of what we mean by saying that the defendant's conduct was outrageous is that severe distress is likely to follow. Consequently, when reasonable persons could find that the defendant's conduct is outrageous, they can usually also find that the plaintiff's distress was caused by the outrage and is severe. In such cases, the question of causation and severity is for the jury.[3]

Severity; physical impact, harm, symptoms. Neither the Restatement[4] nor most of the cases require proof of physical symptoms for all cases, much less proof of physical harm or impact.[5] Some courts, however, have carried over the requirement of physical manifestation or symptoms from the law of negligent infliction of distress.[6] And all courts require some kind of evidence of severe distress. When the defendant's conduct is extreme enough, that fact tends to prove severe distress.

425, 901 P.2d 112 (1995); cf. Retherford v. AT & T Communications, Inc., 844 P.2d 949 (Utah 1992) (claim based on retaliation for complaining of sexual harassment was preempted in part by Labor Management Relations Act).

23. Doe v. Purity Supreme, Inc., 422 Mass. 563, 664 N.E.2d 815 (1996) (claims against employer for rape by coemployee and allegations of sexual harassment barred by exclusive remedy provision); but cf., Estate of Underwood v. National Credit Union Admin., 665 A.2d 621 (D.C.1995) (when distress arises from sexual harassment, workers' compensation does not apply to bar tort suit).

§ 306

1. E.g., McQuay v. Guntharp, 331 Ark. 466, 963 S.W.2d 583 (1998).

2. See Stump v. Ashland, Inc., 201 W.Va. 541, 499 S.E.2d 41 (1997); cf. Smith v. Norwest Financial Acceptance, Inc., 129 F.3d 1408 (10th Cir.1997) (same, Title VII); Human Rights Com'n v. LaBrie, Inc., 164 Vt. 237, 668 A.2d 659 (1995) (medical evidence would be needed to establish causation of distress if link was obscure, but medical evidence is not usually required for violation of antidiscrimination statutes).

3. See, e.g., Savage v. Boies, 77 Ariz. 355, 272 P.2d 349 (1954). It is, of course, for the court to determine whether the evidence would warrant reasonable people in finding severe distress. Hatch v. State Farm Fire and Cas. Co., 930 P.2d 382 (Wyo.1997).

4. Restatement § 46, cmt. k.

5. See Knierim v. Izzo, 22 Ill.2d 73, 85, 174 N.E.2d 157, 164 (1961) ("jurors from their own experience will be able to determine whether outrageous conduct results in severe emotional disturbance"); Curtis v. Firth, 123 Idaho 598, 601, 850 P.2d 749, 752 (1993) ("Although evidence of physical harm may bear on the severity of emotional harm, it is clear that evidence of physical injury or manifestation is not a required element for the claim of intentional infliction of emotional distress"); Blakeley v. Shortal's Estate, 236 Iowa 787, 20 N.W.2d 28 (1945); Vicnire v. Ford Motor Credit Co., 401 A.2d 148 (Me.1979).

6. Vallinoto v. DiSandro, 688 A.2d 830 (R.I.1997).

When the defendant's conduct is not so extreme, the plaintiff may need proportionately stronger evidence that her distress is severe.[7] By itself, testimony that the plaintiff cried and was upset is simply insufficient.[8]

Some decisions, however, seem to be exceptionally demanding on the severity issue, with the result that a very serious wrongdoer is shielded from responsibility, although he no doubt intended to cause distress and caused it in fact. The Virginia Supreme Court held that 340 hang-up phone calls to a woman from a man she dated only once was not actionable because the plaintiff had shown no physical injury from the stress, had not sought medical attention, and had not lost income.[9] Some other cases have held that proof of a deteriorated sex life[10] and humiliation at constant on-the-job mimicking of a speech impediment[11] is not enough evidence to show severe distress.

§ 307. Emotional Distress of Third Persons

Third person injury pattern. A familiar pattern in the law of torts arises when a defendant acts tortiously toward A but in fact harms B. The pattern appears in the intentional infliction of distress cases as well as elsewhere. Suppose that the defendant threatens to kill a person, A, and makes the threat credible by drawing a pistol. The threatened person may have an action in such a case, possibly one for assault, possibly one for intentional infliction of distress. Now suppose that B is watching the pending murder with increasing fear and apprehension. The question is whether B has an action against the defendant for intentional infliction of emotional distress.

Restatement's conditions for recovery. The Restatement's rule would allow B to recover if either of two conditions is met. First, B could recover if she is "present" when the defendant's conduct takes place and suffers bodily harm as a result of her distress. (This is not a requirement in other kinds of intentional infliction cases). Second, B could recover if she is present and a the defendant's conduct is directed at a member of her family, regardless of any bodily harm.[1]

Rejecting transferred intent. The Restatement's requirement of "presence" is a rejection of the "transferred intent" rule traditionally applied in cases of trespassory torts like battery and assault. The transferred intent rule allows recovery of all damages resulting from battery, assault, false imprisonment and the like, whether those damages were foreseeable or intended or not. But it has no application in negligence cases, or to intentional torts that do not threaten immediate

7. See Stump v. Ashland, Inc., 201 W.Va. 541, 499 S.E.2d 41 (1997) (recognizing the evidentiary relationship between outrageous conduct and severe distress); cf. Millington v. Kuba, 532 N.W.2d 787 (Iowa 1995) (noting court's doubt about outrageousness and holding distress not sufficiently severe).

8. E.g., Hatch v. State Farm Fire and Cas. Co., 930 P.2d 382 (Wyo.1997).

9. Russo v. White, 241 Va. 23, 400 S.E.2d 160 (1991).

10. Vaughn v. Ag Processing, Inc., 459 N.W.2d 627 (Iowa 1990).

11. Harris v. Jones, 281 Md. 560, 380 A.2d 611, 86 A.L.R.3d 441 (1977).

§ 307

1. Restatement § 46 (2).

invasion of a physical interest. If transferred intent rules applied in stand-alone emotional distress claims, presence of the third person would not be required. Because the claim for stand-alone emotional distress is not a traditional trespassory tort like battery, the Restatement is coherent in rejecting transferred intent in these cases.

Accepting substantial certainty intent. On the other hand, the defendant who inflicts harm upon a primary victim knowing that another person is present may have every reason to know that the other person will also suffer emotional harm. By definition, the defendant intends not only the results that he desires to achieve, but also the results he knows to a substantial certainty will follow from his conduct. If he knows that his immediate victim's spouse is watching his attack, terrified that the victim will be killed or tortured, he intentionally inflicts harm on the spouse as well as the immediate victim. So the Restatement, in allowing a claim by one who is present, probably assumes that the defendant is aware of that presence and that his conduct demonstrates that he intends harm in the substantial certainty sense.[2]

Conduct intended to harm those not present. If the defendant's conduct is sufficiently outrageous and intended to inflict severe emotional harm upon a person who is not present, no essential reason of logic or policy prevents liability. So courts have sometimes imposed liability when the defendant tells the plaintiff he will kill her husband and then does so out of her presence,[3] or when the defendant kills himself by slitting his own throat in the plaintiff's kitchen but out of her presence.[4] But millions of people who are not present might conceivably suffer emotional harm if they watch the torture or murder of the President on television. That possibility pushes courts to draw the line against recovery close to home. In a good many cases, courts find it convenient to draw the line against recovery by excluding those who are not present and who have not had an immediate or nearly immediate sensory perception of the primary injury.[5]

Relationship of defendant to plaintiff. When the defendant is in a special relationship with the plaintiff, the relationship rather than the plaintiff's presence may best prescribe the limits of liability. Most states have abolished the alienation of affections or criminal conversation

2. The reasoning in Restatement § 46, cmt. a and the impact of Illustrations 21 and 22 make this clear. See Christensen v. Superior Court (Pasadena Crematorium of Altadena), 54 Cal.3d 868, 903, 820 P.2d 181, 202, 2 Cal.Rptr.2d 79, 100 (1991) (must "occur in the presence of a plaintiff of whom the defendant is aware").

3. Knierim v. Izzo, 22 Ill.2d 73, 174 N.E.2d 157 (1961).

4. Blakeley v. Shortal's Estate, 236 Iowa 787, 20 N.W.2d 28 (1945).

5. Nancy P. v. D'Amato, 401 Mass. 516, 517 N.E.2d 824 (1988) (parent could not recover for sexual abuse of child when parent did not have "substantially contemporaneous knowledge of the outrageous conduct"); H.L.O. v. Hossle, 381 N.W.2d 641, 54 A.L.R.4th 85 (Iowa 1986) (similar, presence required); but cf. Croft v. Wicker, 737 P.2d 789 (Alaska 1987) (allegations that Wicker sexually touched the plaintiff's 14–year-old daughter with resulting distress to the daughter and then to the parents who were nearby but not present and almost immediately learned of it). A claim for loss of filial consortium is now possible in a good many states. See § 310.

actions, and consequently a therapist who seduces his patient has no obligation to the patient's spouse and is not liable for the spouse's emotional injury when the seduction is discovered.[6] But when both spouses are patients of the therapist, the therapist's seduction of one may be an intentional or reckless infliction of distress upon the other in the light of the therapists undertaking to care for both.[7] Possibly also, a therapist who implants in his patient the false belief that her father sexually abused her may be liable for the parent's emotional distress at losing his child's affections.[8]

Bodily harm resulting. When emotional harm is inflicted by conduct "directed at" the plaintiff, the Restatement requires proof of severe emotional harm but does not require any bodily injury resulting from the emotions. When the defendant "directs" his acts at another person, however, the Restatement requires the non-family plaintiff to prove not only the distress but resulting bodily harm. The rule seems to have been adopted from the negligence cases, presumably because the American Law Institute believed that emotional harm to third persons would be less likely or less severe and that bodily harm would guarantee the reality or the extent of the emotional harm. Neither proposition seems necessarily so. A woman who watches deliberate injury to or murder of her husband is likely enough to be distressed. Proof of a resulting rash adds nothing to the reality or the extent of the injury. Such a requirement is being rejected by some courts even in negligent infliction cases,[9] and probably should be discarded in these third person cases as well.

Topic C. Negligent Infliction of Emotional Harm

§ 308. General Rules of Liability for Negligent Infliction of Emotional Harm

Original rule denying recovery. As already indicated, damages for emotional distress are recoverable in connection with many torts, includ-

6. Homer v. Long, 90 Md.App. 1, 599 A.2d 1193 (1992).

7. See Horak v. Biris, 130 Ill.App.3d 140, 474 N.E.2d 13, 85 Ill.Dec. 599 (1985); Rowe v. Bennett, 514 A.2d 802 (Me.1986); cf. Destefano v. Grabrian, 763 P.2d 275 (Colo.1988) (clergy person providing marriage counseling to both spouses and who has sexual intercourse with one of them is liable to the other for outrageous infliction of distress). Something similar has applied in negligence cases. See Marlene F. v. Affiliated Psychiatric Med. Clinic, Inc., 48 Cal.3d 583, 770 P.2d 278, 257 Cal.Rptr. 98 (1989) (therapist treating both mother and son liable to mother for molestation of son); cf. Christensen v. Superior Court (Pasadena Crematorium of Altadena), 54 Cal.3d 868, 820 P.2d 181, 2 Cal.Rptr.2d 79 (1991) (negligent infliction of distress in light of contractual relationship to treat dead body properly, but, paradoxically, no intentional infliction claim since plaintiffs were not present).

8. See Joel Jay Finer, Therapists' Liability to the Falsely Accused for Inducing Illusory Memories of Childhood Sexual Abuse—Current Remedies and a Proposed Statute, 11 J. L. & Health 45 (1996–97) (suggesting liability when therapist creates substantial risks of engendering false memories and false accusations); see § 443.

9. See Molien v. Kaiser Found. Hosps., 27 Cal.3d 916, 167 Cal.Rptr. 831, 616 P.2d 813, 16 A.L.R. 4th 518 (1980), modified, Burgess v. Superior Court, 2 Cal.4th 1064, 831 P.2d 1197, 9 Cal.Rptr.2d 615 (1992).

ing ordinary personal injury cases.[1] When the defendant's negligent act caused emotional distress alone, without causing personal injury, courts at one time simply denied all recovery unless the defendant's act amounted to some other tort such as libel or slander.[2] They tended to think of the emotional harm claim as one for fright or shock, a characterization that still seems to shape some of the rules.[3]

Rationale for denial. Reasons for the complete denial of emotional distress recoveries have tended to sound less persuasive over the years. Lawyers argued that the emotional harm was simply not cognizable in courts of law, that it was not a proximate result of the defendant's negligent act, that it could not be measured in dollars, that it might not be real, and that fraudulent or exaggerated claims might proliferate. These reasons counsel nothing more than the usual trial to determine the reality and extent of the claim and the usual judicial control over excessive verdicts; they do not support an absolute rule against recovery for emotional distress. Consequently, courts today recognize many cases for recovery even while they impose many constraints.

Contemporary allowance of the claim for negligent infliction of distress. When the defendant was negligent and emotional harm was foreseeable and caused in fact by his negligence, most courts today do allow many recoveries for stand-alone emotional harm.[4] At the same time, they remain deeply concerned to impose a limit. Many courts impose special limitations when the plaintiff's distress results from harm to another person.[5] They may correspondingly relax the special demands when the defendant has assumed a duty to the plaintiff or one is imposed by law because of the relationship between the plaintiff and defendant.[6]

These cases aside, most courts hold that the plaintiff can recover only if a normally constituted person would suffer,[7] and the plaintiff in fact suffered severe distress.[8] In addition, they adopt one of the additional restrictions stated below.

1. *Telegraphic death messages and dead bodies. The plaintiff can recover for distress arising only where the defendant negligently transmits or fails to deliver telegraphic messages (wrongly an-*

§ 308

1. § 302.

2. Some of the many articles discussing the rule, usually criticizing it, are listed in § 302.

3. See § 311.

4. Texas insists that the claim for negligent infliction of distress may proceed only if there is a tort to someone, so it may allow the claim of a bystander who witnesses a tort to someone else, but not a claim for distress inflicted more directly. See Boyles v. Kerr, 855 S.W.2d 593 (Tex.1993).

5. § 309.

6. See § 312.

7. See § 313.

8. Bovsun v. Sanperi, 61 N.Y.2d 219, 461 N.E.2d 843, 473 N.Y.S.2d 357 (1984); Johnson v. Ruark Obstetrics and Gynecology Assocs., P.A., 327 N.C. 283, 304, 395 S.E.2d 85, 97 (1990) ("the term 'severe emotional distress' means any emotional or mental disorder, such as, for example, neurosis, psychosis, chronic depression, phobia, or any other type of severe and disabling emotional or mental condition which may be generally recognized and diagnosed by professionals trained to do so"); Heldreth v. Marrs, 188 W.Va. 481, 425 S.E.2d 157 (1992).

nouncing a death, for example)[9] *and sometimes in cases of mishandling of dead bodies.*[10] In both kinds of case, the contractual relationship and its implicit undertakings undoubtedly play a large part in liability.

2. *Physical impact followed by distress. The plaintiff can recover for distress in the first category and those in which distress results from a negligently inflicted physical injury, or at least a physical impact to her body.* A negligently inflicted physical impact to the plaintiff would ordinarily result in enough physical harm to count as a tort in itself, so that emotional harm would be recoverable as parasitic damage. Put differently, once a personal injury is inflicted, emotional harm would not be stand-alone harm but would instead represent an element of damages for the physical injury. But courts ceased to consider whether the impact itself was actionable and mechanically held that if any impact occurred, emotional distress damages could be recovered.[11] Even so, the impact rule would preclude recovery where runaway horses almost ran down the plaintiff, but stopped inches away. Under this rule, a subsequent physical harm such as the plaintiff's miscarriage resulting from the emotional distress did not aid the plaintiff.[12] The rule did not draw the line against liability at a satisfactory place, and it has now been abolished in most states in favor of quite different limitations.[13]

3. *No impact required, but emotional distress followed by physical manifestation or symptom of distress. The plaintiff can recover in the first two categories and also when there is no impact, but the plaintiff's emotional harm must in turn cause or be followed by bodily harm or physical symptoms of the emotional harm.*[14] For

9. E.g., Russ v. Western Union Tel. Co., 222 N.C. 504, 23 S.E.2d 681 (1943).

10. Christensen v. Superior Court (Pasadena Crematorium of Altadena), 54 Cal.3d 868, 820 P.2d 181, 2 Cal.Rptr.2d 79 (1991); cf. Chelini v. Nieri, 32 Cal.2d 480, 196 P.2d 915 (1948) (breach of contract to preserve body). The majority rule probably still rejects recovery for negligent, as opposed to intentional, mishanding of a dead body. See Washington v. John T. Rhines Co., 646 A.2d 345 (D.C.1994).

11. See Rickey v. Chicago Transit Auth., 98 Ill.2d 546, 457 N.E.2d 1, 75 Ill.Dec. 211(1983) (reviewing some of the cases and concluding that in the light of the mechanical or formal application of the rule, impact should not be required).

12. Mitchell v. Rochester Ry. Co., 151 N.Y. 107, 45 N.E. 354 (1896).

13. E.g., Battalla v. State, 10 N.Y.2d 237, 176 N.E.2d 729, 219 N.Y.S.2d 34 (1961); Rickey v. Chicago Transit Authority, 98 Ill.2d 546, 457 N.E.2d 1, 75 Ill.Dec. 211(1983); Niederman v. Brodsky, 436 Pa. 401, 261 A.2d 84 (1970), modified, Sinn v. Burd, 486 Pa. 146, 404 A.2d 672 (1979). All states permitting recovery to a parent who witnesses serious injury or death to her child necessarily reject the impact rule. See § 309. However, although Hawai'i does not require impact to the plaintiff, it says it requires impact to some person or thing. Ross v. Stouffer Hotel Co., 76 Hawai'i 454, 879 P.2d 1037 (1994). Some states retain the impact rule, then create particular exceptions for cases deemed worthy. E.g.,Tanner v. Hartog, 696 So.2d 705 (Fla.1997).

14. Metro–North Commuter R.R. Co. v. Buckley, 521 U.S. 424, 117 S.Ct. 2113, 138 L.Ed.2d 560 (1997) (at least in toxic exposure cases symptoms are required to sustain the action); Keck v. Jackson, 122 Ariz. 114, 593 P.2d 668 (1979); Reynolds v. Highland Manor, Inc., 24 Kan.App.2d 859, 954 P.2d 11 (1998) (fear of AIDS after touching a condom); Simmons v. Pacor, Inc., 543 Pa. 664, 674 A.2d 232 (1996) (pleural thickening, an objectively determined result of ex-

instance, when a man fired a shotgun in a nightclub, killing and injuring people, the plaintiff narrowly escaped harm and attempted to deal with the man. The plaintiff had nightmares, frequent headaches, dizziness, depression, nervousness, weight loss, and poor appetite and was medically diagnosed as suffering from a recognized post-traumatic stress disorder. Nevertheless, his emotional harm claim was rejected because he demonstrated no objectively verifiable physical symptoms.[15] Sometimes, however, courts that require physical symptoms are ready to find such symptoms in fairly transient physical phenomena, as where one plaintiff, confronted with a shock, lost control of bladder and bowel.[16]

Courts requiring objective symptomology argue that the requirement is necessary to establish that the emotional harm is real and, implicitly, that a purely mental disturbance is not worth compensating for mere negligence. The second argument is completely irrelevant to the requirement of symptoms or physical manifestation; emotional harm as such is worth no more or less because of physical symptoms that accompany it. The first argument logically requires the court to reject cases in which the plaintiff fails to prove emotional harm by a preponderance of the evidence, but does not logically require a rule of law. In a Rhode Island case, the defendant negligently delivered the plaintiff's child, causing the child overwhelming brain damage. Although the mother would live with the burden of caring for a child nearly totally devastated in mind and body, the court insisted that if the mother had no physical symptoms of emotional harm she could not recover because emotional harm is too easy to feign.[17]

4. *Evidence of distress or severe distress is required, but physical symptoms of harm is not required. The plaintiff can recover for negligently inflicted emotional harm in any of the categories listed above and also when the plaintiff's evidence shows by a preponderance of the evidence that she in fact suffered serious or severe emotional harm, even if the plaintiff has no physical manifestations or symptoms of that harm.* Courts taking this position argue that the requirement of physical symptoms is overinclusive because it allows trivial and transient symptoms to support the emotional harm claim, and underinclusive because it "mechanically denies" convincing claims for emotional distress. They also point out that the nature of the defendant's conduct is often a better guarantee of genuine emotional harm than mechanical symptoms.[18]

posure to asbestos, is not itself an impact or injury that will support the emotional distress claim); Hougum v. Valley Mem'l Homes, 574 N.W.2d 812 (N.D.1998); First National Bank in Sioux Falls v. Drier, 574 N.W.2d 597 (S.D.1998); Restatement § 436A.

15. Wilson v. Sears, Roebuck & Co., 757 F.2d 948 (8th Cir.1985).

16. Armstrong v. Paoli Mem'l Hosp., 430 Pa.Super. 36, 633 A.2d 605 (1993).

17. Reilly v. United States, 547 A.2d 894 (R.I.1988).

18. Molien v. Kaiser Found. Hosps., 27 Cal.3d 916, 167 Cal.Rptr. 831, 616 P.2d 813, 16 A.L.R.4th 518 (1980), modified, Burgess v. Superior Court, 2 Cal.4th 1064, 831 P.2d

This list of the basic rules does not complete the picture. Emotional harm resulting from risk or injury to another person is treated in a special category of its own. In addition, some courts have also begun to exclude or substantially condition recovery for emotional harms that do not result from a sudden event or threat of an impact. On the other hand, the limiting rules adopted for claims among strangers may not apply when the defendant is under some caretaking duty to the plaintiff. These topics are considered in order.

§ 309. Emotional Harm Arising from Risks or Harms to Others

When the plaintiff is a bystander and not in any special relationship with the defendant,[1] courts have added special other limitations on the plaintiff's recovery for emotional harm. In bystander cases, the plaintiff's emotional harm results from her awareness that another person is in danger or is actually harmed. A mother might fear for her daughter's life if she sees a speeding car bearing down on the daughter; she might suffer shock if she sees the car strike her daughter or discovers the body afterwards.

Traditional rule. Courts have thought of these cases in terms of fear, fright, or shock at another's peril or injury. They originally denied recovery altogether. They argued that when a child was at risk from the defendant's negligence, emotional harm to the mother was "unforeseeable" or that difficulties of proving emotional harm made the claim unjust, or that arbitrary lines would have to be drawn if liability were imposed, so that liability was denied.[2] That view is now almost universally rejected.

Zone of danger/fear for ones' self. The case was different if the mother herself were physically endangered along with her child. If mother and child are both in a crosswalk in the speeder's path, the mother might fear for her own bodily safety as well for that of her child. With the impact rule abolished, the mother could recover for the fear for her own safety, at least if physical symptoms resulted. Given that her cause of action was thus established, she could recover all her damages

1197, 9 Cal.Rptr.2d 615 (1992). Accord: Taylor v. Baptist Med. Ctr., Inc., 400 So.2d 369 (Ala.1981); Corgan v. Muehling, 143 Ill.2d 296, 158 Ill.Dec. 489, 574 N.E.2d 602 (1991) (therapist sex-with-patient case, physical harm not required partly because experts can provide analysis of emotional harm claim); Culbert v. Sampson's Supermarkets, Inc., 444 A.2d 433 (Me.1982); James v. Lieb, 221 Neb. 47, 375 N.W.2d 109 (1985) (distress at another's injury), modified, Vosburg v. Cenex-Land O'Lakes Agronomy Co., 245 Neb. 485, 513 N.W.2d 870 (1994); Paugh v. Hanks, 6 Ohio St.3d 72, 451 N.E.2d 759 (1983); Camper v. Minor, 915 S.W.2d 437 (Tenn.1996). When an independent cause of action is shown—invasion of privacy, for example—the requirement of bodily harm is dropped. See, e.g., Fairfax Hosp. v. Curtis, 254 Va. 437, 492 S.E.2d 642 (1997) (medical providers release of plaintiff's confidential records was actionable for emotional harm without physical harm).

§ 309

1. See § 312.

2. The last major explication of these views was in Amaya v. Home Ice, Fuel & Supply Co., 59 Cal.2d 295, 379 P.2d 513, 29 Cal.Rptr. 33 (1963), overruled in Dillon v. Legg, 68 Cal.2d 728, 69 Cal.Rptr. 72 441 P.2d 912 (1968).

resulting from the tortious conduct, including damages resulting because she feared for her child. This zone of danger rule finds support in the Restatement[3] and a number of the decisions that allow the fear-for-another recovery by a person who was in the zone of danger[4] or deny it to a person who was not in that zone or does not fear for own safety.[5] In some, the plaintiff qualifies for recovery if she is in the zone of danger, even if she does not fear for her own safety,[6] but the plaintiff usually must be in a close relationship with the direct victim, the direct victim must suffer or be perceived to suffer serious injury or death, and the plaintiff must manifest some physical symptom of distress.[7] The Supreme Court of the United States has adopted the zone of danger rule for claims under the Federal Employers' Liability Act, but that is not necessarily persuasive for common law cases because the decision turns in part on a construction of the statute.[8]

Rejecting the zone of danger limitation. The zone of danger or fear-for-oneself rule was an improvement but it still excluded recovery for a mother who watches from safety as the tortfeasor runs down and kills her child. It has even been applied to exclude recovery against a hospital responsible for the abduction of the plaintiff's newborn child.[9] In 1968, the California Supreme Court held in *Dillon v. Legg*[10] that foreseeability of emotional harm should be the general test of liability. Most states now appear to have joined *Dillon* in rejecting the zone of danger limitation in favor of some less mechanical limitations.[11]

3. Restatement § 313(2).

4. Keck v. Jackson, 122 Ariz. 114, 593 P.2d 668 (1979); Bovsun v. Sanperi, 61 N.Y.2d 219, 461 N.E.2d 843, 473 N.Y.S.2d 357 (1984) (family members present in auto when husband/father, standing behind the car, was struck by another vehicle; they were within the zone of danger); cf. Rickey v. Chicago Transit Auth., 98 Ill.2d 546, 457 N.E.2d 1, 75 Ill.Dec. 211(1983) (allowing plaintiff to replead to show zone of danger and fear for himself).

5. E.g., Cauman v. George Washington Univ., 630 A.2d 1104 (D.C.1993); Grube v. Union Pac. R.R., 256 Kan. 519, 886 P.2d 845 (1994) (under FELA); Stadler v. Cross, 295 N.W.2d 552 (1980); Leo v. Hillman, 164 Vt. 94, 665 A.2d 572 (1995).

6. Nielson v. AT & T Corp., 597 N.W.2d 434 (S.D.1999).

7. See, e.g., Pekin Ins. Co. v. Hugh, 501 N.W.2d 508 (Iowa 1993); Nielson v. AT & T Corp., supra n. 6.

8. Consolidated Rail Corp. v. Gottshall, 512 U.S. 532, 114 S.Ct. 2396, 129 L.Ed.2d 427 (1994); see Metro-North Commuter R.R. Co. v. Buckley, 521 U.S. 424, 117 S.Ct. 2113, 138 L.Ed.2d 560 (1997).

9. Johnson v. Jamaica Hosp., 62 N.Y.2d 523, 467 N.E.2d 502, 478 N.Y.S.2d 838 (1984).

10. Dillon v. Legg, 68 Cal.2d 728, 69 Cal.Rptr. 72, 441 P.2d 912 (1968).

11. E.g., Tommy's Elbow Room, Inc., v. Kavorkian, 727 P.2d 1038 (Alaska 1986); Zell v. Meek, 665 So.2d 1048 (Fla.1995); Culbert v. Sampson's Supermarkets, Inc., 444 A.2d 433 (Me.1982); Dziokonski v. Babineau, 375 Mass. 555, 380 N.E.2d 1295 (1978); James v. Lieb, 221 Neb. 47, 375 N.W.2d 109 (1985), modified, Vosburg v. Cenex-Land O'Lakes Agronomy Co., 245 Neb. 485, 513 N.W.2d 870 (1994); Portee v. Jaffee, 84 N.J. 88, 417 A.2d 521 (1980); Johnson v. Ruark Obstetrics and Gynecology Assocs., P.A., 327 N.C. 283, 395 S.E.2d 85 (1990); Paugh v. Hanks, 6 Ohio St.3d 72, 451 N.E.2d 759 (1983); Sinn v. Burd, 486 Pa. 146, 404 A.2d 672 (1979); D'Ambra v. United States, 114 R.I. 643, 338 A.2d 524 (1975) (at least in mother-child cases); Kinard v. Augusta Sash & Door Co., 286 S.C. 579, 336 S.E.2d 465 (1985); Ramsey v. Beavers, 931 S.W.2d 527 (Tenn.1996); Boyles v. Kerr, 855 S.W.2d 593 (Tex.1993); Roitz v. Kidman, 913 P.2d 431 (Wyo.1996) (parent who does not see child killed but sees the body immediately thereafter can recover, but not a parent who only sees the body at a hospital); cf. Heldreth v. Marrs, 188 W.Va. 481, 425 S.E.2d 157 (1992) (approving the *Dillon* factors but perhaps requiring contemporaneous sensory perception).

Under *Dillon,* the foreseeability test was to be supplemented by three guidelines. A finding of foreseeable emotional harm would be more likely if (1) the plaintiff was near the scene at which another was injured or threatened, (2) actually knew of the injury or threat to the other, and (3) was closely related. Under that test, no one of the guidelines was conclusive. Consequently, a family member might recover for emotional harm even if she herself was never endangered and even if she did not learn of the injury until after it occurred. For instance, in a New Jersey case,[12] a small boy was trapped between an elevator door and the wall of the shaft. The elevator moved and dragged him. His mother watched rescue efforts for over four hours while he was dying of massive internal hemorrhaging and suffering great pain. The zone of danger rule would have barred the mother's claim, since she was not in physical danger, but the court allowed recovery under the *Dillon* rule.

From guidelines to rules. The California Court that had created the *Dillon* rule later substantially modified it. Under the new version, the "guidelines" in *Dillon* became precise rules. Regardless of foreseeable and actual emotional harm to the plaintiff, she would be denied recovery under the new rule unless she was actually present and witnessed the injury or threat to a close relation. So a mother who heard her son had been struck by a car, and who rushed to the scene to find her son bloody and apparently dead, could not recover for her own distress because she had not been within the zone of danger and had not actually witnessed the injury.[13] Some courts have accepted this modification of *Dillon* or approximated it with modifications of their own. Usually these slightly different formulations of the rule emphasize the importance of a finding family relationship, that the primary victim was seriously injured or killed, that the plaintiff herself suffered serious or severe emotional distress, and that the plaintiff was either at the scene or arrived before substantial changes occurred.[14]

§ 310. Loss of Consortium

Loss of consortium as a species of emotional harm. When one member of a family is injured or killed, others in the family lose something of the injured person's companionship and society. The loss is obviously different from the shock or fright at witnessing injury of a family member, but it is also obviously similar in that both claims address injuries to emotional well-being. Both injuries are real and of the same essential quality, although the general emotional distress claim

12. Portee v. Jaffee, 84 N.J. 88, 417 A.2d 521 (1980).

13. Thing v. La Chusa, 48 Cal.3d 644, 257 Cal.Rptr. 865, 771 P.2d 814 (1989).

14. Clohessy v. Bachelor, 237 Conn. 31, 675 A.2d 852 (1996); Bowen v. Lumbermens Mut. Cas. Co., 183 Wis.2d 627, 517 N.W.2d 432 (1994) (injury to primary victim must be serious or fatal; the plaintiff must witness some extraordinary event, but that might include arriving at the scene of an accident after it had occurred, and the plaintiff must be spouse, parent, child, grandparent or sibling of injured person); Heldreth v. Marrs, 188 W.Va. 481, 425 S.E.2d 157 (1992) (injury to primary victim must be serious or fatal); cf. Gain v. Carroll Mill Co., Inc., 114 Wash.2d 254, 787 P.2d 553 (1990) (must be present, seeing wreck on television news not enough).

may be generated by an immediate shock, while the consortium claim may be generated by a long-term awareness of loss.

Derivation. As a matter of historical derivation, however, loss of consortium seems little related to the claim for emotional distress. The claim originally asserted that the master—of an apprentice, for example—was entitled to recover because his servant or apprentice had been enticed away or injured by the defendant, resulting in the master's loss of services. By crude analogy, the husband was then allowed to recover when the defendant caused him to lose the services of his wife or child. Thus when a wife or child was injured by the defendant's negligence, the husband as well as the primary victim would have a recovery for his own losses.

Contemporary consortium claims. Contemporary loss of consortium claims differ in three important respects. (1) The emphasis has shifted from pure loss of service claims to losses of various intangibles, usually described as services, society, and sexual intercourse. It includes "the mutual right of the husband and wife to that affection, solace, comfort, companionship, society, assistance, and sexual relations necessary to a successful marriage."[1] (2) The claim is no longer the husband's claim alone; the wife may also sue for loss of her husband's services, society and sexual attention.[2] (3) A similar claim for loss of a parent's society, guidance, and the like is actionable by children in a substantial minority of the states.[3] Occasionally a complementary claim is actionable by parents, usually where the child is severely injured.[4]

Limitations. The loss of consortium claim is strictly a family affair; unmarried cohabitants are generally denied such recoveries.[5] Similarly, a spouse cannot claim for loss of consortium based upon injury inflicted upon the other spouse before marriage.[6] In addition to these limits,

§ 310

1. Wal-Mart Stores, Inc. v. Alexander, 868 S.W.2d 322, 328 (Tex.1993).

2. Hitaffer v. Argonne, 87 U.S. App. D.C. 57, 183 F.2d 811, 23 A.L.R.2d 1366 (1950); Millington v. Southeastern Elevator Co., Inc., 22 N.Y.2d 498, 239 N.E.2d 897, 293 N.Y.S.2d 305 (1968).

3. Children's claims for loss of parental consortium began to be recognized in 1980 with the decision in Ferriter v. Daniel O'Connell's Sons, Inc., 381 Mass. 507, 413 N.E.2d 690, 11 A.L.R.4th 518 (1980). Other courts gradually accepted the claim throughout the 1980s and 1990s. At this writing, about 16 courts have done so. See Giuliani v. Guiler, 951 S.W.2d 318 (Ky. 1997) (where mother died and a separate wrongful death suit was pending). Wrongful death statutes now frequently permit recoveries for lost consortium. The leading article is Jean C. Love, Tortious Interference with the Parent–Child Relationship: Loss of an Injured Person's Society and Companionship, 51 Ind. L. J. 591 (1976).

4. Howard Frank, M.D., P.C. v. Superior Court, 150 Ariz. 228, 722 P.2d 955 (1986) (adult child, severe brain damage); Masaki v. General Motors Corp., 71 Haw. 1, 780 P.2d 566 (1989). Recovery by siblings and stepparents was denied in Ford Motor Co. v. Miles, 967 S.W.2d 377 (Tex.1998).

5. Elden v. Sheldon, 46 Cal.3d 267, 250 Cal.Rptr. 254, 758 P.2d 582 (1988). But cf. Dunphy v. Gregor, 136 N.J. 99, 642 A.2d 372 (1994) (emotional distress recovery for cohabitant who witnessed injury).

6. Sawyer v. Bailey, 413 A.2d 165 (Me. 1980); Hite v. Brown, 100 Ohio App.3d 606, 654 N.E.2d 452 (1995); but cf. Planned Parenthood, Inc. v. Vines, 543 N.E.2d 654 (Ind. Ct.App.1989) (marriage partners who are temporarily separated have consortium rights, so that if one is injured during the separation, the other can recover for loss of consortium, presumably to be determined

courts usually say that the consortium claim is derivative, that is, that it will fail if the primary victim's claim would fail, and that damages will be reduced under comparative fault rules if the primary victim's damages would be reduced.[7] To avoid problems of duplication of damages, courts may require that the consortium claim be joined with the injury claim brought by the primary victim.[8]

Absence of special limiting rules. When loss of consortium can be asserted, courts do not concern themselves with zone of danger rules or demands for physical injury or manifestations of emotional harm. They seem willing to assume the reality of injury, at least when the plaintiff testifies to it. Perhaps the disparity between the treatment of consortium and other forms of emotional distress results in part from the fact that the consortium claim cannot be brought except by a spouse or close family member, and in part from the fact that it had and still has a modest economic component in the loss of services claim. Perhaps courts are simply more comfortable with the evidence that supports the consortium claim. Instead of evidence of a plaintiff who is dysfunctional, near an emotional breakdown, or filled with anxiety, they hear evidence of a comfortable homey relationship that has lost its content: one spouse can no longer go dancing,[9] or the injured spouse can no longer recognize the other.[10] For whatever reason, the special rules limiting emotional distress recovery do not apply to the consortium claim.

§ 311. Emotional Harm without Fright, Shock, or Immediate Force—Fear of Harm from Information and Toxic Exposures

Courts initially thought of emotional distress in terms of fright or shock precipitated by a particular act or event. Perhaps because early cases involved a physical risk to the plaintiff, or because the terms themselves suggested physical danger, courts initially conceived of the emotional harm cases very largely in terms of a sudden physical risk to the plaintiff that did not quite eventuate in bodily harm. The zone of danger rule curiously reflected or reinforced this conception of emotional harm by emphasizing immediate physical danger when fear-for-another was in issue.

The result is that as the older requirements of impact and physical manifestation of injury have been gradually discarded, some courts may be developing a new rule to exclude recovery when the plaintiff's emotional distress is not the result of fear or shock from a near-impact, a sudden event, or threat of immediate physical injury. Some seem to have

on the basis of losses likely to occur upon being reunited).

7. White v. Lunder, 66 Wis.2d 563, 225 N.W.2d 442 (1975); contra, Feltch v. General Rental Co., 383 Mass. 603, 421 N.E.2d 67 (1981) (refusing to reduce a wife's consortium recovery because of the husband's contributory fault).

8. See 2 Dan B. Dobbs, Remedies § 8.1 (5) (1993).

9. Rutherford v. State, 605 P.2d 16 (Alaska 1979).

10. Board of Comm'rs v. Nevitt, 448 N.E.2d 333, 344 (Ind.Ct.App.1983).

consciously created such a rule.[1] Others have done the same thing by applying the zone of danger rule to cases in which danger was not the reason for emotional harm in the first place.[2] The assumption or feeling that some immediate physical danger is necessary would exclude liability in all cases based on distressing misinformation or the failure to provide appropriate information. Conversely, it would permit recovery for emotional harm resulting from an actual impact or a near-miss.

Impact or Specific Incident Causing Fear of Future Harm

When the plaintiff is subjected to actual impact or even a specific intangible trauma like excessive X-rays, she may be able to prove by a preponderance of the evidence that some specific harm will eventuate in the future, or, short of that, may be able to claim recovery because her chances of avoiding future harm are seriously reduced.[3] But even if the plaintiff cannot prove that a disease will result in the future, courts have permitted recovery for reasonable fears that the impact will inflict some future disease. She might fear cancer in the case of excessive x-ray doses[4] or exposure to asbestos that has already actually resulted in some physical harm;[5] she might fear brain damage or paralysis in the case of a head injury that caused loss of cerebral fluid.[6] Even if such harms are not necessarily more probable than not, they are fearsome, and courts have allowed recovery readily enough.[7] Such cases fit the pattern of parasitic damages—emotional harm results from an initial injury and is recovered as one element of damages for that injury.

Courts have also sometimes allowed some claims of fear about future harm even when no impact has occurred at all and the rule for parasitic damages could not be invoked. For example, as a result of a negligent reading of a pap smear test, it appeared that the plaintiff needed no treatment. The error was discovered much later and the needed treatment was given, but the delay made future cancer more likely. The court upheld her claim for emotional distress.[8] Two factors

§ 311

1. Metro–North Commuter R.R. Co. v. Buckley, 521 U.S. 424, 117 S.Ct. 2113, 138 L.Ed.2d 560 (1997); Consolidated Rail Corp. v. Gottshall, 512 U.S. 532, 114 S.Ct. 2396, 129 L.Ed.2d 427 (1994) (construing the Federal Employers' Liability Act); Vosburg v. Cenex–Land O'Lakes Agronomy Co., 245 Neb. 485, 513 N.W.2d 870 (1994) (must be a sudden event). Even when there is a sudden event, such as injury to another, the court may insist that the damages be limited to emotional distress immediately resulting from that event and correspondingly may exclude emotional distress resulting from the victim's later suffering or distress in the form of lost society and companionship. See Keck v. Jackson, 122 Ariz. 114, 593 P.2d 668 (1979); Burgess v. Superior Court, 2 Cal.4th 1064, 831 P.2d 1197, 9 Cal.Rptr.2d 615 (1992).

2. See nn. 18–21.

3. See § 178 & 179 on loss of a chance.

4. Ferrara v. Galluchio, 5 N.Y.2d 16, 152 N.E.2d 249, 176 N.Y.S.2d 996 (1958).

5. Eagle–Picher Indus., Inc. v. Cox, 481 So.2d 517 (Fla.Dist.Ct.App.1985) (plaintiff was already suffering asbestosis from exposure, could properly claim fear of future cancer, even though cancer was not likely enough to warrant a recovery for the cancer itself).

6. Davis v. Graviss, 672 S.W.2d, 928 (Ky.1984).

7. See David Carl Minneman, Annotation, Future Disease or Condition, or Anxiety Relating Thereto, as Element of Recovery, 50 A.L.R.4th 13 (1987).

8. Gilliam v. Roche Biomedical Labs., Inc., 989 F.2d 278 (8th Cir.1993).

especially call for relief in such a case. First, as suggested in the next section, the parties are not strangers; on the contrary, the defendant has undertaken to care for the plaintiff professionally and failed to do so. Second, the fear arises from a specific incident rather than, say, gradual environmental exposure. As indicated below, some courts would deny relief when those elements are not present.

Toxic Exposures Causing Fear and Emotional Distress

Exposure of specific persons to AIDS or other toxins. Exposure to toxic substances like the AIDS virus or carcinogens is also likely to lead to serious distress affecting the quality of life but many courts have shown great caution in adjudicating such claims and have tended to deny recovery. Sometimes the courts have insisted that in the absence of physical harm or symptoms, toxic exposure simply does not qualify as grounds for an emotional distress claim when it does not result from a sudden event or immediate force but only reflects the slow absorption of chemicals.[9]

When the defendant has negligently exposed the plaintiff to a toxic substance like the AIDS virus, fear of future harm from AIDS is a virtual certainty. Over a period of time, this fear may subside if tests repeatedly prove negative, but at least during the "window of anxiety," until tests can establish the plaintiff's health, the fear seems to be reasonable in the sense that most people in our culture would suffer a similar fear. Courts have usually insisted, however, that the plaintiff must prove not only that her fear was reasonable but also that she was "actually exposed" to the virus, not merely in a general way, but through a channel that could cause AIDS. For instance, if the plaintiff is negligently stuck with a used hospital needle which cannot be identified and tested, she might reasonably fear contamination and the possibility of AIDS, but if she cannot show that the needle was in fact contaminated, or that she suffers some immediate physical injury, a number of courts hold that she has no claim for emotional distress even though she sustained a physical impact.[10] Or the plaintiff in an emergency room is seated in a pool of unidentified blood. He cannot recover for his fear of AIDS unless he can show that the blood actually entered his body.[11]

Some courts have made this requirement of "actual exposure" quite stringent. In a Minnesota case,[12] the plaintiff's physician had lesions on his hands and forearms. He performed gynecological examinations upon

9. Vosburg v. Cenex–Land O'Lakes Agronomy Co., 245 Neb. 485, 513 N.W.2d 870 (1994). The Federal Employers' Liability Act is construed to impose a similar "near miss" requirement. See Metro–North Commuter R.R. Co. v. Buckley, 521 U.S. 424, 117 S.Ct. 2113, 138 L.Ed.2d 560 (1997) (asbestos exposure without present symptoms).

10. Majca v. Beekil, 183 Ill.2d 407, 701 N.E.2d 1084, 233 Ill.Dec. 810 (1998); Carroll v. Sisters of Saint Francis Health Servs., Inc., 868 S.W.2d 585 (Tenn.1993). Contra, Howard v. Alexandria Hosp., 245 Va. 346, 429 S.E.2d 22 (1993).

11. Barrett v. Danbury Hosp., 232 Conn. 242, 654 A.2d 748 (1995) (rejecting the actual exposure test but concluding as a matter of law that the plaintiff's fear was not reasonable).

12. K.A.C. v. Benson, 527 N.W.2d 553 (Minn.1995).

the plaintiff and others. He tested positive for HIV (the AIDS virus), so there was a risk to his patients in spite of the fact that he used gloves in performing the examinations. The court imported the zone of danger rule from the fear-for-another setting and held that the plaintiff could not recover for emotional distress at her fear that she might suffer AIDS. She had not demonstrated "actual exposure."

Several major decisions have now taken a different view, saying that if the defendant negligently subjected the plaintiff to a reasonable fear of exposure to AIDS, for example if she is stuck by a needle that cannot be tested, that will be enough to warrant a recovery for the period until testing can reasonably assuage that fear.[13] On the other hand, the United States Supreme Court, construing the Federal Employers' Liability Act, concluded that even if the plaintiff had been subjected to actual contact with asbestos dust, that contact could not count as an impact required under the statute.[14]

Environmental contamination and exposures. Some kinds of activities with toxic materials expose many people to risks of future physical harm. For example, if the defendant dumps toxic wastes that leach into the groundwater, many people may be exposed to the contaminated water and some of them may suffer cancer many years later as a result. Have they a present claim based on their fear of future disease? In *Potter v. Firestone Tire & Rubber Co.,*[15] the California Supreme Court addressed just such a case. That court concluded that in the absence of grounds for imposing punitive damages, the claim for fear of future cancer could not proceed unless the plaintiff also proved that cancer was more likely than not to occur.

The logical effect is that the plaintiff cannot recover for emotional distress at the prospect of cancer unless she can recover for the cancer itself. In part, the decision turned on the court's heavily weighted concern that enormous numbers of persons are exposed to toxins everyday, that claims for feared future harm might overwhelm the tort system with its infrastructure of liability insurance, and that manufacturers of useful products like drugs might be so fearful of unfair liabilities that they would reduce the drugs available. The court's own fears applied only to cases of broad exposure, not to cases in which only a limited

13. Faya v. Almaraz, 329 Md. 435, 620 A.2d 327 (1993) (doctor's invasive operations on women without informing patient that he was an HIV carrier, recovery for the window of anxiety period); Hartwig v. Oregon Trail Eye Clinic, 254 Neb. 777, 580 N.W.2d 86 (1998) (distinguishing many cases and noting that if the plaintiff is expected to take safety precautions for the protection of others, she can reasonably fear AIDS); Williamson v. Waldman, 150 N.J. 232, 696 A.2d 14 (1997) (reasonable fear standard, imputing to the plaintiff "that level of knowledge of the disease that is then-current, accurate, and generally available to the public").

14. Metro–North Commuter R.R. Co. v. Buckley, 521 U.S. 424, 117 S.Ct. 2113, 138 L.Ed.2d 560 (1997). Contrast Plummer v. United States, 580 F.2d 72 (3d Cir.1978) where a prisoner was infected with tuberculosis but not suffering from it. Since the tubercle bacili were actually in his body the court found sufficient impact to permit an emotional distress claim based on the fear that it would be activated in the future.

15. Potter v. Firestone Tire & Rubber Co., 6 Cal.4th 965, 25 Cal.Rptr.2d 550, 863 P.2d 795 (1993).

number of specific plaintiffs were exposed. Even so, the court's decision was immediately adopted as a basis for excluding emotional distress recovery from a doctor suffering from AIDS who exposed his patient to that disease in spite of her insistence that she wanted a surgeon who was not infected.[16] On the other hand, the *Potter* approach was rejected where the plaintiff's fear of future cancer allegedly arose because her doctor's delay in diagnosing and removing a cancer made a later recurrence more likely.[17]

Information Causing Emotional Distress without Immediate Physical Injury

Erroneous or inadequate information supplied to the plaintiff. Courts that follow the zone of danger rule sometimes apply it to exclude recovery for harms not based on danger at all, as where a doctor negligently causes his patient to lose the baby she is carrying[18] or harms a child in the course of delivery,[19] or fails to provide appropriate information about genetic defects of a fetus.[20] Such decisions treat physical danger as the single basis for emotional harm and at the same time in effect ignore the duties undertaken by health care professionals.

The same is true when courts reject emotional harm resulting from a misdiagnosis. Suppose the defendants tested the plaintiff for AIDS but negligently and erroneously reported to her that she was infected with the disease when she was not. Since AIDS is presently incurable and almost certainly deadly, the diagnosis is bound to be severely distressing, but the diagnosis itself does not place anyone in danger. Some decisions deny any recovery to the victim of this negligent misdiagnosis because the diagnosis does not endanger the victim in a physical way,[21] although others recognize that emotional harm from this kind of misinformation is foreseeable and worthy of redress.[22]

Erroneous or private information published to others about the plaintiff. Tort law has traditionally recognized that misinformation published *about* the plaintiff can be emotionally and otherwise harmful. Consequently, actions for libel, slander, malicious prosecution, and invasion of privacy, all of which are sometimes based upon publication about the plaintiff, may redress emotional harms. Courts have limited such actions, however, for special reasons of policy that apply to communica-

16. Kerins v. Hartley, 27 Cal.App.4th 1062, 33 Cal.Rptr.2d 172 (1994).

17. Boryla v. Pash, 960 P.2d 123 (Colo. 1998).

18. Tebbutt v. Virostek, 65 N.Y.2d 931, 483 N.E.2d 1142, 493 N.Y.S.2d 1010 (1985).

19. See Carey v. Lovett, 132 N.J. 44, 622 A.2d 1279 (1993) (father denied recovery for his emotional harm).

20. Cauman v. George Washington Univ., 630 A.2d 1104 (D.C.App.1993).

21. R.J. v. Humana of Florida, Inc., 652 So.2d 360 (Fla.1995); Heiner v. Moretuzzo, 73 Ohio St.3d 80, 652 N.E.2d 664 (1995).

22. Chizmar v. Mackie, 896 P.2d 196 (Alaska 1995) (AIDS misdiagnosis); Bramer v. Dotson, 190 W.Va. 200, 437 S.E.2d 773 (1993); cf. Molien v. Kaiser Found. Hosps., 27 Cal.3d 916, 167 Cal.Rptr. 831, 616 P.2d 813, 16 A.L.R.4th 518 (1980) (misdiagnosis of spouse), modified, Burgess v. Superior Court, 2 Cal.4th 1064, 831 P.2d 1197, 9 Cal.Rptr.2d 615 (1992).

tions, for instance, policies associated with free speech and those favoring a report of suspected crime.

Because defamation, privacy and other such actions are available and because they reflect the courts' efforts to balance free speech and other policies against the need for redress, the more general claim for negligent infliction of distress may be inappropriate when the plaintiff is aggrieved by publication to others. The Texas Court denied recovery to a plaintiff whose companion secretly videotaped their sexual acts, then showed the tape to people in the community.[23] Such a betrayal surely warrants a recovery of some kind, but perhaps the rules of privacy invasion or breach of confidence rather than negligence furnish the more suitable approach.[24] Similarly, if the defendant complains to authorities that the plaintiff has stolen his property, the plaintiff may be distressed at the accusation, but recovery probably should be limited by the rules applied in malicious prosecution cases which attempt to balance the need to report suspected crime against the rights of the accused. One court, however, apparently allowed the general emotional distress claim to proceed in such a case.[25]

§ 312. Removing Restrictions on Emotional Harm Claims

Assumed or Independent Duties

Bystander setting. When the plaintiff suffers emotional harm because a stranger creates a risk or causes an injury to another person, almost all courts apply some kind of special rule to limit the cases in which the bystander-plaintiff can recover. Even under the most generous of these rules, the plaintiff ordinarily must be aware of injury when it is happening or soon thereafter.[1] The zone of danger rule and its modern substitutes may now apply, however, when the defendant assumes a duty to the plaintiff or stands in a special relationship to the plaintiff and owes her a duty of care independent of the care owed to others.

Assumed duty under the Burgess rule. A example of a case in which the special bystander rules are not needed and not applied is California's decision in *Burgess v. Superior Court.*[2] Burgess obtained prenatal care from Dr. Gupta and others. After Burgess entered labor, Gupta diagnosed a prolapsed cord, meaning the child would not receive sufficient oxygen. For reasons not explained in the opinion, 44 minutes elapsed before the child was taken by Cesarean Section. By that time, the child had suffered severe brain damage from oxygen deprivation. A suit was

23. Boyles v. Kerr, 855 S.W.2d 593 (Tex. 1993).

24. A privacy claim was supported in Fontaine v. Roman Catholic Church, 625 So.2d 548 (La.Ct.App.1993) (allegations that a priest sexually abused 17–year-old then later published photographs and video tapes).

25. Sacco v. High Country Independent Press, Inc., 271 Mont. 209, 896 P.2d 411 (1995).

§ 312

1. § 309.

2. Burgess v. Superior Court (Gupta), 2 Cal.4th 1064, 831 P.2d 1197, 9 Cal.Rptr.2d 615 (1992).

brought for the child and Burgess brought her own suit for emotional harm. California had repudiated the zone of danger rule, but would still exclude the plaintiff's emotional harm claim unless the plaintiff was contemporaneously aware of the child's injury. Burgess may not have been aware of her child's injury until much later. Nevertheless, the California Court thought that the plaintiff could recover. The key point was that the plaintiff and defendant were already in a physician-patient relationship. The physician's duty to the mother was not derivative of some duty to the child; he owed her a direct duty of care based on the duty he assumed by entering the physician-patient relationship.

Support for the Burgess assumed or independent duty. The *Burgess* idea is relatively new and seems not to have been argued in a number of cases. Some cases quite similar to *Burgess* on their facts have rejected the mother's claim without mentioning the idea that the physician-patient relationship created a duty of care to her that would not otherwise exist.[3] A New Jersey case in a similar factual setting accepted the idea that the physician owed an independent duty to the mother and thus, as in *Burgess,* allowed her claim to proceed even if she had not contemporaneously observed the negligence and the injury. Courts also reach results entirely consistent with the independent duty analysis when they permit recovery for emotional distress in wrongful birth cases.[4] The idea that a contractual or similar relationship can bespeak a duty assumed by the defendant or one imposed by law is itself of respectable lineage. The early allowance of emotional distress damage in suits against carriers, innkeeper, and telegraph companies was based precisely on the consensual relationship between the plaintiff and the defendant.[5]

Rationale. When the defendant owes an independent duty of care to the plaintiff, there is no risk of unlimited liability to an unlimited number of people. Liability turns solely on relationships accepted by the defendant, usually under a contractual arrangement. Consequently, the duty extends only to those for whom the contract was made. When the defendant contracts to provide services for childbirth, he is on notice that negligent acts will likely cause emotional harm. For these two reasons, the zone of danger and contemporaneous awareness rules are not needed to limit liability to an appropriate sphere. An assumed duty or a special relationship with a duty imposed by law might arguably eliminate other restrictive rules, for example, those requiring a physical manifestation or symptom of harm and those requiring a sudden event, but courts have not yet developed the logic of assumed duty.

Other assumed duty cases. Although the childbirth setting is perhaps the most prominent example of the independent duty, the same reasoning can be applied whenever the defendant assumes a duty by contract or otherwise and when that duty encompasses the plaintiff's emotional well-being. A therapist who agrees to treat the plaintiff is assuming a

3. Cauman v. George Washington Univ., 630 A.2d 1104 (D.C.App.1993).

4. See § 291.

5. See § 303.

duty to exercise care for the plaintiff's emotional condition; if he instead negligently inflicts emotional harm, he is responsible.[6] The mortuary contracting to provide appropriate embalming and burial seems to be an obvious example. If the mortuary's work is negligent and it provides a body in a ruinous condition for an open casket service, the case for emotional harm damages to the survivors exactly fits the assumed or independent duty analysis. The duty assumed by the mortuary expressly or impliedly was a duty to take care for the feelings of the survivors and the class of persons who could claim such a duty is limited to those for whom the contract was made. Consequently, it is no surprise to see that California has entertained a claim for emotional distress by survivors when bodies were mishandled by mortuaries.[7] But again, some cases have rejected liability, perhaps because the assumed or independent duty argument was not presented.[8]

Scope of the assumed or independent duty. The scope of the independent duty owed by the defendant "directly" to the plaintiff dictates the limits of liability. If the physician assumes a duty of care to his patient, liability to the patient for negligently inflicted emotional harm seems to follow. But assumption of a duty to the mother does not necessarily mean an assumption of a duty to the father. If the relationship and the concomitant duty are construed narrowly as a physician-patient duty, then the father who suffers emotional harm when the baby is injured at delivery has no claim unless he meets the bystander or loss of consortium rules applied in the particular jurisdiction.[9] The nature and scope of the duty assumed or imposed by law because of the relationship is a matter for the court to decide. A little authority supports a claim for emotional distress by one family member when a physician provides an erroneous and distressing diagnosis to another family member.[10]

Abolishing Restrictive Rules

It is too soon to know whether the assumed or independent duty approach will have a large impact on emotional distress claims. In the meantime, however, at least two courts have expressed a desire to eliminate all the restrictive rules.

6. Corgan v. Muehling, 143 Ill.2d 296, 574 N.E.2d 602, 158 Ill.Dec. 489 (1991).

7. Christensen v. Superior Court, 54 Cal.3d 868, 2 Cal.Rptr.2d 79, 820 P.2d 181 (1991) (particularly abhorrent practices by mortuaries, including harvesting of organs for sale, but liability turned on the assumed duty, not the horrible acts).

8. See Washington v. John T. Rhines Co., 646 A.2d 345 (D.C.1994) (survivors were not in zone of danger from negligent embalming (nobody was), hence could not recover, relying in part on zone of danger cases in which the defendant was a stranger).

9. Carey v. Lovett, 132 N.J. 44, 622 A.2d 1279 (1993). Besides the physician-patient relationship, the court emphasized foreseeability and the unique connection of mother and child.

10. Molien v. Kaiser Found. Hosps., 27 Cal.3d 916, 167 Cal.Rptr. 831, 616 P.2d 813, 16 A.L.R.4th 518 (1980) (health care provider negligently diagnosed syphilis in wife, husband could recover for his distress), modified, Burgess v. Superior Court, 2 Cal.4th 1064, 831 P.2d 1197, 9 Cal.Rptr.2d 615 (1992).

The scope of these decisions, too, remains to be seen. In the first, the Montana Court seemed to hold that the plaintiff could recover for emotional distress incurred when the defendants told authorities that she had stolen goods. The court phrased its new rule broadly: "An independent cause of action for the tort of infliction of emotional distress will arise under circumstances where serious or severe emotional distress to the plaintiff was the reasonably foreseeable consequence of the defendant's negligent or intentional act or omission.... "[11] Because the claim was based in part on a report to authorities that attributed a crime to the plaintiff, the claim would ordinarily be handled under a malicious prosecution theory, with all the special rules that entails. If the negligent infliction claim displaces malicious prosecution (and perhaps other torts), the rules designed to encourage reports to authorities will be substantially undermined. If general foreseeability becomes sufficient to make an emotional distress claim, it may become important to carve out cases that are subject to special rules that apply in cases for malicious prosecution, defamation, privacy invasion and the like.

In 1996 a Tennessee case also abolished special rules for emotional distress. It substituted a general test of foreseeability instead.[12] But that court expressly recognized that the foreseeability test might end up in much the same way as under the restrictive rules. For instance, a plaintiff who was in the zone of danger might be a readily foreseeable victim of emotional distress, while a bystander outside the zone might be required to show some other evidence, such as a close relationship with the injured person, that brought her within the range of foreseeability.[13] It thus remains to be seen whether adoption of the general foreseeability approach, which treats emotional harm like any other injury, will expand liability or whether it will instead be applied to obtain results similar to those the courts now get.

§ 313. Sensitive Plaintiffs

Earlier cases relied on mechanical limitations to exclude recovery for emotional distress. As those limitations have been slightly liberalized, courts have come to insist that the plaintiff demonstrate not only emotional distress, but severe or serious emotional distress. To this they have sometimes added that the defendant's conduct must have been such that it would have severely distressed a reasonable person who is normally constituted.[1]

This requirement that the plaintiff be normally constituted or "reasonable," requires some interpretation. It does not mean that the plaintiff's special vulnerabilities are ignored. If the defendant knows or

11. Sacco v. High Country Indep. Press, Inc., 271 Mont. 209, 220 896 P.2d 411, 418 (1995).

12. Camper v. Minor, 915 S.W.2d 437 (Tenn.1996).

13. See Ramsey v. Beavers, 931 S.W.2d 527 (Tenn.1996).

§ 313

1. E.g., Culbert v. Sampson's Supermarkets, Inc., 444 A.2d 433 (Me.1982); Sinn v. Burd, 486 Pa. 146, 404 A.2d 672 (1979).

should know that he deals with an especially sensitive plaintiff, that is all the more reason for care. Thus a therapist treating a emotionally distressed patient would know of her special vulnerability and be expected to act with reasonable care for that condition. If he does not, liability for her emotional distress is entirely proper.[2]

Neither does the normal person rule mean that the plaintiff is limited to an amount of damages that would be incurred by a normal person. If the defendant's conduct would subject him to liability for severe distress to a normal person, he is also liable for damages to an especially sensitive person, even if those damages are much greater because of the special sensitivity.[3] This rule is merely the familiar thin skull or eggshell skull rule as applied to emotional harm.

On the other hand, the normal person rule excludes compensation for emotional harm when a normal person would suffer no serious emotional harm at all. In a North Carolina case, the defendant negligently struck the plaintiff's car, which could be expected to cause anger or distress, but not severe distress. In fact, however, the plaintiff went into a terrible emotional state, imagining that she had somehow struck a child on a bicycle. She suffered manifestly real harm, but the court denied recovery.[4] Such a result seems logical under the normal person rule. If only transient distress is foreseeable to a normal person and the defendant neither knows nor should know of the plaintiff's special sensitivity, serious distress is by definition not foreseeable.

2. As in Corgan v. Muehling, 143 Ill.2d 296, 574 N.E.2d 602, 158 Ill.Dec. 489 (1991).

3. Miley v. Landry, 582 So.2d 833 (La. 1991). See Steinhauser v. Hertz Corp., 421 F.2d 1169 (2d Cir.1970).

4. Williamson v. Bennett, 251 N.C. 498, 112 S.E.2d 48 (1960); see also McMahon v. Bergeson, 9 Wis.2d 256, 101 N.W.2d 63 (1960).

Chapter 21

Nonaction and Contract: Rescue and Protection

Topic A. The General Rules of Nonaction

§ 314. The No–Duty–To–Act Rule and Its General Exceptions

General rule. Unless the defendant has assumed a duty to act, or stands in a special relationship to the plaintiff, defendants are not liable in tort for a pure failure to act for the plaintiff's benefit. The fact that the defendant foresees harm to a particular individual from his failure to act does not change the general rule. These propositions are widely accepted and acted upon.[1]

Examples. The Restatement illustrates the classic general rule by supposing that the defendant sees an unsighted person about to step in front of an approaching car. The defendant could prevent his injury or death by a word or touch, without danger to the defendant and without delaying the defendant's own progress. But he does nothing to prevent injury, which in fact follows. The general rule applies to relieve the defendant of any liability.[2] The cases are seldom so dramatic, but they accept and apply the rule.[3]

§ 314

1. A notable exception is a Vermont statute requiring assistance when the defendant knows of grave physical danger to another and can assist without danger to himself. Vt.Stat.Ann. Tit. 12, § 519. Another is the decision in Soldano v. O'Daniels, 141 Cal.App.3d 443, 190 Cal.Rptr. 310, 37 A.L.R. 4th 1183 (1983) where the plaintiff alleged that a patron of Happy Jack's Saloon went across the street to the Circle Inn and asked the bartender there to call the police or to permit the patron to do so because a man had been threatened in Happy Jack's. The bartender refused to call or to permit the patron to do so. The plaintiff's father was shot and killed in Happy Jack's Saloon, presumably after the effort to call the police. The court thought that the rule of non-liability for nonfeasance should be re-examined. Circle Inn "displayed a disregard for human life that can be characterized as morally wrong" and the burden of permitting use of the phone in a public place of business would have been minimal.

2. Restatement § 314, Illus. 1.

3. See Yania v. Bigan, 397 Pa. 316, 155 A.2d 343 (1959) (although defendant had challenged a neighbor to jump into a pit of water on the defendant's land, defendant had no duty to save the neighbor when he was drowning); Long v. Patterson, 198 Miss. 554, 22 So.2d 490 (1945) (no duty to warn of dangerous approaching traffic); Krieg v. Massey, 239 Mont. 469, 781 P.2d 277 (1989) (manager of apartment house, who had power to take gun from suicidal tenant, had no duty to do so and is not liable for his death); cf. Rockweit v. Senecal, 197 Wis.2d 409, 541 N.W.2d 742 (1995) (duty is owed to everyone, but as a matter of policy defendant is not liable for failure to put out neighbor's campfire for protection of neighbor's child). The rule frequent-

Supporters and critics. Many scholars have offered their thoughts on the general rule. In favor of the rule, or some version of it, Professor Epstein emphasizes the importance of individual freedom of action, the absence of any moral duty to act, and the very considerable difficulty of administering any general duty to act for the benefit of others.[4] Professor James Henderson thinks a general duty of reasonable rescue would violate important legal process values and would be unmanageable.[5] Many other scholars have expressed differing views in various degrees.[6] One line of thought is that the rule should be rephrased to impose an affirmative duty to act, at least in an "emergency," when reasonable people would do so, or when the defendant has special power to prevent harm with little effort, especially if that power was derived in part from legal rights or privileges.[7] Those who favor a general duty to act when reasonable people would do so believe the law should reflect virtues like compassion as well as a central interest in liberty.[8]

Exceptions. There are relatively few cases as simple at the Restatement's illustration, but the rule is not limited to emergencies or failure to rescue. For example, the rule is embedded in the question whether the defendant owes a duty to protect the plaintiff from harms inflicted by others.[9] In the context of rescue, where the rule is normally discussed, however, litigation is apt to turn, not on the existence of the rule, but its scope and exceptions. In fact, it may be that properly understood exceptions have the effect of creating a duty to act in most instances where a reasonable person would feel compelled to act.

The exceptional cases in which a duty of care may require reasonable affirmative steps by the defendant include: (1) the defendant or his instrumentalities, innocently or not, have created risks or caused harm to the plaintiff; (2) the defendant is in a special relationship to the plaintiff that is deemed to create a duty of care that encompasses affirmative action; (3) the defendant takes affirmative action that is either cut short or performed negligently; and (4) the defendant has

ly takes on a somewhat different form in the insistence that the defendant is under no duty to control others to save the plaintiff. See §§ 322–332.

4. Richard Epstein, A Theory of Strict Liability, 2 J. Leg. Studies 151, 198 ff. (1973).

5. James A. Henderson, Jr., Process Constraints in Tort, 67 Cornell L. Rev. 901 (1982).

6. E.g., Adler, Relying upon the Reasonableness of Strangers: Some Observations about the Current State of Common Law Affirmative Duties to Aid or Protect Others, 1991 Wis. L. Rev. 867; Thomas C. Galligan, Jr., Aiding and Altruism: A Mythopsycholegal Analysis, 27 U. Mich. J.L. Ref. 439 (1994); Steven J. Heyman, Foundations of the Duty to Rescue, 47 Vand. L. Rev. 673 (1994); Jean Etling Rowe and Theodore Silver, The Jurisprudence of Action and Inaction in the Law of Tort: Solving the Puzzle of Nonfeasance and Misfeasance from the Fifteenth Through the Twentieth Centuries, 33 Duquesne L. Rev. 807 (1995); Ernest J. Weinrib, The Case for a Duty to Rescue, 90 Yale L. J. 247 (1980).

7. See Marshall S. Shapo, The Duty to Act: Tort Law, Power & Public Policy 69–73 (1977) (summarizing thesis).

8. See Thomas C. Galligan, Jr., supra n. 6; Leslie Bender, A Lawyer's Primer on Feminist Theory and Tort, 38 J. Leg. Educ. 3, 33–36 (1988) (but rejecting a reasonable care standard in favor of a judgment about the defendant's state of mind, which is to be one of conscious care and concern).

9. See Chapter 23.

assumed a duty of affirmative care by action or promise that evinces such an assumption.

These exceptions to the no-duty-to-act rule do not impose strict liability. When courts recognize a duty to act affirmatively for the plaintiff's benefit, they only impose a duty to act when reasonable people would do so. Consequently, the officer need not rescue occupants of a burning car if to do so would subject him to unreasonable danger. The rules of causation likewise apply. The courts' conclusion that the defendant is under a duty to act is thus not a resolution of the case. It is rather a step that permits evaluation of the negligence and causal issues.

§ 315. Scope of the Rule Protecting Nonaction

The meaning of nonaction, or "nonfeasance"[1] as it is often called, may seem self-evident. However, many omissions to act are not regarded as nonfeasance at all but as only a part of some larger action. If, driving your car, you fail to apply your brakes when you approach a person in a crosswalk, you cannot defend his claim for injury by saying you did nothing. In such a case, you drove a car and did it very badly and will be chargeable with a negligent act, not merely with nonfeasance.

Similarly, if a contractor acting under public authority digs a hole in the highway, then fails to light it at night, courts do not think that failing to light it is nonfeasance. The failure to light is merely one part of a course of affirmative conduct—digging improperly without lighting or guarding the excavation.[2]

With cases like these in mind, courts very often instruct the jury that negligence includes "the omission to do something" a reasonable person would do as well as the doing of something a prudent person would not do.[3]

But no rule has been formulated to prescribe whether courts are to characterize conduct as affirmative action with an embedded omission or as simple nonaction. In *Jackson v. City of Joliet,*[4] an officer encountered a flaming car that had gone off the road. He called the fire department and directed traffic, but did nothing to rescue the occupants of the car or to call an ambulance. One occupant, an expectant mother, died. Quite possibly the officer's actions were reasonable in the light of the risks to himself. However, the court did not even consider whether the officer was negligent or not. It concluded that, at least in a civil rights claim,

§ 315

1. "Nonfeasance" is older terminology meaning nonaction or nondoing. Unfortunately for diligent law students, some dictionary definitions say that nonfeasance means nonaction *when there is a duty to act*. That definition is accurate under a very particular set of statutes that impose liability upon public officers or their bondsmen for nonfeasance. In ordinary tort terms, however, nonfeasance means only nonaction; and the question whether there is a duty to act is a separate question.

2. Newton v. Ellis, 5 El. & Bl. 115, 119 Eng. Rep. 424 (K.B. 1855).

3. Many cases have adopted this language from Blyth v. Birmingham Waterworks Co., 11 Ex. 781, 156 Eng.Rep. 1047 (1856).

4. Jackson v. City of Joliet, 715 F.2d 1200 (7th Cir.1983).

the officer's conduct had to be viewed as a failure to prevent death, not as an affirmative act causing death.

Since there are no settled criteria for distinguishing pure nonaction from conduct that includes a negligent omission, the *Jackson* court may have been right. But it would be just as plausible to say that the officer's failure would be like the contractor's failure to light the excavation, not a case of nonfeasance at all. That view would lead a court to consider whether, under the circumstances, the officer was negligent or not. In contrast, if the no-duty rule applies, courts do not determine whether the defendant's conduct was unreasonably risky or whether it was justified.

Perhaps the cases as a whole would justify the unsurprising and not so helpful conclusion that judges avoid extremes in characterizing conduct. They do not characterize conduct by segregating highly specific omissions (like failing to brake a car) from closely related conduct (like driving). On the other hand, they do not characterize conduct at its most abstract level, either. A water company's failure to provide water to a fire hydrant is not likely to be viewed as a case of running a water company in a negligent way but as a case of mere nonfeasance for which there is no liability in the absence of an exceptional duty.[5]

TOPIC B. GENERAL DUTIES TO ACT AFFIRMATIVELY

§ 316. Defendant Innocently Creates Risk or Harm

Defendant innocently causing harm. The defendant who knows or should know that he has caused physical harm to the plaintiff, even if caused without fault, owes a duty of reasonable care to avoid further harm.[1] If reasonable care requires it, he must act affirmatively to minimize the harm he has innocently caused and he is subject to liability for the additional harm caused by his failure to do so. The defendant is subject to liability for the entire harm done if he was negligent in the first place; but even if he acted innocently in causing the initial harm, he is subject to liability for the added harm he could have avoided by taking reasonable steps.[2] For instance, if the defendant's railroad train runs over the plaintiff and severs a limb, the defendant may not refuse to provide assistance even if the railroad was not negligent to begin with and even if the plaintiff himself was contributorily negligent.[3]

Defendant innocently risking harm. The same principle has been applied when the defendant knows or should know that he has innocently created a risk to others and the defendant has an opportunity to

5. H.R. Moch Co. v. Rensselaer Water Co., 247 N.Y. 160, 159 N.E. 896 (1928), discussed in § 321.

§ 316

1. Restatement § 322.

2. L.S. Ayres & Co. v. Hicks, 220 Ind. 86, 40 N.E.2d 334, 41 N.E.2d 195 (1942) (injury innocently caused by defendant's instrumentality, or by master or invitor); South v. National Railroad Passenger Corp., 290 N.W.2d 819 (N.D.1980) (railroad employees refused to assist victim of crossing accident, liability).

3. Maldonado v. Southern Pac. Transportation Co., 129 Ariz. 165, 629 P.2d 1001 (Ct. App. 1981).

minimize the risk before harm actually eventuates.[4] For instance, if the defendant, without fault, collides with and kills a horse on the highway, reasonable care may oblige him to take steps to warn others or have the animal removed. If he does not do so and a second driver is later injured in striking the carcass or attempting to avoid it, the defendant is again subject to liability if he failed to exercise reasonable care.[5]

§ 317. Defendant's Relationship to the Plaintiff Creates a Duty

Scope. Sometimes the defendant is under a duty to use reasonable care to rescue the plaintiff because the defendant stands in a special relationship to the plaintiff or to a person causing harm to the plaintiff.[1] This section summarizes the general kind of plaintiff-defendant relationship needed to generate such a duty in a rescue situation.

Categorical relationships imposing a duty of affirmative action. Some relationships between plaintiff and defendant have been formalized by practice and by judicial decisions. The Restatement recognizes five kinds of formal relationship that require the defendant to use reasonable care for the plaintiff's safety, including reasonable affirmative efforts to rescue.[2] The relationships are those of (1) the carrier-passenger, (2) innkeeper-guest, (3) landowner-invitee,[3] (4) custodian-ward, and (5) employer-employee. These same relationships and others also play a part when the issue is the defendant's duty to protect the plaintiff from third persons.[4]

Examples. For example, if an employee-seaman goes overboard, the captain is required to conduct a search even if there is little hope.[5] A landowner whose invitee becomes ill may have a duty to summon care or at least to provide shelter until the invitee improves.[6] Under the rubric of custodian and ward, if the operator of a day-care center finds that a child in his care is injured or ill, he is obliged to use reasonable care to obtain appropriate medical attention.[7] Under the same principle, a jailer must secure medical aid and otherwise protect those held in custody. If

4. Restatement § 321.

5. Pacht v. Morris, 107 Ariz. 392, 489 P.2d 29 (1971).

§ 317

1. See generally Marshall S. Shapo, The Duty to Act: Tort Law, Power & Public Policy (1977).

2. Restatement §§ 314A & 314B.

3. Or any entrant where the categories have been abolished. See § 237.

4. See §§ 322–332.

5. Gardner v. National Bulk Carriers, Inc., 310 F.2d 284, 91 A.L.R.2d 1023 (4th Cir. 1962). The Restatement extends the duty only to servants, thereby excluding independent contractors. See Restatement § 314B; Hosein v. Checker Taxi Co. Inc., 95 Ill.App.3d 150, 50 Ill.Dec. 460, 419 N.E.2d 568 (1981).

6. See Lundy v. Adamar of New Jersey, Inc., 34 F.3d 1173 (3d Cir.1994) (recognizing duty of business to provide available medical care and summon assistance when invitee suffered heart attack); cf. Depue v. Flateau, 100 Minn. 299, 111 N.W. 1 (1907) (host refused to allow ill dinner guest to spend the night, but turned him out; the court found a jury case for negligence); Tiedeman v. Morgan, 435 N.W.2d 86 (Minn. App.1989) (family's duty of care to daughter's boyfriend, who was known to have heart problems).

7. See Applebaum v. Nemon, 678 S.W.2d 533 (Tex.App.1984); Restatement § 314A, Illus. 7.

he fails to do so, he is subject to liability as a matter of common law[8] and also in a civil rights action under the Eighth Amendment.[9] In the absence of custody, however, duties of rescue or protection under civil rights statutes may be quite limited.[10]

Other categorical relationships. The Restatement's list of relationships is incomplete in two ways. First, there is no reason to think that the list of categorical relationships that will impose an affirmative duty is necessarily closed or complete.[11] For example, although ignored by the Restatement, the relationship of a parent to a minor child almost certainly imposes an affirmative duty upon the parent to use reasonable care to rescue the child from a known danger.[12] Schools may owe something of the same kind of duty.[13]

Ad hoc relationships. Another way in which the Restatement list may be incomplete is that highly transient relationships that cannot be categorized may be sufficient to impose a duty. A well-known Michigan case, *Farwell v. Keaton*,[14] involved two teen-aged young men who had a few beers on a summer evening and attempted without success to engage some young women in conversation. This unsuccessful attempt led friends of the young women to beat Farwell severely. His companion, Siegrist, found him and put ice on his head. Farwell went "to sleep" in the backseat of the car while Siegrist drove him around for two hours. Siegrist then left him in the car parked in front of his grandparents' house, but did not notify anyone. Farwell died three days later. The Michigan Court held that Siegrist was under a duty of care to Farwell, at least in part because they were "companions on a social venture" with an implicit undertaking to aid one another. That was a sufficient special relationship. As *Farwell* shows, the parties may form their own relationship and that relation, or the assumptions that go with it, may form the basis for an affirmative duty.[15]

Yet courts have not always accepted such duties. For example, in some cases, the defendant was a woman who arranged a date or a tryst at her house with the plaintiff, but did not warn the plaintiff that a jealous friend or husband might attack. But, unlike the *Farwell* court, these courts concluded that the "companions on a social venture" owed

8. See Brownelli v. McCaughtry, 182 Wis.2d 367, 514 N.W.2d 48 (1994).

9. Estelle v. Gamble, 429 U.S. 97, 97 S.Ct. 285, 50 L.Ed.2d 251 (1976). See § 48.

10. See § 327.

11. The Restatement itself provides a caveat that there may be other relations that would have the same effect. It also implies that other relationships, such as spousal relationships, were not listed simply because no cases had arisen. Restatement § 314A, cmt. b.

12. When the issue is protection from third persons, courts often implicitly so recognize. E.g., A.R.H. v. W.H.S., 876 S.W.2d 687 (Mo.App.1994) (grandmother); Hite v. Brown, 100 Ohio App.3d 606, 654 N.E.2d 452 (1995) (mother, relationship to child seemingly the focus).

13. Mirand v. City of New York, 84 N.Y.2d 44, 614 N.Y.S.2d 372, 637 N.E.2d 263 (1994) (school owed duty to students like that of parents). See § 326.

14. Farwell v. Keaton, 396 Mich. 281, 240 N.W.2d 217 (1976).

15. See §§ 317–319. Restatement § 314A, cmt. b notes that the law seems to be "working slowly toward a recognition of the duty to aid or protect in any relation of dependence or of mutual dependence."

no duty, not even the elemental duty of a warning.[16] Perhaps they thought the reasonable expectations of the parties were not like those in *Farwell;* all's fair in love and war.

Breach of duty. Even if a duty to take reasonable action is recognized, liability is by no means a foregone conclusion. The exact conduct that reasonable care would demand may vary according to the relationship and circumstances. If a landowner owes an invitee a duty of affirmative aid in a medical emergency, it is very unlikely that the duty is violated by failure to have a large stock of medical supplies on hand, so a casino is not liable to a patron for failure to provide intubation equipment when the patron suffered a heart attack.[17]

§ 318. Defendant's Affirmative Action Creates a Duty; Rescue

When the defendant acts affirmatively to aid a person who is helpless, he must of course act with reasonable care. It will not do to lift the stranded plaintiff from an ice gorge in a helicopter and then negligently drop her. Liability for injuries incurred in the drop would appear to be based upon negligent action, not upon any exception to the nonaction rule. The Restatement's § 324 recognizes this liability in its first paragraph.[1]

If the defendant discontinues his rescue before the plaintiff is saved, it is not so clear that the same analysis can be applied. The second paragraph of the Restatement's § 324, however, has it that the defendant who takes charge of a helpless person cannot discontinue his aid if discontinuance leaves the victim in a position worse than when the defendant took charge.[2]

Making matters worse is evidently not a matter of negligently causing injury, because that is covered in the Restatement's first paragraph. The Restatement's only hint about what counts as making matters worse is the suggestion that the rescuer could not remove the victim to a position of safety and then put him back in the original danger or in a new danger. This view is supported by authority,[3] but it leaves the possibility that the would-be rescuer might be free to give up the effort so long as he does so before bringing the helpless person to a position of safety. The rescuer who throws a rope to a drowning woman, pulls her toward shore, then decides to go for a beer, leaving the victim

16. Fiala v. Rains, 519 N.W.2d 386 (Iowa 1994); Wilkins v. Siplin, 13 Cal. Rptr.2d 634 (Ct. App. 1992) (unpublished).

17. Lundy v. Adamar of New Jersey, Inc., 34 F.3d 1173 (3d Cir.1994).

§ 318

1. Restatement § 324 (a).

2. Restatement § 324 (b). Section 324 is peculiar in several ways. The Restatement says that § 324 is an application of § 323, but this does not seem accurate. Section 323 bases liability upon an undertaking when the plaintiff relies upon the undertaking or suffers greater harm because of its negligent performance. Reliance is not specifically required under § 324, although reliance is one of the ways in which the plaintiff might be worse off because of the defendant's withdrawal of aid.

3. Parvi v. City of Kingston, 41 N.Y.2d 553, 362 N.E.2d 960, 394 N.Y.S.2d 161 (1977).

to drown has not made her peril any greater, so the taking charge rule as conceived by the Restatement does not seem to impose any legal responsibility in such a case. The Restatement does, however, issue a caveat, leaving open the possibility of responsibility.

The rescuer who discontinues aid could also make matters worse because his efforts dissuade other potential rescuers from acting or because his efforts create the appearance that no rescue is needed. But matters will not be worse for the helpless victim unless someone relies on the appearance of safety or rescue. Perhaps courts are willing to accept very sparse evidence of reliance. When a customer became ill, a department store put her in its infirmary for six hours but provided no medical attention. The court assumed that had the store done nothing, some good hearted bystander would have provided an ambulance.[4] When the Coast Guard misread its incoming messages and wrongly informed people that a vessel in distress had arrived safely, its negligence dissuaded a private person from a search by ship, and the court was seemingly willing to assume that the search would have been successful.[5]

Perhaps these cases are best explained by saying that, when it comes to the rescue situation, courts apply a kind of lost chance reasoning[6]—that is, that loss of a chance will count as a worsening position even if they cannot be confident that the chance of being saved was a very good one. To say that loss of a chance of rescue is enough to show worsened position is not, of course, to say that the court must accept loss of the chance or increased risk reasoning generally.[7]

§ 319. Defendant's Undertaking Creates a Duty

Undertaking or Assuming a Duty

Undertaking as promise or commitment. Special relationships that impose a duty may arise from status, as in the case of parent and child, or jailer and prisoner. Special relationships may also arise from voluntary contracts or undertakings.[1] An undertaking in this sense is a kind of explicit or implicit promise, or at least a commitment,[2] conveyed in words or in conduct. The "taking charge" cases discussed in the immediately preceding section may be regarded as species of commitment expressed in conduct. The general rule that undertakings can create a duty of care is often expressed by saying one who voluntarily assumes a

4. Zelenko v. Gimbel Bros., 158 Misc. 904, 287 N.Y.S. 134 (1935).

5. United States v. DeVane, 306 F.2d 182 (5th Cir.1962); see also Fochtman v. Honolulu Police and Fire Departments, 65 Haw. 180, 649 P.2d 1114 (1982) (private person would have investigated frantic flashlight signal if police had not assured him they would check it out).

6. See §§ 178 & 179.

7. In particular, it is not to say that the Restatement's § 323 supports lost chance claims. See § 319.

§ 319

1. The conclusion that "social contract theory ... favors tort over contract", Gregory C. Keating, The Idea of Fairness in the Law of Enterprise Liability, 95 Mich. L. Rev. 1266 (1997), seems aimed at disclaimers of responsibility rather than at acceptance of added responsibility considered in this chapter.

2. See E. Allan Farnsworth, Decisions, Decisions: Some Binding, Some Not, 28 Suffolk U. L. Rev. 17 (1994).

duty must then perform that duty with reasonable care.[3] Whether the principle applies when the defendant commits no act toward performance is considered in the next section.

Safety undertakings and tort. Undertakings expressed verbally and those expressed by action or implication may be equally enforceable. Some undertakings may be enforceable as contracts but undertakings relating to physical safety of person or property usually suggest that the rules and policies of tort law should apply.[4]

Duty created by undertaking. The Restatement provides that undertakings can create a duty to act affirmatively and with reasonable care. Section 323 specifically recognizes that the undertaking may create a duty of care to perform in accordance with the undertaking, even if no consideration is given. Liability is imposed, however, only if the plaintiff suffers physical harm[5] from the defendant's negligent performance and only if one of two other conditions is met: (1) the defendant's negligent performance (or withdrawal from performance) must increase the risk to the plaintiff or else (2) the plaintiff must have relied upon performance.[6]

The Increased Risk Avenue

Increased risk distinguished from liability for lost chance. These two conditions of liability warrant comment. The defendant may be subjected to liability if he increases the risk by his negligent performance. Some courts have treated § 323 as if it supported a loss of the chance recovery.[7] There are two objections to that reading. The first is that § 323 does not address rules of causation or damages but rules of duty. Specifically, it addresses the creation of a duty to act where none existed without the undertaking. The second is that § 323 does not impose liability for increased risk. Instead, increased risk is really a limitation on liability, which is imposed only if the defendant's negligent performance causes the harm complained of.[8] The increased risk rule in § 323, then, is a rule limiting liability to the scope of the risk created by failure to use due care. If negligent nonperformance causes harm, but the harm caused is not the result of any increased risk, liability is inappropriate.

The double relevance of increased risk. Increased risk in an undertaking case is important in two ways. First, an undertaking might actively work to create risks. In that case the undertaking is itself an affirmative act of negligence and it rightly suffices as a basis for liability.

3. See, e.g., Trull v. Town of Conway, 140 N.H. 579, 669 A.2d 807 (1995); Florence v. Goldberg, 44 N.Y.2d 189, 375 N.E.2d 763, 404 N.Y.S.2d 583 (1978).

4. See § 320.

5. The physical harm requirement excludes cases in which the plaintiff's harm is purely intangible economic loss without physical injury to person or property. However, some authority has gone beyond that in permitting claims for negligent spoliation of evidence. See Boyd v. Travelers Ins. Co., 166 Ill.2d 188, 652 N.E.2d 267, 209 Ill.Dec. 727 (1995).

6. Restatement § 323.

7. Discussed in §§ 178–179.

8. The defendant is subject to liability only "for physical harm resulting from his failure to exercise reasonable care to perform his undertaking," and then only if either increased risk or reliance is shown. "Resulting from" is of course a causal requirement.

For example, if one of two workers at a day care center assures the other worker that he will take a comatose child to the emergency room, his assurance or undertaking creates the risk that the other will not take needed action. In such a case the child at risk does not rely; she is comatose. Nevertheless, the risk to the child is increased as a result of the undertaking and its nonperformance, and that is enough.[9]

Second, the increased risk clause limits liability to harms resulting from the risk that the undertaking was intended or reasonably expected to protect against. A New Jersey case[10] illustrates the point. The plaintiff's band contracted to play at the defendant's place of business and the defendant contracted to provide helpers to unload band equipment. The defendant breached this provision and the plaintiff had to load equipment himself. While he was doing so, he slipped and suffered injury. The defendant's nonperformance of his undertaking to provide helpers to do the loading was a cause in fact of the harm. But the undertaking was not about avoiding falls and liability grounded on the undertaking was inappropriate.

The Reliance Avenue

Action as undertaking. The Restatement's § 323 also imposes a duty to act affirmatively (and with reasonable care) when the defendant undertakes action and the plaintiff relies upon the undertaking.[11] An undertaking assuredly includes an express promise,[12] but it also includes actions that express an intention or commitment to act. If a city always provides crossing guards for children walking to school, that action is an undertaking to continue the protection until notice to the contrary.

Reliance by the plaintiff. Under the reliance alternative, as distinct from the increased risk alternative, the plaintiff must show reliance upon the defendant's undertaking or assumed duty.[13] Perhaps the reliance must be foreseeable or justified,[14] but at least reliance in fact is

9. Increased risk will often result from the reliance upon the undertaking by the plaintiff or someone acting upon her behalf, as where the city undertook to maintain a fence between a playground and a river and a mother relied upon the integrity of the fence in allowing her child to play. Nelson v. Salt Lake City, 919 P.2d 568 (Utah 1996). The separate provision for increased risk as well as for reliance, allows courts to recognize a duty even if the plaintiff herself or her agent did not rely.

10. Coyle v. Englander's, 199 N.J.Super. 212, 488 A.2d 1083 (1985).

11. Restatement § 323 (b).

12. See Sabia v. State, 164 Vt. 293, 669 A.2d 1187 (1995) (promise and statutory duties). As to whether a promise alone will suffice, without any affirmative steps, see § 320.

13. E.g., Wiseman v. Hallahan, 113 Nev. 1266, 945 P.2d 945 (1997) (plaintiff who fell on ice on public walk at defendant's building did not rely on defendant's custom of clearing ice and could not recover for the defendant's failure to clear ice that day); Zima v. North Colonie Central School District, 225 A.D.2d 993, 639 N.Y.S.2d 558 (1996) (plaintiff who saw ice could not have relied on defendant's clearing or sanding it); Morin v. Traveler's Rest Motel, Inc., 704 A.2d 1085 (Pa.Super.1997) (plaintiff who did not know part of parking lot ice had been salted could not have relied on her portion being salted); Staples v. Duell, 329 S.C. 503, 494 S.E.2d 639 (Ct.App.1997) (if plaintiff did not know of defendant's undertaking to inspect trees and cull those likely to fall, she did not rely on it and there was no duty under § 323).

14. Heard v. City of New York, 82 N.Y.2d 66, 623 N.E.2d 541, 603 N.Y.S.2d 414 (1993).

required. If a child is struck in an unguarded crosswalk where guards have always been provided before, liability for negligently failing to provide the guard follows if the parents relied on the guard. Reliance is possible only when the parent has knowledge of the undertaking and a choice whether to provide some other means of protection. Testimony that the parents knew that a guard was regularly provided and would have taken the child to school themselves if they had known that guards would be withdrawn shows reliance and permits recovery.[15]

In the same circumstances, however, the reliance requirement can defeat the claim for the child's injury if the child's parent did not know that guards had been provided. The reliance requirement would also defeat liability if the parent knew of the guards but, because she was working the early shift, could not have taken the child to school herself or found other means of protection. In that case, the parent would have no choice and could hardly be said to have relied on the guard since she could not have changed her actions even if she had known that the guards had been withdrawn. So if two children are struck in the same crosswalk at the same time because the protection of a crossing guard had been discontinued, only the one whose parents could have themselves escorted the child could recover for withdrawal of the guard.

New York has applied the reliance requirement stringently and even added an additional requirement, at least when the claim is asserted against a public entity. In *Kircher v. City of Jamestown*,[16] witnesses saw the plaintiff, a woman, being accosted by Blanco, then forced into a car, screaming. The witnesses followed the car and obtained the license number before losing it. They reported the facts and the license to an officer, who promised to call it in, but did not. Blanco repeatedly raped and beat the plaintiff, causing severe injuries. But the police officer's undertaking was not sufficient to impose a duty upon the city to act, since, although the witnesses relied upon the promise, the plaintiff herself did not.[17]

Such cases demonstrate that the reliance requirement, which sounds abstractly appropriate, is not always benign. Cases like *Kircher*, however, reflect the protective policies of many courts when it comes to suits against public entities or officers, perhaps more than they reflect concepts of duty, for there are certainly other cases denying relief against peace officers or entities who do not keep their promises to protect citizens.[18] Apart from the protective policies for public entities, the increased risk avenue may still be open in cases like *Kircher*. The

15. Florence v. Goldberg, 44 N.Y.2d 189, 196, 375 N.E.2d 763, 767, 404 N.Y.S.2d 583, 587 (1978) ("the police department voluntarily assumed a particular duty to supervise school crossings").

16. Kircher v. City of Jamestown, 74 N.Y.2d 251, 544 N.Y.S.2d 995, 543 N.E.2d 443 (1989).

17. *Kircher* turned ultimately upon the public duty rule, which allows a plaintiff to claim against a public entity for failure to provide police protection, but only when the public duty of protection had been focused upon the individual by a special relationship. The New York Court treated the special relationship in *Kircher* as turning on the reliance by the victim and also direct contact.

18. Hamilton v. City of Omaha, 243 Neb. 253, 498 N.W.2d 555 (1993) (suggesting specific acts of reliance are required but going off on a pleading requirement that

officer's act of telling the witnesses that he would call in the case, coupled with his failure to do so, undoubtedly worsened the plaintiff's chances of rescue and thus increased the risk to her, because the witnesses would have otherwise sought help from more reliable sources.

What duty is undertaken? A number of cases that accept the Restatement's § 323 in principle end up concluding that the duty undertaken was not one that would have saved the plaintiff and consequently that the plaintiff cannot recover.[19] For example, in another crossing-guard case, the school provided guards in the afternoons after school, but that was not construed as an undertaking to provide guards when the kindergarten children walked home much earlier, so the school breached no duty to such a kindergartner who was struck at the dangerous and unguarded crossing.[20] Actions without promises are often ambiguous ways of showing an undertaking. It may go too far, however, to say that the defendant only undertakes what he actually does. That would eliminate the promissory effect of an undertaking.[21]

Reasonable care. So far as tort law is concerned, the defendant's obligation to act is not absolute. The obligation is to act with reasonable care under the circumstances, even though the undertaking itself is unqualified and might be strictly enforced in contract law. Reasonable care in active performance requires the defendant to use the skill and competence he appears to have, or to correct misleading appearances of competence he does not possess.[22] If the defendant undertakes to guarantee performance or accept strict liability by a valid contract, however, he may be held liable under contract principles.[23]

§ 320. Complete Nonperformance of Gratuitous Undertakings

The general rule is that the defendant is under a duty to perform undertakings made for safety purposes and is liable for physical harm he

specific acts of negligence be alleged); Barillari v. City of Milwaukee, 194 Wis.2d 247, 533 N.W.2d 759 (1995) (police promise did not create ministerial duty to protect).

19. E.g., Tollenaar v. Chino Valley School District, 190 Ariz. 179, 945 P.2d 1310 (Ct. App. 1997) (students were injured in driving off campus during school day, but plaintiff failed to show that school's closed campus policy, which it failed to enforce, was intended to protect against such events); Davis v. Westwood Group, 420 Mass. 739, 652 N.E.2d 567 (1995) (racetrack's arrangement for officers to control traffic at the crossing from parking facility was under an undertaking to provide safe crossing, but only to perform the "the discrete task" of traffic direction); Trull v. Town of Conway, 140 N.H. 579, 669 A.2d 807 (1995) (officer's request that another warn highway department of dangerous ice condition was not an undertaking to get the message through, semble); Morin v. Traveler's Rest Motel, Inc., 704 A.2d 1085 (Pa. Super. Ct. 1997) (salting one portion of parking lot ice is not an undertaking to salt all of it, semble).

20. Jefferson County School District R–1 v. Gilbert, 725 P.2d 774 (Co.1986).

21. In Paulson v. Andicoechea, 926 P.2d 955 (Wyo.1996) the defendant had customarily cleared snow but had not done so after the last snowfall. The court appeared to say that the defendant's prior actions in clearing snow only reflected an undertaking to clear snow on the days he actually cleared it and that he would be under no duty to clear it on the day the plaintiff was injured unless he had actually begun to do so that day.

22. Restatement § 323, cmt. b.

23. See St. Joseph Light & Power Co. v. Kaw Valley Tunneling, 589 S.W.2d 260 (Mo. 1979).

causes the plaintiff by negligently performing or quitting performance once it has begun.[1] Under that rule, a duty may arise when the defendant's undertaking appears as an express or implied promise that amounts to an enforceable contract.[2] However, some authority holds that the duty to act in accord with the promise is not to be recognized when the defendant's promise is gratuitous and he has not taken any action in performance of it. The Restatement expresses no opinion on this point.[3]

The leading case against a duty when the defendant does nothing toward performance of a gratuitous promise is an economic harm case.[4] For that reason that authority should bear little or no weight in the case of promises meant to enhance personal safety.[5] When the gratuitous promise is one aimed at the plaintiff's physical safety, contemporary authority does not seem to exclude the duty merely because the defendant has not entered into performance.[6] The cases of more recent vintage are sometimes explicable on other grounds, but they are at least consistent with the idea that a gratuitous promise creates a duty of reasonable care even when very little action[7] or none at all has been

§ 320

1. § 319.

2. See Hiser v. Randolph, 126 Ariz. 608, 617 P.2d 774 (Ct. App. 1980), partially overruled on other grounds; Thompson v. Sun City Community Hospital, Inc., 141 Ariz. 597, 688 P.2d 605 (1984) (doctor's contract with hospital to provide on-call emergency room services obligated him to treat emergency room patient).

3. Restatement § 323, Caveat (1). When the plaintiff claims that actions rather than promises by the defendant constitute an undertaking, the issue of complete nonperformance does not normally arise, since the actions that constitute the undertaking are also actions in performance of it.

4. Thorne v. Deas, 4 Johns. (N.Y.) 84 (1809) (Kent, Ch.). The defendant promised to secure insurance on a vessel owned by the plaintiff and defendant together, but did not do so. The ship was destroyed at sea. The plaintiff sued for his share of the insurance but all recovery was denied because the promise was unsupported by consideration. Notice that the promise would not have made the ship safer; it would only have secured indemnity. Even in the case of such gratuitous promises not involving safety, courts require little in the way of action. When the defendant gratuitously promised to obtain insurance on goods to be gratuitously bailed and then accepted the goods, it was obliged to get insurance or make it good when the goods burned. Siegel v. Spear & Co., 234 N.Y. 479, 138 N.E. 414, 26 A.L.R. 1205 (1923). Under the modern view of the Restatement Second of Contracts, a promise coupled with reasonable reliance would be sufficient even in economic harm cases. In Brunelle v. Nashua Building & Loan Ass'n., 95 N.H. 391, 64 A.2d 315 (1949) a promise to see that the plaintiff would get good title was enforceable when the plaintiff relied upon the promise and was left with only a quit claim deed and encumbered property.

5. Cf. Warren A. Seavey, Reliance upon Gratuitous Promises or other Conduct, 64 HARV. L. REV. 913, 915, 916 (1951) (recognizing that courts treat economic harm differently from personal injury and noting the tacit representation behind product liability).

6. The most recent personal injury case cited by PROSSER & KEETON § 56 as excluding liability is Long v. Patterson, 198 Miss. 554, 22 So.2d 490 (1945), but that case does not seem to exclude the duty of care merely because the gratuitous promisor has not begun performance. After quoting the First Restatement §§ 323 & 325, it goes off on the point that the defendant who made the promise was an infant and could not be held to his promise for that reason. In any event, the case may implicitly support liability for an unperformed gratuitous promise. HARPER, JAMES & GRAY § 18.6 also cite *Long*, seemingly as support for the idea that a promise can create a duty of care, even where there is no performance. When the defendant is a public officer or entity promising protection or warning, however, courts are apt to insist that the promise is not actionable. See § 319.

7. See Crowley v. Spivey, 285 S.C. 397, 329 S.E.2d 774 (Ct.App.1985) (children's

taken towards its performance.[8] The duty is only one of reasonable care, so the defendant is not strictly liable in tort for nonperformance, nor even for negligence unless the plaintiff relied upon the promise.

Why does complete nonperformance matter if the duty is based upon a promise? First, standard thinking is that tort duties are created by law independent of contract.[9] When the statement is unqualified, it seems to imply that there is no tort duty and no tort if the claim is founded in part on a contract and perhaps that could be extended to mean that there is no tort duty when the claim is founded in part on a promise that is *not* an enforceable contract. The standard distinction between tort and contract, however, is not decisive. It is certainly true that tort duties are created by law, but it is not always true that contract is irrelevant in establishing or measuring the duty. Without controversy, courts often create tort duties that would not arise except for a contract. In varied terms, courts tell us in effect that the tort duty is "implied by law as a result of a contractual undertaking."[10]

Second, in theory, the duty is in doubt in complete nonperformance cases because (a) the defendant is under no duty apart from the undertaking and (b) the undertaking, being gratuitous and without consideration, itself could not be enforced as a contract. The thinking is that the nonfeasance rule excludes tort recovery and that, since the

grandparents promised to supervise children's visit with their schizophrenic mother and did search for the mother's gun; they were liable for the mother's killing of the children); cf. Bloomberg v. Interinsurance Exchange of the Automobile Club of Southern California, 162 Cal.App.3d 571, 207 Cal. Rptr. 853 (1984) (allegations that after a car breakdown on a freeway, defendant dispatched a truck, but its driver negligently failed to locate the boys, who were struck by an intoxicated driver; this was sufficient undertaking); Wilmington General Hospital v. Manlove, 54 Del. 15, 174 A.2d 135 (1961) (hospital completely refused any emergency treatment, even a cursory examination of obviously ill baby who later died; held, hospital with emergency room had duty to provide service to patient presenting unmistakable emergency, if the patient has relied upon a custom of the hospital to render aid in such a case); Lyons v. Grether, 218 Va. 630, 239 S.E.2d 103 (1977) (physician making appointment to see a person not previously a patient was under a duty to treat). In many of these cases, however, it may be inferred that the defendant was in the business of providing services or that some consideration was paid or implicitly promised. Even in *Crowley,* supra, the promise was made to induce the children's father to permit a visit.

8. Morgan v. County of Yuba, 230 Cal. App.2d 938, 41 Cal.Rptr. 508 (1964) (peace officers, before and after arresting man who had threatened woman's life, promised to warn her when he was released on bail; they didn't and the man killed her when he was released; cause of action based on nonfeasance stated if the plaintiff can show reliance); Marsalis v. LaSalle, 94 So.2d 120 (La. App. 1957) (without the defendant's fault, his cat scratched the plaintiff, a customer; defendant promised to keep the cat up for fourteen days to determine whether it had rabies, but took no steps whatever to do so and the cat escaped and could not be found, as a result of which the plaintiff had to undergo the painful Pasteur treatment; later the healthy cat reappeared; held, the promise created a duty of care to keep the cat locked up).

9. See, e.g., Kansas Public Employees Retirement System v. Reimer & Koger Associates, Inc., 262 Kan. 110, 936 P.2d 714 (1997).

10. E.g., Breck v. Moore, 910 P.2d 599 (Alaska 1996) (describing the basis for professional malpractice claims); see also Michaelis v. Benavides, 61 Cal.App.4th 681, 687, 71 Cal.Rptr.2d 776, 779 (1998) ("A contractual obligation may create a legal duty the breach of which will support a tort action").

contract is not to be enforced in contract, it should not be enforced in tort either.

On the surface, the Restatement's doubts seem well-founded. It would seem to be poor policy to lock the contract door but open the tort door. If the promise is partly performed, on the other hand, we can think that, in a somewhat sketchy way, the defendant's liability is predicated in part upon something more than mere nonfeasance. If he has not performed at all, we might think that contract rules should not be subverted by recognizing a duty in tort.

The reasoning is sound for some cases but not all. There are two reasons why a gratuitous promise that is not performed might create a tort duty. One of them is that some gratuitous promises are now enforceable as contracts under the Contracts Restatement § 90, which recognizes the plaintiff's reliance as a substitute for consideration.[11] In fact, the distinguished Reporter of the Restatement Second of Contracts has suggested that a number of the undertaking cases could be brought as contract claims.[12] If the promise is enforceable in contract, and relates to physical safety of persons or things, then there is no universal objection to enforcing it in tort.

The second reason why tort liability might be predicated upon a gratuitous and unperformed undertaking is more significant but more complicated. It is that differences in tort law and contract law might warrant tort law enforcement of an undertaking to act even when enforcement in contract is not available. If the tort rules are different enough from contract rules, the policy of contract law against enforcement in contract might not apply to bar enforcement under the rules and limits of tort law. Some of the differences between tort and contract rules and enforcement include the following:

1. Tort law aims, policies, and rules are well-adapted to deal with physical harms to persons and property and hence with undertakings to provide physical safety.[13] Although contracts can be made on almost any subject, including safety, most contracts deal with economic relationships. The policies, rules, and damages measures of contract law are focused accordingly.[14]

2. Tort law duties based upon a safety undertaking are not necessarily as broad as contract duties. Contract obligations are prima facie strict; the plaintiff need not prove that the defendant negligently breached the contract, only that he breached it. If you promised to deliver corn in September you must pay dam-

11. Restatement Second of Contracts § 90.

12. E. Allan Farnsworth, Decisions, Decisions: Some Binding, Some Not, 28 Suffolk U. L. Rev. 17, 26 (1994).

13. Some tort law deals with economic relationships, but in such cases contractual or consensual elements, or property elements, usually figure strongly in determining duties.

14. Cf. Greenman v. Yuba Power Products, Inc., 59 Cal.2d 57, 27 Cal.Rptr. 697, 377 P.2d 897, 13 A.L.R.3d 1049 (1963) (the commercial rule requiring notice of breach of warranty is inappropriate in the injury setting).

ages if you breach the promise, even if you reasonably tried to perform. Tort obligations are rarely strict. Courts can limit the defendant's obligation to perform a gratuitous undertaking to a duty of reasonable care, no more; and in fact the Restatement does so.[15]

3. Liability may be limited in tort law where courts think it appropriate. While a contract obligation might impose liability for any kind of harm, including pure economic harm, courts can limit the obligation imposed by tort law, even when that obligation is rooted in a promise or undertaking. In fact, the Restatement itself limits the obligation based upon undertakings to physical harms such as personal injuries or property damage. It thereby excludes the largest number of contract cases, those based upon expectancy of pure economic harms without physical injury.[16]

These points can be tested by comparing cases in which the defendant makes a gratuitous and wholly unperformed promise (a) to provide something of economic value and (b) to provide something that reduces the risk of physical harm. In the first category, suppose that marine equipment is on a one-day sale and the defendant gratuitously promises to obtain a new rudder and servo mechanism for the vessel he and the plaintiff own together. The plaintiff reasonably relies upon the promise by not purchasing the equipment herself. The defendant forgets his promise, with the result that the two owners must later pay full price for the equipment. The plaintiff, as part owner, loses her share of the savings that would have been made on the sale price, but she was not physically harmed. No rule about complete nonperformance is relevant in this case. Tort recovery under Restatement § 323 is excluded by the physical harm limitation. On the other hand, modern contract law might treat the defendant's economic promise as an enforceable one under notions of promissory estoppel.[17]

In the case for comparison, suppose that the defendant, who is standing at the highway's edge, promises to signal if traffic approaches as the plaintiff backs his trailer out of a blind driveway. The defendant does not watch and does not signal, and the plaintiff is injured backing into oncoming traffic. Although the promise is gratuitous, the plaintiff's reliance was nevertheless reasonable, and there seems no reason not to enforce the promise as a duty in tort, whether or not it is enforceable in contract. The promise is one about safety of persons and property, not about an economic exchange. The moral understanding and expectation of the community would require its performance and reasonable people would perform it. Finally, nonperformance is unreasonable and negligent; the defendant is held, not merely for breach as in contract cases,

15. Restatement § 323 proposes liability only for "physical harm resulting from ... failure to exercise reasonable care to perform [the] undertaking."

16. See n. 15.

17. Cf. E. Allan Farnsworth, Decisions, Decisions: Some Binding, Some Not, 28 Suffolk U. L. Rev. 17 (1994).

but only for negligent breach that created danger and injury. This is not to say that the promise should not also be enforced in contract under promissory estoppel approaches. If it is enforceable in either tort or contract, the plaintiff might be permitted to choose her theory or to assert them both as grounds for relief, subject to the rule that she can have only one recovery.[18]

The requirement of physical harm coupled with the requirement of negligence protect against excessive tort liability for gratuitous promises. The appealing examples for enforcement of the duty have an immediacy about them that makes danger especially clear and should put the need to act high on the defendant's list of priorities. The defendant who promises to watch for traffic as the plaintiff is backing her rig into the highway is easily negligent if he fails to signal the speeding danger. But that may not be so with a defendant who gratuitously promises but forgets to be present next week to keep watch. Courts can readily control the outcome of such cases by insisting that negligence as well as breach must be proved.[19]

§ 321. Defendant's Undertaking Creating a Duty to Third Persons

The privity rule of Winterbottom v. Wright. In a number of cases, the defendant may undertake a service to A under circumstances that make it foreseeable that B may be injured if the service is not performed. At one time it was said that in such cases the defendant owed B no duty at all, even if the defendant's undertaking was in the form of a valid and enforceable contract. The original explanation for that result was that the defendant had no transaction with B and that a duty of care was

18. There is a small discrete jurisprudence on whether the plaintiff can choose one or both theories or whether the court will decide for itself that the claim should be characterized as tort or as contract. The choice may matter notably on such issues as the statute of limitations and damages, but in particular cases it may affect other issues such as immunities. For statute of limitations purposes, personal injury actions are likely to be characterized as tort, even if they depend upon a contractual relationship; economic claims growing out of a promise tend to be characterized as contract claims. The choices of any particular rule of law do not necessarily depend on the contract-tort distinction. Alaska, after years of trying to determine whether the gravamen of the claim was tort or contract, decided to use the two year "tort" statute for personal injury and the six year "contract" statute for economic claims. The same court was willing to apply the discovery rule in some contract as well as some tort cases. Breck v. Moore, 910 P.2d 599 (Alaska 1996). Some courts still struggle with the characterization of the claim as tort or contract in professional malpractice actions that create economic, not physical harm. See, e.g., Great Plains Federal Savings and Loan Association v. Dabney, 846 P.2d 1088 (Okla.1993) (lawyer's title opinion, contract claim is permissible).

19. The risk-utility balance, §§ 144–146, does not seem to work so well in cases of memory and forgetfulness. Courts sometimes seem to think that the reasonable person forgets nothing in the absence of a distraction. See § 122, but failure to keep a gratuitous promise to act in the distant future, whether from forgetfulness or not, might not be negligent if the promisor could expect that the promisee would protect himself against the risk by other means. When the week elapses and the promisor is not present to warn of traffic, the promisee would ordinarily secure a substitute watcher or refuse to back into the traffic. If that is what the promisor reasonably foresees, he is not negligent in failing to keep his promise, for the risk he has created is the risk of the promisor's inconvenience or economic loss, not physical injury.

owed only to those "in privity." The famous case was the 1842 decision in *Winterbottom v. Wright*,[1] where the plaintiff was injured when a coach supplied by the defendant to the plaintiff's employer broke down and threw the plaintiff to the ground. The defendant had not only supplied the coach but had failed to repair it as required by the contract between the defendant and the employer. However, Lord Abinger, in deciding the case, insisted that as there was no privity between the injured employee and the defendant, the defendant owed no duty at all. Liability would, he insisted, lead to the "most absurd and outrageous consequences."

The requirement of privity itself has long since ceased to control negligence claims.[2] When the defendant causes physical harm through misfeasance—affirmative acts of negligence—rather than nonfeasance, he is liable to the foreseeably injured person for that harm. When the defendant's only duty arises from his contract with or undertaking to A, however, and his complete nonperformance results in harm to B, the same nonfeasance rules seen in earlier sections may prevent liability in some cases.

Enforceable contracts with A not intended for B's protection against physical harm. If the defendant's promise or undertaking is not enforceable by A as a contract, then it creates no duty to B, either. But some cases have gone beyond this logic to say that even if the defendant's contract with A is enforceable by A as a contract, as where it is fully supported by consideration, the contract ordinarily creates no duty of care to B unless the contract was intended to be for B's benefit. Cardozo's opinion in the *Moch*[3] case is the leading discussion.

The Moch case. In *Moch* a city contracted with the defendant to supply water to the city for various purposes, including water at appropriate pressure for fire hydrants. The city paid $42.50 annually for the water supply at each hydrant. A building caught fire. Because the defendant, although notified of the fire, did not supply sufficient water pressure at the hydrants, the fire spread and destroyed the plaintiff's warehouse and contents. Although the contract was valid and enforceable, Judge Cardozo concluded that the contract was not intended to make the defendant answerable to individuals who might be injured. Since the contract was not a third party beneficiary contract, it created no duty to the plaintiff. The only question, then, was whether the defendant had been guilty of some affirmative act of negligence. The court did not think of the defendant as negligently operating a water company but instead thought of it as simply failing to provide the pressure promised. Simply running the business and doing it badly was not enough to count as misfeasance. With no misfeasance and no contract protecting him, the plaintiff lost. On similar facts, most other courts agree.[4]

§ 321

1. Winterbottom v. Wright, 10 M. & W. 109, 152 Eng.Rep. 402 (Exch. Pl. 1842).

2. See § 353.

3. H.R. Moch Co. v. Rensselaer Water Co., 247 N.Y. 160, 159 N.E. 896 (1928).

4. E.g., Rose v. Sapulpa Rural Water Company, 631 P.2d 752 (Okla.1981). Contra, permitting recovery against the water

Contracts priced only for economic protection. The answer would be different if the contract in *Moch* had been enforceable by the plaintiff as a third party beneficiary. In that case, the plaintiff could have recovered contract damages. But on the facts, good reasons might preclude recovery in tort and even recovery in contract for the loss of the warehouse. One reason is that the pricing of water at so much for each hydrant suggests that the water company is guaranteeing a water price but not guaranteeing against loss of buildings. If the water company intended to be liable for loss of buildings when its pressure failed, it would presumably charge a premium adjusted to the risk—either a very high overall charge for water or water priced higher in neighborhoods with higher property values.[5] That line of reasoning suggests that contract damages for failure to supply water might be limited to the value of the water as a commodity and would not include consequential damages such as loss of buildings through the spread of fire.[6] The city might expect, then, to protect itself by fire insurance rather than by paying higher water rates.[7] If such considerations would limit the city's recovery, they would also limit the defendant's duty to the plaintiff, both in tort and in contract. Looked at in this way, the water company's compliance with its contract would have saved the plaintiff from physical harm, but the contract was not a guarantee against physical harm.[8]

Physical harm: nonperformance increasing risk to or creating reliance by third person. When the defendant's undertaking or contract with A is clearly made to protect B from physical harm, however, every reason supports a duty of care to B, both in contract and in tort. Judge Cardozo's decision in *Moch* failed to distinguish between risks of physical harm and risks of economic harm, and consequently he feared infinite downstream economic losses and lawsuits.[9] Under the Restatement's

company, Weinberg v. Dinger, 106 N.J. 469, 524 A.2d 366 (1987) (except to the extent the loss is covered by insurance; the insurer cannot pursue its usual subrogation right); Potter v. Carolina Water Co., 253 N.C. 112, 116 S.E.2d 374 (1960) (contract recovery for negligence breach, analogy made to defective product).

5. See Libbey v. Hampton Water Works Co., 118 N.H. 500, 389 A.2d 434 (1978).

6. Under the contemplation of the parties rules of Hadley v. Baxendale, 9 Ex. 341, 156 Eng.Rep. 145 (1854). See 3 Dan B. Dobbs, The Law of Remedies §§ 12.4 (4)–12.4 (7) (1993).

7. See Weinberg v. Dinger, 106 N.J. 469, 487, 524 A.2d 366, 375 (1987) (recognizing "the concern that the water company's added liability insurance cost, ultimately borne by the consumer, constitutes a less efficient method of insuring against fire loss than is afforded by property insurance").

8. Warren A. Seavey, Reliance upon Gratuitous Promises or other Conduct, 64 Harv. L. Rev. 913, 920–21 (1951) thought Cardozo's opinion in *Moch* might be his "most unsatisfactory opinion in the field of torts." So far as Cardozo treated the very bad performance by the water company as if it were no action at all, that might be a good characterization. However, so far as the result may be justified as comporting with the understanding of the parties to the contract, the decision may not be so bad. Seavey did not address that possibility.

9. For example, Cardozo thought that if liability were imposed in *Moch*, then the manufacturer who contracts to sell to a wholesaler would be liable for breach not only to the wholesaler but to retailers who expected to buy from the wholesaler. He thus feared that "[e]veryone making a promise having the quality of a contract will be under a duty to the promisee by virtue of the promise, but under another duty ... to an indefinite number of potential beneficiaries.... The assumption of one relation will mean the involuntary assumption of a series of new relations.... " H.R. Moch Co. v. Rensselaer Water Co., 247

rules, even if the defendant's promise is not enforceable as a contract, the contract may still furnish the source of a tort duty to protect against physical harm when failure to perform increases the risk to the plaintiff and when the plaintiff reasonably relies upon performance.[10]

Consistent with the Restatement rules, the defendant is of course subject to liability if he assumes a duty by making a safety promise, and then negligently performs it, causing injury. That is a simple case of misfeasance and neither privity nor nonfeasance rules apply.[11] Beyond that, a number of cases have imposed liability when the defendant has promised to inspect or repair traffic signals[12] or elevators[13] that create dangers when they are not properly working. The cases are not always clear whether liability depends upon active negligence or whether nonfeasance would suffice, but liability is imposed and the very fact that courts do not actually notice the distinction is itself evidence that they are entirely willing to impose liability for negligent nonperformance of a safety promise.[14]

When the defendant contractually assumes the existing duty of another person. One additional rule applies when the plaintiff is a third party. It is that the defendant is under a duty to B when the defendant contracts with A to assume A's duty to B.[15] On facts like those in *Moch,* if the city itself owed a duty to citizens to supply water with adequate pressure at the hydrant, then contracted with the water company to fulfill that duty, the water company would owe the duty to citizens and the plaintiff would recover.[16] The result is clearly right. If A owes the

N.Y. 160, 168, 159 N.E. 896, 899 (1928). These reasons are among those for treating economic harms with circumspection, but they do no apply to physical harms, as the Restatement recognizes in this very context. Restatement §§ 323, 324A.

10. Restatement § 324A.

11. Schmeck v. City of Shawnee, 232 Kan. 11, 651 P.2d 585 (1982) (contractor contracted to design and install intersection traffic signals or controls, and began work but a long delay left the intersection inadequately controlled and resulted in plaintiff's injury; contractor could be held on misfeasance and also because it undertook duty owed by city to drivers); Dowis v. Continental Elevator Co., Inc., 241 Neb. 207, 486 N.W.2d 916 (1992). Conversely, if the defendant does nothing toward performance and the plaintiff does not rely, the defendant's promise to a third person does not create a duty to the plaintiff. Fort Bend County Drainage District v. Sbrusch, 818 S.W.2d 392 (Tex.1991) (promise to A to repair bridge was not communicated to B who was injured when it collapsed; since B did not rely, the promise without any steps toward performance created no duty to him).

12. Long v. District of Columbia, 820 F.2d 409 (D.C.Cir.1987); contra, Baca v. Britt, 73 N.M. 1, 385 P.2d 61 (1963) (requiring privity or active negligence, even though the implied promise implicated physical safety).

13. Banaghan v. Bay State Elevator Co., 340 Mass. 73, 162 N.E.2d 807 (1959); Dowis v. Continental Elevator Co., Inc., 241 Neb. 207, 486 N.W.2d 916 (1992) (so assuming); Bollin v. Elevator Const. & Repair Co., 361 Pa. 7, 63 A.2d 19, 6 A.L.R.2d 277 (1949).

14. See Long v. District of Columbia, 820 F.2d 409 (D.C.Cir.1987).

15. Restatement § 324A (b).

16. Lopez v. Arizona Water Co., Inc., 23 Ariz.App. 99, 530 P.2d 1132 (1975) (seemingly on a contract theory). See also Phinney v. Boston Elevated Ry. Co., 201 Mass. 286, 87 N.E. 490 (1909) (railroad contractually assumed city's duty of care and was liable for its failure to act in performance of that duty); Palka v. Servicemaster Management Services Corp., 83 N.Y.2d 579, 589, 611 N.Y.S.2d 817, 822, 634 N.E.2d 189, 194 (1994) (defendant assumed duties owed by A to B was held liable for breach of the duty in part because of the "displacement and substitution of a particular safety function designed to protect persons like this plain-

duty to B, A may avoid liability by taking reasonable precautions to protect B, including a precaution in the form of a contract with another person to provide the protection needed. So A can normally shift responsibility and be relieved of liability by contracting with the defendant to perform.[17] By the same token, however, the defendant must be held to the duty he has assumed, for otherwise the plaintiff's rights would have been determined by the contract of two other people to which he was not a party.

Policy against recognizing a duty in particular cases. To eliminate the privity and nonfeasance rules is not necessarily to impose liability for breach of all contracts when nonperformance leads to harm. As always, the courts' sense of policy and justice bear on the decision to recognize a duty. In a Massachusetts case, a tenant promised the landlord that the tenant would clear snow and ice from the property. The plaintiff was employed on the property, though not by the tenant. She fell on a patch of ice. Since the tenant owed no common law duty to clear the ice, the plaintiff relied upon the tenant's promise to the landlord. But the defendant's promise to the landlord was not intended for the benefit of third persons and Massachusetts had a strong policy against imposing snow clearance duties. So not surprisingly, the court refused to permit the tenant's promise to create a tort duty.[18] Such a result is entirely consistent with a general acceptance of the assumed duty rules recognized by the Restatement in cases that do not involve the same policies.

Scope of assumed duty or undertaking. As observed in another connection,[19] undertakings in the form of actions rather than words are often ambiguous. An adjuster's inspection of a dangerous building to determine whether damage to the building comes within insurance coverage is not necessarily an undertaking to warn neighbors of dangers that the building may collapse on them, or any undertaking to anyone except the insurer who employed him.[20] Similarly, some courts hold that insurers who undertake inspections of property to determine appropriate premiums are not undertaking any duty to find dangers and warn of them.[21]

tiff' and the reasonable expectations of the parties).

17. On the shifting responsibility concept, see § 194. Even if the duty is nondelegable, see § 337, the same result follows, though less directly. In the nondelegable duty case, the city would still be liable to B but would have an action over for indemnity against the water company. The water company would thus ultimately be liable for B's injury. That being so, a direct action by the plaintiff is probably more desirable.

18. Anderson v. Fox Hill Village Homeowners Corporation, 424 Mass. 365, 676 N.E.2d 821 (1997).

19. § 319.

20. Gooch v. Bethel A.M.E. Church, 246 Kan. 663, 792 P.2d 993, 13 A.L.R.5th 974 (1990).

21. Smith v. Allendale Mutual Ins. Co., 410 Mich. 685, 303 N.W.2d 702 (1981). A different reason excludes liability in many cases when the inspection is made by a workers' compensation insurer of the insured employer's premises. In that case, the employer's tort immunity may protect the insurer acting on the employer's behalf. See Frank J. Wozniak, Annotation, Breach of Assumed Duty to Inspect Property as Ground For Liability to Third Party, 13 A.L.R.5th 289 (1994). Where no immunity is involved, some courts do permit recovery against the insurer based upon its under-

Topic C. Duties to Protect the Plaintiff from Herself or Third Persons

§ 322. No Duty to Control Others

In a large number of cases the defendant himself does not directly injure the plaintiff but instead fails to prevent the risk of injury by another. The immediate tortfeasor is sometimes merely negligent but often he carries out a criminal attack on the plaintiff. The question is whether the defendant, who could have prevented the injury by a warning, or by exercising the control he had over the attacker, or otherwise, is under any duty to do so.[1] In the usual case, the problem is not rescue of a plaintiff already in peril; it is rather the use of care to prevent harm in the first place.

For example, when a newly released parolee with a history of violence toward women does not appear at the halfway house or residential center to which he is required to report, the halfway house can minimize the risk that the parolee will commit crimes by warning the prison or the police that he has not appeared as required.

Although a phone call by the halfway house in the example does not seem onerous, given the halfway house's effort to direct criminals into a better path, courts have often conceived of this and a variety of other situations narrowly as a question of the defendant's control over others rather than as a question of the defendant's ability to protect the plaintiff from foreseeable harm. They have frequently said that, with certain exceptions, the defendant owes no duty to control the dangerous person and have taken that premise as grounds for refusing relief to the parolee's victims.[2] Similarly, a church Mission Board, learning that one of its missionaries is sexually molesting his own children, has no duty to

taking. See, e.g., Silva v. Hodge, 583 So.2d 231 (Ala.1991).

§ 322

1. Many cases that fall within this problem have tried to deal with it as a proximate cause problem. For instance, if the defendant leaves his keys in his car, a thief may steal it and drive too fast trying to escape, causing injury in the process. See § 190. Some courts say that the driver's negligence is not a proximate cause and that he is thus not liable. That analysis has created several problems. First, proximate cause issues call for case-by-case analysis, not a categorical rule. Although many thefts are no doubt unforeseeable, it cannot be so that every single theft that can ever arise is in that category. Second, proximate cause issues, including the kind called superseding cause, turn ultimately on foreseeability. To declare that the harm is not foreseeable is to declare that the defendant is not negligent at all and if that is the case, there is no proximate cause issue. The keys-in-the-car cases, like the alcohol provider cases, which also traditionally used proximate cause reasoning, thus appear to be no duty cases so far as they reject all liability.

2. Johnson v. State, 553 N.W.2d 40 (Minn.1996) (Halfway House did not report parolee's failure to arrive upon release from prison; parolee went on a crime spree that included rape and murder for days before anyone noticed, no duty to control rule relieves Halfway House from duty to make a telephone warning of his absence); but cf. Dudley v. Offender Aid and Restoration of Richmond, Inc., 241 Va. 270, 401 S.E.2d 878, 9 A.L.R.5th 1203 (1991) (felon with history of violence in a halfway house never held to rules for remaining in the house, raped and murdered a victim, liability of halfway house established).

help prevent future harm to the same child or others, even by providing a warning to the child's mother before washing its hands of the matter.[3]

In some instances, the defendant has done nothing, so the nonfeasance rule would protect the defendant unless his relationship establishes an affirmative duty to act. However, in many of the cases, the defendant seems to be acting affirmatively and in so doing creating a risk of harm to the plaintiff. Perhaps that is true in the Halfway House example, because it is possible to think that the defendant is operating a Halfway House and doing a very bad job of it, not merely failing to use the telephone. The rule that the defendant has no duty to control others (or to protect the plaintiff) seems to be independent of the nonfeasance rule and to go much further because it immunizes affirmative risky acts in some cases.[4]

The general rule is subject to significant exceptions that fall into three categories.[5] (1) Statutes may impose a duty to take action and to use care to protect others. This is the case with statutes requiring state agencies to investigate and deal with reports of suspected child abuse.[6] (2) The defendant is under a duty to use reasonable care for the plaintiff's safety where the defendant is in a special relationship with the plaintiff. A property owner, for one example, may owe a duty of reasonable care to protect an invitee or other entrant upon the land. (3) The defendant is under a duty to use reasonable care for the plaintiff's safety when the defendant is in a special relationship with the immediate tortfeasor and in a position to control his tortious behavior or at least to minimize risks to the plaintiff by some means. For one example, a jailer or other custodian of a dangerous person owes a duty of reasonable care to prevent that person from harming others.

The rule and its exceptions have generated a substantial body of contemporary litigation summarized in the next sections.

§ 323. Duty Based upon Defendant's Relationship to the Plaintiff

The defendant's relationship to the plaintiff has been recognized as a ground for requiring the defendant to take affirmative acts of reasonable care in a substantial body of cases. Courts frequently speak as if duties are generated only within a list of formal relationships such as the carrier-passenger relationship, but as already indicated in discussing rescue cases,[1] the list is not closed. In any event, since duty is a question of justice and policy, some less formal or describable relationships may

3. See Foreign Mission Board of the Southern Baptist Convention v. Wade, 242 Va. 234, 409 S.E.2d 144 (1991).

4. See § 332 (alcohol providers).

5. See Restatement § 315.

6. See Turner v. District of Columbia, 532 A.2d 662 (D.C.App.1987); Mammo v. State, 138 Ariz. 528, 675 P.2d 1347 (Ct. App. 1983); Jensen v. Anderson County DSS, 304 S.C. 195, 403 S.E.2d 615 (1991); Sabia v. State, 164 Vt. 293, 669 A.2d 1187 (1995).

§ 323

1. § 317.

work in the same way. On the other hand, the duty may not be coextensive with all the recognized formal relationships.

Courts recognize several formal relationships between the defendant and the plaintiff as grounds for imposing a duty of reasonable care. The extent of the duty owed is sometimes debated and in some categories particular courts may reject the duty altogether. In general, the categories today include:

(1) A landowner, usually a business enterprise open to the public, and an invitee or other person properly on the premises. This relationship includes the specific relationships between carrier and passenger and innkeeper and guest. To some extent, as modified by lease covenants, it may include landlord and tenant as well.

(2) Custodian and ward. This category includes jailers and their prisoners, persons institutionalized with severe mental or physical disabilities, and an indeterminate number of other custodial or caretaker relationships.

(3) Schools and students.

(4) Spouses and their spouses; parents and their children.

(5) Employers and their employees.

In each case, a duty of reasonable care may require the defendant to give warnings to the plaintiff, to provide shelter, to call for help, or otherwise as reasonable care may dictate to prevent harm by others.

§ 324. Landowner's Duty to Protect Customers and Others

Recognizing a Duty of Care

Earlier decisions recognized that carriers, innkeepers, theaters, fairs and places of public entertainment owed affirmative duties of reasonable care to protect their customers and sometimes to others rightfully upon their premises. Those duties included the duty to take reasonable steps to protect against acts of third persons.[1] The rule today is usually generalized to include all landowners who open their land to the public for business[2] and to require them to use reasonable care even to protect against criminal acts of third persons.[3] If landowners create dangerous conditions attracting crime, even landowners whose premises are not open to the public may be under a duty of care.[4]

§ 324

1. See Smith v. Cumberland County Agricultural Soc'y., 163 N.C. 346, 79 S.E. 632 (1913) ("fairs, shows and theaters").

2. Restatement § 344. Some courts might still demand heightened care from common carriers and the like. See Kenny v. Southeastern Pennsylvania Transportation Authority, 581 F.2d 351 (3d Cir.1978).

3. E.g., Nallan v. Helmsley–Spear, Inc., 50 N.Y.2d 507, 429 N.Y.S.2d 606, 407 N.E.2d 451 (1980).

4. See Nixon v. Mr. Property Management Co., Inc., 690 S.W.2d 546 (Tex.1985) (vacant apartment with no lock, criminal dragged child in and raped her).

Earlier cases sometimes focused on specific events taking place in the defendant's presence. For example, a tavern that permitted a man to drink all day long and into the night, causing "trouble" from time to time, could be found to have been negligent in failing to deal with the marathon drinker before he finally caused an injury.[5] There are still cases in this pattern. For instance, when one customer hit another in a Taco Bell, then adjourned to the parking lot for a serious beating, Taco Bell was liable because it unreasonably failed to call for police.[6] Some courts continue to limit liability to such cases of imminent harm, and to those in which the defendant's method of doing business attracts crime,[7] but other contemporary decisions go a step beyond these cases by imposing a duty of antecedent care, that is, to use care against harms that are generally foreseeable even when the wrongdoer's presence is not known and the wrongdoer himself not specifically identifiable.

In particular, courts have imposed liability upon landowners when crime against patrons is foreseeable and when the landowner could reasonably have prevented shootings,[8] robberies,[9] beatings, rapes[10] or killings,[11] in office buildings, grocery stores, hospitals and other places of business, or in their parking lots or perimeters.[12]

Foreseeability of Crime

Specific instances not required: the totality of circumstances approach. One major issue that has drawn the courts' attention has been whether the defendant's duty is triggered only when he knows or should know of similar incidents of crime on his own property or nearby. On this point the courts are split. One view is that ordinary negligence rules apply, meaning that foreseeability is a question of fact and turns on the

5. Greco v. Sumner Tavern, Inc., 333 Mass. 144, 128 N.E.2d 788 (1955). Other cases in the same pattern include: Naegele v. Dollen, 158 Neb. 373, 63 N.W.2d 165, 42 A.L.R.2d 1099 (1954) (hardware store owner permitted customer to load a shotgun with predictable injury to others); Hill v. Merrick, 147 Or. 244, 31 P.2d 663 (1934) (business failed to stop children playing tag on the high diving board, customer jostled off); Sinn v. Farmers' Deposit Savings Bank, 300 Pa. 85, 150 A. 163 (1930) (bank failed to use opportunity to warn plaintiff bank customer away from a holdup).

6. Gould v. Taco Bell, 239 Kan. 564, 722 P.2d 511 (1986).

7. Wright v. Webb, 234 Va. 527, 362 S.E.2d 919 (1987) (if the business does not attract or provide a "climate for assaultive crime," the landowner's only duty is to act for the invitee's protection when he knows that criminal assaults against persons are occurring, or are about to occur, on the premises which indicate an imminent probability of harm to an invitee).

8. Nallan v. Helmsley-Spear, Inc., 50 N.Y.2d 507, 429 N.Y.S.2d 606, 407 N.E.2d 451 (1980).

9. Butler v. Acme Markets, Inc., 89 N.J. 270, 445 A.2d 1141 (1982).

10. Madden v. C & K Barbecue Carryout, Inc., 758 S.W.2d 59 (Mo.1988); Small v. McKennan Hospital, 437 N.W.2d 194 (S.D. 1989) (abduction from hospital parking ramp, rape and murder). Women are the victims in a high percentage of these cases.

11. Sharpe v. Peter Pan Bus Lines, Inc., 401 Mass. 788, 519 N.E.2d 1341 (1988).

12. The limit of the owner's property is usually the limit of the owner's obligation, see Simpson v. Big Bear Stores Co., 73 Ohio St.3d 130, 652 N.E.2d 702 (1995). But in Banks v. Hyatt Corp., 722 F.2d 214 (5th Cir.1984), a guest at the defendant's hotel was murdered on a public sidewalk four feet from the hotel's entrance and the court found that "innkeepers" owed a duty to protect against off-premises assault so long as reasonable care would require such protection, as might be the case where, as here, the hotel maintained perimeter patrols.

evidence, not on a rule requiring specific crimes like the one that resulted in harm to the plaintiff. Similarly, violent incidents in the neighborhood might be enough to alert the defendant that it could spread to his own property.[13] Indeed, a business might foresee criminal attacks in a dark parking garage even if none had ever occurred there before,[14] and certainly might foresee attacks in a blind spot in its parking lot adjacent to a place where people loitered to drink and where 60 incidents of other kinds of crime had been noted.[15] Some courts are now calling this approach the "totality of circumstances" approach. The label may suggest that it reflects a special rule, but as the New Jersey Court said, it is only the ordinary rule in negligence cases, which determines foreseeability by considering "all the factors a reasonably prudent person would consider,"[16] no more no less.

Specific similar incidents and other requirements. A more conservative view insists that the landowner has no duty of reasonable care to the customer unless similar incidents had occurred. But even this similar incident requirement does not limit liability to harms that are identical to those that have previously been inflicted on the property or in the neighborhood. So the Supreme Court of Georgia held that a landlord's knowledge of several prior burglaries might be enough to show that rape of a tenant was foreseeable.[17] Perhaps the most demanding rule of all holds that the defendant is under no duty of care unless his business is so operated that it actually attracts wrongdoers or the defendant knows of a presently occurring assault.[18]

Specific similar incidents required when risk is low or cost of safety is high. California has now said that when the defendant's supposed negligence is in failing to have security guards present, "a high degree of foreseeability is required" and that this rule would ordinarily require evidence of "prior similar incidents of violent crime on the landowner's premises."[19] As noted much earlier,[20] locutions that refer to degrees of

13. See Isaacs v. Huntington Memorial Hospital, 38 Cal.3d 112, 211 Cal.Rptr. 356, 695 P.2d 653 (1985).

14. See Small v. McKennan Hospital, 437 N.W.2d 194 (S.D.1989).

15. Clohesy v. Food Circus Supermarkets, Inc. 149 N.J. 496, 694 A.2d 1017 (1997).

16. Clohesy v. Food Circus Supermarkets, Inc. 149 N.J. 496, 507, 694 A.2d 1017, 1023 (1997).

17. Sturbridge Partners, Ltd. v.Walker, 267 Ga. 785, 482 S.E.2d 339 (1997), effectively overruling Savannah College of Art and Design, Inc. v. Roe, 261 Ga. 764, 409 S.E.2d 848 (1991) where the court had said that a college would not be under a duty of care to a student to prevent rape by an intruder, even though the dormitory was located in a downtown crime area that had been plagued with a number of other crimes including burglary and peeping toms. Some cases are difficult to interpret. Baptist Memorial Hospital v. Gosa, 686 So.2d 1147, 1149 (Ala.1996) appears to reject the duty entirely, but it then acknowledges that a "duty may be imposed on a store owner to take reasonable precautions to protect invitees from criminal attack in the exceptional case where the store owner possessed actual or constructive knowledge that criminal activity which could endanger an invitee was a probability." Unless "probability" means "more likely than not," the court's statement seems remarkably close to the Restatement section.

18. Burns v. Johnson, 250 Va. 41, 458 S.E.2d 448 (1995).

19. Ann M. v. Pacific Plaza Shopping Center, 6 Cal.4th 666, 679, 863 P.2d 207, 215, 25 Cal.Rptr.2d 137, 145 (1993).

20. § 143.

foreseeability usually mean risk or probability, so the statement quoted appears to mean that the risk of harm must be high in order to impose a duty that requires an expense such as a security guard. At least one other decision has adopted a similar "balancing" approach under which a more onerous burden would be imposed as probability of harm increases, a balance in which similar incidents play an important but not necessarily determinative part.[21] Conversely, this view leaves room to say that if the plaintiff claims only that low-cost protection should have been afforded—that a warning should have been given or that the parking lot should have been better lighted or covered with a surveillance camera—similar incidents may not be required.

A requirement of similar incidents as a precondition to a duty is an application of the usual risk-utility balance in the sense that it weights costs of safety against the probable harm. It differs from the usual risk-utility balance in two related and important ways. As a precondition to a duty, the balance is performed by judges, not juries, and it is turned into something like a rule of law for all cases rather than a guide to adjudication of particular cases that may arise.

Limiting Duty or Finding No Negligence

Even when risks are entirely foreseeable, the landowner or business is not necessarily liable for crimes against invitees or others, since the duty is only to exercise reasonable care, not to guarantee safety. If the risk of assault upon customers is small (and not generated by the business itself), good lighting alone may satisfy the duty of reasonable care. In other cases, a reasonable business might be expected to give a warning of danger, or to eliminate hiding places from which an assault might be launched, or even to provide security guards. But a manager's informal patrol of the parking lot every half hour may readily satisfy the duty of reasonable care in many situations.[22] To a large extent, the issue of whether the duty of care is breached is for the jury to decide if reasonable people could differ.[23]

Some cases, however, may be carved out for special treatment. When an armed robber demands funds from a business, noncompliance may endanger patrons, but even so, the Supreme Court of California has said that the business has no duty to give in to the robber's demands, and if its resistance provokes the robber to injure the plaintiff standing nearby, the plaintiff has no complaint.[24] Some other authority has taken a

21. McClung v. Delta Square Ltd. Partnership, 937 S.W.2d 891, 901 (Tenn.1996).

22. See Kelly v. Retzer & Retzer, Inc., 417 So.2d 556 (Miss.1982).

23. See Draper Mortuary v. Superior Court, 135 Cal.App.3d 533, 185 Cal.Rptr. 396 (1982) (sexual assault on body in mortuary, jury question whether mortuary had exercised reasonable care to protect against such things).

24. Kentucky Fried Chicken of California, Inc. v. Superior Court, 14 Cal.4th 814, 927 P.2d 1260, 59 Cal.Rptr.2d 756 (1997) ("no duty to comply with a robber's unlawful demands should be imposed on a shopkeeper on the theory that compliance may lessen the danger to other persons on the premises. [California law recognizes] the right of any person to defend property with reasonable force," but active resistance might be different).

similar position on similar facts.[25] Such cases, however, do not reject the landowner's duty of care wholesale; they carve out exceptions.

§ 325. Landlord's Duty of Protection

The landlord's common law tort liability for conditions of the leased premises that cause injury has already been mentioned.[1] That liability, particularly in the case of multi-family dwelling units, is now often affected somewhat by statutes and ordinances. Liability is also affected by the recognition that the lease of modern apartment is not analogous to the medieval lease from which the no-duty rule developed[2] but instead represents a combination of property and services usually provided as a part of the landlord's business. This makes many lessors analogous in some respects innkeeper on the one hand and, less forcefully, to the product provider on the other.[3]

When it comes to the duty of landlords and condominium associations to protect tenants and their guests[4] from attacks or thefts, liability in one class of cases turns on the fact that the landlord actually helped to create a danger, for example, by leasing to dangerous tenants or failing to restrict their dangerous activities.[5]

In a second group of cases, the landlord does not necessarily create the immediate danger but he fails to protect the tenant from an attacker by employing adequate door locks or otherwise. The traditional starting point was that the landlord who did not create the danger owed the tenant no duty to protect the tenant from the criminal acts of third persons. The rule has been under siege for decades now, and many courts have now imposed a duty of reasonable care to maintain the physical condition of the premises so as to minimize the risk of assaults

25. Boyd v. Racine Currency Exchange, Inc., 56 Ill.2d 95, 306 N.E.2d 39 (1973) (robber who demanded that a teller give him money, else he would shoot a customer; the teller didn't and the robber did, killing Boyd; a duty of care on these facts would only benefit criminals, who would then be encouraged to take hostages).

§ 325

1. § 240.

2. See Trentacost v. Brussel, 82 N.J. 214, 412 A.2d 436 (1980).

3. Thus the implied warranty of habitability in residential leases requires some minimum standards for heat and sanitation, for example. New Jersey has explicitly included a minimum standard of security from crime, including security in common areas, as part of the implied warranty. Trentacost v. Brussel, supra n. 2.

4. The duty of landlords and condominiums runs not only to the tenant but to the tenant's guests. Martinez v. Woodmar IV Condominiums Homeowners Association, Inc., 189 Ariz. 206, 941 P.2d 218 (1997).

5. Strunk v. Zoltanski, 62 N.Y.2d 572, 468 N.E.2d 13, 479 N.Y.S.2d 175 (1984) (tenant's vicious dog bit boy rightfully on premises; landlord who knows of dangerous activities before lease had duty to use care, for example by inserting controls in the lease); Samson v. Saginaw Professional Building, Inc., 393 Mich. 393, 224 N.W.2d 843 (1975) (lease to innocuously named mental health clinic whose major clients were convicted criminals on parole; no warning to other tenants, liability for attack by clinic's criminal client); cf. Rosales v. Stewart, 113 Cal.App.3d 130, 169 Cal. Rptr. 660 (1980) (tenant who had the habit of discharging firearms in the backyard killed neighbor child; landlord should have controlled the tenant). Liability for leasing to illicit drug traffickers has been harder to impose. See Muniz v. Flohern, Inc., 77 N.Y.2d 869, 568 N.Y.S.2d 725, 570 N.E.2d 1074 (1991).

and robberies,[6] which often involve rapes and killings of women or sexual molestation of children. It may even be fair to say that the landlord always owes care that is reasonable in the light of all the circumstances.[7] However, what counts as reasonable care will ordinarily depend in part upon the landlord's express or implied undertakings, his representations, and his powers under the lease as well as upon foreseeability of harm.

When a tenant has been attacked in common areas of the premises such as entrance halls, the landlord's control of the area together with foreseeable harm may suffice to impose a duty of reasonable care to provide appropriate doors, locks,[8] and lighting.[9] When the tenant is attacked in her apartment, landlords have been held liable for failure to use reasonable care for the tenant's safety for failing to repair locks or windows as required by the lease[10] or by statute,[11] for misrepresenting safety[12] or failing to disclose known dangers,[13] for failing to provide appropriate lighting of dangerous areas,[14] or otherwise maintaining conditions that would attract violent persons,[15] and for mishandling keys to the apartment.[16]

The landlord's undertaking, express or implied, as a term of the lease or otherwise, is often a basis for the duty to protect the tenant. A leading case[17] was a suit brought by a tenant in a large apartment building after she was attacked by an intruder in the hallway. When she had leased the apartment, the building had been protected by a doorman and other devices. At the time of the attack some years later, the doorman and other protections had been withdrawn, although assaults,

6. See Tracy A. Bateman and Susan Thomas, Annotation, Landlord's Liability For Failure to Protect Tenant From Criminal Acts of Third Person, 43 A.L.R.5th 207 (1996).

7. Sharp v. W.H. Moore, Inc., 118 Idaho 297, 796 P.2d 506 (1990); Tenney v. Atlantic Associates, 594 N.W.2d 11 (Iowa 1999).

8. Trentacost v. Brussel, 82 N.J. 214, 412 A.2d 436 (1980).

9. Duncavage v. Allen, 147 Ill.App.3d 88, 497 N.E.2d 433, 100 Ill.Dec. 455 (1986) (landlord did not properly light exterior by decedent's apartment, allowed vegetation to grow where attackers could be concealed, failed to provide working locks on windows, and even left a ladder in the common area that could be and was used by the attacker to gain access to decedent's apartment where he raped and killed her).

10. Cordes v. Wood, 918 P.2d 76 (Okla. 1996) (lease provisions left landlord in exclusive control of locks; landlord was thus under a duty to repair and liable, when he failed to so, for rape of tenant). But N.W. v. Amalgamated Trust & Savings Bank, Trust No. 4015, 196 Ill.App.3d 1066, 554 N.E.2d 629, 143 Ill.Dec. 694 (1990) refused to impose liability on similar facts unless harm was specifically foreseeable.

11. See Brock v. Watts Realty Co., Inc., 582 So.2d 438, 43 A.L.R.5th 839 (Ala. 1991).

12. See Veazey v. Elmwood Plantation Associates, Ltd., 650 So.2d 712 (La.1994).

13. See O'Hara v. Western Seven Trees Corp., 75 Cal.App.3d 798, 142 Cal.Rptr. 487 (1977).

14. Poor lighting or other conditions outside the apartment may increase the tenant's vulnerability in the apartment. See Duncavage v. Allen, supra n. 9.

15. See Walls v. Oxford Management Company, Inc., 137 N.H. 653, 633 A.2d 103 (1993).

16. Rowe v. State Bank of Lombard, 125 Ill.2d 203, 531 N.E.2d 1358, 126 Ill.Dec. 519 (1988) (no general duty of care, but by retaining a copy of key and then allowing it to get into attacker's hands, landlord breached an implicitly assumed duty of care); Tenney v. Atlantic Associates, 594 N.W.2d 11 (Iowa 1999).

17. Kline v. 1500 Massachusetts Avenue Apartment Corp., 439 F.2d 477, 43 A.L.R.3d 311 (D.C. Cir. 1970).

larcenies, and robberies in common passages were common. The court held that, in the light of the landlord's control over the common passageway, the special character of the modern urban multiple-unit lease, and the notice to the landlord of other attacks, the landlord owed her a duty of care. The acts required of the landlord to fulfill his duty of care, however, was dictated largely by contractual expectations–the landlord was required to provide the degree of protection that he himself had provided when the plaintiff first became a resident.

Apart from the landlord's voluntary undertaking or assumption of a duty,[18] the usual claim depends in part on the foreseeability of harm,[19] and if harm is not foreseeable, no precaution is required. Evidence of prior instances of crime in the general neighborhood is usually sufficient to show that intrusion and assault is foreseeable.[20] It would also seem that the landlord's own use of security guards or other security measures would indicate that crime is foreseeable. A single incident of crime in the neighborhood, coupled with the fact that the tenant's building was secluded and thus a good potential target, would permit a jury to say that the landlord should have repaired the tenant's lock.[21] But even without incidents of crime, it is reasonable to say that harm is always foreseeable when the condition of the landlord's premises or the landlord's careless key management invite or facilitate entry into the tenant's private apartment, so liability has been imposed when landlords fail to repair broken locks or fail to keep track of keys to the tenant's apartment.[22]

Given that criminal attacks on tenants are foreseeable and likely enough to call for some response, liability still does not automatically follow. Instead, the landlord is liable only if he fails to provide protection that is reasonable in the light of foreseeable harm. In many of the cases, this is not a seriously disputed element, for the landlord has refused to provide the most elemental protections, such as locks on doors or appropriate lighting at night[23] and it is easy enough to say that these are

18. When the landlord undertakes a duty of care, his undertaking, not foreseeability is the basis and hence the measure of his responsibility. See E.G. Rock, Inc. v. Danly, 98 Md.App. 411, 633 A.2d 485 (1993).

19. E.g., Trentacost v. Brussel, 82 N.J. 214, 412 A.2d 436 (1980) (75 or more incidents of crime against persons in neighborhood and in apartment house in recent years). A California court, purporting to distinguish "degrees of foreseeability," has demanded a high degree of foreseeability, presumably meaning greater risk or probability of harm, before the landlord of a small property can be expected to exercise care against an intruder. Pamela W. v. Millsom, 25 Cal.App.4th 950, 30 Cal.Rptr.2d 690 (1994). New Hampshire imposes a duty when a defect in the premises attracts the attacker, when the landlord undertakes a duty, and when there is "overriding foreseeability." Walls v. Oxford Management Company, Inc., 137 N.H. 653, 633 A.2d 103 (1993).

20. E.g., Jacqueline S. v. City of New York, 81 N.Y.2d 288, 614 N.E.2d 723, 598 N.Y.S.2d 160 (1993). California requires evidence of similar instances when the plaintiff asserts that security guards were necessary. See n. 24.

21. Gans v. Parkview Plaza Partnership, 253 Neb. 373, 571 N.W.2d 261 (1997).

22. Brock v. Watts Realty Co., Inc., 582 So.2d 438, 43 A.L.R.5th 839 (Ala. 1991) (statutory duty to keep locks in repair, similar incidents not required); Tenney v. Atlantic Associates, 594 N.W.2d 11 (Iowa 1999) (key management).

23. E.g., Johnston v. Harris, 387 Mich. 569, 198 N.W.2d 409 (1972).

unreasonable defects in the premises themselves. However, it is also possible that given sufficient danger, reasonable care will require the landlord to provide security guards or patrols even when the premises themselves are not defective.[24] When the landlord has superior knowledge of danger, other cases may require him to warn the tenant and again this may be so even if the premises are themselves in good physical condition.[25]

The most common case for liability involves the lease of premises for residential purposes, usually in multi-unit properties, but liability has also been imposed upon landlords of commercial premises. The office worker attacked in an elevator[26] or a vacant floor,[27] or while working in her office at night,[28] for example, stands in the shoes of the commercial tenant and is entitled to an equal degree of protection, as does a mall tenant's employee on her way to the employee parking facility.[29]

Although the general trend is to bring the landlord within the normal rules of negligence law by imposing a duty to provide reasonable protection against foreseeable harms, almost every decision for liability has a counterpart somewhere that rejects liability. Of these, some ostensibly rely on the general rule that the landlord owes no duty to protect against third persons.[30] At least some of these, however, seem to be adjudicating particular facts on the negligence issue without rejecting a duty of care that would impose liability in appropriate cases.[31]

24. Martinez v. Woodmar IV Condominiums Homeowners Association, Inc., 189 Ariz. 206, 941 P.2d 218 (1997). California, which brings many adjudications about reasonable care into the duty issue decided by judges, holds that the landlord has no duty to provide security guards unless specific instances of criminal activity make the risk especially probable or highly foreseeable. Ann M. v. Pacific Plaza Shopping Center, 6 Cal.4th 666, 679, 863 P.2d 207, 215, 25 Cal.Rptr.2d 137, 146 (1993). This highly foreseeable test has been extended to landowners owning small properties as well. See n. 19.

25. Smith v. General Apartment Company, 133 Ga.App. 927, 213 S.E.2d 74 (1975) (landlord knew intruders had a passkey but deliberately failed to warn female tenants), overruled on other grounds, Country Club Apartments, Inc. v. Scott, 246 Ga. 443, 271 S.E.2d 841 (1980) (rejecting exculpatory clauses). A Minnesota court has taken the view that no warning is due merely because the landlord knows of the risk of attack. It is only due in Minnesota when the landlord knows of a specific threat to a specific individual. Consequently, in Minnesota, a landlord who knows he has a convicted child molester permanently on the premises and who attracts children of tenants with his rabbits, has no duty whatever to warn the tenants. N.W. by J. W. v. Anderson, 478 N.W.2d 542 (Minn.Ct.App. 1991).

26. Samson v. Saginaw Professional Building, Inc., 393 Mich. 393, 224 N.W.2d 843 (1975) (landlord failed to reveal another tenant's dangerous clients).

27. See Doe v. Dominion Bank of Washington, N.A., 963 F.2d 1552 (D.C.Cir.1992) (extending the *Kline* principle, n. 17, to commercial leases).

28. Gans v. Parkview Plaza Partnership, 253 Neb. 373, 571 N.W.2d 261 (1997).

29. Doe v. Montgomery Mall Limited Partnership, 962 F.Supp. 58 (D.Md.1997).

30. Bartley v. Sweetser, 319 Ark. 117, 890 S.W.2d 250 (1994).

31. See, e.g., Doe v. Grosvenor Properties (Hawaii) Ltd., 73 Haw. 158, 829 P.2d 512 (1992) (invoking the no duty rule, but seemingly because of the court's perception that the attack was unforeseeable on the facts).

§ 326. Custodian's and School's State–Law Duty to Protect Ward or Students

A person who has custody of another owes a duty of reasonable care to protect the other from foreseeable harm.[1] A custodian may thus be held liable for failure to make reasonable efforts to protect a ward from a third person's attack or molestation and even to protect the ward from his own self-destructive inclinations. The defendant may undertake to protect the plaintiff quite apart from custody, but this section speaks only to the duty arising from custody itself.

Jailers and custodians of mentally or physically disabled. Custodians include those who actually exercise control over their charges or who have legal authority to control them. One clear example is the jailer who holds prisoners in custody. By reason of his custody, the jailer owes the prisoner a duty of reasonable protection from attack[2] and from suicide.[3] The same point applies to an officer who takes a person into custody.[4] Indeed, the United States Constitution itself requires no less,[5] so jailers who fail in their duty might be held either under state tort law or under federal civil rights laws. What is true of jailers is equally true of those who have custody of insane or incompetent persons.[6]

Parents. Although the issue has seldom arisen, where parents cannot claim the traditional parental immunity, they undoubtedly owe a duty of care to their unemancipated minor children so long as they have custody.[7] Other family members may also take custody of a child and if they do, they assume the protective obligations of custodians.[8] For instance, they may be obliged to protect a child from sexual abuse by others.[9]

Schools. Common lore has it that while children are in the charge of a school, the school stands in loco parentis, that is, in the role of parents.[10] That would mean that the school, during periods in which it

§ 326

1. See Restatement § 314A (4).

2. See, e.g., Daniels v. Andersen, 195 Neb. 95, 237 N.W.2d 397 (1975).

3. Falkenstein v. City of Bismarck, 268 N.W.2d 787 (N.D.1978).

4. Jackson v. City of Kansas City, 263 Kan. 143, 947 P.2d 31 (1997) (arrestee attacked by his girlfriend while he was handcuffed).

5. Estelle v. Gamble, 429 U.S. 97, 97 S.Ct. 285, 50 L.Ed.2d 251 (1976).

6. Youngberg v. Romeo, 457 U.S. 307, 102 S.Ct. 2452, 73 L.Ed.2d 28 (1982) (federal due process rights); cf. Niece v. Elmview Group Home, 131 Wash.2d 39, 929 P.2d 420 (1997) (group home for developmentally disabled owes a duty of care to patient to protect from staff members, both because of its relation to the staff and its relation to the patient).

7. See Hite v. Brown, 100 Ohio App.3d 606, 654 N.E.2d 452 (1995) (mother, relationship to child seemingly the focus).

8. A.R.H. v. W.H.S., 876 S.W.2d 687 (Mo.App.1994) (grandmother).

9. Frideres v. Schiltz, 540 N.W.2d 261 (Iowa 1995); Werre v. David, 275 Mont. 376, 913 P.2d 625 (1996); Hite v. Brown, supra n. 7; cf. A.R.H. v. W.H.S., supra n. 8 (grandmother who had child in her care); but cf. Robinson v. Robinson, 323 Ark. 224, 914 S.W.2d 292 (1996) (in a state that has not abolished the immunity except for wilful acts, mother was immune as to claim for negligently failing to protect daughter).

10. McLeod v. Grant County School Dist. No. 128, 42 Wash.2d 316, 255 P.2d 360 (1953) ("the protective custody of

has charge of students, would owe them the same duties as their parents, presumably the duty of reasonable care. However, where parents can still claim parental immunity, the same premise suggests, and some courts hold, that the school not only takes the parental duties but also the parental immunities.[11] For this reason, or because of statutory immunities granted in some states to public schools, the question of the school's duty of protection may never be reached.

When no immunity applies, however, decisions have recognized that the school owes its students a duty of reasonable supervision[12] and other forms of reasonable protection, sometimes likened to that which ordinary parents would provide.[13] For breach of such duties, schools may be held responsible for a student's own self-harm or suicide.[14] Schools may likewise be responsible for a student's injury from attack, harassment, or molestation by outsiders,[15] other students,[16] and, in some cases, by teachers or other school staff.[17]

As in most other negligence cases, liability is imposed only if the defendant's negligent conduct caused the harm complained of.[18] And of course the duty imposed under these rules is only a duty of reasonable care, so liability does not follow unless the school breached its duty. If the harm was not reasonably foreseeable, or if the school took reasonable

teachers is mandatorily substituted for that of the parent").

11. Stiff v. Eastern Illinois Area of Special Education, 279 Ill.App.3d 1076, 666 N.E.2d 343, 216 Ill.Dec. 893 (1996); contra, Purzycki v. Town of Fairfield, 244 Conn. 101, 708 A.2d 937 (1998). Other immunities besides the delegated immunity of parents may protect the school. See Henrich v. Libertyville High School, 186 Ill.2d 381, 238 Ill.Dec. 576, 712 N.E.2d 298 (1998) (broad statutory immunity); Allan E. Korpela, Annotation, Modern Status of Doctrine of Sovereign Immunity as Applied to Public Schools and Institutions of Higher Learning, 33 A.L.R.3d 703 (1971).

12. See, e.g., Moore v. Wood County Board of Education, 200 W.Va. 247, 489 S.E.2d 1 (1997)

13. Lunsford v. Board of Education of Prince George's County, 280 Md. 665, 374 A.2d 1162 (1977) (approving instruction that schools duty was "analogous" to parent's).

14. Brooks v. Logan, 127 Idaho 484, 903 P.2d 73 (1995) (although school is not in custodial relationship, statutory relationship creates a duty of reasonable care to take affirmative actions to avoid foreseeable harms, including suicide); Eisel v. Board of Education of Montgomery County, 324 Md. 376, 597 A.2d 447, 17 A.L.R.5th 957 (Ct. App. 1991); cf. Kelson v. Springfield, 767 F.2d 651 (9th Cir.1985) (recognizing civil rights claim under § 1983).

15. Fazzolari v. Portland School Dist. No. 1J, 303 Or. 1, 734 P.2d 1326 (1987) (rape by stranger while student was waiting for school to open).

16. Todd M. v. Richard L., 44 Conn.Sup. 527, 696 A.2d 1063 (1995) (sexual abuse by other students on school bus); Mirand v. City of New York, 84 N.Y.2d 44, 614 N.Y.S.2d 372, 637 N.E.2d 263 (1994) (attack in school, inadequate supervision); McLeod v. Grant County School Dist. No. 128, 42 Wash.2d 316, 255 P.2d 360 (1953) (rape of female student by two 15-year-old students who had been left unsupervised with access to secluded area); but cf. Anderson v. Shaughnessy, 526 N.W.2d 625 (Minn.1995) (duty included safe transportation but terminated when students were safety delivered, although the claim was that the school bus driver should have disarmed a student while he was still on the bus).

17. Marquay v. Eno, 139 N.H. 708, 662 A.2d 272 (1995).

18. E.g., Skinner v. Vacaville Unified School District, 37 Cal.App.4th 31, 43 Cal. Rptr.2d 384 (1995) (school's failure to alert teacher to student's disciplinary record not shown to be a substantial factor in student's assault on another student); Doe v. Coffee County Board of Education, 925 S.W.2d 534 (Tenn.Ct.App.1996) (allowing coach to have locks on door was not a substantial factor in sexual harassment of female students, hence school has liability).

precautions in the light of foreseeable harm, it simply is not negligent and liability cannot be imposed.[19] But harm from third persons may be foreseeable in some situations even if it has not occurred before and if so, reasonable protection is required.[20]

Statutes requiring the report of suspected child abuse, may require teachers as well as others to report incidents of abuse, including those inflicted by third persons entirely outside the school setting,[21] but many courts have held that violation of these statutes is not negligence per se.[22]

Sexual harassment, molestation, or exploitation in schools. Sexual harassment in schools presents complex legal problems which the common law of tort deals with only in part.[23] If a student is sexually molested by a member of the school staff, she presumably has an ordinary battery claim against her molester. Because a teacher's sexual conduct toward students is often regarded as outside the scope of his employment,[24] liability often must be based upon the school's negligence in hiring or retaining a dangerous person[25] or in failing to report or otherwise deal with cases of known or suspected abuse of this kind. Given the purpose of the teacher's vocation and the school's relationship to its students, it is appropriate to impose upon the school a duty of care that includes protection from sexual exploitation and abuse. Reasonable care might, for example, include reasonable supervision of students and teachers; it might require a report to authorities who can control the abuser's conduct or dismiss him.[26] The duty is only one of reasonable care. If the school has no notice that a teacher is a risk for sexual or

19. See Beshears v. Unified School District No. 305, 261 Kan. 555, 930 P.2d 1376 (1997) (after-school, off-grounds fight was unforeseeable and school is not liable for injuries inflicted; expressed as a rule of no duty when the problem was unforeseeable).

20. E.g., Garcia v. City of New York, 222 A.D.2d 192, 646 N.Y.S.2d 508 (1996) (small child allowed to go to bathroom alone in violation of school safety rules was sexually assaulted, judgment for plaintiff affirmed).

21. Kimberly S.M. v. Bradford Central School, 226 A.D.2d 85, 649 N.Y.S.2d 588 (1996); see Landeros v. Flood, 17 Cal.3d 399, 131 Cal.Rptr. 69, 551 P.2d 389, 97 A.L.R.3d 324 (1976) (medical personnel). Distinguish statutes requiring state agencies to investigate reports of child abuse.

22. See Cechman v. Travis, 202 Ga.App. 255, 414 S.E.2d 282 (1991); Perry v. S.N., 973 S.W.2d 301(Tex.1998) (considering a number of factors, including the fact that at common law there was no duty to protect from third persons); Marquay v. Eno, supra n. 17.

23. As to federal civil rights claims against schools for sexual harassment or abuse, see § 327.

24. John R. v. Oakland Unified School District, 48 Cal.3d 438, 256 Cal.Rptr. 766, 769 P.2d 948 (1989); P. L. v. Aubert , 545 N.W.2d 666 (Minn.1996); cf. Tall v. Board of School Comn'rs of Baltimore City, 120 Md.App. 236, 706 A.2d 659 (Md. 1998) (teacher beat Down's Syndrome child for urinating in his pants, this is outside scope of employment and vicarious liability cannot be imposed).

25. See § 331; cf. Randi W. v. Muroc Joint Unified School District, 14 Cal.4th 1066, 60 Cal.Rptr.2d 263, 929 P.2d 582 (1997) (allegation that defendant negligently recommendation sexually dangerous person to a school with resulting molestation of student at the new school).

26. See Marquay v. Eno, supra n. 17 (distinguishing between school personnel who have relationships to students and owe a duty for that reason and school personnel who have responsibility for hiring and firing; the latter may owe duties of care in selecting teachers and discharging them).

other abusive misconduct, the school simply is not negligent and is not liable.[27]

Colleges. Colleges may act in a number of different roles. Either as colleges having a relationship to students, or as landlords of student housing, they may be under a duty to protect their tenants from attack by supplying appropriate door locks or otherwise.[28] They might, again like others, undertake duties of care by promises or representations.[29] On the other hand, college students are regarded as independent adults and courts have refused to impose upon colleges any duty to protect them from the pressures of college life.[30] Some courts have been equally unwilling to require reasonable care from colleges in protecting one college student from another,[31] even when the college knows it has admitted a dangerous student.[32]

§ 327. Caretakers without Custody: Civil Rights

Custody as nonexclusive basis for duty. Many people who undertake the care of others or who accept an assignment of such care are not custodians. As a matter of state tort law, persons in a non-custodial caretaker role, however, may be under a duty of care because of their undertaking or assumed duty or because of some other relationship. A medical doctor, for example, has no custody of patients, but may be under a duty to report evidence of child abuse.[1]

Custody not required in sex discrimination cases. Likewise, custody is not required to establish a federal statutory duty to protect certain persons from sexual discrimination, abuse, or harassment. Title IX prohibits discrimination on account of sex in educational institutions receiving federal funds.[2] This is understood to impose a duty upon officials to stop sexual harassment or molestation by school authorities.[3] Under the same statute, the school is also liable under a "deliberate

27. E.g., Moore v. Berkeley County School District, 326 S.C. 584, 486 S.E.2d 9 (1997) (school knew that teacher ran a lax classroom but had no notice that she was having sex with students; no liability).

28. Mullins v. Pine Manor College, 389 Mass. 47, 449 N.E.2d 331 (1983).

29. George v. University of Idaho, 121 Idaho 30, 822 P.2d 549 (Ct.App.1991). (faculty-student handbook and customs; a university's failure to prevent repeated sexual harassment by a law teacher); Delaney v. University of Houston, 835 S.W.2d 56 (Tex. 1992) (assurance of security, failure to repair broken lock).

30. See Beach v. University of Utah, 726 P.2d 413, 62 A.L.R.4th 67 (Utah 1986); Hegel v. Langsam, 29 Ohio Misc. 147, 273 N.E.2d 351, 55 O.O. 2d 476, 58 O.O.2d 423 (1971); Wilson v. Continental Insurance Companies, 87 Wis.2d 310, 274 N.W.2d 679 (1979).

31. See Tanja H. v. Regents of the University of California, 228 Cal.App.3d 434, 278 Cal.Rptr. 918 (1991) (college's failure to enforce its own drinking rules, allegedly resulting in a dormitory sexual assault).

32. Eiseman v. State, 70 N.Y.2d 175, 518 N.Y.S.2d 608, 511 N.E.2d 1128 (1987).

§ 327

1. First Commercial Trust Co. v. Rank, 323 Ark. 390, 915 S.W.2d 262 (1996).

2. 20 U.S.C.A. § 1681.

3. Franklin v. Gwinnett County Public Schools, 503 U.S. 60, 112 S.Ct. 1028, 117 L.Ed.2d 208 (1992) ("when a supervisor sexually harasses a subordinate because of the subordinate's sex, that supervisor 'discriminate[s]' on the basis of sex"; private action for damages against school which tolerated coach's sexual conduct with students).

indifference" standard if it ignores a known and serious sexual harassment of one student by another.[4] Another federal avenue is the claim that purposeful sexual harassment-discrimination violates Equal Protection and is actionable under the basic civil rights statute, § 1983[5] or that it violates substantive Due Process.[6] However, public entities like schools are not subject to vicarious liability under § 1983 for the unconstitutional acts of teachers or other personnel; the school is liable only if the school itself made an official decision or maintained an unconstitutional policy.[7]

When custody is required to establish a duty to protect under civil rights laws. However, when the claim does not turn on sexual discrimination, abuse, or harassment, and the state does not affirmatively create or enhance danger,[8] formal custody has been of controlling importance in federal civil rights duties to protect from third persons. The United States Supreme Court has recognized that the custodial relationship imposes affirmative duties upon a custodian, both in the case of a prisoner[9] and an involuntarily committed mental patient.[10] But the only relationship the Court has so far recognized is the custodial one.

The DeShaney case. In the famous *DeShaney* case,[11] the county department of social services took temporary custody of a small child, Joshua, because of evidence that he was abused by his father. The department returned the child to his father under an agreement with the father that established the department's right to monitor Joshua's safety. The department in fact regularly sent a caseworker, but in spite of mounting evidence that he was being savagely beaten, the caseworker did nothing to regain control. Joshua's father's beatings finally produced profound brain damage and left Joshua confined for life in an institution for the profoundly retarded. The Supreme Court held, however, that the department did not have custody of Joshua even though it had practical

4. Davis v. Monroe County Bd. of Educ., 526 U.S. 629, 119 S.Ct. 1661, 143 L.Ed.2d 839 (1999).

5. Oona, R.-S. v. McCaffrey, 143 F.3d 473 (9th Cir.1998).

6. Doe v. Claiborne County, Tennessee, 103 F.3d 495 (6th Cir.1996) (sexual abuse at the hands of a public school employee "strips the very essence of personhood. If the right to bodily integrity means anything, it certainly encompasses the right not to be sexually assaulted under color of law").

7. See § 277.

8. As to liability for affirmatively creating or enhancing danger, see, e.g., Kneipp v. Tedder, 95 F.3d 1199 (3d Cir.1996) (police officers stopped severely inebriated woman proceeding on foot on a cold night less than half a block from her home, then later releasing her; she suffered brain damage from the cold; this was sufficient to state a constitutional claim). The *Kneipp* court identified four factors it thought were significant in this non-custodial kind of claim: (1) injury was foreseeable; (2) the officer acted in wilful disregard for her safety; (3) there was a relationship, albeit one that fell short of custody; and (4) defendants used their official authority "to create a dangerous situation or to make [the plaintiff] more vulnerable to danger" than if they had not intervened.

9. Estelle v. Gamble, supra n. 5 (8th Amendment, cruel and unusual punishment).

10. Youngberg v. Romeo, 457 U.S. 307, 102 S.Ct. 2452, 73 L.Ed.2d 28 (1982) (due process).

11. DeShaney v. Winnebago County Dept. of Social Services, 489 U.S. 189, 109 S.Ct. 998, 103 L.Ed.2d 249 (1989).

power of obtaining custody and had taken a number of inadequate steps to protect him.

For the Court, "custody" meant depriving the plaintiff of liberty so that he could not longer protect himself or obtain aid from others. Because Joshua was not in custody in this strict sense, no civil rights action would lie.[12] Although as a matter of ordinary tort law, defendants are often under a duty of care because they voluntarily assumed the duty by acts or promises, *DeShaney* might be read to mean that such undertakings have no constitutional significance unless state action makes the plaintiff worse off than no state action.[13]

Children in foster homes. The strict custody requirement of the *DeShaney* case does not foreclose a constitutionally based duty of care when the public entity actually takes guardianship of a child and then fails to exercise appropriate custodial supervision with the result that the child is injured or killed.[14] For instance, the state officers who take charge of a child and then knowingly or indifferently place her in a dangerous foster home environment are subject to liability for depriving the child of due process rights by causing her harm.[15] "If the fire department rescues you from a fire that would have killed you, this does not give the department a constitutional license to kill you, on the ground that you will be no worse off than if there were no fire department."[16] In addition, the state, having placed a child in a foster home, may be expected to verify that the home continues to be safe for children and may even be held to a standard of professional judgment.[17]

Compulsory schooling and custody. On the other hand, the strict custody requirement has indeed been strict in the constitutional cases. For example, in a Seventh Circuit case, the plaintiff alleged that his blind and developmentally disabled son was subjected to repeated sexual abuse by other students at the Illinois School for the Visually Impaired and that the superintendent did not put a stop to the abuse even after he actually learned of it. But since the child was not taken into custody by the state—he voluntarily attended the school—the court thought there was no constitution-based duty to protect the boy.[18] The case reflects the general view that, compulsory school attendance is not custody[19] and that short of "custody," the constitution does not require any school to

12. The *DeShaney* case did not decide whether a denial of equal protection or a denial of a state-created entitlement without procedural due process would produce a different result. As to the latter, see Meador v. Cabinet for Human Resources, 902 F.2d 474 (6th Cir.1990).

13. See Wyke v. Polk County School Board, 129 F.3d 560 (11th Cir.1997) (a school official, informed of a 13-year old's suicide attempt in school, assured his informant that he would "take care of it," but then only read the boy Bible verses, after which the boy committed suicide; no constitutional duty).

14. Camp v. Gregory, 67 F.3d 1286 (7th Cir.1995).

15. E.g., Meador v. Cabinet for Human Resources, 902 F.2d 474 (6th Cir.1990).

16. K.H. v. Morgan, 914 F.2d 846, 849 (7th Cir.1990).

17. Kara B. v. Dane County, 205 Wis.2d 140 555 N.W.2d 630 (1996).

18. Stevens v. Umsted, 131 F.3d 697 (7th Cir.1997).

19. See cases cited nn. 20–22.

protect one student from another,[20] from himself,[21] or from intruders.[22] In fact, unless the school maintains a policy or custom supporting abusive teachers, or the school is responsible under Title IX, it may escape responsibility under federal law for its teachers' sexual abuse of minor students.[23]

§ 328. Employer's and Others' Duties of Protection

It has been held that fellow employees owe no duty of reasonable care to rescue or otherwise assist a coworker who is attacked.[1] Employers, on the other hand, owe a duty of reasonable care to protect "servants" who are endangered on the job, at least when they are threatened with "imminent danger."[2] Few contemporary cases elaborate this duty because workers' compensation has largely supplanted tort obligations. The old familiar cases reflect the rule of maritime law that a captain must make every effort to rescue a seaman lost overboard[3] and provide medical attention when an employee is helpless.[4]

Beyond that, the employer may be under a duty to use reasonable care to protect the employee from attacks by third persons. The duty may be viewed either as arising from the employment relationship alone or from the employer's implied undertaking to provide appropriate protection.[5] For instance, the duty of care may require the employer to provide a reasonably safe work place by providing appropriate lighting and windows so that a night employee in an isolated place can see to protect herself from attack and the employer who does not do so may properly be found negligent.[6] In some cases the duty might be satisfied by a warning that reveals the danger.[7] Besides providing reasonable protection against third persons, employers whose medical examination of employees and prospective employees reveals a serious medical condi-

20. D.R. v. Middle Bucks Area Vocational Technical School, 972 F.2d 1364 (3d Cir. 1992).

21. Wyke v. Polk County School Board, 129 F.3d 560 (11th Cir.1997).

22. See Johnson v. Dallas Independent School District, 38 F.3d 198 (5th Cir.1994) (student shot randomly by intruder who (a) somehow took a school bus to get to the premises, although he was not a student; (b) entered the building without a student badge as was generally required; (c) passed the metal detectors with his gun because the detectors were not being used, but court viewed school as a non-actor and protected by *DeShaney* rather than as an actor who's conduct, e.g., admission of gun-carrying strangers, was negligent).

23. Doe v. Claiborne County, Tennessee, 103 F.3d 495 (6th Cir.1996).

§ 328

1. Fay v. Assignment America, 666 N.Y.S.2d 304, 245 A.D.2d 783 (1997).

2. Restatement § 314B.

3. Gardner v. National Bulk Carriers, Inc., 310 F.2d 284, 91 A.L.R.2d 1023 (4th Cir. 1962).

4. Szabo v. Pennsylvania R.R., 132 N.J.L. 331, 40 A.2d 562 (1945).

5. See Linda A. Sharp, Annotation, Employer's Liability to Employee or Agent for Injury or Death Resulting from Assault or Criminal Attack by Third Person, 40 A.L.R.5th 1 (1996).

6. Lillie v. Thompson, 332 U.S. 459, 68 S.Ct. 140, 92 L.Ed. 73 (1947).

7. Pratt v. St. Marie, 45 Or.App. 709, 609 P.2d 411 (1980) (defendant hired plaintiff to help evict tenant but did not warn the plaintiff that the tenant might be violent; defendant potentially liable when tenant shot the plaintiff).

tion may be under a duty of care to reveal the condition to the employee or prospective employee.[8]

As in other negligence cases, the duty is one of reasonable care. If danger from a third person is not foreseeable, the employer is not negligent in failing to provide protection.[9] Similarly, the employer is not responsible for employee injuries if the employer is not an actual and legal cause of harm, or if the injuries did not not occur during employment.[10]

Many of the decisions are older ones, and some of these as well as some fairly recent decisions refuse to treat the employment relationship in itself as sufficient basis for a duty of care. These impose liability only when the employer greatly increases the risk or when special or imminent danger is shown.[11] Sometimes decisions assert that the employee assumes the risk of assaults that are normal to the employment.[12]

§ 329. Duty Based upon the Defendant's Relationship to a Dangerous Person

The immediately preceding sections covered cases in which the defendant owes a duty to protect the plaintiff from third persons because the defendant and plaintiff stand in a special relationship to one another. A quite distinct ground for imposing such a duty is that the defendant stands in a special relationship to a dangerous person and is in a position to control that person or limit his capacity for harm.

General rule. The usual starting point is that the defendant is under no duty to control a dangerous person in the absence of a special relationship, either with the plaintiff or with the dangerous person. For instance, a passenger in an automobile, perceiving that the driver is dangerously intoxicated, owes no duty to anyone to persuade the driver to stop or relinquish the driving task to others.[1] Frequently, however,

8. See Union Carbide & Carbon Corp. v. Stapleton, 237 F.2d 229, 69 A.L.R.2d 1206 (6th Cir. 1956) (emphasizing employee's reliance, expectation, and the affirmative action of the employer in requiring physical exams); Coffee v. McDonnell–Douglas Corp., 8 Cal.3d 551, 503 P.2d 1366, 105 Cal.Rptr. 358 (1972) (pre-employment exam, relationship of the parties created when defendant undertook the examination); Dornak v. Lafayette General Hosp., 399 So.2d 168 (La.1981) (pre-employment exam).

9. See Habich v. Crown Central Petroleum Corporation, 642 So.2d 699 (Ala.1994) (holding that rape of night employee of a convenience store was not foreseeable, but adding also that there was no special relationship between employer and employee).

10. See Mormino v. Leon Hess, 119 F.Supp. 314 (S.D.N.Y.1953); Farmer v. O/S Fluffy D, 220 F.Supp. 917 (S.D.Tex.1963).

11. E.g., Parham v. Taylor, 402 So.2d 884 (Ala.1981). A later Alabama case, however, seemed to say that either foreseeability of harm or a special relationship would suffice. See Habich v. Crown Central Petroleum Corporation, 642 So.2d 699 (Ala. 1994).

12. Jaynes v. Bush, 136 Ark. 602, 203 S.W. 693 (1918). Contemporary thinking treats this as a case in which the employer has no duty or care or has not breached its duty. See §§ 211–213.

§ 329

1. Martinson v. Cagle, 454 So.2d 1383 (Ala.1984); Olson v. Ische, 343 N.W.2d 284 (Minn.1984). Distinguish the case of a passenger who actively provides alcohol to the driver or encourages him to engage in dangerous behavior. Such passengers may become liable for injuries resulting. See Sneath v. Popiolek, 135 Mich.App. 17, 352

actual custodial *control* of a dangerous person is not really the point.[2] Rather, the relationship of the defendant to the dangerous person may be enough to require the defendant to use reasonable means at his disposal to protect the plaintiff or reduce the risk to her, even if control is impossible. Thus the usual statement of the rule in terms of "control" tends to obscure the possibility that a reasonable defendant might save the plaintiff by the most limited efforts, such as a warning.[3]

Recognized relationships to dangerous person. However that may be, several relationships establish a right, authority, and duty to control dangerous persons, which in turn requires the defendant to exercise care. It must be said once more that the duty under discussion is only a duty to exercise reasonable care under the circumstances, not a duty to guarantee protection. In particular, the Restatement recognizes that the defendant is expected to exercise care to control (1) his minor children,[4] (2) employees using his premises or chattels,[5] (3) dangerous persons in his custody,[6] and (4) those who are subject to his power because they are licensees on his land or using his chattels.[7]

Liability limited to negligence. In each case, the defendant is expected to act only if he knows or should know of his power to do so and knows of the need. If a parent could not foresee that his child would take part in a gay-bashing episode resulting in death, the parent has not breached any duty of care and is not liable.[8]

§ 330. Control through Ownership: Negligent Entrustment

Control of licensees and negligent entrustment. The defendant's ownership and right to control land and chattels imposes upon him a duty to use reasonable care to control permissive users to prevent them from inflicting harm.[1] This obligation is closely related to responsibility

N.W.2d 331 (1984); Shelter Mutual Ins. Co. v. White, 930 S.W.2d 1 (Mo.App.1996).

2. See Hertog v. City of Seattle, 138 Wash.2d 265, 979 P.2d 400, 408 (1999) ("custodial control is not required. The relevant inquiry is the relationship of the officer with the parolee").

3. Thus a wife who knows her husband is a pedophile need not report her husband to authorities or seek his incarceration to protect neighbor children; she can arrange to be present when they are in the home. See J.S. v. R.T.H., 301 N.J.Super. 150, 693 A.2d 1191 (1997). Similarly, a psychiatrist need not commit his dangerous patient if he can protect a potential victim by giving her a warning. Tarasoff v. Regents of University of California, 17 Cal.3d 425, 131 Cal. Rptr. 14, 551 P.2d 334 (1976). Similarly, the owner of a car might not be required to "control" an intoxicated driver by force but could at least make an effort to persuade the driver to return the keys. Casebolt v. Cowan, 829 P.2d 352 (Colo.1992).

4. Restatement § 316.

5. Restatement § 317.

6. Restatement § 319.

7. Restatement § 318.

8. Rodriguez v. Spencer, 902 S.W.2d 37 (Tex.App.1995). Courts may in fact have protected some parents who were in fact negligent because they failed to control children with known aggressive tendencies. See Parsons v. Smithey, 109 Ariz. 49, 504 P.2d 1272, 54 A.L.R.3d 964 (1973) (parents of teenager with long history of aggressive antisocial behavior not liable because they could not have foreseen particular attack with a saw and hammer).

§ 330

1. Restatement § 318. See Huston v. Konieczny, 52 Ohio St.3d 214, 556 N.E.2d

for negligent entrustment of chattels to people who are likely to use the chattel in a dangerous way.[2] The typical case is negligent entrustment of an automobile[3] or a weapon[4] to a person whom the defendant knows or should know is apt to use it in a dangerous way because of his age and inexperience,[5] physical or mental limitations,[6] his character or habits[7], or his actual intoxication[8] or his propensity for it.[9]

Negligence rules applicable. Once the duty of care is imposed, the negligent entrustment case is an ordinary negligence case to which all the principles of negligence law apply.[10] If harm is not a reasonably foreseeable result of the entrustment, the defendant is not negligent at all.[11] Conversely, if harm is foreseeable, liability is appropriate not only when the defendant intentionally "entrusts" the chattel to a dangerous person but also when he negligently leaves the chattel at a place where he should expect that a dangerous person is likely to find and use it.[12] And again because foreseeability of harm is the touchstone, the lender who is not negligent when he entrusts an automobile may come under a duty to terminate the entrustment if he later learns that the borrower is

505 (1990) (parents permitting under-age children to use their house for a New Year's Even party with expectation that some would drink may be liable for injuries resulting from intoxication).

2. Restatement § 308 & Restatement § 390. The former would impose liability when the defendant should know that the user is likely to use the chattel in a way that creates an unreasonable risk. The latter would impose liability when the defendant has reason to know that the user would be incompetent, by reason of inexperience or otherwise. The latter covers commercial transfers as well as friendly loans.

3. E.g., LeClaire v. Commercial Siding and Maintenance Co., 308 Ark. 580, 826 S.W.2d 247 (1992) (but atypically involving a sub-entrustment).

4. Kitchen v. K-Mart Corp., 697 So.2d 1200 (Fla.1997); Bernethy v. Walt Failor's Inc., 97 Wash.2d 929, 653 P.2d 280 (1982) (gun dealer allowed intoxicated man to walk off with rifle). Cf. Hamilton v. Accu-Tek, 62 F.Supp.2d 802 (1999) (injury from illicit handgun; imposing liability upon handgun manufacturers who negligently distributed their products so as to increase the risk of irresponsible sales and criminal use, drawing analogy to negligent entrustment).

5. Ardinger v. Hummell, 982 P.2d 727 (Alaska 1999) (entrusting to 15-year-old unlicensed driver).

6. See Sanders v. Walden, 214 Ark. 523, 217 S.W.2d 357 (1949) (lending automobile to man who could not reach brake pedals and had a bad driving record).

7. Swicegood v. Cooper, 341 N.C. 178, 459 S.E.2d 206 (1995) (bad driving record known to defendant).

8. E.g., Casebolt v. Cowan, 829 P.2d 352 (Colo.1992).

9. See Eagle Motor Lines, Inc. v. Mitchell, 223 Miss. 398, 78 So.2d 482 (1955). Departing from ordinary negligence rules, some cases have required actual intoxication or other disability apparent at the time of the entrustment. E.g., Ellsworth v. Ludwig, 140 Ind.App. 437, 223 N.E.2d 764 (1967).

10. Casebolt v. Cowan, 829 P.2d 352 (Colo.1992); Olguin v. City of Burley, 119 Idaho 721, 810 P.2d 255 (1991). Thus negligent entrustment may show contributory negligence as well as negligence itself. Swicegood v. Cooper, 341 N.C. 178, 459 S.E.2d 206 (1995). But cf. Mackey v. Dorsey, 104 Md.App. 250, 655 A.2d 1333 (1995) (speaking of negligent entrustment as if it were distinct from negligence); Elrod v. G & R Constr. Co., 275 Ark. 151, 628 S.W.2d 17, 30 A.L.R.4th 831 (1982) (rejecting negligent entrustment evidence when the defendant has admitted that he is vicariously liable).

11. E.g., Brewster v. Rankins, 600 N.E.2d 154 (Ind.Ct.App.1992) (no harm foreseeable from allowing child to practice with golf club).

12. Kuhns v. Brugger, 390 Pa. 331, 135 A.2d 395, 68 A.L.R.2d 761 (1957) (child, access to gun); but cf. Mackey v. Dorsey, 104 Md.App. 250, 655 A.2d 1333 (1995) (leaving keys in the car with a stranger who stole the car is not entrusting the car).

using it dangerously.[13] The defendant may even be responsible to the borrower herself where he owes her a duty to protect her from her own incompetence.[14]

Control of chattel required. But the duty of care is not imposed on negligent entrustment grounds unless the defendant has the right to control the chattel. A bailee is not required to withhold the automobile from its owner[15] and a police officer is not required to arrest the intoxicated owner so he can take control of the car.[16] Although some authority holds that the defendant must not even sell or donate a car to a known dangerous driver,[17] others say that the defendant who knows the purchaser or donee is dangerous, has no responsibility to restrict sales of automobiles.[18] When it comes to firearms, however, sellers may be required to deliver them only to properly identified buyers who do not appear to be especially dangerous.[19]

§ 331. Control and other Means of Protecting from Dangerous Persons

Control is sufficient for duty. One in charge of a person who is, or should be recognized as dangerous, is under a duty of reasonable care to control that person to prevent harm.[1] For example, a prison is under a duty of reasonable care not to permit its inmates to escape and do harm.[2] Parole officers may have sufficient relationship if not "control" over dangerous criminals on parole to require them to exercise care in supervision.[3] Similarly, police may have sufficient control over a dangerous person because they are under a duty to enforce an injunction

13. Casebolt v. Cowan, 829 P.2d 352 (Colo.1992).

14. Casebolt v. Cowan, 829 P.2d 352 (Colo.1992); Frain v. State Farm Ins. Co., 421 So.2d 1169 (La.Ct.App.1982); see Ward Miller, Annotation, Negligent Entrustment: Bailor's Liability to Bailee Injured Through His Own Negligence or Incompetence, 12 A.L.R.4th 1062 (1981).

15. E.g., Knighten v. Sam's Parking Valet, 206 Cal.App.3d 69, 253 Cal.Rptr. 365 (1988); Sampson v. W.F. Enterprises, Inc., 611 S.W.2d 333 (Mo.Ct.App.1980). A passenger may relinquish his turn at driving and allow the intoxicated owner to resume driving. Lombardo v. Hoag, 269 N.J.Super. 36, 634 A.2d 550 (1993). But cf. Murray v. Whit Tatum Motors, Inc., 673 F.Supp. 981 (W.D.Ark.1987) (bailee had not been paid and had a right to refuse to release the chattel may be liable); Williams v. Bumpass, 568 So.2d 979 (Fla.Dist.Ct.App.1990) (defendant actually retrieved the owner's gun for him during an altercation between owner and another person; liability).

16. Olguin v. City of Burley, 119 Idaho 721, 810 P.2d 255 (1991); but cf. Ransom v. City of Garden City, 113 Idaho 202, 743 P.2d 70 (1987) (once officer had arrested owner and taken keys, he was under a duty of reasonable care in choosing to make keys available to other dangerous drivers).

17. Vince v. Wilson, 151 Vt. 425, 561 A.2d 103 (1989).

18. Horne v. Vic Potamkin Chevrolet, Inc., 533 So.2d 261 (Fla.1988)

19. Kitchen v. K–Mart Corporation, 697 So.2d 1200 (Fla.1997) (defendant sold gun to intoxicated man who then shot the plaintiff in the neck, rendering her quadriplegic).

§ 331

1. Restatement § 319.

2. Marceaux v. Gibbs, 699 So.2d 1065 (La.1997); State v. Silva, 86 Nev. 911, 478 P.2d 591, 44 A.L.R.3d 891 (1970). Immunity may protect the public entity operating the prison, however. See § 272.

3. Hertog v. City of Seattle, 138 Wash.2d 265, 979 P.2d 400 (1999).

against an abusive husband or father by arrest if necessary to protect the family.[4]

Neither control nor custody are necessary for duty. Cases have not required anything like "custody" of the dangerous person to trigger the duty of reasonable care to protect the plaintiff. Consequently, it would be more accurate as well as less confounding to recognize that "control" is merely one of the ways in which a defendant might act reasonably to minimize the risk of harm to others.

The Pied Piper cases supply an example. A mobile street vendor selling ice cream or the like by attracting children into the street, has no control over dangerous traffic, but the vendor must use reasonable care to protect the small children attracted by his music and his wares and may be liable if a child is struck by a another's car.[5] Gun manufacturers conceivably owe a duty of care to marketing their product so minimize the risk of sales to minors who are likely to kill but over whom they have no direct control.[6] Again without custody, or even immediate control, a landlord with a dangerous tenant[7] and a hospital with a dangerous surgeon[8] may be required to exercise care to prevent harm to others if for no other reason than because they are in a position to "terminate the tenancy" or other privileges. Along the same lines, a wife who knows her husband molests children certainly does not have her husband in custody and probably does not control him, but she is under a duty of care to neighboring children.[9] As usual, the duty is one of reasonable care only; she might satisfy the duty by warning the neighbors but much less disruptive solutions may be reasonably available; she might arrange to be present when neighbor children visit.[10]

Likewise, employers must exercise reasonable care to "control" their employees,[11] which often translates to a duty to use care in hiring,[12]

4. See Sorichetti v. City of New York, 65 N.Y.2d 461, 492 N.Y.S.2d 591, 482 N.E.2d 70 (1985); Nearing v. Weaver, 295 Or. 702, 670 P.2d 137 (1983) (abusive husband subjected to injunction nevertheless continued the abuse; police, under a mandate to arrest such persons, refused; liability supported). Note, however, that absent an injunctive order or the like, courts usually invoke some version of the public duty to relieve police from liability for failure to arrest. See § 271.

5. E.g., Neal v. Shiels, Inc., 166 Conn. 3, 347 A.2d 102 (1974) (duty of ordinary care, ordinary negligence principles govern). See David Rand, Jr., Annotation, Civil Liability of Mobile Vendor for Attracting into Street Child Injured by Another's Motor Vehicle, 84 A.L.R.3d 826 (1978).

6. Hamilton v. Accu-Tek, ___ F.Supp.2d ___ 1999 WL 557261 (1999).

7. Hudson v. Janesville Conservation Club, 168 Wis.2d 436, 484 N.W.2d 132 (1992) (tenant kept ferret, as landlord knew); Rosales v. Stewart, 113 Cal.App.3d 130, 169 Cal.Rptr. 660 (1980) (tenant had a habit of firing gun in the back yard, killed a neighbor); Strunk v. Zoltanski, 62 N.Y.2d 572, 479 N.Y.S.2d 175, 468 N.E.2d 13 (1984) (tenant's dangerous dog); contra: Frobig v. Gordon, 124 Wash.2d 732, 881 P.2d 226 (1994) (landlord not liable for injury resulting from tenant's tiger).

8. Darling v. Charleston Community Memorial Hospital, 33 Ill.2d 326, 211 N.E.2d 253 (1965) (leading case); Strubhart v. Perry Memorial Hospital Trust Authority, 903 P.2d 263 (Okla.1995).

9. See Pamela L. v. Farmer, 112 Cal. App.3d 206, 169 Cal.Rptr. 282 (1980); J.S. v. R.T.H., 155 N.J. 330, 714 A.2d 924 (1998).

10. J.S. v. R.T.H., supra n. 8.

11. Restatement § 317 (duty to control servant on the master's premises or using his chattel where the master knows or has reason to know that he can exert control

supervising,[13] or retaining[14] a dangerous person whose position in employment puts him in a position to harm others, even if in harming others he is not acting within scope of employment. Where the public duty doctrine or other immunities do not protect negligent public employers, they too are subject to a duty of care in hiring, supervising and retaining.[15]

Policy conflicts. Some but not all cases in which the defendant is asked to protect the plaintiff from dangerous persons raise policy conflicts. A duty of reasonable care by definition cannot be an undue burden, but it may still be difficult for a hospital to supervise a physician or a wife to chaperone her husband without risking damage to the relationship. Given a duty of care in such cases, liability by no means follows. It might be, for example, that the duty of reasonable care is readily satisfied by a hospital's annual review of a physician's performance.

The therapist's dangerous patient. The policy conflict in imposing a duty was the strongest argument in one of the famous cases, *Tarasoff v. Regents of the University of California.*[16] In that case, a psychologist concluded that his patient, Poddar, intended to kill Tatiana Tarasoff. He was concerned enough to tell the police, but the police released Poddar after a brief detention. The psychologist and his superiors did not attempt to commit Poddar or even to warn the Tarasoff family. Poddar did in fact kill Tatiana Tarasoff.

In a suit against the psychologist for Tatiana's wrongful death, the defendants argued that it was against good public policy to impose a duty of care upon therapists because it would force them to breach their confidence and undermine what therapists consider to be the essential trust between therapist and patient. The court, however, imposed a duty of reasonable care, at least when a specific, known person was endangered. The therapist is thus required to act only when his own professional judgment indicated that others were in danger. Although some

and that the occasion for control is at hand).

12. Ponticas v. K.M.S. Investments, 331 N.W.2d 907, 38 A.L.R.4th 225 (Minn. 1983) (convicted criminal hired as manager of apartment complex; the investigation required by due care is "directly related to the severity of the risk third parties are subjected to by an incompetent employee." With high risk access to apartments of young women tenants at all times involved, the jury could find negligence in failing to investigate further); J. v. Victory Tabernacle Baptist Church, 236 Va. 206, 372 S.E.2d 391 (1988) (employer hired convicted sexual predator and left him around small girls at the defendant's church, with predictable results; liability even though the predator was not acting within the scope of employment in raping a child).

13. Trahan–Laroche v. Lockheed Sanders, Inc., 139 N.H. 483, 657 A.2d 417 (1995).

14. Welsh Manufacturing, Division of Textron, Inc. v. Pinkerton's, Inc., 474 A.2d 436, 44 A.L.R.4th 603 (R.I. 1984) (supervision, retention of guard hired to protect gold was inadequate, liability). Some cases that formally deny the existence of a duty to supervise, e.g., Roberson v. Allied Foundry and Mach. Co., 447 So.2d 720 (Ala.1984), might be interpreted to mean only that, on the facts of the particular case, the employer was not negligent.

15. E.g., Haddock v. City of New York, 140 A.D.2d 91, 532 N.Y.S.2d 379 (1988)

16. Tarasoff v. Regents of University of California, 17 Cal.3d 425, 131 Cal.Rptr. 14, 551 P.2d 334 (1976).

commentators from the therapeutic community have been negative,[17] the court in *Tarasoff* resolved the policy conflict in favor of the general rule that a duty of care is owed in the absence of compelling reasons to immunize the defendant. A number of states, including California,[18] have adopted the *Tarasoff* duty of reasonable care[19] or have enacted statutes imposing a similar duty.[20] The same rule may apply as well to school counselors and others less well trained, but in that case, they are expected only to make a diagnosis that meets their own professional standards.[21] In *Tarasoff* itself, the psychologist made a correct diagnosis of the patient and knew of the danger. Some cases imposed a duty of care to third persons to make a non-negligent diagnosis in the first place.[22] Other authority takes the view that the duty to diagnose with reasonable care runs only to the patient, so that if the physician never recognizes the danger at all, he is not then responsible for the patient's violence to others.[23]

The medical doctor's contagious or incapacitated patient. Similarly, to protect persons who are not patients,[24] some courts have imposed a duty upon medical doctors to warn their own patients[25] and non-patients as well,[26] that the patient's diseases are contagious or infectious, or to

17. Alan A. Stone, The Tarasoff Decisions: Suing Psychotherapists to Safeguard Society, 90 HARV. L. REV. 358, 368 (1976) (arguing that a warning to protect others would "imperil the therapeutic alliance and destroy the patient's expectation of confidentiality"); Robert F. Schopp, The Psychotherapist's Duty to Protect the Public: The Appropriate Standard and the Foundation in Legal Theory and Empirical Premises, 70 NEB. L. REV. 327 (1991) (arguing that therapists cannot predict danger, so warning would only fortuitously save lives but would regularly damage the therapeutic relationship). But see David B. Wexler, Patients, Therapists, and Third Parties: The Victimological Virtues of Tarasoff, 2 INT. J. OF L. & PSYCHIATRY 1 (1979).

18. CAL. CIV. CODE § 43.92.

19. E.g., Hamman v. County of Maricopa, 161 Ariz. 58, 775 P.2d 1122 (1989); Schuster v. Altenberg, 144 Wis.2d 223, 424 N.W.2d 159 (1988) (both rejecting the specific victim requirement). In Estates of Morgan v. Fairfield Family Counseling Ctr., 77 Ohio St.3d 284, 673 N.E.2d 1311 (1997) the court said it would apply the specific victim requirement only when the act of negligence was a failure to warn. When the therapist fails in his duty to the patient himself—by failing to provide appropriate treatment for example—the therapist is under a duty to all foreseeably injured persons, whether or not they are specifically identified. In this situation, too, the policy conflict disappears, since the therapist can avoid liability simply by properly treating his own patient.

20. See Steven R. Smith, Mental Health Malpractice in the 1990s, 28 HOUS. L. REV. 209 (1991); see also MICHAEL L. PERLIN, MENTAL DISABILITY LAW: CIVIL AND CRIMINAL (3 vols. 1989 & Supps.).

21. See Eisel v. Board of Education of Montgomery County, 324 Md. 376, 597 A.2d 447 (Ct.App.1991).

22. Schuster v. Altenberg, 144 Wis.2d 223, 424 N.W.2d 159 (1988).

23. Van Horn v. Chambers, 970 S.W.2d 542 (Tex.1998).

24. See Tracy A. Bateman, Annotation, Liability of Doctor or Other Health Practitioner to Third Party Contracting Contagious Disease from Doctor's Patient, 3 A.L.R.5th 370 (1992).

25. See Reisner v. Regents of University of California, 31 Cal.App.4th 1195, 37 Cal. Rptr.2d 518 (1995); DiMarco v. Lynch Homes–Chester County, Inc., 525 Pa. 558, 583 A.2d 422 (1990); cf. Pate v. Threlkel, 661 So.2d 278 (Fla.1995) (duty to warn patient that her disease is inheritable so she could warn daughter, but only when medical standard required warning); Safer v. Estate of Pack, 291 N.J.Super. 619, 677 A.2d 1188 (N.J. Super. 1996) (duty to warn patient of genetic danger to her children regardless of medical standard).

26. See Davis v. Rodman, 147 Ark. 385, 227 S.W. 612, 13 A.L.R. 1459 (1921) (but denying liability on causal grounds); McIn-

warn them that prescribed drugs may make driving unsafe for others on the road.[27] So long as the warning is made directly to the patient herself, neither confidentiality nor privacy issues are implicated, so it is difficult to understand a policy basis for cases that refuse to recognize a doctor's duty to warn the patient herself that she carries an infectious disease or that she is not a safe driver.[28]

Warnings to non-patients of medical doctor. When the plaintiff claims that a warning should have been given to a non-patient, however, stronger reasons appear for denying the duty. In some cases, it will be impossible to know who besides the plaintiff should receive a warning. Even when the doctor could identify the person most at risk from the patient's disease, issues of confidentiality and privacy like those raised in *Tarasoff* will be important. But *Tarasoff's* answer—requiring a reasonable warning to endangered non-patients—is not necessarily controlling when the patient himself has expressed no intent to harm others. A warning to the patient that she has an infectious disease, or that she cannot safely drive, would ordinarily reduce the risk to harm to non-patients to tolerable proportions. So cases that deny the duty to warn non-patients[29]—or that deny that the duty was breached—represent intelligible policy decisions .

Failing to control by setting dangerously low standards. A unique case imposed liability upon a trade or professional association that set dangerously low standards for its members. The association of blood banks set standards for screening blood, allegedly knowing that the standards set would fail to screen out AIDS contaminated blood. Some contaminated blood was transfused to the plaintiff who developed AIDS as a result. The New Jersey Court held that the defendant association owed a duty of care to avoid setting dangerously low standards.[30] Although the case has some affinity with products liability cases—the blood was defective in some sense—it also reflects a duty to protect the plaintiff from third persons who donated dangerous blood. Whether it suggests any principle that can generate other ideas about liability remains to be seen.

tosh v. Milano, 168 N.J.Super. 466, 403 A.2d 500 (1979); Bradshaw v. Daniel, 854 S.W.2d 865 (Tenn.1993).

27. Gooden v. Tips, 651 S.W.2d 364, 43 A.L.R.4th 139 (Tex.App. 1983).

28. Kirk v. Michael Reese Hospital and Medical Center, 117 Ill.2d 507, 513 N.E.2d 387, 111 Ill.Dec. 944 (1987); Webb v. Jarvis, 575 N.E.2d 992 (Ind.1991) (absence of privity explains why doctor has no duty to warn patient for benefit of others); Witthoeft v. Kiskaddon, ___ Pa. ___, 733 A.2d 623 (1999) (ophthalmologist failed to tell his patient that her visual acuity was so bad that she could not legally or safely drive; due to her bad vision, she struck and killed a bicyclist, but court asserted that this was "unforeseeable" and liability to recognize a duty of care would be to impose absolute liability).

29. Lemon v. Stewart, 111 Md.App. 511, 682 A.2d 1177 (1996) (AIDS).

30. Snyder v. American Association of Blood Banks, 144 N.J. 269, 676 A.2d 1036 (1996).

§ 332. Enhancing Dangers: Providers of Alcohol and other Substances

Traditional common law rule. Alcohol-impaired driving is a major factor in serious and fatal automobile injuries, and often in other injuries as well.[1] The traditional common law rule, however, was that those who provided alcohol to minors and intoxicated persons had no responsibility whatever for injuries inflicted by those drinkers, for example, injuries inflicted by the intoxicated person who drives negligently after consuming the defendant's alcohol.

Proximate cause rationale. The rule was usually explained on the ground that the consumption of alcohol, not its provision, was "the" proximate cause of the subsequent injury and that injury was "too remote."[2] Since the drinker's intoxication and subsequent negligent acts would be entirely foreseeable, and the risk created by the defendant–intoxicated driving–is exactly the risk that comes about, proximate cause reasoning seems inappropriate at best. For this reason, and because courts made a flat rule of law that did not depend upon circumstances of individual cases, the common law rule looked like a no-duty rule rather than a proximate cause rule tailored to particular facts.[3]

Effect of regulatory statutes. Two kinds of statutes potentially affected liability of the alcohol provider. First, regulatory statutes usually criminalize the sale of alcohol to intoxicated persons, minors, or habitual drunkards. Regulatory statutes also put the provider's license in jeopardy when he makes such sales. The usual rule that violation of a statute is negligence per se or prima facie negligence, however, was not applied to these statutes, so their violation had no effect at all in the tort suit.[4] That left the victim of an intoxicated driver without rights against the provider who knowingly supplied alcohol to a minor or intoxicated person.

Dram shop or civil damage acts. The second kind of statute was known as a Dram Shop or Civil Damage Act. These statutes, enacted in a small number of states, did not merely regulate the sale of alcohol. Instead, they provided expressly for civil liability of alcohol providers. Dram shop statutes sometimes imposed strict liability upon the provider

§ 332

1. Susan P. Baker, Brian O'Neill, Marvin J. Ginsburg, & Guohua Li, The Injury Fact Book 251 (2d ed. 1992) (53% of adult drivers were intoxicated; alcohol was associated with deaths of 25% of all children killed in car crashes).

2. E.g., Carr v. Turner, 238 Ark. 889, 385 S.W.2d 656 (1965), overruled in Shannon v. Wilson, 329 Ark. 143, 947 S.W.2d 349 (1997); Olsen v. Copeland, 90 Wis.2d 483, 280 N.W.2d 178 (1979), overruled in Sorensen v. Jarvis, 119 Wis.2d 627, 350 N.W.2d 108 (1984).

3. A proximate cause rule turning on particular facts, for example, might have inquired into foreseeability that the drinker would drive, the time of day and traffic conditions, the time between drinking and the injury and other such factors. But none of this was relevant. As is characteristic of a duty rule, it covered all cases in the general model of facts without regard to circumstances.

4. See, e.g., Mills v. City of Overland Park, 251 Kan. 434, 837 P.2d 370 (1992) (statute forbidding sale of liquor to incapacitated persons "was intended to regulate the sale of liquor and was not intended to impose civil liability").

(and sometimes upon the lessor of the premises where alcohol was sold as well). On the other hand, liability in such cases might be limited to a rather small sum.[5]

Reversing the common law rule. Dram Shop statutes aside, the courts began reversing themselves about 1960.[6] Most courts without a Dram Shop statute now recognize a common law duty of reasonable care and impose liability when the licensed seller of alcohol negligently sells to a minor or intoxicated person who, as a result, causes injury to the plaintiff.[7] If the harm is foreseeable, liability is not to be avoided merely because the provider furnished alcohol to a minor indirectly.[8]

The new common law regime is not one of strict liability; the plaintiff must prove negligence. This ordinarily takes the form of evidence that, in violation of liquor regulations, the defendant negligently provided alcohol to a person whom the seller should have recognized as being a minor or intoxicated. The plaintiff must also prove proximate cause as in other negligence cases. The negligent provider who supplies alcohol to teenagers or intoxicated persons enhances the risk that the drinker will drive dangerously, but he does not necessarily create a risk that the drinker will set a house afire[9] or commit rape and murder.[10] But the proximate cause issue, as in other negligence cases, is for the jury where reasonable people could differ.

Duty to and responsibility of the intoxicated person. With the reversal of the traditional rule, new issues have arisen. The provider's liability to the intoxicated person does not, of course, displace the intoxicated

5. Il St Ch 235 § 5/6–21 (liability not limited to serving intoxicated or minor persons; liability limited to $45,000 for injury, $55,000 for death in 1999, with increases thereafter keyed to consumer price index).

6. See Rappaport v. Nichols, 31 N.J. 188, 156 A.2d 1,75 A.L.R.2d 821 (1959).

7. E.g., Shannon v. Wilson, 329 Ark. 143, 947 S.W.2d 349 (1997); Ontiveros v. Borak, 136 Ariz. 500, 667 P.2d 200 (1983); Rappaport v. Nichols, 31 N.J. 188, 156 A.2d 1,75 A.L.R.2d 821 (1959); Brigance v. Velvet Dove Restaurant, Inc., 725 P.2d 300 (Okla. 1986); Young v. Caravan Corp., 99 Wash.2d 655, 663 P.2d 834 (1983); Sorensen v. Jarvis, 119 Wis.2d 627, 350 N.W.2d 108 (1984). By statute, California rejected decisions imposing liability, which it limited to cases in which alcohol was provided to an obviously intoxicated minor. See Strang v. Cabrol, 37 Cal.3d 720, 691 P.2d 1013, 209 Cal.Rptr. 347 (1984). Contra, retaining the traditional common law rule: Snyder v. Viani, 110 Nev. 1339, 885 P.2d 610 (1994). See Joel E. Smith, Annotation, Common-law Right of Action For Damage Sustained by Plaintiff in Consequence of Sale or Gift of Intoxicating Liquor or Habit-forming Drug to Another, 97 A.L.R.3d 528 (1980).

8. Petolicchio v. Santa Cruz County Fair and Rodeo Ass'n, Inc., 177 Ariz. 256, 866 P.2d 1342 (1994) (one minor foreseeably stole from liquor licensee and foreseeably provided alcohol to driver of car which caused death of decedent); Tobin v. Norwood Country Club, Inc., 422 Mass. 126, 661 N.E.2d 627 (1996) ("hand to hand" sale not required, liability for death of non-purchasing minor); Schooley v. Pinch's Deli Market, Inc., 134 Wash.2d 468, 951 P.2d 749 (1998) (similar); but cf. Wiener v. Gamma Phi Chapter of Alpha Tau Omega Fraternity, 258 Or. 632, 485 P.2d 18, 53 A.L.R.3d 1276 (1971) ("conduit" who merely furnishes alcohol to social host not liable when host provided it to minor whose subsequent intoxication caused harm).

9. Griesenbeck v. Walker, 199 N.J.Super. 132, 488 A.2d 1038 (1985) (alcohol provider not liable for fire caused by intoxicated smoker).

10. Phan Son Van v. Pena, 990 S.W.2d 751 (Tex.1999); cf. Kunza v. Pantze, 531 N.W.2d 839 (Minn.1995) (intoxicated drinker attacked his wife, who was injured in trying to escape, provider not a proximate cause).

person's own liability to the injured victim. Even so, some courts have held that the alcohol provider is liable to the drinker when the drinker injures himself instead of others.[11] Other courts have rejected any such liability.[12] The same division of opinion prevails under Dram Shop or Civil Damage Acts, where some statutes are interpreted to exclude liability to the drinker himself.[13]

Some authority has distinguished between adults and minors, holding that the alcohol provider owes a duty of care to the minor drinker but not to the intoxicated adult.[14] Other distinctions are possible. Some courts have imposed a duty upon a college organization that drew on its prestige to induce participation of freshman students and then required extreme intoxication as a condition to membership. Such courts have said that the college organization owes a duty to the drinker himself, who may thus have a claim of his own if he suffers serious injury as a result of the intoxication and the alleged callous disregard of his condition. At the same time, these courts have said that an ordinary alcohol provider would not share responsibility to the drinker.[15]

Where courts recognize a duty to the drinker himself, a further question arises. Must the drinker's fault reduce damages or bar the drinker's claim? If the provider has violated a statute intended to protect such drinkers against their own fault or incompetence, then the drinker's fault may be disregarded and full recovery allowed.[16] Most courts, however, seem to have insisted that the plaintiff's recovery is to be reduced under comparative fault regimes for the plaintiff's own fault in drinking.[17]

Duty of social hosts. Are social hosts under a duty of reasonable care to those who might be injured when they provide alcohol to intoxicated

11. See Brannigan v. Raybuck, 136 Ariz. 513, 667 P.2d 213 (1983) (superseded in part by statute); Ellis v. N.G.N. of Tampa, Inc., 586 So.2d 1042 (Fla.1991) (sale of 20 drinks to habitual drunkard who suffered permanent brain damage in car crash); Busby v. Quail Creek Golf and Country Club, 885 P.2d 1326 (Okla.1994) (minor injured as a result of drinking alcohol provided by defendant, citing many cases).

12. Cory v. Shierloh, 29 Cal.3d 430, 629 P.2d 8, 174 Cal.Rptr. 500 (1981) (by statute); Bertelmann v. Taas Associates, 69 Haw. 95, 735 P.2d 930 (1987).

13. Jackson v. PKM Corporation, 430 Mich. 262, 422 N.W.2d 657 (1988) (dram shop statute is exclusive remedy and it does not create liability to the drinker himself).

14. *Compare* Young v. Caravan Corp., 99 Wash.2d 655, 663 P.2d 834 (1983) (duty to minor drinker) *with* Kelly v. Falin, 127 Wash.2d 31, 896 P.2d 1245 (1995) (no duty to adult drinker).

15. Quinn v. Sigma Rho Chapter of Beta Theta Pi Fraternity, 155 Ill.App.3d 231, 507 N.E.2d 1193, 107 Ill.Dec. 824, 68 A.L.R.4th 215 (1987); Nisbet v. Bucher, 949 S.W.2d 111 (Mo.App.1997). See also Cheryl M. Bailey, Annotation, Tort Liability of College, University, Fraternity, or Sorority for Injury or Death of Member or Prospective Member by Hazing or Initiation Activity, 68 A.L.R.4th 228 (1989).

16. See Loeb v. Rasmussen, 822 P.2d 914 (Alaska 1991). The underlying principle is typically but not exclusively invoked in favor of minors or against caretakers like hospitals dealing with incompetents. See § 200.

17. Sage v. Johnson, 437 N.W.2d 582 (Iowa 1989); Tobin v. Norwood Country Club, Inc., 422 Mass. 126, 661 N.E.2d 627 (1996); Lee v. Kiku Restaurant, 127 N.J. 170, 603 A.2d 503 (1992).

or minor guests? A few courts have imposed liability upon the host fraternity or similar organization,[18] sometimes even to the drinker himself,[19] especially in the case of minor drinkers. And some courts have gone beyond this compelling case, extending liability to hosts at parties, banquets, and ordinary home gatherings.[20] But liability of social hosts has proved to be unpopular with many courts[21] and legislatures. Social host liability today remains the exception rather than the rule.

Legislative reaction. The devastating and deadly role of alcohol in a high percentage of traffic accidents, not to mention a number of intentional injuries, led Professor LeBel to propose a tax on alcoholic beverages to be paid by the industry, with the resulting income going to a compensation fund for victims who otherwise would be uncompensated.[22] Legislatures have not gone so far. In a number of states, legislatures have confirmed the new common law liability by amending the old regulatory statutes, but frequently enough also imposed some modification or limitation.[23] The modified regulatory statutes are now often called Dram Shop statutes, too. Where a true Dram Shop statute has been enacted, the statute is sometimes read to exclude the development of common law liability,[24] though a number of courts hold that it is not the exclusive remedy and hence now also permit an ordinary common law negligence action.[25]

18. Wiener v. Gamma Phi Chapter of Alpha Tau Omega Fraternity, 258 Or. 632, 485 P.2d 18, 53 A.L.R.3d 1276 (1971).

19. Quinn v. Sigma Rho Chapter of Beta Theta Pi Fraternity, 155 Ill.App.3d 231, 507 N.E.2d 1193, 107 Ill.Dec. 824, 68 A.L.R.4th 215 (1987).

20. Hart v. Ivey, 332 N.C. 299, 420 S.E.2d 174 (1992) (party; ordinarily principles of the negligence case apply); Kelly v. Gwinnell, 96 N.J. 538, 476 A.2d 1219 (1984) (home; superseded in part by statute); Koback v. Crook, 123 Wis.2d 259, 366 N.W.2d 857 (1985) (superseded in part by statute). By statute, Iowa imposes social host liability for providing alcohol to minors, but not for providing it to adults. Iowa Stat Ann. § 123.92. New Hampshire imposes liability when the social host is reckless in providing alcohol. Hickingbotham v. Burke, 140 N.H. 28, 662 A.2d 297 (1995). Cf. Rust v. Reyer, 91 N.Y.2d 355, 693 N.E.2d 1074, 670 N.Y.S.2d 822 (1998) (large keg party for minors who paid to enter). See the paragraph, *Legislative reaction*, below.

21. E.g., Bankston v. Brennan, 507 So.2d 1385 (Fla.1987) (issue should be left to the legislature); Dowell v. Gracewood Fruit Co., 559 So.2d 217 (Fla.1990); Andres v. Alpha Kappa Lambda Fraternity, 730 S.W.2d 547 (Mo.1987) (arguing that social hosts "do not realize any pecuniary gain from the furnishing of alcoholic beverages and for this reason they likewise have no incentive to encourage excessive consumption" that "the typical social host lacks the expertise required to evaluate the quantity of alcohol a guest can safely consume." and that social hosts could not insure against liability); D'Amico v. Christie, 71 N.Y.2d 76, 518 N.E.2d 896, 524 N.Y.S.2d 1, 62 A.L.R.4th 1 (1987); Settlemyer v. Wilmington Veterans Post No. 49, American Legion, Inc., 11 Ohio St.3d 123, 464 N.E.2d 521(1984). See Edward L. Raymond, Jr., Annotation, Social Host's Liability For Injuries Incurred by Third Parties as a Result of Intoxicated Guest's Negligence, 62 A.L.R.4th 16 (1989).

22. Paul LeBel, John Barleycorn Must Pay: Compensating the Victims of Drinking Drivers, 211–222 (1992).

23. E.g., Ariz. Rev. Stat. § 4–311(recognizing liability of liquor licensee for dispensing to intoxicated persons and minors).

24. D'Amico v. Christie, 71 N.Y.2d 76, 518 N.E.2d 896, 524 N.Y.S.2d 1, 62 A.L.R.4th 1 (1987) ("As an exception to the common law, the statute must of course be construed narrowly"). The statute itself may so provide. See Tex. Alco. Bev. Code Ann. § 2.03.

25. E.g., Kowal v. Hofher, 181 Conn. 355, 436 A.2d 1 (1980) (where sale is reckless or wanton). The statute itself may so provide, as in Minn. Stat. Ann. § 340A.801.

Most legislation passed in response to the new common law decisions was restrictive. In particular, a number of statutes limited or abolished liability of social hosts,[26] or abolished their liability to the adult drinker himself.[27] Some impose evidentiary restrictions, limiting liability to cases in which the adult drinker was visibly intoxicated, for example.[28] Others go beyond that, limiting liability to specific situations or to a comparative fault share.[29] The California statute was the most extreme, abolishing all liability of alcohol providers except those who furnish alcohol to an obviously intoxicated minor.[30]

Providing other substances of abuse or danger. When the defendant provides to a user a substance that is dangerous because it is defective in some way, liability is based upon the product's defect, not upon a failure to protect from others.[31] When a substance is dangerous by nature—like alcohol or street drugs—the product is not usually considered defective and the provider's liability, if any, is based upon his duty to withhold the substance to protect third persons from abuse by the user. A court that recognizes a duty to protect third persons or the user himself in the case of alcohol presumably would recognize the same duty in the case of dangerous drugs.[32] Some states have enacted statutes intended to impose liability for the distribution of illegal drugs that cause harm, extending liability not only to the immediate provider but to anyone who distributes drugs of the same general type.[33] As already indicated, one who provides firearms to a dangerous user may be held on a negligent entrustment theory,[34] and perhaps courts will also hold that manufacturers of weapons whose marketing strategy permits guns regularly to fall into the hands of teenagers will also be liable for injuries caused by the guns.[35]

26. Ariz. Rev. Stat. § 4–301; Cal. Civ. Code § 1714.

27. N. J. Stat. Ann. § 2A:15–5.7 (social host not liable to adult drinker for his own injury).

28. Ga. Code Ann.§ 51–1–40.

29. N.J. Stat. Ann. § 2A:15–5.8.

30. Cal. Bus. & Prof. Code §§ 25602 & 25602.1.

31. See Chapter 24, Products Liability.

32. Cf. Zerby v. Warren, 297 Minn. 134, 210 N.W.2d 58 (1973) (seller of glue liable for harm done by sniffing).

33. E.g., Okla Stat. Ann. Tit. 63, § 2–422; see 109 Harv. L. Rev. 699 (1996).

34. § 330, supra.

35. Hamilton v. Accu–Tek, 62 F.Supp.2d 802 (1999) so held but appeal is almost certain.

*

SUBPART C. INNOCENT INTERFERENCE WITH PERSON OR PROPERTY. STRICT LIABILITY

CHAPTER 22

VICARIOUS LIABILITY OF THE INNOCENT PRINCIPAL

§ 333. Vicarious Liability

Major Instances of Vicarious Liability

Vicarious liability is liability for the tort of another person. Such liability is an important exception to the usual rule that each person is accountable for his own legal fault but in the absence of such fault is not responsible for the actions of others. The most common kind of vicarious liability is based upon the principle of respondeat superior. Under that principle, private and public employers[1] are generally jointly and severally liable along with the tortfeasor employee for the torts of employees committed within the scope of employment. The principle does not apply among employees themselves—employees are not liable for the torts of the employer or other employees.[2] But respondeat superior may apply to impose liability upon the employer for contracts made by an agent within his authority and also for many kinds of torts, including fraud and other torts that do not entail physical harms. This chapter only addresses vicarious liability for torts like negligent driving or medical malpractice that cause physical harm.

A set of terminology, somewhat strange in today's world, sets up some fundamental distinctions. Broadly speaking, employers are principals and employees are agents. Some employees are only agents in the sense that they can make contracts or sell goods for the employer. As to these agents, the employer may be liable on the contract signed by the agent but not for the agent's torts. Other employees are called "servants." These employees are expected to carry out physical tasks, not merely to negotiate contracts. In his role as employer of servants, the employer is a "master," so we still see cases digested under the title "master and servant." The terms distinguish not only between servants and other agents, but also between servants and independent contrac-

§ 333

1. E.g., Mary M. v. City of Los Angeles, 54 Cal.3d 202, 814 P.2d 1341, 285 Cal.Rptr. 99 (1991). However, federal civil rights claims against public entities cannot be based upon respondeat superior. See § 277.

2. See Lyon v. Morphew, 424 Mass. 828, 678 N.E.2d 1306 (1997); Connell v. Hayden, 83 A.D.2d 30, 443 N.Y.S.2d 383 (1981). An employee, supervisory or not, may be liable for acts of co-employees when they act in concert or in a conspiracy. See Jones v. City of Chicago, 856 F.2d 985 (7th Cir.1988).

tors. The master is liable in tort for the torts of servants committed within the scope of their employment, but the employer is not ordinarily liable for the torts of independent contractors.

Respondeat superior liability has ancient roots in Roman law and may have been in continuous use in some form more or less since the Norman Conquest of England.[3] The ordinary instances of it today are non-controversial. The bus company's driver negligently drives the company's bus into the plaintiff's car. The negligent driver is of course liable;[4] under the principle of respondeat superior, the bus company itself is treated as a tortfeasor as well. As a practical matter, that means that the plaintiff will be able to collect her judgment against the business company and will not be left without remedy merely because the driver himself could not pay.

Respondeat superior is not the only kind of vicarious liability. Conspirators, those who act in concert, partners, and joint enterprisers are all vicariously liable for the acts of each other committed as part of their expressly or tacitly agreed-upon activity. These forms of vicarious liability come in for more attention later, but the main problems are associated with respondeat superior and it deserves attention first.

Distinguishing Vicarious from Personal Liability

A defendant who is vicariously liable can be at fault. An employer, for example, might have negligently hired, trained, or supervised a dangerous employee. In that case, the employer might be liable for his own negligence in hiring or supervising. Such liability, however, is not vicarious liability. Vicarious liability is not based upon the defendant's own fault. Rather, it is based upon the principle that he must stand good for the wrong of another person.

From the employer-defendant's point of view, vicarious liability is strict liability, since he is liable without personal fault. That is not quite the case from the plaintiff's point of view. The plaintiff must prove that the employee committed a tort and was acting within the scope of employment when he did so. For the great majority of cases, the plaintiff must thus prove fault, although not necessarily the personal fault of the employer.

Employer's Right of Indemnity against Employee

When the employer who is not personally chargeable with tort is held vicariously liable for the tort of an employee, the employer has a right of indemnity from the employee.[5] If this right were regularly pursued, it would mean that the employer's vicarious liability would really only make the employer a guarantor of the employee's solvency. So long as the employee was solvent or insured, he could pay the tort

3. See O.W. Holmes, Agency, 4 Harv. L. Rev. 345 (1891). Respondeat superior was probably not a widespread or generalized rule until the 18th century, however.

4. Restatement Second of Agency § 343 (except where agent is exercising a privilege of the principal and in similar cases).

5. Restatement Second of Agency § 401, cmt d.

judgment and the employer would not be liable. Or if the employee did not initially pay the judgment, the employer who paid it would recover its costs from the employee.

In fact, however, indemnity is almost never sought against negligent servants.[6] There are probably several reasons. First, the employer's liability insurance is likely to cover servants as well as employers. The employer thus has no direct loss and the insurer has no complaint against the employee, for it will have paid only what it contracted to pay on his behalf. Second, servants as a group are often not in a position to pay a large judgment, perhaps not even a small one. An indemnity claim against an uninsured and insolvent employee would be a waste of time and money.

A third possible reason for the non-use of indemnity claims is different. It may be that our culture now often believes that fairness requires the business enterprise, not the servant to pay. From the point of view of individual responsibility, such a proposition is difficult to understand. Yet in at least two major instances, legal rules take the view that the business, not the individual, is the "right" defendant. The Federal Tort Claims Act now protects all federal employees from liability; either the government alone is liable or no one is.[7] Workers' compensation rules also protect employees from liability to fellow employees by placing exclusive liability upon the employer.[8]

§ 334. Rationale of Respondeat Superior

It would not be difficult to justify respondeat superior liability if it only meant that the master was liable for torts committed at his specific direction, as where the master tells the servant to drive faster than the speed limit permits.[1] But respondeat superior liability is much broader. The master is liable for the servant's negligent acts even though master did not command those acts and could not foresee them in any specific way. Sometimes, masters are liable even for torts committed by servants in violation of specific directions or rules.

Tort law is assuredly imperfect, but it usually attempts to hold individuals accountable for their wrongs and only for their wrongs. Although pockets of strict liability exist, such liability is relatively rare. Consequently, vicarious liability under the doctrine of respondeat superior, which is strict in the sense that it holds an employer liable without the employer's personal fault, seems to require some explanation.

6. When, under the nondelegable duty rule or otherwise, the employer is held vicariously liable for the wrongs of an independent contractor, the employer may be more likely to seek indemnity, as in Spectron Dev. Lab., Div. of Titan Corp. v. American Hollow Boring Co., 123 N.M. 170, 936 P.2d 852 (Ct.App.1997).

7. § 273.

8. § 395.

§ 334

1. See South Carolina Ins. Co. v. Greene, 290 S.C. 171, 348 S.E.2d 617 (Ct. App.1986) (discussing the early liability of the master for intentional acts he commanded under the maxim "qui facit per alium facit per se"—one who acts by another, acts himself).

Some writers have doubted whether vicarious liability, at least in the form of respondeat superior liability, could be justified.[2] Baty argued that it was merely a way of reaching the deep pockets of target defendants like large corporations.[3] Courts have usually defended strict liability only by emphasizing (1) that an innocent person, either the plaintiff or the employer,[4] must bear the loss, (2) that the employer had formal right of control over the employee's work,[5] or (3) that the employer benefits from the employee's work.[6] The first argument is suspect because it is applied selectively, not as a general principle of tort law. To apply it generally would be to adopt a general regime of strict liability. The other two arguments offer attractive implications that responsibility follows control and that one who intentionally reaps the benefits of an activity must bear the burdens as well. But control is doubtful in many cases and the connection between the employee's tort and the employer's benefit is often tenuous.

Commentators have developed somewhat more elaborate explanations. Morris argued that since employees are often financially unable to pay for harms they do, they will not be deterred by tort suits or the threat of tort suits. The best deterrence is to impose liability upon the employer, who will then seek to avoid his own liability by exercising his considerable control over employees to discourage their torts.[7]

Economic thinkers have argued that enterprise liability—that is, the strict liability of business enterprises for harms perceived to be recurrently associated with their operation—is justified as economically efficient. By this they mean that such liability will tend to provide optimal deterrence of activities that are harmful.[8] Others, argue that enterprise liability provides appropriate "insurance" against harms that are not worth preventing. The enterprise can raise prices or lower dividends and thus distribute or spread the losses resulting from injury to all those who benefit from its activities.[9] In this way, the injured individual does not

2. Oliver Wendell Holmes, Jr., Agency, 5 HARV. L. REV. 1, 14 (1891) ("common-sense is opposed to making one man pay for another man's wrong").

3. T. BATY, VICARIOUS LIABILITY 154 (1916). Baty also thought that "The present is not a very propitious time for withstanding a dogma based on such a [deep pocket] principle" but that "a return to simpler manners will probably bring with it a return to saner views of liability, even if it is not sooner recognized that to injure capital is to injure industry."

4. See South Carolina Ins. Co. v. Greene, 290 S.C. 171, 348 S.E.2d 617 (Ct. App.1986) (recounting historical development).

5. National Convenience Stores, Inc. v. Fantauzzi, 94 Nev. 655, 658, 584 P.2d 689, 691 (1978) ("Nevada's policy rationale for the doctrine of respondeat superior is grounded on the theory of control rather than on the entrepreneur theory").

6. Mary M. v. City of Los Angeles, 54 Cal.3d 202, 814 P.2d 1341, 285 Cal.Rptr. 99 (1991).

7. Clarence Morris, The Torts of an Independent Contractor, 29 ILL. L. REV. 339 (1935).

8. See Alan O. Sykes, The Economics of Vicarious Liability, 93 YALE L.J. 1231 (1984); see also The Boundaries of Vicarious Liability: an Economic Analysis of the Scope of Employment Rule and Related Legal Doctrines, 101 HARV. L. REV. 563 (1988) (emphasizing inefficiencies arising out of the agent's insolvency and those arising from the cost of contracting between principal and agent).

9. Young B. Smith, Frolic and Detour, 23 COLUM. L. REV. 444, 456 ff; (1923); see

bear the whole weight of the loss herself. Since no one person bears the whole loss, the loss is not so disruptive. Perhaps more importantly, those subjected to risks of the enterprise are also those who share in the burdens and benefits of its liability. The consumer pays a small sum more for the products of the enterprise, but in return obtains a degree of protection in the form of liability if he is injured.[10]

Still another justification for respondeat superior liability is that it is fair or just. When risks are created randomly by occasional, infrequent acts of individuals, liability is imposed only if the act causing harm is negligent. When an enterprise, individual or corporation, engages in systematic or repeated activity, however, some risks are more or less typical or characteristic of the activity even when no negligence can be shown. The bus company must expect that sooner or later its buses will cause harm, even if drivers are invariably careful. In this sense, bus companies impose risks that are materially greater than or different from the risks that we all impose upon one another by occasional use of motor vehicles. Although the substantial certainty definition of intent has not been carried so far, it is nevertheless reasonable to say that the bus company can be statistically certain that bus injuries will be negligently inflicted and in that sense intends them. Although this is not moral fault, the bus company employer should accept the burdens that go with the benefits of its operation and hence should be responsible for the bus driver's negligence as a matter of justice or fairness.[11]

Judge Friendly had some such ideas in mind in a leading case, *Ira S. Bushey & Sons, Inc. v. United States.*[12] In that case, a seaman returned late at night to his ship, which was in the plaintiff's dry dock. The seaman took it into his head to turn some wheels on the drydock wall. This had the effect of flooding tanks on one side and it partially sank the drydock. The plaintiff as owner sought compensation from the government as the seaman's employer. The Second Circuit upheld a judgment against the United States, but Judge Friendly rejected the argument that liability would be economically efficient or would appropriately motivate the employer to hire more reliable employees. Instead, he reasoned that "a business enterprise cannot justly disclaim responsibility for accidents which may fairly be said to be characteristic of its activities." Characteristic risks of an enterprise, Friendly thought, included risks of foreseeable misconduct of its employees. Many decisions either verbalize similar reasoning or obtain results consistent with it.

George L. Priest, The Invention of Enterprise Liability: A Critical History of the Intellectual Foundations of Modern Tort Law, 14 J. Leg. Stud. 461, 47–83 (1985) (discussing James' thought). Harper, James, and Gray pervasively emphasizes distribution of loss through the tort system as social insurance and even provides an index entry with a number of references.

10. See Fruit v. Schreiner, 502 P.2d 133 (Alaska 1972); Warren A. Seavey, Speculations as to "Respondeat Superior", Harvard Legal Essays in Honor of Joseph Henry Beale and Samuel Williston 433, 450–451 (1934).

11. See Gregory C. Keating, The Idea of Fairness in the Law of Enterprise Liability, 95 Mich. L. Rev. 1266 (1997).

12. Ira S. Bushey & Sons, Inc. v. United States, 398 F.2d 167 (2d Cir.1968).

As this line of reasoning suggests, masters are broadly liable for torts of their servants but not liable for all their torts. When the tort becomes uncharacteristic of the business, liability is not imposed. Legal analysis of this idea is expressed as the rule that the master is liable for the torts of his servants only if those torts are committed within the scope of the servant's employment.

§ 335. Servants: Scope of Employment

General rule. Vicarious liability under the respondeat superior doctrine ordinarily requires some kind of employment relationship or other consensual arrangement under which one person agrees to act under another's control.[1] Employment itself is not enough for vicarious liability. With certain exceptions, vicarious liability attaches for physical harms resulting from conduct of an employee only when the employee acts as a "servant" rather than as an independent contractor.[2] Finally, respondeat superior liability is imposed only for acts of the servant committed within the scope of his employment.[3]

Scope of employment requirements generally. Under the traditional rules, a servant's conduct is not within the scope of his employment unless it is of the same general kind as authorized or expected, or incidental to such conduct, and the servant was acting within the authorized time and space limits. The Second Restatement of Agency adds that the servant's conduct must have been "actuated, at least in part, by a purpose to serve the master"[4] but this rule is rejected in a number of contemporary cases.[5] Where the Restatement's rule is recognized, it is understood as a broad aim rather than as a technical demand. It is also substantially qualified by the rule that the employer is vicariously liable for the employee's acts outside the scope of employment if his employment aided him in accomplishing the tort.[6]

Determining scope of employment. Courts have provided many examples of the broad approach to scope of employment issues. For instance, a

§ 335

1. See Glover v. Boy Scouts of America, 923 P.2d 1383 (1996) (scoutmaster was not an employee of the Boy Scout organization, no vicarious liability for his torts); Restatement Second of Agency §§ 1–2. Thus, apart from statute, parents are not vicariously liable for acts of their children, although they may be responsible for their own negligence in failing to control children. Similarly, someone who merely assists the defendant without subjecting himself to the defendant's right of control is not ordinarily an agent or servant. E.g., Austin v. Kaness, 950 P.2d 561 (Wyo.1997) (adult son feeding cats while parents were away was not agent or servant of parents). The power of guardians and parents to consent to medical attention for children and the like is a partial exception of the rule requiring consent, but the exception is quite limited. Parents cannot ordinarily release a child's cause of action, for instance. E.g., Smith v. YMCA of Benton Harbor/St. Joseph, 216 Mich.App. 552, 550 N.W.2d 262 (1996) ("a parent has no authority, merely by virtue of being a parent, to waive, release, or compromise claims by or against the parent's child").

2. See § 336.

3. E.g., Porter v. Harshfield, 329 Ark. 130, 948 S.W.2d 83 (1997).

4. Restatement Second of Agency § 228 (1) (c).

5. See *Intentional torts* below.

6. Costos v. Coconut Island Corp., 137 F.3d 46 (1st Cir.1998); Restatement of Agency § 219 (2) (d).

cook in a restaurant who is not actually cooking but who is instead talking with a customer and flipping a knife that has nothing to do with his job is within the scope of his employment when the knife accidently strikes the customer.[7] Similarly, an employee-driver does not leave the scope of his employment merely because he acts negligently in violation of his employer's instruction to act with care, or even when he violates his employer's instructions not to take a passenger.[8] Scope of employment questions are usually resolved only by evaluation of many factual details on a case by case basis.[9] Not surprisingly, then, the question whether an employee's act is within the scope of employment is for the jury unless the matter is so clear that reasonable people could not differ.[10]

Time and place limits. The master is not vicariously responsible for the acts of a servant before work begins or after it ends. In particular, the going and coming rule holds that in jobs with a situs such as an office or factory, an employee coming to work or going home from it is not in employment. Consequently, the employer is not liable for, say, automobile accidents of employees of their way to work or after they have left work.[11] The answer is different if the job is broader and requires travel outside the area or the employee is paid for travel time.[12] It is also different when the employee is on a special errand for the employer while on his way to or from work or after regular work hours.[13] Employees like police officers who are always subject to job demands, may be within the scope of employment even when off duty[14] so long as

7. Riviello v. Waldron, 47 N.Y.2d 297, 418 N.Y.S.2d 300, 391 N.E.2d 1278 (1979).

8. Perez v. Van Groningen & Sons, Inc., 41 Cal.3d 962, 719 P.2d 676, 227 Cal.Rptr. 106 (1986).

9. Because factual details count and because the facts require reasonableness evaluations, summary judgment is often inappropriate on the scope of employment issue. See Pyne v. Witmer, 129 Ill.2d 351, 543 N.E.2d 1304, 135 Ill.Dec. 557 (1989).

10. Tuttle v. Muenks, 964 S.W.2d 514 (Mo.App.1998); cf. Russell v. Noullet, 721 So.2d 868 (La.1998) (scope of employment is mixed law-fact question and great deference is given to trier's finding). Some courts say that the question ceases to be for the jury when the facts are not disputed. E.g., Tall v. Bd. of Sch. Comn'rs, 120 Md.App. 236, 706 A.2d 659 (1998). Taken literally, such a statement takes from the jury the inferences from and evaluations of the facts.

11. E.g., Faul v. Jelco, Inc., 122 Ariz. 490, 595 P.2d 1035 (Ct. App. 1979).

12. Hinman v. Westinghouse Elec. Co., 2 Cal.3d 956, 88 Cal.Rptr. 188, 471 P.2d 988 (1970). Sometimes the employee who works out of town may be paid portal-to-portal or may be on call or on duty at all times. See Carroll Air Sys., Inc. v. Greenbaum, 629 So.2d 914 (Fla.Dist.Ct.App.1993); Edgewater Motels, Inc. v. Gatzke, 277 N.W.2d 11 (Minn.1979).

13. Vicarious liability may be imposed because the employer, by general policy or specific command, directed the employee to carry out an employment errand during time that would otherwise have been off the job. See Gutierrez de Martinez v. Drug Enforcement Admin., 111 F.3d 1148 (4th Cir. 1997). The scope of employment may be extended because of the employee's "trouble and time of making the journey, or the special inconvenience, hazard, or urgency of making it in the particular circumstances." See Mayor and City Council of Baltimore v. Jakelski, 45 Md.App. 7, 10, 410 A.2d 1116, 1118 (1980).

14. E.g., Osborne v. Lyles, 63 Ohio St.3d 326, 587 N.E.2d 825 (1992); see Alexander C. Black, Annotation, Liability of Municipal Corporation or Other Governmental Entity For Injury or Death Caused by Action or Inaction of Off-duty Police Officer, 36 A.L.R.5th 1 (1996); cf. Bauldock v. Davco Food, Inc., 622 A.2d 28 (D.C.1993) (off-duty officer working for private employer was obliged as officer to make arrest and was

they are not engaged in purely personal activities.[15]

Frolic and detour. Employees who have arrived at work and begun their jobs can nevertheless physically remove themselves from the job. Not uncommonly, employees indulge in "detours" for their personal amusement. The office messenger delivering a message from the 10th floor to the fifth, might stop off to confirm a date with a friend on the 9th floor, for example. If he takes the stairs rather than the elevator because the 9th floor is only one flight away but negligently knocks the plaintiff down before he reaches the landing, he has physically "deviated" from employment only in taking the stairs rather than the elevator; in terms of his intent, he has a dual motive, part of which is to serve the employer, since he is still on his way.[16] As long as the detour is a slight deviation or is usual, expected, or tolerated in the particular employment, the servant is still acting within the general scope of employment.[17]

On the other hand, if the messenger decides the day is too nice to miss a baseball game and negligently drives into the plaintiff on his way to the ball park, he is almost certainly "on a frolic of his own" and not at all within employment. When the frolicking employee starts back to work after the game is over, the problem is to determine when he has reentered employment. Reentry into employment occurs only when the employee reaches a point reasonably near the authorized time and space limits of the job and the employee has formed an intent to serve the employer's business.[18] Such cases leave a great deal of room for different evaluations about the extent and expectation of deviation from or return to employment. As a result, many such issues will be for the jury to decide.[19]

Personal acts. Although frolic and detour terminology is often associated with an employee's geographical or temporal deviation from employment, employees may depart from employment without leaving the situs of their work. They may do so by undertaking tasks alien to the work they were employed to do. An employee hired to cut down an elm tree on the employer's property undertakes to cut down an oak on the neighbor's land. That may enhance the employer's view and hence benefit the employer in some sense, but it is outside the employment.[20]

therefore not within the scope of employment for private employer); Hudson v. Muller, 653 So.2d 942 (Ala.1995) (caretaker expected to be on farm 75% of her time caused injury while arranging for personal trip; jury question whether she was in employment).

15. See Russell v. Noullet, 721 So.2d 868 (La.1998) (although off-duty officer was permitted to carry sidearms, his attack on woman who was taking his license number was unrelated to police duties and his use of his pistol in self defense was necessary only because of his attack, not because of police duties).

16. See Young B. Smith, Frolic & Detour, 23 Colum. L. Rev. 444, 716, 722 ff. (1923) (discussing mixed motive in detour cases).

17. Pyne v. Witmer, 129 Ill.2d 351, 543 N.E.2d 1304, 135 Ill.Dec. 557 (1989).

18. Prince v. Atchison, Topeka & Santa Fe Ry., 76 Ill.App.3d 898, 32 Il.Dec. 362, 395 N.E.2d 592 (1979); Restatement Second of Agency § 237.

19. Pyne v. Witmer, 129 Ill.2d 351, 543 N.E.2d 1304, 135 Ill.Dec. 557 (1989).

20. See Restatement Second of Agency § 229, Ill. 1.

Employees may also depart from employment by engaging in purely personal acts during working hours. Consensual sexual activity carried on by an employee whose only job is to answer the telephone may not interfere even slightly with performance of the work, but if the employee engaged in such multi-tasking behavior injures his sexual partner, it is unlikely that the employer will be held liable.[21] On the other hand, activities that serve both personal and business purposes do not necessarily count as a departure from employment.[22] Most acts for personal comfort, such as using the toilet[23] and even smoking,[24] and drinking alcohol[25] are now recognized as acts incident to employment, so that the employer is liable when the employee negligently injures another while so engaged.

Intentional torts. In many cases, perhaps most, an employee's intentional torts are personal acts and thus not within the scope of employment. An employee strikes a customer because of his personal grudge. Nothing more appearing, the tort is the employee's tort and the employer is not liable. In recent years the reported cases have often involved sexual assaults or other sexual behavior of an employee. Intentional sexual torts, like other violent conduct, is often personal to the employee, so that quite frequently the employer is not liable.[26]

The Agency Restatement speaks of these cases in terms of motive. It says the tortfeasor must be acting out of motive, at least in part, to serve the employer.[27] But at least since the middle of the 20th century, courts have often rejected the Restatement's formulation by recognizing that intentional torts committed by an employee are within the scope of employment when employment furnishes the specific impetus for or increases a general risk of employee misbehavior.[28] Although the precise tortious act itself is not something the servant was employed to do, it is enough if the general job activity that gave rise to the tortious act was within the scope of employment.[29] The bar bouncer hired to eject unruly

21. Cf. Haybeck v. Prodigy Servs. Co., 944 F.Supp. 326 (S.D.N.Y.1996) (on-line computer service employee engaged customer in extensive communication in service's sex chat room, ultimately had unprotected sexual contact which communicated HIV to her; employer not vicariously liable).

22. Hudson v. Muller, 653 So.2d 942 (Ala.1995).

23. Levine v. Peoples Broadcasting Corp., 149 W.Va. 256, 140 S.E.2d 438 (W.Va. 1965).

24. Edgewater Motels, Inc. v. Gatzke, 277 N.W.2d 11 (Minn.1979).

25. Gutierrez de Martinez v. Drug Enforcement Admin., 111 F.3d 1148 (4th Cir. 1997).

26. E.g., Lisa M. v. Henry Mayo Newhall Mem. Hosp., 12 Cal.4th 291, 48 Cal. Rptr.2d 510, 907 P.2d 358 (1995) (ultra sound technician extended examination in sexual way); Baumeister v. Plunkett, 673 So.2d 994 (La.1996).

27. Restatement Second of Agency § 228 (1) (c) (must be actuated in part by a purpose to serve the master).

28. Ira S. Bushey & Sons, Inc. v. United States, 398 F.2d 167 (2d Cir.1968), discussed in § 334; Carr v. Wm. C. Crowell Co., 28 Cal.2d 652, 171 P.2d 5 (1946); Baumeister v. Plunkett, 673 So.2d 994, 996 (La.1996) ("so closely connected in time, place, and causation to his employment duties as to be regarded as a risk of harm fairly attributable to the employer's business, as compared with conduct instituted by purely personal considerations entirely extraneous to the employer's interest").

29. Plummer v. Center Psychiatrists, Ltd. 252 Va. 233, 476 S.E.2d 172 (1996). Some courts, however, have focused on the precise act or omission. See Haybeck v.

patrons may use excessive force and thus become the author of a battery. Even if that occurs because the bouncer loses his temper or is unnecessarily rough because of an argument with the patron, it is nevertheless the very kind of risk that goes with the work, and the bar owner is vicariously liable.[30]

Counselors, therapists, clergy, youth leaders, and others in a position of trust and confidence often seem to take advantage of innocent or vulnerable patients or parishioners to engage in sexual activity with them, usually to their detriment. Although sexual activity is quintessentially personal, such activity is one of the risks of relationships that generate confidence. Consequently, employers of therapists have been held subject to vicarious liability in such cases.[31] The case of outright rape by an employee who is otherwise carrying out employment duties is more difficult, but sometimes even here the employment creates the risk or impetus of the attack, just as it can create the risk of other physical batteries. A police officer's job, for instance, gives him a great deal of coercive power over citizens who might be subject to arrest and inherent in that power is the potential for abuse. Accordingly, the California Court held that the employer was vicariously responsible for a police officer's rape of a woman he had detained.[32] Even if the rape is not an inherent risk of the type of work, vicarious liability is appropriate when, in the particular case, it arises immediately out of a conflict generated by the employment[33] and even when it is made peculiarly possible by the employment.[34]

Some courts take a much narrower view of vicarious liability, at least in cases where the liability of schools and churches is in issue. In a Maryland case, a public school teacher used a ruler to beat a 9–year-old Down's Syndrome student who had urinated in his pants, but the court

Prodigy Servs. Co., 944 F.Supp. 326 (S.D.N.Y.1996). The logic of that approach appears to reject the idea that vicarious liability is appropriate when employment increases the risk.

30. Mason v. Sportsman's Pub, 305 N.J.Super. 482, 702 A.2d 1301 (1997).

31. Doe v. Samaritan Counseling Ctr., 791 P.2d 344 (Alaska 1990); Marston v. Minneapolis Clinic of Psychiatry, 329 N.W.2d 306 (Minn.1982); Fearing v. Bucher, 328 Or. 367, 977 P.2d 1163 (1999) (priest acting as youth pastor, friend, confessor to minor plaintiff and his family; motive to serve employer in actual act of sexual assault not required if priest's general motives included, initially, a desire to serve the Archdiocese); Lourim v. Swensen. 328 Or. 380, 977 P.2d 1157 (1999) (Boy Scout leader); Plummer v. Center Psychiatrists, Ltd. 252 Va. 233, 476 S.E.2d 172 (1996) (scope of employment a jury question); contra, Bunce v. Parkside Lodge of Columbus, 73 Ohio App.3d 253, 596 N.E.2d 1106 (1991) (counselor's seduction of a patient at a drug rehab center outside the scope of employment).

32. Mary M. v. City of Los Angeles, 54 Cal.3d 202, 285 Cal.Rptr. 99, 814 P.2d 1341 (1991); but cf. Lisa M. v. Henry Mayo Newhall Mem. Hosp., 12 Cal.4th 291, 48 Cal. Rptr.2d 510, 907 P.2d 358 (1995) (semble, the employment must generate not only the risk of sexual misbehavior but its "motivating emotions" as well).

33. See Lyon v. Carey, 533 F.2d 649 (D.C.Cir.1976) (truck driver delivering a mattress got into dispute with customer about whether he was to carry it into the apartment, escalating into a rape of the customer).

34. Costos v. Coconut Island Corp., 137 F.3d 46 (1st Cir.1998) (rape by manager of inn where the plaintiff was staying). This rule may be especially appropriate where the plaintiff has contracted, at least implicitly, for care, as in the case of a doctor's patient or a hotel's guest.

believed that this action was outside the scope of employment because corporal punishment had been forbidden.[35] The Minnesota Court thought a school teacher's sexual activity with a teen-aged student represented a risk that was unforeseeable to the school-employer and hence thought the activity was outside the scope of employment although it occurred in classrooms and at school-related functions.[36] A number of courts have also displayed a determination to relieve churches of liability, often asserting that the First Amendment makes it necessary to relieve them of tort liability and also refusing to impose vicarious liability for the intentional sins of their clergy.[37] It is not clear whether these cases reflect narrow notions of vicarious liability, a preference for the public and religious employers, or merely a lack of information about the kinds of risks associated with the activities involved.

Sexual harassment. Sexual harassment under federal and state statutes is one form of sex discrimination and is actionable under the statutory rules. Under both state[38] and federal statutes,[39] courts have held that employers are liable for the kind of sexual harassment that includes unwelcome sexual advances with an explicit or implicit message that the job or its benefits may depend upon compliance, often called quid pro quo sexual harassment.[40]

Where the supervisory employee inflicts severe or pervasive unwelcome attentions or sexual remarks that do not count as quid pro quo sexual harassment, he may nevertheless create a hostile work environment. That, too, counts as sexual harassment. The Supreme Court has said that the employer is liable for the supervisor's harassment in that case as well as in the quid pro quo case, but with a difference. Where the plaintiff's supervisor causes hostile work environment harassment but tangible job benefits are not at stake, the employer can defend itself by showing that it exercised reasonable care to prevent and promptly correct sexually harassing behavior and that the plaintiff unreasonably failed to take advantage of the preventive or corrective opportunities provided.[41] Although the Court has described this liability-with-a-defense as vicarious liability, the presence of a defense sharply distinguishes it

35. Tall v. Board of School Comn'rs of Baltimore City, 120 Md.App. 236, 706 A.2d 659 (Md. 1998).

36. P.L. v. Aubert, 545 N.W.2d 666 (Minn.1996).

37. Destefano v. Grabrian, 763 P.2d 275 (Colo.1988) (priest, encouraged by church to engage in marriage counseling, also engaged in sexual activity with one of the marital partners he was counseling; church not vicariously liable); Byrd v. Faber, 57 Ohio St.3d 56, 565 N.E.2d 584, 5 A.L.R.5th 1115 (1991) (similar, rejecting vicarious liability unless the church had hired Faber to rape, seduce or otherwise physically assault members of the congregation).

38. Champion v. Nationwide Sec., Inc., 450 Mich. 702, 545 N.W.2d 596 (1996) (rape by supervisory employee, vicarious liability appropriate where rape is accomplished through any use of the supervisor's managerial powers).

39. Karibian v. Columbia University, 14 F.3d 773 (2d Cir.1994).

40. E.g., Karibian v. Columbia University, 14 F.3d 773 (2d Cir.1994).

41. Burlington Industries, Inc. v. Ellerth, 524 U.S. 742, 118 S.Ct. 2257, 141 L.Ed.2d 633 (1998); Faragher v. City of Boca Raton, 524 U.S. 775, 118 S.Ct. 2275, 141 L.Ed.2d 662 (1998). If the employer has no notice of this kind of conduct, it is not liable. Kunin v. Sears Roebuck & Co., 175 F.3d 289 (3d Cir.1999).

from the ordinary case of vicarious liability, where the employer cannot defend by showing reasonableness of its actions.

However, respondeat superior liability in sexual harassment cases usually depends ultimately upon the statute. Under the anti-discrimination statute application to schools receiving federal aid, respondeat superior is not applied; instead, a school is liable under that statute for sexual misconduct of its employees only after an official with power to remedy the harassment has actual notice of it and is then deliberately indifferent to it.[42]

Caretakers. At least since the famous *Ybarra* case,[43] courts have sporadically recognized that those who undertake the care of people who are helpless to care for themselves may fall under special duties. A day-care center that cares for infants and toddlers would be expected to respond in damages for harms done to such a small child even if the child cannot prove how the harm came about.[44] The special duty of caretakers may be expressed in special rules of respondeat superior as well. In fact, common carriers were once treated as caretakers, because during carriage, their passengers were removed from normal sources of support and relatively helpless. Under this approach, carriers were held responsible for injury inflicted upon passengers by servants who were not in the scope of employment.[45]

Should caretakers such as day care centers for infants and institutions for disabled people be subjected to vicarious liability for sexual or physical abuse by their employees? One basis for doing so is that the risk of employees taking advantage of disabled is a normal risk of that kind of business. A similar but narrower reason is that the employment definitely aids the employee in committing a tort.[46]

In an Indiana case,[47] the defendant Children's Center cared for a severely retarded and disabled child of 14, who had the mental capacity of a five-month-old infant. One of its attendants engaged in oral and anal sex with the child. In a suit against the Children's Center, the court held that the jury could find these acts sufficiently related to employment to warrant vicarious liability. The court went on to hold, on analogy to the common carrier rule, that the Children's Center's duty to the helpless could not be satisfied by delegating the duty to others. In a Washington case,[48] the defendant was a home for developmentally disabled persons. A staff member sexually assaulted a young woman with a child's mental ability. The court there rejected vicarious liability of the institution, but

42. Alida Star Gebser v. Lago Vista Independent School Dist., 524 U.S. 274, 118 S.Ct. 1989, 141 L.Ed.2d 277 (1998),

43. See § 158.

44. See § 155.

45. See Worcester Ins. Co. v. Fells Acres Day School, Inc., 408 Mass. 393, 558 N.E.2d 958 (1990). The special carrier rule was repudiated in favor of a scope of employment limitation in Adams v. New York City Transit Authority, 88 N.Y.2d 116, 666 N.E.2d 216, 643 N.Y.S.2d 511 (1996).

46. Restatement § 219(2) (d). On the "aided" point, see also the sexual harassment cases, supra n. 41.

47. Stropes v. Heritage House Childrens Ctr. of Shelbyville, Inc., 547 N.E.2d 244 (Ind.1989).

48. Niece v. Elmview Group Home, 131 Wash.2d 39, 929 P.2d 420 (Wash. 1997).

held that it was under a duty of care to protect its residents from foreseeable sexual assault. Some courts have also imposed special vicarious liability rules upon surgeons and others involved in the care of an anesthetized patient.[49]

§ 336 Independent Contractors

The putative[1] general rule is that employers are not subject to vicarious liability for the torts of carefully selected independent contractors.[2] Independent contractors are contrasted with the kind of employee called servants. An independent contractor—say the person hired to paint your car—might be within the scope of employment when he negligently injures someone, but, unless an exception applies, you are not liable for his tort. As the courts see it, it is the contractor's business, the contractor's tort, and the contractor's liability.

Jurists have found it difficult to formulate a crisp and workable definition of independent contractors, but the concept is easy to understand and in many cases easy to apply as well. Independent contractors are usually persons who are perceived to be operating their own business and hence not subject to the employer's right of control over the manner, means, and details of the work.[3] Instead, the independent contractor's employer has a say-so only about whether the end product is acceptable, not about the exact manner or means used to achieve it. On the other hand, if the employer has a right to control the manner, means, and details of the work, the employee is almost always a servant. Even if the employer does not exercise control over the manner of work but merely has the right to control, the employee is still a servant.[4]

Several kinds of evidence bear on the employer's power of control. The employer's right to discharge the employee, payment of regular wages, taxes, workers' compensation insurance and the like, long-term or permanent employment, and detailed supervision of the work tend to indicate a master-servant relationship. The employee's special skills, the fact that he works for others or is perceived to be in a business of his own, supplies his own tools or instrumentalities, hires and fires his own employees tend to show that the employee is an independent contractor. Many pieces of subsidiary evidence may be relevant. For instance, the fact that the employer is not in business would tend to show that the employee is an independent contractor operating his own business. All these "factors" in one form or another, have been considered in the

49. See § 339.

§ 336

1. Putative because the rule is "riddled with exceptions." Gordon v. Sanders, 692 So.2d 939 (Fla.App.1997). See § 337.

2. Fisher v. Townsends, Inc., 695 A.2d 53 (Del.1997); Restatement § 409. In the Restatement terminology, "employer" includes those who employ independent contractors.

3. E.g., Mavrikidis v. Petullo, 153 N.J. 117, 707 A.2d 977 (1998).

4. See, e.g., McDonald v. Hampton Training Sch. for Nurses, 254 Va. 79, 486 S.E.2d 299 (Va. 1997). If the employer actually exercises control, that fact may be good evidence that he has a right or power to do so.

cases[5] and approved by the Agency Restatement.[6] No one factor or piece of evidence is controlling. The employee's special skill tends to indicate that he is an independent contractor, but nowadays even skilled professionals such as doctors may be "servants" of a hospital for vicarious liability purposes if they are subject to the employer's control.[7]

Perception that the employee's work represents a separate business or that it does not is often important. The fact that an employee works only for a single employer tends to show that he is a servant, not an independent contractor, so a full-time housecleaner or janitor is a servant, while one who provides cleaning services to all comers may be viewed as operating his own business as an independent contractor.[8] A weighmaster who works exclusively for one chicken processor may be an employee even though he provides his own trucks and hires his own chicken-catching crews.[9]

The own-business and control rules are hard to apply in close cases. Working relationships are varied and the circumstances emit mixed signals. In addition, courts may differ in their sense of appropriate policy. Patients might be surprised to find that their hospital has hired an independent contractor to operate its emergency room.[10] A foster parent who is paid by the state to care for one or more children, usually only works for one person—the state. The foster parent is subject to state inspections and some degree of control. Yet the control may not extend to small daily tasks, so the foster parent may be considered an independent contractor.[11] The newspaper carrier who delivers papers to your porch may be rousted out of bed by the employer if he is late, but sometimes courts have treated him as an independent contractor even though he is permitted to work only for the newspaper.[12]

A sawmill could hire full-time employees to cut timber and hall it to the mill, but it could also hire independent contractors who are in the business of cutting and hauling timber. Evidence may present a mixed picture of the relationship. For instance, the sawmill may own timber rights in the land cut and may demand that the timber be cut at a precise distance from the ground. Those factors suggest that the logger is an employee. But the logger may own his own truck for hauling and may also work for other timber buyers at times. Those factors suggest that he

5. E.g., Kime v. Hobbs, 252 Neb. 407, 562 N.W.2d 705 (1997); Mavrikidis v. Petullo, 153 N.J. 117, 707 A.2d 977 (1998).

6. Restatement Second of Agency § 220.

7. See, e.g., McDonald v. Hampton Training School for Nurses, 254 Va. 79, 486 S.E.2d 299 (Va. 1997).

8. See, e.g., Shaw v. C.B. & E., Inc., 630 So.2d 401 (Ala.1993).

9. Fisher v. Townsends, Inc., 695 A.2d 53 (Del.1997).

10. And hospitals have been surprised to find that they are nevertheless liable under doctrines of apparent agency or the like. See § 338.

11. District of Columbia v. Hampton, 666 A.2d 30 (D.C.App.1995).

12. Miami Herald Publ'g Co. v. Kendall, 88 So.2d 276 (Fla.1956); contra, Santiago v. Phoenix Newspapers, Inc., 164 Ariz. 505, 794 P.2d 138 (1990) (analyzing factors in detail); see Mary J. Cavins, Annotation, Newspaper Boy or Other News Carrier as Independent Contractor or Employee for Purposes of Respondeat Superior, 55 A.L.R.3d 1216 (1974) (reflecting diverse results).

is an independent contractor. When the evidence points in both directions, litigation is likely to be required. That litigation is resolved less by rules than by analysis of the evidence pointing to control, with analogies to factually similar cases. When the evidence is substantially mixed, the question is usually one for the jury.[13] But if the undisputed evidence shows that the employer has little control over the means and manner of work, the court may conclude as a matter of law that the worker is an independent contractor.[14]

Service stations, motels, fast food outlets and many other businesses may appear to consumers[15] to be manifestations of a national company with a well-known name. Yet the local operator may be an independent contractor who is a licensee of the national franchisor's trademark. At the same time, the licensee or franchisee is usually subject to somewhat intense control by the franchisor. For this reason, it is sometimes argued that the local enterprise's appearance as an independent contractor is illusory. It is true that although the parties' intent is a factor in determining their status, the fact that they themselves label the agent as an independent contractor does not control.[16] Instead, courts will consider many factual details tending to prove or disprove the employer's right or practical exercise of control over details of the work. Given the employer's interest in protecting its trademark by setting operating standards, courts may tolerate a degree of control over details and still characterize the local operation as an independent contractor.[17]

The local owner or lessee of the gasoline service station, for example, might be subject to many of the national franchisor's company rules, but if he is free to set prices and hours of operation, and free to choose employees, and free to cancel the arrangement, courts are likely to treat him as an independent contractor unless other evidence shows that the franchisor has the right to control details of operation.[18] Similar holdings can be found for fast food restaurants[19] and other franchisees.[20] Sometimes, even taxi drivers who "lease" a cab from the franchisor are regarded as independent contractors.[21] Everything turns on the facts,

13. E.g., Bates v. Legette, 239 S.C. 25, 121 S.E.2d 289 (1961); McDonald v. Hampton Training Sch. for Nurses, 254 Va. 79, 486 S.E.2d 299 (Va. 1997).

14. E.g., Leaf River Forest Prods., Inc. v. Harrison, 392 So.2d 1138 (1981) (facts similar to the logger example, the court emphasizing that the logger financed his own operation, used his own equipment, hired and fired his own workers, and was paid by volume produced, not by the hour and concluding that there was no rational basis for finding a master-servant relationship).

15. On apparent agency or agency by estoppel, see § 338.

16. Santiago v. Phoenix Newspapers, Inc., 164 Ariz. 505, 794 P.2d 138 (1990); Fisher v. Townsends, Inc., 695 A.2d 53 (Del. 1997).

17. See Cislaw v. Southland Corp., 4 Cal.App.4th 1284, 6 Cal.Rptr.2d 386 (1992) (7–11 convenience store).

18. E.g., Miller v. Sinclair Ref. Co., 268 F.2d 114 (5th Cir.1959).

19. O'Banner v. McDonald's Corp., 173 Ill.2d 208, 218 Ill.Dec. 910, 670 N.E.2d 632 (1996); Hoffnagle v. McDonald's Corporation, 522 N.W.2d 808 (Iowa 1994).

20. E.g., Myszkowski v. Penn Stroud Hotel, Inc., 430 Pa.Super. 315, 634 A.2d 622 (1993) (hotel).

21. See Hosein v. Checker Taxi Co., Inc., 95 Ill.App.3d 150, 50 Ill.Dec. 460, 419 N.E.2d 568 (1981); R. L. Martyn, Annotation, Owning, Leasing, or Otherwise Engaging in Business of Furnishing Services for Taxicabs as Basis of Tort Liability for Acts

however; if the franchisor exercises sufficiently detailed control, the court will permit the jury to find that the franchisee is a servant, not an independent contractor.[22]

Quite possibly the national franchisor may have control over some aspects of the operation but not others. For example, local fast food outlets may be subjected to tight contractual control over food ingredients and preparation but not as to security guards on the premises with the odd result that the franchisor might be subjected to liability for some kinds of negligence in food preparation but not for negligent failure to provide adequate premises security.[23]

If employers were always careful to hire solvent and fully insured contractors, the classification as servant or independent contractor would not much matter. However, unless they select incompetent contractors, employers are free to hire contractors who are insolvent and uninsured and to use the independent contractor doctrine to avoid any responsibility for the injury they inflict. Two important exceptions appear in the succeeding sections.

§ 337. Nondelegable Duties

The language and policy of nondelegable duties. Courts have recognized that in spite of the general rule to the contrary, a business enterprise should not always escape responsibility by pursuing its work through independent contractors. When courts conclude that as a matter of policy the enterprise should be responsible for the torts of independent contractors who are carrying out the work of the enterprise,[1] they say that the enterprise had a nondelegable duty of care. What they mean by this is that the enterprise cannot discharge its obligation of reasonable care by hiring independent contractors to fulfill it. They do not mean to say that the independent contractor himself escapes liability. Courts conclude that some duties cannot be transferred or shifted to

of Taxi Driver under Respondeat Superior Doctrine, 8 A.L.R.3d 818 (1967) (reflecting view that drivers are ordinarily servants, but not always).

22. J.M. v. Shell Oil Co., 922 S.W.2d 759, 764 (Mo.1996) (attack on customer at gas station; Shell Oil provided "detailed guidance on such matters as reporting crime, architectural design, approved uniforms, loitering, lighting, display of products, vending machines, hours of operation, adequacy and training of staff, safety and orderliness of the premises, and routine inspections to ensure compliance with Shell's standard operating policies" and could unilaterally change policies; a jury question whether local "independent contractor" was actually a servant); Miller v. McDonald's Corp., 150 Or.App. 274, 945 P.2d 1107 (1997) (McDonald's restaurant, injury from hard object in food). Taxi drivers are often seen to be merely servants of "the company." See E.g., Bates v. Legette, 239 S.C. 25, 121 S.E.2d 289 (1961).

23. See Smith v. Foodmaker, Inc., 928 S.W.2d 683 (Tex.App.1996, no writ).

§ 337

1. Not all independent actors are carrying out the work of the putative employer. Indeed, some are not in any sense the agent of the employer. A retailer who sells Coca–Cola to customers is probably not any kind of employee of the Coca–Cola company. The operator of a service station that uses Texaco signs but does not buy products from or have any contractual relationship with that company is certainly independent, but he is not Texaco's employee. See Bahrle v. Exxon Corp., 145 N.J. 144, 678 A.2d 225 (1996); see also McCubbin v. Walker, 256 Kan. 276, 886 P.2d 790 (1994).

contractors because the enterprise that employs the independent contractor reaps the benefit of his work,[2] and can select competent and financially sound contractors who could bear the costs of their own torts.[3]

Inherent danger. Courts say that the duty of care is nondelegable when the employer engages in activities he knows or has reason to know are inherently or intrinsically dangerous.[4] Such activities are dangerous by nature and not merely because they are carried out in a risky manner.[5] If the enterprise hires an independent contractor to dust crops with poison, it is liable for his negligence in doing so, in spite of the fact that he is undoubtedly a contractor and not a servant.[6] The activity need not be abnormally dangerous or ultrahazardous.[7] Any things that are destructive by nature fall under the same rule, for example, poisons, explosives or fireworks,[8] strong acids,[9] or high voltage lines in an area of public accommodation.[10]

Peculiar risk. The idea has been extended to cover not merely inherently risky work but also work that creates a "peculiar" or special risk of substantial harm in the absence of special precautions.[11] To be peculiar, the risk must be somehow "different"[12] but the peculiarity of the risk may lie in the eye of the beholder. Courts have included or allowed juries to include the risk that use of a brush hog will throw out

2. Haseman v. Orman, 680 N.E.2d 531, 535 (Ind.1997) ("A business should bear its own costs, burdens, and expenses of operation, and these should be distributed by means of the price of the resulting product and not shifted, particularly, to small neighboring property owners for them to bear alone. We can understand no sensible or reasonable principle of law for shifting such expense or loss to persons who are not involved in such business ventures for profit").

3. Miller v. Westcor Ltd. Partnership, 171 Ariz. 387, 831 P.2d 386 (Ct. App. 1991).

4. Restatement § 427; see Francis M. Dougherty, Annotation, Liability of Employer With Regard to Inherently Dangerous Work For Injuries to Employees of Independent Contractor, 34 A.L.R.4th 914 (1981). The concept may be identified with the idea of a nuisance. See Mavrikidis v. Petullo, 153 N.J. 117, 707 A.2d 977 (1998).

5. Arthur v. Holy Rosary Credit Union, 139 N.H. 463, 656 A.2d 830 (1995).

6. Boroughs v. Joiner, 337 So.2d 340 (Ala.1976).

7. Benesh v. New Era, Inc., 207 Ill. App.3d 1049, 566 N.E.2d 779, 152 Ill.Dec. 902 (1991); Restatement § 427, cmt. c. Abnormally dangerous activities are included as activities that are inherently dangerous or at least prompt the same legal result. Restatement § 427A.

8. Miller v. Westcor Ltd. Partnership, 171 Ariz. 387, 831 P.2d 386 (1991); cf. District of Columbia v. Howell, 607 A.2d 501 (D.C.1992) (school chemistry experiment went horribly wrong). Also an acetylene torch. Levy v. Currier, 587 A.2d 205 (D.C. 1991) (fire set by spark or slag).

9. Beck v. Woodward Affiliates, 226 A.D.2d 328, 640 N.Y.S.2d 205 (1996).

10. Saiz v. Belen Sch. Dist., 113 N.M. 387, 827 P.2d 102 (1992).

11. Restatement § 416. Inherent danger and peculiar risk represent the same fundamental idea and courts often treat them as interchangeable terms.

12. See Huddleston v. Union Rural Elec. Ass'n, 841 P.2d 282, 290 (Colo.1992) (the activity must present "a special or peculiar danger to others inherent in the nature of the activity or the particular circumstances under which the activity was to be performed" and that danger must be "different in kind from the ordinary risks that commonly confront persons in the community"); Saiz v. Belen Sch. Dist., 113 N.M. 387, 396, 827 P.2d 102, 111 (1992) (risk must be normal to the work done but not a "routine matter of customary human activity"; it must be "different from one to which persons commonly are subjected by ordinary forms of negligence").

debris that injures bystanders,[13] that sprayed paint will spatter a neighbor's property,[14] that cranes used in construction will drop girders weighing many tons,[15] that demolition of buildings in a crowded city will cause them to fall into adjacent buildings,[16] that door-to-door salesmen, once in a prospect's home to sell vacuum cleaners, will sexually assault the customer,[17] and that logs being hauled will strike another vehicle,[18] and even that a tractor on a grassy slope will turn over.[19] In the usual peculiar risk case, the employer is vicariously liable for the contractor's negligence, but quite distinctly, the employer may be liable for its own negligence in failing to provide in the contract for special precautions or to supervise the contractor's work in cases of special danger.[20]

Beyond this, one who employs a contractor to do work that is likely to involve trespass or creation of a nuisance is liable for the harm resulting from such a trespass or nuisance.[21] Underground coal mining necessarily involves risks that removal of coal will cause the surface to subside to the damage of its owners, so it is appropriate to hold the owner of the mine liable for such harm even if a lessee carried out actual removal of the coal.[22] The same idea has been applied when the work to be done runs substantial risks of harm through breach of the peace or otherwise.[23]

Negligence of contractor. In the ordinary case, the contractor or his employee is negligent, but even if the contractor is not negligent, if he is carrying out an abnormally dangerous activity for which he would be strictly liable, the enterprise, too, may be strictly liable for harms resulting from the abnormally dangerous character of the operation.[24]

13. Falls v. Scott, 249 Kan. 54, 815 P.2d 1104 (1991).

14. Benesh v. New Era, Inc., 207 Ill. App.3d 1049, 566 N.E.2d 779, 152 Ill.Dec. 902 (1991).

15. LaCount v. Hensel Phelps Constr. Co., 79 Cal.App.3d 754, 145 Cal.Rptr. 244 (1978).

16. Majestic Realty Associates, Inc. v. Toti Contracting Co., 30 N.J. 425, 153 A.2d 321 (1959); cf. Rooney v. United States, 634 F.2d 1238 (9th Cir.1980) (painting high radar domes with risk of falling).

17. McLean v. Kirby Co., a Div. of Scott Fetzer Co., 490 N.W.2d 229 (N.D.1992); Read v. Scott Fetzer Co., 990 S.W.2d 732 (Tex. 1998).

18. Doak v. Green, 677 So.2d 301 (Fla. Dist.Ct.App.1996) (jury question, to be resolved on evidence of inherent danger). But an overloaded vehicle is not usually considered an inherent danger; rather it is a danger created by negligence of the loader. See Kime v. Hobbs, 252 Neb. 407, 562 N.W.2d 705 (1997).

19. Williams v. Dep't of Corrections, 224 Ga.App. 571, 481 S.E.2d 272 (1997).

20. Traudt v. Potomac Elec. Power Co., 692 A.2d 1326 (D.C.1997); Gordon v. Sanders, 692 So.2d 939 (Fla.Dist.Ct.App.1997); Restatement § 413.

21. Restatement § 427B. Cf. Axtell v. Kurey, 222 A.D.2d 804, 634 N.Y.S.2d 847 (1995) (employer who directed contractor where to cut trees is liable to owner for the trespass).

22. Haseman v. Orman, 680 N.E.2d 531 (Ind.1997).

23. Hester v. Bandy, 627 So.2d 833, 843 (Miss.1993) (repossession from a debtor ending in breach of the peace; "when one employs another to perform a task in which a serious danger to person or property, a crime, or some tort can reasonably be anticipated in its performance, it is no defense to say the act causing the harm was committed by an independent contractor").

24. See Bahrle v. Exxon Corp., 145 N.J. 144, 156, 678 A.2d 225, 231 (1996); Saiz v. Belen Sch. Dist., 113 N.M. 387, 827 P.2d 102 (1992); Restatement § 427A.

But the enterprise is not liable for the contractor's negligence on an entirely collateral matter not directly or foreseeably resulting from the authorized work.[25]

Public danger. Special danger in the work itself is not the only basis for finding a nondelegable duty. Such duties are imposed as well when the enterprise acts through contractors to carry on construction or the like in public places, for example in excavating or maintaining a public highway.[26]

Landowner-employers. Many employers of independent contractors are landowners contracting for repair or improvements. The duty of a lessor to maintain leased premises in reasonable safety is said to be nondelegable,[27] as it is the possessor's duty to maintain premises in reasonably safe condition, at least for those rightfully upon the land.[28] That duty includes the duty of care imposed when land is held open to the public.[29] In each of these cases, the landowner-employer is subject to liability for the contractor's negligence. For instance, the hotel owner whose independent plumber misconnects the cold water faucet so that a guest is burned in the shower is responsible as if he had done the work himself.[30]

Statutes. Statutes are sometimes construed to provide nondelegable duties. For example, scaffolding acts or the like provide that certain safety standards must be met in structural work and that the landowner who employs a contractor as well as the contractor himself is responsible.[31] But courts have gone further by treating statutory commands as creating nondelegable duties even when the statute itself is not construed to require such a rule.[32] For instance, a creditor who hires a contractor to repossess a delinquent debtor's car is liable if the contractor violates a statute by breaching the peace in making the reposses-

25. Loyd v. Herrington, 143 Tex. 135, 182 S.W.2d 1003 (1944) (as a joke, independent contractor's employee attached dynamite cap to car engine expecting it to explode when the car was started; it didn't, but it exploded when an auto mechanic opened the hood; because the injury was collateral to the contract, the prime contractor was not liable for these acts of the independent contractor's employees).

26. Restatement §§ 417 and cmt. a & 418.

27. Restatement §§ 419–421.

28. Otero v. Jordon Restaurant Enters., 119 N.M. 721, 895 P.2d 243 (Ct.App.1995); Restatement § 422. When a landowner retains a contractor to do construction on the land, there may be factual questions whether the landowner was or was not in possession during construction. See, e.g., Parrish v. Omaha Pub. Power Dist., 242 Neb. 783, 496 N.W.2d 902 (1993).

29. Restatement § 425. Similarly, one who uses a contractor to maintain safety of a chattel supplied to others in the course of business has a nondelegable duty. Id.

30. Id., Ill. 2.

31. See, e.g., Kennerly v. Shell Oil Co., 13 Ill.2d 431, 150 N.E.2d 134 (1958); Gordon v. Eastern Ry. Supply, Inc., 82 N.Y.2d 555, 626 N.E.2d 912, 606 N.Y.S.2d 127 (1993).

32. Williams v. Dep't of Corrections, 224 Ga.App. 571, 481 S.E.2d 272 (1997); Miller v. Lambert, 196 W.Va. 24, 467 S.E.2d 165 (1995) (landfill at river's edge encroached on neighboring property and violated Clean Water Act and other statutes, landowner as well as contractor subject to liability); cf. Maloney v. Rath, 69 Cal.2d 442, 71 Cal.Rptr. 897, 445 P.2d 513 (1968) (car owner responsible for independent contractor's failure to repair brakes properly).

sion.[33] A contract between employer and contractor might have the same effect, so that the contractor cannot escape liability to the employer when his subcontractors cause harm.[34]

Although the rule that statutes create a nondelegable duty is sometimes stated broadly,[35] as if to say that the employer is liable for harm resulting from any statutory violation by the contractor, that is not so; there are certainly cases that refuse to make a duty nondelegable merely because it is one imposed by statute.[36] Courts seem to use statutes as a basis for creating a nondelegable duty when the statute coincides with judicial notions of fairness or policy. Banks that hire contractors to repossess cars are very definitely pursuing their enterprise as lenders and should be liable for the predictable breaches of the peace that accompany this method of enforcing a security interest. A statute against breach of the peace adds little or nothing to such a perception. In other statutory violation cases there is no reason to impose liability upon the contractor's employer. If you take a cab to the airport, you have certainly hired an independent contractor, not a servant; but it is highly improbable that you would be liable to an injured person if the driver causes harm by violating a traffic ordinance.

Collateral negligence. Even when the duty is nondelegable, the employer is not responsible for "collateral negligence" of the independent contractor. Collateral negligence creates a risk that is not a usual or inherent part of the work[37] or is outside the scope of the employer's enterprise.[38] For instance, if the contractor's activity is inherently dangerous because it involves explosives, an injury from explosives is definitely an injury inherent in the risk and the employer of the contractor remains subject to liability.[39] On the other hand, if the injury occurs only because a defective ladder is used in connection with the same work, such an injury is collateral because it is not a result of the inherent danger.[40] Similarly, when the nondelegability rule is based upon the landowner's duty to provide reasonably safe conditions rather than upon inherent danger, the landowner-employer of a contractor will not be responsible for the contractor's negligence in driving negligently to get supplies, but will be liable for harm caused by defective conditions created by the contractor on the land.[41] The affinity of this line of

33. MBank El Paso v. Sanchez, 836 S.W.2d 151 (Tex.1992); accord, Hester v. Bandy, 627 So.2d 833 (Miss.1993).

34. Gordon v. Sanders, 692 So.2d 939 (Fla.Dist.Ct.App.1997) (homeowner retained contractor to remove trees; contractor obtained subcontractors, who caused tree to fall upon the homeowner's house; the contractor was liable because of his contract).

35. See Restatement § 424 (requiring only that the statute impose "specified safeguards or precautions for the safety of others").

36. E.g., Midland Oil Co. v. Thigpen, 4 F.2d 85, 53 A.L.R. 311 (8th Cir. 1925).

37. Restatement § 426.

38. See Clarence Morris, The Torts of an Independent Contractor, 29 Ill. L. Rev. 339, 352 (1935).

39. Miller v. Westcor Ltd. Partnership, 171 Ariz. 387, 831 P.2d 386 (Ct. App. 1991).

40. Cf. Barbera v. Brod–Dugan Co., 770 S.W.2d 318 (Mo.Ct.App.1989) (great heights made work dangerous, but fall was due to defective equipment, not to special danger of heights).

41. See Otero v. Jordon Restaurant Enters., supra n. 28. Collateral negligence is also described as casual negligence or negligence in operational detail rather than in

thought with the scope-of-risk rules of proximate cause seems plain enough.

Retained control. The independent contractor rule does not relieve employers of liability for their own negligence. For example, employers may be negligent in choosing an incompetent and dangerous contractor, or in failing to exercise appropriate supervision and control.[42] The employer is frequently a landowner upon whose land the contractor is working. If the employer retains possession of the land or otherwise retains a degree of control for other reasons, he must exercise that control with reasonable care for the safety of others.[43] The owner who actively directs a contractor's dangerous construction work on his land may thus be held for his own negligence, quite apart from any vicarious liability or nondelegable duty.[44]

Nondelegable duties to the contractor's employees. Some courts hold that a landowner's nondelegable duty may extend to the employees of the independent contractor as well as to others who may be injured by the contractor's negligence.[45] The independent contractor himself, however, is not ordinarily liable in tort to his own employees. Instead, workers' compensation statutes make the compensation benefits the exclusive remedy. Consequently, if the landowner is liable in tort on a nondelegable duty theory, his liability would be greater than and different from the liability of the negligent contractor himself. And the landowner would almost certainly be denied any right of indemnity against the negligent contractor, because to allow him indemnity would be to subvert the exclusive remedy rule that protects the contractor against tort liability to his own workers. With these considerations in mind, most courts hold that the landowner or other employer of an independent contractor is not vicariously liable to the contractor's own employee when the claim is based on nondelegable duty.[46] When the employer's own negligence results in harm to the contractor's employee, the case is entirely different and courts appropriately subject the employer to liability.[47]

plan or general method of work. The fundamental idea, however, is that the landowner's responsibility extends only to features that are characteristic of the work for which he retained the contractor. See Restatement § 426, cmt. a.

42. Restatement §§ 411 (negligent selection); 413 (failing to require contractor to protect against special risks); 414 (negligence in failing to exercise retained control over independent contractor).

43. See Hammond v. Bechtel, Inc., 606 P.2d 1269 (Alaska 1980).

44. E.g., Parrish v. Omaha Pub. Power Dist., 242 Neb. 783, 496 N.W.2d 902 (1993).

45. E.g., Parrish v. Omaha Pub. Power Dist., 242 Neb. 783, 496 N.W.2d 902 (1993).

46. Privette v. Superior Court, 5 Cal.4th 689, 854 P.2d 721, 21 Cal.Rptr.2d 72 (1993); see Francis M. Dougherty, Annotation, Liability of Employer With Regard to Inherently Dangerous Work For Injuries to Employees of Independent Contractor, 34 A.L.R.4th 914 (1981). When the independent contractor fails to obtain workers' compensation coverage, the landowner may remain liable to the contractor's employee. Andreini v. Superior Court., 60 Cal.App.4th 1415, 71 Cal.Rptr.2d 153 (1998) (unpublished).

47. Traudt v. Potomac Elec. Power Co., 692 A.2d 1326 (D.C.1997); cf. Wagner v. Continental Cas. Co., 143 Wis.2d 379, 421 N.W.2d 835 (1988) (employer liable to contractor's employee for employer's affirmative acts of negligence but not for failure to check contractor's credentials). However, if the employer is a statutory employer

Insolvent or uninsured contractors and nondelegable duty. Nondelegable duties operate to inflict liability upon employers of independent contractors only when the employers retain financially irresponsible contractors. If the contractor is financially responsible, his employer may not be sued at all, but even if he is sued and held liable, he will ordinarily be entitled to recover indemnity from the contractor whose negligence caused the plaintiff's harm.[48] The employer can thus protect himself by requiring the contractor to insure or by selecting financially responsible contractors. For this reason, Professor Clarence Morris suggested that the employer should remain liable for the contractor's torts when he selected an incompetent contractor and that incompetence included financial irresponsibility.[49]

The New Jersey Court once signaled some interest in such a rule,[50] and acting on that signal, the Third Circuit applied it to impose liability upon a large developer who employed an essentially insolvent independent paving contractor.[51] Since then, however, it appears that New Jersey would not support such liability.[52] Although other courts have given some weight to the idea that employers should be responsible when they retain uninsured or financially irresponsible contractors,[53] they have not so far adopted a general rule of employer liability.

§ 338. Apparent Authority, Apparent Agency, or Agency by Estoppel

Apparent agency issues arise when an employer retains an independent contractor but creates the appearance that the contractor is acting as his servant. If the plaintiff deals with the independent contractor in the reasonable belief that she is dealing with the employer himself or his servants, she is entitled to hold the employer vicariously liable when she suffers physical harm at the hands of the contractor. In effect, the plaintiff can hold the employer to the appearances he has created.[1] Similarly, if the employer creates the appearance that an employee is acting within the scope of his employment or authority when he is not,

obliged to secure workers' compensation, it might logically claim an immunity even in the case of its own negligence.

48. Spectron Dev. Lab., Div. of Titan Corp. v. American Hollow Boring Co., 123 N.M. 170, 936 P.2d 852 (Ct.App.1997).

49. Clarence Morris, The Torts of an Independent Contractor, 29 Ill. L. Rev. 339, 352 (1935).

50. Majestic Realty Assocs., Inc. v. Toti Contracting Co., 30 N.J. 425, 153 A.2d 321 (1959).

51. Becker v. Interstate Properties, 569 F.2d 1203 (3d Cir.1977).

52. Mavrikidis v. Petullo, 153 N.J. 117, 707 A.2d 977 (1998). See also Robinson v. Jiffy Executive Limousine Co., 4 F.3d 237 (3d Cir.1993).

53. See Huddleston v. Union Rural Electric Ass'n, 841 P.2d 282, 287, n. 6 (Colo.1992)

§ 338

1. See, e.g., Restatement § 429 & Restatement Second of Agency § 267. A verbal representation is not required; any conduct that creates the appearance of agency or "manifests" agency will suffice, so long as the plaintiff in fact believes and believes reasonably that agency exists. See Hansen v. Horn Rapids O.R.V. Park of the City of Richland, 85 Wash.App. 424, 932 P.2d 724 (1997). A Connecticut court has rejected the doctrine on the ground that no precedent in Connecticut had established it. Mullen v. Horton, 46 Conn.App. 759, 700 A.2d 1377 (1997), but the rule is otherwise well established.

the plaintiff who reasonably relies upon the appearance can rightly subject the employer to vicarious responsibility.[2]

For example, suppose the plaintiff wishes to hire a moving or storage company and finds the name "Bekins" in the Yellow Pages. She recognizes the name and calls the listed number. The phone call is answered "Bekins" and when she retains the company, its employees wear uniforms saying "Bekins." One of the employees negligently sets fire to her house, but upon investigation it appears that the company she hired was merely an independent company permitted to use the Bekins name. In such a case, Bekins is subject to liability, for it has created the appearance that the local company was its agent or servant and not merely a licensee of its trade name.[3]

The plaintiff's reliance—whether it is required and what it means in this context—has been a problem. According to some, the Restatement of Agency rule for physical harm cases,[4] often called agency by estoppel, requires reliance by the plaintiff. But, the same jurists say, the Restatement of Torts rule,[5] often called apparent or ostensible agency, allows recovery without reliance.[6] The Torts Restatement specifically requires only the "reasonable belief" that the services are being rendered by the employer.

Actually, the Agency Restatement seems to require only an attenuated kind of reliance. Its illustration supposes that the plaintiff takes a taxi held out as one of the defendant's cabs but in fact driven by an independent contractor. If the driver negligently injures the passenger, the Agency Restatement says, the defendant may be subjected to liability if the passenger relied upon the defendant "as one furnishing safe drivers."[7] The rule so stated does not appear to require full scale, but-for reliance. Although a non-passenger has no basis for recovery against the principal under this rule,[8] the passenger-plaintiff need not prove that, but for the appearances, she would have taken a different taxi. It is enough if she "relied" in the sense that she believed the drivers would be safe because they worked for the defendant as a reputable business.[9] Both Restatements, then, are likely to call for the same result in many tort cases.[10]

2. See Harold Gill Reuschlein and William A. Gregory, The Law of Agency and Partnership § 23 (2d ed. 1990).

3. Independent Fire Ins. Co. v. Able Moving and Storage Co., Inc., 650 So.2d 750 (La.1995).

4. Restatement Second of Agency § 267.

5. Restatement § 429.

6. Jackson v. Power, 743 P.2d 1376 (Alaska 1987).

7. Restatement Second of Agency § 267, Ill. 1. The blackletter is similar; the plaintiff need only show that he relies upon the care or skill of the apparent agent.

8. Restatement Second of Agency § 267, Ill. 1; cf. Myszkowski v. Penn Stroud Hotel, Inc., 430 Pa.Super. 315, 634 A.2d 622 (1993) (plaintiff properly in hotel but not as one who contracted with hotel could not claim hotel's apparent agency for franchisor).

9. See also the excellent discussion of the two levels of reliance in Clark v. Southview Hospital and Family Health Ctr., 68 Ohio St.3d 435, 628 N.E.2d 46, 58 A.L.R.5th 929 (1994).

10. Some of the debates about the correct theory behind apparent authority are generated by contract cases, or by the effort to state universal rules of apparent agency that cover both contract and tort cases. See Harold Gill Reuschlein and William A.

However, the Restatement of Torts shows a greater difference on another issue. The Restatement of Agency—the "estoppel" approach as the courts have labeled it—requires that the employer manifest or create the appearance that the employee is a servant. The Restatement of Torts imposes no such requirement. It requires only that the services be accepted in the reasonable belief that they are delivered by the defendant rather than an independent contractor. The plaintiff's reasonable belief will most often arise because of the defendant's acts in creating the appearance of agency, but perhaps not always.[11] Under the estoppel approach, even the plaintiff who reasonably believes that the independent contractor is the defendant's servant cannot recover without showing that the defendant himself created that belief.[12]

Most courts considering the issue have invoked apparent or ostensible agency when hospitals farm out some of their routine functions to independent physicians.[13] Patients who seek medical assistance in a hospital's regular, full-time emergency room no doubt believe they are getting care provided by the hospital. The hospital, however, may have arranged for physicians' groups to provide emergency room services as independent contractors. In such cases courts have said that the hospital has created the appearance that the emergency room is part of the hospital itself and hence that it is subject to liability for emergency room malpractice under an ostensible agency theory, or at least that the jury could so find from the evidence.[14]

So far as reliance is concerned, these cases resemble the Agency Restatement's taxi example. The plaintiff seeking emergency care relies in a loose or attenuated sense on the hospital's care, but almost certainly does not rely in the sense that the patient would have refused care had she known that the physician providing it was an independent contractor. Nevertheless, this reliance—expectation might be a more accurate

GREGORY, THE LAW OF AGENCY AND PARTNERSHIP § 23 (2d ed. 1990).

11. For example, some courts have said that the appearance must be created by the defendant and not by the putative agent. If this were literally and always true, the plaintiff who sees the defendant's trade name in the Yellow Pages or on a taxicab would not be able to establish apparent agency without showing that defendant himself authorized the use of his name, or that his authorization could be inferred because the name had been publically used for a long period of time so that the defendant must have known and tacitly approved it.

12. Baptist Memorial Hosp. v. Sampson, 969 S.W.2d 945 (Tex.1998).

13. Distinguish "staff physicians" who merely have permission to use hospital facilities but who are retained in the first instance by the patient.

14. Jackson v. Power, 743 P.2d 1376 (Alaska 1987); Clark v. Southview Hosp. and Family Health Ctr., 68 Ohio St.3d 435, 628 N.E.2d 46, 58 A.L.R. 5th 929 (1994); contra, Menzie v. Windham Community Memorial Hospital, 774 F.Supp. 91 (D.Conn.1991) (independent anesthesiology group, one going to emergency room has no choice and hence does not rely); Baptist Memorial Hosp. v. Sampson, 969 S.W.2d 945 (Tex.1998) (requiring act by hospital creating reasonable and justified reliance, no act shown). Health Maintenance or Managed Care Organizations (HMOs or MCOs) may be subject to the same liability when they operate on the "staff model," that is, more like providers and less like insurance or financing companies. See § 256. In addition, it is possible to claim that managed care organizations are liable for physician negligence on the ground that they have warranted ordinary care. See William S. Brewbaker, III, Medical Malpractice and Managed Care Organizations: The Implied Warranty of Quality, 60 L. & CONTEMP. PROBS. 117 (Spring 1997).

word—has been sufficient in emergency room cases, if indeed reliance is required in the physical harm cases.

But courts may not apply this concept of reliance so readily in all cases. Suppose the plaintiff slips and falls in a local McDonald's restaurant. The local restaurant may be owned by an independent contractor, who pays for the privilege of using the McDonald's name and is obliged to follow the franchisor's rules but who is not the servant of the franchisor. Nevertheless, the almost uniform appearance of such restaurants, the use of trademarks and the trade name, the standardized food items and promotions might all give customers the impression that a single entity operates all local restaurants and that the entity is McDonald's, the franchisor. To this kind of claim some courts have answered that the plaintiff did not rely on the franchisor's care, at least with respect to the injuries suffered in the particular case,[15] although others have denied the apparent agency claim on the ground that a franchisor does not hold out the franchisee as an agent merely by licensing the trademark to him.[16]

Everything depends upon the court's assessment of the facts, so in some franchise cases the franchisor is liable because he has created the appearance that the local unit is part of the larger operation.[17] Simple reliance like that in the taxicab example is sufficient for such courts. If injury allegedly results from food in a McDonald's restaurant, the fact that the plaintiff patronized a local McDonald's outlet because she had confidence in McDonald's food would suffice to show reliance.[18]

Perhaps the hospital cases are stronger cases for vicarious liability, not so much because the holding out and reliance are different, but because of public policy concerns with health care. Some courts seem to have been influenced by policy considerations as well as by the appearance created by the hospital.[19] This is borne out by the fact that some courts have imposed upon the hospital a nondelegable duty that does not turn on appearances at all.[20]

§ 339. Borrowed Servants

The problem. The problem of the borrowed (or loaned) servant arises when one person directs his servant, as a part of the job, to do work for

15. O'Banner v. McDonald's Corporation, 173 Ill.2d 208, 218 Ill.Dec. 910, 670 N.E.2d 632 (1996); Myszkowski v. Penn Stroud Hotel, Inc., 430 Pa.Super. 315, 634 A.2d 622 (1993). If the franchisor controlled, say, food preparation, injury from badly prepared food might be different.

16. Mobil Oil Corp. v. Bransford, 648 So.2d 119 (Fla.1995) (service station); Smith v. Foodmaker, Inc., 928 S.W.2d 683 (Tex.App.1996, no writ) (fast food restaurant).

17. Crinkley v. Holiday Inns, Inc., 844 F.2d 156 (4th Cir.1988) (motel bandits at a Holiday Inn franchise, reliance found in part because guest had specifically sought out Holiday Inn).

18. Miller v. McDonald's Corp., 150 Or. App. 274, 945 P.2d 1107 (1997).

19. See Clark v. Southview Hosp. and Family Health Ctr., 68 Ohio St.3d 435, 628 N.E.2d 46, 58 A.L.R. 5th 929 (1994).

20. Jackson v. Power, 743 P.2d 1376 (Alaska 1987); Simmons v. Tuomey Regional Med. Ctr., 330 S.C. 115, 498 S.E.2d 408 (Ct.App.1998); contra: Baptist Memorial Hosp. v. Sampson, 969 S.W.2d 945 (Tex. 1998) (reasoning that nondelegable duty was not needed because patient could sue the negligent physician personally).

another. For example, M may rent heavy equipment to B and furnish the servant as operator. If the servant negligently causes injury to others, the question is whether vicarious liability should be visited upon M as the general employer, or upon B as the special employer, or upon both.

Control test. The answer is such cases usually turns on the familiar control test,[1] perhaps coupled with a sense that "short term cooperation" is not the same thing as a loaned employee.[2] If the general employer retains control, then courts usually say that he and only he is vicariously liable for the loaned servant's tort. On the other hand, if the special employer has the right to direct details of the borrowed servant's conduct, then the special employer is the temporary master and he becomes vicariously liable. In that case, the general employer is not liable under respondeat superior rules.

It is quite possible that the general employer will retain control over some activities of the servant, while the special employer will have control over others, with liability for an act following control, wherever it lies.[3] Although courts say that what counts is control over details, the manner, means, and day-to-day work, control is not a precise concept, and there are usually important ways in which the general employer retains control at the same time that the special employer has control over some particular acts. Facts bearing on control frequently lead to conflicting conclusions, so sometimes courts merely leave the "whose servant" issue to the jury.[4]

The Agency Restatement offers a kind of presumption that in the absence of other evidence, the servant continues to be in general employment.[5] But this presumption is not very useful because some kind of evidence of the special employer's control is always presented in arguable cases.

Courts consider matters besides control when the issue is not respondeat superior liability but the availability of workers' compensation for the borrowed employee. In that setting, the worker's own willingness or reluctance to accept a new, temporary employer, becomes significant.[6]

Treating both lender and borrower as employers. Given the uncertain or conflicting conclusions based upon control, some courts have simply said that both the general and special employers should be treated as

§ 339

1. The evidence to show control or its lack is similar to that used to establish the employee's status as a servant in other cases. Many kinds of evidence are listed in § 336.

2. See Frank L. Maraist and Thomas C. Galligan, Jr., The Employer's Tort Immunity: A Case Study in Post-modern Immunity, 57 LA. L. REV. 467, 487 (1997) (discussing workers' compensation effects of borrowing).

3. New York Cent. R.R. Co. v. Northern Indiana Pub. Serv. Co., 140 Ind.App. 79, 221 N.E.2d 442 (1966); Restatement Second of Agency § 227, cmt. a.

4. E.g., Weaver v. Brush, 166 Vt. 98, 689 A.2d 439 (1996).

5. Restatement Second of Agency § 227, cmt. b (describing it as an inference).

6. The worker's agreement to a substituted employer is especially important in that setting, since the worker may lose either compensation or tort rights or both.

masters of the worker, or at least that they could be so treated in particular cases.[7] On the surface, treating both employers as masters offers a common sense solution to the problem in one setting. Suppose that S is the regular employee of M, but is loaned to B to dig a trench with a backhoe. At B's direction, S digs the trench to a dangerous depth. The trench later caves in and injures the plaintiff, who was employed by B to lay pipe in the trench. From the plaintiff's point of view the maximum benefits can be obtained if (a) he can claim workers' compensation from B, his employer and (b) sue M in tort for damages. If both M and B are deemed masters of the loaned servant who dug the ditch too deeply, the plaintiff will be able to assert both claims.[8]

Those who like this solution may find it less attractive, however, if M's servant S is injured while digging the trench for B. If both B and M are masters, each will owe workers' compensation benefits, but neither will be liable in tort under the rule that workers' compensation is the exclusive remedy for a covered employee.[9] If B negligently caused the injury, the effect of treating both employers as masters in this setting is that B acquires an immunity in tort. The decision that the lender, borrower, or both are employers may have some other unexpected effects as well.[10]

Captain of the ship doctrine. One variation on the borrowed servant theme occurs in a medical malpractice setting when a nurse or resident employed by a hospital is directed to assist an independent surgeon in an operation. When the nurse negligently causes harm to the patient, some courts have said that, because the surgeon was "captain of the ship" and temporarily had the right to control the nurse's work, the surgeon would be liable for the negligence of hospital employees assisting him in the operating room,[11] or that the hospital would not be because its employee had become the servant of the surgeon.

If the doctrine imputed control to the surgeon as a matter of law and without regard to the facts, it was more stringent than the borrowed servant doctrine because the borrowed servant doctrine would treat the

7. Kastner v. Toombs, 611 P.2d 62 (Alaska 1980); see New York Cent. R.R. Co. v. Northern Indiana Pub. Serv. Co., 140 Ind.App. 79, 221 N.E.2d 442 (1966); Harold Gill Reuschlein and William A. Gregory, The Law of Agency and Partnership § 53 (2d ed. 1990); cf. Restatement Second of Agency § 226 (an employee can be the servant of two masters, even though they are not joint employers, if the service to one does not entail abandonment of the service of the other).

8. See Kastner v. Toombs, supra n. 7. Such a solution would also assist the plaintiff if neither employer were negligent, if his only claim was for workers' compensation, and if one of the employers was insolvent and lacking insurance.

9. See § 395.

10. For example, the Westfall Act has provided employees of the federal government with a statutory immunity from tort liability that is not dependent upon any corresponding liability of the government itself. See § 273. If a lender's employee is borrowed by the federal government, he might acquire that immunity, sometimes with the result that the plaintiff's claim would be defeated entirely. Or vice versa, a federal employee, if loaned to a private person, might lose the immunity, or alternatively keep it if courts adopt the view that both lender and borrower remain "employers."

11. McCullough v. Bethany Med. Ctr., 235 Kan. 732, 683 P.2d 1258 (Kan. 1984); McConnell v. Williams, 361 Pa. 355, 65 A.2d 243 (1949) (originating the metaphor).

surgeon's control as a question of fact to be determined case by case. Some courts have rejected the doctrine so far as it automatically held the surgeon liable, but have left room for ordinary applications of the borrowed servant rule, so that if the surgeon in fact has control of hospital employees in the operating room, he is vicariously liable, otherwise not.[12]

The basis for the surgeon's liability is sometimes confusing. Some cases have purported to ground the surgeon's liability in res ipsa loquitur, but the borrowed servant doctrine might be a better ground for such liability because the borrowed servant rules do not suggest, as some res ipsa loquitur cases have, that everyone in the operating room would be liable.[13] When courts automatically impose liability upon the surgeon for acts of hospital personnel, the case appears to be one of a nondelegable duty,[14] perhaps grounded upon the special duties undertaken by those who care for helpless persons[15] rather than upon control. When a court imposes a nondelegable duty as a matter of policy, the law will be clarified by dropping the captain terminology.

Such a nondelegable duty may be less compelling than it was when hospitals had the protection of blanket charitable immunities so that they could not be sued for their employee's negligence. But immunities have made a strong if incomplete comeback in the form of damage caps if nothing else.[16] In addition, doctors and hospitals are in a position to contract for indemnity of the surgeon in such cases, so a nondelegable duty, recognized as such or imposed under the captain of the ship doctrine is not without some purpose to the plaintiff.

§ 340. Other Bases for Vicarious Liability

Partnership. Partners are agents for each other within the scope of the partnership business and consequently each is vicariously liable for the others' torts committed within the scope of the partnership. Tort claims against partners are commonly associated with economic torts such as fraud rather than physical injury torts,[1] but the rule makes each partner individually liable for torts based on ordinary negligence as well.[2]

12. Starcher v. Byrne, 687 So.2d 737 (Miss.1997); Harris v. Miller, 335 N.C. 379, 438 S.E.2d 731 (1994); Holger v. Irish, 316 Or. 402, 851 P.2d 1122 (1993); Sparger v. Worley Hosp., Inc., 547 S.W.2d 582 (Tex. 1977).

13. See §§ 158 & 249.

14. See Long v. Hacker, 246 Neb. 547, 520 N.W.2d 195 (1994) (surgeon's liability for radiologist's X-ray interpretation).

15. As to special responsibility of those who undertake to care for the helpless, see §§ 155 & 335. In McConnell v. Williams, 361 Pa. 355, 65 A.2d 243 (1949) where the captain terminology originated, the court, after analogizing the surgeon's control to that of the captain, emphasized that the unconscious patient was entitled to special protection "by reason of her trust and confidence in, and necessary reliance upon, the surgeon she employed to take care of her and her child when born."

16. See § 282.

§ 340

1. E.g., Duggins v. Guardianship of Washington, 632 So.2d 420, 35 A.L.R. 5th 909 (Miss. 1993) (one attorney vicariously responsible for associated co-counsel's misappropriation of client's funds).

2. Gilpin v. Lev, 70 Ill.App.2d 66, 217 N.E.2d 477 (1966).

Liability of general partners is joint and several.[3]

Joint enterprise. A joint venture is a species of partnership. It characteristically involves a sharing of profits and losses by those who undertake it, but is usually limited in time and devoted to a single purpose. A special version of the joint venture in turn is the joint enterprise, which does not necessarily involve a profit and loss sharing arrangement. The joint enterprise is found to exist when two or more persons tacitly or expressly undertake an activity together—usually an automobile trip—with common purpose, community of interest and an equal right to a voice in the control.[4]

When a joint enterprise exists, each member is an agent for all others. If the enterprise is an automobile trip, the passenger, who ordinarily has no responsibility for the safe operation of the vehicle, may thus be liable to an injured third person if the driver negligently causes harm.[5] However, in most of the cases, the effect is different. The negligence of the driver is imputed to the injured passenger and treated as contributory negligence so that the passenger's claim against a negligent third person is barred or reduced.[6]

Older cases sometimes found a joint enterprise when friends went on a social outing and shared expenses or driving chores.[7] Courts have long since generally adopted a more restrictive view, parsing the elements of joint enterprise somewhat carefully and most often finding that the facts did not permit application of the doctrine.[8] Most courts, tacitly or expressly, now restrict the doctrine to cases in which the parties have a community of pecuniary, not merely social, interest, so that a shared fishing trip or the like will not be a joint enterprise.[9] Another restriction

3. Uniform Partnership Act § 306. The rule is different for limited liability partnerships, which share some of the characteristics of corporations.

4. Carboneau v. Peterson, 1 Wash.2d 347, 95 P.2d 1043 (1939). According to this classic statement, community of interest differs from common purpose because a common purpose might be in the interest of only one of the parties. Many statements de-emphasize the community of interest. The *Carboneau* court referred to the tacit or express undertaking as "contract," but agreement or undertaking is acceptable.

5. As in Straffus v. Barclay, 147 Tex. 600, 219 S.W.2d 65 (1949). When vicarious liability is asserted against a passenger, courts have very often found grounds for saying that no joint enterprise exists. E.g., Farmers Ins. Exch. v. Parker, 936 P.2d 1088 (Utah Ct.App.1997).

6. Lyon v. Ranger III, 858 F.2d 22 (1st Cir.1988).

7. E.g., Johnson v. Fischer, 292 Mich. 78, 290 N.W. 334 (1940), overruled to disallow imputation of negligence between members of the enterprise, Bostrom v. Jennings, 326 Mich. 146, 40 N.W.2d 97 (1949). Some of the decisions appear to conflate joint enterprise and owner-in-the-car-with-control theories. At a time when owner-in-the-car more or less automatically resulted in vicarious liability of the owner, the confusion of the two tended to produce a ready finding of joint enterprise. See Mayer v. Sampson, 157 Colo. 278, 402 P.2d 185 (1965). Understandably, such courts might also fail to mention the requirement of a common right to a voice in the control of the car, since they tended to emphasize the owner's control.

8. E.g., Dimond v. Kling, 221 N.W.2d 86 (N.D.1974) (negligence of one child not to be imputed to the other since they are subject to different "standards" at different ages). See Martin J. McMahon, Annotation, Modern Status of Rule Imputing Motor Vehicle Driver's Negligence to Passenger on Joint Venture Theory, 3 A.L.R.5th 1 (1993) (reflecting many cases holding that no joint enterprise was involved).

9. E.g., Stephens v. Jones, 710 S.W.2d 38 (Tenn.Ct.App.1984); Blount v. Bordens, Inc., 910 S.W.2d 931 (Tex.1995); Farmers

on the doctrine is that even when a joint enterprise is found to exist, the enterprisers are not barred from suits among themselves. When the passenger sues the driver, for example, the driver's fault is not imputed to the passenger.[10]

Bailment. When the owner merely gave another person permission to use the car, the owner was in the position of a bailor, not a master. As always, the owner might be personally negligent in entrusting the car to a known incompetent driver,[11] but under the general rule for bailments, the bailor was not vicariously liable for the bailee's negligence in operating the automobile unless the bailor and bailee also happened to be master and servant.[12] However, courts and legislatures at one time or another imposed liability in several exceptional cases.

Owner in the car. At one time courts thought that if the owner was a passenger in his own car, there was no bailment. The owner, they thought, was necessarily in control of the car and liable for the driver's negligence either vicariously or because of his own negligence in failing to exercise control. Contemporary courts have come to recognize that while owners should be subject to liability if they are actually in a master-servant relationship with the driver and likewise if they are personally negligent, there is no justification for a rule of law that ignores the facts of individual cases. Accordingly, they hold that the owner is not usually liable today merely because he is a passenger in a negligently driven car.[13]

Owner consent statutes. Statutes in a number of states, however, have imposed liability upon owners for injuries negligently inflicted by the permitted use of their automobiles.[14] Under such statutes, the existence and scope of the owner's consent becomes significant, since the owner is not responsible if he has not consented at all nor if he consented to a different use.[15] States without such general owner-consent statutes nevertheless may impose liability in particular situations. One

Ins. Exch. v. Parker, 936 P.2d 1088 (Utah Ct.App.1997).

10. E.g., Gilmer v. Carney, 608 N.E.2d 709 (Ind.Ct.App.1993); Restatement § 491 (2).

11. See § 330.

12. E.g., Smalich v. Westfall, 440 Pa. 409, 269 A.2d 476 (1970).

13. See Holman v. McMullan Trucking, 684 So.2d 1309, 1312 (Ala.1996) ("the negligence of a driver may be imputed to the owner of the vehicle only upon the finding of a master-servant or joint enterprise relationship"); Reed v. Hinderland, 135 Ariz. 213, 660 P.2d 464, 37 A.L.R.4th 555 (1983); Kalechman v. Drew Auto Rental, Inc., 33 N.Y.2d 397, 308 N.E.2d 886, 353 N.Y.S.2d 414 (1973); Smalich v. Westfall, 440 Pa. 409, 269 A.2d 476 (1970); Painter v. Lingon, 193 Va. 840, 844, 71 S.E.2d 355, 357–358 (1952) ("The owner's presence in an automobile driven by another is not alone sufficient to make him responsible for the operator's negligence. Such presence may be an element tending to prove agency, or that the operation was under the owner's control, so that the negligence of the driver would be imputable to him. The fact that the parties are husband and wife does not change this rule"). Some of the decision involved imputed contributory negligence, as to which see § 341.

14. E.g., Cal. Vehicle Code § 17150; N.Y. Vehicle & Traf. Law § 388.

15. E.g., Moore v. Leaseway Transp. Corp., 49 N.Y.2d 720, 402 N.E.2d 1160, 426 N.Y.S.2d 259 (1980) (owner who forbids user to accept passenger is not liable to passenger).

example is the liability of parents who sign a minor's application for driver's license.[16]

Family relationships and the family purpose doctrine. Another exception to the bailment rule was recognized in more than a dozen states that accepted the family purpose doctrine. That doctrine is also an exception to the usual rule that parents are not vicariously liable for the torts of their children in the absence employment relationship, joint enterprise or the like.[17] The parent may of course be liable for his own tort in failing to control a minor child[18] and he may be liable under special statutes which are usually limited to harms wilfully caused by a minor child and which usually limited the parent's liability.[19] The earlier common law made husbands liable for the torts of their wives, but that liability has long since been rejected and today a spouse not generally liable for the torts of the other spouse.[20] However, the family purpose or family car doctrine subjects the owner of a car to vicarious liability when the owner provides an automobile for the general use by members of the family for non-business[21] purposes and when the vehicle is so used by a family member.[22] Courts have sometimes said that the rule was based on agency principles, but it is now usually recognized that the doctrine represents a social policy generated in response to the problem presented by massive use of the automobile. Frequently the doctrine is formulated to apply only if the owner was "head" of the family.[23] In any event, it applies only to "owners"[24] or those who "furnished" the car for family

16. See David B. Sweet, Annotation, Construction and Effect of Statutes Which Make Parent, Custodian, or Other Person Signing Minor's Application for Vehicle Operator's License Liable for Licensee's Negligence or Willful Misconduct, 45 A.L.R.4th 87 (1987). Many states also make parents liable for a child's malicious torts, or malicious torts of certain kinds. E.g., CONN. GEN. STAT. § 52–572.

17. E.g., Bunn v. Landers, 230 Ga.App. 744, 498 S.E.2d 109 (1998).

18. § 329.

19. E.g., ORE. REV. STATS. § 30.765 (intentional or reckless acts of child, $7500 limit).

20. E.g., Seeger v. Canale, 241 Ill. App.3d 177, 607 N.E.2d 687, 180 Ill.Dec. 618 (1993) (wife-passenger not responsible for negligence of husband-driver). *Community property*: In community property states this rule is sometimes circumvented when the community property is subjected to execution for the tort of one spouse who was not acting for the community in committing the tort. See Grolemund v. Cafferata, 17 Cal.2d 679, 111 P.2d 641 (1941); cf. CAL. FAM. CODE § 1000 (b) (2). In other instances the interest of the innocent spouse in community property is protected, a result more consistent with the rule that spouses are not vicariously liable for one another's torts. See Keene v. Edie, 131 Wash.2d 822, 935 P.2d 588 (1997) (permitting execution upon the tortfeasor's interest in the community property only).

21. If the vehicle is used for business, ordinary agency rules may impose vicarious liability. If it is used both for family business and family convenience and pleasure, there is no reason not to apply the doctrine. See Heenan v. Perkins, 278 Or. 583, 564 P.2d 1354 (1977).

22. See R. E. Barber, Annotation, Modern Status of Family Purpose Doctrine with Respect to Motor Vehicles, 8 A.L.R.3d 1191 (1967).

23. See, e.g., Ramirez v. Ramirez, 122 N.M. 590, 929 P.2d 982 (Ct.App.1996).

24. E.g., Barber v. George, 144 Or.App. 370, 927 P.2d 140 (1996) (fact that parents paid for car in son's name does not show parents are owners, hence they are not liable under family purpose doctrine); Thompson v. Michael, 315 S.C. 268, 433 S.E.2d 853 (1993) (jury question whether defendant was owner where he retained title but had "given" the car to a daughter).

members in the same household.[25] The doctrine does not apply to impose liability upon the owner unless the driver used the car with the owner's express or implied permission or consent and for the purposes authorized.[26]

Concert of action or conspiracy. Those who cooperate, tacitly or expressly, in particular conduct to pursue a common illegal design (or a legal design by illegal acts) are said to be acting in concert. Each of those acting in concert is liable jointly and severally for all of the intended or foreseeable resulting harm. The classic examples are cases of intentional and illegal harm. A and B go to the plaintiff's house to steal his goods. A breaks down the door and B beats the plaintiff. A is liable for is own acts and for B's as well.[27] In one unusual case, the court applied a similar idea, holding an entire industry liable where individual manufacturers in effect jointly controlled the risk created by their product (dynamite caps) through industry-wide custom or practices.[28] Sometimes pleaders and courts use the more stringent language of conspiracy to describe the voluntary participation of several people in a tortious enterprise. Conspiracy is not a tort in itself; it reflects the conclusion that each participant should be liable for the tortious course of conduct.[29]

A contemporary example of concerted action is the case of drivers who agree, tacitly or otherwise, to an illegal race on the public streets. In the course of the race, A loses control and crashes into the plaintiff. B, on the other hand, safely comes to a stop some distance away. Given an agreement to race, perhaps a "challenge and response" inferred from the speed and relative positions of the automobiles and from similar behaviors,[30] both drivers are acting tortiously in concert. They are jointly and severally liable to the plaintiff, although only one of them actually made contact with the plaintiff's car.[31]

Vicarious liability explains these cases—the parties are engaged in a kind of partnership or joint venture for illegal or tortious purposes[32]—

25. See Brown v. Stogsdill, 140 Ariz. 485, 682 P.2d 1152 (Ct. App. 1984) (son who lived in parents' guest house paying rent, but at less than rental value could be considered family member; parent might have "furnished" the car even though it was registered in the son's name); Jackson v. Reed, 229 Ga.App. 433, 494 S.E.2d 52 (1997) (adult who had her own car and was merely house sitting was not family member).

26. E.g., Leonard v. Wilson, 238 Neb. 1, 468 N.W.2d 604 (1991).

27. Restatement § 876, Ill. 1.

28. Hall v. E.I. DuPont De Nemours & Co., 345 F.Supp. 353 (E.D.N.Y.1972).

29. See Jones v. City of Chicago, 856 F.2d 985 (7th Cir.1988).

30. Nelson v. Nason, 343 Mass. 220, 222, 177 N.E.2d 887, 888 (1961).

31. Bierczynski v. Rogers, 239 A.2d 218 (Del.1968); Clausen v. Carroll, 291 Ill. App.3d 530, 684 N.E.2d 167, 225 Ill.Dec. 692 (1997) (question of fact whether race was over at time of the collision and whether, if so, the collision was nevertheless a foreseeable result of the race); A. E. Korpela, Annotation, Liability of Participant in Unauthorized Highway Race for Injury to Third Person Directly Caused by Other Racer, 13 A.L.R.3d 431 (1968).

32. Several cases suggest that a drag race is a joint venture, although the same cases may suggest that liability is based on the direct negligence of each defendant in creating a risk of harm. See, e.g., Clausen v. Carroll, 291 Ill.App.3d 530, 684 N.E.2d 167, 225 Ill.Dec. 692 (1997).

but other explanations are often equally or more plausible. In at least some of the drag race cases, each racer is negligent. Each creates an unreasonable risk that one of the racers will lose control. Although causal apportionment is possible in such cases, both defendants are at fault and both created the risk of the very harm that came about. A jurist who rejects vicarious liability altogether could support liability of both defendants in these cases as well as in more common cases of joint and several liability.

On the other hand, the Restatement of Apportionment has recognized that the concert of action rule may be appropriately expanded in the light of two contemporary developments in joint and several liability and in comparative responsibility. In particular, if comparative fault rules are applied to a landlord who negligently creates dangers that tenants will be criminally attacked,[33] the landlord may escape any significant liability on the ground that his fault is minuscule in comparison to the rapist who attacks the tenant, at least where joint and several liability is also abolished.[34] Such a morally unacceptable result is perhaps not inevitable, since some reasonable people may think a great deal of responsibility should be assigned to the landlord, but it is a result that is all too likely. With cases like this in mind, one draft of the Apportionment Restatement suggested that the concert of action rules can be expanded so that the landlord and those similarly situated would be subjected to full liability, jointly and severally with the criminal, even in jurisdictions that have abolished joint and several liability generally.[35]

Aiding, abetting, encouraging. One who knowingly provides substantial aid or encouragement to another's commission of a tort is also jointly and severally liable for it along with the person who actually carries out the tortious acts. The Restatement so provides.[36] One who aids, abets or encourages a tort need not participate in it to be liable, but the aid or encouragement must be substantial.

In *Halberstam v. Welch*,[37] Welch was a career burglar who was quite successful for years until, in the line of work, he killed Halberstam. In a suit for Halberstam's death, the plaintiff sought recovery against Linda Hamilton as well as Welch. Hamilton lived with Welch and kept books on his sales of the goods. Hamilton did not participate in this nor any of the many earlier burglaries, but she knew "the reality." The court upheld a judgment of $5 million against Hamilton partly on the ground that she was a conspirator or acting in concert, but also on the ground that she substantially aided the illegal activity. Although killing was not her purpose, it was a foreseeable result of the illegal activity she supported.

33. On comparative fault allocations between negligent and intentional tortfeasors, see § 206.

34. See §§ 389 & 390.

35. Restatement of Apportionment § 24, cmt. b (Proposed Final Draft 1998).

36. Restatement § 876 (b).

37. Halberstam v. Welch, 705 F.2d 472 (D.C.Cir.1983).

What counts as substantial aid or encouragement no doubt depends heavily on the facts. In a New Mexico case,[38] one Cadena, in his uncle's home, beat the plaintiff. The plaintiff's evidence was that Cadena's uncle shouted "Kill him!" and "Hit him more!" once the attack had begun. This was sufficient to subject the uncle to liability. But we may suspect that the same words shouted from a distance by a stranger or a small child who had no relation to any of the parties would not count as substantial aid or encouragement.

§ 341. Imputed Contributory Negligence

Under vicarious liability rules, the negligence of one person is imputed or attributed to another. The servant's negligence is imputed to the master, for example, and the master is subject to liability for it. Should contributory negligence be imputed as well, either to bar the plaintiff or to reduce her damages in a comparative fault regime? Cases fall initially into two broad categories.

Imputation of negligence of a person for whose acts the plaintiff is not vicariously liable. In the first category the negligent defendant argues that the plaintiff's claim is barred or reduced because of the negligence of T, even though T is not an agent of the plaintiff and the plaintiff would not be vicariously liable for T's torts. On the face of it, this sounds wrong, but at one time courts imputed the negligence of husband to wife or parent to child.[1] Under such a rule, the negligent defendant might escape liability to a child he injured on the ground that the child's mother was also negligent and that the negligence of the mother would be imputed to the child. Similar rules were applied as between husband and wife. As reflected in the Restatements,[2] these rules have now been completely abandoned.[3]

Courts also at one time imputed the negligence of a driver to the passenger-owner of the car on the theory that the passenger, as owner, was necessarily in control, so that the driver was his servant or else was engaged in a joint enterprise with him. This was counterproductive. It relieved the negligent defendant of liability. At the same time, the negligent driver of the plaintiff's car would either avoid responsibility as well, or would pay more than his proportionate share.[4] With this recog-

38. Rael v. Cadena, 93 N.M. 684, 604 P.2d 822 (Ct.App.1979).

§ 341

1. E.g., Lash v. Cutts, 943 F.2d 147 (1st Cir.1991). Contributory negligence is also effectively imputed under the usual rule that the claim of a family member for loss of consortium is derived from the claim of the injured person and comes with all its defects, so that if the injured person's claim is reduced by his contributory fault, the family member's claim is similarly reduced. See § 310.

2. Restatement § 485; Restatement Third of Torts: Apportionment § 5 (Proposed Final Draft 1998).

3. LaBier v. Pelletier, 665 A.2d 1013 (Me.1995); Graham v. Keuchel, 847 P.2d 342 (Okl.1993).

4. Although negligence is imputed to joint enterprisers when they sue third persons, the normal rule is that the driver's negligence is not imputed to the passenger in suits between themselves. Restatement § 491 (2). In states that recognize this rule, the driver might thus have been liable for the entire damages while the other tortfea-

nized, courts now usually hold that no presumption of control or of a master-servant relationship arises from the fact that the owner is in the car while another is driving it.[5] The rule now holds that a bailor of goods is not chargeable with the bailee's negligence in the absence of an agency relationship.[6]

Imputation of negligence of a person for whose acts the plaintiff is vicariously liable. The owner-passenger in a car is no longer to be treated as a master merely by virtue of his ownership. In some cases, however, the injured passenger, whether owner or not, may be a master of the driver for reasons unrelated to ownership. Or the master may own the automobile even if he is not present. Suppose that the ABC Corporation owns a truck used to transport goods for the company and that S, its servant, is driving it in the scope of his employment. T, driving another automobile, and S are both negligent. Together they cause a collision which greatly damages the ABC truck. Since S was acting within the scope of his employment, ABC is subject to liability for the harm he negligently caused. Should its recovery against T for damage to its truck be barred or reduced because of S's negligence? The traditional answer is yes, the rule of vicarious responsibility applies "both ways," to impose liability and to charge the master with contributory fault of its servant.[7]

As a general principle the both ways rule seems right and it has been reaffirmed by the new Apportionment Restatement.[8] If the enterprise is vicariously responsible, it should be accountable for its total share of the total damage, not merely for its share of the third person's damages. Indeed, that seems to be the principle of comparative negligence, at least in its pure form.

One well-known case, *Weber v. Stokely–Van Camp, Inc.*,[9] rejected the both ways rule. The Minnesota Court abolished the rule of imputed contributory negligence in automobile cases altogether, even when the plaintiff would have been vicariously liable for the servant's negligence. The result was that the master (who was an individual) would be permitted to recover from a negligent third party for damage to his automobile and for his own personal injury. The court's idea was that vicarious liability of the master or the company would be justifiable as a means of reaching a solvent defendant to pay for injuries, but not justifiable when it prevented recovery of a person who was not personally at fault. South Dakota may have joined in this view, at least to a large

sor would escape all liability. In states that failed to notice the rule against imputation among enterprisers, the driver would escape liability too, with the result that the victim, who was not at all at fault, would be barred while two tortfeasors both escape any responsibility.

5. Reed v. Hinderland, 135 Ariz. 213, 660 P.2d 464, 37 A.L.R.4th 555 (1983); Watson v. Reg. Transp. Dist., 762 P.2d 133 (Colo.1988).

6. E.g., Perry v. Tendal, 538 N.W.2d 296 (Iowa 1995); see Atlantic Mutual Ins. Co. v. Kenney, 323 Md. 116, 591 A.2d 507 (Ct. App.1991).

7. Restatement § 486.

8. Restatement Third of Torts: Apportionment of Liability, § 5 (Proposed Final Draft 1998).

9. Weber v. Stokely–Van Camp, Inc., 274 Minn. 482, 144 N.W.2d 540 (1966).

extent.[10] Some others courts have condemned imputed contributory negligence in rather broad terms, but mostly in the course of rejecting imputation based upon ownership rather than imputation based on a master-servant relationship.[11]

Perspective. Courts rightly rejected the fictive agency of parent and child, husband and wife, and car owner and driver. However, changes in other aspects of the law may make the whole issue of imputed negligence less important for many cases.

In a state equipped with the full panoply of modern procedures and contemporary tort rules, an employer injured by the concurrent negligence of his servant and another tortfeasor can ordinarily sue both his employee and the third person tortfeasor. If both are proved to be negligent causes of the employer's harm, the employer in a joint and several liability system can recover from either or both. (The employee may be covered by the employer's liability insurance.) If either pays more than his proportionate share, he can in turn recover contribution from the other. This procedure involves no question of imputed negligence, yet each tortfeasor (probably by way of his insurance) pays his appropriate share and the plaintiff's own recover is not inappropriately diminished.

In states that no longer permit joint and several liability, each of the two defendants would be liable for his proportionate share only and no contribution would be needed. Some rules can defeat this scenario. Immunities and workers' compensation might alter the complexion of the case. However, in the light of the contemporary systems for apportioning loss, it may be possible to see that the question of imputed contributory negligence can be put aside so long as comparative fault and contribution are permitted.

10. Berry v. Risdall, 576 N.W.2d 1 (S.D. 1998) appears to hold that when the master sues a third person, the negligence of the master's servant will not be imputed to the master unless the master actually had time to control the specific action of the driver that contributed to a collision. That is not the usual meaning of control in master-servant cases, so it may be that South Dakota should be counted as fully supporting the *Stokely* case.

11. Kalechman v. Drew Auto Rental, Inc., 33 N.Y.2d 397, 308 N.E.2d 886, 353 N.Y.S.2d 414 (1973).

CHAPTER 23

STRICT LIABILITY FOR ANIMALS, ABNORMAL CONDITIONS, AND SPECIAL DANGERS

TOPIC A. TYPES OF STRICT LIABILITY

§ 342. Types of Strict Liability

Strict liability is liability without fault. The defendant is subject to liability for conduct that amounts neither to negligence nor to any intentional tort. The kind of strict liability seen in the last chapter—vicarious liability for the fault of another, justified either on grounds of fairness or economic analysis—is by no means the only kind of strict liability. An even older form was found in early tort law, which, according to traditional views, imposed strict liability for all direct and forcible harms to person or property[1] and perhaps for the spread of fire as well.

In 1850, with the decision in *Brown v. Kendall*[2] the court expressly adopted fault and rejected strict liability based upon direct or forcible harm. Negligence or intentional invasions would thereafter become the normal basis for tort liability. Some writers associated this shift with industrial development, seeing the shift from strict liability to negligence law as a partial immunity for economic activity, a kind of subsidy for business.[3] Other scholars have sought to demonstrate that subsidy was no part of the motivation and indeed that there was not even much strict liability before the decision in *Brown v. Kendall*.[4] In form at least, the older English cases do in fact seem to rest upon strict liability for direct harms involving physical force.[5] But strict liability may not have been congenial to Americans, who had no chancellors issuing original writs and who may have seen fault as an appropriate moral basis for decision, at least in suits between strangers whose duty was not shaped by a particular relationship. In any event, early 19th century cases show that the cases could turn on fault even when direct force was applied.[6] If that

§ 342

1. See § 111 & 112, supra.

2. Brown v. Kendall, 60 Mass. 292, 6 Cush. 292 (1850), discussed in § 112, supra.

3. See MORTON HORWITZ, THE TRANSFORMATION OF AMERICAN LAW, 1780–1860 97–101 (1977); Gregory, Trespass to Negligence to Absolute Liability, 37 VA. L. REV. 359, 368 (1951).

4. Gary Schwartz, Tort Law and the Economy in Nineteenth–Century America: A Reinterpretation, 9 YALE L.J. 1717 (1981); Gary Schwartz, The Character of Early American Tort Law, 26 U.C.L.A. L. REV. 641 (1989); Stephen Young, Reconceptualizing Accountability in the Early Nineteenth Century: How the Tort of Negligence Appeared, 21 CONN. L. REV. 197 (1989).

5. See §§ 111 & 112, supra.

6. The burden might be placed upon the defendant to show he was not at fault, but this is not strict liability in the sense that

is correct, *Brown v. Kendall* was important because it gave the first really clear expression of a fault-based system with the burden of proof upon the plaintiff.

The shift to a fault-oriented system, however, was not always straightforward. Sometimes courts found reasons to retain or develop pockets of strict liability. The cases of strict liability discussed in this chapter have in common the fact that the defendant creates or introduces a dangerous condition not commonly accepted or reciprocated in the social unit. The risk introduced is not necessarily a very large one, but it is always generated by an activity not commonly pursued in the relevant community or neighborhood. The cases fall roughly into two factual settings. In one, the defendant introduces wild animals into a community. In the other, the defendant uses explosives or other forces that are abnormal to the community so that the defendant subjects the members of the community to risks that are quite different from the risk the community imposes upon the defendant.

Topic B. Strict Liability for Animals

§ 343. Strict Liability for Trespassing Animals

Common law strict liability for trespassing animals. In early England, if a cattle owner drove his cattle onto your land so that your crops were trampled, he would easily be liable under the writ of Trespass, since he directly caused an entry onto your land.[1] However, if the cattle merely escaped and wandered onto your land, the entry looks indirect and thus does not sound like a good case for the Trespass writ. When these claims first arose, however, courts had to use the Trespass writ or nothing, because Case, with its idea of negligence, had not yet been invented. Courts opted to permit the claim, although the cattle owner did not sponsor any direct entry upon the plaintiff's land. The writ of Trespass carried strict liability with it, so that, with some exceptions,[2] the owner of wandering cattle was strictly liable, just as he was strictly liable in other cases where the writ of Trespass was used.[3] The rule stuck

fault or lack of it is irrelevant. See Foot and Reynolds v. Wiswall, 14 Johns. 304 (N.Y. 1817). In that case, the plaintiff's sloop was damaged by a steamboat on the Hudson River on a dark night in 1812. The trial judge instructed the jury that (1) the defendant was prima facie liable for the injury, but (2) he could exonerate himself by proof that he was free of negligence; and (3) that the plaintiff's failure to light their own sloop was no defense to the defendant except so far as that showed unavoidable accident or no fault in the defendant. The jury found for the defendant. On a bill of exceptions the court affirmed, on the only issue presented: whether negligence was a question of fact for the jury or law for the judge. The court rejected the plaintiff's argument that it was a question of law for the judge, saying it was a mixed question. So the parties seem to have accepted the substantive and burden of proof points in the charge to the jury.

§ 343

1. The rules for the writ of Trespass and the distinction between Trespass and Case are explained in § 111.

2. There were exceptions for cattle being driven along a public way; in that case, liability was imposed only for negligence. See Restatement § 505.

3. This account is based upon L. Glanville Williams, Liability for Animals (1939).

even after the writ of Case became available. The rule of strict liability applied to barnyard animals generally.[4] It did not apply to pets like dogs and cats,[5] although the keeper of such animals might be liable for negligently or intentionally causing them to enter the land.[6]

American rules. The rule of cattle-owner liability put the economic burden upon cattle owners to protect crop-growers, perhaps by building fences to keep cattle in. This rule has commended itself to some courts.[7] Under this rule, strict liability is imposed for trespass to land. It is not imposed for personal injuries except those that directly resulted from the trespass.[8]

But in some places in America, it may have been easier and cheaper for crop-growers as a group to fence cattle out than for ranchers as a group to fence them in. In the dry west, where many acres were required to sustain a cow, open grazing was essential. On the prairies, timber for fencing was unavailable. Populist resentment of absentee landowners may also have suggested the need for open range country.[9] For these and perhaps other reasons, many states substantially reversed the common law strict liability rule. Under many statutes, for example, the landowner could recover for harm done by trespassing cattle only if the landowner had first erected a fence that met statutory standards—a "fencing out" rule.[10] That left the rancher liable for intentionally driving his cattle upon the land of others, but not strictly liable and not liable for ordinary negligence.[11]

4. E.g., Gresham v. Taylor, 51 Ala. 505 (1874) (hogs); Adams Bros. v. Clark, 189 Ky. 279, 224 S.W. 1046, 14 A.L.R. 738 (1920) (chickens); Nixon v. Harris, 15 Ohio St.2d 105, 238 N.E.2d 785 (1968) (cow); Morgan v. Hudnell, 52 Ohio St. 552, 40 N.E. 716 (1895) (horse).

5. Van Houten v. Pritchard, 315 Ark. 688, 870 S.W.2d 377 (1994) (tomcat running at large, and "spraying" the plaintiff's property, no liability for its bite resulting in multiple surgeries).

6. See Pegg v. Gray, 240 N.C. 548, 551, 82 S.E.2d 757, 759 (1954) ("in deference to this natural instinct of dogs ... [the law allows] a reputable dog a modicum of liberty to follow his roaming instincts without imposing liability on its master," but owner of pack of foxhounds who engaged in a chase adjoining the plaintiff's farm would be liable for the damage they caused if he sent them out knowing they would enter the land); Baker v. Howard County Hunt, 171 Md. 159, 188 A. 223 (1936) (similar).

7. See King v. Blue Mountain Forest Ass'n, 100 N.H. 212, 123 A.2d 151, 57 A.L.R.2d 234 (1956).

8. See Williams v. River Lakes Ranch Dev. Corp., 41 Cal.App.3d 496, 116 Cal. Rptr. 200 (1974) (liability for unprovoked attack by bull trespassing in plaintiff's garden; reviewing cases considering whether injuries were a direct result of the trespass); Restatement § 504 (2); James L. Rigelhaupt, Jr., Annotation, Liability for Personal Injury or Death Caused by Trespassing or Intruding Livestock, 49 A.L.R.4th 710 (1987).

9. See Delaney v. Errickson, 10 Neb. 492, 6 N.W. 600 (1880) (many owners, by virtue of an "entry at the distant land-office" were not and did not expect to inhabit the territory; and "timber for fencing was not to be had"). Barbed wire was not commercially manufactured until about 1874.

10. E.g., Colo. Rev. Stat. § 35–46–102. Ellickson concluded that the fencing out rule became the dominant rule in the 19th century and was not limited to western states. Robert C. Ellickson, Of Coase and Cattle: Dispute Resolution among Neighbors in Shasta County, 38 Stan. L. Rev. 623, 660, n. 94 (1986).

11. Garcia v. Sumrall, 58 Ariz. 526, 121 P.2d 640 (1942) (noting a division of opinion as to what constitutes willful trespass and holding that mere foreseeability is not enough). Intent or willful trespass was found by some courts when so many cattle

As some areas became more settled and fencing more practical, however, legislatures partly returned to the common law rule by imposing liability upon ranchers for livestock trespasses unless the rancher could show he had built an adequate fence to contain them.[12] Frequently enough, statutes provide for open range and free grazing without liability for areas where cattle ranching is dominant, but adopt a different rule for other localities or permit a kind of local option.[13] Local control over the issue is also furthered by contracts or easements assigning grazing rights, and—informally—by local customs.[14] However, a great deal of public land owned and managed by the federal government is leased or allotted for grazing. Rights of the government against trespassing grazier are not dependent upon the state rules.[15]

Interpreting the livestock rules. The cattle trespass rules can be understood at various levels or through various perspectives. One view might be that local norms are so dominant that the actual choice of legal rule—strict liability or not—does not much matter.[16] On the other hand, it is possible to construct an idealized view. If the cattle owners in a given community were relatively wealthy individuals who imposed risks upon the relatively poorer gardeners, strict liability might be seen as reflecting an ideal of equality—one who introduces an unequal or non-mutual risk must bear its costs.

When gardeners are the unusual elements in the community and cattle ranching is normal, the fencing out rule may become more suitable. The same rule might also be understood as a reflection of substantial mutuality; no one is liable because every member of the community will inflict and suffer trespasses, so that in the end the "accounts balance."[17] For skeptics, perhaps the rule changes reflect little more than the power of a dominant group, or the effectiveness of legislative lobbies.

Highway cases. Under any of the rules, injuries inflicted by livestock loose on a public highway represent a different problem. If a motorist is injured in colliding with a cow, there is no trespass to land and hence no strict liability claim. In most instances, the defendant responsible for an animal who strays onto the highway is liable for negligence and only for negligence. Such liability is imposed even when the defendant is entitled

were placed on land that trespass upon adjoining lands became substantially certain.

12. See, e.g., Williams v. Goodwin, 41 Cal.App.3d 496, 116 Cal.Rptr. 200 (1974) (recounting history); CAL. FOOD & AGRIC. CODE § 17122 (limiting victim's rights unless he had a strong fence).

13. E.g., ARIZ. REV. STATS. § 3–1421 (taxpayers may petition to establish a district to reverse the fence-out rule).

14. See Robert C. Ellickson, Of Coase and Cattle: Dispute Resolution among Neighbors in Shasta County, 38 STAN. L. REV. 623 (1986).

15. See John S. Harbison, Hohfeld and Herefords: the Concept of Property and the Law of the Range, 22 N.M. L. REV. 459, 484 ff. (1992).

16. See Robert C. Ellickson, Of Coase and Cattle: Dispute Resolution among Neighbors in Shasta County, 38 STAN. L. REV. 623 (1986) (local norms or informal standards prevail over formal legal rules in the cattle trespass cases studied).

17. This is one explanation for the informal norms Ellickson found. See Ellickson, Of Coase and Cattle: Dispute Resolution Among Neighbors in Shasta County, 38 STAN. L. REV. 623 (1986).

to graze animals on open range.[18] Some courts, however, have taken the position that the animal owner owes no duty at all to those on the highway and hence is not liable, even for negligence.[19]

§ 344. Strict Liability for Abnormally Dangerous Domestic Animals

Strict liability for personal injury caused by domestic animals. The common law rule already discussed made owners of livestock strictly liable for the trespasses of such animals, but that rule did not impose strict liability for personal injuries inflicted by livestock except as injury might be a direct result of trespass. Domestic animals like dogs and cats were treated differently; their owners or keepers[1] were not strictly liable for the animals' trespasses at all but under limited conditions could be strictly liable for personal injuries inflicted by such animals. Strict liability is imposed when the keeper of the animal knows or has reason to know that his animal is abnormally dangerous in some way and injury results from that danger.[2]

For example, if a dog owner knows that his dog has an abnormal or vicious propensity to attack and bite,[3] or his horse to kick,[4] he is liable for the dog's biting and the horse's kicking. The owner would be liable for ordinary negligence or an intentional tort,[5] but strict liability based upon the owner's knowledge of a dangerous propensity differs from ordinary negligence. Although the knowledge or scienter requirement necessarily means that harm is foreseeable in light of the animal's known propensity, liability is imposed even if the defendant exercised reasonable care to keep the dog penned and horse stabled.[6]

18. Carrow Co. v. Lusby, 167 Ariz. 18, 804 P.2d 747 (1990); contra: Kendall v. Curl, 222 Or. 329, 353 P.2d 227 (1960).

19. Douglass v. Dolan, 286 Ill.App.3d 181, 675 N.E.2d 1012, 221 Ill.Dec. 588 (1997) (no common law duty, but recovery if the plaintiff can bring herself within a statute imposing liability upon those in charge of animal); James L. Rigelhaupt, Jr., Annotation, Liability of Owner of Animal for Damage to Motor Vehicle or Injury to Person Riding Therein Resulting from Collision with Domestic Animal at Large in Street or Highway, 29 A.L.R.4th 431 (1981).

§ 344

1. A temporary caretaker such as a babysitter may not qualify as a keeper or possessor of the animal, but even such a person would be subject to liability for negligent failure to control. See Trager v. Thor, 445 Mich. 95, 516 N.W.2d 69 (1994). Similarly, an employer who merely permits an employee to bring his dog to a job site is not a keeper or harborer of the dog. Falby v. Zarembski, 221 Conn. 14, 602 A.2d 1 (1992).

2. Marshall v. Ranne, 511 S.W.2d 255 (Tex.1974); Jividen v. Law, 194 W.Va. 705, 461 S.E.2d 451 (1995); Restatement § 509. Courts sometimes speak of mischievous or vicious propensities of the animal, but the dog's good faith is not an issue and the plaintiff need only show his dangerous tendency. See Restatement § 509, cmt. c.

3. Moura v. Randall, 119 Md.App. 632, 705 A.2d 334 (1998); cf. Marshall v. Ranne, 511 S.W.2d 255 (Tex.1974) (vicious hog biting plaintiff).

4. Cf. Bauman v. Auch, 539 N.W.2d 320 (S.D.1995) (horse rearing up when plaintiff attempted to mount). Because the question of an animal's vicious propensity is relevant both to strict liability and to negligence, decisions may permit the claim to go to the jury without specifying the basis. E.g., Zboray v. Fessler, 154 A.D.2d 367, 545 N.Y.S.2d 844 (1989).

5. See Restatement § 518.

6. See Van Houten v. Pritchard, 315 Ark. 688, 870 S.W.2d 377 (1994).

Normal dangers of the species. Some dog bites and horse kicks are entirely normal to the species; strict liability is imposed, if at all, when the animal has an abnormal propensity to bite, kick or otherwise cause harm. For example, there is nothing abnormal about a bull that is aggressive and charges people or a horse that is frisky. The keeper of an aggressive bull or frisky horse is thus not strictly liable for injuries inflicted as a result of those characteristics unless some added and abnormal quality is shown.[7]

Keeper's knowledge or notice. In addition, the keeper of the animal must have knowledge or at least notice of the dangerous tendencies that resulted in harm. The fact that a bull has "acted up" does not show that he has abnormally dangerous propensities for a bull.[8] The fact that a dog has bitten people before and that the keeper knows it will often tend to show the keeper's knowledge of a dangerous propensity, but not necessarily.[9] On the other hand, the rule does not entitle every animal one bite; the keeper may discover the animal's propensity by observing its traits long before it bites anyone.[10]

Injury resulting from animal's abnormal characteristics. Strict liability is limited to cases in which the animal's dangerous propensity is a cause of the plaintiff's harm. The fact that the plaintiff is injured by an abnormally dangerous animal is not relevant if the injury results from some normal trait or from a danger of which the keeper had neither knowledge nor notice.[11] For example, if a dog's keeper knows of his vicious tendency to bite but not of his tendency to chase bicycles, the keeper is not strictly liable for injuries resulting because the dog chased a bicycle.[12] However, if the tendency to bite includes the likelihood that the dog will chase his targeted victim in order to bite him, the chase victim's injury from a fall may well be within the risks imposed by the abnormally dangerous animal. Likewise, knowledge of some traits is capable of generalization—a nervous, agitated horse who is known to bite may be equally likely to kick, in which case strict liability is again appropriate.[13]

Negligence claims. Although in some states courts have approached domestic animal cases on a negligence analysis,[14] the plaintiff is usually permitted to assert her claim under either a theory of strict liability or a

7. Duren v. Kunkel, 814 S.W.2d 935 (Mo.1991) (bull); Jividen v. Law, 194 W.Va. 705, 461 S.E.2d 451 (1995) (horse); cf. Dunnings v. Castro, 881 S.W.2d 559 (Tex. Civ. App. 1994, writ denied) (dog who lunged at letter carrier was not shown to have tendencies abnormal to his species).

8. Duren v. Kunkel, 814 S.W.2d 935 (Mo.1991).

9. Trager v. Thor, 445 Mich. 95, 516 N.W.2d 69 (1994) (defendant knew dog had bitten before but believed the bite was in response to an attack).

10. See Van Houten v. Pritchard, 315 Ark. 688, 870 S.W.2d 377 (1994) (rejecting a one-bite rule).

11. Restatement § 509, cmt. i.

12. McNair v. Jones, 137 Ga.App. 13, 14, 223 S.E.2d 27, 28 (1975) ("it is necessary that he have reason to know of its propensity to do harm of the type which it inflicts").

13. Restatement § 509, cmt. i.

14. See Griner v. Smith, 43 N.C.App. 400, 259 S.E.2d 383 (1979).

theory of negligence or both.[15] The plaintiff may of course establish negligence by showing that the keeper of an animal knew of its abnormally dangerous propensities, but negligence might be shown in other ways as well. For example, if the owner of a horse encourages small children to play alone with the horse, he may be negligent even though the horse is not abnormally dangerous, because his conduct put the children at risk even from normal behavior of a horse.[16]

Dogs. Under the common law rules, the keepers of a dog were not strictly liable for harms caused by the dog unless they knew of the animal's abnormal propensity to cause harm. But statutes and ordinances often contribute to much larger liabilities for dog owners or keepers. Some statutes, for example, provide expressly or by implication that the owner of a dog is liable for a bite regardless of whether the dog was vicious or known to be vicious, so long as the plaintiff was in a public place where she could lawfully be.[17] Ordinances and leash laws potentially imposing liability are also common.[18] South Carolina adopted this form of strict liability for dog bites as a matter of common law.[19] Although the statutes usually leave room for defenses based upon provocation or trespass by the plaintiff,[20] the effect is that in many instances, an unconditional strict liability is imposed for dog bite injuries.

§ 345. Strict Liability for Wild Animals

Rule and Scope

General rule. Animals wild by nature and by the customary understanding of the community are treated differently from domestic animals. The English rule held that keepers of wild animals were strictly liable for harm caused by such animals.[1] That is, liability is imposed even if the keeper exercised the utmost care to keep the animal confined and safe.[2] The rule has long been recognized by most American decisions[3]

15. The plaintiff can usually proceed on either theory or both. See Jividen v. Law, 194 W.Va. 705, 461 S.E.2d 451 (1995).

16. Williams v. Tysinger, 328 N.C. 55, 399 S.E.2d 108 (1991); cf. Duren v. Kunkel, 814 S.W.2d 935 (Mo.1991) (owner failed to guard against normal dangers of a bull; negligence shown); Sybesma v. Sybesma, 534 N.W.2d 355 (S.D.1995) (failure to warn or instruct novice about ordinary dangers in herding cows; negligence shown).

17. Cal. Civ. Code § 3342; 510 ILCS 5/16; Mont. Code Ann. § 27–1–715.

18. See, e.g., Moura v. Randall, 119 Md. App. 632, 705 A.2d 334 (1998) (leash law, violation would be evidence of negligence); Clo v. McDermott, 239 A.D.2d 4, 668 N.Y.S.2d 743 (1998) (violation of ordinance requiring dogs to be under control in public places would be evidence of negligence when dog ran in front of bicycling plaintiff, causing a fall).

19. Hossenlopp v. Cannon, 285 S.C. 367, 329 S.E.2d 438, 51 A.L.R.4th 439 (1985).

20. See Stroop v. Day, 271 Mont. 314, 896 P.2d 439 (1995) (plaintiff's act of chasing dog four weeks earlier was not provocation, nor was plaintiff's act of leaning on fence where dog was penned).

§ 345

1. W.V.H. Rogers, Winfield & Jolowicz on Tort 475 ff. (14th ed. 1994); cf. May v. Burdett, 9 Q.B. 101 (1846) (liability for monkey known to be of mischievous nature even if defendant exercised care to keep him safely).

2. Smith v. Jalbert, 351 Mass. 432, 221 N.E.2d 744 (1966).

3. See, e.g., Irvine v. Rare Feline Breeding Ctr., Inc., 685 N.E.2d 120 (Ind.App. 1997); American States Ins. Co. v. Guillermin, 108 Ohio App.3d 547, 671 N.E.2d 317

and is accepted by the Restatement,[4] although strict liability for animals is sometimes rejected when it comes to public entity defendants such as public zoos.[5] The strict liability rule applies even if the animal is not known to have

vicious or abnormal propensities to cause harm.[6] Strict liability is, however, limited to harm that results from the wild or dangerous character of the animal or from dangerous traits of which the keeper knows or should know.[7]

Keepers and harborers. The Restatement extends strict liability to those who harbor as well as those who own, possess, or keep the animal.[8] For instance, a parent who permits a child to keep a lion on the parent's premises may not possess the lion but harbors it nonetheless and is responsible accordingly.[9] The emphasis shifts from possession and control of the animal to possession and control of the premises. But of course this does not mean that a landowner is strictly liable for injuries inflicted by a wild animal that intrudes upon the property. In that case, liability will be imposed only if the landowner was negligent, for example by negligently failing to repel the animal or to protect guests.[10]

Defining Wild Animals

The list of animals considered by the courts to be wild runs from Ape[11] to Zebra.[12] It obviously includes such animals as lions and tigers and bears,[13] but courts have classified many others animals, such as elephants, snakes and wolves, as wild,[14] although it is possible that some

(1996) (lion); contra: Vaughan v. Miller Bros. "101" Ranch Wild West Show, 109 W.Va. 170, 153 S.E. 289, 69 A.L.R. 497 (1930).

4. Restatement § 507 (1).

5. See William E. Shipley and Sonja A. Soehnel, Annotation, Governmental Liability from Operation of Zoo, 92 A.L.R.3d 832 (1980) (reflecting decisions both ways). The general rule applied in other cases is that public entities are not strictly liable.

6. E.g., Smith v. Jalbert, 351 Mass. 432, 221 N.E.2d 744 (1966) (zebra).

7. Restatement § 507 (2).

8. Restatement § 514.

9. See American States Ins. Co. v. Guillermin, 108 Ohio App.3d 547, 671 N.E.2d 317 (1996).

10. See Woods–Leber v. Hyatt Hotels of Puerto Rico, Inc., 124 F.3d 47 (1st Cir.1997) (rejecting statutory strict liability where hotel was invaded by a rabid mongoose which bit a sunbathing guest; there was no evidence of negligence); Overstreet v. Gibson Prod. Co., Inc. of Del Rio, 558 S.W.2d 58 (Tex.Civ.App.1977, writ ref'd n.r.e.) (snake on premises but not harbored, no strict liability).

11. Normand v. City of New Orleans, 363 So.2d 1220 (La.Ct.App.1978).

12. Smith v. Jalbert, 351 Mass. 432, 221 N.E.2d 744 (1966).

13. *Lion:* American States Ins. Co. v. Guillermin, 108 Ohio App.3d 547, 671 N.E.2d 317 (1996); *tiger:* Irvine v. Rare Feline Breeding Ctr., Inc., 685 N.E.2d 120 (Ind.Ct.App.1997); *bear:* City of Mangum v. Brownlee, 181 Okla. 515, 75 P.2d 174 (1938).

14. *Coyotes:* Collins v. Otto, 149 Colo. 489, 369 P.2d 564 (1962); *deer* (male): Hudson v. Janesville Conservation Club, 168 Wis.2d 436, 484 N.W.2d 132 (1992); *elephants:* Filburn v. People's Palace & Aquarium Co., Ltd., 25 Q.B.D. 258 (1890); *ferrets:* Gallick v. Barto, 828 F.Supp. 1168 (M.D.Pa. 1993); *monkeys:* Whitefield v. Stewart, 577 P.2d 1295 (Okla.1978) (pet wooly monkey was a "tamed wild animal" and in analogy to dog statute, owner would be strictly liable if it bit without provocation); *rattlesnakes:* Keyser v. Phillips Petroleum Co., 287 So.2d 364 (Fla.Dist.Ct.App.1973); *wolves:* Hays v. Miller, 150 Ala. 621, 43 So. 818 (1907).

of these might become domesticated.[15]

The term wild animals might be thought to imply that only violent, highly dangerous animals are included in the category. It might also be thought that strict liability is imposed for such animals only because of their extraordinary danger and to provide the owner an incentive to remove the tiger from his backyard.[16] But great danger does not in fact seem to be a necessary element in this form of strict liability. Probably no one living in Springfield, Massachusetts would rate zebra danger as one of the major risks of living in that city, but zebras count as wild animals in Massachusetts and their owners are strictly liable for harms done.[17] Perhaps, however, the wild animal must be dangerous enough that liability would be imposed if the owner intentionally allowed it to roam.

The theme that runs through the definition of wild animals and that explains the rule is that these animals and the risks they bring with them are uncommon or abnormal in the community and therefore not mutual or reciprocal. Whether the abnormal quality of risks associated with wild animals is such that strict liability is justified, the theme of abnormality can be seen in the way the wildness of wild animals is determined. An animal is not regarded as wild merely because it is excessively dangerous nor as domesticated because it is generally safe. An animal is instead wild or domesticated according to whether, by local custom, it is devoted to the service of mankind[18] or commonly treated by the community as a tame or domestic animal.[19]

An illustration frequently mentioned is the elephant, which may be regarded as a domestic animal in parts of the former British Empire[20] but not in England itself.[21] Bees are wild in the sense that they have not been trained and also in the sense that they can sometimes be quite dangerous, but beekeeping is commonly practiced almost everywhere and strict liability is not imposed for bee stings.[22]

15. Swain v. Tillett, 269 N.C. 46, 152 S.E.2d 297 (1967); cf. Abrevaya v. Palace Theatre & Realty Co., 25 Misc.2d 600, 197 N.Y.S.2d 27 (1960) (fact question whether monkey had become domesticated).

16. G.J. Leasing Co., Inc. v. Union Elec. Co., 54 F.3d 379, 386 (7th Cir.1995) (Posner, J.).

17. Smith v. Jalbert, 351 Mass. 432, 221 N.E.2d 744 (1966).

18. Restatement § 506. An animal that serves mankind only because it is ferocious and can be used to eat other and undesirable animals is not necessarily domesticated. See Gallick v. Barto, 828 F.Supp. 1168 (M.D.Pa.1993) (ferret).

19. Some courts have emphasized other elements. Wisconsin, in a somewhat unusual decision, suggested that wild animals are those which are untamable by disposition, who live outdoors, and who live without human assistance. Hudson v. Janesville Conservation Club, 168 Wis.2d 436, 484 N.W.2d 132 (1992). Some courts have used statutory definitions of wild or domestic animals even though such definitions were not created for the purpose of establishing liability but for regulating game or establishing an immunity. See Gallick v. Barto, 828 F.Supp. 1168 (M.D.Pa.1993).

20. Maung Kyaw Dun v. Ma Kyin, 2 Upper Burma Rul. 570 (1897).

21. Filburn v. People's Palace & Aquarium Co., Ltd., 25 Q.B.D. 258 (1890).

22. See, e.g, Ferreira v. D'Asaro, 152 So.2d 736, 737 (Fla.Dist.Ct.App.1963); David B. Harrison, Annotation, Liability For Injury or Damage Caused by Bees, 86 A.L.R.3d 829 (1978).

Topic C. Strict Liability for Abnormal Dangers

§ 346. Strict Liability for Abnormal Dangers and the Rule in Rylands v. Fletcher

The Restatement supports liability for activities that are abnormally dangerous, characteristically those that are highly dangerous and that are not commonly pursued in the community.[1] Cases are in accord, so liability without fault is imposed, for example, when carefully handled explosives cause harm. The idea is not necessarily to deter such activities altogether but to make them "pay their way" by charging them with liability for harms that are more or less inevitably associated with the activity.[2]

The nuisance background. The law of strict liability for abnormally dangerous activities seems to have originated in problems between neighbors arising from their incompatible uses of their lands. Incompatible land use has long been the subject of nuisance law. Liability for nuisance may be imposed when the defendant creates an unusual condition or carries out unusual activities on his land that interfere with neighbors' use and enjoyment of their lands. Nuisances typically involve an invasion of neighboring properties by intangibles like gases, smokes, sound, and light. Many nuisances are intentional in the sense that the defendant knows to a substantial certainty that he is causing a noxious invasion.

Location and reciprocity. The focus in many nuisance cases has often been on the claim that the defendant is using his land in a way that is inappropriate to the time and place. A noisy factory in a residential neighborhood is an example. The same factory in an area devoted to factories is no nuisance at all. A theme in many nuisance cases is that the defendant has imposed a nonreciprocal or non-mutual harm upon the plaintiff and one that is out of line with the character and customs of the neighborhood. The noisy factory in a residential neighborhood, for example, substantially impedes the residential neighbors in the enjoyment of their property (and their sleep), but the residential neighbors impose no similar limiting upon the factory owner's enjoyment of his factory.

Abnormal activities on the land: Rylands v. Fletcher. Since 1862, when Baron Bramwell relied upon non-reciprocity as a ground for liability in nuisance,[3] courts have from time to time supported liability

§ 346

1. Restatement §§ 519–520. See § 347.

2. See Spano v. Perini Corp., 25 N.Y.2d 11, 17, 302 N.Y.S.2d 527, 531, 250 N.E.2d 31, 34 (1969) (liability does not "exclude the defendant from blasting and thus prevent desirable improvements," nor does it mean that blasting is unlawful; it merely determines who should bear the cost of harms it causes). Because negligence may be difficult to prove, however, strict liability may nonetheless reduce risks. See Mark Geistfeld, Should Enterprise Liability Rules Replace the Rule of Strict Liability for Abnormally Dangerous Activities?, 45 UCLA L. Rev. 611 (1998).

3. Bamford v. Turnely, 3 B & S 66, 122 Eng.Rep. 25 (Exech. Ch. 1862) (Judgment

for the unusual, non-mutual or "abnormal" activity or condition on land which interferes with the use of other lands. The unusual and abnormal have appeared in various guises and under various names.

Several years after Baron Bramwell advanced his arguments, the House of Lords decided the famous *Rylands v. Fletcher* case.[4] In *Rylands,* the defendant retained an independent contractor to construct a pond in Lancaster, England. Beneath the land were old mine shafts that had long since been filled or covered. Neither the contractor nor the landowner discovered any reason for concern. The ponded water eventually broke through the debris in the shafts and flowed into them, then through horizontal shafts to flood the plaintiff's mine. The House of Lords held that the landowner who was not negligent at all would be strictly liable. On its face, *Rylands* dealt with a nuisance or something very much like it and in any event it adjudicated rights arising from incompatible land uses.

The two strands in Rylands. The Lords in *Rylands* advanced two strands of thought. One was that a person who introduces something to the land that is not naturally there and likely to do mischief if it escapes must be held strictly liable for foreseeable harms resulting if it does in fact escape.[5] The focus here seemed to be on the natural state of the land itself and its alteration by humans.

The second strand of thought could be understood quite differently to focus on non-natural use of the land, that is, a use of the land that was not natural or normal in the community or an activity that was incompatible with surrounding land use. The focus of this line may have been on the community's usage and custom, not on the natural condition of the land itself. That would be understandable on the observation that mining had been conducted in Lancaster from very early times and that of necessity you must mine minerals where they are, while mill ponds can be built in many places in a country full of rivers and streams.

Limiting Rylands v. Fletcher. Although Rylands did not require special danger—ponded water is not destructive by nature or design—it did require that the substance escape from the land. Personal injury to a person on the defendant's land, for example, was not covered.[6] Some thinkers expressed dismay at such a holding, but the holding itself merely served to emphasize that *Rylands* was a land-use case, closely aligned with the concerns of nuisance law.

A second limitation arose out of and developed the second strand of *Rylands'* thought. Non-natural use could mean a use of the land that was out of line with the custom or normal uses in the community, and

of Bramwell, B.). Bramwell's ideas were rooted in considerations much like those in earlier wild animal cases.

4. Rylands v. Fletcher, L.R. 3 H.L. 330 (1868).

5. This version (more fully stated) is seen as the rule in *Rylands* in W.V.H. Rogers, Winfield & Jolowicz on Tort 443–444 (14th ed. 1994). In the intermediate court, the Exchequer Chamber, the rule was said to derive from the same principle as liability for cattle trespass.

6. Read v. Lyons, [1947] A.C. 156.

the English courts came to accept some such view. Thus strict liability would be imposed only in the case of "some special use bringing with it increased danger;" landowners would be not be liable for "ordinary" uses of the land. Waters and their storage tanks are not on the land in a state of nature, but they are natural in the sense that they reflect ordinary use, so escape of household water of this kind is not a non-natural use.[7]

Contemporary authority suggests that while strict liability would be imposed for accumulations of dangerous chemicals or the like, no general English doctrine of strict liability is to be developed out of *Rylands*.[8] In America, however, the Restatements have attempted to go beyond *Rylands* itself and to generate a general doctrine of strict liability and one that does not necessarily fully match either strand of thought in *Rylands*.

§ 347. The Restatement Formulations: Abnormally Dangerous Activities

Conflicts in American cases. Rylands v. Fletcher imposed liability without fault upon landowners who put their land to non-natural uses and as a result caused harm to neighbors.[1] Although some 19th Century American courts accepted *Rylands*,[2] others rejected it because they interpreted it to impose liability without fault even when the land use was perfectly normal.[3] However, courts did impose liability for nuisance-type invasions[4] and, on the theory of trespass, for harm done by use of explosives.[5]

The First Restatement. The First Restatement of Torts attempted to reconcile the different strands by providing that strict liability would be imposed for harms resulting from "ultrahazardous" activities, that is,

7. Rickards v. Lothian, [1913] A.C. 263, 280 (Privy Council); See W.V.H. Rogers, Winfield & Jolowicz on Tort 451–454 (14th ed. 1994).

8. See Cambridge Water Co. Ltd. v. Eastern Counties Leather, [1994] 1 All ER 53 (H.L.); W.V.H. Rogers, Winfield & Jolowicz on Tort 452 (14th ed. 1994).

§ 347

1. § 346.

2. Ball v. Nye, 99 Mass. 582 (1868) (percolating filth, a case that seems to be based upon the substantial certainty type of intent).

3. Brown v. Collins, 53 N.H. 442 (1873) (defendant's horse frightened by a train, knocked down the plaintiff's lamppost); Marshall v. Welwood, 38 N.J. Law 339 (1876) (boiler explosion damaged neighboring property); Losee v. Buchanan, 51 N.Y. 476 (1873) (same). In all probability, *Rylands* would not impose liability on the facts of any of these cases. Something similar happened much later, when Texas rejected *Rylands* in Turner v. Big Lake Oil Co., 128 Tex. 155, 96 S.W.2d 221 (1936). In that case a pond of salt water used in oil well work collapsed and caused damage to neighboring lands. Those facts were in a sense the reverse of the *Rylands* facts, since drilling for oil is "natural" wherever oil is or is likely to be. So again, *Rylands* might actually have supported a judgment for the defendant in all these cases.

4. Ball v. Nye, 99 Mass. 582 (1868).

5. See Sullivan v. Dunham, 161 N.Y. 290, 55 N.E. 923 (1900) (blasting of stumps, one flew through the air and struck and killed decedent, a trespass to the person). As these cases did not involve any intent to enter the land or to harm the person of another, the trespass explanation was either a fiction or a leftover from the days before *Brown v. Kendall* adopted the fault basis of liability.

activities that were especially dangerous and could not be made safe even by the exercise of the utmost care. Strict liability would be imposed, however, only if the activity in question was not a matter of common usage.[6]

The Second Restatement's factors. The Second Restatement modified this formulation. It characterized the problem as one involving "abnormally dangerous activities" rather than "ultrahazardous activities."[7] It then eliminated the elements of strict liability imposed in the First Restatement and turned them, along with some other matters, into factors to be considered. Under this factors approach, strict liability is more likely to be imposed if the defendant's activity (a) creates a high risk, (b) with a likelihood of great harm, (c) that cannot be avoided by reasonable care, and if (d) the activity is uncommon and (e) inappropriate at the particular site. Strict liability is less likely to be imposed if (f) the activity has value to the community which outweighs its dangerous attributes.[8] The judge, not the jury, is to weigh these factors and to determine whether strict liability applies.[9]

Criticisms of the Second Restatement. The first Restatement permitted strict liability only if the activity was both especially hazardous and also uncommon in the community. In contrast, the second Restatement permits strict liability upon consideration of six factors, none of which is a necessary element. The high risk of an activity as well as its abnormality in the community are important but strict liability could be imposed under the Restatement's factor approach even if the activity was not especially risky or uncommon. In addition, these factors look like a poorly disguised negligence regime, balancing such things as the value of the defendant's activity to the community. If strict liability is determined by the same factors that determine negligence cases, this form of strict liability is needless at best and probably should be subjected to Occam's razor. Put the other way around, if strict liability is to be retained, the factors represent a poor way to delineate its contours. Commentators have mentioned all these points and offered somewhat varied criticisms and suggestions for improvement.[10] It has been said also that the factors

6. Restatement of Torts § 520 (1938). The common usage requirement was criticized as a "subtle tactic" to stifle development of strict liability as a means of loss spreading in Virginia E. Nolan and Edmund Ursin, The Revitalization of Hazardous Activity Strict Liability, 65 N.C. L. Rev. 257, 259, 265 ff. (1987).

7. The concept of abnormally dangerous activities is not necessarily identical to the similar concept of special dangers or inherently dangerous activities and related concepts used in determining whether an employer is under a nondelegable duty. See § 337.

8. Restatement § 520.

9. Restatement § 520, cmt. l.

10. See Harper, James & Gray § 14.4, pp. 212–214 (criticizing the idea that the activity's utility is a factor); Prosser & Keeton § 78, pp. 554–556 (criticizing the similarity to negligence and also the absence of a firm requirement that the activity be highly dangerous); William K. Jones, Strict Liability for Hazardous Enterprise, 92 Colum. L. Rev. 1705 (1992) (proposing liability of all hazardous enterprises so long as the plaintiff has no significant control over extent or incidence of harm); Virginia E. Nolan and Edmund Ursin, The Revitalization of Hazardous Activity Strict Liability, 65 N.C. L. Rev. 257, 259, 270 (1987) (asserting that the second Restatement "retained" the restrictive features of the first and added others, even though neither special hazard nor un-

cannot be appropriately applied because the Restatement has furnished no intelligible rationale for this form of strict liability[11] and that strict liability decisions should be made by directly considering the goals of strict liability.[12]

The Restatement and Rylands. Both Restatements differ from *Rylands*. By its setting and its language, *Rylands* anchored strict liability in the law of nuisance or competing land uses, in a concern about the effect that land use could have upon neighbors.[13] The Restatement weighed that anchor. Subject to defenses, the Restatement's strict liability is a free-floating principle hovering over the carrier of abnormal dangers wherever he goes, prescribing liability for whomever he injures. Yet the Restatement provides no reasons for a liability shaped by the factors it names.

§ 348. Contemporary Abnormal Danger Cases

General recognition of strict liability for abnormally dangerous activities. A few states still reject *Rylands* and the abnormally dangerous activity forms of strict liability.[1] But most of the major decisions rejecting such strict liability have now been overruled.[2] Courts now have generally accepted the principle that for some activities involving special dangers, especially those not commonly pursued, liability can be imposed without fault, often adopting[3] the Restatement's formulation.[4]

At the same time, the Restatement's multi-factor approach—a kind of discussion agenda rather than a test or analytical tool—almost inevitably promulgates uncertainty. Aside from a few clear cases such as those involving the use or storage of explosives, the decisions do not seem harmonious. Frequently enough, they reject strict liability in particular cases because the evidence does not demonstrate whether the activity in issue is highly dangerous or whether it can be made safe by the exercise of care.[5]

common usage are absolute requirements under the Second Restatement).

11. See Mark Geistfeld, Should Enterprise Liability Replace the Rule of Strict Liability for Abnormally Dangerous Activities?, 45 UCLA L. Rev. 611 (1998).

12. Joseph H. King, Jr., A Goals–Oriented Approach to Strict Tort Liability for Abnormally Dangerous Activities, 48 Baylor L. Rev. 341 (1996). As to goals or rationales, see § 351.

13. Rabin thinks there is no hint of enterprise liability in *Rylands* and related cases but rather an emphasis upon doing right by neighbors. Robert Rabin, Some Thoughts on the Ideology of Enterprise Liability, 55 Md. L. Rev. 1190, 1194–1195 (1996).

§ 348

1. Turner v. Big Lake Oil Co., 128 Tex. 155, 96 S.W.2d 221 (1936). See Moulton v. Groveton Papers Co., 112 N.H. 50, 289 A.2d 68, 51 A.L.R.3d 957 (1972).

2. State Dep't of Envtl. Protection v. Ventron, 94 N.J. 473, 468 A.2d 150 (1983) (268 tons of mercury); Splendorio v. Bilray Demolition Co., Inc., 682 A.2d 461 (R.I. 1996) (accepting the Restatement Second formula but holding that the activities of asbestos removal were not abnormally dangerous in the particular instance).

3. E.g., Valentine v. Pioneer Chlor Alkali Co., Inc., 109 Nev. 1107, 864 P.2d 295 (1993); Peneschi v. National Steel Corp., 170 W.Va. 511, 295 S.E.2d 1 (1982).

4. § 347.

5. E.g., Valentine v. Pioneer Chlor Alkali Co., Inc., 109 Nev. 1107, 864 P.2d 295 (1993) (chlorine gas); Doundoulakis v. Town of Hempstead, 42 N.Y.2d 440, 368 N.E.2d 24, 398 N.Y.S.2d 401 (1977) (hy-

Courts also reject strict liability in particular cases on the ground that the activity is one commonly pursued in the community.[6]

Strict liability for explosives and high energy activities. Strict liability seems most readily imposed when physical harm results from the defendant's use[7] or storage[8] of dynamite or other materials intended to cause explosions. The idea has been extended to the case of an oil well that blew out and showered the plaintiff's home with debris for 24 hours[9] and to explosions of large quantities of gasoline or propane carried as cargo on the highways,[10] on private property,[11] or railroads.[12] One court has even imposed strict liability for fireworks injuries.[13] As courts dropped the older trespass theories of liability for explosions, they recognized that strict liability could be imposed for vibration damage generated by explosives, even when the explosion did not throw objects upon the land or into persons.[14] From here, some courts have gone on to hold that strict liability applies to other large forces causing vibration damage to property, in particular to vibrations caused by testing a large rocket[15] and those caused by pile driving.[16]

draulic dredging and filling with much water impounded near the plaintiffs' homes, leading to subsidence).

6. E.g., Mahowald v. Minnesota Gas Co., 344 N.W.2d 856 (Minn.1984) (natural gas is common and is valuable to community, no strict liability); Grube v. Daun, 213 Wis.2d 533, 570 N.W.2d 851 (1997) (underground storage tanks for gasoline on farms were common, no strict liability for contaminating leak).

7. E.g., Spano v. Perini Corp., 25 N.Y.2d 11, 18, 302 N.Y.S.2d 527, 532, 250 N.E.2d 31, 35 (1969); see Annotation, Liability for Property Damage by Concussion from Blasting, 20 A.L.R.2d 1372 (1951). Some authority accomplishes much the same thing by holding that it is negligent to engage in an abnormally dangerous activity. Harper v. Regency Dev. Co., Inc., 399 So.2d 248 (Ala.1981).

8. Yukon Equip. v. Fireman's Fund Ins. Co., 585 P.2d 1206 (Alaska 1978). When injury results from stored explosives, not intentionally detonated by the defendant, the Restatement's location factor may be read to discourage strict liability. See William K. Jones, Strict Liability for Hazardous Enterprise, 92 COLUM. L. REV. 1705, 1717 (1992). However, *Yukon Equipment*, supra, held that location and other factors were not to be balanced at all in explosives cases.

9. Green v. General Petroleum Corp., 205 Cal. 328, 270 P. 952, 60 A.L.R. 475 (1928) (advancing a trespass theory).

10. Siegler v. Kuhlman, 81 Wash.2d 448, 502 P.2d 1181 (1972).

11. Zero Wholesale Gas Co., Inc. v. Stroud, 264 Ark. 27, 571 S.W.2d 74 (1978) (propane delivery truck at propane depot).

12. National Steel Serv. Ctr. Inc., v. Gibbons, 319 N.W.2d 269, 31 A.L.R.4th 650 (Iowa 1982).

13. Klein v. Pyrodyne Corp., 117 Wash.2d 1, 810 P.2d 917 (1991); cf. Miller v. Westcor Limited Partnership, 171 Ariz. 387, 831 P.2d 386 (Ct. App. 1991) (vicarious liability for fireworks put on by independent contractor under special danger exception).

14. Exner v. Sherman Power Constr. Co., 54 F.2d 510, 80 A.L.R. 686 (2d Cir. 1931); Spano v. Perini Corp., 25 N.Y.2d 11, 17, 302 N.Y.S.2d 527, 532, 250 N.E.2d 31, 35 (1969); Guilford Realty and Ins. Co. v. Blythe Bros. Co., 260 N.C. 69, 131 S.E.2d 900 (1963); Lobozzo v. Adam Eidemiller, Inc., 437 Pa. 360, 263 A.2d 432 (1970).

15. Smith v. Lockheed Propulsion Co., 247 Cal.App.2d 774, 56 Cal.Rptr. 128, 29 A.L.R.3d 538 (1967).

16. Caporale v. C.W. Blakeslee and Sons, Inc., 149 Conn. 79, 175 A.2d 561 (1961); Vern J. Oja & Assocs. v. Washington Park Towers, Inc., 89 Wash.2d 72, 569 P.2d 1141 (1977); contra: In re Chicago Flood Litigation, 176 Ill.2d 179, 680 N.E.2d 265, 223 Ill.Dec. 532 (1997) (neither pile driving nor maintenance of tunnel under a river is abnormally dangerous activity, at least where pile driving was necessary to maintain bridges and could only be done at the particular place).

Rejecting strict liability for use or storage of explosives and similar activities. It is difficult to reconcile all of the decisions. Materials like gasoline, propane, and natural gas have explosive and flammable potential. In line with what has already been said, some authority supports strict liability when such items are stored or accumulated in unusual volume.[17] Many decisions, however, have rejected such liability or applied a negligence standard in the case of explosions resulting from the storage of such materials.[18] Apparently all of them have rejected it for explosions of natural gas in connection with its transmission in mains or pipes.[19] Likewise, strict liability has been rejected when such substances as propane or gas are used as fuel for vehicles, factories, or homes.[20]

Courts ordinarily impose no strict liability for the spread of fire not associated with explosive or high-energy materials.[21] Electricity, especially at high voltage, can be compared to explosives but transmission of electricity in uninsulated power lines is not regarded as an abnormally dangerous activity and strict liability is rejected.[22] Although the law of products liability sometimes imposes strict liability upon manufacturers of products that are dangerous because they are defective, courts have almost always said that neither manufacturers of handguns nor manufacturers of especially destructive ammunition are strictly liable under an abnormal danger theory.[23]

The reasons given for rejecting strict liability in these cases is often that the activity is socially useful,[24] or is a matter of common usage, or

17. McLane v. Northwest Natural Gas. Co., 255 Or. 324, 467 P.2d 635 (1970); Siegler v. Kuhlman, 81 Wash.2d 448, 502 P.2d 1181 (1972) (gasoline being hauled in tank truck).

18. E.g., Continental Building Corporation v. Union Oil Co. of California, 152 Ill.App.3d 513, 504 N.E.2d 787, 105 Ill.Dec. 502 (1987) (hundreds of drums of explosives and flammables with low flash point stored in warehouse; warehouse was in a warehouse district and hence not in an inappropriate place); see Barron C. Ricketts, Annotation, Liability in Connection with Fire or Explosion Incident to Bulk Storage, Transportation, Delivery, Loading, or Unloading of Petroleum Products, 32 A.L.R.3d 1169 (1971); cf. 750 Old Country Road Realty Corp., v. Exxon Corp., 229 A.D.2d 1034, 645 N.Y.S.2d 186 (1996) (no strict liability for contamination gasoline storage).

19. See, e.g., Mahowald v. Minnesota Gas Co., 344 N.W.2d 856 (Minn.1984).

20. E.g., Allison v. Ideal Laundry & Cleaners, 215 S.C. 344, 55 S.E.2d 281 (1949) (explosion of propane tank where propane was used by defendant for fuel, strict liability broadly rejected); see Siegler v.Kuhlman, 81 Wash.2d 448, 502 P.2d 1181 (1972).

21. King v. United States of America, 53 F.Supp.2d 1056 (D. Colo. 1999) (no strict liability for forest fire resulting from campfire, which is common activity); Koger v. Ferrin, 23 Kan.App.2d 47, 926 P.2d 680 (1996). Statutes may regulate outdoor burning and may impose special liabilities. In Koos v. Roth, 293 Or. 670, 652 P.2d 1255 (1982), strict liability was imposed for an intentionally set field fire that got out of hand. Statutes and the scale of the fire played a part.

22. Kent v. Gulf States Utils. Co., 418 So.2d 493 (La.1982).

23. E.g., Copier v. Smith and Wesson Corp., 138 F.3d 833 (10th Cir.1998). Judge Calabresi suggested that bullets designed to do as much damage as possible to the human body might qualify for abnormal danger type strict liability in McCarthy v. Olin Corp., 119 F.3d 148 (2d Cir.1997) (Calabresi, J., dissenting from refusal to certify questions).

24. Martinez v. Grant County Pub. Util. Dist. No. 2, 70 Wash.App. 134, 851 P.2d 1248 (1993) (distribution of electricity). Social usefulness of the activity is perhaps the most doubtful of the Restatement factors, since it in effect uses a kind of risk-utility weighing that arguably relates only to negligence issues.

can be made reasonably safe by the exercise of care,[25] but sometimes on the broad ground that strict liability is not acceptable. Older decisions that reject strict liability across the board may stand with somewhat dubious authority in the light of later decisions accepting strict liability.[26]

Poisons and toxic materials. Strict liability for abnormally dangerous activities has been imposed when the defendant has used toxic materials commercially to kill pests[27] or protect crops.[28] Hazardous materials (often wastes or byproducts of industrial processes) may contaminate lands, water, and air, and may cause death or serious bodily harm. Strict liability for accumulation, escape, percolation, or disposal of such wastes seems to be especially appropriate. Some cases do in fact support such liability even when toxic materials cause contamination of land rather than bodily harm.[29] This approach is in line with the strict liability imposed under some state and federal environmental statutes, although the statutes usually deal with contamination and cleanup costs rather than with personal injury or property damage.[30]

On the other hand, when the release of dangerous materials is not intended, recent decisions have sometimes emphasized that the activity, not merely the substance, must be an abnormally dangerous one.[31] The idea is that although the substance may be dangerous—asbestos and chlorine gas are examples—some activities dealing with the substance can be carried out with reasonable safety, thereby precluding strict liability.[32] For example, Rhode Island refused to apply strict liability

25. Hartford Fire Ins. Co. v. Public Serv. Co. of Colorado, 676 P.2d 25 (Colo. Ct. App. 1983); New Meadows Holding Co. v. Washington Water Power Co., 102 Wash.2d 495, 687 P.2d 212 (1984).

26. *Compare* Allison v. Ideal Laundry & Cleaners, 215 S.C. 344, 55 S.E.2d 281 (1949) (rejecting strict liability for propane tank's explosion because *Rylands v. Fletcher* was not accepted) *with* Wallace v. A.H. Guion & Co., 237 S.C. 349, 117 S.E.2d 359 (1960) (accepting the Restatement's strict liability formula for blasting).

27. Luthringer v. Moore, 31 Cal.2d 489, 190 P.2d 1 (1948); Old Island Fumigation, Inc. v. Barbee, 604 So.2d 1246 (Fla.Dist.Ct. App.1992).

28. Loe v. Lenhardt, 227 Or. 242, 362 P.2d 312 (1961); Langan v. Valicopters, Inc., 88 Wash.2d 855, 567 P.2d 218 (1977); see Jonathan M. Purver, Annotation, Liability For Injury Caused by Spraying or Dusting of Crops, 37 A.L.R.3d 833 (1972) (reflecting cases in which courts have imposed liability on theories of negligence and trespass as well as strict liability).

29. See Albahary v. City and Town of Bristol, Connecticut, 963 F.Supp. 150 (D.Conn.1997) (landfill operator would be strictly liable for contamination of adjacent lands by hazardous wastes); Yommer v. McKenzie, 255 Md., 220, 257 A.2d 138 (1969) (gasoline percolated through the ground and contaminated the plaintiff's water); T. & E. Indus. Inc. v. Safety Light Corp., 123 N.J. 371, 587 A.2d 1249 (1991) (radium accumulated on the defendant's land); State Dep't of Envtl. Protection v. Ventron, 94 N.J. 473, 468 A.2d 150 (1983) (283 tons of mercury escaped from defendant's property).

30. See William K. Jones, Strict Liability for Hazardous Enterprise, 92 Colum. L. Rev. 1705, 1742 (1992) (succinct discussion of several statutes).

31. E.g., Valentine v. Pioneer Chlor Alkali Co., Inc., 109 Nev. 1107, 864 P.2d 295 (1993).

32. G.J. Leasing Co., Inc. v. Union Elec. Co., 54 F.3d 379 (7th Cir.1995) (sale of building containing asbestos, no strict liability, partly because danger could be "adequately contained by taking care" so that elimination of activity was not necessary); Grube v. Daun, 213 Wis.2d 533, 570 N.W.2d 851 (1997) (underground storage tank for farm gasoline was common and could be made safe by reasonable care, no strict liability for groundwater contamination from leaking tank). Most of the cases on leaks from underground storage tanks go off on

rules to inspections of asbestos, although some other asbestos-related activities might well warrant strict liability.[33] Alabama has similarly said that disposal of masses of batteries for recycling, although it raises risks of lead contamination, is not dangerous enough to be an abnormally dangerous activity.[34] Courts may also find it easy to characterize the activity as common and thus to support a conclusion that liability must be based upon fault.[35]

Ground damage from aircraft. The Restatement addresses the problem of ground damage from aircraft in a separate section.[36] It prescribes strict liability for physical harms resulting from ascent, descent, or flight of aircraft or from things dropped or falling from aircraft. At one time, unintended entry upon land could be conceived as a trespass to land and liability imposed for that reason.[37] With the general adoption of a fault requirement, the trespass theory has become obsolete and if strict liability is to be imposed for injuries from falling aircraft it is for some other reason. A few states prescribe strict liability by statute,[38] but otherwise the cases today expressly reject strict liability[39] and proceed on a negligence theory.[40] Even so, the case for strict liability is a strong one. Aviation is now common and not especially hazardous, but it also presents non-reciprocal risks to those on the ground. The risks are exactly characteristic of the activity and are in no way produced, enhanced, or reciprocated by the victims.[41]

Impoundments of water. Rylands v. Fletcher[42] itself involved escape of water from a mill pond and consequent harm to a neighbor. Building a mill pond hardly sounds like an activity of special hazard like explosives; and whatever may have been true in the mining neighborhood where it was built, it was hardly an uncommon activity in the country as a whole. Not surprisingly, American courts have generally rejected *Rylands* as a basis for liability for the sudden escape of impounded water.[43] But, on

negligence or nuisance theories. See William B. Johnson, Annotation, Tort Liability for Pollution from Underground Storage Tank, 5 A.L.R.5th 1 (1993).

33. Splendorio v. Bilray Demolition Co., Inc., 682 A.2d 461 (R.I.1996).

34. Thompson v. Mindis Metals, Inc., 692 So.2d 805 (Ala.1997).

35. See, e.g., Mahowald v. Minnesota Gas Co., 344 N.W.2d 856 (Minn.1984); Grube v. Daun, 213 Wis.2d 533, 570 N.W.2d 851 (1997).

36. Restatement § 520A.

37. See § 54.

38. S.C. CODE. § 55–3–60.

39. Boyd v. White, 128 Cal.App.2d 641, 276 P.2d 92 (1954) (operation of an airplane in the year 1954 is not "ultrahazardous"); Crosby v. Cox Aircraft Co. of Washington, 109 Wash.2d 581, 746 P.2d 1198, 73 A.L.R.4th 397 (1987).

40. Some courts have invoked res ipsa loquitur in air crash cases. See § 155. Res ipsa loquitur may obtain the same result as strict liability if the jury draws the permissible inference, but its premise is that negligence is the most likely explanation, while strict liability for abnormal dangers is premised in part on the idea that care *cannot* make the activity safe.

41. See William K. Jones, Strict Liability for Hazardous Enterprise, 92 COLUM. L. REV. 1705, 1748 (1992).

42. Rylands v. Fletcher, L.R. 3 H.L. 330 (1868), discussed in § 346.

43. See Chicago and North Western Ry. v. Tyler, 482 F.2d 1007 (8th Cir.1973); Bowling v. City of Oxford, 267 N.C. 552, 148 S.E.2d 624 (1966) (stream dammed, negligence required); cf. Turner v. Big Lake Oil Co., 128 Tex. 155, 96 S.W.2d 221 (1936) (escape of ponded salt water). Even more clearly in the case of water escaping from mains. Summit Hill Assocs. v. Knoxville

one theory or another, strict liability has sometimes been imposed for escape of toxic substances,[44] for overflow of a natural waterway due to the defendant's obstruction,[45] for percolation of harmful substances[46] and for intentional release of wastes.[47] A thoughtful commentator has suggested that strict liability is rightly rejected in dam-bursting cases except where the reservoir is unconnected to natural waterways and a very high volume of water is impounded.[48]

Lateral and subjacent support. Adjacent landowners owe a duty of lateral support for the adjoining lands. So if a landowner removes soil, causing the adjacent lands to subside of their own weight, he becomes strictly liable for the harm done.[49] Similarly, the owner of mineral rights owes the surface owner a duty not to remove necessary support for the surface, and again is strictly liable if he does.[50] The Torts Restatement explains such rules as reflecting a property right and does not treat them as part of the abnormal danger rules.[51] Although the factual settings are in a sense the reverse of the *Rylands* setting—something is removed, not added to the defendant's land—the strict liability rule seems to be *Rylands'* twin. In the case of subjacent support, the usual case is removal of minerals by a person who owns or leases the mineral rights but not the surface. In that kind of case, enterprise liability arguments may be persuasive—the mineral owner must swallow the sour of liability along with the sweet of profit.[52]

§ 349. Limitations on Strict Liability

Proximate cause or the limited scope of strict duties. Strict liability is not unlimited liability. The defendant's strict liability activities must at least be a cause in fact of the plaintiff's harm. Beyond that, the defendant's activities must be a proximate or legal cause of that harm. In the case of animals known to have mischievous propensities, the harm must result from that propensity and not from some other characteristic of the animal. For example, if the defendant's dog has a known propensity to bite house guests, the defendant will be strictly liable for the dog's

Utils. Bd., 667 S.W.2d 91 (Tenn.App.1983); Tillery v. West Side Canal, Inc., 719 P.2d 1384 (Wyo.1986). Possibly some courts would still permit a recovery for "trespass" in dam bursting or washout cases without requiring intent. See Cooper v. Horn, 248 Va. 417, 448 S.E.2d 403 (1994) (where, however, the defendant seems not to have objected to an instruction that permitted a trespass finding without requiring intent).

44. See Cities Serv. Co. v. State, 312 So.2d 799 (Fla.Dist.Ct.App.1975) (escape of billions of gallons of phosphate slimes).

45. See Amish v. Walnut Creek Dev., Inc. 631 S.W.2d 866 (Mo.App.1982); Gossner v. Utah Power & Light, 612 P.2d 337 (Utah 1980).

46. Branch v. Western Petroleum, Inc., 657 P.2d 267 (Utah 1982) (citing cases).

47. Atlas Chemical Industries, Inc. v. Anderson, 514 S.W.2d 309 (Tex. Ct. App. 1974), aff'd, 524 S.W.2d 681 (Tex.1975).

48. William K. Jones, Strict Liability for Hazardous Enterprise, 92 Colum. L. Rev. 1705, 1737 (1992).

49. Prete v. Cray, 49 R.I. 209, 141 A. 609, 59 A.L.R. 1241 (1928) (but not extending liability to subsidence caused by weight of structures on the land).

50. Haseman v. Orman, 680 N.E.2d 531 (Ind.1997) (holding the lessor of mineral rights liable for damage to surface owner caused by lessee's removal of coal).

51. Restatement §§ 817 (lateral support) & 820 (subjacent support).

52. See Haseman v. Orman, 680 N.E.2d 531 (Ind.1997).

bites, but not strictly liable when the dog merely gets in the plaintiff's way and causes a fall.[1]

Similarly, in the case of abnormally dangerous activities, the harm must result from the characteristic that prompted strict liability in the first place. For example, the defendant will be strictly liable for impacts caused by use of explosives and also for vibration damage, but not for the loss of mink pelts resulting because the noise of explosion drives mother mink to eat their young.[2]

The Restatement provides one specific rule as an instance of this principle: the defendant is not strictly liable for harms resulting from abnormally dangerous activities if those harms would not have resulted but for the abnormal sensitivities of the plaintiff's own activities.[3] The case of the mother mink illustrates that particular rule as well as the more general principle.

Intervening acts. When it comes to the intervening acts of third persons, the Restatement provides that innocent, negligent, and even reckless acts of third persons present no barrier to strict liability—nor do forces of nature.[4] This leaves the possibility that intentional intervening wrongs of third persons might at times suffice to insulate the defendant from strict liability. In a Missouri case, a striker caused a large explosion by firing a rifle at the defendant's tractor-trailer loaded with dynamite. The court held that the defendant was not strictly liable for harms done by the explosion.[5] On the other hand, accumulations of dynamite run risks of explosions for the very reason that absolute control is impossible. For this reason, the Alaska Court reached the opposite result, holding that a defendant who stored dynamite would be liable for harms done by an explosion deliberately set.[6]

Perhaps the fundamental question is whether the risks that led courts to impose strict liability included risks that third persons would participate in or trigger the harm. If storage of dynamite runs no special risks that others will set it off, then the Missouri court was right to absolve the defendant. The Restatement in effect takes the view that intervention of others is a part of the risk of abnormally dangerous activity, at least when the intervening actor is not guilty of intentional harm. Some courts, however, have in effect rejected the Restatement view by eliminating strict liability when intervening actors trigger harm.[7] Courts have also said that sometimes a force of nature or Act of God will cut off liability.[8]

§ 349

1. See Restatement § 509 (2).

2. See Foster v. Preston Mill Co., 44 Wash.2d 440, 268 P.2d 645 (1954).

3. Restatement § 524A.

4. Restatement § 522.

5. Pecan Shoppe of Springfield, Missouri, Inc. v. Tri–State Motor Transit Co., 573 S.W.2d 431 (Mo.App.1978).

6. Yukon Equip. v. Fireman's Fund Ins. Co., 585 P.2d 1206 (Alaska 1978).

7. See, e.g., Bianchini v. Humble Pipe Line Co., 480 F.2d 251, reh'g denied, 478 F.2d 1402 (5th Cir.1973).

8. Trotter v. Callens, 89 N.M. 19, 21, 546 P.2d 867, 869 (Ct.App.1976). However, it often turns out here and elsewhere in tort law that the Act of God or force of nature rule is a disguised version of the

These cases deserve some skepticism. It would be downright silly to say, for example, that crop dusting is an abnormally dangerous activity because no one can completely control the spread of pesticides through the air, yet to relieve the duster of liability on the ground that an unusual wind blew the dust. The inability to predict and control the drift is the reason for strict liability, not a reason against it. The same kind of comment applies when a third person intervenes. At best, case by case analysis is required to determine whether the harm is any less characteristic of the activity merely because a third person intervenes.[9]

Plaintiff's status on the defendant's land. Rylands v. Fletcher formulated a strict liability for the escape of things from the defendant's land.[10] With the American expansion of strict liability to include abnormally dangerous activities generally, liability could be imposed even if the dangerous activity took place in public (as with blasting for highway construction) or remained entirely upon the defendant's own land and did not escape at all. When the danger remained on the defendant's own land, however, there was little reason to give the intentional or negligent trespasser the benefit of a strict liability rule. The Restatement thus excludes strict liability to such trespassers, both in the case of dangerous animals[11] and in the case of other strict liability activities.[12] Strict liability is imposed in both cases for injuries to those who are properly upon the land as invitees or licensees or otherwise.[13]

In claims by an entrant upon land based upon negligence, a fair number of statutes have eliminated the licensee category and some of them even the trespasser category.[14] That change, where it has occurred, does not have any logical bearing on the question of strict liability policy. Intentional or negligent trespassers who are entitled to reasonable care in spite of their trespasses, do not necessarily have any claim to recover from a faultless defendant. The states have also enacted recreational use statutes that alter landowners' duties to those who use the land without paying, generally providing an immunity. These statutes almost certainly preclude strict liability where the immunity is granted.[15]

but-for rule of cause in fact. In *Trotter,* the court said that "an Act of God applies only to such an extraordinary and unexpected manifestation of the forces of nature as cannot be prevented by human care, skill or foresight; that is, *such a cause as would have produced the injury independent of the defendants' actions.* However, if the resulting injury is in part produced by the wrongful or negligent act of the defendant he will be held liable." [emphasis added]. The effect of the definition, especially the italicized portion, is that the defendant is relieved only if the injury would have occurred even without the defendant's activity. That means the defendant is relieved only when the defendant's activity is not a but-for cause.

9. See Klein v. Pyrodyne Corp., 117 Wash.2d 1, 17, 810 P.2d 917, 925 (1991), amended, 117 Wash.2d 1, 817 P.2d 1359 (1991) (defendant relieved of liability "only if those acts were unforeseeable in relation to the extraordinary risk created by the activity").

10. § 346.

11. Restatement § 511.

12. Restatement § 520B.

13. Restatement §§ 515, 520C.

14. § 237.

15. See Stuart v. City of Morgan City, 504 So.2d 934 (La.App.1987).

§ 350. Defenses to Strict Liability

Assumed risk, contributory negligence, and comparative fault. Under the Restatement view, the defendant who was subject to strict liability either because he possessed an animal that caused harm[1] or because he carried on abnormally dangerous activities[2] could not assert ordinary contributory negligence as a defense. For instance, if the plaintiff negligently failed to discover the danger, he was not barred by his fault.[3] However, except where statutes provide otherwise,[4] the defendant could defend on the ground that the plaintiff assumed the risk[5] or was guilty of contributory negligence by knowingly and unreasonably subjecting himself to the risk of harm from the strict liability activity.[6]

The Restatement justifies permitting recovery by a plaintiff whose own fault contributed to her injury on a purely formal reason. It says that since the strict liability action is not founded on the defendant's fault in the first place, the plaintiff's fault should furnish no defense.[7] The conclusion that contributory negligence is no defense is explained by rephrasing the conclusion as "the policy of the law" but without asserting any reason for the supposed policy. The result is that the person who is at fault in causing the harm recovers from the person who is not at fault in causing it.

The rule seems wrong. If the plaintiff negligently contributes to her own injury, that means she necessarily has some control of the risks. In that case, the risks cannot be said to be entirely those fostered by the defendant's activities. Even one who speaks for expanded strict liability might support the use of the contributory negligence defense, at least in the present world of comparative fault,[8] and in the case of strict products liability, many courts have rejected the rule protecting plaintiffs from their own fault.[9]

Although it seems wrong to impose a rule of law that exculpates negligent plaintiffs in all cases, it must be remembered that the plaintiff is not necessarily negligent in relying upon the safety of the defendant's activity. For example, it is not negligent to visit a zoo any more than it is negligent for the defendant to operate one; the risk of escaping animals is simply not an unreasonable one if the zoo is well-maintained. Even the

§ 350

1. Restatement § 515.

2. Restatement § 524.

3. Matkovic v. Shell Oil Co., 218 Mont. 156, 707 P.2d 2 (1985).

4. Statutes and ordinances often control liability for injuries by dogs and may equally prescribe and limit the defenses available. See Donner v. Arkwright–Boston Mfrs. Mut. Ins. Co., 358 So.2d 21 (Fla.1978) (error to instruct on assumed risk in dog bite case; only the statutory provocation defense is available).

5. Restatement § 523 (assumption of risk as to abnormally dangerous activities).

6. Restatement § 524 (knowing exposure to risk of abnormally dangerous activities); Restatement § 515 (knowing exposure or assumed risk as to animals); cf. Rickrode v. Wistinghausen, 128 Mich.App. 240, 340 N.W.2d 83 (1983) (willful provocation of an animal is a defense).

7. Restatement § 515, cmt. b; Restatement § 524, cmt. a.

8. See William K. Jones, Strict Liability for Hazardous Enterprise, 92 Colum. L. Rev. 1705, 1756–1757 (1992).

9. See § 369.

plaintiff who knows of the danger is not necessarily at fault in refusing to move her home or business to avoid it. If she is entitled to be where she is, she is not at fault in being there.[10] Finally, in some cases, no doubt rare ones, the defendant may be under a duty to protect the plaintiff from her own fault, in which case the plaintiff's fault is no defense.[11]

An entirely different question arises when the facts show that the plaintiff knowingly and unreasonably encountered the danger. The Restatement recognizes such behavior as a defense to the strict liability claim. The defense looks a good deal like what used to be called assumption of the risk, which the Restatement also recognizes as a defense. The problem is that with the general adoption of comparative fault rules in the United States, assumed risk in negligence cases is now usually treated like contributory negligence so that it no longer invariably bars recovery but usually only reduces damages. At the same time, however, some cases that were once decided for the defendant on an assumed risk analysis, may now be decided for the defendant on the ground that the defendant owed no duty to the plaintiff or did not breach the duty he owed. The result is that some former assumed risk cases are now matters of comparative fault with a reduction in recovery, while others are now matters of no duty with a complete denial of all recovery.[12]

The difference in the treatment of the plaintiff who confronts known danger lies largely in the question of contract, consent, or apparent consent. In the context of strict liability, the person who foolishly tries to pet the defendant's tiger is assuredly foolish and her recovery should probably be reduced, but she has almost certainly not consented to accept the risk and to relieve the defendant of all responsibility.[13] In contrast, the plaintiff who accepts employment as trainer of the defendant's wild animals apparently consents to the abnormal risks that entails and hence should not recover on a strict liability basis;[14] certainly this is true if she expressly contracts to assume the risk.[15]

Privileges or immunities. Governmental entities are almost never held strictly liable even when immunities of public entities are otherwise

10. See Leroy Fibre Co. v. Chicago, Milwaukee & St. Paul Railway Co., 232 U.S. 340, 34 S.Ct. 415, 58 L.Ed. 631 (1914); William K. Jones, Strict Liability for Hazardous Enterprise, 92 Colum. L. Rev. 1705, 1756–1757 (1992); cf. Gary T. Schwartz, Rylands v. Fletcher, Negligence, and Strict Liability in Peter Cane and Jane Stapleton, Essays in Celebration of John Fleming 209, 224 (1998).

11. See § 200.

12. See §§ 211–214.

13. Cf. Leiner v. First Wythe Ave. Serv. Station, Inc., 121 Misc.2d 559, 468 N.Y.S.2d 302 (1983), aff'd, 127 Misc.2d 794, 492 N.Y.S.2d 708 (N.Y. Sup. App. 1985) (plaintiff's conduct toward vicious dog treated as comparative fault).

14. Cf. Peneschi v. National Steel Corp., 170 W.Va. 511, 295 S.E.2d 1 (1982) (acceptance of job dealing with abnormally dangerous activities is assumption of risk barring a strict liability recovery).

15. See Integrated Waste Servs., Inc. v. Akzo Nobel Salt, Inc., 113 F.3d 296 (2d Cir.1997) (conclusion that defendant owed no duty because contractual allocations of rights between the parties bars strict liability as well as negligence claims).

abolished.[16] Does this or any governmental immunity pass down to independent contractors carrying out contracts with the government in accord with specifications? Suppose, for example, that a contractor is blasting for a highway. He in no way violates specifications of the contract but, without negligence, the blasting causes vibration harm to nearby buildings. Where blasting is not prescribed by specification, only a little authority supports the contractor's immunity from strict liability.[17] Other cases have held that the contractor does not share the government's immunity in abnormal danger/strict liability cases.[18]

One similar but distinct immunity is sometimes asserted. The Restatement recognizes an immunity of one who, as a public officer or common carrier acting with reasonable care performs a duty imposed by law.[19] This rule would immunize a common carrier from strict liability for harms resulting from the transportation of explosives as long as it had a public duty to accept all freight and it has been followed in a number of cases.[20] It has been rejected in a few cases on the ground that the carrier, though acting under compulsion of law in accepting the hazardous cargo, is nonetheless a good risk distributor or on the ground that the carrier's freight rates can reflect the potential liability.[21]

§ 351. Rationales and Comments

The variety of settings in which strict liability may be imposed for abnormally dangerous activities is matched by the divergence in the holdings. It is somewhat dismaying to read that impoundment of water leads to strict liability in England but not America, and that storage of dynamite may lead to strict liability but that storage of natural gas may not. The variety of factors introduced by the Restatement contributes to the differences in decisions and to uncertainty about what strict liability for abnormal dangers is all about. Theorists might explain such differences, but as it turns out theorists and commentators have quite divergent views of their own.

Deterrence. One view is that strict liability can reduce risks of harm and encourage actors engaged in abnormally dangerous activities to find safer methods or at least a safer place for dangerous activities.[1] The

16. See, denying strict liability claims against the federal government, Laird v. Nelms, 406 U.S. 797, 92 S.Ct. 1899, 32 L.Ed.2d 499 (1972).

17. Pumphrey v. J.A. Jones Constr. Co., 250 Iowa 559, 94 N.W.2d 737 (1959).

18. Smith v. Lockheed Propulsion Co., 247 Cal.App.2d 774, 56 Cal.Rptr. 128, 29 A.L.R.3d 538 (1967) (distinguishing cases not based on abnormal danger); Lobozzo v. Adam Eidemiller, Inc., 437 Pa. 360, 263 A.2d 432 (1970). As to other claims in which the contractor may assert the government's immunity, see § 274.

19. Restatement § 521.

20. See Actiesselskabet Ingrid v. Central R. of New Jersey, 216 F. 72 (2d Cir. 1914); Annotation, Carrier's "Public Duty" Exception to Absolute or Strict Liability Arising out of Carriage of Hazardous Substances, 31 A.L.R.4th 658 (1981).

21. Chavez v. Southern Pac. Transp. Co., 413 F.Supp. 1203 (E.D.Cal.1976); National Steel Serv. Ctr., Inc., v. Gibbons, 319 N.W.2d 269, 31 A.L.R.4th 650 (Iowa 1982).

§ 351

1. See Mark Geistfeld, Should Enterprise Liability Replace the Rule of Strict Liability for Abnormally Dangerous Activities?, 45 UCLA L. Rev. 611 (1998); cf. G.J.

suggestion is that there is more room to reduce risk with high risk activities than with others. But it may not be so clear that strict liability does in fact reduce risk[2] or that it is more important to reduce the small danger of useful high-risk activities like blasting than to reduce the more pervasive risk of activities like automobile driving to which no strict liability attaches. And it may be difficult to know whether risk-reduction by strict liability comes at too high a price, by over-deterring, for example.[3] Furthermore, some risks simply cannot be reduced. Even the repeated suggestion that the defendant might move the activity to a safer location, if that is somehow different from a question of negligence, will not always work. One might give up recreational blasting lest he be held strictly liable, but contractors cannot very well give up blasting for subways, tunnels, and highways, nor can they consider moving the site for those activities. The requirement that the activity be an uncommon or "non-natural" one would be puzzling, too, if deterrence or risk-reduction were the goal of strict liability.[4]

Compensation; good risk distributors. The enterprise liability approach takes a different tact. It is rooted in the belief that even when an enterprise is not at fault, it should "pay its way." This view is often associated with the idea that a business enterprise is a good risk distributor, meaning that the enterprise can pay for the harms with less dislocation than individuals. It might, for example, pass on the costs to its customers in the form of higher prices, or might absorb some or all of the costs itself as part of the expense of doing business. The idea of the good risk distributor was very popular at one time and still has ardent supporters.[5] However, it has been argued that life today is not much like life in the Great Depression of the 1930s. Individuals today are often very good risk distributors because they (or their employers) can purchase their own insurance against some risks much more efficiently than enterprises can purchase liability insurance and defend law suits.[6] For

Leasing Co., Inc. v. Union Elec. Co., 54 F.3d 379, 386 (7th Cir.1995) (Posner, J.: we want one who keeps a tiger in his backyard to "consider seriously the possibility of getting rid of the tiger altogether").

2. See Joseph H. King, Jr., A Goals–Oriented Approach to Strict Tort Liability for Abnormally Dangerous Activities, 48 Baylor L. Rev. 341, 353–354 (1996).

3. King, supra n. 2, 48 Baylor L. Rev. 341, 355 (1996). Writers have sometimes argued that strict liability might be a good deterrent because in many cases the defendant is in fact negligent but the negligence cannot be proved. See, e.g., King, ibid. This argument seems to imply that judges can make a good judgment that the defendant is at fault in an entire class of cases when they cannot make such a judgment in particular cases the facts of which are actually before the court.

4. It has been argued, however, that a common activity is one with high utility and also that the deterrence effect would be limited with common activities. Geistfeld, supra n. 1, 45 UCLA L. Rev. 611, 653 (1998). In addition, Judge Posner suggested that with common activities "it is unlikely either that its hazards are perceived as great or that there is no technology of care available to minimize them; so the case for strict liability is weakened." Indiana Harbor Belt R.R. Co. v. American Cyanamid Co., 916 F.2d 1174, 1177 (7th Cir.1990).

5. Virginia E. Nolan and Edmund Ursin, The Revitalization of Hazardous Activity Strict Liability, 65 N.C. L. Rev. 257 (1987).

6. See King, supra n. 2, 48 Baylor L. Rev. 341, 351 (1996) (less than half of premium dollars for liability insurance reach victims); Geistfeld, supra n. 1; David G. Owen, the Moral Foundations of Products Liability Law: Toward First Principles, 68 Notre Dame L. Rev. 427, 504 (1993). Howev-

the many individuals who cannot protect themselves from harms that occur without negligence—including some well above the poverty line[7]—an inadequate but still enormous range of social support now exists through both private and public programs.[8] In this setting, use of the judicial system to secure support for victims of non-negligent harms may be less attractive than it once was.

Fairness or justice. Enterprise liability can be justified, however, on different and broader grounds not limited to profit-making business or ability to absorb loss suffered by others. It can be argued that as a matter of fairness or justice an actor ought to pay for the costs that are uniquely or recurrently a result of his acts so long as the community as a whole does not create or tolerate similar risks and the plaintiff himself contributes nothing to it.[9] Activities that are common or "natural" in the community come under the rule of live and let live, so that liability is imposed in those cases only if the activity is carried out negligently.[10] Although such activities may cause harms, they do not represent costs that can be especially identified with the defendant's operations, only with those of the community at large.

In contrast, when the defendant carries out some activity that carries with it unique, typical, or recurrent risks, different from those imposed by activities shared by others in the community, strict liability may be fair and just. In that case the defendant takes the benefit of his activity and must similarly pay the tolls that are regularly associated with that activity.

Fairness rationales like others are incomplete or suffer from weak spots. Quite arguably, new technology with its new risks should not automatically produce strict liability and it is noteworthy that when railroads were built, posing new risks unlike any others, the courts created the law of negligence, not the law of strict liability.

Common usage. Whatever its weaknesses and strengths, fairness reasoning shows why common usage is as important as high risk. The risk in *Rylands v. Fletcher* that impounded water will by its weight make the ground below it give way leading to a flood of an unknown mine is surely a very low order risk. The risk that carefully conducted mining

er, even financially well-off people may have difficulty providing against risks like the contamination of all the community's water supply, so broad generalizations are chancy.

7. See 2 Barry R. Furrow, Thomas L. Greaney, Sandra H. Johnson, Timothy S. Jost, & Robert L. Schwartz, Health Law 562–63 (1995).

8. See Geistfeld, supra n. 1. 45 UCLA L. Rev. 611, 626–627 (1998).

9. Cf. William K. Jones, Strict Liability for Hazardous Enterprise, 92 Colum. L. Rev. 1705, 1713 (1992) (proposing strict liability when "neither the incidence nor the extent of the harm is subject to significant control by the injured party in the normal course of events"); Gary T. Schwartz, Rylands v. Fletcher, Negligence, and Strict Liability in Peter Cane and Jane Stapleton, Essays in Celebration of John Fleming 209 (1998).

10. See Bamford v. Turnley, 3 B & S 67, 122 Eng.Rep. 27 (Exch. Ch. 1862). Important thinkers have considered this idea and variations in detail. See Richard A. Epstein, A Theory of Strict Liability, 2 J. Leg. Stud. 151 (1973); Richard A. Epstein, Nuisance Law: Corrective Justice and Its Utilitarian Constraints, 8 J. Leg. Stud. 49 (1979); George P. Fletcher, Fairness and Utility in Tort Theory, 85 Harv. L. Rev. 537 (1972).

will cause the surface of the land to subside is likewise a small risk. Even storage of dynamite presents a relatively small risk if it is placed in a remote area of Alaska. All these and other cases of not-very-risky activities have invoked strict liability, however. The explosives cases, where liability was originally imposed on entirely different reasoning,[11] led those who tried to synthesize the law to the wrong emphasis. A special hazard requires a greater quantum of care—you handle explosives quite differently from the way you handle flour—but not strict liability. What requires strict liability is that the risks of the defendant's activity are special to that activity and not common to similar activities carried on generally in the community. A broader formulation would be that risks unilaterally imposed by the defendant entail strict liability, while risks generated by interaction of the plaintiff and defendant on an equal footing do not.[12]

Characterization. All the rationales require more explication than can be given here and all have their own strengths and weaknesses. One problem common to any approach is that courts have no principled method for characterizing the activity in question. Yet their characterization of the activity foreordains the outcome because, depending on how you describe the activity, it may or may not seem to be abnormally dangerous or uncommon. In one claim, the plaintiff asserted that she was exposed to paints containing dangerous heavy metals and other compounds and suffered some injuries as a result. The paints were used by the defendant in his occupation as an artist in his own home. The court characterized the activity as "painting in one's house," which made it a certainty that the activity was a common usage.[13] If the court had characterized the activity as "exposing others to dangerous fumes" the activity might have seemed both hazardous and uncommon.

Similarly, in a Minnesota case,[14] the plaintiff sued the city after suffering loss in a multi-car collision caused by a high speed police chase. The trial court found the city not negligent, but thought that the costs of such chases ought to be internalized. That is, the trial judge thought that the costs of such chases were peculiar or regular incidents to the operation of police departments and the department ought to pay its way. Consequently, the trial judge imposed strict liability. The Minnesota Supreme Court rejected this approach in part because the use of automobiles was a matter of common usage.[15] But if the court had characterized the activity as "high-speed chases" rather than as the use of automobiles, both special hazard and uncommon use would have been established.

11. Sullivan v. Dunham, 161 N.Y. 290, 55 N.E. 923 (1900); cf. Colton v. Onderdonk, 69 Cal. 155, 10 P. 395 (1886) (trespass theory with talk of intrinsic danger).

12. Jones, Strict Liability for Hazardous Enterprise, 92 Colum. L. Rev. 1705 (1992).

13. Humphreys v. Humphreys, 949 F.Supp. 1014 (E.D.N.Y.1997).

14. Cairl v. City of St. Paul, 268 N.W.2d 908, 100 A.L.R.3d 807 (Minn. 1978).

15. The court also relied on the exclusion of liability of public officers carrying out a public duty.

To some extent these problems in characterization can be minimized if courts shift the inquiry slightly to ask whether the risk was peculiarly identified with the defendant's activity or not the result of interaction with a plaintiff who had some control over the risks.[16] A one-way risk, imposed by a defendant upon whom similar risks are not imposed by others, would be a good candidate for strict liability.

16. See Jones, Strict Liability for Hazardous Enterprise, 92 COLUM. L. REV. 1705 (1992).

CHAPTER 24

PRODUCTS LIABILITY

TOPIC A. THE COMING AND PARTIAL GOING OF STRICT LIABILITY

§ 352. The Province and Theories of Products Liability

The field of products liability has enjoyed an enormous vogue in legal circles since about 1963, partly because jurists were challenged by the new idea of strict liability that began to be developed about that time.[1] Scores of books, many of them multi-volume treatises,[2] as well as hundreds of law review articles[3] have argued the theory and the rules. The potentials of products liability touched nerves and ignited hopes. Many writers have made products problems the focus of their theories, ideologies, or social concerns.

In court, products liability claims have had an important impact on safety and health. Some claims may have driven manufacturers to despair, but others have revealed seriously defective products and sometimes malign corporate behavior. Some products have produced mass injuries. Among these are the Dalkon Shield, asbestos, and cigarettes. Sub-specialities in mass torts, involving products like asbestos and cigarettes, themselves consume enormous resources and generate volumes of legal materials.[4] In some such

cases, products liability suits have played an important role in public awareness of the danger and in getting greater safety. But it is not all rosy. Courts need to cull both silly and abusive claims and silly and

§ 352

1. See § 353.

2. See ROBERT E. CARTWRIGHT, JERRY J. PHILLIPS, PRODUCTS LIABILITY (1988); LOUIS R. FRUMER & MELVIN I. FRIEDMAN, PRODUCTS LIABILITY; M. STUART MADDEN, PRODUCTS LIABILITY (2d ed. 2 vols. 1988); MARSHALL S. SHAPO, THE LAW OF PRODUCTS LIABILITY (3d ed. 2 vols. 1994); AMERICAN LAW OF PRODUCTS LIABILITY 3D (Looseleaf).

3. Among the earliest writers who shaped the field were William Prosser, Page Keeton, and John Wade. Among the next generation of writers shaping the field were James A. Henderson and Aaron D. Twerski (Reporters for the Restatement of Products Liability), Richard Epstein, David Fischer, David G. Owen, Jerry Phillips, and Gary Schwartz, Victor Schwartz, and Marshall Shapo. Trenchant and effective commentary was provided by many others.

4. See Robert L. Rabin, A Sociolegal History of the Tobacco Tort Litigation, 44 STAN. L. REV. 853 (1992) (an engaging though chilling account of the first two waves of tobacco litigation, with summaries of asbestos litigation). For a discussion of the current status in tobacco litigation, see Richard L. Cupp, Jr., A Morality Play's Third Act: Revisiting Addiction, Fraud and Consumer Choice in "Third Wave" Tobacco Litigation, 46 U. KAN. L. REV. 465 (1998). Other major mass tort products included the Dalkon Shield, DES, and Agent Orange, each with its own literature.

abusive defenses. Courts have been challenged to develop rules and judicious attitudes that will permit good claims and defense while cutting out the bad ones.

Illustrations of a products liability claim. A new passenger car is engulfed with flames when it is in a moderate collision with another car, injuring or killing occupants.[5] A machine, not equipped with a safety device, lops off a worker's fingers.[6] A consumer becomes ill as a result of drinking contaminated milk.[7] A drug prescribed for arthritis causes the patient to go blind.[8] A car's steering fails and a bystander is injured when the driver cannot control it.[9] Cigarettes are addictive in some important sense and deadly as well.[10] In many cases like these, the victim has recovered in tort suits against manufacturers and distributors. In some cases, evidence pointed to horrendous negligence or even much worse.[11] In others, the manufacturer is not shown to be negligent all, but under strict liability rules is fully liable nonetheless. Yet liability is not a foregone conclusion because a number of rules protect manufacturers and distributors.

Scope of the field. The field of products liability concerns the bases for, defenses to, and scope of liability of manufacturers and others who are in the business of selling or supplying goods for harms caused by defective tangible products. The focus has been on products that do not meet safety standards or expectations. While a manufacturer might be held liable for marketing a product in a way that puts it in the hands of a person who is dangerous to himself or others,[12] such cases do not involve defective products and are not traditionally considered under the rubric of products liability. For defective products, the field includes claims against a product manufacturer asserted on any theory ranging from negligence to strict liability in tort. Plaintiffs in fact often assert a number of theories such as breach of implied warranty and strict tort liability as bases for their claims. Sometimes they prevail upon one theory even though they fail on the others.[13] An important aspect of

5. Grimshaw v. Ford Motor Co., 119 Cal.App.3d 757, 174 Cal.Rptr. 348 (1981) (the infamous Pinto case in which Ford knowingly produced a car that could burst into flames or explode on impact when an expenditure of a few dollars per car would have made it safe; strict liability for design defect).

6. Reid v. Spadone Mach. Co., 119 N.H. 457, 404 A.2d 1094 (1979), over'd on other ground, 129 N.H. 561, 534 A.2d 689.

7. Cooper v. Borden, Inc., 709 So.2d 878 (La.Ct.App.1998) (penicillin in milk, causing allergic reaction).

8. Cochran v. Brooke, 243 Or. 89, 409 P.2d 904 (1966).

9. Henningsen v. Bloomfield Motors, Inc., 32 N.J. 358, 161 A.2d 69 (1960).

10. See, e.g., Richard L. Cupp, Jr., A Morality Play's Third Act: Revisiting Addiction, Fraud and Consumer Choice in "Third Wave" Tobacco Litigation, 46 U. Kan. L. Rev. 465 (1998) (considering addiction and assumed risk arguments).

11. See Gary T. Schwartz, Reality in the Economic Analysis of Tort Law: Does Tort Law Really Deter?, 42 UCLA L. Rev. 377, 406 (1994) (giving several examples).

12. See Hamilton v. Accu–Tek, 62 F.Supp.2d 802 (1999) (gun manufacturers held liable for negligently marketing handguns so that teenagers would be too likely to acquire them and commit crimes of lethal violence); cf. Zerby v. Warren, 297 Minn. 134, 210 N.W.2d 58 (1973) (liability for marketing glue to child too likely to damage himself by sniffing); see also the alcohol provider cases, § 332.

13. E.g., Lee v. Crookston Coca–Cola Bottling Co., 290 Minn. 321, 188 N.W.2d 426 (1971) (although jury found against plaintiff on negligence and warranty claims,

product safety not directly considered in this chapter lies in state and federal regulation, especially regulation of drugs through the Food and Drug Commission[14] and the Consumer Product Safety Commission.[15] There is also a special statute for injuries resulting from childhood vaccinations.[16]

The main theories. As a practical matter the plaintiff has often found it useful to assert negligence in the manufacture or sale of a product. Although the Restatement Second collects more than a dozen rules directed at the liability of chattel suppliers for negligence,[17] the rules reflect general negligence principles and require little separate discussion here.

So far as the plaintiff claims a breach of express or implied warranty, that claim is often associated with contract liability. Liability for breach of warranty is ordinarily strict liability: liability results from breach even if the defendant used reasonable efforts to perform. To a large extent, the law of implied warranty gradually merged with strict tort liability. For the purpose of drafting a complaint and presenting alternative theories to the court, warranty theories must be separated from others. For the purpose of outlining contemporary products liability law, however, it is often possible to treat cases that arise under a warranty theory pretty much as cases that arise under a strict tort liability theory.

The misrepresentation claim is little different. The idea is that the plaintiff relies upon a representation, perhaps on a label. For example, the plaintiff might use a ladder relying on the label that proclaims it can hold 500 pounds. If the ladder collapses with a load of 200 pounds, the plaintiff has a misrepresentation claim and perhaps a warranty claim as well.[18] Neither claim requires proof that the defendant was at fault in making or designing the ladder.

Since around 1963, plaintiffs have frequently asserted that the manufacturer or distributor is strictly liable, not as matter of warranty or misrepresentation but as a matter of tort law. The claim has been that it is enough for liability that the ladder is defective and its defective condition causes harm. It is the strict liability theory that captured most

trial judge erred in failing to instruct on strict tort liability as well); Denny v. Ford Motor Co., 87 N.Y.2d 248, 662 N.E.2d 730, 639 N.Y.S.2d 250 (1995) (plaintiff who lost on strict tort liability theory could prevail on warranty theory). When the plaintiff claims a design or warning defect, however, the negligence, warranty, and strict liability claims may turn on tests so similar that it would unduly emphasize the plaintiff's side of the case to submit both those theories to the jury and it may be permissible if not necessary to instruct the jury on strict liability only. See Chestnut v. Ford Motor Co., 445 F.2d 967 (4th Cir.1971); Hyundai Motor Co. v. Rodriguez, 995 S.W.2d 661 (Tex. 1999).

14. For an excellent brief description of the FDA process of approving a new drug, see Michael D. Green, Safety as an Element of Pharmaceutical Quality: The Respective Roles of Regulation and Tort Law, 42 St. Louis U. L.J. 163 (1998).

15. Created by 15 U.S.C.A. § 2053. Under 15 U.S.C.A. § 2072 a federal claim is created for knowing or wilful violation of a Commission's safety rule.

16. See § 399.

17. Restatement §§ 388–402.

18. See Restatement § 402B.

of the thinking and generated most of the developing jurisprudence after about 1963. One of the issues today is whether, or to what extent, strict liability is actually imposed.

The 1998 Restatement of Products Liability has provided a convenient language for discussion of all product liability claims. No manufacturer or distributor is liable for harm caused by a product unless the product is defective. The language of defectiveness encompasses negligence, warranty, and strict tort liability. Although each theory was historically of separate importance, the Restatement's "defect" analysis makes it possible to discuss the rules of liability without necessarily identifying the negligence or warranty basis for them.

Stand-alone economic or commercial harm. Products can cause economic harm without causing any kind of physical harm to persons or to property. For example, buyer of a grain storage tank may be compelled to expend money in purchasing a new tank when the tank develops cracks. The purchaser of engines for a ship may be required to pay damages to shippers whose goods are delayed when the engines function poorly. These are important products cases, but because they involve economic rather than physical harm, courts usually subject them to special rules, limiting liability according to the contract between buyer and seller. That puts commercial harm cases beyond the scope of this chapter because it excludes both strict tort liability and negligence claims, leaving only the plaintiff's claim under the contract itself and subject to its limitations.[19]

However, some claims for economic loss result directly from physical harms to persons. That is so with wrongful death claims—the survivors are suing for their economic losses, not for their own physical injury—and with claims by the states for recompense from tobacco companies for their expenses in dealing with individual citizens injured by smoking. In these cases physical injury is the essence of the claim, even though the claim is in form a claim for economic loss. Consequently, such claims should be treated under the rules for physical injury cases.

§ 353. Development, Rationales, and Decline of Strict Products Liability

The Early Development and the Privity Rule

The privity requirement. The steps that brought about a measure of

19. East River Steamship Corp., v. Transamerica Delaval, Inc. 476 U.S. 858, 106 S.Ct. 2295, 90 L.Ed.2d 865 (1986) (ship's engines); Seely v. White Motor Co., 63 Cal.2d 9, 45 Cal.Rptr. 17, 403 P.2d 145 (Cal.1965); Moorman Mfg. Co. v. National Tank Co., 91 Ill.2d 69, 61 Ill.Dec. 746, 435 N.E.2d 443 (1982) (grain storage tank). Economic loss is the characteristic problem discussed in Part IV of this book. There are some exceptions. Plaintiffs usually recover their economic losses for asbestos cleanup costs, even though the asbestos has caused no injury. See Shooshanian v. Wagner, 672 P.2d 455 (Alaska 1983); 80 South Eighth St. Ltd. Partnership v. Carey–Canada, Inc., 486 N.W.2d 393 (Minn.1992); Northridge Co. v. W.R. Grace and Co., 162 Wis.2d 918, 471 N.W.2d 179 (1991) (on the theory that physical harm was caused to property by minute asbestos particles).

strict liability for defective products have been traced well and often.[1] In brief, they begin with *Winterbottom v. Wright*,[2] a decision of an English court in 1842 holding that a negligent manufacturer was definitely *not* subject to liability for a defective product when the injured victim was not the person who had purchased the product. If the plaintiff was not in contractual privity with the defendant, he had no claim. The privity requirement continued to protect negligent manufacturers until well into the 20th century,[3] with exceptions allowing recovery when the manufacturer was guilty of fraud or misrepresentation or dangerous mislabeling and also when the product itself was inherently or intrinsically dangerous.[4]

MacPherson v. Buick Motor Co. Judge Cardozo substantially abolished the privity rule for negligence cases in the famous *MacPherson* case, decided in 1916. In that case a wheel on the plaintiff's new car collapsed and the plaintiff was injured. The plaintiff was not in privity with the manufacturer—he had purchased the car from a retailer, not from the manufacturer—but Judge Cardozo permitted his claim against the manufacturer to proceed. Imminent, inherent, or intrinsic danger was no longer required to avoid the privity limitation. "If [the manufacturer] is negligent where danger is to be foreseen, a liability will follow."[5] Over the years, other courts came to accept *MacPherson*.

Limits of MacPherson and development of implied warranties. After *MacPherson*, injured plaintiffs could recover against manufacturers for negligence, but negligence of a manufacturer or even a retailer remained difficult to prove. To avoid this difficulty, plaintiffs sometimes sued for breach of express warranty. If breach were established, the defendant would have been liable in contract without proof of fault. Few manufacturers expressly guarantee that the product will produce no injury, so plaintiffs began to urge that the sale of goods *implied* a warranty. As ultimately codified, a sale of goods impliedly carried a warranty that the goods were merchantable, that is, that they were what they seemed to be and fit for the ordinary purposes for which such goods were sold. Likewise, if the seller knew of particular purposes of the buyer, the seller impliedly warranted them to be fit for those purposes as well. Implied warranties were codified as rules of law in the the Uniform Sales Act and

§ 353

1. David Owen, Products Liability Law Restated, 49 S.C.L. Rev. 273 (1998); William L. Prosser, The Assault upon the Citadel (Strict Liability to the Consumer), 69 Yale L. J. 1099 (1960); William L. Prosser, The Fall of the Citadel (Strict Liability to the Consumer), 50 Minn. L. Rev. 791 (1966); 1 M. Stuart Madden, Products Liability § 1.2 (2d ed. 1988).

2. Winterbottom v. Wright, 10 M. & W. 109, 152 Eng. Rep. 402 (Exch. Pl. 1842). Later, *Winterbottom* could be perceived to turn on nonfeasance more than on privity. See § 321.

3. See, e.g., Losee v. Clute, 51 N.Y. 494 (1873) (defendant negligently made a boiler and sold it to the plaintiff's neighbor; the plaintiff was injured when it exploded, but the plaintiff had no contractual relationship with the manufacturer-defendant so the privity rule barred recovery); see Field v. Empire Case Goods Co., 179 App.Div. 253, 166 N.Y.S. 509 (1917) (purchase from a retailer, no privity with manufacturer).

4. Thomas v. Winchester, 6 N.Y. 397 (1852) (deadly poison mislabeled creating "imminent danger").

5. MacPherson v. Buick Motor Co., 217 N.Y. 382, 390, 111 N.E. 1050, 1053 (1916).

later in the Uniform Commercial Code. Since an implied warranty claim suggested that the manufacturer had implicitly contracted to provide a reasonably safe product, the plaintiff was not required to prove fault. On the other hand, the privity rule, which had been abolished by *MacPherson* for negligence cases, still applied to bar the express and implied warranty claims except when the plaintiff sued his immediate seller.

The best of both worlds: avoiding the privity rule. For a period, courts developed some special exceptions to the privity rule, allowing the plaintiff who was not in privity to recover on an implied warranty claim against a manufacturer of deleterious food[6] and sometimes of other products intended for intimate bodily use or considered to be in some way especially dangerous. The Uniform Commercial Code went a little further, eliminating the privity requirement for members of the product purchaser's household, so a daughter could recover on warranty if her mother had purchased the product from the defendant. It also provided more liberal options for expanding warranty liability.[7]

Then in 1960, New Jersey rendered a famous decision in *Henningsen v. Bloomfield Motors.*[8] In that case the plaintiff was injured when the steering failed in a new automobile. The court held that the implied warranty extended not only to items like food, but to any item. Neither the absence of privity nor the presence of contractual limitations on the manufacturer's responsibility would bar the claim. A new era seemed to be opening up.

Development of Strict Liability in Tort

Strict liability in tort. The chief problems with strict liability under an implied warranty theory is that the term itself implies a contractual liability with privity limitations. In 1963, this objection was eliminated by the new leading case, *Greenman v. Yuba Power Products.*[9] In *Greenman*, Justice Traynor held that strict liability would be imposed upon manufacturers of defective products. It was to be imposed by courts as a matter of tort law, not by implied warranty as a matter of contract law. Since the claim was now to be perceived as one brought in tort, privity was not required. Furthermore, as it turned out, strict liability in tort also meant that the plaintiff's claim would not be barred by the defendant's contractual disclaimers or limits on liability. Dean Prosser, drafting the Restatement Second of Torts, picked up *Greenman's* idea and incorporated it in a new section, § 402A. It was formally promulgated in 1964 and published in the bound volume in 1965. Section 402A provided

6. Davis v. Van Camp Packing Co., 189 Iowa 775, 176 N.W. 382 (1920) (ptomaine poisoning from canned beans); Jacob E. Decker & Sons, Inc. v. Capps, 139 Tex. 609, 164 S.W.2d 828 (1942) ("implied warranty" imposed by law as a matter of public policy).

7. UCC § 2–318. One option provision allowed anyone to recovery who might be expected to use or be affected by goods sold in breach of warranty, not merely household members, but only in cases of personal injury. Another option allowed claims by corporations and for harms other than personal injury.

8. Henningsen v. Bloomfield Motors, Inc., 32 N.J. 358, 161 A.2d 69 (1960).

9. Greenman v. Yuba Power Prods., Inc., 59 Cal.2d 57, 27 Cal.Rptr. 697, 377 P.2d 897 (1963).

that if a product was defective and the defect caused harm, liability would be imposed upon the manufacturer and distributors, whether or not they were at fault and whether or not they were in privity with the plaintiff. Courts widely adopted § 402A and regarded it as their guide, philosopher, and friend.[10]

Rationales of Strict Liability

The common law in the twentieth century has operated mainly on a fault system. Courts on the whole have struggled to better attain liability for fault and only for fault, by abolishing immunities, for example, or by substituting reasonable care rules for categorical rules of nonliability in the case of landowners. Why did courts take so quickly and happily to strict liability for product defects?

Current thinkers tend to emphasize one of two or three rationales for holding a manufacturer or distributor strictly liable for defective products. These are:

(1) Compensation, loss spreading, or enterprise liability. This line of reasoning holds that manufacturer liability is socially desirable as a means of spreading losses that would be a hardship upon individuals but that can be passed on by enterprises through insurance and increased prices.[11] A different version of enterprise liability emphasizes that strict liability is just in imposing liability for harms that are statistically associated with the enterprise. This view is that the enterprise should "pay its own way." This view is easiest to sustain when safety does not require care by the product user.

(2) Deterrence, greater safety. This view holds that manufacturers will tend to make products safer if strict liability is imposed. This rationale is usually grounded in economic analysis. It is sometimes associated with the idea that liability will require manufacturers of products either to make them safer or to raise prices and that either action would promote safety. Higher prices would promote safety because the higher prices would reflect true costs (including losses resulting from injuries) and buyers, to save money, would often seek cheaper substitutes, which would tend to be safer.[12] A related proposition is that the manufacturer is, or sometimes is, in the best position to weigh risks and utilities and is therefore the "cheapest cost avoider."[13] It has also been suggested that the cost of contracting for appropriate safety and the cost of regulation may be so high

10. A few retained a kind of implied warranty theory that was regarded as largely coincident and congruent with liability under § 402A. See Ex parte Chevron Chem. Co., 720 So.2d 922 (Ala. 1998); Commonwealth v. Johnson Insulation, 425 Mass. 650, 682 N.E.2d 1323 (1997) (also noting the advent of the new Restatement of Products Liability but not passing on its effect on the Massachusetts warranty law).

11. See, e.g., Virgina E. Nolan and Edmund Ursin, Enterprise Liability and the Economic Analysis of Tort Law, 57 Ohio St. L. J. 835 (1996) (one of numerous publications by the authors).

12. See Guido Calabresi, The Costs of Accidents (1970).

13. Guido Calabresi and Jon T. Hirschoff, Toward a Test for Strict Liability in Torts, 81 Yale L. J. 1055 (1972).

that it may be efficient to decide after injury whether the defendant should be liable,[14] which of course is the common law method.

(3) Representation. Manufacturers at least implicitly represent their products as healthy and safe, and consumers are entitled to rely upon that appearance.[15]

A number of other ideas have received less attention.[16] The main ideas—enterprise liability, deterrence or economic efficiency, and justified consumer expectations—all have their supporters and some of them have occasionally been stated by courts, along with some doubtful variations.[17] Most observers believe that none of the strict liability theories is applied across the broad spectrum of tort law and probably not even in cases that are nominally strict liability cases.[18] Most of the rationales are subject to questions, and they have been thoughtfully challenged.[19]

A long time student of products liability, David Owen, has more recently advanced a complex set of ideas about strict products liability, emphasizing freedom and equality.[20] Since costs of products liability will be passed on to the manufacturer's shareholders and to other consumers, their interests must be counted equally with those of injured consumers. That means that an overall regime of strict liability is inappropriate because it fails to respect everyone equally. Injured consumers, too, bear some responsibility in Owen's view. They not only choose products but may contribute to their own injury by the way they use them. Owen concludes that strict liability is not justified for design defects, but that it is definitely justified for product flaws—unintended

14. See William M. Landes and Richard A. Posner, A Positive Economic Analysis of Products Liability, 14 J. LEG. STUDIES 535 (1985).

15. MARSHAL S. SHAPO, THE LAW OF PRODUCTS LIABILITY (3d ed. 1994); William L. Prosser, The Assault upon the Citadel (Strict Liability to the Consumer), 69 YALE L. J. 1099, 1123 (1960).

16. These include the notions that (4) strict liability is justly imposed upon those who inflict non-mutual or nonreciprocal risks upon others, even if they do so innocently; and less philosophically, that (5) the manufacturer of a defective product is probably negligent anyway, so strict liability merely simplifies the process of imposing liability; and (6) that since the retailer would be liable on an implied warranty and if liable would recover indemnity from the manufacturer, the law can properly take a short cut directly to the manufacturer.

17. E.g., Doe v. Miles Laboratories, Inc., Cutter Labs. Div., 927 F.2d 187, 191 (4th Cir.1991) ("the fundamental purpose underlying the theory of strict tort liability is to force hazardous products from the market"); Sternhagen v. Dow Company, 282 Mont. 168, 935 P.2d 1139 (1997) (adopting both enterprise liability and deterrence rationales, along with some minor ideas); Brooks v. Beech Aircraft Corp., 120 N.M. 372, 902 P.2d 54 (1995) (discussing several rationales).

18. See See Gary T. Schwartz, The Beginning and the Possible End of the Rise of Modern American Tort Law 26 GA. L. REV. 601(1992); cf. Robert L. Rabin, A Sociolegal History of the Tobacco Tort Litigation, 44 STAN. L. REV. 853 (1992) (discussing effective limits of tort law). George L. Priest, The Invention of Enterprise Liability: A Critical History of the Intellectual Foundations of Modern Tort Law, 14 J. LEG. STUD. 461 (1985) argues that enterprise liability has been widely influential.

19. See, e.g., Richard Epstein, Products Liability: The Search for the Middle Ground, 56 N.C.L. REV. 643 (1978); David G. Owen, Rethinking the Policies of Strict Products Liability, 33 VAND. L. REV. 681 (1980).

20. David G. Owen, The Moral Foundations of Products Liability Law: Toward First Principles, 68 NOTRE DAME L. REV. 427 (1993).

departures from the product's design. Owen's normative system may also be a good description of the direction in which products liability is moving.

Development and Decline of Strict Liability Theory

As the cases worked out the details of strict liability, many observers began to think that strict liability for design defects, as distinct from occasional product flaws, was wrong in principle. Indeed, many came to believe that the courts were often using the language of strict liability but effectively determining liability on negligence standards. Opponents of strict liability language and strict liability results, along with perennial defendants, gradually developed a critical mass. In 1973, James A. Henderson, Jr., published a strong attack on any kind of judicially imposed liability for design defects.[21] Others, reinforced by Henderson's stream of articles on products liability, added their criticisms.[22] By 1979 the Commerce Department published a "Model Uniform Product Liability Act" as a potential guide to the states and aimed mainly at clarifying and limiting liability.[23] Principally in the 1980s many states passed products liability statutes limiting liability in one regard or another.

In 1998, the American Law Institute published the Restatement Third, Torts: Products Liability. The Products Restatement drops all references to strict products liability. Its view is that courts have mostly come to apply negligence standards in determining design and warning defects, even when they maintained the language of strict liability. The effect, although not the language of the Products Restatement is that strict liability is retained when it comes to product flaws, but negligence or something very much like it, is the test of liability when it comes to design and warning defects. The effect on existing rules and the development of new rules remains largely in the future.

Topic B. Liability for Defective Products

Subtopic 1. Requirement of Defectiveness

§ 354. Requirement of Defect Causing Harm

Requirement of defect. Although some writers have argued that product manufacturers should be liable for harms caused even by perfectly made and designed products,[1] § 402A of the Restatement Second

21. James A. Henderson, Jr., Judicial Review of Manufacturers' Conscious Design Choices: The Limits of Adjudication, 73 Colum. L. Rev. 1531.

22. E.g., James A. Henderson & Aaron D. Twerski, Doctrinal Collapse in Products Liability: The Empty Shell of Failure to Warn, 65 N.Y.U. L. Rev. 265 (1990); Sheila L. Birnbaum, Unmasking the Test for Design Defect: From Negligence [to Warranty] to Strict Liability to Negligence, 33 Vand. L. Rev. 593 (1980); David A. Fischer, Products Liability—Functionally Imposed Strict Liability, 32 Okl. L. Rev. 93 (1979) (arguing for more judicial control); Aaron D. Twerski, Seizing the Middle Ground Between Rules and Standards in Design Defect Litigation: Advancing Directed Verdict Practice in Law of Torts, 57 N.Y.U. L. Rev. 521 (1982) (arguing for more judge-control of decisions).

23. See 44 Fed. Reg. 62714 (1979).

§ 354

1. Virginia E. Nolan and Edmund Ursin, Understanding Enterprise Liability 168 (1995) ("a common law of enterprise liabili-

imposed strict liability only for harm caused by products that were defective and unreasonably dangerous. The Restatement of Products Liability agrees that liability, whether or not it is strict, requires a defect in the product.[2]

Under § 402A, the burden is upon the plaintiff to prove that (a) the defendant was in the business of selling products, (b) he sold or otherwise supplied the product in question, (c) the product was expected to and did reach the plaintiff without substantial change, (d) the product was defective when it left the defendant's hands, and (e) the product's defect was a cause in fact of physical harm to the plaintiff[3] and (f) a proximate or legal cause as well.[4] The more recent Restatement of Products Liability does not use the terminology of either strict liability or negligence, but in effect it requires the same essential elements and adds that in the case of claimed design and warning defects, the risks of harm must be foreseeable.[5]

Danger and negligence. Under § 402A, the plaintiff could show a defect in a product without showing negligence of its manufacturer.[6] The focus, as courts said many times over, is upon the condition of the product, not the act of the defendants.[7] Thus the defendant is liable for a defective product even though he is entirely without fault.[8] At the same time, the fact that a product is dangerous does not render it defective. Knives are not defective merely because they are sharp, nor guns because they propel projectiles.[9] The Restatement tried to capture this idea by saying that the product had to be both unreasonably dangerous and defective.[10] The point of requiring unreasonable danger was not to

ty should dispense with the defect requirement and limit recoverable damages").

2. Restatement of Products Liability § 1.

3. The physical harm requirement has been read to exclude strict liability to a bystander. Pasquale v. Speed Products Eng'g, 166 Ill.2d 337, 654 N.E.2d 1365, 211 Ill.Dec. 314 (1995); contra, allowing such a claim, Walker v. Clark Equipment Co., 320 N.W.2d 561 (Iowa 1982). The physical harm requirement at least eliminates stand-alone economic harm. See § 352.

4. See, e.g., Price v. Blaine Kern Artista, Inc., 111 Nev. 515, 517, 893 P.2d 367, 369 (1995) (legal cause required both in negligence and strict liability); Voss v. Black & Decker Mfg. Co., 59 N.Y.2d 102, 450 N.E.2d 204, 463 N.Y.S.2d 398 (1983). To everyone's confusion, proximate cause issues have at times been treated as defenses. See § 370.

5. Restatement of Products Liability § 1 provides for liability of one engaged in the business of selling or distributing products and a sale or distribution. The same section requires a defect. Sections 2 (b) & (c) require foreseeable risks of harm when the claim is for design or warning defects. In the design defect case, § 2 (b) also requires proof of a reasonable alternative design. See § 361. As to foreseeable users and uses, see § 370.

6. The Restatement of Products Liability also requires a defect, but imposes strict liability in only some of the cases. See § 355.

7. E.g., Lewis v. Coffing Hoist Div., Duff–Norton Co., Inc., 515 Pa. 334, 528 A.2d 590 (1987).

8. Restatement § 402A(2).

9. E.g., Moss v. Crosman Corp., 136 F.3d 1169 (7th Cir.1998); cf. McCarthy v. Olin Corp., 119 F.3d 148 (2d Cir.1997) (Black Talon bullets designed to bend upon impact in order to inflict maximum harm to organs of a person were intended to be dangerous but were not defective).

10. Restatement § 402A, cmt. i. See John W. Wade, On the Nature of Strict Tort Liability for Products, 44 Miss. L. J. 825 (1973). The Restatement of Products Liability uses the term "not reasonably safe" instead of "unreasonably dangerous." See Restatement of Products Liability § 2 (c) & (d).

import negligence thinking; it was rather to insist that risky products were not necessarily defective and that a defect was indeed required.[11]

After the promulgation of § 402A, courts and writers began to think that three types of product defect should be distinguished from one another. These were (1) manufacturing defects or production flaws, (2) design defects, and (3) information or warning defects, also called "marketing" defects.[12] Courts initially attempted to retain the language of strict liability for all these claims, but they increasingly used negligence principles and approaches to decide design and warning defects claims, leaving strict liability to cases of product flaws or manufacturing defects.

§ 355. Defects: Manufacturing, Design, and Marketing Defects

Production flaws or manufacturing defects. A product has a production flaw or manufacturing defect when it disappoints consumer expectations by departing from its intended design.[1] A manufacturing defect—the term means the same as production flaw—is a random failing or imperfection. The defect lies in the production or distribution of the particular item, not in the design of the product line.

Examples of production flaws or manufacturing defects include the soft-drink bottle that explodes because of a microscopic crack in that particular bottle,[2] a blade of an electric saw that shatters because the metals in the blade are not fully bonded together,[3] and food or drink that is contaminated with foreign or dangerous matter.[4] The manufacturer or other distributor may be held strictly liable in such cases for harm caused by the manufacturing defect. For manufacturing defect claims, the product is tested against the consumer's reasonable safety expectations. Consumers reasonably expect that food will not be contaminated, so strict liability is imposed when it is. A major and striking exception to the rule of strict liability for manufacturing defects is that suppliers of

11. Because of the danger of confusion with negligence, California refused to permit the "unreasonably dangerous" phrase in jury instructions. Cronin v. J.B.E. Olson Corp., 8 Cal.3d 121, 104 Cal.Rptr. 433, 501 P.2d 1153 (1972). The requirement that the product be in a "defective condition" was an afterthought, to head off liability for cigarettes and whiskey, see Daniel Givelber, Cigarette Law, 73 Ind. L. J. 867 (1998), but defect has long since been the core of analysis.

12. These categories are now generally recognized. See, e.g., Banks v. ICI Americas, Inc., 264 Ga. 732, 450 S.E.2d 671 (1994).

§ 355

1. See Restatement of Products Liability § 2 (a).

2. See Welge v. Planters Lifesavers Co., 17 F.3d 209 (7th Cir.1994) (permitting inference of some such defect when glass jar of peanuts shattered); Lee v. Crookston Coca-Cola Bottling Co., 290 Minn. 321, 188 N.W.2d 426 (1971) (inferring some such defect).

3. Van Deusen v. Norton Co., 204 A.D.2d 867, 612 N.Y.S.2d 464 (1994).

4. E.g., Jackson v. Nestle-Beich, Inc., 147 Ill.2d 408, 168 Ill.Dec. 147, 589 N.E.2d 547 (1992); Restatement of Products Liability § 7.

blood and blood products contaminated by viruses are universally protected against strict liability both by courts[5] and by legislatures.[6]

Blood cases aside, the defendant is subject to liability for manufacturing defects even though he has exercised the utmost care. The defect in manufacturing flaw cases can be determined with relative ease because, as often observed, the defect can be judged by comparing the product to its intended design.[7] The defect in manufacturing flaw cases also justifies strict liability most readily because the flawed product violates the intention of both the manufacturer and the consumer to sell and buy a standardized product with standard value, utility, and safety features.[8]

Design defects. In contrast to the manufacturing defect that unintentionally appears in isolated or occasional product items, a design defect occurs when the intended design of the product line itself is inadequate and needlessly dangerous.[9] If an automobile is designed in an unsafe and defective way, the entire product line is defective, so the potential for liability in design defect cases can be very great indeed.

"Design" includes chemical formulations and natural, inherent characteristics of a product like asbestos.[10] Prescription drugs that risk cancer when others drugs could provide the same benefit with less risk are defectively designed.[11] Badly conceived products that carry needless danger are designed defectively. For example, a powered machine furnished without a readily available safety device,[12] an off-road vehicle with a roll-bar that doesn't protect against end-over-end rolls,[13] and an electric pot that cooks liquid hot enough to destroy a child's skin for a lifetime but isn't equipped with a lockable lid[14] are all defectively designed products.

The design defect, like the product flaw, may result from negligence, but under the rule of Restatement § 402A and many cases that followed it, the liability was said to be strict. The plaintiff was thus not required to prove negligence. As will appear, however, courts have now generally adopted a risk-utility test to determine whether a harmful design is also a defective design.[15] When a risk-utility test is applied, the courts seem to

5. Merck & Co. v. Kidd, 242 F.2d 592 (6th Cir.1957); see Restatement of Products Liability § 19 (c), and cmt. c.

6. E.g. LA. STAT. ANN. § 9:2797; N.H. STATS. ANN. § 507:8–b; 42 PA. CONSOL. STATS. ANN. § 8333.

7. E.g., Dart v. Wiebe Mfg., Inc., 147 Ariz. 242, 709 P.2d 876 (1985).

8. David G. Owen, The Moral Foundations of Products Liability Law: Toward First Principles, 68 NOTRE DAME L. REV. 427, 467 (1993). Owen also supports strict liability for flaws because the manufacturer has the sole power of control over flaws, even if they are unavoidable. See Id. at 473–74.

9. The tests for design defect require special attention below. See §§ 356 & 357.

10. E.g., Adkins v. GAF Corp., 923 F.2d 1225 (6th Cir.1991) (design defect in asbestos).

11. E.g., Brochu v. Ortho Pharm. Corp., 642 F.2d 652 (1st Cir.1981).

12. E.g., Knitz v. Minster Mach. Co., 69 Ohio St.2d 460, 432 N.E.2d 814 (1982).

13. Leichtamer v. American Motors Corp., 67 Ohio St.2d 456, 424 N.E.2d 568 (1981). Other crashworthiness or enhanced injury cases are considered in § 370.

14. Moulton v. Rival Co., 116 F.3d 22 (1st Cir.1997).

15. Adoption of risk utility test: § 357.

be requiring negligence or at least some similar species of fault. The point is controversial, but the Restatement of Products Liability adopts the risk-utility test of defectiveness and discards the strict liability way of looking at design defects.[16]

Warning and information defects. Some products are reasonably safe and not defective if they are accompanied by a warning of their dangers or by information needed to use them safely. Those same products may become unreasonably dangerous and defective if no information explains their use or warns of their dangers. Such products suffer from information or warning defects. For example, it is perfectly reasonable to market full-strength glucose, but since it is dangerous to babies unless diluted, the manufacturer should not market it in a baby bottle with a nipple, or if it does, must give parents a warning to dilute it.[17]

§ 356. Consumer Expectation Test of Product Defect and the Problem of Obvious Danger

Adoption and Application of the Test

Consumer expectation test under § 402A. The test of defectiveness under § 402A was the consumer expectation test. The product was defective if, considering its reasonably foreseeable use, it left the seller's hands in an unreasonably dangerous condition "not contemplated by the ultimate consumer."[1] For example, consumers rightfully expect that food will not be contaminated with foreign matter[2] or even with some inappropriate and dangerous part of the food item such as a shell in pecan candy.[3] The consumer expectation test may work best in cases like these, involving product flaws rather than products with bad designs. Many courts have adopted and applied the consumer expectation test, both in breach of warranty[4] and in strict tort liability cases.[5] Some allow the plaintiff to use a risk-utility test if the consumer expectation test does not show a defect.[6] Others use the consumer's expectations, not as a test, but as only one factor among several used to determine a product's defectiveness.[7]

16. Restatement of Products Liability § 2 (b).

17. Ross Labs., Div. of Abbott Labs. v. Thies, 725 P.2d 1076, 79 A.L.R.4th 265 (Alaska 1986).

§ 356

1. Restatement § 402A, cmt. g.

2. Restatement of Products Liability § 7.

3. Jackson v. Nestle–Beich, Inc., 147 Ill.2d 408, 168 Ill.Dec. 147, 589 N.E.2d 547 (1992); Goodman v. Wenco Foods, Inc., 333 N.C. 1, 423 S.E.2d 444 (1992) (on breach of warranty theory, foreign-natural distinction relevant on issue of consumer expectations but is not controlling); Restatement of Products Liability § 7, cmt. b. Contra: Mexicali Rose v. Superior Court, 1 Cal.4th 617, 4 Cal.Rptr.2d 145, 822 P.2d 1292 (1992) (one-inch chicken bone in chicken enchilada was natural to the product, no strict liability).

4. Denny v. Ford Motor Co., 87 N.Y.2d 248, 662 N.E.2d 730, 639 N.Y.S.2d 250 (1995).

5. E.g., Potter v. Chicago Pneumatic Tool Co., 241 Conn. 199, 694 A.2d 1319 (1997) (with supplemental risk-utility test in some cases).

6. E.g., Barker v. Lull Eng'g Co., 20 Cal.3d 413, 143 Cal.Rptr. 225, 573 P.2d 443 (1978).

7. American Tobacco Co., Inc. v. Grinnell, 951 S.W.2d 420 (Tex.1997).

Application of the test. The consumer expectation test reflects the contract side of strict liability, derived from its warranty history.[8] It may also reflect the fact that manufacturers make a good many representations about their products, sometimes directly, and sometimes by the product's appearance or by soothing words designed to inspire confidence.[9] The test has worked especially well in the case of non-obvious product flaws, as distinct from design defects. If the grocer displays cartons of milk, the buyer has every reason to think she is buying milk and not milk with human toes in it. The seller in turn knows the buyer's expectation. Both parties understand that the seller is to provide pure milk, not that he will merely exercise care. Even if the producer could not discover the impurity, this makes liability is appropriate.[10]

Products Restatement's general rejection of the test. The 1998 Restatement of Products Liability rejects any general use of the consumer expectation test, reserving it only for food[11] and to a limited extent used products;[12] in all other cases, the consumer's expectation is merely one factor to consider in determining whether a product is defective.[13] Some commentators have disfavored the Products Restatement on this (and related) points, partly because the consumer expectation test is sometimes regarded as a consumer-favorable test, while its chief rival, the risk-utility test, is regarded as industry-favorable.[14] But as will be seen, either of these tests can assist the plaintiff in some cases and defeat the plaintiff in others.

The Open and Obvious Danger Problem and Other Difficulties with the Consumer Expectation Test

Although many courts have approved and continue to use the consumer expectation test, in the design defect cases they have found several distinct kinds of difficulties with the test.

(1) Vagueness and ambiguity. The detailed structure of the consumer expectation test has not been worked out in the cases and to a large extent it is vague or ambiguous where it is most needed. About all that can be said is that the test may not work so well when safety depends upon complex, scientific, or technical information,[15] and is likely to work

8. Under the UCC, the test is comparable. Goods breach the warranty of merchantability unless they are fit for the ordinary purposes for which the goods are used. See UCC § 2–314.

9. On representational background of products liability, see MARSHAL S. SHAPO, THE LAW OF PRODUCTS LIABILITY § 1.02 and passim (3d ed. 1994).

10. See § 359.

11. Restatement of Products Liability § 7.

12. Restatement of Product Liability § 8.

13. Restatement of Products Liability § 2, cmts. g & h.

14. Marshall S. Shapo., In Search of the Law of Products Liability: The ALI Restatement Project, 48 VAND. L. REV. 631 (1995); Rebecca Korzec, Dashing Consumer Hopes: Strict Products Liability and the Demise of the Consumer Expectations Test 20 B.C. INT'L & COMP. L. REV. 227 (1997); John F. Vargo, The Emperor's New Clothes: The American Law Institute Adorns a "New Cloth" for Section 402A Products Liability Design Defects—A Survey of the States Reveals a Different Weave, 26 U. MEMPHIS L. REV. 493 (1996).

15. See, e.g., Biosera, Inc. v. Forma Scientific, Inc., 941 P.2d 284 (Colo.Ct.App. 1996), aff'd on other grounds, Forma Scientific, Inc. v. Biosera, 960 P.2d 108 (1998).

best when widely-shared, well-defined "everyday experience" leads to somewhat specific safety expectations.[16] A new bridge should not fall when the first car crosses it, but we need no test at all to tell us so.

(2) Overbreadth. The consumer expectation test could also be overbroad according to Dean Keeton.[17] If the test means that any injury consumers would not expect—say an unpredictable reaction to a new drug—demonstrates a product defect, liability would follow from almost all product injuries. Although some advocates prefer this kind of total liability, tort law has never gone that far.

(3) Consumer's knowledge of dangers precluding liability. The consumer expectation test could also foreclose liability for unnecessarily dangerous products if consumers knew of the product's dangerous quality. For example, a cigarette lighter can be made child-resistant, but if consumers do not know that, they understand that children might ignite the lighter and cause fires and burns. The consumer's ignorance of safer designs hardly seems like a good reason to deny liability if a safer design is in fact cheap and useful, but the consumer expectation test has been used in just that way.[18] In the case of tobacco, it is argued that consumers already know that cigarettes are unhealthy, perhaps deadly. Consumers thus do not expect safety, so ordinary cigarettes are not defective under the consumer expectation test.[19] Even when the product is not generally known to be dangerous, the product's dangers may be apparent to the consumer when the product is purchased or used. This is most likely the case when the product is badly or dangerously designed, as where it obviously lacks safety devices. In such cases, courts once thought that the product was not defective under the consumer expectation test and some still do.[20]

The open and obvious nature of the danger is no doubt a factor in determining design defect but not necessarily a conclusive one.[21] It is best applied when the plaintiff can see the nature or structure of the product and that structure is directly related by everyday experience to the danger in question and has full choice whether to confront it. For example, it might make sense to say that the dangers of a convertible automobile are obvious, at least once the consumer envisions an over-

16. See Soule v. General Motors Corp., 8 Cal.4th 548, 34 Cal.Rptr.2d 607, 882 P.2d 298 (1994); Ray v. BIC Corp., 925 S.W.2d 527 (Tenn.1996).

17. See Prosser & Keeton § 99, p. 698.

18. Todd v. Societe Bic, 21 F.3d 1402 (7th Cir.1994).

19. American Tobacco Co., Inc. v. Grinnell, 951 S.W.2d 420 (Tex.1997) (ruling as to marketing or warning defects only; but the addictive qualities of tobacco were not necessarily known and the product may be defective for that reason).

20. Haddix v. Playtex Family Prods. Corp., 138 F.3d 681(7th Cir.1998); Lamke v. Futorian Corp., 709 P.2d 684 (Okla.1985) (allegations of victim of cigarette fire that cigarettes had been treated to make them burn more intensely or longer were insufficient to show consumer expectations were defeated, especially where consumers know that cigarettes can start fires).

21. But see Patricia Marschall, An Obvious Wrong Does Not Make a Right: Manufacturers' Liability for Patently Dangerous Products, 48 N.Y.U. L. Rev. 1065 (1973) (attacking both the rule of law and the factor approach).

turned car,[22] and equally to say that an officer who wears a bullet-resistant vest must recognize the obvious fact that she remains exposed to projectiles in areas not covered by the vest.[23] These are cases in which the consumer need not absorb or synthesize information or make a series of deductions in order to perceive the existence and extent of danger and also cases in which the consumer knows both the nature and extent of the risk.

But some courts have thought that the consumer expectation test would go much further. They believe that the test would bar the plaintiff whose work required her to use a machine that lacked a safety device, because it would be "obvious" that the device was not present. For instance, some courts have said that the operator of a bulldozer not equipped with a canopy or cage would understand the danger that bulldozed trees might fall upon the operator.[24] Courts have also held that workers who did not purchase the dangerous machine and who had little choice but to face its dangers would have no claim if its dangers were open and obvious to the employer or other purchaser.[25] Similarly, children have been denied recovery if the danger was obvious to their parents or the product was safe for the intended adult use.[26]

When coupled with the open and obvious danger rule, the consumer expectations test can defeat sound claims for strict liability. In particular, some products are needlessly dangerous and could be made safe quite cheaply. Workers, children, and bystanders who are injured by products may lack any real choice in facing their dangers. Even if all product-injured people had full information, free choice, and the market power to reject dangerous products, the open and obvious danger rule did nothing to encourage the manufacturer to provide safer products.[27] For this and similar reasons, most courts have rejected any automatic application of the open and obvious danger rule.[28] Instead, the obviousness of the danger in a design defect claim is merely one factor in

22. Delvaux v. Ford Motor Co., 764 F.2d 469 (7th Cir.1985) (danger of a convertible—as a roofless car—is open and obvious, as a matter of law not defective under consumer expectation test).

23. See Linegar v. Armour of Am., Inc., 909 F.2d 1150 (8th Cir.1990); House v. Armour of Am., Inc., 929 P.2d 340, 345 (Utah 1996).

24. Orfield v. International Harvester Co., 535 F.2d 959 (6th Cir.1976).

25. Gray v. Manitowoc Co., Inc., 771 F.2d 866 (5th Cir.1985); Spangler v. Kranco, Inc., 481 F.2d 373 (4th Cir.1973).

26. Brawner v. Liberty Indus., Inc., 573 S.W.2d 376 (Mo.Ct.App.1978); cf. Moss v. Crosman Corp., 136 F.3d 1169 (7th Cir. 1998) (judging obvious danger of air gun by appearances to parent, semble); but cf., Price v. Bic Corp., 142 N.H. 386, 702 A.2d 330 (1997) (product with dangers obvious to adults, the intended users, could nevertheless be defective under a risk-utility test if it was foreseeable that children would use the product).

27. As many courts observed. E.g., Byrns v. Riddell, Inc., 113 Ariz. 264, 550 P.2d 1065 (1976). The same is true when courts permit a warning of the danger, which is usually equivalent to obvious danger, to substitute for a safer product. See Howard Latin, "Good" Warnings, Bad Products, and Cognitive Limitations, 41 U.C.L.A. L. Rev. 1193 (1994).

28. Pike v. Frank G. Hough Co., 2 Cal.3d 465, 467 P.2d 229, 85 Cal.Rptr. 629 (1970) (negligent design claim); Camacho v. Honda Motor Co., Ltd., 741 P.2d 1240 (Co. 1987) (strict liability design defect); Ogletree v. Navistar Int'l Transp. Corp., 269 Ga. 443, 500 S.E.2d 570 (1998) (under risk-utility balancing test).

determining whether a defect exists. Such a view suggested, however, that consumer expectations were only part of the test of liability.

§ 357. The Risk–Utility Test for Design Defects

Adoption of risk-utility test of defect with or without an option to use the consumer expectation test. As the courts and many commentators saw it, the consumer expectation test covered both too much and too little, potentially imposing liability for sound products and excluding liability for needlessly dangerous products.[1] Largely as a result of the work of Page Keeton[2] and John Wade,[3] many courts came to believe that an additional test of strict liability was required. A number of courts have adopted a risk-utility test of defectiveness, especially where the plaintiff alleged a design defect rather than a product flaw.[4] Statutes also sometimes prescribe a risk-utility test.[5] The Restatement of Products Liability has likewise adopted a similar system.[6] Some courts adopt the risk-utility test as one part of a two-part test which allows the plaintiff to show a defect in the product's design if the product fails *either* the risk-utility test *or* the consumer expectation test.[7]

Contents and application of risk-utility test. Under the risk-utility test courts attempt to balance the risks of the product as designed against the costs of making the product safer. Costs of making the product safer include not only the expenditures required but also any loss of product utility. Risks of the product include not only the likelihood of harm but also its magnitude. Dean Wade once listed seven factors and courts have often referred to them for guidance: (1) the usefulness and desirability of the product; (2) probability and magnitude of potential injury; (3) availability of substitutes; (4) manufacturer's

§ 357

1. § 356.

2. Page Keeton, Product Liability and the Meaning of Defect, 5 St. Mary's L. J. 31 (1973); Page Keeton, Manufacturer's Liability: The Meaning of "Defect" in the Manufacture and Design of Products, 20 Syracuse L. Rev. 559 (1969).

3. See, among several articles, John W. Wade, On the Nature of Strict Tort Liability for Products, 44 Miss. L. Rev. 825 (1973).

4. E.g., Warner Fruehauf Trailer Co., Inc. v. Boston, 654 A.2d 1272 (D.C.1995); Barker v. Lull Eng'g Co., 20 Cal.3d 413, 143 Cal.Rptr. 225, 573 P.2d 443 (1978); Barton v. Adams Rental, Inc., 938 P.2d 532 (Colo. 1997); Ogletree v. Navistar Int'l Transp. Corp., 269 Ga. 443, 500 S.E.2d 570 (1998); St. Germain v. Husqvarna Corp., 544 A.2d 1283 (Me.1988); Voss v. Black & Decker Mfg. Co., 59 N.Y.2d 102, 450 N.E.2d 204, 463 N.Y.S.2d 398 (1983); Knitz v. Minster Mach. Co., 69 Ohio St.2d 460, 432 N.E.2d 814 (1982); Ray v. BIC Corp., 925 S.W.2d 527 (Tenn.1996) (Tennessee's "prudent manufacturer" test is a risk-utility test). "Danger-utility" and "cost-benefit" are among the terms referring to risk-utility analysis.

5. N. C. Gen. Stat. § 99B–6 (b) (as with many formulations, listing a number of factors all of which could be subsumed under risk or utility); Ohio Rev. Code Ann. § 2307.7.

6. See Restatement of Products Liability § 2, cmt. a, cmt. f; see David Owen, Products Liability Law Restated, 49 S. C. L. Rev. 273 (1998).

7. See Barker v. Lull Eng'g Co., 20 Cal.3d 413, 143 Cal.Rptr. 225, 573 P.2d 443 (1978), discussed in § 358; Ontai v. Straub Clinic and Hosp., Inc., 66 Haw. 237, 659 P.2d 734 (1983); Soproni v. Polygon Apartment Partners, 137 Wash.2d 319, 971 P.2d 500 (1999). Far less clear are those decisions that attempt to weave a single fabric from both tests, saying, for example, that the consumer expects a reasonable risk-utility balance. See, e.g., Falk v. Keene Corp., 113 Wash.2d 645, 782 P.2d 974 (1989).

ability to eliminate the unsafe character; (5) the user's ability to avoid danger; (6) the user's probable awareness of the danger; and (7) the manufacturer's ability to spread the loss.[8]

Except for the seventh, these factors are essentially the factors routinely considered in determining negligence.[9] Given the use of a risk-utility test, nominal strict liability now appears to most observers to be ordinary negligence liability with the possible exception of extraordinary cases.[10]

The seventh Wade factor, the manufacturer's loss-spreading capacity, does not address risk-utility factors but the overall policy of imposing strict liability. To the extent that the risk-utility approach dissolves strict liability into negligence law, this seventh factor now seems to have little if any relevance.[11] The manufacturer's economic losses or reduction in employment from liability are of course equally irrelevant.

Risk-utility assessments are often straightforward and simple. Suppose a manufacturer produces an industrial press that delivers 60 tons of force. Such a press creates a risk that the operator's hand may be crushed if the press is accidentally activated when the operator is handling material in the press bed. The manufacturer can cheaply eliminate the risk by designing the press so that it can be activated only when the operator presses two separate buttons away from the press area. Courts can easily find that the press is defective under the risk-utility balance because a large reduction in risk can be achieved at a relatively small cost.[12] Conversely, if the risk were low and the cost of avoiding it high, the product would not be defective, and the defendant would not be liable either on a negligence or a "strict liability" theory.[13]

The Products Restatement and the reasonable alternative design requirement. Many courts adopting the risk-utility test also retained the consumer expectation test, allowing the plaintiff to recover if a product defect could be shown under either test.[14] The Restatement of Products

8. John W. Wade, On the Nature of Strict Tort Liability for Products, 44 Miss. L. Rev. 825, 837 (1973). See Restatement of Products Liability § 2, cmt. f.

9. Because they are particular pieces of the risk-utility balance used in negligence cases generally. See §§ 144–146. However, some courts and writers have insisted that the risk-utility test does not import negligence standards. E.g., Dart v. Wiebe Mfg., Inc., 147 Ariz. 242, 709 P.2d 876 (1985).

10. See, e.g., Zaza v. Marquess and Nell, Inc., 144 N.J. 34, 49, 675 A.2d 620, 628 (1996).

11. Cf. Fiorino v. Sears Roebuck & Co., Inc., 309 N.J.Super. 556, 707 A.2d 1053 (1998) (jury should almost never be instructed on the seventh factor). The Products Restatement's discussion of factors, § 2, cmt. f, does not mention the seventh factor.

12. E.g., Knitz v. Minster Mach. Co., 69 Ohio St.2d 460, 432 N.E.2d 814 (1982).

13. See § 360.

14. Ontai v. Straub Clinic and Hosp., Inc., 66 Haw. 237, 659 P.2d 734 (1983); see Lamkin v. Towner, 138 Ill.2d 510, 563 N.E.2d 449, 150 Ill.Dec. 562 (1990) (but window screens that did not prevent child from falling out were not defective under either test). A few courts have attempted to combine the two into a single test. See Price v. BIC Corp., 142 N.H. 386, 702 A.2d 330 (1997) ("Whether a product is dangerous to an extent beyond that which would be contemplated by the ordinary consumer is determined by the jury using a risk-utility balancing test"). In still others, the consumer's lack of expectation of safety (because the danger was open and obvious) may operate to veto liability under a risk-utility test. See Todd v. Societe Bic, S.A., 21

Liability, however, supports the consumer expectation test only with respect to food and in a limited way with used products.[15] For other cases, the consumer expectation test is merely one factor to consider. In design and warning defect claims, the Products Restatement indirectly requires a kind of risk-utility balancing. With limited exceptions, it also requires the plaintiff to show that the manufacturer could have avoided or reduced the danger of the product by adopting a reasonable alternative design.[16]

Similarity to or identity with negligence. After the adoption of the risk-utility test for design defect cases, liability remained strict for product flaws or manufacturing defects, but looked like ordinary negligence liability in the case of design defects. However, depending upon the precise rules adopted, some differences between products liability and negligence liability might remain. For example, in products cases the burden of proof might be shifted to the defendant,[17] rules of evidence might be different,[18] and defenses that applied to negligence claims might be rejected.[19] Products cases could also differ from ordinary negligence cases if the manufacturer could be held liable for unknowable risks in a design.[20] A few states have adopted one or more of these distinguishing rules,[21] but in the main the courts appear to use the risk-utility balance as they do in ordinary negligence cases.

§ 358. Shifting the Burden of Proof in Design Defect Cases

Three states have shifted the burden to the defendant to justify the design of a product once the plaintiff shows that a design feature caused injury.[1] The leading case is *Barker v. Lull Eng'g Co.*[2] The plaintiff there was operating a high-lift industrial loader. The load was high; the loader began to vibrate as if it were about to tip over. The plaintiff scrambled out and was injured by lumber falling from the load. The loader had two design characteristics that made it arguably defective. First, it had no outriggers to steady it; second, it had no protective canopy to shield the operator from objects falling from the load. The court held that the plaintiff could recover if the product was defective under either the

F.3d 1402 (7th Cir.1994); Kirk v. Hanes Corp., 16 F.3d 705 (6th Cir.1994); Cooper v. General Motors Corp., 702 So.2d 428 (Miss. 1997).

15. § 376.

16. Restatement of Products Liability § 2 (b). See § 361.

17. § 358.

18. The defendant's post-injury remedial measures are admitted in some strict liability cases but not in negligence cases. See, e.g., Caprara v. Chrysler Corp., 52 N.Y.2d 114, 417 N.E.2d 545, 436 N.Y.S.2d 251 (1981) ("spirit of strict liability" and desire to aid plaintiff in proof make blanket exclusion in strict liability cases inappropriate).

19. See § 369.

20. § 359.

21. See §§ 358 & 359.

§ 358

1. Caterpillar Tractor Co. v. Beck, 593 P.2d 871 (Alaska 1979); Barker v. Lull Eng'g Co., 20 Cal.3d 413, 143 Cal.Rptr. 225, 573 P.2d 443 (1978); Ontai v. Straub Clinic and Hosp., Inc., 66 Haw. 237, 659 P.2d 734 (1983).

2. Barker v. Lull Eng'g Co., 20 Cal.3d 413, 143 Cal.Rptr. 225, 573 P.2d 443 (1978).

consumer expectation or the risk-utility test. Under the risk-utility test the plaintiff gained an added benefit: once the plaintiff proved that "the product's design proximately caused his injury" the defendant had to prove that the design was justified under a risk-utility approach.

The effect of the *Barker* holding was that the plaintiff was not required to prove that the design could have been made safer at a reasonable cost. It would be up to the defendant to establish the negative. For example, a plaintiff who fell from her seat to the floor of a public bus made a prima facie case against the bus manufacturer by showing that no hand-hold was within reach of her seat.[3]

Where the burden shifting rule is adopted, strict liability under the risk-utility test does indeed differ from negligence under the same test, because the burden of proof is different. Most courts to consider it have rejected this approach, however,[4] as has the Restatement of Products Liability.[5]

§ 359. The Risk–Utility Test and Unknowable and Unavoidable Dangers

The Products Restatement's Fault Requirement in Design Cases

The Restatement of Products Liability. The Restatement of Products Liability effectively adopts a risk-utility test as the sole basis of liability for design defects.[1] Under this rule, liability for design defects can be imposed only if the risk of harm was reasonably foreseeable when the product was distributed. Such a rule necessarily means that if the risk was scientifically unknowable at the time the product was distributed, the manufacturer is not liable for design features that failed to avoid that risk.[2] The substantial effect is that manufacturers are strictly liable for manufacturing flaws and food products, but liable only for negligence in design defect cases.[3]

The Restatement Second's Comment k. The earlier Restatement Second approached the matter differently. It envisioned a rule of strict products liability for defective products generally, but the well-known Comment k provided an exception for unavoidably unsafe products. Manufacturing flaws and warning defects did not obtain Comment k's dispensation. Under Comment k, some courts discarded strict liability for design defects of a product only after a determination in each

3. Campbell v. General Motors Corp., 32 Cal.3d 112, 184 Cal.Rptr. 891, 649 P.2d 224 (1982).

4. E.g., Ray v. BIC Corp., 925 S.W.2d 527 (Tenn.1996) (describing the burden shift as an aberration).

5. See Restatement of Products Liability, § 2 (b) & cmts. c, d & f.

§ 359

1. Restatement of Products Liability § 2.

2. A post-sale duty to warn of risks that were or should have been discovered later is not necessarily foreclosed by this rule. See § 368.

3. See David G. Owen, Defectiveness Restated: Exploding the "Strict" Products Liability Myth, 1996 U. Ill. L. Rev. 743 (1996).

individual case that the particular product was unavoidably unsafe.[4] Others went further by discarding strict liability for all cases of prescription drugs.[5] Either way, the net result was that strict liability was not imposed for unavoidably dangerous products if a proper warning was given.

The Restatement of Products Liability and the special rule for prescription drugs and medical devices. The Products Restatement, by requiring foreseeable harm in all design defect claims, has made Comment k's special rules obsolete. The Products Restatement has also added entirely new provisions for prescription drugs that had been dealt with under the Second Restatement only by Comment k. Recovery is permitted only if the foreseeable risks of such drugs or medical devices are so great in comparison to benefits that a reasonable medical provider would not have prescribed the drug for "any class of patients."[6] Manufacturers remain liable for manufacturing defects (a contaminated drug, for example)[7] and for failure to provide proper warnings to physicians who prescribe the drugs.[8]

Reasonably dangerous and unavoidably dangerous products. No separate rule about unavoidable dangers is required under the Products Restatement. Instead, the question is whether the product is reasonably safe. Although no separate rule about unavoidable danger is required, the fact that danger is unavoidable bears heavily on the question whether a product's risks outweigh its utilities. Knives, guns, alcohol and nicotined tobacco are dangerous by nature—unavoidably dangerous. The same is true with prescription drugs that carry irreducible dangers of adverse side effects. If the utility of these products outweighs these irreducible risks, they are not defective. If dangers outweigh the unavoidable risks, the logic of the risk-utility is that they are defective.[9] They are also defective if they are not accompanied by a feasible and reasonable warning when one is needed.

Unknowable Dangers

The concept of unknowable dangers refers to products that appear to be safe as judged by scientific, medical, or technical knowledge existing at the time the product leaves the manufacturer's hands and after reasonable testing that reveals no reason to investigate further. In

4. See, e.g., Tansy v. Dacomed Corp., 890 P.2d 881 (Okla.1994).

5. Brown v. Superior Court, 44 Cal.3d 1049, 245 Cal.Rptr. 412, 751 P.2d 470 (1988).

6. Restatement of Products Liability § 6(c). See, supporting this provision, Aaron D. Twerski, Inside the Restatement, 24 Pepp. L. Rev. 839 (1997), and questioning it, Teresa Moran Schwartz, The Impact of the New Products Liability Restatement on Prescription Products, 50 Food & Drug. L. J. 399 (1995).

7. Restatement of Products Liability § 6 (b) (1) (prescription drugs). The cases are in accord. E.g., Toner v. Lederle Labs. Div. of Am. Cyanamid Co., 112 Idaho 328, 336, 732 P.2d 297, 305 (1987) Some courts seemingly have been unaware of the distinction, however. See Doe v. Miles Labs., Inc., Cutter Labs. Div., 927 F.2d 187 (4th Cir. 1991).

8. Restatement of Products Liability § 6 (d).

9. The Restatement is not keen on this idea, however. See the discussion of manifestly dangerous designs in § 361.

a formal and logical sense, unknowable danger cases are a subset of unavoidably unsafe products. However, they differ from the classic case of unavoidable danger in one important respect. With the classic unavoidably unsafe product, the risk is known even though it cannot be avoided; because the risk is known, the consumer can and must be warned of it. With the unknowable danger case, the risk is not known and the consumer cannot be warned of it.

New drugs and other new chemical products are the best representatives of this class of cases. These cases arise when a properly tested product appears to be safe and its dangers are discovered only after a period of use in which the plaintiff is injured. The properly tested and approved new drug may provide profound benefits but time may reveal that it also causes serious harm to some users. For example, a newly approved prescription drug may work effectively to relieve debilitating arthritis, but after a period of public use, some consumers using the drug begin to have visual difficulties and some eventually lose all vision. By the time suit is brought, it is clear that the drug created a risk and caused a harm, but at the time the drug was marketed, the manufacturer, after all appropriate investigation, had no knowledge of the danger and no reason to suspect it.[10]

For a period, distinguished commentators argued for strict liability of manufacturers in such cases, either because the product's design was (unknowably) defective or because the manufacturer had not given a warning of the unknowable defect. The idea was that scientific knowledge acquired much later could be legally imputed to the manufacturer and that the risk-utility test would be then be applied as if the manufacturer had known all the risks.[11] That construct preserved strict liability even when the risk-utility test was used. The effect was to place the risks of scientifically unknowable dangers upon the manufacturer rather than upon the afflicted individual.

Since the manufacturer could ordinarily spread the costs among all consumers of the product by charging more for it, the very same people who are themselves at risk for unknown dangers are ultimately the people who pay the costs of those risks. In addition, in the case of unavoidable dangers, a warning can be given to the consumer at risk, but in the case of unknowable dangers, a warning is impossible and the consumer enters into a commercial transaction without knowing the risks. For these reasons, and because the concept of unknowable dangers is soft-edged,[12] strict liability for design defects might be more attractive in the case of unknowable dangers than in the case of classic unavoidable dangers. Some cases antedating the Products Restatement did in fact

10. See Cochran v. Brooke, 243 Or. 89, 409 P.2d 904 (1966) (no liability).

11. See Dart v. Wiebe Mfg., Inc., 147 Ariz. 242, 249, 709 P.2d 876, 883 (1985); Page Keeton, Products Liability—Inadequacy of Information, 48 Tex. L. Rev. 398, 404 (1970); John W. Wade, On the Nature of Strict Tort Liability for Products, 44 Miss. L. J. 825 (1973).

12. See Beshada v. Johns–Manville Prods. Corp., 90 N.J. 191, 447 A.2d 539 (1982) (scientific knowability depends in part on the manufacturer's investment in research).

support strict liability for unknowable dangers in a design or formula of a product, although later decisions or legislation may impair their authority in some instances.[13]

Over the years, however, the tide shifted. Deans Keeton and Wade came to the conclusion that imputing knowledge of unknowable risks was a bad idea.[14] Most decisions now directly or indirectly reject liability for warning defects that cause harms if the risks were unknowable when the product was distributed.[15] The rejection logically applies as well to design defects, and most of the cases, using several different legal devices, reject liability based on design defect claims when the risks are unknowable. In some states, the fact that the risk was unknowable at the time of distribution is an affirmative defense by statute, often associated with the highly ambiguous "state of the art" language.[16] In other instances, courts or legislatures have left the burden upon the plaintiff to prove a knowable risk in the first place.[17] Knowability of the risk is critical in still other cases because it bears on feasibility of design or consumer expectations.[18] Some courts have rejected strict liability for unknowable risks on the assumption that unknowable risks are like unavoidably unsafe products and governed by Comment k and thus call for proof of negligence in the first instance.[19] Finally, some states by statute or judicial decision require proof of a feasible alternative design,[20] a requirement that very largely entails a knowable risk. As already noticed, the Restatement of Products Liability takes a strong stand against liability for scientifically unknowable risks by imposing liability for design or information defects only in the case of foreseeable harm.[21]

The rule against liability for scientifically unknowable risks does not necessarily foreclose all liability. First, the plaintiff may be able to prove

13. E.g., Dart v. Wiebe Mfg., Inc., 147 Ariz. 242, 249, 709 P.2d 876, 883 (1985); Johnson v. Raybestos–Manhattan, Inc., 69 Haw. 287, 740 P.2d 548 (1987); Elmore v. Owens–Illinois, Inc., 673 S.W.2d 434 (Mo. 1984) ; Sternhagen v. Dow Co., 282 Mont. 168, 935 P.2d 1139 (1997).

14. Prosser & Keeton, § 99, p. 697–98, n. 21; John W. Wade, On the Effect in Product Liability of Knowledge Unavailable Prior to Marketing, 58 N.Y.U.L. Rev. 734 (1983) (preferring a negligence approach to design defects, but where strict liability has been adopted, preferring an approach that judges defects in the light of knowledge at the time of distribution).

15. See § 363.

16. § 372.

17. E.g., Leslie v. Cincinnati Sub–Zero Prods., Inc., 961 S.W.2d 799 (Ky.Ct.App. 1998) (state of the art statute merely left the burden where it always was, upon the plaintiff, to prove a knowable risk in the product at the time of distribution). See § 372.

18. See Potter v. Chicago Pneumatic Tool Co., 241 Conn. 199, 694 A.2d 1319 (1997) (reviewing many cases).

19. Ackley v. Wyeth Labs., Inc., 919 F.2d 397 (6th Cir.1990); Cochran v. Brooke, 243 Or. 89, 409 P.2d 904 (1966). As indicated above, Comment k seemed directed only to cases of a known danger, which permitted a warning to the plaintiff, the very thing that could not be given if the danger was unknown.

20. § 361.

21. Restatement of Products Liability § 2 (b) & (c). Comments assert that other means may be used to show a defect, but these turn out not to resemble exceptions. One is a species of res ipsa loquitur, permitting an inference of defect when the "incident" was the kind that ordinarily occurs as a result of a defect. Id., § 3. The other is that a production violating a product safety statute or regulation may be treated as defective. Id., § 4. Each of these has its parallel in ordinary negligence law and neither seems to undercut the foreseeability requirement.

that the risk could have been reasonably understood on the basis of existing knowledge, or that existing knowledge at least would require reasonable manufacturers to investigate further before marketing the product. Second, defendants may come under some duty of care to provide a post-sale warning.[22] And third, as in the case of unavoidably unsafe products, strict liability for manufacturing defects or production flaws is retained even when the manufacturer could not foresee harm from his product.[23] To the extent that the consumer expectation test is applied outside the manufacturing defect cases, strict liability for unknowable risks remains possible there, too.[24]

SUBTOPIC 2. PROVING DESIGN AND FLAW DEFECTS

§ 360. Proving Design Defects: Risks and Utilities of the Product

Burden of proof. Under the risk-utility test, the plaintiff in most states has the burden of proving that the design was defective[1] and that its defective character was a cause in fact[2] as well as a legal cause of the plaintiff's injury.[3]

Manifest defects, statutory violation, and circumstantial evidence. The plaintiff's burden may be easily met if the product is manifestly too risky in the light of its low utility.[4] The plaintiff may also show a defect in the product by showing that its design violated a safety statute as to risks the statute aimed to prevent.[5] Sometimes it is said that a product's dangerous malfunction may itself suffice to show a defect, as where the brakes fail on a new car,[6] but more likely such proof will show a manufacturing, not a design, defect.[7]

22. § 368.

23. Restatement of Products Liability § 2(a).

24. See Ellen Wertheimer, Unknowable Dangers and the Death of Strict Products Liability: The Empire Strikes Back, 60 U. CIN. L. REV. 1183, 1197 (1992).

§ 360

1. E.g., Hayes v. Ariens Co., 391 Mass. 407, 462 N.E.2d 273, 41 A.L.R.4th 1 (1984), overruled on other grounds, Vassallo v. Baxter Healthcare Corp., 428 Mass. 1, 696 N.E.2d 909 (1998); see § 358 for the minority view.

2. E.g., Kearney v. Philip Morris, Inc., 916 F.Supp. 61 (D.Mass.1996) (evidence that a different paper and other design elements in defendant's cigarette would have reduced its capacity to ignite a cotton test fabric did not show that a design change would also have reduced its capacity to ignite a couch covered by thermoplastic materials; summary judgment for defendant).

3. See § 370.

4. Restatement of Products Liability § 2, cmt. e. Likewise, the plaintiff may be defeated if the product's utilities obviously outweigh its risks. E.g., Bravman v. Baxter Healthcare Corp., 984 F.2d 71 (2d Cir.1993) (heart valve implant that had life-prolonging history could not be considered defective merely because it was excessively noisy).

5. See, e.g., Orthopedic Equip. Co. v. Eutsler, 276 F.2d 455, 79 A.L.R.2d 390 (4th Cir. 1960); Restatement of Products Liability § 4. Industrial standards and non-binding governmental standards, though not controlling, may be admissible as evidence bearing on defectiveness. Hansen v. Abrasive Eng'g and Mfg., Inc., 317 Or. 378, 856 P.2d 625 (1993).

6. E.g., Tweedy v. Wright Ford Sales, Inc., 64 Ill.2d 570, 357 N.E.2d 449, 2 Ill. Dec. 282 (1976). See § 362.

7. Cf. Dancy v. Hyster Co., 127 F.3d 649, 653 (8th Cir.1997) ("Initially, we note that this res ipsa loquitur-like doctrine is

Estimates of risks and utilities. In the great majority of cases, the plaintiff must provide evidence from which the trier can reasonably estimate risks of the product and the utilities or advantages that would be lost if it were made safer. That burden does not necessarily mean that the plaintiff must adduce either quantified or expert evidence.[8] Juries will frequently be able to estimate dangers and benefits of a product design based on descriptions of familiar products or familiar kinds of risks. For example, the jury could easily conclude that sharp, protruding, propeller-like blades on a hubcap would be unreasonably dangerous to anyone who might accidentally come into contact with the spinning blades in a vehicular accident or otherwise. Jurors could also conclude that the utility of such blades is virtually zero, at best serving only someone's peculiar aesthetic sense by creating serious risks of harm to others.[9] In such cases, the plaintiff's burden is satisfied without any special testimony about the degree of risk or the lack of utility.

Expert testimony. An expert's quantified or unquantified estimates of the risk, the feasibility of an alternative and safer design,[10] testimony about the benefits of the product, and testimony about costs of obtaining greater safety would all be relevant. An expert's testimony that the defendant's product is unsafe for specific reasons and that safer products are actually available should ordinarily suffice.[11]

A decision[12] of the Supreme Court affecting federal trials has made it difficult for some plaintiffs to get expert testimony admitted on scientific matters. The Court has said that federal trial judges are gatekeepers who must not only make sure that testimony is adequate to support a jury finding but who must also keep out scientific expert testimony altogether unless it adequately reflects scientific methods. Federal courts may consider a number of factors, including whether the methodology behind the testimony is generally accepted in the field, whether it is based upon published and peer reviewed studies, and whether it can be applied to the facts in issue.

Cash costs. Sometimes the cost of greater safety can be spelled out in testimony as cash costs. Evidence showing exceedingly small costs to avoid an occasional horrifying injury may suffice to get the plaintiff past a summary judgment or directed verdict. In the Ford Pinto case,[13] the

ill-suited to cases involving defective design for failure to include a safety device").

8. Restatement of Products Liability § 2, cmt. f recognizes that an expert is not required "in every case," but asserts that an expert will be required in "many" cases. Its illustrations rely heavily upon expert testimony.

9. See Passwaters v. General Motors Corp., 454 F.2d 1270 (8th Cir.1972) (holding evidence of the spinning blades protruding from the hubcap was sufficient).

10. As in Garnsey v. Morbark Indus., Inc., 971 F.Supp. 668 (N.D.N.Y.1997).

11. As in Violette v. Smith and Nephew Dyonics, Inc., 62 F.3d 8 (1st Cir.1995).

12. Daubert v. Merrell Dow Pharm., Inc., 509 U.S. 579, 113 S.Ct. 2786, 125 L.Ed.2d 469 (1993). Kumho Tire Co., Ltd. v. Carmichael, 526 U.S. 137, 119 S.Ct. 1167, 143 L.Ed.2d 238 (1999) went on to hold that the principle was the same when expert testimony was based upon technical knowledge or experience in the field, but that the trial judge might apply different factors or apply them differently.

13. Grimshaw v. Ford Motor Co., 119 Cal.App.3d 757, 174 Cal.Rptr. 348 (1981).

plaintiff was able to show a number of items that could have helped prevent the Pinto's eruption into flames upon a mild impact. Some of the safety improvements would have cost as little as $1.80 per car, and although a number of improvements might have been required to insure safety, the totals seem small in comparison to the terrible death and suffering that Ford risked. In some cases even general testimony that costs of a safety device would have been small has been sufficient.[14] The fact that costs of better safety are small does not establish that the product is defective, because the risk of the product may be even smaller than the costs or the utility of the product may be very great.[15] Testimony about the cost of safety is not the same as testimony about the profits of the manufacturer, which would not normally be admissible except on the issue of punitive damages.[16]

Inferring reasonable costs. Evidence that other products have safer designs should almost always suffice to show that the safer design is feasible, at least in the absence of specialized purposes for the defendant's design.[17] In this respect, the use of safer designs by other manufacturers or by the defendant on other models resembles evidence of custom in an ordinary negligence suit. At the very least, a widespread practice tends to show that the customary practice is feasible, even though the custom does not set a standard of care.[18]

Costs in loss of productive utility. Cash costs are not the only costs associated with getting a safer product. If adding a safety feature to a product reduces the product's capacity to function, that also is a cost. A bullet-proof vest for police officers would protect more of the body if it were a full-length coat, but only at a considerable loss of utility because such a design would restrict movement at the very time agility might be most needed.[19] If industrial machinery can be made safer only by slowing it to half speed, the costs in reduced production may be quite high.[20]

14. Soler v. Castmaster, Div. of H.P.M. Corp., 98 N.J. 137, 484 A.2d 1225 (1984). Conceivably, some cases reporting only general "small cost" testimony may be summarizing more precise evidence.

15. Riley v. Becton Dickinson Vascular Access, Inc., 913 F.Supp. 879, 889 (E.D.Pa. 1995) (harmful product costs $0.78 per unit, arguably safer product costs $1.40 per unit); Beaver v. Howard Miller Clock Co., Inc. 852 F.Supp. 631 (W.D.Mich.1994) (safety strap to stabilish grandfather clock would have cost $1.75 per clock).

16. See Ake v. General Motors Corp., 942 F.Supp. 869 (W.D.N.Y.1996).

17. Restatement of Products Liability § 2, cmt. f acknowledges that evidence of alternative designs already on the market is relevant.

18. See Clarence Morris, Custom and Negligence, 42 Colum. L. Rev. 1147 (1942); §§ 163 & 164.

19. See Linegar v. Armour of Am., Inc., 909 F.2d 1150 (8th Cir.1990).

20. E.g., Bolduc v. Colt's Mfg. Co., Inc., 968 F.Supp. 16 (1997) (decedent killed himself with gun after magazine had been removed; a proposed "magazine disconnect" would have prevented firing while the magazine was removed but that would interfere with the ability of police to fire while reloading; the gun was not defective). Similarly, Black Talon bullets are designed to peel open on impact, cutting and tearing maximum areas of the human body. They can be made safer by making them like ordinary bullets, but since doing maximum damage is the whole point, they have not been regarded as defective, even if they are socially undesirable when sold to the general public. McCarthy v. Olin Corp., 119 F.3d 148 (2d Cir.1997).

Similarly, a safety improvement in some products used in the workplace may impose the cost of extensive re-training and supervision.[21]

Costs in increased risks to others. Still another kind of cost that might attend a product's improvement is the cost of new risks the improvement would introduce.[22] Suppose the defendant manufactures a drug that saves victims of a certain kind of cancer but risks blindness to one person out of one million. The drug could be reformulated to eliminate the risk of blindness, but the reformulation would introduce an even greater risk of total paralysis. In that case, the new drug would be safer for blindness but at the cost of inflicting even more injury upon others. The present drug with its small risk of blindness probably has more utility than the alternative drug with its high risk of total paralysis.

Proving presence or absence of risks. As in ordinary negligence cases, issues about risk fall into two large categories. The first is associated with probability and foreseeability; how likely is it that the product will cause harm? The second is associated with the magnitude of the harm likely to befall a victim if harm in fact results. A risk that has a low probability of occurrence might nevertheless represent a defect in the product if the harm threatened is devastating bodily injury or death.

Courts and juries have routinely made judgments about foreseeability of harm in deciding negligence issues, frequently on the basis of ordinary experience in life and without any special evidence. If the product's design does not create any foreseeable risk of harm, or the plaintiff has failed to persuade judges that harm was foreseeable, the product is not defective under the risk-utility test, even if greater safety was in fact possible.[23] Some decisions have clearly demanded evidence about the magnitude of the risk and the utility of proposed alternatives, although quite possibly those decisions are meant to be nothing more than assessment of the evidence in particular cases.[24] But in some cases the risk is demonstrable; anyone can foresee that harm can result when workers must place their hands in or near moving presses that are not equipped with safety devices. And in other cases the plaintiff may sometimes be able to show both the risk and its foreseeability by proving that similar injuries had occurred before and that the manufacturer knew it.[25]

21. Riley v. Becton Dickinson Vascular Access, Inc., 913 F.Supp. 879, 889 (E.D.Pa. 1995).

22. See Self v. General Motors Corp., 42 Cal.App.3d 1, 8, 116 Cal.Rptr. 575, 579 (1974), overruled on other grounds, Soule v. General Motors Corp., 8 Cal.4th 548, 34 Cal.Rptr.2d 607, 882 P.2d 298 (1994) ("Protection gained against a head-on collision may be at the expense of protection against one that is broadside, for like an army in battle the vehicle can't be uniformly strong at all points and under all conditions").

23. Grzanka v. Pfeifer, 301 N.J.Super. 563, 694 A.2d 295 (1997) (traffic signal's control box was vandalized, disabling signal and resulting in collision; vandalism not shown to be foreseeable, even though a better-protected control box was feasible).

24. Owens v. Allis–Chalmers Corp., 414 Mich. 413, 326 N.W.2d 372 (1982) (forklift without seatbelts turned over and crushed operator; evidence did not reveal magnitude of the risks, judgment for defendant affirmed).

25. Ryan v. KDI Sylvan Pools, Inc., 121 N.J. 276, 579 A.2d 1241 (1990); Laing v.

Evidence that in one year small objects or toys caused eleven choking deaths in small children does not by itself show high probability that such harm will occur; but it is enough to show that brightly colored blocks less than an inch wide are dangerously defective for small children when slightly larger blocks can easily avoid the risk.[26] In some cases the parties can go further and provide actual estimates of probability. The risk of a needle-stick injury with a medical catheter may be demonstrably small, the risk of an AIDS infection from a needle stick even smaller.[27] Sometimes, estimates are not quantified in any formal way and courts can only identify factors that tend to reduce or increase risk. For example, the presence of an effective warning may reduce the risk that would otherwise be imposed by a product, but an ineffective one may not.[28] Likewise, danger may be so obvious that users will be likely to protect themselves, leaving only a small net risk.[29]

The plaintiff is no longer automatically barred in all cases merely because the product's danger is open and obvious. But obviousness of danger bears on the product's risks because a product that is excessively dangerous when its dangers are hidden may be much less dangerous when its dangers are known. Harm is less likely to eventuate if the user is aware of danger and can protect herself. The manufacturer's warnings are likewise relevant as bearing on the user's awareness and ability to avoid danger.[30] So if the manufacturer can expect that people will generally recognize the risk and either avoid it or take feasible safety precautions, the risk may be so low that the product is not defective at all. With common everyday objects whose dangers are not only obvious but well known, courts may even conclude as a matter of policy that liability should be rejected.[31]

§ 361. Proving Design Defects: Reasonable Alternative Design

Putting the Burden upon the Plaintiff to Show Reasonable Alternative Design

The Products Restatement's reasonable alternative design rule. Under the risk-utility analysis, a product is not design-defective unless its

American Honda Motor Co., Inc. 628 So.2d 196 (La.App.1993).

26. Metzgar v. Playskool, Inc., 30 F.3d 459 (3d Cir.1994).

27. Riley v. Becton Dickinson Vascular Access, Inc., 913 F.Supp. 879, 885 (E.D.Pa. 1995) (design of catheter could have been safer but at the loss of some utility and risk was low; summary judgment for defendant).

28. See Warner Fruehauf Trailer Co., Inc. v. Boston, 654 A.2d 1272 (D.C.1995).

29. Beaver v. Howard Miller Clock Co., Inc. 852 F.Supp. 631 (W.D.Mich.1994) (cost of $1.75 to attach a safety strap to a tall grandfather clock to prevent tipover on small children; design not defective in light of obvious danger) (perhaps a dubious application of the principle, but one that may have been compelled by authority).

30. See Warner Fruehauf Trailer Co., Inc. v. Boston, 654 A.2d 1272 (D.C.1995) ("the risk side of the equation is comprised of the danger of death or serious injury presented by the use of a single-cylinder liftgate with no safety backup, less the extent to which that danger might have been reduced by the warning decals routinely placed on the liftgates").

31. Kearney v. Philip Morris, Inc., 916 F.Supp. 61 (D.Mass.1996).

design makes harm reasonably foreseeable.[1] But foreseeability of harm, though necessary, is not sufficient. The Restatement of Products Liability provides that a product is design-defective when the product's "foreseeable risks of harm could have been reduced or avoided by the adoption of a reasonable alternative design" and the failure to adopt the alternative leaves the product "not reasonably safe."[2] More specifically, the existence of a reasonable and safer design does not necessarily prove that the product is defective,[3] but the plaintiff may often be required to prove that a safer alternative design is reasonable. Thus subject to the exceptions listed below, the Products Restatement contemplates that the plaintiff must produce evidence that a safer reasonable alternative design was available.

Exceptions to the requirement; manifestly unreasonable designs. The Products Restatement acknowledges that a reasonable alternative design need not be shown when a defect is shown by circumstantial evidence, where the design violates a safety statute, or where it is manifestly unreasonable.[4] A few cases have said or implied that a product may be so dangerous and so useless that it should not be made at all, even if no alternative exists,[5] and some commentators believe that the potential for such liability should remain. For example, if no alternative exists for asbestos, asbestos is still a very bad product.[6] Although production of addictive and lethal cigarettes might be negligent or worse,[7] it may be difficult to imagine a reasonable alternative design.[8] In a warily subjunctive mood, the Products Restatement recognizes without approval the possibility that the design or constant features of some products may be defective and unsafe even if no alternative design is available.[9]

Proving a reasonable alternative design. The Products Restatement does not specifically allocate the burden of proving a design defect to the plaintiff, but seemingly assumes that the plaintiff has the traditional burden to prove a defect. Given that burden, one might expect that the plaintiff would be required to prove that an alternative design would

§ 361

1. See §§ 359 & 360.

2. Restatement of Products Liability § 2 (b).

3. Slisze v. Stanley–Bostitch, 979 P.2d 317 (Utah. 1999) (nail from pneumatic nailer ricocheted, pierced plaintiff's skull; but fact that the same company produced a safer nailer was not sufficient to show this one was defective).

4. Restatement of Products Liability § 2, cmt. b and § 360, supra.

5. Halphen v. Johns–Manville Sales Corp., 484 So.2d 110 (La.1986) (product unreasonably dangerous per se when the danger-in-fact outweighs the utility of the product, regardless of any other factors); O'Brien v. Muskin Corp., 94 N.J. 169, 185, 463 A.2d 298, 306 (1983). Statutes in both states have since materially affected liability rules.

6. Marshall S. Shapo, in Search of the Law of Products Liability: The ALI Restatement Project, 48 Vand. L. Rev. 631 (1995).

7. See Daniel Givelber, Cigarette Law, 73 Ind. L. J. 867 (1998).

8. Some say, however, that safer cigarettes were possible and actually developed but then suppressed. See Givelber, supra n. 7 at 891.

9. Restatement of Products Liability § 2, cmt. e (a toy pellet gun that can cause harm; if toys shooting soft gel are not alternatives, and court "were to ... deem the capacity to cause injury an egregiously unacceptable quality in a toy ... it could conclude that liability should attach without proof of a reasonable alternative design").

probably have reduced or avoided injury, and that the design was not only theoretically possible but also feasible or reasonable. The last point might seem to require some kind of evidence about the alternative design's costs and utilities. If so, the requirement seems to be rather general because the Products Restatement provides that "the plaintiff is not required to establish with particularity the costs and benefits associated with adoption of the suggested alternative design."[10] In line with this, cases have held the plaintiff's evidence adequate when experts testified, apparently in general terms, that a specific improvement would be safer and could be used without impairing the usefulness of the product or imposing undue costs.[11]

Perhaps the clearest evidence of a reasonable alternative design is evidence that other products already have safer designs. If a car roof is weakly supported and deforms downward into the passenger compartment when a side impact occurs, testimony that other mass-marketed vehicles have stronger roof supports that would have avoided the injury seems to establish prima facie a reasonable alternative design.[12] The defendant's own subsequent design change might also show that other designs are feasible. Evidence of a defendant's subsequent repairs of a dangerous condition is usually excluded in negligence cases, but some decisions have admitted it in strict liability claims.[13] If a reasonable alternative design is to be a required element of the plaintiff's proof, the defendant's own subsequent design changes becomes critically relevant evidence to show that a design change was feasible.

The Products Restatement specifically recognizes that a reasonable alternative design can be established without adducing expert testimony and that the plaintiff need not necessarily build a prototype of the proposed alternative. At the same time, however, it suggests that experts will often be required to establish the nature and feasibility of an alternative design.[14] From the plaintiff's point of view, this could be a serious impediment to recovery. One reason for this is that the cost of expert preparation is likely to drive out smaller claims where the potential recovery is not predictably sufficient to pay the costs of experts. Another is that, in some courts, expert testimony must often be but-

10. Restatement of Products Liability § 2, cmt. f.

11. Soler v. Castmaster, Div. of H.P.M. Corp., 98 N.J. 137, 484 A.2d 1225 (1984). Some courts may be rather more demanding, however. See Smith v. Keller Ladder Co., 275 N.J.Super. 280, 645 A.2d 1269 (1994).

12. Cf. Green v. General Motors Corp., 310 N.J.Super. 507, 709 A.2d 205 (1998) (evidence, including evidence of defendant's earlier, safer design, considered along with other evidence as supporting jury's finding of defect); Restatement of Products Liability § 2, cmt. f (other products already on the market may serve as reasonable alternatives).

13. Ault v. International Harvester Co., 13 Cal.3d 113, 528 P.2d 1148, 117 Cal.Rptr. 812, 74 A.L.R.3d 986 (1974); McFarland v. Bruno Mach. Corp., 68 Ohio St.3d 305, 626 N.E.2d 659 (1994); see also Caprara v. Chrysler Corp., 52 N.Y.2d 114, 417 N.E.2d 545, 436 N.Y.S.2d 251 (1981) (rejecting blanket exclusion). Others have rejected such evidence even in design defect claims. E.g., Kelly v. Crown Equip. Co., 970 F.2d 1273 (3d Cir.1992).

14. Restatement of Products Liability § 2, cmt. f.

tressed by scientific study that is not likely to be available when the issue is one of ordinary engineering principles.[15]

What counts as an alternative design. One of the objections to the requirement of RAD evidence can be meliorated if it we understand "design" broadly to include constant features of the product (and its proffered alternative). The objections can also be meliorated if the court can consider as alternatives not only a modified product but also a substitute product.[16] If a reasonable alternative design means that the product must remain the same except for minor tinkering, there will be few reasonable alternatives, since any substantial modification will result in a new and different, not merely altered product. On the other hand, if a broad conception of the product is permissible, a wide range of safer functional alternatives or substitutes might be safer than the defendant's product.

For example, in the narrow view, asbestos is asbestos; you can't change its design and hence there is no reasonable alternative. But you don't have to characterize a product by its specific name or its chemical compound.[17] The important design characteristic of asbestos is that it furnishes very good insulation. If you characterize asbestos as insulating material, you can find very good substitutes that can easily count as reasonable alternative designs. The Products Restatement recognizes this point. However, adjudication of this point will present some difficulties. If three-wheeled all terrain vehicles are unsafe, probably the plaintiff should be permitted to prove that four-wheeled vehicles could provide a reasonable substitute and would be safer.[18] If the product is "blouses" not "blouses made from the same flammable material used by defendant" the plaintiff can prove a safer alternative, but of course could prove nothing of the sort if the she was required to prove a safer

15. See, refusing to admit expert testimony, Peitzmeier v. Hennessy Indus. Inc., 97 F.3d 293, 297 (8th Cir.1996) ("he has never designed, built, or tested a platform that has been shown to reduce the launch effect of an exploding tire and wheel assembly while adequately supporting the tire and wheel assembly during the tire-changing process" and "not one of Milner's proposed changes to the tire-changing machine has been subjected to peer review"). The supposed importance of publication and peer review is derived from language in Daubert v. Merrell Dow Pharms., Inc., 509 U.S. 579, 113 S.Ct. 2786, 125 L.Ed.2d 469 (1993), discussed in § 360; see also Kumho Tire Co., Ltd. v. Carmichael, ___ U.S. ___, 119 S.Ct. 1167, 143 L.Ed.2d 238 (1999).

16. Cf. Brown v. Superior Court, 44 Cal.3d 1049, 245 Cal.Rptr. 412, 751 P.2d 470 (1988); Restatement of Products Liability § 2, cmt. e.

17. Brown v. Superior Court, 44 Cal.3d 1049, 751 P.2d 470, 245 Cal.Rptr. 412 (1988) ("plaintiff might be able to demonstrate at trial that a particular component of DES rendered it unsafe as a miscarriage preventative and that removal of that component would not have affected the efficacy of the drug. Even if the resulting product, without the damaging component, would bear a name other than DES, it would do no violence to semantics to view it as a 'redesign' of DES. ¶ Or plaintiff might be able to prove that other, less harmful drugs were available to prevent miscarriage; the benefit of such alternate drugs could be weighed against the advantages of DES in making the risk/benefit analysis of Barker.... [D]efendants' attempt to confine the issue to whether there is an 'alternative design' for DES poses the problem in an 'unreasonably narrow' fashion").

18. See Richard L. Cupp, Jr., Defining the Boundaries of "Alternative Design" under the Restatement (Third) of Torts: the Nature and Role of Substitute Products in Design Defect Analysis, 63 Tenn. L. Rev. 329, 348 (1996).

flammable blouse.[19] Courts should be permitted to characterize the product broadly or, much the same thing, to consider substitute products that have similar functions[20] or those that would be accepted by consumers as substitutes.[21]

Objections to the Requirement of RAD Evidence

The reasonable alternative design requirement has been controversial and much-criticized, sometimes on the ground that some products are too dangerous to market even if no alternative is available,[22] sometimes because the requirement reflects a risk-utility approach and rejects liability for unknowable dangers[23] or fails to implement enterprise liability notions.[24]

Other objections to the RAD requirement are much narrower. One is that the need for RAD evidence is case specific. The RAD requirement is a rule of law that limits the inferences to be drawn from evidence before the evidence has been presented. In some cases the plaintiff should be permitted to prove a technically possible alternative design and leave it to the defendant to show that it is too costly or that it suffers from other disutilities. In this view RAD evidence is an important factor in the assessment, but no rule made in advance could appropriately either require or dispense with it in all cases.[25] A variation on this viewpoint emphasizes fairness and efficiency rather than the value of the legal process. In at least some cases, it will make sense and do justice if courts leave it to the defendant to show that cash costs or disutilities of the proposed alternative will be excessive. Defendants will ordinarily be

19. The court in Hollister v. Dayton Hudson Corp., 5 F.Supp.2d 530, (E.D.Mich. 1998) (Michigan law) may have thought that "rayon", not "blouses" was the product; it rejected the plaintiff's claim because she could not prove that, years earlier when the blouse was purchased, some form of rayon was safer.

20. When a product is purchased chiefly for its aesthetic appeal or fashion, that appeal could be considered to be its "function." Toys and games, appealing to senses that are not easily described in terms of function or aesthetics, present special challenges, especially where a degree of danger is part of the attraction for users.

21. See Richard L. Cupp, Jr., Defining the Boundaries of "Alternative Design" Under the Restatement (Third) of Torts: the Nature and Role of Substitute Products in Design Defect Analysis, 63 Tenn. L. Rev. 329, 365 (1996) ("cross-elasticity of demand").

22. Marshall S. Shapo, in Search of the Law of Products Liability: The ALI Restatement Project, 48 Vand. L. Rev. 631, 671 ff. (1995).

23. See Ellen Wertheimer, Unknowable Dangers and the Death of Strict Products Liability: The Empire Strikes Back, 60 U. Cin. L. Rev. 1183, 1243 (1992) ("Like the state of the art doctrine, the alternative feasible design doctrine transforms products liability law into a negligence-based doctrine").

24. Frank J. Vandall, The Restatement (Third) of Torts: Products Liability Section 2(b): The Reasonable Alternative Design Requirement, 61 Tenn. L. Rev. 1407, 1423 (1994) ("the reasonable alternative design requirement, in shifting losses to the consumer, assumes that the consumer is as well-insured as the seller. In truth, about one quarter of consumers lack health insurance").

25. See John F. Vargo, The Emperor's New Clothes: The American Law Institute Adorns a "New Cloth" for Section 402A Products Liability Design Defects—A Survey of the States Reveals a Different Weave, 26 U. Memphis L. Rev. 493, 549 (1996) (risk-utility balancing requires treatment of alternative designs as a factor only); cf. Warner Fruehauf Trailer Co., Inc. v. Boston, 654 A.2d 1272, 1277 (D.C. .. 1995) (risk-utility balancing is case specific).

in a position to produce such evidence with relative ease.[26] Indeed, if the manufacturer is a rational economic actor, he will already have had such information as a part of his design decision process.

Specific defect proof. Perhaps the plaintiff should be required to show a specific defect rather than a reasonable alternative design. Design defect claims are certainly more plausible when the plaintiff can identify the particular defect and less plausible when the plaintiff can only say that the product should somehow have been designed not to cause injury. When the plaintiff can point to specific defects, she can almost always suggest an alternative design. If the claimed defect is that a machine's blades or pulleys keep turning dangerously for minutes after the machine is shut off, the jury does not need evidence to conclude that there is some reasonable way to brake the machine automatically when it is switched off; most people have seen instant braking on kitchen appliances.[27] Unless the defendant comes forward with convincing evidence that costs or other disutilities are significant, it is reasonable enough to conclude that the brakeless machine is defective. It is not necessary to require the plaintiff to invent a new design for the defendant's business.[28]

The Reasonable Alternative Design in the Courts

Critics of the Products Restatement's RAD requirement have asserted that most courts do not support it.[29] The Restatement's Reporters respond by saying some of the cases discarding the requirement actually fall within exceptions recognized by the Restatement.[30] Assessments of the cases are difficult partly because some are less than precise about what they require, and a number touch the issue only tangentially or collaterally.

Several states do support the RAD requirement,[31] but, statutes aside, perhaps not all of them support it to the hilt. The New York decision cited as supporting the RAD requirement actually only required the plaintiff to show that "it was feasible to design the product in a safer manner"[32] a statement that literally falls short of requiring proof about the costs and potential disadvantages of an alternative. Some cases are in line with this narrowed interpretation of the New York requirement, holding that the plaintiff must prove a safer design is feasible but not

26. See Rahmig v. Mosley Mach. Co., Inc., 226 Neb. 423, 462, 412 N.W.2d 56, 81, 75 A.L.R.4th 397 (1987) ("A requirement that a plaintiff prove feasibility, as a part of the plaintiff's burden of proof in a case based on strict liability for design defect, weighs down the plaintiff with the onus to provide evidence of those matters which are usually within the knowledge of the manufacturer, and is restoration of the exact burden to be avoided by the doctrine of strict liability in tort for a product's design defect").

27. Garnsey v. Morbark Indus., Inc., 971 F.Supp. 668 (N.D.N.Y.1997).

28. See Frank J. Vandall, supra n. 24.

29. Frank J. Vandall, supra n. 24.

30. See Restatement of Products Liability § 2, cmt. b.

31. See, e.g., Tex. Civ. Prac. & Rem. Code § 82.005 (a); General Motors Corp. v. Sanchez, 997 S.W.2d 584 (Tex.1999).

32. Voss v. Black & Decker Mfg. Co., 59 N.Y.2d 102, 450 N.E.2d 204, 463 N.Y.S.2d 398 (1983)

requiring evidence about its costs and disadvantages.[33] Perhaps some of the cases requiring RAD evidence were not creating a rule of law but were merely holding that such evidence was necessary on the facts of the particular cases.[34] A good many cases, probably the largest single group, have said that the possibility of a safer design or product is only one of the factors to be considered in making a risk-utility analysis.[35] By treating reasonable alternative design as a factor only and not determinative in itself, these decisions may imply that RAD evidence is not required, and sometimes courts have expressly said that it is not.[36] Two other groups of courts would necessarily reject any flat requirement that the plaintiff prove a reasonable alternative design. Those courts that apply a pure consumer expectation test in design defect cases necessarily reject the requirement,[37] as do those courts that shift the burden of proof to the defendant to justify his design.[38]

§ 362. Proving Manufacturing Defects

The plaintiff who asserts a product flaw or manufacturing defect need not prove that the manufacturer or distributor was negligent. However, the plaintiff must prove by a preponderance of the evidence that (a) the product was defective, (b) at the time it left the defendant's hands, and (c) the product caused harm.

Defect. The plaintiff may show a defect by direct evidence that points to the defect and identifies it as a departure from the defendant's intended design.[1] For example, evidence that parts in a tool had measurements outside the tolerance prescribed by the defendant's own specifications shows a manufacturing defect.[2] Similarly, the plaintiff might show that a hand tool or a scaffolding plank had unintended cracks likely to cause it to break, or that food contained dangerous foreign matter. Such evidence of specific, identified defects might be made by direct observation or through expert testimony.

In many cases, however, the plaintiff seeks to prove a defect circumstantially by evidence that the product malfunctioned or miscarried in a way unlikely to occur if the product had been properly made. Sometimes

33. Dancy v. Hyster Co., 127 F.3d 649 (8th Cir.1997). The *Dancy* court may have imposed a worse requirement for the plaintiff—that an alternative design "actually exists."

34. See Owens v. Allis–Chalmers Corp., 414 Mich. 413, 326 N.W.2d 372 (1982).

35. E.g., Dart v. Wiebe Mfg., Inc., 147 Ariz. 242, 709 P.2d 876 (1985); Banks v. ICI Americas, Inc., 264 Ga. 732, 736, 450 S.E.2d 671, 674 (1994) ("the trier of fact may consider" safer alternative designs)

36. E.g., Potter v. Chicago Pneumatic Tool Co., 241 Conn. 199, 219, 694 A.2d 1319, 1333 (1997); Kallio v. Ford Motor Co., 407 N.W.2d 92 (Minn.1987); cf. Wilson v. Piper Aircraft Corp., 282 Or. 61, 577 P.2d 1322 (1978) (requiring proof on the facts of the case but recognizing others in which no proof would be required).

37. Cf. Rahmig v. Mosley Mach. Co., Inc., 226 Neb. 423, 412 N.W.2d 56, 75 A.L.R.4th 397 (1987) (a consumer expectation case rejecting the RAD requirement).

38. § 358.

§ 362

1. Restatement of Products Liability § 2 (a).

2. McKenzie v. S K Hand Tool Corp., 272 Ill.App.3d 1, 650 N.E.2d 612, 208 Ill. Dec. 918 (1995).

courts say that a mere malfunction does not itself prove a defect.[3] Dozens of other opinions have said that the plaintiff need not prove a specific or identifiable defect but may rely upon circumstantial evidence somewhat analogous to the evidence presented in a good res ipsa loquitur case.[4]

Neither statement is to be taken as a rule of law for all product flaw cases. The effect of a product's malfunction is case-specific because malfunction sometimes tends to show a defect and sometimes not.[5] Evidence that a product miscarries or malfunctions is sufficient to show a manufacturing defect when either expert testimony or common experience teaches that, under the circumstances, the malfunction is probably inconsistent with a properly made product.[6] For instance, if a new tire blows out and causes injury when it is being inflated to normal pressures for the first time, the trier can conclude that a defect was the likely explanation.[7] On the other hand, if the product has been subjected to a number of forces that would cause a well-made product to malfunction, the inference of a product defect is weakened and may disappear altogether.[8] Consequently, the plaintiff must ordinarily show not only a malfunction but must also negate the probability that other forces caused it. The judicial problem is to assess evidence in each case, and close cases can produce results in either direction.[9]

Defect when product left the defendant's hands. The plaintiff may need to negate outside forces affecting the product for another reason. The plaintiff must always present evidence sufficient to show that the defect existed at the time the product left the defendant's hands.[10] That

3. E.g., Sears, Roebuck & Co., Inc. v. Haven Hills Farm, Inc., 395 So.2d 991(Ala.1981) (tire blowout after 30,000 miles on a truck).

4. E.g., Murray v. Farmers Ins. Co., 118 Idaho 224, 796 P.2d 101 (1990); McKenzie v. S K Hand Tool Corp., 272 Ill.App.3d 1, 650 N.E.2d 612, 208 Ill.Dec. 918 (1995); Myrlak v. Port Authority of New York and New Jersey, 157 N.J. 84, 723 A.2d 45 (1999); accord: Restatement of Products Liability § 3.

5. See Christopher H. Hall, Annotation, Strict Products Liability: Product Malfunction or Occurrence of Accident as Evidence of Defect, 65 A.L.R.4th 346 (1989).

6. See, e.g., Murray v. Farmers Ins. Co., 118 Idaho 224, 227, 796 P.2d 101, 104 (1990); ("the product liability plaintiff may rely upon circumstantial evidence, including 'proof of the malfunction of a part for which the manufacturer alone could be responsible, ... or the elimination of other likely causes by satisfactory evidence' "); Anderson v. Chrysler Corp., 184 W.Va. 641, 646, 403 S.E.2d 189, 194 (1991) ("so long as the evidence shows that a malfunction in the product occurred that would not ordinarily happen in the absence of a defect").

7. Colboch v. Uniroyal Tire Co., Inc., 108 Ohio App.3d 448, 670 N.E.2d 1366 (1996). Age of the product alone is not conclusive; it is a matter of assessing the likelihood that a defect, not other forces, caused the harm. See Myrlak v. Port Authority of New York and New Jersey, 157 N.J. 84, 98, 723 A.2d 45, 52 (1999).

8. E.g., Winter v. Brenner Tank, Inc., 926 F.2d 468 (5th Cir.1991) (ladder welded to truck broke, but it could have been weakened over time by impacts, jury verdict for defendant was permissible).

9. *Compare* Kerr v. Corning Glass Works, 284 Minn. 115, 169 N.W.2d 587 (1969) (exploding Pyrex plate could have resulted from use) *with* Lee v. Crookston Coca–Cola Bottling Co., 290 Minn. 321, 188 N.W.2d 426 (1971) (exploding soft-drink bottle, inference of defect permissible).

10. See, e.g., Campbell Soup Co. v. Gates, 319 Ark. 54, 889 S.W.2d 750 (1994). In *Campbell Soup*, the plaintiff ate some soup prepared from a dried package, then discovered it had little worms, which turned out to be the larvae of the Trogoderm beetle. She became ill. The court reasoned that the larvae could have entered at any time after manufacture a month earlier and

can be done by evidence negating any interference with the product. For example, evidence showing that the plaintiff handled a glass jar of peanuts carefully at all times and that it was stored in a safe place in her home tends to show that when the jar shattered in ordinary use its defect must have been present when the defendant made the jar and not introduced later.[11] Expert evidence may also point to the manufacturing process as the source of the defect.[12]

Causation of harm. The existence of a defect when the product left the hands of the defendant often carries with it the reasonable conviction that the defect also caused the harm of which the plaintiff complains, but causation is analytically a separate item and one not to be overlooked. For example, when an automobile bursts into flames in the plaintiff's garage, the circumstances make it plausible to believe the car was defective. But if the owner claims lung damage from the smoke, the mere fact of the malfunction does not prove that damage, much less the amount.[13]

Subtopic 3. Warning Defects

§ 363. Requirement of Warnings

Under the Restatement of Products Liability, a product is defective not only when it suffers from a manufacturing flaw or design defect but also when its manufacturer or distributor fails to provide a reasonable warning for reasonably foreseeable harm.[1]

Strict Liability vs. Negligence

The jurisprudence of strict liability developed under the Restatement Second's § 402A conceived of warning failures not merely as negligence but as grounds for strict liability. The theory was that the product itself was not reasonably safe if it could be made safer by the reasonable addition of warnings or instructions. Since only reasonable warnings were required, however, a failure to warn or instruct claim always had a strong affinity with an ordinary negligence claim. The two theories, strict liability and negligence, would be distinguishable if the

hence dismissed the claim. Apparently no one raised the possibility that if larvae could so easily enter, then the packaging itself might be defective or else that a warning would be required.

11. Welge v. Planters Lifesavers Co., 17 F.3d 209, 210–211 (7th Cir.1994) ("Chicago is not Los Angeles; there were no earthquakes ... Elves may have played ninepins with the jar of peanuts while Welge and Godfrey were sleeping.... [but] [t]he plaintiff in a products liability suit is not required to exclude every possibility, however fantastic or remote, that the defect ... was caused by someone other than one of the defendants").

12. Van Deusen v. Norton Co., 204 A.D.2d 867, 612 N.Y.S.2d 464 (1994) (parts of power saw improperly bonded).

13. Ford Motor Co. v. Reed, 689 N.E.2d 751 (Ind.Ct.App.1997) (but inferring causation largely on the basis of sequence and timing).

§ 363

1. Restatement of Products Liability § 2 (c). In most states, no warning is required for unforeseeable harms. See §§ 359 & 370 (unforeseeable misuse).

manufacturer were required to give warnings about scientifically unknowable dangers, but the cases held overwhelmingly that warnings against unknowable risks are not required.[2] The result is that warning claims gravitated toward a negligence approach even while courts were using the language of strict liability.

Under the Products Liability Restatement, the manufacturer's duty is only to provide reasonable warnings against foreseeable risks of harm. Liability is imposed only if the danger could have been reduced or avoided by the omitted information and if the product without warnings was not reasonably safe.[3] In effect, warning claims are negligence claims,[4] as a number of courts agree.[5] Some courts continue to apply the terminology of strict liability in warning cases,[6] but even so, the actual evidence and analysis usually invokes negligence principles of reasonableness.[7] Accordingly, this chapter does not distinguish between negligence and strict liability in discussing warning duties.

The Role of and Necessity for Warning

The role of warnings and design safety. When a product is unavoidably dangerous, a warning permits the consumer to make informed choices whether to accept the product. When the danger is avoidable, a warning may reduce the risk or magnitude of harm by permitting the consumer to use the product with greater safety.

Some warnings will predictably fail to induce better safety. A warning to a worker not to place hands in the operating area of a machine will predictably fail to protect all workers all of the time because fatigue, repetitious work, and other elements make it almost certain that some workers will be harmed. If a reasonably priced safety device could have been built into the product, the product is defective in design. In such cases, even the very best warning does not remedy the design defect.[8] If no safety device is practicable, on the other hand, a good warning must do the whole job of achieving safety. For example, if an industrial cleaner

2. E.g., Anderson v. Owens–Corning Fiberglas Corp., 53 Cal.3d 987, 810 P.2d 549, 281 Cal.Rptr. 528 (1991); Vassallo v. Baxter Healthcare Corp., 428 Mass. 1, 696 N.E.2d 909 (1998) (prospectively overruling Hayes v. Ariens Co., 391 Mass. 407, 462 N.E.2d 273 (1984)); Bernier v. Raymark Indus., Inc., 516 A.2d 534 (Me.1986); Feldman v. Lederle Labs., 97 N.J. 429, 479 A.2d 374 (1984); see Charles C. Marvel, Annotation, Strict Products Liability: Liability For Failure to Warn as Dependent on Defendant's Knowledge of Danger, 33 A.L.R.4th 368 (1981).

3. Restatement of Products Liability § 2(c).

4. See David G. Owen, Defectiveness Restated: Exploding the "Strict" Products Liability Myth, 1996 U. Ill. L. Rev. 743 (1996).

5. Whitted v. General Motors Corp., 58 F.3d 1200 (7th Cir.1995) (design); Olson v. Prosoco, Inc., 522 N.W.2d 284 (Iowa 1994) (warning defect); Crislip v. TCH Liquidating Co., 52 Ohio St.3d 251, 556 N.E.2d 1177 (1990) (but noting that under the Ohio rule, the defense of contributory negligence is not available in strict liability claims).

6. E.g., Carlin v. Superior Court, 13 Cal.4th 1104, 920 P.2d 1347, 56 Cal.Rptr.2d 162 (1996).

7. See Olson v. Prosoco, Inc., 522 N.W.2d 284, 289 (Iowa 1994).

8. Howard Latin, "Good" Warnings, Bad Products, and Cognitive Limitations, 41 U.C.L.A. L. Rev. 1193 (1994) argues that too many cases have in effect treated warnings as a substitute for reasonably safe design.

can be made safer only by substantially reducing its effective cleaning power but users can easily protect themselves by using rubber gloves, an adequate warning may mean that the product is not defective, although a warning would not suffice if the product's danger could be eliminated without cost or loss of utility.

Necessity of warning against foreseeable risks. The Products Restatement requires warnings only when foreseeable risks make the product "not reasonably safe" without a warning.[9] For two reasons, this formulation of the rule is arguably too narrow. First, even a reasonably safe product might be safer with a reasonable warning. Second, the warning sometimes provides information analogous to that required of a physician in informed consent cases.[10] In the physician cases, some states require physicians to provide all information that would be material to patients.[11] A little authority might support a similar approach in product liability suits for failure to warn.[12] The Products Restatement's formulation rules out any responsibility for warnings that would be material and might lead the consumer to forgo using the product.

Risk-utility analysis. The Restatement of Products Liability subjects warning defect claims to a risk-utility analysis.[13] Under that test, now commonly used in ordinary negligence and in design defect cases, it might seem that warnings would almost always be required, since manufacturers can usually provide them quite cheaply; even a remote risk deserves a line of print on the product label.[14] But it has been argued that there are costs in providing detail in warnings because detail takes time for consumers to read,[15] and because when confronted with too much detail, consumers may ignore all the warnings.[16] If true, that is definitely a cost to be considered, but the information overload claim does not apply to all warning cases, since added detail is not always necessary to improve a warning or to change its misleading characteris-

9. Restatement of Products Liability § 2(c); accord, Young v. Key Pharms., Inc., 130 Wash.2d 160, 922 P.2d 59 (1996) (rejecting the plaintiff's argument that the manufacture of a prescription drug should provide information the prescribing physician would wish to know).

10. § 250.

11. § 251.

12. Davis v. Wyeth Labs., Inc., 399 F.2d 121, 129–130 (9th Cir.1968) ("When, in a particular case, the risk qualitatively (e.g., of death or major disability) as well as quantitatively, on balance with the end sought to be achieved, is such as to call for a true choice judgment, *medical or personal*, the warning must be given") (emphasis added).

13. See Restatement of Products Liability § 2, cmt. i (Subsection (c) on warnings adopts a reasonableness test that parallels Subsection (b), on design defects) and cmt. k (risk-utility balance in allergy cases reflects risk-utility balance used in warnings cases generally).

14. See Ross Labs. Div. of Abbott Labs. v. Thies, 725 P.2d 1076, 79 A.L.R.4th 265 (Alaska 1986).

15. See Cotton v. Buckeye Gas Prods. Co., 840 F.2d 935, 938 (D.C.Cir.1988).

16. James A. Henderson, Jr. & Aaron D. Twerski, Doctrinal Collapse in Products Liability: The Empty Shell of Failure to Warn, 65 N.Y.U. L. Rev. 265, 296 (1990); see also Mark Geistfeld, Inadequate Product Warnings and Causation, 30 U. Mich. J.L. Ref. 309 (1997) (supporting risk-utility analysis in warnings cases, with detailed workout on costs and proposed interrogatories to the jury). The information overload argument has been applied in determining what disclosures are required in securities cases. See TSC Indus., Inc. v. Northway, Inc., 426 U.S. 438, 449, 96 S.Ct. 2126, 2132, 48 L.Ed.2d 757 (1976).

tics. Where information overload is established, however, it raises a genuine risk-utility issue that is quintessentially one that must be determined on the particular facts of individual cases. In most instances a case-by-case decision is required to determine the reasonableness of a warning. Unless the matter is so clear that reasonable people cannot differ, that assessment is for the jury.[17]

Known or obvious risks. One reason a warning may not be required is that the risks involved are either generally known or are obvious to a purchaser or user. One function of a warning is to alert the product user to risks. A warning may not be needed if people already know of the risks. In this respect, the warning problem differs greatly from the design problem. If a manufacturer can make a press that is safe just as cheaply as it can make one that is dangerous, its choice to manufacture the dangerous version is unjustified and the machine is defective, even if its danger is open and obvious.[18] But if the machine as designed is reasonably safe and its unavoidable dangers are known or obvious, the consumer is already warned by her knowledge so that reasonable care does not ordinarily require the manufacturer to provide a separate warning.[19] In the case of simple products, courts sometimes say that there is no duty to warn of obvious danger.[20] The question of obviousness is for the jury if reasonable people can differ.[21] Nevertheless courts have sometimes concluded that risks are obvious as a matter of law because rational thinkers would be able to figure them out.[22] Such an approach may too readily relieve manufacturers of warning obligations. Beyond this, warnings may have another function. They may alert the user to safer alternatives that are far from obvious. "Do not use meat grinder without its safety attachment" not only warns of the obvious danger but informs the user that a safety device is available. In such cases, the fact that danger is obvious does not negate the need for a warning.[23]

17. See Restatement of Products Liability § 2, Illus. 11.

18. See § 356.

19. E.g., Ex parte, Chevron Chem. Co., 720 So.2d 922 (Ala.1998); Caterpillar, Inc. v. Shears, 911 S.W.2d 379 (Tex.1995); Restatement of Products Liability § 2, cmt. j. Although cases may state the rule flatly as a rule of law, it is conceivable that reasonable care would require a warning of generally known or obvious dangers in some cases.

20. Glittenberg v. Doughboy Recreational Indus., 441 Mich. 379, 491 N.W.2d 208 (1992).

21. E.g., Keogh v. W.R. Grasle, Inc., 816 P.2d 1343 (Alaska 1991) (jury found ordinary user would recognize danger of high voltage system, judgment for defendant affirmed); Smith v. Minster Mach. Co., 233 A.D.2d 892, 649 N.Y.S.2d 257 (1996) (obviousness a jury question; summary judgment denied); see Maneely v. General Motors Corp., 108 F.3d 1176 (9th Cir.1997) (stating rule; risk of riding in pickup truck bed was obvious as a matter of law).

22. Maneely v. General Motors Corp., 108 F.3d 1176, 1180 (9th Cir.1997) ("If the public recognizes that traveling in the passenger compartment of an automobile without a seatbelt is dangerous, it only follows as night the day that the public also recognizes that riding in the cargo bed of a pickup, where seatbelts and other occupant packaging are conspicuously absent, presents even greater risks;" "[a]t some point, manufacturers must be relieved of the paternalistic responsibility of warning users of every possible risk that could arise from foreseeable use of their product").

23. See Liriano v. Hobart Corp., 170 F.3d 264 (2d Cir.1999) (Calabresi, J., explaining the two warning functions and why obvious danger does not eliminate the need for the informative warning in certain cases).

The allergy rule. So far as courts adopt a risk-utility analysis in warnings claims, no occasion arises to single out allergy cases for any special rules. The risk-utility test would ask whether the manufacturer should foresee harm and whether the risk of harm was significant enough to require a warning, with whatever costs that entailed. If no harm is foreseeable, then no warning is due. If only a small number of people would suffer minor temporary allergies from a product, it may still be true that no warning is needed. But if a small number would suffer serious harm, reasonableness requires a warning, just as it does when a large number are at risk for less significant harm.

However, beginning with early warranty cases, some courts asserted that a manufacturer need not warn of the risk of allergic or hypersensitive reactions to the product unless such reactions are (a) reasonably foreseeable to (b) an appreciable class of persons.[24] Such a rule violates the risk-utility approach because it makes the size of the threatened group determinative without considering the other elements—the magnitude of threatened harm and the cost of avoiding it. Some cases have rejected the appreciable class rules.[25] The best solution, at least where any kind of negligence or risk-utility approach is adopted, is to drop any purported special rule about allergies. If the risk to the small group is skin irritation for an hour, a warning might not be required, while if the risk is paralysis or death, a warning is almost surely necessary.[26]

§ 364. Adequacy of Warning

Whether warnings are defective because they are inadequate is a question for the jury if evidence would permit reasonable people to differ,[1] but judges often conclude as a matter of law that warnings in a particular case are adequate.[2] Warnings can be defective in several distinct ways under a risk-utility analysis—in factual content, in expression or communication, and in the form or mode of communication.[3]

Adequacy of content and expression. Warnings must contain facts necessary to permit reasonable persons to understand the danger[4] and in some cases how to avoid it.[5] Warnings and instructions for use are not

24. Presbrey v. Gillette Co., 105 Ill. App.3d 1082, 435 N.E.2d 513, 61 Ill.Dec. 816 (1982); Kaempfe v. Lehn & Fink Prods. Corp., 21 A.D.2d 197, 249 N.Y.S.2d 840 (1964); Esborg v.Bailey Drug Co., 61 Wash.2d 347, 378 P.2d 298 (1963). See Marshall S. Shapo, The Law of Products Liability § 8.05[5] (3d ed. 1994).

25. Sterling Drug, Inc. v. Cornish, 370 F.2d 82 (8th Cir.1966); Tomer v. American Home Prods. Corp., 170 Conn. 681, 368 A.2d 35 (1976).

26. Davis v.Wyeth Labs., Inc., 399 F.2d 121 (9th Cir.1968); Simeon v. Doe, 618 So.2d 848 (La.1993) (raw oysters).

§ 364

1. E.g., East Penn Mfg. Co. v. Pineda, 578 A.2d 1113 (D.C. . . 1990).

2. Town of Bridport v. Sterling Clark Lurton Corp., 166 Vt. 304, 693 A.2d 701 (1997).

3. Brochu v. Ortho Pharm. Corp., 642 F.2d 652, 657 (1st Cir.1981).

4. See Fuller v. Chemical Specialties Mfg. Corp., 702 A.2d 1239, 1241 (D.C.1997) (must provide the user of the attendant risks and specific directions for safe use).

5. See Wood v. Old Trapper Taxi, 286 Mont. 18, 952 P.2d 1375 (1997) (manufacturer of radio tower failed to warn against erection without guy wires).

reasonable unless they are of sufficient clarity and also sufficient force and intensity to convey the nature and extent of the risks to a reasonable person.[6] A manufacturer's techniques in promoting the product,[7] inconsistencies or undue qualifications in stating the warning or directions,[8] and depictions of uses that run counter to warnings[9] may each nullify or dilute the warnings provided in printed literature. Unless the warning taken as a whole is so clear and forceful that it overrides the dilutions and inconsistencies, the diluted warning may be quite inadequate.[10] Neither the warning itself nor the marketing style should imply a safety that does not exist.[11] The defect in many warnings is that they are not warnings at all, merely directions. A decal on a child's motor bike that says "no passengers" gives no warning that passengers would be burned.[12] Unless the warning specifies the risk, it may be wholly ineffective, but this point has been overlooked in some cases.[13] When possible harm is severe, quite specific information may be required.[14] A drug warning about possible blood clotting may disguise rather than reveal the possibility of a stroke.[15]

Adequacy of form, location or display. When the warning is addressed to the user, is should be sufficiently conspicuous and so located as to attract the user's attention.[16] Fine print won't do. Neither will a warning in the wrong place.[17] On the other hand, the mere fact that the

6. D'Arienzo v. Clairol, Inc., 125 N.J.Super. 224, 230, 310 A.2d 106, 110 (1973) (warning must be "reasonably calculated to bring home to the reasonably prudent person the nature and extent of the danger"); Martin v. Hacker, 83 N.Y.2d 1, 11, 628 N.E.2d 1308, 1313, 607 N.Y.S.2d 598, 603 (1993) (language of the warning in drug case must be "direct, unequivocal and sufficiently forceful to convey the risk").

7. Incollingo v. Ewing, 444 Pa. 299, 282 A.2d 206 (1971) (drug company's promotion of drug to doctors may have "nullified" its printed warnings).

8. McFadden v. Haritatos, 86 A.D.2d 761, 448 N.Y.S.2d 79 (1982) (prescription drug; warning was diluted by statement that adverse reactions disappear when drug is discontinued).

9. Yamaha Motor Co. v. Arnoult, 114 Nev. 233, 955 P.2d 661 (1998) (manufacturer of ATV warned against "jumping" with vehicles but depicted its use in rough desert terrain).

10. See Martin v. Hacker, 83 N.Y.2d 1, 628 N.E.2d 1308, 607 N.Y.S.2d 598 (1993) (inconsistencies may dilute warning, but whether it is adequate depends upon overall clarity; the force of the warning may be strong enough to outweigh inconsistencies).

11. See Ross Laboratories, a Division of Abbott Laboratories v. Thies, 725 P.2d 1076, 79 A.L.R.4th 265 (Alaska 1986) (undiluted glucose marketed in baby bottle with nipple). Thus lawn darts that can readily pierce a child's skull and enter the brain should not be marketed as toys. See First National Bank of Dwight v. Regent Sports Corp., 803 F.2d 1431 (7th Cir.1986). They are now banned altogether. See 16 C.F.R. § 1306.4 and 16 C.F.R. § 1500.18.

12. Evridge v. American Honda Motor Co., 685 S.W.2d 632 (Tenn.1985).

13. See Davis v. Berwind Corp., 547 Pa. 260, 690 A.2d 186 (1997) (a meat grinder-mixer directed users to keep fingers out of specified areas, but did not warn that the blades continued to revolve for a substantial time after the machine was turned off; the direction to keep fingers out was treated as a full warning, although the plaintiff lost her fingers in attempting to clean the machine after it was off).

14. See Fyssakis v. Knight Equip. Corp., 108 Nev. 212, 826 P.2d 570 (1992) (corrosive cleaner should warn that blindness can result).

15. MacDonald v. Ortho Pharm. Corp., 394 Mass. 131, 475 N.E.2d 65 (1985).

16. Town of Bridport v. Sterling Clark Lurton Corp., 166 Vt. 304, 693 A.2d 701 (1997); D'Arienzo v. Clairol, Inc., 125 N.J.Super. 224, 310 A.2d 106 (1973).

17. Bloxom v. Bloxom, 512 So.2d 839 (La.1987) (Pontiac Firebird must be parked on pavement because its exhaust system

warning could be brighter or bigger does not in itself show that it is inadequate.[18]

English-only warnings. Children, illiterate adults, and adults who read only or mainly a foreign language cannot be warned by an English-only label. In a California case, an aspirin manufacturer targeted Spanish-speaking groups with its Spanish advertising, but its aspirin contained no Spanish warnings that aspirin could cause small children severe neurological damage, blindness, spastic quadriplegia and mental retardation. The court thought that the legislature, by affirmatively requiring warnings in English, negatively implied that no others could be required.[19] A few other cases have gone the other way, considering that when illiterate users are foreseeable, symbols or pictographs may be necessary in the warning.[20]

Statutes. Increasingly, statutes have required warnings and have prescribed either content or expression. Sometimes the statutory requirement is taken to mean that no additional information can be required by reasonable care rules. When the statute is a valid federal statute, it may impose the same result because it preempts state law altogether and makes federal law the only law on point. The federal statute requiring warnings on cigarette packages is like this. It preempts state tort law that would require a more adequate warning.[21] In broader perspective, the question is whether tort obligations should be decided exclusively by administrative regulations or statutes where they exist.[22]

§ 365. Prescription Drugs, Medical Device Warnings

Prescription drugs, medical devices. Courts almost always hold that a prescription drug manufacturer's warning to the doctor who prescribes a drug is sufficient to warn the doctor's patient as well. If the doctor fails to inform the patient of the risks, the patient has a claim against the doctor, but not against the manufacturer of the drug.[1] This is usually referred to as the learned intermediary doctrine, and it is usually

will ignite leaves or grass, but the only warning was burried in the 100-page owner's manual); cf. Payne v. Soft Sheen Prods., Inc., 486 A.2d 712, 58 A.L.R.4th 15 (D.C. 1985) (chemicals for hair treatment in multiple steps provided warning of burns only at the end of the instructions, after the instructions had guided operator through each step).

18. See General Motors Corp. v. Saenz, 873 S.W.2d 353 (Tex.1993).

19. Ramirez v. Plough, Inc., 6 Cal.4th 539, 25 Cal.Rptr.2d 97, 863 P.2d 167 (1993).

20. Hubbard-Hall Chem. Co. v. Silverman, 340 F.2d 402 (1st Cir.1965) (suggesting skull and crossbones on deadly poison used by agricultural workers); Campos v. Firestone Tire & Rubber Co., 98 N.J. 198, 485 A.2d 305 (1984) ("In view of the unskilled or semi-skilled nature of the work and the existence of many in the work force who do not read English, warnings in the form of symbols might have been appropriate"). See Marjorie A. Caner, Annotation, Products Liability: Failure to Provide Product Warning or Instruction in Foreign Language or to Use Universally Accepted Pictographs or Symbols, 27 A.L.R.5th 697 (1995).

21. Cipollone v. Liggett Group, Inc., 505 U.S. 504, 112 S.Ct. 2608, 120 L.Ed.2d 407 (1992).

22. See § 373.

§ 365

1. E.g., Stone v. Smith, Kline & French Labs., 447 So.2d 1301 (Ala.1984); Humes v. Clinton, 246 Kan. 590, 792 P.2d 1032 (1990) Restatement of Products Liability § 6 (d). Although the doctor is not chronologically an intermediary between pharmacist and patient, the doctor is the final and

conceived of as a rule of law rather than a matter of balancing risks and utilities in each case.[2] The rule applies not only to drugs but also to medical devices and bodily implants that are usually accompanied by medical advice and supervision.[3]

Reasons for the learned intermediary rule. Courts have asserted several reasons for the learned intermediary rule.[4] They have said for example that warnings to the consumer are not feasible, that warnings would interfere with the doctor-patient relationship, or that they would drive some patients to hysteria. The central reason, however, is the belief that the manufacturer can reasonably rely upon the physician to pass on the warnings and correspondingly that the patient relies upon the physician, not the manufacturer.[5]

Critics have attacked these reasons. Most significantly, Professor Teresa Moran Schwartz has pointed to evidence that doctors do not pass on sufficient information about drugs, in particular about side effects,[6] so manufacturers may not be so reasonable in relying upon learned but busy intermediaries. Correspondingly, patients need more information about dangers they might avoid.

Exceptions to the learned intermediary doctrine. Three possible exceptions to the learned intermediary rule have been advanced. The first is that a direct warning to the patient, if feasible, is required in the case of mass inoculations and other instances of unsupervised dispensation of prescription drugs. This idea is pretty well accepted.[7]

Second, with birth control prescriptions and devices, a few cases have held that a warning must be given to the patient directly.[8] This accords with the FDA treatment of birth control prescriptions, which

only decision-maker about the choice of drug. Hence the pharmacist is traditionally not liable for failure to warn about inherent dangers of the drug. See Coyle v. Richardson–Merrell, Inc., 526 Pa. 208, 584 A.2d 1383 (1991); § 251.

2. See Richard C. Ausness, Learned Intermediaries and Sophisticated Users: Encouraging the Use of Intermediaries to Transmit Product Safety Information, 46 Syracuse L. Rev. 1185 (1996).

3. E.g., Craft v. Peebles, 78 Hawai'i 287, 893 P.2d 138 (1995) (breast implant).

4. See, summarizing these reasons, Teresa Moran Schwartz, Consumer-directed Prescription Drug Advertising and the Learned Intermediary Rule, 46 Food Drug Cosm. L.J. 829 (1991).

5. See MacDonald v. Ortho Pharm. Corp., 394 Mass. 131, 136, 475 N.E.2d 65, 68 (1985). Sometimes courts say the physician's failure to pass on the warning was a superseding cause, see, e.g., Ferrara v. Berlex Labs., Inc., 732 F.Supp. 552 (E.D.Pa. 1990) (doctor's failure was "the causal link"), but the underlying point seems to be a judgment about the manufacturer's reasonableness, not about causation.

6. Teresa Moran Schwartz, Consumer-directed Prescription Drug Advertising and the Learned Intermediary Rule, 46 Food Drug Cosm. L.J. 829, 830 (1991).

7. Restatement of Products Liability, § 6, Cmt. e. But cf. Macias v. State, 10 Cal.4th 844, 42 Cal.Rptr.2d 592, 897 P.2d 530 (1995) (manufacturers of poison sold to state for widespread spraying by helicopter had no duty to correct state's widely publicized misinformation about dangers).

8. MacDonald v. Ortho Pharm. Corp., 394 Mass. 131, 475 N.E.2d 65 (1985) appears to be the only decision of a state's highest court. See also Hill v. Searle Labs., Div. of Searle Pharms., Inc., 884 F.2d 1064 (8th Cir.1989) (IUD; no real individualized medical judgment with many birth control prescriptions, hence no learned intermediary rule; predicting Arkansas law); Diane Schmauder Kane, Annotation, Construction and Application of Learned-intermediary Doctrine, 57 A.L.R.5th 1 (1998).

requires the manufacturer to include warnings in a package insert in or with each prescription intended to reach a user.[9] Perhaps courts that acknowledge this exception would apply it in any case in which a warning directly to the consumer is required by statute or regulation. Oklahoma has taken this view, holding that the learned intermediary rule does not bar a claim for failure to warn the consumer directly of the overdose dangers of a nicotine patch.[10] But other courts hold that a warning to the physicians alone is sufficient, even though physicians may routinely fail to discuss the dangers of birth control measures with patients individually.[11]

Third, some writers have argued that when prescription drugs are advertised directly to the consumer, direct warnings must be given in the same medium.[12] At this writing, a few cases have noted the possibility of such a warning obligation but have not applied it.[13]

§ 366. Warning through Sophisticated Users and Other Intermediaries

In many cases, the manufacturer or distributor sells goods to people in the trade who work with such goods regularly or who for other reasons can be expected to know their dangers. Because the danger is already known, a warning for the buyer's protection may not be required at all. In many cases, however, the goods, although sold to buyers in the trade, will foreseeably be used by or affect others who may not be knowledgeable. When it is foreseeable that other, less sophisticated users may be endangered, the questions are whether the manufacturer can omit warnings altogether because of the immediate buyer's sophistication, and whether, if a warning is required, it must be made directly to those who will be endangered.

Raw Materials and Goods Sold in Bulk

Raw materials and component parts. Sellers of raw materials and component parts, who expect their buyers to fashion a product from such materials, are subject to liability if they supply defective materials or parts.[1] However, such sellers are seldom required to warn ultimate users of dangers that may result from the way their raw materials or compo-

9. 21 C.F.R. § 310.501.

10. Edwards v. Basel Pharms., Div. of Ciba–Geigy Corp., 933 P.2d 298 (Okla. 1997).

11. Martin v. Ortho Pharm. Corp., 169 Ill.2d 234, 661 N.E.2d 352, 214 Ill.Dec. 498 (1996); see West v. G.D. Searle & Co., 317 Ark. 525, 879 S.W.2d 412 (1994) (stating that no direct warning was given but also stating that the defendant complied with the regulatory requirements).

12. See Teresa Moran Schwartz, Consumer–Directed Prescription Drug Advertising and the Learned Intermediary Rule, 46 Food Drug Cosm. L.J. 829 (1991); Barbara J. Tyler, Robert A. Cooper, Blinded by the Hype: Shifting the Burden When Manufacturers Engage in Direct to Consumer Advertising of Prescription Drugs, 21 Vt. L. Rev. 1073 (1997).

13. Garside v. Osco Drug, Inc., 764 F.Supp. 208, 211 (D.Mass.1991), rev'd on other grounds, 976 F.2d 77 (1st Cir.1992); The idea was flatly rejected in Perez v. Wyeth Laboratories, Inc., 313 N.J.Super. 646, 713 A.2d 588 (N.J.Super.L.1997).

§ 366

1. Restatement of Products Liability § 5.

nent parts are integrated into a final product.[2] For example, a manufacturer, A, who supplies nondefective chemicals to B who in turns uses them to manufacture silicone breast implants, is not liable to C, the ultimate purchaser who is injured because the material is allegedly inappropriate for implantation in the human body,[3] unless perhaps the manufacture of silicone knows the use to which the material will be put and knows it to be unsuited.[4]

Bulk materials, sophisticated buyers. Sellers of bulk materials to intermediaries are seldom required to warn end-users of the product's dangers. Bulk materials include items like natural or propane gas, shipped in pipeline to a local distributor, or bulk tanks of chemicals. When sale to an intermediary is in bulk, without packaged objects, a warning to the end-user is difficult to provide.[5] The difficulty bears on the seller's reasonableness in failing to provide a warning. But perhaps the more important point is that the bulk supplier can ordinarily expect that his purchaser is a sophisticated user who knows the dangers and will pass on warnings about the product's dangers. Where that is in fact the case, courts say that warnings to the buyer-intermediary are not required.[6]

The bulk seller must take reasonable steps to warn the buyer or the ultimate user in two situations. First, when the seller knows or has reason to think that the buyer is ignorant of the danger, or inadequately trained, a warning to the buyer may be required.[7] Second, when the seller knows or has reason to think that the product will be dangerous to the user and that the buyer will not transmit warnings to the end-user, the seller may owe an obligation of reasonable care to warn the end-user if that is reasonably feasible.[8]

Sales for Use in Employment or Construction

Products sold to employers for use by employees or contractors. One of the most troubling problems of intermediary warning arises in sales of

2. E.g., Brennaman v. R.M.I. Co., 70 Ohio St.3d 460, 639 N.E.2d 425 (1994).

3. Artiglio v. General Elec. Co., 61 Cal. App.4th 830, 71 Cal.Rptr.2d 817 (1998).

4. In re Silicone Gel Breast Implants Products Liability Litigation, 887 F.Supp. 1455 (N.D.Ala.1995) .

5. Thus the infeasibility of a warning to the ultimate consumer is emphasized in some of the bulk sale cases. E.g., Jones v. Hittle Serv., Inc., 219 Kan. 627, 549 P.2d 1383 (1976) (propane gas).

6. Purvis v. PPG Indus., Inc., 502 So.2d 714, 722, 70 A.L.R.4th 1 (Ala. 1987) ("reliance is permitted, so long as the manufacturer has a reasonable basis to believe that the distributor will pass along the product information or warnings").

7. Restatement § 388 and cmt. n (seller who knows or has reason to know of danger and has no reason to believe user will realize the danger must exercise reasonable care to inform user, but reasonable care may require only a warning to immediate buyer); cf. Stuckey v. Northern Propane Gas Co., 874 F.2d 1563 (11th Cir.1989) (seller of odorized propane gas to intermediary who supplied it to customers owed a duty to warn intermediary that odor could fade if intermediary did not know that fact).

8. See Purvis v. PPG Indus., Inc., 502 So.2d 714, 70 A.L.R.4th 1 (1987) (seller can rely on buyer-intermediary so long as seller can reasonably believe warnings will be passed on to ultimate user); Restatement § 388, cmt. n. But see Jones v. Hittle Serv., Inc., 219 Kan. 627, 639, 549 P.2d 1383, 1394 (1976) (perhaps implying that the seller can rely absolutely upon a knowledgeable and trained intermediary regardless of likelihood that a warning would be passed on).

dangerous goods to employers or to contractors whose work subjects others to risks from the manufacturer's product.[9] Many employers are woefully careless of their employees' safety. Many remove safety devices to enhance production; others actively encourage unsafe practices that violate safety instructions. The prospect that a manufacturer's warnings to the employer will be passed on to employees obviously varies from employer to employer. When neither the employees nor the employer can be expected to know the risks, however, the manufacturer must warn someone and the question is whether a warning to the employer alone will suffice.

The rule-oriented approach. The employer who buys goods from a manufacturer or distributor is a sophisticated buyer when the employer can be expected to know the danger of those goods. Some courts hold as a matter of law that if the employer is a sophisticated buyer, no warning at all need be given, either to the buyer-employer or to his employees.[10] Even if a buyer is not knowledgeable of the danger before he is warned, a warning to him converts him to a sophisticated buyer so that no further warning to his employees is required.[11] This approach does not weigh risks and utilities in particular cases. Even if the warning directly to a buyer's employees is easy because it can be placed on packaging, for example, the manufacturer would have no duty to warn the employees. Some commentators favor this approach for its clarity, administrative ease, and efficiency.[12]

Ironically, the rule-of-law approach is a cousin to the accepted work doctrine, derived from privity rules. In the leading accepted work case, builders who constructed a theater that had been accepted by the landowner were not liable when it collapsed on the audience. Their negligent construction was irrelevant once the theater had been accepted by the "buyer."[13] Courts have since then either abolished the doctrine[14] or liberalized it.[15] The sophisticated user doctrine shifts responsibility in

9. See Swan v. I.P., Inc., 613 So.2d 846 (Miss.1993) (manufacturer supplied chemical to contractor; contractor working on a school, seriously injured teacher by exposing her to the product); Randy R. Koenders, Products Liability: Liability of Manufacturer or Seller as Affected by Failure of Subsequent Party in Distribution Chain to Remedy or Warn against Defect of Which He Knew, 45 A.L.R.4th 777 (1987).

10. Davis v. Avondale Indus., Inc. 975 F.2d 169 (5th Cir.1992); Singleton v. Manitowoc Co., Inc., 727 F.Supp. 217 (D.Md. 1989).

11. E.g., Vines v. Beloit Corp., 631 So.2d 1003 (Ala.1994); Younger v. Dow Corning Corp., 202 Kan. 674, 682, 451 P.2d 177, 184 (1969) (manufacturer who warns immediate buyer, an industrial user, has no duty to warn buyer's employees); Whitehead v. Dycho Co., Inc., 775 S.W.2d 593 (Tenn.1989).

12. See Richard C. Ausness, Learned Intermediaries and Sophisticated Users: Encouraging the Use of Intermediaries to Transmit Product Safety Information, 46 Syracuse L. Rev. 1185 (1996).

13. Ford v. Sturgis, 14 F.2d 253 (D.C.Cir. 1926).

14. E.g., Johnson v. Equip. Specialists, Inc., 58 Ill.App.3d 133, 373 N.E.2d 837, 15 Ill.Dec. 491 (1978); Pierce v. ALSC Architects, 270 Mont. 97, 890 P.2d 1254 (1995); accord: Restatement § 385.

15. See, e.g., Blake v. Calumet Constr. Corp., 674 N.E.2d 167 (Ind.1996) (exceptions paralleling those leading to MacPherson v. Buick Motor Co.). However, where the only applicable exception is for latent defects, the accepted work doctrine becomes quite similar to the sophisticated user rule—the builder is absolved because the defect is open and obvious and the landown-

the same way, but it has become more popular.[16]

Fact-adjudication approaches. Many cases on warnings have avoided enunciating flat rules of law excluding a duty in all cases and have instead attempted to determine in each case whether the manufacturer was reasonable in failing to warn employees directly. The Restatement Second followed this approach, inviting courts to consider the usual factors in determining whether the manufacturer had exercised reasonable care. The seriousness of the risk, the magnitude of potential harm, the ease or difficulty of giving a warning directly to employees, and the probability that the employer, if warned, would pass the warning on were all relevant considerations.[17]

Under this approach, as contrasted with the rule-of-law approach, the court might hold that an asbestos supplier should warn employees directly of dangers, considering the ease in which a warning could be attached to packaged products and the grave risks presented by asbestos. Even if the employer was a sophisticated buyer, the asbestos manufacturer in such a case could not automatically avoid liability for that reason. Instead, the asbestos supplier could justify the failure to warn employees only if it actually had reason to think that their employer would warn them.[18] Feasibility of a warning to the employees is of course highly relevant in any risk-utility balancing. A manufacturer cannot easily warn the buyer's employees about the qualities of powders or liquids shipped by the railroad carload except by a notice on the railroad car itself. But if goods could be shipped in bags or drums, it is feasible to place a warning on the package that could be seen by the buyer's employees.[19]

Comments. Whether the seller-manufacturer is justified in shifting responsibility to the buyer to give warnings is a question of legal policy.[20] Whether the buyer, sophisticated or not, can be expected to pass along a warning is not a legal policy question but a species of fact question. Unfortunately, questions about the buyer's knowledge have been lumped together with questions about the buyer's reliability.[21] Buyer-employers

er knows about it. See Sanchez v. Swinerton & Walberg Co., 47 Cal.App.4th 1461, 55 Cal.Rptr.2d 415 (1996). In such a case, the plaintiff can proceed against the negligent contractor only if the court allows the jury to find the defect to be "latent." E.g., U.S. Lodging of Jacksonville, Ltd. v. H.B. Daniel Constr. Co., 617 So.2d 448 (Fla.Dist.Ct.App. 1993).

16. Distinguish actual discovery of a defect by the buyer as a possible ground for shifting responsibility or for invoking superseding cause rules against liability. See § 370.

17. See Restatement § 388 and cmt. n. See also supporting an assessment of reasonableness in many cases, Restatement of Products Liability § 2, cmt. i.

18. Willis v. Raymark Indus., Inc., 905 F.2d 793 (4th Cir.1990). But the Tennessee Court believes that manufacturers could not foresee that an employer would fail to pass on a warning. Whitehead v. Dycho Co., Inc., 775 S.W.2d 593 (Tenn.1989).

19. See Eagle–Picher Indus., Inc. v. Balbos, 326 Md. 179, 220, 604 A.2d 445, 465 (1992).

20. See § 194.

21. Whitehead v. Dycho Co., Inc., 775 S.W.2d 593, 598 (Tenn.1989) ("Magnavox clearly knew ... of the dangers.... It was, therefore, reasonable for the Defendants to rely upon Magnavox to convey the information about the hazards of naphtha to its employees.... ").

may have incentives to enhance rather than minimize risks, since safety practices may reduce production or necessitate overtime pay. A rule of law approach ignores this risk by focusing solely upon the buyer's sophistication.

Sometimes, however, the rule-of-law approach is favored on the grounds that the manufacturer can rely upon the employer because the employer owes a duty of care to warn the employees[22] or on the ground that the sophisticated user defense actually encourages the employer to provide the warning.[23] However, if the employer is under a duty, it is a most peculiar one because it cannot ordinarily be enforced by a tort action. Workers' compensation immunizes the employer from tort liability in most instances. Negligent employers who can hide behind their workers' compensation immunity are unfair to employees and manufacturers alike. If the question is whether employers are likely to omit warnings in a substantial number of cases, the answer seems to be that they are. No amount of theoretical duty to protect the employee is likely to change that as long as the legal system provides them immunity.

§ 367. Causation in Warning Cases

At least in theory, the plaintiff has the burden of proving that the product defect was a cause in fact and a legal or proximate cause of the harm claimed. In warning cases, the plaintiff must show that, if a proper warning had been given, the injury would have been avoided. Presumably the plaintiff must also show that the reason a better warning was needed was to guard against the forces and types of harm that the plaintiff in fact suffered and that no superseding cause insulates the defendant from liability.[1]

The Heeding Presumption or Inference

No warnings. The most common cause in fact problem arises with the question whether the plaintiff would have read and also heeded the warning if it had been given or given adequately. When no warning at all is given, a few courts have said that the plaintiff must prove that she would have read and heeded a warning had it been given.[2] Many more have been willing to presume or infer that the plaintiff would have heeded a warning.[3] Similarly where the defendant fails to warn an

22. See Joel Slawotsky, The Learned Intermediary Doctrine: The Employer as Intermediary, 30 Tort & Ins. L. J. 1059 (1994).

23. See Richard C. Ausness, Learned Intermediaries and Sophisticated Users: Encouraging the Use of Intermediaries to Transmit Product Safety Information, 46 Syracuse L. Rev. 1185 (1996); Kenneth M. Willner, Note, Failures to Warn and the Sophisticated User Defense, 74 Va. L. Rev. 579 (1988).

§ 367

1. Superseding cause arguments are often dealt with under the rubric of misuse and modification. As to these, see § 370.

2. E.g., Riley v. American Honda Motor Co., Inc., 259 Mont. 128, 856 P.2d 196 (1993).

3. See, e.g., Eagle–Picher Indus. Inc. v. Balbos, 326 Md. 179, 604 A.2d 445 (1992) (infer); Coffman v. Keene Corp., 133 N.J. 581, 628 A.2d 710 (1993) (presume); See generally, Benjamin J. Jones, Annotation, Presumption or Inference, in Products Lia-

intermediary, the presumption is that a properly warned intermediary would have passed on a warning to the plaintiff.[4] Either the presumption or the inference would normally get the plaintiff to the jury on the cause in fact issue unless other evidence makes it clear that the plaintiff would not in fact have read and heeded an appropriate warning.[5] Perhaps the best ground for invoking the presumption is that the plaintiff could seldom prove convincingly that he would have read a warning, so that the manufacturer's duty to warn would be effectively avoided in almost all cases. In this view, the presumption represents a policy decision to enforce the duty to warn.[6]

Inadequate warnings, read and unread. (a) When a warning is in fact given but it is inadequate in its expression or content, the plaintiff who actually read the warning but did not understand it can plausibly claim that an adequate warning would have protected her. However, if the plaintiff failed to read the content-inadequate warning, it is frequently difficult to see how a more adequate warning would have made any difference in the outcome. In such a case the presumption that the plaintiff would have read and heeded an adequate warning may not arise or if it arises it may be rebutted by a finding that the plaintiff did not read the warning that was available.[7] Nevertheless, in some cases the evidence may warrant the belief that even though the plaintiff did not personally read the label, her employer or co-workers did so and would have advised the plaintiff of the dangers if they had been adequately represented.[8]

(b) If the warning's inadequacy lies in its display rather than its content, the story is different. In that case, the plaintiff's whole point is that an adequately displayed warning would have caught her eye and she

bility Action Based on Failure to Warn, That User of Product Would Have Heeded an Adequate Warning Had One Been Given, 38 A.L.R.5th 683 (1996).

4. Eagle–Picher Indus., Inc. v. Balbos, 326 Md. 179, 604 A.2d 445 (1992); Coffman v. Keene Corp., 133 N.J. 581, 628 A.2d 710 (1993) (presumed that warnings to employer will be heeded, although in a given case the defendant may show that the employer would not have passed on the warning).

5. Some courts treat the presumption as a bursting bubble that disappears as soon as any rebutting evidence is introduced. See Daniel v. Ben E. Keith Co., 97 F.3d 1329 (10th Cir.1996). Even so, the inference of causation may remain after the presumption has vanished. See General Motors Corp. v. Saenz, 873 S.W.2d 353 (Tex.1993). On presumptions and inferences generally see § 152.

6. Coffman v. Keene Corp., 133 N.J. 581, 599, 628 A.2d 710, 718 (1993) ("The heeding presumption thus serves to reinforce the basic duty to warn"). Some courts have said that Restatement § 402A, cmt. j supported the presumption. Whether that is true or not, the policy basis, not the textual meaning of Comment j seems to be the relevant point. Ironically, other courts have said the presumption should be used to relieve the plaintiff of the burden of offering inherently subjective and unreliable evidence as to whether she would have heeded the warning.

7. Daniel v. Ben E. Keith Co., 97 F.3d 1329 (10th Cir.1996); Bushong v. Garman Co., 311 Ark. 228, 843 S.W.2d 807 (1992) (apparently treating warning as content-inadequate). Somewhat similarly, if the plaintiff is already aware of the dangers the causal importance of a warning may be doubtful even when the defendant owes a duty to warn of known or obvious dangers. See, e.g., Peitzmeier v. Hennessy Indus., Inc., 97 F.3d 293 (8th Cir.1996); Coffman v. Keene Corp., 133 N.J. 581, 628 A.2d 710 (1993).

8. Ferebee v. Chevron Chem. Co., 736 F.2d 1529 (D.C.Cir.1984); East Penn Mfg. Co. v. Pineda, 578 A.2d 1113 (D.C.1990).

would have avoided the danger. If such evidence is accepted, courts can apply the presumption in the same way they apply it where no warning at all was given.[9]

Rebuttal or evidence that warning would not have been read or heeded. Besides the evidence that the plaintiff did not read the warnings given, defendants can attempt to show that the plaintiff would not have heeded the warning if read. For instance, evidence that the plaintiff disregarded warnings he did receive may persuade the court or the trier that the plaintiff would likewise have disregarded the missing warning.[10] Although the fact that the plaintiff already knew of the danger does not necessarily show that a warning would not have reminded her, it is at least cogent evidence on the causal issue. When the plaintiff acts out of a momentary inadvertence rather than out of ignorance, the court may conclude that a warning would have made no difference at all.[11]

Medical Causation and Scope of Risk

The warning failure must be a cause in fact of the plaintiff's harm. If the plaintiff would not have heeded an adequate warning, failure to warn is not a cause in fact or but-for cause of her harm. In addition, scientific or medical causation may be an issue. The plaintiff who is not properly warned that asbestos can cause respiratory disorders must show that she would have heeded a warning and also that she in fact has such a disorder resulting from asbestos exposure.[12]

As a matter of proximate or legal cause, superseding causes can sometimes insulate the defendant from liability for failing to warn.[13] More centrally, the injury suffered must be within the class of injury that the warning requirement was meant to avoid. For example, the plaintiff, if properly warned that asbestos might cause cancer, might have ceased to work around asbestos. A failure to give such a warning could result in liability if the plaintiff did develop cancer as a result of asbestos exposure. But the failure to provide such a warning would not result in liability if the plaintiff, not being warned, kept her job and lost a hand in a job-related machine accident. In that example, failure to warn would be a cause in fact—the plaintiff would have been elsewhere, not working at the machine, if a proper warning had been given—but it is not a proximate or legal cause. It is not, in other words, within the risk that a warning was designed to avoid.[14]

9. See East Penn Mfg. Co. v. Pineda, 578 A.2d 1113, 1124 (D.C.1990); Town of Bridport v. Sterling Clark Lurton Corp., 166 Vt. 304, 693 A.2d 701 (1997).

10. Gosewisch v. American Honda Motor Co., 153 Ariz. 400, 737 P.2d 376 (1987), overruled on other grounds, Jimenez v. Sears, Roebuck and Co., 183 Ariz. 399, 904 P.2d 861 (1995).

11. Conti v. Ford Motor Co., 743 F.2d 195 (3d Cir.1984) (driver in a moment of inadvertence started standard transmission car in reverse gear while wife was getting in car, warning would not have avoided wife's injury).

12. Coffman v. Keene Corp., 133 N.J. 581, 628 A.2d 710 (1993).

13. See § 370.

14. Cf. Little v. Liquid Air Corp., 37 F.3d 1069 (5th Cir.1994) (warning of nasal fatigue might have protected plaintiff who did not smell dangerous gas, but plaintiff could recover on that basis only if his fail-

§ 368. Post–Sale Warnings and Recalls

Duty to give a post-sale warning. A few states impose upon manufacturers a duty to warn of dangers that were not knowable at the time of sale.[1] Those states in effect attribute to the manufacturer all the technical knowledge developed after sale. Most states do not impose a liability for dangers unknowable at the time of sale but many do impose a duty of reasonable care to issue post-sale warnings of newly discovered dangers or to advise of better safety technology.[2] The Restatement of Products Liability adopts this view.[3] The warning is due if the seller knows or should know that the product poses a risk, if the risk outweighs the burden of providing a warning, and if a warning can be effectively communicated and acted upon. The duty of care does not disappear when the product line is discontinued.[4] The Restatement adds that the risk must be "substantial." Presumably, however, the "substantial" requirement is not meant to override the risk-utility balancing but rather to emphasize the that the risk must be "sufficiently great to justify the burden of providing a warning."[5]

Courts rejecting or limiting the duty. Some courts reject the whole idea of a post-sale duty to provide a reasonable warning.[6] On a different tact with largely the same result, some reject any requirement of reasonable care to make a warning when the product was not defective at the time of sale.[7] Finally, some authority also rejects a duty to pass on information about later-developed safety improvements as distinct from newly discovered dangers in the product itself.[8] The Restatement's formulation of the rule takes a case-oriented approach, recognizing that reasonable care will sometimes require a warning even when the product was not originally defective and might even require the manufacturer to advise of newly discovered safety technology.

Duty to keep abreast of the field. Courts have said that reasonableness may require the manufacturer to keep abreast of the field. If

ure to smell the gas was due to nasal fatigue and not other causes).

§ 368

1. E.g., Ayers v. Johnson & Johnson Baby Prods. Co., 117 Wash.2d 747, 818 P.2d 1337 (1991). See § 359.

2. Patton v. Hutchinson Wil–Rich Mfg. Co., 253 Kan. 741, 861 P.2d 1299 (1993); see Crowston v. Goodyear Tire & Rubber Co., 521 N.W.2d 401 (N.D.1994) ("a post-sale duty to warn about dangers associated with the use of their products"); Timberline Air Serv., Inc. v. Bell Helicopter–Textron, Inc., 125 Wash.2d 305, 884 P.2d 920 (1994). Many cases formulate the duty more narrowly, to require a warning when the manufacturer learned of the danger. This formulation probably reflects the facts of the case before the court in most instances, not a studied intent to reject a reasonable care rule that would require a warning when the manufacturer should have learned of the danger but did not.

3. Restatement of Products Liability § 10.

4. Owens–Illinois, Inc. v. Zenobia, 325 Md. 420, 601 A.2d 633 (1992).

5. Restatement of Products Liability § 10 (b) (4).

6. Birchler v. Gehl Co., 88 F.3d 518 (7th Cir.1996) (Illinois law).

7. E.g., Gregory v. Cincinnati Inc., 450 Mich. 1, 538 N.W.2d 325 (1995).

8. Williams v. Monarch Mach. Tool Co., Inc., 26 F.3d 228 (1st Cir.1994); Wilson v. United States Elevator Corp., 193 Ariz. 251, 972 P.2d 235 (Ariz.App.1998); Bragg v. Hi–Ranger, Inc., 319 S.C. 531, 462 S.E.2d 321 (S.C.Ct.App.1995).

substantial new risks are discovered, or should have been discovered in keeping abreast, reasonable care would then be required to provide a warning.[9] Most of the cases are prescription drug cases, but courts have mentioned the requirement, perhaps ambiguously, in other cases as well.[10]

Recall or retrofit. When the product's design risks are not knowable at the time of sale, the manufacturer is not required to recall, repair, or retrofit the product in the absence of a statutory or regulatory duty to do so.[11] In line with the general rule on undertakings, the manufacturer who undertakes a recall or repair must act with reasonable care.[12] When the product was defective at the time of sale, the manufacturer's failure to recall is not so much the basis for an independent cause of action as grounds for asserting punitive damages[13] or perhaps for postponing the statute of limitations.

TOPIC C. "DEFENSES"

§ 369. Contributory (Comparative) Negligence and Assumed Risk

Emerging orthodoxy. Differences among the courts make a statement of the rules of comparative fault and assumed risk unreasonably complicated. But the mainstream thought now seems to be more straightforward. That thought in products liability actions presently holds that (1) conduct amounting to contributory fault reduces the plaintiff's damages under the comparative fault rules, and (2) assumed risk is now ordinarily regarded as a species of fault also treated under the comparative fault rules, except that (3) some "assumed risk" may turn out upon analysis to be an obscure way of saying that the product was not defective or that a superseding cause insulates the manufacturer from liability. The history, variations, and debates about these rules and their alternatives provides a more detailed picture.

Comparative fault rules generally applied. Under the Restatement Second of Torts, contributory negligence, in the sense of failure to

9. Schenebeck v. Sterling Drug, Inc., 423 F.2d 919 (8th Cir.1970); Proctor v. Davis, 291 Ill.App.3d 265, 682 N.E.2d 1203, 225 Ill.Dec. 126 (1997); Baker v. St. Agnes Hosp., 70 A.D.2d 400, 421 N.Y.S.2d 81 (1979). If, in the course of keeping abreast, the drug manufacturer is put on notice of possible dangers, the manufacturer may need to institute further investigations, tests, or studies of its own. Barson v. E.R. Squibb & Sons, Inc., 682 P.2d 832 (Utah 1984).

10. See Cover v. Cohen, 61 N.Y.2d 261, 461 N.E.2d 864, 473 N.Y.S.2d 378 (1984).

11. Burke v. Deere & Co., 6 F.3d 497 (8th Cir.1993); Tabieros v.Clark Equip. Co., 85 Hawai'i 336, 944 P.2d 1279 (1997); Restatement of Products Liability § 11. See also Lisa Anne Meyer, Annotation, Products Liability: Manufacturer's Postsale Obligation to Modify, Repair, or Recall Product, 47 A.L.R.5th 395 (1997). A number of statutes permit federal agencies to order recalls or repairs. E.g., see 49 U.S.C.A. § 30118 (motor vehicles); 15 U.S.C.A. § 2064 (d) (Consumer Products Safety Commission).

12. Restatement of Products Liability § 11; cf. Gracyalny v. Westinghouse Elec. Corp., 723 F.2d 1311 (7th Cir.1983) (manufacturer warned and provided a new safety device but did not install it; liability for the jury).

13. See Reed v. Ford Motor Co., 679 F.Supp. 873, 880 (S.D.Ind.1988).

discover a product's defect, was not a bar to recovery on a strict liability theory. On the other hand, "assumed risk," in the sense of a voluntary and unreasonable exposure to a known danger was a complete bar.[1] With the advent of comparative fault systems in all but four states,[2] courts and legislatures have now usually said that the plaintiff's comparative negligence can be raised as an affirmative defense and applied to reduce damages, both when the plaintiff asserted negligence and when she asserted strict liability.[3] The Restatement of Products Liability adopts this position.[4] A major commentator has concluded that comparative fault reductions are morally just in principle.[5] Not every foible counts at plaintiff fault, however. For instance, workers who have little choice but to work with dangerous machinery on the job are not necessarily guilty of either comparative fault[6] or assumed risk when they do so.[7]

Assumed risk. What used to be treated as a separate defense of assumed risk is now largely subsumed in comparative fault.[8] In products cases, assumed risk is often defined as a voluntary and unreasonable encounter with a known danger. There is no real reason to distinguish this form of plaintiff-fault from, say, negligently using a product like an automobile. Thus, the driver who negligently crashes his car and is thrown from it may be able to show that the car had a defective door latch, but his damages will be reduced for his fault whether that fault is denominated contributory negligence or assumed risk.[9]

However, some courts still treat assumed risk as a separate and complete defense, barring the risk-assuming plaintiff entirely.[10] In addi-

§ 369

1. Restatement § 402A cmt. n. The two categories do not match the full range of either contributory negligence or assumed risk. Contributory negligence includes matters besides failure to discover. Assumed risk may apply even when the plaintiff's conduct is fully reasonable.

2. Of those four, two hold or provide that contributory negligence is a defense (and a complete defense) in a products action. See Uniroyal Goodrich Tire Co., v. Hall, 681 So.2d 126 (Ala.1996); N.C. Gen. Stat. § 99B–4. The other two disregard contributory negligence. Ellsworth v. Sherne Lingerie, Inc., 303 Md. 581, 495 A.2d 348, 52 A.L.R.4th 247 (1985); Wood v. Bass Pro Shops, Inc., 250 Va. 297, 462 S.E.2d 101 (1995) (warranty theory; also disregarded assumed risk, but recognizing product misuse as a complete defense).

3. E.g., Butaud v. Suburban Marine & Sporting Goods, Inc., 555 P.2d 42, (Alaska 1976); Daly v. General Motors Corp., 20 Cal.3d 725, 575 P.2d 1162, 144 Cal.Rptr. 380 (1978). A number of statutes also specifically prescribe use of comparative fault reductions in products cases. E.g., Colo. Rev. Stats. § 13–21–406.Where a comparative fault statute by its terms addresses "negligence" cases only, courts must determine whether to judicially supplement the statute at all and if so whether to do so in cases conceived of as strict liability cases.

4. Restatement of Products Liability § 17.

5. David G. Owen, The Moral Foundations of Products Liability Law: Toward First Principles, 68 Notre Dame L. Rev. 427, 505 (1993).

6. See Jurado v. Western Gear Works, 131 N.J. 375, 387, 619 A.2d 1312, 1318 (1993); Theer v. Philip Carey Co., 133 N.J. 610, 622, 628 A.2d 724, 730 (1993).

7. Carrel v. Allied Prods. Corp., 78 Ohio St.3d 284, 677 N.E.2d 795 (1997); cf. Green v. Edmands Co., 639 F.2d 286 (5th Cir. 1981) (no alternative way to accomplish job task, no assumed risk).

8. See generally § 211.

9. Cf. Daly v. General Motors Corp., 20 Cal.3d 725, 575 P.2d 1162, 144 Cal.Rptr. 380 (1978) (driver killed, comparative fault rule adopted).

10. E.g., Kupetz v. Deere & Co., Inc., 435 Pa.Super. 16, 644 A.2d 1213 (1994).

tion, if the product's danger is objectively obvious, the risk it presents may be a reasonable one because users could reasonably be expected to protect themselves. In that case, the product may not be defective at all and the plaintiff will be denied recovery for that reason.[11] On the other hand, when the manufacturer should reasonably foresee that the user will have little choice but to deal with the risky product, as is usually the case with machinery used in employment, even an obviously dangerous product may be unreasonably dangerous and therefore defective.[12] In that case, no good grounds appear for a complete bar as distinct from a comparative fault reduction in damages.

The known risk rule. Before the system of comparative fault was generally adopted, most courts refused to recognize the defense of contributory negligence in strict liability actions.[13] Even after the advent of comparative fault, some courts apply a similar rule, so that a voluntary and unreasonable exposure to a known risk can count against the plaintiff as a bar or in reduction of damages but other forms of plaintiff-fault count for nothing.[14] For brevity, this rule can be called the known risk rule. The point here is not what does affect the plaintiff's claim but what does not.

An example of the known risk rule is *Bowling v. Heil Co.*[15] The bed of a dump truck did not return to the down position after the load had been deposited. The decedent put his head under the raised truck bed and manipulated a lever, whereupon the truck bed fell, causing the decedent's instant death. Since the jury found that the decedent was chargeable with contributory fault but that he had not assumed the risk, the court refused to reduce recovery for the defect in the hoist mechanism. On the other hand, if the jury had characterized the decedent's conduct as assumed risk, the claim would have been completely barred.[16]

11. Cases finding no defect because danger was generally known are like this. E.g., Farnham v. Bombardier, Inc., 161 Vt. 619, 640 A.2d 47 (1994) (snowmobile dangers); Elliott v. Brunswick Corp., 903 F.2d 1505 (11th Cir.1990) (motorboat motor's propeller not defective because dangers were inherent and known).

12. See Carrel v. Allied Products Corp., 78 Ohio St.3d 284, 677 N.E.2d 795 (1997).

13. See Gary D. Spivey, Annotation, Products Liability: Contributory Negligence or Assumption of Risk as Defense Under Doctrine of Strict Liability in Tort, 46 A.L.R.3d 240 (1973).

14. Bowling v. Heil Co., 31 Ohio St.3d 277, 511 N.E.2d 373 (1987); Kimco Dev. Corp. v. Michael D's Carpet Outlets, 536 Pa. 1, 637 A.2d 603 (1993); Smith v. Smith, 278 N.W.2d 155 (S.D.1979). In some states, statutes have displaced judicial decisions that once so held. Among the four states that still use the traditional rather than the comparative fault system in tort law generally, one treats assumed risk as a complete bar but disregards contributory fault in strict liability cases. Another allows neither assumed risk nor contributory fault to bar the strict liability claim but bars the claim for product misuse. See n. 2, supra.

15. Bowling v. Heil Co., 31 Ohio St.3d 277, 511 N.E.2d 373 (1987).

16. Onderko v. Richmond Mfg. Co., 31 Ohio St.3d 296, 511 N.E.2d 388 (1987) (assumed risk is a complete bar to strict liability claim but is treated as comparative negligence if the plaintiff sues for negligence). Accord, that assumed risk is a complete bar. Jimenez v. Sears, Roebuck & Co., 183 Ariz. 399, 904 P.2d 861 (1995). Ohio also holds that an encounter with known danger as required by employment does not count as assumed risk. Carrel v. Allied Prods. Corp., 78 Ohio St.3d 284, 677 N.E.2d 795 (1997).

And if the court characterizes the plaintiff's conduct as a superseding cause or the like (rather than comparative fault), she is likewise barred.[17]

The failure to discover rule. Many courts say that no comparative fault reductions should be made when the plaintiff's only fault is failure to discover the product's defect.[18] This rule can be called the failure-to-discover rule. The failure to discover rule may come down to saying that the plaintiff is not at fault in trusting the defendant's product until the plaintiff has notice that requires investigation of it. That is ordinarily correct. The plaintiff who bites into a Mr. Goodbar candy has no reason to inspect its insides for worms and eggs.[19] Consumer expectations, whether a test of product defectiveness or not, are at least relevant to show that the consumer behaved reasonably in accepting the product at face value.[20]

Beyond this, it should be said that a good many acts by product users that are less than optimal do not appear to constitute plaintiff negligence. In a South Dakota case,[21] a power saw suddenly started up. The startled plaintiff moved his hand in response to this unsuspected event and in so doing lost his fingers. His movement was not the optimal response, but in the sudden danger created by the defect, as in emergency, it would be hard to say that he was guilty of negligence.

If all plaintiff fault consists of either failure to discover or voluntary exposure to a known risk, the failure to discover rule is merely a negative statement of the known risk rule. But it is fair to say that between the two categories lies a very large group of cases that do not fit well in either. The plaintiff's fault in failing to wear a safety harness while working on high-rise steel girders does not depend upon either failure to discover a girder defect or upon exposing oneself to it. In such a case, the plaintiff presumably has not in fact discovered the girder's defect that will cause a fall, but his fault does not consist in failure to discover it; it consists in failure to use a safety harness that would protect against a fall caused by any reason. Similarly, the essence of the plaintiff's fault in driving an automobile while intoxicated does not turn either upon discovery of a defect in the door latch or exposure to known danger. In such in-between cases, the plaintiff's fault appropriately reduces recovery. The Texas Court made this point when a defective parking gear design permitted a truck to pop out of gear and roll,

17. Davis v. Berwind Corp., 547 Pa. 260, 690 A.2d 186 (1997).

18. E.g., Jimenez v. Sears, Roebuck & Co., 183 Ariz. 399, 904 P.2d 861 (1995); Coney v. J.L.G. Indus., Inc., 97 Ill.2d 104, 454 N.E.2d 197, 73 Ill.Dec. 337 (1983); General Motors v. Sanchez, 997 S.W.2d 584 (Tex. 1999). Some statutes so provide. E.g., Idaho Code § 6–1305. Sometimes courts will describe this rule by saying that contributory negligence, meaning failure to discover and only failure to discover, is no defense. This kind of locution runs substantial risk of confusing the issue, because other forms of plaintiff fault that historically would have been called contributory negligence, are compared.

19. Kassouf v. Lee Bros., Inc., 209 Cal. App.2d 568, 26 Cal.Rptr. 276 (1962).

20. Cf. Mary J. Davis, Individual and Institutional Responsibility: A Vision for Comparative Fault in Products Liability, 39 Vill. L. Rev. 281 (1994) (emphasizing relationship of parties, special knowledge of manufacturer, trust of the consumer).

21. Smith v. Smith, 278 N.W.2d 155 (S.D.1979).

crushing the owner. While the court held that mere failure to discover a product defect is not contributory fault that will bar or reduce recovery, it also held that the user might be chargeable with fault in parking unsafely quite independent of the defect, and that if so, his damages would be reduced accordingly.[22]

Rejecting reductions in defective safety device cases. Some courts refuse to reduce the plaintiff's recovery when the product was defective for the very reason that it failed to guard the plaintiff against her own momentary lapse, inattentiveness or other fault. Many machines expose users to moving parts that can crush a hand, amputate an arm or leg, or even kill. In each case, the user can avoid such terrible injuries by staying away from moving parts. Yet it is entirely foreseeable that eventually almost all users will be too close to the moving machinery. Some will do so because of inadvertence, some because of confidence born of past good experience with machinery, some because of job pressures to produce. Given this foreseeable harm, the machine is easily counted as defective if it omits a feasible safety device that would avoid such injuries. These cases illustrate the rule, recognized by some courts, that when the product should have been designed to prevent the act or omission that triggers harm, that act should not count as contributory fault.[23] It is a contradiction to say that the defendant has a duty to provide the safety device but then to say that in all cases where it is needed, the plaintiff is guilty of contributory fault.

Deterrence argument for ignoring plaintiff-fault. Among the arguments for ignoring the plaintiff's comparative fault in strict liability cases,[24] the most common is based upon the need to deter production of defective products. If manufacturers systematically get a reduction in damages because many plaintiffs will be guilty of some degree of fault, manufacturers will not have appropriate incentives to invest in safety.[25] This argument asserts that deterrence operates differentially: when the plaintiff's damages are reduced, defendants will be less careful, but plaintiffs will not be more careful.[26] The net result in this view is a

22. General Motors v. Sanchez, 997 S.W.2d 584 (Tex. 1999).

23. Bexiga v. Havir Mfg. Corp., 60 N.J. 402, 412, 290 A.2d 281, 286 (N.J.1972); cf. Bell v. Jet Wheel Blast Div. of Ervin Indus., 462 So.2d 166 (La.1985) (no comparative fault reduction when machine manufacturer failed to include safety device).

24. Two other arguments are that strict liability is not predicated upon the defendant's fault so the plaintiff's fault should not be considered, either, see § 350, and that enterprise liability principles require the manufacturer to pay for all harms, regardless of plaintiff fault. Rejecting this, see Coney v. J.L.G. Indus., Inc., 97 Ill.2d 104, 116, 454 N.E.2d 197, 202, 73 Ill.Dec. 337, 342 (1983) ("no reason to spread the cost of the loss resulting from plaintiff's own fault on to the consuming public"); Duncan v. Cessna Aircraft Co., 665 S.W.2d 414, 425 (Tex.1984) ("[a]n ideal tort system should impose responsibility on the parties according to their abilities to prevent the harm" and that safety is the joint responsibility of all those who can prevent harm).

25. Johnson, J., dissenting in Webb v. Navistar Int. Transp. Corp., 166 Vt. 119, 692 A.2d 343, 356 (1996); cf. Mosk, J., dissenting in Daly v. General Motors Corp., 20 Cal.3d 725, 760, 575 P.2d 1162, 1183, 144 Cal.Rptr. 380, 401 (1978) ("The defective product is comparable to a time bomb ready to explode; it maims its victims indiscriminately, the righteous and the evil, the careful and the careless").

26. See Howard A. Latin, Problem-Solving Behavior and Theories of Tort Liability, 73 Calif. L. Rev. 677, 732 (1985) (em-

forecasted increase in injuries. However, if comparative fault reductions represent the right way to account for the plaintiff's fault in, say, a case brought for negligent repairs to a building or negligent medical practice, it is not clear why the plaintiff's fault should be disregarded in product cases merely because the defendant's liability is strict or nominally strict.

Apples and oranges argument. On a rather different plane, it has been argued that courts cannot compare apples and oranges—the fault of the plaintiff and the non-faulty defect of the defendant's product. The answer has been to treat the objection as a purely practical one and to recognize that juries can come up with some kind of "equitable" (or perhaps intuitive) apportionment of responsibility.[27] An intuitive approach of this kind will make meaningful appellate review quite difficult, but as the Texas Court later said, juries could compare causation rather than fault so that in strict liability cases the rule is comparative causation rather than comparative fault.[28] The idea seems to be that the causal role of the defendant's product can be compared on the same scale as the causal role of the plaintiff in causing harm.[29] The Restatement of Apportionment prefers the vague term "comparative responsibility"[30] and a system that invites the trier to consider virtually anything, including mental states in assigning responsibility. Under this approach, the definitions of negligence that have been built over generations seem to have little use.

Related materials. To recapitulate briefly: some courts consider "assumed risk" as comparative fault while others consider it a distinct defense. Of these, some use assumed risk to bar the plaintiff entirely, while others treat it as grounds for reducing damages. Sometimes, even further distinctions are drawn; the defense can be quite different if the plaintiff is injured by a product used in employment. A few courts still

phasizing that most accidents are due to momentary lapses); Howard Latin, "Good" Warnings, Bad Products, and Cognitive Limitations, 41 UCLA L. Rev. 1193, 1254 (1994) (people can learn about risks but product engineers can learn better). Some proponents of this view think consumers are always, or almost always, guilty of some contributory fault. See Webb v. Navistar Int. Transp. Corp., 166 Vt. 119, 692 A.2d 343 (1996) (Johnson, J., dissenting). Those who favor applying comparative fault rules may take a more optimistic view. David G. Owen, the Moral Foundations of Products Liability Law: Toward First Principles, 68 Notre Dame L. Rev. 427, 505 (1993) ("most consumers are generally capable of acting reasonably," consumers are morally accountable).

27. Daly v. General Motors Corp., 20 Cal.3d 725, 734, 144 Cal.Rptr. 380, 385, 575 P.2d 1162, 1167 (1978); Coney v. J.L.G. Indus., Inc., 97 Ill.2d 104, 454 N.E.2d 197, 73 Ill.Dec. 337 (1983).

28. Duncan v. Cessna Aircraft Co., 665 S.W.2d 414 (Tex.1984).

29. The language is relatively new to the law and perhaps confusing. It does not refer to cause in fact. Perhaps comparative causation is best understood as an effort to rate causal significance. Instead of concluding that one actor's contributions have no causal significance at all, as juries might do in finding "no proximate cause," juries can estimate the importance of each cause—the plaintiff's conduct and the defendant's defective product. Theorists have worked up ways in which this could be done, but their work is not aimed at instructing the jury. See, e.g., Mario J. Rizzo and Frank S. Arnold, Causal Apportionment in the Law of Torts: An Economic Theory, 80 Colum. L. Rev. 1399 (1980); Robert N. Strassfeld, Causal Comparisons, 60 Fordham L. Rev. 913 (1992).

30. Restatement of Apportionment § 8, cmt. a.

bar the plaintiff completely if she is chargeable with contributory fault; others reduce damages; still others ignore it altogether. Some courts consider some forms of contributory fault but not others. If all this seems to require too many distinctions, bad news lies ahead; more distinctions are required. Some assumed risk may not after all count as comparative fault because it may negate the existence of a defect altogether. And some contributory fault can be characterized as product misuse and treated as a separate defense or as defeating the claim on proximate cause or no-defect grounds. The stout-hearted may touch upon those issues in sections that follow.

§ 370. Unforeseeable Misuse, Alteration, and Modification

Introductory Summary

Sometimes courts speak of "misuse" or the "misuse defense" as though the term refers to a doctrine or rule distinct from the more familiar concepts of tort law. In truth, the term refers to a pattern of facts, not a rule of law. Depending on the facts, evidence of the plaintiff's unforeseeable misuse may tend to show that (a) the product is not defective at all; or (b) the defective product was not a proximate cause of harm, or, where the product is defective, that (c) the plaintiff was chargeable with comparative fault.[1] Evidence of misuse is not exclusively relevant to any one of these issues alone. Its probative value on any of them depends on the facts. Alterations of a product by the plaintiff can have the effect of misuse. Much the same thing can be said about risk-enhancing alterations of a product by third persons.[2] In the end, analysis would be clearer if the term misuse were dropped and courts approached the issues of defectiveness, comparative fault, and proximate cause directly.

Misuse Bearing on Defectiveness of the Product

Unforeseeable misuse. A product is defective in design or warning only if harm is reasonably foreseeable. Hence the product is not defective at all if the plaintiff's unforeseeable misuse is the sole cause of the harm. For instance, if the evidence is that the plaintiff was injured because the tread separated on a tire manufactured by the defendant, a tire defect might be the probable explanation. However, if the defendant can show that the tire was eight years old and had suffered numerous punctures and major patches or plugs, the inference that the tire was defective at the time it left the defendant's hands is considerably lessened, perhaps destroyed.[3] The point of misuse in this kind of case is not that the

§ 370

1. See Jurado v. Western Gear Works, 131 N.J. 375, 619 A.2d 1312 (1993); Restatement of Products Liability § 2, cmt. p.

2. See Jurado v. Western Gear Works, 131 N.J. 375, 619 A.2d 1312 (1993); Amatulli v. Delhi Constr. Corp., 77 N.Y.2d 525, 571 N.E.2d 645, 569 N.Y.S.2d 337 (1991) (above-ground pool installed in-ground and provided with a deck, giving the appearance of a deeper pool; alteration precluded manufacturer liability).

3. Korando v. Uniroyal Goodrich Tire Co., 159 Ill.2d 335, 637 N.E.2d 1020, 202 Ill.Dec. 284 (1994).

plaintiff or a third person was at fault but that no defect has been shown to exist. A tire that blows out after its useful life is over simply doesn't seem to be defective.[4] Whether the evidence is convincing on the issue of defectiveness of course turns on the facts of the particular case. For example, misuse that does not cause or enhance the injury does not ordinarily affect the inference of a defect.[5] Since the plaintiff has the burden of proving a defective product in the first instance, misuse in this kind of case is not properly speaking a defense at all; it is instead evidence that bears on and tends to negate an element of the plaintiff's prima facie case.[6]

Foreseeable misuse. Some cases say that foreseeable misuse is not misuse at all. Whether or not that is the most helpful locution, the cases have generally acknowledged the rule that foreseeable misuse does not negate the defectiveness of the product.[7] That is because manufacturers are obliged to design products and give warnings with realities of use in mind. Put otherwise, the product must be reasonably safe for foreseeable misuses;[8] the plaintiff proves defectiveness by proving that the product was not reasonably safe for normal use, including foreseeable misuse.[9] Children, for example, may be expected to use some products in dangerous ways, and while manufacturers can sometimes rely upon parents to protect children, experience teaches that parents do not supervise children at all times, so that if a safer design is within economic reach, the manufacturer should utilize it to protect against a child's misuse.[10]

Enhanced injury or crashworthiness cases. An important example of the rule that designs should take reasonable account of foreseeable misuse is the case of the overturned or crashed automobile. Manufacturers do not intend their automobiles to be crashed, but they do foresee that vehicles will be subjected to crashes and overturns resulting from

4. See Jurado v. Western Gear Works, 131 N.J. 375, 388, 619 A.2d 1312, 1318 (1993). ("When someone is injured while using a product for an unforeseeable purpose or in an unforeseeable manner, the misuse sheds no light on whether the product is defective, because a manufacturer is not under a duty to protect against unforeseeable misuses").

5. Sears, Roebuck & Co. v. Harris, 630 So.2d 1018, 1027 (Ala.1993) ("A manufacturer or seller remains liable if the alteration or modification did not in fact cause the injury").

6. See Ellsworth v. Sherne Lingerie, Inc., 303 Md. 581, 495 A.2d 348, 52 A.L.R.4th 247 (1985); Jurado v. Western Gear Works, 131 N.J. 375, 619 A.2d 1312 (1993). Again, however, statutes may treat misuse as an affirmative defense without drawing the distinction between misuse that is a form of comparative fault and misuse that is a way of negating defects in the product.

7. E.g., Sears, Roebuck & Co. v. Harris, 630 So.2d 1018 (Ala.1993); Hart–Albin Co. v. McLees, Inc., 264 Mont. 1, 870 P.2d 51 (1994). At one time courts said that when a product was not used as "intended," no strict liability would be imposed. That term still appears from time to time. High v. Westinghouse Elec. Corp., 610 So.2d 1259 (Fla.1992). But most courts now recognize that it is the manufacturer's foresight of use, not its intent, that counts.

8. E.g., Ellsworth v. Sherne Lingerie, Inc., 303 Md. 581, 495 A.2d 348, 52 A.L.R.4th 247 (1985); Reid v. Spadone Mach. Co., 119 N.H. 457, 404 A.2d 1094 (1979), overruled on other ground, Daigle v. City of Portsmouth, 129 N.H. 561, 534 A.2d 689 (1987).

9. Reilly v. Dynamic Exploration, Inc., 571 So.2d 140 (La.1990).

10. See Jerry J. Phillips, Products Liability for Personal Injury to Minors, 56 Va. L. Rev. 1223 (1970).

misuse and otherwise. Consequently the vehicle's design must take such eventualities into account. The vehicle need not be crash-proof but it must use reasonable safety features. If, upon slight impact, a roof collapses, a gas tank spews burning gasoline on the passengers, or a restraint system permits occupants to be thrown from the vehicle, the automobile is not designed reasonably, and it is defective.[11] This rule necessarily means that the manufacturer remains liable for a proven defect even if other causes contribute to or concur in causing the injury.[12]

However, when the defect does not cause the impact itself but only adds to the injury, the manufacturer is subject to liability only for the portion of the injury that would have been avoided by a nondefective product if that portion can be established by evidence.[13] Who has the burden of proving how much the injury was enhanced by the defect? One group of courts hold that the plaintiff must prove both that the defect caused the enhanced injury and also the amount of that injury.[14] Some others hold that the plaintiff must prove that the product defect caused enhancement of the injury but the defendant then has the burden of how much of that injury would have occurred even with a non-defective product.[15] The Products Restatement provides that if evidence shows that additional harm did in fact occur but does not permit the trier to distinguish between increased harm caused by the product and the harm that would have occurred anyway, the defendant is liable for the whole amount.[16] An alternative to all these solutions is to apportion liability by fault rather than by causation, that is, to estimate the fault of each party rather than to estimate the amount of increased harm caused by the manufacturer's bad design.[17]

Foreseeability does not invariably prove defect. The rule that designs must take foreseeable use into account does not relieve the plaintiff of proving a defect in the product. The defendant must design reasonably with the product's use in mind, but the manufacturer cannot avoid all foreseeable abuses. It is certainly foreseeable that some drinkers will misuse alcohol, but—so far, at least—uncontaminated alcoholic beverages are not regarded as defective.[18] The plaintiff's misuse of alcohol may

11. See Turner v. General Motors Corp., 584 S.W.2d 844 (Tex.1979); Slone v. General Motors Corp., 249 Va. 520, 457 S.E.2d 51 (1995).

12. Jurado v. Western Gear Works, 131 N.J. 375, 619 A.2d 1312 (1993).

13. Mazda Motor Corp. v. Lindahl, 706 A.2d 526 (Del.1998).

14. Huddell v. Levin, 537 F.2d 726 (3d Cir.1976) heads this list.

15. Polston v. Boomershine Pontiac–GMC Truck, Inc., 262 Ga. 616, 423 S.E.2d 659 (1992).

16. Restatement of Products Liability § 16.

17. This was approved in Hillrichs v. Avco Corp., 514 N.W.2d 94 (Iowa 1994). For discussion of the differences between causal and fault apportionment see §§ 170, 203 & 204. Fault of the plaintiff (or third persons) in causing the accident would ordinarily be compared to the fault of the manufacturer in enhancing injuries. E.g., Whitehead v. Toyota Motor Corp., 897 S.W.2d 684 (Tenn. 1995). Contra, Reed v. Chrysler Corp., 494 N.W.2d 224 (Iowa 1992).

18. See Dauphin Deposit Bank and Trust Co. v. Toyota Motor Corp., 408 Pa.Super. 256, 596 A.2d 845 (1991); Joseph E. Seagram & Sons v. McGuire, 814 S.W.2d 385 (Tex.1991).

be foreseeable, but that will not assist the plaintiff unless she can demonstrate that alcohol is defective.

Misuse, Alteration and other Conduct as a Superseding Cause

The plaintiff's own unforeseeable negligence, misuse, or alternation of the product, if it is one of the causes of her injury, may be a superseding cause that relieves the manufacturer of liability for the defective product, even in states that refuse to reduce recovery for the plaintiff's comparative fault.[19] The same is true with the unforeseeable negligence, misuse, or alteration by others.[20]A common case is an employer's removal of safety devices from machinery used by workers. If the alternation is unforeseeable, the manufacturer is not liable to the injured worker.[21] But if the alteration or misuse is itself foreseeable as a potential increase in the risk of harm, it is not a superseding cause and is not a ground for avoiding liability if the product is defective.[22] As usual, where reasonable people could differ, foreseeability is a jury question.[23] Likewise if the alteration or misuse did not in fact cause the harm, it is of no consequence.[24]

Some older cases in particular go much further by holding that discovery of the danger by an intervening actor who continues to use the product[25] or sells it without repair is a superseding cause.[26] The rule is, however, that if misuse, alteration, or failure to repair is foreseeable, the intervening conduct is not a superseding cause and the manufacturer remains liable. Earlier cases tended to find very little to be foreseeable

19. General Motors Corp. v. Wolhar, 686 A.2d 170 (Del.1996) (seatbelt non-use admissible to show non-use as supervening cause of injury); Monsanto Co. v. Reed, 950 S.W.2d 811 (Ky.1997). Some statutes, at least in form, prohibit all recovery when the product has been altered even if the alteration was foreseeable. See KY. REV. STATS. § 411.320 (1).

20. Statutes may immunize manufacturers even when the defective product is one of the proximate causes of harm. In La Plante v. American Honda Motor Co., Inc., 27 F.3d 731 (1st Cir.1994) the court held that by statute, a third person's failure to do routine maintenance on an ATV was "alteration" so that manufacturer would not be liable even if a defect was one of the contributing causes of harm. See generally, Frederick E. Felder, Annotation, Products Liability: Alteration of Product After it Leaves Hands of Manufacturer or Seller as Affecting Liability For Product-caused Harm, 41 A.L.R.3d 1251 (1972).

21. E.g., Sikorski v. Link Elec. & Safety Control Co., 117 Ohio App.3d 822, 691 N.E.2d 749 (1997); Davis v. Berwind Corp., 547 Pa. 260, 690 A.2d 186 (1997).

22. E.g., Witthauer v. Burkhart Roentgen, Inc., 467 N.W.2d 439 (N.D.1991). New York once barred recovery even when misuse was foreseeable, but appears to be in a process of cautiously withdrawing from this extreme position. See Liriano v. Hobart Corp., 132 F.3d 124 (2d Cir.1998) (certifying question).

23. As in Price v. Blaine Kern Artista, Inc., 111 Nev. 515, 893 P.2d 367 (1995).

24. See Johnson v. Niagara Mach. & Tool Works, 555 So.2d 88, 91 (Ala.1989)

25. Stultz v. Benson Lumber Co., 6 Cal.2d 688, 59 P.2d 100 (1936) (defective lumber was sold for use in scaffolding; the plaintiff's employer discovered the danger but used the lumber anyway, which resulted in collapse of the scaffold and injury to the plaintiff; held, the employer's discovery and use is a superseding cause).

26. Ford Motor Co. v. Wagoner, 183 Tenn. 392, 192 S.W.2d 840 (1946) (discovering a defect, Ford sent dealers a free part replacement to make it safe; the dealer offered it to the original purchaser, who declined the repair; the original purchaser then sold the unrepaired car to B, whose driver was injured as a result of the defect; held, the original purchaser is a superseding cause; the court declared that the original purchaser's failure to accept repair was unforeseeable).

and consequently contracted liability. Contemporary cases more often tend to leave the question of foreseeability of intervening negligence, misuse, or modification to the jury.[27]

Misuse as Comparative Fault

In some cases a product is defective and its defect is a concurring cause of the harm suffered by the plaintiff. In these cases, evidence of the plaintiff's misuse that is a concurring cause of the harm may be relevant on the issue of comparative fault, even though it does not negate a defect or causation. [28]

For example, if the product is an automobile, it might be considered a kind of misuse to drive it drunkenly at high speeds, but since such uses are foreseeable, manufacturers must nevertheless include seatbelts and other reasonable crash protection designs. If they do not do so, the product is defective. If the driver is killed because no protection was available when she crashed the car, the defect was one of the causes of harm. But the driver's fault is also one of the causes of harm and where comparative fault systems are used in products cases, the plaintiff's conduct warrants a reduction of damages whether the driver's speed is considered to be misuse or some other brand of fault.[29]

§ 371. Disclaimers and Limitations on Liability

Products manufacturers and distributors can limit implied warranties of merchantability, subject to limits imposed by the Uniform Commercial Code and a federal statute known as the Magnuson–Moss Act. The Magnuson–Moss Act mainly standardizes some conceptions of warranty and requires clarity and honesty, but does not directly affect personal injury claims.[1] The UCC permits disclaimer of warranties by clear and conspicuous language.[2] So far as a personal injury case is considered to be a warranty case under the UCC and not a strict tort claim in disguise, the disclaimer or limitation of the implied warranty might preclude suit.[3] The UCC also permits the seller to limit remedies for breach of warranty in stand-alone economic harm cases, but a

27. Springmeyer v. Ford Motor Co., 60 Cal.App.4th 1541, 71 Cal.Rptr.2d 190 (1998) (purchaser did not respond to recall/repair offer, sold truck to L, whose employee was injured by defect; superseding cause a jury question); Holmes v. Wegman Oil Co., 492 N.W.2d 107 (S.D.1992) (dealer who had replaced defective parts as part of manufacturer's recall, used one of the replaced parts in another repair, resulting in a number of burns and one death; jury question whether dealer's conduct was superseding cause).

28. Jimenez v. Sears, Roebuck & Co., 183 Ariz. 399, 904 P.2d 861 (1995); Coney v. J.L.G. Indus., Inc., 97 Ill.2d 104, 454 N.E.2d 197, 73 Ill.Dec. 337 (1983).

29. Thus on similar facts the driver's fault could count toward a comparative fault reduction in Daly v. General Motors Corp., 20 Cal.3d 725, 575 P.2d 1162, 144 Cal.Rptr. 380 (1978). Some courts reject comparative fault altogether. Where that rule is followed it would bar comparative fault reduction but that is independent of any misuse rule. See § 369.

§ 371

1. 15 U.S.C.A. § 2301. For a brief discussion, see James J. White & Robert S. Summers, Uniform Commercial Code § 9–12 (3d ed. 1988).

2. UCC § 2–316(2).

3. Ford Motor Co. v. Moulton, 511 S.W.2d 690 (Tenn.1974).

limitation as to damages for personal injury is prima facie unconscionable and unenforceable.[4]

Under the 1964 Restatement Second, manufacturers had no power to disclaim strict liability for personal injury by contractual provisions accompanying the product's sale.[5] Even when claims were pursued under a theory of implied warranty, courts that perceived warranty claims as essentially tort suits held that the manufacturer's disclaimer or limitation of the implied warranty was ineffective so long as the claim was for injury rather than for commercial loss.[6] That is the rule adopted by the Restatement of Products Liability as well.[7]

Although disclaimers will not absolve the defendant of liability for a defective product, adequate warnings may make some products reasonably safe. As a matter of substance, an attempted disclaimer of any liability for burns resulting when a chemical product touches the skin also gives a warning. If the risk of burns is unavoidable, a good warning might suffice to make such a product reasonably safe. Courts (and the UCC) have insisted that warnings be direct, specific, and properly conspicuous, so a warning formulated as a disclaimer probably is not sufficient. On the other hand, the manufacturer may accomplish some of its goals by drafting a warning instead of a disclaimer.

Product descriptions and sales of products for limited purposes may also function to limit liability. If I sell bulk milk described as milk, it had better be safe for human consumption. If I sell the same item as a soil amendment that can add calcium to the soil, there is no reason to make it safe for drinking unless I can foresee that the buyer will consume it or offer it to others for consumption. Similarly, to say the product is a used product is to reduce consumer expectations. In fact, in the case of used products, a seller's formal disclaimer—I'm selling this car as is, with all defects—may be considered as one factor bearing on the defectiveness of the used product.[8]

§ 372. Statutory Defenses

As a part of the tort reform movement, most states have now enacted statutory limitations on liability for product defects. To a large extent, these statutes provide rules substantially in accord with the rules developed by judicial decision in most states. Such statutes may, for example, provide that damages are to be reduced for plaintiff fault and that unforeseeable alteration which is the proximate cause of the harm relieves the defendant of liability, as does some kinds of product misuse. Special protective statutes of limitations are included as well,[1] and

4. UCC 2–719 (3).

5. Restatement of Torts § 402A, cmt. m.

6. Henningsen v. Bloomfield Motors, Inc., 32 N.J. 358, 161 A.2d 69, 75 A.L.R.2d 1 (1960).

7. Restatement of Products Liability § 18 (no exculpatory provision bar or reduce otherwise valid products claim "for harm to persons").

8. See Restatement of Products Liability § 8

§ 372

1. § 374.

damages caps may be imposed either specially in products actions or as part of broad limitations on recoveries.[2]

Eliminating liability for unknowable dangers. One of the most important substantive provisions in the statutes eliminates any potential for liability for unknowable risks. These provisions respond to those cases that impose liability for design and warning defects even when the dangers of the product could not have been known at the time the product was distributed.[3] The statutes, along with most cases, in effect invoke a negligence standard, holding the manufacturer responsible for a design defect if it should reasonably have known of an avoidable risk, but not otherwise. The statutes achieve this result by a variety of provisions ranging from a direct statement that liability is limited to negligence to a provision exculpating the manufacturer if the product met the "state of the art".[4]

Scientific knowability or industry standards? Do the state of the art statutes make industry custom the standard of care, contrary to the general tort rule on the effect of custom?[5] Or do they only mean to foreclose liability for scientifically unknowable risks? Most of the statutes rather clearly foreclose liability for scientifically unknowable risks but definitely do not adopt the industry's own standards as the governing test.[6] Other statutes may allow the industry to set its own standards for its products. One statute presumes the product nondefective if it conformed either to "generally recognized and prevailing standards" *or* to the state of the art, a disjunction that distinguishes prevailing standards from state of the art and exculpates the product if either is established.[7] Others provide that the defendant is not liable if the product design and its method of manufacture, testing and labeling conformed to "the state of the art" at the time.[8] In the absence of a definition or implications to the contrary, such a statute conceivably could mean that the industry's own practices set the limits of the industry's liability. But some such statutes have been construed to establish feasibility as the standard rather than the industry's own

2. E.g., Ohio Rev. Code § 2323.54 .

3. § 359.

4. Ariz. Rev. Stats § 12–683 (state of art); N.C. Gen. Stat. § 99B (liability only for negligence); Mich. Stat. § 600.2946 (2) (requiring feasible alternative design, probably implicitly requiring knowable risks); N.J. Stats. Ann. § 2A:58C–3 (similar); Ohio Rev. Code Ann. § 2307.75(A) (invoking risk-benefit test).

5. See §§ 163 & 164.

6. See, e.g., Ark. Code Ann. § 16–116–104 ("consideration" of industry practice); Colo. Rev. Stats. § 13–21–403 (rebuttably presumed that product is nondefective if product conformed to the state of the arm "as distinguished from industry standards"); Kan. Stat. Ann. § 60–3307 (evidence of industry's improvements inadmissible); La. Rev. Stats. § 2800.59; N.H. Stat. Ann., § 507:8–g (a defense if risks were not discoverable using "prevailing research and scientific techniques"); Tenn. Code Ann. § 29–28–105 (scientific knowledge available to the manufacturer at the time "is applicable," but consideration is also given to industry custom and standards).

7. Ky. Rev. Stats. § 411.310 (2).

8. Ariz. Rev. Stats. § 12–683 1; Ind. Code § 34–20–5–1 (rebuttable presumption when product conforms to "generally recognized state of the art").

custom, even though evidence of industry custom is admissible as tending to show what may be feasible.[9]

Burden of proof. The state of the art statutes, including those that do not actually use that term, also raise questions about the burden of proof. Some of them, referring to a "defense," impliedly or perhaps explicitly put the burden on the defendant to show that the product met the state of the art.[10] Others leave the question in doubt.[11] So far as the statute merely provides for admissibility of state of the art evidence without prescribing a substantive rule, the statute does not indicate anything about the burden of proof.

Flaws. The case of manufacturing flaws, as distinguished from design and warning defects, is now the core case for strict liability, because if a product's risk is unknowable, the design and warning claims now generally fail. But knowability of risks is logically no part of the manufacturing defect case; product flaws are happenstantial, so the fact that the flaw was not known or reasonably knowable seems to be irrelevant as a common law matter. But some state of the art statutes can be read to bar the strict liability claim for product flaws as well as other defects.[12] Other statutes limit the state of the art defense in some way and appear to permit strict liability in manufacturing defect claims.[13]

§ 373. Compliance with or Preemption by Statute

Compliance with Statute, Regulations, or Specifications

Under the common law, the defendant's compliance with a statute is not in itself a defense to a negligence action.[1] If the defendant is driving only 50 miles per hour in a 55 mph zone, he may still be negligent in driving too fast for the circumstances as well as negligent in failing to keep a lookout. The common law rule in products cases is the same—evidence of compliance with statute or regulation is relevant to judg-

9. Hughes v. Massey–Ferguson, Inc., 522 N.W.2d 294 (Iowa 1994).

10. Ariz. Rev. Stat. § 12–683 ("if the defendant proves"); Mo. Stat. § 537.764 2 ("defense" in warning claims); Iowa Code § 668.12 (no fault assigned to one who pleads and proves state of the art); La. Rev. Stat. Ann. § 2800.59 ("if the manufacturer proves"); Neb. Rev. Stat. § 25–21,182 ("defense").

11. Colo. Rev. Stat. Ann. § 13–21–403 (product rebuttably presumed nondefective if it conformed to state of the art) (difficult to interpret since the product is already "presumed" to be nondefective in the sense that the plaintiff has the burden of production and persuasion).

12. Iowa Code § 668.12 (design, manufacturing and warning claims all included); Ky. Rev. Stat. § 411.310 (if design, methods of manufacture and testing conformed to prevailing standards, product "presumed" nondefective).

13. Miss. Code Ann. § 11–1–63 (requiring that the manufacturer should have known danger in warning and design defect case but making no such requirement in manufacturing defect cases); Mo. Stat. § 537.764 (2) (state of the art is a complete defense and relevant evidence in strict liability failure to warn claims); Neb. Rev. Stat. § 25–21,182 (state of art is a defense in action for negligence, defective design, testing or labeling, no mention of manufacturing defect).

§ 373

1. § 247.

ments about the product's alleged design or warning defects and hence admissible[2] but not by any means conclusive.[3]

From time to time critics have proposed statutory change so that a manufacturer's compliance with statute or regulation would furnish some kind of defense or semi-defense.[4] Other commentators have usually observed that such a statutory change would create a number of problems because regulatory standards are often too general, or ambiguous, or insufficiently up to date.[5] Frequently, regulations are intended to provide a floor or a minimum level of safety, not an optimal level or a ceiling on safety precautions. In addition, even if legislatures and regulatory agencies are not "captured" by the industries they regulate, statutes and regulations may reflect the heavy influence of the regulated industry as much as judicious concerns with safety. Most federal law is regulatory in nature; regulators are not likely to think through tort issues when they formulate rules that may be appropriate from an administrative viewpoint but not from a tort law viewpoint. Finally, a compliance defense is likely to shift the forms and the focus of the judicial inquiry from the merits to technical questions of compliance with and meanings of regulations, with no gain in justice and no savings in litigation costs.[6]

Some states have enacted statutes attempting to provide some kind of protection for manufacturers whose products could be found defective even when they have complied with federal statutes. A few of these merely provide that evidence of compliance is admissible as tending to show that the product is not defective or negligently made.[7] A few others provide that when compliance is proven, the product is rebuttably "presumed" non-defective.[8] Neither group appears to change much. The plaintiff already has the burden of proving that the product is defective, which is to say that the product is "presumed" nondefective until the plaintiff sustains that burden. Statutes could, however, meaningfully provide that the presumption resulting from compliance is rebutted only by some especially demanding level of proof, such as clear and convincing evidence.[9] Finally, a few statutes eliminate punitive damages when

2. E.g., Dillon v. Nissan Motor Co., 986 F.2d 263 (8th Cir.1993).

3. Bammerlin v. Navistar Int'l Transp. Corp., 30 F.3d 898 (7th Cir.1994); Restatement of Products Liability § 4.

4. Richard C. Ausness, The Case for a "Strong" Regulatory Compliance Defense, 55 Md. L. Rev. 1210 (1996).

5. Teresa Moran Schwartz, The Role of Federal Safety Regulations in Products Liability Actions, 41 Vand. L. Rev. 1121 (1988).

6. See Michael D. Green, Statutory Compliance and Tort Liability: Examining the Strongest Case, 30 U. Mich. J.L. Ref. 461 (1997) (examining FDA regulations of prescriptive drugs as the strongest case for a defense).

7. Ark. Code Ann. § 16–116–105; Rev. Code Wash. § 7.72.050.

8. Colo. Rev. Stat. Ann. § 13–21–403; Tenn. Code Ann. § 29–28–104.

9. See James A. Henderson, Jr., Manufacturers' Liability for Defective Product Design: A Proposed Statutory Reform, 56 N.C. L. Rev. 625, 632 (1978) (proposing to bar the plaintiff if the product complied with a mandatory standard or regulation unless the plaintiff proved "by clear and convincing evidence" and by "other facts" than already required to prove her case, that the standards were inadequate).

compliance with statute or regulation is demonstrated.[10]

Preemption of State Tort Law

Although the state compliance statutes described above do not appear to have much effect, federal statutes sometimes preempt or entirely displace state law, including tort law.[11] The effect is that when a manufacturer complies with a federal statute, no tort claim can be pursued, so in that case compliance is a complete defense. As already discussed, manufacturers who produce major products to government specification are often accorded the same protection.[12]

Federal statutes may preempt state law, either expressly or impliedly. Implied preemption may occur if a federal statute or set of valid regulations either occupies the regulated field or conflicts with state law. In any such cases, the federal law preempts or displaces state law.[13] Federal lawmaking culture is oriented to regulation, not to private tort rights. Only a few federal statutes create private tort claims for personal injury.[14] In many instances when state tort rights are displaced, no new comparable federal tort right is substituted. Instead, the manufacturer is subjected to regulation without being subjected to liability.

Since preemption requires courts to interpret federal regulatory statutes that are themselves far from clear, preemption issues have bred a good deal of litigation. A given statute may preempt some tort claims but not others. A good example arises under the tobacco labeling act. Congress requires cigarette packages to bear a health warning label. The statute forbids additional advertising requirements but says nothing about common law tort claims. However, the Supreme Court held that a common law tort claim based on failure to warn would be an additional advertising requirement. Hence no tort claim could be pursued based solely upon the the manufacturer's failure to give a better warning than required by the Congress. On the other hand, a claim based upon negligent research or upon express warranty would not be preempted.[15]

A number of federal statutes set products standards or regulate products and may include provisions that arguably expressly or impliedly preempt state tort claims. These include, besides the tobacco labeling

10. Or. Rev. Stats. § 30.927 (as to regulated prescription drugs).

11. The preemption effect is not limited to products cases. It may include such diverse matters of the safe (or unsafe) operation of railroads and the denial of medical benefits due under employment medical plans. See §§ 224 & 256 for examples.

12. See § 274.

13. Robert B. Leflar and Robert S. Adler, The Preemption Pentad: Federal Preemption of Products Liability Claims After Medtronic, 64 Tenn. L. Rev. 691 (1997) proposed a problem-solving type of analysis that is also finer-tuned in hopes of dealing with chaotic preemption jurisprudence. These authors recognize a "dictate preemption" in which state law is preempted when federal law commands that a product be made in a particular way and no other.

14. The Federal Employers Liability Act and its maritime companion are two of the few that eliminate state-law rights and at the same time furnish a federal substitute remedy. See 45 U.S.C.A. § 51; 46 U.S.C.A. § 688.

15. Cipollone v. Liggett Group, Inc., 505 U.S. 504, 112 S.Ct. 2608, 120 L.Ed.2d 407 (1992).

act, statutes on flammable fabrics,[16] on insecticides and other poisons,[17] on hazardous substances, and on motor vehicle safety standards.[18] Food and drugs are regulated heavily, but with no obvious preemptive intent.[19] However, medical devices such as pacemakers and penile implants, are regulated under the same general scheme and as to these devices the statute contains preemptive language.[20] The Consumers Products Safety Commission Act[21] and the the Occupational Health and Safety Act regulating job safety are less likely to generate substantial preemption defenses.[22] Whether a given claim is preempted depends upon statutory language, which itself may emanate contradictory signals.[23]

The result is that a case by case analysis is required to determine whether a claim is preempted, not only because statutes themselves may differ from each other, but because some claims under a given statute may be preempted while others are not. And courts differ among themselves on a number of claims.

The Supreme Court has held that the absence of a regulation on anti-lock brakes is not itself a declaration that manufacturers are free to omit anti-lock brakes. Thus the federal motor vehicle regulations do not preempt a tort claim based on the absence of anti-lock brakes.[24] But a number of courts have held that regulations give manufacturers the option of omitting airbags, so that a tort claim for failure to have airbag protection is preempted.[25] Others have said that the vehicle regulations preempt neither claims based upon the absence of airbags [26]nor those

16. 15 U.S.C.A. § 1203 (with exceptions, states may not prescribe different standards to protect against same risks as covered by statute) (part of the Flammable Fabrics Act).

17. 7 U.S.C.A. § 136v (state may not be more permissive in its regulations and may not alter federal labeling or warning requirements) (part of the Federal Insecticide, Fungicide, and Rodenticide Act (FIFRA)).

18. 49 U.S.C.A. § 30103(b) & (e) ("a State may prescribe ... a standard applicable to the same aspect of performance of a motor vehicle or motor vehicle equipment only if the standard is identical to the standard prescribed under this chapter" but "[c]ompliance with a motor vehicle safety standard prescribed under this chapter does not exempt a person from liability at common law") (part of the National Traffic and Motor Vehicle Safety Act).

19. See e.g., David R. Geiger & Mark D. Rosen, Rationalizing Product Liability for Prescription Drugs: Implied Preemption, Federal Common Law, and Other Paths to Uniform Pharmaceutical Safety Standards, 45 DePaul L. Rev. 395 (1996) (complaining that the absence of preemption is "patently unfair").

20. 21 U.S.C.A. § 360k (states may not impose any requirement for a medical device different from the federal requirement).

21. 15 U.S.C.A. § 2075(b) by its terms permits more demanding regulation.

22. See § 133.

23. See, e.g., Wood v. General Motors Corp., 865 F.2d 395 (1st Cir.1988); Hernandez–Gomez v. Leonardo (Volkswagen of America, Inc.), 185 Ariz. 509, 917 P.2d 238 (1996).

24. Freightliner Corp. v. Myrick, 514 U.S. 280, 115 S.Ct. 1483, 131 L.Ed.2d 385 (1995).

25. Pokorny v. Ford Motor Co., 902 F.2d 1116 (3d Cir.1990) (since manufacturer had option under regulations to use airbag or not, tort requirement of airbag would undermine the "regulatory framework"); Irving v. Mazda Motor Corp., 136 F.3d 764 (11th Cir. 1998) (similar).

26. Wilson v. Pleasant, 660 N.E.2d 327 (Ind.1995); Tebbetts v. Ford Motor Co., 140 N.H. 203, 665 A.2d 345 (1995); Drattel v. Toyota Motor Corp. 92 N.Y.2d 35, 699 N.E.2d 376, 677 N.Y.S.2d 17 (1998) (noting that most federal decisions favoring preemption antedated Freightliner Corp. v.

based upon the need for better safety harness systems than those prescribed by regulations.[27]

A similar story, with varying degrees of preemption, can be told of other statutes. In the medical device area, the Supreme Court has held that the plaintiff's design and warning defect claims in connection with a heart pacemaker were not preempted, where the pacemaker had been approved under a grandfather clause and not actually regulated by specific federal requirements.[28] It may be uncertain how far the case can be generalized. Certainly some implants and devices, including pacemakers,[29] have been protected by preemption. Preemption in the device cases applies only when state law conflicts with the specific federal regulation because compliance with both state and federal rules is impossible or because compliance with the state law would impede enforcement of the federal.[30] For that reason, preemption is most likely when federal regulation is extensive or specific and when the state law "requirement" is also specific in its conflict.[31]

Under a statute requiring certain labeling for poisons and the like, the claim for failure to warn adequately of the product's danger is usually[32] but not always[33] held to be preempted. On the other hand, courts usually say that the Flammable Fabrics Act does not preempt the common law tort claim.[34]

§ 374. Statutes of Limitation

To a large extent what has already been said about the statute of limitations in negligence cases applies in product liability cases as well.[1] The traditional rule starts the statute of limitations running at the time of injury; the discovery rule starts the statute running only when the plaintiff discovered or should have discovered injury and causation; the

Myrick, 514 U.S. 280, 115 S.Ct. 1483, 131 L.Ed.2d 385 (1995) and other major Supreme Court decisions).

27. E.g., Hyundai Motor Co. v. Alvarado, 974 S.W.2d 1(Tex.1998).

28. Medtronic, Inc. v. Lohr, 518 U.S. 470, 116 S.Ct. 2240, 135 L.Ed.2d 700 (1996).

29. Martin v. Telectronics Pacing Sys., Inc., 105 F.3d 1090 (6th Cir.1997) (pacemaker); Papike v. Tambrands Inc., 107 F.3d 737 (9th Cir.1997) (tampon, inadequate warning claim preempted); Fry v. Allergan Med. Optics, 695 A.2d 511 (R.I.1997) (implant).

30. See Worthy v. Collagen Corp., 967 S.W.2d 360 (Tex.1998).

31. Class III medical devices, the most dangerous, are the most heavily and specifically regulated. The premarket approval process (applicable only to some Class III devices) has been regarded as a specific federal regulation with the result that the tort claim is preempted for products that have undergone that process. Mitchell v. Collagen Corp., 126 F.3d 902 (7th Cir.1997) (but express warranty claim not preempted).

32. King v. E.I. Dupont De Nemours and Co., 996 F.2d 1346 (1st Cir.1993).

33. Etcheverry v. Tri–Ag Service, Inc., 65 Cal.App.4th 467, 76 Cal.Rptr.2d 466 (1998) review granted 78 Cal.Rptr.2d 524, 962 P.2d 886 (1998).

34. Wilson v. Bradlees of New England, Inc., 96 F.3d 552 (1st Cir.1996) ("The current flammability standard is not one adopted by the federal agency after a searching inquiry into what best serves the public interest. It is an industry devised standard that has been perpetuated by CPSC inaction in the teeth of some indications that the standard is not adequate").

§ 374

1. See §§ 216–223.

new statutes of repose put an outer limit on the discovery rule by providing that after a stated period, the statute bars the claim even if the injury has not yet occurred and even if it could not have been discovered. Products cases, however, tend to highlight several specific considerations.

Time of accrual. The cause of action for strict tort liability is usually treated under the rules applicable to negligence,[2] so accrual begins when injury occurs,[3] subject to the discovery rule [4]and statutes of repose where applicable. The claim for breach of warranty, however, can arguably accrue at the time the product was sold on the ground that warranty claims are based on contract, which is breached at the time of sale if the product is defective. That rule is especially adapted to commercial or economic loss cases and it is accepted by the Uniform Commercial Code.[5] A number of courts have gone further by applying a time-of-sale rule to personal injury cases brought on a warranty theory.[6] Such an approach can bar the claim before injury occurs.[7] Not surprisingly, other courts have rejected this time-of-sale rule. They say that even if the claim for personal injury is constructed on a warranty theory, the claim is essentially one in tort and governed by the tort statute of limitations.[8] Neither the contract nor the tort approach consistently favors one party or the other. The plaintiff who buys a product that immediately causes a known injury will be benefitted by the longer warranty statute of limitations, although it begins to run immediately.[9] When the state has enacted a specific products liability statute, that statute may control regardless of the legal theory.[10]

Statutes of repose. Statutes of repose are especially popular in products and related cases. A plaintiff may be injured today by a product manufactured in 1930. Likewise, the plaintiff may be injured today by a product manufactured only last year, but the injury may not become apparent for ten or twenty years, especially with toxic injuries. These possibilities have led to widespread use of statutes of repose in products cases, typically cutting off all liability after an easily ascertainable time,

2. See Sheldon R. Shapiro, Annotation, Products Liability: What Statute of Limitations Governs Actions Based on Strict Liability in Tort, 91 A.L.R.3d 455 (1980).

3. Ogle v. Caterpillar Tractor Co., 716 P.2d 334 (Wyo.1986) (date of injury);

4. E.g., Bendix Corp. v. Stagg, 486 A.2d 1150 (Del.1984) (asbestosis, a disease of long latency; statute begins to run when disease manifested itself and became physically ascertainable). Some courts have rejected the discovery rule in products actions. See Jane Massey Draper, Annotation, Statute of Limitations: Running of Statute of Limitations on Products Liability Claim Against Manufacturer as Affected by Plaintiff's Lack of Knowledge of Defect Allegedly Causing Personal Injury or Disease, 91 A.L.R.3d 991 (1980).

5. UCC § 2–725 (2).

6. Ogle v. Caterpillar Tractor Co., 716 P.2d 334 (Wyo.1986) (good discussion of cases on both sides).

7. E.g., Rufo v. Bastian–Blessing Co., 417 Pa. 107, 207 A.2d 823 (1965).

8. Rubino v. Utah Canning Co., 123 Cal. App.2d 18, 266 P.2d 163 (1954).

9. As in Sinka v. Northern Commercial Co., 491 P.2d 116 (Alaska 1971).

10. See Oats v. Nissan Motor Corp., 126 Idaho 162, 879 P.2d 1095 (1994) (statute of repose applied to warranty claim, which was regarded as essentially a strict tort liability claim).

such as six, eight, or ten years after the product was first sold for consumption.[11]

A few courts have held that statutes of repose violate their respective state constitutions,[12] but such statutes have been mostly upheld.[13] The most extreme result would foreclose the plaintiff's claim before she was even injured. The repose rule may be meliorated in narrow circumstances by allowing additional time to sue so long as the injury itself occurred within the repose period[14] or by declaring the rule unconstitutional only so far as it bars the claim before it arises.[15] The plaintiff may also sidestep the statute of repose by asserting that injury resulted from failure to provide a postsale warning,[16] or that it was a result of fraud, or that the more favorable statute of another state applied. But such possibilities arise only occasionally and randomly.

TOPIC D. PARTIES AND PRODUCTS COVERED

§ 375. Commercial Distributors Subject to Liability

Commercial sellers and distributors. The Restatement of Products Liability applies its liability rules for personal injury and property damage to those who are in the business of either selling or distributing products. The business of the defendant must include distribution of products of the same kind that caused harm.[1] In addition, the defendant must have actually distributed the particular item that caused the harm.[2] The rule makes all sellers in the chain of distribution—retailers, for example—subject to the rules of liability and defenses[3] except so far

11. NEB. REV. STATS. § 25–224 (ten years from first sale or lease for consumption); TENN. CODE ANN. § 29–28–103 (six years from injury, ten years from purchase for consumption, one year after anticipated life of product, whichever is shortest period). Statutes may also protect those contributing to improvements on real property. N.C. G.S. § 1–50 (six years for improvement to real property). Sometimes the manufacturer of a product can claim the repose offered by those statutes. See, e.g., Covington v. W.R. Grace–Conn., Inc., 952 P.2d 1105 (Wyo.1998) (question of fact whether product was sufficiently permanent to count as an improvement so as to qualify for the repose).

12. E.g., Hazine v. Montgomery Elevator Co., 176 Ariz. 340, 861 P.2d 625 (1993); see also § 219.

13. E.g., Daily v. New Britain Machine Co., 200 Conn. 562, 512 A.2d 893 (1986); see Jay M. Zitter, Annotation, Validity and Construction of Statute Terminating Right of Action for Product Caused Injury at Fixed Period after Manufacture, Sales, or Delivery of Product, 30 A.L.R.5th 1 (1995).

14. See Davis v. Toshiba Mach. Co., America, 186 Ill.2d 181, 237 Ill.Dec. 769, 710 N.E.2d 399 (1999).

15. Diamond v. E.R. Squibb and Sons, Inc., 397 So.2d 671 (Fla.1981).

16. Cf. Chrysler Corp. v. Batten, 264 Ga. 723, 450 S.E.2d 208 (1994) (state of repose did not apply to failure to warn claim).

§ 375

1. Restatement of Products Liability § 1.

2. See Foster v. American Home Prods. Corp., 29 F.3d 165 (4th Cir.1994) (originator of drug and author of its warnings was not subject to liability for harm done by generic equivalent which copied the drug and its warnings, even though such practice was common and foreseeable). Market-share liability is the main exception. See § 176.

3. See Restatement of Products Liability § 20.

as statutes may provide special protections.[4] On the other hand, the requirement of commercial distribution means that some persons closely involved with the product, such as those who service or recondition it[5] and casual individual sellers[6] are not subject to the Product's Restatement's rules of liability for defective products. Such persons may of course be liable on contract or negligence grounds for supplying dangerous services or products.[7]

Indemnity. In the absence of an agreement to the contrary, the non-negligent retailer who satisfies a judgment for the plaintiff has a right of indemnity or full reimbursement against the manufacturer or the intermediate distributor.[8] When the retailer is at fault, however, contribution or partial reimbursement based upon comparative fault or comparative responsibility is more appropriate.[9]

Successors to the manufacturer. A manufacturer who is subject to liability for defective products may dispose of its business by sale of its assets or by merger with a successor corporation. When that happens, persons injured by the first manufacturer's products may be left without redress. The usual rule has it that the injured plaintiff may subject the successor corporation to liability only if the successor has agreed to assume the predecessor's liabilities, the transfer is fraudulent, the two corporations merge or consolidate, or the successor is essentially a continuation of the predecessor.[10] Merger and continuation with some identity of shareholders justify liability for the predecessor's debts. Some courts, however, go further by imposing liability upon the successor when it merely continues the product line after acquiring substantially all the manufacturing assets, even if no shareholders or directors are the same.[11] In addition, a successor corporation may be obliged to provide a postsale warning if it knows of a danger in its predecessor's products.[12]

4. Under a number of statutes, the non-manufacturing defendant is protected if he has no knowledge of the defect and if the manufacturer is subject to service of process and can satisfy a judgment. E.g., Kan. Stats. Ann. § 60–3306. Under a few, non-manufacturing sellers are wholly exempt from "strict liability in tort." Ga. Code § 51–1–11.1.

5. Rolph v. EBI Companies, 159 Wis.2d 518, 464 N.W.2d 667 (1991). But a rebuilder or remanufacturer may be held as if it were the original manufacturer. Michalko v. Cooke Color & Chem. Corp., 91 N.J. 386, 451 A.2d 179 (1982).

6. E.g., Elley v. Stephens, 104 Nev. 413, 760 P.2d 768 (1988).

7. See Goldman v. Packaging Indus., Inc., 144 A.D.2d 533, 534 N.Y.S.2d 388 (1988). Restatement Second §§ 388–390 collectively impose liability for known and foreseeable harm from chattels.

8. Koehring Mfg. Co. v. Earthmovers of Fairbanks, Inc., 763 P.2d 499 (Alaska 1988); Mettinger v. Globe Slicing Mach. Co., Inc., 153 N.J. 371, 380, 709 A.2d 779, 783 (1998).

9. Horowitz v. Schneider Nat'l, Inc., 992 F.2d 279 (10th Cir.1993); Dunn v. Kanawha County Bd. of Educ., 194 W.Va. 40, 459 S.E.2d 151 (1995). Cf. Emery v. Hussey Seating Co., 697 A.2d 1284 (Me.1997) (seller designed product for manufacturer and sold it as his own, no indemnity).

10. Restatement of Products Liability § 12.

11. See, e.g., Mettinger v. Globe Slicing Mach. Co., Inc., 153 N.J. 371, 709 A.2d 779 (1998).

12. See Restatement of Products Liability § 13.

§ 376. Products and Transactions Covered

What counts as a product can be important even in claims for design or warning defect where the plaintiff must, under the 1988 Restatement, prove negligence much as in other cases. First, the say that the defendant distributes a product is a formal way of invoking the duties of product distributors that might not apply to others. For example, publishers are not responsible for the non-defamatory, non-fraudulent content of their publications. Second, where strict liability remains, as with product flaws, it applies only to things within the definition of product. Third, a unique set of terminology, concepts, and statutory limits is invoked for products and not for other liabilities.

Products

Tangible vs. intangible. The Restatement of Products Liability defines products as commercially distributed tangible personal property or as items sufficiently analogous to warrant application of the same rules.[1] The emphasis on tangibility describes the mainstream of products liability, but some tangible items are not treated as products and some intangible items are. Electricity, which seems to fit any definition of an intangible, has been treated as a product and strict liability imposed for such things as excessive voltage that occurs after it reaches the consumer's meter.[2] On the other hand, blood and blood products are quite tangible, but commercial producers are universally given statutory protection against strict liability.[3] Blood suppliers do remain liable for their proven negligence, but even on this they may be given the benefit of a professional standard of care rule that immunizes careless handling of the AIDS danger so long as they followed practices of other blood suppliers.[4]

Service and "hybrid transactions." Strict liability does not attach to defective services in spite of some arguments for it.[5] A physician is not

§ 376

1. Restatement of Products Liability § 19.

2. Stein v. Southern California Edison Co., 7 Cal.App.4th 565, 8 Cal.Rptr.2d 907 (1992) (overload at meter causing a fire; electricity became a product when it left the defendant's control); Beacon Bowl, Inc. v. Wisconsin Elec. Power Co., 176 Wis.2d 740, 501 N.W.2d 788 (1993) (spikes in electricity caused fire; consumer expectation test); accord, Restatement of Products Liability § 19.

3. E.g., N.H. Stats. Ann. § 507:8–b; 42 Pa. Consol. Stats. Ann. § 8333. The Restatement provides the same protection by its proposed common law rule. Restatement of Products Liability § 19 (c) and cmt. c.

4. Brown v. United Blood Servs., 109 Nev. 758, 858 P.2d 391 (1993). A few cases have rebelled against such a rule, indirectly reaching a reasonable person standard of care. United Blood Servs. Div. of Blood Sys., Inc. v. Quintana, 827 P.2d 509 (Colo.1992); Advincula v. United Blood Servs., 176 Ill.2d 1, 678 N.E.2d 1009, 223 Ill.Dec. 1 (1996); cf. Snyder v. American Ass'n of Blood Banks, 144 N.J. 269, 676 A.2d 1036 (1996) (blood banks' trade association promulgating inadequate standards to protect against AIDS would be subject to liability).

5. See William C. Powers, Jr., Distinguishing Between Products and Services in Strict Liability, 62 N.C. L. Rev. 415 (1984) (noting that some service transactions met some of the rationales for strict liability); Michael M. Greenfield, Consumer Protection in Service Transactions—Implied Warranties and Strict Liability in Torts, 1974 Utah L. Rev. 661; Barry Furrow, Defective Mental Treatment: A Proposal for the Application of Strict Liability to Psychiatric Services, 58 B.U. L. Rev. 391 (1978).

strictly liable when a medical procedure goes wrong,[6] not even if a patient is injured by a defective product supplied by her physician.[7] In a few "hybrid transactions" involving both service and transfer of a product to the plaintiff, the provider of the service-product has been held strictly liable, as where a hairdresser provided a defective hair solution that burned the customer.[8] Similarly, a contractor who builds and sells a house may be strictly liable for defects in its appliances, though not for his services.[9] Some courts have said that in hybrid transactions, strict liability will not attach unless the tangible product aspect was "predominant."[10]

Publications and games leading to physical harms. Publications, games, and charts, as distinguished from toys,[11] can lead to physical harm in a number of ways, for example, by inciting the commission of a crime or a dangerous act, or by providing false information in a navigational chart. In the first category, strict liability is generally denied and even negligence claims may be doubtful under the First Amendment or under proximate cause reasoning.[12] However, so far as a book or navigational charge misrepresents precise factual information that can lead to harm, strict liability is not implausible and sometimes has been accepted.[13] In any event the plaintiff misled by a navigational chart may have a claim for misrepresentation.[14]

Raw materials and component parts. Sellers of raw materials and component parts to be used by others to manufacture finished goods are

6. Hoven v. Kelble, 79 Wis.2d 444, 256 N.W.2d 379, 100 A.L.R.3d 1184 (1977)

7. Magrine v. Krasnica, 94 N.J.Super. 228, 227 A.2d 539 (1967), aff'd sub nom., Magrine v. Spector, 100 N.J.Super. 223, 241 A.2d 637 (1968), aff'd 53 N.J. 259, 250 A.2d 129 (1969) (dentist's needle); In re Breast Implant Prod. Liab. Litig., 331 S.C. 540, 503 S.E.2d 445 (1998) (breast implants); but cf. Shaffer v. Victoria Station, Inc., 91 Wash.2d 295, 588 P.2d 233 (1978) (patron in restaurant suffered injury when wine glass broke in his hand; defect may arise in product, or from foreign objects, from decay, or as in this case from packaging); contra: Bell v. Poplar Bluff Physicians Group, Inc., 879 S.W.2d 618 (Mo.Ct.App. 1994) (temporomandibular implant "purchased" by plaintiff from defendant for $283 and for which the defendant paid $154, strict liability is appropriate on the ground that the defendant is a seller, although profit on the medical implant was not necessary to that conclusion).

8. Newmark v. Gimbel's Inc., 54 N.J. 585, 258 A.2d 697 (1969). Cf. Brokenshire v. Rivas and Rivas, Ltd., 142 Or.App. 555, 922 P.2d 696 (1996) (contractor who installed new and allegedly defective floor in bakery was selling a product, not merely performing a service).

9. See State Stove Mfg. Co. v. Hodges, 189 So.2d 113 (Miss.1966).

10. Hill v. Rieth–Riley Constr. Co., Inc., 670 N.E.2d 940 (Ind.App.1996) .

11. Toys: Lugo v. LJN Toys, Ltd., 75 N.Y.2d 850, 552 N.E.2d 162, 552 N.Y.S.2d 914 (1990) (toy doll, Voltron–Defender of the Universe; Voltron on television threw his shield at enemies and the doll's shield was detachable, with predictable copycat results causing injury; jury question whether Voltron was defective).

12. Winter v. G.P. Putnam's Sons, 938 F.2d 1033 (9th Cir.1991) (book on mushrooms lead to injury; book is a product but its information is not); Watters v. TSR, Inc., 904 F.2d 378 (6th Cir.1990) (claim that Dungeons and Dragons game induced boy to commit suicide; held, strict liability cannot apply to words or pictures); Sakon v. Pepsico, Inc., 553 So.2d 163 (Fla.1989); DeFilippo v. National Broad. Co., 446 A.2d 1036 (R.I.1982) (First Amendment)

13. Saloomey v. Jeppesen & Co., 707 F.2d 671 (2d Cir.1983).

14. See Restatement of Products Liability § 19, cmt. d.

subject to the products rules and liable for defects in what they sell, but as already observed, the raw material is not defective merely because the manufacturer to whom it is sold uses it in a badly designed product.[15] If, however, the manufacturer of a component part substantially participates in integrating his component product into another's defective product, he may become liable as if he had sold the integrated product.[16]

Used goods. Used goods represent a special case. First, strict liability would not be imposed for flaws in used goods unless they were distributed commercially or as part of an enterprise. If you sell your car, you are not strictly liable for its flaws. Second, a failing in a used product is not necessarily a defect. Consumers expect used products to have a shorter working life, to need repairs more often, and to pose other risks peculiar to the specific product. Some courts reject,[17] and some accept[18] strict liability for used goods. The Products Restatement takes consumer expectations into account to limit liability in used goods cases.[19] Under its rule, liability is mainly imposed when the reasonable buyer would expect the used product to present no greater risk of a defect than a new product. Liability is also imposed when the defendant has "remanufactured" the used goods. Used goods that are commercially leased, however, are treated like new goods.[20] The special rules for used goods, if special they are, related to strict liability only. The special concerns do not affect the seller's liability for negligent failure to warn.[21]

Real property. Real property was traditionally off limits for strict liability and even negligence liability was limited. Once a builder or repairer of real property had turned the work over to the owner and it had been accepted, liability, even liability for negligence, was at an end.[22] Where this rule—usually in a modified form—still obtains, the builder or contractor who is not liable for his negligence is assuredly not strictly liable either.[23] The accepted work doctrine, however, is now in disrepute. Either because it is rejected or because an exception applies, contractors

15. Petrucelli v. Bohringer and Ratzinger, GMBH, 46 F.3d 1298 (3d Cir.1995); LaMontagne v. E.I. Du Pont De Nemours & Co., Inc., 41 F.3d 846 (2d Cir.1994); Rynders v. E.I. Du Pont De Nemours & Co., 21 F.3d 835 (8th Cir.1994). *Distinguish* Fleck v. KDI Sylvan Pools, Inc., 981 F.2d 107 (3d Cir.1992) (pool liner that had no depth marking on it had but one purpose, to be incorporated into a pool where depth marking was essential, liability). See § 366.

16. Buonanno v. Colmar Belting Co., Inc., 733 A.2d 712 (R.I. 1999); Restatement of Products Liability § 5.

17. Peterson v. Lou Bachrodt Chevrolet Co., 61 Ill.2d 17, 329 N.E.2d 785 (1975).

18. Jordan v. Sunnyslope Appliance Propane & Plumbing Supplies Co., 135 Ariz. 309, 660 P.2d 1236 (Ct. App. 1983); Nelson v. Nelson Hardware, Inc., 160 Wis.2d 689, 467 N.W.2d 518 (1991) (retailer who took gun in on a trade strictly liable for injury caused by defect in gun arising from manufacture).

19. Restatement of Products Liability § 8. The Restatement also recognizes ordinary negligence liability and liability for violation of a safety statute or regulation.

20. See Perton v. Motel Properties, Inc., 230 Ga.App. 540, 497 S.E.2d 29 (1998)

21. Timberline Air Serv., Inc. v. Bell Helicopter–Textron, Inc., 125 Wash.2d 305, 884 P.2d 920 (1994) (original manufacturer may be obliged to provide a postmanufacture warning to ultimate purchaser of used military helicopter).

22. See § 366.

23. Easterday v. Masiello, 518 So.2d 260 (Fla.1988) (relying both on the accepted work doctrine and the rule that real property is not a product).

and builders have been held strictly liable for defects in prefabricated and mass-produced housing[24] and also for defects in appliances and others items they incorporated in a building.[25] Suppliers of asbestos materials for a building have been put in this category.[26] The Products Restatement accepts real property as a product in such cases.[27]

Transactions

Lessors and other suppliers of products as sellers. At one time courts thought that only a literal sale could trigger the rules of product liability. It is now clear that neither a seller nor a sale transaction is required, as long as the product is supplied as part of a business or institutional operation. In particular, commercial lessors,[28] bailors,[29] and suppliers of goods for promotions and otherwise as incident to an enterprise[30] are all suppliers of products and subject to the products rules. Perhaps it would be better to say that any enterprise, profit or nonprofit, that is significantly involved in distribution of the goods, is subject to the product rules.[31] Casual sellers and others suppliers who do not regularly supply goods of the kind in question are not subject to the products liability rules but are subject to ordinary negligence rules.[32] As a matter of form, the Restatement of Products Liability achieves results largely in line with these rules by imposing liability upon sellers and distributors[33] and then defining sellers and distributors of products to include suppliers like lessors and promoters.[34]

Leases of real property, hoteliers. When a tenant is injured by a defective appliance or article of furniture included with the leased premises, some courts have imposed strict liability on the view that the

24. The leading case is Schipper v. Levitt & Sons, Inc., 44 N.J. 70, 207 A.2d 314 (1965). See also Blagg v. Fred Hunt Co., Inc., 272 Ark. 185, 612 S.W.2d 321 (1981) (house built by builder is a product); Kaneko v. Hilo Coast Processing, 65 Haw. 447, 654 P.2d 343 (1982) (prefab building).

25. Berman v. Watergate West, Inc., 391 A.2d 1351 (D.C.1978) (air conditioning); O'Laughlin v. Minnesota Natural Gas Co., 253 N.W.2d 826 (Minn.1977) (floor furnace grate); cf. Blagg v. Fred Hunt Co., Inc., 272 Ark. 185, 612 S.W.2d 321 (1981) (house built by builder is a product, implied warranty claim for odorous carpet is valid).

26. United States Gypsum Co. v. Mayor and City Council of Baltimore, 336 Md. 145, 647 A.2d 405 (Ct.App.1994).

27. Restatement of Products Liability § 19.

28. E.g., Perton v. Motel Properties, Inc., 230 Ga.App. 540, 497 S.E.2d 29 (1998); Kemp v. Miller, 154 Wis.2d 538, 453 N.W.2d 872 (1990) (lessor of automobile strictly liable for defects arising in design or manufacture and for those arising later).

29. Bainter v. Lamoine LP Gas Co., 24 Ill.App.3d 913, 321 N.E.2d 744 (1974) (LP gas tank furnished without separate charge by seller of gas). Use of the defendant's property on the defendant's premises is arguably different because traditional premises liability rules limit liability to negligence. See, e.g., Dixon v. Four Seasons Bowling Alley, Inc., 176 N.J.Super. 540, 424 A.2d 428 (1980).

30. E.g., Perton v. Motel Properties, Inc., 230 Ga.App. 540, 497 S.E.2d 29 (1998) (hotel facilitated sailboat rental for to guests).

31. See Ridenour v. Bat Em Out, 309 N.J.Super. 634, 642, 707 A.2d 1093, 1096 (1998) ("others having a significant role in the chain of distribution to strict products liability responsibility").

32. See Sukljian v. Charles Ross & Son Co., Inc., 69 N.Y.2d 89, 503 N.E.2d 1358, 511 N.Y.S.2d 821 (1986) (sale of surplus equipment).

33. Restatement of Products Liability § 1.

34. Restatement of Products Liability § 20.

landlord leased the defective chattel as well as the premises themselves.[35] Most courts, however, refuse to impose strict liability for injuries resulting defects in the leased premises themselves.[36] Similarly, but more surprisingly, courts have also refused to impose strict liability upon hoteliers for premises defects.[37] The current common law authority for strict landlord liability consists of a carefully considered but lonely decision of a lower court in New York.[38] Many states recognize an implied warranty of habitability, but that turns out not to impose strict tort liability.[39] Most courts have even rejected strict liability of landlords who fail to remove toxic paint where children are living.[40]

35. E.g., Fakhoury v. Magner, 25 Cal. App.3d 58, 101 Cal.Rptr. 473 (1972).

36. Armstrong v. Cione, 69 Haw. 176, 738 P.2d 79 (1987); See Francis M. Dougherty, Annotation, Strict Liability of Landlord for Injury or Death of Tenant or Third Person Caused by Defect in Premises Leased for Residential Use, 48 A.L.R.4th 638 (1987).

37. Peterson v. Superior Court, 10 Cal.4th 1185, 899 P.2d 905, 43 Cal.Rptr.2d 836 (1995)

38. Kaplan v. Coulston, 85 Misc.2d 745, 381 N.Y.S.2d 634 (1976). Strict liability is also imposed under Louisiana's civil law statutes. See Marcantel v. Karam, 601 So.2d 1(La.App.1992). California once adopted a strict liability rule, Becker v. IRM Corp., 38 Cal.3d 454, 698 P.2d 116, 213 Cal.Rptr. 213 (1985), but has since repudiated it. Peterson v. Superior Court, 10 Cal.4th 1185, 43 Cal.Rptr.2d 836, 899 P.2d 905 (1995).

39. See § 241.

40. Gore v. People's Sav. Bank, 235 Conn. 360, 665 A.2d 1341 (1995); Richwind Joint Venture 4 v. Brunson, 335 Md. 661, 645 A.2d 1147 (1994). See Sonja Larsen, Annotation, Landlord's Liability for Injury or Death of Tenant's Child from Lead Paint Poisoning 19 A.L.R.5th 405 (1995).

*

Part III. Operating and Altering the Tort System in Personal Injury Cases

Chapter 25

Damages

§ 377. Basic Compensatory Damages for Personal Injury[1]

Terms and Elements of Damages

In cases of intentional torts to the person and property—assault, battery, false imprisonment, for example—the tort itself is regarded as harmful and the plaintiff is always entitled to recover at least nominal damages and often entitled to recover a substantial sum without proof of any specific loss other than the tort itself.[2] In negligence cases, damages are an essential element of the plaintiff's claim.[3] Unless she has suffered legally recognized harm, she has no claim for damages and cannot recover even a nominal sum.

The term damages refers to the monetary award for legally recognized harm. Damages is distinct from restitution and injunction, both of which are also occasionally available in tort cases. Restitution, when available, requires the defendant to restore any gains he made in a transaction;[4] injunction, when available, forbids threatened actions or requires the defendant to alter harmful conduct or repair its consequences.[5]

In personal injury cases the normal remedy is compensatory damages, awarded in a lump-sum, for all losses that have proximately resulted from the tort and all losses that will so result in the future. The plaintiff has the burden of proving both past and future damages by the preponderance of the evidence. Punitive damages may be added in

§ 377

1. Damages in wrongful death and survival actions are considered in §§ 296–298. Damages for wrongful pregnancy and wrongful birth are considered in §§ 292 & 293.

2. See § 42.

3. See § 166.

4. See generally, 1 Dan B. Dobbs, Remedies §§ 4.1–4.9; a prominent example is recovery "in assumpsit" for conversion. See Dobbs, supra § 5.18.

5. See, e.g., 1 Dan B. Dobbs, Remedies §§ 5.7 (relief from nuisances) & 5.10 (injunction to remove encroaching structures); 2 Dobbs, supra, §§ 6.4 (5) (injunctions against trademark infringement); 7.3 (5) (dignitary rights generally); 7.4 (4) (constitutional rights).

limited cases.[6]

Elements of damages recoverable. Properly proven, the plaintiff is entitled to recover damages under three basic categories. (1) Time losses. The plaintiff can recover loss of wages or the value of any lost time or earning capacity where injuries prevent work. (2) Expenses incurred by reason of the injury. Under one of the avoidable consequences rules, expenses reasonably incurred to minimize damages are recoverable.[7] Expense recovery in personal injury cases are usually medical expenses and kindred items. (3) Pain and suffering in its various forms, including emotional distress and consciousness of loss. The basic damages recovery, comprising all these elements of past and future damages, is subject to various adjustments[8] and sometimes to limits on the total award.[9] In the absence of statute, the prevailing plaintiff does not recover for her attorney fees. A number of civil rights statutes do specifically provide for recovery of attorney fees, however.[10]

Lost Earnings and Earning Capacity

Lost earnings. If the plaintiff is wholly or partly unable to carry out gainful activity as a result of tortiously inflicted injury, she is entitled to recover for actual wages[11] and fringe benefits[12] lost or that will be lost in the future. Evidence of earnings[13] before and after the injury would be relevant, though it is also important to establish that the reduction is a proximate result of the injury.[14] Pre-injury earnings may understate the actual loss. If future wage increases are to be expected, either because of general increase in industrial productivity or because of the plaintiff's reasonably expected advancement, those increases have also been lost and are thus recoverable as damages.[15]

Lost earning capacity. At least under some circumstances, the plaintiff is entitled to claim lost earning capacity instead of actual or prospective lost earnings. Lost earning capacity reflects the value of work the plaintiff could have done but for the injury. If the plaintiff was not working when injured and had no plans to do so, she has no immediate lost income, but her injury nevertheless reduces her earning *capacity.* The most sympathetic case for such a claim is the domestic partner or family member who does not work in the labor market but works without pay in the family business or in the household. Such persons are allowed to recover for their lost capacity to work although they have no

6. § 381.

7. See 1 Dan B. Dobbs, The Law of Remedies § 3.9 (2d ed. 1993).

8. § 380.

9. § 384.

10. E.g., 42 U.S.C.A. § 1988 (general federal civil rights fee statute); Mass. Gen. L. Ann. 266 § 127B. On attorney fees generally, see 1 Dan B. Dobbs, Law of Remedies § 3.10.

11. E.g., Fuqua v. Aetna Cas. & Sur. Co., 542 So.2d 1129 (La.App.1989).

12. E.g., Rivera v. Philadelphia Theological Seminary of St. Charles Borromeo, Inc., 510 Pa. 1, 507 A.2d 1 (1986).

13. Earnings do not include investment profits. See Trushcheff v. Abell–Howe Co., 239 N.W.2d 116 (Iowa 1976).

14. See Robinson v. Greeley and Hansen, 114 Ill.App.3d 720, 725, 70 Ill.Dec. 376, 380, 449 N.E.2d 250, 254 (1983).

15. See Henry v. National Union Fire Ins. Co., 542 So.2d 102, 107 (La.App.1989).

income loss and cannot project any future income losses.[16] The same rule applies to religious persons who have taken a vow of poverty[17] and to children and unemployed persons.[18] Lost earning capacity claims are entirely just in many cases; recovery reflects opportunity cost[19] or provide excellent evidence of the value of non-income work. In extreme cases, as where the plaintiff took early retirement the day before injury, courts can view lost earning capacity claims with healthy skepticism.[20]

Medical and Other Expenses

Medical and non-medical expenses. The injured plaintiff is entitled to recover reasonable medical and other expenses proximately resulting from tortious injury and those that will probably result in the future. The reasonable charges of health care professionals for relief of pain or for treatment are recoverable, including reasonable charges for diagnostic tests, drugs, medical devices and artificial limbs used.[21] Non-medical expenses are also recoverable if they proximately result from the injury.

Proof of reasonable value. The measure of recovery is not the cost of services or appliances needed but their reasonable value,[22] and then only if the services are reasonably required as a result of the injury.[23] Because reasonable value of the services and goods provided is the measure, recovery does not depend on whether the plaintiff has actually paid the doctor's bills.[24] On the other hand, that measure of damages means that if the plaintiff was charged more than the going rate, or fails to prove that the charges were reasonable, she cannot recoup all of her actual medical expenses.[25] In large cases, plaintiffs' attorneys may welcome this rule because it affords an opportunity to detail each medical procedure in the case and its value. But attorneys with small or moderate cases may find the rule unduly complicates the case and may even be a trap for the

16. E.g., American Nat'l Watermattress Corp. v. Manville, 642 P.2d 1330 (Alaska 1982) (76–year old pinned under waterbed that rolled off its pedestal, lost 48–hours a week working in family business for which she was paid only nominal salary; plaintiff was entitled to recover full lost earning capacity).

17. McLaughlin v. Chicago, M., St. P. & P. Ry. Co., 31 Wis.2d 378, 143 N.W.2d 32 (1966).

18. Bishop v. Poore, 475 So.2d 486 (Ala. 1985); cf. Rubio v. Davis, 231 Ga.App. 425, 500 S.E.2d 367 (Ga.Ct.App.1998) (three-year-old's arm amputated, evidence of earing capacity before and after injury not required; damages are in the jury's sound discretion).

19. See 2 Dan B. Dobbs, Law of Remedies § 8.1 (2) (2d ed. 1993).

20. Cf. Saul Levmore, Self–Assessed Valuation Systems for Tort and Other Law, 68 Va. L. Rev. 771, 803–05 (1982) (expressing doubts about earning capacity recovery).

21. E.g., Atlanta Transit System, Inc. v. Nowell, 138 Ga.App. 443, 226 S.E.2d 286 (1976) (diagnosis); Haudrich v. Howmedica, Inc., 169 Ill.2d 525, 662 N.E.2d 1248, 215 Ill.Dec. 108 (1996) (knee replacement); see 2 Dan B. Dobbs, Law of Remedies § 8.1 (3).

22. See, e.g., Steinauer v. Sarpy County, 217 Neb. 830, 843, 353 N.W.2d 715, 724 (1984).

23. See Kempner v. Schulte, 318 Ark. 433, 885 S.W.2d 892 (1994).

24. Eg., Roland v. Krazy Glue, Inc., 342 So.2d 383 (Ala.Civ.App.1977); Ramsey v. Williams, 625 S.W.2d 196 (Mo.Ct.App. 1981).

25. In re Gloria T., 73 Md.App. 28, 33, 532 A.2d 1095, 1097 (1987); Delta Air Lines, Inc. v. Gibson, 550 S.W.2d 310 (Tex. Civ.App.1977). See L.C. DiStasi, Jr., Annotation, Necessity and Sufficiency, in Personal Injury or Death Action, of Evidence as to Reasonableness of Amount Charged or Paid for Accrued Medical, Nursing, or Hospital Expenses, 12 A.L.R.3d 1347 (1967).

unwary, since attorneys frequently seem to assume that proof of the medical expenses by itself is adequate. With these and similar considerations in mind, some courts permit juries to consider the amounts charged or paid as evidence of reasonableness.[26]

Medical surveillance or monitoring. When the plaintiff has been tortiously exposed to a toxic substance that may result in disease after a long latency period, the best way to minimize the harm is to maintain regular periodic medical checkups. Recovery of monitoring expense, once a tort has been established, appears to be in accord with the usual rules of personal injury damages for diagnostic expenses and also with the rule that permits recovery of expenses incurred to minimize damages. Some courts have not only allowed for such periodic future monitoring expenses,[27] but, in line with commentators,[28] have sometimes suggested that the defendant might be required to set up a special fund to finance such medical checkups as they arise.[29] Courts have shown caution, however, sometimes establishing a number of conditions to be met before damages can be recovered for monitoring. One sensible condition is that the plaintiff must be at significant risk; others may be related to proof that monitoring is likely to help discover disease and that early discovery is likely to help.[30] But if the plaintiff has incurred no detectible harm, there is contrary authority denying the recovery of medical monitoring expense altogether.[31]

Mental and Physical Pain and Suffering and Loss of Enjoyment

Entitlement to recovery. The plaintiff is entitled to recover for all forms of suffering proximately caused by tortious injury, including future suffering. The pain for which recovery is allowed includes virtually any form of conscious suffering, both emotional[32] and physical.[33] Pain

26. Palmer Park Gardens, Inc. v. Potter, 162 Colo. 178, 425 P.2d 268 (1967); cf. Wright v. Fox–Stanley Photo Products, 639 S.W.2d 407 (Mo.Ct.App.1982) (reasonableness could be inferred from plaintiff's payment). Statutes may make the bills themselves prima facie evidence of reasonableness. See Ohio Rev. Code § 2317.42.1 (medical bills prima facie reasonable in amount where copies timely delivered to opposing counsel).

27. Hagerty v. L. & L. Marine Servs., Inc., 788 F.2d 315 (5th Cir.1986); Elam v. Alcolac, Inc., 765 S.W.2d 42, 209 (Mo.Ct. App.1988); Ayers v. Jackson Tp., 106 N.J. 557, 525 A.2d 287 (1987).

28. Note, Increased Risk of Disease from Hazardous Waste: A Proposal for Judicial Relief, 60 Wash. L. Rev. 635, 647–52 (1985) (suggesting that the court should use its equitable powers to require the defendant to provide an insurance policy covering the group at risk).

29. Friends For All Children, Inc. v. Lockheed Aircraft Corp., 241 U.S. App. D.C. 83, 746 F.2d 816, 46 A.L.R.4th 1113 (D.C.Cir. 1984) (preliminary injunction ordered defendant to fund medical monitoring program); see Ayers v. Jackson Tp., 106 N.J. 557, 525 A.2d 287 (1987) (medical surveillance costs for those exposed to toxic chemicals, courts should encourage use of court-ordered medical surveillance funds, but lump-sum award here because case was tried that way).

30. E.g., Bourgeois v. A.P. Green Indus., Inc., 716 So.2d 355 (La.1998).

31. Metro–North Commuter Railroad Co. v. Buckley, 521 U.S. 424, 117 S.Ct. 2113, 138 L.Ed.2d 560 (1997).

32. E.g., Wood v. Mobil Chemical Co., 50 Ill.App.3d 465, 8 Ill.Dec. 701, 365 N.E.2d 1087 (1977) (anxiety and depression following brain injury); Alphonso v. Charity Hosp. of Louisiana at New Orleans, 413 So.2d 982 (La.Ct.App.1982) (post-traumatic stress disorder following rape, along with other serious problems).

from medical treatments that are themselves required by the injury is also recoverable, so long as it can be deemed a proximate result of the tort.[34] Expert testimony can address pain, but frequently the physical injury itself and the kind of medical attention needed, permit or require an inference that the plaintiff suffered physically or emotionally. Awards for pain are not easy to evaluate because there is no objective criterion for judgment. For the same reason, it is difficult to set rational limitations on awards. The claim of pain is therefore a serious threat to the defendant since, lacking any highly objective components, it permits juries to roam through their biases in setting an award. At the same time, an award for pain is not intended to be a matter largesse or discretion any more than the award for medical expense or wage loss is. If pain is established, some courts have therefore insisted that the award be made once physical harm is shown.[35]

Forms of suffering included. Courts have said that the award of pain and suffering includes the sensation of physical pain itself, and the inconvenience, pain and sense of loss that may be built on physical injury. Loss of a bodily member[36] and loss of bodily functions,[37] for example, would be likely to entail considerable further pain and inconvenience all of which is well within the definition of pain and suffering. Compensable suffering also includes emotional anguish or distress resulting from injury.[38] Any form of unpleasant emotional reactions to the injury or its consequences, so long as it is proximately related to the tort, is a basis for the pain and suffering recovery. Disfigurement, for example, may cause mental pain or embarrassment, even if the disfigurement could not normally be seen by others.[39] Other unpleasant emotional states are covered by the rule: terror at an approaching injury,[40] worry

33. Sears, Roebuck & Co. v. Hartley, 160 F.2d 1019 (9th Cir.1947) (past pain plus pain of recalling it). See, Plant, Damages for Pain and Suffering, 19 Ohio St. L. J. 200 (1958) (discussing purely subjective pain).

34. See Abrams v. City of Mattoon, 148 Ill.App.3d 657, 101 Ill.Dec. 780, 499 N.E.2d 147 (1986) (side effects of drugs prescribed as result of injury). Self-inflicted pain may also qualify. Alphonso v. Charity Hosp. of Louisiana at New Orleans, 413 So.2d 982 (La.Ct.App.1982) (mental patient/rape victim mutilated herself to prevent further attacks).

35. See, e.g., Jones v. Wal–Mart Stores, Inc., 870 F.2d 982 (5th Cir.1989) (including future mental anguish); American States Ins. Co. v. Audubon Country Club, 650 S.W.2d 252, 55 A.L.R.4th 177 (Ky. 1983) (generally but not invariably an award of future medical expense would indicate that future pain and suffering damages should also be awarded).

36. Mileski v. Long Island R.R., 499 F.2d 1169 (2d Cir.1974) (eye).

37. Excretory and sexual functions for example. Kenton v. Hyatt Hotels Corp., 693 S.W.2d 83 (Mo.1985).

38. E.g., Boryla v. Pash, 960 P.2d 123 (Colo.1998). See § 302.

39. Jones v. Wal–Mart Stores, Inc., 870 F.2d 982 (5th Cir.1989) (re covery must be awarded for disfigurement even if scar is not visible and plaintiff is not embarrassed).

40. E.g., Blum v. Airport Terminal Servs., Inc., 762 S.W.2d 67 (Mo.Ct.App. 1988) (decedent had been aware that plane would crash; "Blum's pre-impact awareness of the impending disaster can also be considered as well as the fact that as an experienced pilot he was uniquely aware of the impending crash and its probable result to him"); Yowell v. Piper Aircraft Corp., 703 S.W.2d 630 (Tex.1986) (preimpact distress damages allowed when decedents' plane broke up and they fell 10,000 feet to an immediate death).

about whether a dog bite will lead to rabies or a burn to cancer[41] are examples of suffering over the future course of an injury already inflicted. Depression, anxiety, and hysterical or conversion reactions are all covered so long as they proximately result from the tortious injury.[42]

Loss of enjoyment of life. The rules permitting recovery for suffering are easily broad enough to permit recovery for the plaintiff's mental reactions to pain and to her sense of loss. If the plaintiff's injury makes it impossible for her to see a sunset, or hear music, engage in sexual activity, or pursue a chosen vocation, she may have no physical sensation of pain but she is suffering. Almost without exception, loss of enjoyment of life in this sense is as compensable as any other emotional state.[43] Older cases that denied recovery for lost enjoyment now appear to be obsolete.

Unknown losses of enjoyment. The controversy today is not whether the plaintiff can recover for suffering in the form of lost enjoyment but whether she can recover for lost enjoyment as an item of damage independent of suffering. For instance, if the plaintiff is in an irreversible coma, she will no longer be able to play the violin or enjoy the sunset, but she is not aware of her loss and never will be. In such a case ordinary language permits us to say that she has lost enjoyment of life but it does not permit us to say she suffers because she is aware of that loss. If loss of enjoyment is merely an aspect of suffering, she cannot recover for lost enjoyment. If it is an independent element of damages, she can. The traditional assumption was that where loss of enjoyment was recoverable, it was an element of pain and suffering. Consequently, some courts faced with this issue have denied recovery.[44] A little authority goes the other way.[45]

A related but quite distinct issue is whether the jury should be instructed to make an award for pain and suffering and another for loss of enjoyment. Some courts permit this over the defendants' objections

41. E.g., Ferrara v. Galluchio, 5 N.Y.2d 16, 176 N.Y.S.2d 996, 152 N.E.2d 249, 71 A.L.R.2d 331 (1958) (worry about cancer). Anxiety about AIDS exposure is a special problem for some courts. See § 311.

42. See 2 Dan B. Dobbs, Law of Remedies § 8.1(4) (2d ed. 1993).

43. E.g., Thompson v. National Railroad Passenger Corp., 621 F.2d 814 (6th Cir. 1980); McAlister v. Carl, 233 Md. 446, 197 A.2d 140, 15 A.L.R.3d 496 (1964)(vocation); Kenton v. Hyatt Hotels Corp., 693 S.W.2d 83 (Mo.1985) (emphasizing plaintiff's loss of ability to play tennis, ski, jog, and carry on other athletic activities). See Annotation, Loss of Enjoyment of Life As A Distinct Element or Factor in Awarding Damage for Bodily Injury, 34 A.L.R.4th 293 (1984). See also 2 Dan B. Dobbs, Law of Remedies § 8.1 (4) (2d ed. 1993).

44. McDougald v. Garber, 73 N.Y.2d 246, 257, 538 N.Y.S.2d 937, 940, 536 N.E.2d 372, 376 (1989).

45. Holston v. Sisters of the Third Order of St. Francis, 247 Ill.App.3d 985, 618 N.E.2d 334, 187 Ill.Dec. 743 (1993); Flannery v. United States, 171 W.Va. 27, 297 S.E.2d 433, 34 A.L.R.4th 281 (W.Va. 1982); see Ocasio v. Amtrak, 299 N.J.Super. 139, 159, 690 A.2d 682, 692 (1997) ("A jury assigned the responsibility of determining the value of a loss of enjoyment of life should have had the opportunity to consider evidence that the Ocasio's mental and physical functions, customary activities and capacity to enjoy the pleasures of life were already restricted by a long-term addiction to drugs."); cf. Marcotte v. Timberland/Hampstead Sch. Dist., 733 A.2d 394 (N.H. 1999) (death case; loss of life recovery permitted under statute).

that this unduly emphasizes suffering and might result in duplicative recoveries.[46]

"Hedonic" damages. In the 1980s lawyers began to use the term "hedonic damages." Hedonic comes from the Greek word referring to pleasure. As with other newly coined legal terms, this one was used in different ways. At times it suggested a recovery for lost pleasures, but at other times it suggested a recovery for lost pleasures of which the plaintiff was not aware. At other times the word hedonic was associated with a third idea. The third idea was that the plaintiff could actually introduce economic testimony to prove the "value" of life or life's pleasures. An economist or team of economists and accountants would conduct empirical studies to determine what people actually pay for pleasures or to protect them and what premiums employers pay for people in risky jobs. The argument was that from such studies, coupled with statistical analysis, you could figure out the real market value of pleasure or of life itself. Something like this was a logically essential element in any recovery for a plaintiff who was unaware of loss, for without this, the trier would have neither actual suffering to estimate nor any other basis for fixing damages. A federal district court approved testimony along these lines in 1985.[47] Otherwise, courts have refused to admit this kind of testimony.[48]

§ 378. Compensatory Damages for Invasion of Constitutional Rights

When the defendant's violation of the plaintiff's constitutional right causes physical harm to the plaintiff, courts can grant ordinary compensatory damages equivalent to those awarded in common law tort cases. Many constitutional invasions closely parallel common law invasions, which furnish good guides on such matters as the causation required and on damages. Police misconduct such as an unjustified strip search, for example, could amount to a common law battery, or false imprisonment as well as potentially a violation of the Fourth or Eighth Amendments. For physical harms, the civil rights plaintiff is entitled to recover for any proven physical disability, pain, or suffering resulting from the civil rights tort,[1] and also for any proven emotional distress that results from

46. Andrews v. Mosley Well Servs., 514 So.2d 491 (La.Ct.App.1987); Eyoma v. Falco, 247 N.J.Super. 435, 589 A.2d 653 (1991); Kirk v. Washington State University, 109 Wash.2d 448, 746 P.2d 285 (1987).

47. Sherrod v. Berry, 629 F.Supp. 159 (N.D.Ill.1985), overruled on other grounds, Sherrod, 856 F.2d 802 (7th Cir.1988).

48. Mercado v. Ahmed, 974 F.2d 863 (7th Cir.1992); Montalvo v. Lapez, 77 Hawai'i 282, 884 P.2d 345 (1994). West Virginia, which approved recovery for lost enjoyment of which the plaintiff was not aware, has nevertheless rejected this kind of testimony, Wilt v. Buracker, 191 W.Va. 39, 443 S.E.2d 196 (1993), leaving an element of recovery for which there is no known measure or estimate.

§ 378

1. E.g., Spell v. McDaniel, 824 F.2d 1380 (4th Cir.1987) (though medical expenses were only $2,000, an award of $900,000 was upheld where police officer had kneed plaintiff in the groin, damaging a testicle, which "enlarged five to seven times its normal size," with "the outer covering torn and the internal contents passing through the tear").

it.[2] In such cases, substantial damages may be awarded.[3] However, it is difficult to escape the impression that in a number of cases juries or judges have valued intangible damages in civil rights cases on a lower scale.

In a number of common law actions associated with intentional torts, the violation of the plaintiff's right has generally been regarded as a kind of legal damage in itself. The plaintiff who proves an intentional physical tort to the person or to property can always recover nominal damages. Sometimes she can recover something more, simply because her rights have been invaded by an assault or battery or false imprisonment that has not caused physical harm at all.[4] The Supreme Court of the United States has held that this approach does not apply to civil rights claims that do not cause "actual" damages. So

a denial of due process[5] and a denial of free speech rights[6] are actionable for any actual harms and for nominal damages if the plaintiff suffers no actual damages. But the right itself is not usually regarded as having value that can be recovered, nor can such damages be presumed.[7] Nonetheless, the court recognized that actual harm might include proven emotional harm in some cases and also that damages might be presumed if harm was especially likely to have occurred but damages would be hard to prove.[8]

§ 379. Damages for Harms to Property

Two basic rules. Harms to property are complex, partly because, besides physical injury to property itself, its owner may suffer loss of use because he is dispossessed, or loss of enjoyment because of the defendant's activities outside the property.[1] When the defendant's tort has physically damaged real or personal property without severing and taking any part of it,[2] courts usually measure damages by one of two rules. The first rule is the diminished value rule. It gives the plaintiff the difference between the value of the property immediately before harm was done and the value immediately afterwards.[3] This measures the loss in capital value of the land or chattel. The second rule is the cost rule. It

2. E.g., King v. Wells, 760 F.2d 89 (6th Cir.1985); Blackburn v. Snow, 771 F.2d 556 (1st Cir.1985) (extreme emotional reactions based on her predisposition).

3. E.g., Blackburn v. Snow, 771 F.2d 556 (1st Cir.1985); Levka v. City of Chicago, 748 F.2d 421 (7th Cir.1984).

4. See § 42.

5. Carey v. Piphus, 435 U.S. 247, 98 S.Ct. 1042, 55 L.Ed.2d 252 (1978).

6. Memphis Community Sch. Dist. v. Stachura, 477 U.S. 299, 106 S.Ct. 2537, 91 L.Ed.2d 249 (1986).

7. See generally, 2 Dan B. Dobbs, Remedies, § 7.4 (2); Jean C. Love, Damages: A Remedy for the Violation of Constitutional Rights, 67 Cal. L. Rev. 1242 (1979).

8. See 2 Dan B. Dobbs, Remedies § 7.4 (2) (2d ed. 1993).

§ 379

1. See 1 Dan B. Dobbs, Remedies §§ 5.8, 5.9 (damages and restitution for loss of exclusive possession of real property), § 5.6 (2d ed. 1993).

2. As to severance of minerals, timber or the like, see 1 Dan B. Dobbs, Remedies § 5.3.

3. E.g., McKinney v. Christiana Community Builders, 229 Cal.App.3d 611, 280 Cal.Rptr. 242 (1991); Ross v. A Betterway Rent–A–Car, Inc., 213 Ga.App. 288, 444 S.E.2d 604 (1994).

gives the plaintiff the cost of repair or replacement (subject to appropriate adjustments for salvage).[4] This measures the potential cash impact upon the plaintiff. When the property is either converted or totally destroyed by negligence, a special version of the diminished value rule applies; the plaintiff recovers the value of the property at the time it was destroyed or converted,[5] or, in the case of conversion, at a reasonable time thereafter.[6]

Choosing the right rule for the case. Neither rule works well in all cases. If the cost of repair is much higher than the diminished value, sometimes the diminished value should impose a ceiling on recovery because if repair costs are higher that will usually mean that repairs would be economically foolish. For example, if I own a car worth $500 it would be foolish to spend $1,000 on repairs. It would be far better to salvage the car and buy another for something in the neighborhood of $500. There is no good reason to make the defendant pay for foolish repairs. On the other hand, sometimes the damaged property has such important personal significance or social value that I might be justified in spending more in repair than the property is worth on the market. That might be so if the defendant has negligently bulldozed my shade trees or my vegetable garden[7] or damaged a church building used for low-income housing.[8] It makes sense to assume that the diminished value rule will apply unless special reasons justify using the repair cost rule. However, evidence of the cost of repairs will often be admissible as bearing on probable value.[9]

Repairs enhancing value of the property. In deciding whether to apply the repair cost rule courts must also consider the next step. Whether or not repair costs exceed diminished value, repair costs might add new value. If my car was worth $500 before the defendant damaged it, worth $100 afterwards, and worth $600 after repair, then regardless of how much the repair cost, my car is worth more than before. Even if the defendant might in some cases be liable for repair costs in excess of diminished value, he must not be made to give me a better car than before. So when repair cost is used, a reduction must be made for increased value.[10] When that value appears as extended life of a productive chattel like a machine used in business, accounting conventions about depreciation can be used to estimate the increased life resulting

4. E.g., Falcone v. Perry, 68 Wash.2d 909, 416 P.2d 690 (1966).

5. Chlopek v. Schmall, 224 Neb. 78, 396 N.W.2d 103 (1986); Daughen v. Fox, 372 Pa.Super. 405, 539 A.2d 858 (1988).

6. See 1 Dan B. Dobbs, Law of Remedies § 5.13 (2) (2d ed. 1993).

7. See, e.g., Andersen v. Edwards, 625 P.2d 282, 288 (Alaska 1981); Restatement § 929, cmt. b; 1 Dan B. Dobbs, Law of Remedies , § 5.2 (2) (2d ed. 1993).

8. Roman Catholic Church of the Archdiocese of New Orleans v. Louisiana Gas Service Co., 618 So.2d 874 (La.1993) (church-managed property used for low-income housing, costly repair costs represented appropriate measure of damages).

9. E.g., Beggs v. Stalnaker, 237 Ark. 281, 372 S.W.2d 600 (1963).

10. E.g., Freeport Sulphur Co. v. S/S Hermosa, 526 F.2d 300 (5th Cir.1976); 1 Dan B. Dobbs, Law of Remedies § 5.2 (7) (2d ed. 1993).

from repair, again with the aim of relieving the defendant of responsibility for any part of the repair cost that increased the chattel's value.[11]

Consequential damages. A tort to property may not only harm the property itself but may cause consequential losses resulting because the property cannot be used during repair or replacement period. Consequential damages such as lost profits or other forms of lost use are recoverable in appropriate cases,[12] but the existence and amount must be proven with reasonable certainty and must also be a proximate result of the tort.[13] If the plaintiff recovers the market value of a destroyed or converted chattel used in making profits, the fair market value recovery may often reflect something about the chattel's profit making potential, so an added separate recovery for lost profits may be dubious in some cases.[14] Courts have generally denied emotional harm resulting from damage or destruction of a chattel, even such personal chattels as pets,[15] but intentional harm to a pet might qualify as an intentional infliction of emotional distress, for which emotional harm damages could be recovered.[16] One consequential item is generally recoverable: the reasonable expenditures made to minimize damages.[17]

§ 380. Adjustments in Basic Compensatory Damages

The basic estimate of compensatory damages is subject to a number of downward adjustments. Two of these reflect major new policies. Comparative negligence rules—including the avoidable consequences rules for minimizing damages—can substantially reduce the recovery. The avoidable consequences rule has been discussed in connection with comparative fault.[1] Absolute caps on the recovery or some elements of it simply ignore actual damages after they reach a stated level and refuse to permit their recovery.[2] Caps on recoveries require separate attention. The remaining issues about adjusting damages awards are narrower.

Adjustments in Awards for Future Losses[3]

Fixing a loss period. When the plaintiff claims that she will suffer losses in the future, she must prove by a preponderance of the evidence that those losses will in fact be incurred in the future. She must also prove duration. If she will endure pain for the rest of her life, the trier

11. See 1 Dan B. Dobbs, Law of Remedies § 5.14 (3) (2d ed. 1993).

12. E.g., Walker v. Brown, 501 So.2d 358 (Miss.1987); Chemical Express Carriers, Inc. v. French, 759 S.W.2d 683 (Tex. App.1988) (insurance agent's income dropped when he could not use airplane to transport clients).

13. 1 Dan B. Dobbs, Law of Remedies § 3.4 (2d ed. 1993).

14. See McPherson v. Schlemmer, 230 Mont. 81, 84, 749 P.2d 51, 52 (1988) ("Fair market value generally includes a component for present valuation of future profits").

15. E.g., Nichols v. Sukaro Kennels, 555 N.W.2d 689, 61 A.L.R.5th 883 (Iowa 1996).

16. Richardson v. Fairbanks North Star Borough, 705 P.2d 454, 456 (Alaska 1985).

17. See 1 Dan B. Dobbs, Law of Remedies § 3.9 (2d ed. 1993).

§ 380

1. §§ 204 & 205.

2. § 384.

3. See generally, Dan B. Dobbs, Law of Remedies § 8.5 (2d ed. 1993).

must have some basis for estimating her life expectancy. If her injury is permanent and will never allow her to work, the trier must have some basis for estimating how long the plaintiff would have worked if she had not been injured. Such periods may be very long, easily thirty or forty years in some cases.

Reduction to present value. Courts have said that damages awarded for losses that will occur in the future should be reduced to present value.[4] They believe an unreduced award would overcompensate.[5] The reduced award permits the plaintiff to invest that portion of the award attributable to future losses, then use the award and its investment income when those losses actually occur at some time in the future. Perhaps the best-considered view is that no reduction is required for pain and suffering damages.[6]

Once the appropriate interest rate and the time of the future losses are determined, the reduction is simply mathematical, to be made by using tables, a formula, or a software program. The most critical element in the reduction is the discount or interest rate. If courts assume that the plaintiff can earn 10% on the investment of the award, a much smaller award is required to provide compensation than if courts assume the plaintiff can earn only 2%. The "legal rate" of interest is not a good guide here. Courts have said the rate should be what an unsophisticated investor can safely earn in such investments as a savings account or something equally safe.[7]

Adjusting for inflation. The long period of future losses also implicates the problem of inflation. Courts once refused to make any adjustment for inflation.[8] If inflation occurs, however, the dollars awarded in today's lawsuit will be worth less and the plaintiff will be undercompensated unless inflation is accounted for by some means. In the last generation, courts have increasingly been willing to take inflation into account. Inflation can be accounted for in a number of ways. The three main ones are these:

4. E.g., Monessen Southwestern Ry. Co. v. Morgan, 486 U.S. 330, 108 S.Ct. 1837, 100 L.Ed.2d 349 (1988); Green v. General Motors Corp., 310 N.J.Super. 507, 709 A.2d 205 (1998).

5. For example, suppose that future losses will occur at the rate of $10,000 a year for 20 years. The plaintiff's total loss would be $200,000. Paid this sum at the end of a trial, the plaintiff can invest it. At 5% the investment would produce $10,000 annually, thus taking care of the plaintiff's losses as they occurred. At the end of the 20–year loss period, the plaintiff will have been compensated for his losses and will have an additional $200,000 still invested.

6. E.g., Cox v. Crown CoCo, Inc., 544 N.W.2d 490 (Minn.Ct.App.1996); Friedman v. C & S Car Servs., 108 N.J. 72, 527 A.2d 871 (N.J. 1987).

7. See Chesapeake & O. Ry. v. Kelly, 241 U.S. 485, 490, 36 S.Ct. 630, 632, 60 L.Ed. 1117, 1122 (1916).

8. Zaninovich v. American Airlines, Inc., 26 A.D.2d 155, 271 N.Y.S.2d 866 (1966). Distinguish increased productivity. If the inflation rate is 3% but the rate of growth in the industry in which the plaintiff works is 9%, only 3% of the growth is due to inflation. If the plaintiff would have shared in the increased productivity, or would have had wage increases due to his own increased value, those would be accounted for in the basic calculation of damages and do not represent an adjustment for inflation.

(1) Make a straightforward estimate of probable future inflation, then formally or informally apply that estimate to increase the award. Evidence of average past inflation rate or other bases for estimating future inflation would be required.[9]

(2) Use a very low interest rate in computing the reduction to present value but make no separate adjustment for inflation. The theory is that interest rates at a given time reflect estimated inflationary risks as well as "real" interest. To account for inflation, you can exclude that part of the interest rate that is based on investors estimates of inflation. That would leave a very low discount rate, say, 1.5% instead of 4 or 5% or more. The effect of a low discount rate is to require a greater award, since less investment income would be earned to help pay for losses. This can indirectly provide an adjustment for inflation without any separate calculation or even mention of the word.[10]

(3) Let the present value and inflation adjustment wash each other out. The judge would make no reduction to present value and no addition for inflation. Since the whole process is based upon estimates about the future in any event, this solution might be not only acceptable but desirable.[11]

Gains or Savings Resulting from Injury

The collateral source rule. In many cases, the injured plaintiff receives some compensation for injuries from sources that have nothing to do with the defendant. The plaintiff's own insurance, job benefits, or donations by friends may all operate to reduce the plaintiff's loss. The traditional rule is that compensation from "collateral sources" is none of the defendant's business and does not go to reduce the defendant's obligation to pay damages, either in negligence[12] or in strict liability cases.[13] Thus if the plaintiff has an injury causing loss of $100,000 and but $50,000 of that injury is covered by the plaintiff's own insurance, the defendant must still pay the full $100,000. The plaintiff will, theoretically, be better off as a result of the injury; he will be fully compensated and also have $50,000.

Rationales. The overcompensation is often more theoretical than real. In many instances, the collateral source rule only operates to preserve the subrogation rights of an insurer. To the extent an insurer pays the plaintiff under an insurance policy, the insurer acquires the

9. See See Schleier v. Kaiser Found. Health Plan, 876 F.2d 174 (D.C.Cir.1989).

10. See Doca v. Marina Mercante Nicaraguense, S.A., 634 F.2d 30, 37 (2d Cir. 1980); Feldman v. Allegheny Airlines, Inc., 524 F.2d 384 (2d Cir.1975). The Supreme Court thought that some such approach would be permissible. Jones & Laughlin Steel Corp. v. Pfeifer, 462 U.S. 523, 103 S.Ct. 2541, 76 L.Ed.2d 768 (1983).

11. See Beaulieu v. Elliott, 434 P.2d 665 (Alaska 1967).

12. Helfend v. Southern California Rapid Transit Dist., 2 Cal.3d 1, 84 Cal.Rptr. 173, 465 P.2d 61, 77 A.L.R.3d 398 (1970); Mahoney v. Nebraska Methodist Hosp., 251 Neb. 841, 560 N.W.2d 451 (1997) (pension); Restatement §§ 920A & 920 (1979); 2 Dan B. Dobbs, Law of Remedies § 8.6 (3).

13. Gypsum Carrier, Inc. v. Handelsman, 307 F.2d 525, 4 A.L.R.3d 517 (9th Cir. 1962); Tebo v. Havlik, 418 Mich. 350, 343 N.W.2d 181 (1984).

plaintiff's rights to sue. If the collateral source rule were reversed so that payment of the plaintiff's loss by his own insurer eliminated the plaintiff's right to recover damages for such items, the insurer, who only stands in the plaintiff's shoes, would lose the right to recover. The collateral source rule is sometimes justified on the ground that it protects the insurer's subrogation right, without which the insurance premiums would presumably rise.[14] It is also argued that the plaintiff has, after all, paid for his insurance coverage. When he receives donations rather than insurance, it is said that donors do not intend a donation to the defendant but to the plaintiff. Supporters of the rule have also argued that the defendant should not get a windfall.

Because first party insurance (the plaintiff's) is usually cheaper than liability insurance (the defendant's) the effect of the collateral source rule is to draw on the most expensive kind of insurance and to add the costs of subrogation suits in the bargain. Considering the matter prospectively rather than after the fact, it may well be that compensation could be more cheaply secured without the collateral source rule.[15]

Abolishing the collateral source rule. As part of a tort reform program, around half the states have abolished or limited the collateral source rule for specified claims, frequently medical malpractice claims and those against public entities. Some statutes cover all tort actions or even all actions for damages.[16] Others cover claims against favored defendants, such as health care providers or public entities.[17] One approach simply authorizes admission of evidence of collateral benefits;[18] another specifically requires the trier or the judge to deduct collateral benefits from the award.[19] When the award is reduced because the plaintiff has received payments from her own insurance company, the plaintiff may be allowed to add back into the award some of the sums she expended in premiums for that insurance.[20] Some states abolishing the collateral source rule reduce the plaintiff's award only if no insurance company is subrogated to the plaintiff's rights. Those states protect the subrogation rights of the plaintiff's insurer by retaining the collateral source rule as to the insurer.[21] A few courts have held these statutes unconstitutional under provisions of state constitutions.[22] Other courts

14. Cates v. Wilson, 321 N.C. 1, 361 S.E.2d 734 (1987).

15. See Alfred E. Conard, The Economic Treatment of Automobile Injuries, 63 MICH. L. REV. 279, 311 (1964); 2 DAN B. DOBBS, LAW OF REMEDIES § 8.6 (3) (2d ed. 1993).

16. E.g., MONT. CODE ANN. § 27–1–308 (actions for injury or death where total award exceeds $50,000).

17. E.g., 231 MASS. GEN. LAWS ANN. § 60G; N.H. STAT. § 507–C:7, or to medical malpractice actions and some other discrete category of cases. N.Y. CPLR § 4545 (malpractice and actions against public employers). Iowa's statute covers only payments received for medical care, so that the plaintiff's disability payments do not reduce recovery. Collins v. King, 545 N.W.2d 310 (Iowa 1996).

18. E.g., ALA. CODE § 12–21–45.

19. E.g., N.J. STAT. ANN. 2A:15–97.

20. MONT. CODE ANN. § 27–1–308 (premiums paid for five years before injury, those paid from injury to judgment, and the value of those to be paid in the next three years); N.H. STAT. § 507–C:7 (all premiums paid).

21. ALA. CODE § 12–21–45; MICH. COMP. LAWS ANN. 600.6303 (2) & (4).

22. Farley v. Engelken, 241 Kan. 663, 740 P.2d 1058, 74 A.L.R.4th 1 (1987) (discrimination against medical malpractice vic-

have upheld the statutes.[23]

Direct benefits. The collateral source rule does not apply to all benefits received by the plaintiff as a result of the injury. If the benefit results from the injury itself or is compensated by the defendant or those representing him, the defendant gets credit for the benefit gained by the plaintiff.[24] For example, if the defendant's medical pay insurance makes payments to the plaintiff for medical costs, the defendant is entitled to a credit against his liability.[25] When the very act of injury also produces a benefit, the defendant is again entitled to a credit, at least if the benefit is one the plaintiff wants. A surgeon who operates on the wrong ear may have committed a technical battery, but he is entitled to reduce his liability to the extent that the operation was in fact a medical benefit.[26]

The direct benefits rule raises a number of difficult questions. For example, if the defendant is a taxpayer, he contributes to public funds. If public funds are used to help compensate the injured plaintiff, the defendant can claim that the benefit derived from those funds was ultimately traceable in part to him and that his liability should therefore be reduced by the amount of any public funds used to succor the plaintiff because of injury. The answer may depend upon the benefit program involved, but in general defendants have not been able to claim a reduction in damages merely because public funds assisted the plaintiff.[27]

Limits on direct benefits offsets—or not. The direct benefits rule must be applied with caution. First, the rule should not give the defendant a credit for benefits the plaintiff does not want, or at least not in intentional tort cases.[28] Second, the benefit credit should apply only when the benefit received is of the same order or affects the same interest that was harmed.[29] However, courts have ignored both these limitations at times, especially in wrongful birth and wrongful pregnancy cases. For instance, if the plaintiff's medical doctor performs a medical procedure to prevent conception but the patient conceives and bears a child because of the doctor's negligence, a number of courts insist, as a matter of law, that the parents' emotional benefit in having an unwanted child is to be credited to the defendant and then add that the benefits

tims); Thompson v. KFB Insurance Co., 252 Kan. 1010, 850 P.2d 773 (1993) (discrimination against victims with greater harm); O'Bryan v. Hedgespeth, 892 S.W.2d 571 (Ky.1995) (admission of evidence is judicial function, statute violated separation of powers).

23. Eastin v. Broomfield, 116 Ariz. 576, 570 P.2d 744 (1977); see James J. Watson, Annotation, Validity And Construction of State Statute Abrogating Collateral Source Rule as to Medical Malpractice Actions, 74 A.L.R.4th 32 (1990).

24. Restatement §§ 920A (1), 920 (1979).

25. Aragon v. Brown, 93 N.M. 646, 603 P.2d 1103 (N.M.Ct.App.1979).

26. See Mohr v. Williams, 95 Minn. 261, 104 N.W. 12 (1905), overruled on other grounds, Genzel v. Halvorson, 248 Minn. 527, 80 N.W.2d 854 (1957).

27. E.g., Bennett v. Haley, 132 Ga.App. 512, 208 S.E.2d 302, 77 A.L.R.2d 353 (1974) (Medicaid payments, tax supported, could not reduce recovery); see Dan B. Dobbs, Law of Remedies, § 8.6 (2) (2d ed 1993); Dag E. Ytreberg, Annotation, Collateral Source Rule: Receipt of Public Relief or Gratuity as Affecting Recovery in Personal Injury Action, 77 A.L.R.3d 366 (1977).

28. See 1 Dan B. Dobbs, Law of Remedies §§ 3.8 (2) & 4.9 (2d ed. 1993).

29. Restatement § 920 & Comments a & b (1979) .

necessarily exceed the costs of rearing the child so that all substantial damages are eliminated.[30] If benefits were offset only against corresponding types of harm, the emotional benefit of having a child would be offset only against the emotional harm done by having an unwanted child.

Tax savings.[31] Under the United States Revenue Code, the personal injury plaintiff pays no taxes on compensatory damages for physical injury.[32] When the injured plaintiff is entitled to recover for loss of wages or earning capacity, the tax gift to the plaintiff raises two questions. First, should the defendant's liability be reduced to reflect the tax savings so that the plaintiff is not overcompensated? Second, if the answer is no and the defendant is liable for full wage loss even though some of that loss is recovered through the tax gift, should the jury be warned not to add anything for taxes? The traditional answer to both questions highly favored the plaintiff. Courts permitted the plaintiff to recover the full wage loss, which replaced taxable wages with untaxable substitute funds.[33] Courts also usually refused to instruct the jury on this topic, leaving a substantial probability that many juries would "add something" because of supposed taxation.[34] In 1980, the Supreme Court rejected the traditional rule, holding that in suits under the Federal Employers Liability Act the basic computation should be reduced to account for the plaintiff's tax savings so that the plaintiff would recover full compensation, no more.[35] So far, however, this holding has not influenced states to change their rules.[36]

Interest[37]

Prejudgment interest denied. "Prejudgment interest" is interest on losses incurred by the plaintiff from the time of injury until the time of judgment. The common law rule denied prejudgment interest altogether except for claims that were liquidated or ascertainable. A liquidated claim is one for a specific amount of money, such as $100 due for past services. An ascertainable claim is one that yields a specific sum by simple calculation, such as a claim for two hours work at the agreed rate of $50 per hour. Most tort damages were not considered liquidated or ascertainable. Thus prejudgment interest was denied on personal injury claims, even if they arose under a statute.[38] Interest began to accrue only

30. See § 293.

31. See generally 2 DAN B. DOBBS, LAW OF REMEDIES § 8.6 (4) (2d ed 1993).

32. 26 U.S.C.A. § 104 (a).

33. E.g., Marcel v. Placid Oil Co., 11 F.3d 563 (5th Cir.1994) (Louisiana law, although it has little to recommend it in either economics or justice); Johnson v. Manhattan & Bronx Surface Transit Operating Auth., 71 N.Y.2d 198, 524 N.Y.S.2d 415, 519 N.E.2d 326 (1988).

34. E.g., Klawonn v. Mitchell, 105 Ill.2d 450, 86 Ill.Dec. 478, 475 N.E.2d 857 (1985) (saying there is no evidence that jury would add to the award on the erroneous assumption that it would be heavily taxed).

35. Norfolk & Western Ry. v. Liepelt, 444 U.S. 490, 100 S.Ct. 755, 62 L.Ed.2d 689 (1980).

36. E.g., Spencer v. A-1 Crane Service, Inc., 880 S.W.2d 938 (Tenn.1994).

37. See generally 1 DAN B. DOBBS, LAW OF REMEDIES § 3.6 (2d ed. 1993).

38. Monessen Southwestern Ry. Co. v. Morgan, 486 U.S. 330, 108 S.Ct. 1837, 100 L.Ed.2d 349 (1988) (Federal Employers Liability Act claim, statute construed in light of common law rule, prejudgment interest not permissible).

when a judgment was entered. Although interest can properly be denied on noneconomic damages such as damages for pain and punitive damages,[39] the denial of interest on economic harms was unjust. The rule allowed the defendant free use of monies at the same time it left the plaintiff without those monies. The rule was also impolitic; it encouraged defendants to postpone settlement or trial as long as possible, since at worst delay would be cost-free to the defendant, who might actually profit by the delay because the defendant (or his insurer) could keep earnings from the invested sums.

Statutes. Some states have now enacted statutes modifying the common law rule against prejudgment interest. Some of these are aimed specifically at personal injury or tort actions and only at such actions.[40] Some are narrower and cover only wrongful death actions,[41] or claims involving cases of fraud, malice or oppression.[42] Others appear to cover claims generally,[43] while still others focus on some particular claims, not necessarily in tort.[44] Pennsylvania allows a penalty that is similar to prejudgment interest against defendants who fail to make settlement offers approximating the final judgment.[45]

§ 381. Punitive Damages and Their Bases

Availability, Purpose, and Nature

In the great majority of states,[1] the common law rule permits but does not require juries to assess punitive damages in special cases.[2] In a relatively few cases juries have done so. Punitive (or "exemplary") damages represent a sum in excess of any compensatory damages, and are usually available only when the tortfeasor has committed quite serious misconduct with a bad intent or bad state of mind such as malice. Because punishment does not adequately describe the bases for such damages, they are sometimes called extracompensatory damages.

39. A number of cases so hold. E.g., Greater Westchester Homeowners Ass'n v. City of Los Angeles, 26 Cal.3d 86, 160 Cal. Rptr. 733, 603 P.2d 1329 (1979).

40. N.J. Rules of Court 4:42–11(b) (date of institution of action or six months after cause of action arises, whichever is later).

41. "Interest upon the principal sum recovered by the plaintiff from the date of the decedent's death shall be added to and be a part of the total sum awarded." N.Y. ESTATES, POWERS AND TRUSTS LAW § 5–4.3. But other New York statutes cover some other claims. See N.Y. CIV. PRAC. L. & R. § 5001.

42. See CAL. CIV. CODE § 3288 (non-contract damages based on fraud, malice, oppression; interest is discretionary).

43. NEV. REV. STATS. § 17.130 (unless the law or the judgment itself specifies otherwise, "the judgment draws interest from the time of service of the summons and complaint until satisfied"); N.H. REV. STAT. ANN. §§ 524:1–a, 524:1–b.

44. Cf. CAL. CIV. CODE § 3287 (interest on ascertainable damages generally, but if in contract, interest may be given on unliquidated damages in courts' discretion).

45. See Laudenberger v. Port Auth. of Allegheny County, 496 Pa. 52, 436 A.2d 147 (1981) (holding the court rule on which the penalty is based to be constitutional).

§ 381

1. Several states reject or purport to reject punitive damages altogether, e.g, Killebrew v. Abbott Labs., 359 So.2d 1275 (La. 1978), but some of these smuggle in awards under statutes in particular cases. See 1 DAN B. DOBBS, LAW OF REMEDIES § 3.11 (1).

2. Smith's Food & Drug Centers, Inc. v. Bellegarde, 114 Nev. 602, 958 P.2d 1208 (Nev. 1998) (even if jury finds malice, it is not required to assess punitive damages).

No cause of action exists for punitive damages as such; they are available only when the plaintiff has suffered legally recognized harm and can recover at least nominal damages.[3]

Courts usually emphasize that punitive damages are awarded to punish or deter.[4] The idea of punishment or retribution is that it is just for the defendant to suffer for his misconduct. The idea of deterrence is quite different. It is that a sufficient sum should be exacted from the defendant to make repetition of the misconduct unlikely. In some major punitive damages cases, deterrence is necessary because the defendant's activity is profitable or the defendant retains gains even after compensatory damages are paid.[5]

Punitive damages raise unique problems. Sometimes they resemble criminal fines, sometimes civil damages. Courts are divided, for instance, whether an employer can be vicariously liable for punitive damages short of management complicity in or ratification of the actor's misconduct.[6] Likewise, some courts hold that liability insurers may cover punitive damages[7] while others hold they may not.[8] Courts have faced a number of particular punitive damages issues such as liability of a minor or the estate of a decedent.[9] Many articles,[10] and books[11] have addressed puni-

3. 1 Dan B. Dobbs, Law of Remedies § 3.11 (10) (2d ed. 1993).

4. Courts have also sometimes considered punitive damages as a source of funds to aid in financing costly litigation, see Dan B. Dobbs, Law of Remedies § 3.11 (3) (2d ed. 1993), as an emphatic expression of community values, and as a sum added when it is difficult to be sure that the compensatory award was sufficient and the defendant's conduct has no redeeming value. See Kemezy v. Peters, 79 F.3d 33 (7th Cir.1996).

5. See, elaborating this idea and constructing a theory for punitive awards and their measure, A. Mitchell Polinsky, Steven Shavell, Punitive Damages: an Economic Analysis, 111 Harv. L. Rev. 869 (1998).

6. Smith's Food & Drug Ctrs., Inc. v. Bellegarde, 114 Nev. 602, 958 P.2d 1208 (1998) (requiring management level complicity); Restatement § 909 (1979) (requiring management complicity or ratification); see also, Model Punitive Damages Act § 6 (adopting and spelling out the complicity rule limiting vicarious liability); Stroud v. Denny's Restaurant, Inc., 271 Or. 430, 532 P.2d 790 (1975) (ordinary vicarious liability rules apply to punitive liabilities). See 1 Dan B. Dobbs, Law of Remedies § 3.11 (6) (2d ed. 1993).

7. Whalen v. On–Deck, Inc., 514 A.2d 1072, 1074 (Del.1986); Lunceford v. Peachtree Cas. Ins. Co., 230 Ga.App. 4, 495 S.E.2d 88 (1997) .

8. Northwestern Nat'l Cas. Co. v. McNulty, 307 F.2d 432 (5th Cir.1962); cf. Flint Hills Rural Elec. Coop. Ass'n v. Federated Rural Elec. Ins. Corp., 262 Kan. 512, 941 P.2d 374 (1997) (not permissible to insure against punitive liability for one's own act but permissible to insure against vicarious punitive liability).

9. Most courts reject punitive damages against the estate of a deceased tortfeasor, but some allow the award, as in G.J.D. v. Johnson, 552 Pa. 169, 713 A.2d 1127 (1998). See generally 1 Dan B. Dobbs, Law of Remedies § 3.11 (2d ed. 1993).

10. Among a great many, see Dan B. Dobbs, Ending Punishment in "Punitive" Damages: Deterrence-measured Remedies, 40 Ala. L. Rev. 831, 871–888 (1989); See Dorsey D. Ellis, Jr., Fairness and Efficiency in the Law of Punitive Damages, 56 S. Cal. L. Rev. 1 (1982); David G. Owen, The Moral Foundations of Punitive Damages, 40 Ala. L. Rev. 705 (1989); A. Mitchell Polinsky, Steven Shavell, Punitive Damages: an Economic Analysis, 111 Harv. L. Rev. 869 (1998); Cass R. Sunstein, et al., Assessing Punitive Damages (With Notes on Cognition and Valuation in Law), 107 Yale L.J. 2071 (1998); Symposium, The Future of Punitive Damages, 1998 Wis. L. Rev. 1(eleven articles).

11. J. Ghiardi & J. Kircher, Punitive Damages Law and Practice (2 vols. 1995 & Supps.); K. Redden, Punitive Damages (2 vols. 3d ed. 1997) (with L. Schlueter); see 1 Dan B. Dobbs, Law of Remedies § 3.11 (2d ed. 1993).

tive damages. They are currently controversial because of the claims that they are unpredictable or excessive.[12]

Judicially speaking, the many punitive damages issues can be grouped under three headings: (1) What are the conditions under which punitive damages can be awarded? (2) How should punitive damages be calculated or measured? (3) What processes should be used to determine the first two issues?

Basis for Awarding

Defendant's conduct and state of mind. Courts have traditionally agreed that punitive damages can be awarded only when the tortfeasor causes harm by conduct "that constitutes an extreme departure from lawful conduct"[13] and that is motivated by or evinces an antisocial mental state as well.[14] The exact mode of expressing this requirement has varied somewhat. Some courts insist upon malice, ill-will, and intent to injure, evil motive or the like,[15] while others have found it sufficient that the defendant engages in wanton misconduct with its conscious indifference to risk.[16] A great many other terms without much legal or descriptive content have been used to characterize the conduct permitting a punitive award. For instance it has been said that the defendant may be held for punitive damages if he is oppressive, evil, wicked, guilty of wanton or morally culpable conduct, or shows flagrant indifference to the safety of others.[17] Perhaps the defendant's abuse of power or of a special relationship is another marker for punitive awards.[18]

Occasional statements that personal ill-will is required to justify punitive damages can be discounted, at least in some jurisdictions, as judicial hyperbole.[19] In fact, courts have been willing to award punitive

12. § 384.

13. David Owen's phrase, David G. Owen, The Moral Foundations of Punitive Damages, 40 ALA. L. REV. 705, 730 (1989). The conduct itself, as distinct from the state of mind, is in fact almost always serious. But to some extent, the conduct may seem egregiously bad because of the defendant's bad purpose or bad state of mind. A federal statute authorizes punitive damages against an employer who engages in intentional discriminatory practices "with malice or with reckless indifference to the federally protected rights of an aggrieved individual." The Supreme Court has held that the statute does not require any egregious misconduct aside from the intended discrimination. Kolstad v. American Dental Ass'n, ___ U.S. ___, 119 S.Ct. 2118, ___ L.Ed.2d ___ (1999). The court also used broader language suggesting that serious misconduct was never required, only a sufficiently reckless or malicious state of mind.

14. See Smith v. Wade, 461 U.S. 30, 103 S.Ct. 1625, 75 L.Ed.2d 632, (1983).

15. Owens–Illinois, Inc. v. Zenobia, 325 Md. 420, 601 A.2d 633 (1992).

16. E.g., Johnson v. Rogers, 763 P.2d 771 (Utah 1988); Philip Morris, Inc. v. Emerson, 235 Va. 380, 407, 368 S.E.2d 268, 283 (1988).

17. E.g., First Nat'l Bank of Pulaski, Tenn. v. Thomas, 453 So.2d 1313, 1320 (Ala.1984) ("rudeness, wantonness, recklessness, or an insulting manner, or accompanied by circumstances of fraud and malice, oppression, aggravation, or gross negligence"); Martsch v. Nelson, 109 Idaho 95, 99, 705 P.2d 1050, 1054 (Idaho Ct.App. 1985) (only when conduct is "wanton, malicious or gross and outrageous or the facts imply malice and oppression").

18. See Owen, Civil Punishment and the Public Good, 56 S. CAL. L. REV. 103, 104 (1982–83).

19. Shugar v. Guill, 304 N.C. 332, 337–38, 283 S.E.2d 507, 510 (1981) requires personal ill will in one passage but in another said that the requirement was "an

damages when the defendant intentionally indulges in serious risk-taking, without requiring an actual intent to inflict harm.[20] The various descriptions of evil mind and egregious misconduct do not point to attributes of the defendant or his conduct that can be verified by the senses, so inevitably they can only suggest rather than determine the specific cases for punitive awards. In addition, so far as deterrence is the purpose of a punitive award, the defendant's evil mind may not be significant at all.[21]

Examples. Punitive damages have been approved at least in principle in a wide variety of cases, both against defendants engaged in economic activity (manufacturing products that sometimes cause harm for example) and against individual defendants who act in anti-social ways for personal gratification.[22]

Courts have approved punitive damages in principle in a variety of cases, including those in which the defendant is guilty of battery,[23] environmental harm,[24] breach of fiduciary duty,[25] fraud,[26] repeated misconduct,[27] or even driving a vehicle in an extremely dangerous manner.[28] A deliberate policy of corporate misconduct[29] may suffice. The A.H. Robins Company marketed its Dalkon Shield IUD knowing it was dangerous to women and presumably hoping that profits would exceed liability. Punitive damages were of course appropriate.[30] A number of

element of aggravation such as malice, or oppression, or gross and willful wrong, or a wanton and reckless disregard of plaintiff's rights."

20. See Smith v. Wade, 461 U.S. 30, 47–48, 103 S.Ct. 1625, 1636, 75 L.Ed.2d 632, 646 (1983) ("Most cases under state common law, although varying in their precise terminology, have adopted more or less the same rule, recognizing that punitive damages in tort cases may be awarded not only for actual intent to injure or evil motive, but also for recklessness, serious indifference to or disregard for the rights of others, or even gross negligence").

21. See A. Mitchell Polinsky, Steven Shavell, Punitive Damages: An Economic Analysis, 111 Harv. L. Rev. 869 (1998).

22. See § 382.

23. E.g., Hough v. Mooningham, 139 Ill. App.3d 1018, 487 N.E.2d 1281, 94 Ill.Dec. 404 (1986) (defendant struck plaintiff with shovel).

24. See Potter v. Firestone Tire and Rubber Co., 6 Cal.4th 965, 863 P.2d 795, 25 Cal.Rptr.2d 550 (1993). By statute punitive damages can be recovered by the United States in certain cases. 42 U.S.C. § 9607(c)(3).

25. E.g., Coster v. Crookham, 468 N.W.2d 802 (Iowa 1991). If a restitutionary remedy is granted for breach of fiduciary duty or fraud, however, some courts may still refuse punitive damages.

26. E.g., Talent Tree Personnel Services v. Fleenor, 703 So.2d 917 (Ala.1997) (either intentional misrepresentation or concealment of facts defendant was obliged to disclose, if oppressive or malicious).

27. Thus although a single intentional misrepresentation may not warrant punitive damages, a deceitful course of conduct over a two years period does. West v. Western Cas. & Sur. Co., 846 F.2d 387 (7th Cir.1988).

28. E.g., Campbell v. Van Roekel, 347 N.W.2d 406 (Iowa 1984) (single vehicle accident); Cabe v. Lunich, 70 Ohio St.3d 598, 640 N.E.2d 159 (1994) (evidence that driver had consumed alcohol prior to accident is relevant and bears on malice).

29. E.g., Torres v. North Am. Van Lines, Inc., 135 Ariz. 35, 658 P.2d 835 (Ct. App. 1982) (company's failure to monitor driving-time logs of drivers); see Loughry v. Lincoln First Bank, 67 N.Y.2d 369, 378, 494 N.E.2d 70, 74–75, 502 N.Y.S.2d 965, 970 (1986) (employer liable for punitive damages if "the wrong was in pursuance of a recognized business system" of the employer).

30. Tetuan v. A.H. Robins Co., 241 Kan. 441, 738 P.2d 1210 (1987).

scandalous cases have turned on corporate concealment of serious danger.[31]

In the category of those who abuse their power or a special relationship are insurers who do not pay off on their policies,[32] utilities who stop their services,[33] those who attempt to obtain the plaintiff's property without payment or and without using their eminent domain powers,[34] and employers guilty of wrongful discharge.[35] Although punitive damages are not assessed against public entities, public officials who abuse their power to cause harm are liable for such damages[36] as are employers who refuse to protect their own employees against known sexual harassment.[37]

In the end, however, neither broad tests of punitive liability like "malice" nor examples of particular cases can substitute for analysis of cases as they arise. The inquiry must always be whether the defendant's conduct merits punishment as just dessert or shows the need for deterrence.

§ 382. The Amount of Punitive Damages

Traditional factors. As will appear, statutes may limit punitive damages.[1] The traditional common law punitive damage awards are open ended, however, without any particular limit in amount. No objective measure for such damages exists.[2] Courts have tried to provide a framework for assessing punitive damages by considering several factors. In the absence of legislation restricting punitive damages, the main factors have included (1) the reprehensibility of the defendant's misconduct, (2)

31. See Cynthia R. Mabry, Warning! The Manufacturer of this Product May Have Engaged in Cover–Ups, Lies, and Concealment: Making the Case for Limitless Punitive Awards in Product Liability Lawsuits, 73 Ind. L.J. 187, 216–234 (1997) (detailing Dalkon Shield, asbestos, tobacco and other cases).

32. E.g., Hawkins v. Allstate Ins. Co., 152 Ariz. 490, 733 P.2d 1073 (1987); Eichenseer v. Reserve Life Ins. Co., 682 F.Supp. 1355 (N.D.Miss.1988), aff'd, 934 F.2d 1377 (5th Cir.1991).

33. E.g., Haynam v. Laclede Elec. Coop., 889 S.W.2d 148 (Mo.Ct.App.1994).

34. Collens v. New Canaan Water Co., 155 Conn. 477, 234 A.2d 825 (1967); cf. Cumberland Tel. & Tel. Co. v. Poston, 94 Tenn. 696, 30 S.W. 1040 (1895) (utility cut trees after asking permission from one who was not the owner; recklessness found in spite of honest belief in right to cut).

35. E.g., Flanigan v. Prudential Fed. Sav. & Loan Ass'n., 221 Mont. 419, 720 P.2d 257 (1986) ($1.3 million punitive award). If the wrongful discharge claim is based on contract rather than tort theory, punitive damages are typically denied. When the employee is represented by a union, federal preemption of the wrongful discharge claim may eliminate the state law claim altogether.

36. Kemezy v. Peters, 79 F.3d 33 (7th Cir.1996) (police officer beat the plaintiff); Criado v. IBM Corp., 145 F.3d 437 (1st Cir.1998) (termination of employee with disability rather than accommodation is a violation of Americans with Disabilities Act and intent required under that Act to establish claim was sufficient to establish grounds for punitive damages).

37. Deters v. Equifax Credit Information Servs., Inc., 981 F.Supp. 1381 (D.Kan. 1997) (under Title VII); Ford v. Revlon, Inc., 153 Ariz. 38, 734 P.2d 580 (1987) (under state tort law).

§ 382

1. § 384.

2. Multiple damages statutes, authorizing, say, treble damages, may have punitive effects but only fortuitously will a fixed multiple reflect either appropriate deterrence levels or appropriate retribution. As to caps, see § 384.

the defendant's wealth, (3) the profitability of the misconduct, (4) litigation costs, (5) the aggregate of all civil and criminal sanctions against the defendant and (6) the ratio between the harm caused or potentially caused by the defendant's misconduct and the losses suffered by the plaintiff.[3]

Economic vs. personal gratification activity. One large class of potential punitive damage cases involves defendants engaged in economic activity that causes harm. Firms that cause pollution or produce products that cause harm are examples. A second class involves defendants, usually individuals rather than corporations, who obtain personal gratification out of tortious anti-social behavior. Individuals who beat or rape others or who drive while intoxicated are examples. Some of the factors used in estimating appropriate amounts of the punitive award may be more relevant to one class of punitive damages than another. If the objective is to deter the manufacture of known dangerous products, for example, personal ill-will and even corporate wealth will be unimportant or at least less important than finding an award that will deter without overdeterring.[4]

Ratio rules. The ratio factor holds that the punitive award should bear some reasonable (but unspecified) relationship to either (a) the potential for harm created by the defendant's conduct or (b) the actual damages suffered by the plaintiff.[5] If the rule addresses the potential for harm created by the defendant's conduct, it looks less like a separate factor than a piece of evidence bearing on the reprehensibility of the defendant's misconduct. If it addresses the actual harm caused or the amount of compensatory damages awarded, as it does in some statements of the rule, it does not seem especially relevant at all. The defendant who fires a bullet at the plaintiff's head but only breaks a cheap pair of glasses has caused little apparent harm, but it makes no sense at all to suggest that the $50 pair of glasses is somehow mathematically related to any purpose of punitive awards, since it does not measure either just punishment or needed deterrence.[6] In those circum-

3. Labonte v. Hutchins & Wheeler, 424 Mass. 813, 678 N.E.2d 853 (1997); Garnes v. Fleming Landfill, Inc., 186 W.Va. 656, 413 S.E.2d 897 (1991). The Model Punitive Damages Act § 7 lists similar factors and others, including "any adverse effect of the award on innocent persons."

4. See A. Mitchell Polinsky, Steven Shavell, Punitive Damages: An Economic Analysis, 111 Harv. L. Rev. 869 (1998). Polinsky and Shavell argue that corporate defendant will be properly deterred without punitive damages if all victims sue and recover but that punitive damages are needed to achieve proper deterrence when the defendant, through lack of detection or otherwise, is escaping some compensatory liabilities. This implies that the proper amount of punitive damages would be reached by multiplying the plaintiff's compensatory damages by ("a factor reflecting the probability of his escaping liability"). A polluter who causes $100,000 in damages to the plaintiff but is caught in only one case out of four would end up paying $400,000, total. Id. at 874–75. When the defendant merely likes to beat up other people, punitive damages are justified even if the defendant does not escape any compensatory liabilities. See id. at 908–909.

5. E.g., Palmer v. Ted Stevens Honda, Inc., 193 Cal.App.3d 530, 238 Cal.Rptr. 363 (1987); see generally Dan B. Dobbs, Law of Remedies § 3.11 (11).

6. Distinguish the use of compensatory damage multiples under the Polinsky–Shavell theory. See n. 4, supra.

stances, the relevant ratio is the relationships between the amount of potential harm from the defendant's conduct and the punitive award.[7]

Defendant's financial status. The defendant's financial status is a factor in determining the right amount of punitive damages.[8] The theory is that the trier must know something about the defendant's financial condition in order to inflict a liability that will have an appropriate sting,[9] and proof may show either a wealthy defendant or a poor one.[10] In the case of personal ill-will or evil disposition as where the defendant beats or rapes another person, the defendant's financial condition is obviously of some relevance, since a small punitive award against a very wealthy person may have little effect while a large award against a person with little wealth might fail to deter if all the defendant's assets are exhausted so that he has nothing left to lose. On the other hand, when a tort is committed by income-producing activity—by deliberately selling dangerous products, for example—profitability of the tortious activity is probably more significant for deterrence than wealth.[11]

Aggregate punishment. Punitive damages awards in some cases run the risk that the defendant will be punished several times over, perhaps because he is criminally liable and perhaps because he has been or will be subjected to other punitive damages judgments. Punitive damages awards are not subject to the prohibition against double jeopardy,[12] but the aggregate of punishments is a clear and even a constitutional concern in determining the justification for and amount of punitive awards.[13] It is difficult to see a good way to obtain and use all the relevant information, however. The manufacturer who may be held punitively liable in the future probably does not wish to argue to the jury that others will also punish him. The other extreme would permit only a single punitive award, even though the defendant's reckless or malicious behavior has injured many people.[14] Perhaps the best that can be done is to permit the judges in reviewing a jury verdict of punitive damages to consider past and potential punitive awards, although as to future awards, this necessarily seems speculative.

7. See Bowden v. Caldor, 350 Md. 4, 40, 710 A.2d 267, 285 (1998).

8. See 1 Dan B. Dobbs, Law of Remedies, § 3.11 (5) (2d ed. 1993).

9. See. e.g., Zarcone v. Perry, 572 F.2d 52, 56 (2d Cir.1978) ("A $60,000 award may bankrupt one person and be a minor annoyance to another"); Thiry v. Armstrong World Indus., 661 P.2d 515 (Okla.1983).

10. See Michael v. Cole, 122 Ariz. 450, 595 P.2d 995 (1979); Hardin v. Caldwell, 695 S.W.2d 189 (Tenn.Ct.App.1985).

11. See Dan B. Dobbs, Ending Punishment in "Punitive" Damages: Deterrence-measured Remedies, 40 Ala. L. Rev. 831, 871–888 (1989) (proposing punitive damages to equal the amount needed to deter, either the wrongdoer's profits from the tortious activity or where that measure is not feasible, a reasonable attorney fee for the plaintiff, not limited to a percentage of recovery).

12. J. Ghiardi & J. Kircher, Punitive Damages Law and Practice § 3.02 (2 vols. 1995 & Supps.).

13. See Pacific Mut. Life Ins. Co. v. Haslip, 499 U.S. 1, 20, 111 S.Ct. 1032, 1045, 113 L.Ed.2d 1, 21 (1991).

14. This was dictated in Ga. Code § 51–12–5.1, held unconstitutional as discriminatory in McBride v. General Motors Corp., 737 F.Supp. 1563 (M.D.Ga.1990).

§ 383. The Common Law and Constitutional Process of Determining Punitive Damages

Because the law is vague in describing the occasions for punitive damages and equally vague in prescribing the proper level of such damages, the legal process for making the awards becomes especially important. Yet, the process of determining punitive awards has sometimes itself been subject to criticism and more recently, subject to many reform efforts. The process elements include discovery, burden of proof, trial, evidence, and guidelines for assessment of the issues and amounts.

Trial and Pre-trial

Burden of proof. The plaintiff has the burden of proving the factual basis for punitive damages by a preponderance of the evidence. Some courts and legislatures have now altered this to require clear and convincing evidence[1] or even proof beyond a reasonable doubt.[2]

Handling wealth evidence; bifurcation. The traditional assumption was that although evidence of the defendant's financial condition was admissible, nothing compelled the plaintiff to produce such evidence. California and Wyoming have held that the plaintiff must produce evidence of the defendant's wealth if she is to recover any punitive award,[3] a view not generally shared and one surgically dissected and discarded by Judge Posner.[4] If evidence of the defendant's wealth is admitted, it might induce some jurors to find against the defendant on the more basic issue of liability for compensatory damages. In some states by judicial decision or statute the trial of the basic liability issues is held before any evidence of the defendant's wealth is admitted. Only if the defendant is found to have committed a tort is the jury to consider punitive damages, sometimes only after compensatory damages have been determined as well.[5] The procedure that requires two trial segments is called bifurcation.[6]

Discovery. The problem that suggests bi-or trifurcation of trials begins even earlier when the plaintiff seeks to discover the defendant's financial information. Because financial information is relevant, discovery is permitted,[7] but privacy and confidentiality issues suggest that discovery of financial data is inappropriate until the plaintiff can convince the judge that she has a prima facie case for recovery of punitive

§ 383

1. E.g., Linthicum v. Nationwide Life Ins. Co., 150 Ariz. 326, 723 P.2d 675 (1986); See Lee R. Russ, Annotation, Standard of Proof as to Conduct Underlying Punitive Damage Awards—Modern Status, 58 A.L.R.4th 878 (1987).

2. Colo. Rev. Stat. § 13–25–127.

3. Adams v. Murakami, 54 Cal.3d 105, 284 Cal.Rptr. 318, 813 P.2d 1348 (1991); Adel v. Parkhurst, 681 P.2d 886 (Wyo. 1984).

4. Kemezy v. Peters, 79 F.3d 33 (7th Cir.1996).

5. E.g., Campen v. Stone, 635 P.2d 1121, 32 A.L.R.4th 410 (Wyo. 1981); Cal. Civ. Code § 3295 (d); N.C. Gen. Stat. § 1D–30 (jury first determines liability and compensation, then punitive damages).

6. Trifurcation with separate segments for liability, compensation, and punitive awards is also a possibility.

7. See Lunsford v. Morris, 746 S.W.2d 471 (Tex.1988).

damages. The Model Punitive Damages Act so provides[8] and some courts have so held.[9]

Constitutional Limits

Process requirements. The Supreme Court of the United States has held that awards of punitive damages do not in themselves violate the Eighth Amendment[10] or Due Process requirements.[11] But due process exacts some requirements. First, some kind of guidance must be given to the jury about the purpose of punitive damages as retribution or deterrence, perhaps along with an instruction that an award is not required.[12] Second, courts must provide post-trial review of punitive awards.[13] Guidance and review on the basis of factors already mentioned[14]—reprehensibility of the defendant's conduct being the chief—was initially held to be sufficient.[15]

Excessive awards. In 1996, the Supreme Court went several steps further. In *BMW of North America v. Gore*,[16] the Court did not stop at the question of judicial process. Although it placed no caps on the punitive award,[17] it held that the amount of a punitive award could be so grossly excessive that it would in itself violate due process. In so holding, the Court examined some factors that are not in the traditional list. The facts may have shaped a good deal of the opinion. Gore had purchased from BMW a "new car", which as it turned out had been damaged while still in BMW's possession, probably from acid rain. BMW repainted the car and sold it as a new car without disclosing the repair. The fact that it had been repainted before being delivered to a customer might have reduced its resale value by $4,000. The jury awarded $4 million in punitive damages. The Alabama Court reduced that to $2 million.

The United States Supreme Court struck the award on the ground that it was grossly excessive and a violation of due process. The Supreme Court first considered the scope of the state's interests in imposing punitive damages. The state had no interest in imposing sanctions for conduct outside the state or changing the defendant's behavior in other states. Its interest was in its own citizens and its justification for a punitive award was circumscribed accordingly. In other words, a large

8. Model Punitive Damages Act § 4.

9. Larriva v. Montiel, 143 Ariz. 23, 691 P.2d 735 (Ct. App. 1984); Gierman v. Toman, 77 N.J.Super. 18, 185 A.2d 241 (1962).

10. Browning–Ferris Indus. of Vermont, Inc. v. Kelco Disposal, Inc., 492 U.S. 257, 109 S.Ct. 2909, 106 L.Ed.2d 219 (1989).

11. Pacific Mut. Life Ins. Co. v. Haslip, 499 U.S. 1, 111 S.Ct. 1032, 1043, 113 L.Ed.2d 1 (1991).

12. Id.

13. See Honda Motor Co. Ltd. v. Oberg, 512 U.S. 415, 114 S.Ct. 2331, 129 L.Ed.2d 336 (1994).

14. See § 382.

15. Pacific Mut. Life Ins. Co. v. Haslip, 499 U.S. 1, 20, 111 S.Ct. 1032, 1045, 113 L.Ed.2d 1, 21 (1991). See also TXO Production Corp. v. Alliance Resources Corp., 509 U.S. 443, 113 S.Ct. 2711, 125 L.Ed.2d 366 (1993).

16. BMW of North America v. Gore, 517 U.S. 559, 116 S.Ct. 1589, 134 L.Ed.2d 809 (1996).

17. In Montgomery Ward v. Wilson, 339 Md. 701, 664 A.2d 916 (1995), the defendant argued that when punitive damages are awarded in the first trial, the amount awarded provides a constitutional cap on the punitive award to be applied if the defendant appeals and secures a retrial. The court rejected this argument.

punitive award could not be justified on the ground that such a large award was necessary to change the defendant's conduct elsewhere. There is room for uncertainty as to the scope of this rule. In a personal injury suit against a manufacturer who risks harm to people in all states, perhaps there is still room to consider the full breadth of the potential harm when considering whether the manufacturer acted reprehensibly and also when considering the ratio of punitive damages to potential harm.

Second, the Court insisted that the defendant could not be subjected to punishment unless it had fair notice of the conduct that was subject to sanction and also notice of the severity of the penalty. This point turned out to be complex. The Court examined three "guideposts," somewhat but not entirely similar to the factors it had previously recognized in determining what kind of judicial review had to be accorded punitive awards. Here the guideposts were used to determine whether the defendant had received adequate notice of the magnitude of the sanction. The guideposts were: (a) the degree of reprehensibility of the nondisclosure; (b) the disparity between the harm or potential harm suffered by Dr. Gore and his punitive damages award;[18] and (c) the difference between this remedy and the civil penalties authorized or imposed in comparable cases. This third guidepost, however, is one that may raise substantial impediments to deterrence-measured punitive awards. In *BMW*, the Court compared the punitive award with statutory fines for similar conduct, with the inevitable result that the punitive award was considered grossly excessive.

§ 384. "Tort Reform" Statutes Affecting Compensatory and Punitive Damages

The drive to restrict tort liability has generally been referred to as "tort reform." Whether reform is needed or desirable is hotly debated.[1] However, tort reform has succeeded in many states by imposing preconditions to suit, shortening statutes of limitations, modifying the collateral source rule, abolishing joint and several liability, raising the plaintiff's burden of proof, and, most directly, limiting compensatory and punitive damages. The last is the topic of this section.

Capping statutes. The most severe tort reform statutes put a limit or cap on recovery of compensatory damages. Well over half the states have enacted some kind of cap on damages recoverable. In some instances the cap applies only to particular kinds of tort claims, such as claims for professional malpractice,[2] suits against public entities,[3] or suits against

18. BMW of North America v. Gore, 517 U.S. at 575, 116 S.Ct. at 1598 speaks of the ratio of punitive damages to potential harm. Later the Court speaks of the ratio of punitive to actual damages as the ratio to consider. See 517 U.S. at 580, 116 S.Ct. at 1601. When the Court explicates the principle, it comes back to the potential harm idea. See 517 U.S. at 581, 116 S.Ct. at 1602.

§ 384

1. The arguments on both sides are considered in § 391.

2. E.g., Cal. Civ. Code § 3333.2 .

3. E.g., Me. Rev. Stat. Ann. tit. 14 § 8105.

alcohol providers.[4] In others, the cap applies to all tort claims.[5] The statutes are diverse in other ways, too, sometimes capping damages but providing the plaintiff with substitute claims against a fund to care for extreme cases.[6] Statutes may impose an absolute cap on all damages[7] or may impose a cap only on "noneconomic" damages like those awarded for pain and suffering.[8] The statutory cap on recovery varies from state to state. Utah says alcohol providers cannot be liable for more than $500,000.[9] California's cap for pain and suffering is $250,000.[10]

Researchers are beginning to investigate various effects that caps might have in settlement negotiation and other aspects of practice.[11] Broadly speaking, however, caps have at least two distinct potential effects on a given plaintiff's recovery. The obvious one is that the ultimate recovery in larger cases will be reduced by the cap. The other one is that since the recovery finances the lawyer's work through contingent fees, a reduced recovery may mean that some cases requiring heavy work and great expense may not be brought at all, or if brought may be settled even more cheaply than the cap itself suggests.

Objections. In practice, the most central objection probably is that reduction of damages actually suffered eliminates appropriate compensation and reduces appropriate levels of deterrence. In principle, the most central objection to caps is that, assuming that damages should be limited in some way, a cap is exactly the wrong way to do so, since the cap gives a full recovery to the least injured but only a limited portion of the damages suffered by the most seriously injured. Defendants have supported caps on the theory that by reducing liabilities they can reduce insurance premiums. But if damages were correctly figured before caps were introduced, that argument translates to an argument that seriously injured individuals must suffer without compensation for the benefit of the others.[12] It makes A pay so B can save money.

Constitutionality. Plaintiffs have presented several arguments that damages caps are unconstitutional. They have asserted rights to jury trial, equal protection, due process, and separation of powers under state constitutional provisions and others. A number of courts have found particular statutes unconstitutional on one ground or another.[13] Other

4. E.g., Utah Code Ann. § 32A–14–101(5) ($500,000 cap).

5. Md. Ann. Code, Ct. & Jud. Proc. § 11–108.

6. See, e.g., Butler v. Flint Goodrich Hospital, 607 So.2d 517 (La.1992).

7. Colo. Rev. Stat. § 13–64–302; Va. Code § 8.01–581.15 ($1 million cap on total damages against health care provider).

8. Cal. Civ. Code § 3333.2 ; Md. Ann. Code, Ct. & Jud. Proc. § 11–108.

9. Utah Code Ann. § 32A–14–101(5).

10. Cal. Civ. Code § 3333.2 .

11. E.g., Linda Babcock & Greg Pogarsky, Damage Caps and Settlement: A Behavioral Approach, 28 J. Leg. Stud. 341 (1999) (concluding that caps increase the likelihood of settlement, even though some negotiators might truncate their estimates of the case's value at the cap level while others might recalibrate their estimates completely).

12. See Morris v. Savoy, 61 Ohio St.3d 684, 691, 576 N.E.2d 765 , 771 (1991) (cap imposes "the cost of the intended benefit to the general public solely upon a class consisting of those most severely injured by medical malpractice").

13. Moore v. Mobile Infirmary Ass'n,592 So.2d 156 (Ala.1991) (malpractice noneconomic damage cap denied right to

courts have upheld caps. Some of these broadly reject due process and equal protection arguments,[14] but others have upheld the caps only because the legislature provided the victim with some substitute remedy such as a claim against a Patient Compensation Fund when damages were higher than the cap.[15]

Limiting pain and suffering damages without caps. The tort reform statutes have so far attempted to limit compensatory damages only through raw caps, but students of the problem have been developing others kinds of limits for pain and suffering damages, not to create a windfall for tortfeasors but because such damages are inherently difficult to estimate. One kind of limitation would reverse the cap effect and exclude small rather than large claims by imposing a minimum threshold. Much as a collision insurance policy might not cover the first $100 dollars of the loss, this kind of rule would disallow pain and suffering damages that were not significant in amount.[16] The second kind of limitation would ask jurors to compare the case they heard with a set of ten or so other standardized scenarios ranging from very little injury and pain to the most serious.[17] The law could fix damages for each scenario and the jury's decision that their case was worse than scenario 5 and not so bad as scenario 6 would narrow the available pain and suffering damages. A more complicated version would not assign pre-set values to the scenarios, but rather to advise the jury of the national or state average awards for cases similar to each scenario. Several other variations on this approach can be imagined.[18]

The most recent research came up with a surprising finding.[19] In many mock trials, jurors of diverse wealth, education, gender and ethnicity came to almost complete agreement about punitive damages issues when they were allowed to rate the conduct on a given scale, say one to six. Their agreement disappeared when they tried to convert to dollars. The indication is that a set of scenarios or even a scale of one to

jury trial and equal protection; statute created favored class of defendants); Smith v. Department of Ins., 507 So.2d 1080 (Fla. 1987); Best v. Taylor Mach. Works, 179 Ill.2d 367, 413, 689 N.E.2d 1057, 1080, 228 Ill.Dec. 636, 659 (1997) (noneconomic damages generally capped at $500,000; the statute "undercuts the power, and obligation, of the judiciary to reduce excessive verdicts" and violates separation of powers provisions); Carson v. Maurer, 120 N.H. 925, 424 A.2d 825, 12 A.L.R.4th 1 (1980) (medical malpractice cap denies equal protection); Morris v. Savoy, 61 Ohio St.3d 684, 576 N.E.2d 765 (1991) (medical malpractice cap was irrational and arbitrary and violates due process).

14. Fein v. Permanente Med. Group, 38 Cal.3d 137, 695 P.2d 665, 211 Cal.Rptr. 368 (1985); Murphy v. Edmonds, 325 Md. 342, 601 A.2d 102 (1992); Robinson v. Charleston Area Med. Ctr., Inc., 186 W.Va. 720, 414 S.E.2d 877 (1991).

15. University of Miami v. Echarte, 618 So.2d 189 (Fla.1993) (caps apply only when defendant accepts arbitration, regarded as an offsetting benefit); Butler v. Flint Goodrich Hosp., 607 So.2d 517 (La.1992) (patient's compensation fund).

16. See II American Law Institute, Reporter's Study, Enterprise Responsibility for Personal Injury 230 (1991).

17. Randal R. Bovbjerg, et. al, Valuing Life and Limb in Tort: Scheduling "Pain and Suffering", 83 Nw. L. Rev. 908 (1989) considers variations and details.

18. See § 397 (the grids used in social security claims).

19. Cass R. Sunstein, et al., Assessing Punitive Damages (With Notes on Cognition and Valuation in Law), 107 Yale L.J. 2071 (1998).

ten would increase predictability of awards for both punitive and pain and suffering damages. These studies offer considerable opportunity for eliminating the occasional run-away verdict without imposing caps that make the most injured absorb the costs.

Limiting and Redirecting Punitive Damages

Caps. Quite apart from caps on compensatory damages, a number of statutes place limits on the amount of punitive recoveries, often as part of legislation that also constrains punitive recoveries in other ways as well.[20] Several forms of limitation have been enacted. An uncommon form appears in a federal statute governing punitive damages for employment and disability discrimination. That statute combines punitive damages and nonpecuniary damages and limits the total. The top amount recoverable is graduated, not according to the wealth of the defendant but according to the number of persons the defendant employs.[21] The Kansas cap is the highest gross income of the defendant in the preceding five years or $5 million, whichever sum is smaller.[22] In other states, capping legislation puts flat dollar limits on punitive damages or caps punitive damages by limiting them to a multiple of compensatory damages.[23] Or a combination of a flat dollar limit and a multiple of compensatory damage may be used.[24]

So far as a cap is effective, the punitive award will be calibrated to neither the defendant's aggravated misconduct nor the need for deterrence. And caps don't necessary accomplish much. They can prevent excessive punitive awards that are also higher than the cap, but they do not address the problem of excess awards at lower levels.[25] In close cases, judges and juries may actually tend to balloon the award to the cap level.[26] Finally, caps on punitive damages, like an outright prohibition of punitive damages, can protect against excessive awards, but the cap necessarily protects those tortfeasors who are perceived by the trier to be the most guilty of the most aggravated misconduct.

20. E.g., by limiting vicarious liability, requiring bifurcation of trials, imposing higher burdens of proof, requiring proof of specific malice.

21. 42 U.S.C.A. § 1981a (b)(3).

22. Kan. Stat. Ann. § 60–3701(e).

23. Colo. Rev. Stats. Ann. § 13–21–102 (may not exceed compensatory damages); Conn. Gen. Stat. Ann. § 52–240b (products liability cases, twice the compensatory damages awarded); Fla. Stat. Ann. § 768.73 (three times compensatory, with an escape clause). Multiple damages have long been authorized by statutes, but not necessarily as punitive awards. See 1 Dan B. Dobbs, Law of Remedies § 3.12.

24. N.J. Stat. Ann. 2A:15–5.14 ("five times the liability of that defendant for compensatory damages or $350,000, whichever is greater").

25. A cap of, say, $250,000 on punitive damages does not at all touch the median punitive award in many counties. An American Bar Foundation study found that the median punitive award was as low as $10,-000 in some counties with a top of $204,00 in San Diego. See Michael L. Rustad, Unraveling Punitive Damages: Current Data and Further Inquiry, 1998 Wis. L. Rev. 15, 20–30.

26. Cf. Luciano v. Olsten Corp., 110 F.3d 210 (2d Cir.1997) (the maximum is not the ceiling on a scale, so trier can fix the award at the maximum even if the misconduct is not the worst imaginable).

Reallocation of punitive damages. Several states provide for allocation of a portion of the punitive award to a state agency.[27] From the point of view of the plaintiff, this reallocation operates like a cap. From the defendant's point of view, this reallocation does nothing to minimize punitive damages awarded. The defendants' protection from statutes like this comes much earlier. The limitation on punitive damages may cut the funds from which attorneys' fees and litigation costs can be paid, with the result that some suits will not be pursued at all. When suits are not pursued because it is financially infeasible under these statutes, the defendants who most deserve punishment or deterrence will be the ones who escape liability altogether.

27. Iowa Code Ann. § 668A.1 (75% or more to a state agency except when tort is "directed at" the plaintiff); Kan. Stat. Ann. § 60–3402 (50%); Ore. Rev. Stats. § 18.540 (60% to state agency).

*

CHAPTER 26

APPORTIONMENT OF RESPONSIBILITY AMONG PARTIES

§ 385. Causal Apportionment and Joint and Several Liability

In the great majority of states, responsibility for injury is apportioned between plaintiff and defendant on a comparative fault basis.[1] But that does not end the problems of apportionment because in a very large number of tort cases liability must also be apportioned somehow among two or more defendants.

Fundamental traditional rules. Apart from statutory changes, four fundamental rules governed the apportionment of responsibility among multiple tortfeasors and the plaintiffs.

(1) Apportionment required. Except for cases of concerted action and vicarious liability, apportionment is required if the harms done by two or more tortfeasors were separable or divisible as where A caused the plaintiff's broken arm and B caused the plaintiff's broken leg. Each tortfeasor is liable for the harm he caused, no more, no less. This is causal apportionment.[2]

(2) Indivisible injury. If the injury was indivisible in nature (a death or a single broken arm for examples), then each tortfeasor who contributed proximately to that injury was liable for the entire judgment, although the plaintiff could not collect more than one full recovery.[3] This is often referred to as a rule for concurrent torts, but concurrence in time is not required. The essence of the rule is that each tortfeasor is liable in full for an indivisible injury.[4] At one time this rule was cluttered with procedural problems in joinder, but all parties can now usually be joined.

(3) Actions in concert, vicarious liability. Whether or not the injury was indivisible, if the defendants acted in concert, or one defendant acted tortiously and the other was vicariously liable, each defendant was liable for the entire injury.[5]

§ 385

1. § 201.

2. See Restatement of Apportionment § 50.

3. For examples, see § 174.

4. See Watts v. Smith, 375 Mich. 120, 134 N.W.2d 194 (1965) & § 174.

5. E.g., Bierczynski v. Rogers, 239 A.2d 218 (Del.1968); Restatement of Apportionment § 24; see § 340.

(4) Contribution. Apportionment is completed under the rule that when one tortfeasor paid more than his appropriate share of liability, he could ordinarily obtain contribution from the other tortfeasors, a rule generally followed in the latter part of the 20th century.[6]

The meaning of joint and several liability. Joint and several liability has been recognized since the 1700s.[7] When two or more tortfeasors are jointly and severally liable, each defendant is subject to liability for all of the plaintiff's damages. The plaintiff can obtain a judgment against all defendants and then enforce it against any one of them, or partly against one and partly against another.[8] The effect is to provide the plaintiff with more than one source of funds but not more than one complete satisfaction. If tortfeasor A has few assets and is underinsured, or A enjoys an immunity or partial immunity, the plaintiff may be able to enforce the judgment against tortfeasor B. If the plaintiff enforces a judgment against one tortfeasor for more than his fair share of the liability, today's law usually permits that tortfeasor contribution or other adjustments from the non-paying tortfeasor.

§ 386. Contribution and Indemnity in a Joint and Several Liability System

Contribution and Indemnity

History. Under the rule originally adopted by the courts, when the plaintiff enforced a joint and several judgment entirely against A, A was not allowed to recover contribution from B for any part of what he had paid.[1] The result was that although both A and B were at fault, A paid all the damages and B paid none. The rule grew up in the day when joint and several liability applied only to tortfeasors who acted in concert to carry out intentional torts. In that setting, denial of contribution was equivalent to saying that an intentional tortfeasor cannot use the courts to enforce an equitable loss sharing.

General recognition of contribution rights. However, either by statute or judicial decision, a right of contribution is now a generally accepted part of the joint and several liability system[2] except that contribution is still denied to intentional tortfeasors.[3] Early statutes authorized contribution only when one tortfeasor satisfied a judgment

6. See §§ 386 & 387.

7. See Merryweather v. Nixan, 101 Eng. Rep. 1337 (1799) (reflecting one tortfeasor's payment of the entire liability).

8. Restatement of Apportionment § 27A; John W. Wade, Should Joint and Several Liability of Multiple Tortfeasors Be Abolished?, 10 Am. J. Trial Advoc. 193 (1986).

§ 386

1. See Robert A. Leflar, Contribution and Indemnity Between Tortfeasors, 81 U.Pa. L. Rev. 130 (1932).

2. E.g., Cal. Civ. Proc. Code § 875; 740 ILCS § 100/3; Iowa Code Ann. § 668.5; Mich. Stats. § 600.2925a; Uniform Contribution Among Tortfeasors Act § 1.

3. The Uniform Contribution Among Tortfeasors Act § 1 reflects the current view in permitting contribution in favor of one who has paid more than his "pro rata share."

for the plaintiff; the same tortfeasor's settlement with the plaintiff would not support a contribution claim against the other tortfeasors. These statutes have in effect been broadened by judicial decisions creating a contribution right even in cases of settlement, somewhat misleadingly called "equitable indemnity."[4] Other statutes specifically authorize contribution in favor of a tortfeasor who satisfies the plaintiff's claim, whether by paying a judgment or effecting a settlement that releases the other tortfeasors.[5]

Traditional indemnity. Indemnity differs from contribution. While contribution contemplates that two defendants will share in the ultimate liability, indemnity contemplates that one will fully repay the other. Indemnity was and is permitted in only a few situations. If A is liable only vicariously and not because he participated in or ratified B's tort, A can obtain indemnity from B, even if contribution is not permitted. Employers are thus theoretically entitled to indemnity from employees when the employer satisfies a judgment for the employee's tort, although this is a right seldom asserted.[6] Retailers who are held liable without fault for products defective when they left a manufacturer's hands are also entitled to indemnity against the manufacturer.[7] Somewhat similarly, if A acted on directions of B, or on B's misrepresentation, and believed he was acting properly, B is required to indemnify A.[8] Business enterprises dealing with each other often provide that one will indemnify the other for any liability arising out of particular operations.[9]

Active-passive indemnity. Before the days of comparative fault and generally available contribution, courts sometimes awarded indemnity to a tortfeasor who was thought to be significantly less responsible because he was in some sense "passive." That was an all or nothing solution, not a share of responsibility in proportion to fault. That active-passive kind of indemnity is now in disrepute and probably has little or no future in apportioning responsibility among tortfeasors.[10]

Requirements for contribution. Under the liberal modern system, the tortfeasor who pays more than his appropriate share is entitled to recover contribution from other tortfeasors, by separate suit or by asserting third party claims against them in the plaintiff's suit. The tortfeasor claiming contribution must ordinarily prove that he and the other tortfeasors shared a common liability to the plaintiff. This means that if A and B negligently cause the plaintiff's harm, but B is not liable to the plaintiff because he is immune, A is not entitled to contribution

4. See, e.g., See American Motorcycle Ass'n v. Superior Court, 20 Cal.3d 578, 146 Cal.Rptr. 182, 578 P.2d 899 (1978). Traditional indemnity in contrast is not a system for dividing responsibility but for shifting it entirely to one of the tortfeasors.

5. E.g., Mass. Gen. L. Ann. ch. 231B § 1 (a).

6. § 333.

7. § 375.

8. Restatement § 886B (2).

9. E.g., Potlatch Corp. v. Missouri Pac. R.R., 321 Ark. 314, 902 S.W.2d 217 (1995).

10. Miller v. American President Lines, Ltd., 989 F.2d 1450 (6th Cir.1993); Victor Schwartz, Comparative Negligence § 16.9 (3d ed. 1994 & Supp.).

from B.[11] An important example is the case of the employer who is covered by workers' compensation laws. If the employer, A, and a third person, B, negligently injure an employee, the employer is immune to tort liability; the employee recovers only against B, the third person. Because of the employer's immunity, it shares no common liability with the third person and thus is not liable for contribution.[12] The common liability rule also means that one tortfeasor can obtain contribution from the other only if both were legally liable to the plaintiff, so that a tortfeasor seeking contribution must prove his own liability where that liability has not been established by a judgment.

Contribution was traditionally sought by one negligent tortfeasor against another. However, contribution is now allowed in favor of or against tortfeasors who are not negligent at all but only strictly liable.[13] Contribution has even been allowed as between a tortfeasor and a contract breacher whose breach was one of the causes of harm.[14]

The claims for contribution and indemnity are subject to statutes of limitation, but a number of courts have held that defendant A may assert a cross-claim for contribution or indemnity against defendant B even though the plaintiff's claim against B is barred by the statute of limitations.[15]

§ 387. Measures of Contribution in a Joint and Several Liability System

Comparative responsibility among tortfeasors. A joint and several liability system today is usually coupled with a system that permits a tortfeasor who has paid more than his appropriate share of liability to obtain contribution from other tortfeasors. The traditional rule of contri-

11. See, e.g., Stencel Aero Eng'g Corp. v. United States, 431 U.S. 666, 97 S.Ct. 2054, 52 L.Ed.2d 665 (1977) (governmental immunity); Ascheman v. Village of Hancock, 254 N.W.2d 382 (Minn.1977); Coburn v. Reiser, 254 Neb. 495, 577 N.W.2d 289 (1998) (guest statute immunity); Holodook v. Spencer, 36 N.Y.2d 35, 364 N.Y.S.2d 859, 324 N.E.2d 338 (1974) (limited parental duty to child barring contribution against parents); cf. Gaertner v. Holcka, 219 Wis.2d 436, 580 N.W.2d 271 (1998) (failure of adult to secure child with seatbelt as required by statute not actionable by the child, semble, hence adult is not liable for contribution to tortfeasor causing injury).

12. See, e.g., Henning v. General Motors Assembly Div., 143 Wis.2d 1, 419 N.W.2d 551 (1988); Joel E. Smith, Annotation, Modern Status of Effect of State Workmen's Compensation Act on Right of Third-Person Tortfeasor to Contribution or Indemnity From Employer of Injured or Killed Workman, 100 A.L.R.3d 350 (1980). A more policy-explicit statement of the rule would point out that the immunity would be subverted if contribution were allowed.

13. E.g., Safeway Stores, Inc. v. Nest–Kart, 21 Cal.3d 322, 146 Cal.Rptr. 550, 579 P.2d 441 (1978).

14. Dunn v. Praiss, 139 N.J. 564, 656 A.2d 413 (1995).

15. E.g., Willmar v. Short–Elliott–Hendrickson, Inc., 512 N.W.2d 872 (Minn.1994) (city's claim against manufacturer of component was barred by UCC 4–year statute of limitations, but city's claim against consulting engineer on project that used the component was not barred and engineer's cross-claim against the manufacturer would not be barred merely because the city could not recover against the manufacturer). But cf. Johnson v. Core–Vent Corp., 264 Ill. App.3d 833, 201 Ill.Dec. 294, 636 N.E.2d 726 (1993) (dentist and patients joined in suing implant manufacturer after implants broke in patient's mouths; manufacturer's counterclaim for contribution was barred by statute).

bution among tortfeasors divided the loss equally among them, so that if one of two tortfeasors paid the full judgment of $10,000, he would recover $5,000 in contribution from the other.[1]

Where comparative fault was adopted, however, this division seemed irrational, for as between the plaintiff and the defendants, responsibility was apportioned according to relative fault, while as between defendants it was apportioned equally among tortfeasors regardless of their respective fault. Statutes and decisions have altered the traditional rule to adopt a comparative fault apportionment among tortfeasors, apportioning ultimate responsibility among tortfeasors according to their respective shares of fault.[2] So if A and B are chargeable with 25% and 75% of the fault respectively and A pays the plaintiff's judgment in full, A can recover 75% of his payment as contribution from joint tortfeasor B. The modified comparative fault system used in many states deny the plaintiff recovery against a defendant when the plaintiff's negligence is greater than (or sometimes merely equal to) the defendant's. This approach has been rejected, however, for contribution claims by a defendant who seeks contribution from a co-defendant whose negligence is less.[3] Thus if B, chargeable with 75% of the fault, paid the entire judgment, he would be entitled to recover 25% from A.

Comparative responsibility in strict liability cases. When one or more of the tortfeasors is strictly liable, it is not literally possible to compare fault.[4] However, courts can and do allocate responsibility as between strictly liable and negligent defendants in much the same way they allocate responsibility between negligent defendants so that, for example, one might be chargeable with 80% of the responsibility while the other is chargeable with only 20%.[5] Sometimes it is said that this must be comparative causation. The Restatement of Apportionment prefers the term "comparative responsibility."[6]

§ 387

1. National Health Labs., Inc. v. Ahmadi, 596 A.2d 555 (D.C.1991) (equal shares in the absence of a comparative negligence system); see Uniform Contribution Among Tortfeasors Act § 2 (pro rata but not percentage fault allocation).

2. E.g., Iowa Code Ann. § 668.5; American Motorcycle Ass'n v. Superior Court, 20 Cal.3d 578, 146 Cal.Rptr. 182, 578 P.2d 899 (1978); Cartel Capital Corp. v. Fireco, 81 N.J. 548, 410 A.2d 674, 19 A.L.R.4th 310 (1980); Bervoets v. Harde Ralls Pontiac–Olds, Inc., 891 S.W.2d 905 (Tenn.1994); Mackey v. Irisari, 191 W.Va. 355, 445 S.E.2d 742 (1994). Where a statute leaves a choice, the comparative fault allocation seems preferable. See Martignetti v. Haigh–Farr Inc., 425 Mass. 294, 680 N.E.2d 1131 (1997) (general contribution statute rejected comparative fault allocation, but court adopted it under the unclear provisions of an environmental harm statute).

3. Liberty Mutual Ins. Co. v. General Motors Corp., 65 Haw. 428, 653 P.2d 96 (1982); Sitzes v. Anchor Motor Freight, Inc., 169 W.Va. 698, 289 S.E.2d 679 (1982).

4. See § 369 (discussing the argument that comparing strict liability with fault is like comparing apples and oranges).

5. Safeway Stores, Inc. v. Nest–Kart, 21 Cal.3d 322, 146 Cal.Rptr. 550, 579 P.2d 441 (1978) (Safeway, negligent, was chargeable with 80%, the manufacturer of a product causing injury, strictly liable, chargeable with 20%).

6. Restatement of Apportionment § 8, cmt. a (Proposed Final Draft 1998). This Restatement invites an unweighted consideration of broadly stated factors, including states of mind. It may invite jurors to decide more of their preferences for the parties than their judgment of conduct.

Comparative responsibility with joint and several liability. The mere adoption of comparative fault apportionment among tortfeasors does not necessarily change joint and several liability rules.[7] Suppose the trier finds that the plaintiff suffered $100,000 in damages and was chargeable with 10% of all the negligence, thus reducing her judgment to $90,000 under comparative negligence rules. The jury also finds that A was chargeable with 60% of the fault and B with 30%. If the plaintiff enforces her judgment entirely against A under a joint and several liability system, A will pay $90,000 but will be entitled to $30,000 in contribution from B.

As always with the traditional joint and several liability system, A may get a judgment for contribution from B but may not be able to collect it. If the plaintiff was wholly without legal fault, this result would be sound, for it would require the negligent tortfeasor rather than the innocent plaintiff to bear the risks of another tortfeasor's insolvency. However, when the plaintiff herself is also at fault, it seems more logical to require that the plaintiff and tortfeasor A share the risk of B's insolvency in proportion to their respective fault shares.[8] Since A's negligence was 60% of the total and the plaintiff's 10%, they would presumably absorb B's share of liability between them in the same proportion, six to one. The same figure results if you use that ratio for the $100,000 damages figure, ignoring B altogether. A's liability would then by 6/7 of the $100,000 and the plaintiff would absorb 1/7 of that sum.

§ 388. Settlement in a Joint and Several Liability System

Judgment, Release and Covenant Not to Sue

Judgment. When a defendant fully pays a judgment for all of the plaintiff's damages, the plaintiff's claim is satisfied and he has no further claim for the same injury. In a joint and several liability system, the tortfeasor by his satisfaction of the judgment acquires a right of contribution against joint tortfeasors responsible for the same injury. If, however, one tortfeasor pays less than all of the judgment, and less than his appropriate share, the plaintiff retains the right to enforce the balance of the judgment against either or both tortfeasors. So far as injuries are divisible and the defendant satisfies the claim only for his divisible share, as where physician B negligently enhances a tortious injury caused by A and satisfies a judgment for that injury, the satisfac-

7. A number of courts so held, e.g., American Motorcycle Ass'n v. Superior Court, 20 Cal.3d 578, 146 Cal.Rptr. 182, 578 P.2d 899 (1978), but statutes in some states now alter joint and several liability and some courts have initiated the same program. See § 389.

8. See Martignetti v. Haigh–Farr Inc., 425 Mass. 294, 680 N.E.2d 1131 (1997) (where plaintiff and defendants are all responsible for release of hazardous materials plaintiff who bore the cost of cleanup can get contribution from others, but orphan shares of responsibility due to insolvency of any defendant must be borne equitably among all parties); Restatement § 886A, cmt. c (fact that one tortfeasor is insolvent may affect contribution among others).

tion does not affect the plaintiff's claim against A for the remainder and does not create a right of contribution in B.[1]

Releases and covenants. In a joint and several liability system, settlement with one of two or more tortfeasors requires careful preparation. Defendants often settle tort claims by paying the plaintiff a sum of money in exchange for a release of all claims. The release was conceived of, not as a contract but as a document somewhat like a deed—it relinquished the plaintiff's cause of action much as a deed relinquishes Blackacre. This conception led courts to say that if the plaintiff released Tortfeasor A, that automatically released B as well, since the cause of action, being relinquished, no longer existed. When the plaintiff settled with A for part of her damages, hoping to recover the remainder from B, a release would defeat the plaintiff's purposes. Lawyers developed a contract or covenant not to sue to be used in such cases. The covenant not to sue promised A as the settling defendant that the plaintiff would not sue him, and provided some guarantees for that promise; it did not release the cause of action. Consequently the plaintiff who gave covenant not to sue to A could proceed with her suit against B.

The contemporary view rejects the idea that a release of A automatically releases others as well. That view is represented in the Uniform Contribution Among Tortfeasors Act § 4, which provides that a release of one tortfeasor no longer discharges any other tortfeasor unless the release specifically so provides.

Credits to Nonsettling Tortfeasors

Settlement permitting A to seek contribution. When one tortfeasor, A, settles the plaintiff's claim but the other does not, two possibilities open up. First, the plaintiff may release B as well as A. In that case, A, by settling, has bought protection for B and is entitled to contribution against him under whatever measure of contribution is applicable. This is not so common a scenario, but it is an available strategy and sometimes used.[2]

Settlement to permit plaintiff to proceed against nonsettling tortfeasor. Second, in the more common case, the plaintiff and A can come to a settlement if the plaintiff is permitted to pursue her claim for additional compensation from B. In that case, the parties can be sure that the settlement document does not release B by using a covenant not to sue or a release governed by provisions like those in the Uniform Contribution Among Tortfeasors Act. However, this scenario raises two new problems.

Safeguarding the settling tortfeasor from contribution claim. Suppose A and the plaintiff can reach an agreement under which A pays the plaintiff $300,000, perhaps because that exhausts A's assets or insur-

§ 388

1. All of this is succinctly stated in Restatement of Apportionment § 41 (Proposed Final Draft 1998).

2. As in Bervoets v. Harde Ralls Pontiac–Olds, Inc., 891 S.W.2d 905 (Tenn.1994).

ance, and the plaintiff is free to sue B. It is entirely possible that the jury in that suit would assess the plaintiff's total damages at $900,000. If that happens, B might seek contribution against A, arguing that A's payment is far less than his appropriate share of liability. If A can foresee such a development, he will not settle with the plaintiff, for settlement would not terminate his potential liability or exposure to the expense of suit. Since settlement is desirable, statutes often protect A from B's contribution suit,[3] and where they fail to do so, the plaintiff herself may guarantee A against further liability.[4]

Guaranteeing fairness to the nonsettling tortfeasor. When the statute takes away the nonsettling defendant's right of contribution against the settling defendant, it compensates by reducing the nonsettling defendant's liability by some kind of credit applied against the judgment. The credits are mostly of two types, although it is possible to combine different approaches[5] and to make complex contractual arrangements as well.[6]

(a) The pro tanto credit. One kind of credit to B as the non-settling tortfeasor is the *pro tanto* credit. This credit reduces B's liability to the plaintiff by the amount paid by A.[7] One problem with the pro tanto credit is that if the plaintiff settled with A for a small sum such as $10,000, then recovered $1 million against B, B would be liable to the plaintiff in the sum of $990,000 even though his fault may have been considerably less than A's fault. California attempts to deal with this problem by limiting A's protection to cases of good faith settlement and holding judicial review to determine good faith.[8] On the other hand, if A's assets and insurance are limited, it may be that B is no worse off, since a large contribution judgment would be useless if it could not be enforced.

(b) The pro rata credits. The second kind of credit is called *pro rata* and enjoys the support of the Uniform Contribution Among Tortfeasors Act.[9] When the right of contribution was to equalize the shares of all

3. E.g., ARK. CODE ANN. § 16–61–202.

4. The so-called Pierringer release, from Pierringer v. Hoger, 21 Wis.2d 182, 124 N.W.2d 106 (1963). In this kind of settlement with A, plaintiff guarantees that A will not be subjected to a contribution claim from B. If the judgment against B is so large that contribution would otherwise be appropriate, the plaintiff will reduce her claim against B so that he will not be liable for more than his share.

5. See Williams v. Niske, 81 N.Y.2d 437, 615 N.E.2d 1003, 599 N.Y.S.2d 519 (1993) (reflecting difficulties with a New York statute requiring credit in the amount actually paid by the settling tortfeasor or his "equitable share," whichever is greatest).

6. Notably through some form of the Mary Carter agreement. In this type of arrangement, A agrees to guarantee a minimum recovery against B and other tortfeasors. If the plaintiff then recovers more than the minimum from B, she does not collect, or does not fully collect damages from A. If the plaintiff does not recover the minimum from B, she accepts A's guarantee and relieves him of liability. This arrangement is generally but not always permissible. See, e.g., City of Tucson v. Gallagher, 108 Ariz. 140, 493 P.2d 1197, 65 A.L.R.3d 597 (1972); Mackey v. Irisari, 191 W.Va. 355, 445 S.E.2d 742 (1994).

7. E.g., CAL. CODE CIV. PROC. § 877.

8. See Tech–Bilt, Inc. v. Woodward–Clyde & Assocs., 38 Cal.3d 488, 213 Cal. Rptr. 256, 698 P.2d 159 (1985).

9. Uniform Contribution Among Tortfeasors Act § 2.

tortfeasors, the *pro rata* credit in the case of two tortfeasors would be one-half. If A settled for $10,000 and the plaintiff then recovered $1 million from B, B's liability to the plaintiff would be reduced to $500,-000. With the advent of comparative fault, some statutes and judicial decisions have held that the *pro rata* credit should be measured by the percentage of fault attributable to the settling tortfeasor[10] rather than by an equal shares method.

For example, suppose a case in which A settles by paying the plaintiff $5,000, and the jury in B's case fixes the plaintiff's damages at $20,000 and B's fault at 40%. B is entitled to a credit that reduces the judgment to $8,000 (40% of the $20,000 damages). Perhaps A got a bargain; his share would seem to be 60% or $12,000. But as B pays no more than his proportionate share, he has no complaint. The shoe fits the other foot as well. If A had settled for $50,000, and the jury found in B's case that damages were only $20,000, B would still be liable for his proportionate share—40% in this example. As the Texas Court said,[11] the plaintiff takes both the burdens of her bargain with A (as in the first example) and the benefits (as in the second), but B as the nonsettling tortfeasor never pays more than his comparative fault share.

Intractable problems. No form of credit to B avoids all problems. The *pro tanto* credit leaves B exposed almost whimsically or requires an additional impediment to settlement in the form of pre-settlement judicial review. On the other hand, the *pro rata* credit, whether based on equal shares or on comparative fault shares, requires the plaintiff to give up the advantages of joint and several liability if she settles. For example, if A has limited insurance and the plaintiff can settle for the full amount of A's policy, settlement is desirable both to A and to the plaintiff. Yet settlement for the full insurance amount means that the plaintiff's recovery against B will be reduced by A's "share" of liability, not merely by the amount A paid. To retain the full benefit of joint and several liability, the plaintiff in a *pro rata* jurisdiction must forgo the conventional settlement.[12]

§ 389. Abolishing or Modifying Joint and Several Liability

Until the tort reform movement appeared, joint and several liability was not controversial. Principally in the 1980s, joint and several liability was attacked on the ground that it was inconsistent with the adoption of comparative fault and that it forced one tortfeasor to pay without regard to the degree of his culpability. A third attack suggested that much of

10. Dobson v. Camden, 705 F.2d 759 (5th Cir.1983) (civil rights action); Cartel Capital Corp. v. Fireco, 81 N.J. 548, 410 A.2d 674, 19 A.L.R.4th 310 (1980); Bervoets v. Harde Ralls Pontiac–Olds, Inc., 891 S.W.2d 905 (Tenn.1994) (in spite of the statute's rejection of percentage fault allocations); Restatement of Apportionment § 25 (Proposed Final Draft 1998).

11. Duncan v. Cessna Aircraft Co., 665 S.W.2d 414 (Tex.1984).

12. A Mary Carter Agreement in which A guarantees a minimum recovery but does not necessarily pay anything may help the plaintiff keep advantages of join and several liability. See supra n. 6.

the problem lay with immunities enjoyed by many tortfeasors.[1] If the law decided that some tortfeasors should be immune, it would be unfair to saddle solvent tortfeasors with the burden of conduct that the law has in a sense approved.

Perhaps all these points are easily overrated. At best, they apply to some categories of joint and several liability but not others. When the plaintiff is not chargeable with any fault, the adoption of comparative negligence suggests no reason to dispense with the rule of joint and several liability,[2] although it does suggest how contribution among tortfeasors should be measured. If the problem is that immunities of some tortfeasors throw the burden disproportionately upon nonimmune defendants under a joint and several liability system, the adoption of several liability merely shifts the burden to the injured plaintiff; and if the problem lies with immunities and other departures from a fault-based liability, the right response is to return to liability based upon fault.

As to the liability disproportionate to culpability, liability has always attached for actual damages, no matter how high they might be, even when the defendant's fault was quite limited, perhaps a second's distraction. In other words, damages have never been proportioned to fault and to suggest that they must be is to confuse tort liability with the criminal law of proportionate penalties. The criticism of joint and several liability also mistakenly identified *comparative* fault with *degree* of fault. The defendant's fault may be small by comparison to other tortfeasors, especially if the defendant can identify a large number of wrongdoers, but his fault may be extensive nonetheless. In no case is the defendant liable for damages unless (a) he was a cause in fact of those damages and (b) a proximate or legal cause.[3]

Finally, critics often failed to recognize different categories of joint and several liability. In some types of joint and several liability the defendant's negligent conduct was sufficient by itself to cause the plaintiff's harm and would have caused it in the same degree even if no other tortfeasor had appeared on the horizon. In cases like this, neither the defendant's fault nor his causal impact is less in any degree merely because other tortfeasors also participated.[4] In such cases, no logic

§ 389

1. See Aaron D. Twerski, The Joint Tortfeasor Legislative Revolt: A Rational Response to the Critics, 22 U.C. Davis. L. Rev. 1125 (1989).

2. Most courts so held. E.g., American Motorcycle Ass'n v. Superior Court, 20 Cal.3d 578, 146 Cal.Rptr. 182, 578 P.2d 899 (1978); Coney v. J.L.G. Indus., Inc., 97 Ill.2d 104, 454 N.E.2d 197, 73 Ill.Dec. 337 (1983); Sitzes v. Anchor Motor Freight, Inc., 169 W.Va. 698, 289 S.E.2d 679 (1982). But there were notable exceptions. See McIntyre v. Balentine, 833 S.W.2d 52 (Tenn.1992).

3. See John W. Wade, Should Joint and Several Liability of Multiple Tortfeasors Be Abolished?, 10 Am. J. Trial Advoc. 193 (1986); Richard W. Wright, The Logic and Fairness of Joint and Several Liability, 23 Mem. St. U. L. Rev. 45 (1992).

4. For example, A and B separately set fire to the plaintiff's house with a blowtorch and a gallon of gasoline. Either fire would have burned the house down. See Richard W. Wright, The Logic and Fairness of Joint and Several Liability, supra n. 3 at 59.

suggests why the appearance of a second tortfeasor should provide the defendant a windfall; he is no less at fault and he has caused no less harm. In some other cases, something better might be said for abolishing joint and several liability,[5] but the critics have generally lumped all joint and several liability cases together.

In any event, most states have now altered or abolished joint and several liability rules for certain classes of cases or for certain kinds of damages. They replace it with several liability of each individual actor proportioned to his fault. In the late 1990s about 18 states retained substantial joint and several liability rules. The remaining states can be classified in four groups.[6] (1) Joint and several liability is generally abolished, although exceptions may apply.[7] (2) Joint and several liability is abolished, but when it appears at some point that the plaintiff cannot collect a judgment against one of the tortfeasors, that tortfeasor's share of liability is reallocated among the parties, including the plaintiff, on the basis of comparative responsibility.[8] (3) Joint and several liability is abolished, but only for tortfeasors whose comparative fault is below a stated threshold.[9] (4) Joint and several liability is abolished for noneconomic damages like pain and suffering but retained for economic damages like medical expenses or lost wages.[10]

Some states have abolished joint and several liability without any explicit exception or qualification.[11] Other statutes provide specific exceptions[12] and may retain joint and several liability for tortfeasors whose liability is vicarious and those who act in concert.[13] Some statutes also retain joint and several liability when the plaintiff herself is not at fault.[14] In addition, the abolition statute may implicitly retain joint and several liability for some torts besides personal injury by defining its scope to include only injury, property damage, and death actions, thus leaving the joint and several liability rules intact for economic torts.[15] The statutes do not touch federal contribution rights such as those under environmental statutes.[16]

5. Supporters of joint and several liability don't necessarily think so. See Richard Wright, supra n. 3 at 56–57.

6. See Restatement of Apportionment § 26, cmt. a (summarizing); Edward J. Kionka, Recent Developments in the Law of Joint and Several Liability and the Impact of Plaintiff's Employer's Fault, 54 La. L. Rev. 1619 (1994).

7. E.g., Ariz. Rev. Stats. § 12–2506; Kan. Stats. Ann., § 60–258a. About 14 states, by legislation or judicial decision, broadly abolish joint and several liability, but with exceptions.

8. Conn. Gen. Stat. Ann. § 52–572h (g) & (h); Mich. Comp. L. Ann. § 600.6304 (6)(b).

9. E.g., N.Y. CPLR § 1601 (50%); Ohio Rev. Code § 2307.31 (as to economic losses, for tortfeasors chargeable with less than 50% of the negligence). About 14 states use a threshold at some level, sometimes, as in Ohio, in combination with a distinction between economic loss and noneconomic loss.

10. Cal. Civ. Code § 1431.2; Neb. Rev. Stats. § 25–21,185.10.

11. Ky. Rev. Stats. § 411.182; 12 Vt. Stats. Ann. § 1036.

12. E.g., Fla. Stats. Ann. §§ 768.81 (pollution cases); Or. Rev. Stats. § 18.485 (environmental harm cases of various kinds).

13. Ariz. Rev. Stats. § 12–2506; N.Y. CPLR § 1602.

14. E.g., Mich. Comp. L. Ann. § 600.6304 (6) (a).

15. E.g., Mich. Comp. L. Ann. § 600.6304.

16. 42 U.S.C.A. § 9607 creates liability of various parties for release of hazardous substances, while 42 U.S.C.A. § 9613 au-

§ 390. Effects of Abolishing Joint and Several Liability

The most obvious effect of statutes abolishing joint and several liability is the effect the statutes were intended to achieve. The defendant's liability is reduced because others were also at fault in producing injury. If more people were at fault, it is likely than the defendant's comparative share is less. It becomes important to know whose fault may be considered. If many tortfeasors caused the plaintiff's harm, the fault share of any one defendant is very likely to be small. That is of no great consequence if the plaintiff can identify, sue, and collect from each of the many tortfeasors. However, if the fault of, say, an immune tortfeasor is to be weighed in determining the remaining defendant's comparative share, the plaintiff will collect less from the defendant and nothing at all from the immune tortfeasor. So defendants have an interest in asserting that all fault must be considered, including the fault of nonparties, the fault of insolvent and immune tortfeasors, and the fault of intentional tortfeasors. Plaintiffs wish to argue that in weighing the comparative significance of the defendant's fault, the court should consider only the fault of parties and persons against whom suit is possible.

Settling Tortfeasors

In a several liability system, the nonsettling tortfeasor is held only for his comparative fault share. In determining the percentage responsibility of the nonsettling tortfeasor, jurors must determine the comparative share of every tortfeasor, including those who have settled. However, a determination that A's fault was 50% and B's fault was 50% does not affect A's settlement or his liability. It merely means that B is liable for 50%, no more, no less. If A paid more than 50% of the damages, that was his decision. If he paid less, the plaintiff made a bad bargain, but none of this matters to B's liability.

Immune and Nonparty Tortfeasors

Employers who provide workers' compensation benefits to employees are generally immune to tort liability, so they are not liable in tort even if they negligently injure an employee. The injured employee is still free to sue others, such as product manufacturers who contribute to her harm. The question is whether the fault of such a defendant should be judged in comparison to the fault of the immune employer or whether the fault of the employer should be ignored. The fault of the product manufacturer or other defendant may be relatively small in comparison to that of the employer, but relatively large (or total) if the employer's negligence cannot be considered. Where liability is several only, this issue can be critical. The states are substantially divided, many holding that the negligence of immune persons must be considered,[1] many others

thorizes contribution. This is a system of joint and several liability. Bedford Affiliates v. Sills, 156 F.3d 416 (2d Cir. 1998).

§ 390

1. E.g., Y.H. Investments, Inc. v. Godales, 690 So.2d 1273 (Fla.1997); Powers v. Kansas Power & Light Co., 234 Kan. 89, 671 P.2d 491 (1983).

holding that it must not be.[2] To make matters less certain, some of the decisions were rendered when joint and several liability was still applied and ongoing statutory changes may well put some of the authorities in question.

A similar issue arises for similar reasons with nonparties, a category that may include the plaintiff's employer (since, given immunity, the plaintiff cannot maintain a suit against him), but may include others as well. A few courts have excluded nonparties or immune tortfeasors from the comparative negligence calculus,[3] the right result under a joint and several liability system[4] but not clearly so under a several liability system. A few others have excluded the fault of tortfeasors who are not or cannot be joined as defendants.[5] The immunity issue aside, most courts in several liability systems appear to consider the fault of any tortfeasor, whether or not joined as a party.[6] Statutory language may imply a statutory answer in a number of cases.

Strategically, the defendant's interest in this system is to assert the negligence of many other persons regardless of immunity. That is because all liabilities are comparative, not absolute, so that when fault is attributed to other tortfeasors, that reduces the fault attributable to the defendant. The plaintiff's interest, in contrast, is to assert that nonparties and persons who are immune are not in fact at fault.[7]

Defendant Negligently Risks Another's Intentional Harm

One kind of case that has created special concern arises when one defendant negligently creates a risk that another defendant will cause harm. Although this pattern occurs in ordinary negligence cases, it is more dramatic when A creates a risk that B will commit an intentional tort. For example, if A leaves dynamite where children can steal it, the risk is that they will do so and cause injury to others. Older cases might have disposed of such a case by concluding that A was not liable because the children's act constituted a superseding cause.[8] Contemporary cases tend to say that defendants cannot escape liability for foreseeable risks, so in a joint and several liability regime today both A and the children would be liable in many such cases.

Perhaps the most notable version of the problem occurs when a landlord or a business fails to use reasonable care to prevent a robbery or a rape of a customer or tenant. In the joint and several liability

2. See Varela v.American Petrofina Co., 658 S.W.2d 561 (Tex.1983)

3. See Ridings v. Ralph M. Parsons Co., 914 S.W.2d 79 (Tenn.1996) (excluding immune employer whose liability was limited to workers' compensation).

4. See Restatement of Apportionment § 28A, cmt. d.

5. Pepper v. Star Equipment, Ltd., 484 N.W.2d 156 (Iowa 1992).

6. Wells v. Tallahassee Mem. Regional Med. Ctr.Inc., 659 So.2d 249 (Fla.1995) (negligence of nonparty considered); see § 210.

7. Cf. Restatement of Apportionment § 28B, cmt. e (Proposed Final Draft 1998) (noting that sometimes "immunity" appears in reality to be a case of no-negligence or no duty, in which case the joined defendant cannot attribute part of the negligence to the "immune" person).

8. See § 190.

system, the careless handler of dynamite, the business, or the landlord would be liable for the plaintiff's damages resulting from the explosion, the robbery or the rape. When joint and several liability has been abolished, the question is whether negligent actors like the landlord who refuses to repair a broken lock can escape full liability when a rapist takes advantage of the disrepair to rape the plaintiff in her unprotected apartment.

The question is quite distinct from the question whether the plaintiff's own comparative negligence should reduce her recovery against an intentional wrongdoer like the rapist.[9] Authority is limited. Some implies that the negligent actor's fault is compared with that of the intentional actor; the negligent actor is only severally liable for his comparative fault.[10] Other authority refuses to permit the negligent tortfeasor to reduce his liability by comparing the fault of the intentional tortfeasor whose acts he risked. In this view, the negligent tortfeasor is entirely liable.[11] In the undeveloped state of the law at this juncture, there are at least three possible grounds on which the landlord or others in his position can be held liable for all or a substantial part of the plaintiff's damages (subject always to his right of contribution against the criminal actor).

First, courts could refuse to compare intentional harm with negligence. That was the traditional view on the distinct issue of contributory negligence; the plaintiff was not barred by her contributory fault when she sued an intentional tortfeasor. Whether or not that remains the rule when the plaintiff's fault is compared to the defendant's, several courts have held that in determining the appropriate responsibility as between two or more defendants, the negligence of one can be compared to the intentional misconduct of another. Authority at this point is quite limited, but the proposed Restatement of Apportionment lends its weight to that viewpoint. If that viewpoint ultimately prevails, juries would compare the negligence of the landlord with the intentional crime of rape and on this comparison might find the landlord to be comparatively innocent, so that his liability would be minuscule. Again, that would matter not if the rapist can be found and has significant assets, but that is highly unlikely.

Second, it can be argued that some statutes and the Restatement of Apportionment envision an amorphous assignment of responsibility rather than a comparison of fault. In that system of thought, negligence does not necessarily count for less fault than an intentional tort or even a serious intentional crime. One rational reason for such a view is that when the negligent actor creates a risk of an intentional tort, especially when the foreseeable tortfeasor is likely to escape or to have no assets,

9. See § 229.

10. Cf. Barth v. Coleman, 118 N.M. 1, 878 P.2d 319 (1994) (bar manager, though assuring the plaintiff of protection from violent customer, permitted him to attack the plaintiff; the bartender is not liable jointly and severally, but liable only for comparative fault share, comparing intentional tort of the attacker).

11. Veazey v. Elmwood Plantation Assocs., Ltd., 650 So.2d 712 (1994); Turner v. Jordan, 957 S.W.2d 815 (Tenn.1997).

his negligence encompasses that tort and plausibly can be considered worse in some sense. It is far too soon to know how courts and juries will handle this argument, but at least one court has already recognized that a negligent tortfeasor who risks an intentional tort by another may be counted more significantly at fault.[12] Somewhat similarly but more firmly, the Louisiana Court held that a landlord could be entirely liable for the entire judgment when it negligently created risks of a tenant's rape. Comparison of the rapist's fault was deemed inappropriate in the particular case, even though in some cases, comparison of intent with negligence would be permitted.[13]

Third, the Restatement of Apportionment has suggested that tortfeasors who create a risk of intentional harm to the plaintiff might be counted as tortfeasors acting in concert or aiding and abetting the intentional tortfeasor. Liability of one who acts in concert is at least partly vicarious. In concerted action cases, joint liability presumably remains.[14] If so, the landlord acting in concert with the rapists would be liable for the entire damages. Whether the landlord's negligence can count as concerted action, however, has yet to be adjudicated.

Indivisible Injury

The traditional rule held that if two or more tortfeasors cause an indivisible injury, they were jointly and severally liable for the entire damages. Where joint and several liability is abolished, that rule no longer obtains. However, the fact that the plaintiff suffered an indivisible injury remains significant, for the defendants' percentage of fault liability is measured by the total of the plaintiff's indivisible injury damages.[15] On the other hand, when injury is divisible, so that tortfeasor A causes a broken leg and tortfeasor B a broken arm, each tortfeasor remains liable for 100% of the damages he separately caused.

12. Hutcherson v. City of Phoenix, 192 Ariz. 51, 961 P.2d 449, 452 (1998) ("jury may apportion fault among defendants and nonparties, without distinguishing between intentional and negligent conduct or requiring that a minimum percentage of responsibility be assigned to the former").

13. Veazey v. Elmwood Plantation Associates, Ltd., supra n. 11. See also Blazovic v. Andrich, 124 N.J. 90, 590 A.2d 222, 18 A.L.R.5th 1031 (1991).

14. Restatement of Apportionment § 24. Some of the joint and several liability statutes say so, some do not.

15. Piner v. Superior Court, 192 Ariz. 182, 962 P.2d 909 (1998). This may lead to quite complex calculations if there are multiple parties in two or more separate injuries that lead to an indivisible result.

*

CHAPTER 27

CRITICISMS AND CHOICES IN TORT LAW

TOPIC A. CRITICISMS

§ 391. Criticisms of the Tort System

Criticisms and Concerns

Critics of the tort system have appeared on all sides. The traditional view is that tort law should both compensate victims of wrongful behavior and deter that behavior. Ideally, defendants required to make full compensation would make their behavior safer. In the case of intentional torts, punitive damages might be invoked to do the job.

Inefficiency and inadequacy of compensation and deterrence. One wave of criticism variously asserted that the tort system in fact (1) does not adequately compensate because many injuries are uncompensated or under compensated, (2) does not deter or does not deter adequately, either because deterrence simply is not accomplished by legal rules and liabilities or because actual liability systematically tends to be less than theoretically required; (3) is inefficient in its use of resources and in its use of costly liability insurance. Related criticisms pointed to delays that prevented recovery when it was needed and to the limited resources provided by the pool of liability insurance that was sometimes exhausted by recoveries for pain, leaving nothing for what was regarded as more essential—basic economic harms such as wage loss.

Quite a few studies amply supported most of these criticisms except that the deterrence effects remain controversial. One of the earliest empirical studies showed that of 86,000 persons who suffered economic loss, some 20,000 received no compensation, and most of those who were compensated did not draw their compensation from the tort system.[1] While undercompensation has been common for many serious harms, overcompensation frequently occurs for small losses. This overcompensation is dreadfully costly because so many small losses occur. On top of this, liability insurance, which fuels most of the tort system, is said to be relatively inefficient because for each dollar paid in premiums only about 40 cents goes to payment for injuries. The uncertainties of tort litigation contribute to the feeling that it is largely a lottery rather than a system for redressing wrongs or assuring compensation.[2] These and many relat-

§ 391

1. ALFRED F. CONARD, JAMES N. MORGAN, ROBERT W. PRATT, JR., CHARLES E. VOLTZ & ROBERT L. BOMBAUGH, AUTOMOBILE ACCIDENTS COSTS AND PAYMENTS (1964).

2. See Marc A. Franklin, Replacing the Negligence Lottery: Compensation and Se-

ed concerns have led acute observers to suggest that many tort problems should be allocated to some other kind of system to be resolved by regulation, by social welfare programs or social insurance, or administrative agencies.[3]

Excessive liability. A second wave of criticism, associated with "tort reform" mainly of the 1980s, has asserted that the tort system is out of control, that Americans have become law-suit prone and greedy, suing over every little injury, and driving up the cost of doing business. Critics in this wave argue that insurance has become too costly as a result of overcompensating the injured, and that in some cases insurance has become unavailable. They also say that some valuable products like prescription drugs and vaccines may be driven from the market because of the tort liabilities they produce. These criticisms have already affected tort law in most jurisdictions. Many states have imposed caps on compensatory and punitive damages, reintroduced, expanded or created new immunities, barred some claims before they have accrued, or abolished joint and several liability. Overall, the reforms make the individual and the individual case less important by making the facts about liability and damages less significant and categorical rules more significant.[4]

Much of the support for the tort reform criticisms is anecdotal and impressionistic.[5] There is not much good evidence that litigation has increased overall when population increases are taken into account.[6] In fact, the percentage of tort cases today may actually be smaller than it was in earlier years.[7] Similarly, there is not much reason to think that damages awards have generally increased. Economic tort litigation has grown, but that is largely litigation by business enterprises among themselves, not personal injury claims by individuals.[8] As to insurance costs, it is assuredly true that in some periods premiums have risen, and this was especially painful to health care providers. However, increased premium costs is a complex matter. Premiums are raised at least in part when insurance investment income is reduced in a slow economy, not

lective Reimbursement, 53 VA. L. REV. 774 (1967).

3. E.g., STEPHEN SUGARMAN, DOING AWAY WITH PERSONAL INJURY LAW (1989); Richard B. Stewart, Crisis in Tort Law? The Institutional Perspective, 54 U. CHI. L. REV. 184 (1987); Viscusi, Toward a Diminished Role for Tort Liability: Social Insurance, Government Regulation, and Contemporary Risks to Health and Safety, 6 YALE J. REG. 65 (1989). There is also skepticism about proposed solutions. See JERRY MASHAW & DAVID HARFST, THE STRUGGLE FOR AUTO SAFETY (1990); Michael J. Trebilcock, Requiem for Regulators: The Passing of a Counter-Culture, 8 YALE J. REG. 497 (1991).

4. See Kenneth S. Abraham, What Is a Tort Claim? An Interpretation of Contemporary Tort Reform, 51 MD. L. REV. 172 (1992) (noting also that some changes favorable to plaintiffs do the same).

5. And some of the anecdotes reporting absurd awards were not true. See Joseph A. Page, Deforming Tort Reform, Book Review of Peter W. Huber, Liability: The Legal Revolution and Its Consequences (1988), 78 GEO. L. J. 649 (1990).

6. David J. Nye & Donald G. Gifford, The Myth of Liability Insurance Claims Explosion: An Empirical Rebuttal, 41 VAND. L. REV. 909 (1988).

7. See Michael J. Saks, Do We Really Know Anything About the Behavior of the Tort Litigation System—And Why Not?, 140 U. PA. L. REV. 1147 (1992).

8. The Roscoe Pound Foundation reported in 1995 that the corporate members of the American Tort Reform Association and Product Liability Alliance brought 38,000 law suits in 1991–1994 in five populous states alone.

necessarily because of tort claims. The data available are always limited and can never be fully current, but overall they suggest that in fact, many people with very good claims do not sue or even assert a claim.[9] The question whether the tort system has serious problems and how to resolve them has been highly politicized by interest groups.[10] Neutral and objective reporting of the facts and assessment of the arguments is very difficult to obtain.[11]

Mass torts. The development of mass tort litigation in the 1980s—hundreds of thousands of asbestos claims, for example[12]—has generated a third set of critic-observers and a large body of literature.[13] Mass torts claims have clogged courts. Critics say the system has been inefficient, expensive, unfair.[14] Tort law grew out of judicial efforts to resolve cases one by one. That setting enhanced the courts' commitment to the rights of both parties based on the unique facts of each claim and defense. With the development of mass tort litigation, lawyers may carry large "inventories" of claims against a product manufacturer or others—perhaps as many as 10,000 claims aggregated and settled in a batch. Some of the dangers, including collusive settlements that benefit primarily lawyers and defendants but not plaintiffs,[15] may be obvious, but even in the absence of venal behavior, individuals are likely to be submerged in the mass claim. Yet some individuals' only hope of success may be through the enhanced investment and services they obtain as part of the lawyer's inventory of cases. Some critics have even suggested that injured individuals should be permitted to sell their claims to brokers who would amass claims in a group for more efficient handling.[16] Others suggests that

9. See Localio, Lawthers, Brennan, Laird, Hebert, Peterson, Newhouse, Weiler & Hiatt, Relation Between Malpractice Claims and Adverse Events Due to Negligence, 325 N.Eng. J. Med. 245 (July 25, 1991) (study by health care providers of negligence in health care).

10. See, describing one legislative process, Joseph Sanders and Craig Joyce, "Off to the Races": The 1980s Tort Crisis and the Law Reform Process, 27 Hous. L. Rev. 207 (1990).

11. See Marc Galanter, Shadow Play: The Fabled Menace of Punitive Damages, 1998 Wis. L. Rev. 1, 13–14 (reporting that one group tried to get the American Bar Association to repudiate a conference discussing pros and cons of tort reform and then boycotted it); Jerome B. Meites, Steven F. Pflaum, Carolyn H. Krause, Justice James D. Heiple: Impeachment and the Assault on Judicial Independence, 29 Loy. U. Chi. L.J. 741 (1998) (reporting impeachment investigation after the Supreme Court of Illinois held a tort reform statute unconstitutional and an attack on the court by the Illinois Manufacturers' Association).

12. See Deborah R. Hensler, Mark A. Peterson, Understanding Mass Personal Injury Litigation: A Socio-legal Analysis, 59 Brook. L. Rev. 961 (1993) (defining mass torts partly with reference to commonality of issues and interdependence that distinguishes the half million automobile accident cases disposed of each year).

13. John C. Coffee, Jr., Class Wars: The Dilemma of The Mass Tort Class Action, 95 Colum. L. Rev. 1343 (1995) (an excellent summary of facts, issues, and viewpoints).

14. The factual case histories in many instances bear out criticisms. For factual histories of a number of mass tort litigations, see Deborah R. Hensler, Mark A. Peterson, Understanding Mass Personal Injury Litigation: A Socio-legal Analysis, 59 Brook. L. Rev. 961 (1993); Francis E. McGovern, Resolving Mature Mass Tort Litigation, 69 B.U. L. Rev. 659 (1989).

15. See John C. Coffee, Jr., Class Wars: The Dilemma of The Mass Tort Class Action, 95 Colum. L. Rev. 1343, 1367–1384 (1995) (summarizing various forms of "collusion" between plaintiffs' lawyers and defendants in mass tort settlements).

16. The original idea, see Robert Cooter and Stephen D. Sugarman, A Regulated Market in Unmatured Tort Claims: Tort

mass torts be removed from the tort system for some kind of alternative resolution, either one more individually oriented[17] or one less so.[18] A variation is to preserve the tort system until the mass claim is mature, then invoke some kind of administrative or "claims center" approach for remaining issues.[19]

Alternatives

Deep-seated criticisms assert that the tort way of resolving disputes, providing compensation, and seeking deterrence is so inadequate that alternative systems should be sought out. A number of different systems are actually now in place. They do not displace the tort system over a wide spectrum. Instead, they supplement it in providing some degree of relief for injury when tort law provides none or an inadequate amount, or provide a more efficient (and less individualized) system for administering compensation. The alternatives in place always provide caps or limits on compensation, too. Some alternatives are limited welfare systems, providing for emergency medical care[20] or funds for rehabilitation.[21] In mass tort cases, the bankruptcy court has also become a kind of alternative for administering relief.[22] Alternative dispute resolution (ADR), emphasizing party control of the dispute, mediation, and negotiation, and, quite distinctly, arbitration,[23] also represent possible approaches to claims now allocated to the tort system.

Four alternative systems are especially important because they represent some of the divergent approaches that may suggest the pitfalls and advantages of different alternative systems. At the same time, these four systems are not only in place but are sometimes critical in determining tort rights and liabilities and consequently deserve notice of tort lawyers. These four systems are (1) workers' compensation, (2) social security disability or welfare rights, (3) private insurance such as that found in no-fault plans, and (4) a system for taxing dangerous activities

Reform by Contract, in New Directions in Liability Law 174 (Walter Olson ed.1988), was not about mass torts, but can be adapted to deal with the mass tort problem. See Peter H. Schuck, Mass Torts: an Institutional Evolutionist Perspective, 80 CORNELL L. REV. 941 (1995).

17. Cf. Carrie Menkel–Meadow, Taking the Mass Out of Mass Torts: Reflections of a Dalkon Shield Arbitrator on Alternative Dispute Resolution, Judging, Neutrality, Gender, and Process, 31 LOY. L.A. L. REV. 513 (1998) (discussing ADR with mediation and story-telling as part of a mass tort resolution).

18. Cf. Robert L. Rabin, Some Thoughts on the Efficacy of a Mass Toxics Administrative Compensation Scheme, 52 MD. L. REV. 951, 981 (1993) (expressing cautious attitude about substituting administrative compensation systems for mass tort litigation, but also suggesting that if another major wave of mass tort litigation is to be foreseen, the case for a no-fault administrative compensation system would be very strong).

19. Francis E. McGovern, Resolving Mature Mass Tort Litigation, 69 B.U. L. REV. 659 (1989).

20. See § 255.

21. See 29 USCA § 701 et seq. (Structuring a vocational rehab program).

22. John C. Coffee, Jr., Class Wars: The Dilemma of The Mass Tort Class Action, 95 COLUM. L. REV. 1343, 1387 (1995).

23. See William P. Zdancewicz, The Alternative Dispute Resolution in the Personal Injury Forum, 26 U.MEM. L. REV. 1169 (1996) (supporting mediation or arbitration in personal injury context); Harold Brown, Alternative Dispute Resolution, 30 SUFFOLK U. L. REV. 743 (1997) (expressing concerns in the area of commercial ADR).

and using the fund created by the tax to pay for harms. Each of these alternatives could be adopted as a way of dealing with some personal injuries. In fact, three of the four have actually been substituted for the tort system somewhere. Each has advantages and disadvantages in the kind of deterrence that might be generated, the extent and appropriateness of compensation, and the kind of process used. Whether they are deemed better than the tort system or worse, they all throw a strong sidelight on it.

Topic B. Other Injury Systems

§ 392. The Workers' Compensation System

Common Law and the Adoption of Workers' Compensation

Common law liabilities of employers. Nineteenth century employers owed a duty of care to employees, usually described in specific terms as a duty to provide employees with a reasonably safe place in which to work, reasonably safe tools and appliances, warnings of dangers likely to be unknown to employees, a sufficient number of suitable fellow servants, and rules that would make work safe.[1] However, the ordinary rules of vicarious liability did not apply; under the fellow servant rule, the employer was not liable for injuries to an employee caused by the negligence of another employee.[2] In addition, injured employees were barred by contributory negligence and a broad application of assumed risk. Beyond this, much of the work around machinery was unavoidably dangerous, so that injuries occurred often enough even without provable fault. All these things plus the delay and uncertainty of compensation made life for the injured worker almost intolerably difficult, especially in a day when no welfare backup of any kind was available.

There were niches of liability. Admiralty law recognized a kind of judge-made no-fault compensation system for seamen, who would be entitled to maintenance and care during a recuperative period, that is, basic support and medical attention.[3] In addition, a few statutes were passed to require safer working places, but these were construed narrowly to avoid liability in many instances.[4] Congress provided for automatic couplings and other safety devices on railroad trains.[5] The Federal Employers' Liability Act established a rule of comparative negligence and eliminated the bar of contributory fault and assumed risk for

§ 392

1. See Glass v. Hazen Confectionery Co., 211 Mass. 99, 97 N.E. 627 (1912) (instructions, suitable appliances); Carriere v. Merrick Lumber Co., 203 Mass. 322, 89 N.E. 544 (1909) (safe place); Thomas M. Cooley, Law of Torts 647–662 (2d ed. 1888).

2. Priestly v. Fowler, 3 M. & W. 1, 150 Eng. Rep. 1030 (Exch. 1837); Farwell v. Boston & Worcester R.R., 45 Mass. (4 Metc.) 49 (1842).

3. Thomas Schoenbaum, Admiralty and Maritime Law §§ 4–28 through 4–35 (1994).

4. E.g., Jaeger v. Evangelical Lutheran Holy Ghost Congregation, 219 Wis. 209, 262 N.W. 585, 101 A.L.R. 405 (1935) (safe place requirement did not apply to transient conditions like a dangerous stack of chairs that might fall upon the plaintiff).

5. 27 Stat. 531 (1893); the coupling requirement now appears as 49 U.S.C.A. § 20302.

employees of interstate railroads,[6] but at best these statutes applied only to railroad workers.

Development of workers' compensation. Given the limited hopes a worker might have under the common law rules, workers' compensation statutes represented progressive reform. However, it originated in Germany, as Bismarck's defense against Marxism[7] and workers' compensation ever since has shown a side favorable to workers and another side quite favorable to employers. In 1910 New York became the first state to enact a workers' compensation statute. This was held unconstitutional as a taking of property without due process because it imposed liability without fault,[8] but with an amendment of its constitution New York got a statute that held up. Other states followed, most of them quickly. All states now have workers' compensation statutes. A federal compensation plan provides for federal workers[9] and another for longshoremen.[10] Workers' compensation plans reflect the clearest expression of the enterprise liability ideas—that enterprise should bear the costs it systematically produces, including the costs of injury. But they also show a strong intent to limit significantly the employers' liabilities.

The Architecture of Workers' Compensation

Workers' compensation requires employers to pay benefits for disability caused by accidental injuries arising out of and in the course of employment and for injuries resulting from an occupational disease incurred in employment, subject to some careful exclusions. Some employments and some types of employees are excluded by statute[11] and some statutes still permit workers or employers to opt out of a workers' compensation system. The incentives favor staying within the system and few elect to return to the common law system. Otherwise, workers' compensation is generally mandatory. It may even impose responsibility upon "statutory employers" whose "employees" are actually independent contractors.[12] The structure of workers' compensation statutes in most states runs something like this:

The employer (1) is strictly liable for injury incurred in the course and scope of employment and (2) is required to purchase private insurance or participate in a state-managed insurance fund to guarantee payments of benefits as required by the statute; (3) can not limit liability by reason of the workers' contributory negligence or assumed risk, or under the fellow servant rule, although he is not liable for an employee's self-inflicted intentional injury; (4) is benefitted by limited liability (for example, in the case of an employee's total disablement, two-thirds of her average wage for a limited period of years plus medical expenses, but notably not for pain and suffering); (5) pays benefits (through the

6. 45 U.S.C.A. § 53. The Jones Act did the same for seamen. 46 U.S.C.A. § 688.

7. See ARTHUR LARSON & LEX K. LARSON, WORKERS' COMPENSATION § 5.10.

8. Ives v. South Buffalo Ry. Co., 201 N.Y. 271, 94 N.E. 431 (1911).

9. 5 U.S.C.A. § 8101 et seq.

10. 33 U.S.C.A. § 901 et seq.

11. Employers of agricultural workers, casual and domestic workers, and a few employees may be exempted from workers' compensation coverage.

12. E.g., Pinter Construction Co. v. Frisby, 678 P.2d 305 (Utah 1984).

insurer or state fund) periodically and immediately, with payment processed automatically.

Enforcement is ordinarily in the hands of an administrative agency, so there is no jury trial in most states. The role of courts in reviewing the administrative decision is to determine issues of law and the sufficiency of evidence to meet the legal requirements. The workers' compensation remedy is exclusive; the worker cannot recover from the employer in tort, even if the employer is negligent. Moreover, the employee cannot recover unless she suffers medically treatable harm or a disability. Some states do permit a tort recovery against the employer for his intentional torts, however. Occupational disease and disability without external injury may be treated much more cautiously.

Workers' Compensation as a Model for Changing Tort Law?

In comparison to the individualized approach of the tort system, workers' compensation is highly standardized. In workers' compensation, the fact of injury is a matter to be determined individually, case by case, but the amount of compensation and its cap is standardized. The issue of negligence simply does not arise. Standardization and severely limited benefits yield efficiency in the sense that a relatively high percentage of dollars invested in insurance are returned as benefits. Yet the original hope that lawyers would be unnecessary has proved to be too optimistic. A high percentage of claims are disposed of without serious dispute or administrative resolution, but in disputed claims, lawyers are quite often needed. The original hope that payments would be prompt has sometimes been disappointed, too, although the system performs far better in that regard than the tort system.

Some critics object that benefits are too low and too limited; others object that the system, efficient as it is, costs too much. Recent statutes in some states reflect some doubts; they have made it permissible for the first time for unions and employers to provide themselves with an alternative dispute resolution (ADR) system in certain employments.[13]

The workers' compensation system is problematical also in the way it relates to the tort system. The exclusive remedy provision bars claims even against the egregiously negligent employer and it also protects the employer against liability for contribution when third persons are held liable.[14] Employer-oriented criticisms, however, suggest that the exclusive remedy is not exclusive enough because employees can "circumvent" workers' compensation and sue in tort when the employer is guilty of an intentional tort and several other instances.[15]

Workers' compensation systems have not been well-coordinated with other systems of liability. Federal statutes providing protections against

13. See Ellyn Moscowitz, Victor J. Van Bourg, Carve-outs and the Privatization of Workers' Compensation in Collective Bargaining Agreements, 46 SYRACUSE L. REV. 1 (1995).

14. See § 395.

15. Joan T.A. Gabel, Nancy R. Mansfield, Robert W. Klein, The New Relationship Between Injured Worker and Employer: An Opportunity for Restructuring the System, 35 AM. BUS. L.J. 403 (1998).

sex discrimination may preempt workers' compensation, creating a different set of employer obligations. State statutes on job discrimination based on gender or disability may or may not supersede workers' compensation exclusive remedy rules. At the very least, coordination requires adjudication.[16] The Americans with Disabilities Act[17] also adds to employers' obligations to those who are disabled and in the eyes of some employers erodes the exclusive remedy provision.[18] Since a high percentage of workers' compensation costs or benefits come in the form of medical expense, the coming of managed care raises still other possibilities for changes in workers' compensation.[19]

To all these concerns can be added those that arise from the day to day administration of the compensation limits as summarized in the sections that follow.

§ 393. Workers' Compensation: Injury Arising Out of and in the Course of Employment

Course of employment. The statutes provide for benefits only for accidental injury occurring in the course of and arising out of employment. Course of employment refers mainly to time and place; injuries that occur going from or coming to work are not covered[1] unless the employee is on a special errand or holds a traveling job for the employer, in which case injury during the travel falls within the course of employment.[2] There are many borderline cases requiring adjudication, as where the employee is injured in the company parking lot on the way to work.[3]

Arising out of employment. An injury is not necessarily compensable because it occurs in the course of employment; it must also arise out of

16. E.g., City of Moorpark v. Superior Court, 18 Cal.4th 1143, 77 Cal.Rptr.2d 445, 959 P.2d 752 (1998) (worker's compensation provision for dealing with discrimination based upon injury or disability is not exclusive; plaintiff could sue in tort under a general state statute prohibiting discrimination based on disability).

17. 42 U.S.C.A. § 12101 et seq. The principle is that "No covered entity shall discriminate against a qualified individual with a disability because of the disability of such individual in regard to job application procedures, the hiring, advancement, or discharge of employees, employee compensation, job training, and other terms, conditions, and privileges of employment." 42 U.S.C.A. § 12112.

18. See Joan T.A. Gabel, et al., supra n. 15. The authors also discuss the Family Medical Leave Act, 29 U.S.C.A. § 2601 et seq. In at least some instances the employers may use a claim for compensation to defeat the ADA claim on the ground that they entail inconsistent assertions (disability vs. ability). Cf. McConathy v. Dr. Pepper/Seven Up Corporation, 131 F.3d 558 (5th Cir.1998) (claim for social security benefits predicated upon disability defeated a later claim for discrimination under ADA).

19. It has been claimed that the workers' compensation system is more costly for medical benefits than managed care. If so, that suggests the medical portions of workers' compensation could be merged into a managed care plan. See Lisa A. Krouse, Managed Care And Workers' Compensation, 33 Tort & Ins. L.J. 849 (1998).

§ 393

1. E.g., Heath v. Montana Mun. Ins. Auth., 959 P.2d 480 (Mont.1998).

2. E.g., Olsten–Kimberly Quality Care v. Parr, 965 S.W.2d 155 (Ky.1998) (worker who completed health care visit for employer in patient's home was injured on her way to her own home; she was in employment and covered).

3. Cf. Jaeger Baking Co. v. Kretschmann, 96 Wis.2d 590, 292 N.W.2d 622 (1980) (statute making travel between parking lot and work site compensable did not apply to worker who arrived by bus and

employment. That is, the injury must be associated with risks of employment. Broadly speaking, the issue is like the scope-of-risk issue in proximate or legal cause cases, except that since liability for workers' compensation is strict, the risk need not be negligently created or even foreseeable. It is enough if it is a risk associated with employment, even if the risk itself is small or unexpected. In the main, the arising out of employment rule excludes personal risks. If an employee acting in the course of employment is attacked by a stranger, or by a fellow employee in a job-related dispute, the injury arises out of employment.[4] But if the employee is attacked by her spouse because of marital difficulties, the injury arises from the employee's personal life.[5] Horseplay on the job is often customary and accepted as part of the job, so injury resulting from innocent horseplay with no personal animus is often injury arising out of employment,[6] but not if the horseplay is a substantial deviation from employment.[7]

When the risk that eventuates in injury is "neutral," neither especially personal nor especially job-related, courts sometimes have difficulty in determining whether the injury arose out of employment. If the employment increased the risk,[8] or in some states, if the employment was merely a but-for cause of the harm, the employer will owe compensation in neutral risk cases, as where the employee merely slips and falls.[9]

Many variations on the theme arise, almost always turning on factual details that help associate or disassociate the injury from employment risks. Frequently, parallel rules of tort or vicarious liability law provide guidance. For example, an employer may be vicariously liable in tort for an employee's negligence, even if the employee was doing a prohibited act at the time. Similarly, the fact that a worker is injured while violating a company rule does not necessarily mean his injury was not arising out of employment.[10]

§ 394. Workers' Compensation: Accident vs. Disease

Accidental Injury

Intent. Occupational disease aside, compensation statutes also require "accidental injury," or as sometimes phrased, "injury by accident."

was on the parking lot-to-work route but never in the parking lot).

4. Hartford Accident & Indem. Co. v. Cardillo, 112 F.2d 11 (D.C. 1940).

5. Guillory v. Interstate Gas Station, 653 So.2d 1152 (La.1995); Brookhaven Steam Laundry v. Watts, 214 Miss. 569, 59 So.2d 294 (1952) (lover's spouse shot employee). Factual details are determinative and there are many factual variations.

6. Leonbruno v. Champlain Silk Mills, 229 N.Y. 470, 128 N.E. 711 (1920).

7. Clodgo v. Rentavision, Inc., 166 Vt. 548, 701 A.2d 1044 (1997).

8. E.g., Brady v. Louis Ruffolo & Sons Constr. Co., 143 Ill.2d 542, 578 N.E.2d 921, 161 Ill.Dec. 275 (1991) (if risk is not related to employment it must be peculiar or increased by employment).

9. Circle K Store #1131 v. Industrial Com'n of Arizona, 165 Ariz. 91, 796 P.2d 893 (1990); cf. Wilson v. State Farm Ins., 326 Or. 413, 952 P.2d 528 (1998) (tendon injured when employee carrying out normal tasks "skip stepped").

10. Union Colliery Co. v. Industrial Com'n, 298 Ill. 561, 132 N.E. 200 (1921).

The requirement of an accident certainly implies that an injury intentionally self-inflicted would not qualify for compensation. However, when a third person attacks the employee on the job, the injury remains an accident from the point of view of both the employee and the employer, so compensation is awarded in such cases if the attack arose out of employment,[1] and the same kind of reasoning has led courts to treat co-employee attacks as compensable accidental injuries so far as the employer is concerned.[2]

Definite occasion. The requirement of accidental injury or injury by accident may imply not only an unintended injury but (1) a definite occasion or time when injury occurred and (2) an external event. Injuries that occur through repetitive stress over a long period do not fit the definite occasion rule, and some courts have excluded compensation for such injuries.[3] However, in many cases courts ignore or depart from the definite occasion rule and permit compensation for repetitive stress injuries or allergies that grow up in an exposure over time.[4] Others may address such problems under the rubric of occupational disease.

External event. The employer takes the employee with all her preexisting conditions. A compensable injury may therefore result if an accident aggravates or triggers a preexisting condition.[5] On the other hand, courts may narrow the road to compensation for heart attacks, hernias, or strokes on the job by saying that an internal bodily breakdown is not an external event and thus not an accident unless the heart attack or the like is triggered by some unusual activity such as heavy lifting.[6] A more liberal view permits compensation if the job exertion contributes in part to the attack or stroke, whether or not the exertion is unusual.[7]

§ 394

1. E.g., Mullins v. Tanksleary, 376 P.2d 590 (Okla.1962); Barkley v. Corrections Div., 111 Or.App. 48, 825 P.2d 291 (1992).

2. Wal–Mart Stores, Inc. v. Reinholtz, 955 P.2d 223 (Okla.1998) (supervisor raped plaintiff, employer responsible to make compensation for resulting psychological harm).

3. Nelson v. Ponsness–Warren Idgas Enters., 126 Idaho 129, 879 P.2d 592 (1994) (carpal tunnel syndrome not "accident," not compensable); Young v. Melrose Granite Co., 152 Minn. 512, 189 N.W. 426 (1922) (atrophy of muscles through years of vibration working at a machine not compensable).

4. Schlup v. Auburn Needleworks, Inc., 239 Neb. 854, 479 N.W.2d 440, 14 A.L.R.5th 963 (1992) (carpel tunnel syndrome compensable when it developed over a few months); Johannesen v. New York City Dept. of Hous. Preservation and Dev., 84 N.Y.2d 129, 638 N.E.2d 981, 615 N.Y.S.2d 336 (1994) (asthma from office smoke could be an accident); cf. Noble v. Lamoni Prods., 512 N.W.2d 290 (Iowa 1994) (carpel tunnel syndrome compensable where "accident" was not a statutory requirement).

5. See Martinez v. Indus. Com'n of Arizona, 192 Ariz. 176, 962 P.2d 903 (1998); Bright v. Sheehan Pipeline, 960 P.2d 1009 (Wyo.1998) (employment injury compensable if it "aggravated, accelerated, or combined with preexisting condition to produce disability")

6. Wyoming Workers' Compensation Div. v. Harris, 931 P.2d 255 (1997) (changing tire on a large trailer sufficient); Virginia Elec. & Power Co. v. Cogbill, 223 Va. 354, 288 S.E.2d 485 (1982) (sitting in a bent position all day too similar to employee's ordinary work, not compensable).

7. Bush v. Industrial Comn., 136 Ariz. 522, 667 P.2d 222 (1983).

Both external event and definite occasion rules may foreclose a claim for emotional harm that arises out of long continued job stress not focused on a particular event.[8] Some courts have said compensation for emotional disability is compensable if but only if the emotional disability results from a physical trauma.[9] However, many courts recognize disability based upon unusual stress even if it is not inflicted on a single occasion.[10] Statutes may similarly require unusual stress.[11] On the other hand, compensation will be denied if the emotional harm is not disabling and requires no medical attention, since no award is made for pain or suffering.[12]

Occupational Disease

Although a work-related disease can sometimes count as an injury by accident,[13] the definite occasion and external event rules often exclude compensation for diseases. Earlier workers' compensation statutes had no provisions for occupational disease, as distinct from injury, or at best recognized only a limited number of diseases. Modern statutes allow compensation for disability resulting from occupational diseases, but compensation is usually permitted only if the disease is distinctively related to the employee's occupation or the employee was subjected to some unusual exposure. For example, in a New York case, the court refused to entertain a social worker's claim of occupational disease for an eye disorder brought about by exposure to cigarette smoke in a poorly ventilated room on the ground that the disease must derive "from the very nature of the employment, not a specific condition peculiar to the employee's place of work."[14]

Multiple Employers and the Alternative to Joint Liability

When injury or disability results from a compensable disease to which the employee was exposed in two or more employments, the compensation statutes use a remarkable rule for allocating liability among the employers that is quite different from any of the common law apportionment rules. They simply allocate all liability to the last employ-

8. Seitz v. L. & R. Indus., Inc., 437 A.2d 1345 (R.I.1981).

9. See Boutwell v. Domino's Pizza, 25 Kan.App.2d 110, 959 P.2d 469 (1998).

10. E.g., City of Fort Smith v. Brooks, 40 Ark.App. 120, 842 S.W.2d 463 (1992) (police officer forced to kill a man in the line of duty suffered disability when later abnormal job stresses added to the strain); see Donald M. Zupanec, Annotation, Mental Disorders as Compensable Under Workmen's Compensation Acts, 97 A.L.R.3d 161 (1980).

11. See Williams v. State Dept. of Revenue, 938 P.2d 1065 (Alaska 1997) (applying such a statute).

12. Scheduled injuries, under which a fixed sum is paid for, say, loss of a thumb, may be regarded as a partial exception. Some statutes also allow a relatively small payment for bodily disfigurement to take care of cases in which, for example, a worker is castrated but is not disabled from working.

13. Johannesen v. New York City Dept. of Hous. Preservation and Dev., 84 N.Y.2d 129, 638 N.E.2d 981, 615 N.Y.S.2d 336 (1994) (exposure to second-hand tobacco smoke aggravating previous condition compensable as accident under rule that gradual development over a reasonably definite time period is sufficient).

14. Mack v. County of Rockland, 71 N.Y.2d 1008, 1009, 525 N.E.2d 744, 745, 530 N.Y.S.2d 98, 99 (1988).

ment in which the employee suffered injurious exposure.[15] In line with other features of workers' compensation that standardize benefits and liabilities, this one economizes by eliminating the need for individualized and complex factual evidence. In the long run, the rule may work out to approximately the right set of ultimate costs for the employer because so long as the employment characteristically exposes workers to a disease, as asbestos-related employments did, an employer liable in one case for all compensation will escape liability entirely in another case.

§ 395. Workers' Compensation: Exclusive Remedy and Third Parties

Barring the tort claim. One of the most difficult problems in meshing workers' compensation with tort law arises from the common provisions that the employee's compensation remedy is her exclusive remedy against the employer. The effect is to immunize the employer from tort liability for negligence, not only to the employee but to those who might assert derivative claims like consortium.[1] (It does not bar independent claims such as those of a fetus injured by the employee-mother's exposure to toxic substances on the job.)[2] The employer's immunity is usually shared by co-employees who negligently cause on-the-job injury[3] so long as the co-employee has not departed from the scope of his employment by committing an intentional tort unrelated to his employment.[4]

Tortfeasor's contribution claim against employer. The exclusive remedy provision does not bar the injured employee's tort claim against third parties like manufacturers of defective products that contributed to the workplace harm. However, when a suit can be maintained against a third party, issues arise about the fair allocation of responsibility among third parties and the employer. In one situation, the tortfeasor, liable to the employee for an injury also covered by workers' compensation, seeks contribution from the employer. A few courts require the employer to make contribution to the tortfeasor but never in excess of the employer's workers' compensation liability.[5] This preserves the employer's tort immunity. Most courts, however, reject contribution claims against the immune employer altogether.[6] The result is that the negligent employer

15. Union Carbide Corp. v. Industrial Com'n, 196 Colo. 56, 581 P.2d 734 (1978); cf. Bouse v. Fireman's Fund Ins. Co., 932 P.2d 222 (Alaska 1997) (last employer responsible if second injury was a substantial factor in causing disability).

§ 395

1. E.g., Singhas v. New Mexico State Highway Dept., 124 N.M. 42, 946 P.2d 645 (1997).

2. Snyder v. Michael's Stores, Inc., 16 Cal.4th 991, 945 P.2d 781, 68 Cal.Rptr.2d 476 (1997); Pizza Hut of America, Inc. v. Keefe, 900 P.2d 97 (Colo.1995).

3. Mitchell v. Sanborn, 536 N.W.2d 678 (N.D.1995).

4. O'Connell v. Chasdi, 400 Mass. 686, 511 N.E.2d 349 (1987) (co-employee liable for assault, battery, intentional infliction of emotional distress).

5. Kotecki v. Cyclops Welding Corp., 146 Ill.2d 155, 166 Ill.Dec. 1, 585 N.E.2d 1023 (1991); Lambertson v. Cincinnati Corp., 312 Minn. 114, 257 N.W.2d 679, 100 A.L.R. 3d 335 (1977).

6. Joel E. Smith, Annotation, Modern Status of Effect of State Workmen's Compensation Act on Right of Third-Person Tortfeasor to Contribution or Indemnity from Employer of Injured or Killed Workman, 100 A.L.R.3d 350 (1980).

pays the limited amount required as workers' compensation while the third party in a joint and several liability system pays full tort liability. Where joint and several liability has been completely abolished, the tortfeasor will pay only his own comparative fault share.[7] But that means that the employee must bear the loss to the extent that it is caused by the employer's fault and is not fully compensated by workers' compensation. Thus if an employer and tortfeasor are each chargeable with 50% of the fault and the damages are $100,000, the workers' compensation payments might be, say, $10,000 only. That leaves the employee recovering $50,000 from the tortfeasor and $10,000 in compensation payments; she must bear the remaining $40,000 loss herself unless the court reinstates joint and several liability for this situation.[8]

Employer's claim against tortfeasor for reimbursement. Workers' compensation statutes provide that the employer or its insurance carrier will be reimbursed from the recovery available from the tortfeasor to the extent it has or will pay compensation. They create a lien against the tort recovery to protect this right of reimbursement. Some cases have allowed reimbursement from the tort recovery even when the damages recovered are only for pain and suffering for which no compensation at all was paid.[9] Where joint and several liability has been abolished, this system, too, raises problems because the employee would recover from the tortfeasor only a percentage of her damages reflecting the tortfeasor's proportionate share. Her recovery, then, is reduced by the employer's negligence. If she must then fully reimburse the negligent employer for compensation paid, the employer bears no share at all of the injury and the employee bears the burden of paying for the employer's share. Some courts feel that the problem must be resolved by statutes, but others have concluded that the employer's reimbursement right should be limited to exclude its proportionate share of fault.[10]

Permitting tort suit against employer. When no third party tortfeasor is in the picture, workers' compensation systems provide a great deal of assurance that injured employees will receive financial assistance in the event of physical injury causing work loss or medical expenses. On the other hand, the employee has no tort claim even if the employer was negligent and if the injury is serious. Consequently, employees have sought exceptions to the exclusive remedy rule. They have found several, though they are not adopted everywhere. At least some states have recognized an employee's right to sue the employer in tort, even though injury was inflicted arising out of employment, in these cases:

(1) Fraudulent concealment, bad faith. When the employee's on-the-job injury is aggravated because the employer fraudulently conceals it

7. Allied–Signal, Inc. v. Fox, 623 So.2d 1180 (Fla.1993); DaFonte v. Up–Right, Inc., 2 Cal.4th 593, 7 Cal.Rptr.2d 238, 828 P.2d 140 (1992).

8. See Ridings v. Ralph M. Parsons Co., 914 S.W.2d 79 (Tenn.1996) (holding third-person tortfeasor fully liable).

9. United States v. Lorenzetti, 467 U.S. 167, 104 S.Ct. 2284, 81 L.Ed.2d 134 (1984).

10. Aitken v. Industrial Com'n, 183 Ariz. 387, 904 P.2d 456 (1995).

and thus delays treatment.[11] Similarly, the employer's bad faith in delaying benefits due is actionable in some states.[12]

(2) Dual capacity. When the employer causes harm while acting in some capacity other than an employer. For example, if the employer is a manufacturer and the employee is injured by the employer's defective product, courts can think of the employer as having two roles or capacities, one as manufacturer of a product and one as employer. In this view, the employee can sue the employer in tort in its capacity as a product manufacturer.[13] Similarly, if the employer is a health care provider and negligently causes injury while it is acting in that capacity, a common law suit may be permitted.[14] Some reject the dual capacity idea altogether.[15]

(3) Intentional physical harms. When the employer causes injury by an intentional tort. A number of statutes[16] and some courts independent of statute have held that the exclusive remedy provision does not bar a tort claim against an employer guilty of an intentional tort. Some of the decisions recognize the traditional alternative definitions of intent,[17] so that the employer will be liable in tort if he has either purpose to harm or a substantial certainty that harm will follow.[18] Others, perhaps reacting to the danger that high risk could easily be treated like substantial certainty,[19] have rejected the substantial certainty rule altogether and have held the employer liable in tort only when he had a purpose to harm.[20]

Non-injury torts. Many torts can involve an element of intent without producing a disabling injury. For instance, an employer might falsely imprison an employee. If the employee is not disabled and has no medical expense, there would normally be no workers' compensation benefits payable. In these circumstances, the California Court has held that the exclusive remedy clause did not bar a tort recovery because such

11. Martin v. Lancaster Battery Co., Inc., 530 Pa. 11, 606 A.2d 444 (1992).

12. Falline v. GNLV Corp., 107 Nev. 1004, 823 P.2d 888 (1991) (action for negligent or fraudulent delay in payment permitted).

13. Bell v. Industrial Vangas, Inc., 30 Cal.3d 268, 637 P.2d 266, 179 Cal.Rptr. 30 (1981). CAL.LABOR CODE § 3602 (b) (3) now limits this to cases in which the product was sold by the employer-manufacturer to third persons.

14. Duprey v. Shane, 39 Cal.2d 781, 249 P.2d 8 (1952). Contra where the employer furnishes medical care causing injury but is not itself a health care provider, Garcia v. Iserson, 33 N.Y.2d 421, 353 N.Y.S.2d 955, 309 N.E.2d 420 (1974). A California statute has trimmed the use of the dual capacity doctrine in that state. See CAL. LABOR CODE § 3602.

15. E.g., Johnson v. Rental Uniform Serv. of Greenville, S.C., Inc., 316 S.C. 70, 447 S.E.2d 184 (1994).

16. E.g., N.J. STAT. ANN. § 34:15–8.

17. § 24.

18. See Miller v. Ensco, Inc., 286 Ark. 458, 692 S.W.2d 615 (1985) (finding only risk, not substantial certainty).

19. The court in Blankenship v. Cincinnati Milacron Chems., Inc., 69 Ohio St.2d 608, 433 N.E.2d 572 (1982) thought that substantial certainty intent could be shown if the employer knew certain diseases were being contracted in plant with noxious fumes. The Ohio legislature apparently took a different view in enacting OHIO REV. CODE ANN. § 2745.01.

20. Bercaw v. Domino's Pizza, Inc., 258 Ill.App.3d 211, 196 Ill.Dec. 469, 630 N.E.2d 166 (1994); Baker v. Westinghouse Electric Corp., 637 N.E.2d 1271 (Ind.1994).

cases were outside the workers' compensation "bargain" or basic plan.[21] The same kind of argument can be applied to permit a tort suit for fraud by the employer that imposes economic costs but not physical injury,[22] or a libel that harms reputation without causing disablement.[23] Some sexual harassment or assault may present a special case of this kind of tort.

§ 396. Workers' Compensation: Sexual Harassment or Attack

Claims under antidiscrimination statutes. So far as an employee claims a right to recover for sexual harassment or other discrimination under a federal statute, the exclusive remedy provision of the workers' compensation system cannot be used to bar the claim.[1] When the plaintiff asserts a common law tort claim for emotional distress, assault or battery from sexual harassment or attack arising out of employment,[2] the exclusive remedy clause may or may not bar the suit, depending largely on whether the asserted harm is of the general type compensable under the workers' compensation statute.

Intangible harms. Sexual harassment may be intolerably demeaning without causing disability, work loss, or medical expenses. When the worker suffers no work-related disability, workers' compensation would usually offer zero compensation. If sexual harassment is outside the scope of workers' compensation—because it does not involve accident or injury and is not the kind of workplace tort the compensation system was intended to handle—a tort recovery against the employer is logically appropriate.[3] However, some courts have refused to permit the tort suit, a result that may be implicitly required by systems that make intentional torts and emotional harms fully compensable.[4]

Suit against co-employee. When a tort suit is brought against a co-employee for sexual harassment that causes no physical injury, the case for the plaintiff is easier. It is sometimes said that the co-employee loses his immunity because by his misconduct he has stepped out of employment,[5] but it may be better to recognize that this is a kind of claim that

21. Fermino v. Fedco, 7 Cal.4th 701, 30 Cal.Rptr.2d 18, 872 P.2d 559 (1994).

22. See Coleman v. American Universal Ins. Co., 86 Wis.2d 615, 273 N.W.2d 220 (1979).

23. Howland v. Balma, 143 Cal.App.3d 899, 192 Cal.Rptr. 286 (1983); Foley v. Polaroid Corp., 381 Mass. 545, 413 N.E.2d 711 (1980).

§ 396

1. Nichols v. Frank, 732 F.Supp. 1085 (D. Ore. 1990) (federal employees' compensation no bar to Title VII action).

2. The sexual attack or conceivably sexual harassment may be "personal" as opposed to job-related and hence may not arise out of employment. See § 393.

3. Ford v. Revlon, Inc., 153 Ariz. 38, 734 P.2d 580 (1987) (tort suit against employer upheld, not "accident" and hence not barred by workers' compensation statute); Kerans v. Porter Paint Co., 61 Ohio St.3d 486, 575 N.E.2d 428 (1991) (suit against employer permissible, sexual harassment on the facts was not injury covered by workers' compensation statute).

4. Konstantopoulos v. Westvaco Corp., 690 A.2d 936 (Del.1996); Green v. Wyman–Gordon Co., 422 Mass. 551, 664 N.E.2d 808 (1996).

5. See Popovich v. Irlando, 811 P.2d 379 (Colo.1991) (co-employee loses immunity if his harassment results from "personal" or neutral sources rather than employment sources); O'Connell v. Chasdi, 400 Mass. 686, 511 N.E.2d 349 (1987).

was never within the system in the first place. The logical result is that when the plaintiff does not assert physical harm or disabling injury resulting from sexual harassment, the exclusive remedy clause is be no bar to the tort suit.[6]

The employer's vicarious liability and liability for its own tort. The exclusive remedy provision is not the employee's only problem. Sexual harassment by a co-worker, if serious enough, may be outside the scope of employment, so that the employer would not be vicariously liable for it. If the employer himself is guilty of sexual harassment or fails to deal with sexual harassment by others, however, the plaintiff has a strong claim for tort liability based on intentional infliction of emotional distress or the like.[7]

Physical attacks or harms. When the employee is physically harmed or her bodily integrity invaded by on-the-job sexual harassment or a sexual attack such as rape, workers' compensation would normally cover the injury itself and whatever disability for resulting emotional harm that might be recognized in the particular jurisdiction.[8] If the injury is compensable, the exclusive remedy clause normally applies to bar a tort suit against the employer if not the attacking co-employee.[9] If the sexual attack by a co-employee is regarded as outside the scope of employment, the employer would not be liable for workers' compensation, since the injury would not have arisen out of employment. But the employer would not be vicariously liable in tort either, and for the same reason.

In the light of these difficulties, federal or state sexual harassment or anti-discrimination statutes may provide a better solution than the common law tort suit. The exclusive remedy provision is widely regarded as an essential element of workers' compensation and part of the "bargain" under which employers and employees each gave up rights and gained advantages. Nevertheless, it would be possible to design a two-tier system with no-fault limited liability like that in the present system for minor and moderate injuries, and a second tier tort system for very serious injuries, or injuries like sexual harassment that are not well handled in the compensation system.

§ 397. Social Security Disability

Social security disability benefits resemble workers' compensation in several respects. Like workers' compensation, it is a no-fault system and it is enforced ultimately in administrative hearings (before federal administrative law judges by a limited review of their decisions, in the case of social security).[1] As in workers' compensation systems, the fact of

6. Arthur Larson and Lex K. Larson, Workers' Compensation Law § 68.34(d) (multi-volume, looseleaf).

7. See cases cited n. 3, supra.

8. City of Springfield v. Industrial Com'n, 291 Ill.App.3d 734, 685 N.E.2d 12, 226 Ill.Dec. 198 (1997).

9. Knox v. Combined Ins. Co. of America, 542 A.2d 363 (Me.1988).

§ 397

1. See 2 Harvey McCormick, Social Security Claims and Procedures 3 (4th ed. 1991 and 1996 Supp.) (available electronically on Westlaw) (flow chart).

disability that prevents work is the critical fact to be determined in social security claims. Likewise, social security determinations are highly standardized, leaving no room to individuate benefits and little room to individuate findings of disability. In contrast to workers' compensation systems, social security is universal; it is not limited to injury cases at all, much less to on-the-job injuries. One of the most notable differences is that although workers' compensation is a no-fault system, the enterprise that in some important sense causes the harm is also the one who pays the costs. With social security disability benefits, payments, like social security retirement payments, are ultimately derived from tax funds.[2] (Individual contributions to the system, in the form of social security taxes, are insufficient to pay the retirement or disability benefits.)

Disability. Social security disability payments are viewed as early retirement payments. Disability is not partial or momentary; only persons whose impairment prevents "any substantial gainful activity" are entitled to benefits, and then only if the disability has lasted or will last at least a year or can be expected to result in death.[3] Medical impairment is only half of the story. An impairment that might not prevent a trained lawyer from practicing might completely eliminate an uneducated worker from the job market. The statute specifically recognizes that disability is determined partly by medical impairment and partly by education, training and the like. However, the statute also provides that if the claimant can perform any type of work that exists in the national economy, she is not disabled, even if that work is not available locally and even if no actual job vacancy exists.[4] By definition, disability need not result from injury. Frequently the impairment that leads to disability is disease like multiple sclerosis or mental limits or breakdown.[5] Pain resulting from a medically determinable condition may lead to a disability.[6]

Standardizing: listings. Because disability requires both an impairment and an inability to work, hearings on disputed claims at one time routinely involved a good deal of vocational testimony as to jobs available and how they matched the claimant's physical or mental abilities. Much of this was repetitious and wasteful and the governing administrative

2. Under the portion called OASI, individuals have paid social security taxes, but these taxes are not sufficient to pay the retirement or disability benefits. Under the portion called SSI, the system is a form of welfare for persons of inadequate means.

3. 42 U.S.C.A. § 423 (d) (1) (B). Blind persons over 55 years of age are defined as disabled if blindness prevent substantial gainful employment using the skills they previously used.

4. 42 U.S.C.A. § 423 (d)(2)(A). The type of work for which the claimant is qualified must, however, exist either in the "region" where she lives or in several regions of the country.

5. E.g., McLain v. Schweiker, 715 F.2d 866 (4th Cir.1983) (nervous disorders, inadequate personality); Foreman v. Callahan, 122 F.3d 24 (8th Cir.1997) (limited intellectual ability).

6. See 42 U.S.C.A. § 423 (d)(5)(A); Kelley v. Callahan, 133 F.3d 583 (8th Cir. 1998). Professor Pryor believes that too little scope is given for findings of disability based upon pain. She argues that pain professionals can detect malingering and that no special rules are needed to fence-out that possibility. See Ellen Smith Pryor, Compensation and the Ineradicable Problems of Pain, 59 Geo. Wash. L. Rev. 239 (1991).

regulations now contain "listings" of impairments that automatically qualify as a disability.[7] The listings work in favor of the claimant but cannot be used to automatically exclude a disability finding.[8]

Standardizing: the grids. A quite different form of standardizing utilizes the medical-vocational guidelines or "The Grids." When the listings do not show an automatic disability finding, the grids are invoked to provide a disability profile of the claimant by applying a table of several factors. The administrative law judge is required to make a rough finding about the degree of "residual functional capacity" considering impairment. For example, the claimant might be limited to light work or medium work. The ALJ also makes findings about other categories in the table—age, previous work experience, and education. When those findings are plugged in, the table provides the ultimate conclusion—disability or not. The table or grid provides an automatic finding of disability in some cases, as where the claimant is approaching advanced age, has no skilled work experience. But the grids may also automatically determine that the claimant is not disabled, as where a 45-year-old has the same impairment and education. The Supreme Court has upheld the grids, noting that the claimant still gets individualized adjudication on the specific components such as impairment, age, and education.[9]

Social security as a model for tort law change? Some torts scholars doubt the capacity of tort law either to deter wrongdoing or to provide appropriate compensation to victims. Consequently, they argue for an out and out welfare program for injured or disabled persons.[10] Those who hope or believe that tort law is part of the culture that helps deter wrongdoing, indirectly if not directly, on the other hand, would prefer that benefits be provided by someone in a position to reduce injury. In that respect, social security seems to offer no lessons for improving tort law. Its use of standardizing techniques and their acceptance in the courts, on the other hand, point to ways in which efficiencies may be gained for some aspects of tort law, or alternatively, may provide cautionary examples against too much streamlining.

§ 398. The Private Insurance Alternative

So far as personal injury results from automobile accidents—and a very large amount does—the tort system is largely fueled by liability insurance. If the defendant has liability insurance, it will pay his legal liability for harm he causes (and will also investigate and defend the suit against him). Liability insurance is costly, not only in relation to the earnings of many people, but also in the sense that most of the premium dollar is used up in cost of administration, investigation, and trial. Liability insurance as the financial backbone of tort law has some other

7. 20 C.F.R. part 404, Subpart P, Appendix I.

8. See Sullivan v. Zebley, 493 U.S. 521, 110 S.Ct. 885, 107 L.Ed.2d 967 (1990).

9. Heckler v. Campbell, 461 U.S. 458, 103 S.Ct. 1952, 76 L.Ed.2d 66 (1983).

10. Stephen D. Sugarman, Doing Away with Personal Injury Law (1989).

limitations. No matter how much liability insurance you buy, it will not help you when you yourself are injured. And you have no control over whether the person who injures you has purchased any insurance at all or what amount. A number of states now make liability insurance compulsory, but enforcement is difficult and the limits of the insurance purchased severely limit the damages recoverable. Persons who want protection from others' negligence are forced to purchase uninsured motorist insurance, or accident insurance in addition their own liability insurance.

These problems, coupled with the problems of delay and uncertainty and injustice in tort litigation, led Professor Robert Keeton (now Judge Keeton) and Professor Jeffrey O'Connell to work up a detailed plan that would guarantee everyone injured from use of an automobile some minimal protection against wage loss and medical expense.[1]

The Keeton–O'Connell Plan, also called no-fault auto insurance, set up a system under which no one had to rely exclusively upon others to purchase insurance. Instead, each auto owner would be required to purchase insurance that would provide two tiers of benefits. In the first tier, the insurance would pay the owner, his passengers, and pedestrians injured by his automobile, for wage loss and medical expenses, but not pain and suffering. The amounts to be paid were limited. As long as the limit was not exhausted, no tort suit was permitted.

If damages were greater than the coverage, the injured person could go to the tort tier. There he would recover for damage greater than those paid for by his insurance in the first tier. In a two-car collision, if each driver were injured, each would recover the benefits he had paid for from his own insurer. If one or both drivers were negligent, and their damages high enough, they might also litigate tort claims against each other for the excess.

Since the great bulk of claims are small claims that could fall exclusively within the first tier, litigation might be reduced if the first tier was big enough. Basic losses would be paid in all cases, but pain and suffering would be paid only if basic losses were high and tort rules would permit recovery.

The Keeton–O'Connell plan provided a detailed model and a number of states adopted some form of it.[2] To make the plan work well, however, it is necessary to exclude tort claims in the first tier and to make the first tier large enough to cover a very large number of cases. That is, the threshold for entrance to the second or torts tier must be high enough to make sure that most relatively small injuries would be resolved in the no-fault tier. If legislation established a $1,000 top damage in the first tier the plan would fail to insure against substantial losses in the first tier and would fail to reduce tort litigation by any significant amount. If

§ 398

1. Robert E. Keeton and Jeffrey O'Connell, Basic Protection for the Traffic Victim (1965).

2. See Roger C. Henderson, No–Fault Insurance for Automobile Accidents: Status and Effect in the United States, 56 Ore. L. Rev. 287 (1977).

legislation merely permitted you to buy accident insurance without eliminating the tort suit in the first tier, it would have no beneficial effects at all, since you could already buy accident insurance. A number of states that adopted no-fault plans either used an inadequate first tier or merely provided for add-on insurance, with the result in either case that the plan failed to work. A very few states adopted no-fault plans with substantial first-tiers. For instance, New York uses $50,000 as the cap on economic damages recoverable in the first or no-fault tier. If economic damages exceed that sum or injury is otherwise "serious" as defined in the statute, the injured person can then sue in tort.[3]

The Keeton–O'Connell no-fault plan differed more from the workers' compensation and social security systems than it did from the tort system. In one respect it was like neither. It envisioned that most claims in the no-fault tier would not require litigation. The claimant would be claiming against his own insurer, just as she would with a fire insurance or collision policy. The terms of the plan left little to dispute and provided a penalty if the insurer did not properly pay claims. So the bureaucratic or administrative hearings contemplated by workers' compensation and social security had no place in the no-fault plan. The plan was perhaps best adapted to the automobile injury problem. Even if it became popular there, it might not readily furnish a model for general improvements to the tort system. But even if the idea of self-insurance in the no-fault tier is totally rejected, the two-tier structure might prove to be quite useful in managing tort claims. For instance, the strategy of standardizing of damages and disability seen in workers' compensation and social security systems may be more acceptable for tort cases if it were limited to the lower tier of claims. Compared to caps that harm the most seriously injured, a two-tier system of torts that standardized and limited damages in the first tier might prove much more desirable.

§ 399. Other Systems

Many programs affect injured people and might well be taken into account in revising the tort system. One type of program that has been used in limited circumstances taxes dangerous substances and uses the fund created by the tax to pay for injuries that result from those substances. Congress did this with one of the stages provided for in the Black Lung Act[1]

The substance tax is also the approach taken more recently in the National Childhood Vaccine Injury Act.[2] That statute confronts the fact that vaccines mandated by statute and by public health policy do regularly cause devastating injury to vaccinated children. The injury occurs, not because the vaccines are defective, but because some adverse reactions are unavoidable. Taxing vaccines is likely to raise their costs to

3. See N.Y. INS. LAW § 5104; § 5102(d) (defining serious injury).

§ 399

1. 30 U.S.C.A. § 901 et seq.

2. 42 U.S.C.A. § 300aa–1 et seq.

public health agencies that provide them and to private users. This increased cost can be limited if the benefits provided are limited and the liabilities standardized. The vaccine act does both of those things, but leaves the victim the option to go into the tort system if the award under the statute is unacceptable. The compensation for pain is limited to $250,000 and the compensation for death the same. Other types of compensation include medical expense and loss of earnings. The claim must be pursued in the Vaccine Court before a tort suit is possible. If the claimant ultimately does seek a tort recovery, she cannot recover for unavoidable side effects.[3]

The act's standardizing techniques as well as its financing are especially interesting. The plaintiff is permitted to establish that the vaccine actually caused her injury by the usual method of medical evidence if she can. However, as with the listings in social security disability claims, the plaintiff can rely instead upon a predetermined list of injuries or symptoms correlated with each type of vaccine. For example, if the vaccine is the basic DPT vaccine and anaphylaxis or anaphylactic shock occurs within 24 hours, the table establishes that the vaccine is a cause. For the same vaccine, however, if the harm is encephalopathy or encephalitis, causation is established if the problem is first manifest anytime up to three days after vaccination.[4] The table does not resolve all problems[5] and assuredly leaves it open to the plaintiff to prove causation, the only issue, in other ways.

Whether the tax-created injury fund would be suitable for the great mass of tort cases is open to doubt. Its best use may be for those cases in which liability is doubtful or would likely be financially destructive. The idea has been raised, however, as a possible solution for alcohol related injuries.[6] The injured victims of a drunk driver can seldom enforce a substantial judgment against the drinker and often cannot do so against the alcohol provider. In those circumstances, an injury fund created by taxes on the substance may prove a useful solution, especially if, as in the Vaccine Injury Act, the victim still has an option to seeking redress in the tort system.

3. Judge (now Justice) Bryer summarized the act succinctly in Schafer v. American Cyanamid Co., 20 F.3d 1 (1st Cir.1994).

4. The table is enacted and codified at 42 U.S.C.A. § 300aa–14.

5. See Shalala v. Whitecotton, 514 U.S. 268, 115 S.Ct. 1477, 131 L.Ed.2d 374 (1995) (holding against the claimant where evidence indicated that the condition in question existed before the vaccination). See also Russell G. Donaldson, Annotation, Construction and Application of National Childhood Vaccine Injury Act (42 U.S.C.A. §§ 300aa et Seq.), 129 A.L.R. Fed. 1 (1996).

6. Paul LeBel, John Barleycorn Must Pay: Compensating the Victims of Drinking Drivers 135–148 (1992).

*

PART IV. ECONOMIC AND DIGNITARY INJURY

Note to Part IV

Part IV radically departs from the subject matter that has gone before. Part IV reflects an important and growing part of tort law that does not deal at all with personal injury or even with property damage. It deals rather with torts that cause stand-alone economic harm or dignitary harm. That is, it deals with torts that ordinarily do not cause physical harm of any kind. (One partial exception is nuisance, which is primarily an economic tort but does at times result in personal injury.) In all of these torts, the interest protected is the interest is financial or dignitary rather than the interest is personal security or safety of tangible property.

Many of the torts considered in this Part derive from sources disconnected from negligence law. They are also disconnected from trespassory intentional torts, in which direct physical force was an essential element. Because they are independently derived, they resist reduction to the negligence formula and usually display a set of rules that differ from those hitherto encountered. Broadly speaking, the plaintiff who claims a stand-alone commercial or economic tort must usually (but not invariably) prove intent rather than negligence. And liability-expanding rules like those of transferred intent do not apply to broaden liability for economic torts like misrepresentation.

Policy differences abound as well. Many of the commercial or economic torts turn on communication and hence potentially raise issues of free speech, implicating either direct constitutional concerns or the broader policies underlying the First Amendment. Many of the torts are associated with business transactions, sometimes raising questions whether contract rather than tort should control the decision. Others, like those involving interference with family relations, are intensely personal. Most of these torts cause harms to either business or personal relationships; they are relational torts as well as communicative and economic torts.

Torts in this Part sometimes overlap each other, with the result that lawyers often bring suits alleging several torts resulting from the same conduct. This is common with defamation, privacy, and interference with contract. Sometimes these torts also overlap with broad general torts like intentional infliction of emotional distress. One difficult problem with multiple tort theories is to avoid duplicative damages. Another is to determine whether the policy reasons barring a cause of action for one of the overlapping torts should defeat an action under other theories of recovery upon the same essential facts. If the tort consists of a communi-

cation but is defeated by defamation rules, can the plaintiff sidestep the rules of defamation by recasting the tort as one for emotional distress, privacy invasion, or interference with contract? The problem represented by this question is growing partly because courts and lawyers have not always recognized that conflicting tort rules require attention.

Scope. Several kinds of economic interference have been excluded mainly because of space limitations but partly because they are now well-developed specialties. Regretfully, this book omits any substantial coverage of torts based upon intellectual property such as copyright. Similarly, unfair competition and torts embedded in labor law are given only limited treatment.

Chapter 28

Defamation

Topic A. Common Law Requirements

§ 400. Introducing Defamation

Scope of defamation law. The interest of people in their reputation among others, though not a constitutionally protected interest,[1] is highly regarded by the law. Defamation law, executed through the law of libel and slander, aims at protecting reputation and good name against false and derogatory communications.[2] Where the defendant has no defense under the common law rules, for example, if a newspaper editorial accuses the plaintiff of child abuse, the plaintiff is defamed and can recover damages for all harms proximately caused by injury to her reputation. Harm to reputation or good name is the essence of libel and slander, so the plaintiff can have no recovery in libel or slander for emotional distress or economic loss unless her reputation is implicated. Other torts may address stand-alone emotional harm or economic loss, but the law of defamation addresses only those harms that result from reputational injury. To a very large extent it is also true that defamation law is the exclusive law covering injuries resulting from derogatory publications.[3] The plaintiff cannot, for example, sue for negligent harm to reputation; she must prove the elements of defamation and she is subject to its limits.[4]

History. Reputational harm has not always been the focus. Primitive law may have been concerned more with insult or dishonor that could lead to blood feud.[5] Legal redress for harsh words or name-calling formalized the victim's vengeance and made the violence of revenge unnecessary. In the medieval English law, oral statements demeaning to others were punished as sin in the Church courts, which is to say that the priest demanded a penance. Eventually, however, common law torts

§ 400

1. Paul v. Davis, 424 U.S. 693, 96 S.Ct. 1155, 47 L.Ed.2d 405 (1976) (thus no action may be brought under § 1983 for defamation carried out under color of state law).

2. E.g., Little Rock Newspapers, Inc. v. Dodrill, 281 Ark. 25, 660 S.W.2d 933 (1983). For various kinds of reputation and injury to it, see David A. Anderson, Reputation, Compensation, and Proof, 25 Wm. & Mary L. Rev. 747 (1984).

3. Exceptions: false light invasion of privacy, see § 428, and a *Firestone*-type claim for emotional harm without claiming reputational loss, a claim that is rejected by a number of courts. See § 422.

4. See Texas Beef Group v. Winfrey, 11 F.Supp.2d 858, 864 (N.D.Tex.1998).

5. Words of "shame" may have once been central. The capacity of libel to incite to a breach of the peace was given as one reason for imposing criminal liability in Coke's De Libelis Famosis, 50 Co.Rep. 125a, 77 Eng. Rep. 250 (Star Chamber 1605).

in the 1500s took over the slander actions and converted them into actions for damages.[6]

The history of libel based on printed or tangible communications such as those found in pamphlets is quite different. By 1600 or before, the printed word was considered a threat to political stability. Printers had to be licensed and to give a bond. At that time a libel included any criticism of the English government or even of "great men."[7] Truth was no defense;[8] even to laugh at a libel was a crime.[9] This ruthless program of suppression was carried out by the Court of the Star Chamber, called by Alexander Hamilton "the most dangerous Court to the Liberties of the People of England, that ever was known in that Kingdom.... "[10]

After the English Civil War and the restoration of the monarchy in the 17th century, libel law was somewhat tamed. The system of licensing printers was abolished and common law courts took over libel. Its history had molded it, however. In the new rules for libel, the old preoccupation with sin, sedition and insult survived in a number of particulars.

One English governor in colonial America is notorious for using seditious libel as his forbears did, to silence political opposition. New York's British-appointed Governor Cosby controlled the only newspaper in the state, a fountain of propaganda for himself, his party, and the British. Citizens set up a politically independent paper, *The New York Weekly Journal*, printed by John Peter Zenger, to criticize Cosby. The *Journal* reported the Governor's misdemeanors–he seems to have been quite corrupt–and pointed out his attempts to cover up his shady dealings. The governor responded by prosecuting Zenger for libel. Zenger was forced to spend nine months in prison awaiting trial because his bail was set so high. (Anna Catherine Zenger published the paper while her husband was incarcerated.) Ultimately, Alexander Hamilton came to Zenger's defense. Hamilton attacked the Star Chamber's doctrine that a citizen could be imprisoned for sedition because he published the truth. Although the judge did not agree with Hamilton, Hamilton nevertheless secured the jury's acquittal in 1735.

Zenger's acquittal did not establish a free press in the Colonies, but it has ever since been a rallying point against the scheme of criminal punishment for truthful words. Today, libel is still a crime on the books of some states, but largely obsolete in practice. When criminal libel prosecutions are instituted, they cannot succeed without proof that the words used by the defendant were untruthful and where public issues are involved, that they were uttered as knowing or reckless falsehoods.[11] Under President John Adams, the American Congress itself went back to

6. On all this early development see R.H. Helmholz, Introduction, Select Cases on Defamation to 1600 xiv-xv (Selden Society 1985).

7. Punishment for defamation of important persons goes back to a statute of 1275. Unimportant persons were not so protected for centuries.

8. De Libelis Famosis, 50 Co.Rep. 125a, 77 Eng. Rep. 250 (Star Chamber 1605).

9. S.F.C. Milsom, Historical Foundations of the Common Law 389 (2d ed.1981).

10. See Vincent Buranelli, The Trial of Peter Zenger 103 (1957); Leonard Levy, Freedom of the Press from Zenger to Jefferson 45 (1966).

11. Garrison v. Louisiana, 379 U.S. 64,

Star Chamber days by passing the Sedition Act requiring prosecution for criticisms of government; but Congress soon repented and the act was later held unconstitutional.[12] As the South Carolina Court said in 1818, the proper tribunal for judging an alleged libel on government or its officials was the electorate itself, not the courts.[13]

In the 19th and 20th centuries, defamation law has been largely private and civil. The states received a good deal of English law on the subject of defamation. In particular, the American courts thought from the beginning that written defamation is to be treated differently from oral defamation; the categories that limit liability for slander do not apply when the defamation is in writing.[14] American courts also adopted some obscure and even bizarre doctrines best left for later discussion.[15] Although the private or tort law of defamation aims to protect reputation and good name, some of its particular rules seem derived from the roots of defamation in sin, sedition, dishonor and punishment.

The history of libel and slander forecasts the concern of contemporary law to balance reputational interests against the interest of the individual defendant and of society at large in free speech. Since 1964, the Supreme Court of the United States has attempted to effect an appropriate balance of those interests under the First Amendment's free speech guarantee.[16] This has required changes in some of the common law rules for many cases, although those rules remain important for others.

The history of libel and slander also makes a narrower point. Defamation law long antedated the development of general negligence law. Liability for defamation under the common law rules thus did not depend upon proof of negligence. Equally, an ordinary negligence action cannot be maintained for loss of reputation.[17] Defamation law is also wholly unrelated to those intentional torts like battery and assault that are derived from the writ of trespass and that entail direct application of force. The law of defamation, true to its unhappy history, developed its own complex rules unrelated to the law of negligence and intent.

§ 401. Elements of Defamation–Common Law and Constitution

The Common Law

The First Amendment to the United States Constitution today requires the plaintiff to establish some kinds of fault, falsity of publica-

85 S.Ct. 209, 13 L.Ed.2d 125 (1964).

12. New York Times v. Sullivan, 376 U.S. 254, 84 S.Ct. 710, 11 L.Ed.2d 686 (1964).

13. Mayrant v. Richardson, 1 Nott & McC. (S.C.) 347 (1818). This case anticipates the Supreme Court's decision in New York Times v. Sullivan, 376 U.S. 254, 84 S.Ct. 710, 11 L.Ed.2d 686 (1964), advancing some similar ideas and even similar language.

14. Clark v. Binney, 19 Mass. 113 (1824).

15. The doctrines of libel per quod and innocent construction, see § 409.

16. New York Times v. Sullivan, 376 U.S. 254, 84 S.Ct. 710, 11 L.Ed.2d 686, 95 A.L.R.2d 1412 (1964). See § 417.

17. Lawrence v. Grinde, 534 N.W.2d 414 (Iowa 1995).

tion, and sometimes actual damages in order to recover for defamation. Those are not the requirements of the common law. As many common law rules remain intact, or intact in a portion of the defamation cases, those rules are stated first, with constitutional questions postponed until the common law foundation has been laid.

Defamation by writing and by contemporary means analogous to writing such as movies is libel. Defamation communicated orally is slander. Communication in any form can be defamatory, but defamation is most commonly communicated in words, pictorial elements, acts or some combination, and for convenience this chapter often uses the term words or the like to include any form of communication. Traditional common law rules in the case of both libel and slander required the plaintiff to prove (1) defendant's publication to a third person (2) of defamatory material (3) of and concerning the plaintiff. Contemporary law in certain cases may require the plaintiff to prove additionally (4) that the statement was false and (5) some degree of fault on the part of the publisher and sometimes (6) actual damages.

In the case of slander, the plaintiff must also prove either (a) special (pecuniary) damages or (b) a publication meaning that the plaintiff has committed a serious crime, that the plaintiff has a character trait or a practice incompatible with her trade, business, or profession, or that the plaintiff suffers an incurable and communicable disease.[1]

In the case of libel, courts said that once a publication was shown to be defamatory in the sense that it would diminish the esteem in which the plaintiff is held, then three presumptions would carry the day for the plaintiff. The defendant was presumed to have published in malice, the words were presumed to be false, and the plaintiff was presumed to have suffered damages. Translated from the idiom of presumptions, this means that the plaintiff could recover without proof of any fault by the defendant, without any proof that the publication was false, and without any proof of actual damages. Nor were damages merely nominal; substantial sums are recovered in libel cases without proof of any economic loss. The presumption of falsity was different from the others because the defendant was eventually allowed to assert truth as an affirmative defense, but he could not escape liability by showing that he published innocently, reasonably, or in good faith.

So far as the prima facie case at common law was concerned, defamation was a strict liability tort except that with slander the plaintiff often had to prove actual damages. However, as will appear, a number of privileges could be asserted by the defendant for special situations.[2] When a privilege could be asserted, liability would be depend, after all, upon some kind of fault of the defendant.

§ 401

1. Unchastity is a fourth category once recognized, but perhaps no longer. See § 408.

2. §§ 412–415.

The Constitution

Since 1964, the structure of the common law defamation case has been radically altered by constitutional rulings based upon defendants' rights to free speech. All three of the common law presumptions–fault, falsity, and damages–have been reversed by constitutional decisions governing a substantial number of cases.[3] Although some issues remain undecided, the constitutional rules probably cover the following territory: (1) If the plaintiff is a public official or a public figure, she must now prove that the defendant published a knowing or reckless falsehood, but she may still recover presumed damages. (2) If the plaintiff is a private person but the issue involved in the publication is one of public concern, the plaintiff is required to prove some fault (usually negligence) plus actual damages. Upon such proof, she cannot recover punitive damages and without such proof she cannot recover anything. (3) If the plaintiff is a private person and the alleged defamation is of no public concern, the plaintiff can recover presumed damages; probably the states are free to invoke common law strict liability rules as well.

Where falsity is required, the effect is to protect opinion statements that cannot be said to be either true or false.[4] Even where the constitutional limitations may not apply, some states have now adopted some of these constitutional limitations as a part of their common law.[5] The constitutional rules increased the rationality of defamation law, but they have also added their own complexity to the existing intricacies of defamation.

§ 402. Requirement of Publication

Publication.[1] The plaintiff claiming either slander or libel must prove that the defendant published defamatory material about the plaintiff to a third person. Publication is a word of art. It includes any communication, by any method to one or more persons who can understand the meaning.[2] Books and newspapers are publications and so are oral personal remarks made to a neighbor over the back fence. Suggestive questions as well as declaratory statements can communicate defam-

3. §§ 417–420.

4. § 420.

5. See, e.g., United Ins. Co. of America v. Murphy, 331 Ark. 364, 961 S.W.2d 752 (1998) (prospectively abolishing presumed damages); Thomas v. Jacksonville Television, Inc., 699 So.2d 800 (Fla.App.1997) (fault is element of defamation); Simpson v. Mars Inc., 113 Nev. 188, 929 P.2d 966 (Nev. 1997) (same); Hupp v. Sasser, 200 W.Va. 791, 490 S.E.2d 880 (1997) (listing falsity as element).

§ 402

1. The concept of publication is not merely an element in the claim for defamation; it is also a concept utilized in determining what law applies, whether the statute of limitations has run, and other procedural-remedial matters. See § 421.

2. Words spoken in a foreign language to a person who does not understand that language is not a publication. See Economopoulos v. A.G. Pollard Co., 218 Mass. 294, 105 N.E. 896 (1914). New Mexico has taken the unusual view that there is no publication if the recipient knows the statement is false. Silverman v. Progressive Broadcasting, Inc., 125 N.M. 500, 964 P.2d 61 (App. 1998) (perhaps also treating recipient's lack of belief in the statement in the same way).

atory meaning.[3] Pictures, songs, movies, and computer communications can all count as publications. Even some signs or actions without words can communicate a defamatory falsehood.[4] The communication must reach at least one person other than the plaintiff.[5] Nothing requires a mass audience, although if the publication reaches only a few persons, damages may be limited. A communication made only to the plaintiff herself may conceivably give rise to a claim for emotional distress, but it does not give rise to a claim for libel or slander unless others also learn of the statement.[6] Publication to an agent of the plaintiff who is acting for her in matters touched by the defamation may be considered to be no more than publication to the plaintiff herself.[7]

Intent and negligence. The defendant need not be the author of published material to be responsible, but he must publish it. That means he must communicate the material intentionally or negligently.[8] If he is under a duty to remove or prevent a publication, a negligent or intentional failure to do so counts as a publication.[9] Negligent publication is relatively rare, but possible. If I write in my diary that you robbed the bank there is no publication at all, but if I leave the diary open on the coffee table where guests might read it, I am a negligent publisher if one of them does so.[10]

The traditional requirement of intent or negligence has sometimes been misunderstood as a requirement of fault. However, the intent required is an intent to publish, that is, communicate, not an intent to harm or even an intent to relay a falsehood. Although fault in some more substantive sense may be required in some cases under the constitution,

3. E.g., Lara v. Thomas, 512 N.W.2d 777 (Iowa 1994) (does she have a drug problem?).

4. K–Mart Corp. v. Washington, 109 Nev. 1180, 866 P.2d 274 (1993) (marching suspect through store in handcuffs was slander per se). The exact limits on defamation by conduct have not been systematically explored. In Bolton v. Department of Human Services, 540 N.W.2d 523 (Minn. 1995) the court rejected liability for defamation by conduct that did not rise to the level of dramatic pantomime. In Lee v. Bankers Trust Co., 166 F.3d 540 (2d Cir.1999) the court recognized that conduct could be defamatory, but, noting that some conduct had no communicative content, concluded that the conduct in question (searching an employee's desk) had no defamatory meaning. Some First Circuit cases have struggled with the idea that the plaintiff might recover for reputational loss resulting from the defendant's negligence, even if the defendant's conduct was essentially non-communicative. See the discussion and cases cited in Jorgensen v. Massachusetts Port Authority, 905 F.2d 515 (1st Cir.1990).

5. E.g., Brauer v. Globe Newspaper Co., 351 Mass. 53, 217 N.E.2d 736 (1966). Publication may be inferred from circumstances, as where a defamatory article is on display in a library, but the inference may be rebutted. LaMon v. City of Westport, 44 Wash. App. 664, 723 P.2d 470 (1986).

6. Downs v. Waremart, Inc., 324 Or. 307, 926 P.2d 314 (1996).

7. Delval v. PPG Industries, Inc., 590 N.E.2d 1078, 1081 (Ind.App.1992).

8. Restatement § 577 (1).

9. Hellar v. Bianco, 111 Cal.App.2d 424, 244 P.2d 757, 28 A.L.R.2d 1451(1952) (remarks about the plaintiff's sexual activity, along with her home phone number, written on the restroom wall of a bar; liability for failure to remove promptly after learning the content); Restatement § 577 (2) cf. Tacket v. General Motors Corp., 836 F.2d 1042 (7th Cir.1987) (liability based on theory that defendant implicitly adopted the defamatory statement; adoption could not be found without a significant time in which to remove the defamatory material).

10. See Restatement § 577, cmt. k and Ills. 4–6; see also id., cmt. l (mistaken identity of recipient).

the role of fault in determining whether the defendant published material does not touch issues of truth, justification, or reasonableness of the publication. If I tell a friend that you took a gun into the bank, I am a publisher even though I believe in the truth of my statement and see no harm in it. If the statement can be construed to mean that you robbed the bank, I am subject to liability for my publication.

Original publishers and repeaters. A publisher is responsible for all harms proximately caused, including harms resulting from a repeater's foreseeable publication, provided always that the publications are defamatory and unprivileged.[11] The repeater of defamatory material is also a publisher and subject to liability for the publication.[12] For example, unless a newspaper or television broadcaster enjoys a privilege,[13] it is fully responsible in libel for material it prints, even though it is merely quoting or accurately repeating what others have said.[14] The same rule applies to oral repetition.[15] Where constitutional limitations apply, however, the repeater will not be liable unless he is at fault in stating a falsehood and may not be at fault if he reasonably relied upon the original publication.[16]

Transmitters, distributors, or disseminators of information. Many persons who deliver, transmit, or facilitate defamation have only the most attenuated or mechanical connection with the defamatory content. Some primary publishers like newspapers are responsible as publishers even for materials prepared by others, as in the case of advertisements.[17] On the other hand, many others such as telegraph and telephone companies, libraries and news vendors are regarded as mere transmitters or disseminators rather than publishers. As to these, it seems clear that liability cannot be imposed unless the distributor knows or should know of the defamatory content in materials he distributes.[18]

The question remains whether the neutral distributor such as a library is liable even if the distributor knows of the defamation. An English case decided in 1900 held that such liability was appropriate and

11. Barnette v. Wilson, 706 So.2d 1164 (Ala.1997); Trentecosta v. Beck, 703 So.2d 552 (La.1997); Restatement § 576 (also recognizing liability where repeater was privileged to repeat).

12. Restatement § 578.

13. People, including newspapers, enjoy a privilege to report accurately on public documents and meetings of public officials. See § 415.

14. E.g., Snitowsky v. NBC Subsidiary (WMAQ–TV), Inc., 297 Ill.App.3d 304, 696 N.E.2d 761, 231 Ill.Dec. 465 (1998) (reporting principal's allegations against teacher); Cassidy v. Daily Mirror Newspapers, Limited, [1929], 2 K.B. 331, 69 A.L.R. 720.

15. Baskin v. Rogers, 229 Ga.App. 250, 493 S.E.2d 728 (1997) (argument that the repeater did not assert the defamation as the truth but only as something he heard is no defense).

16. See, e.g., Appleby v. Daily Hampshire Gazette, 395 Mass. 32, 478 N.E.2d 721 (1985).

17. Triangle Pubs., Inc. v. Chumley, 253 Ga. 179, 317 S.E.2d 534 (1984); Pettengill v. Booth Newspapers, Inc., 88 Mich.App. 587, 278 N.W.2d 682 (1979).

18. Cubby, Inc. v. CompuServe, Inc.,776 F.Supp. 135 (S.D.N.Y.1991) (computer "library" treated as disseminator like other libraries); Hartmann v. American News Co., 171 F.2d 581 (7th Cir.1948); Restatement § 581; Annotation, Liability of Telegraph or Telephone Company for Transmitting or Permitting Transmission of Libelous or Slanderous Messages, 91 A.L.R.3d 1015 (1980).

that the defendant had the burden of proving he neither knew nor should have known of the defamation.[19] But both time and place make the decision doubtful authority for American consumption. English law imposes a very wide liability upon all associated with publication, including the employee of a printer who merely locks up the presses.[20] Contemporary American ideas about liability for speech seem to be quite different.[21] Injunctions are denied against libel for the very reason that private censorship is not desirable.[22] The same reason cautions against liability of libraries and newsdealers, even when they know of a claimed libel.

Protection for distributors who merely carry the publications of others, or furnish a forum in which others may be heard, seems increasingly accepted in the United States. In the case of radio and similar broadcasts, statutes today frequently immunize the broadcaster who merely provides a forum for the speech of others by leasing air time.[23] A federal statute similarly immunizes the Internet users and providers so that they are not responsible for material posted by others[24] and have no duty to remove it even when notified of its defamatory content, since any such duty would tend to eliminate nondefamatory as well as defamatory speech.[25]

Causing or permitting others to publish. One who causes others to publish is ordinarily himself a publisher. If I write a letter to the editor, I have published it to the editor and become liable for that publication and for the editor's foreseeable republication as well.[26]

Traditional self-publication. One peculiar kind of case is strangely labeled as self-publication. In this kind of case, the defendant directly

19. Vizetelly v. Mudie's Select Library, Ltd., [1900] 2 Q.B. 170, 69 L.J.Q.B. 645 (C.A.)

20. See PATRICK MILMO & W.V. H. ROGERS, GATLEY ON LIBEL AND SLANDER ¶ 6.17 (9th ed. 1998).

21. American statements of the rule imposing liability upon a distributor who knows of the content usually rely upon (1) English authority and (2) American cases like those cited in note 18 that *refuse* to impose liability when the distributor has no knowledge of the content. Cases of this sort at best support liability of distributors who know defamatory content only in dicta.

22. See § 422.

23. E.g., Cal. Civ. Code § 48.5; N.Y. Civ. Rights Law § 75. Before the statutes, common law decisions were divided on the point. For example, Sorensen v. Wood, 123 Neb. 348, 243 N.W. 82 (1932) (liability); Kelly v. Hoffman, 137 N.J.L. 695, 61 A.2d 143, 5 A.L.R.2d 951 (1948) (broadcaster leasing time is disseminator only). Broadcasters are forbidden by law to censor political candidates' speeches and hence are immunized from liability for the content of such speeches. Farmers Educational and Cooperative Union of America v. WDAY, Inc., 360 U.S. 525, 79 S.Ct. 1302, 3 L.Ed.2d 1407 (1959).

24. "No provider or user of an interactive computer service shall be treated as the publisher or speaker of any information provided by another information content provider." 47 U.S.C.A. § 230(c)(1). Before the statute, Cubby, Inc. v. CompuServe, Inc., 776 F.Supp. 135 (S.D.N.Y.1991) got the same result.

25. See Zeran v. America Online, Inc., 129 F.3d 327, 333 (4th Cir.1997).

26. Tuman v. Genesis Associates, 894 F.Supp. 183 (E.D.Pa.1995) (allegations that defendant therapists implanted false and defamatory memories in their patient that resulted in publication). Most claims against therapists for causing their patients to have and communicate false memories defamatory to others have been pursued on negligence or alienation of affections grounds. See § 444.

communicates defamatory material about the plaintiff only to the plaintiff herself. That is ordinarily not publication in the law of defamation, since publication requires communication to a third person. However, in some cases, the defendant can foresee that the plaintiff will feel compelled to communicate the defamatory materials to others. For instance, if the defendant hands a written defamation to an unsighted person, the defendant can expect that the recipient will have others read it.[27] If the defendant makes defamatory accusations about a child to the child herself, the defendant can expect that the child may seek guidance from others and necessarily repeat the remarks.[28] In such cases the defendant, because he can foresee publication to third persons resulting from his act, is himself a publisher.

Self-publication in employment. The defendant's liability for compelled and foreseeable self-publication became controversial when it was applied to employers who gave defamatory reasons for discharging employees. In such cases, the discharged employee seeking employment elsewhere will predictably will be asked why she was discharged. A refusal to answer will make further employment almost impossible. An honest answer will likely be as bad. If the employee attempts an honest answer, he must repeat the defamatory accusations and attempt to explain or deny them. On the surface this seems to fall within the rule that the defendant who initiates the communication is liable for foreseeable publication. A few cases have accepted this idea where the plaintiff has actually published the employer's defamatory remarks to prospective new employers. Courts accepting this have emphasized that the publication by the plaintiff must not only be foreseeable but also compelled by circumstances.[29] Other cases, said to be the majority, however, have expressly rejected the whole idea as applied in employment cases and said that the employer is simply not the publisher at all.[30]

One additional element not formally related to publication must be understood to evaluate this dispute. To find publication is not to impose liability. The employer normally has a conditional privilege to convey negative references about an employee. The privilege is lost only if the employer acts with malice in some sense.[31] To the extent that the employer is privileged to give defamatory references directly to prospective employers, he is also privileged in self-publication cases.[32] Thus courts may accept the principle of self-publication but may still often hold for the employer under the privilege.[33] In addition, it would be

27. Lane v. Schilling, 130 Or. 119, 279 P. 267 (1929).

28. Hedgpeth v. Coleman, 183 N.C. 309, 111 S.E. 517 (1922) (accusations of crime and threat of punishment to 15–year-old, with demands for payment).

29. Lewis v. Equitable Life Assurance Soc'y of the United States, 389 N.W.2d 876, 62 A.L.R.4th 581 (1986) (a leading case); David P. Chapus, Annotation, Publication of Allegedly Defamatory Matter by Plaintiff ("Self-publication") as Sufficient to Support Defamation Action, 62 A.L.R.4th 616 (1989).

30. Sullivan v. Baptist Mem. Hosp., 995 S.W.2d 569 (Tenn. 1999); Bettinger v.Field Container Co., 221 Wis.2d 221, 584 N.W.2d 233 (Wis.App.1998).

31. See § 416.

32. See Lewis, supra n. 29.

33. E.g., Duffy v. Leading Edge Products, Inc., 44 F.3d 308 (5th Cir.1995).

plausible to argue that the employer is a publisher but that he enjoys a privilege to speak directly to the employee unless he is guilty of an intentional or reckless falsehood.

Publication analysis vs. privilege analysis. Because defamation was prima facie a strict liability tort under the common law rules, moral and policy issues arose mainly with the assertion of a privilege. Hence privileges are an essential and major part of defamation law. When courts consider privileges, they directly address their moral and policy concerns. Some of the work of privileges can be done by defining publication to exclude liability in certain cases. However, this approach may cloud the concept of publication without directly addressing the real concerns of privilege. Examples are communications to a spouse, to a stenographer, and to others engaged in the same corporate enterprise. Sometimes courts have said such communications did not count as publications.[34] The contemporary view is that they are indeed publications but that, in appropriate circumstances, these publications are privileged.[35] The difference in the two approaches is that if there is no publication, the plaintiff will have no claim even when the statement is defamatory, does harm, and is unnecessary to the conduct of corporate business. If the communication is a publication that is privileged when appropriate, the plaintiff will be allowed to recover when the privilege is exceeded or abused.

§ 403. The Requirement of Defamatory or Derogatory Content

Defamatory content required. No action for libel or slander lies unless the plaintiff can prove that the defendant has published something of a defamatory nature about her. Publications that are expected to harm and do in fact harm the plaintiff may count as some other tort but they cannot count as libel or slander unless they have defamatory quality.[1] Under the traditional common law rules, proof that the defendant published defamatory matter gave rise to presumptions that the publication was false, malicious, and untrue. Those presumptions have largely if not completely been discarded by constitutional decisions, but courts continue to insist that the defendant's publication must be of a defamatory nature and not merely foreseeably harmful.

Definitions of "defamatory." Under the classic English definition, words had a defamatory quality if they exposed the plaintiff to hatred,

34. Hanson v. New Technology, Inc., 594 So.2d 96 (Ala.1992).

35. Staples v. Bangor Hydro–Elec. Co., 629 A.2d 601 (Me.1993); Simpson v. Mars Inc., 113 Nev. 188, 929 P.2d 966 (Nev. 1997); see Peter Bennett, Dana N. Levitt, Craig J. Marton, Julie M. Ward, Defamation Claims Arising out of the Employment Relationship, 33 TORT & INS. L.J. 857 (1998); Restatement § 577, cmts. e, h, i, and j. The spousal communication is absolutely privileged, the others conditionally so.

§ 403

1. Frinzi v. Hanson, 30 Wis.2d 271, 140 N.W.2d 259 (1966). Nondefamatory statements may at times be actionable under theories of infliction of emotional distress, interference with contract or economic prospects, and the civil version of malicious prosecution.

ridicule,[2] or contempt.[3] American decisions added that defamation included anything that subjected the plaintiff to obloquy, odium, shame, disgrace or other forms of discredit or harm to reputation.[4] They also recognized that a publication would be defamatory if it caused the plaintiff to be shunned or avoided by others, even if she were not discredited or subjected to disgrace.[5] Courts have generally come to adopt the Restatement's more accurate statement[6] that a communication is defamatory if it tends to harm the plaintiff's reputation, lowering her in the esteem of the community or deterring people from associating or dealing with her.[7] Tendency to harm, however, is an estimate of the judges and jurors from their experience in life; it is almost never a matter of evidence or poll-taking.[8] When reasonable people could differ as to whether a communication is defamatory, the question is left to the jury.[9]

Right-thinking people. Even the Restatement's definition does not adequately explain why recovery is excluded in some cases. In a diverse society, almost any statement about the plaintiff would tend to lower the plaintiff in the esteem of someone. Statements that the plaintiff cooperated with police or voted for one party or another in an election are not accepted as defamatory,[10] but some people will feel that such conduct is disgraceful and contemptible. Courts, especially in New York, once attempted to deal with this problem by saying that to be defamatory the statement must lower the plaintiff in the esteem of right-thinking people,[11] but as there is no standard for determining what right-thinking people would rightly think, and since a democratic and individualistic society recognizes all people's right to hold their own opinions, the right-thinking test is at best unhelpful. The test has sometimes been expressly rejected[12] and in the last generation, the right-thinking people test not been widely used outside of New York. The best courts have been able to do with the problem is to say that the publication is not defamatory unless it would cause a substantial number in the community to reduce

2. Liability for ridicule is now doubtful in many instances. See § 420.

3. Parmiter v. Coupland, 151 Eng. Rep. 340 (Exch. Pleas 1840).

4. E.g., Thomas v. Jacksonville Television, Inc., 699 So.2d 800 (Fla.App.1997) (distrust); Brock v. Thompson, 948 P.2d 279 (Okla.1997) (obloquy). All the terms refer to the same general idea.

5. Katapodis v. Brooklyn Spectator, 287 N.Y. 17, 38 N.E.2d 112 (1941). See notes 25–29.

6. Restatement § 559.

7. Based on Peck v. Tribune Co., 214 U.S. 185, 29 S.Ct. 554, 53 L.Ed. 960 (1909). Courts may use the Restatement's test alone or use it as the primary definition followed by references to the older language. E.g., Hupp v. Sasser, 200 W.Va. 791, 490 S.E.2d 880 (1997).

8. See Lyrissa Barnett Lidsky, Defamation, Reputation, and the Myth of Community, 71 Wash. L. Rev. 1, 18 (1996).

9. E.g., Frinzi v. Hanson, 30 Wis.2d 271, 140 N.W.2d 259 (1966).

10. See Saunders v. Board of Directors, WHYY–TV, 382 A.2d 257 (Del.Super.1978) (to identify plaintiff as an FBI informer is not defamatory even though the plaintiff was a prison inmate at the time).

11. See Foster v. Churchill, 87 N.Y.2d 744, 665 N.E.2d 153, 642 N.Y.S.2d 583 (1996).

12. Herrmann v. Newark Morning Ledger Co., 49 N.J.Super. 551, 140 A.2d 529 (1958).

dealings with the plaintiff or to hold her in less esteem.[13] This does not mean, however, that the plaintiff must show that anyone actually believed the defamatory statement.[14] Under the presumed damages rule, it is enough that the publication is of a defamatory nature, even if no actual harm is demonstrable.

Categories and examples of defamatory content. The tests of defamation permit courts to judge each case on its facts without limiting recovery to any artificial categories. However, as a matter of description, most defamation cases involve publications imputing to the plaintiff (1) a serious crime involving moral turpitude or a felony; or (2) a character trait that makes her unfit for, or conduct incompatible with, her business, trade, or profession; (3) acts or views opposing some deeply held moral standard of the community, even when no crime has been asserted; (4) physical or other traits that show no violation at all of community standards but would nevertheless induce others to shun the plaintiff or avoid dealing with her. The first two categories are used in the law of slander for somewhat different purposes, but they also describe the patterns in a great many libel actions.[15]

Examples of the first two categories are easy to imagine. A publication asserting that the plaintiff committed murder is certainly defamatory. Publications asserting or implying that a physician is not trained in his work, or is incompetent to do it[16] or that he does medically unnecessary surgeries[17] are examples of the second category. Courts have also extended this category to include assertions that may damage the plaintiff's credit because they bear upon the plaintiff's ability or willingness to pay her debts.[18]

Examples of the third group include a few cases finding defamatory quality in assertions that the plaintiff is a liar,[19] that the plaintiff holds views deeply repugnant to many members of the community,[20] and that the plaintiff engages in or supports sexual activity that members of the

13. Burns v. McGraw–Hill Broadcasting Company, Inc., 659 P.2d 1351 (Colo.1983); Brauer v. Globe Newspaper Co., 351 Mass. 53, 217 N.E.2d 736 (1966).

14. See Plumley v. Landmark Chevrolet, Inc., 122 F.3d 308 (5th Cir.1997); but cf. Silverman v. Progressive Broadcasting, Inc., 125 N.M. 500, 964 P.2d 61 (App.1998) (publication to one who knows statement is untrue is no publication at all, perhaps treating recipient's belief in truth as the same thing).

15. See § 408.

16. Saunders v. VanPelt, 497 A.2d 1121 (Me.1985) (that psychologist not competent to work with children is defamatory).

17. Slaughter v. Friedman, 32 Cal.3d 149, 649 P.2d 886, 185 Cal.Rptr. 244 (1982).

18. E.g., Alaska Statebank v. Fairco., 674 P.2d 288 (Alaska 1983). The Fair Credit Reporting Act imposes some special duties on credit reporting agencies and also preempts some defamation claims. See 15 U.S.C.A. § 1681h; Cushman v. Trans Union Corp., 920 F.Supp. 80 (E.D.Pa.1996).

19. E.g., Paxton v. Woodward, 31 Mont. 195, 78 P. 215 (Mont. 1904). Most "liar" accusations may imply crime or unfitness for a vocation and hence may be actionable on one of those grounds, depending on the facts. See Cook v. Winfrey, 141 F.3d 322 (7th Cir.1998); Edwards v. National Audubon Soc'y, Inc., 556 F.2d 113 (2d Cir.1977).

20. Grant v. Reader's Digest Ass'n, Inc., 151 F.2d 733 (2d Cir.1945) (perhaps implying sympathy for the Communist Party); MacElree v. Philadelphia Newspapers, Inc., 544 Pa. 117, 674 A.2d 1050 (1996) ("the David Duke of Chester County").

community regard as fundamentally wrong, even when that activity is not a crime at all.[21] Similarly, the implication that an African–American politician makes deals that reduce the power of blacks in the community has been considered defamatory.[22] At least in one era, imputations of communist sympathy, though again not illegal, were held to be defamatory.[23] This third group is quite amorphous. What falls within it is likely to vary with time and place.[24] The third group can also sometimes be subsumed within the second, since any character trait that deeply offends the prevailing views may also be regarded as affecting the plaintiff's fitness for her calling.

In the fourth group are cases in which the plaintiff is not said to have done or even thought anything discreditable by anyone's standards but is held to be defamed nonetheless. For example, it may be defamatory to assert that the plaintiff is insane[25] or mentally impaired,[26] that she has a contagious disease through no fault of her own,[27] that the plaintiff is an African American,[28] or even that the she has been a victim of rape.[29] Such decisions can be troubling because they may seem to institutionalize various forms of bigotry and ignorance. On the other hand, the plaintiff's harm in a world where ignorance and bigotry exist can be very real. The defendant whose negligent or intentional falsehood causes that harm is not necessarily entitled to benefit from a judicial condemnation of the prejudice that he himself has invoked. Perhaps the plaintiff is

21. See Nazeri v. Missouri Valley College, 860 S.W.2d 303, 312 (Mo.1993) ("homosexuality is still viewed with disfavor, if not outright contempt, by a sizeable proportion of our population.... a false allegation of homosexuality is defamatory in Missouri"); Rejent v. Liberation Publications, Inc., 197 A.D.2d 240, 611 N.Y.S.2d 866 (1994); cf. Plumley v. Landmark Chevrolet, Inc., 122 F.3d 308 (5th Cir.1997) (homosexuality, where homosexual acts would be misdemeanor only). Contra as to imputations of homosexuality, Hayes v. Smith, 832 P.2d 1022, 1025 (Colo.App.1991) ("A court should not classify homosexuals with those miscreants who have engaged in actions that deserve the reprobation and scorn").

22. Wilder v. Johnson Pub. Co., Inc., 551 F.Supp. 622 (E.D.Va.1982); cf. State Press Co. v. Willett, 219 Ark. 850, 245 S.W.2d 403 (1952) (implication that African American minister vilified African Americans to please whites); but cf. Moore v. P.W. Pub. Co., 3 Ohio St.2d 183, 209 N.E.2d 412 (1965) (statement that plaintiff, a an African American, was an "Uncle Tom" was not defamatory per se).

23. Grant v. Reader's Digest Ass'n, Inc., 151 F.2d 733 (2d Cir.1945) (asserting that plaintiff was a lobbyist for the communist party); see Gregory G. Sarno, Imputation of Allegedly Objectionable Political or Social Beliefs or Principles as Defamation, 62 A.L.R.4th 314 (1989).

24. See Schermerhorn v. Rosenberg, 73 A.D.2d 276, 284, 426 N.Y.S.2d 274, 282 (1980) (charge of racism).

25. E.g., Powers v. Gastineau, 568 N.E.2d 1020 (Ind.Ct.App.1991); Annotation, Libel and Slander: Actionability of Imputing to Private Person Mental Disorder or Incapacity, or Impairment of Mental Faculties, 23 A.L.R.3d 652 (1969).

26. Brauer v. Globe Newspaper Co., 351 Mass. 53, 217 N.E.2d 736 (1966) (defendant's concession).

27. See McCune v. Neitzel, 235 Neb. 754, 457 N.W.2d 803 (1990) (assertion that plaintiff had AIDS).

28. Bowen v. Independent Pub. Co., 230 S.C. 509, 96 S.E.2d 564 (1957). But see Lyrissa Barnett Lidsky, Defamation, Reputation, and the Myth of Community, 71 Wash. L. Rev. 1, 30–31 (1996) (asserting that after 1950 such claims began to disappear but also that modern cases tend to assume that the allegation is not defamatory; apparently finding no actual decisions to that effect).

29. Youssoupoff v. Metro–Goldwyn–Mayer Pictures, Ltd., 50 T.L.R. 581, 99 A.L.R. 864 (C.A. 1934).

entitled to maintain her reputation and good relationship even with people who hold wrong-thinking opinions on particular subjects.

Examples of nondefamatory content. On the other hand, a good many publications may cause actual harm without being defamatory. Ridicule was once considered to carry a defamatory quality, although it might be privileged on occasions. Constitutional decisions, however, have protected ridicule and other communications that do not falsely assert facts.[30] The common law also rejected suits based upon name-calling,[31] although it must be apparent that in many groups name-calling can be quite destructive of the plaintiff's reputation.[32] Beyond ridicule and name-calling, many assertions can cause harm to the plaintiff's reputation but are not defamatory. It is not actionable to assert that the plaintiff is a Republican or supports Senator Hatch when she does not,[33] that a democratic candidate is not really a Democrat,[34] or that another candidate voted to raise taxes.[35] In some cases the plaintiff is falsely accused of doing something socially useful but inimical to the interests of the plaintiff's own group. In a well-known case,[36] a truck-stop owner was accused of reporting truckers' violations to the Interstate Commerce Commission, and naturally enough lost the truckers' business as a result. Since supporting the interests of the larger community was not reprehensible, the court found the communication not defamatory. This result seems to contradict the premise suggested for the third group, that the plaintiff is entitled to good relationships even with people whose own attitudes are antisocial.

Comment: limiting the issue of defamatory quality. Traditional common law gave a preeminent place to the issue of defamatory quality. If, but only if, the publication was defamatory, the plaintiff could proceed without proving falsity of the publication, without proving any fault on the defendant's part, and without proving any actual damages. The determination that a communication was defamatory was critical. Since 1964, Constitutional decisions have very largely undercut liability without fault.[37] The plaintiff is now often required to prove falsity of the publication and very often to prove actual damages. Some states have adopted some of these reforms as a matter of state law. These changes raise the question whether a determination about the defamatory char-

30. See Hustler Magazine v. Falwell, 485 U.S. 46, 108 S.Ct. 876, 99 L.Ed.2d 41 (1988).

31. E.g., Bullock v. Jeon, 226 Ga.App. 875, 877, 487 S.E.2d 692, 695 (1997) (term "mother fucker" "is a degrading insult, but it has not been interpreted as an actual accusation that the object of the remark has committed an illegal sexual act"); Finck v. City of Tea, 443 N.W.2d 632 (S.D.1989) (statement that police chief was a dumb son of a bitch not actionable). See § 420.

32. "Racist" of a white professor, "sexist" of an employer, "Uncle Tom" of an African American are among the possibilities for serious harm. See supra n. 22.

33. Cox v. Hatch, 761 P.2d 556 (Utah 1988).

34. See Frinzi v. Hanson, 30 Wis.2d 271, 140 N.W.2d 259 (1966).

35. Tatur v. Solsrud, 167 Wis.2d 266, 481 N.W.2d 657 (1992). But cf. Wilder v. Johnson Pub. Co., Inc., 551 F.Supp. 622 (E.D.Va.1982) (defamatory to assert that African-American had swung vote against black leader).

36. Connelly v. McKay, 176 Misc. 685, 28 N.Y.S.2d 327 (1941).

37. § 417.

acter of the publication is any longer necessary. A defendant who intentionally publishes a falsehood that will foreseeably harm the plaintiff is not a good candidate for special benignity of the law. The many public interests clustered under the umbrella of free speech may warrant protection, but the best way to lose focus on that issue is to try to resolve the case by asking whether the communication is defamatory. Perhaps the courts should concentrate primarily on proof of falsity, existence and extent of actual harm, serious fault of the defendant, and issues of privilege and free speech.[38]

§ 404. Interpreting Meaning and Effect

Logically speaking, courts can determine the defamatory content of a publication discussed in the last section only after they have first determined its meaning. The meaning of words, pictures or other communicative elements is critical not only on the issue of defamatory quality but also on the issue of truth or falsity.

Judge and jury. The first question is whether the words used are capable of bearing a defamatory meaning. This question is for the judge to decide. If the answer is no, judgment must go for the defendant.[1] If the answer is that reasonable people could find a defamatory meaning, the jury must decide what meaning the words conveyed and whether that meaning was defamatory.[2] Those questions are ordinarily decided on the basis of the jurors' own experience and understanding rather than on the basis of expert testimony.[3] No rule requires that all people would understand the words in a defamatory sense. The logic is that if only some people would understand the words in a defamatory sense, the damages award should be smaller than otherwise.

Meaning vs defamatory quality. The meaning of words raises a question distinct from their defamatory quality. A statement that a police officer tested positively for drugs but that his friends in the department falsified the test would clearly be a statement having the quality of defamation. But a statement that the police department did not follow required procedures in testing the same police officer may not mean the same thing at all because the department's failure to follow procedures may or may not imply falsification. The second statement

38. But cf. Lyrissa Barnett Lidsky, Defamation, Reputation, and the Myth of Community, 71 Wash. L. Rev. 1, 30–31 (1996) (in rejecting liability for actual harm courts can symbolize public opposition to, e.g., homophobic attitudes).

§ 404

1. E.g., Rippett v. Bemis, 672 A.2d 82 (Me.1996); Golub v. Enquirer/Star Group, Inc., 89 N.Y.2d 1074, 681 N.E.2d 1282, 659 N.Y.S.2d 836 (1997).

2. Belli v. Orlando Daily Newspapers, Inc., 389 F.2d 579 (5th Cir.1967); Long v. Durnil, 697 N.E.2d 100 (Ind.App.1998).

3. See Seropian v. Forman, 652 So.2d 490, 498 (Fla.App.1995) ("If influence peddling conveyed the obloquy that plaintiff suggests, that fact should be readily understood by the ordinary jury without a political scientist swearing that it does"); contra, Weller v. American Broadcasting Companies, Inc., 232 Cal.App.3d 991, 283 Cal.Rptr. 644 (1991) (permitting expert testimony). It is possible to distinguish cases like Fong v. Merena, 66 Haw. 72, 655 P.2d 875 (1982) (expert on unusual locution).

raises a problem about the meaning of the words used; once that is resolved, the question whether the words were defamatory may become quite simple.

The meaning of meaning. Under the Restatement, the meaning (as distinct from the defamatory quality) of a publication is either (1) that which the publisher intended or (2) that which the recipient of the publication reasonably understood to have been intended.[4] Under the first part of this definition, the meaning is that intended by the defendant even if that meaning differs from that conveyed by the words themselves.[5] Under the second part of the definition, the recipients' own reasonable understanding of the words controls. Courts consider not only the meaning recipients would attach to individual words,[6] but the recipients' "habits of deduction,"[7] subject, however, to judicial limits on irrational interpretations.

Factors in assessing meaning. Courts tend to consider questions of meaning (as distinct from questions of defamatory quality) by taking into account (1) the words themselves, especially where the meaning is precise and standardized, together with reasonable implications; (2) the literary context, that is, the entire message; (3) the social context, that is, events, disputes, purposes of the communication and other factors outside the publication itself; and (4) the group feelings or culture of the recipients.

Literal words and implications. Sometimes words mean what they say, no more, no less, but ambiguities and shifts in word usage over time[8] complicate interpretations. When words are ambiguous, with one possible meaning defamatory and one not, most courts permit the jury to resolve the issue. Both judges and juries are to go by the plain and natural meaning as persons of ordinary intelligence would understand it.[9] Much of the difficulty comes when the defamation, if there is any, arises from an implied meaning carried by the literal words. A literal statement that is false but not literally defamatory[10] may imply a further false statement that is entirely defamatory. Some implications are analytically inescapable. To deny a factual assertion made by the plaintiff

4. Restatement § 563.

5. See White v. Fraternal Order of Police, 909 F.2d 512, 521 (D.C.Cir.1990) (one of the publications "provided a clear signal from which a reader could conclude, rightly or wrongly, that the defamatory inference was intended or endorsed").

6. See Wildstein v. New York Post Corp., 40 Misc.2d 586, 243 N.Y.S.2d 386 (1963) (to say the police questioned plaintiff as one of the women "associated" with a murdered man may imply meretricious relationship because the word associated was placed in quotation marks).

7. Herrmann v. Newark Morning Ledger Co., 48 N.J.Super. 420, 440, 138 A.2d 61, 72 (1958)

8. See Bryson v. News America Publications, Inc., 174 Ill.2d 77, 96, 672 N.E.2d 1207, 1218, 220 Ill.Dec. 195, 206 (1996) (discussing shifted meanings of slut and fag).

9. Ramunno v. Cawley, 705 A.2d 1029 (Del.1998). Illinois, however, is a partial exception, preferring innocent constructions in many cases. See Bryson v. News America Publications, Inc., 174 Ill.2d 77, 672 N.E.2d 1207, 220 Ill.Dec. 195 (1996).

10. As to *true* statements carrying defamatory implications, see § 411.

may imply that the plaintiff was lying. If a company has a rule against extending credit, then to say that the plaintiff extended the company's credit to a customer inescapably says that the plaintiff violated company rules.[11]

Many other implications cannot be derived analytically from the published language. The defendant's statement that a former employee is no longer available to serve clients might be understood by someone to mean that the employee was discharged for wrongdoing, but the statement neither says nor implies anything of the kind.[12] When the plaintiff cannot show defamatory implication from the words themselves, however, she may be able to do so by pointing to materials outside the words, that is, to literary or social context.

Literary or internal context. Courts frequently recognize the importance of literary context by observing that a defamatory publication must be judged as a whole.[13] Literary context (as distinct from social context) is often critical in interpreting both defamatory and nondefamatory publications. Trying to focus on the defamatory words alone would be like trying to appreciate a pointillist painting by Seurat with a magnifying glass–the telling pattern would be lost in a maze of dots.[14] Beyond that, courts have recognized that context (including tone and type of publication) may show that language is asserting no defamatory fact because context can show that the words should not be understood as literal statements but as whimsy, irony, hyperbole, or meaningless invective.[15]

One context issue arises with headlines that read alone may be construed to mean something defamatory but that are not defamatory when the entire story is considered. Courts have usually said that the headline must be interpreted by reading it with the accompanying story, which may negate its defamatory meaning.[16] The point of examining context, however, is to assist in determining meaning, not to make a rule. In some cases a sensational headline (or television teaser) will overwhelm the more detailed text, while in others the nature of the headline and story are such that many readers will not read or absorb the supposedly redemptive text. Similarly, if a photograph of the plaintiff is erroneously identified as the perpetrator of a crime, the visual impact may overwhelm the more accurate identification contained in the accompanying newsstory. Not surprisingly, then, in some cases defamatory

11. Quartana v. Utterback, 789 F.2d 1297 (8th Cir.1986).

12. McCullough v. Visiting Nurse Service of Southern Maine, Inc., 691 A.2d 1201 (Me.1997).

13. See, e.g., White v. Wilkerson, 328 S.C. 179, 493 S.E.2d 345 (1997).

14. Chapin v. Knight–Ridder, Inc., 993 F.2d 1087 (4th Cir.1993).

15. E.g., Morse v. Ripken, 707 So.2d 921(Fla.App.1998); § 420.

16. E.g., Blomberg v. Cox Enterprises, Inc., 228 Ga.App. 178, 491 S.E.2d 430 (1997); but cf. Burgess v. Reformer Pub. Corp., 146 Vt. 612, 618, 508 A.2d 1359, 1362 (1986) ("If the headline is a fair index of an accurate article, it is not actionable. If it is not a fair index then the headline must be examined independently to determine whether it is actionable under general principles of libel").

headlines and photographs have been sufficient for liability in spite of qualifications that might be found in accompanying text.[17]

Social or external context. Social context of a publication includes a wide variety of facts extrinsic to the publication itself. A statement that the butcher shop sells bacon or that the woman is engaged to marry Mr. Arbuckle carries no defamatory implications on its face. But when facts extrinsic to the publication are added, serious implications may arise. If the butcher is an Orthodox Jew or the young woman is already married, the first publication implies a violation of religious tenets or practices[18] and the second implies a violation of sexual standards strongly held in many communities.[19] A number of publications that do not obviously mean anything defamatory may be understood to convey additional and defamatory meanings when the full dispute and background issues that led to publication are shown.[20] Some courts required proof of special damages when extrinsic facts are necessary to show the defamatory quality of the communication,[21] but bare meaning itself is often gleaned from the social context of the publication.

Recipient's culture or outlook. The recipient's culture, outlook, and knowledge clearly shape his reaction to the published message, but they may also shape his interpretation of the words used. This is most obviously true with the recipients' knowledge, which may vary from time to time and place to place. To say that the plaintiff is the David Duke of Chester County harbors no meaning except to those who know or think they know something about David Duke.[22] Different cultures may also attribute different meanings to words or styles of communication.

§ 405. Qualifying as Plaintiff in a Defamation Suit: Requirement that Defamation Must Be "Of and Concerning" the Plaintiff

Defamation of others. A defamatory publication is actionable only by the person or persons to whom recipients reasonably or correctly believe it refers.[1] Although a defamatory publication about B may incidentally

17. Kaelin v. Globe Communications Corp., 162 F.3d 1036 (9th Cir.1998) (jury could find that headline 17 pages from text of the story and implying plaintiff was suspected of murdering Nicole Brown Simpson, was libelous because text so far removed would not clean up the headline); Little Rock Newspapers, Inc. v. Fitzhugh, 330 Ark. 561, 954 S.W.2d 914 (1997) (wrong photo); Schermerhorn v. Rosenberg, 73 A.D.2d 276, 426 N.Y.S.2d 274 (1980) (headline); Sprouse v. Clay Communication, Inc., 158 W.Va. 427, 211 S.E.2d 674 (1975) (where the publisher systematically, repeatedly, and intentionally printed misleading political headlines). See Rodney A. Smolla, Law of Defamation § 4.07 (looseleaf regularly supplemented).

18. See Braun v. Armour & Co., 254 N.Y. 514, 173 N.E. 845 (1930) (cause of action stated).

19. Sydney v. MacFadden Newspaper Pub. Corp., 242 N.Y. 208, 151 N.E. 209 (1926).

20. E.g., Ramunno v. Cawley, 705 A.2d 1029 (Del.1998) (long lasting community dispute).

21. See § 409.

22. See MacElree v. Philadelphia Newspapers, Inc. 544 Pa. 117, 126, 674 A.2d 1050, 1055 (1996) (".... the statement could be construed to mean that appellant was acting in a racist manner").

§ 405

1. Restatement § 564.

harm A, A has no defamation claim resulting solely from defamation of another.[2] As Professor Smolla says, there is no vicarious defamation.[3] For example, a publication about A's spouse may harm A because of the association, but A is not defamed merely because her spouse is.[4] The commissioner of police is not defamed by defamatory criticisms of police under the commissioner's command,[5] nor are all police officers defamed when one is.[6] In a North Carolina case, the allegation was that the defendant had faked and published a disgusting and quite defamatory photograph of a teenager. The young man's parents had no claim.[7] There are of course cases in which defamation of one person defames another as well. That might be the case if the publication falsely accuses B of fraudulently depositing government funds into the business account of the A–B partnership; such a statement clearly defames B and perhaps by implication defames A as well.

Identity of defamed person. The problem commonly raised is that the publication does not fully or explicitly identify the plaintiff as the person defamed. Depending upon the surrounding facts or evidence internal to the publication, recipients of the defamatory material may reasonably identify the plaintiff as the person referred to even if the plaintiff is not named or is incorrectly named.[8] Likewise, if the publication refers to another person of the same name, some recipients may reasonably believe it refers to the plaintiff and not to others.[9] Sometimes the words almost unavoidably implicates an unnamed plaintiff. To say that home buyers were swindled almost certainly is to be understood as asserting that the seller was a swindler.[10] In addition, the internal context of the publication may suffice to identify the plaintiff, as where in one portion of a broadcast the defendant mentions the plaintiff by name as a former

2. See Johnson v. Southwestern Newspapers Corp., 855 S.W.2d 182 (Tex.App. 1993).

3. Rodney A. Smolla, Law of Defamation § 4.11 [2].

4. A may, however, have a loss of consortium claim attendant to the accused spouse's defamation claim, provided such loss can be proved. See Hudnall v. Sellner, 800 F.2d 377 (4th Cir.1986).

5. New York Times v. Sullivan, 376 U.S. 254, 84 S.Ct. 710, 11 L.Ed.2d 686 (1964).

6. Arcand v. Evening Call Pub. Co., 567 F.2d 1163 (1st Cir.1977). See the topic Group Defamation below.

7. See Gillikin v. Springle, 254 N.C. 240, 118 S.E.2d 611 (1961) and Gillikin v. Bell, 254 N.C. 244, 118 S.E.2d 609 (1961); cf. Sarwer v. Conde Nast Publications, Inc., 237 A.D.2d 191, 654 N.Y.S.2d 768 (1997) (not defamatory to assert that the plaintiff is a victim of child abuse; article was directed at the plaintiff's father, not at plaintiff).

8. Donati v. Queens Ledger Newspaper Group, 240 A.D.2d 696, 659 N.Y.S.2d 306 (1997) (Wislowski for Wesolowski with other identifying factors).

9. Cf. Little Rock Newspapers, Inc. v. Fitzhugh, 330 Ark. 561, 954 S.W.2d 914 (1997) (photograph of the wrong Fitzhugh in article on Whitewater investigation). Fictional names that happen to be identical to the plaintiffs do not call for liability unless something specific suggests that the name is not in fact fictional. See Smith v. Huntington Pub. Co., 410 F.Supp. 1270 (D.Ohio 1975), aff'd per curiam, 535 F.2d 1255.

10. Grinaldo v. Meusburger, 34 App. Div.2d 586, 307 N.Y.S.2d 974 (1970); cf. Taj Mahal Travel, Inc. v. Delta Airlines, Inc., 164 F.3d 186 (3d Cir.1998) (Delta's refusal to honor plaintiff's airline ticket, purchased from plaintiff travel agency, coupled with its statement that the ticket had been stolen was sufficient to permit jury to conclude that statement defamed plaintiff, although plaintiff was not named).

employee and in a later portion of the broadcast refers, without names, to employees discharged for stealing.[11]

Unless the publication identifies the plaintiff or carries internal clues to the plaintiff's identity, extrinsic evidence will be required to show that the publication was reasonably or correctly understood as referring to her.[12] Such extrinsic facts, if known to at least one recipient of the publication, may demonstrate that it referred to the plaintiff.[13] For example, when the defendants circulated a cartoon in the workplace depicting a sexual act between an identified man and an unidentified woman, the plaintiff was able to introduce evidence of workplace discussions preceding the cartoon that would lead people in the workplace to think she was the woman in the cartoon, who was depicted in jeans, which the plaintiff also wore.[14]

Even works of fiction may be understood as referring to the plaintiff.[15] In *Bindrim v. Mitchell*,[16] the setting for a novel was a nude therapy group conducted to help people shed inhibitions and led by a therapist called Dr. Simon Herford in the novel. Dr. Herford was presented as using crude, unprofessional terms and otherwise in an unpleasant light. Although Dr. Herford was described as "a fat Santa Claus type with long white hair" a real nude therapist was permitted to recover on the ground that it referred to him. The claim was supported by evidence that the real nude therapy sessions attended by the author were closely parallel to scenes in the novel.

Whether the extrinsic evidence, once admitted, establishes a reference to the plaintiff is a matter of factual analysis and judgment and in many cases the plaintiff is unable to establish that the publication is of and concerning her.

§ 406. Qualifying as the Plaintiff in a Defamation Suit: Defaming the Plaintiff by Defaming a Group

An Illinois criminal statute against group defamation was once upheld[1] and "veggie libel laws" create claims for all producers of a

11. Riss v. Anderson, 304 F.2d 188 (8th Cir.1962).

12. See, e.g., Smith v. Long Island Youth Guidance, Inc., 181 A.D.2d 820, 581 N.Y.S.2d 401 (App.Div.1992) (assertion that girl had sold herself on the street from the age of eleven to support a crack habit did not imply that the habit was her mother's in the absence of extrinsic evidence).

13. E.g., Marr v. Putnam, 196 Or. 1, 246 P.2d 509 (1952) ("radio racket" describing repairers who picked up radios and did not return them could refer to plaintiffs who did repairs on a pick-up basis).

14. Linebaugh v. Sheraton Michigan Corp., 198 Mich.App. 335, 497 N.W.2d 585 (1993).

15. Bryson v. News America Publications, Inc., 174 Ill.2d 77, 672 N.E.2d 1207, 220 Ill.Dec. 195 (1996) (plaintiff identified 25 similarities between herself and the fictional character described as a slut; jury question whether plaintiff was referred to).

16. Bindrim v. Mitchell, 92 Cal.App.3d 61, 155 Cal.Rptr. 29 (1979), disapproved on other grounds, McCoy v. Hearst Corp., 42 Cal.3d 835, 727 P.2d 711, 231 Cal.Rptr. 518 (1986).

§ 406

1. Beauharnais v. Illinois, 343 U.S. 250, 72 S.Ct. 725, 96 L.Ed. 919 (1952). The case was decided at a time when it was thought that defamation was not entitled to First Amendment protection, so the case may be

general food that is falsely said to be unsafe.[2] Otherwise, however, defamation of large groups, for example by claims that lawyers are shysters,[3] is almost never actionable by the group itself. Nor do individual members of large groups have a defamation claim.[4] These rules rest partly on practicality but more significantly on a recognition that much group abuse is meaningless invective. It is true that charismatic speakers may induce crowds to accept perverse and unfounded beliefs without ever asserting a provable fact. But the optimism behind free speech guarantees holds that unless more than invective is asserted, the problem is to be solved by speech that appeals to the best rather than the worst in the recipients and not by repression of speakers. That policy and the rule that defamation of another person gives the plaintiff no claim, pretty well rules out recovery based upon general statements about large groups.

When it comes to very small groups, specific defamation (as opposed to general condemnatory statements) about the entire group may conceivably defame each member. It has been said that in groups of 25 or more, the defamation about the group cannot be of and concerning individual members of it.[5] However, in an Oklahoma case, statements construed to mean that all members of the football team take illegal drugs were held to defame members of the team, even though the team included at least 60 persons.[6] The same result would not follow with every group of 60 persons. As the Oklahoma Court later noted, several other factors are important in determining whether an individual member of the group is referred to. The intensity of suspicion, the prominence of the group, and the prominence of the individual plaintiff within the group all bear the question whether the plaintiff is sufficiently identified.[7]

Statements defamatory of only some members of a small group may also be actionable. The question is whether suspicion is cast upon all and hence upon the individual plaintiff.[8] Again, however, intensity of suspicion and other factors may rule out any reference to the plaintiff or to all members of the small group. To say that one member of the police force of 21 officers locked himself and a female companion in the back seat of a squad car and had to radio for help is not to cast suspicion upon all or any substantial suspicion upon any one, nor does it suggest that the conduct of one is typical of all.[9]

outdated. However, with current interest in special punishments for hate speech, the decision may be resurrected before it is officially declared dead. See Rodney Smolla, Law of Defamation § 4.10.

2. E.g., N.D. Cent. Code § 32–44–03. These statutes may be vulnerable to constitutional attack.

3. Cf. Brock v. Thompson, 948 P.2d 279 (Okla.1997) (reflecting on trial lawyers).

4. Restatement § 564A.

5. Thomas v. Jacksonville Television, Inc., 699 So.2d 800 (Fla.App.1997).

6. Fawcett Publications, Inc. v. Morris, 377 P.2d 42 (Okla.1962).

7. McCullough v. Cities Service Co., 676 P.2d 833, 52 A.L.R.4th 609 (Okla. 1984).

8. Neiman–Marcus v. Lait, 13 F.R.D. 311 (D.N.Y.1952) (statement that most of the salesmen, a group of 25, are fairies is actionable by each).

9. Arcand v. Evening Call Pub. Co., 567 F.2d 1163 (1st Cir.1977).

§ 407. Qualifying as the Plaintiff in a Defamation Suit: Defamation of Corporations, Government Entities and the Dead

Corporations; injurious falsehood or disparagement. Corporations and other businesses can and do recover for libel or slander when they have been defamed by charges such as crime or fraud.[1] But defamatory charges commonly made against individuals–adultery, for example–have little relevance to corporations and many of the imputations about corporations are harmful without being defamatory. When the publication asserts that the corporate product is defective, inadequate, or harmful without asserting personal defamation, the traditional view regards the claim as essentially different from the claim for defamation.[2] The same is true if the publication merely says that the plaintiff has gone out of business.[3] This different claim goes under the general name of injurious falsehood.[4] When the publication attacks a product, it is also called trade libel or commercial disparagement.[5] When the publication attacks title to property rather than quality of a product, the claim is likely to be called slander of title.[6]

In all these cases the plaintiff is required to prove much more than was required in a traditional libel claim. To sustain a claim for injurious falsehood (in any of its forms), the plaintiff must prove not only the derogatory publication but also (1) fault, (2) a provably false statement, and (3) pecuniary damages.[7] These rules are more demanding than the traditional rules for libel and somewhat more demanding than the developing contemporary rules for libel as well. The plaintiff in an injurious falsehood claim may be required to prove a knowing falsehood,[8] while the plaintiff who is not a public figure is not invariably required to prove any fault at all or if required to prove fault may be permitted to recover upon proof of negligence.[9] Likewise, the plaintiff in an injurious falsehood claim must prove not only damages, but pecuniary damages, a restriction that does not apply in many claims for libel or even in all claims for slander.

On the other hand, with the expansion of the tort of interference with contract and business prospects, many injurious falsehood claims

§ 407

1. Harwood Pharmacal Co. v. National Broadcasting Co., 9 N.Y.2d 460, 174 N.E.2d 602, 214 N.Y.S.2d 725 (1961).

2. See National Ref. Co. v. Benzo Gas Motor Fuel Co., 20 F.2d 763 (8th Cir.1927).

3. Ratcliffe v. Evans, [1892] 2 Q.B. 524 (C.A.).

4. A good summary of the tort's development, along with recommendations for its use, is found in Paul T. Hayden, A Goodly Apple Rotten at the Heart: Commercial Disparagement in Comparative Advertising as Common–Law Tortious Unfair Competition, 76 Iowa L. Rev. 67 (1990).

5. E.g., Auvil v. CBS "60 Minutes", 67 F.3d 816 (9th Cir.1995).

6. E.g., Rorvig v. Douglas, 123 Wash.2d 854, 873 P.2d 492 (1994).

7. Restatement § 623A. The Restatement requires a knowing or reckless falsehood coupled with harm that is intended or foreseeable.

8. Auvil v. CBS "60 Minutes," 67 F.3d 816 (9th Cir.1995).

9. See § 417.

may be subsumed in those torts.[10] In addition, food suppliers have aggressively lobbied for and obtained legislation sometimes called veggie libel laws or sirloin slander bills. These statutes, using varied language, permit claims based upon false statements about food products. If the defendant publishes a statement that apples are sprayed with a product that can cause cancer and it turns out that the evidence does not support the cancer fear, the statute may permit *all* apple producers to sue for damages.[11] The statutes jeopardize all public discussion of health risks and consequently raise quite serious constitutional issues. Particular statutes differ, but to the extent that they permit a claim by individuals who are not referred to, fail to require knowing or reckless falsehood, put the burden of proving truth upon the defendant, or make opinion actionable they run the risk of constitutional infringement.[12] If the statutes do not run these constitutional risks, they may add little or nothing to the common law of injurious falsehood.

Government entities as plaintiffs. Few cases have been brought by government entities against private individuals. The Supreme Court, recalling the use of criminal libel by the Star Chamber, held that an "impersonal attack on governmental operations" could not constitutionally form the basis for suit.[13] It may be arguable that a false publication of fact harmful financially to a governmental entity should be actionable, if not as defamation then as injurious falsehood. However, the Illinois Supreme Court rejected such a claim, saying that the action "is out of tune with the American spirit, and has no place in American jurisprudence."[14] Somewhat analogously a California court held that a city could not sue for malicious prosecution.[15]

Defamation of the dead. No action lies for defamation of the dead.[16] This means that neither the estate of the deceased person nor her

10. See Chapter 32.

11. N.D. Cent. Code. § 32–44–03. In Auvil v. CBS "60 Minutes," 67 F.3d 816 (9th Cir.1995) suit was brought on behalf of 4700 apple growers, who were unable to show sufficient evidence of falsity. In Texas Beef Group v. Winfrey, 11 F.Supp.2d 858 (N.D.Tex.1998) the plaintiffs were a number of Texas cattle growers suing talk show hostess Oprah Winfrey over a discussion of mad cow disease, although neither the growers nor even the State of Texas was mentioned in the discussion. The judge dismissed the statutory claims.

12. Many law review notes have discussed constitutional issues. E.g., Julie K. Harders, the Unconstitutionality of Iowa's Proposed Agricultural Food Products Act and Similar Veggie Libel Laws, 3 Drake J. Agric. L. 251 (1998); Julie J. Srochi, Note, Must Peaches Be Preserved at All Costs? Questioning the Constitutional Validity of Georgia's Perishable Product Disparagement Law, 12 Ga. St. U. L. Rev. 1223 (1996); Jennifer J. Mattson, Note, North Dakota Jumps on the Agricultural Disparagement Law Bandwagon by Enacting Legislation to Meet a Concern Already Actionable under State Defamation Law and Failing to Heed Constitutionality Concerns, 74 N.D. L. Rev. 89 (1998).

13. New York Times v. Sullivan, 376 U.S. 254, 84 S.Ct. 710, 11 L.Ed.2d 686, 95 A.L.R.2d 1412 (1964).

14. Chicago v. Tribune Co., 307 Ill. 595, 610, 139 N.E. 86, 91, 28 A.L.R. 1368 (1923); see J. A. Bryant, Jr., Right of Governmental Entity to Maintain Action for Defamation, 45 A.L.R.3d 1315 (1972) (reflecting general accord that no such action will be entertained).

15. City of Long Beach v. Bozek, 31 Cal.3d 527, 645 P.2d 137, 183 Cal.Rptr. 86 (1982), reiterated after vacation, City of Long Beach v. Bozek, 33 Cal.3d 727, 661 P.2d 1072, 190 Cal.Rptr. 918 (1983).

16. Gillikin v. Bell, 254 N.C. 244, 118 S.E.2d 609 (1961).

relatives can recover for statements made after her death. Words about deceased persons may sometimes defame the living, and if so the living person will have her own claim for defamation. This might occur, for example, if the publication asserts that the plaintiff bribed the deceased during his lifetime, since such a statement asserts a crime both by the deceased and by the living person. But living people are not defamed when they are not personally implicated, so to accuse the deceased of a crime in which her relatives took no part defames no one.[17]

Survival of defamation actions. As to defamation published before death, whether suit is permitted depends upon the state's survival statute. The common law rule terminated tort actions at the death of either party. Survival statutes changed that rule with respect to claims arising from personal injury and some have done so with respect to defamation claims as well, thus permitting the estate to sue for a defamatory publication made during the deceased's lifetime.[18] Other survival statutes, however, have continued the common law rule with respect to claims for libel and slander. Where that is the case, the claim of a person defamed during her lifetime is terminated at her death,[19] unless, as a little authority has said, the survival statute is unconstitutional insofar as it prescribes a special rule for defamation.[20]

§ 408. The Slander Rules

The damages difference. The traditional common law made much of the distinction between libel and slander. All libel was originally actionable without proof of special damages.[1] Put differently, damages were presumed in the case of libel. General slander, sometimes called slander per quod, however, was not actionable at all unless it caused the plaintiff pecuniary loss, often called special harm or special damages. Harm to reputation that did not show itself in pecuniary loss was insufficient in the case of slander per quod. At the same time, several categories of slander were treated like libel so that damages were in effect presumed. This kind of categorical slander is called slander per se, a term that means the plaintiff need not prove pecuniary loss and that contrasts it with slander per quod.

17. Cf. Decker v. Princeton Packet, Inc., 224 N.J.Super. 726, 541 A.2d 292 (1988) (not defamatory to print obituary of living plaintiff, and children had no action either); Gugliuzza v. K.C.M.C., Inc., 606 So.2d 790 (La.1992) (rejecting a mental anguish claim based on defamation of the dead). Cases on invasion of privacy of the living by dealing with effects of the dead are divided. See Reid v. Pierce County, 136 Wash.2d 195, 961 P.2d 333 (1998) (individual county employees using autopsy photos for their own purposes).

18. See, e.g., Plumley v. Landmark Chevrolet, Inc., 122 F.3d 308 (5th Cir.1997). The results are mixed when the statute does not specify defamation actions either way. See Francis M. Dougherty, Annotation, Defamation Action as Surviving Plaintiff's Death, Under Statute Not Specifically Covering Action, 42 A.L.R.4th 272 (1986).

19. Innes v. Howell Corp., 76 F.3d 702 (6th Cir.1996) (upholding constitutionality of Kentucky statute).

20. Moyer v. Phillips, 462 Pa. 395, 341 A.2d 441 (1975); cf. Thompson v. Estate of Petroff, 319 N.W.2d 400 (Minn.1982) (survival statute was irrational in not permitting survival for intentional torts).

§ 408

1. Restatement § 569.

Distinguishing slander from libel. The core distinction between slander and libel has it that slander is oral, libel is written. That difference is not wholly adequate to distinguish the two forms of defamation today. The Restatement invites courts in close cases to consider several factors: whether the publication is in tangible form, whether it has the potential harmful qualities characteristic of written words, whether it is widely disseminated, and whether it was premeditated.[2] A yes answer in each case tends to indicate that the publication is libel rather than slander. So libel today includes not only writing but all forms of communications embodied in some physical form such as movie film or video tapes, and mass communications through radio broadcasts even if they are not produced from a written script.[3] Most communications by computer are no doubt in the category of libel.[4] Reading aloud from written text may constitute libel.[5] An oral defamatory statement may also result in a libel if the speaker knows, intends, or foresees that it will be reduced to writing or other permanent form, and it is in fact published in such a form. For example, a speaker at a meeting who knows his words are being transcribed and will be printed in the newspaper may be subjected to a libel suit rather than one for slander only.[6]

Slander includes unamplified oral communications and transitory defamatory gestures.[7] The slander-libel distinction prompts endless analysis of close cases such as the loudspeaker in the stadium filled with 50,000 people, but the whole classification process is usually unsatisfactory because it leads to extreme damages rules no matter what classification is adopted.

Slander per se. If the publication is classed as slander rather than libel, a subsidiary classification is required. If the slander is the kind called "per se," then after all it is treated more like libel and the plaintiff will not be required to prove pecuniary damages. In fact, as in traditional libel cases, the plaintiff will be permitted to recover damages without proof of any harm to reputation at all.[8] Slander per se is that which charges a (1) serious criminal offense or one of moral turpitude,[9] (2) a "loathsome" and communicable disease,[10] (3) any matter incompati-

2. Restatement § 568.

3. Restatement § 568A. Statutes, however, may limit the liability of broadcasters to special or actual damages. E.g., N.Y. Civ. Rights Law § 75.

4. See David J. Loundy, E-law 4: Computer Information Systems Law and System Operator Liability, 21 SEATTLE U. L. REV. 1075 (1998). Operators of interactive systems are protected against liability for defamation posted by others. 47 U.S.C.A. § 230(c)(1).

5. See Christy v. Stauffer Publications, Inc., 437 S.W.2d 814 (Tex.1969).

6. See Cohen v. Bowdoin, 288 A.2d 106 (Me.1972) (oral statements reduced to minutes of meeting then passed to newspaper); Bell v. Simmons, 247 N.C. 488, 101 S.E.2d 383 (1958), citing Restatement of Torts § 577 Cmt. f.

7. Restatement § 568 (2).

8. See Biondi v. Nassimos, 300 N.J.Super. 148, 153, 692 A.2d 103, 106 (1997).

9. E.g., Donovan v. Fiumara, 114 N.C.App. 524, 442 S.E.2d 572 (1994); Restatement § 571.

10. McCune v. Neitzel, 235 Neb. 754, 457 N.W.2d 803 (1990) (AIDS); Restatement § 572.

ble with business, trade, profession, or office,[11] and, sometimes, (4) serious sexual misconduct.[12]

Each of these per se categories can prompt its own litigation without getting any closer to the real merits of the claim or defense.[13] Lawyers may find themselves debating whether a charge that the plaintiff is a voyeur charges a crime of moral turpitude.[14] Sometimes the result of working in these categories is surprising. To say that the plaintiff has mob connections and might order a hit upon an adversary does not count as an accusation of crime, for example, because it does not assert that a crime has in fact been committed.[15]

Business, trade or profession. The third category deals with matters incompatible with trade, business, or profession. The category is especially indeterminate and must be defined largely as cases arise. It is probably fair to say that it includes any charges of seriously unprofessional conduct or serious departure from professional ethics,[16] but that a mere conclusion or opinion that the plaintiff is incompetent in her job, without any express or implied assertion of facts, will probably not be accepted as a sufficient basis for a defamation claim.[17]

It has been suggested that either the words or the circumstances must connect the defamatory assertion with the plaintiff's vocation,[18] but if that is too strong, it is at least true that the statements must reflect upon the proper conduct of the business, trade, or profession and not merely upon the plaintiff's general characteristics. For example, the accusation that the plaintiff, a landlord, had threatened the defendant's life and tried to bribe a police officer does not reflect upon the plaintiff's status as a landlord and hence is not actionable without proof of pecuniary damages.[19] Courts seem to be looking for conduct that might be deemed to reflect character or at least habitual misconduct rather than a passing peccadillo. To that end, New York has said that a publication charging professional ignorance or mistake on a single occasion would not be actionable without proof of pecuniary damages.[20] But

11. E.g., Restatement § 573.

12. See, e.g., French v. Jadon, Inc., 911 P.2d 20 (Alaska 1996). Some courts have treated assertions of homosexuality in this category. See cases cited in § 403. At one time the category included slanders imputing unchastity to a woman.

13. Cf. Rodney A. Smolla, Law of Defamation § 7.08.

14. See Gosden v. Louis, 116 Ohio App.3d 195, 687 N.E.2d 481 (1996) (voyeurism might not be crime of moral turpitude but if in writing the charge of any crime would be libel and actionable).

15. Biondi v. Nassimos, 300 N.J.Super. 148, 692 A.2d 103 (1997); cf. Restatement § 571, cmt. c.

16. See White v. Wilkerson, 328 S.C. 179, 493 S.E.2d 345 (1997) (attorney said to have taken over 90% of a settlement); Becker v. Zellner, 292 Ill.App.3d 116, 684 N.E.2d 1378, 226 Ill.Dec. 175 (1997) (paralegals said to have billed $45,000 for a worthless five-page memo).

17. Finck v. City of Tea, 443 N.W.2d 632 (S.D.1989) (statement that police chief was a dumb son of a bitch and incompetent was opinion only and not actionable).

18. Gunsberg v. Roseland Corp., 34 Misc.2d 220, 225 N.Y.S.2d 1020 (1962).

19. Liberman v. Gelstein, 80 N.Y.2d 429, 605 N.E.2d 344, 590 N.Y.S.2d 857 (1992).

20. November v. Time, Inc., 13 N.Y.2d 175, 194 N.E.2d 126, 128, 244 N.Y.S.2d 309 (1963). In Holder Const. Co. v. Ed Smith & Sons, 124 Ga.App. 89, 182 S.E.2d 919, 51 A.L.R. 3d 1296 (1971) the court carried this rule over to a case of libel.

sometimes a single action can reflect character or a gross departure from the conduct required by a profession, so the single instance rule is probably not a general rule at all. Even New York courts tend to recognize that a single instance can sometimes show habitual behavior or character.[21]

The special damages rules for slander per quod. Unless the slander falls in one of the four categories, the plaintiff must plead and prove "special harm," meaning specifically identified pecuniary harm resulting from the slander.[22] "Special harm" in this sense is not the same as "actual harm," which includes any actual loss to reputation, whether pecuniary harm results or not.[23] As a result of the special harm rule, the plaintiff who suffers no loss of anything of pecuniary value but suffers a proven loss of reputation and resulting emotional harm has no slander claim at all.[24] The rule equally implies, however, that if the plaintiff can prove some slight pecuniary loss, she recovers all her damages, including loss of reputation and emotional harm. Pecuniary loss is easy to find in the loss of a job[25] and in the loss of customers or business income[26] but it can take the form of "any material loss capable of being measured in money", such as the loss of a free cruise.[27] Anticipated loss that has not actually occurred at the time of trial, however, is insufficient to permit the slander per quod action.[28]

Reform. Both the damages rules for libel and those for slander are extreme in different ways. The libel rules might be reformed by eliminating the presumption of harm and requiring some evidence that actual harm occurred. The slander rules might be reformed in the other direction, by permitting the plaintiff to prove a real loss of reputation even if it did not result in pecuniary harm, at least where the plaintiff

21. E.g., cf. Daniel Goldreyer, Ltd. v. Van de Wetering, 217 A.D.2d 434, 630 N.Y.S.2d 18 (1995) (statement that restorer of painting masterpiece used house paint and a roller; single instance rule did not bar the claim); Rutman v. Giedel, 67 A.D.2d 662, 411 N.Y.S.2d 960 (1979) (statement that officer was drunk on duty); but cf. Larson v. Albany Med. Center, 252 A.D.2d 936, 676 N.Y.S.2d 293 (App. Div. 1998) (statement that nurse refused to assist in a medical procedure not actionable without special damages).

22. A general allegation of economic loss is usually insufficient. See Becker v. Zellner, 292 Ill.App.3d 116, 684 N.E.2d 1378, 226 Ill.Dec. 175 (1997); contra, Johnson v. Bollinger, 86 N.C.App. 1, 356 S.E.2d 378 (1987). Authorities on special harm in analogous libel per quod and injurious falsehood cases have sometimes insisted that the plaintiff must prove such items as the loss of named customers.

23. Actual harm is required by the constitutional decisions to establish certain defamation claims. See § 422.

24. Terwilliger v. Wands, 17 N.Y. 54 (1858); Scott v. Harrison, 215 N.C. 427, 2 S.E.2d 1(1939); Restatement § 575, cmt. b.

25. Leonardo v. Sley System Garages, Inc., 166 Pa.Super. 633, 74 A.2d 712 (1950).

26. Claims for lost profits and the like arise equally in slander per se, libel and injurious falsehood cases, which provide many of the authorities on evidence required. See, e.g., Erick Bowman Remedy Co. v. Jensen Salsbery Labs., Inc., 17 F.2d 255 (8th Cir.1926) (injurious falsehood, with emphasis on the need to show loss of specific customers in some cases); Schoen v. Washington Post, 246 F.2d 670 (App.D.C. 1957) (libel with claims of lost customers; plaintiff would be required to segregate losses due to true portion of the publication); Van Gundy v. Wilson, 84 Ga.App. 429, 66 S.E.2d 93 (1951) (slander per se as to eating establishment but not as to other businesses operated in the same place).

27. Restatement § 575 and Ill. 4.

28. Scott v. Harrison, 215 N.C. 427, 2 S.E.2d 1(1939).

must also prove that the defendant was guilty of publishing a knowing, reckless, or negligent falsehood. Major commentators have suggested one or more of these reforms[29] and Kansas[30] and Missouri[31] courts have said that proof of actual damages is now required in all cases, including cases traditionally designated as slander per se cases. Some other states may be open to similar reforms.[32]

§ 409. Libel Per Quod: When Special Harm Is Required in Libel Cases

Rule that All Libel Is Libel Per Se

The common law rule was that all libel was actionable without proof of harm; harm to reputation was conclusively presumed once defamatory content was published. In addition, the plaintiff could of course recover for any actual damages proved, including actual loss of reputation and distress, whether or not the plaintiff suffered pecuniary loss. The rule can be expressed by saying that all libel is libel per se. That remains the rule followed in most courts[1] and by the Restatement[2] where the constitutional decisions do not compel a different result. The rule authorizes the jury to award substantial damages even if no loss of reputation has been proved,[3] although the defendant may present evidence tending to show that damages were limited.[4]

The Rule of Libel Per Quod

However, in the 19th century, a number of courts began to say that some libel was "per quod," meaning that after all the plaintiff would be required in libel as well as in slander cases to prove pecuniary loss in order to recover. But these courts did not provide a parallel set of rules for libel and slander. Slander per quod was any slander not falling into one of the special categories, while libel per quod was any libel that was not defamatory "on its face."[5]

29. David A. Anderson, Reputation, Compensation, and Proof, 25 WM. & MARY L. REV. 747 (1984) (requiring actual harm which could sometimes be inferred from other facts); See also RODNEY A. SMOLLA, LAW OF DEFAMATION § 7.08.

30. Zoeller v. American Fam. Mut. Ins. Co., 17 Kan.App.2d 223, 834 P.2d 391 (1992).

31. Nazeri v. Missouri Valley College, 860 S.W.2d 303 (Mo.1993).

32. Ward v. Zelikovsky, 136 N.J. 516, 643 A.2d 972 (1994) (leaving open the question of reform). In Illinois, libel and slander are "unified" but this is hardly a reform, since that entails importing the slander per se categories into libel cases and then combining the that with Illinois unique innocent construction rule. See Bryson v. News America Publications, Inc., 174 Ill.2d 77, 672 N.E.2d 1207, 220 Ill.Dec. 195 (1996).

§ 409

1. Vanover v. Kansas City Life Ins. Co., 553 N.W.2d 192 (N.D.1996) (repudiating earlier authority supporting the per quod rule); Ryan v. Herald Ass'n, Inc., 152 Vt. 275, 566 A.2d 1316 (1989) (recognizing presumed damages when constitutional limits do not apply to the facts).

2. Restatement § 569.

3. See Poulston v. Rock, 251 Va. 254, 467 S.E.2d 479 (1996) (trial judge erred in reducing award from $10,000 to $1,000 merely because no harm had been shown).

4. Williams v. District Court, 866 P.2d 908 (Colo.1993)

5. But confusion is the norm for defamation cases; some courts now describe "defamation per se" with reference to the slander categories even when the publication counts as a libel. E.g., Bryson v. News

For example, if the defendant published a statement that the plaintiff was the only person present at T's home during the entire day yesterday, the statement on its face seems innocuous. However, if the recipient of the statement knows that T was murdered at his home during the day yesterday, the statement can be understood to accuse the plaintiff of murder. Under a libel per quod rule the plaintiff would be required to prove pecuniary harm even though the statement was in the form of libel and when properly understood accused the plaintiff of a felony.[6]

It may be that only a few courts have ever adopted the rule of libel per quod and that many of the cases that were once identified with the rule were actually cases of injurious falsehood, where pecuniary harm is regularly required.[7] Whether few or many, the cases have managed to add technicalities and complications to a body of law already known as a lawyer's labyrinth.

One line of confusion turns on the ambiguity in the per quod rule itself. That rule only applies to require proof of special harm when a publication is not defamatory on its face. There are three distinct ways in which someone might think that the publication is not "defamatory on its face." These ways correspond to three types of additional material that might be adduced to show actionable defamation. These three kinds of additional material are roughly but inconsistently associated with now-obsolete pleading terms, *innuendo*, *inducement* and *colloquium* more or less in this order:

> (1) The reader might not know the defamatory meaning of words used because they were technical or unusual usage or because the words were ambiguous and needed explanatory clarification.
>
> (2) The reader might not be able to see that anything wrong was charged against the plaintiff until additional, extrinsic facts were shown. The statement that the plaintiff spent the day at T's house is like this; the defamatory meaning can only be understood when the fact that T was murdered is shown.
>
> (3) The reader might understand the words and see their defamatory import but might not be able to determine who was defamed by reading the publication alone. But again, extrinsic facts might be adduced to show that the plaintiff was the person referred to.

America Publications, Inc., 174 Ill.2d 77, 672 N.E.2d 1207, 220 Ill.Dec. 195 (1996).

6. See Ilitzky v. Goodman, 57 Ariz. 216, 112 P.2d 860 (1941); Bryson v. News America Publications, Inc., 174 Ill.2d 77, 103, 672 N.E.2d 1207, 1221, 220 Ill.Dec. 195, 209 (1996) ("a per quod claim is appropriate where the defamatory character of the statement is not apparent on its face, and resort to extrinsic circumstances is necessary to demonstrate its injurious meaning").

7. See Laurence H. Eldredge, The Law of Defamation § 24 (1978). Prosser and Eldredge heavily debated the question of "how many" authorities support the rule. See Prosser, Libel Per Quod, 46 Va. L. Rev. 839 (1960); Eldredge, The Spruious Rule of Libel Per Quod, 79 Harv. L. Rev. 733 (1966); Prosser, More Libel Per Quod, 79 Harv. L. Rev. 1629 (1966). See also Henn, "Libel-by-Extrinsic Fact," 47 Cornell L. Q. 14 (1961).

The most obvious case for applying the libel per quod rule–requiring proof of pecuniary harm–would be the middle or inducement case. On its face the statement is harmful to no one and the most conscientious editor would have no reason to question it. In the world of strict liability, courts might naturally seek to provide a little relief for faultless publishers of apparently innocent material.

The least likely case for applying the per quod rule was the first case, an ambiguous publication that could be understood both in a defamatory sense and in an innocent sense. In *MacLeod v. Tribune Pub. Co., Inc.*[8] Justice Traynor firmly rejected the idea that the per quod rule would apply to a publication merely because it was ambiguous and capable of an innocent construction. Illinois, however, has a long line of jurisprudence that prefers an innocent construction. That state currently insists that if an innocent construction is reasonably possible, special damages must be proven.[9]

A poor candidate for the per quod rule's special damages requirement is the case of a publication that contains plainly defamatory material but does not identify the person defamed. An editor considering such matter before publication would realize that it is derogatory of someone and that some readers might identify the person even though the publication itself does not do so. The editor is accordingly on notice that the if the published statements are false, a reputation may be harmed. In fact, however, courts have seldom distinguished carefully among these different senses in which a publication is not defamatory on its face. Some authority may approve application of the per quod rule to situations like this one.[10]

Rationales for a per quod rule are also poorly developed. One possibility, suggested above, is that in one type of libel per quod–when extrinsic facts are required to show any defamatory meaning at all–the publisher is not likely to be at fault and perhaps should not be held strictly liable unless the plaintiff suffers some special damages. Another is that when libel is not apparent on the face of the publication, the plaintiff is likely to suffer little harm; in that case, so the reasoning might go, it is reasonable to require proof of special damages.

Both rationales are now deficient. First, the requirement of pecuniary loss rather than actual harm to reputation is as artificial here as it is with slander. Second, fault is now often required by constitutional and even common law decisions; when it is required, the artificial technicalities of libel per quod cannot be justified as an indirect and complicated

8. MacLeod v. Tribune Pub. Co., Inc., 52 Cal.2d 536, 343 P.2d 36 (1959).

9. See Bryson v. News America Publications, Inc., 174 Ill.2d 77, 90, 672 N.E.2d 1207, 1215, 220 Ill.Dec. 195, 203 (1996) ("Even if a statement falls into one of the recognized categories of words that are actionable per se, it will not be found actionable per se if it is reasonably capable of an innocent construction").

10. Illinois wrenched its innocent construction rule into a kind of libel per quod rule applicable when the publication could "reasonably be interpreted as referring to someone other than the plaintiff." Chapski v. Copley Press, 92 Ill.2d 344, 352, 442 N.E.2d 195, 199 (1982).

way of preventing strict liability. If fault is the hidden issue in libel per quod cases, the court can simply require proof of fault in all cases or at least when extrinsic facts are required to show defamatory meaning.[11] Third, the extrinsic facts that show defamatory quality may be well known to both the publisher and the readers. The "common-sense idea [is] that a fact not expressed in the newspaper but presumably known to its readers is part of the libel"[12] so in all such cases the requirement of special damages is out of place.

TOPIC B. DEFENSES

§ 410. Truth or Falsity

Burden of proof. Under the common law view of defamation, a publication was presumed false once it was shown to be defamatory.[1] Under the original English practice of using criminal libel suits to punish political dissent, it was said that the greater the truth, the greater the libel, and even in some American states it was said that truth was no defense if libel was published maliciously. That idea is obviously at odds with the whole American notion of freedom and is substantially obsolete, and perhaps unconstitutional,[2] although a few ragged threads of that idea can occasionally be found.[3] The mainstream common law thus recognizes truth as an affirmative defense with the burden upon the defendant to prove it. If he succeeds he is not liable. Constitutional decisions have shifted the burden of proof on the issue of truth or falsity in cases involving certain public officials, public figures, or public-concern issues[4] and some states have now said that falsity of the publication is an element of defamation and hence to be proved by the plaintiff.[5] The underlying issues about truth remain.

Substantial truth. The publication need not be literally true to receive protection. It is enough if the publication is substantially true. That means the gist or sting of the defamation must be true even if details are not.[6] Even if the defendant intentionally misquotes the

11. As in Reed v. Melnick, 81 N.M. 608, 471 P.2d 178, 49 A.L.R.3d 156 (1970), overruled on other grounds, Marchiondo v. Brown, 98 N.M. 394, 649 P.2d 462 (1982).

12. Hinsdale v. Orange County Publications, Inc., 17 N.Y.2d 284, 290, 217 N.E.2d 650, 653, 270 N.Y.S.2d 592 (1966).

§ 410

1. E.g., Post Pub. Co. v. Moloney, 50 Ohio St. 71, 33 N.E. 921 (1893); Bird v. Hudson, 113 N.C. 203, 18 S.E. 209 (1893).

2. Shaari v. Harvard Student Agencies, Inc., 427 Mass. 129, 691 N.E.2d 925 (1998) (statute allowing truth defense only for nonmalicious statements unconstitutional).

3. See Young v. First United Bank of Bellevue, 246 Neb. 43, 516 N.W.2d 256 (1994).

4. See Philadelphia Newspapers, Inc. v. Hepps, 475 U.S. 767, 106 S.Ct. 1558, 89 L.Ed.2d 783 (1986); § 420.

5. E.g., Simpson v. Mars Inc., 113 Nev. 188, 929 P.2d 966 (Nev. 1997) (listing falsity as an element of the claim).

6. Williams v. WCAU–TV, 555 F.Supp. 198 (E.D.Pa.1983); see Read v. Phoenix Newspapers, 169 Ariz. 353, 819 P.2d 939 (1991). Some earlier cases were contrary. Sharpe v. Stephenson, 34 N.C. 348 (1851) (a charge that the plaintiff had sexual intercourse at one time and place is not proved to be true by proving a different time or place).

plaintiff, that does not necessarily show a deviation from substantial truth.[7] To say that the plaintiff evicted a wounded Marine is substantially true if the plaintiff actually evicted the Marine's family with whom the marine resided.[8] Statements about crimes are often technically incorrect but substantially true. To laypersons, "theft" may mean any wrongful taking, including such distinct crimes as embezzlement. A statement that the plaintiff is serving time for a crime is shown to be substantially true if the plaintiff was convicted of the crime but has not yet entered prison.[9] A statement that the plaintiff has been disbarred is substantially true even if a motion for rehearing is pending and the judgment is not final.[10] A statement that the plaintiff, booked for a crime, had been identified by his own children is substantially true if he was identified by his former wife's children.[11]

These cases suggest that if (a) the publication states facts similar to the truth and (b) the sting of the publication is substantially equivalent to the sting of the truth, the truth defense should ordinarily apply. To say that the plaintiff robbed the A Bank when in fact he robbed the B Bank is substantially true because the sting is similar in both cases. Perhaps the truth defense should be rejected if there is a substantial likelihood that readers will combine the published statement with their own knowledge and conclude that the plaintiff robbed both banks, but this is surely a rare case.

Evidence of truth. Some defamation charges the plaintiff with specific conduct like perjury in a trial (or specific condition such as a disease). Other defamation attributes to the plaintiff a general character trait, as where the plaintiff is said to be a liar or incompetent at her profession.

If the defamation charges specific conduct, the only admissible evidence of truth is specific evidence of that conduct or conduct substantially similar and carrying the equivalent sting. Evidence of general bad reputation does not tend to prove specific charges. The plaintiff may have a bad reputation as an alcoholic but that does not prove she passed out in an alcoholic stupor last Saturday at the tavern.[12] When the defamation attributes an ongoing course of behavior to the plaintiff, however, evidence of such behavior on particular occasions will tend to show truth and is admissible.[13] Likewise, if the defamation attributes a

7. See Masson v. New Yorker Magazine, Inc., 501 U.S. 496, 111 S.Ct. 2419, 115 L.Ed.2d 447 (1991).

8. Harnish v. Herald–Mail Co., 264 Md. 326, 286 A.2d 146, 49 A.L.R.3d 1056 (1972).

9. Fendler v. Phoenix Newspapers, Inc., 130 Ariz. 475, 636 P.2d 1257 (Ariz.App. 1981).

10. Hamilton v. Lake Charles Am. Press, Inc., 372 So.2d 239 (La.App.1979) .

11. Rouch v. Enquirer & News of Battle Creek Michigan, 440 Mich. 238, 487 N.W.2d 205 (1992).

12. See Rule 404 (a), Fed. R. Evid. (subject to exceptions, "Evidence of a person's character or a trait of character is not admissible for the purpose of proving action in conformity therewith on a particular occasion").

13. Guccione v. Hustler Magazine, Inc., 800 F.2d 298, 300 (2d Cir.1986) (if the statement published could be read as asserting adultery in 1983, proof of adultery at some other time would not show truth, but statement here was more general, asserting ongoing marriage and ongoing adultery, so proof of adultery at one time was sufficient to show the truth).

character trait to the plaintiff, evidence of either specific misconduct that manifests the trait charged or opinion or reputation evidence concerning the trait in question will be admissible.[14]

Older cases especially required exact truth. The truth of a publication that the plaintiff committed adultery under an oak tree was not proved by proving adultery under a myrtle bush.[15] Although this older attitude no longer represents the substantive law, it has sometimes been perpetuated by attaching its underlying attitude to evidence rules. The point of the evidence rule, however, is not to preserve the old literal truth requirement but to distinguish between proof of specific acts and proof of general reputation or character. Consequently, when the plaintiff stands charged with specific conduct, evidence of very similar specific conduct should be admissible to show the truth. Perhaps there is a material difference between stealing a watch and stealing two clocks, but unless that difference can be identified and articulated, a two-clock theft ought to be admissible to prove the substantial truth of a one-watch theft.

Truth vs. limited damages. It may seem odd, but the problem of truth can sometimes be confused with problems of privilege on the one hand and problems of damages on the other. Read literally, some judicial statements seem to say that a publication is true if it generates no more opprobrium or distaste in the readers' minds than the truth. That may make good sense only when the published statement and the truth are factually similar. Benedict Arnold's treason was more shameful than shoplifting but it is not true that he was a shoplifter merely because he was guilty of more serious misbehavior.[16] Arnold's treason is too factually different from shoplifting to show the truth of the shoplifting charge. But there is another possibility.

Even when the defendant cannot show the truth of the charge, he may be able to show that actual harm to reputation was small because the plaintiff's reputation in the community was already bad. This argument does not bar the claim; it only permits the trier to consider evidence on the damages issue.[17] For this purpose, evidence of the plaintiff's conduct on specific occasions would not be admissible,[18] but

14. See Rule 405 (a) & (b), Fed. R. Evid. ("proof may be made by testimony as to reputation or by testimony in the form of an opinion.... In cases in which character or a trait of character of a person is an essential element of a charge, claim, or defense, proof may also be made of specific instances of that person's conduct").

15. Cf. Sharpe v. Stephenson, supra n. 6.

16. See Scalia, J. in Liberty Lobby, Inc. v. Anderson, 746 F.2d 1563, 1568 (D.C.Cir. 1984) (Scalia, J.), vacated, as to applicable standard on summary judgment, 477 U.S. 242, 106 S.Ct. 2505, 91 L.Ed.2d 202 (1986).

17. See Marcone v. Penthouse International Magazine for Men, 754 F.2d 1072, 1079 (3d Cir.1985) (widespread negative publicity before defamation was published); McBride v. New Braunfels Herald–Zeitung, 894 S.W.2d 6 (Tex.App.1994) (if plaintiff's earlier convictions of theft and burglary were well known, that would affect damages but would not justify a summary judgment for the defendant).

18. See Shirley v. Freunscht, 303 Or. 234, 735 P.2d 600 (1987); Towle v. St. Albans Pub. Co., Inc., 122 Vt. 134, 165 A.2d 363 (1960). However, evidence of specific misconduct may be discoverable because it may lead to reputation evidence. On the

evidence of the plaintiff's general reputation would be admissible,[19] at least aspects of reputation affected by the defamation.[20] Indeed, it is sometimes argued that the reputation of some plaintiffs is so bad that no award at all could be justified, even when the publication is defamatory and untrue.[21]

False and defamatory implications embedded in a literally true statement.[22] Several kinds of statement may be literally or formally true yet contain an explicitly false and defamatory statement. Examples of embedded defamation are: (1) "John told me that Pat robbed the bank on Friday," where it is true that John made the statement but false that Pat robbed the bank; (2) "In my opinion, Linda is an embezzler," where it is true that the speaker holds the opinion but false that Linda is an embezzler; (3) "Either I added incorrectly or the cashier stole $10" where it is true that one of the two conditions must exist but false that the cashier stole the money. In all such cases the defamatory statement may do its dirty work even though the non-defamatory portion of the statement is true. If truth is to be a defense in such cases, it must be truth as to the defamatory sting. So if Pat did not rob the bank and Linda is not an embezzler, the defendant cannot avoid liability under the truth defense.[23] The same idea applies to other cases of embedded defamation. If the defendant asks the question "Did Phil attempt to bribe the juror?" he conveys the thought that he believes Phil may have attempted bribery. To assert truth, the defendant would be required to show that Phil did indeed attempt bribery.[24] The truth issue is sometimes confused with the issue of privilege. The fact that the publisher truthfully attributes defamatory statements to others does not raise the truth defense, but he may be privileged to convey information gleaned from others.[25]

other hand, privacy concerns may warrant a restriction of discovery of specific misconduct where the specific acts are not themselves admissible. See Williams v. District Court, 866 P.2d 908 (Colo.1993).

19. E.g., Dunagan v. Upham, 214 Ark. 66, 214 S.W.2d 786 (1948).

20. Gosden v. Louis, 116 Ohio App.3d 195, 687 N.E.2d 481 (Ohio App. 1996).

21. As to the libel-proof plaintiff, see § 422.

22. The reverse case is one in which a truthful and defamatory meaning is embedded in a literally false statement, as where the publication asserts that the plaintiff killed 28 boys when in fact he killed only 27. See § 422.

23. See Restatement § 581A, Cmt. e. Put the other way around, the repeater is liable for the defamatory statement and does not escape this liability merely because he has repeated the statement with precision. E.g.,Taj Mahal Travel, Inc. v. Delta Airlines, Inc., 164 F.3d 186 (3d Cir.1998); Owens v. CBS, Inc., 173 Ill.App.3d 977, 994, 123 Ill.Dec. 521, 527 N.E.2d 1296, 1308 (1988). An opinion that Linda is an embezzler, stated without more, implies unstated and defamatory facts in support of the opinion. It is those facts that must be true.

24. See Lutz v. Watson, 136 A.D.2d 888, 525 N.Y.S.2d 80 (1988); Meaney v. Loew's Hotels, Inc., 29 A.D.2d 850, 288 N.Y.S.2d 217 (1968). Not all questions, even about wrongdoing, carry defamatory implications. See Schupmann v. Empire Fire & Marine Ins. Co., 689 S.W.2d 101, 53 A.L.R.4th 445 (Mo. App. 1985) (question whether plaintiff was pregnant was not implication of unchastity).

25. See, e.g., § 415.

§ 411. Truth of Factual Statements Implying False and Defamatory Facts

Some discussions of defamation seem to suggest that defamation by implication is a peculiar or suspect category of liability. In fact, much defamation is accomplished in whole or in part by implication.[1] For instance, if A asserts that B promised to share the business profits and B denies it, B's denial may imply that A is a liar. If A then repeats his assertion, A may be implying that B is both a liar and a cheat. At least three kinds of defamation by implication can be identified.[2] The defendant may publish (1) false assertions of fact that are not in themselves defamatory but that may be interpreted to imply false and defamatory facts;[3] (2) true assertions of fact that are not in themselves defamatory but that may be interpreted to imply a negative feelings or opinions that are not provably false and not actionable;[4] (3) true and accurate statements of fact that imply a false and defamatory fact.

The first instance, already encountered in this chapter, is actionable under ordinary common law rules and does not intersect with the truth issue, since both the assertion of fact and its implication are false. The second instance is more complicated if only because "opinions" that imply no provably false assertions are not ordinarily actionable at all. The third instance of implied defamation, where true statements create a false implication, has caused difficulties in analysis.[5] Can the defendant avoid liability on the ground that the factual statements are true? Or can the plaintiff prevail on the ground that the implications are false and defamatory?

Two case examples show the difficulty. In the first, the defendant published statements that the plaintiff, a police officer, had been given a drug test before his promotion to captain, that it had tested positive, and that, following some irregular procedures, the first test and a then a second showed no sign of drugs. The detailed statements about the procedures were true and accurate. But those statements could be read to suggest that someone had tampered with the test specimens and perhaps that the officer had indeed used drugs. Readers who drew such inferences would be rational and if the inference was false, the officer's

§ 411

1. See Toney v. WCCO Television, 85 F.3d 383 (8th Cir.1996).

2. Distinguish embedded defamation, as where the defendant repeats a defamatory remark made by another. See § 410.

3. See § 404. *Example*: the defendant falsely states that the plaintiff worked at the office all night, a falsehood that is non-defamatory standing alone but one that may imply a defamatory falsehood that the plaintiff was the person who altered the company books.

4. On the actionability of derogatory "opinions" or the like, see § 420. *Example*: the defendant truthfully points out that a judge sentencing police officers had represented the police officers' association before becoming a judge. The truthfully stated facts may support a negative feeling about the the judge but not a provably false assertion. Rappaport v. VV Pub. Corp., 163 Misc.2d 1, 618 N.Y.S.2d 746 (Sup. Ct. 1994), aff'd, Rappaport v. VV Pub. Corp., 223 A.D.2d 515, 637 N.Y.S.2d 109 (1996).

5. See Dienes and Levine, Implied Libel, Defamatory Meaning, and State of Mind: The Promise of New York Times Co. v. Sullivan, 78 Iowa L. Rev. 237 (1993) (extensive discussion).

reputation would likely suffer. On the other hand, the facts were correctly stated even if some inferences that could be drawn were false. If the facts cannot be correctly stated without liability, that means the topic cannot be honestly discussed at all. The District of Columbia Circuit recognized the problem and counseled caution about implied libel claims. In the particular case, however, the court thought that the defendants' communication did more than state the facts; it impliedly asked the reader to draw the defamatory inference and for that reason truth of the underlying facts was no defense.[6] Similarly, when the publication states facts correctly but omits known facts necessary to exclude a defamatory implication, courts have recognized that liability is appropriate.[7] Likewise liability has been held appropriate when the defendant artificially juxtaposes a series of facts so as to convey a defamatory falsehood,[8] although merely highlighting or emphasizing a particular truthful statement is not by itself enough.[9]

A second example reflects the idea of artificial juxtaposition of truthful statements. In *Michaelis v. CBS, Inc.*,[10] the plaintiff was a pathologist who performed an autopsy upon the body of a young woman. Investigators concluded that her death had been suicide, but the media questioned that conclusion and noted a number of questions about the investigation. The publication said, correctly, that the plaintiff was not board certified as a forensic pathologist, then said: "We tried to talk with the doctor about her qualifications to handle a suspicious case like this one. She hung up on us. Twice." The court believed that the quoted language should be read together with other statements it had already held to be protected because they were accurate reports of public proceedings. When so read, the statements were capable of meaning that the plaintiff was professionally unqualified. All of the statements were seemingly true or privileged, but the court concluded that the "defendant does not avoid liability by simply establishing the truth of the individual statement. Instead, the defendant must also defend the juxtaposition of the two statements or the omission of certain facts."[11]

When, as in *Michaelis,* liability is imposed for quite true statements of fact, new and uncomfortable meaning is given to the repressive English adage: the greater the truth, the greater the libel. Some courts, like the Eighth Circuit in *Michaelis,* seem unperturbed, but others have expressed reluctance to impose liability when the claimed defamation results from accurate statement of facts. At least where the publication

6. White v. Fraternal Order of Police, 909 F.2d 512 (D.C.Cir.1990).

7. Pep Boys v. New World Communications of Tampa, Inc., 711 So.2d 1325 (Fla. App.1998); Memphis Publishing Co. v. Nichols, 569 S.W.2d 412 (Tenn.1978).

8. Toney v. WCCO Television, 85 F.3d 383, 387 (8th Cir.1996) ("the touchstone of implied defamation claims is an artificial juxtaposition of two true statements or the material omission of facts that would render the challenged statement(s) non-defamatory.... the defendant must ... defend the juxtaposition of two statements or the omission of certain facts").

9. Smith v. Maldonado, 72 Cal.App.4th 637, 85 Cal.Rptr.2d 397 (Cal.App.1999).

10. Michaelis v. CBS, Inc., 119 F.3d 697 (8th Cir.1997).

11. Accord by implication, Church of Scientology of California v. Flynn, 744 F.2d 694 (9th Cir.1984).

relates to issues involving public concerns, a number have refused to base liability upon accurate factual statements with defamatory implications,[12] while others have insisted that the publisher may be subjected to liability only if it actually intended the defamatory implication.[13] In those cases in which truth of the literal factual statement is actionable in spite of the courts' concern, issues of privilege and constitutional protection become central.

§ 412. Absolute Privileges

Meaning of absolute privilege. Although the common law defamation plaintiff could make out a case without proof of fault, the defendant might defeat the claim if he had either an absolute or qualified privilege. A privilege is described as "absolute" when it is not defeated by the defendant's malice, which under common law notions involved ill-will, spite, improper purpose or the like. The privilege is in effect a complete immunity. Although it protected malicious statements as well as others, it must be remembered that even the defendant who spoke with ill-will might nevertheless have believed and believed reasonably in the truth of what he said.

Absolute privileges listed. The absolute privilege applies, subject to limitations, principally to (1) judicial proceedings; (2) legislative proceedings; (3) in some cases to executive publications; (4) publications consented to, (5) publications between spouses;[1] (6) publications required by law.[2] In addition, some states give special protections to public participation in affairs that counts as "petitioning" of government.

Judicial and quasi-judicial proceedings. The absolute privilege in judicial and quasi-judicial proceedings protects judges and other judicial officers with respect to statements made in the performance of judicial functions and having some relationship to those functions.[3] The privilege also protects defamatory matter in pleadings,[4] and statements made by attorneys, parties, witnesses, and jurors so far as they are involved in and related to judicial proceedings.[5] As this privilege perhaps implies,

12. Strada v. Connecticut Newspapers, Inc., 193 Conn. 313, 323, 477 A.2d 1005, 1010 (1984) (except where clarifying facts are omitted); Pietrafeso v. D.P.I., Inc., 757 P.2d 1113 (Colo.App.1988); Schaefer v. Lynch, 406 So.2d 185 (La.1981); Locricchio v. Evening News Ass'n, 438 Mich. 84, 476 N.W.2d 112 (1991) (perhaps limiting liability to cases in which the factual statements as well as the implications are false); cf. Diesen v. Hessburg, 455 N.W.2d 446 (Minn.1990)(possibly a plurality).

13. Chapin v. Knight–Ridder, Inc., 993 F.2d 1087, 1092–93 (4th Cir.1993) (proof must suggest "that the author intends or endorses the inference"); Dodds v. American Broadcasting Co., Inc., 145 F.3d 1053 (9th Cir.1998).

§ 412

1. Restatement § 592.

2. Restatement § 592A; Stecks v. Young, 38 Cal.App.4th 365, 45 Cal.Rptr.2d 475 (1995) (mandatory child abuse reports); see Farmers Educational and Cooperative Union of America v. WDAY, Inc., 360 U.S. 525, 79 S.Ct. 1302, 3 L.Ed.2d 1407 (1959).

3. Restatement § 585.

4. Prokop v. Cannon, 7 Neb.App. 334, 583 N.W.2d 51 (1998).

5. E.g., Bird v. W.C.W., 868 S.W.2d 767 (Tex.1994) (psychologist's affidavit concluding that child had been sexually abused by custodial parent); Restatement §§ 586–589.

there is no separate tort of perjury.[6] Attorneys, parties, and their representatives, as well as witnesses may also be absolutely protected from liability for communications made in preparation for trial[7] or in connection with post-trial determinations.[8] The privilege has been extended to administrative proceedings that are adversary and quasi-judicial, that is, when they apply law to facts and are subject to judicial review.[9] It has sometimes been extended to private quasi-judicial proceedings such as a university's formal investigation of charges against its president.[10]

The publication is not protected by the absolute privilege unless both the occasion for publication and the content of the publication have some relation to the proceeding. The judge who makes a defamatory remark at lunch or in the course of hiring or firing an employee is not absolutely privileged.[11] Nor is any participant in a contract suit who simply takes the occasion to let the world know what he thinks of a business rival who is in no way involved.[12] However, the idea of relatedness is very broad, and the privilege protects statements that bear on the case even if they would not be admissible in evidence or would be counted as improper argument.[13]

The purpose of absolute privilege in this context is to immunize participants in the judicial process so as to assure all concerned that they can speak truly (or in their client's interest in the case of a lawyer) without fear of personal liability or an expensive lawsuit.[14] The immunity may sometimes protect scoundrels and liars, but it has always been thought necessary, because if each case is judged on its own merits, honest witnesses and other participants in the trial cannot be assured of protection from suit.

Legislative business. Similar policies apply to legislative proceedings. The United States Constitution provides "for any Speech or Debate in either House," members of Congress "shall not be questioned in any

6. See Eagle, Civil Remedies for Perjury: A Proposal for a Tort Action, 19 Ariz. L. Rev. 349 (1977).

7. Kelley v. Bonney, 221 Conn. 549, 606 A.2d 693, 708 (1992) (lawyer questioning potential witness before trial); Hawkins v. Harris, 141 N.J. 207, 661 A.2d 284 (1995); but cf. Fridovich v. Fridovich, 598 So.2d 65 (Fla.1992) (malicious prosecution suit based on statements made in the course of investigating before trial, qualified privilege only).

8. Van Eaton v. Fink, 697 N.E.2d 490 (Ind.App.1998). Prokop v. Cannon, 7 Neb. App. 334, 583 N.W.2d 51 (1998) goes much further in protecting a comment made by an attorney after the cases had been dropped.

9. E.g., Allan and Allan Arts Ltd. v. Rosenblum, 201 A.D.2d 136, 615 N.Y.S.2d 410 (1994).

10. Gattis v. Kilgo, 128 N.C. 402, 38 S.E. 931 (1901).

11. Cf. Forrester v. White, 484 U.S. 219, 108 S.Ct. 538, 98 L.Ed.2d 555 (1988) (distinguish judicial from administrative capacity of judge; judge who violates constitutional rights in the course of discharging an employee does not enjoy absolute, only qualified, protection).

12. Cf. Post v. Mendel, 510 Pa. 213, 507 A.2d 351 (1986) (lawyer's letter attacking opposing counsel; copy to the judge, written and received during trial was not absolutely privileged as part of the proceeding).

13. See Irwin v. Ashurst, 158 Or. 61, 74 P.2d 1127 (1938).

14. See Rosenberg v. Helinski, 328 Md. 664, 616 A.2d 866 (1992).

other Place."[15] State constitutional provisions, statutes, or common law provides essentially the same immunity for state legislators[16] and sometimes to local council members.[17] The legislative privilege extends to aides engaged in assisting legislators.[18] Legislative functions covered by the privilege include not only speeches on the floor but committee and other work related to the business of the legislature.[19] They do not, however, include electioneering or the communication of defamatory material to constituents outside the business of the legislature. As to that, the absolute legislative privilege has no application.[20]

In the view of the Restatement and a number of courts, the privilege also covers witnesses at legislative hearings.[21] This view is most easily supported when the proceeding has a formal character and procedural safeguards and when the witness is subpoenaed or gives testimony under oath.[22] When the proceeding merely asks members of the public to offer their opinion, some courts have rejected the absolute privilege for witnesses, limiting their protection to the qualified privilege.[23]

Executive branch business. The executive branch, including police, administrators at all levels, and most other governmental employees, is quite different from the judicial and legislative branch. Except in quasi-judicial proceedings where the absolute judicial privilege would apply, employees in the executive do not regularly operate in structured forums like the Congress or the judiciary; they are not often subject to institutional, professional, or even regular political constraints; and they seldom if ever have need of privileges not enjoyed by the citizens they serve. To the extent that they defame other officials, they are protected by the rules developed under the First Amendment. To the extent that they defame citizens, immunity is questionable at best. Apart from statute, executive branch employees were not traditionally afforded the same broad and absolute immunity granted to the judicial and legislative branches.

At the federal level, however, Congress has immunized all federal employees for all torts within the scope of their employment.[24] In doing so, it substituted the government itself as a potential defendant, but only under the terms of the Federal Tort Claims Act, which leaves the government itself immune in many instances and specifically in suits for libel or slander.[25] Congress did not abrogate the constitutional con-

15. U.S. Const. Art I, § 6, Cl. 1

16. E.g., Colo. Rev. Stats. Ann. § 2-2-304; Conn. Const. Art. 3, § 15; Ind. Const. Art. 4, § 8; Restatement § 590.

17. Sanchez v. Coxon, 175 Ariz. 93, 854 P.2d 126 (Ariz. 1993); contra, Mills v. Denny, 245 Iowa 584, 63 N.W.2d 222 (1954).

18. Gravel v. United States, 408 U.S. 606, 92 S.Ct. 2614, 33 L.Ed.2d 583 (1972).

19. See Gravel v. United States, supra n.18.

20. Hutchinson v. Proxmire, 443 U.S. 111, 99 S.Ct. 2675, 61 L.Ed.2d 411 (1979).

21. DeSantis v. Employees Passaic County Welfare Ass'n, 237 N.J.Super. 550, 568 A.2d 565 (1990) (allegedly defaming public official); Restatement § 590A.

22. As in Kelly v. Daro, 47 Cal.App.2d 418, 118 P.2d 37 (1941).

23. Vultaggio v. Yasko, 215 Wis.2d 326, 572 N.W.2d 450 (1998).

24. 28 U.S.C.A. § 2679. See § 273.

25. 28 U.S.C.A. § 2680(h).

straints upon federal officials,[26] so the defamed plaintiff may have a direct constitutional claim against the official.[27] However, the Supreme Court has held that defamation alone does not violate any constitutional right.[28] The effect is that the federal official is absolutely free to defame citizens and that neither he nor the government is liable in a common law or constitutional action for defamation alone.[29]

As to state executive branch employees and officials, the states have come up with at least four views. (1) Officers or employees have an absolute immunity for acts, including defamation, that fall within the scope of their employment and are considered discretionary;[30] (2) High level officers in the state government are entitled to the absolute privilege; lower-level officers are not.[31] (3) A substantial number of state executive branch employees are protected, including those below cabinet rank;[32] (4) No state officers have an absolute common law privilege to defame; their privilege is qualified and destroyed by malice or knowing falsehood.[33]

Consent. The plaintiff's consent or apparent consent to publication of defamatory materials is a complete bar to the plaintiff's recovery for defamation.[34] The reasons for this rule are in no way related to the reasons given for the immunities of those engaged in legislative and judicial functions. Consent is a bar, not only for reasons of policy, but also for reasons of justice. The ordinary rules for consent and apparent consent apply, so that, for example, if consent is obtained by fraud, that "consent" is no bar to the defamation claim.

One application of the consent rule occurs when the plaintiff authorizes evaluations of her past work to be communicated to a prospective employer.[35] There are elements of economic compulsion in some such cases, so it may be that consent to publish should not be interpreted to permit publication of a knowing or reckless falsehood. In addition, a rule of fair play that warns the plaintiff about the nature of the evaluation before consent is given might also represent good policy.[36] Consent is also

26. § 278.

27. Under the rule in Bivens v. Six Unknown Named Agents of Federal Bureau of Narcotics, 403 U.S. 388, 91 S.Ct. 1999, 29 L.Ed.2d 619 (1971).

28. Paul v. Davis, 424 U.S. 693, 96 S.Ct. 1155, 47 L.Ed.2d 405 (1976).

29. Aversa v. United States, 99 F.3d 1200 (1st Cir.1996).

30. Kendrick v. Fox Television, 659 A.2d 814 (D.C.App.1995).

31. See Bauer v. State, 511 N.W.2d 447 (Minn.1994); Stukuls v. State, 42 N.Y.2d 272, 397 N.Y.S.2d 740, 366 N.E.2d 829 (1977).

32. Cf. Liberty Bank of Seattle, Inc. v. Henderson, 75 Wash.App. 546, 878 P.2d 1259 (1994) (refusing to state a rule, but indicating that officers below the "cabinet rank" are protected).

33. Gibson v. Abbott, 529 So.2d 939 (Ala.1988); Chamberlain v. Mathis, 151 Ariz. 551, 729 P.2d 905 (Ariz. 1986); cf. Aspen Exploration Corp. v. Sheffield, 739 P.2d 150 (Alaska 1987) (governor had only qualified privilege as to defamation; choice between absolute and qualified privilege depends upon the facts).

34. Restatement § 583 and cmt. c.

35. Smith v. Holley, 827 S.W.2d 433 (Tex.App.1992). When the plaintiff has not consented to a reference, former employers are often protected by a conditional or qualified privilege, destructible if abused by malice or the like. Statutes sometimes offer specific protection. E.g., Ga. Code § 34–1–4.

36. See Horkan, Note, Contracting around the Law of Defamation and Employment References, 79 VA. L. REV. 517 (1993).

implied when the plaintiff accepts or applies for membership in an organization contemplating an investigation of the plaintiff and report to membership or governing boards[37] or other publications about the plaintiff.[38]

Petitioning activity. The First Amendment guarantees the right to petition government. Petitioning activity is understood in a broad sense to include all kinds of public participation in issues facing governmental bodies and even issues that may face them in the future. It is constitutionally protected in the same way as other forms of speech. It does not enjoy an absolute immunity.[39] However, following a series of articles and speeches claiming that individuals who speak out on public issues are subject to retaliatory lawsuits on a vast scale,[40] about nine states have enacted statutes providing special immunities or near-immunities to citizens who exercise their right to petition by speaking on public issues.[41] In a frequently given example, citizens object to rezoning or some similar action in favor of a developer. The developer retaliates by suing the citizens for defamation or interference with business opportunities or the like. The retaliatory suit is called a SLAPP suit, an acronym for Strategic Lawsuits Against Public Participation. The statutes also provide for a halt to discovery and for speedy dismissal without much if any factual development, thus raising the question whether they adequately protect the defamation plaintiff's right to petition by way of a lawsuit.[42] New Hampshire has held that such a statute would be unconstitutional as a deprivation of jury trial rights.[43]

37. Rosenberg v. American Bowling Congress, 589 F.Supp. 547 (M.D.Fla.1984).

38. O'Connor v. Diocese of Honolulu, 77 Hawai'i 383, 885 P.2d 361 (1994).

39. McDonald v. Smith, 472 U.S. 479, 105 S.Ct. 2787 86 L.Ed.2d 384 (1985).

40. See George W. Pring and Penelope Canan, SLAPPs: Getting Sued for Speaking Out (1996); Penelope Canan and George W. Pring, Studying Strategic Lawsuits Against Public Participating: Mixing Quantitative and Qualitative Approaches, 22 L. & Soc'y Rev. 385 (1988); George W. Pring, SLAPPs: Strategic Lawsuits Against Public Participation, 7 Pace Envt'l L. Rev. 3 (1989); George W. Pring and Penelope Canan, "Strategic Lawsuits Against Public Participation" ("Slapps"): An Introduction for Bench, Bar and Bystanders, 12 Bridgeport L. Rev. 937 (1992).

41. Some statutes appear to afford an absolute immunity by protecting all petitioning activity unless it is a sham in the sense that it is not really aimed at procuring favorable government action. R.I. Gen. L. § 9–33–2 (labeling the immunity conditional, however). The literal meaning seems to be that the public participant would be free to engage in knowing falsehood as long as he intended to affect government action. The Massachusetts statute may be subject to a similar interpretation, but might be read to bear a more moderate meaning. See E.g., Mass. Gen. L. Ann. 231 § 59H. Some statutes offer a qualified immunity only, defeasible if the public publishes in bad faith. Nev. Rev. Stats. § 41.650; Rev. Code. Wash. Ann. § 4.24.510. The Delaware and New York statutes definitely do not grant an absolute immunity but merely invoke, on behalf of public participants, the constitutional rules requiring proof of knowing or reckless falsehood. 10 Del. Code Ann. § 8136; N.Y. Civ. Rts. L. § 76–a. Somewhat strangely, Minnesota offers an immunity "unless the conduct or speech constitutes a tort," or constitutional violation. Minn. Stat. Ann. § 554.03. Like most other statutes, California's halts discovery and grants a motion to strike the claim unless the plaintiff can show she will probably prevail. See Cal. Code Civ. Proc. § 425.16 (b). This has worked out to be an absolute immunity or something close to it in some instances. See Dixon v. Superior Court, Scientific Resource Surveys, Inc., 30 Cal.App.4th 733, 36 Cal.Rptr.2d 687 (1994).

42. See Joseph W. Beatty, The Legal Literature on Slapps: A Look Behind the Smoke Nine Years after Professor Pring and Canan First Yelled "Fire!", 9 U. Fla. J. L. & Pub. Pol'y 85 (1997).

§ 413. Qualified Privileges at Common Law

When a defendant asserts a qualified privilege to publish material that turns out to be defamatory, two kinds of legal issues are raised. First, did the defendant have a privilege to publish the material? Second, was the privilege abused? The second issue usually raises issues of fault. The traditional common law approach was that the fault required to show abuse of privilege was "malice" meaning spite, ill-will, or improper purpose. The courts may be in the process of shifting to a different standard of fault, one that emphasizes knowing, reckless, or negligent publication of a falsehood rather than improper purpose.

Under the common law rule, the plaintiff was not required to show that the defendant was at fault in any way in publishing defamatory material, so the claim of privilege was the only way a defendant could assert his innocence. Under the constitutional decisions developed since 1964, the fault issue is now often one of the elements of the plaintiff's case, not merely a defense under the rubric of privilege. Where fault is required in the first instance, either because the constitution so requires or because state courts have voluntarily added a fault requirement, the privilege analysis might be regarded as superfluous. At the very least, the role of privilege could be reduced without substantially changing the defendant's ultimate liability.

There are four basic qualified privileges. (1) The public interest privilege, to publish materials to public officials on matters within their public responsibility; (2) the privilege to publish to someone who shares a common interest, or, relatedly, to publish in defense of oneself or in the interest of others; (3) the fair comment privilege;[1] and (4) the privilege to make a fair and accurate report of public proceedings.

§ 414. The Interest Privileges

The "legal, moral, or social duty." The qualified privilege to publish to protect one's own interest, the interest of a recipient or the public, or in a common interest is often introduced in the cases with antique language: "A communication, made in good faith, on a subject matter in which the person communicating has an interest, or owes a duty, legal, moral, or social, is qualifiedly privileged if made to a person having a corresponding interest or duty."[1] The language of moral or social duty is

43. See Opinion of the Justices (SLAPP Suit Procedure), 138 N.H. 445, 641 A.2d 1012 (1994).

§ 413

1. Fair comment at common law is now largely subsumed in the constitutional rule that statements that are not provably false are not actionable. The common law privilege is discussed in connection with the constitutional rule in § 420.

§ 414

1. E.g., Great Coastal Express, Inc. v. Ellington, 230 Va. 142, 153, 334 S.E.2d 846, 853 (1985). This form of expression originated in Toogood v. Spyring, 1 C.M. & R. 181 (1834). See PATRICK MILMO & W.V.H. ROGERS, GATLEY IN LIBEL AND SLANDER ¶ 14.5 (9th ed. 1998).

little more than a chant; it seems almost impervious to analysis and at best begs the question what moral and social duties one might have.[2] It seems particularly strange to say that one might have a "a legal or moral duty ... to protect his own interests" by speaking out.[3] A better approach is to identify particular interests to be served by a publication that turns out to be defamatory and to weigh those interests against the risk of reputational loss.

Public interest–charges made to public officials. Citizen complaints about supposed crime of an identifiable person are necessarily defamatory, but so long as the complaint is made to appropriate officials who have authority to deal with the case, the publication is qualifiedly privileged.[4] When the same charge is made as part of a judicial process, the absolute judicial privilege applies instead. Some cases do not plainly fall in the judicial category and thus call for policy judgment. Courts can regard a communication to a prosecuting attorney in an ongoing investigation, for example, as similar to statements before a grand jury and thus judicial; or, especially when no subpoena has been issued and no oath administered, they can regard communications to the prosecutor as reports to a law enforcement officer. Accordingly they may provide an absolute privilege[5] or only a qualified one.[6]

Perhaps the qualified privilege should extend to cases in which the defendant seeks guidance from governmental agents in locating the official with jurisdiction over the case. The qualified privilege to report crime may cut off liability for defamation but it may leave the victim of a false accusation the possibility of a malicious prosecution suit if the defamatory charge actually results in a prosecution without probable cause and other elements of that tort are shown.[7]

Publication in self-interest. Anyone who has, or reasonably believes he has an important interest at stake, is conditionally privileged to protect that interest by relevant communications to appropriate recipients.[8] For example, one who is defamed by another may reply to the defamation in any way that appears reasonable so long as the privilege is

2. A *legal* duty to publish, of course provides a privilege and in fact an absolute one. See Restatement § 592A.

3. Powers v. Carvalho, 117 R.I. 519, 531, 368 A.2d 1242, 1249 (1977).

4. E.g., Hutchinson v. New England Tel. And Tel., 350 Mass. 188, 214 N.E.2d 57 (1966) (erroneous identification to police). The privilege may be codified in some cases, as with child abuse reports. See F.A. v. W.J. F., 280 N.J.Super. 570, 656 A.2d 43 (1995).

5. Bergman v. Hupy, 64 Wis.2d 747, 221 N.W.2d 898 (1974).

6. Toker v. Pollak, 44 N.Y.2d 211, 376 N.E.2d 163, 405 N.Y.S.2d 1 (1978)

7. See § 430 for all the elements of malicious prosecution.

8. Richmond v. Southwire Co., 980 F.2d 518 (8th Cir.1992) (where it was widely known that a number of employees had been discharged, the employer was privileged to state that they discharged for possession of controlled substances); Williams v. Garraghty, 249 Va. 224, 455 S.E.2d 209 (1995); Restatement § 594; cf. Gregory's Inc. v. Haan, 545 N.W.2d 488 (S.D.1996) (conditional privilege to file lien of record, although this is not considered a judicial proceeding). Other privileges may of course apply, as where self-interest publication are made in a judicial proceeding. Frank Pisano & Associates v. Taggart, 29 Cal.App.3d 1, 105 Cal.Rptr. 414 (1972) (mechanic's lien filing deemed part of official proceedings and absolutely privileged).

not abused.[9] What is reasonable depends in part on the importance of the interest at stake, in part on the need for publication.[10] The privilege to make a response of this kind is a species of the self-defense privilege, and like its physical counterpart, it authorizes the defendant to meet the attack, not to launch a new one of his own on the same or a different subject.[11]

Publication in the interest of a recipient or third person. The same kind of principle applies to publications made to protect the interests of the recipient.[12] The recipient's interest, however, must be important enough to justify the defamatory communication and sometimes that turns on the relationship between the defendant and the recipient.[13] A stranger might enjoy a privilege to warn the recipient that the plaintiff was planning to kill him,[14] but might not enjoy a privilege to tell him that his wife was flirting with men at the tavern.[15] The interest of a prospective employer of the plaintiff is sufficient to justify a former employer in providing negative evaluations.[16]

Common interest. Many publications are privileged because they are made in the common interest of the publisher and recipient. Common interests are usually found among members of identifiable groups in which members share similar goals or values or cooperate in a single endeavor. Churches, labor unions, families, and business enterprises are examples. The idea is to promote free exchange of relevant information among those engaged in a common enterprise or activity and to permit them to make appropriate internal communications and share consultations without fear of suit. Employers and employees share many interests in the employment, so an employee may be privileged to communicate information about third persons involved with the business[17] and certainly to communicate information about fellow employees.[18] Equally, the shared interest warrants the employer's privilege to explain to its employees why some of them were discharged.[19] An insurer and its

9. E.g., Dickins v. International Bro. Teamsters, Etc., 171 F.2d 21 (D.C.Cir. 1948); Gattis v. Kilgo, 128 N.C. 402, 38 S.E. 931(1901); see J. A. Bryant, Annotation, Libel and Slander: Qualified Privilege of Reply to Defamatory Publication, 41 A.L.R.3d 1083 (1972).

10. Cf. Foretich v. Capital Cities/ABC, Inc., 37 F.3d 1541 (4th Cir.1994) (plaintiffs, previously accused of child abuse in highly publicized case, had privilege to respond with attacks on accuser and did not become public figures under constitutional rules by so responding).

11. See Reynolds v. Pegler, 223 F.2d 429 (2d Cir.1955) (choice example of Pegler's wide-ranging attack).

12. Restatement § 595.

13. Restatement §§ 595 & 597.

14. See Restatement § 595, cmt. g.

15. Cf. Watt v. Longsdon, [1930] 1 K.B. 130 (1929) (no privilege to communicate all the gossip one hears at "men's clubs or women's bridge parties" to the spouses affected).

16. See Sigal Construction Corp. v. Stanbury, 586 A.2d 1204 (D.C.App.1991). This is sometimes treated as a common interest privilege, but the main interest seems to be that of the recipient.

17. Van Eaton v. Fink, 697 N.E.2d 490 (Ind.Ct.App.1998) (paralegal).

18. Ikani v. Bennett, 284 Ark. 409, 682 S.W.2d 747 (1985) (supervisory employees stating defamatory material among themselves); Gautschi v. Maisel, 565 A.2d 1009 (Me.1989) (tenured professor reported something heard about non-tenured teacher up for review).

19. Schrader v. Eli Lilly and Co., 639 N.E.2d 258 (Ind.1994); Olson v. 3M Company, 188 Wis.2d 25, 523 N.W.2d 578 (Wis. App.1994).

insureds may share a common interest,[20] as do church members, who are therefore privileged to discuss among themselves the supposed proclivities of their ministers.[21] Even neighbors may have a common interest privilege to discuss neighborhood concerns with each other.[22] Possibly the privilege permits publication to a limited segment of the public where the common interest is a strong one,[23] but it has not been broad enough to justify a defamatory report to the general public merely because the material is newsworthy.[24] The privilege does not arise in the first place unless the communication relates in some degree to the common interest, and once the privilege arises it is lost if it is abused by malice or excessive publication.

Dueling privileges. Employees are of course privileged to communicate to their employer as well as to officials that they have been sexually harassed or otherwise unlawfully discriminated against in violation of statute. Under the ordinary self-interest privileges, the employer or supervisor would be qualifiedly privileged to answer the charges in self defense and that might include an attack on the truthfulness and motives of the employee who made the charge. Since a charge of discrimination is a serious one in most employment environments, the supervisor or employer who is so charged might also bring a defamation suit against the employee. The policy problem is that if the employee who makes a charge of discrimination will be subject to either a defamation suit or a privileged attack on her motives, employees may be forced to forgo their rights against discrimination lest they lose all in defending a lawsuit.

Some antidiscrimination statutes prohibit not only primary discrimination such as sexual harassment but also discrimination against an employee who has filed or supported a claim of harassment or the like.[25] This has been interpreted to mean that the employer cannot discharge an employee for publishing false charges of discrimination to the enforcement agency.[26] As this rule suggests, the employer's defamation suit violates the anti-retaliation provision if the suit is either based upon charges filed with the enforcing agency,[27] or founded on a purpose to retaliate for the discrimination claim.[28] On the other hand, the employer or supervisor is free to sue the employee for defamatory accusations not made to the enforcing agency, so long as the suit is not maintained to

20. Turner v. Welliver, 226 Neb. 275, 411 N.W.2d 298 (1987).

21. See Rasmussen v. Bennett, 228 Mont. 106, 741 P.2d 755 (1987).

22. See Christenson v. Gutman, 249 A.D.2d 805, 671 N.Y.S.2d 835 (App. Div. 1998) (accusation that plaintiff yelled at and abused child).

23. Cf. Richmond v. Southwire Co., 980 F.2d 518 (8th Cir.1992) (self-defense privilege allowed company to report to public of a small town the putative reasons for substantial numbers of firings).

24. Draghetti v. Chmielewski, 416 Mass. 808, 626 N.E.2d 862 (1994).

25. E.g., 42 U.S.C.A. § 2000e–3 (a).

26. Pettway v. American Cast Iron Pipe Co., 411 F.2d 998 (5th Cir.1969).

27. Equal Employment Opportunity Com'n v. Virginia Carolina Veneer Corp., 495 F.Supp. 775 (W.D.Va.1980).

28. Equal Employment Opportunity Com'n v. Levi Strauss & Co., 515 F.Supp. 640 (N.D.Ill.1981).

retaliate for the discrimination charge.[29] In this situation, the employee may also have a defamation claim–based on the employer's countercharges.[30] The employee will hold one of the interest privileges while the employer will hold at least the privilege to defend himself. In the end, such litigation will almost certainly boil down to arguments over abuse of privilege that call the truth of the charges and countercharges into question.

§ 415. Reports of Public Proceedings and News

Public Proceedings and Documents

Privilege scope and loss. The common law did not traditionally recognize a privilege to report newsworthy events. The common law does, however, recognize a qualified privilege to provide a fair and accurate report of public proceedings and documents and even to report meetings open to the public and dealing with matters of public concern.[1] The privilege is lost if the report is inaccurate or unfair, although even in that case constitutional rules may protect the defendant.[2] Even if the reporter knows the underlying facts are false, as where he reports a false statement in a legislative document, he does not lose the privilege, since he is a conduit for information that citizens have a right to see for themselves.[3] "Accuracy means 'substantially correct,' while fair means balanced."[4] Fairness requires that the report must substantially represent the matter contained in the public records or proceedings[5] and provide appropriate context for statements reported so that the inevit-

29. Herlihy v. Metropolitan Museum of Art, 214 A.D.2d 250, 633 N.Y.S.2d 106 (1995) (volunteer-employees charged superior with racial epithets; in the superior's suit for defamation, they are protected by qualified privilege only); Williams v. Garraghty, 249 Va. 224, 455 S.E.2d 209 (1995) (employee had qualified privilege to charge sexual harassment; privilege was found to have been abused).

30. Wilson v. UT Health Center, 973 F.2d 1263 (5th Cir.1992).

§ 415

1. Restatement § 611; but cf. Greenbelt Cooperative Pub. Ass'n v. Bresler, 253 Md. 324, 252 A.2d 755 (1969) (suggesting the privilege might not apply to report of an open city council meeting as contrasted an official report by the same council), rev'd on other grounds, Greenbelt Cooperative Publishing Ass'n v. Bresler, 398 U.S. 6, 90 S.Ct. 1537, 26 L.Ed.2d 6 (1970).

2. If the plaintiff is a public figure, she will be required to show knowing or reckless falsehood. If she is a private person and the issue is one of public concern, she will be required to show at least negligence. See § 417.

3. Wright v. Grove Sun Newspaper Co., Inc., 873 P.2d 983 (Okla.1994); Restatement § 611 cmt. a. Some jurisdictions have held, inconsistently with the rationales of the privilege, that it is lost if the defendant publishes with spite or ill-will or with knowledge that the reported statements are false. See Schiavone Construction Co. v. Time, Inc., 735 F.2d 94 (3d Cir.1984) (New Jersey law generated under the First Restatement). Where such holdings are not compelled by statute, they may be a result of confusion between fair report and true conditional privileges, or it may be one of the many leftovers from the days when defamation law under the English approach sought to root out sin and sedition.

4. Green Acres Trust v. London, 141 Ariz. 609, 618, 688 P.2d 617, 626 (1984).

5. Northland Wheels Roller Skating Center, Inc. v. Detroit Free Press, Inc., 213 Mich.App. 317, 539 N.W.2d 774 (1995). But a report of a witness' testimony need not include a comprehensive report of the entire trial. Rosenberg v. Helinski, 328 Md. 664, 616 A.2d 866 (1992).

able summary and omissions do not distort the overall picture.[6] Some authority adds that the privilege does not arise unless the public proceeding or document is referred to in the report and the reporter actually knows about and relies upon the document or proceeding.[7]

Application. The privilege to report public proceedings protects fair and accurate reports of judicial,[8] legislative,[9] and official executive proceedings or reports[10] arrests,[11] and official hearings or meetings of public bodies.[12] The privilege also applies to reports of documents open to public inspection, including recall petitions,[13] police reports,[14] and pleadings[15] and others.[16] An unsupported comment of the Restatement[17] notwithstanding, the privilege has even been applied to protect "self-reports"–publication by a witness or pleader of his own testimony or pleadings–so long as they are not corruptly designed to foster protected defamation.[18]

Rationales. The privilege is based in part on the principle that government activities must always be conducted in the daylight of public scrutiny and in part on the right of members of the public to read public materials for themselves–the reporter being a kind of agent for the readers who as a practical matter cannot always exercise their rights to be present or to read public documents on file.[19]

The judicial action rule for pleadings. The Restatement and some courts implicitly reject the second ground by insisting that pleadings cannot be reported, even accurately and fairly, until they have been subjected to some kind of judicial action.[20] The fear behind the Restatement's version is that intentional defamers will file defamatory pleadings protected by the absolute judicial immunity, and then spread the defa-

6. See Costello v. Ocean County Observer, 136 N.J. 594, 643 A.2d 1012 (1994).

7. See Dameron v. Washington Magazine, 779 F.2d 736 (D.C.Cir.1985); Bufalino v. Associated Press, 692 F.2d 266 (2d Cir. 1982);

8. E.g., Rushford v. New Yorker Magazine, Inc., 846 F.2d 249 (4th Cir.1988).

9. E.g., Cresson v. Louisville Courier–Journal, 299 Fed. 487 (6th Cir.1924).

10. E.g., Brandon v. Gazette Pub. Co., 234 Ark. 332, 352 S.W.2d 92 (1961) (governor's press conference reporting official actions and bases).

11. Trentecosta v. Beck, 703 So.2d 552 (La.1997) (the fact of the arrest and investigation but not evidence that is no part of a public record).

12. Bray v. Providence Journal Co., 101 R.I. 111, 220 A.2d 531 (1966) (school committee meeting).

13. Herron v. Tribune Pub. Co., Inc., 108 Wash.2d 162, 736 P.2d 249 (1987).

14. Dinkel v. Lincoln Pub. (Ohio), Inc., 93 Ohio App.3d 344, 638 N.E.2d 611 (1994) (under statutory version of the privilege); cf. Gist v. Macon County Sheriff's Dept., 284 Ill.App.3d 367, 671 N.E.2d 1154, 219 Ill.Dec. 701 (1996) (newspaper published sheriff's "most wanted" flyer accurately stating warrant existed for plaintiff); Wright v. Grove Sun Newspaper Co., Inc., 873 P.2d 983 (Okla.1994) (district attorney's press conference about drug investigation by his office).

15. E.g., Newell v. Field Enterprises, Inc., 91 Ill.App.3d 735, 415 N.E.2d 434, 47 Ill.Dec. 429, 20 A.L.R.4th 551 (1980).

16. E.g., the contents of search warrants. Pearce v. Courier–Journal, 683 S.W.2d 633 (Ky.App.1985).

17. Restatement § 611, cmt. c ("A person cannot confer this privilege upon himself").

18. Rosenberg v. Helinski, 328 Md. 664, 616 A.2d 866 (1992) (relying in part on Harper, James and Gray).

19. See Cox Broadcasting Corp. v. Cohn, 420 U.S. 469, 491–492, 95 S.Ct. 1029, 1044–45, 43 L.Ed.2d 328 (1975) .

20. Restatement § 611, cmt. e.

mation by reporting those pleadings under the protection of the qualified privilege to report public documents.

The drawback of the Restatement's position is that its rule aims to cover the small risk of contrived defamation while doing nothing for the much larger risk that the public will be deprived of practical access to information about their public processes. At the same time, the Restatement rule does little or nothing to protect against the unlikely results it fears, since no kind of judicial action will make a defamatory complaint less so and many kinds of judicial action–rejecting a motion to dismiss, for example–will tend to validate the complaint in the public eye. The case support for the Restatement's narrow view of the privilege is found mostly in older decisions;[21] most of the more recent decisions hold that the privilege applies as soon as the action is commenced.[22]

Meetings open to the public. A few cases have extended the privilege to report public documents and proceedings to cover private meetings open to the public if issues of public concern are discussed.[23]

Newsworthiness or Neutral Reportage

Traditionally, the common law recognized no privilege to report defamatory matter simply because it was newsworthy. The absence of a privilege, combined with the rule that repeaters are liable for defamation, meant that a newspaper could be held liable for reporting a newsworthy event or accusation if it was also defamatory. The fact that events or accusations took place in public would not itself provide a privilege.

However, in *Edwards v. National Audubon Society,*[24] the court held that at least under some circumstances, the press would be privileged to report serious and defamatory charges made against a public figure by responsible organizations as part of a controversial public issue. The court appeared to have in mind an analogy to the fair reporting privilege for public proceedings and documents; the reporter's doubts about the truth of the statements would be irrelevant. "What is newsworthy about such accusations is that they were made. We do not believe that the press may be required under the First Amendment to suppress newsworthy statements merely because it has serious doubts regarding their truth."[25] The *Edwards* court called its rule a privilege of "neutral reportage" and based it upon the First Amendment.

A number of courts have rejected the neutral reportage privilege.[26] The Supreme Court has not passed on it. A few courts have adopted the

21. See John E. Theuman, Annotation, Libel and Slander: Reports of Pleadings as Within Privilege for Reports of Judicial Proceedings, 20 A.L.R.4th 576 (1981).

22. See Newell v. Field Enterprises, Inc., 91 Ill.App.3d 735, 415 N.E.2d 434, 47 Ill.Dec. 429, 20 A.L.R.4th 551 (1980); Rodney A. Smolla, Law of Defamation 8.10 [3].

23. Phoenix Newspapers, Inc. v. Choisser, 82 Ariz. 271, 312 P.2d 150 (1957) (Junior Chamber of Commerce open forum for candidates, newspaper had privilege to report highly defamatory material asserted by some); Restatement § 611, cmt. i.

24. Edwards v. National Audubon Society, Inc., 556 F.2d 113 (2d Cir.1977).

25. Id. at 120.

26. E.g., Dickey v. CBS, Inc., 583 F.2d 1221 (3d Cir.1978); Young v. The Morning

privilege.[27] Courts would be free to maintain it as a matter of state law even if it turns out that the Constitution does not its dictate such a privilege. The idea is not preposterous. Many cases have used both ordinary and arcane doctrine–innocent construction, libel per quod, for example–to relieve defendants of liability. Other decisions more directly seek protection by expanding the fair report privilege to include report of things like a witness' repetition for television cameras of testimony he gave in court,[28] a governor's press conference,[29] a private meeting,[30] and even to unofficial remarks of a congressman.[31] Such decisions come increasingly close to a newsworthiness privilege, so frank adoption of the privilege seems quite possible.

If the neutral reportage privilege is to be adopted, its contours almost certainly require further thought. If the leader of a mob publicly bellows defamation of the plaintiff while the mob bombs and ransacks buildings, it is hard to believe that the press could not report the whole event including the defamation. It is hard to believe, too, that the right to print this news should be forfeited because the defamed plaintiff was a private person rather than a public figure as *Edwards* might require. Likewise, notwithstanding *Edwards'* proposed limitations, it is irrelevant that the mob leader is not a responsible person or organization. The central point of *Edwards* was that the statement quoted was newsworthy because it was made, not because its content was true. If the privilege is to be adopted, some way must be found to formulate the privilege to further that idea.[32]

§ 416. Abuse or Loss of Privilege

Common Law

In some instances the claimed privilege never arises because the publication is outside its scope. If members of a church are privileged by common interest to discuss the putative shortcomings of their minister, they do not have the same privilege to discuss the minister's mother.[1] If the defendant shows that the publication was privileged, however, he is

Journal, 76 Ohio St.3d 627, 669 N.E.2d 1136 (1996).

27. Krauss v. Champaign News Gazette, Inc., 59 Ill.App.3d 745, 375 N.E.2d 1362, 17 Ill.Dec. 78 (1978); Gist v. Macon County Sheriff's Dept., 284 Ill.App.3d 367, 671 N.E.2d 1154, 219 Ill.Dec. 701 (1996) (applied to bar plaintiff who seemingly was not a public figure).

28. Rosenberg v. Helinski, 328 Md. 664, 616 A.2d 866 (1992).

29. Brandon v. Gazette Pub. Co., 234 Ark. 332, 352 S.W.2d 92 (1961).

30. Phoenix Newspapers, Inc. v. Choisser, 82 Ariz. 271, 312 P.2d 150 (1957).

31. Chapin v. Knight–Ridder, Inc., 993 F.2d 1087 (4th Cir.1993); Coleman v. Newark Morning Ledger Co., 29 N.J. 357, 149 A.2d 193 (1959) (report of a press conferences held by Senator Joseph McCarthy about a secret congressional committee meeting).

32. Cf. Robert D. Sack & Sandra S. Baron, Libel, Slander and Related Problems 401, n. 150 (1994) (emphasizing that the identity of neither the speaker nor the person defamed is central).

§ 416

1. Cf. Emo v. Milbank Mutual Ins. Co., 183 N.W.2d 508 (N.D.1971) (insurer canceling policy would have been privileged to state concerns about insured but was not privileged to explain putative crime of her husband).

not subject to liability unless the plaintiff then sustains the burden of proving that the defendant abused the privilege.[2] Abuse is usually shown by proving some species of fault. However, depending upon the privilege asserted, abuse can take several forms.

Excessive publication. When the facts or the nature of the privilege calls for publication only to a limited group, the privilege is lost by excessive publication.[3] For example, if the defendant has a common interest privilege to discuss church affairs with fellow church members, the privilege would be lost if he published defamatory material about church affairs on a radio talk show. What is excessive is determined in part by the nature of the privilege, in part by practicality. A defendant is entitled to use a method of publication that involves an incidental communication to persons not within the scope of the privilege. Hence if an employer is privileged to communicate materials to its employees in a company newsletter, the fact that the employees will sometimes circulate the letter in the community at large does not necessarily reflect excessive publication.[4]

Inaccuracy in reporting public documents and proceedings. The privilege to report public documents and proceedings fairly is lost by substantial inaccuracy or unfair or slanted reporting, regardless of the publisher's intent.[5]

Common law malice. When the publisher had a privilege to publish in his own interest, the interest of others, or in a common interest, the privilege was lost if he published with malice.[6] The same rule was even applied to the public interest privilege, so that a report to police of a suspected crime would be actionable if the report was motivated by ill-will.[7] Malice at common law referred to a state of mind such as spite, ill-will, or any purpose other than the one for which the privilege was intended to serve.[8] Malice in this sense could be shown by evidence that the defendant's chief motivation in publishing the defamation was based upon "ill will, hostility, threats, rivalry,"[9] a direct intent to injure, or a

2. E.g., Ikani v. Bennett, 284 Ark. 409, 682 S.W.2d 747 (1985); Gattis v. Kilgo, 128 N.C. 402, 38 S.E. 931(1901).

3. Elliott v. Roach, 409 N.E.2d 661(Ind.Ct.App.1980) (jury might conclude privilege to communicate to licensing board may have been abused by circulating communication to others); Restatement § 604.

4. Zinda v. Louisiana Pacific Corp., 149 Wis.2d 913, 440 N.W.2d 548 (1989).

5. The privilege may not arise unless the public document or proceeding is actually referred to and forms the basis of the report. See § 415.

6. Courts have more rarely said that the privileged was lost if the defendant was negligent. See Muresan v. Philadelphia Romanian Pentecostal Church, 154 Or.App. 465, 473, 962 P.2d 711, 715 (1998) (lacked objectively reasonable grounds for belief).

7. Otten v. Schutt, 15 Wis.2d 497, 113 N.W.2d 152 (1962) (report of shoplifting incident to police chief based on mistaken identity; jury could find ill-will and hence liability).

8. See, e.g., Coleman v. Newark Morning Ledger Co., 29 N.J. 357, 375, 149 A.2d 193, 202 (1959) ("the privilege is lost if the publication is not made primarily for the purpose of furthering the interest which is entitled to protection" (quoting Prosser)); Brehany v. Nordstrom, Inc., 812 P.2d 49 (Utah 1991).

9. Clark v. America's First Credit Union, 585 So.2d 1367, 1371 (Ala.1991).

reckless disregard of the reputational consequences.[10] When a privilege exists, the common law presumption of malice from the mere publication of defamation disappears. Nevertheless, courts have sometimes said that extreme defamatory language may lead to an inference of malice in fact.[11]

However, evidence of ill will is not by itself enough; the trier must have a basis for believing that the ill will motivated the publication. "If the defendant's statements were made to further the interest protected by the privilege, it matters not that defendant also despised plaintiff."[12] Even if one of the motives for publication was improper, the privilege is not lost unless the improper motive is the predominant one.[13]

Under the conception of fault embodied in the common law malice rules, a publisher could be liable even if he believed reasonably that he was publishing the truth and even if he published under a privilege, since his personal animus would destroy the privilege. This made sense if the purpose of the courts was to punish sinful states of mind as in the early cases of slander, or to imprison political enemies as in the 16th and 17th century libel cases. Some courts continue to emphasize that privileges can be lost for malice in this sense. However, the malice terminology induces courts to focus on the wrong things in many cases.

Potential Impact of Constitutional Cases

Two differences in constitutional fault. In a series of decisions beginning in 1964, the Supreme Court has held that the First Amendment's free speech guarantee requires the libel suit plaintiff to prove fault in a wide band of cases described in the next section. For constitutional purposes, the treatment of fault is changed in two distinct ways. First, the common law privileges introduced fault defensively, but under the constitutional decisions, the plaintiff must prove the defendant's fault as part of the plaintiff's prima facie case. If the plaintiff's proof of fault in her prima facie case is sufficient to defeat any privilege, the privilege issue becomes superfluous in these cases. Second, the fault sufficient to defeat the common law privilege was often a matter of motive or a bad state of mind, not desire to utter a falsehood, but under the constitutional decisions fault to be proven is the defendant's fault with respect to accuracy. In particular the plaintiff must prove either knowing or reckless falsehood or something like negligence with respect to the truth, but in neither case is the fault determined by motive. This difference is important because under the constitutional decisions a defendant's subjective motives are of not interest as long as he believed (or sometimes reasonably believed) he was publishing the truth.

10. Kuwik v. Starmark Star Marketing and Administration, Inc., 156 Ill.2d 16, 30, 619 N.E.2d 129, 135, 188 Ill.Dec. 765, 771 (1993)

11. Bauer v. State, 511 N.W.2d 447 (Minn.1994).

12. Liberman v. Gelstein, 80 N.Y.2d 429, 439, 605 N.E.2d 344, 350, 590 N.Y.S.2d 857, 863 (1992) .

13. Caudle v. Thomason, 992 F.Supp. 1(D.D.C.1997).

Potential common law responses. To avoid needless complexity, the common law could respond to these constitutional changes by (1) putting the burden upon the plaintiff to prove fault in the first instance and dropping the whole privilege-defense approach in the case of the interest privileges; and (2) using the fault concepts and terminology used in the constitutional cases and dropping the malice and motive approaches to fault on the ground that one set of fault principles is quite sufficient. This response would help simplify and modernize libel law. Under this approach, if the plaintiff proves the requisite fault as part of her case, there is no need to reconsider fault again in a defense. If she does not prove fault, she loses and the issue of privilege is again unnecessary.

Protecting speech without investigating motive. The policy of protecting the defendant can be fully implemented by requiring the plaintiff to prove constitutionally required fault–negligence in some cases, knowing falsehood in others–without investigating the defendant's malicious motives. Thus if the plaintiff must constitutionally prove knowing or reckless falsehood, traditional privilege analysis adds nothing, or nothing that is worth the complications it introduces. If the plaintiff is constitutionally required to prove only negligence, the court might wish to establish greater protection for the defendant's speech on some occasions, in which case it can require the plaintiff to prove knowing or reckless falsehood as part of her case. And again, with fault as part of the plaintiff's case, no defense based on the same issue is required.

The Restatement. The Second Restatement take a view something like this in providing that where common law malice formerly destroyed a privilege, it would now be destroyed only by proof that the defendant knowingly or recklessly published a falsehood.[14] And where proof of knowing or reckless falsehood as part of the plaintiff's prima facie case would also destroy any of the interest privileges,[15] the whole privilege analysis would become superfluous in those cases. None of this applies, however, to the privilege of fair reporting of public materials, which turns on accuracy and fairness.

Authorities. The implications of the constitutional changes have not been universally recognized and the jurisprudence of privilege has not fully developed these ideas. Some courts have not altered their approach to the common law privilege in the light of the constitutional decisions. Among those courts that have modified their abuse of privileges rules, some, with the Restatement, drop common law malice out of the picture and hold that the interest privileges are destroyed only by knowing or reckless falsehood.[16] Alternatively, courts may require the plaintiff to

14. Restatement § 600.

15. See Haworth v. Feigon, 623 A.2d 150 (Me.1993) (trial judge charged jury that the plaintiff had to prove knowing or reckless falsehood, consequently it was not reversible error that trial judge failed to charge on privilege).

16. De Leon v. Saint Joseph Hospital, Inc., 871 F.2d 1229 (4th Cir.1989); Hagler v. Proctor & Gamble Mfg. Co., 884 S.W.2d 771 (Tex.1994); See Green Acres Trust v. London, 141 Ariz. 609, 616, 688 P.2d 617, 624 (1984) (but also stating in boilerplate that improper purpose will destroy the privilege). Some cases seem to have used a

prove knowing or reckless falsehood as part of her prima facie case, so that the issue of privilege is implicitly decided before it is reached even when constitutional rules do not require such a result.[17] A third reaction to the constitutional decisions treats either knowing or reckless falsehood or common law malice as sufficient to destroy the privilege.[18]

TOPIC C. CONSTITUTIONAL LIMITATIONS ON RECOVERY

§ 417. Constitutional Fault and Damage Requirements Generally

Beginning in 1964, the Supreme Court recognized that the First Amendment's free speech provisions imposed limits on common law strict liability for defamation. The common law rules did not require a defamation plaintiff to prove fault, falsity, or actual damages. Each of these elements, sometimes all of them, is now constitutionally required in some cases, depending largely upon the status of the plaintiff. The rules developed for each category can be summarized as follows.

1. *Public official and public figure plaintiffs.* Under the rule developed in and after *New York Times Co. v. Sullivan*,[1] when the plaintiff is a public official, a candidate for public office, or a public figure suing for defamation, the plaintiff's claim must be established by proving whatever is required under state tort law *and,* as a constitutional requirement, that the defendant published (a) a falsehood, (b) knowing it to be false or acting in reckless disregard whether it was true or false. The constitutionally required elements must be proved with "convincing clarity."[2] This rule does not require proof of actual harm to reputation.[3]

The *Times-Sullivan* rule also applies in criminal prosecutions for libel of public officials[4] and an analogous rule has been used as gatekeeper rule to limit defamation claims in labor disputes subject to the jurisdiction of the National Labor Relations Board.[5]

recklessness standard in applying their common law malice rules. See Sigal Construction Corp. v. Stanbury,586 A.2d 1204 (D.C.App.1991).

17. Turf Lawnmower Repair, Inc. v. Bergen Record Corp., 139 N.J. 392, 655 A.2d 417 (1995) (recognizing knowing or reckless falsehood standard for some cases, negligence for others).

18. Schrader v. Eli Lilly and Co., 639 N.E.2d 258 (Ind.1994); Haworth v. Feigon, 623 A.2d 150 (Me.1993); Liberman v. Gelstein, 80 N.Y.2d 429, 605 N.E.2d 344, 590 N.Y.S.2d 857 (1992).

§ 417

1. New York Times Co. v. Sullivan, 376 U.S. 254, 84 S.Ct. 710, 11 L.Ed.2d 686 (1964) (public officials); Curtis Publishing Co. v. Butts, 388 U.S. 130, 87 S.Ct. 1975, 18 L.Ed.2d 1094 (1967) (public figures).

2. New York Times Co. v. Sullivan, supra n. 1, 376 U.S. at 285–86, 84 S.Ct. at 729. Although *Times-Sullivan* required knowing or reckless falsehood, some judges have suggested that the convincing clarity requirement applied only to the knowing or reckless elements and that falsity could be proved by a preponderance of the evidence. See Ayala v. Washington, 679 A.2d 1057 (D.C.App.1996).

3. New York Times Co. v. Sullivan, 376 U.S. 254, 84 S.Ct. 710, 11 L.Ed.2d 686 (1964).

4. Garrison v. Louisiana, 379 U.S. 64, 85 S.Ct. 209, 13 L.Ed.2d 125 (1964).

5. See Linn v. United Plant Guard Workers of America, Local 114, 383 U.S. 53, 86 S.Ct. 657, 15 L.Ed.2d 582 (1966).

Statements about limited purpose public figures must be germane to their public figure status,[6] but when it comes to public officials, almost anything is relevant to the public official's qualifications, including misbehavior that is remote in time or considered minor by many people.[7] The Supreme Court has applied the rule even when the publication does not mention the plaintiff's official capacity,[8] and some courts have agreed that reference to the plaintiff's public capacity is not required.[9] However, several courts have refused to apply the knowing or reckless falsehood rule when the plaintiff's official status is not mentioned in the publication, at least where the plaintiff is not well-known in the community.[10]

The rule is not a constitutional version of the fair comment privilege, which protects only comment and not errors of facts and which leaves the burden upon the defendant. Because the burden under the *Times-Sullivan* rule is upon the plaintiff, it is not even helpful to think of the rule as a privilege.

2. *Private persons suing for defamation on issues of public concern.* Under the *Gertz* rule, when a private person who is neither a public official nor a public figure sues for defamation arising from publication of matters of public concern she must prove whatever is required under state tort law *and* that the defendant (a) published a falsehood; (b) that he was negligent or otherwise at fault in failing to ascertain or state the truth; (c) and that the plaintiff suffered actual harm to reputation as a result. Not only must the plaintiff prove actual harm, but she is limited to a recovery of "actual damages." Consequently, the plaintiff cannot recover either presumed or punitive damages unless she proves a knowing or reckless falsehood described in the preceding paragraph.[11] A few doubts remain about the exact scope of the rules, for example, whether they apply only to media publications.[12] In addition, a few states by statute protect speakers who address issues on which governmental action may be forthcoming.[13]

3. *Private persons suing for defamation on issues not of public concern.* Under the *Dun & Bradstreet* rule, when a private person who is neither a public official nor a public figure sues for defamation arising from publication of matters not of public concern, she need not prove actual damages.[14] Several decisions have said or assumed that in the *Dun*

6. See § 418.

7. Monitor Patriot Co. v. Roy, 401 U.S. 265, 91 S.Ct. 621, 28 L.Ed.2d 35 (1971) (charge that plaintiff candidate was former small-time bootlegger; charge of criminal conduct, no matter how remote, is protected by the rule).

8. Ocala Star–Banner Co. v. Damron, 401 U.S. 295, 91 S.Ct. 628, 28 L.Ed.2d 57 (1971).

9. Stone v. Essex County Newspapers, Inc., 367 Mass. 849, 330 N.E.2d 161 (1975).

10. Bufalino v. Associated Press, 692 F.2d 266 (2d Cir.1982); Hinerman v. Daily Gazette Co., Inc., 188 W.Va. 157, 423 S.E.2d 560 (1992).

11. Gertz v. Robert Welch, Inc., 418 U.S. 323, 94 S.Ct. 2997, 41 L.Ed.2d 789 (1974).

12. Francis M. Dougherty, Annotation, Defamation: Application of New York Times And Related Standards to Nonmedia Defendants, 38 A.L.R.4th 1114 (1981).

13. See § 412.

14. Dun & Bradstreet, Inc. v. Greenmoss Builders, Inc., 472 U.S. 749, 105 S.Ct. 2939, 86 L.Ed.2d 593 (1985).

& Bradstreet category, all of the common law rules are intact.[15] Perhaps that means that falsity as well as damages can also be presumed in a *Dun & Bradstreet* claim. Professor Smolla thinks that the logic and the policy of Justice Powell's plurality opinion in *Dun & Bradstreet* would apply to the fault as well as to the damages issue, so that, after all, courts could continue to impose strict liability for defamation when the plaintiff is a private person and the issue under discussion is not one of public concern.[16] If he is right, the law of defamation will be complicated further because courts in all public figure cases will be required to act as arbiters determining what counts as a matter of public concern.[17]

Bases for the constitutional rules. (a) Public officials. The constitutional basis for rules requiring fault and falsity lies in the First Amendment to the United States Constitution, which broadly protects free speech against constraints imposed either by federal or state governments through legislation or judicial decisions. Because libel judgments, or even the possibility of a libel suit, can chill criticism of government and other public discussion and can lead to self-censorship, defamation actions potentially infringe rights of speech and association and even the right to petition government. This is most especially true when the plaintiff is a public official suing for a publication that may throw light on governmental operations. Since criticism of government is at the very heart of the free speech right and since such criticism most often is focused on a particular official, and since some factual error is inevitable in robust debate, the strict liability imposed at common law is inappropriate. In a sense, the public in a democratic society is always the judge of information about public officials, not the courts. These are ideas developed at length in the landmark 1964 decision, *New York Times Co. v. Sullivan.*[18]

(b) Public figures. Three years after the *Times-Sullivan* decision, the Supreme Court extended its knowing or reckless falsehood rules to cover publications about public figures who were not public officials.[19]

15. See Dombey v. Phoenix Newspapers, Inc., 150 Ariz. 476, 724 P.2d 562 (1986); Cox v. Hatch, 761 P.2d 556 (Utah 1988).

16. Rodney A. Smolla, Law of Defamation § 3.02 [5].

17. See Robert D. Sack & Sandra S. Baron, Libel, Slander and Related Problems § 5.9.5 (2d ed. 1994).

18. New York Times Co. v. Sullivan, 376 U.S. 254, 84 S.Ct. 710, 11 L.Ed.2d 686 (1964). *New York Times Co. v. Sullivan* arose out of the controversies and feelings of the civil rights struggle in the 1960s. A group of responsible persons published an advertisement in the New York Times soliciting donations, in part to defend Dr. Martin Luther King, who stood charged with perjury in Alabama. The advertisement asserted that those upholding civil rights were being subjected to a "wave of terror," and that "Southern violators" had bombed King's home and that "They have arrested him seven times.... " The police commissioner of Montgomery, Sullivan, sued the New York Times claiming defamation. He argued that the advertisement implicitly identified those who arrested King as Southern violators who also bombed his home. Since the police commissioner was supervisor of the police, he claimed the advertisement libeled him even though he was not named. The Alabama Supreme Court affirmed a judgment against the New York Times for $500,000. It was this judgment that was reversed by the Supreme Court's requirement of a knowing or reckless falsehood.

19. Curtis Publishing Co. v. Butts, 388 U.S. 130, 87 S.Ct. 1975, 18 L.Ed.2d 1094 (1967)

The reason given in Chief Justice Warren's opinion was that public figures can exercise informal power and influence over government and social decisions that may be as important as the power exercised by officials. However, the Court also seemed to say that public figures had ready access to media so that they could counter criticism, and later the Court seemed to put a great deal of emphasis on the fact that public figures are ordinarily in the public eye because they choose to be.[20]

(c) Private persons, issues of public concern. Observers might doubt whether the public figure's assumed risk or ability to reply to criticism would count as a constitutional reason to invoke the knowing or reckless falsehood rules. It might seem instead that the rules were constructed to foster free speech about public issues rather than public figures. In 1971, in *Rosenbloom v. Metromedia,*[21] a plurality of the Court adopted the view that publications about matters of public concern fell under the *Times-Sullivan* protections. However, three years later, in *Gertz,*[22] the Court firmly rejected the *Rosenbloom* decision. The *Gertz* argument for the proposition that "some" fault was enough in private plaintiff cases turned on its view that First Amendment values had to be accommodated to the states' interests in redressing defamation. The *Gertz* Court thought the state's interests in redressing defamation of private persons was much stronger than its interests in redressing defamation of public figures, who, after all, would ordinarily have chosen the limelight and its risks of defamation. Given the Court's balancing of the states' general interest and the First Amendment concerns, the Court hit on "some fault" plus actual damages as the appropriate compromise or "accommodation" of those interests.

(d) Private persons, issues not of public concern. In the case of private plaintiffs suing for defamation that does not involve public concern issues, the same balancing of state interests against the First Amendment led the Court to hold in *Dun & Bradstreet*[23] that the states were free to revert to the common law of presumed damages.

The constitutional rules requiring fault, falsity, and damages held a potential for rationalizing and simplifying the law of defamation. In fact, however, because the rules vary in each category, much of the dispute in libel cases now turns on how to categorize the plaintiff. The result is that new layers have been added to the law of defamation and that it has become more, not less complex.

20. Gertz v. Robert Welch, Inc., 418 U.S. 323, 94 S.Ct. 2997, 41 L.Ed.2d 789 (1974).

21. Rosenbloom v. Metromedia, Inc., 403 U.S. 29, 91 S.Ct. 1811, 29 L.Ed.2d 296 (1971).

22. Gertz v. Robert Welch, Inc., 418 U.S. 323, 94 S.Ct. 2997, 41 L.Ed.2d 789 (1974).

23. Dun & Bradstreet, Inc. v. Greenmoss Builders, Inc., 472 U.S. 749, 105 S.Ct. 2939, 86 L.Ed.2d 593 (1985).

The Matrix of Speech Protections after Dun & Bradstreet

	Persons	
	Public	Private
Public Concern	1 *Times-Sullivan* rules: knowing or reckless falsehood required. Damages may be presumed.	2 *Gertz* rules: "some fault plus actual damages required unless *Times-Sullivan* knowing or reckless falsehood is established.
Private Concern	3 Unknown.	4 *Dun & Bradstreet* rules: damages may be presumed; uncertainty: must plaintiff prove fault and/or falsity? Publications not germane to limited purpose public figure status may fall in this category.

§ 418. Who Are Public Officials and Public Figures

Public officials and public figures come under the same substantive rule: both must prove knowing or reckless falsehood. The determination of public official[1] and public figure[2] status on any given set of facts is for the judge, not the jury. Public officials are, however, defined differently from public figures.

Public Officials

Definitions and limitations. States sometimes have their own definitions of "official" but those definitions do not control the constitutional rule. Under the Supreme Court's decision in *Rosenblatt v. Baer*,[3] public officials include all government employees who have substantial responsibility in government affairs. In addition, a governmental employee is a public official if there is a public interest in the qualifications for her position apart from the general public interest in the qualifications of all employees. The definition does not limit the public official category to government employees who issue orders or those who are at upper levels of the political hierarchy. There is, however, a limit. The plaintiff is not a public official under the *Times-Sullivan* rule unless she holds a position that "would invite public scrutiny and discussion of the person holding it, entirely apart from the scrutiny and discussion occasioned by the particular charges in controversy." *Rosenblatt* itself included former

§ 418

1. See Rodney A. Smolla, Law of Defamation § 2.29 (1).

2. Costello v. Ocean County Observer, 136 N.J. 594, 643 A.2d 1012, 44 A.L.R.5th 799 (1994); Krueger v. Austad, 545 N.W.2d 205 (S.D.1996).

3. Rosenblatt v. Baer, 383 U.S. 75, 86 S.Ct. 669, 15 L.Ed.2d 597 (1966).

officials in the same category and candidates for government positions were later included as well.[4]

Examples. A number of persons in governmental positions easily qualify as public officials because of their substantial responsibility in the conduct of government affairs. Federal, state, and local elected officials would almost always count as public officials.[5] So would a good many others who act in positions of authority, management, or independence in their sphere of operation.[6] Police officers, with their potential for substantial effects on lives of citizens, are usually held to be public officials.[7] But the same reasoning is not always applied, for a few cases have held that public school teachers and even school principals, whose effect on the lives of citizens for good or bad is profound, are not public officials.[8] Other courts insist that as public education is a vital matter to society, public school principals and teachers are public officials whose capacities can be discussed under the *Times-Sullivan* rule.[9] Numerous other government employees have litigated these issues with similar differences in results.[10]

Public Figures

Public figures as well as public officials come under the *Times-Sullivan* rule. A public figure is often an individual, but various organizations including businesses,[11] public interest groups,[12] charities,[13] and religious organizations[14] may also count as public figures who are required to prove knowing or reckless falsehood in defamation suits.

4. Monitor Patriot Co. v. Roy, 401 U.S. 265, 91 S.Ct. 621, 28 L.Ed.2d 35 (1971) (candidates could be considered either public officials or public figures).

5. See Ocala Star–Banner Co. v. Damron, 401 U.S. 295, 91 S.Ct. 628, 28 L.Ed.2d 57 (1971) (mayor); Krueger v. Austad, 545 N.W.2d 205 (S.D.1996) (state senator); cf. Lewis v. Coursolle Broadcasting of Wisconsin, Inc., 127 Wis.2d 105, 377 N.W.2d 166 (1985) (former legislative activity, public *figure*).

6. Barnett v. Mobile County Personnel Bd., 536 So.2d 46 (Ala.1988) (town clerk in charge of payroll); Demby v. English, 667 So.2d 350 (Fla.Dist.Ct.App.1995) (director of animal control).

7. Moriarty v. Lippe, 162 Conn. 371, 378, 294 A.2d 326, 330–331 (1972) (although low-ranking, "a patrolman's office, if abused, has great potential for social harm and thus invites independent interest in the qualifications and performance of the person who holds the position"); Costello v. Ocean County Observer, 136 N.J. 594, 643 A.2d 1012, 44 A.L.R.5th 799 (1994).

8. True v. Ladner, 513 A.2d 257, 264 (Me.1986); see McCutcheon v. Moran, 99 Ill.App.3d 421, 424, 425 N.E.2d 1130, 1133, 54 Ill.Dec. 913, 916 (1981).

9. Johnson v. Robbinsdale Ind. Sch. Dist. No. 281, 827 F.Supp. 1439, 1443 (D.Minn.1993) ("Education of children is of vital importance to our society.... A contrary holding would stifle public debate about important local issues"); Sewell v. Brookbank, 119 Ariz. 422, 581 P.2d 267 (Ct. App.1978); Kelley v. Bonney, 221 Conn. 549, 606 A.2d 693, 709 (1992).

10. See Danny R. Veilleux, Annotation, Who Is "Public Official" For Purposes of Defamation Action, 44 A.L.R.5th 193 (1996).

11. E.g., Steaks Unlimited, Inc. v. Deaner, 623 F.2d 264 (3d Cir.1980).

12. E.g., Friends of Animals, Inc. v. Associated Fur Manufacturers, Inc., 46 N.Y.2d 1065, 390 N.E.2d 298, 416 N.Y.S.2d 790 (1979).

13. National Foundation for Cancer Research, Inc. v. Council of Better Business Bureaus, Inc., 705 F.2d 98 (4th Cir.1983).

14. E.g., Reader's Digest Ass'n v. Superior Court, 37 Cal.3d 244, 690 P.2d 610, 208 Cal.Rptr. 137 (1984) (church).

All purpose and limited purpose public figures. In *Gertz v. Robert Welch, Inc.*,[15] the Supreme Court recognized two kinds of public figures.

(1) Some public figures are all purpose public figures. As to these, a wide range of discussion would be relevant and protected under the *Times-Sullivan* rule. To prove that the plaintiff is this kind of public figure, the defendant would rely upon proof that the plaintiff enjoyed "pervasive power and influence" or "pervasive fame and notoriety" in public affairs.[16] With this kind of public figure, the plaintiff's role in society seems to be the central concern. Some people–a famous sports figure, perhaps–may attain public figure status by reason of their position alone.[17]

(2) Most are limited purpose public figures. They are public figures only with respect to some particular controversy or set of events.[18] To prove the plaintiff is a limited purpose public figure, the defendant must ordinarily show that the plaintiff voluntarily thrust herself into the controversy,[19] or at least is drawn into it[20] and attempted to influence its outcome. The *Gertz* Court thought the plaintiff would be a public figure in these cases because (a) she assumed the risk of public scrutiny by her voluntary involvement in issues and (b) she would have access to media and hence to self-defense against defamatory publications.

Those who thrust themselves into public controversy. The defamation plaintiff is not ordinarily a limited purpose public figure merely because she is herself newsworthy or involved in a newsworthy event.[21] Courts often conclude that the plaintiff is not a limited purpose public figure unless (a) there was a preexisting public controversy[22] and (b) the plaintiff injected herself into that controversy by voluntary action.

The plaintiff in *Gertz* itself was a lawyer involved with a case that caught public attention and he had participated in various civic activities in the course of his career, but as the Court held, that did not make him a general purpose public figure. And although he handled a controversial case, Mr. Gertz did not "thrust himself into the vortex of this public

15. Gertz v. Robert Welch, Inc., 418 U.S. 323, 94 S.Ct. 2997, 41 L.Ed.2d 789 (1974). The earlier emphasis had been on the importance of public figures in influencing public affairs. Curtis Pub. Co. v. Butts, 388 U.S. 130, 163, 87 S.Ct. 1975, 1996, 18 L.Ed.2d 1094 (1967) (opinion of Warren, C.J.).

16. 418 U.S. at 345, 351, 94 S.Ct. at 3009, 3013.

17. Curtis Pub. Co. v. Butts, 388 U.S. 130, 155, 87 S.Ct. 1975, 1991, 18 L.Ed.2d 1094 (1967) (Harlan, J.)

18. Gertz, supra n. 15, 418 U.S. at 351, 94 S.Ct. at 3013 ("a public figure for a limited range of issues").

19. 418 U.S. at 345, 94 S.Ct. at 3009.

20. Gertz, supra n. 15, 418 U.S. at 351, 94 S.Ct. at 3013 ("an individual voluntarily injects himself or is drawn into a particular public controversy and thereby becomes a public figure for a limited range of issues")

21. See Marcone v. Penthouse International Magazine for Men, 754 F.2d 1072 (3d Cir.1985). But see Dameron v. Washington Magazine, 779 F.2d 736 (D.C.Cir.1985) ("involuntary public figure" because involved in air crash).

22. The idea is that the publisher cannot create a controversy by his defamatory publication and then rely upon that as a defense. See Hutchinson v. Proxmire, 443 U.S. 111, 135, 99 S.Ct. 2675, 2688, 61 L.Ed.2d 411 (1979); Waldbaum v. Fairchild Pubs., Inc., 627 F.2d 1287, 1297 (D.C.Cir. 1980); Gannett Co., Inc. v. Re, 496 A.2d 553 (Del.1985).

issue, nor did he engage the public's attention in an attempt to influence its outcome."[23] He was thus not a limited purpose public figure either. Representing controversial clients is not enough to put a lawyer in the public figure category,[24] but the same lawyer may become a public figure if she is involved in controversy outside the courtroom or takes public stands about the case.[25]

Similarly, participants in litigation are not necessarily public figures. In *Time, Inc. v. Firestone,*[26] the Supreme Court held that the plaintiff did not become a public figure merely because she was married to the scion of a famous industrial family. And although she was involved in a publicized divorce, she did not choose freely to publicize the issues about the propriety of her married life. Consequently she was not required to show that the defendant's defamatory publication was a knowing or reckless falsehood, only a negligent one. Even a plaintiff who has been charged with crime may escape public figure status. In *Wolston v. Reader's Digest Ass'n, Inc.*[27], the Supreme Court held that a man who voluntarily refused to obey a subpoena and who had been held in criminal contempt as a result, was not a public figure, partly because his participation in the controversy was not voluntary.

Public activity alone does not force the plaintiff into the public figure category. A business, for example, may be a public figure, but not merely because it does business with the public or publicly sells its stock,[28] or because it is important and regulated.[29] Those who contract to provide goods or services to government may be public figures,[30] but not simply because they are recipients of public funds.[31]

Public figure status without voluntary involvement in controversy. The Supreme Court's decisions on limited purpose public figures have put a great deal of emphasis on the plaintiff's voluntary participation in controversy or public issues, but it is not clear that either a pre-existing controversy or voluntary participation in it is required in all cases. In justifying its rule for public figures, the Court in *Gertz* relied on the

23. Gertz, supra n. 15, 418 U.S. at 352, 94 S.Ct. at 3013.

24. See Spence v. Flynt, 816 P.2d 771 (Wyo.1991).

25. Finkelstein v. Albany Herald Pub. Co., Inc., 195 Ga.App. 95, 392 S.E.2d 559 (1990) (plaintiff had entered controversy surrounding district attorney's office and thus became a public figure; defendant's publication highlighting colorful incidents in plaintiff's own career were not made with knowing or reckless falsehood).

26. Time, Inc. v. Firestone, 424 U.S. 448, 96 S.Ct. 958, 47 L.Ed.2d 154 (1976).

27. Wolston v. Reader's Digest Ass'n Inc., 443 U.S. 157, 99 S.Ct. 2701, 61 L.Ed.2d 450 (1979).

28. Bank of Oregon v. Independent News, Inc., 298 Or. 434, 693 P.2d 35 (1985).

29. Blue Ridge Bank v. Veribanc, Inc., 866 F.2d 681 (4th Cir.1989).

30. Green v. Northern Pub. Co., Inc., 655 P.2d 736 (Alaska 1982) (doctor under contract to provide services to jails); Dombey v. Phoenix Newspapers, Inc., 150 Ariz. 476, 724 P.2d 562 (1986); Ferguson v. Watkins, 448 So.2d 271(Miss.1984); but see Saunders v. Van Pelt, 497 A.2d 1121 (Me. 1985) (psychologist contracting with school districts for examinations of students not a public figure).

31. Hutchinson v. Proxmire, 443 U.S. 111, 99 S.Ct. 2675, 61 L.Ed.2d 411 (1979) (leaving open the possibility that one who receives grant funds for government research is a public official even though not a public figure); Lundell Manufacturing Co. v. American Broadcasting Companies, Inc., 98 F.3d 351 (8th Cir.1996).

factual supposition that public figures would likely have access to the media and on the value judgment that they should be held to have assumed the risk of increased scrutiny. Those underlying reasons do not suggest that public figure status requires controversy or even public issues, since many public figures not involved in controversy of any kind have access to media and also assume the risks of fame. If controversy is required, it is not clear how it fits with voluntary participation. For example, it is not clear whether more controversy can make up for less voluntary participation.

It is clear, however, that courts have recognized public figure status in some cases even when the defamation plaintiff did not inject herself into public issues and also when no controversy was involved In one case, an air traffic controller on duty when a plane crashed was held to be a public figure with respect to events surrounding the crash, even though he had not thrust himself into any controversy about it.[32] In another case, doctors who were paid to supply services to a community hospital were public figures so that the defendant would enjoy *Times-Sullivan* protection for speech about their income even though no controversy existed.[33]

Fame without a preexisting controversy; a third category? Sometimes a defamation suit plaintiff is important in society or famous even though there is no preexisting controversy and though she does not attempt to influence society about a specific issue. The all-purpose public figure category includes those who enjoy pervasive fame as well as those who enjoy pervasive influence, so well-known entertainers and sports figures among others* have been classified as public figures. Perhaps courts have silently recognized a third category that amalgamates elements of the first two–a category based upon fame rather than the plaintiff's involvement in a controversy, yet with the limitation that discussions of the famous plaintiff are protected only if they are germane to her fame.

Some decisions seem consistent with such a view. In a suit by a professional football player, the court held that his fame was enough to place him in the public figure category although he did not attempt to influence preexisting public issues. But the court also implied that he might be a public figure only for purposes of discussions about his football career.[34] Courts have also said that sometimes the plaintiff's actions invite discussion although they have not engaged in controversy. A charity that massively solicits donations becomes a public figure on the basis of its voluntary action although it did not enter any preexisting controversy.[35] Persons associated in some way with major criminal

32. Dameron v. Washington Magazine, 779 F.2d 736 (D.C.Cir.1985).

33. Ferguson v. Watkins, 448 So.2d 271, 278 (Miss.1984) ("We emphasize that the matter of legitimate public interest need not produce actual controversy. It is enough that the matter is in the public domain").

34. Chuy v. Philadelphia Eagles Football Club, 595 F.2d 1265, 1280 (3d Cir.1979) ("was a public figure, at least with respect to his ability to play football").

35. National Foundation for Cancer Research, Inc. v. Council of Better Business Bureaus, Inc., 705 F.2d 98 (4th Cir.1983).

activity,[36] and those who have become major entertainment figures[37] have likewise been classed at times as public figures., although they have not pushed themselves to the forefront of any public controversy. Unless something can be made of a third category–limited public figures based on fame rather than controversy–courts may be forced to make the public figure concept even more slippery by using lists of factors.[38]

§ 419. Proving Constitutional Levels of Fault

Under the Knowing or Reckless Falsehood Rule

Rule. Under *New York Times Co. v. Sullivan*[1] public officials and public figures suing for defamation are required to prove with convincing clarity[2] that the defendant was guilty of publishing a knowing or reckless falsehood. Some courts believe this rule is limited to suits against media defendants,[3] while others reject any such special disability for individual speakers.[4] The Supreme Court has never resolved that issue.

"Actual malice." Unfortunately, the Court initially said that knowing or reckless falsehood amounted to "actual malice." For a period, courts confused this requirement with common law malice based on spite, ill-will or the like.[5] The *Times-Sullivan* rule, however, clearly requires that the plaintiff must prove more than common law malice; she must prove fault with respect to the substantial truth of the defamatory statement, that is, knowing or reckless falsehood.[6]

Insufficiency of negligence; subjective standard. Under the knowing or reckless falsehood rule, the defendant who negligently fails to investigate or otherwise ascertain the truth of a defamatory statement is not

36. Marcone v. Penthouse International Magazine for Men, 754 F.2d 1072 (3d Cir. 1985) (indictment in connection with drug operation that gained much notoriety was a factor in public figure determination as was social contract with Pagans motorcycle gang).

37. E.g., Brewer v. Memphis Pub. Co., Inc. 626 F.2d 1238 (5th Cir.1980); see Rodney A. Smolla, supra n. 1, § 2.21[4].

38. Rodney A. Smolla, The Law of Defamation § 2.09 [3] discusses a number of factors, mainly variants on the controversy and thrusting factors.

§ 419

1. New York Times Co. v. Sullivan, 376 U.S. 254, 84 S.Ct. 710, 11 L.Ed.2d 686 (1964).

2. Id., 376 U.S. 254, 286, 84 S.Ct. 710, 729, 11 L.Ed.2d 686. Presumably convincing clarity can be equated with the familiar clear and convincing evidence standard.

3. Denny v. Mertz, 106 Wis.2d 636, 318 N.W.2d 141 (1982) (holding, over a dissent by Judge Abrahamson, that a magazine publishing a quotation from an individual was protected by the *Gertz* rule but that the individual who supplied the quotation was not).

4. In Jacron Sales Co., Inc. v. Sindorf, 276 Md. 580, 592, 350 A.2d 688, 695 (1976) (as a matter of tort law, it would be bizarre to impose strict liability upon individuals while relieving an enterprise).

5. See, e.g., Greenbelt Cooperative Pub. Ass'n v. Bresler, 253 Md. 324, 252 A.2d 755 (1969) (reversed partly because trial judge instructed on ill will or spite as malice); Mobile Press Register, Inc. v. Faulkner, 372 So.2d 1282 (Ala.1979) (similar).

6. Literal falsity is not enough to meet the constitutional demand. If the publisher knows the statement he is publishing is literally false, as in the case of a known misquotation, the defendant is still not liable if the statement is substantially true in the sense that it caused no more injury to the plaintiff's reputation than a similar and true statement. See Masson v. New Yorker Magazine, Inc., 501 U.S. 496, 111 S.Ct. 2419, 115 L.Ed.2d 447 (1991).

liable to a public official or public figure plaintiff.[7] The defendant is not reckless merely because he is very negligent in failing to discover the truth. Rather, he is reckless when he publishes a statement with a high degree of awareness of its probable falsity. "There must be sufficient evidence to permit the conclusion that the defendant in fact entertained serious doubts as to the truth of his publication."[8] The standard is subjective; a credulous reporter taken in by source is not guilty of reckless falsehood.[9]

Evidence of knowing or reckless falsehood. Although a negligent failure to investigate is not ground for liability under the *Times-Sullivan* rule and does not prove knowing or reckless falsehood, the defendant's negligent conduct may be an outward reflection of the defendant's inner knowledge or awareness of probable falsity. If he publishes an inherently improbable story or one based upon an unverified anonymous telephone call, the jury may at times be permitted to conclude that he in fact knew or at least seriously doubted his own statements.[10] The trier may infer that the publisher who interviews all witnesses except the one witness who could show that the defamatory material is false purposefully avoided the truth and was thus highly aware of probable falsity.[11]

Under the "Some Fault" Standard for Private Persons

Negligence vs. other standards. Under the *Gertz*[12] rule, even a private person suing for defamation–or perhaps media defamation–is constitutionally required to prove "some fault" when the defamation touches an issue that is not of purely private concern.[13] *Gertz* leaves the states free to set the level of fault required, but presumably it must be fault in publishing a falsehood, not "fault" in the sense of common law malice such as hatred or ill-will.[14] The states have overwhelmingly adopted negligence as the standard of fault to be required when a private person sues.[15] Several states have adopted the stronger standard based upon knowing or reckless falsehood when speech touches public con-

7. New York Times Co. v. Connor, 365 F.2d 567 (5th Cir.1966); Davis v. Borskey, 660 So.2d 17 (La.1995); but cf. Curtis Publishing Co. v. Butts, 388 U.S. 130, 87 S.Ct. 1975, 18 L.Ed.2d 1094 (1967) (some Justices found reckless disregard of the truth largely because of slipshod investigation of serious allegation and a source regarded as untrustworthy).

8. St. Amant v. Thompson, 390 U.S. 727, 731, 88 S.Ct. 1323, 1325, 20 L.Ed.2d 262 (1968).

9. See McCoy v. Hearst Corporation, 42 Cal.3d 835, 727 P.2d 711, 231 Cal.Rptr. 518 (1986).

10. St. Amant v. Thompson, 390 U.S. 727, 88 S.Ct. 1323, 20 L.Ed.2d 262 (1968).

11. Harte–Hanks Communications, Inc. v. Connaughton, 491 U.S. 657, 109 S.Ct. 2678, 105 L.Ed.2d 562 (1989); but cf. McFarlane v. Sheridan Square Press, Inc., 91 F.3d 1501 (D.C.Cir.1996).

12. Gertz v. Robert Welch, Inc., 418 U.S. 323, 94 S.Ct. 2997, 41 L.Ed.2d 789 (1974).

13. Dun & Bradstreet, Inc. v. Greenmoss Builders, Inc.,472 U.S. 749, 105 S.Ct. 2939, 86 L.Ed.2d 593 (1985).

14. See Hustler Magazine v. Falwell, 485 U.S. 46, 108 S.Ct. 876, 99 L.Ed.2d 41 (1988) (expressing the view that fault must relate to falsehood in a privacy claim).

15. E.g., Peagler v. Phoenix Newspapers, Inc., 114 Ariz. 309, 560 P.2d 1216 (1977); Embers Supper Club v. Scripps–Howard Broadcasting Co., 9 Ohio St.3d 22, 457 N.E.2d 1164 (1984); Restatement § 580B; Rodney A. Smolla, Law of Defamation § 3.10 (looseleaf).

cerns.[16] States adopting that rule will not be required to draw the fine line between public figures and private persons but will still be required to determine whether the speech involves matters of public concern. On speech arguably of public concern, New York imposes liability only for gross departure from ordinary standards of investigation and dissemination.[17]

Negligence or no negligence as a matter of law. It is difficult to transfer the negligence concept from the physical world to the world of words. In a few cases courts can rule out negligence as a matter of law. The defendant probably is not negligent unless the published statement "makes substantial danger to reputation apparent" so that the publisher would be on notice that investigation or other care is especially important.[18] A number of courts have also said that a publisher can ordinarily rely on reputable wire services or similar sources of information and is not negligent in publishing their content without further investigation.[19] The other end of the same stick is that something like *res ipsa loquitur* could conceivably apply in some cases. But as the Restatement suggests, great caution should be exercised here less false analogies from cases of physical injury nullify a constitutional right to speak and publish or reimpose the strict liability that is now forbidden.[20]

Professional vs. ordinary care standard. A media publisher's negligence is perhaps most easily imaginable when the publisher fails to investigate facts and when such a failure can be evaluated by professional standards of journalists. It would be possible to adjudicate such cases under what Professor Smolla calls the professional malpractice model of negligence.[21] Some of the cases have in fact stated that the professional standard would control.[22] Other cases speak with more caution, saying that the standard is reasonable care, but professional standards or customs are evidence bearing on that issue, just as they are in ordinary negligence cases.[23] Still other authority seems ambiguous or vague about the role of professional standards.[24] Finally, a number of decisions adopt

16. Diversified Management, Inc. v. Denver Post, Inc., 653 P.2d 1103, 33 A.L.R.4th 193 (Colo. 1982) (but rejecting the subjective test of reckless disregard); AAFCO Heating and Air Conditioning Co. v. Northwest Pubs., Inc., 162 Ind.App. 671, 321 N.E.2d 580 (1974). New Jersey has subdivided public concern, using the knowing or reckless falsehood standard for some issues of public concern but not others. See Turf Lawnmower Repair, Inc. v. Bergen Record Corp., 139 N.J. 392, 655 A.2d 417 (1995).

17. Chapadeau v. Utica Observer–Dispatch, Inc., 38 N.Y.2d 196, 341 N.E.2d 569, 379 N.Y.S.2d 61 (1975).

18. See Gertz v. Robert Welch, Inc., 418 U.S. 323, 348, 94 S.Ct. 2997, 3011 41 L.Ed.2d 789 (1974).

19. E.g., Appleby v. Daily Hampshire Gazette, 395 Mass. 32, 478 N.E.2d 721 (1985).

20. See Restatement § 580B, cmt. g.

21. Rodney A. Smolla, Law of Defamation § 3.25.

22. Gobin v. Globe Pub. Co., 216 Kan. 223, 531 P.2d 76, 84 (1975); Seegmiller v. KSL, Inc., 626 P.2d 968 (Utah 1981); cf. Triangle Pubs., Inc. v. Chumley, 253 Ga. 179, 317 S.E.2d 534 (1984) (stating a professional standard but also stating that professional custom is not controlling).

23. Appleby v. Daily Hampshire Gazette, 395 Mass. 32, 37, 478 N.E.2d 721, 724 (1985) ("Customs and practices within the profession are relevant" but "custom is not controlling").

24. The Restatement attempts to adopt the professional standard as controlling "to

the ordinary care or reasonable person standard[25] or at least reject any requirement of professional expert testimony on the standard of care.[26]

The theoretical effect of a true professional malpractice standard would be to give professional custom or standards determinative weight,[27] and, if the analogy to medical malpractice was carried out, to require expert testimony to establish the standard in the case of a media publication.[28] Unless journalists have established a specific applicable custom or standard, the practical effect may be that journalists testifying about the standard will supplant the normal role of judge and jury. Many subsidiary questions arise as well. If the analogy is to professional standards in medical malpractice, it may be that journalistic specialties will each have their own standards; those of supermarket tabloids might conceivably differ from those of a national news magazine. No doubt courts will reject any application of the professional standard that exonerates the most negligent journalists, but the point suggests the conceptual weakness of the general idea.

The ordinary care standard contrasts sharply with the professional standard, but it has many disadvantages of its own, not the least of which is that rights to speak freely may be conditioned upon wholly unknowable expectations of the trier of fact imposed ex post facto. However, the debate about the "standard of care" is in reality a debate about several distinct issues: (1) Will expert testimony be *required* to establish journalistic negligence? (2) Is expert evidence *admissible* as bearing on the appropriate journalistic standard? (3) Will the jury be instructed to judge fault by the standard of the reasonable prudent person in similar circumstances or by the standard of journalists? Broken down in this way, the questions may be much easier to answer.

As to expert testimony, there seems little reason to require it in every case; in some cases the trier can easily find negligence without it. At the same time, a trial judge assessing the evidence may conclude that in particular cases expert testimony is required to establish a plausible claim. While a rule of law requiring professional testimony is not necessary, assessment of the evidence is. By the same token, as in other negligence cases, the customary practice or standard of care of the industry almost always has some bearing on the fault issue and should be admitted. If those observations are right, then the instruction to the jury should be to judge fault under the reasonable and prudent person or ordinary care standard, and should add such additional guidance as the courts may think is required. Directed verdicts and summary judgments

a substantial degree," yet maintains the traditional rule that custom of nonprofessionals is only relevant, not controlling. Restatement § 580B cmt. g.

25. Memphis Pub. Co. v. Nichols, 569 S.W.2d 412 (Tenn.1978)

26. Little Rock Newspapers, Inc. v. Dodrill, 281 Ark. 25, 660 S.W.2d 933 (1983). See Robert D. Sack & Sandra S. Baron, Libel, Slander, and Related Problems, § 5.9.1.2 (2d ed. 1994).

27. See §§ 242 & 246.

28. See Seegmiller v. KSL, Inc., 626 P.2d 968 (Utah 1981) (suggesting that such testimony would be required unless negligence was flagrant).

would still be in order if the evidence is not rationally sufficient to show negligence.

Risks and benefits. The ordinary analysis of negligence weighs risks and benefits of the defendant's action.[29] If this approach were carried out in a defamation case, courts would be required to weigh the harm to reputation that would be foreseeable from publishing the defamation, perhaps as discounted by the probability that such harm would result. Against such harm, courts would be required to weigh the value of the information the defendant reasonably thought it was publishing.

Although the Restatement suggests that this can be done in rather gross ways[30]–the value of gossip is less than the value of hard news–there are two major reasons not to proceed in this way. First, it is impossible to set a value on any particular published item or its part in the cumulative value of information. It is definitely impossible to set a value on the loss of further items of information that may follow if liability is imposed too readily. Second, except perhaps in the most extreme cases, courts cannot rightly judge the value of information; the readers must do that. Relatedly, any judicial declaration that information about a matter of public concern is of little value might well turn out to be unconstitutional. These objections and difficulties make it likely that any risk-benefit analysis of publications will be unsatisfactory in every possible way.

Types of fault. Much of the discussion of negligence under the *Gertz*-fault standard has been directed to, or assumed, that the fault involved was a failure to verify or check information. Failure to check further does indeed represent one kind of publication error, but it is not the only kind. A reporter might credit his sources when some people would not do so; he might make erroneous deductions or inferences (possibly without knowing he was drawing inferences at all); he might misunderstand legal or other terminology. In addition, the publication may be defamatory because of mechanical or typographical errors.[31] Finally, the act of writing itself may utilize accurate information but convey the wrong idea.

The negligence concept is not well adapted to any of the conduct leading to these errors, but it is harder to apply to some than others. Errors of inference, ambiguous articulation, and other communicative errors are almost inevitable; they occur not only in journalistic but also in almost any kind of communication, including judicial opinions and learned treatises. Reports of someone else's report–for example, what the police said about a shooting,[32] what the judge held in a divorce suit[33]–are

29. See §§ 144 & 145.

30. Restatement § 580B, cmt. h.

31. All of the items in this list are adapted from a longer list found in Rodney A. Smolla, Law of Defamation § 3.28 [3].

32. See, e.g., Memphis Pub. Co. v. Nichols, 569 S.W.2d 412 (Tenn.1978) (report of a shooting that failed to indicate the number of persons present and as a result permitting a reader to think that an adulterous affair was going on).

33. Time, Inc. v. Firestone, 424 U.S. 448, 96 S.Ct. 958, 47 L.Ed.2d 154 (1976) (divorce judge granted divorce to husband after discussing husband's claim that wife

routine, but all such reports "can contain an almost infinite variety of shadings"[34] and many opportunities for imperfection. Even a reviewer's own experience listening to music on a sound system might be translated into words in a variety of different ways, some of which may seem defamatory to the manufacturer of the system.[35] If negligence is to be the basis for liability in such cases, it does not look very much like the negligence we see in cases of physical injury and perhaps a different terminology should be developed. Certainly caution is required in applying a negligence test of liability for speech.

§ 420. Constitutional Falsity Requirement and Opinion Statements

The Burden of Proving Falsity

The common law presumed that defamatory statements were false, thus putting the burden upon the defendant to justify the statement by proving truth. *New York Times v. Sullivan*[1] held that under the First Amendment, a public official suing for defamation would be required to prove knowing or reckless falsehood. To prove a knowing falsehood, the plaintiff would seemingly be required to prove a falsehood, so it looked as if the common law presumption of falsity had been abolished for public official (and later) public figure plaintiffs.

That result was confirmed and extended in *Philadelphia Newspapers, Inc. v. Hepps.*[2] In that case, the plaintiff was a private, not a public figure. The defendant newspaper, discussing matters of public concern, said that the plaintiff had links with organized crime. The Court held, over dissents, that the burden of proving falsity fell upon the private plaintiff suing for public concern speech as well as upon the public figure plaintiff.

The result seems logical and indeed unavoidable if the plaintiff must show knowing, reckless, or negligent falsehood. Only if the Constitution would countenance liability for fault unrelated to falsity–ill-will, for example, or negligence not bearing on the truth of the statement–would it be possible to prove defendant's fault without also proving falsity. Up until *Hepps*, courts seem to have agreed that the fault required was directed at the question of truth and falsity, so that fault and falsity

committed adultery and saying that there was testimony of extramarital escapades; magazine thought this meant divorce was granted for adultery and so reported; legal analysis showed that the divorce was granted for cruelty).

34. Time, Inc. v. Pape, 401 U.S. 279, 285, 91 S.Ct. 633, 637, 28 L.Ed.2d 45 (1971).

35. Bose Corporation v. Consumers Union of United States, Inc., 466 U.S. 485, 104 S.Ct. 1949, 80 L.Ed.2d 502 (1984) (suit against Consumer Reports for a review that said the plaintiff's speakers made the sound seem to wander around the room when the reviewer actually meant that the sound seemed to move back and forth along a wall).

§ 420

1. New York Times Co. v. Sullivan, 376 U.S. 254, 84 S.Ct. 710, 11 L.Ed.2d 686 (1964).

2. Philadelphia Newspapers, Inc. v. Hepps, 475 U.S. 767, 106 S.Ct. 1558, 89 L.Ed.2d 783 (1986).

went hand in hand.[3] Yet four Justices dissented, saying that defendants would be adequately protected by the fault requirement without also requiring the plaintiff to prove falsity. Some of the Justices may also have implied that the constitutional protections extended only to media publishers. These features of *Hepps* may suggest that, as a practical matter, the states will remain free to presume falsehood when a private person sues on a publication that is not about issues of public concern.

Provably False Statements

Protection of non-factual statements under fair comment rules. Earlier common law offered no general doctrine protecting non-factual statements such as statements of opinion[4] or statements ridiculing the plaintiff without the use of any false factual statement.[5]

Sometimes, however, a distinction was drawn between statements about verifiable facts on the one hand and characterization of facts such as opinion or comment on the other. The distinction appeared mainly in the fair comment cases. The fair comment privilege protected the defendant's statement of opinion about matters of public interest,[6] provided the defendant truly stated the facts upon which the opinion was based. The privilege in effect protected the publisher willing to expose his irrational opinions as well as the publisher whose opinions might be justified by the facts. If the opinion was ventured without a statement of the facts upon which it was based, no privilege attached.[7] The courts also

3. All of the discussions seem to have assumed or implied that the fault required was fault because it led to untruthful publications. In *Time, Inc. v. Firestone*, 424 U.S. 448, 458, 96 S.Ct. 958, 967, 47 L.Ed.2d 154 (1976) the Court said: "[D]emonstration that an article was true would seem to preclude finding the publisher at fault.... "

4. Restatement (First) of Torts § 566 ; see Christie, Defamatory Opinions and the Restatement (Second) of Torts, 75 Mich. L. Rev. 1621 (1977). The First Restatement's illustration has it that one making a political speech and truthfully describing the plaintiff's actions with particularity is guilty of defamation is he characterizes the plaintiff's acts as like those of a murderer. It leaves open the possibility of a privilege, however. The Second Restatement, however, restated the rule of § 566 to say that an opinion statement would be actionable only if it implied the allegation of undisclosed defamatory facts.

5. Burton v. Crowell Pub. Co., 82 F.2d 154 (2d Cir.1936) (by accident of lighting and composition photo made it appear that a piece of the plaintiff's saddle was a part of the plaintiff and that he was exposing himself; although any viewer would recognize that this was not in fact the case, viewer might still laugh and the plaintiff would suffer from the ridiculous association); see also Spence v. Flynt, 816 P.2d 771 (Wyo. 1991) (labeling plaintiff as "asshole of the month" and offering other epithets was actionable). Courts also held that a privilege to publish would be destroyed if the defendant's purpose was to ridicule the plaintiff. Hogan v. New York Times Co., 313 F.2d 354 (2d Cir.1963) (misstatements of fact; reference to police as "Keystone Cops" showed abuse of privilege because of intent to ridicule and thus abuse of privilege); Triggs v. Sun Printing & Publishing Ass'n, 179 N.Y. 144, 71 N.E. 739 (1904). *Distinguish* ridicule based upon factual misstatements. E.g., Powers v. Durgin–Snow Pub. Co., 154 Me. 108, 144 A.2d 294 (1958) (alleged misstatement that plaintiff was building his own coffin and digging his own grave with comment on his thrift in saving burial expense).

6. The fair comment privilege was recognized not only for comments about political and governmental figures but also for comments about those who submitted their work for public approval, including restaurants, authors, solicitors for charities and others.

7. A.S. Abell Company v. Kirby, 227 Md. 267, 176 A.2d 340, 90 A.L.R.2d 1264 (1961) (referring to the "infamous Kirby" without

sometimes refused to impose liability for name-calling and invective, largely on the ground that it was meaningless and not defamatory.[8] The name-calling rule and the fair comment privilege, now largely superseded by the constitutional protections for speech about public figures, marked the main boundary of common law protection for opinion statements.

Constitutional requirement of falsity. The Constitutional protection for truthful speech has led to a constitutional principle that the liability may not be imposed for any speech of public concern unless the defendant's publication contains statements that are "provably false."[9] Although the Court in so holding rejected any separate protection for "opinion," a statement of opinion that implied no facts at all would not be provably false and hence would be constitutionally protected.

Value-judgment opinions vs. "opinions" about matters of fact. This point is demonstrated in the cases that led to the provably false standard test. *Gertz* itself has asserted that there is no such thing as a false idea.[10] A statement that one who accepts the teachings of Marx and Lenin is abysmally ignorant is protected as an idea or evaluation of the teachings of Marx and those who accept them. But a statement that, in the writer's opinion, "Mayor Jones is a liar" is not protected.[11] That statement is not an evaluation of stated facts or an "idea," but rather an assertion that some facts exist to show Jones is a liar.

Rhetorical hyperbole. Even before *Gertz* was decided, the Court had decided a closely related point. In *Greenbelt Cooperative Publishing Ass'n v. Bresler,*[12] the plaintiff was a developer trying to secure zoning variances from the city. At the same time, the city was trying to purchase other land from the plaintiff. At a city council meeting, some citizens feared the plaintiff could obtain the variances because the city wanted his other land. They characterized the plaintiff's leverage by calling him a blackmailer. The defendant newspaper published an account of the meeting and the blackmailer language. The Maryland Court treated "blackmailer" as if it were a defamatory accusation of crime,[13] although it would have been apparent to anyone who read the story that "blackmail" merely described Bresler's negotiating strength with the city. The Supreme Court held that liability could not be imposed for the report because "even the most careless reader must have perceived that the

stating facts upon which publisher's opinion of infamy was based). Conversely, if the basis for the opinion is clear, the comment is protected. E.g., People for the Ethical Treatment of Animals v. Bobby Berosini, Ltd., 111 Nev. 615, 895 P.2d 1269 (1995) (after showing a video tape of the plaintiff handling animals defendant said the tape showed animal cruelty, protected opinion).

8. E.g., Ward v. Zelikovsky, 136 N.J. 516, 643 A.2d 972 (1994) ("she's a bitch" and even a ruinous accusation of bigotry, "They don't like Jews").

9. Milkovich v. Lorain Journal, 497 U.S. 1, 110 S.Ct. 2695, 111 L.Ed.2d 1 (1990).

10. Gertz v. Robert Welch, Inc., 418 U.S. 323, 339, 94 S.Ct. 2997, 3007, 41 L.Ed.2d 789 (1974).

11. Milkovitch, supra n. 9, 497 U.S. at 20, 110 S.Ct. at 2706.

12. Greenbelt Cooperative Publishing Ass'n v. Bresler, 398 U.S. 6, 90 S.Ct. 1537, 26 L.Ed.2d 6 (1970).

13. Greenbelt Cooperative Pub. Ass'n v. Bresler, 253 Md. 324, 252 A.2d 755 (1969).

word was no more than rhetorical hyperbole, a vigorous epithet used by those who considered Bresler's negotiating position extremely unreasonable."[14] Rhetoric or epithet that implies no fact that can be falsified is thus constitutionally protected. So far as this is a constitutional rule, it seems to be derived from the requirement that the plaintiff prove a falsehood and presumably covers the same cases covered by that requirement. So far as it is a common law rule, it appears to cover all cases.

Ridicule without factual implications. Hustler Magazine v. Falwell,[15] presented the Supreme Court with an exceptionally scurrilous publication. It depicted a public figure as having had an incestuous encounter with his own mother in an outhouse. The publication was a tasteless parody on a series of "First Time" ads for Campari, but it was clear that the publisher did not intend to assert any fact about the plaintiff and clear as well that no one would view the cartoon as an assertion of fact. Since no factual assertion was found, a libel recovery seemed out of the question. The plaintiff attempted to avoid this limitation by asserting that the publication amounted to an intentional infliction of emotional distress. But the Supreme Court held that so far as this tort was based upon publication, the plaintiff would be required to show knowing or intentional falsehood. Since there was no falsity, the claim failed.

The provably false standard. As all these cases were summed up in *Milkovitch*, the plaintiff could recover only if she could show a provably false statement. Perhaps this means that the statement must be the kind that could be verified or falsified through the senses if witnesses had been present at all times. In contrast, statements that could be judged and evaluated but not neutrally determined by touch, vision, or hearing, would not be provably false. Although circumstantial evidence might be required to prove falsity of some statements, the circumstantial evidence itself would presumably have to be factual rather than evaluative. In adopting the provably false standard, *Milkovitch* appears to have rejected the complicated analyses that determine what counted as protected "opinion" by considering whether the statement was important to public debate and the type of publication and type of language used.[16] States courts are, of course, free to add their own protections and hence to protect publication of statements whose "tone" or "apparent purpose" somehow suggest that they constitute a non-factual statement.[17] Somewhat surprisingly, this has led one court to protect a publication "imagining" that the plaintiff was guilty of a murder, on the ground that it was mere conjecture and not "factual."[18]

14. Greenbelt, supra n. 12, 398 U.S. at 14, 90 S.Ct. at 1542.

15. Hustler Magazine v. Falwell, 485 U.S. 46, 108 S.Ct. 876, 99 L.Ed.2d 41 (1988).

16. See Ollman v. Evans, 750 F.2d 970 (D.C.Cir.1984); Janklow v. Newsweek, Inc., 788 F.2d 1300 (8th Cir.1986).

17. Immuno AG. v. Moor–Jankowski, 77 N.Y.2d 235, 567 N.E.2d 1270, 566 N.Y.S.2d 906 (1991).

18. Levin v. McPhee, 119 F.3d 189 (2d Cir.1997) (distinguished author's report of statements of various persons interviewed; perhaps the case supports the neutral reportage privilege without saying so).

Opinion that implies provably false statements. The *Milkovitch* Court recognized that some statements couched in the language of opinion might imply provably false statements of fact. To say that anyone who attended a wrestling meet "knows in his heart that Milkovich and Scott lied at the hearing after each having given his solemn oath to tell the truth" is to imply a factual assertion, a contradiction between facts that witnesses could have observed and statements under oath which witnesses could have and did hear.

Statement of facts upon which opinion is based. It is often difficult to determine whether an evaluative statement implies defamatory facts. Meaning always depends in part upon context as well as syntax and definition. "She's a crook" in some contexts is merely meaningless invective but in others such a statement implies that there are facts showing a violation of law by theft or the like. However, when the publication states all of the facts upon which the evaluative comment is based, the comment itself does not imply facts and is presumably fully protected under the constitutional rules.[19] Suppose the statement referring to the plaintiff is that "she left work thirty minutes early; that makes me think she's a crook." The listener or reader cannot reasonably think that the plaintiff is charged with anything more than leaving work early; full revelation of the publisher's reasoning negates all other implications. If the fact is that the plaintiff left work early, then the defendant's view that leaving work early is "crooked" is not actionable. If the facts themselves are misstated then the protection is lost.[20]

TOPIC D. PROCEDURES, REMEDIES, AND ALTERNATIVES

§ 421. Procedural Incidents

Two or three procedural points are of special significance in defamation suits.

Single publication rule. Publication is not only an element of the cause of action; it is also the trigger for the statute of limitations. If a book was published in 1950, a one-year statute of limitations would run in 1951. Because most states did not apply the discovery rule to defamation, the statute would run even if the plaintiff did not become aware of the defamation until much later.[1]

On the other hand, the common law concept of publication treated each new communication, such as sale of a single copy of a book, as a new publication. If the publisher of a book originally sold in 1950 later

19. See, e.g., Levin v. McPhee, 119 F.3d 189 (2d Cir.1997).

20. E.g., Afro-American Pub. Co. v. Jaffe, 366 F.2d 649 (D.C.Cir.1966).

§ 421

1. E.g., Palmer v. Westmeyer, 48 Ohio App.3d 296, 549 N.E.2d 1202 (1988) ; contra, Allen v. Ortez, 802 P.2d 1307 (Utah 1990); see Francis M. Dougherty, Annotation, Limitation of Actions: Time of Discovery of Defamation as Determining Accrual of Action, 35 A.L.R.4th 1002 (1981).

sold a copy in the year 2000, persons defamed by the book could sue in that year although they would have been barred in 1951. By statute or judicial decision, most states now follow the single publication rule. That rule treats any mass publication such as an edition of a book or newspaper as a single publication for which only one suit is authorized.[2] The plaintiff can recover in one suit for all damages incurred at home or abroad. Concomitantly, the statute begins to run when that publication occurs.[3]

The concept of a single publication also seems to suggest that a single state's law would control even if damages were inflicted in all states and other political units. That would normally be the state of the plaintiff's domicile or, in the case of procedural incidents, the state where the claim is tried. However, the mysteries of choice of law and jurisdiction in defamation cases must be left to more specialized treatises.

Pleading, summary judgment and discovery. At one time courts required the plaintiff to plead the exact words used in a libel and occasionally still do,[4] but contemporary pleading rules ordinarily require only that the gist of the libel be pleaded.[5] Discovery is commonly pursued in media defamation cases in any event, usually with the hope that the issue can be resolved on summary judgment. Under the rule in *New York Times v. Sullivan*[6] (applicable to public official and public figure plaintiffs) the plaintiff must prove a knowing or reckless falsehood, a subjective test that warrants discovery about what the defendant knew or believed to be true.[7] The *New York Times* rule requires the public official and public figure plaintiff not only to prove knowing or reckless falsehood, but to do so by clear and convincing evidence. That burden of proof affects summary judgment as well as standards for directed verdict and instruction to the jury. Consequently if the undisputed facts presented on summary judgment motion do not present a case from which a jury could find knowing or reckless falsehood by clear and convincing evidence, the defendant's motion should be granted.[8]

2. Keeton v. Hustler Magazine, Inc., 131 N.H. 6, 549 A.2d 1187 (1988); see Uniform Single Publication Act; Restatement § 577A.

3. Possibly publication does not occur for this purpose until the defamation reaches the plaintiff's domicile. See Applewhite v. Memphis State University, 495 S.W.2d 190 (Tenn.1973). Some publications might count as continuing torts so that, on a one-year statute of limitations, the plaintiff could sue belatedly and recover for all damages incurred during the preceding year. Cf. Dominiak v. National Enquirer, 439 Pa. 222, 266 A.2d 626, 42 A.L.R.3d 798 (1970) (similar).

4. Lichtor v. Missouri Board of Registration for the Healing Arts, 884 S.W.2d 49 (Mo.App.1994).

5. Mittelman v. Witous, 135 Ill.2d 220, 552 N.E.2d 973, 142 Ill.Dec. 232 (1989).

6. New York Times v. Sullivan, 376 U.S. 254, 84 S.Ct. 710, 11 L.Ed.2d 686 (1964).

7. Herbert v. Lando, 441 U.S. 153, 99 S.Ct. 1635, 60 L.Ed.2d 115 (1979).

8. See Anderson v. Liberty Lobby, Inc., 477 U.S. 242, 106 S.Ct. 2505, 91 L.Ed.2d 202 (1986).

§ 422. Remedies

Damages

Actual damages under common law and the Gertz rule. The common law rule, which still governs many cases, allows juries to presume that a defamatory publication of libel has caused harm to reputation and then to award substantial sums of money even in the absence of evidence on the point. The rule may be headed for extinction. Commentators have attacked it and some states have abandoned it even when the Constitution a does not require them to do so.[1] And the First Amendment bars the recovery of presumed damages in one instance–when the plaintiff is a private person defamed on a topic of public concern and proves fault short of knowing or reckless falsehood. In such a case, the plaintiff can recover only her "actual" damages. The rule excludes both the common law presumed damages and punitive damages. On the other hand, "actual" damages permitted in such cases are not limited to special or pecuniary damages required by the common law rules in slander cases. They may include any harm to reputation and also emotional harm.[2]

Elements of damages. Except for presumed damages, *Gertz* presumably permits recovery of all compensatory damages recognized under common law decisions.

In addition to damages for estimated loss of reputation, the award may include damages for pecuniary losses, so long as they are proximately caused by the defamatory publication.[3] For example, the plaintiff may recover for loss of employment resulting from the defamation.[4] The plaintiff may also recover for emotional distress[5] and resulting bodily harm,[6] at least where it is a result of reputational loss,[7] and for costs of corrective advertising by the plaintiff[8] and other expenses incurred in defending his reputation.[9] Courts have even allowed loss of consortium recovery by the spouse of a defamed person.[10] So far as the plaintiff claims actual damages, she must of course prove them. If the publication has caused loss of business, she may be required to show how much of

§ 422

1. United Ins. Co. of America v. Murphy, 331 Ark. 364, 961 S.W.2d 752 (1998); see David Anderson, Reputation, Compensation, and Proof, 25 WM. & MARY L. REV. 747, 758 (1984).

2. Gertz v. Robert Welch, Inc., 418 U.S. 323, 350, 94 S.Ct. 2997, 3012 41 L.Ed.2d 789 (1974).

3. Lara v. Thomas, 512 N.W.2d 777 (Iowa 1994) ("natural and probable consequences").

4. E.g., Sigal Construction Corp. v. Stanbury, 586 A.2d 1204 (D.C.App.1991).

5. Prozeralik v. Capital Cities Communications, 188 A.D.2d 178, 593 N.Y.S.2d 662 (1993), reversed on other grounds, 82 N.Y.2d 466, 626 N.E.2d 34, 605 N.Y.S.2d 218 (1993).

6. Vinson v. Linn–Mar Community Sch. Dist., 360 N.W.2d 108 (Iowa 1984).

7. See text below at nn. 22–26.

8. Den Norske Ameriekalinje Actiesselskabet v. Sun Printing and Pub. Assn., 226 N.Y. 1, 122 N.E. 463 (1919).

9. Bolduc v. Bailey, 586 F.Supp. 896 (D.Colo.1984).

10. Hudnall v. Sellner, 800 F.2d 377 (4th Cir.1986); Garrison v. Sun Printing & Publishing Ass'n., 207 N.Y. 1, 100 N.E. 430 (1912)

the business loss was due to true portions of the defamation and how much due to the untrue and defamatory portion.[11]

Harm to reputation itself, though often not quantifiable, is the chief item for which recovery is permitted. The traditional common law rule did not require the plaintiff to prove that any person believed the defamatory publication,[12] but evidence that it was believed and that people held the plaintiff in lower esteem as a result is relevant to show harm to reputation and equally evidence that no one believed it tends to show that little harm was inflicted.[13] Testimony may also substantiate and explain the negative feelings induced by those who read the defamation.[14] Other factors bear on the assessment of reputational loss: Was the accusation specific or vague, did it touch highly emotional issues or charge serious departures from well-established and important community standards, would it tend to be permanent and have repeated effects, did it reach a large audience or one especially relevant to the reputational issue? Perhaps the source of the defamation itself is an important factor. Defamation contained in a magazine with a poor reputation will perhaps have less effect than defamation contained in a respected news magazine.[15] The plaintiff's own existing reputation is of course central to the estimate of damages and that requires further attention.

Effect of plaintiff's existing bad reputation; libel-proof plaintiffs. If the defamation plaintiff already has a bad reputation on the topic involved in the defamation, her damages are at least arguably less than if she enjoyed a good reputation or no reputation at all. Consequently, evidence of the plaintiff's reputation prior to publication of defamatory material is highly relevant in most cases to show that damages should be limited.

The main argument is whether some plaintiffs have such terrible reputation that the judge should deny all recovery as a matter of law. Such a plaintiff is referred to as a libel-proof plaintiff; nothing said can make her reputation worse. Some courts have in fact barred the plaintiff's defamation claim altogether on this ground,[16] sometimes saying that the plaintiff should be denied even nominal damages.[17] The libel-proof plaintiff doctrine might even be used to bar the claim when the plaintiff's reputation is ruined by true or privileged statements in the defamatory publication itself, so that the untrue and unprivileged por-

11. See Schoen v. Washington Post, 246 F.2d 670 (App.D.C.1957).

12. E.g., See Plumley v. Landmark Chevrolet, Inc., 122 F.3d 308 (5th Cir.1997).

13. E.g., Gazette, Inc. v. Harris (Fleming v. Moore), 229 Va. 1, 48, 325 S.E.2d 713, 745, 54 A.L.R. 4th 685 (1985). Some courts have refused to admit such evidence. E.g., Clay v. Lagiss, 143 Cal.App.2d 441, 448, 299 P.2d 1025, 1030 (1956).

14. Poleski v. Polish American Pub. Co., 254 Mich. 15, 235 N.W. 841 (1931) (testimony showing how the plaintiff's Polish-ancestry constituency reacted to defamation associating plaintiff with the Klan).

15. See 2 Dan Dobbs, Law of Remedies § 7.2 (7) (2d ed. 1993).

16. Cardillo v. Doubleday & Co., Inc., 518 F.2d 638, 639 (2d Cir.1975); see Note, The Libel-Proof Plaintiff Doctrine, 98 Harv. L. Rev. 1909 (1985); Note, Libel Proof Plaintiffs—Rabble without a Cause, 67 B.U.L. Rev. 993 (1987).

17. See Guccione v. Hustler Magazine, Inc., 800 F.2d 298, 303 (2d Cir.1986).

tion of the defamation is thought to add little or nothing to the harm already caused by portions of the publication that are not actionable.[18]

Some of these cases, though reasoned as libel-proof plaintiff cases, might be viewed as cases of substantial truth which forms a complete defense. If the community already knows that the plaintiff murdered 27 boys and the defendant asserts that she also murdered a 28th, libel-proof plaintiff reasoning suggests that the plaintiff had no reputation left to lose and should not recover. But a publisher who says the defendant murdered 28 rather than 27 probably has the complete defense of substantial truth in any event. A different fact pattern also suggests a connection with the truth defense. If the publisher says that the defendant had burglar tools in his car, the fact that this is false and defamatory hardly seems significant if in fact the plaintiff is a burglar.[19]

But truth issues do not intersect all potential libel-proof plaintiff cases. Suppose the defendant accuses an officer of (a) treasonous spying for the enemy and also (b) shoplifting. If the officer is in fact a traitor but not a shoplifter, the shoplifting charge can hardly qualify as true merely because treason is worse. Not surprisingly, the libel-proof plaintiff doctrine, disconnected from anything that might resemble a truth defense, has been rejected in some cases in this pattern.[20] Even so, the treasonous plaintiff may have little reputation left to protect. It is true that he might betray his country and still be honest with respect to shopkeepers, and that the two things reflect different dimensions of personality; nevertheless, juries can reasonably conclude that harm to reputation must be quite small and damages limited accordingly.

Although various patterns can be discerned and various justifications offered or rejected,[21] it is fair to say that only seldom should judges grant summary judgment when the only question is the amount of harm to reputation. That is preeminently a fact question for the jury. When the libel proof plaintiff case approximates a case of the truth defense, however, the judge may be justified in dismissing the claim altogether.

Emotional harm damages without reputational loss. The plaintiff's claim for emotional harm is usually that she suffered anxiety, depres-

18. See Herbert v. Lando, 781 F.2d 298 (2d Cir.), cert. denied, 476 U.S. 1182, 106 S.Ct. 2916, 91 L.Ed.2d 545 (1986); Simmons Ford, Inc. v. Consumers Union of the United States, Inc., 516 F.Supp. 742 (S.D.N.Y. 1981).

19. Cf. Herbert v. Lando, 781 F.2d 298, 312 (2d Cir.1986) ("not be actionable if they merely imply the same view, and are simply an outgrowth of and subsidiary to those claims upon which it has been held there can be no recovery"); but cf. Crane v. New York World Telegram Corp., 308 N.Y. 470, 126 N.E.2d 753 (1955) (semble, evidence that the defendant was guilty in fact of crime did not tend to prove truth of publication that plaintiff was under indictment).

20. See Liberty Lobby, Inc. v. Anderson, 746 F.2d 1563, 1568 (D.C.Cir.1984) (Scalia, J.), vacated, as to applicable standard on summary judgment, 477 U.S. 242, 106 S.Ct. 2505, 91 L.Ed.2d 202 (1986) Cf. Schiavone Const. Co. v. Time, Inc., 847 F.2d 1069 (3d Cir.1988) (plaintiff had a bad reputation for a connection with Mafia or "mob," but defendant's publication might be read also to charge a connection with the Hoffa "execution," libel-proof plaintiff doctrine does not apply).

21. See 2 Dan Dobbs, Law of Remedies § 7.2 (9) (2d ed. 1993); Note, The Libel–Proof Plaintiff Doctrine, 98 Harv. L. Rev. 1909 (1985).

sion, or other emotional harm because her reputation was damaged. The question is whether the plaintiff can sever her claim for emotional distress and avoid constitutional requirements and defenses. The Supreme Court has held that an emotional harm claim cannot be asserted for brutal satire that does not include false statements.[22] However, in the *Firestone* case the Court permitted the plaintiff to drop the defamation claim and proceed on an emotional distress claim standing alone.[23] In that case, Time Magazine said the plaintiff's husband had divorced her for adultery. This was not true, although the trial judge had mentioned evidence of extramarital escapades. In a defamation case a private person like the plaintiff cannot recover presumed damages without proof of knowing or reckless falsehood.

One risk of the stand-alone emotional harm claim based upon publication is that presumed damages may be allowed under the name of emotional harm.[24] Another possibility is that if a plaintiff is permitted to drop the defamation claim but recover for stand-alone emotional harm, evidence of the plaintiff's reputation would be excluded on the ground that it would be highly relevant to the defamation claim but not relevant to emotional harm.[25] The result would be that some plaintiffs might recover damages based upon a loss of reputation they did not enjoy in the first place. A number of state courts have avoided these results.[26]

Punitive damages. When the plaintiff proves a knowing or reckless falsehood, punitive damages are constitutionally permissible. This is the level of fault required under the *Times-Sullivan* rule for public officials and public figures to recover even compensatory damages,[27] so, constitutionally, no additional fault is required when such plaintiffs claim punitive damages.

When the plaintiff is a private person defamed in connection with a matter of public concern, she may recover proven compensatory damages under *Gertz* upon proof of some fault such as negligence. But she cannot recover punitive damages on such proof. Only if she goes further and proves knowing or reckless falsehood can she recover punitive damages. Although knowing and reckless falsehood suffices to meet the constitutional standard for punitive damages, New York has held that something more is required–a malicious motive for publishing the falsehood.[28]

When the plaintiff is a private person defamed on a matter that is of no public concern, *Dun & Bradstreet* permits the plaintiff to recover both

22. Hustler Magazine v. Falwell, 485 U.S. 46, 108 S.Ct. 876, 99 L.Ed.2d 41 (1988).

23. Time, Inc. v. Firestone, 424 U.S. 448, 96 S.Ct. 958, 47 L.Ed.2d 154 (1976).

24. David Anderson, Reputation, Compensation, and Proof, 25 WM. & MARY L. REV. 747, 758 (1984); see also 2 DAN DOBBS, LAW OF REMEDIES § 7.2 (6) (1993).

25. See 2 DAN DOBBS, LAW OF REMEDIES § 7.2 (6) (2d ed. 1993).

26. See Little Rock Newspapers, Inc. v. Dodrill, 281 Ark. 25, 660 S.W.2d 933 (1983); Gobin v. Globe Pub. Co., 232 Kan. 1, 649 P.2d 1239, 36 A.L.R.4th 797 (1982); accord, Richie v. Paramount Pictures Corporation, 544 N.W.2d 21 (Minn.1996).

27. See § 417.

28. Prozeralik v. Capital Cities Communications, Inc., 82 N.Y.2d 466, 626 N.E.2d 34, 605 N.Y.S.2d 218 (1993).

common law presumed damages and punitive damages without constitutional restriction.[29]

States are free to impose more restrictive rules on the grant of punitive damages. New York has held that something more than knowing or reckless falsehood is required to establish a claim for punitive damages in a defamation case. A malicious motive for publishing the falsehood is also required.[30] In addition, the Supreme Court has held that due process requires certain judicial scrutiny of all punitive awards and that some punitive awards may be stricken as constitutionally excessive.[31]

Restitution

Many people have been confused by the word restitution and some of them appear to believe that the measure of restitution is the same as the measure of damages. This may be true in the criminal cases where the offender is required to "make restitution" to his victim. More generally, however, restitution refers to the defendant's liability to disgorge gains he has made from wrongdoing. Liability is measured by the defendant's gain, not, as with damages, by the plaintiff's loss. That makes restitution an attractive measure of liability when the defendant's tort provides him extraordinary gain in excess of the plaintiff's loss. The publisher of a book, for example, might make great profits from it and if the book's premise and theme defames the plaintiff, the plaintiff might conceivably prefer to recover the book's profits rather than ordinary damages. The limited authority on this point, however, excludes restitutionary recovery[32] and that is indeed in accord with free speech concerns, at least in the absence of knowing or reckless falsehood.

Injunctions

Quite apart from constitutional constraints, a long tradition has it that equity will not enjoin defamation.[33] To a large extent the precedents against injunction are the products of state law based upon judicial reluctance to censor speech and sometimes upon state constitutions.[34] To some extent, however, "prior restraint" on speech is a violation of the

29. Dun & Bradstreet, Inc. v. Greenmoss Builders, Inc., 472 U.S. 749, 105 S.Ct. 2939, 86 L.Ed.2d 593 (1985).

30. Prozeralik v. Capital Cities Communications, Inc., 82 N.Y.2d 466, 626 N.E.2d 34, 605 N.Y.S.2d 218 (1993).

31. § 383.

32. Hart v. E.P. Dutton & Co., 197 Misc. 274, 93 N.Y.S.2d 871 (1949), aff'd, 277 A.D. 935, 98 N.Y.S.2d 773 (1950); Cason v. Baskin, 155 Fla. 198, 20 So.2d 243 (1944) (in a right of privacy claim); cf. Simon & Schuster, Inc. v. Members of the New York State Crime Victims Board, 502 U.S. 105, 112 S.Ct. 501, 116 L.Ed.2d 476 (1991) (statutes allocating profits criminal makes from writing about his crime toward payment of victims unconstitutional).

33. E.g., Kramer v. Thompson, 947 F.2d 666 (3d Cir.1991) (even though jury has first found statements libelous and awarded damages, no injunction and no compulsory retraction); High Country Fashions, Inc. v. Marlenna Fashions, Inc., 257 Ga. 267, 357 S.E.2d 576, 577 (1987). See generally, Dan B. Dobbs, Law of Remedies§ 7.2 (14) (2d ed. 1993); Rodney A. Smolla, Law of Defamation § 9.13.

34. See Willing v. Mazzocone, 482 Pa. 377, 393 A.2d 1155 (Pa. 1978); Robert A. Leflar, Legal Remedies for Defamation, 6 Ark. L. Rev. 423 (1952).

United States Constitution.[35] However, courts have sometimes in effect issued injunctions against publishing by ordering that public records be sealed or even actually expunged.[36]

Retraction and Reply

The damages action for defamation is expensive to defendants, risks a chill on free speech, and is so clogged with distinctions and decision points it cannot be counted upon to clear the plaintiff's name, to provide measured redress of her rights, or fully protect the rights of speakers and society. Critics have often proposed reforms, but most of these have their deficits, too.

Retraction. The common law recognized that the defendant's full and fair retraction of the defamatory statement would be admissible in evidence as tending to show that harm to reputation may have been minimized[37] and as tending to negate grounds for punitive damages.[38] Most states have enacted statutes governing retraction by media publishers.[39] If no statutory demand is made for retraction or if a statutory retraction is published, then damages may be limited, for example, by eliminating presumed damages. The statutes do not require retraction and almost certainly could not constitutionally do so, partly for reasons that appear in the next paragraph and because an official, governmentally prescribed "truth" would raise even more fundamental questions. The retraction statute cases litigate various collateral issues such as the sufficiency of the demand for retraction, or the retraction itself, the timing, and other statutory terms.[40]

Right of reply. Conceivably a statute might structure some kind of intelligible right of reply to media defamation in lieu of a damages recovery. Florida once had a rather inadequate version of such a statute, triggering a right of reply whenever the plaintiff was "assailed" in a newspaper, which was then required to devote equal space to the plaintiff's reply. The Supreme Court held this to be an unconstitutional

35. See Near v. State of Minnesota, 283 U.S. 697, 51 S.Ct. 625, 75 L.Ed. 1357 (1931). The exact scope of the rule against prior restraints is debated.

36. See In re Smith, 63 Misc.2d 198, 310 N.Y.S.2d 617 (1970) (physical obliteration of the names from all records to prevent employer's knowledge that juveniles had been arrested); § 427.

37. Webb v. Call Pub. Co., 173 Wis. 45, 180 N.W. 263 (1920). In Whitcomb v. Hearst Corp., 329 Mass. 193, 107 N.E.2d 295 (1952) the court approved an instruction that told the jury it could find the retraction reduced damages to a nominal level, did not reduce them at all, or reduced them to some extent in between.

38. Kehoe v. New York Tribune, 229 A.D. 220, 241 N.Y.S. 676 (1930) (admissible to reduce punitive but not compensatory damages). The defendant's refusal to retract after being fully informed of the facts is evidence of common law malice, e.g., Myers v. Pickering Firm, Inc., 959 S.W.2d 152 (Tenn.App.1997), but not necessarily evidence of knowing or reckless falsehood. New York Times Co. v. Sullivan, 376 U.S. 254, 84 S.Ct. 710, 11 L.Ed.2d 686 (1964).

39. See Robert D. Sack & Sandra S. Baron, Libel, Slander and Related Problems, Appendix 2 (2d ed. 1994) (setting out all of the retraction statutes).

40. See Robert D. Sack & Sandra S. Baron, Libel, Slander and Related Problems § 9.2 (2d ed. 1994). Arizona held its statute unconstitutional in Boswell v. Phoenix Newspapers, Inc., 152 Ariz. 9, 730 P.2d 186 (1986).

intrusion upon the editorial decisions of the press, a kind of compelled speech.[41]

§ 423. Reform Proposals

Declaratory judgment and defamation law reform. The possibility that a declaratory judgment could be substituted for a damages award in defamation cases has fascinated some thinkers.[1] A declaratory judgment about the truth of a statement raises fundamental issues whether official truth is tolerable in a free society. Nevertheless, major reform proposals envision an ultimate declaratory judgment. The Annenberg Libel Reform Proposal, resulting from a substantial study,[2] would attempt to resolve the libel controversy through retraction or reply. If that was unsuccessful, then declaratory judgment would become a possibility.

The Uniform Correction and Clarification of Defamation Act. In 1993 the Commissioners on Uniform State Laws offered a statute embodying some of the same ideas.[3] Under that statute, the plaintiff is almost always barred altogether unless she had made a timely and adequate request for correction or clarification.[4] The plaintiff may recover only economic loss, that is, "special, pecuniary loss caused by the publication" if a publisher makes a timely and sufficient clarification or correction. This recovery is "mitigated" by the correction itself.[5] Economic loss is also the level of recovery when the plaintiff fails to supply the publisher with evidence that the publication was false and the publisher makes no correction.[6] The plaintiff may recover litigation expenses, either as the sole monetary recovery or in addition to the economic loss in certain specific situations.[7] The statute does not directly specify any case in which full common law damages would be available. Implicitly, however, common law damages (as limited by any applicable constitutional rules), would be available if the correction or clarification is not timely or sufficient and if the publisher does not take advantage of the offer provisions.

In many cases, the statute is likely to shift the focus from the falsity and defamatory content of the publication to issues about timeliness and sufficiency of the correction or clarification. A number of its provisions are addressed to such issues and to information the plaintiff must furnish on request. The statutes thus create a number of issues that

41. Miami Herald Pub. Co. v. Tornillo, 418 U.S. 241, 94 S.Ct. 2831, 41 L.Ed.2d 730 (1974). But cf. PruneYard Shopping Center v. Robins, 447 U.S. 74, 100 S.Ct. 2035, 64 L.Ed.2d 741 (1980) (state could compel privately owned shopping center to permit people to distribute leaflets on its property).

§ 423

1. See Restatement § 623, Special Note (recognizing a number of problems with this remedy); Robert A. Leflar, Legal Remedies for Defamation, 6 Ark. L. Rev. 423 (1952).

2. See Rodney A. Smolla, The Annenberg Libel Reform Proposal: The Case for Enactment, 31 Wm. & Mary L. Rev. 25 (1989) and Rodney A. Smolla, The Law of Defamation § 9.13 [4].

3. Uniform Correction or Clarification of Defamation Act (UCCDA).

4. UCCDA § 3 (a).

5. UCCDA § 5.

6. UCCDA § 4 (a).

7. UCCDA § 8 (a) (1) & (b); UCCDA § 8 (c).

promote defensive litigation opportunities without going directly to the merits of the original defamatory statement at all. This is because the drafters see correction as a full remedy, so that demanding correction in a proper way, publishing it in a suitable medium, and with a suitable content become, for the drafters, something very close to the merits.

What counts as a correction, however, is quite problematical and the correction rules of the statute appear to alter substantially some substantive rules of defamation. The general provision is that the correction is sufficient if it refers to and "corrects the [defamatory] statement." But if the defamation does not arise from express language, then the correction is sufficient if it merely "disclaims an intent to communicate that meaning or to assert its truth.... "[8] If the defamation lies in a statement attributed to another person, the correction is sufficient if it "identifies the person and disclaims an intent to assert the truth of the statement."[9] This appears to effectively undermine the traditional rules concerning the truth defense, which hold that a publisher does not escape liability by truthfully attributing a defamatory statement to another person; instead, the underlying statement must itself be true in order to invoke the truth defense. A number of troubling cases might arise, for example, if a fictional magazine story portrays a character committing illegal acts and the character closely resembles the plaintiff in name, locale, and personal qualities. It looks as if under § 6(b)(ii) the publisher might escape even the limited liability provided in the act by saying that the character is not intended to refer to the plaintiff. At this writing only North Dakota has adopted the Uniform Act.[10]

Other reforms. The English Defamation Act of 1996[11] uses correction and the publisher's offer to make amends as a central feature, leading, the drafters hope, to an agreed correction and damages. If the parties cannot agree on damages, the court determines damages without a jury. The statute permits the judge granting summary relief to order both a correction and apology, something that would be unconstitutional in the United States.

8. UCCDA § 6(b)(2)(ii).

9. UCCDA § 6(b)(2)(iii).

10. N.D. Cent. Code §§ 32–43–01 et seq.

11. Defamation Act, [1996, c. 31]. The Act is reprinted in Patrick Milmo & W. V. H. Rogers, Gatley on Libel and Slander 997 (9th ed. 1998) and discussed where relevant throughout that work.

CHAPTER 29

PRIVACY

§ 424. Introducing Privacy Rights

A degree of privacy is probably required for full human development. It is essential to personal autonomy and liberty and it is treasured, even by the most open and gregarious people, as important to the quality of life, valuable in itself. In addition, the privacy of individuals reflectively asserts a limit on the power of other individuals, corporations, and government entities.

Rights of privacy have been protected by law for a very long time incident to other torts. Tort liability for trespass to land, for example, protected not only against damage to the physical integrity of the land itself but against intrusions upon the possessor's privacy. Common law copyright offered at least some protection against publication of private writings. The Fourth Amendment of the United States Constitution protects against unjustified government intrusions.

Nevertheless, a systematic right of privacy was developed only in the twentieth century. The impetus, or at least the most obvious impetus, was a law review article by Samuel D. Warren and Louis D. Brandeis published in 1890.[1] Brandeis and Warren were mainly concerned at the intrusive press and the resulting gossip. They proposed a new tort to protect privacy against the trashier interests of both the press and its readers.

The New York Court of Appeals rejected any such right a few years later,[2] whereupon the New York legislature enacted a statutory right of privacy, but one covering only the use of the plaintiff's picture in advertising or trade without the plaintiff's consent.[3] In the meantime, other states had begun to recognize a common law right of privacy, at least when the defendant had used the plaintiff's likeness in advertising.[4] Cases that once had been brought on other theories or on no discernible theory at all gradually coalesced around the privacy idea. Most states by legislation or judicial decision have now recognized some form of privacy invasion, but not necessarily all its forms.

§ 424

1. Louis D. Brandeis and Samuel D. Warren, The Right to Privacy, 4 HARV. L. REV. 193 (1890).

2. Roberson v. Rochester Folding Box Co., 171 N.Y. 538, 64 N.E. 442 (1902) (defendant who used plaintiff's picture in advertisements without the plaintiff's knowledge or consent violated no right of the plaintiff).

3. N.Y. CIV. RTS. L. §§ 50–51 (picture used for advertising without consent).

4. Beginning with Pavesich v. New England Life Ins. Co., 122 Ga. 190, 50 S.E. 68 (1905) (use of the plaintiff's picture in advertising).

Sometimes it is said that the right of privacy is the right to be let alone, but the phrase does not reflect the varieties of privacy invasion. Scholars eventually posited four forms of privacy invasion (or four different torts), only one of which was rooted in the original advertising scenario. Harper, James, and Gray analyzed privacy as entailing interests in (a) seclusion, (b) personal dignity and self-respect, (c) name and likeness, and (d) sentimental associations.[5] A different set of categories was sponsored by Prosser and the Restatement. As the Restatement puts it, privacy is invaded by (a) an unreasonable intrusion upon the plaintiff's seclusion, (b) the appropriation of the plaintiff's name or likeness, (c) unreasonably giving publicity to the plaintiff's private life, and by (d) publicizing the plaintiff in a false light.[6]

So expressed, the right of privacy leaves a good many problems in its wake. So far as privacy is said to be violated by publication or communication, the free speech considerations that limit liability for defamation may have similar application when the plaintiff switches to the privacy theory.[7] So far as privacy is violated by intrusion, the tort looks much like a specific form of infliction of emotional distress, but again without the stated limits of that tort. And so far as privacy rights turn on commercial use of the plaintiff's name or likeness in an advertisement or the like, the claim is often a commercial claim and dealt with as such.

§ 425. Appropriation of the Plaintiff's Personality

Gist of the tort. The early cases establishing privacy as a separate tort were based upon the defendant's use of the plaintiff's name or likeness in commercial advertising.[1] It later became apparent that appropriation of the plaintiff's identity for any purpose would be actionable, whether advertising was used or not.[2] Since the gist of the tort is the appropriation of the plaintiff's identity or reputation, or some substantial aspect of it, no element of falsity is required.

Dignitary tort vs. property right. The earliest plaintiffs were mostly private individuals, not public figures. The emphasis was personal and dignitary. The individual had liberty interests at stake; she could associate with others or not according to her personality and preferences; she might be humiliated if people thought she sold her picture for advertising. Later cases adapted this form of privacy invasion to the case of public figures who do not seek privacy but on the contrary seek out opportunities for public exposure and who wish to use their name, likeness, voice or other aspects of "identity" as a property to be sold.[3] In

5. Harper, James & Gray § 9.6.

6. Restatement §§ 652A–652E.

7. See § 427.

§ 425

1. Pavesich v. New England Life Ins. Co., 122 Ga. 190, 50 S.E. 68 (1905); Kunz v. Allen, 102 Kan. 883, 172 P. 532 (1918); Flake v. Greensboro News Co., 212 N.C. 780, 195 S.E. 55 (1938).

2. Hinish v. Meier & Frank Co., Inc., 166 Or. 482, 113 P.2d 438 (1941) (signing plaintiff's name to a communication to the governor).

3. The Restatement treats all appropriation cases as "property" cases, although it recognizes that personal feelings and emotional distress of the plaintiff were part of

this form, the claim is sometimes strangely called a right of publicity.[4] The recent appropriation cases of note have been of this kind and are closer to the fields of intellectual property, unfair competition, and trademarks than to the purely dignitary torts.[5] Some courts have apparently rejected the earlier emphasis upon the plaintiff's personal rights and liberties. These refuse to allow a recovery for appropriation of the plaintiff's name or likeness unless the plaintiff was a famous person who could sell her identity for endorsements or the like.[6]

Intent and appropriation. The Restatement Second is not specific about the intent required to support the appropriation tort. It requires "appropriation," which perhaps implies that intent to utilize the plaintiff's identity is required.[7] But the Restatement also characterizes the plaintiff's right as one of property, perhaps as if to say that even an innocent taking of that property right in identity is actionable. Some authority might be read to support liability even if the defendant does not intend to appropriate the plaintiff's identity or reap the benefits of her fame.[8] However, the defendant does not appropriate the plaintiff's identity by incidental mention.[9] A public figure may be mentioned in a work of fiction if her identity is not used to tout a product or imply her sponsorship and if the work is clearly not a factual report about the public figure. So fictional work involving Notre Dame and its mention of its President does not offend the rights of either the school or the individual, and even more clearly so if the work is one of criticism or satire.[10]

Newsworthiness. In any event, reporting of matters that are newsworthy or of public concern is not an appropriation for which liability is imposed, even though the reported matter increases circulation or profits of the publisher.[11] In privacy law, newsworthiness is a broad concept that

the reason for recognizing the right in the first place. See Restatement § 652C, cmt. a.

4. See J. Thomas McCarthy, The Rights of Publicity and Privacy (1998) (expansive definitions of right of publicity).

5. E.g., Midler v. Ford Motor Co., 849 F.2d 460 (9th Cir.1988) (voice imitation); Carson v. Here's Johnny Portable Toilets, Inc., 698 F.2d 831 (6th Cir.1983) (phrase used to introduce famous television person). See § 460.

6. Cox v. Hatch, 761 P.2d 556 (Utah 1988) (Senator Hatch posed for photos with federal postal workers, then used pictures in his political campaign; workers had no claim as their likeness had no intrinsic value).

7. Restatement § 652C. See Tropeano v. Atlantic Monthly Co., 379 Mass. 745, 400 N.E.2d 847 (1980) (contrasting incidental use which is not actionable with an effort "deliberately to exploit" the plaintiff's likeness for advertising).

8. See Kerby v. Hal Roach Studios, Inc., 53 Cal.App.2d 207, 127 P.2d 577 (1942) (plaintiff's name was same as fictional movie character; the name was "signed" to printed and suggestive letters advertising the movie; no intent was required, but the case might be a false light case if that matters).

9. Tropeano v. Atlantic Monthly Co., 379 Mass. 745, 400 N.E.2d 847 (1980) (photo of several unidentified people to illustrate [?] "sociological commentary" on the sexual revolution was not effort to sell goods but only an incidental use of the plaintiff's likeness).

10. University of Notre Dame Du Lac v. Twentieth Century–Fox Film Corp., 22 A.D.2d 452, 256 N.Y.S.2d 301 (1965), aff'd, 15 N.Y.2d 940, 207 N.E.2d 508, 259 N.Y.S.2d 832.

11. Freihofer v. Hearst Corp., 65 N.Y.2d 135, 480 N.E.2d 349, 490 N.Y.S.2d 735 (1985).

includes much more than hot news,[12] so a magazine article discussing a public figure or a newsworthy or educational topic is free to use names and photographs as much as a newspaper.[13] In the same way, nothing limits the right to publish a biography of a public figure so long as it is not fictionalized or false.[14]

First Amendment. Although the First Amendment's protection of free speech requires proof of falsity as a prerequisite to recovery in defamation cases and in some other kinds of privacy cases,[15] no such requirement has been imposed in the appropriation cases. Perhaps that is partly because commercial speech is sometimes given less First Amendment protection and partly because the plaintiff's right in her own identity is treated as a species of property. It is especially easy to think of the plaintiff's right as one analogous to intellectual property when the plaintiff has created a public personality, style, or characteristic performance. In that kind of case, at least, the Supreme Court has held that states may impose liability when the defendant appropriates the plaintiff's entire public performance.[16] Although falsity is probably never required to establish a claim, it appears unlikely that an accurate report on a newsworthy matter or one of public concern could be actionable without a very substantial appropriation indeed.

§ 426. Intrusion upon Private Life

Intrusive invasion of privacy is a rule desert; such rules as there are turn out to be shimmering mirages. The Restatement's illusion of a rule is that an intentional intrusion upon the solitude or seclusion of another or upon her private affairs is subject to liability if the intrusion would be highly offensive to a reasonable person.[1] As this implies, the plaintiff must have a reasonable expectation of privacy in the place, the materials involved, or the subject matter.[2] Something less than an expectation of complete privacy may be sufficient, so long as the limited privacy

12. See Shulman v. Group W Productions, Inc., 18 Cal.4th 200, 955 P.2d 469, 74 Cal.Rptr.2d 843 (1998).

13. E.g., Rozhon v. Triangle Pubs., 230 F.2d 359 (7th Cir.1956).

14. See Spahn v. Julian Messner, Inc., 18 N.Y.2d 324, 221 N.E.2d 543, 274 N.Y.S.2d 877 (1966), on reargument after review in the Supreme Court, Spahn v. Julian Messner, Inc., 21 N.Y.2d 124, 233 N.E.2d 840, 286 N.Y.S.2d 832, 30 A.L.R.3d 196 (1967) (biography protected but fictionalized biography of famous baseball pitcher actionable as use of personality for trade or business). There is a dispute whether right of privacy or publicity survives and passes to the estate of the deceased. Where it does not, even a fictionalized biography of a deceased person is permissible. Guglielmi v. Spelling–Goldberg Prods., 25 Cal.3d 860, 603 P.2d 454, 160 Cal.Rptr. 352 (1979). By statute, California treats rights in personality, voice, likeness and so on as property rights that can be transferred at death or otherwise. See Cal. Civ. Code § 990.

15. See §§ 427 & 428.

16. See Zacchini v. Scripps–Howard Broad. Co., 433 U.S. 562, 97 S.Ct. 2849, 53 L.Ed.2d 965 (1977) (defendant broadcast video of the plaintiff's entire act as a human cannonball, state may impose liability).

§ 426

1. Restatement § 652B.

2. E.g., Cheatham v. Paisano Pubs., Inc., 891 F.Supp. 381 (W.D.Ky.1995) (at a large public bikers' event, plaintiff wore clothing that partly revealed her "bottom;" a photograph made at the event was not an intrusive invasion of privacy).

expected excludes the kind of intrusion launched by the defendant.[3] Given a reasonable expectation of privacy, the intentional intrusion that defeats the expectation is itself tortious. If carried out under color of law, the intrusion may violate the standards of the Fourth Amendment or Due Process clause and may be actionable as a civil rights tort under § 1983.[4] Liability does not turn upon publication of any kind. For that reason, liability for intrusion alone would not ordinarily raise free speech considerations that may concern other forms of privacy invasion. In particular, an intrusion upon privacy is not justified by newsworthiness of material that may be gained.[5]

It is almost impossible to sketch the lineaments of the intrusion tort except perhaps to say that the defendant's conduct is often either harassing or has the purpose or potential for obtaining or perpetuating data about the plaintiff. Peeping and eavesdropping are prime examples.

Courts say that intrusive invasion of privacy is independent of any other tort such as trespass, but in fact a number of privacy cases could be resolved under better-defined rules of trespass, battery, Fourth Amendment violation, or the like. No doubt a defendant who enters the plaintiff's home on the basis of a "consent" procured by deceit should be liable on a close analogy to trespass.[6] In 1881 ,the Michigan Court held that a doctor was liable for bringing an untrained man into the room where the plaintiff was delivering a child.[7] The plaintiff's "consent" was not valid because she had been under the mistaken belief that the man was a doctor or medical student, so recovery could have been justified on a trespass theory as well as any other. A well-known Missouri case is only a little different because the plaintiff was in a hospital room rather than her home; journalists invaded the room over her express objection, photographed her in bed against her will, and published the photograph with a story about her disease. This was said to be an invasion of privacy, but its substantial core is only a technical variation on trespass in which the plaintiff lacked a present possessory interest in the hospital room.[8] Courts have also said that the right to reject medical treatment or

3. See Sanders v. American Broadcasting Companies, Inc., 20 Cal.4th 907, 85 Cal.Rptr.2d 909, 978 P.2d 67 (1999).

4. Wilson v. Layne, 526 U.S. 603, 119 S.Ct. 1692, 143 L.Ed.2d 818 (1999) (establishing the principle that officers violate the Fourth Amendment by inviting media representatives to enter the plaintiff's home while officers executed a warrant); see Sepulveda v. Ramirez, 967 F.2d 1413 (9th Cir.1992) (male officer watching female parolee urinate for drug test); York v. Story, 324 F.2d 450 (9th Cir.1963) (police required nude photos of assault victim); James v. City of Douglas, Ga., 941 F.2d 1539 (11th Cir.1991) (video tape of sexual conduct of the plaintiff seized by police from another person was not logged in as evidence but kept in a drawer and viewed by various persons). Distinguish false light privacy invasions that are not actionable as constitutional violations. See Paul v. Davis, 424 U.S. 693, 96 S.Ct. 1155, 47 L.Ed.2d 405 (1976).

5. See Shulman v. Group W Prods., Inc., 18 Cal.4th 200, 955 P.2d 469, 74 Cal. Rptr.2d 843 (1998).

6. E.g., Dietemann v. Time, Inc., 449 F.2d 245 (9th Cir.1971).

7. De May v. Roberts, 46 Mich. 160, 9 N.W. 146 (1881).

8. Barber v. Time, Inc., 348 Mo. 1199, 159 S.W.2d 291 (1942); cf. Froelich v. Adair, 213 Kan. 357, 516 P.2d 993 (1973) (defendant paid hospital orderly to obtain plaintiff's body tissue from a discarded bandage).

the like is grounded in a privacy right when they could as well have said that forced medical treatment is a battery.[9]

The Restatement's version of this tort requires intent, presumably intent to commit the act that the court considers an intrusion. However, it provides little guidance as to what counts as protected seclusion or private affairs or what conduct that is not already some other tort would offend a reasonable person. The cases clearly allow recovery for intrusive invasions where the defendant commits a virtual trespass, entering the plaintiff's possession or domain by electronic means such as tapping telephones or using other listening devices,[10] and statutes provide an independent ground for relief in the case of wiretapping.[11] But while many of the cases involve close analogies to a trespass, not all of them do. The California Supreme Court has held that if A covertly records his own conversation with B that is also heard by others, the recording itself can violate B's "limited" expectation of privacy and may be actionable. The theory is that although B can have no expectation of confidentiality, she has an expectation that it will not be recorded.[12]

Some forms of the intrusive privacy action appear to be especially like the claim for intentional infliction of emotional distress. In a Washington case,[13] individual county employees retained for their personal use autopsy photos of deceased persons. Relatives were allowed to claim an invasion of privacy although their claim for intentional infliction of emotional distress failed because they were not present when the defendants took or used the photos. Likewise, harassment—repeated and unwanted attentions—may be characterized as an intrusive invasion of privacy rather than as an intentional infliction of emotional distress. A bill collector hounds a debtor,[14] an employer repeatedly broaches sexual questions to an employee,[15] or a stalker repeatedly follows or threatens the object of his obsession;[16] all are subject to liability for invasion of privacy.

Employee rights of privacy vis-a-vis employers has developed into something of a speciality itself.[17] A federal statute now prohibits employers from administering, demanding, or even suggesting a polygraph test to employees and creates a federal cause of action against employers who

9. In re Schuoler, 106 Wash.2d 500, 723 P.2d 1103 (1986).

10. E.g., Hamberger v. Eastman, 106 N.H. 107, 206 A.2d 239 (1964); Roach v. Harper, 143 W.Va. 869, 105 S.E.2d 564 (1958).

11. 18 U.S.C. § 2520.

12. Sanders v. American Broadcasting Companies, Inc., 20 Cal.4th 907, 85 Cal. Rptr.2d 909, 978 P.2d 67 (1999).

13. Reid v. Pierce County, 136 Wash.2d 195, 961 P.2d 333 (1998).

14. A federal statute now heavily regulates debt collection. 15 U.S.C.A. § 1692.

15. Phillips v. Smalley Maintenance Servs., 435 So.2d 705 (Ala.1983); Cf. McSurely v. McClellan, 753 F.2d 88 (D.C.Cir.1985) (wife's pre-marriage relations with others revealed to husband).

16. Rumbauskas v. Cantor, 138 N.J. 173, 649 A.2d 853 (1994).

17. See Matthew W. Finkin, Privacy in Employment Law (1995 & 1997 Supp.); Pauline T. Kim, Privacy Rights, Public Policy, and the Employment Relationship 57 Ohio St. L.J. 671 (1996).

violate the statute.[18] Drug testing by employers as a condition of employment or by schools and private associations as a condition to participation in sports or other activities,[19] is a different matter. So far as the employer is a governmental entity, the Fourth Amendment forbids unreasonable searches (including drug testing). A search is reasonable when there is reasonable ground for suspicion of wrongdoing and when compelling governmental interests and special needs outweigh privacy concerns. Compelling interests and special needs have been found in a number of cases,[20] but not all.[21]

Private employers are generally constitutionally free to enforce rules requiring employee searches and to discharge employees who do not comply. Even so, states are free to hold that privacy rights trump the employer's right to discharge an employee. Some states have thus held that private employers may not discharge an employee for refusing to accept a suspicionless drug test unless safety issues made such testing reasonable.[22] Other courts and statutes, however, have left little or no room for claims based upon private employer drug testing.[23]

§ 427. Publicizing Private Life

Although truth was a complete defense in latter-day libel actions and under the constitutional decisions the plaintiff is often required to prove falsehood of defamatory statements, these restrictions may be ignored under the Restatement's private facts privacy claim.

Elements. As the Restatement states the rule, the "private facts" category of privacy invasion occurs when the defendant publicly discloses a private fact about the plaintiff when disclosure would be highly offensive to a reasonable person and is not of legitimate public concern.[1] The Restatement rule does not require falsity, so the defendant may be held liable for publicizing the truth. The action lies, however, only when there is a "publicity," meaning publication to the public at large or to a substantial group of people.[2] The facts published about the plaintiff must also be "private," which at least means that they must not be generally known.[3]

18. The Employee Polygraph Protection Act of 1988, 29 U.S.C. §§ 2001–2009 (1994).

19. As to testing as a condition of sports see Hill v. National Collegiate Athletic Ass'n, 7 Cal.4th 1, 865 P.2d 633, 26 Cal. Rptr.2d 834 (1994) (testing college athletes permissible).

20. Skinner v. Railway Labor Executives' Ass'n, 489 U.S. 602, 109 S.Ct. 1402, 103 L.Ed.2d 639 (1989).

21. Chandler v. Miller, 520 U.S. 305, 117 S.Ct. 1295, 137 L.Ed.2d 513 (1997).

22. Twigg v. Hercules Corp., 185 W.Va. 155, 406 S.E.2d 52 (1990); see Hennessey v. Coastal Eagle Point Oil Co., 129 N.J. 81, 609 A.2d 11 (1992); Edward L. Raymond, Jr., Annotation, Liability for Discharge of At-will Employee for Refusal to Submit to Drug Testing, 79 A.L.R.4th 105 (1991).

23. See Ariz. Rev. Stat. § 23–493.04; Roe v. Quality Transp. Servs., 67 Wash.App. 604, 838 P.2d 128 (1992).

§ 427

1. Restatement § 652D. Perhaps "deeply shocking" rather than "highly offensive" would better express the requirement. See Haynes v. Alfred A. Knopf, Inc., 8 F.3d 1222 (7th Cir.1993).

2. Restatement § 652D, cmt. a.

3. See Rodney A. Smolla, Law of Defamation § 10.04; cf. Barbara Moretti, Outing: Justifiable or Unwarranted Invasion of Pri-

Because this action always entails communication to others, it runs squarely into the issue of free speech and the First Amendment. The Restatement's version of the rule attempts to stay within the limits of the First Amendment by restricting liability to publications that are not newsworthy or of legitimate public concern, since truthful communications on matters of public concern and matters involving public figures appear to be constitutionally protected.[4] One thinker has gone so far as to say that the "shocking character of the disclosure" is a sufficiently good basis for liability, even in the light of First Amendment considerations.[5]

Wrongfully obtained information. Some cases that may be thought to support the Restatement's broad liability are actually much narrower. Those cases impose liability for revelation of private facts when the defendant obtained the private information by wrongful means such as trespass, deceit, betrayal, or breach of confidence.[6] Such cases do not seem to raise First Amendment or common law free speech issues because the information itself is obtained by wrongdoing. A number of cases imposing liability can be justified on the ground that the published information was itself obtained by wrongdoing. In *Dietemann v. Time, Inc.*,[7] journalists got into the plaintiff's den by deceit and secretly photographed and recorded events, then published. The tort was the deceitful intrusion, but the proximate damages included harm resulting from publication. In *Barber v Time, Inc.*,[8] journalists forced their way into the plaintiff's hospital room over her protests and then by trickery photographed her and published the photograph. In the famous *Sidis* case,[9] a former child prodigy turned into an obsessive recluse who valued privacy above all was the subject of a *New Yorker* profile that subjected him to merciless treatment. The court went off on a newsworthiness issue, but if the interviewer had gained entry into Sidis' room and mind by deceit and breach of confidence, liability of the interviewer would have been entirely appropriate. Such cases need not turn on such subjective criteria as the shocking nature of the disclosure or the private quality of the facts. Liability would be appropriate because the informa-

vacy? The Private Facts Tort as a Remedy for Disclosures of Sexual Orientation, 11 Cardozo Arts & Ent. L.J. 857 (1993) (arguing that although the fact of dating a person is not a private fact to heterosexual persons, it should be considered private as to gays and lesbians because it goes to core identity).

4. See § 420 (reflecting the rule that even defamatory publications are protected if true and related to public figures or matters of public concern).

5. Alfred Hill, Defamation and Privacy under the First Amendment, 76 Colum. L. Rev. 1205, 1258 (1976).

6. Humphers v. First Interstate Bank of Oregon, 298 Or. 706, 696 P.2d 527 (1985) (doctor's breach of confidence in disclosing child's identity was actionable as breach of confidence, not as privacy invasion); MacDonald v. Clinger, 84 A.D.2d 482, 446 N.Y.S.2d 801 (1982) (similar); Horne v. Patton, 291 Ala. 701, 287 So.2d 824 (1973) (medical information in breach of confidence); Doe v. Roe, 93 Misc.2d 201, 400 N.Y.S.2d 668 (1977) (therapist's book made her patient recognizable).

7. Dietemann v. Time, Inc., 449 F.2d 245 (9th Cir.1971).

8. Barber v. Time, Inc., 348 Mo. 1199, 159 S.W.2d 291 (1942).

9. Sidis v. F–R Publ'g Corp., 113 F.2d 806 (2d Cir.1940).

tion was gained by a wrong to the plaintiff.[10]

Rightfully obtained information. Other cases, however, have gone far, far beyond liability for publishing wrongfully obtained information. The most notable and extreme cases once held the defendant liable for publishing truthful information gleaned from records open to the public. In *Melvin v. Reid*,[11] the defendants made a movie in which true incidents of the plaintiff's life and her involvement in a murder trial were shown and her real name was used so that she could be identified. Although the court conceded that the defendants could use the incidents from the public record, it thought it was "unnecessary" and uncharitable to give the plaintiff's name. On this ground it held that the plaintiff stated a cause of action. The California Supreme Court reached a similar result when a magazine article truthfully identified the plaintiff as a person who committed a hijacking and shooting eleven years earlier. Like the *Melvin* court, the California Supreme Court made its editorial judgment a rule of law—the publication of the plaintiff's name, it thought, would serve little public purpose and emphasized that the plaintiff had rehabilitated himself.[12]

Newsworthiness/public concern. Cases like these raise serious constitutional questions first because they decide what the public has a right to know—in these particular cases, about crimes and criminals—and second because they penalize publication of the truth. Courts do, however, recognize that newsworthy events are matters of public concern and that the defendant may publicize those events even when they relate to private persons who are involuntarily involved in them. For example, a television broadcaster may provide a videotaped report of an auto accident showing the victims[13] or even a frantic woman covered only with a dishtowel escaping from her husband's attack.[14] The freedom to report truthfully on newsworthy events or matters of public concern does not depend upon the plaintiff's preexisting public figure status, and in that respect it differs from the false defamatory report. Newsworthiness, moreover, is a shorthand expression rather than a precise description; the term is defined broadly to include many matters of public interest

10. Distinguish Pearson v. Dodd, 410 F.2d 701 (D.C.Cir.1969) (publishers, who did not obtain information by trespass or betrayal and did not authorize such conduct, nevertheless published the information; publishers not liable). In Shulman v. Group W Prods., Inc., 18 Cal.4th 200, 955 P.2d 469, 74 Cal.Rptr.2d 843 (1998), however, the court held that the jury could find an intrusive invasion of privacy but that the defendant would not be liable for publishing information obtained in the intrusion. Professor Hill suggested that if the intrusion turned up the plaintiff's current criminal activity the plaintiff might have no privacy interest the law would protect. Alfred Hill, Defamation and Privacy under the First Amendment, 76 Colum. L. Rev. 1205, 1282 (1976). Equally, some intrusive behavior—surveillance in public places, for example—that would invade privacy when conducted by a business rival may not invade privacy at all when conduct by an investigative reporter. See Id. at 1284–85.

11. Melvin v. Reid, 112 Cal.App. 285, 297 P. 91(1931).

12. Briscoe v. Reader's Digest Ass'n, Inc., 4 Cal.3d 529, 483 P.2d 34, 93 Cal.Rptr. 866 (1971).

13. Shulman v. Group W Prods., Inc., 18 Cal.4th 200, 955 P.2d 469, 74 Cal. Rptr.2d 843 (1998).

14. Cape Publications, Inc. v. Bridges 423 So.2d 426 (Fla.Dist.Ct.App.1982).

that are by no means news, including educational and entertaining materials, and the quotidian details of life involving births, deaths, personal heroism and tragedy.[15]

Broad as the newsworthiness defense may be, however, it does not necessarily provide clear rights for speakers and publishers or clear protections for privacy. Perhaps it is not even capable of definition.[16] For example, Oliver Sipple, otherwise a private citizen, obstructed an effort to shoot former President Gerald Ford and became famous for it. Two days later, a columnist publicly revealed that Sipple was a homosexual. Sipple suffered various humiliations, some at the hands of his own family, but his privacy claim was rejected, in part because his sexual preference was regarded as newsworthy. "Newsworthy" turned out to be a matter of the publisher's subjective motive. The court thought that the publisher's purpose to dispel false ideas about gays by using Sipple's life as an example showed that the publisher had no motive based upon sensational prying, and that, for the court, seemed to make the story newsworthy as a matter of law.[17] On the other hand, revelation that a student body president involved in a dispute with a college was a transsexual was thought not to be newsworthy as a matter of law,[18] and some argue that private sexual matters are seldom or never newsworthy.[19] Both speech and privacy represent fundamental values sometimes given constitutional protection. Whether newsworthiness or public concern is a concept capable of sufficient development to protect either remains to be seen.

Public information. The Supreme Court of the United States has considered the First Amendment's impact in a series of cases in which the media lawfully obtained information about the plaintiff from public records and then publicized it. In each of the cases so far, the media's right to publish the information was upheld. Some of the claims for the plaintiff are especially sympathetic. In two, the plaintiffs were rape victims. Revealing names of rape victims will often compound the grievous injury; and it may at times also endanger the victims further. In the first case, *Cox Broadcasting Corp. v. Cohn,*[20] the Court held that the state could not prohibit publication of a rape victim's name when the name was obtained by the media from an indictment available for inspection. Part of the reason was that the press served as a kind of

15. See the good list in Rodney A. Smolla, Law of Defamation § 10.04 [2][b].

16. The term itself is not treated as a mere description of what the public wants to know, but a normative term standing for the court's willingness to protect the publication. See Shulman v. Group W Prods., Inc., 18 Cal.4th 200, 955 P.2d 469, 74 Cal. Rptr.2d 843 (1998). Willingness to protect the publication does not, however, appear to turn upon any objectively determinable fact and often permits the court to wade around in the defendant's supposed motivations.

17. Sipple v. Chronicle Publ'g Co., 154 Cal.App.3d 1040, 1049, 201 Cal.Rptr. 665, 670 (1984).

18. Diaz v. Oakland Tribune, Inc., 139 Cal.App.3d 118, 188 Cal.Rptr. 762 (1983).

19. See John P. Elwood, Note, Outing, Privacy, and the First Amendment 102 Yale L.J. 747 (1992).

20. Cox Broad. Corp. v. Cohn, 420 U.S. 469, 95 S.Ct. 1029, 43 L.Ed.2d 328 (1975).

agent for individual members of the public who would have a right to inspect public records for themselves. Public scrutiny was particularly important as a means of helping to guarantee fair trials.

The Court later went beyond trial records. It has said that media may publish the names of juveniles charged with a crime when the names are obtained by listening to police band radio and may publish rape victims' names obtained from police reports (as distinguished from trial records). When "a newspaper lawfully obtains truthful information about a matter of public significance then state officials may not constitutionally punish publication of the information, absent a need to further a state interest of the highest order."[21]

Restricting access to public information. These Supreme Court decisions recognize two potential conditions in which a truthful report of public records might be actionable. First, if there is a state need of the highest order, the state might forbid publication of records that are otherwise open to public access. Second, the state might restrict public access to records. The first instance is hard to imagine in the light of the second, and the second raises a new realm of concern. If government can be carried out secretly by invoking privacy rights of individuals, government will not be open or democratic. This point has led to concerns when courts or legislatures seal or expunge records, although their purpose is always said to be laudable.[22]

Statutes. State and federal statutes provide a mixed response to these concerns, some guaranteeing access to public records and meetings, others providing for various degrees of privacy for individuals named in governmental records. For instance, the federal Freedom of Information Act[23] provides a detailed scheme for obtaining information from the federal government, but creates a number of exemptions to protect privacy. The federal Privacy Act[24] on the other hand purports to require government agencies to protect privacy, but not where freedom of information requires disclosure. Other state and federal statutes address particular situations,[25] sometimes with a privacy orientation, sometimes with a disclosure orientation, but often with lapses and litigational possibilities.[26] In some cases the privacy orientation may be

21. The Florida Star v. B.J.F. 491 U.S. 524, 109 S.Ct. 2603, 105 L.Ed.2d 443 (1989) (police report) (quoting Smith v. Daily Mail Publishing Co., 443 U.S. 97, 99 S.Ct. 2667, 61 L.Ed.2d 399 (1979) (police radio)).

22. See Franklin & Johnsen, Expunging Criminal Records: Concealment and Dishonesty in an Open Society, 9 Hofstra L. Rev. 733 (1981). In some cases even those litigating against a person may be denied access to relevant arrest records, see State ex rel. Herget v. Circuit Court for Waukesha Co., 84 Wis.2d 435, 267 N.W.2d 309 (1978), but this may deny due process in some instances. Cf. Davis v. Alaska, 415 U.S. 308, 94 S.Ct. 1105, 39 L.Ed.2d 347 (1974).

23. 5 U.S.C.A. § 552.

24. 5 U.S.C.A. § 552a.

25. E.g., The Family Educational Rights and Privacy Act of 1974, 20 U.S.C.A. § 1232g (penalizing educational institutions receiving federal funds if they do not follow privacy rules of the statute, which generally protects student educational records from disclosure).

26. See Bauer v. Kincaid, 759 F.Supp. 575, 112 A.L.R. Fed. 671 (W.D. Mo. 1991).

deadly, as where statutes forbid disclosure of the plaintiff's AIDS condition to those who are at risk for exposure.[27]

Rejecting the tort. All in all, the privacy invasion tort most closely related to the Brandeis and Warren proposal has proved to be a serious problem. Neither adjudications nor statutory solutions have proved entirely satisfactory. Not surprisingly, commentators have argued against this form of the privacy right.[28] New York, with a statutory right of privacy limited to appropriation cases, rejects the private facts version of privacy invasion.[29] Oregon has held that publication about the plaintiff is not actionable "unless the manner or purpose of defendant's conduct is wrongful in some respect apart from causing the plaintiff's hurt feelings,"[30] and a plurality decision in Indiana agreed, noting that emotional injuries from disclosure were not worse than other emotional injuries, so that the plaintiff should recover, if at all, for intentional infliction of emotional distress.[31] North Carolina flatly rejected the private facts tort with the observation that at best it was constitutionally suspect.[32] Such decisions leave potential for liability when the defendant is a wrongdoer in some respect other than in publishing the truth, as where he breaches confidence or obtains information wrongfully, and where he intentionally inflicts severe emotional distress. Otherwise, the intrusion tort rather than the publicity tort may come closer to the core privacy value.

§ 428. False Light

Elements. The fourth privacy tort recognized by the Restatement and conventional wisdom is the false light tort. The tort is established only if the plaintiff proves that (a) the defendant publicized a matter about the plaintiff to a substantial group of persons or to the public; (b) the matter put the plaintiff in a false light; (c) the false light would be highly offensive to a reasonable person; and (d) the defendant knew of the falsity or acted in reckless disregard whether the matter was false or not.[1]

False light and defamation. The tort theoretically goes beyond defamation because the objectionable false light is not necessarily a defamatory one, only false and offensive. For example, a false light claim was established when a newspaper feature article made false statements

27. See Doe v. Marselle, 236 Conn. 845, 675 A.2d 835 (1996) (approving potential liability under an AIDS-confidentiality statute for disclosure made to the discloser's own sons who were at risk from the plaintiff's AIDS).

28. Diane L. Zimmerman, Requiem for a Heavyweight: a Farewell to Warren and Brandeis's Privacy Tort, 68 Cornell L. Rev. 291 (1983).

29. Freihofer v. Hearst Corp., 65 N.Y.2d 135, 480 N.E.2d 349, 490 N.Y.S.2d 735 (1985).

30. Anderson v. Fisher Broad. Companies, Inc., 300 Or. 452, 469, 712 P.2d 803, 814 (1986) (Linde, J.).

31. Doe v. Methodist Hosp., 690 N.E.2d 681 (Ind.1997).

32. Hall v. Post, 323 N.C. 259, 372 S.E.2d 711 (N.C. 1988).

§ 428

1. Restatement § 652E.

about the plaintiff's poverty and her stoic attitude following the death of her husband in a disaster.[2] Likewise, a false light claim was made out when a television program, by splicing shots, falsely depicted the plaintiff as a hunter who shot wild geese on the ground rather than in flight.[3] Possibly, but not certainly, these are cases in which defamation could not be established.

On the other hand, many of the false light cases appear to be cases of defamation or infliction of emotional distress under another name. Where the defamation claim requires derogatory content that would lower the plaintiff in the esteem of others, the false light privacy claim requires that the content would be highly offensive to a reasonable person. If a reasonable person would find the publication highly offensive, it is quite likely that the content is also defamatory under contemporary definitions. Not surprisingly then, the Supreme Court, after holding that defamation under color of state law violated no constitutional rights, held that false light publicity violated none either.[4]

False light as element of damage resulting from other torts. Sometimes conduct that in fact puts the plaintiff in a false light is actionable for entirely different reasons, so that the false light is merely one element of damages resulting from some other tort. In a Minnesota case,[5] the plaintiff alleged that a photo-developer retained a copy of a photo showing the plaintiff and another person in a shower together, then circulated the photo to others. The plaintiff alleged that as a result, some people questioned her sexual orientation. The court concluded that no false light claim would be permitted but remanded for trial to determine the plaintiff's intrusion and appropriation claims. In an Oregon case, the defendant signed the plaintiff's name to a petition sent to the governor. The court held the claim actionable, but as fraud and an appropriation of the plaintiff's name, not as a false light tort.[6]

Perhaps most of the cases of false light are cases of defamatory communications, appropriation of name or likeness, intrusive invasion of privacy followed by publication of matters wrongfully gained in the intrusion, or some other tortious activity. In all of these cases the plaintiff would be entitled to recover for the harms done by placing her in a false light, even if there were no separate false light tort. Consequently, a serious question is raised whether the false light tort is a helpful addition to the armory or merely another piece of baggage that gets in the way. In addition, the false light claim always involves publication or publicity and hence is either entitled to some kind of constitutional and common law free speech protection or else is merely an evasion of those constitutional protections.

2. See Cantrell v. Forest City Pub. Co., 419 U.S. 245, 95 S.Ct. 465, 42 L.Ed.2d 419 (1974) (in effect reinstating a jury verdict).

3. Uhl v. Columbia Broad. Systems, Inc., 476 F.Supp. 1134 (W.D.Pa.1979).

4. Paul v. Davis, 424 U.S. 693, 96 S.Ct. 1155, 47 L.Ed.2d 405 (1976).

5. Lake v. Wal–Mart Stores, Inc., 582 N.W.2d 231 (Minn.1998).

6. Hinish v. Meier & Frank Co., Inc., 166 Or. 482, 113 P.2d 438 (1941).

Rejecting the false light tort. With these considerations in mind, the highest courts of at least two states have flatly rejected any false light tort.[7] Others doubted that the tort should be recognized and so far refused to do so[8] or suggested special impediments to it.[9] The Supreme Court of Arizona, on the other hand, has insisted that even when the plaintiffs allege that the publication accused them of incompetence in office, illegal activities, misuse of public funds, and police brutality, all clearly defamatory, the plaintiff could assert the false light tort and would not be limited to a defamation action.[10] One potential advantage in retaining the false light claim is that it can be and has been used to avoid some of the more arcane and complex rules of defamation.[11] That hardly seems to be a justification for the false light claim, however, when it would be more clear and more just to abolish the undesirable defamation rules.

Constitutional constraints. In any event, where the false light tort is recognized the Constitution imposes limits in the interest of free speech, just as it does in libel cases. Under the rule for defamation cases, the plaintiff who is a public official or public figure must prove knowing or reckless falsehood and do so by clear and convincing evidence.[12] A more lenient rule applies to libel cases brought by private figures; in that case, the plaintiff is required to show "some fault" such as negligence and can recover only actual damages.[13] The Supreme Court handed down its initial false light privacy decision before the more lenient rule for private plaintiffs had been announced and consequently required a knowing or reckless falsehood without regard to the plaintiff's status as a private figure.[14] Because of the parallel to libel cases, it may well be that a negligent falsehood would suffice in a false light claim by a private person,[15] provided that such a plaintiff could only recover actual dam-

7. Renwick v. News & Observer Pub. Co., 310 N.C. 312, 312 S.E.2d 405 (1984); Cain v. Hearst Corporation, 878 S.W.2d 577, 579 (Tex.1994) (false light tort rejected because "it largely duplicates other rights of recovery," and because "it lacks many of the procedural limitations that accompany actions for defamation, thus unacceptably increasing the tension that already exists between free speech constitutional guarantees and tort law").

8. Lake v. Wal–Mart Stores, Inc., 582 N.W.2d 231 (Minn.1998); cf. Sullivan v. Pulitzer Broad. Co., 709 S.W.2d 475 (1986) (plaintiff could not evade defamation statute of limitation by casting claim as one for false light privacy). See Russell G. Donaldson, Annotation, False Light Invasion of Privacy—Cognizability and Elements, 57 A.L.R.4th 22 (1988).

9. See Colbert v. World Pub. Co., 747 P.2d 286, 292 (Okla.1987) (linking the tort to intentional infliction of emotional distress and requiring a knowing or reckless falsehood).

10. Godbehere v. Phoenix Newspapers, Inc., 162 Ariz. 335, 783 P.2d 781 (1989).

11. See, e.g., Zechman v. Merrill Lynch, Pierce, Fenner & Smith, Inc., 742 F.Supp. 1359, 1373 (N.D.Ill.1990) (Illinois' innocent construction rule and distinction between per se and per quod defamation avoided by false light privacy claim). But other courts have carried over the per quod rules of defamation to privacy claims as well. Fellows v. National Enquirer, Inc., 42 Cal.3d 234, 721 P.2d 97, 228 Cal.Rptr. 215, 57 A.L.R.4th 223 (1986).

12. § 417.

13. § 417.

14. Time, Inc. v. Hill, 385 U.S. 374, 87 S.Ct. 534, 17 L.Ed.2d 456 (1967).

15. Such a rule has been applied. See Wood v. Hustler Magazine, Inc., 736 F.2d 1084 (5th Cir.1984) (Texas law before Texas rejected false light claims altogether). To complete the parallel, the plaintiff would be limited to a recovery of actual damages in such a case.

ages.[16] The Supreme Court has implied that the question is open for consideration.[17] However, states may require the plaintiff to prove not merely negligence but a knowing or reckless falsehood even when a private person sues, and some, in line with the Restatement's rule, have done so.[18]

16. Haynes v. Alfred A. Knopf, Inc., 8 F.3d 1222 (7th Cir.1993).

17. Cantrell v. Forest City Pub. Co., 419 U.S. 245, 95 S.Ct. 465, 42 L.Ed.2d 419 (1974).

18. See Pfannenstiel v. Osborne Publ'g Co., 939 F.Supp. 1497 (D.Kan.1996) (predicting Kansas law to this effect and citing a number of cases); Colbert v. World Publ'g. Co., 747 P.2d 286 (Okla.1987); ROBERT D. SACK & SANDRA S. BARON, LIBEL, SLANDER AND RELATED PROBLEMS § 10.3.6.2 (2d ed. 1994 & 1998 Supp.) (reviewing cases on all positions).

*

CHAPTER 30

PROCESS RIGHTS: MISUSING AND DENYING JUDICIAL PROCESS

§ 429. Tortious Use of the Legal Process: Policies and Immunities

The integrity of the legal system can be undermined by the innocent, negligent, or intentional conduct of many people, including lawyers, litigants, witnesses, judges, and juries. A judge who makes a palpably erroneous ruling, a witness who commits perjury, and a litigant who brings wholly unjustified suits all inflict harm on the legal system and the public interest. They may also inflict private harm upon others in the process. This chapter addresses that private harm.

In the most common kind of case, the plaintiff is complaining because the defendant unjustifiedly instigated an earlier suit or criminal prosecution against the plaintiff, causing the plaintiff expense and perhaps loss of reputation. The injustice felt by one who has been wrongly prosecuted is clear enough. The chief policy against redress for such a victim is that prosecutions of the arguably guilty should not be discouraged by the threat that the complaining witness will be held liable in damages. Moreover, if a second court could impose liability for what was done in the first, then a third court could question the second, and a fourth could question the third. Much more substantially, the first court's resolution of the issues represents the appropriate solution to the dispute. These policies translate into great caution about imposing liability upon those who instigate criminal or civil litigation or utilize the process of the courts.[1]

The policy of limiting liability of those involved in legal processes is expressed in two major ways. First, courts protect many actors in the legal process by recognizing privileges or immunities. Second, courts require the plaintiff who asserts harm resulting from litigation to prove a series of difficult elements to make out a prima facie case summarized in the next section.

§ 429

1. See Sheldon Appel Co. v. Albert & Oliker, 47 Cal.3d 863, 872, 765 P.2d 498, 501, 254 Cal.Rptr. 336, 340 (1989) ("the tort has the potential to impose an undue 'chilling effect' on the ordinary citizen's willingness to report criminal conduct or to bring a civil dispute to court"; it is "a disfavored cause of action"); Richey v. Brookshire Grocery Co., 952 S.W.2d 515, 517 (1997) ("Malicious prosecution actions involve a delicate balance between society's interest in the efficient enforcement of the criminal law and the individual's interest in freedom from unjustifiable and oppressive criminal prosecution").

Almost everyone directly involved in litigation enjoys an absolute immunity from liability for communications made in the litigation or even in preparation for it[2] lest the voices of the honest be stilled by fear of liability.[3] Beyond that, judges are immune from suit based upon their rulings in a case over which they have jurisdiction, even if the ruling is erroneous or malicious,[4] and the witness who testifies to a knowing falsehood equally avoids liability to those harmed by his testimony, either on the ground that perjury is not a tort or that the witness is absolutely immune.[5] And no civil rights action lies even though the lying witness is a government official.[6] Official prosecutors,[7] grand juries,[8] and those in similar roles[9] are absolutely immune for their decision to prosecute as well as for their in-trial conduct.

As to private citizens and police officers, however, common law case patterns reflect a radical distinction between misconduct that takes place after proceedings have begun and misconduct that induces or affects the proceedings, with liability limited to the latter case.[10] For instance, although perjury is not ordinarily actionable, pre-litigation spoliation of evidence sometimes is.[11] More central in this chapter, citizens and officers who procure the institution of a prosecution, civil suit, or even misuse a process within the suit may be held liable if they have done so wrongfully.[12] Attorneys fall under the same rule. They are not liable vicariously for the acts of their clients, but for their own decisions to sue when the known facts show that there is no probable cause to do so, and for their own abuse of process, they enjoy no more immunity than others[13] and are subject to liability.[14]

2. See § 412.

3. See Briscoe v. LaHue, 460 U.S. 325, 333, 103 S.Ct. 1108, 1114, 75 L.Ed.2d 96 (1983) ("A witness's apprehension of subsequent damages liability might induce two forms of self-censorship. First, witnesses might be reluctant to come forward to testify. And once a witness is on the stand, his testimony might be distorted by the fear of subsequent liability"); § 412.

4. See, e.g., K.D. v. Bozarth, 313 N.J.Super. 561, 713 A.2d 546 (1998).

5. E.g., Schmidt v. State Aerial Farm Statistics, Inc., 62 Ohio App.2d 48, 403 N.E.2d 1026 (1978); Cooper v. Parker–Hughey, 894 P.2d 1096 (Okla.1995). Some authority permits an action based upon perjured testimony before a grand jury. See Wheeler v. Satilla Rural Elec. Membership Corp., 103 Ga.App. 401, 119 S.E.2d 375 (1961). Bribery of a judge may also be actionable as a civil rights violation. See Dennis v. Sparks, 449 U.S. 24, 101 S.Ct. 183, 66 L.Ed.2d 185 (1980).

6. Briscoe v. LaHue, 460 U.S. 325, 103 S.Ct. 1108, 75 L.Ed.2d 96 (1983).

7. Imbler v. Pachtman, 424 U.S. 409, 96 S.Ct. 984, 47 L.Ed.2d 128 (1976) (immunity of state prosecutor extends to federal civil rights actions under § 1983).

8. Crawford v. Busbee, 164 Ga.App. 559, 298 S.E.2d 278 (1982).

9. The absolute immunity follows the function rather than the status of the prosecutor. When the prosecutor becomes a complaining witness, the immunity becomes qualified. Kalina v. Fletcher, 522 U.S. 118, 118 S.Ct. 502, 139 L.Ed.2d 471 (1997).

10. The privilege is qualified to the extent that, in a suit for abuse of process, a suitor's statement made in the course of litigation is admitted to show the suitor's ulterior motive to pervert the court's process. See Baglini v. Lauletta, 315 N.J.Super. 225, 717 A.2d 449 (1998).

11. E.g., Henry v. Deen, 310 N.C. 75, 310 S.E.2d 326 (1984); as to constraints on this tort, see § 451.

12. However, some states may provide a non-traditional immunity for officers guilty of malicious prosecution. See Cal. Gov. Code § 821.6.

13. Mozzochi v. Beck, 204 Conn. 490, 529 A.2d 171 (1987); Baglini v. Lauletta, 315 N.J.Super. 225, 717 A.2d 449 (1998).

However, in lieu of the immunity invoked once litigation begins, all those who instigate litigation are given partial protection by the rules that require a plaintiff claiming malicious prosecution to show improper purpose, a lack of probable cause for the suit or prosecution, and other elements considered in the sections that follow.

§ 430. Elements of Malicious Prosecution

A malicious prosecution suit asserts that the plaintiff was formerly prosecuted and that the prosecution was wrongfully instigated by the now defendant. It differs from false arrest in that the prosecution does not necessarily involve any detention of the plaintiff at all and in that any detention that does occur is the result of legal process that would defeat a false imprisonment claim. Malicious prosecution focuses upon the elements necessary to show that the process is wrongful; detention or confinement is no part of the issue, although the plaintiff who has a malicious suit may also have a false arrest action. Malicious prosecution always involves defamation, since it entails charging the now plaintiff with a crime, but a defamation action as such would be defeated by the privilege to report suspected crimes to appropriate authorities. In the usual view, malicious prosecution also differs from abuse of process, which requires misuse of legal process after it has been rightly issued.

A common illustration of the malicious prosecution case goes something like this: a store manager believes the plaintiff has secreted merchandise on her person and has left the premises without paying. The manager swears out a warrant charging the plaintiff with shoplifting or some similar crime. The jury returns a not guilty judgment. The plaintiff then sues the store for malicious prosecution. A retailer's bad check charge, a lender's or partner's charge of criminal fraud, an employer's charge of embezzlement or indeed any charge of crime can produce a tort claim that the accused was maliciously prosecuted.

The plaintiff who is unjustifiably prosecuted suffers a number of harms that are worthy of redress, but redress does not come easily. The malicious prosecution claim must assert that the plaintiff's wrongful prosecution was (1) directly or indirectly instigated or continued by the defendant,[1] (2) without probable cause, (3) with improper purpose ("malice"), and (4) terminated favorably to the plaintiff.[2] The plaintiff is also required to prove damages, but that is seldom a problem. Since all of these elements are required to establish the claim, there is no such thing as a valid claim for negligent prosecution.[3] It is difficult to prove all four

14. See Sheldon Appel Co. v. Albert & Oliker, 47 Cal.3d 863, 765 P.2d 498, 254 Cal.Rptr. 336 (1989) (recognizing potential liability); Vazquez v. Reeves, 138 Or.App. 153, 907 P.2d 254 (1995).

§ 430

1. This can be broken into two elements: (a) a prosecution must be commenced, for example, a mere charge to authorities is not a commencement; and (b) the accuser must be legally responsible for it.

2. See Restatement § 653.

3. See Lawson v. Kroger Co., 997 F.2d 214 (6th Cir.1993).

of the required elements and it is meant to be, since those who report a perception of crime should not be led by fear of liability to withhold information from police and prosecutors.

The tort of malicious prosecution is paralleled by a civil rights version when the instigator of the prosecution such as a police officer acts under color of state law.[4] The tort rules furnish an appropriate starting place for formulating rules in such claims, which are treated in a quite similar manner.[5]

§ 431. Malicious Prosecution—Instigating or Continuing the Prosecution or Proceeding

Criminal proceeding required. Malicious prosecution can be established only if the defendant has instigated a criminal proceeding. The Restatement rightly points out that a criminal proceeding must be formally begun by issuance of criminal process, by an indictment, or at least by an official arrest on a criminal charge.[1] Almost any kind of criminal proceeding will qualify, and most courts say that a proceeding has been instituted even if the court lacks jurisdiction.[2] On the other hand a mere complaint to authorities that never results in arrest, indictment or information does not initiate a criminal proceeding.[3]

But-for and legal cause required. Although everyone agrees that the defendant is not responsible unless he instituted or instigated criminal proceedings, the issue of instigation itself has not always been given the attention it deserves. The instigation requirement is a requirement that the defendant must be both a cause in fact and a legal cause of the prosecution or, more rarely, its continuance.[4] For instance, the defendant does not cause or continue the prosecution by testifying at trial, and he is not subject to liability for such testimony, even if it is perjured.[5]

Reporting facts to prosecutor or officer. To be an instigator, the defendant must necessarily make a complaint, induce another to do so,[6]

4. E.g., Malley v. Briggs, 475 U.S. 335, 106 S.Ct. 1092, 89 L.Ed.2d 271 (1986); Lippay v. Christos, 996 F.2d 1490 (3d Cir.1993) (adopting state law of malicious prosecution for the civil rights claim). Although those who carry out prosecutorial functions are immune in doing so, police officers do not ordinarily qualify for that immunity.

5. See Heck v. Humphrey, 512 U.S. 477, 114 S.Ct. 2364, 129 L.Ed.2d 383 (1994).

§ 431

1. Restatement § 654.

2. See, e.g., Calhoun v. Bell, 136 La. 149, 66 So. 761 (1914).

3. Restatement § 654.

4. Restatement § 655. This covers the case in which the defendant initiates proceedings by honestly swearing out a complaint, then later discovers facts exculpating the accused but nevertheless continues to assert his guilt.

5. § 429.

6. See Restatement § 653, cmt. d. In everyday language, the defendant does not himself "initiate" a criminal proceeding but he may procure its initiation by inducing officers to make a complaint or prosecutors to file an information or seek an indictment. He thus instigates the proceeding when he provides false information or uses improper influence to induce prosecution. Occasionally the defendant moves back one step by inducing another private person to make the complaint and if so this is actionable under the same conditions. But as in the more direct case, mere advice or encouragement is not enough. Cf. Chapman v. Grimm & Grimm, 638 N.E.2d 462 (Ind.Ct. App.1994) (civil malicious prosecution).

or otherwise communicate directly or indirectly[7] with the prosecutor; and prosecution must in fact follow. But while that is necessary, it is not sufficient. If the officer or prosecutor makes his own decision to prosecute, it is he, not the complaining witness, who is regarded as instituting the action. The defendant is free to report the facts to the prosecutor. The defendant's provision of facts leaves the decision to the prosecutor, and the defendant is not responsible for his decisions to prosecute.[8] Similarly, if the prosecutor makes his own independent investigation of the facts and makes his decision to prosecute uninfluenced by the defendant's complaint, the defendant has not instigated the prosecution.[9]

Falsity, inaccuracy, or undue influence required. As these limitations imply, the defendant can be regarded as an instigator of the proceeding only if (a) he communicates material information falsely or inaccurately and the prosecutor relies upon his statement,[10] or (b) the defendant uses his power or position to influence the prosecutor in favor of prosecution.[11] An inaccurate statement of facts can be found when the defendant omits material information such as exculpatory evidence that might induce a prosecutor not to proceed.[12]

7. In rare cases, the person who committed the crime with which the plaintiff was charged has been held liable for the plaintiff's prosecution, see Seidel v. Greenberg, 108 N.J.Super. 248, 260 A.2d 863, 40 A.L.R.3d 987 (1969) (arson under circumstances that made it likely that the plaintiff would come under suspicion for the crime, arsonist liable to plaintiff who was prosecuted); cf. Singer v. Jefferies & Co., Inc., 160 A.D.2d 216, 553 N.Y.S.2d 346 (1990) (plaintiff as an employee was asked to sign an invoice to Boesky Corporation which later brought him under suspicion).

8. Bankston v. Pass Road Tire Ctr., Inc., 611 So.2d 998 (Miss.1992); Lester v. Buchanen, 112 Nev. 1426, 929 P.2d 910 (1996); Johnson v. Weast, 123 N.M. 470, 943 P.2d 117 (1997) (a civil rights claim); Restatement § 653, cmt. g; see Dan B. Dobbs, Belief and Doubt in Malicious Prosecution and Libel, 21 Ariz. L. Rev. 607 (1979) (arguing that the citizen-accuser should be free to rely upon officers to make the appropriate decision). In Correllas v. Viveiros, 410 Mass. 314, 572 N.E.2d 7 (1991) the defendant confessed that she had taken $4,000, but stated (a) that the plaintiff had conceived the plan to take money and (b) that she "believed" the plaintiff took the other half. Although statement (a) appears to be a factual statement and the plaintiff claimed it was false, the court held that the defendant had not instituted the criminal action against the plaintiff merely by transmitting information to officers.

9. But the defendant who provides the prosecutor with an inaccurate picture may remain liable if the investigation itself is prejudicially colored by the defendant's inaccurate presentation, as in Thrift v. Hubbard, 974 S.W.2d 70 (Tex.App.1998); cf. Interiors v. Petrak, 188 Cal.App.3d 1363, 234 Cal.Rptr. 44 (1987) (investigation on different aspect did not terminate liability of defendant for providing false information).

10. Matthews v. Blue Cross and Blue Shield of Michigan, 456 Mich. 365, 385, 572 N.W.2d 603, 613 (1998) ("Unless the information furnished was known by the giver to be false and was the information on which the prosecutor acted, the private person has not procured the prosecution"); see Thrift v. Hubbard, 974 S.W.2d 70, 78 (Tex.App. 1998).

11. Cases sometimes suggest that a demand for prosecution, or even advice or encouragement might suffice, e.g., Pugach v. Borja, 175 Misc.2d 683, 670 N.Y.S.2d 718 (Sup.Ct. 1998); Browning–Ferris Indus., Inc. v. Lieck, 881 S.W.2d 288 (Tex.1994); see Restatement § 653, cmt. g. But while encouragement or the like might evince pressure, it does not seem sufficient by itself to show that the prosecutor's decision to prosecute was not his own independent choice.

12. Jones v. City of Chicago, 856 F.2d 985 (7th Cir.1988) (identification of plaintiff as perpetrator worthless; this and other exculpatory evidence suppressed by police); McCraney v. Barberi, 677 So.2d 355 (Fla. Dist.Ct.App.1996) (debt collector complaining of bad check failed to reveal that it had been made good immediately and that only a $20 store charge for bad checks was due).

Unintended falsehood. An important question arises when the defendant believes that he has reported the information accurately to the prosecutor but it is in fact false, so that by honest error the prosecutor is misled. The Restatement and most cases protect the defendant who honestly believes the information he has furnished the prosecutor, even if it turns out to be false.[13] For example, if the defendant honestly identifies the plaintiff as the person who committed a crime, the plaintiff is not an instigator of the prosecution and not liable even though the identification is in fact false.[14] In effect, this requires a knowing or reckless falsehood. The danger of penalizing one who cooperates with law enforcement is so great that it is appropriate to require more than negligence. Some authority, however, may support the view that the accuser is adequately protected by the rules of probable cause and malice, so that knowing falsehood is not required to say that he is an instigator of the prosecution.[15]

Police officers' liability. Police officers, like others, are subject to liability for malicious prosecution unless they are performing purely prosecutorial duties. If they initiate a criminal proceeding by presentation of false statements, or by withholding exculpatory information from the prosecutor, for example, they are clearly instigators. If the prosecution proceeds and all the other elements of the tort are proven they are liable for malicious prosecution in the same way as civilians.[16] When a police officer acts on a judicially issued warrant that is fair on its face, he is usually fully protected; the warrant itself gives him probable cause to arrest according to its terms. However, when the officer is the complaining witness seeking a warrant from the magistrate, he is no more privileged to shade the facts than a private person and in spite of the judge's decision to issue the warrant, is responsible for instituting the proceeding.[17]

The Supreme Court in a civil rights case seems to have gone a step further by holding the officer responsible for a prosecution initiated without probable cause, even though the officer had seemingly presented the magistrate with a fair statement of the facts and obtained a warrant. The officer was expected to make a correct probable cause determination, and the judge's failure to do so did not relieve the officer.[18]

13. Lester v. Buchanen, 112 Nev. 1426, 1429, 929 P.2d 910, 913 (1996) (defendant "cannot be held liable for commencing the criminal action because they merely reported information they believed to be true"); Restatement § 653, cmt. g (information furnished and acted upon was "known to be false").

14. E.g., Cedars–Sinai Med. Ctr. v. Superior Court, 206 Cal.App.3d 414, 253 Cal. Rptr. 561 (1988).

15. Browning–Ferris Indus., Inc. v. Lieck, 881 S.W.2d 288 (Tex.1994) (so saying but perhaps only meaning that undue pressure upon the prosecutor would suffice, not that a statement of honest belief would by itself).

16. E.g., Jones v. City of Chicago, 856 F.2d 985 (7th Cir.1988) (civil rights and state law malicious prosecution claim reflecting terrifyingly unconstitutional behavior); Martin v. City of Albany, 42 N.Y.2d 13, 396 N.Y.S.2d 612, 364 N.E.2d 1304 (1977).

17. See Jones v. City of Chicago, 856 F.2d 985 (7th Cir.1988); Bender v. City of Seattle, 99 Wash.2d 582, 664 P.2d 492 (1983).

18. Malley v. Briggs, 475 U.S. 335, 106 S.Ct. 1092, 89 L.Ed.2d 271 (1986).

§ 432. Malicious Prosecution—Want of Probable Cause

Requirement. The plaintiff must prove that the defendant instigated criminal proceedings without probable cause. Probable cause turns on reasonableness of the accusation made against the plaintiff but not on the accuser's improper purpose or malice, which is entirely distinct. If the defendant had probable cause to procure the prosecution, the fact that he harbored malice or improper purpose will not avail the plaintiff. The accuser's malice, as the saying goes, does not permit an inference that probable cause was lacking.[1]

Definitions. Many courts have defined probable cause in similar language. One version of the definition says that probable cause is a state of facts known to the accuser that would permit a person of ordinary prudence to believe that the accused committed the *offense* charged,[2] although the facts need not show guilt beyond a reasonable doubt.[3] A second version, perhaps more accurately, says that the facts must permit a reasonable person to believe that the accused committed the *act* of which the accuser complains.[4] The first version suggests that a citizen-accuser is responsible for failing to name the crime correctly[5] except that in very unusual cases he can avoid liability because of an honest mistake of law.[6] The second suggests that he need only state the facts accurately.

Which definition? The first version may be more appropriate when the accuser is an officer who should know or find out the appropriate charge. The second version is more appropriate when the accuser is a private person whose responsibility should be limited to accurate reporting of the facts. Sometimes, however, the accusation of a crime implies the assertion of some specific facts. If a reasonable person would not believe the implied assertions of fact, then probable cause is lacking even under the second version. For instance, a storekeeper might accuse someone of larceny when the crime actually shown by the facts is only a crime called shoplifting. The second version of the probable cause definition does not require the storekeeper to take the risk that his legal language is inappropriate but it does require reasonable grounds for believing facts. But the charge of larceny, like the more accurate charge

§ 432

1. E.g., Cordes v. Outdoor Living Ctr., Inc., 301 Ark. 26, 781 S.W.2d 31 (1989); Restatement § 669A.

2. E.g., Adams v. Sussman & Hertzberg, Ltd., 292 Ill.App.3d 30, 684 N.E.2d 935, 225 Ill.Dec. 944 (1997); Bacon v. Towne, 58 Mass. (4 Cush.) 217 (1849).

3. E.g., Strickland v. University of Scranton, 700 A.2d 979, 984 (Pa.Super.1997).

4. See Lawson v. Kroger Co., 997 F.2d 214, 216 (6th Cir.1993) ("without probable cause to believe the facts upon which the claim was based")(Tennessee law); Lindenman v. Umscheid, 255 Kan. 610, 624, 875 P.2d 964, 974 (1994); cf. Miller v. East Baton Rouge Parish Sheriff's Dept., 511 So.2d 446 (La.1987) (belief that accused committed "an" offense).

5. See Restatement § 662, Ill. 1, based upon Parli v. Reed, 30 Kan. 534, 2 P. 635 (1883).

6. See Restatement § 662, cmt. i (limiting the mistake of law defense to such cases as those in which a statute that is facially valid is later held unconstitutional and suggesting that mistake of law will seldom assist a layman because he should ordinarily know he doesn't know the law).

of shoplifting, implies grounds for believing that the accused took something. If the facts do not warrant such a belief by a reasonable person, probable cause is lacking under either version of the definition.

Factual analysis. Under any definition, the determination of probable cause or its absence usually requires detailed factual analysis. A shopper's concealment of merchandise coupled with prompt departure may warrant an inference of theft, but a customer's departure with openly carried merchandise may not.[7] There are, of course, easy cases in which courts can simply say that the defendant was irrational in drawing an inference of guilt. The officer who overhears A say he smoked marijuana in B's presence can hardly rationally conclude that B possessed marijuana.[8] The officer who relies upon contradictory and uncertain statements of a child who has been beaten so badly he cannot talk coherently to identify the plaintiff as a criminal when all other evidence exculpates him obviously has no probable cause for accusing the plaintiff.[9]

Reasonable appearance and advice of counsel. Probable cause—the reasonableness of inferences of guilt—is to be judged by facts as they appeared at the time, not by later-discovered facts.[10] When liability is based upon continuance rather than initiation of the prosecution, probable cause must be judged on appearances at the time the accuser acts to continue the prosecution, as where he refuses to withdraw his complaint even after he has learned of the accused's innocence.[11] Non-lawyers may judge appearances by relying in good faith upon advice of fully informed counsel who is admitted to the bar in the state or otherwise appears to be reasonably competent.[12]

Further investigation required. When appearances leave heavy doubts, or create serious ambiguities, and when they indicate that other information is available that will confirm or dispel suspicions, an accusation made without further investigation may be premature and lacking in probable cause. For example, when a store customer walks out with an unpaid-for item of merchandise, courts often say that the inference of theft is reasonable, so the store manager has probable cause to prosecute,[13] but when the evidence is ambiguous or doubtful, the accuser's failure to investigate, or at least to utilize all the evidence at hand, may be enough to indicate a want of probable cause. The store security guard who sees ambiguous acts of a shopper should clear up doubts by viewing

7. Gustafson v. Payless Drug Stores Northwest, Inc., 269 Or. 354, 525 P.2d 118 (1974).

8. Cf. Malley v. Briggs, 475 U.S. 335, 106 S.Ct. 1092, 89 L.Ed.2d 271 (1986) (on similar facts).

9. Jones v. City of Chicago, 856 F.2d 985 (7th Cir.1988).

10. Richey v. Brookshire Grocery Co., 952 S.W.2d 515 (1997)

11. Branson v. Donaldson, 206 Ga.App. 723, 426 S.E.2d 218 (1992).

12. Schnathorst v. Williams, 240 Iowa 561, 36 N.W.2d 739 (1949) (full information not given to prosecutor, reliance on "advice of counsel" therefore not justified); Strickland v. University of Scranton, 700 A.2d 979 (Pa.Super.1997); Restatement § 666.

13. E.g., Richey v. Brookshire Grocery Co., 952 S.W.2d 515 (1997); cf. Lester v. Buchanen, 112 Nev. 1426, 929 P.2d 910 (1996) (no record of return of rented video tape, probable cause to believe it was not returned).

the store's video tape or verifying the shopper's version if he can.[14] Similarly, an officer who has only an unsupported accusation of the plaintiff from a felon with a motive for revenge should not lodge a serious charge of armed robbery when further leads remain to be investigated.[15] On the other hand, the mere fact that some evidence can be found that tends to exculpate the accused does not eliminate probable cause to believe in guilt.[16]

Objective vs. subjective judgments of reasonableness. The reasonableness standard of probable cause is an objective standard.[17] If the citizen-accuser only states facts to an officer or prosecutor, and he honestly believes those facts, the whole matter is left to the prosecutor, and the accuser is not an instigator of the prosecution at all.[18] However, when it comes to the issue of probable cause, the accuser's own honest belief in guilt is not sufficient; the facts must warrant a reasonable person's belief in guilt.[19] However, a formula recited by a number of courts implies or states that while the accuser's subjective belief in guilt is not enough to show probable cause, his subjective belief in the accused's innocence is enough to show the lack of it.[20] If the facts warrant prosecution, however, the citizen's belief in innocence seems irrelevant. A completely objective test would be more appropriate,[21] and some recent decisions have explicitly rejected subjective elements.[22] Perhaps in most cases the citizen-accuser would be protected because he is not an instigator at all.

Presuming a want of probable cause from judicial actions. Since the criminal trial itself does not deal with the issue of probable cause but with the issue of ultimate guilt beyond a reasonable doubt, an acquittal of the accused at trial does not tend to prove that the accuser lacked probable cause.[23] Some courts, however, have said that when the examining magistrate finds no probable cause, or the grand jury rejects an indictment, a rebuttable presumption or an inference arises that the accuser lacked probable cause.[24] Some have even said so when the public

14. Cf. Soares v. Ann & Hope of Rhode Island, Inc., 637 A.2d 339 (R.I.1994) (reciting failure to check video and allegedly switched price tag, but not specifically stating why a want of probable cause could be found).

15. Miller v. East Baton Rouge Parish Sheriff's Dept., 511 So.2d 446 (La.1987).

16. E.g., Gray v. State, 624 A.2d 479 (Me.1993) (evidence of mother's child abuse justified reasonable belief in her guilt, although some therapists could pose alternative explanations for the evidence).

17. Matthews v. Blue Cross and Blue Shield of Michigan, 456 Mich. 365, 572 N.W.2d 603 (1998); Jordan v. Bailey, 113 Nev. 1038, 944 P.2d 828 (1997).

18. § 431.

19. Bacon v. Towne, 58 Mass. (4 Cush.) 217 at 238 (1849) ("Probable cause is such a state of facts in the mind of the prosecutor as would lead a man of ordinary caution and prudence to believe, or entertain an honest and strong suspicion, that the person arrested is guilty").

20. Torian v. Ashford, 216 Ala. 85, 112 So. 418 (1927); see Hitson v. Sims, 69 Ark. 439, 64 S.W. 219 (1901).

21. See Dan B. Dobbs, Belief and Doubt in Malicious Prosecution and Libel, 21 Ariz. L. Rev. 607 (1980).

22. Sheldon Appel Co. v. Albert & Oliker, 47 Cal.3d 863, 765 P.2d 498, 254 Cal. Rptr. 336 (1989); Matthews v. Blue Cross and Blue Shield of Michigan, 456 Mich. 365, 572 N.W.2d 603 (1998); Roberts v. Federal Express Corp., 842 S.W.2d 246 (Tenn.1992).

23. E.g., Banks v. Montgomery Ward & Co., Inc., 212 Md. 31, 128 A.2d 600 (1957).

24. Schnathorst v. Williams, 240 Iowa 561, 36 N.W.2d 739 (1949); Tritchler v. West Virginia Newspaper Pub. Co., 156 W.Va. 335, 193 S.E.2d 146 (1972).

prosecutor enters a nolle prosequi or abandons the prosecution.[25] Other courts have rejected such presumptions.[26]

The presumption or inference is usually a diversion. At best, it puts the burden upon the defendant to show he had probable cause and hence places upon him the risk of uncertainty. It may promote a substantial diversion from the merits because the presumption may be attacked on the ground that the magistrate's discharge was not upon the merits, or was a mistaken adjudication of the ultimate guilt rather than probable cause, or was based upon misconduct.[27] If the evidence bearing upon probable cause is before the court, the presumption satisfies no need, especially under the usual rule that the probable cause issue is for the judge, not the jury.[28] In addition, if the court indulges a presumption that the defendant lacked probable cause because a magistrate so determined at a preliminary criminal hearing, the court is binding the present defendant by the results of a proceeding in which the defendant was not a party. If that is not actually unconstitutional, it is at least unfair[29] and since it is also unneeded, such presumptions could be dropped without loss.

Presuming the presence of probable cause. The converse case is one in which the accused is bound over by the magistrate, or indicted by the grand jury. Courts in these cases have held that such determinations make a prima facie showing that the accuser had probable cause,[30] rebuttable by proof that the magistrate in fact made the determination on some other ground.[31] The requirement of favorable termination of the criminal proceeding bars the accused who is found guilty at trial and does not succeed in reversing the conviction; but even if the conviction is reversed on appeal, the now-reversed guilty finding has been treated as establishing prima facie evidence of probable cause.[32]

Judge and jury. Under the traditional view, the jury determines any disputed facts bearing on the issue of probable cause, but the question whether the facts so determined count as probable cause or not is a question of law for the judge.[33] Some courts reject this view and leave both the facts and the ultimate issue of probable cause to the jury;[34]

25. Thompson v. Harris, 603 So.2d 1086 (Ala.Civ.App.1992).

26. Miessner v. All Dakota Ins. Assocs., Inc. 515 N.W.2d 198 (S.D.1994) (nolle prosequi or abandonment creates no presumption); Roberts v. Federal Express Corp., 842 S.W.2d 246 (Tenn.1992) (grand's jury's refusal to indict creates no presumption).

27. See Restatement § 663.

28. As recognized in Palmer Ford, Inc. v. Wood, 298 Md. 484, 471 A.2d 297 (1984).

29. See Davis v. McMillan, 142 Mich. 391, 105 N.W. 862 (1905) (rejecting the presumption on the ground that an act that is not the defendant's cannot bind him).

30. E.g., Lewis v. White, 222 Ga.App. 842, 476 S.E.2d 602 (1996); Miessner v. All Dakota Ins. Assocs., Inc. 515 N.W.2d 198 (S.D.1994).

31. E.g., Rodgers v. W.T. Grant Co., 341 So.2d 511 (Fla.1976) (magistrate bound the accused over because she would not release her potential civil action; this was not a determination of probable cause).

32. E.g., Ex Parte City of Gadsden, 718 So.2d 716 (Ala.1998).

33. Palmer Ford, Inc. v. Wood, 298 Md. 484, 471 A.2d 297 (1984); Matthews v. Blue Cross and Blue Shield of Michigan, 456 Mich. 365, 381, 572 N.W.2d 603, 611 (1998); Restatement § 673 (1).

34. Schnathorst v. Williams, 240 Iowa 561, 576, 36 N.W.2d 739, 747 (1949).

others sometimes use an ambiguous formulation that may leave the roles of judge and jury in doubt.[35]

The traditional view is sometimes regarded as anomalous because the probable cause issue, turning as it does on a kind of reasonableness, is sometimes compared to the issue of negligence, which is usually left to the jury so long as reasonable people could differ. But the judgments to be made in the two kinds of cases are quite different, as are the risks of error. Reasonableness in negligence cases ordinarily turns on an assessment of a risk, and most often a risk of physical harm. Reasonableness in the probable cause issue usually turns, literally, on reasoning. The question is whether inferences of guilt are justified from known facts. The risk of error in probable cause determinations is an especially sensitive matter for reasons already summarized. So understandably enough, courts have retained control over probable cause decisions, even if the rule is sometimes forgotten by trial and even appellate judges.

The judge's role in determining probable cause is a problem, however, when facts are disputed. In the negligence case, the judge defines negligence for the jury, which then resolves factual disputes and applies the definition to the facts it finds. But such a procedure in a malicious prosecution case would effectively leave the probable cause issue to the jury and displace the judge's traditional role. To avoid that, a judge could conceivably ask the jury a large number of special interrogatories about very precise facts and then utilize the answers to determine probable cause. Alternatively, the judge might outline a number of factual scenarios the jury might find and instruct the jury as to whether each one does or does not show probable cause.[36]

§ 433. Improper Purpose or "Malice"

Requirement of improper purpose. The malicious prosecution plaintiff must prove, in addition to the other elements, that the now defendant instigated the earlier prosecution for an improper purpose—for a purpose other than to bring the accused to justice, as the Restatement puts it.[1] This is the element traditionally referred to as "malice." As long as evidence supports a finding, this element, unlike the probable cause element, is for the jury's determination.[2]

35. Courts often state that probable cause is for the judge unless facts are not in dispute, but that if facts are disputed, the issue becomes one of mixed law and fact to be resolved by the jury. Thrifty Rent–A–Car v. Jeffrey, 257 Ark. 904, 520 S.W.2d 304 (1975); Richey v. Brookshire Grocery Co., 952 S.W.2d 515 (1997). Conceivably such a statement means only that the hard facts are to be resolved by the jury with the judge then deciding probable cause on the basis of the jury's factual determination. Sometimes courts that advance such a formula in fact go on to clarify it by saying as much, e.g., Dutt v. Kremp, 111 Nev. 567, 894 P.2d 354, 61 A.L.R.5th 801(1995).

36. Montgomery Ward v. Wilson, 339 Md. 701, 664 A.2d 916 (1995); Shoemaker v. Selnes, 220 Or. 573, 349 P.2d 473, 87 A.L.R.2d 170 (1960).

§ 433

1. Restatement § 668.

2. E.g., Lambert v. Sears, Roebuck & Co., 280 Or. 123, 570 P.2d 357 (1977); see Nassar v. Concordia Rod and Gun Club, Inc., 682 So.2d 1035 (Miss.1996).

Mixed motives. All tests that turn on the defendant's supposed motive or purpose raise difficult problems, first because motives can only be guessed at from actions, and second because motives are usually quite mixed. The Restatement resolves the mixed motive problem by providing that the accuser must act "primarily" for a purpose other than to bring the supposed offender to justice.[3] For example, there is a good deal of abuse of the criminal process by merchants who use it as a means of collecting bad checks, but the fact that a merchant prosecutes those who bounce checks partly because the merchant hopes to collect the check is not enough to show malice.[4] The primary purpose test may be less suited than a but-for test used in some other circumstances. Under a but-for test, the prosecutor's supposed improper purpose would not count against him if he would have instituted the prosecution even without the improper purpose.[5]

Improper purposes. The mixed-motive problem aside, the Restatement takes the view that any purpose other than to bring the offender to justice is improper and establishes the "malice" element of malicious prosecution. Use of the criminal process solely to enforce a supposed debt or to extort money from the accused shows improper purpose,[6] and so does personal hostility or ill-will,[7] or impersonal hostility based upon race or other group characteristics.[8] In some of the cases malice seems more like oppressive behavior or abuse of power or authority than anything else.[9] Courts can easily infer malice if the accuser knowingly asserts falsehoods. On the other hand, it is difficult to see how he can be malicious if he honestly reports facts pointing toward guilt, even if he does not believe the inference of guilt. The Restatement flatly states, however, that the accuser who does not believe in guilt is necessarily malicious.[10] This seems wrong because an honest citizen can believe it is his duty to report facts even if he does not believe their negative implications.[11]

Relation to probable cause. Courts sometimes appear to confuse or conflate probable cause and malice issues. The most serious problem arises in applying the old saw that while malice is not evidence of a lack of probable cause, a lack of probable cause is evidence of malice.[12] The

3. See Restatement § 668, cmt. c.

4. Lawson v. Kroger Co., 997 F.2d 214 (6th Cir.1993).

5. Mt. Healthy City Sch. Dist. Bd. of Educ. v. Doyle, 429 U.S. 274, 97 S.Ct. 568, 50 L.Ed.2d 471 (1977) (discharge for both unconstitutional and constitutional reasons); Greenwich Citizens Comm., Inc. v. Counties of Warren and Washington Ind. Dev. Agency, 77 F.3d 26 (2d Cir.1996).

6. Hodges v. Gibson Prods. Co., 811 P.2d 151(Utah 1991); Restatement § 668, cmt. g.

7. Restatement § 668, cmt. f.

8. Lippay v. Christos, 996 F.2d 1490 (3d Cir.1993).

9. See Lippay v. Christos, 996 F.2d 1490 (3d Cir.1993); Martin v. City of Albany, 42 N.Y.2d 13, 396 N.Y.S.2d 612, 364 N.E.2d 1304 (1977) (civil rights claim adopting state law; oppressive behavior may warrant finding of malice); Lambert v. Sears, Roebuck & Co., 280 Or. 123, 570 P.2d 357 (1977).

10. Restatement § 668, cmt. e.

11. Dan B. Dobbs, Belief and Doubt in Malicious Prosecution and Libel, 21 Ariz. L. Rev. 607 (1979).

12. See, e.g, Montgomery Ward v. Wilson, 339 Md. 701, 664 A.2d 916 (1995); Moore v. Evans, 124 N.C.App. 35, 476 S.E.2d 415 (1996).

inference of malice from a want of probable cause has been permitted even when the want of probable cause itself is merely "presumed" from a grand jury's refusal to indict.[13] But if malice or improper purpose can be inferred anytime probable cause is lacking, then malice does not look like an independent element of the plaintiff's case at all. The Restatement has accordingly attempted to limit the inference to cases in which the lack of probable cause shows the accuser did not believe the charges he brought.[14] Perhaps as Judge Linde argued, it would be more accurate to say that the same evidence that shows a want of probable cause might sometimes show malice as well.[15] If the evidence is that the accuser reported incriminating facts he knew to be false, for example, instigation, want of probable cause, and presence of malice can all reasonably be inferred from the knowing falsehood.

§ 434. Termination of the Prosecution

The malicious prosecution plaintiff must show not only that the criminal prosecution of which he complains has been terminated but also that it has been terminated in his favor.[1] The requirement of termination serves to minimize a threat of civil liability that might chill testimony in the criminal action and to avoid litigation that may become needless if a conviction is obtained and upheld. The additional requirement that termination must be in favor of the accused—the malicious prosecution plaintiff—serves a different purpose. If the accused was convicted, a malicious prosecution action should be impermissible because courts should not be permitted to collaterally attack the conviction.[2]

An acquittal of the accused after a trial or on a dispositive motion is of course a termination favorable to the accused.[3] Short of that, courts have looked for dispositions that tend to show the accused's innocence or at least a determination that a criminal case could not be proved,[4] saying with Prosser that a mere procedural victory would not suffice.[5] Maybe it would be more accurate to say that a disposition of the criminal proceedings that probably entailed some judgment about the merits will count as a favorable termination. Consistent with that approach, a favorable termination may occur even though the termination is not "final"

13. Schnathorst v. Williams, 240 Iowa 561, 36 N.W.2d 739 (1949).

14. Restatement § 669.

15. Lambert v. Sears, Roebuck & Co., 280 Or. 123, 570 P.2d 357 (1977) (Linde, J., concurring).

§ 434

1. Restatement § 658.

2. See Heck v. Humphrey, 512 U.S. 477, 486, 114 S.Ct. 2364, 2372, 129 L.Ed.2d 383 (1994). Perhaps this is what courts have in mind when they occasionally say that the favorable termination requirement is imposed to assure that probable cause was lacking. See DeVaney v. Thriftway Mktg. Corp., 124 N.M. 512, 518, 953 P.2d 277, 283 (1997).

3. Restatement § 659.

4. Jaffe v. Stone, 18 Cal.2d 146, 114 P.2d 335 (1941); MacFawn v. Kresler, 88 N.Y.2d 859, 666 N.E.2d 1359, 644 N.Y.S.2d 486 (1996); Ash v. Ash, 72 Ohio St.3d 520, 651 N.E.2d 945 (1995).

5. E.g., Foshee v. Southern Finance and Thrift Corp., 967 S.W.2d 817 (Tenn.Ct.App. 1997) (on this basis and others holding that a dismissal of the first action on double jeopardy grounds was not a favorable termination).

because the prosecution can be revived or reinstituted. For example, if a magistrate determines that no probable cause has been shown and discharges the accused, jeopardy has not attached and the same charge may be laid again.[6] Nevertheless, a magistrate's discharge and a grand jury's refusal to indict count as sufficient terminations.[7]

When the criminal prosecution is terminated because of a mere lapse of time or because the accused has left the jurisdiction,[8] because of a compromise settlement,[9] or for other reasons that do not bear even remotely upon the merits,[10] courts have held that the termination is not favorable to the accused, with the result that he cannot bring a malicious prosecution action based upon the criminal proceeding. Sometimes a nol pros reflects a compromise or mercy or some other reason for abandoning the prosecution that does not touch the merits and hence leaves the accused without a favorable termination.[11] Some courts have assumed that the unexplained nol pros is a compromise;[12] others have permitted or required evidence to show the reasons for the nol pros.[13] Still others have tacitly or expressly treated a nol pros as a termination.[14]

§ 435. Special Defenses

Aside from immunities[1] and ordinary defenses such as those based upon the statute of limitations,[2] two special defenses may be raised.

Guilt in fact. First and most important is the defense of guilt in fact. If the defendant instigated a prosecution of the plaintiff without proba-

6. United States v. Levy, 268 U.S. 390, 45 S.Ct. 516, 69 L.Ed. 1010 (1925).

7. Jaffe v. Stone, 18 Cal.2d 146, 114 P.2d 335 (1941); but cf. MacFawn v. Kresler, 88 N.Y.2d 859, 666 N.E.2d 1359, 644 N.Y.S.2d 486 (1996) (dismissal of criminal charge on the ground that facts as stated were not sufficient to show a crime was not a sufficient termination).

8. Halberstadt v. New York Life Ins. Co., 194 N.Y. 1, 86 N.E. 801 (1909).

9. Cimino v. Rosen, 193 Neb. 162, 225 N.W.2d 567 (1975).

10. Restatement § 660 (listing compromise, accused's misconduct that prevents a proper trial, mercy, a new proceeding for the same offense instituted).

11. See Restatement §§ 660 & 661; cf. O'Brien v. Alexander, 101 F.3d 1479 (2d Cir.1996) (voluntary dismissal).

12. Tucker v. Duncan, 499 F.2d 963 (4th Cir.1974) (after a conference in the back room, a nolle prosequi entered; compromise assumed).

13. Alamo Rent-A-Car, Inc. v. Mancusi, 632 So.2d 1352, 1356 (Fla.1994) ("when a plaintiff establishes that an underlying criminal case was nol prossed and presents evidence that the nol pros was not the result of a negotiated plea or bargain, the burden then shifts to the defendant to present evidence to the contrary and the issue becomes one for a jury to decide"); Grand Union Co. v. Miller, 232 Ga.App. 857, 503 S.E.2d 49 (1998) (covenant not to sue given at time of nol pros showed compromise).

14. Sometimes courts have even held that a nol pros is evidence that probable cause was lacking. See Thompson v. Harris, 603 So.2d 1086 (Ala.Ct.Civ.App. 1992).

§ 435

1. E.g., McEachern v. Black, 329 S.C. 642, 496 S.E.2d 659 (1998) (judge who issued show cause order for contempt then dismissed it upon attorney's request was immune).

2. The malicious prosecution action normally accrues upon termination of the criminal prosecution and the statute begins to run at that point. Campo v. Wolosin, 211 A.D.2d 660, 622 N.Y.S.2d 291 (1995); Patrick v. Howard, 904 S.W.2d 941 (Tex.App. 1995) (the fact that the accused did not know the prosecution's lack of probable cause until long after termination did not trigger the discovery rule; knowledge of the injury from prosecution plus termination triggers the statute).

ble cause but with malice, and the plaintiff was fully vindicated by a favorable termination, it is still possible that the plaintiff was in fact guilty of the crime for which she was prosecuted or one quite similar. Authorities agree that in such a case, the plaintiff cannot recover for malicious prosecution.[3] The rule is essentially similar to the rules applied in defamation and false arrest cases, relieving the defendant of all liability when the defamation turns out to be true[4] or the arrest justified because the arrested person is guilty in fact.[5] A different rule applies to the case of a discriminatory discharge from employment, which is not justified by the later discovery of non-discriminatory grounds for discharge; but even here, the employer-accuser is liable only for a limited remedy.[6]

The guilt-in-fact rule does not exactly permit a collateral attack, since the earlier criminal action only determines that guilt has not been proven beyond a reasonable doubt, while the later malicious prosecution suit determines that guilt is established by a preponderance of the evidence.

Release. Public prosecutors not uncommonly agree to drop criminal charges in exchange for the accused's release of all claims against the prosecutor and others who have participated in the prosecution. If the release is valid, it forecloses legitimate complaint as well as frivolous complaints of malicious prosecution or analogous civil rights violations. The New York Court of Appeals held that such releases were invalid because they invaded the integrity of the legal system. If the accused was guilty, he went free, while if he was innocent the prosecutor was under an ethical duty to dismiss in any event.[7] That is not a popular view, however and some other states have held that such releases are not per se invalid.[8] The Supreme Court of the United States, in a decision governing federal civil rights claims for malicious prosecution, took the position that such releases were not necessarily invalid, but might be held so in particular cases. The Court implied that the release would be valid if there were no prosecutorial misconduct, a public interest supported the prosecutor's use of a release, and if the release were given voluntarily.[9]

3. Wal-Mart Stores, Inc. v. Blackford, 264 Ga. 612, 449 S.E.2d 293 (1994) (theorizing that guilt in fact eliminates damages and describing it as a "defense"); Rogers v. Hill, 281 Or. 491, 576 P.2d 328 (1978); Restatement §§ 653 & 657 (respectively appearing to treat the plaintiff's innocence as element to be proved by the malicious prosecution plaintiff and as an affirmative defense to be shown by the defendant).

4. See § 410. For further comparison of defamation and malicious prosecution, see § 430; see also 1 Harper, James & Gray, § 4.11.

5. Restatement § 119(a). Similarly, if a client is convicted because of a lawyer's malpractice but the client is in fact guilty of the crime, that is a defense to the lawyer. See § 489.

6. McKennon v. Nashville Banner Pub. Co., 513 U.S. 352, 115 S.Ct. 879, 130 L.Ed.2d 852 (1995).

7. Cowles v. Brownell, 73 N.Y.2d 382, 538 N.E.2d 325, 540 N.Y.S.2d 973 (1989) .

8. Hoines v. Barney's Club, Inc., 28 Cal.3d 603, 620 P.2d 628, 170 Cal.Rptr. 42 (1980).

9. Newton v. Rumery, 480 U.S. 386, 107 S.Ct. 1187, 94 L.Ed.2d 405 (1987).

Following that lead, federal courts have developed a small jurisprudence of release law.[10] They have held that the prosecutor would be required to show a public interest favoring the release in the particular case so that a blanket policy of obtaining releases in all cases of abandoned prosecution would not be valid.[11] They have also considered whether particular releases were given voluntarily, taking into account a variety of factors. The release is less likely to be voluntary if the accused signs it while in custody, is not represented by counsel, is unsophisticated and is not fully informed about its effects.[12] Several courts have said that the burden of proof to show the validity of the release is upon the prosecutor.[13] Where police misconduct is part of the underlying civil rights claim, the release may deserve special scrutiny, since police might file charges as bargaining chips when their own misconduct is called into question.[14]

§ 436. Wrongful Civil Litigation and Tactics

Wrongful institution of a civil action is actionable under rules similar to those for malicious prosecution of a criminal proceeding. Where it is necessary to draw a distinction between the two, the claim based upon a wrongful civil action may be called malicious prosecution of a civil suit, or "malicious use of process," wrongful civil litigation or the like. The policy of protecting the right to resort to court, analogous to if not grounded in the First Amendment's right to petition government, applies to protect a certain amount of wrongful civil litigation, a point recognized under federal law as well as under the common law.[1] On the other hand, wrongful civil suits can destroy a livelihood, devastate a business, or chill debate on public issues.[2] Balance between these competing and core concerns is critical, and the rules aim with varying success at striking that balance.

Elements. The analogy to malicious prosecution led lawyers and courts to focus on wrongful initiation or continuation of civil proceedings or wrongful assertion of a counterclaim,[3] rather than wrongful or unjustified defensive tactics.[4] Under the traditional view, then, the elements of the plaintiff's claim for wrongful civil proceedings were variations on

10. See David B. Sweet, Annotation, Validity, as Against Claim under 42 U.S.C.A. § 1983, of Accused's Release Etc., 139 A.L.R. Fed. 1 (1997).

11. Cain v. Darby Borough, 7 F.3d 377, 139 A.L.R. Fed. 677 (1993).

12. Livingstone v. North Belle Vernon Borough, 12 F.3d 1205 (3d Cir.1993).

13. E.g., Lynch v. City of Alhambra, 880 F.2d 1122 (9th Cir.1989).

14. Coughlen v. Coots, 5 F.3d 970 (6th Cir.1993).

§ 436

1. Professional Real Estate Investors, Inc. v. Columbia Pictures Indus., Inc., 508 U.S. 49, 113 S.Ct. 1920, 123 L.Ed.2d 611 (1993) (all but "sham" litigation [essentially that brought without probable cause and with malice] is protected from claims that litigation is used to violate antitrust laws).

2. On special SLAPP statutes see § 439.

3. E.g., Harrison v. Springdale Water & Sewer Com'n, 780 F.2d 1422 (8th Cir.1986) (public entity's counterclaim, § 1983 civil rights action was viable).

4. For changes in this view see § 439.

those in malicious prosecution.[5] The plaintiff can recover if the defendant had instigated a civil proceeding[6] or even a quasi-judicial administrative proceeding,[7] without probable cause and for an improper purpose, provided that the proceeding had been terminated favorably to the now plaintiff. A substantial number of states add a requirement not found in malicious criminal prosecution cases: the plaintiff cannot recover unless she suffers special injury, which turned out to mean that her person or property was seized in the former action.[8]

Circumventing rules by pleading other torts. As with the malicious prosecution of a criminal charge, the plaintiff cannot avoid the burden of proving these elements by claiming on a theory of negligence.[9] The protections for court access erected by the rules for wrongful litigation claims presumably cannot be avoided by claim under a theory of defamation, privacy invasion, outrage, interference with contract, or professional negligence of lawyers, either. In fact, courts have rejected such claims under the rules for those particular torts.[10] But some courts have allowed plaintiffs to circumvent the rules protecting access to courts. If the plaintiff alleges that a lawsuit caused emotional harm[11] or interference with prospective economic relations,[12] a few cases have allowed the claim to proceed without evidence that the lawsuit was brought without probable cause. For this reason, it is important to recognize straightforwardly that no alternative theory can be permitted to subvert the rules by permitting liability for maintaining a suit when the conduct involved would not show wrongful civil litigation. The original suitor's lawyer

5. Courts sometimes also invoke "presumptions" based on judicial determinations in the prior litigation. See Hornstein v. Wolf, 67 N.Y.2d 721, 490 N.E.2d 857, 499 N.Y.S.2d 938 (1986).

6. Two qualifications: (1) One court has excluded all family law proceedings from the rules of malicious prosecution, saying that sanctions by the family law court would suffice. Bidna v. Rosen, 19 Cal. App.4th 27, 23 Cal.Rptr.2d 251 (1993). This was attacked and rejected in Vazquez v. Reeves, 138 Or.App. 153, 907 P.2d 254 (1995), holding that a guardianship proceeding brought without probable cause was actionable. (2) Although the wrongful litigation tort requires institution of a proceeding, acts committed prior to institution may count as some other tort such as abuse of process by issuing process before suit, or a violation of the federal Fair Debt Collection Act by certain threats.

7. Hardy v. Vial, 48 Cal.2d 577, 311 P.2d 494, 66 A.L.R.2d 739 (1957); Restatement § 680.

8. § 437.

9. O'Toole v. Franklin, 279 Or. 513, 569 P.2d 561 (1977).

10. See, e.g., Tappen v. Ager, 599 F.2d 376 (10th Cir.1979) (physician who won malpractice action had no claim based upon libel, privacy invasion, and intentional infliction of emotional distress); Bidna v. Rosen, 19 Cal.App.4th 27, 23 Cal.Rptr.2d 251 (1993) (intentional infliction of emotional distress claim would require acts other than those supporting malicious prosecution). But cf. Sacco v. High Country Independ. Press Inc., 271 Mont. 209, 896 P.2d 411 (Mont. 1995) (seemingly allowing an emotional distress claim on facts that suggest malicious prosecution rules should limit the claim). Absolute privilege would almost always protect against liability on a libel or privacy theory for a pleading or words used in litigation. Presumably the same is true with intentional infliction of emotional distress.

11. Green Bay Packaging, Inc. v. Preferred Packaging, Inc., 932 P.2d 1091 (Okla. 1996).

12. Green Bay Packaging, Inc. v. Preferred Packaging, Inc., 932 P.2d 1091 (Okla. 1996). See also Nesler v. Fisher and Company, Inc., 452 N.W.2d 191 (Iowa 1990); cf. Voorhees v. Guyan Machinery Co., 191 W.Va. 450, 446 S.E.2d 672 (1994) (threat of litigation actionable as interference with contract without a showing that the litigation itself was without probable cause).

owes a duty of care only to his client, so although he may be liable for malicious prosecution or abuse of process, he is not liable to his client's adversary for negligence or violation of the Code of Professional Responsibility.[13] Taken together, these rules are a formidable barrier to recovery in many cases. For example, almost all of the physicians' countersuits against lawyers and former patients for bringing unjustified medical malpractice actions have been defeated by at least one of these rules.[14]

Probable cause. The special injury rule aside, one of the chief differences between the claim for malicious prosecution and the claim for wrongful civil litigation is that "probable cause" in the civil context means only that the original suitor must believe in the facts he asserts and that a civil claim is plausible, or he has a good chance at establishing the case to the satisfaction of judge and jury,[15] or that he "may" have a claim.[16] In this respect, he may rely upon advice of apparently competent and unbiased counsel after full disclosure of all relevant facts.[17] When the lawyer himself is sued for his part in instigating the former civil action, the lawyer is held to a kind of objective professional standard and liable only if the claim he fosters is not legally tenable.[18] A lawyer who files a medical malpractice suit on behalf of a client, for example, may be justified even though he has not consulted medical experts and though discovery will later show the suit to be without merit.[19] This lenient approach to probable cause reflects the fact that in American litigation courts are constantly drawing distinctions, modifying formulations of rules, and recognizing new claims and defenses, so that even arguments that have been previously rejected are not necessarily untenable and the further fact that much of the evidence in complex cases must be developed by discovery rather than before suit is commenced.

Malice. The requirement of improper purpose (or "malice") is again similar to its analog in malicious prosecution cases. The suitor is not liable for his failed suit unless he brought it for an improper purpose—that is, "primarily" for any purpose other than securing proper adjudication of the claim.[20] Spite itself is not enough; few tort suits are brought without a degree of rancor.[21] A motive that includes a spiteful desire to

13. Friedman v. Dozorc, 412 Mich. 1, 312 N.W.2d 585 (1981).

14. See Linda A. Sharp, Medical Malpractice Countersuits, 61 A.L.R.5th 307 (1998).

15. Bradshaw v. State Farm Mut. Auto. Ins., 157 Ariz. 411, 417, 758 P.2d 1313, 1319 (1988).

16. Restatement § 675.

17. E.g., Neumann v. Indus. Sound Eng'g, Inc., 31 Wis.2d 471, 143 N.W.2d 543 (1966).

18. Sheldon Appel Co. v. Albert & Oliker, 47 Cal.3d 863, 765 P.2d 498, 254 Cal. Rptr. 336 (1989).

19. Dutt v. Kremp, 111 Nev. 567, 894 P.2d 354, 61 A.L.R.5th 801 (1995); but cf. Bull v. McCuskey, 96 Nev. 706, 615 P.2d 957 (1980) (successful abuse of process claim against lawyer who sued physician, went to trial without consulting any medical experts, and offered nuisance settlement), overruled on other grounds, Ace Truck v. Kahn, 103 Nev. 503, 746 P.2d 132 (1987). Once investigation shows facts that eliminate reasonable grounds for suit, however, the lawyer must not continue the litigation.

20. Restatement § 676.

21. See DeVaney v. Thriftway Mktg. Corp., 124 N.M. 512, 522, 953 P.2d 277, 287 (1997).

harass or a calculated desire to extort a settlement by a suitor who knows that the facts do not support his claim will suffice, however.[22] And a complaint based upon knowing or reckless falsehoods shows improper purpose, but mere negligence of a lawyer in failing to discover that he has no case does not.[23] At the same time, purposeful avoidance of the evidence might show a knowing or reckless falsehood in libel cases;[24] a lawyer's complete lack of evidence in support of a claim might be understood to show that his motive for suit was primarily extortionate, not colorably legitimate. It should go without saying that a lawyer's contingent fee arrangement assuredly does not show malice in bringing the suit.[25] As in the malicious prosecution cases, courts say that malice may be inferred from a want of probable cause.[26] The same objections can be raised as in malicious prosecution cases.

Termination. Termination of the former civil suit is important in two ways. First, the wrongful litigation claim accrues at termination of the former suit, so that the statute of limitations begins running at that time.[27] Second, favorable termination of the former suit is a substantive element of the plaintiff's claim for wrongful litigation.[28] The termination requirement leads courts to say that wrongful civil litigation cannot be challenged by a counterclaim in the same action, since that litigation could not have terminated when the counterclaim is filed.[29]

Favorable termination is not necessarily a termination on the merits, but it is usually a termination that tends to reflect probable merits. A disposition of the former suit that is on appeal is not regarded as a sufficient termination until the appeal is decided.[30] Otherwise, however, a determination on the merits that the defendant in the prior suit is not liable is sufficient to show favorable termination, whether the termi-

22. E.g., Bradshaw v. State Farm Mut. Auto. Ins., 157 Ariz. 411, 417, 758 P.2d 1313, 1319 (1988) (insurer induced insured to file a suit as part of strategy to defend against a valid claim; this shows "malice").

23. Spencer v. Burglass, 337 So.2d 596 (La.Ct.App.1976)

24. See Harte–Hanks Communications, Inc. v. Connaughton, 491 U.S. 657, 109 S.Ct. 2678, 105 L.Ed.2d 562 (1989); § 419.

25. Miskew v. Hess, 21 Kan.App.2d 927, 910 P.2d 223 (1996).

26. One Thousand Fleet Ltd. Partnership v. Guerriero, 346 Md. 29, 694 A.2d 952 (1997).

27. Christian v. Lapidus, 833 S.W.2d 71 (Tenn.1992) (abandonment of claim by filing a complaint not naming the present plaintiffs terminated the action and started the statute of limitations running).

28. New Mexico, consolidating the wrongful litigation and abuse of process torts, treats favorable termination as evidence bearing on probable cause but not as a separate element. See DeVaney v. Thriftway Mktg. Corp., 124 N.M. 512, 521, 953 P.2d 277, 286 (1997).

29. Bismarck Hotel Co. v. Sutherland, 175 Ill.App.3d 739, 529 N.E.2d 1091, 125 Ill.Dec. 15 (1988); Anello v. Vinci, 142 Vt. 583, 458 A.2d 1117 (1983). A counterclaim asserting a wrongful provisional remedy preceding the main suit can be entertained, however, if the provisional remedy has been terminated. Blankenship v. Staton, 348 S.W.2d 925 (Ky.1961). Beyond that, it seems logically possible to file a contingent counterclaim, to be determined only after the main action had terminated or even better to award attorney fees to the wrongfully sued defendant in lieu of a separate action for wrongful litigation. New Mexico permits counterclaims provided lack of probable cause can be proved by clear and convincing evidence. See DeVaney v. Thriftway Mktg. Corp., supra n. 28.

30. One Thousand Fleet Ltd. Partnership v. Guerriero, 346 Md. 29, 694 A.2d 952 (1997).

nation is based upon trial or upon summary judgment or other motion.[31] But courts have said that a dismissal of the prior suit because the statute of limitations has run does not reflect the innocence of the defendant in the former suit and hence does not show favorable termination.[32] The Restatement view is that a dismissal for failure to prosecute the former suit is a sufficiently favorable termination and that a withdrawal or voluntary dismissal by the plaintiff in that suit is likewise.[33] However, a voluntary dismissal is analogous to the prosecutor's nol pros of a criminal action. To the extent that the nol pros reflects a compromise or settlement, it it not a favorable determination[34] and the same may be said about the voluntary dismissal of a civil action.[35]

§ 437. Special Injury or Special Grievance Requirement

Special injury or grievance requirement. According to most counts, a majority of American courts allow the plaintiff to pursue the wrongful civil litigation claim without showing any special kind of injury.[1] A substantial number of courts, however, permit the action for wrongful civil proceedings only when the plaintiff has suffered "special injury" or "special grievance" as a result of the wrongful litigation.[2] And many cases that purport to ignore special injury requirements are actually decided on facts consistent with such requirements.[3]

Special injury or grievance generally. Courts say that special injury must be something more than the expense, distress, and reputational loss that is ordinarily suffered as a result of wrongful litigation. The fact that the plaintiff suffers damage to his property, business, or reputation as a result of the suit is not sufficient to show special grievance or injury; the interference must result directly from the suit itself or the court's pre-judgment orders.[4] The wrongful litigation claim is allowed when the

31. Restatement § 674, cmt. j.

32. Lackner v. Lacroix, 25 Cal.3d 747, 602 P.2d 393, 159 Cal.Rptr. 693 (1979); Miskew v. Hess, 21 Kan.App.2d 927, 910 P.2d 223 (1996). Arguably the termination is sufficient and the real issue is probable cause. To the extent that the statute of limitations turns on factual determinations to be made at trial, the lawyer may have had a tenable case even though it was ultimately dismissed on statute of limitations ground. The difference between a probable cause and a termination analysis is that the former specifically addresses the propriety of the former suit rather than the propriety of its underlying claim.

33. Restatement § 674, cmt. j; accord, Cult Awareness Network v. Church of Scientology Int'l, 177 Ill.2d 267, 685 N.E.2d 1347, 226 Ill.Dec. 604 (1997).

34. § 434.

35. Frey v. Stoneman, 150 Ariz. 106, 722 P.2d 274 (1986) (also suggesting other reasons for voluntary dismissal that would not amount to a confession that the suit was without basis).

§ 437

1. DeVaney v. Thriftway Mktg. Corp., 124 N.M. 512, 953 P.2d 277 (1997). Statutes may so provide. See ORE. REV. STATS. § 30.895(1).

2. Robb v. Chagrin Lagoons Yacht Club, Inc., 75 Ohio St.3d 264, 662 N.E.2d 9 (1996) (prejudgment seizure of property required); Friedman v. Dozorc, 412 Mich. 1, 312 N.W.2d 585 (1981).

3. E.g., Ackerman v. Kaufman, 41 Ariz. 110, 15 P.2d 966 (1932) (rejecting the special injury requirement where facts actually showed many harassing prior suits that would count as special injury); Greenberg v. Wolfberg, 890 P.2d 895 (Okla.1994) (similar).

4. Thus the fact that the victim of wrongful litigation takes voluntary bankruptcy does not show special grievance,

defendant has repeatedly brought unjustified suits.[5] It is also allowed when a single suit directly results in pre-judgment impairment or suspension of the plaintiff's rights in property, income, or credit, or detention of the plaintiff's person.[6] Unjustified insanity proceedings are actionable, at least when they constrain the plaintiff's person for examination or otherwise,[7] while unjustified bankruptcy proceedings are actionable because they put the plaintiff's property under the control of the bankruptcy court.[8]

Provisional remedies. Provisional remedies almost always impose constraints on person or property before trial on the merits. These remedies include injunction, replevin, garnishment, attachment and receivership. Statutes almost always require the original suitor seeking such provisional relief to post a bond and make the bond liable for damages if the suit fails.[9] In addition, however, the original suitor is liable for wrongful civil litigation if provisional remedies are maliciously obtained without probable cause.[10]

Lis pendens and the like. Similar considerations might control when the original suitor files an unjustified lis pendens,[11] which clouds or encumbers the plaintiff's title to property and impairs its marketability. Consequently, some courts have permitted the victim to recover[12] on a

since it results only indirectly from the wrongful litigation. Venuto v. Carella, Byrne, Bain, Gilfillan, Cecchi & Stewart, P.C., 11 F.3d 385 (3d Cir.1993).

5. Cult Awareness Network v. Church of Scientology Int'l, 177 Ill.2d 267, 685 N.E.2d 1347, 226 Ill.Dec. 604 (1997) (21 allegedly meritless suits in 17 months in various jurisdictions sufficient showing of special injury); Restatement § 679.

6. O'Toole v. Franklin, 279 Or. 513, 516, 569 P.2d 561, 563 (1977) ("immediate interference with the person, property, income, or credit of the subsequent complainant, apart from the ultimate judgment, as in the use of garnishment"); Daniels v. Conrad, 331 S.W.2d 411 (Tex.Civ.App. 1959).

7. Pellegrini v. Winter, 476 So.2d 1363 (Fla.Dist.Ct.App.1985); Fowle v. Fowle, 263 N.C. 724, 140 S.E.2d 398 (1965). When there is no detention of the person, the action may nevertheless be allowed on the ground that insanity proceedings are analogous to criminal proceedings so that the special injury requirement does not apply. See Hill v. Carlstrom, 216 Or. 300, 305, 338 P.2d 645, 648 (1959).

8. Balsiger v. American Steel & Supply Co., 254 Or. 204, 212, 458 P.2d 932, 933 (1969) (even if "there is no actual seizure of property or appointment of a trustee, the alleged bankrupt's property is in limbo, because the trustee's title, if and when appointed, reverts back to the date of the filing of the petition in bankruptcy"). Some courts, however, require an actual seizure of the property. See Peter G. Guthrie, Annotation, Action For Malicious Prosecution Based on Institution of Involuntary Bankruptcy, Insolvency, or Receivership Proceedings, 40 A.L.R.3d 296 (1971).

9. See Dan B. Dobbs, Law of Remedies § 2.11 (3) (2d ed. 1993).

10. See O'Brien v. Alexander, 101 F.3d 1479 (2d Cir.1996) (listing remedies and many cases); Blankenship v. Staton, 348 S.W.2d 925 (Ky.1961) (attachment); Mayflower Indus. v. Thor Corp., 15 N.J.Super. 139, 83 A.2d 246 (1951) (injunction); Shute v. Shute, 180 N.C. 386, 104 S.E. 764 (1920) (injunction; bond is not exclusive remedy); Novick v. Becker, 4 Wis.2d 432, 90 N.W.2d 620 (1958) (garnishment). An actual levy, not merely commencement of proceedings for attachment, may be required. Horner v. Savannah Valley Enters., Inc., 138 Ga.App. 117, 225 S.E.2d 458 (1976).

11. Lis pendens is an official record notifying prospective purchasers of real property that a suit is pending asserting a legal interest in the property. It is not authorized merely because the suitor has a claim for money damages that might ultimately be enforced against the property. See National City Bank, Indiana v. Shortridge, 689 N.E.2d 1248 (Ind.1997).

12. Wyatt v. Wehmueller, 163 Ariz. 12, 785 P.2d 581 (Ct. App. 1989), rev'd on other

wrongful litigation or some other theory[13] when a lis pendens is filed improperly or without probable cause. In the case of lis pendens, however, some other courts have rejected the action on the ground that the special injury rule requires physical seizure[14] or on the ground that the filing of a lis pendens is absolutely privileged as a judicial act, at least where it is based upon underlying litigation that claims title to the disputed land.[15] Excessive attachments and wrongful lien filings create similar problems, but are usually dealt with under the abuse of process theory[16] or under statutes[17] rather than as wrongful civil litigation.

§ 438. Abuse of Process

Distinguishing wrongful civil litigation. The gist of the abuse of process tort is said to be the misuse of legal process primarily to accomplish a purpose for which it was not designed,[1] usually to compel the victim to yield on some matter not involved in the suit. The abuse of process tort could readily be integrated with the malicious prosecution and wrongful litigation torts,[2] but the traditional view treats them as separate torts with distinct elements. If the plaintiff can show instigation of a suit for an improper purpose without probable cause and with a termination favorable to the now plaintiff, she has a malicious prosecution or a wrongful litigation claim, not a claim for abuse of process.[3]

grounds, 167 Ariz. 281, 806 P.2d 870 (1991) (filing lis pendens when statutory criteria were clearly not met, statutory penalty); Cok v. Cok, 558 A.2d 205 (R.I.1989) (both wrongful litigation and abuse of process theories); Kensington Dev. Corp. v. Israel, 142 Wis.2d 894, 419 N.W.2d 241 (1988).

13. Courts have analyzed unjustified filing of lis pendens under theories of interference with contract, see National City Bank, Indiana v. Shortridge, 689 N.E.2d 1248 (Ind.1997), slander of title, see Montecalvo v. Mandarelli, 682 A.2d 918 (R.I.1996), abuse of process, and wrongful civil litigation, see Cok v. Cok, 558 A.2d 205 (R.I. 1989) (both abuse of process and malicious use of process).

14. Sharif–Munir–Davidson Dev. Corp. v. Bell, 788 S.W.2d 427 (Tex. Ct. App. 1990).

15. Ringier America, Inc. v. Enviro–Technics, Ltd. 284 Ill.App.3d 1102, 673 N.E.2d 444, 220 Ill.Dec. 532 (1996); cf. Manders v. Manders, 897 F.Supp. 972 (S.D.Tex.1995) (lis pendens absolutely privileged in slander of title claim, but perhaps suggesting that privilege would not apply in a wrongful civil litigation claim). The privilege may be limited, however, to cases in which the lis pendens is related to the property in question or the underlying action that supports it. Birdsong v. Bydalek, 953 S.W.2d 103 (Mo.Ct.App.1997). The analogy is to the absolute privilege against liability for defamation in the course of judicial proceedings. The analogy is incomplete, however, because the special grievance cases almost always entail the use of legal process to detain property or person. Although the plaintiff may be defamed thereby, the action is not based upon loss of reputation but upon detention of person or property. Second, many of the special grievance cases turn the original suitor's abuse of his ex parte powers to impose legal effects upon the plaintiff or her property before a trial, as in the case of temporary restraining orders, attachments, lis pendens and the like. Such differences suggest that the blanket immunity seen in libel cases is at least distinguishable and perhaps inappropriate.

16. E.g., White Lighting Co. v. Wolfson, 68 Cal.2d 336, 66 Cal.Rptr. 697, 438 P.2d 345 (1968); see § 438.

17. See New York Lien Law § 39–a (authorizing damages recovery for exaggerated lien).

§ 438

1. See Restatement § 682.

2. See DeVaney v. Thriftway Mktg. Corp., 124 N.M. 512, 953 P.2d 277 (1997), discussed in § 439.

3. Some cases have taken this view so far as to exclude the abuse of process claim

Conversely, if the plaintiff cannot show those elements, she may still have a good abuse of process claim. Specifically, the abuse of process claim permits the plaintiff to recover without showing the traditional want of probable cause for the original suit and without showing termination of that suit. The abuse of process claim may also permit the plaintiff to avoid the requirement of special grievance applied in some wrongful litigation cases.

Elements and example. The elements of the abuse of process claim can be stated in slightly different ways, but, however stated, they are both vague and simple: first, the original suitor must have a primary purpose to use the criminal or civil process for an end for which it was not designed; and second, he must use that process in a way not proper in the regular course of the proceeding,[4] or in other words, bad motive plus some use of the court's process. Some courts add that actual seizure of person or property is also required,[5] but in most cases motive or purpose is the centerpiece of the tort. In one of its common versions, the suitor attempts to use the suit itself or some process issued after suit has commenced as a form of extortion.[6] For example, a suitor may attach all the plaintiff's property so that the plaintiff cannot operate her business; the suitor then explicitly or implicitly offers to drop the attachment if the plaintiff will pay the suitor money she does not owe.[7]

The meaning of process. In its broadest sense, legal process includes the whole legal order and all the steps involved in invoking and applying it. We have in mind a broad sense of legal process when we speak of process values or the integrity of the legal process. Such a broad meaning is not invoked in abuse of process cases; merely filing a complaint in court does not institute any process, although procuring a summons does.[8] In its narrowest sense, process refers to enforceable court orders, although many of these are in fact issued routinely by the clerk of court. These include the summons, subpoenas, attachments, garnishments, replevin or claim and delivery writs, arrest under a

based on attachment that was not wrongful by itself but that was issued in a suit brought without probable cause. Ladd v. Polidoro, 424 Mass. 196, 675 N.E.2d 382 (1997); cf. McGrew v. Heinold Commodities, Inc., 147 Ill.App.3d 104, 497 N.E.2d 424, 100 Ill.Dec. 446 (1986) (garnishment issued on claim of debt brought without probable cause, action must be for wrongful civil litigation).

4. E.g., Simpson v. Laytart, 962 S.W.2d 392 (Ky.1998); Yaklevich v. Kemp, Schaeffer & Rowe Co., 68 Ohio St.3d 294, 626 N.E.2d 115 (1994) (a legal proceeding has been set in motion with probable cause but the proceeding has been perverted to accomplish an ulterior purpose for which it was not designed); Nevada Credit Rating Bureau, Inc. v. Williams, 88 Nev. 601, 503 P.2d 9 (1972).

5. See Parks v. Neuf, 218 Ill.App.3d 427, 578 N.E.2d 282, 161 Ill.Dec. 155 (1991); Lee v. Mitchell, 152 Or.App. 159, 953 P.2d 414 (1998).

6. See, e.g., Fuller v. Local Union No. 106, United Bhd. of Carpenters and Joiners of America, 567 N.W.2d 419, 421 (Iowa 1997).

7. Cf. Grainger v. Hill, 4 Bing. N.C. 212, 132 Eng.Rep. 769 (1838) (the classic case; the original suitor had the plaintiff arrested under civil process available at that time in order to induce the plaintiff to yield control of the vessel by which the plaintiff earned his livelihood).

8. Potter, Prescott, Jamieson & Nelson, P.A. v. Campbell, 708 A.2d 283 (Me.1998); cf. Fuller v. Local Union No. 106, United Bhd. of Carpenters and Joiners of America,

warrant, injunctive orders, and other orders directly affecting obligations of persons or rights in property. Abuse of any of these processes is actionable upon appropriate proof.[9] Between these two extreme versions of process, the term can refer to judicial procedures of various kinds that do not actually entail a court order or a writ.[10] Some courts have in mind the narrowest conception of process and hold that filing a wrongful lis pendens is not a tort because lis pendens is not a process.[11] Other courts, taking process to include all the procedures in the litigation process, include lis pendens as process, so that abuse is actionable.[12] Such a view holds that repeated filings in the wrong venue[13] and even abusive discovery techniques or oppressive litigation tactics can be an abuse of process.[14]

Abuse by coercive process plus offer to abandon it for illegitimate objective. Abuse appears in several forms. In the most commonly mentioned case, the original suitor offers to release or withdraw a justly procured process such as attachment or arrest in exchange for some collateral advantage unrelated to the law suit or which the court itself would be powerless to order.[15] For example, the original suitor may procure an arrest of the plaintiff pursuant to a warrant and then offer to have the prosecution dismissed if the plaintiff will work in the suitor's fertilizer factory. Since the only purpose of a criminal prosecution is punishment of crime, the use of the prosecution as a means of extorting payment of a debt is an abuse for which the action lies, even if the prosecution itself was proper.[16] Even if the offer for an illicit exchange is not explicit, the improper purpose to release the process in exchange for

567 N.W.2d 419 (1997) (falsely reporting that officer misbehaved is not process).

9. E.g., White Lighting Co. v. Wolfson, 68 Cal.2d 336, 66 Cal.Rptr. 697, 438 P.2d 345 (1968) (attachment); Spellens v. Spellens, 49 Cal.2d 210, 317 P.2d 613 (1957) (claim and delivery or replevin); Czap v. Credit Bureau of Santa Clara Valley, 7 Cal. App.3d 1, 86 Cal.Rptr. 417 (1970) (garnishment); Board of Educ. of Farmingdale Union Free Sch. Dist. v. Farmingdale Classroom Teachers Ass'n, Inc., Local 1889, 38 N.Y.2d 397, 403, 343 N.E.2d 278, 283, 380 N.Y.S.2d 635, 642 (1975) (subpoena); Ellis v. Wellons, 224 N.C. 269, 29 S.E.2d 884 (1944) (arrest under warrant); Fordham v. Eason, 131 N.C.App. 226, 505 S.E.2d 895 (N.C.App.1998) (preliminary injunction). But cf. Union Nat'l Bank of Little Rock v. Kutait, 312 Ark. 14, 846 S.W.2d 652 (1993) (bank's offer to drop suit against Kemel if Kemel would persuade Ed to drop a different suit against the bank was not actionable since this did not abuse summons or other specific process).

10. Nienstedt v. Wetzel, 133 Ariz. 348, 352, 651 P.2d 876, 880, 33 A.L.R.4th 635 (1982) (process "encompasses the entire range of procedures incident to the litigation process").

11. Podolsky v. Alma Energy Corp., 143 F.3d 364 (7th Cir.1998); Stahl v. St. Elizabeth Med. Ctr., 948 S.W.2d 419 (Ky.Ct.App. 1997).

12. National City Bank, Indiana v. Shortridge, 689 N.E.2d 1248 (Ind.1997); Cok v. Cok, 558 A.2d 205 (R.I.1989); Broadmoor Apartments of Charleston v. Horwitz, 306 S.C. 482, 413 S.E.2d 9 (1991).

13. Barquis v. Merchants Collection Ass'n of Oakland, Inc., 7 Cal.3d 94, 496 P.2d 817, 101 Cal.Rptr. 745 (1972).

14. A number of courts have said so, see, e.g., Simon v. Navon, 71 F.3d 9 (1st Cir.1995), but usually find that, in the particular case before the court, the discovery abuse is not actionable, partly because those abuses can usually be addressed by the court at the time they occur.

15. See Robb v. Chagrin Lagoons Yacht Club, Inc., 75 Ohio St.3d 264, 271, 662 N.E.2d 9, 14 (1996).

16. Palmer Ford, Inc. v. Wood, 298 Md. 484, 471 A.2d 297 (1984); Ellis v. Wellons, 224 N.C. 269, 29 S.E.2d 884 (1944).

improper benefit may be inferred from what is said or done.[17]

Other forms of abuse of process. In a number of cases, abuse of process can be found even though the original suitor makes no express extortionate demand at all. At least three patterns or explanations can be found for these cases. (1) Excessive attachments[18] and wrongful lis pendens[19] often amount to an abuse of process regardless of any extortionate demand.[20] Many or all of these can be explained on the ground that the suitor's act is, in the circumstances, an implicit proposal to abandon the process in exchange for an obvious quid pro quo. (2) In other cases, the process itself seems to be inherently or definitionally wrongful and that seems to be sufficient, even if the suitor commits no further act. Wrongful lis pendens and excessive attachment cases may fall in this category as well as in the category of implicit threats. The abuse in such cases lies in the "illegitimate use of the attachment process to tie up more property than is reasonably necessary to secure the attaching creditor's claim," and no improper threat or bargaining is required.[21] Even a process server's falsification of an affidavit of service without more has been held to be an abuse of process.[22] (3) In some cases intended detriment to the adversary without any necessary benefit to the suitor may suffice,[23] as where the suitor repeatedly garnishes the plaintiff's wages solely to induce the harassed employer to fire the plaintiff,[24] or the suitor subpoenas all the teachers in a school system to impose financial hardship on the school[25] or sues debtors in the wrong venue in hopes of obtaining more default judgments.[26]

Collateral advantage. When the claim for abuse of process rests upon the suitor's attempt to use the court's process to extort some special advantage, courts usually say that the advantage sought must be collateral, meaning that it is not a benefit to the suitor that the process was designed to secure. However, emphasis on the collateral character of

17. See, e.g., Tranchina v. Arcinas, 78 Cal.App.2d 522, 178 P.2d 65 (1947); Robb v. Chagrin Lagoons Yacht Club, Inc., 75 Ohio St.3d 264, 662 N.E.2d 9 (1996).

18. Nevada Credit Rating Bureau, Inc. v. Williams, 88 Nev. 601, 503 P.2d 9 (1972); see Thomas J. Goger, Annotation, Liability of Creditor for Excessive Attachment or Garnishment, 56 A.L.R.3d 493 (1974).

19. E.g., Cok v. Cok, 558 A.2d 205 (R.I. 1989); see also § 437.

20. E.g., Broadmoor Apartments of Charleston v. Horwitz, 306 S.C. 482, 413 S.E.2d 9 (1991).

21. White Lighting Co. v. Wolfson, 68 Cal.2d 336, 66 Cal.Rptr. 697, 438 P.2d 345 (1968).

22. Parks v. Neuf, 218 Ill.App.3d 427, 578 N.E.2d 282, 161 Ill.Dec. 155 (1991).

23. Board of Educ. of Farmingdale Union Free Sch. Dist. v. Farmingdale Classroom Teachers Ass'n, Inc., Local 1889, 38 N.Y.2d 397, 403, 343 N.E.2d 278, 283, 380 N.Y.S.2d 635, 642 (1975) (defendant must seek collateral advantage or a "corresponding detriment to the plaintiff which is outside the legitimate ends of the process").

24. Peterson v. Worthen Bank & Trust Co., 296 Ark. 201, 753 S.W.2d 278 (1988) (repeated wage garnishments pursued to induce employer to fire the employee).

25. Cf. Board of Educ. of Farmingdale Union Free Sch. Dist. v. Farmingdale Classroom Teachers Ass'n, Inc., Local 1889, 38 N.Y.2d 397, 403, 343 N.E.2d 278, 283, 380 N.Y.S.2d 635, 642 (1975) (subpoena of 87 teachers to appear at the same time, forcing school to hire substitutes, although not all could appear on any one day).

26. Barquis v. Merchants Collection Ass'n of Oakland, Inc., 7 Cal.3d 94, 496 P.2d 817, 101 Cal.Rptr. 745 (1972) (debt collection agency's pattern of filing claims in wrong venue to impose hardship and make default judgment more likely).

the advantage sought can be misleading. First, the advantage need not always be collateral in the sense that it would be outside the court's power to grant. An attempt to gain a nuisance value settlement for a bad medical malpractice suit was regarded as sufficient in *Bull v. McCuskey*,[27] although a money judgment for the same small amount would easily be within the court's jurisdiction. On the other side of the coin, even when the demand is for collateral advantage, it is not necessarily a wrong. A collateral demand may reflect nothing more than an insistence upon a comprehensive settlement of all disputes among the parties. In a California case,[28] a husband had the wife's property seized under claim and delivery or replevin proceedings. He then offered to drop the proceedings if the wife would drop her suit to establish the validity of their marriage. That was held an abuse of process. The husband's offer clearly sought an advantage that was collateral to his claim and delivery suit, and perhaps the detailed facts warranted liability. But the case can hardly reflect a rule of law that makes it tortious to work out a comprehensive settlement of all disputes between the parties.[29]

Characterization of wrongful process cases. As a matter of language, courts could regard excessive attachment and other coercive process cases as a sub-species of malicious prosecution or wrongful civil litigation in which the suit may be brought with probable cause but the particular process invoked is not.[30] The suitor might have probable cause to claim a $10 debt, but no probable cause to think that he needs to attach a million dollars in property to secure such a claim. There are justifications and advantages to treating this kind of tort as an abuse of process, as most courts do in fact.[31] Excessive attachment is inherently coercive and lends itself to extortion, so the abuse element is distinctly present. And by regarding the claim as one for abuse, courts can permit the victim to counterclaim for relief without waiting for a formal termination of the whole suit,[32] a reform much to be desired in the civil side of tortious litigation cases.[33]

27. Bull v. McCuskey, 96 Nev. 706, 615 P.2d 957 (1980), overruled on other grounds, Ace Truck v. Kahn, 103 Nev. 503, 746 P.2d 132 (1987). The facts were convincing. A lawyer brought a medical malpractice suit, apparently without the slightest reason. He consulted no physicians before suit or after. He got to the verge of trial without medical evidence and offered a nuisance value settlement. He was subjected to liability.

28. Spellens v. Spellens, 49 Cal.2d 210, 317 P.2d 613 (1957).

29. In Baglini v. Lauletta, 315 N.J.Super. 225, 717 A.2d 449 (1998), A refused to settle his suit against B unless B would drop an entirely different suit in which A was interested. This was considered a sufficient "further act" or misuse of the process, but apparently only because A's suit was itself brought without probable cause.

30. See Simon v. Navon, 71 F.3d 9, 15 (1st Cir.1995) (malicious prosecution claim challenges "the whole of a lawsuit ... while abuse of process covers the allegedly improper use of individual legal procedures after a suit has been filed properly").

31. See Thomas J. Goger, Liability of Creditor for Excessive Attachment or Garnishment, 56 A.L.R.3d 493 (1974).

32. E.g., Yaklevich v. Kemp, Schaeffer & Rowe Co., 68 Ohio St.3d 294, 626 N.E.2d 115 (1994) (counterclaim for abuse of process is permissive, not compulsory).

33. See DeVaney v. Thriftway Mktg. Corp., 124 N.M. 512, 953 P.2d 277 (1997) (creating a unitary tort for tortious civil litigation and dropping the termination requirement). See § 439.

Act after process has issued. A number of courts have said that abuse of process is shown by showing the original suitor's ulterior purpose and his willful use of the process in a way not proper in the regular conduct of the proceeding or words to that effect.[34] As such formulations imply, the very issuance of the process may be abusive in some cases without additional acts.[35] But courts have repeatedly quoted or paraphrased[36] Prosser's comment[37] that the defendant is not liable if he has done nothing more than to carry a process to its authorized conclusion, even if he acted with bad intentions. That observation is similar to the added requirement adopted in some courts that the suitor must commit some further act after the process has issued.[38] In either form, the point applies only to one kind of abuse of process.

Melton v. Rickman[39] is an example of the added "act after" requirement. The plaintiff there alleged that a moneylender loaned the plaintiff $25 for two weeks (at an interest at the rate of 65%). The lender, knowing that the plaintiff had no bank account, nevertheless took a check as "evidence" of the debt, but in fact solely to permit him to use the criminal processes to collect the debt. Although the plaintiff had fully paid all but the usurious interest charges, the moneylender then instigated a warrant for the plaintiff's arrest on a bad check charge. The Justice of the Peace found the plaintiff guilty but withheld judgment for a week to permit payment, which the plaintiff then made. The arrest warrant was clearly "process," but according to the court, the moneylender had done nothing after the warrant was issued to abuse that process. Only if the moneylender had offered to obtain the plaintiff's release in exchange for payment would there have been abuse after process was issued.

The added requirement of post-process wrongdoing does not make much sense in *Melton v. Rickman*, but it can make sense in a few cases. First, a mere threat to sue or to attach property involves no process at all and is not an abuse of process. Second, where the gist of the tort is the use of coercive process coupled with an illegitimate bargain for collateral advantage, the defendant must somehow communicate the offer to abandon the process in exchange for his illegitimate objective. *Melton v. Rickman* carried the post-process requirement much further than either of these sensible goals suggests. The inference is almost inescapable in *Melton* that the moneylender was implicitly offering to drop the prosecution if the debt was paid and that the offer stood open

34. E.g., Yaklevich v. Kemp, Schaeffer & Rowe Co., 68 Ohio St.3d 294, 626 N.E.2d 115 (1994) (a legal proceeding has been set in motion with probable cause but the proceeding has been perverted to accomplish an ulterior purpose for which it was not designed); Nevada Credit Rating Bureau, Inc. v. Williams, 88 Nev. 601, 503 P.2d 9 (1972).

35. Mills County State Bank v. Roure, 291 N.W.2d 1, 5 (Iowa 1980) (refusing to protect the tortfeasor "where the issuance of the process alone is sufficient to accomplish the collateral purpose").

36. E.g., Cabletron Sys., Inc. v. Miller, 140 N.H. 55, 662 A.2d 304 (1995).

37. Prosser & Keeton, § 121, p. 898.

38. See Baglini v. Lauletta, 315 N.J.Super. 225, 230, 717 A.2d 449, 452 (1998).

39. Melton v. Rickman, 225 N.C. 700, 36 S.E.2d 276 (1945).

after the arrest was effected. For another, the process—arrest under a warrant—was itself wrongful on the facts as a means of collecting a private debt. As shown by those cases allowing a recovery for excessive attachment or wrongful lis pendens, the requirement of a post-process act has no place when the process is itself wrongful.

§ 439. Reforms and New Directions

One source of difficulties in abusive litigation cases is that there is no comprehensive or integrated set of responses to abuse. Concerns over abusive litigation have already led to recent changes both in the tort rules and in some procedures that may affect abuse, but so far no jurisdiction has adopted a systematic plan to utilize all approaches.

Fast-tracking abusive suits and procedures. Many abuse of process cases reflect the fact that in our legal system, individuals not only have the power to invoke legal processes but to do so without supervision by responsible judges or notice to the opposing party. In 1991, the Supreme Court held that a statute permitting ex parte attachment before judgment was unconstitutional for want of notice to and opportunity to be heard by the owner.[1] Notice to the owner is the first step in early termination of an abusive suit. A much more aggressive solution calls for early dismissal in certain cases and some states have so provided in the case of the so-called SLAPP suits. These are suits for defamation or the like brought against individuals whose discussion of public issues allegedly defames the plaintiff. As already indicated in discussing defamation privileges,[2] some states put these suits on a fast track, terminating discovery early and making dismissal especially easy. Some of the statutes are themselves subject to abuse, but, right or wrong, they point to the possibility that abusive litigation can be dealt with at the point of abuse, not later in a tort suit.

Sanctions at the point of abuse. A closely related means of dealing with abusive litigation tactics is to permit sanctions for abuse during the trial itself. Sanctions can include attorney fee awards to the victim for the costs of dealing with abusive process such as excessive attachment or even harassing delay, for example.[3] To the extent that sanctions are imposed, separate suits for abusive litigation may be unnecessary and courts might even bar such suits where sanctions have proved adequate.[4]

Permitting counterclaims for wrongful civil litigation. If dealing with abuse when it occurs rather than later is a good idea when it comes to sanctions or dismissal, it is also a good idea to permit counterclaims in

§ 439

1. Connecticut v. Doehr, 501 U.S. 1, 111 S.Ct. 2105, 115 L.Ed.2d 1 (1991).

2. See § 412.

3. Linscott v. Foy, 716 A.2d 1017 (Me. 1998) (court ordered sanctions against recalcitrant litigant who refused to obey court's orders and this properly included attorney fees for his adversary).

4. Bidna v. Rosen, 19 Cal.App.4th 27, 23 Cal.Rptr.2d 251 (1993), barred wrongful litigation suits in family court matters in favor of a complete sanctions approach. Without going this far, sanctions and fee awards might be seen as an option for the victim rather than an exclusive remedy.

civil cases for wrongful litigation. Under the present rule, a counterclaim can be asserted for abuse of process but not for wrongful litigation. That prohibition in turn results from the requirement that the unjustified original action must have terminated favorably to the now plaintiff. The favorable termination rule makes good sense when the plaintiff complains of a unjustified criminal prosecution, but it serves no useful purpose when the plaintiff complains of a former civil suit. On the contrary, the original suit is by far the best place to resolve the issues, although bifurcation of trial might be required when a particular counterclaim raises serious dangers of prejudice.

In 1997, the Supreme Court of New Mexico eliminated the termination requirement and permitted counterclaims for wrongful civil litigation.[5] It restructured the wrongful litigation and abuse of process torts as a single tort requiring an overt wrongful act and improper motive. The wrongful act might be, as in traditional wrongful litigation claims, a suit brought without probable cause; or it might be "procedural abuse" of the kind associated with traditional abuse of process claim. Under the tort as restructured, termination is not required, so a defendant aggrieved by either an unjustified suit or unjustified procedures, can assert a counterclaim. Alternatives to the counterclaim are possible. For instance, courts could award attorney fees for wrongful litigation on motion, as part of an award of costs or otherwise and could provide that if such fees are claimed and awarded, no separate tort action could be brought for the wrongful litigation or abuse of process.

Malicious or abusive defenses. Courts traditionally recognized tort claims for abusive criminal prosecutions, civil suits, and misuse of judicial process, but they did not recognize a claim for wrongful or abusive defenses and seldom for harassing tactics within such actions. In 1995, following the proposal of an earlier article,[6] New Hampshire recognized a claim for malicious defense knowingly asserted without probable cause and asserted primarily for a purpose other than to secure the proper adjudication of the claim, provided the suit so defended has terminated in favor of the now plaintiff and that it caused damages.[7]

§ 440. Damages

Damages awardable for malicious prosecution, wrongful civil litigation and abuse of process are dependent upon the facts and upon proof of losses, but when evidence shows the harm claimed, the principles of damages are essentially the same with all three torts:[1] the plaintiff is

5. DeVaney v. Thriftway Mktg. Corp., 124 N.M. 512, 953 P.2d 277 (1997).

6. Jonathan K. Van Patten & Robert E. Willard, The Limits of Advocacy: A Proposal for the Tort of Malicious Defense in Civil Litigation, 35 HAST. L. REV. 891 (1984).

7. Aranson v. Schroeder, 140 N.H. 359, 671 A.2d 1023 (1995).

§ 440

1. Bull v. McCuskey, 96 Nev. 706, 615 P.2d 957 (1980), overruled on other grounds, Ace Truck v. Kahn, 103 Nev. 503, 746 P.2d 132 (1987).

entitled to recover for all harms adequately proven and proximately caused.

Compensatory damages. Compensatory damages for tangible losses or harm normally include reasonable attorney fees and other expenses incurred in defending the wrongful criminal or civil litigation[2] or avoiding or quashing abusive process,[3] other consequent losses such as lost earnings,[4] damages for dispossession of or cloud on the title of property[5] and for physical illness or pain resulting from the tort,[6] subject to the usual limitations that they must result proximately from the wrong and that damages will not be awarded for speculative or conjectural items of loss.[7] Intangible damages recoverable include damages for harm to reputation[8] and damages for emotional harm[9] both in wrongful litigation and abuse of process cases. In jurisdictions that require special injury or grievance as a prerequisite to a suit for wrongful litigation, the full range of damages is recoverable once special grievance is shown to exist.[10]

Attribution of damages to the abusive litigation. Although the plaintiff is entitled to recover for all harms proximately resulting from actionable forms of abusive litigation, recovery is limited to those harms fairly attributable to the defendant's wrongful acts. Recovery does not include items like counsel fees that result from legitimate claims asserted or processes invoked by the defendant, nor from the plaintiff's own counterclaims in the original suit.[11] Damages recoverable for malicious prosecution include damages for detention that results,[12] but if the plaintiff was first subjected to a false arrest, damages for the arrest itself terminate when a legitimate prosecution has begun and the plaintiff is detained by rightful process rather than under the unwarranted arrest.[13]

2. Ziobron v. Crawford, 667 N.E.2d 202 (Ind.Ct.App.1996) (allowing fees to pro se attorney).

3. Hewes v. Wolfe, 74 N.C.App. 610, 330 S.E.2d 16 (1985); Davis v. Rudolph, 243 Iowa 744, 52 N.W.2d 15 (1952) (in suit on attachment bond).

4. Thrift v. Hubbard, 974 S.W.2d 70 (Tex.Ct.App. 1998) (almost $10,000 in lost earnings during court appearances).

5. Kleinschmidt v. Morrow, 642 A.2d 161 (Me.1994) (lost rental value resulting because of excessive lien claim); Ruiz v. Varan, 110 N.M. 478, 797 P.2d 267 (1990) ("nominal" damages of $5,000 when wrongful lis pendens clouded title but did not result in any loss of use).

6. Avildsen v. Prystay, 204 A.D.2d 154, 611 N.Y.S.2d 188 (1994).

7. E.g., MTW Inv. Co. v. Alcovy Properties, Inc., 228 Ga.App. 206, 491 S.E.2d 460 (1997) (land tied up by lis pendens, but owner's claims that he would have subdivided land and made profit was too speculative).

8. Papa v. City of New York, 194 A.D.2d 527, 598 N.Y.S.2d 558 (1993); Junior Food Stores, Inc. v. Rice, 671 So.2d 67 (Miss. 1996); MTW Investment Co. v. Alcovy Properties, Inc., 228 Ga.App. 206, 491 S.E.2d 460 (1997).

9. E.g., Kmart Corp. v. Kyles, 723 So.2d 572 (Ala.1998); Ford Motor Credit Co. v. Hickey Ford Sales, Inc., 62 N.Y.2d 291, 465 N.E.2d 330, 476 N.Y.S.2d 791 (1984) (wrongful attachment); Avildsen v. Prystay, 204 A.D.2d 154, 611 N.Y.S.2d 188 (1994) ($225,000).

10. See Texas Beef Cattle Co. v. Green, 921 S.W.2d 203, 209 (Tex.1996).

11. Bertero v. National Gen. Corp., 13 Cal.3d 43, 118 Cal.Rptr. 184, 529 P.2d 608, 65 A.L.R.3d 878 (1975) (victim was forced to defend wrongful litigation but also asserted a counterclaim raising same issues; attorney fee expense must be allocated between fees for defense and fees for counterclaim).

12. See Erp v. Carroll, 438 So.2d 31(Fla.Dist.Ct.App.1983).

13. Asgari v. City of Los Angeles, 15 Cal.4th 744, 937 P.2d 273, 63 Cal.Rptr.2d 842 (1997) (officer liable for false arrest but

Punitive damages. Since malicious prosecution, wrongful civil litigation, and abuse of process all entail abuse of the legal system itself and a supposed intent to harm or "malice," punitive damages can often be awarded against the tortfeasor,[14] subject to all the rules governing such awards in the particular jurisdiction.[15] For purposes of establishing liability, courts in malicious prosecution cases have often permitted juries to infer the defendant's malice from his lack of probable cause.[16] Even if that rule is sound, however, it does not necessarily apply to permit punitive damages. Because the law of abusive litigation is foremost concerned with providing redress for wrong without discouraging proper use of the legal system, courts can properly require something more than the malice supposedly inferred from a want of probable cause.[17]

immune by statute from liability for malicious prosecution); Broughton v. State, 37 N.Y.2d 451, 335 N.E.2d 310, 373 N.Y.S.2d 87 (1975) (damages for false imprisonment terminate with arraignment or indictment); cf. Smiddy v. Varney, 665 F.2d 261 (9th Cir.1981) (arresting officer liable under § 1983 only for damage accrued from false arrest to time of prosecution unless officer deprived prosecutor of independent judgment).

14. E.g., Harold McLaughlin Reliable Truck Brokers, Inc. v. Cox, 324 Ark. 361, 922 S.W.2d 327 (1996); Alamo Renta-A-Car, Inc. v. Mancusi, 632 So.2d 1352 (Fla. 1994). Contra as to abuse of process, Snellings v. Sheppard, 229 Ga.App. 753, 494 S.E.2d 583 (1997).

15. See § 382 & 383.

16. See § 433.

17. Cf. Montgomery Ward v. Wilson, 339 Md. 701, 664 A.2d 916 (1995) (because Maryland requires clear and convincing evidence of actual malice to justify a punitive award, malice inferred from want of probable cause is not sufficient).

*

CHAPTER 31

INTERFERENCE WITH FAMILY RELATIONSHIPS

§ 441. Tort Law and the Family

Families and family relationships have been important in tort law in a number of ways. Family immunities have been dissolved or relaxed in most states,[1] leading to suits between family members and new questions about the way tort claims must be tailored to fit with divorce.[2] The family is much involved in issues of vicarious liability[3] and statutes of limitations, which might treat long-term spousal abuse differently from a single battery.[4] Fetal injury through toxins[5] and claims for wrongful birth and wrongful pregnancy also raise significant issues affecting the family.[6] In addition, physical injury to any member of the family unit may implicate the emotional or financial interests of other family members, and thus lead to claims for loss of society or consortium discussed in connection with emotional harm claims.[7]

The present chapter focuses upon none of these matters. Its concern is instead the potential liability of those who interfere with family relationships where physical harm is no part of the claim. "Relational injury" or injury to the family relationship itself with the concomitant emotional harm and loss of well-being is the essential concern here. The most notable historical example is the claim by a spouse that the defendant has alienated the affections of the other spouse, but contemporary custody battles and the seduction of children by religious groups has raised issues about "interference" and alienation in new contexts.

§ 442. Husband and Wife: Alienation of Affections and Criminal Conversation

At one time the common law treated a husband and father as the master of his wife and children. If the defendant injured a servant or enticed him away from service, the master would have a cause of action for the loss.[1] Similar rules applied if the master's wife was injured or enticed away.[2] By the latter part of the 19th century courts developed two or three semi-distinct torts from this beginning. Together they

§ 441

1. See Chapter 16.
2. § 281.
3. See § 340.
4. See § 220.
5. § 289.
6. §§ 291–293.
7. § 310.

§ 442

1. See § 447.
2. See 3 Bl. Com. 139–139.

protected the husband's interest in his wife's services, society, affection, and honor against interference by others. Later, courts became more even-handed and provided wives with the same rights. These interference torts are now abolished in most states,[3] but lawyers sometimes attempt to resurrect them under another label.

Criminal conversation. Criminal conversation merely meant adultery or sexual relations. The defendant who engaged in adultery with the plaintiff's spouse would be liable to the plaintiff. The authorities state the elements of the tort with almost alarming simplicity: the tort is said to consist of having sexual relations with one spouse.[4] "The fact that the wife consented, that she was the aggressor, that she represented herself as single, that she was mistreated or neglected by her husband, that she and her husband were separated through no fault of her own, or that her husband was impotent, were not valid defenses."[5] The only defense was the nonparticipating spouse's own consent.[6] In other words, the defendant was liable to the husband although he had committed no tort to the wife and was guilty of no fraud, force, or deception.

Alienation of affections. If the defendant deprived one spouse of the other's affections but did not engage in sexual relations, that, too, became a tort by the latter half of 19th century.[7] The defendant here must ordinarily have known of the marital relationship and acted for the purpose of affecting it adversely,[8] but neither sexual nor romantic involvement was required. Indeed, the defendant could be held liable though he was only a minister or a family member who, without a privilege,[9] urged one spouse to leave the other.[10] The defendant was not subject to liability unless his conduct was a substantial factor, along with other causes, for the alienation[11] and of course there was no alienation if no affection remained in the marriage at the time of the defendant's conduct.[12] However, causation and wrongful intent were both elements that might be proved by circumstances.[13] As with criminal conversation,

3. See *Abolishing the Torts* below.

4. See Brown v. Hurley, 124 N.C.App. 377, 477 S.E.2d 234 (1996) (actual existing marriage plus sexual intercourse); Russo v. Sutton, 310 S.C. 200, 422 S.E.2d 750 (1992) (same); Restatement § 685.

5. Kline v. Ansell, 287 Md. 585, 587, 414 A.2d 929, 930 (1980).

6. Restatement § 687.

7. See, e.g., Foot v. Card, 58 Conn. 1, 18 A. 1027 (1889) (also recognizing that the right to sue for alienation extended to the wife).

8. Restatement § 683.

9. Under Restatement § 686, a parent or near relative had a privilege to give advice in good faith and reasonably to advance the interest of the alienated spouse, but not for the purpose of "appropriating the affections" of that spouse. But cf. Poulos v. Poulos, 351 Mass. 603, 222 N.E.2d 887 (1967). (mother who aggressively tries to persuade her son to leave his wife and tells him nine times that the marriage is a disgrace may be liable for abusing her privilege by going further than is "reasonable").

10. Boland v. Stanley, 88 Ark. 562, 115 S.W. 163 (1909) (parents of alienated spouse); Carrieri v. Bush, 69 Wash.2d 536, 419 P.2d 132 (1966) (minister who taught that God had come to separate husband from wife).

11. Norton v. Macfarlane, 818 P.2d 8 (Utah 1991) (controlling or primary cause as opposed to incidental cause).

12. See Pickering v. Pickering, 434 N.W.2d 758, 763 (S.D.1989).

13. See Kirk v. Koch, 607 So.2d 1220 (Miss.1992).

the defendant would be liable without a tort to the person whose affections were alienated and without any kind of falsehood.

Enticement. A defendant who abducted the plaintiff's spouse might be liable to the abducted spouse for false imprisonment, and the other spouse might plausibly claim loss of consortium as in the case of other physical harms. Historically, courts took a shortcut across such reasoning by holding simply that one who abducted a spouse would be liable to the other spouse, and by extension of this, that one who enticed one spouse to separate from the other would also be liable. In line with this history the Restatement recognized enticement as a separate tort.[14] It is apparent, however, that enticement is merely one form of, or at most an extension of, alienation of affections and like alienation, turns on an intent to disrupt the marriage.[15]

Abolishing the torts. Criminal conversation[16] and alienation of affections[17] have now been abolished in the great majority of states, either by explicit legislation or by judicial decision. Only four or five states have continued to give full scope to the alienation action and some of those have abolished the criminal conversation claim.[18] Three other states seem not to have passed on the issue. The reasons to abolish the torts are numerous and they run deep.[19]s

Courts and legislatures have been moved in part by the conclusion that these torts lent themselves to blackmail and to vindictiveness pursued by a spouse whose marriage is over and who seeks merely to inflict harm. With the advent of no fault divorce everywhere and the decriminalization of adultery in many states, these torts also came to seem illogical and inimical to the reforms enacted in divorce and criminal laws.[20] Beyond this, the torts have become offensive because they have, sometimes quite explicitly, treated a spouse as the property of the other spouse and because they are thoroughly inimical to the freedom of

14. Restatement § 684.

15. Restatement § 684(2) and cmt. f.

16. By statute in most states, e.g., Ore. Rev. Stats. § 30.850; Va. Code § 8.01–220. Among decisions abolishing criminal conversation see Bearbower v. Merry, 266 N.W.2d 128 (Iowa 1978); Thomas v. Siddiqui, 869 S.W.2d 740 (Mo.1994); Feldman v. Feldman, 125 N.H. 102, 480 A.2d 34 (1984).

17. Statutes abolishing the tort have been enacted in most states. E.g., N.Y. Civ. Rts. L. § 80–a; Tex. Fam. Code § 1.107. Among judicial decisions abolishing the tort, see O'Neil v. Schuckardt, 112 Idaho 472, 733 P.2d 693, 67 A.L.R.4th 1065 (1986); Hoye v. Hoye, 824 S.W.2d 422 (Ky. 1992); Russo v. Sutton, 310 S.C. 200, 422 S.E.2d 750 (1992).

18. Kirk v. Koch, 607 So.2d 1220 (Miss. 1992); Hellmann v. Walsh, 965 S.W.2d 198 (Mo.App.1998); Brown v. Hurley, 124 N.C.App. 377, 477 S.E.2d 234 (1996); Norton v. Macfarlane, 818 P.2d 8 (Utah 1991). South Dakota has retained the action but rejects an action for emotional distress based on the same facts. Pickering v. Pickering, 434 N.W.2d 758 (S.D.1989). A limited recovery is theoretically possible in Illinois, but suits are discouraged as a practical matter by statutes limiting recovery to "actual damages," 740 ILCS § 5/2, and forbidding recovery of the normal damage elements such as injury to the plaintiff's feelings, shame, or the like. 740 ILCS § 5/4.

19. See Kay Kavanagh, Note, Alienation of Affections and Criminal Conversation: Unholy Marriage in Need of Annulment, 23 Ariz. L. Rev. 323 (1981).

20. On the relation of these and other tort claims to divorce, see Ira Mark Ellman & Stephen D. Sugarman, Spousal Emotional Abuse as a Tort?, 55 Md. L. Rev. 1268 (1996).

every human being to choose their associations and to depart dangerous, stultifying, or deeply unhappy homes if they choose. These torts could also operate unjustly by punishing the defendant for conduct to which both participants consent. Finally, some of the cases turned on nothing more than words that were by no means false and thus punished speech. The grounds for abolishing the torts are thus ample but the question now arises whether their abolition also prevents recovery on other theories.

Alternative theories after abolition. After the abolition of the interference torts, lawyers began to assert claims on the same facts but under other theories. For instance, a spouse might assert that the defendant's adultery with the other spouse was an intentional or negligent infliction of distress or an interference with contract. Courts have rejected both the emotional harm[21] and interference with contract claims[22] as mere disguises for the alienation and criminal conversation claims. Negligent interference was never enough to show alienation of affections and is of course not enough once the tort has been abolished.[23] Even if the claim adds aggravating facts not necessary to the alienation or criminal conversation theory, it has still been denied when the underlying facts are in the patterns of those torts.[24]

When a therapist or counselor has sexual relations with the spouse who is his patient, the patient herself may well have a claim for malpractice.[25] But the spouse who is not a patient has no malpractice claim of her own for the very reason that professional duties are ordinarily owed only to patients or clients.[26] With the claim for criminal conversation abolished, that leaves the non-patient spouse with no claim at all. The same analysis is made when a clergyman has an affair with a parishioner to the dismay of the parishioner's spouse.[27] However, the story is different if the therapist owes an independent duty to both spouses or to the complaining spouse. For instance, when a counselor or minister gives marriage counseling to both of the marital partners as his patients his duty is independent of the duty a stranger would have owed under the old criminal conversation or alienation torts. Having under-

21. R.E.R. v. J.G., 552 N.W.2d 27 (Minn.Ct.App.1996); Lotring v. Philbrook, 701 A.2d 1034 (R.I.1997).

22. E.g., Speer v. Dealy, 242 Neb. 542, 495 N.W.2d 911 (1993).

23. Helena Labs. Corp. v. Snyder, 886 S.W.2d 767 (Tex.1994). Distinguish negligence arising in a violation of a duty owed to the whole family unit or to the aggrieved spouse, as where a physician to both husband and wife negligently reports that the wife has syphilis, resulting in disruption of the marriage. See Molien v. Kaiser Found. Hosps., 27 Cal.3d 916, 167 Cal.Rptr. 831, 616 P.2d 813, 16 A.L.R.4th 518 (1980), as modified in Burgess v. Superior Court, 2 Cal.4th 1064, 831 P.2d 1197, 9 Cal.Rptr.2d 615 (1992).

24. Koestler v. Pollard, 162 Wis.2d 797, 471 N.W.2d 7 (1991) (emotional distress claim alleging that defendant's sexual intercourse with the plaintiff's wife resulted in conception and birth of a child, which, after a period of the defendant's concealment, the plaintiff discovered; the added facts were not sufficient to make the claim anything but a criminal conversation claim).

25. See §§ 102 & 307.

26. Smith v. Pust, 19 Cal.App.4th 263, 23 Cal.Rptr.2d 364 (1993).

27. Cherepski v. Walker, 323 Ark. 43, 913 S.W.2d 761 (1996). See § 258 on clergy malpractice, including claims based on sexual relations in therapy.

taken to professionally treat the marital problems of both spouses, he may be liable for professional negligence if sexual relations or romantic affairs with one of them violates the duty owed to both.[28]

§ 443 Interference with Parental Custody and Other Rights in Children

Early common law recognized a right in the father of a child to have the child's services and hence a right to recover for loss of those services when the defendant abducted or injured the child. This approach is largely obsolete, first because rights in the parent-child relationship are no longer those of the father alone but belong to the mother as well, and second because loss of services is no longer the essence of the loss.[1] In most cases a full range of damages for the loss of society and affection and other values in the relationship is now permitted. So far as the parent-child relationship is damaged by negligent physical injury to the child, only a few courts have accepted the parent's claim for loss of the child's society and affection.[2] This section addresses the remaining issues—interference with relationships in the family by abduction, alienation of affections of a child or parent and the like.

Enticing, abducting or harboring; interference with custody rights. When the minor child is enticed, or abducted, or "harbored," the parents having custody of the child are entitled by common law or statute to recover.[3] The claim is not for alienation of affections, but for deprivation of physical custody.[4] On the other hand, damages are no longer limited to an award for loss of the child's services, but may include awards for the parents' distress, their loss of the child's society, and the expenses incurred in recovering custody as well as punitive damages in an appropriate case.[5] The action can be characterized as an intentional and unjustified interference with the parental right of custody of a minor.[6] As this implies, the defendant must have notice of the plaintiff's custodial rights. The consent of the child is of course no defense to the parents' action[7] but the defendant is not liable unless he takes some affirmative

28. Richard H. v. Larry D., 198 Cal. App.3d 591, 243 Cal.Rptr. 807 (1988), overruled on other grounds, John R. v. Oakland Unified Sch. Dist., 48 Cal.3d 438, 769 P.2d 948, , 256 Cal.Rptr. 766 (1989); Figueiredo-Torres v. Nickel, 321 Md. 642, 584 A.2d 69 (1991); Rowe v. Bennett, 514 A.2d 802 (Me. 1986). See also § 307. The point seems not to have been addressed in some of the cases. See Strock v. Pressnell, 38 Ohio St.3d 207, 527 N.E.2d 1235, 75 A.L.R.4th 729 (1988). As to supposed constitutional limitations on clergy liability see § 258.

§ 442

1. Pickle v. Page, 252 N.Y. 474, 169 N.E. 650, 72 A.L.R. 842 (1930).

2. See § 310.

3. Magnuson v. O'Dea, 75 Wash. 574, 135 P. 640 (1913); Restatement § 700.

4. See Murphy v. I.S.K. Con. of New England, Inc., 409 Mass. 842, 860, 571 N.E.2d 340, 351 (1991).

5. Murphy v. I.S.K. Con. of New England, Inc., 409 Mass. 842, 571 N.E.2d 340 (1991); Howell v. Howell, 162 N.C. 283, 78 S.E. 222 (1913); Kessel v. Leavitt, 204 W.Va. 95, 511 S.E.2d 720 (W.Va. 1998).

6. See Anonymous v. Anonymous, 672 So.2d 787 (Ala.1995).

7. Surina v. Lucey, 168 Cal.App.3d 539, 214 Cal.Rptr. 509 (1985).

steps to take or restrain the child or seeks to induce the child to leave or remain away from home.[8]

The claim by its terms covers out-and-out abduction with criminal intent to harm or ransom, as well as cases of sexual enticement,[9] but most of the contemporary cases are more complex. When an outsider provides a haven for the child in the reasonable suspicion that the child is abused at home,[10] or merely exercises his religious freedom in speaking to the minor,[11] he may be guilty of no wrongdoing at all or may be protected by a privilege or a constitutional right.

Suits between parents and abetters. One important group of cases arises when a parent or other family member kidnaps a child following a divorce and a lost custody battle. This last group has spurred conflict. Most courts dealing with the issue have recognized the action brought by the custodial parent against the non-custodial parent or family members who aid and abet the kidnaping.[12] A Minnesota case is the principal authority rejecting the action against a parental kidnaper.[13] The Minnesota Court did so on the theory that it would not be best for the child to undergo such litigation. Supporters of this view have suggested that statutes enhancing power over the kidnaper who flees the jurisdiction,[14] coupled with other litigation against the kidnaper, may ameliorate the problem. But the other litigation approved by this view includes criminal felony prosecutions, contempt of court, and tort claims for infliction of emotional distress[15] which are not obviously any less harmful to the child

8. Robbins v. Hamburger Home for Girls, 32 Cal.App.4th 671, 38 Cal.Rptr.2d 534 (1995) (no liability for providing shelter when defendant neither induced child to leave home nor induced her to remain).

9. Surina v. Lucey, 168 Cal.App.3d 539, 214 Cal.Rptr. 509 (1985) (allegations that uncle took minor child and engaged in sexual relations with her).

10. Robbins v. Hamburger Home for Girls, 32 Cal.App.4th 671, 38 Cal.Rptr.2d 534 (1995); Restatement § 700, cmt e.

11. Cf. Murphy v. I.S.K. Con. of New England, Inc., 409 Mass. 842, 571 N.E.2d 340 (1991) (emotionally disturbing religious arguments not actionable as intentional infliction of distress).

12. Stone v. Wall, 734 So.2d 1038 (Fla. 1999); Wood v. Wood, 338 N.W.2d 123 (Iowa 1983); Weirich v. Weirich, 833 S.W.2d 942 (Tex.1992); William B. Johnson, Annotation, Liability of Legal or Natural Parent, or One Who Aids and Abets, for Damages Resulting from Abduction of Own Child, 49 A.L.R.4th 7 (1987); see Kessel v. Leavitt, 204 W.Va. 95, 511 S.E.2d 720 (W.Va. 1998) (recognizing claim where plaintiff has sole custody right and applying it to mother's adoption placement of child out of the country).

13. Larson v. Dunn, 460 N.W.2d 39 (Minn.1990); two other cases reach a similar result. Mantooth v. Richards, 557 So.2d 646 (Fla.Dist.Ct.App.1990) (without discussion); Friedman v. Friedman, 79 Misc.2d 646, 361 N.Y.S.2d 108 (1974). Politte v. Politte, 727 S.W.2d 198 (Mo.App.1987), expressed doubts about the action but apparently went off on the fact that the plaintiff had no custodial rights. Zaharias v. Gammill, 844 P.2d 137 (Okla.1992), was not a suit against a former spouse but the court expressed approval of the *Larson* approach, at the same time saying that the tort of abduction was recognized in Oklahoma and that an intentional infliction of emotional distress claim would be allowable. *Mantooth,* supra, was effectively set aside by the decision in Stone v. Wall, 734 So.2d 1038 (Fla. 1999), which allowed a common law action.

14. Parental Kidnapping Prevention Act (PKPA), 28 U.S.C.A. § 1738A; Unif. Child Custody Jurisdiction & Enforcement Act. Support of an international convention is reflected in 42 U.S.C.A. § 11601. Expenses and attorney fees can be recovered under § 312 of the Uniform Act where that act applies.

15. See Larson v. Dunn, 460 N.W.2d at 46, 47 (emotional distress claim might be entertained); Joseph R. Hillebrand, Parental Kidnapping and the Tort of Custodial

than the interference claim based upon the same loss of custody. To some extent this conflict may represent a conflict of two legal cultures, one associated with tort practice and emphasizing rights and responsibilities, the other associated with family law practice and emphasizing a kind of social work role for judges and court staff.

Custody required; joint custody. The right protected in these cases is the right to custody of the child. If the plaintiff does not have custody rights, she has no claim.[16] The Restatement, in a passage accepted by a number of courts, takes the position that when parents have joint custody of a child, neither may recover from the other for denying access to the child.[17] Although the rule makes sense if it only means that joint custody does not give either parent an absolute right to sole custody of the child for a percentage of the time, but if joint custody means anything, it must mean that one parent cannot be the sole custodian. When a father carries children abroad and hides them, it seems absurd to say that he is respecting the mother's right of joint custody. The Restatement rule might protect others besides the joint-custody parent. A third person who assists the joint-custody father in permanently hiding the children from the mother can not logically be aiding and abetting a tort if it would be no tort for the father to do the same things by himself. Some authority is in line with this analysis,[18] although some other courts have supported claims against those who aid a joint-custody parent in abducting the child.[19]

Visitation rights. Where the one parent interferes with the other's rights of visitation rather than rights of custody, some courts have refused to permit a tort recovery,[20] at least for what they considered to be minor infringements of visitation rights remediable by injunction or contempt proceedings.[21] When the custodial parent totally removes the child from the jurisdiction and hides him, the other parent's right of visitation is completely destroyed and the action has been approved[22] in some cases, but not in others.[23] The difficulty of justly monitoring the seething relations between former spouses and their various allies warrants a refusal to entertain actions for the kind of minor guerrilla warfare that regularly occurs, but when the defendant's action is a substantial and long-term interference, courts should not lightly put aside their own fundamental purposes to do justice nor too readily

Interference: Not in a Child's Best Interests, 25 Ind. L. Rev. 893, 915 (1991) (proposing tougher enforcement of criminal laws against kidnaping).

16. Stevens v. Redwing, 146 F.3d 538 (8th Cir.1998).

17. Restatement § 700, cmt. c.

18. Marshak v. Marshak, 226 Conn. 652, 628 A.2d 964 (1993).

19. Rosefield v. Rosefield, 221 Cal. App.2d 431, 34 Cal.Rptr. 479 (1963); cf. Kessel v. Leavitt, 204 W.Va. 95, 511 S.E.2d 720 (W.Va. 1998) (unwed father have no custody rights but prevailed against child's grandparents who helped place the child for adoption outside the country as soon as he was born).

20. Politte v. Politte, 727 S.W.2d 198 (Mo.App.1987).

21. Hixon v. Buchberger, 306 Md. 72, 507 A.2d 607 (1986).

22. Brown v. Denny, 72 Ohio App.3d 417, 594 N.E.2d 1008 (1991) (under statute); Hershey v. Hershey, 467 N.W.2d 484 (S.D.1991).

23. Cosner v. Ridinger, 882 P.2d 1243 (Wyo.1994).

assume that a tort action will be against the child's long term best interest.

Seduction of a minor child. When a minor female child was seduced, old common law recognized a claim by the father both for medical expenses and or loss of his daughter's services resulting from the seduction.[24] The seduction claim belonged to the father, not the child.[25] The loss of services here became the fictional basis of the action which in reality was a reflection of judicial outrage coupled with the belief that the father had legal rights in his female children. Social change brought more independence to women and procedural reforms required suit to be brought by the real party in interest. After these changes and sometimes as a result of explicit statutes, courts began to permit the seduced woman to bring her own suit.[26] The effect was to convert the relational injury claim into a kind of battery claim, or perhaps one for fraud,[27] but either way to be pursued by the immediate victim. In a battery claim, the plaintiff's valid consent would bar the claim, but not if the consent had been procured by fraud.[28] So far as the relational injury claim remains distinct from the victim's personal claim, courts now recognize that its earlier formulation was discriminatory in allowing the claim only to women and in vesting the claim in the father.[29] But in any event, the parental claim for anything more than obligatory medical expenses may be abolished along with the alienation and criminal conversation claims.[30]

§ 444. Alienation of a Parent's or Child's Affections

Alienation of a child's or parent's affections. A parent or anyone else who is libeled by the defendant can recover for loss of esteem or standing in the eyes of the community and with friends and family.[1] In such a case, alienation of a child's affections is merely one item of damages. Children in some states can also recover for loss of society and other

24. Restatement § 701.

25. On the wrongs of this system, see Lea Vandervelde, The Legal Ways of Seduction, 48 Stan. L. Rev. 817 (1996).

26. See Piggott v. Miller, 557 S.W.2d 692 (Mo.Ct.App.1977); Lee Vandervelde, supra n. 25.

27. Many discussions treat the claim as one of "fraud," focusing on the misrepresentation required to invalidate the plaintiff's consent. See Jane E. Larson, "Women Understand So Little, They Call My Good Nature 'Deceit' ": A Feminist Rethinking of Seduction, 93 Colum. L. Rev. 374 (1993) (proposing a tort of sexual fraud). With consent invalidated, however, the sexual touching perfectly fits the definition of battery as well. Where seduction is not specifically covered by the statute of limitations (or is covered only as to the old common law action brought by the father), conceptualizing the case as one for fraud rather than battery might be decisive on the limitation issue.

28. See § 100; Jane E. Larson, supra n. 27.

29. See Franklin v. Hill, 264 Ga. 302, 444 S.E.2d 778 (1994) (statute applying only to men unconstitutional).

30. N.Y. Civ. Rts. L. § 80–a; 76 Okl.St. Ann. § 8.1 (as to persons of legal age and sound mind).

§ 444

1. E.g., Tuman v. Genesis Assocs., 894 F.Supp. 183 (E.D.Pa.1995) (therapist allegedly implanted false memories in child-patient of abuse by parents, potential liability for defamation when child foreseeably published).

consortium values when a parent is physically injured, and in fewer states a parent can similarly recover when a child is injured.[2]

The usual rule, however, is that there is no independent action for the defendant's acts alienating the affections of either a parent[3] or a child.[4] The child's claim, asserted against a parent's new spouse or lover, seems inconsistent with the general abolition of alienation claims and also with the right of the parent to obtain a divorce. If the rule against a recovery for alienation of a parent's affections is to be effective, courts must also deny the claim when it is asserted on the same essential facts under the theory of privacy invasion, or interference with contract, or intentional infliction of emotional distress.[5]

The parents' claim for alienation of a child's affection might stand on substantially higher ground and at least one notable case supports it.[6] So far as the claim is asserted against the child's other parent or against the child's custodian, however, the problem of monitoring the persistent destructive behavior of divorced parents may make it difficult to be confident that adjudications would produce just results with appropriate consistency. On the other hand, when the issue is not tort recovery but custody of the child, courts have been perfectly willing to consider whether one parent has been guilty of alienating the child's affections for the other.[7]

Liability of therapists for alienating a child's affections. When therapists induce an adult to believe falsely that a parent sexually abused her as a child, standard doctrine holds that the therapist is not liable to the parent for mere negligence in diagnosis because a professional's duty of care ordinarily runs to the patient or client, not to others, and because so far as the therapist reports suspected child abuse, he may be privileged as well.[8] Expressed in policy terms, a professional's duty of care should not run to his client's or patient's adversary lest his professional

2. § 310.

3. Taylor v. Keefe, 134 Conn. 156, 56 A.2d 768 (1947); Whitcomb v. Huffington, 180 Kan. 340, 304 P.2d 465 (1956). See Jeffery F. Ghent, Annotation, Right of Child or Parent to Recover for Alienation of Other's Affections, 60 A.L.R.3d 931 (1975). Contra: Johnson v. Luhman, 330 Ill.App. 598, 71 N.E.2d 810 (1947); Miller v. Monsen, 228 Minn. 400, 37 N.W.2d 543 (1949).

4. Stevens v. Redwing, 146 F.3d 538 (8th Cir.1998) (holding also that this rule is not to be circumvented by allowing an emotional distress claim); Restatement § 699. Cf. Mackintosh v. Carter, 451 N.W.2d 285 (S.D.1990) (defendants providing shelter to child when they reasonably thought she was in danger).

5. See Kane v. Quigley, 1 Ohio St.2d 1, 203 N.E.2d 338 (1964). Defamation of a family member, however, is distinguishable because, unlike the claim for interference and emotional harm, it now requires at least a publication of a falsehood. See Tuman v. Genesis Associates, n. 1.

6. Strode v. Gleason, 9 Wash.App. 13, 510 P.2d 250, 60 A.L.R.3d 924 (1973). Hershey v. Hershey, 467 N.W.2d 484 (S.D. 1991), allowed recovery where the child was taken from the jurisdiction and hidden until he reached adulthood, calling the claim one for alienation of affections.

7. E.g., Stevens v. Stevens, 977 S.W.2d 305 (Mo.App.1998).

8. J.A.H. v. Wadle & Assocs., 589 N.W.2d 256 (Iowa 1999) (public policy: confidentiality and divided loyalties of therapist would ensue if liability is imposed; in any event, no negligent treatment was proven); Bird v. W.C.W., 868 S.W.2d 767 (Tex.1994). Contra: Montoya v. Bebensee, 761 P.2d 285 (Colo.Ct.App.1988).

conduct be shaped by fear of liability rather than by duty to his patient or client.[9]

However, the literature is full of accounts of quite serious misbehavior by talk therapists (as distinct from those who use drugs to correct chemical imbalances) and some of this might count as something a good deal worse than mere negligence. Some seem to lack the professional training a patient might expect of a person permitted to manipulate the minds of others.[10] Some therapists have used hypnotism and other aggressively manipulative techniques to implant "memories" of sexual abuse.[11] One scholar, summarizing many of the wrongful therapeutic practices in falsifying "memory," proposes modest statutory liability where hypersuggestive techniques are used recklessly or in willful blindness to the probability of implanting false memories.[12] But, not surprisingly, the claim is made that there is good therapy and that such therapy will be harmed if therapists are liable for their wrongs.[13]

Some courts have refused to entertain an action against therapists for alienation of a minor child's affections by erroneous diagnosis of sexual abuse[14] or by unspecified means,[15] but such decisions may not exclude liability for implanting or encouraging false memories by aggressive suggestion. Some decisions have favored the falsely accused parent against a therapist who uses suggestive techniques that encourage false memories.[16] Those who oppose the injustice and emotional devastation

9. See Zamstein v. Marvasti, 240 Conn. 549, 561, 692 A.2d 781, 787 (1997); Doe v. McKay, 183 Ill.2d 272, 700 N.E.2d 1018, 233 Ill.Dec. 310 (1998) (also arguing that confidentiality would be imperiled).

10. See, e.g., Borawick v. Shay, 68 F.3d 597 (2d Cir.1995) (patient allegedly hypnotized by one Valerian St. Regis began to "recall" abuse by an aunt and uncle and hosts of others, including ritual sexual abuse inflicted by Masons, and scenes in which she was forced to drink blood and do things with a dead pig, incense, and people dressed in black gowns. Valerian St. Regis had a high school education and no formal training in therapy or hypnotic technique before becoming a hypnotist at Pacific Medical Center).

11. Therapists have been found liable in direct suits by their patients as distinguished from suits by the falsely accused. See Sheila Taub, Legal Treatment of Recovered Memories of Child Sexual Abuse, 17 J. Legal Med. 183 (1996).

12. Joel Jay Finer, Therapists' Liability to the Falsely Accused for Inducing Illusory Memories of Childhood Sexual Abuse—Current Remedies and a Proposed Statute, 11 J. L. & Health 45 (1996–97).

13. Cynthia Grant Bowman and Elizabeth Mertz, A Dangerous Direction: Legal Intervention in Sexual Abuse Survivor Therapy, 109 Harv. L. Rev. 549 (1996). The therapeutic community has also reacted negatively to proposals for a statute requiring therapists to obtain informed consent of patients before practicing some kinds of "trauma search therapy." See Sheila Taub, supra n. 11 at 201.

14. Zamstein v. Marvasti, 240 Conn. 549, 692 A.2d 781 (1997); cf. Doe v. McKay, 183 Ill.2d 272, 700 N.E.2d 1018, 233 Ill.Dec. 310 (1998) (accused claimed accusation was false but opinion reflects only a generic claim for interference with family relationship rather than assertions of deliberate or reckless acts).

15. Sahid v. Chambers, 237 A.D.2d 175, 655 N.Y.S.2d 20 (1997) (alleging a conspiracy by therapist to brainwash, but as reported no claim of implanting false memories).

16. Sawyer v. Midelfort, 227 Wis.2d 124, 595 N.W.2d 423 (1999) (parent asserted that therapist negligently performed hypnosis, and"implanted and reinforced false memories" in the patient; court noted that the therapist is not threatened unless he fails to comply with the duty of care he already owes the patient); see, reporting trial court decisions, Joel Jay Finer, supra n. 12 at 56; Sheila Taub, supra n. 11 at 210.

wreaked by therapists's sponsorship of false accusations do not, of course, oppose well-founded identification of child abusers.

*

CHAPTER 32

INTERFERENCE WITH CONTRACT AND ECONOMIC OPPORTUNITY GENERALLY

§ 445. Intentional Interference with Contract and Other Economic Opportunities

In many instances the defendant can inflict economic harm upon the plaintiff without causing any harm at all to the plaintiff's person or property. One way of inflicting stand-alone economic harm is to interfere with the plaintiff's contracts or business opportunities with others. Interference is sometimes tortious under the rules of, say, defamation or copyright infringement or some other named tort. In such cases, interference with the plaintiff's economic interests is merely an element of damages resulting from the named tort, not a separate tort called interference. When the defendant has committed no named tort (such as defamation), lawyers argue that the intended interference with economic interests is a tort in itself. Courts originally accepted that idea, treating intended interference itself as a prima facie tort.[1] Some courts today require a little more—intended interference by improper means or by perfectly legitimate means accompanied by a bad motive. Liability follows even if the defendant has done nothing that is otherwise tortious at all.

The interference torts always involve three persons—the plaintiff, a person with whom he has a valuable economic relationship, and the defendant who disrupts that relationship.[2] They are quite different from almost all other torts in several ways. For one thing, the rules of liability do not describe specific wrongful conduct like fraud or trespass; they only proscribe "wrongful" interference with economic rights. For another, when the defendant induces a third person to breach a contract with

§ 445

1. Holmes' idea was that intended infliction of harm is prima facie tortious without regard to whether some specific tort could be identified. See Aikens v. Wisconsin, 195 U.S. 194, 204, 25 S.Ct. 3, 5, 49 L.Ed. 154, 158 (1904). The idea is criticized in Dan B. Dobbs, Tortious Interference with Contractual Relationships, 34 ARK. L. REV. 335 (1980). A few states have recognized a prima facie tort even when no specific wrong or tort has been committed. See Schmitz v. Smentowski, 109 N.M. 386, 785 P.2d 726 (1990); Advance Music Corp. v. American Tobacco Co., 296 N.Y. 79, 70 N.E.2d 401 (1946). Professor Gergen thinks the idea is the real source of liability for interference, see Mark P. Gergen, Tortious Interference: How It Is Engulfing Commercial Law, Why This Is Not Entirely Bad, and a Prudential Response, 38 ARIZ. L. REV. 1175 (1996).

2. Bad faith breach of contract and public policy wrongful discharge do not involve three identified persons but for convenience are discussed in §§ 453 & 454.

the plaintiff, the plaintiff is not required to pursue her rights against the breaching third party; she may instead seek tort damages, sometimes including punitive damages, from the defendant whose "wrong" may have been only to advise a breach.

So far, at least, the vague rules of the interference torts have not worked well. At best, they emphasize that the intent must be "wrongful," but do not define the term and certainly do not always limit liability to cases of activity that is independently tortious. They have invited many, many suits which must be dismissed, or worse, fully tried and then dismissed. Liability has received a degree of support from some scholars,[3] but others have been critical. One criticism is that liability for interference with contract undercuts the efficient breach principle, the idea that except for specifically performable contracts, you should be free to breach your contract and pay the damages if a better opportunity appears. Another criticism has more to do with the judicial process and appropriate scope of the defendant's economic activity; it holds that courts should not make liability turn on the character or motive of the defendant rather than his acts.

Critics have suggested that at least in large part the interference torts should be abolished in favor of torts like fraud, defamation, or restraint of trade that focus on identifiable wrongful acts,[4] misappropriation of the plaintiff's contract relations rather than mere interference with them,[5] or at least be limited so as not to interfere with appropriate competition.[6] It might also be suggested that courts could minimize resort to the vague rules of interference by recognizing that in many cases the defendant has committed a specific tort and that interference is relevant only because it is an element of damages, not because it is a separate tort.[7]

§ 446. Mainstream Patterns and Principles of Liability

The Patterns

Interference cases can be classed in a number of different ways, for example, according to whether the interference is anticompetitive or

3. Marina Lao, Tortious Interference and the Federal Antitrust Law of Vertical Restraints, 83 Iowa L. Rev. 35 (1997) (arguing against certain limits in federal antitrust law and suggesting that the common law interference torts can to some extent supply the claimed deficiency in antitrust law). Lillian R. BeVier, Reconsidering Inducement, 76 Va. L. Rev. 877 (1990) supports the liability for one range of cases, but thinks it is not justified for another. Some other supporters of liability are discussed in David A. Anderson, Torts, Speech, and Contracts, 75 Tex. L. Rev. 1499 (1997).

4. Dobbs, supra n. 1; Harvey S. Perlman, Interference with Contract and Other Economic Expectancies: A Clash of Tort and Contract Doctrine, 49 U. Chi. L. Rev. 61 (1982).

5. See Mark P. Gergen, Tortious Interference: How It Is Engulfing Commercial Law, Why This Is Not Entirely Bad, and a Prudential Response, 38 Ariz. L. Rev. 1175 (1996).

6. Gary Myers, The Differing Treatment of Efficiency and Competition in Antitrust and Tortious Interference Law, 77 Minn. L. Rev. 1097 (1993).

7. A reading of cases suggests that in many instances a real and specific tort lies behind the interference and sometimes it is quite explicit. E.g., Tamiami Trail Tours, Inc. v. J.C. Cotton, 463 So.2d 1126 (Fla. 1985). (battery and other torts).

whether it is economically efficient.[1] The Restatement's rules are arranged around four simple patterns. These are:

(1) The defendant induces breach or otherwise interferes with performance by plaintiff's promisor or fiduciary. For example, the defendant intentionally and without justification induces the plaintiff's employee to breach his employment contract and work for the defendant instead of the plaintiff; alternatively, he facilitates the employee's breach.

(2) The defendant makes the plaintiff's performance impossible or more burdensome. For example, the defendant intentionally and without justification interferes with his tenant's right to assign the lease, making it impossible for the tenant to sell his business to a buyer.[2]

(3) The defendant interferes with the plaintiff's economic prospects or opportunities that are not embodied in contract. For example, the plaintiff has no contract but does have a prospective buyer for her business. The defendant without justification induces the would-be buyer to choose a cheaper alternative.[3] This pattern can be called interference with prospective advantage or interference with opportunity. Special privileges and limitations apply to the interference with opportunity claim and the plaintiff must prove damages resulting from the interference.[4]

(4) The defendant does not intentionally interfere but does so negligently. For example, the defendant negligently spills a dangerous chemical, requiring the neighborhood to be evacuated with resulting loss of business to the plaintiff. A few courts have recognized such claims, but negligently caused economic harm is generally not actionable.[5]

Although each of these patterns is distinct and may call for distinct rules, the most significant difference in the patterns is the one between interference with an existing and enforceable contract on the one hand and interference with an opportunity or prospective advantage on the other, mainly because courts permit a greater range of interference with economic opportunities that are not reduced to contract.

The Principles

Elements. The traditional view holds that actionable interference is shown prima facie by showing intentional and improper interference with the plaintiff's contract or economic opportunity with another.[6] Sometimes courts spell out several of the elements implicit in that brief statement: the plaintiff must show (1) the existence of a contract (or economic opportunity) involving the plaintiff and another, (2) the defen-

§ 446

1. See Lillian R. BeVier, Reconsidering Inducement, 76 VA. L. REV. 877 (1990) (concluding that certain patterns, such as those involving relational contracts, economically warrant liability for breach inducement).

2. E.g., Campbell v. Westdahl, 148 Ariz. 432, 715 P.2d 288 (1985).

3. Scallywags, Inc. v. Sweeney, 84 B.R. 303 (Bkrtcy.D. Mass. 1988) (landlord suggested that buyer lease directly from landlord and pay nothing for business, then evicted the would-be seller and dealt directly with the prospective buyer).

4. See § 450.

5. § 452.

6. See Restatement §§ 766–766B.

dant's knowledge of it, (3) the defendant's malicious, improper, or intentional interference with it, (4) breach of the contract or other legally cognizable disruption of economic opportunity, and (5) resulting damage to the plaintiff.[7] The defendant cannot "interfere" with his own contract.[8] He can instead breach his own contract in ways that may cause a disruption in the plaintiff's contracts or opportunities with others for which the defendant is liable. But, in many such cases, the defendant's liability for his own breach, even in bad faith, is properly for breach of contract, not for the interference tort.[9]

Burden of proof. Courts traditionally held that proof of intentional interference was by itself prima facie proof of the tort. In effect, they presumed that the defendant had acted with wrongful motive or by improper purposes when he intentionally interfered with the plaintiff's contract or economic opportunity. Under that rule, the defendant could escape liability only by showing a privilege and shouldering the burden of justifying the interference.[10] Even if the defendant showed a privilege, the privilege could be defeated if the plaintiff showed the defendant was guilty of malice.[11] A number of important contemporary cases have begun to put the burden of proof where it normally is by requiring the plaintiff to show first that the defendant's interference was improper or wrongful.[12]

Nature of intent required. The keystone element is the third one in the list above. Sometimes courts state that mere intended interference suffices. Intended interference necessarily means that the defendant must be aware of the plaintiff's contract or opportunity and that the defendant's words or deeds will interfere with it. Knowledge of the contract or opportunity can be proved by circumstantial evidence,[13] and the defendant need not know the detailed terms of the contract if he knows enough to understand its nature and that his conduct is substantially certain to interfere with the agreement.[14] Intent may be found if his primary purpose was to interfere, but intent can be found as well if the defendant acts with a substantial certainty that interference will

7. Quelimane Co., Inc. v. Stewart Title Guar. Co., 19 Cal.4th 26, 960 P.2d 513, 77 Cal.Rptr.2d 709 (1998); Foster v. Churchill, 87 N.Y.2d 744, 665 N.E.2d 153, 642 N.Y.S.2d 583 (1996).

8. See § 449.

9. See §§ 453 & 454.

10. Alyeska Pipeline Serv. Co. v. Aurora Air Serv., Inc., 604 P.2d 1090 (Alaska 1979).

11. See Langer v. Becker, 176 Ill.App.3d 745, 751, 531 N.E.2d 830, 834, 126 Ill.Dec. 203, 207 (1988) (for this purpose requiring "actual malice," defined as "a desire to harm which was unrelated to the interest he was presumably seeking to protect by bringing about the contract breach").

12. Wagenseller v. Scottsdale Mem. Hosp., 147 Ariz. 370, 710 P.2d 1025 (1985); Mason v. Wal-Mart Stores, Inc., 333 Ark. 3, 969 S.W.2d 160 (1998) (interference with contract); Penna v. Toyota Motor Sales, U.S.A., Inc., 11 Cal.4th 376, 902 P.2d 740, 45 Cal.Rptr.2d 436 (1995) (interference with opportunity); Top Serv. Body Shop, Inc. v. Allstate Ins. Co., 283 Or. 201, 582 P.2d 1365 (1978); Leigh Furniture and Carpet Co. v. Isom, 657 P.2d 293 (Utah 1982); see Restatement Third of Torts (Unfair Competition) § 1, cmt. a (1995).

13. Texaco, Inc. v. Pennzoil Co., 729 S.W.2d 768 (Tex.App.1987).

14. See Guard-Life Corp. v. S. Parker Hardware Mfg. Corp., 50 N.Y.2d 183, 193, 406 N.E.2d 445, 450, 428 N.Y.S.2d 628, 634 (1980).

result.[15] Courts have at times said that the defendant's act must be malicious, but on inspection, this often turns out to be an old-fashioned way of saying only that the intent must be improper in some way.[16] Consequently, courts either require the plaintiff to show that the interference is somehow "improper" or they permit the defendant to offer an affirmative defense that the interference was privileged.

Rightful, justified, or privileged interference. Whoever has the burden of proof, the interference must be wrongful or unjustified. Two rules are clear. It is not wrongful to induce another to breach a marriage contract, and it is not wrongful to compete lawfully for opportunities not embodied in an existing contract. Beyond that, an agent acting within the scope of his employment is free to advise his employer to breach.[17] The Restatement and the cases recognize that the defendant who has an economic interest of his own is free to protect his interests by advising a termination or avoidance of relations with the plaintiff[18] or by bringing or threatening a bona fide suit to protect his own interests.[19] If the defendant's subjective purpose is to further his own legitimate ends, some courts express the idea that his interference is justified by saying that interference is only incidental and is protected for that reason.[20] The defendant is also free to advise breach when the defendant has taken responsibility for the third person's welfare, as where the defendant advises a friend to breach a contract that is dangerous to his health.[21] Somewhat strangely in the light of liability for honest persuasion to breach, the Restatement also recognizes that the defendant is free to provide truthful information and honest advice within the scope of a request.[22]

When interference is accomplished by means of some specific tort like defamation, the interference represents an element of damages in that tort. Accordingly, the rules of the specific tort should ordinarily govern liability. For example, if the defendant's derogatory publications cause a third person to breach a contract with the plaintiff or terminate her employment, the defendant should not ordinarily be liable for

15. Restatement § 766, cmt. j.

16. See, e.g., Carroll Anesthesia Assocs., P.C. v. Anesthecare, Inc., 234 Ga.App. 646, 507 S.E.2d 829 (1998); Nesler v. Fisher and Co., Inc., 452 N.W.2d 191 (Iowa 1990); see Restatement § 766, cmt. s. When "malice" is asserted to defeat a privilege, it may mean action taken outside the scope of the privilege. See Langer v. Becker, supra n. 11.

17. E.g., Lachenmaier v. First Bank Sys., Inc., 246 Mont. 26, 803 P.2d 614 (1990). When the agent acts exclusively in his own interests and outside the scope of his employment, however, this justification does not apply. E.g., Ives v. Guilford Mills, Inc., 3 F.Supp.2d 191 (N.D.N.Y.1998).

18. Restatement § 769; Langer v. Becker, 176 Ill.App.3d 745, 531 N.E.2d 830, 126 Ill.Dec. 203 (1988).

19. Restatement § 773; Westfield Dev. Co. v. Rifle Inv. Assocs., 786 P.2d 1112 (Colo.1990) (asserting claim by filing lis pendens); contra, Voorhees v. Guyan Mach. Co., 191 W.Va. 450, 446 S.E.2d 672 (1994) (not citing the Restatement anywhere).

20. See, reviewing cases, K & K Management, Inc. v. Lee, 316 Md. 137, 557 A.2d 965 (1989).

21. Restatement § 770 and ill. 4.

22. Restatement § 772. See Allen v. Safeway Stores, Inc., 699 P.2d 277 (Wyo. 1985) (truthful information given by customer or business contact about treatment by business employee is fully protected whether requested or not).

interference if the defamation rules protect the defendant's right to publish.[23] But some courts, long attuned to liability for bad motive, seem to have overlooked the point and to have imposed liability for conduct that might be protected under defamation[24] or malicious prosecution rules.[25]

Wrongful means, wrongful motive and competition. When no specific rule governs, what is improper is determined largely by considering (a) the defendant's motive or purpose for his intentional interference and (b) the means he used to interfere as judged by a number of factors.[26] In contract interference cases courts have thought that either improper motive or improper means could show wrongful interference. In interference with opportunity cases, some courts have said that bad motive won't suffice to permit liability and improper means is required instead.[27] Some other courts, however, have emphasized bad motives as well as improper means even in opportunity interference cases.[28] Even so, competition is held to be a good rather than a bad motive in the opportunity cases, so improper means rather than improper motive is often required in interference with opportunity cases.[29] As the Restatement of Unfair Competition says, the public benefits from competition do not correlate with the defendant's motivation.[30] In competition for opportunity cases, then, motive is largely irrelevant even if it can be properly considered in interference with existing contract cases.

23. See Levin, Middlebrooks, Mabie, Thomas, Mayes & Mitchell, P. A. v. United States Fire Ins. Co., 639 So.2d 606 (Fla. 1994) (absolute privilege for communications in litigation applied to interference claim, but not a case involving injurious falsehood); Caruso v. Local U. No. 690, Int. Bro. of Teamsters, 100 Wash.2d 343, 670 P.2d 240 (1983) (defamation free speech rules protect against interference liability as well).

24. Centro Nautico Representacoes Nauticas, LDA. v. International Marine Co-op, Ltd., 719 So.2d 967 (Fla.Dist.Ct.App. 1998) (liability for interference by statements not shown to be false); Magnum Radio, Inc. v. Brieske, 217 Wis.2d 130, 577 N.W.2d 377 (Wis.Ct.App.1998) (in the FCC radio station licensing process, the defendant objected to licensing radio station to plaintiff; the absolute defamation privilege applied in judicial and administrative litigation was not applied).

25. Voorhees v. Guyan Mach. Co., 191 W.Va. 450, 446 S.E.2d 672 (1994) (threat of litigation actionable when it caused interference without analysis showing that the threatened litigation would itself be tortious; some language suggesting that negligence in determining validity of suit would suffice).

26. See the paragraph *Restatement "factors"* below.

27. Peace v. Conway, 246 Va. 278, 435 S.E.2d 133 (1993); see Pratt v. Prodata, Inc., 885 P.2d 786, 789, n. 3 (Utah 1994) (the "improper-purpose test creates a trap for the wary and unwary alike: business practices that are found to be 'proper means' by a finder of fact and may otherwise be regarded as wholly legitimate under our capitalistic economic system may be recast through a jury's unguided exercise of its moral judgment into examples of spite or malice"; suggesting that in an appropriate case the improper means test be "recast").

28. In extreme cases, courts have been influenced to impute bad motives when they felt the defendant was making enough return on investment without interference, see Cherberg v. Peoples Nat'l Bank of Washington, 88 Wash.2d 595, 564 P.2d 1137 (1977), or when they felt that the defendant's decision to discourage dealer alliances was not an appropriate business decision. See Smith v. Ford Motor Co., 289 N.C. 71, 221 S.E.2d 282, 79 A.L.R.3d 651 (1976).

29. See Guard-Life Corp. v. S. Parker Hardware Mfg. Corp., 50 N.Y.2d 183, 406 N.E.2d 445, 428 N.Y.S.2d 628 (1980).

30. Restatement Third of Unfair Competition § 1, cmt. c (1995).

In neither the interference with contract nor interference with opportunity torts have courts been able to provide any concept of what counts as wrongful or improper. Many decisions are so vague about what is "wrong" that the judicial process itself is sometimes dubious in these cases. The rules risk bias and even a wrong emphasis upon the defendant's character rather than his conduct.[31]

Mixed motives. The defendant's liability frequently turns on the courts' estimate of the defendant's subjective motive and the courts' characterization of that motive as proper or improper. Motives, purposes, and attitudes are usually mixed. Some authority suggests that when liability turns on the defendant's bad motive, the bad motive must be the sole motive[32] or at least the primary or predominant motive.[33] If subjective motive must be considered at all, however, the kind of approach taken by the Supreme Court with analogous motive issues seems better.[34] This approach would ask whether the interference would have taken place even without the bad motive, that is, whether the acceptable motive would have produced the same interference. If so, the bad motives are to be ignored because they were not but-for causes of the interference.

Restatement "factors." The Restatement provided a list of factors to aid in determining whether interference was wrongful or improper. Judges are to consider the nature of the defendant's conduct, his motive, the interests of the plaintiff and those of the defendant as well as social interests, the proximity of the defendant's conduct and the relationship between the parties.[35] Somewhat more specifically, courts consider relevant business ethics, customs, and practices as well.[36] The named factors are so abstract that they might apply to almost any decision in torts. The result is that the rules are vague and indeterminate. The problem is not merely one of predictability but whether a process of decision that

31. See Penna v. Toyota Motor Sales, U.S.A., Inc., 11 Cal.4th 376, 902 P.2d 740, 45 Cal.Rptr.2d 436 (1995) (Mosk, J., concurring).

32. See Los Angeles Airways, Inc. v. Davis, 687 F.2d 321 (9th Cir. 1982).

33. Alyeska Pipeline Serv.Co. v. Aurora Air Serv., Inc., 604 P.2d 1090 (Alaska 1979); Leigh Furniture and Carpet Co. v. Isom, 657 P.2d 293 (Utah 1982).

34. See Mt. Healthy City Sch. Dist. Bd. of Ed. v. Doyle, 429 U.S. 274, 97 S.Ct. 568, 50 L.Ed.2d 471 (1977) (discharge of public employee partly for the illegitimate reason that he exercised First Amendment rights and partly for legitimate reasons, no civil rights action by employee if the legitimate reasons were sufficient to cause the discharge); Price Waterhouse v. Hopkins, 490 U.S. 228, 109 S.Ct. 1775, 104 L.Ed.2d 268 (1989) (similar with discharge partly for discriminatory and partly for nondiscriminatory reasons); cf. McKennon v. Nashville Banner Pub. Co., 513 U.S. 352, 115 S.Ct. 879, 130 L.Ed.2d 852 (1995) (wrongful motive, but after-acquired evidence would have provided acceptable motive, remedy limited); but cf. 42 U.S.C. 2000e–2 (unlawful employment practice is established by proof that discrimination was motivating factor even if there were other motives). In the case of employment sex discrimination, however, 42 U.S.C.A. § 2000e–2(m) now provides that if discriminatory motives are established for any employment practice, that practice is unlawful even if other factors also motivated it.

35. Restatement § 767.

36. Saglioccolo v. Eagle Ins. Co., 112 F.3d 226 (6th Cir.1997); Restatement § 767, cmt. j.

cannot describe the wrongful acts it condemns is either judicial or entirely fair.[37]

§ 447. Intentional Interference with the Performance of the Plaintiff's Promisor

Liability for inducing the promisor's breach. A 14th century English statute passed in response to the labor shortage caused by the plague prohibited ordinary agricultural laborers from quitting their present work and marketing their labor elsewhere. To back up the prohibition, the statute provided that no other employer could hire a laborer who did so.[1] The effect, of course, was to reinforce a system of serfdom. The modern liability for interference with contract extended that approach in part to other employees. *Lumley v. Gye*[2] is the classic modern case. The plaintiff there had contracted for a series of performances by an opera singer. The defendant, a competing producer, "enticed" the singer to cease further performances for the plaintiff in breach of her contract. The court held the defendant liable for interference. In effect, courts converted a contract right between A and B into a property right that binds everyone who knows of the contract.[3]

Scope and acceptance. Subject to the exception for marriage contracts and the possibility that some inducements are justified, this kind of interference with the promisor's contracted-for performance is actionable almost everywhere[4] so long as the interference is improper or unjustified and causes at least partial breach of the contract.[5] Liability may be imposed for such intentional interference with any kind of contract including those for the sale of goods or property,[6] for sale of a business,[7] for the services of brokers,[8] doctors,[9] and lawyers[10] among many others. Inducing breach of a fiduciary duty falls under the same

37. See Dan B. Dobbs, Tortious Interference with Contractual Relationships, 34 ARK. L. REV. 335, 346 (1980).

§ 447

1. The Ordinance of Labourers, 23 Edw. III (1349); see 3 Bl. Com. 142 (beating or hiring the servant actionable).

2. Lumley v. Gye, 2 El. & Bl. 216, 118 Eng.Rep. 749 (1853).

3. See Johnson v. Gustafson, 201 Minn. 629, 632, 277 N.W. 252, 254 (1938).

4. Restatement § 766. See generally M. C. Dransfield, Liability for Procuring Breach of Contract, 26 A.L.R.2d 1227 (1952). Louisiana has rejected the tort. See Lagarde v. Allstate Ins. Co., 515 So.2d 1147 (La.App.1987).

5. In Pettit v. Paxton, 255 Neb. 279, 583 N.W.2d 604 (1998) the seller contracted to sell a ranch to the plaintiffs. The defendant offered a greater sum. The seller used this offer to jack up the original contract price. Expressing doubts about the causal connection between interference and the raised price, the court concluded that the original sale contract had not been breached and the buyers had no claim for interference. When courts are willing to recognize the claim that the defendant interfered with the plaintiff's own performance, breach is not required. See § 448.

6. Duff v. Engelberg, 237 Cal.App.2d 505, 47 Cal.Rptr. 114 (1965) (real property); Mooney v. Johnson Cattle Co., Inc., 291 Or. 709, 634 P.2d 1333 (1981) (cattle sale contract).

7. Campbell v. Westdahl, 148 Ariz. 432, 715 P.2d 288 (Ct.App. 1985).

8. Graff v. Whitehouse, 71 Ill.App.2d 412, 219 N.E.2d 128 (1966).

9. Okusami v. Psychiatric Inst. of Washington, Inc., 959 F.2d 1062 (D.C.Cir.1992).

10. E.g., Adler, Barish, Daniels, Levin and Creskoff v. Epstein, 482 Pa. 416, 393 A.2d 1175, 1 A.L.R.4th 1144 (1978).

rules.[11] The defendant must know of the contract or fiduciary duty, else he could not intend to interfere with its performance, but liability is not limited to cases of malice, much less to cases of falsehood or threat.

Coercive threats inducing breach. In many cases, the promisor breaches his contract with the plaintiff because he feels coerced to do so. Not all coercion is objectionable. For instance, if you threaten me with a legitimate lawsuit, I may feel coerced to yield to your demands but it is highly desirable that I feel coerced by legitimate demands and that I consequently offer an appropriate settlement. In some cases, however, courts have assumed that coercion is necessarily wrongful, with the result that liability is imposed for acts that may be entirely justifiable. To threaten a lawsuit without probable cause is a tort—a version of malicious prosecution—but defendants have been held liable for interfering with a contract by threatening a lawsuit even though the plaintiff has not shown that the suit would have been tortious if brought.[12]

Coercive refusal to deal. A refusal to deal with the plaintiff's promisor is sometimes called a boycott. A refusal to deal or a threat to refuse to deal in the future, may also induce the promisor to breach. "I will refuse to sell you the goods you need for your manufacturing business unless you repudiate your contract with the plaintiff." Refusals to deal raise a problem. On the one hand people are generally free to refuse to do business with others.[13] On the other, some refusals to deal will tend to operate as restraints on trade or to create monopolies that are wrongful both under common law and under antitrust laws. The Restatement purports to recognize the principle that people are free to refuse dealings with others; but then it dithers. It suggests that the defendant who refuses to deal with the promisor must not tell the promisor his reason, lest he induce the promisor to breach his contract. Yet the Restatement goes on to suggest that after all he can admit his reason for refusing to deal if he is answering a direct question.[14] The distinction between telling the truth in the first place and answering a direct question seems unjustified on principle and unreliable as a basis for evidence in trial.

Anticompetitive interference. What is justified is the general principle that, political and social boycotts aside,[15] a group boycott that tends to restrain trade or produce monopoly or predatory destruction of a competitor is actionable, not because of motive but because of the anticompetitive results. The rational inquiry is thus not merely whether the defendant interfered by refusing to deal or whether he had a bad motive

11. Hannex Corp. v. GMI, Inc., 140 F.3d 194 (2d Cir.1998) (agent as fiduciary under a duty to act in principal's best interests, liability for inducing breach of this duty).

12. Voorhees v. Guyan Mach. Co., 191 W.Va. 450, 446 S.E.2d 672 (1994) (defendant's threat to enforce a non-competition covenant led defendant's competitor to discharge the plaintiff).

13. See, e.g., Lyon v. Campbell, 120 Md. App. 412, 707 A.2d 850 (Md. Ct. Spec. App. 1998).

14. Restatement § 766, cmt. l and ills. 1 & 2. This was accepted as good law in Uptown Heights Assocs. Ltd. Partnership v. Seafirst Corp., 320 Or. 638, 891 P.2d 639 (1995).

15. Free speech considerations justify these boycotts. See NAACP v. Claiborne Hardware Co., infra n. 24.

but whether the interference had substantial anticompetitive effects. That may occasionally be the case when the defendant excludes the plaintiff from economic competition through the defendant's use of his own economic power.[16] Much more clearly, anticompetitive effects can be shown when the defendant engages in a concerted refusal to deal to induce interference. If all lumber yards agree with each other that they will not do business with saw mills that sell lumber to lumber brokers, their threatened refusal to deal interferes with lumber brokers' ability to compete and the concerted action is plainly anticompetitive.[17] The competitive or anticompetitive character of the defendant's acts cannot be found in the defendant's motive but in the nature of his acts and its results. Nevertheless, courts frequently assess motive rather than anticompetitive results. They may characterize the defendant's motive as improper even if competition is not reduced by the defendant's act. Once judges condemn the motive, they are likely to regard competitive behavior as tortious.[18]

Persuasion and free speech. Cases like *Lumley* impose liability for persuading or offering a better deal to the plaintiff's promisor.[19] Liability has been consistently imposed in such cases.[20] But in the absence of falsehood or coercion, free speech considerations suggest caution about liability. Although liability for inducing breach has been defended as well as attacked, it is not so easy to see why liability can be imposed for

16. See Tuttle v. Buck, 107 Minn. 145, 119 N.W. 946 (1909) (predatory pricing driving out only competitor in town). Under antitrust laws, competitive pricing is regarded as anticompetitive only if the price is below the defendant's costs. For a comparison of this and other antitrust doctrines, see Gary Myers, The Differing Treatment of Efficiency and Competition in Antitrust and Tortious Interference Law, 77 MINN. L. REV. 1097 (1993).

17. E.g., Jackson v. Stanfield, 137 Ind. 592, 36 N.E. 345 (1894) (lumber yards combined economic power to force sawmills to refuse to sell to lumber brokers, held actionable). The same result might be obtained under federal antitrust laws, see Eastern States Retail Lumber Dealers' Ass'n v. United States, 234 U.S. 600, 34 S.Ct. 951, 58 L.Ed. 1490 (1914), and in fact antitrust claims are often asserted with interference claims.

18. E.g., Deauville Corp. v. Federated Dept. Stores, Inc., 756 F.2d 1183 (5th Cir. 1985) (rejecting antitrust claims but allowing the interference claim to go to the jury because the defendant's motive in obtaining an anchor tenant might have been to harm a competitor); Hannigan v. Sears, Roebuck and Co., 410 F.2d 285 (7th Cir.1969). In *Hannigan*, T, as a supplier of goods called lawn lockers, contracted to provide the lockers exclusively to the plaintiff as a distributor. Sears, an economic power, was a major purchaser of other goods from T. Sears threatened to cease purchasing from T unless T could supply lawn lockers. This induced T to renegotiate its contract with the plaintiff in a deal that left the plaintiff with less profit. The plaintiff was allowed to recover from Sears. The court's result may be more anticompetitive than Sears' threat. Dean Perlman has offered measured criticism of that case. Harvey S. Perlman, Interference with Contract and Other Economic Expectancies: a Clash of Tort and Contract Doctrine, 49 U. CHI. L. REV. 61, 109 (1982). Professor BeVier, however, argues that tort liability is justified when the defendant induces a breach of relational contracts that set up long term relationships and those that require pre-contract investment to obtain information about the contract that would be useless in other contracts. See Lillian R. BeVier, Reconsidering Inducement, 76 VA. L. REV. 877 (1990).

19. American Airlines v. Christensen, 967 F.2d 410 (10th Cir.1992) (defendant was in the business of brokering frequent flyer awards, which, under the contract between airline and its passengers were not saleable; liability was proper).

20. E.g., Texaco, Inc. v. Pennzoil Co., 729 S.W.2d 768 (Tex. Ct. App. 1987). See Lillian R. BeVier, Reconsidering Inducement, 76 VA. L. REV. 877 (1990).

truthful persuasion to do an act that it is not itself criminal or tortious,[21] especially since the plaintiff as promisee of a breached contract retains her full rights under the contract and can sue for its breach.[22] Historically, the interference torts were used to condemn and enjoin peaceful union activity and picketing on the ground that it interfered with business.[23] This is no longer possible under modern labor laws, and cases have now gone on to protect the right to speech that interferes with contracts or opportunities when that speech addresses political or social issues. For example, interfering with business by picketing and boycotting to protest alleged discrimination or consumer prices is protected activity.[24] The Supreme Court now recognizes a substantial degree of protection for commercial speech and a distinguished commentator has suggested that liability for speech in cases like *Lumley* may invade constitutional free speech rights if the speech is not false, does not contain coercive threats, and does not violate a fiduciary duty.[25]

Interference without inducement to breach. The defendant's liability for interference with the promisor's performance is not limited to cases of inducement in the sense of persuasion. Suppose a landowner uses economic power to force a contractor to reduce his price. To make up the losses, the contractor insists that subcontractors must reduce their price as well. The subcontractor may be permitted to recover for interference with his contract with the contractor if the landowner's action is considered to be wrongful.[26] Similarly, buyers and sellers sometimes

21. See Lillian R. BeVier, Reconsidering Inducement, supra n. 18. Marina Lao, Tortious Interference and the Federal Antitrust Law of Vertical Restraints, 83 Iowa L. Rev. 35 (1997), mainly argues that the common law tort need not parallel antitrust law or goals and that interference liability is based upon fair play.

22. The argument that the promisor may be insolvent seems to be an unsatisfactory response. The promisee has many ways of contracting that will tend to secure performance. Cf. Mark P. Gergen, Tortious Interference: How It Is Engulfing Commercial Law, Why This Is Not Entirely Bad, and a Prudential Response, 38 Ariz. L. Rev. 1175, 1231 n. 345 (1996) (transaction specific investments can be protected by contract mechanisms such as stipulated damage clauses). The promisee who seeks rewards by doing business with doubtfully solvent promisors and by avoiding the costs of securing performance must take the bitter losses with the sweet successes. The insolvency of the promisor is no more reason to impose liability upon others than in any other case. In any event, as Professor Anderson has pointed out, tort liability is not limited to cases of insolvent promisors. See David A. Anderson, Torts, Speech, and Contracts, 75 Tex. L. Rev. 1499, 1528 (1997).

23. E.g., O'Brien v. People ex rel. Kellogg Switchboard & Supply Co., 216 Ill. 354, 75 N.E. 108 (1905) (unlawful for union to persuade workers to strike as that would interfere with business); A.S. Beck Shoe Corp. v. Johnson, 153 Misc. 363, 274 N.Y.S. 946 (1934) (picketing a store in African-American neighborhood that refused to hire African-American employees was tortious and enjoined).

24. NAACP v. Claiborne Hardware Co., 458 U.S. 886, 102 S.Ct. 3409, 73 L.Ed.2d 1215 (1982) (politically motivated boycott, including picketing, assembly, and petitioning activity is constitutionally protected against a claim for intentional interference); cf. Organization for a Better Austin v. Keefe, 402 U.S. 415, 91 S.Ct. 1575, 29 L.Ed.2d 1 (1971) (no prior restraints against leaflets allegedly invading the plaintiff's privacy); Stansbury v. Beckstrom, 491 S.W.2d 947, 62 A.L.R.3d 222 (Tex.Civ.App. 1973) (no injunction against picketing of a doctor's office with signs claiming he charged too much).

25. David A. Anderson, Torts, Speech, and Contracts, 75 Tex. L. Rev. 1499 (1997).

26. Cf. Hannigan v. Sears, Roebuck and Co., 410 F.2d 285 (7th Cir.1969) (major purchaser/supplier/supplier's subsupplier).

attempt to defeat a broker's commission on the sale by constructing a sham sale to a person who was not produced by the broker. The helpful friend who plays the role of the buyer in the charade has induced no one to do anything, but he has definitely interfered with the broker's commission and is liable for the broker's loss.[27] Even an employer who innocently hires an employee may be liable for interference with an earlier employer's rights if the second employer continues to pay the employee after discovering that she was in breach of her contract with the first.[28]

Pseudo-interference. Sometimes, however, cases that might seem to turn on interference with contract, are only pseudo-interference cases because the defendant has committed some particular tort such as a trespass or negligence or fraud that results in disruption of the plaintiff's contracts with others[29] or has breached a contract of which the plaintiff is a third party beneficiary.[30] Although the harm in such cases encompasses the harm from a disrupted contract, the ground for recovery lies in the defendant's commission of some named tort. It is misleading to say that these are cases of interference with contract rather than cases in which a tort results in damages that include interference. This point cuts both ways. If the court characterizes the case as a claim for interference with contract, negligent interference is ordinarily not enough and the plaintiff will lose. But if the court characterizes the case as negligent damage to property (or a trespass to it) it may impose liability for all proximate harms, including the plaintiff's loss of a contract. Similarly, if the real claim is that the defendant has breached his own contract, it is misleading to say that the plaintiff's claim is one for the tort of interference, which may carry punitive damages with it.[31]

Improper vs. justified inducement or interference. Occasionally the defendant can escape liability because he can justify interfering or inducing a breach. In some courts, the plaintiff must prove in the first place that the interference is improper. In others, the older rule still

27. Johnson v. Gustafson, 201 Minn. 629, 277 N.W. 252 (1938) (friend aiding the buyer to deceive seller and broker); cf. Hangar One, Inc. v. Davis Assocs., Inc., 121 N.H. 586, 431 A.2d 792 (1981) (individual aiding corporate seller to convey to buyer without broker's knowledge).

28. Fowler v. Printers, II, Inc., 89 Md. App. 448, 598 A.2d 794 (1991) (restrictive covenant prohibited employee from working for competitor after employment with first employer was terminated; defendant hired the employee knowing nothing of the covenant but discovered it later; defendant was liable because he continued the employment after learning of the first employer's rights).

29. See Edwards v. Travelers Ins. of Hartford, Connecticut, 563 F.2d 105 (6th Cir.1977) (defendant's fraud on client led client to terminate attorney's representation); Zarrow v. Hughes, 282 P.2d 215 (Okla.1955) (the defendant's pollution of the plaintiff's ranch resulted in the plaintiff's loss of a grazing contract with a third person).

30. Just's Inc. v. Arrington Constr. Co., Inc., 99 Idaho 462, 583 P.2d 997 (1978).

31. See Wasserman v. NRG Realty Corp., 118 A.D.2d 495, 500 N.Y.S.2d 109 (1986) where a tenant had a contract to sublet the premises which was lost because the landlord breached a lease covenant by refusing to consent to subletting. The court spoke of the case as one for interference with contract but also as one of breach.

prevails and the defendant can escape liability only if he affirmatively persuades the court and jury that his conduct is privileged.[32]

No authoritative rule adequately describes conduct that is privileged. When the plaintiff has an existing, valid contract that is not merely an at-will contract, the defendant cannot justify interference on the ground that he is competing. Nor can he justify intended interference that is accomplished by committing some other tort, or by acts that themselves improperly coerce, threaten, or restrain trade. But the defendant's intentional interference by advising a breach is often not improper if the advice is given at least in part[33] for purposes or with motives the courts approve, sometimes even if the advice is given with malice.[34] It is in these cases in particular that motive or purpose may be a dominant consideration. The defendant may advise and induce a breach to protect his own existing financial interests,[35] the interests of another for whom he can properly take responsibility,[36] the interests of an employer[37] or those of a client.[38] The Restatement says he can also safely provide truthful information,[39] but presumably does not mean to include the information that the defendant is prepared to offer a better deal. The Restatement, following a theme it pursues in defamation cases and elsewhere, also recognizes a privilege to give advice apart from those cases already mentioned, but only if the advice is requested.[40] Under the free speech rules, he can also take a position on social and political issues, even though the position will induce others to cease all dealings with the plaintiff and even if that is the purpose of his advocacy.[41]

§ 448. Intentional Interference with the Plaintiff's Contractual Performance

The Restatement rule and its support. In § 766A, the Restatement recognizes a tort not only when the defendant improperly interferes with the performance due to the plaintiff but also when he interferes with the performance due from the plaintiff to another. If interference with the plaintiff's performance makes that performance more burdensome to the plaintiff, the action will lie unless the defendant's conduct is privileged or justified.[1] Some courts have expressly approved the Restatement's rule of liability[2] or at least assumed or implied it was acceptable.[3]

32. See § 446.

33. Mixed motives: see § 446.

34. Johnson Enters. Of Jacksonville, Inc. v. FPL Group, Inc., 162 F.3d 1290 (11th Cir.1998).

35. Johnson Enters. Of Jacksonville, Inc. v. FPL Group, Inc., 162 F.3d 1290 (11th Cir.1998) (corporate stockholder); Restatement § 769.

36. Restatement § 770.

37. Foster v. Churchill, 87 N.Y.2d 744, 665 N.E.2d 153, 642 N.Y.S.2d 583 (1996) (directors of a corporation).

38. Los Angeles Airways, Inc. v. Davis, 687 F.2d 321 (9th Cir. 1982).

39. Restatement § 772.

40. Restatement § 772 (b).

41. NAACP v. Claiborne Hardware Co., supra n. 24.

§ 448

1. Restatement § 766A.

2. See Plattner v. State Farm Mut. Auto. Ins. Co., 168 Ariz. 311, 812 P.2d 1129 (Ct. App. 1991); Herman v. Endriss, 187 Conn. 374, 446 A.2d 9 (1982); Callis, Papa, Jensen, Jackstadt & Halloran, P.C. v. Nor-

Rejection of and doubts about the Restatement rule. Interference torts are always formulated broadly, but the rule in § 766A may be broader than many courts will accept. Given that wrongfulness of interference lies in the eye of the beholder and that interference is intentional if the defendant is substantially certain that it will result from his acts, thousands of acts could intentionally interfere with the plaintiff's contract relations by making the contract more difficult to perform. Even the bus driver who sleeps late one morning might be intentionally interfering with his passengers' performance of their employment contracts. No court would hold the driver liable, but that merely shows that liability can not well be based upon the logic of § 766A. Some court's have doubted the rule's propriety,[4] avoided passing on it,[5] or rejected it outright in favor of a rule that breach or termination of the business relationship is required.[6]

Narrow support for the liability. Some cases that might be read to support the Restatement rule are actually only cases in which the defendant has breached his contract with the plaintiff.[7] These cases call for separate attention.[8] Still other cases relied upon by the Restatement itself to support its rule are just as consistent with a narrower band of liability. These cases, and some in which liability seems to be overstated, at best provide only soft support for the Restatement's position. The cases cited by the Reporter in support of the broad rule of § 766A, when they are on point at all,[9] mainly support the non-controversial rule that

folk Southern Corp., 292 Ill.App.3d 1003, 686 N.E.2d 750, 226 Ill.Dec. 967 (1997); Magnum Radio, Inc. v. Brieske, 217 Wis.2d 130, 577 N.W.2d 377 (1998) (defendant's complaint to FCC delayed plaintiff's ability to complete purchase of radio station); cf. Pettit v. Paxton, 255 Neb. 279, 583 N.W.2d 604 (1998) (dictum suggesting approval of § 766A although in § 766A type cases breach or termination of relationship would be required).

3. Westfield Dev. Co. v. Rifle Inv. Assocs., 786 P.2d 1112 (Colo.1990) (implicitly recognizing that if lis pendens was improperly filed without a privilege so as to impede seller's sale of land, the claim would be actionable).

4. Windsor Sec., Inc. v. Hartford Life Ins. Co., 986 F.2d 655 (3d Cir.1993) (counseling caution and noting that liability for interfering with a promisee's own performance would not provide incentives to bargain that might be provided by liability for interfering with a promisor's performance).

5. See Burns Jackson Miller Summit & Spitzer v. Lindner, 59 N.Y.2d 314, 451 N.E.2d 459, 464 N.Y.S.2d 712 (1983). The New York Court of Appeals has repeatedly counseled caution in interference claims and has said that breach was required, e.g., NBT Bancorp Inc. v. Fleet/Norstar Fin. Group, Inc., 87 N.Y.2d 614, 664 N.E.2d 492, 641 N.Y.S.2d 581 (1996). That requirement may not have been directed at § 766A claims, but D'Andrea v. Rafla–Demetrious, 146 F.3d 63 (2d Cir.1998), predicted that New York would reject such claims.

6. St. Louis Convention & Visitors Com'n v. Nat'l Football League, 154 F.3d 851 (8th Cir.1998) (interpreting Missouri law); Price v. Sorrell, 784 P.2d 614 (Wyo. 1989).

7. E.g., Trimed, Inc. v. Sherwood Med. Co., 977 F.2d 885 (4th Cir.1992).

8. §§ 449 & 453.

9. The Restatement claimed the support of South Central Livestock Dealers, Inc. v. Security State Bank, 551 F.2d 1346 (5th Cir.1977), which only held that if plaintiffs had beneficial interests in a fiduciary account held in A's name, the bank could not rightfully use the funds as an offset against fiduciary's personal liability to the bank. The Restatement erroneously cites this case as if the fiduciary were the plaintiff. It also claimed Harber v. Ohio Nat'l Life Ins. Co., 512 F.2d 170 (8th Cir.1975), which held for the defendant and did not seem to have in mind interference with the plaintiff's performance but interference with his agent's ability to sell life insurance on which the plaintiff took a percentage.

if you commit a specific tort like trespass, you are liable for all proximately caused damages, including such items as the foreseeable increased cost incurred by the plaintiff in carrying out her contracts with others. In other words, liability in many of the cited cases simply reflects liability for some specific tort like conversion,[10] or intentional damage to property.[11]

In one version of these cases, the defendant commits a specific tort to T that causes loss to P. For example, the plaintiff is a contractor obliged by contract to complete or repair a private bridge for T, her promisee. When the work is partially completed, the defendant damages the work so that the plaintiff must reconstruct the work on the bridge. The plaintiff has been permitted to recover in some such cases,[12] but that hardly supports a general rule of liability for interfering with the plaintiff's performance. From the defendant's point of view, this kind of case introduces no new liability at all; it only redirects the recovery to the person injured. In fact, the case could be understood as an ordinary subrogation case in which the plaintiff has paid for the property owner's loss and is now permitted to stand in his shoes to recover from the tortfeasor. Be that as it may, when courts do allow the contractor a recovery, the narrowness of the subrogation fact pattern hardly suggests the breadth of the Restatement's rule.

The Restatement also relied upon a Minnesota case[13] in which the defendant, a stockyards company, allegedly (a) refused to permit the plaintiff to enter its land and (b) prohibited employers operating in the yards from continuing the plaintiff's employment. The plaintiff, who had been employed by a commission merchant in the stockyards, consequently either lost his employment or was prevented from performing his job and either way lost his wages. The court did not distinguish the two types of interference but in a one-page per curiam opinion concluded without explanation that the complaint stated a cause of action for interference with contract relations. If the case means that by contracting with another person I can acquire the right to enter and use your land against your will, the principle is foreign to American law; it supports the Restatement like a pillar of jelly. If the case turns on some narrower rule unrevealed by the opaque opinion—perhaps on notions of discrimination, restraint of trade, or the obligations of a public utility—it suggests some narrow rule quite unlike the Restatement's global one. Some other cases relied upon by the Restatement also interfered with

10. Sidney Blumenthal & Co. v. United States, 30 F.2d 247 (2d Cir.1929) (loss of goods and conversion).

11. Coonis v. Rogers, 429 S.W.2d 709 (Mo.1968) (defendant put sugar in competitor's garbage truck gas tank).

12. Piedmont Cotton Mills, Inc. v. H.W. Ivey Const. Co., 109 Ga.App. 876, 137 S.E.2d 528 (1964). Perhaps there are reasons to deny even this kind of recovery in some cases. The California Court said so in Fifield Manor v. Finston, 54 Cal.2d 632, 7 Cal.Rptr. 377, 354 P.2d 1073 (1960), where the the plaintiff was under contract to provide medical care to T, who was personally injured by the defendant's negligence. The court thought that subrogation in a personal injury case was inappropriate.

13. Bacon v. St. Paul Union Stockyards Co., 161 Minn. 522, 201 N.W. 326 (1924).

the plaintiff's performance by first inducing a breach by another and thus fell at least partly within § 766.[14]

§ 449. Intentional Interference by a Contracting Party

Courts have commonly said that it is not a tort to interfere with one's own contract. Sometimes they use stronger expression: only a stranger to the contract can be liable for any species of interference. However, expressed, the rule generates two sets of issues.

Interference by Persons Identified with a Contracting Party

Agents and those identified with a contracting party. First, some courts have considered that agents of a contracting party are so identified with that party's interests that the agents should be treated as if they were also parties to the contract.[1] The result is that agents cannot be liable for interfering with the contract between their principals and the plaintiff. The idea has been expanded in some courts to treat all those with a financial interest as if they were parties and hence to protect them from liability. Stockholders and partners, for example, can advise the promisor to breach so long as they are acting in part in the interest of the promisor and not adversely to him.[2] The Supreme Court of Georgia has said that a defendant is not liable unless he is not only a stranger to any contract involved but also a stranger to the entire set of interwoven contractual or business relationships involved.[3]

Other courts have tackled the problem of the liability of agents and others who are financially involved by turning to the concepts of privilege, justification, or wrongfulness. Under this approach, courts say that an agent is not acting improperly at all (or is privileged) when he advises his principal to breach a contract, so long as he does so within the scope of his employment and not solely for malevolent purposes, but that once his motive ceases to include his employer's interest, he becomes liable.[4]

Interference by Contracting Party

Interference claim against contracting party. The rule that the defendant is not liable to the plaintiff in tort for interfering with the

14. White v. Massee, 202 Iowa 1304, 211 N.W. 839 (1927); Rinaldi v. Tana, 252 Md. 544, 250 A.2d 533 (1969).

§ 449

1. E.g., Daniel Adams Assocs., Inc. v. Rimbach Publ'g, Inc., 360 Pa.Super. 72, 519 A.2d 997 (1987).

2. E.g., Broussard v. Meineke Discount Muffler Shops, Inc., 155 F.3d 331 (4th Cir. 1998) (parent corporation of promisor).

3. Atlanta Mkt. Ctr. Management Co. v. McLane, 269 Ga. 604, 610, 503 S.E.2d 278, 283 (1998) ("one must be a stranger to both the contract at issue and the business relationship giving rise to and underpinning the contract").

4. Los Angeles Airways, Inc. v. Davis, 687 F.2d 321 (9th Cir. 1982); Storm & Assocs., Ltd. v. Cuculich, 298 Ill.App.3d 1040, 1051, 700 N.E.2d 202, 210, 233 Ill. Dec. 101, 109(1998) ("The proposition that an agent can never be held liable for wrongfully interfering with his principal's contracts is far too broad. Even in circumstances where an agent is cloaked with a qualified privilege, a claim for tortious interference may lie where the agent's actions in interfering with the principal's contract are unjustified or malicious, such as where the agent's conduct is totally unrelated or antagonistic to the principal's interests").

plaintiff-defendant contract is perhaps best interpreted as an overstatement that can be spelled out more precisely and more workably like this:

(1) Interference with promisee's relations with others. The defendant cannot interfere with the contractual rights between himself and the plaintiff; that is merely breach. However, he can interfere with rights between the plaintiff and other persons such as the plaintiff's customers. For instance, a creditor to whom a business owes money may interfere with the debtor's relation with her customers by driving them away, to the detriment of the debtor's business and a suit to recover damages for that interference would be permissible[5] because it would not be a suit to recover expectancy damages under the contract.[6]

(2) Interference by breach of contract. (a) Limiting liability to contract. If the defendant's "interference" between the plaintiff and others is accomplished merely by breach of the plaintiff-defendant contract, liability should ordinarily be the liability imposed for breach of contract. With an exception to be mentioned,[7] tort liability for the stand-alone economic consequences of a breach is almost always inappropriate, although breach of a safety contract that leads to physical harm is a different matter. Contracting parties expect the contract to express the scope of their responsibilities on matters governed by the contract, so courts honor the contract by limiting the liability for breach to a contract action.[8] One effect of this is to say that the plaintiff cannot recover emotional harm and punitive damages that are normally available only in tort actions. Thus courts can rightly hold that breach of contract alone does not establish either improper purpose or improper means, even though the defendant can foresee that his breach will interfere with the plaintiff's relations with others.[9] Likewise, if the contract limits the recovery to liquidated damages, the defendant who "interferes" by breaching should be limited to the liability provided for in the liquidated damages clause.[10]

(b) Breach leading to tort liability. In spite of what has just been said, courts have sometimes treated contract breach as a tort for which punitive and emotional distress damages may be recovered. Some have said that although the defendant is not liable for breaching his own

5. Leigh Furniture and Carpet Co. v. Isom, 657 P.2d 293 (Utah 1982); see K & K Management, Inc. v. Lee, 316 Md. 137, 160, 557 A.2d 965, 976 (1989) ("the breach or threatened breach of the P–D contract may be the instrument selected by D for the purpose of interfering with the P–T contract").

6. See Mark P. Gergen, Tortious Interference: How It Is Engulfing Commercial Law, Why This Is Not Entirely Bad, and a Prudential Response, 38 Ariz. L. Rev. 1175, 1184, n. 48 (1996).

7. § 453.

8. Colorado Nat'l Bank of Denver v. Friedman, 846 P.2d 159 (Colo.1993) (applying the rule to the personal representative of a deceased party).

9. See Applied Equip. Corp. v. Litton Saudi Arabia Ltd., 7 Cal.4th 503, 515, 869 P.2d 454, 460, 28 Cal.Rptr.2d 475, 481 (1994) ("Conduct amounting to a breach of contract becomes tortious only when it also violates an independent duty arising from principles of tort law"); K & K Management, Inc. v. Lee, 316 Md. 137, 557 A.2d 965 (1989).

10. Memorial Gardens, Inc. v. Olympian Sales & Management Consultants, Inc., 690 P.2d 207 (Colo.1984).

contract, he becomes liable when he breaches it in conspiracy with others.[11] Otherwise, courts have used two different theories when imposing liability in tort for breach of contract: first, that bad faith breach of some covenants is a tort, an idea summarized later; and, second, that breach of a contract can be an improper interference with the plaintiff's business or contracts with others. For example, although it was unnecessary to the decision, the Utah Supreme Court concluded that breach of a contract plus a bad motive taken together would be grounds for tort liability against the breacher[12] and some other courts have said the same.[13] Where the defendant uses improper means in addition to the breach, or uses the breach to capture for himself the part of the contract's harvest allocated by the contract itself to the plaintiff, liability is easier to support, since in that case it is grounded in something more than breach and bad attitudes. Some cases of tort liability for interference by breach seem to be justified on those grounds.[14] However, some authority seems to treat breach of a contract as itself a wrongful interference, thus potentially converting all contract breaches into tort.[15]

(3) Interference by exercising a right. If the defendant's "interference" represents the exercise of a right the defendant has under the contract or otherwise, the plaintiff ordinarily has no claim for either breach or tortious interference. On the face of things, it seems logically and morally impossible for a court to impose liability for exercise of a right. As the Oregon Court said, exercise of an express contractual remedy by definition reflects the reasonable expectations of the parties and tort liability may not be imposed simply because the defendant had a bad motive for exercising his right.[16] But some authority has taken the position that interference with the plaintiff's contract or prospects is actionable even when the only interference is the exercise of defendant's own contract rights or remedies.[17]

11. See, summarizing this authority, Joseph P. Caulfield & Assocs., Inc. v. Litho Prods., Inc., 155 F.3d 883 (7th Cir.1998). Conspiracy liability is firmly rejected in other cases. See Applied Equip. Corp. v. Litton Saudi Arabia Ltd., 7 Cal.4th 503, 869 P.2d 454, 28 Cal.Rptr.2d 475 (1994).

12. Leigh Furniture and Carpet Co. v. Isom, 657 P.2d 293 (Utah 1982). A later Utah decision suggests that the role of motive should be reconsidered. Pratt v. Prodata, Inc., 885 P.2d 786, 789 n. 3 (Utah 1994).

13. Cherberg v. Peoples Nat'l Bank of Washington, 88 Wash.2d 595, 564 P.2d 1137 (1977) (lessor's refusal to repair structural defects in leased premises was a constructive eviction and also an interference with tenant's business).

14. Buxbom v. Smith, 23 Cal.2d 535, 145 P.2d 305 (1944) (defendant contracted for plaintiff to leave his business and set up a distribution network for defendant, sharing certain profits; once the network was in place, defendant breached the contract by terminating it, then took over the network). Such cases may also be explained on economic analysis. See Lillian R. BeVier, Reconsidering Inducement, 76 Va. L. Rev. 877, 932–33 (1990).

15. Trimed, Inc. v. Sherwood Med. Co., 977 F.2d 885 (4th Cir.1992).

16. Uptown Heights Assocs. Ltd. Partnership v. Seafirst Corp., 320 Or. 638, 651, 891 P.2d 639, 647 (1995).

17. Woody v. Tamer, 158 Mich.App. 764, 405 N.W.2d 213 (1987) (seller agreed that buyer of business would (a) pay in installments but (b) would not be personally liable upon default, leaving the land as security; buyer defaulted, seller could not make his own debt payments, and seller lost the land; held an actionable interference). This case and others are discussed in detail in Mark P. Gergen, Tortious Interference: How It Is Engulfing Commercial Law, Why This Is Not Entirely Bad, and a Prudential Response, 38 Ariz. L. Rev. 1175 (1996).

§ 450. Intentional Interference with Economic Opportunity

Characteristics of the tort. As with the other claims discussed in this chapter, the claim for interference with economic opportunity or prospects refers to stand-alone economic loss without physical harm either to person or property. It differs from the claim for interference with contract in that the defendant does not interfere with an existing and enforceable contract but merely with the plaintiff's probable economic advantage, such as a likely prospect of selling goods to a buyer who was willing to purchase. The plaintiff need not have a prospect of obtaining a contract; it is enough if she has a probable prospect of economic gain.[1]

Opportunity vs. contract rules. The rules for the tort are similar to those invoked in interference with contract cases. However, the defendant has greater freedom to pursue his own economic interests by interfering with the plaintiff's economic opportunity than by interfering with the plaintiff's contracts.[2] In addition, some courts that put the burden upon the defendant to justify an interference with contract reverse the burden and require the plaintiff to prove that interference was wrongful in the opportunity cases.[3] For these reasons, interference with economic opportunity or prospects can be considered a separate tort for purposes of identifying elements and defenses.[4] Under various names, the tort is now generally recognized.[5]

Scope; at will and unenforceable contracts. The mainstream idea today is that an at will contract represents a protectible interest. In one case, a defendant who merely explained to a landlord that she had a right to evict a tenant and procured a lawyer to initiate an eviction was held liable, although he apparently only assisted the landlord in exercising her rights and the tenant lost nothing she had a right to keep.[6] Although courts do protect at will contracts, most appear to treat them realistically as merely reflecting business opportunities or prospective advantage. At will contracts therefore come under the rule protecting competitors and limiting liability to cases of interference by improper means.[7] Unenforceable contracts, so long as they are not illegal and do

§ 450

1. Hannex Corp. v. GMI, Inc., 140 F.3d 194 (2d Cir.1998).

2. E.g., NBT Bancorp Inc. v. Fleet/Norstar Fin. Group, Inc., 87 N.Y.2d 614, 664 N.E.2d 492, 641 N.Y.S.2d 581 (1996).

3. Compare Penna v. Toyota Motor Sales, U.S.A., Inc., 11 Cal.4th 376, 902 P.2d 740, 45 Cal.Rptr.2d 436 (1995) with Quelimane Co., Inc. v. Stewart Title Guar. Co., 19 Cal.4th 26, 960 P.2d 513, 77 Cal.Rptr.2d 709 (1998).

4. Sometimes courts cluster all the interference torts together under the rubric "tortious interference," viewing them as a single, expansive tort with different branches. E.g., Lake Shore Investors v. Rite Aid Corp., 67 Md.App. 743, 509 A.2d 727 (1986). This may be appropriate for the purpose of pleading, assessing damages, or interpreting old language in the cases. But because substantive tort policies, elements, and defenses differ among the various interference torts, it is convenient if not essential to speak of separate torts.

5. See James O. Pearson, Liability For Interference With At Will Business Relationship, 5 A.L.R.4th 9 (1981).

6. Fossett v. Davis, 531 So.2d 849 (Ala. 1988) (tenant moved out upon second eviction notice, no indication that landlord lacked right to evict).

7. Storm & Assocs., Ltd. v. Cuculich, 298 Ill.App.3d 1040, 1051, 700 N.E.2d 202, 210, 233 Ill.Dec. 101, 109 (1998); Silverman

not promote an illegal objective,[8] are logically in the same category, which is to say they represent prospects, not existing contracts and they fall under the rules for opportunities rather than the rules for contracts.[9]

Basing liability upon assertedly bad motive. Although changes may be in the air,[10] courts have sometimes held interference with economic opportunity actionable when the defendant's interference is improperly motivated, even when the defendant's acts are objectively proper and within the defendant's rights. Among several extreme cases allowing relief for proper acts done with a motive the court condemns,[11] *Deauville*[12] furnishes a simple illustration of the motive problem. Federated was actively developing a large shopping mall and had some anchor tenants. It induced Ward, a retailer, to sign on, knowing that Ward had earlier signed on with a competing mall, but knowing also that Ward had the right to withdraw from that contract. Ward did withdraw and the competing mall developer, Deauville, sued Federated for interfering with its contract with Ward. The court concluded that Federated and Deauville were competitors for Ward's tenancy and that Ward was not contractually committed to remain with Deauville. Nevertheless, the court held that a jury could find that Federated's motive was "only to harm Deauville" and that if the jury so found, Federated would be liable. Decisions like this can chill appropriate competition. Even if courts have a roving commission to root out bad thoughts and inspect the inner purposes of economic actors, liability for motive alone is an especially bad idea when it comes to competitive behavior that is otherwise permissible. As the Restatement of Unfair Competition says, the public benefits of competition do not correlate with the defendant's motivation.[13]

v. Progressive Broadcasting, Inc., 964 P.2d 61, 125 N.M. 500 (1998); Guard–Life Corp. v. S. Parker Hardware Mfg. Corp., 50 N.Y.2d 183, 406 N.E.2d 445, 428 N.Y.S.2d 628 (1980). Perhaps a contract that can be terminated only after notice and a waiting period should be treated as a durational rather than an at will contract. See Ahern v. Boeing Co., 701 F.2d 142 (11th Cir.1983) (describing such as contract as an at will contract but holding that interference was not privileged).

8. E.g., Thomas v. Ratiner, 462 So.2d 1157 (Fla.Dist.Ct.App.1984) (attorney-doctor illegally obtained retainer from hospital patient, defendant firm could not be liable for interfering with that contract).

9. Bed, Bath & Beyond of La Jolla, Inc. v. La Jolla Village Square Venture Partners, 52 Cal.App.4th 867, 60 Cal.Rptr.2d 830 (1997) (oral agreement to lease unenforceable under statute of fraud, competition privilege to compete without wrongful means applied to protect defendant interferer); Guard–Life Corp. v. S. Parker Hardware Mfg. Corp., 50 N.Y.2d 183, 406 N.E.2d 445, 428 N.Y.S.2d 628 (1980).

10. See the paragraph, *Rejecting or ameliorating motive-based liability* below.

11. Alyeska Pipeline Serv. Co. v. Aurora Air Serv., Inc., 604 P.2d 1090 (Alaska 1979) (defendant exercised its contract option to terminate a contract, which led contractor to exercise its option to terminate the plaintiff's subcontract, defendant liable) (criticized in Dan B. Dobbs, Tortious Interference with Contractual Relationships, 34 Ark. L. Rev. 335 (1980)); Smith v. Ford Motor Co., 289 N.C. 71, 221 S.E.2d 282, 79 A.L.R.3d 651 (1976) (although Ford dealership had a right to terminate the plaintiff's employment, Ford itself could be held liable for inducing the dealership to do so, in spite of Ford's belief that its business interests were at stake; emphasis on "bad" motive).

12. Deauville Corp. v. Federated Dept. Stores, Inc., 756 F.2d 1183 (5th Cir.1985).

13. Restatement Third of Unfair Competition § 1, cmt. c (1995).

Rejecting or ameliorating motive-based liability. It is difficult to be sure, but courts may be moving away from motive-based liabilities. Important decisions have now begun to insist that the plaintiff has the burden of proving improper interference by "conduct that was wrongful by some legal measure other than the fact of interference itself."[14] Courts increasingly appear to recognize that the defendant's pursuit of economic gain deserves as much protection as the plaintiff's and that the defendant is free to compete with the plaintiff for economic opportunity so long as the defendant does not use improper means and the interference does not create an illegal restraint of trade or monopoly.[15] Improper means include physical violence and any conduct that is independently tortious such as bribery, unfounded litigation, fraud, misrepresentation, defamation, duress, undue influence, misuse of inside or confidential information, or breach of a fiduciary relationship.[16]

Competition. Competition itself represents both lawful means and good motive that suffices to justify the defendant's competitive action. Even if the defendant's psyche was tinged with dislike of the plaintiff or similar "bad" motive, courts will protect the defendant against liability if he also had justifiable motives such as competition.[17] Thus as a practical matter most courts probably do not now impose liability for lawful competition even if it is accompanied by some bad motive. In fact, courts may directly recognize that the defendant is simply free to compete without using unlawful or wrongful means.[18]

Under these rules, you are thus free to induce my customers, employees, or suppliers to deal with you instead of me, as long they are not bound to me by contract and your conduct does not restrain trade. Without a rule recognizing the rightfulness of competition, "the whole competitive order of American industry" would be "prima facie illegal."[19] Beyond this, many cases that still use the language of malice and motive now also speak of the defendant's "economic interest," not merely his competition, that justifies interference.[20] Thus if the defendant has an

14. Penna v. Toyota Motor Sales, U.S.A., Inc., 11 Cal.4th 376, 902 P.2d 740, 45 Cal.Rptr.2d 436 (1995).

15. Restatement § 768.

16. Peace v. Conway, 246 Va. 278, 281, 435 S.E.2d 133, 135 (1993)

17. The defendant is not liable even under the more stringent cases when his *predominant* motive is justifiable. See Alyeska Pipeline Serv. Co. v. Aurora Air Serv. Inc., supra n. 11. A rule more favorable to competition is that the defendant is not liable for conduct amounting to competitive interference with bad motive unless the bad motive is the *sole* motive. See PPX Enters., Inc. v. Audiofidelity Enters., Inc., 818 F.2d 266, 269 (2d Cir.1987); Silverman v. Progressive Broadcasting, Inc., 125 N.M. 500, 964 P.2d 61 (1998). A third view rejects liability if the justifiable motive would have produced the same conduct by the defendant. See See Mt. Healthy City Sch. Dist. Bd. of Ed. v. Doyle, 429 U.S. 274, 97 S.Ct. 568, 50 L.Ed.2d 471 (1977) and § 446.

18. E.g., Bed, Bath & Beyond of La Jolla, Inc. v. La Jolla Village Square Venture Partners, 52 Cal.App.4th 867, 60 Cal. Rptr.2d 830 (1997).

19. See 46 ALI PROCEEDINGS 201 ("foreign lawyers reading the Restatement . . . would find it astounding that the whole competitive order of American industry is prima facie illegal") (statement of Professor Carl Auerbach).

20. Langer v. Becker, 176 Ill.App.3d 745, 531 N.E.2d 830, 126 Ill.Dec. 203 (1988) (defendant can interfere to protect his own equal or greater economic interest); Foster v. Churchill, 87 N.Y.2d 744, 665 N.E.2d 153, 642 N.Y.S.2d 583 (1996) (defendant's economic interest is a "defense" even to

economic interest to pursue, his right to "interfere" may be protected in the same way, even if he is not classed as a "competitor."[21]

Remaining liability risks. Decisions that reject motive-based liability provide an improvement, but defendants actively pursuing their own economic interests often remain at risk for liability. One reason is that some courts have been quick to find that the defendant used improper means even when the defendant's "interference" would not be independently tortious[22] and would likely have been protected by a privilege under the rules for defamation.[23]

Another remaining risk is that the court may characterize the plaintiff's economic prospects as an existing contract, thus excluding the defendant's right to compete. In the famous *Texaco v. Pennzoil* case,[24] Getty Oil and Pennzoil had an arrangement not reduced to writing, but intended to lead to the complex sale or merger of the two oil companies. Texaco offered Getty shareholders a better price. Pennzoil recovered almost $10 billion against Texaco for interference with its Getty contract. The court thought that a jury could find the oral agreement, which might look only like a prospect of a contract to outsiders, was actually an enforceable contract. Hence the competitor's privilege would not apply and liability could be imposed. As *Texaco* shows, competitors are at risk for utter destruction if the judge or jury draw mistaken inferences, potentially a serious chill on competition.[25]

§ 451. Intentional Interference with Noncommercial Opportunities

Courts have extended liability for interference with economic opportunity to some but not all noncommercial opportunities. Liability is

interference with existing contracts unless he is guilty of "malice or illegality"); St. Benedict's Dev. Co. v. St. Benedict's Hosp., 811 P.2d 194 (Utah 1991) (but recognizing that liability might be imposed if desire to harm was predominant purpose).

21. See Lyon v. Campbell, 120 Md.App. 412, 431, 707 A.2d 850, 860 (Md.Ct. Spec.App. 1998) ("Tortious or deliberate intent to harm a plaintiff's business relationship is not alone sufficient to support an intentional interference claim. There also must be proof that the defendant's conduct in interfering with contract or business relations was accomplished through improper means"); Peace v. Conway, 246 Va. 278, 281, 435 S.E.2d 133, 135 (1993) (improper means required); cf. Central Bank of Lake of the Ozarks v. Shackleford, 896 S.W.2d 948 (Mo.App.1995) (bank's financial interest gave it a privilege such that it would be liable only if interference was accomplished by independently wrongful means).

22. Voorhees v. Guyan Mach. Co., 191 W.Va. 450, 446 S.E.2d 672 (1994) (threat of suit; no finding that suit would have been abuse of process or wrongful civil suit, but liability for interference resulting from the seemingly honest threat).

23. See Centro Nautico Representacoes Nauticas, LDA. v. International Marine Co-op, Ltd., 719 So.2d 967 (Fla.Dist.Ct.App. 1998) (critical statements about promisee induced promisor's breach but court does not demonstrate that the statements would be actionable as slander); Magnum Radio, Inc. v. Brieske, 217 Wis.2d 130, 577 N.W.2d 377 (Wis.Ct.App.1998) (objections to FCC license for plaintiff's proposed radio station, not demonstrated to be actionable as a libel).

24. Texaco, Inc. v. Pennzoil Co., 729 S.W.2d 768 (Tex. Ct. App. 1987).

25. Cf. Matsushita Elec. Ind. Co. Ltd. v. Zenith Radio Corp., 475 U.S. 574, 594, 106 S.Ct. 1348, 1360, 89 L.Ed.2d 538, 545 (1986) (discussing the risks of mistaken inferences of conspiracies in restraint of trade; such inferences "are especially costly, because they chill the very conduct the antitrust laws are designed to protect").

sometimes imposed for interference with a reasonably expected gift or inheritance and for interference with a good opportunity to recover in a lawsuit. Even so, in the few decisions on point, courts have been loath to permit recovery for interference with elections and sporting events that does not involve some specific tort.

Interference with gift, devise, or inheritance. Courts have recognized a cause of action against defendants who prevent the plaintiff from receiving an inheritance or gift she would otherwise have received, provided the defendant uses undue influence, duress, or tortious means such as fraud or murder.[1] The form of the property interest does not control the right, but may affect the remedy. Interference with inheritance, devise, trust, life insurance, or rights of survivorship will all be actionable if the plaintiff is tortiously deprived.[2] Many acts can count as improper interference. Preventing a testator from making or revoking a will, inducing him to make a new one, or murdering an ancestor or cotenant to accelerate inheritance[3] will all suffice. The defendant might even induce the would-be testator to give away all his property during his lifetime, and some decisions have allowed the plaintiff to sue the tortfeasor in such cases even though the would-be testator is still alive and would be able to recover the donation himself if it had been procured by tortious means.[4] Liability turns on proof that the defendant used tortious means, or at least duress or undue influence. In this respect it differs from the usual case of interference with commercial interests where bad motive or vaguely improper means is often enough to impose liability.

The plaintiff must prove that the defendant's tort caused her loss. That is, the plaintiff must prove that, more likely than not, she had an expectancy and would have received it but for the defendant's tort. Sometimes her burden is expressed by saying that she must prove the expectancy and its loss to a reasonable certainty.[5] Since the transmission of property at death is often a matter committed to specialized tribunals such as probate courts, the tort action may itself interfere with orderly procedure, so some courts have also said that the tort action should not lie in the case of interference with inheritance if the matter can be adequately handled in a will contest or the like.[6]

§ 451

1. E.g., Nemeth v. Banhalmi, 99 Ill. App.3d 493, 425 N.E.2d 1187, 55 Ill.Dec. 14 (1981); Bohannon v. Wachovia Bank & Trust Co., 210 N.C. 679, 188 S.E. 390 (1936); Restatement § 774B; Sonja A. Soehnel, Annotation, Liability in Damages for Interference with Expected Inheritance or Gift, 22 A.L.R.4th 1229 (1981).

2. See the varieties of property right listed in Dan B. Dobbs, Law of Remedies § 6.7 (2d ed. 1993).

3. Statutes usually control when the interference is by way of murder. See Dan B. Dobbs, Law of Remedies § 6.7 (2d ed. 1993). A number of different remedial measurements are possible when a cotenant is murdered. See Id.

4. Harmon v. Harmon, 404 A.2d 1020 (Me.1979).

5. See, e.g., Estate of Mocny, 257 Ill. App.3d 291, 630 N.E.2d 87, 196 Ill.Dec. 390 (1993); Restatement § 774B, cmt. d.

6. See Moore v. Graybeal, 843 F.2d 706 (3d Cir.1988); Sonja A. Soehnel, Annotation, Liability in Damages for Interference with Expected Inheritance or Gift, 22 A.L.R.4th 1229 (1981); but cf. Plimpton v. Gerrard, 668 A.2d 882 (Me.1995) (Superior

When the claim is fashioned as a tortious interference claim, the normal remedy is damages representing the plaintiff's lost expectancy. As always, the expectancy must be reasonably certain, but the trier is permitted to estimate that certainty from circumstantial evidence.[7] Instead of damages, the plaintiff may recover a constructive trust in appropriate cases,[8] and often may attack a transaction that interferes with inheritance by a will contest rather than by a tort suit.

Interference with evidence; "spoliation" by a party. When a party to litigation alters or destroys physical evidence or documents relevant to the litigation, courts have said that his adversary may be entitled to a presumption (or permissible inference) that the evidence was favorable to her and unfavorable to the evidence destroyer. Because the presumption and other in-trial sanctions will at least roughly remedy the problem, courts have usually said that in such cases the plaintiff has no independent tort action against the adversary who destroyed evidence.[9]

Spoliation by a non-party. When it comes to destruction by non-parties, the problem is surprisingly complex. A third person's destruction of evidence clearly does not warrant a presumption against a defendant who had nothing to do with the destruction,[10] so in that case, a tort action may be the plaintiff's only hope. If the physical evidence is property rightfully owned or possessed by the plaintiff, T's intentional destruction will ordinarily be actionable as a conversion or trespass, but proximate cause and reasonable certainty rules of damages may tend to limit liability to the value of the property as a tangible good unless T

Court and probate court had concurrent jurisdiction, and plaintiff could get a jury trial in Superior Court on the tort claim; theoretical adequacy of probate contest is no bar to the tort claim in Superior Court).

7. E.g., Nemeth v. Banhalmi, 99 Ill. App.3d 493, 425 N.E.2d 1187, 55 Ill.Dec. 14 (1981) (prior wills in favor of the plaintiff plus an obligation to plaintiff).

8. See 1 Dan B. Dobbs, Law of Remedies § 6.7 (2d ed. 1993).

9. Cedars–Sinai Med. Ctr. v. Superior Court, 18 Cal.4th 1, 954 P.2d 511, 74 Cal. Rptr.2d 248 (1998) (when the destroyer is a party and the destruction or loss of evidence is discovered in time to claim the presumption); Trevino v. Ortega, 969 S.W.2d 950 (Tex.1998) (not passing on spoliation by non-parties); but cf. Hazen v. Municipality of Anchorage, 718 P.2d 456 (Alaska 1986) (claim that prosecuting authorities in a criminal case altered a tape to make it incriminating); contra, allowing the tort action against one who is a party-defendant, Bethea v. Modern Biomedical Servs., Inc., 704 So.2d 1227 (La.Ct.App. 1997). See generally Thomas G. Fischer, Intentional Spoliation of Evidence, Interfering With Prospective Civil Action as Actionable, 70 A.L.R.4th 984 (1990). Distinguish physical harm resulting from destruction of a thing or information: defendant destroys information that would show the antidote to a poison and plaintiff suffers needlessly because the information is not available. This is an ordinary negligence or intentional harm case. See La Raia v. Superior Court, 150 Ariz. 118, 722 P.2d 286 (1986).

10. Cf. Boyd v. Travelers Ins. Co., 166 Ill.2d 188, 652 N.E.2d 267, 209 Ill.Dec. 727 (1995) (refusing also to apply a presumption against the third person that the loss of evidence caused loss of the suit). If the third person is the defendant's agent acting within his employment, the presumption against the defendant may be appropriate. In some cases the third person is apparently not an agent for the defendant but stands in some special relationship to him such that one might reasonably suspect that the third person has acted for the defendant's benefit. Hospitals which "lose" innumerable records may be protecting staff doctors from malpractice suits; employers who destroy their harm-causing property may be protecting their subsidiary from a products suit. See Austin v. Consolidation Coal Co., 256 Va. 78, 501 S.E.2d 161 (Va. 1998).

knew of its importance in existing or probable litigation. However, even if the plaintiff does not own the destroyed property, T's intentional destruction of it with knowledge of its importance in litigation has been held to be a tort warranting damages for lost litigation opportunities.[11] But there are numerous concerns that have led the California Court to reject the whole idea of a tort against third persons for intentional destruction of evidence.[12] Relitigation by disappointed losers, the speculative nature of the claim, the potential for confusion are among the reasons given for rejecting the claim. In addition, it may be noted that when the destroyed evidence consists of property that has not been subjected to the court's process and is owned outright by the alleged non-party spoliator, ordinary property rules permit the defendant to destroy the property as he wishes.[13]

Negligent spoliation. Liability for negligent interference with the plaintiff's lawsuit prospects is perhaps even more problematical. As with intentional interference, damages are likely to be speculative. In addition, courts are generally cautious about imposing a duty of reasonable care to protect a plaintiff's purely economic prospects. Consequently, liability of a third person for negligent interference with evidence is frequently rejected,[14] unless the third person undertakes to preserve the evidence,[15] a statute requires him to do so,[16] or other special circumstances warrant imposition of a duty.

Causation and value of the chance in spoliation cases. Causation and damages raise difficult issues in all spoliation cases. The plaintiff must contend that the spoliator has destroyed evidence that would have allowed the plaintiff to recover in the underlying suit and that she cannot recover because the evidence is missing. But if the plaintiff does not know what the evidence would show, she cannot possibly show that it would have saved her suit. If she can prove indirectly what the evidence would have shown, she could presumably have proved the same thing in the underlying suit. Perhaps some of the courts that recognize

11. Coleman v. Eddy Potash, Inc., 120 N.M. 645, 905 P.2d 185 (1995) (intent to disrupt lawsuit as well as to significantly alter evidence, even when the evidence consisted of the defendant's own property); Smith v. Howard Johnson Co., Inc., 67 Ohio St.3d 28, 615 N.E.2d 1037 (1993) (no mention of ownership in recognizing the tort).

12. Temple Community Hospital v. Superior Court, 20 Cal.4th 464, 84 Cal.Rptr.2d 852, 976 P.2d 223 (1999) (a 4–3 decision).

13. E.g., Austin v. Consolidation Coal Co., 256 Va. 78, 501 S.E.2d 161 (Va. 1998) (employer who had paid workers' compensation destroyed instrumentality causing harm, which interfered with plaintiff's action against manufacturer, but property was the employer's so its destruction was not actionable).

14. Coleman v. Eddy Potash, Inc., 120 N.M. 645, 905 P.2d 185 (1995).

15. Holmes v. Amerex Rent–A–Car, 710 A.2d 846 (D.C.1998); Boyd v. Travelers Ins. Co., 166 Ill.2d 188, 652 N.E.2d 267, 209 Ill.Dec. 727 (1995) (saying that this is not a separate tort but ordinary negligence based upon an assumed duty of care); Callahan v. Stanley Works, 306 N.J.Super. 488, 703 A.2d 1014 (1997) (voluntary assumption of a duty to preserve would be a jury question where defendant placed evidence tag on harmful instrumentality then lost it); cf. Smith v. Superior Court, 151 Cal.App.3d 491, 198 Cal.Rptr. 829 (1984) (promise to preserve evidence).

16. Bondu v. Gurvich, 473 So.2d 1307 (Fla.Dist.Ct.App.1984) (hospital required to maintain medical records, cause of action stated for negligent loss which resulted in loss of plaintiff's malpractice suit; hospital was a defendant in the underlying suit).

the tort claim assume that the normal burden of proof is to be relaxed. The District of Columbia Court has said that the plaintiff need only prove "that the underlying lawsuit was significantly impaired, that the spoliated evidence was material to that impairment, and that the plaintiff enjoyed a significant possibility of success in the underlying claim." Recovery would then be limited to the value of the chance of recovery.[17]

Interference with game or contest. The Restatement suggests that interference with one's chance of winning a game or contest of economic value would be actionable if the chances of winning before the interference were quite substantial.[18] While some courts may be forgiving when it comes to proof of causation in spoliation cases, the plaintiff who loses a game or contest after the defendant tortiously interferes may face tougher resistance. The California Supreme Court has held that the plaintiff is required to prove that, but for the interference, she would have won and that, as a matter of law such proof could not be made, at least in the ordinary horse race. The same court thought that as a matter of public policy, courts should not be judging games and sports when the claim was one for prospective economic loss rather than physical injury.[19] It may be, however, that when the defendant not only tortiously interferes with the plaintiff's opportunity but also himself profits from the interference, the plaintiff would be permitted in some cases to recover the defendant's gain.

§ 452. Negligent Interference with Contract or Economic Interests

Disfavoring Liability

General rule. When economic harm results from harm to person or property, ordinary negligence rules apply. When commercial or economic harm stands alone, divorced from injury to person or property, courts have not imposed a general duty of reasonable care.[1] They have instead imposed a duty of reasonable care in commercial harm cases mainly when the parties are in a special relationship and the defendant has implicitly undertaken such a duty. Lawyers and accountants whose malpractice may inflict economic harm upon their clients are examples of a duty undertaken.[2] In contrast, defective products may cause economic

17. Holmes v. Amerex Rent–A–Car, 710 A.2d 846 (D.C.App.1998) (if plaintiff would have had 60% chance of recovering $100,-000 given the missing evidence, plaintiff's recovery for its destruction would be $60,-000).

18. Restatement § 774B, Special Note.

19. Youst v. Longo, 43 Cal.3d 64, 729 P.2d 728, 233 Cal.Rptr. 294, 85 A.L.R.4th 1025 (1987). For various factual situations involving contests, see Lisa A. Ferguson, Annotation, Recovery in Tort for Wrongful Interference with Chance to Win Game, Sporting Event, or Contest, 85 A.L.R.4th 1048 (1991).

§ 452

1. E.g., Misany v. United States, 873 F.2d 160 (7th Cir.1989) (Wisconsin law, intent required for interference with contract or prospects); AFM Corp. v. Southern Bell Telephone & Tel. Co., 515 So.2d 180 (Fla. 1987) (negligent failure to list telephone numbers, no liability in negligence for economic harm).

2. See § 484. Negligent misrepresentation may be actionable as well, but usually only when some special relationship is established. See § 472. Libel has a wholly different history and liability even today

loss if they do not work well; but so long as they do not cause physical harm to person or property, most courts do not impose liability in tort. In those cases, courts limit the manufacturer's liability to contract or warranty claims.[3] Since a duty of reasonable care is not ordinarily owed to protect against purely commercial loss, courts do not generally impose liability for negligent interference with contract or with opportunities. Liability attaches only for intentional interference.[4]

Bases of the rule. Reasons for the economic or commercial loss rule are of at least two general kinds. First, financial harm tends to generate other financial harm endlessly and often in many directions. Liability in most pure commercial harm cases would be onerous for defendants and burdensome for courts. Second, where commercial loss is suffered by parties to a transaction, contract law is adequate to deal with the problem and also usually more appropriate.[5] In particular, imposition of duties in tort at odds with the contract rights established between the parties would undermine contract law.[6]

Physical harm to A with economic harm to B. In one kind of case, the defendant negligently causes physical harm to A which results in economic harm to B. The economic loss rule has been applied to prevent a recovery by B. In the classic kind of case, the defendant negligently damages A's factory, with the result that B and other factory workers have no job until the factory is repaired. Although the defendant had caused physical damage to A, and is liable for it, he is not liable for B's purely economic loss.[7] The same is true if the worker is injured and the employer loses his services with resulting economic harm; the employer's stand-alone economic loss is not actionable as an interference with the employer's contract with her employee or otherwise.[8] Others may suffer

may not require intent, but in that case, elements of personal indignity often predominate over purely economic loss. See Chapter 28.

3. E.g., East River Steamship Corp., v. Transamerica Delaval, Inc., 476 U.S. 858, 106 S.Ct. 2295, 90 L.Ed.2d 865 (1986); Moorman Mfg. Co. v. National Tank Co., 91 Ill.2d 69, 61 Ill.Dec. 746, 435 N.E.2d 443 (1982). Some authority goes further, imposing only contract liability even when a defective product causes harm to other property in some instances. Neibarger v. Universal Cooperatives, Inc., 439 Mich. 512, 486 N.W.2d 612 (1992).

4. See, e.g., Offshore Rental Co. v. Continental Oil Co., 22 Cal.3d 157, 168, 583 P.2d 721, 728, 148 Cal.Rptr. 867, 874 (1978); Alvord and Swift v. Stewart M. Muller Constr. Co., Inc. 46 N.Y.2d 276, 281, 385 N.E.2d 1238, 1241–1242, 413 N.Y.S.2d 309, 312 (1978).

5. All–Tech Telecom, Inc., v. Amway Corp., 174 F.3d 862 (7th Cir.1999).

6. See the discussion of the bad faith tort in § 453.

7. Stevenson v. East Ohio Gas Co., 73 N.E.2d 200 (Ohio Ct.App.1946); United Textile Workers of America, AFL–CIO v. Lear Siegler Seating Corp., 825 S.W.2d 83 (Tenn.Ct.App.1990) (similar).

8. I.J. Weinrot and Son, Inc. v. Jackson, 40 Cal.3d 327, 708 P.2d 682, 220 Cal.Rptr. 103 (1985) (statute did not permit the action of employer for (a) lost profits or (b) out of pocket expenses incurred because of employee's injury); Fischl v. Paller & Goldstein, 231 Cal.App.3d 1299, 282 Cal.Rptr. 802 (1991) (general negligence principles did not permit the action); Gonzalez v. Yancey, 939 P.2d 525 (Colo.Ct.App.1997) (injured person's professional corporation had no action); Morton v. Merrillville Toyota, Inc., 562 N.E.2d 781 (Ind.Ct.App.1990); Edward F. Heimbrock Co., Inc. v. Marine Sales & Serv., Inc., 766 S.W.2d 70 (Ky.Ct. App.1989); Champion Well Service, Inc. v. NL Indus., 769 P.2d 382 (Wyo.1989).

The common law recognized a claim by the master per quod servitium amisit—that is, for loss of services of a servant injured

economic loss when an individual is negligently injured, as for example, those who have contracted to provide his upkeep. They are in the same boat.[9]

The leading case, often discussed, is *Robins Dry Dock & Repair Co. v. Flint.*[10] In that case the plaintiff had chartered a vessel but the owner was entitled to and did put it in dry dock during the charter period. The plaintiff was not entitled to compensation for the loss of use while the vessel was in dry dock under this provision. While there, the defendant negligently damaged the vessel so that the plaintiff was delayed resuming possession for commercial use. The plaintiff sued for loss of use. Justice Holmes thought the plaintiff had no property interest in the ship and that the negligent defendant would not be liable for his loss. Perhaps the case warranted relief when some others do not, but it remains as a bulwark against liability for negligent interference with economic interests.

Environmental or public harm with economic harm to another. In a number of cases the plaintiff has rights to use public waters and is in fact using them for commercial fishing or the like. If the defendant negligently pollutes the waters or prevents access to them, commercial fishers have been allowed recovery for their purely economic losses.[11] Such cases are sometimes viewed as public nuisance cases with special private harm, a category of recovery permitted to a limited group of plaintiffs under nuisance law.[12] Liability to the commercial fishers is perhaps reconcilable with the general rule against recovery for negligently inflicted economic loss because the right to use public waters coupled with actual usage might be tantamount to a limited property interest in the waters. Whatever the explanation for those cases, however, the recovery has not been extended to others. In one of the longest discussions of the problem, a divided court permitted recovery by commercial

by the defendant's battery. This was extended in some cases to negligent injuries of the servant as well as intentional ones. See Jones v. Waterman S.S. Corp., 155 F.2d 992 (3d Cir.1946). The recovery was pervasively understood as a reflection of the master's property interest in menial servants. So far as the employer might claim actual out of pocket expense (as in *Jones v. Waterman S.S. Corp.*), the claim may be understood, not as one based upon property in the servant, but upon subrogation or indemnity rights. Some such right may be in fact recognized in favor of the employer's workers' compensation carrier. Nevertheless, the contemporary cases have made the old per quod action obsolete.

Distinguish the spouse or family member's claim for loss of consortium resulting from injury of other and the statutory action for wrongful death.

9. Fifield Manor v. Finston, 54 Cal.2d 632, 7 Cal.Rptr. 377, 354 P.2d 1073, 78 A.L.R.2d 813 (1960). By statute, however, the federal government may recover against a tortfeasor for medical expenses it incurs in treating someone such as a member of the armed forces who is injured by a tortfeasor. See Medical Care Recovery Act, 42 U.S.C.A. § 2651.

10. Robins Dry Dock & Repair Co. v. Flint, 275 U.S. 303, 48 S.Ct. 134, 72 L.Ed. 290 (1927).

11. Union Oil Co. v. Oppen, 501 F.2d 558 (9th Cir.1974); Carson v. Hercules Powder Co., 240 Ark. 887, 402 S.W.2d 640 (1966) ("public nuisance" on a non-navigable stream or bayou, plaintiff had permission of riparian owners to fish there and earned his living doing so; polluter was subject to liability); Hampton v. North Carolina Pulp Co., 223 N.C. 535, 27 S.E.2d 538 (1943).

12. § 467.

fishers affected by a chemical pollution of the Mississippi River but firmly denied recovery by others who suffered economic losses such as seafood restaurants on the shore.[13] Similarly, a business may lose customers because traffic is reduced after the defendant's negligence requires closure of a bridge but no claim for economic loss lies against the negligent defendant[14] unless the business owner's property right is invaded by denial of access to her land.[15] Under the same general principle, a contractor whose work is delayed because of the pollution is denied recovery for his purely economic loss.[16]

Favoring Liability

In spite of the general rule, some cases have imposed liability for negligent interference with economic interests and perhaps liability would be justified in a few others. In addition, some statutes have imposed liability for economic harm, most notably in the case of oil spills in navigable waters.[17] There is also a federal statute, the Medical Care Recovery Act, which allows the federal government to recover its expenses in treating a member of the armed forces who is injured by a tortfeasor.[18]

Rejecting the general rule. Two or three cases have proposed a general modification of the rule against recovery for negligently inflicted economic harm. In the most important, *People Express*,[19] the defendant was allegedly negligent in the management of highly dangerous chemicals. The area nearby, including the plaintiff's airline office, had to be evacuated, with resulting loss of profits and business operations for the airline. No physical harm ever occurred. The New Jersey Supreme Court did not attempt to justify liability on the ground that the plaintiff had been denied access to its property. It concluded instead that the general rule against liability was wrong. It held that the defendant would owe a duty of reasonable care to protect against economic harm when "particular plaintiffs or plaintiffs comprising an identifiable class" suffered stand-alone economic harm, provided the defendant knew or had reason to know that such harm was likely. The court emphasized that it was not enough, however, that the class of plaintiffs was foreseeable; it had to be something more. The class would have to be "particularly foreseeable in terms of the type of persons or entities comprising the class, the certainty or predictability of their presence, the approximate numbers of those in the class, as well as the type of economic expectations disrupt-

13. Louisiana ex rel. Guste v. M/V Testbank, 752 F.2d 1019, 88 A.L.R.Fed. 239 (5th Cir. 1985).

14. Nebraska Innkeepers, Inc. v. Pittsburgh–Des Moines Corp., 345 N.W.2d 124 (Iowa 1984).

15. Denial of access to property invades a property right, see Restatement § 821C, cmt. f. Consequently liability for denial of access to an abutting owner is appropriate. Stop & Shop Companies, Inc. v. Fisher, 387 Mass. 889, 444 N.E.2d 368 (1983).

16. Garweth Corp. v. Boston Edison Co., 415 Mass. 303, 613 N.E.2d 92 (1993).

17. 33 U.S.C.A. § 2702 (b) (2) (E).

18. 42 U.S.C.A. § 2651.

19. People Express Airlines, Inc. v. Consolidated Rail Corp., 100 N.J. 246, 495 A.2d 107, 65 A.L.R.4th 1105 (1985).

ed."[20] Alaska has at least partially approved the idea[21] and in a much looser opinion, a federal court has favored a general regime of negligence liability for economic harm.[22]

Duty of care based upon undertaking or special relationship. In a few decisions, courts appear to favor a more eclectic approach, recognizing the general rule but also recognizing that in some instances the defendant must exercise reasonable care because of his special relationship with the plaintiff or because he actually undertook to exercise care. In some of these, the defendant undertakes a duty of care directly to the plaintiff, as in the ordinary case of lawyer malpractice. In others, however, the defendant contracting with A may be understood as undertaking a duty of care toward B. Some such cases might be best understood as third party beneficiary cases. But even if the case is not formally a third party beneficiary case, the defendant who is hired to work cooperatively with others and not as an adversary may be expected to exercise reasonable care for the interests of others in the project. So courts have said that an engineer or architect hired to design or supervise a construction project is liable for negligence in doing so, and not only liable to the owner who hired him but also to contractors whose work becomes economically burdensome as a result of his negligence.[23]

The famous *J'Aire* case[24] is not quite in this pattern but has some kinship. The plaintiff there operated a restaurant in premises leased in an airport building. The lease permitted the landlord-airport to improve the air conditioning system, even though the construction disrupted the tenant's business. The defendant, hired to carry out the construction, failed to prosecute the work with reasonable diligence, as a result of which the plaintiff restaurant was inoperable for a longer period than necessary. The plaintiff was allowed to recover for the contractor's negligence. Commentators have suggested that the plaintiff in *J'Aire* could properly recover on something like a third party beneficiary contract.[25]

Comment. When the parties are not in a contractual relationship, the reason to deny relief for negligently inflicted economic harm turns on the importance of a bright line rule in a world where economic harm

20. People Express Airlines, Inc. v. Consolidated Rail Corp., 100 N.J. 246, 264, 495 A.2d 107, 116 (1985).

21. Mattingly v. Sheldon Jackson College, 743 P.2d 356 (Alaska 1987) (confusingly holding that the plaintiff employer cannot recover for negligent injury to the employee that causes loss of services or loss of profits but that he can recover for negligently caused economic loss, which is evidenced by the same injury to the same employee).

22. Petitions of Kinsman Transit Co., 388 F.2d 821 (2d Cir.1968) (dictum disapproving of the general rule; holding that the economic injury was too remote anyway).

23. Donnelly Constr. Co. v. Oberg/Hunt/Gilleland, 139 Ariz. 184, 677 P.2d 1292 (1984); Tommy L. Griffin Plumbing & Heating Co. v. Jordan, Jones, & Goulding, Inc., 320 S.C. 49, 463 S.E.2d 85 (1995).

24. J'Aire Corp. v. Gregory, 24 Cal.3d 799, 598 P.2d 60, 157 Cal.Rptr. 407 (1979).

25. See Robert L. Rabin, Tort Recovery for Negligently Inflicted Economic Loss: A Reassessment, 37 STAN. L. REV. 1513, 1521 (1985); Gary Schwartz, Economic Loss in American Tort Law: The Examples of J'Aire and of Products Liability, 23 SAN DIEGO L. REV. 37 (1986).

can cause infinite chain reactions of other economic harm. The restaurant owner, unable to operate because of the contractor's negligence, stops ordering flour, sugar, and meat. His suppliers reduce their purchases from their suppliers, and so on. That reason does not apply in some cases, however. Suppose that the defendant negligently damages a bridge on private property. It happens that the plaintiff has contracted with the bridge owner to keep it in repair and because of the defendant's negligence the plaintiff must now spend more money to do so. The defendant's liability in such a case is probably for the cost of repairs. He is liable either to the bridge owner or to the plaintiff who contracted to keep it in repair. No threat of an infinite or even an extended chain of liability appears in such a case. The only real question in that case is not about the economic loss rule. The real question is one of practicality. Courts can allow the plaintiff to recover and deny recovery to the bridge owner or vice versa. If they allow recovery to the bridge owner, they can allow the plaintiff to recover from him on an unjust enrichment theory if nothing else. Which route to take depends on the court's assessment of procedural and litigation issues unrelated to the economic loss rule.[26]

In some cases the threat of extended chains of liability may or may not be present, depending upon the measure of damages sought by the plaintiff. In the famous *Robins* case,[27] the plaintiff deprived of the use of the vessel he had chartered could reasonably claim loss of profits. But loss of profits is more than the vessel's owner could claim; the vessel's owner, in the business of chartering vessels, not operating them, could claim only the reasonable rental or charter value of the vessel for the time it was negligently tied up. If the plaintiff reduced the claim from "lost profit" to "reasonable rental value" it would be clear that the negligent tortfeasor need never be subjected to more than one liability. Further, his liability would be no more than his admitted liability to someone, either the owner or the charterer. If the court should choose to permit the charterer rather than the owner to recover, as in subrogation cases, the tortfeasor would have no complaint. In such cases the rule against recovery for negligently inflicted economic harm has no place. It may still be true, however, that the vessel's owner (or the bridge owner) can most efficiently effect recovery, but that is a very different question.

§ 453. Bad Faith Breach of Contract as a Tort

Theoretically, bad faith breach of one's own contract is not an interference with contract. Yet the idea sometimes advanced that a defendant can be liable for interfering with his own contract can often be understood as nothing more than a bad faith breach of contract. For that reason, the bad faith cases belong with the discussion of interference.

The implied covenant of good faith. Courts generally recognize that contracting parties are under a duty to act in good faith so as not to deprive the other party of the benefits expressly or implicitly allocated to

26. See Fifield Manor v. Finston, supra n. 9.

27. Supra n. 10.

him by the contract and contemplated by the parties.[1] This is usually called an implied covenant of good faith and fair dealing. For example, if the defendant buys the plaintiff's business, payment to be made only from the business profits, the contract implies and the parties contemplate that the defendant will in fact operate the business in good faith. Under the traditional rule, the defendant who breaches the implied covenant of good faith is liable in contract, not in tort, and the remedies are circumscribed accordingly.[2]

Liability in tort; third-party insurance. Two lines of insurance cases recognized that an insurer's breach of contract obligation to its insured would be a tort under certain circumstances. The earliest cases involved a liability insurer whose insured was faced with a large claim but whose policy had relatively low limits. The insured would be personally liable to the extent that the injured person secured a judgment in excess of the policy limits. In such a case, courts held that the liability insurer should accept a reasonable opportunity to settle within its policy limits, or at least act in good faith in deciding whether to settle, considering the insured's interests as well as its own.[3] The insurer would of course be required to honor its contractual obligation to defend the insured as well as to pay judgments against him up to the policy limits. If the insurer breaches these obligations, so that the insured is subject to liability beyond the policy limits, the insurer is liable in tort, not merely in contract. That means it could be liable for the entire judgment the injured party obtained against its insured, without respect to policy limits.[4]

First-party insurance. In the 1970s, courts began to impose tort liability, including potential liability for punitive damages and emotional distress, for bad faith breach of first-party insurance contracts such as fire insurance policies. The original case, *Gruenberg v. Aetna Insurance Co.*,[5] for example, held that a fire insurer who unreasonably and in bad faith withheld payment of a claim covered by its policy would be liable, not merely on contractual provisions of the policy, but in tort and for tort damages. Since that time many states have adopted similar views

§ 453

1. See Restatement Second of Contracts § 205 (1979) (every contract "imposes" the duty of good faith and fair dealing).

2. Texas rejected the contract claim based upon an implied covenant of good faith in English v. Fischer, 660 S.W.2d 521 (Tex.1983), but accepts tort claims based on the relationship created by the contract. See Mark Gergen, A Cautionary Tale about Contractual Good Faith in Texas, 72 Tex. L. Rev. 1235 (1994) (arguing that it should be the other way around).

3. See Stephen S. Ashley, Bad Faith Actions: Liability and Damages §§ 2.04 & 2.05 (2d ed. 1997 & Supp.) (discussing negligence and bad faith theories of the claim).

4. Comunale v. Traders & Gen. Ins. Co., 50 Cal.2d 654, 328 P.2d 198, 68 A.L.R.2d 883 (1958). The exact scope of the duty and the conditions under which it applies vary somewhat. See, e.g., Soto v. State Farm Ins. Co., 83 N.Y.2d 718, 635 N.E.2d 1222, 613 N.Y.S.2d 352 (1994) (insurer who grossly ignores insured's interest is liable for entire judgment against insured except that it is not liable for punitive damages); Trinity Universal Ins. Co. v. Bleeker, 966 S.W.2d 489 (Tex.1998) (duty not invoked unless offer to settle all claims within policy limits).

5. Gruenberg v. Aetna Ins. Co., 9 Cal.3d 566, 510 P.2d 1032, 108 Cal.Rptr. 480 (1973).

and the bad faith liability is extended to cover other acts of the insurer besides withholding of payment, although courts differ somewhat as to the exact scope of the duty.[6] Wisconsin has extended the idea to Health Maintenance Organizations, which function somewhat like insurers, with the result that an HMO will be liable in tort for bad faith breach if it refuses needed and covered medical care for cost containment reasons.[7] The tort claim is grounded in the special duties undertaken in the insurance contract, so there is no reverse bad faith claim against an insured who make a false or bad faith claim, although such an insured may well be subjected to contractual liabilities or defenses or for fraud if he is guilty of that.[8]

Expanded bad faith liability in tort: commercial dealings generally. Breach of contract normally leads only to contract liability, not liability in tort for punitive damages and emotional distress. Nevertheless, once the bad faith tort gained roots in insurance cases, it spread to others. In 1984, the California Supreme Court created a tort based upon the defendant's bad faith denial that it had a valid contract to supply oil to the plaintiff.[9] This kind of expansion of liability provoked Judge Kozinski to say that "we will next be seeing lawsuits seeking punitive damages for maliciously refusing to return telephone calls or adopting a condescending tone in interoffice memos."[10]

Restricted tort liability. By the 1990s, however, courts were thinking that bad faith breach should ordinarily give rise to a contract but not tort action. Montana announced that although every contract contained the implied covenant of good faith, breach would ordinarily entail contract analysis and contract liability. Tort liability would be limited to cases in which the parties were inherently in unequal positions and sought something besides economic advantage (like peace of mind in the insurance contract).[11] Upon consideration, California first refused to apply the bad faith tort to breach of employment contracts,[12] and then concluded that the tort should be limited to (a) cases of insurance contracts and (b) cases in which some independent tort was committed.[13]

6. See Roger C. Henderson, The Tort of Bad Faith in First–Party Insurance Transactions after Two Decades, 37 Ariz. L. Rev. 1153 (1995).

7. McEvoy v. Group Health Cooperative of Eau Claire, 213 Wis.2d 507, 570 N.W.2d 397 (1997). The claim will be for medical malpractice instead if it is based upon a lapse in medical judgment. The facts in *McEvoy* involved "out of network" care, but the principle appears to cover any administrative as distinct from medical decision that violates the plaintiff's contract rights to medical care. See also Kathleen J. McKee, Annotation, Liability of Third-party Health-care Payor for Injury Arising from Failure to Authorize Required Treatment, 56 A.L.R.5th 737 (1998).

8. Agricultural Ins. Co. v. Superior Court, 82 Cal.Rptr.2d 594, 70 Cal.App.4th 385 (1999).

9. Seaman's Direct Buying Serv. Inc. v. Standard Oil Co. of California, 36 Cal.3d 752, 206 Cal.Rptr. 354, 686 P.2d 1158 (1984). As to the demise of this position, see text at nn. 12 & 13 below.

10. Oki Am. Inc. v. Microtech Int'l, Inc., 872 F.2d 312 (9th Cir.1989).

11. Story v. City of Bozeman, 242 Mont. 436, 791 P.2d 767 (1990) (also separately requiring that contract damages be inadequate and that the plaintiff was vulnerable and the defendant knew it).

12. Foley v. Interactive Data Corp., 47 Cal.3d 654, 254 Cal.Rptr. 211, 765 P.2d 373 (1988).

13. Freeman & Mills, Inc. v. Belcher Oil Co., 11 Cal.4th 85, 900 P.2d 669, 44 Cal. Rptr.2d 420 (1995).

Courts have also now stressed that the duty of good faith must be tied to some specific contract provision[14] and that it is not violated merely because the defendant insists upon a right he has under the contract.[15] Put differently, the obligation of good faith and fair dealing cannot be used to negate an express term of the contract or the defendant's rights under it.

Franchisees such as local dealers for auto manufacturers or local fast-food restaurants doing business under a national trademark and business style, may be able to assert antitrust claims against franchisors in some cases, and in others they may enjoy special franchisee protections under statutes.[16] Otherwise, however, they, too, generally come under the rule that the covenant of good faith cannot create a right at variance with the express provisions of the contract.[17]

In lender liability cases, some courts have found surprisingly concrete duties of good faith that appear to be at variance with the contract, but these duties are enforced as contract obligations, not in tort.[18] A leading student of bad faith actions concluded that the tort cause of action for bad faith breach had almost completely collapsed by the late 1990s[19] and the cases now assert that breach of contract simply is not a tort outside the insurance context.[20] It presently seems likely that courts will generally reject the tort claims based upon breach of contract unless there is at least a special relationship between the parties that implies fiduciary or similar duties.

Remaining bad faith claims. Some cases impose liability upon lessors who unreasonably refuse to permit their tenants to sublease, especially when it is apparent that the lessor is attempting to use the occasion to extract a higher rent than the one promised. Although courts may treat the lessor's breach as an interference with his own contract,[21] liability is easiest to understand as liability for bad faith breach. And tort

14. Duquesne Light Co. v. Westinghouse Electric Corp., 66 F.3d 604 (3d Cir. 1995).

15. Wagenseller v. Scottsdale Mem. Hosp., 147 Ariz. 370, 710 P.2d 1025 (1985) (duty of good faith not violated by discharge of at-will employee); Uptown Heights Assocs. Ltd. Partnership v. Seafirst Corp., 320 Or. 638, 891 P.2d 639 (1995) (lender did not breach good faith duty by foreclosing as it was entitled to under contract, although foreclosure was unnecessary).

16. E.g., the Automobile Dealers' Franchise Act, 15 U.S.C.A. § 1221 (broadly defined good faith duty); Petroleum Marketing Practices Act, 15 U.S.C.A. § 2802 (franchisor cannot terminate franchise or fail to renew it except upon terms provided in detail by the statute).

17. See Beraha v. Baxter Health Care Corp., 956 F.2d 1436 (7th Cir.1992) (implied covenant of good faith creates no independent liability; instead it guides construction of contract terms). In re Vylene Enters., Inc., 90 F.3d 1472 (9th Cir.1996), decided without substantial discussion, appears to be contra, but might be justified on narrower grounds.

18. E.g., K.M.C. Co., Inc. v. Irving Trust Co., 757 F.2d 752 92 A.L.R.Fed. 661(6th Cir. 1985) (in a relational contract for financing a wholesale business, court found a duty of objective good faith owed by lender to borrower to notify in advance when the lender intended to exercise its right to refuse further loans).

19. Stephen S. Ashley, Bad Faith Actions: Liability and Damages § 11.01(2d ed. 1997 & Supp.).

20. Quinn Companies, Inc. v. Herring–Marathon Group, Inc., 299 Ark. 431, 773 S.W.2d 94 (1989).

21. Campbell v. Westdahl, 148 Ariz. 432, 715 P.2d 288 (1985).

rather than contract liability may be warranted in such cases to prevent the landlord's opportunistic behavior. The language of bad faith has also appeared in some of the wrongful discharge cases, but the mainstream of thought in those cases has turned to public policy and contract rules, leaving little of a bad faith claim.

§ 454. Wrongful Discharge from Employment

Common Law Claims

Breach of contract. In the absence of statute, the traditional view holds that employees are employed at will unless their contract specifies otherwise.[1] Thus employers are free to discharge employees for any reason or no reason. The discharged employee has a breach of contract action if employment was for a particular duration or if the contract of employment permitted discharge only for just cause. In contemporary practice, employees are sometimes able to establish from employee handbooks or other means that the employee had an implied right to the job and could be discharged only for specific causes.[2] This claim is an ordinary contract claim, although the contract rights are proved circumstantially rather than by explicit terms.

Bad faith. At one time it appeared that courts would also treat discharge of an at will employee as a tort based upon the employer's breach of an implied covenant of good faith and fair dealing.[3] Although courts can reasonably perceive an implied covenant of good faith, the content of such a covenant is another matter. In particular, it would not be logically possible to say that an at will contract, which gives both parties the right to terminate at any time, also implies a covenant to retain the employee indefinitely.[4] Most decisions have now rejected the whole idea that employers of at will employees can be liable in tort for a termination in bad faith or for bad motives alone[5] or have shifted the

§ 454

1. For a summary of some of the arguments over at will employment and support for contract-based good faith obligations, see Stewart J. Schwab, Life-cycle Justice: Accommodating Just Cause and Employment at Will, 92 Mich. L. Rev. 8 (1993).

2. E.g., Witkowski v. Thomas J. Lipton, Inc., 136 N.J. 385, 643 A.2d 546 (1994).

3. Monge v. Beebe Rubber Co., 114 N.H. 130, 316 A.2d 549, 62 A.L.R.3d 264 (1974). Liability has also been imposed *in contract* for breach of the implied covenant. See Fortune v. National Cash Register Co., 373 Mass. 96, 364 N.E.2d 1251 (1977). As to the covenant of good faith, see § 453.

4. See Wagenseller v. Scottsdale Mem. Hosp., 147 Ariz. 370, 710 P.2d 1025 (1985).

5. Foley v. Interactive Data Corp., 47 Cal.3d 654, 254 Cal.Rptr. 211, 765 P.2d 373 (1988) (no action in tort for breach of employment contract, but contract action will lie if there is an implied term restricting discharge); cf. Tatge v. Chambers & Owen, Inc., 219 Wis.2d 99, 579 N.W.2d 217 (1998) (no tort action for misrepresentation inextricably tied to breach). Some courts have said that there simply is no covenant of good faith in employment at will contracts. Burk v. K–Mart Corp., 770 P.2d 24 (Okla. 1989). Others have said that there is a covenant of good faith but that good faith cannot require the employer to give up his right to terminate employment in an at will contract. See Wagenseller v. Scottsdale Mem. Hosp., supra n. 4. Contract liability based upon a fair reading of the contract's implications does not seem objectionable. See Fortune v. National Cash Register Co., supra n. 3. K Mart Corp. v. Ponsock, 103 Nev. 39, 732 P.2d 1364 (1987), is sometimes cited as supporting the bad faith claim but that case did not involve an at will contract and did involve a plain breach of the agreement.

ground for liability from the employer's bad faith to the employer's violation of some particular public policy.[6]

Public policy. With the bad faith breach claim largely eliminated from the tort repertoire, the claim of tortious wrongful discharge today is now commonly predicated upon a specific and identifiable public policy against discharge on the particular facts of the case. A few courts have limited this claim to a contract theory and exclude tort damages[7] but most treat it as a tort. In most cases the employer fires the at will employee for refusing to engage in illegal conduct,[8] for blowing the whistle on the employer's illegal conduct,[9] or for asserting her rights, as where she claims workers' compensation benefits for an employment injury.[10] One who conspires to procure a discharge in retaliation for the employee's participation in a federal prosecution or investigation may similarly find himself liable under federal statutes.[11] In all these cases, employers have been held liable or potentially liable in tort for wrongful discharge. Sometimes courts refer to the discharge in such cases as retaliatory discharge.

Some cases have gone a little further, finding very broad or at least less obvious public policies. In one, the employer was liable for discharging an employee who may have actively sought jury service that interfered with employment duties and from which she might have been excused.[12] In another, the employer was liable for discharging the guard in an armored truck who violated specific rules by leaving the truck unguarded to save a woman's life from a bank robber, the policy being the importance of human life.[13]

Public policy about employee rights. The exact policy in cases like these may be arguable, but if it exists at all, it is largely independent of any employment relationship. For instance, quite apart from any employment relation, public policy favors a report of crime and opposes inducements to crime. Courts are in effect saying that one must not be permitted to subvert or encumber the state's policy, whether by discharging employees or by some other means. A few cases have gone beyond this protection of external public policy by recognizing a public policy about the conditions of employment or the employment relation itself. For instance, some cases have held that an employer who discriminates on the basis of race or gender by discharging an employee violates

6. Howard v. Dorr Woolen Co., 120 N.H. 295, 414 A.2d 1273 (1980) (limiting the bad faith approach of Monge v. Beebe Rubber Co., supra n. 3 to discharge in violation of public policy). See MONT. CODE ANN. § 39–2–904. Courts sometimes say that the claim lies for breach of "implied covenants of good faith and fair dealing" but then add that the discharge must violate an important public policy. See Lewis v. Cowen, 165 F.3d 154 (2d Cir.1999).

7. Brockmeyer v. Dun & Bradstreet, 113 Wis.2d 561, 335 N.W.2d 834 (1983).

8. Tameny v. Atlantic Richfield Co., 27 Cal.3d 167, 610 P.2d 1330, 164 Cal.Rptr. 839 (1980).

9. Sheets v. Teddy's Frosted Foods, Inc., 179 Conn. 471, 427 A.2d 385 (1980).

10. Shick v. Shirey, 552 Pa. 590, 716 A.2d 1231 (1998).

11. Haddle v. Garrison, 525 U.S. 121, 119 S.Ct. 489, 142 L.Ed.2d 502 (1998).

12. Nees v. Hocks, 272 Or. 210, 536 P.2d 512 (1975).

13. Gardner v. Loomis Armored Inc., 128 Wash.2d 931, 913 P.2d 377 (1996).

public policy as declared by statute and is thus liable for the wrongful discharge.[14] Several courts have held that it violates public policy to require employees to undergo lie detector or polygraph tests.[15] Although these cases are rooted deeply in specific statutes forbidding use of polygraph tests in employment, they suggest that courts may enforce some employee privacy interests by finding a public policy limiting employer invasion of privacy.[16]

Rejecting or limiting the tort. A few cases have rejected the public policy wrongful discharge tort, sometimes on the ground that liability is at odds with the at will contract.[17] That view seems exaggerated. The mainstream cases imposing liability merely hold that the employer cannot use his right of discharge to defeat or encumber public policy. The cases do not require the employer to show just cause for discharge or even a good reason for it.[18] Courts have recognized that employers retain wide latitude to protect their own business, for example by discharging employees who refuse to sign non-competition covenants.[19] The employer is free to fire an employee who refuses to carry out the company program even though the employee believes that program is unethical, so long as the policy does not violate a legally recognized public policy.[20]

Likewise, vague and evanescent public policy will not support the plaintiff's claim in most jurisdictions. On the contrary, the public policy must provide a "clear mandate" and a specific one.[21] Although some courts may find a public policy that exists quite apart from any specific statute,[22] others insist that any public policy must derive from constitutions or statutes[23] or administrative regulations.[24] And even when a statute declares policy, it may not be a basis for liability, since the statute may regulate merely private rights or may declare only a minor policy. On the other hand, some statutes that do not seem very important in themselves are nevertheless important enough that the employee

14. Tate v. Browning–Ferris, Inc., 833 P.2d 1218, 21 A.L.R.5th 831 (Okla. 1992); Shaw v. Titan Corp., 255 Va. 535, 498 S.E.2d 696 (1998) (although public policy was grounded in Human Rights Act, the claim is the common law claim in tort for wrongful discharge based on race, gender, or age).

15. Perks v. Firestone Tire & Rubber Co., 611 F.2d 1363 (3d Cir.1979); Cordle v. General Hugh Mercer Corp., 174 W.Va. 321, 325 S.E.2d 111 (1984).

16. Cf. Ozer v. Borquez, 940 P.2d 371 (Colo.1997) (law firm could be held for invasion of former employee's privacy if it publicized his homosexuality and depending upon facts developed on remand might be liable for wrongful discharge).

17. Martin v. Tapley, 360 So.2d 708 (Ala.1978) (discharge in retaliation for claiming workers' compensation not actionable).

18. Sheets v. Teddy's Frosted Foods, Inc., 179 Conn. 471, 427 A.2d 385 (1980).

19. Tatge v. Chambers & Owen, Inc., 219 Wis.2d 99, 579 N.W.2d 217 (1998).

20. Pierce v. Ortho Pharm. Corp., 84 N.J. 58, 72, 417 A.2d 505, 512, 12 A.L.R.4th 520 (1980).

21. Pierce v. Ortho Pharm. Corp., supra n. 20.

22. E.g., Gardner v. Loomis Armored Inc., 128 Wash.2d 931, 913 P.2d 377 (1996) (value of human life).

23. Brockmeyer v. Dun & Bradstreet, 113 Wis.2d 561, 335 N.W.2d 834 (1983).

24. Green v. Ralee Eng'g Co., 19 Cal.4th 66, 960 P.2d 1046, 78 Cal.Rptr.2d 16 (1998) (federal regulatory standards for airplane parts embodied public policy; employee who complained internally of violations asserted valid state-law claim for discharge).

should not be compelled to violate them on pain of losing her job. A statute against public exposure of private parts may or may not apply to mooning, but be that as it may, no employee should be compelled to bare her buttocks in order to keep her job.[25]

Statutory Claims

Antidiscrimination statutes. A number of federal statutes create employee job rights, usually against discrimination based on race, gender, age, or disability.[26] Such statutes forbid not only discriminatory discharge but also other forms of job discrimination. They thus provide broader protection than has so far been provided under the common law public policy wrongful discharge tort. On the other hand, some federal statutes deny the plaintiff a jury trial,[27] require the plaintiff to exhaust administrative remedies before bringing suit,[28] and limit punitive and emotional harm damages.[29] Another group of federal statutes deals specifically with the rights of whistleblowers, forbidding discrimination against an employee who has reported or testified about particular law violations by employers.[30] Under these, an employee can recover if she is discharged for reporting or alleging discrimination or other specified law violations.[31] A number of state statutes impose parallel obligations but may not include the same money remedies. All such statutes must be considered as offering potential alternatives or additions to the common law claim. Statutory regulation of employment has become a large field in itself and even the subset involving wrongful discharge generates volumes of explanation and commentary[32] far beyond the scope of this work. A few additional cautionary words are required, however.

Effects of antidiscrimination statutes on common law tort claim. State and federal job rights statutes can have several different effects on the common law wrongful discharge claim. Besides the possibility that they may simply add specific rights or remedies, statutes may represent a public policy that can be the basis of a claim that discharge in violation

25. Wagenseller v. Scottsdale Mem. Hosp., 147 Ariz. 370, 710 P.2d 1025 (1985) (employee allegedly refused supervisor's request to "moon" in a skit; statute against publicly exposing genitalia may not have been violated but its policy was).

26. The best known are Title VII of the 1964 Civil Rights Act, 42 U.S.C.A. §§ 2000e et seq; the Age Discrimination Act (ADEA), 29 U.S.C.A. § 621 et seq.; and the Americans with Disabilities Act (ADA), see 42 U.S.C.A. § 12112. There are many, many other statutes affecting employment and employment discrimination.

27. See DAN B. DOBBS, LAW OF REMEDIES § 6.10 (5) (2d ed. 1993).

28. Title VII requires that plaintiffs first go through an administrative process, sometimes both state and federal, before they can receive a right to sue letter. See 42 U.S.C.A. §§ 2000e–5(e) & 2000e–5(f).

29. In 1991, Title VII was amended to permit punitive and emotional harm damages in the case of intentional discrimination. Both are subject to some special caps under 42 U.S.C.A. § 1981a (b).

30. E.g., 43 U.S.C.A. § 7622 (employees reporting employer pollution); 42 U.S.C.A. § 5851 (employees testifying in proceedings to enforce nuclear energy statutes).

31. E.g., McCue v. State Dept. Human Resources, 165 F.3d 784 (10th Cir.1999) (plaintiff's claim for sexual harassment was time-barred, but her claim that she was discharged for complaining about harassment was not).

32. E.g., HENRY H. PERRITT, JR., EMPLOYEE DISMISSAL LAW AND PRACTICE (4th ed. 1998) (3 vols.); PAUL H. TOBIAS, ET AL., LITIGATING WRONGFUL DISCHARGE CLAIMS (3 vols. 1998 and Supps.).

of statute is a violation of public policy. On the other hand, some statutes may be construed to provide the exclusive remedy, in effect preempting the common law wrongful discharge remedy.[33] The main federal statutes probably do not preempt the common law claim,[34] but preemption and exclusivity of the statutory remedy is a matter of construction, so particular statutes must be consulted.[35] Courts may also shape the common law right in the light of existing statutes, not as a matter of statutory construction but as a matter of their own sense of policy. In doing so, they may limit the common law right to cases not covered by the statute.[36] Finally, statutes may require the plaintiff to exhaust administrative remedies before suit can be filed, thus imposing costs and delays.[37]

Other preemption problems. The employment relationship may invoke a number of preemption problems quite apart from antidiscrimination statutes. A state's workers' compensation law, with its exclusive remedy provision, may bar the common law claim for wrongful discharge where physical or emotional injury results from the discharge, although statutory claims for the discharge will probably remain viable.[38] Federal labor laws applicable mainly to employees covered by collective bargaining agreements at times preempt the wrongful discharge claim,[39] although not when the claim can be adjudicated without interpreting the collective bargaining agreement.[40] The federal statute intended to protect employee retirement benefits (ERISA) also preempts state wrongful discharge claims if they relate to any benefit plan.[41] So if the employee claims she was fired by an employer seeking to avoid paying covered benefits, she has no common law wrongful discharge case but must pursue non-tort ERISA remedies for enforcement of the benefit plan.[42]

33. E.g., Vaughn v. Ag Processing, Inc., 459 N.W.2d 627 (Iowa 1990).

34. See 42 U.S.C.A. § 12201(b) (Americans with Disability Act: nothing limits rights and remedies under more favorable laws); California Fed. Sav. & Loan Ass'n v. Guerra, 479 U.S. 272, 107 S.Ct. 683, 93 L.Ed.2d 613 (1987) (Title VII does not preempt state statutory claim furthering same goals); Cancellier v. Federated Dept. Stores, 672 F.2d 1312 (9th Cir.1982) (Age Act does not preempt state law wrongful discharge claim); Ellenwood v. Exxon Shipping Co., 984 F.2d 1270 (1st Cir.1993) (rehabilitation act does not preempt state statutory remedies).

35. See also Kimberly C. Simmons, Annotation, Pre-emption of Wrongful Discharge Cause of Action by Civil Rights Laws, 21 A.L.R.5th 1 (1995) (using the term preemption broadly).

36. See Greene v. Union Mut. Life Ins. Co., 623 F.Supp. 295 (D.Me.1985); Makovi v. Sherwin–Williams Co., 316 Md. 603, 561 A.2d 179 (1989) (wrongful discharge claims limited to cases in which the public policy is not vindicated by other means); Allen v. Safeway Stores, Inc., 699 P.2d 277 (Wyo. 1985); cf. Sands Regent v. Valgardson, 105 Nev. 436, 777 P.2d 898 (1989) (age discrimination against public policy but that policy is not strong enough to support a common law claim by at will employee, leaving only statutory claims with limited "liquidated" damages). Courts are not always clear about whether they are construing a statute or enunciating common law rules.

37. See note 28.

38. Shoemaker v. Myers, 52 Cal.3d 1, 801 P.2d 1054, 276 Cal.Rptr. 303 (1990).

39. Monroe v. Missouri Pac. R.R., 115 F.3d 514 (7th Cir.1997).

40. Lingle v. Norge Div. of Magic Chef, Inc., 486 U.S. 399, 108 S.Ct. 1877, 100 L.Ed.2d 410 (1988).

41. 29 U.S.C.A. 1144(a).

42. Ingersoll–Rand Co. v. McClendon, 498 U.S. 133, 111 S.Ct. 478, 112 L.Ed.2d 474 (1990).

Ironically, the impact of the many statutes intended to benefit employees as a group may make it extremely difficult to pursue a modest or mid-size claim because the amount of legal work required in dealing with numerous and complex issues of preemption may be incommensurate with the expected financial return. Perhaps the net result is that public policy wrongful discharge cases will continue to represent a very small niche in tort law.

§ 455. Remedies

The threat of tortious interference with contract has been enjoined in some cases,[1] and the contract itself may be protected from interference by specific performance decrees where it involves real property or a unique or special subject matter.[2]

The damages remedy is more popular than the injunctive remedy with most plaintiffs who claim interference with contract or economic opportunities. Courts have said repeatedly that some damage is required to sustain the action,[3] but that statement probably is not meant to preclude the equitable relief already mentioned or restitution based on the defendant's gains rather than damages based upon the plaintiff's losses, because courts have required the defendant to disgorge profits he made by interfering with the plaintiff's contract,[4] even when the plaintiff has suffered no losses.[5] Courts seem to feel that the contract breacher and the interfering defendant are more or less like joint wrongdoers, even though the contract breacher has committed no tort. Perhaps for this reason, courts have not required the plaintiff to seek specific performance of the contract in order to minimize damages, although damages actually paid by the breacher will reduce the defendant's liability.[6] Presumably the defendant's liability will also be reduced if, because of the interference and breach, the plaintiff captures other opportunities that he would not have gained but for the breach.[7]

Compensatory damages could be measured as they are often measured in contract cases, by the difference between the contract price and the market value of the breacher's promised performance.[8] But quite often, plaintiffs assert the claim as one for consequential damages. Under that heading, the plaintiff can recover the loss of profit or other income that was not directly promised by the contract but that would

§ 455

1. E.g., Adler, Barish, Daniels, Levin and Creskoff v. Epstein, 482 Pa. 416, 393 A.2d 1175, 1 A.L.R.4th 1144 (1978). See 2 Dan B. Dobbs, Law of Remedies § 6.6 (4) (2d ed. 1993).

2. Duff v. Engelberg, 237 Cal.App.2d 505, 47 Cal.Rptr. 114 (1965).

3. E.g., K & K Management, Inc. v. Lee, 316 Md. 137, 557 A.2d 965 (1989).

4. Zippertubing Co. v. Teleflex Inc., 757 F.2d 1401 (3d Cir.1985); National Merchandising Corp. v. Leyden, 370 Mass. 425, 348 N.E.2d 771, 5 A.L.R.4th 1266 (1976); 2 Dan B. Dobbs, Law of Remedies § 6.6 (3).

5. Federal Sugar Ref. Co. v. United States Sugar Equalization Board, 268 F. 575 (S.D.N.Y.1920).

6. Restatement § 774A (2).

7. See Dan B. Dobbs, Law of Remedies § 12.6 (2) (2d ed. 1993).

8. International Minerals and Resources, S.A. v. Pappas, 96 F.3d 586 (2d Cir.1996).

have been probable if the contract had been performed,[9] or conversely, the losses incurred on collateral matters because the contract was breached. Such consequential damages might be denied under the little authority that uses the contract measure of damages with its limitation to damages in the parties' contemplation.[10] Most courts award damages under tort principles, however, with damages limits based upon proximate cause rather than contemplation of the parties. Under this view, the plaintiff can recover all proximately caused damages, including consequential damages, even if those damages were greater than the damages the plaintiff could recover against the contract breacher.[11] In many cases there is probably no real difference except on emotional harm damages.

As always with consequential damages, the plaintiff must prove the loss (and usually its amount) with a reasonable certainty. The plaintiff must show that, but for the wrongful interference, she would have been able to realize the economic opportunity involved.[12] If the plaintiff loses customers after the defendant's wrongful interference, the plaintiff must still prove that the loss was a result of the interference and not something else.[13] Claims for lost profits in a business are viewed with a degree of scepticism here as elsewhere,[14] but if an established profit was probable but for the defendant's interference, the loss of profit is recoverable.[15] In wrongful discharge cases, the plaintiff can recover the contract benefits, including future earnings, but only if it was reasonably certain that the employment would have continued indefinitely.[16] Even then, the normal rule requires the plaintiff to minimize damages by seeking and accepting other available employment.

Courts have sometimes allowed recovery for foreseeable emotional

9. E.g., Brookeside Ambulance, Inc. v. Walker Ambulance Service, 112 Ohio App.3d 150, 678 N.E.2d 248 (1996). An alternative way of attempting to measure the loss is to award the loss in capital value of the plaintiff's business where that is traceable to the interference. See Creek v. Village of Westhaven, 144 F.3d 441 (7th Cir.1998).

10. Swaney v. Crawley, 133 Minn. 57, 157 N.W. 910 (1916).

11. See Horchheimer v. Prewitt, 33 N.M. 411, 268 P. 1026 (1928) (cost of hiring and transporting new laborers); Collins Music Co., Inc. v. C.W. Smith, 332 S.C. 145, 503 S.E.2d 481 (Ct.App.1998). In Texaco, Inc. v. Pennzoil Co., 729 S.W.2d 768, 859–60 (Tex.Ct.App. 1987) the plaintiff was not limited to difference between contract price and value of stock promised but was allowed to recover the amount of cost savings the plaintiff would effected by having the assets of the target company. See Douglas Laycock, The Remedies Issues: Compensatory Damages, Specific Performance, Punitive Damages, Supersedeas Bonds, and Abstention, 9 Rev. Litigation 473 (1990). A little authority has asserted that there is no limit on damages and that the plaintiff can recover for all harms, whether they are foreseeable or not. Duff v. Engelberg, 237 Cal.App.2d 505, 47 Cal.Rptr. 114 (1965).

12. Medical Mut. Liability Soc'y of Maryland v. B. Dixon Evander & Assocs., Inc., 339 Md. 41, 660 A.2d 433 (1995).

13. Bayley Prods., Inc. v. Cole, 720 So.2d 550 (Fla.Dist.Ct.App.1998); Restatement § 774A (1) (c).

14. See generally Dan B. Dobbs, Law of Remedies §§ 3.3 (4) & 3.4 (2d ed. 1993).

15. E.g., Girsberger v. Kresz, 261 Ill. App.3d 398, 633 N.E.2d 781, 198 Ill.Dec. 940 (1993).

16. See Hummer v. Evans, 129 Idaho 274, 923 P.2d 981 (1996) (bad faith discharge is a contract, not tort action, but future damages could have been recovered if she had been able to prove them to a reasonable certainty).

distress resulting from interference with contract or opportunities[17] or, somewhat more cautiously, for emotional distress that is "a common and predictable result of disrupting" the particular type of contract or relationship.[18] Similarly, courts have supported recovery for harm to reputation,[19] although the rules of libel and slander should probably dictate the limits of any recovery based upon speech. The anomaly in the recovery for emotional and reputational harms is that they result from a breach of contract, for which such damages are permitted only rarely. A Texas court has held that emotional harm damages cannot be recovered in an interference with contract claim.[20]

Punitive damages are now subject to a constitutional and other constraints,[21] but within those limits, courts have also said that punitive damages are recoverable for tortious interference with contract or opportunity when the facts are said to show malice or other states of mind that warrant such damages.[22] Punitive damages may also be allowed in the public policy wrongful discharge cases[23] and, where bad faith breach is a tort, for that as well,[24] always providing that the defendant's conduct and state of mind were sufficiently egregious.

17. Stafford v. Puro, 63 F.3d 1436 (7th Cir.1995); Nesler v. Fisher and Co., Inc., 452 N.W.2d 191 (Iowa 1990); Rite Aid Corp. v. Lake Shore Investors, 298 Md. 611, 471 A.2d 735, 44 A.L.R.4th 1063 (1984).

18. Mooney v. Johnson Cattle Co., Inc., 291 Or. 709, 634 P.2d 1333 (1981).

19. Restatement § 774A (1)(c).

20. Delgado v. Methodist Hosp., 936 S.W.2d 479 (Tex.Ct.App. 1996).

21. See § 383.

22. Texaco, Inc. v. Pennzoil Co., 729 S.W.2d 768 (Tex.App.1987) ($1 billion for the outrage of interfering with a contract by offering a seller more money than the plaintiff had offered); Continental Trend Resources v. OXY USA, Inc., 101 F.3d 634 (10th Cir.1996) (discussing constitutional limits); Sara L. Johnson, Annotation, Punitive Damages for Interference with Contract or Business Relationship, 44 A.L.R.4th 1078 (1987).

23. O'Day v. McDonnell Douglas Helicopter Co., 191 Ariz. 535, 959 P.2d 792 (1998) (punitive damages even when after-acquired evidence justifies the discharge); Shaw v. Titan Corp., 255 Va. 535, 498 S.E.2d 696 (1998).

24. Carter v. Catamore Co., Inc., 571 F.Supp. 94 (N.D.Ill.1983).

CHAPTER 33

HARMS TO INTERESTS IN INTANGIBLES AND UNFAIR COMPETITION

§ 456. Introducing Rights in Intangibles

Most wealth today is represented in whole or in part by a wide range of intangibles that receive a degree of legal protection. These include trademarks and other means of identifying a business or its products; inventions; creative works including music, arts, and writings; trade secrets; and even aspects of a public personality. The best single volume dealing with all of this is the lucid Restatement of Unfair Competition. Each of these topics, however, is the subject of multi-volume speciality works.

At a minimum, intangible rights may be protected against specific wrongful acts such as deceptive trade practices, restraints on trade, or the misappropriation of trade secrets. In some instances, however, intangible rights are treated more like property so that courts focus more on the scope of the right and less on finding specific wrongful acts by the defendant.

Strong policies favor protection of intangible values. In some cases, protection is needed to encourage development of intangibles like inventions, for without legal protection, the inventor will not reap rewards of invention.[1] Likewise, protection of trademarks is a part of the competitive system that permits consumers to choose among competitive brands because their trademarks clearly denote the source of the goods. In some cases, protection seems important regardless of encouragement; "natural law" permits the artist to reap the rewards of his work[2] and have it attributed to him rather than to others. In still other cases, protection directly serves public interests, as it does when public confusion is minimized by forbidding competitors from using the plaintiff's trademark.

There are also strong policies against excessive protection. Protection creates a form of monopoly in the protected materials. That is what assures the plaintiff that she will reap her reward and that the public

§ 456

1. See, discussing and criticizing "encouragement theory," Wendy J. Gordon, An Inquiry into the Merits of Copyright: the Challenges of Consistency, Consent, and Encouragement Theory, 41 STAN. L. REV. 1343 (1989).

2. See Wendy J. Gordon, A Property Right in Self-expression: Equality And Individualism in The Natural Law of Intellectual Property, 102 YALE L.J. 1533 (1993) (exploring Locke's approach to property and liberty as applied to intellectual property).

will not be confused by pirated trademarks. At the same time, our society values both free competition and freedom of ideas. In the economic as well as in the artistic sphere, my original idea is transformed in your hands and achieves new economic or artistic value. Similarly, free speech interests suggest that broad communication of ideas is not only appropriate but necessary.

The balance of policies. Given this balance of policies, the law does not protect general ideas; ideas are free as the air, and competitors may copy as well as breathe. The balance of the policies is at risk when courts approach intangible rights under novel theories. For example, expanding the tort of conversion to cover intangibles runs the risk that a judge will offer protection to general ideas that would not be protected by copyright or patent and that should not be protected. The same was once done under what is called the misappropriation doctrine. In the famous INS case, a competitor was not permitted to copy uncopyrighted materials and then use them in competition with their author.[3] To a very large extent, this case has been superseded by the view that rights in intangibles must depend upon independent wrongdoing such as fraud, breach of confidence as in the case of trade secrets, infringement of the time-delimited monopolies of patent and copyright statutes, or invasions of rights of personality.[4]

§ 457. Unfair Competition, Trademark Infringement and Dilution[1]

Unfair competition is a general term that includes deceptive trade practices, acts such as trademark infringement, and appropriation of trade values or rights in publicity.[2] All of these are torts under common law rules. Some are enhanced or limited by statutory provisions. When unfair competition claims involve appropriation of trade values, as in cases of product design copying, issues of intellectual property or ownership rights arise, implicating the law of patent and copyright.

False advertising. The defendant who falsely disparages the products of a competitor may be liable for the injurious falsehood.[3] If, instead of disparaging his competitor's products, he advertises or otherwise misrepresents material qualities of his own goods, he might also be liable to the purchaser who is deceived. But in that case, earlier law tended to deny competitors any recovery on the ground that they could not show any direct losses.[4] The Lanham Trademark Act's famous § 43(a)[5] has

3. International News Service v. Associated Press, 248 U.S. 215, 39 S.Ct. 68, 63 L.Ed. 211 (1918).

4. See Restatement of Unfair Competition § 38.

§ 457

1. Among the multi-volume treatises discussing this topic is J. THOMAS MCCARTHY, TRADEMARKS AND UNFAIR COMPETITION (4th. ed. vols. 1998).

2. Restatement of Unfair Competition § 1.

3. See § 407.

4. E.g. American Washboard Co. v. Saginaw Mfg. Co., 103 Fed. 281 (6th Cir.1900). For history and exceptions, see Restatement of Unfair Competition § 2, cmt. b.

now made it clear that a competitor has a claim against defendants who falsely represent the qualities of their own goods as well as their source. State statutes may do the same.[6] A recovery of damages and/or an accounting for profits[7] is appropriate if the plaintiff's loss or the defendant's gain from the false advertising is proved with sufficient certainty,[8] and § 43(a) permits trebling of the recovery "as compensation."[9] If damages cannot be proved, the aggrieved competitor can at least enjoin the false representations.[10]

Passing off. In the passing off cases, the defendant is likely to mislead purchasers by misrepresenting that his goods are produced or sponsored by the plaintiff, or by representing himself as an agent or affiliate of the plaintiff.[11] For example, if a customer orders "Coca–Cola" but the restaurant provides Pepsi–Cola without warning of the substitution, the restaurant is passing off Pepsi for Coca–Cola.[12] Passing off can be done in more sophisticated ways by creating an appearance that one product is another. These cases can best be discussed in connection with trademark and trade dress cases.

Trademark. Any words, symbols, or designs can qualify as a protected trademark if they sufficiently distinguish one person's goods or services from another's.[13] Labels, packaging, even the design of the product itself, can count as trademarks if they are distinctive and nonfunctional.[14] Trade names–the name by which an enterprise is known–receive similar protection.[15] At one time courts distinguished between technical trademarks and other identifiers that were entitled to less protection. These distinctions are no longer necessary except for the purpose of interpreting older decisions,[16] but it is true that some trademarks may be protected more broadly than others. For brevity, the term trademark will be used here to stand for all identifiers of goods, including tradenames. In the original passing off or unfair competition cases, courts tended to make liability depend upon the defendant's wrongful

5. 15 U.S.C.A. § 1125(a).

6. See Uniform Deceptive Trade Practices Act § 2.

7. Accounting for profits permits a recovery of the gains obtained by the defendant as a result of the tort and presents special problems of measurement. See 2 Dan B. Dobbs, Law of Remedies § 6.4 (4) (2d ed. 1993).

8. Tim Torres Enterprises, Inc. v. Linscott, 142 Wis.2d 56, 416 N.W.2d 670 (1987). The plaintiff may be aided by a presumption of causation when false representations about the defendant's goods are combined with potentially disparaging representations about the plaintiff's goods, always a possibility with comparative advertising. See Porous Media Corp. v. Pall Corp., 110 F.3d 1329 (8th Cir.1997).

9. See 2 Dan B. Dobbs, Law of Remedies § 6.4 (3) (2d ed. 1993).

10. See Id., § 6.4 (5).

11. Restatement of Unfair Competition § 4.

12. E.g., Coca–Cola Co. v. Overland, Inc., 692 F.2d 1250 (9th Cir.1982).

13. See Restatement of Unfair Competition § 9.

14. Restatement of Unfair Competition § 16; see § 458 below.

15. Restatement of Unfair Competition § 12. Other recognized marks are "collective marks" Id. § 10 and "certification marks", id. § 11.

16. See 1 J. Thomas McCarthy, Trademarks and Unfair Competition Chapter 4 (4th ed. 1998) (listing and discussing archaic and modern usage of various terms) (hereafter McCarthy Trademarks).

conduct such as intentional deceit.[17] In contrast, contemporary law holds that any valid mark is infringed by similar marks if they in fact are likely to cause customer confusion about the source of the marked goods.[18] Nontrademark uses, as where the plaintiff's product is named by reference to its trademark in comparative advertising or otherwise, is not ordinarily an infringement.[19]

Acquisition of rights. Rights in trademarks are usually acquired only by using the mark to identify goods with the plaintiff as their source.[20] Once used, the mark may be registered under federal and state statutes. Registration affords the mark's owner some evidentiary and procedural advantages in litigation and may help forestall imitation by others. Once the mark is established, it may be sold or licensed with the product.

Arbitrary, fanciful, or inherently distinctive marks. As already indicated, a mark is valid only if it is distinctive, that is, capable of unambiguously identifying goods as those of the mark's owner in the minds of a large number of consumers. The mark is distinctive either because it is arbitrary or because from public usage it has come to identify the owner's goods in the public mind. For example, Kodak is an arbitrary word coined as a trademark; when coined, it had no meaning except as a trademark. By itself, it describes nothing about the product. It is thus quite distinctive as an identifier and protectible without proof that the public associates it with a particular producer of goods. Marks that are not arbitrary or fanciful but are suggestive without being descriptive may also be distinctive and protected on the same basis.[21]

Descriptive marks, secondary meaning. Other words or symbols are not naturally distinctive because they have existing meaning that tends to describe the plaintiff's product or its characteristics. The Restatement illustration is helpful: TRAQ as a trademark for steel girders is fanciful or arbitrary and distinctive without further proof. On the other hand RIGID may be taken to describe some characteristic of the girders and is not by itself distinctive.[22] Similarly, the personal name of the producer and geographical terms describing origin are descriptive and have no arbitrary meaning that makes them distinctive.[23] Such descriptive

17. See McCarthy Trademarks § 5:2.

18. With trade names, collective and certifying marks, the relevant confusion is confusion about the business, collective, or certifying organization. See Restatement of Unfair Competition § 20.

19. Pebble Beach Company v. Tour 18 I Limited, 155 F.3d 526 (5th Cir.1998); New Kids on the Block v. News America Publishing, Inc., 971 F.2d 302 (9th Cir.1992) (newspapers could run contests asking readers to answer a poll about a trademark).

20. McCarthy, Trademarks §§ 16:1, 16:4. This is qualified in a limited way by a federal provision that establishes priority from the time a trademark is applied for, provided actual registration follows. 15 U.S.C.A. § 1057.

21. See Zatarains, Inc. v. Oak Grove Smokehouse, Inc., 698 F.2d 786 (5th Cir. 1983) (discussing the categories and noting that secondary meaning is not required for suggestive marks like Coppertone for a tanning product). Words that do have an existing meaning but not even remotely in relation to the product may also be regarded as arbitrary or fanciful. Even words that remotely suggest the product or its qualities may be in this category. See Restatement of Unfair Competition § 13, cmt. c.

22. Restatement of Unfair Competition § 13, Ills. 1 & 4.

23. Restatement of Unfair Competition § 14.

marks, however, can become distinctive if consumers generally come to identify the mark with the owner's products. In such a case, the mark is said to acquire distinctiveness through secondary meaning. Once it is found to be distinctive, it can be protected against infringement by others.

Generic terms and loss of distinctiveness. There is a limit to acquired distinctiveness: no one can acquire rights in words understood to be generic descriptions of a category of goods. Bank and camera are examples.[24] More than this, a once-distinctive mark may cease to be distinctive if the public comes to use the trademark as a generic description. Aspirin is a traditional example. Once a fanciful term, it is now used as a generic name for a type of pain reliever, regardless of the manufacturer. The term is no longer distinctive of a particular manufacturer and is thus no longer a trademark.

Infringement: likelihood of confusion. A defendant infringes a mark by using the same mark or one that is sufficiently similar to make it likely that consumers will be confused about the source or sponsorship of the marked goods.[25] Judgments about the likelihood of confusion draw upon sophisticated analysis. Similarity itself may take several forms; even if a spelling is different, the phonetic similarity may indicate a danger of confusion. The nature of the market for the goods matters, too; if two disparate groups of consumers purchase the plaintiff's and defendant's goods respectively, confusion may not be likely in spite of similarities in two marks.[26]

Sponsorship confusion. Trademark protection originally aimed to redress or prevent a diversion of trade that would occur if customers intended to purchase the plaintiff's product but mistakenly chose the defendant's product with a confusingly similar mark. This was called source confusion because the purchaser might believe that the plaintiff was the source of the defendant's product. That would mean that if A sold a magazine called Seventeen and B sold girdles called Seventeen, the likelihood of confusion was practically nil, since hardly anyone would think a magazine was a girdle or vice versa. Nevertheless courts came to say that confusion about sponsorship of a product would suffice to show infringement. So if a prospective girdle purchaser might think that Seventeen Girdles were somehow sponsored or approved by Seventeen Magazine, the girdle manufacturer's use of the term Seventeen would infringe the magazine's trademark.[27] Sometimes this idea is taken to the edge or perhaps invoked as a conscious fiction for something else. In one case,[28] a pornographic movie depicted young women who wished to

24. Restatement of Unfair Competition § 15 & cmt. a.

25. Slightly different kinds of confusion are entailed with trade names, and with collective and certification marks. See Restatement of Unfair Competition § 20.

26. See Restatement of Unfair Competition § 21 (listing a number of evidentiary considerations).

27. Triangle Publications, Inc. v. Rohrlich, 167 F.2d 969 (2d Cir.1948), overruled on other grounds by Monsanto Chem. Co. v. Perfect Fit Products Mfg. Co., 349 F.2d 389 (2d Cir.1965).

28. Dallas Cowboys Cheerleaders, Inc. v. Pussycat Cinema, Ltd., 604 F.2d 200 (2d Cir. 1979).

become "Texas Cowgirl" cheerleaders and who wore a uniform similar to that worn by cheerleaders for the Dallas Cowboys football team. The court granted a preliminary injunction against showing the movie on the likelihood that the uniform was a trademark and that the movie infringed it because the viewers of pornographic movies might believe that the Dallas Cowboys Cheerleaders, Inc. had authorized use of the similar uniforms.

Dilution. As the sponsorship confusion cases show, trademark protection underwent a mutation. What began as a protection against customer confusion and diversion of trade became an effort to enhance or maintain the selling power of trade symbols. Since around 1950, state[29] and federal[30] anti-dilution statutes have explicitly embraced this selling-power ideal[31] by protecting trademarks against "dilution" of a mark even when no confusion of any kind is to be found. For instance, "the proliferation of various noncompetitive businesses utilizing the name Tiffany's" dilute "the public's association of the name Tiffany's solely with fine jewelry."[32] This type of dilution is known as the "blurring" or "whittling down" kind. The claim for dilution is appropriate, however, only when the plaintiff's mark is highly distinctive[33] or, in the terms of the federal statute, famous. A mark containing the phrase "Blue Ribbon" or "Allied" is not distinctive and cannot be diluted.[34]

Tarnishment. Tarnishment of the plaintiff's trademark can occur when it or a similar mark is used for products that are inconsistent with the image the plaintiff's goods or their mark seeks to project. Use of a bank's trademark for a place of adult entertainment[35] or a beer's trademark for an insecticide[36] tends to tarnish the original trademark and such use is enjoinable. Where the plaintiff's trademark is used, not to identify goods or services but as commentary, satire, or parody, protection is inappropriate. Similarly, discussion or comparative advertising that uses an unaltered mark must be permitted.[37] Consequently, the Restatement provides that if the defendant uses the mark to disparage it without using it to identify goods, liability may be appropriate only under the rules of defamation or injurious falsehood, not under trade-

29. E.g., Mass. Gen. L. Ann. 110B § 12.

30. 15 U.S.C.A. § 1125 (c) (effective from January 1996).

31. See Allied Maintenance Corp. v. Allied Mechanical Trades, Inc., 42 N.Y.2d 538, 542, 369 N.E.2d 1162, 1164, 399 N.Y.S.2d 628 (1977) (reflecting legislative purpose to stop "the whittling away of an established trade-mark's selling power and value through its unauthorized use by others upon dissimilar products").

32. Allied Maintenance Corp. v. Allied Mechanical Trades, Inc., 42 N.Y.2d 538, 545, 369 N.E.2d 1162, 1166, 399 N.Y.S.2d 628 (1977)

33. Restatement of Unfair Competition § 25.

34. Allied Maintenance Corp. v. Allied Mechanical Trades, Inc., 42 N.Y.2d 538, 369 N.E.2d 1162, 399 N.Y.S.2d 628 (1977) ("Allied" not strong enough to be diluted).

35. E.g., Community Fed. Sav. & Loan Ass'n v. Orondorff, 678 F.2d 1034 (11th Cir.1982) (bank's "cookie jar" mark for ATM diluted by use of "Cookie Jar" for place of adult entertainment); cf. Dallas Cowboys Cheerleaders, Inc. v. Pussycat Cinema, Ltd., supra n. 27.

36. Chemical Corp. of America v. Anheuser–Busch, Inc., 306 F.2d 433, 2 A.L.R.3d 739 (1962).

37. See Deere & Co. v. MTD Products, Inc., 41 F.3d 39 (2d Cir.1994).

mark law.[38] And since the rules for defamation, injurious falsehood, and privacy invasion take account of free speech interests, satiric or parodic use of the plaintiff's mark may not be actionable.[39] Speech rights may be undermined in tarnishment cases, however, if the court declares that confusion is likely and brings the case within the framework of traditional trademark infringement.[40] The Internet has brought dilution problems as well as many others.[41]

§ 458. Product Design, Trade Dress, and Functional Features

Trade dress. In contemporary law, a distinctive overall appearance of a container, label, or means of packaging a product can work as a trademark independent of any specific trademark accompanying such packaging.[1] This kind of overall appearance is often called trade dress. The fundamental rules of trademark apply: trade dress is protected as a trademark only when it is inherently distinctive or acquires distinctiveness through secondary meaning and identifies the product's source or sponsorship.[2] A wide range of attributes, including restaurant decor,[3] the special color of pads for dry cleaners,[4] the shape and texture of a bottle in which a product is marketed,[5] and many others can count as protectible trade dress, so long as the total look distinguishes the plaintiff's goods or services from others. A product's design itself can also function as a trademark and is also sometimes called trade dress. Special limits apply when trade dress, and especially product design, is claimed as a trademark.

Functional features. Functional features cannot be protected as trademarks.[6] This means that competitors can copy any feature of a product's design that is functional and not protected by patent. Although

38. Restatement of Unfair Competition § 25 (2).

39. L.L. Bean, Inc. v. Drake Publishers, Inc., 811 F.2d 26 (1st Cir.1987); see Deere & Co. v. MTD Products, Inc., 41 F.3d 39, 44 (2d Cir.1994). The U.S. Olympic Committee enjoys special statutory protection so that its trademark will not be diluted or tarnished. See San Francisco Arts & Athletics, Inc. v. United States Olympic Committee, 483 U.S. 522, 107 S.Ct. 2971, 97 L.Ed.2d 427 (1987).

40. See Mutual of Omaha Ins. Co. v. Novak, 775 F.2d 247 (8th Cir.1985) (affirming injunction on trial court's finding that "Mutant of Omaha" used on clothing by opponent of nuclear war would confuse purchasers).

41. See Daniel R. Pote, A Domain by any other Name: The Federal Trademark Dilution Act of 1995 Applied to Internet Domain Names, 37 Jurimetrics J. 301 (1997).

§ 458

1. Restatement of Unfair Competition § 16.

2. See McCarthy, Trademarks § 8:1.

3. See Two Pesos, Inc. v. Taco Cabana, Inc., 505 U.S. 763, 112 S.Ct. 2753, 120 L.Ed.2d 615 (1992).

4. Qualitex Co. v. Jacobson Products Co., Inc., 514 U.S. 159, 115 S.Ct. 1300, 131 L.Ed.2d 248 (1995).

5. E.g., Nora Beverages, Inc. v. Perrier Group of America, Inc., 164 F.3d 736 (2d Cir.1998).

6. E.g., American Greetings Corporation v. Dan–Dee Imports, Inc., 807 F.2d 1136 (3d Cir.1986); Restatement of Unfair Competition § 16. A combination of functional features, however, might not be functional in toto even if each feature is. See Pebble Beach Company v. Tour 18 I Limited, 155 F.3d 526 (5th Cir.1998); Publications International, Ltd. v. Landoll, Inc., 164 F.3d 337 (7th Cir.1998).

functionality can be defined in varied formulas,[7] the general idea is that a feature is functional if it makes the product more workable, useful, or efficient than reasonable alternatives, or if it affects the quality or cost of the product. For example, the first automobile might have had a distinctive appearance, "but if its distinctiveness was due to the fact that it had an engine in front instead of horses, and a crank, radiator grill, and steering wheel, the producer would not be able to claim that this combination of functional features constituted trade dress; for that would give him a monopoly of the production of automobiles, and trademark law is not intended to confer product monopolies."[8] A product might even have aesthetically functional features, features that command a premium in the market because they appeal to tastes.[9]

Policy and effect of the functionality rule. The functionality rule is a part of the balance between free competition and protection of identifying marks. Copying of useful ideas and designs not protected by patent laws is entirely desirable and permissible. It is in fact a part of the balance dictated by the patent laws. Under the Constitution, federal patent laws are the exclusive source for rights in inventions.[10] They grant inventors of useful items a monopoly or patent for a period of years, after which anyone may copy the invention and go into competition with the inventor. The laws restrict patents to specific devices; general ideas are not patentable.[11] In addition, the device must be inventive and novel and not merely an extension of earlier ideas.[12] Trademark protection for functional features of a product that is not protected by a patent would subvert the balance of competition and property rights struck by the patent laws. That is because trademark of functional items would provide protection for devices that patent laws might refuse to protect altogether, and would provide protection in perpetuity where patent laws would at most protect for 20 years.[13]

Preemption of state patent-like laws. With these ideas in mind, the Supreme Court has held that federal patent laws preempt state laws that attempt to create patent-like rules to forbid copying of products that are not protected by federal patent law. In one of the leading cases, the

7. Qualitex Co. v. Jacobson Products Co., Inc., 514 U.S. 159, 165, 115 S.Ct. 1300, 1304, 131 L.Ed.2d 248 (1995) ("if it is essential to the use or purpose of the article or if it affects the cost or quality of the article"); Restatement of Unfair Competition § 17 (a feature is functional if it affords benefits in marketing independent of the feature's value as indicating the source of the goods and if those benefits are important in effective competition and if they cannot be captured in other ways); McCarthy, Trademarks § 7:69.

8. Publications International, Ltd. v. Landoll, Inc., 164 F.3d 337, 340 (7th Cir. 1998).

9. Restatement of Unfair Competition § 17. Judge Posner gave this example: "Mink coats are normally sold dyed. The dye does not make the coat any warmer, but it makes it more beautiful, and, once again, it could not be claimed as trade dress by the first furrier to have hit on the idea." Publications International, Ltd. v. Landoll, Inc., 164 F.3d 337 (7th Cir.1998).

10. U.S. Const., Art. I, § Cl. 8; Bonito Boats, Inc. v. Thunder Craft Boats, Inc., 489 U.S. 141, 109 S.Ct. 971, 103 L.Ed.2d 118 (1989) (preemption of patent-like laws).

11. Gottschalk v. Benson, 409 U.S. 63, 93 S.Ct. 253, 34 L.Ed.2d 273 (1972).

12. See 35 U.S.C.A. §§ 102 & 103.

13. 35 U.S.C.A. § 154 (with some variation in the term depending upon circumstances and patent type).

defendant made a mold of the plaintiff's boat design, then cast copies and competed with the plaintiff. Since the boat design was not patented, copying was not only permitted but, under the patent scheme, desirable as a means of promoting competition. A state statute that attempted to prohibit such copying was thus invalid.[14] Earlier cases had taken a similar view about copying of lamp designs.[15]

Federal law claims and functionality. The preemption analysis does not apply to claims for trademark infringement under the federal trademark laws, which permit a claim for infringement of trademarks in trade dress and product design.[16] But the policy behind the patent preemption decisions applies to federal claims by way of the functionality rules: a functional feature cannot count as a trademark, even if it also identifies the plaintiff as producer of the goods.[17] The plaintiff must protect functional features under the law of trade secrets or patents or not at all.

§ 459. Ideas and Trade Secrets[1]

Ideas not protected. Ideas as such are not protected either by statutes or by the common law. Newton did not own gravity. If the idea is sufficiently inventive and novel and also reduced to a specific useful design, it may be patented for a limited period of years, otherwise not.[2] A person with an idea may exploit it by going into business using the idea, but she cannot prevent others from using it as well once she reveals it. In such a case, her rewards for developing a good idea must come from the fact that she is the first to exploit it and from her efficient use of it, not from static ownership.

Protection from breach of confidence or contract. However, ideas and information can be protected to some extent by divulging them only to fiduciaries, or in confidence, or pursuant to a contract. A stranger or an employee may suggest improvements to a business, which may be liable if it contracts to pay for ideas and perhaps on an implied contract if it uses the idea,[3] but otherwise liability must be founded upon the trade secret rules[4] or not at all.[5]

14. Bonito Boats, Inc. v. Thunder Craft Boats, Inc., 489 U.S. 141, 109 S.Ct. 971, 103 L.Ed.2d 118 (1989). As to boat hulls specifically, Congress itself has now provided protection against copying in 1998. 17 U.S.C.A. § 1301.

15. Sears, Roebuck & Co. v. Stiffel Co., 376 U.S. 225, 84 S.Ct. 784, 11 L.Ed.2d 661 (1964); Compco Corp. v. Day–Brite Lighting, Inc., 376 U.S. 234, 84 S.Ct. 779, 11 L.Ed.2d 669 (1964).

16. See McCarthy Trademarks § 7:58.

17. Two Pesos, Inc. v. Taco Cabana, Inc., 505 U.S. 763, 112 S.Ct. 2753, 120 L.Ed.2d 615 (1992); Publications International, Ltd. v. Landoll, Inc., 164 F.3d 337 (7th Cir.1998).

§ 459

1. See Roger M. Milgrim, Trade Secrets (4 vols. 1998).

2. Gottschalk v. Benson, 409 U.S. 63, 93 S.Ct. 253, 34 L.Ed.2d 273 (1972).

3. See Phillips v. Frey, 20 F.3d 623 (5th Cir.1994) (prospective seller enthusiastically revealed too much; buyers implicitly accepted the information in confidence).

4. See Restatement of Unfair Competition § 39, cmt. h.

5. Joyce v. General Motors Corp., 49 Ohio St.3d 93, 551 N.E.2d 172 (1990) (employee not entitled to compensation under the terms of employee suggestion program); Martin v. Little Brown and Company, 304

Rights in trade secrets. Trade secret protection works in essentially the same way. A trade secret is any kind of secret information used in an enterprise for actual or potential economic advantage,[6] at least if it has independent value because it is secret. It must not be readily ascertainable[7] or widely known.[8] But it is protected though it is not novel enough to justify a patent,[9] and though it is not actually used by the plaintiff.[10] It is often a formula or a compilation of information used in business. Sometimes it is a process or a combination of elements each of which is publicly known although the combination is not.[11] Liability turns on a finding that the defendant misappropriated the information by tortious or improper means such as fraud, theft, or the like,[12] or the finding that he was guilty of, or took advantage of, a breach of confidence.[13] For example, if the owner of a trade secret discloses it in confidence to the defendant as a prospective buyer of the business, the defendant's use of the trade secret without making the purchase is a breach of confidence and a wrongful use of the trade secret.[14] The same is true when the plaintiff discloses the trade secret to employees who must use it in their work.[15] Because the focus is on wrongdoing and breach of confidence, a person who acquires the trade secret from a wrongdoer without knowledge of the wrong is not subject to liability.[16]

Enforcement. If a trade secret is misappropriated or revealed in breach of confidence, the owner may have relief measured by her own damages or by the defendant's unjust enrichment; where future revela-

Pa.Super. 424, 450 A.2d 984 (1981) (stranger not entitled to compensation for notifying publisher that its copyright had been infringed by others); cf. Copy–Data Systems, Inc. v. Toshiba America, Inc., 755 F.2d 293, 302 (2d Cir.1985). Hamilton Nat'l Bank v. Belt, 210 F.2d 706, 708, 93 U.S. App. D.C. 168 (1953) treats ideas as property when they have sufficient concreteness, but this appears to be out of line with the patent cases and others limiting ideas protection to contract and confidence cases. *Hamilton* is discussed in 2 Dan B. Dobbs, Law of Remedies § 6.5 (2) (2d ed. 1993).

6. Restatement of Unfair Competition § 39.

7. See Uniform Trade Secrets Act § 1 (4); Buffets, Inc. v. Klinke, 73 F.3d 965 (9th Cir.1996); Aetna Building Maintenance Co., Inc. v. West, 39 Cal.2d 198, 246 P.2d 11 (1952) (prospective customers readily discoverable).

8. Many courts have tried to resolve trade secret disputes through a determination whether a trade secret existed rather than through a focus upon the defendant's wrongful conduct. In so doing, they have often emphasized a number of factors including the extent to which the information is known outside of his business and even inside the business. E.g., Wilson Certified Foods, Inc. v. Fairbury Food Products, Inc., 370 F.Supp. 1081 (D.Neb.1974).

9. Dionne v. Southeast Foam Converting & Packaging, Inc., 240 Va. 297, 397 S.E.2d 110 (1990).

10. Restatement of Unfair Competition § 39, cmt. e. Older authorities sometimes did require use and even "continuous use."

11. Integrated Cash Management Services, Inc. v. Digital Transactions, Inc., 920 F.2d 171 (2d Cir.1990).

12. E.I. duPont deNemours & Co. v. Christopher, 431 F.2d 1012 (5th Cir.1970) (overflights with photography to reveal plant structure which in turn would reveal nature of secret process).

13. See generally Restatement of Unfair Competition § 40. The Restatement adds that the defendant is also liable for misappropriation if discovers the trade secret by accident or mistake and knows it to be a trade secret.

14. E.g., Roton Barrier, Inc. v. Stanley Works, 79 F.3d 1112 (Fed.Cir. 1996).

15. See the paragraph *Employees joining a competitor* below.

16. See Forest Laboratories, Inc. v. Pillsbury Co., 452 F.2d 621 (7th Cir.1971); Restatement of Unfair Competition § 40 (b) & cmt. d.

tion is threatened, the owner may frequently obtain an injunction.[17] Damages may include lost profits resulting because use of the trade secret permitted the defendant to sell goods in competition with the plaintiff and also erosion of prices made necessary by the competition founded on misappropriation of the trade secret.[18] The Uniform Trade Secret Act embodies the common law rules protecting trade secrets[19] and a federal statute makes misappropriation of trade secrets a crime.[20] One great advantage for the owner of a trade secret is that, unlike patents, it does not expire at the end of a fixed term. A company that developed a formula or process in 1900 and never divulged it, may still be exploiting that process to its competitive advantage today.

Losing rights in trade secrets. Trade secret protection is lost when the secret becomes publicly or widely known, either because of the plaintiff's divulgence or in spite of the plaintiff's best efforts to keep it secret.[21] Furthermore, the defendant is free to develop the same information covered by a trade secret, so long as he does not take advantage of a breach of confidence or commit an independent tort to do so. In particular, he is free to analyze or reverse engineer the plaintiff's products and to acquire the secret in that manner if he can.[22] These rules reflect disadvantages of trade secret ownership compared to patents. They also reflect the fact that trade secrets are property protected by tort law[23] mainly in the limited sense that tort law will impose liability for breach of confidence or some independent tort.[24]

Employees joining a competitor. The breach of confidence issue often arises when employees who are knowledgeable about the employer's trade secrets set up a competing business or go to work for an existing competitor. The employee owes a fiduciary duty to his employer,[25] so it is

17. For all these remedies, see 2 Dan B. Dobbs, Law of Remedies § 10.5 (3) (2d ed. 1993).

18. Roton Barrier, Inc. v. Stanley Works, 79 F.3d 1112 (Fed.Cir. 1996).

19. Uniform Trade Secret Act. Punitive damages are also permissible but limited by the act to double the compensatory damages. See § 3(b).

20. 18 U.S.C.A. § 1831–1839.

21. Religious Technology Center v. F.A.C.T.NET, Inc., 901 F.Supp. 1519 (D.Colo.1995) (secret works of Scientology's founder had escaped into the public domain, although the Church had worked hard to keep the works secret).

22. Roboserve, Ltd. v. Tom's Foods, Inc., 940 F.2d 1441 (11th Cir.1991); see Restatement of Unfair Competition § 43.

23. A contract between the parties, an employer and employee, for example, might provide greater terms of protection, as in the case of a non-competition agreement.

24. The famous Holmes' statement is that "The word 'property' as applied to trademarks and trade secrets is an unanalyzed expression of certain secondary consequences of the primary fact that the law makes some rudimentary requirements of good faith. Whether the plaintiffs have any valuable secret or not the defendant knows the facts, whatever they are, through a special confidence that he accepted. The property may be denied, but the confidence cannot be. Therefore the starting point for the present matter is not property or due process of law, but that the defendant stood in confidential relations with the plaintiffs.... " Holmes, J. in E.I. du Pont de Nemours Powder Co. v. Masland, 244 U.S. 100, 37 S.Ct. 575, 61 L.Ed. 1016 (1917). There are indisputably some property aspects; for example, trade secrets may also be "taken" by the government and if so due process requires compensation. See Ruckelshaus v. Monsanto Co., 467 U.S. 986, 104 S.Ct. 2862, 81 L.Ed.2d 815 (1984).

25. Restatement Second of Agency §§ 395, 396 (1959).

clear that he cannot take the employer's secret information. On the other hand, in the absence of a valid agreement to the contrary, the employee is entitled to take her own skills and general knowledge with her to another employment. If a customer list is a trade secret—sometimes they are, sometimes not[26]—the employee may still be entitled to use his memory of faces and names in his new job.[27] The conflict between the employee's right to work with her own skills and the employer's right to protect trade secrets leads to difficult decisions. In extreme cases, the developing inevitable disclosure doctrine permits the court to enjoin the former employee from working for a competitor for a period of time on the theory that he would inevitably reveal trade secrets.[28]

§ 460. Rights in Personality and Publicity[1]

The earliest right of privacy claims sought relief because the defendant, without permission, had used the plaintiff's name or picture in commercial advertising.[2] Privacy invasion claims with their dignitary emphasis remain valid to redress dignitary harms such as personal distress. When the claim is that the defendant has appropriated the plaintiff's "identity" for commercial purposes, the harm is different; it is economic harm to the plaintiff (or unjust economic gain to the defendant). In that case, the tort can be viewed as an invasion of privacy in which damages happen to be economic, or as a separate tort for the commercial appropriation of identity or personality or as a vindication of the "right of publicity."[3] A fair number of states so provide by statute, the terms of which are sometimes exclusive.[4]

The broad term identity here means the plaintiff's name, likeness, or other singular or notable characteristics associated peculiarly with the

26. E.g., Leo Pubs., Inc. v. Reid, 265 Ga. 561, 458 S.E.2d 651 (1995) (tangible list made in employment must be returned but defendant can use the information contained therein); Rugen v. Interactive Business Systems, Inc., 864 S.W.2d 548 (1993) (customer list and accompanying information was trade secret where it was kept confidential); K. H. Larsen, Annotation, Former Employee's Duty, in Absence of Express Contract, Not to Solicit Former Employer's Customers or Otherwise Use His Knowledge of Customer Lists Acquired in Earlier Employment, 28 A.L.R.3d 7 (1970).

27. Carl A. Colteryahn Dairy, Inc. v. Schneider Dairy, 415 Pa. 276, 203 A.2d 469 (1964).

28. PepsiCo, Inc. v. Redmond, 54 F.3d 1262 (7th Cir.1995) (marketing strategies, six month injunction against work for direct competitor). See Integrated Cash Management Services, Inc. v. Digital Transactions, Inc., 920 F.2d 171 (2d Cir. 1990); Novell Inc. v. Timpanogos Research Group Inc., 46 U.S.P.Q.2d 1197 (Utah Dist.Ct.1998) (nine month injunction from developing software that could use plaintiff's trade secrets, partly because "negative knowledge" defendants learned while working for plaintiff would inevitably show them what avenues *not* to explore); 2 Dan B. Dobbs, Law of Remedies § 10.5 (3) (2d ed. 1993). In this setting, employee covenants not to compete take on special significance.

§ 460

1. The leading treatise on this topic is J. Thomas McCarthy, Publicity and Privacy (2 vols. looseleaf, supplements).

2. See § 425.

3. See Restatement of Unfair Competition §§ 46–49; J. Thomas McCarthy, The Rights of Publicity and Privacy (1998). If the plaintiff's identity has become associated with goods or services he produces, he may have a trademark interest it as well.

4. See Stephano v. News Group Pubs., Inc., 64 N.Y.2d 174, 474 N.E.2d 580, 485 N.Y.S.2d 220 (1984).

plaintiff.[5] The forbidden commercial use includes use of the plaintiff's identity in an advertisement, as where the plaintiff's name,[6] voice[7] or likeness[8] is used or imitated in an advertisement and where the plaintiff's identity is used as part of the defendant's trademark,[9] or sold directly as a poster, tee shirt, or statuette or the like.[10] The emphasis is on the fact that the plaintiff's identity has commercial value, so plaintiffs in such cases are usually celebrities. But even a little-known recluse may have a reasonable claim if her identity has commercial value, and in any event such a person may have a claim for emotional or other dignitary harm on right of privacy grounds.[11]

Extending identity or style. One kind of problem case involves the plaintiff's claim to protection for her public style or distinctive performing persona rather than her name or likeness, that is, to a combination of demeanor, dress, and truly intangible aspects of personality. Courts have held that an Elvis Presley imitation infringed rights of publicity,[12] and that a TV news publication depiction of the late Zacchini's entire cannon-ball act would be an infringement, even though the tape was legitimately made.[13] The Ninth Circuit held that a parodic ad showing a robot dressed in clothes similar to those worn by a television person, Vanna White, was an infringement of her right of publicity.[14] The robot also had similar hair and jewelry. The reference to Vanna White was unmistakable to those who watch TV game shows. Although White did not own the exclusive right to dress and bejewel herself in that particular way, the court thought the advertiser could be liable for using her "identity" for commercial purposes. Proof that defendant published a TV commercial in which a bandleader is shown playing Auld Lang Syne on New Year's Eve, with the tempo and gestures of Guy Lombardo, was sufficient to create a factual question whether the defendant was guilty

5. Cf. Cheatham v. Paisano Pubs., Inc., 891 F.Supp. 381 (W.D.Ky.1995) (doubting that the plaintiff could establish sufficient distinctiveness in a representation of her semi-bare backside).

6. Hirsch v. S.C. Johnson & Son, Inc., 90 Wis.2d 379, 280 N.W.2d 129 (1979) (nickname).

7. Midler v. Ford Motor Co., 849 F.2d 460 (9th Cir.1988).

8. Ali v. Playgirl, Inc., 447 F.Supp. 723 (S.D.N.Y.1978) (seemingly realistic drawing or cartoon depicting Mohammed Ali nude); Onassis v. Christian Dior–New York, Inc., 122 Misc.2d 603, 472 N.Y.S.2d 254 (1984). So far as an advertisement implies the plaintiff's endorsement by using a look-alike actor, the advertiser may also be guilty of false advertising or passing off. Allen v. National Video, Inc., 610 F.Supp. 612 (S.D.N.Y.1985) (Woody Allen look-alike in ad).

9. Carson v. Here's Johnny Portable Toilets, Inc., 698 F.2d 831 (6th Cir.1983).

10. E.g., Comedy III Productions, Inc. v. Gary Saderup, Inc., 68 Cal.App.4th 744, 80 Cal.Rptr.2d 464 (1998) (T-shirts with likeness of Three Stooges), *review granted*, 83 Cal.Rptr.2d 533, 973 P.2d 512; Martin Luther King, Jr. Center for Social Change, Inc. v. American Heritage Products, Inc., 250 Ga. 135, 296 S.E.2d 697 (1982) (bust of Dr. Martin Luther King infringed right of publicity). Once the plaintiff has licensed use of her identity on items like tee-shirts, the purchaser of the tee-shirt is entitled to use it and even to resell it. See Allison v. Vintage Sports Plaques, 136 F.3d 1443 (11th Cir.1998).

11. See Restatement of Unfair Competition § 49, cmt. b.

12. Presley's Estate v. Russen, 513 F.Supp. 1339 (D.N.J.1981).

13. Zacchini v. Scripps-Howard Broadcasting Co., 433 U.S. 562, 97 S.Ct. 2849 53 L.Ed.2d 965 (1977).

14. White v. Samsung Electronics America, Inc., 971 F.2d 1395 (9th Cir.1992).

of a commercial appropriation of Lombardo's identity.[15] Other cases have given actors rights in their portrayal of fictional characters, even though the actors do not own the copyright on the script and did not create the set in which they acted.[16] Such cases raise questions whether the defendant has appropriated something of the plaintiff's personality or has merely appropriated the role she was playing, which, in the medieval metaphysics of intellectual property, is owned by someone else altogether.

Descendability. Some courts and legislatures have expanded[17] the right of publicity in another direction by holding that the right of publicity survives the death of the person whose identity is used, permitting the estate of performers like Elvis Presley or their licensees to control the uses of the image and even the general style of the performer long after the performer's death.[18] Some other states, by statute or otherwise, have limited the right of publicity to the protection of living persons,[19] but the majority have permitted descent of the right to heirs or devisees.[20]

Criticisms and alternatives. The leading treatise author on the subject strongly favors the right of publicity,[21] but some thinkers have suggested that protection ought to extend mainly to use of name or likeness. One potential limitation upon the more expansive forms of publicity right is that the federal copyright statute could be interpreted to preempt some publicity rights, as the 7th Circuit actually held.[22] More recently, it has become possible to see that protection of intangible rights in a performer's persona apart from name and likeness is really not protection of identity but protection for creative efforts. Protection for creative efforts, it can be argued, should be left to copyright laws when the creation is fixed in a tangible medium, otherwise left to confidentiality agreements or to the public domain.[23] Behind the desire to restrict liability for less tangible aspects of persona are concerns for free speech and free competition. In addition, as has been noted in connection with copyright issues, art historically builds on art, even if it uses ideas or

15. Lombardo v. Doyle, Dane & Bernbach, Inc., 58 A.D.2d 620, 396 N.Y.S.2d 661 (1977)

16. Wendt v. Host International, Inc., 125 F.3d 806 (9th Cir.1997) ("Norm" and "Cliff" of Cheers fame).

17. Rights of privacy and reputation traditionally die with the person, so that, for example, there is no liability for "defaming" the dead.

18. Cal.Civ.Code § 990 (only specifying name, voice, signature, photograph or likeness); Presley's Estate v. Russen, 513 F.Supp. 1339 (D.N.J.1981) (performance style and pose); Martin Luther King, Jr. Center for Social Change, Inc. v. American Heritage Products, Inc., 250 Ga. 135, 296 S.E.2d 697 (1982).

19. New York's statute refers specifically to living persons and this statute has been held to be the exclusive source of rights in New York. Stephano v. News Group Pubs., Inc., 64 N.Y.2d 174, 474 N.E.2d 580, 485 N.Y.S.2d 220 (1984).

20. J. Thomas McCarthy, 1 The Rights of Publicity and Privacy § 9.5 [B].

21. J. Thomas McCarthy, The rights of Publicity and Privacy.

22. Baltimore Orioles, Inc. v. Major League Baseball Players Ass'n, 805 F.2d 663 (7th Cir.1986).

23. See David W. Melville, Harvey S. Perlman, Protection for Works of Authorship Through the Law of Unfair Competition: Right of Publicity and Common Law Copyright Reconsidered, 42 St. Louis U. L.J. 363 (1998).

forms peculiarly associated with others artists. Too much restriction on the ability of one artist such as an Elvis impersonator may not only reward fame; it may defeat creativity as well.

§ 461. Copyright[1]

Rights of authorship. As with the other topics mentioned in this chapter, copyright is a specialized field, but its broad outlines can be sketched. The Constitution specifically provides for federal control of patents and copyrights,[2] and federal statutes preempt state laws except for works like performances that are not reduced to a tangible form.[3] Patent law protects rights in inventions. Copyright law protects rights in all original works of authorship fixed in any tangible medium of expression.[4] That includes books, musical compositions, sculptures, paintings, movies and a long list of other tangible expressions of authorship. The copyright endures for the life of the author plus 70 years.[5] Authorship of a work in a tangible medium coupled with a copyright notice secures the copyright without more; but registration enhances remedies and facilitates proof.[6] Specialized rules govern and specialized problems beset some particular copyrights, as in the case of musical reproductions and computer software, the Internet, satellite transmission and others.

Scope. Copyright gives the author the exclusive right to make derivative works from the copyrighted material, for example, a movie from a novel.[7] Otherwise, however, copyright protects the particular form of expression, not the underlying idea.[8] I can copyright a photograph or painting of a pregnant nude, but I do not thereby own the idea of representing a nude pregnant woman. You infringe my photograph only if you photographed a pregnant nude in the same pose, with the same lighting, skin color and other detail.[9] Similarly, I cannot copy and sell your copyrighted newspaper story or law review article, but I can describe it and report its essential contents.[10] Similarly, copyright does not protect a process, procedure, or facts.[11] On the other hand, while

§ 461

1. Leading multivolume treatises include MELVILLE B. NIMMER & DAVID NIMMER, COPYRIGHT (10 vols. 1998) (hereafter Nimmer on Copyright); PAUL GOLDSTEIN, COPYRIGHT (4 vols. 2d ed. 1999).

2. U.S. Const. Art. 1, § 8, cl. 8.

3. 17 U.S.C.A. § 301. The issue can be convoluted, however. See National Basketball Ass'n v. Motorola, Inc., 105 F.3d 841 (2d Cir.1997) (no copyright in games but a copyright in stimultaneous broadcasts; nevertheless, state misappropriation claims would be preempted so that Motorola was free to broadcast to its pagers sports scores it obtained from watching TV).

4. 17 U.S.C.A. § 102.

5. 17 U.S.C. § 302 (a).

6. See 2 DAN B. DOBBS, LAW OF REMEDIES § 6.3 (2d ed. 1993).

7. 17 U.S.C.A. § 106.

8. 17 U.S.C.A. § 102 (b).

9. See Leibovitz v. Paramount Pictures Corp., 137 F.3d 109, 116 (2d Cir.1998) ("the particular way the body of Moore is portrayed, rather than the fact that the ad copies the appearance of a nude, pregnant body").

10. See National Basketball Ass'n v. Motorola, Inc., 105 F.3d 841 (2d Cir.1997).

11. See Feist Publications, Inc. v. Rural Tel. Service Co., Inc., 499 U.S. 340, 111 S.Ct. 1282, 113 L.Ed.2d 358 (1991)

copyright will protect a work only if it originates with an author, the work itself need not be novel or inventive as with a patent.[12]

Infringement. Copyright is infringed if the plaintiff owns the copyright and the defendant copied original elements of the copyrighted work. Copying is frequently shown by the fact that the defendant had access to the work and that the defendant's publication was substantially similar,[13] even though some parts are also dissimilar.[14] Neither total nor literal reproduction is required to establish copying. A publisher may infringe a copyrighted work by quoting several hundred words.[15] An artist may infringe a copyrighted photograph by "copying" it to a three dimensional sculpture.[16]

Free speech, fair use, and parody. Copyright ownership is sometimes asserted to to stifle speech, thought, and cultural interchange.[17] The copyright system attempts to protect free speech and competition in part by refusing protection to events, facts, and ideas and thus permitting both information and concepts to reach the public freely. The copyright statute itself also provides some protection for speech interests by recognizing a right of fair use. The statute specifically provides that "fair use" of copyrighted materials is not an infringement. It then provides that fair use is to be determined by considering four factors: (1) the purpose and character of the use, in particular whether it was for commercial use or on the contrary for nonprofit educational purposes; (2) the nature of the copyrighted work; (3) the amount and substance of the portion used in relation to the copyrighted work as a whole, and (4) the effect of the use upon the potential market for the copyrighted work.[18]

The broad "purpose and character" factor invites courts to consider whether the use of copyrighted materials "adds something new, with a further purpose or different character, altering the first with new expression, meaning, or message."[19] In particular, use for criticism, commentary, or news reporting would be new or transformative uses and would weigh in favor of a fair use finding. Parody has transformative value; it may shed light on the original and in the process create a new work.[20] The use of copyrighted works to satirize–to throw light on something else altogether–does not necessarily require the use of the copyrighted work and may have less claim to fair use.[21] But neither

12. See NIMMER ON COPYRIGHT § 2.01.

13. E.g., Williams v. Crichton, 84 F.3d 581 (2d Cir.1996).

14. Rogers v. Koons, 960 F.2d 301 (2d Cir.1992).

15. Harper & Row, Publishers, Inc. v. Nation Enterprises, 471 U.S. 539, 105 S.Ct. 2218, 85 L.Ed.2d 588 (1985).

16. Rogers v. Koons, 960 F.2d 301 (2d Cir.1992).

17. See Wendy J. Gordon, a Property Right in Self-expression: Equality And Individualism in The Natural Law of Intellectual Property, 102 YALE L.J. 1533 (1993) (giving examples and explaining why a natural rights view of copyright would provide significant protection for free speech).

18. 17 U.S.C.A. § 107.

19. Campbell v. Acuff–Rose Music, Inc., 510 U.S. 569, 579, 114 S.Ct. 1164, 1171, 127 L.Ed.2d 500 (1994) (hereafter Campbell).

20. Campbell, supra n. 18.

21. Campbell, supra n. 18, 510 U.S. at 581, 114 S.Ct. at 1173; Dr. Seuss Enters. v. Penguin Books USA, Inc., 924 F.Supp. 1559 (S.D.Cal 1996) (using rhymes and pictures

parody nor commercial use is controlling; each factor counts. Perhaps the purpose and character factor invites other considerations as well, for instance whether the defendant used the copyrighted material to defend himself from attacks by the copyright holder.[22]

The nature of the copyrighted work counts as a factor. If it lies outside the core of copyright protection, as where it has high factual content, a fair use finding may be more likely.[23] The significance as well as the amount copied[24] is likewise a factor, but again not controlling. Taping a complete copyrighted TV program at home for home use is permissible,[25] but a hefty quotation from an unpublished work is likely not to be.[26] One reason for the difference lies in the last factor, the effect of copying upon the market for the original. Copying from an unpublished work may destroy the copyright holder's right of first publication, with a significant effect on the marketability. In contrast, a transformative parody of a published work may not affect the market at all.

Moral rights. French law developed and continental law adopted versions of the *droit moral*, which gives authors a bundle of rights with respect to their works even after they have sold the work itself and even when they no longer own the copyright.[27] The term itself has nothing to do with morality; it refers to rights in intangibles. By adhering to the Berne Convention in 1988, the United States has imported some of these moral rights for artists.

Moral rights in the United States. The Visual Artists Rights Act, effective in 1991,[28] provided artists with a number of post-sale rights unless the artist merely produced the work for hire.[29] Under that version of moral rights, the artist creating a work of visual art such as sculpture, paintings, limited edition prints, or photographs[30] has rights to attribution. That is, authorship must be accurately represented. More surprisingly, the artist can also claim a right of integrity so that even after an

similar to famous children's stories to comment on O.J. Simpson murder trial not fair use, while using the same to question values in the children's books themselves is fair use).

22. Wendy J. Gordon & Sam Postbrief, On Commodifying Intangibles (Book Reviews), 10 Yale J.L. & Human. 135, 158, n. 106 (1998) ("transactional fairness").

23. See Campbell, supra n. 19, 510 U.S. at 586, 114 S.Ct. at 1175.

24. See Harper & Row, Publishers, Inc. v. Nation Enterprises, 471 U.S. 539, 105 S.Ct. 2218, 85 L.Ed.2d 588 (1985).

25. Sony Corp. of America v. Universal City Studios, Inc., 464 U.S. 417, 104 S.Ct. 774, 78 L.Ed.2d 574 (1984).

26. Harper & Row, Publishers, Inc. v. Nation Enterprises, supra n. 23.

27. The bundle is said to include (1) the right to disclose or not disclose the work; (2) the "right of paternity," accurate reflection of authorship, and perhaps under some circumstances a forced publication; (3) the right of integrity, that is, to prevent change in the work. Other moral rights may include the right to prevent "excessive criticism" and "assaults" upon the artist's personality. These components are discussed in Roberta Rosenthal Kwall, Copyright and the Moral Right: Is an American Marriage Possible?, 38 Vand. L. Rev. 1 (1985).

28. Largely codified in 17 U.S.C.A. § 106A.

29. 17 U.S.C.A. § 101; see Roberta Rosenthal Kwall, How Fine Art Fares Post Vara, 1 Marq. Intell. Prop. L. Rev. 1 (1997) (favoring extending moral rights to cover works made for hire).

30. Motion pictures and a number of other items are excluded by definition in 17 U.S.C.A. § 101.

unqualified sale, an intentional "distortion, mutilation, or modification" of an author's work of visual art infringes the artist's rights. In addition, if the work is of "recognized stature," a grossly negligent destruction of the work also infringes the artist's right.[31] Although the statute utilizes the copyright framework, the artist's right is independent of copyright and independent of ownership of the work itself. However, the artist may waive her moral rights.[32] A number of state statutes, if not preempted, provide somewhat similar moral rights protections, although some of them may put more emphasis on cultural preservation.[33]

Extending or restricting moral rights? Many writers favor not only the moral rights accorded by the statute but an extension of them.[34] Under the statute, an artist could prohibit a purchaser of a black and white print from adding color to it.[35] The extended right of integrity that is afforded elsewhere more significantly prevents the purchaser and owner of the copyright from altering a *reproduction* of the purchased art: the heirs of Picasso might prevent distribution or making of a motion picture that showed paintings Picasso sold years earlier because they did not like the screenplay.[36] This extensive right of integrity is rejected in the federal statute,[37] perhaps because it conflicts not only with normal property rights and the freedom of others, but also with egalitarian values.[38] The extended version of the right of integrity may also stifle creation by others in order to give a cachet and "honor" to the first artist.[39] But Manet did not dishonor Giorgione by rendering his own version of *The Concert*; on the contrary, he added to the world's stock of art without harming the Giorgione at all. The integrity right could interfere with freedom of religion as well as with speech and creativity. In a pre-statutory case, a church overpainted an art work in the church because the church believed it conveyed the wrong perception of religious doctrine. The artist attempted to require removal of the overpainting. To be required to publish anything is at least potentially an offense to free speech,[40] and to be required to publish a religious belief that is

31. 17 U.S.C.A. § 106A (a).

32. Under American law, waiver is permitted, although transfer of the moral right is not. 17 U.S.C.A. § 106A (e). Waiver is defended, for this time and place, in Thomas F. Cotter, Pragmatism, Economics, and the Droit Moral, 76 N.C. L. Rev. 1 (1997).

33. E.g., Cal. Civ. Code § 987; see Nimmer on Copyright § 8D.07 (listing and discussing state statutes).

34. See, e.g., Roberta Rosenthal Kwall, How Fine Art Fares Post Vara, 1 Marq. Intell. Prop. L. Rev. 1 (1997).

35. Under French law, motion pictures are included in the protection and a French court actually held that colorization was an infringement of moral rights. See describing this and other decisions, Thomas F. Cotter, Pragmatism, Economics, and the Droit Moral, 76 N.C. L. Rev. 1, 13–14 (1997).

36. See, reporting this event and others, Richard Hurowitz, Surviving Copyright Infringement: Fair Use of Protected Works in "Biopics", 22 Colum.-VLA J.L. & Arts 247 (1998).

37. See 17 U.S.C.A. § 106A (c) (3).

38. Sheldon W. Halpern, of Moral Right and Moral Righteousness, 1 Marq. Intell. Prop. L. Rev. 65 (1997).

39. See Beyer, Intentionalism, Art, and the Suppression of Innovation: Film Colorization and the Philosophy of Moral Rights, 82 NW. U. L. REV. 1011 (1988).

40. See Miami Herald Pub. Co. v. Tornillo, 418 U.S. 241, 94 S.Ct. 2831, 41 L.Ed.2d 730 (1974) (right of reply in libel cases unconstitutional); Wooley v. Maynard, 430 U.S. 705, 97 S.Ct. 1428, 51 L.Ed.2d 752 (1977).

odious to the publisher seems an offense to religious freedom as well. Not surprisingly, the court refused to compel removal of the paint.[41]

41. Crimi v. Rutgers Presbyterian Church, 194 Misc. 570, 89 N.Y.S.2d 813 (Sup.Ct. 1949).

*

CHAPTER 34

NUISANCE

§ 462. Introducing Nuisance Law

Scope and related fields. Private nuisance law deals primarily with the plaintiff's right to use and enjoy her land free from intangible invasions that can be loosely called pollution. Private nuisance almost always involves incompatible uses of two parcels of land. The use-and-enjoyment side of nuisance law is now supplemented heavily by statutes and ordinances providing for zoning and land-use development, backed by specialized legal literature,[1] which in turn may take lawyers into the law of unconstitutional takings of property by regulation.[2]

The pollution side of nuisance law has its limits; it cannot deal with pollution common in the environment such as the pollution from auto emissions. Environmental statutes and regulations have developed a specialized law and literature on environmental protection and recovery,[3] including a growing sub-speciality in environmental justice with concerns to distribute the burdens of unremedied pollution fairly in society.[4] Sometimes nuisance law and regulation work together, each supplementing the other.[5] At other times regulation displaces nuisance law, leaving the individual victim to hope that regulators adequately protect her interest.[6] Legislatures have also intervened to immunize special interest groups from liability for nuisance, as in the case of Right to Farm laws in many states.[7] This chapter addresses only the common law private nuisance and the public nuisance causing special private harm.

§ 462

1. E.g., EDWARD H. ZIEGLER, JR. ET AL., RATHKOPF'S LAW OF ZONING AND PLANNING (5 vol. 1995 & Supps.).

2. See Louise A. Halper, Untangling The Nuisance Knot, 26 B.C. ENVTL. AFF L. REV. 89 (1998).

3. See, e.g., WILLIAM H. RODGERS, JR., ENVIRONMENTAL LAW (2d ed. 1994 & Supp.).

4. Largely developing after ROBERT D. BULLARD, DUMPING IN DIXIE: RACE, CLASS, AND ENVIRONMENTAL QUALITY (1990), there is already a substantial literature with divergent viewpoints and emphases. Some use the term "environmental racism." For a brief summary of the viewpoints and literature in an article recent at this writing, see Alice Kaswan, Environmental Laws: Grist for the Equal Protection Mill, 70 U. COLO. L. REV. 387 (1999).

5. E.g., New York v. Shore Realty Corp., 759 F.2d 1032 (2d Cir.1985) (CERCLA and nuisance).

6. San Diego Gas & Elec. Co. v. Superior Court, 13 Cal.4th 893, 920 P.2d 669, 55 Cal.Rptr.2d 724 (1996) (nuisance claim based upon invasion by electromagnetic fields would be inconsistent with public utility commission regulation).

7. See, e.g., Pure Air and Water Inc. of Chemung County v. Davidsen, 246 A.D.2d 786, 668 N.Y.S.2d 248 (1998) (shielding the defendant with the immunity); Neil D. Hamilton, Right-to-farm Laws Reconsidered: Ten Reasons Why Legislative Efforts to Resolve Agricultural Nuisances May Be Ineffective, 3 DRAKE J. AGRIC. L. 103 (1998). It has also been said that a public utility cannot be a nuisance. Kuper v. Lincoln–

Prosser's jungle. At one time the law of nuisance was the jungle Prosser described.[8] This was in part because of the peculiar history of nuisance,[9] but more often for other reasons. Older decisions employed broad, almost meaningless definitions[10] and bewildering terminology that can now be largely discarded.[11] The term nuisance itself, which in a lay sense means only annoyance, was applied quite variously to a wide variety of seemingly unrelated cases.[12] Judges and commentators approached nuisance with different philosophical orientations. Public and private nuisance were not carefully distinguished, and the distinction between the damages remedy and the abatement remedy was not observed.[13]

Formal distinctions of an earlier era also make nuisance confusing to contemporary observers. For instance, what might seem like an ordinary trespass by backed up waters or sewage might be called a nuisance in many cases,[14] because under formalistic thinking of an earlier era, the entry would not qualify as a trespass, because under contemporary rules it was not intended, or because by describing a tort as a nuisance the plaintiff could penetrate the defendant's governmental immunity. To classify a problem as nuisance rather than trespass is to invoke a regime of reasonable accommodation between conflicting uses and to reject absolute rights associated with trespass. So airplane overflights, a trespass under older views, may be analyzed under the nuisance rules in which the landowner's right to enjoy her property is weighed against the defendant's rights.[15]

Quite different kinds of nuisances arise because when legislatures wish to terminate a given land use, they often first declare that the use is a nuisance. For example, statutes may declare that use of land for prostitution is a nuisance.[16] Still other cases involve interferences with

Union Elec. Co., 557 N.W.2d 748 (S.D. 1996).

8. Prosser & Keeton § 86 at 616.

9. Nuisance was often loosely associated with strict liability. The emphasis was also often upon abatement rather than upon damages.

10. See § 463.

11. *Absolute nuisance* means any interference for which courts would impose liability without regard either to the defendant's fault or to the gravity and unreasonableness of the harm done. Under contemporary rules recognizing negligent, intentional, and strict liability nuisances, the term can be dropped. See Highview North Apartments v. County of Ramsey, 323 N.W.2d 65 (Minn.1982). A *nuisance per se* is an activity or condition that is a nuisance in itself and not permissible under any circumstances. This category mainly, or perhaps, solely consists of uses prohibited by statute or regulation, E.g., Tiegs v. Watts, 135 Wash.2d 1, 954 P.2d 877 (1998), but some courts use the term much more broadly. A lawful business, by definition, is not a nuisance per se. A *nuisance in fact* or *per accidens* is the ordinary private nuisance, an activity or condition that is out of place or is a nuisance because of the particular way it is carried on. See § 465.

12. Among discussions of this, Copart Indus., Inc. v. Consolidated Edison Co. of New York, Inc., 41 N.Y.2d 564, 362 N.E.2d 968, 394 N.Y.S.2d 169 (1977).

13. See Louise A. Halper, Untangling The Nuisance Knot, 26 B.C. Envtl. Aff. L. Rev. 89 (1998).

14. E.g., Fletcher v. City of Independence, 708 S.W.2d 158 (Mo.App.1986) (sewer backup); Bible Baptist Church v. City of Cleburne, 848 S.W.2d 826 (Tex.App.1993) (same).

15. See Atkinson v. Bernard, Inc. 223 Or. 624, 355 P.2d 229 (1960).

16. E.g., Cal. Penal Code § 11225

the common right and are said to be "public nuisances," as where a public stream is polluted, a condition that may lead to a private right of action in certain instances.[17] These diverse examples suggest that nuisance could not be clearly defined.

Clearing a path. Two increasingly clear perceptions assisted understanding of nuisance law. First, if public and statutory nuisance cases are set aside for separate analysis, some paths can be marked in the remaining private nuisance tort. Second, private nuisance does not describe any particular conduct of the defendant, but a type of harm suffered by the plaintiff—impaired enjoyment of rights in land.[18] These perceptions make possible a reasonably coherent understanding of private nuisance, so some of the main features of Prosser's jungle can be mapped in the succeeding sections.

§ 463. Defining and Illustrating Private Nuisance

Definitions of private nuisance. A private nuisance today is a condition[1] or activity[2] that interferes with the possessor's[3] use and enjoyment of her land by incorporeal or non-trespassory invasions[4] to such an extent that the landowner cannot reasonably be expected to bear without compensation.[5] What the plaintiff can reasonably be expected to bear it often determined by the character of the neighborhood, but the utility of the defendant's activity is also relevant.[6] The interference may cause tangible harm to the land, diminution in its market value, or personal discomfort to its occupants. The interference must be one that would

17. See § 467.

18. See Graber v. City of Peoria, 156 Ariz. 553, 753 P.2d 1209 (Ct. App. 1988).

§ 463

1. E.g., Rodrigue v. Copeland, 475 So.2d 1071 (La.1985) (Christmas display drawing heavy traffic).

2. E.g., Bowers v. Westvaco Corp., 244 Va. 139, 419 S.E.2d 661 (1992) (continual loading and moving of trucks a few feet from the plaintiff's house).

3. E.g., a lessee. Nichols v. Mid-Continent Pipe Line Co., 933 P.2d 272 (Okla. 1996); but not a mortgagee. Stevensen v. Goodson, 924 P.2d 339 (Utah 1996). The possessor's family is usually included if they suffer individual illness or discomfort. Mere guests or adult children may be excluded, however. See Arnoldt v. Ashland Oil, Inc., 186 W.Va. 394, 412 S.E.2d 795, 25 A.L.R.5th 890 (1991). If the nuisance does permanent harm, the owner out of possession may also have a claim. Restatement § 821E., cmt. f.

4. Restatement § 821D. Judicial formulations have evolved over the years. Much broader definitions can be found in older cases. For example, a nuisance is sometimes defined as anything done to the hurt, annoyance, or detriment of the lands or hereditaments of another, and not amounting to a trespass. Such broad definitions are unworkable. When similar definitions are found in statutes, the statute is usually treated as a statement of general principle, not a precise rule formulation. See Mel Foster Co. Properties, Inc. v. American Oil Co., 427 N.W.2d 171 (Iowa 1988) (statute does not modify common law rules). The same observation has been made about the maxim that supposedly founds nuisance law, sic utere tuo ut alienum non laedas, meaning you must so use your property as not to injure your neighbor. See Amphitheaters, Inc. v. Portland Meadows, 184 Or. 336, 198 P.2d 847, 5 A.L.R.2d 690 (1948) (giving a small collection of criticisms of the maxim).

5. Usually put in short form: the interference must be substantial and unreasonable. E.g., San Diego Gas & Elec. Co. v. Superior Court, 13 Cal.4th 893, 920 P.2d 669, 55 Cal.Rptr.2d 724 (1996). Nuisance does not, however, require unreasonable actions by the defendant, only that the plaintiff cannot reasonably be expected to bear the harm. See § 465.

6. § 465.

interfere with the normal use and enjoyment of a normal person; the interference is not a nuisance if it interferes only with especially sensitive persons or uses.[7] Proof that the nuisance has resulted in a diminution of the land's market value shows or tends to show that the harm is not merely the result of the plaintiff's sensitivity, since loss of market value necessarily means that potential buyers would also be affected by the nuisance.

Examples of private nuisance. The issue of nuisance often arises because the defendant's activity causes pollution of air, water, or land by dust or smoke,[8] odors,[9] chemicals,[10] or noise.[11] Heavy traffic in a neighborhood[12] or an intense light shone directly into the plaintiff's bedroom might constitute a nuisance.[13] If the defendant's electromagnetic radiation[14] or stray voltage[15] invades the land, it is a nuisance if it is any tort at all.[16]

Distinguishing trespass. Possession vs. enjoyment. If I enter your land or deposit a boat upon it, I may be a trespasser and liable for interference with your possession, even if your land is not harmed.[17] But if I invade your land with smells and stenches, pollution or electromagnetic radiation, I am no trespasser under traditional law, for I have not interfered with your possession. In such cases, I am liable if at all for interference with your use and enjoyment, that is, for nuisance. Some contemporary cases have been impatient with these distinctions between visible and invisible interferences and have treated some invasions by polluting particles as micro-trespasses that invade possessory rights.[18] At the same time, they have sometimes used the word trespass to describe the tort but have then proceeded to apply at least some of the rules of nuisance.[19]

7. Amphitheaters, Inc. v. Portland Meadows, 184 Or. 336, 198 P.2d 847, 5 A.L.R.2d 690 (1948) (lights from a race track interfered with drive-in movie by casting glow on the screen, but outdoor movie represented an abnormally sensitive use, no recovery).

8. Boomer v. Atlantic Cement Co., 26 N.Y.2d 219, 309 N.Y.S.2d 312, 257 N.E.2d 870, 40 A.L.R.3d 590 (1970) (cement dust, remedy limited to damages, however); Smith v. Wallowa County, 145 Or.App. 341, 929 P.2d 1100 (1996) (smoke, dust, odors).

9. Penland v. Redwood Sanitary Sewer Serv. Dist., 156 Or.App. 311, 965 P.2d 433 (1998).

10. Scribner v. Summers, 84 F.3d 554 (2d Cir.1996) (barium draining onto the plaintiff's land); Mel Foster Co. Properties, Inc. v. American Oil Co., 427 N.W.2d 171 (Iowa 1988) (gasoline percolation to the plaintiff's land).

11. E.g., Rose v. Chaikin, 187 N.J.Super. 210, 453 A.2d 1378, 36 A.L.R.4th 1148 (1982); Mandel v. Geloso, 206 A.D.2d 699, 614 N.Y.S.2d 645 (1994).

12. Rodrigue v. Copeland, 475 So.2d 1071 (La.1985).

13. Greene v. Spinning, 48 S.W.2d 51(Mo.App.1931).

14. San Diego Gas & Elec. Co. v. Superior Court, 13 Cal.4th 893, 920 P.2d 669, 55 Cal.Rptr.2d 724 (1996) (common law claim could not be pursued because of regulation of administrative agency).

15. Vogel v. Grant–Lafayette Elec. Coop., 201 Wis.2d 416, 548 N.W.2d 829 (1996).

16. See Kuper v. Lincoln–Union Elec. Co., 557 N.W.2d 748 (S.D.1996) (holding that stray voltage of a public utility is not a nuisance in the absence of negligence).

17. §§ 50 & 56.

18. Bradley v. American Smelting and Refining Co., 104 Wash.2d 677, 709 P.2d 782 (1985).

19. See Borland v. Sanders Lead Co., Inc., 369 So.2d 523, 2 A.L.R.4th 1042 (Ala. 1979) (invasion of possessory interest is not

Regimes of rights vs. regimes of accommodation. The significant point, however, is that the terms trespass and nuisance stand for two different approaches to handling interference with rights in land. To say the case is for trespass is to declare that the rights of the plaintiff landowner brook no interference, not even a little, not even if it is reasonable, not even if it does no physical harm. To say that the case is for nuisance is to insist that with some kinds of interference, liability must be limited not only to cases of actual harm but also to cases in which the harm is unreasonable. The question where to draw the line between these two regimes is perhaps less important than the realization that courts can consciously adopt one set of rules or the other as the facts seem to demand.[20]

Distinguishing harm caused to the land by predecessors in title. Private nuisance is traditionally a claim based upon activities outside the land by a stranger to the title, for instance, based upon a neighbor's noise or pollution. When a landowner complains that her vendor contaminated the land before she purchased, the nuisance action does not traditionally lie.[21] In such a case, the vendor is liable for fraudulent representations that induce the land's purchase, but if the purchaser wishes further assurance she must bargain for it so that her contract and deed place responsibility upon the vendor. However, a few recent cases have imposed liability upon the vendor where his pre-sale activities on the land caused abnormally dangerous[22] or at least a serious and destructive contamination of the land.[23] And Wisconsin has held a nuisance claim can be asserted against a defendant who is rightfully supplying electricity to the land if stray voltage causes harm to cattle.[24] Some environmental statutes also impose liability upon the predecessor in title among others.

determined by size of particles, but if the trespass is indirect (with microscopic particles), then actual damages must be proven); Martin v. Reynolds Metals Co., 221 Or. 86, 342 P.2d 790 (1959) (treating microscopic particles as trespass but excluding liability when the harm is de minimis); Bradley v. American Smelting & Refining Co., 104 Wash.2d 677, 709 P.2d 782 (1985) (requiring "actual and substantial" damages). See also Scribner v. Summers, 84 F.3d 554 (2d Cir.1996) (physical contamination of land with barium particles called a trespass, but the liability was for actual damages, not for presumed damages of trespass); Mercer v. Rockwell International Corp., 24 F.Supp.2d 735 (W.D.Ky.1998) (physical harm required, economic loss not enough); Chance v. BP Chemicals, 77 Ohio St.3d 17, 670 N.E.2d 985 (1996) (deep underground injection of wastes migrated to the plaintiff's land but was not an interference so no liability for "trespass").

20. The two torts may overlap on some facts, See Restatement § 821D, cmt. e. But that only means that in some cases courts will allow the plaintiff to have the advantage of the more favorable rules, usually the rules of the trespass regime.

21. Philadelphia Electric Co. v. Hercules, Inc., 762 F.2d 303 (3d Cir.1985); Rosenblatt v. Exxon Co., 335 Md. 58, 642 A.2d 180 (1994) (also rejecting strict liability based upon abnormally dangerous activity).

22. T & E Industries, Inc. v. Safety Light Corp., 123 N.J. 371, 587 A.2d 1249, 13 A.L.R.5th 1041 (1991).

23. Newhall Land and Farming Co. v. Superior Court, 19 Cal.App.4th 334, 23 Cal. Rptr.2d 377 (1993) (where the vendor did not disclose its contamination and the purchaser could not factor the contamination into the purchase price).

24. Vogel v. Grant–Lafayette Elec. Coop., 201 Wis.2d 416, 548 N.W.2d 829 (1996).

§ 464. Intent, Negligence and Strict Liability

The idea of a private nuisance is that the plaintiff is being subjected to an invasion of her interest in use and enjoyment of land that she cannot reasonably be required to suffer. Because a finding of nuisance is based upon the plaintiff's harm and not necessarily upon the defendant's conduct,[1] the defendant's liability may be based upon strict liability principles as well as upon intentional or negligent interference.[2] Indeed, as a practical matter, the question of negligence vs. strict liability is seldom determinative.

Negligence. So far as a supposed nuisance rests upon proof of the defendant's negligence, the case proceeds largely as any other negligence case, and the nuisance label adds little to the analysis. For example, courts have said repeatedly that when the defendant's negligent conduct is the basis for liability in nuisance, the plaintiff's contributory or comparative fault is a defense or partial defense as in other negligence cases,[3] although the plaintiff's contributory fault, short of willful misconduct or the like, will not defeat other nuisance claims.[4] However, if the court conceives of the case as one for nuisance rather than negligence, it may reject immunities that would otherwise apply.[5] In addition, to find a nuisance is to say that the plaintiff can recover for loss of enjoyment, a kind of chronic emotional harm that might be viewed more cautiously without a finding of nuisance.[6]

Strict liability. One unusual form of strict liability appears when the landowner is held responsible for abating a nuisance on his land that was created by someone else.[7] In some such cases, the landowner may be at fault, but his fault is not necessarily a requirement, provided abatement is actually feasible. Except for this kind of vicarious responsibility, the Restatement rule imposes strict liability only if the plaintiff can show that the defendant maintained or pursued an abnormally dangerous condition or activity.[8] This view finds support in the cases that deny liability when the defendant unintentionally discharges fumes or the like on a single occasion without knowing of the harm until after it has occurred. If the fumes are not regarded as abnormally dangerous, many

§ 464

1. E.g., Highview North Apartments v. County of Ramsey, 323 N.W.2d 65 (Minn. 1982); Branch v. Western Petroleum, Inc., 657 P.2d 267 (Utah 1982).

2. Restatement § 822.

3. See Copart Indus., Inc. v. Consolidated Edison Co. of New York, Inc., 41 N.Y.2d 564, 362 N.E.2d 968, 394 N.Y.S.2d 169 (1977); Vogel v. Grant–Lafayette Elec. Coop., 201 Wis.2d 416, 548 N.W.2d 829 (1996); Restatement § 840B (1).

4. See Batick v. Seymour, 186 Conn. 632, 443 A.2d 471 (1982) (willful misconduct required to defeat "absolute" nuisance); Turner v. Thompson, 102 Ill.App.3d 838, 430 N.E.2d 157, 58 Ill.Dec. 215 (1981) (nuisance so declared by statute, contributory fault irrelevant); Restatement § 840B (2) & (3). Coming to the nuisance, though not usually a matter of contributory fault, may defeat the plaintiff for other reasons. See § 465.

5. See § 269.

6. See § 308 (reflecting limitations on emotional harm recoveries).

7. New York v. Shore Realty Corp., 759 F.2d 1032 (2d Cir.1985); Nassr v. Commonwealth, 394 Mass. 767, 477 N.E.2d 987 (1985); Restatement § 839.

8. Restatement § 822; as to strict liability for abnormal danger, see § 347.

such cases require the plaintiff to prove negligence.[9] Some thinkers believe that some strict liability should be imposed more broadly, even when the defendant's activity is not abnormally dangerous,[10] and some cases have stated the same view.[11] Although it does not impose strict liability for a single, unintended escape of substances that are not abnormally dangerous, the Restatement does impose liability upon reasonable and careful defendants who repeatedly or continuously discharge substances that deprive the plaintiff of her rights of use and enjoyment. It imposes that liability, however, on a theory of intentional invasion.

Intent and strict liability effects. The defendant intends the invasion not only when he has a purpose to invade the plaintiff's land but also when he is substantially certain that his activities will cause such an invasion.[12] The defendant who attracts indigents to a neighborhood and knows that they continuously invade the rights of neighbors is responsible for the nuisance he has fostered, though his own acts and motives are entirely praiseworthy.[13] An industrial nuisance might begin innocently, but once the defendant is apprised of its effect upon the plaintiff's use and enjoyment, it is intentional if the defendant continues the harmful condition. In such cases, the fact that the defendant exercises care or uses the best technology available does not relieve it of responsibility for activity that unreasonably invades the plaintiff's rights to use and enjoy her land.[14] Although the industrial nuisance can be regarded as an intentional invasion, it works as a soft version of strict liability because even extraordinary care by the defendant does not defeat the claim. It may be, however, that social utility of the defendant's activity and its economic value to the community, will protect the defendant from a damages award[15] or an injunction.[16]

§ 465. Substantial and Unreasonable Interference Required

Unreasonable interference required. The invasion that affects the plaintiff's use and enjoyment must be unreasonable as well as substan-

9. E.g., Wright v. Masonite Corp., 368 F.2d 661 (4th Cir.1966); see Waschak v. Moffat, 379 Pa. 441, 109 A.2d 310 (1954); see William K. Jones, Strict Liability for Hazardous Enterprise, 92 Colum. L. Rev. 1705, 1737 (1992).

10. See Robert E. Keeton, Restating Strict Liability and Nuisance, 48 Vand. L. Rev. 595 (1995).

11. Washington Suburban Sanitary Com'n v. CAE–Link Corp., 330 Md. 115, 622 A.2d 745 (1993). Many of these cases in fact involve intent in the Restatement sense. A number state that neither negligence nor intent is required, but those do not necessarily show the adoption of a broader strict liability rule than proposed by the Restatement.

12. Copart Indus., Inc. v. Consolidated Edison Co. of New York, Inc., 41 N.Y.2d 564, 362 N.E.2d 968, 394 N.Y.S.2d 169 (1977); Jost v. Dairyland Power Cooperative, 45 Wis.2d 164, 172 N.W.2d 647 (1969); Restatement § 825.

13. Armory Park Neighborhood Ass'n v. Episcopal Community Services in Arizona, 148 Ariz. 1, 712 P.2d 914 (1985); cf. Shamhart v. Morrison Cafeteria Co., 159 Fla. 629, 32 So.2d 727 (1947) (cafeteria attracting customers who lined up on the sidewalk, blocking other businesses).

14. Parker v. Barefoot, 130 N.C.App. 18, 502 S.E.2d 42 (1998); Jost v. Dairyland Power Cooperative, supra n. 12.

15. § 465.

16. § 468.

tial. "Unreasonable" in nuisance law is not like "unreasonable" in the law of negligence, for it does not refer to risk-creating conduct of the defendant but to the reasonable expectations of a normal person occupying the plaintiff's land. Reasonable expectations must take into account the fact that others, too, must have the right to use their land. For this reason, even an intentional invasion is not necessarily a nuisance. The defendant may know that the noise of his church bells or the smells of his baking bread invade the plaintiff's land and are offensive to the plaintiff, but the invasion would seldom be unreasonable.[1] Similarly, the fact that the defendant's activity diminishes the value of the plaintiff's land does not necessarily show that the defendant's activity is a nuisance. In a neighborhood of mansions, a small home may diminish the value of the large homes nearby, but a small home is not in itself a nuisance. What is unreasonable depends upon a number of considerations discussed below.

Character of the neighborhood or social expectations. In the absence of physical harm to the plaintiff's land or person or prohibited activity like toxic dumping, courts almost always consider, directly or indirectly, the character, custom, and culture of the neighborhood or community in determining whether the defendant's legal activities cause unreasonable and substantial harm and thus count as a nuisance.[2] The obligatory observation is that a nuisance may be the right thing in the wrong place, like a pig in the parlor instead of the barnyard.[3] Noise, odors, or sights that are consistent in nature and extent with the neighborhood's legitimate use patterns are seldom if ever a nuisance.[4] The same invasions are likely to be nuisances if they are out of character with the neighborhood. A factory in a residential district may well be a nuisance, but a factory in the factory district operating like others usually is not. In line with this, the fact that the defendant is in compliance with a zoning ordinance, although not ordinarily conclusive, is at least a relevant factor in

§ 465

1. See Langan v. Bellinger, 203 A.D.2d 857, 611 N.Y.S.2d 59 (1994) (church bells liked by some neighbors were not a nuisance).

2. Weinhold v. Wolff, 555 N.W.2d 454 (Iowa 1996) (location a major factor); Clinic & Hospital v. McConnell, 241 Mo.App. 223, 236 S.W.2d 384 (1951) (noise exceeding level of neighborhood); Robie v. Lillis, 112 N.H. 492, 299 A.2d 155 (1972) (incompatible with the surrounding neighborhood); Rose v. Chaikin, 187 N.J.Super. 210, 453 A.2d 1378, 36 A.L.R.4th 1148 (1982) (noise nuisance; "Its intrusive quality is heightened because of the locality. The neighborhood is quiet and residential."); Penland v. Redwood Sanitary Sewer Serv. Dist., 156 Or.App. 311, 965 P.2d 433 (1998); O'Cain v. O'Cain, 322 S.C. 551, 473 S.E.2d 460 (Ct. App.1996) (pigs in front of house a nuisance); cf. Rassier v. Houim, 488 N.W.2d 635 (N.D.1992) (coming to the nuisance may have different effects depending upon the character of neighborhood). In many instances, the character of the neighborhood or locality is a way of summarizing the kinds of reciprocal harms that are acceptable; so long as neighbors impose similar harms upon each other, there is no nuisance. See Bamford v. Turnely, 3 B & S 66, 122 Eng.Rep. 25 (Exch. Ch. 1862) (Judgment of Bramwell, B.).

3. Village of Euclid, Ohio v. Ambler Realty Co., 272 U.S. 365, 388, 47 S.Ct. 114, 118, 71 L.Ed. 303, 54 A.L.R. 1016 (1926).

4. This is one of the foundations of the rule that often bars a plaintiff who moves to the neighborhood where activities like those of the defendant are carried on. See Erbrich Products Co., Inc. v. Wills, 509 N.E.2d 850 (Ind.App.1987).

determining a nuisance.[5] Environmental justice advocates might argue that the emphasis on the neighborhood's character tends to distribute environmental burdens unfairly to neighborhoods that are already carrying more than their fair share of pollution.[6] This may suggest that courts will need to work out responsibility for cumulative pollution,[7] but it is also true as explained in the next paragraph that a defendant could be held under present rules if he causes more harm than is reasonably expected in the neighborhood.

Magnitude, frequency, or duration exceeding neighborhood norms. The defendant's use of his land may be broadly consistent with the uses to which the neighborhood is dedicated, yet because of the magnitude, frequency, or duration , the use may constitute a nuisance.[8] For example, pigs are part of rural life, but an excessive concentration of them in a small area with inadequate drainage and ventilation may produce a stench that is unbearable and unreasonable even in a farming community.[9] The same is true with the frequency of invasions; an occasional invasion may be tolerated as reasonable and within the neighborhood norms but continuous, repeated, or frequent invasions may not be.[10] An understanding of the neighborhood character, customs, and values suffices to determine whether the pig odor is a nuisance. Even if the defendant's activity has high social utility and is well-intended, there are some invasions the landowner should not be required to bear.[11]

Priority in time; "coming to the nuisance." Courts resolving nuisance disputes consider priority in time as an important factor. The defendant who moves hog production to an established residential neighborhood will need mighty justifications to escape liability.[12] In the reverse situation, when a plaintiff moves her residence to a neighborhood of nonresidential uses such as a neighborhood of small factories,

5. E.g., Prah v. Maretti, 108 Wis.2d 223, 321 N.W.2d 182, 29 A.L.R.4th 324 (1982). A California statute requires a finding of unreasonable operation before an industry can be found a nuisance while operating in an expressly permitted zone. CAL.CODE CIV.PRO. § 731a.

6. See Kathy Seward Northern, Battery and Beyond: a Tort Law Response to Environmental Racism, 21 WM. & MARY ENVTL. L. & POL'Y REV. 485 (1997).

7. See § 171, n. 6 (collective responsibility for nuisance).

8. Clinic & Hospital v. McConnell, 241 Mo.App. 223, 233, 236 S.W.2d 384, 391 (1951) ("alleged music" on loudspeaker in business district; "these annoyances and discomforts must not be more than those ordinarily to be expected in the community or district").

9. Weinhold v. Wolff, 555 N.W.2d 454 (Iowa 1996). Right to farm laws may jeopardize this example as well as the environment generally. See Neil D. Hamilton, Right-to-farm Laws Reconsidered: Ten Reasons Why Legislative Efforts to Resolve Agricultural Nuisances May Be Ineffective, 3 DRAKE J. AGRIC. L. 103 (1998).

10. See, e.g., Rose v. Chaikin, 187 N.J.Super. 210, 453 A.2d 1378, 36 A.L.R.4th 1148 (1982) (constant noise of windmill in quiet residential neighborhood); Penland v. Redwood Sanitary Sewer Serv. Dist., 156 Or.App. 311, 965 P.2d 433 (1998). Nuisance is often associated with conditions or with continuing activities rather than with harms caused on a particular occasion.

11. Jost v. Dairyland Power Cooperative, 45 Wis.2d 164, 172 N.W.2d 647 (1969); see Robert E. Keeton, Restating Strict Liability and Nuisance, 48 VAND. L. REV. 595 (1995); Restatement § 826 (b) (if the harm is serious and compensation is feasible).

12. Cf. Weinhold v. Wolff, 555 N.W.2d 454 (Iowa 1996) (extensive hog production and smells in rural but residential neighborhood).

the nonresidential uses are not often a nuisance.[13] Prior use in that case has stamped the neighborhood with its character, so that the residents must reasonably expect the kind of factory operations that were present when the residents chose to move in. A second reason for denying relief to one who moved to the nuisance is that the price the plaintiff paid for the land reflects factory neighborhood prices, not upscale suburban prices. She has, in a sense, already been paid for the inconvenience she may suffer because that inconvenience is reflected in the reduced purchase price.

Limits on coming to the nuisance rules. Such conclusions are not inevitable, however. First, the factory may substantially change its operation to make it more detrimental, as where a factory begins operating at night after the plaintiff moves to the neighborhood. Second, the factory may accidentally discharge toxic materials that cause personal injury distinct from any nuisance. Liability in that case will turn on ordinary rules of negligence or strict liability. Third, the first landowner to arrive upon the scene should not be permitted to rule out all other uses, in effect unilaterally zoning his neighbor's land for the uses he has adopted by his own. In a dynamic country, a certain amount of change must be expected in many communities and neighborhoods. In one famous case,[14] suburban developments expanded outward until they came close to a cattle feed lot that produced large amounts of manure and attracted flies to the neighborhood. Although the feed lot was there first, the growth of cities must be expected and permitted, so the feed lot was a nuisance in spite of its priority. Its priority did limit the remedies available, however.

Gravity of harm. Character of the neighborhood does not always cast direct light upon the nuisance issue. When the nuisance is invasive and seriously affects the physical integrity of the land itself, as where toxic chemicals percolate into the groundwater, it may be a nuisance as a matter of law and without regard to the neighborhood's character.[15] In many instances, the gravity has been weighed by legislators and administrators under federal or state environmental laws. Statutes or regulations may thus establish that the defendant's chemical pollution is a nuisance or may create a claim independent of common law nuisance. Courts may also consider gravity of harm in determining whether the harms caused by the defendant's activity go beyond those sanctioned by neighborhood usage, as in the case of excessive odors from a hog farm in a rural area.[16]

Lack of utility of the defendant's activity. If the defendant's activity is conducted at an inappropriate location[17] or causes harm that is

13. See Erbrich Products Co., Inc. v. Wills, 509 N.E.2d 850 (1987) (statutory version of coming to nuisance rule).

14. Spur Industries, Inc. v. Del E. Webb Development Co., 108 Ariz. 178, 494 P.2d 700, 53 A.L.R.3d 861 (1972).

15. E.g., New York v. Shore Realty Corp., 759 F.2d 1032 (2d Cir.1985).

16. Weinhold v. Wolff, 555 N.W.2d 454 (Iowa 1996).

17. Restatement §§ 828 & 831.

reasonably avoidable,[18] it can count as a nuisance regardless of its social utility. Even when the defendant's land use is properly conducted and at a proper location, however, the fact that it has little or no social utility compared to the harm it causes classes the activity as a nuisance.[19] That is the case of malicious nuisances such as spite fences erected solely to obstruct the plaintiff and for no other purpose.[20]

Utility of the defendant's activity. Discounting social utility. The more debated question deals with the converse situation, where the defendant's activity causes harm that cannot be eliminated by reasonable care but is also socially useful. Should the utility or social value of the activity relieve the defendant of liability? When the harm is severe, the Restatement says not.[21] An important body of opinion supports that view.[22] To find a nuisance even when the social utility of the activity outweighs the harm, courts must also find that the activity would count as a nuisance if its utility is disregarded.[23] The Restatement and some other authorities also imply that the defendant must be able to capture enough of the activity's utility (in profits) to pay damages without going out of business,[24] but even if the defendant's activity is a charity or conducted in the public interest and not for profit, its social utility will not necessarily be enough to justify the harm it causes.[25] The remedy of injunction is a different matter, however; while the useful nuisance may subject the defendant to damages, courts may require payment of damages and allow it to continue.[26]

18. Highview North Apartments v. County of Ramsey, 323 N.W.2d 65 (Minn. 1982) (socially useful sewer system could have been placed to avoid sewage backup harming the plaintiff); Restatement §§ 828 & 830.

19. See Restatement § 829A.

20. Thus courts may treat a fence that blocks the plaintiff's view as a nuisance if it serves no purpose other than to inflict harm. Welsh v. Todd, 260 N.C. 527, 133 S.E.2d 171 (1963). If the fence has utility to the defendant, however, it is no nuisance.

21. Restatement § 829A as read with § 826.

22. See Jost v. Dairyland Power Cooperative, 45 Wis.2d 164, 172 N.W.2d 647 (1969); Bamford v. Turnley, 3 B & S 66, 122 Eng.Rep. 25 (Exch. Ch. 1862) (Judgment of Bramwell, B.); Restatement §§ 826 (b) & 829; 1 Harper, James & Gray § 1.24 (but criticizing the Restatement's patchwork solutions and preferring "incomplete privilege" based upon the private necessity cases).

23. Thus, courts have found no nuisance at all when an industry without negligence accidentally emits a noxious gas on a single occasion and the gas is not abnormally dangerous. See § 464. The defendant's activity is no more of a nuisance if it is socially useful. Likewise when the activity is appropriate to its location, or when the plaintiff comes to the nuisance.

24. Restatement § 826 (b). On the idea that profits of the business should pay for the harm done by the business, see especially the discussion in Bamford v. Turnley, supra n. 22.

25. See Armory Park Neighborhood Ass'n v. Episcopal Community Services in Arizona, 148 Ariz. 1, 712 P.2d 914 (1985) (church organization provided free meals to indigents, whose misbehavior became a nuisance to residents; the law does not allow "the costs of a charitable enterprise to be visited in their entirety upon the residents of a single neighborhood. The problems of dealing with the unemployed, the homeless and the mentally ill are also matters of community or governmental responsibility"); Rose v. Chaikin, 187 N.J.Super. 210, 453 A.2d 1378, 36 A.L.R.4th 1148 (1982) (windmill socially useful in creating alternative power sources, but still a noise nuisance in a residential neighborhood).

26. § 468.

Counting social utility. In spite of what has just been said, the social utility of the defendant's activity is important at least in the sense that if the activity is useful to the community or to society, the plaintiff might reasonably expect to put up with more annoyance.[27] Consequently, courts as well as the Restatement do attempt to consider the usefulness of the defendant's activity.[28] On the issue of nuisance vel non, however, courts do not seem to assess social utility in a quantitative way.[29] So the weighing of social utilities does not mean that a plaintiff with a low-value residence will always lose her claim against a defendant whose factory has great economic importance. On the contrary, the high value of the defendant's operation may suggest that the factory should pay damages or buy the plaintiff's property. Beyond this, it is now apparent that the cost of cleaning up toxic wastes produced by some industries is astronomical; so high, in fact, that courts may well be uncertain that a given industry's social value exceeds the harm it causes.

§ 466. Non–Invasive Nuisances

The Restatement speaks of private nuisances as "invasions."[1] Courts often speak of nuisances as "interferences."[2] Most private nuisances in fact involve invasion of the plaintiff's land by matter, sound, or light. For example, a light shone upon the plaintiff's property is an invasion that may count as a nuisance.[3] A plume of contamination deep under the plaintiff's land is an invasion, and if permanent and serious enough, can count as a nuisance, even though the landowner cannot directly perceive it and is harmed only because the value of her land is reduced by its presence.[4] In some cases, however, the plaintiff's discomfort arises because light or air is blocked by the defendant's structures,

27. See Fleming James, Jr., Memorandum: The Element of Fault in Private Nuisance, Appendix, Restatement Second of Torts Tentative Draft #16, 132, 140–141 (1970).

28. Carpenter v. Double R Cattle Co., Inc., 108 Idaho 602, 701 P.2d 222 (1985) ("the interests of the community, which would include the utility of the conduct, should be considered in the determination of the existence of a nuisance");Louisville Refining Co. v. Mudd, 339 S.W.2d 181 (Ky. 1960) (among other factors in determining existence of nuisance, the importance of the defendant's industry to the community); Kopecky v. National Farms, Inc., 244 Neb. 846, 510 N.W.2d 41 (1994) (evidence of social utility of swine raising in general should have been admitted, even though defendant proffered no evidence of the utility of its particular installation).

29. See Pendoley v. Ferreira, 345 Mass. 309, 187 N.E.2d 142, 2 A.L.R.3d 924 (1963) (injunction appropriate because, although "dollar loss to the plaintiffs is much smaller than that of the [defendant] ... the injury affects their residences and their reasonable enjoyment of them.")

§ 466

1. E.g., Restatement § 822. But "invasion" here is not clearly a requirement that physical matter intrude. Epstein, constructing a general theory of nuisance law, devotes a good deal of attention to the necessity for a physical invasion. Richard A. Epstein, Nuisance Law: Corrective Justice and Its Utilitarian Constraints, 8 J. LEG. STUD. 49, 56–65 (1979).

2. E.g., Robie v. Lillis, 112 N.H. 492, 299 A.2d 155 (1972).

3. Greene v. Spinning, 48 S.W.2d 51(Mo.App.1931); Firth v. Scherzberg, 366 Pa. 443, 77 A.2d 443 (1951) (noise and lights at night). In Golen v. Union Corp., U.C.O.-M.B.A., Inc., 718 A.2d 298 (Pa.Super.1998), the court thought light was not invasive but could be a nuisance because it could be perceived by a person on the land.

4. Bradley v. Armstrong Rubber Co., 130 F.3d 168 (5th Cir.1997).

or because the defendant's activities are aesthetically repugnant, or because they generate fear of future harm without any invasion at all. Plaintiffs have fared less well in such cases unless the defendant acts with "malice."

Blocking light, air or view. When the defendant erects a useful structure on his own land, the plaintiff will seldom be able to show a nuisance merely because her view or air are blocked.[5] However, when the defendant's structure interferes with the the plaintiff's view, light, or air for no purpose useful either to others or to the defendant himself, many courts have been willing to find a nuisance.[6]

Aesthetic nuisances. The unsightliness of the defendant's property may be considered in balancing the rights of the plaintiff and defendant.[7] But, because tastes differ and criteria for aesthetic judgment are deemed unreliable, courts have been reluctant to say that an inappropriate and ugly sight can be a nuisance.[8] So when the one neighbor mounted a toilet "seat and its lid on a piece of plywood placed atop a post overlooking his neighbors' land" with a brown spot alleged by the plaintiff to represent human excrement, the victim of this continuing visual assault had no right to abate the nuisance.[9] Vagaries of taste do indeed make it difficult to pass judgment upon outdoor sculptures and architectural disasters, but neighborhood character may permit a court to say with confidence that a front yard full of junked autos[10] or a mortuary[11] can constitute a nuisance where it is wholly inconsistent with the neighborhood's character, even though its impact derives solely from visual perception and distaste.[12]

5. Cf. Richmond Bros., Inc. v. Hagemann, 359 Mass. 265, 268 N.E.2d 680 (1971) (no nuisance even if defendant's building interfered with operation of the plaintiff's radio station); but cf. Prah v. Maretti, 108 Wis.2d 223, 321 N.W.2d 182, 29 A.L.R.4th 324 (1982) (law of nuisance to be used to determine whether defendant's house unreasonably blocked solar access for plaintiff's solar home). The plaintiff may have rights under statute or zoning ordinance. See Thomas R. Trenkner, Annotation, Zoning Regulations Prohibiting or Limiting Fences, Hedges, or Walls, 1 A.L.R.4th 373 (1981).

6. Sundowner, Inc. v. King, 95 Idaho 367, 509 P.2d 785 (1973) (listing many authorities); Welsh v. Todd, 260 N.C. 527, 133 S.E.2d 171 (1963). Some states deal with spite fences by statute, with the result that if the defendant meets the requirements of the statute, no nuisance action will lie. See Wernke v. Halas, 600 N.E.2d 117 (Ind.App. 1992).

7. Robie v. Lillis, 112 N.H. 492, 299 A.2d 155 (1972).

8. Raymond Robert Coletta, the Case for Aesthetic Nuisance: Rethinking Traditional Judicial Attitudes, 48 Ohio St. L.J. 141 (1987).

9. Wernke v. Halas, 600 N.E.2d 117 (Ind.App.1992).

10. Foley v. Harris, 223 Va. 20, 286 S.E.2d 186 (1982). Courts refusing to recognize a purely aesthetic nuisance may be willing to find one in cases of ugliness plus a little more. See Talley v. Borough of Trainer, 38 Pa.Cmwlth. 441, 394 A.2d 645 (1978) (finding that junked cars on the defendant's property were not only unsightly but constituted a public hazard in some unspecified way).

11. Mitchell v. Bearden, 255 Ark. 888, 503 S.W.2d 904 (1974).

12. Epstein argues against liability for all non-invasive annoyances including aesthetic nuisances, on the ground that corrective justice principles require a certain view of causation and that causation requires an invasion. In part, this includes the idea that the plaintiff's annoyance is chargeable to the plaintiff's "own independent judgment about an external state of affairs," not to the defendant's act. See Richard A. Epstein, Nuisance Law: Correc-

Recovery for nuisances creating anticipated harm without invasion.[13] Many activities outside the land that threaten future harm are non-invasive. Some cases have been willing to impose liability, as when the defendant's building threatens to harm the plaintiff's nearby building through increased snow-load,[14] when the defendant's stored explosives create a reasonable fear and depreciate the value of the plaintiff's property,[15] when toxic materials contaminated a general area or nearby land,[16] and when a halfway house in a residential neighborhood presents a serious danger that convicted felons on early release will cause harm.[17] When a degree of invasion can be found, the plaintiff may be able to recover parasitically for the accompanying fear, as where the noise of automatic weapon fire next door is itself invasive and also creates anticipation of harm.[18] In addition, contamination of the defendant's land may count as a public nuisance that can be abated by public action even though none of the hazardous materials have escaped.[19]

Denying recovery for anticipated harm without invasion. But many recent cases have denied recovery for conditions that diminish the plaintiff's property value but do not physically invade or physically harm the property. It should go without saying that if the defendant's waste is not the cause of the contamination complained of, the plaintiff's loss in property value is not the defendant's responsibility,[20] but a number of decisions have gone far beyond this by refusing to treat fear-creating activities as a nuisance in the absence of an actual invasion upon or physical harm to the land. Some have done so even when the activity actually causes depreciation in the plaintiff's land value, so-called stigma damages. In a Michigan case,[21] the defendant allegedly contaminated ground water near the plaintiffs' residences, but the contamination, although nearby, would flow away from, not toward the plaintiffs' land. The court thought that fear of contamination was unfounded so that although the land had depreciated in value because of the defendant's

tive Justice and Its Utilitarian Constraints, 8 J. Leg. Stud. 49 (1979).

13. See Furrow, Governing Science: Public Risks and Private Remedies, 131 U. Pa. L. Rev. 1403 (1983).

14. Omega Chemical Co., Inc. v. United Seeds, Inc., 252 Neb. 137, 560 N.W.2d 820 (1997).

15. Cumberland Torpedo Co. v. Gaines, 201 Ky. 88, 255 S.W. 1046 (1923) (depreciation of value due to fear, not fear itself is the basis); Comminge v. Stevenson, 76 Tex. 642, 13 S.W. 556 (1890). Most of the explosives storage cases, however, involve an actual explosion.

16. Gray v. Westinghouse Elec. Corp., 624 N.E.2d 49 (Ind.Ct.App.1993) (PCBs in adjacent landfill); Exxon Corp. v. Yarema, 69 Md.App. 124, 516 A.2d 990 (1986) (nearby groundwater contaminated, recovery without invasion if this substantially reduced plaintiff's use and enjoyment); Allen v. Uni–First Corp., 151 Vt. 229, 558 A.2d 961 (1988).

17. Arkansas Release Guidance Foundation v. Needler, 252 Ark. 194, 477 S.W.2d 821 (1972); cf. Smith v. Gill, 293 Ala. 736, 310 So.2d 214 (1975) (halfway house for mental patients).

18. Cf. Kolstad v. Rankin, 179 Ill. App.3d 1022, 534 N.E.2d 1373, 128 Ill.Dec. 768 (1989) (preliminary injunction issued, to be modified as to scope).

19. See New York v. Shore Realty Corp., 759 F.2d 1032 (2d Cir.1985); on public nuisances, § 467.

20. Anglado v. Leaf River Forest Products, Inc., 716 So.2d 543 (Miss.1998) (rejecting stigma damages where defendant did not produce the contaminating dioxin).

21. Adkins v. Thomas Solvent Co., 440 Mich. 293, 487 N.W.2d 715 (1992).

contamination, the plaintiffs could not recover. Perhaps similar thinking has prompted some other decisions that have refused claims of "stigma" damages without clearly stating reasons.[22]

Denying recovery without regard to reasonableness of the fear. The Connecticut Court discounted a fear that seems entirely reasonable when it held that a half-way house for felons, placed in a residential neighborhood, was not a nuisance until the felons actually engaged in "specific acts." The court refused relief even though the plaintiff's claimed that the presence of felons would depreciate the value of their property.[23] Some other opinions, mostly in toxic pollution cases, have asserted broadly that a nuisance exists only when there is an invasion that is harmful to the land or its occupants or at least is perceptible to one on the land.[24] Variations on the theme assert that fear of future harm cannot count as a nuisance[25] and that no nuisance can exist when the land is wholly unmarketable because of adjacent deadly contamination, so long as the plaintiff can actually use the land.[26] Ironically, courts may impose upon the victimized homeowner a duty to reveal the pollution or danger when she attempts to sell to another,[27] thus guaranteeing that the homeowner will realize the loss in market value.

Abating the nuisance or the fear. The strongest case for recognizing a nuisance and awarding damage is one in which (1) the fear is reasonable at least in the sense that it is understandable and (2) the market value of the property has diminished because potential buyers would pay less for the property due to the threat. Something is to be said for recognizing a nuisance even if the fear is not reasonable, but in that case courts may not have confidence that damages can be calculated fairly. That is because if the fear is unreasonable, it may also be ephemeral; as the facts about danger become better known, the fear may dissipate and the market value may be recovered. The same point arises if the nuisance is likely to be abated by court order or otherwise. In that case, damages based upon permanently diminished property value will not be in order because, again, at least something of the value will be

22. Chance v. BP Chemicals, 77 Ohio St.3d 17, 670 N.E.2d 985 (1996) (stigma damages not recoverable on the facts of the case, no other explanation).

23. Nicholson v. Connecticut Half-Way House, Inc., 153 Conn. 507, 218 A.2d 383, (1966). The court did not say the fears were unreasonable or unfounded but that they were speculative and intangible. All fear is intangible, and uncertainty of harm is also commonly the case with fear, so the court's comment is, at best, puzzling.

24. See Adams v. Star Enterprise, 51 F.3d 417 (4th Cir.1995); Wilson v. Amoco Corp., 33 F.Supp.2d 981 (D.Wyo.1998); In re Chicago Flood Litigation, 176 Ill.2d 179, 205, 680 N.E.2d 265, 278, 223 Ill.Dec. 532, 545 (1997).

25. Koll–Irvine Center Property Owners Ass'n v. County of Orange, 24 Cal.App.4th 1036, 29 Cal.Rptr.2d 664 (1994).

26. Golen v. Union Corp., U.C.O.-M.B.A., Inc., 718 A.2d 298 (Pa.Super.1998).

27. Reed v. King, 145 Cal.App.3d 261, 193 Cal.Rptr. 130 (1983) (home seller required to disclose fact that multiple murders were committed in the house if that would in fact affect market value); Strawn v. Canuso, 140 N.J. 43, 657 A.2d 420, 41 A.L.R.5th 859 (1995) (in selling land, developer and broker must disclose existence of nearby landfill that may affect land's market value).

recovered when the nuisance is abated.[28]

Observations. (a) In the case of an aesthetic offense in a neighborhood, the defendant's conduct is not usually tortious apart from its arguable status as a nuisance. But in the case of toxic dumping, the defendant's conduct may be wrongful independent of its nuisance effects upon the plaintiff. In that case, liability for genuine depreciation in the market value of the plaintiff's property does not seem extreme.

(b) Reduced market value is an objective measure of loss in the quality of life for those in possession of the property. If market value is actually reduced, that means that as a practical matter no buyer can be found to pay the property's pre-nuisance value. If that is because of the defendant's tortious dumping, both a tort and an objectively measured loss have been established.

(c) But diminution in market value may not last. Fear of the contamination may evaporate with time. The real problem, then, may be to estimate with care the probable actual diminished value over time.[29] This might be a situation for new remedies that treat such invasions as we treat conversion of personal property; permit the plaintiff to force a sale to the tortious defendant, who then must bear the risks that the market will not recover, but who will not suffer if it does.

§ 467. Public Nuisance

Definitions. A public nuisance, as distinct from a private nuisance, is a substantial and unreasonable interference with a right held in common by the general public, in use of public facilities, in health, safety, and convenience.[1] A wide range of specific activities are often declared to be a public nuisance by criminal statutes. A public nuisance may be abated or enjoined by public authorities, even if it is not specifically declared to be a nuisance or a crime by statute.[2] Public as well as private nuisance theories may supplement environmental statutes as a tool for dealing with hazardous wastes and other environmental contaminations.[3] Much

28. Santa Fe Partnership v. ARCO Products Co., 46 Cal.App.4th 967, 54 Cal. Rptr.2d 214 (1996). This implicates the permanent nuisance/continuing nuisance dichotomy. See § 57 generally and § 468, this chapter. For a nuisance that will be abated in the future, diminished rental value during the remediation period is the appropriate property measure. If abatement will not be complete, damages can be calculated on the residual loss in market value.

29. See Alex Geisinger, Nothing but Fear Itself: a Social-psychological Model of Stigma Harm And its Legal Implications, 76 Neb. L. Rev. 452 (1997).

§ 467

1. Restatement § 821B. Sometimes courts emphasize that a public nuisance interferes with the rights of a sizeable number of persons, a formula that may lose the idea of a public right.

2. Armory Park Neighborhood Ass'n v. Episcopal Community Services in Arizona, 148 Ariz. 1, 712 P.2d 914 (1985); People ex rel. Gallo v. Acuna, 14 Cal.4th 1090, 929 P.2d 596, 60 Cal.Rptr.2d 277 (1997) (enjoining certain activities of street gangs).

3. Some writers express disappointment at the low success rate of federal environmental statutes, See Tom Kuhnle, Note, The Rebirth of Common Law Actions for Addressing Hazardous Waste Contamination, 15 Stan.Envtl. L. J. 187 (1996). See also Kathleen Ann O'Neill, Note, Chemical Nuisance: Application of Public Nuisance Theory as a Remedy for Environmental Law Violations, 26 Suffolk U. L. Rev. 51 (1992); Michael C. Skotnicki, Note, Private

of public nuisance law arises in this public litigation or in related suits about public regulatory activity and its limits.[4] Apart from whatever is declared by statute to be a public nuisance, the common law generally recognized public rights in health, safety, and comfort, and in particular the right to use public ways and waters. A condition may count as a public nuisance without causing any loss of enjoyment in the use of private land.

Public nuisance causing special harm or private nuisance. In the absence of a statute allowing citizens to enforce the public's rights,[5] those rights are normally enforced only by public authorities. The "private attorney general," welcomed in civil rights litigation, is given little place in protecting public environmental rights. However, a private tort action is available to redress private harm resulting from a public nuisance if (1) the public nuisance is also a private nuisance to the plaintiff because it substantially and unreasonably diminishes her use and enjoyment of her land,[6] or (2) the nuisance is a public nuisance that causes special harm to the plaintiff in the exercise of the public right,[7] and that harm differs in kind from the harm caused to other members of the public generally.[8]

Obstructions of public streets and ways. General rule. Traditional examples involved obstruction of public streets or ways. The mere presence of an obstruction might be a public nuisance. But the fact that the inconvenienced plaintiff used the street more than other people would not give her standing to sue. Her inconvenience might be greater than that suffered by people generally but it would be of the same general kind, and that is not enough. The abortion protester who is dampened by a sprinkler that sprays partly on the public sidewalk thus has no claim based upon public nuisance.[9]

Actions for Damages Resulting from an Environmental Public Nuisance: Overcoming the Barrier to Standing Posed by the "Special Injury" Rule, 16 AM. J. TRIAL ADVOC. 591 (1992).

4. Whether public regulation constitutes a taking of property for which compensation must be made may depend in part upon whether the property could have been regulated as a nuisance. See Louise A. Halper, Untangling The Nuisance Knot, 26 B.C. ENVTL. AFF. L. REV. 89 (1998).

5. FLA. STAT. ANN. § 60.05 permits such suits. In Kirk v. United States Sugar Corp., 726 So.2d 822 (Fla.App.1999), the court held that a suit was maintainable by private citizens who alleged that officials were not enforcing existing environmental laws.

6. See Armory Park Neighborhood Ass'n v. Episcopal Community Services in Arizona, 148 Ariz. 1, 712 P.2d 914 (1985); Restatement §§ 821B, cmt. h and 832C, cmt. e. (instancing a bawdy house next door to a private residence.) When the public nuisance actually substantially interferes with the integrity of the land itself or causes personal injury to its occupants, it would almost always qualify as a private nuisance and also demonstrate special harm different in kind from that suffered by the public generally.

7. Philadelphia Electric Co. v. Hercules, Inc., 762 F.2d 303 (3d Cir.1985) (plaintiff's vendor contaminated the riparian land, which in turn contaminated the river; although contamination of the river was a public nuisance, plaintiff's harm did not result from exercise of rights in the river, but from direct contamination of the land, as to which caveat emptor applied).

8. Lower Commerce Ins. Inc. v. Halliday, 636 So.2d 430 (Ala. 1994); Newhall Land and Farming Co. v. Superior Court (Mobil Oil Corporation), 19 Cal.App.4th 334, 23 Cal.Rptr.2d 377 (1993); Restatement § 821C (1).

9. Hartford v. Womens Services, 239 Neb. 540, 477 N.W.2d 161 (1991); cf. See Schroder v. City of Lincoln, 155 Neb. 599,

Travelers and abutting owners. In fact, the street obstruction cases are ordinarily maintained only by abutting owners whose property is denied access to or from the public way.[10] Although courts have sometimes talked of public nuisance in these cases, the relevant right seems to be the plaintiff's own right of access as a property owner, not the public right.[11] If access is made substantially more burdensome, the blockage need not occur at the property line.[12] However, when a remote street is blocked so that the property owner's access is merely inconvenienced, her claim cannot rest upon her property right but must instead be founded on a public nuisance. Yet as a public nuisance claim it must fail if she suffers mere inconvenience in travel, since that is a harm shared by other members of the public when a street is blocked. Remote obstructions are therefore not likely to be actionable.[13] By the same token, relatively few cases support a claim based upon public nuisance when the plaintiff is merely a traveler on the streets and not an abutting owner.[14]

52 N.W.2d 808 (1952) (bank teller machine on the sidewalk, citizen had no standing to sue).

10. E.g., Hall v. Polk, 363 So.2d 300 (Ala.1978); Brown v. Florida Chautauqua Ass'n, 59 Fla. 447, 52 So. 802 (1910); Shamhart v. Morrison Cafeteria Co., 159 Fla. 629, 32 So.2d 727, 2 A.L.R.2d 429 (1947); Missouri–Kansas–Texas R.R. v. Neuhoff Bros., 297 S.W.2d 316 (Tex.Civ.App.1956) (railroad's standing trains repeatedly obstructed the only road to the plaintiff's plant in violation of a statute limiting trains standing at crossings to five minutes).

11. "The fact that the injury was common to all other property holders on the street would not bar the plaintiff's right of recovery. The plaintiff sues for a special damage to his own property by reason of defendant's having impaired the use of the street upon which it fronts. It does not affect his right to recovery that the owners of property fronting on the same street have been injured in the same manner." Powell v. Houston & T.C. R.R., 104 Tex. 219, 223, 135 S.W. 1153, 1155–1156 (Tex. 1911) (quoting). In many of the cases the main discussion centers on the nature of the plaintiff's easement or other property right of access. E.g., Burrell v. Kirkland, 242 S.C. 201, 130 S.E.2d 470 (1963); Lindsay v. James, 188 Va. 646, 51 S.E.2d 326, 7 A.L.R.2d 597 (1949).

12. See Restatement § 821C, cmt. f.

13. See Taylor v. Barnes, 303 Ky. 562, 198 S.W.2d 297 (1946) (distinguishing abutting owner from others); Burrell v. Kirkland, 242 S.C. 201, 130 S.E.2d 470 (1963). In Hall v. Polk, 363 So.2d 300 (Ala.1978), obstruction of the road did not deny plaintiff access from property to public street, but it did obstruct the only convenient access to a nearby river, presumably itself a public facility that the plaintiff was entitled to access. If the blockage is negligent, plaintiffs sometimes assert claims for negligent interference with economic opportunities.

14. Prosser & Keeton 648, n. 49 cited Wiggins v. Boddington, 172 Eng.Rep. 539, an English trial judge's instruction to the jury, which permitted the jury to find for the plaintiff whose way was repeatedly blocked because the defendant at various times each day would open a swing bridge for an unreasonable length of time. The plaintiff was hauling sand and other goods for construction on the wharves and was allowed to recover for the increased costs he suffered from the delays. The case neither alludes to nor applies any rule of law; neither the judge nor counsel cite any case. Statutes that limit the time that standing trains can block a street might create a claim for delayed users. Patterson v. Detroit, Lansing & Northern Railroad, 56 Mich. 172, 22 N.W. 260 (1885), allowed a blocked traveler to recover because the delay made him miss a train. Although he was a landowner, his claim did not seem to turn primarily upon access to his own land but upon use of the public facilities. If the train violates the statute and also blocks the only entrance to the plaintiff's property, liability can easily be imposed without resort to public nuisance doctrine, although courts may label the blockage a nuisance. See Missouri–Kansas–Texas R.R. v. Neuhoff Bros., 297 S.W.2d 316 (Tex.Civ.App.1956). When a railroad's blockage in violation of statute causes personal injury, liability may again

Public waters. The same rules apply to public waters. An interference with public waters, if substantial enough, will count as a public nuisance. For example, if the defendant contaminates public waters by chemical spills or the continuous discharge of noxious effluent, he may have created a public nuisance (and may have violated environmental statutes as well). Those who suffer "special harm" different in kind from that suffered by the public generally can recover for the harms suffered in their exercise of the public right. This includes direct users such as those engaged in commercial fishing,[15] but does not include pleasure users who suffer harm in common with the public generally or even owners of nearby businesses who suffer economic loss when pollution of the waters reduces tourism.[16] A federal statute creates liability (with a damages cap) for oil spills upon navigable waters. It extends liability to all those who suffer actual economic harm from damage to natural resources.[17] That would appear to include, say, a nearby motel owner whose business declines when the river is polluted.

Personal injury. When a land occupant or her family suffers personal injury such as illness from a private nuisance, recoverable damages may include an award for personal injury. Public nuisances causing personal injury are different. First, legislatures can declare almost low-grade crime to be a nuisance, and the court holding that violation of such a statute is actionable may adopt the statutory term and declare that the defendant is liable for a nuisance.[18] Second, a public nuisance is actionable under the common law only if the plaintiff's enjoyment of a public right is diminished and her injury differs in kind from injury to the general public. Thus, the defendant who substantially pollutes the air or public waters commits a public nuisance, and is liable if a few people suffer personal injury as a result,[19] but if the defendant's pollution causes respiratory problems for everyone in town, the plaintiff's respiratory harm does not differ in kind from that suffered by others and she cannot recover on a public nuisance theory.[20] Third, talk of public

be appropriate, but again seems to have little to do with nuisance, public or private. Terry v. New Orleans Great Northern Railroad, 103 Miss. 679, 60 So. 729 (1912).

15. Union Oil Co. v. Oppen, 501 F.2d 558 (9th Cir.1974) (commercial fishers could recover; court did not specifically rely upon public nuisance doctrine); Hampton v. North Carolina Pulp Co., 223 N.C. 535, 27 S.E.2d 538 (1943); cf. Carson v. Hercules Powder Co., 240 Ark. 887, 402 S.W.2d 640 (1966) ("public nuisance" on a non-navigable stream or bayou, plaintiff had permission of riparian owners to fish there and earned his living doing so; polluter was subject to liability).

16. See Louisiana ex rel. Guste v. M/V Testbank, 752 F.2d 1019, 88 A.L.R.Fed. 239 (5th Cir. 1985).

17. 33 U.S.C.A. § 2702 (b) (2) (E).

18. Corgan v. Muehling, 143 Ill.2d 296, 574 N.E.2d 602, 158 Ill.Dec. 489 (1991) (psychologist would be liable for nuisance if he engaged in sexual activities with patient without holding a current registration as required by "nuisance" statute).

19. Anderson v. W. R. Grace & Co., 628 F.Supp. 1219 (D.Mass.1986) (leukemia victims of groundwater contamination in Woburn, Massachusetts).

20. Venuto v. Owens-Corning Fiberglas Corp., 22 Cal.App.3d 116, 99 Cal.Rptr. 350 (1971); cf. In re The Exxon Valdez, 104 F.3d 1196 (9th Cir.1997) (massive oil spill; " 'the right to obtain and share wild food, enjoy uncontaminated nature, and cultivate traditional, cultural, spiritual, and psychological benefits in pristine natural surroundings' is shared by all Alaskans" and hence Native Americans suffered no special harm).

nuisance in personal injury cases can be confusing when the plaintiff claims damages rather than abatement. If the defendant should be liable for the injury, it is because he has intentionally caused personal injury, carried on an abnormally dangerous activity, violated a statute aimed at protecting the plaintiff, or was negligent. To label the case as one of nuisance adds nothing to the clarity of decision-making or policy.[21] Plaintiffs usually assert a public nuisance causing personal injury for strategic reasons, for example, to avoid the effect of their own contributory fault. But as Cardozo said in the leading case, "whenever a nuisance has its origin in negligence, one may not avert the consequence of his own contributory fault by affixing.... the label of a nuisance."[22] In personal injury cases, the law will be clarified by dropping the public nuisance label and by directly considering the rules and policies of negligence and strict liability.[23]

§ 468. Remedies

The main remedies. The remedies potentially available for a private nuisance (or a public nuisance with special harm to the private plaintiff) are (1) compensatory damages, (2) punitive damages in egregious cases, and (3) injunctions abating or modifying the nuisance and (rarely) (4) a "compensated injunction" that abates the nuisance but requires the plaintiff to pay the costs of that abatement. Some of the confusion about nuisance arises when the liability question (is there a nuisance?) is confused with the remedy question (what remedy should be permitted?). The choice among remedies has a good deal of impact, however, and has generated a good deal of analysis.

Abatement and modification.[1] *Injunctive relief available.* On the ground that the damages remedy is inadequate to protect rights in property, courts often issue injunctions compelling the defendant to abate private as well as public nuisances.[2] Injunctions may be tailored narrowly to fit the nuisance. If a factory operation is a nuisance because of noise, it may be that an injunction closing the factory is unnecessary and that the nuisance can be remedied by an injunction that bars or limits the noise. Such an approach would properly match the remedy to the wrong.

Denying injunction for useful nuisances. Courts may also limit or even refuse injunctions in private nuisance cases for reasons that have

21. Thus in Corgan v. Muehling, supra n. 18, if the psychologist seduced his patient he should be responsible for the harm done by his malpractice even if the statute had not labeled his unregistered practice as a nuisance.

22. McFarlane v. City of Niagara Falls, 247 N.Y. 340, 160 N.E. 391 (1928).

23. The use of the nuisance label to evade public entity immunities is more complicated because the immunities are so often overstated in the first place. Ideally, the nuisance label would be dropped when the plaintiff asserts personal injury and the immunity reformulated more narrowly.

§ 468

1. See generally 1 Dan B. Dobbs, Law of Remedies §§ 5.7 (2)–5.7 (4) (2d ed. 1993).

2. E.g., Bishop Processing Co. v. Davis, 213 Md. 465, 132 A.2d 445 (1957) (injunction to avoid escape of noxious gases that interfere with plaintiff's use and enjoyment of property); see 1 Dan B. Dobbs, Law of Remedies § 5.7 (2) (2d ed. 1993).

nothing to do with matching the remedy to the right.[3] The main one is that if the defendant is carrying on an activity that is so socially useful or economically important, the injunction closing the defendant's operation may do more harm than good. Unavoidable industrial nuisances, for example, may have great value to the public because of the products that result or the jobs they foster. Courts may weigh the good against the harm and conclude that the injunction should be refused but that the defendant must nevertheless pay the plaintiff's damages. In a leading modern case, *Boomer v. Atlantic Cement Co.*,[4] the defendant was a cement plant that constantly produced high levels of cement dust that clogged the homes of neighboring residents. The operation was a nuisance as the courts found, but the defendant employed 300 persons and had invested $45 million in the plant. The total damage to the neighbors was $185,000. The court concluded that the injunction should be denied if the defendant paid the damages, bringing New York law into line with the practice in a number of other states.[5]

Limiting the injunction to avoid closing a useful business. To deny the injunction is to permit the defendant to take rights in the plaintiff's property at a valuation determined by judges or juries. Even if their valuation is an accurate estimate of the market, it may not represent the price at which the plaintiff would voluntarily sell the property right. The effect is to give the defendant a power much like the power of eminent domain. So denial of injunction is a serious matter. For this reason, the injunction is definitely granted when the defendant harms the plaintiff willfully or when he could reasonably avoid doing so.[6] And courts may find a middle ground by ordering the defendant to minimize or eliminate the nuisance without shutting down the defendant's operation,[7] for example, by reducing the amount of dynamite in any one quarry explosion,[8] or reducing nighttime activities.[9] Courts can also order the defendant to experiment with alternative processes or procedures as potential means of minimizing the harm.[10]

The compensated injunction. One other way of avoiding an injunction that closes the defendant's business but still manages some relief for the plaintiff is most unusual. The compensated injunction is illustrated

3. As to equitable doctrines affecting injunctive relief, including adequacy of legal remedy, equities between the parties, laches, and hardship, see 1 DAN B. DOBBS, LAW OF REMEDIES § 5.7 (2) (2d ed. 1993).

4. Boomer v. Atlantic Cement Co., 26 N.Y.2d 219, 257 N.E.2d 870, 309 N.Y.S.2d 312 (1970).

5. E.g., Northern Indiana Pub. Serv. Co. v. Vesey, 210 Ind. 338, 200 N.E. 620 (1936); Riter v. Keokuk Electro-Metals Co., 248 Iowa 710, 82 N.W.2d 151 (1957) (factory furnishing work in the community); Madison v. Ducktown Sulphur, Copper & Iron Co., 113 Tenn. 331, 83 S.W. 658 (1904) (jobs in community plus enormous increase in tax assessments in county due to defendants' smelters); see Jonathan M. Purver, Annotation, Modern Status of Rules as to Balance of Convenience or Social Utility as Affecting Relief From Nuisance, 40 A.L.R.3d 601 (1971).

6. See Mobile & O.R. R. v. Zimmern, 206 Ala. 37, 89 So. 475 (1921).

7. See 1 DAN B. DOBBS, LAW OF REMEDIES § 2.4 (6) (2d ed. 1993).

8. Beecher v. Dull, 294 Pa. 17, 143 A. 498 (1928).

9. Smith v. Staso Milling Co., 18 F.2d 736 (2d Cir.1927).

10. Restatement § 941 Comment e.

in a famous Arizona case where suburban development gradually pushed so close to a massive feed lot that life quickly became intolerable to the residents. The developer was granted an injunction forcing the feed lot to move further away from inhabited areas, but only on condition that the costs of the move were borne by the developer.[11]

Damages.[12] *Permanent nuisances and diminished market value.* Since damages are intended to compensate the plaintiff for actual harm done, the award may be measured in different ways according to the evidence. If the harm done by the nuisance will not terminate or be abated, the nuisance is said to be permanent. In that case, one traditional measure of damages awards the plaintiff the diminished market value of her land.[13] That might be the case if the land is irremediably contaminated for an indefinite time, for example.[14]

Temporary nuisance and loss of rental value, cost of restoring land. On the other hand, if the harm is temporary, the parallel measure of damages would be an award for loss of use, usually based upon the reduction of rental value of the land while the nuisance lasts.[15] With some nuisances, the harm is abated when the defendant's activity is abated. That is true, for example, if the nuisance is noise inflicted upon the plaintiff. When the noise stops, the plaintiff has nothing to repair. But if the nuisance is a toxic contamination of groundwater or land, the harm does not terminate when the defendant stops dumping toxins. In cases like that, the plaintiff is entitled to have her land restored if that is feasible, and if the defendant does not restore it, the plaintiff is entitled to the cost of doing so in addition to her recovery for diminished rental value for the period until the cleanup is completed.[16]

11. Spur Industries, Inc. v. Del E. Webb Development Co., 108 Ariz. 178, 494 P.2d 700, 53 A.L.R.3d 861 (1972). See Calabresi & Melamed, Property Rules, Liability Rules, and Inalienability: One View of the Cathedral, 85 Harv.L.Rev. 1089 (1972). The compensated injunction, first recognized by Calabresi & Melamed, supra, aroused a good deal of academic interest. Some of the views are discussed in 1 Dan B. Dobbs, Law of Remedies § 5.7 (3) (2d ed. 1993).

12. On the damages rules for nuisance, see 1 Dan B. Dobbs, Law of Remedies § 5.6 (2) (2d ed. 1993).

13. See, e.g., Tri–County Investment Group, Ltd. v. Southern States, Inc., 231 Ga.App. 632, 500 S.E.2d 22 (1998).

14. Weinhold v. Wolff, 555 N.W.2d 454 (Iowa 1996).

15. E.g., Superior Const. Co. v. Elmo, 204 Md. 1, 102 A.2d 739, 48 A.L.R.2d 932 (1954) (plaintiff could not occupy land for period of nuisance, recovery for rental value during that period). With temporary nuisances, courts may say that the plaintiff can recover only those damages suffered up to the time of suit. E.g., Plonley v. Reser, 178 Cal.App.2d Supp. 935, 3 Cal.Rptr. 551, 80 A.L.R.2d 911 (1960). The real point, however, is that the plaintiff can*not* recover diminished market value. If the evidence shows that the nuisance will terminate one month after trial, and permits nonspeculative calculation of damages for the entire period, a recovery of diminished rental value for the entire period of the nuisance is appropriate. Some authority has insisted that diminished rental value is not an appropriate measure unless the land is held for rental purposes. See Reeser v. Weaver Bros., Inc., 78 Ohio App.3d 681, 605 N.E.2d 1271 (1992). But if the land can be rented, diminished rental value furnishes an objective measure and also a measure of the plaintiff's opportunity cost in holding the land for other purposes. For both these reasons, evidence of diminished rental value should always be considered in temporary nuisance cases.

16. Scantlin v. City of Pevely, 741 S.W.2d 48 (Mo.App.1987); Reeser v. Weaver Bros., Inc., 78 Ohio App.3d 681, 605 N.E.2d 1271 (1992). In the case of a private nuisance without threat of public harm, such

Personal illness or the like. Courts recognize that the occupants of land may suffer a loss in quality of life and perhaps even physical illness, discomfort, and annoyance as a result of a nuisance, and they have allowed recovery for such items.[17] However, some care should be exercised not to overlap awards if the plaintiff claims diminished value based upon conditions that produce discomfort and also claims discomfort as a separate item of damages.[18]

To enjoin or not to enjoin? Efficiency and externalizing. A great deal of analysis, far more than can be summarized here, has gone into the question whether courts should always, never, or sometimes enjoin socially useful nuisances.[19] One reason not to weigh social utilities is that accurate weighing may be unlikely or at least expensive. The interest in efficiency may suggest to some that if more value can be generated by keeping the nuisance and paying the damages, the injunction should be denied, but it may be that this should be accomplished by routinely denying the injunction rather than by weighing utilities. On the other hand, if we are sure that the cost of, say, running a rocket laboratory is the disposal of toxic wastes it generates, the rocket facility should not be able to dump the fuel where it will cause harm to others; in doing so, it would be externalizing its costs, forcing others to bear costs of its business.[20]

Strategic behavior. One approach might be to leave the whole matter to party bargaining. If nuisances are not enjoined, the defendant is permitted to buy rights to interfere with the plaintiff's land as a price fixed by courts but not one agreed to by the plaintiff. People who do not commit nuisances are not permitted to take rights in the plaintiff's land except by paying a price the plaintiff will accept, so it is somewhat anomalous that the defendant who commits a nuisance is able in effect to compel a sale. Yet if nuisances are enjoined, the community may lose enormously, or alternatively the plaintiff may be able to sell the injunction back to the defendant (by agreeing not to enforce it) at an extortion-

as waters backed up onto the plaintiff's land without toxic deposits, recovery of repair or cleanup costs may be limited so that they do not exceed the diminution in value that would occur if the nuisance were allowed to recur. See Stratford Theater, Inc. v. Town of Stratford, 140 Conn. 422, 101 A.2d 279, 41 A.L.R.2d 1060 (1953).

17. E.g., Woodmen of World, Unit Number 3 v. Jordan, 231 Ga.App. 517, 499 S.E.2d 900 (1998) ("The measure of damages for discomfort, disrupted peace of mind, unhappiness and annoyance caused by a nuisance is for the enlightened conscience of the jury"); Gorman v. Sabo, 210 Md. 155, 122 A.2d 475 (1956).

18. See Dan B. Dobbs, Law of Remedies § 3.3 (7) (2d ed. 1993).

19. See, e.g., Robert C. Ellickson, Alternatives to Zoning: Covenants, Nuisance Rules, and Fines as Land Use Controls, 40 U.Chi.L.Rev. 681 (1973); W. Page Keeton and Clarence Morris, Notes on "Balancing the Equities", 18 Tex. L. Rev. 412 (1940); Jeff L. Lewin, Compensated Injunctions and the Evolution of Nuisance Law, 71 Iowa L.Rev. 775 (1986); A. Mitchell Polinsky, Resolving Nuisance Disputes: The Simple Economics of Injunctive and Damages Remedies, 32 Stan.L.Rev. 1075 (1980); Edward Rabin, Nuisance Law: Rethinking Fundamental Assumptions, 63 Va.L.Rev. 1299 (1977). Some of the writings on this subject are discussed in 1 Dan B. Dobbs, Law of Remedies § 5.7 (4) (2d ed. 1993).

20. For an excellent short discussion of the efficiency-externality point, see Marshall S. Shapo, Basic Principles of Tort Law § 36.04, p. 157 (1999).

ate price that is far in excess of the plaintiff's loss and the plaintiff's own subjective valuation. Extortionate behavior is possible on either side.

Damages measured to provide appropriate incentives. If an injunction is denied and the damage is awarded for diminished value of the plaintiff's property, the defendant will in effect have purchased an easement to commit the nuisance forever. In a world of changing technology, some of which might in the future permit the defendant to operate without causing harm to others, it may be unwise to remove the incentive to invest in technology. A better measure of damages for some cases would be the temporary measure (lost rental value), which would allow the plaintiff to sue periodically as long as the nuisance continues. Given accurate damages measures, however, a refusal to enjoin a nuisance like the cement-dust may often turn out well even under the permanent or diminished market value measure. If the defendant pays the true loss in value of the plaintiffs' homes, the plaintiffs will be able to sell them to purchasers who, because of the cheaper price, are willing to put up with the nuisance. Alternatively, if the plaintiffs prefer to remain neighbors to the cement plant, they themselves are evidently satisfied to have less comfort and more cash. This optimistic view, however, will work only if the court can be confident that its estimate of damages is an accurate one.

Chapter 35

Misrepresentation and Nondisclosure

§ 469. The Scope of Misrepresentation

The bargaining or exchange context of misrepresentation. This chapter deals with common law liability for commercial harm caused by the plaintiff's justifiable reliance upon material misrepresentations of fact that lead to contracts, transfers of property, or other bargains. Misrepresentation of a fact includes deception created by nondisclosure in some instances, but it is distinct from a contractual promise. Sometimes the bargaining context is real but less than obvious because the defendant acts in the role of a fiduciary who is giving friendly counsel. Even third persons, who are not themselves involved in the transaction, may make and be liable for misrepresentations that affect a transaction with others.[1] Statutes covering particular situations such as securities[2] and consumer transactions[3] have helped create specialized and sometimes intricate fields that may or may not offer more protection against fraud than the common law.

Examples of tortious misrepresentation include the homeowner who induces a sale by falsely representing that the basement does not flood;[4] the employer who recruits desirable employees by falsely representing that it had no plans to move or close[5] or who induces older employees to quit by falsely representing retirement options;[6] the adjuster who falsely says that a release to be signed by an injured person is merely a receipt;[7] and even the HMO that induces members to join by falsely representing that it will expeditiously arbitrate disputes when in fact it stonewalls

§ 469

1. Special rules for negligent third persons: § 480.

2. Of many statutes, 15 U.S.C.A. § 78j is perhaps the most used and best known. See generally 7 & 8 Louis Loss and Joel Seligman, Securities Regulation, Chaps 9 & 10 (fraud and manipulation) (3d ed. 1991 & Supps.).

3. Some consumer protection law is public law, but most state statutes recognize a private right of action for misleading or deceptive practices. See, listing all state statutes, Restatement of Unfair Competition § 1, Reporter's Note. There are many statutes covering particular consumer problems, for instance, the federal Interstate Land Sales Full Disclosure Act, 15 U.S.C. §§ 1701 et seq., the Truth and Lending Act, 15 U.S.C. § 1601 et seq. and others. Many statutes aim at more than providing full and accurate information, sometimes forbidding particular practices that are deemed coercive or unfair.

4. Cf. Wasson v. Schubert, 964 S.W.2d 520 (Mo.App.1998) (similar).

5. Cf. Meade v. Cedarapids, Inc., 164 F.3d 1218 (9th Cir.1999) (similar).

6. Cf. Voilas v. General Motors Corp., 170 F.3d 367 (3d Cir.1999) (similar claim not preempted by labor laws).

7. Cf. Lubin v. Johnson, 169 Ariz. 464, 820 P.2d 328 (1991) (similar).

even the dying patient.[8] If such representations are culpably false, the plaintiff who justifiably relies upon them may have a claim for damages or, in some cases, for equitable relief such as rescission of the transaction.

"Misrepresentation" as a tort. Fraudulent misrepresentation is a stand-alone economic or commercial tort that causes financial harm without causing physical harm either to person or to property. Negligent misrepresentation may also be actionable in some cases, but only when the defendant is under a duty to use care in communicating, as where the defendant is in a special relationship with the plaintiff. Strict liability is also possible if the defendant's representation is a warranty or strict responsibility is imposed by statute.

"Misrepresentation" as description of a fact relevant in some other tort. The terms fraud, deceit, and misrepresentation are used as the name of a tort. However, these terms can also be used to describe an actual event or the communication of a statement that does not accord with the facts. In that descriptive sense, many misrepresentations are important in establishing legal liability for some other tort, one that has nothing to do with the kind of misrepresentation covered in this chapter. A former employer might subject others to danger by recommending a sexual predator for a job with children.[9] A physician might cause emotional distress by representing to a patient that she has a disease when she does not.[10] A driver might cause a collision by giving signals representing that it is safe to pass when it is not. A manufacturer might infringe a trademark by offering its goods under a counterfeit of the plaintiff's trademark, in effect misrepresenting the origin of the goods. None of these cases invoke the tort of fraud or misrepresentation. In the first three examples the misrepresentation is merely a way in which personal injury or direct emotional harm is inflicted. They do not entail stand-alone economic harm at all and do not invoke the rules of misrepresentation but the rules of personal injury, property damage, or emotional harm. For that reason, the defendant's negligence may be a sufficient basis for liability. The third example differs in that the trademark owner who sues is not the person who is misled by the counterfeit, so the owner's claim is not for fraud but for trademark infringement and governed by the rules for that tort.

Damages vs. rescission and other equitable remedies; constructive fraud. The plaintiff who suffers financial harm from reliance upon a

8. Cf. Engalla v. Permanente Medical Group, Inc., 15 Cal.4th 951, 938 P.2d 903, 64 Cal.Rptr.2d 843 (1997) (similar).

9. Cf. Randi W. v. Muroc Joint Unified Sch. Dist., 14 Cal.4th 1066, 929 P.2d 582, 60 Cal.Rptr.2d 263 (1997) (claim that school failed to qualify its positive recommendation for teacher who allegedly had been subject of previous complaints of sexual impropriety with students; in his new job, teacher allegedly molested a middle school student); cf. Estate of Shinaul v. State Dept. of Social & Health Services, 980 P.2d 800 (Wash. App. 1999) (social worker allegedly gave misleading information leading guardians to place child in allegedly unsafe institution where he met his death).

10. See Molien v. Kaiser Found. Hosps., 27 Cal.3d 916, 167 Cal.Rptr. 831, 616 P.2d 813, 16 A.L.R. 4th 518 (1980), modified, Burgess v. Superior Court, 2 Cal.4th 1064, 831 P.2d 1197, 9 Cal.Rptr.2d 615 (1992).

misrepresentation can frequently seek rescission of any agreement that resulted from that reliance or raise the misrepresentation as a defense when she is sued for breach of the agreement. Sometimes she can capture whatever gains the defendant made from his fraud. The old equity courts applied the term constructive fraud to any conduct that would warrant equitable relief such as rescission or reformation[11] and to any ground for equitable relief against fiduciaries.[12] Constructive fraud in this sense is not actual fraud at all, but any conduct that would warrant equitable relief, including cases of innocent mistake that would justify rescission. The term is perhaps best avoided because it invites lawyers to confuse the rules for equitable relief and fiducial obligation with the rules for damages that traditionally require a knowing falsehood.[13] The rules stated in this chapter are those governing the tort claim for damages except when specifically noted otherwise.

§ 470. Fraudulent Misrepresentation: Elements and Burdens

Courts list anywhere from four to nine elements of the common law fraudulent misrepresentation claim,[1] but whatever the number, they agree in substance that the plaintiff must prove (1) an intentional misrepresentation (2) of fact or opinion (as distinct from a promise) (3) that is material and (4) intended to induce and (5) does induce reasonable reliance by the plaintiff, (6) proximately causing pecuniary harm to the plaintiff. Procedurally, the plaintiff may be required to plead fraud with particularity.[2] Many courts add that fraud must be proved by clear and convincing evidence,[3] although a number say a preponderance of the

11. E.g., Wells v. Schuster-Hax Nat'l Bank, 23 Colo. 534, 48 P. 809 (1897) (conveyance without consideration that could defeat creditors' rights would be fraud in law though there was no specific misrepresentation or even intent); Gibson v. Gibson, 102 Wis. 501, 78 N.W. 917 (1899) (equitable suit to alter record title).

12. See Barger v. McCoy Hillard & Parks, 346 N.C. 650, 488 S.E.2d 215 (1997) (defining constructive fraud); Stanley v. Luse, 36 Or. 25, 58 P. 75 (1899) (self dealing by fiduciary as constructive fraud).

13. See, e.g., Hockett v. Winks, 82 N.M. 597, 485 P.2d 353 (1971); Pugh's IGA, Inc. v. Super Food Services, Inc., 531 N.E.2d 1194 (Ind.App.1988) (discussing but not applying constructive fraud rules in an ordinary damages claim).

§ 470

1. Restatement § 525 requires a (1) fraudulent misrepresentation (2) of fact, opinion, intention, or law, (3) for the purpose of inducing reliance, (4) justifiable reliance. Similar formulations are to be found in some cases. E.g., Walker v. Percy, 142 N.H. 345, 702 A.2d 313 (1997). Courts often add that the misrepresentation must be material, e.g., D'Ambrosio v. Colonnade Council of Unit Owners, 717 A.2d 356 (D.C.Ct. App.1998), but justifiable reliance may be regarded as encompassing materiality. The legal requirements imposed by this list of elements are not changed if the elements are broken down into more detailed parts. For example, the single element of fraudulent representation can be expressed as three elements—(i) a representation, (ii) which is false in fact, and (iii) known to be false. By a process like this, Arizona comes up with nine elements, see e.g., Nielson v. Flashberg, 101 Ariz. 335, 419 P.2d 514 (1966), but they appear to exact essentially the same proof demands required by the Restatement.

2. Hobson v. American Cast Iron Pipe Co., 690 So.2d 341 (Ala.1997); Hames v. Cravens, 332 Ark. 437, 966 S.W.2d 244 (1998).

3. Marriage of Cutler, 588 N.W.2d 425 (Iowa 1999); Richmond Metropolitan Authority v. McDevitt Street Bovis, Inc., 256 Va. 553, 507 S.E.2d 344 (1998). Where heightened standard is imposed, courts usu-

evidence is sufficient, at least under some conditions.[4]

§ 471. Intent Required

Scienter—A False Representation Made Knowingly

Traditional rule. In the leading 19th Century case, *Derry v. Peek,*[1] Lord Herschell laid down a rule that has been widely accepted in American decisions.[2] Lord Herschell said:

> "Fraud is proved when it is shown that a false representation has been made (1) knowingly [*scienter*], or (2) without belief in its truth, or (3) recklessly, careless whether it be true or false."

The second category really includes both the first and the third. If the defendant represents a fact knowing it to be false he is making a representation without belief in the truth of his statement. Likewise, if he falsely asserts a fact without caring whether it is true or not he probably if not certainly lacks a belief in its truth and it is entirely fair to treat the case as an intentional fraud.

The common case falls in the first category—a knowing falsehood. The seller who assures the buyer that the basement has never been flooded when she knows that it has is guilty of a knowing falsehood.[3] But the key principle is expressed in the second category—a statement made without belief in its truth. The language of recklessness in the third category may be misleading to contemporary Americans who might be led to think of highly irresponsible driving. The context makes it clear, however, that the test was not about some extreme form of negligence, but about a lack of belief in the truth of the representation.

Under the rules in *Derry v. Peek*, the defendant may be liable not only for unadorned lies but also for half truths uttered *scienter*,[4] for intentionally misleading ambiguities,[5] and even for misrepresentations of his own present intention to provide benefits in the future.[6] The defendant may also fall under a duty to correct a representation that was true when made but has since become untrue.[7]

ally say the standard applies to all elements of the fraud claim, but some courts have reasonably said that it does not apply to proof of damages. See Kilduff v. Adams, Inc., 219 Conn. 314, 593 A.2d 478 (1991).

4. See Huffman v. Poore, 6 Neb.App. 43, 569 N.W.2d 549 (1997) (preponderance sufficient in actions at law for damages, though not for suits in equity); Clay v. Brand, 236 Ark. 236, 365 S.W.2d 256 (1963) (preponderance sufficient unless the misrepresentation claimed would contradict a solemn writing).

§ 471

1. Derry v. Peek, 14 App.Cas. 337 (H.L. 1889) (judgment of Lord Herschell).

2. E.g., Kimber v. Young, 137 Fed. 744 (8th Cir.1905). Many opinions reflect *Derry v. Peek* in stating the elements of fraud even when the case is not cited.

3. Nielsen v. Adams, 223 Neb. 262, 388 N.W.2d 840 (1986).

4. E.g., Junius Constr. Co. v. Cohen, 257 N.Y. 393, 178 N.E. 672 (1931).

5. Restatement § 527.

6. § 479.

7. See Restatement § 535; § 481.

Circumstantial evidence and the relevance of negligence. Under the *scienter* test, ordinary negligence, such as the defendant's failure to ascertain facts with reasonable care or his failure to formulate representations more accurately, is not enough for liability.[8] On the other hand, short of the defendant's own admission, the plaintiff can ordinarily prove knowing falsehood only by circumstantial evidence. Such evidence must not be merely speculative,[9] but if it is strong enough, it is not only admissible[10] but may meet the clear and convincing standard.[11] If the defendant makes a representation that, given his other knowledge, a reasonable person *should* know to be false, the trier may at times be permitted to infer that he *did* know it to be false and hence that he had made a knowingly false statement.[12]

Conscious ignorance, facts stated of one's own knowledge. In line with the rules in *Derry v. Peek*, the defendant who is consciously aware that he does not know the truth of his representation is held responsible for the falsehood.[13] A similar idea is that the defendant is subject to liability if he (a) asserts something of his own knowledge when he does not know the truth or falsity of the proposition[14] or knows he lacks information necessary to support such a statement,[15] and (b) expects that he will be understood as implicitly asserting knowledge.[16] The seller who

8. VF Corp. v. Wrexham Aviation Corp.,350 Md. 693, 704, 715 A.2d 188, 193 (1998) ("Negligence or misjudgment, however gross, does not satisfy the knowledge element").

9. Four R Cattle Co. v. Mullins, 253 Neb. 133, 570 N.W.2d 813 (1997).

10. See Edwards v. Travelers Ins. of Hartford, Connecticut, 563 F.2d 105 (6th Cir.1977).

11. Kuo Feng Corp. v. Ma, 248 A.D.2d 168, 669 N.Y.S.2d 575 (1998).

12. See Stromberger v. 3M Co., 990 F.2d 974, 978 (7th Cir.1993) ("No doubt some statements are so outlandish that no one in his right mind could think them true when he said them, and then intent to defraud could be inferred from the statement itself"); Ultramares Corp. v. Touche, 255 N.Y. 170, 191, 174 N.E. 441, 449 (1931) ("negligence or blindness, even when not equivalent to fraud, is none the less evidence to sustain an inference of fraud"); Restatement § 526, cmt. d.; Inferred intent is probably the explanation for cases that say on the one hand that liability may be imposed if the defendant "ought to have known" the falsity and yet also say that the tort requires bad faith, as in Parker v. State of Florida Bd. of Regents, Florida State University, 724 So.2d 163 (Fla.Dist.Ct.App. 1998).

13. Borcherding v. Anderson Remodeling Company, Inc., 253 Ill.App.3d 655, 191 Ill.Dec. 699, 624 N.E.2d 887 (1993); Gross v. Sussex Incorporated, 332 Md. 247, 630 A.2d 1156 (1993) (knowingly or in conscious disregard of its truth); *B.O. v. C.O.*, 404 Pa.Super. 127, 590 A.2d 313 (1991).

14. Florenzano v. Olson, 387 N.W.2d 168 (Minn.1986).

15. See Page Keeton, Fraud: The Necessity for an Intent to Deceive, 5 UCLA L. Rev. 583, 592 (1958) (defendant who makes an unqualified representation of fact realizing information was inadequate to justify a feeling of certainty about it).

16. See Schlossman's, Inc. v. Niewinski, 12 N.J.Super. 500, 507–508, 79 A.2d 870, 874 (1951). Sometimes courts seem to think that an unqualified or positive assertion of ascertainable fact by itself implies an assertion that the defendant knows whereof he speaks. See Doyle v. Fairfield Mach. Co., Inc., 120 Ohio App.3d 192, 208, 697 N.E.2d 667, 677 (1997); Baber v. Pioneer Concrete of Texas, Inc., 919 S.W.2d 664 (Tex.Ct.App. 1995). No doubt that is sometimes true, but not always, since context and human relationships may put the assertion in a different light. If the representation is peculiarly a matter of judgment rather than readily ascertainable fact likely to be known by the speaker, for instance, the courts are not ready to treat the statement as one made of the defendant's own knowledge. See Kimber v. Young, 137 Fed. 744, 749 (8th Cir. 1905) Schlossman's, Inc. v. Niewinski, supra.

assures the buyer that the slip covers are washable may imply that he has at least some basis for knowing that their colors will not run and may be liable when they do.[17]

Conceivably such a defendant is honest in the sense that he believes what he has asserted, so that he lacks any intent to deceive even though he knows he lacks knowledge about the facts represented. But even if, as a psychological proposition, such a defendant might be in a sense honest about the fact asserted, he has dishonestly represented at least one thing, namely the extent of his knowledge. He can readily avoid liability if he avoids making a statement as one of known fact, for example, by stating his belief or by indicating the limits of his knowledge. Liability in such cases is not only recognized, it is appropriate.

Slipping into negligence or strict liability. As Harper, James, and Gray point out,[18] the core cases of liability for statements made of one's own knowledge are consistent with the rules in *Derry v. Peek*, but when liability is imposed beyond the core cases, courts may be imposing liability for mere negligence. A part of the problem is that the term knowledge is highly uncertain. Suppose the defendant in possession of a surveyor's map of his property showing ownership of 180 acres relies upon it in representing to a potential buyer that the tract contains such acreage. He has not personally surveyed the area. Does he "know" the acreage? Or suppose he once knew a fact that put the acreage in doubt, such as the surveyor's assumption that a certain marker was the southwest corner, but that he forgot the assumption and relied quite honestly upon the map. A well known older case imposed liability on similar facts[19] (before *Derry v. Peek* was decided), although it would be hard to say that anything more than negligence was involved. Along the same lines, an Arizona opinion, without discussing any basis in logic, justice, or policy, held that a defendant could be subjected to liability for making a representation that proved to be false. It was enough that he was in fact ignorant of the truth; it was not necessary for him to have been conscious of his own ignorance. [20]That formulation necessarily means that the defendant who speaks reasonably and in good faith can be held liable. In other words, the court formulated a rule of prima facie strict liability, perhaps without realizing it.

Intent to Deceive

A number of opinions have said that the defendant must have an intent to deceive. Some statements of the rule appear to use the term

17. Schlossman's, Inc. v. Niewinski, 12 N.J.Super. 500, 79 A.2d 870 (1951) (rescission of the contract).

18. 2 Harper, James & Gray § 7.3, p. 394.

19. Chatham Furnace Co. v. Moffatt, 147 Mass. 403, 18 N.E. 168 (1888).

20. Walters v. First Federal Sav. & L. Assn. of Phoenix, 131 Ariz. 321, 641 P.2d 235 (1982); accord, approving an instruction that fraud was established if the defendant knew or *should have known* the falsity, General Elec. Co. v. Dorr, 140 Ind.App. 442, 219 N.E.2d 206 (1966); cf. South County, Inc. v. First Western Loan Co., 315 Ark. 722, 727, 871 S.W.2d 325, 327 (1994) ("the test for constructive fraud, also called 'legal fraud' or 'fraud in law' has been defined as the making of misrepresentations by one who, not knowing whether they are true or not, asserts them to be true without knowledge of their falsity and without moral guilt or evil intent").

interchangeably with or as a substitute for the *scienter* requirement.[21] Following this view, the Nebraska Court concluded that a separate instruction on intent to deceive was undesirable where an instruction on *scienter* falsehood was also given.[22] Others appear to state intent to deceive as a separate element of the claim, to be proved in addition to the elements listed in *Derry v. Peek*.[23] If intent to deceive is a separate element of the claim, then it may be difficult or impossible to impose liability merely on the ground that the defendant knows he does not know the truth, because a person who knows he does not know may nevertheless hold a strong belief in his statement and may wholly lack any intent to deceive. A court that wishes to enforce the liabilities envisioned in *Derry v. Peek* could modify the intent to deceive language and say instead that the defendant must have an intent to induce reliance. Intent to induce reliance is in fact the language of the Restatement[24] and of some opinions.[25]

§ 472. Negligent Misrepresentation

Courts fully accept liability for personal injury or property damage resulting from negligent misrepresentations. When it comes to stand-alone economic or commercial harm, some courts draw the line, refusing to impose liability for negligent misrepresentations,[1] and the most common case of liability is still for the traditional false representation knowingly made. However, many courts have now recognized that under some restrictive circumstances the defendant may be under a duty of care to make his representations accurately and may be liable for a limited measure of damages[2] to a limited group of persons if his negligent misrepresentations induce justifiable reliance to the plaintiff's loss.

One of the sources of confusion in negligent misrepresentation cases is that the negligence claim may be asserted when the facts support a claim for knowing fraud as that term is traditionally understood. For instance, if the defendant misrepresents to the plaintiff a fact within the defendant's expertise in his business or profession, he is likely to come within the rule that treats an unqualified statement of one's own

21. Johnson v. University Health Services, Inc., 161 F.3d 1334 (11th Cir.1998); Kimber v. Young, 137 F. 744 (8th Cir.1905); Martens Chevrolet, Inc. v. Seney, 292 Md. 328, 439 A.2d 534 (1982). The structure of the rule as envisioned in PROSSER AND KEETON § 107 is that the rule requires intent to deceive, which is then proved by proving a knowing falsehood, or a lack of belief in the statement, or a statement made in conscious ignorance.

22. Nielsen v. Adams, 223 Neb. 262, 388 N.W.2d 840 (1986).

23. Myers & Chapman, Inc. v. Thomas G. Evans, Inc., 323 N.C. 559, 374 S.E.2d 385 (1988).

24. Restatement § 525 (requiring a "purpose" of inducing reliance); Restatement § 531 ("reason to expect" reliance).

25. Foreman v. As Mid-America, Inc., 255 Neb. 323, 586 N.W.2d 290 (1998); Marchant v. Cook, 967 P.2d 551 (Wyo.1998).

§ 472

1. South County, Inc. v. First Western Loan Co., 315 Ark. 722, 871 S.W.2d 325 (1994); cf. Duffin v. Idaho Crop Improvement Ass'n, 126 Idaho 1002, 895 P.2d 1195 (1995) (stating a rule against liability for negligent misrepresentations except for accountants).

2. Restatement § 552B (excluding benefit of the bargain damages).

knowledge as scienter fraud.[3] Although courts do impose liability on a negligence theory in some cases like this,[4] such a result does not suggest expansive liability for negligent misrepresentation because many such cases would be supportable on actual fraud grounds as statements made of the defendant's own knowledge.[5] When the claim is constructed as one for negligent misrepresentation, the first problem is to state the conditions under which a duty of care arises. The second is to determine whether the duty runs to third persons and if so to which ones. The problem of liability to third persons is treated in a separate section.[6]

Exclusions from the duty of care. No precise formula for determining the existence of a duty of care has yet been authoritatively stated. Persons who have no pecuniary interest in the transaction ordinarily have no duty to care and are thus liable only for knowingly false misrepresentations.[7] More broadly, the ordinary commercial adversary bargainer ordinarily has no duty to use care in supplying information to those with whom he bargains.[8] Likewise, one giving an ordinary business reference may be under no duty of care to verify the good qualities he to attributes a job seeker.[9] Rather, a special relationship or some implicit undertaking to exercise care in investigating or communicating information is normally required.[10]

Defendants retained to exercise reasonable care in providing information. The clear cases for a duty of care and concomitant liability for negligent misrepresentations are those in which the defendant has expressly or implicitly undertaken to exercise care for the benefit of the plaintiff. That is ordinarily the case when the defendant is retained for the very purpose of providing accurate information. In such a case, the relationship of the parties suggests that the defendant has implicitly

3. E.g., an insurer's representation about coverage afforded by a policy as in Flamme v. Wolf Ins. Agency, 239 Neb. 465, 476 N.W.2d 802 (1991) (recognizing potential liability for agent's negligent misrepresentation).

4. Mahler v. Keenan Real Estate, Inc., 255 Kan. 593, 876 P.2d 609 (1994) (negligent misrepresentation of real estate broker to buyer).

5. See Greycas, Inc. v. Proud, 826 F.2d 1560 (7th Cir.1987); Keck v. Keck, 54 Ohio App.2d 128, 375 N.E.2d 1256 (1977); cf. Bittel v. Farm Credit Services of Central Kansas, P.C.A., 265 Kan. 651, 962 P.2d 491 (1998) (rejecting negligent misrepresentation claims on the facts because the representation, if false, was deliberately false).

6. § 480.

7. Restatement § 552 (1). Presumably, however, such persons could undertake a duty. See Jackson v. State, 287 Mont. 473, 956 P.2d 35 (1998) (state as adoption agency assumed a duty of reasonable care in representing genetic and behavioral background of parents of prospective adoptee).

8. Haupt v. Miller, 514 N.W.2d 905 (Iowa 1994); Onita Pacific Corp. v. Bronson Trustees, 315 Or. 149, 843 P.2d 890 (1992); see Alfred Hill, Damages for Innocent Misrepresentation, 73 Colum. L. Rev. 679, 685–688 (1973); 2 Harper, James, & Gray § 7.6. A seller who negligently misrepresents his goods, however, may be subject to liability to a buyer who reasonably relies, much as he would be liable for breach of warranty. See Ritter v. Custom Chemicides, Inc., 912 S.W.2d 128 (Tenn.1995) (but rejecting liability on the facts).

9. Hale v. George A. Hormel & Co., 48 Cal.App.3d 73, 121 Cal.Rptr. 144 (1975) (recommending a seller of goods) . Distinguish misrepresentations in a recommendation that affect personal safety of others. Randi W. v. Muroc Joint Unified Sch. Dist., 14 Cal.4th 1066, 929 P.2d 582, 60 Cal. Rptr.2d 263 (1997).

10. See Stillwater Condominium Ass'n v. Town of Salem, 140 N.H. 505, 668 A.2d 38 (1995) (no special relationship existed and defendant did not undertake a duty).

undertaken to use reasonable or professional care. Consequently, their clients[11] can recover for damages inflicted by the negligent misstatements of lawyers,[12] accountants,[13] abstractors,[14] notaries,[15] and others retained or consulted to determine or certify a given state of facts[16] or who assume such duties.[17] Sometimes statutes prescribe particular duties and the liability that follows from breach.[18]

Fiduciaries and other relationships and undertakings. Courts have recognized that a fiduciary, confidential, or other special relationship between the parties implies such an undertaking or expectation that the defendant would exercise reasonable care. Fiduciaries and those in similar confidential relationships are accordingly liable for negligent misrepresentation.[19] When the facts are peculiarly within the knowledge of the defendant and inaccessible to the plaintiff, commercial dealings between the parties must come to a halt unless the plaintiff can put confidence in reasonable accuracy of the defendant's statements. So courts sometimes impose a duty of care when the defendant had peculiar knowledge or expertise.[20] Perhaps in some of these cases the plaintiff has reposed confidence in the defendant's special knowledge and the defendant has accepted that confidence as a basis for their dealings.[21] Similarly, the particular facts or the words or deeds of the defendant may warrant the belief that he has undertaken to exercise care in the

11. As to negligent misrepresentations made on behalf of a client to third persons, see §§ 480 (accountants and others) & 488 (lawyers).

12. When the claim is asserted by the client, it may be conceptualized as one for "malpractice" rather than "misrepresentation," even though based upon a misstatement of fact. Mecca v. Shang, 258 A.D.2d 569, 685 N.Y.S.2d 458 (App.Div. 1999) (negligent misrepresentation claim should have been dismissed as it was but one form of the lawyer malpractice claim and duplicative); Safeway Managing General Agency, Inc. v. Clark & Gamble, 985 S.W.2d 166 (Tex.App.1998) (since insurer who retained attorneys to defend insured was not "client," the claim was not one for malpractice but for negligent misrepresentation).

13. E.g., Cordial v. Ernst & Young, 199 W.Va. 119, 483 S.E.2d 248 (1996).

14. Williams v. Polgar, 391 Mich. 6, 215 N.W.2d 149 (1974).

15. Keck v. Keck, 54 Ohio App.2d 128, 375 N.E.2d 1256 (1977).

16. Barrie v. V.P. Exterminators, Inc., 625 So.2d 1007 (La.1993) (termite inspector's certificate); Glanzer v. Shepard, 233 N.Y. 236, 135 N.E. 275 (1922) (public weighmaster certificate of weight in commercial transaction); Aesoph v. Kusser, 498 N.W.2d 654 (S.D.1993) (insurance agent representing that coverage was not available).

17. Culp Construction Co. v. Buildmart Mall, 795 P.2d 650 (Utah 1990) (title company may have assumed duty of abstractor).

18. E.g., Cal. Civ. Code § 1185 (what notary must do to identify person signing acknowledgment); Cal. Gov. Code § 8214 (liability of notary).

19. See McAuley v. International Bus. Mach. Corp., 165 F.3d 1038 (6th Cir.1999) (ERISA fiduciary's duties); Kimmell v. Schaefer, 89 N.Y.2d 257, 675 N.E.2d 450, 652 N.Y.S.2d 715 (1996) (even though defendant was to gain a commission if the plaintiff invested in project, defendant's expertise and special relation sufficed to require reasonable care). Some cases have stated that New York imposes a duty only upon fiduciaries. See Stewart v. Jackson & Nash, 976 F.2d 86 (2d Cir.1992). This seems inaccurate.

20. See, e.g., Fine Host Corp. Securities Litigation, 25 F.Supp.2d 61(D.Conn.1998) (emphasizing unique knowledge or specialized expertise); Colonial Imports, Inc. v. Carlton Northwest, Inc., 121 Wash.2d 726, 853 P.2d 913 (1993).

21. Confidence reposed and accepted establishes a confidential relationship. See City of Atascadero v. Merrill Lynch, Pierce, Fenner & Smith, Inc., 68 Cal.App.4th 445, 80 Cal.Rptr.2d 329 (1998).

plaintiff's behalf.[22] That may be the case even though on some issues in the transaction the plaintiff and the defendant are bargaining adversely to each other.[23]

Over-and under-stating the duty of care. Some decisions imply more expansive duties while others imply less. On the expansive side, decisions sometimes impose a duty of care upon adversary bargainers,[24] or at least give that impression. That impression may be erroneous because sometimes the defendant simply did not argue the duty issue but only argued instead that negligence could never be a basis for liability. When the court rejects a "never" argument, the defendant who did not address the duty issue is left with a lost cause, but if the court did not address the duty question, it would still be open to the same court later to limit the duty in line with the mainstream views.[25]

On the restrictive side, some decisions have said that no duty of care in supplying information is imposed upon the defendant who is not actually in the business of providing such information,[26] or that negligent misrepresentation of "noncommercial" information, even when given in a business transaction cannot be actionable.[27] Taken literally, such formulations exclude the possibility that fiduciaries and others could actually undertake a duty of care by conduct, contract or relationship.

The Restatement is also probably both too over-and under-inclusive. It provides that anyone who has a pecuniary interest in a transaction is subject to liability for negligently supplied information intended to guide

22. Cf. Lacher v. Superior Court, 230 Cal.App.3d 1038, 281 Cal.Rptr. 640 (1991) (developer, to obtain neighbor's support for development, assured neighbors that buildings would be one story and not block views, public policy imposed duty of care in making representations).

23. See Jackson v. State, 287 Mont. 473, 956 P.2d 35 (1998) (state revealing some information about prospective adoptee in state's custody was undertaking duty to prospective adopting family to exercise care in its representations). Along these lines, cases have held or assumed that a prospective employer, inducing a recruit to accept a job, is under a duty of care and hence liable for negligent misrepresentations. E.g., Van Buren v. Pima Community College Dist., 113 Ariz. 85, 546 P.2d 821 (1976); Pollmann v. Belle Plaine Livestock Auction, Inc., 567 N.W.2d 405 (Iowa 1997); cf. D'Ulisse–Cupo v. Board of Directors of Notre Dame High School, 202 Conn. 206, 520 A.2d 217 (1987) (existing employer alleged to have negligently represented no problems to renewal of teaching contract); but cf. Conway v. Pacific University, 324 Or. 231, 924 P.2d 818 (1996) (university owed no duty of care in its representations about tenure in the absence of some relationship beyond employment).

24. Williams Ford, Inc. v. Hartford Courant Co., 232 Conn. 559, 657 A.2d 212 (1995) (newspaper and its advertisers; the fact that parties are ordinary arms-length bargainers does not eliminate a duty of care but may be considered in determining justifiable reliance).

25. Thus in Martens Chevrolet, Inc. v. Seney, 292 Md. 328, 439 A.2d 534 (1982) the seller of a business was allegedly negligent in supplying financial information. The defendant argued that Maryland did not recognize a negligent misrepresentation claim, not that the duty of care was limited to those in special relationships. The court held that Maryland did recognize negligent misrepresentation but did not purport to decide whether adversaries owed a duty of care. Liability in similar cases may also be justified when the plaintiff can show mutual mistake that would justify rescission or a monetary equivalent. As to that, see § 473.

26. Freeman v. Ernst & Young, 516 N.W.2d 835 (Iowa 1994).

27. Barmettler v. Reno Air, Inc., 114 Nev. 441, 956 P.2d 1382 (Nev. 1998) (employer allegedly stated an intention to keep confidential any employees' participation in chemical dependency programs).

others.[28] As phrased, the Restatement does not require the defendant to be in the business of supplying information, only that he does supply it either in the course of his business or in connection with a transaction in which he is financially interested. Unfortunately, that formulation could be read to include adversary bargainers who do not undertake to exercise reasonable care for the other's informational interests.

The problem of over-and under-statements of the duty can be avoided by recognizing that the duty of care must arise only when the defendant undertakes such a duty, either explicitly or implicitly, through his relationship with the plaintiff, or when the plaintiff is led reasonably to expect reasonable care for her interests.

Clarity in stating and applying the duty can also be improved by recognizing that falsity does not by any means prove negligence. The defendant's representation might be erroneous because the defendant (1) did not know facts he should have known, failed to investigate facts, or investigated them with less than reasonable care; (2) knew the facts but used words or other communicative devices poorly; or (3) unreasonably failed to make statements at all, or failed to make statements needed to clarify the plaintiff's understanding. Quite possibly a defendant might be under a duty of care with respect to one of these items but not all. For instance, my insurance agent might be under a duty to know the available options but under no duty at all volunteer information about appropriate levels of liability coverage.[29] Similarly, it may be that even if there is a duty of care, it is not breached merely because the defendant failed to investigate facts for the plaintiff's benefit.[30] And where the alleged negligence is in the use of words rather than in gathering facts, it might be noted that even lawyers, judges, and legislators, not to mention quires of professors and students, have at times failed to capture their thoughts accurately in their words.

Negligent misrepresentation to a contracting party; the economic or commercial loss rule. Some courts have said that the plaintiff, or at least a sophisticated plaintiff, may not pursue a negligent misrepresentation claim for commercial harm against a defendant with whom he has a contractual relationship.[31] In that view, if the claim cannot be made on grounds of intentional misrepresentation, it must be made as a contract claim or not at all. The idea is that between contracting parties the contract's provisions should control and also that if a point covered by a misrepresentation is important to the plaintiff, she should have it expressed in the contract or suffer the risk of the trier's conclusion that

28. Restatement § 552.

29. Cf. Murphy v. Kuhn, 90 N.Y.2d 266, 682 N.E.2d 972, 660 N.Y.S.2d 371 (1997) (agent owed no duty to volunteer advice as to whether $500,000 was sufficient liability coverage).

30. Bortz v. Noon, 556 Pa. 489, 729 A.2d 555 (Pa. 1999) (real estate broker honestly representing that septic tank test had been completed successfully was not liable for negligent misrepresentation where the plaintiff had not proved that the standard of care for brokers included investigation of facts reported to broker from reliable third parties).

31. E.g., Apollo Group, Inc. v. Avnet, Inc., 58 F.3d 477 (9th Cir.1995) (forecasting Arizona law); see § 482.

it was not so important as she now claims.[32] However, not all agreements between sophisticated bargainers call for the same result. A lawyer's contract with his client, for example, should not preclude recovery by the client for a negligent misrepresentation upon which the client relied to her detriment.[33]

§ 473. Innocent Misrepresentation

Imposing Liability for Innocent Misrepresentation

The general rule requiring a knowing falsehood to support a damages action for misrepresentation implies that negligent and innocent misrepresentations causing commercial harm are actionable only under special conditions. Consumer fraud statutes may impose strict liability within their scope,[1] and beyond that, one group of cases,[2] has broadly stated strict liability rules applicable to contracting parties without regard to the parties' intent or expectations, and sometimes even discarding the parties' own contractual limitations to do so.[3]

If the cases mean to impose a general rule of strict liability independent of the parties' intent or reasonable expectations founded on the facts of the case, the approach is peculiar for at least two reasons. First, except in consumer contracts or the like, it is unusual to ignore the parties' own intent in a consensual transaction. Second, strict liability more onerous than liability for negligence, yet liability for negligent misrepresentation is usually imposed only when the parties are in a special relationship or tacitly understand that care is required. Perhaps many of the cases using broad strict liability language do not entirely mean it. Some, for example, are merely rescission cases[4] that come under the special rule discussed below. Some others have used the broad

32. Cf. All–Tech Telecom, Inc. v. Amway Corp., 174 F.3d 862 (7th Cir.1999) (discussing the concerns).

33. Collins v. Reynard, 154 Ill.2d 48, 180 Ill.Dec. 672, 607 N.E.2d 1185 (1992).

§ 473

1. See, e.g., Gennari v. Weichert Co. Realtors, 148 N.J. 582, 691 A.2d 350 (1997); Winton v. Johnson & Dix Fuel Corp., 147 Vt. 236, 515 A.2d 371 (1986).

2. E.g., Cordial v. Ernst & Young, 199 W.Va. 119, 483 S.E.2d 248 (1996) (elements are falsity in fact of a material statement and justified reliance; knowledge of falsity is not required where there is a duty to know); see cases cited nn. 3, 5, & 6 below. ALA. CODE § 6–5–101 also appears to impose a general rule of strict liability. In spite of broad language, some of the cases may be referring to negligent misrepresentations or even to scienter fraud. See, e.g., the discussion in Horton v. Tyree, 104 W.Va. 238, 139 S.E. 737, 738 (1927).

3. Clements Auto Co. v. Service Bureau Corp., 444 F.2d 169 (8th Cir.1971). Professor Hill traced the antecedents of this case to insouciant use of fraud precedents in innocent misrepresentation cases. See Alfred Hill, Damages for Innocent Misrepresentation, 73 COLUM. L. REV. 679, 682, n. 6 (1973). Professor Hill's scholarly study concluded that these cases are a minority and, contrary to the Restatement, that they have not substantially increased in number since 1936. Some of the strict liability cases simply apply the scienter rules loosely, sometimes without discussion of or even apparent awareness that strict liability is being imposed. See § 471.

4. Swanson v. Domning, 251 Minn. 110, 86 N.W.2d 716 (1957) (broadly stating liability for innocent misrepresentation, although in fact the case was one essentially for rescission and restitution of a downpayment); Halpert v. Rosenthal, 107 R.I. 406, 267 A.2d 730 (1970) (broadly favoring strict liability for innocent "unqualified" representations, but actually only permitting a rescission).

language of strict liability merely in dicta, and in still others the court may have adopted the broad rule of liability without realizing that it imposed strict liability, and certainly without giving a reason for strict liability.[5]

In a court that accepts strict liability for innocent misrepresentation, the critical question may be whether the defendant is to be protected by contract defenses such as disclaimer clauses and the parol evidence rule. Although those defenses may not apply to cases of actual fraud, on principle they avoid liability for innocent misrepresentations,[6] as contemporary cases have recognized.[7]

Limiting Strict Liability

Another group of cases rejects any general rule of strict liability for misrepresentations causing commercial harm but may permit the claim in limited circumstances.[8] Two reasons can be suggested why a wholly innocent misrepresentation might be actionable. (1) The plaintiff is led reasonably to believe that the representation is a guarantee and not merely an honest statement of the defendant's belief. (2) The misrepresentation reflects a mutual mistake that justifies rescission. With these reasons in mind, strict liability for innocent misrepresentations causing only commercial harm is thus most appropriately imposed apart from statute only if (a) the representation is a warranty, or (b) the plaintiff seeks rescission rather than tort damages, or (c) damages that are financially equivalent to the restitution required by a rescission can be fairly awarded. These forms of strict liability would ordinarily apply only to the contracting parties.[9]

Warranty. The defendant may be subjected to liability for innocent misrepresentation causing stand-alone economic harm when the defendant undertakes to guarantee the truth of the matter represented, that is, when his representation is a warranty. Where a warranty is breached, the plaintiff may recover the contract or loss of bargain measure of damages.[10] The most familiar warranties are the UCC warranties by sellers of goods. The UCC treats any affirmation of fact relating to the goods sold as a warranty. Samples, models, and descriptions may have the same effect.[11] In addition, the UCC imposes an implied warranty of merchantability which requires that the goods must be at least able to pass without objection in the trade and that they are fit for the ordinary purposes for which such goods are used.[12] If the seller breaches these

5. Walters v. First Federal Sav. & L. Assn. of Phoenix, 131 Ariz. 321, 641 P.2d 235 (1982).

6. See Alfred Hill, Damages for Innocent Misrepresentation, 73 Colum. L. Rev. 679 (1973).

7. See nn. 15–18.

8. See Bortz v. Noon, 556 Pa. 489, 729 A.2d 555 (Pa. 1999) (recognizing rescission for innocent misrepresentations but rejecting liability in damages).

9. See Restatement § 552C.

10. Johnson v. Healy, 176 Conn. 97, 405 A.2d 54 (1978); see § 483 as to damages measures.

11. UCC § 2–313.

12. UCC § 2–314.

warranties, he is liable for the economic harm suffered as a result, without proof of fraud or even negligence.

So far as commercial losses are concerned, the parties can limit the implied warranty of the chattel seller. The implied warranty described by the UCC is also ordinarily limited to sales of tangible chattels. But an express warranty is still possible in any kind of transaction. For instance, the seller of a business may warrant in writing that the financial records attached to the closing documents are accurate and may be liable without fault of any kind for breach of such a warranty.[13] And some representations, especially by sellers, may be construed as warranties under the particular circumstances of the case.[14]

Apart from the implied warranties in chattel sales, however, an oral representation is not ordinarily construed to be a warranty. Even if an oral representation is construed as a contractual warranty or promise, the parol evidence rule [15]and any valid disclaimer clause[16] will likely bar the warranty claim if the transaction is later reduced to a complete writing. If the oral representation is conceived as a warranty that amounts to a tort, the economic loss rule, which requires courts to focus upon the contractual rights will probably bar the claim.[17] Strict tort liability as distinct from liability under the terms of the contract itself, seems increasingly unlikely. For commercial losses a contracting party must ordinarily be governed by the law of contract.[18]

Rescission for mistake and innocent misrepresentation. Rescission is distinct from the tort action for damages. Rescission voids the transaction and requires each party to restore what he received in it. The defendant's innocent representation may cause or reflect a mutual mistake. If the plaintiff acts promptly,[19] transactions may be rescinded, usually by the buyer, for certain mutual mistakes, but not all.[20] The mistake must go to the basis of the transaction; a mistake about a

13. VF Corp. v. Wrexham Aviation Corp.,350 Md. 693, 715 A.2d 188 (1998).

14. Johnson v. Healy, 176 Conn. 97, 405 A.2d 54 (1978) (homebuilder assertions); Richard v. A. Waldman & Sons, Inc., 155 Conn. 343, 232 A.2d 307 (1967) (real estate developer sold a house and lot with a plot plan showing a 20–foot side yard that complied with zoning regulations; the parties later discovered that the house was so close to the next lot that to enter the house required a trespass; the representation was construed as a warranty). At one time, Alaska imposed strict liability for innocent misrepresentations by real estate sellers, but that has been changed by statute. See Amyot v. Luchini, 932 P.2d 244 (Alaska 1997).

15. Betaco, Inc. v. Cessna Aircraft Co., 103 F.3d 1281 (7th Cir.1996) (if writing fully integrates agreement, parol evidence of other terms is not admissible; disclaimer of warranty and merger clause are among factors indicating integration); Martin & Martin, Inc. v. Bradley Enterprises, Inc., 256 Va. 288, 504 S.E.2d 849 (1998) (enforcing merger clause).

16. Gibson v. Capano, 241 Conn. 725, 699 A.2d 68 (1997).

17. Apollo Group, Inc. v. Avnet, Inc., 58 F.3d 477 (9th Cir.1995).

18. All–Tech Telecom, Inc. v. Amway Corp., 174 F.3d 862 (7th Cir.1999) (discussing importance of adhering to contract analysis, including use of parol evidence rule, in commercial harm cases); see Alfred Hill, Damages for Innocent Misrepresentation, 73 COLUM. L. REV. 679 (1973).

19. Knudsen v. Jensen, 521 N.W.2d 415 (S.D.1994).

20. See 2 DAN B. DOBBS, LAW OF REMEDIES § 11.3 (2d ed. 1993) (mustual mistake as basis for rescission and restitution).

material matter that is not basic or of the essence is insufficient.[21] If the plaintiff has assumed the risk of her own mistake, as where she knows she does not know the facts,[22] or parties have allocated the risk of mistake to the plaintiff,[23] the plaintiff cannot have rescission. If, by disclaimers or otherwise, the contract indicates that the defendant will not be liable for mistakes and the defendant delivers the performance promised by the contract, rescission must be denied if the contract is to be honored.[24] Thus, although rescission may be granted without fault of the defendant, it is not granted in opposition to the contract rights of the innocent defendant. As in the case of a claimed warranty, a written and fully integrated contract will determine the rights of the parties.

The defendant's innocent misrepresentation is one way in which mistakes of the parties may be reflected, reinforced, or generated. To the extent that the defendant, particularly a seller, actually generates the mistake by innocent representation, rescission is arguably more justified than in the case of mutual mistakes caused by neutral means. Accordingly, rescission is to be granted for innocent material misrepresentations upon which the plaintiff reasonably relied.[25] But this is not to say that the recipient of an innocent misrepresentation can acquire a right to rescind that is at odds with the parties' allocation of the risk of error. At least in the case of formal non-consumer contracts, it would seem that the plaintiff cannot justifiably rely upon representations plainly inconsistent with the contract's own provisions or disclaimers,[26] a result also obtained by excluding evidence of prior misrepresentations under the parol evidence rule.[27]

Liability for innocent misrepresentation presents further problems when damages are analyzed. The plaintiff deceived by an innocent misrepresentation is one of two innocent and mistaken parties and at most should recover out of pocket damages on the theory that such a measure would ordinarily be the financial equivalent of rescission.[28] And

21. See 2 Dan B. Dobbs, Law of Remedies § 11.3 (2d ed. 1993).

22. By some definitions, the plaintiff who knows she does not know the facts simply is not mistaken. See 2 Dan B. Dobbs, Law of Remedies § 11.2 (2d ed. 1993).

23. Id.

24. As in, e.g., Knieper v. United States, 38 Fed.Cl. 128 (1997)

25. Hyler v. Garner, 548 N.W.2d 864 (Iowa 1996); Halpert v. Rosenthal, 107 R.I. 406, 267 A.2d 730 (1970); Restatement Second of Contracts § 164; accord, Baker v. Cambridge Chase, Inc., 725 A.2d 757 (Pa.Super.1999); cf. Dudzik v. Leesona Corp., 473 A.2d 762 (R.I.1984) (representation inducing employee to forego stock option actionable on analogy to rescission). Statutes may eliminate this liability. See Amyot v. Luchini, 932 P.2d 244 (Alaska 1997).

26. See Morris v. United States, 33 Fed. Cl. 733, 746 (1995); but cf. Halpert v. Rosenthal, 107 R.I. 406, 267 A.2d 730 (1970) (general merger clause did not prevent rescission for innocent misrepresentation).

27. See Calomiris v. Woods, 353 Md. 425, 727 A.2d 358 (1999) (parol evidence rule bars admission of evidence of prior representations when the plaintiff claims only innocent misrepresentations).

28. Restatement § 552C (limited to sale, rental, or exchanges but purporting to permit out of pocket damages in all such cases of innocent misrepresentation); Anzalone v. Strand, 14 Mass.App.Ct. 45, 436 N.E.2d 960 (1982) (innocent misrepresentation); see § 483. Some opinions seem to have been unaware of the distinction, but possibly because the liability was imposed on the ground of contractually implicit warranty rather than on the basis of the mis-

since the plaintiff could not rescind against a third person who is not a party to the contract, she should not recover damages for innocent misrepresentation against a third person, either.[29] Besides these limitations, some forms of rescission or rescission-equivalent recoveries can have unjust and undesirable effects that are discussed in connection with the topic of remedies.[30]

§ 474. Reliance, Justified Reliance, and Comparative Fault

Requirement of reliance. A representation is not actionable unless the plaintiff in fact relies upon it.[1] To rely, the plaintiff must choose her conduct because of the representation, either acting or refraining from action because or partly because of the representation.[2] For example, the plaintiff who enters into a transaction with the defendant does not rely upon the defendant's misrepresentation if she enters into the transaction without a belief in its truth, or doesn't learn of the misrepresentation until after the transaction has closed, or would have entered the transaction whether or not the misrepresentation had been made.[3] If the misrepresentation is material, however, the plaintiff who acts in accordance with the representation has inferentially or presumptively relied upon it.[4] The requirement of reliance in fact is a requirement that the defendant's representation is one of the causes in fact of the plaintiff's harm, although it need not be the sole cause.[5]

Indirect reliance. One kind of case that has gained much attention involves the claim that although the plaintiff herself never knew of the defendant's misrepresentation, she bought in a market that reacted to that representation by price adjustments and because she relied upon the integrity of the market, she had indirectly relied upon the misrepresentation. The Supreme Court has given limited approval of this "fraud on the market" theory in certain federal securities cases, provided that the fraud did actually affect market price;[6] but the theory would presum-

take-rescission analysis. See Richard v. A. Waldman & Sons, Inc., 155 Conn. 343, 232 A.2d 307 (1967).

29. Norman v. Brown, Todd & Heyburn, 693 F.Supp. 1259 (D.Mass.1988); see M&D, Inc. v. McConkey, 231 Mich.App. 22, 585 N.W.2d 33 (1998) (privity required).

30. § 483.

§ 474

1. Restatement §§ 537(a) (fraudulent representations); 552(1) (negligent representations); 552C (innocent representation).

2. St. Paul Fire & Marine Ins. Co. v. Russo Brothers, Inc., 641 A.2d 1297 (R.I. 1994); Restatement § 537(a).

3. Schaaf v. Highfield, 127 Wash.2d 17, 896 P.2d 665 (1995) (plaintiff-buyer did not rely upon negligent representation about roof because he intended to construct a new roof anyway, and further because he received the representation after purchase, not before).

4. See Vasquez v. Superior Court, 4 Cal.3d 800, 484 P.2d 964, 94 Cal.Rptr. 796, 53 A.L.R.3d 513 (1971).

5. Engalla v. Permanente Medical Group, Inc., 15 Cal.4th 951, 938 P.2d 903, 64 Cal.Rptr.2d 843 (1997); Horton v. Tyree, 104 W.Va. 238, 139 S.E. 737 (1927).

6. Basic Inc. v. Levinson, 485 U.S. 224, 108 S.Ct. 978, 99 L.Ed.2d 194 (1988); cf. Connick v. Suzuki Motor Co., Ltd., 174 Ill.2d 482, 675 N.E.2d 584, 221 Ill.Dec. 389 (1996) (under deceptive practices or consumer fraud statute, manufacturer's misleading statements to a magazine sufficed because reliance was not required). In Mirkin v. Wasserman, 5 Cal.4th 1082, 858 P.2d

ably work only in very strong markets like those represented by major stock exchanges. In other instances, indirect reliance upon statements made to another raise issues more concerned with the scope of the defendant's duty rather than the actuality of reliance.[7]

Requirement of justified reliance. According to most courts, however, bare reliance is not enough. The plaintiff must go on to show that she justifiably relied.[8] Reliance upon the defendant's material representations is ordinarily justified unless the plaintiff is on notice that the statement is not to be trusted or knows the statement to be false.[9] Reliance is not ordinarily justifiable if the misrepresentation (a) is not material; (b) is mere puffing, states an opinion or judgment of one without specialized knowledge and who does not imply assertions of facts; (c) predicts some future course of events over which the defendant has little or no control; (d) states a legal conclusion by one without specialized knowledge and who does not imply assertions of facts.

Comparative fault. Some courts still use the term reasonable reliance and tend to equate it with contributory negligence of the plaintiff.[10] Most courts use the term justifiable reliance and treat that term as something quite different from contributory negligence.[11] Contributory negligence analysis (now governed largely by comparative fault rules) does, however, have a limited place in the resolution of misrepresentation claims. Most decisions say the plaintiff's contributory fault, determined under the objective reasonable person standard, is relevant to bar or reduce damages when the defendant's misrepresentation is merely negligent,[12] but that contributory fault has no effect on the plaintiff's

568, 23 Cal.Rptr.2d 101 (1993) the courts rejected a common law fraud on the market theory but left standing claims under state securities statutes with limited remedies.

7. See § 482 (discussing contractual disclaimers of reliance).

8. E.g., Johnson v. University Health Services, Inc., 161 F.3d 1334 (11th Cir. 1998); Hyler v. Garner, 548 N.W.2d 864 (Iowa 1996). Some authority holds that reliance alone is sufficient. Phinney v. Adelman, 222 Mich.App. 513, 564 N.W.2d 532 (1997) (justification for reliance not required). Some consumer fraud statutes eliminate the justified reliance requirement and may even drop the requirement of reliance in fact. See Gennari v. Weichert Co. Realtors, 148 N.J. 582, 691 A.2d 350 (1997). Justified reliance is a jury issue if reasonable people could differ. Marcus Bros. Textiles, Inc. v. Price Waterhouse, LLP., 350 N.C. 214, 513 S.E.2d 320 (N.C. 1999) ; Doyle v. Fairfield Mach. Co., Inc., 120 Ohio App.3d 192, 697 N.E.2d 667 (1997). But rules on materiality, opinion, law, future predictions, and puffing are often enforced as a matter of law.

9. § 475.

10. See Foremost Ins. Co., Grand Rapids, Michigan v. Parham, 693 So.2d 409 (Ala.1997) (returning to "reasonable reliance" standard when the plaintiff fails to read a document she signed).

11. See Field v. Mans, 516 U.S. 59, 116 S.Ct. 437, 133 L.Ed.2d 351(1995) (discussing and reviewing many authorities).

12. E.g., Williams Ford, Inc. v. Hartford Courant Co., 232 Conn. 559, 657 A.2d 212 (1995) (although comparative fault statute covered only personal injury and property damages, court would use comparative fault approach to the plaintiff's contributory fault in negligent misrepresentation case); ESCA Corp. v. KPMG Peat Marwick, 135 Wash.2d 820, 959 P.2d 651 (1998) (similar). Sonja Larsen, Annotation, Applicability of Comparative Negligence Doctrine to Actions Based on Negligent Misrepresentation, 22 A.L.R.5th 464 (1995). Traditionally, contributory negligence had no role in strict liability claims, but that has changed in products liability suits for injury and property damage. See § 369. Unless the rule of strict liability for misrepresentations is intended to protect the negligent plaintiff from her own fault, comparative negligence

claims or recovery when the defendant is guilty of actual fraud[13] or breach of fiduciary duty.[14] Some courts reject the comparative fault defense even when the defendant's representation is only negligent, on the ground that it is not adapted to commercial transactions and that the defendant should bear the risks, not the plaintiff.[15]

Justifiable reliance and comparative fault. The justified reliance rules, on the other hand, bar the plaintiff whose reliance is unjustified, purportedly even when the defendant is guilty of scienter fraud. What is the function of the justified reliance rule? It is not a rule needed to establish but-for causation; that is established by the plaintiff's reliance in fact, justifiable or not. Nor is unjustified reliance merely a matter of contributory negligence. If it were contributory negligence it would be an affirmative defense, not a matter, like justified reliance, that is part of the plaintiff's case in chief. And as to intentional torts like fraud, the contributory fault of the plaintiff was not even a valid affirmative defense. Finally, if unjustified reliance were merely a matter of contributory fault, a failure to prove such reliance would not be a complete bar to recovery but would only reduce damages in most states. These objections are not eliminated by the suggestion that the justified reliance rule is merely contributory negligence judged subjectively by the plaintiff's personal capacity rather than by the objective reasonable person standard.[16]

Justified reliance as a reflection of the defendant's duty or conduct. The justified reliance requirement, then, looks more like an indirect way of assessing two other issues. (1) Did the plaintiff rely in fact? If reliance would be foolish and unjustified, perhaps the plaintiff did not in fact rely but only claims to have done so to avoid a bad deal.[17] (2) Did the defendant in fact make the representation and if so did he intend to induce reliance? If the plaintiff's reliance would be foolish, perhaps the defendant did not make the representation, and if he did make it, perhaps, since reliance would be so foolish as to be unjustifiable, the defendant did not intend or expect reliance.[18] In the end, the justified

seems as appropriate in innocent as in negligent misrepresentation cases. Comparative fault principles were invoked in Gennari v. Weichert Co. Realtors, 148 N.J. 582, 691 A.2d 350 (1997) as between defendants. Contra, for reasons that may be hard to generalize, Reda v. Sincaban, 145 Wis.2d 266, 426 N.W.2d 100 (Wis.App.1988).

13. See Edwards v. Travelers Ins. of Hartford, Connecticut, 563 F.2d 105 (6th Cir.1977); Greycas, Inc. v. Proud, 826 F.2d 1560 (7th Cir.1987).

14. Neff v. Bud Lewis, Co., 89 N.M. 145, 548 P.2d 107 (1976).

15. Estate of Braswell v. People's Credit Union, 602 A.2d 510, 22 A.L.R.5th 868 (1992).

16. See Restatement § 545A, cmt. b; Prosser & Keeton § 108, p. 751. The term justifiable reliance is meant to convey the subjective standard as opposed to the objective, contributory negligence standard connoted by "reasonable reliance."

17. See Field v. Mans, 516 U.S. 59, 76, 116 S.Ct. 437, 446, 133 L.Ed.2d 351(1995).

18. Note that the defendant will not often know which facts or representations among many played a part in the plaintiff's decision to enter into the transaction. However, if the only conceivable basis for entering into the deal lies in a single misrepresentation of the defendant, the defendant does know that the plaintiff is relying. "I own the Brooklyn Bridge and will let you have it for $100 cash" is a case for liability if the plaintiff relies by paying the $100.

reliance requirement seems less like a separate issue and more like evidence about the plaintiff's actual reliance or the defendant's culpability. Consequently, if the defendant's culpability is established by evidence that he did in fact intend and expect to induce reliance by a fraudulent misstatement, liability is appropriate even if the plaintiff's reliance in fact is utterly foolish. For example, the defendant who takes advantage of the plaintiff's known intellectual limitations[19] or of confidence reposed[20] to sell to the victim worthless stock in a micron mine will be accountable in spite of the plaintiff's foolishness. Courts could, in other words, abolish the separate requirement of justified reliance without changing the outcomes of cases, only the mode of analysis.

§ 475. Justified Reliance: Investigation and Failure to Read

Plaintiff's investigation. If the plaintiff mistrusts the defendant's representations and fully investigates for herself, it is possible that the defendant's misrepresentation has no effect upon her decision to enter into the transaction with the defendant. That is the case if the plaintiff's investigation reveals the whole truth. In that instance the plaintiff, knowing the truth, does not rely at all upon the defendant's statements.[1] When no evidence shows what the plaintiff learned from the investigation, courts may conclude that she did not rely upon the defendant's misrepresentations but upon her own investigation.[2] Perhaps the real point in some such cases is that the trier can conclude that no knowing misrepresentations were made.

But the defendant's representation need not be the sole cause of the plaintiff's decision to act, and if the evidence shows that the plaintiff's investigation does not dispel the representation, she can appropriately rely upon both.[3] On the other hand, if the plaintiff's investigation puts her on notice that the defendant's statements may be false her reliance upon the defendant's statement may be regarded as unjustifiable.[4] Some statements of the plaintiff-investigation rule are much broader, and would bar the plaintiff if she made any investigation at all, even if it appeared to confirm the defendant's fraudulent statements.[5] Some of these broad statements appear to have been based upon inadequate analysis. Others simply reflect a valid exculpatory clause[6] or a starting

19. E.g., Adan v. Steinbrecher, 116 Minn. 174, 133 N.W. 477 (1911) (grossly misrepresenting value of roadhouse to gullible young man).

20. Hyma v. Lee, 338 Mich. 31, 60 N.W.2d 920 (1953) (spiritualist inducing follower's financial transactions by representing that God and the dead were giving advice).

§ 475

1. See Restatement § 541.

2. E.g., McNabb v. Thomas, 190 F.2d 608, 88 U.S.App.D.C. 379 (1951).

3. See Townsend v. Felthousen, 156 N.Y. 618, 625, 51 N.E. 279, 281 (1898); Cordial v. Ernst & Young, 199 W.Va. 119, 132–133 483 S.E.2d 248, 261–262 (1996).

4. Simpson v. Widger, 311 N.J.Super. 379, 709 A.2d 1366 (1998).

5. See Heifetz v. Bell, 101 Cal.App.2d 275, 225 P.2d 231 (1950) (but actually only deciding that a finding of no reliance in fact was justified).

6. As in Kuch & Watson, Inc. v. Woodman, 29 Ill.App.3d 638, 331 N.E.2d 350 (1975) where the exculpatory clause stated

point that is then qualified by substantial exceptions that gobble up the rule.[7]

Plaintiff's failure to investigate. In actual fraud cases, the plaintiff is ordinarily justified in relying upon the defendant's material representations without any investigation at all,[8] even though those representations come from an adverse bargainer[9] and could be checked by examining courthouse records.[10] Commerce thrives when parties can conclude transactions without extensive investigation of representations. So the rule makes sense. At the same time, if the plaintiff wants more detail than has been provided,[11] or is on notice that the representation is doubtful because it is improbable or could not be stated with the precision the plaintiff demands, or because the plaintiff believes the defendant to be dishonest, the trier of fact may be permitted to find that reliance without investigation was not justified,[12] and in some cases, courts may conclude the same as a matter of law.[13] The contract itself may also require the plaintiff to rely upon her own investigation in some instances.[14] In cases of negligent misrepresentation, the contributory negligence standard usually applies, so that the courts may more readily expect the plaintiff to protect herself by investigation.[15]

Failure to read. A special kind of failure to investigate arises when the falsity of the defendant's representation would be disclosed by reading the proposed contract. One who signs a document is bound even though he has not read it.[16] However, the parol evidence rule does not

that plaintiff had inspected for itself and did not rely upon representations. As to these clauses, see § 482.

7. See Wasson v. Schubert, 964 S.W.2d 520 (Mo.App.1998) (exceptions: when the plaintiff relies in part on the misrepresentation, when the plaintiff and defendant are not on equal footing, when the defendant makes distinct and specific representations).

8. Gross v. Sussex, Inc., 332 Md. 247, 630 A.2d 1156 (1993) (excellent discussion of various statements of the rule); Townsend v. Felthousen, 156 N.Y. 618, 51 N.E. 279 (1898); Horton v. Tyree, 104 W.Va. 238, 139 S.E. 737 (1927); Halpert v. Rosenthal, 107 R.I. 406, 267 A.2d 730 (1970) (nothing absurd in statement that house had no termites that would put buyer on notice to investigate). Some early cases took the view that bargainers should distrust and hence investigate everything said. The change in this attitude has been attributed to changed standards of business ethics. See 2 Harper, James & Gray, § 7.12, 460; Prosser & Keeton § 108, p. 751.

9. See Restatement § 541A.

10. Cf. Field v. Mans, 516 U.S. 59, 116 S.Ct. 437, 133 L.Ed.2d 351(1995) (creditor who justifiably relied upon debtor's representations is not barred by debtor's bankruptcy, even if he could readily have learned the truth by checking deed records); see Restatement § 545A, cmt. b.

11. Hays v. Olzinger, 669 So.2d 107 (Ala.1995) (purchaser assumed odor in home was a pet and did not inquire, seller not liable).

12. Sims v. Tezak, 296 Ill.App.3d 503, 694 N.E.2d 1015, 230 Ill.Dec. 737 (1998).

13. See Finn v. Prudential–Bache Securities, Inc., 821 F.2d 581 (11th Cir.1987) (plaintiffs who allegedly knew defendant had defrauded them already, had no right to rely upon the defendant's statements in negotiations over compromising the fraud claim); Esposito v. Saxon Home Realty, Inc., 254 A.D.2d 451, 679 N.Y.S.2d 152 (App.Div.1998) (facts not peculiarly in defendant's knowledge; plaintiff could not rely upon representation as to location of property boundaries).

14. E.g., Danann Realty Corp. v. Harris, 5 N.Y.2d 317, 157 N.E.2d 597, 184 N.Y.S.2d 599 (1959). See § 482.

15. See, e.g., Jardine v. Brunswick Corp., 18 Utah 2d 378, 423 P.2d 659 (1967).

16. E.g., Yee v. Weiss, 110 Nev. 657, 877 P.2d 510 (1994).

bar evidence of actionable misrepresentations.[17] When the defendant has fraudulently induced the plaintiff to execute the contract by materially misrepresenting the written terms, their effect, or the defendant's intention to enforce them, courts have often permitted plaintiffs to defend a suit on the contract or to pursue actions for reformation[18] or rescission[19] or for tort damages.[20] Unless the contract is void for fraud in the factum,[21] however, a bargained-for writing, not prior statements, may represent the real agreement of sophisticated parties. Consequently, courts may conclude in particular cases that as a matter of law the plaintiff's reliance is unjustified when a reading of the document would have revealed the truth,[22] even though on other facts the courts leave the issue of justified reliance to the jury.[23] In some cases the writing seems to best reflect the parties' actual agreement while in others the prior representation does so. The differences in outcome perhaps depends less on "justified reliance" by itself than upon the court's assessment of the parties' probable agreement.

§ 476. Reliance on Immaterial Representations

Materiality. Courts agree that the plaintiff is not justified in relying upon representations that are not material to the transaction.[1] Representations are material if a reasonable person would want to consider the fact represented in determining whether to enter the transaction in question, and also if a reasonable person would not care about the fact but the plaintiff attaches her own idiosyncratic importance to it and the defendant knows it.[2] A house seller who falsely says the roof does not leak has made a material misrepresentation; but if the same seller falsely states that he is a member of the Baptist Church, the misrepresentation is not material[3] unless the seller knows that church membership is a significant factor in the particular buyer's decision to purchase.

17. See Restatement Second of Contract § 214(d), cmt. d (1981).

18. Ruff v. Charter Behavioral Health System of Northwest Indiana, Inc., 699 N.E.2d 1171 (Ind.Ct.App.1998).

19. Lubin v. Johnson, 169 Ariz. 464, 820 P.2d 328 (1991) (release); Bank of Sun Prairie v. Esser, 155 Wis.2d 724, 456 N.W.2d 585 (1990).

20. McEvoy Travel Bureau, Inc. v. Norton Co., 408 Mass. 704, 563 N.E.2d 188, 9 A.L.R.5th 1007 (1990) (representation that defendant did not intend to enforce term in proposed written contract); Godfrey, Bassett & Kuykendall Architects, Ltd. v. Huntington Lumber & Supply Co., Inc., 584 So.2d 1254 (Miss.1991) (representation to bidder that clause in construction contract would be removed); Flamme v. Wolf Ins. Agency, 239 Neb. 465, 476 N.W.2d 802 (1991) (representation as to insurance coverage of policy).

21. See § 482.

22. Maw v. McAlister, 252 S.C. 280, 166 S.E.2d 203 (S.C. 1969).

23. Kantlehner v. Bisceglia, 102 Cal. App.2d 1, 226 P.2d 636 (1951) (whether failure to read will bar claim is ordinarily for the jury).

§ 476

1. Restatement § 538 (1).

2. Gross v. Sussex, Inc., 332 Md. 247, 630 A.2d 1156 (1993); Restatement § 538. Under federal securities laws, an omitted fact is material only "if there is a substantial likelihood that a reasonable shareholder would consider it important in deciding.... " TSC Indus., Inc. v. Northway, Inc., 426 U.S. 438, 449, 96 S.Ct. 2126, 2128, 48 L.Ed.2d 757 (1976).

3. Farnsworth v. Duffner, 142 U.S. 43, 12 S.Ct. 164, 35 L.Ed. 931 (1891).

Some opinions overstate the rule by saying that any fact is material if it induces the plaintiff to act.[4] Other opinions have understated the rule by defining materiality to mean something likely to affect a reasonable person's conduct in the transaction.[5] The overstated version would make membership in the Baptist Church material even if the seller knew nothing of the buyer's peculiar standards for home purchases. The understated version would relieve the seller even if he knew that the representation was of signal importance to the particular buyer. Perhaps over-and under-statements of the rule merely reflect loose formulations.

A misrepresentation may be material because it misstates the physical nature or condition of property or goods.[6] A misrepresentation of facts is also material if it bears on the risk of loss or hopes for gain, or the market value of the items sold. For instance, misrepresentations about the history of property in the transaction[7] or about neighborhood conditions like a landfill nearby are material if they affect the market value of the property.[8] Misrepresentations about the drivers who use a car are material to a liability insurance company because they bear on its risks of loss.[9] When the issue is one on which people could differ, the issue of materiality may be left to the trier of fact.[10]

§ 477. Requirement of Factual Representations: The General Rules of Opinion, Law and Prediction

General rules. Courts have said repeatedly that a claim for misrepresentation lies only for misrepresentation of a fact, or as they say for emphasis, a past or existing fact.[1] An implication of fact rather than an explicit statement of it will do, but, in the absence of a factual assertion or implication, statements that are merely puffing of dealer's talk, statements that are merely opinion, and statements that are merely promises or predictions of the future, do not qualify as representations of fact. These rules turn on the courts' characterization of the representation and may apply whether or not the defendant himself purports to be offering opinion.[2]

4. Lacher v. Superior Court, 230 Cal. App.3d 1038, 1049, 281 Cal.Rptr. 640, 645 (1991).

5. Campbell v. Southland Corporation, 127 Or.App. 93, 871 P.2d 487 (Or. App. 1994).

6. See Watts v. Krebs, 131 Idaho 616, 962 P.2d 387 (1998) (existence or nonexistence of standing timber on the land).

7. Reed v. King, 145 Cal.App.3d 261, 193 Cal.Rptr. 130 (1983) (nondisclosure of fact that home had been site of multiple murders was material). But see MD. CODE OF REAL PROPERTY § 2–120 (no duty to disclose AIDS, homicide, or the like on the property).

8. Strawn v. Canuso, 140 N.J. 43, 657 A.2d 420, 41 A.L.R.5th 859 (1995); cf. Shapiro v. Sutherland, 64 Cal.App.4th 1534, 76 Cal.Rptr.2d 101 (1998) (noisy neighbors may be material fact to homebuyer; "facts are material if they would have a significant and measurable effect on market value").

9. E.g., Colonial Penn Ins. Co. v. Guzorek, 690 N.E.2d 664 (Ind.1997).

10. Ellis v. Liter, 311 Ark. 35, 841 S.W.2d 155 (1992).

§ 477

1. E.g., Edwards v. Travelers Ins. of Hartford, Connecticut, 563 F.2d 105 (6th Cir.1977); Ruff v. Charter Behavioral Health System of Northwest Indiana, Inc., 699 N.E.2d 1171 (Ind.Ct.App.1998).

2. The meaning, not the form of the statement, determines whether it will be counted as non-actionable opinion. See Re-

Exceptions. The rule that requires factual representation and denies liability for opinions and predictions is often broadly stated, but in fact courts recognize a number of undermining exceptions. Courts have expressly said that liability may be imposed for false and material misrepresentations of opinion when the defendant is a fiduciary, when he is a disinterested person or an expert upon whom the plaintiff can justifiably rely, when he has special knowledge, and when the opinion implies material facts.[3]

Examples. For example, the dealer who says that his goods are "first class" is puffing his wares but asserting no fact at all.[4] The securities dealer who tells a client that a stock is bound to rise in the next year, is not asserting a fact but predicting the future.[5] The auction house that says a painting is beautiful is merely expressing an opinion. Since none of these assertions explicitly states a fact and none seem to imply any particular fact, none is actionable.

Reasons for the rule. Three reasons support the rule against liability for non-factual statements, and a fourth bears ii particular upon statements about the future. But the reasons are not always present in particular cases, so not all "opinion" cases can be treated alike.

The reason most prominently addressed is that the plaintiff does not rely upon such statements, or if she relies, she is not justified in doing so.[6] As already suggested, justified reliance analysis may be merely one way of considering whether the defendant is culpable. But if it is a separate ground, the justifications for reliance vary from case to case and do not support an invariant rule against recovery. For instance, the relationship of the parties and their relative knowledge may indicate that reliance is justified. If a court concludes that reliance is justified, it may declare that the statement is one of fact, not opinion.[7]

The second reason supporting the opinion rule is that what courts sometimes have in mind when they classify a statement as one of opinion is that the defendant has not exceeded the rules of the particular kind of bargaining game and hence is not culpable at all. The buyer's assertion that $250 is his top dollar price is to be understood as a step in the process to getting to $300 or some other figure, not as a literal factual statement.

The third reason is that many opinion or puffing statements are not provably false, or rather that they are provably false only in extreme cases. Here again, the defendant may not be culpable because he has attempted to persuade but not to deceive about facts. This, too, varies

statement § 538A, cmt. d. See the detailed analysis in W. Page Keeton, Fraud: Misrepresentations of Opinion, 21 Minn. L. Rev. 643 (1937).

3. See Restatement § 542.

4. Ed Miller & Sons, Inc. v. Earl, 243 Neb. 708, 502 N.W.2d 444 (1993)

5. Kennedy v. Flo–Tronics, Inc., 274 Minn. 327, 143 N.W.2d 827 (1966).

6. The Restatement is organized around the idea that opinion rules are merely an aspect of justified reliance rules.

7. See Transport Ins. Co. v. Faircloth, 898 S.W.2d 269 (Tex.1995).

with the evidence, for as shown below, some statements are false even when they are taken as approximations.

§ 478. Puffing and Statements of Law and Opinion

The opinion rules already stated imply that not all statements that can be called opinion are alike. The effect of opinion varies with the circumstances and with the trust that the plaintiff can reasonably repose in the defendant. It also varies with the way the opinion functions in bargaining. Perhaps the cases would be clearer if courts focused less on supposed rules about opinions and more on the effect that the words would be likely to have in the bargaining transaction before the court, with due regard for the distinction between deception and persuasion. In doing this, courts could resolve many cases by considering whether the statement would be understood to mean something that was provably true or false.

Opinion as approximation. In one type of statement that may be labeled as opinion, the point seems to be that the statement does not exceed the tolerance for error the parties expect. The number of acres in a parcel of land is surely a matter of verifiable fact, but the seller's statement that the tract contains 150 acres may nevertheless be called opinion. What the opinion label means in that context is that both parties must understand that acreage cannot be measured within the narrow tolerances imposed for machine tools, so the defendant's statement must be taken to mean 150 acres, more or less.[1] It might be better not to label such statements as opinion but to recognize instead that they are approximations and not actionable so long as they are what they purport to be—approximately correct. Thus a statement that a horse is sound is not actionable merely because a horse has a bony growth if a horse can have such imperfections and still be considered sound in the trade.[2] On the other hand, a builder's statement that a house is free from structural defects is not even approximately correct if the walls are rotting. Liability is appropriate in such a case.[3]

Opinion as judgment or taste. Some statements that can be labeled opinions merely reflect taste, judgment, personal standards, or social viewpoint, as in "that painting is beautiful" or "the electric chair is inhumane." One may falsely state that he holds such opinions, and conceivably that could be material and actionable by one entitled to rely. The content of such an opinion statement itself, however, could seldom if ever be proved false by application of the senses; a witness could not see, hear, or touch anything that would contradict the opinion. Such opinions, then, are not likely to be actionable.

§ 478

1. See Saxby v. Southern Land Co., 109 Va. 196, 63 S.E. 423 (1909).

2. Simpson v. Widger, 311 N.J.Super. 379, 709 A.2d 1366 (1998).

3. Tate v. Colony House Builders, Inc., 257 Va. 78, 508 S.E.2d 597 (1999); but cf. Holland v. Lentz, 239 Or. 332, 397 P.2d 787 (1964) (house built in workmanlike manner was opinion by anyone but the builder and not actionable).

Opinion as an assessment of facts. The difficult kind of opinion for courts is quite different. It is an assessment of or conclusion from facts. An expert might conclude from style, color, subject matter and other indicia that a canvass was painted by Titian, but the conclusion is a deduction from facts, not a fact demonstrable to the senses. If the expert ventures an opinion but makes it clear that he is substantially uncertain, or not based upon known facts, or that he does not stand by it, he has not misstated any fact.[4] At the same time, however, an unqualified attribution to Titian, at least if made by one who claims to be knowledgeable, impliedly asserts (a) that the speaker holds the opinion and (b) that he has facts to support his judgment.[5] Even if he is not knowledgeable, his opinion statement implies that he knows nothing that makes the opinion fantastic.[6] In this kind of opinion case, the question is not about legal rules but about the implications of fact that can be fairly drawn from the statement and whether those implications are material. The speaker's opinion that a canvass is a Titian would be immaterial if the speaker were merely a lawyer with no training in art, but that same opinion would be critical if the opinion were offered by an expert in Titian paintings. If in such a case the plaintiff could prove that the expert held no such opinion or that he had no factual basis for it, the implications of the statement are provably false and actionable. The distinction between statements that are not provably false (this is a beautiful painting) and those that carry provably false implications is mirrored in the law of libel, which draws essentially the same distinction.[7]

Statements of value or quality. Statements of value and those proclaiming a good buy are often puffing or opinion statements and as such they are not actionable. The seller's claim that merchandise is worth twice the asking price and the buyer's claim that he is paying top dollar are usually like this. In addition, when the item valued is land, or has never been widely marketed and no objective criteria exist for determining value, a statement of value is often fairly described as one of opinion.[8] However, courts have at times gone far beyond this by proclaiming that statements of value are generally opinion and not actionable.[9]

When value statements are actionable. In spite of the purported general rule, statements of value are often entirely factual and quite

4. See Restatement § 538A (belief without certainty); cf. Taggart v. Ford Motor Credit Co., 462 N.W.2d 493 (S.D.1990) (statement that price "might be reasonable" and that price was "probably" close to book value not actionable).

5. See Vulcan Metals Co. v. Simmons Mfg. Co., 248 F. 853 (2d Cir.1918) (the existence of the speaker's opinion is a fact and the question is whether the plaintiff can justifiably rely).

6. See Restatement § 539, cmt. c.

7. The effect, though not the language in libel cases, is that if a statement is not provably false—what might be called pure opinion in fraud cases—no libel action can be pursued, at least not by public figures. But once it carries a provably false implication, it is actionable. See §§ 411 & 420.

8. E.g., Block v. Lake Mortgage Co., Inc., 601 N.E.2d 449 (Ind.App.1992) (appraisal of land was opinion).

9. E.g., Daibo v. Kirsch, 316 N.J.Super. 580, 720 A.2d 994 (1998).

reliable if they are taken to refer to a standardized price or an actual market in the item valued.[10] In addition, there are four qualifications that completely undermine the supposed general rule. The plaintiff is not barred by the opinion rule as to the defendant's statements (1) of facts bearing on value,[11] or when (2) the defendant is a fiduciary, in a position of confidence, or at least disinterested in the transactions, (3) the defendant is an expert or a person with greater knowledge than the plaintiff, or (4) the defendant makes the statement of opinion or value with intent to deceive.[12] The last two, if regularly applied, would largely eliminate the supposed rule that value statements are opinions. It would be more accurate today to ignore the purported general rule and to ask instead whether the defendant's statement contained provably false assertions or implications. When there is a clear market in goods, for example, statements of value may be provably false, while a statement of value of remote land with undetermined resources may not.

Statements of law. Statements of law represent a subset of the opinion problem. Some statements of law may actually state or at least imply facts that are provably false and if so they are actionable on the same grounds as other factual statements. "The court decided the Brown case yesterday" and "the court applied res ipsa loquitur in a medical malpractice case" are statements of a factual nature; if the facts asserted are material, false, and known to be false, liability is appropriate.[13] Other statements of law seem to be only opinions about potential legal consequences of a given action. "You will probably be held liable in tort if you do not settle" and "this lot is zoned industrial" are examples. If false and uttered by a lawyer as an expert, they may be actionable as false statements of fact because they imply that the lawyer both holds the opinion and has a basis for it; uttered by a layman who has no special knowledge or fiduciary obligation it is probably protected as opinion.[14] Even a non-lawyer might be held if his representation is to be interpreted as stating that the matter is settled by an authoritative decision, as where a business advertises that its solar heaters qualify for a tax credit,[15] or if he implies that facts within his knowledge justify the legal

10. Gray v. Wikstrom Motors, 14 Wash.2d 448, 128 P.2d 490 (1942) (new automobile). In some instances, a representation of "market value" may not be meant to assert that there is actually a standard market price. That would explain decisions like Cravens v. Skinner, 626 S.W.2d 173 (Tex.Ct.App. 1981) which say that "market value" representations are opinions.

11. Nisson v. Hood, 140 Cal. 224, 73 P. 981 (1903) (statement about income from crops grown on land for sale); Kotz v. Rush, 218 Ark. 692, 238 S.W.2d 634 (1951); Black v. Iovino, 219 Ill.App.3d 378, 580 N.E.2d 139, 162 Ill.Dec. 513 (1991) (statement implying that car for sale had not been wrecked); see M. L. Cross, Annotation, False Representations as to Income, Profits, or Productivity of Property as Fraud, 27 A.L.R.2d 14 (1953).

12. See Cohen v. S & S Construction Co., 151 Cal.App.3d 941, 201 Cal.Rptr. 173 (1983); Vokes v. Arthur Murray, Inc., 212 So.2d 906, 28 A.L.R.3d 1405 (1968); Shafmaster v. Shafmaster, 138 N.H. 460, 642 A.2d 1361 (1994); Holland v. Lentz, 239 Or. 332, 397 P.2d 787 (1964). The disinterest of the defendant may be sufficient to justify reliance upon his opinion if the fact that he holds the opinion is itself material. Restatement § 543.

13. See generally Restatement § 545 (1).

14. See Restatement § 545 (2).

15. Winton v. Johnson & Dix Fuel Corp., 147 Vt. 236, 515 A.2d 371 (1986).

opinion, as where he states he owes Blackacre.[16] But as with other opinion cases, courts often omit all analysis and content themselves with general statements to the effect that representations of law are not actionable.[17]

§ 479. Predictions of the Future and Statements of Present Intent

The rule that misrepresentations are not actionable unless they state "past or existing facts" is the formal basis for a more specific version: Unless a representation or projection of the future implies existing or past facts, it is not actionable.[1] Representations or predictions about the future may be regarded as a species of opinion, and they may be intended to persuade or deceive, but quite literally, they are not factual assertions and they cannot be false at the time they are uttered.

The policy grounds for excluding liability in cases of prediction or promise include the ground most often mentioned, that the plaintiff is not justified in relying upon such statements. That is often the case. "You should buy this stock, it will double in value this year" is a classic case of puffing by predicting the future, for which, in the absence of a fiduciary relationship or the like, liability should be rejected.[2] In addition, the defendant may not be culpable; he may not expect to deceive by a statement that he obviously cannot know.

However, just as many statements about the past or present imply something about the future, many statements about the future imply something about the present.[3] "You should lease this apartment, by next summer the swimming pool will be installed" is in form a statement about the future but it might be understood to imply that plans have been made and funded for a swimming pool. At the very least, such a statement may be construed as stating or implying one fact, the defendant's present intent to install the swimming pool. And courts agree that the defendant's present intent is a factual matter distinct from promises and predictions, so a false statement of present intention is actionable if it meets all the other requirements for establishing fraud.[4] Unlike the prediction of a rise in stock value, or the prediction of another's con-

16. See W. Page Keeton, Fraud—Misrepresentations of Law, 16 TEX. L. REV. 410 (1937) (discussing superior knowledge cases).

17. E.g., Meyer v. Santema, 559 N.W.2d 251 (S.D.1997)

§ 479

1. E.g., Golden Tee, Inc. v. Venture Golf Schools, Inc., 333 Ark. 253, 969 S.W.2d 625 (1998); Forge v. Smith, 458 Mich. 198, 580 N.W.2d 876 (1998).

2. Cf. Kennedy v. Flo-Tronics, Inc., 274 Minn. 327, 143 N.W.2d 827 (1966) (rejecting liability for similar predictions).

3. The classic article on liability for statements of intention is W. Page Keeton, Fraud—Statements of Intention, 15 TEX. L. REV. 185 (1937).

4. Engalla v. Permanente Medical Group, Inc., 15 Cal.4th 951, 938 P.2d 903, 64 Cal.Rptr.2d 843 (1997); Gerhardt v. Harris, 261 Kan. 1007, 934 P.2d 976 (1997); Formosa Plastics Corp. v. Presidio Eng'rs and Contractors, Inc., 960 S.W.2d 41 (Tex. 1998). The common epigram is that the state of one's mind is as much a fact as the state of one's digestion.

duct,[5] the defendant's addition of a swimming pool is within the defendant's control.

At the same time, the mere fact that the defendant does not add the swimming pool next summer does not prove that he never intended to do so. If his representation amounted to an enforceable contract, the hapless tenant could sue on the contract, but if the representation does not qualify as an enforceable contract, the plaintiff must prove that the statement of intention was false when it was made and nonperformance is not by itself sufficient for that.[6] Direct evidence by way of the defendant's admission by documents showing that defendant planned not to perform,[7] or circumstantial evidence that the defendant could not have raised funds necessary for the construction, or that he had already been denied necessary permits,[8] or even that he had demonstrated a pattern of making representations that were never performed[9] would tend to prove that he lacked the intention he represented.

In the present intention cases, an additional policy surfaces. The statement of a present intention to act in the future functions much like a contractual promise (and may actually be presented in the form of a promise). Unless the defendant's culpability is convincingly established, perhaps this kind of "promissory fraud" should be treated as a contract claim and stand or fall on that ground. And fall it might, if there is a written contract, for the parol evidence rule or disclaimer clauses might exclude contractual liability. That is a topic considered in a later section, but it is not premature to notice that with promissory statements, including those that are in form statements of intention, additional policies arise.

§ 480. Representations Relied upon by Third Persons

Privity not required. It has been settled since the 1700s that privity is not required to support an action for fraudulent misrepresentation. So the defendant who fraudulently induces the plaintiff to enter into a contract with another person is subject to liability for his misrepresentation, although he himself was not a party to the transaction and gained nothing from it.[1]

5. A representation of another person's intention seems to be a form of opinion that implies the defendant has a basis for forming a reasonable belief. Cf. Restatement § 530 (2), cmt. e (treating misrepresentation of another's opinion as representation of fact).

6. E.g., Goodyear Tire & Rubber Co. v. Washington, 719 So.2d 774 (Ala.1998); Bamira v. Greenberg, 256 A.D.2d 237, 682 N.Y.S.2d 174 (App.Div.1998).

7. Gerhardt v. Harris, 261 Kan. 1007, 934 P.2d 976 (1997) (admission); Formosa Plastics Corp. v. Presidio Eng'rs and Contractors, Inc., 960 S.W.2d 41 (Tex.1998) (defendant planned different course of action before contract was signed).

8. Cf. Chesus v. Watts, 967 S.W.2d 97 (Mo.App.1998) (representation that septic tanks could be installed in development after inspector had rejected them because of soil conditions).

9. B.K.W. Enterprises, Inc. v. Tractor & Equip. Co., Inc., 603 So.2d 989 (Ala.1992).

§ 480

1. Pasley v. Freeman, 3 T.R. 51, 100 Eng.Rep. 450 (K.B. 1789).

Reliance by third persons. To dispense with a requirement of privity, however, does not dispense with the requirement of reliance. Although reliance may be indirect,[2] it must be the plaintiff and not merely others who rely upon the misrepresentation. If an employer relies upon the defendant's misrepresentation to discharge an employee, the employee has no action for deceit, since it was the employer, not the employee, who relied upon the representation.[3]

Duty to third persons—fraud. Dispensing with the privity requirement likewise leaves open the fundamental question, the scope of the defendant's duty to persons he did not address or intend to influence. Suppose the defendant misrepresents the condition of his house to A, who passes the information on to B, who buys the defendant's house in reliance. The older view limited the defendant's liability, even for fraudulent representations, to persons to whom the defendant made the representation and intended to influence.[4] It also limited liability to the type of transaction he intended to influence.[5] These rules excluded liability for foreseeable reliance if the defendant did not intend that reliance. Such restrictions were rejected by the Restatement[6] and the contemporary view[7] that the maker of a fraudulent representation should be liable not only to those persons he directly addressed or intended to influence, but also to the entire class of persons he intends or has reason to expect will rely upon the representations.

Duty to third persons—negligence. (a) The problem. Negligent misrepresentation is another matter. If liability for negligent representations extended to all who might foreseeably rely, liability could extend "in an indeterminate amount for an indeterminate time to an indeterminate class." [8]A simple but erroneous news report of a Supreme Court decision, for example, might cause an avalanche of sales and losses in financial markets before it could be corrected minutes later.[9] Such practical concerns are much like those that have led courts to reject or limit liability for negligent interference with contracts and business

2. See § 474 (fraud on the market).

3. Pegram v. Hebding, 667 So.2d 696 (Ala.1995). The employee's may have an action for interference with contract or defamation.

4. Greenville Nat. Bank v. National Hardwood Co., 241 Mich. 524, 217 N.W. 786 (1928) (representations to brokers and to existing stockholders, no liability to members of the public who purchased and to whom no representation was made).

5. Wells v. Cook, 16 Ohio St. 67 (1865) is a well known example. Defendant induced A to purchase sheep for B by false representations to A. A then purchased them from B relying on those representations but could not recover as the representations were not made to influence A's purchase.

6. Restatement §§ 531, 533. The Restatement's § 531, Ill. 8, cautiously avoids commitment on the facts of Well v. Cook, supra n. 5.

7. See, imposing liability for fraudulent representations to those whose reliance is reasonably foreseeable. Bily v. Arthur Young & Co., 3 Cal.4th 370, 11 Cal.Rptr.2d 51, 834 P.2d 745 (1992) (accountant performing audit); Geernaert v. Mitchell, 31 Cal.App.4th 601, 37 Cal.Rptr.2d 483 (1995) (homeowner-seller expecting repetition of falsehood in subsequent sales); Clark v. McDaniel, 546 N.W.2d 590 (Iowa 1996).

8. Ultramares Corp. v. Touche, 255 N.Y. 170, 179, 174 N.E. 441, 444 (1931).

9. See Jaillet v. Cashman, 235 N.Y. 511, 139 N.E. 714 (1923) (erroneous report that Supreme Court had held stock dividends taxable income; no contract or fiduciary relation to the public, no liability).

opportunities.[10] In the case of negligent misrepresentation by one who is retained to make an accurate report, liability to the client is justified for mere negligence because the defendant has undertaken a duty of care to the client. But that is not a reason to say that the duty undertaken to A must also mean a duty to B.

(b) Ultramares. The problem has arisen most prominently in the case of auditors who certify the financial condition of Company A, knowing that the auditor's figures will be used by bankers in deciding whether to loan money and investors in determining whether to invest. In Ultramares Corporation v. Touche,[11] an accounting firm employed by the company certified a substantial net worth when in fact the company was insolvent. Lenders provided loans to the company in reliance upon the audit. When they discovered they could not be repaid, they sued the accountants. Judge Cardozo emphasized that the accountants had assumed no duty to the lenders; the assumption of one duty should not inescapably mean that the accountants were forced to assume others as well. Relatedly, he also emphasized the practical fears of unlimited liability.

(c) The Restatement test. Ultramares was not the last word. By 1977 when the Restatement Second was published, a degree of liability to third persons for negligent misrepresentation seemed more appropriate. The Restatement recognizes a limited kind of liability to third persons for negligent representations. The defendant has no general liability to the public; at most he is liable to small group. The defendant is subject to liability if he intends to supply the information to a small group of which the plaintiff is a member. He is also liable if he knows his client will do so.[12] Even under these conditions, the defendant is not liable if the plaintiff relies on the information in a type of transaction the defendant does not intend to influence.

Most courts adopt the Restatement's position or something close to it.[13] In support of the Restatement position, they have said that expansive potential liability was not justified where the audited client retains a good deal of control of the important records upon which the audit is based and where the plaintiff-lender can seek security for the loan or can arrange to become a client of the auditor if she really wants to rely upon the auditor's work.[14] Unless auditors can charge more when the risk is greater, there is an element of unreality and even unfairness in a scheme

10. § 452.

11. Ultramares Corp. v. Touche, 255 N.Y. 170, 174 N.E. 441 (1931).

12. Restatement § 552 (2).

13. Boykin v. Arthur Andersen & Co., 639 So.2d 504 (Ala.1994); Bily v. Arthur Young & Co., 3 Cal.4th 370, 11 Cal.Rptr.2d 51, 834 P.2d 745 (1992); First Florida Bank, N.A. v. Max Mitchell & Co., 558 So.2d 9 (Fla.1990); Rozny v. Marnul, 43 Ill.2d 54, 250 N.E.2d 656 (1969); Nycal Corp. v. KPMG Peat Marwick LLP., 426 Mass. 491, 688 N.E.2d 1368 (1998); Raritan River Steel Co. v. Cherry, Bekaert & Holland, 322 N.C. 200, 367 S.E.2d 609 (1988); Bethlehem Steel Corporation v. Ernst & Whinney, 822 S.W.2d 592 (Tenn.1991).

14. Bily v. Arthur Young & Co., 3 Cal.4th 370, 11 Cal.Rptr.2d 51, 834 P.2d 745 (1992) (deriving the argument from John A. Siliciano, Negligent Accounting and the Limits of Instrumental Tort Reform), 86 MICH. L. REV. 1929 (1988).

of unlimited liability, all the more so since auditors would seldom be able to estimate anything about their potential liability.[15]

Some courts have said that the Restatement extends liability to all foreseeable or foreseen users of the information furnished,[16] but that is not accurate. The Restatement's point is to protect the defendant against liability to the entire group who may foreseeably rely. Thus the Massachusetts Court concluded that although an auditor might foresee that stock purchasers would rely upon his audit, he was not liable to such a purchaser who was not a member of a limited group for whom he prepared the audit but was merely an unidentified potential investor at the time the audit was prepared.[17] An auditor who merely conducts a normal annual audit when no particular use has been specified is likely to escape liability to any third person under this view.[18]

(d) The near-privity test. The Restatement or middle position is the most popular today, but New York uses a "privity or near privity" rule, imposing liability for negligence only when the defendant has had some actual contact with the plaintiff.[19] Under this rule, the weighmaster who weighs A's beans for the very purpose of certifying their weight to B as buyer, is liable to B for negligently certified weight.[20] But the accountant who prepares an audit for A, knowing that B will rely upon it is not responsible to B in the absence of some actual contact with B. beyond, say, a telephone call.[21] New Jersey by statute imposes a somewhat similar limitation, exculpating the accountant unless he knew of the specific plaintiff and specific transaction for which his work product was intended.[22]

(e) Foreseeability tests. Two states, Mississippi and Wisconsin, have moved away from the Restatement's position in the other direction, imposing liability to the extent of reasonably foreseeable reliance.[23]

(f) Additional limitations. As already indicated, the plaintiff must rely and rely justifiably, before liability will be imposed under any test. Some perfectly justifiable reliance may be outside the scope of the defendant's duty or beyond the limits of proximate cause. In a North

15. See John A. Siliciano, Negligent Accounting and the Limits of Instrumental Tort Reform, 86 MICH. L. REV. 1929, 1949 (1988) (discussing informational asymmetry).

16. See Clark v. McDaniel, 546 N.W.2d 590, 593 (Iowa 1996); Touche Ross & Co. v. Commercial Union Ins. Co., 514 So.2d 315 (1987).

17. Nycal Corp. v. KPMG Peat Marwick LLP., 426 Mass. 491, 688 N.E.2d 1368 (1998).

18. See Bily v. Arthur Young & Co., 3 Cal.4th 370, 11 Cal. Rptr. 2d 51, 834 P.2d 745 (1992).

19. Credit Alliance Corporation v. Arthur Andersen & Co., 65 N.Y.2d 536, 483 N.E.2d 110, 493 N.Y.S.2d 435 (1985).

20. Glanzer v. Shepard, 233 N.Y. 236, 135 N.E. 275 (1922).

21. Security Pacific Business Credit, Inc. v. Peat Marwick Main & Co., 79 N.Y.2d 695, 597 N.E.2d 1080, 586 N.Y.S.2d 87 (1992).

22. NEW JERSEY STAT. ANN. 2A:53A–25.

23. Touche Ross v. Commercial Union Ins., 514 So.2d 315 (Miss.1987);Citizens State Bank v. Timm, Schmidt & Co., 113 Wis.2d 376, 335 N.W.2d 361 (1983). New Jersey took this view in H. Rosenblum, Inc. v. Adler, 93 N.J. 324, 461 A.2d 138 (1983) but the statute, supra n. 22, now rejects it.

Carolina case,[24] the court held that the plaintiff who relied upon the audit only indirectly by relying upon a Dun & Bradstreet report that reflected the audit could not recover from the accounting firm. Even the courts that impose a duty to those who foreseeably rely upon the representation recognize that other limitations may foreclose liability in particular cases. Wisconsin, expressing views that in other states are often identified with proximate cause rules or limited duties, has said that the negligent information giver would not be liable for injuries that are too remote, disproportionate, or burdensome.[25] Mississippi concluded that fraudulent acts of an unforeseeable intervening actor was a superseding cause that relieved the accountant of all liability.[26] More broadly, it may be suggested that no loss would produce liability unless it was the kind of loss risked by the accountant's negligence.

Single loss cases. One kind of case should easily warrant recovery. This is the case in which innumerable third parties may rely, seriatim, upon the defendant's representation but the defendant can only be liable for one loss. Suppose an inspector, abstractor, or surveyor negligently represents the condition of a seller's property or the condition of title, or the boundaries. In reliance, A purchases from the seller and later resells to the plaintiff, who also relies upon the same information. The plaintiff should be permitted to recover directly from the defendant under any of the rules discussed above because in such a case, only one person can suffer the loss, no matter how many times the property is sold.[27] This kind of single loss case is thus not a case of potentially indeterminate liability to an indeterminate class but rather the case of a single liability.

§ 481. Nondisclosure

Liability for concealment. A bargainer's active concealment of a material fact operates like a misrepresentation and liability is imposed accordingly.[1] For example, the house seller who covers up signs of termites by installing wallboard to hide the damage[2] and the car seller who putties over a crack in the engine block[3] are actively concealing material defects in the house and car. If the buyer relied on the false appearances so created, the seller is subject to liability for the effective misrepresentation.

24. Raritan River Steel Co. v. Cherry, Bekaert & Holland, 322 N.C. 200, 367 S.E.2d 609 (1988).

25. Citizens State Bank v. Timm, Schmidt & Co., 113 Wis.2d 376, 387, 335 N.W.2d 361, 366 (1983).

26. Touche Ross v. Commercial Union Ins., 514 So.2d 315 (Miss.1987).

27. Rozny v. Marnul, 43 Ill.2d 54, 250 N.E.2d 656 (1969); Barrie v. V.P. Exterminators, Inc., 625 So.2d 1007 (La.1993). Cf. Schaaf v. Highfield, 127 Wash.2d 17, 896 P.2d 665 (1995) (recognizing liability to the first purchaser but perhaps intimating that later purchasers could not recover). The point of course applies in fraud as well as negligent misrepresentation cases.

§ 481

1. Restatement § 550.

2. Miller v. Bare, 457 F.Supp. 1359 (W.D.Pa.1978).

3. Lindberg Cadillac Co. v. Aron, 371 S.W.2d 651 (Mo.App.1963).

Nonliability for nondisclosure. The traditional rule treats mere nondisclosure differently, holding that the bargainer is not ordinarily obliged to make affirmative revelations of known material facts.[4] The seller could not hide the termite infestation, for that would be concealment, but he was not obliged to mention termites if the buyer did not ask.

Under the traditional rule, the buyer can avoid the problem by asking the right question; if the seller denies the termite damage he knows to exist, he has made a knowingly false representation and is liable. Regulations or customs of real estate brokers may avoid the problem by inspections and formal disclosure statements. Sophisticated buyers now know to inspect for hazardous waste, lest they become liable for its cleanup, and many buyers will be protected in the termite case by asking a question or seeking inspection. But no one could think of all possible questions that would reveal some material defects in a house. That is even more so when it comes to more complex business deals in which the material facts are not about physical defects. So the nondisclosure rule may pose a substantial risk or burden.

Traditional disclosure duties. The nondisclosure rule is subject to several qualifications which permit liability for "fraud by silence." Affirmative duties of disclosure are imposed when (1) statutes so provide;[5] (2) the defendant is in a confidential relationship or under a fiduciary duty to the plaintiff;[6] (3) the defendant has made a representation that is true at the time it was made but that becomes untrue or misleading before the bargain is consummated; the representation is treated as continuing;[7] similarly if the statement was untrue at the time made and the defendant later realizes that it has become material or that the plaintiff is relying upon it;[8] (4) the defendant has communicated a half-truth, that is, a partial or ambiguous statement that is misleading unless additional facts are disclosed,[9] as where the seller of a lot discloses that the city has the right to widen a street bounding the lot but saying nothing about the fact that the city also has the right to open a street that will divide the lot in half.[10]

4. Universal Investment Co. v. Sahara Motor Inn, Inc., 127 Ariz. 213, 619 P.2d 485 (1980) (seller failed to divulge that electrical system in motel was not in compliance with code); Stevens v. Bouchard, 532 A.2d 1028 (Me.1987) (roof leaks).

5. For examples, see n. 17 below.

6. See Burkons v. Ticor Title Ins. Co. of California, 168 Ariz. 345, 813 P.2d 710 (1991) (escrow agent's duty to reveal evidence of fraud by one of the parties upon the other); Pacelli Brothers Transportation, Inc. v. Pacelli, 189 Conn. 401, 456 A.2d 325 (1983) (obligation may continue after relationship terminated);Martin v. Heinold Commodities, Inc., 163 Ill.2d 33, 205 Ill. Dec. 443, 643 N.E.2d 734 (1994) (precontract negotiations to create fiducial relationship required disclosure of special commissions).

7. Refrigeration Indus., Inc. v. Nemmers, 880 S.W.2d 912 (Mo.Ct.App.1994); Shafmaster v. Shafmaster, 138 N.H. 460, 642 A.2d 1361 (1994).

8. Restatement § 551 (d).

9. Meade v. Cedarapids, Inc., 164 F.3d 1218 (9th Cir.1999); St. Joseph Hosp. v. Corbetta Construction Co., Inc., 21 Ill. App.3d 925, 316 N.E.2d 51 (1974).

10. Junius Constr. Co. v. Cohen, 257 N.Y. 393, 178 N.E. 672 (1931) (the ennumeration of "a risk like in kind but vastly greater in degree" tacitly implied there were no others).

Extending disclosure duties; basic facts and known mistakes. Contemporary thought lends a degree of support to the Restatement in adding a fifth obligation of disclosure when the defendant knows that the plaintiff is acting under a mistake that is basic to the transaction and disclosure would reasonably be expected.[11] The seller of a used car would be obliged under that rule to disclose that the engine was so out of date that oil filters were no longer made that would fit it.[12] The seller of a home would be obliged to disclose that the ground beneath it was so contaminated that grass could never grow there.[13] A builder-developer or a real estate broker may be under a duty to disclose the existence of a nearby hazardous waste dump.[14] Some courts might accept this view only with respect to a latent defect not readily observable by the plaintiff,[15] and it seems probable that courts would more readily impose a duty to disclose a condition of the property itself than to disclose other matters such as the vendor's intentions to building apartment houses on adjacent property.[16] With sales of new homes, statutes may require full disclosure in excruciating detail[17] and courts may impose implied warranties of habitability,[18] though not necessarily in commercial property sales.[19] In addition, consumer protection or deceptive practices acts may require disclosure of all material facts in a consumer transaction.[20]

Buyer's nondisclosure. It has been generally thought that buyers are under no duty to disclose material facts to sellers. The leading case on the point held that the buyer was not required to disclose market factors (that peace had been declared),[21] but some other authority has gone on to say that the buyer need not disclose facts about the very property being purchased either.[22] A fiduciary buyer like a fiduciary seller must make full disclosure of material facts.[23]

11. Restatement § 551 (e).

12. Maybee v. Jacobs Motor Co., Inc., 519 N.W.2d 341 (S.D.1994).

13. Griffith v. Byers Constr. Co. of Kansas, Inc., 212 Kan. 65, 510 P.2d 198 (1973); but cf. Futura Realty v. Lone Star Building Centers (Eastern), Inc., 578 So.2d 363 (1991) (no duty to disclose hazardous wastes in commercial as distinct from home sale); see Jane Massey Draper, Annotation, Vendor's Obligation to Disclose to Purchaser of Land Presence of Contamination from Hazardous Substances or Wastes, 12 A.L.R.5th 630 (1993).

14. Strawn v. Canuso, 140 N.J. 43, 657 A.2d 420, 41 A.L.R.5th 859 (1995).

15. See Layman v. Binns, 35 Ohio St.3d 176, 519 N.E.2d 642 (1988).

16. Blaine v. J.E. Jones Construction Co., 841 S.W.2d 703 (Mo.App.1992).

17. See, e.g., Cal. Civ. Code § 1102.1 et seq (requiring disclosures, with formal statements and opportunity by the buyer to rescind). For the items to be disclosed see Id. § 1102.6. In contrast, some information is privatized by other statutes. See Md. Code of Real Property § 2–120 (no duty to disclose AIDS, homicide, and the like on the property).

18. E.g., Theis v. Heuer, 264 Ind. 1, 280 N.E.2d 300 (1972); Stevens v. Bouchard, 532 A.2d 1028 (Me.1987) (only to new homes).

19. Futura Realty v. Lone Star Building Centers (Eastern), Inc., 578 So.2d 363 (Fla. App.1991); see Kathleen McNamara Tomcho, Commercial Real Estate Buyer Beware: Sellers May Have the Right to Remain Silent. 70 S. Cal. L. Rev. 1571 (1997).

20. See, e.g., Connick v. Suzuki Motor Co., Ltd., 174 Ill.2d 482, 675 N.E.2d 584, 221 Ill.Dec. 389 (1996).

21. Laidlaw v. Organ, 15 U.S. (2 Wheat.) 178, 4 L.Ed. 214 (1817).

22. Harrell v. Powell, 249 N.C. 244, 106 S.E.2d 160 (1958).

23. Dolan v. Cummings, 116 App.Div. 787, 102 N.Y.S. 91 (1907), aff'd, 193 N.Y. 638, 86 N.E. 1123 (1908).

§ 482. Contract Defenses or Limitations on Liability

Contract or tort? The claim of scienter fraud and the claim of negligent misrepresentation are claims in tort, invoking obligations imposed by law. When misrepresentation induces a contract, the contract's own limitations on liability and indeed all of the rules of contract could conceivably displace the rule of tort law. Probably the most significant issue under this heading is whether the parol evidence rule, or exculpatory clauses in the contract can furnish defenses to the claim of fraudulent or other misrepresentations.

Exculpatory rules and clauses. Exculpatory rules and clauses may take several forms. If applicable, the parol evidence rule and the merger clause that declares the contract to contain the parties' entire agreement would preclude parol evidence of misrepresentations about the contract obligations themselves. Contract clauses may specify that the seller has made no representations, or that the buyer has relied upon her own investigation and upon nothing said by the seller, or that the buyer accepts the goods or property "as is." Although the parol evidence rule and the merger clause operate by excluding evidence of misrepresentation while a contract disclaimer might operate by negating a representation or reliance upon it, and their scope might differ slightly,[1] they are alike in potentially relieving the defendant of liability. At a minimum, all reflect doubts that representations were made or acted upon, for why would the plaintiff relying upon a material representation sign on to a contract that specifically says otherwise? Even if the contract does not disclaim a representation asserted by the plaintiff, if it is a detailed apparently complete contract, it is hard to believe that the plaintiff was relying upon a representation not included.[2]

Scienter fraud; traditional rule. When the plaintiff's claim is that the defendant induced the contract by scienter fraud, the traditional approach treats the case as a thoroughgoing tort case to which the defenses appropriate to a contract claim do not apply. Under this view, neither the parol evidence rule[3] nor the statute of frauds[4] prevents the plaintiff from presenting evidence that the defendant's oral and fraudulent representations induced the contract. And the contract's own exculpatory clauses, having been brought to life by fraudulent inducements, are equally unavailing to the defendant,[5] who is thus liable if the elements of fraud are proven.

§ 482

1. The scope of these defenses may differ. See, e.g., Stambovsky v. Ackley, 169 A.D.2d 254, 572 N.Y.S.2d 672 (1991) (as is clause related to physical condition of seller's house, not to other matters affecting value).

2. Johnson v. University Health Services, Inc., 161 F.3d 1334 (11th Cir.1998).

3. See Meland v. Youngberg, 124 Minn. 446, 145 N.W. 167 (1914).

4. Tenzer v. Superscope, Inc. 39 Cal.3d 18, 702 P.2d 212, 216 Cal.Rptr. 130 (1985); Burgdorfer v. Thielemann, 153 Or. 354, 55 P.2d 1122 (1936); Restatement § 530, cmt. c.

5. Bening v. Muegler, 67 F.3d 691 (8th Cir.1995) (no reliance clause); Gibb v. Citicorp Mortgage, Inc., 246 Neb. 355, 518 N.W.2d 910 (1994) (as is clause); Travers v. Spidell, 682 A.2d 471 (R.I.1996) (merger clause); Maybee v. Jacobs Motor Co., Inc., 519 N.W.2d 341 (S.D.1994) (as is clause). In

Scienter fraud; contract defenses as a bar. The traditional rule for scienter fraud perhaps makes best sense when the fraudulent representation has little or no promissory element. That view may help explain why some courts have permitted the defendant to invoke contract defenses against a claim of scienter fraud. One argument for this position is that to allow the fraud claim in derogation of the contract provisions would be to nullify the statute of frauds[6] or to strike at the vitals of the parol evidence rule.[7] Alternatively, it is suggested that the plaintiff would have no justification for relying (or maybe did not in fact rely) upon the prior oral representations that were contradicted by the later contract.[8] These reasons do not seem applicable when the defendant is guilty of what is called fraud in the execution or fraud in the factum as distinct from fraud in the inducement. Fraud in the execution deceives the plaintiff about the nature or content of the document she signs, and it is sometimes said that in that case there is no contract at all or that it is void and not merely voidable.[9] If the plaintiff did not in fact read the writing and was justified in not doing so, then it would make sense to admit parol evidence of prior oral representations even under the more restrictive view.

Scienter fraud: specific disclaimers as a bar. When the claimed fraudulent representation directly contradicts the contract's specific disclaimer, some courts have held that the disclaimer prevails, even though the plaintiff claims scienter fraud. Suppose the defendant induces the plaintiff to sign a promissory note by representing that it would not be due or enforced for one year, but the note itself directly contradicts the representation by providing that payment is due in six months or on demand. Because the contradiction is clear and direct, some courts will reject parol evidence of fraud.[10] New York and some other courts have made a somewhat similar point by saying that if a disclaimer or merger clause is specific, it will rule out liability for fraud on the specific topics covered by the clause,[11] while if it is general, or perhaps if it does not

each of these cases and a number of others that allow the fraud claim to proceed, the person claiming fraud is a consumer or small investor while the fraud is alleged against a relatively sophisticated repeat player who is engaged in a business operation.

6. Cassidy v. Kraft–Phenix Cheese Corp., 285 Mich. 426, 280 N.W. 814 (1938).

7. Beers v. Atlas Assur. Co. Ltd., 215 Wis. 165, 253 N.W. 584 (1934), aff'd, 231 Wis. 361, 285 N.W. 794, 123 A.L.R. 372 (1939).

8. Beers v. Atlas Assur. Co. Ltd., supra n. 7.

9. See Rosenthal v. Great Western Financial Securities Corp., 14 Cal.4th 394, 926 P.2d 1061, 58 Cal.Rptr.2d 875 (1996); Haller v. Borror Corporation, 50 Ohio St.3d 10, 552 N.E.2d 207 (1990).

10. Bank of America Nat'l Trust & Sav. Ass'n v. Pendergrass, 4 Cal.2d 258, 48 P.2d 659 (1935).

11. Danann Realty Corp. v. Harris, 5 N.Y.2d 317, 157 N.E.2d 597, 184 N.Y.S.2d 599 (1959); Citibank v. Plapinger, 66 N.Y.2d 90, 485 N.E.2d 974, 495 N.Y.S.2d 309 (1985) (guarantee unconditional, absolute); LaFazia v. Howe, 575 A.2d 182 (R.I. 1990) (contract specifically provided no reliance upon representations about income of seller's business); C & A Investments, Inc. v. Bonnet Resources Corp., 959 S.W.2d 258 (1997) (several factors may affect decision to invoke contract defenses against fraud claim). A test based upon specificity of the disclaimer appears to differ from a test based upon direct or clear contradiction between the representations and contract provisions. In Barash v. Pennsylvania Terminal Real Estate Corp., 26 N.Y.2d 77, 308

specifically contradict the alleged representations, it will not.[12] A different tactic allows the defendant to avoid liability under exculpatory clauses unless the alleged fraud relates to the exculpatory clause itself.[13] Still another approach, and one consistent with many of the decisions rendered on other grounds, considers (a) the extent of the contradiction between disclaimer and representation and (b) the relative strength or sophistication of the parties, tending to allow parol evidence to show fraud when the contradiction is weak or non-obvious and also when the plaintiff is an inexperienced consumer dealing with a sophisticated bargainer or repeat player.[14]

Negligent and innocent misrepresentations. When it comes to liability for negligent or innocent misrepresentations (warranties), it is hard to find a justification for holding the defendant to a representation he has disclaimed in writing. The protection seems to be even broader in many such cases: under the economic loss rule, the plaintiff cannot recover for negligent or innocent misrepresentation at all, only upon the contract itself.[15]

§ 483. Remedies

The main remedies. To some extent the remedies available for misrepresentation depend upon the facts. (1) When the written document does not correctly express the parties' actual agreement because of fraud or mistake, the plaintiff is entitled to reformation of the document to make it reflect the real agreement.[1] (2) When the transaction was induced by fraud or even by innocent misrepresentation of a basic fact,

N.Y.S.2d 649, 256 N.E.2d 707 (1970) the tenant signed a lease specifically limiting air conditioning to times specified by the landlord but claimed a representation that air conditioning would always be available. The contradiction is apparent, but the court thought that as the merger clause was "general," it would not bar the claim (which, however, was barred on other grounds).

12. See Manufacturers Hanover Trust Co. v. Yanakas, 7 F.3d 310 (2d Cir.1993) (guarantee, insufficiently specific) (New York law).

13. See UAW–GM Human Resource Center v. KSL Recreation Corp., 228 Mich. App. 486, 503, 579 N.W.2d 411, 419 (1998). A similar rule is applied when the contract contains an arbitration clause. One claiming the contract was procured by fraud does not avoid the arbitration clause unless she can also show that the clause itself was induced by fraud, Prima Paint v. Flood & Conklin, 388 U.S. 395, 87 S.Ct. 1801, 18 L.Ed.2d 1270 (1967); Ericksen, Arbuthnot, McCarthy, Kearney & Walsh, Inc. v. 100 Oak Street, 35 Cal.3d 312, 197 Cal.Rptr. 581, 673 P.2d 251 (1983), or the entire contract was procured by fraud in the execution. See Rosenthal v. Great Western Financial Securities Corp., 14 Cal.4th 394, 926 P.2d 1061, 58 Cal.Rptr.2d 875 (1996).

14. Pinnacle Peak Developers v. TRW Investment Corporation, 129 Ariz. 385, 631 P.2d 540 (Ariz.App.1980).

15. Duquesne Light Co. v. Westinghouse Electric Corp., 66 F.3d 604 (3d Cir. 1995); Apollo Group, Inc. v. Avnet, Inc., 58 F.3d 477 (9th Cir.1995); Richey v. Patrick, 904 P.2d 798 (Wyo.1995); cf. D.S.A., Inc. v. Hillsboro Ind. Sch. Dist., 973 S.W.2d 662 (Tex.1998) (claim for negligent misrepresentation in inducing contract can be maintained only if plaintiff has an injury independent injury); Richmond Metro. Auth. v. McDevitt Street Bovis, Inc., 256 Va. 553, 507 S.E.2d 344 (1998) (breach of contract and cover-up not actionable as tort, only as breach of contract). Contra, Keller v. A.O. Smith Harvestore Products, Inc., 819 P.2d 69 (Colo.1991) (relying upon cases of actual fraud).

§ 483

1. See 2 Dan B. Dobbs, Law of Remedies § 9.5 (2d ed. 1993) (hereafter in this section Dobbs, Remedies 2d).

the plaintiff may be entitled to rescission, provided circumstances have not so changed as to make rescission inequitable.[2] (3) In all cases in which the misrepresentation is actionable, the plaintiff is entitled to recover damages instead of rescission, but the measure of damages may be less favorable to the plaintiff if the basis for liability is an innocent or negligent representation.[3] (4) When the defendant has gained from a transaction induced by scienter fraud or breach of fiduciary relationship, the plaintiff may be entitled to recover, on a theory of constructive trust or otherwise, the defendant's gains from the transaction, even if those gains exceed the plaintiff's losses.[4]

Market based damages measures. Courts have recognized three potential measures of damages calculated on market or capital values (as distinct from consequential damages).

(1) The loss of bargain measure gives the plaintiff the difference between what she received in value and the value she would have received had matters been as represented. If the misrepresentation induces the plaintiff to pay $5,000 for a car that is worth $5,000 but would have been worth $10,000 had it been as represented, the plaintiff recovers $5,000 under the loss of bargain rule.

(2) The out of pocket measure allows the plaintiff to recover the loss she sustained in the transaction but not her expected gain. Consequential damages aside, that loss is the difference between what the plaintiff paid in the transaction and what she received at the time the transaction was completed. If the misrepresentation induces the plaintiff to pay $5,000 for a chattel worth only $4,000, the plaintiff recovers $1,000. In effect, the exchange is equalized.[5]

(3) The third potential measure has been used almost not at all. It calculates the out of pocket measure at a later date, giving the plaintiff a recovery that resembles the financial effect of a rescission. It is sometimes called rescissory damages. If the plaintiff is induced to buy shares of stock for $100,000 at a time when their market value is $80,000 and does not get a judgment until a year later when the market has dropped and the shares are worth only $50,000, rescissory damages would permit the plaintiff to recover $50,000, not merely the $20,000 authorized by the traditional out of pocket measure.

Intentional fraud. When the defendant's fraud is intentional, a few courts still insist that the plaintiff can recover only the out of pocket measure.[6] Most courts, including some that formerly supported the out

2. 2 Dobbs, Remedies 2d §§ 9.3 (1) & 9.6.

3. See *Negligent misrepresentation* and *Innocent misrepresentation as mistake justifying rescission-equivalent damages* below.

4. 2 Dobbs, Remedies 2d § 9.3 (4).

5. When the misrepresentation induces the plaintiff to forego a transaction or induces the plaintiff to enter into a transaction with some person other than the defendant, none of these market value rules seem to portray the problem. See Trytko v. Hubbell, Inc., 28 F.3d 715 (7th Cir.1994) discussing some such cases. In those instances, the claim can appropriately be viewed as a consequential damages claim involving neither of the market measures.

6. Lama Holding Co. v. Smith Barney, Inc., 88 N.Y.2d 413, 668 N.E.2d 1370, 646 N.Y.S.2d 76 (1996). Cal. Civ. Code § 3343

of pocket measure, now permit the plaintiff to recover the loss of bargain,[7] or choose the measure they deem best to fit the facts,[8] or say with the Restatement that the plaintiff can recover under either loss of bargain or out of pocket, at her option.[9] The plaintiff will usually prefer a loss of bargain measure, but if the transaction would have resulted in a loss to the plaintiff, even had the representations been true, she will prefer the out of pocket measure, which in effect gets her out of a bad contract.[10] The plaintiff may also recover consequential damages such as expenses incurred or profits lost in collateral affairs as a proximate result of the fraud,[11] provided such damages are proved with reasonable certainty and do not duplicate the out of pocket or loss of bargain award.[12] Emotional harm damages are not ordinarily recoverable in a misrepresentation action[13] although they might be recovered in other actions in which misrepresentation is an operative fact.[14] Punitive damages are recoverable if the defendant's intentional fraud qualifies as sufficiently malicious or oppressive.[15]

Negligent misrepresentation. When the defendant's misrepresentation is merely negligent, the Restatement provides that liability is limited to the out of pocket measure and cannot include consequential

begins by imposing the out of pocket rule for transactions within its scope but then permits some loss of bargain elements.

7. E.g., American Family Service Corp. v. Michelfelder, 968 F.2d 667 (8th Cir. 1992); Bechtel v. Liberty Nat'l Bank, 534 F.2d 1335 (9th Cir.1976); Turnbull v. LaRose, 702 P.2d 1331 (Alaska 1985); A number of cases have stated the formula as "the difference between the value of the goods received and the value of the goods as represented." E.g., Lancaster v. Schilling Motors, Inc., 299 Ark. 365, 369, 772 S.W.2d 349, 351 (1989); Slack v. Sodal, 190 Colo. 411, 547 P.2d 923 (1976); Miller v. Appleby, 183 Conn. 51, 438 A.2d 811 (1981); Gerill Corporation v. Jack L. Hargrove Builders, Inc., 128 Ill.2d 179, 131 Ill.Dec. 155, 538 N.E.2d 530 (1989); LeFlore v. Reflections of Tulsa, Inc., 708 P.2d 1068 (Okl.1985); Danca v. Taunton Sav. Bank, 385 Mass. 1, 429 N.E.2d 1129 (1982); Terry v. Panek, 631 P.2d 896 (Utah 1981); Kramer v. Chabot, 152 Vt. 53, 564 A.2d 292 (Vt. 1989).

8. Walston v. Monumental Life Ins. Co., 129 Idaho 211, 923 P.2d 456 (1996).

9. Hall v. Lovell Regency Homes Limited Partnership, 121 Md.App. 1, 708 A.2d 344 (1998); Restatement§ 549; cf. O'Neal Ford, Inc. v. Davie, 299 Ark. 45, 770 S.W.2d 656 (1989) (a preference for loss of bargain but approving a recovery based upon out of pocket).

10. Example: P pays $10,000 for farm machinery after receiving a representation that the machinery is in working order. Had the representation been true, the machinery would not have been worth more than $8,000. The representation was false and the machinery was worth only $7,000. The value of the bargain had the representations been true was negative—a loss of $2,000 on the deal. The plaintiff therefore would opt to recover the out of pocket, $3,000, or to rescind.

11. E.g., Lazar v. Superior Court, 12 Cal.4th 631, 909 P.2d 981, 49 Cal.Rptr.2d 377 (1996) (items like moving expenses in addition to loss of bargain damages for employee fraudulently induced to move to new job). See generally 2 Dobbs, Remedies 2d § 9.2 (3). New York, with a strong policy of limiting damages to out of pocket losses, has rejected some consequential damages on the ground that allowance will tend to match a loss of bargain rule. See Alpert v. Shea Gould Climenko & Casey, 160 A.D.2d 67, 559 N.Y.S.2d 312 (1990).

12. Loss of expected profits and loss of bargain may turn out to be two ways of measuring the same thing. See 2 Dobbs, Remedies 2d § 9.2 (4), p. 558.

13. E.g., Brogan v. Mitchell International, Inc., 181 Ill.2d 178, 692 N.E.2d 276, 229 Ill.Dec. 503 (1998); Jourdain v. Dineen, 527 A.2d 1304 (Me.1987); 2 Dobbs, Remedies 2d § 9.2 (4).

14. § 469.

15. E.g., Midwest Home Distributor, Inc. v. Domco Indus. Ltd., 585 N.W.2d 735 (Iowa 1998).

damages.[16] Earlier cases of negligence did not discuss the damages issue or failed to realize that negligence might call for a milder measure. More recent cases alluding to the issue have lent support to the Restatement.[17] Perhaps it is conceivable in some cases that the defendant might have undertaken a duty to protect the plaintiff against loss of a bargain, but unless such an undertaking is demonstrated, it would be hard to justify imposing a loss of bargain liability for merely negligent statements. On the other hand, it may be reasonable to permit the plaintiff to recover actual collateral expenses as consequential damages in some cases.

Innocent misrepresentation as warranty. The Restatement also provides that the out of pocket measure is to be applied in the case of innocent misrepresentations.[18] There are, however, two logically distinct grounds for imposing liability in innocent misrepresentation cases, and they do not necessarily suggest the same damages measure. The first is that the innocent misrepresentation is a true contractual warranty, that is, an implicit or explicit understanding of the parties. It may be unlikely that the warranty would imply a benefit of the bargain measure of damages, but if it does, it should be honored as part of the parties' agreement.

Innocent misrepresentation as mistake justifying rescission-equivalent damages. The other ground for recognizing innocent misrepresentation as actionable at all is rooted in equitable notions and in the remedy of rescission. Rescission was granted for honest mutual mistakes about truly basic—not merely material—incidents of an agreement. It seemed, therefore, that rescission should equally be granted when the defendant honestly but mistakenly asserted a fact and the plaintiff honestly and mistakenly relied upon it. Once a court goes that far, it is easy to say that if rescission can be granted for an honest misrepresentation if it is important enough, then the court could also grant damages that have a substantially similar impact. Out of pocket damages do have an impact similar to rescission in many cases. You give me $100 for a dog that I honestly and reasonably represent to be pedigreed, but it turns out that I am wrong and the dog is worth only $50. You can rescind the dog deal and get your $100 back. If you recover out of pocket damages, you keep the $50 dog and get damages of $50, ending up with $100 in assets. If damages for innocent misrepresentations are to be justified on the ground that this result approximates a justified rescission, the damages must be limited to out of pocket losses. Perhaps this reason for imposing liability for innocent representations is logically limited as well to contracting parties.

Rescission and delay. Rescission is granted only for very serious or basic mistakes about the transaction and even then is denied unless the parties can be restored to their former position. So delay or lapse of time or change of circumstances may induce courts to refuse to grant rescis-

16. Restatement § 552B.

17. E.g., Trytko v. Hubbell, Inc., 28 F.3d 715 (7th Cir.1994).

18. Restatement § 552C.

sion. The effect of rescission is sometimes minor, but at other times it can be highly disruptive and could permit the plaintiff to speculate at the defendant's expense. Suppose the purchaser pays $100,000 cash for shares of stock in reliance upon the defendant's representation that the company has just received orders to build 100 new commercial airplanes. When the purchaser learns that the representation is false, the purchase still may be a good buy and the value of the shares may rise in the future. The plaintiff's strategy in such a case might be to do nothing immediately, planning to keep the shares if the market rises but to seek rescission if the market drops. With the possibility of this kind of plaintiff speculation in mind, the courts have traditionally been reluctant to rescind after a serious delay and also when circumstances have so changed as to make rescission inequitable.[19]

Rescission-equivalent or rescissory damages for the buyer when value has changed. The reasons that counsel caution about granting rescission to a buyer after a delay also suggest that a damages substitute for rescission should not always fully emulate rescission. Damages that emulate rescission would value assets at the time of rescission (or the damages judgment) and not at the date of the original transfer.[20] In the case of a plaintiff who buys shares for $100,000 at a time when their market value is only $80,000, out of pocket damages are fixed at the time of purchase, but rescissory damages would continue to rise as the market continued to fall. If judgment is entered on a day when the market value has fallen to $50,000, the plaintiff would recover that sum instead of the $20,000 out of pocket. This creates a substantial risk of uncertainty that will prevent settlement, speculation, and manipulation by the plaintiff. In addition, shifting the date for calculating damages undercuts the plaintiff's incentive to mitigate damages.[21] Where delay has occurred in a fluctuating market, and the choice is between out of pocket and rescissory damages, out of pocket would almost always reflect the more prudent measure, which explains why, apart from statute, rescissory damages are not ordinarily given.[22] And in any event rescissory damages (based on values at the date of a hypothetical rescission) should be permitted only against a contracting party, against whom actual rescission could have been granted.[23]

Rescission-equivalent or rescissory damages for the seller when value has changed. When the plaintiff is the seller of property rather than the

19. See 2 Dobbs, Remedies 2d §§ 9.3 (3), 9.4, & 9.6 (restoration required of plaintiff, delay under election of remedies doctrine, & equitable defenses including delay).

20. NL Industries, Inc. v. MAXXAM, Inc., 659 A.2d 760, 776 (Del.Ch.1995).

21. Mitigation or the avoidable consequences rule normally applies only to consequential damages claims because the fixed date for determining damages based on market values builds in an incentive. Any rule that lets the date float affects that incentive.

22. Some securities statutes authorize rescissory damages. See 15 U.S.C.A. § 77l and the cases discuss such damages for the buyer in the securities context.

23. See Standard Chartered PLC v. Price Waterhouse, 190 Ariz. 6, 945 P.2d 317, 346 (Ariz.Ct.App.1996) (permitting out of pocket but holding that rescissory damages cannot be granted except against contracting parties).

buyer, the plaintiff will want to rescind if the value of the property she transferred rises. This kind of claim has traditionally been pursued as a claim for constructive trust, which in effect allows the plaintiff to recover the property she transferred even though it has appreciated in value. If the defendant has sold the property the plaintiff transferred to him, the constructive trust permits the plaintiff to recover the price paid to the defendant, even if it exceeds the plaintiff's out of pocket or loss of bargain. Here the basis for recovery is the defendant's unjust enrichment. These rules can be conceived of as the old equity version of "rescissory damages."[24]

The proximate cause or "loss causation" problem in rescission and damages cases. The plaintiff speculation problem is closely related to the proximate cause problem. The problem arises when the plaintiff suffers financial harm because she relied upon the misrepresentation but the harm is not of a type that would foreseeably result. A dramatic case furnishes the clearest illustration. Suppose the plaintiff purchases shares in the X Rocket Company in reliance upon the defendant's fraudulent misrepresentations that the government has awarded it a valuable contract. No such contract exists, but the next day the company's entire rocket plant is demolished in an explosion and the plaintiff's shares become worthless. It is possible but not certain that the defendant's fraud is a but for or actual cause of the plaintiff's loss. Quite possibly, the plaintiff would have purchased the shares even without the misrepresentation, but would have paid a lower price.

In any event, the loss from the explosion is not the same kind of loss that would foreseeably result from the defendant's misrepresentation. Under the Restatement, the plaintiff cannot recover for "unforeseeable" losses, that is, those different from the losses risked by the misrepresentation.[25] Some cases may be contrary,[26] but a number of decisions have now begun to follow what is essentially the Restatement's rule by saying that "loss causation" as well as "transaction causation" is required.[27] That does not mean, however, that the plaintiff would be denied all recovery in the case of the rocket company. The plaintiff's loss independent of the explosion can be determined as of the moment the transaction is completed and without reference to the explosion. If she paid $1 million for the shares but they were worth only $500,000, the out of pocket measure would give her $500,000. The remainder of her loss (from the explosion) is one she must bear herself under this proximate cause approach.[28]

24. See Barshak v. Buccheri, 406 Mass. 187, 547 N.E.2d 23 (1989) (holding, however, that once the defendant has sold the property, the gain to which the plaintiff is entitled is the price paid the defendant, not the current appreciated value of the property in the hands of the defendant's buyer).

25. Restatement § 548A.

26. See the discussion of approaches in 2 DOBBS, REMEDIES 2d § 9.2 (6).

27. Movitz v. First Nat'l Bank of Chicago, 148 F.3d 760 (7th Cir.1998).

28. See Huddleston v. Herman & MacLean, 640 F.2d 534, 549, n. 25 (5th Cir. 1981) (example of misrepresentation as to capacity of ship that later sunk as a result of extraneous events).

Chapter 36

Lawyer Malpractice

§ 484. Scope, Duties, and Elements

Scope of malpractice. Lawyer malpractice is ordinarily an economic tort, causing financial harm without personal injury or property damage.[1] The topic deals only with violation of a lawyer's duty arising out of the lawyer's representation of a client.[2] Lawyer malpractice, in other words, entails breach of a duty created by the contract or by the relationship with the client. Indeed, in some cases the claim may be brought as a contract claim as well as a negligence claim[3] and the contract itself may not only create duties but limit them.[4] Lawyers may be liable to clients for reasons having nothing to do with malpractice; negligent driving that injures a client is surely actionable, and so is battery. Lawyers may be chargeable with defamation, and malicious prosecution, or indeed, any tort. But while the lawyer-client relationship may facilitate such torts, they are not ordinarily part of the representation and not malpractice.

§ 484

1. Malpractice in a criminal representation can lead indirectly to imprisonment of a client, but even in such cases the analogy is to malicious prosecution rather than to false imprisonment. When the plaintiff claims physical harms resulting from lawyer malpractice, courts tend to say that the malpractice was not a proximate cause or not an actual cause. See Peeler v. Hughes & Luce, 909 S.W.2d 494 (Tex.1995) (malpractice plaintiff convicted of crime cannot recover if he is guilty in fact because in that case his own crime, not attorney malpractice, is the proximate cause of conviction); Roberts v. Healey, 991 S.W.2d 873 (Tex. App.1999) (failure to obtain a protective order not a cause of client's death at the hands of her husband); cf. Bolte v. Joy, 150 Wis.2d 744, 443 N.W.2d 23 (1989) (lawyer failed to produce a witness in client's suit against a fire insurer; the jury believed that the client had set the fire himself and this led to a loss in the client's reputation, for which the client asserts a malpractice claim; denied; there would be no stopping place).

2. Representation of the client may, however, create duties to third persons. See § 488.

3. See e.g., Pancake House, Inc. v. Redmond, 239 Kan. 83, 716 P.2d 575 (1986) ("Where the act complained of is a breach of specific terms of the contract without any reference to the legal duties imposed by law upon the relationship created thereby, the action is contractual. Where the essential claim of the action is a breach of a duty imposed by law upon the relationship of attorney/client and not of the contract itself, the action is in tort"); Ray Ryden Anderson & Walter W. Steele, Jr., Fiduciary Duty, Tort and Contract: A Primer on the Legal Malpractice Puzzle, 47 SMU L. Rev. 235 (1994).

4. Lawyers are forbidden to contract out of malpractice liability. See Restatement of Law Governing Lawyers § 76(1) (Tentative Draft No. 8, 1997). However, the contract or undertaking of the lawyer helps define the boundaries of his duties. For instance, a retainer agreement may limit the scope of the lawyer's representation to particular stages of a case or to certain aspects of a legal problem. See ABA Model Rules of Professional Conduct 1.2(e).

Forms and examples. Malpractice itself takes many forms. For example, fiduciary breach aside, lawyers may fail to recognize a cause of action or may fail to file a claim or defense within the time limits imposed,[5] may inadequately prepare for trial,[6] or use substandard strategies or techniques in trial itself.[7] However, malpractice claims are not confined to litigation malpractice; they can arise in any kind of representation. Lawyers may be negligent in drafting[8] or recording[9] documents, in search of records,[10] negotiating a settlement[11] or advising its acceptance,[12] in giving advice,[13] and possibly even in accepting a case beyond their experience and competence.[14] Each field of law practice tends to have its own unique problems. Representation of several clients jointly—both spouses in preparing wills for example—may run risks that the lawyer will have conflicts of interests or will face dilemmas of confidentiality unlike those routinely faced by, say, a personal injury lawyer.[15]

Elements and rules of liability. The plaintiff must first show a lawyer-client relationship.[16] The contract or relationship establishes the general duty to provide professional care.[17] Given the relationship, the commercial loss rule does not apply to eliminate liability for negligence.[18]

5. E.g., Phillips v. Clancy, 733 P.2d 300, 152 Ariz. 415 (Ct. App. 1986).

6. Waldman v. Levine, 544 A.2d 683, 78 A.L.R.4th 703 (D.C. App. 1988).

7. Wartnick v. Moss & Barnett, 490 N.W.2d 108 (Minn.1992) (lawyer's admission in opening statement).

8. E.g., Lucas v. Hamm, 56 Cal.2d 583, 364 P.2d 685, 15 Cal.Rptr. 821 (1961).

9. See Pizel v. Zuspann, 247 Kan. 54, 795 P.2d 42, 10 A.L.R. 5th 1098 (1990).

10. Cf. Greycas, Inc. v. Proud, 826 F.2d 1560 (7th Cir.1987) (failure to search for UCC filings followed by misrepresentation that none existed).

11. E.g., Meyer v. Wagner, 429 Mass. 410, 709 N.E.2d 784 (1999) (following the usual rule that judicial approval of a settlement does not foreclose the malpractice action based upon the attorney's negligence).

12. Thomas v. Bethea, 351 Md. 513, 718 A.2d 1187 (1998) (reviewing and analyzing a number of settlement cases). Pennsylvania adopted an unique rule forbidding malpractice claims based upon a settlement. Muhammad v. Strassburger, McKenna, Messer, Shilobod and Gutnick, 526 Pa. 541, 587 A.2d 1346 (1991). That rule has been rejected elsewhere, as in Thomas v. Bethea.

13. Conklin v. Hannoch Weisman, 145 N.J. 395, 678 A.2d 1060 (1996) (plaintiff claimed lawyer gave inadequate explanation of subordination agreement).

14. See Battle v. Thornton, 646 A.2d 315 (D.C.App.1994). However, mere acceptance of a case would not necessarily cause harm unless the attorney fell below the standard of care in some particular act.

15. See A. v. B., 158 N.J. 51, 726 A.2d 924 (1999).

16. E.g., Allyn v. McDonald, 112 Nev. 68, 910 P.2d 263 (1996). The relationship arises from the lawyer's undertaking (sometimes implicit) and the client's reasonable expectations. See Restatement of Law Governing Lawyers § 26 (Proposed Final Draft No. 1, 1996). It does not depend upon the client's payment of a fee. See Togstad v. Vesely, Otto, Miller & Keefe,291 N.W.2d 686 (Minn.1980) (consultation about a potential medical malpractice claim; seeking and receiving advice when reasonable person would rely upon it is enough); George v. Caton, 93 N.M. 370, 376, 600 P.2d 822, 828 (1979) (even if no fee); Lieberman v. Employers Ins. of Wausau, 84 N.J. 325, 419 A.2d 417 (1980) (attorney retained by liability insurer to defend medical malpractice suit against doctor was doctor's attorney).

The lawyer-client relationship required is not necessarily a relationship between the lawyer and the plaintiff, since non-clients may be third party beneficiaries entitled to sue for malpractice. See § 488.

17. Collins v. Miller & Miller, Ltd., 189 Ariz. 387, 943 P.2d 747 (Ct. App. 1996); Krahn v. Kinney, 43 Ohio St.3d 103, 538 N.E.2d 1058 (1989).

18. Collins v. Reynard, 154 Ill.2d 48, 180 Ill.Dec. 672, 607 N.E.2d 1185 (1992);

The remaining elements are those of other negligence cases. The plaintiff must prove a breach of the duty,[19] cause in fact,[20] proximate cause,[21] and damages.[22] Additional elements may be required in the case of criminal-case malpractice.[23] The duties include the duties of professional care and competence, but also includes the special duties of fiduciaries[24] and the duty to provide certain information to the client, somewhat analogous to the obligation of medical practitioners to provide patients with information.[25] Lawyers are also liable vicariously for the negligence of their general partners committed within the scope of their agency,[26] and within limits, for the negligence of outside counsel they have associated in the case.[27] If the lawyer practices in a professional corporation, the corporation itself may be vicariously liable, but sometimes the shareholder-lawyers are not.[28] Limited Liability Companies and Limited Liability Partnerships, relatively new business forms, may also turn out to shield lawyers in the firm from vicarious responsibility.[29]

§ 485. Professional Standard of Care and Its Breach

Standard of care. Lawyer codes of conduct or ethics, adopted by the states for disciplinary purposes,[1] may be relevant to a court determining the civil obligations of lawyers, but they do not create a cause of action against lawyers.[2] Instead, subject to slight variations in expression,

Clark v. Rowe, 428 Mass. 339, 701 N.E.2d 624 (1998).

19. Breach may be either failure to use the professional standard of care or a violation of fiduciary obligations. See §§ 485 & 487 respectively.

20. E.g., Gregory v. Hawkins, 251 Va. 471, 468 S.E.2d 891 (1996) (plaintiff failed to show "proximate cause" [in the sense of cause in fact] because same harm could have resulted without the alleged malpractice).

21. See Rohricht v. O'Hare, 586 N.W.2d 587 (Minn.App.1998); see also cases cited n. 1, supra.

22. § 492.

23. Bailey v. Tucker, 533 Pa. 237, 621 A.2d 108 (1993).

24. See § 487; John Leubsdorf, Legal Malpractice and Professional Responsibility, 48 Rutgers L. Rev. 101 (1995).

25. §§ 250 & 251.

26. E.g., Olson v. Fraase, 421 N.W.2d 820 (N.D.1988) (failure to create joint tenancy with concomitant losses to survivor; partner vicariously liable). But not, of course, for actions outside the scope of their employment. Entente Mineral Co. v. Parker, 956 F.2d 524 (5th Cir.1992) (lawyer induced client to sell to him rather than to proposed buyer, first not vicariously liable to the proposed buyer for interference with contract).

27. See Duggins v. Guardianship of Washington, 632 So.2d 420, 35 A.L.R.5th 909 (Miss. 1993) (if the division of responsibility between retained attorney and the attorney he associates "is not clearly spelled out, the client's consent to the association does not prevent vicarious liability between or among counsel when the attorneys share the representation and legal fees"; treating the association as a joint venture or partnership for purpose of the case).

28. Vanderhoof v. Cleary, 725 A.2d 917 (Vt.1998). Statutory language may control this issue, however.

29. On all three forms of business structure for law firms, See Ronald E. Mallen & Jeffrey M. Smith, Legal Malpractice §§ 5.4–5.6 (4th ed. 1996).

§ 485

1. Most have patterned their rules on models drafted by the American Bar Association, the current version of which is found in the ABA Model Rules of Professional Conduct.

2. E.g., Lazy Seven Coal Sales, Inc. v. Stone & Hinds, P.C., 813 S.W.2d 400 (Tenn. 1991); see ABA, Annotated Model Rules of Professional Conduct, (Preamble 1996) ("nothing in the Rules should be deemed to

attorneys owe clients the skill, care, knowledge, and diligence exercised by reasonable and prudent lawyers in similar circumstances.[3] Under this standard, not every professional mistake is negligence.[4] In fact, courts often say that lawyers are not liable for good faith errors in judgment,[5] but taken literally this would virtually eliminate all lawyer liability. The error of judgment statement seems to apply only when reasonable professional judgments could differ, in which case the lawyer simply has not violated the professional standard.[6] The standard is the usual objective standard; good faith of the lawyer is no defense if he violates the standard.[7] As with medical malpractice, specialists may be held to the standard of their speciality rather than to the standard of lawyers generally.[8] The locality rule, however, seems never to have had the major place in lawyer malpractice cases that it once had in the medical cases.[9]

augment any substantive legal duty of lawyers or the extra-disciplinary consequences of violating such a duty"). The rules of conduct for lawyers are perhaps less relevant to ordinary negligence actions than to breaches of fiduciary and other special duties. See § 487.

3. See Boyle v. Welsh, 256 Neb. 118, 589 N.W.2d 118 (1999); Olson v. Fraase, 421 N.W.2d 820 (N.D.1988). Some courts express this by saying said that attorneys must exercise ordinary care or the care of a reasonable person, but they then modify this statement by adding that ordinary care in the case of professionals is the care reasonably expected of other professionals acting under the same or similar circumstances, or by saying that expert testimony is required to establish the particular standard. See Barth v. Reagan, 139 Ill.2d 399, 564 N.E.2d 1196, 151 Ill.Dec. 534 (1990); Waldman v. Levine, 544 A.2d 683, 687, 78 A.L.R.4th 703 (1988). Pennsylvania has said that in criminal-case malpractice, the convicted client must prove reckless or wanton lawyer conduct. See Bailey v. Tucker, 533 Pa. 237, 621 A.2d 108 (1993). Other courts use the reasonable care standard. See RONALD E. MALLEN & JEFFREY M. SMITH, LEGAL MALPRACTICE § 25.6 (4th ed. 1996 & Supps. 1996). Courts also usually require innocence in fact when the client has been convicted of crime. See Wiley v. County of San Diego, 19 Cal.4th 532, 79 Cal.Rptr.2d 672, 966 P.2d 983 (1998); § 489, below.

4. Lucas v. Hamm, 56 Cal.2d 583, 364 P.2d 685, 15 Cal.Rptr. 821 (1961) (rule against perpetuities).

5. E.g., Pugh v. Griggs, 327 Ark. 577, 940 S.W.2d 445 (1997).

6. See Bergstrom v. Noah, 266 Kan. 847, 878–79, 974 P.2d 531, 556 (1999) (quoting the Mallen treatise and American Jurisprudence); Baker v. Fabian, Thielen & Thielen, 254 Neb. 697, 578 N.W.2d 446 (1998) (" not answerable for a mere error of judgment or for a mistake *in a point of law which has not been settled by the court of last resort in his or her state and on which reasonable doubt may be entertained by well-informed lawyers*") (emphasis added); Michael P. Ambrosio & Denis F. McLaughlin, The Use of Expert Witnesses in Establishing Liability in Legal Malpractice Cases, 61 TEMP. L. REV. 1351, 1367–1368 (1988) (error of judgment rule does not insulate lawyer from liability for failure to exercise ordinary care and skill). Even the fact that the law in issue is unsettled does not necessarily mean the lawyer is to be absolved of liability. On the contrary, uncertainty of the law may require the lawyer to take extra precautions. See Collins v. Miller & Miller, Ltd., 189 Ariz. 387, 943 P.2d 747 (Ct. App. 1996).

7. See Meyer v. Wagner, 429 Mass. 410, 709 N.E.2d 784 (1999).

8. E.g., Duffey Law Office, S.C. v. Tank Transport, Inc., 194 Wis.2d 674, 535 N.W.2d 91 (Ct.App.1995) (lawyer who holds himself out as a specialist or expert is held to the specialist's standard).

9. Some cases make no mention of any particular geographic unit, or refer to a large one such as the entire state. E.g., Bye v. Mack, 519 N.W.2d 302 (N.D.1994); Russo v. Griffin, 147 Vt. 20, 510 A.2d 436 (1986); John Leubsdorf, Legal Malpractice and Professional Responsibility, 48 RUTGERS L. REV. 101 (1995). However, a little authority anchors the standard in the "same or similar locality." Progressive Sales, Inc. v. Williams, Willeford, Boger, Grady & Davis, 86 N.C.App. 51, 356 S.E.2d 372 (1987); see also Michael P. Ambrosio & Denis F. McLaughlin, The Use of Expert Witnesses in Establishing Liability in Legal Malpractice Cases, 61 TEMP. L. REV. 1351 (1988).

Expert testimony required. At one time, courts weren't so sure they would even admit expert testimony to establish the standard of care or its breach.[10] That has all passed, and courts now not only admit but generally require expert testimony to show the standard of care.[11] If it is not obvious that the lawyer's conduct breached the standard, then expert testimony may be required to show that breach as well.[12] If a locality rule is used, a court might properly exclude or at least discount expert testimony not based on local practice,[13] but if a statewide or national standard is used, the expert need not know local practice and can testify to the state or national standard instead.[14] Similarly, if the defendant is a specialist, a witness who know the specialist's standards is required or appropriate.[15]

Testimony as to specialists. A dictum in a California case has it that only a specialists can provide evidence of the standard of care for specialists.[16] That is probably right for many cases; a personal injury lawyer could hardly help the trier understand whether a tax lawyer's estate plan met standards or not. However, the usual view is that the standard for specialists is more exacting than the standard for non-specialists, so in some cases, however, proof that the specialist breached the less exacting standard for non-specialists would also show that he breached the more exacting standard for specialists. In *Wright v. Williams*,[17] the lawyer was a specialist in admiralty law. His clients were purchasing a vessel intended for use between American cities. Such a use was prohibited by law and the documents of title because the ship had once been owned by a foreign national. The lawyer did not advise the purchasers of this limitation. The client-purchasers adduced no evidence of any standard of care at all and the only issue was whether the court could say that the lawyer was negligent at a matter of law. Instead of saying that expert testimony was required, the court went further and said that expert testimony of an admiralty specialist was required. Yet many lawyers must advise clients about proposed transactions. If real estate or commercial lawyers think they should advise clients purchasing property that its use is severely limited, that surely establishes a standard about appropriate advice. Only if admiralty law standards were *less* exacting than those governing other purchases, would the testimony

10. Developments in the Law—Lawyers' Responsibilities and Lawyers' Responses, II. Lawyers' Responsibilities to the Client: Legal Malpractice and Tort Reform, 107 Harv. L. Rev. 1557 (1994).

11. Boyle v. Welsh, 256 Neb. 118, 589 N.W.2d 118 (1999); cf. Bent v. Green, 39 Conn.Supp. 416, 466 A.2d 322 (1983) (defending against tax lawyer's suit for fees due, the client urged that the lawyer's advice was poor but offered no expert testimony; held, this defense requires expert testimony).

12. Baird v. Pace, 156 Ariz. 418, 752 P.2d 507 (Ct. App. 1987) (Expert testimony is generally used to establish the standard of care . . . and to determine whether the attorney deviated from the proper standard).

13. See Brett v. Berkowitz, 706 A.2d 509 (Del.1998) (experts must be competent to testify to the standard of care ordinarily employed in the local community).

14. See Russo v. Griffin, 147 Vt. 20, 510 A.2d 436 (1986) (trial judge discounted non-local expert testimony on standards; reversed and remanded).

15. See n.14 below.

16. Wright v. Williams, 47 Cal.App.3d 802, 121 Cal.Rptr. 194 (1975).

17. Supra n.14.

of admiralty experts be important. If the lawyer claims his specialty requires less care than non-specialists ordinarily provide, perhaps the burden should be upon him to prove that unusual point.

Exception to expert testimony requirement. Courts seldom mention *res ipsa loquitur* in lawyer malpractice cases except occasionally to say that it does not apply.[18] However, courts do recognize a common knowledge exception to the expert testimony requirement to cover the case in which the standard and its breach are so clear that no expert testimony is required to establish them. That is the case with one of the most routine kinds of malpractice, failures to act within the time permitted, as where the lawyer with opportunity to do so fails to file a suit within the statute of limitations period.[19] But if the statute of limitations is missed because of a legal judgment is implicated, expert testimony is required to show that the judgment fell below standards.[20]

§ 486. Causation: The Case within the Case

Cause in fact. As in other negligence cases, the malpractice plaintiff must show that she has suffered legally recognized harm and, ordinarily, that it was caused by the defendant's negligence.[1] In many instances, proof of causation is no problem to the plaintiff once she proves negligence, because she can meet the but-for test by showing that her harm is the very kind that professional care would have avoided. If the lawyer does not file a lien that could have secured the plaintiff's right to payment from a debtor, the lawyer's failure to do so is demonstrably a cause of loss when the debtor sells the property and absconds.[2]

Case within the case. In litigation malpractice, however, the plaintiff must frequently prove causation of loss by proving that, had the lawyers (or litigation support personnel[3]) properly carried their roles in the litigation, the client would have won or won more. To do that, the client-plaintiff must often prove her original claim or defense and the amount of damages she would have recovered or avoided.[4] The effect is that the

18. Barth v. Reagan, 139 Ill.2d 399, 564 N.E.2d 1196, 151 Ill.Dec. 534 (1990).

19. Allyn v. McDonald, 112 Nev. 68, 910 P.2d 263 (1996); Little v. Matthewson, 114 N.C.App. 562, 442 S.E.2d 567 (1994), aff'd, 340 N.C. 102, 455 S.E.2d 160 (1995).

20. Boyle v. Welsh, 256 Neb. 118, 589 N.W.2d 118 (1999).

§ 486

1. Courts always state that proximate cause (meaning both cause in fact and proximate cause) is an element of the malpractice claim. E.g., Shaw v. State, 861 P.2d 566 (Alaska 1993). Under the but for test of cause in fact, liability is rejected when the plaintiff's loss would have occurred even had the lawyer not been guilty of malpractice. E.g., Gregory v. Hawkins, 251 Va. 471, 468 S.E.2d 891 (1996). Likewise when the defendant's malpractice in fact caused harm but is not regarded as a proximate cause because the harm was outside the risk or because damages are not recoverable as a matter of policy. E.g., Peeler v. Hughes & Luce, 909 S.W.2d 494 (Tex.1995).

2. Cf. Rhine v. Haley, 238 Ark. 72, 378 S.W.2d 655 (1964) (divorce settlement, attorney failed to require a lien on property of husband, who saw his opportunity and "absconded to Louisiana with his new wife").

3. Mattco Forge, Inc. v. Arthur Young & Co., 52 Cal.App.4th 820, 60 Cal.Rptr.2d 780 (1997). Indeed, anyone who interferes with litigation prospects would seem to fall under the same rule requiring proof of causation.

4. E.g., Thomas v. Bethea, 351 Md. 513, 718 A.2d 1187 (1998); Restatement (Third) of Law Governing Lawyers § 75 (Tentative Draft No. 8, 1997).

plaintiff must stage a "trial within a trial" or "case within a case." The plaintiff must "prove two claims: first, the one that was lost, and also that his attorney's negligence caused that loss."[5] The malpractice plaintiff's former lawyer in turn will argue that he or any lawyer would have lost the case even had he been guilty of no malpractice and in any event that he was not negligent. In many instances, the malpractice plaintiff will be compelled to actually stage the original trial by putting on testimony that should have been put on but for the lawyer's alleged malpractice. If the plaintiff's original suit was a malpractice suit against a surgeon, for example, she would put on evidence of the surgery, the injury following, the doctor's negligence, and medical causation.[6] For this purpose she will ordinarily require one or more medical experts. And to show that her former lawyer was negligent, she will also need a legal expert unless the lawyer's negligence is obvious.

Criticisms and alternatives. Writers and courts have criticized the case within the case approach to causal proof, partly because it makes heavy and perhaps impossible demands upon the plaintiff and partly because the original setting, party alignment and incentives, discovery opportunities, and the like cannot be in fact duplicated. It can also result in expensive tiers of litigation. If the plaintiff's lawyer in the legal malpractice suit loses, the plaintiff might sue him as well, creating a case within a case within yet another case.[7] Similarly, if the alleged malpractice is a failure to perfect an appeal that might have remanded for a new trial, the plaintiff would be required to prove that the lawyer was negligent, that appellate court would or should have ruled favorably, and that upon the supposed retrial the trial court would or should have ruled favorably. A little authority ameliorates the problem by permitting the use of expert testimony to evaluate the probable outcome of the earlier case[8] or its probable settlement[9] but the leading treatise expresses skepticism about the use of such testimony.[10] Some authority has used something like estoppel against the lawyer who selected a statutory cause of action and then argues that the plaintiff has not proved its conditions were met.[11] Perhaps it is possible to interpret some authority as eliminating altogether the but for rule and its case within the case proof.[12] One writer proposed use of lost chance rules to recognize that

5. Bye v. Mack, 519 N.W.2d 302, 305 (N.D.1994).

6. See, e.g., Stanski v. Ezersky, 228 A.D.2d 311, 644 N.Y.S.2d 220 (Sup. Ct. 1996).

7. E.g., Elliott v. Videan, 164 Ariz. 113, 791 P.2d 639 (Ct. App. 1989); see Ronald E. Mallen & Jeffrey M. Smith, Legal Malpractice § 32.1 (4th ed. & Supp. 1996) (listing a number of cases).

8. Lieberman v. Employers Ins. of Wausau, 84 N.J. 325, 419 A.2d 417 (1980); cf. Honeywell, Inc. v. American Standards Testing Bureau, Inc., 851 F.2d 652 (3d Cir. 1988).

9. Scognamillo v. Olsen, 795 P.2d 1357 (Colo.App.1990).

10. Ronald E. Mallen & Jeffrey M. Smith, Legal Malpractice § 32.17 (4th ed. 1996 & Supps., 4th ed. & Supp. 1996).

11. Baker v. Beal, 225 N.W.2d 106 (Iowa 1975).

12. See Cincinnati Ins. Co. v. Byers, 151 F.3d 574 (6th Cir.1998) (interpreting Ohio law, plaintiff relieved of need to show that it would have won appeal had defendant not been guilty of malpractice); Vahila v. Hall, 77 Ohio St.3d 421, 674 N.E.2d 1164 (1997) (using very broad language which might be read both to affirm and reject the need to show but for causation).

when lawyers are guilty of malpractice they compromise the client's opportunities for success even if they do not demonstrably cause losses.[13] None of this is in the mainstream, however.

Scope of the case within the case. Mallen's treatise suggests the scope of the case within the case proof by saying that the evidence should show the result that *should* have been obtained, not the result that *would* have been obtained in the particular case.[14] Surely this is correct about some issues. If the malpracticing lawyer could convincingly prove that the original jury were rogues who would have rejected the client's claim for unwholesome reasons, the lawyer presumably would not escape the liability a reasonable jury would have imposed. Yet some individual circumstances in the case are taken into account. If the plaintiff could not have collected a judgment against the original defendant, the lawyer will not be liable. On the other hand, the fact that every case has a settlement value, even if it is very small, does not mean that the plaintiff-client whose case would have been lost even by the best lawyering should recover a settlement value from her malpracticing lawyer. It is convenient to treat these examples in the discussion of remedies,[15] but they suggest that the case within a case puzzle probably has not been finally solved.

§ 487. Fiduciary and Information Duties

Fiduciary breach as malpractice. Quite apart from the duty of competence and professional care, lawyers are fiduciaries to their clients. Lawyers can thus think of fiduciary breach as a form of professional malpractice or as an entirely separate ground for liability. Whether or not both fiduciary breach and negligence both fit under the umbrella of professional malpractice, the two torts are not the same. "Professional negligence implicates a duty of care, while breach of a fiduciary duty implicates a duty of loyalty and honesty."[1] Thus if breach of fiduciary duty is a form of lawyer malpractice, it is a distinct one with rules that do not necessarily turn on traditional negligence analysis.[2]

Core fiduciary concept. The fiduciary concept was developed in old equity courts which provided equitable remedies like constructive trusts to enforce the fiduciary's duty. However, breach of a fiduciary duty is a

13. Polly A. Lord, Loss of Chance in Legal Malpractice, 61 WASH. L. REV. 1479 (1986). On the lost chance approach, see §§ 178 & 179.

14. RONALD E. MALLEN & JEFFREY M. SMITH, LEGAL MALPRACTICE § 32.2 (4th ed. & Supp. 1996).

15. See § 492 (Remedies).

§ 487

1. Beverly Hills Concepts, Inc. v. Schatz and Schatz, Ribicoff and Kotkin, 247 Conn. 48, 57, 717 A.2d 724, 730 (1998).

2. See generally Ray Ryden Anderson & Walter W. Steele, Jr., Fiduciary Duty, Tort and Contract: A Primer on the Legal Malpractice Puzzle, 47 SMU L. REV. 235 (1994). For statute of limitations purposes, the court may be forced to classify a claim as either one for malpractice *or* one for breach of fiduciary duty. Otherwise, it is helpful to recognize fiducial breach as a distinct form of lawyer malpractice.

tort for which damages may be awarded.[3] At the core of the obligation is the fiduciary's duty to act for the benefit of his beneficiary, not for the fiduciary's own interests.[4] As already noted, rules of professional responsibility do not directly create a cause of action for their breach. But the strong ethical component in the code rules may reflect the profession's own assessments of its responsibilities that can at least provide a guide to fiduciary duties,[5] and violation of the rules may be evidence that a duty was breached.[6]

Confidential information. The fiducial obligation has many ramifications and the exact scope of fiduciary duties is the province of books on legal ethics or professional responsibility.[7] However, a few of the important ideas can be sketched. Lawyers must protect confidential client information from disclosure. Disclosure might conceivably be an invasion of privacy, or something analogous to it, with liability apart from any economic harm.[8] But the cases usually focus on economic loss, or at least a potential for economic loss.[9] Lawyers must not use confidential information for their own advantage[10] and must not reveal confidential information to others in a way that adversely affects the client.[11] Indeed, even without disclosure of confidential information, lawyers must not use client information or other advantages of the lawyer-client relationship adversely to their client,[12] for instance, by buying the client's property at a favorable price.[13]

Use of client's opportunities. Sometimes confidential information is important mainly because it represents an economic opportunity and because lawyers must not use, or permit others to use their client's

3. See Restatement § 874.

4. See Restatement (Third) of Trusts § 2, cmt. b (Tentative Draft No. 1, 1996).

5. See John Leubsdorf, Legal Malpractice and Professional Responsibility, 48 RUTGERS L. REV. 101, 117 (1995).

6. Crookham v. Riley, 584 N.W.2d 258, 266 (Iowa 1998).

7. E.g., CHARLES W. WOLFRAM, MODERN LEGAL ETHICS (1986); see also Restatement of the Law Governing Lawyers (various drafts) (Charles W. Wolfram, Reporter).

8. See § 427, supra. But cf. Madden v. Creative Services, Inc., 84 N.Y.2d 738, 622 N.Y.S.2d 478, 646 N.E.2d 780 (1995) (New York, with a limited right of privacy, rejecting a client's claim against investigators who gained access to attorney's office and photographed but did not develop confidential client documents).

9. Potential because some authority suggests that the rules of causation and damages might be loosened when the defendant commits a fiduciary breach. See Milbank, Tweed, Hadley & McCloy v. Boon, 13 F.3d 537, 543 (2d Cir.1994).

10. See Tante v. Herring, 264 Ga. 694, 453 S.E.2d 686 (1994) (confidential information reflecting client's mental condition used by lawyer to seduce client to her detriment, liability for fiduciary breach); Restatement of the Law Governing Lawyers § 112 (Proposed Final Draft No. 1 1996).

11. Perez v. Kirk & Carrigan, 822 S.W.2d 261 (Tex.App.1991) (revealing client statement to prosecuting attorney, summary judgment for lawyer was error).

12. E.g., Tri–Growth Centre City, Ltd. v. Silldorf, Burdman, Duignan & Eisenberg, 216 Cal.App.3d 1139, 265 Cal.Rptr. 330 (1989) (lawyer allegedly using confidential information to compete with client for purchase of property needed by client); Restatement of the Law Governing Lawyers § 28 (3).

13. See Speckels v. Baldwin, 512 N.W.2d 171 (S.D.1994); cf. Himrich v. Carpenter, 569 N.W.2d 568 (S.D.1997) (the city attorney and another "blatantly ignored their fiduciary duties to City; they should have made a choice between public service and private gain. By choosing both, they acted for self-profit, rather than for the benefit of their client").

economic opportunities.[14] Purchase of property that is the subject matter of the lawyer's representation comes under similar rules. The lawyer who purchases the property from the client is presumptively in breach of his duty and the transaction may be void so that the lawyer is forced to disgorge the profits he made to the client.[15] Likewise, lawyers are at risk if they enter a business venture with clients unless the transaction and its terms are fair to the client and the lawyer fulfills strict disclosure requirements.[16] Even gifts from clients are highly suspect.[17]

Conflicts of interest. One fundamental principle that lies behind some of the rules mentioned above is that lawyers must maintain their ability to devote their best efforts to the client. The lawyer must, therefore, have no interests that are adverse to the client's and that would interfere materially with full and competent representation. In addition, the lawyer may not represent a client whose interests are directly in conflict with those of another client or whose representation would be materially limited by the lawyer's responsibilities to that other client.[18] In an Iowa case,[19] the lawyer represented two minority shareholders, each of whom had claims against the corporation. In settlement negotiations a jury could find that the lawyer advised Client A not to accept the offered settlement. When the Client A rejected the proffered settlement, Client B's settlement was lost, too. Client B had a malpractice claim based upon the attorney's conflict of interest and was able to recover the value of the lost settlement. Former client conflicts re treated more leniently, but even these may raise a problem if the interests are related and materially adverse.[20]

Consent to conflicts. But in many instances clients can consent to the conflict if they are fully informed.[21] Such a consent and the joint representation that follows it are often desirable, for example, in the case of business partners setting up business, two shareholders against a corporation, or marital partners jointly planning their estates. But in such cases, the lawyer may not then represent one against the other.[22]

14. E.g., Tri–Growth Centre City, Ltd. v. Silldorf, Burdman, Duignan & Eisenberg, supra n.12 (lawyer purchasing property he knew client wanted); Milbank, Tweed, Hadley & McCloy v. Boon, supra n.9 (representing competitor of former client seeking to consummate the same transaction in which client was interested).

15. See Hamilton v. Allen, 86 Neb. 401, 125 N.W. 610 (1910) (accounting for profits made when lawyers purchased property concerned in their representation and resold for great profit).

16. See ABA Model Rules of Professional Conduct 1.8. See also Ronald E. Mallen & Jeffrey M. Smith, Legal Malpractice § 14.23 (4th ed. & Supp. 1996); Restatement of the Law Governing Lawyers § 207 (Proposed final Draft No. 1, 1996).

17. Restatement of the Law Governing Lawyers § 208 (Proposed Final Draft No. 1, 1996).

18. Crookham v. Riley, 584 N.W.2d 258 (Iowa 1998); Klemme v. Best, 941 S.W.2d 493 (Mo.1997).

19. Crookham v. Riley, supra n.18.

20. See Restatement of Law Governing Lawyers § 201 (Proposed Final Draft No. 1, 1996) for a general statement of the prohibition and the types of conflict.

21. See Restatement of Law Governing Lawyers § 202 (Proposed Final Draft No. 1, 1996).

22. See Restatement of Law Governing Lawyers § 202, Ill. 1 (Proposed Final Draft No. 1, 1996).

Serious conflicts can arise in such cases. In a New Jersey case,[23] a husband and wife wished to leave their estates to each other, but the wife was unaware that the husband had an illegitimate child who might ultimately take all her assets if she died first. When the firm discovered this fact, the husband insisted upon his right of confidentiality but the firm emphasized the wife's right to be informed and the court, in an adversary proceeding between the firm and the husband, held that the firm could make the disclosure. Sometimes the problem is resolved if the lawyer clearly understands and fully communicates to others the identity of his client. Interests of shareholders and a small corporation, heirs and the personal representative, an insured and her liability insurer, the agent and the principal may initially be aligned, but if conflicts arise, the lawyer who attempts to represent both may find himself liable for violation of fiduciary duty.

Client's information rights. The law of informed consent familiar in medical cases has not been so developed in lawyer malpractice cases, but the principle is clear that lawyers must properly consult with and inform the client of material facts and issues that require client action or decision.[24] Lawyers must ordinarily explain the nature of the transaction they structure for their clients and its attendant risks to the client's interests.[25] In *Moores v. Greenberg*,[26] the court held that lawyers must keep their clients "seasonably apprised of relevant developments, including opportunities for settlement." The client's authorization, agreement, or expectation, however, presumably dictates the scope of the information required.

Basis of liability and defenses. Courts and lawyers have not always thought of fiduciary breach as a malpractice tort and consequently some of the standard questions for tort law have not been firmly answered in fiduciary cases. The Restatement of the Law Governing Lawyers refers to negligent or intentional breach of fiduciary duty,[27] but it is not clear that either negligence or intent has always been proved or required as a basis of liability.[28] It is quite possible to think that some fiduciary duties are strict and that liability will follow whether or not the lawyer was at fault in breaching them.[29] In this view, fiduciary duties might be viewed

23. A v. B, 158 N.J. 51, 726 A.2d 924 (1999).

24. See Restatement of the Law Governing Lawyers § 31 (Proposed final Draft No. 1 1996). The client has the right to decide whether to accept a settlement, or, in a criminal case, whether to enter a given plea, waive a jury trial, or testify is the client's. See ABA Model Rules of Professional Conduct 1.2(a).

25. Conklin v. Hannoch Weisman, 145 N.J. 395, 678 A.2d 1060 (1996) (lawyer retained by seller of land with a low "risk quotient" was under a duty to explain effect of subordination agreement that left seller with no reliable security for unpaid balance of $9 million).

26. Moores v. Greenberg, 834 F.2d 1105 (1st Cir.1987); cf. Krahn v. Kinney, 43 Ohio St.3d 103, 538 N.E.2d 1058 (1989) (failure to communicate prosecutor's offer to dismiss criminal charge in exchange for testimony against another defendant).

27. See Restatement of Law Governing Lawyers § 76A and cmt. d (Tentative Draft No. 8, 1997).

28. See Klemme v. Best, 941 S.W.2d 493, 496 (Mo.1997) ("Proof of an attorney's intent is not required to establish breach of fiduciary duty or constructive fraud").

29. See John Leubsdorf, Legal Malpractice and Professional Responsibility, 48 Rutgers L. Rev. 101, 113 (1995) (noting this possibility).

as specific rules of law to be distinguished from the more general "reasonable care" duties. The specific duty would be defined to the jury in instructions. This would also mean that expert testimony would not be required to establish the duty itself (as distinct from its breach).[30] Similarly, in breach of fiduciary duty cases, courts might hold that damages are to be presumed or that causation might be interpreted liberally in favor of the client,[31] and that the client's comparative fault might not reduced her damages. Most of this seems presently uncertain. When the lawyer profits from his own breach of fiduciary duty, however, traditional concepts of restitution would permit recovery of the lawyer's gains independent of fault, since the basis of liability in that case is unjust enrichment rather than fault.[32]

§ 488. Liability to Nonclients

Privity rule. At one time courts said that lawyers owed no duty to those who were not clients. That is, they asserted a privity requirement to bar a nonclient's claim to reap the benefits of the lawyer-client contract. The convenient model for discussion is the case of the lawyer who negligently drafts his client's will so that it is invalid or fails to pass the client's estate in accord with the client's wishes. The intended beneficiary in such a case is the nonclient plaintiff suing the lawyer-draftsman. Some courts still retain the privity rule or some slightly liberalized version of it.[1] Maryland, for example, permits nonclients to recover only if they fit a narrow definition of third party beneficiaries, but that definition is so narrow that it does not include beneficiaries of a will that is negligently drafted.[2] The reasons for maintaining the privity rule include the assertion that to allow nonclients a recovery would be to risk divided loyalties of the attorney, that the solemnity of wills must be protected, and that liability would be unlimited.

Rejecting the blanket privity rule. The first reason for the privity rule seems inapplicable in the context of will beneficiaries who have lost a devise, since they are asserting nothing more or less than what the lawyer undertook to provide and what the client herself sought to achieve. So far as solemnity of wills is concerned, the attack is not upon the will but upon the lawyer's negligence.[3] Finally, the risk of unlimited

30. See Tante v. Herring, 264 Ga. 694, 453 S.E.2d 686 (1994) (expert affidavit not required for breach of fiduciary duty claim).

31. Milbank, Tweed, Hadley & McCloy v. Boon, 13 F.3d 537, 543 (2d Cir.1994).

32. See generally 1 Dan B. Dobbs, Law of Remedies § 4.1 (1) (2d ed. 1993).

§ 488

1. Texas retains the privity rule, see Barcelo v. Elliott, 923 S.W.2d 575 (Tex. 1996), but if the lawyer's negligence takes the form of a representation to the nonclient, he may be held liable on the ground that liability for a professional misrepresentation is not the same as liability for "malpractice." See McCamish, Martin, Brown & Loeffler v. F.E. Appling Interests, 991 S.W.2d 787 (Tex.1999). Arkansas, controlled by a lawyer immunity statute, adheres to the privity rule but permits a breach of contract action by the personal representative. See McDonald v. Pettus, 337 Ark. 265, 988 S.W.2d 9 (1999).

2. Noble v. Bruce, 349 Md. 730, 709 A.2d 1264 (1998).

3. When the plaintiff's proof would contradict the face of the will, courts might require clear and convincing evidence, see Restatement of the Law Governing Lawyers

liability seems well within the capacity of courts to handle under traditional concepts of duty, causation, and proximate cause. Consequently, most courts today reject the blanket privity rule.[4] Even with the blanket rule abolished, however, the lawyer's professional duty does not extend to all nonclients; but it extends to those the lawyer was retained to benefit, such as the beneficiary of the will, and also to those who are involved in a transaction with the client and who rely upon the lawyer's work after the lawyer has invited them to do so.[5]

Tort and contract. Many cases rejecting the privity rule are understandable on the simple and straightforward ground that the non-client is an intended third-party beneficiary and that the lawyer necessarily knows it. Although the third party beneficiary terminology is the terminology of contract, the essential point holds whether the plaintiff sues on a contract or on a tort theory, since the tort duty grows out of the same contractual relationship.[6] Elimination of the privity rule in such cases is also understandable in terms of basic policy, for to adhere to the privity rule in the wills setting is to allow the lawyer's negligence to work adversely to the client's instructions, defeating the client's wishes and at the same time exculpating the negligent lawyer. Consequently, when the court or jury cannot conceive of the claim as a third party beneficiary contract claim, the court may still recognize a tort duty to the would-be beneficiary.[7]

Duty to adversaries and those with conflicting interests. The privity rule might have been an overstatement of an enduring policy. The lawyer owes no duty of care to his client's adversary. That much is essential to the adversary system and required to prevent conflicts of

§ 73, Ill. 3, or even exclude recovery where extrinsic evidence is required to contradict the will. See Holsapple v. McGrath, 575 N.W.2d 518 (Iowa 1998). But the privity rule would be a blunt instrument to accomplish such a purpose, since it covers cases in which the will shows on its face that the plaintiff was the intended beneficiary but fails because of negligent draftsmanship or because the lawyer arranged improper execution.

4. E.g., Lucas v. Hamm, 56 Cal.2d 583, 364 P.2d 685, 15 Cal.Rptr. 821 (1961) (but finding no negligence on the facts); Stowe v. Smith, 184 Conn. 194, 441 A.2d 81 (1981); Hale v. Groce, 304 Or. 281, 744 P.2d 1289 (1987); Restatement of the Law Governing Lawyers § 73 (2), (3) & (4) (Tentative Draft No. 8, 1997).

5. See Restatement of the Law Governing Lawyers § 73 (2) (Tentative Draft No. 8 1997). Greycas, Inc. v. Proud, 826 F.2d 1560 (7th Cir.1987) illustrates the invited category. The lawyer there, to facilitate loan to client, represented to lender that proffered collateral was not subject to other liens. In fact, the lawyer had not checked the records. The collateral was already subject to other liens, the borrower-client defaulted on the loan, and the lender lost money because it had no effective collateral. The lawyer was held liable for his misrepresentation and subjected to a judgment in excess of $800,000. Texas obtains the same result by saying that negligent misrepresentation by a lawyer is not "malpractice" and does not require privity. See McCamish, Martin, Brown & Loeffler v. F.E. Appling Interests, 991 S.W.2d 787 (Tex.1999).

6. See Mieras v. DeBona, 452 Mich. 278, 299, 550 N.W.2d 202, 211 (1996) (Opinion of Boyle, J.); Hale v. Groce, 304 Or. 281, 744 P.2d 1289 (1987).

7. E.g., Pizel v. Zuspann, 247 Kan. 54, 795 P.2d 42, 10 A.L.R.5th 1098 (1990). The existence of a tort duty to third persons may require a consideration of a number of factors that are also often considered when the duty issue arises in other settings. These include the extent to which the transaction was intended to affect the plaintiffs, foreseeability of harm to the plaintiffs and other similar features. See § 229.

interest. Likewise, the lawyer must owe no duty of care even to friendly third persons where efforts to comply with such a duty would impair the lawyer's obligation to his client.[8]

Non-malpractice liabilities to nonclients. The liability of attorneys to nonclients so far discussed has turned on malpractice—that is, on violation of a duty owed to the client that has caused harm to nonclients as well. In some cases, however, attorneys violate no duty to the client but violate a duty owed directly to the nonclient. That is surely the case if the attorney negligently drives his car on the way to the courthouse and runs down a nonclient in the process. It is also the case when the attorney pursues the client's claim in a way that is forbidden by law. The attorney may become personally liable, for example, if he wrongfully files a lis pendens, in effect tying up the adversary's property without meeting the statutory rules.[9] Equally, he may become liable to his client's adversary if he instigates an action against the adversary in bad faith and without probable cause.[10] Such liability is based upon the rules of malicious prosecution (never upon mere negligence).[11] Under those rules, the attorney is protected from the adversary's suit if the attorney had probable cause to sue, given the facts at hand, or, if he acted in good faith. The malicious prosecution rules (and somewhat similar rules for abuse of process) serve mainly to protect access to the courts without fear of retaliation. In the case of the attorney, they also serve to protect and encourage full and vigorous representation.

§ 489. Defenses: Client Fault

Contributory Negligence/Comparative Fault

Comparative fault a defense. When the malpractice claim is based upon negligence, courts have been quite ready to adopt the defense or partial defense of contributory negligence or comparative fault,[1] although some comparative fault statutes are addressed only to personal injury

8. See Restatement of the Law Governing Lawyers § 73 (Tentative Draft No. 8 1997).

9. Wyatt v. Wehmueller, 163 Ariz. 12, 785 P.2d 581 (Ct. App. 1989), rev'd in part, Wyatt v. Wehmueller, 167 Ariz. 281, 806 P.2d 870 (1991).

10. E.g., Munson v. Linnick, 255 Cal. App.2d 589, 63 Cal.Rptr. 340, 27 A.L.R.3d 1104 (1967); see Bird v. Rothman, 128 Ariz. 599, 627 P.2d 1097 (Ct. App. 1981) (but finding no liability on the facts); see Debra E. Was, Annotation, Liability of Attorney, Acting for Client, for Malicious Prosecution, 46 A.L.R.4th 249 (1987). In malicious prosecution claims, the action must first terminate favorably to the original defendant who is now suing.

11. See Chapter 30. Protection for the attorney may be called an immunity, but it appears that courts simply apply the rules for wrongful litigation, so that "malice" or bad faith, along with a want of probable cause, instigation, and termination are required in malicious prosecution suits, while an improper purpose (something in the nature of extortion) is required in the case of abuse of process.

§ 489

1. Pizel v. Zuspann, 247 Kan. 54, 795 P.2d 42, 10 A.L.R.5th 1098 (1990);Pontiac Sch. Dist. v. Miller, Canfield, Paddock & Stone, 221 Mich.App. 602, 563 N.W.2d 693 (1997); Clark v. Rowe, 428 Mass. 339, 701 N.E.2d 624 (1998); Susan L. Thomas, Annotation, Legal Malpractice: Negligence or Fault of Client as Defense, 10 A.L.R.5th 828 (1993). *Distinguish*: the plaintiff's contributory negligence in the underlying case that might defeat the plaintiff or reduce damages under the case within the case rules.

cases and the like.[2] Relatedly but quite distinctly, courts may sometimes conclude that the plaintiff's conduct is the sole proximate cause of her own harm, in which case recovery is altogether barred.[3] Some thinkers have argued that because lawyers are fiduciaries, the comparative fault defense should not be available in malpractice claims,[4] but only Wyoming seems to have rejected the defense altogether.[5]

Limits on comparative fault defense. With contributory negligence or comparative fault generally accepted as defenses, narrower issues become important. First, the plaintiff's fault is irrelevant unless it relates to the representation and is one of the causes of the plaintiff's harm.[6] Second, as with other cases, the plaintiff's comparative fault may be ignored where the defendant's duty is to protect the plaintiff from her own fault, or put negatively, there will be cases in which the plaintiff has no obligation to protect herself.[7]

A third limitation on the comparative negligence defense recognizes that the client has retained the attorney to protect her. It would seem that the client is not at fault in relying on the attorney's advice, draftsmanship, or strategy unless, tacitly or otherwise, she has accepted a particular responsibility, for example, to review a document.[8] In this respect, individuals might not be expected to read and review complex documents, but a corporate client with his own in-house specialists in the subject matter might.[9] Perhaps the best candidates for a comparative negligence reduction are the clients who fail to provide requested information or to follow the lawyer's instructions.[10] In many of these cases of the plaintiff's contributory negligence may be an awkward way of recognizing that the lawyer was not negligent in the first place.[11] If the client fails to follow the lawyer's good instructions, the lawyer seems not to be at fault; if the lawyer's instructions were bad, the client is not likely to be at fault for failure to follow them.

2. E.g., Ind. Code § 34–6–2–45 ("Fault includes any act or omission that is negligent, willful, wanton, reckless, or intentional toward the person or property of others").

3. E.g., Tushinsky v. Arnold, 195 Cal. App.3d 666, 241 Cal.Rptr. 103 (1987).

4. See Ronald E. Mallen & Jeffrey M. Smith, Legal Malpractice § 20.2 (4th ed. & Supp. 1996).

5. Jackson State Bank v. King, 844 P.2d 1093 (Wyo.1993).

6. McLister v. Epstein & Lawrence, 934 P.2d 844 (Colo.App.1996) (plaintiff's fault in failing to obtain workers' compensation insurance as required by law was irrelevant; it occurred before the representation was established).

7. Pizel v. Zuspann, 247 Kan. 54, 70, 795 P.2d 42, 52, 10 A.L.R.5th 1098 (1990) ("comparative fault principles apply to a legal malpractice action based upon negligence unless as a matter of law the client had no obligation to act on the client's behalf").

8. Cf. Restatement of Law Governing Lawyers § 76, cmt. d (Tentative Draft No. 8, 1997) (client fault to be appraised in light of lawyer's duties, including duties of competence and loyalty).

9. This was seemingly the case in Pontiac Sch. Dist. v. Miller, Canfield, Paddock & Stone, 221 Mich.App. 602, 563 N.W.2d 693 (1997).

10. E.g., Ott v. Smith, 413 So.2d 1129 (Ala.1982).

11. Mallen & Smith, supra n.4 take note of this. The phenomenon is not limited to malpractice cases. See § 209, supra.

Comparative fault in contract and fiduciary claims. Whether comparative fault should apply to fiduciary breach claims or those founded on contract is not so clear.[12] At least if the fiduciary breach is intentional, some courts would reject the comparative negligence reduction because the defense does not apply to intentional torts.[13] And some case authority asserts that the defense has no application to attorney malpractice claims based upon a contract or fiduciary breach analysis.[14] The development of the comparative negligence defense in warranty and other products liability claims, however, is a sufficient warning that the theory of the case may not automatically eliminate the defense. And some courts will insist that the lawyer malpractice claim, though grounded in contract, must be pursued as a negligence claim and subject to negligence rules, so the plaintiff cannot count on avoiding comparative fault defenses by re-labeling the claim.[15]

Guilt in Fact and Pari Delicto

Two defenses involving client fault are quite different from the comparative negligence defense both in their basis and in their effect. First, the pari delicto (sometimes called the unclean hands) defense applies when the client is guilty of highly culpable and illegal conduct and his claim or injury arises in part from that conduct as well as from the lawyer's fault. A lawyer who advises his client to perjure herself is guilty of malpractice; but a client to follows the advice is barred by the pari delicto or unclean hands doctrine.[16] This is not a matter governed by comparative fault rules; it is a complete bar.

The second distinct defense arises when the lawyer's negligent representation of a client charged with a crime results in the client's conviction. When the convicted client sues for malpractice, courts have usually said that, negligent or not, the lawyer is not liable for malpractice if the client was in fact guilty of the crime.[17] Some authority place the burden of proof upon the lawyer, who must show guilt in fact.[18] Most cases on point, however, require the plaintiff to prove her innocence in the first place under a preponderance of the evidence standard.[19] Of

12. One article says flatly without discussion that contributory negligence or comparative fault would not defeat a fiduciary breach claim. Ray Ryden Anderson & Walter W. Steele, Jr., Fiduciary Duty, Tort and Contract: A Primer on the Legal Malpractice Puzzle, 47 SMU L. Rev. 235 (1994). The cases cited deal only with the traditional rule that contributory negligence did not defeat a claim based upon actual fraud or deceit.

13. See Cummings v. Sea Lion Corp., 924 P.2d 1011 (Alaska 1996).

14. Jackson State Bank v. King, 844 P.2d 1093 (Wyo.1993).

15. Barcelo v. Elliott, 923 S.W.2d 575 (Tex.1996).

16. E.g., Blain v. The Doctor's Company, 222 Cal.App.3d 1048, 272 Cal.Rptr. 250 (1990). See Restatement of Law Governing Lawyers § 76, cmt. f (Tentative Draft No. 8, 1997).

17. Bailey v. Tucker, 533 Pa. 237, 621 A.2d 108 (1993); Peeler v. Hughes & Luce, 909 S.W.2d 494 (Tex.1995). The rule has close affinity with the rule in malicious prosecution that the prosecuted plaintiff who is guilty in fact cannot recover even if prosecuted without probable cause. See § 435, supra.

18. Shaw v. State, 861 P.2d 566 (Alaska 1993).

19. Wiley v. County of San Diego, 19 Cal.4th 532,79 Cal.Rptr.2d 672, 966 P.2d 983 (1998); Rowe v. Schreiber, 725 So.2d 1245 (Fla.Dist.Ct.App.1999); Glenn v. Aiken, 409 Mass. 699, 569 N.E.2d 783, 4

courts a number require the convicted client to show that he has been exonerated in a post-conviction proceeding.[20]

§ 490. Immunities

Absolute immunity of prosecutors acting as advocates. The absolute judicial immunity, or at least an analogy to it, is generally extended to public prosecutors acting within the scope of prosecutorial duties as an advocate. This is the common law rule[1] and also the rule in civil rights actions brought under § 1983.[2] The absolute immunity, which protects even the malicious prosecutor, is not much in issue, but its scope or application is. For instance, the absolute immunity protects decisions to prosecute and methods of prosecution, but it does not protect the prosecutor acting in the role of a complaining witness[3] or the role of police officers in acquiring evidence.[4] In such cases, the prosecutor denied the absolute immunity nevertheless receives protection of a qualified immunity, but that immunity is destroyed if the conduct violates clearly established statutory or constitutional rights of which reasonable person would have known. None of this has much relationship to attorney malpractice, because in the typical case the prosecutor is sued by his adversary for malicious prosecution, defamation, or civil rights violation, not by his client for failure to protect the client's interests. However, the immunity has been applied even when the prosecutor's role is to protect a private individual who is at least analogous to a client. For instance, a prosecutor who decides to drop a paternity suit that would have benefitted the plaintiff as mother of a child, has been given an absolute immunity.[5] In the same case, even clerical personnel who gave the mother wrong legal advice are also protected.

Public defenders and court-appointed attorneys. Suits against public defenders and court-appointed defense counsel are true malpractice cases, that is, suits by clients based upon the claim of a breach of duty owed by the lawyer to the client. Although public defenders and court

A.L.R.5th 1060 (1991); Mahoney v. Shaheen, Cappiello, Stein & Gordon, P.A., 727 A.2d 996 (N.H.1999) (civil contempt fines arising from grand jury investigation governed by the rules for criminal conviction).

20. Rowe v. Schreiber, 725 So.2d 1245 (Fla.Dist.Ct.App.1999); Peeler v. Hughes & Luce, 909 S.W.2d 494 (Tex.1995); contra: Krahn v. Kinney, 43 Ohio St.3d 103, 538 N.E.2d 1058 (1989).

§ 490

1. Hirschfeld v. City of New York, 253 A.D.2d 53, 686 N.Y.S.2d 367 (App.Div. 1999); Restatement § 656. Absolute though it is, this immunity has limits; it protects only the prosecutor who is acting as advocate. Defamatory press conferences, false affidavits, and the like may be outside that immunity, just as they would be outside the federal immunity. See Newton v. Etoch, 332 Ark. 325, 965 S.W.2d 96 (1998). Even the prosecutor who acts with a corrupt motive may be acting outside the scope of his duties and lose his privilege. See Koch v. Grimminger, 192 Neb. 706, 223 N.W.2d 833, 79 A.L.R.3d 874 (1974).

2. Imbler v. Pachtman, 424 U.S. 409, 96 S.Ct. 984, 47 L.Ed.2d 128 (1976).

3. Kalina v. Fletcher, 522 U.S. 118, 118 S.Ct. 502, 139 L.Ed.2d 471 (1997).

4. Buckley v. Fitzsimmons, 509 U.S. 259, 113 S.Ct. 2606, 125 L.Ed.2d 209 (1993) (claim that prosecutor conspired to fabricate evidence, no absolute immunity).

5. Gill v. Ripley, 352 Md. 754, 724 A.2d 88 (1999).

appointed attorneys may be paid by a public entity, their client is the individual accused. Indeed, the lawyer owes undivided loyalty to the accused and must act independently of the government. Fear of liability in this situation is not like fear of liability to one's adversary; fear of liability to a client for a bad job is the same fear that a purely private practitioner has and it provides a proper incentive, not an obstacle to good public decision-making. On reasoning of this sort, the Supreme Court held that as a matter of federal law, no absolute immunity attached to lawyers appointed by federal courts to defend those accused of crime.[6] Later, the Court went on to hold that court-appointed counsel also lacked immunity when sued for civil rights violations under § 1983.[7]

When the issue is one of state law, some authority support an immunity on the ground that public defenders or appointed counsel not so much like private practitioners because they cannot reject clients and because, at least with respect to public defenders, they are typically overworked and undersupported.[8] Other state courts have lined up against the absolute immunity.[9] Two sets of rules tend to make the reality more complicated and to provide further protection for public lawyers. First, in some states the public defender may be regarded as a state employee even if he is not entitled to the absolute judicial immunity. As a state employee, he may benefit from whatever immunity or procedural advantage is accorded to state employees by local law.[10] Second, most states provide all criminal-defense attorneys some special advantages by imposing added burdens upon the convicted client who wishes to sue for malpractice.[11]

§ 491. Statute of Limitations

Contract and tort: the occurrence rule. Decisions on the statute of limitations in lawyer malpractice claims are quite diverse if not actually chaotic.[1] Since malpractice arises out of a consensual relationship, the claim has some connection to contract and that connection may affect the statute of limitations defense in two ways. First, if the plaintiff is permitted to sue on a contract rather than negligence theory, the contract statute of limitations may apply as it does in other contract cases.[2] Even when the claim is asserted in tort for negligence, the old

6. Ferri v. Ackerman, 444 U.S. 193, 100 S.Ct. 402, 62 L.Ed.2d 355 (1979).

7. Tower v. Glover, 467 U.S. 914, 104 S.Ct. 2820, 81 L.Ed.2d 758 (1984).

8. Dziubak v. Mott, 503 N.W.2d 771 (Minn.1993). Some public defender or indigent defense statutes support this view. E.g., Tenn. Code Ann. § 8–14–209. See Coyazo v. State, 120 N.M. 47, 897 P.2d 234 (Ct.App.1995).

9. Spring v. Constantino, 168 Conn. 563, 362 A.2d 871 (1975); Donigan v. Finn, 95 Mich.App. 28, 290 N.W.2d 80 (1980).

10. E.g., Wright v. Elston, 701 N.E.2d 1227 (Ind.Ct.App.1998) (public defender entitled to special notice of claim provisions of Tort Claims Act); Bradshaw v. Joseph, 164 Vt. 154, 666 A.2d 1175 (Vt. 1995) (complete immunity).

11. § 489, supra.

§ 491

1. See Francis M. Dougherty, Annotation, When Statute of Limitations Begins to Run upon Action Against Attorney for Malpractice, 32 A.L.R.4th 260 (1981).

2. Zupan v. Berman, 142 Ill.App.3d 396, 491 N.E.2d 1349, 96 Ill.Dec. 889 (App. Ct. 1986).

connection with contract nevertheless led courts to say that the plaintiff could recover nominal damages when the contract was breached by the lawyer's negligent act. That in turn meant that the cause of action would accrue upon breach, not later when damages were inflicted.[3] The occurrence rule can foreclose the plaintiff's claim before harm is done or discovered. In spite of its problems, some contemporary authority has refused to budge from the rule.[4]

The time of harm rule. The conventional negligence case would start the statute at the moment when the defendant's negligence has actually caused damages, whether or not the plaintiff was aware of the harm at the time. Some courts apply this rule in lawyer malpractice cases,[5] especially but not only in cases of drafting errors in the preparation of a will that can cause injury only after the putative testator dies.[6] Even when the time of harm is not itself the ultimate governing rule, the time of harm may be a significant component in some other rule. Time of the harm remains important even under the discovery rule because the plaintiff cannot discover a cause of action that has not accrued.[7]

The discovery rule. In recent years especially, a number of states have adopted some form of the discovery rule for lawyer malpractice cases. This usually postpones the statute's running until the plaintiff-client discovered or could reasonably have discovered both the lawyer's conduct that is negligent and the injury.[8] However, Alaska adopted a version that starts the statute when the plaintiff discovers *either* the lawyer's negligence *or* the injury.[9] One reason for the rule lies in the lawyer's fiduciary obligation to disclose his malpractice.[10] Statutes may adopt the discovery rule in some instances of malpractice but use the occurrence rule in others.[11]

The continuous representation rule. An increasing number of decisions recognize termination of the relationship or representation or some similar time as an appropriate time for starting the statute,[12] unless the

3. See 1 Calvin Corman, Limitation of Actions § 7.4.5 (1991); 2 Ronald Mallen & Jeffrey Smith, Legal Malpractice 21.10 (4th ed. 1996).

4. Cf. Keegan v. First Bank of Sioux Falls, 519 N.W.2d 607 (S.D.1994) (rejecting discovery rule as a substitute but recognizing the continuing representation rule).

5. Tingley v. Harrison, 125 Idaho 86, 867 P.2d 960 (1994); Michels v. Sklavos, 869 S.W.2d 728 (Ky.1994) (in the litigation malpractice, case within the case setting, the plaintiff-client's claim accrues when the first case is terminated, not when the lawyer commits the earlier act of negligence); Uhler v. Doak, 268 Mont. 191, 885 P.2d 1297 (1994).

6. Cf. Pizel v. Zuspann, 247 Kan. 54, 795 P.2d 42, 10 A.L.R.5th 1098 (1990) (trust instrument); 2 Ronald Mallen & Jeffrey Smith, Legal Malpractice 18.11 (1989).

7. See Grunwald v. Bronkesh, 131 N.J. 483, 621 A.2d 459 (1993).

8. Grunwald v. Bronkesh, 131 N.J. 483, 621 A.2d 459 (1993); cf. Murphy v. Smith, 411 Mass. 133, 579 N.E.2d 165 (1991) ("coalescence of discovery and appreciable harm").

9. Beesley v. Van Doren, 873 P.2d 1280 (Alaska 1994).

10. John Leubsdorf, Legal Malpractice and Professional Responsibility, 48 Rutgers L. Rev. 101, 146 (1995).

11. See Nevin v. Union Trust Co., 726 A.2d 694 (Me.1999) (statutory discovery rule for will drafting did not apply to the facts, plaintiff was time-barred under the occurrence rule).

12. O'Neill v. Tichy, 19 Cal.App.4th 114, 25 Cal.Rptr.2d 162 (1993); Murphy v. Smith, 411 Mass. 133, 579 N.E.2d 165

plaintiff actually sues earlier.[13] Termination of the relationship may represent an important starting time for the statute of limitations in litigation malpractice cases for several different reasons, not at all alike. One reason is that the termination may be a good index to the the client's discovery or probable discovery of the elements of a claim against her lawyer.[14] Another is that the lawyer's negligence may be remediable or at least that the damages he inflicts can be minimized if he takes steps to reduce the harm after his initial act of negligence. In that case, it may be that he is guilty of continuing negligence throughout the representation and possibly even afterwards, so that it would be appropriate to postpone the statute's running at least until the lawyer-client relationship terminates.[15]

Underlying action completed and appeals exhausted. When the client believes she discovers negligence of a lawyer in an ongoing litigation, perhaps when the client loses at the trial level, she may discharge the attorney and retain another to seek a new trial or to appeal. The client will often find it difficult to sue in such a case, for she must urge on appeal that she was entitled to win on the record, but in the malpractice suit argue that the lawyer was negligent and caused a loss. The two positions are essentially inconsistent, so some courts have postponed the statute's start until appeals are exhausted.[16] Others have rejected that rule.[17] The New Jersey Court suggested that the problem was minimal because the malpractice plaintiff could sue and then move to stay the mal practice suit until the appeal was completed.[18]

Combined rules. No one of these rules is likely to be apt for all circumstances. For example, the discovery rule should not start the

(1991); Bjorgen v. Kinsey, 466 N.W.2d 553 (N.D.1991); cf. Hughes v. Mahaney & Higgins, 821 S.W.2d 154 (Tex.1991) (tolled until appeals are exhausted). The O'Neill court, supra said: "The continuous representation rule was adopted in order to avoid the disruption of an attorney-client relationship by a lawsuit while enabling the attorney to correct or minimize an apparent error, and to prevent an attorney from defeating a malpractice cause of action by continuing to represent the client until the statutory period has expired.... " (all internal quotation marks omitted). Other cases are listed in Francis M. Dougherty, Annotation, When Statute of Limitations Begins to Run upon Action Against Attorney for Malpractice, 32

13. The continuous representation rule can be conceptualized as a tolling rule rather than an accrual rule. This would permit but not require the plaintiff to sue before actual termination of the representation if she discovered the conduct and harm sooner.

14. Cf. Bailey v. Tucker, 533 Pa. 237, 621 A.2d 108 (1993) (in a litigation malpractice context, "The appropriate starting point is the termination of the attorney-client relationship, since at that point the aggrieved defendant is aware of the injury (i.e., the conviction), and is on clear notice to investigate any alternate cause of that harm which he believes to exist").

15. In Hargett v. Holland, 337 N.C. 651, 447 S.E.2d 784 (1994), the court thought that, on the facts, no continuing duty to review a will, and in the absence of a continuing relationship between lawyer and client, the lawyer's last act under a statute of repose occurred when he drafted the will. If the lawyer had discovered an error in the draft, however, one might speculate that a difference would be recognized and a continuing duty imposed.

16. Hughes v. Mahaney & Higgins, 821 S.W.2d 154 (Tex.1991).

17. See Wettanen v. Cowper, 749 P.2d 362 (Alaska 1988) (date of unfavorable judgment against the malpractice plaintiff in the antecedent litigation, once the plaintiff had discovered his claim).

18. Grunwald v. Bronkesh, 131 N.J. 483, 621 A.2d 459 (1993).

statute running and force a suit before actual harm has occurred.[19] Unless controlled by statute, courts are free to apply the combination of rules that makes sense on the facts. The California statute[20] represents a carefully considered scheme and resolves many of the issues. First, actual fraud cases aside, the statute provides a discovery and repose system. The plaintiff has one year to sue after she discovers or should have discovered "the facts constituting the wrongful act or omission," but not longer than four years from the date of the wrongful act. Second, the statute provides for tolling, without respect to the four year limit. The statute is tolled until actual injury occurs, and during continued representation or wilful concealment by the attorney. It is also tolled for legal or physical disabilities. A separate provision covers documents like wills that will have an effective date depending upon a future event. For these, the statute begins to run upon the happening of the event. This unusually careful statute may provide appropriate guidelines where the statute of a particular state does not compel a different result.

§ 492. Remedies

Compensatory Damages Generally

Principle and limits. Punitive damages aside, the general principle of damages measurement is to provide compensation. The plaintiff is entitled to recover only damages that are reasonably proven and that are proximately caused by the defendant's breach of duty. The measurement of damages is subject to some practical constraints, too. They must be adjusted to reflect any applicable comparative fault, interest, or reduction of present value. Subject to such limitations and adjustments, the plaintiff is entitled to recover a sum that will put her in the financial position she would have been in but for the malpractice.

Three damages layers. Depending upon facts and upon the evidence, the plaintiff can potentially claim three layers of damages: (1) The loss incurred or gain prevented as a result of the defendant's malpractice. (2) Consequential damages, which is to say collateral losses that would have been no part of the recovery in any underlying litigation, potentially including items like loss of credit. (3) Damages based upon costs in the malpractice suit itself, such as fees incurred in pursuing the malpractice claim.

First layer damages. In the first category, many examples are straightforward in principle even if proof is sometimes difficult. The attorney negligently causes the client to lose his property; the client is entitled to recover the value of the property lost.[1] The attorney negli-

19. The actual harm test does not always reveal a bright line, however. See Jordache Enterprises, Inc. v. Brobeck, Phleger & Harrison, 18 Cal.4th 739, 76 Cal.Rptr.2d 749, 958 P.2d 1062 (1998) (if attorneys failed to client assert a timely claim for the client's insurance benefits, client suffered actual harm when attorney's omission occurred, not later when the client settled the insurance claim).

20. Cal. Code Civ. Proc. § 340.6.

§ 492

1. Rafferty v. Scurry, 117 Ohio App.3d 240, 690 N.E.2d 104 (1997).

gently causes a trust in favor of the beneficiary to fail; the beneficiary recovers what she would have taken if the trust had been properly handled.[2] The attorney negligently recommends that the client accept an inadequate settlement on dissolution of her marriage; he is liable to the client for the settlement or recovery that she could have recovered had their advice been appropriate.[3]

Second layer or consequential damages. One example of recoverable consequential damages occurs when the malpractice requires the plaintiff to carry on litigation with others. If the attorney's bad advice or negligent drafting results in a criminal prosecution or civil suit against his client, the client's costs of that collateral litigation are recoverable items of consequential damage.[4] All the reasonable costs of such litigation, including attorneys fees incurred there, are recoverable against the malpracticing defendant.[5]

In keeping with the general attitude toward economic torts, some courts have subjected emotional harm damages to special limitations or have rejected them outright, except under the case-within-a-case rules. For instance, Minnesota has said that emotional harm damages could be recovered in a lawyer malpractice case only if the lawyer directly caused the harm by wilful, wanton, or malicious conduct[6] and a number of other courts have place similar restrictions on the recovery.[7] This result is perhaps more understandable when the malpractice implicates no dignitary interests of the client.[8] But emotional harm damages seem appropriate without respect to physical harm if the defendant's malpractice is the kind that runs the risk of substantial emotional distress, and courts have allowed emotional harm damages in some such cases.[9] The lawyer who

2. As in Pizel v. Zuspann, 247 Kan. 54, 795 P.2d 42, 10 A.L.R.5th 1098 (1990) (subject to comparative fault reduction).

3. E.g., Grayson v. Wofsey, Rosen, Kweskin and Kuriansky, 231 Conn. 168, 646 A.2d 195 (1994) ($1,500,000 recovery).

4. Dessel v. Donohue, 431 N.W.2d 359 (Iowa 1988) (attorney with conflict of interest drafted hold-harmless clause in contract between plaintiff and others, liable for the cost of defending suit based substantially on that clause); Ramp v. St. Paul Fire & Marine Ins. Co., 263 La. 774, 269 So.2d 239, 55 A.L.R. 3d 967 (1972) (client retained new attorneys to reclaim share of estate lost through first lawyer's negligence); First Nat. Bank of Clovis v. Diane, Inc., 102 N.M. 548, 698 P.2d 5 (Ct.App.1985).

5. See Restatement (Second) of Torts, § 914 (2) (1979) for the general principle. See generally 1 Dan B. Dobbs, Law of Remedies § 3.10 (2d ed. 1993).

6. Lickteig v. Alderson, Ondov, Leonard & Sween, 556 N.W.2d 557 (Minn.1996).

7. See Quezada v. Hart, 67 Cal.App.3d 754, 136 Cal.Rptr. 815 (1977) (absent intentional wrong or physical impact, no liability for emotional distress); McClain v. Faraone, 369 A.2d 1090 (Del.Super.1977) (client lost residential property due to lawyer's failure to discover lien in title search, no emotional distress recovery absent physical injury or "direct conscious action" in displacing person from his home); Hamilton v. Powell, Goldstein, Frazer & Murphy, 167 Ga.App. 411, 306 S.E.2d 340 (1983), aff'd, 252 Ga. 149, 311 S.E.2d 818 (1984) (emotional distress claim against lawyers whose advice allegedly led to grand jury investigation, plaintiff must show either physical injury or wanton or intentional misconduct).

8. As in Cornell v. Wunschel, 408 N.W.2d 369 (Iowa 1987).

9. Snyder v. Baumecker, 708 F.Supp. 1451 (D.N.J.1989) (incarcerated client became depressed and committed suicide; no liability for the suicide, but liability for emotional distress); Salley v. Childs, 541 A.2d 1297 (Me.1988); Gillespie v. Klun, 406 N.W.2d 547 (Minn.App.1987); see Kirtland and Packard v. Superior Court, 59 Cal. App.3d 140, 131 Cal.Rptr. 418, 421 (1976).

negligently allows an entirely sane client to be dispatched to a mental hospital would be an obvious example.[10] If malpractice runs the risk of stigmatizing the client or destroying her reputation, emotional distress damages seem entirely appropriate.[11]

Third layer damages: costs of the malpractice litigation. Under the basic American rule, neither party to a litigation is liable to the other for attorney fees incurred in that litigation,[12] although as noted above, costs of collateral litigation is another matter. This rule governs malpractice litigation, except for the potential peculiarity resulting from case-within-the-case proof.

Case within the Case Suit

Elements recoverable. When the lawyer's malpractice allegedly deprived the plaintiff of an appropriate litigation outcome, as where the lawyer fails to file a claim within the statute of limitations period, or negotiates or counsels an inadequate settlement, the malpractice plaintiff must normally prove what she would have recovered had the case been tried and tried properly, or if she was a defendant in the underlying case, what losses she would have avoided by proper representation.[13] This rule impacts damages. For example, if the client would have recovered a fund of money or a share in property, he is entitled to recover its value against the attorney.[14] If the plaintiff would have recovered lost wages[15] and medical expenses,[16] pain and suffering[17] or emotional distress[18] or lost consortium[19] damages, those items of damage are recoverable against the malpracticing lawyer. If prejudgment interest or attorney fees would have been available in the first suit, those items are also recoverable against the lawyer whose fault caused the loss of the

10. Wagenmann v. Adams, 829 F.2d 196 (1st Cir.1987) (a long but fascinating tale of human error, panic, grief and pain). Cf. Lawson v. Nugent, 702 F.Supp. 91 (D.N.J. 1988) (former client alleged attorney permitted guilty plea without inquiring whether there was a basis for it, client suffered "extra" twenty months in prison, emotional distress claim if plaintiff can demonstrate physical harm resulting or "demonstrable psychiatric injury").

11. See Salley v. Childs, 541 A.2d 1297 (Me.1988) (lawyer failed to discover evidence that would exculpate trainer whose license was revoked because a horse was drugged).

12. See 1 Dan B. Dobbs, Law of Remedies § 3.10 (1) (2d ed. 1993).

13. See § 486, supra.

14. Martin v. Northwest Washington Legal Services, 43 Wash. App. 405, 717 P.2d 779 (1986) (divorce, value of husband's pension rights which lawyer failed to claim).

15. E.g., Williams v. Bashman, 457 F.Supp. 322 (E.D.Pa.1978) (loss of wages would have been recovered, but only for part-time work in light of plaintiff's physical ailments).

16. Harris v. Kissling, 80 Or.App. 5, 721 P.2d 838 (1986) (future medical expenses included).

17. Smith v. Pool Offshore Co., 1987 WL 14344 (E.D.La.1987) (not reported in F.Supp.) (pain and suffering, medical expense past and future lost wages, all reduced to reflect plaintiff's contributory negligence).

18. Harris v. Kissling, 80 Or.App. 5, 721 P.2d 838 (1986) (lawyer failed to file suit against hospital which had failed to make routine blood tests for Rh factors, resulting in serious complications for the plaintiff's subsequent pregnancies, emotional distress damages could have been recovered against hospital, therefore recoverable against lawyer).

19. Togstad v. Vesely, Otto, Miller & Keefe, 291 N.W.2d 686 (Minn.1980).

original recovery.[20] Perhaps the same principle applies to punitive damages, so that if such items were recoverable in the first action they would also be recoverable against the attorney, though the attorney was not personally guilty of the kind of malicious behavior that would otherwise warrant a punitive award against him.[21]

Collectibility. The point of all this is that the plaintiff should recover compensation—what she lost—and that point also requires that she recover no more than her loss. For this reason, the plaintiff who claims she would have recovered a judgment (or a high judgment) must ordinarily also establish that it would have been collectible against the adversary in the underlying case.[22] If she cannot establish that, she cannot establish that she has a loss.

Settlement. In the world of what might have happened if the lawyer had not been negligent there is one more important variation: the plaintiff might have settled the case, since after all most cases do settle, or she might have gone to trial. Settlement values vary over the course of a long preparation and negotiation period and verdicts are hard to predict, but if the plaintiff can mount sufficient evidence to provide a basis for estimation, the question is whether the jury should be estimating settlement value or the probable verdict. Perhaps the answer is that it depends upon the evidence. If the plaintiff claims and can offer evidence that she would have gone to trial and received a verdict, then that is the basis for calculating her damages. If, on the other hand, she can show that a settlement was likely in a given amount (or in a given range), then that would be the basis for determining damages.[23]

Attorney fees. If, but for the defendant's malpractice, the plaintiff would have won a collectible verdict and judgment, she would normally have been required to pay her lawyer a fee. If she recovers from the lawyer the amount she would have recovered had the lawyer properly tried the case, she will be more than compensated unless a fee for the lawyer is deducted. For this reason, some courts have deducted a reasonable fee from the malpractice judgment.[24] On the other hand, the lawyer did not earn any fee;[25] far from it, he was guilty of malpractice. In

20. See Glamann v. St. Paul Fire & Marine Ins. Co., 144 Wis.2d 865, 424 N.W.2d 924 (1988).

21. Elliott v. Videan, 164 Ariz. 113, 791 P.2d 639 (Ct. App. 1989).

22. See, e.g., Klump v. Duffus, 71 F.3d 1368 (7th Cir.1995); Thomas v. Bethea, 351 Md. 513, 718 A.2d 1187 (1998).

23. Thomas v. Bethea, 351 Md. 513, 718 A.2d 1187 (1998), appears to support this view. See also Duncan v. Lord, 409 F.Supp. 687 (E.D.Pa.1976) ("amount which plaintiff would have received from a jury or through settlement"); see John H. Bauman, Damages for Legal Malpractice: An Appraisal of the Crumbling Dike and the Threatening Flood, 61 TEMP L. REV. 1127, 1148–1150 (1988).

24. Moores v. Greenberg, 834 F.2d 1105 (1st Cir.1987).

25. Kane, Kane & Kritzer, Inc. v. Altagen, 107 Cal.App.3d 36, 165 Cal.Rptr. 534, 538 (1980) (lawyer "failed to earn" fee and crediting him "rewards his wrongdoing"); Campagnola v. Mulholland, Minion & Roe, 76 N.Y.2d 38, 556 N.Y.S.2d 239, 555 N.E.2d 611 (1990) ("it is especially appropriate to deny credit for a fee where, as here, the defendant attorneys performed absolutely no services in connection with the disputed claim, and thus, even if discharged by plaintiff without cause, would not have been

addition, the plaintiff may have incurred fees to pursue the malpractice claim, so that deduction of the malpracticing lawyer's fee would in effect require the plaintiff to pay fees twice.[26] With such arguments in mind, a number of cases have rejected any reduction.

Punitive Damages

The malpracticing lawyer may be liable for punitive damages in the case-within-the-case scenario on the ground that his negligence cost his client a recovery of such damages from the adversary. Direct punitive liability is a different matter and it ordinarily requires willful, malicious or other serious wrongdoing.[27] The attorney is not liable for punitive damages merely because he is negligent.[28] Bad drafting, inadvertence, or ordinary negligence are insufficient grounds for punitive damages. The more likely kinds of cases for punitive awards include those in which the attorney is guilty of fraud or an unauthorized settlement,[29] or at least a conscious disregard of the client's interests,[30] those in which the attorney breaches a fiducial duty to the client, and those in which the attorney acts adversely to the client[31] or has a conflict of interest.[32]

entitled to any quantum meruit compensation").

26. See Togstad v. Vesely, Otto, Miller & Keefe, 291 N.W.2d 686 (Minn.1980) ("a reduction for attorney fees is unwarranted because of the expense incurred by the plaintiff in bringing an action against the attorney"); Strauss v. Fost, 213 N.J.Super. 239, 517 A.2d 143 (1986); Andrews v. Cain, 62 A.D.2d 612, 406 N.Y.S.2d 168 (App.Div. 1978) ("any fee which plaintiffs may have had to pay the defendant had he successfully prosecuted the suit is canceled out by the attorney's fees plaintiffs have incurred in retaining counsel in the present action").

27. § 3.11 above.

28. E.g., McKinnon v. Tibbetts, 440 A.2d 1028 (Me.1982); Cary v. Fisher, 101 A.D.2d 924, 475 N.Y.S.2d 628 App.Div. 1984).

29. Cf. Rodriguez v. Horton, 95 N.M. 356, 622 P.2d 261 (Ct.App.1980) (misleading as to one settlement, unauthorized as to another, plus excessive fees); Harmening v. Howland, 25 N.D. 38, 141 N.W. 131 (1913) (dismissed claim without authority).

30. Cf. Blegen v. Superior Court, 125 Cal.App.3d 959, 178 Cal.Rptr. 470 (1981) (allegation that attorney failed to file plaintiff's injury claim in time, but even so advised plaintiff not to undergo pain-relieving surgery in order to enhance damages at trial, punitive claim adequately pleaded).

31. See Stinson v. Feminist Women's Health Center, Inc., 416 So.2d 1183 (Fla. App.1982) (evidence supported finding of fee claim in excess of that agreed upon, misrepresentations to client, attorneys tied up recovery for months).

32. Gillespie v. Klun, 406 N.W.2d 547 (Minn.App.1987) (conflict of interest situation).

APPENDIX

RESEARCHING TORT LAW ON WESTLAW®

Analysis

Section 1. Introduction

The Law of Torts provides a strong base for analyzing even the most complex problem involving tort law. Whether your research requires examination of case law, statutes, expert commentary or other materials, West books and Westlaw are excellent sources of information.

To keep you abreast of current developments, Westlaw provides frequently updated databases. With Westlaw, you have unparalleled legal research resources at your fingertips.

Additional Resources

If you have not previously used Westlaw or have questions not covered in this appendix, call the West Group Reference Attorneys at 1–800–REF–ATTY (1–800–733–2889). The West Group Reference Attorneys are

trained, licensed attorneys, available 24 hours a day to assist you with your Westlaw search questions.

Section 2. Westlaw Databases

Each database on Westlaw is assigned an abbreviation called an *identifier*, which you use to access the database. You can find identifiers for all databases in the online Westlaw Directory and in the printed *Westlaw Database Directory*. When you need to know more detailed information about a database, use Scope. Scope contains coverage information, lists of related databases and valuable search tips. To access Scope, click the **Scope** after you access the database.

The following chart lists Westlaw databases that contain information pertaining to tort law. For a complete list of tort law databases, see the online Westlaw Directory or the printed *Westlaw Database Directory*. Because new information is continually being added to Westlaw, you should also check Welcome to Westlaw and the Westlaw Directory for new database information.

Selected Tort Law Databases on Westlaw

Database	Identifier	Coverage
Federal and State Case Law Combined		
Federal & State Case Law	ALLCASES	Begins with 1945
Federal & State Case Law–Before 1945	ALLCASES–OLD	1789–1944
State Case Law		
Multistate Tort Law Cases	MTRT–CS	Varies by state
Individual State Tort Law Cases	XXTRT–CS (where XX is a state's two-letter postal abbreviation)	Varies by state
Multistate Professional Malpractice Cases	MMAL–CS	Varies by state
Individual State Professional Malpractice Cases	XXMAL–CS (where XX is a a state's two-letter postal abbreviation)	Varies by state
Multistate Products Liability–Cases	MPL–CS	Varies by state
Individual State Products Liability Cases	XXPL–CS (where XX is a state's two-letter postal abbreviation)	Varies by state
Federal Case Law		
Federal Case Law	ALLFEDS	Begins with 1945
Federal Case Law–Before 1945	ALLFEDS–OLD	1789–1944
Federal Products Liability–Cases	FPL–CS	Begins with 1789
Federal Products Liability–Supreme Court Cases	FPL–SCT	Begins with 1790
Federal Products Liability–Courts of Appeals Cases	FPL–CTA	Begins with 1891

Federal Products Liability–District Courts Cases	FPL–DCT	Begins with 1789
Statutes and Regulations		
State Statutes–Annotated	ST–ANN–ALL	Varies by state
Individual State Statutes–Annotated	XX–ST–ANN (where XX is a state's two-letter postal abbreviation)	Varies by state
State Administrative Code Multibase	ADC–ALL	Varies by state
Individual State Administrative Code	XX–ADC (where XX is a state's two-letter postal abbreviation)	Varies by state
Code of Federal Regulations	CFR	Current data
United States Code Annotated®	USCA	Current data
Jury Verdicts, Judgments and Settlements		
Combined Jury Verdicts and Settlements	JV–ALL	Varies by source
Association of Trial Lawyers of America ATLA Record	ATLA–JV	Begins with 1984
California Jury Verdicts and Judgments (Trial Digest)	CA–JV	Begins with 1991
Florida Jury Verdict Reporter	FL–JV	Begins with 1987
Jury Verdict and Settlement Summaries	LRP–JV	Begins with 1987
Jury Verdicts Northwest	JVN	Begins with 1988
Verdicts, Settlements & Tactics	VST	Begins with January 1988
Litigation and Current Developments		
All News	ALLNEWS	Varies by source
Andrews AIDS Litigation Reporter	ANAIDSLR	Begins with November 1996
Andrews Asbestos Litigation Reporter	ANASBLR	Begins with January 1996
Andrews Asbestos Property Litigation Reporter	ANAPLR	Begins with November 1996
Andrews Aviation Law Reporter	ANAVIALR	Begins with November 1996
Andrews Breast Implant Litigation Reporter	ANBRIMLR	Begins with November 1996
Andrews Consumer Product Litigation Reporter	ANCPLR	Begins with November 1996
Andrews DES Litigation Reporter	ANDESLR	Begins with November 1996
Andrews Hazardous Waste Litigation Reporter	ANHWLR	Begins with November 1996
Andrews Health Law Litigation Reporter	ANHLLR	Begins with November 1996
Andrews Latex Allergy Litigation Reporter	ANLALR	Begins with July 1997
Andrews Mass Tort Litigation Reporter	ANMTLR	Begins with November 1996
Andrews Medical Devices Litigation Reporter	ANMDLR	Begins with November 1996

Andrews Pharmaceutical Litigation Reporter	ANPHARLR	Begins with November 1996
Andrews Professional Liability Litigation Reporter	ANPLLR	Begins with November 1996
Andrews Repetitive Stress Injury Litigation Reporter	ANRSILR	Begins with November 1996
Andrews Tobacco Industry Litigation Reporter	ANTILR	Begins with November 1996
Andrews Toxic Chemicals Litigation Reporter	ANTCLR	Begins with November 1996
Asbestos MDL 875 Update	ANAMDLU	Begins with November 1996
BNA Product Liability Daily	BNA–PLD	Begins with September 1989
Daubert Citator	DAUBERT	Begins with January 1994
Legal Newspapers	LEGALNP	Varies by publication
Liability Week	LIABWEEK	Begins with January 1992
Mealey's Emerging Drugs and Devices	MLREDD	Begins with January 1996
Mealey's Emerging Toxic Torts	METT	Begins with January 1993
Mealey's Litigation Reports: Asbestos	MLRASB	Begins with January 1993
Mealey's Litigation Reports: Biotechnology	MLRBT	Begins with September 1996
Mealey's Litigation Reports: Breast Implants	MLRBI	Begins with January 1993
Mealey's Litigation Reports: Fen–Phen/Redux	MLRFPR	Begins with November 1997
Mealey's Litigation Reports: Latex	MLRLTX	Begins with May 1997
Mealey's Litigation Reports: Lead	MLRLEAD	Begins with October 1991
Mealey's Litigation Reports: Patents	MLRPAT	Begins with June 1993
Mealey's Litigation Reports: Superfund	MLRSF	Begins with January 1993
Mealey's Litigation Reports: Tobacco	MLRTOBAC	Begins with May 1995
Westlaw Topical Highlights–Products Liability	WTH–PL	Current data

Law Reviews, Legal Texts and Periodicals

Texts & Periodicals–All Law Reviews, Texts & Bar Journals	TP–ALL	Varies by publication
Tort Law–Law Reviews, Texts & Bar Journals	TRT–TP	Varies by publication
Restatement of the Law–Torts	REST–TORT	Current data
Litigation–Law Reviews, Texts & Bar Journals	LTG–TP	Varies by publication
Products Liability–Law Reviews, Texts & Bar Journals	PL–TP	Varies by publication
Professional Malpractice–Law Reviews, Texts & Bar Journals	MAL–TP	Varies by publication

Punitive Damages: A State-by-State Guide to Law and Practice	PUNITIVE	Current through 1999 pocket part
West Legal Directory®		
West Legal Directory–Personal Injury and Torts	WLD–PI	Current data
West Legal Directory–Products Liability	WLD–PL	Current data
West Legal Directory–Professional Malpractice	WLD–MAL	Current data

Section 3. Retrieving a Document with a Citation: Find and Hypertext Links

3.1 Find

Find is a Westlaw service that allows you to retrieve a document by entering its citation. Find allows you to retrieve documents from anywhere in Westlaw without accessing or changing databases. Find is available for many documents, including case law (state and federal), the *United States Code Annotated*, state statutes, administrative materials, and texts and periodicals.

To use Find, simply access the Find service and type the citation. The following list provides some examples:

To Find This Document	Access Find and Type
Palsgraff v. Long Island R. Co., 248 N.Y. 339, 162 N.E. 99 (1928)	**162 ne 99**
Medtronic, Inc. v. Lohr, 116 S. Ct. 2240 (1996)	**116 sct 2240**
42 U.S.C.A. § 1983	**42 usca 1983**
21 C.F.R. § 312.23	**21 cfr 312.23**
Fla. Stat. Ann. § 768.19	**fl st s 768.19**
42 Pa. Cons. Stat. Ann. § 8301	**pa st ti 42 pa csa 8301**

For a complete list of publications that can be retrieved with Find and their abbreviations, consult the Publications List after accessing Find.

3.2 Hypertext Links

Use hypertext links to move from one location to another on Westlaw. For example, use hypertext links to go directly from the statute, case or law review article you are viewing to a cited statute, case or article; from a headnote to the corresponding text in the opinion; or from an entry in a statutes index database to the full text of the statute.

Section 4. Searching with Natural Language

Overview: With Natural Language, you can retrieve documents by simply describing your issue in plain English. If you are a relatively new Westlaw user, Natural Language searching can make it easier for you to retrieve cases that are on point. If you are an experienced Westlaw user, Natural Language gives you a valuable alternative search method.

When you enter a Natural Language description, Westlaw automatically identifies legal phrases, removes common words and generates variations

of terms in your description. Westlaw then searches for the concepts in your description. Concepts may include significant terms, phrases, legal citations or topic and key numbers. Westlaw retrieves the 20 documents that most closely match your description, beginning with the document most likely to match.

4.1 Natural Language Search

Access a database, such as Multistate Tort Law Cases (MTRT–CS). In the text box, type a Natural Language description such as the following:

does a spectator assume the risk of injury at a sporting event

4.2 Next Command

Westlaw displays the 20 documents that most closely match your description, beginning with the document most likely to match. If you want to view additional documents, use the Next command.

4.3 Natural Language Browse Commands

Best Mode: To display the best portion (the portion that most closely matches your description) of each document in your search result, click the **Best Selection** arrow at the bottom of the window or page.

Standard Browsing Commands: You can also browse your Natural Language search result using standard Westlaw browsing commands, such as citations list, Locate, page mode and term mode. When you browse your Natural Language search result in term mode, the five portions of each document that are most likely to match your description are displayed.

Section 5. Searching with Terms and Connectors

Overview: With Terms and Connectors searching, you enter a query, which consists of key terms from your issue and connectors specifying the relationship between these terms.

Terms and Connectors searching is useful when you want to retrieve a document for which you know specific details, such as the title or the fact situation. Terms and Connectors searching is also useful when you want to retrieve documents relating to a specific issue.

5.1 Terms

Plurals and Possessives: Plurals are automatically retrieved when you enter the singular form of a term. This is true for both regular and irregular plurals (e.g., **child** retrieves *children*). If you enter the plural form of a term, you will not retrieve the singular form.

If you enter the nonpossessive form of a term, Westlaw automatically retrieves the possessive form as well. However, if you enter the possessive form, only the possessive form is retrieved.

Automatic Equivalencies: Some terms have alternative forms or equivalencies; for example, *5* and *five* are equivalent terms. Westlaw

automatically retrieves equivalent terms. The *Westlaw Reference Manual* contains a list of equivalent terms.

Compound Words, Abbreviations and Acronyms: When a compound word is one of your search terms, use a hyphen to retrieve all forms of the word. For example, the term **along-side** retrieves *along-side, alongside* and *along side.*

When using an abbreviation or acronym as a search term, place a period after each of the letters to retrieve any of its forms. For example, the term **l.l.c.** retrieves *llc, l.l.c., l l c* and *l. l. c.* Note: The abbreviation does *not* retrieve *limited liability company*, so remember to add additional alternative terms to your query such as "**limited liability company**".

The Root Expander and the Universal Character: When you use the Terms and Connectors search method, placing the root expander (!) at the end of a root term generates all other terms with that root. For example, adding the ! to the root *negligen* in the query

standard /s negligen!

instructs Westlaw to retrieve such terms as *negligent, negligence* and *negligently.*

The universal character (*) stands for one character and can be inserted in the middle or at the end of a term. For example, the term

withdr*w

will retrieve *withdraw* and *withdrew*. Adding three asterisks to the root *elect*

elect* * *

instructs Westlaw to retrieve all forms of the root with up to three additional characters. Terms such as *elected* or *election* are retrieved by this query. However, terms with more than three letters following the root, such as *electronic,* are not retrieved. Plurals are always retrieved, even if more than three letters follow the root.

Phrase Searching: To search for an exact phrase, place it within quotation marks. For example, to search for references to *res ipsa loquitur*, type "**res ipsa loquitur**". When you are using the Terms and Connectors search method, you should use phrase searching only if you are certain that the terms in the phrase will not appear in any other order.

5.2 Alternative Terms

After selecting the terms for your query, consider which alternative terms are necessary. For example, if you are searching for the term *admissible,* you might also want to search for the term *inadmissible.* You should consider both synonyms and antonyms as alternative terms. You can also use the Westlaw thesaurus to add alternative terms to your query.

5.3 Connectors

After selecting terms and alternative terms for your query, use connectors to specify the relationship that should exist between search terms in your retrieved documents. The connectors are described below:

Use:	To retrieve documents with:	Example:
& (and)	both terms	**trespass! & consent!**
or (space)	either term or both terms	**malpractic! negligen!**
/p	search terms in the same paragraph	**strict! /p explosive**
/s	search terms in the same sentence	**defect! /s design!**
+s	the first search term preceding the second within the same sentence	**burden +s prov! proof**
/n	search terms within "n" terms of each other (where "n" is a number)	**risk /3 assum!**
+n	the first search term preceding the second by "n" terms (where "n" is a number)	**contributor! +3 negligen!**
" "	search terms appearing in the same order as in the quotation marks	**"federal tort claims act"**

Use:	To exclude documents with:	Example:
% (but not)	search terms following the % symbol	**battery % criminal**

5.4 Field Restrictions

Overview: Documents in each Westlaw database consist of several segments, or fields. One field may contain the citation, another the title, another the synopsis and so forth. Not all databases contain the same fields. Also depending on the database, fields with the same name may contain different types of information.

To view a list of fields for a specific database and their contents, see Scope for that database. Note that in some databases not every field is available for every document.

To retrieve only those documents containing your search terms in a specific field, restrict your search to that field. To restrict your search to a specific field, type the field name or abbreviation followed by your search terms enclosed in parentheses. For example, to retrieve a New York case entitled *Morrison v. National Broadcasting Co.,* access the New York Tort Law Cases database (NYTRT–CS) and search for your terms in the title field (ti):

ti(morrison & "national broadcasting")

The fields discussed below are available in Westlaw databases you might use for researching tort law issues.

Digest and Synopsis Fields: The digest (di) and synopsis (sy) fields, added to case law databases by West's attorney-editors, summarize the main points of a case. The synopsis field contains a brief description of a

case. The digest field contains the topic and headnote fields and includes the complete hierarchy of concepts used by West's editors to classify the headnotes to specific West digest topic and key numbers. Restricting your search to the synopsis and digest fields limits your result to cases in which your terms are related to a major issue in the case.

Consider restricting your search to one or both of these fields if

- you are searching for common terms or terms with more than one meaning, and you need to narrow your search; or
- you cannot narrow your search by using a smaller database.

For example, to retrieve state cases that discuss status as a public figure for purposes of defamation actions, access the Multistate Tort Law Cases database (MTRT–CS) and type the following query:

sy,di(defam! /p status /p public private /s figure)

Headnote Field: The headnote field (he) is part of the digest field but does not contain topic numbers, hierarchical classification information or key numbers. The headnote field contains a one-sentence summary for each point of law in a case and any supporting citations given by the author of the opinion. A headnote field restriction is useful when you are searching for specific statutory sections or rule numbers. For example, to retrieve headnotes from state cases that cite 42 U.S.C.A. § 1983, access the Multistate Tort Law Cases database (MTRT–CS) and type the following query:

he(42 +5 1983)

Topic Field: The topic field (to) is also part of the digest field. It contains hierarchical classification information, including the West digest topic names and numbers and the key numbers. You should restrict search terms to the topic field in a case law database if

- a digest field search retrieves too many documents; or
- you want to retrieve cases with digest paragraphs classified under more than one topic.

For example, the topic Torts has the topic number 379. To retrieve state cases that discuss questions of law, as opposed to questions of fact, in the context of torts, access the Multistate Tort Law Cases database (MTRT–CS) and type a query like the following:

to(379) /p question /5 law legal

To retrieve cases classified under more than one topic and key number, search for your terms in the topic field. For example, to retrieve recent cases discussing scope of employment, which may be classified to Automobiles (48A), Employers' Liability (148A), Master and Servant (255), Municipal Corporations (268) or States (360), among other topics, access the Multistate Tort Law Cases database (MTRT–CS) and type a query like the following:

to(scope /5 employment) & da(aft 1998)

For a complete list of West digest topics and their corresponding topic numbers, access the Key Number Service or the Key Number Center.

> *Note*: Slip opinions, cases not reported by West and cases from topical services do not contain the digest, headnote and topic fields.

Prelim and Caption Fields: When searching in a database containing statutes, rules or regulations, restrict your search to the prelim (pr) and caption (ca) fields to retrieve documents in which your terms are important enough to appear in a section name or heading. For example, to retrieve federal regulations regarding lead-based paint, access the Code of Federal Regulations database (CFR) and type the following:

pr,ca(lead! /s paint)

5.5 Date Restrictions

You can use Westlaw to retrieve documents *decided* or *issued* before, after, or on a specified date, as well as within a range of dates. The following sample queries contain date restrictions:

da(1998) & "pedicle screw"

da(aft 1995) & sy,di(duty /5 warn /p open /5 obvious)

da(1/22/1997) & electromagnetic magnetic /5 field /p cancer leukemia

You can also search for documents *added to a database* on or after a specified date, as well as within a range of dates. The following sample queries contain added-date restrictions:

ad(aft 1995) & "repetitive stress" "carp*l tunnel" /p key-board typ!

ad(aft 2-1-1998 & bef 2-17-1998) & minor juvenile /p tobacco cigarette /p fire

Section 6. Searching with Topic and Key Numbers

To retrieve cases that address a specific point of law, use topic and key numbers as your search terms. If you have an on-point case, run a search using the topic and key number from the relevant headnote in an appropriate database to find other cases containing headnotes classified to that topic and key number. For example, to search for cases containing headnotes classified under topic 313A (Products Liability) and key number 91 (Farm implements), access the Multistate Products Liability Cases database (MPL–CS) and enter the following query:

313ak91

For a complete list of West digest topic and key numbers, access the Key Number Service or the Key Number Center.

> *Note*: Slip opinions, cases not reported by West and cases from topical services do not contain West topic and key numbers.

Section 7. Verifying Your Research with Citator Services

Overview: A citator service is a tool that helps you ensure that your cases are good law; helps you retrieve cases, legislation or articles that cite a case, rule or statute; and helps you verify that the spelling and format of your citations are correct.

7.1 KeyCite

KeyCite is the citation research service from West Group.

KeyCite for cases covers case law on Westlaw, including unpublished opinions.

KeyCite for statutes covers the *United States Code Annotated* (USCA®), the *Code of Federal Regulations* (CFR) and statutes from all 50 states.

KeyCite Alert monitors the status of your cases or statutes and automatically sends you updates at the frequency you specify when their KeyCite information changes.

KeyCite provides the following:

- Direct appellate history of a case, including related references, which are opinions involving the same parties and facts but resolving different issues
- Negative indirect history of a case, which consists of cases outside the direct appellate line that may have a negative impact on its precedential value
- The title, parallel citations, court of decision, docket number and filing date of a case
- Citations to cases, administrative decisions and secondary sources on Westlaw that have cited a case
- Complete integration with the West Key Number System® so you can track legal issues discussed in a case
- Links to session laws amending or repealing a statute
- Statutory credits and historical notes
- Citations to pending legislation affecting a federal statute
- Citations to cases, administrative decisions and secondary sources that have cited a statute or federal regulation

7.2 Westlaw As a Citator

For citations not covered by KeyCite, including persuasive secondary authority such as restatements and treatises, use Westlaw as a citator to retrieve cases that cite your authority.

For example, to retrieve state cases citing the law review article "Handguns and Products Liability," 97 Harv. L. Rev. 1912, access the Multistate Products Liability Cases database (MPL–CS) and type a query like the following:

handguns /s 97 +5 1912

Section 8. Researching with Westlaw—Examples

8.1 Retrieving Law Review Articles

Recent law review articles are often a good place to begin researching a legal issue because law review articles serve 1) as an excellent introduction to a new topic or review for a stale one, providing terminology to help you formulate a query; 2) as a finding tool for pertinent primary authority, such as rules, statutes and cases; and 3) in some instances, as persuasive secondary authority.

Suppose you need to gain background information on the liability of business owners for criminal acts of third parties.

Solution

- To retrieve recent law review articles relevant to your issue, access the Tort Law–Law Reviews, Texts & Bar Journals database (TRT–TP). Using the Natural Language search method, enter a description like the following:

  liability of business owner for criminal acts of a third party

- If you have a citation to an article in a specific publication, use Find to retrieve it. For more information on Find, see Section 3.1 of this appendix. For example, to retrieve the article found at 50 Ark. L. Rev. 521, access Find and type

  50 ark l rev 521

- If you know the title of an article but not which journal it appeared in, access the Tort Law–Law Reviews, Texts & Bar Journals database (TRT–TP) and search for key terms using the title field. For example, to retrieve the article "When Sticks and Stones May Break Your Bones: An Overview of Texas Premises Liability Law for Business Owners," type the following Terms and Connectors query:

  ti(stick & stone & break & bone)

8.2 Retrieving Case Law

Suppose you need to retrieve Texas case law dealing with a physician's liability for failure to warn a patient of a drug's side effects.

Solution

- Access the Texas Professional Malpractice Cases database (TXMAL–CS). Type a Natural Language description such as the following:

liability of physician for failure to warn a patient of drug side effects

- When you know the citation for a specific case, use Find to retrieve it. (For more information on Find, see Section 3.1 of this appendix.) For example, to retrieve *Helms v. Gonzalez*, 885 S.W.2d 535 (Tex. App. 1994), access Find and type

885 sw2d 535

- If you find a topic and key number that is on point, run a search using that topic and key number to retrieve additional cases discussing that point of law. For example, to retrieve cases containing headnotes classified under topic 299 (Physicians and Surgeons) and key number 15(8) (Disclosure to patient), type the following query:

299k15(8)

- To retrieve cases written by a particular judge, add a judge field (ju) restriction to your query. For example, to retrieve cases written by Judge Day that contain headnotes classified under topic 299 (Physicians and Surgeons), type the following query:

ju(day) & to(299)

8.3 Retrieving Statutes and Regulations

Suppose you need to retrieve federal statutes and regulations specifically addressing lead as a toxic substance.

Solution

- Access the United States Code Annotated database (USCA). Search for your terms in the prelim and caption fields using the Terms and Connectors search method:

pr,ca(lead! & toxic!)

- When you know the citation for a specific section of a statute or regulation, use Find to retrieve it. For example, to retrieve 40 C.F.R. § 745.87, access Find and type

40 cfr 745.87

- To look at surrounding sections, use the Table of Contents service. Click a hypertext link in the prelim or caption field, or click the **TOC** tab in the left frame. You can also use Documents in Sequence to retrieve the section following § 745.87, even if that subsequent section was not retrieved with your search or Find request.
- When you retrieve a statute on Westlaw, it will contain a message if legislation amending or repealing it is available online. To display this legislation, click the hypertext link in the message.

Because slip copy versions of laws are added to Westlaw before they contain full editorial enhancements, they are not retrieved with Update. To retrieve slip copy versions of laws, access the United States Public Laws database (US–PL) or a state's legislative service database (XX–LEGIS, where XX is the state's two-letter postal abbreviation). Then type **ci(slip)** and descriptive terms, e.g., **ci(slip) & lead**. Slip copy documents are replaced by the editorially enhanced versions within a few working days. Update also does not retrieve legislation that enacts a new statute or covers a topic that will not be incorporated into the statutes. To retrieve this legislation, access US–PL or a legislative service database and enter a query containing terms that describe the new legislation.

8.4 Using KeyCite

Suppose one of the cases you retrieve in your case law research is *American Cyanamid Co. v. Frankson*, 732 S.W.2d 648 (Tex. App. 1987). You want to determine whether this case is good law and to find other cases that have cited this case.

Solution

- Use KeyCite to retrieve direct history and negative indirect history for *American Cyanamid Co. v. Frankson.*
- Use KeyCite to display citing references for *American Cyanamid Co. v. Frankson.*

8.5 Following Recent Developments

As the products liability specialist in your firm, you are expected to keep up with and summarize recent legal developments in this area of the law. How can you do this efficiently?

Solution

One of the easiest ways to stay abreast of recent developments in products liability law is by accessing the Westlaw Topical Highlights–Products Liability database (WTH–PL). The WTH–PL database contains summaries of recent legal developments, including court decisions, legislation and materials released by administrative agencies in the area of products liability law. Some summaries also contain suggested queries that combine the proven power of West's topic and key numbers and West's case headnotes to retrieve additional pertinent cases. When you access WTH–PL you will automatically retrieve a list of documents added to the database in the last two weeks.

Table of Cases

A

B

C

D

E

Foster v. South Carolina Dept. of Highways and Public Transp., 306 S.C. 519, 413 S.E.2d 31 (S.C.1992)—**§ 148, n. 9.**
Fotos v. Firemen's Ins. Co. of Washington, D.C., 533 A.2d 1264 (D.C.1987)—**§ 65, n. 25, 43.**
Fouldes v. Willoughby, 151 Eng.Rep. 1153 (1841)—**§ 59, n. 7; § 65, n. 50.**
Four R Cattle Co. v. Mullins, 253 Neb. 133, 570 N.W.2d 813 (Neb.1997)—**§ 471, n. 9.**
Fouts v. Builders Transport, Inc., 222 Ga. App. 568, 474 S.E.2d 746 (Ga.App. 1996)—**§ 207, n. 5.**
Fowle v. Fowle, 263 N.C. 724, 140 S.E.2d 398 (N.C.1965)—**§ 437, n. 7.**
Fowler v. Key System Transit Lines, 37 Cal.2d 65, 230 P.2d 339 (Cal.1951)—**§ 165, n. 13.**
Fowler v. Printers II, Inc., 89 Md.App. 448, 598 A.2d 794 (Md.App.1991)—**§ 447, n. 28.**
Fowler v. Roberts, 556 So.2d 1 (La.1989)—**§ 272, n. 1.**
Fowler v. Seaton, 61 Cal.2d 681, 39 Cal. Rptr. 881, 394 P.2d 697 (Cal.1964)—**§ 155, n. 22; § 156, n. 10.**
Fox v. City and County of San Francisco, 47 Cal.App.3d 164, 120 Cal.Rptr. 779 (Cal. App. 1 Dist.1975)—**§ 117, n. 1; § 120, n. 10.**
Fox v. Dannenberg, 906 F.2d 1253 (8th Cir.1990)—**§ 157, n. 11.**
Fox v. Smith, 594 So.2d 596 (Miss.1992)—**§ 25, n. 3; § 103, n. 6; § 250, n. 9, 15.**
Fox v. Travis Realty Co., 262 Ill.App.3d 1071, 200 Ill.Dec. 199, 635 N.E.2d 538 (Ill.App. 1 Dist.1994)—**§ 192, n. 7.**
Fox v. Warner-Quinlan Asphalt Co., 204 N.Y. 240, 97 N.E. 497 (N.Y.1912)—**§ 77, n. 12.**
Fraguglia v. Sala, 17 Cal.App.2d 738, 62 P.2d 783 (Cal.App. 1 Dist.1936)—**§ 70, n. 14.**
Frain as Tutrix of Beason v. State Farm Ins. Co., 421 So.2d 1169 (La.App. 2 Cir. 1982)—**§ 330, n. 14.**
Franco v. Bunyard, 261 Ark. 144, 547 S.W.2d 91 (Ark.1977)—**§ 136, n. 1; § 192, n. 15.**
Franconia Associates v. Clark, 250 Va. 444, 463 S.E.2d 670 (Va.1995)—**§ 149, n. 3.**
Franklin v. Collins Chapel Connectional Hosp., 696 S.W.2d 16 (Tenn. Ct. App. 1985)—**§ 155, n. 23.**
Franklin v. Gwinnett County Public Schools, 503 U.S. 60, 112 S.Ct. 1028, 117 L.Ed.2d 208 (1992)—**§ 21, n. 2; § 259, n. 10; § 275, n. 9; § 327, n. 3.**
Franklin v. Hill, 264 Ga. 302, 444 S.E.2d 778 (Ga.1994)—**§ 443, n. 29.**
Franklin v. United States, 992 F.2d 1492 (10th Cir.1993)—**§ 267, n. 12.**
Frank Pisano & Associates v. Taggart, 29 Cal.App.3d 1, 105 Cal.Rptr. 414 (Cal. App. 1 Dist.1972)—**§ 414, n. 8.**
Franz v. Lytle, 997 F.2d 784 (10th Cir. 1993)—**§ 47, n. 4.**
Frazier v. Metropolitan Dade County, 701 So.2d 418 (Fla.App. 3 Dist.1997)—**§ 299, n. 9.**
Frazier By and Through Frazier v. Norton By and Through Norton, 334 N.W.2d 865 (S.D.1983)—**§ 98, n. 23; § 124, n. 6.**
Frederick v. Philadelphia Rapid Transit Co., 337 Pa. 136, 10 A.2d 576 (Pa. 1940)—**§ 232, n. 7, 16.**
Fredericks v. Castora, 241 Pa.Super. 211, 360 A.2d 696 (Pa.Super.1976)—**§ 122, n. 19.**
Fred Howland, Inc. v. Morris, 143 Fla. 189, 196 So. 472 (Fla.1940)—**§ 287, n. 6.**
Freehauf v. School Bd. of Seminole County, 623 So.2d 761 (Fla.App. 5 Dist.1993)—**§ 133, n. 13.**
Freeman v. Davidson, 105 Nev. 13, 768 P.2d 885 (Nev.1989)—**§ 296, n. 5.**
Freeman v. Ernst & Young, 516 N.W.2d 835 (Iowa 1994)—**§ 472, n. 26.**
Freeman v. Martin, 116 Ga.App. 237, 156 S.E.2d 511 (Ga.App.1967)—**§ 119, n. 8.**
Freeman & Mills, Inc. v. Belcher Oil Co., 44 Cal.Rptr.2d 420, 900 P.2d 669 (Cal. 1995)—**§ 453, n. 13.**
Freeport Sulphur Co. v. S/S Hermosa, 526 F.2d 300 (5th Cir.1976)—**§ 379, n. 10.**
Freeway Park Bldg., Inc. v. Western States Wholesale Supply, 22 Utah 2d 266, 451 P.2d 778 (Utah 1969)—**§ 80, n. 8, 15.**
Freeze v. Congleton, 276 N.C. 178, 171 S.E.2d 424 (N.C.1970)—**§ 194, n. 4; § 236, n. 7.**
Freightliner Corp. v. Myrick, 514 U.S. 280, 115 S.Ct. 1483, 131 L.Ed.2d 385 (1995)—**§ 373, n. 24, 26.**
Freihofer v. Hearst Corp., 490 N.Y.S.2d 735, 480 N.E.2d 349 (N.Y.1985)—**§ 425, n. 11; § 427, n. 29.**
French v. Ehrenfeld, 180 A.D.2d 895, 579 N.Y.S.2d 480 (N.Y.A.D. 3 Dept.1992)—**§ 164, n. 13.**
French v. Jadon, Inc., 911 P.2d 20 (Alaska 1996)—**§ 408, n. 12.**
French v. Sunburst Properties, Inc., 521 N.E.2d 1355 (Ind.App. 1 Dist.1988)—**§ 233, n. 7.**
Fresno Traction Co. v. Atchison, T. & S.F. Ry. Co., 175 Cal. 358, 165 P. 1013 (Cal. 1917)—**§ 134, n. 7.**
Frey v. Kouf, 484 N.W.2d 864 (S.D.1992)—**§ 24, n. 1; § 26, n. 1; § 28, n. 7.**
Frey v. Stoneman, 150 Ariz. 106, 722 P.2d 274 (Ariz.1986)—**§ 436, n. 35.**
Frideres v. Schiltz, 540 N.W.2d 261 (Iowa 1995)—**§ 326, n. 9.**
Fridovich v. Fridovich, 598 So.2d 65 (Fla. 1992)—**§ 412, n. 7.**

G

H

I

J

K

L

M

N

O

P

Q

R

S

T

Tranchina v. Arcinas, 78 Cal.App.2d 522, 178 P.2d 65 (Cal.App. 1 Dist.1947)—**§ 438, n. 17.**

Transamerica Ins. Co. v. Royle, 202 Mont. 173, 656 P.2d 820 (Mont.1983)—**§ 280, n. 20.**

Transamerica Ins. Group v. Meere, 143 Ariz. 351, 694 P.2d 181 (Ariz.1984)—**§ 70, n. 11.**

Transport Ins. Co. v. Faircloth, 898 S.W.2d 269 (Tex.1995)—**§ 477, n. 7.**

Traudt v. Potomac Elec. Power Co., 692 A.2d 1326 (D.C.1997)—**§ 337, n. 20, 47.**

Travers v. District of Columbia, 672 A.2d 566 (D.C.1996)—**§ 244, n. 10; § 246; § 246, n. 9, 10.**

Travers v. Spidell, 682 A.2d 471 (R.I. 1996)—**§ 482, n. 5.**

Travis v. City of Mesquite, 830 S.W.2d 94 (Tex.1992)—**§ 180, n. 4; § 190, n. 15.**

Travis v. Ziter, 681 So.2d 1348 (Ala.1996)—**§ 222, n. 25.**

Traxler v. Varady, 16 Cal.Rptr.2d 297 (Cal. App. 1 Dist.1993)—**§ 106, n. 4.**

Trentacost v. Brussel, 82 N.J. 214, 412 A.2d 436 (N.J.1980)—**§ 325, n. 2, 8, 19.**

Trentecosta v. Beck, 703 So.2d 552 (La. 1997)—**§ 402, n. 11; § 415, n. 11.**

Trevino v. General Dynamics Corp., 865 F.2d 1474 (5th Cir.1989)—**§ 274, n. 9.**

Trevino v. Ortega, 969 S.W.2d 950 (Tex. 1998)—**§ 451, n. 9.**

Trevino v. United States, 804 F.2d 1512 (9th Cir.1986)—**§ 261, n. 12.**

Triangle Publications v. Rohrlich, 167 F.2d 969 (2nd Cir.1948)—**§ 457, n. 27.**

Triangle Publications, Inc. v. Chumley, 253 Ga. 179, 317 S.E.2d 534 (Ga.1984)—**§ 402, n. 17; § 419, n. 22.**

Tri–County Inv. Group, Ltd. v. Southern States, Inc., 231 Ga.App. 632, 500 S.E.2d 22 (Ga.App.1998)—**§ 468, n. 13.**

Triggs v. Sun Printing & Publishing Ass'n, 179 N.Y. 144, 71 N.E. 739 (N.Y.1904)—**§ 420, n. 5.**

Tri–Growth Centre City, Ltd. v. Silldorf, Burdman, Duignan & Eisenberg, 216 Cal.App.3d 1139, 265 Cal.Rptr. 330 (Cal. App. 4 Dist.1989)—**§ 487, n. 12.**

Trimarco v. Klein, 451 N.Y.S.2d 52, 436 N.E.2d 502 (N.Y.1982)—**§ 163, n. 4; § 164, n. 16; § 165, n. 10.**

Trimed, Inc. v. Sherwood Medical Co., 977 F.2d 885 (4th Cir.1992)—**§ 448, n. 7; § 449, n. 15.**

Trindle v. Wheeler, 23 Cal.2d 330, 143 P.2d 932 (Cal.1943)—**§ 244, n. 7; § 247, n. 2.**

Trinity Universal Ins. Co. v. Bleeker, 966 S.W.2d 489 (Tex.1998)—**§ 453, n. 4.**

Triple Elkhorn Min. Co., Inc. v. Anderson, 646 S.W.2d 725 (Ky.1983)—**§ 55, n. 4.**

Tri–State Wholesale Associated Grocers, Inc. v. Barrera, 917 S.W.2d 391 (Tex. App.-El Paso 1996)—**§ 184, n. 14.**

Tritchler v. West Virginia Newspaper Pub. Co., Inc., 156 W.Va. 335, 193 S.E.2d 146 (W.Va.1972)—**§ 432, n. 24.**

Tropeano v. Atlantic Monthly Co., 379 Mass. 745, 400 N.E.2d 847 (Mass. 1980)—**§ 425, n. 7, 9.**

Trotter v. Callens, 89 N.M. 19, 546 P.2d 867 (N.M.App.1976)—**§ 191, n. 3; § 349, n. 8.**

Troy, Town of v. Cheshire R. Co., 23 N.H. 83 (N.H.1851)—**§ 57, n. 9.**

True v. Ladner, 513 A.2d 257 (Me.1986)—**§ 418, n. 8.**

Trujeque v. Service Merchandise Co., 117 N.M. 388, 872 P.2d 361 (N.M.1994)—**§ 155, n. 15; § 157, n. 15, 16; § 159, n. 3.**

Trull v. Town of Conway, 140 N.H. 579, 669 A.2d 807 (N.H.1995)—**§ 319, n. 3, 19.**

Truman v. Thomas, 165 Cal.Rptr. 308, 611 P.2d 902 (Cal.1980)—**§ 251, n. 32.**

Truman v. United States, 26 F.3d 592 (5th Cir.1994)—**§ 267, n. 7, 9.**

Trushcheff v. Abell–Howe Co., 239 N.W.2d 116 (Iowa 1976)—**§ 377, n. 13.**

Trytko v. Hubbell, Inc., 28 F.3d 715 (7th Cir.1994)—**§ 483, n. 5, 17.**

TSC Industries, Inc. v. Northway, Inc., 426 U.S. 438, 96 S.Ct. 2126, 48 L.Ed.2d 757 (1976)—**§ 363, n. 16; § 476, n. 2.**

Tubell v. Dade County Public Schools, 419 So.2d 388 (Fla.App. 3 Dist.1982)—**§ 259, n. 20.**

Tucker v. Duncan, 499 F.2d 963 (4th Cir. 1974)—**§ 434, n. 12.**

Tucker v. Lombardo, 47 Cal.2d 457, 303 P.2d 1041 (Cal.1956)—**§ 128, n. 3, 12; § 211, n. 1.**

Tucson, City of v. Gallagher, 108 Ariz. 140, 493 P.2d 1197 (Ariz.1972)—**§ 388, n. 6.**

Tucson, City of v. Wondergem, 105 Ariz. 429, 466 P.2d 383 (Ariz.1970)—**§ 297, n. 12.**

Tulkku v. Mackworth Rees, Division of Avis Industries, Inc., 406 Mich. 615, 281 N.W.2d 291 (Mich.1979)—**§ 200, n. 25.**

Tuman v. Genesis Associates, 894 F.Supp. 183 (E.D.Pa.1995)—**§ 402, n. 26; § 444, n. 1.**

Tunkl v. Regents of University of Cal., 60 Cal.2d 92, 32 Cal.Rptr. 33, 383 P.2d 441 (Cal.1963)—**§ 213, n. 6.**

Tunnell v. Hicks, 574 So.2d 264 (Fla.App. 1 Dist.1991)—**§ 65, n. 12.**

Turcotte v. Fell, 510 N.Y.S.2d 49, 502 N.E.2d 964 (N.Y.1986)—**§ 212, n. 1; § 215, n. 10, 12, 15.**

Turek v. Saint Elizabeth Community Health Center, 241 Neb. 467, 488 N.W.2d 567 (Neb.1992)—**§ 245, n. 2.**

Turf Lawnmower Repair, Inc. v. Bergen Record Corp., 139 N.J. 392, 655 A.2d 417 (N.J.1995)—**§ 416, n. 17; § 419, n. 16.**

U

V

W

Y

*

Index

References are to page numbers, including footnotes. If the topic continues or resumes in immediately succeeding pages, the reference is to the page on which discussion begins.